75|

DICTIONARY

OF

NATIONAL BIOGRAPHY

1931–1940

THE
DICTIONARY
OF
NATIONAL BIOGRAPHY

Founded in 1882 by

GEORGE SMITH

1931-1940

Edited by L. G. Wickham Legg

With an Index covering the years 1901–1940
in one alphabetical series

OXFORD UNIVERSITY PRESS

Oxford University Press, Amen House, London E.C.4

GLASGOW NEW YORK TORONTO MELBOURNE WELLINGTON
BOMBAY CALCUTTA MADRAS KARACHI LAHORE DACCA
CAPE TOWN SALISBURY NAIROBI IBADAN ACCRA
KUALA LUMPUR HONG KONG

FIRST PUBLISHED NOV. 1949
REPRINTED 1950, 1961

PRINTED IN GREAT BRITAIN
AT THE UNIVERSITY PRESS, OXFORD
BY VIVIAN RIDLER
PRINTER TO THE UNIVERSITY

PREFATORY NOTE

THE Supplement to the Dictionary of National Biography which is now offered to the public contains the names of King George V and 729 of his subjects who died during the decade from 1931 to 1940. The Editor has endeavoured to follow in the steps of his predecessors and to keep a mean between too much stiffness in refusing and too much easiness in admitting names, bearing in mind that the purpose of the Dictionary (as he conceives it) is to assist the student by opening its doors as widely as circumstances and reason will permit.

Between the earliest birth and the latest death recorded in this volume there is a space of 104 years. The senior in the list is Archdeacon J. M. Wilson, mathematician, schoolmaster, and antiquary, whose name is the only one to come down from the reign of King William IV; the junior is 'Gino' Watkins, the Arctic explorer, who, with Humfry Payne, the archaeologist, represents the many who were born in the twentieth century and called away out of due time. All the others are men and women born under Queen Victoria, in almost the middle of whose reign comes the birth of King George V. Round him are here clustered stars of the very first magnitude. Of all in this galaxy the brightest are those who belong to the constellations of natural science. First and foremost are two physicists, alike both in the hopes and in the apprehensions which their labours have aroused, Rutherford and J. J. Thomson. The future alone can reveal their true place in the history of mankind; it is easier to assess the place of other scientists. In prophylactics, it needs no great imagination to realize the measure of relief to human suffering that is associated with the names of David Bruce, Ronald Ross, and W. J. R. Simpson. And it is surely no disparagement of the work of such men as Sharpey Schafer in physiology, or of Henry Head and Robert Philip in therapeutics, or of Robert Jones, Moynihan, and Trotter in surgery, if those who have cause to bless their memories are, in mere numbers, far fewer than those who should remember with gratitude the invention of Henry Wellcome. Among biologists, Karl Pearson may well rank as the founder of a new school; the important work of William Pope will show the lay reader that 'wonders of modern science' is a phrase which the nomenclature of biochemistry raises into the very province of letters. Among the practical engineers, Charles Parsons, held by some to be the most original engineer produced by this country since James Watt, takes rank in historical significance with R. J. Mitchell, the designer of those 'Spitfires' in which a band of heroes saved their country from subjugation in the Battle of Britain. And let it be remarked in passing that the senior veteran of all the fighting men here commemorated is an engineer, Colonel R. E. B. Crompton, who as a boy of eleven earned the Crimean war medal by a visit to the trenches before Sebastopol. It is of course from younger generations that are drawn the warriors whose names appear in these pages, for they include almost the last of those great admirals and generals who by the aid of the inventions of the engineers led their men to victory in the war of 1914–1918: Beatty and Jellicoe at sea, Allenby, Byng, Plumer, and Robertson on land, together with that master of irregular warfare, the soldier-scholar 'Lawrence of Arabia', whose capture of the imagination of the world should not obscure the services of Percy Cox in the Middle East, nor the career of Reginald Johnston in China, nor the 'saga' of 'the most picturesque Scotsman of modern times', 'Don Roberto' Cunninghame Graham of Ardoch. In days when man's view of the world is ever more distorted by the fog of mechanics, and enterprise is discounted by the yearning for social security, these men showed that something not unlike Elizabethan adventure could still be open to those born in the nineteenth century.

Whether in the region of art, letters, and politics there are names which can be compared with the great lights of natural science is a question which does not call for discussion here. Critics will doubtless long dispute over the value of the compositions of Delius and Elgar, and of Tovey's contributions to musical learning; but none who heard Melba in her prime will deny her supremacy among the singers, nor will those who saw Mrs. Patrick Campbell contest her pre-eminence in the theatre. Roger Fry taught the public to see beauty where the light of nature unaided would not reveal it, but it may be that Tonks exercised an even greater influence on rising artists of his day. Yet it may well be questioned whether their teaching did more for the survival of a true aesthetic in this country than did those great successors of the old aristocratic patrons, the merchant collectors like Eumorfopoulos or great dealers like Duveen. They at any rate have now, in museums and elsewhere, held up standards of former days before a generation which, striving towards originality in technique, is as yet uncertain of the line to be drawn between the beautiful and the bizarre.

Of those who in political life helped to shape the destinies of the subjects of the Crown, we here find the names, not only of two prime ministers of Great Britain, Ramsay MacDonald and Neville Chamberlain, but also of Lyons in Australia and Borden in Canada. Round the first two, fierce fires of party strife will blaze for many a year. Subordinate statesmen like Austen Chamberlain, Grey of Fallodon, and Arthur Henderson at the Foreign Office, with others like Lothian and Reading, all strove to promote harmony in the world and a better understanding between the mother country and all her daughters. In contrast to the moderating influence exerted, not in parliament only, by Speaker Whitley, the names of Carson, Healy, Plunkett, and Snowden will recall bitter controversy, and so, too, will those of O'Dwyer in India and Percy FitzPatrick in South Africa; but if statesmanship is to be measured by peace brought to the greatest number of human beings, the palm may well be awarded to Hubert Murray, the great Australian administrator of Papua. Nor can those be overlooked who have advanced the development of features characteristic of modern society: Goodenough and Schuster among the bankers of London, Boot and Lipton in the development of the multiple shop, Tata in the growth of a steel trust, Ellerman and Inchcape in shipping, all helped to illustrate the old adage that competition tends to monopoly; and readers will here find some attempt to pay tribute to another characteristic of our life to-day in recording the achievements of Guy Nickalls on the river, of John Ball on the links, and of 'K. S. Ranjitsinhji' on the cricket field.

In the region of letters, the star of Kipling shines with a lustre which no political detraction can dim. As a poet he stands beside Henry Newbolt and William Watson, as a writer of fiction beside Arnold Bennett and John Buchan, to say nothing of Galsworthy and Barrie who as playwrights as well as novelists call to mind the contemporary Irish literary movement here represented by 'AE', Lady Gregory, George Moore, and W. B. Yeats. Among essayists, it is not easy to find a rival to Chesterton, and journalism has good reason to remember with honour the names of G. E. Buckle and C. P. Scott, who maintained its high traditions in days when they began to be seriously menaced. Andrew Bradley and Saintsbury as critics in English literature may not unfairly be mentioned in the same breath with such a giant as A. E. Housman in the classics, while the uncanny cleverness of D. S. Margoliouth both in Greek and in oriental scholarship is balanced by the rigid accuracy of A. A. Bevan. If the versatility of H. A. L. Fisher makes it uncertain whether he should be classed among the historians, the statesmen, or the educationists, there can be no such doubt about Firth, the last survivor of a generation of great historians, and one of the most prolific and most valued contributors to this DICTIONARY. In any age, the contribution of Frederick Pollock to the science of jurisprudence would stand conspicuous, as judges like Buckmaster, Scrutton, Sumner, or Trevethin would be the first to recognize. In philosophy Samuel Alexander and Seth-Pringle-Pattison gained reputations comparable to that of Mohammed Iqbal in India. In theology Gore's chapter in *Lux Mundi* first revealed how far the younger disciples of the tractarian movement had broken away from the fundamentalism of Pusey and Liddon. Nor was this field wanting in practical workers: Cardinal Bourne and Archbishop Edwards of Wales were both champions of the interests of their own flocks, and Donald Fraser, Robert Laws, and E. de M. Rudolf in the missionary and social fields are of them that have left a name behind them for many years to come.

Like his predecessors, the Editor must first and foremost give grateful recognition to the help given by his sub-editors in the preparation of this volume. Without the experience of Miss Margaret Toynbee, her accurate eye for detail, and her tenacious memory, it would have been impossible for the Editor to overcome the many difficulties that have been attendant on the preparation of this volume. He would also like to express his thanks to Mrs. Christopher Ritchie who for some months assisted in the work of sub-editing. For help and advice given from all quarters with great liberality, the Editor is under an obligation too multifarious to be acknowledged in its entirety, but he would like especially to mention the information and advice tendered by the late Sir Hugh Allen, Dr. E. H. Alton, Mr. C. T. Atkinson, Sir Vincent Baddeley, Mr. A. M. Binnie, Mr. Martin S. Briggs, Sir Frank Brown, Mr. B. Burdekin, the late Sir Richard Burn, the late Mr. L. Burpee, Sir Patrick Cadell, Lord David Cecil, Dr. R. W. Chapman, Dr. G. N. Clark, Dr. Hugh Clegg, Dr. Alexander Cooke, Mr. R. C. K. Ensor, Professor M. G. Fisher, Mr. Hamilton Fyfe, Professor H. A. R. Gibb, Mrs. E. S. Goodrich, Sir C. N. Hinshelwood, Mr. R. H. Hodgkin, the Rev. Dr. Hodgson, Lord Horder, Sir Robert Hutchison, Mr. E. A. A. Joseph, Professor R. W. Lee, the late Sir H. V. Lovett, the Very Rev. John Lowe, the Very Rev. Dr. Norman Maclean, Dr. C. A. Malcolm, Sir Dougal Malcolm, Colonel K. Mason, the Rev. Dr. N. Micklem, Sir Humphrey Milford (whose reading of the proofs has put the Editor under a special obligation), Mr. John Parker, Mr. K. T. Parker, Lord Eustace Percy, Mr. A. L. Poole, Professor G. V. Portus, Dr. D. R. Pye, Sir Bruce Richmond, the late Admiral Sir Herbert Richmond, Sir David Ross, Mr. Albert Rutherston, Sir Charles Sherrington, Professor Nevill Sidgwick, the late Dr. W. T. S. Stallybrass, Mr. C. W. Stanley, Mr. J. A. Stevenson, the Hon. W. Downie Stewart, Rear-Admiral H. G. Thursfield, Mr. J. R. H. Weaver, Mr. Geoffrey Whitworth, and the Hon. Hugh Wyndham. He also asks his contributors who by their courtesy and forbearance have lightened the burden of his work to accept this expression of his thanks; but a very special meed of gratitude is due from the Editor to the secretary and staff of the Clarendon Press. Help so generously given enables this lexicographer to say that, whether harmless or not, he has never been a drudge.

L. G. W. L.

January 1949.

LIST OF CONTRIBUTORS

ADAMS, William George Stewart:
Plunkett.
ADY, Cecilia Mary:
Paget, Violet (Vernon Lee); Toynbee.
ALLEN, Walter Godfrey:
Simpson (J. W.).
ALTRINCHAM, Edward William Macleay
Grigg, Baron:
Hichens; Poynder (Islington).
ANDERSON, David:
Mott.
ANDERSON, John George Clark:
Ramsay.
ANDREWS, Hilda:
Terry (R. R.).
ANDREWS, John Miller:
Craig (Craigavon).
ARBER, Agnes:
Scott (D. H.).
ARMFIELD, Maxwell Ashby:
Wilkinson (N.).
†ARMSTRONG, Edward Frankland:
Cross.
ATKINS, John Black:
Butler (E. S.).
ATKINS, William Ringrose Gelston:
Young.
ATKINSON, Christopher Thomas:
Butler (R. H. K.); Cobbe; Fortescue;
Hunter (A.); Methuen.

BADDELEY, Sir Vincent Wilberforce:
Backhouse; Colville; Douglas; Henderson
(R. G. H.); Madden; Milne; Murray
(O. A. R.); Pakenham; Wemyss (Wester
Wemyss).
BAERLEIN, Henry:
Dillon (E. J.).
BAILEY, Cyril:
Conway (R. S.).
BAILLIE, Donald Macpherson:
Mackintosh.
BAILLIE, John:
Kennedy.
BAIRD, Matthew Urie:
Gordon, I. M. (Aberdeen). See under
Gordon, J. C. (Aberdeen).
BAKER, Charles Henry Collins:
Holmes (C. J.).
BAKER, John Randal:
Bourne (G. C.).
BALLARD, Philip Boswood:
Adams.
BALSTON, Thomas:
Gertler.
BARBER, Eric Arthur:
Farnell.
BARBOUR, George Freeland:
Gordon, J. C. (Aberdeen).
BARRY, Frank Russell, Bishop of Southwell
(Fr. Southwell):
Dearmer.

BARTLETT, Frederic Charles:
McDougall.
BARTON, Sir William Pell:
Mysore.
BATTISCOMBE, Georgina:
Anderson (Benson, S.); Caine; Ford; Harri-
son (Lucas Malet); McNeile (Sapper).
BEAZLEY, Sir John Davidson:
Payne.
BEHARREL, Sir John George:
Geddes (E. C.).
BELL, Sir Harold Idris:
Hunt (A. S.).
BENIANS, Ernest Alfred:
Tanner.
BENTLEY, Edmund Clerihew:
Lawson (Burnham).
BETHUNE-BAKER, James Franklin:
Barnes (W. E.); Burkitt.
BISHOP, William John:
Dudgeon; Kettle; McLeod; McMurrich;
Robertson (G. M.).
BLACKER, Lady Doris:
Peel.
†BLAKISTON, Herbert Edward Douglas:
Jones (H. Stuart).
BOLITHO, Henry Hector:
Greville (Warwick).
BONHAM-CARTER, Sir Edgar:
Wilson (A. T.).
BONNEY, Victor:
Sutton.
BOSANQUET, Ellen Sophia:
Bosanquet.
†BOTTOMLEY, Gordon:
Shannon.
BOWLEY, Arthur Lyon:
Foxwell.
BOYCOTT, John Agg:
Boycott.
†BRADBY, Henry Christopher:
Vaughan.
BRAITHWAITE, Richard Bevan:
Johnson.
BRAMWELL, John Crighton:
Bramwell.
BRAND, Robert Henry Brand, Baron:
Kerr (Lothian).
BRIGGS, Martin Shaw:
Champneys; Dawber.
†BROWN, Alfred Barratt:
Furniss (Sanderson).
BROWN, Sir Frank Herbert:
Bhownagree; Butler (S. H.); Fuller; Nehru;
Yate.
BROWN, Sir Harold Arthur:
Oram.
BUCKNILL, Sir Alfred Townsend, Lord Justice
Bucknill:
Hill.
†BURMESTER, Sir Rudolf Miles:
Calthorpe.

BURNETT, Richard George:
Hocking (J. and S. K.).
BURROW, Thomas:
Rapson.
BURTON, Herbert:
Anstey; Lyons; Quick; Ryrie.
BUTLER, Harold Edgeworth:
Clark; Deller; Foster (T. G.).

CADELL, Sir Patrick Robert:
Baroda; Besant; Nawanagar.
†CALLENDER, Sir Geoffrey Arthur Romaine:
Jellicoe, J. R. (Earl).
CALMAN, William Thomas:
McIntosh.
CANTELUPE, Dorothy Jeffreys, Viscountess:
Louise (Argyll).
CARLYLE, Edward Irving:
Banbury; Buxton; Cavendish (Devonshire); Dyke; Evans (L. Worthington); Ewing; Ferguson (Novar); Hicks (Brentford); Macnamara; Russell, A. O. V. (Ampthill); Shortt; Thomson (B. H.).
CARNEGIE, Moir:
Mackenzie (A. C.).
CECIL, Algernon:
Bailey (J. C.).
CECIL, Lord Edward Christian David Gascoyne:
Morrell; Strachey (G. L.).
CHALMERS, William Scott:
Beatty.
CHAMPION, Harry George:
Troup.
CHANDLER, Noel Raymond:
Royce.
CHAPMAN, John Alexander:
Ross (E. D.).
CHAPMAN, Sydney:
Lamb.
CHAPMAN-HUSTON, Desmond:
Low.
CHARLTON, George:
Tonks.
CHAUNDY, Theodore William:
Elliott; Rogers (L. J.).
CHOKSI, Rustum:
Tata.
CHRISTIE, Ella Robertson:
Haldane (E. S.).
CHRISTOPHERS, Sir Samuel Rickard:
Bruce (D.); Ross (R.).
CLAPPERTON, Gladys Laura:
Yapp.
CLARK, George Norman:
Firth; Montague; Poole (R. L.).
CLARK, Sir Kenneth McKenzie:
Fry.
CLEGG, Hugh Anthony:
Herringham.
CLEVELAND-STEVENS, William:
Dibdin.
COBB, John William:
Smithells.
COBHAM, John Oldcastle:
Hoskyns.
†COCHRANE, Alfred:
Baillie, C. W. A. N. R. Cochrane- (Laming-

ton); Boot (Trent); Buchanan, J. (Woolavington); Clarke, G. S. (Sydenham); Coleridge; Falkner; Guest (F. E.); Guest, I. C. (Wimborne); Harris, G. R. C. (Lord); Hawke; Lunn; Mills (B. W.); Nawanagar; Noble; Philipps, J. W. (St. Davids); Philipps, O. C. (Kylsant); Vestey.
COCHRANE, Sir Arthur William Steuart:
Charrington; Howard of Penrith; King; Nathan.
COCKERELL, Sir Sydney Carlyle:
Walker (E.).
COFFEY, Diarmid:
Campbell, J. H. M. (Glenavy).
COHEN, Sir Lionel Leonard, Lord Justice Cohen:
Warrington.
COOK, Stanley Arthur:
Bevan; Kennett.
COOK, William Lewis:
Hartshorn.
CORBYN, Ernest Nugent:
Currie (J.).
†COULTON, George Gordon:
Fowler (H. W.).
COUPLAND, Sir Reginald:
Thesiger (Chelmsford).
COWEN, Zelman:
Duffy.
CRAIG, Maurice:
Devlin.
†CREWE, Robert Offley Ashburton Crewe-Milnes, Marquess of:
Birrell; Paul.
CRITCHLEY, Macdonald:
Wilson (S. A. K.).
CUNDELL, Edric:
German; Ronald.
CUNNINGHAM, William Ross:
Rait.
CURGENVEN, Sir Arthur Joseph:
Sankaran Nair.
CURLE, Alexander Ormiston:
Macdonald (G.).
CURTIS, William Alexander:
Paterson.

DALE, Sir Henry Hallett:
Andrewes.
DAMPIER, Sir William Cecil Dampier:
Glazebrook; Leathes.
DANBY, Herbert:
Cooke; Montefiore.
†DARK, Sidney:
Waggett.
DARLINGTON, William Aubrey:
Drinkwater; Robertson (J. Forbes-); Wyndham (Moore).
DARWIN, Bernard:
Ball; Hutchinson (H. G.).
†DAUKES, Sidney Herbert:
Wellcome.
DAVIDSON, Sir Nigel George:
Lawrence, A. T. (Trevethin).
†DAVIES, Sir Alfred Thomas:
Hopkinson.
DAVIES, David:
Horridge.

DAWES, George:
  Tucker.
DAWKINS, Richard MacGillivray:
  Giles (P.).
DE LA MARE, Walter:
  Newbolt.
DENNY, Sir Maurice Edward, Bart.:
  Denny.
DENT, Edward Joseph:
  Baylis.
DESCH, Cecil Henry:
  Carpenter; Hadfield; Rosenhain.
DILLING, Walter James:
  Cash.
†DILNOT, Frank:
  Wallace.
DINGLE, Herbert:
  Fowler (A.).
DIXON, Henry Horatio:
  Joly.
DOUGLAS, Claude Gordon:
  Haldane (J. S.); Pembrey.
DOUGLAS, James Archibald:
  Sollas.
DRIVER, Godfrey Rolles:
  Cowley; Langdon.
†DUGDALE, Blanche Elizabeth Campbell:
  Sidgwick.
DUGGAN, George Chester:
  Pollock (H. M.).
DUNCAN, George Simpson:
  Milligan.
DUNCAN, Leslie:
  Laws.
DUNCAN-JONES, Arthur Stuart:
  Edwards.
DUNSANY, Edward John Moreton Drax Plunkett, Baron:
  Watson.

EASON, Herbert Lightfoot:
  Perry.
EDMONDS, Sir James Edward:
  Snow.
EGERTON, Sir Alfred Charles Glynn:
  Bone.
ELLIOTT, Thomas Renton:
  Bradford; Fletcher (W. M.).
ELLIS, Lionel Frederic:
  Barnett.
ELTON, Godfrey, Baron:
  MacDonald (J. R.).
†ELTON, Oliver:
  Abercrombie; Sampson (J.).
EMMET, Dorothy Mary:
  Stocks.
ENSOR, Robert Charles Kirkwood:
  Birrell; Dalziel; Ellis; Hobhouse; Sidebotham; Snowden.
ENTHOVEN, Reginald Edward:
  Temple.
ERVINE, St. John Greer:
  Du Maurier; Kendal; McNeill, R. J. (Cushendun); Pinero.
ESDAILE, Arundell James Kennedy:
  Wise.

FALLS, Cyril Bentham:
  Allenby; Byng.

FARMER, Herbert Henry:
  Oman.
FERGUSON, Allan:
  Lodge (O.).
†FFOULKES, Charles John:
  Dillon, H. A. (Viscount).
FIELD, Guy Cromwell:
  Morgan (C. L.).
†FISHER, Edwin:
  Goodenough.
FISHER, Matthew George:
  Johnston, C. N. (Sands).
FLETCHER, Sir Frank:
  Page (T. E.).
FLEURE, Herbert John:
  Haddon.
FORDYCE, Christian James:
  Lindsay (W. M.).
FOSS, Hubert James:
  Tovey.
FRANCKENSTEIN, Sir George:
  De Bunsen.
FRENCH, Sir James Weir:
  Barr.
FYFE, Henry Hamilton:
  Donald; Harmsworth (Rothermere); Marlowe; Riddell.

GALBRAITH, Vivian Hunter:
  Clarke (M. V.); Lyte.
GARROD, Heathcote William:
  Allen (P. S.).
GARVIN, Viola Gerard:
  Wolfe.
GEDDES, Arthur:
  Geddes (P.).
GIBB, Sir Claude Dixon:
  Parsons.
GIBB, Hamilton Alexander Rosskeen:
  Iqbal; Poole (S. Lane-).
GIBSON, Charles Stanley:
  Pope.
GILLON, Stair Agnew:
  Buchan (Tweedsmuir).
GIRDLESTONE, Gathorne Robert:
  Jones (R.).
GODFREY, Walter Hindes:
  Burnet.
GODLEY, Hon. Eveline Charlotte:
  Godley (Kilbracken).
GOLD, Sir Harcourt Gilbey:
  Nickalls.
GOOCH, George Peabody:
  Temperley.
GORE, John:
  Holland (Knutsford).
GRAHAM-CAMPBELL, Archibald Rollo:
  Brooke.
GRAHAM-SMITH, George Stuart:
  Nuttall.
GRAVES, Philip Percival:
  Cox (P. Z.).
GRAY, Basil:
  Eumorfopoulos.
GREENWOOD, Major:
  Pearson (K.).
GREG, Walter Wilson:
  McKerrow.

GRENSTED, Laurence William:
Knox; Streeter.

GRIER, Lynda:
Hadow (G. E.).

GRIFFITHS, Ezer:
Griffiths.

GRIMSDITCH, Herbert Borthwick:
Dyson (W. H.); Grahame; Jagger; László; Lipton; Orage; Rackham; Ramsden; Speyer; Thornton; Wilkinson (N. R.); Wyllie.

†GUBBAY, Moses Mordecai Simeon:
Mackay (Inchcape).

GUNN, George Battiscombe:
Griffith (F. L.); Peet; Sayce.

GUNN, James Andrew:
Dixon (W. E.).

GUTTERIDGE, Harold Cooke:
De Montmorency.

GWYER, Barbara Elizabeth:
Rogers (A. M. A. H.).

HACKETT, Felix Edward Walsh:
Orr.

HADLEY, Patrick Arthur Sheldon:
Delius.

HADLEY, William Waite:
Chamberlain (A. N.).

HAMILTON, Mary Agnes:
Henderson (A.); Lansbury; Smillie.

HAMILTON-EDWARDS, Gerald Kenneth Savery:
Stevens.

†HAMMOND, John Lawrence Le Breton:
Scott (C. P.).

HANBURY, Harold Greville:
Buckley (Wrenbury); Dreyer; Eve; McCardie.

HANNON, Sir Patrick Joseph Henry:
Ashley (Mount Temple).

†HARDY, Godfrey Harold:
Hobson (E. W.); Mercer.

HARE, Tom:
Hobday.

HARINGTON, Charles Robert:
Barger.

HARRIS, Henry Albert:
Smith (G. E.).

HARRISON, John Vernon:
Gregory (J. W.).

HARVEY, Godfrey Eric:
Keith; Scott (J. G.).

HAY, Agnes Yelland, Lady Dalrymple-:
Hay.

†HAYNES, Edmund Sidney Pollock:
Bottomley.

†HEADLAM, Arthur Cayley:
Nairne.

HEADLAM, Maurice Francis:
Chalmers; Heath; Murray (G. H.).

HEATON, Trevor Braby:
Thomson (A.).

HETHERINGTON, Sir Hector James Wright:
MacAlister.

HIELD, Robert:
Colvin.

HILL, Archibald Vivian:
Hardy.

HILL, Walter Scott:
Dixon (R. B.).

HINKSON, Pamela:
Harrell.

HIRST, Francis Wrigley:
Cox (H.).

HODGSON, Stuart:
Lygon (Beauchamp); Maclean.

HODSON, Henry Vincent:
Dove.

HOLLINS, Clara Joyce Elizmar:
McCormick.

HONE, Joseph Maunsell:
Graves; Healy (T. M.); McNeill (J.); Sexton (T.); Yeats.

HORNER, Norman Gerald:
Sprigge.

HORNYOLD-STRICKLAND, Henry:
Strickland.

HOWES, Frank:
Dolmetsch.

HUMPHREYS, Sir Travers:
Avory.

HURD, Sir Archibald:
Beardmore (Invernairn); Isherwood; Ismay.

HURD, Sir Percy Angier:
Hewins.

HUTTON, John Henry:
Balfour (H.).

HUXLEY, Elspeth Josceline:
Cholmondeley (Delamere).

HYAMSON, Albert Montefiore:
Gaster; Sutro.

ILLINGWORTH, Charles Frederick William:
Wilkie.

IRVINE, Sir James Colquhoun:
Morgan (G. T.).

JAMES, Howell Ewart:
Evans (E. V.).

JAMES, Sir William Milburne:
Bayly; Custance.

JAMISON, Evelyn Mary:
Lodge (E. C.); Wordsworth.

JEFFERY, George Barker:
Filon.

JENKINS, Claude:
Robertson (A.); Robinson; Sheppard.

JENYNS, Roger Soame:
Johnston (R. F.).

JOHNSON, Charles:
Crump.

JOHNSTONE, Alfred Ernest:
Runciman.

JONES, Bernard Mouat:
Baker.

JONES, Sir Harold Spencer:
Brown (E. W.); Dyson (F. W.).

JORDAN, Karl:
Rothschild.

KENYON, Sir Frederic George:
Lindsay, D. A. E. (Crawford); Warner; Wright.

KING, William Bernard Robinson:
Marr.

KNOWLES, Dom Michael David:
Butler, E. J. A. (Dom Cuthbert).
KNOX, Edmund George Valpy:
Lucas (E. V.); Reed; Seaman.
KNOX, Ronald Arbuthnott:
Fraser, S. J. (Lovat).

†LAIRD, John:
Alexander; Pattison.
LAMB, Sir John:
Gilmour.
LANDON, Philip Aislabie:
Astbury; Mathew.
LASKI, Harold Joseph:
Robertson (J. M.).
LASKI, Neville Jonas:
Darling.
LATHAM, Sir John Greig:
Murray (J. H. P.).
LAVER, James:
Gilbert; Greiffenhagen; Jones (A.); Tweed.
LAVRIN, Janko:
Maude.
LAWRENCE, Sir Henry Staveley:
Patel.
LAYTON, Thomas Bramley:
Symonds.
LEATHES, John Beresford:
Mellanby.
LEE, Amice:
Macdonell.
LEE, Robert Warden:
Jenks.
LE FANU, William Richard:
Ballance; Moynihan.
LEGG, Leopold George Wickham:
Bourne (R. C.).
LEVIEN, John Mewburn:
Butt; Cowen; Melba.
LEVY, Reuben:
Le Strange.
LITTLEWOOD, Samuel Robinson:
Asche; Greet; Poel.
LOCKHART, John Gilbert:
Wood (Halifax).
†LOVETT, Sir Sackville Hatton Harrington Verney:
Besant; Craddock; O'Dwyer.
†LOWINSKY, Thomas Esmond:
Philpot; Ricketts.
LUCE, Arthur Aston:
D'Arcy.
LUNN, Arnold:
Conway of Allington.
LYND, Sylvia:
Hinkson (Tynan).

MACALISTER, Sir Ian:
Caroë.
MACARTHUR, Sir William Porter:
Keogh.
McDOWALL, Robert John Stewart:
Halliburton.
MACKENZIE, Agnes Mure:
Terry (C. S.).

MACKIE, John Duncan:
Fleming.
†MacKINNON, Frank Douglas, Lord Justice MacKinnon:
Hamilton (Sumner); Scrutton; Talbot (G. J.).
MACLAGAN, Michael:
Gibbs.
McLAREN, Martin John:
McLaren (Aberconway).
MACLEAN, Norman:
Balfour (F.); Fisher (R. H.).
MACMILLAN, Hugh Pattison Macmillan, Baron:
Horne; Shaw, T. (Craigmyle).
MACMUNN, Sir George Fletcher:
Plumer.
MACNAGHTEN, Hon. Sir Malcolm Martin:
Clarke (E. G.).
MacNALTY, Sir Arthur Salusbury:
Balfour (A.); Buchanan (G. S.).
MAGEE, William Kirkpatrick:
Russell, G. W. (AE).
MAINE, Basil Stephen:
Elgar.
MAJOR, Henry Dewsbury Alves:
Gardner (P.).
MALCOLM, Sir Dougal Orme:
Joel (S. B. and J. B.); Oliver.
MANSBRIDGE, Albert:
McMillan (M.).
MANSON, Thomas Walter:
Charles.
MARRIOTT, Charles:
Collier; Mackennal; McKenzie (R. T.); Ouless.
†MARRIOTT, Sir John Arthur Ransome:
Horton.
MARSHALL, Francis Hugh Adam:
Schafer.
†MARTEN, Sir Clarence Henry Kennett:
Fletcher (C. R. L.).
MARTIN, Sir Alec:
Duveen.
MARTIN, Sir Charles James:
Harden.
MARTIN, Thomas:
Jackson (H.).
MARYON-WILSON, Sir George Percy Maryon, Bart.:
Jellicoe (J. B. L.).
†MASON, Alfred Edward Woodley:
Barrie; Hawkins (Anthony Hope).
MASON, Kenneth:
Bruce (C. G.).
MASTERMAN, Lucy:
Lyttelton.
MAUCHLINE, John:
M'Fadyen.
MAURICE, Sir Frederick Barton:
Birch; Marshall; Robertson (W. R.).
MAWSON, Sir Douglas:
David.
MAXWELL, Sir Alexander:
Ruggles-Brise.
MAYOR, Henry Bickersteth:
Wilson (J. M.).

RIVETT, Sir Albert Cherbury David:
Masson.
ROBBINS, Lionel Charles:
Cannan.
†ROBERTSON, Sir Charles Grant:
Bain; Lodge (R.); Muirhead.
ROBERTSON, Donald Struan:
Housman; Pearson (A. C.).
†ROBERTSON, Sir Robert:
Mond; Petavel.
ROBINSON, Lennox:
Gregory (I. A.).
RODD, Ernest Harry:
Armstrong.
†ROLLESTON, John Davy:
Browne; Cheyne; Crawfurd; Garrod; Head;
Whitla.
Ross, Hugh Munro:
Brennan; Buchanan (G. C.); Clerk; Dew-
rance; Edge; Hunter (G. B.); Mills (W.);
Snell.
Ross, Sir William David:
Phelps; Smith (J. A.).
†ROWE, Frederick Maurice:
Perkin.
RUDMOSE BROWN, Robert Neal:
Freshfield; Jackson (F. G.); Watkins; Wild.
RUDOLF, Cyril de Montjoie:
Rudolf.
RUSSELL, Geoffrey William:
Buckmaster.

SADLEIR, Michael:
Benson (E. F.); Harraden; Savage (Ethel
M. Dell).
†SANKEY, John Sankey, Viscount:
Duke (Merrivale); Talbot (E. S.).
SANSOM, Sir George Bailey:
Eliot.
SAUNDERS, Hilary Aiden St. George:
Houston.
SAVORY, Douglas Lloyd:
Carson.
SCHOLFIELD, Alwyn Faber:
James.
SCHUSTER, Claud Schuster, Baron:
Schuster (F. O.).
SCOTT, John Waugh:
Mackenzie (J. S.).
†SEYMOUR, Sir Edward:
Victoria.
†SHAW, Richard James Herbert:
Healy (J. E.).
SHEPHERD, Edwin Colston:
Mitchell; Salmond; Samson; Smith
(C. E. K.).
SHERA, Frank Henry:
Hadow (W. H.).
SHEWRING, Walter:
Gill.
SHUCKBURGH, Sir John Evelyn:
Dobbs.
SIEPMANN, Harry Arthur:
Blackett.
SIMON, John Allsebrook Simon, Viscount:
Isaacs (Reading).
SIMPSON, David Capell:
Lock.

SIMPSON, Sir George Clarke:
Schuster (A.).
SIMPSON, Percy:
Herford.
SINGLETON, Sir John Edward:
Swift.
SITWELL, Sir Osbert, Bart.:
Sassoon.
SMITH, David Nichol:
Saintsbury.
SMITH, John Sandwith Boys:
Creed.
SMITH, Sidney:
Budge.
SMITH, Walter Campbell:
Hutchinson (A.); Thomas.
SOUTHWELL, Richard Vynne:
Jenkin.
SPARKS, Hedley Frederick Davis:
White (A. J.).
SPENCE, James Calvert:
Murray (G. R.).
SPENCER, Leonard James:
Tutton.
STANLEY, Carleton Wellesley:
Borden; Gordon, C. W. (Ralph Connor);
Parker.
STENTON, Sir Frank Merry:
Childs.
STEVENSON, John Alexander:
Foster (G. E.); Graham, H. (Atholstan);
McLennan; Macphail.
STEWART, Hon. William Downie:
Bell.
STORRS, Sir Ronald:
Lawrence (T. E.).
†STURT, Henry:
Schiller.
SUTHERLAND, Halliday Gibson:
Philip.
SWAN, Kenneth Raydon:
Steel-Maitland.
SWINNERTON, Frank Arthur:
Bennett; Harris, J. T. (Frank).
SWINTON, Sir Ernest Dunlop:
Wilkinson (H. S.).

TATE, Sir Robert William:
Ross (J.).
TATLOW, Tissington:
Fraser (D.).
TAWNEY, Richard Henry:
Hobson (J. A.); Postan (Power).
TAYLOR, Frank Sherwood:
Gunther.
TEMPLE, Reginald Cecil:
Aston; Paris.
TENNANT, Frederick Robert:
Sorley.
TENNYSON-D'EYNCOURT, Sir Eustace Henry
William, Bart.:
Biles; Yarrow.
THOMAS, Frederick William:
Waddell.
THOMAS, Ivor:
Heath.
THOMAS, Mary Gwyneth Lloyd:
Newall (Phillpotts).

THOMPSON, Alexander Hamilton:
Baillie (J. B.); Frere.
THOMPSON, John Eric Sidney:
Gann.
THOMSON, Gladys Scott:
Russell, H. A. and M. du C. (Duke and Duchess of Bedford).
THURSFIELD, Henry George:
Duff; Fisher (W. W.); Jerram; Kelly; Ottley; Phillimore.
TILLEY, Cecil Edgar:
Harker.
TIZARD, Sir Henry Thomas:
Rutherford; Threlfall.
TOBIAS, Theodore Cronhelm:
Atkinson.
TOMLIN, James William Sackett:
Welldon.
TOMLINSON, Henry Major:
Graham (R. B. C.).
TOYNBEE, Jocelyn Mary Catherine:
Gardner (E. A. and P.).
TOYNBEE, Margaret Ruth:
Finberg; Wain.
TREVELYAN, George Macaulay:
Grey.
TREWIN, John Courtenay:
Campbell (Mrs. P.); Terry (F.).
TUCKER, Bernard William:
Jourdain.
TWYMAN, Frank:
Taylor.

UNWIN, Sir Stanley:
Macmillan (F. O.).
†UTHWATT, Augustus Andrewes Uthwatt, Baron:
Tomlin.

VAUGHAN WILLIAMS, Ralph:
Holst.

WALKER, Edward George:
Unwin (W. C.).
†WALKER, Ernest:
Maitland.
WALLACE, William Stewart:
Grenfell.
WALSHE, Francis Martin Rouse:
Trotter.
WAND, John William Charles, Bishop of London (W. Londin.):
Donaldson.
WARD, Maisie (Mrs. Sheed):
Chesterton.

WATERMEYER, Ernest Frederick, Chief Justice:
Kotzé.
WATERS, Sir George Alexander:
Macpherson (Strathcarron).
WATSON, James Anderson Scott:
Somerville.
WATSON, Sir Malcolm:
Simpson (J. W. R.).
†WATTS, William Whitehead:
Sollas.
WEAVER, John Reginald Homer:
Hunt (W.).
WELLINGTON, Hubert Lindsay:
Orpen.
WHAYMAN, William Matthias:
Oram.
WHEARE, Kenneth Clinton:
Morris; Ward, W. H. (Dudley).
WHEELER, Sir Henry:
Carlyle.
WHITTAKER, Sir Edmund Taylor:
Macdonald (H. M.); Sampson (R. A.).
WHITWORTH, Geoffrey Arundel:
Fagan; Playfair.
WILLIAMS, Alwyn Terrell Petre, Bishop of Durham (Alwyn Dunelm.):
Gore.
WILSON, Sir Horace John:
Shackleton; Whitley.
WILSON, James Bromley:
Wilson (H. W.).
WILSON, Sir James Steuart:
Greene; Henschel.
WINFIELD, Percy Henry:
Amos.
WOOD, Hon. Marion Evelyn:
Ashton of Hyde.
WOOD, William John:
Bourne (F. A.).
WOODRUFF, John Douglas:
Guthrie (F. Anstey).
WRIGHT, Robert Alderson Wright, Baron:
Pollock (F.).
†WROTTESLEY, Sir Frederic John:
Pollock, E. M. (Hanworth).
WYNDHAM, Hon. Everard Humphrey:
Bridges; Bulfin.
WYNDHAM, Hon. Hugh Archibald:
Bailey (A.); FitzPatrick.

YOUNG, George Malcolm:
Kipling.
YOUNG, Robert Arthur:
Fowler (J. K.).

ZIMMERN, Sir Alfred Eckhard:
Wallas.

DICTIONARY

OF

NATIONAL BIOGRAPHY

(TWENTIETH CENTURY)

PERSONS WHO DIED 1931–1940

ABERCONWAY, first BARON (1850–1934), barrister and business man. [See McLAREN, CHARLES BENJAMIN BRIGHT.]

ABERCROMBIE, LASCELLES (1881–1938), poet and critic, the fifth son, and the eighth of nine children, of William Abercrombie, stockbroker, of Ashton-upon-Mersey, by his wife, Sarah Ann Heron, was born at Ashton 9 January 1881. Even in boyhood he was devoted to music and letters; his taste was fostered at a preparatory school, and also at Malvern College, where he read Greek and Latin eagerly. From 1900 to 1902 he read science at the Owens College, Manchester, but then turned to journalism for a living and to poetry for his vocation. He reviewed much in the Liverpool daily press; his first poem, 'Blind', appeared in 1907 and his first volume of verse, *Interludes and Poems*, in 1908. In 1909 he married Catherine, daughter of Owen Gwatkin, surgeon, of Grange-over-Sands; they had three sons and one daughter. After a stay of more than a year in Birkenhead he and his wife migrated first to Herefordshire and then (1911) to Gloucestershire, where, inspired by happiness and by the noble scenery, he published some of his best verse. It included *Mary and the Bramble* (1910), *The Sale of St. Thomas*, Act I (1911), and also some poetic plays in *New Numbers*, i–iv (1914), a periodical privately issued in partnership with Rupert Brooke, John Drinkwater [qq.v.], and Mr. Wilfrid Gibson.

Abercrombie now came to be recognized as a leading poet of the new generation, distinguished for his lyrical power and speculative daring. He was praised by Robert Bridges for his lucid exposition of difficult themes. He responded profoundly to natural beauty; his love-poetry was ardent and exalted; and the mystical and 'metaphysical' strain was never far away.

It is heard again in the prose of *Speculative Dialogues* (1913), with its musings on life and love and on the Last Things; and also in several dramatic poems, such as *Deborah* (1912), which were not designed for the stage. But several were acted; of these the most notable is *The End of the World* (published in *New Numbers*), in which some homely folk are terrified by a false alarm that doomsday has arrived.

Abercrombie was still to write his best verse, but his richest period of poetic production was over. The war of 1914–1918 came as a grievous interruption. Although a keen patriot he was not strong enough for military service and laboured in Liverpool as an examiner of munitions. When peace came he was at a loss for employment, but after a while funds were found for a lecturership in poetry at Liverpool University; this appointment, which he held from 1919 to 1922, was an event that was to affect his whole career. He spoke upon his own craft; he held public audiences, not least by his rare gift for reading aloud; and he taught small classes the outlines of literary criticism and of its history. Abercrombie now devoted himself chiefly to prose, and published many critical studies, often based on the public lectures which he gave at Cambridge, at Baltimore, to the British Academy, and elsewhere. They include *An Essay towards a Theory of Art* (1922), *Principles of English Prosody* (1924), and *Romanticism* (1926). *Poetry, its Music and Meaning* (1932) is a felicitous statement of his artistic and critical convictions. The article on Thomas Hardy in this DICTIONARY is eloquent of a lifelong admiration.

A very active professor, Abercrombie rose quickly in the academic world. He occupied the chair of English literature at Leeds University from 1922 to 1929 and was Hildred Carlile professor of English literature in London University, at

Bedford College for Women, from 1929 to 1935. In 1935 he became Goldsmiths' reader in English at Oxford and a fellow of Merton College. He received honorary degrees from the universities of Cambridge, Manchester, and Belfast; held several special lecturerships, including the Clark lecturership at Trinity College, Cambridge, in 1923, and was elected a fellow of the British Academy in 1937. But his health declined, and he died in London 27 October 1938.

In 1930 the Oxford University Press published (in 'The Oxford Poets') Abercrombie's collected *Poems*, all but one, the richest and maturest of all, the completed *Sale of St. Thomas* (1931). Here, in a style which often rises to grandeur, he proclaims his faith in an omnipresent divine spirit embodying the law of ideal beauty. Abercrombie deepened and ennobled English 'metaphysical' poetry. He charged it anew with his passionate feeling for the essential beauty of nature and of human nature. The symbolism may be now and then excessive, or too difficult; yet again and again, as in some of his early lyrics, in the stately choruses of 'Peregrinus', in 'Marriage Song', and never better than in 'The Death of a Friar', he achieves either beauty, or strength, or magnificence, or all these in harmony.

[*The Times*, 28 October 1938; Oliver Elton, *Lascelles Abercrombie, 1881–1938* in *Proceedings* of the British Academy, vol. xxv, 1939 (portrait and bibliography); Wilfrid Gibson in *English*, vol. ii, No. 10, 1939; private information; personal knowledge.]

OLIVER ELTON.

ABERDEEN AND TEMAIR, first MARQUESS OF (1847–1934), statesman, and ABERDEEN AND TEMAIR, MARCHIONESS OF (1857–1939). [See GORDON, JOHN CAMPBELL.]

ADAMS, SIR JOHN (1857–1934), educationist, was born at Glasgow 2 July 1857, the son of Charles Adams, of that city, by his wife, Barbara McCallum. From St. David's School he entered the Jordanhill Training College and the university of Glasgow (1875), where he graduated with a first class in mental and moral science. He became headmaster of Jean Street school, Port-Glasgow, and afterwards rector of Campbeltown Grammar School. This experience of school practice formed a sound basis for his subsequent work as a trainer of teachers and as a university lecturer in education. In 1890 he was appointed principal of the Free Church Training College, Aberdeen, and in 1898 became rector of the Free Church Training College, Glasgow. Here his connexion with university teaching began, for he then held the lecturership in education in the university of Glasgow.

The year 1897 was noteworthy in Adams's career; he not only had the local distinction of being president (from 1896) of the Educational Institute of Scotland, but gained much wider fame by the publication of a provocative little book the forbidding title of which, *Herbartian Psychology applied to Education*, belied the sprightliness of its contents.

The year 1902 was another important landmark in Adams's career. He visited Canada; published an account of the Protestant schools of the province of Quebec; was appointed principal of the London Day Training College; and became the first professor of education in the university of London. For the next twenty years London was the main field of his labours. He was pre-eminently the teacher of London teachers—not only teachers in training, but also teachers at work. For he lectured abundantly in the evenings as well as in the day-time. After he had, in 1922, retired from training college work and become emeritus professor, he set out on his journeys overseas, and by the delivery of series of lectures in the United States of America, South Africa, Australia, and New Zealand he became an international figure in the world of education.

Adams published many books, the most important of which, in addition to *Herbartian Psychology*, are *Exposition and Illustration in Teaching* (1909), *The Evolution of Educational Theory* (1912), *The Student's Guide* (1917), and *Everyman's Psychology* (1929). All these works, like his lectures, are characterized by an easy style, a shrewd wisdom, and a 'pawky' humour.

Adams was singularly happy in his marriage in 1893 to Agnes Anne, youngest daughter of John Cook, of Ashley, Aberdeen. There were no children. In 1925 he was knighted for his services to education, and the honorary degree of LL.D. was conferred upon him by St. Andrews University.

As a lecturer Adams was a memorable figure. His impressive bald head, his Scottish accent, his clear, incisive style, and particularly his sly humour, rendered him attractive to audiences all over the British Empire. He died suddenly, as the result of a stroke, at Los Angeles 30 September 1934.

[*The Times*, 2 October 1934; *Times Educational Supplement*, 6 October 1934; Records of the Educational Institute of Scotland; Sir Michael Sadler, *John Adams* (University of London Institute of Education, Studies and Reports, No. vi), 1935; personal knowledge.]

P. B. BALLARD.

A E (pseudonym), Irish writer. [See RUSSELL, GEORGE WILLIAM.]

ALEXANDER, SAMUEL (1859–1938), philosopher, the third son and fourth child of Samuel Alexander, an Australian, by his wife, Eliza Sloman, who came from Cape Town, was born at Sydney, New South Wales, 6 January 1859. His father, a saddler, died of consumption at the age of thirty-eight, shortly before his birth. His mother died in his house at Manchester in 1917, having gone to live with him there, with the rest of her family, in 1903. About 1863 the family left Sydney for St. Kilda, a suburb of Melbourne, and Alexander, after a varied early schooling, entered Wesley College, Melbourne, in 1871. There, and in his two years at the university of Melbourne, where he held an exhibition, he gained all the distinctions open to him. In 1877, without completing his degree, he sailed for England on a voyage lasting 108 days, with the express purpose, bold in view of the family finances, of winning a scholarship at Oxford or Cambridge. Being advised that a scholarship at Balliol College, Oxford, might be beyond his reach, he prudently entered for one at Lincoln College as well, and did not succeed. But he won his scholarship at Balliol. Lincoln made amends by electing him to a fellowship in 1882. Its choice was amply justified by the sustained distinction of Alexander's undergraduate career, for he obtained first classes in mathematical and classical moderations (1879) and in *literae humaniores* (1881). According to the *Jewish Chronicle* (5 May 1882) this was the first election of a professing Jew to a fellowship in either of the ancient English universities.

Alexander retained his fellowship for eleven years, residing in Oxford except for the period between the end of 1888 and the June of 1891. The break, originally designed to be permanent, was due partly to his desire to mingle with a wider world, partly to his determination to increase his proficiency in experimental psychology. In pursuit of the latter aim he studied under Hugo Münsterberg at Freiburg-im-Breisgau; in pursuit of the former, he lectured at Toynbee Hall, Whitechapel, and busied himself in other ways with the popularization of academic subjects. These activities grew out of the settled policy of his mind, in or out of Oxford. In Oxford he was one of the rebels who thought that the course in 'Greats' needed quickening from modern science, especially psychology. He lectured on that subject to any, dons or undergraduates, who were sufficiently interested to attend supernumerary courses. The same policy directed Alexander's occasional writings and his first book, *Moral Order and Progress* (1889), an expansion of his essay for the Green moral philosophy prize which he had won in 1887. It may still be what in its day it was widely believed to be, the best systematic general treatise on evolutionary ethics in the English language. In his preface Alexander expressed his 'present dissent from Green's fundamental principles' and added: 'I have come to the ideas, borrowed from biology and the theory of evolution, which are prevalent in modern ethics, with a training derived from Aristotle and Hegel, and I have found, not antagonism but, on the whole, fulfilment.'

In 1893 Alexander became professor of philosophy at the university of Manchester, where he taught for thirty-one years. It was a happy appointment. Even the physical climate of 'dear old sooty Manchester' was tolerably congenial to him. In its university, while he had rather too many courses to give, their variety stimulated him, and, his classes being small, he could think aloud as he lectured. His academic influence soon extended far beyond his lecture-room. Indeed, he was of the stuff of which legends are made in advance of the subject's actions. His width of interests, his unstudied, notorious, picturesque untidiness, his catholic understanding of whatever was young almost compelled this result. Long before he reached the peak of his fame he had become a focus for admiration and for vast affection in the university and in the city. He was prominent in the university's more public activities, especially in the movement for providing university residences for women. In an extra-academic way his feminist principles made him favour the cause, although not always the tactics, of the lively local advocates of women's suffrage.

As the years passed, many of his friends began to fear that Alexander's wide knowledge and his highly original powers would never find expression in print. A very few articles and an admirable little book on *Locke* (1908) were inadequate counter-evidence. By 1907, however, according to his own modest statement, he had come to believe that he might have something to say. He took his cue, in a measure, from the 'realist' principle of Dr. G. E. Moore's 'Refutation of Idealism' (*Mind*, 1903), but unlike many contemporary 'realists' was never content with polemical forays into the theory of knowledge. He was always bent upon a comprehensive system of ontological metaphysics, and this attitude, at the time, raised exceptional interest and expectation in the small world of technical British philosophy. The interest grew as Alexander in a series of presidential addresses to the Aristotelian Society (1908–1911: he was again president, 1936–1937) and in articles in *Mind* (1912–1913) attempted the exploratory work which, as he always maintained, should precede the composition of a serious philosophical treatise. When the university of Glasgow, shortly before the war of 1914–1918, invited him to become its Gifford lecturer, there was a general belief that he would use the opportunity to complete the huge task for which he had been preparing so sedulously for at least seven years.

An elaborate essay, *The Basis of Realism*, published for the British Academy in 1914, the year after he had been elected a fellow of that body, is an admirable summary of the results which Alexander had reached during this preparatory period. The Gifford lectures themselves, given in the war years 1917 and 1918, were called 'Space, Time, and Deity'. Strenuously revised, but not very much altered, they were published under the same title (although Alexander much preferred the hyphenated form 'space-time') in two substantial volumes in 1920. By that time the issue of 'realism' had become subordinate in the author's philosophy, although, if the name matters, he remained a realist, holding that mind takes its place among the differentiated compresents in space-time. Primarily Alexander was a metaphysician who attempted to describe and 'identify in concrete experience' 'the ultimates which the sciences left over'. Whatever is, he maintained, is a specification of space-time, either a 'categorial' (or wholly pervasive) attribute of space-

time, or, like the neural process which is 'enjoyed' as personal experience, something 'empirical' (i.e. non-pervasive) which nevertheless evolves or 'emerges' from the 'continuum of motions' which is the ultimate matrix space-time. Deity is the stage beyond mind, as yet unaccomplished but descriptive of a nisus in space-time towards a specific accomplishment which, just because it expresses the march of things, should receive the reverent acquiescence of 'natural piety'.

The value of the book has to be estimated by the vision, skill, and resolution with which it pursued its sweeping design. It is only accurate to say that, after Hobbes, no English philosopher, before Alexander, had built in accordance with so ambitious an architectural plan or had given comparable attention to the proportion and solidity of all the parts of his edifice. In less than a decade the general opinion was that the book marked the end of an epoch rather than a fresh beginning, and Alexander himself considered that the future was with A. N. Whitehead, rather than with himself, so far as such a philosophy had a future. He preferred to let his book stand with very few published afterthoughts, although his essay on *Spinoza and Time* (1921) is an important supplement. Probably several decades must elapse before a verdict can be given with the relative finality which such cases permit. Whatever that later verdict may be, it is undeniable, in the interim, that Alexander was a great philosophical architect whose skill and resourcefulness deserve abiding recognition. In himself he was modest although not self-depreciating. He wrote and planned in the grand manner simply because no other manner suited his theme.

Alexander resigned his chair in 1924, but continued to reside in Manchester in honoured and busy tranquillity. Manchester's pride in him seemed to increase with his years. In its university he presented for honorary degrees until 1930, in a memorably delightful way. His fairly frequent public lectures were eagerly attended in Manchester and elsewhere. At philosophical congresses he held as of right the unofficial position of the foremost British philosopher, distinguished in appearance, matter, manner, and beauty of voice, sensitive to the meeting's mind, and overcoming the lifelong handicap of his deafness in the most charming manner imaginable. His main interest in these closing years was in literature and aesthetic theory. This is shown in several of the essays published after his death in *Philosophical and Literary Pieces* (1939) and in his last book, *Beauty and Other Forms of Value* (1933). Here, despite the perils of a refractory and elusive subject, Alexander's delicate ear for verbal music, his love of the illuminating magic of appropriate imagery, and his vivid psychological interest in the mind and methods of great artists in many spheres of art made his book, if not altogether great, something more than merely a great man's book.

Alexander died at Manchester 13 September 1938, and his ashes lie in the section reserved for the British Jewish Reform Congregation in Manchester Southern cemetery. He was unmarried. He received honorary degrees from the universities of St. Andrews, Durham, Oxford, Birmingham, Liverpool, and Cambridge, and was appointed to the Order of Merit in 1930. He was elected an honorary fellow of Lincoln College in 1918 and of Balliol College in 1925. In the latter year his friends presented him with a bust by Jacob Epstein: it is now in the hall of the Arts Building of Manchester University.

[*The Times*, 14 September 1938; *The Times Literary Supplement*, 23 March 1940; J. Laird, *Samuel Alexander, 1859–1938* in *Proceedings* of the British Academy, vol. xxiv, 1938; Memoir prefixed to *Philosophical and Literary Pieces* (containing a bibliography); private information; personal knowledge.]

JOHN LAIRD.

ALLEN, PERCY STAFFORD (1869–1933), president of Corpus Christi College, Oxford, and Erasmian scholar, was born at Twickenham 7 July 1869, the younger son and fourth child of Joseph Allen, a London bill-broker, by his wife, Mary, youngest daughter of Hans David Christopher Satow, and sister of the diplomatist and historian Sir E. M. Satow [q.v.]. Percy Allen was educated at Clifton, and at Corpus Christi College, Oxford, where he was a scholar. He obtained a first class in classical moderations in 1890 and a second class in *literae humaniores* in 1892. In 1893 he travelled with a pupil in Australia and New Zealand. Returning to Oxford at the end of that year, he won the chancellor's prize for a Latin essay in the summer of 1894. In 1896 he became a master at Magdalen School, Oxford, and in 1897 was appointed professor of history in the Government College at Lahore. In the summer of 1898 he visited England, marrying in September his cousin, Helen Mary, daughter of Arthur John Allen, of Chislehurst. They had one child, who died at birth. The climate of India seriously affected the health both of himself and his wife, and in 1901 he resigned his Lahore professorship and returned to Oxford, where the rest of his life was spent. In 1908 he was elected to a fellowship at Merton, which he held for sixteen years, and he was elected an honorary fellow in 1925. In 1924 he was elected president of Corpus. He received honorary degrees from several British and foreign universities, was elected a fellow of the British Academy in 1923, and was a foreign, honorary, or extraordinary member of several Dutch and Belgian academies and learned societies. He died at Oxford 16 June 1933.

Allen's name will always be associated with his masterly edition of the Letters of Erasmus, *Opus Epistolarum Des. Erasmi Roterodami*, of which the first volume appeared in 1906 and the eighth was published posthumously in 1934; he left it to Mrs. Allen (his collaborator since 1922) and Mr. Heathcote William Garrod to complete the last three volumes, for which he had collected the materials, but without furnishing commentary and introductions (vol. ix appeared in 1938, vol. x in 1941, vol. xi in 1947). Allen's interest in Erasmus dated from 1892, when, immediately after taking his first degree, he competed, unsuccessfully, for the chancellor's English essay prize. The subject was Erasmus. A year later (1893–1894) he attended for two successive terms Froude's lectures on 'The Life and Letters of Erasmus'. Froude influenced him profoundly. To the end, he maintained that the *Life and Letters* (published in 1894) was better than any other book on Erasmus. On the day on which Froude died, he began to read the *History of England*; and he was never willing to listen to disparagement of it. His first published book was a volume of *Selections from the Writings of James Anthony Froude*, which appeared in 1901. His errorless scholarship and his gentle, impartial temper make his admiration for Froude seem paradoxical. But he was a man incapable of paradox. The truth is that, on the main issues of the Reformation, he thought that Froude was right.

During his four years in India Froude and Erasmus were always with Allen. While at Lahore he was already projecting his edition of Erasmus's correspondence, for which, indeed, he had made extensive collections in the libraries of Holland and

Germany between the years 1893 and 1896. After his return to Oxford in 1901, he spent the summer of every year (the years of the war of 1914–1918 only excepted) in the libraries of the continent, collating all the known material and bringing to light an immense amount of material hitherto unknown. Every letter was copied fair in the library where the manuscript of it (or the first printed text) was to be found. The copy so made became the 'printer's copy', with no intervening transcript. The proof of each letter was always corrected in the library where the original copy had been made. In the decipherment of difficult fifteenth- and sixteenth-century hands Allen had no rival. There resulted a critical edition of the letters of Erasmus which is perhaps the most accurate book in the world. Text apart, it is, in its commentary and introduction, a treasure-house of unborrowed learning. Nobody knew the texts of the Reformation so well as Allen. To nobody were the lives of the great and little men of the period so intimately familiar. The commentary is full of biographical notices which array in brief all the available material. Often the persons whose lives or works are sketched are persons obscure or insignificant. But Allen knew them and their writings, and anything that anybody else had written about them, at first hand. It was not for nothing that Ingram Bywater [q.v.] in 1915 called him 'the most learned man in Oxford'. The *Opus Epistolarum* is, in truth, one of the great monuments of English learning. As a commentary on the Reformation it has the defect, perhaps, of leaving too much to the reader. Allen was unwilling to make historical judgements, or moral judgements. The student will not discover from Allen (although he may do so from the *Letters*) what kind of a man Erasmus was, or anybody connected with him. The material for judgement is there; but it is presented with a scrupulosity and bareness which sometimes achieves the effect of a *suppressio veri*. Often the reader sighs for something of Froude's partisanship.

Besides the *Opus Epistolarum* Allen published, in 1914, eleven lectures on *The Age of Erasmus*. In 1929 he and his wife edited the *Letters of Richard Fox, 1486–1527*, the correspondence of the founder of Corpus. In 1934 appeared posthumously another volume of Erasmian studies, *Erasmus: Lectures and Wayfaring Sketches*. In 1939 a selection of his letters was pub-

lished, the greater number of them addressed to his lifelong friend Sir Aurel Stein. The letters exhibit happily a scholar of single-minded devotion and a man of lovable and saintly character.

A portrait of Allen, painted by Herbert Olivier in 1929, hangs in the president's lodgings at Corpus Christi College.

[H. W. Garrod, *Percy Stafford Allen, 1869–1933* in *Proceedings* of the British Academy, vol. xix, 1933; *Oxford Magazine*, 12 October 1933; *Letters of P. S. Allen*, edited by H. M. Allen, 1939; P. S. Allen's diaries; personal knowledge.]   H. W. GARROD.

ALLEN, REGINALD CLIFFORD, BARON ALLEN OF HURTWOOD (1889–1939), labour politician, was born at Newport, Monmouthshire, 9 May 1889, the elder son of Walter Allen, a Newport draper, by his wife, Frances Augusta Baker. He was educated at Berkhamsted School, University College, Bristol, and Peterhouse, Cambridge. His political interests were first aroused by hearing J. Keir Hardie [q.v.] as a boy at Newport; and at Cambridge he was chairman of the University Fabian Society. In 1911 he was appointed secretary and general manager of the first official labour daily newspaper, the *Daily Citizen*, until it ceased in 1915. He was also chairman of the University Socialist Federation from 1912 to 1915.

In November 1914 he was one of the founders and the chairman of the 'No Conscription Fellowship', the members of which opposed the military service acts and refused service in the armed forces, some, like Allen, also refusing to perform 'alternative service', on conscientious grounds. While chairman of the fellowship (1914–1918) he was three times imprisoned during the years 1916 and 1917, and the hunger strikes which he sustained almost cost him his life and certainly undermined a naturally frail physique.

In 1920 Allen visited Russia as a member of a delegation representing the independent labour party, of which he was an active officer, serving (1922–1926) as chairman and treasurer, and as chairman of the *New Leader*, its official weekly journal. He contributed by counsel, speech, and pen to the 'Socialism in Our Time' propaganda which the independent labour party conducted in the 'twenties. So long as the official labour movement was solely responsible for its publication he was a director of the *Daily Herald* (1925–1930).

When the labour government dissolved in 1931, Allen joined Ramsay MacDonald in the national labour organization, and approved its collaboration in the 'national' government formed in that year; he was raised to the peerage as Baron Allen of Hurtwood, in Surrey, in 1932. He was a keen and informed supporter of the League of Nations and severed his connexion with the national labour group in 1936, owing to disagreement on this aspect of international policy. After meeting Hitler and Göring in Berlin, in 1935, Allen wrote and spoke extensively in favour of collective security.

Intensely interested in educational affairs, Allen of Hurtwood was chairman of the executive of the Home and School Council and chairman of the New Schools Association. He married in 1921 Marjory, second daughter of George Joseph Gill, and with her conducted a co-educational school on modern lines near Guildford. He published various political works, a preface to *Conscription and Conscience* (1922), *Putting Socialism into Practice* (1924), *Socialism and the next Labour Government* (1925), *Labour's Future at Stake* (1932), *Britain's Political Future* (1934), and *Peace in Our Time* (1936), in addition to many articles in newspapers and reviews.

Suffering from a complete breakdown in 1938, Allen of Hurtwood was taken to Switzerland, and died at Montana-Vermala 3 March 1939. After cremation his ashes, at his own request, were scattered in the Lake of Geneva. His only child was a daughter and the peerage therefore became extinct.

A portrait of Allen of Hurtwood, by Colin Gill, is at Hurtwood House, Albury, Guildford.

[*The Times*, 4 March 1939; private information; personal knowledge.]

J. S. MIDDLETON.

ALLENBY, EDMUND HENRY HYNMAN, first VISCOUNT ALLENBY OF MEGIDDO (1861–1936), field-marshal, was born 23 April 1861 on the estate of his maternal grandfather, Brackenhurst, near Southwell, Nottinghamshire. He was the eldest son and second child of Hynman Allenby, a country gentleman, by his wife, Catherine Anne, daughter of the Rev. Thomas Coats Cane. From the year of their marriage (1859) until that of Edmund's birth his parents had lived at Dartmouth. Soon afterwards they purchased Felixstowe House, in Suffolk, and West Bilney Lodge,

with a considerable estate, in Norfolk. The family thenceforth spent spring and summer at Felixstowe, autumn and winter at West Bilney. Young Allenby grew up in close contact with the life and sport of the countryside. He rode, shot, fished, and sailed, and he early acquired the ornithological and botanical interests which were to remain with him all his life.

Allenby was educated at Haileybury, a new public school founded the year after his birth, and at the Royal Military College, Sandhurst. It had been his original intention to enter the Indian civil service, but he failed to pass the entrance examinations in 1879 and 1880, when there were vacancies for only about one-seventh of the candidates. His next choice was the army. He was not particularly distinguished at work or sport at Haileybury but he passed well into and out of Sandhurst, where he was an under-officer in his last term. In May 1882 he was gazetted to a commission in the Inniskillings (6th Dragoons). He was then a big, strong, good-looking young man, somewhat clumsy in build, although his weight did not increase unduly to his dying day. His eye had been trained for observation of country, and he possessed a strong and dominating character, physical and moral courage, and presence of mind, so that he had good prospects in his career.

The Inniskillings were stationed in South Africa, and Allenby gained invaluable experience in two little expeditions, both bloodless, or nearly so, into Bechuanaland (1884–1885) and Zululand (1888), as well as knowledge of people and country which were to serve him well later on. In 1886 he went home for two years' service at the cavalry depot at Canterbury. He was promoted captain early in 1888, the year of his return, and appointed adjutant next year. It was noted by his brother officers that the new responsibility not only made him take his profession much more seriously but also induced a certain grimness of disposition.

The regiment returned to England in 1890, and in 1896 Allenby passed into the Staff College, by competition, at a time when few cavalrymen entered except by nomination. He made no outstanding mark in his military studies but was popular with his fellow students, and was elected master of the drag hounds in preference to Douglas (afterwards Earl) Haig, a better horseman than himself. He passed out with a good report. While at

Camberley he had been promoted major in May 1897, and qualified as an army interpreter in French. He had also married, in 1896, Adelaide Mabel, daughter of Horace Edward Chapman, of Donhead House, Salisbury. In March 1898 he became what would now be termed brigade-major but was then termed adjutant to the 3rd Cavalry brigade at the Curragh, in Ireland. While he was holding this appointment his only child, a son, was born.

Allenby rejoined his regiment the following year on the outbreak of the South African war. Shrewd and cautious, with knowledge of the character and qualities of his adversary, he fell into none of the traps laid by the Boers, and it was due to his good work in the operations round Colesberg that his squadron was chosen as part of the cavalry division formed under General French for the relief of Kimberley in the early part of 1900. In the numerous small actions or marches with convoys his losses were small.

Early in 1900 Allenby assumed temporary command of his regiment at Bloemfontein and with it took part in the main advance to Pretoria. His great chance came with the final period between January 1901 and May of the following year, when the Boers remaining under arms had been reduced to a handful of picked men, not exceeding 50,000 even at the outset, yet brilliantly manœuvred against the numerous columns sent out to round them up and to clear the country. In these trying operations he commanded a column, generally of two regiments of cavalry, artillery, and half a battalion of infantry. He suffered no reverse and never lost a convoy, and at the end of the war had established a sound if not a spectacular reputation. He received brevet promotion to colonel and was appointed C.B.

Allenby began his home service, which was to last until the outbreak of war twelve years later, in command of the 5th Royal Irish Lancers at Colchester. In October 1905, as a brigadier-general, he took over command of the 4th Cavalry brigade. In September 1909 he was promoted major-general, and after some six months on half-pay, during which he visited South Africa, was appointed inspector-general of cavalry. So far he had been generally popular in the army and with his subordinates, but his always high temper was now becoming even less under control and his roughness of manner was unwelcome to the staffs and regi-

mental officers. On the outbreak of war in 1914 he was appointed to the command of the unwieldy cavalry division, of which the brigades had seldom trained together, to accompany the British Expeditionary Force to France.

Allenby's conduct of his command in the retreat from Mons is a matter which has aroused controversy. By some he is held to have displayed weakness in losing control of a large proportion of it, while others consider that circumstances would have been too much for any commander in his position. It is universally acknowledged, however, that he showed coolness and resolution throughout and that the rear and flanks of the retreating British infantry corps were effectively protected from a superior force of German cavalry. In the advance to the Aisne the cavalry was handled with a prudence approaching timidity, but that was in part founded on orders from British headquarters and in part upon reactions from previous overconfidence, in which, however, Allenby himself had never shared.

Five British cavalry brigades were now formed into two divisions of more manageable size, and after the transfer of the Expeditionary Force from the Aisne to Flanders these became the Cavalry Corps, to the command of which Allenby was appointed. In the first battle of Ypres (19 October–22 November) the cavalry performed magnificent service. One of the decisive elements in the British defence proved to be the skill of the dismounted trooper with the rifle, for which the former inspector-general must be given at least part of the credit. In fighting of this nature there was little that a corps commander could effect beyond maintaining a reserve for the ugliest situations, and this Allenby contrived to do. On 6 May 1915 he took over command of the V Corps in the midst of the second battle of Ypres, which had opened with the German gas attack. Later in the year he carried out local operations in support of offensives farther south, but his efforts were rendered abortive by superior German observation and equipment.

In October 1915 Allenby was appointed to the command of the newly formed Third Army north of the Somme. He was not, however, destined to take part in the battle, as in the following March his army side-slipped northward to relieve the French in front of Arras. He was by this time identified with the costly and somewhat unimaginative methods on which the offensives and counter-attacks had been conducted, but it should be recognized that his loyalty to his superiors was so complete that he always fulfilled his orders to the letter and allowed no criticism even in the bosom of his own military family, his staff. His nickname of 'the Bull', dating from days of peace, had by now become universal.

The outstanding episode in Allenby's military career in Europe was the battle of Arras in 1917. The plan had been to a certain extent compromised by the German retreat to the Hindenburg Line, which extended on its northern flank to the front of his right corps and necessitated an improvisation of dispositions prejudicial to its chances of success. In an effort to obtain a measure of surprise Allenby had decided to cut down the length of the preliminary bombardment, at the same time intensifying it by increasing the rate of fire. This project met with objections from general headquarters resulting in a compromise by which the bombardment was to cover four days instead of the forty-eight hours proposed by him. As the attack was postponed by one day to suit the French, the bombardment was in fact increased to five days. The object of the Third Army's offensive was to break the German defences between Arras and Cambrai while the First Army on the left captured the Vimy ridge. The attack was launched on Easter Monday, 9 April, a day punctuated by squalls of snow and sleet, which, however, blew in the faces of the enemy. Although the right-hand corps made only limited progress, the main attack on the first day was remarkably successful. The maximum advance, just north of the Scarpe, was three and a half miles, believed to be the longest carried out by any belligerent on the western front since trench warfare had set in. As so often in that war, however, the success was not exploited. The complete breach through which it had been hoped to pass the Cavalry Corps was never fully opened or cleared of wire. The Germans made a partial recovery and brought up some reinforcements. The fighting degenerated into costly local actions, until Field-Marshal Sir Douglas Haig, the commander-in-chief, ordered a pause on the 14th to reorganize for a further co-ordinated attack. This, known officially as the second battle of the Scarpe, was launched on 23 April and achieved only limited success after very heavy fighting. A third attempt, on 3 May (the third battle of the Scarpe), was disastrous. Against Allenby's will the assault was carried out in darkness, and the half-trained reinforcements with which the ranks of the divisions had been filled fell into confusion.

Meanwhile a new commander was wanted in Palestine, where the British had suffered a sharp check in April in front of Gaza. Allenby was known as a man of abounding energy and it was considered that he would be more likely to give of his best outside the orbit of Haig. The two men were uncongenial to each other and Allenby always felt himself tongue-tied in the presence of the commander-in-chief. He assumed command of the Egyptian Expeditionary Force at the end of June 1917, and, as soon as the move could be carried out, transferred general headquarters to the Palestine border, close behind the front. He came like a fresh breeze to the somewhat dispirited troops. As he drove from camp to camp for brief visits of inspection he contrived to impress his personality upon them. The independently minded Australians took to him at once and gave him their full confidence. It was a promising beginning to his command. He received most of the reinforcements which he demanded, bringing his army to a strength of seven infantry and three mounted divisions.

Allenby's plan, largely based upon an appreciation put forward by Lieutenant-General Sir Philip Chetwode, and the work of his staff officer, Brigadier-General Guy Payan Dawnay, was to capture Beersheba, on the Turkish left, then roll up the enemy's centre and net the largest possible proportion of the forces between it and the coast by a sweep with his three mounted divisions. It was a difficult operation in which every move depended upon the capture of water supplies for men, horses, and camels. The attack on Beersheba began on 31 October. The opening stages of the offensive were brilliantly successful, but, as so often happens in a campaign of this type, there were some delays and the cavalry became more dispersed than was desirable. As a consequence, although the Turks suffered heavily, their main body escaped envelopment. Meanwhile, however, Allenby's left had broken through at Gaza. He immediately transferred all available transport to this flank, leaving much of the rest of the force temporarily immobilized round the railhead, and drove the enemy northward up the Philistine plain, beyond Jaffa, to the Nahr el Auja.

Allenby then decided to wheel a strong force into the hills and capture Jerusalem —which for religious and political reasons it was important not to harm—by envelopment between this force and another advancing northward from Beersheba up the road through Hebron. He penetrated without excessive difficulty almost to the Nablus road, but then his XXI Corps and Yeomanry mounted division became involved in fierce and bloody fighting. To the east progress was blocked; to the north the thinly held British flank was fiercely counter-attacked by the able and energetic hostile commander-in-chief, General (Marshal in the Turkish army) von Falkenhayn. Floods in the plain delayed the movement of supplies. But the flank held and the supply situation gradually improved. Allenby brought up the XX Corps. Another assault proved successful, and on 9 December Jerusalem was surrendered intact to Allenby, who made his impressive ceremonial entry on foot into the holy city on 11 December. During the following days a counter-offensive was defeated and the front advanced to a distance sufficiently far north and east of the city to ensure its safety. The Turks had suffered some 28,000 casualties, almost half as many again as those of the British.

Allenby was called upon by the government to exploit his success to the extent of driving Turkey right out of the war, but his attitude was cautious. Storms prevented the unloading of supplies on the coast. Railway construction was required. While it was in progress he proposed to operate against the enemy beyond Jordan, on the Hejaz railway. His plans were finally approved, but all hope of a major offensive early in 1918 was removed by the success of the German offensives of March and April in France. Heavy demands fell upon the Egyptian Expeditionary Force for reinforcements. Two whole divisions, nine yeomanry regiments, twenty-three infantry battalions, heavy artillery, machine-gun battalions, etc., were withdrawn. Their place was taken by two Indian divisions, and by Indian cavalry regiments and infantry battalions, the latter being in many cases raw and without experienced officers or specialists. The spring and summer were occupied in reorganization and training, and it was not until mid-September that Allenby was ready for his next main stroke. His operations beyond Jordan were not particularly successful, but they caused acute anxiety to the new Turkish commander-in-chief, the German Liman von Sanders. Allenby accentuated this by keeping a strong force in the low-lying Jordan valley despite its torrid heat and other discomforts.

On his arrival Allenby had taken over from his predecessor and strengthened the policy of assisting the Arabs in the Hejaz and Trans-Jordan in revolt against the Turks. He worked through a body of able officers, of whom the most outstanding was Colonel T. E. Lawrence [q.v.]. Much had already been effected in breaching the Hejaz railway and locking up garrisons at Medina, Ma'an, and elsewhere along the line. In his final offensive he called upon the Arabs, now partly organized as semi-regular forces, to keep the Turks engaged round the vital station of Der'a, the junction of the Hejaz and Palestinian systems, to interrupt the traffic in any case, and if possible to block it altogether. It was the one key objective which he could not reach quickly himself. Arab activity also increased Turkish fears of a British thrust on this flank, and they were strengthened by a number of skilful ruses.

It was actually Allenby's intention to attack on the left, in the coastal plain, massing the bulk of his forces of all arms in that sector, carrying out with the infantry of the XXI Corps a huge right wheel to drive the enemy into the hills and open a gateway for three cavalry divisions concentrated immediately in the rear. These were to cross the Samarian ridge which ends with Mount Carmel above the Bay of Acre, sweep down into the Plain of Esdraelon (or Megiddo), and pass through the Valley of Jezreel down to the Jordan near Beisan, thus throwing a net round the Turkish armies. Allenby possessed a superiority of four to one in cavalry, about six to four—the exact figures on the Turkish side are still a matter of dispute—in infantry, and nearly three to two in artillery. He had complete command of the air, so that his concentration could be carried out unobserved. His troops were fit and well found, whereas the Turks were ill supplied and ragged.

The assault was launched at 4.30 a.m. on 19 September with complete success. The two leading cavalry divisions entered the gateway before 9 a.m. They carried out their great drive against only scattered opposition. The hostile commander-in-chief was surprised in his headquarters at

Nazareth and narrowly escaped capture in person. The 4th Cavalry division reached Beisan after covering over seventy miles in thirty-four hours. The Turkish forces west of Jordan were almost completely destroyed. Their transport was smashed by the Royal Air Force in defiles. Those down the Hejaz railway were trapped at Amman, and those east of Jordan harried and hunted by the Arabs. The remnant streamed north towards Damascus. Allenby ordered the cavalry to push on to that city, the Arabs moving parallel to its right flank. Damascus was entered on 1 October. Already malaria was taking a heavy toll, as Allenby had known would be the case when he left an area in which precautions had been taken for country in which there had been none. A wave of influenza followed. Allenby sent on his fittest cavalry division, the 5th, which captured Homs and Tripoli and entered Aleppo on 26 October. Almost immediately afterwards an armistice was signed with Turkey in Mudros harbour on 30 October. Allenby had captured 75,000 prisoners, 360 guns, and taken or destroyed all the enemy's transport. His own casualties were 5,666.

It was the last great campaign of cavalry employed in strategic mass in the annals of war, and one of the most notable. That fact alone would suffice to render Allenby's name immortal. The distances covered were enormous. The 5th Cavalry division marched 550 miles in 38 days, fighting four considerable actions and losing only 21 per cent. of its horses from all causes—there never have been better horse-masters than Allenby's Indians, British yeomanry, Australians, and New Zealanders. And throughout the offensive his inspiration, thrustfulness, and the confidence which he inspired were priceless assets.

Many problems, chief among them the rivalry between French and Arab claims in Syria and the withdrawal of the Turks, were still to be solved, but Allenby was not left to deal with them for long. In March 1919 he was appointed special high commissioner for Egypt, where his former corps commander in Palestine, Lieutenant-General Sir E. S. Bulfin [q.v.], was engaged in stamping out a dangerous revolt. It was a difficult post because Egypt felt herself conscious of nationhood and had found a national champion in the person of the violent Saad Zaghlul. Allenby began with a disputed measure, for which he obtained the rather reluctant approval of the Foreign Office, the release of Zaghlul and three colleagues who had been arrested

and deported to Malta. In September of that year he went on leave to England, which he had not seen since June 1917. He was fêted as one of the great victors of the war. He had already been promoted field-marshal (July 1919); he was now created a viscount (October 1919), received the thanks of parliament, and was given a grant of £50,000, while during the war he had been appointed K.C.B. (1915), G.C.M.G. (1917), and G.C.B. (1918). The allied countries had bestowed upon him their principal decorations. Among the universities which conferred honorary degrees upon him were Oxford, Cambridge, Edinburgh, and Aberdeen. In 1920 he was made colonel of the 1st Life Guards, which included the court appointment of Gold Stick in Waiting.

Back in Egypt, Allenby carried through his task grimly and in face of difficulties in the country and differences of opinion with the Foreign Office. He produced, and persuaded the British government to accept, a declaration abolishing the protectorate and recognizing Egypt as a sovereign state in February 1922. The end of his tenure of office was clouded by the murder of Sir Lee Stack [q.v.], the sirdar, and his indifferent relations with the then foreign secretary, Mr. (afterwards Sir) Austen Chamberlain [q.v.], which brought about his resignation. He left Egypt in June 1925. There may still be discussion as to the value of his work there and by some he is considered to have committed grave mistakes, but on balance the view must be favourable. His moral courage and integrity and his grip of the essence of the Egyptian problem cannot be questioned.

As a field-marshal Allenby remained theoretically on the active list, but the remainder of his life was spent in retirement. His chief public work was done as president (1930) of the British National Cadet Association, which owes him a deep debt. He was able to indulge to the full his hobby of bird-watching, and established an aviary in the small garden of his London home. He fished enthusiastically and travelled extensively. He died very suddenly in London, through the bursting of a blood-vessel in his brain, 14 May 1936. His ashes are buried in Westminster Abbey. His son Michael, a young man of the greatest promise, had been killed in action in France in 1917. His viscountcy passed by special remainder to his nephew, Dudley Jaffray Hynman Allenby (born 1903).

Allenby's worst foe was his violent temper, but he rarely punished except with his tongue, and, like Napoleon, constantly continued to employ men whom he had forcibly abused. It is also true to say that, although he never apologized for fits of unjustified anger, he often made amends for them. He was grateful for good service and generous in rewarding it, and in many respects kindly and thoughtful. Like some other famous soldiers he was devoted to children. The men who knew him best and were brought most closely in touch with him either in the army or during his six years in Egypt were his warmest admirers, and on them he left the impression of a great man. The worst error that can be made about him is to look upon him as an unimaginative, heavy-handed soldier on the western front and a brilliant and inspired soldier in Palestine. Doubtless he expanded and gained confidence in independent command, but essentially he remained the same. The difference was in the conditions. This is not to say that his plan and performance in Palestine, especially in the final offensive, were not masterly. As a man he was ever animated by the highest sense of duty, simple and sincere, thorough in everything. The strength of his character may be exemplified by the fact that he imposed upon himself restraint in indulgence in the pleasures of the table, to which he was at one time addicted, because he feared they were injuring his health, just as he gave up smoking because he thought the habit might affect his remarkable eyesight, which he considered a professional asset. Although he had never been a scholar he was a man of considerable cultivation, widely read, and a passable Grecian and Latinist. But the most significant thing to be said of him is that he stands in the tradition of the great cavalrymen and, if the term be confined to horsemen, that he is the last of the line.

A portrait of Allenby is included in J. S. Sargent's picture, 'Some General Officers of the Great War', painted in 1922. There is also a chalk drawing (likewise in the National Portrait Gallery) by Eric Kennington.

[*The Times*, 15 May 1936; Viscount Wavell, *Allenby: a Study in Greatness*, 2 vols., 1940–1943; Cyril Falls, (Official) *History of the Great War. Military Operations. France and Belgium, 1917*, 1940, and *Egypt and Palestine*, vol. ii, 1930; private information.]

CYRIL FALLS.

AMOS, SIR (PERCY) MAURICE (MACLARDIE) SHELDON (1872–1940), jurist and judge in Egypt, was born in London 15 June 1872, the only son of Sheldon Amos [q.v.], a judge of appeal in Egypt, and grandson of Andrew Amos [q.v.]. His mother was Sarah Maclardie, daughter of Thomas Perceval Bunting, of Manchester. After private education in Egypt and a brilliant career as a scholar of Trinity College, Cambridge—he was awarded a first class in both parts of the moral sciences tripos (1893 and 1895) and the Cobden prize (1895)—he was called to the bar by the Inner Temple in 1897. The chief part of his life was spent in Egypt where, in 1903, he was appointed a judge of the Cairo Native Court, and in 1906 was promoted to the Native Court of Appeal. In these offices, but quite apart from his ordinary judicial functions, he established close contact with the leaders of the French Law School and the foreign judges of the Egyptian mixed courts, and he took a prominent part in attacking administrative and social problems with which the country was beset. He retired from the bench in 1912 in consequence of a decision of his relating to an assault on an English child which, although creditable to his views as to equality of administration of the law, excited the disapprobation of the local English community.

For the next two years (1913–1915) Amos was director of the Khedivial School of Law. In 1915 he returned to England and accepted the post of adviser on foreign contracts to the Ministry of Munitions. His familiarity with the law and language of France and other countries made his work of great value to the government. In 1917 A. J. Balfour enlisted his services in a mission to the United States of America in connexion with the prosecution of the war, and his visit there sharpened his interest in the American constitution, which often formed the subject of lectures that he gave in later years. From 1917 to 1919 he was acting judicial adviser to the government of Egypt, and thereafter he returned to Cairo as judicial adviser and held this office until 1925. Here again he gave proof of his abilities by taking a prominent part in the discussions which led to the treaty of 1922 between Great Britain and Egypt which terminated the British protectorate and, subject to certain conditions, made Egypt an independent state. Another successful achievement was his work at the end of the war of 1914–1918 as counsel for Great Britain before a mixed arbitration tribunal at Constantinople; he was also the chief British delegate to the International Committee of Experts on Private Aerial Law from 1933 until his death.

Amos's later years were spent in England where he had a house in Cambridge and another at Ulpha, near Broughton-in-Furness. From 1932 to 1937 he held the Quain professorship of comparative law at University College, London. He was appointed K.B.E. in 1922, took silk in 1932, and in 1923 was awarded the grand cordon of the Order of the Nile. He received the honorary degree of LL.D. from Lausanne University in 1936. His chief publication is *The English Constitution* (1930). He married in 1906 Lucy, elder daughter of Colonel Sir Colin Campbell Scott-Moncrieff, R.E., and had two sons and three daughters. He died at Ulverston 10 June 1940.

The most impressive characteristics of Amos were his intense intellectual curiosity and the wide range of interest that was its natural consequence. His friends might occasionally differ from his point of view, but they could never ignore the arguments by which he supported it. Conversation with him, whether on professional or social topics, always provided a mental stimulus.

[*Journal of Comparative Law*, vol. xxii, 1940; personal knowledge.]

P. H. WINFIELD.

AMPTHILL, second BARON (1869–1935). [See RUSSELL, ARTHUR OLIVER VILLIERS.]

ANDERSON, STELLA (1892–1933), better known as STELLA BENSON, novelist, was born at Lutwyche Hall, Shropshire, 6 January 1892, the younger daughter and third child of Ralph Beaumont Benson, of Lutwyche Hall, by his wife, Caroline Essex, second daughter of Richard Hugh Cholmondeley, rector of Hodnet, later of Condover Hall, Shropshire, and younger sister of the novelist Mary Cholmondeley.

Being a delicate child Stella Benson was educated at home. After eighteen months spent in Switzerland she sailed in 1912 on a voyage to the West Indies, an experience which supplied the material for her first book, *I Pose* (1915). On her return (1913) she took up social work in Hoxton, where for a time she carried on a small business for the sale of paper bags in partnership with a local woman, finding time meanwhile to continue her writing and to take a part in the women's suffrage movement early in 1914.

During the war of 1914–1918 Stella Benson worked for eighteen months in east London and afterwards for a time on the land; but her health was never good and in 1918 she left England under doctor's orders for California. Here she stayed for two years, making many friends and supporting herself by a strange variety of occupations until in January 1920 she sailed for England by way of the East. On this adventurous journey she found herself teaching in a mission school in Hong-Kong, working in the X-ray department of the Rockefeller Institute in Peking, and escaping from the dangers of civil war in Chungking.

In September 1921 Stella Benson was married in London to James Carew O'Gorman Anderson, of the Chinese customs service, only surviving son of Brigadier-General Sir Francis Anderson, R.E., of Ballydavid, co. Waterford. There were no children of the marriage. With the exception of visits to England, the United States of America, and the Bahamas, the rest of her life was spent in China. Whilst living in Hong-Kong she helped to organize a successful campaign against the system of licensed prostitution then existent in that colony.

Between 1915 and 1931 Stella Benson published several novels, short stories, travel sketches, and poems, but her great popular success came with the appearance of *Tobit Transplanted* (1931), a novel which won for her in 1932 the Femina Vie Heureuse prize and the A. C. Benson silver medal of the Royal Society of Literature. She was now at the height of her powers, but in that same year she had a severe illness and she died of pneumonia at Hongay, Tongking, in northern Indo-China, 6 December 1933.

Stella Benson's genius is paradoxical; she combines fantasy with realism and satire with a profound pity. Her unfinished novel *Mundos* (published posthumously 1935) shows that had she lived she would have surpassed her already notable achievement. English literature is the poorer for her early death.

A portrait of Stella Benson by Cuthbert Orde is in the possession of her brother, Major George Reginald Benson, and Mr. J. C. O'G. Anderson owns two drawings by the same artist and a drawing by Wyndham Lewis.

[*The Times*, 8 December 1933; R. Ellis Roberts, *Portrait of Stella Benson*, 1939;

S. J. Kunitz and H. Haycraft, *Twentieth Century Authors; a Biographical Dictionary* (New York), 1942.]
                                    GEORGINA BATTISCOMBE.

ANDREWES, SIR FREDERICK WILLIAM (1859–1932), pathologist and bacteriologist, was born at Reading 31 March 1859, the eldest of the four sons of Charles James Andrewes, J.P., by his second wife, Charlotte Parsons. The father was engaged in business connected with ironworks and was a substantial and respected citizen of Reading, of which he was sometime mayor, but Andrewes held the opinion that his inheritance of special ability came chiefly from his mother's side.

Andrewes began his education at Oakley House School, Reading, and among his schoolfellows there were (Sir) Edward Bagnall Poulton, W. F. R. Weldon [q.v.], and (Sir) Owen Seaman [q.v.]. Andrewes formed then, and kept throughout his life, a special friendship with Poulton; they had like interests, as boys and young men, in field entomology and geology, and shared many expeditions in school holidays and, later, in vacations. Andrewes always retained these interests of a field naturalist, and Poulton records with pride that he was able later to include in the University Museum at Oxford entomological varieties of great interest which Andrewes had taken in school holidays when he was between thirteen and fourteen years old, showing thus precociously a skill and alertness of observation which were later to serve him well in other fields.

Andrewes entered Christ Church, Oxford, in 1879 as a junior student; his essay is said to have made an especially favourable impression upon his examiners. In 1881, with biology as his subject, he was placed alone in the first class of the final honours school of natural science. In 1883 he was awarded the Burdett-Coutts university scholarship in geology. In 1886 he was elected to the Sheppard fellowship at Pembroke College, the holder of which was under obligation to study either law or medicine. Owing to his biological background he had already chosen medicine as his career, having won an open entrance scholarship at St. Bartholomew's Hospital and entered upon his studies there in 1885.

After Andrewes had qualified in medicine he spent a short time in Vienna as a preliminary to entering upon a career as a consulting physician, graduating M.B. and becoming F.R.C.P. in 1895. Meanwhile he had become increasingly interested in pathology and bacteriology. The latter, undergoing vigorous development on the continent through the schools of Pasteur and Robert Koch, had reached Great Britain rather late, one of its pioneers in this country being Edward Emanuel Klein, who was lecturer on physiology at St. Bartholomew's Medical School. When Andrewes first made contact with the pathological laboratory there, in 1885, Klein was already examining material from the wards for the tubercle bacillus, discovered by Koch some three years earlier. In 1893 Alfredo Auturus Kanthack was appointed lecturer in pathology and pathologist to the hospital, and Andrewes worked in increasingly close association with him until, on Kanthack's departure to Cambridge in 1897, Andrewes was appointed to succeed him.

During the thirty years (1897–1927) in which he held the post of lecturer in pathology (which was raised to that of professor by the university of London in 1912) at St. Bartholomew's Hospital, Andrewes saw the department change from a single laboratory to a separate building with three floors of laboratories and an additional one for post-mortem examinations. His tenure of office had begun at a time when pathology, and especially the new science of bacteriology, were developing an essential relation to public health and to clinical medicine, and he was an important agent of that development. His reputation, which grew steadily with the years, depended more on his influence as a teacher, on his wide knowledge and experience, and on his care and wisdom as an expert and consultant on special problems, than on such new developments of knowledge as arose from the researches which he had always in hand. On the side of pathology he added something of permanent value to the differential histology of lymphadenoma and to a more exact knowledge of arteriosclerosis. In bacteriology he took particular interest in variations within a bacterial species, as recognized by reactions with specific, immune sera. During the war of 1914–1918 he made a valuable classification on these lines of the variant strains of dysentery bacilli, and at the time of his death in London, 24 February 1932, was engaged upon a similar but more complex problem, presented by the haemolytic streptococci. At an earlier stage he had been one of the first to recognize the importance of healthy or mildly affected persons as carriers of such infections as that of diphtheria.

Andrewes was a man of quiet, friendly personality, readily accessible, generous with his help, and prone to flavour his wisdom with a sly humour. Throughout life, in work and recreation, his instinct and habit were those of a born naturalist; in his later years especially, these tastes found expression in the creation and tending of a rock-garden, well known to all his friends. He had a great gift for the effective, though apparently free and informal, exposition of intricate problems, and was known as a forceful lecturer outside his own department. To the Royal College of Physicians he delivered the Dobell (1906) and the Croonian (1910) lectures, as well as the Harveian oration (1920). His deep knowledge and wide experience made him a valuable member of various public committees and of the Medical Research Council. In 1919 he was appointed O.B.E. in recognition of his services during the war of 1914–1918, and was knighted in 1920. He was elected F.R.S. in 1915. He married in 1895 Phyllis Mary, daughter of John Hamer, J.P., publisher, and had a son and a daughter; the son is head of the department of bacteriology and experimental pathology at the National Institute for Medical Research, Hampstead.

[*The Times*, 25 February 1932; *Obituary Notices of Fellows of the Royal Society*, No. 1, December 1932 (portrait); *Journal of Pathology and Bacteriology*, vol. xxxv, 1932; personal knowledge.] H. H. DALE.

ANSTEY, F. (pseudonym), humorous writer. [See GUTHRIE, THOMAS ANSTEY.]

ANSTEY, FRANK (1865–1940), Australian journalist and politician, was born of English parents in Blackfriars, London, 18 August 1865, the posthumous and only child of Samuel Anstey, a dockworker from Devon, by his wife, Caroline Gamble. Frank Anstey helped to support his mother through a great part of her life.

The poverty of Anstey's early life left a deep impression. At twelve he obtained employment in the Blackwall clipper, *Melbourne*, running to Australia. He saw something of 'black-birding' in the Pacific, and became a staunch supporter of the 'White Australia' policy. He worked as a labourer, and as a caretaker, but his gift of oratory soon won him a place in the Melbourne Trades Hall Council, and later in parliament. He represented East

Bourke boroughs (1902–1904) and Brunswick (1904–1910) in the Victorian assembly. He wrote much for the *Tocsin* (later *Labor Call*), and frequently acted as editor. In 1907 he worked his passage to England to see his mother. As the outstanding member of the Victorian labour party, he seemed destined to become its leader, but in 1910 he won the Bourke (Victoria) seat in the Commonwealth parliament and held it for twenty-four years.

In Commonwealth politics Anstey became a close friend of Mr. William Morris Hughes. But when the labour party split in 1916, Mr. Hughes made the strongest personal attacks on Anstey as one of the chief opponents of conscription. Anstey objected to conscription of men without conscription of wealth. He attacked the 'money power' in the *Kingdom of Shylock* (1917), the distribution of which was ineffectively prohibited by the Commonwealth. This was revised, expanded, and reprinted in 1921 as *Money Power*. In 1918 Anstey worked his passage to the United States of America and London, and joined an Australian press mission to the western front. After visits to France, Switzerland, and Scandinavia he returned to Australia in June 1919; his book *Red Europe* appeared in September. From 1922 to 1927 he held the position of deputy leader of the parliamentary labour party, and when labour came into office in 1929 he became minister for health and repatriation. In the depression (1930) he fought for compulsory reduction of interest and compulsory conversion of loans. When this policy was rejected by his party in March 1931 he had to leave the ministry; he retired from politics in 1934.

Anstey married in 1888 Catherine, daughter of John McColl, police officer, of Sale, Victoria, and had two sons. He died at Melbourne 31 October 1940.

Anstey's gift of oratory was unusual; during his term in parliament no one equalled his power of holding the House. He spoke with a passionate sincerity, lightened by wit and irony. His forceful writings also had a wide public. Although generally regarded as too unstable for the highest offices, he proved a most able minister of health. His attachment to his principles earned him the respect even of political opponents, but brought him little material advancement.

[Melbourne newspapers, *Argus*, *Age*, *Labor Call*, *passim*; E. O. G. Shann and D. B. Copland, *The Crisis in Australian Finance*,

1929–1931, 1931; *Commonwealth Parliamentary Handbook, 1901–1930*, 1930; private information.]   HERBERT BURTON.

ARMSTRONG, HENRY EDWARD (1848–1937), chemist and educationist, was born 6 May 1848 at Lewisham, where he resided during the whole of his life. He was the eldest son of Richard Armstrong, a commission agent and importer, by his wife, Mary Ann Biddle.

Armstrong went to Colfe Grammar School, Dartmouth Hill, and began to study chemistry in 1865 at the Royal College of Chemistry in Oxford Street under (Sir) Edward Frankland [q.v.], and within a very short time was assisting his teacher in devising methods for water analysis, particularly for detecting and estimating sewage contamination. The methods which they devised were subsequently used by Frankland in a survey of the whole British drinking water supply, which put this country ahead of all others in the provision of safe drinking water. In 1867 Armstrong went to Leipzig to study chemistry under Adolphe Wilhelm Hermann Kolbe, returning in 1870 with the degree of Ph.D. and a passion for research which never left him. After holding teaching appointments at St. Bartholomew's Hospital (1870–1882) and at the London Institution as professor of chemistry (1871–1884) he became associated in 1879 with the City and Guilds of London Institute, first at their Finsbury School in Cowper Street where he organized classes in technical chemistry, and in 1884 as professor of chemistry at the new Central Institution at South Kensington which became in 1893 the Central Technical College. Here he and his colleagues W. E. Ayrton and W. C. Unwin [qq.v.] were pioneers in designing courses for higher technical education for engineers and chemists. The chemistry school was a small one, but it was the first in this country to give such a training to chemists as would equip them for work in a factory, and the first to produce what are now called chemical engineers.

Armstrong's interests as a scientist ranged over a wide field of chemistry. His researches in the chemistry of naphthalene were of fundamental importance when this substance was becoming increasingly used as a starting material for the manufacture of intermediates for dyestuffs. The value of this work was especially appreciated in Germany. Concurrently he carried out research into the laws of substitution in benzine derivatives, suggesting the well-known 'centric' formula to explain its chemical behaviour. His 'quinone' theory of the colour of organic compounds was a guiding principle for students of dyestuffs until it became superseded in recent times by more comprehensive ideas. The theory of aqueous solution was another subject to which Armstrong devoted much attention, and upon which he carried out a great deal of experimental work. He contested hotly the dissociation theory of Svante August Arrhenius and Wilhelm Ostwald on the justifiable ground that that theory took insufficient account of the part played by the solvent and of the complex character of water. Armstrong's mathematical equipment was inadequate to give his alternative ideas a quantitative basis, but in its modern form the dissociation theory has been modified so far as to justify his criticism. Other subjects of research in Armstrong's laboratory were the constitution of camphor and its derivatives, the study of plant enzymes, and the crystallography of organic compounds, of which he realized the fundamental importance, for as early as 1886 he invited (Sir) H. A. Miers to give instruction in the subject. In all this research work Armstrong was assisted by a succession of students, many of whom subsequently made their mark in academic and industrial spheres, carrying his influence with them. He was also an accomplished geologist, and his long association with the Rothamsted Research Station, where he was a member of the Lawes Agricultural Trust Committee from 1889 and eventually chairman in 1937, testified to his keen interest in the development of agriculture.

Armstrong was elected F.R.S. in 1876 and received the Davy medal in 1911. He was a fellow of the Chemical Society for nearly seventy years, and served as secretary for eighteen years, as president from 1893 to 1895, and as councillor for over sixty years. He received the honorary degree of LL.D. from the university of St. Andrews and that of D.Sc. from the universities of Melbourne and Madrid. He was awarded the Messel medal of the Society of Chemical Industry (1922), the Albert medal of the Royal Society of Arts (1930), and the Horace Brown medal of the Institute of Brewing (1926). He spoke and wrote much upon matters of public interest in which the application of science was involved, and was a frequent contributor to *The Times*. After his retirement on the closing of the chemistry school in 1913 he maintained his activity as a critic, writer, and lecturer and came to be regarded as the doyen of British chemistry.

Armstrong was a man of forceful personality who, once having formed an opinion on a subject, held to it strongly and advocated it vigorously. He undoubtedly rendered great service by the reforms which he caused to be brought about in the teaching of science, at both the elementary and the advanced stages. The elementary teaching of science was studied closely by committees of the British Association under Armstrong's inspiration, between 1884 and 1891. He believed that children could at an early age be made to think for themselves if properly guided, and he was one of the strongest advocates of the heuristic method. He rendered most valuable service to Christ's Hospital as the Royal Society representative on the council of almoners. It was largely through his influence that the school was moved from Newgate Street to West Horsham in 1902, and under his guidance it became one of the best-equipped schools in the country for the teaching of science. His many reports and essays on the teaching of science are collected in his book *The Teaching of Scientific Method* (1903, 2nd ed. reprinted 1925). Other essays are published in *The Art and Principles of Chemistry* (1927).

Armstrong married in 1877 Frances Louisa (died 1935), daughter of Thomas Howard Lavers, and had four sons and three daughters. He died at Lewisham 13 July 1937. His eldest son, Edward Frankland, achieved a prominent position as an industrial chemist and died in 1945.

A portrait of Armstrong, by T. C. Dugdale (1927), is in the possession of the Royal Institution, Albemarle Street.

[*The Times*, 14 July 1937; *Obituary Notices of Fellows of the Royal Society*, No. 9, January 1941 (portrait); *Journal* of the Chemical Society, July 1940 (portrait); *The Central*, Armstrong memorial number, 1938; *Chemistry and Industry*, vol. lx, 1941; *Nature*, 24 July 1937; personal knowledge.]

E. H. RODD.

ARTHUR FREDERICK PATRICK ALBERT (1883–1938), prince of Great Britain and Ireland, the only son and second child of Prince Arthur William Patrick Albert, first Duke of Connaught (1850–1942), the third son of Queen Victoria, by his wife, Princess Louise Margaret Alexandra Victoria Agnes, daughter of Prince Charles Frederick of Prussia, was born at Windsor Castle 13 January 1883. During the absence of their parents in India he and his two sisters were much with Queen Victoria, who showed them great affection and afterwards continued to invite them to Osborne and Balmoral. From 1893 their home was with their parents at Bagshot Park.

Prince Arthur was educated at Farnborough School, Hampshire, at Eton, and at the Royal Military College, Sandhurst. In 1899 he joined in his father's renunciation of the succession to the Duchy of Saxe-Coburg-Gotha, then held by his uncle, Prince Alfred, Duke of Edinburgh [q.v.].

Prince Arthur received his commission in the 7th Hussars in 1901 and joined the regiment in South Africa, where he saw active service. In 1907 he was promoted captain in the Royal Scots Greys, of which regiment he became colonel-in-chief in 1921. He also held that rank in the Royal Army Pay Corps. In the war of 1914–1918 he was aide-de-camp successively to Sir John French, Sir Douglas Haig, and Sir Charles Monro, commanding the First Army, was twice mentioned in dispatches, was promoted major and was appointed C.B. (1915), and retired in 1919 as brevet lieutenant-colonel after serving with the army of occupation on the Rhine. In 1920 he became an honorary major-general.

Prince Arthur undertook state missions on behalf of King Edward VII and King George V to two successive Emperors of Japan in 1906, 1912, and 1918, and represented the King on state occasions in Portugal (1908) and in Russia, Bavaria, and Italy (1911). During King George's absence in India (1911–1912) he was one of the four counsellors of state.

In 1920 Prince Arthur was appointed governor-general of the Union of South Africa in succession to S. C. Buxton, first Earl Buxton [q.v.], and arrived in Cape Town in November. While no outstanding constitutional issues arose during his three years in the Dominion, several notable events occurred which find their place in Union history. In 1919 parliament had authorized the government to accept the League of Nations' mandate for German South-West Africa and this involved legislation to provide for its administration as an integral part of the Union. There were negotiations in 1921 between Southern Rhodesia, then under a chartered company, and the Union government on the possibility of the incorporation of the country in the Union, but as a result of a referendum in Southern Rhodesia in which the majority voted against the Union's offer, Southern Rhodesia in 1923 received responsible government. During all these years General Smuts was premier and it was during his term of office that the industrial unrest and discontent, which had been manifest immediately before the war of 1914–1918, now made themselves felt on a larger scale than ever before, leading to an outbreak on the Rand which was only suppressed by the government after the declaration of martial law, General Smuts himself leaving Cape Town to take charge of the situation. In the matter of the Indian problem in South Africa the governor-general, on the advice of the Union ministers, withheld his assent to a Natal ordinance of 1921 depriving Indians of the municipal franchise; but after the Imperial Conference of 1923 was over Indians were deprived of this franchise by ordinances passed subsequent to the termination of his governorship in that year. It was during Prince Arthur's term of office that the Union undertook the entire responsibility for its own defence, except that, by an agreement of 1921, under which the United Kingdom transferred to the Union government the freehold of the lands and buildings of the naval base of Simonstown, a servitude was registered against the freehold in favour of the Admiralty as perpetual user for naval purposes. Accordingly the historic castle at Cape Town was handed over to the defence officers of the Union and the United Kingdom command was withdrawn.

In 1923 Prince Arthur became chairman of the Middlesex Hospital and presided regularly over its building committee and over the 'appeal committee' formed to provide for a great expansion of its work. For this he personally worked so hard and successfully that nearly two million pounds were raised by and under him, and the Middlesex became one of the greatest of the teaching hospitals with first-rate laboratories, a new out-patients' building, and a new nurses' home.

Prince Arthur was appointed G.C.V.O. (1899), K.G. (1902), K.T. (1913), and G.C.M.G. (1918). He was sworn of the Privy Council in 1910. He was an Elder Brother of the Trinity House (1910) and high steward of Reading (1935). He

married in 1913 his first cousin once removed, Princess Alexandra Victoria Alberta Edwina Louise, by special remainder Duchess of Fife, elder daughter of Alexander William George Duff, first Duke of Fife (died 1912), by his wife, Louise Victoria Alexandra Dagmar, princess royal [q.v.], eldest daughter of King Edward VII. Their only child, Alastair Arthur, Earl of Macduff (born 1914), succeeded his grandfather as second Duke of Connaught in 1942, and died 26 April 1943. Prince Arthur died in London 12 September 1938.

[Dominions Office papers: private information; personal knowledge.]   E. B. PHIPPS.

ASCHE, (THOMAS STANGE HEISS) OSCAR (1871–1936), actor, manager, author, and producer, was born at Geelong, Victoria, Australia, 24 January 1871, the third son of Thomas Asche, by his second wife, Harriet Emma, daughter of William Trear, licensed victualler, of Sunderland, co. Durham. Thomas Asche, a Norwegian from Christiania, was proprietor of Mack's Hotel, and was himself a man of remarkable character and physical strength, able to squeeze a pewter pot in one hand. Oscar Asche was educated at Melbourne Grammar School, which he left at the age of sixteen. Shortly afterwards he went with a school friend on a sailing trip to China. The voyage lasted six months and had an undoubted influence in giving the boy a taste for adventure. On his return he tried his hand as a storekeeper and at other occupations without much satisfaction, and then went on a trip with another friend to Fiji. While still in his 'teens he decided to make his way to Norway with a view to adopting the stage as a profession. In Christiania he studied under Bjørn Bjørnson, the famous author's son. He met Ibsen, who gave him an introduction to William Archer [q.v.], and told him that, as an English-speaking actor, he should go to England.

Asche made his first appearance on the stage in London at the Opéra Comique in 1893, when he played a small part in *Man and Woman* under the management of Arthur Dacre. He himself has left a candid record of his early struggles—of sleeping on the Embankment and calling cabs outside theatres in which he afterwards appeared. He had the good fortune in the same year to join the Benson Repertory Company on the strength of having played cricket and been a wicket-keeper. He was with (Sir) Frank Benson [q.v.] for eight years, acting every kind of part, from Biondello in *The Taming of the Shrew* and Pistol in *Henry V* to the King in *Hamlet*. While he was with Benson he married, in 1898, Lily, daughter of John Grindall Brayton, physician and surgeon, of Hindley, Lancashire, who joined the company three years after. Both were engaged after Benson's Lyceum season in 1900, Oscar Asche to appear as Maldonado in (Sir) A. W. Pinero's *Iris* at the Garrick Theatre in 1901, and Lily Brayton as Viola in *Twelfth Night*, but she played Mariamne during Maud Jeffries's illness in Stephen Phillips's *Herod* with (Sir) Herbert Beerbohm Tree [q.v.] at Her Majesty's Theatre (October 1900); here Asche was himself to arrive to play Antinous in Phillips's *Ulysses* in 1902.

In 1904 both Asche and Lily Brayton joined their old Bensonian comrade, Otho Stuart, in the management of the Adelphi Theatre, where memorable productions were given of J. B. Fagan's *The Prayer of the Sword*, of *A Midsummer Night's Dream*, *The Taming of the Shrew*, and *Measure for Measure*, with Asche as Bottom, Christopher Sly, Petruchio, and Angelo, and of Mr. Rudolf Besier's first play, *The Virgin Goddess*. In 1907 Asche went into management at His Majesty's Theatre, producing Laurence Binyon's *Attila*, with himself in the title-part, and several Shakespearian revivals, notably *Othello*, Asche proving one of the best Othellos of his generation. It was at the Garrick Theatre in 1911 that he created Hajj, the philosophic beggar in Edward Knoblock's *Kismet*, an oriental study which paved the way for his own *Chu Chin Chow* at His Majesty's five years later. The libretto of this was written in order to fill up time during a rainy week in Manchester. With the help of Mr. George Frederic Norton's tuneful score it achieved what was long the record run of 2,238 performances (August 1916 to July 1921). In 1917 Asche was concerned as producer with Mr. Frederick Lonsdale's *The Maid of the Mountains*, which ran for 1,352 performances at Daly's Theatre.

Asche was not destined to enjoy another popular triumph. The £200,000 to which his share of the *Chu Chin Chow* profits amounted dwindled in his always lavish hands, and losses on a Gloucestershire farm were an added trouble in his later years. Some experiments, such as his presentation of *The Merry Wives of Wind-*

sor in modern dress in 1929, were hardly the result of sincere artistic conviction. Between 1909 and 1922 he made three extended tours of his native Australia, meeting with an enthusiastic welcome, and in 1913 he visited South Africa. At the Shakespeare tercentenary celebration at Drury Lane in 1916 he appeared as Casca in *Julius Caesar*. He died at Marlow 23 March 1936. He had no children. Lily Brayton survived him, afterwards marrying (1938) Douglas Chalmers Watson, a Scottish physician.

Although his huge stature naturally limited the parts which he could take, Asche had a distinct creative imagination of his own and sympathetic understanding, both as actor and as author. He made no literary pretensions; but he did much to break down the artificiality of Victorian and Edwardian 'romance'. In *Chu Chin Chow* he touched the old pantomime-story of Ali Baba and the Forty Thieves with personal memories of the East. His adaptation, *Mameena*, of Sir Henry Rider Haggard's *Child of Storm* (Globe Theatre, 1913), strove to do the like for native life in Africa. His appreciation of Shakespeare was genuine and fruitful. His character, with its curious blend of masterful shrewdness on the one hand and love of sport and readiness for any sort of gamble on the other, found full expression both in his life and in his art. His publications include an autobiography which tells his story with characteristic frankness, and two works of fiction, *The Joss-sticks of Chung* and *The Saga of Hans Hansen* (1930).

[*The Times*, 24 March 1936; *Oscar Asche. His Life by Himself*, 1929; Lady Benson, *Mainly Players: Bensonian Memories*, 1926; personal knowledge.]   S. R. LITTLEWOOD.

ASHBY, THOMAS (1874–1931), archaeologist, was born at Staines 14 October 1874, the only child of Thomas Ashby, a member of the well-known Quaker family which owned Ashby's brewery at Staines, by his wife, Rose Emma, daughter of Apsley Smith. Young Ashby was an exhibitioner at Winchester, where, possibly by some stroke of schoolboy genius, he was almost immediately dubbed by the lasting nickname of 'Titus'. When he was sixteen his father settled in Rome, there to become an enthusiastic explorer of the Campagna and an associate of Rodolfo Lanciani. Learning and enthusiasm won him a scholarship at Christ Church, Oxford, where he was a pupil of F. J. Haverfield [q.v.] and (Sir) John Linton Myres, and was awarded a first class in classical moderations (1895) and in *literae humaniores* (1897). In the latter year he was awarded a Craven fellowship, thereafter devoting himself to studies of Roman antiquities, on which he obtained the Oxford degree of D.Litt. (1905) and the Conington prize for classical learning (1906).

Ashby was the first student of the British School at Rome in 1901, contributing to its *Papers* detailed topographical studies of the Roman roads of Italy. He became a master of Rome's urban topography, and derived from early literature and prints a unique knowledge of the vicissitudes of the city's monuments and artistic treasures. While the former mastery was evinced by articles eventually running into hundreds, the latter was demonstrated by his treatment of such varied themes as Eufrosino della Volpaia's map of the Campagna (1547), the sixteenth-century architectural drawings of Antonio Labacco, the topographical studies of Étienne du Pérac (1581), Giovanni Battista de' Cavalieri's *Antiquae Statuae Urbis Romae*, and the Windsor Castle, Soane Library, and Eton College collections of drawings and paintings. To topographical and bibliographical lore was added excavation, in the Romano-British town of Caerwent (1899–1910) and the megalithic monuments of Malta and Gozo (1908–1911). It is not surprising that he became assistant director (1903) and director (1906–1925) of the British School at Rome, which he made a centre of topographical studies and of international comity, and which, assisted by Mrs. Arthur Strong, he saw embrace after 1915 not only archaeology but art and architecture in a new building in the Valle Giulia. After 1925 he set himself to complete three standard works: a valuable revision of the second part of W. J. Anderson and R. P. Spiers, *The Architecture of Greece and Rome* (1927); a thoroughly revised edition of S. B. Platner's *Topographical Dictionary of Ancient Rome* (1929); and his own *Aqueducts of Ancient Rome*, published posthumously in 1935. He also published a slighter but valuable work on *The Roman Campagna in Classical Times* (1927). In 1915 he offered his services to the War Office, but later in that year joined the Red Cross where for his most remarkable intrepidity on the Asiago plateau he was mentioned in dispatches.

Ashby was a member of the Accademia Pontificia (1914) and of the Reale Società Romana di Storia Patria (1923), a foreign member of the Accademia dei Lincei (1918), an honorary member of the Reale Accademia di San Luca (1925), an honorary A.R.I.B.A. (1922), and a fellow of the British Academy (1927). His figure was stocky, his head tall and forceful, with a neat beard first red and later white. He spoke equally brusque English and Italian, the latter with an undisguised British accent. He was shy with strangers, blunt with acquaintances, and devoted to his friends. He married in 1921 Caroline May, eldest daughter of Richard Price-Williams, civil engineer. There were no children of the marriage. He died 15 May 1931, accidentally falling from a train between Malden and Raynes Park, Surrey.

A painting of Ashby, by (Sir) George Clausen (1925), and a bronze bust, by David Evans, are in the possession of the British School at Rome. A drawing by Clausen (the first study for the painting) is in the National Portrait Gallery.

[A. H. Smith, *Thomas Ashby, 1874–1931* in *Proceedings* of the British Academy, vol. xvii, 1931; *Archivio della R. Società Romana di Storia Patria*, vol. l, 1927 (bibliography to 1926); personal knowledge.] IAN A. RICHMOND.

ASHLEY, WILFRID WILLIAM, BARON MOUNT TEMPLE (1867–1938), politician, was born in London 13 September 1867, the only son of (Anthony) Evelyn Melbourne Ashley [q.v.], by his first wife, Sybella Charlotte, second daughter of Sir Walter Rockcliffe Farquhar, third baronet. He was a grandson of Anthony Ashley Cooper, seventh Earl of Shaftesbury [q.v.]. He was educated at Harrow and Magdalen College, Oxford, and served in the Ayrshire Militia (1886–1889), the Grenadier Guards (1889–1898), and the Hampshire Militia (1899–1903).

By family tradition, environment, and temperament it was inevitable that Ashley should enter upon a political career. In addition to military training and experience he was an extensive traveller, and had made a particular study of the social, economic, and political life of the United States of America and the British Dominions and Colonial Empire. Through his great-grandmother, Lady Palmerston, he inherited Broadlands, and as high steward of Romsey he could claim the town as part of his estate. He was *par excellence* the county squire and the country gentleman; with a lofty sense of public duty he became justice of the peace, deputy lieutenant, and alderman of the county of Hampshire. He became early attached to the conservative party, but always entertained broad and discriminating views on imperial and foreign affairs during his whole political life. He was elected member of parliament for Blackpool at the general election in 1906, and sat for that constituency until the general election of 1918, when he became member for the Fylde division of Lancashire until 1922. In that year he transferred to the New Forest division of Hampshire, which he represented until 1932, when he was raised to the peerage as Baron Mount Temple, of Lee, in the county of Southampton.

Ashley served as a conservative whip in the years preceding the war of 1914–1918, and from 1914 to 1915 commanded the 20th battalion of the King's Liverpool Regiment. In 1915 he became parliamentary private secretary to the financial secretary to the War Office. He first reached office in 1922 when he became parliamentary secretary to the Ministry of Transport, and in the following year was appointed under-secretary of state for war. From 1924 to 1929 he was minister of transport, and was responsible for the reorganization and practical operative structure of that ministry. He planned the introduction of the 'round-about' scheme of one-way traffic in London and the larger provincial cities. He was for several years chairman of the Anti-Socialist Union and president of the Navy League, and was one of the founders of the Comrades of the Great War, from which arose the national movement of the British Legion. In 1924 he was sworn of the Privy Council.

The Irish estate, Classiebawn, on the west coast of Ireland, also inherited from Palmerston, received Ashley's constant attention. He was twice married: first, in 1901 to Amalia Mary Maud (died 1911), only child of Sir Ernest Joseph Cassel [q.v.], and had two daughters, the elder of whom, Edwina, married Lord Louis Mountbatten (later Admiral Earl Mountbatten of Burma); secondly, in 1914 to Muriel Emily, elder daughter of the Rev. Walter Spencer, of Fownhope Court, Hereford, and formerly wife of Arthur Lionel Ochoncar Forbes-Sempill, fifth son of the seventeenth Baron Sempill. He died at Broadlands, Romsey, 3 July 1939 and the peerage became extinct.

What has been said of the previous owner of Broadlands may be applied with more justice to Ashley, that he possessed 'pluck combined with remarkable tact, unfailing good temper associated with firmness almost amounting to obstinacy'.

In addition to a picture and a crayon drawing of Mount Temple in childhood by Edward Clifford there are also at Broadlands a crayon drawing by Eva Sawyer, a picture by Mrs. Blakeney Ward, and another by Emil Fuchs.

[*The Times*, 4 July 1939; personal knowledge.]   P. J. HANNON.

ASHTON, THOMAS GAIR, first BARON ASHTON OF HYDE (1855–1933), industrialist, philanthropist, and politician, was born at Fallowfield, Manchester, 5 February 1855, the eldest son of Thomas Ashton, of Hyde, Cheshire, by his wife, Elizabeth, daughter of Samuel Stillman Gair, who belonged to Rhode Island, U.S.A., and whose English residence was Penketh Hall, Liverpool. Thomas Ashton's second daughter became the wife of James (afterwards Viscount) Bryce [q.v.]. The Ashtons were well known, during generations, for singularly humane treatment of the work-people in their cotton mills, and, after his education at Rugby and University College, Oxford (of which he was elected an honorary fellow in 1923), Thomas Gair Ashton was connected with the family business in Manchester and Hyde for forty years, carrying on this tradition, which coloured his whole life. He was liberal member of parliament for the Hyde division from 1885 to 1886 (losing the seat in the latter year and failing to regain it in 1892) and for the Luton division from 1895 to 1911. During that period he sat on various royal commissions, was chairman of the House of Commons Railway and Canal Traffic Committee in 1909 and of the Standing Orders Committee in 1910, and became notable in the House for his wide knowledge of finance.

Ashton's care for education was also displayed by his guarantee to make good any losses sustained in its first three years by the county secondary school at Hyde, and by his support of the Hyde Technical School and the free library, so that for a time both chiefly depended upon him. He was a governor of Manchester University, the first honorary secretary of the Manchester Technical School, and a member of the governing body of the Whitworth Institute. He also took a keen interest in the history and antiquities of Sussex, where he lived after 1902.

Ashton was raised to the peerage in 1911 as Baron Ashton of Hyde, and, during the war of 1914–1918, was chairman of the

Cotton Exports Committee, which controlled the amount of cotton allowed to pass through the blockade to neutral nations bordering Germany. The work derived importance from the fact that cotton was then a raw material for munitions.

Ashton was sagacious, far-sighted, widely read, and widely travelled, with excellent judgement of men and affairs, and an immense capacity for work, but his extreme reserve and modesty hid his real capabilities from those not closely acquainted with him. He had a most exacting sense of duty in all public affairs, and was entirely incapable of self-advertisement, never pushing his own claims and interests. Nor for one moment did he support any views merely because of their popularity. For instance, he advocated home rule for Ireland before Gladstone pronounced in its favour. But, owing to his profound shyness, he struck even those knowing him well as curiously impersonal, a fact which militated perhaps against due recognition of his deep feeling for the causes which he served so faithfully.

Ashton married in 1886 Eva Margaret (died 1938), second daughter of John Henry James, of Watford, who belonged to a Cumberland family. They had two sons, the elder of whom died as a child, and two daughters. He died at his home at Robertsbridge 1 May 1933 and was succeeded as second baron by his younger son, Thomas Henry Raymond (born 1901).

[*Manchester Guardian*, 2 May 1933; personal knowledge.]   MARION WOOD.

ASTBURY, SIR JOHN MEIR (1860–1939), judge, was born at Broughton, near Manchester, 14 June 1860, the eldest son of Frederick James Astbury, J.P., chartered accountant, of Hilton Park, Prestwich, Lancashire, by his wife, Margaret, daughter of John Munn, of Manchester. He was educated at Manchester Grammar School and at Trinity College, Oxford, where he graduated with a second class in jurisprudence in 1882: in the following year he was the only candidate placed in the first class in the B.C.L. examination, and in 1884 he won the Vinerian law scholarship. In the last-named year he was called to the bar by the Middle Temple (of which Inn he became a bencher in 1903 and treasurer in 1926), and entered practice on the Chancery side at the local bar at Manchester. He took silk in 1895 and migrated to London, attaching himself first to the court of Sir E. W. Byrne [q.v.] and later to that of Sir H. B. Buckley (later Lord Wrenbury, q.v.) 'going special' in 1905, with a large business in patent litigation, which increased greatly after John Fletcher Moulton [q.v.] became a lord justice of appeal in 1906. In that year he stood as liberal candidate for the Southport division and defeated (Sir) E. Marshall Hall [q.v.], but he was not greatly interested in politics and retired from parliament in January 1910. In 1913 Lord Chancellor Haldane offered him, and he accepted, the judgeship in the Chancery division recently vacated by the promotion of Sir Charles Swinfen Eady [q.v.]. For the next sixteen years he discharged the duties of this position with efficiency and firmness, though without any great distinction.

Astbury was best known to the general public and will be remembered by future historians for the part which, as judge, he played during the General Strike of 1926. The litigation in question is reported as *National Sailors' and Firemen's Union of Great Britain and Ireland* v. *Reed and others*. This union, composed of loyal merchant seamen, under the wise direction of its secretary J. Havelock Wilson [q.v.], had little sympathy with the attempt of the strikers to subvert democratic government, and when certain local branches called upon members to cease work the union immediately applied to the High Court of Justice for an injunction prohibiting its subordinate officials from usurping the functions of the union as a whole. The case was in Astbury's list on 11 May, and he gave his decision at once, not confining himself to the technical point as to the relations between the union and its branches, but declaring in forcible language that the whole General Strike was illegal and that the court would use its powers, by injunction, to prevent any action which might further its objective. On the previous night Sir Henry Slesser, at that time a leading lawyer amongst the labour members of parliament, had declared in the House of Commons that the question of the legality of the strike was one to be decided by the courts of justice, and that 'whatever the decision of this tribunal, we shall all, as law-abiding citizens, obey it'. When the House met on the following evening, Sir John Simon, with a copy of Astbury's judgement, given earlier in the day, in his hand, in a trenchant speech charged the leaders of the strike as law-breakers. On the following morning Mr. Baldwin made the announcement

22

that the strike had been called off. There can be little doubt, in view of this sequence of events, that Astbury's judgement played an important part in bringing about the collapse of the whole movement. This is not the place to estimate the validity of the judgement as an exposition of the law: at the time it had the general approval of lawyers, although it was subsequently attacked by Professor A. L. Goodhart.

In 1929 Astbury's eyesight began to fail and in October he resigned his judgeship: in December he was sworn of the Privy Council. His last years were saddened by his blindness and by the death in a motor accident of his only child, a daughter by his first marriage. He died at Sandwich 21 August 1939. He was twice married: first, in 1888 to Evelyn (died January 1923), daughter of Paul Susman, merchant, of Manchester; secondly, in August 1923 to Harriet, daughter of George William Holmes, of Philadelphia, U.S.A., and widow of Captain Morrell Andrew Girdlestone. By his will, he directed that the ultimate residue of his estate should be devoted to legal education.

Astbury was elected in 1923 an honorary fellow of Trinity College, Oxford, which possesses a portrait of him by the Austrian artist Kopek.

[*Law Reports. National Sailors' and Firemen's Union of Great Britain v. Reed and others*, 1926, ch. 536; *Law Quarterly Review*, vol. xliii, 1926; A. L. Goodhart, *Essays in Jurisprudence and the Common Law*, 1931; Hansard, *Parliamentary Debates*; private information; personal knowledge.]

PHILIP A. LANDON.

ASTON, SIR GEORGE GREY (1861–1938), major-general, was born in Cape Colony 2 December 1861, the youngest son of Lieutenant-Colonel Henry Aston, Indian Army (retired), by his wife, Katherine, daughter of the Rev. Abraham Faure, of the Cape of Good Hope. Educated at Westminster and at the Royal Naval College, Greenwich, he joined the Royal Marine Artillery in 1879.

In 1884, while serving in the Mediterranean flagship, Aston landed at Suakin with the Royal Marine battalion and was present at the battles of El Teb and Tamai. In 1886, in recognition of his marked ability, he was appointed to the Foreign Intelligence Committee, Admiralty, the forerunner of the Naval Intelligence Department, and after completing the course at the Staff College, Camberley, in 1891, he held a succession of staff appointments with conspicuous success and growing reputation. The more important of these were professor of fortification at the Royal Naval College, Greenwich (1896–1899); deputy-assistant-adjutant-general (Intelligence) 8th division in South Africa (1900); instructor at the Staff College (1904–1907); brigadier-general on the staff of P. S., Lord Methuen [q.v.], commander-in-chief in South Africa (1908–1913). For his services in the South African war he was promoted brevet lieutenant-colonel. On relinquishing his appointment in 1913 he received from the government of the Union of South Africa an expression of thanks for the zeal and ability displayed in carrying out his duties. Lord Methuen, reporting on him, said: 'I have seldom served with an officer of such rare ability combined with such great zeal.' He was specially promoted to colonel 2nd commandant for meritorious services, particularly those in South Africa.

On the outbreak of war in 1914 Aston was appointed to command a Royal Marine brigade, landing with it at Ostend and subsequently at Dunkirk. A breakdown in health led to his relief by Brigadier-General (Sir) Archibald Paris [q.v.] in September, and from then onwards he served as colonel commandant Royal Marine Artillery until the termination of the appointment in 1917, when he was retired at his own request and promoted major-general.

Aston now devoted himself to writing, contributing articles to *The Times* and publishing several books, including *Memories of a Marine* (1919), *The Navy of To-day* (1927), and *Biography of Marshal Foch* (1929). He was appointed C.B. in 1902 and K.C.B. in 1913. He was appointed aide-de-camp to the king in 1911, and in 1925 he was awarded a good service pension.

Aston was dark, of medium height and slender build. He had a very quick brain and great store of nervous energy which, in conjunction with a ready pen, assured his success as a staff officer. He married in 1909 Dorothy Ellen, daughter of Vice-Admiral William Wilson, of Clyffe Pypard, near Swindon, and had three sons and two daughters. He died at Woodford, Salisbury, 2 December 1938.

[*The Times*, 3 December 1938; Sir George Aston, *Memories of a Marine*, 1919; Official records at the Royal Marine office, Admiralty; personal knowledge.]   R. C. TEMPLE.

ATHOLSTAN, BARON (1848–1938), newspaper proprietor. [See GRAHAM, HUGH.]

ATKINSON, JOHN, BARON ATKINSON, of Glenwilliam (1844–1932), judge, was born at Drogheda, co. Louth, 13 December 1844, the elder son of Edward Atkinson, physician, of Glenwilliam Castle, co. Limerick, and Skea House, Enniskillen, by his first wife, Rosetta, daughter of John Shaw McCulloch. From the Royal Belfast Academical Institution he entered Queen's College, Galway (a constituent college of the old Royal University of Ireland), where he gained scholarships in his first three years, in his fourth a senior scholarship in mathematics, and in his fifth a senior scholarship in natural philosophy. He graduated with first class honours in 1861 and in 1862 he entered as a student both in King's Inns, Dublin, and at the Inner Temple. In 1865 he was called to the Irish bar, and in the same year took the LL.B. degree with honours, becoming a bencher of King's Inns in 1885. He joined the Munster circuit, of which he remained a member until his appointment as a law officer. He was called to the English bar by the Inner Temple in 1890, and was elected a bencher in 1906. Meanwhile his practice in Ireland was increasing and became large. In 1880, at an exceptionally early age, he took silk, and after appointment in 1889 as solicitor-general for Ireland and in 1892 as attorney-general, he was sworn of the Irish Privy Council that same year, but the fall of Lord Salisbury's administration put a speedy period to his tenure of office. It was not until 1895 that he entered the House of Commons as conservative member for North Londonderry, having earlier in the year been once more chosen to be attorney-general for Ireland. He continued in that office until, in 1905, he was appointed a lord of appeal in ordinary with the title of Lord Atkinson, of Glenwilliam, co. Limerick, and was sworn of the English Privy Council. In office his knowledge of land and social problems in Ireland rendered him a highly valued adviser to the chief secretary for Ireland, Gerald Balfour (later second Earl of Balfour) in the framing and passing of the Irish Land Act of 1896 and the Local Government Act of 1898.

Atkinson was the first Irish barrister to go direct from his practice at the bar to the House of Lords. His appointment called forth criticism on the ground that the room of a great lawyer like Lindley should not have been filled by one better known as a politician than as a legist, but the sequel did not justify the doubts about his competence as a judge. Not that he was a profound lawyer—he was the last man to have made such a claim; but he was a ready speaker, an energetic worker possessing an instinctive and sincere passion for justice, and, above all, endowed with the gifts of courage both physical and moral, and an inflexible sense of duty, which enabled him to steer undaunted a straight course through the stormy seas of Irish political life during a period when navigation was by no means easy, and to resist the strong pressure put upon him to resign by the first coalition government in order to satisfy the requirements of the political party leaders. He resigned his seat as a lord of appeal in 1928.

Atkinson married in 1873 Rowena Jane (died 1911), daughter of Richard Chute, M.D., of Tralee, co. Kerry, and had four sons, the three elder of whom predeceased their father. He died in London 13 March 1932. An excellent portrait, by John St. Helier Lander, hangs in the dining-hall of King's Inns, Dublin.

[*The Times*, 14 and 15 March 1932; private information.]   THEODORE C. TOBIAS.

AVORY, SIR HORACE EDMUND (1851–1935), judge, was born in London 31 August 1851, the second son of Henry Avory, clerk of the court at the Central Criminal Court (a post to which Henry Kemp Avory, Horace's elder brother, succeeded in due course), by his wife, Margaret Kemp. Horace was educated at Gothic House College, Clapham, King's College, London, and Corpus Christi College, Cambridge, where he was a scholar and was awarded a third class in the law tripos of 1873: he was captain of the college boat club in 1872. He was called to the bar by the Inner Temple in 1875 and read for a time in the chambers of E. T. E. Besley, one of the leaders of the criminal bar. He joined the South-Eastern circuit and regularly attended the Surrey sessions held at Newington in addition to the monthly sessions of the Central Criminal Court where he had the opportunity of 'devilling' for such men as (Sir) Harry Poland, Montagu Williams, and (Sir) Edward Clarke [qq.v.] as well as Besley. He soon came to be known as a sound lawyer as well as an astute and courageous if not eloquent advocate. His practice grew rapidly and in 1889 his name was included with those of (Sir) Forrest Fulton, (Sir) C. W. Matthews [q.v.], and (Sir) C. F. Gill, as one of the official prosecuting counsel at the Central Criminal Court. For the next twelve years he was engaged in most of the important criminal trials in London, and in 1899 he became senior prosecuting counsel to the Crown at the Central Criminal Court. When he was not required to act for the Crown he was frequently briefed for the defence as junior to some fashionable Queen's Counsel, his role being to deal with any legal point which might arise. He was counsel for the prosecution in the trials in 1893 of Jabez Balfour and his co-directors of the Liberator group of companies, the failure of which in 1892 with liabilities of eight millions caused widespread ruin.

By 1901 Avory considered that his practice in the civil courts, particularly in rating and licensing cases, justified him in applying for silk, and he was included in the first batch of King's Counsel to be appointed by King Edward VII. His success as a leader was immediate. His arguments were always listened to with close attention by the judges, for he never indulged in irrelevance or repetition, while his direct and lucid method of stating his case appealed to a jury. He quickly acquired a leading practice in 'Crown paper' matters and had a fair share of briefs at *nisi prius*. The *Law Reports* are the best evidence of his activities at this period, but it may be mentioned that he advised the prosecution of Whitaker Wright [q.v.] after the law officers had stated in the House of Commons that in their opinion Wright had committed no criminal offence. The subsequent conviction of Wright (1904) showed Avory's view to be correct. In 1902 Avory was appointed recorder of Kingston, an office involving no work and carrying no salary, but, as a compliment, much appreciated by the holder.

In the summer of 1909 Avory was appointed commissioner of assize for the South-Eastern circuit and when, in January 1910, he was again appointed commissioner, this time for the Northern circuit, it was realized that his elevation to the bench was only a matter of time. The opportunity occurred in the same year, and in October he was sworn in as a judge of the King's Bench division. It is as a judge that Avory will be best remembered. Always dignified and courteous, his control of a case was perfect.

Prolixity, irrelevance, and levity were alike discouraged in his court. For the most part a silent judge, what he did say was always to the point and expressed in the simplest language. His judgement on any question of law is invariably treated as deserving the utmost respect. His summing up to a jury in a criminal trial was usually a model of lucidity and accuracy. He made mistakes, as all judges must, but the accused who relied upon facts always had his defence fully and fairly put, while he or she who relied upon sentiment found Avory unsympathetic. His manner was cold and at times stern, but if the accused was convicted it was by the logic of facts not as the result of any undue pressure from the bench, and many convicted persons, including the two murderers of Police-Constable Gutteridge, in 1927, Guy Frederick Browne and William Henry Kennedy, went out of their way to acknowledge the fairness of their trials before him. As a member of a divisional court Avory's knowledge of magisterial law was invaluable, while in the Court of Criminal Appeal his opinion usually prevailed with the other members of the court.

On the retirement of Sir Charles (later Lord) Darling [q.v.] in 1923 Avory became senior judge of the King's Bench division. During the absence through ill health of Lord Hewart, the lord chief justice, he discharged the official duties of that office and in 1932 he was sworn of the Privy Council. He continued to sit in court regularly until the end of the Easter sittings of 1935 when he left London for the Dormy House Club at Rye. There he died suddenly 13 June. In the previous January he had celebrated the diamond jubilee of his call to the bar.

Avory was chairman of the committee which was responsible for the codification of the law to be found in the Perjury Act (1911), the Forgery Act (1913), and the Larceny Act (1916). The Indictments Act (1915) and its rules were largely his work and his hand is clearly traceable in the Criminal Justice Act (1925) and in other statutes dealing with criminal law.

Avory received the honorary degree of LL.D. from the university of Cambridge in 1911 and was elected an honorary fellow of Corpus in 1912. He also became a fellow of King's College, London, in 1912. He was elected a bencher of the Inner Temple in 1908 and treasurer in 1929. He was fond of riding and in his youth hunted with the Surrey Union hounds. Later he took up golf, which he played accurately and very seriously. He regularly attended the meetings and dinners of the Pegasus Club, of which he was an original member, becoming president in 1911. His fellow members of the Garrick and United University clubs found him a pleasant and, when he chose, an amusing companion. His life, however, was devoted to the law, which was his hobby as well as his profession. He did not court publicity and preferred the society of a limited circle of friends. He married in 1877 Maria Louisa (died 1937), daughter of Henry Castle, of Wandsworth, and had a son and a daughter.

A cartoon of Avory, by 'Spy', appeared in *Vanity Fair* 2 June 1904.

[*The Times*, 14 June 1935; F. W. Ashley, *My First Sixty Years in the Law*, 1936; private information; personal knowledge.]
                                TRAVERS HUMPHREYS.

BACKHOUSE, SIR ROGER ROLAND CHARLES (1878–1939), admiral of the fleet, the fourth son (twin with his brother Miles) of (Sir) Jonathan Edmund Backhouse, first baronet, a descendant of well-known Quaker forebears, by his wife, Florence, youngest daughter of Sir John Salusbury Salusbury-Trelawny, ninth baronet, the head of a famous and ancient Cornish family, was born at The Rookery, Middleton Tyas, Yorkshire, 24 November 1878. He entered the training-ship *Britannia* at Dartmouth as a naval cadet in 1892, and passing out after two years was appointed to the *Repulse* battleship in the Channel squadron, being promoted midshipman in 1894. A year later he was transferred to H.M.S. *Comus*, a small third-class cruiser which was commissioned to join the Pacific squadron, an opportunity for seeing the New World in the days of 'showing the flag' all down the American coast from Alaska to Patagonia. In her he remained until she returned to England in 1898, being promoted sub-lieutenant in March of that year. Exactly one year later he was promoted lieutenant with a prize of £10 for gaining five first class certificates. After a year in the battleship *Revenge* in the Mediterranean he rapidly became recognized as a gunnery expert, winning the Egerton prize in 1902. He divided his last remaining nine years as lieutenant equally between the staff of the gunnery-school ship *Excellent* at Portsmouth and appointments as gunnery officer of battleships afloat, including the new *Dreadnought* with its great advance in gun power. On promotion to commander at the end of 1909 he left the *Dreadnought* to return to the *Excellent* as experimental officer for a year, and then began a long period of staff work at sea. From March 1911 until August 1914 Backhouse was flag-commander to three successive Home Fleet commanders-in-chief, Sir F. C. B. Bridgeman, Sir G. A. Callaghan, and Sir John (afterwards Earl) Jellicoe [qq.v.], in their flagships *Neptune* and *Iron Duke*. After the outbreak of the war of 1914–1918 he was specially promoted captain (1 September), and at once reappointed to Jellicoe's staff for special service. Jellicoe, when first sea lord, placed on record the assistance of the greatest value rendered by Backhouse as flag-commander and captain on the staff from August 1914 to October 1915, both as gunnery expert and in the compilation of battle orders, and directed that this notice was to be treated as a 'mention in dispatches'.

In November 1915 Backhouse was for the first time in command of a ship, the *Conquest*, light cruiser, in the Harwich force under Commodore (Sir) Reginald Yorke Tyrwhitt. He had an exciting year and incidents were numerous. When German battle cruisers bombarded Lowestoft on 25 April 1916 the commodore, flying his broad pennant in the *Conquest*, intervened with three light cruisers and sixteen destroyers and drew off the enemy's fire. In turning to retire the *Conquest* was hit by four or five 12-inch shells; twenty-three of her crew were killed and sixteen wounded, and a serious fire broke out. Backhouse's conduct in leaving the bridge directly the shellfire had ceased and taking personal charge of the operation was given official approbation by the Board of Admiralty; 'by his personal efforts he saved his ship from destruction'.

In November 1916 Jellicoe left the Grand Fleet to become first sea lord. Sir David (afterwards Earl) Beatty [q.v.] succeeded to the chief command and took his staff and many of the officers from the battle-cruiser *Lion* to the battleship *Iron Duke* which had been Grand Fleet flagship since March 1914. Sir W. C. Pakenham [q.v.] succeeded Beatty in command of the battle-cruisers, and Backhouse went to the *Lion* as his flag-captain and for gunnery duties in the battle-cruiser force. In the summer of 1918 ill health compelled him to come ashore, but he recovered before the armistice (11 November) and was able to take up special duties at the Admiralty. These included membership of several committees, including the post-war problems committee. While still on duty in Whitehall Backhouse was appointed director of naval ordnance in September 1920, a post for which his record clearly marked him out. He went to sea again in January 1923 for twenty months' command of the battleship *Malaya*, in the Atlantic Fleet, and then underwent senior officers' courses at Portsmouth during which he reached flag rank in April 1925. In May 1926 he hoisted his flag in the veteran *Iron Duke* as rear-admiral commanding the third battle squadron Atlantic Fleet for the usual one year of command, and then had a well-earned rest at home on half-pay.

In November 1928 Backhouse succeeded Vice-Admiral Sir Alaric Ernle Montacute (afterwards Lord) Chatfield as third sea lord and controller of the navy in William Clive (afterwards Viscount) Bridgeman's Board and remained under Mr. Albert Victor Alexander through the following labour administration (1929–1931), through the financial and political crisis of 1931, and under Sir Bolton Meredith Eyres-Monsell (afterwards Viscount Monsell) until March 1932. He had been promoted vice-admiral in October 1929. His tenure of office as controller was a difficult time of stringent economy. Naval expenditure fell by eight millions between 1917 and 1932, and of this drop over four and a quarter millions came from the armament votes under the controller's supervision. It was a time when 'disarmament' was the international atmosphere and aggression had scarcely begun to show its head. Provision for the navy was not welcome to the labour government, and the coalition of 1931 was pledged to a general reduction of public expenditure. The Board of Admiralty had a prolonged struggle to maintain what they considered to be the minimum standard of efficiency, and in this Backhouse's sane judgement and unrivalled knowledge of the material needs of the navy were a tower of strength in preventing economy from going too far.

From his place on the Board Backhouse went to take command of the first battle squadron, with his flag in the *Revenge*, and to be second-in-command of the Mediterranean Fleet, first under Admiral Chatfield and then under Admiral Sir W. W. Fisher [q.v.]. He was promoted admiral in February 1934, was relieved of his command three months later, and in

August 1935 became commander-in-chief, Home Fleet, with his flag in the *Nelson*, one of the two newest and most powerful ships. At the coronation review in May 1937 the whole assembled fleet was under his command. He was relieved in April 1938, having been selected to succeed Lord Chatfield as first sea lord and chief of the naval staff. This office he took up in September, having in the meantime been appointed first and principal aide-de-camp to the king. It was a critical moment in world affairs, and the first sea lord was immediately plunged into business of the most exacting kind and had to be prepared to give professional advice on issues of major importance. But early next year his health began to fail; he relinquished his duties in May, was placed on the retired list in June, and a serious illness developed from which he died in London 15 July 1939. With the King's approval he had been specially promoted to admiral of the fleet a week previously.

Backhouse was a man of striking appearance, six feet four inches tall, with charming manners and a winning personality, of great strength of character and unswerving devotion to duty. His tireless love of his work and justifiable confidence in his own judgement led him somewhat to overlook the advantage of devolution to trusted assistants, both in high command afloat and in office administration, while keeping the control of policy and the ultimate decision in his own hands. He was recognized throughout the service as one of the ablest and most eminent sea officers of his time, and his premature death on the eve of the outbreak of the war of 1939–1945 was regarded as a national calamity. He was beloved by all who knew him well.

Backhouse was appointed C.B. (civil) in 1914, C.B. (military) in 1928, C.M.G. for war service in 1917, K.C.B. in 1933, G.C.V.O. at the coronation review in 1937, and G.C.B. in 1938. He married in 1907 Dora Louisa, sixth daughter of John Ritchie Findlay, of Aberlour, Banffshire, and had two sons and four daughters. The elder son, John Edward (born 1909), succeeded his uncle as third baronet in January 1944 and was killed in action in Normandy the following August.

[Admiralty records; personal knowledge.]
VINCENT W. BADDELEY.

BAILEY, SIR ABE, first baronet (1864–1940), South African financier and statesman, was born at Cradock, Cape Colony,

6 November 1864, the only son of Thomas Bailey, of Keighley, Yorkshire, who became a general storekeeper at Queen's Town, Cape Colony, and represented it in the legislative assembly. His mother was Ann Drummond, daughter of Peter McEwan, of Muthill, Crieff, Perthshire. Bailey was sent to England to be educated at the Keighley Trade and Grammar School and at Clewer House, Windsor. Returning to the Cape in 1881 he worked at his father's business until he left for the Barberton gold-fields in the Transvaal, arriving there in July 1886. He began dealing in shares with a capital of £100. Losing it he borrowed £10 from a friend, took out a licence, and setting up as a broker on the Stock Exchange, began to make his way. Leaving Barberton in March 1887, he went to the Rand in order to continue his sharebroking and to become secretary of the Gipsey and Kleinfontein mines. As soon as his fortune warranted it he abandoned broking and the secretary-ship and began acquiring and developing properties. In the end his business inter-ests comprised the chairmanship of the fourteen subsidiary companies in the Abe Bailey and London and Rhodesian mining group, a directorship of the Central Mining and Investment Corporation con-trolling twenty-four subsidiary companies, and several other company directorships. He became one of the largest breeders and owners of race-horses both in England and in South Africa. His most famous horse, Son-in-Law, won the Cesarewitch and the Goodwood Cup, was founder of a line of stayers including Foxlaw, Trimdon, Fox-hunter, and Tiberius, and was sire of Straitlace, winner of the Oaks in 1924. Bailey himself won the Oaks in 1936 with Lovely Rosa and was second in the Derby of 1935 with Robin Goodfellow. He also carried on large farming operations in the Colesberg district of the Cape.

Bailey began his public service in the Johannesburg Staatsraad before the Jame-son Raid of 1895. He was a member of the 'reform committee' and was sen-tenced, for the raid, to two years' im-prisonment, afterwards commuted to a fine of £2,000. In the South African war he served in the Intelligence Division and helped to raise and equip Gorringe's Horse and the City Imperial Volunteers. In 1902, after the war, he entered the Cape House of Assembly as 'progressive' repre-sentative of Barkly West, Cecil Rhodes's old constituency. This seat he resigned in 1905 and, after the grant of responsible government to the Transvaal in 1906, he was elected in 1907 to the legislative assembly at Pretoria as member for Krugersdorp, holding the seat until 1910 and becoming whip of the opposition to the administration of General Louis Botha [q.v.]. He was an active worker for South African union, helping to finance the *State*, the organ of the Closer Union Society which was founded to popularize the cause.

In 1915 Bailey re-entered politics as member for his old constituency, Krugers-dorp, taking his seat in the Union House of Assembly as an independent, but sitting with General Botha's South African party. He retained the seat until his defeat at the general election of 1924. Party politics and debate were not the sources of his influence. That lay rather in the bound-less hospitality which he dispensed at Rust-en-Vrede at Muizenberg, near Cape Town, and at his London residence, 38 Bryanston Square. His dispassionate per-sonality, his skill and tact as host, made his houses centres where men of all shades of opinion and experience intermixed and exchanged views. At times they acted as neutral territories for the settlement of political difficulties. The critical meeting of 3 December 1916 which led to the super-session in the premiership of Asquith by Lloyd George was held at 38 Bryanston Square. In March 1933 General Smuts and General James Barry Munnik Hertzog met at Rust-en-Vrede to form a national government for the Union of South Africa, although Bailey personally took no part in these deliberations.

Bailey was appointed K.C.M.G. in 1911 for his services in promoting South African union, and created a baronet in 1919. He died at Rust-en-Vrede 10 August 1940, after having suffered the amputation of both legs, the first in July 1937 and the second in April 1938. In his will he left a quarter of his estate to an Abe Bailey Trust to be applied by the trustees for the advancement and strengthening of the South African people, and his pictures at Bryanston Square in trust for them also. He bequeathed £100,000 or £5,000 a year to the Royal Institute of International Affairs, for research.

Bailey was twice married: first, in 1894 to Caroline Mary (died 1902), elder daughter of John Paddon, a Kimberley merchant; secondly, in 1911 to Mary, only daughter of Derrick Warner William Westenra, fifth Lord Rossmore. By his first wife he had a son, John Milner (born 1900), who succeeded him as second baronet, and one daughter; by his second wife he had two sons and three daughters.

There is a portrait of Bailey, by Oswald Birley, at the Royal Institute of International Affairs. A cartoon of him, by 'Spy', appeared in *Vanity Fair* 9 September 1908.

[*The Times*, 12 August 1940; *African World Annual*, 1941; personal knowledge.]

H. A. WYNDHAM.

BAILEY, JOHN CANN (1864–1931), critic and essayist, the third son of Elijah Crosier Bailey, solicitor, clerk of the peace for Norwich, by his wife, Jane Sarah, daughter of William Robert Cann, of Cavick House, Wymondham, Norfolk, was born at Norwich 10 January 1864. He was educated at Haileybury and at New College, Oxford, where he obtained second classes in classical moderations (1884) and *literae humaniores* (1886), and was called to the bar by the Inner Temple in 1892. He came to London with private means sufficient to enable to him stand for parliament (he unsuccessfully contested the Sowerby division of Yorkshire in the conservative interest in 1895 and 1900), but with little in the way of social acquaintance, other than that which he had formed at the university. Bailey's easy, agreeable, and intelligent conversation, however, gave him a ready entrance into the metropolitan society of the 'nineties; and his marriage in 1900 to Sarah Kathleen (died 1941), the eldest daughter by his second marriage of G. W. Lyttelton, fourth Lord Lyttelton [q.v.], herself a spirited conversationalist, gave him not only a very happy home life but the association of several brothers-in-law of exceptional distinction. These included Arthur Temple Lyttelton, suffragan bishop of Southampton, and Alfred Lyttelton [qq.v.], the lawyer and statesman. He made many friends, was a constant and valued member of the Literary (dining) Society, of which he eventually became president, and, as might be expected of so ardent a Johnsonian, was immensely gratified by his election to 'the Club'.

Bailey's intense pleasure in good talk may possibly have restricted his literary output, but his literary ambition was always circumscribed. He related that when people asked him to write a *magnum opus* he used to counter by inquiring: 'If I write it, will you buy it and will you read it?' It is arguable that his best work was, in fact, slight in compass. He himself may have rated his little book on *Milton*

(1915) highest, but there are many good judges who would hold that *Dr. Johnson and his Circle* (1913) gave his particular powers their fullest scope. Bailey's other publications include *Studies in Some Famous Letters* (1899), *An Anthology of English Elegies* (1899), *The Poems of William Cowper* (edited with an introduction and notes, 1905), *The Claims of French Poetry* (1907), *Some Political Ideas and Persons* (1921), *The Continuity of Letters* (1923), *The Diary of Lady Frederick Cavendish* (2 vols., 1927), and *Shakespeare* ('English Heritage' series, 1929). For the rest, he was a constant contributor to *The Times Literary Supplement*, for which he did much important though anonymous work; to the *Quarterly Review*, of which he was deputy-editor in 1907–1908 and again in 1909–1910; to the *Edinbugh Review* and the *Fortnightly Review*; and to the *London Mercury*. Tributes in distinguished quarters attested his critical powers. Among these an observation attributed to A. J. Balfour (first Earl of Balfour, q.v.) to the effect that Bailey, whilst tending to take traditional views in literature which were generally the true views, would invest them with freshness and interest, is perhaps worth preserving as an estimate of his place in literary criticism.

As chairman (1912–1915) and president (1925–1926) of the English Association, Bailey made a further contribution to the study of English letters, and as chairman (1923–1931) of the executive committee of the National Trust for places of historic interest or natural beauty and also of the Fulham branch of the Charity Organisation Society, he disclosed a practical interest in things of beauty and in matters of social welfare. Never a strong man physically, Bailey died in London 29 June 1931 in the plenitude of his intellectual powers. He lies buried in the churchyard of Wramplingham near Wymondham, as befits one who valued both his connexion with the county of Norfolk and his membership of the Church of England. His outlook was that of a broad churchman. He had three daughters, the youngest of whom predeceased him.

[*The Times*, 30 June 1931; *John Bailey, 1864–1931, Letters and Diaries*, edited by his wife (containing a bibliography of Bailey's writings), 1935; personal knowledge.]

A. CECIL.

BAILLIE, SIR JAMES BLACK (1872–1940), vice-chancellor of the university of Leeds, was born at Haddington 24 October

29

1872, the second of the four sons of William Baillie, of Haddington, by his wife, Agnes Black. Educated at Haddington School, the university of Edinburgh, where he obtained the Baxter scholarship and Hamilton fellowship, and the Ferguson scholarship and Shaw fellowship in philosophy, and at Trinity College, Cambridge, he subsequently studied at Halle, Strasburg, and Paris. For a time he was lecturer in philosophy at University College, Dundee, until, in 1902, he was appointed professor of moral philosophy at the university of Aberdeen. During the war of 1914–1918 he served for two years in the Intelligence division of the Admiralty, developing administrative talent which, from 1917 to 1919, was exercised in the work of arbitration and conciliation in industrial disputes at the Ministry of Labour. In 1919 he was appointed to the panel of chairmen of arbitration courts, and in 1920 became chairman of the board appointed for the jute, flax, hemp, and kindred industries. He resigned this post and his professorship in 1924, when he was chosen to succeed Sir Michael Sadler as vice-chancellor of the university of Leeds.

During the fourteen years in which he filled this office Baillie was busily occupied with increasing the number of professorships and lecturerships and with the promotion of a building scheme, including the library given by Lord Brotherton in 1930, and laboratories for the chemical and other scientific departments which were completed by the time of his retirement under the age-limit in 1938. In 1929 he became a member of the royal commission on the civil service. He continued his work on arbitration committees, and after his retirement went for a time to Trinidad as chairman of the arbitration tribunal set up to inquire into disputes in the oil-fields. He died at Weybridge 9 June 1940.

Baillie married in 1906 Helena May, youngest daughter of John Gwynne Jones, of Aylstone Hill, Hereford; there were no children of the marriage. He was knighted in 1931, appointed O.B.E. in 1918, and in 1933 was made a knight commander of the Order of the Crown of Italy. He received the honorary degree of LL.D. from the university of Aberdeen, and was an honorary freeman of the Company of Clothworkers and a freeman of the City of London. He was Hibbert lecturer in 1931. His chief published works are The Origin and Significance of Hegel's Logic (1901) and a translation of Hegel's Phäno-

menologie des Geistes (2 vols., 1910, 2nd ed. 1931), An Outline of the Idealistic Construction of Experience (1906), and Studies in Human Nature (1921).

A portrait of Baillie, by G. Fiddes Watt, is in the possession of his widow, and will eventually become the property of Leeds University.

[The Times, 11 June 1940; private information; personal knowledge.]

A. HAMILTON THOMPSON.

BAILLIE, CHARLES WALLACE ALEXANDER NAPIER ROSS COCHRANE-, second BARON LAMINGTON (1860–1940), was born in London 29 July 1860, the only son of the politician and author Alexander Dundas Ross Wishart Cochrane-Baillie, first Baron Lamington [q.v.], by his wife, Annabella Mary Elizabeth, elder daughter of Andrew Robert Drummond, of Cadland, Hampshire. He was educated at Eton and Christ Church, Oxford. In 1885 he became assistant private secretary to Lord Salisbury, and after an unsuccessful candidature at North St. Pancras in the same year, he entered parliament as conservative member for that constituency in 1886. He was only four years in the House of Commons, for he succeeded his father in 1890.

An enthusiastic sportsman, Lamington was fond of travel, and made a notable journey from Siam to Tongking in 1890–1891. In 1895 he was appointed governor of Queensland. There he made substantial contributions to the cause of Imperial unity, which bore fruit later in the federation of Australia. When the South African war broke out, he raised volunteers, and on their sailing, bade them farewell with stirring speeches. His state was at the time afflicted by a long drought which lasted seven years and caused much hardship. In order to understand the disaster, and to promote means of alleviation, Lamington, as no other governor had done, traversed the length and breadth of Queensland.

Lamington returned to his Lanarkshire estates in 1901, and two years later his interest was directed to the East by his selection as governor of Bombay in succession to H. S. Northcote, Lord Northcote [q.v.]. He sought in western India to understand the needs of all classes and to provide for them. The viceroy of India at the time was his old Oxford friend, Lord Curzon, whose love of dominance might have created difficulties but for Lamington's fairness, moderation, and good sense. The latter, however, was obliged in 1907, after three and a half years' service, to resign his governorship on account of the serious illness of his wife. Lady Lamington gave her husband steadfast support in all his public activities, which were numerous. One of them was his constant interest in the Territorial movement. He was lieutenant-colonel of the Lanarkshire Yeomanry, and an honorary colonel of the 6th battalion of the Scottish Rifles (Cameronians). He was also captain of the Royal Company of Archers, the king's bodyguard for Scotland. During the war of 1914–1918 he vigorously encouraged recruiting, and in 1919 he went to Syria as commissioner of the British relief unit.

In the House of Lords Lamington spoke on many subjects. He was always ready to support the claims of minorities and smaller nations struggling to be free. But the main interest of his life was the welfare of the British Empire, and the advocacy of a good understanding between the British government and eastern peoples. He was a member of many organizations concerned with oriental well-being, and diligent in his attention to them, as indeed he was to all his public work.

On 13 March 1940 Lord Lamington was present at a meeting of the Royal Central Asian Society at the Caxton Hall. It was at this meeting that a man in the audience rose and fired several shots at the occupants of the platform, killing Sir Michael O'Dwyer [q.v.] and wounding others, of whom Lord Lamington was one. In spite of the shock, his injury, which was in the forearm, seemed to make him more than ever zealous on behalf of Indian reform.

Lamington was appointed G.C.M.G. in 1900 and G.C.I.E. in 1903. He married in 1895 Mary Haughton, youngest daughter of William Wallace Hozier, first Baron Newlands, and had a son and a daughter. He died at Lamington House, Lanarkshire, 16 September 1940, and was succeeded as third baron by his son, Victor Alexander Brisbane William (born 1896), who was awarded the M.C. in the war of 1914–1918.

A portrait of Lamington as a boy, by Henry Richard Graves (1868), and another, as a young man (1895), are in the possession of the family.

[*The Times*, 18 September 1940; private information.]   ALFRED COCHRANE.

BAIN, FRANCIS WILLIAM (1863–1940), scholar and writer, the third son of Joseph Bain, archivist and antiquary, of Sweethope, Bothwell, Lanarkshire, by his wife, Charlotte, daughter of Edward Piper, of Alston, Cumberland, was born at Bothwell 2 April 1863. He was elected an exhibitioner (1877) and a scholar (1878) on the foundation of Westminster, and went up as a Westminster scholar to Christ Church, Oxford, in 1882. He obtained a second class in classical moderations (1884) and a first class in *literae humaniores* (1886), and was also a 'blue' for association football for four years from 1883 to 1886, captaining the team in his fourth year. In 1889 he obtained a fellowship (which he held until 1896) at All Souls College; in 1890 he married Helen Margarita, daughter of Henry Blandford, of Blandford, Dorset; and, in 1892, to the surprise of many of his friends, he took a post in the Indian educational services as professor of history and political economy at the Deccan College at Poona, where he remained until his retirement in 1919, after serving, in addition, as junior principal in 1908, and as senior principal in 1911. He was appointed C.I.E. in 1918, and when he left Poona he received an address in a silver casket expressing the enthusiastic appreciation of many hundreds of former students not only for his teaching but for his deep sympathy with, and insight into, the higher elements in Indian life and thought; he was regarded 'not only as a professor but also as a prophet and a philosopher'.

After 1919 Bain lived quietly in London, paying frequent visits to All Souls, where, as in the years before 1914, he was always an eagerly awaited guest; but deeply affected by the death of his wife (1931) and of his only child, a daughter (1934), he retired into a self-imposed isolation, broken with difficulty even by his most intimate friends, which continued until his death. This took place in London 24 February 1940.

Bain, as an undergraduate, developed the views on life, philosophy, politics, and literature which he maintained with increasing tenacity to the end. Aristotle was for him 'the master of the wise'; in politics he was a tory with a creed based on his interpretation of Bolingbroke and Disraeli; for whigs, liberals, and modern conservatives he had a profound contempt; in modern physical and natural science he saw only a perversion of judgement and the facts; the classical economists and most historians he regarded as ability corrupted by original sin; but into imaginative literature of all types he had a wonderful insight. As a teacher he could expound with fascinating lucidity views which he was convinced were fundamentally wrong, and instruct his Indian students that 'this is what they must say' and then demonstrate its perversity and errors. Deep in Bain's mind was an inspiring mystical element which at Poona was richly nourished by his study of Indian life, religion, and the Sanskrit classics.

In his early years Bain published two or three volumes of fiction, philosophical pamphlets, and a remarkable essay on *The English Monarchy and its Revolutions* (1894), full of penetrating observations, all of which attracted no attention; but in 1899 he found the right scope for his genius when he published *A Digit of The Moon*, a Hindu love-story, professing to be a translation from a Sanskrit manuscript. Even experts were at first taken in, but its quality both in imagination and style captured a large and critical public, which rightly hailed it as unique in English literature. It was followed by twelve other similar Hindu love-stories, the last of which, *The Substance of a Dream* (1919), was as successful as its predecessors. He then ceased to write.

Bain's personality was even more impressive than his best writing. Strikingly handsome, when stirred by his company he exercised almost a witchery over his friends; and in the common room at All Souls his conversation in that congenial atmosphere, discussing any and every topic, and soaring at times into flights of imaginative eloquence, was an experience impossible to describe, but thrilling to have shared. His loyalty to the college and to a limited circle of friends earned from all an affection as strong as was the admiration of his genius. Copies of most of Bain's writings, long out of print and never reprinted, are in the Codrington library at All Souls. Besides those mentioned above there may be noted his biographical study of *Queen Christina of Sweden* (1890), *On the Realisation of the Possible and the Spirit of Aristotle* (1899), and the essay *De vi physica et imbecillitate Darwiniana* (1903) which summarizes his homage to Aristotle and his views on 'modern science'.

[*The Times*, 26 February 1940; personal knowledge.] CHARLES GRANT ROBERTSON.

BAKER, HERBERT BRERETON (1862–1935), chemist, was born at Livesey, near Blackburn, 25 June 1862, the second son of John Baker, curate in charge of Livesey, afterwards vicar of St. John's church, Blackburn, by his wife, Caroline Slater. Ill health developed in him the habits of a student: he could read before he was four years old and by the time that he was ten he had read through most of his father's library. He was educated first at Blackburn Grammar School and then at Manchester Grammar School, and, changing from the classical to the science side, he came under the influence of Francis Jones, often referred to by him as 'the best of all teachers'. A Brackenbury scholarship at Balliol College and a school Brackenbury award enabled him to go to Oxford where, with Harold Baily Dixon as his tutor, he in 1883 obtained a first class in natural science. From 1883 to 1885 he was demonstrator in chemistry at Balliol and private assistant to Dixon, who communicated to him his own enthusiasm for investigation and led him into that field of research to which later he contributed so notably—the influence of moisture on chemical change. In 1886 he went as chemistry master and head of the science side to Dulwich College. Here he built up a most successful science side and many of his pupils have testified to the excellence of his teaching and to the interest in research which the knowledge that he himself was engaged in important investigations inspired in them. Baker is indeed to be regarded as one of the few schoolmasters who have become eminent both in scholastic and in scientific work. Some of his most remarkable results were obtained while he was at Dulwich and he was elected F.R.S. in 1902 while there. In the same year he was appointed headmaster of Alleyn's School, Dulwich, a secondary school on the same foundation, but shortly afterwards (1904) he returned to Oxford as Lee's reader in chemistry at Christ Church, of which he was elected a student and tutor. Here he was responsible for the teaching of inorganic chemistry in the university and his experimentally illustrated lectures were highly popular. In 1912 he accepted the chief professorship of chemistry at the Imperial College of Science and Technology, South Kensington, in succession to Sir T. E. Thorpe [q.v.], and held this post until his retirement in 1932.

In April 1915 Baker was called upon by the rector of the Imperial College, Sir Alfred Keogh [q.v.], who in the previous year had become director of medical services at the War Office, to advise on the steps to be taken to meet the serious menace of the German gas attacks. For his valuable services in this and other scientific duties undertaken for the war departments he was appointed C.B.E. in 1917.

Baker's claim to fame rests on his achievements as an experimentalist rather than as a theoretical chemist. His exceptional skill in the preparation and manipulation of intensively dried substances enabled him to achieve results which others, with less mastery of the technique, were sometimes at first unable to repeat. Perhaps his most outstanding achievements in this field were the demonstration that dried ammonium chloride does not dissociate when volatilized by heat: that hydrogen and oxygen prepared by the electrolysis of pure barium hydroxide do not combine on heating when carefully dried; and that while very dry nitrogen trioxide does not break up on vaporization, the slightest trace of moisture causes the gas to dissociate completely into nitric oxide and nitrogen peroxide. He demonstrated the slowing down or complete stoppage of chemical action in numerous other instances and his remarkable success in demonstrating this effect led chemists to refer to the relative dryness of things as dry, very dry, or 'Baker dry'.

In 1923 Baker was awarded the Davy medal of the Royal Society, and in 1912 the Longstaff medal of the Chemical Society, of which he was elected president in 1926. In 1926 the university of Aberdeen conferred upon him the honorary degree of LL.D. In 1905 he married Muriel, only child of Harry James Powell, partner in the Whitefriars glass-works. She too was a trained chemist and collaborated with her husband in a number of his researches. They had one son, who predeceased his father, and one daughter. Baker died at his home at Gerrards Cross 27 April 1935.

[*Obituary Notices of Fellows of the Royal Society*, No. 4, December 1935 (portrait); *Journal* of the Chemical Society, 1935, part ii (portrait); personal knowledge.]

B. MOUAT JONES.

BALDWIN BROWN, GERARD (1849–1932), historian of art. [See BROWN.]

BALFOUR, SIR ANDREW (1873–1931), expert in tropical medicine and public health, and novelist, was born in Edinburgh 21 March 1873, the eldest son of Thomas Alexander Goldie Balfour,

M.D., of Edinburgh, by his wife, Margaret, daughter of Peter Christall, of Elgin. He was educated at George Watson's College and at the university of Edinburgh, graduating M.B., C.M. in 1894 and M.D. in 1898 with a thesis on the 'toxicity of dye-stuffs and river pollution' for which he received a gold medal. After a short period of private practice he entered Gonville and Caius College, Cambridge, as an advanced student in 1895. He took the D.P.H. there in 1897 and the B.Sc.(Edin.), in public health, in 1900. During the South African war he served (1900–1901) as a civil surgeon and gained the Queen's medal with three clasps. In 1901 the counsel and friendship of (Sir) Patrick Manson [q.v.] interested him in tropical medicine, in which he made his reputation. In 1902 he became director of the Wellcome Tropical Research Laboratories at Khartoum and local medical officer of health. His knowledge of Arabic, his popularity with the Sudanese, and his untiring energy resulted in the banishment of malaria from Khartoum and made it a modern and sanitary city. His work there earned the support and approbation of the British administrative triumvirate, Lord Cromer [q.v.], Lord Kitchener [q.v.], and Sir Reginald Wingate, and he strongly advocated that the care and health of native communities were essential features of modern rule.

In addition to the duties of organization Balfour made several important discoveries in protozoology. These included work on spirochaetosis of birds and of man, the study of the life-history of these organisms in the tick, and the identification of a leishmanoid disease of the skin. In order to study protozoa he explored the upper reaches of the White Nile in a floating laboratory. All this scientific work was published in the four reports of the Wellcome Research Laboratories (1904–1911). In 1913 he returned to England and became the founder of the Wellcome Bureau of Scientific Research.

During the war of 1914–1918 Balfour, with the rank of lieutenant-colonel, Army Medical Service, rendered conspicuous service. First, as president of the medical advisory committee of the Mediterranean Expeditionary Force in Mudros, Salonika, Egypt, and Mesopotamia, and then as scientific adviser in East Africa, he organized sanitary reforms throughout these theatres of war. Subsequently he was asked to reorganize the health service of Egypt, and later in 1918, at the request of General Sir Edmund (later Viscount) Allenby [q.v.], he examined and reported on anti-malarial measures in Palestine.

At the conclusion of the war Balfour resumed scientific research at the Wellcome Bureau, but he was soon called away from his laboratory. In 1921 and again in 1923 he visited Mauritius and Bermuda to advise the Colonial Office on health reform in these islands. In 1923 he was appointed director of the London School of Hygiene and Tropical Medicine and for seven years worked with boundless energy towards the perfecting of the school and on government committees. The predominant place which this school has taken in the teaching of and research into preventive medicine owes much to Balfour's initial administration.

Balfour contributed extensively to medical literature. The following are of permanent value: *Public Health and Preventive Medicine* (with C. J. Lewis, 1902); *Memoranda on Medical Diseases in Tropical and Sub-Tropical Areas* (1916); *War Against Tropical Disease* (1920); *Reports to the Health Committee of the League of Nations on Tuberculosis and Sleeping Sickness in Equatorial Africa* (1923); *Health Problems of the Empire* (with H. H. Scott, 1924).

Early in his career Balfour achieved fame as a novelist. His novels of historical adventure, 'wild tales' as he called them, show the influence of R. L. Stevenson, but he had a distinctive and vigorous style of his own. He wrote *By Stroke of Sword* (1897), *To Arms* (1898), *Vengeance is Mine* (1899), *Cashiered and Other War Stories* (1902), and *The Golden Kingdom* (1903).

Balfour was appointed C.M.G. in 1912, C.B. in 1918, and K.C.M.G. in 1930. Honorary degrees were conferred upon him by the university of Edinburgh and by the universities of Johns Hopkins and Rochester, U.S.A. He was elected F.R.C.P. (London and Edinburgh). In 1920 he was awarded the Mary Kingsley medal and from 1925 to 1927 was president of the Royal Society of Tropical Medicine and Hygiene. He was endowed with qualities which brought him distinction in various paths of life. He was a fine athlete, and played Rugby football for both Edinburgh and Cambridge, obtaining his 'blue' at the latter university. He won his international cap for Scotland (1896, 1897). He was a noted boxer, a keen fisherman, and a big-game shot. He was of a kindly and modest disposition. An old friend describes him as 'a rock of a man, handsome of mien and fine of figure'. His conversation and speeches were adorned with wit and humour: his work in tropical medicine and public health was of outstanding merit.

Balfour married in 1902 Grace, third daughter of George Nutter, of Sidcup, Kent, and had two sons. His health broke down in 1929 under the strain of overwork and he died near Tonbridge 30 January 1931.

[*The Times*, 2 February 1931; *British Medical Journal*, 1931, vol. i, p. 245 (portrait); *Lancet*, 1931, vol. i, p. 325; *Nature*, 21 February 1931; private information; personal knowledge.]   ARTHUR S. MACNALTY.

BALFOUR, LADY FRANCES (1858–1931), churchwoman, suffragist, and author, was born at Argyll Lodge, Kensington, 22 February 1858, the fifth daughter of George Douglas Campbell, eighth Duke of Argyll [q.v.], by his first wife, Lady Elizabeth Georgiana, eldest daughter of George Granville Leveson-Gower, second Duke of Sutherland. Her early days were passed at Roseneath Castle, Dunbartonshire, and Inveraray Castle, Argyll. In 1879 she married (Colonel) Eustace James Anthony Balfour (died 1911), youngest brother of A. J. Balfour (afterwards first Earl of Balfour, q.v.), of Gerald William Balfour (afterwards second earl), of F. M. Balfour [q.v.], and of E. M. Sidgwick [q.v.]. They had two sons and three daughters. She received honorary degrees from the universities of Durham (1919) and Edinburgh (1921). She died in London 25 February 1931, and was buried at Whittingehame, East Lothian.

Lady Frances Campbell was cradled in the religious disputes which shook the heart of the men of those days. In her veins flowed the blood of Archibald Campbell, first and only Marquess of Argyll [q.v.], and in her home she felt the strength of these controversial currents. For while her father had strenuously worked to prevent the disruption of the Scottish Church in 1843, her nurse, Elizabeth King, a remarkable woman, was a stern Calvinist who harrowed her charges with the tales of the martyrs on the moors and had 'come out' at the disruption. But R. H. Story [q.v.], who was minister of Roseneath from 1860 to 1886, overcame the antagonism thus created, and inspired Lady Frances with a love for the Church of Scotland which was the ruling passion of her life; but to the end, when Lady Frances denounced innovations (as she often did) and upheld the old order, it was Elizabeth King and not Dr. Story who spoke. The achievement of which she may well have been most justly proud was the rebuilding of Crown Court church (the church of the Scottish ambassador in London prior to 1603), for which she collected the money and for which her husband was the architect. It was her happiness to see the Church reunited in 1929, and in spite of infirmity she came to Edinburgh, to 'keep tryst', as it were, with her father, with the Marquess, and with all those of her race who had died for conscience' sake. In this one life was focused the history of centuries.

Lady Frances Balfour was an unwearied leader in the cause of women's enfranchisement and was a most effective speaker. She worked with Dame Millicent Fawcett [q.v.] in the cause of votes for women. A mistress of invective, she wielded the dagger of sarcastic wit with the same zest as her ancestors had wielded the broadsword. She wrote much for the periodical press and published several memoirs, of which the best are *Lady Victoria Campbell* (an account of her third sister, 1911), *The Life and Letters of the Reverend James MacGregor* (1912), and *Dr. Elsie Inglis* (1918). *The Life of George, fourth Earl of Aberdeen* (2 vols., 1923), *A Memoir of Lord Balfour of Burleigh* (1925), and two volumes of reminiscences, bearing as their title the Argyll motto, *Ne Obliviscaris* (1930), also came from her pen. The books will be of value for historians, especially her autobiographical sketches of life at Inveraray and Whittingehame; but her personality was far greater than her books.

By her marriage Lady Frances Balfour was brought into close touch with both the great political parties. The daughter of one who for more than twenty years was a member of Gladstone's cabinets, she married the nephew of Lord Salisbury, and her eager mind took full advantage of her opportunities. She became the intimate friend of Gladstone, the Cecils, the Asquiths, of Randall Davidson, and Cosmo Gordon Lang. She was equally at home at Lambeth and at the General Assembly in Edinburgh, and she exhorted, corrected, and reproved all, when the necessity occurred. Stories were often told against her, but she had a personal magnetism and a gift of making friends no less remarkable than her courage and her crusading spirit.

A portrait of Lady Frances Balfour, by (Sir) Edward Burne-Jones (1880), is in the possession of Lieutenant-Colonel Francis C. C. Balfour, of The Cleeve, Ross-on-Wye.

[*The Times*, 26 February 1931; Lady Frances Balfour, *Ne Obliviscaris*, 2 vols., 1930; private information; personal knowledge.]   Norman Maclean.

BALFOUR, HENRY (1863–1939), anthropologist, was born at Croydon 11 April 1863, the only son of Lewis Balfour, silk broker, of Croydon, by his wife, Sarah Walker Comber. He was educated at Charterhouse and at Trinity College, Oxford, where he earned a reputation as an oarsman and as an accomplished fencer and obtained a second class in natural science (biology) in 1885. His earlier travels were primarily dictated by his interest in zoology, and he remained all his life a devoted student of birds, but under the influence of H. N. Moseley and of (Sir) E. B. Tylor [qq.v.] he very soon directed his attention to anthropology and in particular to the study of material culture both comparatively and in evolution. Even before he took his degree he and his fellow student (Sir) W. B. Spencer [q.v.] were helping Tylor and Moseley to arrange the ethnological and archaeological collections which General A. H. L. F. Pitt-Rivers [q.v.] had given to the university in 1883. Spencer went to Melbourne in 1887, but Balfour remained in Oxford and in 1891 was appointed curator of the Pitt-Rivers Museum, a post which he held until his death at Headington, Oxford, 9 February 1939.

When the university of Oxford established its diploma course in anthropology in 1907, Balfour undertook all the teaching of technology and of prehistoric archaeology, academic work which brought him into contact not only with undergraduates but with a long succession of colonial civil service probationers, and of officers on leave from service overseas. He lectured in the museum, handling and comparing specimens with characteristic skill and establishing a personal relationship with his pupils which led to a stream of accessions, documented as he desired. But his position as curator of the Pitt-Rivers galleries did not prevent him from travelling widely. In Norway (which he visited five times between 1905 and 1929) he studied the habits of whales, and of whalers; in South Africa he was probably the first to detect palaeolithic implements in the gravels of the Zambezi River and to correlate them to prehistoric European types; in Assam he travelled on foot through the Naga Hills; he visited Lapland early in his career, returning later, and his other travels included a visit to Australia and to New Zealand with calls at various islands in Indonesia and the Pacific, and a return via Japan and the United States of America. In a similar way his visits to South Africa were used to help him to direct knowledge of other parts of that continent.

Balfour was an active fellow of the Royal Geographical Society and was president from 1936 to 1938; he was president of the Folk-Lore Society in 1923–1924, of the Museums Association in 1909, and of the (Royal) Anthropological Institute in 1904; he was elected F.R.S. in 1924. He was also president of the Prehistoric Society of East Anglia, and was an honorary or corresponding member of many foreign societies. He was elected a research fellow of Exeter College, Oxford, for seven years in 1904 and was again elected from 1919 onwards, and in 1935 the university conferred upon him the personal title of professor. In 1887 he married Edith Marie Louise (died 1938), only daughter of Robert Francis Wilkins, of Kingswear, South Devon; she shared his many interests, his work, and often his travels. They had one son.

Balfour was in many respects the ideal curator for an ethnological museum. He combined a useful knowledge of the classics with a working knowledge of German and with fluent French, and his natural inclination towards methodical classification was fortified by his training in zoology. He was a musician, had a lively sense of humour, and very great personal charm, and made many friends, enriching the collections in his charge by their contributions as well as by his own. For his powers of observation were acute, and made him an admirable collector as well as a naturalist. He was perhaps the first to demonstrate that the 'drumming' or 'bleating' of snipe is caused by the vibration of the outer tail-feathers. His range of knowledge of the material culture of primitive peoples has probably never been equalled, and he showed great tenacity in solving problems of the use and provenance of any unfamiliar object brought to him. Besides being a collector and an observer he was himself a craftsman. He drew with great facility, and enjoyed drawing, as witness his illustrated

programmes for the Oxford Fencing Club. He held that to understand primitive or prehistoric craftsmanship it is necessary to learn its methods, and examples of his admirable handiwork in flint may be seen in the Pitt-Rivers Museum, which, arranged typologically instead of geographically and with so many of its exhibits labelled in his firm and clear handwriting, is his chief contribution to human knowledge, and was his chosen means of imparting his own learning to others.

As a writer Balfour left all too little, for his work as a curator engrossed his time, but what he did write he wrote extremely well. *The Evolution of Decorative Art* (1893) was his first important publication, and perhaps the only one in book form, but among his many other publications the following are possibly the most significant: his presidential address to section H (anthropology) of the British Association at Cambridge in 1904, remodelled later as an introduction to Pitt-Rivers's *The Evolution of Culture* (1906); 'The *Goura*' (*Journal* of the (Royal) Anthropological Institute, vol. xxxii, 1902); 'The Relationship of Museums to the Study of Anthropology' (presidential address to the (Royal) Anthropological Institute, 1904); 'Musical Instruments from the Malay Peninsula' (*Fasciculi Malayenses*, 1904); 'The Friction-Drum' (*Journal* of the Royal Anthropological Institute, vol. xxxvii, 1907); 'The Fire-piston' (*Anthropological Essays presented to Edward Burnett Tylor*, 1907, reprinted in the *Report* of the . . . Smithsonian Institution for 1907, Washington, 1910); 'The Origin of West African Cross-bows' (*Journal* of the (Royal) African Society, 1909, similarly reprinted, 1911); 'Kite-Fishing' (*Essays and Studies presented to William Ridgeway*, 1913); 'Frictional Fire-making with a Flexible Sawing-thong' (*Journal* of the Royal Anthropological Institute, vol. xliv, 1914); 'Some Ethnological Suggestions in regard to Easter Island' (*Folk-Lore*, December 1917); *The Archer's Bow in the Homeric Poems* (Huxley memorial lecture for 1921); 'Earth Smoking-pipes from South Africa and Central Asia' (*Man*, May 1922); 'The Origin of Stencilling in the Fiji Islands' (*Journal* of the Royal Anthropological Institute, vol. liv, 1924); 'The Status of the Tasmanians among the Stone-Age Peoples' (presidential address to the Prehistoric Society of East Anglia, 1924, in which Balfour called attention to

the similarity of Tasmanian to Aurigna-
cian and Mousterian forms, which he had
noticed at a time when others spoke of the
Tasmanians as being in an 'eolithic'
stage); 'South Africa's Contribution to
Prehistoric Archaeology' (presidential address to section H of the British Association, 1929); 'The Tandu Industry in
Northern Nigeria and its Affinities Elsewhere' (*Essays presented to C. G. Seligman,*
1934); and *Spinners and Weavers in
Anthropological Research* (Frazer lecture
for 1937, 1938).

[*Obituary Notices of Fellows of the Royal
Society,* No. 8, January 1940 (portrait); *Man,*
May 1939; personal knowledge.]

J. H HUTTON.

BALL, JOHN (1861–1940), golfer, was
born 24 December 1861 at Hoylake,
Cheshire, the second son of John Ball, by
his wife, Margaret Parry. The father was
of yeoman-farmer stock and the owner of
the Royal Hotel at Hoylake, which became
the headquarters of the Royal Liverpool
Golf Club when the course was laid out
in 1869. The boy was therefore brought
up with golf on his doorstep, and his early
promise was such that at the age of sixteen he entered for the open championship in 1878 and finished sixth. His career
in big matches began in 1883, and he
became widely known when the amateur
championship was founded in 1885; but
it was not until 1888 that he came into
his own by beating J. E. Laidlay at Prestwick by 5 and 4 in the final of the amateur
championship. After winning it again at
Hoylake in 1890, in that same year, on
what Dr. Laidlaw Purves called 'a great
day for golf', he won the open championship at Prestwick with a score of 164,
beating all the professionals, a feat hitherto deemed impossible for an amateur. In
1892 he tied for second place in the open
championship at Muirfield which was won
by another Hoylake amateur, Harold
Hilton; and he also won the amateur
championship for the third time at Sandwich. In 1894 he won it for the fourth
time at Hoylake, and again in 1899 at
Prestwick. After the South African war,
when he served with the Denbighshire
Yeomanry, his play showed no perceptible
falling off; but it was not until 1907 that
he won the amateur championship again,
this time at St. Andrews. In 1910 at
Hoylake he won it for the seventh time,
and in 1912 at Westward Ho! for the
eighth time, a record wholly without
parallel. Of these matches, the most

memorable were that of 1894 at Hoylake
with S. Mure Fergusson, in which he
played a famous brassy shot over the
cross bunkers to the Dun (then the 17th)
hole and won by a hole, and that of 1899
against his great Scottish competitor F. G.
Tait, when he won at the 37th hole. Having
been at one time in the morning round five
down, he gradually retrieved himself and
was one up with two to play. Both played
historic shots from the bunker at the Alps
(the 17th), Tait from water, Ball from hard
wet sand close to the boarded edge of the
bunker. Tait saved the match with a
three at the home hole, but at the 37th
Ball laid an iron shot about eight feet from
the hole and holed the putt for three. In
1912 he beat Abe Mitchell, later a famous
professional, at the 38th hole, but perhaps
the finest golf he ever played in his later
years was in the final of 1910, when he beat
Collinson Charleton Aylmer by 10 and 9.
His lesser successes were innumerable:
he was three times Irish open amateur
champion (1893, 1894, and 1899); he won
the St. George's Cup at Sandwich four
years running (1888 to 1891); and he
regularly played for England against Scotland from the first international match in
1902 until 1911.

Ball's style was eminently characteristic, with a peculiar underhand grip of
the right hand, but the swing was a perfect
model of grace and rhythm. He was a
magnificent iron player and he set up a
new standard of accuracy in long iron shots
hit right up to the flag. If he had a comparatively weak spot, it was on the green;
he was inclined to miss short putts. As a
match player he had the most indomitable
spirit and seemed to revel in a close finish.
A quiet, reserved man, he had a great
dislike of publicity, but withal a remarkable power for inspiring hero-worship,
especially at Hoylake. In his later years
he parted with his interest in the Royal
Hotel there, and went to live at Lygan-y-
wern in Flintshire, where he died 2 December 1940. Late in life he married Nellie
Williams.

A portrait of Ball by R. E. Morrison
hangs in the club-house of the Royal
Liverpool Golf Club at Hoylake.

[*Golf* (Badminton Library), 1890; G. B.
Farrar, *The Royal Liverpool Golf Club, 1869–
1932,* 1933; *The Golfing Annual* and *The
Golfer's Year Book* (*passim*); personal knowledge.]   BERNARD DARWIN.

BALLANCE, SIR CHARLES AL-
FRED (1856–1936), surgeon, was born

at Taunton 30 August 1856, the eldest son and second child of Charles Alfred Ballance, silk-throwster, later of Stanley House, Lower Clapton, by his wife, Caroline Hendebourck, daughter of Samuel Hendebourck Pollard, of Taunton. Sir Hamilton Ballance was his youngest brother. He was educated at Taunton College, in Germany, and at St. Thomas's Hospital, where he graduated M.B. (Lond.) with first class honours in every subject. He became aural surgeon at St. Thomas's in 1885, as well as assistant surgeon to the West London Hospital, and was among the first to succeed in radical mastoid operation. In 1882 he proceeded M.S. with a gold medal. He was elected assistant surgeon in 1891, surgeon in 1900, and consulting surgeon in 1919; and was surgeon with (Sir) Victor Horsley [q.v.] at the National Hospital for the Paralysed and Epileptic, Queen Square (1891–1908). During the war of 1914–1918 he was a consultant with rank of colonel, Army Medical Service, in Malta and was appointed C.B. in 1916 and K.C.M.G. in 1918. He was president of the Medical Society of London in 1906, a member of the council (1910) and vice-president (1920–1921) of the Royal College of Surgeons, and the first president of the Society of British Neurological Surgeons in 1927. He was chief surgeon to the Metropolitan Police from 1912 to 1926.

Ballance approached surgical problems through experiment on the living animal, in the tradition of John Hunter [q.v.], seeking physiological authority for new operations. All his research related to urgent questions. His methods were in some cases superseded in his lifetime, for instance his technique for ligation of large arteries, which had marked a distinct advance. His work with (Sir) Charles Sherrington, in the *Journal of Physiology*, on the formation of scar-tissue (1889), made a real addition to knowledge. Ballance was a general surgeon who favoured the 'splendid branches' of aural and neurological surgery. His *Some Points in the Surgery of the Brain and its Membranes* (1907) surveys a field where he had been an early worker, and his scholarly *Essays on the Surgery of the Temporal Bone* (2 vols., 1919) records his valuable contributions over thirty years. But the repair of nerves was his chief interest. With (Sir) James Purves-Stewart he wrote *The Healing of Nerves* (1901) and applied their findings in successful treatment of facial palsy. In 1919 he gave the Brad-

shaw lecture to the Royal College of Surgeons on 'The Surgery of the Heart'. When age precluded him from practice, he made experimental nerve-anastomoses in monkeys, with results of great help to surgery. In the United States of America, in 1932, he studied the development of nerve-grafts, and finally in London he worked at delicate and complicated cross-suture of divided nerves. In 1933 he gave the Lister memorial lecture and was awarded the Lister memorial medal. He received honorary degrees from the universities of Glasgow and Malta.

Ballance was large and imposing. A slow, deliberate manner hid his cultivation and charm. He married in 1883 Sophie Annie (died 1926), only daughter of Alfred Smart, of Blackheath, and had one son, a doctor, who predeceased his father, and five daughters. Ballance died in London 8 February 1936.

[*The Times*, 10 February 1936; *British Medical Journal*, 1936, vol. i, p. 339; *Lancet*, 1936, vol. i, pp. 396 and 450 (portrait); *St. Thomas's Hospital Gazette*, vol. xxxv, p. 337, 1936 (photograph); personal knowledge.]

W. R. LE FANU.

BANBURY, FREDERICK GEORGE, first BARON BANBURY OF SOUTHAM (1850–1936), politician, was born in London 2 December 1850, the eldest son of Frederick Banbury, of Shirley House, Surrey, by his wife, Cecilia Laura, daughter of William Cox, of Woodford Hall, Essex. He was educated at Winchester and afterwards abroad. In 1872 he was elected a member of the Stock Exchange and was head of the firm of Frederick Banbury & Sons, stockbrokers, from 1879 until his retirement in 1906. At the general election of 1892 he entered the House of Commons as conservative member for the Peckham division of Camberwell and retained that seat until the liberal triumph of 1906: within six months of his defeat he was returned at a by-election for the City of London and retained his seat until he entered the House of Lords in January 1924 as Baron Banbury of Southam in Warwickshire. In 1903 he was created a baronet and was sworn of the Privy Council in 1916.

Although Banbury never held office, he made for himself a unique position as an opponent of legislation which appeared to him unnecessary and of change which he did not regard as progress. This was facilitated by his ability to talk at any length at any moment on any subject.

He declared that in his opinion there was too much legislation and he generally opposed bills proposed by private members. His long experience in the City made him an able critic of finance bills, on which he was an undoubted authority, and he also did much useful work for the Public Accounts Committee by carefully scrutinizing estimates. He was a member of the Select Committee on National Expenditure. He earned esteem by his technical knowledge, and his criticism of his own party was seldom resented. A master of House of Commons procedure, he was dexterous in raising points of order. 'Punctual in his attendance, he came to be regarded in his corner of a back bench as the uncompromising champion of the old order. . . . He was always most carefully dressed, and with his formal frock-coat and tall hat, and his slow dignified carriage he would walk to his seat and look round at the increasingly slipshod attire of his colleagues with sad disapproval. The advent of women members into the House he regarded as nothing short of an outrage. Banbury, in fact, became an institution.'

Banbury was for many years a member, and sometime chairman, of the council of the Royal Society for the Prevention of Cruelty to Animals; was sometime a director and chairman of the Great Northern Railway, and a director of the London and Provincial Bank. He married in 1873 Elizabeth Rosa (died 1930), daughter and co-heir of Thomas Barbot Beale, of Brettenham Park, Suffolk, and had one son, who was killed in action in 1914, and one daughter. He died at Warneford Place, Highworth, Wiltshire, 13 August 1936, and was succeeded as second baron by his grandson, Charles William (born posthumously 1915).

There is a portrait of Banbury, by John Collier, in the board-room of the old London and North Eastern Railway Company, and a replica at Warneford Place, Wiltshire, in private possession.

[*The Times*, 14 August 1936.]

E. I. CARLYLE.

BARGER, GEORGE (1878–1939), chemist, was born at Manchester 4 April 1878, the elder son of Gerrit Barger, a Dutch engineer, by his wife, Eleanor Higginbotham. He received his school education at Utrecht, and at the age of sixteen obtained a scholarship to University College, London, which he entered in 1896. After two years' study in London he proceeded in 1898 to King's College, Cambridge, with an entrance scholarship, and in 1901 he was placed in the first class in part ii of the natural sciences tripos in both chemistry and botany. On leaving Cambridge he was appointed demonstrator in botany under Leo Errera, of Brussels, and in 1903 he returned to England to join the staff of the Wellcome Physiological Research Laboratories. In 1909 he was appointed head of the department of chemistry at the Goldsmiths' College, New Cross, and in 1913 became professor of chemistry at the Royal Holloway College, Englefield Green. In 1914 he joined the staff of the Medical Research Committee (later Medical Research Council), and in 1919 he was appointed the first professor of chemistry in relation to medicine in the university of Edinburgh, where he remained until, in 1937, he accepted regius chair of chemistry in the university of Glasgow, an appointment which he held for the rest of his life.

Barger's scientific work followed two main lines, namely, studies of alkaloids and investigations of simpler nitrogenous compounds of biological importance: both arose from his studies of ergot initiated in the Wellcome Physiological Research Laboratories. His main achievements in alkaloid chemistry were the isolation of ergotoxine from ergot, the elucidation of the constitutions of carpaine, physostigmine, and of a group of aporphine alkaloids, and an important contribution to the chemistry of yohimbine.

Barger's identification of tyramine, as one of the compounds responsible for the biological activity of ergot extracts, led to a series of studies of bases similarly derived from naturally occurring amino-acids; among such bases isolated both from ergot and from mammalian tissues was histamine, a compound which later proved to be of the greatest physiological significance. Barger's close association in this field with (Sir) H. H. Dale led to the joint development of the important conception of the sympathomimetic amines.

In the early part of work by others leading to the synthesis of thyroxine and of vitamin B_1, Barger's contribution was considerable. His lifelong interest in ergot found expression in *Ergot and Ergotism* (1931), a masterly monograph covering all aspects of the subject; this was based on his Dohme lectures delivered in 1928 at Johns Hopkins University, Baltimore. In addition to many scientific papers he published three other books: *The Simpler Natural Bases* (1914); *Some Applications of Organic Chemistry to Biology and Medicine* (1930); and *Organic Chemistry for Medical Students* (1932; 2nd ed. 1936; Spanish translation 1935).

An expert linguist and enthusiastic traveller, Barger had close scientific contacts in many countries, which he used with all his power to promote his ideal of free intercourse between scientists of different nations. In his own work he was essentially an experimentalist and his scientific outlook was mechanistic. He was uncompromisingly honest and outspoken, not over-patient, but most generous of himself to his friends and pupils.

Barger was a fellow of King's College, Cambridge, from 1904 to 1910 and was elected F.R.S. in 1919, receiving the society's Davy medal in 1938. He was vice-president of the Chemical Society in the year in which he died, and had been Longstaff medallist in 1936; he was Hanbury medallist of the Pharmaceutical Society (1934) and president of section B of the British Association (1929). He received honorary degrees from the universities of Liverpool, Padua, Heidelberg, Utrecht, Michigan, and Lausanne.

Barger married in 1904 Florence Emily, daughter of Alfred William Thomas, and had two sons and one daughter. He died at Aeschi, Switzerland, 6 January 1939.

A portrait of Barger, by Frank Morley Fletcher (1923), belongs to Mrs. Barger.

[*The Times*, 7 January 1939; *Obituary Notices of Fellows of the Royal Society*, No. 8, January 1940 (bibliography and portrait); *Journal* of the Chemical Society, April 1939; private information; personal knowledge.]

C. R. HARINGTON.

BARLING, SIR (HARRY) GILBERT, baronet (1855–1940), surgeon and academic administrator, was born at Newnham-on-Severn 30 April 1855, the fourth son of William Barling, farmer and veterinary surgeon, of Newnham-on-Severn, by his wife, Eliza Sharpe. He was educated at a boarding-school at Weston, near Bath. The agricultural depression precluded his succeeding his father as a farmer, and lack of funds his adoption of a medical career. He was therefore apprenticed when almost sixteen years of age to a chemist in Manchester, where he learnt little of value and was used by his principal as a drudge and errand-boy; nevertheless, he qualified as a chemist and passed the matriculation examination of London University.

In 1874 Barling became a student at St. Bartholomew's Hospital, where poverty compelled him to take part-time employment. Finding that this occupied too much of his time, he decided to act as coach to his more junior colleagues. One of his pupils chanced to be the son of a Birmingham surgeon who so much appreciated the kindness shown to his son that he promised to help Barling if the opportunity ever occurred. Shortly after graduating M.B. (Lond.) in 1879, the opportunity did occur, and Barling obtained the appointment of resident pathologist at the General Hospital, Birmingham. Five years later (1885), having in the meantime been elected F.R.C.S. (1881), he was appointed assistant surgeon and in 1891 full surgeon, a position which he occupied until his retirement from the active staff at the age of sixty, in 1915, when he was appointed consulting surgeon. Whilst he was an assistant surgeon he drew up a scheme for rebuilding the hospital which was accepted, and the present General Hospital was opened in 1897.

Barling's surgical career began in the early Listerian days and covered a revolutionary period in surgery; he was the first surgeon on the staff of his hospital to remove the appendix, the kidney, the gall-bladder, and tumours from the brain and spinal cord. Although he was not a brilliant surgical genius like his contemporaries R. L. Tait [q.v.] and Jordan Lloyd, yet by his knowledge and skill he probably contributed more than any other man to the reputation of Birmingham as a surgical centre.

Barling's association with the university of Birmingham was as important as that with the General Hospital. In 1885 he was appointed demonstrator of anatomy at Queen's College, where the medical school was housed until its transfer to Mason College, the precursor of the university. He was the first holder of the chair of pathology, to which he was appointed in 1886, and in 1893 he was made professor of surgery. After seven years' tenure of the deanship of the medical faculty, he resigned it in 1912 in order to have more time for surgical research and for writing. The leisure period was, however, a brief one, since in 1913 he was elected vice-chancellor, a title changed to pro-chancellor in 1927, and held that office for twenty years, during which time under his stimulus the university research departments in mental diseases and cancer were founded. As a result of his financial skill and ability to influence generous donors, the university, when he retired, was free from debt, and had a greatly increased income despite the great developments in staffing and in buildings which had taken place during his tenure of office.

During the greater part of the war of 1914–1918, except from October 1916 until August 1917, when he was consulting surgeon in France, Barling was consulting surgeon to the Southern Command of the British army. For these services he was twice mentioned in dispatches, was appointed C.B. in 1917 and C.B.E. in 1919, and in the latter year was created a baronet.

Barling took a leading part in the early negotiations for the union of the two voluntary teaching hospitals in Birmingham (the Queen's and the General Hospitals) into one body, the United Hospital, and he was also chairman of the committee which launched the Hospitals Centre Scheme. This scheme planned the building of a hospital teaching centre and a new medical school in close proximity to the main university buildings at Edgbaston. Unfortunately in 1926 a serious illness compelled his retirement from this committee, but he lived to see the first part of the scheme fulfilled and the opening of a large new general hospital, the Queen Elizabeth Hospital, and a well-equipped medical school. Although he retired from the active staff in 1915 his interest in the General Hospital never flagged, and for four years (1924–1927) he was its president. His last appearance at any public function, five days before his death at Edgbaston 27 April 1940, was at the annual meeting of the United Hospital, when he was presented with an address of congratulation on his completion of sixty years' active service with the hospital.

Barling was a talented administrator, teacher, and speaker; he was a loyal friend, and a methodical and hard worker. He expected hard work from his assistants but always acknowledged their help. His record of hospital, university, and other public service was recognized in 1935 by the presentation of the gold medal of the Birmingham Civic Society; the university conferred upon him the honorary degree of LL.D. in 1937.

Barling married in 1884 Katharin Jaffray (died 1920), second daughter of Henry Edmunds, bank manager, of Edgbaston, and had two daughters.

A portrait of Barling, by Edward F. Harper (1915), hangs in the board-room of the General Hospital, Birmingham; another, in oils, by G. Fiddes Watt (1924), was presented to him by the university in 1925 and hangs in the great hall of the university.

[*The Times*, 29 April 1940; *British Medical Journal*, 1940, vol. i, p. 748; *Lancet*, 1940, vol. i, p. 947; private information; personal knowledge.]   LEONARD G. PARSONS.

BARNES, GEORGE NICOLL (1859–1940), statesman, was born at Lochee, Dundee, 2 January 1859, the second of the five sons of James Barnes, a Yorkshireman, then a journeyman machine-maker at Lochee, by his wife, Catherine Adam Langlands, a native of Kirriemuir, Angus. In 1866 the family moved to Tranmere on the Mersey and thence in the following year to Ponders End, Middlesex. Educated at a Church school at Enfield Highway, when eleven years old George became a clerk in a jute mill at seven shillings a week. At thirteen he was apprenticed to engineering at a Lambeth factory for woodwork-machinery and completed his time in Dundee. As an unemployed journeyman he found work at the shipyard at Barrow-in-Furness and later on the construction of the Royal Albert Dock on the Thames. He studied drawing and machine construction and subsequently worked for eight years with a firm in Fulham. He finished his period in the workshops with a year or two at Woolwich Arsenal. Joining the Amalgamated Society of Engineers, he associated with John Burns and Tom Mann, and in 1887 took part in the Trafalgar Square demonstration that led to the historic riot. He was greatly influenced by the dock strike of 1889, which marked the inauguration of the 'New Unionism', giving similar status to skilled and unskilled labour in the trade union world. He was elected to the executive of the Amalgamated Society of Engineers in 1889 and became assistant secretary in 1892.

Barnes was drawn to socialism by William Morris [q.v.], whose meetings he attended at Kelmscott House and elsewhere in Hammersmith. Joining the independent labour party, he was an active colleague of J. Keir Hardie [q.v.], and in 1895 stood unsuccessfully for Rochdale under the auspices of that party. In 1896 he was elected general secretary of the Amalgamated Society of Engineers, a post which he held until 1908, when he resigned owing to differences with his executive. His first year of office was notable for the dispute that arose from the Engineering Employers' Federation locking out the London members of the union over the eight hours controversy. The remaining 75 per cent. of the union members, in the provinces, struck work from July 1897 to January 1898. While the strike failed in its immediate objective, it was followed by the adoption of collective bargaining on conditions of employment.

Barnes visited Germany in 1898, Denmark and Sweden in 1899, and as a member of the Mosley industrial commission he travelled widely in the United States of America in 1902. He was a delegate when the labour representation committee (afterwards the labour party) was formed in 1900, and throughout his career was an active propagandist for trade unionism, socialism, and co-operation. He was chairman of the national committee of organized labour for old-age pensions, which pioneered that social reform prior to the passing of the Act in 1908. In 1906 he won the Blackfriars division (Glasgow) from A. Bonar Law [q.v.], and was one of the original twenty-nine members of the parliamentary labour party, of which he was chairman in 1910. He held Blackfriars at the general elections in January and December 1910, and in 1918 when, following redistribution, it became the Gorbals division. He served on the King's civil list committee (1910) and proposed the nationalization of the duchies of Lancaster and Cornwall. He was also active in the promotion of labour exchanges and legislation for the provision of work or maintenance for the unemployed.

At the outbreak of war in 1914 Barnes recruited many men for the services and afterwards visited Canada and Flanders in order to withdraw mechanics for the munition industries. He served on the appeal board for conscientious objectors, and was an effective member of the statutory committee on service pensions. Appointed first minister of pensions in Lloyd George's coalition government in December 1916, he was largely responsible for the more enlightened policy that characterized that ministry.

In 1917 Barnes succeeded Arthur Henderson [q.v.] upon the latter's resignation from the War Cabinet, and assisted in promoting measures for miners' welfare, women's suffrage, and educational advance. When the labour party withdrew support from the coalition before the general election of December 1918, Barnes resigned from the party and remained in

office with the avowed object of influencing the peace terms. He attended the Peace Conference in Paris as minister plenipotentiary, and, while protesting against the reparation clauses of the Treaty of Versailles, was chiefly responsible for the institution of the International Labour Organization as an integral section of the League of Nations. He represented Great Britain at the first International Labour Organization conference, held at Washington in October 1919, when delegates attended from forty-one countries, including Germany and Austria, and he considered that the greatest achievement of his career was the inauguration of the organization's headquarters at Geneva, with Albert Thomas as director. After signing the Treaty of St. Germain with Austria on 10 September 1919, Barnes resigned from the government in January 1920, but, in company with A. J. Balfour and H. A. L. Fisher [qq.v.], he attended the first Assembly of the League of Nations at Geneva later in that year, when he pleaded unsuccessfully for the admission of Germany. He retired from parliament in 1922. He had been sworn of the Privy Council upon attaining cabinet rank in 1916, and was appointed C.H. in 1920. He afterwards visited Egypt, Palestine, and South Africa and pursued literary and peace interests during his retirement, almost up to his death, which took place at his home in London 21 April 1940.

In addition to his autobiography, *From Workshop to War Cabinet* (1923), Barnes wrote, besides pamphlets, *The History of the Amalgamated Society of Engineers* (1901), *An Eastern Tour* (1921), *Industrial Conflict: The Way Out* (1924), and *The History of the International Labour Office* (1926).

Barnes married in 1882 Jessie, daughter of Thomas Langlands, of Dundee, and had two sons and one daughter. The elder son was killed in action in 1915.

A portrait of Barnes, by Murray Urquhart, was presented to the International Labour Office, Geneva, by a committee of public men. Another portrait, by Sir William Orpen, is in the City Art Gallery, Bradford.

[G. N. Barnes, *From Workshop to War Cabinet*, 1923; private information; personal knowledge.]   J. S. MIDDLETON.

BARNES, WILLIAM EMERY (1859–1939), divine, was born in London 26 May

1859, the younger son of Samuel Emery Barnes, a linen draper, of London, by his wife, Charlotte Ann Noss. He was educated at Islington Proprietary School and from there in 1877 went up to Peterhouse, Cambridge. He was placed in the first class of the theological tripos of 1881 and he won the Jeremie prize (septuagint), the Crosse scholarship (divinity), and the Tyrwhitt scholarship (Hebrew). In 1883 he was ordained to a curacy at St. John's church, Lambeth, returning to Cambridge in 1885 as lecturer in Hebrew at Clare College and afterwards in Hebrew and divinity at his own college, Peterhouse, of which he was elected a fellow in 1889. He was Hulsean professor of divinity at Cambridge from 1901 to 1934, when he resigned and retired to live at Canterbury, continuing, however, as warden of the Central Society of Sacred Study for the diocese of Canterbury, to promote this study by taking classes and giving occasional lectures. While doing this at Exeter he was seized with illness and died there 17 August 1939. He had married in 1890 Georgina de Horne, daughter of Alexander Bevington, of Lloyd's. She died, without children, in 1917.

Barnes was a fine scholar in Hebrew, Rabbinic (in which he had read extensively), and Syriac, and he had a working knowledge of several other languages. When pressed in his latter years to begin the study of Persian, he replied that he already kept seven languages going and could not add another. His most substantial contributions to scholarship were in Syriac. After the death of R. L. Bensly [q.v.] Barnes edited his unfinished work on *The Fourth Book of Maccabees and Kindred Documents in Syriac* (1895), himself writing the general introduction and making the translation of four of the six documents included. He published a useful *apparatus criticus* to the Peshitta text of Chronicles (1897) and an edition of Samuel Lee's Syriac Pentateuch (in collaboration, 1914), and in 1904 a fine edition of the Peshitta text of the Psalms. What was wanted for younger students he gave at its best in his editions of Chronicles (1899) and Kings (1908), and of Haggai, Zechariah, and Malachi (1917) in the 'Cambridge Bible'.

As joint-editor with C. H. Turner [q.v.] of the *Journal of Theological Studies* at its inception in 1899 Barnes helped to set the high standard of method and style of that journal and ever after contributed to it articles, notes, and reviews which were often of high value. He remained joint-editor (from 1902 with Henry Austin Wilson) until 1903.

Always averse from controversy and unwilling to commit himself, Barnes accepted the new learning of his time and the new approach to the literary and historical study of the Old Testament, but used it very cautiously in his own work. Much of the new literature of the subject he regarded as 'wild' and he disliked intensely the way in which some scholars cut texts about; but he took full notice of their arguments and reasons and weighed them before he put them aside. With his strong conservative and devotional tendencies and his respect for time-honoured tradition he was happiest in drawing out the moral and spiritual values of the books on which he commented, as he did in his edition of the Psalms for the 'Westminster Commentaries', published, with an admirable introduction, in 1931.

Bishop Arthur Mesac Knight, who was a younger contemporary of his at school, remembered Barnes as at that time 'a trim and somewhat prim little figure, precise, careful, but with strength of character . . . and he had his own opinions'. That description was true of him all through his later life. Gentle and quiet, with entire sincerity and integrity, kindly disposed and mildly humorous, he was a good friend to different types of people whom he liked to gather together to luxurious lunches in Peterhouse. As a teacher he was painstaking and simple, anxious not to be above the heads of his pupils.

In rather quaint contrast with Barnes's small stature and slight physique was his eager interest in warfare. In his early days he joined the University Volunteers when they had very little support, and almost to the end of his time in Cambridge he would go up to the butts to fire off his rounds. Military history, strategy and tactics, were his hobby, and in discussions of them in combination room he would sometimes correct the master of his college, that master being Lord Birdwood. Another subject which attracted him was the revision of English spelling, and he wrote letters to *The Times* and other papers to promote the common-sense reformation which he desired, but he objected to having his own name spelt without the *e*. He also liked to make excursions into fields of study other than those with which he was most familiar, with something of his own to illustrate the subject.

A drawing of Barnes, by Sir William Rothenstein (1933), hangs in the Ward Library at Peterhouse.

[*The Times*, 19 August 1939; private information; personal knowledge.]

J. F. BETHUNE-BAKER.

BARNETT, DAME HENRIETTA OCTAVIA WESTON (1851–1936), social reformer, was born at Clapham 4 May 1851, the daughter of Alexander William Rowland, of Clapham, by his wife, Henrietta Monica Margaretta Ditges. Fond of country pursuits and a keen horsewoman, she early showed for the poor and needy an eager concern which became the guiding passion of her long and active life and gave purpose to the organizing ability and tireless energy which were the outstanding traits of her character. In 1873, at the age of twenty-one, after some experience of work with Octavia Hill [q.v.] in the parish of St. Mary's church, Bryanston Square, she married S. A. Barnett [q.v.], at that time a young curate of St. Mary's. By their marriage his rare spiritual gifts, fine mind, and sensitive nature were joined with Mrs. Barnett's robust energy and assertive personality. It is impossible to measure what she owed to her husband's influence, and the story of their work together is best sought in the account of his life; but Mrs. Barnett's personal activities were noteworthy. She was the first nominated woman guardian, in 1875, and was manager of Forest Gate district school from 1875 to 1897. Her further experience as a member of a departmental committee appointed to inquire into 'the condition of Poor Law children' led to the formation in 1896 of the State Children's Association with Mrs. Barnett as honorary secretary. Twelve years later Asquith spoke of her as 'the unofficial custodian of the children of the State'. From 1876 to 1898 she was honorary secretary of the Whitechapel branch of the Metropolitan Association for Befriending Young Servants. In 1877 she arranged country holidays for nine ailing children, and out of that experience developed the Children's Country Holidays Fund, of which she was a co-founder in 1884, and through which hundreds of thousands of London children have benefited. In 1884 also she founded the London Pupil Teachers' Association, of which she was president from 1891 to 1907. In 1901 she was closely associated with Barnett in the foundation of the Whitechapel Art Gallery, of which she remained a trustee until her death.

Throughout this time, while she ardently supported her husband in the development of Toynbee Hall, Mrs. Barnett was an active advocate of the settlement ideal in the United States of America. There it took root quickly and it has borne much fruit. In 1920 the 480 American settlements which were already established paid her a remarkable tribute by electing her, an Englishwoman living in England, to be honorary president of the American Federation of Settlements. Toynbee Hall had been conceived as a bridge between learning and labour and between 'the East End' and 'the West End' at a time when the former term connoted toil and poverty and the latter leisure and riches. It expressed a protest against class separation and the ugliness of ignorance. Much of its activity marked the Barnetts' faith in the uplifting nature of art and beauty, and the same philosophy inspired Mrs. Barnett's subsequent work at Hampstead. First she raised £43,000 to save eighty acres of the heath for public enjoyment. Then, in 1903, she formed the Hampstead Garden Suburb Trust which raised funds for the purchase of a further 240 acres on which to lay out the houses and grounds, and in 1907 work was begun. Mrs. Barnett had experienced in Whitechapel the evils of class segregation and unregulated urban development. The new garden suburb was designed to provide homes for all classes, and these ranged from cottages with small weekly rents to houses with an annual rent of several hundred pounds. Development was to be carefully controlled and facilities for worship, for education, and for recreation were to be open to all alike. It was a pioneer venture, and it has influenced town planning in this and other countries. The Dame Henrietta Barnett School, which she founded at Hampstead, and Barnett House, Oxford, both owed much to her, as did the National Association for Promoting the Welfare of the Feeble Minded, the National Union of Women Workers, and the Play and Pageant Union.

In 1918 Mrs. Barnett, who had already written a good deal, both alone and in collaboration with her husband, published *Canon Barnett, His Life, Work and Friends* in two volumes; in 1923, at the age of nearly seventy-two, she began painting and had a picture hung in the Royal Academy. She was appointed C.B.E. in

1917 and D.B.E. in 1924. She died, child-less, at Hampstead 10 June 1936.

[Dame Henrietta Barnett, *Canon Barnett*, 2 vols., 1918, and *Matters that Matter*, 1930; *The Times*, 11 June 1936.]   L. F. ELLIS.

BARODA, SIR SAYAJI RAO, MAHA-RAJA GAEKWAR OF (1863–1939), was born at Kavlana in the Nasik district of Bombay 17 March 1863, and originally named Gopalrao, the second son of a village headman, belonging to the Gaek-war family which founded a dynasty in Guzerat. In 1875 the ruling Maharaja was deposed for continued misconduct. The widow of his brother and predecessor, being allowed to adopt an heir to the chiefship, chose the boy, who was placed on the *gadi* in May 1875, with the name of Sayaji Rao III. He was at this time entirely illiterate, but, with an English tutor, he was carefully educated so that it was possible to invest him with govern-ing powers in December 1881 when he was not yet nineteen years of age. The state had a sad record of misgovernment, but its soil was rich and its commercial situation excellent, with very favourable arrangements with the government of India for the receipt of customs duties at its ports. These elements only needed the good government which the young ruler supplied. As he later said of himself: 'Work was his hobby and administration his passion.' His attention to detail, in-deed, led to a great degree of centraliza-tion and, on the part of his officials, a fear of responsibility, while his excessive caution was liable to approach suspicious-ness. In 1887 he wrote to the viceroy: 'I hate the idea of an absentee maharaja': yet his travels and residence overseas became prolonged. They were originally due in large part to the insomnia and ner-vous irritability from which he believed himself unable to obtain relief in India, but were extended by his restlessness and intellectual curiosity. He was a close ob-server of systems and institutions in the countries which he visited and sought to introduce such as seemed desirable into his state. His close touch with the affairs of his state was maintained, but the unwil-lingness of his officials to make decisions on their own motion was thereby in-creased. The frequency of his journeys led the viceroy, Lord Curzon, to issue in 1900 a circular on the absence of rulers from their states which was directed at the Gaekwar, and was deeply resented by him. The fact that the Baroda territory was

interspersed with lands under the Bom-bay government and with small states over which Baroda had originally claimed suzerainty afforded other grounds for friction. The Maharaja objected in par-ticular to any appearance of interference with his administration. This accounted for his attitude on the question of imperial service troops which the other leading states were glad to maintain, while the Gaekwar rejected them because of the necessary technical inspection by British officers. His state was thus unable to play so conspicuous a part in the war of 1914–1918 as the other Indian states, although in every other way the Maharaja gave all the help in his power. Before the end of his reign he agreed to the maintenance of such troops, afterwards called the Indian State Forces, in his state. Another source of friction was the Maharaja's somewhat detached attitude to complaints that sedi-tious movements against the British Indian administration were hatched, and were insufficiently checked, in his terri-tory. This had the result of making him popular with the nationalist elements in British India which regarded him as sympathizing with their aims. This doubt-less lessened their criticism of his con-stant attacks on weaknesses in the Indian social system such as general illiteracy, infant marriages, prohibition of widow re-marriage, and the disabilities of out-castes and backward tribes. The fact that the penalties enacted for breaches of his social legislation were imperfectly enforced led to a belief that the reforms were not very real. The Maharaja, however, held that reforms could not far outstrip public opinion, and that reliance should be placed upon a widening of outlook rather than upon penalties.

An unfortunate incident at the Delhi Durbar of 1911 affected for a time the public estimation of the Gaekwar. His apparent disrespect to the King-Emperor, attributed by his own friends to nervous-ness and *gaucherie*, may have been also partly due to the irritability already noted. The surroundings of the incident gave it greater notoriety than it deserved.

With increasing age the Maharaja's character mellowed, and he became a force as an elder statesman. At his jubilee in 1925 it could be truly claimed that he had raised Baroda from chaos to the position of a model state. He took a prominent part in the first and second Round Table Conferences, with an increasingly conservative outlook. His foreign absences continued, but he became more willing to leave details of administration to his dewan and council. Although he returned to India in November 1938, he was unable to reach Baroda, and died in Bombay 6 February 1939, after a reign of nearly sixty-four years.

The Maharaja was appointed G.C.S.I. in 1887 and G.C.I.E. in 1919. He was twice married: first, in 1881 to Lakshimibai (died May 1885), of the Tanjore family, by whom he had one son, who predeceased his father, and a daughter; secondly, in December 1885, to Gajnabai, later styled Chimnabai II, of a branch of the Ghatge family settled in the Dewas state, and had three sons, the two elder of whom predeceased their father, and one daughter. He was succeeded by his grandson, the son of his eldest son, Pratapsingh.

A cartoon of the Maharaja, by 'M. R.', appeared in *Vanity Fair* 3 January 1901.

[*The Times*, 7 February 1939; P. W. Sergeant, *Ruler of Baroda*, 1928; P. Stanley Rice, *Life of Sayaji Rao III, Maharaja of Baroda*, 2 vols., 1931.]   PATRICK CADELL.

BARR, ARCHIBALD (1855–1931), inventor of range-finders, was born at Glenfield House, Abbey, near Paisley, Renfrewshire, 18 November 1855, the third son of Archibald Barr, yarn merchant, by his wife, Jeanie Stirrat, of Paisley. From Paisley Grammar School he entered the works of Messrs. A. F. Craig & company, manufacturers of spinning and weaving machinery, of that town, as an engineering apprentice under the Scottish 'sandwich' system, which enabled him to attend the winter sessions of Glasgow University, from which he graduated in 1876.

During the following eight years Barr remained there as assistant to James Thomson [q.v.] until in 1884, having graduated D.Sc., he was called to the chair of civil and mechanical engineering at the Yorkshire College, later Leeds University, where he founded the first engineering laboratories of Great Britain. Glasgow University recalled him in 1889, in succession to Thomson, as regius professor of civil engineering and mechanics, the oldest chair of engineering science in the world; this gave him the privilege of continuing his important consultative business. As he found no facilities for research at the university, he set himself to build and equip the James Watt laboratories, which were opened in 1900

and, at that time, were recognized as being the most complete in Britain.

At Leeds Barr met the colleague of his lifetime, William Stroud, the young regius professor of physics, with whom his name is widely associated as the pioneer of naval range-finding and gunnery and as the founder of the firm of manufacturers of optical and mechanical instruments of precision which bears their name. Under his chairmanship the firm did great service to the country in its designs for naval range-finders, which were adopted by the Admiralty and by nearly all foreign powers. His great knowledge of mechanics also led to inventions of height-finders in anti-aircraft services and for fire-control instruments, as well as aerial survey apparatus. Owing to the rapid growth of the factory established at Anniesland, Glasgow, he found it necessary to resign from his chair in 1913, becoming emeritus professor.

Barr was elected F.R.S. in 1923, and received the honorary degree of LL.D. (1914) from the university of Glasgow. He was president of several learned societies. He married in 1885 Isabella (died 1928), eldest daughter of John Young, wood merchant, of Priory Park, Castlehead, Paisley; they had three sons, the second of whom was killed in action in France in 1915, and a daughter. He died at his home, Westerton of Mugdock, Milngavie, near Glasgow, 5 August 1931.

In 1913 Barr was presented with two portraits, painted by G. Fiddes Watt, one of which hangs in the engineering department of the university of Glasgow, the other being in the possession of the family. They represent the professor in a mood of seriousness which was rarely evident to his students.

[*The Times*, 7 August 1931; *Obituary Notices of Fellows of the Royal Society*, No. 1, December 1932 (portrait); *Nature*, 22 August 1931; personal knowledge.]
   JAMES WEIR FRENCH.

BARRIE, SIR JAMES MATTHEW, baronet (1860–1937), playwright and novelist, was born at Kirriemuir, Forfarshire, 9 May 1860, the ninth child and third and youngest son of David Barrie, hand-loom weaver, of Kirriemuir, by his wife, Margaret, daughter of Alexander Ogilvy, stonemason. He was educated first at Glasgow Academy, where his brother Alexander was a teacher, and, from 1873, when Alexander was appointed inspector of schools of the district, at

Dumfries Academy. He matriculated at Edinburgh University in 1878, and graduated M.A. in 1882. From his boyhood he had determined to write, and in January 1883 he was appointed leader-writer and sub-editor on the *Nottingham Journal*. His articles were thorough and complete within the required length and he had enough spare time for sketches and stories which he dispatched at a venture. Some, in which Kirriemuir was disguised as 'Thrums', were published anonymously in the *St. James's Gazette*, of which Frederick Greenwood [q.v.] was editor.

Against Greenwood's advice Barrie moved to London in March 1885 and again lived without struggling. He wrote for many magazines and now (Sir) W. Robertson Nicoll [q.v.] began his staunch support of his brother Scot by publishing serially (1887–1888) over the signature of 'Gavin Ogilvy' in the *British Weekly* Barrie's 'When A Man's Single, A Tale of Literary Life'. Barrie published his first book, *Better Dead*, in November 1887 at his own expense. It was an immature joke, cost one shilling, but almost paid its expenses. The years 1888 and 1889 were memorable ones in the author's life. In 1888 Messrs. Hodder and Stoughton published *Auld Licht Idylls*, sketches of Thrums, and *When A Man's Single* under Barrie's own signature. 'Gavin Ogilvy' was expiring. He died in December after signing his name to *An Edinburgh Eleven*, a skit on his professors, published by Nicoll in paper covers as a Christmas extra to the *British Weekly*. In 1889 Hodder and Stoughton published *A Window in Thrums*, a companion volume of Scottish episodes, and Donald Macleod accepted 'The Little Minister' for serial publication in *Good Words*. In 1890 *My Lady Nicotine* was published. It aroused comment because of its pleasant humour and a growing curiosity to know what, if any, brand of smoking mixture was disguised as Arcadia.

In 1891 Barrie's bent towards the stage began to unfold. In April a play by himself and Henry Brereton Marriott Watson, *Richard Savage*, was produced at a matinée. In May *Ibsen's Ghost* was put on as a front piece by J. L. Toole [q.v.] at the suggestion of (Sir) Henry Irving [q.v.], and in July the *British Weekly* brought out a sixteen-page illustrated supplement, *J. M. Barrie, a Literary and Biographical Portrait*. It was early, perhaps, for so recently fledged an author to achieve a recognition from the press so noticeable. At the year's end, Toole paid £200 for a three-act farce, *Walker, London*, which ran for 511 consecutive performances from 25 February 1892. But more profitable was Barrie's first novel, *The Little Minister*. Its publication in book form in October 1891 was secured for Messrs. Cassell by (Sir) T. W. Reid [q.v.], who, always alert to fresh talent, had attached Barrie to the staff of his new weekly paper the *Speaker* with (Sir) Arthur Thomas Quiller-Couch, H. W. Massingham [q.v.] and Augustine Birrell [q.v.]. *The Little Minister* was an instantaneous success.

But Barrie was looking to the stage as a means of expression. He collaborated with (Sir) A. Conan Doyle [q.v.] in a libretto for Richard D'Oyly Carte's opera company at the Savoy Theatre, *Jane Annie; or, The Good Conduct Prize* (May 1893), without success; and, commissioned by Irving, he completed *The Professor's Love Story* in the autumn of 1892. Irving was not satisfied and the play went the round of West End managers. The American rights were secured by Edward Smith Willard for £50 and he played in it in the United States with marked success. Under new arrangements, for Barrie now had Arthur Addison Bright as his agent, Willard produced *The Professor's Love Story* at the Comedy Theatre, London, in June 1894 and transferred it to the Garrick Theatre. It had a combined run of 144 performances.

In that year (1894) Barrie married Mary, daughter of George Ansell, a licensed victualler in Bayswater. She was a young actress who had played Nanny O'Brien in *Walker, London*. After a honeymoon in Switzerland they settled in 1895 in Gloucester Road, South Kensington, where they remained for seven years. There were no children of the marriage.

Meanwhile Barrie was working upon a tribute to his mother, *Margaret Ogilvy* (1896), written with a frankness of affection from which a good many authors would have shied and which took and held the favour of his more tender admirers; and upon two novels of Scottish life, *Sentimental Tommy* (1896) and its sequel, *Tommy and Grizel* (1900). The two books make an odd story and contain an analysis of a tortured literary mind and the tragical consequences to which it might lead, with a glimpse, by the way, of the Peter Pan who was to be. A fanciful description of a Scottish boy, Tommy, in a slum of south London, his mother's renunciation of Aaron Latta, the coward to whom she had been betrothed, and her flight from Thrums to London with Sandys, her braggart husband, her struggle to bring up her two children, Tommy and Elspeth, Tommy's inventions and stories of a Scottish village which he had never seen, and the rescue of himself and Elspeth by Latta on their mother's death are the bare bones of the first book. But it is in the analysis of the boy dramatizing himself and in his invented stories of the unknown but wonderful small town in which the interest lies. From London the two children are transplanted to Thrums, where Tommy becomes the leader of the village boyhood, always playing a part, now Elspeth's protector, now the champion of Griselda, the Painted Lady's daughter, now Charles Stuart on the run in the heather, now the antagonist of Cathro the schoolmaster, but sometimes with a laugh as he catches a glimpse of what he really is and contrasts it with the heroic figure which he cannot but make himself out to be. *Tommy and Grizel* carries on the account. These were the last novels which Barrie wrote. *The Little White Bird* (1902), *Peter Pan in Kensington Gardens* (1906), and *Peter and Wendy* (1911) are all variations upon the theme of Peter Pan.

At this time Charles Frohman, the American impresario, was seeking a play which would give an opportunity to Maude Adams, a young actress in whom he had great faith. A dramatized version by Barrie of *The Little Minister* followed the book too closely to appeal to Frohman; but Barrie changed the character and origin of the heroine, and *The Little Minister* appeared successfully at Washington in September 1897. Mr. Cyril Maude and Frederick Harrison produced it at the Haymarket Theatre (November 1897) with Maude as the Little Minister and Winifred Emery, his wife, as Lady Babbie. It ran for a year and Barrie acknowledged afterwards that between England and America this play brought him £80,000.

A cricket-match arranged by Barrie at Shere in 1887 with players who mostly had played little cricket before included Joseph Thomson [q.v.], the explorer of Morocco. He invented for the team the name of Allahakbarrie. For four or five summers the Allahakbarries played not too strenuous cricket at Broadway, Shere, and other places. Later, county cricketers and really fast bowlers were admitted, two-day matches were played, and the team foundered. The summer months were spent at Black Lake Cottage, a small house opposite to Moor Park by Farnham which Barrie, in 1900, had given to his wife, and, cricketing being over, Barrie gave himself to the writing of plays and the building up, among the pine-trees above the garden in company with the five little boys of Arthur Llewelyn Davies, of the story of *Peter Pan*. But other work was completed first. *The Wedding Guest*, produced by Arthur Bourchier [q.v.] at the Garrick Theatre in September 1900, was hardly a success and certainly not a failure. It ran for 100 performances—a play in the fashionable mould, a problem play, as the saying went. An artist marries the daughter of the great house and a witness is brought in from outside according to Scottish custom, a woman who a year ago was the mistress of the artist. She now carries a baby. The disclosure, the intolerant ignorance of the girl-wife, the gradual compromise by which the crisis is smoothed over are all in the fashion of the day. The wise old spinster is the kindly Felice of *The Little Minister* and a family relationship exists between the Earl of Rintoul and Mr. Fairbairn, but there is more of Barrie in *Sentimental Tommy* than in either of these plays.

Quality Street was first performed at Toledo, Ohio, in October 1901 and was transferred to the Knickerbocker Theatre, New York, with Maude Adams as Phoebe Throssel. Barrie was now established as a successful dramatist in both England and America, and *Quality Street*, a sentimental comedy set in a small English town during Napoleonic days, had an equal success in both countries. In London at the Vaudeville Theatre (September 1902) Phoebe Throssel was played by Miss Ellaline Terriss and Valentine Brown, the dashing young doctor, by her husband, (Sir) Seymour Hicks. The comedy was not for everyone. There were playgoers who felt moments of embarrassment at the more cloying passages, but the play with its twists of plot and humour kept the stage for 459 performances, was revived at the Haymarket Theatre in August 1921, and, translated into German as *Qualität Strasse*, ran for months in Berlin during the war of 1914–1918.

Three months before *Quality Street* was produced in London, Barrie moved to a small regency house, Leinster Corner, facing the Bayswater Road, with a stable behind which he turned into a study. Across the road were Kensington Gardens to which Barrie obtained a much-treasured private key from the first commissioner of Works. There, with Luath, his New-foundland, almost as big as himself, he might be seen on any day dreaming over *Peter Pan*.

A more ambitious play, *The Admirable Crichton*, was presented by Frohman in November 1902 at the Duke of York's Theatre. Here was that valuable touch of acidity which keeps plays alive. It is the story of a radical peer with a tory soul, the Earl of Loam, who believes at 5 o'clock once a month in the equality of the classes, and a butler, Crichton, who believes that rank is the order of nature. The first act shows Lord Loam and his daughters having tea in the drawing-room with their servants. In the second act they have been wrecked upon a deserted Pacific island and nature begins to put Crichton, the ingenious butler, in his rightful place. In the third act he is king of the island. The house which he has built is lit with electricity, a chain of bonfires round the coast awaits only the movement of a switch to burst into flames, and the daughters, great hunters and good cooks, with the invaluable Cockney Tweeny, all aspire to Crichton's hand. Crichton's choice is Lady Mary, the eldest daughter, but as he is on the point of announcing his choice a ship is seen on the horizon and its hooter is heard. Crichton is faced with a problem: do nothing, and the ship will go: reply, and once more he is a butler. With a pull of the lever he sets the bon-fires burning, and as the officers of the rescue ship enter the house he replies to a timid word from Lady Mary, 'Milady'. In the fourth act the old order has uncom-fortably returned. A book has been writ-ten about the family experiences in which Crichton is hardly mentioned. He gives notice of his intention to marry Tweeny and take a public-house, 'The Case Is Altered'. After the war of 1914–1918, Barrie changed the last act to the play's disadvantage by leaving Crichton's fate uncertain. A pity, for the reader may be quite sure that within two years 'The Case Is Altered' would have become a Grand Hotel. No doubt both Lord Loam and Crichton are larger than life, just as are so many of the characters of Dickens, but it does not follow, any more than in the case of Dickens's characters, that they are untrue. This play, with an admir-able cast—(Dame) Irene Vanbrugh, (Sir) Gerald du Maurier [q.v.], Henry Brodribb Irving, and Henry Kemble [q.v.]—ran for 328 performances and was followed, in September 1903, by an odd comedy, *Little Mary*. The crêche boxes of children (to reappear, children and all, in *A Kiss For Cinderella*) at the back of the parlour of a chemist's shop, and the dialogue between the twelve-year-old granddaughter of the chemist and the Earl of Carlton open the play in the true Barrie fashion. It owed its success to some excellent scenes between the Earl of Carlton and his son Cecil and the alacrity with which the public took up the phrase 'Little Mary' as a euphemism for 'stomach'.

Peter Pan had grown to full stature in the pinewoods behind Black Lake Cot-tage and now sought for his shadow in the nursery of the Darlings at the Duke of York's Theatre on 27 December 1904. Nana, the dog-nurse, Tinker Bell, Wendy, the Never Never Land, the kindly Red Indians, the furious pirates, Smee, Starkey, with Captain Hook at their head, and, above all, the crocodile with the eight-day clock ticking away inside of him are house-hold words to-day, but in 1904 no one but Barrie had any faith in them. (Sir) H. Beer-bohm Tree [q.v.] thought that Barrie had gone mad. Frohman wanted to defer the production. Barrie himself from the begin-ning was confident that *Peter Pan* would not only attract but would be produced at Christmas-time year after year. For a fortnight it looked as if Tree and Frohman were going to be justified. Then children of all ages flocked to the play until it closed on 1 April 1905, to be revived at nearly every Christmas season afterwards. The lagoon scene was added for the first revival. It explains why the Red Indians protected the children from the pirates. Was not Tiger Lily rescued by Peter Pan at the risk of his life? 'To die', he said with a shaking voice, 'will be an awfully big adventure.' The line is to be remem-bered if only because it was quoted by Barrie's great friend Frohman as he plunged to his death in the *Lusitania*.

Four days after *Peter Pan* was shelved for the summer *Alice-Sit-by-the-Fire* was produced at the same theatre. It was written for Ellen Terry [q.v.], but the theme had little life in it and she never felt easy in her part. Nevertheless, it ran for 115 performances, a satire upon the social play of the times which has not been revived. The year 1906 was the cause of another satire still less successful.

A friend of Barrie was standing for the liberal party in the heart of the tariff reform area and won the seat. Barrie was present at the final meetings and on his return to London wrote with considerable enjoyment *Josephine*. It is a political burlesque and Barrie admitted that he had been so careful to baffle the censor, who banned political plays, that he had made it quite unintelligible to any audience. Frederick Harrison of the Haymarket Theatre nibbled at it and refrained. Gerald du Maurier, cast for Josephine, refused to act the part. Frohman the faithful came to the rescue and with two one-act plays put on the first triple bill at the Comedy Theatre in April. It failed completely and all three plays have ceased to exist in any form.

None the less, the idea of a play with a political environment clung, and two words spoken by his friend from a balcony out of an expiring throat after his election were an inspiration. *What Every Woman Knows* opens with a flawless first act. John Shand, the young ticket-collector-student, enters into a contract with the father, Alick Wylie, to marry Maggie, sister of David and James Wylie, the girl without charm, in five years if called upon to do so, in return for £300. In the second act Shand is returned to parliament. He has the support of two aristocratic friends, the Comtesse de la Brière and her niece, Lady Sybil Tenterden (originally Lazenby). Maggie proposes to cancel their contract. This he declines to do. In the third act he is married but is caught by Maggie in an avowal of passion to Lady Sybil. Maggie determines to fight for her man. Her method is to send him for a holiday to the country house of the Comtesse de la Brière where Lady Sybil is staying. In the fourth act the cards have been stacked in favour of Maggie. Lady Sybil and John Shand thrown together are unutterably bored. The Cabinet minister, responsible for a speech to be made by Shand at a big political rally, finds the draft shown to him unworthy of the occasion: and then 'all's well' is reached by the emergence of Maggie with a new draft containing the quips which had made Shand famous, the delight of the Cabinet minister, and the reconciliation of husband and wife. The play was one of Barrie's greatest successes in London. It opened in September 1908 at the Duke of York's Theatre.

Barrie's enthusiasm for the stage then dwindled for a time. In October 1909 he obtained a divorce from his wife and in November moved to a flat in Adelphi Terrace overlooking the river. In March 1910 he was responsible for a triple bill at the Duke of York's Theatre consisting of his own *Old Friends* and *The Twelve-Pound Look*, and *The Sentimentalists* by George Meredith [q.v.]. Meredith's one-act play failed and was replaced by Barrie's *A Slice of Life*. Repertory seasons were in the air and with this triple bill *Justice* by John Galsworthy [q.v.], *The Madras House* by Harley G. Granville-Barker, and *Misalliance* by Mr. Bernard Shaw were alternatively staged. The season was unsuccessful. Again there was an interval.

In May 1912 occurred something which, on account of its astuteness, no survey of Barrie's life can disregard. There appeared by the water in Kensington Gardens a bronze statue of Peter Pan blowing his pipes. There was no unveiling ceremony. Barrie had thought of it, had commissioned Sir George Frampton [q.v.] to make it, had paid for it, and had arranged with the first commissioner of Works to have it privately erected. A question was asked about it in parliament when it was discovered; but the statue was so appropriate and so clearly an embellishment that authority did not disturb it.

In the autumn of 1912 came another triple bill at the Duke of York's Theatre of which Barrie's play *Rosalind* alone found favour. Next year (1913) the King created him a baronet, and in the autumn he finished at last a play in three acts, *The Adored One, A Legend of the Old Bailey*. It treated a trial for murder as a lark. Some, like Sir John Hare [q.v.] who played the judge, had doubts of its success, but if Barrie could get away with *Little Mary*, why not with *The Adored One*? Mrs. Patrick Campbell [q.v.], a tower of strength, was the murderess, but even during the first act the author felt the temperature of the house falling and knew that the play had failed. It was altered in vain and languished for ten weeks from 4 September 1913, before it died. All that remains of it now is a one-act play, *Seven Women*. On the outbreak of war in 1914, Barrie's help was called upon and given. For special charity performances he wrote one-act plays of which many have disappeared for ever. In 1915 soldiers returning for forty-eight hours' leave from the squalor of the trenches wanted music, gaiety, bright lights, faces, and frocks—revues, not Ibsen. Barrie wrote *Rosy Rapture, The Pride of the Beauty Chorus*. Gaby Deslys, a French actress, famous for her acrobatic dancing, played Rosy, but the revue, which included some cinematography, wobbled. Frohman in New York was sent for to pull it together, but he went down in the *Lusitania* and once more a Barrie play had a short run.

In 1916, however, he took new life with Gerald du Maurier. *A Kiss For Cinderella*, produced at Wyndham's Theatre in March, ran to full houses for 156 performances and was revived that Christmas at the Kingsway Theatre. The babies in boxes had crept in from *Little Mary* and the 'slavey' from *Alice-Sit-by-the-Fire*, but du Maurier, as Robert the policeman one moment and Prince Charming of the pantomime the next, was new, and Cinderella's dream of a state ball at Buckingham Palace was as brilliantly funny a scene as its author ever wrote.

For a good many years Barrie had had in his mind the theme that if people had a second chance they would in their new environment make the same mistakes which they had made before. The idea was taken out and dusted, as it were, and put back again. But in the spring of 1917 he set to work upon it and in October *Dear Brutus* was produced—again by du Maurier—at Wyndham's Theatre. Barrie had added the poetry of a midsummer night, the mystery of a magic wood, and Lob from old English folk-lore as a host. In the first act the drawing-room curtains are torn aside to reveal the magic wood and one by one the ill-assorted guests wander out through the French windows into their other life. In the third act they gradually come to themselves, except in the case of Dearth, the artist, to whom must be attributed the triumph of the play. In the first act his wife, Alice, who was his model, and Dearth, who drinks, are estranged. During the imaginary other life he is shown painting with a daughter to keep him company and the long scene between these two charmed everyone who saw it. In the last act Dearth and his wife are reconciled and, in a subtle piece of theatre, are seen crossing the window arm in arm with the dream child following them. The play ran for 365 performances.

Mary Rose, with a fantastic sub-title, *The Island That Wants To Be Visited*, followed at the Haymarket Theatre in April 1920. It is a romantic theme with embarrassing moments for those too fastidious for the emotional frankness with which Barrie could always write but never speak, some admirably drawn characters, and one or two vital scenes which brought people again and again to the theatre: that scene, for instance, where the elderly husband and wife admit to each other that, although they had believed themselves heartbroken, happiness would keep breaking through.

During the past ten years Barrie had written a great number of one-act plays, many of which, like *The Twelve-Pound Look* (1910), *The Old Lady Shows Her Medals* (1917), and *Shall We Join the Ladies?*, were masterpieces of construction. *Shall We Join the Ladies?* was first performed with a star cast at the opening of the new theatre of the Dramatic Academy (May 1921). A simpleton, as his twelve guests think, announces that his brother has been murdered and that the murderer is among his guests. One after another they fall into traps which the simpleton has laid for them, and at the end it seems that any one of them might be guilty. Possibly the author himself was no more aware which one than the audience.

There remains of his plays *The Boy David*, a dramatization of the biblical story. It opened in London in December 1936 in a theatre probably too large (His Majesty's), was long enough delayed to outlive expectation, and was too thin in characterization. It ran for only 55 performances, a pity, since it was the last work which Barrie did.

In this tale of rare failure and much achievement, Barrie only thrice owed his inspiration to the circumstances of the day: *Josephine*, the political skit, *The Wedding Guest*, the problem play, and *The Well-Remembered Voice* (1918), the war hunger for lost sons. In two other one-act plays, *The Old Lady Shows Her Medals* and *The New Word* (1915), he was merely using the war as a background for his own ideas. Few authors have been more individual.

Barrie died in London 19 June 1937. He received honorary degrees from the universities of St. Andrews (1898), Edinburgh (1909), Oxford (1926), and Cambridge (1930); was elected lord rector of St. Andrews University in 1919 and chancellor of Edinburgh University in 1930; and was appointed to the Order of Merit in 1922.

There is a drawing of Barrie, by

W. T. Monnington, which has been placed in the National Portrait Gallery.

[Denis Mackail, *The Story of J. M. B.*, 1941; *The Plays of J. M. Barrie*, edited by A. E. Wilson, 1942; personal knowledge.]

A. E. W. MASON.

BARTLET, JAMES VERNON (1863–1940), ecclesiastical historian, was born at Scarborough 15 August 1863, the only son of George Donald Bartlet, an English Presbyterian minister who had a private school at Scarborough from 1862 to 1864 and was headmaster of Mill Hill from 1864 to 1868, by his wife, Susan Robe McNellan, of Alloa, near Stirling. Vernon Bartlet was educated at his father's private school in Highgate and at Highgate School, whence he proceeded in 1882 with a scholarship to Exeter College, Oxford. He obtained a first class in classical moderations (1883), a second class in *literae humaniores* (1886), and a first class in theology (1887). He won the senior Hall-Houghton Greek Testament prize in 1889. In that year he became a tutor and the first librarian at the newly established Mansfield College, Oxford, which he had entered in 1887 and where he studied under A. M. Fairbairn [q.v.]; and at Mansfield College he remained until his retirement in 1928, being senior tutor from 1890 to 1900 and thereafter professor of church history. He received the honorary degree of D.D. from St. Andrews University in 1904. He was twice married: first, in 1900 to Mary Elizabeth (died 1904), daughter of Robert Edward Gibson, surgeon, of Norwich; secondly, in 1906 to Sarah, daughter of James Burgess, Congregational minister, of Little Baddow, Essex. By the first marriage there were two sons, the younger of whom died in infancy. Bartlet died at Oxford 5 August 1940.

In 1900 Bartlet published *The Apostolic Age: its Life, Doctrine, Worship and Polity.* He contributed commentaries on *The Acts* (1901) and on *St. Mark* (1922) to the 'Century Bible' series. His Birkbeck lectures, delivered at Trinity College, Cambridge, in 1924, were edited by Dr. Cecil John Cadoux and published posthumously (1943) as *Church-Life and Church-Order During the First Four Centuries.* He was a frequent contributor to symposia, encyclopaedias, and theological journals, his work being marked by careful learning and his own emphasis. For Bartlet the prophetic character of original Christianity, expressed in terms of the Holy Spirit on the divine side, and of

moral personality on the human, was definitive; and he was always sensitive to manifestations of this character in later piety, whether in orthodox or in heretical circles. His presentation was strictly historical in its perspectives: neither to terms nor to the thought-forms which they represent did he allow finality. This presentation the Oxford Society of Historical Theology, of which Bartlet was secretary from 1894 until 1936, did much to nurture. Its applications are shown with penetration in the chapters contributed by Bartlet to *Christianity in History. A Study of Religious Development* (1917), in which he collaborated with Alexander James Carlyle.

Keenly interested in Christian reunion, Bartlet took a prominent part in the World Conference on Faith and Order held at Lausanne in 1927. Although never ordained, he was regarded as a recognized leader in the Congregational churches. Tall, dignified in bearing, delicate, and of valetudinarian habits, he was a vehement teetotaller; tobacco was abhorrent to him. Yet his personal influence on generations of students was incalculable. The length of his words and sentences bewildered, even offended, the less patient and reflective; his gentleness, sincerity, and deep devotion won the affection of all.

[C. J. Cadoux, Biographical Memoir prefixed to J. V. Bartlet, *Church-Life and Church-Order During the First Four Centuries*, 1943 (bibliography and portrait); *Mansfield College Magazine*, January 1941; personal knowledge.]

GEOFFREY F. NUTTALL.

BATESON, SIR ALEXANDER DINGWALL (1866–1935), judge, was born at Allerton, near Liverpool, 30 April 1866, the youngest of the six sons of William Gandy Bateson, a partner in a well-known firm of shipping solicitors in Liverpool, by his wife, Agnes Dingwall, daughter of Sir Thomas Blaikie, of Aberdeen. He was educated at Rugby and Trinity College, Oxford, being in his youth both a footballer and a cricketer. Called to the bar by the Inner Temple in 1891, he began his professional career in the chambers of (Sir) Joseph Walton [q.v.]. With such backing and under such a mentor he had no long wait for practice: he quickly specialized in shipping work, mainly in salvage and collision cases in the Admiralty division, occasionally in the Commercial Court. His progress was steady rather than eventful, but before long he had secured the confidence of the maritime business community more by his accuracy in every detail of his cases and by his capacity for decision than through any profound legal learning. With a pleasing voice, incisive in manner and speech, his advocacy was lucid and businesslike.

In 1909 Bateson was appointed junior counsel to the Admiralty for Admiralty division work: in 1910, with his friend and principal rival in the Admiralty Court, (Sir) E. M. Hill [q.v.], he took silk, and thereafter there were few cases in the Admiralty division in which he was not on one side or the other. He was elected a bencher of his Inn in 1920. Under the Administration of Justice Act (1925) power was given to appoint an additional judge of the Probate, Divorce, and Admiralty division, and with the universal approbation of the bar, in a wide circle of which Bateson had great personal popularity, the lord chancellor (Viscount Cave) in the May of that year selected him for appointment to the office. Entirely conversant as Bateson was with maritime law and practice, the probate and matrimonial jurisdiction in which he was thus also launched was an uncharted sea for him, but, although perhaps he never quite mastered all the historical principles of the earlier ecclesiastical law, his very sound common sense stood him in good stead, and his innate modesty enabled him to take full advantage of assistance proffered by the bar. Dignified, courteous to all, and probing carefully into the facts of each case, Bateson was rarely misled by any witness, and he continued to show that supreme judicial qualification, the capacity for decision. In the result he gave full satisfaction not only to the shipping community but also to other litigants and to the bar. He seldom reserved a judgement, and he disliked anything which attracted public attention to himself.

Bateson's outside interests included agriculture, forestry, and shooting, and for many years he farmed in the county of Kirkcudbright. He married in 1893 Isabel Mary (died 1919), fourth daughter of William Latham, Q.C., and had four sons and two daughters. He died in London, while still upon the bench, 11 January 1935.

[*The Times*, 12 January 1935; private information.]   NOEL MIDDLETON.

BAYLIS, LILIAN MARY (1874–1937), theatrical manager, was born in London 9 May 1874, the eldest daughter of Edward William Baylis, singer, by his wife, Elizabeth Cons, singer and pianist. She was educated at home and trained at an early age as a violinist under J. T. Carrodus [q.v.], appearing in public when only seven years old at the entertainments organized by her aunt Emma Cons in the 'Royal Victoria Coffee Music Hall', as it was then called. Miss Cons had secured a lease of the theatre in Lambeth originally (1818) called the Royal Cobourg Theatre and renamed (1833) the Victoria Theatre, familiarly known as the 'Old Vic': she reopened it as the Royal Victoria Coffee Music Hall on 27 December 1880. Miss Cons, a social worker closely associated with Charles Kingsley, John Ruskin, and Octavia Hill [qq.v.], seems to have been led to take this step by John Hollingshead [q.v.], the famous manager of the Gaiety Theatre: their idea was to open a popular music-hall for the working classes in which no alcoholic liquor should be obtainable. In 1890 the Baylis family emigrated to South Africa, where they toured the country giving musical entertainments under great difficulties of transport. Lilian Baylis eventually settled in Johannesburg, where she taught music and trained a ladies' orchestra; but in 1898 Miss Cons persuaded her niece to return to England to assist her in the management of the Royal Victoria Hall. Hitherto the entertainments had consisted of oratorio and ballad concerts interspersed with variety and scientific lectures, as well as temperance meetings. Plays and operas could not be given under the lord chamberlain's regulations, but in the case of opera these were evaded by presenting selections from operas with *tableaux vivants* in costume. Lilian Baylis became acting manager in 1898 and in 1899 engaged Charles Corri as musical director. This partnership lasted for over thirty years, during which time the musical activities of the hall were considerably developed, although symphony concerts were financially unsuccessful. Miss Baylis was one of the first to seize on the cinematograph as a popular entertainment, especially for children, but dropped it after a few years when it became a general commercial enterprise which presented films which she considered unsuitable for the young.

Miss Cons died in 1912 and Lilian Baylis became sole manager of the hall. Miss Cons's interests had been primarily social and religious; her niece shared these interests but was now free to raise the whole artistic standard of her theatre, which she advertised as 'The People's Opera House'. William Poel [q.v.], who had been manager from 1881 to 1883, had offered to bring his own dramatic company in 1906, but this offer had had to be refused owing to the lord chamberlain's regulations; an offer of Shakespeare recitals in costume made by Mr. George Owen and Mr. William Bridges-Adams in 1911 came to nothing. After 1912 the restrictions seem to have been lifted; a few plays of a popular type were performed, but with little success. In April 1914 Miss Rosina Filippi presented Shakespeare for the first time, and also *The School for Scandal*. She had wished to perform Mr. Bernard Shaw's *Candida*, but this play was abandoned, probably because no suitable actress was available for the name part.

The development of the Old Vic as the 'home of Shakespeare' was first made possible by the war of 1914–1918, which rendered all theatrical enterprise so precarious that actors of distinction were glad to join a Shakespeare company at the Old Vic at very modest salaries for the sake of a secure engagement. Between 1914 and 1923 all the plays of Shakespeare were performed there under various producers; Miss Baylis took no part in production but limited herself to general management. By the end of the war the Old Vic had become one of London's leading theatres, drawing audiences from all parts of the capital, and Miss Baylis began to be aware that she was now doing what should have been the work of a national theatre. Sadler's Wells Theatre in Islington was acquired and rebuilt, mainly through the energy of (Sir) Reginald Rowe, and reopened in 1931 as an 'Old Vic' for north London; after a short time it was found more practicable to confine performances there to opera and ballet, drama being given at the Old Vic. Miss Baylis found herself obliged to delegate much of the management to others, but controlled the two theatres to the end of her life. She died at Stockwell 25 November 1937.

Lilian Baylis's achievement was the creation of a true people's theatre and opera-house out of what had begun as a philanthropic temperance institution. She had the reputation of being a hard woman, because she was always struggling with inadequate resources: she herself admitted that she was ill-educated, but she had a sure instinct for finding the right collaborators. She was devoutly religious, full of broad-minded humanity, and she kept her theatres going mainly by the intense personal affection and idealism which she inspired in all who worked with her.

Miss Baylis was appointed C.H. in 1929 and received honorary degrees from the universities of Oxford (1924) and Birmingham (1934).

A chalk drawing of Miss Baylis, by (Sir) William Rothenstein (1922), and an oil painting, by Ethel Gabain, are at Sadler's Wells Theatre. A third portrait, by Charles E. Butler, hangs in the Old Vic Theatre.

[*The Times*, 26, 29, and 30 November 1937; Sybil and Russell Thorndike, *Lilian Baylis*, 1938; Lilian Baylis and Cicely Hamilton, *The Old Vic*, 1926; E. G. Harcourt Williams, *Four Years at the Old Vic, 1929–1933*, 1935; *Vic-Wells. The Work of Lilian Baylis*, edited by E. G. Harcourt Williams, 1938; E. J. Dent, *A Theatre for Everybody*, 1945; Norman Marshall, *The Other Theatre*, 1947; *Who's Who in the Theatre*, 1936.]   EDWARD J. DENT.

BAYLY, SIR LEWIS (1857–1938), admiral, was born at Woolwich, 28 September 1857, the third son of Captain Neville Bayly, of the Royal Horse Artillery, by his wife, Henrietta Charlotte, fourth daughter of General Charles George Gordon, of the Royal Artillery, and great-nephew of Admiral Sir Richard Keats [q.v.]. He was educated in the *Britannia*, passing out in 1872 as a navigating cadet, but he was promoted to sub-lieutenant for navigating duties in 1876, when the navigating branch was abolished and changed over to the executive branch; he became lieutenant in 1881. He served in the Ashanti campaign (1873) and in the Congo expedition (1875) in the *Encounter*, and in the Egyptian war of 1882. In 1883 he specialized in torpedo, but his first important appointment was as naval attaché to the United States of America in June 1900; in the two years there he gained experience which was to stand him in good stead in his last appointment.

In 1907, after having commanded the cruiser *Talbot* on the China station and the battleship *Queen* in the Mediterranean, Bayly was selected for the command of the destroyer flotillas in the Home Fleet, with the rank of commodore, in the *Attentive*. In Bayly's own words, 'destroyers were then a comparatively new arm, and their capabilities when working in flotillas were not very well understood'. A fine seaman and a hard taskmaster, he completed an immense programme of exercises during the next two years and laid solid foundations for the future handling and administration of flotillas. In 1908 he was appointed president of the War College, at Portsmouth, and promoted to flag rank; he held the presidency until 1911 when he was given the command of the first battle-cruiser squadron (flag in the *Indomitable* and later in the *Lion*); this was followed by the command of the third battle squadron (1913–1914, flag in the *King Edward VII*), and, in 1914, by that of the first battle squadron (flag in the *Marlborough*). This squadron was part of the Grand Fleet assembled at Scapa Flow on the outbreak of war in August 1914. In September Bayly was promoted vice-admiral and in December he was appointed to command the recently strengthened Channel Fleet (flag in the *Lord Nelson*), but a few days later was relieved of his command because, during exercises, one of his battleships, the *Formidable*, was sunk by torpedo. He asked for a court martial, but this was refused, and he was appointed president of the Royal Naval College, Greenwich. With that appointment his active career appeared to have ended, but his greatest work still lay ahead of him. In July 1915 he was appointed to command the Western Approaches with base at Queenstown and in the beginning of 1916 was raised to the position of commander-in-chief. The German submarine campaign was at its height and the frequent sinkings in the Western Approaches could only be checked by extremely vigorous defence measures and by exploiting new methods of attacking the submarines. Bayly had all the qualities for conducting the anti-submarine campaign, but for the first two years he never had sufficient ships for the large area for which he was responsible, until, in 1917, welcome reinforcements from the United States began to arrive.

Bayly, who had been promoted admiral in 1917, proved the ideal commander of a mixed Anglo-American force. He made the senior United States officer (Captain Joel Roberts Poinsett Pringle, afterwards vice-admiral) his chief of staff, the first foreign naval officer to hold such an appointment, and he mixed the ships of the two navies in his flotillas and squadrons so that after a few months they were all one navy. Although in his own service his reputation was that of a hard taskmaster with a brusque, intolerant manner, the American navy discovered a human side which led him to be known to all American sailors as 'Uncle Lewis'. It is no exaggeration to say that by the time the war was over, he was as well known in the United States as in his own country. It was the joint practice of naval warfare that broadened and deepened into a sympathetic understanding between Bayly and Pringle and all those who served under them, and this understanding spread to wider reaches and helped materially to cement friendship between the two English-speaking countries.

In 1921 Bayly, who had retired in July 1919, visited the United States as the guest of the Queenstown Association, a club formed by officers who had served under him from 1915 to 1918, and of which he was vice-president. In 1934 he was again the guest of the American navy when, at the Naval Academy at Annapolis, he unveiled a memorial, which the Secretary of the Navy had granted him permission to erect, to his American chief of staff, Vice-Admiral Pringle.

Bayly was appointed C.V.O. in 1907, C.B. in 1912, K.C.B. in 1914, and K.C.M.G. in 1918. He received the Grand Cross of the Dannebrog in 1912 and the American D.S.O. He married in 1892 Yves Henrietta Stella, daughter of Henry Annesley Voysey; there was no issue of the marriage. He died in London 16 May 1938.

[*The Times*, 17 May 1938; Sir Lewis Bayly, *Pull Together!*, 1939 (portraits); personal knowledge.]   W. M. JAMES.

BEARDMORE, WILLIAM, BARON INVERNAIRN (1856–1936), shipbuilder, was born at Greenwich 16 October 1856, the eldest son of William Beardmore, of Parkhead, Glasgow, by his wife, Sophie Louisa Holfman. He was educated at Glasgow High School and Ayr Academy and completed his studies at the Royal Technical College, Glasgow, and at the Royal School of Mines, South Kensington. He served his apprenticeship at Parkhead Forge, which, founded by David Napier [q.v.], had passed under the control of his father eleven years before. Working for long hours by day, he attended evening classes at Anderson's College, specializing in chemistry and mathematics. On the death of his father he became in 1879 a partner with his uncle, Isaac Beardmore, and on the latter's retirement founded the firm of William Beardmore & company, which gained world-wide fame, not only for the building of men-of-war and merchant ships, but for the construction of the R. 34, which was the first airship to make the double crossing of the Atlantic. During the war of 1914–1918 the Beardmore shipyard, engine shops, and foundries rendered great service to the nation, for it was recognized as the best-equipped and most efficient establishment in the world. Some conception of its activities may be formed when it is stated that in the years 1906 to 1919 the firm built four battleships, seven cruisers, twenty-one destroyers, thirteen submarines, twenty-four hospital ships, and one seaplane-carrier. For some years after the war the firm continued its activities successfully, being responsible for such notable ships as the *Empress of France*, *Lancastria*, *Cameronia*, *Conte Rosso*, *Conte Verde*, *Largs Bay*, *Esperance Bay*, and *Duchess of Atholl*, and in April 1925 the largest vessel ever to leave the Beardmore slip-ways was floated, the first-class passenger and cargo steamer *Conte Biancamano*, 23,121 tons, for the Lloyd Sabaudo. The firm also built the 9,730-ton cruiser *Shropshire* and two submarines.

Soon after the launching of this large man-of-war, the most serious depression affecting both warship and merchant ship construction began and the huge establishment which Beardmore had created and managed so successfully suffered in common with other firms. Shipping, as well as ship-building, was affected by the depression. The Admiralty had ceased to place contracts for men-of-war and Beardmore could not secure sufficient mercantile work to keep the large body of technicians, draughtsmen, and workmen employed. The firm entered the field of locomotive construction and made motor-cars and commercial vehicles. But these experiments were not a success. It was one of the tragedies of the after-war period that the splendidly equipped ship-yards, engine shops, and foundries were without work. Eventually, in 1930, the shipyard was acquired by National Shipbuilders' Security Limited, under an agreement which laid down that it might not be used for a period of forty years. One year before this development Beardmore had severed his connexion with the firm. He was an autocrat in his relations with his employees, but was regarded as a fair and just employer.

For many years Beardmore was chairman of the Industrial Welfare Society in the activities of which he took a keen interest. In 1917 he was president of the Iron and Steel Institute. He encouraged Antarctic exploration, his name being given by Sir Ernest Shackleton [q.v.] to a glacier discovered on one of his voyages to the Antarctic regions. He was also a keen sportsman. In 1914 he was created a baronet and in 1921 raised to the peerage as Baron Invernairn, of Strathnairn, Inverness-shire. He married in 1902 Elspeth Stiven, eldest daughter of David Tullis, of Glencairn, Rutherglen, Lanarkshire; there were no children of the marriage. He died at Flichity, Inverness-shire, 9 April 1936.

[*The Times*, 10 April 1936; David Kirkwood, *My Life of Revolt*, 1935.]

ARCHIBALD HURD.

BEATTY, DAVID, first EARL BEATTY (1871–1936), admiral of the fleet, was born at Howbeck Lodge, Stapeley, near Nantwich, Cheshire, 17 January 1871, the second son in a family of four sons and one daughter of Captain David Longfield Beatty, of the 4th Hussars, by his first wife, Katherine Edith, daughter of Nicholas Sadleir, of Dunboyne Castle, co. Meath, a remarkable woman who more than once prophesied that England would ring with David's name. The Beattys were of old Irish stock; the admiral's grandfather was long master of the Wexford hounds, and his parents, when they settled in Cheshire, devoted themselves to hunting and training the horses sent over from the family estates at Borodale in county Wexford. It is not therefore surprising that Beatty's favourite sport was hunting, or that he wrote to his sister about the battle of Jutland as if it had been a hunt. 'I describe the battle to you thus because only in this way would you understand it.'

Sea and ships had always greatly fascinated young Beatty, and there was never any doubt that he was destined for the navy. At thirteen years of age he passed into the *Britannia*, and on passing out two years later he was posted to the *Alexandra*, flagship of Prince Alfred, Duke of Edinburgh [q.v.], commander-in-chief of the Mediterranean Fleet, and he served practically the whole of his time as midshipman in this ship. During the period from 1890 to 1892 he was under training ashore at Portsmouth and at the Royal Naval College, Greenwich, as acting sub-lieutenant, emerging with a first-class certificate in torpedo, a second class in seamanship, gunnery, and pilotage, and a third class in navigation. He was promoted lieutenant in August 1892, and spent his watch-keeping days in the training corvette *Ruby*, and the battleships *Camperdown* and *Trafalgar*, for the most part in the Mediterranean.

Beatty's early enthusiasm for the navy was damped at this time by the monotony of service routine; but his opportunity came in 1896, when Kitchener asked for a small force of gunboats to operate on the Nile in support of his expedition for the recovery of the Sudan. (Sir) Stanley Colville [q.v.], commander of the *Trafalgar*, chose his shipmate Beatty as second-in-command of this little expedition in stern-wheel gunboats. Only three of these boats, one of which was Beatty's, passed the Third Cataract, and immediately above it they were hotly engaged by the Dervishes, not without artillery. Colville, severely wounded, handed over the command to Beatty who immediately decided to attempt the daring manœuvre of leading the flotilla upstream beyond the Arab position. He was assisted in this by the army, which, thanks to the action of the gunboats, had been able to establish artillery and infantry within close range. Beatty, however, pressed on at full speed to Dongola, and after another stiff fight won for the navy the honour of being the first to occupy the town. The enemy were by now in full retreat, but Beatty continued to harass them and did not give up the pursuit until he reached the Fourth Cataract. This gallant piece of leadership was highly praised by Kitchener, Beatty was appointed to the D.S.O., and his name was noted for early promotion.

After a brief spell at home, Beatty, at Kitchener's special request, was again lent, in 1897, to the Egyptian government for operations on the Nile in a flotilla reinforced by specially designed gunboats. He had a narrow escape when, on 4 August, his ship, the *Hafir*, capsized at the Fourth Cataract. During the advance on Omdurman in 1898 he was constantly in action, and commanded a rocket battery ashore at the battle of the Atbara (8 April). After the battle of Omdurman (2 September) Beatty was in one of the gunboats that escorted the sirdar to Fashoda, on his return from whence he received special promotion to commander (November) at the early age of twenty-seven, over the heads of 395 senior officers on the lieutenants' list.

After a winter spent at home in the hunting field, Beatty was appointed (April 1899) to the China station as commander of the battleship *Barfleur*, commanded by Colville. In spite of his youth, Beatty won the respect of both officers and men. After twelve months of normal duty he found himself again on active service in the Boxer rebellion. Sir Edward Seymour [q.v.], the British naval commander-in-chief, made a gallant attempt to reach Pekin with an international force but was compelled to return to Hsiku, where he was completely surrounded. The foreign settlement at Tientsin, six miles to the south, was also besieged, and Beatty landed from the *Barfleur* to reinforce the garrison. In this he succeeded and was continuously employed in sorties; in one across the river he was ambushed. Wounded and in severe pain, he nevertheless brought his men back in good order, remaining with the rearguard until all the wounded had been embarked. While still suffering from his wounds, he accepted the command of a naval detachment which eventually assisted in extricating Seymour from Hsiku. For his services in this campaign he was promoted captain (November 1900). The average age of a captain being then forty-three, his promotion at twenty-nine caused considerable stir.

As captain, Beatty commanded (1902–1910) the cruisers *Juno*, *Arrogant*, *Diana*, and *Suffolk*, and the battleship *Queen*. His marriage had made him independent of the service and his rapid promotion brought him to the head of the list of captains before he had completed the six years' service at sea required for promotion to flag rank. Nevertheless, in view of the time lost on account of the wounds which he had received in China and his war services, he was promoted rear-admiral by order in council on 1 January 1910, the youngest flag-officer for over a hundred years, being just under thirty-nine years of age, whereas Nelson on his promotion was a few months over thirty-eight. This promotion created even greater stir than the previous one, and with perhaps more justification in view of the length of time during which he had been on half-pay.

Beatty was far more interested in the proper employment of the fleet in war than in its technicalities, and soon after Mr. Churchill, with his 'mind full of the dangers of war', became first lord of the Admiralty in October 1911, he chose Beatty, in spite of naval advice to the contrary, for his naval secretary (1912). They were admirably suited to each other; and, probably in order to confound the critics of Beatty and to test his capacity as a flag-officer, the first lord gave him the command of a cruiser squadron in the important manœuvres of 1912. Clearly Beatty fulfilled Mr. Churchill's expectations, for in the spring of 1913 he appointed Beatty 'over the heads of all' to command the battle-cruiser squadron. Beatty hoisted his flag in the *Lion* in March 1913, and when war broke out on 4 August 1914 he was in northern waters in command of the scouting forces of the Grand Fleet based at Scapa Flow under Sir John (later Earl) Jellicoe [q.v.].

When, on 22 September 1914, the three cruisers *Cressy*, *Hogue*, and *Aboukir* were torpedoed with great loss of life off the Dutch coast, the shock to a fleet which had not wholly appreciated the potentialities of the submarine was such that the commander-in-chief, apprehensive about the security of the Grand Fleet at Scapa Flow, decided to take the fleet to ports on the west coast of Scotland and Ireland until Scapa could be properly defended. Although Beatty recognized the need for this decision, the result of government improvidence was more than he could bear, and he lost no time in pressing his views in the strongest terms by private letter to Mr. Churchill. Believing Scapa to be too distant from the enemy, he urged that Cromarty and Rosyth should also be equipped and defended as operational bases, and these defences were completed by the end of the year.

It has been a matter for wonder why the Germans did not take fuller advantage of the awkward predicament in which the Grand Fleet found itself at this time. The answer is supplied by the success of the offensive movement into the Heligoland Bight, carried out by Beatty, (Sir) Reginald Yorke Tyrwhitt, and Roger John Brownlow (later Lord) Keyes, during the first month of the war. The plan designed by the Admiralty was, briefly, that Tyrwhitt with his destroyers should penetrate deeply into the Bight under cover of darkness and sweep out at dawn from east to west with the object of destroying all enemy ships encountered, while Keyes with his submarines lay off the mouths of the German rivers in suitable positions to attack enemy heavy ships if they came out. Two older battle-cruisers from the Humber under Rear-Admiral Sir Archibald Gordon Henry Wilson Moore were to act in support. Jellicoe, uneasy as to the adequacy of this support, directed Beatty to proceed to Heligoland with the battle-cruisers *Lion*, *Queen Mary*, *Princess Royal*, and Commodore (Sir) William Edmund Goodenough's six light cruisers. The weather was calm, but visibility was bad. Beatty's first

move was to make contact with the Humber battle-cruiser force, which he did at daylight on 28 August, and he was thus able to obtain detailed information of the movements of the other units. The presence of British forces in the Bight having become known, the enemy sent out cruisers and destroyers to reinforce their patrols. In the thick weather, the British flotillas lost touch with one another, the situation became confused, and it was difficult to distinguish friend from foe. In several fleeting actions, the German cruiser *Mainz* and a destroyer were sunk. Just before noon, Tyrwhitt's flagship *Arethusa*, which had been badly damaged a short time previously, was attacked by four enemy cruisers. Captain W. F. Blunt in the *Fearless*, with a division of destroyers, came to her support, but could do little against such a superior force. At this critical moment, to the north-westward out of the mist, Beatty appeared with his battle-cruisers steaming at high speed to the rescue. Sundry other British forces rallied towards the battle-cruisers, and in a hot pursuit of the enemy into the Bight, the *Köln* and *Ariadne* were sunk. The two remaining German cruisers, *Strassburg* and *Stralsund*, made their escape. At 1.10 p.m. Beatty made the general signal 'Retire'.

There is no doubt that by his prompt action Beatty turned what would certainly have been a disaster into an important success. It is interesting to note how he arrived at his decision, which was no easy one in view of the risks involved in the face of mines, submarines, and enemy heavy ships. At 10 a.m., realizing that the whole position was confused, Beatty broke wireless silence and informed all concerned where he was and what he was doing. He became very uneasy, and on receipt of various signals for assistance he decided to disregard the dangers and proceed at high speed in support of the *Arethusa*. His reasons for this are given in his own dispatch: 'The situation appeared to me to be extremely critical . . . there was the possibility of a grave disaster. At 11.30 I therefore decided that the only course possible was to take the battle-cruiser squadron at full speed to the eastward . . . I had not lost sight of the danger to my squadron.' Here he enumerates the risks and discounts them methodically one by one, a good example of Beatty's power of tempering boldness with caution but, once the situation had been weighed, acting with vigour and determination. No British ship was lost in an action which, although a marked success, disclosed grave deficiencies in staff work and system of command. Nevertheless, the moral effect was profound: the German navy in particular was severely shaken, and the inactivity of the enemy from August to September enabled the defences of the British bases to be completed and the position of the Grand Fleet in the North Sea was consolidated.

December 1914 was an anxious month for the British command. Owing to the commitments in other seas, only three battle-cruisers were available. There were signs of German naval activity and on 14 December the Admiralty reported that the enemy battle-cruisers were about to carry out a 'tip and run' raid on the east coast of England. As it was impossible to ascertain where the enemy would choose to attack, a strong British force, including the second battle squadron under Admiral Sir George Warrender [q.v.] and the first battle-cruiser squadron under Beatty, were dispatched to a point between Heligoland and Flamborough Head, where they would be in a good position to intercept the enemy on his return.

At dawn on 16 December, when the British forces were in process of concentrating, news was received that Scarborough, Whitby, and Hartlepool were being bombarded. The weather was thick and the situation was complicated by the fact that a German mine-field lay between the British fleet and the five bombarding battle-cruisers. Aided by mist and the mine-field, the enemy slipped through the British forces and escaped. It was an exasperating day for the British admirals who were frustrated because there was no scientific means of locating the enemy or of synchronizing the movements of the four British squadrons groping blindly for their prey. The success of the raid emphasized the need for basing strong British forces farther south. Accordingly Beatty's battle-cruisers were stationed at Rosyth, and they had not long been there before Beatty found himself speeding across the North Sea to intercept Admiral Hipper, who, according to Admiralty intelligence, was expected to be near the Dogger Bank with four battle-cruisers, accompanied by cruisers and destroyers, on the morning of 24 January. So accurate was this intelligence that the British scouting forces sighted the enemy, as if at a pre-arranged rendezvous, at 7.30 a.m. on that day.

Beatty pressed forward at full speed to attack with the *Lion*, *Tiger*, and *Princess Royal*. Rear-Admiral Moore with the older and slower *Indomitable* and the *New Zealand* began to fall astern. Hipper turned to run for home but Beatty was overhauling him and had a good chance to destroy the enemy ships before they could reach their base. But it was not to be. At 9 a.m. the British ships opened fire, the *Seydlitz* was severely damaged, and the *Blücher*, the rear ship of the enemy, very soon fell out of line and was abandoned to her fate. On the other hand, Beatty's flagship *Lion* became the target for the concentrated fire of the German squadron and after two hours' fighting received a blow which stopped one engine and caused her to list heavily to port. The other ships swept past her, and Beatty, who could no longer lead his squadron, was obliged to issue instructions by flag signals.

The British squadron had now lost some distance on account of a turn to avoid a reported submarine. Beatty has been criticized for having ordered this turn, but he was no doubt influenced by the fate which had befallen the three cruisers in September. In order to continue the pursuit and get his guns to bear on the fleeing enemy, Beatty gave the order to his signal officer: 'Course north-east—attack the rear of the enemy.' But the *Lion* had only two signal halyards left, and the arrangement of the signals as hoisted conveyed the meaning 'Attack the rear of the enemy bearing north-east', and so it was interpreted by Moore, the second-in-command. The effect was tragic, for by coincidence the *Blücher*, now well separated from her consorts, bore north-east: consequently the whole of the British squadron attacked and destroyed her. The *Lion* by now had dropped well astern, and Beatty was at a loss to know why his squadron was not continuing the pursuit of the main German force. He accordingly gave the order to use Nelson's signal 'Engage the enemy more closely', but was told that it had been omitted from the signal book. The modern substitute 'Keep nearer to the enemy' was then hoisted, but by this time the *Lion* was so far away that the signal could not be read. He transferred to a destroyer and gave chase: but it was too late: the enemy had escaped. So ended an action, which, although acclaimed as a British victory, was not so satisfactory as it might have been had Beatty been able to retain his leadership.

In December 1915 Beatty, now promoted to vice-admiral, had under his command ten battle-cruisers organized into three squadrons, three light cruiser squadrons, and the thirteenth destroyer flotilla, with the *Lion* as fleet flagship. As that year wore on it was clear that the Germans had no intention of challenging British sea power in the North Sea, and no major action took place, but in January 1916 Admiral Scheer, the new commander-in-chief of the German fleet, announced his intention of coming to 'close grips with England'. He implemented his threat by carrying out some ineffective 'tip and run' raids at scattered points on the east coast, hoping that public indignation would cause dispersal of the British fleet. He was disappointed; so he planned a more ambitious operation in which his light forces were to attack trade off the Norwegian coast and in the Skagerrak while the High Sea Fleet remained fifty miles to the south ready to pounce on any British detachment which might be sent to deal with the raiders. Before putting this plan into action, he placed strong forces of submarines in positions where they could intercept British units coming out from Rosyth, Cromarty, and Scapa.

The date selected was 31 May, and by an extraordinary coincidence Jellicoe had also prepared for 2 June an operation which was in essence the same as Scheer's, namely, to draw the German forces into the Skagerrak and destroy them with the Grand Fleet. Towards the end of May the fleet had taken up its disposition for the impending operation, and as the third battle-cruiser squadron under Rear-Admiral (Sir) H. L. A. Hood [q.v.] happened to be at Scapa for routine gunnery practice, Jellicoe sent Rear-Admiral (Sir) H. Evan-Thomas [q.v.] with the fifth battle squadron to replace it in Beatty's fleet at Rosyth.

On 30 May the Admiralty warned Jellicoe that the enemy intended to go to sea by way of Horn's Reef on 31 May; on the evening of the 30th the Grand Fleet sailed from Scapa, and Beatty left Rosyth with six battle-cruisers and the fifth battle squadron. Jellicoe's plan was that the Grand Fleet should pass through a position 200 miles east of Kinnaird Head on a southerly course. Beatty was to take his force to a point seventy miles south of this, and, if nothing was sighted, to turn north and take up his position ahead of the Grand Fleet. The whole fleet would then sweep south towards Horn's Reef with the cruiser screen ahead covering a wide front.

Scheer left the Jade the same night, but neither Beatty nor Jellicoe had any definite information that the enemy was at sea. About noon on the 31st, the Admiralty incorrectly informed Jellicoe and Beatty that the German flagship was still in the Jade. Beatty reached his rendezvous at 2 p.m., and having sighted nothing he turned his whole force to the north to meet Jellicoe. He stationed the fifth battle squadron five miles to the northward of him so that it could be conveniently situated to drop into its normal position ten miles north of the battle-cruisers when the whole fleet had finally concentrated, and was proceeding to the southward in accordance with Jellicoe's plan. A few minutes later Commodore (Sir) Edwyn Sinclair Alexander-Sinclair in the *Galatea*, scouting to the eastward, reported the presence of enemy cruisers and destroyers. Beatty immediately turned to south-south-east to place himself between the enemy and his base. Evan-Thomas with the fifth battle squadron did not turn to follow Beatty until six minutes later, partly because he had not at the moment received the report of the enemy, and partly because smoke had prevented him from seeing the turning signal. This, opening the distance between the two squadrons, caused Beatty to go into action without the support of the four battleships. It has been suggested that he should have waited for Evan-Thomas, but his primary duty was to locate the enemy, and, if in superior force, to destroy him. In view of the Admiralty intelligence received two hours previously, he had every reason to believe that he would be in superior force, and he had six battle-cruisers against Hipper's five.

At 3.25 p.m. Beatty sighted the German battle-cruisers and reported their position to Jellicoe, at this time about sixty miles to the northward. The two squadrons closed, and at 3.48 p.m. a fierce battle began on a southerly course at high speed. The British were unfavourably placed for wind and light, and the Germans quickly found the range. The *Lion* was repeatedly hit, and twenty minutes after the battle was joined the *Indefatigable*, which was struck by two plunging salvoes, blew up. Twenty minutes later the *Queen Mary* blew up, which caused Beatty to remark to his flag-captain: 'There seems to be something wrong with our bloody ships to-day, Chatfield.' In spite of these two disasters, Beatty kept at close action range; meanwhile Evan-Thomas, by cutting corners and cramming on maximum speed, had skilfully managed to bring his squadron into action against the rear of the enemy. At this critical moment, Beatty threw his destroyers into the attack. Hipper did the same, and a brisk destroyer battle took place between the lines in which the British attack was the more successful, for a torpedo struck the *Seydlitz* and Hipper was forced to turn away. The German attack failed completely, and this gave the British a slight breathing space and from now onwards their fire began to tell. 'Nothing', reported Hipper, 'but the poor quality of the British bursting charges saved us from disaster.'

At 4.40 p.m. with dramatic suddenness the scene changed. A forest of masts appeared on the southern horizon where for the moment visibility was good. This was the High Sea Fleet, reported for the first time seven minutes previously by Commodore Goodenough, who had been scouting ahead of the battle-cruisers. Beatty's duty was clear. He must retire to the northward at once and endeavour to lead Scheer into Jellicoe's clutches. Accordingly he reversed his course and after another hour and a half of dogged fighting, in which the fifth battle squadron bore the brunt, he sighted the Grand Fleet. During this time the two British squadrons inflicted very heavy damage on the German battle-cruisers, all the turrets of the *Von der Tann* being put out of action.

At 5.35 p.m. Beatty, realizing that Jellicoe was not far off, turned sharply to the eastward in order to bend back Hipper's van and prevent him from sighting the main British battle-fleet. This manœuvre gave Beatty improved visibility and after a sharp encounter the enemy withdrew from the action behind a smoke screen. Of this action, the German official account says: 'Hard pressed and unable to return the fire, the position of the German battle-cruisers soon became unbearable.'

And now the battleships of the Grand Fleet appeared out of the mist in six columns to the northward, and Beatty found himself streaking across their front. In spite of conflicting reports as to the position of the enemy battle fleet, Jellicoe deployed into line of battle in the nick of time on an easterly course, with the object of getting between the enemy and his base, and Beatty was able to take up his position in the van while Evan-Thomas proceeded to his alternative battle-station in the rear. By 6.30 p.m. the main battle fleets were in action, and Beatty was joined a little later by the two remaining battle-cruisers out of the three that composed the third battle squadron under Hood, who at 6.34 had been lost in the *Invincible*. At 8.25 p.m., Beatty, who was conforming as arranged with the movements of the Grand Fleet, got a sight of the German battle-cruisers and one of their battle squadrons. He immediately closed and opened fire; but the Germans, having no spirit for further fighting, turned away and were lost in the mist.

Although Beatty's force had sustained heavy losses, he had by nightfall under his command, ready for action next day, six battle-cruisers, whereas Hipper had only one. To Evan-Thomas Beatty gave full credit in his dispatch for the part played by the fifth battle squadron in achieving this result.

Professional investigations at the Royal Naval War College and Staff College over many years confirm the view expressed in Jellicoe's dispatch that Beatty carried out the duties assigned to him with conspicuous success. Despite heavy losses, he located the enemy battle fleet and led it to a position where the Grand Fleet could engage it. He also, at the critical moment, prevented Hipper from sighting the British main fleet and so enabled Jellicoe to complete his deployment unobserved in the right direction while Beatty himself took up his position in the van of the British line of battle in accordance with the commander-in-chief's plan. It is true that reports of the enemy's positions coming in from Beatty and his cruisers were misleading to Jellicoe. The main reason for this (apart from bad visibility) was that each ship's position was based upon her own individual calculations, and no means then existed for synchronizing these estimates on a common basis. Errors of omission can be accounted for by the fact that Beatty was hotly engaged most of the time, and the *Lion*'s wireless was inoperative. It was only natural, therefore, that there should have been recriminations, arising mainly from the fact that in the conditions of visibility prevailing, no two commanders got the same view of the action, and that, although 250 ships took part, there were never more than three or four enemy ships in sight at the same time from any point in our line of battle. It must always be remembered that a complete bird's-eye view of the battle was denied to those who took part, and particularly to the commander-in-chief, who that day bore on his shoulders the responsibility for possibly losing the war in an afternoon.

At the end of 1916 Jellicoe became first sea lord, and Beatty, at the age of forty-five, when most of his contemporaries were still on the captains' list, was appointed with the acting rank of admiral to command the most powerful fleet in history. Early in 1917 he chose the *Queen Elizabeth* as his flagship because she had the speed to enable him to get to the most favourable position for exercising supreme command in battle. He immediately set to work to enforce the lessons of Jutland. To make his system of leadership clear to all, he changed the title 'Battle Orders' to 'Battle Instructions', thereby implying that senior officers could use their own initiative to the fullest extent in translating into action the general intentions of the commander-in-chief. Being determined that the confusion in information experienced at Jutland should not recur, he introduced a system of plotting the positions of British and enemy units upon a synchronized basis. He always believed in aircraft and arranged for kite balloons to be flown by various selected units. Ships were taken in hand by the dockyards to improve their magazine protection, and meanwhile the Admiralty had designed a really effective projectile and was hastening its supply to the fleet.

The anti-submarine campaign of 1917 aroused Beatty's hunting instincts. While keeping a sharp look-out for a sortie by the German fleet—there was indeed one abortive attempt—he used every means in his power to combat the menace. He was a firm believer in the convoy system, and, growing impatient with the Admiralty slowness in organizing it, asked and obtained permission to run convoys under his own direction to and from Norway. Over 4,000 ships sailed in convoy in the North Sea with negligible loss in six months. But it was only a question of time before one of the Norwegian convoys would be located by fast enemy surface ships, using the hours of darkness to evade the British patrols. This happened on two occasions in the autumn of 1917 and the following winter. Fortunately neither convoy was large and the total loss was sixteen merchant ships, four destroyers, and four armed trawlers. It was, nevertheless, only

to be expected that the enemy would try again, so Beatty decided to send larger convoys at longer intervals, but escorted by a division of battleships. The inherent hope that this would entice the enemy to send out still stronger forces to attack the convoys was nearly fulfilled, for Scheer, in April 1918, did make one more sortie, but he miscalculated the date and dared not prolong his stay in waters where Beatty might be met.

The advent of a squadron of United States battleships under Admiral Hugh Rodman diminished the strain on the Grand Fleet. Beatty and Rodman worked in perfect harmony and in a very short time the American squadron became an integral part of Beatty's battle fleet. In 1918 the added strength of the United States navy enabled more effective measures to be brought against enemy submarines, and the patrols round the coasts of Great Britain became so effective that the enemy was compelled to look for targets far out at sea, only to be frustrated by the convoy system. By midsummer the submarine danger was definitely mastered, but in October there were indications that Scheer might take a 'death-ride' with his fleet. Beatty countered the German move of concentrating all their submarines in the North Sea in positions where they could attack the Grand Fleet on its way to battle, by massing all available anti-submarine vessels at the threatened points. Then he dispatched Rear-Admiral (Sir) Arthur Cavenagh Leveson with the second battle-cruiser squadron and a strong destroyer force on a high-speed sweep through the submarine-infested waters towards the Skagerrak. When Leveson reported on his return that only one torpedo had been fired at his force, it was evident that the morale of the German navy was broken, and this opinion was confirmed by the news that the High Sea Fleet had mutinied and refused to obey orders to sail.

Two days after the signing of the armistice on 11 November, the German cruiser *Königsberg* arrived at Rosyth, having on board Rear-Admiral Meurer and a 'soldiers' and workmen's council' which claimed to have plenipotentiary powers. Beatty made it clear that he would only negotiate with a naval officer of flag rank. The delegates could not but agree, and Meurer, while thanking Beatty at the conference table, stated that this was the first time that his rank had been recognized during the last two months. The necessary arrangements were made on 15 and 16 November, and on 21 November the Grand Fleet escorted the High Sea Fleet to its anchorage in the Firth of Forth. A service of thanksgiving was held in every ship, and that evening Beatty made the famous signal: 'The German flag will be hauled down at sunset, and will not be hoisted again without permission.' On 1 January 1919 Beatty was promoted admiral and on 3 April admiral of the fleet: four days later he hauled down his union flag and the Grand Fleet ceased to exist.

On 1 November 1919 Beatty succeeded Admiral of the Fleet Sir R. Wemyss (later Lord Wester Wemyss, q.v.) as first sea lord, and was immediately confronted with the problem of reducing the navy in order to reconcile the demands of economy with the maintenance of sea power adequate for national security. The presentation of the freedom of many cities gave him a fine opportunity of impressing on the public the need for a strong navy. At the Washington Conference, which assembled in November 1921, although he agreed generally with the principle of parity with the United States, he insisted upon Great Britain retaining the right to have the number of cruisers necessary for her own peculiar needs. He succeeded in getting the British case accepted, and it was not until he had left the Admiralty that the minimum of seventy cruisers for Britain was abandoned. Wrapped up with this problem was that of overseas bases, and Beatty, with his eye on Japan, succeeded in convincing the Cabinet that if the fleet was to operate in Far Eastern waters a strongly defended base with full docking facilities must be established at Singapore. There were some warm controversies with the Air Ministry over this and other problems, including that of the status of the Fleet Air Arm which the Air Ministry considered should be retained within its own organization, including responsibility for providing material and training air personnel, but which the Admiralty maintained must be an integral part of the navy. The dispute was ended by the government decision of 1937 by which the administration, operating, and training of the Fleet Air Arm were put almost wholly under naval control. Experience in the war of 1939–1945 proved that Beatty's view was correct.

Beatty's experience of naval warfare convinced him of the value, which he had learned under Mr. Churchill, of a trained body of staff officers to assist admirals in all the ramifications of war. He approved and encouraged the Naval Staff College, and re-established the war course for senior officers only. To ensure common doctrine both were established at Greenwich. At the Admiralty he made the naval staff responsible for seeing that construction and armaments were designed to meet fighting requirements, in which he was ably assisted by Rear-Admiral (Lord) Chatfield. He confirmed the creation of the Department of Scientific Research advocated by Rear-Admiral (Sir) William Coldingham Masters Nicholson and established the Admiralty experimental laboratory at Teddington. He played a leading part in the inauguration of the Chiefs of Staffs Committee which has since proved to be a most efficient instrument for the conduct of war under the prime minister. He was first sea lord for seven and a half years, a longer period than any of his predecessors, and all the time he had to resist continual assaults aimed at reducing British naval strength. Yet he left the Admiralty in July 1927, not only with the goodwill and admiration of the navy, but with the thanks of the government for invaluable assistance 'during a period of exceptional difficulty'.

On retirement Beatty went back to the hunting field, where he had a serious accident which necessitated his lying for three months with a broken jaw tightly screwed. Some years afterwards, while suffering from a severe attack of influenza, he rose from a sick bed against all medical advice, to attend Jellicoe's funeral in November 1935. During a halt in Fleet Street a member of the staff of a newspaper office, noticing how ill he looked, kindly revived him with a glass of brandy, and he marched on with the procession. Barely four months later he died in London 11 March 1936, and was buried in St. Paul's Cathedral on the 16th.

Beatty took a deep interest in the welfare and recreation of the ships' companies and devoted much time and energy to improving their domestic and service conditions. An increase of pay being long overdue, he created two committees under Rear-Admiral Sir Lionel Halsey and Admiral Sir T. H. M. Jerram [q.v.] to investigate the question, and as a result of their report the pay of officers and men was substantially raised in 1919 for the first time for many years. This well-timed measure did much to alleviate distress and successfully checked any discontent which might have arisen during the dangerous period of transition from war to peace. Of the many honours done to him none pleased him more than the invitation issued to him in 1919 by the men of the fleet to be their guest at a banquet at Portsmouth, where amid a vociferous reception, gun teams dragged his car through the streets. Ordinary honours were legion. He was appointed M.V.O. in 1905, C.B. in 1911, K.C.B. in 1914, K.C.V.O. and G.C.B. in 1916, and G.C.V.O. in 1917. In 1919 he was appointed to the Order of Merit and later in that year he was raised to the peerage as Earl Beatty, at the same time receiving the thanks of both Houses of Parliament and a grant of £100,000. In 1927 he was sworn of the Privy Council. He received honorary degrees from the universities of Oxford and Aberdeen and was lord rector of Edinburgh University from 1917 until his death. His numerous foreign decorations included that of grand officer of the Legion of Honour.

Beatty married in 1901 Ethel (died 1932), only daughter of Marshall Field, of Chicago, and formerly wife of Arthur Magic Tree, of the United States of America. They had two sons, the elder of whom, David Field (born 1905), succeeded as second earl.

In the course of his naval career, Beatty was sometimes the target of ill-informed criticism, but he never spoke a word in reply, being content to abide by the verdict of his countrymen and of history. He was neither impetuous nor rash; his judgement was sound and his decisions were the result of careful reflection and forethought. During the war he never took any leave, and, although his wife and family lived close to Rosyth, he slept in his flagship every night. He landed every afternoon while in harbour for physical exercise and maintained perfect health throughout, nor did he ever show the slightest sign of the strain imposed upon him. In moments of crisis his brain worked with absolute clarity and he never had cause to reverse an important decision. Above all was his dauntless courage, both moral and physical.

A portrait of Beatty is included in Sir A. S. Cope's picture 'Some Sea Officers of the Great War', painted in 1921, in the National Portrait Gallery. Another portrait is that in Sir John Lavery's 'Surrender of the German Fleet' in the Imperial War Museum. Other portraits include a full-length in captain's uniform, by Hugh Riviere (1909), a full-length in evening dress, by Cowan Dobson (1930), and a head (black and white), by J. S. Sargent (1919), all in the possession of the second Earl Beatty; a head, by P. A. de László, belonging to the Hon. Peter Beatty; and a painting in admiral's uniform, by an unknown artist, at the Naval and Military Club, Pall Mall. There is a bust, by Feredah Forbes, at Brooksby Hall, near Leicester.

[Official dispatches; Staff College records; Admiralty office memoranda, The German official account of the Battle of Jutland; Winston Churchill, *The World Crisis*, 1923; Sir E. H. Seymour, *My Naval Career and Travels*, 1911; Geoffrey Rawson, *Beatty*, 1930; private information; personal knowledge.]

W. S. Chalmers.

BEAUCHAMP, seventh Earl (1872–1938), politician. [See Lygon, William.]

BEDFORD, eleventh Duke of (1858–1940) and BEDFORD, Duchess of (1865–1937). [See Russell, Herbrand Arthur.]

BELL, Sir FRANCIS HENRY DILLON (1851–1936), New Zealand lawyer and statesman, was born at the residency of the New Zealand Company at Nelson 31 March 1851. He was the eldest of the six sons of (Sir) Francis Dillon Bell, by his wife, Margaret, daughter of Abraham Hort, a leading member of the Jewish community in Wellington. The Bell family was descended from Robert Barclay, of Ury [q.v.], the Quaker apologist, and its members were thus collateral relations of Edward Gibbon Wakefield [q.v.] and Elizabeth Fry [q.v.]. Bell's father was a member of the Bell–Sewell ministry (1856) which was the first New Zealand ministry under responsible government. He held many high public positions in New Zealand and was decorated for distinguished services by Great Britain and France.

Bell was educated at the Auckland Grammar School and the Otago Boys' High School at Dunedin (1864–1869), being dux of the latter for five years. In 1869 he entered St. John's College, Cambridge; he was a college prizeman (1871) and a senior optime in the mathematical tripos of 1873. He read law in the chambers of (Sir) John Gorst [q.v.] and (Sir) John Holker [q.v.], and was called to the bar by the Middle Temple in June 1874. He spent his vacations at the home of Lord Kitchener's father at Dinan, in company with the future field-marshal.

Returning to New Zealand at the end of 1874, Bell began practice at Wellington in partnership with C. B. Izard. He rose rapidly in his profession, and was crown solicitor in Wellington from 1879 to 1911 (except for the years 1893 to 1896 when he was in parliament). His conduct of many important appeals to the Privy Council won high praise from Lord Haldane and Lord Macnaghten. For nearly forty of his sixty years of practice he was the acknowledged leader of the New Zealand bar, and in his first year he initiated the *Colonial Law Journal* and later other law reports. He took silk in 1907. He declined a judgeship offered him by the Atkinson government of 1887–1891. As mayor of Wellington (1891–1893 and 1896–1897) he carried out important municipal reforms.

In 1893, after two unsuccessful attempts (1890 and 1892) to enter parliament, Bell was elected one of the three members for Wellington as an opponent of the Seddon liberal–labour government, but he did not seek re-election in 1896. When W. F. Massey [q.v.] became prime minister in July 1912 he was made leader of the legislative council and minister of internal affairs and immigration. He soon raised the council to its proper place as a revising chamber, and his reforming zeal found ample scope. After three years' effort (1911–1914) he carried a measure making the council elective on a basis of proportional representation, but, owing to the outbreak of war, this Act was suspended and is still in abeyance. Bell continued as a minister during the national government (1915–1919), the new Massey ministry (1919–1925), and the Coates ministry (1925–1928). From 1918 to 1926 he was attorney-general. Among his notable reforms were a system of state forestry (1919–1922), which earned for him the title of 'the Father of Forestry' in New Zealand, and the extension of the land transfer system to bring all lands under state control (1924). As minister for external affairs (1923–1926), he enacted important health and education reforms for the natives under the mandate. With the solicitor-general, Sir John Salmond, he drafted much intricate war legislation which served as a model for some other countries. At his first visit to Geneva as representative of New Zealand at the League of Nations (1922) he challenged the right of the Mandates Commission to criticize publicly the administration of the Samoan mandate, claiming that the Assembly alone could do so, and that New Zealand had the right to be heard in her own defence. In 1921 and 1923 he acted as prime minister during Massey's absence at Imperial Conferences.

On the death of Massey in 1925 Bell became prime minister, but held office for only a brief period (14–30 May) pending the election by the 'reform party' of a new leader. He remained leader of the legislative council until the defeat of the Coates ministry in 1928. In 1926 he attended an Imperial Conference with Mr. Coates, and also (at the request of the Foreign and Colonial Offices) a conference at Geneva called to deal with the question of the International Court of Justice at The Hague. He was a vice-president and a member of the drafting committee, and he sought to persuade the United States of America to participate in the work of the court, but, on the ground that they were purely domestic issues, he strongly objected to disputes between different parts of the British Empire being subject to the court. At the 1926 Assembly of the League of Nations Bell viewed with alarm the claim of some Dominions to a seat on the Council of the League, fearing that this practice would enable a Dominion (e.g. Ireland) to veto British proposals. Colour was lent to his view in 1937 when a clash threatened between Mr. Anthony Eden and the New Zealand representative on the Council. In like spirit, at the Imperial Conference of 1926, with Mr. Coates he reluctantly acquiesced in the Balfour formula for the sake of uniformity. Bell thought that the formula and the Statute of Westminster (1931) were a grave danger to imperial unity. He was equally hostile to the formation of an Empire Consultative Council, and regarded conferences of prime ministers as the true Imperial Council and 'much superior to any conclave or cabal of Ministers of second rank in London'. He remained a member of the legislative council until his death, which took place at his home at Lowry Bay, near Wellington, 13 March 1936.

During his public life Bell's influence in politics was so great that a labour member once described him as 'the uncrowned king of New Zealand and one of the ablest men in the southern hemisphere'. On all legal and constitutional questions he was recognized as a consummate authority, and he was confidential adviser to successive governors-general. Sometimes he appeared brusque when deputations proved long-winded, but he had a kindly and generous disposition. He was one of the ablest administrators that New Zealand has ever had, and he served the British Empire with passionate devotion.

Bell married in 1878 Caroline (died 1935), third daughter of William Robinson, of Cheviot, Runholder, a member of the legislative council, and had four sons, of whom only the youngest survived him, and four daughters. The second son was killed in action in France in 1917. He was appointed K.C.M.G. in 1915 and G.C.M.G. in 1923, and he was sworn of the Privy Council in 1926.

There are portraits of Bell by A. F. Nicoll in the National Gallery, Wellington, in the Parliament House, and at the Wellington Club.

[W. Downie Stewart, *The Right Honourable Sir Francis H. D. Bell, His Life and Times*, 1937; personal knowledge.]

WM. DOWNIE STEWART.

BENNETT, (ENOCH) ARNOLD (1867–1931), novelist, playwright, and man of letters, was born at Hanley, Staffordshire, 27 May 1867, the eldest child in a family of three sons and three daughters of Enoch Bennett, solicitor, of Hanley, by his wife, Sarah Ann, elder daughter of Robert Longson, a Derbyshire weaver who afterwards settled as a draper in the Potteries. His father, before becoming a solicitor, had been potter and schoolmaster; while in a part of the house in Hope Street there was carried on for a time a pawnbroking business. The Bennetts, although rigid Wesleyan Methodists, were uncommonly musical, artistic, and bookish for the Potteries of that day, and had the habit attributed to the Orgreaves, in *Clayhanger*, of playing classical music arranged as pianoforte duets. Arnold and his brother Frank, the most ardent musician of them all, likewise acquired a good working knowledge of French which in Arnold's case proved of cardinal importance. He was educated at the Burslem Endowed School, and the Middle School, Newcastle-under-Lyme, attended a local art school (he painted charming, rather pale water-colours to the end of his life), and in 1885 entered his father's office in order to finish preparing for matriculation at London University and to study for a law degree which he never took.

At the age of twenty-one (1888) Bennett left Staffordshire to become clerk to Messrs. Le Brasseur & Oakley, a firm of London solicitors, at a salary of twenty-five shillings a week. He had already made precocious experiments in local journalism and, without success, in sensational fiction combining the grimness of Zola with the airy romance of Ouida; and in London, where he enjoyed the society of young artists, he was encouraged by their belief in his talent to become a writer. Some unambitious trifles for the press were followed by a short story entitled 'A Letter Home', which, rejected by a popular weekly as below its literary standard, was published in *The Yellow Book* (July 1895). Bennett thereupon resolved to write a novel, which 'was to be unlike all English novels except those of one author' (George Moore); and, 'life being grey, sinister, and melancholy, the novel must be grey, sinister, and melancholy'. His own life, he subsequently remarked, was at this time not at all grey or sinister or melancholy. The book was at first called 'In the Shadow': but when accepted and published, in 1898, by John Lane [q.v.], upon the recommendation of his reader, John Buchan [q.v.], it had become, much less greyly, *A Man from the North*. Meanwhile Bennett, forsaking the tedium of a solicitor's office, and the belatedly confessed humiliations of free-lance journalism, had in 1893 become assistant editor, later (1896) editor, of the weekly journal *Woman*, thereby founding an assurance about feminine clothes and psychology which he retained throughout life.

Bennett possessed immense confidence in his own judgement, and from reviews and dramatic criticism for *Woman* passed to reviews and critical articles for the *Academy*, at that time the second critical journal in the country, which regularly employed, among others, E. V. Lucas [q.v.], Wilfred Whitten, Francis Thompson [q.v.], Thomas William Hodgson Crosland, and (Sir) Edmund Kerchever Chambers. Then, having as editor to buy serial fiction at low prices, he offered boastfully to write for Tillotsons' Newspaper Syndicate, which sold him such fiction, a sensational serial story which should surpass all rivals. This story, which he called 'For Love and Life', was sold outright for £75, and, with a later performance of the same order, but of lower quality, 'Teresa of Watling Street', greatly embarrassed the author when, after the great serial success of 'The Grand Babylon Hotel' (also sold outright to Tillotsons), he failed to prevent publication in book form. 'For Love and Life' appeared in 1907 as *The Ghost*; and, again to Bennett's embarrassment, was long afterwards made the first volume in a French translation of his novels published by *La Nouvelle Revue Française*.

In 1900 Bennett resigned the editorship of *Woman*, and went to live at Trinity Hall Farm, on Watling Street, near the village of Hockliffe in Bedfordshire, with his parents and his youngest sister. He had shown facility in two slight books, *Journalism for Women* (1898) and *Polite Farces for the Drawing Room* (1899), and, besides doing much journalistic work and 'reading' for the firm of Pearson, was writing plays, alone and in collaboration with Arthur Hooley, short stories, and the first of those serious novels about life in the Potteries upon which his fame as an author rests. *Anna of the Five Towns*, begun in 1896, was finished in 1901 and published almost simultaneously with *The Grand Babylon Hotel* in 1902. By this simultaneous publication Bennett showed, either modestly or in bravado, or perhaps by mere chance, that the opposed styles in which he had experimented as a youth, the styles of Zola and of Ouida (now, more accurately, those of George Moore and Eugène Sue), still irresistibly attracted him. He was to be at the same time an artist and a professional writer. And, as Moore and Sue had both been distinguished Parisians, it is not surprising that by the end of 1902 Bennett himself was in Paris. There, and at Fontainebleau, he lived for ten happy, supremely influential years. Having been briefly engaged to an American girl, he married in Paris in 1907 a Frenchwoman, Marie Marguerite Soulié. They had no children.

Bennett maintained in France his habit of regular industry. Writing steadily, continuing dramatic collaborations with Mr. Eden Phillpotts, with whom he also wrote two romances, he contributed shrewd advisory self-help articles to *T.P.'s Weekly* (a periodical founded by T. P. O'Connor [q.v.], but edited by Bennett's old colleague on the *Academy*, Wilfred Whitten) which were afterwards (1908) printed in book form under such significant titles as *How to Live on Twenty-four Hours a Day* and *Mental Efficiency*. He continued to release his natural sense of fun in such works as *The Truth About an Author* (1903) and *A Great Man* (1904); and at this time was perhaps doing too many things not quite well enough to consolidate a single reputation. Although it was in 1903 that he saw in a restaurant in Paris the ungainly elderly woman who first inspired his best novel, *The Old Wives' Tale*, he did not begin writing that book until four years later, and meanwhile all his industry made little public impression, so that his earnings from novels remained small, usually under £100 apiece.

But *The Old Wives' Tale* (1908) changed everything. Whereas his former tales of Staffordshire types had lacked attractive characters and Bennett's characteristic humour, this book represented all his gifts. It was both generous and minute; it was thoroughly English; and it brimmed over with the author's compassionate merriment. Although the publishers were at first rueful at its length, and although its first sales, by present-day standards, would be considered small, *The Old Wives' Tale* caused Bennett to be accepted, with H. G. Wells and John Galsworthy [q.v.], as one of a dominating triumvirate of novelists. It made him an influence in British letters, and potentially a rich man. And while the first volume of the *Clayhanger* trilogy, published in 1910, confirmed his rank as a serious novelist, *The Card*, the best sustained of his comic inventions, written in two months in 1909 during a Swiss holiday, but not published until 1911, endeared him to those who may have found *Clayhanger* a little slow. 'Meticulous' was the word most used of his method at this time by reviewers who thus met objectors half-way. Bennett, however, was not at the end of his dangerous versatility; and some pungent and adventurous brevities about books which, as 'Jacob Tonson', he contributed between 1908 and 1911 to the *New Age*, the brilliant weekly edited by A. R. Orage [q.v.], gave him still another fame. A visit paid to the United States of America in 1911 had a success unequalled by that of any English author since Dickens, and inevitably produced a lively book, *Those United States* (1912). Finally, his plays, *What the Public Wants* (1909), *Milestones* (written in collaboration with Edward Knoblock, 1912), and *The Great Adventure* (1913), a dramatization of his own novel, *Buried Alive* (1908), brought him for a time almost unlimited theatrical popularity. In 1912 he left France and returned to England for good, buying, restoring, and lavishly furnishing in the Empire style an oldish house at Thorpe-le-Soken in Essex. He was an outstandingly successful man; critically, his prestige was at its zenith.

When the war of 1914–1918 began, Bennett became less a novelist and dramatist than a public servant and a public figure. He at once engaged in powerful journalism, the object of which was to instruct and hearten the nation and to carry assurance of British effort to allied and neutral countries, and served on various committees such as those for War Memorials and Wounded Allies Relief. His home at Thorpe-le-Soken, which, as a yachtsman, he had bought because of its nearness to the Essex waterways, became a military and political centre for the district. He was sent to France in 1915 to describe, very discreetly, conditions at the front, and the collected impressions appeared in a little book called *Over There* (1915). When Lord Beaverbrook became minister of information in 1918, Bennett was given charge of propaganda in France, and he later succeeded Lord Beaverbrook for a few weeks as head of the organization. His associates were no longer only the stimulating writers and artists of former years, but, in addition to the large number of those with whom he was in natural sympathy, the wealthy men and women of social and political power whom he satirized in *The Pretty Lady* (1918) and *Lord Raingo* (1926). Such men and women offended the rigid Wesleyan Methodist (the supremely 'decent' man of Mr. Aldous Huxley's sketch in *The Times*, 31 March 1931) who lived at the core of Bennett's nature; but the more superficial Bennett was flattered and impressed by them. Much of his later work suffered from a loss, not of the craftsman's integrity, but of certainty in the author's mind that it had ultimate importance. *The Pretty Lady* showed the conflict in progress; *Lord Raingo* a restoration of values; but neither equalled *These Twain* (1916), that stubborn completion of a task confidently undertaken after the success of *The Old Wives' Tale*, when, at the age of forty-one, Bennett planned with lighthearted ambition to tell in three volumes the whole life-stories of Edwin Clayhanger and Hilda Lessways, his wife.

After the war Bennett became still further involved in large affairs. He lived entirely in London, and between 1919 and 1930 successively rented the upper portion of a house in George Street, Hanover Square, and a house in Cadogan Square, where he entertained in the grand style. He began an intimate association with the stage by partnering (Sir) Nigel Playfair [q.v.] and Alistair Tayler in the management of a new enterprise at the Lyric Theatre, Hammersmith, where *Abraham*

Lincoln by John Drinkwater [q.v.] and a production of *The Beggar's Opera* decorated by C. L. Fraser [q.v.] caught different moods of the post-war spirit. Endless social engagements; inexhaustible patronage of musicians, actors, poets, and painters; the maximum of benevolence to friends and strangers alike, marked the last ten years of his life. He wrote the best, and worst, of his later novels amid this hurly-burly, and a number of plays, some of which were not even produced, while the rest were received with critical hostility and public indifference; and he contributed week by week to the *Evening Standard* the most readable and most highly priced literary causerie of the time. In 1921 he was legally separated from his wife; and in the following year he met and fell in love with an English actress, Miss Dorothy Cheston, by whom, in 1926, he had one daughter. At the end of 1930 he visited France, returned to London in January 1931, ill with what, at first diagnosed as influenza, proved to be typhoid fever, and, after a long struggle for life, died in his flat at Chiltern Court, Marylebone, at night, 27 March 1931.

Any assessment of Bennett's work is complicated by the problems of his versatility and capacity to perform at different levels of seriousness. In part this versatility was due to conflict between his temperament, his early training, his later artistic enthusiasms, and his unlimited sense of fun. Temperamentally, he was a puritan; intellectually, he was a liberal; personally, he was a humorist. In addition, he was naturally diffident; from childhood he was handicapped by an impediment which was not so much a stammer as a total inability to utter the word which he proposed to use, which word, nevertheless, owing to pride and determination, he would never abandon. As a child he had suffered from the rigours of a strict religious upbringing in a denomination which he several times harshly derided; and, although a fine swimmer and a formidable opponent at lawn tennis, he had little taste, as child, boy, and man, for violent physical activity. He claimed to be incapable of moral indignation; his work suggests that he was either incapable of passion or incapable of allowing it to master him. He might be grim, or sardonic; he was always restrained; and the fun to be seen in his happiest works lightened all that close observation upon which realists depend for the effect of veracity, and overflowed into the wit of his abrupt speech and careless plays and 'frolics'. He was as scrupulously a realist as humour and kindness of vision allowed in such novels as *A Man from the North, Anna of the Five Towns, Leonora* (1903), *Whom God Hath Joined* (1906), *The Old Wives' Tale, Clayhanger, Hilda Lessways* (1911), *The Price of Love* (1914), *These Twain, Riceyman Steps* (1923), *Lord Raingo,* and *Imperial Palace* (1930). He was a *farceur* in *A Great Man, Buried Alive, The Card, The Regent* (1913), and *Mr. Prohack* (1922). His plays suffered as a rule from the lack of a strong central idea, and, having entertained for an evening by verbal adroitness, were quickly scorned. His criticism startled, amused, and annoyed, as it was meant to do. His short stories ranged from the trivial to rich and delightful cameos of provincial life. His utilitarian homilies were as natural to him as his fun. His sensational tales, such as *The Grand Babylon Hotel* and *Hugo* (1906), enjoying great ingenuities of incidental invention, were robbed of vehemence and suspense by that same fun. He passed from one type of writing to another, without warning, without progress; and critics coming to such varied activities have found it hard to draw lines between the good, the bad, and the indifferent. Bennett could not have helped them. His pride never allowed him to admit a failure.

For this reason there were always books or plays or articles or short stories from Bennett's industrious pen which offered excellent targets for detractors. There were always books, and in particular the most ambitious of all his later novels, *Imperial Palace,* which could be represented as illustrating a legendary Bennett, a vulgar, gaping provincial with a passion for money and gilded luxury. It did not matter that his sensitiveness to beauty in character and all the arts was beyond question. It did not matter that the foundation of *Imperial Palace* was his delight in microcosms and his enthusiasm at the emergence of servants to any microcosm as mysterious individual human beings whose souls were free. The fact remained that there were writings by Arnold Bennett which had been produced at different levels of seriousness; and it is undeniable that his reputation suffered from their existence.

It is therefore necessary to remember that, at his very best, in *Whom God Hath Joined, The Old Wives' Tale, Clayhanger, These Twain,* and the directly personal parts of *Lord Raingo,* Bennett was a highly scrupulous artist and a profoundly wise and resolute truth-teller. No novelist of his day had a greater, or perhaps an equal, integrity. The kind of life described in these books came perfectly within the range of his comprehension, and his portrayal of it was warmed and made beautiful by exceptional understanding. He did not at any time surpass *The Old Wives' Tale,* because that book, alone among his novels, had an inspired and inspiring design, which was to show the moulding of character by experience, and the tragic inevitability of old age. *Clayhanger* was in a sense to repeat that design, the middle portion of the book, *Hilda Lessways,* approximating to the Paris chapters about Sophia, and the third, *These Twain,* to that reunion of the sisters in which *The Old Wives' Tale* rises to its height. But the design of the *Clayhanger* trilogy remains mechanical; and for the poignancy of the reunion is substituted, first Edwin's 'terrible gloom which questioned the justification of all life', and secondly Edwin's realization that 'the conflict between his individuality and Hilda's would never cease'. Nevertheless, while the other books are fragmentary, or are based, as *Imperial Palace* is based, upon a conception of material rather than spiritual coherence, they hold innumerable scenes in which the author's ruthless vision is courageously expressed. If the *Clayhanger* trilogy had been written continuously, without knowledge of the expectations formed by readers of *The Old Wives' Tale,* the mechanical nature of its design would have been redressed, and its execution exactly proportioned to the design. Events intervened; the first enthusiasm for its plan was lost; and the strain of imaginatively living and writing *These Twain* in the first years of a terrible war was even physically too much for Bennett. It is all the more to his credit that this third volume contains superb scenes from provincial life and the most powerful and truthful picture ever painted in England of the conflict of wills in inharmonious marriage.

The defect in the *Clayhanger* trilogy, as in all Bennett's novels and plays, excepting *The Old Wives' Tale,* arises from meagre or insufficiently considered design. He had great resource in arrangement and incidental invention; he would never shirk the truth of his perceptions, and so was never sentimental; but he could not conceive life as tragedy, and modesty forbade him to plan any work as epic. His strength lay in the unique degree of his love for simple people, and in his ability to see interest and beauty in much that to the superficial eye is squalid or tedious. That love and perception were best informed when he described life in the Five Towns, and accordingly it is as the profound and comic dramatist and historian of life in the Potteries that Bennett, for all his versatility, his brilliance, and his position between 1914 and 1930 as an adored English figure, will live as long as English novels are read.

A drawing of Bennett, by (Sir) William Rothenstein (1920), is in the City Art Gallery, Stoke-on-Trent; another drawing, by W. E. Tittle (1923), and a plasticine medallion, by Theodore Spicer-Simson, are in the National Portrait Gallery.

[Arnold Bennett, *The Truth about an Author*, 1903; *The Journals of Arnold Bennett, 1896–1928* (edited by Newman Flower), 3 vols., 1932–1933; Margaret Locherbie-Goff, *La Jeunesse d'Arnold Bennett (1867–1904)*, 1939; private information; personal knowledge.]   FRANK SWINNERTON.

BENSON, EDWARD FREDERIC (1867–1940), author, was born at Wellington College 24 July 1867, the third son of Edward White Benson, afterwards archbishop of Canterbury [q.v.], by his wife, Mary Sidgwick. He was a younger brother of A. C. Benson and an elder brother of R. H. Benson [qq.v.]. He was educated at Marlborough and at King's College, Cambridge, where he was exhibitioner (1888) and scholar (1890); after taking his degree with first classes in both parts of the classical tripos (1890, 1891) he worked in Athens for the British School of Archaeology (1892–1895) and in Egypt for the Society for the Promotion of Hellenic Studies (1895). Latterly he lived for the greater part of each year at Lamb House, Rye, which had been the home of Henry James [q.v.]. He was mayor of Rye from 1934 to 1937. He was elected an honorary fellow of Magdalene College, Cambridge, in 1938. As a young man he was a considerable athlete, particularly as a skater and winter sportsman. He never married; and many of his novels suggest that he had a generalized dislike of women. He died in London 29 February 1940.

As a writer Benson was uncontrollably prolific: he published at least ninety-three books (not counting collaborations), of which about twenty are plays, biographies, sporting or political, and the rest fiction and reminiscences. This was his first misfortune. The second was that his first story, *Dodo* (1893), had a great success. In consequence—because he wrote too much and too quickly, and because the adolescent thrill of being in 'society' matured into a witty and malicious delight in mocking fools and climbers—his genuine talents as a novelist seldom achieved the perfection of form or the permanence of interest of which they were certainly capable. A few of his books are so nearly first rate that the reader becomes regretfully aware that none quite reaches that level. A further result of his easy, careless writing, added to his obsession with the artificialities of socially ambitious women, was that he became repetitive. He would re-use one of his series of groupings, embellishing it with new and amusing dialogue, with new and crushing incidental detail, yet in fact writing the same story two, three, or even four times over.

In one of his books of family recollections Benson claims for himself a retentive, observational memory, even of things hardly noted at the time; and this is perhaps his most remarkable quality. In non-fiction and fiction alike, he shows an extraordinary power of recalling scenes and individuals over the whole period of his adult life. This capacity gives to his works of reminiscence (e.g. *Account Rendered*, 1911; *Our Family Affairs, 1867–1897*, 1920; *As We Were*, 1930; *As We Are*, 1932; *Final Edition*, 1940) real value as sources for social history and personal anecdote, even though the student may hesitate to take them literally. Those of his novels—and they are the majority—which applaud or scarify smart London, or literary, or provincial society, give so strong an impression of carefully distorted portraiture that, just as the 'Dodo' series (*Dodo, Dodo the Second*, 1914, *Dodo Wonders*, 1921) is generally assumed to centre on Margot Tennant, who became Lady Oxford; just as *Secret Lives* (1932), one of his best novels, can hardly have been based on anyone but Marie Corelli; just as the 'Lucia' series (the first two, *Queen Lucia*, 1920, and *Lucia in London*, 1927, are the best) are said to be *romans à clé*, so it is natural to suspect real people everywhere. It is hardly worth while to wonder on whom are based the chattering West End exhibitionists in such remembered but inferior books as *Scarlet and Hyssop* (1902), *Sheaves*, and *The Climber* (1908); but the reader might well like to know from whom are derived the more modest provincial *intrigantes* in such far superior stories as *Mrs. Ames* (1912) and *Miss Mapp* (1922).

Apart from social satire Benson made repeated experiments in two other fictional directions. The first comprises stories of public school, university, and immediately post-university life. These are so over-sweetened as to be almost intolerable. From the tedious sparkle of *The Babe, B.A.* (1897), an early product of 'dodoism' in undergraduate terms, through the 'Blaize' books to *Colin II* (1925), the tales pile wholesome fun on saccharine sentimentalism, until the reader sickens of the clean-limbed young Apollos, for all the frequent wit with which they are presented. The second group, that of stories of horror and of the supernatural, contains much excellent work. *The Luck of the Vails* (1901) perhaps hardly qualifies, as nearly half of it is a lavish picture of rich, selfish folk, painted with the admiring relish which Benson at this early period undoubtedly felt for persons of the kind; but the second portion of the story is at once dramatic and brilliant, terror and wit being perfectly fused. *The Room in the Tower* (1912) shows him mastering the technique of *macabre* writing, although he still overdoes the details of spendthrift luxury and too often lets the climax of his tale dissolve in sentiment. *Visible and Invisible* (1923) is 'horror' in perfect training, proficient, inventive, but, save in the final story, queerly devoid of feeling. *Spook Stories* (1928) and *More Spook Stories* (1934) mark the closing stages of a highly efficient, coldly unemotional excursion into the realm of ghosts and marvels.

[*The Times*, 1 March 1940; *The Times Literary Supplement*, 9 March 1940; *Final Edition: Informal Autobiography*, 1940; private information.]   MICHAEL SADLEIR.

BENSON, SIR FRANCIS ROBERT ('FRANK') (1858–1939), actor-manager, was born at Tunbridge Wells 4 November 1858, the third son and fourth child of William Benson, barrister, of Alresford, Hampshire, by his wife, Elizabeth Soulsby, daughter of Thomas Smith, of Colebrooke Park, Tonbridge. He was educated at Winchester and New College, Oxford, but gained no academic honours. He became famous at the university as an all-round athlete, devoting himself to football, cricket, rowing, and running, his greatest achievement being the winning of the three-mile race against Cambridge.

Always attracted to the theatre, Benson became one of the leaders of the movement which led in 1884 to the foundation of the Oxford University Dramatic Society. In the hall of Balliol College, in June 1880, he took part in a performance of the *Agamemnon* of Aeschylus, in which he played the part of Clytemnestra with considerable success. This performance was repeated at the St. George's Hall, London, in September of the same year, and his success turned Benson's thoughts to the adoption of the stage as his profession. In July 1881 he took the Imperial Theatre, London, for a single performance of *Romeo and Juliet*, and appeared as Romeo. He then studied voice production under Emil Bencke and Hermann Vezin [q.v.], and at the invitation of Ellen Terry [q.v.], who had witnessed his performance of Clytemnestra, he was invited in July 1882 to take part in a private Shakespearian reading of *Much Ado About Nothing*, at the house of Sir Theodore Martin [q.v.], appearing as Don Pedro, with (Sir) Henry Irving [q.v.] as Benedick and Lady Martin (Helen Faucit, q.v.) as Beatrice.

Benson made his first appearance on the professional stage at the Lyceum Theatre in September 1882, when he played Paris in Irving's production of *Romeo and Juliet*, with Ellen Terry as Juliet. On her advice, he then joined the Shakespearian company of Miss Alleyn and Charles Bernard, in order to gain experience, and a few months later he was a member of a company under the management of Walter Bentley, a well-known Shakespearian actor. This manager became involved in financial difficulties, and Benson, with monetary aid from his father, promptly acquired the company. He opened under his own management in a hall at Airdrie, Lanarkshire, in May 1883, with *The Corsican Brothers* and *Cramond Brig*, and in this modest way the famous Benson repertory company came into being.

It was not long before Benson had established a sound reputation and the Benson company became an important factor in the provincial theatre. He gathered together a very capable band of actors, and by 1886 his company was of sufficient importance to be invited to provide the Shakespearian festival at the Memorial Theatre, Stratford-on-Avon, where he appeared for the first time, in April of that year, playing Richard III. During the next thirty-three years he provided the plays for twenty-eight spring festivals and some half-dozen summer festivals at the theatre, in the course of which period he presented all Shakespeare's plays except *Titus Andronicus* and *Troilus and Cressida*. In addition he presented many old comedies and one or two modern plays. In recognition of his services to Stratford-on-Avon, Benson received the freedom of the borough in 1910, an honour only once previously conferred on an actor, namely, David Garrick, in 1769. He appeared as director of the Stratford festival for the last time in 1919, and at the birthday celebrations that year he was presented with a handsome gift by Stratfordonians and festival patrons.

Benson's first London season was given at the Globe Theatre, where, in December 1889, he opened with a revival of *A Midsummer Night's Dream*, which was performed 110 times, a record at that date. Revivals of *The Taming of the Shrew*, *Hamlet*, and *Othello* were also presented. His next London season, the most important of his eight London ventures, began at the Lyceum Theatre in February 1900, with a revival of *Henry the Fifth*. Subsequent seasons were given at the Comedy (1901), Adelphi (1905), St. James's (1910), Shaftesbury (1914), Court (1915), and St. Martin's (1920) theatres. At the height of his success there were no fewer than three of his companies touring the country. In addition, he toured in Canada and the United States of America, in 1913–1914, and in South Africa, in 1921. During his Canadian tour Montreal University conferred upon him the honorary degree of LL.D.

At the Shakespeare tercentenary performance, given at Drury Lane Theatre on 2 May 1916, Benson appeared in the title-role of *Julius Caesar*, and at the conclusion of the performance was knighted by King George V, in the stage-box, the only occasion on which an actor had been knighted in a theatre. The ceremony was performed with a 'property' sword, no other being available.

Although he was nearing the age of sixty, from 1916 to 1918 Benson served in France as an ambulance-driver, and received the French croix de guerre. In June 1925, in the picture-gallery of the Stratford Memorial Theatre, Dame Ellen Terry unveiled the stained-glass windows to Old Bensonians, including one in memory of the ten players of the company who had fallen in the war.

Benson was never a great actor, and he was handicapped somewhat by defects of voice and gait. Richard II and Petruchio in *The Taming of the Shrew* were among his best performances. His Richard had much grace and dignity and his Petruchio was full of excellent touches. He also gave a notable performance as Caliban in *The Tempest*. Many of the numerous parts which he undertook, including Hamlet, Othello, Shylock, and Henry V, were quite uninspired. It was not his acting which made Benson great, nor his teaching. His genius lay in the opportunities which he afforded to the many capable young artists whom he gathered round him, many of whom achieved greater fame than Benson himself. His company became the nursery for the English stage. It is truly said of him that he gave the best years of his life to spreading the love of Shakespeare throughout the world. In his efforts he exhausted the whole of his considerable personal fortune, and in July 1933 he was granted a civil list pension of £100.

Benson made his last appearance in London in 1933; this was at the Winter Garden Theatre, as Dr. Caius in *The Merry Wives of Windsor*. He published his reminiscences, *My Memoirs* (1930), and a short work entitled *I Want to Go on the Stage* (1931). In July 1886 he married Gertrude Constance, daughter of Captain Morshead Fetherstonhaugh Samwell, of the Indian army, and had a son and a daughter. Lady Benson was a capable actress, and played leading parts in his company for many years. Their son was killed in action in France in 1916. Benson died in London 31 December 1939.

An early portrait of Benson, by Hugh Riviere, hangs in the picture gallery of the Shakespeare Memorial Theatre. Of a drawing of him as Mark Antony, by Will Ledbury, and of another by R. G. Eves (1927), the whereabouts are uncertain.

[*The Times*, 1 January 1940; *Who's Who in the Theatre*, 1939; Sir F. Benson, *My Memoirs*, 1930; Lady Benson, *Mainly Players*, 1926; personal knowledge.]

JOHN PARKER.

BENSON, STELLA (1892–1933), novelist. [See ANDERSON, STELLA.]

BESANT, ANNIE (1847–1933), theosophist, educationist, and Indian politician, was born in London 1 October 1847, the only daughter of William Persse Wood, man of business, of London, by his wife, Emily Mary Roche, daughter of James

Morris, of Clapham. Her father, who was Irish on his mother's side, belonged to an elder branch of the Woods of Tiverton, which included Sir Matthew Wood, W. P. Wood, Lord Hatherley, Sir Henry Evelyn Wood [qq.v.], and Mrs. O'Shea *née* Wood, later the wife of C. S. Parnell. Her mother's family was Irish. She was educated by Miss Marryat, a sister of the novelist, and in 1867 married Frank Besant, later vicar of Sibsey in Lincolnshire until his death in 1917, and a younger brother of Sir Walter Besant [q.v.]. They had a son and a daughter. The mother lost her religious faith, left Sibsey in 1873, and was legally separated from her husband.

In 1874 Mrs. Besant joined the National Secular Society, of which she became vice-president, and formed a close friendship with Charles Bradlaugh [q.v.], to whose paper she contributed, acting some time as co-editor. In 1878, as authoress of the *Gospel of Atheism* (1877) and a champion of neo-Malthusianism, she was deprived by the courts of the custody of her daughter who, like her son, returned to her later. In 1885 she joined the Fabian Society and the Social Democratic Federation. She was present at the famous meeting in Trafalgar Square (1886), organized the matchmakers' strike (1888), and formed their union. But drifting apart from Bradlaugh she announced her conversion to theosophy as taught by Madame Blavatsky, who with Colonel H. S. Olcott had founded an association in the United States for 'the study and elucidation of occultism, the Kabbala, etc.', with branches in London, India, and Ceylon. After Madame Blavatsky's death Mrs. Besant visited India in 1893, and speedily discovered that she had often been incarnated in that sacred land. She announced that she had received 'phenomenally' letters from the mahatmas, but on this point she quarrelled with W. Q. Judge who with her was one of the two 'heads' of the Esoteric section, and the quarrel led to the secession from the Theosophical Society of the major part of the American members. In 1895 she became absolute head of the inner organization, being elected president of the society in 1907.

From 1895 onwards India was the scene of Mrs. Besant's activities. She devoted herself to representing theosophy as compatible with the ancient Hindu religion, philosophy, and morality. These, she said, were on a higher plane than the West had ever reached, and she urged the Hindus to sympathize with the cause of the 'Indian National Congress', first convoked in 1885 under the guidance of A. O. Hume [q.v.]. In 1899 she persuaded the Maharaja of Benares to give her foundation, the Central Hindu College, a fine site and buildings, and by her energy, zeal, eloquence, and powers of organization the college, with a girls' school founded at Benares in 1904, became the nucleus of a Hindu university in 1916. But in 1909 she put forward the strange claim that her adopted son, a young Madrasi, named Krishnamurti, had been revealed to her as the vehicle of the world teacher or Messiah. The claim (only renounced by the young man in 1932) led to Mrs. Besant's resignation of the presidency of the Central Hindu College, and she shifted her headquarters to the Theosophical Institution at Adyar near Madras.

In September 1916, when Lord Chelmsford had succeeded Lord Hardinge of Penshurst as viceroy, and the British Empire was fighting for its life, Mrs. Besant thought fit to initiate a Home Rule for India League. From Adyar she proclaimed herself 'an Indian tomtom waking all the sleepers so that they may work for their Motherland'. As some of her pamphlets and speeches were considered by the Madras government likely to inflame racial feeling, she was called on under the Press Act to give pecuniary security for her better conduct. She deposited, but soon forfeited, the large sum. At least one governor refused her admission to his province, and in 1917 the governor of Madras interned her, but allowed her to direct her home rule campaign. But on 20 August 1917 the famous declaration had been issued, and India was to be placed on the path to responsible government by stages. In order to create the calm atmosphere requisite for the investigations of E. S. Montagu [q.v.], the secretary of state, and the viceroy, Mrs. Besant was released from internment. Politically minded Hindus caused her to be elected president of the Indian National Congress which met at Bombay in December 1918. Although the year 1919 began with the end of the war and ended in December with the Government of India Act, it also saw the rise of Gandhi's 'civil disobedience' and 'passive resistance' movement against the Rowlatt legislation, the consequent riots, and the Amritsar tragedy. The riots of April 1919 shocked Mrs. Besant into sober reflection. Before Gandhi began to move she had found it desirable to point out in the press that India depended on England for safety: that was the plain brutal truth, and no amount of shouting could alter it. When after order had been restored and some moderates of the central legislature did not condemn the doings of Gandhi's followers with downright emphasis, she declared herself vigorously: 'None, I presume, will contend that government should look on while mobs murdered, wrecked banks, fired railway stations. Do [the critics] then think that it is more merciful to give a mob its head than to attack it at the very outset of violence, at the cost of a score of lives, or will the critics say at what stage the government should interfere? Let us in the time of danger drop all criticism of government action and stand firmly against revolution, which means bloodshed at home and invasion from abroad.' Such doctrine alienated the extremist Congress politicians: even her own Home Rule League rejected her as president in favour of Gandhi, and for a time she seemed to have tired, for she took no action against an outspoken exposure (*The Evolution of Mrs. Besant*) published in 1918 by Dr. T. M. Nair, the leader of the non-Brahmans of Madras. In 1925 she brought a Commonwealth of India bill to England where it was twice introduced into the House of Commons and obtained the active support of the labour party, which she joined. Late in life she travelled by air, and often kept her intellectual powers long on the stretch, but in 1931 her health failed, and she lived in retirement at Adyar where she died 20 September 1933 and was cremated on the sea-shore.

The influence of Mrs. Besant on the growth of nationalist feeling in India was at one time considerable, largely because she painted the India of the fabled past in attractive colours, and associated theosophy with Hinduism in a manner flattering to the beliefs of intellectual Hindus, while her prestige was increased by her successful effort to found the Hindu College and University. When, moreover, in the early stages of the war of 1914-1918, Indian politicians generally agreed to suspend such agitation as might impede the war effort, Mrs. Besant put no such restriction on her activities, and thereby gained an advantage which she fully exploited. Her facile but somewhat shallow eloquence also increased her following. She thus influenced both in Upper India and in Madras several rising politicians who afterwards reached prominence. But her influence, at least in political life, was short-lived: the courageous stand which she made after the riots of 1919 turned even the students of Madras against her. Her share in the foundation and control of the Hindu University was regarded with jealousy by a section of the orthodox Hindus; her position in the theosophical world was prejudiced by a scandal that was attached to the principal of the institution near Madras, by the sponsoring of Krishnamurti, and by the lengthy proceedings by which the boy's relatives sought to recover his custody. Her name will be remembered among Indian theosophists, but these are no longer a political body and tend to become one more among the sects of Hinduism.

[*The Times*, 21 September 1933; H. V. Lovett, *History of the Indian Nationalist Movement*, 1920; private information.]

H. V. LOVETT.
PATRICK CADELL.

BEVAN, ANTHONY ASHLEY (1859-1933), orientalist and biblical scholar, was born at Trent Park, Barnet, 19 May 1859, the eldest of the three sons of Robert Cooper Lee Bevan, of Fosbury House, Wiltshire, and Trent Park, head of the great banking-house later known as Barclay & company, by his second wife, Emma Frances, daughter of P. N. Shuttleworth, bishop of Chichester [q.v.]. The youngest son was the archaeologist and Hellenist Edwyn Robert Bevan. Ashley Bevan was educated at Cheam, Surrey, the Gymnase Littéraire, Lausanne, and the university of Strasburg, where he studied under Theodor Noeldeke, the greatest of scholars in the field of oriental studies. He entered Trinity College, Cambridge, in 1884, and obtained a first class in the Semitic languages tripos of 1887. In 1888 he gained a Tyrwhitt Hebrew scholarship and the Mason prize for biblical Hebrew, and two years later was elected a fellow of his college and appointed lecturer in oriental languages. In 1893 he became lord almoner's professor of Arabic at Cambridge, a post previously held by his brother-in-law I. G. N. Keith-Falconer and by R. L. Bensly [qq.v.]. The post was abolished after his death. He was elected a fellow of the British Academy in 1916, resigning in 1928.

Bevan was 'one of the dozen most learned Arabists, not of England and Europe only, but of the whole world. He was almost equally distinguished for his knowledge of Hebrew and Old Testament literature. He knew Syriac thoroughly and other Semitic languages well, and he had an excellent acquaintance with Persian language and literature' (F. C. Burkitt in *Cambridge Review*, 27 October 1933). He also had a knowledge of Sanskrit, and was fluent in French, Italian, and German. His published work was relatively small, but what there is of it is of the highest scholarship. His edition of the satirical poems the *Naḳa'id of Jarir and al-Farazdak* (Arabic text, 3 vols., 1905–1912), was a tribute to his teacher, the famous orientalist William Wright [q.v.]; and in an exhaustive volume of indexes and addenda to the *Mufaḍḍaliyāt* (1924) he completed the edition of the poems edited by Sir C. J. Lyall [q.v.]. He was interested in classical Arabic rather than later Mohammedan literature, in a knowledge of which his more enthusiastic colleague E. G. Browne [q.v.] excelled. But among various articles contributed to the *Journal of Theological Studies* he wrote one on 'The Beliefs of Early Mohammedans respecting a Future Existence' (October 1904). He was also interested in Manichaeism, and besides contributing an article on the subject to Hastings's *Encyclopaedia of Religion and Ethics*, completed, with F. C. Burkitt [q.v.] in 1912, under the title *St. Ephraim's Refutations*, the collections of St. Ephraim's writings on that and allied sects which C. W. Mitchell had prepared before his death. Mention must also be made of his edition of the Gnostic Syriac *Hymn of the Soul Contained in the Syriac Acts of St. Thomas* ('Cambridge Texts and Studies', vol. v, No. 3, 1897).

Bevan's *Short Commentary on the Book of Daniel* (1892) was the first work in English to demonstrate the Maccabean date of this perplexing document, and was regarded as a masterpiece. Besides articles in the *Encyclopaedia Biblica*, he contributed an important 'Essay on Historical Methods in the Old Testament' to *Essays on Some Biblical Questions of the Day* (edited by H. B. Swete, 1909). These and various reviews exhibit his keen critical faculty and incisive judgement. Classical Hebrew was his interest, and although he was an enthusiastic pupil of Solomon Marcus Schiller-Szinessy, the university reader in Talmudic and rabbinic literature and a remarkable figure in his day, Bevan's attitude to medieval New Hebrew literature was not sympathetic. Throughout he was fastidious and scrupulously careful: as he observed in the course of one of his typically uncompromising reviews, 'even slight inaccuracies are liable to become sources of confusion'. His friends and pupils could well believe the story that he was almost reduced to tears on discovering a misprint in one of his own works.

If Bevan's output was slight he spared himself no pains in assisting his colleagues, among other ways by reading their proofs: many, including his brother Edwyn, were indebted to his scholarship. Even the inner circle stood a little in awe of his immense erudition and the authority which it gave him. He did much teaching, and as a teacher surprised his pupils by his methods and by his readiness to confess his inability to translate some Hebrew passage which they thought that they had mastered from their knowledge of the Authorized Version. But he was hospitable and at his ease with undergraduates, with soldiers and policemen, and especially with humbler folk. A hater of tobacco, he freely provided excellent cigars; witty, with a characteristic laugh and with a tongue like a rapier, he was a man of unbounded kindness and sympathy. Unostentatious, no one was ever more determined to prevent his left hand from knowing what his right hand was doing.

Bevan had had an extremely evangelical upbringing, which led to later reaction; he was liberal and outspoken in his opinions. Slightly built and of middle height, he was scrupulously neat and tidy in dress and demeanour, and his politeness was almost a byword. He was over-particular about his food and over-anxious as to his health. He died, unmarried, at Cambridge 16 October 1933.

[*The Times*, 17 and 20 October 1933; *Cambridge Review*, 27 October 1933; private information; personal knowledge.]

S. A. Cook.

BHOWNAGGREE, Sir MANCHERJEE MERWANJEE (1851–1933), Indian lawyer and politician, was born at Bombay 15 August 1851, the son of Merwanjee N. Bhownaggree, a Parsee merchant of that city, who belonged to a family of Persian origin, by his wife, Cooverbai. He was educated at Elphinstone College, Bombay, and Bombay University. After a brief apprenticeship to journalism, he succeeded, on the death of his father in 1875 to the agency in Bombay for the Kathiawar State of Bhavanagar. At this time he published a translation into Gujerati of Queen Victoria's *Leaves from the Journal of our Life in the Highlands*. In 1881 he came to London in order to study law, and in 1885 was called to the bar by Lincoln's

Inn. Thereafter as judicial counsellor in Bhavanagar, he introduced far-reaching reforms in law administration. Appointed C.I.E. in 1886, he was advanced to K.C.I.E. in 1897. He had settled in London, and at the general election of 1895 was returned to parliament for North-East Bethnal Green, in the conservative interest. His only Indian predecessor in the House of Commons, elected in 1892 as a radical reformer and now defeated, was Dadabhai Naoroji, one of the founders of the Indian National Congress and a severe critic of British rule. Bhownaggree, on the other hand, was a sound and practical imperialist. His resourceful advocacy of the removal of disabilities suffered by Indians in South Africa and other parts of the British Empire deeply impressed the House. After ten years in parliament he was among the unionists who were swept away by the tide of liberal victories in the general election of January 1906. Yet another Parsee, Shapurji Saklatvala [q.v.], was a third—and so far the last—Indian to sit in the House of Commons.

Over a long period of years Bhownaggree was the leading Indian permanently resident in Great Britain. Among many other institutions which he served he was dominant as chairman of the Parsee Association of Europe, the Northbrook Society, and the Indian Social Club. Under the title of *Verdict of India* he published in 1916 a booklet repelling German falsehoods as to British rule in his native land. In memory of his only sister, Ave Bhownaggree, he founded a nurses' home in Bombay and provided the Bhownaggree corridor to the east wing of the Imperial Institute in London. He married in 1872, and his wife ordinarily resided in Bombay as she could not keep well in the variable English climate. He was predeceased by the elder of his two sons, and his daughter married a distinguished Bombay physician, Dr. J. N. Bahadurjee. He died at his London house 14 November 1933.

A portrait in oils of Bhownaggree, by Mrs. Radcliffe Beresford, was presented to him in 1927 by the Parsee Association of Europe, and is now in the possession of his daughter in Bombay.

[*The Times*, 15 November 1933 and 27 July 1928; Hansard, *Parliamentary Debates*; personal knowledge.]   F. H. BROWN.

BIGGE, ARTHUR JOHN, BARON STAMFORDHAM (1849–1931), private secretary to King George V, was born at Linden Hall, near Morpeth, Northumber-land, 18 June 1849, the fourth of the five sons of John Frederick Bigge, vicar of Stamfordham in the same county, by his wife, Caroline Mary, only daughter of Nathaniel Ellison, barrister and commissioner in bankruptcy, of Newcastle-upon-Tyne. He was educated at Rossall School and at the Royal Military Academy, where he was a fellow cadet with Prince Arthur, later Duke of Connaught. In 1869 he obtained a commission in the Royal Artillery, from which he retired as lieutenant-colonel (1892) in 1898. A few years after he entered the army there was attached to his battery the Prince Imperial, the only son of Napoleon III, and the close friendship which sprang up between the two young men determined Bigge's career.

Serving in the Kaffir and Zulu wars of 1878–1879, Bigge was mentioned in dispatches after the battle of Kambula on 29 March 1879: the part played by the Horse Artillery battery in which he was serving is thus commended by Sir (Henry) Evelyn Wood [q.v.] (*From Midshipman to Field-Marshal*, vol. ii, p. 59): 'I have never known a battery so exceptionally fortunate in its subalterns.... Both Bigge and Slade were unsurpassable; they with their gunners stood up in the open from 1.30 p.m. till the Zulus retreated at 5.30 p.m.' Later in that year the Prince Imperial was killed in South Africa and Bigge had the melancholy task of escorting the body of his friend back to England. He went to Abergeldie to tell the Empress Eugénie of the circumstances in which the Prince had been killed, and while staying there he had several interviews at Balmoral with Queen Victoria, who wrote of him to her eldest daughter (24 October): 'He is a charming person, of the very highest character, clever, amiable and agreeable, as well as good looking.' Three days later the Queen recorded in her diary: 'After tea saw Lieut. Bigge, with whom I had a long talk. He was at Inhlobane and Kambula, his horse being killed under him at the latter. ... After Kambula Lieut. Bigge became very ill indeed and the Prince Imperial came to see him in hospital, when he said he hoped they would meet again soon. This was only a week before the Prince was killed, and humanly speaking it seemed more likely that Lieut. Bigge should die than that the other should happen. He cautioned and begged the Prince to be very careful, which he promised he would. ... We spoke of the Empress' wish, indeed determination, to go to South Africa to visit the spot where her dear son fell, which will be difficult to carry out, but not impossible.'

On 1 January 1880 the Queen appointed Bigge a groom-in-waiting to herself, giving him leave first to accompany Wood, to whom he was at that time aide-de-camp, and who had undertaken to conduct the Empress to the scene of the tragedy. Bigge went ahead, on 11 March, to make arrangements. On their return from South Africa at the end of July he went for two nights to Osborne to report to the Queen, who immediately appointed him assistant private secretary and assistant privy purse, 'as both Sir Henry Ponsonby and I think no-one better fitted than him' (Diary, 2 August). This association with Sir Henry Ponsonby [q.v.] proved most happy on both sides, and Bigge carried with him to the grave an unstinted admiration for his former chief. He resigned as groom in May 1881, having been appointed equerry in the previous month. He was made C.B. in 1885 and C.M.G. in 1887. In May 1895 he was advanced to K.C.B. upon succeeding Ponsonby as private secretary to the Queen, a post which he held until the close of her reign.

King Edward VII came to the throne already provided with a private secretary in the person of Sir Francis (later Viscount) Knollys [q.v.]. But when the heir to the throne, Prince George, Duke of Cornwall and York, made his famous tour through the British Dominions in 1901, Bigge accompanied him as private secretary. At the close of the tour Bigge was appointed G.C.V.O. and K.C.M.G. He retained the post of private secretary to the Prince of Wales throughout King Edward's reign and accompanied him to India in 1905. He was appointed K.C.S.I. in 1906.

On his accession in 1910 King George V at first made use of the services and experience of both Knollys and Bigge as joint private secretaries. Knollys retired in 1913, and Bigge, who had been raised to the peerage as Baron Stamfordham in 1911, remained until his death eighteen years later principal private secretary. He was sworn of the Privy Council in 1910, attended the King to India in 1911, and was appointed G.C.I.E. in 1911 and G.C.B. in 1916. He also received several foreign decorations, including the Legion of Honour, and in 1906 the university of Durham conferred upon him the honorary degree of D.C.L.

Among Stamfordham's few but distinguished predecessors in his office his place is deservedly high. As private secretary to two sovereigns he revealed qualities of tact and wisdom, a sure grasp of affairs, and an unswerving rectitude. Politically he was at once less eager and less radical than either of his immediate forerunners. The affinity between Ponsonby and Gladstone, or that between Knollys and Asquith, found its natural parallel in the intimacy which for nearly fifty years linked Stamfordham with Randall Davidson [q.v.]. His impartiality was never questioned. Upon vacating office in December 1916 Asquith wrote to him: 'Our intercourse, official and personal, during all these years, is one of the pleasantest memories of my public life. The times have not been easy, and of late more than difficult, but our task has been lightened by complete mutual confidence and ever-growing friendship.'

Stamfordham was a man of persistent industry, making it his practice to finish the day's work within the day, whatever the cost in leisure or the physical burden. This towards the close of Queen Victoria's life became heavy, for her eyes began to fail, and by 1895 the task of writing to her legibly had become so exacting that the prime minister permitted himself to communicate with her through Bigge, dictating his letters to an amanuensis with a clear handwriting (Lord Crewe, *Lord Rosebery*, vol. i, p. 508). For his part, Bigge used to dry his submissions in a stove of ingenious design instead of blotting them; and he taught himself afresh to write. It was thus that he acquired the bold script which remained to the end the joy and envy of his correspondents. His letters were largely handwritten; if they lack the astringency and sparkle of Ponsonby's they are marked by a like economy of phrase.

Against the wiles of the importunate he knew well how to guard himself, and fashionable company he resolutely eschewed. A certain austerity which he had imbibed in the north-country vicarage mellowed in later years to a gentler tolerance, and he came to be regarded by his colleagues with a love which perhaps never wholly cast out fear. But the young, the shy, and the inexperienced were drawn towards him by the candour and the simplicity of his bearing. 'I shall never forget', wrote Ramsay MacDonald after his death, 'the kindness he shewed to my colleagues and myself when we were but prentices in 1924. The country has lost a devoted servant who for many years bore delicate responsibilities with a sagacity and resourcefulness which smoothed many a difficult road and enabled change to come gently and be accepted without misgiving as a thing belonging to the natural flow of time.'

Stamfordham had learnt his trade in the service of an aged queen, of towering personal ascendancy, unrivalled experience, and marked political capacity. It was to a different scene that he returned a decade later, at a period of strong civil ferment, the intermediary this time between a reticent and untried sovereign and a resourceful prime minister. It was Stamfordham's solicitude which brought confidence to the new king at the same time as his experience brought counsel in statecraft. There was in him an absence of self-esteem which responded to a like quality in his master, establishing between them more than a merely professional relationship throughout the thirty years of their association. On the day of his death at St. James's Palace 31 March 1931, the King wrote in his diary: 'Dear Bigge passed peacefully away at 4.30 to-day. I shall miss him terribly. His loss is irreparable.'

Stamfordham married in 1881 Constance (died 1922), second daughter of William Frederick Neville, vicar of Butleigh, Somerset, and had one son, who was killed in action in 1915, and two daughters. He had but one grandchild, Major Michael Adeane.

A portrait of Stamfordham, by H. A. Olivier (1927), is in the possession of the family, and a charcoal drawing, by Francis Dodd (1931), is in the Royal Library, Windsor Castle. A poor cartoon of him, by 'Spy', appeared in *Vanity Fair* 6 September 1900.

[*The Times*, 1 April 1931; published *Letters*, and unpublished diary, of Queen Victoria; P. H. Emden, *Behind the Throne*, 1934; private information; personal knowledge.]

OWEN MORSHEAD.

BILES, SIR JOHN HARVARD (1854–1933), naval architect, was born at Portsmouth 6 January 1854, the third son of John Biles, an official at Portsmouth dockyard, by his wife, Margaret, second daughter of William Groombridge, of Ernehill, Kent. His childhood was spent at Portsmouth, where in his early years his interest in ships was quickened and his natural bent for mechanics encouraged by the very nature of his surroundings. He was educated at G. L. Oliver's school (now the Mile End House School), Portsmouth,

from which he passed to serve his apprenticeship at Portsmouth dockyard, at a period during which the use of wood in warship construction was being largely superseded by steel, and sails were giving place to mechanical power. The *Devastation*, on which he was chiefly engaged, was the first of the modern ships built entirely by the new methods.

In 1872, at the age of eighteen, Biles was placed first on the list of candidates for a scholarship at the Royal School of Naval Architecture and Marine Engineering, moving in 1873 to the Royal Naval College, Greenwich, where he finished his three-year course in 1875. As was customary with all students of the school, at the end of his course he returned to the dockyards for practical experience, mainly at Pembroke, until in 1876 he was appointed Admiralty overseer at the Landore ironworks in South Wales, where he gained intimate knowledge of steel manufacture. Biles's ability was soon recognized, and on joining the Admiralty in 1877 he was given full opportunity to use his growing skill and knowledge. At this time no great importance was attached to the investigations of William Froude [q.v.] in estimating resistance of ships' models, but Biles, with his quick perception and vision, rightly judged the value of Froude's work, and studied its possibilities whilst he was still at the Admiralty. In 1880 he was offered the post of chief designer to Messrs. J. and G. Thomson, of Clydebank (later Messrs. John Brown & company), where his reputation as a naval architect was soon established. Under his guidance the firm became famous for the building of both naval and mercantile ships, and his study of Froude's work led to improvements in hull form which resulted in increasing speed in passenger vessels. The *City of Paris* and *City of New York*, built in 1887, were revolutionary in design and construction, demonstrating the advantages of lighter construction coupled with adequate strength, made possible by scientific design.

In 1891 Biles was appointed to the chair of naval architecture in Glasgow University, a post which he held for thirty years. Here he was extremely popular, not only for his talent for teaching but for his sympathetic understanding of his students, many of whom became distinguished naval architects in later life. During this period Biles combined lecturing at the university with practical work on designs for various firms, and gave his students practical experience by allowing them to help in the working out of the plans. In 1907 he opened offices in Broadway, Westminster, as a consulting naval architect and engineer. His reputation was almost world-wide: he travelled widely, particularly in North and South America and in India, where his work was so highly thought of that on the death of Sir E. J. Reed [q.v.], in 1906, he was appointed consulting naval architect to the India Office. The British Admiralty called him in as a consultant on many occasions, and he was associated with the development of river and shallow-draft vessels for use in Mesopotamia during the war of 1914–1918.

Among the many government committees on which Biles served were the dry-dock experiments on the *Wolf* (1901–1903) to test for the first time by actual measurements the stresses on the hull of a destroyer, a highly successful piece of experimental work; the Board of Trade departmental committee on boats and davits (1912) after the disaster of the *Titanic*; the ship designs committee (1904–1905) appointed by Lord Fisher [q.v.], from which there emerged the design of the *Dreadnought*, completed under Sir Philip Watts [q.v.], director of naval construction at the Admiralty. For his services on these and other committees he was knighted in 1913 and appointed K.C.I.E. in 1922. He was elected a member of council of the Institution of Naval Architects in 1889, vice-president in 1905, and honorary vice-president in 1919. His first paper, 'Some Results of Curves of Resistance and Progressive Measured Mile Speed Curves', was read to the institution in 1881, and his last, 'Draught and Dimensions of the Most Economical Ship', in 1931. For many years he served on the court of the Worshipful Company of Shipwrights and was master of the company in 1904. He published *The Marine Steam Turbine* in 1906 and *The Design and Construction of Ships* in 1908. The honorary degree of LL.D. was conferred upon him by the universities of Yale (1901) and Glasgow (1922), and of D.Sc. by Harvard (1908). He was an honorary member of the Japanese Society of Naval Architects, and was decorated with the Egyptian order of Osmanieh in 1906.

Biles was a man of remarkable vitality, genial disposition, and possessed of a physical stamina which enabled him to use his mental powers to the full in his professional capacity. That his work did not absorb the whole of his energy is shown by his filling in his spare time when working on the *Devastation* reading the whole of Alison's *History of Europe* while seated in the double bottom of the ship. A keen yachtsman, he won many prizes at Cowes, Dublin, and the Clyde regattas with his yawls *Caress* and *Lais*, and he presented one of these trophies to the Shipwrights' Company.

Biles married in 1876 Emma Jane (died June 1933), only child of Richard Hoskyn Lloyd, of Pembroke, and had one son and two daughters. He died at Virginia Water, Surrey, 27 October 1933.

A portrait of Biles, by Maurice Greiffenhagen, is in the possession of the family.

[*The Times*, 28 October 1933; *Nature*, 4 November 1933; private information.]

E. H. T. D'EYNCOURT.

BIRCH, SIR (JAMES FREDERICK) NOEL (1865–1939), general, was born at Llanrhaiadr, Denbighshire, 29 December 1865, the second son of Major Richard Frederick Birch, J.P., of Maes Elwy, St. Asaph, by his wife, Euphemia Mercer, eldest daughter of James Somerville, of Edinburgh. Educated at Giggleswick, Marlborough, and the Royal Military Academy, he was commissioned in the Royal Artillery in 1885. An exceptionally fine horseman and whip, he quickly gained his Royal Horse Artillery 'jacket' and in 1894 became aide-de-camp to the general commanding the Woolwich district. In 1895–1896 he took part in the Ashanti expedition, and in South Africa he served with his Royal Horse Artillery battery in the Cavalry division under the command of Sir John French [q.v.], taking part in the relief of Kimberley, the operations in the Orange Free State and the Transvaal, and being present at the battle of Diamond Hill. He was promoted major in June 1900, and in 1901 was given command of a battalion of Imperial Yeomanry, which he led in the operations in Cape Colony from December 1901 to the conclusion of hostilities. He was in command of the Riding Establishment at Woolwich from 1905 to 1907.

Promoted lieutenant-colonel in 1912, Birch commanded the 7th brigade, Royal Horse Artillery, and took it to France in August 1914, serving with the Cavalry division under the command of Sir Edmund (later Viscount) Allenby [q.v.], in the retreat from Mons and in the battles of the Aisne and of Ypres–Armentières. In January 1915 he was appointed brigadier-general on the general staff of the Cavalry Corps, and a few months later C.R.A. of the 7th division, going in the same position in July to the I Corps, then commanded by Sir Douglas Haig [q.v.]. In May 1916 Haig brought him to general headquarters as artillery adviser, and he held that post until the end of the war. He was promoted major-general in 1917 and lieutenant-general in 1919. In 1920 he became director of remounts at the War Office and had regretfully to supervise the changes required by the development of mechanical transport. In the following year he was appointed director-general of the Territorial Army and concerned himself actively with the development of cadet corps. In 1923 he was appointed master-general of the Ordnance and fourth military member of the Army Council. He held this position until 1927, during a period when important experiments, followed by equally important developments in artillery, were in progress, and his long experience of artillery in war, from the fighting front to general headquarters, was of great value. He was promoted general in 1926 and retired from the army in the following year in order to become a director of Vickers-Armstrong.

Birch was made a colonel commandant of the Royal Artillery in 1919 and in 1923 a colonel commandant of the Royal Horse Artillery. He was appointed C.B. in 1916, K.C.M.G. in 1918, K.C.B. in 1922, and G.B.E. in 1927, and received numerous foreign honours. He published two books, *Modern Riding* (1909) and *Modern Riding and Horse Education* (1912). He married in 1903 Florence Hyacinthe (died 1938), youngest daughter of Sir George Chetwode, sixth baronet, of Oakley, Staffordshire, and Chetwode, Buckinghamshire, and had two sons. He died at his home in London 3 February 1939.

A portrait of Birch, by Oswald Birley, is now in the possession of his son, Lieutenant-Colonel Nigel Birch, M.P.

[*The Times*, 4 February 1939; personal knowledge.]   F. MAURICE.

BIRRELL, AUGUSTINE (1850–1933), author and statesman, born at Wavertree, near Liverpool, 19 January 1850, was the younger son of Charles Morton Birrell, minister of Pembroke Baptist chapel there, by his wife, Harriet Jane, daughter of Henry Grey [q.v.], Free Church minister, of Edinburgh. Thus he was reared in the tradition of liberal nonconformity which reckons education to be one of the orna-

ments of a good life. On leaving Amersham Hall School, Caversham, in 1866, he became an articled clerk in a solicitor's office in Liverpool; but a fortunate legacy enabled his father to send him to Trinity Hall, Cambridge, and it seemed as though he had burned his last boat on Merseyside, and would qualify for a profession elsewhere. He began university life in dingy lodgings near the Hall, and his preference for retaining them throughout his whole career at Cambridge indicates the quiet studious life which he led in the company of a few special friends, not engaging in college competitions on field or river, but carrying on a modest existence, varied by occasional rides on the broad grass verges of roads ending on Newmarket Heath, and working hard enough to obtain the good second class in the law tripos of 1872 which he thought represented his merits and his prospects, for without affectation of humility he was never ambitious, or believed that the glittering prizes of life were there for him to grasp. He was elected an honorary fellow of Trinity Hall in 1899.

At the age of twenty-five Birrell was called to the bar by the Inner Temple. The excitements of the Common Law bar and going on circuit had no attractions for him, and with some advantages at the start, he settled down to quiet Chancery business, securing before long enough work to enable him in 1878 to marry Margaret, daughter of Archibald Mirrielees, of St. Petersburg, to whom he had long been attached. This happy union was broken up by her death after thirteen months, and his younger sister came to live with him for the next nine years, during which his practice grew steadily but not on a great scale, and he was able to devote his leisure to reading, of infinite variety, but not in the direction of an increased study of the classics, or the acquisition of modern languages, although he was able to enjoy not a few expeditions to European countries.

In time Birrell became known as a capable and versatile reviewer. A persistent exception to the catholicity of his reading was his inability to enjoy a novel: he read but few, and never reviewed one until the persuasion of a younger esteemed critic induced him to crown the popular admiration already given to Miss Margaret Kennedy's *The Constant Nymph* (1924). In 1884 he became a public character by the appearance of a collection of essays on various subjects, including one 'On the

Alleged Obscurity of Mr. Browning's Poetry', 'A Rogue's Memoirs' (Benvenuto Cellini), a note on Carlyle, and another on Falstaff, thus covering a wide field. *Obiter Dicta* was published at a time when an influential section of fashionable society had become ashamed of appearing only to frequent Melton and Newmarket, and the book's fascinating style and its small bulk made it easy to carry about from country house to country house and discuss under the trees on a fine afternoon. A second series was published in 1887 and many years later *More Obiter Dicta* (1924). His literary reputation was further enhanced by the publication in 1887 of *Charlotte Brontë*, which he describes as a biographical sketch, in no way intended to supersede Mrs. Gaskell's authoritative memoir, but so to be called because it is impossible to criticize her work without telling something of the story of her life.

Some critics were disposed to regard Birrell's literary judgements as somewhat superficial. The term 'Birrelling' was devised to describe a sort of literary flute-playing, agreeable to listen to, but not to be compared with mastery of the violin or pianoforte. This was unfair: during his Liverpool years he had absorbed a vast quantity of sixteenth- and seventeenth-century literature, including the *arcana* of long-forgotten divinity and social history. This enabled him to write entertainingly on a dull subject, the reverse practice to that of some of his critics, who did not contribute anything fresh or novel to a subject known to be exciting in itself. He made no claim to the profound erudition of his friend W. P. Ker [q.v.], but neither that scholar nor others who enjoyed Birrell's essays expected it of him. Among British essayists probably none found it so needless to follow a single path for information or study.

In 1888 Birrell married Eleanor Mary Bertha, widow of Lionel Tennyson, younger son of the poet laureate. This alliance encouraged fresh intimacies in the region governed by the Muses, for she was the daughter of Frederick Locker, later Locker-Lampson [q.v.]. She was a woman of much charm and mental capacity, with a sense of humour that chimed in happily with Birrell's, and she became a favourite in many political and social circles. She died in 1915 after a happy married life of twenty-seven years. Two sons were born of this marriage.

In 1885 and again in 1886 the liberal barrister had been an unsuccessful candidate for the Walton division of Liverpool, and it was not until 1889 that a by-election for the West Fife division offered the chance which one or two fortunate accidents enabled Birrell to grasp. He became a loyal follower of Gladstone's government in 1892 and afterwards of Rosebery's briefer leadership (1894–1896), and in the following years shared the political views of Campbell-Bannerman. In 1895 he took silk, and from 1896 to 1899 he held the Quain professorship of law at University College, London. In 1900 he was unfortunately persuaded to abandon West Fife and fight a losing battle for the North-East division of Manchester, so that he was absent from parliament during the later stages of the South African war and took no part in the acrimonious discussions on the education bill of 1902, in which he was destined to be so deeply interested. The resignation of the Balfour government in 1905 brought about the formation of Campbell-Bannerman's administration, in which Birrell, who was to be elected member for North Bristol at the general election of 1906, accepted the presidency of the Board of Education. It was a particularly important post at the moment, for the Education Act of 1902 had not only infuriated the great nonconformist bodies, but had convinced liberals of all shades that the legislation of 1870 was being tampered with in a spirit of undue favouritism towards Church of England elementary schools. Birrell's upbringing pointed him out as being especially qualified to redress the balance, while his broad sympathies and a sense of humour which pervaded all his speeches and writings saved him from being identified with the extreme section of dissenting spokesmen, of whom Dr. John Clifford [q.v.] was the most conspicuous. The education bill of 1906 was accordingly framed on lines designed to restore equality of treatment, notably in single-school areas. The fight in the House of Commons was long and bitter; Birrell did not enjoy the support of the Irish members, many of whom were Roman Catholics, while all were irritated at finding that their grievance was not set in the forefront of reforms to be dealt with. But the measure passed on to the House of Lords, and there its doom was sealed in spite of the qualified support of some members of the opposition, of whom the Duke of Devonshire was the most notable, and the efforts of the archbishop of Canterbury to state the Church case moderately. After long conferences between the Houses the bill was lost by a large majority.

Birrell was only thirteen months at the Board of Education, and in 1907 was nominated chief secretary for Ireland, in succession to James (afterwards Viscount) Bryce [q.v.]. It was felt that Birrell's qualities were predominantly fitted to the task, as minister in charge of Ireland. Thus three eminent men of letters, Morley, Bryce, and Birrell were nominated by liberal prime ministers to the chief secretaryship: it may be held by some that experienced administrators in India or Africa might have been able to cope more appropriately with the situation in Dublin, since they would begin by recognizing the deep-seated and sometimes unplumbed divergencies between the two races. Be that as it may, Birrell accepted the chief secretaryship with little hope of scoring a triumphant success during his term of office, but he was stimulated by the hope of doing something to set education in Ireland, particularly religious education, on a sounder footing than it had enjoyed since the Act of Union, most of all in its higher branches. The creation of a really representative Roman Catholic university, facing on equal terms Trinity College, the great and honoured foundation emblematic of Protestant ascendancy, would mean triumph for the liberal administration of Ireland such as it had not achieved for many years. He set to work at once on the complicated details of this measure, and amid much criticism and some disappointments became responsible for the new National University of Ireland, with three constituent colleges in Dublin, Cork, and Galway, established in 1908. Trinity College was of course not included, but submitted to a vague connexion of affiliation, while the university of Belfast satisfied the *amour propre* of Northern Ireland.

The old landlord and tenant system had broken down, and both English parties, especially the conservatives, had engaged in vast purchase schemes for the benefit of occupying ownership. Reviewing his Irish experiences in later years, Birrell was able to claim that he had completed this task.

Birrell remained chief secretary for over nine years, but he never became a leading member of the Cabinet, even for Irish affairs. The home rule bill of 1912 was not his work, but that of the prime minister, Asquith; and it was Asquith who introduced it, piloted it, and during the two years of its stormy career was responsible for the negotiations carried on from time to time with Carson and John Redmond [qq.v.]. It is significant that when on the eve of the outbreak of war in 1914 a supreme effort was made to settle the home rule problem by a four-day conference at Buckingham Palace, the Irish chief secretary was not one of the eight statesmen who composed it. His position, well understood, was different. He was not responsible for high policy as Forster, Morley, Balfour, and Wyndham had been in their times, but merely for the day-to-day administration of Dublin Castle. Even that was slackly performed, and on terms which (as the Larne gun-running in 1914 showed) impaired the efficiency of the Royal Irish Constabulary. His qualities for his task were good nature and humour; his defect was indolence.

As time went on, Birrell saved himself much trouble by following a single prescription—to act on the advice of the Irish leader John Redmond. There was much to be said for it; Redmond was not only a great Irish patriot, but a good friend to England and a loyal ally of the liberal government; and since he was cast for the part of Ireland's future ruler, why not leave it to him to prepare the ground? Unfortunately he was not a reliable mentor. Living mainly in England he had no longer an inside knowledge of Irish movements, and especially after August 1914 failed to realize either the shock to nationalist sentiment through the shelving of home rule or the power of Sinn Fein to overthrow his own position. John Dillon [q.v.] was much better informed on these subjects, but he had not Birrell's ear. Despite warnings the chief secretary did nothing whatever to counter the plotting of the Sinn Feiners, until at Easter 1916 they launched in collusion with Germany their open, armed rebellion. The long-term effects which that famous rising would leave on the history of Irish separatism could hardly be foreseen at the moment. But what was obvious to everybody was the military danger of an Irish revolt at the height of a great European war, and Birrell's complete blindness to its coming until it came. The condemnation passed on him was universal. He did not challenge it; his resignation speech in the House of Commons was a frank and penitent admission of the facts. As such it evoked respect and sympathy on all sides; but his political career was ended. There could be no question of public responsibilities being entrusted to him again, and he did not seek re-election to parliament at the general election of 1918.

Birrell survived this catastrophe by over seventeen years. He settled quietly in Chelsea, surrounded by the care of the Locker-Lampson brothers and of his wife's sons by her first marriage. He resumed writing; a sketch of his father-in-law, Frederick Locker-Lampson, appeared in 1920, followed by two volumes of collected essays and one of reminiscences, the last published posthumously in 1937. These neither raised nor lowered his literary reputation, which rests essentially on the two earlier volumes of *Obiter Dicta*.

Birrell died in London 20 November 1933. He was not a great nor even a fortunate statesman. But as a writer he has stronger claims, being one of that happy fellowship who, by recording good lives of the past and adorning their tale with scintillant wit and kindly humour, have helped to make goodness attractive to the less gifted of their own and future generations.

A portrait of Birrell, which hangs in the National Gallery of Ireland, Dublin, was painted by Sir William Orpen who also executed a chalk drawing of him (1909) which is in the National Portrait Gallery, London; a portrait by Roger Fry (1928) was sold when Birrell's effects were dispersed. A small version is in the possession of Mr. Charles Tennyson. A cartoon by 'Spy' appeared in *Vanity Fair* 18 January 1906.

[*The Times*, 21 November 1933; Augustine Birrell, *Things Past Redress*, 1937.]

CREWE.
R. C. K. ENSOR.

BLACKETT, SIR BASIL PHILLOTT (1882–1935), financial administrator, was born 8 January 1882 in Calcutta, where both his parents (the Rev. William Russell Blackett, at that time principal of a theological training college, and later of another in London, and his wife, Grace Anne Phillott), were missionaries. They returned to England shortly afterwards and in 1893 the father died, leaving his widow in straitened circumstances, with five children of whom Basil was the eldest son. He went to Marlborough as a foundation scholar and was elected to a classical scholarship at University College, Oxford, where he obtained a first class in *literae humaniores* in 1904. In the same year he entered for the civil service examination, intending to go to India, but being placed

first he chose the Treasury. On the outbreak of war ten years later he was in the financial division, and had been secretary to the royal commission on Indian finance and currency (1913–1914). Foreign exchange problems took him to America for the first time in October 1914 and he went again a year later as a member of the Anglo-French financial commission, so that when the United States entered the war he was the natural choice for the post of representative of the British Treasury in Washington; this he held from 1917 to 1919. On his return he became the first controller of finance at the Treasury, and in 1922 he went to India as finance member of the viceroy's council.

Blackett's work in India during the next five years showed him to be not only an exceptional but an outstanding financial administrator. Within a twelvemonth he had initiated and put through three major financial reforms. The Indian railways were ripped out of the central budget and placed on an independent footing; the charges for the repayment or avoidance of public debt were concentrated into a statutory sinking fund; and the eight provincial finance members were brought together for the first time in a conference, which has been repeated annually, to compare and co-ordinate their problems and to discover means of reducing, if not abolishing, the provincial contributions to the central revenues. The same principles of conference and co-ordination were applied by the finance member to the vexed political questions with which, more and more, he came to be concerned in virtue of his personal prestige. That prestige was enhanced by the fact that, although he lacked both talent and experience as a debater, he taught himself the art and became leader of the legislative assembly, in which he introduced six successive budgets and fixed the value of the rupee at eighteen pence.

When Blackett returned to England in 1928, by way of Australia, New Zealand, China, Japan, and North America, he was a marked man for whom a future had been prepared outside the civil service. His friend Mr. Montagu (later Lord) Norman, then governor, sponsored his election to the court of directors of the Bank of England in 1929; a merger of cable and wireless services provided an opportunity for placing him in charge of the new Imperial and International Communications Company; and a place was waiting for him in London from which his influence could be brought to bear on colonial currency problems. In order to undertake this triple task he left the Treasury for the City. But within three years the crisis of 1931 and the devaluation of sterling created a breach of continuity in which he found himself on the side of the future rather than of the past. His attention was increasingly engaged by national problems and he became a convert to planned money (on which he published a book under that title in 1932) and to budgeting for a deficit. He was a prophet of the 'sterling area'—a phrase which he popularized if he did not invent it. He also stood for parliament as an unofficial conservative candidate for the St. Marylebone division in 1932, but was not elected. In the same year he resigned the chairmanship of the Imperial and International Communications Company and joined the board of De Beers Consolidated Mines. He also took a keen interest in the British Social Hygiene Council, of which he was president.

Blackett died in hospital at Marburg, Germany, as the result of a motor accident 15 August 1935. While he was still at Marlborough an injury to his leg had caused him to spend a period of enforced idleness in a visit to Germany which roused an interest that did not end with his membership of the international committee on reparations which produced the Young Plan in 1929, and when he died he was on his way to lecture at Heidelberg University. A volume of translations published posthumously in 1937 bears witness to his abiding scholarship and particular interest in Byzantine Greek, acquired from his father. A window in Durham Cathedral—the Blacketts are a Durham family—and the school observatory at Marlborough preserve his memory.

Blackett was twice married: first in 1905 to Marion Enid, daughter of David Provan Graham, of Glasgow; secondly, in 1920 to Beatrice, daughter of Edward Henry Bonner, of New York. He had no children. He was appointed C.B. in 1915, K.C.B. in 1921, and K.C.S.I. in 1926.

[*The Times*, 16 August 1935; private information; personal knowledge.]

H. A. SIEPMANN.

BLAND-SUTTON, SIR JOHN, baronet (1855–1936), surgeon. [See SUTTON.]

BLOOD, SIR BINDON (1842–1940), general, was born near Jedburgh 7 November 1842, the eldest son of William Bindon Blood, of Cranaher, co. Clare,

civil engineer, by his first wife, Margaret, daughter of Robert Stewart, of Hawick. He was a descendant of Colonel Thomas Blood [q.v.] who attempted to seize the crown jewels in 1671. He was educated at the Royal School, Banagher, and Queen's College, Galway, whence he went to the Indian Military Seminary at Addiscombe, near Croydon, and in 1860 received his first commission as temporary lieutenant in the Royal Engineers. For the next ten years he specialized in signalling and pontoon bridge construction. He was responsible for the design of the boats which replaced the old sausage system of pontoons, and he became the first commander of the R.E. Telegraph Troop formed in 1870. He embarked for India in 1871, and, except for short periods of active service in Zululand and South Africa, served there for thirty-five years. On arrival in India he was posted to the Bengal Sappers and Miners at Roorkee where he remained for the next few years enjoying much sport and big-game shooting.

In 1873 Blood was promoted captain, and served on the committee under Sir F. (later Earl) Roberts [q.v.] which arranged for the ceremony to proclaim Queen Victoria Empress of India in 1877. Towards the end of that year he commanded on the North-West Frontier part of a punitive expedition against the Jowaki Afridis (1877–1878) for which he received the medal and clasp. In August 1878 he came home on leave, but on the outbreak of the Zulu war he was drafted to Africa early in 1879 as commanding royal engineer, 1st division Zulu Field Force. He was made brevet major and received the medal and clasp for his services in the campaign. On his return to England at the end of 1879 he found orders awaiting him to proceed to Kabul, where he arrived in 1880 a few months after the outbreak of the second Afghan war. He took very little part in the actual fighting and returned to Roorkee towards the end of the year with the medal of the campaign. He left India in 1882 and was posted to command the 26th Field Company, Royal Engineers, at Shorncliffe, but after only a few months was ordered on active service to Egypt, where his sappers took part in the battle of Tel-el-Kebir. This campaign brought him promotion to brevet lieutenant-colonel (1882), the medal and clasp, and the Osmanieh Egyptian medal.

Blood returned to England in 1883 but soon succeeded in getting himself posted once more to India, rejoining the Sappers and Miners as commandant in Simla in 1885. Seven years later he was promoted brigadier-general and in 1894 colonel on the staff in command of the garrison at Rawalpindi. In the following year he was made chief staff officer of the Chitral relief force. For these services he received the medal and clasp and was appointed K.C.B. He came home in 1896 but returned before the end of the year to command the Malakand Field Force and the Buner Field Force (1897–1898). He was promoted major-general in 1898. Owing to Blood's skilful handling the campaign was speedily brought to an end. Returning to India from short leave, he commanded the Meerut division for the next two years, but early in 1901 Lord Kitchener [q.v.] asked for his services in South Africa, and as lieutenant-general he commanded the troops in the Eastern Transvaal with headquarters at Middelburg and for some months was engaged on various 'rounding-up' operations. Late in the year he returned in order to take up the important military command of the Punjab. This appointment he held, having been promoted full general in 1906, until he retired in November 1907 when he settled in London, continuing to lead a very active life.

In 1909 Blood was appointed G.C.B. and in 1914 colonel-commandant, Royal Engineers. For the next sixteen years his activities were largely concerned with the interests of the corps, but he found time for recruiting work in connexion with the war of 1914–1918. When he was ninety years of age (1932) he was appointed G.C.V.O., and four years later he was the first officer to fill the re-created post of chief royal engineer.

Blood's great popularity earned him many friends. His successes were due to his brilliant staff work and strategy and his carefully acquired knowledge of the habits and temperament of opposing forces.

Blood married in 1883 Charlotte Elizabeth, second daughter of Sir Auckland Colvin [q.v.], a distinguished Indian and Egyptian administrator, and had one daughter. He died in London 16 May 1940, at the great age of ninety-seven, his name having appeared in the Army List for eighty years.

[The Times, 17 May 1940; Sir Bindon Blood, Four Score Years and Ten, 1933; Journal of the Royal Engineers, vol. liv, 1940; Sir J. F. Maurice and M. H. Grant, (Official) History of the War in South Africa, 1899–1902, 1906–1910.]   C. V. OWEN.

BONE, WILLIAM ARTHUR (1871–1938), chemist and fuel technologist, was born at Stockton-on-Tees 19 March 1871, the eldest son of Christopher Bone, tea merchant, of Stockton, by his wife, Mary Elizabeth Hutchinson. He was educated at Middlesbrough High School, and then at the Friends' School at Ackworth whence he entered Stockton High School; there the science master was a particularly inspiring teacher. Bone's uncle, T. C. Hutchinson, was manager of the Skinningrove iron-works, in which the boy spent much of his spare time. These two influences led him towards a scientific career. Before entering the Owens College, Manchester, in 1888, he spent a year at the Leys School, Cambridge. After graduation in chemistry three years later, he continued to work in Henry Baily Dixon's laboratory at the Owens College and his first paper, entitled 'The behaviour of ethylene on explosion with less than its volume of oxygen', was published in 1892. In 1896 he went to study for a year in Victor Meyer's laboratory at Heidelberg and worked there on the Indoxazen derivatives. Returning to England, he was head of the chemistry department at the Battersea Polytechnic for two years. In 1898 he went back to the Owens College as lecturer in chemistry and metallurgy and worked along with W. H. Perkin [q.v.] on various carboxylic acids. During the next ten years Bone continued researches in organic chemistry and published a number of papers with collaborators. Whatever Bone undertook, he pursued with relentless vigour; nevertheless his early interests were at this time drawing him back to study the chemistry of combustion, which became his life's work.

In 1906 Bone was appointed professor of fuel and metallurgy, and in 1910 first Livesey professor of coal, gas, and fuel industries at the university of Leeds. After six years of activity, he was called to London in 1912 to establish at the Royal College of Science, South Kensington, a department of fuel technology, and became professor of chemical technology in the university of London; he retired in 1936. He was a fine experimentalist and the founder of a flourishing school of fuel technology at the Imperial College of Science and Technology. Bone continued the supervision of researches on blast furnace reactions there after his retirement, but a serious illness ended his life's work and he died in London 11 June 1938. He was elected F.R.S. in 1905, received the Davy medal in 1936, and delivered the Bakerian lecture in 1932. He received the Melchett medal of the Institute of Fuel in 1931, and the medal of the Society of Chemical Industry in 1933.

Most of Bone's work was published along with collaborators in the *Philosophical Transactions* and *Proceedings* of the Royal Society and the *Journal* of the Chemical Society. He summarized the main content of his life's work in a lecture delivered to the Society of Chemical Industry in 1933: his early interests in iron smelting combined with the influence of Dixon at the Owens College enabled him to envisage combustion from both the technical and the scientific points of view. His early work on combustion was in support of some long neglected experiments of John Dalton [q.v.], which showed that in hydrocarbon combustion the hydrogen was not burnt preferentially: during this work he investigated the explosive combustion of ethylene, acetylene, cyanogen, hydrogen, and pentane. Perhaps the most important section of his whole work was that on the slow combustion of the hydrocarbons which began in 1902 and continued until the end of his career. As a result of these researches, Bone formulated an hypothesis, known as the hydroxylation theory of hydrocarbon combustion. Although more recent work on the reactions of hydrocarbons and oxygen shows that the 'hydroxylation theory' does not truly represent all that happens, nevertheless the hypothesis was a useful guide in the pioneer work which he carried out in this field, and he staunchly defended it.

While he was at Leeds, Bone carried his researches on gaseous combustion to high pressures and he continued this work at South Kensington in collaboration with Dr. Dudley Maurice Newitt and Dr. Donald Thomas Alfred Townend, and they eventually reached initial pressures of 750 atmospheres and explosion pressures as high as 7,000 atmospheres. The combustion of carbon monoxide and the influence of water on its combustion became the subject of an elaborate series of investigations which illustrate the exceptional pertinacity possessed by Bone. He eventually proved that carbon monoxide could be burnt without the intervention of any water vapour. Quite early in his career he set about studying the catalytic combustion at surfaces of various kinds. At one period of this work (1908–1912), along with C. D. McCourt, he developed the incandescent surface combustion process (to which the name Bonecourt was given). The process was adapted to crucible and muffle furnaces, to steam-raising in multi-tubular boilers, etc. He was also known for the improvements which he introduced in methods for the accurate analysis of gases.

Bone and his collaborator, R. P. Fraser, from about 1930 onwards carried out the most remarkable series of photographic investigations of flame propagation which had been made up to that date.

Bone had a very wide knowledge of coal and its treatment and his advice was widely sought by industry. In 1919 he began to publish his researches on the constitution of coal. He proved that the benzenoid constituents increase with the maturity of the coal. Of his other books, the last, written jointly with G. W. Himus and entitled *Coal, its Constitution and Uses*, was published in 1936.

Bone's early interest in blast furnace technology culminated in studies with his assistant, H. L. Saunders, on the chemical reactions within the blast furnace; the importance of the direct reduction of ore by carbon was established.

Bone was twice married: first, in 1893 to Kate (died 1914), daughter of Richard Hind, J.P., who was twice mayor of Stockton, and had one son and two daughters; secondly, in 1916 to Mabel Isabel (died 1922), daughter of John Edward Liddiard, civil engineer, of Swindon. Like his father, Bone was fiercely independent, and forceful in expression. Rugged in appearance and above the average in stature, he had a positive and dominant personality which inevitably led him into controversies; nevertheless many of those who disagreed with him admired his character. He had wide interests and a memory richly stocked with knowledge. He was a staunch supporter of the policy of free trade.

[*The Times*, 13 June 1938; *Obituary Notices of Fellows of the Royal Society*, No. 7, January 1939 (portrait); personal knowledge.]

A. C. EGERTON.

BOOT, JESSE, first BARON TRENT (1850–1931), man of business and philanthropist, was born in Nottingham 2 June 1850, of humble origin. His lineage has been traced back to one Richard Boote of Diseworth, Leicestershire, who died in 1577. But he himself liked to recall that he was the grandson of an agricultural labourer: his family had lived for over 150 years in various Nottinghamshire villages.

He was the only son of John Boot, by his second wife, Mary, daughter of Benjamin Wills, of Nottingham. His father traded as a herbalist in Nottingham, and died when his son was ten years old. Three years later Jesse left school and took complete control of the shop. He devoted all his spare time to the study of pharmacy, but it was not until he was twenty-seven that he opened his first chemist's shop in an adjoining street. His untiring energy made this venture a success, and after turning his business into a limited liability company in 1888, he went on opening new shops until he had built up the largest retail chemists' undertaking in the world.

In middle age Boot had a complete breakdown in health. A description which he gave of his early days, of the work which he did, and of the hours which he kept, makes it no surprise that his health gave way, but remarkable that he lived at all. He says that after being busy all day in the shop, he had usually hours of writing to do. Later on when there were branches to manage, he would work at stocktaking all through the night for a fortnight on end. He was so worn out that when he was thirty-six, anyone could have bought his business very cheap. When he was fifty an insidious disease, ossification of the muscles, set in, crippling him so hopelessly that he had to be carried about like a child. But this disability did not affect his working powers: his business and philanthropic labours increased with his malady. He owed much to his wife, for she was a woman of remarkable judgement and business capacity, and her assistance was of the greatest value to him.

In 1892 Boot's company began the manufacture of its own drugs and other commodities. Large modern factories were built at Nottingham, and the business, both retail and wholesale, grew rapidly. A new idea was the opening in his shops of other 'lines', circulating libraries, restaurants, jewelry, silver, and art departments. During the war of 1914–1918 the company rendered notable service by supplying the troops with effective respirators for resisting poison gas, and millions of tablets for sterilizing water. In 1920 Boot sold the controlling interest in his Pure Drug Company to the United Drug Company of America, and a few years later he retired from business, to be succeeded as chairman of all his companies by his only son.

Boot's benefactions to Nottingham were on the most munificent scale, and cannot have fallen far short of £2,000,000. His greatest gift was the new University College at Highfields, together with the park of several hundred acres in which it stands. Part of this park was devoted to the public, and used for sports and games. He made other gifts to the city, and contributed handsomely to other good causes. In recognition he received the freedom of Nottingham in 1920. He was a man of plain, straightforward character, and his wealth afforded him welcome opportunities of extended social service.

Boot was knighted in 1909 and created a baronet in 1917. In 1929 he was raised to the peerage as Baron Trent, of Nottingham. He married in 1886 Florence Anne, daughter of William Rowe, of St. Heliers, Jersey, and had one son and two daughters. He died at Millbrook, Jersey, 13 June 1931, and was succeeded as second baron by his son, John Campbell (born 1889).

Portraits of Boot, by Denholm Davis, at the ages of sixty and seventy, are respectively in the possession of the second Lord Trent and of the Dowager Lady Trent. A bust, by C. L. J. Doman, stands outside the Nottingham University College gates.

[*The Times*, 15 June 1931.]

ALFRED COCHRANE.

BORDEN, SIR ROBERT LAIRD (1854–1937), Canadian statesman, was born on a farm near Grand Pré in Nova Scotia 26 June 1854, the eldest surviving son of Andrew Borden, by his wife, Eunice Jane, daughter of John Laird, schoolmaster, of Grand Pré, who was of Scottish descent. His father, a farmer at the time of Robert's birth, was later station-master on the railway at Grand Pré. His great-grandfather, Perry Borden, of Kentish descent, emigrated from Massachusetts to Nova Scotia about 1763. His mother's father was a classical scholar and mathematician. Robert Borden was educated at Acacia Villa Academy, Horton, and taught classics and mathematics in Nova Scotia and New Jersey at an early age. At nineteen he was apprenticed to the law in Halifax, where he later practised. He was called to the bar in 1878 and took silk in 1891. At twenty-eight his income was large and, despite his political preoccupations, he remained a practising lawyer until his fifties.

An industrious and able lawyer, Borden hoped for a judicial position. He entered parliament reluctantly (as conservative member for the city and county of Halifax in 1896), and never found it congenial, but he soon became a front-bencher, and, in 1901 at the age of forty-seven, on the resignation of Sir Charles Tupper [q.v.], leader of the conservative party, then in opposition. He always called himself a liberal conservative, being at heart a reformer. He was fascinated by the long constitutional development towards Canadian nationhood, a process which accelerated during his lifetime. He wanted a civil service free from patronage and doubted whether any real advance could have been made except under his so-called union government, which showed little 'enthusiasm'. He wanted railways and water-powers nationalized. Even in opposition he secured the initiation of free rural mails, and curbed corruption in elections. His Halifax manifesto (1907) called for other reforms: reform of the Senate; closer supervision of immigration; nationalization of telephones and telegraphs; a public utilities commission closely controlling corporations with national franchises; control of their natural resources by the western provinces; a protective tariff. Except that last named, such ideas did not attract conservatives; Borden had to face mutinies in his own party. Besides, the great prosperity of Canada since 1896 had made the liberals, under Sir Wilfrid Laurier [q.v.], very strong.

Two clouds now appeared in the political sky: the threat of national bankruptcy through extravagant railway building and the threat of war in Europe. The election of 1908 revealed an ebb in liberal fortunes. In the 1909 session a further loan to the Grand Trunk Pacific Railway was keenly debated, Borden maintaining that since the taxpayers had put about $250,000,000 into the enterprise—nine-tenths of the cost—the government should expropriate. But the question of naval defence overshadowed all others. To a conservative resolution Laurier proposed a less definite amendment which, however, gave assurance that Canada, in emergency, would make any sacrifice required. Borden, urging a Canadian navy, feared that a crisis might come before it could be built. Laurier accordingly modified his amendment, which was passed unanimously. From the Imperial Conference of July 1909 two plans for a Canadian fleet unit emerged, one to cost £400,000 annually, the other £600,000. It soon appeared that Quebec conservatives were taking the same stand as Quebec nationalists in opposing any immediate action. This hardly justified the charge that 'the conservative party of

Canada allied with Quebec isolationists to oust Laurier'. Borden had as much difficulty with conservatives elsewhere as with Quebec conservatives. The latter wanted him to do nothing; the former denounced his support, for unanimity's sake, of the resolution put forward by Laurier, who was experiencing the same division between Quebec liberals and liberals elsewhere. The double aspect of the case, the political necessity that the fleet unit, however small, be Canadian, preferably built in Canada, and the possibility of the outbreak of war before this unit could be ready, lent plausibility to the 'die-hards' of all parties. Few could be so isolated as to escape the din of Germany's naval preparations, but the government, in touch with the Admiralty, could best judge the risks.

The naval defence bill of 1910, providing for eleven ships, to cost $11,000,000, passed by a majority of forty-one. During the same session a conservative cabal, outside Quebec, made Borden consider resignation. Meanwhile Laurier, touring the western provinces, was being heckled on his failure to redeem his promise of free trade. Now, it happened that in March 1910 the United States of America had offered the Canadian government better tariff relations. Early in 1911 the Canadian minister of finance divulged the famous reciprocity proposals. These were so close to what both parties had long sought that they seemed an overwhelming triumph for Laurier. But presently the banks, manufacturers, and railways began a crusade against them; indiscreet utterances of American public men set the Canadian heather afire; although the cabal against Borden was broken, there was a strong defection of liberals from the government. At the general election in September the conservatives won by a large majority, and Borden became prime minister: he held this position until his resignation, owing to ill health, in July 1920. The naval bill of 1912–1913, providing for an emergency contribution of capital ships to the British navy, was rejected by the Senate, still strongly liberal.

Borden has frequently been blamed for 'splitting' Canada, especially by his conscription measure during the war of 1914–1918. The wisdom of conscription in 1917 was certainly debatable in view of Canada's sudden industrialization, added to her great agricultural output. In the more perilous war of 1939–1945 a liberal government avoided it; but it may be doubted whether this latter course allayed sectional odium: certainly rioting in Quebec itself was not diminished. From Laurier's point of view it was an invitation to political suicide to decide upon conscription and then ask him to join a union government to enforce it. Nevertheless, Borden ran risks in forming in October a government equally divided, except for the premiership, between both parties. This government was given a mandate, in a general election, to proceed with conscription. If Borden erred, he erred with the large majority.

In view of the frequent unqualified statement that it was Borden who 'split' Canada it may be best to set forth here his own considered statement, made at the close of his days, and before the outbreak of war in 1939: 'The comparative failure of recruiting in Quebec was due, like most human events, to a variety of causes, and it would be difficult, in fact impossible, to assign to each cause its proportionate influence.

'The Canadian of French descent is essentially a most desirable and useful citizen. He is devout, industrious, hardworking and frugal, thoroughly devoted to his people and his province and deeply attached to his family, his friends and his neighbours. To leave them for military service beyond the seas, to cross the ocean in unknown adventure made no appeal and seemed undesirable and indeed desperate. Naturally his vision was not very wide and sometimes it did not extend far beyond the boundaries of his parish. He had an unbounded belief in the invincible power of Great Britain and regarded the co-operation of Canada as useless and futile as well as burdensome. It was no lack of courage that held back these people from enlistment. Those who went overseas proved themselves worthy of their descent from a fighting and heroic race.

'One might suppose that the savagery of German warfare against the French people would have aroused her kindred in Quebec, but the clergy had been alienated from their natural sympathy by confiscation of religious houses and property and by the growth of atheistic outlook and tendency in France. The Quebec peasant was sometimes told that the sufferings of the French people were just retribution for the unholy spoliation and humiliation of the Church in France.' [*Memoirs*, pp. 612–613.]

From 1763 onward the 'split' has been there. It was not just chance that Borden,

a native of Grand Pré, whence the French settlers, or Acadians, were expelled, failed, despite great efforts, to bridge the rift between Quebec and the rest of Canada. Quebec has dominated all Canadian life in war and peace. The French-Canadians—Laurier was a notable exception, and there have been thousands of other exceptions, among the less eminent—have adopted all the liberties and constitutional privileges won in the secular development in Great Britain, but have adopted them to their own purposes, showing little consciousness of the responsibility entailed. The legacy of modern France they have never acknowledged. Few patriotic men have been so little tainted with bigotry, religious or racial, as Borden, who loved the French, read their literature from an early age, and finally spoke their language fluently. He and Laurier respected one another highly.

It was Laurier's fortune, early in his premiership, to experience an 'Imperial' war in the southern hemisphere. The expediency and morality of that war were debated far more in Great Britain itself than in Canada. But it was not a war requiring a levy *en masse*, nor did it bring Britain's naval supremacy into question. It was Borden's fortune to be premier when a long expected war broke out, a war which threatened Britain's very existence, but which was fought largely on French soil, on behalf of the French people. If any war, short of the invasion of Quebec itself, could have united Canada it was the war of 1914–1918. Its failure to do so does not reflect on Borden's statesmanship. Indeed, few Canadians have so richly deserved the title of 'statesman' as did he; few Canadians have played so large a part in making Canada a nation, and for the consummation of unity in Canada no idle word of his will have to be forgotten, no mistaken action to be forgiven.

One marked characteristic merits an added word. Steady judgement and critical power are not common virtues, especially in public men. Borden was a critic and a courageous one. No one described more trenchantly than he the withering away of interest in education in his native province, or the general phlegmatic unconcern of Canadians about the evils of corruption, and the spoliation of the public domain. Generous with praise, putting the best construction on the motives of others, ready to work with men of every type for the common good, he yet recorded, even of men still living while he wrote, faults which made them dangerous. Sometimes he did not mince words, but the wickedest Canadian he met in high places was blasted with an understatement: 'untrustworthy'.

Borden attended the Imperial Conference of 1917. He was chief Canadian plenipotentiary at the Paris Peace Conference in 1919 and he represented Canada at the Washington Conference of 1921–1922 and Great Britain in the arbitration with Peru conducted in Paris in 1922. He also represented Canada on the Council of the League of Nations, and was chief Canadian delegate at the Assembly in 1930. He was the author of several books, including *Canadian Constitutional Studies* (1921), *Canada in the Commonwealth* (1929), and his *Memoirs* up to the year 1920 (published posthumously in 1938). He was sworn of the Privy Council in 1912 and appointed G.C.M.G. in 1914. His many academic and other distinctions included the chancellorship of McGill University (1918–1920) and of Queen's University, Kingston (1924–1929), and honorary degrees from numerous British and Canadian universities. He married in 1889 Laura (died 1940), youngest daughter of Thomas Henry Bond, of Halifax, and had no children. He died at Ottawa 10 June 1937.

There is a portrait of Borden by Dorothy Vicagi (1925) in the Law Courts, Halifax, Nova Scotia, and another, by John Macgillivray, is at Acadia University, Wolfville, Nova Scotia.

[*The Times*, 11 June 1937; *Robert Laird Borden, his Memoirs*, edited by H. Borden, 2 vols., 1938; O. D. Skelton, *Life and Letters of Sir Wilfrid Laurier* (New York), 1922; R. M. Dawson, *The Civil Service of Canada*, 1929; 'Borden and Canadian Nationhood' in *Canadian Forum*, July 1937; Hansard, *Parliamentary Debates*; personal knowledge.]

CARLETON STANLEY.

BOSANQUET, ROBERT CARR (1871–1935), archaeologist, was born 7 June 1871 in London where his father, Charles Bertie Pulleine Bosanquet, of Rock Hall, near Alnwick, the eldest brother of Bernard Bosanquet [q.v.], was then acting as honorary secretary to the recently formed Charity Organisation Society. His mother, Eliza Isabella, eldest daughter of Ralph Carr (afterwards Carr-Ellison), belonged to a well-known Northumbrian family, the Carrs of Dunston Hill, co. Durham, and Hedgeley, Northumberland. Robert was the elder son in a family of eight children.

After a brilliant career as a king's scholar at Eton, where he won the Newcastle scholarship, Bosanquet, as a scholar of Trinity College, Cambridge, attracted attention by his light verse, the felicities of which lived long in the memories of his contemporaries, and was awarded a first class in both parts of the classical tripos (1892 and 1894). As Craven student (1895–1897) he went to Greece and visited museums on the continent, following this with the excavation of Housesteads on the Roman Wall in 1898, the results of which he published in 'The Roman Camp at Housesteads' (*Archaeologia Æliana*, vol. xxv, 1904). These activities led to his being offered the post of assistant to Ernest Gardner [q.v.], then director of the British School of Archaeology in Athens, and in 1900 he himself became director. The next six years were spent almost entirely in Greek lands, developing the activities of the school in Athens and supervising its excavations on the islands of Melos (Phylakopi), Crete (Praesos and Palaikastro), and on the mainland of Greece (Sparta).

In 1905 the death of his father made it advisable for Bosanquet to live within reach of the Northumbrian estate to which he now succeeded. He therefore resigned the post at Athens and in 1906 he was appointed to the newly established chair of classical archaeology in the university of Liverpool. With congenial colleagues and generous financial backing an Institute of Archaeology was soon built up. Although Egypt, Greece, and Crete were the chief fields of research, a beginning was also made on the excavation of Roman sites in Wales, his appointment enabling him to spend one term in travel or excavation.

When, therefore, war broke out in 1914, Bosanquet was involved in a variety of interests, domestic and professional, and he had gained a European reputation. He at once put his knowledge of the Near East at the disposal of the War Office, but met with no response, and he was glad to be attached to that part of the Friends' Emergency Committee which was working for the defeated Serbs in Albania and Corfu. In July 1916 he was sent to Salonika as agent of the Serbian Relief Fund and remained there until his health broke down after attacks of malaria and enteric. For this mission and for his work in Greece he received the Serbian order of St. Sava and the Greek order of the Redeemer.

In 1920 Bosanquet resigned his chair at Liverpool and thenceforth until his death, which took place at Newcastle-upon-Tyne 21 April 1935, he lived at his Northumbrian home, Rock Moor, an adapted farmhouse on the estate, in a 'retirement' which never gave him the leisure which he needed to write the books on Roman trade routes and on the Covenanters in Northumberland for which he had collected material.

Bosanquet married in 1902 Ellen Sophia, third and youngest daughter of Thomas Hodgkin, the historian [q.v.], and had two sons and four daughters.

[Personal knowledge.]

E. S. Bosanquet.

BOTTOMLEY, HORATIO WILLIAM (1860–1933), journalist and financier, the only son of William King Bottomley, a tailor's foreman, and his wife, Elizabeth, daughter of George Holyoake, engineer, of Birmingham, and sister of George Jacob Holyoake [q.v.], was born in his father's house in Bethnal Green 23 March 1860. Sidney Theodore Felstead writes that some little time before he died, Bottomley told James Douglas that he was in fact though not in law the son of Charles Bradlaugh [q.v.] whom he strikingly resembled, but his birth certificate is reproduced by Henry James Houston, who describes him as deeply attached in earlier years to the memory of his father W. K. Bottomley. He lost both parents before he was five years old and was placed by his uncle G. J. Holyoake in the Sir Josiah Mason Orphanage at Erdington. He ran away at the age of fourteen, and after a year or two as an errand boy served in a London solicitor's office for five years and as a shorthand writer in the Supreme Court of Judicature for three further years; this, supplemented by Bradlaugh, who introduced him to the world of books, was the effective part of his education.

In 1880 Bottomley married Eliza, daughter of Samuel Norton, a debt-collector, of Battersea (where Bottomley was then living, whence they moved to the City, and then to Clapham where he was 'a pillar of the Methodist Church' and in private a virulent atheist. He entered the printing business and in 1884 started a small suburban weekly, the *Hackney Hansard*. Its success encouraged him to establish others of the same nature, and in 1889 he promoted the Hansard Publishing Union with a capital of £500,000. It failed in 1891 and left him bankrupt. He was charged with conspiracy to defraud and, stimulated by Bradlaugh's example,

he defended himself and was acquitted. Mr. Justice Hawkins (afterwards Lord Brampton, q.v.) who tried the case (January–April 1893) was so much impressed by Bottomley's conduct of it that he urged him to study law, but not obtaining admission to any Inn of Court, he plunged with surprising audacity into finance. He founded the Joint Stock Trust and Institute and floated a number of gold-mining companies (Associated Gold Mines of West Australia, Great Boulders Proprietary Gold Mines, West Australian Loan and Finance Corporation, etc.) and other enterprises (one appropriately called Nil Desperandum Mines) few of which paid the shareholders. In little over ten years he promoted nearly fifty companies with a total capital of over £20,000,000, and he says that his name 'constantly cropped up in the Courts', rarely with reverence. In five years (1901–1905) sixty-seven bankruptcy petitions and writs were filed against him. In 1897 his photograph appeared in a series of 'Men of Millions' in the *Financial Times*. It was estimated that he made £3,000,000 by promoting companies.

Bottomley's astonishing success made him equally reckless in venture and expenditure. He started a racing stable in 1898 and although he won the Cesarewitch, the Stewards' Cup, and other prizes of the turf, squandered very large sums on racing and gambling, theatrical adventures, newspaper enterprises, lawsuits, a very costly country house, The Dicker, at Hailsham in Sussex, a luxurious flat in Pall Mall, and a villa in France, all of which, together with lavish expenditure on travelling, entertaining, and gifts, absorbed most of his income. According to his secretary, their joint expenses on the journey to Brighton and back would amount to £25. Apart from finance, Bottomley was a journalist and speaker of great ability, and by these gifts alone could have made a very large income. He bought the *Sun* in 1898 and he founded *John Bull* with an expenditure of £96,000 (a large part of which was supplied by Ernest Terah Hooley) in 1906. When the *Sunday Pictorial* was established in 1915 he was engaged at £100 an article. He got this increased later, though he now employed others to write articles for him at one-fourth of his fee, and he sacrificed his position to found an illustrated weekly of his own which failed. He had no aptitude for the business management of a newspaper. He was elected liberal member for South Hackney in 1906; but his financial methods were now being gravely questioned, and in 1907 the shareholders of the Joint Stock Trust petitioned for the liquidation of the concern. The officials spent eighteen months in examining his books, the more important of which were missing, but when he was charged with fraud at the Guildhall in 1909 he secured an acquittal. His skill and wit in court drew crowds at all his cases and generally baffled leading counsel, but he lost a case in which Mrs. Curtis sued him for £50,000 which he had got from her aged father and lost his appeal.

By 1911 Bottomley's financial position was so desperate that he presented a petition in bankruptcy disclosing liabilities to the extent of £233,000 and £50,000 assets and in 1912 he applied for the Chiltern Hundreds. His country house and French villa were found to be in his wife's name, and he made large sums by organizing lotteries and sweepstakes on sporting events. The outbreak of war in 1914 gave him a new opportunity. He told friends that he would break with his 'sordid past' and his innumerable patriotic speeches (for each of which he got at least £50) and the articles in the *Sunday Pictorial* gave him a national reputation. His popularity stimulated again his financial audacity and in 1915 he began to organize the enterprises which eventually ruined him. He received subscriptions to the extent of nearly £900,000 and in 1918 he paid off his old creditors, was relieved from his bankruptcy, and again won his seat at South Hackney, this time as an independent, with a huge majority. But the very complicated affairs of his new enterprises were already arousing suspicion, and demands for repayment began to pour in. An associate with whom he quarrelled issued a very defamatory pamphlet and in the course of his action for criminal libel, in which he did not succeed, there were ominous revelations. When friends warned him he said that if there were any proposal to prosecute him, fifty thousand ex-servicemen would march on Westminster. Chancery appointed a receiver to examine his enterprises and in March 1922 he was charged at Bow Street with fraudulent conversion and was committed for trial. In May he was found guilty on twenty-three counts out of twenty-four and sentenced to seven years' penal servitude. On his appeal being rejected, he was formally expelled from the House of Commons in August. He was released in 1927, but all his confident efforts at rehabilitation, which included founding a new weekly, *John Blunt* (1928), failed, and his wife, who had always loyally supported him, died in 1930. He passed into want and obscurity, and died in London 26 May 1933. He had one daughter.

[*The Times*, 27 May 1933; *Bottomley's Book* (his autobiography), 1909; H. J. Houston, *The Real Horatio Bottomley*, 1923; S. T. Felstead, *Horatio Bottomley*, 1936; personal knowledge.]   E. S. P. HAYNES.

BOURNE, FRANCIS ALPHONSUS (1861–1935), cardinal, was born at Clapham 23 March 1861, the younger child and son of Henry Bourne, a principal clerk in the Post Office, by his wife, Ellen, daughter of John Byrne, a Dublin merchant. Religious interests dominated in their home. St. Cuthbert's College, Ushaw, near Durham, was the school chosen for the two brothers, but after the death in 1874 of the elder boy, Francis was removed in the following year to St. Edmund's College, Ware. After reading philosophy he went, in 1880, to St. Thomas's seminary at Hammersmith to begin his theological course, and thence to St. Sulpice in Paris. The training there had a marked influence on his spiritual development. He was a painstaking student though not marked by great depth of learning. In Paris he was ordained deacon by (Cardinal) Richard, archbishop of Paris, in 1883, and after some months spent at Louvain University, he received the priesthood at St. Mary's church, Clapham, in 1884.

After several brief curacies, Bourne went, in 1887, to West Grinstead, Sussex, where his work included some responsibility for the boys of an orphanage. He took a personal interest in his charges and gave Latin lessons to some who seemed likely to be suitable candidates for the priesthood. The bishop of Southwark, John Butt, had decided to found a college for the training of his future clergy, but had difficulty in finding suitable teachers. Bourne was recommended to him as one interested in fostering vocations among boys, and the bishop opened a house of studies at Henfield Place, Sussex, in 1889 and put Bourne in charge. He took with him a few of the boys whom he had begun to teach at West Grinstead. Meanwhile a permanent college was being built at Wonersh, near Guildford. In 1891 the Henfield school was transferred there and Bourne became the first rector of the new diocesan seminary. He was appointed a domestic prelate to Pope Leo XIII at Easter 1895.

Bishop Butt was in failing health and petitioned the Holy See for a coadjutor with the right of succession to the bishopric of Southwark. Bourne, his nominee, was consecrated titular bishop of Epiphania by Herbert Cardinal Vaughan [q.v.] in 1896. He was thirty-five years of age and quite unknown to the diocesan clergy. He remained at Wonersh as rector while assisting in the episcopal oversight of the diocese. Within a year Butt resigned and Bourne succeeded him. This necessitated his residence in south London where the work of the large parishes was new to him. Although shy and reserved, he gave himself entirely to his many new tasks with much success.

In August 1903, while still the youngest bishop on the bench, Bourne was translated to the archiepiscopal see of Westminster in succession to Cardinal Vaughan. There he had to deal with larger problems, for he was now leader of the Roman Catholic bishops of England and Wales, Westminster until 1911 being the only archiepiscopal see of the Roman Catholic Church in this country. His new duties brought him into contact with various government departments and he had to represent the Holy See in its relations with the British government when Roman Catholic interests within the Empire were at issue. Westminster Cathedral was not yet open for divine service and Bourne was not enthroned until December 1903.

The education question loomed large throughout Bourne's episcopate and caused him much anxiety. Some measure of justice had been done to the voluntary schools by the Balfour Act of 1902, but the liberal government of 1906 was pledged to important changes. Bourne's steady leadership saved the voluntary schools for forty years.

In September 1908 the International Eucharistic Congress was held at Westminster and its great success was due to the organizing ability of the archbishop. June 1910 saw the consecration of Westminster Cathedral.

Bourne was created cardinal priest with the titular church of Santa Pudenziana at the consistory of November 1911. He was twice legate of the pope, in May 1931 at Rouen for the Joan of Arc celebrations, and at the consecration of Buckfast Abbey church in August 1932.

A man of prayer and of deep spirituality, Bourne's conception of the episcopal office was very high. He was a great pastor. No orator, his straightforward utterances were everywhere received with respect. His only published work, apart from sermons and pastoral letters, was his book *Ecclesiastical Training* (1926). He received honorary degrees from the universities of Louvain and Oxford.

After occupying the see for over thirty-one years Bourne died at Westminster 1 January 1935 and was buried at St. Edmund's College, Ware. He had a great love for the college, where part of his studies had been made and where the Westminster clergy are trained. His benefactions to it were of princely munificence and he may well be called its second founder.

A portrait of Bourne, by A. Chevallier Tayler (1934), is at Archbishop's House, Westminster.

[Ernest Oldmeadow, *Francis, Cardinal Bourne*, 2 vols., 1940–1944; personal knowledge.]   W. J. WOOD.

BOURNE, GILBERT CHARLES (1861–1933), zoologist and oarsman, was born at Grafton Manor, Worcestershire, 5 July 1861, the second son of Lieutenant-Colonel Robert Bourne, 54th Regiment, of Cowarne Court, near Ledbury, by his wife, Anna Eliza, youngest daughter of Samuel Baker, of Lypiatt Park, Gloucestershire. He was educated at Eton and at New College, Oxford, where he gained an exhibition in natural science. He rowed in the winning university crews of 1881 and 1882. While still an undergraduate he studied at Freiburg-im-Breisgau under August Weismann. On his return to Oxford he obtained a first class in natural science in 1885. After making a scientific study of the atoll of Diego Garcia, in the Indian Ocean, he was elected to a fellowship at New College in 1887. Shortly afterwards he acted for two years as the first director of the Marine Biological Laboratory at Plymouth. He returned to Oxford and in 1906 was elected to the Linacre chair of zoology and comparative anatomy with a fellowship at Merton College, both of which he held until 1921, when he succeeded to his father's property in Herefordshire.

Bourne's early researches in Diego Garcia were concerned with the origin of coral reefs. He attributed the formation of atolls in the Indian Ocean to the rapid growth of corals round the edges of submerged banks. He denied Darwin's theory of reef-formation by subsidence, and considered that the lagoon within an atoll was present from the time when the growing coral first reached the surface in a ring. Bourne's later zoological interests were largely determined by his visit to Diego Garcia. He made important studies on the structure, development, and classification of corals and related animals, and much of his work in this field has passed into the text-books. He also made detailed morphological studies of certain groups of mollusca. Although in later years his researches were mainly in morphology, yet his interests remained wide. He entered into the preformation-epigenesis controversy and wrote two articles of lasting value in defence of the cell-theory against the attack of Adam Sedgwick [q.v.]. His *Introduction to the Study of the Comparative Anatomy of Animals* (1900–1902) provided a fresh and readable approach to a subject that is often drily presented. He was a contributor to the *Treatise on Zoology* (1900–1909) by (Sir) E. R. Lankester [q.v.]. His writing was crisp, vigorous, and scholarly, and the illustrations to his morphological papers show considerable artistic ability. He was a stimulating teacher, and some of those who studied under him passed on to particularly successful careers in zoology. He served as a member of the advisory committee on fisheries of the development commission, and in 1931 was appointed chairman. He was elected F.R.S. in 1910.

Apart from his scientific pursuits, Bourne devoted much time to boats and oarsmanship. He was an outstanding figure in the rowing world as an oarsman and subsequently as an expounder of the theory and practice both of oarsmanship and the design of racing boats. He had imbibed at Eton the principles of Edmond Warre [q.v.], the founder of the orthodox style of rowing, but it is as a coach that he achieved renown. To his teaching of the correct method of applying muscular power is to be attributed the high position held by his college on the river for some fifty years, and many university crews owed much to his coaching in the early days of their training. His *Text Book on Oarsmanship* (1925), a masterpiece of careful detail, was compiled with the help of mechanical experts and mathematicians who worked out innumerable experiments for him. By developing Warre's theories on the lines of racing eights, and from his own observations of the streamlines of fish, he considered that the racing boat should have its greatest beam and draught much

farther forward than was usual, so that the waves thrown off by the boat's entry into the water met exactly at the stern. This would eliminate any suction to impede the boat's progress, and undue friction on its sides. The main features of his design are now adopted by several designers of racing eights.

Always a keen soldier, Bourne rose to be second in command of the 4th battalion of the King's Shropshire Light Infantry during the South African war. He represented the university of Oxford on the committee appointed by the War Office in 1906 to consider the provision of an Officers' Training Corps, which proved of the greatest value on the outbreak of war in 1914. In that war he was appointed superintending officer of the young officers' company of the 12th Reserve Infantry Brigade.

Bourne married in 1887 Constance Margaret Graham, eldest daughter of Sir John Frederick Croft, second baronet, of Dodington Place, Kent, and had a son, Robert Croft Bourne [q.v.], and a daughter. He died at Tubney Warren House, near Abingdon, 9 March 1933.

[*The Times*, 10 March 1933; G. C. Bourne, *Memories of an Eton Wet Bob of the Seventies*, 1933; *Obituary Notices of Fellows of the Royal Society*, No. 2, December 1933 (portrait); private information; personal knowledge.]

JOHN R. BAKER.
C. M. PITMAN.

BOURNE, ROBERT CROFT (1888–1938), politician and oarsman, was born at Dodington Place, Kent, 15 July 1888, the only son of Gilbert Charles Bourne [q.v.]. At Eton he rowed in the eights of 1906 and 1907; at New College, Oxford, where he obtained a second class in modern history (1911), his chief renown was gained on the river, as he was the first stroke of a university crew to win the boat race in four successive years. In April 1909, at the end of his third term, Bourne confounded the riverside critics by winning the race with a spurt which revealed at once his powers of leadership, his immense reach, and his nice sense of rhythm. His last university race (1912) became famous by both boats being swamped in the prevailing hurricane, and was called off when Oxford, who at the Meadows were overcome by the fate that had befallen Cambridge at Harrod's, were given unsolicited help by over-zealous spectators. The race was decided two days later. At Henley Bourne won the Stewards' Cup three times

(1912–1914) and in 1912 stroked his college crew in the final of the Olympic regatta at Stockholm.

After being called to the bar by Lincoln's Inn (1913), Bourne went in 1915 with his territorial battalion of the Herefordshire regiment to the Mediterranean and had one hand crippled and a lung seriously injured at Suvla Bay in August. Further active service being impossible (he had also while at school lost the sight of one eye when playing rounders during the summer holidays) Bourne, now a captain, served on the Claims Commission (1917) and on the Herefordshire County Council (1922). In 1923 he contested Oxford City as a conservative, and, on his opponent being unseated on petition, was returned at the resultant by-election (1924). He retained the seat until his death. In the House of Commons, where he rose to be deputy chairman of ways and means (1931), Bourne's name was canvassed as a possible Speaker, for, although on the platform he filled his speeches with too much information for a popular audience, he earned the respect of all parties by his mastery of the rules of procedure, the clearness and quickness of his rulings, his skill as a draftsman, and, above all, by that same strict impartiality which had secured for him as president of the Oxford University Boat Club the complete confidence of his fellow oarsmen in the justice of his choices when making up his crews. He was sworn of the Privy Council in 1935. On 7 August 1938, while walking on the moors near Strontian, Argyll, he suddenly fell dead.

Bourne married in 1917 Lady Hester Margaret, eldest daughter of Wilfrid Dallas Cairns, fourth Earl Cairns, and had two sons and one daughter who all survived him.

A cartoon of Bourne by 'Ape Junior' appeared in *Vanity Fair* 29 March 1911.

[*The Times*, 9 August 1938 ; private information ; personal knowledge.]

L. G. WICKHAM LEGG.

BOYCOTT, ARTHUR EDWIN (1877–1938), pathologist and naturalist, was born at Hereford 6 April 1877, the third son of William Boycott, solicitor, by his wife, Eliza Mellard. He was educated at Hereford Cathedral School, and gained a classical scholarship at Oriel College, Oxford, where, however, he read natural science, being awarded a first class in physiology in 1898. After election to a senior demyship at Magdalen in 1900, he completed his medical training at St. Thomas's Hospital in 1902. In the last-named year he was elected to one of the last prize fellowships at Brasenose. The influence of three of his Oxford teachers, Sir J. S. Burdon-Sanderson [q.v.], J. S. Haldane [q.v.], and James Ritchie, fellow of New College, later first professor of bacteriology at Edinburgh University, never left him.

Shortly after qualifying B.M. in 1902 Boycott assisted Haldane in an inquiry into hookworm disease among Cornish miners (the subject of his Milroy lectures to the Royal College of Physicians in 1911), and later joined him in his investigations into the physiological effects of compressed and rarefied atmospheres. Between 1904, when he graduated D.M., and 1907 he was on the staff of the Lister Institute and published papers on the bacteriology of diphtheria and of the paratyphoid fevers. In 1907 he returned to Guy's Hospital (where he had been for a short time in 1903–1904) as Gordon lecturer in pathology and there began a series of investigations on the physiology and pathology of the blood which continued intermittently until his retirement. Independently, and with Dr. Claude Gordon Douglas, he studied the blood volume and its response to changes in environment and to disease. In later life he used to say that the experiment which had pleased him most was the demonstration that the rate of blood regeneration after haemorrhage was in inverse proportion to the size of the animal. He returned to this subject many years later and showed that oxygen tension was the factor controlling haematopoiesis. It was on the basis of these and related observations that he postulated the 'erythron', the circulating blood and haematopoietic tissues considered as a single organ. In 1912 he was appointed professor of pathology in the university of Manchester and there he continued the work begun earlier on the function of the kidney in controlling the volume and composition of the blood. The war of 1914–1918 coincided with his appointment, in 1915, to the Graham chair of pathology in the university of London, which is held at University College Hospital. After serving on the Health of Munition Workers Committee he was commissioned in the Royal Army Medical Corps to work at the Chemical Warfare Experimental Station at Porton. He co-operated with (Sir) Joseph Barcroft and others in extensive experiments on the physiological action of toxic gases, but it was for him, a pacificist by conviction, a most unhappy time. After the war he returned to University College Hospital where he spent the remainder of his working life; he retired, owing to ill health, in 1935. In his later years he published some addresses of a speculative nature which gave an accurate picture of his width of interest and originality of inquiry.

Pathology was half of Boycott's life; natural history, conchology in particular, was the other. At the age of fifteen he published a catalogue of Herefordshire mollusca and until his death his chief recreation was the oecology of British land and freshwater snails, on which he published numerous papers. An offshoot of this interest was an inquiry into the genetics of left-handed twist in the shell of *Lymnaea peregra* which occupied several years and involved breeding over one million snails.

Boycott was elected F.R.S. in 1914 and F.R.C.P. in 1926. In 1924 McGill University conferred upon him the honorary degree of LL.D. For fifteen years he was assistant editor and for eleven editor of the *Journal of Pathology and Bacteriology*. He was fluent and lucid as a writer and speaker but he was not a magnetic teacher of undergraduates and had little influence on current medical practice. Apart from his contributions to knowledge his desire that pathology should be recognized as a science in its own right found expression in the *Journal* which he edited for so long and in the work of his pupils and close associates. He enjoyed well-mannered controversy but was a man of firm convictions and some odd prejudices.

Boycott married in 1904 Constance Louisa, daughter of Colonel William Agg, of the (51st) King's Own Yorkshire Light Infantry, of Prestbury, near Cheltenham, and had two sons. He died at Ewen, Cirencester, 12 May 1938.

[*The Times*, 18 May 1938; *Obituary Notices of Fellows of the Royal Society*, No. 7, January 1939 (portrait); *British Medical Journal*, 1938, vol. i, p. 1133 (portrait); *Journal of Pathology and Bacteriology*, vol. xlvii, 1938 (bibliography); private information; personal knowledge.]   J. A. BOYCOTT.

BRADFORD, SIR JOHN ROSE, baronet, of Mawddwy (1863–1935), physician and physiologist, was born in London 7 May 1863, the only son of Abraham Rose Bradford, by his wife, Ellen, daughter of Nicholas Littleton. Both parents came from Saltash, near Plymouth, where Littletons had for generations been general practitioners in the neighbourhood; Abraham Bradford was a surgeon in the navy, finally attaining the rank of deputy inspector-general of hospitals.

Bradford was educated at University College School, London, and after a year spent at Bruges in learning French, he entered University College in 1881 as a medical student with an exhibition and began the close association with the college and hospital which lasted unbroken until his death. Here he met the inspiring teaching of (Sir) E. R. Lankester [q.v.], in zoology, in which he gained a first class in 1883 when he graduated B.Sc. The subject fascinated him; to the end of his life he was a nature lover, and he would have preferred to continue that study had not lack of means compelled him to adhere to his original choice of medicine as a securer way to livelihood. Gold medals in anatomy and physiology in 1884 were followed in 1889 by the gold medal in medicine when he proceeded M.D. (Lond.). But time was also seized for laboratory research, and in 1885 (Sir) William Bayliss [q.v.] and he, young men of twenty-five and twenty-two respectively, published in the *Proceedings* of the Royal Society the first of a series of excellent papers on the electrical changes accompanying nervous stimulation of the salivary glands.

Allowing for a brief period of residence in 1886 as house physician, teaching in anatomy and research in physiology continued to be Bradford's main occupation until 1889 when he was appointed to the staff of University College Hospital as assistant physician, with (Sir) Henry Head [q.v.] as his first clinical clerk. Thenceforward he gave first place to his clinical duties, and even sought special acquaintance with nervous diseases by joining the staff of the National Hospital for Diseases of the Nervous System, Queen Square, as assistant physician from 1893 to 1896. But still he continued to press forward eagerly with fundamental researches in physiology that had no immediate reference to clinical problems, and freedom to do so was given him by his success in obtaining certain research studentships, rareties at that time in London. Starting from the great scheme of the anatomical distribution of spinal nerves to viscera that had been unfolded in the illuminating paper of W. H. Gaskell [q.v.], in 1886, Bradford sought to analyse in precise detail the physiology of this nervous supply. He began with the innervation of the blood-vessels of the lungs, and then passed to those of the kidneys. But he was soon outpaced by J. N. Langley [q.v.], who had also taken Gaskell's field for experimental study and, in advance on the routine methods of nerve stimulation, could also use his own discovery of the power of nicotine to paralyse and thus identify ganglion cells on the paths of the visceral nerves.

Bradford now moved towards pathology and began a laborious study on dogs of the general changes caused by removal of a portion of the kidney substance. This was designed to answer some of the questions arising from clinical experience in man; it focused his attention on kidney diseases, and in that branch of medicine he was thenceforward recognized as an authority. As professor-superintendent of the Brown Animal Institution from 1895 to 1903 he carried on the great tradition of Sir Victor Horsley [q.v.] and (Sir) Charles Sherrington. The high quality of Bradford's physiological studies led to his election in 1894 as F.R.S. at the early age of thirty-one. He was elected F.R.C.P. in 1897, and delivered the Goulstonian lecture in 1898, the Croonian lectures in 1904, and the Harveian oration in 1926.

In 1900 Bradford became full physician with charge of wards at University College Hospital, and soon afterwards he ceased all sustained research. It was not that he sought time to secure the rewards of consulting practice, for after his marriage he no longer needed them, but he now seemed to prefer to devote himself to teaching duties and especially to the advance of scientific thought in medicine through work by other hands than his own. In both of these directions his influence was of high importance for British medicine. He served on his hospital staff until 1923, and was one of the greatest clinical teachers in the history of that distinguished school. His formal lectures, delivered with never a note or illustrative diagram, had that perfection of clarity and emphasis which makes an audience understand as well as remember. He always sought to make men think, and think with scientific exactitude resting on observed facts. In the wards there was no overbearing dogma, but rather an encouraging comradeship in the way in which he would seek to help his students. On one principle he stood firmly, that while medicine needed all possible aid from such ancillary sciences

as physiology or pathology, nothing could be accepted from animal experiments except by analogy: in the last resort clinical science could only rest on what was proved to occur in man himself. That point of view was not commonly held either by clinicians or scientific workers of his period in medicine.

Friendship with (Sir) David Bruce [q.v.] aroused Bradford's interest in tropical medicine, and he sought clinical experience in that direction by serving as physician at the Seamen's Hospital at Greenwich from 1905 to 1919. In 1907 he became a member of the tropical diseases committee of the Royal Society, and in 1908 he was foremost in planning the Sleeping Sickness Bureau which developed into the Tropical Diseases Bureau of the London School of Tropical Medicine. He was senior medical adviser to the Colonial Office from 1912 to 1924.

In the Royal Society itself Bradford had the rare distinction of serving from 1908 to 1915 as secretary on the biological side, a post that had not been entrusted to a practising physician for over eighty years. This enabled him to advance still further the relationship of the society with government departments, especially with regard to the study of tropical diseases. He was on the governing body of the Lister Institute from 1899 to 1918 and chairman from 1912 to 1914, and the creation of the Beit Trust for fellowships in medical research in 1909 was entirely due to the guidance of Bradford and (Sir) James Kingston Fowler [q.v.].

On the outbreak of war Bradford relinquished all his interests in London and served in France from 1914 to 1919 as consulting physician to the British Expeditionary Force, with the rank of major-general, Army Medical Service, being appointed C.B. in 1915 and C.B.E. in 1919. Towards the end of that time he attempted a bacteriological study of some of the non-suppurative diseases prevalent in the army, and published his belief that his laboratory colleagues and he had discovered the viruses of trench fever, nephritis, and influenza. Faulty technique was soon proved to have spoiled the observations. This was the only error in all Bradford's scientific work; he felt it deeply.

Returning to London, Bradford no longer took a chief part in the projects for the advancement of medical research. But his authority among clinicians was confirmed by his election as president of the Royal College of Physicians (1926–1931) and it was a happy turn of fortune that in 1928 one with his true reverence for science conducted the College celebrations of the tercentenary of the publication of Harvey's *De Motu Cordis*. He was vice-chairman of the governing body of University College, London, from 1922 to 1932, and chairman in 1932. He was appointed K.C.M.G. in 1911 and created a baronet in 1931. The universities of Cambridge, Edinburgh, Durham, Dublin, and Christiania conferred honorary degrees upon him. In 1924 he unsuccessfully contested the parliamentary seat of the university of London.

Tall and austerely erect, with an air of authority in his approach, Bradford was surprisingly found to be a man of the warmest human feelings and ready accessibility. Organization was easy to him, for he united a most retentive memory with a clear judgement, and was not lightly swayed when once his resolution was formed.

In 1899 Bradford married Mary (died 1937), daughter of Thomas Ffoulkes Roberts, of Llanidloes, Montgomeryshire, sometime mayor of Manchester, and niece of the physician Sir William Roberts [q.v.]; there was no issue of the marriage. He died in London 7 April 1935.

A posthumous portrait of Bradford, by Randolph Schwabe, is in the library of University College Hospital medical school.

[*The Times*, 8 April 1935; *Obituary Notices of Fellows of the Royal Society*, No. 4, December 1935 (portrait); *British Medical Journal*, 1935, vol. i, p. 805; *Lancet*, 1935, vol. i, p. 906; personal knowledge.]   T. R. ELLIOTT.

BRADLEY, ANDREW CECIL (1851–1935), literary critic, was born at Cheltenham 26 March 1851, the fourth and youngest son of Charles Bradley [q.v.], vicar of Glasbury, Brecknockshire, and incumbent of St. James's chapel, Clapham, by his second wife, Emma, daughter of John Linton, stockbroker, of Clapham. His father, of Yorkshire stock on both sides, was a distinguished cleric and notable preacher. Andrew Bradley was a younger brother of F. H. Bradley [q.v.], and a half-brother of G. G. Bradley [q.v.], who was in succession (head) master of Marlborough, master of University College, Oxford, and dean of Westminster.

Bradley was educated at Cheltenham College, and in 1869 went up to Balliol College, Oxford, as a classical exhibitioner. He was awarded a second class in classical moderations in 1871, but he followed this up with an excellent first class in *literae humaniores* in 1873. In 1874 he was elected to a fellowship at Balliol, and in 1875 won the chancellor's English essay prize for an essay on 'Utopias, Ancient and Modern'. Next year he was appointed a lecturer of the college, at first in English, and then, until 1881, in philosophy. In this work he was in close contact with T. H. Green [q.v.], and, like all who came within the orbit of that wise and selfless teacher and had the temper to estimate him rightly, Bradley was deeply influenced. The Balliol of those days, under Jowett in his prime, was a brilliant and stimulating college, but the stimulus was perhaps at times a little feverish, and the atmosphere not wholly congenial to all, even among the ablest, of its members.

In 1882 Bradley became the first occupant of the chair of literature and history at University College, Liverpool, and threw himself with ardour into a new and very busy life, grasping eagerly the rich opportunities which it offered, especially those of sharing with men and women whose lines had been cast in less pleasant places all that his own life and education had given him. On his evening classes and everything that had to do with adult education he spent himself unsparingly, and his lectures, on the testimony of many who heard them, were a revelation. To this period of his life belong his edition of T. H. Green's *Prolegomena to Ethics* (1883), with an analysis, and his *Commentary on Tennyson's 'In Memoriam'*, which, although not published until 1901, was an expansion of lectures delivered to one of his evening classes at Liverpool.

After eight strenuous years at Liverpool Bradley was elected to the chair of English language and literature at Glasgow University, where, as a Glasgow student wrote, his 'brilliant dark eyes lighting up his pale black-bearded face and a voice that matched it in gentle sweetness, not less than his great intellectual gifts, gave him quite an unusual sway over the minds of his students'. In 1897 he edited, with a biographical sketch, the first volume of the *Philosophical Lectures and Remains* of R. L. Nettleship [q.v.]. In 1900 he retired to London, proposing to devote himself to his critical work in a leisure which his two professorships had precluded. But in 1901 he was elected to the professorship of poetry at Oxford, and to that election we owe, at least in part, one of the great works of English criticism. Bradley was in the full maturity of his powers, and doubtless *Shakespearean Tragedy* (1904) would have been a notable work under whatever conditions it had been written. But the professorship of poetry, light though its duties are if computed by the number of lectures that must be delivered, none the less imposes the duty of lecturing, and *Shakespearean Tragedy*, if written purely to be read, would have been a different work. Bradley needed precisely the stimulus of exposition before a living audience to put the last fine edge on his work. He was always a philosopher as well as a literary critic, and subtle intellectual distinctions were to him a delight, sometimes a temptation. But the challenge of an audience which was to be convinced by the spoken, not the written, word evoked from him the subtle persuasiveness of the orator, and enforced that limpid, relentless clarity of presentation in which he had no rival.

Re-election to the chair of poetry in 1906 was, to the general regret, statutorily impossible. He was offered the new King Edward VII chair of English literature at Cambridge, but declined it, and devoted the rest of his life to quiet work in London, with holidays spent among his beloved Alps, which were one of the passions of his life. In 1907 and 1908 he delivered two courses of Gifford lectures at Glasgow University, the former of which was published posthumously in 1940 as *Ideals of Religion*. In 1929 he published his *Miscellany*, from which, in spite of one brilliant paper on Tennyson, the fire had noticeably departed. He died, unmarried, in London 2 September 1935. He received honorary degrees from the universities of Glasgow, Edinburgh, Liverpool, and Durham, and was elected a fellow of the British Academy in 1907. At Balliol College, of which he was elected an honorary fellow in 1912, he founded by his will a research fellowship, the aim of which is characteristic of his wisdom and his humanity. Looking back at his own career, he determined to secure for at least a few young men, who might later have some contribution to make to English letters, two or three unhurried years immediately after graduation in which to find themselves, and not be rushed by economic pressure into posts which might be unsuitable, and which, even if academic, were likely, through pressure of administrative and tutorial routine, to cramp their development. He took a prominent part in the creation in 1906 of the English

Association, of which he was president in 1911.

Bradley was one of the greatest of the English critics of Shakespeare, possibly the greatest. Even those who disapprove alike of his aims and of his methods reluctantly admit his stature, and his position is secure, above the shifting currents of critical fashion. But it was criticism of Shakespeare alone that showed him at his best. As a critic of other writers he was workmanlike, penetrating, and often illuminating. It needed an outstanding artist and a full man to elicit the deepest powers of his keen mind and human heart. It is significant that in *Oxford Lectures on Poetry* (1909), together with a number of other pieces of able criticism, there are three lectures on Shakespeare which are of a different calibre and temper from the rest. One of them indeed, that on *Antony and Cleopatra*, is perhaps his crowning achievement.

Bradley never forgot that Shakespeare was a brilliantly successful Elizabethan playwright. But he also never forgot, as some modern criticism is apt to forget, that he was a man of the most comprehensive soul who put into his plays far more than was needed for his 'fellows' and Burbage to make a resounding box-office success. To censure Bradley for 'finding in Shakespeare what Shakespeare never meant' is to mistake the way in which a great creative artist works. Of course Shakespeare put into his greater plays more than was needed for the two hours' traffic of the stage and the suffrages of the contemporary public. He put it there because he was Shakespeare, creating men and women, not marionettes. And it was with this overplus that Bradley was largely concerned. In the perhaps unexpected company of Johnson he felt Shakespeare's characters to be human beings with an existence of their own, and was eager to show Hamlet or Macbeth or Othello in his habit as he lived, not merely as he postured for the groundlings. The test of Bradley's method is the purely pragmatical test that it works, as with a more mechanical artist than Shakespeare it would not work. Of all English critics of Shakespeare he is the surest expositor of the 'supererogatory' Shakespeare, of all that makes Shakespeare one of the supreme interpreters of the human soul.

Bradley always based his criticism on a precise and exhaustive knowledge of the text, so that even when a reader disagrees with the conclusions he cannot deny the premisses. His method is the Socratic method, 'let us see where the *logos* leads us'. The manner in which he presented his conclusions was, it may be supposed, inherited from his father. Like his father's sermons, Bradley's lectures are marked by 'singular simplicity and force, and sustained dignity and purity of language'. Every now and then he rises to greater heights. The last paragraph of his lecture on *Antony and Cleopatra* (even though it contains an odd geographical blunder) has a fire and a secure complication of cadence that should ensure its inclusion in any anthology of English prose.

There is a portrait of Bradley, by George Henry, in Glasgow University.

[*The Times*, 4 September 1935; J. W. Mackail, *Andrew Cecil Bradley, 1851–1935* in *Proceedings* of the British Academy, vol. xxi, 1935; J. W. Mackail in *Oxford Magazine*, 17 October 1935; personal knowledge.]

M. Roy Ridley.

BRAMWELL, Sir BYROM (1847–1931), physician, was born at North Shields 18 December 1847, the eldest son of John Byrom Bramwell, M.D., by his wife, Mary Young. At the age of eleven he was sent to Cheltenham College, where he spent seven years. On leaving school in 1865 he went to Edinburgh University, in order to study medicine, and there boarded for some time with William Stewart, the author of *The Practical Angler*, whose name has become even more familiar as the inventor of Stewart tackle. To Stewart, no doubt, he owed some of his skill as a fisherman. This hobby was destined to become his chief recreation during the busy years of his professional life. At Edinburgh he graduated with honours in 1869, and captained the university cricket eleven.

After serving his time as house surgeon to James Spence [q.v.], in 1870 Bramwell refused the appointment of assistant to the professor of medicine as he felt it his duty to return to North Shields to assist his father, who was in poor health, in a busy general practice.

When only twenty-five years of age Bramwell was appointed lecturer in medical jurisprudence at University College, Durham, and in 1877 was awarded a gold medal for his thesis for the degree of M.D. In 1874 he went to live in Newcastle-upon-Tyne, having been appointed physician and pathologist to the Newcastle Royal Infirmary, and having started practice as a consulting physician. Five years later he resigned his appointments in Newcastle on going to Edinburgh, where he was the first physician to start practice as a pure consultant. These early years in Edinburgh were an uphill struggle. Edinburgh was then very conservative, and it was quite contrary to tradition for an Englishman to migrate and settle in practice north of the Tweed. In his first twelve months his total income from consulting practice amounted to but five guineas, but this very fact was partly responsible for his subsequent success, since it gave him ample time for study and writing. In 1879 he gave his first course of lectures on medicine at the Extra-mural School. In 1882 he was appointed pathologist, in 1885 assistant physician, and in 1897 physician, to the Edinburgh Royal Infirmary, where his clinic became one of the most popular in the medical school. He retired in 1912. Amongst therapeutic experiments for which he was responsible were the use of arsenic in pernicious anaemia, massive doses of iron in anaemia, and thyroid in psoriasis.

During these strenuous years Bramwell's pen was never idle. In addition to some 160 scientific papers he wrote several books on different branches of medicine, of which that on *Diseases of the Spinal Cord* (1881) was translated into German, French, and Russian, while several editions were published in the United States of America. His books on *Diseases of the Heart and Thoracic Aorta* (1884), *Intracranial Tumours* (1888), and *Anaemia and some of the Diseases of the Blood-forming Organs and Ductless Glands* (1899) were widely read at the time, and his *Atlas of Clinical Medicine* (3 vols., 1892–1896) contains many beautiful coloured lithographic illustrations. *Clinical Studies*, published in eight volumes from 1903 to 1910, approached the subject from an original aspect, and their vitality gained for them a wide popularity throughout the English-speaking world.

The universities of Edinburgh, St. Andrews, Birmingham, and Durham conferred honorary degrees upon Bramwell. He was elected F.R.S. (Edin.) in 1886. In 1910 he was elected president of the Royal College of Physicians of Edinburgh, of which he had been a fellow since 1880, and in 1923 president of the Association of Physicians of Great Britain and Ireland. He was elected F.R.C.P. (London) in 1923 and was knighted in 1924 for his services to medicine. He was a foreign corresponding member of the Neurological Society of Paris and of the German and Philadelphia Neurological clubs.

Bramwell was a man of robust physique and boundless energy, a clear thinker with a flair for sifting evidence, picking out the important facts, and discarding those which were irrelevant. These gifts rendered him a born diagnostician and a brilliant clinical teacher, one who became outstanding even in the Edinburgh school. A keen athlete in his youth, and an expert trout fisherman, in the autumn of his life he enjoyed nothing better than watching cricket at Lords or an international Rugby match at Murrayfield. Although he did not suffer fools gladly, he inspired admiration and affection in his subordinates, some of whom later attained considerable eminence in the profession. Their visits to his home in Edinburgh were always a joy to him.

In 1872 Bramwell married his second cousin, Martha (died 1919), only child of Edwin Crighton, of North Shields, to whose lifelong unselfish devotion and able support he owed much of his success in the years to come. They had three sons and two daughters, the younger of whom predeceased her father. Clear in mind to the very end, the closing years of a full and happy life were absorbed by interest in his children and grandchildren, to whom he was intensely devoted. He died in Edinburgh 27 April 1931.

Bramwell was presented in 1923 with his portrait, by David Alison, which hangs in the hall of the Royal College of Physicians of Edinburgh.

[*The Times*, 28 April 1931; *Proceedings* of the Royal Society of Edinburgh, 1930–1931, vol. li, p. 224; *British Medical Journal*, 1931, vol. i, p. 823 (portrait); *Lancet*, 1931, vol. i, pp. 1057 and 1108 (portrait); private information; personal knowledge.]

J. CRIGHTON BRAMWELL.

BRENNAN, LOUIS (1852–1932), mechanical engineer, the son of Thomas Brennan, by his wife, Bridget McDonnell, was born (according to his own statement) at Castlebar, co. Mayo, 28 January 1852 where he was christened Luis 2 April 1852. While still a boy he was taken to Australia, and it was when he was living in Melbourne as a watchmaker that he devised the dirigible torpedo for coast defence for which his name is chiefly known.

The invention was brought to the notice of the British government in 1880 by Commodore J. C. Wilson, and Brennan was invited to come to England. He was provided with facilities on the Medway for the development of the weapon, re-ceiving an annual grant of £1,000 with a preliminary award of £5,000. In 1885 the torpedo was adopted by the government, which a year or two later purchased the exclusive rights for over £100,000. This figure was criticized as being excessive, but the commission which recommended the payment justified it on the ground that it was important not to allow the device to pass into the hands of other countries. In 1887 Brennan was appointed superintendent of the government factory at Gillingham, Kent, established for the manufacture of the torpedo, and held that position until 1896, subsequently acting, until 1907, as consulting engineer. His torpedo had two screws, revolving in opposite directions, and drums mounted on each propeller shaft were wound with wires the ends of which were connected with a high-speed engine on shore. Steering was effected by varying the rate at which the wires were unwound from one or other of the drums by the engine, so varying the relative speed of rotation of the screws.

After the torpedo Brennan turned his attention to a monorail system of transport which depended on the use of self-propelled vehicles travelling on a single rail, or even a tightly stretched cable, and maintained upright by a high-speed gyrostat rotating in a vacuum. He showed a model of this arrangement at a conversazione of the Royal Society in 1907 and later carried out trials with full-scale equipment, but the system did not come into practical use.

During the war of 1914–1918 Brennan was employed in the munitions inventions department of the Ministry of Munitions, and from 1919 to 1926 he worked for the Air Ministry at the Royal Aircraft Establishment, Farnborough, on the development of helicopter flying machines. He was appointed C.B. in 1892 and elected an honorary member of the Royal Engineers' Institute in 1906, and he was a founder member of the National Academy of Ireland (1922). He married in 1892 Anna Mary (died 1931), daughter of Michael Quinn, of Castlebar, and had one son and two daughters. He died suddenly at Montreux 17 January 1932.

[*The Times*, 21 and 26 January 1932; *Engineering* and *Engineer*, 29 January 1932; *Nature*, 13 February 1932; G. E. Armstrong, *Torpedoes and Torpedo-Vessels*, 2nd ed., 1901.]

H. M. ROSS.

BRENTFORD, first VISCOUNT (1865–1932), statesman. [See HICKS, WILLIAM JOYNSON-.]

BRIDGES, SIR (GEORGE) TOM (MOLESWORTH) (1871–1939), lieutenant-general, was born at Park Farm, Eltham, Kent, 20 August 1871, the third son of Major Thomas Walker Bridges, R.A., who was an elder brother of Robert Bridges, the poet laureate [q.v.]. His mother was Mary Anne, daughter of Frederick Theodore Philippi, of Belfield Hall, near Rochdale, Lancashire, a naturalized Englishman whose family came from Usingen in Germany. Tom Bridges, as he was commonly called, was educated at Newton Abbot College and the Royal Military Academy, was gazetted second lieutenant in the Royal Artillery in 1892, and spent the early part of his service in India. In August 1898 he was posted to the new formation of the armed forces of Central Africa at Zomba, Nyasaland, where he was when the South African war broke out. Between 1899 and 1901 he served with the Imperial Light Horse, taking part in the relief of Ladysmith, and being severely wounded. He was promoted captain in April 1900. Between May and July 1901 he commanded the 5th and 6th West Australian Mounted Infantry. Subsequently he took part in the operations in the Orange River Colony, on the Zululand frontier of Natal, and in Cape Colony. He was twice mentioned in dispatches, and was given a brevet majority in August 1902.

Between 1902 and 1904 Bridges served in East Africa and took part in operations in Somaliland, being in command of the Tribal Horse (which he raised), and being again severely wounded. He was again mentioned in dispatches and he received the D.S.O. During 1905 and 1906 he passed through the Staff College and was employed in the Military Intelligence Directorate at the War Office in 1907 and subsequently as chief instructor at the Cavalry School at Netheravon. In 1908 he transferred to the 4th Dragoon Guards as a major. Between 1910 and 1914 he was military attaché at Brussels, The Hague, Copenhagen, and Christiania.

In August 1914 Bridges went out to France with the British Expeditionary Force in command of a squadron of his regiment. On 22 August his squadron was the first unit of the British Expeditionary Force to meet the Germans, near the village of Soignies. On 27 August there occurred at St. Quentin the incident for which he is perhaps best known. He found in the town two British battalions the commanding officers of which had given written assurances to the mayor that they would surrender with their units in order to save the town from bombardment. Bridges rallied the men of these battalions with a tin whistle and a toy drum purchased at the local toy-shop and led them back into contact with the remainder of the British forces.

On 3 September Bridges was given command of the 4th Hussars, but a month later was appointed head of the British military mission at the headquarters of the Belgian army, where he remained until December 1915, being wounded on the Yser. He then commanded the 19th division until April 1917, when he was sent on a mission to the United States of America for two months, after which he resumed command of the 19th division until he lost a leg at Passchendaele in September 1917. He had been promoted major-general in the previous January.

In the spring of 1918 Bridges headed another mission to the United States. Between January and November 1919 he was employed, with the rank of temporary lieutenant-general, as chief of the British military mission to the army of the Orient with headquarters at Salonika and subsequently at Constantinople. In 1920 he was sent to Novorossisk, where he arranged the evacuation of the remnants of General Denikin's White Russian army. Subsequently he was at Smyrna with the Greeks when they were driven out of Asia Minor by the Turks. He retired from the army in 1922, with the rank of honorary lieutenant-general, and was governor of South Australia from that year until 1927. From 1920 to the time of his death he was colonel of the 5th Inniskilling Dragoon Guards and was also colonel of the 9th Australian Light Horse and the 43rd Australian Infantry.

During the war of 1914–1918 Bridges was nine times mentioned in dispatches, and was appointed C.M.G. (1915), C.B. (1918), and K.C.M.G. (1919), besides receiving numerous foreign decorations. In 1925 he was appointed K.C.B. He received honorary degrees from the universities of McGill and Adelaide.

In 1907 Bridges married Janet Florence (died 1937), second daughter of Graham Menzies, of Hallyburton House, Cupar Angus, Forfarshire, and widow of Major Wilfred George Howard Marshall, Grenadier Guards. There was one daughter of the marriage. In 1938 he published a book of reminiscences entitled *Alarms and Excursions*. In 1939 he was compiling, for the use of the fighting forces, an anthology entitled *Word from England*, which was published posthumously in 1940. In 1939, also, some of his paintings were exhibited in London. He died at Brighton 26 November 1939.

[*The Times*, 27 November 1939; Sir G. T. M. Bridges, *Alarms and Excursions*, 1938; Official records; private information.]

E. H. WYNDHAM.

BRIGHTMAN, FRANK EDWARD (1856–1932), liturgiologist, was born at Bristol 18 June 1856, the second of the three sons of Charles Brightman, a Bristol business man, by his wife, Emma, daughter of Isaac Brown. From Bristol Grammar School he obtained a scholarship at University College, Oxford, in 1875, and after being awarded a first class in mathematical moderations (1876) and a second class in classical moderations (1877), *literae humaniores* (1879), and theology (1880), he won in 1882 both a Denyer and Johnson theological scholarship and the Hall-Houghton Senior Septuagint prize. He was ordained deacon in 1884, and priest in 1885, after having been admitted in 1884 an original librarian of Pusey House, Oxford, an office which he held until the year after his election to a fellowship at Magdalen in 1902. There he continued to live until his sudden death in college 31 March 1932. He was unmarried.

Brightman was one of the most learned of the band of liturgical scholars who flourished in England at the turn of the century; but whereas the majority devoted themselves to the study of Latin liturgies, Brightman's name was generally associated among them with oriental rites, and it is significant that his amplification of C. E. Hammond's *Liturgies, Eastern and Western* did not go beyond the first volume on Eastern liturgies (1896). But his knowledge was extremely wide and, if his output was disappointingly small, one cause was the unbounded generosity with which he gave help to students, and another the exactness and labour which he devoted to nearly thirty years' (1904–1932) joint editing of the *Journal of Theological Studies*. His learning did not go unrecognized, for he was an adviser to the leaders of the Church of England, and in the controversy over Anglican orders he was consulted in the compilation (1897) of the reply to the bull *Apostolicae Curae*. On a kindred subject, but away from mere controversy, his essay on 'The Terms of Communion and the Ministration of the Sacraments in Early Times' (published in *Essays on the Early History of the Church and the Ministry*, edited by H. B. Swete, 1918) was such as no other liturgical scholar then alive could have written. In the narrower sphere of the Church of England, Brightman's contributions to learning were his editions of the *Preces Privatae* (1903) and the *Manual of the Sick* (1909) of Lancelot Andrewes [q.v.] and a monumental work in two volumes, *The English Rite* (1915), a synopsis in which he set out the sources of the Book of Common Prayer and the changes made from 1549 to 1662. On the question of the revision of the Prayer Book in 1927 a devastating article from his pen in the *Church Quarterly Review* influenced church opinion against the new book.

Brightman was little of stature and walked with his head bent as if avoiding notice; but his finely domed head, ascetic face, and grave but kind eyes marked him out from other men. He was very shrewd, and his rare sermons were made deeply arresting by their moral earnestness. He detested publicity, but honours came to him nevertheless. Bishop Edward King [q.v.] collated him in 1902 to a prebend in Lincoln Minster; the university of Louvain conferred upon him the honorary degree of Doct. Phil. in 1909, and the university of Durham that of D.D. in 1914. In 1926 he was elected a fellow of the British Academy. Shy and reticent with strangers, he attracted undergraduates of the most varied types, who soon forgot in his rooms the disorder of the books as they listened to his conversation with its touches of irony and keen sense of humour.

[*The Times*, 1 April 1932; H. N. Bate, *Frank Edward Brightman, 1856–1932* in *Proceedings of the British Academy*, vol. xix, 1933; *Journal of Theological Studies*, July 1932; *Oxford Magazine*, 5 May 1932; personal knowledge.]

S. L. OLLARD.

BRISE, SIR EVELYN (JOHN) RUGGLES- (1857–1935), prison reformer. [See RUGGLES-BRISE.]

BROOKE, ALAN ENGLAND (1863–1939), biblical scholar and provost of King's College, Cambridge, was born at Spring Grove, Middlesex, 1 September 1863, the youngest of the four sons of Richard England Brooke, perpetual curate of St. Mary's church, Spring Grove, and honorary canon of Manchester Cathedral, afterwards successively vicar of Hull and rector of Bath, by his wife, Harriet, daughter of

William Bonner Hopkins, of Limber Grange, Lincolnshire. A scholar first of Eton and then of King's College, Cambridge, Alan Brooke was awarded a first class in part i of the classical tripos of 1885, a second class in part ii (1886), a first class in part ii of the theological tripos of 1888, and several university prizes. In 1889 he was elected a fellow of his college, at a time when Brooke Foss Westcott [q.v.] was at the height of his influence at Cambridge. It was Westcott's influence, with that of Joseph Armitage Robinson [q.v.], which largely determined the direction of his life's work. Ordained deacon in 1891 he served for a few months as curate at Gayton, Northamptonshire; his scholarly interests, however, soon drew him back to Cambridge. His first published work was an edition of *The Fragments of Heracleon* (1891), which was followed by an edition of *The Commentary of Origen on St. John's Gospel* (2 vols., 1896). But he had already been chosen, with (Dr.) Norman M'Lean, to edit the larger Cambridge edition of the Septuagint, and this vast and self-denying task, calling for discriminating judgement and close attention to detail, occupied him for the rest of his life, and remained unfinished at his death. The first volume of *The Old Testament in Greek*, of which the first part was published in 1906, was completed in 1917; the second in 1935; the final volume, of which the first part appeared in 1940, shortly after Brooke's death, is still incomplete, although much work had been done upon it.

Meanwhile Brooke was for twenty-four years (1894–1918) dean of his college and lecturer in divinity. The claims of the Septuagint precluded much independent authorship, but his *Critical and Exegetical Commentary on the Johannine Epistles* (1912) is a distinguished work which illustrates not only his thoroughness and fine critical judgement but something too of his spiritual insight which appears also in his sermons. He was ordained priest in 1904. In 1916 he was elected Ely professor of divinity at Cambridge. This meant also a stall in Ely Cathedral, and he valued the opportunity which his canonry afforded of taking part in the wider life of the Church, especially of visiting the village churches in the Fens. He was appointed a chaplain to the king in 1918. In 1926 he was elected provost of King's (whereupon he became an honorary canon of Ely) and for seven years during the transitional period after the royal commission on the university he was head of the college, which owed much to his wise counsel and shrewd judgement, as also to his generosity. After his retirement in 1933 he continued to work at the Septuagint until his death at Cambridge 29 October 1939. Elected a fellow of the British Academy in 1934, he was in 1939 awarded the Burkitt medal for biblical studies. His marriage in 1901 to Frances Rachel (died 1919), daughter of Nicholas John Dunn, J.P., D.L., of St. Florence, near Tenby, Pembrokeshire, brought him much happiness. There was one son. Rupert Brooke [q.v.] was his nephew.

There is a portrait of Brooke, by Henry Lamb, at King's College, Cambridge.

[*The Times*, 31 October 1939; *Cambridge Review*, 18 November 1939; J. F. Bethune-Baker, *Alan England Brooke, 1863–1939* in *Proceedings* of the British Academy, vol. xxvi, 1940 (portrait); private information.]

A. R. GRAHAM-CAMPBELL.

BROWN, ERNEST WILLIAM (1866–1938), mathematician and astronomer, was born at Hull 29 November 1866, the second child and elder son of William Brown, farmer, and later a lumber merchant of Hull, by his wife, Emma Martin. Educated at the Hull and East Riding College, he entered Christ's College, Cambridge, as a scholar in 1884. He was sixth wrangler in the mathematical tripos of 1887 and was elected a fellow of Christ's in 1889. At the suggestion of (Sir) George Darwin [q.v.], he took up in 1888 the study of G. W. Hill's papers on the lunar theory.

This led Brown to what was to prove his lifework: for the next twenty years he gave little thought to other research and during the thirty years that followed it remained his favourite subject. In 1891 he went to the United States of America as professor of applied mathematics at Haverford College, Pennsylvania; in 1907 he was appointed professor of mathematics at Yale University, retiring in 1932, on account of ill health, with the title of emeritus professor. But he retained his connexion with Cambridge and with Christ's College, spending a part of almost every summer there. He was elected an honorary fellow of Christ's in 1911.

In 1896 Brown published *An Introductory Treatise on the Lunar Theory*, containing a critical examination of the various methods. His own theory of the motion of the moon was a development of Hill's method. The main results were published in five parts in the *Memoirs* of the Royal Astronomical Society between 1897 and 1908. For an essay on the direct planetary perturbations of the moon he was awarded in 1907 the Adams prize in the university of Cambridge. The heavy task of reducing the theory to tables was begun in 1908, the numerical values of the constants used in the tables being obtained from comparison of the theory with the Greenwich observations of the moon (some 20,000 in number) from 1750 to 1900. His monumental *Tables of the Motion of the Moon* in three volumes were published in 1919. These tables have been used for the calculation of the moon's place in the *Nautical Almanac* since 1923.

The completeness and accuracy of Brown's theory enabled one of the most pressing problems in gravitational astronomy to be decided. Comparison between the moon's observed positions and the earlier theory of Petrus Andreas Hansen had shown large fluctuations, which could not be explained by any known gravitational cause but which might have arisen from errors or incompleteness in the theory. Comparison with Brown's *Tables* soon showed that the moon's observed positions were not accurately represented by the theory. Brown suggested that the cause was a variable rate of rotation of the earth and obtained evidence in support of this view, which has since been conclusively established. In order to improve the observed positions of the moon, he organized a world-wide programme for the observation and reduction of occultations of stars by the moon. In his later years he made significant contributions to various problems in celestial mechanics, mainly concerned with planetary theory.

Brown was elected F.R.S. in 1897. He was awarded the gold medal of the Royal Astronomical Society in 1907 ; the Pontecoulant prize of the Paris Academy of Sciences in 1909 ; a Royal medal of the Royal Society in 1914 ; the Bruce medal of the Astronomical Society of the Pacific in 1920 ; and the Watson medal of the National Academy of Sciences, Washington, in 1937. He received honorary degrees from the universities of Adelaide (1914), Yale (1933), Columbia (1934), and McGill (1936). He was never married. He died at New Haven, Connecticut, 22 July 1938.

[*Obituary Notices of Fellows of the Royal Society*, No. 8, January 1940 (portrait); private information ; personal knowledge.]

H. SPENCER JONES.

BROWN, GERARD BALDWIN (1849–1932), historian of art, was born in London 31 October 1849, the only son of James Baldwin Brown, a leading nonconformist divine, who was at the time minister of Brixton Independent chapel, by his wife, Elizabeth, daughter of William Gerard Leifchild, of Moorgate Street and Wanstead, and a sister of the sculptor H. S. Leifchild [q.v.]. Gerard was educated at Uppingham under Edward Thring [q.v.] and at Oriel College, Oxford, where he graduated in 1873 with a first class in *literae humaniores*. In 1874 he was awarded the chancellor's prize for an English essay and was elected to a fellowship, which he held until 1877, at Brasenose. In his thirty-first year (1880) he went to Edinburgh University to fill the newly established Watson Gordon chair of fine art. He held it for fifty years, resigning in 1930, two years before his death at Edinburgh 12 July 1932. In 1882 he married Maude Annie (died 1931), daughter of Robert Hull Terrell, of Exeter ; they had no children.

Although his earliest lectures at Edinburgh had Greek art as their main topic, and although, throughout his career, Baldwin Brown maintained a close association with the school of classical studies, his first book, *From Schola to Cathedral* (1886), deals with a subject which was subsequently to serve as the theme for his main life's work. Its sub-title, *A Study of Early Christian Architecture and its Relation to the Life of the Church*, indicates the line of his approach, in which art is considered as a manifestation of the life and culture of its age, and where great importance is always given to the connexion between art and its social background. The same method of approach characterizes a later book, *The Arts and Crafts of Our Teutonic Forefathers* (1910), wherein Baldwin Brown made public studies which must have formed the basis for parts of his great work on the dark ages in this country, *The Arts in Early England*, the first volume of which appeared in 1903 and the second part of the sixth and last, completed by Eric Hyde Lord Sexton, in 1937. Some of Baldwin Brown's opinions as expressed in this, his most important, work will no doubt be questioned as knowledge advances, but the ground covered is so extensive and the research so thorough that the book should always retain its place as the standard work on the subject. It may be supplemented by articles and monographs, but it can hardly be replaced by a similar general study.

Other of Baldwin Brown's publications, *The Fine Arts* (1891, 4th ed. 1916), *William Hogarth* (1905), *Rembrandt* (1907), and *The Art of the Cave Dweller* (1928), all bear witness to his method of approach. But, more than that, they illustrate the author's habit of making himself familiar at first hand with the subjects of his study, whether pots, pictures, or buildings. His abilities as a draughtsman and photographer helped him in this, and his understanding of the nature and value of craftsmanship, learnt in his uncle's studio and at the South Kensington School of Art before going to Edinburgh, enabled him to maintain a contact with the object, the absence of which often constitutes a serious blemish in the more purely theoretical studies of the fashionable modern German school of historians of art.

From his appointment to the Watson Gordon chair until his death, Baldwin Brown made Edinburgh his home, but he travelled extensively in Great Britain and western Europe and attended numerous congresses at home and abroad. Personal memories and written records attest the enhanced value that his presence lent to such gatherings. It was, however, probably as professor that the fullest scope was given for the expression of his shy though delightful personality. His energy, enthusiasm, and kindliness were proverbial; he was always ready to make his wide knowledge available to others.

The titles of Baldwin Brown's publications, which also include *The Care of Ancient Monuments* (1905) and *The Glasgow School of Painters* (1908), denote the catholic nature of his interests and the titles of the books in his library, which he bequeathed to the department of fine art at Edinburgh University, further illustrate the breadth and freshness of his tastes. This breadth of outlook influenced the lives of many generations of Edinburgh graduates, and, through them and similar contacts, did much to encourage the spread of liberal tastes in the city.

Baldwin Brown contributed a number of papers to learned journals: 'The Origin of Roman Imperial Architecture', read before the Royal Institute of British Architects in 1889, is among the more important of them. He was elected a corresponding fellow of a large number of learned societies, and received honours from numerous bodies both at home and abroad, including two honorary degrees from Edinburgh University. These honours were crowned by his election to an honorary fellowship at Oriel College, Oxford, in 1923 and to a fellowship of the British Academy in 1924.

A bronze bust of Baldwin Brown, by C. d'O. Pilkington Jackson, presented to him in 1930, belongs to Edinburgh University.

[*The Times*, 14 July 1932; Sir George Macdonald, *Gerard Baldwin Brown, 1849–1932* in *Proceedings* of the British Academy, vol. xxi, 1935; private information; personal knowledge.]   D. TALBOT RICE.

BROWNE, SIR JAMES CRICHTON- (1840–1938), physician and psychologist, was born in Edinburgh 29 November 1840, the eldest son of William Alexander Francis Browne, the first medical superintendent of the Crichton Royal Institute at Dumfries, by his wife, Magdalene Howden, daughter of Andrew Balfour, a highly cultured woman and a Shakespearian scholar. James's second Christian name, which he afterwards adopted as part of his surname, was derived from Dr. James Crichton, of Crichtons' Carse, who left a sum of about £100,000 for the foundation of the institute. Like David Skae [q.v.], of the celebrated Edinburgh asylum at Morningside, Dr. Crichton was one of the pioneers of the early treatment of mental breakdown.

Crichton-Browne was educated at Dumfries Academy, Trinity College, Glenalmond, and Edinburgh University where his teachers were Joseph (later Lord) Lister, Lyon (later Lord) Playfair, Sir Robert Christison, James Syme, John Goodsir, and Thomas Laycock [qq.v.]. From an early stage of his career he showed an interest in medical psychology. In his third year of student life he presented a paper to the Royal Medical Society of Edinburgh on 'The Psychical Diseases of Early Life', and in his fourth year delivered his valedictory address to the society on 'The Clinical Teaching of Psychology'. He qualified L.R.C.S. (Edinburgh) in 1861 and graduated M.D. with a thesis on 'Hallucinations' in the following year. He began practice in 1865 by serving as assistant medical officer of the Devon, Derby, and Warwick county asylums and subsequently was appointed medical superintendent at Newcastle-upon-Tyne City Asylum, where he lectured on mental disease at the Newcastle College of Science. In 1866 he became medical director of the West Riding Asylum at Wakefield and gave a similar course of lectures at the Leeds School of Medicine and also founded and edited the annual *West Riding Lunatic Asylum Medical Reports*. These reports, which were the first of their kind in this country, contain contributions from J. Hughlings Jackson, (Sir) T. C. Allbutt, (Sir) T. L. Brunton [qq.v.], and Crichton-Browne himself among others. He was also co-editor of *Brain* from 1878 to 1885.

In 1875 Crichton-Browne was appointed lord chancellor's visitor in lunacy and held that post until he retired in 1922. During these years he was concerned with the supervision of the wards and the proper administration of their estates. In 1883 he was elected F.R.S., and six years later he became treasurer of the Royal Institution.

Crichton-Browne was one of the first to emphasize the importance of the recognition of the prodromal symptoms of mental disease. Besides work of this kind he was particularly interested in public health and education, and published a large number of addresses, reports, and letters to the press on these subjects, of which the most interesting is a parliamentary paper on 'Elementary Schools'. Subsequently he supported the campaign for the open-air treatment of tuberculosis, the control of venereal disease, and the better housing of the working classes. During his last years he published a number of popular and humorous reminiscences such as *Victorian Jottings* (1926), *What the Doctor Thought* (1930), *The Doctor's Second Thoughts* (1931), *The Doctor's Afterthoughts* (1932).

Crichton-Browne received many distinctions at home and abroad. He was knighted in 1886 and received honorary degrees from the universities of Aberdeen, St. Andrews, Edinburgh, and Leeds, as well as being president of the following learned societies: the Medico-Psychological Association, the Neurological Society, the Medical Society of London, and the National Health Society. He was also a fellow of the New York Academy of Medicine. He was granted the freedom of Dumfries. Apart from considerable deafness and gradual impairment of vision, he retained his faculties until his death at Dumfries 31 January 1938.

Crichton-Browne was twice married: first, in 1865 to Emily (died 1903), youngest daughter of John Halliday, surgeon, of Seacombe, Cheshire, and had a son, who predeceased him, and a daughter; secondly, in 1912 to Audrey Emily, eldest daughter of General Sir Edward Bulwer [q.v.] and great-niece of Edward Bulwer-Lytton [q.v.]; there were no children of the second marriage.

[*The Times*, 1 February 1938; *Obituary Notices of Fellows of the Royal Society*, No. 7, January 1939; *British Medical Journal*, 1938, vol. i, p. 331; *Lancet*, 1938, vol. i, p. 906.]

J. D. ROLLESTON.

BRUCE, CHARLES GRANVILLE (1866–1939), soldier, mountaineer, and traveller, was born in London 7 April 1866, the younger son of Henry Austin Bruce, afterwards first Baron Aberdare [q.v.], by his second wife, Norah Creina Blanche, youngest daughter of Lieutenant-General Sir William Napier [q.v.]. He was educated at Harrow and Repton, and was commissioned, through the militia, in the Oxfordshire and Buckinghamshire Light Infantry in 1887. He first saw active service with the Military Police in Burma and in 1889 transferred to the 5th Gurkha Rifles, the regiment with which he served for most of his career. Stationed with it at Abbottabad, he saw much service on the North-West Frontier of India: in Black Mountain (Hazara), 1891, Miranzai, 1891, Chitral, 1893, Waziristan, 1894–1895, and Tirah, 1897–1898, receiving in all six clasps to his two frontier medals, three mentions in dispatches, and a brevet-majority in 1898. After being adjutant and second-in-command of the 5th Gurkha Rifles he was promoted lieutenant-colonel in May 1913, and appointed in May 1914 to command the 6th, the friendly rivals of his old regiment; it was with the 6th that he went to Egypt for the defence of the Suez Canal on the outbreak of war in 1914. For his services there and later in Gallipoli, where he commanded the depleted battalions of the 29th Indian brigade, including the 5th and 6th Gurkhas at Gurkha Bluff, he was thrice mentioned in dispatches and promoted brevet-colonel in November 1915. Severely wounded in the leg, he was evacuated before the withdrawal, and on discharge from hospital was appointed general officer commanding the Independent Frontier brigade at Bannu (1916–1919). He commanded the North Waziristan Field Force in 1917, and served in the Afghan war of 1919. In these operations he was mentioned twice in dispatches. No longer young, his health was at last undermined by strenuous work during these hot-weather seasons on the frontier, and he was invalided out of the service with the honorary rank of brigadier-general in

1920, after thirty-two years of distinguished service.

Bruce had all the qualities of a great traveller and fine soldier. From the moment he joined the Gurkhas he studied their language and became the foremost authority on their customs and ways of life. Having learnt to get behind their thoughts, he taught them how to make the best of their qualities and personally evolved their system of training for mountain warfare. It was Bruce who originated and trained the Frontier Scouts, and incidentally it was largely due to him that 'shorts' were introduced into the Indian army, after he had tried them and proved them useful with the Scouts. Bruce's mountaineering travels covered the whole extent of the Himalaya from end to end. On all his journeys he took and trained Gurkhas from his own regiment, and on all he studied and made friends with the natives of the districts through which he travelled. He was on the expedition of Martin Conway (later Lord Conway of Allington, q.v.) to the Hispar and Biafo glaciers in the Karakoram in 1892, and with A. F. Mummery [q.v.] and John Norman Collie on the first ill-fated attempt to climb Nanga Parbat in 1895 when Mummery was killed. He explored and climbed many lesser known summits in Khagan, Kashmir, Kulu, and Lahoul, and prepared plans for the exploration of Mount Everest in both 1907 and 1910, although both projects had to be abandoned for political reasons. It was not until after the war of 1914–1918, when he had been invalided out of the army, that, at the age of nearly fifty-six, he was able to carry out this ambition. He was the organizer and leader of both the 1922 and 1924 Mount Everest expeditions, and although he was then too old to attempt the final assaults, his remarkable knowledge of Gurkhas, Sherpas, and Tibetans, and his own qualities of cheerfulness and joviality, were assets that contributed much to the success of these expeditions. This love of adventure and fun and his command of Himalayan lore were the secret of his success among Himalayan folk, for his hearty laugh was known and mimicked in many parts. Many stories will be handed down of his phenomenal strength and endurance, and of the vast appetite of his early days; not all will be far from the truth. It is, for instance, a fact that he often wrestled with two Indian wrestlers at a time and on one occasion threw three opponents simultaneously; it is also true that in his early days, in order to keep fit, he would daily carry his orderly up the hills of the Khyber on his back.

Bruce married in 1894 Finetta Madeline Julia (died 1932), third daughter of Colonel Sir Edward Fitzgerald Campbell, second baronet; their only child, a son, died in infancy. Mrs. Bruce accompanied her husband on his mountain expeditions and was the author of Kashmir (1911). Bruce was appointed M.V.O. in 1903, and C.B. in 1918. The Royal Geographical Society awarded him the Gill memorial prize in 1915 and the Founder's gold medal in 1925. He was president of the Alpine Club in 1923, an honorary member of the leading continental climbing clubs, and an enthusiastic founder member of the Himalayan Club. He was the author of four books relating his Himalayan experiences: *Twenty Years in the Himalaya* (1910); *Kulu and Lahoul* (1914); *The Assault on Mount Everest, 1922* (1923); and *Himalayan Wanderer* (1934). He received the honorary degree of D.Sc. from the universities of Oxford and Wales, of D.C.L. from Edinburgh, and of LL.D. from St. Andrews. In 1931 he was appointed colonel of the 5th Gurkha Rifles, to the delight of all ranks of his old regiment. Thereafter, almost until his death in London 12 July 1939, he regularly revisited India and his regiment and was always greeted with enthusiasm.

A portrait of Bruce, by G. P. Jacomb-Hood, belongs to the Hon. Alice Bruce.

[*The Times*, 13 July 1939; C. G. Bruce, *Himalayan Wanderer*, 1934; *Geographical Journal*, October 1940; *Alpine Journal*, May 1940; personal knowledge.]

KENNETH MASON.

BRUCE, SIR DAVID (1855–1931), discoverer of the causes of Malta fever and sleeping sickness, was born in Melbourne, Australia, 29 May 1855, the only son of David Bruce, who came from Edinburgh, by his wife, Jane, daughter of Alexander Hamilton, of Stirling. The father was presumably an engineer as he went to Australia during the gold-rush in order to instal a crushing plant in a gold-field near Sandhurst, some hundred miles distant from Melbourne. When he was five years old David's parents returned to Scotland and settled in Stirling, David being sent to the Stirling High School where he continued until he was fourteen. As a boy and young man he was a keen naturalist,

roaming the country of the Scottish Highlands and being especially interested in
observing the habits of wild birds. On
leaving school he was placed with a business firm in Manchester, but in 1876, at
the age of twenty-one, he entered the
university of Edinburgh with the intention
of studying zoology. However, on the
advice of a friend, he decided to read
medicine and he graduated M.B., C.M. in
1881. After qualifying he became assistant
to Dr. Herbert Stanley Stone, a practitioner in Reigate. It was here that he met
his wife, Mary Elizabeth, daughter of John
Sisson Steele, M.R.C.S., Stone's predecessor
in the Reigate practice, and he married
her in 1883.

Shortly after his marriage Bruce obtained
a commission in the Army Medical Service,
being first on the passing-out list. In the
following year he was ordered to Malta.
At this time the naval and military hospitals at Malta contained large numbers of
cases of an obscure continued fever with
a high mortality rate and even in the
milder cases associated with prolonged
ill health and disability. So seriously was
the incidence of this disease regarded that
the naval and military medical officers
were at the time engaged in collecting all
available information on the clinical
nature and epidemiology of the disease.
Bruce worked on the pathological and
bacteriological aspects. Bacteriology was
then in its infancy and the introduction
by Robert Koch in 1880 of solid media
and other technical methods of isolating
organisms and the recent discoveries of
the organisms of enteric fever, tubercle,
and cholera had stimulated Bruce to attack
the problem of Malta fever by these new
methods. Within two years he had found
in the spleen of fatal cases an organism to
which he gave the name of *Micrococcus
melitensis* now known as *Brucella melitensis*. Bruce proved conclusively as a result
of his researches that this organism was
the cause of Malta fever.

In 1888 Bruce left Malta on leave which
he spent working with his wife in Koch's
laboratory in Berlin. On his return to
England he was appointed assistant professor of pathology in the Army Medical
School at Netley. In this post, which he
held from 1889 to 1894, he did much to
introduce modern methods in pathology.
In 1894, again in the ordinary course of
military duty, Bruce received orders to
proceed abroad, this time to South Africa,
where he was posted to the garrison at
Pietermaritzburg in Natal. In Zululand

at this time a fatal disease was devastating
the domestic animals of the native population and settlers, and the governor of the
Colony, Sir Walter Hely-Hutchinson, who
had been lieutenant-governor of Malta at
the time of Bruce's successful researches
on Malta fever, requested that Bruce
might be seconded to investigate the cause
of the mortality. Two months later Bruce
was able to report the discovery of an
organism, later named *Trypanosoma brucei*,
in the blood of infected animals and that
this was the cause of both tsetse-fly disease
and nagana, then thought to be two distinct diseases. This led to Bruce being
seconded in December 1896 for a further
period, and he and his wife returned for
two years to a wild and isolated camp life
in the bush in Zululand, where they lived
like pioneers in wattle and daub huts and
on wild game which they themselves shot.
The result was the complete working out
of the main facts as they are now known
regarding trypanosomiasis in domestic
and wild animals and the tsetse-fly which
transmits the organism. Bruce's reputation as a scientific worker of remarkable
capacity was now established and whilst
still absent in South Africa he was elected
a fellow of the Royal Society (1899). In
the South African war in 1899 the Bruces
were shut up in Ladysmith where Bruce,
among other experiences in active service,
was in command of a large military hospital and acted as an operating surgeon,
whilst his wife was sister-in-charge of the
operating theatre.

In 1901 Bruce returned to England, but
in February 1903 he was seconded by the
War Office at the request of the Royal
Society to undertake the supervision and
control of the commission which the
society in 1902 had dispatched to Uganda
to investigate a serious outbreak of sleeping sickness that was decimating the lake
shore population. Success in determining
the nature and cause of this disease
quickly followed.

As so often happens, the actual discovery of the cause of sleeping sickness
was not wholly attributable to any one
individual, although it was Bruce who,
with his extraordinary power of systematic
research, first established the nature and
cause of this deadly disease. Trypanosomiasis due to *T. brucei* very fortunately did
not affect man. But while J. E. Dutton
[q.v.] was working in West Africa he was
shown by Dr. Robert Michael Forde parasites in the blood of a case of sleeping sickness which he recognized as a trypanosome

and which in 1902 he named *T. gambiense*. In 1903 Aldo Castellani, a member of the commission originally sent out by the Royal Society to Uganda in 1902, had found shortly before Bruce's arrival from England trypanosomes in the cerebro-spinal fluid of five out of fifteen cases of sleeping sickness. Castellani informed Bruce of this fact and in the three weeks before leaving for England found these organisms in twenty out of twenty-nine further cases. Bruce at once recognized the implications of Castellani's observations and grasping the resemblance of the conditions to those with which he was so familiar in Zululand, immediately began collecting all available information about the distribution of the disease and of tsetse-fly and setting up, as in Zululand, fly-feeding experiments. By August 1903, when Bruce and his wife returned to England, he had proved that sleeping sickness was a trypanosome disease carried by tsetse and that it could be transmitted from sick to healthy individuals by the bite of this insect.

Bruce, assisted always by his wife, made other successful investigations. In 1904 he revisited Malta as head of the Royal Society's Malta Fever Commission, proving this time that the source of infection in Malta fever was the goat, infection in man being contracted by drinking goat's milk. In 1908 Bruce again visited Uganda and in 1911 carried out investigations on trypanosomal disease in Nyasaland. He was specially promoted surgeon-general in 1912 for his eminent scientific services. During the war of 1914–1918 he was commandant of the Royal Army Medical College, Millbank, and rendered great service to the army by directing research on the aetiology and control of trench fever and tetanus. Bruce retired in 1919 and for reasons of health spent the winters in Madeira. He continued, however, to keep in touch with research at home and to give to workers the benefit of his experience and advice.

In all his work Bruce was assisted by his wife who accompanied him throughout his foreign service, working in the laboratory and taking charge of camp arrangements and much else. Bruce on his deathbed laid stress on the great service which she had rendered him and expressed the wish that her part in his scientific work should be recognized. She received the Royal Red Cross for her work with the wounded in the siege of Ladysmith, and was appointed O.B.E. for her work for the committees on trench fever and tetanus during the war of 1914–1918.

Of the many honours which Bruce received only some can be mentioned here. In 1904 he was awarded by the Royal Society a Royal medal and in 1922 the Buchanan medal. He was the recipient of the Mary Kingsley medal of the Liverpool School of Tropical Medicine in 1905, of the Leeuwenhoek medal of the Dutch Academy of Sciences in 1915, of the Manson medal of the Royal Society of Tropical Medicine and Hygiene (of which he was president from 1917 to 1919), and of the Albert medal of the Royal Society of Arts in 1923, besides honorary degrees from four universities and honorary memberships of several foreign academies and societies. He was Croonian lecturer of the Royal College of Physicians in 1915 and president of the British Association in 1924. He was appointed C.B. in 1905, and, having been knighted in 1908, K.C.B. in 1918. He died in London 27 November 1931 during the funeral of Lady Bruce four days after her death. He had no children.

Bruce was a man of strong physique and forceful mind. He was one of the great pioneers in medical research, a highly trained investigator exploring new fields in the causation of disease. Few investigators have had such a record of successes to their name. His approach to the problems which he undertook to solve was extraordinarily simple, logical, vigorous, and direct, and this was backed by a remarkable, seemingly intuitive, perception of the essential point for attack. In his personal relations, whilst he is said to have been somewhat reserved and self-contained, all agree as to his loyalty and integrity of mind and purpose.

[*The Times*, 28 November 1931; *Transactions* of the Royal Society of Tropical Medicine and Hygiene, vol. xxv, 1931–1932 (portrait); *Obituary Notices of Fellows of the Royal Society*, No. 1, December 1932 (portrait).]

S. R. CHRISTOPHERS.

BUCHAN, JOHN, first BARON TWEEDS-MUIR (1875–1940), author, and governor-general of Canada, born at Perth 26 August 1875, came of mainly Border lowland stock, being the eldest child in the family of four sons and one surviving daughter (the novelist 'O. Douglas') of John Buchan, minister of the Free Church of Scotland, by his wife, Helen, daughter of John Masterton, farmer, at Broughton Green, Peebles-shire. Buchan's father, who had been brought up in the atmosphere of the Disruption, served congregations at Kirkcaldy and at John Knox's church, in the Gorbals district of Glasgow, and the impression made by these rather different places can be easily traced in his son's writings. Perhaps an even greater influence on Buchan was wielded by his mother, a woman sentimental yet shrewd, contemplative but alert, able to hold her own in any company, who lived to see her son surrounded by the pomp of Holyrood and the splendour of Ottawa. In 1895, after attendance at Hutcheson's Boys' Grammar School at Glasgow and at lectures at Glasgow University, he was awarded a scholarship at Brasenose College, Oxford, and thenceforth his life was bound up with England, South Africa, and Canada. Nevertheless, Scotland always 'haunted him like a passion', and he never lost the impress of his home and native land; he remained throughout his life a Christian who said his prayers, read his Bible, and knew the *Pilgrim's Progress* almost by heart.

At Oxford, Buchan won in 1897 the Stanhope historical essay prize on the subject of 'Sir Walter Raleigh' and in 1898 the Newdigate prize for English verse with the 'Pilgrim Fathers' as its theme. He was president of the Union in 1899 and was awarded a first class in *literae humaniores* that same year. Having one or two books already to his credit, he was commissioned by his college to write its history for the Robinson series of 'College Histories'. It appeared in 1898 while he was yet an undergraduate, and called forth severe criticism from antiquarian reviewers unaccustomed to so unconventional a style of historical writing. Disappointed of a prize fellowship, Buchan went to London, where he widened the large circle of his friends and was called to the bar by the Middle Temple in 1901, earning his living by journalism, and reading with J. A. Hamilton (later Lord Sumner, q.v.) and (Sir) Sidney Rowlatt. But his legal career was cut short when, after his call to the bar, Lord Milner [q.v.] summoned him to South Africa as one of his assistant private secretaries.

Although Buchan spent only two years (1901–1903) in South Africa, the appointment was the most important step in his career. He gained enormously from daily association with Milner and from his modest tasks in the resettlement of the country, where his warm human desire to make friends with the Boers and bury the hatchet gave him horizon and a sense of

size, and his imperialism, cleansed of vulgar jingoism, became elevated above the patronizing 'trust' conception into an association of free peoples in loyalty to a common throne. So Pieter Pienaar, resourceful and true, becomes one of the heroes of his adventure novels. Indeed he was eager for a career in Egypt under Lord Cromer [q.v.] when his work in South Africa was over. For the second time and again for the good he was disappointed. Yet it may be affirmed with confidence that, without apprenticeship in Africa, there would have been no governor-generalship of Canada, for Buchan had there learned to think as statesmen think.

In 1903 Buchan returned to the bar in London, 'devilling' for Rowlatt and 'noting' for Sir R. B. (later Viscount) Finlay [q.v.] who, while assessing his mind as not exact enough for supremacy at the bar, admired his abilities and character. He wrote 'opinions', one, for instance, on the legality of Chinese labour (after the liberal victory of 1906) in which his seniors were Arthur Cohen, Finlay, and Rufus Isaacs (later Marquess of Reading) [qq.v.]. But this episode was a backwater. In 1907 T. A. Nelson the publisher, a friend from Oxford days, invited him to join the firm as 'literary adviser' and as a limited partner. He was to reside in London and superintend the issue of, *inter alia*, the sevenpenny edition of *The Best Literature*. He accepted and was in his element. He could never have mortified the flesh as he describes Milner doing, nor could he have given himself body and soul to the bar. His admirable, but ephemeral, *Law relating to the Taxation of Foreign Income* (1905), written at the instance of R. B. (later Viscount) Haldane [q.v.], remains as his testament to the Middle Temple, which elected him a bencher in 1935. He was also engaged to be married to one of that world which had fascinated him since his Oxford days by its ease and grace. With her he enjoyed unclouded happiness for thirty-three years. Being free from drudgery he could, as a man of letters, give scope to the dominating activity of his life. Hitherto his books, some written before he ever came to Oxford (*Sir Quixote of the Moors*, 1895, *Scholar Gipsies*, 1896, *Grey Weather*, 1899, *The Half-Hearted*, 1900, and *The Watcher by the Threshold*, 1902), had contained the freshness of youth and were charming harbingers of even better to come. These had been followed by the African books, *The African Colony* (1903) and *A Lodge in the Wilderness* (1906), more interesting perhaps as autobiography than as literature, while *Prester John* (1910) begins the long series of his books of adventure. Except for the Stanhope essay, *Sir Walter Raleigh* in dramatic form (1911) is the first sign of his turn towards history, and then, after two more adventure stories, came *The Marquis of Montrose* (1913), now out of print and not included in his collected works. This was Buchan's first serious attempt at writing history and a good deal of it was history, and very good history, the most impressive feature being the power which he exhibited of describing marches and battles and their wild natural settings. But zeal for his idolized 'discovery' (although the tragedy of the 'great Marquess' had pointed many a moral and adorned many a tale) led him to commit so many elementary blunders, all of which invariably told in favour of Montrose and against Argyle and the Estates, tinged with a certain 'acerbity' and an air of omniscience, that he was severely taken to task by D. H. Fleming [q.v.] in a review printed in *The British Weekly* of 12 February 1914. No reply was or could be made. *Montrose* (1928) is the sequel: the blemishes complained of are gone, but whether we have the final Marquess 'in his faults and failings, in his virtues and valour' (Hay Fleming) is open to question among those for whom historic truth is all in all, and brilliant writing no more than decoration.

The outbreak of war in 1914 found Buchan, on the eve of his thirty-ninth birthday, seriously ill for the first time since his childhood, when at the age of five he had fallen out of a carriage and a wheel passing over the side of his skull had left its mark for life. He had then lain for a year in bed and had to learn once more how to walk. He grew to be about 5 feet 8 inches in height, lean, sinewy, well knit, and active as a chamois. A daring and expert cragsman, he had sampled many rock climbs in Skye and Austria, and he had literally climbed into the Alpine Club. He was a keen fisherman but an indifferent shot, and his riding was purely utilitarian, preferring as he did Shanks's mare, a nimble, sure steed which never tired. Games, accomplishments, and parlour tricks were outside his activities.

Compelled to keep his bed, Buchan wrote. He made a start with his well-known *History of the Great War*, which occupied twenty-four volumes of the 'Nelson Library' series; but he also wrote *The Thirty-Nine Steps* (1915) which fairly stormed the reading world with its combination of excitement and sensation, written as only a master of English can write. He was well enough by 1915 to be on the staff of *The Times* on the western front, and by 1916 he had joined the army as a major in the Intelligence Corps and enjoyed confidential innominate duties at general headquarters at Montreuil-sur-Mer, which brought him into personal touch with another Borderer by extraction, Sir Douglas Haig, whom he admired as a great man and soldier. Summoned to London in 1917, he made such a personal success of the new Department of Information that it became a ministry with Buchan as subordinate director until the armistice. With renewed successes his pen consoled him for irritating drudgery and unreasonable people: *Greenmantle* (1916) and *Mr. Standfast* (1919) completed the trilogy on the war opened by *The Thirty-Nine Steps*. In *Poems, Scots and English* (1917) some of the poems are topical of the front, but the book is at once a monument of detachment from ugly actuality and a source of regret that he did not write more verse. Buchan loved poetry and had it in his bones.

Private life resulted in settlement at Elsfield Manor, near Oxford, purchased in 1919 after deliberation of several years. That 'ivory tower' was so unlike Buchan's native land that nostalgia was not aroused, and in this phase of his life there was a copious output of books. *The History of the South African Forces in France* and the memoir of *Francis and Riversdale Grenfell* (1920) were the aftermath of the war, together with the *History of the Great War* which was revised, compressed, and republished in 1921–1922 and the complete regimental *History of the Royal Scots Fusiliers* (1925), a valuable tribute to the memory of his youngest brother, Alastair, killed in 1917.

The excellence of the tribute to the Grenfells may have led to his life of *Lord Minto* (1924) which proved to be the forerunner of the historical biographies, on which he undoubtedly intended that his future fame should rest. By an interesting chance it familiarized him with a stage on which, as a successor to Minto, he was destined to play his part. Meantime novel after novel poured from his pen. *Huntingtower* (1922) opened a new series based on Glasgow memories and the scout movement, with a coy candidature of Peeblesshire. *Midwinter* (1923) was an historical novel linking Elsfield with Samuel Johnson just as Elsfield and Henry VIII were drawn together in *The Blanket of the Dark* (1931). *Witch Wood* (1927) links Tweeddale with Montrose and Philiphaugh and is a by-product of the preparation for *Montrose*. But the majority were the yarns (as he called them) spun easily for his own and an eager public's enjoyment.

It is remarkable that he went on writing in the last phase of his life, when he was a public man. The almost inspired literary criticism of his *Sir Walter Scott* (1932) and the sympathetic understanding of the spiritual side of the Protector in *Oliver Cromwell* (1934) show Buchan at his best. At a by-election in 1927 he was elected conservative member of parliament for the Scottish Universities, and held the seat until his elevation to the peerage in 1935. He fitted the constituency like a glove. He loved the House of Commons and the House listened to him. Moreover he had achieved fame in America chiefly as an historian and a novelist. He was a member of the Pilgrim Trust and in that capacity he did good service to Oxford City and Oxford University. And then, in 1933 and 1934 the elder of St. Columba's church at Oxford was appointed lord high commissioner to the General Assembly of the Church of Scotland. In that illustrious office, eloquent of the history of the struggles between church and state since the Reformation, Buchan was supremely happy both in his manner and in his utterances, as befitted the joint author (with Sir George Adam Smith) of the masterly little treatise *The Kirk in Scotland, 1560–1929* (1930). And it was again Ramsay MacDonald who in 1935 advised the appointment of Buchan to the governor-generalship of Canada, the supreme opportunity of Buchan's life, to show of what mettle he was made.

That Lord Tweedsmuir (the appropriate title conferred upon Buchan) had qualities which fitted him in no common degree for the office was shown by *The King's Grace: 1910–1935* (1935). The auspices, save in the matter of his health, were good. He was a Scot, a Presbyterian, and his wife was descended from the two noble houses of Grosvenor and Stuart-Wortley, and in her ancestry she could count more statesmen than most people. His vigour was undiminished and in 1937 *Augustus* brought to a close his studies in ancient history and the humanities.

As governor-general Tweedsmuir had to face the change in the position of the representative of the crown made by the Statute of Westminster (1931). He therefore requited a warm welcome with unwearied devotion to duty on ceremonial occasions, courts, reviews, the delivery of addresses and lectures, not only in English but in French, for he took a special interest in Lower Canada and the French-Canadian culture. Moreover, he was discreet and tactful, and he possessed charm in both its forms, sympathy with the interlocutor or audience, and sympathy of bearing. He was made a Red Indian chief. The author of *The Last Secrets* (1923) never neglected a chance of exploration and he travelled to visit all sorts and conditions of men throughout the Dominion.

But Tweedsmuir overtaxed his strength, and the anxiety inseparable from the visit of the King and Queen in 1939 strained it in spite of the excellence of the arrangements. Any chance of a needed rest was lost by the outbreak of war in September. His death, which took place at Montreal 11 February 1940, was followed by a spontaneous outburst of sorrow from all quarters of the free world. It was felt in Canada that his public services in voicing the spirit of Canadian loyalty, in promoting recruiting, and showing a gallant front had, as Cardinal Villeneuve said, been a factor in cementing national unity in Canada. Nor was his influence confined to Canada. Since 1937 at least he had been on terms of real friendship with President Roosevelt, and, with Lord Lothian [q.v.] at Washington, another member of Milner's South African 'kindergarten', he played his part in maintaining relations with the United States on the right plane.

Tweedsmuir married in 1907 Susan Charlotte, elder daughter of Captain Norman de l'Aigle Grosvenor, third son of the first Lord Ebury [q.v.], and had three sons and one daughter. He was succeeded as second baron by his eldest son, John Norman Stuart (born 1911). His honours, public and academic, came freely. He was sworn of the Privy Council in 1937, and was appointed C.H. in 1932, G.C.M.G. in 1935, and G.C.V.O. in 1939. He was elected chancellor of Edinburgh University in 1937 and an honorary fellow of Brasenose College in 1934, and he received honorary degrees from three of the four Scottish universities, and from Oxford, Harvard, Yale, and most of the Canadian universities.

A portrait of Lord Tweedsmuir, by Sholto Johnstone-Douglas (1900), is in the possession of Mr. J. W. Buchan, Bank House, Peebles, who also owns a bust by T. J. Clapperton. A posthumous portrait, by Alphonse Jongers, was presented to Lady Tweedsmuir by the women of Canada.

[*Manchester Guardian*, 12 February 1940; *The Times*, 12 and 15 February 1940; John Buchan, *A Lost Lady of Old Years*, 1899, and *Memory Hold-the-Door*, 1940; Hon. A. C. Murray, *Master and Brother*, 1945; Anna Buchan (O. Douglas), *Ann and her Mother*, 1922; *Unforgettable: Unforgotten* (1945); *John Buchan*, by his wife and friends, 1947; personal knowledge.]

S. A. GILLON.

BUCHANAN, SIR GEORGE CUNNINGHAM (1865–1940), civil engineer, was born at Islington 20 April 1865, the eldest son of George Buchanan, of Westminster, also a civil engineer, by his wife, Emily, youngest daughter of Thomas Boosey, of London. He was trained on the Tyne from 1882 until 1886, first under J. Watt Sandeman and then under P. J. Messent, chief engineer to the Tyne Improvement Commission. From 1886 he was associated for ten years with railway and other works in many parts of the world, Venezuela, Nova Scotia, Argentina, Spain, and Jamaica. On his return to England in 1895 he became resident engineer for the construction of a graving dock at Blyth, and in the following year he was appointed chief engineer to the Dundee Harbour Trust.

In 1901 Buchanan left Dundee to become chairman and chief engineer of the Rangoon Port Trust, and during the fourteen years for which he held that position designed new port works and carried out extensive training works on the river (for which he received the Watt gold medal from the Institution of Civil Engineers in 1916). At the end of 1915 he went to Basra as adviser to Sir John Nixon [q.v.], the commander-in-chief of the Mesopotamian campaign, on all matters connected with the port, its administration, engineering works, and river conservancy, and in 1917 attained the rank of brigadier-general. For his work at Basra, which he described in his book *The Tragedy of Mesopotamia* (1938), he was twice mentioned in dispatches, and his services and powers of organization were acknowledged by the government of India to have 'sensibly promoted' the ultimate success of British arms in Mesopotamia. His war services also included membership of the Indian Munitions Board (1917–1919).

After the war Buchanan entered into partnership with C. S. Meik and was appointed consulting engineer for the Back Bay reclamation scheme at Bombay, which provided for the reclamation of over 1,100 acres of land by the construction of a sea wall four miles long, the area within it being filled with silt dredged from the sea bed outside. In this undertaking he had less than his usual success, for his estimates proved faulty and his plans miscarried.

In 1922 Buchanan visited South Africa at the request of the Union government to report on the transport problems of the country, particularly in connexion with ports and harbours, and in 1925 he undertook a similar mission in Australia for the Commonwealth government, preparing a report on the development and administration of Northern Australia.

Buchanan was appointed C.I.E. in 1911, and after having been knighted in 1915, K.C.I.E. in 1917. He was twice married: first, in 1894 to Elizabeth Isabelle (died 1926), younger daughter of William Mead, of Plymouth, and had a son and a daughter; secondly, in 1930 to Joan, second daughter of Lieutenant John George Haggard, R.N., later consul at Malaga. He died at Ditchingham, Norfolk, 14 April 1940.

[*The Times*, 15 April 1940; *Engineer* and *Engineering*, 19 April 1940.]

H. M. ROSS.

BUCHANAN, SIR GEORGE SEATON (1869–1936), expert in public health, was born in London 19 February 1869, the elder son of Sir George Buchanan [q.v.], by his second wife, Alice Mary Asmar, daughter of E. C. Seaton, M.D. [q.v.]. He was educated at University College School, University College, London, and St. Bartholomew's Hospital, graduating M.B., with a gold medal in 1891 and proceeding to M.D. in 1893.

After holding hospital appointments, Buchanan became in 1895 a medical inspector of the Local Government Board where his early work was directed to the investigation of food-poisoning epidemics. He was chief inspector of foods from 1906 until 1911 and chief assistant medical officer from 1911 until 1919. During the war of 1914–1918 he was attached to the Army Sanitary Committee with the honorary rank of lieutenant-colonel and was a member of the Medical Advisory Committee, both to the British Mediterranean Expeditionary Force (1915–1916) and to the Mesopotamian Expeditionary Force

(1916–1917). This work entailed a considerable amount of service abroad. He was appointed C.B. in 1918.

Buchanan became a senior medical officer of the new Ministry of Health in 1919. He dedicated the rest of his active life to the promotion of co-operation in international health, and in 1934 he gave the Milroy lectures on *International Co-operation in Public Health, Its Achievement and Prospects* (published in the same year) to the Royal College of Physicians. He was vice-president of the international health organization of the League of Nations, president of the League's cancer commission, and in 1929 a member of the commission for the reorganization of the public health services of Greece. In 1932 he received the signal honour of being elected president of the Office International d'Hygiène Publique, of which he had been a member since 1914.

Buchanan was knighted in 1922, elected F.R.C.P. in 1925, and was master of the Society of Apothecaries in 1934–1935. He married in 1896 Rhoda Agnes, fifth daughter of Thomas Atkinson, of Plumgarths, Westmorland, and had one son, who predeceased him, and one daughter. He retired from office in 1934 and died in London 11 October 1936.

Buchanan was an indefatigable worker and had few interests outside his official duties. He effected much abroad through the respect evoked by his high qualities and personality, and he had considerable social gifts which aided him in making clear the British point of view on international health matters to foreign colleagues. His minutes and reports in their finished form were models of clarity and excellence.

Buchanan had been brought up in the atmosphere of public health and learned much from his father. His mind, therefore, was a storehouse of precedents and epidemiological knowledge. He asked much from those who worked under him, but was ever ready to acknowledge their contributions, to promote their interests, and to delight them by his wit and courtesy.

Save for the Milroy lectures and certain special reports and addresses, Buchanan made few contributions to medical literature. His vast knowledge and administrative ability are either buried in office files or are to be found in blue-books and in the reports of the health organization of the League of Nations. Inheriting and maintaining great traditions, Buchanan was the last of a famous generation of public servants.

[*The Times*, 12 October 1936; *British Medical Journal*, 1936, vol. ii, p. 788; *Lancet*, 1934, vol. i, p. 142, and 1936, vol. ii, p. 947 (portrait); personal knowledge.]

ARTHUR S. MACNALTY.

BUCHANAN, JAMES, BARON WOOLAVINGTON (1849–1935), philanthropist and racehorse owner, was the youngest son of Alexander Buchanan, of Glasgow, by his wife, Catharine, daughter of William Mclean. He was born at Brockville, West Canada, 16 August 1849 and was brought to Scotland when he was a year old. Of delicate health, he was educated privately, and he was still quite a young man when he went to London to sell whisky for a Scottish firm of distillers. The turning-point in his life came when a friend, struck by his grit and perseverance, offered him some capital to open business on his own account, and in 1880 he established the firm of James Buchanan & company in a small office in Bucklersbury. After a hard struggle he managed to repay all that had been lent to him, and, as soon as he was master of his own business, he arranged various combinations and amalgamations which assisted him to build up a considerable fortune. An unusual feature of his career was that, although he lived to a great age, he was always a delicate man, constantly obliged to nurse his health. He made many friends wherever he went, and not one had anything but good to say of him. They described him as never having taken an unfair advantage of anybody, and as always ready to help those in trouble or difficulty.

Buchanan's experiences on the turf covered nearly forty years. He began to race about the end of the nineteenth century, and owned horses that won him many good races. His first classic victory was in the St. Leger of 1916, when, owing to the war, the race was run at Newmarket instead of at Doncaster. Buchanan was training with F. Darling at Beckhampton at the time, and it was to him that he sent Hurry On, a yearling which he had bought for 500 guineas. As a two-year-old Hurry On could not be trained owing to unsoundness, but as a three-year-old he ran in six races and won them all. Not only was he Buchanan's first classic winner, but he sired for him the Derby winners of 1922 and 1926, Captain Cuttle and Coronach. The last-named was probably the best horse that Lord Woolavington, as he had then become, ever owned. Although his debut as a two-year-old was only modest, the triumphs of Coronach as a three-year-old in the Derby, the Eclipse Stakes, and the St. Leger were resounding. In 1927 Woolavington was elected a member of the Jockey Club, and the last time that his colours were carried to victory was in a race at Worcester a few days before his death.

Much of the wealth which he derived from his business was devoted by Woolavington to philanthropy. He gave away large sums both to public objects and to charity. He bought the log-book of the *Victory*, written in the sailingmaster's own hand, and presented it to the British Museum, and when an appeal was made for funds to fit out the old *Implacable* as a training ship, he sent a cheque for the £4,000 needed for the purpose. He showed his love of animals when, in 1926, he gave £10,000 to Edinburgh University for its animal breeding research department: the university conferred upon him the honorary degree of LL.D. In 1928 he gave £125,000 to the Middlesex Hospital in memory of his wife, and at the same time placed £50,000 at the disposal of the King for the restoration of the nave of St. George's Chapel, Windsor. Not only did he give many other sums to good causes, but his private life was full of kind and generous actions known only to those who benefited by them.

Buchanan was created a baronet in 1920, was raised to the peerage as Baron Woolavington, of Lavington, Sussex, in 1922, and was appointed G.C.V.O. in 1931. In 1891 he married Annie Eliza Bardolph, widow, daughter of Thomas Pounder, upholsterer. She was a hospital nurse, and he met her on one of the voyages undertaken for the sake of his health. Her sudden death in 1918 was due perhaps to overwork in nursing the wounded in London hospitals. The only child of the marriage was a daughter. Woolavington died at Lavington Park, Petworth, Sussex, 9 August 1935.

A portrait of Woolavington, by (Sir) J. J. Shannon, was exhibited at the Royal Academy in 1918. A cartoon of him, by 'Spy', appeared in *Vanity Fair* 20 November 1907.

[*The Times*, 10 August 1935.]

ALFRED COCHRANE.

BUCKLE, GEORGE EARLE (1854–1935), editor of *The Times* newspaper and man of letters, was born at Twerton-on-Avon, near Bath, 10 June 1854, the eldest of the four sons of George Buckle, successively fellow of Oriel College, Oxford, vicar of Twerton-on-Avon, rector of Weston-super-Mare, and canon and precentor of Wells Cathedral, by his wife, Mary Hamlyn Earle, sister of the philologist John Earle [q.v.]. He was educated at Honiton Grammar School, whence he gained a scholarship at Winchester and afterwards was elected a scholar of New College, Oxford. There he read classical and mathematical moderations, won the Newdigate prize (1875), and was awarded a first class in *literae humaniores* (1876) and in modern history (1877). From 1877 to 1885 he was a fellow of All Souls. At Lincoln's Inn he read in the chambers of (Sir) John Rigby [q.v.]. Journalism, however, to which he was no stranger, in that his father had been a regular contributor to the *Guardian*, offered him an opportunity almost at once, for he was recommended for the post of assistant editor to the *Manchester Guardian* by Mandell Creighton [q.v.], but the offer was declined. Five months before being called to the bar in November 1880, his name had been put before John Walter III [q.v.] by Sir William Anson [q.v.] for the post of assistant to the editor of *The Times*, Thomas Chenery [q.v.], on whose death, in February 1884, Buckle, still under thirty, was appointed editor.

Buckle's predominant interest was in home politics, and he carried on readily the tradition of *The Times* to give support, general but critical, to the government of the day; but this tradition was soon broken by the home rule controversy, which led up to the Parnell commission. The responsibility for accepting the forged letters lay with the proprietor and the manager, and the true source of the letters was not known to Buckle until shortly before the appearance of Richard Pigott [q.v.] in the witness-box. After the proceedings he offered to assume responsibility for the publication and tendered his resignation. This was declined; and Buckle, whose instincts lay in carrying on the paper on the lines on which he had found it, was confronted with the necessity of many administrative changes. His general attitude towards innovations was that they were probably dangerous; but he was prompt and generous in adopting any innovation (except the telephone) when he saw that it would work. But the prosperity of the paper had to be restored, and the establishment of a foreign department tended to withdraw a large portion of the paper from his immediate supervision, though not from his control. In other directions also the increasing size of the daily paper made for decentralization; and so when the change in proprietorship came (1908), with the new ideas of separate departments under separate directors and of the editor being limited to leading articles and general political direction, Buckle, who considered himself personally responsible for all that appeared in the paper, found his position increasingly difficult. Nevertheless he loyally set himself to make new arrangements work, until, to his surprise, it was informally conveyed to him that his resignation would be welcomed. He accordingly resigned at once (August 1912). To his efforts to hold to the inherited idea of general support for the government of the day and keeping open the correspondence columns to both sides of controversy, many tributes reached Buckle from political opponents and notably from Haldane, Grey, and Morley.

What might then have seemed to be the end of a career proved to be the prelude to two others. On the death in 1912 of W. F. Monypenny [q.v.] the Beaconsfield trustees commissioned Buckle to continue the *Life of Benjamin Disraeli*; and the labours of the next eight years were devoted to the last four of its six volumes (published 1914–1920). For one who followed the vicissitudes of home politics and public life with something of a sportsman's zest, the career of Disraeli could not but be engrossing; and the book has become a classic, and a quarry. Many years later Lord Morley wrote to him: 'We have each of us done his best to keep public life and public opinion on a wholesome and self-respecting level: and we have done our best to make the two great political rivals immortal.'

A few months after the completion of the *Life of Disraeli*, King George V chose Buckle to continue the selection and editing of the *Letters of Queen Victoria* which had been carried to 1861 by A. C. Benson and Viscount Esher [qq.v.] in 1907. Two series, each of three volumes, appeared between 1926 and 1932. Of the first series (1862–1885) perhaps the most salutary effect was the dispelling of legends and misunderstandings that had grown up during the years of the Queen's self-imposed seclusion, and the tracing of the gradual recovery of public trust, culminating in the jubilees of 1887 and 1897. Buckle showed in this work a reassuring

quietness of judgement combined with a spirit of discriminating hero-worship. He did not shrink from revealing the limitations of the Queen, her cloistered upbringing, her self-centredness and vehemence, but he brought out clearly her shrewd political interest, devotion to duty, and wide sympathy with all classes. Buckle's editing was a triumph of self-suppression, and an eminent judge declared the six volumes to be 'a masterpiece by a dumb historian'. But the editor's guidance to the reader is always there.

The remaining three years of Buckle's life were passed quietly in London with occasional visits to his former haunts where he helped in the preparation of the first volume of the *History of The Times* (1935). He died in London, after a very short illness, 13 March 1935.

When Buckle retired from the editorship of *The Times*, a journal politically opposed to it used words that might well have come from any member of his large and devoted staff. 'In appearance he is a typical Englishman of the upper classes, intellectualized and refined. In character, too, he is thoroughly English, sound and wholesome to the core, not too idealistic, inflexibly just, moderate and judicious in his views and spirit, honest as the day, and with serious and lofty views of life and duty.' With these qualities were combined a robust body, a robust voice, a hearty boyish manner (concealing a certain shyness), and a natural buoyancy which carried him through laborious nights and days. An enduring taste for an English holiday (golf or exploratory walks) enabled him to pass at once from work to complete relaxation and, in middle life, to treat a serious operation almost with contumely. His tastes were those naturally formed by a boy of his upbringing, and they remained those of the man: a preference for the well-established and a cautious welcome to the new.

Buckle was offered a baronetcy by A. J. Balfour, but declined it: he received honorary degrees from the universities of St. Andrews (1899) and Oxford (1932). He was twice married: first, in 1885 to Alicia Isobel (died 1898), third daughter of the novelist James Payn [q.v.]; secondly, in 1905 to his first cousin Beatrice Anne (died 1938), second daughter of John Earle. A son and a daughter were born of the first marriage.

[*The Times*, 13 March 1935; private information; personal knowledge.]

BRUCE L. RICHMOND.

BUCKLEY, HENRY BURTON, first BARON WRENBURY (1845–1935), judge, was born in London 15 September 1845, the fourth of the six sons of John Wall Buckley, vicar of St. Mary's church, Paddington Green, by his wife, Elizabeth, daughter of Thomas Burton. He went in 1854 to Merchant Taylors School, from which he obtained a scholarship at Christ's College, Cambridge. He was ninth wrangler in the mathematical tripos of 1868, having won, in 1866, the Tancred law studentship at Lincoln's Inn. From 1868 to 1882 he was a fellow of Christ's. He was called to the bar by Lincoln's Inn in 1869, and became a bencher in 1891. He took silk in 1886, and in 1900 was appointed a judge of the Chancery division. In 1906 he was promoted to the Court of Appeal, where he sat assiduously until his retirement, and was sworn of the Privy Council. On his retirement in 1915 he was raised to the peerage as Baron Wrenbury, of Old Castle, Surrey. He soon showed that he by no means intended to retire from the active life of the law, for he continued for many years to sit, as a peer who had held high judicial office, on appeals before both the House of Lords and the Judicial Committee of the Privy Council. He was elected an honorary fellow of his college in 1901.

Some years before he obtained forensic success, he had become well known to the legal profession as the author of the classic 'Buckley on Companies'. The first edition of *The Law and Practice under the Companies Acts* appeared in 1873, and the most recent (eleventh) edition, the compilation of which was necessitated by the passage of the Act of 1929, in 1930. Although (Sir) Francis Beaufort Palmer's work on *Company Law*, which first appeared in 1898, was to prove a formidable and more popular rival, nevertheless Wrenbury's book has retained its authority undimmed. Its character differs from that of Palmer's in that it takes the form of a commentary on the Act, section by section, and in showing continuity of authorship throughout the editions it has one definite advantage over the later work, for in the preparation even of the eleventh edition Wrenbury himself, then in his eighty-fifth year, was able to render personal assistance.

Although his forte naturally lay in company law, Wrenbury had a very firm grasp of every side of equity. In the field of Common Law, with which in the higher courts he was not infrequently called upon to deal, he was perhaps less generally happy, but here too his alert mind, his sound common sense, and his capacity for the absorption of the details of a problem, were great assets, both to himself and to his colleagues on the bench.

In the course of a thirty-five years' tenure of judicial office, Wrenbury's output of judgements was of course enormous, and the choice of a few for especial mention is a task of more than ordinary difficulty. In 1915 he was one of the majority of a divided Court of Appeal which decided *Hurst* v. *Picture Theatres*, the case which has perhaps given rise to more comment and controversy than has fallen to the lot of any other decision of this century. The court laid down that one who has paid for his seat and taken it in a theatre, and has been ejected from it although his behaviour has in no way called for blame, is, as the result of the Judicature Act (1873), entitled, not only to nominal damages for breach of contract, but to substantial damages for assault. Opinion, both professional and academic, has on the whole been unfavourable to the decision in that, by a spurious use of equitable principle, it in effect elevates a mere licence to the status of a licence coupled with interest, or of an easement. But Buckley's judgement, although it has failed to command agreement, is everywhere recognized as a monument of learning. When he went to the House of Lords it was noticeable that Lord Wrenbury showed an independence of judgement that had hardly been a characteristic of Lord Justice Buckley. Although no man was ever less cantankerous or less prone to dissent for the mere sake of dissent, he was never reluctant to utter a strong dissenting speech when he was convinced that his colleagues were in the wrong. Perhaps the two most famous cases in which he was in a minority of one were *Bourne* v. *Keane* (1919) and *Stopes* v. *Sutherland* (1925). The former laid down that bequests for masses for the souls of the dead are not now void as directed to superstitious uses. The latter was an action for libel, brought by Dr. Marie Stopes against the defendant, who had published strong disapproval of her campaign for instruction in birth control. The jury negatived fair comment, and the Court of Appeal upheld that verdict. In the House of Lords Wrenbury took the isolated view that the order of the Court of Appeal should be upheld or, alternatively, that there should be a new trial.

Wrenbury interested himself not only in the judicial but also in the legislative work of the House of Lords. He was a very valuable member of the Joint Committee of Lords and Commons on the bill for consolidating the various statutory provisions relating to income tax, which ultimately passed into law as the Income Tax Act (1918). He was greatly interested in political economy, and in 1904 founded a scholarship in that subject, tenable at Cambridge. The same interest led him to contribute in April 1924 an article to *The Times* on the important subject of trade unions, in which he advanced the eminently practical proposition that every class should be educated to understand the difficulties of every other class. His was a life packed throughout its long duration with painstaking and useful work for humanity.

Wrenbury married in 1887 Bertha Margaretta, third daughter of Charles Edward Jones, of South Kensington, and had four sons, the second of whom died in infancy, and four daughters. He died in London 27 October 1935, at the age of ninety, and was succeeded as second baron by his eldest son, Bryan Burton (1890–1940).

Two portraits of Wrenbury, by John Collier (1897 and 1907), are in the possession of his widow.

[*The Times*, 28 October 1935.]

H. G. HANBURY.

BUCKMASTER, STANLEY OWEN, first VISCOUNT BUCKMASTER (1861–1934), lord chancellor and statesman, was born at Slapton, Cheddington, Buckinghamshire, 9 January 1861, the third of the four sons of John Charles Buckmaster, of Slapton, afterwards of Wandsworth, by his wife, Emily Anne, eldest daughter of George Goodliffe, of Trumpington, near Cambridge. John Buckmaster was a remarkable man who, beginning life as an agricultural labourer, became successively a joiner, a well-known platform speaker in the cause of free trade, and, under the patronage of the Prince Consort whom he had advised and helped in the matter of the Great Exhibition of 1851, an inspector in the Department of Science and Art at South Kensington, which has since developed into the Imperial College of Science and Technology.

Stanley Buckmaster was sent to Aldenham School where he remained until 1879, living a life so hard that he never forgot its hardships. He then went, with a junior studentship, to Christ Church, Oxford, where he obtained a second class in mathematical moderations (1881) and in the final mathematical school (1882).

Buckmaster was a devoted liberal and, as his father had been, an ardent free trader. In 1906 he was returned to parliament for the borough of Cambridge: in January 1910 he lost that seat, which, in the following December, he again unsuccessfully contested; but at a by-election in October 1911 he was returned for the Keighley division of the West Riding of Yorkshire. Under the leadership first of Campbell-Bannerman and afterwards of Asquith, Buckmaster was a supporter of the government. But often he would speak, albeit from the government benches, from the experience of a practising lawyer rather than as a party man, and such speeches as the defence of Sir William Grantham [q.v.], a strong conservative, in connexion with a petition in respect of the election at Yarmouth in 1906, and his criticisms of the criminal appeal bill (1907) came from him as a lawyer's guidance of the House.

It was not, however, until he reached the House of Lords in 1915 that Buckmaster's powers as a parliamentary debater, and as a parliamentary orator, reached their height and that he became a leader of debate. While he was on the woolsack he took the ordinary part of a lord chancellor in debate and was sometimes the most prominent speaker for the government; and afterwards he often availed himself of the benefit of the custom by which an ex-lord chancellor, as distinct from the other law lords, is granted by the House full liberty to take part, and even a leading part, in general political debate. He spoke thus on many subjects, including finance, industrial unrest, disarmament, the treatment of Germans after the war of 1914–1918, the government's Irish policy, the reform of the House of Lords, many times on the reform of the divorce laws (a subject always much in his mind), birth control, and women's suffrage: what he said always compelled the respect of the House and the manner of his saying it its admiration. During the same years he made many important speeches outside parliament, a number of which, especially the speeches which he made in 1925 to lawyers in Canada and the United States of America, will be remembered. As a platform orator he was regarded by many as supreme in his time.

In 1884 Buckmaster was called to the bar by the Inner Temple and in 1902 became a member of Lincoln's Inn. He was made a bencher of Lincoln's Inn in 1910 and was treasurer in 1934. He practised first on the Common Law side, largely on the Oxford circuit and in county courts, and it was because he did there, as a young man, so much litigation work, unled, that he learnt to lean on his own judgement about a case as a whole, and so, when he went over into Chancery and as a junior was soon engaged in cases involving different questions and more important amounts, he was competent from experience, and bold from having known responsibility, to determine, and to advise without waiting for a leader, not only on the law and the form of the pleadings, but on the merits of the case and the strategy and tactics for the court. On the Chancery side he had a large practice as a junior and in 1902 he took silk. In those days the King's Counsel practising on the Chancery side were 'attached' to the courts of particular judges of that division and he went to Sir H. B. Buckley (afterwards Lord Wrenbury, q.v.). In 1907 he 'went special' and so for a special fee could, and did, practise before any Chancery judge. Like every great success at the bar, Buckmaster's was gained by hard work and thoroughness: he was by nature and training a good lawyer; he learnt and understood what equity might be necessary; he was quick enough and industrious enough to scrutinize the facts put before him, and had skill and judgement in the selection and presentation of what among those facts was material. He never sought to evade a difficulty by pretending that it was not there; it was a precept of his that before you put together the stones of which a house is to be built you must look all round each stone to see whether there is a beetle underneath it.

In 1913 Buckmaster was appointed solicitor-general in succession to Sir John Simon. His work as a law officer earned much commendation from the bench, the bar, and the departments, but soon after the outbreak of war he was given additional duties as director of the Press Bureau. To a press accustomed to freedom and a public whose curiosity was insatiable, his methods appeared too drastic, nor did his explanations always command satisfaction in the House of Commons or in the country.

On the reconstruction of Asquith's government into a coalition ministry in May 1915, and the retirement of Haldane as lord chancellor, the great seal was given to Buckmaster, who the same day was sworn of the Privy Council. He took the title of Baron Buckmaster, of Cheddington, in Buckinghamshire. When the coalition ministry fell in December 1916, Buckmaster, who had been lord chancellor for only eighteen months, was succeeded by R.B., Lord Finlay [q.v.] With the exception of some time passed in the City, in 1925–1926, in a crusade against what he regarded as an injustice (for which time he relinquished his pension) he spent the rest of his life as an appellate judge in the House of Lords and the Judicial Committee of the Privy Council and often presided in those tribunals.

Buckmaster was probably best known as an orator, but the work which he did as a judge is the work that will be remembered longest. It was not the work which he most enjoyed, but it was done under the compulsion of a stern sense of duty and the recognition, when sitting as a judge in the highest tribunals of the Empire, that justice, which had always been the ruling motive of his life, was now best served by statement of the law as it was. Any temptation to find a construction of the law which would 'right a wrong' in the particular case or would mitigate a hardship caused by the law itself was resolutely resisted. No one ever saw more clearly that hard cases make bad law, and that the cure in such cases was for parliament. Lord Birkenhead said of him that he was 'a consummately equipped judge'; and when Lord Dunedin was asked: 'Whom do you regard as the greatest colleague you have had?', he answered: 'You will be surprised when I tell you—Buckmaster; I have not and I never have had any sympathy with Buckmaster's political ideas and performances and I think him to be a sentimentalist—unless he is sitting on his arse on the bench; there he is one of the most learned, one of the most acute, and the fairest judge I ever sat with; and he will leave much in the books.'

Buckmaster was appointed G.C.V.O. in 1930 and advanced to a viscountcy in 1933: the step in the peerage was made, certainly in the opinion of the profession, particularly in order to enable him, after he had ceased to be lord chancellor, to preside in appeals in which some other law lord or member of the Judicial Committee, junior to him but a viscount, might be sitting: it was a legal, not a political, nor a social, advancement. He was counsel to Oxford University from 1910 to 1913; was elected an honorary student of Christ Church in 1917; and received honorary degrees from the universities of Toronto (1925) and Oxford and Edinburgh (1933). He held a very special position in regard to the boot and shoe trade as umpire for determining wages and disputes about conditions. He had held this position for three years before his appointment as a law officer, and in 1925 was re-appointed and held the office until his death. In 1923 he became chairman of the governing body of the Imperial College of Science and Technology, an appointment of which, for the sake of his father's memory, he was most proud.

Buckmaster was much beloved by his friends and particularly at the Garrick Club of which he was a member from 1909 until his death. He seldom said a witty thing and seldom told a good story, but his speeches at the famous Sunday dinners of the club were delightful in their always kindly humour. Perhaps the best of his talk was when, on a fishing holiday beside the Spey, he would be lying on the bank with a friend, often his faithful and much-loved gillie, waiting for the sun to go off the pool.

Buckmaster married in 1889 Edith Augusta (died 1935), fourth daughter of Spencer Robert Lewin, of Widford, Hertfordshire; they had one son and two daughters, the elder of whom predeceased her father. He died in London 5 December 1934, and was succeeded as second viscount by his son, Owen Stanley (born 1890).

A portrait of Buckmaster, by Thomas McKegger, is in the possession of Dr. Dorothy Tasker. Another (posthumous) portrait, in his lord chancellor's robes, by Reginald Eves, hangs in the hall of Christ Church, Oxford.

[*The Times*, 6 and 7 December 1934; *A Village Politician. The Life-Story of John Buckley* (edited by J. C. Buckmaster whose autobiography it is), 1897; James Johnston, *An Orator of Justice. A Speech Biography of Viscount Buckmaster*, 1932; private information; personal knowledge.]

GEOFFREY RUSSELL.

BUDGE, SIR (ERNEST ALFRED THOMPSON) WALLIS (1857–1934), Assyriologist and Egyptologist, came of Cornish Quaker stock engaged in Indian and Chinese trade. He was born 27 July 1857. While still a child at an elementary school run by a relative, he became interested in Hebrew; employed at an early age by W. H. Smith & Son, in his scanty

leisure he studied Hebrew and Syriac with Charles Seager [q.v.]. The intense interest aroused by the Assyrian discoveries of George Smith [q.v.] led to an introduction to Samuel Birch [q.v.] at the British Museum, and to opportunities for study which he generously provided. Gladstone, appealed to by Seager in 1874, arranged for funds to send the boy to Cambridge as a non-collegiate student under William Wright [q.v.] in 1878. In 1879, following John Peile's suggestion, Budge won the Otway exhibition at Christ's College where he was elected scholar in 1881. Wright, an unsparing critic of decipherers of cuneiform, was much incensed by the appearance of two books on Assyrian texts, destined to remain useful for forty years, from the pen of an undergraduate, but later he became a firm friend, whose counsel was sought and followed until his death in 1889. After taking the Semitic languages tripos in 1882, Budge won the Tyrwhitt Hebrew scholarship, and a year later (1883), in accordance with Gladstone's desire, accepted appointment as assistant in Birch's department (oriental antiquities) at the British Museum.

This appointment led to Budge's abandonment of Assyriology owing to the jealousy of a colleague. This was a bitter blow, but his training proved constantly useful. At the request of Sir H. C. Rawlinson [q.v.] the trustees sent Budge on three missions to Mesopotamia, partly to conduct excavations strictly limited in scope, but chiefly to clear up unsatisfactory arrangements made by Hormuzd Rassam [q.v.], involving payment of guards on sites where pillage was rife. Budge's reports, leading to the dismissal of the guards, were displeasing to Sir A. H. Layard [q.v.], who had recommended Rassam, and two interviews led to an action for slander by Rassam against Budge, tried before Mr. Justice Cave in 1893. The award of £50 damages and the consequent costs were only met with the assistance of colleagues, indignant that official reports should ultimately have become the subject of a private action. In 1897, when in Egypt, Budge had an opportunity to purchase tablets from Amarna, and his knowledge enabled him to form a more correct opinion of this surprising find than did others. His long acquaintance with Assyriologists is recorded in *The Rise and Progress of Assyriology* (1925).

Before Birch's death in 1885 Budge was

competent to read Egyptian texts. In 1886 he dug at Assuan, and between 1897 and 1905 he went five times for short periods to examine sites in the Sudan. It was there that he contracted glaucoma; one eye was rendered useless for reading. In sixteen official visits to Egypt, from 1886, his purchases greatly extended the range and representative character of the collections not only of his own, but also of other departments of the Museum; among them were celebrated Greek papyri, the Ἀθηναίων πολιτεία, the mimes of Herodas, and the odes of Bacchylides. In 1892, while still an assistant, Budge was put in charge of the department, now re-named Egyptian and Assyrian Antiquities, and in 1894 he was appointed keeper, remaining so until his retirement in 1924. Owing to structural alterations and the war of 1914–1918, the heavy task of rearranging the collections had to be carried out three times. The toil of introducing order into chaotic disorder, and of maintaining it in spite of such adverse conditions, and of extensive acquisitions, not easily appreciated by those not concerned, did not prevent necessary and extensive publication. Catalogue-guides, essential for students and visitors, came from Budge's own pen. Official publications of copies of cuneiform and hieroglyphic texts were devised by him as a result of his practical knowledge of printing. He himself edited two volumes of reproductions of hieratic papyri with explanatory introductions and translations, and numerous ancient copies of the Book of the Dead. He created a thoroughly efficient department and left it in good working order.

Wright had impressed upon Budge the duty of speedy publication of texts, and the desirability of publishing translations with the texts, even if imperfect, to assist others, and Budge accomplished a remarkable volume of work in following these precepts. In Syriac a long series begins with the Book of the Bee in 1886 and ends with the Syrian Chronicle of Bar Hebraeus in 1932. The first Coptic text which he published was the History of Isaac of Tiphre (1884); the last were the Miscellaneous Texts (1915). His work in Ethiopic began with the Contendings of the Apostles (1898) and ended with the Bandlet of Righteousness (1929). There were also translations for the first time into English of texts published by others. Time and trouble were freely spent in finding money; during his later years he paid for publication himself. Editions and translations produced under such pressure called for, and received, considerable criticism; in so far as the criticism promoted knowledge more quickly than would otherwise have been possible, Budge's purpose was served.

Among Egyptologists Budge was the best Semitic scholar of his generation. He sturdily refused to accept two theories which became fashionable, namely, the grammatical interpretation of certain forms of the Egyptian verb by analogy with the Semitic verb, and transliteration based upon the unprovable phonetic theory that the hieroglyphic writing represents always only consonants as in Semitic languages. His work accordingly found no favour in contemporary academic schools, but it has been of great assistance to the self-taught. His most important original work lay in the deciphering of the hieratic papyri in the Museum, above all the remarkable Teaching of Amenemapt (1924), and in the edition of a standard text of the Book of the Dead (1898). His reading books, devised to enable private students to read, were the best introductions to hieroglyphs in English for thirty years. The Egyptian Hieroglyphic Dictionary (1920), a remarkable achievement for one man, is still useful, even after the appearance of the Berlin Wörterbuch. His ephemeral books, intended to place general information on his subjects before the reading public, were numerous and useful in their time; some still retain their value, for instance The Mummy (edition of 1925), The Egyptian Sudan, Its History and Monuments (1907), A History of Ethiopia, Nubia, and Abyssinia (1928).

Budge had great physical energy and zest for life. He was a notable raconteur, and his company was appreciated by excellent judges. Impatient of idleness, pretentiousness, and humbug, he made many enemies and rejoiced in sincere friendships, sympathizing rather with the soldier than with the diplomat. A man of wide learning, he was critical of most of the 'critical' methods of modern scholarship; intensely interested in the main lines of development in his subjects, he was less impressed by insistence on accuracy in minutiae than by sound judgement and real discoveries due to pioneer work. His private life was exceptionally happy; he married in 1888 Dora Helen, daughter of Titus Emerson, rector of Allendale, Northumberland, and he tended and obeyed her with great gentleness until her death in 1926. They had no children. On his death his estate provided for a memorial to her in the form of two foundations for the encouragement of Egyptology, the one at his own college, the other at University College, Oxford, to which he belonged owing to the friendship of Reginald Walter Macan. He was knighted in 1920. He died in London 23 November 1934.

[Autobiographical material in *By Nile and Tigris*, 1920; bibliography in *Who was Who, 1929–1940*, 1941; private information; personal knowledge.]   SIDNEY SMITH.

BULFIN, SIR EDWARD STANIS-LAUS (1862–1939), general, was born in Dublin 6 November 1862, the second son of Patrick Bulfin, of Woodtown Park, Rathfarnham, co. Dublin, by his wife, Teresa Clare, daughter of John Carroll, of Dublin. He was educated at Stonyhurst and Trinity College, Dublin, and entered the army through the militia in which he served in the 3rd battalion, the Royal Irish Fusiliers. In 1884 he joined the Yorkshire Regiment (the Green Howards). He was promoted captain in 1895 and held the appointment of assistant military secretary and aide-de-camp to the general officer commanding in South Africa from November 1898 until November 1899. The South African war broke out in October 1899 and he continued to serve on the staff until 1901, taking part in the advance on Kimberley and the battles at Belmont, Enslin, Modder River, and Magersfontein. In December 1901 he was given command of a mobile column with which he served until the conclusion of the campaign in 1902. He was three times mentioned in dispatches, and received the brevets of major and lieutenant-colonel, the Queen's medal with four clasps, and the King's medal with two clasps.

In November 1903 Bulfin was given a majority in the Manchester Regiment, but he never served with that regiment as he held the appointment of deputy-assistant-adjutant-general, the I Army Corps, from October 1902 until October 1904, when he transferred to the Royal Welch Fusiliers. In 1906 he returned to South Africa as assistant-adjutant and quartermaster-general, Cape Colony district. In this same year he was made a brevet colonel, reaching the substantive rank in 1908. He remained in South Africa until 1910. Between 1911 and the outbreak of war in 1914 he commanded successively the Essex Infantry brigade of the Territorial Force and the 2nd brigade at Aldershot, which he took out with the British Expeditionary Force to France. On 14 Sep-

tember, during the battle of the Aisne, he fought a successful action with his brigade near Troyon. On 26 October he was promoted major-general and, in command of a number of units temporarily put together under the title of 'Bulfin's force', he played a prominent part in repelling the German attacks during the first battle of Ypres, being wounded on 1 November.

In December Bulfin was given command of the 28th division, which he took out to France in January 1915. His division was on the flank of the Canadian division when the latter met the full force of the first German gas attack at Ypres in April. Under Bulfin's resolute leadership the 28th division bore a very heavy burden throughout the second battle of Ypres and suffered very heavily. He remained in command of this division until October 1915, when he took over the 60th division and served with it in France, at Salonika, and with the Egyptian Expeditionary Force until August 1917, when he received command of the XXI Army Corps, which also formed part of the Egyptian Expeditionary Force. He thus took part as a corps commander in the successful campaign in Palestine of Sir Edmund (later Viscount) Allenby [q.v.], whereby Turkey was put out of the war. He retained command of the XXI Army Corps until November 1919 and was subsequently employed as commissioner for the disposal of surplus stores in India and Iraq from the end of 1921 until August 1923. He was promoted lieutenant-general in 1919 and full general in 1925. He retired in 1926.

During the war of 1914–1918 Bulfin was seven times mentioned in dispatches and was promoted both to major-general and to lieutenant-general for distinguished conduct in the field. He was appointed C.V.O. in 1910, K.C.B. in 1918, and received numerous foreign decorations, and the honorary degree of LL.D. from Trinity College, Dublin, in 1920. He was colonel of the Green Howards from 1914 until his death.

Bulfin married in 1898 Frances Mary (died 1947), only daughter of Francis William Lonergan, of London, and had one son and one daughter; his son, Captain James Joseph Bulfin, M.C., died in Palestine in 1929 while serving with the 2nd battalion, the Green Howards. Bulfin died at Boscombe, Bournemouth, 20 August 1939.

A portrait of Bulfin, by St. Helen Lauder, is in the officers' mess of the depot of the Green Howards at Richmond, Yorkshire.

[*The Times*, 22 August 1939; Official records; private information.]

E. H. WYNDHAM.

BUNSEN, SIR MAURICE WILLIAM ERNEST DE, baronet (1852–1932), diplomatist. [See DE BUNSEN.]

BURKITT, FRANCIS CRAWFORD (1864–1935), professor of divinity, was born in London 3 September 1864, the only child of Crawford Burkitt, who was in business there. Francis Burkitt's grandfather had migrated to London from Sudbury in Suffolk, and founded the business which his father carried on so successfully that the son had no need to make a living for himself. This grandfather married a sister of the philanthropist William Crawford [q.v.] whose unworldliness and reforming spirit were seen again in some measure in his great-nephew. His mother was Fanny Elizabeth Coward, of a Somerset family connected with Chilcompton.

Being supposed to need special care Burkitt was sent to a day school near his home. In 1878 he went to Harrow, on the modern side, and in 1883 entered Trinity College, Cambridge, of which he was elected a scholar in 1885. He graduated as a wrangler in part i of the mathematical tripos of 1886, but he turned at once from mathematics to the study of Hebrew. The natural way of doing this in the Cambridge of that time was to read for the theological tripos. This involved a course of scientific study of the Old and the New Testament and the early history of Christian thought and institutions, which gave him a good foundation for his later work in the domain of the beginnings of Christianity. He won several university prizes and the second Tyrwhitt scholarship (1889) and was placed in the first class in part ii of the tripos of 1888.

In the last-named year Burkitt married Amy Persis, daughter of William Parry, rector of Fitz, Shropshire, and granddaughter of Sir Edward Barnes [q.v.]. They settled down in Cambridge and had one son, the archaeologist, Mr. Miles Burkitt. It was not until 1903 that he held any academic office—a university lectureship in palaeography previously held by James Rendel Harris—and not until after the promulgation of the university statutes of 1926 that he was elected a fellow of his college, although he had been Norrisian

professor of divinity (combined with the Hulsean professorship in 1934) since 1905. So he had his whole time at his own disposal and he set to work to study other oriental languages, Syriac in particular. It was as a Syriac scholar that he first became widely known, especially in connexion with the textual criticism of the Gospels. He was the first to recognize the importance of the Syriac palimpsest of the four Gospels in the convent of St. Catherine on Mount Sinai and was one of the party that transcribed it in 1893 [see LEWIS, AGNES]. The two-volume edition of the old Syriac Gospels which he published in 1904 with the title *Evangelion da-Mepharreshe: the Curetonian Version of the Four Gospels, with the Readings of the Sinai Palimpsest and the Early Syriac Patristic Evidence edited, collected and arranged* will always be indispensable to the student of the Syriac versions of the New Testament.

Similarly as regards the Old Testament, although the conditions are different, Burkitt's article 'Text and Versions' in the *Encyclopædia Biblica* (1903) is a masterly survey which remains without an equal. He lived through the years when the new literary and historical criticism of the Old Testament was fighting its way, and he took an active part in expounding its main results. But it was in the field of critical study of the New Testament that his own chief contributions were made. In this sphere Burkitt was, for English students at least, one of the pioneers, especially by his book *The Gospel History and its Transmission* (1906), but scarcely less so by his acceptance of the teaching of Johannes Weiss as to the meaning of 'the kingdom of God' in the message of Jesus. Burkitt made himself at once the champion in England of the 'eschatological', 'apocalyptic', interpretation of the aims and teaching of Jesus. It was mainly at his instigation also that Albert Schweitzer's great book *Von Reimarus zu Wrede* (1906) was translated by William Montgomery and made known to English readers under the title *The Quest of the Historical Jesus* (1910). It must be counted as one of his chief services to the history of Christianity that he took a lead in showing the inadequacy of the Liberal Protestant ideas of the nineteenth century as regards Jesus and His Gospel and recalled students to the fact that Jesus shared the apocalyptic conceptions current in some circles of religious Jews of His time and in His teaching never envisaged a future for human society in the world as it has actually been. Burkitt's mastery of the conditions of the transition from the reformed religion of Israel to the Jewish-Christian conditions of the first century A.D. was shown in his Schweich lectures for 1913, *Jewish and Christian Apocalypses* (1914).

In common with other students Burkitt held that the Christ of the Catholic creeds and institutions was the product of epigenesis, in the course of which the historical Figure had been transformed. But he was convinced that really scientific criticism applied to the Gospels revealed an historical Person with a *substratum* of His actual doings and sayings adequate to account for the origin and the later developments of the Christian Church. So he found the new school of *formgeschichtlich* criticism unacceptable as leaving one of the greatest of historical phenomena—the rise of Christianity—in the air, without foundation in events and happenings in actual human experience (*Jesus Christ: an Historical Outline*, 1932). He made valuable contributions also to Franciscan studies (notably in an essay on 'The Study of the Sources of the Life of St. Francis' in the volume *St. Francis of Assisi* edited by Walter Seton in 1926), and to the history and significance of Christian worship in *Eucharist and Sacrifice* (1921) and in vol. iii (1930) of *The Christian Religion: its Origin and Progress*, edited by J. F. Bethune-Baker, as well as in numerous articles on special points. His books on Manichaeism and Gnosticism, *The Religion of the Manichees* (1925) and *Church and Gnosis* (1932) are fresh and original surveys of well-worn themes.

A list of Burkitt's published writings (books and pamphlets and articles in various magazines) occupies ten pages of small print in the *Journal of Theological Studies* for October 1935, arranged under the headings Syriac Studies, Textual Criticism, The Latin Bible (*Old Latin* and *The Latin Vulgate*), Hebrew and Old Testament Studies, New Testament Studies (*The Gospels* and *Acts and Epistles*), Early Christian Literature and Life, On Gnosticism, On Mandaeism, on Manichaeism, Liturgical Studies (*General* and *Hymns*), Franciscan Studies, Archaeological Studies, Philological, The Past and The Present, Biographical.

Such a list shows the wide range of Burkitt's learning. All his writings bear the mark of a mind of unusual acumen as well as equipment. He was a vivid and attractive personality, full of interests other than those of the mere scholar—an eager fisherman and occasional gardener, a skilled pianist and musician (with Bach as his standard of perfection), a player of patience and other such games, a rapid solver of the crossword puzzles in *The Times* (he 'knew the way the man's mind worked')—no great reader of poetry or novels. Poetry and philosophy were scarcely in his orbit, although he could make truly poetical versions (*Ecclesiastes. Rendered into English Verse*, 1922, *The Song of Brother Sun in English Rime*, 1926) and he sometimes threw light on philosophical 'questions' by reference to facts which had escaped the philosophers' attention. 'Facts' always came first with him and he had an unfailing memory for detail.

A practising member of the Church of England of the modernist school (regularly reading the lessons at a church of the 'liberal evangelical' type near his home) he had members of most of the great Christian denominations, and Jews and other non-Christians, among his intimate friends, and would take endless pains with students—younger or older—who consulted him. He conducted a seminar of his own and was a constant attendant and speaker at congresses and meetings of various kinds.

Always on the track of something, always alert, Burkitt's gifts of spirit and mind were kept in fruitful exercise all his life. While he was still apparently as alert and active as ever, in his seventy-first year, after a full day's work, as he was about to go to sleep, at his home at Cambridge, a blood vessel in the brain gave way and without recovering consciousness he died in the early morning of 11 May 1935.

Burkitt received honorary degrees from the universities of Edinburgh and Dublin (1907), St. Andrews and Breslau (1911), Oxford (1927), and Durham (1934). He was elected a fellow of the British Academy in 1905.

A portrait of Burkitt, by Mrs. Proffit, is in the possession of his son.

[J. F. Bethune-Baker, *Francis Crawford Burkitt, 1864–1935*, in *Proceedings* of the British Academy, vol. xxii, 1936; *Journal of Theological Studies*, July and October 1935; personal knowledge.]

J. F. BETHUNE-BAKER.

BURNET, SIR JOHN JAMES (1857–1938), architect, was born at Glasgow 31 May 1857, the youngest son of John

Burnet, architect, of Glasgow, by his wife, Eliza Hay Bennet. He was educated at the Western Academy, Glasgow. In his eighteenth year he went to Paris to study architecture at the École des Beaux Arts, joining the atelier of Jean Louis Pascal where he qualified for the *diplôme du gouvernement* in the unusually short period of three years. On his return his father took him into partnership and he immediately distinguished himself by winning the competition for the galleries of the (Royal) Glasgow Institute of Fine Arts. In this design Burnet, at the early age of twenty-one, showed the mastery in handling plan, elevation, material, and detail as a coherent whole which was to characterize all his subsequent work. Commissions came to him quickly, in great number and variety. Public buildings (Glasgow Athenaeum and Edinburgh International Exhibition, 1886), business premises (Clyde Navigation Trust, Glasgow, 1883–1886, and many others in Glasgow and Edinburgh), churches (Barony church, Glasgow, 1886–1889, Arbroath parish church, 1894–1896, etc.), hospitals, railway stations, and private houses engaged him during his thirty years' practice in Glasgow and gained him his immense reputation in Scotland. He had succeeded in investing commercial architecture with a new vigour and *rationale* and in hospital planning he laid the foundation for the modern advance that has revolutionized hospital design. Burnet's strongly developed sense of composition explains his lifelong interest in sculpture, and in the Glasgow Savings Bank (1895) he gave (Sir) George Frampton [q.v.] his first important architectural commission.

In 1904 the trustees of the British Museum commissioned Burnet to erect the King Edward VII galleries in Montague Place. The result is by common consent one of the most important contributions to the architecture of this century. The great single order of twenty Ionic columns, between their flanking pylons, achieves the maximum of dignity and repose. The composition is much more than a brilliant exercise on a classic theme; every subtlety of varying diameter, intercolumniation, and inclination of verticals was employed to secure grace and homogeneity and it is justly acclaimed for its modern vigour and originality. On its completion in 1914 Burnet was knighted and the Paris Salon conferred upon him its bronze medal. The gold medal followed in 1922 and the Royal Institute of

British Architects, of which he had been elected a fellow in 1897, awarded him its Royal gold medal in 1923. He was elected A.R.A. in 1921 and R.A. in 1925. In 1910 the university of Glasgow conferred upon him the honorary degree of LL.D.

After 1905 Burnet moved to London, the Glasgow office being carried on separately in partnership with Mr. Norman Dick. Important commissions multiplied in England and Scotland and notable works in London were the offices of the General Accident Fire and Life Assurance Company in Aldwych (sculptor, Albert Hodge), the Institute of Chemistry, Russell Square, and (in association with Mr. T. S. Tait) the Kodak building, Kingsway, Adelaide House, London Bridge, Vigo House, Regent Street, and Unilever House, Blackfriars. He assisted the War Graves Commission, Palestine, and designed the Indian war memorials (Gulf of Suez and Cape Helles), the Cavalry War Memorial, Hyde Park, and the Glasgow cenotaph.

Burnet married in 1886 Jean Watt, daughter of the legal and historical writer (Sir) James David Marwick [q.v.], and died without issue, at Colinton, Edinburgh, 2 July 1938. A portrait bust by Sir William Reid Dick is in the possession of Lady Burnet.

[*The Times*, 4 July 1938; *Journal* of the Royal Institute of British Architects, 18 July and 15 August 1938; personal knowledge.]

WALTER H. GODFREY.

BURNHAM, first VISCOUNT (1862–1933), newspaper proprietor. [See LAWSON, SIR HARRY LAWSON WEBSTER LEVY-.]

BUTLER, EDWARD JOSEPH ALOYSIUS (in religion DOM CUTHBERT) (1858–1934), Benedictine abbot and scholar, was born in Dublin 6 May 1858, the only child of Edward Butler, barrister, by his wife, Mary, sister of the well-known Dublin physician Sir Francis Cruise. His father was professor of mathematics in the recently established Roman Catholic university in Dublin of which Cardinal Newman was rector from 1854 to 1858. Educated at Downside from 1869 to 1875, Butler entered the Benedictine novitiate at Belmont Priory, Hereford, in 1876, taking in religion the name of Cuthbert. Returning in 1880 to Downside, where the young Dom Aidan Gasquet [q.v.] was prior, and the scholar Edmund Bishop [q.v.] a frequent visitor, he was ordained priest in 1884 and taught in the school, of which he was first prefect from 1888 to 1892. But his principal interest was the contemporary movement to win for Downside and the other monasteries of the English Benedictine Congregation autonomy and full monastic discipline and observance. This end was in large part achieved in 1900, when Downside became an abbey and the Congregation was organized on traditional Benedictine lines.

Meanwhile, Butler was sent in 1896 to Cambridge as superior of Benet House, where he edited the *Lausiac History of Palladius* (1898, 1904); during these years he owed much in different ways to friendships with J. A. Robinson [q.v.] and Friedrich von Hügel [q.v.]. Returning to Downside as subprior in 1904, he was elected abbot in 1906, and was re-elected in 1914. He did much to develop the monastic life of the house, and was abbot president of the English Benedictine Congregation from 1914 to 1921. While in office at Downside he published a critical edition of the Rule of St. Benedict (1912), and wrote *Benedictine Monachism* (1919), the fruit of a life's experience and thought, and *Western Mysticism* (1922). In this last year he resigned the abbacy, and thenceforward lived at Ealing Priory, writing *The Life and Times of Bishop Ullathorne* (2 vols., 1926), *The Vatican Council* (1930), and other books. He died suddenly of heart failure at Clapham on Easter Day, 1 April 1934, and was buried at Downside.

Tall and of striking appearance, Butler conveyed an instantaneous impression, which further acquaintance did not belie, of intellectual distinction and unaffected benevolence. By temperament a scholar rather than a ruler, he failed on occasion both in judgement and in decision, without ever forfeiting the respect which his sincerity and genuine piety inspired. Towards the end of his life his work won wide recognition as that of a candid and judicious scholar; his real monument, however, must be sought in the liturgical and intellectual life of Downside in his day.

Butler received the honorary degree of doctor of letters from Trinity College, Dublin, in 1908. A portrait of him, by W. C. Symons, is at Downside.

[*Downside Review*, July 1934; private information; personal knowledge.]

M. D. KNOWLES.

BUTLER, ELIZABETH SOUTHERDEN, LADY (1846–1933), painter, was born at the Villa Claremont, Lausanne,

3 November 1846, the elder daughter of Thomas James Thompson, by his second wife, Christiana, daughter of Thomas Edward Weller. The younger daughter was Alice Meynell, the poet and essayist [q.v.]. Thompson undertook entirely the early education of these two daughters; and as he believed that travel and languages are the sovereign means for acquiring an historical sense, the family lived at that time nearly as much abroad, particularly in Italy, as in England. The daughters derived their sensitive response to beauty not only from him but also from their mother, an accomplished pianist and a sketcher in water-colour. Between the ages of nineteen and twenty-one Elizabeth Thompson studied at the South Kensington School of Art, which she entered early in 1866, distinguishing herself in water-colour. In 1869 she became a pupil of Giuseppe Bellucci in Florence, and she also studied in Rome. On her return to England she continued zealously painting in oils and in 1872 made an inspiring contact with the army through watching some manœuvres. About 1873 she was received into the Roman Catholic Church whither her mother and her sister Alice had preceded her. In 1874 fame came to her suddenly when she exhibited 'The Roll Call' at the Royal Academy. The picture had to be specially protected from the pressure of the 'sight-seeing' crowds and it was reproduced in numberless engravings. It was bought from the original purchaser by Queen Victoria and is now in St. James's Palace. Thenceforward the painter of 'The Roll Call' was held, sometimes against her will, almost exclusively to military subjects. Among her best-known pictures may be mentioned 'Quatre Bras' (1875, now in the National Gallery, Melbourne), 'The Remnants of an Army' (1879, Tate Gallery), 'The Defence of Rorke's Drift' (1880, Windsor Castle), 'Scotland for Ever!' (1881, Leeds Art Gallery), 'The Dawn of Waterloo' (1896, in private hands), and 'Steady the Drums and Fifes' (1896, Depot of the Middlesex Regiment). Ruskin described 'Quatre Bras' as 'Amazon's work' and as 'the first fine pre-Raphaelite picture of battle that we have had'. The precision of her painting was prized by the army for its faithful recording of regimental deeds and dress, but a later generation has preferred to find her real merit in her masterly draughtsmanship with its unfailing sense of movement. Few artists have equalled her drawing of horses. Her water-colours

have a softness that suggests a reaction from the clash of arms.

In 1877 Elizabeth Thompson married Major (afterwards Lieutenant-General Sir) William Francis Butler [q.v.]. They had three sons and three daughters, the eldest of whom died in infancy. In person Lady Butler was notable for a combination of dignity and humility; she was always reticent in the presence of public curiosity. Her friends were gratefully familiar with the droll inventiveness of her conversation. After her husband's death in 1910 she continued to live for a time at Bansha, co. Tipperary, where they had settled on his retirement, but her last years were spent at Gormanston Castle, co. Meath, the home of her youngest daughter, where she died 2 October 1933.

There is a portrait of Lady Butler, by Louis Desanges, in the possession of her eldest son.

[Lady Butler, *Letters from the Holy Land*, 1903, *From Sketch-book and Diary*, 1909, and *An Autobiography*, 1922; Viola Meynell, *Alice Meynell*, 1929; Wilfrid Meynell, *The Life and Work of Lady Butler* (Christmas number of the *Art Journal*), 1898; private information.]
J. B. ATKINS.

BUTLER, SIR RICHARD HARTE KEATINGE (1870–1935), lieutenant-general, was born, possibly abroad, 28 August 1870, the son of Colonel E. R. Butler, Army Medical Service. He was educated at Harrow and the Royal Military College, Sandhurst. He was commissioned in the Dorsetshire Regiment in 1890, becoming lieutenant in 1892 and captain in 1894. He became adjutant of the 2nd battalion in 1896 and held that post most efficiently during the operations of January and February 1900 for the relief of Ladysmith. During the withdrawal from Spion Kop he went back across the Tugela to rescue a wounded man and was actually the last man to recross the river. He again distinguished himself the following June when the Boers were cleared out of northern Natal, the 2nd Dorsets storming the key of the Boer position at Alleman's Nek. Transferring in August to the 5th division's Mounted Infantry, he saw much service in Natal, the south-east Transvaal, and the Zululand border. He played a prominent part in the successful defence of Fort Itala (September 1901) against Louis Botha [q.v.], being severely wounded. His services brought him a brevet as major (1900) and two mentions in dispatches.

After passing the Staff College in 1906, Butler was a brigade-major at Aldershot, obtaining his regimental majority in 1910; a year later he returned to Aldershot as G.S.O. 2 and received a brevet as lieutenant-colonel in 1913. He was selected in June 1914 for the command of the 2nd Lancashire Fusiliers but was to be retained at Aldershot until the end of the training season. He therefore did not take his battalion to France, only joining it in September 1914 for the fighting on the Lys in October and November, where he acquitted himself so well that he was given the 3rd brigade (1st division) in November. Here again he made his mark as a fighting soldier in the winter operations round Givenchy but was appointed in February 1915 to succeed Brigadier-General J. E. Gough [q.v.] as brigadier-general, General Staff, I Corps, becoming in June major-general, General Staff, First Army. This brought him again under Sir Douglas Haig [q.v.], who had known him at Aldershot and wished to have him as chief of staff when he himself succeeded Sir John French (later Earl of Ypres, q.v.) in December. Butler was considered too junior for this post but was appointed deputy chief of the staff in 1915, a post which he retained until February 1918. His long tenure of this important post testified to Haig's confidence in him, but the qualities of vigour, resolution, and drive which made him so successful in command of troops and in fighting were less calculated to ensure his success at general headquarters. His energy made him apt to be impatient and not always very helpful with subordinates and their problems. He himself would have gladly relinquished his post for an active command, but Haig would not part with him and wished him to become chief of staff when Lieutenant-General Sir Launcelot Kiggell relinquished that post. However, in 1918 Butler was at last given a corps, the III Corps.

In the attack of March 1918 the III Corps (on the right of the Fifth Army's long line and astride the Oise, south of St. Quentin) had a longer front than any other, 31,000 yards to hold with only thirty battalions, but it was not on this front that the chief German successes were achieved. Thanks largely to Butler's dispositions and handling of his forces the III Corps did remarkably well, and though events on its left forced it back over the Crozat canal and towards Noyon, still more ground was lost after the French had replaced the depleted units. Afterwards Butler and his staff temporarily relieved that of the XIX Corps (5 April) and he was in command in front of Amiens when the final German offensive in this quarter was checked at Villers-Bretonneux (24–25 April). Reverting to his own corps but continuing in this area, Butler took part in the opening of Haig's offensive on 8 August, his corps attacking north of the Somme and playing a big part in the advance past Péronne to Epéhy and Vendhuile: before it was relieved at the end of September it had sustained 30,000 casualties and taken 10,000 prisoners. It was then transferred to the Fifth Army in the Douai region. During the war of 1914–1918 he was mentioned in dispatches nine times, received a brevet as colonel, and special promotion to major-general (June 1916). He was appointed C.B. in 1917, K.C.M.G. in 1918, and K.C.B. in 1919.

Butler subsequently commanded the Lowland division on the Rhine and the 1st division at Aldershot (November 1919 –February 1923). He was promoted lieutenant-general in 1923 and was general officer commander-in-chief, Western Command, from June 1924 to June 1928, retiring at his own request in 1929. He married in 1894 Helen Frances, second daughter of Major William Benjamin Battiscombe, of the Argyll and Sutherland Highlanders, and had a son and a daughter. He died at Shrewsbury 22 April 1935.

[*The Times*, 23 April 1935; *Army Quarterly*, July 1935; Sir J. F. Maurice and M. H. Grant, (Official) *History of the War in South Africa, 1899–1902*, 1906–1910; Sir J. E. Edmonds (Official) *History of the Great War. Military Operations. France and Belgium, 1914–1918*, 1922–1940; regimental information.]

C. T. ATKINSON.

BUTLER, SIR (SPENCER) HARCOURT (1869–1938), Indian administrator, born in London 1 August 1869, was the second of the nine sons of Spencer Perceval Butler, barrister, of Lincoln's Inn, conveyancing counsel to the Office of Works, by his wife, Mary, only child of the Rev. Nicholas Kendall, of Bodmin. He was elder brother of Sir G. G. G. Butler [q.v.]. Butler was educated at Harrow, then under the headmastership of his uncle, H. M. Butler [q.v.], and after passing the Indian civil service examination of 1888 spent his probation at Balliol College, Oxford. In October 1890 he entered upon his Indian career in the

North-West Provinces (renamed in 1902 the United Provinces of Agra and Oudh). He first came into notice as secretary in 1901 of the famine commission presided over by Sir Antony (afterwards Lord) MacDonnell [q.v.]. The report which he drafted remains the standard authority on Indian famine prevention and relief. For this work he was appointed C.I.E., and later C.S.I. (1909), K.C.S.I. (1911), G.C.I.E. (1923), and G.C.S.I. (1928).

As deputy commissioner of Lucknow district (1906–1908) Butler enhanced the beauty and amenities of the capital of Oudh. At the close of 1907 the viceroy, Lord Minto [q.v.], took him from this post to be secretary of the Foreign Department, which then had charge both of external relations and those with the Indian states. Three years later (1910) he was appointed to the viceroy's executive council in charge of the new department of education, which included within its scope public health, local self-government, archaeology, and several minor branches. In 1913 he formulated a memorable government resolution which reviewed and reshaped educational policy.

In 1915 Butler went to Rangoon as lieutenant-governor of Burma. By his development for the use of the Allies of the output of wolfram concentrates from the Tavoy fields he broke the virtual monopoly which the Germans had acquired in the manufacture of tungsten, a valuable agent in the production of munitions. Butler also did much to awaken a new spirit in Burma, notably by raising a large sum by public subscription for the foundation of the teaching Rangoon University, thereby ending the inconvenient and unsatisfactory affiliation of the colleges of Burma to the Calcutta University, across the Bay of Bengal.

Early in 1918, when his term in Burma had run only half its course, Butler went as lieutenant-governor to that part of India where he was best known and most highly esteemed—the United Provinces. Serious agrarian unrest in Oudh was allayed by his ability to reconcile the landowning *taluqdars* to a policy of tenancy reform. The Montagu-Chelmsford reforms, coming into force under the 1919 Government of India Act on 1 January 1921, initiated the system of provincial 'dyarchy', and the heads of provinces became governors. Like Lord Willingdon in Madras, Butler encouraged joint consultations between the two halves of his government— the 'reserved', with executive councillors, and the 'transferred', with ministers responsible to the legislature.

Butler had the unique experience of introducing the 'dyarchical' system into two great provinces. The second of these was Burma, where the reforms took effect two years later than in peninsular India. As governor from the beginning of 1923, he nursed the country into a measure of adolescence, but never concealed from higher authority the dangers of instability and the need for less exiguous defence measures. He took prompt steps to bring to an end slavery and human sacrifice practised by the Nagas in the wild unadministered territory bordering on the Hukwang Valley, which he himself visited in 1925.

On leaving Rangoon at the end of 1927 Butler accepted the chairmanship of the Indian States Committee. Reporting in 1929 it reaffirmed the doctrine of paramountcy, but laid down guiding principles on its application and on equitable financial relations. In 1931 he accepted the chairmanship of the governing body of the School of Oriental and African Studies, London University. He joined the boards of the Peninsular and Oriental Steamship Company, the National Provincial Bank, and other concerns. His occasional writings include his concise and fascinating description of *India Insistent* (1931).

Butler married in 1894 Florence, daughter of Francis Nelson Wright, I.C.S., and had one son. He died in London 2 March 1938. There are statues of him raised by public subscription at Lucknow and Rangoon, the former equestrian, both by George Harvard Thomas.

Butler's gifted personality was well summed up by Sir John Hewett, one of the most distinguished of his predecessors in the headship of the United Provinces: 'He had a brilliant intellect, boundless energy, and wonderful capacity for getting at the root of a matter, ability to express his conclusions so as to be clear to all, and a very practical head in carrying them out. Butler was a wonderful host. His fondness for music added greatly to the charm of his entertainments.'

[*The Times*, 3 and 7 March 1938; *Journal* of the Royal Central Asian Society, April 1938; private information; personal knowledge.]

F. H. Brown.

BUTT, Dame CLARA (1873–1936), singer, whose married name was Clara Ellen Kennerley Rumford, was born at Southwick, near Brighton, 1 February 1873, the eldest daughter and eldest surviving child of Henry Butt, a captain in the Mercantile Marine, by his wife, Clara Hook, great-granddaughter of Theodore Hook [q.v.]. Both her parents sang, and Clara, beginning with piano lessons, was encouraged by them also to take advantage of some minor opportunities to cultivate her voice, which was soon discovered to be of remarkable richness and great compass. Miss Cook, the headmistress of the South Bristol High School at which Clara was educated (her parents having settled in Bristol in 1880), accidentally hearing some of Clara's already splendid low notes, got Daniel Rootham, a fine bass singer, conductor of the Bristol Festival Choir, to hear her, and he began her training, although she was still in her early 'teens. Soon she was singing in the Bristol Festival Choir and hearing famous soloists. In January 1890, when sixteen years old, she won a valuable scholarship, which was also open to instrumentalists, at the Royal College of Music, but she had to wait until she had attained the regulation age of seventeen before she could take up residence and begin her studies, which were directed by John Henry Blower. The college authorities extended her scholarship for a fourth year and then sent her for a three months' course to Duvernoy in Paris, Queen Victoria defraying the cost. Later in her career Clara Butt studied with Bouhy in Paris, and with Etelka Gerster in Berlin, and in Italy. She made her début at the Royal Albert Hall in the comparatively small contralto part of Ursula in Sir Arthur Sullivan's cantata *The Golden Legend* on 7 December 1892, and three days later sang the name part in Gluck's *Orfeo* at a performance given by pupils of the Royal College of Music at the Lyceum Theatre.

On both occasions Clara Butt's success was complete, her magnificent voice and splendid appearance (she was six feet two inches in height) launching her on a career of almost unexampled popularity. Confining herself to the concert platform (with the exception of some appearances as Orfeo at Covent Garden under Sir Thomas Beecham in 1920), she sang at all the principal festivals in England and at concerts (many of them her own, with her husband, Robert Kennerley Rumford, baritone, whom she married in 1900) at home, all over the British Empire, and in America, with striking success. Sir Edward Elgar [q.v.] composed 'Sea Pictures', his cycle of five songs for contralto solo with orchestral accompaniment, for Clara Butt, and she produced them at the Norwich festival in 1899. Elgar also wrote the music of the Angel in *The Dream of Gerontius* with Clara Butt in mind; and it was a suggestion from her that brought from the future master of the king's musick the patriotic song 'Land of Hope and Glory'. What has become a classic of its kind, the setting of 'Abide with Me', was composed by Samuel Liddle, her fellow student at the Royal College of Music, for Clara Butt, who sang it with an appeal of great poignancy. Her singing was remarkable for its broad effect rather than for its artistic finesse, and there could not be a greater contrast in style than between her and Patti when they appeared on the same concert platform. Her activity and generosity in organizing and singing at concerts during the war of 1914–1918 for charities—the Red Cross, Three Arts Club women's unemployment fund, etc.—knew no bounds: a week of Elgar's music at the Queen's Hall was notable as an artistic as well as a charitable achievement; and for these services she was appointed D.B.E. in 1920. She died at North Stoke, Oxfordshire, as the result of an accident in 1931, after a long and painful illness, 23 January 1936. Both her sons predeceased her, but she was survived by her husband and her daughter.

[Winifred Ponder, *Clara Butt. Her Life-Story*, 1928; *Grove's Dictionary of Music and Musicians*, 4th ed., vol. i, edited by H. C. Colles; H. Saxe Wyndham and Geoffrey L'Epine, *Who's Who in Music*, 1913; *Musical Times*, March 1936; personal knowledge.]

J. MEWBURN LEVIEN.

BUXTON, SYDNEY CHARLES, EARL BUXTON (1853–1934), statesman, was born in London 25 October 1853, the younger son of the liberal politician Charles Buxton [q.v.], by his wife, Emily Mary, eldest daughter of the physician Sir Henry Holland [q.v.]. He was grandson of the philanthropist Sir T. F. Buxton [q.v.]. He was educated at Clifton and Trinity College, Cambridge. He served on the London School Board from 1876 to 1882, and after unsuccessfully contesting Boston as a liberal in 1880 was returned for Peterborough at a by-election in 1883. He was defeated at the general election of 1885, but sat for the Poplar division of the Tower Hamlets from 1886 to 1914. In 1880 he made his first mark in politics by publishing his *Handbook to Political Questions of the Day* which passed through

eleven editions. He was under-secretary of state for the Colonies from 1892 to 1895 and the first Matabele war brought him into contact with native problems in Africa. In 1905 he was appointed postmaster-general, with a seat in the Cabinet, and sworn of the Privy Council. He introduced penny postage to the United States of America, the Canadian magazine post, and cheap postage for the blind. Appointed president of the Board of Trade in 1910, he introduced and passed the Copyright Act of 1911, the unemployment section of the National Insurance Act of 1912, the Miners' Minimum Wage Act of 1912, and the Bankruptcy Act of 1913, and, in the last-named year, extended the Trade Boards Act to other trades. After the loss of the *Titanic* in 1912 he issued stringent regulations for the preservation of life at sea.

In February 1914, on appointment as governor-general of the Union of South Africa, Buxton was appointed G.C.M.G., and in May was raised to the peerage as Viscount Buxton, of Newtimber, in Sussex. He arrived at the moment of the outbreak of war and was at once faced with the very serious crisis of the rebellion, which for a moment threatened to cut him off in Pretoria from the rest of the Union. But General Louis Botha [q.v.] had taken the momentous decision to side with Great Britain in the struggle. Buxton and Botha worked together most cordially. They saw harmony restored within the Union, carried through the campaign in South-West Africa, and supported both the long campaign in East Africa and the valuable contribution made by South Africa on the western front in France. Although Buxton's presence was needed at Cape Town and Pretoria, he travelled frequently and acquired great influence with the Dutch backveld farmers, who found him accessible and sympathetic, and appreciated his receptions of their synods and assemblies; while Lady Buxton took an active part in the work of adapting social conditions, especially in Cape Town, to the conditions of war. Buxton's term of office was extended until 1920, and at his retirement there were striking demonstrations of the feeling of affection which he and Lady Buxton had inspired. The University of Cape Town conferred an honorary degree upon him, and on his return to England he was raised to an earldom. Of his work as governor-general, General Smuts has said: 'His close personal friendship with General Botha gave him

131

a special position, and I know how much General Botha was influenced by his wise counsel and ripe experience. . . . Self-government in Rhodesia was largely due to his favourable report, and time has justified his wise advice.' After his return he continued to work for South Africa, largely through the Africa Society, of which he was president from 1920 to 1933 and the gold medal of which was awarded to him in 1930.

Although his sympathy with the working classes led him to modify his earlier strictly Gladstonian views, Buxton supported the liberal party, and remained in full sympathy with his old friend and colleague Lord Grey of Fallodon. In 1924 he spoke against the labour scheme for nationalizing the Bank of England. His publications include *Mr. Gladstone's Irish Bills* (1886), *Finance and Politics: an historical study 1783-1885* (2 vols., 1888), *Mr. Gladstone as Chancellor of the Exchequer* (1901), *Fishing and Shooting* (1902), *The Arguments on either side of the Fiscal Question* (1903), and *General Botha* (1924).

Owing to an injury to his knee as a schoolboy, Buxton, at the age of seventy-seven, had to suffer the amputation of his leg. He died at Newtimber Place 15 October 1934 and was buried at Newtimber. He was twice married: first, in 1882 to Constance Mary (died 1892), second daughter of John Lubbock, first Lord Avebury [q.v.], and had two sons, who both predeceased their father, the younger in childhood, and one daughter; secondly, in 1896 to Mildred Anne, elder daughter of Hugh Colin Smith, governor of the Bank of England, of Mount Clare, Roehampton, and had one son, who was killed in action in 1917, and two daughters, the elder of whom predeceased her father.

A portrait of Buxton, by Edward Roworth, is in the House of Assembly at Cape Town. A cartoon, by 'Spy', appeared in *Vanity Fair* 2 January 1907.

[*The Times*, 16 and 17 October 1934; Lord Buxton, *General Botha*, 1924; private information.]   E. I. CARLYLE.

BYNG, JULIAN HEDWORTH GEORGE, VISCOUNT BYNG OF VIMY (1862-1935), field-marshal, was born at Wrotham Park, Barnet, 11 September 1862, the youngest of the four sons of George Stevens Byng, second Earl of Strafford, by his second wife, Harriet Elizabeth, younger daughter of Charles Compton Cavendish, first Lord Chesham. His grandfather, John Byng, first Earl

of Strafford [q.v.], had commanded a brigade at Waterloo and ended his career as a field-marshal. Julian Byng was educated at Eton, entered the army through the militia (7th battalion, the King's Royal Rifle Corps), and was gazetted to the 10th Hussars in January 1883. The 10th Hussars was an expensive regiment, and Byng had a very small allowance, so that for many years he could afford no social gaieties. As, however, he had no taste for them, this was not a deprivation, and, the regiment being stationed in India, he was able to enjoy all the polo that he could desire. Being a good horseman and player, ponies bought cheaply became speedily of increased value after being acquired by him. Since he was extremely popular, he also had at his disposal good mounts lent by friends. The 10th Hussars was on its way home in 1884 when it was landed at Suakin for the campaign in the eastern Sudan against Osman Digna; so that by unexpected good fortune Byng, at an early stage in his career, saw active service and took part both in the historic charge at El Teb (29 February) and in the fierce struggle at Tamai (13 March). In 1886 he became adjutant to his regiment. In 1894 he passed the Staff College and in 1897 was appointed deputy-assistant-adjutant-general at Aldershot. He was promoted captain in 1889 and major in 1898.

On the outbreak of the South African war in 1899 Byng was sent out to serve in the first instance in a provost marshal's appointment. In November 1900 he raised the South African Light Horse which he commanded until April 1901. A strict disciplinarian by instinct and coming from a British regiment where discipline was of the strictest, he none the less readily adapted himself to the unconventional and free-and-easy atmosphere of his new command. He was soon on as good terms with it as he had been with his own regiment. His sense of humour helped him when he was confronted with eccentricities, and he became a leader of ir-regular light horse of the highest quality. He was employed in command of a column, and later on of more than one, throughout the period when this form of warfare was practised. At one period Mr. Winston Churchill acted as his galloper. Byng received successively the brevet rank of lieutenant-colonel and of colonel, and was on five occasions mentioned in dispatches.

After the war had come to an end Byng

was appointed to command his regiment, the 10th Hussars, and remained at its head for the next two years. In 1902 he married Marie Evelyn, only child of (Sir) Richard Charles Moreton, of Crookham House, near Fleet, Hampshire, ninth son of H. G. F. Moreton, second Earl of Ducie [q.v.], and thus gained an ideal partner who was to give him invaluable support in the years of his public life. From 1904 to 1905 he was commandant of the Cavalry School at Netheravon. From 1905 to 1907 he commanded the 2nd Cavalry brigade in the Eastern Command, and was appointed C.B. in 1906. From 1907 to 1909 he commanded the 1st Cavalry brigade at Aldershot, but in April of the last-named year he was promoted major-general and in October 1910 returned to the Eastern Command to command the Territorial East Anglian division. Now for the first time he had a home, near Dunmow, which was then something of a literary centre. Byng took pleasure in the society of the London editors and novelists who were his neighbours. He was an intense reader himself, but for the most part of utilitarian subjects connected with his profession.

In October 1912 Byng was appointed to the command in Egypt, and was there when war broke out in August 1914. He was soon recalled, and late in September appointed to the command of the 3rd Cavalry division. In the first battle of Ypres he proved himself as sound and as determined a commander as the best judges had foretold, and this in adverse circumstances, the hardest test of a general. His division gave brilliant support to the I Corps and was repeatedly called upon to restore ugly situations at the shortest notice and in the most unfavourable conditions. In March 1915 he was appointed K.C.M.G. and in May took over command of the Cavalry Corps with the temporary rank of lieutenant-general. In the following August he was sent out to the Gallipoli Peninsula to command the IX Corps at Suvla, where the opportunities of a new landing had been frittered away. It was a thousand pities that General Sir Ian Hamilton's request for Byng's services to conduct that landing had been refused, since now he came too late. No senior officer was more strongly in favour of evacuation than he. He began, in fact, to study the problem almost immediately after his arrival, proof of remarkable detachment in a commander who had been summoned in the hope that he would redeem a failure. He considered,

too, contrary to the general belief, that withdrawal need not be costly, provided that it was carried out before more German forces and material arrived on the scene and before the weather broke. He drew up the plan, but left the detail to two reliable divisional commanders, Major-Generals (Sir) E. A. Fanshawe and (Sir) F. S. Maude [q.v.]. The withdrawal was completely successful, and Byng was appointed K.C.B. (1916).

After a brief spell in Egypt in the Suez Canal defences and in command of the XVII Corps in France from February to May 1916, Byng took over command of the Canadian Corps in the latter month. This was a fine appointment, since, whereas other army corps were simply headquarters to which divisions were attached as required, the commander of the Canadian Corps could always count on having the Canadian divisions under his command. Within a week, on 2 June, he had to deal with an ugly situation, when the Germans attacked at Mount Sorrel, Hill 62, and Sanctuary Wood, in the Ypres sector, and captured some valuable ground. Local counter-attacks failed, but on the 11th the situation was righted by a successful counter-offensive, which was, however, unpleasantly expensive. Byng had an extraordinary gift for impressing his gay and friendly personality upon the troops under his orders, and he gained not only the confidence but also the affection of the Canadian Corps. It is hardly too much to say that nowhere in the world at war was there a formation so large in which the links between the commander and the troops were so strong. The Canadian Corps distinguished itself on the Somme in the battle of Flers-Courcelette in mid-September, and again at the end of the month in the Thiepval ridge operations, but its greatest feat, which will ever be inseparably connected with its name, was the capture of Vimy ridge in April 1917.

In June of that year, Byng, although loth to leave his Canadians, was appointed to command the Third Army in succession to General Sir Edmund (later Viscount) Allenby [q.v.] who went to command the Egyptian Expeditionary Force. Byng passed straight to preparation for the most daring and original operation yet undertaken by the British on the western front, the Cambrai offensive. This depended on two factors, the use of tanks operating independently and in unprecedented strength to open gaps in the enemy's wire without the need for a preliminary bombardment such as had hitherto rendered surprise impossible, and —as a further element in surprise—the employment of 'predicted' fire from the massed artillery, without preliminary registration. The objects were to capture the wooded height of Bourlon and to roll up the German front towards the Sensée marshes to the north, and at the same time to thrust eastwards, capture Cambrai, and exploit in the direction of Valenciennes. The first stage of the assault, launched on 20 November, was brilliantly successful; but serious hitches occurred, and the available reserves could not maintain the momentum. At the end of the month the Germans counter-attacked the salient created by the British advance. On the north they were generally held, but they broke the southern flank, and the situation was not stabilized until after hard touch-and-go fighting. As an operation Cambrai was a disappointment, but it pointed to the road to victory.

That, however, was still some way ahead. The German offensive of March 1918 fell heavily upon the Third Army, though less heavily than upon the Fifth on its right. The Third put up a splendid resistance, lost relatively little ground, and smashed the offensive round Arras. Byng had, however, to make a rapid withdrawal, which got temporarily out of hand, from the remains of the Cambrai salient. That autumn the Third Army played a great part in the offensive which decided the issue of the war. Its first attack was launched on 21 August. By a series of heavy blows, in conjunction with the Fourth Army on its right and the First Army on its left, it drove the enemy back to the Hindenburg Line and on 27 September broke that position. In the space of eighty days it advanced sixty miles—a fast pace for that war—and took 67,000 prisoners and 800 guns. Byng's qualities of leadership were unquestionably high, and the only two episodes which can possibly create controversy on this subject are his aims in the battle of Cambrai and his delay in evacuating the Cambrai salient in March 1918. It has been suggested that in the former instance he was unduly optimistic, refusing to modify an ambitious plan when it was found impossible to put at his disposal resources as large as originally intended because they had been used up at Passchendaele and in Italy. It may be

so, but it should be recalled that plans were carefully scrutinized by the commander-in-chief, Field-Marshal Sir Douglas Haig [q.v.], who was not the man to give army commanders their heads if he considered them rash. It is probable that Byng's judgement was more questionable in the second case than in the first, but his conduct of the final offensive showed him to be as capable in command of a big army as he had been in command of a column, a division, and an army corps.

In 1919 Byng, who had been gazetted to the full rank of general in 1917, was appointed G.C.B., raised to the peerage (October) as Baron Byng of Vimy, of Thorpe-le-Soken, in Essex, and received the thanks of parliament and a grant of £30,000. He received, on various occasions, a number of other honours, British and foreign, including honorary doctorates from Cambridge (1919) and Oxford (1931). In 1919, also, he was offered the Southern Command, but asked leave to retire and make way for a younger man. While he was in Egypt before the war his wife had bought Thorpe Hall, Thorpe-le-Soken. This old house she restored and enlarged, making it into a beautiful home with a widely famed garden. There was good shooting, and shooting was now his favourite sport. But he was far from idle, and took over the trying and delicate task of administering the United Service Fund.

In June 1921 Byng was appointed governor-general of Canada. Needless to say, the choice was largely dictated by his prestige and popularity in the Dominion, where his name was known to everyone. Yet even those who had hoped most from it were astonished by the success which he made of his mission. Well supported by Lady Byng, he kept up the requisite state and entertained on a large scale, but was otherwise unconventional, mixing with people as had none of his predecessors. He travelled widely and developed a talent for making brief and telling speeches which did not contain the platitudes too common on official occasions. The theme to which he constantly returned, in terms sometimes approaching admonition, was the need for unity in the Dominion and for eliminating the bitterness of political strife. His popularity, great from the first, never ceased to grow. In his last year there was a widespread desire that he should serve a second term, but this he would not consider.

Just before he was due to return to England, in June 1926, Byng became involved, by reason of his office, in a painful political crisis. The prime minister, Mr. W. L. Mackenzie King, had in the previous September sought and obtained from the governor-general a dissolution of parliament, with the stipulation that it could not again be granted in similar circumstances. The general election which followed had seriously worsened Mr. King's position, and he had since carried on the government with his own liberal party in a minority dependent on outside support. Now, having to face a vote of censure, certain to go against him, he asked for a second dissolution. Byng refused it, and called upon Mr. Arthur Meighen, the conservative leader, who believed that he could command a majority. Had he been right in this, the affair would not have created an inordinate stir, but he was defeated by a single vote, owing to the breaking of his 'pair' by a pledged supporter. Byng then granted him a dissolution, and in the subsequent election the liberals were victorious. The affair was complicated by the fact that when Mr. Meighen took office there was an interregnum because the liberals had left their offices, so that there was no ministry. If the new ministers had now accepted offices of profit they would have had to vacate their seats and seek re-election. To avoid this until the session was ended, Mr. Meighen decided that there should be no appointment to offices and no emoluments, but that a small number, who had already taken the oath of privy councillors, should carry on as ministers without portfolio. This procedure was strongly reprobated by the liberal party. Byng's last days in Canada were clouded by this episode, although Mr. King himself and all the more responsible of his adherents refrained from criticizing the governor-general's motives and expressed their appreciation of his sincerity. Yet it was with unfeigned affection and deep regret that the people of Canada said farewell to him. It has been asserted that the decision of the Imperial Conference which was held shortly after Byng's return proved that he had been in error in his handling of the crisis; but this is an over-simplification of the problem. What the Imperial Conference decided was that the governor-general is the representative of the king, not of the British government, and that the constitutional relationship between him and the prime minister of Canada is the same as that between the king and the British prime minister. Byng had, in fact,

acted in accordance with this principle. He believed, as did Mr. Meighen, that, in similar circumstances, the king would have acted as had Byng.

In June 1928 Byng was asked by the home secretary, Sir William Joynson-Hicks [q.v.], to become chief-commissioner of the metropolitan police. He strove to excuse himself on the grounds of age and indifferent health, but strong pressure was put upon him, and he gave way. There was need at Scotland Yard for an able man with high prestige and a combination of tact and ruthlessness. The public was becoming disquieted about what appeared to be inefficiency and by certain unsavoury scandals. But Byng, the least politically minded of men, became once more the subject of a political controversy. The appointment was strongly resented by the labour opposition in the House of Commons, and a heavy attack was made upon it by one of the labour leaders, Philip Snowden [q.v.]. This agitation presently died down. Byng's reforms were widespread and fundamental. He retired a number of senior officers, not because he suspected them of complicity in the scandals but because he considered that the force was in need of fresh and vigorous blood. He reorganized the system of patrolling, abolishing the conventionality and clock-like regularity to which the malefactor had become accustomed. He instituted police telephone boxes and extended, if he cannot be said to have instituted, the use of police cars. He tightened up discipline. Yet his reforms were not resented, as had at first seemed possible, in the force, over which he established as strong a hold as he had done over every other body of men whom he had commanded. When the labour government took office in 1929, mindful of the criticism with which his appointment had been received, he went to the home secretary, Mr. John Robert Clynes, and told him that he was prepared to resign, although he would be glad to continue at his post if the government so desired. Mr. Clynes informed him that he possessed the confidence of the government and that he could rely upon its support. Byng's health deteriorated towards the end of his term of office, and he resigned in September 1931.

Byng had been appointed G.C.M.G. in 1921 and advanced to a viscountcy in 1928, but the highest honour of the career of arms had so far eluded him. Although not an ambitious man, his hopes had been set upon the field-marshal's baton. A former secretary of state had decided that it should not be accorded to a retired officer, despite the fact that Byng would probably have had it had he remained two or three years longer on the active list and not retired voluntarily to make way for youth. To his great satisfaction, he received it in October 1932. He died suddenly at Thorpe Hall 6 June 1935, leaving no issue, and his peerage therefore became extinct.

Byng had developed, through careful self-preparation and experience, from a somewhat shy young officer, avoiding when he could all society except that most congenial to him, to a public figure at home in any society and able to impress his personality upon multitudes. Yet he was to the end essentially simple-minded, and his greatest weakness was a guileless belief in the integrity of mankind. Since he never suspected an ulterior motive in any action, men less scrupulous than himself could on occasion take advantage of his trustfulness. Yet the man who expects most from his fellow men generally gets more from them than does the suspicious man, and this was the case with Byng. He had a genius for friendship and many friends in all walks of life. As a soldier he was thoroughly competent as well as personally inspiring. He never held independent command in the field, and it is doubtful whether he possessed the scope or the forcefulness of Haig. On the other hand, he did well what he was called upon to do, and the manner in which he first welcomed and then developed the draft scheme for the Cambrai offensive proves that as a commander he was lacking neither in open-mindedness nor in imagination.

There is a portrait of Byng, by P. A. de László, at 5 St. James's Square, and another, in field-marshal's uniform, by the same artist, at Thorpe Hall. A third portrait is included in J. S. Sargent's picture, 'Some General Officers of the Great War', painted in 1922, in the National Portrait Gallery.

[Sir J. E. Edmonds, Cyril Falls, and Wilfred Miles, (Official) *History of the Great War. Military Operations, France and Belgium, 1914–1918*, 1922–1940; C. F. Aspinall-Oglander, (Official) *History of the Great War. Military Operations, Gallipoli*, vol. ii, 1932; Lady Byng, *Up the Stream of Time*, 1945; E. A. Forsey, *The Royal Power of Dissolution of Parliament in the British Commonwealth*, 1943; private information.]

CYRIL FALLS.

CAINE, SIR (THOMAS HENRY) HALL (1853–1931), novelist, was born at Runcorn, Cheshire, 14 May 1853, the eldest son of John Caine, a ship's smith, of Ballaugh, Isle of Man, by his wife, Sarah, daughter of Ralph Hall, of Whitehaven. John Caine had migrated to Liverpool from Ramsey in an attempt to better his fortunes, but much of Hall Caine's childhood was spent in the Isle of Man.

Leaving an elementary school in Liverpool at the age of fourteen, Hall Caine became the pupil of a local architect, but when he was about seventeen, owing to ill health, he abandoned work for a time and revisited the Isle of Man, where he succeeded his uncle as schoolmaster at Kirk Maughold Head. Returning to Liverpool after nearly a year, he contributed articles to the *Builder* and the *Building News*, and soon became assistant to a builder. These essays in architectural criticism won him the notice of John Ruskin [q.v.], whilst his membership of the 'Notes and Queries' Society brought him into touch with many famous men, including (Sir) Henry Irving and the poet (Sir) William Watson [qq.v.]. Later in life he became an intimate friend of the Manx writer T. E. Brown [q.v.].

Hall Caine's most important literary contact was with Dante Gabriel Rossetti [q.v.]. In 1878 he delivered a lecture in Liverpool on Rossetti's poetry which, on its publication the next year, was the beginning of a friendship described in his *Recollections of Dante Gabriel Rossetti* (1882; new and enlarged version 1928). When, in 1881, Hall Caine decided to devote himself entirely to writing, Rossetti invited him to live at his house and he remained the poet's constant friend and companion until Rossetti's death in 1882. In the latter year Hall Caine married Mary (died 1932), daughter of William Chandler, of Walthamstow. There were two sons of the marriage.

Shortly after Rossetti's death Hall Caine was offered a post on the *Liverpool Mercury* and, whilst still living in London, he worked for a time as one of its leader-writers. His first novel, *The Shadow of a Crime* (1885), appeared as a serial in the *Liverpool Weekly Mercury*, but he soon abandoned journalism and settled in the Isle of Wight. The publication in 1887 of *The Deemster*, a story set in the Isle of Man, which Rossetti had suggested as a good subject for fiction, marked the beginning of his extraordinary popularity.

His books were translated into many languages and several, including *The Bondman* (1890), were adapted for the stage. His success helped to popularize the shorter one-volume format which he adopted in preference to the traditional three volumes.

In 1892–1893 Hall Caine visited Poland and the frontier towns of Russia at the request of the Russo-Jewish Committee in order to investigate the facts of the Jewish persecutions, and in 1895 he was sent on behalf of the Incorporated Society of Authors and the Colonial Office to Canada where he conducted successful negotiations with the Dominion government on the subject of Canadian copyright. From 1901 to 1908 he was a member of the Manx House of Keys, associating himself with the reforming party.

During the war of 1914–1918 Hall Caine devoted his energies to Allied propaganda in the United States of America. He also edited *King Albert's Book* (1914), a service for which he was made an officer of the Belgian Order of Leopold. He was appointed K.B.E. in 1918 and C.H. in 1922. He died at his home, Greeba Castle, Isle of Man, 31 August 1931, leaving unfinished a *Life of Christ* which was published posthumously in 1938.

Hall Caine's novels are remembered chiefly for their astonishing popularity. Over a million copies were sold of *The Eternal City* (1901), and *The Christian* (1897) was hardly less popular, but the success of books such as these should not obscure the genuine merit of some of his Manx novels, notably *The Manxman* (1894). He had a real knowledge of the Manx people, their history and customs, and in the Isle of Man he found a setting, hitherto unknown to novelists, which exactly suited his romantic and picturesque stories.

Two portraits of Hall Caine, one by Annie Louisa Swynnerton, the other by Alfred Jonniaux, are in the possession of the family. A bust, by Joseph William Swynnerton, is in the Douglas Free Library. A drawing by Sir Bernard Partridge appeared in *Punch* 27 October 1926.

[Hall Caine, *My Story*, 1908, and *Recollections of Rossetti*, 1928 ; Samuel Norris, *Two Men of Manxland*, 1947 ; C. F. Kenyon, *Hall Caine: the Man and the Novelist*, 1901 ; William Gaunt, *The Pre-Raphaelite Tragedy*, 1942 ; *The Times*, 1 September 1931 ; private information.]   GEORGINA BATTISCOMBE.

CALTHORPE, SIR SOMERSET ARTHUR GOUGH- (1864–1937), admiral of the fleet, the younger son of Somerset Frederick, seventh Lord Calthorpe, by his wife, Eliza Maria, only child of Captain Frederick Chamier, R.N. [q.v.], and widow of Captain Frederick Crewe, was born in London 23 December 1864.

Calthorpe entered the Royal Navy from the training-ship *Britannia* in 1878. He soon made his mark, gaining special promotion to lieutenant in 1886 for meritorious examinations. In 1887 he was posted to the *Vernon* in order to qualify in torpedo. He was promoted to commander in 1896 for active service on the Africa station ; he served in the latter rank for six years, five of which were spent at sea, and was promoted post-captain in 1902. As a captain he was for three years naval attaché to Russia, Sweden, and Norway, after which he commanded the cruiser *Roxburgh*, the battleship *Hindustan*, and was captain of the fleet (commodore 1st class) of the Home Fleet until his promotion to rear-admiral in 1911. He was rear-admiral of the first battle squadron (1912–1913) with his flag in the *St. Vincent*, rear- and vice-admiral in command of the second cruiser squadron (1914–1916) (flag in the *Shannon*), second sea lord and admiral commanding coastguard and reserves (1916–1917), and British commander-in-chief, Mediterranean (1917–1919) (flag in the *Egmont*, *Superb*, and *Iron Duke*). He was promoted to admiral in 1919 and was commander-in-chief, Portsmouth, from 1920 to 1923. In July 1924 he became first and principal naval aide-de-camp to King George V and held this, his last service appointment, until his promotion to admiral of the fleet in May 1925. This was an exceptional record of continuous service and testifies to the esteem in which he was held by his superior officers afloat and at the Admiralty. As a lieutenant he was perhaps fortunate in seeing active service when such opportunities were rare. As commander he was a highly successful executive officer, and as captain he was noted for handling his ships well and for getting the best results from his officers and men.

Having spent part of his boyhood in France Calthorpe spoke French fluently and was a student of French history. This was to prove a great asset to him when naval attaché in Russia and in the high appointments which he held later. When captain of the fleet to Sir W. H. May [q.v.], who initiated great advances in the battle tactics of a modern fleet, he was an invaluable adviser and assistant to his chief, who made handsome acknowledgement of the fact. In 1912, as a result of the *Titanic* disaster, a Board of Trade committee was appointed to make recommendations for the increased safety of life at sea. J. C. Bigham, Viscount Mersey [q.v.], was president and Calthorpe was the Admiralty's representative. Their conclusions were of great practical value and were adopted and passed into law without delay or amendment.

In the battle squadron and cruiser squadron commands that Calthorpe held as a rear-admiral no signal opportunities of distinction presented themselves, but in August 1917 he was given command of all the British naval forces in the Mediterranean. Supreme command was vested in the Allied (French) commander-in-chief, Admiral Gauchet, but this officer was never active in direction or guidance and Calthorpe, as president of a mixed commission at Malta of French, Italian, and Japanese admirals, bore the main responsibility for the defence of Allied trade throughout the Mediterranean, and the operations against Turkey. He controlled, in addition to vessels of those nations and of the United States of America and Greece, over a thousand ships, large and small, flying the white ensign. His measures were successful, and as the climax of the war approached the probability of a Turkish capitulation became evident.

On 22 October 1918 Calthorpe was empowered by the Admiralty to conclude an armistice with Turkey, acting as sole negotiator on behalf of all the Allies. His position in so doing was a delicate one. French agreement to this procedure was apparently lacking and expostulations were immediately forthcoming from the French government and, what made matters still more difficult, from his nominal superior officer, Gauchet. Prescience had, however, already taken Calthorpe to Mudros, the Turkish plenipotentiaries were fetched by a British cruiser, the discussions were expedited by his skilful and rapid diplomacy, and the armistice was signed on 30 October. The *fait accompli* was perforce accepted, and it is not surprising that the Allied fleet, British, French, Italian, and Greek, which passed the Dardanelles and anchored off Constantinople on 13 November was led by the British flagship and commanded by the British commander-in-chief. He was at once also nominated British high commissioner in Turkey and fulfilled the

duties of both appointments with striking success, in the face of Turkish intrigues, Allied dissensions, a French naval mutiny, and a spasmodic state of war with Bolshevist Russia until his relief a year later.

Calthorpe's subsequent service as commander-in-chief, Portsmouth, and as Admiralty representative on the armament commission of the League of Nations, although less momentous, was in the highest traditions of the naval service, and his promotion to admiral of the fleet was a fitting recognition of all that he had accomplished for the navy and the nation. His character was an admirable blend of simplicity and sagacity, moderation and firmness, prudence and prompt decision; he had great charm of manner, and was the soul of honour. Self-seeking ambition or advertisement were wholly alien to his nature, and he commanded the complete confidence and affection of his colleagues and subordinates in the Royal Navy, and of the many foreign officers of high rank who served with him, or under his direction, in the war of 1914–1918.

Calthorpe was awarded many British and Allied decorations, including the C.V.O. (1910), the G.C.M.G. (1919), the G.C.B. (1922), and the highest orders of France, Italy, Greece, Rumania, China, Japan, and the United States.

On his retirement from the navy in 1930 Calthorpe resided in the Isle of Wight where he was a D.L. and a J.P. and a notable supporter of all good causes in that locality. He married in 1900 Effie, daughter of Robert Dunsmuir, of Victoria, British Columbia, and had no issue. He died at Ryde 27 July 1937.

There is a portrait of Calthorpe by Philip Connard, painted on board the *Superb* in 1919, at the Imperial War Museum.

[*The Times*, 28 July 1937; Admiralty records; personal knowledge.]

R. M. BURMESTER.

CAMPBELL, BEATRICE STELLA (1865–1940), better known as MRS. PATRICK CAMPBELL, actress, was born in Kensington 9 February 1865, the youngest daughter and child of John Tanner, the son of an army contractor to the British East India Company and a descendant of Thomas Tanner, bishop of St. Asaph [q.v.]. Her mother was Maria Luigia Giovanna, daughter of Count Angelo Romanini, an Italian political exile. Beatrice Tanner was educated at Brighton and Hampstead, and in Paris, and studied for a short time at the Guildhall School of Music. In 1884, when she was nineteen, she eloped to marry Patrick Campbell, who had then a small post in the City: his father owned property at Stranraer.

In October 1888 Mrs. Patrick Campbell went upon the professional stage, making her first appearance in a play called *Bachelors* at the Alexandra Theatre, Liverpool. After touring in the company of (Sir) Phillip Ben Greet [q.v.] (Rosalind and Viola were among her parts), she arrived in London in March 1890, playing Helen in *The Hunchback* at the Adelphi Theatre. During the following year the Gattis engaged her for the Adelphi where she acted between August 1891 and the spring of 1893 in such melodramas as *The Trumpet Call* and *The Black Domino*. Shortly after *The Black Domino* opened she received a fortnight's notice from the Gattis (who were paying her £8 a week) on the grounds that her voice and gestures were ineffective and that nothing she said or did 'got over the footlights'. It was at this time that her performance was seen by Mrs. Alexander and Graham Robertson, the artist, who knew that (Sir) George Alexander [q.v.] wanted an actress to play the part of Paula Tanqueray in the new drama, *The Second Mrs. Tanqueray*, by (Sir) A. W. Pinero [q.v.] at the St. James's Theatre. Negotiations followed, made difficult by the attitude of the Gattis who wished to keep Mrs. Campbell when they heard that she was sought for the St. James's. At last she was released, and, thanks to the generosity of Elizabeth Robins, who had been cast meantime for Paula and withdrew in Mrs. Campbell's favour, this almost unknown player—'the fragile creature of Italian origin', as Pinero called her—had her chance. From the moment that she walked upon the stage of the St. James's on the night of 27 May 1893, her success was astonishing. Mrs. Campbell had a dark Italian beauty and a rich and expressive voice: it was soon realized that none of her contemporaries had her gift for portraying passionate, complex women, 'the flash and gloom, the swirl and the eddy, of a soul torn by supposed intellectual emotion', as (Sir) Edmund Gosse put it in a letter to her written in 1895. She might fail in the simplicities, but properly cast she was unexampled. William Archer wrote of her Paula: 'Never was there a more uncompromisingly artistic piece of acting. It was incarnate reality, the haggard truth.' John Davidson in a letter to her written

in 1901 said: '"Paula" is like an opal of many hues and lustres, with stains of life, and wounds of passion through which the disastrous fires glow that shatter it in the end.' Although, as Mr. Hamilton Fyfe has noted, Davidson did not attribute this merit entirely to the actress, no other player of Paula has left the same impression or shown the same temperamental brilliance.

Later during the 'nineties, when her fame was at its height, Mrs. Campbell appeared in such parts as Dulcie Larondie in Henry Arthur Jones's strong, romantic play, *The Masqueraders* (St. James's, April 1894); Agnes Ebbsmith, who threw the Bible into the fire, in Pinero's *The Notorious Mrs. Ebbsmith* (Garrick Theatre, March 1895); Fédora, in the play of that name (Haymarket Theatre, May 1895); Juliet to the Romeo of (Sir) Johnston Forbes-Robertson [q.v.] at the Lyceum Theatre (September 1895), a part to which she was less fitted; and Magda in Sudermann's drama of that name, also at the Lyceum (June 1896), in which she was superb in revolt and indignation. Although the play failed on its first production, she acted in it often during her later career. In November 1896 she appeared at the Avenue Theatre as the Rat Wife in Ibsen's *Little Eyolf*. She was generally considered to have been miscast as Ophelia to Forbes-Robertson's Hamlet at the Lyceum (September 1897), although Mr. Bernard Shaw defended her in the *Saturday Review*. 'Mrs. Patrick Campbell,' he wrote, 'with that complacent audacity of hers which is so exasperating when she is doing the wrong thing, this time does the right thing by making Ophelia really mad. The resentment of the audience at this outrage is hardly to be described. . . . Playgoers naturally murmur when something that has always been pretty becomes painful; but the pain is good for them, good for the theatre, and for the play.' Nine months after this, in June 1898, Mrs. Campbell had one of her most memorable successes as a Mélisande of haunting beauty in Maeterlinck's *Pelléas and Mélisande* (Prince of Wales's Theatre, June 1898), with (Sir) John Martin Harvey as Pelléas. Her Lady Macbeth (Lyceum, September 1898) was played with what A. B. Walkley [q.v.] termed 'a mysterious sensuous charm'.

In September 1899 Mrs. Campbell went into management at the Prince of Wales's, opening with a failure, Chester Bailey Fernald's Japanese play, *The Moonlight*

Blossom. The financial loss was heavy. In April of the next year Mrs. Campbell had a deep personal grief when her husband was killed fighting in South Africa. Her management remained unfortunate financially, but she had a run of artistic successes in such parts as Mrs. Daventry (Royalty Theatre, October 1900) in the play *Mr. and Mrs. Daventry*, based by Frank Harris [q.v.] on a scenario of Oscar Wilde; Mariana in a revival of José Echegaray's play of that name (Royalty, May 1901); and Mrs. Clara Sang, the bedridden wife in Björnstjerne Bjørnson's *Beyond Human Power* (Royalty, November 1901). During January 1902 she acted for the first time in New York, as Magda. When she returned to London she appeared in a series of unimportant productions interrupted by one famous revival: that in which she played Mélisande in French to the Pelléas of Sarah Bernhardt (Vaudeville Theatre, July 1904). According to W. L. Courtney [q.v.] in the *Daily Telegraph*, Mrs. Campbell's Mélisande was 'in its French form more gracious and childlike and poetic than we have ever seen it before'. After 'a nightmare', Mrs. Campbell's word for the melodrama *The Bondman* by (Sir) Hall Caine [q.v.] (Drury Lane Theatre, September 1906) in which she appeared as Greeba, there came the triumph of a few Court Theatre matinées of Ibsen's *Hedda Gabler* (March 1907). Mrs. Campbell, physically nothing like Ibsen's description, was a mistress of heat and light and sound; she saw Hedda as 'a proud, intelligent woman, a well-bred woman in the highest sense. A vital creature, suffocated by the commonplace.' Another visit to the United States of America followed, and then an English tour. Next Mrs. Campbell gave matinées at the New Theatre (November 1908) of Arthur Symons's version of Hugo von Hofmannsthal's *Elektra* and of Yeats's *Deirdre*. In January 1909 she played Olive in Rudolf Besier's *Olive Latimer's Husband* (Vaudeville), and in September of that year Mieris in the ill-fated *False Gods* by J. B. Fagan [q.v.], with Sir H. Beerbohm Tree at His Majesty's Theatre.

Mrs. Campbell spent the year 1910 in America. Back in London she opened at the Haymarket (March 1911) in Besier's *Lady Patricia*. Here it was said of her that she burlesqued with much humour both herself as an actress and the kind of woman she had been impersonating for so long. At the St. James's (December 1911)

she appeared with Sir George Alexander for the first time in seventeen years: the part—one she had refused more than once and never liked—was Mrs. Chepstow in the drama *Bella Donna*, by Fagan and Mr. Robert Hichens. After a revival at the St. James's (June 1913) of *The Second Mrs. Tanqueray* and her performance of Leonora in *The Adored One* by Sir J. M. Barrie [q.v.] (Duke of York's Theatre, September 1913), Mrs. Campbell found one of her last major successes, Eliza Doolittle, the flower-girl Galatea of Mr. Bernard Shaw's *Pygmalion*. 'I invented a Cockney accent and created a human Eliza' she wrote later of a part that she played first at His Majesty's (April 1914) and afterwards in the United States. Mr. Shaw was always a firm friend: his letters to her are the crown of the autobiography which she published in 1922.

During the rest of her career Mrs. Campbell's star slowly waned. She had such effective parts as Rosalie la Grange in *The Thirteenth Chair* (Duke of York's, October 1917), George Sand in *Madame Sand* (Duke of York's, June 1920), and Anastasia in *The Matriarch* (Royalty, May 1929). There were also revivals of *Macbeth* (Aldwych Theatre, November 1920, with the American actor James K. Hackett); *Hedda Gabler* (Everyman Theatre, May 1922); and Ibsen's *Ghosts* (in which she played Mrs. Alving, Wyndham's Theatre, March 1928). But much of her time was spent in touring and her new parts were few and unimportant. She never regained her full hold on the West End stage, and during the last years of her life she was engaged chiefly in minor film work in America. To the end she retained her sense of humour and cutting wit. Off the stage she was tempestuous, tactless, and good-hearted; upon it she was an actress in the grand manner. A modern critic, James Agate, said of her at her death: 'In my life I have seen six great actresses, and six only. These are Bernhardt, Réjane, Mrs. Kendal, Ellen Terry, Duse, and Mrs. Patrick Campbell.' She died of pneumonia at Pau 9 April 1940. In 1914 she had married, as his second wife, (Major) George Frederick Myddleton Cornwallis-West. By her first husband she had a son, who was killed in action in France in 1917, and a daughter, Stella Patrick Campbell, an actress who appeared often with her mother.

A portrait of Mrs. Campbell as Paula Tanqueray was painted by Solomon J.

Solomon in 1894, and another was painted by Prince Pierre Troubetzkoy.

[*The Times*, 11 April 1940; Mrs. Patrick Campbell, *My Life and Some Letters*, 1922; H. Hamilton Fyfe, *Sir Arthur Pinero's Plays and Players*, 1930; G. Bernard Shaw, *Our Theatres in the Nineties*, vol. iii, 1932; A. E. W. Mason, *Sir George Alexander and the St. James' Theatre*, 1935; James Agate, *Ego 4*, 1940; *Who's Who in the Theatre*, 1939.]

J. C. TREWIN.

CAMPBELL, JAMES HENRY MUS-SEN, first BARON GLENAVY (1851–1931), Irish lawyer and politician, was born at Terenure, Dublin, 4 April 1851, the youngest son of William Mussen Campbell, an officer in the Dublin metropolitan police, by his wife, Delia, daughter of Henry Francis Graham Poole, of Newtown Abbey, co. Kildare. He was educated at Kingstown, co. Dublin, and at Trinity College, Dublin, where he won a classical scholarship and was a senior moderator in both classics and history. As a speaker he was outstanding, and won the college historical society's gold medal for oratory.

Called to the Irish bar (King's Inns, Dublin) in 1878 Campbell rapidly became a leading junior on the North-Eastern circuit. His oratory won him distinction among such brilliant advocates as T. M. Healy, Edward Carson [qq.v.], and Seymour Bushe. He took silk in 1892 and was made a bencher of King's Inns in 1894. He was called to the English bar by Gray's Inn in 1899, and became a bencher in 1901 and K.C. in 1906, but practised little in England.

Like most Irish barristers Campbell was a politician. He became prominent as a unionist. Elected to parliament for the St. Stephen's Green division of Dublin at a by-election in 1898, he lost this seat to the nationalists in 1900. In 1903, at another by-election, he was returned as one of the two members for Dublin University, Carson having been the other member since 1892. This seat Campbell held until he was raised to the bench in 1916. An effective member, his speeches were praised by A. J. Balfour. He held office as solicitor-general for Ireland from 1901 to 1905 and as attorney-general for a short time in December 1905. He was sworn of the Irish Privy Council in the last-named year.

During the home rule controversy of 1912 to 1914 Campbell, deeply involved in the Ulster unionist movement, was a member of Carson's provisional government. He was re-appointed attorney-general in April 1916 a few days before the Sinn Fein rising. In December 1916 he was made lord chief justice of Ireland, was created a baronet in 1917, and in June 1918 was appointed lord chancellor of Ireland. In the last scramble for office before the setting up of the Irish Free State in 1921 he was induced to retire in favour of Sir John Ross [q.v.], and was raised to the peerage as Baron Glenavy, of Milltown, co. Dublin.

Campbell's experience as potential rebel in the Ulster provisional government and attorney-general after the rising of 1916 had considerably modified his views on home rule. During the years 1918 to 1921, as head of the Irish judiciary while the country was in active rebellion, he had come to see that a change was inevitable. Accordingly when the Irish Free State was established he accepted the new régime and was made a member of its first senate of which he was elected chairman in 1922. He was a dominating figure, perhaps too strong for a chairman, and did not allow the senate to develop its independence. He was even known to adjourn the House to suit his own convenience. In the words of his fellow senator, W. B. Yeats [q.v.], 'handsome, watchful, vigorous, dominating, courteous, he seemed like some figure from an historical painting'. The chairmanship of the senate was his last office. In 1928 he did not seek re-election.

Glenavy was a convinced member of the Church of Ireland and served on its synod. In private life he was a keen golfer and bridge player. He married in 1884 Emily (died 1939), second daughter of John MacCullagh, resident magistrate, of Newry, co. Down, and niece of the mathematician James MacCullagh [q.v.]. They had three sons, the youngest of whom was killed in the war of 1914–1918, and one daughter. Glenavy died in Dublin 22 March 1931, and was succeeded as second baron by his eldest son, Charles Henry Gordon (born 1885).

There is a portrait of Glenavy, by Sir William Orpen, at Gray's Inn, and another, by Leo Whelan, is in the possession of his son.

[*The Times*, 23 March 1931; private information; personal knowledge.]

DIARMID COFFEY.

CANNAN, EDWIN (1861–1935), economist, was born at Funchal, Madeira, 3 February 1861, the younger son of David Alexander Cannan, a native of Kirkcudbrightshire, who held a business post in Australia at the time of the Victoria gold rush, and in Edwin's boyhood resided at Bournemouth. His mother, Jane Dorothea Claude, who died eighteen days after his birth, was the daughter of a Liverpool merchant, of Huguenot descent. He was brother of Charles Cannan [q.v.].

Cannan was educated at Clifton and Balliol College, Oxford. At Balliol, owing to illness and a consequent voyage round the world, he did not take an honours degree but, in the pass school, took political economy as one of his subjects. In 1885 he won the Lothian essay prize. In the introduction to his *Economic Outlook* (1912), he gave a characteristic account of the evolution of his studies as an economist. An essay, which was unsuccessfully submitted for the Cobden prize in 1886, was turned partly into his first book, *Elementary Political Economy* (1888), partly into a paper on 'The Bearings of Recent Economics on Individualism, Collectivism, and Communism' (republished in *The Economic Outlook* under the title 'Economics and Socialism') which was read to the Fabian Society in 1889, and contained the germs of much that was most characteristic in his approach to the problems of economic policy. There followed three years' study of the works of earlier economists. This resulted in 1893 in *A History of the Theories of Production and Distribution in English Political Economy from 1776 to 1848*, a work which, in spite of some protest at the sharpness of its strictures on the masters of the past, established his standing in the profession.

On the strength of these writings and perhaps partly because it was believed that his attitude to the main tradition of English political economy was much more unorthodox than in fact it actually was, when the London School of Economics and Political Science was founded in 1895, he was among those who were invited to lecture on economics. Thenceforward, although, by a deliberate choice which sprang from the enjoyment of independent means, his appointment was never on a full-time basis and he resided all his life at Oxford, his teaching at the school was the main preoccupation of his life. He was not created professor of political economy in the university of London until 1907. But throughout this whole period he was the effective head of the economics department and played an essential part in building up the main tradition of the school. He retired in 1926 and devoted himself first to the preparation of *A Review of Economic Theory* (1929), which embodies the substance of his great sixty-lecture course on principles of economics at the school, and is as much a running disquisition on past theories and their genesis as an exposition of contemporary doctrine. He then turned to a number of miscellaneous works, some arising from the presidency of the Royal Economic Society to which he was elected in 1932. The universities of Glasgow (1901) and Manchester (1927) conferred honorary degrees upon him. He died at Bournemouth 8 April 1935. He married in 1907 his second cousin, Margaret Mary, eldest daughter of David Cullen, deputy-surgeon-general, of Cheltenham. The only child of the marriage died in boyhood.

The concern with the history of economic thought, which showed itself in Cannan's first major work, was an abiding interest throughout his whole career. In 1895 he had the supreme good fortune to discover a set of student's notes of Adam Smith's Glasgow lectures which he published with a learned introduction and notes the next year (*Lectures on Justice, Police, Revenue and Arms delivered in the University of Glasgow by Adam Smith . . . in 1763*). In 1904 he published, in two volumes, what is acknowledged to be the standard edition of the *Wealth of Nations*. Later there came an edition of the *Bullion Report* (*The Paper Pound of 1797–1821*, 1919).

Cannan was a severe critic of the classical economists. Many would say that he was too severe and that, in some instances at least, a better case could be made out for his victims than he was prepared to concede. Nevertheless, he was deeply imbued with the spirit of the classical outlook—its long views, its wide perspectives, the broad humanity and cosmopolitanism of its approach. The questions which seemed to him to be important were the questions to which the classical economists attempted to provide an answer: the question regarding the main causes of the increase of wealth and the conditions determining its distribution. His text-book *Wealth: A Brief Explanation of the Causes of Economic Welfare* (1914) is still probably the best introduction to the study of the economic system from this point of view. He was much less interested in the questions of equilibrium and disequilibrium which have been the main preoccupation of the present generation of economists. He had a strong dislike of the mathematical approach, and an almost passionate conviction that the important economic truths could be expressed, as he tried so hard to express them, in language which would be intelligible to laymen. Coupled with this was a sturdy suspicion of any speculative excursion which did not seem to have a more or less direct concern with practice. While he would have rightly repudiated the suggestion that he was a classical economist *malgré lui*, for that would have suggested affiliations with the Ricardians with their lack of a sense of history, it is probable that he would not have resented the suggestion of some continuity of outlook, if not of doctrine, with that of the author of the *Wealth of Nations*.

Cannan's work in economics was not confined to the exposition and history of general theory. From a very early stage he took a lively interest in policy; and he played a prominent part in the public discussion of the practical problems of the day. For many years he reviewed current governmental publications for the Oxford *Economic Review*; and he served a term of office on the Oxford city council. At an early stage, also, his interest in demography led to a prediction, many years ahead of other experts, of 'The Probable Cessation of Growth of Population in England and Wales' (*Economic Journal*, 1895, reprinted in *Economic Scares*, 1933). His profound knowledge of local government and its history received classic expression in his *History of Local Rates in England* (1896: the second edition, published in 1912, contains very important additional matter). His criticisms and disquisitions on various aspects of economic policy during and immediately after the war of 1914–1918, reprinted in *An Economist's Protest* (1927), are marked by great practical insight and expository skill. It was in this last connexion that he became involved in the great monetary controversies of the day—inflation, stabilization, rate of interest, the role of bank credit, and the like; and the vigour of his polemics on some of these topics, especially in regard to the nature of bank credit and the return to the gold standard, is probably responsible for the disproportionate attention which has been given to his attitude towards these questions, to the neglect of his more solid and enduring contributions.

As a teacher Cannan was outstanding.

In lectures his delivery was poor. But his sense of the architecture of his subject was superb; and his complete disinterestedness and great learning and good sense, disguised behind a somewhat jaunty informality which endeared him greatly to the young, exercised a profound influence upon all who came into contact with him. In the years following his death, owing partly to his lack of interest in those aspects of pure theory which were the main focus of attention in this country in the inter-war period, and partly to his identification in the public mind with certain practical policies in regard to money which, in their results, proved to be unfortunate, his reputation has tended to be somewhat under a cloud. But his contributions to pure scholarship and to our knowledge of the evolution of incentives and institutions are of lasting value. If it is fair to say that he ignored much that was good in the intellectual developments of the inter-war period, it is equally fair to say that in his own work there is much that is novel and true that has not yet received full recognition.

Cannan was a man of strong personality. A mordant wit and an abrupt manner concealed a character of strong attachments and infinite gentleness and sympathy. He possessed in a marked degree that characteristic British determination to assert his individual rights as a citizen which has done so much for the rule of law in this country; and, although not litigious, if he thought that a principle was involved, he would go to any trouble and expense to defend it. He had little feeling for the arts, save for the modes of the sweet, wholesome English prose that he himself handled with such distinction. But he had a great interest in the day-to-day history of the face of England and he was a leading authority on roads which he studied for many years, first as an ardent cyclist, and then as a driver of a 'baby' Austin which he learned to drive at the age of sixty-six.

[*Economic Journal*, June 1935; *Clare Market Review*, vol. xv, No. 3, and vol. xvi, No. 1, 1935; personal knowledge.]

LIONEL ROBBINS.

CARLYLE, SIR ROBERT WARRAND (1859–1934), Indian civil servant and scholar, was born at Brechin 11 July 1859, the elder son of James Edward Carlyle, minister of the Free church at Brechin, subsequently successively Free Church chaplain in Bombay, Berlin, and Pietermaritzburg, by his wife, Jessie Margaret, daughter of James Milne, of Huntly, Aberdeenshire. The original spelling of the name, Carlile, was altered by Robert's grandfather, a kinsman of the famous Thomas Carlyle and brother-in-law of Edward Irving [q.v.] through Robert's grandmother,

Robert Carlyle was educated privately and at Glasgow University and Balliol College, Oxford. He passed the Indian civil service examination of 1878 and in 1880 was posted to the old undivided province of Bengal. Here he spent his junior years in attaining the sound grasp of district administration which stood him in good stead thereafter. In 1897 he was collector of Darbhauga during one of the last serious Bihar famines, and was conspicuous for his untiring personal supervision of relief operations over a wide area, his excellent work being recognized by his appointment as C.I.E. in 1898. His next important appointment was that of inspector-general of police (1902), in which he gained the respect of all ranks. This was followed by promotion (1904) to the difficult post of officiating chief secretary to the government of Bengal (the appointment was confirmed in 1905), and thence to that of secretary to the government of India in the revenue and agricultural department at Simla (1907). He became a member of the governor-general's council in 1910, and was serving in that capacity during the viceroyalty of Lord Hardinge of Penshurst at the time of the momentous removal, in 1911, of the headquarters of the government of India from Calcutta to Delhi. Of the wisdom of that change he always entertained doubts.

Secretariat work was never particularly congenial to Carlyle. His handwriting was curiously illegible, and he had no liking for debates in the legislative council. His strength lay in his thorough knowledge of administration, the soundness of his judgement, the fearless expression of his views, and the attractiveness of his personality. He was held in high regard by all, both British and Indian, and always commanded the loyalty of those who served under him. He was appointed C.S.I. in 1910 and K.C.S.I. in 1911.

Carlyle retired in 1915 and went to live in Essex. Thenceforward his main interest lay in collaboration with his brother, Alexander James Carlyle, in the writing of *A History of Mediaeval Political Theory in the West* (6 vols., 1903–1936). He also wrote an article on 'The Political Theories of St. Thomas Aquinas', which appeared erroneously above his brother's name, in the *Scottish Review* for January 1896. He was a member of the Central Tribunal to consider adjustments between war service and necessary industrial activities (1916–1918) and a trustee of the King's Fund (1919).

Carlyle married in 1903 Isabel Jane, daughter of James Barton, of Farndreg, Dundalk, co. Louth. Lady Carlyle, whose house was always a gracious social centre, was indefatigable in organizing much needed comforts for the troops engaged in the Mesopotamian campaign, for which work she received the Kaiser-i-Hind gold medal in 1916. There were no children of the marriage. After his retirement both Carlyle and his wife were much interested in the work of his cousin, Prebendary Wilson Carlile, founder of the Church Army. Carlyle died at Florence 23 May 1934.

[*The Times*, 28 May 1934; private information; personal knowledge.]

HENRY WHEELER.

CARÖE, WILLIAM DOUGLAS (1857–1938), architect, was born at Great Crosby, near Liverpool, 1 September 1857, the younger son of Anders Kruise Caröe, Danish consul at Liverpool and a naturalized British subject, by his wife, Jane Green. He was educated at Ruabon Grammar School and Trinity College, Cambridge, where he was a senior optime in the mathematical tripos of 1879.

Caröe was articled to J. L. Pearson [q.v.], and after completing his articles he remained on in Pearson's office on a gradually diminishing part-time basis while he built up his own practice. It was at this period that he was responsible under Pearson for a great deal of the detailing of Truro Cathedral. His own practice at that time included a large amount of work in Ireland—houses, farm buildings, and stables—and his church work in England grew rapidly. In 1895 he was appointed architect to the Ecclesiastical Commissioners and the Charity Commission and held the post until his death. A vast amount of ecclesiastical work passed through his hands in these years. He acted as consulting architect to the diocesan boards of finance of Lichfield, Canterbury, Bath and Wells, and Newcastle-upon-Tyne. He was architect to the cathedrals of Canterbury, Durham, Southwell, St. Davids, Brecon, and Jerusalem, and to many churches, including Great Malvern Priory, Tewkesbury Abbey,

Romsey Abbey, and St. Peter's, Wolverhampton. He built or reconstructed the archbishop's palace at Canterbury, and the bishops' palaces at Abergwili, Southwell, Bristol, St. Albans, Llandaff, Rochester, and Wolvesey (Winchester). He was also the designer, among other buildings, of the University College of South Wales and Monmouthshire at Cardiff, the Teddington laboratories of the National Physical Laboratory, the offices of the Ecclesiastical Commissioners in Millbank, Wycombe Abbey School, Sherborne School for Girls, North Foreland School, Broadstairs, new buildings for Pembroke College, Cambridge, and the churches of St. David, Exeter, St. George, Leicester, SS. Andrew and Patrick, Elveden, Suffolk, St. Helen, St. Helens, Lancashire, and St. Ninian, Douglas, Isle of Man. He designed internal fittings for many hundred medieval churches, including St. Mary's, Weston Zoyland, Winchester College Chapel, and St. Mary's, Cardigan, and between the years 1887 and 1937 he was responsible for the structural restoration of many medieval buildings including the churches of St. Hilda, Hartlepool, and St. Michael, Stanton Harcourt; he also did important restoration work at Christ Church, Oxford. He designed the monuments to Archbishop Temple in Canterbury Cathedral, to Bishop Owen in St. David's Cathedral, to Bishop Satterlee and Bishop Harding in Washington Cathedral, U.S.A., and to Bishop Ridding in Southwell Cathedral. He was a member of the first commission on St. Paul's Cathedral in 1912, when he signed a minority report with (Sir) Horace Darwin [q.v.], and acted as adviser to the Norwegian government on Trondhjem Cathedral. He received the Order of St. Olaf of Norway, and was elected a fellow of the Royal Institute of British Architects in 1890.

Caröe's publications include two books, *Sefton* (1893) and *King's Hostel, Trinity College, Cambridge* (1909). He edited ' *Tom Tower*', *Christ Church, Oxford. Some Letters of Sir C. Wren to J. Fell* (1923). He married in 1891 Grace Desborough (died 1947), daughter of John Randall, barrister, of London, and had two sons and one daughter. He died at the house which he had built at Kyrenia in Cyprus 25 February 1938.

Caröe was a man of forceful character and great energy and business capacity. He was a faithful representative of what may be considered the closing phase of the Gothic revival which reached its climax in the work of his master, Pearson, and of G. F. Bodley [q.v.], and gave way in its turn to later developments which aimed at the spirit of Gothic architecture rather than at the close reproduction of period methods and details.

A crayon drawing of Caröe is in the office of his firm at 3 Great College Street, Westminster.

[*The Times*, 1 and 4 March 1938; *Journal* of the Royal Institute of British Architects, 11 April 1938; *Builder* and *Architect*, 4 March 1938; private information.]

IAN MACALISTER.

CARPENTER, SIR (HENRY CORT) HAROLD (1875–1940), metallurgist, was born at Clifton, Bristol, 6 February 1875, the second son of William Lant Carpenter, engineer, of Bristol, by his wife, Annie Grace Viret. He was a grandson of W. B. Carpenter [q.v.] and a great-great-grandson of Henry Cort [q.v.], the inventor of the puddling process for iron. Owing to his father's early death, his mental development was much influenced by his uncle, J. Estlin Carpenter [q.v.]. He was educated at St. Paul's School and at Eastbourne College for a year and in 1893 entered Merton College, Oxford, as a postmaster. Having obtained a first class in natural science in 1896, he studied organic chemistry at Leipzig and took his Ph.D. at the end of two years. He then worked with W. H. Perkin [q.v.] at the Owens College, Manchester, until 1901, when he was appointed to take charge of the new departments of chemistry and metallurgy at the National Physical Laboratory. His interest soon shifted from organic chemistry to metallurgy, and from 1905 he confined his work to that subject, his first original contribution, with B. F. E. Keeling, being a study of the alloys of iron and carbon, involving accurate measurements in the range of high temperatures. This difficult investigation, establishing the main features of the system, was followed by studies of the structure of other alloys, especially the complex alloys of copper with aluminium.

In 1906 Carpenter was invited to occupy the new chair of metallurgy in the university of Manchester, where he built up a school of research, investigating tool steels and various complex alloys containing copper and aluminium. The 'growth' of cast iron was traced to the penetration of oxygen along the surface of the flakes of graphite. He left Manchester in December 1913 for the chair of metallurgy at the

Royal School of Mines, South Kensington, but before taking up the duties he made a six months' tour of Canada and the United States of America in order to study metallurgical operations on a large scale. At the Royal School of Mines, however, he devoted himself mainly to the metallographic side of the subject. In a series of papers, mostly in collaboration with Miss C. F. Elam (Mrs. Tipper), he followed the process of recrystallization of metals which had been deformed, in the course of which means were devised for growing crystals of metals, especially aluminium, large enough to allow of a study of their mechanical properties. This research laid the foundation of later work on single crystals. Other papers, in collaboration with Mr. John Monteath Robertson, described, more minutely than before, the changes of structure in carbon steels when heated or cooled through the critical range of temperature. The production of well-formed crystals of oxide of iron heated under a reduced pressure of oxygen was also studied, as was the structure of native metals, these subjects being linked by a common interest in the processes of growth of crystals.

Carpenter successively filled the presidential chairs of the three principal metallurgical institutes, being president of the Institute of Mining and Metallurgy (1934), of that of Metals (1918–1920), and of that of Iron and Steel (1935–1937). He had been instrumental in founding the Institute of Metals, and as chairman of a Treasury committee was responsible in 1929 for a report which resulted in improving the status of professional men in government service. He was elected F.R.S. in 1918 and knighted in 1929. He received the honorary degree of D.Met. from the university of Sheffield and that of D.Sc. from the university of Wales. He also received numerous gold medals, including the Japanese Honda medal (1940).

Carpenter married in 1905 Ethel Mary, daughter of George Henry Lomas, of Brooklands, Cheshire; there were no children of the marriage.

In the war of 1914–1918 Carpenter served on the Admiralty Board of Invention and Research. On the outbreak of war in 1939 the metallurgical department of the Royal School of Mines was transferred to Swansea, and it was while on a country walk that he succumbed to heart failure 13 September 1940.

Carpenter's numerous publications in-clude only one book, a two-volume work on *Metals*, written in collaboration with Mr. J. M. Robertson and published in 1939, remarkable for its clear exposition of the main facts of the structure of metals and alloys.

[*The Times*, 16 September 1940; *Obituary Notices of Fellows of the Royal Society*, No. 10, December 1941 (portrait); *Journal* of the Iron and Steel Institute, vol. cxlii, 1940; *Metallurgia*, October 1940; personal knowledge.]   C. H. DESCH.

CARSON, EDWARD HENRY, BARON CARSON, of Duncairn (1854–1935), Ulster leader and lord of appeal in ordinary, was born in Dublin 9 February 1854, the second son of Edward Henry Carson, a civil engineer practising in that city, by his wife, Isabella, daughter of Captain Peter Lambert, of Castle Ellen, Athenry, co. Galway, a descendant of General John Lambert [q.v.]. He was educated at Portarlington School and at Trinity College, Dublin, where he studied law, although his first inclination was towards architecture. After taking his degree, he was called to the Irish bar (King's Inns, Dublin) in 1877 and by 1880 had become known to solicitors as 'a desirable junior', so that three years later he was much in demand both in the Dublin courts and on the Leinster circuit. In 1887 he became junior counsel to the attorney-general, John Gibson, on whose elevation to the bench in 1888 Peter O'Brien (afterwards Lord O'Brien, q.v.) continued Carson as his counsel. As junior crown prosecutor he conducted several important criminal trials until, in 1889, he took silk. At the instance of A. J. Balfour, who had formed a high opinion of him, he was appointed solicitor-general for Ireland in June 1892, only two months before the end of Lord Salisbury's second administration. In July he was returned to parliament as one of the members for Dublin University, a seat which he continued to hold for twenty-six years. He then determined to explore the wider field open to talent across St. George's Channel, and he was called to the English bar by the Middle Temple in 1893, becoming Q.C. the following year. In due course he was elected a bencher (1900) and treasurer (1922) of his Inn; he had been a bencher of King's Inns since 1891.

Carson's first success at the English bar was in the libel action brought in 1895 by Oscar Wilde [q.v.] against the Marquess of Queensberry, which caused him to be acknowledged by common consent as one of the foremost advocates at the bar. Although he was invited to take office when the unionists gained power in 1895, Carson refused: he was at the height of his powers as an advocate, and he felt it necessary to devote himself to his professional career. In 1900, however, having been sworn of the Irish Privy Council in 1896, he became solicitor-general for England, an office which involved a knighthood and which he held until the fall of the unionist administration in December 1905, when he was sworn of the Privy Council. In January 1910 he was chosen as leader of the Irish unionists in the House of Commons on the retirement of W. H. (afterwards Viscount) Long [q.v.] from that position. On the resignation of Balfour himself from the leadership of the opposition in the next year, Carson was one of the four men canvassed as possible successors, but he refused to allow his name to go forward, preferring to devote all his energies to the service of Irish unionism. Many years afterwards he said: 'From the day I first entered parliament up to the present, devotion to the union has been the guiding star of my political life.'

Even though the liberals had promised that no home rule bill should be introduced during the parliament elected in 1906, Carson saw that a liberal administration constituted a grave menace to the union, and he promoted to the best of his ability the close organization of the rank and file of the loyalists of Ulster; in 1907 he vigorously opposed the devolution scheme which, as it was also rejected by the nationalists, remained stillborn. In the battle over the parliament bill (1910–1911), his speeches were directed to showing the effect that this measure would have on the Irish problem, for if the veto of the House of Lords were abolished, the passage of home rule was assured.

In 1911 the Ulster Unionist Council appointed a commission 'to take immediate steps, in consultation with Sir Edward Carson, to frame and submit a constitution for a provisional government in Ulster'. For this post of Ulster leader, Carson had all the qualities necessary; readiness to accept responsibility, insight, courage, resource, and single-minded sincerity for the cause. At a great demonstration on 23 September, at Craigavon, near Belfast, he was welcomed as the new leader, and in a speech in reply to addresses declaring for resistance to the jurisdiction of a Dublin parliament, he declared that the people of Ulster and he joined together would yet defeat 'the most nefarious conspiracy that has ever been hatched against a free people' and called on them to be ready themselves 'to become responsible for the government of the Protestant Province of Ulster'. The appeal was heard, and in spite of extreme provocation and threats, the discipline maintained by him prevented any outbreak of disorder in Ulster.

In 1912 the Ulster Volunteer Force was raised, and application was made to the magistrates for permission to drill. It was granted, and soon battalions sprang up all over the province to form the nucleus of the body which gave substance to the declaration that Ulster intended to govern the districts over which she had control. On 9 April 1912, at a great demonstration at Balmoral, near Belfast, Bonar Law, after assuring Ulster of the support of English unionists, shook hands with Carson as a visible sign of the pledge amid great enthusiasm.

When in the committee stage of the home rule bill an amendment was put down by Thomas Charles Reginald Agar-Robartes, liberal member for St. Austell, to exclude the counties of Antrim, Down, Derry, and Armagh from the jurisdiction of the Dublin parliament, Carson advised that it should be supported. His colleagues had doubts, but their faith in his judgement was such that they unanimously supported him. Once more, at a gathering at Blenheim on 29 July, Bonar Law pledged the support of the unionists of England, and Carson announced that the people of Northern Ireland would shortly challenge the government to interfere with them if they dared, and would await the result with equanimity. This was followed by the drafting of a bond or sacred obligation, which at first was intended to be worded according to the Scottish national covenant of 1581; but this was found to be impracticable, and a new covenant was drawn up which was to be signed all over the province on 28 September, known as 'Ulster day'. Carson described the covenant as a step forward, not in defiance, but in defence, not in a spirit of aggression nor of ascendancy, but with a full knowledge that Ulster would carry out everything which it meant, whatever the consequences. Following this up, Carson moved, in January 1913, the exclusion of the whole province of Ulster from the scope of the bill. The amendment was defeated, although Carson's speech made a powerful impression, and on 16 January the bill was read a third time. A fortnight later it was defeated in the Lords by a majority of 257, but it had only to be passed again in two succeeding sessions in order to become law, and therefore preparations were pushed forward in Ulster, plans were adopted for a provisional government, and Carson, accepting the chairmanship of the central authority, said Ulster might be coerced into submission, but in that case she would have to be governed as a conquered country. To the guarantee fund of £250,000 for members of the Ulster Volunteer Force and their dependents who might suffer as a result of their services, Carson subscribed immediately £10,000.

The importation of arms and ammunition into Ireland having been prohibited by royal proclamation in December 1913, correspondence took place between Carson and the prime minister, H. H. Asquith, which many people looked upon as the forerunner of some concessions on the part of the government. Carson, however, knowing how much the government was in the hands of the nationalists, had no illusions on the subject, and his scepticism was shown to be well founded when, on the second reading of the bill on 9 March 1914, the prime minister was only able to offer 'county option' with a time limit of six years. Carson described the offer as 'sentence of death with a stay of execution', but he noted with satisfaction that the government had admitted the principle of exclusion. The debate was adjourned, but on 14 March at Bradford Mr. Winston Churchill made a grave speech clearly hinting that if Ulster refused the offer of the prime minister, force would be employed, and concluded: 'Let us go forward together and put these grave matters to the proof.' What this meant was revealed when it was announced that warships had been dispatched to Lamlash in the Isle of Arran, and that extra troops were to be rushed into Ulster. The immediate sequel was the 'Curragh incident' (20 March), and the imminence of civil war was brought home to the world. Lastly, when the gun-running at Larne (24 April) was denounced by Asquith as a grave and unprecedented outrage, Carson replied that he took full responsibility for everything that had been done. The prime minister then assured the House of Commons that the government would, without delay, take proper steps to vindi-cate the authority of the law; but there the matter ended, for no steps whatever were taken.

The promised amending bill was introduced and passed the Commons (25 May), but on 8 July the Lords substituted the permanent exclusion of the whole province of Ulster in the place of 'county option'. Rumours reached Carson that there were differences of opinion in the Cabinet over the amending bill. At the subsequent conference of party leaders opened at Buckingham Palace on 21 July, Carson and James Craig (afterwards Viscount Craigavon, q.v.) attended as the Ulster representatives, and when, on 24 July, it broke down on the question what portion of Ulster should be excluded, the amending bill, with 'county option', was put down for second reading on 30 July. By then, however, the country was on the brink of war, and at Asquith's request, in order to avoid domestic controversy at such a crisis, Carson and Bonar Law consented to the postponement of the proceedings on the amending bill, on the express assurance of the prime minister that 'this was of course without prejudice to its future'. War having broken out in August, a party truce was proclaimed on the terms that no controversial measures were to be taken, but the prime minister provoked the protest of the whole unionist party by advising the royal assent to the home rule bill, although at the same time announcing a bill suspending its operation until after the war, and saying that 'as an integral part of the proposals' the government would introduce an amending bill before the Irish government bill could possibly come into operation. In the same speech Asquith declared the coercion of Ulster to be 'an absolutely unthinkable thing' which he and his colleagues 'would never countenance or consent to'.

Together with the rest of the unionist party, Carson considered the government to have been guilty of a flagrant breach of faith in thus passing the home rule bill into law; nevertheless, he offered it the services of the Ulster Volunteer Force. In Belfast, on 30 September, he explained to the Ulster Unionist Council the position in regard to the postponement of the amending bill, and said that however unworthily the government had acted, their own duty was to think of their country. Their country and the Empire were in danger; England's difficulty was their difficulty and England's sorrows had been, and always would be, their sorrows. He therefore said to the Ulster volunteers: 'Go and help to save your country; go and win honour for Ulster and for Ireland.' Next morning he marched at the head of the North Belfast volunteers to the Old Town Hall where they were enrolled as the first unit of the now famous 36th (Ulster) division.

In Asquith's administration of May 1915, Carson was appointed attorney-general. In the eighteen months of its existence, he became more and more dissatisfied with the way in which the government was being conducted, holding strong views about the delay in applying conscription, the necessity of a retreat from the Dardanelles, and the dishonour of Great Britain's abandonment of Serbia after the pledges given by Sir Edward Grey. The exigencies of war having still required the further postponement of the amending bill, Asquith renewed his pledge on the matter, but after the Easter rebellion in Dublin in 1916, the government, to the astonishment of everyone, proposed that negotiations should be opened for an arrangement for bringing the Home Rule Act into immediate operation, subject to an amending bill excluding the whole or a portion of Ulster. On behalf of the government, Lloyd George asked Carson to go to Belfast to try to persuade the people there to agree to the exclusion of the six counties. Carson consented, solely, as he said, 'on account of the representations made to me as to the urgency of the matter for the prosecution of the war and the encouragement of America to join the Allies. The Ulster people, with equal reluctance, authorised me to assent on their behalf, while protesting that their devotion to the union remained unimpaired.'

Before leaving on this difficult mission, Carson had received a letter from Lloyd George 'assuring him that the six county area would be permanently excluded from the act of 1914'. Meanwhile the nationalist leaders had persuaded their followers to agree to this policy of exclusion, but they maintained that a promise as to its temporary character had been made to them. On this misunderstanding the negotiations broke down. On 24 July Lloyd George gave another assurance that under no conditions did the present government or any member of it contemplate forcing the six counties into a home rule government against their will.

Carson's resignation from office in October 1916 heralded the break up of Asquith's administration. Under Lloyd George, who became prime minister in December 1916, Carson accepted office as first lord of the Admiralty. His admiration for the men of the navy was unbounded and he avowed that the glory of success belonged only to the officers and men of the ships. His whole duty lay in serving them, in seeing that they got all that they required for their support in guns, ammunition, and comfort.

Carson had said: 'I myself would never have accepted office in [Lloyd George's] government except on the distinct understanding that no attempt would be made to violate these reiterated pledges not to put Ulster under Home Rule.' Nevertheless, T. P. O'Connor [q.v.] once more raised the question in the Commons on 7 March 1917, and Lloyd George in his speech on that occasion pointed out that 'in the north-eastern portion of Ireland you have a population as hostile to Irish rule as the rest of Ireland is to British rule, as alien in blood, in religious faith, in traditions, in outlook—as alien from the rest of Ireland in this respect as the inhabitants of Fife or Aberdeen'. In May, under pressure from the prime minister, Carson consented to the setting up of a convention of representative Irishmen under the chairmanship of Sir Horace Plunkett [q.v.], and it was said by Lloyd George that if this body could propose a settlement 'by substantial agreement', the government would introduce legislation to give effect to it. But after it had sat for many months, the prime minister admitted that in the report of the convention there was no 'substantial agreement'. In January 1918, on learning that Lloyd George was intending to introduce a home rule bill for the whole of Ireland, which it was generally assumed would be based on the majority report from which all the Ulster delegates had dissented, Carson, who had left the Admiralty in order to become a member of the War Cabinet in July 1917, resigned from the government.

The joint letter issued by Lloyd George and Bonar Law on the eve of the general election of December 1918 gave a solemn pledge that only when the condition of Ireland was sufficiently settled would the Home Rule Act of 1914 be put into force, and that the policy of the government, if again returned to power, was to exclude the six counties of north-east Ulster from its operation. Carson was shown this letter and asked if he agreed with it. He replied in the affirmative, and in response to representations from Belfast, consented to return to Westminster for the newly created Duncairn division of Belfast. No one realized more than Carson that the danger to Ulster was as great as ever and that while the Home Rule Act of 1914 was likely to come into force at any time after the legal end of the war had been determined, no provision had been made for the amending bill. In December 1919 Lloyd George, stating that three-fourths of the people of Ireland were bitterly hostile and were at heart rebels against the Crown and government, but that Ulster was a complete contrast which would make it an outrage to place her people under the rest of Ireland, announced that these were the considerations upon which he based his proposed legislation for the next session.

When the Government of Ireland bill had been introduced on 25 February 1920, Carson went to Belfast and after a speech from him, the Ulster Unionist Council adopted a resolution disclaiming responsibility for the bill, but declaring that as there was no prospect of securing the repeal of the Act of 1914, the Ulster parliamentary representatives should not assume the responsibility of attempting to defeat it. Therefore when the rejection of the bill was moved on 31 March 1920, Carson rose and reiterated his opposition to the very end to the whole policy of home rule for Ireland: 'It will be fraught with disaster to your country and to mine. . . . The truth of the matter is there is no alternative to the union, unless separation, and anybody who will think out the circumstances will necessarily come to that conclusion. . . . What you are really going to do, and I wish to put it on record as my opinion, is to give a lever to your enemies by which they may, under the guise of constitutional law, attain results which you know in your hearts will be absolutely fatal to your whole Empire.' But he went on: 'If I help to kill this bill, I bring automatically into force the Act of 1914', and he added, 'It may turn out, as the leader of the House said yesterday, that under this bill, if it passes, the only part of Ireland which will have a parliament is the part that never asked for it. . . . . One thing I will promise you, that Ulster will do her level best with her parliament.' And to the lord chancellor, F. E. Smith, Lord Birkenhead [q.v.], he wrote a letter which the latter read to the House of

Lords on 22 November 1920. 'We have agreed therefore, and have made up our minds that in the interests of Ireland, Great Britain and the Empire, the best and only solution of the question is to accept the present bill and endeavour to work it loyally.' When therefore Government of Ireland bill became law on 23 December 1920, many people believed that the great struggle had at last come to an end.

Carson now felt that his place should be taken by a younger man, and at a meeting of the Ulster Unionist Council held on 4 February 1921 he announced his resignation as leader of the Ulster unionists. An urgent request to him to continue in office was met by the plea that it was a case of age and energy, and that he felt himself unequal to the task of undertaking the initiation and establishment of the new Northern Ireland parliament. Three months later (24 May) he left the House of Commons on appointment as a lord of appeal in ordinary. As a compliment to his old constituency he took the title of Baron Carson, of Duncairn, and from his seat in the House of Lords he never ceased to guard the interests of Ulster. He strongly protested against handing over the southern loyalists to their enemies under the 'treaty' of 6 December with Sinn Fein. He also, on 11 May 1922, spoke very strongly in support of measures taken by the government for the protection of the old Royal Irish Constabulary, and once more he called attention to the treatment by Sinn Fein of British subjects in Ireland. At the end of October 1929 he resigned his office as lord of appeal in ordinary.

In October 1926, in the course of a fortnight's stay in Ulster, Carson received the honorary degree of LL.D. from Queen's University, Belfast, and his last two visits were for the opening of the new parliament buildings at Stormont by the Prince of Wales in 1932 and for the unveiling of his own statue in front of these buildings in July 1933.

Soon after his eightieth birthday (1934) Carson fell very seriously ill with bronchitis, and although he recovered, his health was undermined and he died at Cleve Court, Minster, Kent, 22 October 1935. He was given a state funeral in Belfast and was buried in St. Anne's Cathedral.

Carson was twice married: first, in 1879 to Sarah Annette Foster (died 1913), adopted daughter of Henry Persse Kirwan, of Triston Lodge, co. Galway, and had two sons and two daughters of whom the elder son and younger daughter predeceased their father; secondly, in 1914 to Ruby, elder daughter of Lieutenant-Colonel Stephen Frewen (afterwards Frewen-Laton), of Winton and Sigston Castle, Yorkshire, formerly commanding the 16th Lancers, and had one son, who was elected conservative member of parliament for the Isle of Thanet in July 1945.

Carson was one of the most remarkable and powerful advocates that the bar has ever produced, and one of the most conscientious and fearless in defence of his clients' interests. He had a shrewd and wide insight into human nature and his persuasive influence was enhanced by the charm of his attractive personality. As a lawyer he was at his best in cross-examination and in his appeal to a jury, of which he was an acknowledged master. His gift of searching cross-examination was aided by his piercing eyes and the height of his thin sinewy frame. He was certainly not a bully, as his enemies sometimes suggested, but he overpowered a witness with his penetrating eyes and the impression of commanding power. He was liked by all the juniors at the bar and respected by them, because he was never overbearing, pompous, or remote. He would never take a case unless he could give his whole time to it. He cared nothing for money if it stood in the way of what he conceived to be his duty. In the Archer-Shee case (1910), in which he vindicated the honour of a young Osborne cadet against all the forces of the Crown and its law-officers, he devoted ten days to the case for a nominal fee and turned away a brief for 1,500 guineas. He said to a friend after he had become a lord of appeal in 1921: 'I died on the day I left the House of Commons and the bar.' As a judge, he was fearless in his championship of right and in his passionate desire to do justice and prevent oppression and wrong.

Carson was a great orator—perhaps the greatest of his time, if the test of oratory is its power to move men to the very depths of their souls—but he never attempted to be oratorical. He never prepared set speeches. Lord Morley said to a friend in reference to the greatest oration which Carson ever made (the speech in the House of Lords on the capitulation, as he regarded it, of the government to Sinn Fein): 'It was so overwhelming in its passionate sincerity that if a division had been taken at that moment I should have trembled for the result.' But Carson told the same friend: 'I had prepared nothing, because I had a heavy case in the courts that day.'

To the eloquence, courage, and capacity of Carson in critical years, Ulster owes her existence, for it can be truly said that by his determined refusal to allow Ulster to be driven out of the union, he saved the province from being coerced into a separation from all that it held dear. His services to Ulster were made at great personal sacrifice without the slightest consideration of the cost or the risk involved, and he was distinguished by a moral grandeur of character of which everybody was conscious except himself.

Probably the best portrait of Lord Carson is that by P. A. de László in the Middle Temple. An oil-painting by Sir John Lavery, executed in 1921, is in the Belfast Museum and Art Gallery. A picture by the American artist Robert MacCameron is in the possession of Lady Carson, as well as a portrait of Carson as a young man by Julia Falkard. There is also a portrait by Sir Edward Burne-Jones in the possession of Mr. Walter Carson. In the National Portrait Gallery, and also in the Belfast Museum and Art Gallery, there is an etching of the head by John George Day (1914) which is a striking likeness. The statue which stands in the grounds of the parliament buildings at Stormont is by L. S. Merrifield, who also executed a marble bust now in the possession of the Belfast Corporation. In *Vanity Fair*, 9 November 1893 appeared a cartoon by 'Lib' entitled 'Dublin University', which is considered an excellent likeness and was reproduced by Edward Marjoribanks as the frontispiece to his biography.

[Edward Marjoribanks, *The Life of Lord Carson*, vol. i, 1932; Ian Colvin, *The Life of Lord Carson*, vols. ii and iii, 1934, 1936; private information; personal knowledge.]

D. L. SAVORY.

CARTER, HOWARD (1874–1939), painter and archaeologist, was born in London 9 May 1874, the youngest son of Samuel John Carter, animal-painter, of South Kensington, by his wife, Martha Joyce Sandys. He was educated privately and trained by his father to be a draughtsman. At the age of seventeen (1891) he went to Egypt as assistant draughtsman on the staff of the Archaeological Survey of Egypt then being carried out by the

Egypt Exploration Fund. Early in 1892 Carter joined (Sir) W. M. Flinders Petrie at El-Amarna and under him received four months' training in the art of excavating. In the autumn of the same year he was appointed draughtsman on the staff of the Archaeological Survey and worked in the tombs of Beni Hasan and El-Bersheh in Middle Egypt. Late in 1893 he joined at Deir el-Bahari the staff of Edouard Naville with whom he remained six years making line-drawings of the sculptured scenes and inscriptions in the temple of Queen Hatshepsut; these drawings were published by the Egypt Exploration Fund in six volumes with letterpress by Naville (1896–1908). At the end of 1899 Carter was appointed by the Egyptian government to be inspector-in-chief of the monuments of Upper Egypt and Nubia with headquarters at Thebes. In 1902 he began excavations in the Valley of the Tombs of the Kings, discovered the sepulchres of Hatshepsut (as sovereign) and Tuthmosis IV, and installed electric lighting in several of the larger royal tombs at Thebes and in the rock-temple at Abu Simbel in Nubia. In 1903 Carter was transferred to the inspectorate of Lower Egypt with headquarters at Tanta, but soon afterwards, owing to an incident with foreigners in which he asserted that he had done no more than his duty, he resigned and devoted himself to water-colour painting as a profession.

Five years later (1908), at the urgent request of (Sir) Gaston Maspero, then director-general of the Service of Antiquities of Egypt, Carter returned in order to superintend the excavations in the necropolis at Thebes being conducted by George Herbert, fifth Earl of Carnarvon [q.v.]. During the war of 1914–1918, among other discoveries, he found and cleared the long sought for tomb of Amenophis I. On 4 November 1922 he made the great discovery which will always be associated with his name, the tomb of King Tutankhamūn with its extraordinary wealth of artistic treasures. Carter's records of the objects found and his handling and packing of them for transport down the Nile to Cairo were a most brilliant achievement and occupied no less than ten seasons (1922–1932). He published The Tomb of Tut-ankh-Amen (3 vols., 1923–1933, vol. i in collaboration with A. C. Mace) and he had hoped to publish the full catalogue of all objects found, but his health failed and the work was unfinished. He died in Kensington after a grievous illness 2 March 1939. He was unmarried.

[The Times, 3 March 1939; Journal of Egyptian Archaeology, vol. xxv, 1939; personal knowledge.]   PERCY E. NEWBERRY.

CASH, JOHN THEODORE (1854–1936), physician, was born at Manchester 16 December 1854, the younger son of John Walker Cash, who retired from business and took up farming near Leeds, by his wife, Martha Midgley. He was educated at Bootham School, York, and the Edinburgh Collegiate School, and studied medicine at the university of Edinburgh, where he qualified M.B., C.M., and M.R.C.S. (Eng.) in 1876 and gained a gold medal for his M.D. thesis in 1879. After graduation he studied the methods of pharmacological research in Berlin, Vienna, and Paris. He was then house physician at the Edinburgh Royal Infirmary, but returned to Berlin and afterwards moved to Leipzig. On coming to London he began researches with (Sir) T. L. Brunton [q.v.] at St. Bartholomew's Hospital and from 1880 to 1884 published many valuable pharmacological papers which are representative of a new and accurate scientific approach to the elucidation of the actions of drugs. His elaborate and precise researches upon the various alkaloids of aconitum, begun prior to 1886, paved the way for his pioneer endeavours, by researches on the substituted ammonias and benzene compounds, to lay the foundations of a relationship between chemical constitution and pharmacological action: this investigation, published jointly with Brunton in the Philosophical Transactions of the Royal Society (1885, 1892), indicated to synthetic chemists paths towards the discovery of new remedies.

The high scientific standard of Cash's researches led to his appointment to the regius chair of materia medica and therapeutics in Aberdeen University in 1886 and to his election as a fellow of the Royal Society in the following year. He was a skilled experimentalist, ingenious in devising recording apparatus, and imbued with the axiom that, in order to obtain true results, the least disturbance of the tissues was of paramount importance. His gracious manner and cultured language as a lecturer inspired honourable work by his students and his scientific example encouraged A. R. Cushny [q.v.] to adopt pharmacology as his lifework.

Cash was dean of the faculty of medicine at Aberdeen University and from 1911 to 1919 a member of the General Medical Council when he took a large share in editing the *British Pharmacopœia* of 1914. He received the honorary degree of LL.D. from the universities of Edinburgh and Aberdeen.

Cash's chief recreation was a passionate devotion to salmon and trout fishing: he was an expert on the pathology of diseases of the salmon, and a particular salmon-fly bears his name. The opening of the salmon fishing season could always be dated by his disappearance from the laboratory after months of continuous research. He retired from his chair in 1919 and settled at Hereford where, on the Wye, he enjoyed his favourite pastime but continued to be keenly interested in pharmacological researches. He died at Hereford 30 November 1936 and is buried there.

Cash married in 1881 Margaret Sophia (died 1924), youngest daughter of the statesman John Bright [q.v.], and had two sons and two daughters. His accomplished wife painted the beautiful water-colours used to illustrate his lectures on materia medica.

[*Obituary Notices of Fellows of the Royal Society*, No. 6, January 1938 (bibliography and portrait); *Aberdeen University Review*, vol. xxiv, 1937; *British Medical Journal*, 1936, vol. ii, p. 1238; *Lancet*, 1936, vol. ii, p. 1429.]

WALTER J. DILLING.

CAVENDISH, VICTOR CHRISTIAN WILLIAM, ninth DUKE OF DEVONSHIRE (1868–1938), was born in London 31 May 1868, the eldest son of Lord Edward Cavendish, youngest son of William Cavendish, seventh Duke of Devonshire [q.v.], by his wife, Emma Elizabeth, fourth daughter of William Saunders Sebright Lascelles, third son of Henry Lascelles, second Earl of Harewood [q.v.]. He was a nephew of Lord Frederick Cavendish [q.v.]. He was educated at Eton and Trinity College, Cambridge. When he came down from Cambridge, where he had been president of the Amateur Dramatic Club, he went into a firm of accountants in the City in order to gain experience, and in order to obtain a knowledge of legal principles he entered the Inner Temple. On the death in 1891 of his father who had represented West Derbyshire as a unionist, he succeeded him unopposed, becoming the youngest member of the House of Commons. In 1892 he married Lady Evelyn Emily Mary, elder daughter of H. C. K. Petty-Fitzmaurice, fifth Marquess of Lansdowne [q.v.]. They lived chiefly at Holker Hall in Lancashire where he carried on traditions of the famous Holker herd of shorthorns. A popular member of the House of Commons he was appointed treasurer of the household in 1900, and in 1901 he undertook the duties of a whip. From 1903 to 1905 he was financial secretary to the Treasury. On the death in 1908 of his uncle S. C. Cavendish, eighth Duke of Devonshire [q.v.], he succeeded to the dukedom, and in 1916 he was appointed governor-general of Canada in succession to the Duke of Connaught.

During his tenure of the governor-generalship the Duke of Devonshire toured through the Dominion from east to west, from Nova Scotia to Vancouver. Without courting popularity he was exceedingly well liked and gained the confidence of the Meighen government without forfeiting the friendship of the liberals and agrarians. In 1922, the year after his return home, he declined the secretaryship of state for India in Lloyd George's coalition government, but when at the end of that year Bonar Law offered him the office of secretary of state for the Colonies he accepted and thereby became involved in the preparations for the British Empire Exhibition held at Wembley in 1924, the fortunes of which owed an immense debt to him for the particular care which he gave to it both before and after its opening. Without the knowledge of the public, he was a principal financial guarantor for its success. Relieved in the spring of 1925 of the double strain of office and of the exhibition, he took continuous and violent exercise on his Irish estate, which caused a sudden collapse which endangered his life and left him something of an invalid for the rest of his days.

When Cavendish succeeded to the dukedom he decided to live at Chatsworth as far as possible. But the Duke was careful to arrange that the public should have access to the house and grounds, and he continued the same traditions at Bolton Abbey, where, as at Chatsworth, he was visited by King George and Queen Mary. In 1926 he presented Pevensey Castle to the nation. In 1932 he was elected president of the Royal Agricultural Society of England, and he was vice-president of the Navy League from 1909.

The Duke of Devonshire was sworn of the Privy Council in 1905, and appointed G.C.V.O. in 1912 and K.G. and G.C.M.G.

in 1916. He was high steward of Cambridge University from 1923, and chancellor of Leeds University from 1909. He died at Chatsworth 6 May 1938, and was survived by his two sons and five daughters. He was succeeded as tenth duke by his elder son, Edward William Spencer, Marquess of Hartington (born 1895), whose elder son, William John Robert, Marquess of Hartington, was killed in action in France in 1944.

A portrait of the Duke of Devonshire wearing the robes of chancellor of Leeds University, by P. A. de László (1928), is at Chatsworth: one of several copies is at Leeds University.

[*The Times*, 7, 9, 11 May 1938.]

E. I. CARLYLE.

CHALMERS, ROBERT, BARON CHALMERS, of Northiam (1858–1938), civil servant and master of Peterhouse, Cambridge, was born in London 18 August 1858, the only son of John Chalmers, of Aberdeen, by his wife, Julia, daughter of Robert Mackay. He was educated at the City of London School under Edwin Abbott [q.v.], and in 1877 entered Oriel College, Oxford, as a classical scholar. He obtained a first class in classical moderations in 1878 and a second class in natural science (biology) in 1881.

Chalmers secured in 1882 the first place in the open competitive examination for the upper division of the civil service and was appointed a second-class clerk in the Treasury. He was promoted first-class clerk in 1894, principal clerk in 1899, and assistant secretary in 1903. In 1907 he accepted the post of chairman of the Board of Inland Revenue, where he was largely responsible for the rearrangement under which, by the Finance Act of 1908, excise was transferred from the Inland Revenue department to the Board of Customs which now became the Board of Customs and Excise. In 1911 he returned to the Treasury as permanent secretary and auditor of the civil list. Two years later Chalmers was appointed governor of Ceylon, a country in which he was interested, as one of his *parerga* was the study of Pali, Ceylon's ancient language. But his time as governor was a troubled one. his 'spiritual home' was the Treasury, and he was glad to return there in 1916 as joint permanent secretary with Sir T. L. Heath [q.v.] and Sir John (afterwards Lord) Bradbury. Almost immediately, however, at Mr. Asquith's request, he accepted, in May, the post of under-

secretary to the chief secretary of Ireland, on the retirement of Sir Matthew Nathan [q.v.] after the Easter rebellion of that year. This was only a temporary appointment, and he returned in September to his former office at the Treasury, which he held until his retirement in March 1919, his period of service being prolonged from August 1918 at the personal request of Bonar Law. He had been sworn of the Irish Privy Council in 1916. On Chalmers's retirement the chancellor of the Exchequer, (Sir) Austen Chamberlain, recorded in a Treasury minute: 'There cannot be many instances in the long line of his distinguished predecessors where tasks of such difficulty and diversity have been heaped in quick succession on the shoulders of a single man.'

In 1924, on the death of Sir Adolphus Ward [q.v.], Chalmers, who had been raised to the peerage in 1919 as Baron Chalmers, of Northiam in the county of Sussex, accepted the mastership (which he retained until 1931) of Peterhouse, Cambridge, a college with which he was already identified: his younger son, who had died of wounds in May 1915, had been an undergraduate there, and he himself had resided and taken an *ad eundem* degree from there in 1920. From 1920 to 1922 he was a member of the royal commission on the universities of Oxford and Cambridge.

Chalmers was twice married: first, in 1888 to Maud Mary (died 1923), daughter of John George Forde Pigott; secondly, in 1935 to Iris Florence, elder daughter of Sir John Biles [q.v.], and widow of Robert Latta, professor of logic at Glasgow University. By his first wife he had two sons, the elder of whom was killed in May 1915, and one daughter. He died at Oxford 17 November 1938, when the peerage became extinct.

Chalmers was appointed C.B. in 1900, K.C.B. in 1908, and G.C.B. in 1916. He was elected an honorary fellow of Oriel College in 1918, and academic honours were showered upon him. He received honorary degrees from the universities of Glasgow (1913), Oxford (1923), Cambridge (1924), and St. Andrews (1930). He was a trustee of the British Museum (1924–1931); was elected a fellow of the British Academy (1927); and was president of the Royal Asiatic Society (1922–1925), years which included the society's centenary). Besides his works on Pali he was the author of a *History of Currency in the British Colonies* (1893).

Chalmers was a many-sided man, and the side which he presented to the official world, and to the world of Ceylon, Ireland, and Cambridge, was not always his most attractive side. It is a testimony to his merits that this did not affect his career. Those who knew him soon discovered that his mask of pomposity and cynicism concealed not only genuine kindness of heart and unostentatious generosity often secretly exercised, but an intense inward sensitiveness to misfortune and suffering. He felt bitterly, although he never showed it, the deaths of his two sons, of whom he was very proud. Few of his younger colleagues at the Treasury knew that, as a young man, he had lived in the East End where he worked under Samuel Barnett [q.v.], then vicar of St. Jude's, Whitechapel, giving up all the time not required by his official duties at the Treasury to the social work of St. Jude's and helping by personal contact the poor and the sick. If, in the civil service as a whole, his strict guardianship of the public purse made him respected rather than loved, his absolute integrity in the high positions which he occupied was generally recognized. In the Treasury itself his profound knowledge of financial procedure was a valuable asset; and he had the faculty, such as few seniors possessed, of communicating, by influence and example, his methods and his energy, if not his own powers, to those of his juniors who were able to profit by them. As master of Peterhouse, although he did not take a prominent part in the life of the university, he proved, in spite of his mannerisms, a real acquisition to his college as an institution, and a generous benefactor to the poorer scholars whom he helped lavishly by his hospitality, and from his private purse.

[*The Times*, 18, 19, 26, and 28 November 1938; P. E. Matheson, *Lord Chalmers, 1858–1938* in *Proceedings* of the British Academy, vol. xxv, 1939 (portrait); official records; personal knowledge.] MAURICE HEADLAM.

CHAMBERLAIN, (ARTHUR) NEVILLE (1869–1940), statesman, was the youngest of three members of his family who, in two successive generations, played great parts at the highest level of British statesmanship. He was born at Edgbaston, Birmingham, 18 March 1869, the only son of Joseph Chamberlain [q.v.], by his second wife, Florence, daughter of Timothy Kenrick, of Birmingham. His half-brother (Sir Joseph) Austen Chamberlain [q.v.], being set apart for a political career, passed from Rugby to Cambridge. Neville, who was to go into business, returned home from Rugby and took commercial courses at Mason College, which was afterwards converted into Birmingham University. There he studied metallurgy and engineering design. From Mason College he entered the office of a firm of accountants where his mental alertness and quick mastery of financial problems were soon noted.

In 1890 Joseph Chamberlain bought 20,000 acres on the island of Andros in the Bahamas where he was advised that sisal could be profitably grown. There Neville went at the age of twenty-one (November 1890) to take charge of the development of the estate. For seven years he planned and toiled in the attempt to bring the enterprise to success. It was a life of extreme hardship, and all in vain: the soil was too thin for the crop. In the complete social isolation of those years, he found comfort in books, reading steadily and well in history, biography, and science. While his character was strengthened, the extreme loneliness of the life must have intensified the natural shyness and reserve which handicapped him for a time when he entered public life.

Back at Birmingham in 1897, Chamberlain began the business career which for many years absorbed all his energies. Although he then had no ambition for a parliamentary career, he was an ardent politician with a lively interest in local public affairs. No one could be of the household of Joseph Chamberlain and remain indifferent to the problems of government or to the individual's civic responsibilities. But his father and brother were fully occupied by their public duties and, after the loss of precious time in the Bahamas, Neville felt that he must concentrate on business until he had established an independent position. He soon became one of the outstanding figures in the industrial life of Birmingham and took an active part in the proceedings of the influential chamber of commerce. At the same time his lifelong interest in health questions was stimulated by work for the General Hospital, of which he became chairman. His life was broadening as Joseph Chamberlain's had done a generation before. There is, indeed, a remarkable resemblance between father and son, not only in the several main stages of their careers—business, city government, parliament, Cabinet—but (allowing for the seven lost years) in the timing of them.

Chamberlain was elected to the Birmingham city council in 1911, the year of his marriage to Annie Vere, daughter of Major William Utting Cole, 3rd Dragoon Guards, of Woodhay House, Newbury, who became an unfailing help in all phases of his public as of his private life. To city government he brought new vitality and enterprise. Under his chairmanship of the town planning committee, two Birmingham schemes for planning in built-up areas were the first to be sanctioned in this country. A still more notable personal achievement was the establishment in 1916, against the strong opposition of banking interests, of the first municipal savings bank. Although it succeeded beyond expectation, it remains the only municipal institution of its kind in the country.

Chamberlain's very exceptional record in city government was noted outside Birmingham and soon widened his responsibilities. In 1915 he was appointed a member of the Central Control Board (Liquor Traffic). A hapless experience in national war administration followed. In December 1916 Lloyd George, who had just succeeded Asquith as prime minister, proposed to relieve the strain on manpower by voluntary recruitment of labour for war industries. Chamberlain was made director-general of national service to organize and direct the work. In order that he might give his full time to the post, he resigned the lord mayoralty of Birmingham, to which he had been elected for a second term in the previous month. His efforts were fruitless. Within a few days of the appointment Lloyd George conceived a dislike of him and he was left without authority or equipment for his difficult task. He said afterwards that he was without instructions and without powers. After seven months of futility he resigned and returned to Birmingham.

This unhappy episode was a turning-point in Chamberlain's life. He was not the man to sit down quietly under failure that was not due to fault of his own. His mind was at last fixed on a career in national politics and, at the general election of December 1918, he was returned to the House of Commons as conservative member for the Ladywood division of Birmingham. He was then in his fiftieth year: there is no other instance of a prime minister who entered parliament so late.

For four years Chamberlain supported the coalition government of which his brother Austen was a leading member. He spoke seldom but always well. Voice, pose, and a lucid and incisive style recalled memories of his father. He was chairman of several departmental committees but rejected a suggestion of Bonar Law that he should accept government office; he no longer had any confidence in Lloyd George and would not serve under or with him. On the Irish 'treaty' of December 1921 he supported the government.

When the coalition fell in October 1922, Chamberlain was on his way home from a holiday in Canada. For the first time he and his brother were in different camps. Austen was the chief defender of the coalition at the Carlton Club meeting (19 October) which destroyed it; and he continued for a time longer his co-operation with Lloyd George. Bonar Law pressed Neville to join the new government and, having become definitely anti-coalition, he accepted office as postmaster-general. At once the prime minister was greatly impressed by his sound judgement and fine administrative gifts. Promotion came swiftly, and he rose easily to each successive post. There were four posts in a little over a year (1922–1924): after the Post Office, the paymastership-general, the Ministry of Health (where he passed an important housing bill), and the chancellorship of the Exchequer. He was sworn of the Privy Council in 1922.

In his first term at the Treasury (1923–1924), Chamberlain was a chancellor without a budget. Baldwin, who succeeded Bonar Law as prime minister in May 1923, having announced a policy of tariff reform, decided—against the advice of most of his colleagues, including Chamberlain—to appeal to the country in the autumn. The conservative majority was lost and, with liberal help, Ramsay MacDonald [q.v.] formed the first labour government in January 1924.

It was a sharp disappointment to Chamberlain that when the conservatives secured a great majority in the following October, the party was once more committed against a general tariff. Baldwin offered him the Exchequer again but he preferred to return to the Ministry of Health; Mr. Churchill, who had just rejoined the conservative party, went to the Exchequer. His first budget provided the finance of the widows, orphans, and old-age pensions bill. This measure was suggested to Baldwin by Chamberlain while in opposition in 1924 and it was he who piloted the bill through the House in 1925.

Chamberlain's four and a half years (1924–1929) at the Ministry of Health raised the department's status and his own. Masterly conduct of the difficult Rating and Valuation Act of 1925 (which gave relief to agriculture and industry) put him in the first rank of parliamentarians. By securing the full co-operation of private builders as well as of the local councils, he solved the immediate housing problem: nearly a million houses had been built when he left office. In 1929 he passed the very important Local Government Act which reformed the Poor Law (boards of guardians were abolished) and recast the financial relations of the State and local authorities.

At the general election of May 1929 Chamberlain was returned for the Edgbaston division of Birmingham, and held the seat until his death. With labour in office again, he, at Baldwin's request, turned his attention to the re-organization of the conservative central office. A research department was set up and at once gave special consideration to the question of tariffs. The party leadership also came under review and, as chairman of the central office, he presented a critical memorandum which Baldwin so much disliked that for a short time it was thought that he would resign.

In the financial crisis of August 1931, which destroyed the labour government, it was Chamberlain who, until Baldwin returned from abroad, represented the conservative party in negotiations preceding the formation of the provisional all-party government. In that he was again minister of health, but he succeeded Philip Snowden [q.v.] as chancellor of the Exchequer when the government was reconstituted in November after the general election, and he held the office for five and a half years. Drastic economies were necessary for several years before normal expenditure and revenue could be balanced. Throughout that trying period he directed policy with courage and sound judgement. Upon him also fell the brunt of negotiation and decision on war reparations, war debts, and Empire trade policy, this last being dealt with at the memorable Imperial Economic Conference held at Ottawa in 1932.

Although, in the general election, the government was not committed on the fiscal question, Chamberlain secured Cabinet approval for a general tariff which, at a common standard of 10 per cent., was more for revenue than protection. The free trade system, initiated eighty-six years before with the repeal of the Corn Laws, was thus ended in 1932; and the settlement has not since been seriously challenged. In the same year a great saving in debt charges was effected by the conversion of £2,000,000,000 of the 5 per cent. war loan to a 3½ per cent. stock.

By 1935 there seemed to be a good prospect of substantial tax reductions; but hope of that vanished when, in the following year, the government proposed an expenditure of £1,500,000,000 on rearmament within five years. This had been delayed to the point of danger, partly because of hostile public opinion, partly because a disarmament policy was still being pursued in the League of Nations, and partly because the financial crisis in the early 'thirties was held to be, for the time, more important. As soon as that anxiety was relieved Chamberlain's was the chief political initiative in increasing the air estimates in 1934. He thought that Baldwin exaggerated the strength of labour opposition in the country and he desired to make rearmament the main issue at the general election in 1935.

Dangers multiplied. Italy invaded Abyssinia in October 1935; Hitler's aggressions had already begun; the Spanish civil war broke out in July 1936; the Japanese menace continually disturbed the Far East. Foreign affairs occupied more and more of the time of the Cabinet, and Chamberlain took an active part in the discussions. Labour party hostility to him, which reached the depth of bitterness after the Munich conference of 1938, was intensified in the Abyssinian war when, quite wrongly, he was widely regarded as pro-Italian and anti-League of Nations. He had been in fact a stout upholder of the League and in the Abyssinian crisis was ready, if the French had been willing to co-operate, to prevent or stop war. He supported League sanctions against Italy, and called for their abandonment only when their failure was manifest.

In the summer of 1936 Baldwin, worn by the labours and anxieties of the time, decided to resign the premiership after the coronation in the following May. There was no rival to Chamberlain as his successor and, within the inmost circle of high politics, it was known for months before that he would be the next prime minister. It was with the warm approval and goodwill of all his colleagues that he entered upon the office on 28 May 1937.

Chamberlain had thus been able to ponder, months in advance, over the grave responsibilities awaiting him. The paramount, inescapable problem now was national defence. German militarism, and its aggressive political direction, menaced the peace of the world. Great Britain was unprepared to meet it: and danger was so near that it had become imprudent to reveal her military weakness. The labour party's opposition to rearmament still continued.

The position was one of extraordinary difficulty. British and French military weakness was an incitement to German aggression, and prejudiced every effort by negotiation to stop the drift towards war. Could Germany and Italy be brought back into the comity of nations? In no other way could war be averted. It was the way which for nearly two years Chamberlain resolutely pursued. He knew the difficulties and, in particular, was not unaware of the sinister qualities of Hitler and Mussolini. But the pacification of Europe, which was the aim of his policy, could not be achieved without their collaboration, and not to seek it was to admit failure which he would not do while any hope of success remained. He often said that he would take no responsibility for war until he had done everything possible to prevent it.

Conversations with the Berlin government were opened in the early days of the new premiership. The German foreign minister accepted an invitation to come to London in June; but events in the Spanish civil war angered Hitler and the visit was never paid. Chamberlain then turned to Rome. Through the foreign secretary, Mr. Eden, he sent a message to Mussolini who, in a friendly reply, suggested the expansion of the Anglo-Italian 'gentleman's agreement' of the previous January. It was arranged to begin negotiations in September, but here also the Spanish war barred the way.

In November direct contact with Hitler came about in a curious manner. Lord Halifax, who was a master of foxhounds as well as lord president of the Council, went to Berlin for a national hunting exhibition. While there he was invited to meet the Führer at Berchtesgaden. They had what Lord Halifax called a 'free, frank, informal and confidential talk'. There was in this no movement away from France, whose government was at once informed of what

happened. M. Chautemps, the premier, and M. Delbos, the foreign minister, came to London for discussion of the European situation; and, shortly afterwards, M. Delbos exchanged views with von Neurath in Berlin. The way appeared to be clearing for Anglo-German negotiations. Sir Nevile Henderson, the British ambassador in Berlin, came to London for consultation and returned with full instructions. At the same time von Ribbentrop, already counted an enemy of Great Britain, was appointed foreign minister in the German government. A month passed before Hitler received the ambassador. He was, Henderson reported, in a bad temper, very angry with British newspapers, and resentful of any criticism of his relations with Austria.

Hitler's designs upon Austrian independence alarmed Mussolini who at this turning-point (February 1938) informed the British government that he was ready to open discussions covering all matters in dispute between Great Britain and Italy. Chamberlain felt that if this offer were spurned the Hitler-Mussolini association would be strengthened and the risk of war increased. Mr. Eden objected to the procedure proposed on the ground that there should be no negotiation with Italy until she had withdrawn a substantial part of her forces from Spain. Chamberlain's undertaking that no agreement should take effect until that condition was complied with did not satisfy the foreign secretary; and, after close discussion at three meetings of the Cabinet, he resigned on 20 February. Lord Halifax succeeded him at the Foreign Office, and negotiations with Italy began at once. Three weeks later Hitler invaded Austria, destroyed its government, and proclaimed it a province of the German Reich. British protests, ignored in Berlin, were repeated in parliament: Chamberlain spoke of the profound shock to the friends of peace and the setback to hopes of international co-operation. The Germans gave a general undertaking that there would be no further aggression, and a particular assurance that they had no designs against Czechoslovakia. But confidence was everywhere weakened.

The British Cabinet considered the position and, on 24 March, Chamberlain gave to the House of Commons a detailed review of the country's liabilities abroad. As to Czechoslovakia, he quoted with approval a statement made by Mr. Eden, when foreign secretary, that 'nations cannot be expected to incur automatic military obligations save for areas where their vital interests are concerned'. But that, Chamberlain continued, must not be interpreted as meaning that Britain would in no circumstances intervene. Ought Britain to assure France forthwith of full military support if she were called upon, by reason of German aggression, to go to the aid of her ally, Czechoslovakia? The Cabinet had decided against that but, said Chamberlain, 'legal obligations are not alone concerned and, if war broke out ... it would be well within the bounds of probability that other countries besides those which were parties to the original dispute would almost immediately become involved. This', he added, 'is especially true in the case of two countries like Great Britain and France, with long associations of friendship, with interests closely interwoven, devoted to the same ideals of democratic liberty and determined to uphold them.'

While the labour opposition condemned this speech, Mr. Churchill welcomed it as 'a very considerable advance on any previous declaration'. In effect, he said, there was evidently a defensive alliance with France and he was for declaring it openly and making it effective by a military convention. This view was not accepted. The Dominion governments approved the policy announced, but they did not wish to widen their obligations; and it would not have been easy at that time, nor even when events became more critical later in the year, to bring them into war on any issue which had then arisen in central Europe.

Within Czechoslovakia the situation rapidly worsened throughout the summer. Discontent among the three million Germans in the Sudeten border districts was whipped by Nazi agents into fierce agitation. Concessions by the Prague government were met by demands for more and still more. Border 'incidents', invented or distorted, were reported with provocative headings in all the German newspapers. The position was already dangerous when, towards the end of July, Chamberlain persuaded Lord Runciman to go to Prague as mediator. After weeks of negotiation with both sides he submitted a plan of home rule for the Sudeten areas on the Swiss cantonal model, and it was accepted by the Czech government. It was too late. Henlein, the Sudeten leader, threw off disguises and was seen to be Hitler's tool. The orders now came

direct from Hitler. At Nuremberg, on 12 September, he demanded self-determination for the Sudetens and promised them the support of the Reich. Powerful German forces were ready for action. Lord Runciman could do no more and returned to London on 16 September.

The French government had approved the Runciman mission. France was pledged by treaty to defend the Czechs against aggression. At Lanark on 27 August, Sir John Simon, speaking for the government, repeated Chamberlain's declaration of 24 March which was, in effect, that if France were involved in war with Germany because she went to the aid of the Czechs, Britain would be at the side of France. Nevile Henderson also repeated this in an official communication to the German foreign minister. But France was unready. Many French newspapers, of all parties, favoured the German minority claims and blamed the Czech government for dilatoriness. Public opinion generally was apathetic. After information that the German army was ready to strike, the French Cabinet met on 13 September and the announcement was made that 'more reserves may be called up'. It was evident that France would not then fulfil her treaty obligations to the Czechs. M. Daladier, the premier, afterwards said that he suggested to Downing Street some 'exceptional procedure'.

Chamberlain had already considered what, in such a situation, his exceptional action should be. On the evening of 14 September the world was startled by the news that he had just sent a message to Hitler proposing that they should meet the next day to discuss a peaceful settlement. Hitler agreed, and on Thursday, 15 September, Chamberlain flew to Berchtesgaden. His action was everywhere approved. Hitler demanded an immediate assurance that the British government accepted the principle of self-determination for the Sudeten Germans. Chamberlain said that he would consult the Cabinet about that if Hitler gave an assurance that Germany would, meantime, refrain from hostilities. The assurance was given.

Chamberlain returned to London on the Friday, the same day that Lord Runciman arrived from Prague. The Cabinet sat for five hours on the Saturday, and on the Sunday there were long discussions with M. Daladier and M. Bonnet, the French foreign minister. It was then announced that the two governments were 'in complete agreement'. The demand for self-determination had been conceded. British labour leaders condemned the decision and sought common action against it with French labour only to find that their French friends were not prepared to risk a war to preserve the integrity of Czechoslovakia.

On Thursday, 22 September, Chamberlain met Hitler a second time, at Godesberg, and was able to tell him that self-determination was accepted not only by Britain and France but also by Czechoslovakia. Moreover, arrangements for the transfer of territory had already been worked out. Hitler denounced these arrangements as dilatory and said that the German flag must fly over Sudetenland within a few days. Having considered this overnight, Chamberlain sent a letter to Hitler, protesting against any threat of force and adding that the Czechs could not withdraw their armed forces so long as they were faced with the prospect of invasion. Hitler replied a few hours later with a violent attack on the Czechs. Germany's decision was irrevocable. Chamberlain's curt rejoinder was that he proposed to return home at once. He asked for a memorandum and a map showing the areas in which it was proposed that plebiscites should be taken. These were not received and at half-past ten that night he saw Hitler again. He was then shown the memorandum. It provided for Czech evacuation of the Sudeten frontier districts within forty-eight hours. This moved Chamberlain to anger. He called it an ultimatum. Talk continued for several hours without removing the deadlock. But Hitler did say that 'this was the last of his territorial ambitions in Europe, and that he had no wish to include in the Reich people of any other race than the Germans'. On Saturday, 24 September, Chamberlain returned to London.

Before the Godesberg conference ended, the Prague government was informed that the British and French governments could no longer take the responsibility of advising it not to mobilize. French opinion stiffened and M. Daladier said that if Czechoslovakia were attacked France would take measures to help her. The Czech government rejected the German terms. War appeared to be certain. British military and civil defence preparations were pressed forward with all speed.

But Chamberlain refused to abandon his peace efforts. On 26 September he sent Sir Horace Wilson to Berlin with a letter to Hitler suggesting that German and Czech representatives should together consider how the territory to be ceded should be handed over. The letter was delivered to Hitler the same day by Sir Horace and the British ambassador. Next morning Sir Horace saw Hitler again and gave him this message from the British prime minister: 'If, in pursuit of her treaty obligations, France became actively engaged in hostilities against Germany, the United Kingdom would feel obliged to support her.' 'It is Tuesday to-day', Hitler retorted, 'and by next Monday we shall be at war.' But he replied to the prime minister with an assurance that the Czechs' fears were groundless and that their 'economic organism' would be stronger than before. Chamberlain thereupon appealed to him not to risk a world war when settlement was within reach in a few days. At the same time he asked Mussolini to support his proposal for further negotiation; and the Duce asked Hitler and Ribbentrop to delay action for twenty-four hours.

The next afternoon, Wednesday, 28 September, the prime minister reported to the House of Commons. From no quarter was there any ray of hope that war would be averted. The speech, heard in sombre silence, was near its end when a note from Lord Halifax was passed along the Treasury bench and handed to Chamberlain who read it and, with scarce a pause, announced that Hitler had invited him to a conference at Munich on the following day. Mussolini and Daladier were also invited. 'I need not say what my answer will be', he added. The relief was indescribable. For the moment differences were forgotten, and the goodwill of the whole House was with him as he left for the last stage of these momentous events.

Many people, perhaps most, failed to apprehend the limited range of the Munich conference. Settlement was possible only on the basis of self-determination, which meant the cession of the Sudeten districts in which Germans were a majority of the population. That had already been agreed: it was Hitler's assumption of the rights of a victor in war that the Czechs, supported in this by Great Britain and France, found intolerable. In a few hours at Munich the Godesberg terms were so modified that the Czech government accepted them. The evacuation of the Sudeten areas, which was to have been completed on 1 October, was extended over ten days. It was agreed that the limits of the territory to be occupied by the Germans after the first four days should be defined by an international commission. An international force was to occupy the plebiscite areas. Hitler withdrew his demand that the evacuating Czechs should take none of their goods with them. The release of Germans from the Czech army was to be completed, not in one day but in four weeks; and a right of option into or out of the transferred territories might be exercised at any time within six months after the date of the agreement. So, for the time, was peace saved.

The agreement was signed at 12.30 a.m. on Friday, 30 September. Later the same morning Chamberlain saw Hitler for the last time and they both signed a declaration which, taken at its face value, was of immense importance. The agreement on Czechoslovakia just signed was said to be 'symbolic of the desire of our two peoples never to go to war again'; and 'the method of consultation shall be the method adopted to deal with any other questions that may concern our two countries'. This document had been prepared by Chamberlain in advance, with the thought in his mind that, if it were violated, it would effectually damn Hitler. A similar declaration, on behalf of Germany and France, was signed in Paris several weeks later.

In the evening of 30 September Chamberlain was welcomed back to London by vast crowds of cheering people. The newspapers of all parties on the Saturday and Sunday acclaimed him as the saviour of peace: the British press had never been more united on any great public occasion. The churches were crowded at services of thanksgiving. From all parts of the world messages of congratulation poured into Downing Street. The statesmen of the Dominions and Colonies were fervent in their praise. 'A great champion has appeared in the lists', General Smuts said at Johannesburg. . . . 'He risked all and I trust he has won all.'

But there was criticism, much of it strident and bitter, in the House of Commons during the four days' debate in the following week. With a few notable exceptions, the labour party was solidly hostile; and a small conservative minority which condemned the Munich settlement included Mr. Churchill. Yet nearly every speaker swelled the chorus of praise of the prime minister's courageous struggle for peace. All deplored the terms of settlement. The government's justification was put in one sentence by Sir John Simon: 'How many amongst us are there who, if we could undo what was then done, would reject the settlement to which the prime minister put his hand on Friday, and instead—because it was the only alternative—would fling the world into the cauldron of immediate war?' Chamberlain said: 'By my action I did avoid war. I feel equally sure that I was right in doing so.'

On 6 October, by 366 votes to 144, the House of Commons declared confidence in the government. There was no division in the House of Lords, and the speeches there, spread over three days, nearly all supported Chamberlain's policy. It was remarkable, moreover, that in the French Chamber the Munich settlement was approved, except for the communists, by an all but unanimous vote.

Chamberlain had the support of a great majority of the nation. He said in the Commons debate that he would not snatch party advantage by capitalizing the thankfulness for peace; he would not advise an early general election unless some new issue arose which required a fresh mandate from the country, or he lost the confidence of his supporters. One other sentence showed that on the morrow of Munich he realized the grave uncertainties of the future. 'It is possible', he said, 'that we may want great efforts from the nation in the months to come, and if that be so the smaller our differences the better.' He had insisted that rearmament would be pressed forward.

The European prospect worsened throughout the autumn. A dreadful pogrom against Jews in Germany horrified civilized people everywhere. Hatred of Hitler and his works spread among all classes in Britain. But Chamberlain would not yet abandon his peace efforts: if there was to be war let the country be ready for it. He could not, of course, persist in his attempt to turn the Germans from their evil ways and, at the same time, tell the world what he thought of their leader. The restraints which his policy imposed were misunderstood, and the prejudice against him, fostered by political opponents, deepened from this time on.

With Italy relations had temporarily improved. The negotiations that followed Mr. Eden's resignation soon led to a comprehensive agreement. It was approved by the House of Commons on 2 May 1938. The condition that it should not take effect until there had been a substantial withdrawal of Italian forces from Spain was, however, insisted upon and the agreement did not come into full operation until November. In January 1939 Chamberlain and Lord Halifax went to Rome for discussions with the Italian government, but without any fixed agenda and the visit had no lasting effect.

In the same month, at Birmingham, Chamberlain spoke of political tension in Europe. There was talk of German designs on the free city of Danzig which was in the Polish customs system; but Ribbentrop countered that with the assurance at Warsaw on 26 January that enmity no longer existed between Germans and Poles. This was the prelude to a war of nerves against the Czechs. President Hacha was summoned to Berlin on 14 March and there bullied hour after hour until he signed a document in which he 'placed the fate of the Czech people in the hands of the Reichsführer'. Czechoslovakia was simultaneously invaded and, in a few hours, the Prague Cabinet surrendered.

The policy of appeasement was dead— 'wantonly shattered', Chamberlain said at Birmingham. Hitler stood before the world a man forsworn, whose word no one could trust, from whose lawless aggression no neighbour of Germany was safe. The Poles at once consulted the British and French governments, and a provisional understanding was reached. On 31 March Chamberlain announced in the House of Commons that Britain and France would give all the support in their power to Poland if her independence were threatened while negotiations were in progress.

Even before that announcement there were more aggressions: Hitler had seized Memelland from Lithuania and demanded the incorporation of Danzig in the Reich. On Good Friday, 7 April, Italy invaded Albania, three days after an official denial that military action was intended against that country. The British government thereupon gave assurances of support to Greece and Rumania, and made a long-term agreement with Turkey.

As early as March it was found that Poland and Russia could not be brought into one alliance. But obviously Britain's new agreements in Europe would be strengthened by a good understanding with the Soviet government. Anglo-French negotiations to secure it were begun at Moscow early in the summer. One obstacle

was Russia's demand that Britain should recognize her annexation of the three Baltic republics, Latvia, Esthonia, and Lithuania. This could not be squared with the British policy of protecting small nations against aggression. Yet on 24 May Chamberlain told the House of Commons that he hoped for early and full agreement. Discussions continued, and at the beginning of August British and French military missions went to Moscow. As this was done on Russia's invitation, a painful shock was caused by the announcement on 21 August that she had signed a non-aggression pact with Germany.

German propagandist reports that Britain would now abandon Poland were at once denied by Chamberlain. If the need arose, he said, British forces would be fully engaged in support of our Allies. Yet he continued the most strenuous exertions to prevent war and intensified these efforts when, in the last week of August, the hour of decision was felt to be near. But Hitler was bent on war, and on the morning of Friday, 1 September, German armies invaded Poland. British and French demands for suspension of hostilities being ignored, Chamberlain, at 11.15 in the morning of Sunday, 3 September, broadcast from 10 Downing Street the announcement that 'this country is at war with Germany. . . . It is the evil things we shall be fighting against—brute force, bad faith, injustice, oppression and persecution—and against them I am certain that right will prevail.' France declared war on Germany six hours later.

Chamberlain's wish that the war-time government should represent all parties was thwarted by the refusal of the labour leaders and of liberals led by Sir Archibald Sinclair to serve under him. But there were some notable recruits, Mr. Churchill and Mr. Eden among them. Emergency measures were passed quickly with the support of all parties.

The opening stages of the war were very different from what had been expected. U-boat attacks on British and Allied shipping began on the first day but many months passed before enemy air raiders bombed London, and there were only minor clashes between the opposing armies on the Franco-German frontier. After the quick defeat of Poland, there were no important land operations until the invasion of Denmark and Norway on 9 April 1940. As the British fleet, owing to air attacks, could not remain in the Skagerrak, there was no effective check upon enemy reinforcements for Norway, and the small British forces landed to help the Norwegian defence were mostly re-embarked within two or three weeks.

This was the first and not the worst British disaster in the war but it made a greater impression upon parliament than any that followed. On 7 and 8 May the withdrawal from Norway was debated in the House of Commons. In the division forced by the labour party the government was given a majority of 81—the figures were 281 to 200—but 40 ministerialists were in the minority and many abstained. Chamberlain thereupon considered his position and, when he was informed on 10 May that labour members still refused to serve under him, he at once tendered his resignation and advised the King to commission Mr. Churchill to form a new administration. The change was announced in a broadcast by Chamberlain that night.

Chamberlain joined the new government as lord president of the Council and for several months worked in full harmony with his successor. In August he underwent an operation which was believed to be successful and he resumed his official duties, but only for a short time: illness returned and on 1 October he resigned from the War Cabinet, knowing that his public life was over. Titular honours (including the Garter) he declined, preferring to remain plain Mr. Chamberlain. He was a freeman of Birmingham; the freedom of the City of London death prevented him from accepting, and the scroll was presented to Mrs. Chamberlain in 1941. Honorary degrees were conferred upon him by the universities of Oxford, Cambridge, Birmingham, Bristol, Leeds, and Reading; and he was elected a fellow of the Royal Society (1938). He died at Highfield Park, Heckfield, near Reading, on 9 November. His ashes were interred in Westminster Abbey. His son and daughter survived him.

Chamberlain's career has some remarkable features. Coming to parliament in his fiftieth year, without a reputation in national politics, he excelled in every office entrusted to him and was given the premiership for the best of all reasons, because he was the most trusted man in his party. He owed nothing to social influence. He was temperamentally unfitted for the arts of self-advertisement. The lucid speech of which he was a master was on simple, straight lines: and the style was the man. On the business side of the premiership he was exceptionally efficient. Occasionally his appointments to government office were criticized, but his leadership of the Cabinet was strong and masterful; and his colleagues knew that in all affairs that came before them he was animated by a lofty sense of public duty. To this all his varied interests were subordinate. Gardening and bird life attracted him all through his life. Music was a joy to him and he did much to foster public interest in the art. Family love and loyalty were deep and strong. His leadership of the conservative party did not mean repudiation of essentials in the radical faith in which he was brought up, and it was a grief to him that war prevented far-reaching social reforms upon which his heart was set. The failure to maintain peace was not, however, a complete failure; for, as Mr. Churchill said on the first day of the war, his resolute struggle for peace was of the highest moral and practical value and secured 'the wholehearted concurrence of scores of millions of men and women whose co-operation was indispensable'.

Of portraits of Chamberlain, one, by Sir William Orpen, is in the possession of Mrs. Chamberlain; another, by Oswald Birley, is in the Birmingham Art Gallery; and a third, by James Gunn, is at the Carlton Club.

[Keith Feiling, *The Life of Neville Chamberlain*, 1946; private information; personal knowledge.]   W. W. HADLEY.

CHAMBERLAIN, SIR (JOSEPH) AUSTEN (1863–1937), statesman, was born at Birmingham 16 October 1863, the only son of Joseph Chamberlain [q.v.] by his first wife, Harriet, daughter of Archibald Kenrick, of Berrow Court, Edgbaston. His mother died at his birth, and his father subsequently remarried twice: (Arthur) Neville Chamberlain [q.v.] was his half-brother. Austen Chamberlain was educated at Rugby and Trinity College, Cambridge; he took his degree in 1885. On leaving Cambridge he was sent to France for nine months, and it was then that he developed the love of that country which was to influence him so greatly for the rest of his life. In Paris he attended at the École des Sciences Politiques, and among those whose acquaintance he made was Clemenceau. In February 1887 he went to Germany for twelve months, and he never revisited the country, although he had arranged to do so in the summer of 1914. Chamberlain went regularly to

Treitschke's lectures on Prussian history, but they disquieted him. Berlin did not attract him as Paris had done, and he found it 'slightly provincial'. What was true of the German capital equally applied to the Germans themselves, and from these early days his preference was always for the French.

When Chamberlain came home from Germany the first step that his father took was to find him a constituency, and he was duly adopted as prospective candidate for the Border Burghs. He nursed the seat for four years, when something more attractive, and nearer Birmingham, offered itself, namely, East Worcestershire, and he was returned unopposed as a liberal unionist at a by-election in March 1892. Parliament was dissolved shortly afterwards, and Chamberlain did not make his maiden speech until after the ensuing general election, when he was re-elected. In April 1893, however, Gladstone is found writing to Queen Victoria that Austen Chamberlain had 'delivered one of the best speeches which has been made against the bill [the second home rule bill], and exhibited himself as a person of whom high political anticipations may reasonably be entertained'. The liberal unionists were returned forty-seven strong at the election of 1892, and Chamberlain was appointed their junior whip. When the conservatives came back to office in 1895 he was made a civil lord of the Admiralty, a post which he held until 1900 when he became financial secretary to the Treasury; as usual, that soon led to high office, in his case the postmastership-general with a seat in the Cabinet and a Privy Councillorship. In 1903 he was appointed chancellor of the Exchequer, when both his father and the free traders left Balfour's administration.

This appointment had been very largely made in order that the breach between Joseph Chamberlain and Balfour should not be widened unnecessarily, and Austen was to be a link between his father and the prime minister. But the new chancellor found Balfour by no means easy to understand, and if he acted as a link, it was as one which often had to stand a very severe strain. He was responsible for two budgets during his first tenure of office as chancellor of the Exchequer, but the circumstances in which he was appointed precluded him from applying the principles of tariff reform and imperial preference in which he had come to believe, and he had to do the best he could with the exist-

ing fiscal system. Nevertheless, although neither of his budgets was sensational, they were both well received. In December 1905 the administration resigned, and at the general election of the following month its supporters were routed at the polls, although East Worcestershire remained faithful to Austen Chamberlain.

Shortly afterwards, Joseph Chamberlain was incapacitated from taking any further active part in political life, and in opposition his son had now a difficult part to play. In theory, the conservatives and liberal unionists were still distinct, but as only a small number of the latter had survived the election Chamberlain's immediate following hardly mattered: his task was to leaven the conservative mass with the doctrine of tariff reform, and to ensure that when next the party obtained a majority protection would be carried into effect. This brought him into conflict with other sections of the party, and not infrequently with Balfour himself. In the fight against the parliament bill in 1911 he was numbered among the 'die-hards', although in later years he admitted that it had been a mistake for the House of Lords to throw out the budget in the first instance.

In November 1911 Balfour resigned the leadership of the conservative party and Chamberlain and Walter Long (afterwards Viscount Long of Wraxall, q.v.) were rival candidates for the succession. However, as the voting was likely to be close, they both stood down in favour of Bonar Law, who was elected unanimously. Whether this compromise was really in the best interests of the party and the country is a moot point, and Chamberlain was to have differences at least as serious with his new leader as those which he had experienced with his old. At first Bonar Law relied upon him to a very large extent, but before long, to quote Chamberlain himself in *Down the Years*, he 'turned more and more to Sir Edward Carson' and Chamberlain doubted the wisdom of concentrating the party's energies so largely upon opposition to the third home rule bill, to the exclusion of educational work for tariff reform. There was, in particular, a sharp difference of opinion between the two men over the advisability of postponing the imposition of taxes on food in the event of a conservative victory, a course advocated by Bonar Law.

Chamberlain played a prominent part during the days immediately preceding the outbreak of the war of 1914–1918 in inducing the opposition leaders to bring pressure upon the government to stand by France and Russia, and to assure Asquith of conservative support. When the coalition was formed in May 1915 he became secretary of state for India, and he retained that office for two years. His resignation was brought about by the mismanagement of the campaign in Mesopotamia, for the commission which inquired into it revealed a very disquieting state of affairs, particularly where the medical services were concerned. There was never any suggestion that blame attached to Chamberlain, but he was secretary of state for India, and as it was his department which was involved he felt it to be his duty to resign in July 1917.

Until April 1918, when he became a member of the War Cabinet, Chamberlain remained out of office, although his services were by no means wasted, for he did valuable work on a committee to control the dollar expenditure of all departments. When Lloyd George reorganized his government after the general election of 1918 he offered Chamberlain the post of chancellor of the Exchequer, which was accepted (January 1919) on condition that there should be an early return to the old Cabinet system which had been suspended during the war. During this second period at the Treasury Chamberlain was confronted with a very difficult situation, not least owing to the industrial unrest which was the aftermath of the war, and the three budgets for which he was responsible went a long way towards placing the national finances on a sound footing. For two years he remained chancellor of the Exchequer, with Bonar Law as lord privy seal and leader of the conservative party. In March 1921 Bonar Law retired on account of ill health, and Chamberlain succeeded him in the conservative leadership: the Exchequer he vacated in favour of Sir Robert Horne (afterwards Viscount Horne of Slamannan, q.v.).

Chamberlain was leader of the conservative party in the House of Commons from the spring of 1921 until the autumn of the following year, and his task was no easy one. The rank and file was showing every day a more marked desire to break away from the coalition, and was arguing that in view of the unpopularity of the government this was the only course for the conservative party to pursue if it was not to go down to disaster with Lloyd George at the next general election. Chamberlain

did not share this opinion. He had no confidence in his party's ability to win an independent majority of its own, and in view of the strength of the disruptive forces up and down the country the fall of the existing administration might well be the prelude to revolution. From the beginning, therefore, there were sharp differences between the new leader and many of his followers.

The great dissolvent of conservative unity was the problem of Ireland. Chamberlain was, in October 1921, one of the British representatives at the conferences which then began with Sinn Fein. He also signed the Irish 'treaty' itself on 6 December. His next task was to obtain the assent of his followers to the settlement, and although he secured a substantial majority at the party conference in Liverpool his difficulties were increased rather than diminished. The 'die-hards', as the irreconcilable element was again termed, became increasingly dissatisfied with his continued support of Lloyd George, and during the year 1922 his position and that of the government was still further weakened by the murder of Sir Henry Wilson [q.v.] and by the situation in the Near East where war with Turkey was narrowly averted.

With the approach of autumn the crisis within the conservative party reached its height, and the head of the machine, Sir George Younger (afterwards Viscount Younger of Leckie, q.v.), was at open variance with his chief. Accordingly a meeting of conservative members of parliament was convoked at the Carlton Club on 19 October, and Chamberlain recommended that the existing government as then constituted under the leadership of Lloyd George should go to the country; it would be time to talk of changes when the victory had been won. A motion was at once proposed to the effect that the party 'should fight the election as an independent party with its own leader and its own programme', and this point of view was backed by Stanley Baldwin. It was, however, the reappearance of Bonar Law that decided the issue, for he gave his support to the motion, which was then carried by 187 votes to 87. Chamberlain refused, as he put it, 'to send to the prime minister a message of dismissal', and he consequently ceased to be leader of the conservative party.

Chamberlain, in common with Lord Birkenhead and others who had supported him at the Carlton Club, did not take office under either Bonar Law or Baldwin, but assumed an attitude of benevolent neutrality. This attitude, so far as Chamberlain was concerned, was in no small measure due to the presence of his half-brother, Neville Chamberlain, in the administration, and he is found writing, 'If Neville had not joined this Government, I'd have had them out in six months.' Chamberlain disapproved of the precipitancy of Baldwin in going to the country in 1923 on a protectionist policy without adequate preparation, but the labour victory at the polls soon reunited the conservative party. When, therefore, Baldwin, on the formation of his second government in November 1924, offered Chamberlain the foreign secretaryship he gladly accepted.

Chamberlain took office in circumstances of peculiar difficulty, in view of the estrangement of France from Germany over the occupation of the Ruhr, although he had the advantage of enjoying that free hand which Baldwin gave to all his ministers. His first task was to denounce the protocol of Geneva, which had been approved by the previous government. The proposal had met with a hostile reception in many quarters in Great Britain and the Empire overseas, and was especially disliked by Chamberlain's own party. Something, nevertheless, had to be put in its place, and an offer by Stresemann, then German foreign minister, to guarantee the existing territorial position on the Rhine, gave Chamberlain an opportunity to initiate the negotiations which later resulted in the Locarno pact. His patience in overcoming obstacles, both on the part of Germany and of France, was remarkable, for although the scheme was first envisaged in January 1925, it was not until the following 16 October that the Locarno pact was actually signed. It was very largely Chamberlain's work, and the recognition of this fact came in the form of the Garter, which was conferred upon him at this time, an honour bestowed upon only two commoners, Sir Edward Grey and A. J. Balfour, since the award to Castlereagh in 1814. If it be objected that the Locarno pact did not go far enough, especially where Germany's eastern frontiers were concerned, the answer must be that it was as far as Chamberlain could then have persuaded his fellow countrymen to go, and that it did give Europe a breathing-space.

Chamberlain was the first foreign secretary to make a habit of attending regularly the meetings of the Council of the League of Nations, and in 1926 his presence at Geneva was very necessary to ensure for Germany that seat on the Council which she had been promised at Locarno. It was not only in Europe that Chamberlain had difficulties to surmount. He had hardly taken office when he was confronted with the murder of Sir Lee Stack [q.v.], and during his tenure of the foreign secretaryship he was continually endeavouring to put the admittedly unsatisfactory Anglo-Egyptian relations upon a sounder footing. In 1927 matters got so far as a draft treaty, but these hopes were wrecked upon the rock of Wafd opposition. In China, too, the British position became extremely serious in face of an outbreak of xenophobia on the one hand and the refusal of the Japanese to co-operate on the other. Chamberlain was much criticized for making no effort to regain the British concession at Hankow, which had been captured by the Chinese in January 1927, but he knew that the country was not prepared for a campaign in the interior of China; nevertheless he persuaded the Cabinet to send a strong force to Shanghai to prevent a repetition there of the events which had taken place at Hankow.

During the greater part of 1928 Chamberlain was ill, and so was unable to be present at the signing of the Kellogg pact in Paris on 27 August of that year. At the general election of May 1929 the conservative government was defeated, and although Chamberlain urged Baldwin to meet parliament, the prime minister decided otherwise, and the administration resigned.

Of the various offices which Chamberlain held during the course of his career he is best remembered for his foreign secretaryship. In this connexion he would seem to have two claims to distinction; he never took a step without preparing the way very carefully indeed, and his historical sense rendered him profoundly aware of the mistakes of his predecessors. It has been said that he was little more than the mouthpiece of the Quai d'Orsay, and, alternatively, that he was the dupe of Stresemann. These accusations are mutually contradictory, and neither of them is true. As foreign secretary he was above all else a great realist; he never hankered after the unattainable, but he did his best with the tools that he had. When he laid down office the world was far more settled than it had been when he became foreign secretary four and a half years earlier.

For a time Chamberlain was under a cloud; he was returned for West Birmingham, the seat to which he had succeeded on his father's death in 1914, and which he never lost, by the narrow majority of 43: his policy of solidarity with France was temporarily unpopular in many quarters; and a number of conservative members of parliament had asked Baldwin for a promise that Chamberlain would not go back to the Foreign Office when their party returned to power. He had, however, no longer any ambitions for himself, and, the ties between himself and his brother being as strong as they were, all his political hopes were based upon Neville succeeding Baldwin in the leadership, and thus eventually becoming prime minister.

When the all-party government came to be formed in August 1931, and Chamberlain was asked to co-operate, he willingly agreed, but he was bitterly disappointed that it was the Admiralty and not the Foreign Office which was offered to him. He felt that at the latter he might have been of real assistance, whereas at the Admiralty 'except to a few I appear not as someone who gives all he can to help in a crisis but as an old party hack who might be dangerous outside and so must have his mouth stopped with office'. His tenure of office as first lord of the Admiralty was not destined to be of long continuance, but it was marked by one important event, namely, the naval mutiny at Invergordon in September. It has, however, nowhere been suggested either that Chamberlain was in any way responsible for this incident, or that his attitude was other than scrupulously correct. After the general election of October 1931 he wrote to Baldwin to say that he waived all claim to inclusion in the new administration which was in process of formation. By no means the least cogent of the motives by which he was actuated was the desire to help his brother. 'I hope', he wrote, 'that my elimination will make Neville's accession to the Chancellorship easier to secure.'

When Chamberlain left office for the last time he had still five and a half years to live, and his position, politically, recalled that of his father between 1886 and 1895 in that he exercised over the House of Commons a control which had not been his when he was a minister. Advancing years may have prevented him from that participation in the daily round at Westminster which had characterized him during the earlier part of his career, but he was rarely absent when foreign policy was the subject to be discussed. Nor did he treat the House of Commons as if it were a mere platform from which to address the country, for he listened to others with the courteous attention that he expected from his listeners. He refused to indulge in any factious criticism of the government of the day, but as the German danger became ever more manifest he neglected no opportunity of warning his fellow countrymen against it. Another task which occupied a good deal of his time was the work of the joint select parliamentary committee on Indian constitutional reform which was set up in 1932, and of which he was a member.

Chamberlain took part at this time in a number of non-political activities. He was chancellor of Reading University (1935–1937), and chairman both of the court of governors of the London School of Hygiene and Tropical Medicine and of the governing body of the British Postgraduate Medical School; he was also chairman of the board of governors of Rugby School: in all of these capacities he worked extremely hard, for to the very end he displayed all his old zeal on behalf of any cause with which he was associated. In addition, he formed a number of business connexions, and also wrote from time to time for the British, French, and American press. It was during this period, too, that he published two books of an autobiographical character.

The last occasion on which Chamberlain appeared in the centre of the political stage was in December 1935, after the conclusion of the Hoare–Laval pact, which he criticized severely. It was said that at first the government had intended to stand by the pact, and that what decided Baldwin to take the opposite course, even at the price of dropping his foreign secretary, was the fear that Chamberlain would attack him, although in actual fact Chamberlain had not decided what line to adopt. In the ensuing debate Chamberlain supported the government, but he believed, with considerable justification, that 'after S. B.'s miserably inadequate speech and the initial blunder' he could 'have so reduced his majority as to force his resignation'. On the following day Baldwin asked Chamberlain to join the administration as minister of state without a department, as he considered that he was too old to go to the Foreign Office again. Chamberlain refused, as he believed that all that Baldwin wanted was 'the use of my name to help patch up the damaged prestige of his government'.

Chamberlain died suddenly in London 16 March 1937. To turn from the statesman to the man, all who knew him can bear witness to his devotion to his family and to his sociability. He married in 1906 Ivy Muriel, daughter of Colonel Henry Lawrence Dundas, of Datchet, and had two sons and one daughter. He was a devoted husband and father, and it was the happiness of his home life which enabled him to emerge unscathed from the storms of his public career. He was a scholar, and throughout his life he read widely, which was apparent in all that he did and said. He was also a lover of nature and of rural pursuits, and possessed a very considerable knowledge of flowers. Nothing gave him greater pleasure than to stroll through woods and fields in spring picking primroses and cowslips, and when he was able to cultivate a rock-garden in Sussex, he spent many hours attending to his precious Alpines on which he became quite an authority. Owing to his poor sight and immaculate attire Chamberlain often conveyed to strangers an impression of austerity which was very far from being the case. Actually, he was the most 'clubbable' of men, was naturally sociable, and delighted in company. He was an extremely interesting and agreeable talker, for he had stored up in a exceedingly retentive memory a host of reminiscences which he told well. He had an even temper which was always under control, and an inborne generosity which led him to acknowledge without reserve any mistakes which he had made. He delighted in travel and sight-seeing, especially if he had the opportunity of studying pictures and works of art, in which he took great pleasure. He spoke French easily and well, and although his German became rather rusty, he could understand most of a conversation in that language. He had a large acquaintance among people of many nations, and he liked to invite them to his house in London, and to exchange views with them upon international politics.

The chief portraits of Chamberlain are a full-length in Garter robes by I. M. Cohen in the Cordwainers' Company's hall; one as chancellor of Reading University by Sir William Rothenstein at Reading; and one by P. A. de László in the robes of chancellor of the Exchequer in private possession.

[*The Times*, 17 March 1937; Austen Chamberlain, *Down the Years*, 1935, *Politics from Inside*, 1936, and *Seen in Passing*, 1937; E. Stern-Rubarth, *Three Men Tried*, 1939; Sir Charles Petrie, *Life and Letters of the Right Hon. Sir Austen Chamberlain*, 2 vols., 1939–1940; personal knowledge.]

CHARLES PETRIE.

CHAMPNEYS, BASIL (1842–1935), architect and author, was born in London 17 September 1842, the third of the five sons of William Weldon Champneys, rector of St. Mary's church, Whitechapel, afterwards dean of Lichfield [q.v.], by his wife, Mary Anne, fourth daughter of Paul Storr, of Beckenham, Kent. He was an elder brother of Sir F. H. Champneys [q.v.].

Champneys was educated at Charterhouse School, then in London; and at Trinity College, Cambridge, where he obtained a second class in the classical tripos of 1864. He then studied architecture under John Prichard, diocesan surveyor of Llandaff, who was 'an uncompromising medievalist, and stickler for the letter of Gothic'. He began private practice in 1867 and continued it for forty years. The long list of his buildings includes the Indian Institute, Mansfield College, the Robinson Tower at New College, new buildings for Oriel and Merton Colleges, the library of Somerville College, and the church of St. Peter-le-Bailey, all at Oxford; the Archaeological Museum, the Divinity and Literary Schools, and Newnham College (at intervals from 1875 to 1910), all at Cambridge; new buildings for Bedford College, in Regent's Park, London; King's Lynn Grammar School; the Butler Museum at Harrow School; the chapel at Mill Hill School; the museum at Winchester College; the Harpur Girls' School at Bedford; churches at Slindon (Staffordshire), Hastings, and Kentish Town; much work at Manchester Cathedral; and, most important of all, the John Rylands Memorial Library in Deansgate, Manchester, which took nine years (1890–1899) to build and equip. This remarkable and costly monument was raised to the memory of John Rylands [q.v.] by his widow, as a worthy repository for the fine collection of early books and manuscripts (the 'Althorp Library') which he had purchased from Lord Spencer. Mrs. Rylands seems to have admired the small library of Mansfield College, one of Champneys's most successful buildings, and to have asked him to develop it on a far more lavish and magnificent scale. In spite of its cramped position on a mean street, the Rylands Library is a really noble design carried out in every detail with consummate skill in late Gothic style and with considerable regard for practical requirements. Champneys was happiest when working in stone rather than in brick, and in late Gothic rather than in neo-Jacobean or some form of Renaissance design. His work was always scholarly; and, if not invariably original, was at least more original than that of some of his contemporaries.

The Royal Institute of British Architects paid tribute to Champneys's great talents by awarding him the Royal gold medal for architecture in 1912, but he never became a member of that institute or took any part in professional politics, being himself a pronounced individualist who regarded architecture as an art rather than a profession. However, he was by no means a recluse and had a wide circle of friends, among them Coventry Patmore [q.v.], whose *Memoirs and Correspondence* he published in 1900. It is said that he divided his time fairly equally between architecture and literature, and as early as 1875 he produced a little book on the then unfrequented district around Rye and Romney Marsh under the title *A Quiet Corner of England*. In later life he published (1915) a *Retrospect and Memoir* of his mother-in-law, Adelaide Drummond, and also wrote many delightful articles on historic towns and buildings.

Champneys married in **1876** May Theresa Ella, second daughter of Maurice Drummond, a descendant of William Drummond, fourth Viscount Strathallan [q.v.], and had two sons and two daughters. He died at his home at Hampstead 5 April 1935, at the age of ninety-two.

[*The Times*, 6 April 1935; *Manchester Guardian*, 8 April 1935; *Builder* and *Architect*, 12 April 1935; *Journal* of the Royal Institute of British Architects, 27 April 1935.]

MARTIN S. BRIGGS.

CHARLES, ROBERT HENRY (1855–1931), archdeacon of Westminster and biblical scholar, was born at Cookstown, co. Tyrone, 6 August 1855, the fifth of the seven sons of David Hughes Charles, M.D., J.P., of Cookstown, by his wife, Annie Elizabeth, second daughter of John Allen. He was an elder brother of Sir Richard Havelock Charles, first baronet [q.v.]. His education was begun at a private school near his home; but he became dissatisfied with the quality of the instruction, and, at his own request, he was transferred to Belfast Academy. Here he made rapid progress, and entered Queen's College, Belfast, in 1874. Concentrating on classics, he won the first of five scholarships, and graduated B.A. (1877) and M.A. (1880), both with first class honours. During his undergraduate years at Belfast he passed through a spiritual crisis, one of the results of which was his resolve to seek ordination. He accordingly entered Trinity College, Dublin, where he had a brilliant career in classics and theology. At the end of his courses he spent some time in Germany and Switzerland; and it was during a stay at Heidelberg that he met Mary Lilias, daughter of William Bence-Jones, of Lisselan, co. Cork. They were married in 1886; and, although they had no children, their house was the home of a number of nieces whom they brought up as their own children.

Charles was ordained deacon in 1883 and priest in 1884 and during the six years from 1883 to 1889 served curacies in Whitechapel, Kensington, and Kennington with such zeal and energy that his health was seriously impaired and prolonged rest became necessary. With his wife he went to Germany for a year. During this visit he began the study of the religious developments within Judaism in the period between the Testaments, and particularly the exposition of the Apocalyptic literature both Jewish and Christian.

On their return Charles settled in Oxford and incorporated at Exeter College in 1891. At Oxford began the publication of a long series of works of first-rate importance. It opened with an English translation of the *Book of Enoch* (1893, 2nd ed. 1912) and was crowned by the massive edition of the Apocalypse of St. John (2 vols., 1920) and the great *Critical and Exegetical Commentary on the Book of Daniel* (1929). In the intervening years he published English translations, with commentaries, of many important Apocalypses. More important still, he provided scholars with reliable information about the texts. For this purpose it was necessary to command not only Hebrew, Greek, and Latin, but also Syriac, Armenian, and Ethiopic. Charles did it all: his mastery of classical Ethiopic was outstanding and universally recognized. His critical editions of the *Book of Jubilees* (Ethiopic, 1895) and *Enoch* (also Ethiopic,

1906), and *The Testaments of the Twelve Patriarchs* (Greek, 1908) are indispensable. Indeed, nothing of his on Apocalyptic literature can safely be ignored. While pursuing his own researches with characteristic zeal he gathered about him a band of scholars with similar interests, and the result of their joint labours was the great Oxford edition of *The Apocrypha and Pseudepigrapha of the Old Testament in English* (2 vols., 1913), in which, besides the general editorship, Charles had a large share of the detailed work. He brought together his conclusions on the Apocalyptic literature and its main ideas in two important articles, 'Apocalyptic Literature' and 'Eschatology', published in the *Encyclopaedia Biblica*; in his Jowett lectures for 1898–1899, *A Critical History of the Doctrine of a Future Life in Israel, in Judaism and in Christianity* (1899, 2nd revised and enlarged ed. 1913); and in his *Religious Development between the Old and the New Testaments* (1914). In 1916 he made a valuable contribution to Byzantine studies by producing an English edition of the *Chronicle of John, Bishop of Nikiu*.

Charles's great scholarship obtained due recognition. He received honorary degrees from the universities of Belfast (1923) and Oxford (1928). He was professor of biblical Greek in Trinity College, Dublin (1898–1906); Grinfield lecturer on the Septuagint (1905–1911) and Speaker's lecturer in biblical studies (1910–1914) at Oxford; Warburton lecturer in Lincoln's Inn Chapel from 1919; and Schweich lecturer of the British Academy (1919–1920). He was elected a fellow of the British Academy in 1906 and of Merton College, Oxford, in 1910. In 1925 he was the first recipient of the British Academy's medal for biblical studies. In 1913 he was appointed a canon of Westminster, and became archdeacon in 1919. Here he applied himself with his customary zeal to the duties of his office, especially the preaching. His sermons were solid and scholarly deliverances on important matters of Christian life and doctrine: many of them appeared in print. In the last eighteen months of his life he was gravely handicapped by injuries sustained in a road accident. He died at his home in Little Cloisters 30 January 1931. He was a benefactor of Ripon Hall, Oxford, the library of which inherited many of his books. His portrait, painted in oils by M. Grixoni, was given to the hall by his nephew, Sir Havelock Charles.

Of Charles's work on the Apocalyptic literature, on which his fame chiefly rests, two things fall to be said. He was a man of powerful intellect and unflagging industry who, by years of concentrated study, made himself master of the language of the Apocalypses. His knowledge was vast in extent and accurate in detail; and his commentaries are a wonderful storehouse of exact information. Yet there was a sense in which the language of Apocalyptic remained a foreign language to him. He could never be completely at home in the world of the Apocalyptists. And this made it impossible for him to achieve that perfect understanding which demands sympathy as well as knowledge. Further, his editions of the texts stand as models of scholarship. The materials are set out with far greater completeness and accuracy than ever before; and those who find themselves compelled to dissent from some of Charles's conclusions usually do so on the basis of evidence which Charles himself supplies. The making available of so much material was an immense service to biblical scholarship, and further progress in this field must inevitably be based on Charles's work.

[*The Times*, 2 February 1931; F. C. Burkitt, *Robert Henry Charles, 1855–1931* in *Proceedings of the British Academy*, vol. xvii, 1931; Memoir by Dr. C. F. D'Arcy prefixed to the posthumous volume of Charles's sermons, *Courage, Truth, Purity*, 1931 (portrait); private information.]   T. W. MANSON.

CHARRINGTON, FREDERICK NICHOLAS (1850–1936), philanthropist and temperance reformer, was born in London 4 February 1850, the eldest son of Frederick Charrington, brewer, by his wife, Louisa, daughter of Huxley Griffith, of Stepney. After two terms at Marlborough in 1864, he left and a year later was sent to Brighton College. On leaving school after two years he travelled on the continent, and afterwards went into a brewery at Windsor with a view to learning the details of that trade. A place was then found for him in his father's firm of Charrington & company, but this he soon relinquished, sacrificing the prospect of a large fortune in order to take up the cause of Christianity and temperance in the district surrounding the brewery in the East End.

Charrington was at that time (1870) aged twenty, and his action created a considerable impression. At a meeting of the Band of Hope over which he presided there was a crowded audience. The early meetings of the Tower Hamlets mission which he founded were held in a tent. The work made great progress. A conference hall was built, and later the great assembly hall in Mile End Road to hold 4,000 people. Here every Sunday Charrington provided a free tea for 700 hungry men and women of the district, and in 1909 King George V, then Prince of Wales, gave the first of an annual series of free teas. The lord mayor and sheriffs of London on lord mayor's day have contributed to this charitable hospitality since 1887.

Charrington's ardent advocacy of the causes which he championed led at times to some criticism and opposition from a section of the public and the press. But the very publicity that ensued brought the conditions of life in the poorer quarters of London to the notice of many who became his devoted friends and supporters. A man of great muscular strength, he never made any attempt to avoid violence in the strange quarters which he frequented by day and night and from the strange characters with whom he had to do. Although quite capable of giving as good as he got, he was more than once severely injured by assaults from his opponents. At times it must be admitted that he allowed his fervent enthusiasm to carry him to fantastic lengths. On 18 May 1915, when the House of Commons was discussing the report of a select committee on pensions, Charrington, wearing evening dress, an overcoat, and a silk hat, dashed into the House from the members' lobby, seized the mace from the Speaker's table, and began to protest against the drinking bar inside the lobby being used by members. He was arrested, but released after two hours' detention.

Charrington was one of the original members (1889–1895) of the London County Council, a member of the old Mile End guardians and vestry, and later of the Stepney borough council. He died, unmarried, in London 2 January 1936. He left his body to the medical school of the London Hospital.

A portrait of Charrington was presented to him in 1930 and is now at the Tower Hamlets Mission.

[*The Times*, 3 January 1936; Guy Thorne (C. A. E. R. Gull), *The Great Acceptance*; the *Life Story of F. N. Charrington*, 1912.]

ARTHUR COCHRANE.

CHELMSFORD, first VISCOUNT (1868–1933), viceroy of India. [See THESIGER, FREDERIC JOHN NAPIER.]

CHESTERTON, GILBERT KEITH (1874–1936), poet, novelist, and critic, was born on Campden Hill, London, 29 May 1874, the elder son of Edward Chesterton, head of the well-known Kensington firm of auctioneers and estate agents. His mother, Marie Louise Grosjean, was of French and Scottish blood, and her maternal ancestors, the Keiths of Aberdeen, gave Chesterton his middle name. He was educated at St. Paul's School from 1887 to 1892. At sixteen he started the junior debating club and a magazine known as 'The Debater' which contains startlingly good work for a boy of that age—a boy, moreover, who was almost two years behind his contemporaries in his school work. The practical side of producing and distributing the paper was altogether beyond Chesterton's powers and was taken care of by one of his most intimate friends, later his wife's brother-in-law, Lucian Oldershaw. He was already the kind of being that he was to remain all his life: absent-minded, good-natured almost to weakness, yet of a rock-like strength in holding and maintaining his ideas. Some of those ideas were inherited: love of freedom, belief in human equality and in all that is generally known as liberalism; others he was now slowly acquiring. As he sat at his desk, a tall, clumsy, unbrushed, untidy scarecrow, drawing all over his blotter and his books, his mind was deeply concentrated, not on his lessons, but on the deepest problems of reality. Of this mental travail he has given some notion in *Orthodoxy* and it is confirmed by his note-books and the memories of his friends.

Chesterton's drawings at this time showed so much talent that it was decided that he should go, not to Oxford, but to the Slade School of Art, continuing at the same time to study English literature at London University. It soon became abundantly clear that writing, not drawing, was his primary talent. But that he could and still did draw may be seen from his illustrations to Mr. Hilaire Belloc's novels: he would often complete the sketches for one of these in a couple of hours: at all times he would draw and paint while he talked or thought. In *The Coloured Lands*, published in 1938 after his death, may be seen a fair sample of his work at different periods.

Although Chesterton's headmaster had spoken of him to his mother as a genius, neither she nor his father dreamed of a livelihood made by writing alone. Obviously unfitted for the career of an estate agent, he worked for a time in two publishing houses and thence moved gradually into journalism. This became his profession, and in later years when his fame was at its height he would claim no other title than that of journalist.

Chesterton in 1899 was working on the *Speaker* with a group of young liberals of the same general outlook as his own. His friendship with Mr. Belloc had begun, and this meant much for his social thinking. He had fallen in love and was engaged to Frances, eldest daughter of George William Blogg, a London diamond merchant. She was an Anglo-Catholic, and this meant much for his religious thinking. His first published volumes were both verse. *The Wild Knight*, financed by his father, won wide acclaim as poetry. *Greybeards at Play*, illustrated by the author, was highly successful fooling. Both were published in 1900. He was married in 1901. Public events were shaping in a fashion that stimulated at once his patriotism and a fierce criticism of the country that he loved. The South African war came like a flash of lightning separating liberal from liberal—Chesterton, for instance, from Mr. Bernard Shaw: separating brother from brother—Chesterton, for instance, from his brother Cecil: and casting a vivid light on thoughts that had not yet been fully outlined even, perhaps, to himself.

Rightly or wrongly, Chesterton thus accepted the war and his own possible unpopularity as a pro-Boer as a test of his social and political views. He hated imperialism: he was what has been called a 'little Englander': and he wrote *The Napoleon of Notting Hill* (1904) in fantastic illustration of this thesis, outlining it more soberly in his long introductory chapter to *England a Nation* (also 1904), a symposium of young liberal thinking with the sub-title 'Papers of a Patriots' Club', edited by Oldershaw.

During the period 1900 to 1910 the whole of Chesterton's philosophy was outlined and illustrated in twenty books and innumerable articles. He published over one hundred volumes in the course of a lifetime, greatly enriching and deepening but in no fundamental altering that philosophy. There were vigorous controversies in the religious field with Robert Blatchford and Joseph McCabe, in the social field with Mr. Bernard Shaw and H. G. Wells; criticism in the national field

of Rudyard Kipling and the imperialists made of *Heretics* (1905) a brilliant display of fireworks that drew all eyes. He had long contributed art criticism to the *Bookman*, and in 1904 he published *G. F. Watts*. In the field of pure letters his studies of *Robert Browning* (1903) and of *Charles Dickens* (1906) won him another sort of fame: it seemed that he might choose—poet, fantastic novelist, artist and art critic, political pamphleteer, essayist, sociologist, philosopher, and theologian. He chose them all and he chose, too, to remain in style and manner a journalist, to be careless of his facts and references, to avoid solemnity, to laugh at the experts and at himself, to puzzle his fellow journalists alike by his earnestness and his frivolity, to prove that 'there is foam on deep water'.

Orthodoxy (1908) was called by Chesterton 'a sort of slovenly autobiography'. It was, he said, 'an attempt to utter the unutterable things . . . my ultimate attitude towards life'. As against the various 'prophets' of the period—Ibsen, Mr. Shaw, Wells, Kipling, and the rest, each of whom was stressing some one element or tendency—Chesterton saw the riddle of a vast variety in the universe and he came to see Christianity as its only answer. Christianity made a new balance that was also a liberation: it 'made moderation out of the still crash of two impetuous emotions', 'got over the difficulty of combining furious opposites by keeping them both furious'. It taught 'terrible ideals and devouring doctrines': it managed to make the lion lie down with the lamb and yet keep his royal ferocity. *Orthodoxy* was 'a thrilling romance'. It was not the philosophy created by one man to fit himself, and hence too small even to satisfy that self. 'God and humanity made it and it made me.'

Soon after the publication of *Orthodoxy* the Chestertons moved from their little flat in Battersea and went to live at Beaconsfield where they remained for the rest of their lives, at first in a small rented house, later in one built to suit their ideal, a house with a few small bedrooms and one vast living-room where they could have parties for young and old, act charades, or show plays in Chesterton's favourite toy theatre. He spent much time in painting and cutting out figures and scenery for this theatre and in making drawings for guessing games in the invention of which he showed an endless fertility. Grieved at having no child of their own the Chestertons surrounded themselves with children: nieces and nephews, godchildren and young neighbours. His wife created a lovely garden in which Chesterton took a vague pleasure and which often appears in the background of his stories. He began to write about Father Brown, the little priest-detective (*The Innocence of Father Brown* was published in 1911). He took his wife with him and motored over the King Alfred country planning *The Ballad of the White Horse*. He saw his many friends, sometimes in London, sometimes at Beaconsfield: he appeared in pageants as Dr. Johnson: he grew fatter every year and became more and more a figure of legend, wearing a large flapping hat and an ample cloak, carrying a sword-stick and getting lost on every possible and impossible occasion. Setting out from home to give a lecture in some midland town he telegraphed to his wife: 'Am in Market Harborough. Where ought I to be?'

'Father Brown' was actually Father (afterwards Monsignor) O'Connor who, despite his Irish name, is a Yorkshireman, in whose house part of the *White Horse* was written and who, in long walks over the Yorkshire moors, helped Chesterton to thrash out the ideas that beset him. Both Father O'Connor and Mr. Belloc were deeply concerned with the social angle of Christianity's answer to the riddle of the universe. And as with *Orthodoxy* so, too, with Chesterton's social philosophy the battle against the opposing ideas held by Mr. Shaw and others brought Chesterton's own thoughts into clearer focus. In 1909 he published his brilliant sketch of Mr. Shaw. 'I liked it very much,' wrote Mr. Shaw, 'especially as it was so completely free from my own influence.' This book cleared the ground for *What's Wrong with the World?* (1910) much as *Heretics* and the controversy with Blatchford had cleared it for *Orthodoxy*.

Starting life as a liberal by inheritance Chesterton said in these years: 'as much as ever I did, more than ever I did I believe in Liberalism. But there was a rosy time of innocence when I believed in Liberals.' It seemed to him that while no medical doctor says: 'we've had too much scarlet fever, let's try a little measles for a change', that was precisely what the sociological 'doctors' were saying. Capitalism was a failure: he agreed that it was a disease: but when they said: 'let's try a little socialism for a change', it seemed to him that for lack of a clear picture of health one disease was being offered as remedy for another.

In *What's Wrong with the World?* Chesterton suggests some root thought on the nature of man, of sex, of the child and its education. Historically and of his nature man needs the family, for its protection the family needs property which capitalism destroys no less than socialism. 'It is the negation of property that the Duke of Sutherland should have all the farms in one estate: just as it would be the negation of marriage if he had all our wives in one harem.' Property in its true meaning is also a condition for the ordinary man's development: 'Property is the art of the democracy.' He goes on to define 'the functions of father, mother and child as such' and to show the limits that a free family would set to the power of the State. The book is Chesterton's social credo: later on he wrote *The Superstition of Divorce* (1920), *Eugenics and Other Evils* (1922), *The Outline of Sanity* (1926). These and his essays deepen and enrich his social thinking but they add nothing in essentials to *What's Wrong with the World?*

The Ballad of the White Horse was published in 1911 and in 1912 *Manalive*, which is among the best of Chesterton's fantastic stories, expressing as it does supremely the intense zest which he brought to the business of living. *The Victorian Age in Literature* (1913) showed him still brilliant in the field of pure literature. The same year, goaded by Mr. Shaw, he produced a play, *Magic*, which, despite admiring reviews, was a stage failure.

Then came the war of 1914–1918 and Chesterton's almost mortal illness. He had been overworking, overeating, and drinking—('absent-mindedly' as a friend said, for it was only necessary to fill his plate or glass while he talked for him to empty it again). Cecil Chesterton had stood his trial for a libel action which had worried his elder brother more than himself: the war had come as a final blow. 'I wonder', the doctor heard him murmur as he was lifted into a water bed, 'if this bally ship will ever get to shore.' He lay for many months unconscious between life and death. His wife nursed him devotedly and brought him back to full life and vigour. 'I am afraid', he wrote at once to Mr. Shaw, 'you must reconcile yourself to the dismal prospect of my being more or less like what I was before; and any resumption of my ordinary habits must necessarily include the habit of disagreeing with you.'

In 1917 appeared Chesterton's fascinating, sketchy, and inaccurate *Short History of England*. It exasperated historians, yet 'He's got at something we hadn't got' wryly confessed a professor of history to one of Chesterton's friends. In 1919 came *Irish Impressions* and in 1920 *The New Jerusalem*. These books all mark stages in that mental voyage of discovery in which Chesterton, historically and in the contemporary world, was approaching nearer and nearer to the Roman Catholic Church. Externally he was at once urged forward and held back by the circumstances of his life. Cecil Chesterton had with Mr. Belloc some years earlier started a newspaper, first (1911) the *Eye Witness*, later (1912) the *New Witness*, to combat corruption in public life and to uphold and restore the liberties of the poor against a growing bureaucracy. On Cecil's joining the army in 1916 Gilbert took over the editorship. Cecil died in France in December 1918, and his brother continued to edit the paper until its termination in 1923. It was revived under his editorship in 1925 as *G. K.'s Weekly*, which survived until 1938. Added to all that he already had in hand, this editorship produced a chronic condition of overwork. On the other hand a journey to Jerusalem gave fresh inspiration to his thinking, and lecture tours in Holland and the United States of America strengthened his awareness of the Church's universality. All his thinking—directly religious, philosophical, sociological—brought him to the same conclusion, and in 1922 he overcame the largely physical problem posed for him by overwork, physical lethargy, and the habit of depending on his wife for all practical decisions. Chesterton was received into the Roman Catholic Church by Father O'Connor in July 1922. His wife followed him four years later.

The two best known of the books which quickly followed Chesterton's reception are *St. Francis of Assisi* (1923) and *The Everlasting Man* (1925). Of these the former is by far the more popular, the latter the more important. In *Orthodoxy* Chesterton had traced his own discovery of Christianity, in *The Everlasting Man* he traced rather what that discovery, that revelation, had meant for mankind as a whole. Like Wells writing his *Outline of History*, Chesterton claimed 'the right of the amateur to do his best with the facts the specialists provide'. Unlike Wells: 'I do not believe', says Chesterton, 'that the best way to produce an outline of history is to rub out the lines.' But his own aim was not merely to draw an outline but to show something that seemed stale and dusty and old as it really was, fresh and new everlastingly. He asked men to read the Gospels like their daily paper, not merely as good but as *news*. 'I desire to help the reader to see Christendom from the outside in the sense of seeing it as a whole against the background of other historic things; just as I desire him to see humanity as a whole against the background of natural things. And I say that in both cases when seen thus, they stand out from their background like supernatural things.'

When *The Everlasting Man* was published Chesterton had only eleven years to live. They were years of little external action, of amazing productivity. He travelled: to Europe fairly often, to America once more (1930–1931) where he gave courses at Notre Dame University, Indiana, and lectured throughout the country and in Canada. He wrote another play (*The Judgment of Dr. Johnson*, 1927), essays innumerable, more detective stories, more poems (especially *The Queen of Seven Swords*, 1926), literary works, of which by far the best was his *R. L. Stevenson* (1927), theology and philosophy, books of travel. His *St. Thomas Aquinas* (1933) was called by Etienne Gilson 'the best book on St. Thomas that has ever been written'. The pages of *G. K's Weekly* are littered with brilliant matter never reprinted, but from them and from his scattered papers were gathered posthumously (1940) *The End of the Armistice* which cast, like his *William Cobbett* (1925) written during the same period, an almost lurid light of prophecy on the horrors that have followed. Never did Chesterton give in to the 'rather weakminded reaction', the mood of pacificism and appeasement that followed the war of 1914–1918.

Added to Chesterton's other activities in his last years were several series of radio talks for the British Broadcasting Corporation. Both his own purely literary talks and his contributions to various series ('The Spice of Life', 'Seven Days Hard') were received with rare enthusiasm. In these talks and in his writings down to the hour of his death an element was present that has caused the most fundamental disagreement as to Chesterton's character and his place in history. A note of youth, of high spirits, of fooling, present when he entered letters as a young journalist, was as audible in the mature man broadcasting his last message to his countrymen

They may go out with a whimper,
But I will go out with a bang.

'Chesterton the Child' was the supreme attribute given to Chesterton by Walter de la Mare when the sword of the warrior and the pen of the thinker had been laid aside. There was nothing childish in Chesterton, nothing callow in his youthful high spirits. The conception of Chesterton as a Peter Pan who never grew up accords ill with the books and ideas which led philosophers to welcome him as one of their own calibre, poets to give him front rank among themselves, and men of letters to acclaim his *Dickens*, his *Browning*, and his *Stevenson* as showing the insight of genius.

Chesterton died at Beaconsfield 14 June 1936; his wife survived him until 1938.

A painting of Chesterton, Maurice Baring, and Mr. Hilaire Belloc (1932), by James Gunn, belongs to Mr. Hugh Balfour, Foss House, Pitlochry. There is a plasticine medallion, by Theodore Spicer-Simson, in the National Portrait Gallery, which also owns a bronze bust by Maria Petrie.

[G. K. Chesterton, *Autobiography*, 1936; Maisie Ward, *Gilbert Keith Chesterton*, 1944; personal knowledge.]   MAISIE WARD.

CHEYNE, SIR (WILLIAM) WATSON, first baronet (1852–1932), bacteriologist and surgeon, was born at sea, off Hobart Town, Tasmania, 14 December 1852, the only son of Andrew Cheyne, of Ollaberry, Shetland, captain in the mercantile marine, by his wife, Eliza, daughter of William Watson, minister of the united parishes of Fetlar and North Yell. He was educated at the grammar school and King's College, Aberdeen, and at Edinburgh University, where he graduated with first class honours in medicine in 1875. He went the same year to Vienna, where he attended the lectures of A. C. Theodor Billroth, Ernest Wilhelm von Brücke, Anton Politzer, Ferdinand R. von Hebra, and Siegmund Exner, and the following spring spent three months with the great pathologist Friedrich Daniel von Recklinghausen at Strasburg.

Shortly after his return to Edinburgh Cheyne became house-surgeon to Joseph (afterwards Lord) Lister [q.v.], who invited him to accompany him to King's College Hospital, where Lister had been appointed professor of clinical surgery in 1877. At first, Lister and Cheyne received only a cold welcome which, however, enabled Cheyne to pursue his study of bacteriology, including the translation of two German works on bacteriology for the New Sydenham Society, namely, Robert Koch's *Etiology of the Traumatic Infective Diseases* (1880) and Carl Flügge's *Micro-organisms, with Special Reference to the Etiology of the Infective Diseases* (1890). Gradually, however, Cheyne received due recognition, and in 1882 he published an important work entitled *Antiseptic Surgery: its Principles, Practice, History and Results*, an enlargement of his thesis for the Jacksonian prize, awarded by the Royal College of Surgeons in 1881, followed three years later by *Lister and his Achievements* (1885), which formed the subject of the first Lister memorial lecture delivered at the Royal College of Surgeons of England in 1924, when he was awarded the Lister medal. In 1880 Cheyne was appointed assistant-surgeon at King's College Hospital, becoming full surgeon in due course, professor of the principles and practice of surgery in 1891, and professor of clinical surgery in 1902. He was Hunterian professor at the Royal College of Surgeons from 1888 to 1890.

On the outbreak of the South African war in 1899 Cheyne was appointed civil consulting surgeon to the forces and was appointed C.B. for his services, and in 1908 he was created a baronet. When war broke out in 1914 he was made consulting surgeon to the navy and in 1915 became temporary surgeon-general, and was appointed K.C.M.G. in 1916. He retired from active practice at the end of the war.

The importance of Cheyne's work lies in the fact that not only was he a pioneer in antiseptic surgery and was one of Lister's most active followers, but he also emphasized the value of preventive medicine in clinical practice. When Cheyne began his bacteriological investigations at Edinburgh 'there was no staining of bacteria, no oil immersion lenses, no solid cultivating media, no proper incubators— in fact, everything was in its infancy'.

In 1917 Cheyne was elected member of parliament for the universities of Edinburgh and St. Andrews and from 1918 to 1922 he was a member for the combined Scottish Universities. In 1919 he was gazetted lord-lieutenant of Orkney and Shetland, an office from which he resigned in 1930. He was elected in 1879 a fellow of the Royal College of Surgeons, was president from 1914 to 1916, and Hunterian orator in 1915. In 1894 he was elected F.R.S. He received honorary degrees from the universities of Oxford, Edinburgh, and Birmingham.

Cheyne was twice married: first, in 1887 to Mary Emma (died 1894), daughter of the Rev. William Servante, of Plumstead, Kent, and had two sons and one daughter, who died in infancy; secondly, in 1894 to Margaret (died 1922), daughter of George Smith, of Lerwick, Shetland, and had one son and two daughters, all of whom predeceased him. He retired in 1922 to Fetlar where he died after a prolonged illness 19 April 1932, and was succeeded as second baronet by his eldest son, Joseph Lister Cheyne, M.C. (born 1888), colonel, 16th Lancers.

[*The Times*, 20 April 1932; *Obituary Notices of Fellows of the Royal Society*, No. 1, December 1932 (portrait); *British Medical Journal*, 1932, vol. i, p. 821 (portrait); *Lancet*, 1932, vol. i, p. 963.]   J. D. ROLLESTON.

CHILDS, WILLIAM MACBRIDE (1869–1939), educationist, was born at Carrington, near Boston, Lincolnshire, 3 January 1869, the second son of William Linington Childs, vicar of Carrington and Frith Ville, who in 1879 became vicar of St. George's church, Portsea, by his wife, Henrietta Fowles Bell. He was educated at Portsmouth Grammar School and at Keble College, Oxford, of which he was a scholar; he obtained a second class in modern history in 1891. In 1892 he became assistant private secretary to (Sir) A. H. D. Acland [q.v.], but a career in official service did not attract him, and, in 1893, he accepted a lecturership in history at a college in Reading which had recently been opened at the instance of Christ Church, Oxford, as a centre for education of the university extension pattern. Within a few years Childs had become convinced that this college (which in 1902 received the title of University College, Reading) would offer a field for the work of his whole life. In 1897 he married Emma Catharine, daughter of Alfred Whiting Pollard; he fixed his home in Reading, and he neither sought nor accepted employment elsewhere. In 1903, on the resignation of (Sir) Halford John Mackinder, the first principal of the college, Childs, who had become vice-principal in 1900, succeeded him, and thenceforward until his retirement he devoted himself unreservedly to its interests.

It was Childs's achievement to inspire and direct the efforts which in little more than twenty years converted the obscure college of 1903 into an independent university. No one could have reached this end without many helpers, and Childs was remarkably successful in bringing together a group of persons who, like himself, believed in the future of the college. But the initiative in its development was always with him, and its expansion was made possible by his personal qualities. It was his obvious sincerity which won him the support of those whose aid he needed. His advocacy was made more effective by his conviction that a college which aimed at the character of a university must establish an ordered form of common life for its students. A series of halls of residence was an integral part of the college which he was planning, and few events in his career gave him greater satisfaction than the opening, in 1908, of Wantage Hall, a foundation for men students of the type traditional in the older English universities.

By the end of 1911 Childs had obtained an endowment which made possible the ultimate independence of the college. Progress was delayed by the war of 1914–1918 and the necessary work of reconstruction, but the end was reached in 1926, and Childs became the first vice-chancellor of the new university of Reading. In 1929, feeling that the main object of his work had been secured, he retired from office. He died at Hermitage, near Newbury, 21 June 1939, survived by his wife and their four sons. He received honorary degrees from the universities of Liverpool (1928), Oxford (1929), and Reading (1935).

There are two portraits of Childs, one by Morley Fletcher, the other by Eric Kennington, in the university of Reading.

[W. M. Childs, *Making a University*, 1933; personal knowledge.]   F. M. STENTON.

CHOLMONDELEY, HUGH, third BARON DELAMERE (1870–1931), pioneer settler in Kenya, was born in London, 28 April 1870, the only son of Hugh Cholmondeley, second Baron Delamere, by his second wife, Augusta Emily, eldest daughter of Sir George Hamilton Seymour [q.v.]. Educated at Eton, he inherited the title with the estate of Vale Royal, Cheshire, at the age of seventeen. He served for a time in the 3rd battalion, The Cheshire Regiment, and in the Cheshire Yeomanry. As a young man he organized five expeditions to Somaliland in pursuit of big game; the fifth took him from Berbera into the unsettled desert region through which the Kenya–Abyssinia border now runs. He reached the highlands of what is now Kenya Colony in 1897, the first Englishman to traverse this route.

Delamere could not settle down to the life of a country gentleman at Vale Royal, and in January 1903 he returned to the East Africa Protectorate and decided to take up land. The highlands were still wild and partly uninhabited, but the newly built Uganda railway connected Lake Victoria with the coast.

The commissioner, Sir Charles Eliot [q.v.], was then embarking on a policy of attracting white settlers. Delamere received a ninety-nine-years' lease on 100,000 acres in the Njoro district, and immediately set about importing rams from England and New Zealand in order to improve the native sheep. At this time he was suffering from severe injuries to the spine as a result of several bad falls and arrived at his new estate on a stretcher. When the land proved unsuitable for sheep he turned to cattle and finally, after these too had died, to wheat, on which he inaugurated East African research into the breeding of rust-resistant varieties. Although not the first settler in East Africa, he was the first to experiment on a large scale and to sink considerable capital (mostly borrowed, for he was never well off) in these untried farming lands.

Delamere's fiery and autocratic temper, his quickness in debate, his generosity, and his passionate belief in the civilizing mission of white settlement in Africa fitted him for leadership of the settlers in their frequent tussles with colonial officials and their attacks on bureaucratic restrictions and delays. He was elected the first president of the Farmers' and Planters' Association in 1903 (which became the Colonists' Association in 1904), and was one of two unofficial members nominated to the first legislative council in 1907. During the war of 1914–1918 he was at first employed on intelligence work among the Masai along the German border. The strenuous life and severe malaria did his heart an injury which was ultimately to cause his death, and he was forced to give up active service. After six months in England he returned to his ranch, Soysambu, on which he had been able to realize his ambition of breeding, on a large scale, high-grade merino sheep.

After the war the European community was enfranchised and Delamere was elected member for the Rift Valley in 1920. He held this position until his death and became, in addition, leader of the elected members, and one of two unofficial members of the governor's executive council. In 1923 he headed a deputation to the Colonial Office to resist proposals to enfranchise Indians on a common roll with Europeans and to allow their unrestricted immigration.

Delamere's guiding faith was his belief in the need for strong and permanent settlements of British families in the highlands of Africa. After the conquest of 'German East' he hoped to see this policy extended to Tanganyika Territory, and a chain of European settlements forged from Kenya to the Cape. He envisaged the eventual creation of an East African Dominion, working towards the goal of self-government already reached by the white communities of South Africa and Southern Rhodesia, and he persistently pressed for the grant of an unofficial majority in the Kenya legislative council. In 1925 he organized, at his own expense, an unofficial conference of delegates from Kenya, Tanganyika, Northern Rhodesia, and Nyasaland, held at Tukuyu (southern Tanganyika), to promote the 'solidification of the white ideal'. Two other conferences followed, in Livingstone and Nairobi, in 1926 and 1927. The economic crisis, however, put an end to these and other projects for the strengthening of white settlement in Tanganyika and the Central African territories. In 1929 Delamere was appointed K.C.M.G. for his public services.

By now the British government had veered from a belief that 'the main object of our policy and legislation should be to found a white colony' (1920), to a declaration that 'primarily, Kenya is an African territory, and . . . the interests of the African natives must be paramount' (1923). With this latter statement Delamere could never agree, and in 1930 he headed his last deputation to London to put forward the colonists' point of view to the labour government. By this time he was a sick man, and on his return to Kenya the strain of reorganizing his heavily indebted farms to meet the catastrophic fall in prices, superimposed on exacting political duties, proved too much for a system which he had never spared. He died of angina at Loresho, near Nairobi, 13 November 1931, and was buried on his estate at Soysambu, near Lake Elmenteita.

Delamere was twice married: first, in 1899 to Florence Ame (died 1914), fourth daughter of Lowry Egerton Cole, fourth Earl of Enniskillen, and had one son;

secondly, in 1928 to Gwladys Helen (died 1943), daughter of Rupert Evelyn Beckett, formerly wife of Sir Charles Markham, second baronet. He was succeeded as fourth baron by his son, Thomas Pitt Hamilton (born 1900).

A portrait of Delamere by F. R. Copnall, hangs in the chamber of the Legislative Council, Nairobi. A statue, by Lady Kennet, stands at the junction of Delamere Avenue and Government Road, Nairobi.

[*The Times*, 14 November 1931; Elspeth Huxley, *White Man's Country: Lord Delamere and the Making of Kenya*, 2 vols., 1935; private information; personal knowledge.]

ELSPETH HUXLEY.

CLARK, ALBERT CURTIS (1859–1937), classical scholar, born at Salisbury 21 February 1859, was the eldest son of Albert Charles Clark, writing-master at Haileybury College, by his wife, Ellen Curtis. He was educated at Hertford Grammar School and Haileybury College, and afterwards at Balliol College, Oxford, of which he was an exhibitioner. After a brilliant undergraduate career, during which he gained first classes in classical moderations (1879) and *literae humaniores* (1881), the Ireland (1879) and the Craven (1882) scholarships, Clark was elected (1882) to a classical fellowship at Queen's College, where, first as lecturer (1882–1887), and then as tutor (1887–1913), he not only proved himself a teacher and lecturer of exceptional ability, but won a world-wide reputation by the distinction and originality of his work upon the text of Cicero's orations.

In 1895 Clark produced a full-scale edition of the *Pro Milone* (with English notes), which was followed by four volumes containing the text of the following speeches: *Pro Milone, Caesarianae, Philippicae* (1900); *Pro Sex. Roscio, de imperio Cn. Pompei, pro Cluentio, in Catilinam, pro Murena, pro Caelio* (1905); *Pro Quinctio, pro Roscio Comoedo, pro Caecina, de lege agraria, pro C. Rabirio, pro Flacco, in Pisonem, pro Rabirio Postumo* (1909); *Pro Tullio, pro Fonteio, pro Sulla, pro Archia, pro Plancio, pro Scauro* (1911). To these must be added his edition of Asconius (1907). These volumes reveal scholarship, learning, and industry of the highest quality. Clark made a thorough collation and classification of the manuscripts, and threw new light upon their history and value in his *Collations from the Harleian MS. of Cicero 2682* (1891), *The Vetus*

Cluniacensis of Poggio (1905), and the *Inventa Italorum* (1909). Of these *The Vetus Cluniacensis* is his *chef d'œuvre*, a masterpiece of erudition, detective ability, and constructive power.

Clark had in 1909 been appointed university reader in Latin, a deserved tribute to the distinction of his work, and when in 1913 the Corpus Christi professorship of Latin fell vacant, his claim to the succession was universally acknowledged. Three minor works of considerable interest belong to the period of his readership: the *Fontes Prosae Numerosae* (1909), a collection of ancient evidences for Latin prose rhythms; *The Cursus in Mediaeval and Vulgar Latin* (1910), a fascinating study showing that the rhythms of classical oratory were preserved in medieval Latin, with this difference that, whereas the classical rhythm was based on quantity, the medieval was based on stress accent; and *Prose Rhythm in English* (1913) wherein he sought to relate the Latin rhythms with those of English.

The works published by Clark during his tenure of the chair, despite their erudition and ingenuity, are on the whole less convincing. They are largely concerned with the application of stichometry to textual problems presented by the Greek Testament, a field in which he moved with less security, while his interest in this method had become almost an obsession. In his *Primitive Text of the Gospels and Acts* (1914) he employed it to explain the difference between the two main families of manuscripts, contending that the longer text of the *Codex Bezae* and its kindred represented the primitive form, and that the shorter version given by the *Codices Sinaiticus* and *Vaticanus* was due to line-omissions. To this scheme Clark returned in the elaborate edition of *The Acts of the Apostles* published in 1933; there, however, he laid less emphasis on stichometric principles and held that the shorter version of the Acts was largely due to deliberate revision. He also sought to show that the *Codex Bezae* came not from the West but from Egypt, and that the author of the Acts was not the author of St. Luke's Gospel. Between the publication of these two works Clark had returned to his first love in a learned and valuable work, *The Descent of Manuscripts* (1918), illustrated in the main from the text of Cicero, but extending its survey to the manuscripts of Plato and Demosthenes. Here again the importance of stichometry is perhaps overstressed.

In 1934 ill health and failing sight led Clark to resign his chair: he retired to London where he died, unmarried, 5 February 1937. He received honorary degrees from the universities of Durham, Dublin, Manchester, and Oxford, and was elected an honorary fellow of his three colleges (Balliol, Queen's, and Corpus Christi) and a fellow of the British Academy (1916). But he was something more than a great scholar: he was a delightful human being who could carry his learning lightly, the best of company, full of humour and of wit, a perfect raconteur; above all, he was courteous, warm-hearted, and kindly, ready with his help and counsel for all who sought it. As a scholar he won admiration; as a man, affection and regard.

[*The Times*, 6 February 1937; Cyril Bailey, *Albert Curtis Clark, 1859–1937* in *Proceedings* of the British Academy, vol. xxiii, 1937; personal knowledge.]

H. E. Butler.

CLARKE, Sir EDWARD GEORGE (1841–1931), lawyer and politician, was the eldest son and third of the six children of Job Grey Clarke, by his wife, Frances, daughter of Henry George, of Bath. His father, who came from Axbridge in Somersetshire, kept a small silversmith's shop in King William Street in the City of London, in the rooms over which he lived with his family, and there Clarke was born 15 February 1841. At the age of ten he was sent for two years as a boarder to College House, Edmonton, where his health, previously delicate, was set up for life. In December 1854 he was taken from the City Commercial School in Lombard Street, where he had spent another two years, to assist his father in the shop: and he remained in that uncongenial occupation until nearly the end of 1858. In February 1859 he took up a clerkship in the India Office, which had been recently established on the dissolution of the old East India Company. He obtained the clerkship by examination. There were 400 candidates and Clarke was placed seventh on the list, a very remarkable achievement considering how scanty had been his opportunities for education. He had, however, made the most of those opportunities. When serving in the shop he spent any spare time in reading and, after the shop was closed, he attended evening classes regularly, becoming, in 1858, the first associate in arts of the university of Oxford. Moreover, he was gifted with a

very retentive memory and his industry never flagged.

Clarke found that the life of a clerk in a government office was as little to his liking as that of a shop assistant. In 1860 he happened to hear the aged Lord Lyndhurst make one of his last speeches in the House of Lords and was fired with ambition to be called to the bar and to make such a career for himself. Accordingly, when, later that same year, the government, desiring to reduce the clerical staff at the India Office, offered compensation to clerks who were willing to resign, Clarke sent in his resignation and received £253 by way of compensation. It was an act of great courage and self-confidence—qualities which Clarke displayed throughout his life—to give up an assured competence for the hazards of a career at the bar, more especially since several years would necessarily elapse before he could be called and begin to earn an income at that profession. During those years he supported himself by reporting law cases and parliamentary debates and by writing literary reviews: but in addition to those sources of income he obtained, in 1861, one of the Tancred studentships at Lincoln's Inn which provided him with an income of £95 for six years. In June 1861 he was admitted as a student of Lincoln's Inn: in November 1864 he was called to the bar: and in 1880 he took silk. He became a bencher of his Inn in 1892 and was treasurer in 1906. From the time when he became a Q.C. he was beyond all question one of the most eminent, if not the most eminent, of the leaders of the Common Law bar. He was an admirable forensic orator in jury cases, and for many years he was engaged on one side or the other in most of the important cases on the Common Law side of the High Court.

From the time when he quitted the India Office Clarke took an active interest in politics. He was a strong conservative and an enthusiastic admirer of Lord Beaconsfield. In February 1880 he stood as the conservative candidate at a by-election for the borough of Southwark and won a notable victory over his liberal opponent. He was defeated at the general election which took place in April of that year; but he was elected at a by-election for Plymouth in July, and for the next twenty years he represented that constituency in the House of Commons.

While making a name for himself at the bar Clarke worked hard for the conservative cause both in parliament and in the country and when, in the summer of 1885, Lord Salisbury formed his first administration, Clarke had reasonable grounds for thinking that he might be appointed one of the law officers. His claims were, however, disregarded. Richard Webster, subsequently Viscount Alverstone and lord chief justice of England [q.v.], who was not then and had never been a member of parliament, was appointed attorney-general. On hearing a rumour that Webster would be appointed attorney-general Clarke actually wrote to Lord Salisbury that it would be a mistake to make such an appointment and at the same time with characteristic frankness he sent a copy of the letter to Webster himself. In the following year, when Lord Salisbury, after the defeat of Gladstone's first home rule bill, was again called upon to form a government, Clarke's claims were recognized and he was appointed solicitor-general, an office which he continued to hold until 1892 when the government resigned and Gladstone formed his last administration. The position which Clarke had by that time attained in the House of Commons, where eminent barristers are often apt to fail, is shown by the fact that he was chosen to answer the speech of Gladstone when he introduced his second home rule bill in February 1893.

The general election of 1895 gave the unionist party a clear majority over the combined forces of the liberals and the Irish nationalists and Lord Salisbury became prime minister for the third time. He invited Clarke to resume the office of solicitor-general subject, however, to the condition, which Webster as attorney-general had accepted, that he would not take any private practice so long as he held the office. Clarke refused the office on that condition. Two years later Lord Salisbury offered Clarke the important judicial office of master of the Rolls, but Clarke declined that office also, because it would have precluded him from taking any part in politics. During the parliament which sat from 1895 to 1900 Clarke, although sitting as a private member on the government side of the House, seems to have developed a cross-bench mind. He criticized the conduct of the Foreign Office in the matter of the Venezuelan boundary dispute; he crossed swords with the chancellor of the Exchequer, Sir Michael Hicks Beach [q.v.], on the subject of Irish taxation; and he denounced the conduct of the colonial secretary, Joseph Chamberlain [q.v.], with regard to the Boer Republics. He even went so far as to suggest that Lord Salisbury should himself take over from Chamberlain the management of South African affairs. His speeches on these subjects—for Clarke considered it his duty to express his opinions publicly—were very displeasing to many of his supporters in Plymouth. He was asked in 1900 to resign his seat, and thereupon did so.

At the general election of 1906 Clarke was elected as the senior member for the City of London; but in May he resigned his seat ostensibly on the ground that his health was no longer good enough for both his work at the bar and his parliamentary duties. Thus at the age of sixty-five he abandoned the political ambition which he had formed when he was a clerk at the India Office. He continued in practice at the bar until 1914, retiring nearly fifty years after the date of his call. The position which he had attained in the profession is marked by the fact that in 1908 he was sworn of the Privy Council, and that on his retirement the bench and bar gave him a dinner in Lincoln's Inn hall, at which the prime minister, H. H. Asquith, presided.

Clarke was a staunch supporter of the Church of England, and in 1894 had built at his sole expense a church beside the river at Staines, dedicated in honour of St. Peter, and on his retirement from the bar he lived at a house called Peterhouse which he had built adjacent to the church. There he died 26 April 1931 in his ninety-first year. On the following day there appeared in *The Times* newspaper a long obituary notice which he had himself written and sent to *The Times* eighteen years before with a covering letter expressing the remarkable opinion that an obituary notice of a man who has reached old age should be written by himself.

Clarke was twice married: first, in 1866 to Ann (died 1881), eldest daughter of George Mitchell, builder, of Camberwell; secondly, in 1882 to Kathleen Mathilda, daughter of Augustus William Bryant. By his first wife he had one son and three daughters, the eldest of whom died in infancy and the second as a child. By his second wife he had two sons, the younger of whom died at birth.

A portrait of Clarke, painted by S. J. Solomon and presented to him by the bar of England, was given by him to the Royal Courts of Justice and hangs there.

Cartoons by 'Spy' appeared in *Vanity Fair* 13 March 1880 and 11 June 1903.

[*The Times*, 27 April 1931; D. Walker-Smith and E. Clarke, *The Life of Sir Edward Clarke*, 1939; Sir Edward Clarke, *The Story of My Life*, 1918, and *Selected Speeches, with Introductory Notes*, 1908.]

MALCOLM M. MACNAGHTEN.

CLARKE, GEORGE SYDENHAM, BARON SYDENHAM OF COMBE (1848–1933), administrator, was born at Swinderby, Lincolnshire, 4 July 1848, the eldest of the five sons of Walter John Clarke, vicar of Swinderby, later of Knoyle House, Folkestone, by his wife, Maria Frances, daughter of Joseph Mayor, rector of South Collingham, Nottinghamshire. His mother was a first cousin of J. E. B. Mayor [q.v.]. After being sent successively to Repton, Rossall, Haileybury, and finally Wimbledon, he passed both first into and first out of the Royal Military Academy, being gazetted to the Royal Engineers in 1868. In 1871 he was appointed lecturer on practical geometry and engineer drawing at the newly established Royal Indian Engineering College at Coopers Hill, near Staines, where he remained until 1880.

Although he took part in the Egyptian expedition of 1882 and the eastern Sudan campaign of 1885, Clarke saw little active service, and his promotion was slow, for the military authorities of those days had little regard for scientific young officers with progressive views. In other quarters, however, his gifts were fully appreciated, and he was given numerous missions abroad for investigating and reporting on technical questions, in one of which the correctness of his judgement was afterwards to be startlingly proved when armoured cupolas, on which at Bucharest he had reported unfavourably in 1885, collapsed before the German guns at Liège and Namur in 1914. As an alternative he advocated earthwork defences such as had done good service for the Turks at Plevna, and his views carried great weight with the Colonial Defence Committee to which he was secretary from 1885 to 1892. As secretary to the royal commission on navy and army administration (1888–1890), he became an earnest advocate of closer ties between the mother-country and its overseas possessions in matters naval and military, as well as between the navy and the army. It was indeed to Clarke's room at the Horse Guards that for the first time a naval officer was brought from the

Admiralty for joint discussion of imperial strategy. Moreover, during his seven years (1894–1901) as superintendent of the royal carriage department at Woolwich Arsenal, he had realized sooner than anyone else what a strain a war, such as the South African, would put upon the resources of the Empire in the production of war material; and when during that war the need was recognized for reorganizing the War Office, Clarke was made in 1900 a member of the committee entrusted with the preparation of a scheme of reform, and in 1903 he was summoned home to serve, with Lord Esher and Lord Fisher [qq.v.], on the War Office reconstitution committee set up by the conservative government. This committee [see BRETT, REGINALD, VISCOUNT ESHER] reported within two months, in March 1904, recommending the establishment of a general staff, later known as the Army Council, and this led on eventually to the Imperial General Staff and the Haldane reforms. The report was immediately adopted and Clarke was appointed to the Committee for Imperial Defence.

As early as 1901 Clarke had interrupted his labours on military organization by accepting the office of governor of Victoria. At Melbourne he made himself popular and respected by all, but the constitutional checks imposed by his position on a masterful spirit might have led to early retirement but for his summons home in 1903. In 1907, however, on the recommendation of Campbell-Bannerman, he was appointed governor of Bombay, and this ushered in the period of his life in which he received most fame and obloquy.

Clarke was a lifelong liberal, and, as often happens to men of that temper, his views came to be identified at the end of his life with hide-bound toryism. Given co-operation with Indians, he expected to do much to advance the political life of India, but he was soon disillusioned. His appeals for co-operation, which caused him to be looked upon as 'dangerously pro-native', fell upon deaf ears, and believing as a liberal that it was his paramount duty to maintain law and order without distinction of race or colour or creed, he formed the deepest suspicion of the motives of the Indian political leaders and of the result to the unvocal millions of the races of India if democratic institutions were introduced. When therefore Tilak, the popular Brahman leader, advocated the use of the bomb, Clarke had him prosecuted, but on his conviction, commuted his transportation to imprisonment at Mandalay. The prosecution was regarded, even by Morley, no believer in popular government for India, as unwise; nevertheless, when he resigned in 1913, Clarke left India as one who had brought great improvements, moral and material, to Bombay, who had paved the way for the construction of the great Sukkur barrage, and who left a memory of a 'great, fearless, and upright' governor whom Indians would visit in his retirement in Kent and ask for his advice in their political problems. He was raised to the peerage on his retirement as Baron Sydenham of Combe, of Dulverton, Somerset.

It was a profound disappointment to Sydenham that his services were not called upon by the government in the war with Germany in 1914, but he had been appointed in 1913 chairman of a royal commission on venereal diseases, the duties of which he carried out most judiciously. Other notable services which he rendered were as chairman (1915–1916) of the central tribunal hearing appeals from local committees administering the National Service Act, and as a member (1918) of Lord Bryce's conference on the second chamber. After the war he became more and more mistrustful of the opinions apparently dominant, and both in ample writings and in speeches in the House of Lords he made it no secret that he regarded the future of the Empire and of civilization with the deepest pessimism. He died in London 7 February 1933.

Sydenham was twice married: first, in 1871 to Caroline Emily (died 1908), eldest daughter of General Peregrine Henry Fellowes, and had one daughter, who predeceased her father; secondly, in 1910 to Phyllis Angelina Rosamond, youngest daughter of George Morant, Grenadier Guards, resident at Shirley House, Carrickmacross, co. Monaghan, and widow of Captain Arthur Reynolds, East Surrey Regiment. There were no other children and the title became extinct. He was appointed C.M.G. (1887), K.C.M.G. (1893), G.C.M.G. (1905), G.C.I.E. (1907), G.C.S.I. (1911), and G.B.E. (1917). He was elected F.R.S. in 1896.

A portrait of Sydenham by a Hungarian artist, Miss Schulz, is in the possession of his widow.

[*The Times*, 8, 9, 11, and 15 February 1933; Lord Sydenham, *My Working Life*, 1927, and *Studies of an Imperialist*, 1928.]

ALFRED COCHRANE.

CLARKE, MAUDE VIOLET (1892–1935), historian, was born in Belfast 7 May 1892. In 1903 her father, Richard James Clarke, rector of Trinity church, Belfast, later archdeacon of Connor, accepted the living of Carnmoney on the outskirts of the city, and here, in an atmosphere of religion and scholarship, Maude, the second child and only daughter, and her three brothers grew up. Her mother was Anne Nugent, daughter of John Thomas Jessop, J.P., of Mount Jessop, co. Longford.

After being educated at a school in Belfast and later at Alexandra School and College, Dublin, Miss Clarke graduated with a first class in history at the university of Belfast. She then went with a scholarship to Lady Margaret Hall, Oxford, where she was awarded a first class in modern history in 1915. The three years from 1916 to 1919 were spent in Belfast, deputizing for the professor of modern history, (Sir) Frederick Maurice Powicke, and in the last-named year she returned to Oxford as history tutor of Somerville College. The rest of her life was divided between Coole Glebe (the rectory house of Carnmoney) and Somerville College, of which she became a fellow in 1922 and vice-principal in 1933. With a witty Irish tongue masking a deeply religious nature, and an iron will, she made an indelible impression upon her pupils and contemporaries, living a free social life and extending open hospitality to a wide circle of friends. She lived, in fact, at full pressure in these years, making for herself a many-sided reputation as a college tutor and administrator, as a university lecturer (1930), and, not least, as a scholar. A fine future seemed to lie ahead when, in 1933, she was smitten with cancer, and she died at Carnmoney 17 November 1935, working almost to the last after a stoical resistance to the disease.

Although the best was still to come— a projected history of fourteenth-century England—Miss Clarke had achieved at her death an established reputation by a number of articles of which 'The Origin of Impeachment' (1934) and a brilliant paper on the Wilton Diptych (1931), now in the National Gallery, are outstanding. An elaborate study of the *Modus tenendi parliamentum* was also finished just before her death and published posthumously (1936) under the title of *Medieval Representation and Consent*. Equally sure in its treatment of both the English and the Irish material, the book is an important contribution to the history of parliament at a critical phase in its development. A collection of her papers was published as *Fourteenth Century Studies* (edited by L. S. Sutherland and M. McKisack, 1937). Although written for the scholar these articles are uniformly stimulating and at times provoking. With their great learning lightly borne, close reasoning, and clear cut conclusions they are eminently original, and even the unproved hypothesis will be found to have thrown light on the problem.

A distinguished personality and a tireless worker, Miss Clarke advanced knowledge by her own work and through that of her pupils. Her premature death was incontestably a loss, not easily measured, to later medieval studies in England.

[*The Times*, 18 November 1935; Memoir by E. L. Woodward prefixed to M. V. Clarke, *Fourteenth Century Studies*, 1937 (portrait); personal knowledge.]   V. H. GALBRAITH.

CLERK, SIR DUGALD (1854–1932), mechanical engineer, was born at Glasgow 31 March 1854, the eldest son of Donald Clerk, machinist, of Glasgow, by his wife, Martha Symington, second daughter of John Brown, of Glasgow. He was about fifteen years old when he began his training in the drawing office of Messrs. H. O. Robinson & company, of Glasgow, and in his father's works, also attending classes at the West of Scotland Technical College; and from 1871 to 1876 he studied at Anderson's College, Glasgow, and the Yorkshire College of Science, Leeds, under the chemist (Sir) T. E. Thorpe [q.v.], who made him one of his assistants and set him to work on the fractionation of petroleum oils, an exercise which proved of great value to him in his subsequent investigations. He had intended to become a chemical engineer, but his attention was drawn to the gas engine by seeing one of the Lenoir type at work in a joiner's shop in Glasgow, and it, with other forms of the internal-combustion engine, became the leading interest of his life.

After his return to Glasgow from Leeds Clerk was for a short time assistant to E. J. Mills, the Young professor of technical chemistry at the Royal Technical College; he then devoted himself to research on the theory and design of the gas engine with the Glasgow firm of Messrs. Thomson, Sterne & company from 1877 to 1885 and with Messrs. Tangyes, of Birmingham, from 1886 to 1888. In the latter year he joined his friend (Sir)

George Croydon (later Lord) Marks in the firm of Messrs. Marks and Clerk, consulting engineers and patent agents; this partnership lasted for the rest of his life. From 1892 to 1899 he was engineering director of Messrs. Kynoch, of Birmingham, for whom he designed machinery for the manufacture of ammunition, and from 1902 he was a director and from 1929 until his death chairman of the National Gas Engine Company, of Ashton-under-Lyne.

Clerk began his work on the gas engine at the end of 1876. His first patent, taken out in 1877, was followed by a second in 1878, and in 1881 he patented an engine working on what became known as the Clerk (two-stroke) cycle, in which the main crankshaft received an impulse at each revolution, in contrast to the Otto (four-stroke) engine in which there was one impulse for each two revolutions. Engines of the Clerk type were manufactured in considerable numbers, but their popularity waned for a time after the lapse of the Otto patent in 1890. The Clerk cycle, however, came into extensive use for gas engines of the larger sizes.

The long series of researches carried out by Clerk on the internal-combustion engine, the specific heat of gases, and the explosion of gaseous mixtures won him an international reputation. He embodied his results in a book, *The Gas Engine* (1886), which subsequently appeared as *The Gas, Petrol and Oil Engine* (1909), and in many communications to scientific and technical societies, particularly the Institution of Civil Engineers, to which, between 1882 and 1928, he contributed five papers, besides two James Forrest lectures (1904 and 1920). The second of these lectures, dealing with coal conservation in the United Kingdom, was of wider scope than his other contributions, and with it may be coupled his Thomas Hawksley lecture to the Institution of Mechanical Engineers in 1915, on the world's supplies of fuel and motive power. In 1917 he delivered the first Trueman Wood lecture to the Royal Society of Arts.

During the war of 1914–1918 Clerk was director of Engineering Research at the Admiralty (1916–1917) and served on many committees concerned with the war effort. He was also chairman of the water power resources committee of the conjoint board of scientific societies (1917) and a member of the water power resources committee appointed by the Board of Trade in 1918. Other activities included chairmanship of the Delegacy of the City and Guilds College, South Kensington (1918–1919), and membership of the University Grants Commission and of the Carnegie Trust for Scotland. He was frequently a judge at the reliability trials which were fashionable in the early days of the motor-car.

Clerk, who was appointed K.B.E. in 1917, received honorary degrees from the universities of Glasgow, Leeds, Liverpool, Manchester, and St. Andrews. The Royal Society of Arts awarded him the Albert medal in 1922, and the Royal Society, of which he was elected a fellow in 1908, a Royal medal in 1924. For the papers which he read before the Institution of Civil Engineers he received the Watt medal (1882), Telford prize (1882 and 1886), and Telford gold medal (1907). He was president of many engineering societies, and would have been president of the Institution of Civil Engineers for the session of 1932–1933 had not ill health prevented him from assuming office. He married in 1883 Margaret (died 1930), elder daughter of Alexander Hanney, of Helensburgh. He died at his home at Ewhurst, Surrey, 12 November 1932.

[*Obituary Notices of Fellows of the Royal Society*, No. 2, December 1933 (portrait); *Engineer and Engineering*, 18 November 1932 (portraits); *Proceedings*, vol. ccxxxv, 1932–1933, and *Journal*, vol. xii, 1938–1939, of the Institution of Civil Engineers; *Proceedings* of the Institution of Mechanical Engineers, vol. cxxiii, 1932; *Nature*, 24 December 1932.]

H. M. Ross.

COBBE, Sir ALEXANDER STAN-HOPE (1870–1931), general, was born at Naini Tal, India, 5 June 1870, the second son of Lieutenant-General (Sir) Alexander Hugh Cobbe, 17th regiment, by his wife, Emily Barbara, daughter of Captain G. Stanhope Jones, 59th regiment. He was educated at Wellington and Sandhurst. Commissioned in the South Wales Borderers in 1889, he was promoted to lieutenant in 1892 but transferred to the Indian Staff Corps that year, his appointment being confirmed in 1894. He was attached to the 32nd Sikh Pioneers, with whom he saw active service in Chitral in 1895, taking part in Colonel (later Major-General) F. H. Kelly's great march to the relief of the Agency. He subsequently served in Nyasaland in 1898 and 1899 in various minor operations and with the Central African regiment in Ashanti in 1900, was wounded, and awarded the D.S.O. He was again on active service in 1902, in Somaliland, and won the V.C. at

Erego 6 October for good work with a Maxim gun when left alone in front of the line at a critical moment, while later he went out under heavy fire and brought in a wounded man. He had received his captaincy in 1900 and became major and brevet lieutenant-colonel in 1907.

Between 1902 and 1914 Cobbe held several staff appointments in India and at the War Office and was made aide-de-camp to the king and brevet-colonel in 1911. He went to France in October 1914 as general staff officer of the Lahore division, transferred to the staff of the Indian Corps in June 1915, and was later brigadier-general, General Staff, I Corps. Returning to India in January 1916 as director of staff duties and military training, he took over the Meerut 7th Indian division in Mesopotamia the following June, becoming major-general, and two months later succeeded General Sir Stanley Maude [q.v.] in the III Indian Corps, which he commanded in the operations of December 1916–February 1917 for the recapture of Kut al Amara, being particularly concerned with the clearance of the Khudhaira bend and the capture of the Sannaiyat position. He was later in charge of the operations which resulted in substantial success at Mushahida (March 1917) and Istabulat and the capture of Samarra (April) and also of the advance to Tikrit in October. In 1918 his corps carried out the advance upon Mosul which culminated after sharp fighting at Sharqat and on the Lesser Zab in the surrender of the main Turkish field force. Difficulties of supply and transport were great but Cobbe's plans resulted in an outstanding success.

Cobbe was appointed C.B. in 1915, K.C.B. in 1917, C.S.I. in 1918, and K.C.S.I. in 1919, becoming lieutenant-general in that year. From October 1919 to June 1920 and again in 1921 and 1922 he was military secretary at the India Office; he was general officer commanding-in-chief, Northern Command in India from 1926 to 1930, and had returned to his old post at the India Office shortly before he died. He had been promoted full general in February 1924, being the youngest holder of that rank in the army, and was made aide-de-camp general to the King and appointed G.C.B. in 1928. To the great pleasure of his old regiment he had been made colonel of the South Wales Borderers in 1922. An accomplished, as well as a gallant and popular, soldier, he had a fine record both as a staff officer and in command in the field and he inspired confidence as well as liking and respect.

Cobbe married in 1910 Winifred Ada, eldest daughter of Sir Albert Edward Bowen, first baronet, of Colworth Park, Bedfordshire, and had one son, who was killed in the war of 1939–1945 as an officer in the Royal Air Force, and two daughters. He died in London, after an operation, 29 June 1931.

[*The Times*, 1 July 1931; J. W. B. Merewether and F. Smith, *The Indian Corps in France* (1918); (Official) *History of the Great War. The Campaign in Mesopotamia*, vols. iii and iv, 1925–1927; regimental information.]

C. T. ATKINSON.

COCHRANE-BAILLIE, CHARLES WALLACE ALEXANDER NAPIER ROSS, second BARON LAMINGTON (1860–1940). [See BAILLIE.]

COCHRANE, DOUGLAS MACKINNON BAILLIE HAMILTON, twelfth EARL OF DUNDONALD (1852–1935), lieutenant-general, was born at Auchentoul House, Banff, 29 October 1852, the second son of Thomas Barnes Cochrane, eleventh Earl of Dundonald, a soldier, by his wife, Louisa Harriet, daughter of William Alexander Mackinnon of Mackinnon. He was a grandson of Thomas Cochrane, tenth Earl of Dundonald [q.v.].

Dundonald (then Lord Cochrane) was educated at a private school at Walton-on-Thames and at Eton, and in 1870 entered the army as cornet and sub-lieutenant in the 2nd Life Guards. During the following fifteen years he visited Germany and South America and in 1884 was sent in command of a contingent of the 2nd Life Guards to relieve General Gordon [q.v.] at Khartoum. He took part in the battles of Abu Klea and Gubat in 1885. His rides with dispatches across the desert to announce the seizure of Gakdul Wells and again to tell of the death of Gordon and the fall of Khartoum made him famous at the time. During this campaign he succeeded to the title (1885). For his services in Egypt he was mentioned in dispatches and promoted lieutenant-colonel on his return early in 1885. Four years later he became a brevet colonel. In 1890 he was made captain of the Queen's Guard, and in 1895 he took command of the 2nd Life Guards. Four years later the Boers attacked Natal, and, although his period of command had in the meantime expired, within a few weeks (October 1899) he landed at Cape Town and offered

his services to Sir Redvers Buller [q.v.] and was given command of the South Natal Field Force. With it he was engaged at Colenso, and early in 1900, in command of the 2nd Cavalry brigade, he took part in the Tugela fighting and on 28 February 1900 entered Ladysmith. Later the same year he commanded the combined 3rd Mounted and Natal Volunteer brigades in the fighting on the Biggarsberg, and at Laing's Nek and in the eastern Transvaal. When Buller resigned the command of the Natal army in October 1900 the brigade was broken up and Dundonald returned to England. For his services in the campaign he was mentioned in dispatches six times and promoted major-general (1900).

In December 1900 Dundonald sat on the Yeomanry Reorganization Committee which brought about many changes, particularly in replacing the sword by the rifle. In 1902 he was invited to take command of the Canadian Militia with a view to its reorganization and he accordingly proceeded in July to Ottawa where two years of inspections resulted in a scheme for a Canadian citizen army. He was author of *Cavalry Training, Canada* (1904). Owing, however, to political conflict, his work came to an end and he returned to England in 1904, and in 1906 served on the committee for the reorganization of the Territorial Army under the chairmanship of R. B. (Lord) Haldane [q.v.]. In 1906 he was promoted lieutenant-general and retired from the army in 1907. During the next few years he exerted himself in the interests of ex-servicemen and the work of their national association. He had, in 1897, designed a light machine-gun and a light ambulance, but neither was adopted for army use.

When war broke out in 1914 Dundonald was prevented by age from active participation, but he served his country as chairman of the Admiralty committee on smoke screens (1915), making use of plans drawn up by his grandfather, the proposals of which bore fruit in 1918. In 1921 he served as special ambassador on the occasion of the Peruvian centenary. He was appointed C.B. in 1896, K.C.V.O. in 1907, and K.C.B. in 1913.

In 1878 Dundonald married Winifred (died 1924), daughter of Robert Bamford-Hesketh, 2nd Life Guards, of Gwyrch Castle, Abergele, Denbighshire. They had two sons and three daughters. Although as a young officer in Africa he suffered an injury that somewhat handicapped him thereafter, he remained active to a late age, and at the age of seventy-seven he sailed a 14-ton boat across the Atlantic to South America. He died at his residence at Wimbledon Park, London, 12 April 1935, and was succeeded as thirteenth earl by his elder son, Thomas Hesketh Douglas Blair (born 1886).

A cartoon of Dundonald by 'Spy' appeared in *Vanity Fair* 8 May 1902. He is also included in the cartoon 'A General Group' by 'Spy', which appeared in *Vanity Fair* 29 November 1900.

[*The Times*, 13 April 1935 ; Lord Dundonald, *My Army Life*, 1926.]

C. V. OWEN.

COLERIDGE, STEPHEN WILLIAM BUCHANAN (1854–1936), author and anti-vivisectionist, was born in London 31 May 1854, the second son of John Duke (afterwards first Baron) Coleridge, lord chief justice of England [q.v.], by his first wife, Jane Fortescue, daughter of the Rev. George Turner Seymour, of Farringford, Isle of Wight. He was brother of the judge B. J. C. Coleridge, second Baron Coleridge [q.v.], and of Mr. Gilbert Coleridge, assistant master of the Crown Office from 1892 to 1921.

Stephen Coleridge did not go, as did his brothers, to Eton. He graduated from Trinity College, Cambridge, and after a year (1879–1880) spent in travel, became private secretary to his father (1884–1890). In 1886 he was called to the bar by the Middle Temple. In 1890 the lord chief justice appointed him clerk of assize for the South Wales circuit. His natural kindness and courtesy made him popular with the members of the circuit.

An inherited rhetorical faculty characterized Coleridge's writings both in prose and in verse. He appreciated good literature, and was an acceptable lecturer. His large output includes *A Morning in my Library* (1914), *An Evening in my Library among the English Poets* (1916), and other books of the same kind. He also published four volumes of *Letters to my Grandson* (1921–1923), telling him of the world about him, the happy life, and the glory of English prose and poetry. He had a pleasing amateur skill in painting, and showed at various exhibitions.

Coleridge was best known to the public for his outspoken attacks upon vivisection. Hatred of cruelty in all forms, especially to children and animals, was a marked feature of his character. He was one of the founders, in 1884, of the National Society for the Prevention of Cruelty to Children.

Although fond of games and outdoor pursuits, he disliked any sport that involved the taking of animal life, and became president of the League for the Prohibition of Cruel Sports. But he reserved his most violent denunciations for experiments, conducted in the interests of medical science, on living animals. In the opinion of many he carried his prejudices to unreasonable extremes. He would listen to no arguments which demonstrated the lifesaving value of the discoveries founded on vivisection, and went so far as to say that, even if the examples given to him were true, they were no justification for the practice. He even maintained that knowledge and reason were miserable bases on which to build conduct, character, and life. Such statements may well be thought to have damaged rather than furthered the cause which he advocated, and perhaps they did, but at the same time there must be hesitation in accepting this view without some qualification. Vivisection is not now the detestable and almost unmentionable horror that it was to the masses in the far-off days when Coleridge attacked it, but, on the evidence of those acquainted with the subject, is practised with more care for the alleviation or removal of animal suffering by the use of anaesthetics.

Coleridge was twice married: first, in 1879 to Geraldine Beatrix (died 1910), daughter and co-heir of Charles Manners Lushington, of Norton Court, Kent, and niece of Sir Stafford Northcote, first Earl of Iddesleigh [q.v.]; secondly, in 1911 to Susan, second daughter of Allan Duncan Stewart, of Bun Rannoch and Inverhadden, Perthshire. By his first marriage he had three sons, the eldest of whom predeceased his father. Coleridge died at his home at Chobham, Surrey, 10 April 1936.

A cartoon of Coleridge by 'Elf' appeared in *Vanity Fair* 27 July 1910.

[*The Times*, 11 April 1936; Stephen Coleridge, *Memories*, 1913.]

ALFRED COCHRANE.

COLLIER, JOHN (1850–1934), painter and writer on art, was born in London 27 January 1850, the younger son of the judge Robert Porrett Collier, afterwards first Lord Monkswell [q.v.], by his wife, Isabella Rose, daughter of William Rose Rose, of Wolston Heath, near Rugby, and Daventry. He was educated at Eton and then went abroad to study French and German, the latter at Heidelberg, with the intention of entering the diplomatic service, but instead he went into the City office of Sir John Pender [q.v.], chairman of the Telegraph Construction and Maintenance Company, whose trade-mark of the flying horse Collier designed. From May 1916 to December 1918 he served as a temporary clerk at the Foreign Office.

Collier's father did not oppose his desire to become a painter but introduced him to (Sir) Lawrence Alma-Tadema [q.v.] who, however, could not take him as a pupil, so Collier went to the Slade School of Art, afterwards studying in Paris and Munich. He began to exhibit at the Royal Academy at the age of twenty-five and continued to do so almost without a break until the year of his death. He was at his best in portraiture. He was vice-president of the Royal Society of Portrait Painters, and he is represented at the National Portrait Gallery by no fewer than eleven works, the subjects including Charles Darwin and T. H. Huxley. At the Tate Gallery he is represented by two pictures, 'The Last Voyage of Henry Hudson', a Chantrey purchase of 1881, and 'Henrietta Anne Huxley, aetat. LXXX', presented in 1928.

Collier's popular reputation rested upon his so-called 'problem pictures', which, under such titles as 'The Cheat' and 'The Fallen Idol', appeared at the Academy from time to time. He himself disliked the description and said that he merely depicted little tragedies of modern life and always endeavoured to make their meaning perfectly plain. Perhaps the fairest judgement of Collier as a painter is to say that he was concerned with accuracy rather than with truth in the artistic meaning of the word, which implies a certain amount of emotional deformation. Not that he was indifferent to feeling, but he recorded it in the subject rather than expressed it in the treatment. In portraiture he achieved a sober veracity slightly reminiscent of Frank Holl [q.v.]. If his publications, *A Primer of Art* (1882), *A Manual of Oil Painting* (1886), and *The Art of Portrait Painting* (1905), be taken into account, it is difficult to resist the conclusion that Collier had the scientific rather than the artistic habit of mind.

In personal relations Collier, who was a thin, bearded man, gave the impression of quiet tenacity and a sort of polite ruthlessness. He devoted much time and thought to the causes of Rationalism and divorce law reform. He was twice married: first, in 1879 to Marian, second daughter of Thomas Henry Huxley and sister of

Leonard Huxley [qq.v.], who herself drew portraits (she died in 1887, shortly after the birth of their only child, a daughter); secondly, in 1889 in Norway, to Ethel Gladys, fifth daughter of T. H. Huxley, the marriage being regularized in England by the passing of the Deceased Wife's Sister Act of 1907. By his second wife Collier had a son and a daughter. He died at his home in Hampstead 11 April 1934.

A self-portrait of Collier hangs in the Uffizi Gallery, Florence.

[*The Times*, 12 April 1934; personal knowledge.]   CHARLES MARRIOTT.

COLVILLE, SIR STANLEY CECIL JAMES (1861–1939), admiral, was born in London 21 February 1861, the second son of Charles John Colville, tenth Lord Colville of Culross, later Viscount Colville of Culross, chamberlain to Queen Alexandra both as Princess of Wales and as Queen (1873–1903). He was grandson of General Sir Charles Colville [q.v.]. His mother was Cecile Katherine Mary, only child by his first wife of Robert John Carrington, second Lord Carrington. After a short time at Marlborough, he entered the training ship *Britannia* as a naval cadet in 1874 and in 1876 was appointed as midshipman to the *Sultan* in the Mediterranean under Prince Alfred, Duke of Edinburgh [q.v.], and remained with the Duke when in 1878 he transferred to the *Black Prince* in the Channel squadron and afterwards on the North America and West Indies station. Next year he was sent to the *Boadicea*, wearing the broad pennant of Commodore (afterwards Admiral Sir) F. W. Richards [q.v.], at the Cape, and served on shore in the Zulu war. Promoted sub-lieutenant in 1880, he underwent the usual examinations at Portsmouth. In July 1882 he joined the *Alexandra*, flagship of Sir F. B. P. Seymour (afterwards Lord Alcester, q.v.) in the Mediterranean, being promoted lieutenant in November: thus he was present at the bombardment of Alexandria (11 July) and took part in the subsequent land operations. In 1883 he was appointed to the *Canada*, North America station, in which Prince George (afterwards King George V) was midshipman. From 1884 to 1885 Colville was again in the Mediterranean for service with the Nile flotilla during the Gordon relief expedition, and after a short spell at home in the royal yacht *Osborne*, resumed his service for three years under the Duke of Edinburgh, now commander-in-chief, Mediterranean, with his flag in the *Alexandra*. From 1889 to 1892 he was first lieutenant of the royal yacht *Victoria and Albert* and thus earned his promotion to commander (August 1892).

After three years as commander of Admiral (Sir) Compton Domvile's flagship *Trafalgar* in the Mediterranean, Colville was at the Sirdar's request lent to the Egyptian government for operations on the Nile, and while in command of the flotilla in the Dongola campaign (1896) was severely wounded [see BEATTY, DAVID, EARL]. For this service he was specially promoted captain in October, and appointed C.B. In 1897–1898 he filled his only office appointment in London as naval adviser to the inspector-general of fortifications at the War Office, and then went as flag-captain to Admiral Penrose Fitzgerald, in the *Barfleur*, in China for eighteen months. Next he was flag-captain to Sir Frederick Bedford, in the *Crescent*, on the North America station for two years, followed by three more as chief of staff to Domvile in the *Bulwark*, Mediterranean Fleet. For one year (1906) he had his only independent captain's command in the *Hindustan*, Atlantic Fleet, and reached flag-rank in November at the early age of forty-five. In 1908 he hoisted his flag in the *Bulwark* as rear-admiral of the Nore division of the recently formed Home Fleet under Sir Francis Bridgeman [q.v.]. A year later he was appointed to the first cruiser squadron, then part of the Channel Fleet under Lord Charles Beresford [q.v.] just before that great officer's dispute with Lord Fisher [q.v.] ended in his being ordered to haul down his flag.

Colville's squadron and the rest of the Channel Fleet was then absorbed into the expanded Home Fleet under Sir William May [q.v.], and he soon found himself in charge of the first three great battle cruisers of the *Dreadnought* era, with his flag in the *Indomitable*. He completed two years in that command, was promoted vice-admiral in April 1911, and a year later went to sea again as vice-admiral commanding the first battle squadron, Home Fleet. He completed the usual two-year term in June 1914, and thus was ashore on half-pay when war broke out. He naturally wished for a new command afloat but, nothing being available, he was offered the shore command of vice-admiral, Orkneys and Shetlands. During August Admiral Sir John (afterwards Earl) Jellicoe [q.v.] had found the detailed work of arranging for the protection of the un-

defended base at Scapa Flow, where the main Grand Fleet was stationed, too great a burden and asked for the appointment of a senior flag-officer who should be responsible for the general defences of the islands and base, and for the control of patrol vessels and minesweepers and the placing of obstacles to prevent the entry of enemy submarines. Colville in accepting the post asked that he should be treated as junior in rank to Jellicoe to whom he was senior in the flag-list by five months. The chief peril which he had to face was the entry of German submarines into the anchorage and his measures were so successful that, although there were several reports of such intrusion, in fact none did get in, but one of Colville's patrol vessels rammed and sank one outside the Hoxa entrance.

In 1916 Jellicoe reported in a dispatch that it was largely due to Colville that the work at the northern base was so cheerfully and energetically carried out, and official appreciation of the Admiralty was duly expressed. In February 1916 he succeeded Sir Hedworth Meux [q.v.] as commander-in-chief at Portsmouth, having been promoted admiral soon after going to Scapa in September 1914. He held that important post for the rest of the war, and finally hauled down his flag in March 1919. He was appointed first and principal aide-de-camp to the king in the following July and was placed on the retired list in April 1922.

In 1927 Colville was appointed rear-admiral of the United Kingdom and in 1929 vice-admiral of the United Kingdom and lieutenant of the Admiralty, ancient offices which had fallen into desuetude but were revived in 1901 by King Edward VII as high court appointments, corresponding to the military Silver Stick and Gold Stick in Waiting. He died at Crawley Down, Sussex, 9 April 1939.

Colville was a fine type of the 'salt horse' naval officer: without any pretensions to brilliance or scientific eminence he had a thorough knowledge of his profession, and possessed the complete confidence of his seniors. His lifelong energy and activity in everything concerned with the welfare of the navy were greatly appreciated by all ranks. He made no mistakes and was popular and trusted throughout the service. Although owing something no doubt to his association with the royal family, he well deserved his fortunate career in the Royal Navy.

Colville was appointed C.V.O. in 1902,

K.C.B. in 1912, and G.C.V.O. on the occasion of the King's visit to Scapa in July 1915, G.C.M.G. in 1919, and G.C.B. in 1921. Of foreign honours he received the Japanese Order of the Rising Sun, the Russian Order of St. Stanislaus, and the Order of the Crown of Siam, and he was a grand officer of the Legion of Honour. He married in 1902 Lady Adelaide Jane, youngest daughter of Admiral of the Fleet Richard James Meade, fourth Earl of Clanwilliam [q.v.], and had four sons.

An oil portrait of Colville, painted by Sir William Llewellyn (1927), is in private possession. A tinted charcoal drawing of him by Francis Dodd is in the Imperial War Museum.

[Admiralty records; private information.]
VINCENT W. BADDELEY.

COLVIN, IAN DUNCAN (1877–1938), journalist, biographer, and poet, was born at Inverness 29 September 1877, the second son of Duncan Colvin, Free Church minister, by his wife, Grace Macpherson Strother. He was educated at Crieff Academy and Inverness College, and was for a short time with the *Inverness Courier* before going in 1897 to Edinburgh University, where he studied under the professor of rhetoric and English literature, G. E. B. Saintsbury [q.v.], and won the gold medal for history and literature.

Having left Edinburgh for London, where he served for a time in the London office of the Allahabad *Pioneer*, Colvin went to India in 1900 to join the staff of that journal. Three years later he passed (suffering shipwreck on the way) to the *Cape Times* under (Sir) Maitland Park. Apart from his leading articles, he became famous there for his political verse and tales signed 'Rip van Winkle'.

In 1907 Colvin returned to London and in 1909 became leader writer of the *Morning Post*, his name being associated with its leading articles for the next twenty-eight years. Here his knowledge of imperial questions became blended with stern conservatism and a deadly satiric touch. Lord Morley is reported to have said of Colvin's writings: 'There has been nothing like it since Junius.' Colvin's industry and inspiration also found scope in historical work. During the war of 1914–1918 he wrote *The Germans in England 1066–1598* (1915) and *The Unseen Hand in English History* (1917), which traces the struggle between the Merchant Adventurers and the Hanseatic League; and subsequently appeared a book of his

on protection, *The Safety of the Nation* (1919).

After the war Colvin engaged vigorously in the party controversies which agitated the next two decades. On nearly all these questions he was severely critical of the official policies of the day, irrespective of the party in power. He denounced Lloyd George's Irish 'treaty' of December 1921, and was implacable in hostility towards the Indian Round Table Conference of 1931. He had no sympathy with the compromises and concessions with which successive governments sought to stave off awkward questions. They affronted the 'passionate logic' by which he claimed to test their worth. His last campaign was inspired by the civil war in Spain, where his sympathies were whole-heartedly on the side of General Franco. Assuredly he well deserved the title that was bestowed upon him by those who came under the lash of his satire and censure: 'keeper of the tory conscience'. He was never inconsistent or unstable. He never 'paltered with the truth to serve the hour'; but was as faithful to his friends as unsparing to his adversaries, however overborne the former and however highly placed the latter.

In 1922 Colvin published the *Life of Jameson*, in 1929 the *Life of General Dyer*, whose action at Amritsar in 1919 he championed; and, in 1934 and 1936 respectively, vols. ii and iii of the *Life of Lord Carson*, of which vol. i by Edward Marjoribanks had appeared in 1932. His other works include *South and East Africa* (1910) and *The Cape of Adventure* (1912); his satirical verse is collected in *Party Whips* (1912), *Intercepted Letters* (1913), and *A Wreath of Immortelles* (1924). *The Leper's Flute* (1920), a tragedy in blank verse, was later produced as an opera. His lyrical translations *After the Chinese* appeared in 1927, and he contributed many political and literary articles to the periodicals of his day. During the six years from 1931 to 1937 his journalism was interrupted by intermittent ill health, and his death occurred in a nursing home at Ealing 10 May 1938.

Colvin married in 1909 Sophie, daughter of the Rev. George Robson, of Edinburgh, and had three sons and one daughter.

[Private information; personal knowledge.]
ROBERT HIELD.

CONNOR, RALPH (pseudonym), divine and author. [See GORDON, CHARLES WILLIAM.]

CONWAY, ROBERT SEYMOUR (1864–1933), classical scholar and comparative philologist, the eldest son of Samuel Conway, Congregational minister, by his wife, Amy Curling, was born at Stoke Newington 20 September 1864. He was educated at the City of London School under Edwin Abbott [q.v.], from whom he learned accuracy in detail, an interest in comparative philology, and a broad outlook on literature. Proceeding to Cambridge as a scholar of Gonville and Caius College, he obtained first classes in both parts of the classical tripos (1885, 1887). He was distinguished in part ii for an essay on *Verner's Law in Italy* (published 1887). Conway was appointed classical lecturer at Newnham College, Cambridge, where he met Margaret Mary, daughter of William Hall, an iron-master in the Midlands, whom he married in 1891. Shortly after this appointment he was elected a fellow of his college. In 1893 he became professor of Latin at University College, Cardiff, and in 1903 Hulme professor of Latin in the university of Manchester, where he remained until his resignation in 1929. He improved the teaching of Latin and established a final honours examination in Latin alone.

In 1897 Conway published *The Italic Dialects* (2 vols.), which was followed after many years by *The Prae-Italic Dialects of Italy* (with Joshua Whatmough and Elizabeth Johnson, 3 vols., 1933). While at Manchester he undertook an edition of Livy. He set about his task with enthusiasm and examined many manuscripts, especially in Italy. Three successive volumes were published (Books i–v, 1914; vi–x, 1919; xxi–xxv, 1929) in collaboration with William Charles Flamstead Walters, after whose death he produced a fourth volume (Books xxvi–xxx, published posthumously, 1935), with the help of Stephen Keymer Johnson. The work is very thorough but unnecessarily detailed. Conway's other great interest was in Virgil: or, as he always insisted on spelling it, 'Vergil'. In 1907 he published in collaboration with J. B. Mayor and William Warde Fowler [q.v.] a small but important book on *The Messianic Eclogue*; and many papers on Virgilian subjects came from his pen, including an attempt to find a new site for Virgil's farm (*Where was Vergil's Farm?*, 1923). The edition of the *Aeneid*, Book I, published in 1935 after his death by his son Geoffrey Seymour Conway is perhaps his happiest piece of work, for it combines all his main interests.

Conway was an accurate scholar in his own fields, but they were somewhat limited. He never lectured or wrote on a Greek author, and outside Livy, Virgil, and Cicero his acquaintance with Latin authors was not comprehensive. But he had great enthusiasms and a power of instigating his pupils to research on their own account. Conway's frequent visits to Italy gave him a deep love of the country, and it was a high pleasure to him when in 1929 he was made Commander of the Order of the Crown of Italy. Among other distinctions he received honorary degrees from the universities of Dublin (1921), Padua (1922), and Oxford (1928); and he was elected an honorary fellow of Gonville and Caius College in 1920 and a fellow of the British Academy in 1918. He was a founder of the Classical Association, and its president in 1927.

Conway died in London 28 September 1933. He had one son and four daughters.

[*The Times*, 29 September 1933; Cyril Bailey, *Robert Seymour Conway, 1864–1933*, in *Proceedings* of the British Academy, vol. xxii, 1936; personal knowledge.]

CYRIL BAILEY.

CONWAY, WILLIAM MARTIN, BARON CONWAY OF ALLINGTON (1856–1937), art critic and collector and mountaineer, was born at Rochester 12 April 1856, the only son of William Conway, vicar of St. Nicholas's church, Rochester, afterwards rector of St. Margaret's church, Westminster, by his wife, Elizabeth, daughter of Adam Martin, M.D., of Rochester. Martin Conway was educated at Repton and Trinity College, Cambridge, where the counter attraction of the Fitzwilliam Museum robbed him of that first class in the historical tripos to which he had good reason to aspire. The university librarian, Henry Bradshaw [q.v.], who became his greatest friend, was delighted by his interest in woodcuts and early printed books. 'This is the most wonderful thing that has happened to me', he exclaimed, 'here have I been for twenty-five years studying the early printed books, and hitherto not one individual has taken the smallest interest in the subject.' Bradshaw financed the journeys on which Conway collected the material for his *Woodcutters of the Netherlands in the Fifteenth Century* (1884), which was to rank as the most important of his thirty books. After leaving Cambridge, where he was a university extension lecturer from 1882 to 1887, Conway lectured and wrote a book on *Early Flemish Artists* (1887), a masterly and beautifully written contribution to art criticism, republished in 1921 as *The Van Eycks and their Followers*.

Conway became Roscoe professor of art at University College, Liverpool, at the early age of twenty-nine (1885), and held the post until 1888. He was Slade professor of fine art at Cambridge from 1901 to 1904, and in 1917 was appointed director-general of the Imperial War Museum. He was the first to realize the value of a systematic and comprehensive collection of photographic records of architecture and works of art. He presented his collection of 100,000 carefully classified photographs to the Courtauld Institute of Art, in which the Conway library has a house to itself.

Conway first saw the Alps at the age of sixteen, and from 1872 to 1901 he missed very few Alpine seasons. He was not a natural athlete, or a good rock climber, and the ideal mountaineer whom he extolled in a famous paper read before the Alpine Club was, by an odd coincidence, very like Conway himself. He was one 'who loves first and foremost to wander far and wide among the mountains, does not willingly sleep two consecutive nights in the same inn, hates centres, gets tired of a district, always wants to see what is on the other side of any range of hills, prefers passes to peaks, but hates not getting to the top of anything he starts for; chooses the easiest and most normal route, likes to know the names of all the peaks in view, and cannot bear to see a group of peaks, none of which he has climbed'.

Passes always moved Conway to more enthusiasm than peaks, and inspired the most effective of his mountain writing. His tastes found expression in that long Alpine journey which is recorded in *The Alps from End to End* (1895). In 1892 he mapped 2,000 square miles of the Karakoram (Himalayas) range, an achievement which earned him his knighthood in 1895. He made the first crossing of Spitsbergen in 1896, and his experiments with ski on that occasion placed him among the pioneers of British ski-ing. In 1898 he visited the Bolivian Andes and climbed Illimani, Sorate, and Aconcagua (22,900 ft.). He was president of the Alpine Club from 1902 to 1904, and first president of the Alpine Ski Club in 1908.

Conway's *Zermatt Pocket Book* (1881) is the ancestor of an immense and inter-national family of technical guides for the climber, and in particular for the guideless climber. By chronicling the routes which had been climbed, he indirectly gave an impetus, as has been remarked, to the pioneering of new routes. Conway was responsible for many beautiful mountain names, such as Wellenkuppe, Windjoch, and Dent du Requin. His gift of conveying in words the elusive qualities of a painting explains the evocative power of his best mountain writing. He looked at peaks and glaciers with the trained eye of a connoisseur of colour and form, quick to note not only the more dramatic effects, but also the elusive beauty of some apparently featureless snowfield, such as the Plaine Morte, the theme of one of the finest descriptive passages in Alpine literature, his contributions to which are also marked by his keen, discerning interest in the peoples and historic traditions of the countries in which he climbed. His swan song as a mountaineer and his favourite book, *Mountain Memories*, was published in 1920.

Conway, who received honorary degrees from the universities of Durham and Manchester in 1919, represented the combined English Universities as a unionist from 1918 until he was raised to the peerage as Baron Conway of Allington in 1931. He would not have welcomed 'the century of the common man', for he did not believe in the infallibility of the majority, and the Conway who, as a young man, referred with contempt to 'the insane cry of "Liberty, Equality and Fraternity" under the echoes of which the revolutionaries of Paris banished the reality of all three from the soil of Europe', expressed his mature mind in his depreciatory diagnosis of *The Crowd in Peace and War* (1915). He considered this to be his best book. Conway was indulgent to human folly, and felt, to paraphrase Montaigne, that it was paying a man's views too high a compliment to burn with indignation because of them. His political friends were drawn indiscriminately from all parties. He was a genuine conservative but he was created a peer by Ramsay MacDonald, and he was on such friendly terms with Leonid Borisovich Krassin that he was among the first to obtain permission to visit the new Russia, where the Bolshevists surrendered to his charm and gave him every facility to collect material for his book *The Art Treasures in Soviet Russia* (1925). In the mountaineering world he had the distinction of being the only eminent mountaineer with whom W. A. B. Coolidge [q.v.] found it impossible to pick a quarrel. Few men had a larger circle of friends, and few men could have felt less need for the more intimate and enduring forms of friendship. 'Whether in the Alps or the Himalayas his friendships seldom remained coherent for very long.'

Conway was twice married: first, in 1884 to Katrina (died 1933), the beautiful daughter of Charles Lambard, of Augusta, Maine, U.S.A., builder of the Chicago and Western Railway; secondly, in 1934 to Iva, daughter of Daniel Christian and widow of Reginald Lawson, of Saltwood Castle, Kent. By his first marriage he had one daughter. He died in London 19 April 1937.

[Lord Conway, *Episodes in a Varied Life*, 1932, and *A Pilgrim's Quest for the Divine*, 1936; *Alpine Journal*, November 1937; private information; personal knowledge.]

ARNOLD LUNN.

COOK, ARTHUR JAMES (1883–1931), miners' leader, was born at Wookey, Somerset, 22 November 1883, the eldest son in a family of three sons and seven daughters of Thomas Cook, by his wife, Selina Brock. His mother had been a travelling dressmaker, and as his father spent twenty-one years in the 20th Foot (Lancashire Fusiliers), all the family except Arthur were born in English or Irish barracks. As a child he had learned to beat the drum and blow the bugle, but at the age of twelve, in rebellion against paternal discipline, and aided by his mother, he was smuggled from the Curragh in a vessel bound for Bristol. Farm work at half a crown a week preceded mining, and migrating to South Wales he spent twenty-one years in underground work. Christian Endeavour and Band of Hope membership shaped him as a boy preacher, who at sixteen was conducting singing missions among the Baptists. The independent labour party claimed him in 1905 and he was kept out of many pulpits as a result of his socialist enthusiasm. Association with the South Wales Miners' Federation afforded him a scholarship to study Marxian economics at the Central Labour College in 1911 and 1912. After filling various lodge offices, he was appointed agent for Rhondda No. 1 district and a member of the South Wales Federation executive in 1919. He also represented the Welsh miners on the Miners' Federation of Great Britain, and, upon the resignation of Frank Hodges, in 1924, was elected secretary and at the same time secretary of the International Miners' Federation. For a time he served on the Rhondda Urban District Council and was a governor of the Porth Schools. Mining disputes in 1918 and 1921 led to his imprisonment on two occasions; the second time he was charged with incitement to revolutionary rioting. He was a member of three coal commissions and was a government delegate to the coal conference held under the auspices of the International Labour Organization at Geneva in 1930.

Cook became a national figure, engaging extensively in trade union and socialist propaganda, and in particular voicing the claims of the miners before the wider public. Associated with the South Wales Miners' unofficial reform committee which issued *The Miners' Next Step* (1912), Cook was attracted to the syndicalist policy and was a leading figure in the General Strike in 1926, by which the unions affiliated to the Trades Union Congress endeavoured to compel support for the miners after the government subsidies to the industry had ceased and demands were being made for reduced wages and longer hours. After nine days, during which the country generally had been caused not a little inconvenience, the strike collapsed and Cook was among the minority who opposed the miners' continuing the struggle alone. Nevertheless, accepting the majority decision, he worked strenuously with his colleagues throughout the seven months which elapsed before defeat had to be acknowledged. He was elected to the general council of the Trades Union Congress in 1927.

Having suffered an injury to his leg in his early mining days which was aggravated in later life, Cook underwent amputation for cancer in the summer of 1931. He persisted in his work, but the cancer re-appeared and he died in hospital at Hampstead 2 November 1931. In 1906 he married Annie Edwards, and had one son and two daughters.

Cook was portrayed by the press as a national menace in his later days, but his immediate colleagues, recognizing that he was more of an agitator than a negotiator, held him in regard for his warm-hearted though impulsive nature and his dogged determination to make the public realize the actualities of mining life.

[*The Times*, 3 November 1931; personal knowledge.]   J. S. MIDDLETON.

COOKE, GEORGE ALBERT (1865–1939), regius professor of Hebrew and canon of Christ Church, Oxford, was born in London 26 November 1865, the elder son of George Isaac Foster Cooke, barrister, of Lincoln's Inn, by his wife, Agnes Marian, daughter of Stephen Mackenzie, a surgeon, and sister of Sir Morell Mackenzie and Sir Stephen Mackenzie [qq.v.]. He was educated at Merchant Taylors School (where Hebrew was still taught as a school subject) and in 1884 gained a Hebrew scholarship at Wadham College, Oxford. He was awarded a second class in theology (1888) and won the second Pusey and Ellerton Hebrew scholarship (1886), the junior Kennicott Hebrew scholarship (1888), and the Houghton Syriac prize (1889). In 1889 he was ordained and licensed by the bishop of Oxford to the curacy of Headington, and St. John's College appointed him senior scholar and Hebrew lecturer. He became chaplain (1890) and fellow (1892–1899) of Magdalen College, serving meanwhile as curate to Cosmo Lang at the university church (1894–1896) and as rector of Beaconsfield (1896–1899). He was private chaplain at Dalkeith to the Duke of Buccleuch (1899–1908), warden of the Community of St. Andrew of Scotland (1904–1908), and canon of St. Mary's Cathedral, Edinburgh (1907–1908). He received the honorary degree of D.D. from Edinburgh University in 1911.

Returning to Oxford in 1908, Cooke succeeded T. K. Cheyne [q.v.] as Oriel professor of the interpretation of Holy Scripture, canon of Rochester Cathedral, and fellow of Oriel College. In 1914 he succeeded S. R. Driver [q.v.] as regius professor of Hebrew and canon of Christ Church. This position he voluntarily resigned in 1936 to become rector of the tiny parish of Bettiscombe-with-Pilsdon, near Bridport. He died suddenly at Cheltenham 9 September 1939, while undergoing an operation. He married in 1897 Frances Helen (died 1932), daughter of Patrick Anderson, a man of business in Dundee, and had four daughters.

Cooke's most valuable work is a *Text-book of North-Semitic Inscriptions* (1903) which opened up the field of Hebrew and Aramaic epigraphy to English-speaking students and still remains unsuperseded. Following on smaller commentaries (for the 'Cambridge Bible') on the Books of Judges and Ruth (1913) and Joshua (1918),

he wrote a large-scale *Critical and Exegetical Commentary on the Book of Ezekiel* (1937) and, in an attempt to combine Coverdale's style with accuracy of rendering, *The Prayer Book Psalter Revised* (1939). His standard of scholarship was high and his writing conspicuous for kindliness and caution: the scholar in him never overcame the instincts of the conscientious parish priest.

There is a portrait of Cooke by Hugh Riviere (1935) in the lodgings of the Professor of Hebrew, Christ Church.

[*The Times*, 11 and 13 September 1939; *Oxford Magazine*, 26 October 1939; private information; personal knowledge.]

H. DANBY.

COWEN, SIR FREDERIC HYMEN (1852–1935), composer and conductor, whose original name was HYMAN FREDERICK COWEN, was born at Kingston, Jamaica, 29 January 1852, the younger son of Frederick Augustus Cowen, who later became secretary to William Ward, first Earl of Dudley, and treasurer to Her Majesty's Opera in London, by his wife, Emily, second daughter of James Davis, of Kingston. Brought by his parents to England at the age of four, Frederic Cowen early displayed his musical capacity by composing a waltz (which was published) when six, and an operetta, *Garibaldi*, when eight, to a libretto by his sister, aged seventeen: this latter was privately printed. Becoming a pupil of (Sir) John Goss and (Sir) Julius Benedict [qq.v.], in 1863 he gave a piano recital at Her Majesty's Theatre, and in 1864 played Mendelssohn's D minor concerto at Dudley House, (Sir) Charles Santley [q.v.] and Joseph Joachim also taking part in the concert. A year later he won the Mendelssohn scholarship, the blue riband of British musical scholarships, but relinquished it, as his parents wished to retain control of his education. They took him to Leipzig, where he entered the conservatorium and became a pupil of Louis Plaidy, Ignaz Moscheles, Carl Heinrich Garstin Reinecke, Ernst Friedrich Eduard Richter, and Moritz Hauptmann. In 1867 he went to the Stern Conservatorium in Berlin, where he studied under Friedrich Kiel and laid the foundations of his skill as a conductor.

Returning to England in 1868, Cowen made a name as a pianist, playing at concerts of the Philharmonic Society and elsewhere, and became noted as an accompanist, assisting Sir Michael Costa [q.v.] in that capacity at Her Majesty's Opera at Drury Lane Theatre, and on tour, under the management of J. H. Mapleson [q.v.], from 1871 to 1877. His gifts as a conductor led to his appointment as conductor of the Covent Garden promenade concerts in 1880 and to an engagement for five concerts of the Philharmonic Society in 1884; from 1888 to 1892 he was the society's permanent conductor in succession to Sir Arthur Sullivan [q.v.]. The unprecedented fee of £5,000 was paid him to go to Australia to conduct the daily orchestral concerts at the Melbourne Centennial Exhibition for six months (August 1888–January 1889). He conducted the Hallé Orchestra in Manchester from 1896 to 1899 ; and among other conductorships which Cowen held were those of the Liverpool Philharmonic Society, the Bradford Festival Choral Society, and the Scottish Orchestra. He returned to the Philharmonic Society from 1900 to 1907, and conducted the famous triennial Handel festivals at the Crystal Palace from 1903 to 1912, and again in 1920 and 1923.

As a composer, Cowen wrote a number of operas, one of which, *Signa*, was first produced at Milan in 1893, but they have not held the stage: his oratorios and cantatas, often written for festivals and produced there, have been of use to choral societies, and his orchestral works display marked fancy, and are excellently scored, his skill in this respect owing nothing to instruction. His 'Scandinavian' symphony(1880),which owed its origin to three tours in Sweden, Denmark, and Norway as accompanist to the famous mezzo-soprano Zelia Trebelli, may be mentioned as presenting imaginative use of orchestral colouring then new to English audiences, and the suite 'The Language of Flowers' (also 1880), may be cited as an example of individual fantastic grace. Cowen composed nearly three hundred songs: quite a number of them deserve remembrance for their lyrical art: others, Victorian ballads of sentiment, among which may be named 'The Better Land' and 'The Children's Home', achieved a 'best-selling' success which was at times embarrassing.

Cowen was knighted in 1911, and received honorary degrees from the universities of Cambridge (1900) and Edinburgh (1910). He married in 1908 Frederica Gwendoline, only daughter of Frederick Richardson, of London ; there was no issue of the marriage. He died in London 6 October 1935, and was buried in the Jewish cemetery at Golders Green.

[*The Times*, 7 October 1935; Sir F. H. Cowen, *My Art and My Friends*, 1913 ; *Grove's Dictionary of Music and Musicians*, 4th ed., vol. i, edited by H. C. Colles ; H. Saxe Wyndham and Geoffrey L'Epine, *Who's Who in Music*, 1913 ; *Oxford Companion to Music*, edited by Percy Scholes, 6th ed., 1945 ; *Musical Times*, November 1935 ; personal knowledge.]   J. MEWBURN LEVIEN.

COWLEY, SIR ARTHUR ERNEST (1861–1931), orientalist and Bodley's librarian, the fourth son among the seventeen children of Frederick Thomas Cowley, of Forest Hill, Sydenham, by his wife, Louisa Emily Boddy, was born at Forest Hill 13 December 1861, and educated at St. Paul's School and at Trinity College, Oxford, where he was an exhibitioner. He graduated without high honours because his interests even from schooldays had come to lie not in the classics but in oriental, notably the Semitic, languages. There being then no school of oriental languages at Oxford Cowley was practically self-taught, and his early departure from Oxford precluded his competing for any of the prizes offered in such subjects. After taking his degree in 1883 he studied at Lausanne and later taught French and German, in which he had unusual proficiency, at Sherborne and at Magdalen School, Oxford. This last appointment enabled him to follow up his study of Samaritan liturgies in the British Museum and put within his reach the Semitic collections of the Bodleian Library. From being quite unknown as an orientalist, Cowley saw his reputation rapidly grow, and in 1892 he was sent by the university to examine (along with Mr. John Frederick Stenning) the library of St. Catherine's monastery on Mount Sinai. The fruits of the expedition were not commensurate with the expectations, but may be seen in *Anecdota Oxoniensia* (Semitic series, vol. i, part ix, 1896).

In 1896 Cowley was appointed assistant to Adolf Neubauer [q.v.] in the Bodleian Library, and in 1899 succeeded him as sub-librarian in charge of the oriental department ; and in 1902 he was elected a fellow of Magdalen College and charged with the duty of giving instruction in Rabbinic Hebrew literature, on which he became the leading non-Jewish authority in the world. In 1919 he succeeded Falconer Madan as Bodley's librarian, holding that office until his resignation in July 1931.

Cowley's librarianship was marked by academic agitation, not always based on experience, for wider facilities for access to shelves. With these movements there was coupled the question of the enlargement and future site of the library, and the present compromise was adopted during his last illness in May 1931. Much of his administrative work aimed at objects wholly desirable, such as uniform administration of various collections scattered all over Oxford and the inauguration of a much-needed printed catalogue.

Cowley was, however, pre-eminent as a scholar and a friend. Besides brief articles, he published important work falling under three heads: Hebrew, Aramaic, and Hittite. In the first of these categories he published (with Neubauer) *The Original Hebrew of a Portion of Ecclesiasticus* (1897) followed by *Facsimiles of the Fragments hitherto recovered of the Book of Ecclesiasticus in Hebrew* (1901) which gathered together everything then known of this long-lost text. He edited (with Neubauer) the second volume of the *Catalogue of Hebrew Manuscripts in the Bodleian Library* (1906) and (as sole editor) the *Concise Catalogue of the Hebrew Printed Books in the Bodleian Library* (1929), two works indispensable to all students of Hebrew literature and important works of scholarship. In this class translations of two successive German editions of F. H. W Gesenius's *Hebrew Grammar* (1898, 1910) may be included. The second category contains equally important work in a very different field; the two volumes of *The Samaritan Liturgy* (1909); a volume edited from Aramaic papyri of the fifth century B.C. presented to the Bodleian Library by A. H. Sayce [q.v.], and published by Cowley and Sayce as *Aramaic Papyri discovered at Assuan* (1906); finally, joining to this an edition of the documents which had gone to Berlin, he was able in 1923 to publish a corpus entitled *Aramaic Papyri of the 5th Century B.C.* in which he presented the Aramaic text of every known document of this class with translation, notes, and glossary. The last category contains his attempts, in the Schweich lectures for 1918 (*The Hittites*, 1920), to decipher Hittite hieroglyphic texts, but his lack of success here is not surprising as the task was one for which he was not adequately equipped either by temperament or scholarship.

Cowley's strength as a scholar lay not so much in high originality as in a complete mastery of the field to which he had devoted himself, with an accuracy so painstaking and thorough that some of the texts which he edited may never require to be done again. His knowledge of Hebrew and Aramaic was exhaustive, and he coupled with it a sound knowledge of Arabic and some acquaintance with Accadian literature. On problems of biblical criticism his views were somewhat conservative; but his outlook was in the strictest sense scientific. He was a single-minded scholar, entirely free from self-seeking or self-assertion, but he also stood out for his remarkable talent for friendship with old and young alike, being quickly on easy terms with all sorts and conditions of men. He was much in demand for attendance at international conferences where his knowledge of languages and powers of conciliation made him a more than usually valuable member. He represented the Royal Asiatic Society at an orientalist meeting of the American Academy of Arts and Science at Boston (1921) and the university of Oxford at the centenary of the Société Asiatique in Paris (1922). He was an enthusiastic freemason.

Of the academic honours conferred upon him, Cowley was especially proud of his corresponding membership of the Institut de France. He was Sandars reader in bibliography at Cambridge for 1912–1913 and was elected F.B.A. in 1914. In 1931 he was nominated for knighthood, but his death at Oxford after a long illness, on 12 October of that year, anticipated his receiving the accolade. He married in 1913 the owner of the historic priory of St. Osyth, near Colchester, Mabel Beatrice, second daughter of William Longmore Watts, rector of Boxted, Essex. He adopted two sons but had no issue of his body. He bequeathed his estate to the Bodleian Library, where a portrait by Harry Collison hangs in the curators' room.

[*The Times*, 13 October 1931; T. W. Allen, *Arthur Ernest Cowley, 1861–1931* in *Proceedings* of the British Academy, vol. xix, 1933; personal knowledge.]   G. R. DRIVER.

COX, HAROLD (1859–1936), economist and journalist, was born at Wimbledon, 16 August 1859, the second son of Homersham Cox, a county court judge. He was educated at Tonbridge School, whence he obtained a mathematical scholarship at Jesus College, Cambridge. He was president of the Union in 1881, and after graduating as a senior optime in the mathematical tripos of 1882, became a university extension lecturer in Yorkshire. Coming under the influence of Edward Carpenter [q.v.], according to his own account he spent nearly a year working as an agricultural labourer in Kent and Sussex 'in order to gain an insight into the life of English labourers'. From 1885 to 1887 he taught mathematics in the Mohammedan Anglo-Oriental College at Aligarh in India.

On his return to England in 1887 Cox joined Gray's Inn and read for the bar, but, turning to journalism and authorship, he was appointed secretary of the Cobden Club in 1899, and in that position took an active part in opposing the tariff reform proposals of Joseph Chamberlain [q.v.]. He resigned the secretaryship in 1904 and in recognition of his services to free trade he was adopted as candidate by the liberal party in Preston, and won the seat at the general election in 1906. But in 1909, when Lloyd George's 'people's' budget brought up new issues, Cox took a line of his own which was unsatisfactory to the local liberals, and he did not stand for parliament again. His independence attracted admiration and in 1909 he was honoured by a dinner given by the British Constitutional Association 'in recognition of his great services in the late Parliament to the cause of personal liberty and personal responsibility'. Lord Rosebery, who presided, described Cox as 'embodying the very principle of liberty', in an oration which one of those present pronounced to be 'the most brilliant after-dinner speech I have ever heard'. Cox, in a long reply, set forth at length the duties of a member of parliament. 'Excellent, but impracticable', was the whispered comment of one guest to another; and this observation marked a defect in Cox's fine qualities, which often made it difficult for others to co-operate with him in public life.

After his retirement from parliament Cox constantly spoke and wrote against the growth of public expenditure and of bureaucracy. Although in early life he had been friendly with Sidney Webb and had collaborated with him in a book on the *Eight Hours Day* (1891), he was now an uncompromising opponent of socialism; and his book on *Economic Liberty* (1920) is an admirable exposition of the case. His public work included membership (1914–1915) of the inquiry into alleged German atrocities in Belgium held under the chairmanship of Lord Bryce and (1916)

of the Committee on Public Retrenchment. From 1910 to 1912 he was an alderman of the London County Council, and on the death of A. R. D. Elliot [q.v.] in 1912 he was appointed editor of the *Edinburgh Review*, a post which he held until 1929 when it ceased to be published. He was elected an honorary fellow of Jesus College, Cambridge, in 1913.

Cox married Helen Clegg; she died childless in 1930 after they had removed from Gray's Inn to Old Kennards, Leigh, near Tonbridge, where he also died 1 May 1936. One of his neighbours there writes: 'He was a scholar, but without a trace of pedantry, and a most attractive speaker. I was very fond of him. He had great personal charm and maintained to the last his interest in a wide range of public problems. One of his obsessions was the new phonetic spelling. Gardening was his favourite hobby in his charming cottage at Old Kennards.'

[*The Times*, 2 May 1936; *Economic Journal*, September 1936; private information; personal knowledge.]

FRANCIS W. HIRST.

COX, SIR PERCY ZACHARIAH (1864–1937), soldier, administrator, and diplomatist, was born at Herongate, Essex, 20 November 1864, the youngest of the three sons of Arthur Zachariah Cox (formerly surnamed Button), of Harwood Hall, Essex, deputy-lieutenant of the county, by his wife, Julienne Emily, younger daughter of Richard Saunders, of Largey, co. Cavan, and Hawley House, Kent. He was educated at Harrow and the Royal Military College and was commissioned to the 2nd Cameronians, then stationed in India, in 1884. He took his profession seriously, learnt oriental languages quickly, became an excellent rider and shot, and studied geography and natural history with ardour. In 1889 he married Louisa Belle, youngest daughter of Surgeon-General John Butler Hamilton, of the Royal Army Medical Corps, after joining the Indian Staff Corps as a stepping stone to the Political Department. After holding minor political appointments in the Mahratta states of Kolhapur and Savantwadi he accepted in 1893 the post of assistant political resident at Zeila in the British Somaliland Protectorate in the hope that he would enjoy more responsibility and independence in that primitive country than a junior could expect to do in India.

Cox's chance came in May 1895 after his transfer to Berbera in the previous year. The Rer Hared clan had closed the trade routes and was terrorizing the coastal tribes. Lieutenant-Colonel William Butler Ferris, the resident, decided without official authorization to send an expedition against the tribesmen. He put Cox, now captain, in command of 52 trained Indian and Somali camelry and 1,500 irregulars whom Cox's diary shows to have been as absurdly unreliable as Falstaff's braves. Taking Lieutenant (afterwards Sir John) Harrington as his second-in-command, Cox in six weeks defeated the Rer Hared, detached their allies, and forced their surrender. This unauthorized 'little war' gave the Protectorate several years of peace and established Cox's reputation for decision and ability.

Later in 1895 Cox was appointed assistant to the governor-general's agent in Baroda. In 1899 he was preparing to join the American explorer and hunter A. Donaldson-Smith in an expedition to the then unknown regions between Lake Rudolf and the Nile, when Lord Curzon offered him the post of political agent and consul at Muscat which he took up in October. He had a delicate task to perform. Great Britain and France had recognized the independence of Muscat, but in 1891 the Indian government had signed a secret convention with its ruler, Sultan Feisal, who bound himself not to alienate any territory except to the British government. Meanwhile, French agents distributed French flags and papers to Muscat shipowners—thus in effect giving French protection to their traffic in slaves and arms—and in 1898 persuaded Feisal to lease a coaling station to the French government. An over-hasty ultimatum from Calcutta was modified, but Feisal, who had been ordered on board the *Eclipse*, the guns of which were trained on his palace, and who had lost his subsidy from the government of India, was left with a grievance. Cox's first care was to restore good relations with the Sultan, whom his knowledge of Arabic, his dignity, courtesy, and Wellingtonian presence had impressed favourably at their first meeting. He secured the restoration of the subsidy, defeated several French attempts to cajole or bully Feisal into further concessions, and persuaded him to send his son Taimur to the Delhi Durbar of 1903. Curzon's visit to Muscat and the investiture of Feisal with the G.C.I.E. in November marked the triumph of Cox's masterly diplomacy.

Early in 1904 Cox, a major and C.I.E. since 1902, was promoted to acting political resident in the Persian Gulf and consul-general for the Persian provinces of Fars, Luristan, and Khuzistan with the Persian coasts and islands of the Gulf. He was gazetted resident in 1909. As consul-general he was charged, under the British minister in Teheran, with the defence of this country's interests in a region where the Persian revolution of 1905–1907 promoted lawlessness to an extent which compelled the British government to land sailors at Bushire in 1909, and to dispatch Indian troops to Shiraz in 1911. An exception to the general disorder was the autonomous Arab district of Mohammera bordering on Turkey in the Euphrates Delta. Cox won the friendship of its stern but intelligent ruler, Sheikh Khazaal, secured him British support when Turkey threatened aggression, and in 1909 negotiated an agreement whereby Khazaal leased a frontage on the navigable Euphrates estuary (Shatt-el-Arab) to the Anglo-Persian Oil Company for the construction of refineries and the terminus of its pipeline. As political resident Cox combined the powers of an official guardian and an ambassador to the small Arab states on the southern shores of the Gulf, and it was well for them and for the British and Indian governments that their common interests were placed in his skilled charge. Local politics mirrored changes in the European balance of power, and while the Anglo-French and Anglo-Russian agreements had dissipated one threat to the beneficent naval paramountcy of Great Britain in the Gulf, the Turco-German thrust towards its waters constituted a more serious danger. At Kuweit, an important strategic position, Cox strengthened British ties with its ruler, Mubarak ibn Sabah, and through him opened relations with a greater figure, Abdulaziz ibn Saud, who had regained his ancestral throne in Nejd. Cox recognized his commanding abilities, and in 1906 suggested that the British government should conclude a treaty with the ambitious Wahabi ruler. The suggestion found no favour with the liberal government which feared oriental entanglements. Cox, however, managed to maintain good relations with ibn Saud, and he must be given the entire credit for having been the first British diplomatist to foresee the ascendancy of that warrior statesman and the first to urge the importance of securing his confidence and friendship.

Such were the most striking of Cox's achievements during his ten years of almost continuous service in an appalling climate which could not sap his energies. There were others to his credit. The lighting of the Gulf from end to end, the re-survey of its coasts, the erection of wireless installations, the suppression of the arms traffic were changes in which he played an important part. British trade in the Gulf had more than doubled since he took up its defence in 1904. Above all, his single-minded devotion to the public service, his unerring choice of subordinates, the methodical accuracy of his official reports and letters—for whether he wrote in Arabic, Persian, or English his meaning was always clear—and the confidence which he inspired among all races and classes were of immense service to his country in the troubled years to come.

In 1911 the K.C.I.E. was conferred upon Cox, who had been appointed C.S.I. in 1909 and promoted lieutenant-colonel in 1910. Early in 1914 he was appointed secretary to the government of India in the Foreign Department. When it was decided to send Indian Expeditionary Force 'D' to the Gulf he accompanied it, in October, as chief political officer, and on the outbreak of war with Turkey (31 October) he took charge in that capacity of the army's political relations in Mesopotamia, where his prestige and experience were invaluable. His influence on ibn Saud enabled him to negotiate a treaty tantamount to an alliance with that ruler in December 1915, and subsequently to prevent the rivalry between the Wahabi Amir and King Hussein of the Hejaz from becoming dangerous. He saw several engagements during the campaign, accompanying Major-General (Sir) Charles Townshend [q.v.] to Ctesiphon, and being promoted honorary major-general (1917), but his chief tasks were administrative and he proved a first-class administrator, adapting and improving the Turkish system with rare skill. At the beginning he worked almost alone, but he gradually assembled and trained an admirable team of political and administrative officers which included (Sir) Arnold Wilson [q.v.] and was joined later by Gertrude Bell [q.v.], who became oriental secretary. The Iraqi Arabs admired him and not least for his silences—for Cox, although by no means taciturn, never talked for talking's sake. Cox's relations with the military authorities were good until the appointment of Major-General Sir F. S.

Maude [q.v.] as army commander, in August 1915. Maude's reluctance to permit his chief political officer to furnish the British government with information and to safeguard its declared Arab policy would have caused Cox's resignation but for Curzon's decisive intervention in the War Cabinet on a warning received from Gertrude Bell. He was appointed K.C.S.I. in 1915 and G.C.I.E. in 1917.

Shortly before the armistice Cox was sent as acting-minister to Teheran. The position there was difficult since Persia's neutrality had not prevented British, Russian, and Turkish military operations on Persian territory. After the armistice Cox negotiated an Anglo-Persian treaty by which Curzon set great store. Unfortunately, it never became effective, partly owing to Persian fears that it involved a surrender of national independence but still more to Curzon's over-emphasis of its importance. In June 1920 Cox was summoned to London by Curzon who informed him that his appointment as high commissioner of Iraq under the British mandate would be announced in order to pacify nationalist discontent. The announcement came too late to prevent a tribal rising. Asked his opinion whether Great Britain should abandon Iraq and the mandate or set up a national government, Cox told the government that he considered evacuation to be unthinkable and that the risk involved in setting up an Arab government was, 'without over-confidence', worth running.

Cox, who had been appointed K.C.M.G. in August, arrived in Bagdad in October to undertake the most difficult task in his career. It was first necessary to form a provisional government and to pacify the disturbed districts. Next, a ruler must be chosen. The British government favoured the candidature of Amir Feisal, son of King Hussein. Cox agreed, provided that the candidate was not imposed upon the Iraqis. Feisal came to Iraq in June 1921, and soon won widespread support. A referendum held in July gave him a comfortable majority, and he was enthroned on 23 August. The next step was to conclude a treaty embodying the obligations of Great Britain to Iraq under the mandate. Here difficulties arose largely owing to the weakness of King Feisal who allowed himself to be manœuvred into opposition to the mandate and his own ministers by extremist politicians who wished to substitute the treaty for the mandate. On 25 August 1922 Feisal fell dangerously ill. The council had resigned. To the general relief, Cox immediately took over the government. On his recovery Feisal realized his mistake and agreed to accept the British requirements. The treaty of alliance was signed on 10 October. This done, Cox went to meet ibn Saud whose tribesmen had been raiding Iraqi territory, and fixed the boundary between the two Arab states. In April 1923, when he was about to retire, he signed the protocol to the treaty of alliance. He left Iraq on 4 May. He had been appointed G.C.M.G. in 1922.

In retirement Cox, as chairman of the Mount Everest Committee and president (1933–1936) of the Royal Geographical Society, kept in touch with some of the interests of his active career. He received honorary degrees from the universities of Oxford (1925) and Manchester (1929). He died in the hunting field near Bedford 20 February 1937. His wife, who endured the heat of the Gulf and Iraq for so many years and is gratefully remembered for her hospitality, survived him: she was appointed D.B.E. in 1923. His only son was killed in action in 1917, and his only daughter died at birth. In memory of him children in Iraq are still called 'Kokkus'.

[*The Times*, 22 February 1937; P. P. Graves, *The Life of Sir Percy Cox*, 1941; private information; personal knowledge.]

PHILIP P. GRAVES.

CRADDOCK, SIR REGINALD HENRY (1864–1937), Indian civil servant, the youngest son of Surgeon-Major William Craddock, of the Bengal Medical Establishment, by his wife, Mary Charlotte, daughter of Francis Spencer Hawkins, born at Dharmsala, Punjab, 11 March 1864. Educated at Wellington and at Keble College, Oxford, he passed the open competition for the Indian civil service in 1882 and the final examination in 1884, when he proceeded to India, being posted to the Central Provinces which had then been constituted less than a quarter of a century and were far more remote from the main currents of Indian life than they are to-day. Craddock rose rapidly in the interesting work and congenial air of the Provinces where so many interests and a robust, vigorous life could be had for the asking. As a settlement and district officer, as a very capable and industrious chief secretary to the chief commissioner, he was plainly the coming man of the Provinces. In 1907 he was made chief commissioner by Lord Minto [q.v.], and, in a

time of considerable unrest, won general appreciation from all classes and was appointed K.C.S.I. at the coronation Durbar of 1911. He was then (1912) advanced to be home member of the viceroy's executive council on which he served for the rest of Lord Hardinge of Penshurst's term of office and for a few months of Lord Chelmsford's. In 1917 he was promoted to be lieutenant-governor of Burma, but left at the end of 1922 on the eve of the change under which Sir (Spencer) Harcourt Butler [q.v.] returned as governor to that province. The Rangoon University scheme was initiated by Craddock, who was the first chancellor.

Craddock retired in 1923 and was appointed G.C.I.E.; and soon afterwards became chairman of the Indian Civil Service (Retired) Association. In 1923–1924 he served as a member of the royal commission on the superior civil services in India under the chairmanship of Lord Lee of Fareham. In 1931 he entered parliament as a conservative member for the Combined English Universities. From 1932 to 1934 he served on the joint select parliamentary committee on Indian constitutional reform and spoke often in committee on the bill in 1935. He had an uphill battle to fight, but he remained popular with his fellow members.

Craddock married in 1888 Frances Henrietta (died 1932), younger daughter of General Henry Ralph Browne, and had one son and two daughters. He was elected an honorary fellow of Keble College in 1931. He died in London 10 February 1937. In *The Dilemma in India* (1929) Craddock left a valuable record of his work and his views on affairs in India. It was written to be of service at the time when the constitution then existing was under consideration, but it deserves to be studied for other reasons. It is the work of a man who knew India exceptionally well, was thoroughly respected and appreciated by all with whom he came into contact, and was a tower of strength in Lord Hardinge's successful administration in years of crisis.

[*The Times*, 11 and 13 February 1937; R. H. Craddock, *The Dilemma in India*, 1929; personal knowledge.] H. V. LOVETT.

CRAIG, JAMES, first VISCOUNT CRAIGAVON (1871–1940), statesman, was born at Sydenham, a suburb of Belfast, 8 January 1871, the youngest of the six sons of James Craig, J.P., of Craigavon and Tyrella, co. Down, a successful business man in Belfast, by his wife, Eleanor Gilmour, daughter of Robert Brown. Educated at a private school at Holywood in county Down and afterwards at Merchiston Castle, Edinburgh, he became a stockbroker.

After the South African war, in which he served with distinction, Craig turned to politics, and at the general election of 1906, after an unsuccessful candidature in North Fermanagh (1903), he was elected member for East Down and held the seat until 1918. He was member for Mid-Down from 1918 to 1921. His sagacity, honesty of purpose, and courage were fully recognized at Westminster, and he served as parliamentary secretary to the Ministry of Pensions (1919–1920) and as parliamentary and financial secretary to the Admiralty in 1920–1921. He resigned on becoming, in June of the last-named year, under the Government of Ireland Act of December 1920, the first prime minister of Northern Ireland. Thenceforth he sat as one of the members for county Down in the parliament of Northern Ireland

Craig's time at Westminster was mainly occupied in a struggle against the Irish separatist movement, which was relegated to the background in the general election of 1906 and by the majority given then to the liberals in the House of Commons. But the constitutional crisis following on the rejection of the finance bill of 1909 by the House of Lords, involved two appeals to the electorate (January and December 1910), the outcome of which was to make the nationalist vote a decisive factor in parliament. Thereupon the liberal government committed itself to another home rule bill, and in the bitter struggle which followed Craig took a leading part as the chief lieutenant of Sir Edward Carson [q.v.], the Ulster leader.

Both leaders knew well the difficulties and dangers of the task that lay ahead, but they also knew that the loyalists of Ulster would never surrender their birthright as citizens of the United Kingdom. Ulster people were convinced that home rule for Ireland would lead to an Irish republic, disloyal to the Empire, and that Ulster's industries would be seriously affected by legislation promoted by men unacquainted with its industrial affairs.

Between the two leaders it was agreed that Carson would mainly devote himself to upholding Ulster's interests at Westminster and on public platforms throughout the kingdom, and that Craig would chiefly deal with organizing the means of

resistance which, it was felt, must be adopted. The intention was that if the home rule bill became law, Ulster should be held in trust, in the King's name, until the Act was repealed. To this end a provisional government, with a judiciary, was planned, the Ulster Volunteer Force was brought into existence and armed, and the Ulster Covenant was signed (28 September 1912) by almost half a million people who pledged themselves to shirk nothing which might be required to prevent dismemberment of the kingdom.

In 1914 there followed a crisis of supreme gravity marked by the gun-running incident at Larne (24 April), but the war of 1914–1918 supervened, and at Carson's call the Ulster Volunteer Force, to the military qualities of which Kitchener afterwards paid tribute, became the Ulster Division and won undying glory in France.

Meanwhile the home rule bill had been placed on the Statute Book, but with a stay on its operation. With the advent of peace, however, the Irish question (complicated by the Sinn Fein rising at Eastertide 1916) again became a very dangerous issue, and after the provisional 'settlement' of 1920, promoted by Lloyd George as head of the coalition government, had been repudiated by the Southern Irish, the 'treaty' of 6 December 1921 led to immediate 'opting out' by Northern Ireland. Craig, a baronet since 1918, remained prime minister of Northern Ireland. He faced a task of great difficulty. The members of his government had to be chosen for the most part from men with no former parliamentary experience; a new police force had to be brought into being; and order established. Lawlessness was rampant at the time, murder and outrage of almost daily occurrence, and ministers carried on their work at great personal risk. In an attempt to make government impossible, nationalists boycotted the new parliament and the new Royal Ulster Constabulary Force and demanded a revision of the Ulster boundary. In due course a boundary commission was set up by the British government but its report was never published, the *status quo* being maintained as a result of a financial deal between the ministers of London and Dublin.

For nineteen years, until his death, Craig, who was raised to the peerage as Viscount Craigavon, of Stormont, co. Down, in 1927, remained prime minister of Northern Ireland, slowly and surely steering the small ship of state into relatively calm waters, and setting himself to strengthen its defences against future storms. During his premiership parliament passed many measures such as those maintaining social services similar to those in Great Britain, providing for improved housing and drainage, and creating a new educational system, as well as legislation designed to further the establishment of new industries and improve the agricultural position.

As parliamentarian and statesman, Craigavon possessed qualities of a very high order. He was a man of undaunted courage, high character, sound judgement, and devotion to duty, and his powers of leadership were conspicuous. He was a great organizer. He trusted his colleagues and his colleagues trusted him.

Craigavon died suddenly at Glencraig, co. Down, 24 November 1940, and was buried in the grounds of the parliament with the establishment of which his name is peculiarly connected. The aftermath of his work has been described in Mr. Churchill's commentary on the part played by Ulster since the outbreak of war in 1939. 'Only one great channel of entry remained open. That channel remained open because loyal Ulster gave us the full use of the Northern Irish ports and waters, and thus ensured the free working of the Clyde and the Mersey. But for the loyalty of Northern Ireland and its devotion to what has now become the cause of thirty governments or nations, we should have been confronted with slavery and death, and the light which now shines so strongly throughout the world would have been quenched.'

Craig married in 1905 Cecil Mary Nowell Dering, only child of Sir Daniel Alfred Anley Tupper, an officer of the King's household, and had twin sons and a daughter all of whom survived him. He was succeeded as second viscount by his elder son, James (born 1906). He was sworn of the Irish Privy Council in 1921, and of that of Northern Ireland in 1922. He received the honorary degree of LL.D. from Queen's University, Belfast, in 1922, and that of D.C.L. from Oxford in 1926. A statue of Craigavon by L. S. Merrifield was placed in the Northern Ireland House of Commons at Stormont in 1945.

[*The Times*, 25 November 1940; Hugh Shearman, *Not an Inch. A Study of Northern Ireland and Lord Craigavon*, 1942; St. John Ervine, *Craigavon, Ulsterman*, 1948; personal knowledge.]   JOHN M. ANDREWS.

CRAIGAVON, first VISCOUNT (1871–1940), statesman. [See CRAIG, JAMES.]

CRAIGMYLE, first BARON (1850–1937), lawyer and politician. [See SHAW, THOMAS.]

CRAWFORD, twenty-seventh EARL OF (1871–1940), politician and art connoisseur. [See LINDSAY, DAVID ALEXANDER EDWARD.]

CRAWFURD, SIR RAYMOND HENRY PAYNE (1865–1938), physician and scholar, was born at East Grinstead, Sussex, 9 November 1865, the sixth son of the Rev. Charles Walter Payne Crawfurd, by his wife, Mary, daughter of James Adey Ogle, regius professor of medicine at Oxford [q.v.]. He was educated at Winchester, New College, Oxford, and King's College Hospital, at all of which he gained scholarships or prizes. He qualified B.Ch. (Oxon.) in 1894 and M.D. (Oxon.) in 1896. After holding resident appointments at his hospital and the Victoria Hospital for Children, Chelsea, he became in 1898 assistant physician to King's College Hospital and later (1905) full physician, as well as lecturer there and at the London School of Medicine for Women. He continued with active work at King's College Hospital until 1930.

Crawfurd took a keen interest in the history of medicine and played a leading part in the foundation of the section of history of medicine of the Royal Society of Medicine, of which section he became president. He contributed to the *Proceedings* of the society many interesting papers such as 'Martial and Medicine' (1913), 'Oliver Goldsmith and Medicine' (1914), and 'Superstitions concerning Menstruation' (1915). He also published a monograph entitled *The Last Days of Charles II* (1909). Besides his historical work he was the author of a thesis on exophthalmic goitre, and was joint editor with (Sir) Farquhar Buzzard of Burmoy Yeo's *Manual of Medical Treatment* (1913).

Crawfurd took an active part in the affairs of the Royal College of Physicians, of which he was elected a member in 1894, a fellow in 1901, and registrar in 1925, holding this post until his death in 1938. He also gave the Fitzpatrick lectures in 1911–1912 which were expanded and published as *The King's Evil* (1911) and as *Plague and Pestilence in Literature and Art* (1914), and delivered the Harveian oration in 1919. His skill as an organizer, for which he was knighted in 1933, was shown by the active part which he took in the removal of King's College Hospital from its position near the Strand to its present site on Denmark Hill. Reference should also be made to his administrative ability as regards Epsom College of which he was the ideal chairman of the council for many years (1923–1936).

Crawfurd married in 1898 Ethelberta Ormrod, youngest daughter of Colonel Arthur Bailey, J.P., of Bolton, and had three sons. He died in London, after a few days' illness, 9 March 1938.

[*The Times*, 10 March 1938 ; *British Medical Journal*, 1938, vol. i, p. 651 (portrait) ; *Lancet*, 1938, vol. i, p. 697 (portrait).]

J. D. ROLLESTON.

CREED, JOHN MARTIN (1889–1940), divine, was born at Leicester 14 October 1889, the eldest son of Colin John Creed, vicar of All Saints' church, Leicester, and later rector of Farthinghoe, Northampton-shire, by his wife, Etheldreda Wright, daughter of Frederick Robert Spackman, M.D., of Harpenden, Hertfordshire. He was educated at the Wyggeston Grammar School, Leicester, and in 1908 went as a scholar to Gonville and Caius College, Cambridge, where he was a Bell scholar in 1909 and obtained first classes in part i of the classical tripos (1911) and in part ii of the theological tripos (1912). In 1913 he was ordained to an assistant cur-acy at St. Paul's church, Manningham, Bradford, and in the following year was elected a fellow of his college, to which he returned as chaplain in 1915. From 1917 to 1919 he was a chaplain to the forces in France. In the last-named year he was elected a fellow of St. John's College, Cam-bridge, and appointed dean and lecturer in theology. In 1926 he succeeded A. E. Brooke [q.v.] as Ely professor of divinity and in the canonry of Ely Cathedral annexed to the chair, and he held these offices until his death at Cambridge 17 February 1940. He was elected a fellow of the British Academy in 1939. In 1927 he married May Geraldine, younger daughter of Alfred Leslie Lilley, canon of Hereford, and had one son and three daughters, the youngest of whom pre-deceased her father.

In his exact scholarship and historical outlook Creed inherited and maintained the Cambridge theological tradition which had come down from the time of J. B. Lightfoot [q.v.]. His principal contribu-tions to theology lay in the field of the New Testament and the early Christian age.

His work in this field is represented by *The Gospel according to St. Luke. The Greek Text with Introduction, Notes, and Indices* (1930), a critical commentary con-cerned especially with the composition of St. Luke's narrative and the stage which it marks in the development of the Gospel tradition, and by articles in the *Journal of Theological Studies*, of which he became an editor towards the end of 1935, and elsewhere. Noteworthy amongst these articles is a discussion of the early Christian document known as the *Didache* (*Journal of Theological Studies*, October 1938). A second field of study, to which he devoted himself increasingly, was the history of religious thought in the eighteenth and nineteenth centuries. Although widely separated in time, these periods were not dissociated in his thought, both because the later period gave him the background against which to view the modern study of the earlier and the problems to which it had given rise, and because his strong historical sense led him always to ap-preciate the continuity, yet changing con-ditions, of Christian theology. His work in the later field is represented by *Reli-gious Thought in the Eighteenth Century Illustrated from Writers of the Period* (1934), prepared in collaboration with the Rev. J. S. Boys Smith, and by his Hulsean lectures delivered at Cambridge in 1936 and published in 1938 under the title of *The Divinity of Jesus Christ. A Study in the History of Christian Doctrine since Kant*, which illustrates the characteristic lucidity of his thought and his gift of literary presentation.

Creed was always deeply interested in the history and nature of the Church of England, and as a churchman he repre-sented, as well perhaps as any man of his time, its central tradition, liberal in out-look and resting upon sound learning. He knew that the intimate association of the Church of England with the history and people of England is integral to the idea of the historic Church of England. In his view, a national Church was a natural counterpart to the political and social order of a world in which the nation was the fundamental political and cultural unit. It was thus a proper, though not the only legitimate, form of Church polity, fitted to express a catholic tone and temper and able to preserve the religious and the non-religious activities of man in their true and organic relation. The association of Church and State in England had fostered this wholesome contact between the sacred and the secular, which was characteristic of the special ethos of the Church of England and of the religion of the English people. This position, stated in a number of published articles and sermons and supported by wide learning and with notable fairness of mind, gave to Creed's outlook a representative importance, and it added weight to the part which he played as a member of the Archbishops' Commission on Christian Doctrine, the Report of which was published in 1938 as *Doctrine in the Church of England*.

[*The Times*, 21 and 22 February 1940; J. F. Bethune-Baker, *John Martin Creed, 1889–1940* in *Proceedings* of the British Academy, vol. xxvi, 1940 (portrait); *Journal of Theological Studies*, April 1940; *Cambridge Review*, 1 March 1940; *The Eagle* (magazine of St. John's College, Cambridge), vol. lii, pp. 51–54, 1941; private information; personal knowledge.]   J. S. Boys Smith.

CRICHTON-BROWNE, Sir JAMES (1840–1938), physician and psychologist. [See Browne.]

CROMPTON, ROOKES EVELYN BELL (1845–1940), engineer, was born at Sion Hill, near Thirsk, 31 May 1845, the fourth son and youngest child of Joshua Samuel Crompton, by his first wife, Mary, daughter of Sir Claud Alexander and a friend and pupil of Mendelssohn. The names Rookes Evelyn record his kinship through the Rookes, his grandmother's family, with the diarist John Evelyn.

During the Crimean war Crompton was allowed to accompany Captain (Sir) William Houston Stewart [q.v.], his mother's cousin, commander of the *Dragon*; and was officially enrolled as a naval cadet. He visited his elder brother in the trenches and actually came under fire; thus at the age of eleven he had the Crimean medal and Sebastopol clasp.

School at Elstree prepared Crompton for Harrow (1858–1860). During his holidays he built, in a workshop at home, a full-size steam-driven road engine; but before his true engineering career began he served for four years in India (1864–1868) as an ensign in the Rifle Brigade. Even there, however, he equipped a travelling workshop and had his machine tools sent out from England. His strong views on the inefficiency and slowness of the bullock trains impressed R. S. Bourke, Earl of Mayo [q.v.], then viceroy, and within a short time Crompton introduced steam road-haulage, receiving a government grant of £500 for his services.

Returning in 1875, Crompton left the army and bought a partnership in a Chelmsford engineering firm, and, when adviser at the Stanton iron-works belonging to the Derbyshire branch of his family, purchased some of the new Gramme dynamos in order to improve the lighting of the foundry. Their success provided a turning-point; from that date (1878) electricity and engineering became for him almost inseparable. Co-operating with Emil Bürgin, of Basle, who was then working on dynamo design, Crompton obtained the rights of manufacture and sale of Bürgin's machine, improved it, and developed it to commercial success. He began making electric light plant, and carried out many installations, those at the Mansion House and the Law Courts in London and the Ring Theatre in Vienna being especially notable. In 1881 the firm of Crompton's was awarded the first gold medal ever given for electric lighting plant.

Towards the end of 1886 Crompton formed the Kensington Court Company, financed by a few friends, for electricity supply to neighbouring premises. This pioneer enterprise, one of the first of its kind, became the Kensington and Knightsbridge Electric Supply Company. Crompton advocated the direct current system; S. Z. de Ferranti [q.v.], engineer of the London Electric Supply Corporation, believed in alternating current and led the opposing school. The resulting 'battle of the systems', with these two as friendly antagonists, has its place in electrical history.

Between 1890 and 1899 Crompton revisited India, advising the government on electrical projects. On his return he took charge of a volunteer corps of Electrical Engineers, and by May 1900 was in South Africa with his men, whose efficiency in maintaining communications and skill in emergencies won high praise. Crompton had gone out as captain; on his return, later that year, he was promoted lieutenant-colonel, appointed C.B., and retained as consultant to the War Office on the development of mechanical transport.

Although electrical matters still claimed much of his time, Crompton became increasingly occupied with road transport. He had been a founder-member of the Royal Automobile Club in 1896, and was one of the judges in 1903 at the first motor show; as engineer-member of the Road Board appointed by the government in 1910, he improved road construction practice and materials. In the early part of the war of 1914–1918 Mr. Churchill consulted Crompton upon the design of an armoured vehicle capable of crossing trenches, and he was responsible for producing a type of 'landship' which later evolved, under various hands, into the tank.

In his laboratory at 'Thriplands', his Kensington home, Crompton spent many hours at research. He served on the committee of the National Physical Laboratory, and his advocacy of a closer understanding between all countries on electrical affairs resulted in the founding of the International Electrotechnical Commission in 1906, of which he was the first secretary.

In 1927 the firm of Crompton's became merged with another under the title of Crompton, Parkinson, & company, Limited. 'The Colonel' was then over eighty, but still active, and he retained a directorship in the new concern. A dinner in his honour, held in London in 1931, was attended by probably the largest gathering of distinguished scientists and engineers ever recorded at a personal function. Each of the three principal engineering bodies, the Civil, Mechanical, and Electrical, made him an honorary member; he was twice president of the Institution of Electrical Engineers, in 1895 and again in 1908. He was awarded the Faraday medal in 1926 and was elected F.R.S. in 1933. His ninetieth year was celebrated by another banquet, at which Sir James Swinburne presented him with his portrait by George Harcourt, which is now in the possession of the Institution of Electrical Engineers.

Professionally, Crompton was the expert, commanding respect and admiration; socially, a host of friends regarded him with affection. Young men benefited by his cheerful attitude to life, his resource and originality, and often by his generous help.

Crompton married in 1871 Elizabeth Gertrude (died 1939), daughter of George Clarke, of Tanfield, near Ripon, his father's other estate in Yorkshire; they had two sons, one of whom predeceased his father, and three daughters. His wife was his constant companion, keenly interested in all his enterprises. He died at Azerley Chase, Ripon, 15 February 1940.

[R. E. B. Crompton, *Reminiscences*, 1928; J. H. Johnson and W. L. Randell, *Colonel Crompton* (British Council 'Science in Britain' series), 1945; *Obituary Notices of Fellows of the Royal Society*, No. 9, January 1941 (bibliography and portrait); *Journal* of the Institution of Civil Engineers, vol. xiv, April 1940; personal knowledge.]

WILFRID L. RANDELL.

CROSS, CHARLES FREDERICK (1855–1935), analytical chemist, was born at Brentford, Middlesex, 11 December 1855, the second son of Charles James Cross, J.P., of Brentford, who was at first a schoolmaster and later a director of T. B. Rowe & Sons, soap-makers, of that town, by his wife, Ella Mendham. He was educated at King's College, London (where he graduated B.Sc. in 1878), Zürich University and Polytechnikum, and the Owens College, Manchester (1878–1879). He thus had as teachers Georg Lunge and (Sir) H. E. Roscoe [q.v.]. He devoted his life to the field of cellulose technology, and in 1885 set up in business in Lincoln's Inn in partnership with Edward J. Bevan, his fellow student at Manchester, who died in 1921, as analytical and consulting chemists.

The reputation of Cross is based upon many achievements. With the public, especially with women, he must rank among the greatest of all practical chemists since, by his discovery in 1892 of viscose, he made possible artificial silk, afterwards called rayon. His achievement, which led to the making of textiles, silk stockings for example, from wood cellulose, is no less esteemed by chemists. The discovery consisted in treating cellulose with aqueous caustic soda and then with carbon bisulphide, producing a golden yellow viscous liquid. This liquid when projected or spun through fine nozzles into a precipitating bath of sulphuric acid yielded fibres. These, after further treatment to remove the sulphur, left a pure regenerated cellulose. His patent remained a chemical master patent for its full term of years and was extended for a further term in view of its outstanding merit.

Cross was also a pioneer in the production of viscous films, now universal, as well as in that of cellulose acetate, later associated in the public mind with the name Celanese: he took out the first industrial patent for the manufacture of this in 1894. Although less spectacular, his work was likewise of remarkable influence in the development of the paper trade.

Cross, who was far ahead of his time in working with a substance so essentially mystic and intangible in its chemical behaviour, never ceased to be actively interested in the theoretical chemistry of cellulose. He published his researches in book form as well as in contributions to scientific journals. His book *Cellulose* (written in collaboration with Bevan, 1895) is unique; full of imagination and inspiration, with ideas, often only partly expressed, tumbling over one another. He also published four volumes of *Researches on Cellulose*, 1895-1921 (1901-1922), the first three in collaboration with Bevan, the last with Charles Dorée. Although he achieved so much on the technical side, at heart he was a scientist, chiefly interested in the pursuit of pure knowledge.

Cross was elected F.R.S. in 1917 and was awarded the medal of the Society of Chemical Industry (1916), the research medal of the Worshipful Company of Dyers (1918) and the Perkin medal of the Society of Dyers and Colourists (1924). Owing to ill health he retired to Hove about eight years before his death, which took place there 15 April 1935. He married in 1890 Edith Vernon, daughter of Major-General Charles Roper Stainforth, Madras Cavalry, and had two sons and one daughter. He was fortunate in his artistic temperament and happy in his musical gifts: he was an organist of ability. A man of striking appearance, cultured, and with broad interests, he was widely popular.

[*The Times*, 16 and 22 April 1935; *Obituary Notices of Fellows of the Royal Society*, No. 4, December 1935 (portrait); personal knowledge.]   E. F. Armstrong.

CRUMP, CHARLES GEORGE (1862-1935), archivist, born at Wyke Regis, near Weymouth, 9 April 1862, was the eldest son of Charles Ashbrook Wright Crump, barrister, of the Inner Temple, then an instructor in the training-ship *Britannia*, by his wife, Helen Ann Crane. His parents left England with their family in 1872, and lived at San Remo until 1885. Charles, like his brothers Harry and Louis, was educated by his father, who also took private pupils, for the Indian civil service, and obtained seventh place in the examination of 1880, whereupon he entered Balliol College, Oxford, as a civilian in training. After graduating in jurisprudence in 1883 he proceeded to India, but after six months at Cawnpore he was invalided home for good, retiring in 1886. On recovering, he aimed at a post in the home civil service, and while waiting to compete, worked under Sir J. A. H. Murray [q.v.] on the *Oxford English Dictionary*. In 1887 he obtained a post as

clerk in the secretary's department of the General Post Office, from which in 1888 he was transferred as a junior clerk to the Public Record Office. Here he remained until his retirement with the rank of senior assistant keeper (which he had held since 1916) in 1923.

Crump's earliest considerable work was an edition of the works of W. S. Landor (1891-1893), but the historical and economic interest of his official duties led him away from purely literary tasks. He contributed to (Sir) Robert Harry Inglis Palgrave's *Dictionary of Political Economy* (1891-1899) and to *Social England* (1893-1897) by H. D. Traill [q.v.]. With two colleagues, he edited in 1902 the *Dialogus de Scaccario* of Richard FitzNeale [q.v.], superseding the 1711 text of Thomas Madox [q.v.], and he was co-editor of the essays entitled *The Legacy of the Middle Ages* (1926). His extremely acute mind and attractive character are reflected in some degree in *The Logic of History* (1919), *History and Historical Research* (1928), and his one novel, *The Red King Dreams* (1931). His official work will be found in such publications as the *List of Foreign Accounts* (1900), *Calendar of Charter Rolls* (1903-1927), and the *Book of Fees* (1920-1931). He was an active member of the advisory committee appointed in 1912 by the master of the Rolls to bring the Record Office into closer touch with historical scholars; but his greatest service to history was his insistence on the need for the study of records in their proper setting as products of an administrative machine, and not merely as evidence of isolated facts. In this respect the historians and archivists of to-day are all in a sense his pupils.

Crump married in 1890 Lucy (died 1946), younger daughter of George Birkbeck Hill, sister of Sir (Edward) Maurice Hill, and sister-in-law of Sir W. J. Ashley [qq.v.], and had a son and a daughter. He died in London 11 December 1935.

[*The Times*, 13 December 1935; Official records of the Public Record Office; private information; personal knowledge.]   Charles Johnson.

CUNNINGHAME-GRAHAM,ROBERT BONTINE (1852-1936), traveller, scholar, etc. [See Graham.]

CURRIE, Sir ARTHUR WILLIAM (1875-1933), general, was born at Napperton, Adelaide, Ontario, Canada, 5 December 1875, the son of William Garner

Currie, of Strathroy, Ontario, by his wife, Jane Patterson. Both his parents were Canadian born, but their families originally migrated from Scotland and Ulster. The first years of Currie's life were spent on his father's farm and in his education at Strathroy Collegiate Institute and Strathroy Model School, but in 1894 he became a schoolmaster in Sydney, Vancouver Island, and later in Victoria, following this profession for the next five and a half years. He then abandoned teaching and in 1900 opened a brokerage and insurance business. Soon after reaching his new home, however, he joined the militia (1897) as a gunner. He became a lieutenant in 1900 and such was his energy and enthusiasm that by 1909 he was commanding the 5th Regiment Canadian Garrison Artillery.

In 1913 Currie left the unit to command the newly formed 50th Regiment Gordon Highlanders of Canada; and so, when war broke out in 1914, he was prepared and volunteered for service, and was given command of the 2nd Canadian Infantry brigade. With this brigade he withstood the onslaught of superior forces at St. Julien in 1915 and in the same year was promoted successively colonel and brigadier-general. When the Canadian Corps was formed in September 1915 Currie was given command of the 1st Canadian division, and with the rank of major-general led his men on the Somme and at Vimy Ridge. When, in 1917, Sir Douglas Haig [q.v.] brought him from the division to lead the Canadian Corps, with the rank of lieutenant-general, the appointment was questioned by the Army Council and the Canadian government, but Haig was satisfied with the enterprise and initiative of his civilian officer and insisted on his selection standing. Subsequent events fully justified such a bold decision on the part of the commander-in-chief. Currie planned and carried through the battle of Hill 70 (August 1917) and led his Corps at Passchendaele (October). During his first year in command of the Corps he had a number of British staff officers serving under him, a sufficient testimony, if any were needed, to the esteem in which he was held. His and the Corps' great test was the battle of Amiens (August 1918) where they greatly distinguished themselves. Currie himself was mentioned in dispatches nine times, was appointed C.B. in 1915, K.C.M.G. in 1917, K.C.B. in 1918, and G.C.M.G. in 1919. He received many foreign decorations.

After the armistice Currie remained for a time in command of the Canadian forces on the Rhine and upon his return to Canada was promoted general, and made inspector-general, Canadian Militia, and principal military councillor (1919). From soldiering his thoughts returned very largely to education when in 1920 he became principal and vice-chancellor of McGill University. He also gave his services unsparingly to the Canadian Legion of British Empire Service League of which he was grand president, to the Carnegie Foundation for the Advancement of Teaching, of which he was a trustee, to the governorship of the Montreal General and Royal Victoria Hospitals, and to the directorship of the Bank of Montreal. Eighteen universities in Great Britain, Canada, and the United States of America conferred honorary degrees upon him.

Currie was a big, well-built, soldierly man, and was a courageous and resourceful commander possessed of great initiative and a thorough grasp of strategy. He exemplified and interpreted the war-time genius of the Canadian people, and on his death at the Royal Victoria Hospital, Montreal, 30 November 1933, Canadian tributes were paid to his memory and achievements by Sir Robert Borden [q.v.] and Mr. B. B. (later Viscount) Bennett. He married in 1901 Lucy Sophia, youngest daughter of William Chaworth Chaworth-Musters, of Nottingham, England, and had a son and a daughter.

A portrait of Currie is included in J. S. Sargent's picture, 'Some General Officers of the Great War', painted in 1922, in the National Portrait Gallery.

[*The Times*, 1 and 5 December 1933; *Canadian Defence Quarterly*, vol. xi, 1933-1934; Sir J. E. Edmonds, (Official) *History of the Great War. Military Operations. France and Belgium, 1914-1918*, 1922-1939.] C. V. OWEN.

CURRIE, SIR JAMES (1868-1937), educationist, was born in Edinburgh 31 May 1868, the eldest son of the Rev. James Currie, principal of the Church of Scotland Training College, Edinburgh, by his wife, Jane Lyall, daughter of George Key, of St. Vigeans, Angus. He was educated at Fettes and at Edinburgh University, from which he transferred to Oxford in 1888 on his election to a classical scholarship at Lincoln College.

Holding an idealistic view of the claims of the national system of education on the highly educated, after taking his Oxford degree Currie went back to Edinburgh to teach in one of the Scottish Education Board's schools. This gave him a firm basis of practical educational experience which later stood him in good stead. In 1899 he joined the Egyptian education service, where his originality and strength of character attracted the attention of Lord Cromer [q.v.], who sent him in 1900 to be the first director of education in the Sudan and first principal of Lord Kitchener's newly founded Gordon Memorial College. Here he had a remarkable opportunity of original work of lasting benefit to the Sudan. The country had been left a *tabula rasa* by thirteen years of Dervish tyranny, following on sixty-four years of Egyptian misrule. The sullen Arabs, defeated in war, had to be won. Justice, education, and medicine were the keys to confidence, and one of these was entrusted to Currie. The people soon saw that he came with his hands full of gifts, the gifts of careers for their sons. Before he left, in March 1914, the Gordon College was an established Sudanese national institution, and the country was covered with a network of schools from which the college was fed. He was in advance of other tropical administrators in realizing also the importance of scientific research for the health and welfare of the people. It was on his initiative that the Wellcome Medical Research Laboratories were installed in Khartoum under (Sir) Andrew Balfour [q.v.] and that agricultural and entomological research laboratories and a geological survey were added to his department and housed in Gordon College. He was a member of the governor-general's council, established in 1910, and the Medjidieh and Osmanieh decorations were conferred upon him.

The war of 1914–1918 brought Currie into government service when, in 1916, the training of munition workers was entrusted to him as voluntary director of a new Labour Supply Department. As a result thousands of semi-skilled workers were made available for the manufacture of implements of war. In 1918 he joined the Ministry of Labour, again in a voluntary capacity, as controller of the training department. He originated government instructional factories and training centres for the disabled, in which, when he retired in 1921, over 25,000 disabled ex-servicemen had been qualified for renewed usefulness.

At the general election of 1918 Currie stood unsuccessfully for the Devizes division. An Asquithian liberal, he regarded with dislike those liberals who had deserted Asquith. He later became a national liberal, but did not again seek election.

In 1922 Currie was appointed director of the newly formed Empire Cotton Growing Corporation. This gave yet another opportunity for his special originality and knowledge. Cotton was to be grown in a dozen different countries, each with a different climate and different physical conditions. There would be no uniform cotton seed which would suit them all. First must come research in each country, experimental farms, knowledge of constituents of soils. He therefore had to concentrate on soil chemists and plant breeders before he could supply seed which would not bankrupt Empire farmers. It was this extension of his activities into tropical agriculture which brought him first membership and, in 1927, the chairmanship of the governing body of the Imperial College of Tropical Agriculture, Trinidad. By sending young men appointed to the service of his corporation for training there, he had initiated a plan which was later followed by the Colonial Office for the training of cadets for Colonial agricultural service. He was also a leading member of the colonial secretary's advisory committee for education in the Colonies.

As chairman of the governors of Dauntsey's School, Devizes, Currie took a leading part in converting a small local grammar school into a modern and scientific school which attracted a largely increased number of pupils even from remote regions. He was also a member of the governing council of Marlborough College, and a governor of the Imperial College of Science and Technology, South Kensington. He was appointed C.M.G. in 1912, K.B.E. in 1920, and K.C.M.G. in 1933. After his return to England, in 1914, he developed a keen interest in farming.

Currie married in 1913 Hilda Beatrice, only daughter of Sir Thomas Hanbury, of La Mortola, Ventimiglia, Italy, and had a daughter, who died in childhood. He died at Cambridge 17 March 1937.

A bust of Currie by Sir Goscombe John is in the Gordon College at Khartoum; a replica was in his own possession. A stone memorial plaque recording his love of the Sudan, provided by his former pupils of Gordon College, is affixed to a wall in Dauntsey's School.

[*The Times*, 18 March 1937; *Nature*, 10 April 1937; private information; personal knowledge.]   E. N. CORBYN.

CUSHENDUN, BARON (1861–1934), Irish politician. [See McNEILL, RONALD JOHN.]

CUSTANCE, SIR REGINALD NEVILLE (1847–1935), admiral, was born in Belfast 20 September 1847, the eldest son of General William Neville Custance, by his second wife, Mary, eldest daughter of Thomas Meggison, of Walton, Northumberland. He was educated in the *Britannia*, and in 1863 was present, as a midshipman in the *Euryalus*, at the naval action off Kagoshima and next year at that off Shimonoseki. After the ordinary promotions he was appointed in 1886 to the post of assistant-director of Naval Intelligence, which he held until he was appointed to command the cruiser *Phaeton* in 1890. He held this post for three years and in 1895 he was appointed captain of the battleship *Barfleur*, having in the interval served as naval attaché in Washington and Paris. From 1899 to 1902 he was director of Naval Intelligence, and in the latter year he was appointed rear-admiral, Mediterranean Fleet (flag in the *Venerable*), where he remained for two years. He was promoted vice-admiral in 1906 and from 1907 to 1908 he was second in command of the Channel Fleet (flag in the *Hibernia*), being promoted admiral in 1908. Although Custance's rare mastery of professional topics and wide attainments were expected to lead to his preferment to the highest appointments in the navy, he proved to be totally out of sympathy with Admiralty policy in the early years of the twentieth century, and as he did not hesitate to express his views, he was retired in 1912, and his career ended after his service in the Channel Fleet.

During the early part of Custance's career the navy was in the transition period between sail and steam, and naval designers were still seeking for a battleworthy type of ship in which speed, armament, armour protection, and seaworthiness were balanced to the greatest advantage. It was also a period when there was little prospect of war with another maritime power. So whilst much attention was given to harbour drills and equal-speed manœuvres few naval officers made any serious study of war. Custance was one of the few exceptions. A lifelong student of the theory and practice of sea-warfare, he called attention to the importance of studying war in *Naval Policy; a Plea for the Study of War* which was published in 1907 under the nom de plume 'Barfleur'. His main thesis, to which he returned in several subsequent publications, was that the naval mind had become divided into two schools—the historical and the *matériel*, and that a consequence of the *matériel* school being in power was that the principles governing warship design were entirely wrong.

Believing that 'offence is the best defence', Custance deprecated sacrificing gun-armament for speed or armour protection, and advocated fleets of many ships of moderate tonnage, powerful armament, and slow speed in preference to a few very large, fast ships with relatively weak armament. With his wide knowledge of war and battle-tactics, he was a powerful advocate, and his first book and two subsequent pamphlets, *The Fighting Power of the Capital Ship* (1909) and *Military Growth of the Capital Ship* (1910), aroused much interest. But his was a voice crying in the wilderness. Once the *Dreadnought* was launched, there could be no turning back. All maritime powers followed the lead given by British designers and the process of increasing speed and armour in each new class, which filled Custance with misgiving in the pre-*Dreadnought* era, began again.

To later generations of naval officers Custance's trenchant criticism of the large armoured cruiser, which he aptly described as an excessively costly inferior class of battleship, seems to be better founded, and few will disagree that he was on solid ground when he emphasized the dangers of design being entirely in the hands of a *matériel* school and unrelated to battle tactics and the lessons of history. After retirement he wrote under his own name three books of value to the student of naval warfare; *The Ship of the Line in Battle* (1912), a study of tactics from Trafalgar to Tsushima; *War at Sea, Modern Theory and Ancient Practice* (1919), a study of the campaign of Salamis and the Peloponnesian war; and *A Study of War* (1924).

Although his courageous effort to influence the design of warships failed, Custance aroused the navy to the importance of studying war and to him the Naval Staff College and various war courses of to-day owe not a little. He was very reserved and social activities made little appeal to him. He demanded, and received, a high standard of service from officers and men who served under him. Although not a man who could gather round him a band of brothers, his high sense of duty and tireless energy maintained the ships and squadrons under his command at a high standard of efficiency.

Custance was appointed C.M.G. in 1900, C.V.O. in 1903, K.C.M.G. in 1904, K.C.B. in 1908, and G.C.B. in 1913. The honorary degree of D.C.L. was conferred upon him by Oxford University in 1913. In 1868 he was awarded the silver medal of the Royal Humane Society. He died, unmarried, at Broadclyst, Devon, 30 August 1935.

[*The Times*, 2 September 1935; personal knowledge.]   W. M. JAMES.

DALRYMPLE-HAY, SIR HARLEY HUGH (1861–1940), civil engineer. [See HAY.]

DALZIEL, JAMES HENRY, BARON DALZIEL OF KIRKCALDY (1868–1935), politician and newspaper proprietor, was born at Borgue, Kirkcudbrightshire, 24 April 1868, the second son of James Dalziel, shoemaker, of Borgue, by his wife, Margaret Emily Davies. He was educated at Borgue Academy, Kirkcudbrightshire, at Shrewsbury High School, and at King's College, London. From an early age he worked as a London journalist, and getting into the press gallery became known to the liberal whips. Thus it was through their support that in March 1892 he was adopted as liberal candidate at a by-election in the Kirkcaldy District, and won the seat by a large majority. The constituency remained faithful to him for twenty-nine years, and he only abandoned it to go to the House of Lords.

Entering parliament so young as an advanced radical with a hard Scottish head, Dalziel was expected to rise high in politics. But he exemplified the rule that when men combine journalism with a seat in the House of Commons, their journalism gains by the combination, but their politics lose. He had rare parliamentary gifts; he was a clever debater, a deadly asker of questions; and he had that sixth sense which divines just how far in any particular direction the House will go. But he used his early success at Westminster to effect the difficult transition from the writing side of journalism to the proprietorial side, and thereafter became increasingly immersed in business, although on occasions he was formidable in the House to the end. His chief newspaper property was *Reynolds' Weekly Newspaper*, an old radical periodical which he converted into a prosperous Sunday paper of the lower grade.

An old ally of Lloyd George, from 1916 onwards Dalziel was enormously valuable to that statesman as a radical supporter of his coalition government. In 1918 Lloyd George with his help and that of wealthy friends bought the *Daily Chronicle*, then the morning paper with the largest circulation south of the Trent. Dalziel, who had been knighted in 1908 and sworn of the Privy Council in 1912, was rewarded with a baronetcy and made chairman and political director of the paper. In this post, however, he was not a success; and in 1921 he was raised to the peerage as Baron Dalziel of Kirkcaldy, but replaced as political director by Philip Henry Kerr (afterwards Marquess of Lothian, q.v.). His complete retirement came a year and a half later (December 1922); he then sold out his other newspaper interests (including, besides *Reynolds' Newspaper*, the *Pall Mall Gazette*, the *Era*, and some trade newspapers), and left active life.

A bachelor until he was sixty, Dalziel married in 1928 Amy Thackeray, daughter of Fossey Thackeray, and widow of Donald MacRae, of Wicklow. Her sudden death, which took place 26 June 1935, greatly affected him, and he died at Hove 15 July, nineteen days later.

[*The Times*, 16 July 1935; personal knowledge.]   R. C. K. ENSOR.

D'ARCY, CHARLES FREDERICK (1859–1938), archbishop of Armagh and primate of all Ireland, was born at Rehoboth House, Dublin, 2 January 1859, the eldest son of John Charles d'Arcy, assistant cashier in the Great Southern and Western Railway Company's service, by his wife, Henrietta Anna, daughter of Thomas Brierly, of Rehoboth House. He was descended from John Darcy [q.v.], lord justice of Ireland in the reign of Edward III. D'Arcy's childhood and youth were passed in Dublin. He attended the high school, and in 1877 entered Trinity College where he spent seven years, studying chiefly mathematics, philosophy, and divinity, and graduating with a senior moderatorship in logics and ethics. In 1884 he was ordained for St. Thomas's church, Belfast. There he remained for six years. In 1890 d'Arcy was appointed to the country parish of Billy, near the Giant's Causeway, moving in 1893 to the industrial town of Ballymena, co. Antrim. Here he laid the foundation of his career and reputation, publishing *A Short Study of Ethics* (1895) which went through two editions and was reprinted in 1912. In 1899 he published his first set of Donnellan lectures (delivered at Trinity College in 1897–1898) under the title *Idealism and Theology*. This was his best book; in it he argues boldly that the current idealism cannot bridge the gulf between the self and society, that idealism, if it is to survive, must transcend itself and mere theism, and must accept substance, at once personal and supra-personal, i.e. the Christian Trinity.

D'Arcy was now recognized as the leading religious thinker of his country, and preferment came his way every three or four years. He returned to Belfast in 1900 as vicar of the city and dean of the newly founded cathedral; three years later he was raised to the bench as bishop of Clogher. In 1907 he was translated to the southern see of Ossory, Ferns, and Leighlin. In 1911 he returned to the north to preside over the populous see of Down and Connor and Dromore. Those were anxious days for Ulster and for all Ireland. The home rule agitation was at its height, and the clouds of civil war were gathering. D'Arcy after some hesitation took his stand openly with Sir Edward (afterwards Lord) Carson [q.v.], and the Ulster Unionist Council, and signed the Ulster Covenant (28 September 1912). (By the Larne gun-running on 24 April 1914 the Ulster Volunteer Force secured arms; but in August the European war broke out, and civil war was averted.) D'Arcy's political views were strongly with Ulster, and he had taken a firm line in the crisis; but he understood well the feelings of southern Protestants, and was *persona grata* in both north and south. When in 1919 the archbishopric of Dublin fell vacant, he was elected to fill the see; but he was not to rule for long in his native city, for in the following year he was called to the highest office in the Church of Ireland, becoming archbishop of Armagh and primate of all Ireland.

D'Arcy's eighteen years' tenure of the primacy was outwardly uneventful; he was not confronted with any acute crisis, nor called upon to take any far-reaching decision; but the problem of preserving an undivided Church in a divided land was present and urgent, if in the background. D'Arcy avoided word or act which might accentuate the acute division of political sentiment consequent on the recent partition of the country; thus he rendered a signal service to his Church at a critical period. His liberal outlook in theology and his personal qualities helped to foster good relations between north and south.

As primate d'Arcy soon became well known in England both in ecclesiastical circles and in the learned societies. He was prominent at the Lambeth Conferences of 1920 and 1930, and at the Lausanne Conference of 1927. In 1927 also he was elected a fellow of the British Academy. In 1936 he was chosen to represent the Anglican communion at the centenary of the consecration of W. G. Broughton [q.v.] as first bishop of Australia. In the summer of 1937 his health began to fail, and he had thoughts of resignation, but he remained primate to the day of his death, which occurred at Armagh 1 February 1938.

D'Arcy had a fluent pen, never idle for long. He was not in the first rank as a littérateur, but his writings possess considerable interest, covering as they do the best part of half a century, and as a leader of Christian thought he exerted through his books no little influence upon speculative theology and philosophy. His writings fall into two periods. In his younger days he was the metaphysician and moralist seeking along academic lines to harmonize faith and reason in the spheres of thought and practice. Later in life science in its theoretical aspects occupied his attention, and in a series of books, *Science and Creation* (1925), *The Christian Outlook in the Modern World* (1929), *God in Science* (1931), he endeavoured to reconcile the doctrine of evolution with Christian faith and practice. His views found their best expression in his last serious work, *Providence and the World Order* (1932, Alexander Robertson lectures delivered at Glasgow University in that year); here he argues that what to God is creation, to man is evolution, and that the ascending orders of reality, physical, biological, psychical, etc., constitute 'the splendid epic of creation'.

D'Arcy married in 1889 Harriet le Byrtt (died 1932), elder daughter of Richard Lewis, of Comrie, co. Down, and had one son and three daughters. A portrait of him by Frederic Whiting is at the Palace, Armagh.

[*The Times*, 2 February 1938; C. F. d'Arcy, *The Adventures of a Bishop* (his autobiography), 1934; A. A. Luce, *Charles Frederick D'Arcy, 1859–1938* in *Proceedings* of the British Academy, vol. xxiv, 1938 (containing a bibliography of his writings and appreciations of the more important works); personal knowledge.]   A. A. LUCE.

DARLING, CHARLES JOHN, first BARON DARLING, of Langham (1849–1936), judge, was born at Abbey House, Colchester, 6 December 1849, the elder son of Charles Darling, afterwards of Langham Hall, Essex, a member of a Border family, who managed estates and farmed on his own account in the neighbourhood of Colchester, by his wife, Sarah Frances, daughter of John Tizard, of Dorchester. In childhood he suffered much from very delicate health which isolated him from other children and prevented him from going to school. His education was given to him by a private tutor and added to by his own omnivorous reading, but he does not seem to have been possessed of ambition. Under the patronage of a rich uncle, by whom he was eventually left a most comfortable competence, Darling was at first articled to a firm of Birmingham solicitors. After a short time with them he joined the Inner Temple as a student and became the pupil in 1872 of John Welch, of King's Bench Walk, a pleader by profession. In these chambers he read for two years and was called to the bar in 1874, being made a bencher of the Inner Temple in 1892. He began by 'devilling' for (Sir) John Huddleston [q.v.] in Crown Office Row and joined the Oxford circuit. His early years were marked by much journalism, particularly in connexion with the *St. James's Gazette*, the *Pall Mall Gazette*, and the *Saturday Review*. His circuit life followed the usual round and was not such as to call for any particular mention. Indeed until his appointment as a judge Darling was never a prominent figure at the bar and his practice was almost wholly confined to his circuit. In 1885 he took silk and married Mary Caroline (died 1913), elder daughter of Major-General William Wilberforce Harris Greathed, R.E., a veteran of the Indian Mutiny, and granddaughter of Caroline Clive [q.v.]. He had one son, who predeceased his father, and two daughters.

In December 1885 Darling contested South Hackney as a conservative, and after a further unsuccessful contest there (July 1886) against Sir Charles Russell (afterwards Lord Russell of Killowen, q.v.) he was returned at a by-election in February 1888 for Deptford and retained the seat until his elevation to the bench in 1897. His interventions in debate were those of a competent party man rather than of a politician with any original contributions to make. He mostly spoke on legal matters and on home rule for Ireland and was silent on social and economic issues. Apparently during nearly ten years in the House of Commons Darling never entered the smoke-room, its social centre. He gave as his reason that he was a non-smoker.

In the autumn of 1896 Darling was appointed commissioner of assize on his own circuit and did his work competently. The liberal party made the appointment a political issue on the ground that this place of profit under the Crown vacated his seat. The issue came to nothing when Darling pointed out that he had stipulated that no fee should be paid to him for his services. In October 1897 rumours spread that the lord chancellor, Lord Halsbury, was intending to appoint Darling to the High Court bench. On 26 October *The Times* devoted a leading article to the rumours and stated, without mentioning a name, that the subject of the rumour was a man of 'acute intellect and considerable literary power', but that he had given 'no sign of legal eminence . . . if he is raised to the Bench, it will be on political grounds'. Two days later Darling's appointment to the Queen's Bench division was announced. *The Times* returned to the charge; Asquith gave expression to his doubts; much indignation was expressed in the Temple, but the *Law Journal* was prescient in writing: 'He will prove a far better judge than some of his critics believe.' Darling remained a judge until 1923. He was not a great judge. His summing-up in a criminal case and his judgements in the Court of Criminal Appeal were on the whole excellent; his judgements being particularly characterized by close reasoning and being always expressed in admirable English. In a murder trial he was very good. Unfortunately, in charges of less gravity he often allowed himself to behave with a levity quite unsuited to the trial of a criminal case, thinking erroneously that he could thereby induce the jury to bring in the right verdict by an eventual careful and accurate summing-up. In fact he had frequently lost the respect of the jury to such an extent that they ignored or paid little attention to the judge. The Pemberton Billing case (1918) was a shocking example and went far to lower the status of the bench. In this instance he insisted on trying the case against the wish of the defendant, who alleged, without contradiction, that a few weeks before in a civil case Darling had said of him that he did not believe him on his oath. Darling often allowed himself as a judge to be grossly insulted by witnesses and laughed with them and at them. He presided over the notorious Steinie Morrison (1911) and Armstrong (1922) cases, *Douglas* v. *Ransome* and *Wootton* v. *Sievier* (1913), the Romney picture case (1917), and the Mond libel case (1919) amongst others, and was much concerned with the court career of Horatio Bottomley [q.v.]. In the Court of Criminal Appeal Darling presided over the Crippen (1910) and Casement (1916) appeals.

When R. D. Isaacs, Lord Reading [q.v.] went to the United States of America as ambassador during the war of 1914–1918, Darling as senior puisne of the King's Bench division served as his deputy and his work was recognized by the distinction, unusual in the case of a serving judge, of being sworn of the Privy Council (1917). It was at one time in some quarters thought that he would succeed Lord Reading as lord chief justice, but on being passed over by the appointment of A. T. Lawrence, Lord Trevethin [q.v.], he is said characteristically to have remarked that he supposed he was not old enough. Darling retired from the bench in November 1923, an event which was marked by a public farewell in court. A few months later (January 1924) he was raised to the peerage as Baron Darling, of Langham. He spoke in the House of Lords on matters of legal interest; he took part in Privy Council cases as a member of the Judicial Committee; and as late as 1931 he returned to the King's Bench division in order to assist in reducing arrears. In 1926 he made a six weeks' tour of Canada as guest of the Canadian Bar Association. His last three years were lived quietly, and he died at the age of eighty-six at his home at Lymington 29 May 1936.

On the bench Darling was not a profound lawyer, nor was he a good judge for a commercial or lengthy case. He was interested in life and human beings and had sound common sense. His status as a wit was an established one, but how far his impromptus were prepared cannot be determined. They certainly were sometimes. But his literary sense and rapidity of literary allusion were due to a vast reading and deep appreciation of English and French literature.

Darling was a member of the royal commission on the working of the King's Bench (1912), and chairman of the committees on courts martial (1919), on the moneylenders bill (1925), and on national

marks (1928). As a conversationalist, particularly in the Benchers' room of the Inner Temple, he was pleasant, amusing, and often really witty, and was a delightful companion on a walk. He wrote *Scintillae Juris* (1877), which is rich in gnomic wisdom and sharp satire, and *On the Oxford Circuit and Other Verses* (1924), amongst other works of distinct literary, although at times somewhat slight and precious, character.

Darling was succeeded as second baron by his grandson, Robert Charles Henry (born 1919).

A portrait of Darling by Charles Furse (1890) is in the National Portrait Gallery, and another by Aidan Savage (1924) is in the possession of the family. A cartoon by 'Spy' appeared in *Vanity Fair* 8 May 1907.

[*The Times*, 30 May 1936; D. Walker-Smith, *Life of Lord Darling*, 1938; Evelyn Graham, *Lord Darling and his Famous Trials*, 1929; Dudley Barker, *Lord Darling's Famous Cases*, 1936; personal knowledge.]

NEVILLE LASKI.

DAVID, SIR (TANNATT WILLIAM) EDGEWORTH (1858–1934), geologist, was born at St. Fagans, Cardiff, 28 January 1858, the eldest son of William David, rector of St. Fagans, by his wife, Margaret Harriette Thomson. The family claimed to be of the same stock as James Ussher, archbishop of Armagh, the Abbé Edgeworth de Firmont, Richard Lovell Edgeworth, and Maria Edgeworth [qq.v.]. He was educated at Magdalen School, Oxford, where, although studious, he did not neglect athletics, and at New College, Oxford, of which he was a scholar. He was awarded a first class in classical moderations (1878), but having for reasons of health been absent during five terms on a voyage which took him to Australia, he graduated in the pass schools.

David's original desire to take holy orders gradually yielded to an interest in geology under the influence of (Sir) Joseph Prestwich [q.v.]. Under John Wesley Judd at the Normal School of Science and Technology (later the Royal School of Mines) he continued to study that science. In 1882 he took up an appointment in Sydney as assistant geological surveyor to the government of New South Wales, being for the most part concerned during the following years with the mapping of the Sydney–Newcastle basin, and although his *Memoir on the Geology of the Hunter River Coal Measures* did not appear until

1907, he paved the way to the establishment of a great coal industry, and greatly extended his own fame by his ability and clarity of diction in scientific matters.

In 1891 David was appointed to the chair of geology at Sydney University, and there he built up a famous school of geology, becoming a leading figure in the investigation and exploration of permocarboniferous glacial phenomena in Australia, while his oratorical fervour and talent spread his influence far beyond the university.

Besides his interest in past geological climates, David was deeply interested in the problem of the origin of coral atolls, and in 1897, accompanied by his wife, he led the second of the expeditions sponsored by the Royal Society for the solution of the problem, at Funafuti. He was awarded the Bigsby medal of the Geological Society in 1899, and was elected F.R.S. in 1900. In 1906, on his way to the Geological International Congress in Mexico, he visited areas in India where the famous Talchir glacial boulder-heads are developed.

But it is in Antarctic research that David's name will best be remembered. He was invited to join the British Antarctic expedition of 1907–1909 led by (Sir) Ernest Shackleton [q.v.] in the *Nimrod* to the Ross Sea, and his sterling qualities so deeply impressed Shackleton that he was invited to become a full-time member of the expedition. His chief exploits as a member of the first party to reach the summit of Mount Erebus (10 March 1908) and, with (Sir) Douglas Mawson, to reach and record, after a hazardous sledge journey, the south magnetic pole on 16 January 1909, made him widely known, and he was appointed C.M.G. in 1910.

During the war of 1914–1918 David, at the age of fifty-seven, enlisted and helped to raise a mining battalion of Australian Tunnellers. He reached France, as a major, in 1916, and full use was made of his experience both in tunnelling and in the supply of water. He was responsible for the great mining operation under Messines Ridge. In 1918 he was promoted lieutenant-colonel, was awarded the D.S.O., mentioned in dispatches, and withdrawn to general headquarters in order to act as chief geological adviser to the British armies. In 1920 he was appointed K.B.E.

After a short stay in England, David returned to Sydney and became engrossed in the compilation of his comprehensive *Geology of the Commonwealth of Australia*

(2 vols. with maps, edited by Dr. W. R. Browne; these are still in the press). In order to enable him to prosecute this great work he was freed at the end of 1922 from all teaching duties, and, in 1924, he resigned his chair. The very wide scope of this work prevented any publication until 1932, when a volume appeared entitled *Explanatory Notes to accompany a new Geological Map of the Commonwealth of Australia*, but unfortunately further progress was interrupted by David's rather sudden death in Sydney 28 August 1934, and by the outbreak of war in 1939.

As a senior and leading scientist of the Commonwealth, David repeatedly held high office in scientific societies and he showed remarkable powers of organization on the occasion of the visit of the British Association to Australia in 1914. He was awarded the Clarke memorial medal of the Royal Society of New South Wales, of which he was twice president (1895 and 1911). The progress of natural science in Australia during the last forty years of his life owes a great deal to his advocacy and the charm of his personality. Shackleton indeed said of him that he could charm a bird off a bough. With charm he combined unfailing courtesy, kindness, and modesty. Besides the honours already mentioned, he received honorary degrees from the universities of Oxford, Manchester, Cambridge, Wales, and St. Andrews. He was elected in 1926 an honorary fellow of his college at Oxford.

David married in 1885 Caroline Matilda, daughter of Samuel Mallet; she had gone out to New South Wales as head of the Training College for Teachers. He had one son and two daughters.

A portrait of David by Norman Carter hangs in the Science House, Sydney University; a copy of this, by Norman Carter, is in the City Hall, Cardiff.

[*Sydney Mail*, 5 September 1934; *The Times*, 29 August 1934; Mary Edgeworth David, *Professor David*, 1937; *Obituary Notices of Fellows of the Royal Society*, No. 4, December 1935 (bibliography and portrait); *Geological Magazine*, vol. lix, 1922 (bibliography up to 1920); *Journal and Proceedings* of the Royal Society of New South Wales, vol. lxix, 1935; E. H. Shackleton, *The Heart of the Antarctic*, 1909; Mrs. Edgeworth David, *Funafuti*, 1899; private information; personal knowledge.] DOUGLAS MAWSON.

DAVIES, WILLIAM HENRY (1871–1940), poet and author, was born at his paternal grandfather's public-house, Church House Tavern, Newport, Monmouthshire, 3 July 1871, the younger son of Francis Davies, a moulder, by his wife, Mary Ann Evans. William's father died when his son was very young, and on his mother's remarriage, he and his sister and imbecile brother were adopted by their grandparents. The grandfather, a native of Cornwall, had been master of a small schooner. William was an unruly schoolboy, but had a passion for reading. Later on, in *Who's Who*, under the item of 'Education', he chose to describe himself as having 'picked up knowledge among tramps in America, on cattle boats, and in the common lodging-houses in England'. On leaving school he was apprenticed to a picture-frame maker, but having been left an allowance of ten shillings a week by his grandmother, at the age of twenty-two he obtained from his trustee an advance of £15 for passage-money to the United States of America, reaching New York with only a few dollars. He then began that career which he later described in his *Autobiography of a Super-Tramp* (1908), tramping thousands of miles in the United States in five or six years, most often begging, but sometimes working at fruit-picking; riding illicitly on freight trains; and making eight or nine trips to England as a cattle-man. He then returned home for a few months, in which time half of his allowance, none of which he had touched since he had been in America, and which had accumulated to £120, was spent. He now determined to go to the gold-diggings in the Klondike, and at Renfrew, Ontario, while attempting to board a moving train, he fell, and the wheel severed his right foot at the ankle. It was found necessary to amputate the leg at the knee, but he was well nursed and was able to return to Wales within five weeks. He soon moved to London, where he lived in common lodging-houses on his allowance, less two shillings which he sent back every week to Newport. After more than two years in London, which he continued to make his base, he made several walking tours as a pedlar of laces, pins, and needles, sometimes varying this life by singing hymns in the streets.

By 1905 Davies's poems had been rejected by publisher after publisher, until he approached Messrs. C. A. Watts & company, bringing with him a letter of recommendation from George R. Sims. Recognizing the merit of the poems, they agreed to pay for the printing of *The Soul's Destroyer, and other poems* partly on the assurance that Davies would do his ut-

most to dispose of copies among likely purchasers. He sent them to various people, requesting each of them either to send him half a crown or to return the book. Among the recipients was Mr. Bernard Shaw, who became most actively interested. At Mr. Shaw's suggestion Davies sent copies to Philip Edward Thomas, Israel Zangwill [qq.v.], Edward Garnett, St. John Adcock, editor of the *Bookman*, and others. Favourable reviews appeared: Davies mentions with especial gratitude notices by Arthur Symons and Arnold Bennett. Edward Thomas, he says, 'gave me a fine boom in several influential papers . . . and became a practical friend, finding me a small cottage in the Weald of Kent [at Sevenoaks] . . . my rent, coal and light being paid mysteriously by Thomas and his friends'. Following upon the reviews, one newspaper wrote up his story.

At Sevenoaks Davies wrote his *Autobiography*, which was published with a preface by Mr. Bernard Shaw at the suggestion of Garnett and Thomas. Mrs. Shaw paid for the typesetting and for the casting of the plates, of which she made a present to Davies. It was the preface, doubtless, that made Davies known to a large public, but it was, Mr. Shaw states, for the sake of the poems that he wrote the preface to the prose book. He had recognized at once that Davies was a poet: it was with some amusement that he wrote of the placid style of the prose book in which tramps 'argue with the decorum of Socrates, and narrate in the style of Tacitus', and in which Davies's loss of a leg is mentioned with the utmost casualness.

In *Who's Who* Davies says that he became a poet at the age of thirty-four and had remained one ever since. He must have been born a poet, but between 1905 and 1939 he produced a score of little books of verse: the *Collected Poems* of 1943 contain 636 pieces (and an introduction by Sir Osbert Sitwell).

Besides these Davies wrote four novels, two of which, *The True Traveller* (1912) and *The Adventures of Johnny Walker, Tramp* (1926), should be read rather as autobiography, bridging the gap between the *Super-Tramp* and *Later Days* (1925). In 1924 he wrote an introduction to Defoe's *Moll Flanders*, with which book his other novels are akin. In 1923 he published *True Travellers: a Tramp's Opera in Three Acts* in prose with interspersed lyrics. This was to have been produced at the Lyric Theatre, Hammersmith, where *The Beg-*

gar's *Opera* had been revived so successfully, but the scheme fell through. Other prose books are *Beggars* (1909), *Nature* (1914), and *My Birds* and *My Garden* (1933). He selected and edited two anthologies, *Shorter Lyrics of the Twentieth Century, 1900 to 1922* (1922) and *Jewels of Song* (1930, reissued 1938). He was joint editor, with Mr. Austin Osman Spare, of a monthly magazine *Form* (October 1921 to January 1922), himself contributing the editorials, each with incidental poems.

In 1919 Davies was granted a civil list pension which was twice increased. In 1926 the university of Wales conferred upon him the honorary degree of Litt.D. In 1923 he married Helen Matilda, daughter of William Payne, farmer, who came from Sussex: his happiness with her is recorded and reflected in *The Lover's Song-Book* (thirty poems, 1933), reprinted as *Love Poems* (1935) with the number of poems increased to fifty. He died, childless, at Nailsworth, Gloucestershire, 26 September 1940.

The contrast between Davies's outer life and the apparently effortless ease, delicacy, and perfection of almost every poem is remarkable. He speaks of himself as a drinking man, with a great interest in pugilism. His poetry puts him with the happiest of the Elizabethans, with Blake in the *Songs of Innocence and of Experience*, with Wordsworth at his simplest. His inexhaustible store of happy similitudes is peculiar to himself.

A bust of Davies by Jacob Epstein is in the Newport (Mon.) Art Gallery, and a painting, by Augustus John, is in the National Gallery of Wales. A pencil sketch by Augustus John (1918) and a plasticine medallion by Theodore Spicer-Simson (1924) are in the National Portrait Gallery. There are other portraits, by Harold Knight, Laura Knight, Sir William Rothenstein, and Walter Sickert.

[*The Times*, 27 September 1940; Thomas Moult, *W. H. Davies*, 1934; W. H. Davies, *The Autobiography of a Super-Tramp*, 1908, *The True Traveller*, 1912, *Later Days*, 1925, and *The Adventures of Johnny Walker, Tramp*, 1926.]   FREDERICK PAGE.

DAWBER, SIR (EDWARD) GUY (1861–1938), architect, was born at King's Lynn, Norfolk, 3 August 1861, the younger son of John Stockdale Dawber, of King's Lynn, by his wife, Lois Ellen Edwards.

Dawber was educated at King's Lynn Grammar School, and was then articled for four years to William Adams, an architect practising in that town. Chance led to his subsequent migration to Dublin, where he became an assistant in the office of Sir Thomas Deane [q.v.]. Here Dawber spent his spare time in measuring and sketching the fine Georgian buildings of the city. He had only been there a year when political troubles caused an interruption in building, so he went to London with a roll of drawings under his arm and was fortunate enough to join the staff of (Sir) Ernest George [q.v.]. That well-known architect had already established a reputation as a designer of imposing mansions in the country and picturesque houses in the West End; and his office became noted as a nursery of genius. In his evenings, at this period, Dawber attended the Royal Academy Schools. In 1887, however, overwork strained his eyes, and George therefore sent him to be clerk of works on a great house at Batsford in Gloucestershire. This apparent interruption to his career proved, in fact, to be his opportunity; for he applied himself with his usual zest to an intensive study of the beautiful but then little-known architecture of the Cotswolds. Soon he decided to begin practice on his own account in that delightful district, and for his office hired a room in the village institute at Bourton-on-the-Hill, at a rent of ninepence a week. Small commissions began to come to him at once, and in 1891 he opened an office in London. From that date up to the time of his death a steady stream of attractive designs, especially although not exclusively for country houses, flowed from his versatile and painstaking pencil. A complete list of them is given in the *Journal* of the Royal Institute of British Architects for 9 May 1938; but here it is only possible to mention a few typical examples: Nether Swell Manor, Burdocks, and Eyford Park in Gloucestershire; Conkwell Grange, Purton Manor, and Hamptworth Lodge in Wiltshire; Ashley Chase in Dorset; Tuesley Court and Dutton Homestall in Surrey; Stowell Hill in Somerset; and the Foord Almshouses at Rochester. The last-named building was the first to be accorded a preservation order under the Town and Country Planning Act.

Honours came freely to Dawber in later life. He was elected A.R.A. in 1927 and R.A. in 1935; he served as president of the Royal Institute of British Architects in 1925–1927; and was awarded the Royal gold medal for architecture in 1928. He was knighted in 1936. He took a prominent part in establishing in 1926 the

Council for the Preservation of Rural England of which he became vice-president and chairman, and England was always his first love although he travelled extensively abroad. A friendly, genial man, looking more like a country squire than an artist, he seemed to typify in his person the spirit of rural England which he understood so well; and his charming country houses and gardens invariably melted into their natural surroundings.

Apart from his consummate skill in the English tradition and his sensitive handling of all the building crafts, Dawber was a talented painter in water-colour, his sketches showing a luminous quality far removed from prosaic architectural drawing. He contributed notes and sketches to two books illustrating *Old Cottages and Farm-houses in Kent and Sussex* (1900) and *Old Cottages, Farm-houses, and other Stone Buildings in the Cotswold District* (1905).

Dawber married in 1896 Mary, daughter of Alexander Eccles, of Roby, near Liverpool, who survived him. There were no children of the marriage. He died in London 24 April 1938. His portrait by Sir William Orpen is at the Royal Institute of British Architects.

[*The Times*, 25 April 1938; *Builder*, 29 April 1938; *Journal* of the Royal Institute of British Architects, 23 June 1928 and 9 May 1938; private information; personal knowledge.] MARTIN S. BRIGGS.

DEARMER, PERCY (1867–1936), divine, was born in London 27 February 1867, the younger son of Thomas Dearmer, artist and drawing master, who died when Percy was ten years old, by his wife, Caroline Miriam Turner. He was educated at Streatham School, at Westminster (1880–1881), at a private school at Vevey, and at Christ Church, Oxford, where he read modern history.

At Christ Church Dearmer began to absorb the two dominant interests of his life—Christian art and the Christian 'social movement'. He was much influenced as a young man by James Adderley, Charles Gore [q.v.], and others of their circle, and threw himself into the work of the Christian Social Union, of the London branch of which he was secretary from 1891 to 1912. But fundamentally he was an artist; his most creative work lay in this field and his most permanent contribution both to the Church and to national life is to be found in his understanding of the true relation between religion and art. He saw that art is not mere decoration but an essential and integral expression of the worship offered to God in religion. No one man did more to raise the standards of art in public worship, and he is believed to be the only clergyman to have been awarded the distinction of the honorary A.R.I.B.A.

Dearmer was ordained deacon in 1891 and priest in 1892, and after serving four curacies (which ranged from St. Anne's, South Lambeth, to Berkeley Chapel, Mayfair), he was appointed in 1901 to the vicarage of St. Mary's, Primrose Hill, where he remained until 1915, and there he put his convictions into practice. Leading artists of all kinds gathered round him, and St. Mary's became known throughout the country. His *Parson's Handbook* (1899, 12th ed. 1931) was an attempt to recall the Church to the native English tradition in matters of liturgy and ceremonial. He made vigorous and imaginative efforts to improve the quality of church music, and was largely responsible for editing the *English Hymnal* (1906), *Songs of Praise* (1925), and the *Oxford Book of Carols* (1928), which revolutionized congregational hymn-singing.

During the war of 1914–1918 Dearmer was chaplain to the British Red Cross ambulance unit in Serbia where his wife, Jessie Mabel, daughter of Surgeon-Major William White, whom he had married in 1892, died of enteric fever in 1915. She was a novelist and playwright. In 1916 he married Nancy, only daughter of Arthur Knowles, and after the war resided in Chelsea and busied himself in manifold activities. He was first professor of ecclesiastical art at King's College, London (1919–1936) and was lecturer in art there (1924–1932). In 1920 he became secretary (chairman, 1921–1936) of the recently founded League of Arts, and, along with Miss Maude Royden, with whom he worked until 1924, he established the Guildhouse. In 1931 he was nominated to a canonry at Westminster Abbey, where—perhaps too late in life—his gifts had full scope and opportunity. He made a distinctive contribution to the preaching and ceremonial in the Abbey and developed remarkable powers as a broadcaster of services for children. He died suddenly at his residence in the Little Cloister 29 May 1936, and was buried in the cloister.

Striking in appearance and highly 'individual' in speech and manner, Dearmer was an original, independent thinker, informed by a thorough scholarship in his own subjects, although in later life this tended to be dissipated by an overgreat and somewhat ephemeral output.

By his first wife Dearmer had two sons, the younger of whom died of wounds received at Gallipoli in 1915; by his second wife, who survived him, he had one son, who was killed in 1942, and two daughters.

A drawing of Dearmer by David Rolt (1935) is in the possession of Lady Sykes (formerly Mrs. Dearmer).

[Nan Dearmer, *Percy Dearmer* (with bibliography), 1940.]   F. R. SOUTHWELL.
(F. R. BARRY.)

DE BUNSEN, SIR MAURICE WILLIAM ERNEST, baronet (1852–1932), diplomatist, was born in London 8 January 1852, the second son of Ernest Christian Ludwig de Bunsen, of Abbey Lodge, Regent's Park, and grandson of the well-loved Baron von Bunsen who was Prussian minister in England from 1841 to 1854 and had married an Englishwoman. His father, a soldier, courtier, and mystical writer, became a British subject in 1849. His mother, Elizabeth Sheppard, daughter of Samuel Gurney [q.v.], of Ham House, West Ham, Essex, bill discounter and philanthropist, was one of the Gurneys of Earlham and a remarkable character; she was a niece of Elizabeth Fry [q.v.], with whom she travelled abroad. He was brought up with a Quaker background in the cultured and cosmopolitan atmosphere of Abbey Lodge, and was educated at Rugby and Christ Church, Oxford.

De Bunsen entered the diplomatic service in 1877. In his third post, at Madrid, he was commended for his dignity and discretion when left in charge of the legation at a difficult time. After three years (1891–1894) as secretary of legation in Japan, he was, in 1894, appointed chargé d'affaires and consul general at Bangkok, where he was in the confidence of the King and the Siamese authorities in their struggle against French pressure. He was first secretary at Constantinople (1897–1902) in the days of Abdul Hamid and the Cretan troubles, and was then transferred to Paris as first secretary. He was appointed C.B. in 1895, C.V.O. in 1903, and K.C.V.O. in 1905. In the last-named year he went as minister to Lisbon.

In 1906 de Bunsen was sworn of the Privy Council and appointed K.C.M.G., G.C.V.O., and ambassador at Madrid, where he and his wife were popular and enjoyed the friendship and confidence of King Alfonso XIII and his Queen. Perhaps de Bunsen's most conspicuous diplomatic achievement was his unofficial mediation, in 1911–1912, at the invitation of both parties, in the dispute over Morocco between France and Spain, which materially helped to bring about a peaceful settlement. He was appointed G.C.M.G. in 1909. In 1913 he succeeded Sir Fairfax Cartwright as ambassador at Vienna, where he kept the British government in close touch with the complicated political developments preceding the outbreak of war.

De Bunsen worked in the Foreign Office until 1918, when he headed a mission to the states of South America, which was a remarkable success. After its close, he retired, at the end of 1918, from the diplomatic service to spend thirteen busy years as a City man and a prominent member of many societies in London, where he died in harness at the age of eighty 21 February 1932.

De Bunsen's good looks and appearance went well with his courtesy, fearless character, and complete honesty. In the service he stood out among his contemporary diplomats for his ability to reconcile opposing parties and to bring the representatives of clashing interests to discuss their differences with reason and temper. He was looked upon as the ideal chief, for kindness, example, and hospitality. A keen sportsman and a good shot, he was also a lover of literature and well informed on many subjects. His most notable accomplishment was in public and personal relationships and in the art of living.

De Bunsen's family life was a happy one. In 1899 he married Berta Mary, elder daughter of Armar Henry Lowry-Corry, who was in the Foreign Office; she was a niece of M. W. Lowry-Corry, Lord Rowton [q.v.], private secretary to Disraeli from 1866 to 1881. They had four daughters. De Bunsen was created a baronet in 1919.

A portrait of de Bunsen by Emil Fuchs (1912), in diplomatic uniform and the robes of a G.C.M.G., is in the possession of his daughter, Mrs. Salisbury Jones.

[*The Times*, 22 February 1932; E. T. S. Dugdale, *Maurice de Bunsen: Diplomat and Friend*, 1934; *British Documents on the Origins of the War*, edited by G. P. Gooch and H. W. V. Temperley, vol. xi; private information; personal knowledge.]
GEORGE FRANCKENSTEIN.

DELAMERE, third BARON (1870–1931), pioneer settler in Kenya. [See CHOLMONDELEY, HUGH.]

DE LÁSZLÓ, PHILIP ALEXIUS (1869–1937), painter. [See LÁSZLÓ DE LÖMBÖS.]

DELIUS, FREDERICK (1862–1934), musician, was born at Bradford 29 January 1862, the second son in a family of four sons and ten daughters of Julius Delius, a well-to-do wool merchant, of Bradford, by his wife, Elise Pauline, daughter of Christian Kroenig, of Bielefeld, Westphalia. Both his parents were German-born but his father, who was also from Bielefeld, had become a naturalized Englishman in 1850. There was much music-making, both amateur and professional, in the home. The young Frederick soon began to prefer Chopin and Grieg to Mozart and Beethoven, a trend of taste which remained undeviating to the end.

After receiving some education at Bradford Grammar School and the International College at Isleworth (1876–1879) Delius, who wished to make music his career, was ordered into the family business and there was actually a brief period of unavailing endeavour in the woollen industry until the domestic crisis so familiar in the lives of artists came to a head. In this case the unusual compromise, reached after some heat, was that Frederick Delius, aged twenty-two, should go out and plant oranges in Florida. There the solitude of the grove, the resplendent tropical scenery, and the strange music of the negroes combined to set the youth's imagination ablaze. He must get a pianoforte. While negotiating for this in Jacksonville he fell in with a convalescent Brooklyn organist, T. F. Ward, who returned to the grove with Delius and the pianoforte to become his informal teacher. This six-months' course proved of greater value than all the formal instruction which Delius was subsequently to undergo. In 1885 he left the grove and set up as a teacher of pianoforte and violin first at Jacksonville and later at Danville, Virginia.

Meanwhile Delius's parents had altogether lost touch with their errant and now independent offspring. But they eventually succeeded in causing a message to reach him in which they offered terms of well-nigh unconditional surrender. At all events in August 1886 Delius became installed as a student at the Leipzig Conservatorium. Now at last he could hear orchestras and operas to his heart's content and live for nothing but music. There

was also the formal instruction at the conservatorium, but no trace of this can be found in his subsequent output except in certain of the weaker passages. The great event of this sojourn was the meeting with Grieg, who was probably the second person—Ward being the first—to perceive the genius in the younger man. In the spring of 1888 an orchestra was hired with the contents of a barrel of beer to play a suite by Delius called 'Florida'. The conductor was Hans Sitt, one of Delius's masters; the audience, Grieg, Christian Sinding, and the composer. The new work received an enthusiastic ovation. Delius, after about eighteen months in Leipzig, accompanied Grieg to London where he was giving some concerts. Now there was arranged a special dinner party at which Grieg finally persuaded Julius Delius of his son's quality. This auspicious occasion marks the end of parental opposition to Frederick's musical career. When Grieg died in 1907 Delius 'felt that he had lost his best friend'.

Delius then (1888) became a whole-time composer. He never did anything else. He moved to France where he lived for the rest of his life. He worked mostly in Paris for eight years, consorting with literary folk, painters, and sculptors—notably Gaugin and Strindberg—rather than with French musicians with whom he had but little in common; to this day his music is unknown in France. In 1897 two friends of his, girl students of painting, invited him for the week-end to a house which they had taken for the summer at Grez-sur-Loing, near Fontainebleau. He accepted and stayed on until death. So did one of the young ladies, Jelka Helen (von) Rosen, whom shortly afterwards he married. Born of a German diplomatic family, she had linguistic talent and a rare literary and artistic perception. Wonderful though she was as a wife, particularly during her husband's last stricken years, she was more than that. She helped in the selection and arrangement of the words for most of the choral output of his best years, a literary task which, unaided, the composer was not at all well qualified to perform. Notable too were her wit and charm, which even life with Delius failed to impair.

From then until 1921 all the great works were composed in the quiet home at Grez with the garden running down to the river. Here the couple mostly remained except when the war came too dangerously near for comfort. Then having buried the wine, they sought the temporary shelter of these shores. Otherwise there would merely be trips to Germany and England in order to hear Delius's works performed, and to the Norwegian mountains for the summer holidays. He had learnt to love these in youth during one of his wool-trade visits to Sweden.

It is a tale of toil, frustration, gradual recognition, and ultimate triumph. Before the end of the century faint signs of recognition were stirring. Hans Haym and Alfred Hertz, of Elberfeld, and Julius Buths, of Düsseldorf, began to show interest. In 1899 Delius gave a choral-orchestral concert in the St. James's Hall, London. Hertz came over to conduct the programme which included the tone poem 'Over the Hills and Far Away' (which had already been given at Elberfeld under Haym), the music which now forms the close of 'A Mass of Life', and excerpts from the opera *Koanga*, the negro opera inspired by his sojourn in Florida. Press and public gave this concert a fairly good though puzzled reception; yet the general impression remains that a considerable curiosity to hear more of this unknown composer was aroused.

Nevertheless, it was left to Germany to carry on the good work with performances of 'Appalachia' (choral-orchestral variations on an old slave song, also inspired by Florida) at Düsseldorf (1905), 'Sea-Drift' (cantata with words taken from a poem by Walt Whitman) at Essen (1906), and the opera *A Village Romeo and Juliet* at Berlin (1907). Delius's renown was established in Germany by virtue of these three works alone, and his subsequent compositions were repeatedly played with abundant success up and down the country ('Brigg Fair' for instance was in 1910 alone played by thirty-six different orchestras) until the outbreak of war in 1914.

But about 1910 a young conductor called Thomas Beecham had already appeared to put English lovers of music in general and of Delius in particular under an unlimited debt. He was the first to discover the key to this composer's *tempi* and to his peculiar mode of utterance. Fortunately he has directed the recording of most of Delius's large works for the concert hall. These are the authoritative renderings ecstatically approved throughout by the composer, so that there can never be any excuse for future arbitrary individual 'readings', for the tradition is now established once and for all. But the list is still (1945) incomplete.

Soon after 1924 Delius lost his sight and the use of his limbs. It seemed that his muse must be stilled for ever. Meanwhile there was a steady increase in performances of Delius, although Sir Thomas Beecham was at that time in temporary self-imposed retirement. In 1920 there occurred at the Queen's Hall the first performance of 'The Song of the High Hills' under Albert Coates, and later (1925) the first post-war performance of 'A Mass of Life' under Paul Klenau, both at concerts of the Royal Philharmonic Society. Sir Henry Wood also was including certain smaller works in his promenade and Saturday symphony concerts at the Queen's Hall, while (Sir) Hamilton Harty in the north was doing good work. But with Sir Thomas Beecham's return in 1926 the composer rapidly became—what his most fervent admirers had never envisaged—a genuine popular success. That he had at last won the ear of the musical multitude was proved by the six-day Delius festival held at the Queen's Hall in the autumn of 1929 under Beecham and in the presence of the composer in his bathchair. With the disappointing exception of 'The Song of the High Hills' the cream of his orchestral output with and without *soli* and chorus was included. In the same year the King appointed Delius a C.H. In 1932 he received the freedom of the city of Bradford and in 1933 an honorary degree from Leeds University. In 1929 the university of Oxford invited him to come and receive the honorary degree of D.Mus., but at the last moment he was unable to visit Oxford.

In 1928 Mr. Eric Fenby, a young Yorkshire musician, offered his services as amanuensis and they were gratefully accepted. The task consisted largely in constructing finished articles from previously existing sketches, but there was also actual invention of new material. The process of dictation evolved by this unique partnership is fascinatingly described in Mr. Fenby's book *Delius as I knew him* (1936). The most outstanding work realized by this collaboration is 'Songs of Farewell' for double chorus and orchestra given at a Courtauld–Sargent concert in 1932.

Delius died at Grez-sur-Loing 10 June 1934. After temporary burial in Grez churchyard, his body was next year removed to Limpsfield in Surrey. At the service on that occasion Sir Thomas Beecham read the funeral oration and conducted a detachment of picked orchestral players in certain Delius pieces fitting for the occasion. Delius's widow was placed beside her husband a few days later. There were no children of the marriage.

'But it's not music' expostulated Delius one day, humming a misquotation from Beethoven. His bitterly caustic tongue, at strange variance with his music, in a harsh almost rasping accent, half Bradford, half foreign, would thus give pungent expression to his distaste for the classics. Another violent antipathy was towards the verbal discussion of composition technique. A notable English pundit was one day holding forth upon this subject in a musical company until Delius, bearing it no longer, interpolated the observation 'Well, at any rate music is a thing to be listened to, not talked about.' Both these traits explain to some extent his curious isolation in musical realms, for apart from a superficial affinity with Grieg's his music derives from nothing and leads nowhere. Professional critics have decried his lack of 'form' and amateur listeners have complained of monotony of texture. Both strictures are half just. He disdained the use of mechanical expedient to secure semblance of 'form', so that the innocent listener, deprived of such adventitious aids to sustained attention, cannot always follow the composer's thought and tends to become drowsy with the sheer sensuous beauty of sound from moment to moment. So with his operas, which are not 'dramatic' according to any hitherto known conventions. Yet the carefully wrought and beautiful performances under Beecham at the Royal College of Music of *A Village Romeo and Juliet* (1934) convinced the audiences of the work's innate though highly individual dramatic purpose. Intensely susceptible to the beauties of nature and to the emotions, joys, and sorrows of life, Delius made these the inspiration of all his most lovely works, the titles of which usually indicate the character of each one.

There are three portraits of Delius by James Gunn: a painting which represents him listening to his 'Mass of Life' (1929) is in the possession of the City Art Gallery, Bradford; a sketch in oils (1932) and another portrait (also 1932) are in private possession.

[Philip Heseltine, *Frederick Delius*, 1923; Clare Delius, *Frederick Delius. Memories of my Brother*, 1935; Eric Fenby, *Delius as I knew him*, 1936; R. H. Hull, *Delius*, 1928; Arthur Hutchings, *Delius*, 1948; *Grove's Dictionary of Music and Musicians*, 4th ed., vol. ii, edited by H. C. Colles; personal knowledge.]

PATRICK HADLEY.

DELL, ETHEL MARY (1881-1939), novelist. [See SAVAGE.]

DELLER, SIR EDWIN (1883-1936), principal of the university of London, was born at Paignton, Devon, 16 March 1883, the son of Edwin Deller, carpenter, of Paignton, by his wife, Mary Ann Stone. He was educated at local schools up to the age of fourteen, when he began work as a clerk for an uncle at Paignton. He came to London at the age of about twenty and was engaged on clerical work in various offices before joining the Kent education committee, with which he stayed until 1912, when he became a secretary in the academic department of London University. He was already a member of the university, for he had matriculated in 1908 as an evening student at King's College, graduating LL.B. in 1911. He obtained the degree of LL.D. in 1916 with a thesis entitled 'The Liberty of the Subject', as a student of University College. He had also studied at the London School of Economics. His career on the staff of the university was rapid. In 1921 he became academic registrar, in which post he made his mark, and in 1929 he was elected principal of the university.

Great things were expected of Deller and he fulfilled those expectations; for he had many gifts. He was a born administrator and a man of great culture and knowledge of the world, while his quickness of intuition made him singularly skilful in handling men and situations. He seldom intervened in debate, but when he did, he would settle a point by a few brief words, wise and tactful, and often touched with a quiet and irresistible humour. He had a quick eye for the heart of any problem, and an equability of temper that was of the utmost value in handling the often heated controversies which confronted him during his term of office. Above all, he was a man of striking personality and charm, and won the enduring affection of those with whom he worked. His open-hearted friendliness and his quiet wisdom diffused a much needed spirit of goodwill and co-operation in the university, upon which the erection of the central buildings in Bloomsbury set the crown. In the organization of these buildings and the general policy of the development of the site Deller made a great contribution, although he was not destined to see their completion, dying in London 30 November 1936 from the effects of an accident when visiting, three days earlier, the great tower, then in the course of construction.

Outside the university, Deller played a great part in founding the British Institute in Paris. In 1926 he visited the United States of America, and on his return wrote an excellent book *Universities in the United States* (1927). He was made a chevalier of the Legion of Honour in 1932 and was knighted in 1935. Among other distinctions he was elected an honorary bencher of the Inner Temple in 1933. He married in 1914 Winifred Lilian (Betty), eldest daughter of Benjamin Willey Betts, embosser and chaser, of Hornsey, and had a son.

[*The Times*, 1, 2, 4, and 5 December 1936; personal knowledge.] H. E. BUTLER.

DE MONTMORENCY, JAMES EDWARD GEOFFREY (1866–1934), legal scholar, was born at Greenwich 6 December 1866, the third son of James Lodge de Montmorency, a member of the hospital staff there, by his wife, Susan Kiddel. Educated at Blackheath Proprietary School, he was admitted to Peterhouse, Cambridge, in 1886, and graduated B.A. in 1889 and LL.B. in 1890: in 1909 he was awarded the Seatonian prize for an English poem on a sacred subject. In 1892 he was called to the bar by the Middle Temple and went into chambers on the Chancery side. He had a strong inclination towards the more academic aspects of the law and, at an early stage in his career, was inspired with enthusiasm for comparative legal studies by the influence of (Sir) John Macdonell [q.v.], Quain professor of comparative law in the university of London. In 1902 he was Quain prizeman in comparative law at University College, London, and in 1911 and 1912 King Edward VII legal research scholar of the Middle Temple. In 1920 he succeeded Macdonell as Quain professor and he held the chair until his retirement in 1932. From 1930 to 1932 he was also dean of the faculty of laws in the university of London.

De Montmorency's activities covered a wide area and, in addition to those already mentioned, he was for many years literary editor of the *Contemporary Review*. He acted as assistant secretary of the royal commission on divorce and matrimonial causes (1910–1912) and as joint secretary and member of the attorney-general's committee of inquiry into breaches of the laws of war (1918–1920). He was a prolific writer, but much of his published work is of a somewhat miscellaneous and transient

character. He was one of the principal contributors to the series of monographs published by the Society of Comparative Legislation under the title of 'Great Jurists of the World' and he wrote the section on 'Sea-Policy and the Alabama Claims' in the *Cambridge History of British Foreign Policy*, vol. iii (1923). Selections of the articles which he contributed to *The Times* and the *Contemporary Review* were published under the titles of *The Never-Ending Road* (1916), *The White Riders* (1918), and *The Admiral's Chair* (1921).

De Montmorency met with considerable success as a teacher of the law. He was of a warm-hearted and generous disposition, which endeared him to students, and he was untiring in his efforts to assist them. A keen churchman, he was invaluable as a governor and manager of Church schools. He married in 1899 Caroline Maud Saumarez, third daughter of Major-General James de Havilland, and had one son and two daughters. He died at Blackheath 9 March 1934.

[Private information; personal knowledge.] H. C. GUTTERIDGE.

DENNY, SIR ARCHIBALD, first baronet (1860–1936), shipbuilder and engineer, was born at Dumbarton 7 February 1860, the fourth son of Peter Denny, of Helenslee, Dumbarton, shipbuilder, by his wife, Helen, eldest daughter of James Leslie, of Dumbarton. Educated at the Dumbarton Burgh Academy until the age of fourteen, he spent two years at the École Cantonale at Lausanne, and then began his apprenticeship in the shipbuilding department of the family business of William Denny & Brothers, shipbuilders and engineers. During this period he qualified for entrance to the Royal Naval College, Greenwich, and for three years combined academic and practical training. On the completion of these courses he served for a short time on the Liverpool staff of Lloyd's Register of Shipping.

In 1883 Denny became a partner in his father's firm, and quickly assumed responsibility for the technical side of the undertaking. He was particularly identified with the development of the experiment tank in the Leven shipyard, which was installed in 1883, the first in the world in a private establishment; his name is probably best known to the public as a designer and builder of high-speed passenger vessels, particularly those of the cross-Channel type. On the scientific side of his profession he was an acknowledged leader, and was freely consulted by government departments and other interests. He played a prominent part in the counsels of the Institution of Naval Architects, and for long was chairman of the technical committee of the British Corporation Register of Shipping. He was chairman of the British Engineering Standards Institution for nine years; of the Board of Trade committee on the subdivision of ships from 1920 to 1924; and of the committee appointed to investigate the *Titanic* disaster (1912–1915), and also during this period, of the International Conference on the Safety of Life at Sea. He also acted as chairman or served as a member of many other governmental and official commissions or committees.

An enthusiastic volunteer, Denny served for many years (ultimately as second in command) in the local battalion of the Argyll and Sutherland Highlanders.

For his professional services to the country and his profession Denny was created a baronet in 1913. He received the honorary degree of LL.D. from the universities of Glasgow (1911) and Cambridge (1927).

In 1885 Denny married Margaret, second daughter of John Tulloch, engineer, of Dumbarton, a partner in the engineering department of the firm. He had five sons and one daughter. He died in London 29 May 1936, and was succeeded as second baronet by his eldest son, Maurice Edward (born 1886).

A portrait of Denny by Maurice Greiffenhagen is the property of Sir Maurice Denny.

[Leven Ship Yard office papers; personal knowledge.]   MAURICE DENNY.

DEVLIN, JOSEPH (1871–1934), Irish politician, was born in Hamill Street, Belfast, 13 February 1871, the fourth son of Charles Devlin, car-driver, of Belfast, by his wife, Elizabeth King. His parents, recent immigrants from the Lough Neagh district, were Roman Catholics, and at the age of six he entered the Christian Brothers' Schools, Divis Street. While still very young he became a pot-boy in a public house. He showed an early aptitude for public speaking, and at the age of fifteen was elected chairman of a debating society formed to commemorate the victory of Thomas Sexton [q.v.] over his unionist opponent at West Belfast in 1886. From 1891 until 1893 Devlin was a journalist on the *Irish News*, the Belfast

nationalist paper, and in the last-named year became Belfast correspondent of the *Freeman's Journal*. He soon became secretary of the Belfast Young Ireland Society, which he represented at the convention held in Dublin in 1897. This led to a post at the party headquarters in Dublin. In 1902 he went to the United States of America as secretary of the United Irish League, and on five later occasions visited the United States on political missions. He also visited Australia in 1905. He was returned unopposed for North Kilkenny at a by-election in February 1902, and in 1906 regained the seat for West Belfast which Sexton had lost in 1892, holding it until 1918. During this period he refounded the Ancient Order of Hibernians, of which he was president from 1905 until his death. In 1913 he was a leading organizer of the National Volunteers in opposition to the Ulster Volunteers of Sir Edward (later Lord) Carson [q.v.]. He was a member of the Irish Convention of 1917–1918, and his difference with J. E. Redmond [q.v.] over the customs question contributed to the failure of the convention. On Redmond's death in 1918 he was offered the chairmanship of the party, but gave way in favour of John Dillon [q.v.]. In that year he defeated Mr. de Valera in the Falls division of Belfast (Imperial parliament), holding the seat until 1922, when he unsuccessfully contested the Exchange division of Liverpool. In 1921 he was returned for county Antrim and West Belfast in the new Northern Irish parliament. He did not take his seat (West Belfast only) until 1925, and, after holding this seat until 1929 and being returned for Central Belfast in 1930, with the other nationalist members withdrew in 1932, having won concessions for his co-religionists in the Education Act of 1930. From 1929 onwards he was senior member for Fermanagh and Tyrone at Westminster, and was again elected for Central Belfast in the Northern Irish parliament in 1933. He died, unmarried, in Belfast 18 January 1934, and his body was followed to the grave by representatives of both Irish governments.

Devlin, who was small and thick-set, with a large head and coal-black hair, was loved by all creeds and parties, accessible to all his constituents, generous and active on behalf of the poor and oppressed. He founded a holiday home for working-women near Belfast. In debate he was witty but intellectual, a ready improviser and, although very nervous, a powerful platform speaker. He was called by T. M. Healy [q.v.] 'the duodecimo Demosthenes' and by Belfastmen 'Wee Joe'. He was the last eminent survivor of the Irish party, and Northern nationalism has had no such leader since.

A portrait of Devlin by Sir John Lavery hangs in the Municipal Gallery, Belfast, and a bronze head by Francis Doyle-Jones is at Charlemont House, Dublin.

[*Irish News, The Times, Irish Times, Belfast Telegraph,* 19 January 1934; *Christian Brothers' Souvenir* (Derry), 1927; *Hibernian Journal,* January 1947; private information.]

MAURICE CRAIG.

DEVONPORT, first VISCOUNT (1856–1934), business man. [See KEARLEY, HUDSON EWBANK.]

DEVONSHIRE, ninth DUKE OF (1868–1938). [See CAVENDISH, VICTOR CHRISTIAN WILLIAM.]

DEWRANCE, SIR JOHN (1858–1937), mechanical engineer, was born at Peckham, London, 13 March 1858, the only son of John Dewrance, of Greenhills, Tilford, Surrey, who erected the locomotive *Rocket* for George Stephenson [q.v.] and was on its footplate with him during the famous trials at Rainhill in 1829, by his wife, Elizabeth, daughter of Joseph Curtis, of Tilford. He was educated at Charterhouse and King's College, London, where he paid special attention to chemistry, and was a pupil of his step-father, Colonel John Davis. On coming of age he took control of the engineering business of Dewrance & company, which had been left him by his father, who died in 1861. In this business, which was opened in London in 1835 by Joseph Woods, brother of Edward Woods [q.v.], the elder Dewrance became a partner and on the death of Woods in 1842 changed its name to Dewrance & company, which it still bears.

Dewrance had a 'great affection' for scientific research, which he said was implanted in him by the electro-metallurgist George Gore [q.v.], and in 1880 he started a research laboratory, taking over Professor Frederick Barff's assistants and apparatus and working up his process for protecting iron from rust by treatment with superheated steam. In this laboratory he produced, in 1882, an ingot of aluminium by electrolysis, and carried out extensive investigations, notably on lubri-

cation and the corrosion of marine boilers. Some of his results were described in two papers which he read before the Institution of Civil Engineers; the first, on mechanical bearings, won him a Telford premium in 1896, and the second, on the corrosion of boilers, a Watt gold medal and a Telford premium in 1900. Some years before the war of 1914–1918 he gave up this laboratory, which by then had developed into a two-acre factory with a pier on the Thames, and with it what he called individualistic research. His interest in research, however, continued, and hoping by team work to accomplish more for the benefit of industry than could be done by working alone, he became a member of many research committees, particularly those of the Institution of Mechanical Engineers on alloys and cutting tools, of both of which he was chairman. Increase of co-ordinated research work, standardization, and mass production was the prescription which he offered in 1923 for the future prosperity of British industry.

Dewrance was a prolific inventor who took out more than a hundred patents, mainly relating to steam fittings and boiler mountings. He was also an able administrator and man of business. From 1899 until a few months before his death he was chairman of Babcock & Wilcox, Ltd., and from 1914 of Kent Coal Concessions, Ltd., and allied companies; aspersions cast by a shareholder on his conduct of these coal companies led him to take legal action, and in 1924 the offender was convicted of defamatory libel. In 1923 he was president of the Institution of Mechanical Engineers and from 1926 to 1928 of the Institute of Metals. He was also president of the Engineering and Allied Employers' National Federation (1920–1926), master of the Armourers' and Braziers' Company (1923), and a fellow of King's College, London (1929). He was appointed K.B.E. in 1920 and G.B.E. in 1928. In 1882 he married Isabella Ann (died 1922), second daughter of Francis Trevithick, of Penzance, and granddaughter of Richard Trevithick [q.v.], the 'father of the locomotive'; they had a son and a daughter. He died at his home, Wretham Hall, Thetford, Norfolk, 7 October 1937.

[*The Times,* 8 October 1937; *Engineer* and *Engineering,* 15 October 1937 (portraits); *Proceedings* of the Institution of Mechanical Engineers, vol. cxxxvi, 1937; *Journal* of the Institution of Civil Engineers, vol. ix, 1937–1938.]

H. M. ROSS.

DIBDIN, Sir LEWIS TONNA (1852–1938), ecclesiastical lawyer, judge, and administrator, was born in London 19 July 1852, the third son of the Rev. Robert William Dibdin, by his wife, Caroline, only child of William Thompson, barrister, of the Temple. He was grandson of Charles Dibdin the younger, of Sadler's Wells Theatre, who was a natural son of Charles Dibdin the dramatist and song-writer, and nephew of the musician Henry Edward Dibdin, [qq.v.]. His father enjoyed considerable popularity for many years as a preacher at West Street chapel, Seven Dials, which, as La Tremblade, had been one of the earliest Huguenot churches in London and at a later date was a regular preaching place of John Wesley.

Dibdin, after being educated at home, entered St. John's College, Cambridge, in 1869, and graduated as a senior optime in the mathematical tripos of 1874. He was called to the bar by Lincoln's Inn in 1876 and from 1895 to 1901 was official counsel to the attorney-general in charity matters. His main interest, however, had from an early date been ecclesiastical law and history, and he was appointed chancellor of the dioceses of Rochester (1886), Exeter (1888), and Durham (1891). In 1899 he was engaged in the Lambeth hearings on incense and reservation. He took silk in 1901. Next year he appeared for the Crown in the proceedings arising out of the appointment of Charles Gore [q.v.] to the see of Worcester; his services had been sought by all four other parties. From 1903 to 1934 he was dean of the Arches, master of the Faculties, and official principal of the Chancery Court of York, and from 1925 to 1934 he was vicar-general of the province of Canterbury.

In 1907 the Deceased Wife's Sister's Marriage Act was passed; next year Dibdin had to decide its effect in the memorable litigation known as the Deceased Wife's Sister case, which, in its various phases, lasted from 1908 to 1912. His judgement was upheld in the divisional court, the Court of Appeal, and the House of Lords, and the principle was settled that the Deceased Wife's Sister's Marriage Act of 1907 validates for all purposes a marriage between a man and his deceased wife's sister, wherever and whenever contracted. In view of his evangelical upbringing, several of his decisions in the Court of Arches came as a welcome surprise to the Anglo-Catholic party and strengthened its position.

Dibdin's main occupation, however, from his appointment as first Church estates commissioner in 1905 until his resignation in 1930 was the direction of the business of the Ecclesiastical Commission. During that time he bore the chief responsibility for its policy and, with Lord Phillimore [q.v.], for initiating the many schemes for the benefit of the clergy which eventually took statutory shape in the measures beginning with the clergy pension and episcopal pension measures of 1926. To him, too, are largely attributable the numerous measures relating to the Ecclesiastical Commission and to patronage and episcopal endowments. Combining with his office of commissioner that of an active governor and chairman of committees of Queen Anne's Bounty, he eliminated much of the overlapping of functions and the competition which had formerly existed.

Dibdin had taken a prominent part in the deliberations of the House of Laymen of the Convocation of Canterbury almost from the formation of the House in 1886 and he was for a time its vice-chairman. Immediately on the establishment of the Church Assembly in 1920 he took a very active share in its work, both in his personal capacity and as the spokesman of the ecclesiastical commissioners, and he was largely responsible for a great many of its measures. There is probably no one to whom the assembly is more heavily indebted for its procedure and for the spirit in which its business is conducted.

Dibdin served on many royal and other commissions and committees on Church affairs. The report of the royal commission on ecclesiastical discipline (1904–1906) was mainly his work. As a signatory of the minority Report of the royal commission on divorce (1909–1912) he, together with the archbishop of York (Cosmo Lang) and Sir William Anson [q.v.], recommended no alteration in the existing law other than equality of treatment for the sexes. In 1914 he presided over the Archbishops' Ancient Monuments (Churches) Committee, which led to the formation of the diocesan advisory committees. The historical section of the Report of the Archbishops' Committee on Church and State was prepared by Dibdin and A. L. Smith, master of Balliol College, Oxford [q.v.], and published in 1916; on this Report were based the constitution of the Church Assembly and the proposals which received statutory form in the Church of England (Assembly) Powers Act, commonly called the Enabling Act, of 1919. Between 1923 and 1926 he served on the ecclesiastical courts commission. In 1934 illness compelled his resignation from the commission on the relations between Church and State, appointed in 1930 after the rejection by the House of Commons of the 1928 Prayer Book. At the same time he resigned all his offices, legal and administrative.

Dibdin was knighted in 1903; in 1891 he received the honorary degree of D.C.L. from Durham University; he was elected a bencher of Lincoln's Inn in 1908 and an honorary fellow of St. John's College, Cambridge, in 1924. Other honours were offered him and were refused. He died at his home at Dormansland, Surrey, 12 June 1938. He married in 1881 Marianne Aubrey (died 1927), eldest daughter of Humphrey Senhouse Pinder, rector of Bratton Fleming, North Devon. He was survived by three of his five sons and by his two daughters; the eldest son, Mr. Lewis George Dibdin, became secretary of the Church Assembly in 1939.

Dibdin combined in a very rare degree the qualities of lawyer, judge, and administrator, and this, together with his great experience, gave him a unique position for a layman in Church affairs. Archbishop Benson relied greatly upon him and when Archbishop Davidson was at Lambeth Dibdin advised him almost daily on practically everything except patronage.

Dibdin wrote or edited a number of legal and other works including *The Livery Companies of London* (1886), *Monasticism in England* (1890), and *The Ecclesiastical Commission* (1919). His *Establishment in England* (1932), a collection of essays written over a period of fifty years, emphasizes his strong support of the Establishment.

[*The Times*, 13 and 16 June 1938; *Church Times*, 17 June 1938; *Guardian*, 3 August 1887; G. K. A. Bell, *Life of Archbishop Davidson*, 2 vols, 1936; Records of St. John's College, Cambridge, and of Lincoln's Inn; Reports of royal commissions; *Law Reports*, *passim*; private information.]

WILLIAM CLEVELAND-STEVENS.

DICKINSON, GOLDSWORTHY LOWES (1862–1932), humanist, historian, and philosophical writer, was born in London 6 August 1862, the third child and younger son of Lowes (Cato) Dickinson [q.v.], portrait-painter, by his wife, Margaret Ellen, daughter of William Smith Williams, who, as the literary adviser of Messrs. Smith, Elder & company, discovered Charlotte Brontë for that firm. He was educated at Charterhouse and went to King's College, Cambridge, as an exhibitioner in 1881; in 1884 he was awarded a first class in the classical tripos and the chancellor's English medal for a poem on Savonarola, and was elected into a fellowship at his college three years later with a dissertation on Plotinus.

Against the grain Dickinson forced himself to begin to qualify as a physician, believing it to be his duty to do practical service to his fellow men. He passed his first M.B. examination in 1887 and his second in 1888, but he then had to admit that medicine was not his *métier*, and he saw that he could better discharge his duty in life by giving a practical application to his own qualities of mind and spirit. He had already given courses of university extension lectures and he now turned to modern history, regarding this as the field in which his pursuit of truth could best be brought to bear on the practical problems of humanity. The first fruits of this decision were *Revolution and Reaction in Modern France* (1892) and *The Development of Parliament during the Nineteenth Century* (1895), and when his fellowship was permanently renewed in 1896, it was as an historian that he was appointed, holding the post of lecturer in political science from then until 1920, when he retired with a pension fellowship for life.

During the next fifteen years Dickinson's lectures, tuition, and the discussion society which he founded kindled the imagination and the inquiring spirit of the young in the tradition handed down at King's from Oscar Browning [q.v.]. But besides thus fulfilling his practical obligations, Dickinson, established in those benign surroundings which were, in no ordinary sense, his spiritual home, felt free to devote himself to the studies which had always been nearest to his heart. Plato and the Greeks had been his first love, and this love he now commemorated in *The Greek View of Life* (1896) which was for long the finest appreciation of the Greek genius in English, and this was followed by a series of dialogues in the Socratic tradition, written in pure English yet tinged with pervasive poetry and lit by the love of plain truth: *The Meaning of Good* (1901), *A Modern Symposium* (1905), and *Justice and Liberty* (1908).

Dickinson helped to found the *Independent Review* in 1903, and in the following years he contributed a number of articles, some of which were reprinted in *Religion. A Criticism and a Forecast* (1905) and *Religion and Immortality* (1911). He made two lecture tours in the United States of America in 1901 and 1909, and in 1912 he became the first holder of the Albert Kahn travelling fellowship, which took him to India, China, and Japan. India he did not like, but China, which he had already celebrated from intuition rather than knowledge in *Letters from John Chinaman* (1901), answered all his expectations, and the mandarin's cap which he brought back and wore as indoor head-gear for the rest of his life symbolized his affection for a civilization which stood second only to Greece in his spiritual loyalties.

The outbreak of war in 1914 abruptly closed this golden period and brought Dickinson sharply back to his own sternest conception of his tasks. He was not a conscientious objector and he did not think that the war could have been avoided, but all his hopes for humanity seemed to have been brought to nought. Yet he threw himself at once into practical activity in the cause of preventing future wars. Within the first fortnight of the war he drafted schemes for a 'League of Nations' (a phrase which he may have invented) and played the leading part in founding the group of pacificist internationalists known as the Bryce group, which later became one of the nuclei of the League of Nations Union and promulgated some of the actual provisions of the covenant of the League. Dickinson worked hard throughout the war in these organizing and propagandist activities: he attended a pacificist conference at The Hague in 1915, and lectured in America the following year: he also produced a large number of books and pamphlets of which the most considerable are *The European Anarchy* (1916) and *The Choice Before Us* (1917). These were the forerunners of the far more authoritative work, *The International Anarchy, 1904–1914* (1926), with which he brought to consummation and put on record his labours to unravel the true causes of the war and to show by contrast the principles on which alone peace could be built for the future.

With this publication Dickinson entered what was perhaps the happiest period of his life. The war years and their aftermath had been a time of great bitterness, and he had only allowed himself one interlude from his sterner labours—the poetic fantasy of *The Magic Flute* (1920)—

but his remaining six years were a kind of St. Martin's summer which he devoted to his old loves of Plato, poetry, and the pursuit of truth. The new generation of undergraduates, comparatively untouched by the war, took Dickinson to its heart, and he, emerging from his loneliness, found that the college, which had never ceased to shelter him during the stress of war, sought him as a companion of both young and old in the concerns and occasions of its daily life. Under these influences of balm and stimulus, Dickinson wrote *After Two Thousand Years: a Dialogue between Plato and a Modern Young Man* (1930), a last flowering from the old roots, which he himself described as his *Nunc Dimittis*.

It was characteristic of Dickinson that, at a time when he might well have felt that his work was done, he found a new activity and became a broadcaster, to whom the response was wide enough for repeated contributions to be invited. The themes which he chose were those nearest to his heart: Goethe (a lifelong devotion), Plato, and the hope of throwing the light of clear thought on the ways of the world. *Plato and his Dialogues* (1931) is an expansion of one of these broadcast series. His last work, *The Contribution of Ancient Greece to Modern Life* (1932), was a lecture delivered at a Cambridge summer school a few weeks before he died in London 3 August 1932. He was unmarried.

As a young man Dickinson had been a member of that Cambridge Society in which Roger Fry [q.v.], his oldest friend, J. M. E. M'Taggart [q.v.], and Nathaniel Wedd were then the moving spirits. This society meant much to Dickinson all his life; but no searcher after truth less deserved the name of 'highbrow' or fitted less into a coterie than Dickinson. Never was anyone less pompous, less of a prig, or more charming: he was a loved and honoured member of the intellectual élite of the time, but he thought his own thoughts and went his own way. In a rationalist age he was interested in mysticism, and his sense of the mystical was never far below the surface, although he himself had no experience of ecstasy. He was at no time tempted to swerve from agnosticism into Christianity, but his scepticism was of the true unresting kind and would never find in suspension of judgement a relief from the necessity of further thought. There could be no doubt of his seriousness on any important subject, but there was no trace of the puritan in his nature or his work. He loved gaiety and humour, he felt the cold intensely, he suffered from a kind of amused exasperation with inanimate objects; but he cared for first things first and did honour over a lifetime to truth, beauty, and love.

A portrait of Dickinson by Roger Fry (1925) hangs in the hall at King's College, Cambridge; another portrait by the same artist (1893) is in the National Portrait Gallery.

[E. M. Forster, *Goldsworthy Lowes Dickinson* (with a bibliography by R. E. Balfour), 1934; *Cambridge Review*, 14 October 1932; unpublished letters and papers; personal knowledge.]   P. D. PROCTOR.

DICKSON-POYNDER, SIR JOHN POYNDER, sixth baronet, and BARON ISLINGTON (1866–1936). [See POYNDER.]

DILLON, EMILE JOSEPH (1854–1933), philologist, author, and journalist, was born in Dublin 21 March 1854, the only son of Michael Dillon, a cutlery and hardware merchant, by his wife, Mary Byrne. He ardently desired that his son should enter the priesthood; and after visiting the Carmelite School and Holy Cross College, Clonliffe, the young man spent some time at Pantasaph Monastery in Wales, the Grande Chartreuse, the Seminary of St. Sulpice, and the Paulist College, New York. But theology attracted Dillon much less than oriental languages, to which he devoted himself under Ernest Renan at the Collège de France. Inspired by that great man's enthusiasm and erudition, he continued his linguistic studies at the universities of Innsbrück, Leipzig, Tübingen, Louvain, St. Petersburg, and Kharkoff. At three of these institutions he obtained his doctorate in oriental languages, comparative philology, and philosophy. Sanskrit, Arabic, Hebrew, and Persian were among the languages which he acquired, as well as medieval Scandinavian, Armenian, and Zend. Various modern languages were added, without apparent effort, to his range of learning and, as an example of the correctness with which he spoke them, he went from Germany to act as tutor to the sons of a Russian nobleman and only after five months there was it realized that Dillon was not a German.

Although he wrote learned works on philology and such books as *The Sceptics of the Old Testament* (1895) Dillon's true bent was towards journalism and occasional literature. He published essays and fiction in Russian, translated some of Tolstoy's stories, contributed to the *Fortnightly Review* a series of bold articles, signed 'E. B. Lanin', on Russian affairs, married in 1881 a Russian lady, the daughter of a St. Petersburg civil servant (who bore him three sons and, the marriage having been dissolved, died in 1919), and edited a newspaper in Odessa. Returning to Kharkoff University in 1884 he lectured, of course in Russian, as professor of comparative philology. A journey to Armenia, the language of which fascinated him, resulted in the translation of an ancient Armenian manuscript into Russian and subsequently he was elected—a rare distinction which he shared with Byron—to membership of the Armenian Academy in Venice.

From 1887 to 1914 Dillon was the correspondent in Russia of the *Daily Telegraph*, which frequently entrusted him with special missions elsewhere. If he judged that the situation was critical in any country he could go on the spur of the moment, merely letting the editor know that he had gone. Within a few hours of arriving at his destination he would be sending long and well informed dispatches. In 1894, forbidden by the Sultan to go to Armenia after the massacres, he went in disguise as a Russian officer and was received with military honours; the dispatches which he sent by devious routes created a sensation and won the high approval of Gladstone. In 1897 he watched the Cretan revolt against Turkish misrule and, disguised as an insurgent monk, he went with Eleutherios Venizelos—his friend ever after—on board the flagship of the Allied Fleet, to refuse autonomy instead of annexation to Greece. On leaving the ship the pious Italian admiral asked for his blessing, whereupon, with two fingers on the admiral's head, he muttered a few words of Anacreon, all he could think of at the moment. During the Spanish-American war of 1898 he was in Spain. Next year he reported voluminously the second trial of Alfred Dreyfus, at Rennes. In 1900 he followed the international expedition against the Chinese 'Boxers'. He was ubiquitous and indefatigable. Of medium stature and without marked physical characteristics, Dillon could mingle unnoticed with any oriental crowd, while his linguistic virtuosity disarmed suspicion.

Throughout his long life Dillon remained a man of mystery. He kept secret his methods of gaining information. Not many of his employers or colleagues felt that they knew him, but that did not prevent their admiration. 'He is', said W. T. Stead—no mean authority—'far and away the ablest, most cultured and most adventurous newspaperman I have ever met, with an extraordinary combination of varied faculties, an artist in temperament, a journalist by instinct, a scholar and philosopher by choice, a statesman in ambition.' His most intimate friend among foreign statesmen was Count Serge de Witte, the rough-hewn Russian railway organizer and financial statesman, whose views Dillon sedulously advocated, although it was never clear whether Dillon inspired Witte or Witte Dillon. Witte took Dillon with him as his adviser when he went to take part as first plenipotentiary in the peace negotiations at Portsmouth, New Hampshire, in 1905, and he used Dillon's pen to sign the peace treaty. Witte's resignation of the premiership next year did not prevent the two men from still seeing a great deal of each other, thrashing out with many disagreements (as can be seen from Dillon's very detailed diaries) intricate questions of the past, present, and future. In 1908–1909 Dillon supported Baron von Aehrenthal, the Austro-Hungarian foreign minister, against the Russian foreign minister, Isvolsky, during the Bosnian annexation crisis.

For many years Dillon wrote a monthly article on foreign affairs for the *Contemporary Review* and numerous others (often under a pseudonym) in the *Fortnightly* and the *National Reviews* and in American organs. The publicity which he thus commanded, together with his wide learning and experience, gained him ready access to leading statesmen and diplomatists who were often eager to consult him. Sir Cecil Spring-Rice, for instance, wrote that he was a sort of pupil of Dillon and that from him he had learned more than from anyone else about foreign politics. Yet it cannot be affirmed that he left an abiding mark upon the history of his times. His very versatility may have detracted from his permanent influence. His fame rests upon his linguistic abilities and his remarkable achievements as a copious chronicler of contemporary events. He wrote leading articles in five languages, although he used modestly to say that those in Spanish had to be corrected. Retiring from the *Daily Telegraph* during the war of 1914–1918, he remained very active behind the scenes. Subsequently he went twice to Mexico, on which country he wrote two books. But in his

last book, published posthumously in 1934, he returned to Russia. In *Count Leo Tolstoy* he related his association, pleasant and otherwise, with that great man. In such a book there was scope for his wit and irony, while the floridness once fashionable in the *Daily Telegraph* is absent.

In 1914 Dillon married his second wife, Kathleen, daughter of James Ireland, of Belfast, who survived him. In his old age he bought a house in Barcelona, where he died 9 June 1933. A portrait of him, painted by Sir William Orpen, is in the National Gallery, Dublin.

[*Daily Telegraph*, 10 June 1933; *Fortnightly Review*, July 1933; private information; personal knowledge.]

HENRY BAERLEIN.

DILLON, HAROLD ARTHUR LEE-, seventeenth VISCOUNT DILLON (1844–1932), antiquary, was born in London 24 January 1844, the elder son of Arthur Edmund Denis Dillon-Lee, sixteenth Viscount Dillon, a numismatist (whom he succeeded in 1892), by his wife, Ellen, daughter of James Adderley, of King's county. The Dillon family had held land in Ireland since the twelfth century: several of its members are noticed in this DICTIONARY. The seventh viscount raised the famous Dillon regiment for James II, which at a later date went over to the French service; the eleventh married, in 1744, the heiress of the Lees, of Ditchley, Oxfordshire, through whom Lord Dillon was related to Sir Henry Lee [q.v.], champion to Queen Elizabeth, and descended from Charles II. He was educated at a private school at Eltham from 1855 to 1860, and afterwards at Bonn University. He passed out fourth in the army examination of 1862, and was gazetted as an ensign in the Rifle Brigade. After having been stationed in Canada and India, he retired from the Brigade in 1874, whereupon he was promoted captain in the Oxfordshire Light Infantry (militia battalion), retiring as major in 1891.

After leaving the Rifle Brigade Dillon became interested first in military equipment and dress and later in the history of arms and armour, medieval costume, and kindred subjects, of which he made an exhaustive study. In 1892 he was appointed first curator of the armouries of the Tower of London, a post which he held until 1913. In the course of his researches he travelled much abroad, making frequent visits to France, Belgium, Germany, and Russia. In 1905 he found in Paris a volume of armourer's drawings which enabled him to identify many armours in the Tower, at Windsor, and elsewhere, and on his advice it was purchased for the Victoria and Albert Museum. He never collected armour, as he considered that the keeper of a national armoury should not make a private collection. He took all the important armours in the Tower to pieces in order to learn their construction and made minute studies of the locks and crossbows and firearms. His knowledge of medieval and later periods was encyclopaedic, and inquiries on subjects within these fields came to him from all over the world. He had two maxims, one that 'Duty is doing more than you are paid for', the other being 'Never say you do not know, but find out and then reply'. On one occasion it took him three months and a visit to Germany to deal with a question, but he answered it correctly.

Dillon was responsible for much of the work connected with the Stuart and Tudor exhibitions held at the New Gallery, Regent Street, in 1889 and 1890. As chairman of the trustees of the National Portrait Gallery from 1894 to 1928 his knowledge was of the greatest possible value to that body. From the notable collection at Ditchley he presented to the Gallery in 1925, in memory of his first wife, three portraits of outstanding historical importance, Archbishop Warham, Sir Philip Sidney, and Sir Henry Lee (the last-named by Antonio Moro). He presented and bequeathed other portraits, including the Ditchley Queen Elizabeth, to the gallery.

In any case where finance was involved Dillon was very exact, and he would never give an official signature until he had checked the accounts before him. His knowledge of his own library was such that he could tell the shelf, the colour of the binding, and often the page of the work which was asked for. He would never put forward theories unsupported by evidence, and when at a trial which involved the authenticity of a suit of armour the opposing counsel questioned his opinion he replied: 'My opinions *are* facts.' A true aristocrat, he was equally at home in a royal palace and in a third class carriage of the Great Western Railway by which he travelled from Charlbury to London and back several times a week for many years.

Dillon contributed numerous papers to archaeological and antiquarian journals. He was president of the Royal Archaeo-

logical Institute (1892–1898) and of the Society of Antiquaries (1897–1904); was a trustee of the British Museum (1905–1912) and of the Wallace Collection (1918–1931); and was elected a fellow of the British Academy on its foundation in 1902. He was antiquary to the Royal Academy and was an honorary member of the Armourers' Company of London. He was appointed C.H. in 1921. He was twice married: first, in 1870 to Julia (died 1925), eldest daughter of Isaac Brock Stanton, of Ottawa, and had one son who predeceased him; secondly, in 1926 to Margaret Louisa Everard, daughter of the Rev. Henry Edward Browne ffolkes, and widow of the Rev. John Erasmus Philipps. He died at Ditchley 18 December 1932, and was succeeded as eighteenth viscount by his nephew, Arthur Henry (1875–1934), who sold Ditchley in 1933, when nearly all the remaining pictures in the collection were dispersed.

Lord Dillon possessed a fine head and figure. A portrait by Georgina Brackenbury is in the National Portrait Gallery, and a portrait by Maurice Codner belongs to the Society of Antiquaries. There is a monumental tablet in St. Peter's chapel, Tower of London, and a memorial window depicting his kneeling figure is in Enstone church, Oxfordshire, in the churchyard of which he is buried. A portrait-medal, by Sydney Carline, was struck in 1913.

[*The Times*, 20 December 1932; C. ffoulkes, *Viscount Dillon, 1844–1932* in *Proceedings* of the British Academy, vol. xviii, 1932 (containing a bibliography compiled by J. G. Mann); personal knowledge.]

C. FFOULKES.

DIXON, SIR ROBERT BLAND (1867–1939), engineer vice-admiral, was born at Darlington 30 March 1867, the elder son of Robert Bland Dixon, architect and surveyor, by his wife, Mary Ann Whitecomb Parr. He was the elder brother of Walter Ernest Dixon [q.v.]. He was educated at Queen Elizabeth Grammar School, Darlington, and at the Royal Naval Engineering College at Keyham, then recently established, and was in fact the first student of the college to reach the head of his profession. Thence in 1888 he passed for further training to the Royal Naval College, Greenwich, with the rank of assistant engineer (the equivalent of sub-lieutenant). His first year's progress qualified him for an additional two years' study and for specialization in machinery design and the more scientific side of his profession, with only sea service required to qualify him for successive steps of promotion.

On leaving Greenwich in 1891, Dixon joined the *Hecla*, one of the earliest repair ships, in the Mediterranean. A special feature of her equipment was the carriage of a flotilla of 'second-class torpedo boats' which were hoisted out and exercised together, and provided the initial experience in the evolution of destroyers and destroyer tactics. On promotion to engineer in 1892 he was sent to the battleship *Trafalgar*, and in 1893 to the Royal Naval College, Greenwich, as instructor in applied mechanics to assist J. H. Cotterill.

After two years' service on the China station in the *Centurion* (1896–1898) Dixon came home and was posted successively to Chatham dockyard as assistant to the chief engineer (1899), to the Admiralty, to Portsmouth as first assistant to the engineer manager (1902) and, in 1904, soon after his promotion to chief engineer, he joined the staff of the director of dockyards.

In that same year, owing to the change in naval titles then introduced, Dixon became engineer commander, and as such he spent his last spell of sea service in the battleship *Dominion*, during 1907 and 1908. By then he was recognized by both his seniors and juniors as an exceptionally capable and popular officer, and after three years at Haulbowline yard as chief engineer, he was appointed engineer manager of Portsmouth yard in 1912.

Dixon held this post until 1917, having been promoted engineer captain in 1915, a period which gave his powers of organization and technical judgement a full test on account of the great increase both in men and machinery demanded by first the threat and secondly the outbreak of war. He left Portsmouth in order to become assistant director of dockyards, and he remained at Whitehall until his retirement in 1928, being successively assistant engineer (1919), deputy engineer (1920), and, in succession to Sir George Goodwin, engineer-in-chief of the fleet in 1922, receiving then the usual promotion from engineer rear-admiral (1919) to engineer vice-admiral on appointment.

On retirement in 1928, Dixon became chairman and director of several engineering firms, notably of Messrs. Babcock & Wilcox. He was an active member of several technical societies and was president in 1926 of the Junior Institute of Engineers, and in 1929 of the Marine

Engineers. He served on the Privy Council committee of scientific and industrial research. He took a keen and continuous interest in engineering education, and served on the committee on the training of naval cadets under the chairmanship of Sir Reginald Custance [q.v.] in 1912, and on the education committee of the Mechanical Engineers.

Although no spectacular advance marked Dixon's tenure of high office comparable with the introduction of the water tube boiler and the steam turbine, the British lead in Admiralty engineering was fully maintained. In the *Kent* class, designed to embody the experience of the war of 1914–1918 and to meet the growing menace from the air, the 'unit' system whereby each propeller can have, as required, its own independent supply of steam, with high pressures and temperatures, was, after long opposition, introduced in the *Nelson* and the *Rodney* and is now almost universal in all important vessels. The cure of 'condenseritis' was achieved after prolonged tests by the use of cupronickel tubes, while the introduction of corrugated steam-pipes to provide for expansion successfully met a difficulty in spite of opposition from competent opinion. Another development was the use of electric drive at cruising speeds for auxiliary machinery, but of steam drive with independence of the vulnerable 'ringmain' when in action.

At a time when the German navy had adopted the Diesel engine—notably in the *Deutschland* and *Graf von Spee*—and the United States in the *Maryland* and others —it was largely owing to the representations of Dixon that in face of persistent and repeated pressure the Royal Navy retained its faith in the steam turbine; a faith fully justified, since both countries reverted to British practice.

Further, during Dixon's term of office there largely disappeared the lack of understanding and contact between seagoing engineer officers and the higher engineer officers at the Admiralty of which the former had long been conscious.

Dixon was a man of quiet and retiring disposition, with great tenacity of character. He rarely thrust his views forward, but was always ready, when called upon, with a well weighed and considered opinion. He was appointed C.B. on leaving Portsmouth in 1918 and K.C.B. in 1924. The university of Sheffield conferred upon him the honorary degree of D.Eng. in 1926. Dixon married in 1896 Hettie Alice (died

1936), daughter of Dr. Frank Sextus Tuck, of Aylesford, Kent. He died, without issue, at Sydney, New South Wales, while on a business visit for Messrs. Babcock & Wilcox, 28 July 1939.

[*The Times*, 29 July 1939; Admiralty records; personal knowledge.]

W. Scott Hill.

DIXON, WALTER ERNEST (1870–1931), pharmacologist, was born at Darlington 2 June 1870, the younger son of Robert Bland Dixon, architect and surveyor, by his wife, Mary Ann Whitecomb Parr. He was the younger brother of Sir Robert Bland Dixon [q.v.]. He was educated at Queen Elizabeth Grammar School, Darlington, and entered St. Thomas's Hospital in 1890, graduating B.Sc. (1891) and M.D. (Lond., 1898). In 1899 he was appointed assistant to the Downing professor of medicine at Cambridge. In 1909 he was made lecturer and in 1919 first reader in pharmacology in that university, a post which he held until his death. He also held concurrently until 1919 the chair of materia medica at King's College, London. For his services in the war of 1914–1918, in the Intelligence Department of the Royal Navy, he was appointed O.B.E. in 1919.

When Dixon began to devote himself to pharmacology in 1899, there was no university chair in this subject in England, and the science received scanty attention from the point of view of teaching or research. By the time of Dixon's death, chairs of pharmacology had been established in many English universities and the subject was attaining somewhat nearer to the recognition which its importance for the practice of medicine deserved. In fostering this development, Dixon played a dominant part. He taught pharmacology as an experimental science and as the scientific basis of therapeutics. As a writer, teacher, lecturer, and investigator, he became one of the foremost pharmacologists of the world. He was author of *A Manual of Pharmacology* (1905, 7th ed. 1929) and *Practical Pharmacology* (1920).

Dixon's own original researches, of which only a few can be mentioned, covered a wide field. With the help of various collaborators he investigated the physiology and pharmacology of the bronchial muscles, the pulmonary circulation, and the cerebro-spinal fluid. He was greatly interested in the subject of addiction and tolerance to drugs and in various papers dealt specifically with particular drug habits—tobacco, alcohol, cocaine, morphine, and Indian hemp. His most significant contribution to the foundations of pharmacology was made in 1907, when he suggested that, when a nerve is excited, the resultant effect may be due to the liberation of some chemical substance. Based upon somewhat slender experimental data, this hypothesis gained little credence at the time, but its subsequent verification has completely revolutionized conceptions of the nature of transmission of nerve impulses, and has constituted one of the most far-reaching advances in physiology of this century.

Dixon's impact on his generation would be undervalued by mere consideration of his own contributions to science. He took a wide and participating interest in medical affairs. His witty and persuasive lectures and dogmatic writing had a potent influence in moulding medical thought both within and without the confines of his own university. His buoyant and resolute spirit was a stimulus and example to his fellows.

Dixon was elected F.R.S. in 1911 and F.R.C.P. in 1930. The university of Manitoba conferred upon him the honorary degree of LL.D. in 1930. In 1907 he married Hope, only daughter of Francis Glen-Allan, of Dulwich; they had no children. At their home at Whittlesford, near Cambridge, where scientists from all parts of the world had enjoyed so much hospitality, he died suddenly 16 August 1931.

[*The Times*, 17 August 1931; *Proceedings* of the Royal Society, vol. cx, B, 1932 (portrait); *Journal of Pharmacology*, vol. xliv, 1932 (bibliography); *British Medical Journal*, 1931, vol. ii, pp. 361 and 405; *Lancet*, 1931, vol. ii, p. 429; personal knowledge.] J. A. Gunn.

DOBBS, Sir HENRY ROBERT CONWAY (1871–1934), Indian civil servant and administrator of Iraq, was born in London 26 August 1871, the second son of Robert Conway Dobbs, of Cappoquin, co. Waterford, and Killiney, co. Dublin, by his wife, Edith Julianna, daughter of Henry Fowler Broadwood, of Lyne, Surrey. He was a scholar of both Winchester and Brasenose College, Oxford. He passed the Indian civil service examination of 1890, entered the service in 1892, and was transferred to the political department in 1899. His first 'political' post was in the State of Mysore; but it was not long before he found his way to the North-West Frontier with which so much of his later career was to be associated. Dobbs carried out some adventurous journeys in his earlier years in the political department. In 1902–1903 he travelled across Persia from Bagdad to Seistan: in 1904 he explored the little-known tract of Hazarajat between Herat and Kabul. He paid two further visits to Afghanistan in the course of his career. The first was in 1904–1905, when he was attached as secretary to Sir Louis Dane's mission to Kabul, the outcome of which was the treaty by which the Amir Habibullah renewed the engagements entered into by his predecessor in 1880. The terms of this treaty aroused some criticism at the time; but it stood the test of the war of 1914–1918. Later, in 1920–1921, Dobbs himself headed a mission to Kabul and negotiated a revised treaty with Habibullah's successor, Amanullah.

During the war of 1914–1918 Dobbs saw active service as political officer with the Expeditionary Force in Mesopotamia and was present at the battle of Ctesiphon (22 November 1915). He returned to India at the end of 1916 and served successively as revenue and judicial commissioner (April 1917) and chief commissioner (December 1917) in Baluchistan, and subsequently (1919) as foreign secretary to the government of India. In 1923 he succeeded Sir Percy Cox [q.v.] as high commissioner for Iraq. It was not an easy post to fill; nor was 'Kokkus', with his immense experience and prestige in the Middle East, an easy man to follow. The circumstances of the moment were abnormal. Iraq was in process of recovery from a period of acute unrest. The worst stage was past, for Cox had already laid the foundations of a more stable régime; but the task that awaited his successor—that of raising a durable superstructure—was scarcely less exacting. Dobbs was fond of saying that he liked difficult tasks. He had his full share of them at Bagdad. During the six years of his high commissionership the political sky was seldom clear for many weeks in succession. One political problem followed on the heels of another. The election of a constituent assembly, and subsequently of the Iraqi parliament; the ratification of the Anglo-Iraqi treaty; the control of the Kurdish districts; the Mosul frontier question: these marked the successive stages by which the Iraqi State, under the high commissioner's wise and sympathetic guidance, advanced through adolescence towards maturity. At each stage heavy demands were made upon his tact, patience, and administrative experience. When Dobbs retired in 1929 he left behind him what, compared with the conditions of 1923, could fairly be described as a prosperous and contented country. It was also a country which was to acquire full national status in the following year and to afford a striking illustration—not without significance for the future—of the successful operation of the 'mandatory' system.

Dobbs was appointed C.I.E. in 1905, C.S.I. in 1916, K.C.I.E. and K.C.S.I. in 1921, K.C.M.G. in 1925, and G.B.E. in 1929. He married in 1907 Esmé Agnes, eldest daughter of George Rivaz, of Canterbury, late Indian civil service, and had two sons and two daughters. The last years of his life were spent at his family home at Cappoquin, where he died, after a long illness, 30 May 1934.

There is a portrait of Dobbs by G. F. Kelly in the Embassy at Bagdad: a copy is in the possession of the family.

[*The Times*, 1 June 1934; *Annual Register*, 1934; Colonial Office records.]

J. E. SHUCKBURGH.

DOLMETSCH, (EUGENE) ARNOLD (1858–1940), musician and musical craftsman, was born at Le Mans, France, 24 February 1858. He came of a family of musicians. His grandfather, of Bohemian origin, settled in Zürich in 1808. There his father, Rudolf Arnold Dolmetsch, was born and became a pianoforte maker but was himself a musician who played Bach's fugues on the clavichord. His mother was Marie Zelie Guillouard. Arnold was the eldest son. He was thus early apprenticed to the craft of instrument making and the art of playing. After his father's death he went to the Brussels Conservatoire for a general musical education and studied the violin with Henri Vieuxtemps. In 1883 he entered the newly founded Royal College of Music in London and was encouraged by its director, Sir George Grove [q.v.], not only in his professional career as music master at Dulwich College but in his investigations into the early English instrumental music which he found in the British Museum in 1889.

Thereafter the study of old music, the way to play it, the instruments on which to play it, how to play them, and, when the stock of old specimens ran out, the making of new lutes, virginals, clavichords, harpsichords, recorders, and ultimately of viols and violins, became

Dolmetsch's lifework. His chief contributions to the English musical renaissance, which throughout his lifetime was growing from roots pushed into native soil by the revivals of folk-music and Tudor music, was the rediscovery of a school of English composers for consorts of viols, of whom the chief were John Jenkins (1592–1678) and William Lawes [qq.v.], and the re-establishment of the recorder (first made by him in 1921) as an instrument of popular music. In 1915 he published *The Interpretation of the Music of the Seventeenth and Eighteenth Centuries.* He soon after settled at Haslemere, Surrey, and established workshops there. In 1925 he founded an annual summer festival of chamber music at which old music unearthed from many a library was performed on the instruments for which it had been composed and in the right style. These performances by his family and pupils were not always highly polished in execution, but Dolmetsch was unabashed. He formulated his principles in these words: 'This music is of absolute and not antiquarian importance; it must be played as the composer intended and on the instruments for which it was written with their correct technique; and through it personal music-making can be restored to the home, from which two centuries of professionalism have divorced it.' His sons and daughters, who were all four turned by him into versatile executants, certainly formed a domestic consort. His restoration of the recorder opened a new line of amateur effort. His improved harpsichords encouraged the use of that instrument for the *basso continuo* of eighteenth-century operas and oratorios. His work for viols and lute was of the greatest antiquarian, although of less general musical, interest. In the words of Sir Henry Hadow [q.v.] his lifework as a whole certainly 'opened the door to a forgotten treasure-house of beauty'.

In 1928, in honour of Dolmetsch's seventieth birthday, the Dolmetsch Foundation was incorporated for the 'encouragement of the revival of early instrumental music'. In 1937 he was granted a civil list pension; in 1938 he was created a chevalier of the Legion of Honour; and in 1939 he received the honorary degree of doctor of music from Durham University. He was naturalized in 1931. He died at Haslemere 28 February 1940.

Dolmetsch was twice married: first, in 1877 to Marie Morel, of Namur; secondly, in 1903 to Mabel, daughter of John Brookes

Johnston, of Denmark Hill. By his first wife he had a daughter, Hélène (1880–1924), who was a fine player of the viola da gamba. By his second wife he had two sons, the elder of whom was killed in the war of 1939–1945, and two daughters.

There are portraits of Dolmetsch by Sir Max Beerbohm, Sir William Rothenstein, and Nevill Lytton at Haslemere, and by Edmond Xavier Kapp at Bedales Junior School.

[Arnold Dolmetsch, *Dolmetsch and his Instruments* (privately printed at Haslemere), 1929; Robert Donington, *The Work and Ideas of Arnold Dolmetsch*, Dolmetsch Foundation, 1932; *Musical Quarterly*, April 1933; *Grove's Dictionary of Music and Musicians*, 4th ed., vol. ii, edited by H. C. Colles.]

FRANK HOWES.

DONALD, SIR ROBERT (1860–1933), journalist, was born at Corsemaul in the parish of Mortlach, Banffshire, 29 August 1860, the son of Robert Donald, a mason, of Auchindoun, by his wife, Jane (or Jean) McConachie. Donald early took up journalism in Edinburgh and subsequently in the English provinces, Paris, and New York before coming to London where in 1893 he founded the *Municipal Journal* and in 1897 the *Municipal Year Book*, having made a special study of local government. He edited these periodicals until 1902 when he became editor of the London *Daily Chronicle* (subsequently *News Chronicle*) to which he gave a distinctive character, increasing both its circulation and its influence. He made book reviewing one of its strong features and developed its literary side to an importance equal with news and political topics. He was also managing director of United Newspapers with control over several journals outside London. Although never a keen politician, he kept in close touch with liberal party leaders and was a very popular as well as a prominent member of the National Liberal Club.

In 1917, on Donald's recommendation, Lloyd George created the Department (which in 1918 became the Ministry) of Information: he was made a director of it and in that capacity strongly advocated the dropping of leaflets over enemy territory, a device that proved very useful and which he considered the War Office was far too slow in adopting. In 1918 the *Daily Chronicle* was sold without his knowledge to a group representing Lloyd George. Donald at once resigned the editorship, declining to remain under control of the new board. To mark the respect for him which was felt by all journalists irrespective of party ties he was entertained at a luncheon and made a speech in which he accused Lloyd George of trying to 'corner public opinion' and declared that no editor should be expected to work under any conditions save those of 'absolute freedom and independence' such as he had enjoyed. Limitation of that freedom would, he warned his audience, be a national danger. Persons who became newspaper proprietors did not become newspaper men and it was by newspaper men that newspapers should be conducted. The speech attracted much attention and made public a matter which was more and more widely discussed in the years that followed and led eventually to the appointment of the royal commission on the press in 1947.

After his retirement or 'ejection', as he called it, Donald occupied himself more with public affairs than with journalism. He bought a Sunday newspaper, the *Referee*, and an interest in the *Yorkshire Observer*, but neither experiment was successful. Valuable work was done by him, however, as a member of royal commissions and committees on local government, wireless, and transport; as chairman of the publicity committee of the British Empire Exhibition held at Wembley in 1924; and as organizer of Imperial Press Conferences and the Empire Press Union, of which latter he was chairman from 1915 to 1926. For these services he was appointed G.B.E. in 1924, and during a visit to Canada in 1920 he received the honorary degree of LL.D. from Toronto University. During his last years he undertook publicity work for his old friend Ramsay MacDonald and the national labour party, and also wrote several books on subjects connected with European reconstruction in the period 1920–1930, urging that special attention should be paid to what he believed were the 'danger spots of Europe', Poland among others.

In all that he did or wrote Donald gave proof of well balanced judgement, steady industry in collecting information, wise foresight, and sturdy courage. He engaged in many controversies and usually won his point. To him was due the recasting of the original plans for the British Empire Exhibition, on which he made severe public comment. His vigorous, well directed efforts led to many improvements in Post Office and wireless communications. He worked hard to bring about the broadcasting of special programmes to the British Empire, which proved of great value. He married in 1890 Marie-Jeanne, daughter of Professor Garassut, of Paris, and had one daughter. He died in London 17 February 1933.

[*The Times*, 18 February 1933; personal knowledge.]   HAMILTON FYFE.

DONALDSON, ST. CLAIR GEORGE ALFRED (1863–1935), successively archbishop of Brisbane and bishop of Salisbury, was born in London 11 February 1863, the third of the four sons of Sir Stuart Alexander Donaldson [q.v.], first premier of New South Wales, by his wife, Amelia, daughter of Frederick Cooper, of Carleton Hall, Cumberland. He was nephew of the philologist J. W. Donaldson [q.v.]. He was educated at Eton and obtained a scholarship at Trinity College, Cambridge, where he was placed in the first class in both the classical (1885) and the theological tripos (1887). He was trained for the ministry at Wells theological college and was ordained deacon in 1888 and priest in 1889.

Donaldson's first appointment was that of assistant curate at St. Andrew's church, Bethnal Green, in 1888, but later in the same year he became resident chaplain to E. W. Benson, archbishop of Canterbury [q.v.]. He remained at Lambeth for three years and was then placed in charge of the Eton mission at Hackney Wick from 1891 to 1900. In 1901 he was appointed rector of Hornsey, and rural dean of Hornsey in the following year. His thoughts had long dwelt upon the possibility of work overseas and it was in accordance with that leaning that he acted as president of the London Junior Missionary Association. The call came in 1904 when he accepted the invitation to become bishop of Brisbane. He was consecrated in St. Paul's Cathedral, London, on 28 October.

The year after his arrival Brisbane became the archdiocese of the newly constituted province of Queensland, and Donaldson, in spite of his protests, became the first archbishop of that province. The work was of a very varied nature and carried him as far afield as New Guinea and the islands of the Torres Strait. In his own diocese his rule was marked by the foundation of the previously projected Bush Brotherhood, with headquarters at Charleville. He revived his predecessor's project for the building of a cathedral at Brisbane. The choir and transepts with a portion of the nave were built under this fresh impetus and were consecrated in 1910. Later, as a diocesan memorial to the fallen in the war of 1914–1918, he succeeded in founding the St. Martin's Hospital on a closely adjacent site.

On a somewhat larger stage Donaldson showed himself the champion of the Aboriginals. He also took a leading part in the vain effort to disentangle the Church of England in Australia from its 'legal nexus' with the Church at home and to make it completely autonomous. Further, he led the struggle to secure the recognition of the place of religion in the state system of education and succeeded after a referendum in obtaining the right of entry for denominational teachers into the state schools. He founded (1907) St. Francis College, Nundah, for the training of candidates for the ministry, and also St. John's College, an Anglican residential hostel for students at the university of Queensland. His main object in these two latter measures was to build up a body of Australian clergy, trained in their own country. The success of the effort can be seen from the fact that whereas when Donaldson arrived in Queensland there were in his own diocese only fifty-three priests, thirty-eight of whom had been born and trained in England, when he left the number had risen to one hundred and sixteen, all but thirty-two of whom had been born and trained in Australia.

Donaldson was translated to the diocese of Salisbury in 1921. He found the change to a highly complicated system of ecclesiastical administration as trying as have all other bishops from overseas. His reforming efforts to leave the episcopal palace and to divide the somewhat unwieldy diocese were opposed and presently abandoned. In order to meet the difficulty the ancient see of Sherborne was revived as a suffragan bishopric in 1925. This gave Donaldson some freedom to serve the Church outside the borders of his own diocese. When the Missionary Council was created in 1921 he became its chairman and he helped to organize the first missionary schools which were to do a great deal in building up a well informed public opinion about the vast Anglican communion overseas. He held this chairmanship throughout the formative years of the council and only resigned to make way for a younger man in 1933.

Donaldson also served as chairman (1931–1935) of the Canterbury Convocation committee on the Church and marriage and as such signed the report of the joint committees of Canterbury and York which was published in 1935. He took an adequate share in the Lambeth Conference of 1930, showing himself as always alive to new movements of thought while refusing to countenance any large onslaught upon the Church's traditional faith and practice. It was from this point of view that he defended the famous Resolution No. 15 on birth control while drawing attention to the very careful reservations with which it was protected.

Such wider interests did not prevent Donaldson from devising new ways of dealing with his own diocese. He was particularly interested in meeting the needs of youth and of those educated people who sat loose to the claims of orthodoxy. For the former he organized week-end gatherings in his palace, known to the irreverent as the 'bishop's lipstick parties'. For the latter he arranged courses of Lent lectures which were also held at the palace. Invitations to these lectures were eagerly sought and those who attended were not deterred by the quickly earned sobriquet of 'bishop's heathen'.

Donaldson himself published nothing beyond the ephemeral writings which are the duty of every diocesan. However, the intensity of his personal religious life was revealed by the posthumous publication (1937) of a small book entitled *A Meditation on the Acts of the Apostles*, which was compiled from the notes which he left of his daily thoughts and prayers.

Donaldson received several honours. Besides the honorary degree of D.D. conferred upon him by Cambridge University on his elevation to the bench, he was an honorary D.D. of Oxford (1920) and D.C.L. of Durham (1908). In 1923 he was elected an honorary fellow of Magdalene College, Cambridge. In 1933 when he became prelate of the Order of St. Michael and St. George he received the insignia of a knight commander of the order.

Donaldson died, unmarried, at Salisbury 7 December 1935. Valuable as was his work in England, his strongest influence was felt in Australia, where he showed himself the greatest ecclesiastical statesman that country has yet seen. A portrait by Oswald Birley is at Bishop's House, Salisbury.

[C. T. Dimont and F. de Witt Batty, *St. Clair Donaldson*, 1939; personal knowledge.]

Wm. Londin.

(J. W. C. Wand.)

DOUGLAS, SIR (HENRY) PERCY (1876–1939), hydrographer, was born at Dacre Hill, Higher Bebington, Cheshire, 1 November 1876, the second son of Admiral Sholto Douglas, by his wife, Maria Louisa, only daughter of William Bickford, of Stonehouse, Devon. He entered the training ship *Britannia* as a naval cadet in 1890, and in 1892 was appointed to the *Cleopatra* on the North America and West Indies station as midshipman. At the end of 1895 he was transferred to the *Majestic*, flagship of Lord Walter Kerr [q.v.], Channel squadron, and promoted sub-lieutenant in 1896. Then followed the usual courses at Greenwich and Portsmouth; and, having decided to enter the surveying branch, he served in the *Stork*, surveying ship, in the Pacific for nearly three years, being promoted lieutenant in her in 1898.

Until the end of 1906 Douglas was continuously employed on surveying work in the Red Sea, Mediterranean, China, west coast of Africa, and home waters. He then had a short spell ashore as naval assistant to the hydrographer, and in June 1907 joined the *Egeria* at Esquimalt for survey work in the North Pacific. A year later he was selected for command of the *Waterwitch* for the survey of the Malacca Straits and other Far Eastern waters. In March 1910 he was brought to Whitehall to be superintendent of charts in the hydrographic department and held this post for nearly five years, being promoted commander at the end of 1910. By this time Douglas was recognized as one of the ablest of the younger surveying officers, and when Admiral (Sir) John de Robeck [q.v.], at the beginning of the Dardanelles campaign, asked the Admiralty for the addition to his staff of a good surveying officer, Douglas was sent out in February 1915 and joined the *Inflexible*, flagship, and later the *Queen Elizabeth* and *Lord Nelson*. De Robeck's dispatches contain several mentions of his 'work of inestimable value to the fleet'. His expert work was in fact indispensable for successful landing operations and included also the compilation and printing of new local charts and dealt with problems of minefields, ranges, and indirect bombardment. His zeal and ability were recognized by promotion to acting captain in October 1915, confirmed two months later.

In June 1916, after the evacuation of the Gallipoli peninsula, Douglas returned to the hydrographic department and held the new office of director of the naval meteorological service from April 1917 until January 1918. Then Admiral Roger (afterwards Lord) Keyes, who had been chief of staff to de Robeck, asked for Douglas's assistance on his staff at Dover in preparation for the Zeebrugge and Ostend exploits. He was accordingly appointed to the *Arrogant* (Keyes's flagship) for indirect firing duties. Keyes reported that his services were invaluable and his dispatches of May 1918 stated that the preparation of the routes from the starting point of attack by the removal of obstructions and the placing of navigational marks and marks for the long-range bombardments were carried out by Douglas and his assistant. For this service he was appointed C.M.G. and received the Belgian Order of Leopold and the Italian silver medal for valour.

From February 1919 until July 1921 Douglas was assistant hydrographer, and then resumed duty at sea in command of the *Mutine*, and later the *Ormonde* for surveys in British Guiana and the West Indies. He received the official commendation of the governors of Honduras, Jamaica, and Bermuda for surveying work in their waters.

Douglas returned to the Admiralty as hydrographer of the navy in October 1924 and, on completing the normal five years in that office, was offered and accepted an extension for three more years on condition of retiring from the active list. He was appointed C.B. in 1929 and K.C.B. in 1933. He reached flag rank in February 1927 and was promoted vice-admiral on the retired list in 1931. After retirement from the service he was appointed acting conservator of the Mersey and chairman of the Dover harbour board, and on the outbreak of war in September 1939 was employed as commodore superintendent of Dover, where he died the following 4 November; he was buried at sea at his own wish in the Straits of Dover.

Douglas was much interested in the technical side of his professional work and had a probing, inventive mind for the discovery of new aids to navigation. When in command of the *Waterwitch* he developed the Douglas–Schafer sounding gear which did much to facilitate the accurate determination of the depth of water in from twenty to one hundred fathoms, and received the thanks of the Board of Admiralty 'for devising and perfecting a sounding traveller for rapid sounding for ships under weigh' and was given a money prize for this service. He was an enthusiastic advocate of echo-sounding and it is mainly owing to his enterprise that this valuable invention was adopted for general use. Various improvements in surveying apparatus are due to him, especially the development of the 45° prismatic astrolabe.

In hydrography, Douglas's interest was mainly in improvements of instruments and the geodetic and astronomical control of marine surveys and he did much to improve both; he maintained his study of meteorology, begun officially in 1917. He was from 1928 to 1932 Admiralty representative on the *Discovery* executive committee, appointed by the Colonial Office for the promotion of research in the southern and Antarctic seas, and took a leading part in the design, equipment, and manning of the new ship built for that purpose. He gave close and invaluable personal attention to all her proceedings until she was finally laid up shortly before the outbreak of war in 1939. This work led to his being associated with other polar exploration schemes in which his expert help was readily and unobtrusively given. He had many intimate friends particularly in the scientific world and seldom made enemies.

Douglas was a younger brother of Trinity House. He married in 1898 Katherine Chute, second daughter of Captain John Mackenzie, Lincolnshire Militia, of Belmont, near Kirkcudbright, and had one daughter.

[Admiralty records; *Geographical Journal*, April 1940; private information.]

VINCENT W. BADDELEY.

DOVE, JOHN (1872–1934), journalist, was born at Birkenhead 6 November 1872, the second son of John Matthew Dove, managing director of the Liverpool, London and Globe Insurance Company, of Birkenhead and Boreatton Hall, Baschurch, Shropshire, by his wife, Amy Gordon Wood. He was educated at Rugby and New College, Oxford, where he read classics; and after being called to the bar by the Inner Temple (1898), he became in 1903 assistant town clerk, and later town clerk, of Johannesburg; in these posts, and as chairman (1907–1911) of the Transvaal Land Settlement Board, he played an important part in the work of administrative reconstruction after the South African war. In 1918, after serving during the European war in the Intelligence Department of the War Office, Dove became a director of the Commonwealth Trust, a non-profit-making organization formed to take over the sequestrated properties of certain German-Swiss missionary bodies. Despite health which had been permanently injured by an early hunting accident and by dysentery contracted in South Africa, he undertook several arduous journeys in India and Africa for the trust, before returning to England to assume in 1920 the editorship of the *Round Table*, the quarterly review of British Commonwealth and international affairs. The *Round Table* had been founded in 1910 by a number of his friends who, like Dove himself, had belonged to that group of young men, affectionately dubbed 'the kindergarten', whom Alfred, Lord Milner [q.v.] gathered about him in South Africa. He was editor until his death, which took place at North Aston, Oxfordshire, 18 April 1934. He was unmarried.

As editor Dove always took great pains to ensure that nothing which he printed should be inaccurate in facts or faulty in balance. Although he himself wrote very little for publication, he carefully guided the policy of the review, according to his own luminous idealism, which embraced a strong belief in the need for cohesion of the British Commonwealth and for loyal support for the wider League of Nations.

After his death a volume of his personal letters, mostly written on his travels in India and Europe after the war, was edited by his friend Mr. Robert Henry (later Lord) Brand, and published (*The Letters of John Dove*, 1938). They reveal a deep sensitivity and insight into the thoughts and feelings of people of different nations whom he came across, as well as great foresight into the future. He was a man beloved by many friends. Through them, and through the anonymous pages of the *Round Table* and the work of its constituent groups in the Dominions, which he himself had helped to form in 1910, he left his mark modestly but distinctly upon the thought of his time.

[*The Times*, 19 April 1934; *Round Table*, June 1934; *Letters of John Dove*, edited by R. H. Brand, 1938; personal knowledge.]

H. V. HODSON.

DREYER, GEORGES (1873–1934), pathologist, was born at Shanghai 4 July 1873, the second son and third and youngest child of Captain Georg Hannibal Napoleon Dreyer, of the Royal Danish Navy, by his wife, Dagmar Alvilde, daughter of Judge W. T. Qvistgaard, of Fredensborg, a well-known jurist. Their place of residence was Copenhagen, but at the time of Dreyer's birth his father was in Shanghai in the capacity of diplomatic adviser to the Great Northern Cable Company.

Dreyer was sent to school at Borgerdydsskolen at Christiansharn. His unusually rich education in mathematics, physics, and chemistry, and periods of postgraduate research in Denmark, Germany, and England under Carl Julius Salomonsen, Niels Ryberg Finsen, Albert Neisser, and Sir J. Burdon Sanderson [q.v.], with the command of languages which he then acquired, supremely fitted him for a scientific career after he had graduated M.D. at the university of Copenhagen in 1900. During his first appointment as demonstrator of pathology in the university of Copenhagen he laboured long days and nights in research as well as in arduous routine. Here, in collaboration with Thorvald Madsen, he made valuable additions to the knowledge of diphtheria-toxin and anti-toxin, and studied the effects of ultra-violet radiations on micro-organisms. From the beginning a passionate precision of technique and a loathing of slipshod thought characterized all his work, and it was in the accurate quantitative measurement of biological processes that he made many of his most notable contributions to science.

Appointed in 1907, when only thirty-four, to the chair of pathology at Oxford, which he held until his death, Dreyer revolutionized the teaching, and by his vivid personality, enthusiasm, and learning attracted a steady succession of collaborators. Among the varied fields of research which, with his assistants, he pursued at Oxford were the principle and practice of the serological diagnosis of intestinal infections; quantitative studies of blood-volume, the size of the aorta, vital capacity, and their relations to height and weight; the calculation of the dosage of toxins and drugs according to the surface-area of the individual; inoculation against typhoid and paratyphoid fevers, and its effects on the Widal reaction; and methods of serological diagnosis in syphilis. Putting to practical use in the war of 1914–1918 his expert knowledge of enteric fever, he instituted in 1915 the Standards Laboratory at Oxford which for the next thirty years provided this country and the Dominions with scientifically standardized reagents for serological diagnosis. Later came investigations on the quantitative estimation of tuberculin, on variations in the virulence of the tubercle bacillus, and on the preparation and use of immunizing reagents against tuberculosis. He carried out, over a period of some years, a successful field-test of the latter in Danish cattle, which deserved more recognition than it received.

Although in his later years he paid increasing attention to university business and to the building of the Sir William Dunn School of Pathology, which is his monument and his provision for the ampler development of his science, Dreyer's soul was always in research. An extensive study of the action of radiations on bacteria, a revival of an earlier interest, and the devising of quantitative methods for the estimation of bacteriophage-potency were the main activities of this period.

Dreyer was elected a member of the Kongeligi Danske Videnskabernes Selskab in 1909, and in 1913 received the French order of Officier de l'Instruction Publique. From 1915 to 1919 he served with the British Expeditionary Force in France with the temporary rank of lieutenant-colonel, Royal Army Medical Corps. For his war-work on the oxygen supply to high-fliers and on the diagnosis of enteric fever he was appointed C.B.E. in 1919, and he was elected F.R.S. in 1921.

In 1912 Dreyer was elected a fellow of Lincoln College, Oxford, and although a professor's main allegiance belongs to the university he always showed great interest in the college, which profited greatly by his wise counsels. He served for many years on the hebdomadal council where his unusual power of understanding the points at issue, shown in university, college, and scientific matters, caused his opinions and judgement to command respect.

Dreyer married in 1900 Margrete Caroline, daughter of Laurits Jörgersen, of Söllestedgaard Manor, Laaland, Denmark. There was no issue of the marriage. He was naturalized in 1912. He died suddenly at Söllestedgaard 17 August 1934.

[*Georges Dreyer. A Memoir by his Wife*, 1937; E. W. Ainley Walker, *Georges Dreyer. His Scientific Work at Oxford*, 1934; *Obituary Notices of Fellows of the Royal Society*, No. 4, December 1935 (bibliography and portrait); *Journal of Pathology and Bacteriology*, vol. xxxix, 1934 (bibliography and portrait); private information; personal knowledge.] H. G. HANBURY.

DRINKWATER, JOHN (1882–1937), playwright, poet, and actor, was born at Leytonstone, Essex, 1 June 1882, the only son of Albert Edwin Drinkwater, a schoolmaster who came from Oxford and who later turned actor, theatrical manager, and playwright, by his first wife, Annie Beck, only daughter of John Beck Brown, an ironmonger, of Oxford. The father, like many actors, was determined to discourage stage ambitions in his son; and on leaving the Oxford High School at the age of fifteen the boy was put into the service of the Northern Assurance Company at Nottingham. Later he was transferred to an office at Birmingham, where he met (Sir) Barry Jackson, a wealthy young man some three years his senior. Both were enthusiasts for the theatre, and they became co-founders, in 1907, of the Pilgrim Players, an amateur dramatic society. Their work was so good that, in 1909, Mr. Jackson decided to build a professional repertory theatre and invited Drinkwater to become its manager. Drinkwater leapt at the chance to escape from business drudgery, and in the four years before the Birmingham Repertory Theatre took full professional rank (1913) he not only acted many parts but also began to take himself seriously as a writer. He was handicapped at first by lack of a cultural background, but boundless energy and a questing mind soon made up the gaps in his education. By 1917 he had to his credit some lyrics of authentic quality and several verse plays.

Drinkwater now had the idea of writing a series of historical plays, for the first of which he chose Abraham Lincoln as his subject. The play was produced at Birmingham in 1918, and had a success which led to its transfer to London in the following year. It was staged by (Sir) Nigel Playfair [q.v.] during his memorable tenure of the Lyric Theatre at Hammersmith, ran for over a year, and established Drinkwater's fame at a blow.

Although none of the other plays in his historical series—*Mary Stuart* (published 1921, produced 1922), *Oliver Cromwell* (published 1921, produced 1923), and *Robert E. Lee* (published and produced 1923)—enjoyed a similar success, each added to the esteem in which the author was held. Later, in 1928, critics who accused him of over-solemnity were confuted when *Bird in Hand* (published 1927), a comedy of contemporary country life written with the lightest touch, was received with applause in both England and the United States of America. Drinkwater became a busy writer in many fields, besides making occasional appearances on the stage, and although his strength was great, he overtaxed it. He died in London

25 March 1937. He was twice married: first, in 1906 to Kathleen Walpole, who acted in the Birmingham company as Cathleen Orford; this marriage was dissolved in 1924; secondly, in 1924 to a violinist of note, Daisy, daughter of Joseph Arthur Kennedy, schoolmaster, of Norwood, Adelaide, Australia, and formerly wife of Benno Moiseiwitsch, the Russian pianist. There was one daughter of the second marriage.

A bust of Drinkwater by Savd Botzaris is in the possession of his widow.

[John Drinkwater, *Inheritance*, 1931, and *Discovery*, 1932; *Who's Who in the Theatre*, 1936; personal knowledge.]

W. A. DARLINGTON.

DRUCE, GEORGE CLARIDGE (1850–1932), botanist, was born at Potterspury, Northamptonshire, 23 May 1850, the illegitimate son of Jane Druce who came of farming stock from Buckinghamshire. Little is known of his early life: circumstances were evidently difficult for his mother and in 1855 she took a situation in the nearby small village of Yardley Gobion. Two ministers of the Independent chapel at Potterspury, J. and T. B. Slye, took an interest in the boy and his education. From his earliest years Druce had an eye for plants and a remarkable memory of their occurrence. As a child his chief relaxation and interest were found in the collection and study of the insects and flora of the country-side.

In 1866 Druce was apprenticed to P. Jeyes & company, of Northampton, a firm of retail and manufacturing chemists. After long hours in shop and laboratory, in which he was soon given considerable responsibility, he somehow found time for hard study and in 1873 passed all his pharmaceutical examinations with high honours. Once these were out of the way he felt free to give time to field botany. He began to collect a herbarium, to write on the local flora, and helped to found and organize the activities of the Northamptonshire Natural History Club. For six years after qualifying he remained with his employer, but in June 1879 he suddenly broke all connexions with Northampton and took the risk of setting up in business in Oxford, where he invested his savings of about £400 in a chemist's shop at 118 High Street. The cause of this unexpected and complete break with Northampton may perhaps be connected with his parentage. Local tradition has it that he aspired to copy the industrious apprentice too closely and, being reminded of the circumstances of his birth, left, declaring that he would make both money and a name for himself. If these were his ambitions, he succeeded, for he left a considerable fortune and his name is firmly placed in the literature of British floristic botany.

As soon as he was settled in Oxford, Druce began to take part in activities similar to those abandoned at Northampton. In 1880 he helped to found the Ashmolean Natural History Society of Oxfordshire and began to investigate the county flora. In 1886 he published the *Flora of Oxfordshire*. In 1895 recognition came in his appointment as Fielding curator in the department of botany, an appointment which gave him official access to the library and herbarium there. In 1889 he had been given the degree of honorary M.A., and he was matriculated by Magdalen College in 1902. He was granted an M.A. by decree in 1919.

The cares of his business and the pursuit of his hobby did not exhaust Druce's energies. He was prominent in freemasonry and took an active part as a liberal in municipal affairs. He served on the city council from 1892 until his death, was chairman of the public health committee for thirty years, and was sheriff in 1897 and mayor in 1900. He also served on the council of the Pharmaceutical Society of which he was president in 1901 and 1902.

From 1903 until his death Druce was secretary to the British Botanical Exchange Club, the main purpose of which was the exchange of specimens collected in Great Britain. During Druce's period of office the membership grew rapidly, especially among amateurs interested in the wild life of their counties. The secretary's reports gave Druce a medium of publication; as editor he had a journal entirely within his own hands and in its pages his more original and unorthodox views appeared.

Druce was remarkable as a topographical field botanist. He 'visited places not in order to get a rare plant already known to occur there, but to find out what other rare plants that locality afforded and to make notes of such as were absent'. He travelled in all the counties of Great Britain and Ireland and also went several times to the Shetlands and Channel Islands. As the cares of his business became less, and after his retirement, so his opportunities to travel became greater. He accompanied the British Association

to Australia and made independent visits to Mediterranean lands and South America. From his eighteenth year until the end of his long life, Druce, with many characteristics of a keen investigator, noted and collected plants whenever and wherever he could. It is therefore hardly surprising that 'he never studied intensively nor became an authority on a group' of plants. Indeed, the soundness of his taxonomic judgement may often be questioned. In nomenclature, he consistently favoured the earliest name for a plant, whatever the International Rules might decree. He appeared to take delight in showing that the generally accepted name should be replaced by a new combination reviving some older specific epithet. Criticism, of which he was impatient, attacked his fondness for creating '*nov. comb.*' while 'his descriptions were singularly unequal, never orthodox and usually avoided the citation of types'. The results of his wide travels in Great Britain appear in his *Comital Flora of the British Isles* (1932). In compiling this he was greatly helped by the information which came to him from the Botanical Exchange Club.

Druce's best work is to be found in his four books on the *Flora of Oxfordshire* (1st ed. 1886, 2nd ed. 1927), of *Berkshire* (1897), of *Buckinghamshire* (1926), and of *Northamptonshire* (begun in 1873 and published by the Northamptonshire Natural History Club in 1879, revised in 1930). He also collaborated with S. H. Vines [q.v.] in accounts of the two more famous of the ancient herbaria at Oxford, that of Dillenius (1907) and that of Morison (1914).

Druce died at Oxford 29 February 1932. During his long life and as a result of his public service he made many friends and acquaintances. He received the honorary degree of LL.D. from the university of St. Andrews (1919); obtained the D.Sc. of Oxford, by examination (1924); and was elected F.R.S. in 1927. The wide respect and affection which was felt for him was remarkably demonstrated in the celebrations of his eightieth birthday and at his funeral. He left his library and herbarium to the department of botany together with the residue of his estate as an endowment. He was unmarried.

There is a portrait by P. A. de László in the Radcliffe Science Library, and a copy hangs in the City Hall at Oxford; a bronze bust by Frank Lascelles is in the department of botany, Oxford.

[*Obituary Notices of Fellows of the Royal Society*, No. 1, December 1932 (portrait);

Autobiographical notes in *Flora of Northamptonshire*, 1930, p. cxxi, and in *Flora of Buckinghamshire*, 1926, p. cvi; *Journal of Botany*, vol. lxx, 1932; *Kew Bulletin*, 1932, p. 157; *Pharmaceutical Journal and Pharmacist*, January to June, 1932; *The Times*, 1 March 1932; *Oxford Times*, 4 March 1932; *Nature*, 19 March 1932; private information.]

T. G. B. OSBORN.

DUDGEON, LEONARD STANLEY (1876–1938), pathologist, was born in London 7 October 1876, the second son and the youngest of the eight children of John Hepburn Dudgeon, of Haddington, East Lothian, by his wife, Catherine, daughter of Alexander Pond. He was educated at University College School and St. Thomas's Hospital, and qualified in 1899. Close association with Louis Leopold Jenner and S. G. Shattock [q.v.] led him to become one of the earliest workers in pathology and bacteriology as specialized subjects. After acting for a short period as a pathologist at the West London Hospital, he returned in 1903 to St. Thomas's, where he spent the rest of his life, and became superintendent of the Louis Jenner Clinical Laboratory. He found students eager to be taught and colleagues willing to take advantage of the application of pathology and bacteriology to medicine and surgery. His collaboration was constantly sought over obscure cases in the wards, and under his direction the clinical laboratory became one of the most important departments of the hospital. He was appointed director of the pathological laboratory and bacteriologist (1905), professor of pathology in the university of London (1919), curator of the Shattock Museum (1927), and dean of the medical school (1928).

During the war of 1914–1918 Dudgeon served in the Near East as a temporary colonel, Army Medical Services, and carried out valuable investigations of infectious diseases prevalent among the troops. An account of his work on dysentery in Macedonia was published by the Medical Research Council in 1919. For his war services he was thrice mentioned in dispatches and was appointed C.M.G. in 1918 and C.B.E. in 1919, and awarded the Order of St. Sava of Serbia.

As dean of St. Thomas's Hospital Dudgeon enjoyed the full confidence of the staff, and during his term of office the medical school was largely rebuilt and modernized. He was for many years honorary secretary of the Voluntary Hospitals Committee, chairman of the Deans' Committee, and a member of the senate of London University. He was an active member of the Sankey commission on voluntary hospitals which reported in 1937. In these positions he exerted considerable influence on the course of medical education and hospital policy, and in particular took a leading part in securing co-operation for teaching purposes between the voluntary and the London County Council hospitals.

Administration, teaching, and the claims of a large consulting practice left little time for research. Nevertheless, Dudgeon published work that was both sound and original. He was the author of *The Bacteriology of Peritonitis*, in collaboration with (Sir) Percy Sargent (1905), and of *Bacterial Vaccines and their Position in Therapeutics* (1927), and wrote many papers on tropical diseases and on bacteriology and immunity. During the latter years of his life he developed a technique by means of smears for the rapid diagnosis of tumours and for the detection of malignant cells in bodily secretions, which has found wide application. At the Royal College of Physicians, of which he was elected a fellow in 1908, he was Horace Dobell lecturer (1908) and Croonian lecturer (1912). He gave the Erasmus Wilson lecture at the Royal College of Surgeons in 1905 and 1908, and was president of the section of tropical diseases of the Royal Society of Medicine (1923–1925).

Dudgeon was a kindly and humorous man, who endeavoured to disguise his warm humanity by a somewhat brusque manner. He married in 1909 Norah, third daughter of Richard Orpen, of Kenmare, co. Kerry, and had two sons and one daughter. He died in London 22 October 1938.

[*The Times*, 24 October 1938; *Journal of Pathology and Bacteriology*, January 1939 (portrait); *St. Thomas's Hospital Gazette*, December 1938 (portrait); *British Medical Journal*, 1938, vol. ii, p. 922 (portrait); *Lancet*, 1938, vol. ii, pp. 1031 and 1088 (portrait); private information.] W. J. BISHOP.

DUDLEY, second EARL OF (1867–1932), lord-lieutenant of Ireland and governor-general of Australia. [See WARD, WILLIAM HUMBLE.]

DUFF, SIR ALEXANDER (LUDOVIC) (1862–1933), admiral, was born at Knockleith, Aberdeenshire, 20 February 1862, the fourth son and seventh child of Colonel

James Duff, of Knockleith, by his wife, Jane Bracken, daughter of Alan Colquhoun Dunlop, of Edinburgh. He entered the navy in 1875, and served as midshipman in the Mediterranean from 1877 to 1881. He served as sub-lieutenant in the royal yacht *Victoria and Albert*, and was promoted to lieutenant from her in September 1884, serving on the China station for two years in the *Agamemnon*. Having qualified as torpedo lieutenant he served for three years in the *Imperieuse*, flagship of the China station, and afterwards (1891) in the *Blake*, flagship of the North America station, and the torpedo depot-ship *Vulcan*. He was promoted to commander in 1897. After two years in command of the destroyer *Bat* on training service at Devonport, he joined the cruiser *St. George* as executive officer. He was promoted captain in 1902 and became flag captain in the battleship *Albemarle*, flagship of the rear-admiral, first in the Mediterranean and later in the Channel Fleet.

In 1905 Duff became naval assistant to the controller of the navy for three years, returning thence to sea service in command of the battleship *Temeraire*. In 1910 he was appointed commodore of the naval barracks at Portsmouth for a year before becoming director of naval mobilization (entitled director of the mobilization division after the creation of the Naval War Staff in 1912), continuing to hold this appointment after his promotion to rear-admiral in March 1913. In October 1914 he returned to sea service as rear-admiral, fourth battle squadron in the Grand Fleet (flag in the *Emperor of India*). The commander-in-chief, Admiral Sir John Jellicoe, recognizing his great technical abilities, put him in charge, jointly with Rear-Admiral (Sir) Arthur Cavenagh Leveson, of experiments with devices for defending ships from submarine mines and with other inventions; during the battle of Jutland Duff flew his flag in the *Superb*. When in December 1916 Jellicoe left the fleet to become first sea lord in order to cope with the immense problem of the U-boat war, he took Duff with him to the Admiralty as director of the anti-submarine division which was then formed in the Naval Staff. Six months later Duff joined the Board of Admiralty with the title of assistant chief of the Naval Staff and was put in charge of all the divisions dealing with the same problems, being replaced as director of the anti-submarine division itself by Captain (Sir) W. W. Fisher [q.v.]. To his

and Fisher's work in accomplishing the eventual defeat of the U-boat, Jellicoe later paid a handsome tribute in his book *The Crisis of the Naval War* (1920). Duff was promoted vice-admiral in 1918 and appointed K.C.B. On leaving the Admiralty in 1919 he was appointed commander-in-chief of the China station and during his three years tenure of that command he convened a conference with the commanders-in-chief of adjoining stations which recommended the establishment of the naval base at Singapore. He was promoted admiral in 1921 and relinquished the China command the following year. He was appointed C.B. (civil) in 1912 and (military) in 1916, G.C.B. in 1926, K.C.V.O. in 1922, and G.B.E. in 1924. For his services he was awarded, amongst other foreign orders, the commandership of the Legion of Honour and the American D.S.M. He retired in 1925, and settled at Copdock, Ipswich.

Duff was twice married: first, in 1886 to Janet Douglas (died 1908), third daughter of Garden William Duff, of Hatton Castle, Aberdeenshire, and had two daughters; secondly, in 1924 to Marjorie, daughter of Charles Hill-Whitson, of Parkhill, Perthshire; there was no issue of this marriage. He died in London 22 November 1933.

[*The Times*, 23 November 1933; Admiralty records; private information.]

H. G. Thursfield.

DUFFY, Sir FRANK GAVAN (1852–1936), Australian judge, was born in Dublin 29 February 1852, the elder son of the Irish nationalist and colonial politician (Sir) C. G. Duffy [q.v.], by his second wife, Susan, daughter of Philip Hughes, of Newry, co. Down. He was educated at Stonyhurst College and at the university of Melbourne, where he graduated M.A., LL.B. He was called to the Victorian bar in 1874.

Duffy was for some time an officer of the Victorian State Treasury. In his legal practice he devoted himself first to the County Court, where he became a leading practitioner. He subsequently transferred his practice to the Supreme Court, where he became a leader of the bar, being regarded as a brilliant cross-examiner. He took silk in 1901. In the course of a busy practice Duffy found time to lecture in law at the university of Melbourne, and he was the editor of the *Australian Law Times* and subsequently of the *Victorian Law Reports*. In addition he was the author and joint author of several works on legal subjects.

In 1913 Duffy was appointed a justice of the High Court of Australia. The federal character of the Commonwealth constitution is such that the High Court is not infrequently called upon to pronounce upon constitutional issues of far-reaching importance, and Duffy was a member of the court on the occasion of several famous decisions. In the Engineers' case (1920), one of the most famous decisions in the history of Australian constitutional interpretation, the High Court overruled earlier decisions in which it had been held that State instrumentalities were not subject to the operation of federal law. Duffy was the sole dissentient, and in a short and closely reasoned judgement expounded a view of the federal character of the constitution which denied to Commonwealth legislation a general power to bind the States as such.

In an earlier, and almost equally famous, case, *Farey* v. *Burvett* (1916), decided in the course of the war of 1914–1918, Duffy also dissented. The majority there held that the defence power conferred by the constitution upon the Commonwealth supported the fixing of the price of bread. Duffy's view was that while the ambit of defence might be more extensive in time of war than in peace, a power to legislate with respect to the naval and military defence of the Commonwealth did not justify a general regulation of the national economy.

In general it may fairly be said that Duffy was unfavourable to an extended interpretation of Commonwealth powers. The two decisions already cited are perhaps the best illustration of this. Again, in cases involving Commonwealth Arbitration Court powers, there is evident in Duffy's judgements the same tendency to interpret these powers restrictively. On the other hand, towards the close of his judicial career, in the Clothing Factory case (1935), a decision involving the interpretation of the defence power of the Commonwealth, Duffy was a party to the majority decision that the peace-time activities of the Commonwealth Clothing Factory were authorized by the constitution.

Duffy was appointed K.C.M.G. in 1929, and in 1931, on Sir Isaac Isaacs becoming governor-general of the Commonwealth, he was raised to be chief justice of the High Court. He was sworn of the Privy Council in 1932, and resigned the office of chief justice in 1935. He died in Melbourne 29 July 1936.

Duffy married in 1880 Ellen Mary, daughter of John Richard Torr, warehouseman, of Melbourne. He had six sons, three of whom predeceased their father, and one daughter, who also died before him.

There is a portrait of Duffy by W. B. McInnes in the High Court Buildings in Melbourne.

[*Australian Law Journal*, October 1935 and August 1936; *Commonwealth Law Reports*; private information.] ZELMAN COWEN.

DUKE, HENRY EDWARD, first BARON MERRIVALE (1855–1939), judge and politician, was the second son of William Edward Duke, then a clerk at the granite works at Walkhampton, South Devonshire, where Henry was born 5 November 1855. His mother was Elizabeth Ann Lord. Without any advantage of family or fortune, he was educated locally, did not attend any public school, nor was he a member of any university. In early life he was a journalist on the *Western Morning News*, but he came up to London at the age of twenty-five, and entered the press gallery of the House of Commons. While there he read for the bar and was called by Gray's Inn in 1885. He joined the Western circuit and acquired a considerable practice at assizes and in the local courts. His reputation as an advocate soon reached London where he built up a large junior practice and took silk in 1899. He was recorder of Devonport and Plymouth from 1897 to 1900, retaining the recordership of Devonport (which he held until 1914) when he became unionist member of parliament for Plymouth in 1900. He lost his seat in 1906 but was returned for Exeter in January 1910. In December 1910 his opponent headed the poll by four votes, but after a scrutiny Duke was awarded the seat by one vote and held it until 1918.

At the height of his career at the bar Duke found himself opposed to such famous advocates of the day as Sir Edward Clarke, Sir Edward (afterwards Lord) Carson, and Sir Rufus Isaacs (afterwards first Marquess of Reading) [qq.v.]. Although his industry and experience had given him a wealth of legal knowledge, he was better in cases tried by judge and jury than by a judge alone. No one would dispute his claim to be one of the finest *nisi prius* advocates of his time. He understood well the outlook and reactions of the ordinary juryman. Tall, with a commanding presence, he was a slow and deliberate speaker, and had a slight Devonshire accent which attracted attention. In court he was always serious with a profound belief in the cause he was pleading. Above all he was imperturbable and never upset when things appeared to go against him. As a cross-examiner he was formidable, and often turned to the advantage of his client what had seemed to be a damaging answer. Among many famous cases in which Duke was engaged were those of *Adam* v. *Ward* (1914), a libel action brought against the permanent under-secretary of state for war, and the Slingsby baby (1915). In 1915 he was sworn of the Privy Council and was appointed attorney-general to the Prince of Wales, a post which he held until 31 July 1916.

Duke did well in the House of Commons, achieving more success than lawyers usually do in that assembly. During the early days of the coalition government of 1915 he sat on the front opposition bench and greatly advanced his reputation by his speeches. In 1915 he presided over the royal commissions on the defence of the realm losses and on the liquor trade control losses. Meanwhile affairs in Ireland had become critical. A citizen army had been enrolled, and broke out into rebellion on Easter Day 1916. The actual fighting was chiefly street fighting in Dublin and lasted a week, only about 2,000 rebels in all being engaged. The British troops lost 379 men, including 106 killed, while the rebel losses were trifling. The chief secretary for Ireland, Augustine Birrell [q.v.], resigned and the situation was extremely grave. It was in these circumstances that, on 31 July 1916, Asquith appointed Duke chief secretary with a seat in the Cabinet.

The chief secretaryship has been the graveyard of many reputations. Whatever may be said of Duke's tenure and administration of the office, it required high political courage and even a stern sense of duty to accept it at such a time and under such conditions. The government at once set on foot negotiations for an Irish settlement, but they failed, as did also a convention of Irishmen called under government sanction which sat for nearly a year. Matters consequently went from bad to worse. Any attempt at concession or conciliation was regarded by the Sinn Fein party as a sign of weakness. Early in 1917 seditious propaganda had

increased to such an extent that both the military authorities and the police urged the need of strong measures, to which Duke steadily refused his sanction. All the incidents of those troublous times cannot be set out here. It was an impossible task which confronted the chief secretary. Sinn Fein continued to go from strength to strength, an Irish republican army was organized, and in May 1918 Duke resigned. Two views are taken of his Irish administration. Both recognize that 'the verdict on his Chief Secretaryship must be modified by a due appreciation of his position as the representative of Coalition Ministries in a period of unexampled difficulty' [*The Times*, 22 May 1939]. His critics contend that his methods were too conciliatory, that he resorted to clemency when a firm hand was called for. They say that he had no 'imagination or breadth of view' and that he lacked 'appreciation of the Irish psychology. The troubles of that time were not to be met by administrative routine, however conscientiously carried on' [*Ibid.*]. His supporters, and they were many, say that he was a high-minded English gentleman, that he did his best, and earned the esteem of all people of good will. History will probably find far more to commend than criticize in his career as chief secretary. He could not command success and it is difficult to see how he could have done better in the situation in which he found himself.

On his retirement from Ireland, Duke was knighted and made a lord justice of appeal, an office which he held for eighteen months until he was appointed in November 1919 president of the Probate, Divorce, and Admiralty division of the High Court. The presidency is an office of great commercial and social importance, and Duke's appointment was an excellent one. His natural seriousness admirably fitted him for the discharge of the duties of a divorce judge. He was dignified and efficient. There were no 'scenes' in his court, no bandying of jokes, no laughter during the hearing of a case. During his presidency there was passed the Matrimonial Causes Act (1923) which placed the sexes on an equality as regards grounds for divorce. The work increased and necessitated the appointment of an additional judge in 1925. Duke in his summings up and judgements showed great power in clarifying the issues and marshalling the facts. He was an urbane judge, always courteous to counsel. In the Admiralty Court he was satisfactory but had not technical knowledge. It fell to him to wind up the work of the Prize Court. He retired in 1933.

Duke was raised to the peerage in 1925 as Baron Merrivale, of Walkhampton in the county of Devon. He was a devoted member of Gray's Inn, serving as treasurer in 1908 and 1927. He married in 1876 Sarah (died 1914), daughter of John Shorland, of Shrewsbury, and had one son, Edward (born 1883), who succeeded him as second baron, and one daughter. He died in London 20 May 1939.

A portrait of Duke by Sir William Orpen is at Gray's Inn.

[*The Times*, 22 May 1939; *Annual Register*, 1939; E. H. Butcher in *Graya* (Gray's Inn magazine), Easter Term 1940; personal knowledge.]   SANKEY.

DU MAURIER, SIR GERALD HUBERT EDWARD BUSSON (1873–1934), actor-manager, was born 26 March 1873 at Hampstead, where he lived all through his boyhood and young manhood until his marriage in 1903, and whither he returned in 1916 and remained until he died. He was, as he himself said, essentially a cockney, but he was a Hampstead cockney, a cockney entirely different from all others. He was extraordinary among these unique cockneys for several reasons. His father, George Louis Palmella Busson du Maurier [q.v.], although the son of a naturalized British subject, was a Frenchman, born in Paris and married to an Englishwoman, Emma, daughter of William Wightwick.

Gerald du Maurier, the younger son and youngest child in a family of five, was educated at Harrow. At first indeterminate about his career, he decided that as he had been successful in amateur theatrical performances, he might as well go on to the professional stage. The decision was as casual as his style of acting, a deceptive style, since it caused shallow-minded people to think that he 'was always himself' and to overlook the remarkable technique which he brought to this easy, casual performance. His first appearance was made at the Garrick Theatre on 6 January 1894, as Fritz a waiter, in *An Old Jew* by Sydney Grundy. The management was that of (Sir) John Hare [q.v.], and du Maurier appeared under it because his father and Hare were friends. He remained with Hare for six months, went on tour with (Sir) Johnston Forbes-Robertson [q.v.], and then in September 1895 joined (Sir) Herbert Beerbohm Tree [q.v.] at Manchester, to play the part of Dodor in the dramatic version of his father's novel, *Trilby*, which was brought to the Haymarket Theatre, London, in October. He stayed with Tree for just over four years, steadily perfecting his nonchalant style. Two years (1899–1901) with Mrs. Patrick Campbell [q.v.] followed his long engagement with Tree. It was not, however, until November 1902 that he established himself truly. In that month, at the Duke of York's Theatre, he played the part of the Hon. Ernest Woolley in *The Admirable Crichton*, a comedy by (Sir) J. M. Barrie [q.v.], and his nonchalance was now seen to be power. Thus he began an association with Barrie which was to be highly beneficial to both men: his tally of Barrie pieces was eight, including *Peter Pan* (in which he 'created' the parts of Captain Hook and Mr. Darling), *What Every Woman Knows*, and *Dear Brutus*. In 1910 du Maurier joined Frank Curzon in the management of Wyndham's Theatre where he remained for fifteen years, except for a short break in 1918 when he became a cadet in the Irish Guards. After his separation from Curzon, he joined Gilbert Miller at the St. James's Theatre, his first production, Frederick Lonsdale's *The Last of Mrs. Cheyney* (1925), being immensely successful.

Du Maurier was knighted in 1922, and died in London after an operation 11 April 1934. His wife, Muriel, herself an actress, daughter of Harry Beaumont, a solicitor, was playing with him in *The Admirable Crichton* at the time of their engagement. They had three daughters, of whom the second, Daphne, is a widely popular novelist and has written successful plays.

Du Maurier, who, in addition to introducing a style of acting which is now over-common and almost routine, was a very skilful producer of plays, had a singularly successful career in the theatre. His daughter Daphne wrote of him 'he did not know what it was to wait at stage doors to interview managers and beg for a part in a new production'. If his good fortune began to flicker in the last year or two of his life, it was because he became careless of his performance. His moods were unusually variable, but he rallied easily from despondency and was good company, especially when he exercised his gift of mimicry. His family affection was strong, and he was deeply distressed by the death in action in 1915 of his brother Guy, a professional soldier who had, unexpectedly, written a play,

An Englishman's Home, which was remarkably successful when Gerald produced it in 1909; and the deaths of his sisters and of his mother distressed him no less. His standard, as a theatre manager, was good, although not of the highest order. His profile, he declared, was against him, and debarred him from poetic drama and tragedy. But he read poetry aloud very charmingly, and might, if he had trusted himself more, have aspired to greater heights than he achieved.

There are portraits of du Maurier by Harrington Mann and John Collier in the possession of his widow. Another portrait by Collier is in the Public Library at Hampstead. A portrait by Augustus John was last heard of in the United States of America. A cartoon by 'Spy' appeared in *Vanity Fair*, 25 December 1907.

[*The Times*, 12 April 1934; Daphne du Maurier, *Gerald: A Portrait*, 1934; personal knowledge.]   ST. JOHN ERVINE.

DUNDONALD, twelfth EARL OF (1852–1935), lieutenant-general. [See COCHRANE, DOUGLAS MACKINNON BAILLIE HAMILTON.]

DUVEEN, JOSEPH, BARON DUVEEN, of Millbank (1869–1939), art dealer, patron, and trustee, was born at Hull 14 October 1869, the eldest of the ten sons and four daughters of (Sir) Joseph Joel Duveen [q.v.], by his wife, Rosetta, daughter of Abraham Barnett, of Hull. He was educated privately, and at the age of seventeen entered his father's business, which had dealt chiefly with oriental porcelain and objects of art. He quickly visualized the vast possibilities of buying pictures by the great masters from Europe and selling them in America, thus adding enormously to the activities of the business, which became the most prominent in the art trade. His intense energy and salesmanship made him the world's foremost dealer, and his transactions were on a scale that was until then unprecedented. He paid £60,900 for the small Romney portrait of Mrs. Bromley Davenport; £77,700 for the Lawrence portrait of 'Pinkie' (Mary Moulton Barrett); and £73,500 for Gainsborough's 'Harvest Waggon'. Besides these auction purchases he acquired privately whole collections at immense sums, such as those of Oscar Hainauer from Berlin (1906); the Rodolphe Kann collection from Paris (1907); the Maurice Kann collection (Rembrandt and

Boucher rooms, 1909); the Morgan collection of Chinese porcelain, eighteenth-century furniture, and the great Fragonard room which is now in the Frick Museum in New York (1914); Robert Henry Benson's collection of Italian pictures (1927); the Gustav Dreyfus collection of Italian sculpture, bronzes, etc. (1930); and Lord Hillingdon's collection of Sèvres porcelain and furniture (1936); also the two superb Raphael Madonnas of 1504 and 1508 which he purchased from Panshanger (Lady Desborough's collection, 1914 and 1928); Gainsborough's 'Blue Boy' from the Duke of Westminster (1921); and the Giorgione from Lord Allendale (1937). These and many other treasures passed to such prominent collectors as Benjamin Altmann, Jules S. Bache, Henry Clay Frick, Henry E. Huntington, Samuel H. Kress, Andrew Mellon, Mrs. Hamilton Rice, and Joseph E. Widener, and were presented by them either as collections where formed, or as part of the National Gallery of Art, Washington, D.C., and other public galleries and museums in America.

Duveen's art benefactions to this country were on a princely scale. In addition to many valuable pictures and works of art, including Hogarth's 'The Graham Children', Correggio's 'Christ Taking Leave of His Mother', J. S. Sargent's 'Mme. Gautreau', and Mr. Augustus John's 'Mme. Suggia', which he presented to the national collections, he gave to the Tate Gallery in 1926 several galleries for modern foreign art and one devoted to the work of Sargent, and in 1937 a new building comprising three large and two smaller galleries for modern sculpture; to the National Gallery in 1932 a gallery for Italian primitives; to the National Portrait Gallery in 1933 an extension; and to the British Museum a gallery for the Elgin marbles. He also bore the cost of the decorations at the Wallace Collection and of Rex Whistler's mural decorations at the Tate, and was a generous contributor to the National Art-Collections Fund. He founded, financed, and organized the British Artists Exhibitions Organization for the encouragement of lesser known British artists; and in 1931 he endowed a chair for the history of art in London University.

Duveen was a trustee of the Wallace Collection from 1925; of the National Gallery from 1929 to 1936; and of the National Portrait Gallery from 1933. He was an honorary member of the council of the National Art-Collections Fund and of the Council of the British School at Rome. He was director of the American Institute for Persian Art and Archaeology, New York City; a trustee of the Museum of Modern Art, New York; and honorary correspondent of the Commissions of Ancient and Modern Art of the Royal Belgium Museum of Fine Art. In 1929 he was presented with the freedom of the city of Hull. He received foreign decorations from France, Belgium, Holland, Serbia, and Hungary. He was knighted in 1919, created a baronet in 1927, and raised to the peerage as Baron Duveen, of Millbank (commemorating his long association with the Tate Gallery) in 1933.

Duveen married in 1899 Elsie, daughter of Gustav Salamon, of New York. She survived him with their only child, a daughter. The peerage therefore became extinct on his death, which took place in London 25 May 1939.

There is a pencil drawing of Duveen by W. E. Tittle, and also a stone bust by Sir W. Reid Dick, in the National Portrait Gallery.

[*The Times*, 26 May 1939; A. C. R. Carter, *Let Me Tell You*, 1940; Auction and exhibition catalogues; personal knowledge.]

ALEC MARTIN.

DYKE, SIR WILLIAM HART, seventh baronet (1837–1931), politician, was born at East Hall, Orpington, Kent, 7 August 1837, the second son of (Sir) Percyvall Hart Dyke, sixth baronet, of Lullingstone Castle, Eynesford, Kent, by his wife, Elizabeth, youngest daughter of John Wells, of Bickley Park, Kent. He was educated at Harrow and Christ Church, Oxford.

At Oxford Dyke was the most famous rackets player of his day. He played for four years against Cambridge, and won every match, both doubles and singles. In 1862 he challenged Francis Erwood, the professional at Woolwich and holder of the world's championship, and won by four games to two at Woolwich and by four games to one at the old Prince's Club in Hans Place, Chelsea. To him was due the starting of the public schools' rackets championship. He was very fond of tennis and kept up the game at Prince's Club, Knightsbridge, until he was well past his seventieth year. He was also an originator of lawn tennis. In 1873, a year before Major W. C. Wingfield took out a patent for 'Sphairistike', Dyke and two friends laid out a court at Lullingstone Castle and played the first game.

Although Dyke wished to enter the navy, he acquiesced in his father's desire that he should go into parliament. He was elected conservative member for West Kent in 1865 and represented Mid Kent from 1868 to 1885. Before the general election in the last-named year he was candidate for the Medway division, regarded as a safe seat, but he was solicited to contest the Dartford division, considered a probable liberal division, and was returned at the head of the poll; and he sat for Dartford until the liberal revival of 1906, when he was defeated and retired from parliament into private life. In 1868 he was appointed a whip and in 1874 he was promoted to be chief whip as patronage secretary to the Treasury. In this capacity, known as 'Billy Dyke', he had great influence with his party and was esteemed by his opponents. He was sworn of the Privy Council in 1880.

In 1885, when Lord Salisbury came into office for a few months, Dyke was appointed chief secretary for Ireland and sworn of the Irish Privy Council. During this administration the Ashbourne Act was passed. In Salisbury's second administration he was appointed vice-president of the committee of council on education (1887–1892). He established a reputation as an efficient and conscientious administrator and was partly responsible for the code of 1890 which was the first step in the abolition of the system of 'payment by results'. During its passage through the House of Commons he was in charge of the free education bill.

Dyke, who succeeded his father in 1875, spent practically his whole life in Kent, being alderman of the county council as well as deputy-lieutenant. He married in 1870 Lady Emily Caroline, elder daughter of John William Montagu, seventh Earl of Sandwich. They celebrated their diamond wedding. They had three sons, the two elder of whom predeceased their father, the second in infancy, and three daughters. Dyke died at Lullingstone Castle 3 July 1931 in his ninety-fourth year, and was succeeded as eighth baronet by his youngest son, Oliver Hamilton Augustus (born 1885).

[*The Times*, 4 July 1931.]

E. I. CARLYLE.

DYSON, SIR FRANK (WATSON) (1868–1939), astronomer, was born at Measham, near Ashby de la Zouche, 8 January 1868, the eldest child in a family of four sons and three daughters of Watson Dyson, a Baptist minister, by his wife, Frances, daughter of James Dodwell, of Long Crendon, Buckinghamshire. Educated at Bradford Grammar School and Trinity College, Cambridge, being a scholar of the latter, he was second wrangler in the mathematical tripos of 1889 and in 1891 was first Smith's prizeman and was elected a fellow of his college. In 1892 he was awarded an Isaac Newton studentship for research in astronomy. In 1894 he was selected by the astronomer royal, (Sir) W. H. M. Christie [q.v.], to fill the post of chief assistant at the Royal Observatory, Greenwich. The choice proved a singularly happy one and Dyson devoted himself with energy and enthusiasm to the advancement of practical astronomy. His first task was to take charge of the Greenwich share in the great international co-operative scheme for the preparation of a star-catalogue and star-map of the whole sky. This work brought home to him the need of an increase in knowledge of the motions of the stars. He therefore undertook, with William Grasset Thackeray, a new reduction of the 27,000 observations of more than 4,000 circumpolar stars made at Blackheath between 1806 and 1819 by Stephen Groombridge [q.v.]. The stars were re-observed at Greenwich and their motions were derived. This work made an important addition to the knowledge of stellar motions, which it extended to fainter stars.

In 1906 Dyson was appointed astronomer royal for Scotland. He made investigations of stellar motions in relation to the distances and luminosities of the stars and to their distribution in space. He showed that the phenomenon of star streaming, which had been announced by Jacobus Cornelius Kapteyn in 1904, was confirmed by stars of large proper-motion.

In 1910, on the retirement of Christie, Dyson returned to Greenwich as astronomer royal and from then until his retirement in 1933 a description of his work is largely a description of the work of the Royal Observatory at Greenwich. This was extended in many new directions: the determination of stellar parallaxes and proper-motions by photographic methods, of stellar magnitudes, of effective wavelengths, and of temperatures were undertaken. Particular attention was given to the reduction and discussion of meridian observations, the programmes of observation being chosen with care to meet the needs of practical astronomy. Sanction was obtained for the construction of a

new transit circle of the highest modern standard. The time service was greatly improved and clocks of a new type, known as free-pendulum clocks, of much higher precision than earlier clocks, were installed as the standards of time. In 1924 the distribution through the British Broadcasting Corporation of time signals from Greenwich was begun, and in 1927 from the Post Office wireless station at Rugby the transmission of wireless time signals of world-wide range for the benefit of shipping was inaugurated. Dyson was for many years president of the British Horological Institute, which awarded him its gold medal in 1928. He was also twice master of the Clockmakers' Company. Under his direction the prestige of the Royal Observatory was greatly enhanced.

Dyson was keenly interested in total eclipses of the sun. He observed the eclipses of 1900 in Portugal, 1901 in Sumatra, 1905 in Tunis, 1912 in Paris, 1927 at Giggleswick, and 1932 in the United States of America, and he made important contributions to the knowledge of the spectra of the sun's chromosphere and corona. He organized the two expeditions, one from Greenwich and one from Cambridge, to test, at the eclipse of 1919, Dr. Albert Einstein's prediction of the deflexion of star-light in the sun's gravitational field. The successful results obtained by these expeditions confirmed the prediction and did much to secure general acceptance of Dr. Einstein's generalized theory of relativity.

Dyson took a prominent part in the reconstitution of international scientific co-operation after the war of 1914–1918 through the International Research Council and in the formation of the International Astronomical Union, of which he was president for the period 1928–1932. A gift in 1931 by Mr. W. Johnston Yapp to the Royal Observatory of a fine 36-inch reflecting telescope to commemorate the great services of Dyson as astronomer royal was gratefully accepted by the lords commissioners of the Admiralty and is a fitting memorial of his important contributions to astronomy. He was president of the Royal Astronomical Society from 1911 to 1913, and of the British Astronomical Association from 1916 to 1918, and from 1913 to 1914 vice-president of the Royal Society, of which he had been elected a fellow in 1901. He was awarded a Royal medal of the Royal Society in 1921, the Bruce gold medal of the Astronomical Society of the Pacific in 1922, and the gold medal of the Royal Astronomical Society in 1925. He received honorary degrees from the universities of Oxford, Cambridge, Edinburgh, Durham, Leeds, Toronto, Perth, and Melbourne, and was foreign or corresponding member of various academies. He was knighted in 1915 and appointed K.B.E. in 1926.

Dyson was a man of engaging personality and of singular charm of manner. He married in 1894 Caroline Bisset (died 1937), daughter of Palemon Best, M.B., J.P., of Louth, Lincolnshire, and had two sons and six daughters. He died at sea 25 May 1939, when returning from a visit to Australia.

[*The Times*, 26 May 1939; *Obituary Notices of Fellows of the Royal Society*, No. 8, January 1940 (portrait); private information; personal knowledge.]   H. SPENCER JONES.

DYSON, WILLIAM HENRY (WILL) (1880–1938), cartoonist and etcher, was born at Ballarat, Australia, 3 September 1880, the sixth son of George Arthur Dyson, traveller, who came from London, by his wife, Jane, daughter of Ambrose Mayall, cotton spinner, of Ashton-under-Lyne. He was educated at Melbourne. He began with caricatures, working first for the Sydney *Bulletin* and later for *Lone Hand, Gad Fly*, and *Clarion*. In 1909 he came to London as a cartoonist, and his first work to be published in England was in the *New Age* of A. R. Orage [q.v.], who in due course indoctrinated him with the social credit theories of Major Clifford Hugh Douglas, of which he became an ardent and brilliant exponent.

There followed contributions to the *Weekly Dispatch*, the *World*, the *Daily Chronicle*, the *Daily Sketch*, and the *Daily Herald*. In the last-named (in which his first cartoon appeared in 1913) Dyson found his true vehicle, for he had an extremely radical outlook which often expressed itself in bitter attacks on the propertied classes. He was therefore able to lend powerful aid to the *Daily Herald* in its formative years.

During the war of 1914–1918 Dyson became an official artist on the western front, and in 1918 a collection of his war drawings was shown at the Leicester Galleries, London. He returned to the *Daily Herald*, but in 1925 went back to Australia. Although he was on the staff of the *Melbourne Herald*, he had the notion of concentrating upon pure art as an etcher. In 1930 he went to New York with a selection of his etchings,

which were successfully exhibited there; and in November of the same year he showed them at the St. George's Gallery, Hanover Square, London. These etchings display great beauty of line, and many of them are humorous literary commentaries.

But British labour was engaged in fierce political strife, and in August 1931 Dyson gave up all ideas of artistic detachment and rejoined the *Daily Herald*. He remained a valued contributor to that journal up to the day of his death, which occurred from heart failure 21 January 1938 after a morning's painting in his Chelsea studio.

Dyson was an inveterate castigator of greed, snobbery, and militarism, and some of his best cartoons had that power of seeing phenomena *sub specie aeternitatis* which gives distinction to pictorial satire. He was, indeed, one of the noteworthy cartoonists of his age, although his composition was often diffuse and formal design was not his strong point. His bitterness was reserved for causes, and in his personal relationships he was quiet, modest, and friendly.

Dyson was very sensitive to the needs of his less fortunate fellow artists, and was a champion of British art against detractors who seemed to him over-fond of foreign products. His advocacy of social credit found literary expression in a book, *Artist Among the Bankers*, published in 1933.

Dyson married in 1910 Ruby Lindsay, an Australian artist whose works were signed 'Ruby Lind'. She died in 1919, leaving one daughter, Betty, who in her turn became an artist.

A portrait in oils of Dyson by T. C. Dugdale is in the possession of the artist.

[*The Times*, 22 January 1938; *Daily Herald*, 22, 24, and 25 January 1938, 4 November 1930; *Manchester Guardian*, 22 January 1938; W. H. Stevenson in supplement to *Labour*, February 1938.]   HERBERT B. GRIMSDITCH.

EDGE, SELWYN FRANCIS (1868–1940), pioneer motorist, was born at Concord, Sydney, New South Wales, 29 March 1868, the son of Alexander Ernest Edge, by his wife, Annie Charlotte Sharp. He was brought to England in 1871 and educated at Belvedere House College, Upper Norwood, London. He was intended for the army, but was attracted by bicycling, and after winning, at the age of nineteen, the Westerham Hill climb on a 'safety' bicycle, entered the bicycle business, obtaining employment with the Rudge Company and afterwards with the Dunlop Tyre Company, of which he became manager.

Edge left the Dunlop Company in 1896 and turned to the motor-car, which in that year was emancipated from the red flag. Besides introducing foreign makes, such as the De Dion-Bouton and the Gladiator, to the British market, he took a share in promoting the manufacture of motor-cars in this country, where at that time the industry was non-existent, by inducing Montague Stanley Napier, of D. Napier & Son, makers of mint machinery, to take up motor-car manufacture. Through S. F. Edge, Limited, a company in which he was the principal shareholder, he managed the sales of Napier cars, and by driving them in races and competitions and by vigorous use of other arts of publicity did much to increase their popularity. His wide experience as a driver and his knowledge of the trend of public taste also enabled him to influence the Napier firm both in its general policy and in respect of such mechanical details as the number of cylinders in its engines, the adoption of battery and coil in preference to hot-tube ignition, and the use of the propeller shaft in place of chains for the final drive to the rear wheels.

The first Napier engine to be put on the road, a two-cylinder model of 8 h.p., was fitted in the Panhard and Levassor car No. 8 which had obtained second place in the Paris–Marseilles race of 1896. This car was bought by Edge in 1898 and he drove it, with the new engine, in the trials between Southall and Stokenchurch organized by the Automobile Club in 1899. In the following year he drove the first complete Napier car, also of 8 h.p., in the same club's 1,000 miles trials over roads in Great Britain, and in 1902 he won the Gordon-Bennett cup with a four-cylinder Napier of 50 h.p. in a race from Paris to Innsbrück. His powers of physical endurance were shown by his feat in 1907 of driving a six-cylinder Napier of 60 h.p. round the track at Brooklands continuously for twenty-four hours at an average speed of all but sixty-six miles an hour. In motor-boat racing he had several notable successes, boats fitted with Napier engines winning the British International (Harmsworth) trophy at Queenstown with *Napier I* in 1903 and off Ryde with *Napier Minor* in 1904, the Kaiser's Cup at Kiel in 1904, and the Championship of the Sea at Monaco in 1906.

In 1912 Edge sold his interest in S. F. Edge, Limited, to the Napier Company, one condition of the sale being that he should keep out of the motor-car trade for seven years. He then devoted himself to agricultural pursuits in Sussex, in particular the breeding of pedigree pigs on a large scale. A pioneer in the use of mechanical traction on the farm, he was appointed controller of the agricultural machinery department of the Ministry of Munitions in 1917, but did not hold the position long, work in a government office not being congenial to his energetic and impulsive temperament. In 1921 he returned to the motor-car business with the A. C. (Acedes) car, but the venture did not prove a financial success. In 1934 he published *My Motoring Reminiscences*.

Edge was twice married: first, in 1892 to Eleanor Rose (who predeceased him), daughter of John Sharp, warehouseman; and secondly, in 1917 to Myra Caroline, daughter of John Martin, and had two daughters. He died at Eastbourne 12 February 1940.

[*The Times*, 13 February 1940; *Engineer* and *Engineering*, 16 February 1940; S. F. Edge, *My Motoring Reminiscences*, 1934; Claude Johnson, *The Early History of Motoring* [n.d.]; private information.]

H. M. Ross.

EDWARDS, ALFRED GEORGE (1848–1937), successively bishop of St. Asaph and first archbishop of Wales, was born 2 November 1848 at the Bryn, a small manor house used as the rectory of Llanymawddwy, a remote, wide-spreading, mountain parish in Merionethshire. He was the youngest son of William Edwards, later vicar of Llangollen, by his wife, Sarah, daughter of Thomas Wood, of Painswick. Alfred Edwards's family was typically Welsh in its strongly clerical character. His grandfather was a devout churchman, three of whose four sons became clergymen in Welsh parishes. His home background was austere, but cultivated. His father's income never reached £450 a year. Edwards, after only one year (1860–1861) at Llandovery College, went to Jesus College, Oxford, with an exhibition which brought up his income to £75 for his first year; in his last two years it was £140. After taking his degree in 1874 he became second master at Llandovery and in the following year headmaster, an appointment that he owed to his knowledge of Welsh. The task was formidable; but Edwards was equal to it.

In five years' time the numbers had risen from 27 to 178; a large percentage of the boys were going to Oxford and Cambridge; scholarships were won at both universities. After eleven years of strenuous work Edwards, who had been ordained deacon in 1874 and priest in 1875, was, in 1885, appointed chaplain and secretary to Basil Jones, bishop of St. David's, and also accepted one of the two vicarages of Carmarthen.

In 1889 Edwards was chosen bishop of St. Asaph on the recommendation of Lord Salisbury. It was a critical moment in the history of Wales. Social discontents were becoming clamant. In the mid-nineteenth century the small farmers had had a severe struggle to make ends meet; in the coal-mines great fortunes were made, but the lot of the workers was harsh; education was at a low ebb. The social cleavage was accentuated by the difference of ecclesiastical allegiance. By 1889 things had changed vastly for the better. The work of Bishops Connop Thirlwall, Alfred Ollivant, and T. V. Short [qq.v.] had borne fruit in a widespread system of Church schools, restored churches, and quickened religious life. But the evil memory remained. Political strategy canalized these memories by concentrating discontent upon the Established Church. The year before Edwards became bishop of St. Asaph the destruction of 'the English establishment in Wales' had been declared by Stuart Rendel, the leader of the Welsh party in the House of Commons, to be the first objective of the liberal party. This controversy dominated Edwards's episcopate of forty-five years. Even before he became bishop he had been active (in London no less than in Wales) in defending the Welsh Church. The first stage was completed when the fall of Lord Rosebery's government in 1895 swept away a disestablishment bill of a most drastic character.

Edwards took a leading part in another controversy which then came to the fore. The Education Act of 1902 introduced order into the field of education; but it left unsolved the grievances connected with religious instruction. Edwards, as a former schoolmaster, took an independent line. After consultation with Lloyd George and (Sir) Robert Morant [q.v.], he introduced a series of bills designed both to placate the Welsh county councils, which were penalizing Church schools, and also to establish religious instruction on a wider basis. They provided for religious instruction in all schools, freedom for the teacher, and the transference of all buildings to the State. His efforts failed largely because Church opinion thought more of the preservation of Church schools than of the extension of religious teaching to State schools.

The return of the liberal party to power in 1906 brought the question of the disestablishment of the Welsh Church to the front again. To Edwards and to John Owen, bishop of St. David's [q.v.], fell the leadership in the struggle for the defence of the Church in Wales. Once again the task of negotiation with political leaders was left to Edwards. Despite the outbreak of war, the bill disestablishing the Church in Wales and Monmouthshire passed into law in September 1914, although in the following July disestablishment was postponed by an order in council until the end of the war. From that time onwards Edwards devoted his energies to securing better terms for the Church than those which the bill had originally proposed. He was between two fires. The Welsh members of parliament insisted upon the bill. A group of loyal friends of the Church, headed by Lord Robert Cecil, were demanding repeal. In the last stages Edwards maintained close contact with Lloyd George and Bonar Law, having been given complete power to act by the governing body which had been set up for the Church in Wales in October 1917. The Welsh Church Temporalities Act, passed in August 1919, gave more generous terms. If the Welsh Church emerged from the struggle consolidated by reason of its freedom, and, although poorer, not crippled, much of the credit must go to Edwards's skill as a negotiator.

In April 1920 Edwards was elected the first archbishop of Wales. His remaining years were occupied with the heavy task of reorganization, which included the creation of two new sees, Monmouth, and Swansea and Brecon, and the consolidation of the finances of the Church. He retired in 1934, and died at St. Asaph 22 July 1937. In 1920 he received honorary degrees from the universities of Oxford, Cambridge, and Wales, and was elected an honorary fellow of his college. It was fortunate for the Church in Wales that, at the crisis of its fate, it threw up a leader who combined absolute devotion to his Church and the land of his fathers with a determined will, an alert and supple mind, and a wide outlook on the needs of the hour.

Edwards was married three times; first, in 1875 to Caroline Elizabeth (died 1884), daughter of Edward Edwards, of Llangollen, and had three sons and two daughters; the second son and younger daughter predeceased their father; secondly, in 1886 to Mary Laidley (died 1912), youngest daughter of Watts John Garland, of Lisbon and Worgret, near Wareham, Dorset, and had one son, who was killed in action in 1915, and one daughter; thirdly, in 1917 to Margaret, daughter of John Richard Armitstead, vicar of Sandbach.

There is a portrait of Edwards (*aetat.* 45) by (Sir) W. Q. Orchardson in the possession of Captain Harold Edwards, Bryn Arthur, St. Asaph, and a copy by the artist is at the Palace, St. Asaph. Another portrait (*aetat.* 74), by St. Helier Lander, is in the hall of Howell's School, Denbigh.

[*The Times*, 23 July 1937; A. G. Edwards, *Memories*, 1927; George Lerry, *Alfred George Edwards, Archbishop of Wales*, 1940; personal knowledge.]   A. S. DUNCAN-JONES.

ELGAR, SIR EDWARD WILLIAM, baronet (1857–1934), composer, was born at Broadheath, near Worcester, 2 June 1857, the fifth child and eldest surviving son of William Henry Elgar, by his wife, Ann, daughter of Joseph Greening, of Weston, Herefordshire. The father, who came from Dover, settled in Worcester in 1841, and was for many years organist of St. George's Roman Catholic church there. During that time he established a music shop in the city.

Edward Elgar was brought up in a family where there was much talk of music and in a district where there was regular music-making. He often sat with his father in the organ-loft at St. George's and after a time played the organ there, eventually succeeding his father as organist (1885–1889). He went to a local teacher for violin lessons and realized one of his earliest ambitions when, as a violinist, he joined the orchestra of the Worcester Glee Club, and, like his father, played in the orchestra at the meetings of the Three Choirs. Soon after his coming of age, Elgar was conducting some of the local concerts, with members of his family in the orchestra. Works by Mozart, Rossini, and others were played, but first of all had to be arranged by the young conductor for the slender orchestra of the club. By trial and experience he began to learn how to transfer a part written for one instrument to another, and how to treat the orchestral garment at his disposal so that it did not seem too threadbare.

Elgar's education insisted chiefly upon self-reliance. He had been to a kindergarten and later to a boys' school, Littleton House, near Worcester, where during a scripture lesson he formed the first dim resolve to compose one day a work on the subject of Christ's Apostles. He left school at the age of fifteen and for a short time served as an apprentice in a solicitor's office. Then he had the idea of becoming a solo violinist and began to give lessons with the intention of saving enough money to have violin lessons himself in London from a good teacher. Everything had to be worked out carefully in terms of money, and at length in 1877, 'living on two bags of nuts a day', as he himself used to describe the venture, he embarked on a series of violin lessons from Adolf Pollitzer. As a result he found himself gradually coming to the decision that he would devote his life and thought, not to the mastery of the violin, but to the composition of music.

But the knowledge which Elgar had gained was casual. He began to perceive that, if he would realize his dreams, it was not enough to continue arranging music for the Glee Club and the Worcestershire County Asylum band. He studied Mozart and, by stern application, taught himself the externals of symphonic form. He went to Leipzig for two weeks in 1882 and heard all the music available there. Not long afterwards, in 1883, an orchestral composition of his called 'Intermezzo: Serenade Mauresque' was performed at a Birmingham concert.

A visit by Dvořák to England must be regarded as one of the early influences in Elgar's life, not in the matter of style but as an incident which stirred the young composer's enthusiasm. Another influence can be dated from 1886 when Miss Caroline Alice Roberts came to him as a pupil. She was the only daughter of Sir Henry Gee Roberts [q.v.], and they were married in 1889. The Elgars settled in London, but in 1891 they moved to Malvern and thence (1904) to Hereford, where they remained until 1911. In 1912 they made their headquarters at Severn House, Hampstead, where they remained until Lady Elgar's death eight years later.

It was about the time of his marriage that Elgar, encouraged by his wife, decided to give most of his time to composition. Without a doubt, his wife's belief in his genius was a prime factor in his development at this period. The development was not spectacular but very sure. He began to think in terms of the larger forms of composition. For the Worcester festival of 1890 he was ready with the 'Froissart' overture. Three years later (1893) he had finished a work which he described as 'a symphony for chorus and orchestra' called 'The Black Knight', and in another three years (1896) he had completed his first oratorio, 'The Light of Life', and his choral work, 'Scenes from the Saga of King Olaf'. It was in this last work that Elgar became fully confident of his powers, and in 1899 he produced a work, 'Variations on an original theme for orchestra', generally known by the title 'Enigma variations', which left no more doubt in the public estimation of his genius. This fine work, which has become one of the best known of all Elgar's orchestral compositions, was first played under Hans Richter in 1899. When Sir Arthur Sullivan died in 1900 it became apparent to many that Elgar, although a composer of another build, was his true successor as first musician of the land. It was in that year that his masterpiece appeared, the oratorio 'The Dream of Gerontius', a setting of part of Newman's poem. This was first performed on 3 October at the Birmingham festival under Richter. The performance itself was disappointingly below standard, but after the work had been given in Germany with a German translation of the text (at Düsseldorf in 1901 and again in 1902) with Julius Büths as conductor, it was accepted at its proper worth in the composer's own country. It was 'Gerontius' which moved Richard Strauss to drink to the success of 'the first English progressive musician, Meister Elgar'. Meanwhile the university of Cambridge had anticipated this toast by conferring upon Elgar in 1900 the honorary degree of doctor of music.

This was the beginning of Elgar's most sustained period of creative energy and it lasted until 1920, which was the year of his wife's death. From time to time he turned aside to the smaller forms and produced songs, incidental music for plays, and music for occasions (the 'Coronation Ode', 1902, and the 'Coronation March', 1911), but for the most part during these years he was at work upon some full scale orchestral or choral work. The unfolding of his genius showed him to be essentially a symphonic writer. This was already to be discerned in the oratorios 'The Apostles' (1903) and 'The Kingdom' (1906), which

were the first two works of an uncompleted trilogy, and again in a number of orchestral works such as the first four 'Pomp and Circumstance' marches (1901–1907, the first of which contains the popular tune later known as 'Land of Hope and Glory'), the overtures 'Cockaigne' (1901) and 'In the South (Alassio)' (1904), and the superb 'Introduction and Allegro' for strings (1905). But the full flower of his imagination was not shown until the two symphonies and the violin concerto were completed and performed. These achievements, together with the symphonic study 'Falstaff' (1913), with their richness, expansiveness, and majesty, can be truly appraised only against the background of the Edwardian age, although the violin concerto is more contemplative than the others. This concerto was dedicated to Fritz Kreisler who was soloist in the first performance in 1910. The first symphony (Symphony in A flat, 1908) may be thought of as a noble pæan in praise of the Edwardian era, the second symphony (Symphony in E flat, 1911) as an epic, and the violoncello concerto (1919) as an elegy on the same theme. This last-named work and three examples of chamber music plainly reveal the disillusioning influence of the war years of 1914 to 1918, especially the concerto, with its spare orchestration and plangent cadences.

When in 1924 Elgar was made master of the king's musick, it was evident that there were some in authority who heard in his music a voice of exceptional eloquence. But there were others, steadily increasing in numbers, who knew that Elgar was far greater than a mere laureate, and that, like Sibelius, he was a composer whose music, although imbued with national feeling, spoke with universal appeal. English people had been slow to appreciate his work until the 'Enigma variations' was heard, but thereafter approval and understanding increased with almost every composition. He received numerous honours: he was appointed a member of the Order of Merit in 1911 (being the first musician to receive the order), was knighted in 1904, created a baronet in 1931, and appointed K.C.V.O. in 1928 and G.C.V.O. in 1933. Besides his Cambridge doctorate already mentioned, he received honorary doctorates of music from the universities of Durham, Oxford, Yale, and London, and honorary degrees from several others, and among foreign honours are to be reckoned those of corresponding member of the Institut de

France and honorary member of the Regia Accademia di Santa Cecilia.

After Lady Elgar's death, Elgar produced no major work. Some very personal orchestrations of Bach and Handel, some music for the Wembley British Empire Exhibition (1924), some incidental music for a play, No. 5 of the 'Pomp and Circumstance' marches, planned as a set of six (1930), and the 'Nursery Suite' (1931, dedicated to the Duchess of York and the Princesses Elizabeth and Margaret) were almost the only evidence which the public had to indicate that the composer had not completely given up writing music. A few friends knew that he had sketched some music for an opera which was to be based on Ben Jonson's play *The Devil is an Ass*, and on the occasion of his seventy-fifth birthday (1932) it was announced that the British Broadcasting Corporation had commissioned him to write his third symphony. Elgar made some sketches for this work, but before he could come to grips with the great undertaking, a fatal illness overtook him, and he died at Worcester 23 February 1934. He was buried in his wife's grave in the churchyard of St. Wulstan, Little Malvern. He was survived by his only child, a daughter.

Among symphonic composers of all nations, Elgar's name shines because of his orchestral writing, and in this respect he did much to raise the standard of orchestral playing in England. By the members of English orchestras he was greatly beloved, and in turn memories of early days, when he was a humble bandsman, made him deeply appreciative of their work, and led him to take great pains in helping them to understand the intricacies of his scores. His reward has been that the best of the English orchestras have the secret of bowing his melody and of breathing his rich harmony, and have mastered the idiom of his phrase and the curve of his eloquence.

In the history of music Elgar will be remembered as the man who so far lifted the status of English music that the once fashionable description of England as 'the land without music' became an absurdity. 'Falstaff', one of the finest of all works written for a modern orchestra, is called a symphonic study and the symphonic aspect cannot be too much emphasized. The music's behaviour, that is, is guided by an inner logic of its own rather than by a series of scenes and events, although it is still true that the agreement between that inner logic and the 'programme' is a remarkable feature of the music. When Elgar's finely imaginative achievement in 'Falstaff' is contemplated and some of the excellent music which he wrote in an earlier work, the cantata 'Caractacus' (1898), is then recalled, it is impossible not to be set wondering what heights the composer would have reached in the Ben Jonson opera which he was sketching. But, although destiny's plan included no opera by Elgar, the splendid attainments of succeeding English composers, especially in symphonic writing, have been so much the more notably excellent for the vantage-ground gained by Elgar in his oratorios, symphonies, concertos, the 'Enigma variations', the 'Introduction and Allegro' and in 'Falstaff'.

A portrait of Elgar by Talbot Hughes no longer exists, but a drawing by (Sir) William Rothenstein (1910) in the Royal Library at Windsor Castle is reproduced in *Music and Letters*, January 1920. A bronze cast of a bust by Percival Hedley (1927), is in the National Portrait Gallery.

[Basil Maine, *Elgar. His Life and Work*, 2 vols., 1933; R. J. Buckley, *Sir Edward Elgar*, 1904; Ernest Newman, *Elgar*, 1906; W. H. Reed, *Elgar*, 1939; *Grove's Dictionary of Music and Musicians*, 4th ed., vol. ii, edited by H. C. Colles; Louise B. M. Dyer, *Music by British Composers. A Series of Complete Catalogues, No. 2. Sir Edward Elgar*, 1931; personal knowledge.]   BASIL MAINE.

ELIOT, SIR CHARLES NORTON EDGECUMBE (1862–1931), diplomat and orientalist, was born at Sibford Gower, Oxfordshire, 8 January 1862, the eldest son of Edward Eliot, perpetual curate of Sibford Gower, who in 1863 became vicar of Norton Bavant, Wiltshire, by his wife, Elizabeth Harriet Wyatt, younger daughter of Charles Henry Watling, rector of Tredington, Warwickshire (then Worcestershire). He was educated at Cheltenham College and at Oxford, where his career, first as a scholar of Balliol College and later (1884) as a fellow of Trinity College, was a succession of triumphs which almost bears comparison with that of D. S. Margoliouth [q.v.]. He obtained a first class in classical moderations (1881) and *literae humaniores* (1884), and won the Hertford (1881), Boden Sanskrit and Ireland (1883), Craven (1884), and Derby (1886) scholarships, as well as the Houghton Syriac prize (1884). His chief interest at this period, and indeed throughout his life, was the study of languages both ancient and modern. In addition to a great store of classical learning and a familiar knowledge of several modern European languages, he was conversant with Finnish (of which he published the first grammar in English in 1890), Sanskrit, Pali, Hebrew, Syriac, Arabic, Turkish, Persian, Hindustani, and Chinese, besides having acquaintance with many other languages and dialects.

Eliot entered the diplomatic service in 1887 and served as third secretary at St. Petersburg and in several posts in the Near East, where he gained the knowledge which enabled him to write the authoritative *Turkey in Europe* (1900). In 1898 he was appointed C.B. and nominated first secretary at Washington, and the following year was sent to Samoa as British representative on a three-Power commission to consider the future government of the islands. For this work he was appointed K.C.M.G. in 1900. His next post was as consul-general at Zanzibar and commissioner for the British East African Protectorate. He found the work of colonial administration much to his taste, and travelled widely in the regions under his control on tours of observation which enabled him to produce his book, *The East African Protectorate*, in 1905. His service in Africa came to an unhappy end in 1904, through a dispute with the Foreign Office over a question of policy upon which he felt that he must resign.

Eliot now turned to academic life, becoming vice-chancellor (1905–1911) of the newly founded Sheffield University. He spent several long vacations in journeys to India, China, and Japan, which he described in a lively book entitled *Letters from the Far East* (1907). In 1908–1909 he served on the royal commission on electoral systems. He left Sheffield in 1912 in order to become vice-chancellor of the new university of Hong-Kong. In 1918 he accepted the post of British high commissioner in Siberia, but the provisional government supported by the Allies collapsed within a year of his arrival. The Foreign Office having now forgotten or forgiven the East African dispute of 1904, he was offered in 1919 (the year in which he was sworn of the Privy Council) the post of ambassador to Japan, and took up this appointment in the spring of 1920. After the Anglo-Japanese alliance had been allowed to lapse in 1921, Eliot's main task as ambassador was to ensure that Anglo-Japanese relations should be adjusted to the new circumstances without friction. This he carried out with success, thanks to his sympathetic understanding of oriental peoples. He was appointed G.C.M.G. in 1923. It happened that during his term in Japan no acute political issues arose to occupy his attention. He was therefore able to maintain his long-standing interest in marine biology (on which he had written many valuable papers); to complete his greatest work, the profound, erudite, and lucid three-volume *Hinduism and Buddhism* (1921); and to collect further materials for a study of Buddhism in Japan.

Eliot's term of service as ambassador came to an end in 1926. He continued to reside in Japan, but failing health slowed down progress on his last book and it was not quite complete when he died at sea 16 March 1931. It appeared posthumously in 1935, with some minor additions by other hands, under the title of *Japanese Buddhism*. Although not the book that it would have been had he given it the finishing touch, it is nevertheless a worthy ornament to the noble edifice of oriental scholarship which he erected during his life.

Eliot received honorary degrees from the universities of Edinburgh (1905), Durham (1908), Oxford (1923), Hong-Kong (1924), and Sheffield (1926). He was elected an honorary fellow of Trinity College, Oxford, in 1924. He was unmarried.

[Sir Harold Parlett, *In Piam Memoriam* prefixed to C. N. E. Eliot, *Japanese Buddhism*, 1935; personal knowledge.] G. B. SANSOM.

ELLERMAN, SIR JOHN REEVES, first baronet (1862–1933), financier and shipowner, reputed at his death to be possibly the richest man and certainly one of the greatest forces behind shipping that Britain had ever known, was born at Kingston-upon-Hull 15 May 1862, the only son of Johannes Hermann Ellermann, a Hamburg corn-merchant who was naturalized in 1854 and settled in Hull, by his wife, Ann Elizabeth, daughter of Timothy Reeves, of Kingston-upon-Hull. He was left fatherless before he reached his 'teens, but his mother, a gifted woman, encouraged him to follow his bent and train as an accountant, at the same time fostering in him a love of beauty and the arts, a whole-hearted loyalty to family, friends, and country, and a quick response to human need. She lived to see him established in the great Victorian mansion at 1 South Audley Street, Mayfair, and created a baronet in 1905. But she died twelve years before he was appointed C.H. in 1921, a tribute to his work which he dearly prized and the satisfaction in which he would have delighted to share with her.

It was a great moment for Ellerman when he joined the board of the Leyland line in 1892. He had been dealing in shipping in a quiet way, and was to give substantial help to the government in the transport of troops during the South African war. Indeed ships meant romance as well as business to him. His idea of a holiday, and very sensibly he took many, was to cast off from a British port for Egypt, Italy, or the south of France, and the more picturesque the port of entry the better. His house overflowed with mosaics, tapestries, carvings, furniture, and a medley of objects, some of them works of art and others without value, which had caught his fancy in the markets and bazaars of Europe and Africa. He loved showing these to his friends and telling the tale of how he bargained for them. So romance and commerce fused in the board room of Leyland's. It was not long before he became chairman; now he could enter boldly the immense and stimulating field of operations that shipping proved to be for his genius. It might be said here that Ellerman exercised his talent for making money largely for the pure joy of self-expression, and only incidentally for financial advantage. He was at heart an artist, but the financial wizard in him overwhelmed in the end every other creative impulse. Within the decade he had acquired for himself the Mediterranean services of Leyland's after bringing off a complicated deal with John Pierpont Morgan, and founded the Ellerman line (1901). One after the other in order of mention he drew into his orbit that same year, Westcott and Lawrence, which had been founded in 1857, The Papayanni group (1854), the City line (1839), and the Hall line (c. 1863). Later he acquired Bucknalls Steamship Company, the Shaw, Savill, and Albion, and other concerns. In 1916 he created a sensation by absorbing the great Wilson's of Hull, which became known as Ellerman's Wilson line. During the war of 1914–1918 his ships were of immense value to the country because of their numbers and efficient management. At his death the fleets under his control represented about 1,500,000 tons gross.

Newspapers were Ellerman's second favourite investment. At one time he joined Lord Northcliffe as shareholder in *The Times* and in Associated Newspapers,

Limited, and later he took over the bulk of the shares of the 'Big Six', which comprised the *Illustrated London News*, the *Sphere*, the *Tatler*, the *Sketch*, *Eve*, and the *Illustrated Sporting and Dramatic News*. With his immense curiosity and endless appetite for detail, he thoroughly sampled each new field that he entered until he got the 'feel' of it. For example, he surprised editors in the late 'twenties when he began suggesting books for review, drafting out new features, and even interviewing an individual contributor who had attracted his attention. At about the same time he conducted a series of London property deals. Some hundred or more acres changed hands in South Kensington and Chelsea, together with a considerable acreage in the Oxford Circus district. Many guesses have been made, and will still be made, at the total amount of his fortune. He left estate which in September 1936 was resworn at £36,684,994, indicating death duties of about £18,000,000.

Apart from his acknowledged genius for finance, Ellerman's dominant characteristic was his unmitigated determination to keep his private life and that of his family from public knowledge. The more astonishing his financial achievements became, the deeper he burrowed into anonymity. Very few besides relatives and business associates entered the blind-looking door in the heavily curtained frontage of 1 South Audley Street. As a result of this almost morbid passion for secrecy, much material about his business career will never be known, because he obscured his vast transactions in shipping, newspapers, and periodicals, London real estate, breweries, and other interests under the guise of trust companies, the shares of which he held. Only his confidential deputies and managers, who were exceptionally loyal to him, knew the extent of his investments and the number of millions involved. This intimate, tightly knit business concern, its numberless branches fitting with engineering precision into an organic whole, had an advantage not unforeseen by its brilliant founder. His death created scarcely a ripple of disturbance on the surface of London finance, and his organization continues to function almost automatically to-day from the same headquarters at 21 Moorgate, with unimpaired efficiency and steadily rising increment.

Ellerman was not a public benefactor, but encouraged by his wife he poured out money anonymously on causes and individuals known to him. A number of struggling artists were maintained by him, one or two for life. The things he shrank from doing are illuminating: rarely if ever did he dine at a restaurant, or have his photograph taken, or go to a race-meeting or public banquet, make a speech, or accept invitations from any but his few intimate friends, attend a club, public conference, concert, or even a church. His great delight was to bring business friends home to a lunch which he had planned down to the minutest detail in conference with his chef. It remained for his wife only to preside at the table and arrange the flowers. Afterwards he would show his guests his fine library and large collection of paintings of the conventional Royal Academy type. He was jealous as well as proud of his wife's vitality and attractiveness, and to please him she gave up having friends of her own. 'He keeps me in a glass case, but I keep him human', she would say. Ellerman had no lasting interests outside his work and family, and he moved in a routine so rigid as to approach the ritualistic. His weakness was that he made no attempt to understand the new forces working beneath the surface of his time. Generous and sympathetic in his own small circle, he was lacking in a broad humanitarian outlook and had little social imagination.

Ellerman married in 1908 Hannah (Annie), daughter of George Glover; she survived him until 1939. She was, after his mother, the most powerful influence in his life. They had one son and one daughter (a writer of distinction under the name of Bryher). He died suddenly of a stroke at Dieppe 16 July 1933 while on holiday. He was succeeded as second baronet by his son, John Reeves (born 1909).

[*The Times*, 18 July 1933; Robert McAlmon, *Being Geniuses Together*, 1938; private information; personal knowledge.]

LOUISE MORGAN.

ELLIOTT, EDWIN BAILEY (1851–1937), mathematician, was born at Oxford 1 June 1851, the eldest son of Edwin Litchfield Elliott, an Oxford business man, by his wife, Matilda Bailey. He was educated at Magdalen School, Oxford, and in 1869 went up to Magdalen College with a demyship. His mathematical ability was soon recognized and, after having been awarded a first class in moderations (1872) and in the final school (1873), he was in 1874 elected fellow and mathematical

tutor of Queen's College. This post he held for eighteen years; for nine years (1884–1893) he was lecturer in mathematics at Corpus Christi College. In 1892 he was appointed the first Waynflete professor of pure mathematics, a chair carrying with it a fellowship at Magdalen College. After twenty-nine years' tenure of this chair he retired in 1921: he was elected an honorary fellow of Queen's College in 1916. He was an active member of the London Mathematical Society, serving on the council for many years and holding the two-year presidency in 1896–1898. He was elected F.R.S. in 1891.

Elliott served the university as a member of the Hebdomadal Council, a visitor of the Observatory, a delegate of the Common University Fund, and a curator of the University Chest. His opinion was often sought in financial matters, where his strength lay in exactness of detail rather than in boldness of conception. He was a trustee of the Oxford City Charities and a treasurer of the Oxford Eye Hospital. His whole life was spent in Oxford, where he died 21 July 1937. He married in 1893 Charlotte Amelia (died May 1937), daughter of John William Mawer, an Oxford business man; there were no children of the marriage.

Elliott's mathematical life circulated round the twin foci of Oxford and London. Besides his work in formal teaching and lecturing at Oxford he was one of the founders (1888) of the Oxford Mathematical Society, its first secretary, and later its president.

Elliott wrote much for English mathematical periodicals: the *Proceedings* and *Journal* of the London Mathematical Society, the *Quarterly Journal of Mathematics*, and the *Messenger of Mathematics*. To the Royal Society he communicated in 1889 a lengthy memoir on reciprocants (*Philosophical Transactions*, vol. clxxxi, 1890). His most important published work, *An Introduction to the Algebra of Quantics*, appeared in 1895 with a second edition in 1913, and it is by this book that he is most generally known to mathematicians. Arthur Cayley [q.v.], J. J. Sylvester [q.v.], and others, both in England and on the continent, had developed the theory of the invariants under linear substitutions, of homogeneous algebraic expressions (quantics). Elliott's contributions to the theory were important: he gave a fluent and characteristic account of it in his book, which was for long the recognized text-book on the subject. Much work in this field, especially abroad, had been developed by purely symbolic methods; these Elliott eschewed, preferring always to rely on direct and, so to speak, more tangible processes, and his presentation is, in this respect, characteristically English. His work, like all good mathematics, was distinguished by simplicity and naturalness, surprising results being often achieved by the exploitation, with real insight, of ideas in themselves elementary. His earlier study of reciprocants had been in a more limited field concerned with the invariance of differential expressions under a restricted linear substitution. This lacked the completeness of his subsequent algebraic work but doubtless helped to direct his mind to invariant principles and problems.

Elliott's last important contribution to mathematics was made in his seventy-seventh year, a striking challenge to the doctrine, sometimes accepted, that mathematicians do all their best work in their thirties. It concerned an inequality of considerable consequence in the theory of integral equations. Elliott's proof was short and it was decisive: it was obviously the right proof, although it had escaped the notice of contemporary mathematicians of distinction.

Elliott's lesser writings are concerned mainly with algebra, algebraic or pure geometry, and with closely linked regions of analysis such as elliptic functions and the theory of convergence. Here too are to be found the simple unexpectedness and beauty of form of his more important work.

Elliott's other interests lay in music, in natural history, and in literature: he was one of the founders of the Addison Society, the oldest literary society at Queen's College.

In demeanour Elliott was modest and retiring, hesitant in speech, unfailing in his helpfulness to others, a much-loved man. He held by the ancient virtues, deploring many of the changes that he had seen both in the city and in the university. He cared deeply for the integrity of mathematics and had little patience with specious half-proofs or unsupported speculation. For these reasons he did not readily encourage research by the young mathematicians unless, at least, he was certain that they had something of substance to consider. His convictions made him a severe critic of mathematical writing, whether his own or others, and sharpened his style to a certain

austere lucidity. His work looked back to a closing epoch. It was typically English, it could be called Victorian; it lacked sympathy with more recent developments, but it had honesty and dignity and set a fair example to those that follow.

[*The Times*, 23 July 1937; *Obituary Notices of Fellows of the Royal Society*, No. 5, January 1938 (portrait); *St. Edmund Hall Magazine*, 1937; private information; personal knowledge.]   T. CHAUNDY.

ELLIS, HENRY HAVELOCK (1859–1939), pioneer in the scientific study of sex, thinker, critic, essayist, and editor, was born at Croydon 2 February 1859, the only son of Edward Peppen Ellis, by his wife, Susannah Mary, daughter of John Wheatley. His father and his maternal grandfather were both sea-captains, and all his near male relatives lived on or by the sea. He was called after Sir Henry Havelock, the general of the Indian Mutiny [q.v.], who was his maternal grandfather's first cousin. Those were the days of sailing ships, and the father voyaged annually round the world via Australia, taking nine months. When the boy was seven he made the voyage with him; but for the rest he was brought up in the Surrey suburbs of London and educated at private schools at Merton and Mitcham. There he had no chance to become a trained scholar; but the account of his personal reading given in his autobiography shows precocity and a strong literary bent. The first writer to make him conscious of the latter was Scott.

When Ellis was sixteen, alarm was felt about his health, and it was decided that he should make a year's sea-voyage in the ship which his father commanded. But after they reached Australia he settled there as a school-teacher, and eventually stayed four years. A part of this time, which he spent teaching at a lonely school at Sparkes Creek in the New South Wales bush, proved the turning-point in his career. There came to him then what he never afterwards lost, a belief in the unity of scientific and artistic attainment; based doubtless in part on an exceptional dualism in his own nature, equally preoccupied with factual and with aesthetic values. The Sparkes Creek period was one of stormy solitude and bitter self-questioning. He lost his childhood's moorings of evangelical piety, and passed through a tangle of perplexities to attain a kind of peace: not in faith, but in search—the search for scientific truth, which was seen also as the source of artistic satisfaction. In all this he was much helped by the writings of James Hinton [q.v.], whose blending of medical with philosophical studies he resolved to emulate. He first planned to write a book on religion, but then chose as his life's main task the study of sex.

With these ideas Ellis returned in 1879 to England, and eventually became a medical student at St. Thomas's Hospital. A friend of the Hintons lent him £200, and his mother added £100 from a legacy; and thus furnished he embarked upon the seven-year course. But it took him over eight years (1881–1889); for although he worked hard, he had a natural inaptitude for examinations; and in the end, after passing some and missing others and failing to secure the joint qualifications of the Colleges of Physicians and Surgeons, he became a doctor with the licence of the Society of Apothecaries. Afterwards he scarcely practised at all. His sole gain was a scientific grounding, which might, he came to think, have been had otherwise at less cost.

The eight years, however, were not spent on medicine alone. Ellis began writing for the monthly reviews, and found his way into the clubs and haunts where young people with new ideas forgathered. In this way he early became familiar with many English socialists of the 'eighties—John Burns, Henry Hyde Champion, R. B. P. Frost, H. M. Hyndman [q.v.], Ernest Belfort Bax, Mr. Bernard Shaw, and the two Davidsons, Thomas and John Morrison. But he was not carried in their currents; his preoccupations remained literary and scientific. In each of these fields he soon made a name as the editor of a well-known series. On the literary side was the 'Mermaid' series of dramatists—reprints, scholarly and unexpurgated, of all the best plays by Shakespeare's contemporaries, made accessible for the first time to the reading public in octavo volumes at popular prices. The idea was Ellis's own; he showed great skill in selecting his sponsors for the different dramatists; and although after a year, in 1888, the series passed out of his hands, he had made in it a real contribution to English literary culture. His similar success on the scientific side was the 'Contemporary Science' series. Begun when the toil of his examinations neared its climax, this was a surprising venture for a medical student. But again he succeeded in getting the best people to

work for him; many volumes in the series became famous text-books; and the effect of the whole in popularizing scientific progress was outstanding. He continued to be editor until 1915. These two editorial enterprises brought him the friendship of many distinguished men, with at least one of whom, Arthur Symons, he formed a close lifelong connexion.

Meanwhile Ellis developed relations of passionate attachment to two remarkable women, each an authoress. The first was Olive Schreiner [q.v.], famous for *The Story of an African Farm*; the second was Edith Mary Oldham Lees (only daughter of Samuel Oldham Lees, a landed proprietor of Ashton-under-Lyne), who became his wife. Not the least singular feature of these attachments (which are described and documented in his autobiography) was their co-existence. He met Olive Schreiner early in 1884, through the intermediary of Karl Marx's daughter Eleanor, and between then and Miss Schreiner's leaving England in 1889 some thousands of letters passed between them. They were love-letters, and the relation was passionate and exclusive, although the lady decided eventually against marriage. After her return to Cape Colony the letters went on, unabated save by the delays of distance; first he and then she found marriage elsewhere, but neither spouse objected to the relationship continuing; and it did so until Olive Schreiner's death in 1920. Ellis's attachment to Edith Lees did not begin until a year after Miss Schreiner left England, but it led to marriage in 1891. Thomas Davidson, the well-known Scottish-American 'wandering scholar', had in 1883 collected not a few talented people into a 'Fellowship of the New Life', from which the Fabian Society originated in 1884 as an offshoot. Weakened by this hiving-off, the fellowship lasted fourteen years longer; and in its final phases Edith Lees, a young woman of dynamic personality with a bachelor income and pronounced gifts for lecturing and writing, became its chief organizer. On marrying Ellis she let it drop, but in other respects was sedulous to preserve despite wedlock her separate activity. Her literary output includes sketches, short stories, novels, a successful short play, and a good many essays; perhaps she would have chosen to be judged by the volume *Three Modern Seers* (1910), studies of James Hinton, Nietzsche, and Edward Carpenter [q.v.]. Her sincerity and eagerness gave her best work some abiding value, although it was always more vivid than matured.

The common bond which first brought Ellis and his wife together was the influence of Hinton's teaching on sex, for which both were enthusiasts. Their marriage relations were on an unusual footing, which is fully described in Ellis's autobiography, and corresponded to the desire of both parties for freedom and experiment in life. Theirs was a turbulent love, but on its peculiar terms it endured until Edith Ellis's final illness; and although it robbed the husband of peace, it must have stimulated his thinking. They lived together at various places, but for the longest time at Carbis Bay in Cornwall. As he then earned little, while she was an impulsive spender, they were normally short of money; and she died in 1916, leaving him much encumbered. Olive Schreiner attended her funeral.

Meantime Ellis had gone ahead with his chosen life work. It took shape in a series of six volumes, *Studies in the Psychology of Sex*, of which the first appeared in 1897 and the last in 1910. On completing the sixth, he felt, he tells us, like Gibbon finishing his *History*, and wrote in his diary: 'The work that I was born to do is done.' In 1928 he added a seventh; and in 1936 rearranged the whole in four volumes. The earliest in the original series (it was entitled *Sexual Inversion*) was the occasion in 1898 of a notable prosecution, *Reg. v. Bedborough*. Bedborough was not the publisher, but an anarchist bookseller who had stocked the book. A committee was formed, including most of the leading radicals and socialists of the day, and they raised a substantial defence fund; but their guns were spiked by Bedborough himself, who pleaded guilty and was bound over. Ellis remained in a precarious position—not prosecuted but liable to prosecution; and for a short while he left the country. The problem of continuing the *Studies* was solved by publishing them in the United States of America. Although essentially addressed to doctors and psychologists, and not to the public at large, they have since been translated into many languages.

At the same time Ellis poured out a stream of books meant for the general reader. Some of them were by-products of his studies in sex; the best of these, *Man and Woman*, appeared as early as 1894, but was repeatedly revised and enlarged in later editions (the eighth in 1934); others are *The Erotic Rights of Women* (1918), *The Play-Function of Sex* (1921), and notably *Little Essays of Love and Virtue* (1922). Others are on special subjects, such as criminology; and others deal directly with the problem of life and the universe: the best of these, *The Dance of Life*, appeared in 1923. Lastly, he wrote much about literature and the arts, and here his best work is in the three series of *Impressions and Comments* (1914, 1921, and 1924). His appreciation of art was genuine and many sided, but not original; he followed closely, if unconsciously, the art fashions (usually Parisian); and apart from the charm of the style these books are chiefly interesting as reflecting their changes. His posthumously published autobiography, *My Life* (1940), contains much that is of minor concern, but the long account of his marriage is a human document of extraordinary interest. Expansive in youth, he became later in life more of a hermit, seeing few but intimates. His last home was at Hintlesham in Suffolk, the county of his ancestors; and there he died, without issue, 8 July 1939.

A drawing of Ellis by W. Rothenstein (1931) is in the National Portrait Gallery. Busts by J. Davidson (1916) and A. Ströbl (1936) are privately owned, as is a painting by Henry Bishop, of which a replica is at the College of Physicians. A bronze bust by A. G. Walker is in the Ipswich Museum.

[*The Times*, 11 July 1939; H. Havelock Ellis, *My Life*, 1940; Houston Peterson, *Havelock Ellis, Philosopher of Love* (containing a complete bibliography of his writings down to 1928), 1928.]   R. C. K. ENSOR.

ERNLE, BARON (1851–1937), administrator, author, and minister of agriculture. [See PROTHERO, ROWLAND EDMUND.]

EUMORFOPOULOS, GEORGE (1863–1939), collector of Chinese and other works of art, was born at Liverpool 18 April 1863, the eldest son of Aristides George Eumorfopoulos, by his wife, Mariora Scaramanga. His father was a Greek merchant whose family originally came from the island of Chios. George entered the firm of Ralli Brothers, merchants, of London, of which for a time in early life he was representative in south Russia: he rose eventually to be vice-president and retired in 1934. In 1890 he married Julia (died 1943), daughter of George Emanuel Scaramanga, merchant, of Tiltwood, Crawley Down, Sussex. Soon afterwards Eumorfopoulos started collecting: beginning with European porcelain, he was soon led on to Chinese. It was a time when the frontiers of knowledge of Chinese art in the West were about to expand rapidly: railway construction in north China cut into tombs richly furnished with pottery figures and vessels of the first to the tenth century A.D. In his preface to the first of the six volumes of R. L. Hobson's monumental catalogue of his Chinese and other Eastern ceramics (1925–1928) Eumorfopoulos records that it was in 1906 that he saw the first specimens of tomb wares: 'First came the Han, then the T'ang (figures of horses and camels first in 1910), and lastly the Wei.' The collection grew rapidly until it became remarkably representative of the ceramics of the Sung and earlier periods. Not content with this, he launched out into the field of Chinese archaic bronzes and jades, and eventually of sculpture and paintings as well, until it became the greatest of his time. He lived first at Clandon in Surrey and afterwards in London, where he added a two-story museum at the back of 7 Chelsea Embankment. There he and his wife were always ready to show the collection, and their Sunday afternoon receptions became a feature of London life for all those interested in the arts.

Eumorfopoulos had intended to bequeath his collection to the nation, but in 1934 he found it necessary to realize a part; and he offered the national museums all that they required of the Chinese portion for £100,000, a sum which was estimated at the time to be well under half the market value. The money was found, and the division between the British and Victoria and Albert museums made on a basis of three to two. His small frame and stooping shoulders concealed resources of energy, fed by the enjoyment that he received from the 'delighted surprise' with which he saw new works of art. He was indeed an inveterate collector, and continued to buy Chinese antiquities until his death. But his taste was wide, ranging from Islamic and medieval art to modern European painting and sculpture. Archaeological appeal alone, he has recorded, never induced him to acquire an object; while the vitality of his judgement is shown in the remarkable examples of modern work which he acquired, largely through patronage of young painters and sculptors. He also supported archaeological studies and was one of the founders of the Oriental Ceramic Society and the first

president from 1921 until his death in London 19 December 1939. The collections remaining in his hands were sold by auction in Messrs. Sotheby's rooms from 28 to 31 May and on 5 and 6 June 1940 and, after his widow's death, in 1944. He had no children.

A bust of Eumorfopoulos by Ivan Mestrović is in the British Museum, and another, by Dora Gordine, is in the Victoria and Albert Museum.

[*The Times*, 20 December 1939; *Transactions* of the Oriental Ceramic Society, vol. xvii, 1940 (portrait); private information.]

BASIL GRAY.

EVANS, SIR (EVAN) VINCENT (1851–1934), journalist, is reputed to have been born in the parish of Llangelynin, Merioneth, 18 November 1851, the elder son of Lewis Evans, farmer, who removed in 1856 to Tynllyn, Trawsfynydd, in the same county, by his first wife. The registration of the birth cannot be traced. He was for some years a pupil teacher in the national school at Trawsfynydd and later an assistant in the village store. In 1872 he removed to London, where he remained until his death. Some clerical employment brought him into touch with the Chancery Lane Safe Deposit and Offices Company, Limited, the service of which he entered, becoming first secretary and then managing director. He was attracted to journalism, becoming a member of the parliamentary press gallery, and he continued throughout his life his connexion with the press and particularly with the *South Wales Daily News*, for the London letter of which he was for many years largely responsible. He was intimate with the younger members of parliament from Wales and welcomed the advent of his neighbour David Lloyd George to London on his election as member for Carnarvon Boroughs in 1890.

In 1881 Evans became secretary and editor of the publications of the National Eisteddfod Association and in 1884 a member of the Honourable Society of Cymmrodorion, the council of which he joined in 1886. He became secretary in 1887, and later undertook the editorship of the society's publications and may be said to have re-established the society. He retained his offices in both these institutions until his death.

The strong national feeling which manifested itself in Wales during the last two decades of the nineteenth century looked to the 'London Welsh' for guidance, and

Evans's interests and associations connected him with many bodies, and in particular with the university colleges at Aberystwyth and Bangor of the university of Wales, of which he was a governor, and which in 1922 conferred upon him the honorary degree of LL.D. Among other offices he was a governor of the Welsh National Museum and the National Library of Wales; president in 1918 of the Cambrian Archaeological Society; chairman of the executive committee of the Welsh Bibliographical Society; treasurer of the Welsh Folk-Song Society; and he took a large part in organizing and recruiting the London Welsh battalions during the war of 1914-1918. Although he made no claim to scholarship, many articles of useful comment and careful compilation were published by him in the *Cymmrodor* and the *Transactions* of the Cymmrodorion Society.

Evans, who was knighted in 1909 for his services to Wales, and appointed C.H. in 1922, was of sturdy build, somewhat above the middle height, with a large and striking head, typical of the people of the uplands of Merioneth. He married in 1881 Annie Elizabeth (died 1898), daughter of Thomas Beale, of Oxford, and had a son, Mr. Lewis Noel Vincent Evans, C.B., deputy director of public prosecutions, and a daughter. Evans died in London 13 November 1934.

There is a portrait of Evans by William Oliver in the National Museum of Wales at Cardiff. A bust by Sir W. Goscombe John is at the National Library of Wales, at Aberystwyth.

[*The Times*, 15 November 1934; *Transactions* of the Honourable Society of Cymmrodorion, 1933-1935; private information.]

HOWELL E. JAMES.

EVANS, SIR (WORTHINGTON) LAMING WORTHINGTON-, first baronet (1868-1931), politician, was born at Broadstairs 23 August 1868, the elder son of Worthington Evans, of Isleworth, a solicitor in the City of London, by his second wife, Susanna Jane, daughter of James Laming, of Birchington Hall, Kent. He was educated at Eastbourne College, and was articled to his father at the age of seventeen, being admitted a solicitor in 1890 and eventually becoming head of the firm of Worthington Evans, Dauney, & company. He retired from practice in 1910. In 1905 he was appointed a member of the Board of Trade committee for the reform of company law and in 1906 he

unsuccessfully contested the borough of Colchester as a conservative, but at the general election of January 1910 Evans gained the seat (which in 1918 became the Colchester division), and he held it until in 1929 he was returned for St. George's, Hanover Square, by a very large majority.

On the outbreak of war in 1914 Evans served first at York as inspector of administrative services, with the temporary rank of major. In the following year he was appointed parliamentary private secretary to the financial secretary to the War Office, and from January to December 1916 was controller of the foreign trade department of the Foreign Office. He filled offices for short periods from 1918 to 1921; and from February 1921 to October 1922, and again from 1924 to 1929, he was secretary of state for war. He was postmaster-general from 1923 to 1924. In 1929 he accompanied Lord Birkenhead on a visit to the United States of America. Mr. Churchill has described him as 'an experienced parliamentarian, capable of speaking at short notice and of taking an effective part on the spur of the moment in hot debate. . . . He was essentially a House of Commons man.' His real interest lay in finance.

Evans was created a baronet in 1916, when he assumed by royal licence the additional surname of Worthington; he was sworn of the Privy Council in 1918, and was appointed G.B.E. in 1922. He died in London 14 February 1931. In 1898 he married Gertrude Annie, younger daughter of William Hale, of London, and had a son, William Shirley (born 1904), who succeeded him as second baronet, and a daughter.

There is a plaque of Worthington-Evans by Maurice Webb in St. Margaret's church, Westminster.

[*The Times*, 16 February 1931.]

E. I. CARLYLE.

EVE, SIR HARRY TRELAWNEY (1856-1940), judge, was born in London 13 October 1856, the only son of Thomas Eve, a Jamaica merchant. He was educated privately and at Exeter College, Oxford. He early chose the bar as his career, reading in the chambers of Charles Swinfen Eady [q.v.], who had a large practice. Eve was called to the bar by Lincoln's Inn in 1881 and took silk in 1895. He was returned to parliament at a by-election in January 1904 as liberal member for the Ashburton division of Devon, a seat which he retained by a large majority at the general election of 1906. His political career was, however, destined to be of short duration, for in 1907 he was offered, and accepted, a judgeship in the Chancery division. He retired in 1937 and was sworn of the Privy Council. He became a bencher of Lincoln's Inn in 1899, and on his elevation to his judicial office he was elected an honorary fellow of his college. He married in 1879 Beatrice Wright, only daughter of Henry Strangways Hounsell, M.D., of Torquay, and had one son, who was killed in action in 1917, and two daughters, the younger of whom predeceased her father. He died at Farnham, Surrey, 10 December 1940.

Eve was a thoroughly sound judge. His grasp of equity was very comprehensive, and it is one of the most baffling mysteries in the whole history of judicial appointments that he, who was for many years the senior judge in the Chancery division, and sat on many occasions in the Court of Appeal, was always passed over for actual promotion to that court.

One of Eve's earliest decisions was in *Cope* v. *Crossingham* in 1908. It concerned that difficult statutory provision section 4 of the Trade Union Act (1871), which provides that nothing in the Act shall enable any court to entertain any legal proceeding for the object of 'directly enforcing' certain trade union agreements. Here the members of a branch of a trade union passed a resolution that they would secede from the parent society and distribute the funds of the branch among themselves. This resolution was contrary to the rules of the trade union, and its trustees sought a declaration that the resolution was *ultra vires*, and an order that the funds should be paid over to them according to the rules. Eve held that they had sufficient interest in the property of the branch to maintain the action and were not prevented by section 4 from doing so: further, he declared the proposed distribution of the funds to be *ultra vires*, but on the other hand he refused to administer the funds of the union by making any order for the payment over of the funds to the head trustees. He pointed out that the declaration would prevent misapplication of the funds; beyond that he did not feel it his duty to go, by laying down the exact method of appropriation. Other well-known decisions during the course of his career were in *Powell* v. *Hemsley* (1909), an often-cited authority on covenants restrictive of the user of land; *Re Pryce*

(1917), on a covenant in a marriage settlement to settle the after-acquired property of the wife; *Hill* v. *Peters* (1918), on mortgage priorities; *Wise* v. *Whitburn* (1924), on the determination of the moment at which executors cease to hold property in that character and begin to hold it as trustees; *Re Bathe* (1925), on the validity of conditions in wills in partial restraint of marriage; and *Cummins* v. *Bond* (1926), a case which attracted a great deal of attention and in which Eve decided that a spiritualistic medium who had produced a script entitled 'The Chronicle of Cleophas' by automatic writing was the owner of the copyright in it and entitled to restrain a person who was present at the séances at which it had been written from publishing it, annotated by himself, in book form. His judgements must always loom large in any account of the vital subject of charitable trusts. It is, finally, to be noted as one of his outstanding merits that, although his judicial career was well past its meridian in 1926, when the property legislation of 1925 came into force, he was quick in absorbing it and never unduly conservative, as were some of his colleagues on the bench, in its interpretation.

A portrait of Eve by E. C. Wilkinson hangs in the hall of Exeter College, Oxford.

[*The Times*, 11 December 1940.]

H. G. HANBURY.

EWART, ALFRED JAMES (1872–1937), botanist, was born at Liverpool 12 February 1872, the second of the four sons of Edmund Brown Ewart, director of the chemical laboratory of the Liverpool Institute, by his wife, Martha Williams. The father, who was of Scottish descent, was a nephew of the politician William Ewart [q.v.], after whose father Gladstone was named. Alfred was educated at the Liverpool Institute and at the University College (later Liverpool University), where he read for a London degree, graduating B.Sc. with first class honours in botany in 1893. The following year he was awarded an 1851 Exhibition scholarship and proceeded to Leipzig where he studied plant physiology under Wilhelm Friedrich Philipp Pfeffer. There he obtained the degree of Ph.D. in 1896 and an extension to his studentship allowed him to work in the laboratory of the Botanical Garden at Buitenzorg, Java, under Melchior Treub. Returning to England in 1897, he began an association with Mason College, Birmingham (converted in 1900 into Birmingham

University), which lasted until his departure for Melbourne in 1905. During this period he worked at intervals at the Botanic Garden at Oxford, where he matriculated as a non-collegiate student in 1898, graduating B.Sc. in 1906.

For the first sixteen years of his tenure of the Melbourne chair Ewart held the dual office of professor of botany and plant physiology and government botanist. Half of each day he spent in the national herbarium at South Yarra, and the remainder in the university at Carlton on the opposite side of the city. In 1921 the two positions were separated, and in 1929 Ewart achieved one of his ambitions when he moved his department to a new building dedicated to botany: previously he had shared the laboratory with the zoology school. A second ambition was attained in 1930 with the publication of his large illustrated work on *Flora of Victoria*.

Ewart's contributions to botany cover a wide field. Trained as a physiologist, he is remembered as the translator of Pfeffer's *Physiology of Plants* (3 vols., 1900–1906) and as the author of important contributions on *The Physics and Physiology of Protoplasmic Streaming in Plants* (1903) and 'The Ascent of Water in Trees' (*Philosophical Transactions* of the Royal Society, series B, vols. cxcviii and cxcix, 1906 and 1908). After his migration to Australia, work of a taxonomic nature and problems of applied botany had to occupy most of his time. He did much for the education of foresters and in 1925 published *A Handbook of Forest Trees for Victorian Foresters*. Inevitably problems of weed identification and control took a large part in his career as a government botanist. Towards the end of his life he made a useful contribution towards the causes of the poisoning of stock and horses in Central and Western Australia.

Ewart was a man of robust physique and somewhat choleric disposition. Unfortunately he became involved in some bitter controversies which prevented his taking as large a part in the development of botanical work in Australia as might have been expected from one of his ability and standing. He was elected a fellow of the Linnean Society in 1898 and F.R.S. in 1922, and was an active member of the Royal Society of Victoria. A man of simple tastes, he delighted in country life and in good music. He was twice married: first, in 1898 to Florence Maud, daughter of Frederick William Donaldson, accountant; she was an accomplished violinist whom he met in Leipzig: the marriage was dissolved in 1929; secondly, in 1931 to Elizabeth, daughter of David Richard Bilton, grazier, of Craigie, Victoria. There were two sons of the first marriage. He died in Melbourne 12 September 1937.

[*Obituary Notices of Fellows of the Royal Society*, No. 7, January 1939 (portrait); *Proceedings* of the Linnean Society of London, October 1937 to May 1938; *Nature*, 1 January 1938; private information.]

T. G. B. OSBORN.

EWING, SIR (JAMES) ALFRED (1855–1935), engineer, was born at Dundee 27 March 1855, the youngest of the three sons of James Ewing, minister of St. Andrew's Free church, Dundee, by his wife, Marjory, eldest daughter of John Ferguson, a Glasgow solicitor. He was educated at the West End Academy and at Dundee High School. 'In a family', he says, 'whose chief interests were clerical and literary, I took my pleasure in machines and experiments. My scanty pocket money was spent on tools and chemicals. The domestic attic was put at my disposal. It became the scene of hair-raising explosions. There, too, the domestic cat found herself an unwilling instrument of electrification and a partner in various shocking experiences.' In 1871 Ewing was awarded a scholarship in engineering to Edinburgh University, where he studied under H. C. Fleeming Jenkin and P. G. Tait [qq.v.], who both recognized his unusual ability. Jenkin was then engaged with Sir William Thomson (later Lord Kelvin, q.v.) in making and laying submarine telegraphs for the Great Western Telegraph Company, and Jenkin suggested that Ewing should assist in this work during the summer. Ewing accepted this offer and carried out three successive cable-laying expeditions to Brazil and the River Plate, returning to Edinburgh for the university session in the summer.

In 1878 Ewing, on Jenkin's recommendation, was appointed professor of mechanical engineering and physics at the imperial university of Tokyo for three, subsequently extended to five, years. In the winter of 1879 he investigated in Japan the phenomena of earthquakes, and devised instruments for measuring and recording them. He established an observatory in the lowest part of the vale of Gedo. The results of his labours were published in the *Memoirs* of the science department of the university of Tokyo in

1883, the year in which he was appointed professor of engineering in the new university college of Dundee. His researches on magnetic induction and in organic chemistry produced much fruitful work.

In 1890 the professorship of mechanism and applied mechanics at Cambridge fell vacant, and on the advice of John Hopkinson [q.v.] Ewing successfully applied for the chair. During his tenure the school grew at almost an embarrassing rate; a tripos was instituted (1892); a laboratory was founded (1894); and in 1899 a wing was opened in memory of Hopkinson. In 1898 Ewing was elected into a professorial fellowship at King's College. He was offered, but refused, the post of director of the National Physical Laboratory in 1899.

In 1903 Ewing was called to a wider sphere of action. The Admiralty was about to introduce for naval officers a new scheme of education and training promoted by W. W. Palmer, Lord Selborne, and Sir John (later Lord) Fisher [qq.v.], into which a large element of engineering knowledge was to be infused. The post of director of naval education was offered to Ewing and accepted, and he threw himself into his new duties with characteristic enthusiasm. He organized the system of scientific and engineering training and declared his belief that the reorganization would be productive of immense benefit in promoting the efficiency of the service. The teaching was eminently practical and included much experimental work, preliminary to the exposition of theory. He directed the preparation of several textbooks for young officers and continued to supervise the work of naval education until 1916. He was a member of the ordnance board from 1906 to 1908, when Sir Philip Watts [q.v.] was building dreadnoughts; and from 1903 to 1906 a member of the explosives committee which improved the quality and the manufacture of cordite.

But on the day of the outbreak of war in 1914 Ewing was asked by Rear-Admiral (Sir) H. F. Oliver, then director of the intelligence division of the naval staff, to decipher some wireless 'intercepts' from German stations, there being no department to which to refer them. This was the beginning of 'Room 40' in the Old Buildings of the Admiralty where the task of deciphering the German messages under Ewing's supervision was facilitated by the opportune discovery in 1914 of the 'highly confidential' signal book of the German navy in the arms of a drowned signalman of the *Magdeburg*, and led up to the battles of Dogger Bank and Jutland, the arrest of Roger Casement [q.v.], the loss of his armament off Tralee, and the revelation of the Zimmermann telegrams with their effect on the policy of the United States of America.

In May 1916 Ewing was offered the principalship and vice-chancellorship of Edinburgh University. It was intended that he should continue to superintend 'Room 40', but he found after a year that the claims of Edinburgh were too insistent to make the double duty practicable or desirable. Under his headship, from 1916 to 1929, the university passed through an unexampled period of development and expansion. When he received the freedom of the city in 1929, the lord provost, Sir Alexander Stevenson, declared that since 1916 no fewer than thirteen new chairs had been established besides a number of lecturerships; a new degree of commerce had come into being, and the degree of Ph.D. instituted for postgraduate research. The increase in the number of the teaching staff involved an extension scheme of new buildings, known as the King's buildings, on a large area about a mile and a half from the Old College, where independent blocks were erected for chemistry and zoology, while provision was made, and plans prepared, for geology and engineering. These were carried out after Ewing's resignation in 1929, when he retired to Cambridge where, in 1890, as a stranger, he had been 'received with a dispassionate readiness which was as gratifying as it was surprising'; he had been elected an honorary fellow of King's College in 1903.

Ewing was appointed C.B. in 1907 and K.C.B. in 1911; in 1887 he was elected F.R.S. and was awarded a Royal medal by the society in 1895. He was elected F.R.S. (Edin.) in 1878 and was president from 1924 to 1929. He received honorary doctorates in science from the universities of Oxford, Cambridge, Durham, and Sheffield, and in law from Edinburgh, St. Andrews, and Glasgow. He was awarded the Albert medal of the Royal Society of Arts in 1929. He was president of the British Association in 1932, and received the freedom of Dundee in 1933. He gave the James Forest lecture to the Institution of Civil Engineers in 1899 and in 1928; the Rede lecture at Cambridge in 1904 on 'The Structure of Metals'; the second Kelvin lecture to the Institution of Electrical Engineers in 1910; and the Hibbert lecture at Cambridge in 1933. For many years he was associated with the Department of Scientific and Industrial Research; in 1923 he became chairman of the Bridge Stress Committee, besides belonging to several other committees.

Besides the *Treatise on Earthquake Measurement* (1883), Ewing published *Magnetic Induction in Iron and other Metals* (1891), containing his final definition of hysteresis (3rd ed. 1900); *The Steam Engine and other Heat Engines* (1894, 4th ed. 1926); *The Strength of Materials* (1899); *The Mechanical Production of Gold* (1908); and *Thermodynamics for Engineers* (1920).

Ewing was twice married: first, in 1879 at the British Legation in Tokyo to Annie Maria Thomasina Blackburn (died 1909), daughter of Thomas Blackburn Washington, of Claymont, West Virginia, and a great-great-grand-niece of George Washington, and had a son and a daughter; secondly, in 1911 to Ellen Lina, daughter of John Hopkinson [q.v.] and sister of Bertram Hopkinson [q.v.], and had a son. He died at Cambridge 7 January 1935.

A large portrait of Ewing by Henry Lintott hangs in the court room, Edinburgh; another, by the same artist, is in possession of Lady Ewing. A portrait by Douglas Shields (*c.* 1903) is in the board room at the Engineering Laboratory, Cambridge. A bronze bust by Miss Campbell Muirhead is at Toronto, in the possession of his son.

[*The Times* and *Scotsman*, 8 January 1935; A. W. Ewing, *The Man of Room 40. The Life of Sir Alfred Ewing*, 1939; Preface to J. A. Ewing, *An Engineer's Outlook*, 1933; L. F. Bates, *Sir Alfred Ewing* (British Council 'Science in Britain' series), 1946; Winston Churchill, *The World Crisis, 1911–1918*, 1931; Sir J. S. Corbett, (Official) *History of the Great War. Naval Operations*, vol. iii, 1923; Lord Fisher, *Memories*, 1919; S. J. Hendrick, *Life and Letters of W. H. Page*, vol. iii, 1925; *Obituary Notices of Fellows of the Royal Society*, No. 4, December 1935 (portrait); *Nature*, 26 January 1935.]

E. I. CARLYLE.

FAGAN, JAMES BERNARD (1873–1933), actor-manager, producer, and playwright, was born in Belfast 18 May 1873, the elder son of (Sir) John Fagan, surgeon, of Belfast, by his wife, Mary Catherine, daughter of Bernard Hughes, also of Belfast. He was educated at Clongowes Wood College and Trinity College, Oxford, and studied for the bar, but soon joined the company of (Sir) F. R. Benson [q.v.],

making his first appearance on the stage in October 1895. There followed from 1897 to 1899 an engagement with (Sir) Herbert Beerbohm Tree [q.v.] at Her Majesty's Theatre, where he acted in *Katherine and Petruchio*, *A Man's Shadow*, *Julius Caesar*, *The Musketeers*, *Carnac Sahib*, and other plays.

In 1899 Fagan began his career as a dramatist with *The Rebels*, and among his many other plays may be specially noted *The Prayer of the Sword* (a poetical drama, 1904), *Treasure Island* (adapted from R. L. Stevenson's story, 1922), *And So To Bed* (a Pepysian comedy, 1926), and finally *The Improper Duchess* (1931). After fourteen years of retirement from the stage he resumed his career as an actor in 1913, touring in his own play *The Earth* (first produced in 1909), and in March 1917 broke new ground as a producer, when he was responsible in this capacity for the much-discussed performance at the St. Martin's Theatre of *Damaged Goods*, adapted from the French of Eugène Brieux. Thenceforward Fagan threw himself more and more into the work of producer and theatre manager. In October 1923 he opened the Oxford Playhouse in the Woodstock Road, where he gathered round him a company of young and distinguished players, making a real and lasting contribution to the dramatic history of the university. This theatre was transferred in 1938 to a new and more convenient building in Beaumont Street, but its original conception was Fagan's, and to him is due the credit of its foundation. In 1929 he became associated as director with the Festival Theatre, Cambridge, but much of his best work in this department was seen in London at the Court Theatre, the management of which he took over in 1918, and elsewhere, notably in Tchekhov's *The Cherry Orchard* (Lyric Theatre, Hammersmith, 1925), in Mr. Sean O'Casey's *Juno and the Paycock* (Royalty Theatre, 1925), and in Strindberg's *Spook Sonata* (Globe Theatre, 1927).

In middle life Fagan was robust in figure and of a jovial countenance. His very versatility may have prevented the attainment of supreme excellence in any single branch of the art which he practised with such enthusiasm and in so many spheres. But he was always true to his best ideals of acting, authorship, and production, and at a time of growing commercialism in the theatre he manfully upheld high standards. He was twice married: first, in 1897 to the actress

Susan Elizabeth Kirby; the marriage was dissolved; secondly, in 1914, as her second husband, to Ada, daughter of Edward Bevan ap Rees Bryant; she acted under the name of Mary Grey. There was one daughter of the second marriage. He died at Hollywood, California, 17 February 1933.

[*The Times*, 18 February 1933; *Who's Who in the Theatre*, 1933; personal knowledge.]

GEOFFREY A. WHITWORTH.

FAIRBAIRN, STEPHEN (1862–1938), oarsman, was born at Toorak, Melbourne, Australia, 25 August 1862, the fifth of the six sons of George Fairbairn, who, having emigrated from Berwickshire in 1839, owned a large sheep station and (in the 'seventies) started the first canning and meat-freezing works in Australia. The Scottish theologian Patrick Fairbairn [q.v.] was Stephen's uncle. His mother was Virginia, youngest daughter of George Armytage, of Geelong, Victoria, a native of Derbyshire. He was educated at Geelong Grammar School, where he earned distinction in all forms of sport, and at Jesus College, Cambridge, graduating in 1884. He was called to the bar by the Inner Temple in 1886 but did not practise. In 1884 he returned to Australia where, but for an interval in 1886 and 1887 when he was in England, he worked on a sheep station for twenty years. He came back to England in 1905 and thereafter devoted himself almost exclusively to coaching various rowing clubs.

Fairbairn rowed in the Cambridge crews of 1882, 1883, 1886, and 1887 and won many races at Henley and other regattas: but his claim to fame rests on his methods of coaching and the success of the crews which he coached. Some people have tried to add a new word 'Fairbairnism' to the English language as denoting a peculiar style of rowing. That, however, comes from a complete misunderstanding of him. Fairbairn invented no new style and had no desire to invent a style. He wrote: 'There are certain principles underlying rowing, and what is called style is the endeavour to carry them out. Variations are merely failures to carry out the principles. There can be only one true style.' There is little doubt that had he produced his perfect crew it would have been indistinguishable from the perfect crew produced by any other methods. What was different about Fairbairn was the method of coaching by which he tried to arrive at the perfect crew. He turned the pupil's mind to the oar in the water and to moving the boat, regardless of what might happen to various parts of the body, whereas the orthodox coach would concentrate on positioning the body in order to produce certain results on the oar and the passage of the boat.

Fairbairn coached always for looseness and ease. A favourite remark was: 'If you can't do it easily, you can't do it at all.' He would never try to correct by condemnation: anything, if it is to be done successfully, must be done naturally and easily: set before the performer an ideal after which to strive: if in his striving he does some odd things, never mind: be positive in your coaching and encourage rather than criticize. It was inevitable that some of his crews, which had moved only a little way along the road to perfection, showed ungainly attitudes and exaggerations of ideals which earned bitter condemnation from more orthodox coaches.

Fairbairn was an enthusiast and was able to impart his enthusiasm to his pupils. He was ever progressive, ever ready to try out some new idea in coaching or some new device such as long slides or swivel rowlocks. He did much to make rowing popular, particularly in the clubs at Putney, and in 1925 he instituted the 'Head of the River' race on the Putney to Mortlake course. He coached many successful crews of both the London Rowing Club and the Thames Rowing Club, but his old college, Jesus, always took first place in his affections, and for more than thirty-three years he devoted himself to coaching its crews. It was a small college with a small boat club, but Fairbairn brought it many successes. His crews always raced hard and often won against crews which seemed to be better or more experienced.

Fairbairn was known throughout the rowing world as 'Steve', and even those who disagreed with his unorthodox ways admitted his genuine love of rowing, his boundless enthusiasm, his kindliness, and his genius for coaching. His writings include *Rowing Notes* (1926) and an autobiography, *Fairbairn of Jesus* (1931). He married in 1891 Ellen, daughter of Sydney Sherwood, of Aramac, Queensland, and had two sons. He died in London 16 May 1938.

A portrait of Fairbairn by James Quinn is in the possession of Jesus College, Cambridge.

[Private information; personal knowledge.]

H. B. PLAYFORD.

FALKNER, JOHN MEADE (1858–1932), author and antiquary, was born at Manningford Bruce, Wiltshire, 8 May 1858, the eldest of the three sons of Thomas Alexander Falkner, of Manningford Bruce, later curate of Holy Trinity church, Dorchester, and afterwards some time of North Newnton, Wiltshire, by his wife, Elizabeth Grace Meade. He was educated at Marlborough and at Hertford College, Oxford, where he graduated in modern history in 1882, and in 1927 was elected an honorary fellow. After leaving the university, filled with affection for Oxford and the south of England and expressing an extreme distaste for the north and everything connected with it, he went to Newcastle-upon-Tyne as tutor to the sons of (Sir) Andrew Noble [q.v.], the principal figure in the large firm of Messrs. Armstrong & company, armament manufacturers. With the Noble family his association was close, and he soon became an intimate and beloved member of their household, so that when the tuition of his sons came to an end, Noble invited Falkner to become his private secretary, and, on the firm being transformed in 1897 into a limited liability company as Sir W. G. Armstrong, Whitworth & company, Falkner was in due course appointed the first secretary of the board. As an official of the firm he travelled much on the continent in order to negotiate contracts for ships and guns, and, under Noble's guidance, he did much useful work. In 1901 he became a member of the board, and eventually its chairman, a position in which he can hardly be called a success. His genius as well as his tastes followed other lines.

When he first came north Falkner spent all his holidays walking or bicycling, chiefly in Oxfordshire and Berkshire, and he came to know those counties so well that he compiled Murray's handbooks for them (*Oxfordshire*, 1894; *Berkshire*, 1902), and wrote an admirable popular *History of Oxfordshire* (1899). But as the years went by, he found his love for antiquities stirred by the neighbouring city of Durham, and he exchanged his Newcastle lodgings for a house in Durham. Here he interested himself in the cathedral service, its music and ceremonies, as well as in the university library. He became honorary librarian to the dean and chapter, a post much to his liking, and at the university he was appointed honorary reader in palaeography.

Falkner's reputation as a writer of fiction rests upon three novels or romances, each in its way noteworthy. The first appeared in 1895, and the other two in the course of the next ten years. All received a good deal of public appreciation and sold quite satisfactorily. Yet in the curiously discontinuous way which was characteristic of him, he never produced another book. He was said to have begun a fourth story, but lost the manuscript when it was half finished and never resumed it. His first novel, *The Lost Stradivarius*, deals with the discovery of a violin which had been hidden in a secret cupboard behind the panels of an Oxford undergraduate's sitting-room. There is much ghostly and mysterious detail about the plot, which is wonderfully well worked out. His second book (1898) was called *Moonfleet*, and, although it is perhaps not his best, it is decidedly the most popular of his works. Written in the style of Stevenson or Hardy, about smugglers and preventive men and abounding in hair-breadth escapes and exciting adventures, it has delighted every generation since it first appeared. His third and last novel, *The Nebuly Coat* (1903), may well rank as his masterpiece. The theme was after his own heart: the experience of an architect sent to inspect a church which is in danger of collapse owing to the giving way of the arches which support the tower. Heraldry also, as the title suggests, figures largely in the narrative. The book ends with a striking description of the fall of the tower and the dismay and alarm of the villagers. In addition to his novels, Falkner wrote a good deal of admirable poetry which appeared in various periodicals. After his death some attempt was made to collect the poems, and a reprint was circulated privately.

As has already been pointed out, Falkner's main interests were ecclesiastical. He may indeed be said to have adopted a church of his own. In his Oxfordshire rambles he came across the picturesque village of Burford, by which he was much attracted, and the church was for long the centre of his interests. He and his former pupil, Sir John Noble, contributed substantial sums in alterations and additions for the beautifying of the interior, and when he died at Durham 22 July 1932, Falkner was buried in Burford churchyard.

In person, Falkner was an exceptionally tall man, and he may have outgrown his strength in youth, as for many years his heart gave him trouble. Considering all that he did by way of authorship, study, and research, it is remarkable how his powers lasted. In the last phase of his active life he spent much of his time at Bath, a city of which the beauty and traditions had always greatly attracted him, and to the subject of which he devoted a short book, hardly more than a pamphlet, entitled *Bath, in History and Social Tradition* (1918).

Falkner married in 1899 Evelyn Violet, youngest daughter of General Sir John Miller Adye [q.v.]. There were no children of the marriage. He received several foreign decorations.

[*The Times*, 23 and 25 July 1932; personal knowledge.]   ALFRED COCHRANE.

FARNELL, LEWIS RICHARD (1856–1934), rector of Exeter College, Oxford, and classical scholar, was born at Salisbury 19 January 1856, the sixth child and third son of John Wilson Farnell, by his wife, Harriot Pritchard. His father was then established as a draper in Salisbury, but in 1858, involved in the ruin of a brother, had to move his family to London where he eventually became manager for a Bicester brewery. Farnell was educated at the City of London School under E. A. Abbott [q.v.] and entered Exeter College, Oxford, as an open classical scholar in 1874. At Exeter he owed much to the teaching of Ingram Bywater and H. F. Pelham [qq.v.] and, after obtaining a first class in classical moderations (1875) and in *literae humaniores* (1878), was elected a fellow of the college in 1880. Appointed classical lecturer in 1883, he spent the rest of his active life primarily in college teaching and administration, being sub-rector from 1883 to 1893, senior tutor from 1893 to 1913, and rector from 1913 to 1928, in which year he was elected an honorary fellow. From 1903 to 1914 he was university lecturer in classical archaeology, from 1908 to 1911 first Wilde lecturer in natural and comparative religion, Hibbert lecturer in 1911, and Gifford lecturer at St. Andrews University in 1920–1921 and 1924–1925. From 1920 to 1923 he was vice-chancellor.

Despite these activities Farnell, who was an energetic promoter of the degree of D.Litt. and was one of the first to take it in 1901, was able between 1880 and 1893 to make a series of continental tours during which he studied classical archaeology in Berlin and at Munich and visited many museums, and from 1896 to publish a succession of important books concerning Greek religion, a subject to which he had been attracted in the course of his archaeo-

logical studies. Of these the most massive is *The Cults of the Greek States* (5 vols., 1896–1909), completed in 1921 by a supplementary volume, *Greek Hero Cults and Ideas of Immortality* (being his Gifford lectures for 1920). In these volumes the evidence for Greek religion is exhaustively collected and interpreted with judgement, rituals and art-forms being used to illustrate each other. Shorter works, but all marked by wide learning and clear exposition, are *Greece and Babylon* (1911), *The Higher Aspects of Greek Religion* (1912), and *The Attributes of God* (1925, being his Gifford lectures for 1924–1925). His *Outline-History of Greek Religion* (1920) is a constructive summary of high value. In retirement he produced two notable books, *The Works of Pindar* (3 vols., 1930–1932), based upon a lifelong study of that author, and a delightfully written autobiography, *An Oxonian Looks Back* (1934). He was elected a fellow of the British Academy in 1916 and honorary degrees were conferred upon him by the universities of Dublin, St. Andrews, and Geneva.

For many years Farnell played a leading part in the politics of his university. He led or supported many reforms designed to promote learning within its walls and with the same object in view was often found championing the university against the colleges, although he was a devoted *alumnus* and very successful head of his own college and recognized that there were others besides himself who realized his ideal of a college tutor as one who should combine 'the conscientious discharge of tutorial functions with original research and literary production'. As vice-chancellor in the difficult post-war years he was sometimes criticized for excessive strictness, but calmer consideration nearly always admitted that he had been right.

In 1893 Farnell married Sylvia, eighth child and youngest daughter of Captain Christopher Baldock Cardew, of East Liss, Hampshire; she was a granddaughter of the lord chancellor Richard Bethell, first Lord Westbury [q.v.]. They had three sons and one daughter. Farnell died at Parkstone, Dorset, 28 March 1934. His portrait by J. St. H. Lander is in Exeter College hall.

[L. R. Farnell, *An Oxonian Looks Back*, 1934; R. R. Marett, *Lewis Richard Farnell, 1856–1934* in *Proceedings* of the British Academy, vol. xx, 1934; *Oxford Magazine*, 26 April 1934; College records; private information; personal knowledge.]   E. A. BARBER.

FERGUSON, RONALD CRAUFORD MUNRO-, VISCOUNT NOVAR (1860–1934), politician, was born at Kirkcaldy 6 March 1860, the eldest of the three sons of Colonel Robert Ferguson, of Raith, Fife, by his wife, Emma, daughter of James Henry Mandeville, of Merton, Surrey. He was grandson of General Sir R. C. Ferguson [q.v.]. His father took the additional surname of Munro on the death of his first cousin Hugh Andrew Munro in 1864 when he inherited the estates of Novar, Ross-shire, and Muirton, Morayshire. Ronald Munro-Ferguson was educated at home and in 1875 joined the 1st Fife Light Horse, and later, after the course at Sandhurst, was gazetted to the Grenadier Guards in which he served for five years (1879–1884). In the last-named year he was returned at a by-election as liberal member for Ross and Cromarty, but was defeated at the general election of 1885 by a crofter candidate, and in 1886 he unsuccessfully contested Dumbartonshire. But later in that same year he succeeded Gladstone as member for Leith Burghs and retained the seat until 1914. He was private secretary to Lord Rosebery when foreign secretary both in 1886 and in 1892 and accompanied him to India in 1886, and when Rosebery became prime minister in 1894 Munro-Ferguson was appointed a junior lord of the Treasury. In 1910 he was sworn of the Privy Council.

Munro-Ferguson, who in 1889 had married Lady Helen Hermione, eldest daughter of F. T. Hamilton-Temple Blackwood, first Marquess of Dufferin and Ava [q.v.], was appointed, on Asquith's recommendation, to be governor-general of Australia and G.C.M.G. in 1914. He reached the Commonwealth in May and worked amicably with the prime minister, (Sir) Joseph Cook, and his successors, Andrew Fisher [q.v.] and Mr. William Morris Hughes. On the outbreak of war in August the energies of Australia had to be diverted to military matters, to which Munro-Ferguson devoted himself in every form of war work. In this his past military experience was of great service, particularly in the training and dispatch of the Australian Expeditionary Force. In travelling to visit the training camps he made himself very popular everywhere. The nursing and supply of comforts were the especial care of his wife, who was appointed G.B.E. for her services in 1918. Munro-Ferguson's knowledge and experience of afforestation led him to encourage the cultivation of Australian timber and

he considered this to be his 'best legacy to Melbourne'. In 1919 his term as governor-general was extended to 1920 on account of the forthcoming visit of the Prince of Wales, and on his return to Scotland he was raised to the peerage as Viscount Novar, of Raith. In the absence of any effective liberal party in 1922 he supported the Bonar Law and Baldwin administrations, and accepted the office of secretary for Scotland from 1922 to 1924. In 1925 he was appointed chairman of the committee for the review of political honours.

Novar received the honorary degree of LL.D. from the universities of St. Andrews (1911) and Edinburgh (1923) and was appointed K.T. in 1926. He died, without issue, at Raith 30 March 1934. A portrait of him by J. H. Lorimer is at Raith House.

[*The Times*, 31 March 1934.]
E. I. CARLYLE.

FIFE, DUCHESS OF (1867–1931), princess royal of Great Britain and Ireland. [See LOUISE VICTORIA ALEXANDRA DAGMAR.]

FILON, LOUIS NAPOLEON GEORGE (1875–1937), mathematician, was born at St. Cloud, near Paris, 22 November 1875, the only son of Pierre Marie Augustin Filon, littérateur and tutor to the Prince Imperial, by his wife, Marie Jeanne Madeline Poirel. When he was three years old his parents, his father now blind and his mother in delicate health, came to England and settled in Margate. His early education under the personal direction of his father centred mainly round the classics. He went to Herne House School at Margate and in 1894 became a student at University College, London, where he graduated B.A. with first class honours in 1896, and was awarded a gold medal for Greek. He had so far shown no great interest in mathematics and came to it only because it was at that time part of the curriculum for the B.A. degree. This brought him into contact with Karl Pearson [q.v.] and Micaiah Hill for whom he retained throughout life an abiding affection and reverence, and it was their influence which very largely shaped his subsequent career as a mathematician and scientist.

In 1898 (the year in which he was naturalized) Filon went to King's College, Cambridge, as one of the earliest 'advanced students'; he then joined the staff of University College, London, as lecturer in pure mathematics in 1903. In 1912 he succeeded Pearson in the Goldsmid chair of applied mathematics and mechanics, to the work of which he devoted himself for the rest of his life with the exception of the years 1914–1918, when he saw active service in France and later commanded the 2nd battalion London Regiment. From 1929 until his death he was director of the University Observatory.

The results of Filon's mathematical researches are embodied in over fifty memoirs, the publication of which was spread pretty evenly over forty years of a busy life. They are concerned with many aspects of mathematics, but his outstanding contributions were in the field of classical mechanics and particularly the mechanics of continuous media. It is a field that had been well culled over before his time and the problems that were obvious and easy had all been solved. Important and significant problems remained unsolved, but they usually presented formidable technical difficulties. Filon was well equipped both by temperament and training to wrestle with such problems. He had the mathematical courage that will tackle any problem, a resourceful mind in meeting technical difficulties, and the patient and methodical perseverance that can hang on until a solution is reached. His greatest achievement was the theory of 'generalized plane stress' which shows how the average elastic stresses in a thick plate may be determined by the simpler analysis appropriate to two-dimensional problems. A development of this theory shows how the optical measurement of the stresses in a transparent celluloid plate may be used to investigate the stresses in a steel structure. It is the working out of this idea in general theory and in particular cases that constitutes Filon's most important contribution to the advance of mechanics. It was a particular source of gratification to him when, in association with Professor E. G. Coker, he was able to apply the method to the exploration of the stresses in structures actually used in engineering practice.

Filon was a great teacher and, even at times when he was most heavily engaged with other activities, he gave intense care to the preparation and delivery of his lectures. He regarded mechanics as a branch of physics rather than of mathematics. He insisted on the application of rigorous logic to the development of the theory of the subject, while at the same time insisting that theory should yield its results in a form that could be tested by experiment. Thus, his lectures on mechanics were freely illustrated by experiment and he established a mechanics laboratory in which his students carried out experiments for themselves. In prescribing this unusual but profitable experience for the mathematical undergraduate he was a pioneer, and more recent developments have shown how right he was.

Filon took an active part in the affairs of the university of London in the critical phase of its development and unification. He was a member of the senate (1920) and the court and served as vice-chancellor (1933–1935). He worked consistently and unremittingly to maintain academic freedom and to develop teaching and research. The high offices in which he served and the heavy responsibilities that were laid upon him never led him to neglect his primary duty as a teacher. For years he carried a full lecturing time-table every morning and a full programme of committees and councils every afternoon, and still the steady stream of published work flowed on. In all this every lecture was prepared and every document studied with the closest attention to detail, and only his magnificent constitution enabled him to bear the strain for so long. He was elected F.R.S. in 1910, and appointed C.B.E. in 1933.

Filon was vigorous and combative, a man of strong convictions, yet always just and generous, and a constant help and inspiration to those with whom he worked. In 1904 he married Anne, eldest daughter of Professor Philippe Godet, of the university of Neuchâtel, and had one son and two daughters. He died at Croydon 29 December 1937, a victim of a typhoid epidemic prevalent there at that time.

[*The Times*, 30 and 31 December 1937; *Obituary Notices of Fellows of the Royal Society*, No. 7, January 1939 (bibliography and portrait); *Mathematical Gazette*, February 1938 (portrait); *Nature*, 26 February 1938; personal knowledge.]   G. B. JEFFERY.

FINBERG, ALEXANDER JOSEPH (1866–1939), writer on the history of English art, was born in London 23 April 1866, the son of Alexander Abraham Finberg, compositor, by his wife, Susanna Wanstall. He was educated at the City of London College and King's College, London, and studied art at the Lambeth School of Art and in Paris. He did black-

and-white work for the *Graphic* and *Illustrated London News*, and became art critic to several papers, including the *Manchester Guardian* and the *Saturday Review*. In 1905 Finberg, who for many years had made a special study of the work of J. M. W. Turner [q.v.], was commissioned by the trustees of the National Gallery to complete the arrangement of the sketches and water-colours in the Turner bequest, which had been begun by John Ruskin. While he was engaged upon this task, numerous unknown paintings by Turner were brought to light, and they were first exhibited at the Tate Gallery in 1906. The interest excited by them prompted (Sir) Joseph Duveen [q.v.] to present a new Turner wing to the gallery in 1908. Finberg's writings on Turner include *A Complete Inventory of the Drawings of the Turner Bequest* (2 vols., 1909); *The History of Turner's Liber Studiorum with a new Catalogue Raisonné* (1924), which superseded that of W. G. Rawlinson [q.v.]; and *The Life of J. M. W. Turner* (1939), to the composition of which he devoted much of his life and the proofs of which he had finished correcting only a few days before his death.

The Life of Turner is perhaps Finberg's chief, but it is not his only, monument. When he was cataloguing the Turner bequest he discovered among the drawings many which were not by Turner. He set himself to identify the artists of these drawings, but was greatly hampered by lack of books of reference. For whereas the work of foreign artists was receiving searching attention from English scholars, the British school of painting was undeservedly neglected. Accordingly, after much consideration, Finberg in 1911 founded the Walpole Society, the main object of which was 'to continue the work begun by Horace Walpole's *Anecdotes of Painting in England*, viz., "to celebrate the arts" of this country'. Until 1922 he acted as honorary secretary and as editor of the annual volumes of the society which have done so much to encourage the study and promote the knowledge of the history of all aspects of British art, not least by the publication of such indispensable sources as the notebooks of George Vertue [q.v.].

Finberg was twice married: first, in 1899 to Norah Kathleen (whom he divorced in 1913), daughter of William Mutch, cartridge manufacturer, of Holloway; secondly, in 1914 to Hilda Félicité, youngest daughter of Ferdinand Baruch

Ehrmann, wine merchant, of Islington. He had two sons by his first and one by his second marriage. He died at Barnes Common 15 March 1939.

[*The Times*, 16 March 1939; C. E. Hughes, 'A. J. Finberg', in the *Walpole Society*, vol. xxvii, 1938–1939.]   M. R. TOYNBEE.

FIRTH, SIR CHARLES HARDING (1857–1936), historian, was born at Sheffield 16 March 1857, the eldest son of John Firth, of Abbeydale, Sheffield, by his second wife, Charlotte Harding. John Firth, who had been trained as an architect, belonged to the great steel-making firm of Thomas Firth & Sons, of which his brother Mark Firth [q.v.] was the head. In 1870 Charles's mother was living at Clifton and he entered Clifton College as a day-boy. Here he came under the influence of Thomas William Dunn, afterwards headmaster of Bath College, to whom, as he wrote many years later, he owed 'a greater debt than to any other man'. When Dunn opened a boarding-house in the school, Firth became the head of it. Dunn not only taught him accuracy and thoroughness but impressed on him for life Carlyle's gospel of work. He won a copy of Carlyle's *Cromwell* as a school prize. The headmaster, John Percival [q.v.], recommended him to try for a classical scholarship at one of the smaller Oxford colleges, where competition was less keen than at the larger; but he preferred to enter New College as a commoner and to read modern history. In the next year, 1876, on being elected to a Brackenbury scholarship, he migrated to Balliol College. Here he knew as undergraduates a number of men who afterwards became distinguished scholars, and with several of them, notably R. L. Poole, T. F. Tout, W. P. Ker, and S. L. (Sir Sidney) Lee [qq.v.], he began lifelong friendships. The most important influence on his education was that of William Stubbs [q.v.], then regius professor of modern history, five of whose courses of lectures he attended. In 1877 he won the Stanhope essay prize and in 1878 obtained a first class in modern history.

After taking his degree Firth spent some months in Hanover improving his German; subsequently he seldom went abroad and never for more than a few weeks. For a time he lectured at his uncle's foundation, Firth College, in Sheffield, and he had thoughts of giving expression in local politics to a radicalism which he did not retain in middle age. In

1883 he settled in Oxford, to live there for the rest of his life. He was already married, and it was partly for this reason that he did not as yet become a fellow of any college: at that time most of the fellowships still carried with them an obligation to reside within the college walls. Another Balliol man said later that Firth had three disadvantages, bad health, a private income, and a special subject, and this unhandsome remark hit off some of the reasons for his unusual career. He was slightly lame, and so could not take vigorous exercise; asthma often kept him indoors in the winter. His means, which in later life were considerable, enabled him to acquire a magnificent library, kept from 1902 in the house which he built at 2 Northmoor Road. It was preponderantly a collection on the English seventeenth century. His interest centred in this period partly because it was the heroic age of the 'Puritan' business class from which he came and partly through the influence of S. R. Gardiner [q.v.], whose history had been carried down to the outbreak of the Civil war when Firth returned to Oxford. Firth was an insatiable reader, not only of history and historical novels, but of everything that had human interest, and he had an extremely good memory. He gave Gardiner much assistance in his work and occupied himself for about twenty years with editions, articles, and monographs within the same field. He soon developed the characteristics of his mature studies: he delighted and excelled in the handling of historical evidence, and especially in identifying the sources of historical works; he had a fine appreciation of literature, including popular writings, such as ballads. Although always attracted most by the history of action, particularly military and naval affairs, travel and colonization, he had more interest and a better judgement than Gardiner in social and economic matters. He acquired a great knowledge of historical portraits and neglected no branch of genealogical or biographical research. His style was severely restrained, but on occasion his intense sympathy with some great idea would force it into eloquence. Narrower than Gardiner in his command of languages and of continental history, and less apt to relate his immediate subjects to their wider context, he surpassed his master in decisiveness and in the construction of narrative.

In the 'eighties and 'nineties Firth edited a number of texts, of which the most important are the *Memoirs of the Life of Colonel Hutchinson* (1885), the *Life of William Cavendish, Duke of Newcastle* (1886), the *Memoirs of Edmund Ludlow* (2 vols., 1894), and the *Clarke Papers* (4 vols., 1891–1901), the last a new authority of great value. He sometimes annotated so heavily that he used up an amount of learning which would have sufficed for an independent work; but these studies perfected his method. From the third volume, published in 1885, he was a contributor to this DICTIONARY, for which he wrote altogether about 225 lives, nearly all of the seventeenth century. He was also one of the most active of the group of scholars who launched the *English Historical Review* in 1886. In 1900 his *Oliver Cromwell* made him known to a wide reading public and in 1902 he published his admirable volume *Cromwell's Army*. That was the year of Gardiner's death, and in accordance with his wish Firth carried on his great history from the point which it had reached, the summer of 1656, to the death of Oliver Cromwell two years later.

The two volumes of this continuation (*The Last Years of the Protectorate*), which did not appear until 1909, are Firth's best work. He intended to go further, to the Restoration and indeed all through the reign of Charles II, but these plans were never carried out. The intense application of earlier years had perhaps encroached on his staying-power, and the university made increasing claims on his time. From 1883 he had never been without teaching work in Oxford: from 1887 to 1893 he was history lecturer at Pembroke College. In 1900–1901 he was Ford's lecturer, his lectures being the substance of *Cromwell's Army*, and in the next year he succeeded Gardiner as a research fellow of All Souls. When another of his friends, Frederick York Powell, died in 1904 the prime minister, A. J. Balfour, recommended him for appointment as regius professor of modern history. He held this office, which carried with it a fellowship at Oriel, until 1925. In his inaugural lecture he gave an impressive account of the historian's science and art, and he announced a programme for training historians in the use of original authorities. For a generation past there had been a divergence between the 'professorial' point of view and the practice of the teachers of history in the colleges, whose main concern was with a general education, fitting men for any liberal pursuit and tested by the examinations for honours. Most of the college teachers signed a printed reply to the inaugural lecture, and this controversy began a series of disappointments for Firth. He did not enjoy lecturing; he chose limited and sometimes exacting subjects, and his audiences were small. The regulations for the 'research degrees' of B.Litt. (from 1895) and D.Phil. (1917) gave effect to some of his ideas, and he made some progress in providing graduates with instruction in historical method. He persuaded the faculty of modern history to modify the honours examinations, for instance by allowing candidates to submit 'theses', but his criticisms of the system as testing mainly facility and memory were without effect. In some other faculties he found happier co-operation than in his own. From its foundation in 1894 he had been active in building up the honour school of English language and literature; he worked for the establishment of a school of medieval and modern languages, and took part in the lively controversies over the Taylor Institution. The study of geography and the education of women were also among his good causes. He thus sat on many university boards and committees, and he wrote many pamphlets and leaflets, some of them historical *opuscula* of permanent value.

Outside Oxford Firth held a good many appointments, some mainly honorific but others burdensome. From 1910 to 1919 he was a valuable member of the royal commission on the public records, and in 1913 of the Admiralty committee on the battle of Trafalgar. He served as president of the Royal Historical Society (1913–1917) and twice (as first president 1906–1910 and again 1918–1920) of the Historical Association, of which he was a founder. He was a trustee of the National Portrait Gallery from 1908 to 1929 and a member of the Historical Manuscripts Commission.

Firth's only other substantial book in these later years was *The House of Lords during the Civil War* (1910). In 1913–1915 he published a reprint of the text of Macaulay's *History of England*, very fully illustrated, the best example of his great knowledge of portraits and engravings. He continued to write many articles and to edit many documents, extending his range in time from the sixteenth century to the nineteenth. He gave more advice and encouragement to other writers than any other English historian of his day: innumerable prefaces acknowledge his generosity to British, American, and con-

tinental writers, whether beginners or experts. *A Bibliography of the Writings of Sir Charles Firth*, his own work, was published in 1928 and is very nearly complete to that date. In the remaining years of his life he published a pamphlet on *Modern Languages at Oxford, 1724–1929* (1929) and articles in the *English Historical Review*, the *Proceedings* of the British Academy, *History*, and the *Review of English Studies*. Mr. Godfrey Davies, the most intimate of his younger friends, edited three posthumous works, in the last of which he had more than an editorial part: *A Commentary on Macaulay's History of England* (1938); *Essays Historical and Literary* (reprinted pieces, 1938); and *The Regimental History of Cromwell's Army* (2 vols., 1940).

Firth's many honours included doctorates from the universities of Aberdeen, Durham, Cambridge, Sheffield, Manchester, and Oxford, and a knighthood, conferred in 1922. He was elected a fellow of the British Academy in 1903. In 1925 he resigned his chair and was elected an honorary fellow of Oriel; after that he worked quietly in his library, except for a brief but severe illness in 1929, until within a few days of his death at Oxford 19 February 1936. He married in 1880 Frances, daughter of Henry Ashington, vicar of Anwick with Brauncewell, Lincolnshire. She and their only child, a son, survived him. His most important manuscripts and printed books were presented to the Bodleian Library.

The most characteristic likeness of Firth is the photograph reproduced in the *Oriel Record* for June 1936. He was of middle height, a prosperous-looking man, rather heavily built and slow-moving, with a well-trimmed beard and moustache, his expression sometimes thoughtful and in conversation often kindly humorous. He smoked large pipes and many cigarettes. Very much at home in the common rooms of Oriel and All Souls, he enjoyed conversation, speaking slowly, simply, and quietly, and contributing both wit and common sense. He was reticent about himself and his own affairs and seldom expansive, but he had and communicated a sense of immovable confidence. He was completely loyal to his friends and to his side in any contention. He gave money generously to institutions and to people in need, often doing his alms in secret. In later life he had no religious beliefs. Having no liking for speculative thought, and considering how often minds are at the mercy of physiological processes or external accidents, he resigned himself to a kind of materialism; but he lived up to an austere standard of duty.

[*The Times*, 20 and 22 February 1936; G. N. Clark in *English Historical Review*, April 1936; E. S. de Beer in *History*, June 1936; P[ercy] S[impson] in *Oriel Record*, June 1936; Godfrey Davies, *Charles Harding Firth, 1857–1936* in *Proceedings* of the British Academy, vol. xxii, 1936; *Thomas William Dunn, A Memoir* (privately printed), 1934; personal knowledge.]   G. N. CLARK.

FISHER, HERBERT ALBERT LAURENS (1865–1940), historian, statesman, and warden of New College, Oxford, was born in London 21 March 1865, the eldest son of Herbert William Fisher, by his wife, Mary Louisa, daughter of John Jackson, M.D., of the East India Company's service, the leading English physician in Calcutta. One of his younger brothers was Admiral Sir W. W. Fisher [q.v.]. Through his mother he was a first cousin of W. W. Vaughan [q.v.]. His parents were both people of rare culture. His father was by profession a barrister, but when a student of Christ Church, Oxford, he had been tutor to Albert Edward, Prince of Wales, and afterwards was for many years his private secretary. In later life, by gift of the Prince as Duke of Cornwall, he accepted the ancient office of vice-warden of the Stannaries of which he was the last holder. His mother, a daughter of the fourth of the beautiful Pattle sisters, had been the model for the heroine in G. F. Watts's picture of 'Una and the Red Cross Knight'. Fisher was educated at Winchester, where he was (1878–1884) a commoner and took many prizes, and at New College, Oxford, of which he was a scholar. He obtained a first class in classical moderations (1886) and in *literae humaniores* (1888), and was elected a fellow of his college in the latter year.

Fisher was a first-class scholar in pure classics, and his chief interest as a young man was in ancient history, but, under the impression, soon to be strikingly falsified, that ancient history was by that time a closed field, with nothing much more to be discovered, he turned to modern history. It was that subject which Fisher went on to study at the universities of Paris and of Göttingen. He returned particularly impressed by the historical methods of Paris, ranging from the intense technical accomplishment of the École des Chartes to the wide and humane genius of Taine and Renan. The field of the Oxford school of modern history is alarmingly large, and

Fisher felt bound to prepare carefully every period that any pupil might choose to take. At the same time he managed to find leisure for writing. His first work, more difficult perhaps than rewarding, was the revision for a new edition (1892) of *The History of France* by George William Kitchin [q.v.]; this was followed in 1898 by a study of *The Medieval Empire*. Meantime, he was working his way towards that intimate knowledge of the non-military side of the Napoleonic system for which he was afterwards famous. *Studies in Napoleonic Statesmanship: Germany* (1903) was followed by *Bonapartism* (1908), *The Republican Tradition in Europe* (his Lowell lectures at Boston, U.S.A., delivered 1910, published 1911), *Political Unions* (1911), and *Napoleon* in the 'Home University Library' series (1913), which has been described by a French writer as the best short life of Napoleon in any language. Fisher contributed Volume v (1485–1547) to Longman's *Political History of England* (1906). His sketch of his brother-in-law, Professor Frederic William Maitland [q.v.], published in 1910, showed for the first time his special gifts as a biographer. This was followed by an edition (3 vols., 1911) of *The Collected Papers* of Maitland, whose lectures on *The Constitutional History of England* he had already edited in 1908.

In 1912 came an interruption to writing through calls to two more urgent tasks. He was appointed a member of the royal commission on the public services in India, which occupied much of his time until the publication of the Report of the commission in 1917, and he was elected vice-chancellor of the university of Sheffield, where he took up residence in the spring of 1914. The change from intellectual to administrative work came as a rest and refreshment. The university was a new one. The college out of which it grew had been chiefly known for its departments of applied science, metallurgy, and mining, but in 1905 it received a royal charter and was inaugurated with four faculties: arts, pure science, medicine, and applied science. As with most of the provincial universities, much ground had to be made up on the arts side; this, of course, was work for which Fisher was admirably fitted, but he never attempted to redress the balance to the detriment of applied science; on the contrary, he set himself to encourage the application of science to industry. He set up a University Scientific Advisory Committee the function of which was to put manufacturers into communication with scientific and expert opinion. Further, he sponsored the formation in the university of a delegacy for the promotion of research in glass technology, an enterprise which bore abundant fruit. It may be said that he regarded the university as a sort of central power station of the intellectual life of its diocese. A tactful and ready speaker, Fisher soon won respect and popularity in the city of Sheffield as well as in the university. He continued to encourage greater co-operation between the scientific and literary departments of the university, when the nature of the problems before him was changed by the outbreak of the European war in August 1914. He acted at once with the lord mayor and the master cutler in the great work of getting the cutlery industries adapted to the needs of the war. For instance, when a demand arose for iron helmets, objects practically unknown since the seventeenth century, a Sheffield manufacturer whom he had approached said, 'Helmets? Well, I make dish-covers. It is the same idea.' And helmets were duly made.

In the midst of these activities Fisher was suddenly invited by Lloyd George in December 1916 to join his ministry as president of the Board of Education, and without further preparation (he was returned unopposed at a by-election as liberal member of parliament for the Hallam division of Sheffield) entered the House of Commons as a minister. He seemed instantly at home. He knew his subject; he had always been a keen and well-informed politician; he could take on the work of a Cabinet minister as easily as that of a vice-chancellor. His maiden speech in the House (19 April 1917) was actually on the education estimates and occupied a full two hours. Fisher had remarkable collaborators in the Board at that time, some of whom, like (Sir) E. K. Chambers and J. W. Mackail, are better known for their independent literary work than for their services in a government office. He worked hard at visiting schools and getting to know the various parts of the vast educational machine of which he had not had experience. He was impressed by the great scope given by the British system to originality and experiment. Of the London elementary schools he once said that there was more difference between the worst and the best of them than there was between the best of them and Eton or Winchester. He encouraged the enlightened tendencies of the Board when brought into danger by the war-fever. The Board under his guidance refused to consider that to forbid the teaching of German was a useful form of patriotism; nor was it convinced of the educational value to little boys of the decapitation of sparrows. But, of course, he will be chiefly remembered for his Education Act.

One of the paradoxes of war-time is that a nation, just when it is most hard pressed for money, is often more ready to undertake expensive reforms than in periods of peace and prosperity. In 1916 this country had suddenly realized the deficiencies of its national education, and Fisher made skilful use of the opportunity. He succeeded in introducing a system of percentage grants, by which three-fifths of the salary expenditure on teachers was to be found by the Board of Education and only two-fifths by the locality. By this scheme the average salary of the elementary teacher was doubled, and later on the provision for pensions was greatly increased. For the secondary schools also he provided some improvement in salary and pension, and made easier the path to the university by the establishment of a system of state scholarships and by special grants for advanced courses. He also succeeded in substituting for the fifty-five separate entrance examinations which gave access to as many different black-coated occupations a single general examination, the School Certificate, accepted by all.

Among the schemes of progress laid up in the pigeon-holes of the Board there were two noticeable tendencies. Was it better simply to raise the universal age of education up to fifteen, or to provide part-time continuation schools up to eighteen? The former plan looked attractively democratic and equalitarian; but Fisher unhesitatingly supported the latter. A grave flaw in the British system, he considered, was that after enjoying the whole-time care of conscientious teachers up to fourteen, a boy was at that age suddenly flung loose into industry, with little care for his conduct and no provision for his intellectual interests. Up to fourteen nothing but education; after fourteen no education at all. Surely, he argued, what was needed was a more gradual shading off; a provision of some continued chance of studying the subjects, not necessarily technical, in which a boy takes an interest, and some continued association with teachers whom he has learnt to like and respect. This part of the Fisher Act, for reasons over which its author had no control, was never put into force. It involved expense; it called for a great additional number of teachers; various other post-war difficulties stood in its way. But it remains on the Statute Book, and had a preponderant guiding influence on the Butler Act of 1944.

Fisher remained in the Cabinet until the fall of Lloyd George's government in 1922, and kept his seat, which he had held since 1918, in the House of Commons as national liberal member for the Combined English Universities until 1926. When there was a question of his becoming a professor of history, he considered that he was not up to date in his reading. Perhaps he did not realize that his experience of public affairs more than compensated for that deficiency. There are already signs of this in the *Studies in History and Politics* and the essay *An International Experiment*, published in 1920 and 1921 respectively. He took part in the 'International Experiment' as a British delegate to the Assembly of the League of Nations for two years (1920–1922).

There is no doubt that Fisher took naturally to practical politics. He had long enjoyed the friendship of many leading statesmen, particularly those of specially intellectual leanings, such as Morley, Rosebery, Balfour, and Asquith; Lloyd George was of a different type, but Fisher fell rapidly under the charm of his lively genius, and an affectionate intimacy between the two men remained until Fisher's death. When after six years as minister and four as a private member he became warden of his old college and retired from the House, he could not help casting sometimes a 'longing, lingering look behind' towards that 'pleasing anxious being' which he had enjoyed so long in parliament. An historian cannot but be fascinated by seeing the processes by which history is made and taking an occasional hand in making it. It was as an historian that he was elected a fellow of the British Academy in 1907. He served on the council from 1915 to 1918 and again from 1927 to 1928, and was president from 1928 to 1932. He gave only one presidential address, on leaving office in 1932; but his Raleigh lecture in 1928 on *The Whig Historians* began with a section on the work of the Academy in that year.

Although principally an historian, Fisher had a remarkably full knowledge of the progress of all the various studies which are called 'humane', the sort of knowledge that beseemed the president of the British Academy and was often tested in the editor of the 'Home University Library'. He understood foreign nations. He could well have been a great ambassador, like Bryce, or a distinguished governor-general, like Tweedsmuir. The same genuine understanding of human nature gives value to his biographies of Bryce (*James Bryce*, 2 vols., 1927) and Vinogradoff (*Paul Vinogradoff. A Memoir*, 1927).

These wider interests did not distract Fisher from his duties as warden. His knowledge of the larger world made him a stimulating friend and a useful guide to undergraduates. His rebuke to one who, without being exactly vicious, was wasting his time, deserves to be quoted as a model. 'Mr. X, there are forty-two applicants who have had to be refused a place in the college; I think some of them would make better use of it than you.'

Besides various lectures, such as those on *The Whig Historians* and *The Common Weal* (1924), Fisher wrote during these years *Our New Religion* (1929), a study of Christian Science and the life of its founder, Mrs. Eddy. Seldom can destructive criticism have been delivered with greater urbanity. A piece of fancy, perhaps the most brilliant of the series, is his contribution to the collection called *If it had Happened Otherwise* (edited J. C. Squire, 1931), on the theme 'If Napoleon had escaped to America'. He had the happiness to be working efficiently up to the end of his life, and his last serious work, the *History of Europe* (3 vols., 1935), is not only his longest but, by common consent, his best. It is particularly interesting in two ways; for one thing, he writes, especially in the modern period, as one who has practical knowledge of the workings of governments; for another, his book seems to be a definitive utterance of a certain philosophy or faith, of which a later chaotic generation largely lost hold: the spirit of liberalism among forms of thought, of Great Britain among nations, of the nineteenth century among the ages.

Fisher was appointed a member of the Order of Merit in 1937. He was elected a fellow of the Royal Society in 1920 and was a trustee of the British Museum. Honorary degrees were conferred upon him by the universities of Edinburgh (1913), Sheffield (1918), Manchester (1919), Cambridge (1920), Liverpool (1928), and Oxford (1929). But among all his academic honours, of none was he prouder than of his admission in 1937 into the very small band of British historians who were honorary members of the Massachusetts Historical Society. In the same year he was elected an honorary corresponding member of the American Academy of Arts and Letters.

Fisher married in 1899 Lettice, eldest daughter of Sir Courtenay Peregrine Ilbert [q.v.], parliamentary draftsman, and had one daughter. He died in London 18 April 1940, after having been run down several days previously by a lorry while on his way to preside at the appeal tribunal on conscientious objectors to military service.

A portrait of Fisher by William Nicholson hangs in the hall of New College, and a drawing, better as a likeness, by Frances Catherine Dodgson (Mrs. Campbell Dodgson) in the smoking room of the senior common room. A bust (not very satisfactory) in bronze adorns the Milner room at the College. The most characteristic portraits are two photographs, the one taken in his study at New College and forming the frontispiece to the British Academy memoir; the other (at New College) a transparency in colour.

[*The Times*, 19 April 1940; *Oxford Magazine*, 2 May 1940; Gilbert Murray, *Herbert Albert Laurens Fisher, 1865–1940* in *Proceedings* of the British Academy, vol. xxvi, 1940; H. A. L. Fisher, *An Unfinished Autobiography*, 1940; David Ogg, *Herbert Fisher, 1865–1940. A Short Biography*, 1947; H. W. B. Joseph in *New College Record*, 1939–1940; personal knowledge.]   GILBERT MURRAY.

FISHER, ROBERT HOWIE (1861–1934), Scottish divine, was born at Kilmarnock 27 April 1861, the elder son of Matthew Fisher, then minister of Deerness, Orkney, and later minister of Cross and Burness, Orkney, by his second wife, Elizabeth Cunningham, daughter of George Chalmers, of Kilmarnock. Both parents came of good Ayrshire ancestry. Robert Fisher received his early education from a local 'dominie' to whom he later paid high tribute; he was a pupil at George Watson's College, Edinburgh, for only two years; at Edinburgh University his lack of early preparation handicapped his career, but did not prevent him from graduating in 1884 as the first man of his year in divinity. In 1885 he was ordained minister of Skelmorlie, Ayrshire, and was thence successively translated to Jedburgh (1890); the west church of St. Nicholas, Aberdeen (1896); Morningside, Edinburgh

(1900); and St. Cuthbert's parish church, Edinburgh (1914). He was appointed chaplain in ordinary to the king in 1913, and was university lecturer on pastoral theology from 1911 to 1914 and on apologetics from 1913 to 1916. He was Baird lecturer in 1922, and his lectures were published in 1924 under the title of *Religious Experience*. Although he was nominated in the last-named year to the moderatorship of the General Assembly, ill health, which caused him to resign his charge in 1925, prevented his acceptance of this high post. He retired to Oxford where he died 2 November 1934.

It was once said of Fisher that had he chosen the law instead of the ministry for his profession, he might have risen to the highest judicial office. As it was, he came to be one of the most prominent personalities in the Church of Scotland of his day, and in many respects his position was unique. His sermons, delivered in a voice of exceptional beauty, were illumined by wide knowledge of literature, glowed with ethical passion, and were inspired by a belief that the doctrines of the Christian faith could be presented to the modern mind without doing despite to the just demands of reason. Laying great store on visiting his parishioners, he gained the affection of the poor; and what provided the salt of life was an inexhaustible fund of wit and humour. He was also the author of books on *The Four Gospels* (1899) and *The Beatitudes* (1912).

Fisher's most notable service to the Church of Scotland was his editorship, from 1902 to 1925, of its official magazine, *Life and Work*. He was an ideal editor. His vivid style and keen sense of what was interesting made *Life and Work* the leading religious organ in Scotland, and in the two pages of 'Notes and Comments' which he always contributed, he anticipated features conspicuous in modern journalism. Less conspicuous, but hardly less important, was his contribution in the Church Union Committee which brought about the union of the Church of Scotland with the United Free Church in 1929. His very incisive mind helped to solve difficulties and in the course of twenty years of negotiation he never failed to pour oil on troubled waters. Reunion lay very near to his heart, and he would have gladly welcomed an even wider union, had that been feasible, for while he set a great value on history, he was strongly convinced that the Church should not be the slave of its history, and the episcopate would not have been a difficulty to him.

Fisher was twice married: first, in 1886 to Margaret Ada (died 1899), daughter of Robert Hutchison, of Carlowrie, Kirkliston, West Lothian, and had a son, now Professor M. G. Fisher, K.C., and two daughters; secondly, in 1906 to Edith Mary, daughter of Robert Strathern, W.S., and widow of William Percival Lindsay, W.S.

[*Scotsman*, 3 November 1934; R. H. Fisher, *The Outside of the Inside: Reminiscences*, 1919; private information; personal knowledge.]

NORMAN MACLEAN.

FISHER, SIR WILLIAM WORDSWORTH (1875–1937), admiral, was born at Blatchington Court, Seaford, 26 March 1875, the fifth son and eighth child of Herbert William Fisher, vice-warden of the Stannaries. His eldest brother was H. A. L. Fisher [q.v.]. He entered the training ship *Britannia* in July 1888. As midshipman he served on the Cape of Good Hope station for three years, in the *Raleigh*, flagship, which often made the longer passages under sail alone.

As sub-lieutenant (1894) and later as lieutenant (1896), Fisher served in the Mediterranean before qualifying as a gunnery lieutenant in 1900. The next year he joined the *Canopus* in the Mediterranean Fleet. He was already recognized by his contemporaries as a man of great ability and outstanding character, possessing exceptional talents as a leader of men. In 1903 he was appointed a senior staff officer at Whale Island, but having left after a disagreement with Captain (Sir) P. M. Scott [q.v.], he was appointed to the *King Edward VII*, flagship, in January 1905 at the request of the commander-in-chief of the Atlantic Fleet, Vice-Admiral Sir W. H. May [q.v.]. He took a prominent share in the renaissance of scientific naval gunnery then in progress; he was promoted commander in June 1906, at the age of thirty-one, and joined the *Albemarle*, flagship of the rear-admiral of the Atlantic Fleet, as executive officer. Before he joined, her ship's company were slack and discontented, but the new commander in the space of a few months brought about a great improvement and he earned glowing reports from his captain, R. F. Scott [q.v.], later of Antarctic fame, and from both the rear-admiral and the commander-in-chief. In 1908 he was executive officer of the *Indomitable* when she took the Prince of Wales to Canada,

and he was appointed M.V.O. on completion of the voyage. In May 1909 he became flag commander, in the *Dreadnought*, to Admiral May, commander-in-chief of the Home Fleet, a position principally concerned with the gunnery of the fleet but also involving close study of naval tactics, to the development of which the commander-in-chief devoted much of the work of the Home Fleet during his two years in command. Fisher accompanied the admiral when he left the fleet to become commander-in-chief at Plymouth; and was promoted to captain in 1912.

Five months later Fisher was appointed to command the battleship *St. Vincent* in the Home Fleet, then flagship of Rear-Admiral (Sir) S. A. Gough-Calthorpe [q.v.]; he remained in her for four and a half years. By the time war broke out in 1914 he had brought the *St. Vincent* to the highest pitch of efficiency, and moreover was able to maintain the morale of his ship's company at high pitch even in the somewhat depressing conditions which the strategic situation imposed on the Grand Fleet. The *St. Vincent*, which ceased to be a flagship in 1916, was in the battle of Jutland. In May 1917, six months after Sir John Jellicoe [q.v.] left the fleet to become first sea lord, Fisher was called to the Admiralty as director of the recently formed anti-submarine division, in succession to Rear-Admiral A. L. Duff [q.v.], a position which he held with marked distinction up to the end of the war, earning golden opinions from all, civilian men of science who were called in at his suggestion, as well as British and American naval officers. His great share of the credit for the final defeat of the U-boat campaign was recognized by the dedication to him of Sir Henry Newbolt's unofficial *Naval History of the War, 1914–1918* (1920).

In April 1919 Fisher returned to the sea in command of the *Iron Duke*, flagship of the Mediterranean Fleet, and in August 1919, when the new commander-in-chief, Admiral Sir John De Robeck [q.v.], arrived, Fisher became his chief of staff with the rank of commodore, 2nd class. Throughout the troubled times in the Near East he was De Robeck's right-hand man and a particularly valued counsellor in a situation which was never free from problems and difficulties. In 1922 De Robeck transferred from the Mediterranean to the Atlantic Fleet and Fisher continued as his chief of staff, first with the rank of commodore, 1st class and, from November

1922, as rear-admiral. When De Robeck hauled down his flag in 1924 Fisher was appointed rear-admiral in the first battle squadron (flag in the *Barham*) and returned once more to the Mediterranean for an uneventful year.

In August 1926 Fisher was appointed director of Naval Intelligence; but the following April he joined the Board of Admiralty as fourth sea lord. It was promotion in status, but the work was not to his taste and he was delighted when he was translated in 1928 to the even more responsible post, also with a seat on the Board, of deputy chief of the Naval Staff. He had become a vice-admiral three months earlier, and in his new office was directly concerned with naval policy on the highest plane. It was a difficult period for the sea lords, under successive governments committed to disarmament and naval limitation. Fisher was much exercised regarding the moral and constitutional obligations of the sea lords in such a situation, and what action it was their duty to take if their professional judgement regarding standards of security should be overruled on political grounds.

Fortunately, reductions were not pressed beyond those which Fisher felt that he could conscientiously accept. To him, and to the divisions of the Naval Staff working under him, fell the tasks of working out the voluminous technical details involved in the negotiations for the Naval Treaty of London (1930) and of marshalling the strategical arguments against any over-drastic limitations urged for political ends. That the treaty was not more crippling than it proved to be when published, his brother officers attributed chiefly to Fisher's able advocacy.

In the autumn of 1930 Fisher was appointed vice-admiral commanding the first battle squadron (flag in the *Revenge* and the *Resolution*) and second-in-command of the Mediterranean Fleet. That appointment was something of a disappointment to him, since a deputy chief of the Naval Staff could usually expect to become a commander-in-chief on resuming sea service; but he gave no sign of it, and no commander-in-chief could have had a more loyal lieutenant than Admiral Sir Alfred Ernle Montacute (afterwards Lord) Chatfield had in him for the next year and a half. Together they devoted much attention to anti-aircraft gunnery and to the hitherto neglected problems of night fighting between heavy ships. He was now able to exercise to the full his talent for leadership, in a wider sphere than hitherto. That quality stood him, and the ships of the battle squadron under his command, in good stead in 1931, when cuts in naval pay led to the mutiny in the Home Fleet at Invergordon in September. That there was no similar breakdown in the morale or discipline of the Mediterranean Fleet was due in no small measure to Fisher's personal influence on all those under his command.

In July 1932 Fisher was promoted admiral and the following October, after six months unemployed at home, he took over the Mediterranean command from Chatfield (flag in the *Resolution* and later the *Queen Elizabeth*). Within three weeks he was able to say that he had seen practically every officer and man under his command; and within a year he had visited almost every part of his station. He continued the series of exercises and experiments in night fighting begun under his predecessor, and was able to demonstrate the progress achieved in that important province in a spectacular manner in the combined fleet exercises of 1934. His work in that respect bore valuable fruit in the battle of Cape Matapan, fought four years after his death. Wherever he went, whatever country he visited round the Mediterranean, he was received with every honour and left with the friendship and appreciation of all. An example of his talents in this direction was furnished by the affection, born of his insight, understanding, and sympathy, with which he was regarded by the people of Malta, and of one small Maltese village in particular.

In the summer of 1935 Fisher brought the Mediterranean Fleet home for the jubilee review at Spithead, at which he was the senior admiral afloat. Returning to his station after those ceremonies he soon found himself immersed in more serious events, for the Italo-Abyssinian war made it necessary to assemble in the Eastern Mediterranean under his command practically the whole of the Royal Navy outside the Home Fleet. This great fleet had to be concentrated at Alexandria and maintained for months on end in instant readiness for attack, with few if any opportunities for relaxation or recreation for the greatly increased numbers of officers and men, and at first no organized facilities for such alleviations. That the morale and spirit of all men of the fleet remained of the highest was due in great measure to the example, wise conduct, and unrivalled personal influence of Fisher as commander-in-chief, an influence which was even enhanced by the personal tragedy which overtook him at the height of the crisis by the death in a flying accident of his elder son.

It was not until the end of March 1936 that tension had relaxed enough for the government to authorize a change of commander-in-chief. Fisher turned over the command to Admiral Sir Dudley Pound and after only three and a half months' rest was appointed commander-in-chief at Portsmouth. He was a tired man by then and the coronation celebrations in the following May, with another Spithead review, threw an even greater strain upon him. A month later, taking the salute at a King's Birthday parade on Southsea Common, he collapsed from fatigue before it was over. A few days later, 24 June 1937, he died in London and was buried at sea with full naval honours.

Fisher was appointed C.B. in 1918, C.V.O. in 1924, K.C.B. in 1929, and G.C.B. and G.C.V.O. in 1935. He married in 1907 Cecilia, youngest daughter of Francis Warre Warre-Cornish [q.v.], and had two sons and two daughters.

Fisher was one of the most eminent sailors of his day; and if it had fallen to him in time of war to command a fleet or conduct naval operations from the Admiralty, it cannot be doubted that he would have shone as brilliantly as he did in command of his battleship in 1914–1917, or of the Mediterranean Fleet in the crisis of 1935–1936. He stood out not only by great ability but chiefly because of his deep sympathy with, and understanding of, his fellow men in all degrees of life; and his great qualities in that respect were born largely of his wide interests in learning, art, and culture outside the limits of his chosen, and well-loved, profession.

[*The Times*, 26 June 1937; Sir William James, *Admiral Sir William Fisher*, 1943; Admiralty records; private information; personal knowledge.]　　　H. G. THURSFIELD.

FITZMAURICE, BARON (1846–1935). [See PETTY-FITZMAURICE, EDMOND GEORGE.]

FITZPATRICK, SIR (JAMES) PERCY (1862–1931), South African statesman and author, was born at King William's Town, Cape Colony, 24 July 1862, the eldest son of James Coleman FitzPatrick, judge of the Supreme Court, Cape Colony, who came from Nenagh, co. Tipperary, by his wife,

Jenny, daughter of Peter FitzGerald, of Soho House, co. Westmeath. He was educated in England at St. Gregory's College, Downside, near Bath, until 1878, when his father's death recalled him, at the age of sixteen, to the Cape, where in 1880 he entered the service of the Standard Bank of South Africa. To one of his temperament the life soon became irksome and in 1884 he moved to Barberton in the Transvaal, then the principal gold-field, working there first as a storekeeper's assistant and later as a transport-rider and editor of a weekly journal. Barberton, however, was soon eclipsed by the new gold-fields on the Witwatersrand and FitzPatrick moved there in 1889. Two years later he organized the journey made by Lord Randolph Churchill [q.v.] through Bechuanaland and Mashonaland. He then (1892) joined the firm of Hermann Eckstein & company, taking charge of the intelligence department and becoming a partner in 1898. He retired in 1907.

The Uitlander agitation against President Kruger's government was now increasing and FitzPatrick was appointed honorary secretary of the 'reform committee', often acting as intermediary between it and Cecil Rhodes and L. S. Jameson [qq.v.] in Cape Town. *The Transvaal from Within*, a book which greatly influenced public opinion, was a product of his intimate knowledge of events at this period. After the Jameson Raid FitzPatrick was arrested together with the other members of the committee and was sentenced to two years' imprisonment and a fine of £2,000; but he was released in May 1896 on condition of neither directly nor indirectly intermeddling in the politics of the South African Republic for three years. This ban prevented any publication of *The Transvaal from Within* before September 1899. As soon as it had been lifted Fitz-Patrick worked to promote a settlement and played a part in bringing about the conference at Bloemfontein between Sir Alfred Milner [q.v.] and President Kruger (31 May 1899). He was in England when war was declared in October and he remained there for some time as an extra official adviser on South African affairs to the British government. Returning to the Transvaal when Milner had set up his administration FitzPatrick became an unofficial member of the legislative council and of the inter-colonial council responsible for the control of the central South African railways. He continued his connexion with the mining industry, becoming president of the Witwatersrand Chamber of Mines (1902) and a leading supporter of the temporary introduction of Chinese labour.

In the general election of 1907 which followed on the grant of responsible government to the Transvaal FitzPatrick was returned as 'progressive' candidate for south-central Pretoria, defeating Sir Richard Solomon [q.v.] in a memorable contest. He actively promoted the movement for the union of the four South African Colonies, was a member of the Transvaal delegation to the National Convention of 1908–1909 which drew up the South Africa Act of 1909, and made with General J. B. M. Hertzog the settlement on the dual language question which it effected. With union accomplished (1910) he boldly advocated 'a fresh start' in politics and the formation of a 'best man' government to bury the old racial antagonisms. But General Louis Botha [q.v.] formed the first Union Cabinet on party lines and himself stood against FitzPatrick in Pretoria East. Again a memorable contest ended in FitzPatrick's victory, and he held the seat in the Union parliament until 1920. However, the war of 1914–1918 effected that conjunction of the moderate men of both sections which he had proposed.

After the war FitzPatrick travelled abroad, visiting Mexico and California in order to study methods of citrus culture. In France he carried through the purchase of the Delville Wood as a memorial to the South Africans who had given their lives in the war and presented the site as a free gift to the nation. To him also is due the initiation of the two minutes' silence observed on Armistice Day. His last years were largely devoted to developing the Cape Sunday's River Valley as an irrigation and citrus-growing settlement. Here he lived on his farm Amanzi at Uitenhage where every Armistice Day a charge of dynamite was fired as the signal for the two minutes' silence, and where he died after a long illness 25 January 1931. He married in 1889 Elizabeth Lillian (died 1923), daughter of John Cubitt, of Pretoria, and had three sons, all of whom died before him, and one daughter. He was knighted in 1902 and appointed K.C.M.G. in 1911.

FitzPatrick will be well remembered as a short-story writer and as a raconteur of his experiences as a transport-rider and of his wide knowledge of veld lore. His *Jock of the Bushveld* (1907), a classic of its kind, followed *Through Mashonaland with Pick and Pen* (1892) and *The Outspan* (1897). His *South African Memories*, published in 1932, after his death, is prefaced by a short biography.

[*The Times*, 26 January 1931; Biographical Introduction to Sir J. P. FitzPatrick, *South African Memories*, 1932; personal knowledge.]

H. A. WYNDHAM.

FLEMING, DAVID HAY (1849–1931), historian, antiquary, and critic, was born at St. Andrews 9 May 1849, the third and youngest son of John Fleming, china and stone-ware merchant, of St. Andrews, who came of Deeside ancestry, by his wife, Ann, daughter of David Hay, whose forebears belonged to St. Andrews. Educated at Madras College, St. Andrews, he entered the family business, but an early taste for history was fostered by examination of the civic records, and by the successful prosecution of his mother's claim upon an estate in Chancery. The business was sold in 1883, and he gave himself to the study of history.

In 1885 Fleming married Robina Agnes, daughter of James Hart, of St. Andrews, and for the next twenty years he remained there. A series of learned essays on the history of the burgh gave him a reputation more than local, but, although much of his work was embodied in the *Alphabetic Guide Book to St. Andrews* (1881) which (as the *Handbook*) went through six further editions, much also is preserved only in pamphlets and in contributions to the local press. His knowledge of the antiquities of St. Andrews was profound, and his last book, *St. Andrews Cathedral Museum* (1931), describes an institution which he had done much to foster. Fleming's main interest was in ecclesiastical history. He was baptized into the Free Church of Scotland, but in 1899 he and his wife joined the Original Seceders: he ruled his life according to the strict practice of these Churches and thought it his duty to justify their tenets upon historical grounds. In 1891 a review in the *Original Secession Magazine* caught the eye of (Sir) William Robertson Nicoll [q.v.], and thereafter Fleming's contributions to the *British Weekly* and *The Bookman* made him known to a wide public as the champion of the Scottish Reformation and of the Covenanters. He transcribed and edited for the Scottish History Society the *Register of the Ministers, Elders and Deacons of the Christian Congregation of St.*

Andrews . . . 1559–1600 (2 vols., 1889–1890), and in 1901 produced a valuable edition of Patrick Walker's *Six Saints of the Covenant*. Meanwhile, his *Mary, Queen of Scots, from her Birth to her Flight into England* (1897), concise in narrative but enriched with admirable notes, had firmly established his reputation. To Andrew Lang he became 'my friend and constant trouncer'.

In 1905 Fleming moved to Edinburgh, where he became an active member of various learned societies. In 1907 he delivered at Princeton Theological Seminary the Stone lectures which were published in 1910 as *The Reformation in Scotland: Causes, Characteristics, Consequences*, a work of great importance. He edited vol. ii (1529–1542) of the *Register of the Privy Seal of Scotland* (1921), and, although the hoped-for continuation of *Mary, Queen of Scots* and a life of John Knox never appeared, he produced pamphlets for the Knox Club and a steady stream of articles and reviews of which only some are collected in *Critical Reviews relating chiefly to Scotland* (1912).

Fleming died in Edinburgh 7 November 1931. His wife died in 1909; they had no children. He bequeathed to the city of St. Andrews the residue of his estate for the foundation and maintenance of a public reference library of which his own great collection of books should be the core. He wrote, deliberately and frankly, in defence of Protestant principles as he understood them. Some of his criticism was acerb and provocative, but he was personally courteous and all his work is marked by deep learning, sound scholarship, and accurate documentation. His rigid sabbatarianism did not prevent him from being a good raconteur. In his youth he was a bold horseman, and rode on his own horse over the hills to visit his kinsfolk on Deeside. His contribution to Scottish history is of great value.

[H. M. Paton, *David Hay Fleming. Historian and Antiquary* (portraits and bibliography), 1934; personal knowledge.]

J. D. MACKIE.

FLETCHER, CHARLES ROBERT LESLIE (1857–1934), historian, was born in London 22 October 1857, the only child of Alexander Pearson Fletcher, assurance company general manager, by his wife, Caroline Anna, daughter of the painter Charles Robert Leslie [q.v.] and sister of Sir Bradford Leslie [q.v.]. He was a king's scholar at Eton (1868–1876) arriv-ing, according to legend, in an Aberdeen version of an Eton jacket which had to be promptly discarded. In 1876 he went as a demy to Magdalen College, Oxford, obtained a first class in modern history in 1880, and won the chancellor's English essay prize and was elected a fellow of All Souls in 1881.

From 1889 to 1906 Fletcher was fellow and tutor of Magdalen College. In that capacity he was one of a small group comprising A. L. Smith [q.v.], A. H. Johnson, Edward Armstrong [q.v.], and (Sir) Richard Lodge [q.v.] which built up the history school at Oxford. As a tutor and lecturer he was extremely stimulating. He was also unconventional in his methods and never concealed his strong views: he was a fierce Protestant Anglican, a confirmed tory, a 'red-hot free-trader', and, although kind enough to individual women students, an anti-feminist opposed to women having degrees. He was the founder at Magdalen of the undergraduates' history library which he ruled with a rod of iron. In 1905 he became a delegate of the Clarendon Press and was perpetual delegate from 1912 to 1927, and until his death he took a lively interest in everything connected with it—its authors, its staff, its workpeople. His main activity was in the promotion and criticism of books on modern history, and his acute and sympathetic comments were of great value, especially to young writers.

In 1914–1915 and again from 1917 to 1919 Fletcher went back to Eton to help in the teaching of history. He was an inspiring influence there. In 1915, at the age of fifty-seven, he joined the R.N.V.R. for anti-aircraft duties in London, but an attack of lumbago consequent on scrubbing a floor put an end to this enterprise. He died at his Oxford home 30 April 1934. In 1885 he married Alice Katharine (died 1939), elder daughter of W. W. Merry [q.v.], rector of Lincoln College, Oxford, and had three sons, the two younger of whom were killed in the war of 1914–1918.

Fletcher's published works include biographies of *Gustavus Adolphus* (1890) and *Edmond Warre* (1922); an annotated edition of Carlyle's *French Revolution* (3 vols., 1902), containing a mass of information not easily obtainable elsewhere; *Historical Portraits* (in collaboration with Mr. H. B. Butler and (Sir) Emery Walker [q.v.], 1909–1919); *A School History of England* (in collaboration with Rudyard Kipling [q.v.], 1911); and, most popular of all, *An Introductory History of England* (5 vols.,

1904–1923), with its famous description of the 'manor of Tubney'. The unconventional, conversational style of this work, which at the time of its publication seemed 'very strange' to the orthodox, set a fashion for some subsequent writers of popular history. His intimate friends knew him as a racy, original, sparkling letter-writer; a glimpse of this he gave to the public in a collection of letters entitled *Mr. Gladstone at Oxford 1890* (1908), a Boswellized account of the statesman's conversation.

[*Oxford Magazine*, 10 May 1934; private information; personal knowledge.]

C. H. K. MARTEN.

FLETCHER, SIR WALTER MORLEY (1873–1933), physiologist and administrator, was born at Liverpool 21 July 1873, the sixth and youngest son of Alfred Evans Fletcher, by his wife, Sarah Elizabeth, daughter of Richard Morley, of Leeds, and a cousin of the politician and philanthropist Samuel Morley [q.v.] and of H. H. Asquith. Both parents were from Yorkshire, independently minded Congregationalists, who sought to imbue all their ten children with a religious love of beauty and a desire for service to mankind. The father had gained high distinction as a student of chemistry at University College, London, and after being inspector of alkali works under the Local Government Board in Liverpool ultimately became chief inspector in London.

Fletcher went in 1891 from University College School, London, to Trinity College, Cambridge, with a sub-sizarship to study physiology and with the auxiliary aim of medical qualification. His rapidly maturing strength of mind and body soon brought him success and friendships in every aspect of university life, whether intellectual, social, or athletic. Tall and splendidly built, he was fast over the hurdles and a powerful hammer-thrower. His quick attractiveness of manner, his vivid enjoyment of all forms of artistic beauty, and his eager interest in the thoughts of others made men glad to give him their lasting friendship. He obtained first classes in both parts of the natural sciences tripos (1894, 1895); and he was Coutts Trotter student in 1896 and Walsingham medallist in 1897. As the years passed it seemed that he might find all that his spirit desired by remaining at Trinity and working in the physiological laboratories under (Sir) Michael Foster [q.v.].

Election into a fellowship of his college in 1897 was followed by a tutorship from 1905 to 1914; and administrative work for Trinity and the university, with all its human interests, progressively absorbed fully as large a share of Fletcher's mind as did his laboratory research in physiology. But the latter was very fruitful. He had chosen the problems of the 'respiration' of frog's muscle, using an apparatus recently devised by the botanist Mr. Frederick Frost Blackman for measuring the gaseous exchange of leaves. This enabled Fletcher to trace the discharge of small quantities of carbon dioxide during successive brief intervals of time, instead of simply measuring such accumulated end results as had alone been accessible to previous workers. He proved that there is no sudden discharge of carbon dioxide on the contraction of an isolated muscle, and that the main discharge occurs during the phases of recovery of power. This result was opposed to all the accepted teaching of the time. The next step, in collaboration with (Sir) Frederick Gowland Hopkins, was to measure the cycle of changes in lactic acid during and after contraction, and to relate them also to the output of carbon dioxide and the muscle's ability for work. The entire group of experiments has been recognized as classical, because it laid the foundation of the modern ideas of cellular activity that look on much of its material intake and output as never being raised to high levels of biochemical complexity but as being used by the living cell protoplasm in relatively simple ways which are thereby individually accessible to analysis. Fletcher was elected F.R.S. in 1915, and was Croonian lecturer of the society in the same year. At intervals during the earlier years of his researches he had travelled daily to St. Bartholomew's Hospital in London, and so completed in 1900 the medical training that equipped him for the wider tasks of public service to which he was ultimately called.

When the Medical Research Committee was created in 1913 by Lloyd George under the National Insurance Act of 1911, it was essential for its success that the right man should be chosen as its secretary. The selection in 1914 of Fletcher for this new post in London proved to be an ideal appointment, and all his inmost aims quickly found their complete satisfaction in the great hope of guiding scientific work so that it might give its fullest aid for bettering the health of the people. On the outbreak of war the resources of the committee were largely diverted towards help for the services, and the speed with which Fletcher found himself free for action in arranging such work, combined with his policy of friendly co-operation rather than of intrusiveness, soon proved the value of an organization which could, without official delays, concentrate scientific workers upon any urgent problem. The authority of the new committee became recognized everywhere, and Fletcher's services were acknowledged by the award of the K.B.E. in 1918. Civilian problems in the meantime were not neglected and the proof, obtained by work which the committee had promoted during the war, that rickets is a deficiency disease, fully preventable by better feeding, seized Fletcher's imagination and made him eager for the rest of his life to study and plan for improvements in human nutrition.

In 1920 Fletcher saw an important change effected whereby the committee, renamed the Medical Research Council, was freed from any control by the Ministry of Health and placed under the Privy Council with a charter of its own and direct financial support from the Treasury. Its future was now secure, and that position together with its high reputation was undoubtedly due in the main to Fletcher's administrative skill, his ardent enthusiasm, and his wise use of the scientific talent in Great Britain which hitherto had lacked concentration upon problems in medicine.

Fletcher's personal aid became sought in work apart from that of the council. From 1919 to 1922 he was a member of the royal commission on the universities of Oxford and Cambridge. The buildings of the biochemical laboratories at Oxford and Cambridge and of the School of Hygiene and Tropical Medicine in London, together with endowments for the medical sciences in these and other places, were in large measure due to the confidence placed in his advice by the Sir William Dunn trustees and the Rockefeller Foundation. In 1928 he travelled to India as chairman of the Indian government committee for the organization there of medical research, and his visit was followed by the gift in memory of Lady Tata, the wife of Sir Dorabji Tata [q.v.], of £250,000 for research upon leukaemia. He was appointed C.B. in 1929. He received honorary degrees from the universities of Oxford, Leeds, Glasgow, Birmingham, Edinburgh, and Pennsylvania.

In 1904 Fletcher married Mary Frances,

second daughter of Charles James Cropper, of Ellergreen, Kendal; she was great-great-granddaughter of the philanthropist James Cropper [q.v.] and niece of Sydney Holland, second Viscount Knutsford [q.v.]. They had one son and one daughter.

During the war incessant overwork had resulted in a serious attack of pneumonia in the winter of 1915–1916: Fletcher recovered slowly with a damaged lung, and from this came occasional bouts of ill health and at last the sudden infection that, shortly before he had completed his sixtieth year, prematurely ended the life of a man whose long-lived ancestry and personal strength had seemed to promise the fullest span, rich with many further years of excellent service. He died in London 7 June 1933, and was buried at Cambridge.

A posthumous bronze bust of Fletcher by Miss Dora Clarke is in the library of the National Institute for Medical Research, London.

[*The Times*, 8 June 1933; *Nature*, 1 July 1933; *Cambridge Review*, 13 October 1933; *Obituary Notices of Fellows of the Royal Society*, No. 2, December 1933 (portrait); personal knowledge.]   T. R. ELLIOTT.

FORBES-ROBERTSON, SIR JOHNSTON (1853–1937), actor. [See ROBERTSON.]

FORD, FORD MADOX (1873–1939), author and critic, was registered at birth as FORD HERMANN HUEFFER, but adopted the additional Christian names of Joseph Leopold Madox, and in 1919 changed his surname by deed poll to Ford. He was born at Merton, Surrey, 17 December 1873, the elder son of Francis Hueffer [q.v.], by his wife, Catherine, younger daughter of the artist Ford Madox Brown [q.v.]. A noted musical critic, Francis Hueffer came to London from Germany in 1869 and was later naturalized. Mrs. Hueffer's artist sister, Emma Lucy [see ROSSETTI, LUCY MADOX] married W. M. Rossetti [q.v.]. The Hueffers were thus closely connected with the pre-Raphaelite movement.

Hueffer was educated at a private school at Folkestone and at University College School. In 1892 he published a fairy-story entitled *The Brown Owl*, following this with books on *Ford Madox Brown* (1896) and *Rossetti* (1902), and also with essays, poems, and novels, the best known being the historical trilogy *The Fifth Queen* (1906), *Privy Seal* (1907), *The Fifth Queen*

Crowned (1908), and the modern novel *The Good Soldier*, which was not published until 1915. He collaborated with Joseph Conrad [q.v.] in the writing of three books, including *Romance* (1903).

In 1908 Hueffer founded the *English Review*, a periodical of remarkably high literary standard, the contributors to which included such writers as Hardy, Henry James, H. G. Wells, and Galsworthy. Financial difficulties, however, forced Hueffer to sell the *Review* at the end of a year.

In 1894 Hueffer married Elsie (died 1949), daughter of William Martindale, analytical chemist, of London. Two daughters were born of the marriage. In 1910 an order was made against Hueffer for restitution of conjugal rights, and in 1931 Mrs. Hueffer sued the *Throne* newspaper for having described Miss Violet Hunt as 'Mrs. Ford Madox Hueffer'. Judgement was given for the plaintiff and the case, which attracted much publicity, had an unhappy effect upon Hueffer's reputation.

From 1915 to 1919 Hueffer held a commission in the Welch Regiment and saw active service in France, where he was severely gassed. After the war he took up farming in Sussex, but in 1922 he moved to France and the next year settled in Paris, where he became the centre of a group of young authors such as Ezra Pound and Ernest Hemingway, whose work appeared in the *Transatlantic Review*, founded by Ford in 1924. The remainder of his life was divided between Paris, Provence, and the United States of America, where in 1937 he was appointed lecturer in comparative literature at Olivet College, Michigan, and was given the honorary degree of doctor of letters. He died at Deauville, France, 26 June 1939.

Ford was a fine stylist and the series of books written round the character called Tietjens (*Some Do Not*, 1924, *No More Parades*, 1925, *A Man Could Stand Up*, 1926, *Last Post*, 1928) rank among the best novels of the war of 1914–1918. He will be remembered also for his gift of detecting talent in others and for the criticism and encouragement which he gave to two generations of writers.

A portrait of Ford by Janice Biala is in the possession of the dean of Olivet College.

[*The Times*, 27 June 1939; Douglas Goldring, *South Lodge* (containing a bibliography of Ford's writings), 1943, and *The Last of the Pre-Raphaelites: The Life of Ford Madox Ford*, 1948; Stella Bowen, *Drawn from Life*, 1940;

Violet Hunt, *The Flurried Years*, 1926; F. M. Ford, *Thus to Revisit*, 1921, *Return to Yesterday, Reminiscences 1894–1914*, 1931, and *It was the Nightingale*, 1934; S. J. Kunitz and H. Haycraft, *Twentieth Century Authors, a Biographical Dictionary* (New York), 1942.]

GEORGINA BATTISCOMBE.

FORTESCUE, SIR JOHN WILLIAM (1859–1933), military historian, was born in Madeira 28 December 1859, the fifth son of Hugh Fortescue, third Earl Fortescue, by his wife, Georgiana Augusta Charlotte Caroline, eldest daughter of Colonel George Lionel Dawson-Damer, third son of John Dawson-Damer, first Earl of Portarlington. He was descended from Chief Justice Sir John Fortescue [q.v.]. Brought up in country surroundings at Castle Hill, near Barnstaple, he developed a great love of country life and pursuits with a countryman's eye for ground, which stood him in good stead in explaining the battlefields which he described. He was educated at Harrow under H. M. Butler [q.v.], to whose love of English literature he owed much. Short sight curtailed his athletic activities, besides debarring him from a military career; he therefore entered Trinity College, Cambridge, in 1878, intending to read for the bar, but, finding the law uncongenial, in 1880 became private secretary to Sir William Robinson, governor of the Windward Islands; two years in the West Indies aroused his interest in their history and connexion with the army.

After completing his degree at Cambridge Fortescue spent four years in New Zealand (1886–1890) as private secretary to the governor, Sir William Jervois [q.v.], during which he began writing and had several articles accepted by *Macmillan's Magazine*. This led to his contributing a volume on *Dundonald* to Macmillan's 'English Men of Action' series (1896), which was preceded in 1895 by a history of his elder brother Lionel's regiment, the 17th Lancers. Messrs. Macmillan then commissioned him to write a popular one-volume history of the British army. Finding it impossible to do justice to his subject in so brief a compass he obtained the publishers' assent to a more ambitious venture in four volumes. The first two (1899), which reached 1713 and 1763, were at once recognized as a really authoritative contribution to the subject, but when a third (1903) and a fourth (1906) only reached 1792 and 1802 it became evident that the work must extend far beyond the limits contemplated. Finally thirteen volumes appeared, the last (continuing to 1870) in 1930. Few historians have ventured on so large a project, still less accomplished it single-handed.

A work on such a scale, copiously provided with elaborate maps, could not be remunerative and Fortescue would not have been able to complete it had not King Edward VII in 1905 appointed him librarian at Windsor Castle. This post, which he held until 1926, although it involved the rearrangement and care not only of the books but of the pictures and other collections, enabled him to carry on his history, which owed much to the encouragement of the King and his successor. As king's librarian he accompanied the King and Queen to India in 1911 for the coronation durbar, of which he wrote the official account (1912). He was appointed C.V.O. in 1917 and K.C.V.O. in 1926. He was elected an honorary fellow of Trinity College, Cambridge, in 1920, received honorary degrees from the universities of Oxford and Edinburgh, and was awarded the Chesney gold medal of the Royal United Service Institution. He delivered the Ford lectures (1911), published the same year as *British Statesmen of the Great War, 1793–1814*, and the Romanes lecture (1929) at Oxford, and the Lees-Knowles lectures at Cambridge (1914).

Fortescue published many works besides the *History of the British Army*. He edited six volumes of the *Correspondence of King George the Third* (1927–1928) and seven volumes (the first with W. N. Sainsbury, q.v.) of the *Calendar of State Papers, Colonial Series, America and West Indies*, covering the years 1677 to 1698 (1896–1905). His *County Lieutenancies and the Army, 1803–1814* (1909), a short life of *Wellington* (1925), perhaps the least unsatisfactory of the biographies of the Duke, and many other volumes were offshoots of his main work. The *Story of a Red Deer* (1897), written for a nephew of nine years old, shows him in a very different light and is probably his most widely read work.

In 1916 Fortescue undertook a history of the war which was then in progress; based on official sources, it was to be of an interim character, mainly for the general public. He entered upon the work reluctantly, finding it hard to switch from the Peninsula period to the very different conditions, ideas, and methods of 1914, with which he was less familiar, and he was not sorry to be relieved of the task.

Fortescue was an excellent lecturer with a good presence and delivery. He was among the few Ford lecturers at Oxford to attract and retain a large undergraduate audience. He wrote vigorously, lucidly, and graphically. He visited every battlefield which he could reach, and could grasp and explain their important features. He was indefatigable in research and no future writer on British military history will be able to neglect 'Fortescue'. He provided a basis on which others have built and illuminated many obscure corners. He held very definite views and never hesitated to express them, sometimes rather more forcibly than the evidence warranted. He had his share of foibles and preferences and it is easy to find fault with details, but his work remains one of solid and permanent value, one of the really big achievements of his generation.

Fortescue married in 1914 Winifred, elder surviving daughter of Howard Beech, rector of Barlavington, Sussex. Herself something of a writer, her *Perfume from Provence* (1935) contains some very attractive sketches of Provençal life, written with real insight and humour. He died without issue at Cannes 22 October 1933.

[*The Times*, 23 October 1933; Sir John Fortescue, *Author and Curator*, 1933; personal knowledge.]   C. T. ATKINSON.

FOSTER, SIR GEORGE EULAS (1847–1931), Canadian statesman, was born of United Empire Loyalist stock on a farm in the parish of Wakefield, Carleton County, New Brunswick, 3 September 1847, the second son and seventh child of John Foster, of Apohaqui, New Brunswick, whose ancestors came originally from Northumberland. His mother was Margaret, daughter of Eulas Heine, of Pennsylvanian Dutch descent. He was educated at the common and superior schools of King's County and at the university of New Brunswick; he chose teaching as his first profession and in 1871 was appointed to the chair of classical literature and history in the university of New Brunswick; but before taking up this appointment he studied at the universities of Edinburgh (1872–1873) and Heidelberg (1873). But his zeal for temperance reform, which never abated, led him to resign his professorship in 1879 and become a professional lecturer for this cause.

Foster's success in this role led to his election in 1882 as member for King's County to the federal parliament as an independent conservative, and he made his mark so rapidly as a first-rate parliamentarian that Sir J. A. Macdonald [q.v.], having won his steady allegiance, made him minister of marine and fisheries in 1885 when he was sworn of the Canadian Privy Council, and promoted him in 1888 to the Ministry of Finance. The chances which he had of succeeding to the leadership of the conservative party were prejudiced by his first marriage. In 1896 he retired from the ministry and from the constituency of King's County and at the ensuing general election was returned for York County, New Brunswick.

Excluded from parliament by the loss of his seat when he stood for St. John City in 1900, Foster became engaged in financial business and made a platform campaign in Great Britain to support Joseph Chamberlain's crusade for tariff reform and imperial preference. He stood unsuccessfully at a by-election for North Ontario in 1903, but was restored to the front opposition bench at Ottawa as member for North Toronto in 1904; he became its most brilliant debater, and when his party returned to power in 1911 he was appointed minister of trade and commerce, a post which he held until 1921. He played a considerable part in the campaign for founding the Dominion Bureau of Statistics and the National Research Council and served on a royal commission on imperial trade which investigated the resources of the British Empire. During the war of 1914-1918 he rendered invaluable services as the right-hand man of Sir Robert Borden [q.v.]; he served on the Canadian delegation at the Paris Peace Conference (1919) and represented Canada at the first Assembly of the League of Nations (1920) when he was elected vice-president; he also attended the seventh (1926) and ninth (1929) assemblies. He retired in 1921 to a seat in the senate, where he remained a very influential figure until his death at Ottawa 30 December 1931.

A conservative of the Right and an ardent Imperialist during most of his career, Foster became in its closing stages an equally ardent internationalist and on many domestic issues moved to a position of advanced liberalism. He had a better intellectual equipment for politics than most of his Canadian contemporaries, but, great as his services were, they fell short of fulfilling the high promise of his early career. He was never known to make a poor speech and could always gain a hearing, although his academic cast of mind

and his social aloofness were barriers to his personal popularity. He was appointed K.C.M.G. in 1914 and G.C.M.G. in 1918, and in 1916 he was sworn of the Privy Council of Great Britain. He received the honorary degree of D.C.L. from Acadia University (1885) and of LL.D. from the universities of New Brunswick (1894), Queen's, Kingston (1914), and Edinburgh (1920). His *Canadian Addresses*, edited by Arnold Winterbotham, were published in 1914, followed in 1927 by *Citizenship: The Josiah Wood lectures, 1926.*

Foster was twice married: first, in 1889 to Adeline (died 1919), eldest daughter of Milton Davies, banker, of Hamilton, Ontario, and formerly wife of Daniel Black Chisholm, barrister; secondly, in 1920 to Jessie (died 1947), daughter of Sir William Allan, of Gateshead. There were no children of either marriage.

A portrait of Foster by Eyre Macklin (1926) was in the possession of his widow.

[*The Times*, 31 December 1931; W. Stewart Wallace, *The Memoirs of the Rt. Hon. Sir George Foster*, 1933; *Encyclopædia of Canada*, 1935; Augustus Bridle, *Sons of Canada* (with drawing by F. S. Challoner), 1916; *Canadian Men and Women of the Time*, 2nd ed. 1912; *A Cyclopædia of Canadian Biography*, 1886; *Who's Who in Canada*, 1930; personal knowledge.]   JOHN A. STEVENSON.

FOSTER, SIR (THOMAS) GREGORY, first baronet, of Bloomsbury (1866-1931), provost of University College, London, and educationist, was born in London 10 June 1866, the eldest son of Thomas Gregory Foster, barrister, of Clapham and Lincoln's Inn, by his wife, Sophie, daughter of John Farquhar Allday, of Birmingham. He was educated at University College School, and at University College, London, where he graduated with honours in English language and literature (1888). In 1892 he was awarded the degree of Ph.D. by Strasburg University for a thesis on the Old English poem *Judith* (published in the same year). He was a sound philologist, and taught for the English department at University College, first as Quain student (1894-1899), and then as assistant professor (1900-1904). He was also professor of English language and literature at Bedford College for Women, London, between 1897 and 1900.

Foster found his true sphere as an administrator in 1900, when he was appointed secretary to University College. In 1904 he was elected principal: a title which, in 1907, on the occasion of the college becoming an 'incorporated college' of London University, was changed to provost. His appointment came at a difficult time. The university of London had at last become a true university instead of a glorified examining body. The colleges and schools had as yet but little sense of unity and co-operation. There were jealousies and rivalries among them, while there was continual friction between the external and the internal sides of the university. Foster during his long term of office (1904–1929) steered the college with wisdom, vigilance, and courage through all these difficulties. Many important new departments of study were established; the college buildings were increased threefold; and the number of students was trebled. It would be difficult to overrate the part which he played in this development. He may well be regarded as the second founder of the college. His last years of office were clouded by ill health and pain, but he was able, nevertheless, to take an active part in the celebration of the college centenary in 1926 and, just before his retirement in 1929, he was elected vice-chancellor of London University, an office which he filled with dignity and success (1928–1930). He died in London 24 September 1931.

Foster was knighted in 1917 and created a baronet in 1930. He was twice married: first, in 1894 to Fanny Maude (died 1928), daughter of James Sledge, of Hove, by whom he had two sons and two daughters; secondly, in March 1931 to Elise Johanna Emma (died October 1931), daughter of George Peter William Augener. He was succeeded as second baronet by his elder son, Thomas Saxby Gregory (born 1899). A portrait by Sir William Orpen, which was presented to him on his retirement, is in the possession of University College, London.

[The Times, 25 September 1931; personal knowledge.]   H. E. BUTLER.

FOTHERINGHAM, JOHN KNIGHT (1874–1936), historian and authority on ancient astronomy, was born 14 August 1874 at Tottenham, Middlesex, the second son of David Fotheringham, minister of St. John's Presbyterian church, Tottenham, who came of a Forfarshire family, by his wife, Jane, daughter of George Ross, master of the Lancastrian School at Tottenham. Always delicate, he was fortunate in a devout and cultured home, and in his education at the City of London School and at Merton College, Oxford, of which latter he was an exhibitioner. He obtained a second class in classical moderations (1894) and a first class in *literae humaniores* (1896) and in modern history (1897), and was a senior demy of Magdalen College from 1898 to 1902. In 1903 he married Mary Eleanor, daughter of Joseph Atkinson, of Crosby Garrett, Westmorland, who shared his studies, and survived him. There were no children of the marriage.

For a man so learned and self-contained, life was not easy. Fotheringham taught first classics (1904–1909), then ancient history (1909–1912), at King's College, London, and he held a readership in ancient history in London University from 1912 to 1920, living sometimes at Oxford, sometimes at Muswell Hill. His first publications were articles on 'The Formation of the Julian Calendar' and 'The Date of the Crucifixion', both contributed to vol. xxix of the *Journal of Philology* (1903). He completed volume xi (1801–1837) of Longman's *Political History of England* (1906), begun by G. C. Brodrick [q.v.], and collaborated with Mr. Laurence Frederic Rushbrook Williams in a life of *Marco Sanudo* (1915).

But Fotheringham's lifework was done in ancient astronomy and chronology: *The Bodleian Manuscript of Jerome's Version of the Chronicle of Eusebius* (1905) gained him the degree of D.Litt. of Oxford University (1908); and the critical edition *Eusebii Pamphili Chronica Canones latine vertit, adauxit, ad sua tempora produxit S. Eusebius Hieronymus* (1923), completed with the help of a fellowship at Magdalen, which he held from 1909 to 1916, established the text, form, and appearance of this difficult work, and the respective shares in it of Eusebius and Jerome.

In 1918, when war had suspended his London work, Fotheringham accepted a small post under H. H. Turner [q.v.] in the University Observatory at Oxford, and undertook for S. H. Langdon [q.v.] the astronomical interpretation of the Assyrian 'Table of the Movements of the Planet Venus and their Influences'. With help from a German astronomer, Carl Schoch, he corrected the calculations of F. X. Kugler (*Sternkunde und Sterndienst in Babel, 1907–1924*) and published with Langdon and Schoch *The Venus Tablets of Ammizaduga* (1928), which established the chronology of the Babylonian dynasties. But as the movements of Venus recur in cycles, subsequent archaeological research by Dr. Sidney Smith (*Alalakh and Chronology*, 1940) has transferred Babylonian events to a later cycle than that accepted by Langdon, without prejudice to the calculations of Fotheringham and Schoch. Another astronomical discovery—the secular acceleration of the sun and of the moon, and the irregular movements known as 'trepidation'—although repeatedly recorded by Fotheringham, was still imperfectly published at his death.

After failing to become Radcliffe observer at Oxford in 1924, Fotheringham was next year elected to a readership of ancient astronomy and chronology, which was specially created for him, and he was appointed an honorary assistant at the University Observatory. He lectured regularly and dealt punctiliously with a wide range of inquiries. In 1932 he unsuccessfully sought election to the Savilian chair of astronomy, vacant since the death of Turner in 1930, and submitted a review of the position of astronomical research at Oxford, with proposals for future studies. In 1933 he was elected a fellow of the British Academy. He died at his home on Cumnor Hill 12 December 1936, and was buried in the Presbyterian cemetery at Aston Tirrold, Berkshire.

Fotheringham's deep and varied knowledge, fine scholarship, and kindly temperament made him 'a very lovable man', devout and loyal to his Presbyterian training.

[*The Times*, 14 December 1936; J. L. Myres, *John Knight Fotheringham, 1874–1936* in *Proceedings* of the British Academy, vol. xxiii, 1937; *Isis*, vol. xxvii, 1937 (bibliography and portrait); *Archeion*, vol. xix, 1937; private information; personal knowledge.]

JOHN L. MYRES.

FOWLER, ALFRED (1868–1940), astrophysicist, was born at Wilsden, Yorkshire, 22 March 1868, the youngest child and seventh son of Hiram Fowler, by his wife, Eliza Hill. About 1876 the family removed to Keighley, where Alfred attended various schools and later the Trade and Grammar School. In 1882 he proceeded, with the aid of a Devonshire exhibition, to the Normal School of Science (later absorbed into the Imperial College of Science and Technology) at South Kensington, where he gained a first class diploma in mechanics and was enabled to continue his studies through an appointment as 'teacher in training'. His first duties were those of an assistant to (Sir) J. N. Lockyer [q.v.] who in 1879 had set up his Solar Physics Observatory at South Kensington and was conducting astronomical research there in close association with spectrographic work at the college. Thus at the beginning Fowler saw astronomy and spectroscopy as two aspects of a single subject, and his subsequent work was controlled by this view.

Fowler remained with Lockyer (from 1888 onwards as demonstrator in astronomical physics) until the latter's retirement from the college in 1901, when he became assistant professor of physics and assumed charge of the astronomical work. In 1915 he was appointed professor of astrophysics and in 1923 one of the first Yarrow research professors of the Royal Society [see YARROW, SIR ALFRED]. He continued to work at the college, however, although without undergraduate teaching responsibilities, until his retirement in 1934. He died at Ealing 24 June 1940. In 1892 he married Isabella, daughter of John Orr, a designer of dress materials, and had a son and a daughter.

During Fowler's association with Lockyer his work was merged in that of the elder man. Together they amassed much data on the successive spectra emitted by the elements as the exciting stimulus was intensified, a manifestation, in Lockyer's view, of the step-by-step dissociation of the elements into simpler forms. The idea was unpopular, however, and only when Niels Bohr's theory of spectra appeared in 1913 was its essential truth realized. On the astronomical side the outstanding work was the study of the sun's atmosphere during total eclipses, and Fowler went with the British government expeditions of 1893, 1896, 1898, 1900, 1905, and 1914 to various parts of the world for this purpose.

From 1901 onwards Fowler worked on his own responsibility, and a series of papers appeared recording the identification of previously unknown celestial spectra with spectra obtained in the laboratory from sources which he succeeded with marked ability in distinguishing. Among other achievements the absorption bands in the spectra of the red stars were traced to titanium oxide, the bands in the spectra of comets' tails to low pressure carbon monoxide, certain bands in sunspot spectra to magnesium hydride, and the absorption at the shorter wave-length end of celestial spectra to ozone in the earth's atmosphere. Of especial importance was the laboratory production of the spectrum then attributed to 'cosmic hydrogen' and now to ionized helium: this proved of great value in establishing the Bohr theory of spectra.

As that theory developed, Fowler's almost unrivalled knowledge of spectra became of increasing importance, and he displayed a natural ability in classifying spectrum lines comparable with his skill in identifying them.

Fowler played an active part in the administrative work of science, and he was largely responsible for the organization of the International Astronomical Union (founded in 1919), of which he was the first secretary. He was highly successful also as a director of research, and several distinguished men are numbered among his pupils. He was appointed C.B.E. in 1935 and was elected F.R.S. in 1910. He was president of Section A of the British Association in 1926, of the Royal Astronomical Society from 1919 to 1921, and of the Institute of Physics from 1935 to 1937. His numerous other distinctions included honorary degrees from the universities of Bristol, Cambridge, Durham, and Leeds, the Bakerian lecturership of the Royal Society (1914 and 1924), the gold medal of the Royal Astronomical Society (1915), and a Royal medal of the Royal Society (1918).

[*The Times*, 25 June 1940; *Obituary Notices of Fellows of the Royal Society*, No. 9, January 1941 (portrait); personal knowledge.]

HERBERT DINGLE.

FOWLER, HENRY WATSON (1858–1933), lexicographer, was born 10 March 1858 at Tonbridge, where his father, the Rev. Robert Fowler, fellow of Christ's College, Cambridge, from 1854 to 1856, was an assistant master. Robert Fowler was the son of a 'gentleman', so at least he is described in his marriage certificate, to the hearty amusement of the man who has rendered the word 'genteelism' notorious. The elder Henry Fowler was, in fact, a master-carpenter or builder at Buckfastleigh, Devon. The same certificate describes Humphry Watson, the father of the bride, Caroline, as 'yeoman'; he was tenant of the extensive farm buildings at Dartington Hall, near Totnes. Robert Fowler, after four years (1856–1860) at Tonbridge, set up on his own account as a very successful 'military tutor' at Tunbridge Wells. Henry was the eldest of seven sons and one daughter. From his father's death in 1879 he bore the main responsibility for the family. He had gone up to Oxford in 1877 with a senior exhibition from Rugby and a scholarship at Balliol College. He obtained a second class in classical moderations (1878) and in

literae humaniores (1881), but in consequence of his failure to pass the qualifying divinity examination, he took his actual B.A. degree at the same time as his M.A. in 1886.

After a brief temporary mastership at Fettes, Fowler became in 1882 an assistant master at Sedbergh under H. G. Hart who, like himself, had in his day been head of the school house at Rugby, and now strove among the Yorkshire fells to maintain the healthy tradition of Thomas Arnold and Frederick Temple [qq.v.]. He chose his masters with great care and set them a noble example: of these, two of the best were Henry Fowler and his brother Arthur John Fowler.

In term-time, Henry worked steadily for ten hours a day, Sundays included. In the holidays he commonly went to Norway or Switzerland, for he was an excellent walker, climber, skater, and football player. This lasted for seventeen years of unshaken friendship, but then came an irreconcilable difference of principle: Hart held it a strict rule that housemasters should prepare their boys for confirmation, and Fowler's conscience would not allow this. The painful interchange of letters which ensued does equal honour to both men, and the personal friendship remained unbroken. Fowler retired, in 1899, to a hermit's life in London. To a friend, who urged upon him a line of historical research for which his mind and attainments seemed especially fitted, he replied emphatically, 'No, my dear fellow, I'm not going to do anything useful again!' He enjoyed his new freedom in the quiet, remote Paulton's Square, Chelsea. He read voraciously and wrote literary essays, which, collected into volumes, remained always his favourite work (*More Popular Fallacies*, 1904; *Si Mihi–!*, 1907, republished in 1929 as *If Wishes were Horses*; *Between Boy and Man*, 1908; and *Some Comparative Values*, written at this period but not published until 1929).

Fowler's essays in periodical form brought in a steady average of £30 a year; he had his patrimony of £120, neither increased nor diminished by the seventeen years of schoolmastering; and out of this he spared financial help to his landlady, whose husband was an invalid. But he found his true vocation at last under encouragement from the Oxford University Press. In 1905, in conjunction with his brother Francis George Fowler (1870–1918), scholar of Peterhouse, Cambridge, who had obtained a first class in the classical tripos of 1892, he produced a four-volume translation of Lucian, which was well received by reviewers and public. This success paved the way for *The King's English* (1906). The brothers were next engaged by the Oxford University Press to produce an abridgement of the *Oxford Dictionary*, which appeared in 1911 as the *Concise Oxford Dictionary of Current English*. After the outbreak of war in 1914, Henry, who had already belonged to the Inns of Court Volunteers, *splendide mendax*, subtracted thirteen years from his actual age when in 1915 he joined the Sportsmen's battalion as a private of 'forty-four'. Frank, at forty-five, followed his example. Henry's wonderful physique carried him through the training and into the trenches where he was once under fire but fired no shot himself. A crippling attack of gout invalided him in May 1916. Frank also was invalided, and died in 1918 of a consumption probably contracted in the army.

Henry had married in 1908, on his fiftieth birthday, Jessie Marian, daughter of Richard Sydenham Wills; she, aged forty-six, was head of a nursing home in Guernsey, where Henry had gone to live with Frank in 1903. It was an ideal union in spite of picturesque and dramatic contrasts, which he crystallized later in a little volume of poems, *Rhymes of Darby to Joan* (1931). He and Frank, in earlier years of collaboration, had led as bachelors a scholarly life of Spartan regularity; and now Henry lived the same life *à deux*, first at Moulin de Haut near St. Peter Port in Guernsey and then in an equally charming cottage at Hinton St. George, Somerset. He was now in regular employment on different branches of the great *Oxford English Dictionary*; the *Pocket Oxford Dictionary of Current English* appeared in 1924. Side by side with this, he compiled a *Dictionary of Modern English Usage* (1926), a companion volume to *The King's English*, and his most original work. After a few years his wife developed cancer, which gradually defied medical skill and made heavy demands upon his affection: but he bore the double burden unflinchingly. Her death (October 1930) left him with energies noticeably diminished. He gave up his swim before breakfast and his run in all seasons and weathers. He had already lost one eye for some years past and now the other began to fail very seriously. Yet he struggled on with his work, experience making up to some extent for waning strength, until an attack

of influenza, unconfessed for ten days, turned to pneumonia and caused his death from sheer exhaustion, with little pain, at Hinton St. George 26 December 1933. His *Oxford Dictionary* work was continued with fraternal devotion and beaver-like persistence by A. J. Fowler, his junior by ten years, who had retired from a long and valuable career at Sedbergh and died in 1939.

The main characteristics of Henry Fowler's life were his quiet, unpretentious stoicism and his moral and intellectual integrity. Strangers and schoolboys were often impressed by a certain austerity which concealed his deep affections. Both his last years and those of his brother Arthur were darkened by a wife's lingering illness; but the elder brother earned that praise which he had given to his junior: 'He is the most unselfish man I know.' Religious by nature and early training, he broke away finally from all dogma; yet to the last it might be said of him, as of his older fellow-Rugbeian Henry Sidgwick [q.v.], that he was a Christian in all but actual faith. In literature his tastes were catholic; but the one *genre* for which he disclaimed all sympathy was that of '*cruel satire*', with emphasis upon the adjective.

[*The Times*, 28 December 1933; *Meteor* (Rugby School magazine), 7 March 1934; *Sedberghian*, March 1934 and November 1939; *Punch*, 10 January 1934; G. G. Coulton, *H. W. Fowler*, S.P.E. Tract No. xliii, 1934 (portraits), and *A Victorian Schoolmaster: Henry Hart of Sedbergh*, 1923; private information; personal knowledge. Fowler's correspondence with Hart and his war letters of 1915–1916 are preserved complete in the library of St. John's College, Cambridge.]

G. G. COULTON.

FOWLER, SIR JAMES KINGSTON (1852–1934), physician, was born at Woburn, Bedfordshire, 11 March 1852, the fifth son of James Fowler, of Woburn, by his wife, Frances, daughter of Henry Sargeant, of Bedford. After leaving school, Fowler entered King's College, London, in 1870, intending to proceed to Cambridge and prepare for holy orders, but he suddenly decided to study medicine and therefore joined King's College medical school. He qualified in 1874 and was house physician to (Sir) George Johnson and house surgeon to Sir William Fergusson [qq.v.] at King's College Hospital. In 1876 he went, as house physician, to Addenbrooke's Hospital, Cambridge, where he availed himself of the opportunity to enter Gonville and Caius College as an undergraduate, eventually graduating M.A. (1879) and M.D. (Cantab. 1884). Returning to London in 1879 he was for a short period on the staff of Westminster Hospital, but in 1880 left on being elected assistant physician to the Brompton Hospital for Diseases of the Chest and to the Middlesex Hospital, where the wide experience of morbid anatomy gained as pathologist and curator of the museum he applied with great success to the study of disease in the living. In 1891 he became physician. In the wards he was a successful teacher, owing to his methodical and accurate observation, and the care he used to indicate the reasoning by which he arrived at his diagnosis.

Fowler wrote largely on professional subjects. He edited *A Dictionary of Practical Medicine*, published in 1890. In collaboration with (Sir) Rickman Godlee [q.v.] he published in 1898 a treatise on *The Diseases of the Lungs*. He was thus early to recognize the importance of the close co-operation of physician and surgeon in the treatment of chest diseases. In 1921 he published a monograph on *Pulmonary Tuberculosis*, a disease on which he was a recognized authority.

In the reconstitution of London University in 1900 Fowler played a notable part. He was a senior member of the senate and afterwards dean of the faculty of medicine. When (Sir) Otto Beit [q.v.] founded the Beit memorial fellowships, Fowler was made honorary secretary and one of the trustees of the fund.

Fowler received many professional and other distinctions and honours. He was a censor of the Royal College of Physicians in 1908 and 1909 and senior censor in 1913. The honorary degree of D.Sc. was conferred upon him by Sheffield University in 1908. In the previous year he was president of the Medical Society of London. In 1910 he was appointed K.C.V.O. after attendance with (Sir) Alfred Pearce Gould on Prince Francis of Teck in his last illness. He was one of the first members of the Colonial Advisory Medical and Sanitary Committee (formed 1909) and chairman of the Colonial Medical Appointments Board. In 1913 he was made chairman of the West African yellow fever commission.

Early in the war of 1914–1918 Fowler served on the staff of the 3rd London Territorial Hospital, but in 1917 went to the Rouen Base Hospital as consulting physician with the honorary rank of colonel, Army Medical Service. He was

mentioned in dispatches, and appointed C.M.G. in 1919, and K.C.M.G. in 1932 on his retirement from his Colonial Office appointments.

Fowler was unmarried. He made numerous friends, for the most part men of distinction in walks of life other than the medical. Tall, always well dressed and well groomed, he was a distinguished figure in any company. Through his friendship with John, second Lord Montagu of Beaulieu [q.v.] he was appointed warden of Beaulieu Abbey, and in 1911 wrote a *History of Beaulieu Abbey*, which is well illustrated and gives details of the life of the Cistercian monks. In 1928 he published a smaller work on Hayles Abbey, Gloucestershire, of which he was custodian. On retirement he lived in the Warden's House at Beaulieu, where he died 3 July 1934.

[*The Times*, 4 July 1934; *British Medical Journal*, 1934, vol. ii, p. 91; *Lancet*, 1934, vol. ii, p. 104; personal knowledge.]

R. A. YOUNG.

FOXWELL, HERBERT SOMERTON (1849–1936), economist and bibliographer, was born at Shepton Mallet, Somerset, 17 June 1849, the eldest of the four sons of Thomas Somerton Foxwell, of Shepton Mallet, who had a considerable and lucrative business as an ironmonger and later as a slate and timber merchant, by his second wife, Jane Handcock, who was of Irish and Channel Islands descent. Herbert Foxwell was educated at the Wesleyan Collegiate Institute (later Queen's College), Taunton, and graduated B.A. of London University in 1867. Proceeding in the Lent term of 1868 to St. John's College, Cambridge, he was senior in the moral sciences tripos of 1870 and was elected a foundation scholar of his college, being awarded the Whewell scholarship in international law in 1872.

Foxwell lived at Cambridge throughout his adult life, first at St. John's, and, after his marriage in 1898, in Harvey Road, a few doors from Dr. John Neville Keynes. His wife was Olive May (died 1930), eldest daughter of William Edward Dorrington, of a firm of Manchester shippers, and they had two daughters. Foxwell usually spent the summer at Barmouth, where he was a consistent pedestrian and mountaineer. He died at Cambridge 3 August 1936.

Foxwell's university work was threefold; at Cambridge, at University College, London, and at the London School of Economics and Political Science. His interests were also threefold; political economy in general, banking, and the formation of a library of economic literature. Beginning with extension lecturing in 1874, he was, that same year, elected a fellow of St. John's, and first as lecturer and later (1912) as director of economic studies was closely associated with the college for sixty years. During the absence from Cambridge (1877–1885) of Alfred Marshall [q.v.], he took the main share in the honours teaching of economics in the university.

Foxwell was appointed professor of political economy at University College, London, in 1881, and he did not retire until 1927. Until 1902 the only scope afforded for the study of economics in the university was as a compulsory subject for the M.A. degree in philosophy and as an optional one for the D.Sc. For many years Foxwell had the whole range of economics as his field. He lectured on banking and currency from the first session of the London School of Economics (1895–1896) until his retirement in 1922. In 1907 he and Edwin Cannan [q.v.] were appointed professors of political economy in the university of London.

From 1878 Foxwell was a fellow of the (Royal) Statistical Society, and in 1882 he was elected an honorary member of the historic Political Economy Club. In 1890 he was closely connected with the initiation of an economics club at University College, and in 1890–1891 was one of the founders of the British Economic Association, later the Royal Economic Society, and was its president from 1929 to 1931. He was elected a fellow of the British Academy in 1905.

When Foxwell began lecturing in 1874, the economic teaching of J. S. Mill [q.v.] was dominant in England, but a new and wider approach was already appearing in the work of a brilliant group of men born in the period from 1835 to 1855, which included W. S. Jevons, A. Marshall, William Cunningham, Arnold Toynbee [qq.v.], Charles Wicksteed, and Dr. J. N. Keynes. Foxwell described 'The Economic Movement in England' in a very important contribution to the second volume of the *Quarterly Journal of Economics* (October 1887). Here he argued that economics is not a self-contained science, the 'laws' of which are normative and universal, as was implied by the followers of Ricardo and Mill, but is part of the wider study of the development of institutions and governments, which dominates the economic ideas of each nation and genera-

tion, continually growing as conditions change. Although not opposed to pure analysis, when properly limited and defined—for he was a wholehearted admirer of Jevons and appreciated Marshall, who had been his teacher—Foxwell's bent was historical. Partly for this reason he was in opposition to the trend of 'orthodox' English economics, especially in his support (about 1886) of bimetallism and in his partial sympathy with the movement towards imperial preference and tariff reform (about 1903). His early interest in the development of socialism is shown in the above named paper, and in his long historical introduction to the English translation of Anton Menger's *The Right to the Whole Produce of Labour* (1899). He was one of the first economists to realize the tragedies of irregularity of employment, the subject of his lecture, 'Irregularity of Employment and Fluctuations of Prices', published in *The Claims of Labour* (1886).

Although Foxwell never lost his interest in general economics, the subject of which he was complete master was banking. In his university lectures and in those delivered to many public bodies he showed intimate acquaintance with the practice of banking, both at home and abroad, and its relation to industry, based on continual contact with bankers and other business men. During more than a generation there can have been few men seriously interested in the wider problems of banking and currency who did not come under his influence. Unfortunately, the only book which he published on any subject, *Papers on Current Finance* (1919), relates only to the period from 1909 to 1917, save that reprinted in it is an article of 1888 on the inevitability of the growth of monopoly under competition.

Foxwell is best known, however, not for his economic teaching, but for the libraries which he formed on economic and allied subjects, covering the period from about 1740 to 1848. The first was purchased by the Goldsmiths' Company in 1901, and presented in 1903 to the university of London. At that date the catalogue contained 30,000 items, but purchases and gifts have continued, and now (1947), when it is housed in the university buildings in Bloomsbury, the collection has reached some 56,000 items. Its earlier contents are described by Foxwell in the appendix to Sir Robert Harry Inglis Palgrave's *Dictionary of Political Economy*, edited by Henry Higgs, vol. i, pp. 870–872

(1925). Immediately after the disposal of this first library was completed, Foxwell started upon a second collection. In 1929 this was sold to Harvard University, 4,000 volumes at once and the remainder to be delivered after his death. By 1939 it formed a very important part of the Kress Library of Business and Economics at the Harvard business school. It then contained some 42,000 books and pamphlets, and, as compared with the Goldsmiths' library, is particularly strong on the historical side.

Foxwell's charm won him a wide circle of friends and his apparent immunity from fatigue enabled him to indulge his passion for books without ever neglecting his duties. In discussion temperate, but in business intractable, he was embittered in his later years by many obstacles in the transfer of his first library and by disappointment in failing to attain the chair of political economy at Cambridge in 1908.

A portrait of Foxwell by Charles Hopkinson is at Harvard Graduate College of Business Administration. Another portrait by Agatha Shore, is at St. John's College, Cambridge.

[J. Maynard Keynes, *Herbert Somerton Foxwell, 1849–1936* in *Proceedings* of the British Academy, vol. xxiii, 1937; *Economic Journal*, December 1936 (bibliography and portraits); *Journal* of the Royal Statistical Society, vol. xcix, 1936; Audrey G. D. Foxwell, Publication No. 1 of the Kress Library of Business and Economics, Harvard University, 1939; personal knowledge.] ARTHUR L. BOWLEY.

FRASER, DONALD (1870–1933), missionary, was born at Lochgilphead, Argyll, 1 June 1870, the fifth son of William Fraser, minister of the Free church, Lochgilphead, by his wife, Violet Ferguson, of Ardrishaig, Argyll. He was educated at Glasgow High School and University and at the Free Church Hall there. While a student he became one of the pioneers of the Student Volunteer Missionary Union and as its travelling secretary visited the universities and colleges of the British Isles in 1893–1894. He undertook similar work in 1894–1895 for the British College (formerly the Inter-University) Christian Union. These two societies united in 1898 to form the Student Christian Movement of Great Britain and Ireland. Fraser's work among students culminated in the Liverpool Student Volunteer Missionary Union conference (January 1896) where he presided over 715 students together with representatives of the missionary societies of all the non-Roman Catholic Churches.

It was the first gathering of the kind in Great Britain, it attracted widespread attention in the press, and Fraser was the outstanding figure. His eloquence, charm, and spiritual power, combined with his youth, made a deep impression upon all those present. Immediately afterwards he visited by invitation student centres in France, Switzerland, Holland, Denmark, Sweden, Norway, and Germany in order to promote the Student Christian Movement. His spiritual gifts and administrative ability, together with his tenacity of purpose, helped him everywhere to achieve success.

In 1896 Fraser was appointed a missionary of the Free Church of Scotland, was ordained, and sailed for Africa. On his arrival at Cape Town he attended a student conference at Stellenbosch and was there persuaded to visit the schools and colleges of Cape Colony. His link with students was never broken; when on furlough he always renewed his contact with the Student Christian Movement, and to the last year of his life he retained the power to sway student audiences. It was at the close of 1896 that Fraser reached Livingstonia in Nyassaland. The pioneering stage among the warlike Ngoni was closing and constructive work had begun. Fraser was stationed first at Ekwendeni, then at Hora, but when in 1902 the Ngoni trekked southward seeking fresh pastures he went with them and built Loudon (called after a friend of David Livingstone) where he remained for twenty-three years. When he left Loudon it was the centre of an area of 2,000 square miles with 200 sub-stations, schools with 10,000 pupils, and a Christian community of over 10,000. Fraser's personal charm, restless energy, and spiritual fervour won him a unique place as a leader. He was builder, manufacturer, farmer, translator, and pastor. From Loudon radiated influences which made him the founder of a new civilization in Nyassaland and the spiritual father of a people. He married in 1901 Agnes Renton, daughter of the Very Rev. George Robson, D.D., of Perth: they had two sons and two daughters. His wife was a medical graduate: he built a hospital for her, and her work splendidly supplemented his own.

The United Free Church of Scotland elected Fraser moderator for 1922–1923 and in 1925 recalled him to Scotland as one of its foreign mission secretaries. So, after touring South Africa in a United Churches missionary campaign, he left

Africa with marked reluctance, but feeling that as a loyal servant of the Church he could not refuse. As a foreign mission secretary he made his influence widely felt, although he was increasingly hampered by attacks of illness, the result of his years of service in Africa. He had already in 1921, 1922, and 1923 united ten denominations in Scotland in carrying out joint missionary campaigns throughout that country. He was chairman of the Conference of British Missionary Societies in 1922 and 1932, and a member of the British Broadcasting Corporation committee on religious broadcasting. He wrote six books on Africa and its evangelization. Glasgow University conferred upon him the honorary degree of D.D. in 1922. He was appointed chaplain to the king in 1929. He died in Glasgow 20 August 1933. Fraser was a genial companion; humility, humour, and the courage of his convictions marked his character.

[A. R. Fraser, *Donald Fraser of Livingstonia* (portrait), 1934; Tissington Tatlow, *The Story of the Student Christian Movement of Great Britain and Ireland*, 1933; *Life and Work*, October 1933; personal knowledge.]

TISSINGTON TATLOW.

FRASER, SIMON JOSEPH, fourteenth (sometimes reckoned sixteenth) BARON LOVAT and forty-first MacShimi (1871-1933), was born at Beaufort Castle, Beauly, Inverness-shire, 25 November 1871, the second son of Simon Fraser, thirteenth Baron Lovat, by his wife, Alice Mary, fifth daughter of Thomas Weld-Blundell, of Ince Blundell, Lancashire. He was educated by the Benedictines at Fort Augustus Abbey School, at the Oratory School, Edgbaston, and at Magdalen College, Oxford. His elder brother having died in infancy he succeeded his father in 1887. From 1894 to 1897 he served in the 1st Life Guards. He returned from an expedition to the Blue Nile in 1899 with stuffed specimens of seventeen hitherto unknown species of fauna, three of which bear his name. During the South African war he raised, served in, and finally commanded the Lovat Scouts, a corps of Highlanders whose field-craft shattered the legend of Boer invisibility. At an Oxford meeting in 1902 he foreshadowed the formation of the Officers' Training Corps, and was one among a small group which, for twelve years, urged on the government the needs of national defence. He helped to found the *Round Table* in 1910, and originated cotton-planting in

the Sudan. He contributed to *The Grouse in Health and in Disease* (2 vols., 1911), which put together the findings of an important committee on which he served at this time. He commanded the Highland Mounted Brigade in Gallipoli in 1915; then, invalided home, held various commands in France, the most important of which was the directorship of forestry on the western front. He was the first chairman (1919-1927) of the royal commission on forestry, under-secretary of state for the Dominions (1927-1928), and chairman (1928-1929) of the Overseas Settlement Committee. In the difficult years from 1929 onwards he was the immensely popular convener of the Inverness-shire county council.

Lovat's hospitable nature gave him an unrivalled power of dealing with men; his services to the British Empire as soldier and administrator, to his own countryside in promoting forestry, fisheries, and the welfare of the crofter, depended largely on his capacity for getting a team to work together; that he should be its captain was of no importance to him. To his enthusiasm and experience the Forestry Commission and the first Empire Forestry Conference, held in Canada in 1923, owed everything; Canada idolized him. A staunch Roman Catholic, he formed, with men of all creeds, a host of effortless friendships. He was appointed K.T. in 1915, and received many other decorations, British and foreign. He died suddenly at Little Tew, near Chipping Norton, Oxfordshire, 18 February 1933. He married in 1910 Laura, second daughter of Thomas Lister, fourth Lord Ribblesdale, and had two sons and three daughters. He was succeeded as fifteenth baron by his elder son, Simon Christopher Joseph, Master of Lovat (born 1911), who was awarded the D.S.O. and M.C. during the war of 1939-1945.

A portrait of Lord Lovat by Somerled Macdonald is at Beaufort Castle.

[*The Times*, 20 February 1933; Sir Francis Lindley, *Lord Lovat. A Biography*, 1935; private information; personal knowledge.]

R. A. KNOX.

FRERE, WALTER HOWARD (1863-1938), bishop of Truro, was born at Cambridge 23 November 1863, the younger son of the Rev. Philip Howard Frere [q.v.], agriculturist, who was fellow, tutor, and bursar of Downing College, Cambridge, by his wife, Emily, daughter of Henry Gipps, canon of Carlisle Cathedral and vicar of Crosthwaite, Cumberland. He was grandson of William Frere [q.v.]. His parents died during his early childhood and he was brought up by relations. He was educated at Charterhouse, and won a scholarship at Trinity College, Cambridge, where he was awarded a first class in the classical tripos of 1885. In the following year he went to Wells Theological College. He was ordained deacon, with a title to the assistant-curacy of St. Dunstan's church, Stepney, in 1887, and priest in 1889. He remained at Stepney until 1892, when he joined the community of the Resurrection, which moved from Oxford to Radley in 1893 and to Mirfield in 1898: he became the second superior, succeeding Charles Gore [q.v.] in 1902. He held this office until 1913 and again from 1916 to 1922. He was select preacher at Cambridge in 1901 and at Oxford in 1913 and 1914. He was one of the representatives of the Anglican Church at the Malines 'conversations' of 1921–1925. In 1923 he was appointed bishop of Truro and was consecrated in Westminster Abbey in November of that year. He resigned his see in 1935 and retired to Mirfield, where he died 2 April 1938: he is buried in the graveyard of the community.

Frere combined wide and varied learning with practical ability which displayed itself in his work for the Mirfield community and in diocesan administration. His knowledge of ecclesiastical history and his perception of the application of its lessons to present-day needs were conspicuous in his influence, for example, on such bodies as the archbishops' cathedral commission (1925), while his activity as historian and liturgiologist and his musical scholarship made him a leading member of the Church Historical, Henry Bradshaw, and other learned societies. His historical writings include: *The Marian Reaction* (1896); *The English Church in the Reigns of Elizabeth and James I, 1558–1625* (vol. v of W. R. W. Stephens and W. Hunt, *The History of the English Church*, 1904); and *Some Links in the Chain of Russian Church History* (1918). His editions of original documents include three volumes of *Visitation Articles and Injunctions of the Period of the Reformation* (in collaboration with W. P. M. Kennedy, 1910) and three volumes of the *Registrum Matthei Parker* (in collaboration with Miss E. M. Thompson, 1907–1933). In 1901 appeared his *New History of the Book of Common Prayer*, a revised and rewritten edition of the well-known work of Francis

Procter [q.v.]. Among liturgical works his editions of *The Winchester Troper* (1894) and *The Use of Sarum* (2 vols., 1898–1901), and his *Pontifical Services* (1901) are noteworthy examples of his methods.

A portrait of Frere by Harold Knight, presented to him in 1933, is at Lis Escop, Truro: a copy is at Mirfield.

[C. S. Phillips and others, *Walter Howard Frere, Bishop of Truro*, 1947; *Cambridge Review*, 29 April 1938; private information; personal knowledge.]   A. HAMILTON THOMPSON.

FRESHFIELD, DOUGLAS WILLIAM (1845–1934), mountain explorer and geographer, was born at Hampstead 27 April 1845, the only son of Henry Ray Freshfield, solicitor to the Bank of England, by his wife, Jane Quentin, daughter of William Crawford, member of parliament for the City of London. He was educated at Eton and University College, Oxford, and was called to the bar by the Inner Temple in 1870, but having always ample means, he never practised.

Frequent visits to the Alps in his youth developed in Freshfield a passion for mountain travel as an aspect of serious exploration. To him it was not a sport, and he disclaimed any ambitions in mere rock climbing. While still a schoolboy he ascended Mont Blanc and in the 'sixties and 'seventies made at least twenty first ascents, chiefly in the less-known Italian Alps. He also travelled widely over classical ground in the Near East, for second only to his love of mountains was his interest in classical life and lore. In 1868 he explored, with Charles Comyns Tucker, Adolphus Warburton Moore, and his lifelong friend François Devouassoud, the central Caucasus which, except for the lower heights, were then unknown. He made the first ascent of Kazbek (16,546 ft.), Elbruz (18,470 ft.), and several other peaks. After returning to the Caucasus in 1887 and 1889 he published his *Exploration of the Caucasus* (1896), which remains a standard work. In 1899 he made, with Dr. Edmund Johnston Garwood, the circuit of Kangchenjunga through unmapped territory in Sikkim and Nepal, recorded in *Round Kangchenjunga* (1903). Lastly, in 1905, he tried, with A. L. Mumm, to ascend Ruwenzori, or the Mountains of the Moon, but was baffled by weather and mud at 12,000 feet. Later in life he visited many mountains, including the Pyrenees and the Japanese Alps, and was planning an expedition to Chinese Turkestan (Sinkiang) in 1914.

At home Freshfield had many interests in the advancement of geography, especially in connexion with the Royal Geographical Society, of which he was president from 1914 to 1917, Founder's medallist in 1903, and elected a trustee in 1924. Largely owing to his initiative, (Sir) J. S. Keltie [q.v.] in 1884 was commissioned to investigate and report on geographical teaching in Europe, with the result that Oxford, and later Cambridge, started geographical teaching which eventually spread to all other universities in the country. Freshfield was also a strong supporter of the Geographical Association. It was largely due to his advocacy, in the face of strenuous opposition, that women were admitted to the fellowship of the Royal Geographical Society. He edited several editions of *Hints to Travellers* and from 1872 to 1880 the *Alpine Journal*. From 1893 to 1895 he was president of the Alpine Club.

Freshfield's quick, epigrammatic, and often satirical wit made him a doughty champion of the causes which he espoused, and, although essentially a Victorian in outlook, he fought the tyranny of tradition when he felt that its maintenance hindered progress. His numerous books include several privately printed volumes of verse. The honorary degree of D.C.L. was conferred upon him by the universities of Oxford (1916) and Geneva (1923) and he was elected an honorary fellow of University College, Oxford, in 1925.

Freshfield married in 1869 Augusta Charlotte (died 1911), eldest daughter of William Ritchie, advocate-general of Bengal, and sister of Sir R. T. W. Ritchie [q.v.]. They had one son, who died in boyhood, and four daughters. Freshfield died at Wych Cross Place, Forest Row, Sussex, 9 February 1934.

[*The Times*, 10 February 1934; *Geographical Journal*, April 1934 (portrait); *Alpine Journal*, vol. xlvi, 1934 (portrait); H. R. Mill, *The Record of the Royal Geographical Society, 1830–1930*, 1930 (portraits); A. L. Mumm, *The Alpine Club Register, 1864–1876*, 1925; private information. See also, for his early climbs, books by his mother, Jane Freshfield, *Alpine Byways*, by 'A Lady', 1861, and *A Summer Tour in the Grisons*, 1862.]

R. N. Rudmose Brown.

FRY, ROGER ELIOT (1866–1934), art critic and artist, was born at Highgate 14 December 1866, the younger son of the judge (Sir) Edward Fry [q.v.], by his wife, Mariabella, daughter of John Hodgkin (1880–1875, q.v.). Both his parents were members of the Society of Friends, with Bristol connexions, and on his mother's side he was a great-grandson of Luke Howard (1772–1864, q.v.), meteorologist and classifier of the clouds.

Edward Fry's true ambition had always been scientific, and Roger Fry was brought up in an atmosphere of science. The only lasting result of his days at Clifton College was his friendship with J. M. E. M'Taggart [q.v.], the future philosopher, whose precocious intelligence did something to expand the narrow boundaries of Fry's Quaker upbringing. In December 1884 he won an exhibition in science at King's College, Cambridge. He there made friends with Goldsworthy Lowes Dickinson and came under the influence of Edward Carpenter [qq.v.], who completed the liberation from his conventional upbringing which M'Taggart had begun. J. H. Middleton [q.v.], then Slade professor of fine art, encouraged his dawning interest in art. In 1887 he was made a member of the society known as the 'Apostles', and he was awarded first classes in both parts of the natural sciences tripos (1887, 1888).

Although science and the discussion of morals seem to have absorbed most of Fry's intellectual energy while at Cambridge, during his last year he had begun to visit exhibitions of pictures and even to paint himself; and when he left the university he disappointed his father by a desire to take up art rather than science as a profession. At first a compromise was arranged by which he continued his studies of biology but also learned painting under Mr. Francis Bate, but the strain of this divided loyalty made some definite break inevitable, and early in 1891 he left for Italy. His letters to Lowes Dickinson from Rome and Florence, in which he describes his impressions of Raphael and Michelangelo, are the first indication of his true bent. After his return there followed some years of indecision, which included a period of study at the Académie Julian in Paris in 1892, which was a failure. His enthusiasm for Italian renaissance art made it difficult for him to paint in a contemporary idiom, and uneasy in the company of painters; and his pictures were rejected by the New English Art Club. In 1894 he again visited Italy, and this time studied the history of art with far greater thoroughness. He read the works of Giovanni Morelli, and began to take part in the activity known as connoisseurship, then being practised with great brilliance by Mr. Bernhard Berenson. Although Fry's view of art was too humane and intelligent for him to attach great importance to this approach, he recognized its value as a discipline, and later was able to use his *expertise* as a means of livelihood. Much of his time in the next two years was spent in lecturing, and he developed that unique power of communicating to his audience his own sense of discovery and excitement which made him, by common consent, the most enthralling lecturer of his time. His painting also met with rather more success, and in 1896 he married a fellow exhibitor at the New English Art Club, Helen, daughter of Joseph Coombe. It was an ideally happy marriage, but within eighteen months his wife showed the first signs of mental disease. She recovered in 1899, and became the mother of a son and a daughter, but after a long struggle, in which Fry acted with great courage, she became permanently insane.

From 1900 onwards Fry wrote some occasional articles and reviews for the *Athenaeum*, and in 1901 he became its regular art critic. He now also published his first long studies of the old masters, a small book on *Giovanni Bellini* (1899), and two articles on Giotto in the *Monthly Review* for December 1900 and February 1901, the former of which deals with the church of San Francesco at Assisi. The *Bellini* is relatively timid in style, but already shows the balance of technical and theoretical approach which was to be Fry's strength. During the next five years much of his time was spent in writing of its nature ephemeral, but in 1905 he produced a work of lasting value, his edition of Sir Joshua Reynolds's *Discourses*. The theme suited him perfectly. Like Reynolds he wished to show that the classic tradition of European painting was still an essential discipline to the student, and a form from which he could only depart when it had been mastered. Like Reynolds he believed that great art is a thing of the mind, concerned with ideas and not with imitation. And like Reynolds he knew himself to be, as a painter, incapable of carrying out the principles which he recommended, and so could speak of them with a sort of modest detachment. His introduction and notes to the *Discourses* contain the most carefully expressed thought in all his writings. His notes on the illustrations have the further merit of increasing the understanding of a school of painting, the seventeenth-century Italians, then completely out of fashion.

By this time Fry had a considerable reputation as a scholar and expert, and was concerned with many artistic projects of the time. He took an active part in the establishment of the *Burlington Magazine* and the foundation of the National Art-Collections Fund in 1903, and in the reform of the Chantrey Bequest in 1904. In June 1904 he stood for the Slade professorship at Cambridge, but was rejected; and in December of the same year he was invited by John Pierpont Morgan, whom he had already advised as a collector, to visit the United States of America, in the hope that he would become director of the Metropolitan Museum of Art in New York. He hesitated for some time. He could not bring himself to live entirely in America; and the directorship of the National Gallery, for which he was generally regarded as the most suitable candidate, fell vacant early in 1905. Finally he decided to accept the directorship of the Metropolitan, and almost immediately afterwards was offered that of the National Gallery, which he did not feel able to accept. He remained at the Metropolitan until 1910, spending a part of the year in New York, and accompanying Pierpont Morgan on his buying expeditions in Europe.

This American episode coincided with the turning-point in Fry's life. In 1906 he was accepted as a student of the old masters with an exceptionally wide range of knowledge, but his interest in modern painting was more a matter of duty than of conviction. In that year, however, he saw for the first time the work of Cézanne and immediately recognized that this was what he had always been looking for, a painter who could combine the colour of the Impressionists and their sense of contemporary vision with the structural coherency of the old masters. From Cézanne he began to take an interest in those other artists who were in reaction against the merely sensational elements of Impressionism, Gauguin, Van Gogh, and Matisse, and, in sculpture, Maillol; and made them the subject of articles in the *Burlington Magazine*, articles which, on the whole, the last forty years have done nothing to invalidate. This new application of the critical principles was given active expression when, in November 1910, he organized at the Grafton Galleries an exhibition of the modern French painters whom he admired, under the title of Post-Impressionists. The occasion will be remembered as one of the most noteworthy of those recurring outbreaks of mass-hysteria which have marked the course of art during the last seventy years. Fry was widely referred to as a charlatan or a maniac. Official opinion was voiced by Sir W. B. Richmond [q.v.] who wrote that 'Mr. Fry . . . must not be surprised if he is boycotted by decent society'. But far from distressing him these attacks seem to have had a liberating influence. From 1910 onwards his writings gain a new confidence and vitality. He ceased to be a learned expert and became the champion of modern art: a second Post-Impressionist exhibition was organized at the Grafton Galleries in October 1912. This change led to a break with those members of the art world such as Henry Tonks [q.v.] and Dugald Sutherland McColl, who, while Fry was still safely engaged in the study of old masters, had been his friends. In compensation he became a centre of influence among young painters, chief amongst them being Mr. Duncan Grant and Mrs. Clive (Vanessa) Bell.

Fry had long been impressed by the need to reintroduce art into ordinary life, and had expressed his concern with the subject in an article on 'Art and Socialism' (H. G. Wells, *Socialism and the Great State*, 1912) and a paper on 'Art and Life' read before the Fabian Society in 1917 (both reprinted in *Vision and Design*, 1920). These show that, in spite of a different critical outlook, he was the true heir of John Ruskin and William Morris. In 1913 he gave the same practical expression to his beliefs; he founded the Omega workshops in Fitzroy Square for the manufacture of well-designed articles of daily use. The articles produced— chairs, tables, pottery, even stained-glass windows—were designed by those young artists who had felt the influence of the Post-Impressionist movement, and to some extent the Russian ballet, and brought into interior decoration a new boldness of colour and design. The Omega workshops were a success, until the outbreak of the war of 1914–1918, and even during the war they continued to absorb much of Fry's time, both on the business side and in the actual making of pottery. He also worked at his own painting, which had naturally undergone a great change since his discovery of the Post-Impressionists. He had held an exhibition at the Alpine Club Gallery in January 1912, and had been severely criticized for his abandonment of a style reminiscent of Thomas

Girtin in favour of one based on Cézanne and Marchand. During the Omega period his painting was decorative and unrealistic, but he admitted that he was only happy when drawing his inspiration directly from the visible world, and after the war he settled down to a careful, learned naturalism, in which his sense of design seldom involved the alteration of appearances. He contributed regularly to the exhibitions of the London group of which he was one of the founders and a strong supporter. He was at his best as a painter of architecture, where the subject went halfway to meet his desire for structure, and involved a critical as well as a creative approach. A good example is the picture of the antique sculpture gallery in the Louvre which he presented to the Ashmolean Museum in 1933.

It was after the war that Fry's position as a critic was established and he became incomparably the greatest influence on taste since Ruskin. A collection of his writings, hitherto largely inaccessible in the pages of the *Burlington Magazine* and other reviews, was printed under the title *Vision and Design* (1920). Although covering a period of twenty years they are consistent in maintaining that the response to art is a pure, disinterested activity, apart from life, and that this 'aesthetic state' can be induced by combinations of form and colour irrespective of what these are intended to represent. Fry's critical standpoint was subjected to searching attack by D. S. McColl and by Dr. Ivor Armstrong Richards (*Principles of Literary Criticism*, 1924), but he reaffirmed his faith in it in a second collection of papers, published in 1926 under the title *Transformations*, where, in 'Some Questions in Esthetics', he says unequivocally that 'our reaction to works of art is a reaction to a relation and not to sensations or objects or persons or events'. In addition to papers on general questions of aesthetics, these two collections contain many examples of the kind of criticism in which Fry was at his best, those in which his conclusions are drawn directly from the analysis of actual works. The most sustained and convincing example of this is his book on *Cézanne* (1927), the piece of writing to which, since the Reynolds *Discourses*, he had given most pains. Reading it we cannot but regret that a sense of public urgency led him to write practically all his later works in the form of lectures, which, enchanting as they were to their hearers, lack just those qualities of structure and closely wrought texture which he so greatly admired in art. In particular they suffer when a subject of impossible scale has been forced upon him, as in the lectures on the Flemish, French, and British exhibitions at Burlington House, reprinted as *Flemish Art* (1927), *Characteristics of French Art* (1932), and *Reflections on British Painting* (1934). Nevertheless, with these lectures he filled the Queen's Hall, a feat probably never before performed by a speaker on a subject not concerned with politics or religion. More satisfactory are the lectures expanded into short studies of individual artists, such as that on *Henri Matisse* (1930).

Fry had been a candidate for the Slade professorship at Oxford in 1910, but his outlook was too bold for the electors. He applied again in 1927 at the height of his reputation, and was again rejected, on a frivolous pretext. Finally, in 1933, he accepted the Slade professorship at Cambridge. His inaugural lecture was on *Art-History as an Academic Study*, and thereafter he set out to examine the art of the world in chronological order, from pre-Dynastic Egypt to the present day, in the light of two aesthetic qualities to which he attached particular importance, sensibility and vitality. He had got as far as Greek art when he died in London from heart failure following a fractured thigh 9 September 1934. The Cambridge course was afterwards reprinted as *Last Lectures* (1939). Unfortunately, only the first two lectures, in which he defined the qualities under discussion, had been revised: the remainder were only notes and in printed form do not do justice to the range and brilliance of the course.

It is natural that Fry's influence should have diminished since his death. Much of it was due to his personal charm, his sonorous and persuasive voice, and an air of reasonableness with which he could invest the most improbable statements. His attitude of mind, tolerant, rational, and speculative, is out of keeping with the violent thirst for belief of a subsequent generation. He was in the tradition of the Encyclopedists, and like them disguised as science a liberal measure of credulity. Although in some of his work he carries on the tradition of Morris, his critical standpoint was that of Poe, Gautier, and Pater. It is, however, less by theory or learning, than by his power of analysing his unusually vivid and informed responses that Fry's criticism will live.

Fry was elected an honorary fellow of King's College, Cambridge, in 1927, and the honorary degree of LL.D. was conferred upon him by Aberdeen University in 1929.

Portraits of Fry are numerous, and include several admirable self-portraits in private possession, one of which is reproduced in his biography by Virginia Woolf; there is also a remarkable etching by W. R. Sickert, which is a caricature of Fry lecturing, entitled 'Vision Volumes and Recession'.

[Virginia Woolf, *Roger Fry. A Biography*, 1940; *Burlington Magazine*, October and November 1934; *Cambridge Review*, 10 October 1934; *The Times Literary Supplement*, 21 October 1939; private information; personal knowledge.]   KENNETH CLARK.

FULLER, SIR (JOSEPH) BAMPFYLDE (1854–1935), Indian administrator and author, was born at Newton, near Keynsham, Somerset, 20 March 1854, the eldest son of Joseph Fuller, afterwards vicar of Ramsdale, Hampshire, by his wife, Anne Isabella, daughter of Charles Bampfylde, rector of Hemington and Dunkerton, Somerset. He was educated at Marlborough and secured first place in the competitive examination for the Indian civil service in 1873. He went out at the end of 1875 to the North-West (afterwards the United) Provinces, and his brilliance led to early promotion. In 1882 he was transferred to the Central Provinces where from 1885 to 1893 he was in charge of the settlement and agricultural department. Appointed C.I.E. in 1892, he officiated as commissioner in 1894. After acting in 1900 as chief commissioner of Assam he was called in 1901 to headquarters to be secretary of the revenue and agricultural department. An important resolution on the complex subject of land revenue then issued was made memorable by his mastery of the subject in drafting and by final shaping at the hands of the viceroy, Lord Curzon.

In 1902 Fuller went to Assam, first as acting and then as substantive chief commissioner, and won the warm regard of the tea-planting community. In October 1905, on the short-lived partition of Bengal coming into effect, he was appointed lieutenant-governor of the newly constituted province of Eastern Bengal and Assam. The storm of protest and denunciation raised by the Hindus of Bengal and by Congress politicians generally now centred largely upon him. Measures which he deemed necessary to overcome lawlessness and intimidation were magnified beyond all recognition by an unscrupulous press. On the other hand, the Mohammedans, who formed two-thirds of the population under his charge, rallied to his support.

Fuller, who was appointed K.C.S.I. at the beginning of 1906, held charge for only ten unquiet months. The viceroy, G. J. M. K. Elliot, fourth Earl of Minto [q.v.], to quote his biographer, John Buchan, came to the conclusion that the lieutenant-governor 'lacked the qualities of patience and discretion which could alone in time abate the partition ferment'. Buchan adds that in July 1906 'an incident happened which was not quite unwelcome to either Viceroy or Secretary of State' (John Morley). A petulant letter from Fuller hinting that he might have to reconsider his position if his advice on a particular matter were not accepted, was seized upon as a pretext for informing him, to his chagrin, that his 'resignation' had been accepted. Before the exact details of this incident were known the course adopted was stoutly defended in parliament by the secretary of state in reply to critics who complained that the 'man on the spot' had been ill treated.

Fuller, eager to air his grievance on return home, was enthusiastically welcomed by such assemblies as the annual Assam and Calcutta dinners, and later he was vehemently critical of the policy of annulment of the Bengal partition. But he was far too likeable, volatile, and energetic merely to assume the role of a disappointed reactionary. He wrote voluminously and travelled extensively in the Old World and the New, thrice going back to India. At Winchester, where he first made his home, he served on the bench of magistrates and engaged in municipal and philanthropic affairs. In the war of 1914–1918 he was a temporary major in the Army Ordnance Department from 1915 to 1917, and director of timber supplies at the War Office from February of the last-named year.

Fuller's non-controversial *Studies of Indian Life and Sentiment* (1910) and *The Empire of India* (1913) were followed by a long series of philosophical books beginning with *Life and Human Nature* (1914) and ending only a few months before his death with *The Tyranny of the Mind* (1935). His reminiscences under the title of *Some Personal Experiences* appeared in 1930. He died at his home, the Red House, Marlborough, 29 November 1935.

Fuller was thrice married: first, in 1879 to Maria Caldwell (died 1880), fourth daughter of Colonel Henry Aston, of the Bombay Staff Corps; secondly, in 1884 to Sarah Augusta (died 1923), fourth daughter of Arthur Wellesley Critchley; thirdly, in 1924 to Gabrielle Marie Adèle, daughter of Professor Eugène Rousselin. He had no children.

A portrait of Fuller, presented by service colleagues in the Assam commission, is at Government House, Shillong.

[*The Times*, 30 November 1935; *India Office List*, 1934; Sir J. B. Fuller's own writings; Lord Morley *Recollections*, vol. ii, 1917; Mary Countess of Minto, *India: Minto and Morley, 1905–1910*, 1934; John Buchan, *Lord Minto: a Memoir*, 1924; Lord Ronaldshay (afterwards Marquess of Zetland), *Life of Lord Curzon*, vol. ii, 1928; Claud Lovat Fraser, *India under Curzon and after*, 1911.]

F. H. BROWN.

FULLER-MAITLAND, JOHN ALEXANDER (1856–1936), musical critic and connoisseur. [See MAITLAND.]

FURNISS, HENRY SANDERSON, BARON SANDERSON (1868–1939), principal of Ruskin College, was born in London 1 October 1868, the elder son of Thomas Sanderson Furniss, J.P., barrister, of Stratford St. Mary, Suffolk, by his wife, Mary, second daughter of Edward Fisher Sanderson, of New York. His family on both sides was the same as that of Bishop Robert Sanderson [q.v.].

Almost blind from birth, Furniss overcame his affliction with courage and tenacity. After receiving his early education from private tutors, he went up to Oxford, and with the aid of a reader and amanuensis studied modern history at Hertford College and obtained a second class in 1893. In 1905 he settled at Oxford, and in 1907 he was invited to become tutor and lecturer in economics at Ruskin College, which had been founded eight years earlier for the education of adult workers. In 1916 he became principal, and until his retirement in 1925 he devoted himself to the development of adult education not only in the college itself, but in the Workers' Educational Association and the Oxford University Delegacy for Extra-Mural Studies.

Furniss's blindness was compensated by a retentive memory, and he not only planned the teaching work of Ruskin College with thoroughness and balance, but knew his students individually. His lectures, and still more his tutorials in economics were calculated to stimulate in his pupils respect for careful and considered thinking. He had no patience either with windy rhetoric or with thin academic word-spinning. His occasional acidity of comment on the prejudices of persons or the shortcomings of institutions was relieved by an essential kindness and generosity which gained him the affection as well as the respect of his colleagues and his students.

Visits with his wife to Australia, South Africa, and the United States of America for the benefit of his health brought Furniss into contact with educational and labour movements in those countries. Both he and his wife had been brought up in conservative circles, but had moved to liberalism and thence to labour, and in 1918 he stood unsuccessfully for parliament as the first labour candidate for Oxford University. In 1930 he was raised to the peerage as Baron Sanderson, of Hunmanby, Yorkshire, and from 1931 to 1936 he was representative of the labour peers on the parliamentary executive of the labour party. Later his pacificism separated him somewhat from his party, which he left in 1938, but his integrity and sincerity won the respect of all.

In 1902 Sanderson married Averil Dorothy, only daughter of Henry Frederick Nicholl, J.P., of Twyford, Berkshire: there were no children of the marriage. He died suddenly in London 25 March 1939. Portraits of Sanderson by Sir William Rothenstein and A. K. Lawrence are in the possession of Lady Sanderson.

[Lord Sanderson, *Memories of Sixty Years*, 1931, and *Charles Sydney Buxton. A Memoir* (privately printed), 1914; *Manchester Guardian*, 27 March 1939; *Economic Journal*, June 1939; personal knowledge.]

A. BARRATT BROWN.

GALSWORTHY, JOHN (1867–1933), playwright and novelist, was born at Kingston Hill, Surrey, 14 August 1867, the elder son of John Galsworthy, solicitor, of Old Jewry, London, chairman and director of several companies, by his wife, Blanche Bailey, daughter of Charles Bartleet, needlemaker, of Redditch. He was descended on his father's side from an old Devonshire family which was settled at Wembury, near Plymouth Sound, where since the Middle Ages there was a field called Great Galsworthy. He was educated at Harrow, where he was two years a monitor, captain of football, and winner of the mile-and-a-half, and at New Col-

lege, Oxford, where he obtained a second class in jurisprudence (1889). Called to the bar by Lincoln's Inn in 1890, he took up marine law, and for the sake of experience travelled in merchant ships to the Far East. He narrates how once in changing ship in 1893 he was somewhat repelled by his first sight of the new mate, angry, black with coal dust, and speaking imperfect English, who proved to be Joseph Conrad [q.v.], afterwards his lifelong friend and fellow novelist.

Galsworthy began to write in 1897, when he published, under the pseudonym of John Sinjohn, a collection of stories, *From the Four Winds*. His first novels, published under the same pseudonym, were *Jocelyn* (1898), *Villa Rubein* (1900), and *The Island Pharisees* (1904), but it was in 1906 that he secured a double success with his first play, *The Silver Box*, produced by Harley Granville-Barker at the Court Theatre, and his novel *The Man of Property*, which gave the lead to a great sequence, *The Indian Summer of a Forsyte* (1918), *In Chancery* (1920), *Awakening* (1920), and *To Let* (1921), which afterwards appeared as *The Forsyte Saga* (1922). The *Saga* gives a highly critical, but not altogether unsympathetic, description of Victorian upper-class commercial society, narrow in sympathies but strong in will and in the prudential virtues. The same type recurs in most of Galsworthy's work, for example in *The Country House* (1907), *Fraternity* (1909), *The Patrician* (1911), and *The Freelands* (1915). Indeed, the books as a whole depict the decadence or supersession of a strong, though not very amiable, generation by something more free and easygoing, an effect which is deepened by his post-war studies, *The White Monkey* (1924), *The Silver Spoon* (1926), and *Swan Song* (1928), in which Soames Forsyte, the odious 'Man of Property' of 1906 has so mellowed as to appear, in contrast with the younger generation, almost a hero and capable of great self-sacrifice. These studies were republished as a trilogy under the title of *A Modern Comedy* in 1929.

The novels are remarkable for a very sensitive and exact observation of life as well as for purity of style. By temperament and perhaps also by his artistic conscience Galsworthy avoided many appeals to a reader's sympathy which seemed to him not consistent with objective truth. He belonged to no political party and professed to have no political convictions. He does not indulge in political or social ideals, like Mr. Shaw and Wells, nor in philosophic 'meliorism', like George Eliot, still less in high spirits and fun, like Dickens, or in sheer romance, like Conrad. The public causes which appealed to him were either literary, like the reform or abolition of the dramatic censorship, the foundation of the international P.E.N. Club, of which he was the first president, and the English Association, of which he was president in 1924; or else such as responded to his ever-wakeful sense of pity, like aid to prisoners and protection of animals. Pity for the unfortunate is, indeed, the main emotion roused by most of Galsworthy's works, but the only thing which really sweeps him away is mere sympathy with young love and beauty. Here, too, he never pretends that his young lovers have any especially admirable qualities; they long and they suffer, and that is enough. At times on this theme he rises to an almost lyrical beauty, for example in *The Dark Flower* (1913) and some of the short stories, such as 'The Apple Tree' (*Five Tales*, 1918).

Galsworthy's stagecraft, as evidenced by the immediate success of *The Silver Box*, was even more striking. For one thing, in his dialogue he turned right away both from the somewhat stagey style of Sir A. W. Pinero [q.v.] and H. A. Jones [q.v.] and the artificially brilliant epigrams which such writers as Mr. Shaw and Oscar Wilde had made fashionable, much as in an earlier generation Thomas Holcroft and Thomas Morton had turned from the wit of Sheridan. The extreme skill with which he composed a dialogue which was both lifelike and varied, being carefully suited to each individual character, gave him an additional dramatic instrument and explains the highly dramatic quality of many of his most quiet and unemphatic scenes. Secondly, Galsworthy's construction was daringly simple, with no ingenious intrigues or theatrical surprises. A theme is stated, such as the different treatment of rich and poor offenders in *The Silver Box*, the blind way in which the law crushes the weak criminal in *Justice* (1910), the clash between the new rich and the old aristocracy in *The Skin Game* (1920), and is allowed to work itself out logically with fair play and no favour to either side. For, in the plays as in the novels, Galsworthy not only avoids unreally sympathetic heroes and heroines, but equally abstains from showing any side which is definitely right or any clear remedy for the troubles in which his characters find themselves. This sometimes, no doubt, produces a depressing effect, felt even by the author. On coming away from a very moving performance of *Justice* he was heard to murmur, 'I will never see that damned play again.' It may be mentioned that in an early draft of *Justice*, after the suicide there was a line spoken by the simple-minded religious old clerk, 'He's gone to gentle Jesus.' The line had value, but was cut out; the prolonged crushing of the worm, which forms the theme of the play, was kept conscientiously unrelieved.

Owing to this simplicity of construction and dialogue Galsworthy's plays are often considered easy to act, but in reality they require great intelligence and skill; the unthinking actor has no help from rhetoric or 'strong curtains'. In one play, *Escape* (1926), he departed considerably from his ordinary manner by giving a series of exciting adventures to his prisoner escaped from Dartmoor; but the sequence is simple. There is no attempt at theatrical ingenuity. Considering how completely Galsworthy refused to play down to the public by cheap or sensational appeals, it is remarkable what great and widespread success he achieved both in Great Britain and abroad. In Germany, indeed, he was studied with an enthusiasm said to be due to the acceptance of his books as authentic documents admitting and proving in detail the decadence of Great Britain; but that explanation does not apply to the rest of Europe. His *Collected Plays* appeared in 1929.

The war of 1914–1918 did not produce much direct effect upon Galsworthy's work, although it would be an exaggeration to make comparisons with Jane Austen's imperviousness to the Napoleonic conflict. He had made a somewhat prophetic though ineffective appeal, when the aeroplane was invented, for an international agreement not to use the new instrument for military purposes, and during the war he wrote various addresses and short stories, satirical or allegorical. But in such matters his reluctance to take sides or to make up his mind on disputed problems was something of a hindrance.

Galsworthy's one volume of *Collected Poems*, published in 1934 after his death, is enough to suggest that he might have been a considerable poet if he had not already found an instrument for the expression of beauty which suited him better.

A full bibliography of Galsworthy's

writings down to 1928 will be found in H. V. Marrot's *A Bibliography of the Works of John Galsworthy* (1928); those published between 1928 and 1933 are given in the same writer's *The Life and Letters of John Galsworthy* (1935). The following works were published posthumously: *Over the River* (1933), *Forsytes, Pendices, and Others*, an early fictional work (1935), and a volume of miscellaneous essays entitled *Glimpses and Reflections* (1937).

Galsworthy refused a knighthood in 1918. He accepted the Belgian decoration of Les Palmes d'Or in 1919, received honorary doctorates from the universities of St. Andrews, Manchester, Dublin, Cambridge, Sheffield, Oxford, and Princeton, and was elected an honorary fellow of his college in 1926. He was appointed to the Order of Merit in 1929 and awarded the Nobel prize for literature in 1932.

Galsworthy married in 1905 Ada Pearson, daughter of Emanuel Cooper, M.D., of Norwich, and formerly wife of his first cousin, Arthur John Galsworthy: she was a most understanding helper in all his work. They had no children. He died at Hampstead 31 January 1933. There is a crayon portrait of Galsworthy by Sir William Rothenstein at New College, Oxford.

[*The Times*, 1 February 1933; H. V. Marrot, *The Life and Letters of John Galsworthy*, 1935; André Chevrillon, *Trois Études de Littérature Anglaise*, 1922, translated by F. Simmonds, 1923; Leon Schalit, *John Galsworthy*, 1928, translated as *John Galsworthy, a Survey*, 1929; H. L. Ould, *John Galsworthy*, 1934; personal knowledge.]   GILBERT MURRAY.

GANN, THOMAS WILLIAM FRANCIS (1867–1938), archaeologist, was born at Murrisk, Westport, co. Mayo, 13 May 1867, the son of William Gann, of Murrisk and later of Whitstable, by his wife, Elizabeth Rose Garvey. He was educated at the King's School, Canterbury, and the medical school of Middlesex Hospital, London. After practising some time in London and Yorkshire, he was appointed in 1894 a district medical officer in British Honduras, where for nearly thirty years he served in that capacity and occasionally as acting district commissioner. At the time of his retirement in 1923 he was principal medical officer.

Almost from the moment of his arrival in the colony Gann's interest was attracted by the pyramids, mounds, and other vestiges of the ancient Maya civilization, which occur in great abundance in British Honduras, particularly in the Cayo and Corozal districts, in which he was stationed during most of his medical career. In his spare time he began a series of excavations, the first report of which was published as early as 1895 in the *Proceedings* of the Society of Antiquaries of London. For the rest of his life he was constantly engaged in archaeological work and in discovering new groups of ruins.

Among the most outstanding of Gann's discoveries were some mural paintings buried in a small mound at Santa Rita, in northern British Honduras. These were among the finest examples of that type of decorative art yet found in the Maya area, and have supplied many data on costume and religious customs of the late period to which they belong. Other excavations in that vicinity and across the border in the Mexican territory of Quintana Roo brought to light many burials and much mortuary furniture of various periods. Gann discovered or first described a number of important Maya sites, notably Lubaantun, in southern British Honduras, with its magnificent masonry (1904); Coba, in Quintana Roo, a large and extremely important site, the investigation of which radically altered ideas concerning the history of Yucatan (1926); Ichpaatun, Quintana Roo, a walled city with a stele bearing an early date (1926); Tzibanche, also in Quintana Roo, a large site with a peculiar style of architecture (1927); and Noh Mul and nearby Louisville, northern British Honduras, which yielded respectively much pottery and a series of fine portraits modelled in stucco (1936 and 1938).

Gann was the first to excavate and describe the queerly shaped objects of flint and obsidian, known as eccentric flints, which are so typical of the Maya lapidary art. The collections gathered by him are in the British Museum, at the Liverpool Institute of Archaeology (the full damage to which has yet to be ascertained), the Museum of the American Indian, Heye Foundation, New York, and the Middle American Research Institute, New Orleans. He bequeathed the most notable collection of Maya jades in private hands, together with other archaeological material, to the British Museum.

Gann detailed his archaeological work in forty books and articles. A full bibliography, compiled by the present writer, appeared in *Boletín Bibliográfico de Antropología Americana*, vol. iv (Mexico, 1940). Six popular books, written in an interesting, facile style, containing a mixture of travel, adventure, and archaeology, together with articles in the *Illustrated London News* and the *Morning Post* and talks arranged by the British Broadcasting Corporation, did much to acquaint the public, both in Great Britain and the United States of America, with the little known Maya civilization. He was lecturer in Central American archaeology at the university of Liverpool (1919–1938), and adviser to the British Museum expeditions to British Honduras. He married in 1930 Mary, only daughter of Robert Wheeler, of Hazlemere, Buckinghamshire; in his subsequent archaeological work she ably assisted him. There were no children of the marriage. He died in London 24 February 1938.

[*The Times*, 25 February 1938; private information; personal knowledge.]

J. ERIC S. THOMPSON.

GARDNER, PERCY (1846–1937), classical archaeologist and numismatist, was born at Hackney 24 November 1846, the third child and eldest son of Thomas Gardner, of the Stock Exchange, by his wife, Ann, daughter of Peter Pearse. He was educated at the City of London School, which he left at the age of fifteen in order to enter the stockbroking business. This work, however, proved uncongenial, and at the end of two years he was released. In 1865 he matriculated at Christ's College, Cambridge, and immediately found his level with undergraduates who had enjoyed a full classical training at school. He had, however, a strong speculative bent and found the Cambridge emphasis on exact scholarship barren and pedantic. In his spare time, almost unaided, he read philosophy, and in 1869 obtained a first class in both the classical and the moral sciences triposes. Next year he won the Whewell university scholarship in international law. After a period of depression and uncertainty he was appointed in 1871 assistant in the department of coins and medals at the British Museum, and there he discovered his life's work, the scientific study of Greek coins and art in relation to Greek history. He collaborated with R. S. Poole [q.v.] and B. V. Head [q.v.] in producing the British Museum catalogues of Greek coins, the volumes for which he was eventually responsible being those on Sicily (1876), Thrace (1877), the Seleucids (1879), Thessaly to Aetolia (1883), and the Peloponnesus (1887). Other numismatic works of this period are *Samos and Samian Coins*

(1882), *The Types of Greek Coins* (1883), a general work based upon his detailed researches, and *A Numismatic Commentary on Pausanias* in collaboration with F. Imhoof-Blumer (1887), in which he revealed the contribution made by coins to the study of ancient sculpture.

Meanwhile, in 1872, Christ's College had elected Gardner into a fellowship, which in 1874 he forfeited on his marriage to Agnes (died 1933), daughter of John Reid and sister of J. S. Reid [q.v.]. In 1877 he had what was perhaps the most exciting experience of his life when he paid his first visit to Greece, witnessed the actual progress of the German excavations at Olympia, and saw the newly revealed treasures of Mycenae. Under this stimulus he became an enthusiastic promoter of the Hellenic Society, founded in 1879, and edited the *Journal of Hellenic Studies* from 1880, the year in which he was appointed to the Disney chair of archaeology at Cambridge, until 1896.

In 1887 Gardner was elected to the recently founded Lincoln and Merton professorship of classical archaeology at Oxford, where he lived and worked for the remainder of his long life. A researcher *par excellence* and accustomed while at the British Museum to almost daily contact with the world of international learning and discovery, he was inevitably somewhat impatient of the Oxford of that day, with its concentration on the teaching and formation of youth at the expense of knowledge pursued for its own sake. The story of his early struggles for the admission of archaeology as a subject in the classical schools is told in *Classical Archaeology at Oxford* (1889) and *Oxford at the Cross Roads* (1903). The latter work also contains an eloquent plea for the reinstatement of learning and research as the primary function of a university. Gradually, however, his scholarship, devotion, and energy prevailed. He freed the Arundel marbles in the University Galleries from modern restorations, built up an archaeological library and cast collection, and founded a school of pupils, some of whom became most distinguished archaeologists. The modern department of archaeology at the Ashmolean Museum, its international reputation as a centre for the study of Greek vase-painting and Romano-British antiquities, is his monument. Gardner's literary output kept pace, meantime, with his teaching activities. *New Chapters in Greek History* appeared in 1892, *A Manual of Greek Antiquities* (with F. B. Jevons) in 1895, *The Sculptured Tombs of Hellas* in 1896, *The Grammar of Greek Art* (republished as *The Principles of Greek Art* in 1914), and *A History of Ancient Coinage 700–300 B.C.* in 1918. He was a most thorough, painstaking, and helpful, if not pre-eminently stimulating, teacher. He was no less appreciative of the work of his women, than of his men, pupils, but he remained unrepentantly hostile to the admission of women to full membership of the university.

Gardner's general position as an archaeologist can best be gathered from his last substantial work, *New Chapters in Greek Art* (1926). For him classical Greek art between 600 B.C. and 300 B.C. was the ideal norm: on the one hand, he mistrusted any tendency to specialize in pre-historic studies, while, on the other, the great advances in realistic portraiture, historical relief-sculpture, and landscape-painting made by artists of the Roman age were, in his eyes, little more than degenerate and puerile deviations from the fixed standards of earlier times. By his own admission, his approach to ancient monuments was always more historical than aesthetic, and he feared, groundlessly, as it proved, that the detailed study of artistic style pursued by some of the ablest of his pupils might lead to neglect of the spirit and content of Greek sculptures and vase-paintings. But by insisting that archaeological work must ever be firmly anchored in historical, literary, and linguistic knowledge he rendered enduring service to the essential unity of classical studies.

Brought up in a devout Christian home, Gardner possessed a strong moral and spiritual nature. In his younger manhood he was much attracted by Positivism and asserted that he had read every word of Auguste Comte's exposition of his positivist philosophy. He became increasingly aware, however, of a religious need which Positivism failed to satisfy. This religious need was eventually satisfied for him by 'evolutional', not static, Christianity; and the last half of his life was devoted to critical and constructive study and exposition of the Christian religion. This bore fruit in some ten publications between 1899 and 1931, of which the earliest, *Exploratio Evangelica* (1899), was undoubtedly the greatest of Gardner's achievements in this sphere. His scientific criticism of religion, united to his strong and practical faith in the supreme value of Christianity both for the individual and for society, gave his religious life a dual aspect which was reflected in his will, whereby he gave £200 to Ripon Hall and an equal amount to the Salvation Army.

Gardner was elected an honorary fellow of Christ's College, Cambridge, in 1897 and a fellow of the British Academy in 1903; he was a corresponding member of several continental academies, as well as a member of various foreign archaeological institutions. He retired from his professorship in 1925 and died at Oxford 17 July 1937. He had no children.

ERNEST ARTHUR GARDNER (1862–1939), classical scholar and archaeologist, youngest brother of the preceding, the sixth and youngest child of Thomas Gardner, was born at Clapton 16 March 1862. He was educated at the City of London School under Dr. E. A. Abbott [q.v.] and at Gonville and Caius College, Cambridge, which he entered as a scholar in 1880. He obtained a first class in both parts of the classical tripos (1882 and 1884). He was a fellow of his college from 1885 to 1894 and Craven student from 1887 to 1890.

By the time that Gardner started upon his career British scholars had already embarked on scientific field-archaeology in classical lands. He became the first student of the British School of Archaeology at Athens and its director from 1887 to 1895. He excavated at Naucratis in Egypt in 1885–1886 and later at Paphos in Cyprus and on many sites in Greece, including Megalopolis. In 1896 he was elected Yates professor of archaeology in the university of London, where he soon established a school of classical archaeology at University College: he also became Yates lecturer in 1927. In addition to teaching he organized a number of successful vacation tours to Greece and the eastern Mediterranean and collaborated with his brother Percy in arranging vacation courses in archaeology for school-teachers and others in this country. He was one of the editors of the *Journal of Hellenic Studies* from 1897 to 1932 and president of the Hellenic Society from 1929 to 1932. He was also active in university administration, serving as dean of the faculty of arts from 1905 to 1909 and from 1913 to 1915, as vice-chancellor from 1924 to 1926, and as public orator from 1910 to 1932. As lieutenant-commander in the Royal Naval Volunteer Reserve he saw active service at Salonika from 1915 to 1917 and was awarded the gold cross of the Greek Order of the Redeemer in 1918.

The wide scope of Gardner's archaeological interests is attested by his numerous publications. The earliest of these are the chapter on inscriptions in *Naucratis I* (1886) and *Naucratis II* (1888). His *Handbook of Greek Sculpture* (1896–1897), of which a revised and enlarged edition appeared in 1915, is still used by students, although knowledge has advanced, and canons of taste and criticism have shifted very considerably since that day. *The Catalogue of the Greek Vases in the Fitzwilliam Museum, Cambridge*, appeared in 1897, *Ancient Athens* in 1902, *Six Greek Sculptors* and *Religion and Art in Ancient Greece* in 1910. In 1905 he collaborated with E. S. Roberts in the *Introduction to Greek Epigraphy*, of which he wrote part ii, 'The Inscriptions of Attica'. His later works include *The Art of Greece* (1925) and *Greece and the Ægean* (1933).

Gardner retired from his chair in 1929, but retained his lecturership until 1933. Among the distinctions which he received were the honorary fellowship of Gonville and Caius College (1926) and the honorary degree of Litt.D. of Trinity College, Dublin. In 1887 he married Mary (died 1936), daughter of Major John Wilson, of the Scots Greys, and had one son and two daughters, the elder of whom predeceased her father. He died at Maidenhead 27 November 1939.

A full-length portrait of Ernest Gardner, in his robes as vice-chancellor, by Sidney Carline, belongs to the League of the Empire.

[*The Times*, 19 July 1937, 29 November 1939; George Hill, *Percy Gardner, 1846 to 1937* in *Proceedings* of the British Academy, vol. xxiii, 1937; Percy Gardner, *Autobiographica*, 1933; *Oxford Magazine*, 21 October 1937; personal knowledge. There is a bibliography of Percy Gardner's archaeological work at the end of his *New Chapters in Greek Art*.]   JOCELYN M. C. TOYNBEE.
H. D. A. MAJOR.

GARROD, SIR ARCHIBALD EDWARD (1857–1936), physician and biochemist, was born in London 25 November 1857, the fourth and youngest son of Sir Alfred Baring Garrod [q.v.], physician to King's College Hospital and an authority on diseases of the joints, by his wife, Elizabeth Ann, daughter of Henry Colchester, of Ipswich. Garrod was educated at Marlborough and Christ Church, Oxford, where he obtained a first class in natural science in 1880, and received his medical training at St. Bartholomew's Hospital, where he qualified, and afterwards paid a visit to Vienna.

Shortly after returning to England, Garrod was appointed to the medical staff of St. Bartholomew's, becoming casualty physician in 1889 and assistant physician in 1903. He also joined the visiting staff of the West London Hospital, the Hospital for Sick Children, Great Ormond Street, becoming full physician there in 1899, and the Alexandra Hospital for Children with Hip Disease. Promotion at St. Bartholomew's was slow on account of the unusual amount of talent there at this time, and it was not until 1912 that he was appointed full physician. He took an active part in the war of 1914–1918, in which he served first on the staff of the 1st London General Hospital at Camberwell and later, in 1915, he was promoted to the rank of temporary colonel in the Army Medical Service, and went to Malta, where he was consulting physician to the Mediterranean forces until 1919. For his services he was appointed C.M.G. in 1916 and K.C.M.G. in 1918.

On returning to St. Bartholomew's in 1919 Garrod was chosen as the first director of the new Medical Unit. He had not, however, held this new position for more than a year when in 1920 he was nominated regius professor of medicine at Oxford in succession to Sir William Osler [q.v.]; here he remained for seven years. After leaving Oxford he spent some years in Suffolk and then moved to Cambridge, where he died after a short illness 28 March 1936. He married in 1886 Laura Elisabeth, eldest daughter of Sir Thomas Smith, first baronet [q.v.], surgeon to St. Bartholomew's Hospital, and had three sons, all medical men; two were killed in action and one died of influenzal pneumonia at Cologne. He also had one daughter, who is Disney professor of archaeology at Cambridge.

In 1900 Garrod gave the Bradshaw lecture to the Royal College of Physicians on 'Urinary Pigments in their Pathological Aspects'; and to the same college in 1908 the Croonian lectures dealing with the incidence and heredity of 'Inborn Errors of Metabolism', which were published in a revised version in 1909 under the same title. To the Medical Society of London he read the Lettsonian lecture on 'Glycosuria' in 1912; he was Linacre lecturer at Cambridge in 1923, and in 1924 he gave the Harveian oration to the Royal College of Physicians on the 'Debt of

Science to Medicine'. At Charing Cross Hospital in 1927 he gave the Huxley lecture on 'Diathesis', in which the basic principles and several kinds of disposition were discussed; this was published in fuller form as *The Inborn Factors in Disease* (1931).

Garrod's other works include *An Introduction to the Use of the Laryngoscope* (1886); *A Treatise on Rheumatism and Rheumatoid Arthritis* (1890); a translation of Bernard Naunyn's monograph on *Cholelithiasis* (1896); and, in collaboration with (Sir) W. P. Herringham [q.v.] and W. J. Gow, *A Handbook of Medical Pathology, for the Use of Students in the Museum of St. Bartholomew's Hospital* (1894). It is noteworthy that his earlier works were mainly of a clinical character, whereas his later books were more of a biochemical nature. The high opinion held by Osler of his successor is shown by his invitation to Garrod in 1907 to join the editorial board of the *Quarterly Journal of Medicine* (on which he remained until 1927) and to help in the formation of the Association of Physicians of Great Britain. He was co-editor in 1913 with F. E. Batten and Hugh Thursfield of the first edition of *Diseases of Children*, to which he contributed articles on 'Disease as it Affects Children', 'Diseases of Ductless Glands', and 'Disorders of Metabolism'. He contributed also to the *Journal of Pathology* and to the *Proceedings* of the Royal Society. He joined the British Medical Association in 1888 and in 1922 was vice-president of the section of medicine. He was a member of the Medical Research Council from 1923 to 1928.

Garrod received many distinctions besides those already named. In 1910 he was elected a fellow of the Royal Society of which he was vice-president from 1926 to 1928. He received honorary degrees from the universities of Aberdeen, Dublin, Glasgow, Malta, and Padua.

[*The Times*, 30 March 1936; *Obituary Notices of Fellows of the Royal Society*, No. 6, January 1938 (portrait); *British Medical Journal*, 1936, vol. i, p. 731 (portrait); *Lancet*, 1936, vol. i, p. 807 (portrait).]

J. D. ROLLESTON.

GASTER, MOSES (1856–1939), scholar and rabbi, was born in Bucharest 16 or 17 September 1856, the eldest son of Abraham Emanuel Gaster, who was attached to the Netherlands legation in Bucharest, by his wife, Phina Judith Rubinstein. He graduated at the university of Bucharest,

whence he proceeded to the Rabbinical Seminary at Breslau, receiving the rabbinical diploma in 1881. He received the degree of Ph.D. In 1880 he returned to Rumania and became in 1881 a lecturer at the university of Bucharest on the history of Rumanian literature and on comparative mythology, but although his work here and as an inspector of schools and as a member of the council for the examination of teachers gained the approval of the government, his activities on behalf of the Jews in Rumania who were entitled to Rumanian citizenship under the Treaty of Berlin led the government to expel him from Rumania at short notice. The decree was indeed revoked and a reconciliation ultimately followed, but Gaster never returned to his native country as a resident, and for the rest of his life was domiciled in England, where he had connexions with Friedrich Max Müller and Adolf Neubauer [qq.v.]. He was naturalized in 1893.

Gaster was Anglo-Jewry's most versatile scholar, as is attested by only a selection from his writings. Besides the first translation of the Jewish liturgy into Rumanian (1883), he published *Jewish Sources and Parallels to the Early English Metrical Romances of King Arthur and Merlin* (1888); *The Sword of Moses* (1896), an early Hebrew magical work which he discovered; *The Chronicles of Jerahmeel* (1899); *Hebrew Illuminated Bibles of the Ninth and Tenth Centuries* (1901); 'The Hebrew Version of the "Secretum Secretorum"' (*Journal* of the Royal Asiatic Society, 1907–1908); *Rumanian Bird and Beast Stories* (1915); *The Exempla of the Rabbis* (1924); *The Samaritans* (Schweich lectures, 1925); *The Tittled Bible* (1929); *Samaritan Eschatology* (1932); and *Ma'aseh Book* (on Jewish tales and legends, 1934). His *Chrestomatie Română* (2 vols., 1891) is still the basic work for the study of Rumanian language and literature. His learning was recognized outside Jewry by a vice-presidency of the Royal Asiatic Society and of the English Folk Lore Society, of which he was also sometime president, a fellowship of the Royal Society of Literature (1930), honorary membership of the Rumanian Academy (1929), and the Rumanian Orders of the Crown and *Bene Merenti*.

In 1886 Gaster was appointed to deliver the Ilchester lectures, on Greco-Slavonic literature, in Oxford (published in 1887) and in 1891 he was re-appointed. In 1887 he was asked to fill the historic chief rabbinate of the Sephardi Jews in England, of which community he wrote a history (privately printed in 1901); and in 1890 he was chosen to be principal of the Judith Lady Montefiore College at Ramsgate, a theological institution administered by the community, but in 1896 serious differences arose about its management and he resigned. He retained his rabbinate until failing eyesight compelled his retirement at the end of 1918.

These scholarly activities were only one side of Gaster's life. He was a most prominent member of Anglo-Jewry and held active office in many of its principal institutions. For some time after his arrival in England he continued his support of the *Choveve Zion* movement in which he had been active when in Rumania, but with the rise of Theodor Herzl and his new Zionist movement he ranged himself on that side, being a founder and president of the English Zionist Federation and vice-president of four Zionist congresses held in Basel and London between 1898 and 1900. It was at his house in London that the talks were initiated between prominent Zionists and, on behalf of the Foreign Office, Sir Mark Sykes [q.v.], which led up to the issue of the Balfour declaration of November 1917.

In public causes Gaster was a vigorous and outspoken leader, often involved in controversy, in which he showed himself aggressive and courageous, but always with the saving virtue of a strong sense of humour. Both in the pulpit and on the platform he was an arresting orator. To the young and to the newcomer he was exceedingly generous, going to any trouble to assist a beginner and always ready with advice and help.

Gaster married in 1890 Leah Lucy, only child of Michael Friedlander, principal of Jews College, London, and had seven sons and six daughters. He died in a motor-car between Oxford and Reading, whither he was going to address a gathering of Rumanian students, 5 March 1939.

The best portrait of Gaster is that by Moses Maimon at the Spanish and Portuguese Synagogue in Bevis Marks, London. Another (whereabouts unknown) was by Leopold Pilichowski; a third is in the possession of Gaster's daughter Mrs. N. Laski.

[*The Times*, 6 and 16 March 1939; *Transactions* of the Jewish Historical Society of England, vol. xiv, 1940; *Jewish Chronicle*, 10 March 1939; *Encyclopaedia Judaica*; Publications of the American Jewish Historical Society, No. xxxvii, 1947; *Occident and Orient. Gaster Anniversary Volume*, edited by B. Schindler and A. Marmorstein (select bibliography and portrait), 1936.]

ALBERT M. HYAMSON.

GEDDES, SIR ERIC CAMPBELL (1875–1937), politician, administrator, and man of business, was born at Agra, India, 26 September 1875, the eldest son of Auckland Campbell Geddes, civil engineer, of Edinburgh, by his wife, Christina Helen Macleod, daughter of the Rev. Alexander Anderson, of Old Aberdeen. He was educated at Merchiston Castle School, Edinburgh, Edinburgh Academy, and the Oxford Military College, Cowley, where he was athletic and high-spirited rather than studious, but he decided not to join the Royal Engineers, and left for the United States of America at the age of seventeen, gaining in four years a varied experience as a brakesman on freight trains on the Baltimore and Ohio railroad, as a lumberman, and as a labourer in steel works. In 1895 he returned to Scotland with nothing more material in his possession than that which he had taken away.

Geddes then went to India, where he was manager of a forestry estate. This involved the running of fifty miles of light railway, and it gave him an opening in the railway world, for his railway was amalgamated with the Rohilkhand and Kumaon Railway of which he became traffic superintendent. Relying on greater prospects which he saw, he returned in 1906 to England and took a relatively lower post on the North Eastern Railway, of which thus in 1914, before the age of forty, he was deputy general manager and nominated as future general manager.

On the outbreak of war in 1914 Geddes took charge of the mobilization movement in Northern Command, and raised a battalion from the employees of the North Eastern Railway, later known as the 17th Royal Northumberland Fusiliers. It was thus that his great opportunity came to him in 1915, when as deputy director-general of munitions supply he was asked to report on the obstacles which were impeding the flow of munitions to the front. Here he won the complete confidence and friendship of Lloyd George. Consequently in 1916 he was appointed director-general of transportation on the staff of the commander-in-chief of the British army in France, and later inspector-general of transportation for all theatres of war, with the honorary rank of major-general (1917). By the spring of 1917 it was felt that the capacity of ports, railways, roads, and canals was generally equal to the demands made upon them, but at this time an even more serious question of transportation was causing grave anxiety, and in May 1917 Geddes was appointed controller of the navy and an additional member of the Board of Admiralty with the temporary and honorary rank of vice-admiral; Sir Douglas Haig [q.v.], however, insisted that he should be liable to recall to his staff, and thus Geddes became one of the few to hold senior naval and military rank at the same time. In July 1917 he was elected unionist member of parliament for the borough of Cambridge at a by-election, and in September of that year he was appointed first lord of the Admiralty and sworn of the Privy Council.

Thanks to Jellicoe's dispositions in the introduction of the convoy system the losses of merchantmen by submarine had fallen by the end of 1917 to less than half of those suffered in April. Eventually Geddes overcame the suspicion with which the navy had received him, and after the general election in 1918, at which he retained his seat, Sir David (afterwards Earl) Beatty urged Lloyd George, in the interest of the service, to retain Geddes as first lord, but this was not to be, for Lloyd George appointed him to the Imperial War Cabinet, and from 1919 to 1921 Geddes was the first minister of transport with a thorough knowledge of the subject. Thus it was that Geddes conducted the legislation of 1921 which provided for the amalgamation of all the railways of Great Britain into four groups, and for the settlement of the claims of the railways on the government in respect of its possession of them during the war.

Perhaps the work for which Geddes will best be remembered is his chairmanship of the committee on national expenditure, commonly known as the 'Geddes Axe' committee. National expenditure in 1921 was still at far too high a level, and the report made recommendations of detailed cuts amounting to £86,750,000, and indicated further sources of economy which together would yield the hundred millions which were the aim. On the break-up of the coalition in 1922 Geddes left the House of Commons after a brief but highly effective period of service as minister of the Crown.

Geddes now turned to industry and transport. His principal chairmanship was that of the Dunlop Rubber Company, which under his administration rose from serious difficulties to its place as one of this country's outstanding industrial enterprises with interests in all parts of the world. The other great development which owes much to his imagination and leadership is civil aviation. He was the first chairman of Imperial Airways and he soon realized that the proper field of development was the wide communications of the Empire rather than the ferry services across the Channel. Although he did not live to see it in operation, the 'all-up Empire air mail' was his conception and it ranks as one of the greatest steps ever taken for knitting together the Colonies and the Dominions.

Geddes's achievements in war were undoubtedly very great. His capacity for hard work, physical and mental, was abnormal: he asked a great deal, but never more than he gave. The independence of character commonly associated with Scotsmen never left him, and if it did not always make for harmony, he could inspire his collaborators with enthusiasm.

Geddes was knighted in 1916 and was subsequently appointed K.C.B. (mil.) in 1917, G.B.E. in the same year, and G.C.B. (civ.) in 1919, a curious instance of a promotion from the military to the civil ranks of the order; the honorary degree of LL.D. was conferred upon him by Sheffield University in 1920. He was never so happy as when he was out of doors at his country house, Albourne Place, Hassocks, Sussex, where he died 22 June 1937. He married in 1900 in India Ada Gwendolen, daughter of the Rev. Arthur Spokes, schoolmaster, and they had three sons.

A portrait of Geddes by R. G. Eves (1922) hangs in the office of the Dunlop Rubber Company in London. Another portrait, by Irvine McNalty, belongs to Mr. Acland Geddes, of The Manor House, Wye, Kent.

[*The Times*, 23 June 1937; personal knowledge.]   GEORGE BEHARRELL.

GEDDES, SIR PATRICK (1854–1932), biologist, sociologist, educationist, and town-planner, was born at Ballater, Aberdeenshire, at the gateway to the Highlands, 2 October 1854, the youngest son of Alexander Geddes, a Gaelic-speaking native of Strathspey, who was a quartermaster in the Black Watch and later a captain in the militia, by his wife, Janet Stevenson. Patrick was educated at Perth Academy. Then, having served a year in a bank at his father's request and having also laid aside his own thoughts of a career as an artist, he freed himself for his chief aim, the study of life. Early in the 'seventies he undertook a hard apprenticeship with T. H. Huxley [q.v.]. This shocked his Presbyterian father; yet the son never lost the Scottish traditions of family worship and of faith as a lifelong quest. From Huxley, Geddes went to Henri de Lacaze-Duthiers, with whom he studied zoology. In Paris he met with social science and awoke to the vitality of France, and saw, for the first time, the aftermath of war, international and civil, and the meaning of reconstruction. When senior demonstrator at University College, London, from 1877 to 1878, he came to know Charles Darwin and A. R. Wallace [qq.v.].

While exploring in Mexico, when he was twenty-five, Geddes endured the supreme crisis of his intellectual life: an attack of blindness which, although it slowly passed, broke the promise of a career in biology by making it impossible for him to continue microscopy. During his first months at Edinburgh University as demonstrator in botany, the oculist's orders cut down his indoor work to two hours a day. The career of a talented but orthodox biologist might have survived such restrictions: not that of a thinker and teacher whose very unorthodoxy required a mass of supporting concrete research and concentrated induction. Two great compensating experiences emerged from this trial. The first was the development of abstract thinking and the beginning of methods of diagrammatic thought, without which this intensely concrete observer might never have reached philosophic achievement. The second, his rediscovery of mankind and their home, about him, led to the founding of self-governing university halls, linked to rebuilding and the redemption of neighbourhood and community, in Edinburgh's 'Royal Mile'.

The great spiritual adventure of Geddes's life came in 1886 with his marriage to Anna, eldest daughter of Frazer Morton, an Ulster Scot and a merchant in Liverpool, who grafted upon the intellectual challenge of her forebears' faith her own musical and mental gifts. Three months after their marriage the couple made their home in the heart of Old Edinburgh, making friends with all classes, and there they dwelt until they moved to Ramsay Garden on the Castle hill, built co-operatively under Geddes's leadership. In 1892 Geddes acquired the Outlook Tower in Castlehill, and established there 'the world's first Sociological Laboratory'.

From 1889 to 1914 Geddes, whose chief biological interest now lay in botany, was professor of that subject (during summer sessions) at University College, Dundee, with a final session in 1919. Nevertheless, he collaborated with his old student (Sir) J. Arthur Thomson, the zoologist, in writing, from 1889 (*The Evolution of Sex*) to 1931 (*Life: Outlines of General Biology*, 2 vols.). From 1889 he was free for nine months of the year to devote much of his energy to other spheres. These centred more and more on civics and on the planning of country and town, initially in Great Britain, in Cyprus in 1897, and from 1914 to 1923 mainly in India, where, as professor of civics and sociology at the university of Bombay (1920-1923), he organized the postgraduate school. *City Development* appeared in 1904. In sociology he collaborated with Victor Branford. From 1911 Geddes's Cities and Town Planning Exhibition was shown in British cities, on the continent, and in India. In planning he pointed out the disastrous error of ruinously expensive rectilinear street-widening, and he provided for neighbourly life in 'garden and sun-court'. 'Survey before alteration', and 'diagnosis before treatment' with 'conservative surgery' where need required it, were his principles; and he regarded the citizens first, with a care not only for their physical but also for their spiritual health.

When Anna Geddes died in 1917, only three months after the death at the front of their elder son, a wise friend wrote that the disaster was irreparable: although Geddes was the pilot, 'it was she who steered the ship'. Overstrain brought an illness from which he nearly died and from which he never really recovered. In 1924 he settled at Montpellier, where he built an unofficial student residence which he named 'the Scots College', in memory of the Scots College in Paris. In 1928 he married Lilian (died 1936), second daughter of John Armour Brown, of Paisley. He died at Montpellier 17 April 1932, and was survived by his younger son, Arthur, a geographer, and by his only daughter, who married one of his collaborators, Sir Frank Mears, P.R.S.A. He was knighted in 1932; a previous offer of knighthood had been refused, but the honour was accepted in 1931, under the labour government, as his endeavours were now entirely non-professional and altruistic.

One of his own remarks sums up

Geddes's view of life: 'Our greatest need to-day is to grasp life as a whole, to see its many sides in their proper relations; but we must have a practical as well as a philosophic interest in such an integrated view of life.' Never granted a degree, he remained a student all his life, eager to learn, quick to appreciate but also quick to reject teaching wherever the form seemed to him to stifle the spirit. He was a pioneer in many ways. He was an evolutionist; but he reacted from Huxley's Neo-Darwinism, which stressed the elimination of 'unfit' variants, to search afresh into the nature of variation. He conceived of species as tending to differentiate either towards greater anabolism or katabolism—as in plants with emphasis either on vegetation or on reproduction. He stressed the importance of the development of sex as a more profoundly important step in evolution than had yet been realized. Within a species he regarded the female as the more anabolic, the male as the more katabolic. His interest in the forms of life was inseparable from his interest in the functioning of life in its environment. Of his own botanical assistants, more than one turned to geography, notably Andrew John Herbertson; and among his friends were the social geographers Elisée Reclus and Kropotkine. In his Outlook Tower he arranged stories of regional interpretation, from city and region (Edinburgh) through land (Scotland) and cultural environment (the English-speaking world) to continent (Europe) and world. His concept of the relationship Environment—Function—Organism led naturally to the concept of Place—Work—Folk (a rediscovery of Le Play's formula *Lieu, Travail, Famille*). Ever alive to the infinite variety of life about him, Geddes brought together the apparent chaos of contacts by the 'charting' of factors in order to bring out their relationships. Of this 'charting' Thomson wrote: 'To those who find such notations useful'—and Thomson was one of these—'they appear as the most remarkable organa which the mind of man has devised for disclosing all the possible relations of any subject.'

In the near future Geddes's influence will greatly depend upon what is being edited by the Outlook Tower Association. This has already provided the foundation for Philip Boardman's *Patrick Geddes, Maker of the Future* (University of North Carolina Press and Oxford University Press, 1944). Of Geddes's own work, there has so far appeared *Patrick Geddes in India*: selections from Town Planning Reports edited by J. Tyrwhitt, in collaboration with H. V. Lanchester and A. Geddes, with a foreword by L. Mumford (1947).

A bust of Geddes by Charles Pibworth is in the Scottish National Portrait Gallery, Edinburgh.

[Philip Boardman, *Patrick Geddes, Maker of the Future*, 1944; *Nature*, 14 May 1932; personal knowledge. Ten works in preparation include a revision of his *Cities in Evolution*, 1915; *The Charting of Life; Place, Work and Folk*, Geddes's major synthesis; and *Olympus*, an interpretation of phase and sex in human life. It is also hoped to revise his biological theses, and to prepare a volume of his letters.]   ARTHUR GEDDES.

GEORGE V (1865–1936), KING OF GREAT BRITAIN, IRELAND, AND THE BRITISH DOMINIONS BEYOND THE SEAS, EMPEROR OF INDIA, was born at Marlborough House, London, 3 June 1865, the second child of the Prince and Princess of Wales, later King Edward VII and Queen Alexandra. He was baptized at Windsor Castle on 7 July following by the names of George Frederick Ernest Albert. Like Richard I, Henry VIII, Charles I, and other notable sovereigns he was not born to the expectation of kingship: his elder brother, Prince Albert Victor Christian Edward, Duke of Clarence (q.v., known as Prince Eddy), was his senior by seventeen months, and Prince George remained a younger son for the first twenty-six years of his life. Nor at that moment in the history of the monarchy could it have been asserted with confidence that he would have attained to the throne even had he been the elder. There were many still living who remembered the peculiar contribution to the history of their times made by the sons of George III; and although twenty-one years of ideal married life had done much to endear Queen Victoria to her subjects, the period of muffled seclusion which had elapsed since the death of the Prince Consort was already beginning to be the subject of murmuring, and the reported manner of life of the Prince of Wales lent support to the nascent republican sentiment.

But of disquieting possibilities such as these the young princes and their three sisters were unaware as their childhood pursued its course in an atmosphere of sustained happiness and affection. In his attachment to his children the Prince of Wales was only surpassed by their mother; her happiest hours were spent in the nursery, and Prince George's mind was formed from earliest infancy under the spell of her charm and merriment. To her, as also to the memory of his father, he remained devoted throughout life.

An intellectual circle it was not, neither did the arts find place within the sphere of its interests, beyond a certain proficiency at the piano on the part of the mother. But all the ingredients for happiness were there, the family was sufficiently numerous to mitigate the disadvantages of isolation, and with the simple pleasures of childhood the early years passed in uneventful contentment. No undue stress was laid upon book-learning, of which in his youth the Prince of Wales had received a surfeit. They lived while in London at Marlborough House; their seaside visits were based upon Osborne in the Isle of Wight; August and September would find them at Abergeldie adjoining the Balmoral estate in Scotland. But for the most part it was Sandringham House in Norfolk that they regarded as home, the house which his father had built and for which King George himself all his life retained a particular affection. Here in an extensive domain of heath and pine in the bracing east coast air they roamed and played and rode, leading the normal country life of the days before motors, sharing the pride of other Norfolk families in their county and their home.

Within the family circle Prince George was distinguished by an irrepressible fund of spirits: 'so affectionate, though sometimes rather naughty', as Queen Victoria noted in her diary. In later years he would credit his youthful self with a hot temper, the germ perhaps of that occasional irascibility which marked his nature without disguising the essential kindliness beneath. He showed from the first more character than his elder brother. His open manner and twinkling eye brought him in boyhood friendships that endured through life. With the same loyalty he retained an abiding affection for the Rev. John Neale Dalton, his tutor between the ages of six and eighteen. Dalton left to become a canon of Windsor; his death in 1931 terminated an unbroken intimacy of sixty years.

At the age of twelve (1877) Prince George, together with his brother, joined the old wooden training ship *Britannia* at Dartmouth as a naval cadet. Younger than his fellows (indeed the youngest cadet ever admitted) and small even for his age, he underwent the full curriculum, in addition to further instruction in the humanities from Dalton who continued in attendance as tutor. The brothers were allowed to share a special cabin, but their only other distinction, as the King was wont to recall in later years, was that their services were at the command of all who desired a princely fag. Thus with the theory of navigation the future Prince of Wales acquired the practice of *Ich Dien*. To the seamanship he took kindly from the first, enjoying in particular the handling of a boat, in which sphere later on his proficiency was to become marked.

After the prescribed course of two years the brothers passed out in the summer of 1879. Prince George, whose nature always responded to the call of the sea, had already set his heart upon a naval career, and this aspiration found favour both with his father and the Queen. Both brothers were posted in August to the *Bacchante*, a fully-rigged cruiser-corvette with auxiliary engines and a complement of four hundred and fifty. This proved to be their home for the next three years. In it they first made an eight months' cruise to the West Indies by way of Gibraltar and a preliminary excursion into the Mediterranean. Prince Eddy's sixteenth birthday was celebrated when they were at Port of Spain, Trinidad (8 January 1880); the occasion was marked by their being both rated as midshipmen. This brought them level with two of King George's lifelong friends among their shipmates, John Scott (later seventh Duke of Buccleuch) and Rosslyn Wemyss (later Lord Wester Wemyss, q.v.) who was destined to rise to the top of his profession.

From this short cruise the princes returned in May 1880. After two months' leave they set off again in the *Bacchante*, which was now to form part of a flying squadron of five ships of the line detached for an extended training cruise round the Horn to Vancouver and thence to China and Japan, the passages being made largely under sail. Dalton accompanied them as governor, being entered on the ship's books as acting chaplain; and he it was who subsequently edited from the princes' diaries and letters two ponderous volumes, published in 1886, entitled *The Cruise of H.M.S. 'Bacchante' 1879–1882*. In the course of some 1,500 pages every detail of both cruises is recorded, together with a mass of interesting information about the topography and development of the places visited; but the work is conceived in so improving a style as to iron out all traces of individuality in the two princes.

The squadron assembled off Vigo, whence on 31 October (1880) course was set for the River Plate; Monte Video was reached on 22 December. Resuming the cruise on 19 January (1881) they reached the Falkland Islands on the 24th. Here they were intercepted by a signal from home bidding them abandon the projected passage to the Pacific and sail instead to the Cape of Good Hope, there to show the flag at a moment when British prestige in South Africa was at a low ebb. They accomplished this 4,000-mile voyage in three weeks, arriving at the Cape on 16 February, eleven days before the third successive humiliation inflicted by the Boers upon the British, at Majuba Hill.

The squadron was not in the event called upon to land a force. On 9 April it sailed once more, this time on a 5,000-mile trip across the Indian Ocean to Australia. Visits were paid to Albany (15 May), Adelaide, Melbourne, Ballarat (where the brothers descended a gold mine), Sydney, and Brisbane. They left the shores of Australia on 20 August with regret after enjoying the hospitality of its inhabitants for three months. They now set off for Fiji, where they passed a week (3–9 September) before embarking on another voyage of 4,000 miles to Japan. Yokohama was reached on 21 October, and after a month in the country they crossed to Shanghai (22 November) and thence passed down the coast to Hong-Kong (20 December), and so to Singapore (9 January 1882). Returning by Colombo to Suez (1 March), they were able to enjoy a month's sightseeing in Egypt, after which they crossed to Jaffa (28 March) and made their way on horseback through the Holy Land, covering thus close on 600 miles in the course of six weeks. On 6 May they rejoined the *Bacchante* at Beirut and crossed to Athens, where for ten days the brothers were the guests of their maternal uncle, King George of the Hellenes, before returning home through the Mediterranean.

Immediately upon their return to Portsmouth both princes were confirmed by Archbishop Tait in Whippingham church (8 August) in the presence of Queen Victoria. Exactly three years had passed since she had taken leave of Prince George, then a child of fourteen. Now at seventeen he was on the threshold of manhood, more travelled by far than his father at forty; incomparably more so than herself at sixty-three or than any of her predecessors on the throne. Throughout 45,000 miles of voyaging he had shared cheerfully and unselfishly in the hard fare and arduous duties of a young officer at sea, in standards of comfort which would now be regarded as primitive. He had measured himself against the responsibility of every junior officer for the lives of the men in his cutter. When the journey had first been mooted the Queen had noted (Diary, 15 May 1879): 'Mr. Smith and others are afraid lest something might happen if both boys went': her will had prevailed, but something very nearly had happened when the *Bacchante* narrowly escaped shipwreck in a storm off Southern Australia. From the first the understanding had been (Diary, 7 February 1877) that 'Georgie should only enter the Navy if he liked it'. Now he had tasted the salty life of the sea and found it good.

For the next year Prince George remained ashore. After a holiday, of which the most enjoyable part was the shooting at Abergeldie, the two brothers were taken to Lausanne in order to improve their French. Upon their return in the following June (1883) their ways parted: the elder entered the army; the younger, bereft of Dalton's affectionate tutelage, joined the corvette *Canada* for service on the North America station. Her captain, Francis Durrant, became his governor and remained his friend. He stayed with his aunt Princess Louise, whose husband (the Marquess of Lorne) [qq.v.] was governor-general of Canada; and a visit to Niagara just warranted the modest claim made in later years that he had set foot on the soil of the United States of America. Before his return to England in July 1884 he had visited his future dominions in the West Indies for the second time. On his nineteenth birthday (3 June 1884) he had been promoted sub-lieutenant, and on 4 August he was invested with the Order of the Garter by Queen Victoria at Osborne.

In September Prince George joined the Royal Naval College at Greenwich, 'where the work is very hard; nine hours a day' (Queen's diary, 7 December). After six months he secured a first class in seamanship, gunnery, and torpedo work, and he next proceeded to Portsmouth for his course in pilotage. Here, as in the *Britannia*, his advancement owed little to his august station, for Captain (afterwards Admiral of the Fleet Lord) Fisher wrote: 'Prince George only lost his first class at Pilotage by 20 marks. The yarn is that one of his examiners, an old salt-horse sailor, didn't think it would do to let him fancy he knew all about it.' These obstacles negotiated, he was promoted lieutenant.

To his satisfaction Prince George was now appointed as fifth lieutenant to the *Thunderer*, under Captain (Sir) Henry Stephenson, whom he had known all his life, as equerry to his father, as captain of the royal yacht, and as captain of a ship accompanying the *Bacchante* on her long cruise. To him the Prince gave unstinted loyalty and devoted service, and from him he received in return disinterested counsel in the spirit of the father's dictum, 'you can do him no greater service than being very strict with him'.

Prince George remained until November 1888 on the Mediterranean station, where his uncle Prince Alfred, Duke of Edinburgh [q.v.], was commander-in-chief. At the jubilee Queen Victoria appointed him her personal naval aide-de-camp on 21 June 1887. He was in London for this occasion, and again on 1 June 1889 when he received the freedom of the City at Guildhall. A month later he attained his first independent command on commissioning torpedo boat No. 79. In May 1890 he was advanced to the command of a gunboat of the first class, the *Thrush*, which he at once took across the Atlantic to Montreal after towing a torpedo boat out to Gibraltar on the way. Still a lieutenant, he brought his ship home in the following year and was promoted commander in August 1891 on paying her off.

Although he commanded the cruiser *Melampus* in the autumn manœuvres of 1892, the curtain had now fallen on Prince George's cherished naval career, save for a brief reappearance in 1898 when he took the first-class cruiser *Crescent* for a three months' cruise. A stroke of fate, as calamitous at the time as it proved fortunate in the event, substituted for the career of his choice the prospect of a lifelong burden which few would choose. On 14 January 1892 the Duke of Clarence died of pneumonia. Overnight Prince George found himself second in succession to the throne.

The death of his brother fell like a hammer-blow upon Prince George. For the first eighteen years of his life he had hardly been separated for a day from Prince Eddy, with whom he had shared a community of interest both within the circle of a singularly united family and in the turbulent days of their first introduction to naval life. He was himself only just recuperating from typhoid fever. While he had still been confined to bed the betrothal had been announced between the Duke of Clarence

and their cousin, Princess Victoria Mary (May) of Teck. Six weeks later the Duke had in turn fallen ill, and within six days had died.

In the Queen's birthday honours list (1892) Prince George was created Duke of York, with the subsidiary titles of Earl of Inverness and Baron Killarney. He was introduced into the House of Lords on 17 June by his father and his uncle the Duke of Connaught. A suite of apartments was arranged for him in St. James's Palace, together with an unpretentious cottage in the grounds of Sandringham; to these the appellations York House and York Cottage were respectively assigned.

The next year (1893) brought him to another important milestone, his betrothal (3 May) to the Princess who was to have been his sister-in-law. She was the daughter of Prince Francis Paul Charles Louis Alexander, Duke of Teck, a member of the royal house of Württemberg long resident in England, and of Princess Mary Adelaide Wilhelmina Elizabeth of Cambridge, granddaughter of King George III and thus first cousin to Queen Victoria. The marriage took place in the Chapel Royal, St. James's Palace, on 6 July. 'I cannot say how pleased I am', wrote the Queen to her daughter, the Empress Frederick. 'The more I see of her the more I like her. . . . She is really a very dear good sensible girl, and very wise, and so *distinguée*. I feel *very* happy about them.' This union, which the Queen with characteristic discernment had commended, brought to the future King the greatest blessing of his life. Their close companionship, which was to last to the end of his reign, exemplified a lofty standard of family life in an age of loosening domestic ties; and his Consort, by her gentle tact and wisdom, her studied detachment from politics, her informed interest in the royal collections, and her supreme dignity and presence, was destined to reveal herself to the realm and empire as a queen of stature rarely equalled, never surpassed.

The seven years which followed were to prove the quietest period that the Duke was to know. In November 1894 he visited St. Petersburg for the funeral of his uncle the Emperor Alexander III (who had married the Princess of Wales's sister) and the wedding of his ill-fated successor Nicholas II. Between the latter and himself there was a startling physical resemblance and a brotherly affection; the bride, moreover, being a granddaughter of Queen Victoria, was also his first cousin. In

August 1897 and again in April 1899 the Duke and Duchess paid visits to Ireland, where they were received with enthusiasm. For the rest, there were continual engagements and claims, all of which were met with cheerfulness. Now, as ever, the Duke delighted to devote his leisure to various forms of outdoor sport, chief among them being yachting and shooting. During these years too were born his first four children: Prince Edward, later King Edward VIII and Duke of Windsor (23 June 1894); Prince Albert, later Duke of York and King George VI (14 December 1895); Princess Mary, later Princess Royal and Countess of Harewood (25 April 1897); and Prince Henry, later Duke of Gloucester (31 March 1900); to these were subsequently added a further two sons: Prince George, later Duke of Kent (20 December 1902), who was killed on active service 25 August 1942; and Prince John (12 July 1905) who died 18 January 1919.

On 22 January 1901 the death of Queen Victoria brought to a close an epoch both in time and in social outlook. The Duke now became Duke of Cornwall as of right, and eligible for the Principality of Wales when it should please his father to confer it upon him. His new position necessarily involved an increase in his public duties as the only son of a sexagenarian king. Tension between sovereign and heir neither began nor ended in the Victorian age; and a comparison between the dispositions of King Edward VII and his son can have afforded little hope of an amelioration in this traditionally uneasy relationship. But it had been given to Queen Alexandra to forge throughout her family a powerful bond of mutual love, and she was now to witness its happy fulfilment. Unlike though they were in disposition, between King Edward VII and his son there existed on both sides a degree of trust and affection rare in their respective stations, and not a passing cloud disturbed the harmony of their intercourse throughout the reign. Every day the Prince of Wales would discuss current topics with the King; nor, after his own accession, did a day pass without its recollection of a father to whose memory he remained jealously devoted to the end.

The outset of a new reign involves changes and adjustments in the royal household. From the ensuing redistribution the Duke of Cornwall and York (as he now for a short while became) drew the services of Sir Arthur Bigge (later Lord Stamfordham, q.v.), and an association thus began which was to end only with the latter's death thirty years later. Bigge had served a fifteen years' apprenticeship under Sir Henry Ponsonby [q.v], whom in 1895 he had succeeded as private secretary to Queen Victoria. He thus brought to his work for the new heir to the throne an intimate acquaintance with the politics and personalities of the preceding twenty years; and this knowledge of affairs, coupled with a selfless devotion and an immense capacity for work, proved an asset to his master of which it is impossible to overestimate the importance. King George's household was at all times a happy and efficient structure, reflecting his perspicacity in the right choice of men: but the acquisition of Bigge was an uncovenanted stroke of fortune which the King and the ministers of a whole generation were destined to bless.

As early as 1893, a few months after his marriage, the Duke had received an invitation from the various colonies in Australia to make a tour in those parts, and the New Zealand government had raised the question afresh after the diamond jubilee of 1897. For his part he would willingly have acceded, but various circumstances had operated to postpone the plan. In August 1900, however, Queen Victoria had signified her consent, urged thereto by an important development in the structure of the empire which called for a demonstration of her imperial interest. On 18 September a proclamation was issued in London announcing that from New Year's Day 1901 the constituent colonies in Australia, together with Tasmania, would be federated into a single unit: it was the first session of this new Commonwealth parliament that was to provide the occasion for the royal tour. Early in December the Queen sanctioned the extension of the itinerary to include a visit to Canada. Preparations were well advanced when the Queen died. It was decided that the tour should take place as planned, but that mourning should be worn and festivities correspondingly curtailed.

Leaving Portsmouth in the *Ophir* on 16 March 1901 the Duke and Duchess followed the route through the Mediterranean. At Gibraltar they inspected the embryo harbour works then under construction and the subject of controversy at home. At Malta they found a comfortable assurance of security in the fact that no land-battery could be constructed within a range of sixty miles: nevertheless a vigilant Admiralty was experimenting with the new Brennan torpedo, of which a demonstration was witnessed. In the words of Sir Donald Mackenzie Wallace: 'Whether this ingenious instrument would prove a formidable weapon in real warfare the experts alone can decide, but it is certainly a very pretty toy to play with in time of peace.' The inconveniences of distance were already being mitigated by wireless telegraphy, which enabled a message to be received from as far as 180 miles away with the aid of a ship stationed midway; it was evident that it might presently 'in certain circumstances be of enormous assistance to the navy'.

After calling at Suez and Aden the royal party reached Colombo on 12 April, and here in the course of an address the Duke first alluded to the need for increased trade with the mother country which was to prove the keynote of his observations throughout the tour. Thence they proceeded via Singapore to call for the second time in his life at Albany, Western Australia, before passing along the southern coast to Melbourne. Here on 9 May, amid scenes of the greatest enthusiasm, he opened parliament in the Exhibition Building in the presence of 15,000 spectators. After paying tribute to the spontaneous participation of the land and sea forces of Australia in the South African war, he expressed the King's heartfelt satisfaction and thankfulness for the achievement of political union among the Australian colonies. Here, as also at Brisbane and Sydney which they next visited, an enthusiastic ovation was accorded them, and the Duchess won all hearts by her simple dignity and practical interest in all that they were shown. From Sydney they crossed to New Zealand, where particular attention was devoted to the welfare of the Maori population. On the return journey calls were made at Hobart and Adelaide; and so across the Indian Ocean to Mauritius and Durban. At Pietermaritzburg the Duke held a military investiture in the presence of Lord Kitchener, then conducting the final stages of the South African war.

After calling at Cape Town course was set across the Atlantic for Quebec, where the Duke and Duchess landed on 16 September. In the course of the ensuing five weeks they crossed and recrossed Canada in a train specially built by the Canadian Pacific Railway, making many stops on the way. In a series of felicitous speeches the Duke thanked the Canadian people for the timely help accorded to the home country in her hour of need, and was once more impressed by the fervent loyalty to the throne which he had observed on his first visit eighteen years earlier.

Leaving Newfoundland on 25 October, the Duke was received at Portsmouth by the King on 1 November and experienced the joy of seeing his children once more. It had not been easy for the King to spare his services for so long a period at a time when only the Duke of Connaught was available to assist in the functions inseparable from the opening of a new reign. In a letter written on his sixtieth birthday (9 November) King Edward wrote to his son: 'In creating you to-day Prince of Wales and Earl of Chester I am not only conferring on you ancient titles which I bore for upwards of 59 years, but I wish to mark my appreciation of the admirable manner in which you carried out the arduous duties to the Colonies which I entrusted you with. I have but little doubt that they will bear good fruit in the future and knit the Colonies more than ever to the Mother Country. God bless you, my dear boy, and I know I can always count on your support and assistance in the heavy duties and responsible position I now occupy.'

On 5 December, in the course of a memorable speech at Guildhall, the Prince of Wales paid tribute to the intense loyalty which animated the inhabitants of the territories which he had visited; and with this loyalty, he said, were evidences of their readiness to share the burden and responsibility of membership of the Empire. In a passage which attained worldwide attention he then spoke of 'the impression that seems generally to prevail among our brethren across the seas, that the old country must wake up if she intends to maintain her old position of preeminence in her colonial trade against foreign competitors'.

During the nine years of his father's reign the Prince of Wales devoted himself to the public duties incumbent upon the heir to the throne. He was now the only son, and the Duke of Connaught was still pursuing a distinguished military career, largely overseas. Active and intelligent though King Edward VII was, he was no longer young; moreover, he was in the habit of passing a quarter of the year on the continent. In political affairs the Prince had much to learn. The King, his own experience fresh in his mind, saw to it that state papers were at his son's disposal: ministers would come to see him, and he formed the habit of listening to debates in both Houses. How great was his debt during these formative years to the sage and experienced Bigge he acknowledged at Christmas 1907 in a letter which does credit to both: 'I was much touched by your kind letter received this morning. You have nothing to thank us for, it is all the other way. I fear sometimes I have lost my temper with you, and often been very rude, but I am sure you know me well enough by now to know that I did not mean it. . . . For all these past services I offer you my thanks from the bottom of my heart. I am a bad hand at saying what I feel, but I thank God I have a friend like you.'

The Prince lived during these years at Marlborough House when in London. For country retreats he had Frogmore House in the Home Park at Windsor, Abergeldie Castle near Balmoral, and York Cottage at Sandringham—always his favourite home. Here through many a winter day he perfected his shooting, the sport at which he early reached and long retained pre-eminence. In these middle years too he sometimes fished, occasionally rode to hounds, and often played golf and lawn tennis. Cricket and football he always enjoyed as a spectator. But above all he delighted in sailing his famous yacht *Britannia*, the closely contested supremacy of which he noted with statistical pride in his diary. Long experience, coupled with an Englishman's love of the sea, had wrought in him the ideal yachtsman, and he revelled in a sport in which he did not need the advice of any man. For indoor recreation he relied upon his lifelong interest in the postage stamps of the British Empire. Here, as with shooting and yachting, he was an expert in his own right, his knowledge in this specialized field being scientific and detailed. It remained his hobby until the end of his life and served as a relief from the cares of state, particularly during the years of war. Thus, whether indoors or out, he was as amply furnished with internal resources as most men, and this boon contributed not a little to his buoyancy of spirits in a position necessarily lonely.

As Prince of Wales he paid several visits to the courts of Europe, spent twelve days in Ireland in January 1905, and enjoyed yet another visit to Canada in July 1908. But his most important overseas undertaking was the tour which he and the Princess carried out in India under the guidance of Sir Walter Lawrence [q.v.] in the winter of 1905–1906. Reaching Bombay in the *Renown* on 9 November they were immediately involved in a series of visits which took them from the Khyber Pass to Rangoon and Mandalay, across by sea to Madras and up to the Afghan frontier again before re-embarking at Karachi on 19 March. As the guest of Lord Kitchener the Prince had followed the course of the manœuvres in the Frontier country: 'Lord Kitchener is a perfect host', he wrote in his diary; 'I have the greatest admiration for him as a strong man and a good soldier.' He enjoyed the four and a half months of this visit, in the course of which he formed lasting friendships and laid the foundation of that pride and affection which always marked his references to India and its inhabitants.

The death of King Edward VII on 6 May 1910 was an overwhelming sorrow which the pressure of immediate events was powerless to alleviate. The funeral on the 20th was attended by the rulers of Norway, Denmark, Belgium, Germany, Spain, Portugal, Greece, and Bulgaria. As they dispersed to their countries (from which all but the first three were destined to be evicted) it was in no cheerful spirit that the new King turned to face responsibilities which he had never sought. The political climate was such as to tax even his experienced and popular father: he felt himself alone, ill-equipped to handle a complex situation, and little known to his four hundred million subjects. He was, moreover, vexed by the circulation of a story concerning his alleged marriage in 1890 to a lady in Malta, a criminal libel which brought the maximum term of imprisonment to its utterer on 1 February 1911. It was a strange charge to bring against a sovereign of unimpeachable virtue, whose crowning benediction was a happy domestic life.

For the first twelve months of his reign the King was sufficiently occupied in acquiring the habit of sovereignty. There were political problems to master, acquaintances to be made, rulings to be given upon domestic rearrangements. For these purposes he welcomed the respite from public and social functions which the long term of public mourning afforded. But the midsummer pomps of 1911 were the prelude to a period of activity. The coronation ceremony in Westminster Abbey on 22 June was a triumph of careful preparation. Its pageantry and ritual made a profound impression upon all, and not least upon the central figure, who was touched to deep emotion by the solemnity

of the occasion and heartened by the bewildering ovations of his crowded capital.
In the following week Their Majesties
carried out two public drives through
London, attended a thanksgiving service
at St. Paul's Cathedral, gave a party at
the Crystal Palace to 100,000 London
schoolchildren, and reviewed at Spithead
the largest naval fleet ever assembled. A
fortnight after the coronation the King
and Queen set out for Dublin, where they
were accorded an enthusiastic reception
during a five-day visit. Recrossing to
Wales, they spent a similar period in the
Principality, their most memorable function being the investiture of the Prince of
Wales at Carnarvon Castle on 13 July:
'the dear boy did it all remarkably well
and looked so nice', the King recorded in
his diary. From Wales they passed on to
Holyrood, there to be greeted by the
plaudits of loyal Scottish subjects.

Back in London, at a time of strong
political ferment, the King's thoughts
were engaged upon the state visit to his
Indian Empire upon which he had set his
heart. On 11 November 1911 he set out
from Portsmouth with the Queen in the
Medina, escorted by four cruisers, and
with this flotilla (containing little short of
4,000 officers and men) arrived at Bombay
on 2 December. At the ancient capital of
Delhi he was accommodated in an enormous camp of 40,000 tents, and here as
King Emperor he held on the 12th a state
Durbar of matchless magnificence. With
his coronation robes he wore a crown of
diamonds provided by the Indian government in order to obviate the necessity of
transporting the traditional regalia overseas. Enthroned upon a platform set in
a spacious amphitheatre, His Majesty received the homage of the ruling princes
and British governors, and announced the
substantial boons customary upon such
occasions. He then made a dramatic
announcement, the secret of which had
been well kept. Speaking in a clear voice
he declared that the seat of government
was to be transferred from Calcutta to
Delhi and that there was to be established
a governorship of Bengal similar to those
of Madras and Bombay.

These ceremonies concluded, the King
turned to the enjoyment of ten days' tiger
shooting in Nepal, after which he 'took
leave of the kind Maharajah, his sons and
all his people, with much regret. They
have spoilt us with kindness and given us
the best sport in the world.' Their Majesties spent nine days in Calcutta before

re-embarking at Bombay on 10 January
1912. How much this visit had meant
to the King is clear from his diary: 'To-day
I regret to say is our last day in India.
The Legislative Council presented an
address of farewell. I quite broke down
in reading my answer. . . . Our second
visit to India is now over and we can thank
God that it has been an unqualified success
from first to last. It was entirely my own
idea to hold the Coronation Durbar at
Delhi in person, and at first I met with
much opposition. But the result has I
hope been more than satisfactory and has
surpassed all expectations. I am vain
enough to think that our visit will have
done good in India. We have been fully
repaid for our long journey.'

The King, in assuming the troubled inheritance bequeathed to him by his father,
had found himself immediately confronted
with a constitutional crisis of the gravest
character. In order to meet the cost of
the old age pensions and the increased
estimates necessitated by the threat of
German naval competition, the liberal
government had been faced with the task
of levying additional taxation. The budget
of 1909 had consequently raised the
income-tax from 1s. to 1s. 2d. and imposed
a novel supertax of 6d., together with
certain land taxes. The House of Lords,
which had not endeared itself to the
Commons by rejecting several of their
proposed measures of reform, on 30 November had taken the unprecedented step
of throwing out the budget *in toto*, thus
setting the stage for a trial of strength
between the two chambers. The issue was
barely joined before the throne was deprived of a sovereign of exceptional political acumen, and a crucial responsibility
devolved upon his untried and inexperienced successor.

The new King was unaware that within
a month of his father's death important
meetings and conversations had taken
place between the King's private secretary, Lord Knollys, Archbishop Davidson,
Balfour, and Esher, concerning the possibility of King Edward being pressed by
Asquith to give a contingent guarantee
for the creation of peers: he only learned
this in December 1913 [Royal Archives,
sub Home Rule iii. 63]. But it was known
that King Edward had caused an intimation to be conveyed by Knollys (15 December 1909) that in no event would he
consent to an *ad hoc* creation until after a
second general election, in which the issue
should have been placed squarely before

the people. It is a reasonable inference, but no more, that had the condition been fulfilled and the need arisen, King Edward would not have withheld the use of his prerogative. The first election took place immediately upon the Lords' rejection of the budget, upon the text that the Commons alone were to control finance and that any non-financial bill sent up to the Lords in three successive sessions should receive the royal assent. With this mandate the liberals were again returned to power (28 January 1910) with a majority reduced from 335 to the still effective figure of 123. The Lords now (28 April) accepted the budget. But they had been playing for high stakes and were faced with the parliament bill, which limited their powers for the future. It was at this juncture (6 May) that King Edward died.

In the political truce which followed it was at Asquith's suggestion that the question at issue was referred to a constitutional conference consisting of four liberals and four conservatives. The conference met from June until November without achieving agreement, and the prime minister proceeded to fulfil the condition which the late King had postulated. In December 1910, for the second time within a twelvemonth, the country was once more consulted, and again returned the liberals, with a majority of 125. To anticipate the course of events it may here be added that on 10 August 1911, in an atmosphere of political excitement unsurpassed in modern times, the Lords accepted the parliament bill by the narrow majority of seventeen votes.

But before the December election the new King had been placed in an unenviable position. Asquith was unexcelled in the use of language at once precise and enigmatic. On 14 April 1910 he had told the House of Commons: 'In no case would we recommend dissolution except under such conditions as will ensure that in the new parliament the judgement of the people as expressed in the election will be carried into law.' On 11 November he explained the political situation to the King, pointing out that should the Lords remain obdurate a final settlement could only be brought about by the willingness of the Crown to exercise its prerogative. He told the King that he would not ask for any guarantees before the election [Royal Archives, K. 2552 (2). 72]: for the moment he contented himself with stating the case, and left it for consideration [Spender and Asquith, vol. i, p. 296].

None the less, five days later Asquith and Crewe felt constrained to seek from the King at Buckingham Palace (16 November) a secret and 'hypothetical understanding' that sufficient peers would be created should need arise in the parliament that was yet to be elected. 'His Majesty said that his only wish was to do what was right and constitutional and best for the country in the present circumstances. The King then felt with reluctance that it would be impossible not to act upon their advice and therefore agreed to the understanding' [Royal Archives, *ut sup.*]. In the carefully chosen words of Crewe (House of Lords, 8 August 1911), 'We ascertained His Majesty's view that, if the opinion of the country were clearly ascertained upon the parliament bill, in the last resort a creation of peers might be the only remedy, and might be the only way of concluding the dispute. His Majesty faced the contingency and entertained the suggestion as a possible one with natural, and if I may be permitted to use the phrase, in my opinion with legitimate reluctance. But it is altogether inaccurate, and I might use a stronger phrase, to say that at that time we asked His Majesty for guarantees. The whole position was obviously hypothetical.'

Shades of meaning were here involved to which the King's mind was a stranger. It can hardly be matter for surprise that he should feel that he was being expected to underwrite the words uttered in April by the prime minister, and to implement in advance the construction which plain men would place upon them in the constituencies. He felt for the rest of his life that he might have been trusted to take the right step should the occasion have arisen. Asquith, for his part, held the Crown in high veneration: as the case presented itself to him it was not a matter of trusting the King, but of coercing the conservative peers, who were in no mood to be persuaded though one rose from the dead. Even when at a later date (18 July) the secret was by agreement divulged, there were those who declined to believe that the sovereign would indeed subject the constitution to so severe a strain.

The King harboured no resentment either against Crewe, who remained to the end one of his closest personal friends, or against Asquith, for whom he reserved a high, if watchful, esteem. When, in the hour of Asquith's political adversity, the King, of his own mere motion, created his former prime minister one of the now less powerful peers (February 1925) he interpreted with characteristic insight the corporate feeling of the nation, and took a personal pleasure in doing so.

The Parliament Act, in drawing the teeth of the House of Lords, created for the King a difficulty unforeseen, by him at any rate, at the time. Its preamble announced the intention to set up a new second chamber; but since this could not be done at once the Act made provision for restricting the powers of the House of Lords in the meanwhile. Although not intended to affect the position of the sovereign, it nevertheless removed the first check upon the operations of the Commons; and this elimination of one branch of the legislature necessarily increased the responsibility of the King when a bill, thrice rejected by the upper House, came up for the royal assent. No longer could the Lords force a dissolution, even in the few cases where they had that power before the passing of the Act; henceforth the sovereign alone must decide whether a bill which comes from a single chamber is of such gravity that, with all the attendant risks of bringing the Crown into party politics, an appeal to the country against the advice of his ministers would be justified.

This dilemma was not long in making itself felt. Already by the spring of 1912 preparations of a military nature in the province of Ulster were affording grounds for misgiving, and the debates which followed the introduction of the home rule bill on 11 April were carried on in an atmosphere of passion. The same autumn (27 September) Bonar Law, staying at Balmoral, took occasion to indicate the thankless position in which it appeared that the King would find himself. The government, he argued, admitted its responsibility for carrying out the preamble of the Parliament Act, and in the meanwhile the constitution was in suspense: it was doubtful whether the government still had the support of the country: it would once more rely upon the exercise of the royal prerogative to overcome the opposition of the peers. It was the identical quandary expressed in different terms, and it seemed that the King would again find himself compromised.

The home rule bill, forced through the Commons by the aid of the closure and the support of the Irish and labour members, was first rejected by the Lords on 13 January 1913. Re-submitted, it was thrown out afresh on 15 July. Then followed ten months during which the King observed with dismay a worsening situation in which, to the disorders attendant upon the suffragette menace, it seemed certain that an uprising in Ireland was to be added. To imagine that in a time of crisis it is the ministers alone who tender advice to the sovereign would be to overlook the operations of the Post Office and the press. From all sides he was urged to take this course or that: to dismiss his ministers, to impose a dissolution, to demand a referendum, to issue a state paper defining his position and intentions, to grant (or alternatively to withhold) the royal assent. Whatever the nature of the advice there was evident in all quarters a recognition of his impartiality, a desire to safeguard his constitutional position, a disposition to seek a possible solution, and a loyal sympathy in the dilemma in which he was placed.

His course was not made easier by the rosy optimism with which the prime minister appeared to confront the rising storm. The King listened with inward sympathy to those who counselled strong action, but schooled himself in the exercise of a stronger forbearance. An anxious winter gave way to the yet more vexed summer of 1914, and still his voice was heard, now by one leader and now by another, urging patience and restraint in public utterance, suggesting fresh lines of accommodation, a renewal of private negotiation, concession here, conciliation there. Whether Ireland was to have home rule or not, he had told Asquith on 13 December, was for the politicians to settle. But as king he held that it was his duty by every means in his power to prevent the outbreak of civil strife in any part of his kingdom; that was his responsibility and he should do his best to fulfil it.

Space forbids a detailed examination of the part played by the King throughout the long-drawn-out crisis, but a month, that of February 1914, may be chosen as a sample. On the 2nd Stamfordham wrote a letter of reassurance on the King's behalf to Bonar Law, saying that His Majesty was not so pessimistic as he, and that as to any special communication to his ministers the King's action would be guided by time and circumstance. On the 5th the King saw Asquith at Windsor and had a serious conversation about possible trouble in the army, such as eventually occurred at the Curragh, and repeated that he could not allow bloodshed among his loyal subjects without exerting every means in his power to avert it. On the 11th he wrote personally congratulating Asquith upon his moderate and conciliatory speech in the House. On the 12th Stamfordham was sent to ask Asquith whether he thought that it would be helpful for the King to urge moderation upon Bonar Law and Sir Edward Carson [q.v.] in entertaining the government proposals. On the 20th he had members of the opposition to dinner. On the 25th Stamfordham wrote on his behalf to Bonar Law regretting the rasping tone of his speech the night before; and on the following day to Asquith deploring the acrimonious nature of the debates. On the 27th the King had the members of the government to dinner and held long conversations with the prime minister. Next morning he sent Stamfordham to tell Carson that His Majesty had delivered to Asquith the kindly personal messages with which Carson had entrusted him; that Asquith had been touched and would like to reopen negotiations with him; and to express the King's hope that Carson would refrain from making a bitter speech on the following Tuesday. And so it went on for month after month, the King, with a degree of patience formerly to seek in his natural habit of mind, propounding every means that ingenuity could devise for effecting a reconciliation.

On 21 March, after a number of officers at the Curragh had resigned rather than take part in the coercion of Ulster, the King addressed to the prime minister a letter of sharp protest that he had been left to learn of the incident from the public press next day. It was not, as it happened, Asquith's fault; and it proved fortunate in the event since it subsequently cleared the King from the imputation of complicity which in the heat of the moment had been directed against him in certain quarters.

On 1 May the King, on his own initiative, invited Mr. James Lowther (later Viscount Ullswater) to Buckingham Palace and there prevailed upon him to address to the prime minister an offer to invite the various leaders to meet under his presidency, as Speaker, with a view to arriving at a solution. On 22 June (Coronation Day) the King wrote a personal letter to Asquith recalling to his memory a sentence in the message which he had addressed to his subjects on that occasion three years previously. 'Whatever perplexities or difficulties may lie before me and my people', he had then written, 'we shall all unite in facing them resolutely, calmly

and with public spirit, confident that under Divine guidance the ultimate outcome may be to the common good.' 'The perplexities and difficulties', he now wrote, 'have not grown less with time, and there is greater need than ever that they should be met and dealt with in that spirit upon which I then felt I could confidently depend. I know that I can count upon your support in the fulfilment of my hopes and prayers of three years ago.'

The prospect of a conference was discussed on 16 July between Stamfordham and Asquith, with the result that on the following day the latter submitted to the King a request that he might be allowed to announce that His Majesty would invite representatives of all parties to Buckingham Palace for a full and free discussion of the outstanding issues. On the 18th invitations were sent by Stamfordham to Lansdowne and Bonar Law, Carson and Craig, Redmond and Dillon; Asquith and Crewe represented the government, and the Speaker presided. The speech with which His Majesty welcomed the members on the 21st was a model of simple eloquence. 'For months', the King said, 'we have watched with deep misgivings the course of events in Ireland. The trend has been surely and steadily towards an appeal to force, and to-day the cry of civil war is on the lips of the most responsible and sober minded of my people. We have in the past endeavoured to act as a civilising example to the world, and to me it is unthinkable, as it must be to you, that we should be brought to the brink of a fratricidal war upon issues apparently so capable of adjustment as those you are now asked to consider, if handled in a spirit of generous compromise. My apprehension in contemplating such a dire calamity is intensified by my feelings of attachment to Ireland and of sympathy for her people who have always welcomed me with warmhearted affection. Gentlemen, you represent in one form or another the vast majority of my subjects at home. You also have a deep interest in my Dominions overseas, who are scarcely less concerned in a prompt and friendly settlement of this question. I regard you then in this matter as trustees for the honour and peace of all. Your responsibilities are indeed great. The time is short. You will I know employ it to the fullest advantage and be patient, earnest and conciliatory in view of the magnitude of the issues at stake. I pray that God in His infinite wisdom may guide your deliberations so that they may result in the joy of peace and settlement.'

These hopes were not to be fulfilled. After four meetings the conference broke down upon a point insignificant in comparison with the issues involved. But the King had done his best; and if during the lapse of valuable time the forces unleashed in Ireland had become too strong for their leaders, it was due to no inactivity on his part. Events of yet greater moment supervened to avert the immediate consequences, and the controversy was laid aside, as it was hoped, for the duration of the European war. In a letter to the King dated 17 September Asquith wrote: 'He hopes he may be allowed to express his respectful sympathy with, and admiration of, the patience and the strict observance of constitutional practice, together with the tact and judgment, which in a time of exceptional difficulty and anxiety, Your Majesty has never for a moment failed to exercise.'

War on the cosmic scale of that which was now about to break out involves every citizen in strain and distress from which the sovereign is not immune. The rhythm of his work is intensified; the inspection of hospitals brings the horror of the conflict continually before his eyes; he is apprised of perils without, and doubts and dissensions within, of which his subjects are unaware. But from the constitutional point of view war provides few occasions for the intervention of a king who finds himself at the head of a united and harmonious nation, intent upon the pursuit of a common purpose. For months King George had nursed the hope that agreement upon the Irish question would have been reached. Patiently he had studied the timing of his final attempt to produce a settlement. Now, when his conference had failed, it could hardly be otherwise than with a sense of momentary relief that he observed the dramatic unfolding of events. Overnight the nation which had been sliding rapidly into disruption and civil war had braced itself to meet a sterner issue, standing united once more before the threat from without.

Of its implications the King was in no doubt. As early as 8 December 1912 he had written from Sandringham to the foreign secretary: 'My dear Grey, Prince Henry of Prussia paid me a short visit here two days ago. In the course of a long conversation with regard to the present European situation, he asked me point blank, whether in the event of Austria and Germany going to war with Russia and France, England would come to the assistance of the two latter powers. I answered undoubtedly yes under certain circumstances. He professed surprise and regret but did not ask what the circumstances were. He said he would tell the Emperor what I told him. Of course Germany must know that we could not allow either of our friends to be crippled. I think it is only right that you should know what passed between me and the Emperor's brother on this point.'

Now, on 26 July 1914, the day on which the Admiralty cancelled leave and bade the fleet stand by at Portland, it happened that the King received another visit from Prince Henry, then on a holiday in England. At that moment Belgium had not been invaded and the Cabinet was working against wind and tide to avert a European conflict. The King told the prince that England still hoped not to be drawn in, and the Emperor, to whom his brother reported the conversation, interpreted it as an assurance of British neutrality, come what might. The incident is dealt with in a letter from Lord Wigram to *The Times* of 2 June 1938. The German claim subsequently based upon the interview was demolished by the archivist of the House of Hohenzollern, Dr. Kurt Jagow, in the *Berliner Monatshefte* for July–August 1938 [see *The Times*, 30 June 1938, under 'The Word of a King', with leading article].

Most of the war the King spent at Buckingham Palace, visiting Windsor for a month at Easter and six weeks in the late summer; Balmoral was too remote, but at times he enjoyed a few days at Sandringham, occasionally taking out his gun to shoot game which he sent to the hospitals. Early in 1915 he made a gift to the Exchequer of £100,000, an example which was later followed by others. On 6 April 1915 he gave orders that no wine, spirits, or beer should be consumed in the royal household, observing a like abstinence himself; and from February 1917 strict adherence to the new rationing regulations was imposed throughout the palace, from the royal table downwards. The war had not long started when, within the space of little more than a week, there fell in action three members of his personal suite to whom he was especially devoted, Lord Charles Petty-Fitzmaurice, Lord Crichton, and Lord John Hamilton, together with his first cousin Prince Maurice of Battenberg. His own two eldest sons were hostages to fortune, the Prince of

Wales in the army from the outset, Prince Albert in the battle of Jutland in May 1916. The removal in deference to an unreasoning popular outcry in October 1914 of his brilliant cousin by marriage, Prince Louis of Battenberg (afterwards Marquess of Milford Haven, q.v.), from his office of first sea lord, involved the King in a conflict of loyalties. The dramatic loss of Lord Kitchener in June 1916 he felt as something more than a national calamity, for he had long held him in personal affection as well as the highest professional esteem.

The formation of Asquith's coalition government in May 1915 brought the first labour minister into the King's service in the person of Arthur Henderson [q.v.] at the Board of Education. The next change of government, in December 1916, involved the extrusion of Asquith by Lloyd George, to whose talents the King frequently paid generous and encouraging tribute, although on personal grounds he missed the sturdy and unruffled presence of his first prime minister. The fissures and stresses which gave birth to the new administration have been recorded in the leading political biographies, and in great detail in Lord Beaverbrook's *Politicians and the War* (1928). Asquith resigned on 5 December and Bonar Law was invited to form a government. At the instance of the latter the King on the following day held a conference attended by Asquith, Balfour, Bonar Law, Lloyd George, and Henderson; but since Asquith felt unable to serve under his leadership, Bonar Law abandoned the attempt and the King accordingly entrusted the task to Lloyd George. In reply to the King's letter offering him the Garter Asquith wrote: 'I trust that Your Majesty will permit me, in all gratitude and humility, to decline. I have had the honour of serving Your Majesty as Prime Minister continuously from the first day of your reign. Through times of much difficulty and peril Your Majesty has honoured me with unstinted confidence and unwavering support. I desire no higher distinction.'

On 20 June 1917 the following announcement appeared in the press: 'The King has deemed it desirable, in the conditions brought about by the present war, that those princes of his family who are his subjects and bear German names and titles should relinquish these titles, and henceforth adopt British surnames.' In consequence of this decision four new peerages were created. The Duke of Teck and his brother, Prince Alexander, became Marquess of Cambridge and Earl of Athlone; Princes Louis and Alexander of Battenberg became Marquesses of Milford Haven and Carisbrooke; members of the Teck and Battenberg families adopted the surnames Cambridge and Mountbatten respectively. At a meeting of the Privy Council held on 17 July His Majesty announced his intention, embodied in a royal proclamation of the same date, of adopting on his own behalf and that of all his subjects descended from Queen Victoria the name of Windsor for the Royal House and Family. The 'sublime inspiration', as Lord Rosebery called it, came to Lord Stamfordham, who was unaware at the time that King Edward III had been styled 'Sir Edward de Windsor, King of England' in a deed dated 1375 [Record Office, C. 2121]. Finally, by letters patent dated 11 December 1917, the Princely title and its attendant appellation Royal Highness were confined to the children of a sovereign and of the sons of a sovereign (with the addition of the special case of the eldest living son of the eldest son of the Prince of Wales). To the grandchildren of the sons of a sovereign in the direct male line was assigned the style and title of the children of dukes.

The extent of the burden shouldered by the King during the war years was not apparent to the public owing to the secrecy which necessarily cloaked his movements. The record of his activities reveals that he paid 300 visits to military hospitals, each a taxing ordeal for a sensitive nature; nor was the personal distribution of 58,000 decorations accomplished without fatigue. He inspected 300 naval and military formations and a like number of factories engaged upon war work. He paid five visits to the Grand Fleet and seven to his armies in France and Belgium. In October 1915, after the abortive battles of Neuve Chapelle and Loos, murmurs demanding a change in the high command made themselves heard (prime minister's secretary to Stamfordham, 7 October), and the King was able during his tour later in the month to ascertain the views of the leading generals in the field. It was early in December that Sir John French was replaced by Sir Douglas Haig, a change effected by Asquith upon his sole responsibility [Spender and Asquith, vol. i, p. 191]. This same tour in France came to an untimely end when a restive mount, frightened by the cheering of the troops, reared and fell backwards on the King fracturing his pelvis. Such visits to his armies in the field had a stimulating effect upon the troops, none more so than that undertaken at his own instance at the end of March 1918, a week after the opening of the final German onslaught.

The labours of the King during the war had been pursued with an absence of publicity congenial to him, but the conclusion of hostilities brought him to the front once more. The agony and triumph of the past four years were over and with the sudden release of tension the relief of millions found expression in widespread demonstrations of affection and loyalty to the throne. Alike on Armistice Day and in the later celebrations of Peace Day in 1919 it was to the palace that all steps were turned in the exuberance of a common emotion. In a series of public appearances the King and Queen were greeted with a demonstrativeness of affection to which the past afforded no parallel, and the scenes witnessed in the course of six drives through the capital in the days immediately succeeding the armistice were re-enacted at the close of the month both in Edinburgh and in Paris. Particularly notable was the address delivered to both Houses of Parliament on 19 November in which the King dwelt on the dedication of the whole British race to the demands of war and called for a heightened sense of individual and national duty in the years ahead. 'For centuries past', he declared, 'Britain has led the world along the path of ordered freedom. Leadership may still be hers among the peoples who are seeking to follow that path.'

If hostilities had ceased on the continent the case was otherwise in Ireland, where the best that the government could claim was that it had murder by the throat. The Home Rule Act of December 1920, although repudiated by the South, had been accepted by Northern Ireland, and the Ulster parliament was to be opened in June 1921. Despite the untoward aspect of Irish affairs the Cabinet felt that an occasion of such high imperial significance should be marked by the presence of the sovereign in person. The King would have been other than himself had he not readily acceded. 'As is naturally to be expected', Stamfordham wrote to the prime minister of Northern Ireland on 9 June, 'there is a very strong difference of opinion about the King going to Belfast, and many Irishmen, including those residing in that country, tell me that His Majesty is running considerable risk in going. Once the Govern-

ment had expressed the wish that His Majesty should go, you may be quite certain that the King would not look back for one instant: and as to personal risk, I can frankly say that this has not entered into His Majesty's calculations—it would be entirely contrary to his nature for it to do so.' At the last minute the Ulster government expressed the desire that the Queen should go too, and the invitation was accepted with equal alacrity. Their Majesties crossed to Belfast on 22 June and there, in the City Hall, the King delivered a speech striking in its dramatic timing and sincerity of utterance. 'I am emboldened', His Majesty declared, 'to look beyond the sorrow and the anxiety which have clouded of late my vision of Irish affairs. I appeal to all Irishmen to pause, to stretch out the hand of forbearance and conciliation. It is my earnest desire that in Southern Ireland too there may ere long take place a parallel to what is now passing in this hall. The future lies in the hands of my Irish people themselves. May this historic gathering be the prelude of a day in which the Irish people, under one parliament or two, as those parliaments may themselves decide, shall work together in common love for Ireland upon the sure foundation of mutual justice and respect.'

'None but the King', wrote Lloyd George, 'could have made that personal appeal.' It was the more unfortunate that, on the evening before it was uttered, the lord chancellor (Birkenhead) should have held threatening language in the House of Lords, and that on the same day the secretary of state for war should have announced in the Commons that more troops and every soldier available would be sent to Ireland.

Three days later the King sent Stamfordham to urge the prime minister to make fresh overtures to Southern Ireland while the iron was hot. General Smuts, then providentially in London for the Imperial Conference, crossed to Dublin on 5 July; and assuredly there was no one who, from personal experience and elevation of character, was better qualified to act as intermediary. The subsequent interviews in London between Lloyd George and Mr. de Valera were followed by a series of communications which continued into the autumn, the Cabinet insisting that allegiance to the throne and membership of the Commonwealth should be postulates to any conversations.

A critical point had been reached when

Lloyd George, then in Scotland, summoned a Cabinet meeting at Inverness on 7 September to approve the dispatch of a note couched in aggressive language and possibly naming a time limit for the truce which had been in operation since 11 July. It happened that the King was then staying at Moy, twelve miles from Inverness. His Majesty received the prime minister at breakfast on the morning of the Cabinet meeting, and the proposed draft was discussed between them. The King suggested numerous alterations in the text, the elimination of all threats and contentious phrases, and the inclusion of an invitation to the Sinn Fein representatives to meet the prime minister at once. The latter then drew up a fresh draft in the conciliatory tone which the King had advocated, and this was accepted by the Cabinet later in the morning. The Irish delegates came to London in mid-November, and the articles of agreement inaugurating the Irish Free State were signed on 6 December. 'I humbly congratulate Your Majesty', wrote the prime minister, 'on the triumph of the famous Ulster speech from the throne.'

It is the characteristic of King George's reign that his constitutional troubles came early. High seas had been running when the sailor King had put out: the Irish strife, the parliament bill, the embittered struggle over Welsh disestablishment, the bizarre war conducted by the suffragettes against the community, these all had been overwhelmed in the crowning convulsion of the European conflict, with the passing of which it seemed that the storm had spent its force. Difficulties remained, both in the national and international spheres, but with one or two exceptions they were such as called for no personal intervention on the part of the King. To the ceaseless round of duty which is the inescapable lot of the sovereign, he addressed himself with a devotion which bore fruit in the increasing regard and affection of all ranks of his subjects. In a period of disillusionment and moral disintegration the King and Queen were observed by all men to set a course of public service and to uphold the traditional standards of family life. The marriage of Princess Mary in 1922 proved an occasion of rejoicing to the entire nation, and the later marriages of his younger sons brought the King three daughters each of whom in turn greatly endeared herself to him. Always at his easiest with children, he reserved the tenderest affection for Princess Elizabeth,

whose infant presence never failed to ensure his happiness during the closing decade of his life.

The 'coupon' election of December 1918 had given to Lloyd George's coalition a further lease of life until November 1922, when the conservative party was returned and the King sent for Bonar Law. An ailing man at the time, he sank beneath the load in the following May, giving it to be understood that he would prefer not to tender advice as to his successor. The King decided to summon Stanley (later Earl) Baldwin, then little known, in preference to the brilliant and experienced Lord Curzon. To mitigate the disappointment he caused Curzon to be invited to return from the country in order to learn from Stamfordham the reason for the choice. (It is not the case that the King summoned Curzon with the intention of offering him the premiership but was persuaded to the contrary.) Curzon was mortified upon his arrival to find the purpose of the interview to be other than that which his eagerness had led him to expect; but he bore the intimation with nobility and the King spoke words of healing and gratitude to him at their meeting on 29 May. That the blow should have been so bitter reveals the fallibility of human memory and judgement where self-interest is most strongly engaged; for on 24 May 1919 Curzon himself, in a letter to the King concerning his precedence as lord president, had written: 'The Prime Minister, who is commonly a member of the House of Commons, and will in all likelihood almost invariably be so in the future, has already been placed before the Lord President.' If ever there would recur circumstances in which the prime minister might reasonably be a peer it was not now, when labour was the official opposition, and being unrepresented in the Lords would be unable to hear policy expounded by the head of the government.

Five months after taking office Baldwin sought a dissolution in order to obtain a mandate for protection, which Bonar Law had pledged himself not to introduce. The King deprecated a second election within the twelvemonth, but the prime minister 'said that he had committed himself' (King's diary, 12 November 1923) and the King yielded. After the election in December, for the first time a House of Commons was returned in which there were three parties, each prepared to form a government, yet none commanding a majority. Parliament met on 15 January; a week later the government was defeated and Baldwin resigned. The King sent for Ramsay MacDonald [q.v.].

At this first attainment of labour to office there were many croakers. The King was not among them. 'Thank God', he once wrote to a friend, 'I am an optimist, and I believe in the commonsense of the people of this country.' It was by the twin landmarks of character and principle that he had been in the habit of judging men, and in the mirror of working-class opinion he had always found the reflection of his own unassuming dignity and friendliness. 'To-day', recorded Stamfordham on 22 January 1924, 'the King saw Mr. Ramsay MacDonald and entrusted to him the formation of a new Government, which he undertook. He assured the King that, though he and his friends were inexperienced in governing and fully realised the great responsibilities which they would now assume, nevertheless they were honest and sincere, and his earnest desire was to serve his King and country. They may fail in their endeavours, but it will not be for want of trying to do their best. The King told Mr. Ramsay MacDonald that he might count upon his assistance in every way. His Majesty asked only for frankness between them. His Majesty went on to say that, little expecting to occupy his present position, he served in the Navy for fourteen years and thus had opportunities of seeing more of the world and mixing with his fellow creatures than would otherwise have been the case; while during the past fourteen years he had naturally gained much political knowledge and experience of the working of the machine of government under four different Prime Ministers. Mr. Ramsay MacDonald spoke very openly and said he was sure the King would be generous to him and understand the very difficult position he was in.'

With the members of the new administration the King was at once at home. That they might get to know each other's outlook on the world he gave it to be understood that he would like to see them in turn, at their convenience, for a quiet talk, and his diary records twenty such interviews in the month of February. 'He is an extreme socialist', he noted of the minister of health, 'and comes from Glasgow. I had a very interesting conversation with him.' The household arrangements worked smoothly because both parties intended that they should.

The King made it known informally that the question of court dress was one for the ministers to settle as might seem best to them; and judging that it would conduce to the greater convenience of their guests, Their Majesties initiated a series of afternoon parties at the Palace. In his turn the prime minister, unlike Peel in 1839, himself desired the King to take the political appointments in the royal household and deal with them as His Majesty thought fit. It was agreed that after placing the customary whips at the disposal of the government the King should nominate the lord chamberlain, lord steward, master of the horse, the captains of the bodyguard and yeomen, and three of the lords in waiting: but in order to safeguard the constitutional position the submissions continued to be made by the prime minister, and the officials concerned undertook not to speak or vote against the government or participate in political activities outside.

'Some day', declared an eminent scientist as late as 1920, 'we may have the Prime Minister, or even the Monarch himself, addressing by word of mouth, and at one and the same time, all the different parts of the entire British Empire.' This daring forecast came true on St. George's Day 1924, when the King opened the British Empire Exhibition at Wembley; and, thus established, the precedent was followed on several occasions towards the close of the reign. Over a long period of time he had stood for peace and goodwill among the family of nations under his care, and it was natural that he should be in their thoughts at Christmas time. In a series of admirably turned broadcasts each Christmas Day from 1932 onwards his voice found a welcome in British homes throughout the world, establishing a new intimacy between sovereign and subject and kindling in all hearts the proud sense of kinship one with another. He essayed no flights of oratory, being content to greet each family with a personal message of kindliness and to assert a simple faith in the continued guidance of a divine Providence. Recordings of these homely addresses will enable posterity to judge the nature of the man, and go far to explain the singular hold which he established upon the affections of a quarter of the population of the world.

Under a three-party system the lot of a minority government is unenviable, for a nod exchanged between the opposition leaders can terminate its life at any moment: nor for the sovereign is the position free from ambiguity, for the dissolution and re-election of parliament may only prolong the position of stalemate. To a conservative vote of censure on the Campbell case the liberals moved, on 8 October 1924, an amendment calling for the milder step of a committee of inquiry into the withdrawal of the prosecution. But Mac-Donald chose to stand at bay on the first issue. He had only held office for nine months, but he had shown that labour was capable of bearing rule, proved himself an acceptable minister to the King, done well in the vexed sphere of foreign affairs, and equipped his Cabinet with political experience. His numerical strength was insufficient to effect the introduction of socialism in the present parliament, and he was not ill content to declare his innings closed. The King accordingly returned from Balmoral on the morning after the government's defeat (9 October) and received the prime minister, who sought a dissolution. That the Campbell case was in itself insufficient justification for a third general election within two years was manifest, but the circumstances were unusual. To decline the first request of a young and inexperienced party might have exposed the King's impartiality to question; and moreover it was clear that any extension of the government's lease could only be for a term of weeks. The King therefore granted the dissolution, but took the step of recording his reasons in a memorandum addressed to the prime minister. After the election on 29 October he sent for Baldwin, whose government was destined to last for more than four years.

As early as June 1916 Asquith had announced that an Imperial Conference would be held after the war to consider the recasting of the government of the Empire. When the Dominions were enrolled as separate members of the League of Nations the time had come to define that elusive constitution which was the casual offering of the British race to the science of politics. It was Lord Balfour who, with a courageous sweep of onward vision, devised the formula adopted as the Nicene Creed of the Commonwealth in 1926 and embodied in the Statute of Westminster in 1931. No longer was parliament in the home country to control the overseas Dominions: henceforward the King alone was to constitute the bond in a voluntary association of free peoples, whose co-operation would be effective only in so far as it was willingly accorded. The abdication of the sovereign in 1936 still further loosened the attachment of the Irish Free State: the furnace of a second war served but to anneal the links with the remainder of the British Empire. If Great Britain was fortunate in 1926 in having at hand a statesman of the stature of Balfour, she was no less fortunate in the possession of a King fitted alike by character and by experience to retain the allegiance of her sister nations.

The General Strike in May 1926 was a challenge to constitutional government which the Cabinet met with firmness and the nation with good humour. To an informal suggestion that recourse might be had to the precedent of the Buckingham Palace conference of 1914 the King replied that he would take no such action except upon the advice of his prime minister. He grasped the significance of a football match at Plymouth between the police and the strikers; and when the Cabinet was considering 'freezing' trade union funds he observed with dry common sense that men denied the use of their own money were apt to turn to other people's. He took exception to the announcement in the official *British Gazette* that all ranks of the armed forces of the Crown would receive the full support of the government in any action taken in the honest endeavour to aid the civil power. When after nine days the strike collapsed, 'Let us forget', he wrote in a message to his people, 'whatever elements of bitterness the events of the past few days may have created, and forthwith address ourselves to the task of bringing into being a peace which will be lasting because, forgetting the past, it looks only to the future with the hopefulness of a united people.'

Hitherto King George had been blessed with good health. He was no stranger to a passing attack of rheumatism, was a little careful about his food, and was not immune from the common cold: indeed an intractable bout of influenza in the spring of 1925 had even induced him to commission the royal yacht for a month's cruise in the Mediterranean, averse though he was from foreign travel. But apart from his typhoid fever in 1891 he had escaped lightly until, at the age of sixty-three, he contracted an illness of the gravest character. On 21 November 1928 he took to his bed at Buckingham Palace with a streptococcal infection which necessitated a severe operation for the drainage of the chest on 12 December.

A week earlier the King had been able

to execute a warrant appointing six counsellors of state: the Queen, his two eldest sons, the archbishop of Canterbury, lord chancellor, and prime minister. 'Whereas We have been stricken by illness and are unable for the time being to give due attention to the affairs of Our Realm', the preamble stated, any three of the counsellors were empowered to discharge the royal office: but they were not to dissolve parliament, nor confer titles, 'nor act in any manner or thing in which it is signified by Us or appears to them that Our special approval should be previously obtained.' The council was held in a manner identical with that adopted when Queen Victoria was *en retraite* after the death of the Prince Consort (*Letters*, series ii, vol. i, p. 6): the council assembled in the audience chamber adjoining the bedroom, the home secretary read the order paper standing in the communicating doorway, the King assented and signed the document with his own hand.

Throughout the sombre December days crowds kept vigil outside the palace railings; thousands upon thousands read the bulletins and turned silently away. For several weeks death hovered about the sick chamber and kept in doubt the issue upon which the hopes of millions turned. At length patience and courage had their reward, and on 9 February 1929 the patient was taken by ambulance to Craigweil House, near Bognor. Here he remained until 15 May, when he made the journey to Windsor.

The wound, however, was not yet healed and the King was in considerable discomfort when, during the first week in June, he had to deal with a change of ministry. Baldwin's government had reached the end of its course while he had been ill: the labour party had been returned (again in a minority) at the general election on 30 May, and on 8 June the new ministers journeyed to Windsor to receive their seals of office. If it was a strange complexion of political parties, it was a singular council that assembled once more outside the bedroom in which the King was seated in his dressing-gown. On the previous afternoon he had braced himself to receive separately each member of the outgoing ministry, and had accepted the custody not only of their seals of office but also of the great seal of the realm. Sidney Webb (later Lord Passfield) received two separate seals, for the Dominions and for the Colonies, notwithstanding that he was at the time a member of neither House. The King him-

self broke the customary silence with a kindly comment, observing that Miss Bondfield became *ipso facto* a privy councillor as minister of labour, and was the first woman to attain either status.

On 1 July the King returned to London, and on the 7th drove with the Queen to St. Paul's Cathedral for a service of national thanksgiving upon his nominal recovery. But he was not yet out of the wood. Eight days later he was subjected to a further small operation which delayed until the end of August his departure to Sandringham for recuperation in the health-giving and familiar surroundings of home. In the new year (21 January 1930) his voice was once more heard on the wireless when he opened the London Naval Conference, and he broadcast again in the following November at the inauguration of the Indian Round Table Conference. During the years that remained to him he passed for a fit man, although he was induced to take things more easily and to spare himself undue exertion.

It was largely on account of the unemployment position that the labour party had come into power, but it found itself in the grip of forces far transcending the strength of one party in one country. When it took office there were just over a million unemployed in Great Britain; despite all the government's efforts the figure had doubled in the next twelve months, and risen afresh to 2,800,000 by September 1931, when the cost of unemployment benefits exceeded contributions by more than a million pounds a week. As early as October 1930 the grave financial prospect had been engaging the attention of the Cabinet, and early in June 1931 a royal commission had recommended the unpalatable step of saving £24,000,000, partly by increasing workmen's contributions. A crisis was precipitated by the publication on 31 July of the report of the Economy Committee under the chairmanship of Sir George (later Lord) May, calling for the raising of an extra £120,000,000 if the next year's budget was to be balanced; and events proved that even this was an under-estimate by fifty millions. The situation thus revealed spread alarm among foreign nations which had deposited their gold reserves for safety in London, and a rapid series of withdrawals brought the Bank of England to the edge of bankruptcy.

The position was already threatening when on 20 August the King went north to Balmoral: his own inclination was to have postponed his departure, but in order not to disturb public confidence the prime minister advised his adhering to his programme. He arrived there on the Friday morning, but on the Saturday the reports from London were so grave that he decided to return that evening, and he was back at Buckingham Palace by breakfast time on Sunday (23 August). At 10.30 he saw MacDonald, who reported that while he and some of his colleagues favoured a ruthless policy of retrenchment, Henderson and a substantial proportion of the Cabinet were unyielding in their opposition. He accordingly felt that he would have no option but to resign, but the King urged him to remain in office and cheered him with words of encouragement and support. At 12.30 the King saw Sir Herbert (later Viscount) Samuel, acting leader of the liberal party, and was impressed by his clear arguments in favour of an all-party government under MacDonald's leadership. At 3 the King saw Baldwin, who patriotically undertook to sink party differences and serve under MacDonald; or, failing that, to carry on the government with the aid of the liberals, having previously obtained the King's consent to a dissolution as soon as the financial situation had been restored.

At 10.15 the same evening the prime minister returned to the palace to tender the resignation of the Cabinet in view of its continued internal dissension. The King urged him to reconsider his own position in view of the support which the other parties were willing to lend him and the confidence which a united front would inspire among foreign creditors at a moment when the banking resources of the country were to be measured rather in hours than in days. The prime minister asked the King to hold a conference of the three party leaders next morning. At 10 o'clock on the 24th the King accordingly received MacDonald, Baldwin, and Sir Herbert Samuel and requested them to come to some arrangement for carrying on the government; after half an hour His Majesty withdrew, and an hour later was gratified to learn that they had come to a provisional agreement. At 4 MacDonald returned and accepted the commission to form an all-party administration. 'If you will permit me to say so', he wrote on the 29th in answer to a generous letter from the King, 'Your Majesty's own conduct has been a great inspiration and guidance to my colleagues and myself, not only during these recent days of great trouble and heart-searching, but throughout the years when we have had the honour of being your special servants.'

Interpreting the mood of the nation, the King spontaneously gave up £50,000 of his civil list and the other members of the Royal Family made corresponding sacrifices, thus identifying themselves with those of all classes upon whose incomes drastic cuts were now imposed. The flight of capital had been checked, but not wholly stemmed. The economic blizzard was beginning to strike other countries, which were calling home their capital in order to strengthen their own position; moreover, the fundamental issue of a protective tariff could only be solved by a general election, the result of which continued to disturb foreign confidence. It was, however, the mutiny in the Atlantic Fleet at Invergordon in the middle of September, consequent upon the reduction in naval rates of pay, which immediately started a fresh run on the Bank, causing the government to abandon on 20 September the gold standard to which Great Britain had returned in May 1925. The general election on 27 October resulted in an overwhelming endorsement by the nation of the King's action in promoting an all-party government.

In considering advice from Lord Rosebery as prime minister it would have been open to Queen Victoria to observe that she had been on the throne before he was born. In like manner Time, the sovereign's friend, had dealt kindly with King George, whose shadow had lengthened as his day drew in. Those who had moved in public affairs throughout the preceding quarter of a century had learned to repose trust in his disinterested judgement: deprived though he had been of Stamfordham in March 1931, few among his advisers could claim a greater store of political experience, and his later ministers were apt not only to tender but to seek advice. The extent to which he had become the father of his people was disclosed during the silver jubilee celebrations in 1935, on the eve of his seventieth birthday. He had observed the preparations with a detached, even a deprecatory eye, and he was frankly taken aback by the welcome which awaited himself and the Queen on their return to London after the customary Easter residence at Windsor. On 6 May Their Majesties drove to St. Paul's Cathedral through sunlit streets gay with flags and packed with cheering crowds. Although advancing years had taken their toll and he was no longer the man he had been, none discerned in the happy joy-bells the knell of a passing reign. The numerous jubilee functions were hardly concluded when, on 7 June, MacDonald resigned the leadership of the all-party government and the King took leave with regret of one who had been his valued prime minister for over a quarter of his reign. He replaced the conduct of affairs with confidence in the hands of Baldwin and withdrew to Sandringham for a rest. Here, six months later, after an illness short and peaceful in its close, he died 20 January 1936.

Happy alike in the manner and the moment of his passing, King George was well spared the events of the ensuing years. Many and moving were the tributes paid to his memory throughout the world while the life of the Empire was stilled in the silence of a deep and intimate sorrow. For four days and nights his coffin lay in a sublime setting beneath the ancient rafters of Westminster Hall and 800,000 of his subjects waited in the wintry weather to witness a scene breath-taking in its august majesty. On 28 January the funeral took place at Windsor, where in due course a tomb of rare beauty and symbolic simplicity was erected in the nave of St. George's Chapel.

In person King George was slightly below the middle height, neatly made, and impeccably dressed in the style before last. His voice was strong and resonant, his prominent eyes arrestingly blue. Moderate in diet, he drank hardly at all but smoked heavily. His mode of life was of an extreme regularity, his occupations being predictable to the day, almost indeed to the hour, given the precedent of the previous years. His naval training had implanted habits of discipline. Punctual himself, he discountenanced unpunctuality in others. Rules were made to be obeyed, and he was not slow to check infractions of traditional observances and duties, by whomsoever they were committed. His disapproval of the High Court of Parliament assuming the appearance of a dormitory during the course of an all-night sitting was marked by a letter which, but for the vigilance of a subordinate official, would have raised the hoary spectre of the rights of his faithful Commons. So valued a counsellor as Balfour, when betrayed by pressure and inadvertence into undertaking a foreign mission without previously notifying the sovereign, incurred a brisk reminder that the throne was not unoccupied. He did not lack moral courage, as when he bluntly told Lloyd George that he knew nothing of the army, or reminded Birkenhead on one occasion, and Joynson-Hicks on another, that Cabinet ministers were expected to conform to a dignified standard of dress when appearing on a public platform. Such occasions, however, were rare, and he never suffered them to impair the ease and cordiality of his personal intercourse. Towards his labour ministers in particular he revealed a generous consideration.

Although not pietistically inclined, the King was all his life a sound churchman and early formed the habit of daily Bible reading. He attended Sunday morning service wherever he might be; when travelling in India his train used to be stopped for the purpose. Both archbishops of Canterbury (Davidson and Lang) were among his closest personal friends; he secured promising men as preachers and week-end guests, and took pains to inform himself independently about candidates recommended for higher preferment. Among the fighting services the navy never lost the hold which it had early established upon his affections. He loved the ships and their men; he knew the leading officers, read the leading books. If the army ranked second it was by the narrowest of margins. Nearly every summer with the Queen he would enjoy a week at the Royal Pavilion at Aldershot and be among the soldiers from early morning until nightfall. He would ride out to watch the training, visit barracks in the afternoon, and give dinner parties every evening in order to get to know the younger officers and their wives. The occasion (12 June 1922) when the Irish regiments, disbanded after the formation of the Free State, handed to him their colours to be laid up in Windsor Castle was one of the most affecting experiences of his life. It was with pride and admiration that he observed the rise of the Royal Air Force, and he manfully opposed its suggested abolition, during the disarmament phase in the early 'thirties. At the notion of entering an aeroplane himself he would shake his head.

It was with humility that King George recognized his shortcomings in the field of the humanities. He would deplore the technical nature of his education, ruefully wishing that he had been taught Latin instead of trigonometry. In French he was reasonably proficient, in German less so. To the perusal of state documents he applied himself with diligence tempered with distaste; he was concerned on one occasion to find that Baldwin himself had not studied certain papers issued by the Cabinet, and his secretaries had to read the newspaper carefully if they were to escape being similarly ensnared. His private reading amounted to some forty books a year, largely contemporary biographies. Writing he found uncongenial. 'Naturally my language does not approach yours in style or finish', he wrote, in sending to Stamfordham a clear account of a certain interview. It is true that his letters and the diary which he kept throughout his life owed little to the graces of composition or calligraphy; but no one could write a more generous message of encouragement to an overdriven prime minister or an exiled governor-general, and his letters gained in sincerity what they lacked in stylistic virtuosity. One of the most unrewarding fruits of human toil is the weekly letter home of a schoolboy son: he had four such, and to each he would return a hand-wrought reply even at moments of greatest pressure.

In London the King was commonly to be seen in the summer riding in Rotten Row with a friend before breakfast. He often went to the theatre and he enjoyed a musical play and the more familiar operas. He did not like to miss a good Rugby match at Twickenham, a cup-tie final at Wembley, a test match at Lord's, or the lawn tennis championship at Wimbledon: at such spectacles and many others throughout the season no figure was more familiar or more welcome. His nature also responded to such revelations of human endurance as the various attempts upon Mount Everest or the polar regions, and he was apt to send for individual members of the expeditions upon their return in order to ply them with questions.

In private life the King's interests lay in the pursuits associated with the English country gentleman. Apart from those already alluded to, his love of racing far outstripped the meagre successes of his own stable, and he was as faithful to Newmarket, Epsom, and Aintree as to Ascot itself. Farming he both encouraged and practised, although it was never numbered among his more personal hobbies. It is noteworthy, however, that his experimental plot of flax at Sandringham was in 1931 the only example of its cultivation in England, and it was to a large extent due to the King's persistence in this field in the period between the wars that homegrown flax was enabled to contribute towards the needs of the war of 1939–1945. When in the country he was attentive to his social duties and every year would pay a round of calls on his neighbours, tenants, and village friends, many of whom he had known all his life. He almost always had guests in the house and was a gifted host. He had a remarkable memory and was a good raconteur. His recollections of past events were interesting and often of an unreserved frankness; concerning current affairs he observed a more guarded discretion. Beneath a bluff and bantering manner he was a man of marked kindness and geniality, of the type that likes to see others happy. Although he was modest about his own accomplishments, he possessed in fact the range of qualities best calculated to appeal to Englishmen of all classes, not least in his mistrust of cleverness, his homespun common sense, his dislike of pretension, his ready sense of the ludicrous, and his devotion to sport.

King George was served by a household knit together in the fellowship of a common loyalty. Some had been chosen from among the friends of his childhood, not a few from his associates in the navy; others, recruited with care as his establishment increased, were assimilated into a circle from which retirement was rare. The daily round was governed by protocol and precedent. This unwritten code was respected at every level, with the result that contentment reigned, and unhastening order prevailed alike on occasions of ceremonial pageantry and in the well-regulated routine of domestic life. In former times it was the custom to speak of the prince and his 'family': of King George it may truly be said that he had two families, and that he was hardly less devoted to his household than to his children. Affection was thus harnessed to the service of duty in a court remarkable alike for the precision of its arrangements and the harmony of its personal relationships.

King George sat for the following artists in the years shown. Sir Luke Fildes (1912, for the state portrait, Windsor). (Sir) Arthur Cope (1912, for H.M. Queen Mary, the United Service Club, and the Royal Naval College, Dartmouth [destroyed by enemy action in 1942]; 1926, for Windsor; 1928, for the Royal Academy): his portrait for the Royal Yacht Squadron, Cowes, was lost by fire in 1929. (Sir) John Lavery (1913, for the conversation piece, with the Queen, the Prince of Wales, and Princess Mary, National Portrait Gallery).

A. T. Nowell (1920, for the Leys School, Cambridge). Charles Sims (1924, for a portrait which proved unsuccessful). Richard Jack (1926, for Fulham Town Hall and the Junior Constitutional Club). Oswald Birley (1928, for the National Museum of Wales, Cardiff; 1930, for the Royal Yacht Squadron, Cowes; 1932, for the Royal Welch Fusiliers, Wrexham; 1933, for Lincoln's Inn and the Royal Artillery Mess, Chatham; 1934, for Windsor). John Berrie (1931, for the King's Liverpool Regiment; 1935, for the Canberra War Memorial, Australia). Harrington Mann (1932, for the Junior United Service Club). F. W. Elwell (1932, for the throne room at Holyrood).

His Majesty also gave sittings to the following sculptors. Sir George Frampton (1913, for the marble bust in Guildhall, London). (Sir) Bertram Mackennal (1913, for two marble statues for India, presumbaly Delhi and Madras): he also designed the head on the coinage, the reverse of which was the work of G. Kruger Gray. (Sir) W. Reid Dick (1933, for the bust in marble at Buckingham Palace and in bronze at the Mansion House, London): he also executed the memorials in Sandringham and Crathie churches, the recumbent effigy in St. George's Chapel, Windsor, and the statue outside the east end of Westminster Abbey. Kathleen Scott (Lady Kennet) (1935, for the bronze bust for the Hearts of Oak, Euston Road).

[John Gore's *King George V: a Personal Memoir*, 1941, will remain the standard authority on the life of the King, especially in its more intimate aspect. This truthful and revealing book was promoted by King George VI and Queen Mary while the memory of its subject was fresh in the minds of those who had known him: no information was withheld from its author, who received assistance from many of the King's friends. The political background may be conveniently followed in D. C. Somervell's *The Reign of King George the Fifth*, 1935, and John Buchan's *The King's Grace*, 1935. Much further information is contained in the memoirs and biographies of the leading figures of the reign. John Stephenson, *A Royal Correspondence*, 1938; Sir Donald Mackenzie Wallace, *The Web of Empire*, 1902; H. F. Burke, *The Historical Record of the Coronation of King George V and Queen Mary*, 1911; John Fortescue, *Narrative of the Visit to India of King George V and Queen Mary*, 1912; Stanley Reed, *The King and Queen in India*, 1912; J. A. Spender and C. Asquith, *Life of Lord Oxford and Asquith*, 2 vols., 1932; Harold Nicolson, *Curzon, the Last Phase, 1919–1925* (1934), pp. 353 ff.; L. S. Amery, *Thoughts on the Constitution*, 1947, pp. 21, 22; *Journal* of the Royal Society

of Arts, December 1920 and October 1944; Royal Archives; personal knowledge.]

OWEN MORSHEAD.

GERMAN, SIR EDWARD (1862–1936), composer, whose original name was EDWARD GERMAN JONES, was born at Whitchurch, Shropshire, 17 February 1862, the elder son and second child of John David Jones, by his wife, Betsy Cox. His father held the post of organist at the Congregational chapel, and in his early years the son frequently deputized for the father. Edward was educated at Bridge House School, Chester, and on leaving there in 1878 began to study for an engineering career. Teaching himself the violin, he soon led the orchestra of the Whitchurch choral society and his ability impressed the conductor, Professor Walter Hay, of Shrewsbury. Supported by Hay, he persuaded his parents to have him trained for the musical profession, and after studying under Hay's direction, he entered the Royal Academy of Music in September 1880. About this time he adopted his two christian names and gave up the surname of Jones. In 1885 he won the Charles Lucas medal for composition, and became a sub-professor of the violin. An operetta, *The Two Poets*, was produced at the St. George's Hall in December 1886, and was taken on tour with moderate success. Later he changed its name to *The Rival Poets*, and under this title it achieved much popularity. In 1887 his first symphony was performed at a Royal Academy concert in the St. James's Hall.

German succeeded W. G. McNaught as professor of the violin at Wimbledon School, and through the help of Alberto Randegger began conducting in the autumn of 1888 at the Globe Theatre for the production of *Richard the Third* in 1889. His incidental music to this was very favourably received, and shortly after he met (Sir) Henry Irving [q.v.], who commissioned him to write the music for the production of *Henry the Eighth* at the Lyceum Theatre in 1892: the three dances have become famous. There followed a succession of compositions incidental to theatre productions, mostly Shakespearian: they include the overture and incidental music to *English Nell*, by Edward Rose and Anthony Hope (Prince of Wales's Theatre, 1900). *The Emerald Isle*, left unfinished by the death of Sir Arthur Sullivan [q.v.], was completed by German, and produced at the Savoy Theatre in 1901. *Merrie England* (1902) and *A*

Princess of Kensington (1903) followed, and later (1907), *Tom Jones*. In 1904 appeared his 'Welsh Rhapsody'. In 1907 he toured the United States of America, conducting and directing productions. Collaborating with Sir W. S. Gilbert [q.v.], he produced *Fallen Fairies* in 1909, and two years later he was commissioned to write the coronation march and hymn for King George V and Queen Mary. Thereafter little of note took place until 1919, when he wrote 'Theme and Six Diversions' for the Royal Philharmonic Society. From 1922 to 1928, German was busily engaged in conducting and examining, and during those years his compositions were constantly being performed. In 1928 he was knighted. From that time on he lived in comparative retirement (receiving, however, the gold medal of the Royal Philharmonic Society in 1934) and died in London 11 November 1936. He was unmarried.

Highly popular with his fellow musicians, German's work and personality were much admired by such men as Sullivan, Elgar, Parry, Stanford, and Mackenzie. Revolutionary changes in musical thought were taking place during his lifetime. Although striving to keep an open mind on the new tendencies, German admitted that they contained a great deal which he did not and could not understand. During his trip to America he was interviewed by the press on the question and is reported to have said: 'Young England is full of splendid promise, but there is danger ahead in sacrificing the beauties of art to mere sensation.' Of his own work it has been said that he takes a high place among 'those few specially gifted composers who were able to combine artistic achievement with strong popular appeal'.

[*The Times*, 12 November 1936; *Musical Times*, December 1936; W. H. Scott, *Edward German*, 1932; *Grove's Dictionary of Music and Musicians*, 4th ed., vol. ii, edited by H. C. Colles; private information.]

EDRIC CUNDELL.

GERTLER, MARK (originally MARKS) (1891–1939), painter, was born in Spitalfields 9 December 1891 (though he himself always gave 1892 as the date), the third and youngest son of Louis Gertler, of Przemysl, by his wife, Kate Berenbaum. In 1893 the family returned to Austria, to five years of desperate poverty. In 1898, back in London, they settled in Whitechapel. Gertler, still speaking only Yid-dish, attended a rabbi's school until summoned in 1899 to the Deal Lane elementary school. While there, excited by a poster advertising a beef extract and some 'still lifes' by a pavement artist, he began drawing 'still lifes' on the pavement of his home yard. His family gave him water and oil colours and, inspired by reading a life of W. P. Frith [q.v.], he determined to be an artist, and attended classes at the Regent Street Polytechnic. In December 1907 he began work, for five shillings a week, with Messrs. Clayton & Bell, glass-painters, of Regent Street, but in October 1908 the Jewish Educational Aid Society, on the advice of (Sir) William Rothenstein, sent him to the Slade School of Fine Art, where in 1909 he won the Slade scholarship. In 1912 he won the British Institute scholarship, left the Slade, joined the New English Art Club, and received some commissions, including a portrait of Sir George Darwin [q.v.], which was presented in 1923 to the National Portrait Gallery.

Already a marked figure among students and at the Café Royal for his talents, vivacity, and exotic beauty, Gertler early became known to (Sir) Edward Marsh, Mr. Gilbert Cannan, and D. H. Lawrence [q.v.], and also to Lady Ottoline Morrell [q.v.], at whose homes in London and at Garsington, Oxfordshire, he met (Giles) Lytton Strachey [q.v.], Roger Fry [q.v.], and many leading intellectuals: for some years he painted much at Garsington. In January 1914 he showed ten pictures at the Chenil Gallery, but hard work and sociability impaired his health and in the autumn he retired temporarily to Mr. Cannan's windmill at Cholesbury, Buckinghamshire. Mr. Cannan's novel *Mendel* (1916) is based, in many parts verbatim, on Gertler's account of his life; he was always a brilliant raconteur, especially of Whitechapel episodes. In 1915 he left home and established himself at Penn Studio in Hampstead, where he worked for fifteen years. In 1920 he spent the first of several periods in a sanatorium. But painting was the breath of life to him and he worked steadily on, holding frequent one-man shows at the Goupil, Leicester, and Lefevre galleries, contributing regularly to the London Group exhibitions and, from 1932, teaching at the Westminster Technical Institute. He had, however, periods of great depression and on 23 June 1939 he committed suicide at his home in Highgate. He married in 1930 Marjorie Greatorex, daughter of George

Edmund Hodgkinson, a London solicitor, and had a son.

Although he was deeply impressed by Cézanne, and later by Picasso, Gertler's best works are profoundly original, marked by large and firm design, executed with masterly craftsmanship in rich and harmonious colour. Portraits are among them, but, although he painted habitually from models, the necessity of securing a likeness militated against the more generalized vision of form and colour which inspired him.

Five works, including 'The Artist's Mother', are in the Tate Gallery, others in the Manchester, Bradford, Belfast, Pietermaritzburg, and Tel-Aviv collections.

[*Mark Gertler (British Artists of To-Day)*, 1925; Mark Gertler, 'Fragment of Autobiography'; personal knowledge.]

T. BALSTON.

GIBBS, VICARY (1853–1932), genealogist and gardener, was born at Hampstead 12 May 1853, the third, but second surviving, son of Henry Hucks Gibbs, afterwards first Lord Aldenham [q.v.]. He was great-great-nephew of the judge Sir Vicary Gibbs [q.v.] whose dry humour he was supposed to have inherited. His mother was Louisa Anne, third daughter of William Adams, of Thorpe, Surrey, fellow of the College of Advocates, Doctors' Commons. George Edward Cokayne [q.v.], the original compiler of *The Complete Peerage*, who in 1873 changed his name from Adams, was his mother's brother, and also married his father's sister.

Gibbs was educated at Eton and at Christ Church, Oxford, where he obtained a third class in classical moderations (1874). In 1880 he was called to the bar by Lincoln's Inn. He became, however, a partner in the family business of Antony Gibbs & Sons, merchants and bankers. In 1892 he was elected conservative member of parliament for the St. Albans division, but in 1904 he voluntarily vacated his seat, on the ground that his business had accepted an Admiralty contract, and was defeated at the ensuing by-election.

By a family arrangement Gibbs continued to live at Aldenham House, near Elstree, and there he developed gardens the fame of which was world-wide. His tastes were against formal horticulture, and he gradually acquired a magnificent collection of the rarer trees and flowering shrubs, especially of American thorns.

The beauties of his garden were freely shared, for he regularly issued catalogues of his surplus plants at moderate prices. He had himself a keen eye for variations of foliage and habit.

For many years Gibbs had been collecting material for a new edition of *The Complete Peerage*, which he dedicated to his uncle. The first volume was published in 1910, and four volumes had appeared by 1916. In 1920 Gibbs relinquished the editorship to Henry Arthur Doubleday, whose name appears on the title-page of the original issue of vol. v (1921). After the appearance of vol. v he ceased to bear the major part of the expenses of the enterprise; these he had defrayed in full up to 1919. He continued, however, to give valued advice until his death, and excerpts from the copious material which he had prepared will appear over his initials in all the later volumes. By 1945 the work had been carried down to vol. x (Oakham to Richmond). The revised edition treats of medieval peerages with a far higher degree of scholarship than did Cokayne's original work, which relied too much on printed sources, especially on Dugdale's *Baronage*; it also bears witness in its less austere footnotes to the remarkable range of Gibbs's reading and information. He delighted in appropriate quotations which give a thumbnail portrait or a vignette of contemporary manners and often reflect his characteristic sardonic humour. Genealogists and historians are doubly in debt to his learning and his generosity.

Gibbs died, unmarried, at his London house 13 January 1932. A portrait by J. B. Wirgman is in the possession of Lord Aldenham, and another, by R. G. Evans, is the property of the National Provident Institution.

[*The Times*, 14 and 22 January 1932; Hansard, *Parliamentary Debates*, 1904; private information.]   MICHAEL MACLAGAN.

GILBERT, SIR ALFRED (1854–1934), sculptor, was born in London 12 August 1854, the elder son of Alfred Gilbert, musician, by his wife, Charlotte, daughter of James Cole, of Tarrington, Herefordshire. He was educated at the Mercers' School, London, and Aldenham Grammar School, in Hertfordshire, whence his father intended that he should go to Oxford. However, in 1872 he persuaded his father to allow him to enter for the examination of the Royal College of Surgeons, which he passed. Thereafter, while waiting to enter for an open scholarship at the Middlesex Hospital, he began to attend Heatherley's Art School, in Newman Street. When he failed to win a scholarship, he continued to work at Heatherley's, feeling that he had discovered his true vocation, and later went on to the Royal Academy Schools. During this period he was also receiving instruction from (Sir Joseph) Edgar Boehm, the Queen's sculptor [q.v.]. In 1875 he married his cousin, Alice Jane, daughter of Francis Gilbert, of Ottawa, Canada; and in the same year he moved to Paris, where he entered the École des Beaux Arts. He studied there, under P. J. Cavelier, for three years, contriving to live on the sale of works of sculpture and the giving of lessons in Latin and Greek. At the end of this period he took his family, by now consisting of his wife, a son, and a daughter, to Rome and other cities of Italy, to complete his studies. It was in Italy that he produced the early works upon which his reputation was founded: 'The Kiss of Victory', 'Perseus Arming', and 'Icarus', which last was a commission from Sir Frederic (later Lord) Leighton [q.v.].

In 1884 Gilbert brought his family to England, where he had decided to make his home. As a result of his 'Icarus' he was elected A.R.A. in 1887, and there followed a period of considerable prosperity and fame. Through the influence of Boehm he obtained the commission to design a memorial to Lord Shaftesbury; the result of this was the Shaftesbury memorial fountain and its crowning statue, vulgarly known as Eros, which was unveiled in Piccadilly Circus in 1893. Its symbolic nature, as opposed to the more conventional forms of memorial statuary, aroused a certain amount of criticism. A characteristic lavishness led him to exceed the cost for which he had contracted, with the result that he paid a large proportion out of his own pocket.

In 1892 Gilbert was elected R.A. His next important commission was to design and construct a memorial to the Duke of Clarence who died in that year. This took the form of an elaborate sarcophagus, flanked with statuary, which was to be placed in the Albert Chapel, St. George's, Windsor. In 1897 he was appointed M.V.O. In 1901 he was nominated professor of sculpture at the Royal Academy Schools. Although his artistic reputation was now at its zenith, his financial affairs had slipped into a very precarious state. Lavish expenditure on his work, his

friends, and the house which he had built for himself in Maida Vale reduced him to a state of bankruptcy. He was forced to sell his house and pay out all his remaining funds to his creditors. As a solution to his difficulties, he decided in 1904 to leave England altogether, choosing to settle in Bruges, where he was in fact to remain until 1926. In 1908 he resigned his professorship at the Royal Academy and his membership of that and other English societies.

During the twenty years or so which Gilbert spent in Bruges, he was not entirely cut off from his friends in England. Many of them visited him, and he executed commissions for clients in England. During the war of 1914–1918 he remained in Bruges. Thereafter he made two visits to Italy. In 1926 he returned to England, at the express wish of King George V, who desired him to complete the Clarence memorial. He was received back in England with acclamation, and in the same year was awarded the gold medal of the Royal Society of British Sculptors. He was also commissioned to execute a memorial to Queen Alexandra at Marlborough Gate, St. James's, which was unveiled by King George in 1932. In this year Gilbert was knighted and resumed his membership of the Royal Academy.

Gilbert died in London 4 November 1934. By his first wife, who predeceased him in 1916, he had three sons, the youngest of whom was killed in a naval engagement in 1917, and two daughters. He married secondly in 1921 Stéphanie de Bourg, a widow, by whom he had no children.

Some of Gilbert's works have already been mentioned. He made many portrait statues, among which should be noted the statue at Winchester of Queen Victoria (1887), and the John Howard centenary statue at Bedford (1894). He also exercised his gift in the production of smaller works of delicate craftsmanship, of which the Preston mayoral chain, of silver-gilt and enamel (1892), provides a good example. His versatility is shown by the juxtaposition of these works; it was perhaps the result of his lifelong admiration for the ideals of Italian Renaissance craftsmanship, which he embodied sufficiently for Rodin to describe him as the 'English Cellini'. While this is an exaggeration, it must be admitted that Gilbert combined the capacities for delicate and monumental work to an unusual degree: if his sentiment is sometimes inclined to cloy, the blame must fall as much upon the change in taste as upon himself.

A chalk drawing of Gilbert by J. M'L. Hamilton (1887) is in the National Portrait Gallery. Of a painting by G. F. Watts (1889), exhibited at the Royal Academy in 1896; another painting, by J. Seymour Lucas (1891), showing him at work; a water-colour drawing by H. F. W. Ganz (1907), showing him in his studio at Bruges; and a crayon drawing by Mrs. a'Beckett Terrell, reproduced in *The Times* of 5 November 1934, the present whereabouts are uncertain. He is commemorated by a tablet in St. Paul's Cathedral.

[*The Times*, 5 November 1934; Isabel McAlister, *Alfred Gilbert*, 1929; *Art Annual*, Easter 1903; E. Machell Cox, *Commemorative Catalogue of an Exhibition of Models and Designs by the late Sir Alfred Gilbert R.A. held at the Victoria and Albert Museum Autumn 1936*, 1937; H. F. W. Ganz, *Alfred Gilbert at Work*, 1934.]   JAMES LAVER.

GILES, HERBERT ALLEN (1845–1935), Chinese scholar and author, was born at Oxford 8 December 1845, the fourth son of the editor and translator John Allen Giles [q.v.], afterwards rector of Sutton, Surrey, by his wife, Anna Sarah Dickinson. He was educated at Charterhouse and then joined the China consular service, reaching Peking early in 1867. He became vice-consul at Pagoda Island (1880) and at Shanghai (1883); he was consul at Tamsui (1885) and at Ningpo (1891). He left China late in 1892, his resignation dating from 1893, and he lived at Aberdeen until 1897 when he moved to Cambridge on his appointment to succeed Sir T. F. Wade [q.v.] as professor of Chinese there, and he held the chair until his resignation in 1932. His first task was to catalogue the collection of Chinese books which his predecessor had given to the university, a task which he performed perhaps too rapidly and with insufficient knowledge of bibliography. His principal achievement as professor was to win a place for Chinese as a subject both in the previous examination and in the oriental languages tripos. His consular career had been without special opportunity for distinction and his professorship (which was at first unpaid and later rewarded with a meagre honorarium) was a disappointment, except that it gave him abundant leisure for writing; for his pupils were very few and he failed to win popularity for Chinese in university circles.

Giles's title to fame rests on his published writings. With a considerable command of the Chinese language, an unerring instinct for what the public would read, and a clear and graceful English style, he began very early to publish a stream of books which flowed unabated for more than fifty years, ranging from technical works for students, like *Chinese without a Teacher* (1872), his large *Dictionary* (1892, 2nd ed. 1912), and his *Chinese Biographical Dictionary* (1898), to popular books like *Strange Stories from a Chinese Studio* (1880), *Gems of Chinese Literature* (1884), and *Chuang Tzŭ* (1889). But all were based alike on a direct knowledge of the country, people, and language of China; and it was truly said, when he received the triennial gold medal of the Royal Asiatic Society in 1922, that 'beyond all other living scholars he had humanized Chinese studies'. He was probably the most potent influence in replacing the old English regard for things Chinese as merely queer or silly by an intelligent perception of the depth and beauty of the culture of China; but he did not profess the gifts of the profound and minute researcher.

In private life Giles was punctual and methodical, bright in talk and faithful in friendship. An old Chinese admirer described him as 'of the fanatical type, always furiously taking sides no matter right or wrong', and this characteristic inevitably involved him in occasional controversy.

Giles received honorary degrees from the universities of Aberdeen (1897) and Oxford (1924) and was twice awarded the Prix Stanislas Julien by the French Academy, of which he was a corresponding member (1924) and in which he had himself endowed a prize in 1916. He was twice married: first, in 1870 to Catherine Maria (died 1882), daughter of Thomas Harold Fenn, of Nayland, Suffolk; secondly, in 1883 to Elise Williamina (died 1921), daughter of Alfred Edersheim [q.v.]. By his first wife he had six sons and three daughters, and one daughter by his second. Two of the sons followed him in the China service, both reaching the rank of consul-general, a third became a distinguished sinologist and keeper of the department of oriental printed books and manuscripts at the British Museum, and yet another rose to be a colonel in the Royal Engineers. Only the fourth and fifth sons survived their father and the third daughter predeceased him. Giles died at Cambridge 13 February 1935 in his ninetieth year.

[*The Times*, 14 February 1935; *Cambridge Review*, 22 February 1935; *Journal* of the Royal Asiatic Society, July 1935; *Cambridge Chronicle*, 14 December 1932; personal knowledge.]

GILES, PETER (1860–1935), philologist and master of Emmanuel College, Cambridge, was born at Strichen in the district of Buchan, Aberdeenshire, 20 October 1860, the eldest son of Peter Giles, a factor, by his wife, Margaret Eddie Brown, who, on her mother's side, was of Highland descent from Inverness-shire. He was educated first at the parish school of Strichen. In 1878 he proceeded with a bursary to King's College in the university of Aberdeen, and in 1882 with a classical scholarship to Gonville and Caius College, Cambridge. Here he obtained first classes in both parts of the classical tripos (1884, 1887) with the star for distinction in comparative philology and history in part ii; in the historical tripos he was awarded a second class (1885), was Browne medallist (1884), and Whewell scholar for international law and Lightfoot scholar for ecclesiastical history (1885). In 1887 he was elected a fellow of his college, but in 1890 he migrated to Emmanuel College as fellow and classical tutor. In 1891 he was elected university reader in comparative philology, and in 1911 master of Emmanuel: these posts he retained until his death. He was vice-chancellor of Cambridge University from 1919 to 1921.

Giles possessed wide learning, but his chief interest was in comparative philology, a field at Cambridge in which he followed John Peile, master of Christ's College [q.v.]. In 1886 at Freiburg (and again in 1887 at Leipzig) he attended the lectures of Karl Brugmann, who was then expounding the doctrines of the *Neo-Grammatiker*. This led Giles to carry on Peile's work and to produce his main book, the *Short Manual of Comparative Philology for the Use of Classical Students* (1895, 2nd ed. 1901). In 1888 *The Principles of Sound and Inflexion as illustrated in the Greek and Latin Languages* by J. E. King and Christopher Cookson had already brought the new ideas to England, but Giles's book was the first to apply them in a wider survey. He wrote many papers on linguistic, classical, and miscellaneous subjects (including several articles for this DICTIONARY), which are fully enumerated in the British Academy memoir. His views on linguistics appear most clearly in an essay which he contributed to the commemorative volume *Darwin and Modern Science* (edited by A. C. Seward, 1909). Much time was devoted to an edition of Theocritus in collaboration with Dr. A. B. Cook, but pressure of other work, largely administrative, in the university as well as in the college, caused this to be abandoned.

Giles received honorary degrees from the universities of Aberdeen (1903) and Harvard (1927), and was elected an honorary fellow of Gonville and Caius College (1913) and a fellow of the British Academy (1927). He married in 1893 Elizabeth Mary, eldest daughter of Thomas William Dunn, headmaster of Bath College, and had one son and four daughters, one of whom predeceased her father. He died at Cambridge 17 September 1935.

A portrait by Alfred Hayward, painted in 1934, hangs in Emmanuel College: a replica was presented to Giles's family.

[R. M. Dawkins, *Peter Giles, 1860–1935* in *Proceedings* of the British Academy, vol. xxi, 1935; private information; personal knowledge.]
     R. M. DAWKINS.

GILL, (ARTHUR) ERIC (ROWTON) (1882–1940), stone-carver, engraver, typographer, and author, was born at Brighton 22 February 1882, the eldest son and second child of Arthur Tidman Gill, minister of the Countess of Huntingdon's connexion, by his wife, Cicely Rose King. He was for seven years a pupil at Arnold House, Brighton. In 1897 he moved with the family to Chichester. He spent two years at the Art School there, and the planned and ordered city deeply impressed his mind. In 1899 he was articled in London to W. D. Caroë [q.v.]. But he soon felt distaste for current notions of architecture, and in his leisure turned with relief to lessons in masonry and lettering—the latter under Edward Johnston, then just beginning the masterly revival of a languishing craft. By 1903, when he abandoned his architect's office, he was proficient enough to earn a living by letter-cutting, which was to be a dominant interest throughout his life.

Meanwhile Gill had gone to share Johnston's rooms in Lincoln's Inn, remaining there until his marriage in 1904 to Mary Ethel, daughter of Henry Holding Moore, head verger of Chichester Cathedral. He now moved to Battersea, thence to

Hammersmith, and in 1907 back to Sussex, where he settled at Ditchling. His trade was still lettering—stone inscriptions (with heraldic emblems on occasion), painted signs, drawn or engraved titles for books. He began engraving in 1906 or 1907. In 1909 he made his first stone figure, for him an experiment, but for Count Kessler and Roger Fry [q.v.], his friends and patrons, an eventful achievement which broke with convention by being not modelled but carved direct from the stone. He was encouraged to continue, and, aided by Mr. Augustus John, held his first exhibition in 1911 in the Chenil Gallery, Chelsea.

Gill's thought had developed meanwhile. For the world as he now saw it the prime necessity was religion, the rule of God; and there was only one institution which professed to rule the whole world in God's name. In February 1913 he was received into the Roman Catholic church (later he was to become a Dominican tertiary). In the same year he was commissioned to carve the Stations of the Cross in Westminster Cathedral, an important work which occupied him until 1918. He exhibited at the Goupil Gallery in 1914, and from 1919 onwards executed a number of war memorials (village crosses at Bisham, Harting, Trumpington; lettering on a magnificent scale at New College, Oxford, 1921; a relief of the 'Driving out of the Money-changers' at Leeds University, 1923). For St. Cuthbert's church, Bradford, he carved another set of Stations (1920-1924). During this period he was also actively connected with St. Dominic's Press, Ditchling, for which he made some of his earliest illustrations, while to its periodical, The Game, he contributed not only engravings but essays on social matters and on the philosophy of art. He also extended his drawing from working sketches (always beautiful things in themselves) to portraits and studies from the life.

In August 1924 Gill left Ditchling for Capel-y-ffin in the Black Mountain. For the next four years he did little sculpture, although this included two of his finest works, the colossal torso 'Mankind' (1928, later acquired by the Tate Gallery) and his own favourite work, a 'Deposition' in black marble (1925, now at the King's School, Canterbury). An altar-piece for Rossall School chapel (1927) remains his principal carving in wood. He engraved a good deal for the Golden Cockerel Press and designed the first two of his ten printing types, 'Perpetua' (1925) and 'Gill

Sans-serif' (1927). Gill's reputation was now assured. His lettering in stone, with its impersonal grandeur and its finality, was the noblest that had been seen for centuries. His sculpture, mainly in low relief but also in the round, was in the forefront of modern work, though more different than was commonly recognized from that of famous contemporaries, the balance and rhythm admired for their own sake by connoisseurs being for him the mere flowering of rationality in the apt expression of an intelligible idea. His drawings were of great purity and precision, and his illustrations reveal an unequalled sense of the nature of a book and the proper sympathy between engravings and type.

In October 1928 Gill moved to Pigotts, near High Wycombe. In 1929 he published his first full-length book, Art-Nonsense, a collection of essays, lectures, and pamphlets written since 1918. To the next three years belong not only his most ambitious illustrations, the vivacious sequence of 'Canterbury Tales' and his masterpiece the 'Four Gospels', but also his best-known sculptures, those at Broadcasting House. He enriched the practice of printing with five more types and its theory with the searching Essay on Typography (1931).

In 1934 Gill visited Palestine to carve ten panels on the Palestine Museum at Jerusalem. Between 1935 and 1938 he was chiefly engaged on the great relief of the 'Creation of Adam' for the League of Nations council hall at Geneva, but found time besides for one of his most important books, The Necessity of Belief (1936). His mastery in the visual arts had long been recognized, and about this time was winning him public honours: he became honorary A.R.I.B.A. (1935), A.R.A. (1937), and received the honorary degree of LL.D. from Edinburgh University (1938). But he now had also a growing influence as a penetrating thinker and powerful writer on the problems of the modern world. Akin to Ruskin and Morris in some regards, he nevertheless drew less from them than from W. R. Lethaby [q.v.] and Ananda Coomaraswamy, and again from Thomist philosophy and the social encyclicals of modern Popes. Against puritans he defended the holiness of all natural things, against sensualists the primacy of the spiritual, against emotionalists the prerogatives of the intellect. Characteristic theses were: 'Look after goodness and truth, and beauty will look after herself'; 'In a normal society the artist is not a special kind of man, but every man is a special kind of artist'; 'The artist is the responsible workman'. The conception of responsibility indeed coloured his whole thought; and its absence from much of modern life was the root of his lifelong opposition to commercialism and industrialism and his later opposition to war.

Admiring past cultures, Gill detested exploitation of them to veneer and romanticize the present. In architecture, clothing, typography he combated picturesque intrusions and demanded the rational and consistent: he took pleasure in designing such things as a coin or capbadge or postage stamp or the name-plate of a locomotive in conformity with the nature and use of each. In 1938 he collaborated with a professional architect in building a church at Gorleston-on-Sea, planned round a central altar and with arches crossed to make an octagon—an impressive experiment which with longer life he might have developed far.

The year 1940 found Gill busied with writing, lecturing, and the carving of a reredos for a chapel in Westminster Cathedral. But an affection of the lungs which had long been troubling him forced him to enter Harefield hospital near Uxbridge, and there he died 17 November, survived by his wife and their son and three daughters. He was buried in the village churchyard at Speen, Buckinghamshire.

Gill's *Autobiography*, published just afterwards, took its place forthwith among English classics. It includes a self-portrait (1927) and two photographs. Another self-portrait accompanies Mr. James Laver's study of Gill in *Portraits in Oil and Vinegar* (1925), and *Artwork*, Autumn 1930, has a water-colour portrait by David Jones.

[Eric Gill, *Autobiography*, 1940; *Letters of Eric Gill*, edited by Walter Shewring, 1948; private information; personal knowledge.]

WALTER SHEWRING.

GILMOUR, SIR JOHN, second baronet, of Lundin and Montrave (1876–1940), politician, was born at Montrave in the parish of Scoonie, Fife, 27 May 1876, the second, but eldest surviving, son of (Sir) John Gilmour, first baronet (whom he succeeded in 1920), by his wife, Henrietta, second daughter of David Gilmour, of Quebec. He was educated at Trinity College, Glenalmond, Edinburgh University, and Trinity Hall, Cambridge.

Gilmour began his lengthy career of public service as an officer of the Fife and Forfar Yeomanry during the South African war, in which he served with distinction, and as an administrator in 1901, being a member of the county council of Fife until 1910. He unsuccessfully contested East Fife in 1906, as unionist candidate, in opposition to H. H. Asquith, the sitting member. In January 1910 he entered parliament as member for East Renfrewshire, holding the seat until 1918, when he transferred to the Pollok division of Glasgow, for which constituency he sat until his death. Gilmour's parliamentary duties were interrupted by service in the field, where he was awarded the D.S.O. (with bar). However, his appointment in 1919 as Scottish unionist whip gave a prospect of higher responsibilities when his party should return to power. He retained the post until 1922, and held it again in 1924. In 1921 he was appointed a junior lord of the Treasury, in 1922 was sworn of the Privy Council, and in 1924 became secretary for Scotland, the status of the office being raised to a secretaryship of state in 1926. This office he held until 1929. When the all-party government came into power in 1931 Gilmour became minister of agriculture and fisheries. In 1932 he was transferred to the Home Office, and held the position of home secretary until he relinquished it in 1935, when he was appointed G.C.V.O. His next, and last, office was that of minister of shipping, which he held from 1939 until his death the next year.

In 1937, during the interval between his tenure of the Home Office and of the Ministry of Shipping, Gilmour presided over a departmental committee appointed to inquire into the organization of the various Scottish departments of government. The reorganization of these departments in 1939 followed upon the recommendations of his committee.

As the owner of a considerable landed estate and a noted breeder of stock, Gilmour had a deep interest in agriculture and practical knowledge of it. He was master of the Fife foxhounds from 1902 to 1906, captain of the Royal and Ancient Golf Club at St. Andrews in 1927, and a brigadier of the Royal Company of Archers (King's Bodyguard for Scotland). From 1926 to 1929 he was lord rector of Edinburgh University, and he received the freedom of the cities of Edinburgh and Dundee in 1928 and of Glasgow in 1929. In 1938 and 1939 he was lord high commissioner of the General Assembly of the Church of Scotland, of which Church he was a loyal and devoted member.

Gilmour was twice married: first, in 1902 to Mary Louise (died 1919), eldest daughter of Edward Tiley Lambert, of Telham Court, Battle, Sussex, and had one son and one daughter; secondly, in 1920 to Violet Agnes, youngest daughter of Edward Tiley Lambert, and had one daughter. He died in London 30 March 1940, and was succeeded as third baronet by his son, John Edward (born 1912).

Gilmour had most of the qualities which make the good administrator. He possessed a sound judgement, was quick to grasp the essentials of a problem, had power of decision and tenacity of purpose. Fluency of speech and unlimited courage made him an effective debater. Although a strong party man, he was devoid of bitterness and was popular with members of all parties. When, therefore, Scotland regained its secretaryship of state, which had been in abeyance since 1746, members of both Houses of Parliament combined to mark the occasion by the presentation of Gilmour's portrait, finely painted by James Guthrie, to the Scottish Office, where it now hangs.

[*The Times*, 1 April 1940; personal knowledge.]   JOHN LAMB.

GIROUARD, SIR (EDOUARD) PERCY (CRANWILL) (1867–1932), railway engineer and colonial administrator, was born at Montreal 26 January 1867. He was of French Canadian origin, the son of Désiré Girouard [q.v.], a judge of the High Court of Canada, by his second wife, Essie, daughter of Joseph Cranwill. He was educated privately and at the Royal Military College of Canada, Kingston, Ontario, and in 1886 took up engineering in the service of the Canadian Pacific Railway. In 1888 he received a commission in the Royal Engineers, and from 1890 to 1895 was railway traffic manager at the Royal Arsenal, Woolwich. In 1896 he was seconded to the Egyptian army, and as director of the Sudan railways (1896–1898) played an important part in Kitchener's conquest of the Sudan. He served with the Dongola Expeditionary Force in 1896, was mentioned in dispatches, and received the brevet of major and the D.S.O. In 1898 he was appointed president of the Egyptian Railway and Telegraph Administration, and, on the outbreak of the South African war, director of railways for the South African Field

Force, with the local rank of lieutenant-colonel, being promoted brevet-colonel in 1904. Never before the South African campaign had a British army been required to control a vast network of railways, largely through hostile country, and with innumerable columns or other detached forces using it as a base along many thousands of miles. An account of the manner in which this task was carried out is given by Girouard himself in his *History of the Railways during the War in South Africa, 1899–1902* (1903).

In 1900 Girouard was appointed K.C.M.G., and on the conclusion of the war in 1902 was nominated commissioner of railways in the Transvaal and Orange River Colony, a position which he resigned in 1904. On returning home he became staff officer to the chief engineer at Chatham, and in 1906 assistant-quartermaster-general, Western Command. In 1907 he was appointed to succeed Sir Frederick (later Lord) Lugard as high commissioner, and in 1908 as governor, of Northern Nigeria. In this vast new territory there were then no railways and Girouard's first concern was to plan and supervise the construction of a line from Baro on the Niger to Kano, the principal city of Northern Nigeria. This line of 350 miles was subsequently extended to the tin fields of the Bauchi Plateau and to the seaports of Lagos and Port Harcourt. The railway has been a governing factor in the development of Nigeria and has been described as 'the cheapest, most rapid, and in every way the most satisfactory line in tropical Africa' (Lord Lugard in *The Dual Mandate in British Tropical Africa*, p. 448).

Girouard also took a keen interest in the conditions of land tenure in Northern Nigeria and it was due to his initiative that the Northern Nigeria lands committee was constituted in London in 1908, followed by legislation which virtually nationalized the lands of Northern Nigeria and provided a model for land policy in other African territories. His further proposals for instituting a system of land taxation were subsequently rejected in favour of an income-tax.

In native administration Girouard was a faithful follower of the principles of 'indirect rule' laid down by Lugard. These he applied and developed, both in Nigeria and in the British East Africa Protectorate, to which he was transferred as governor in 1909. These principles are well summarized by him in the 1909–1910

Colonial Report for the British East Africa Protectorate, and Lugard observed that few had shown greater insight into problems of native administration than Girouard.

In 1912 Girouard resigned his governorship and became a director of the Elswick works of Armstrong, Whitworth & company. In 1915 he was appointed director-general of munitions supply, but resigned in 1917 in order to return to Elswick. He married in 1903 Mary Gwendolen (died 1916), only daughter of Sir Richard Solomon [q.v.], and had one son. The marriage was dissolved in 1915. He died in London 26 September 1932.

[*The Times*, 27 September 1932; A. C. Burns, *History of Nigeria*, 3rd ed. 1942; C. W. J. Orr, *The Making of Northern Nigeria*, 1911; M. Perham, *Native Administration in Nigeria*, 1937; Lord Lugard, *The Dual Mandate in British Tropical Africa*, 1922; *Colonial Reports for Nigeria*, 1907–1909, and *Colonial Reports for the British East Africa Protectorate*, 1909–1912.]   C. K. MEEK.

GLAZEBROOK, SIR RICHARD TETLEY (1854–1935), physicist, was born at West Derby, Liverpool, 18 September 1854, the eldest son of Nicholas Smith Glazebrook, surgeon, by his wife, Sarah Anne, second daughter of Richard Tetley, also of Liverpool. He was cousin of M. G. Glazebrook [q.v.]. He was educated at Dulwich College, Liverpool College, and at Trinity College, Cambridge, where he was elected a scholar in 1875 and a fellow in 1877. He graduated as fifth wrangler in the mathematical tripos of 1876, and at once began to study physics under James Clerk Maxwell [q.v.] and to carry out researches on the theory of light in the Cavendish laboratory. When J. W. Strutt, third Lord Rayleigh [q.v.], succeeded Clerk Maxwell as Cavendish professor of experimental physics in 1880, Glazebrook and (Sir) Napier Shaw both became demonstrators and later lecturers, with particular responsibility for the teaching of practical physics. In 1883 Glazebrook was appointed secretary of a British Association committee on electrical standards, and, following Rayleigh, carried out many accurate measurements. In 1891 he became assistant director of the Cavendish laboratory.

In 1895 Glazebrook became senior bursar of Trinity College and, as such, showed much business ability. In 1898 he left Cambridge in order to assume the office of principal of University College, Liverpool,

and in the next year was appointed the first director of the National Physical Laboratory, then being formed under the management of the Royal Society. In that institution he found his true field of work, to the benefit of science and of the nation in both peace and war.

The laboratory was placed in Bushy House, Teddington, the ground floor being fitted for experiments and the upper floors being made into a residence for the director. The laboratory space was, of course, quite inadequate, and Glazebrook's first task was to secure extension, which shortage of funds made difficult. In planning the work, priority was given to the construction of units and standards, needed for both science and industry. The experiments of Rayleigh and Glazebrook, at Cambridge, formed a basis for electrical measurements, while thermometry was later on transferred from Kew Observatory. Many other branches of physics were taken up during the first few years, and in 1908 (Sir) Alfred Yarrow [q.v.] presented a large tank for experiments on models of ships, experiments which soon gave much help to the shipbuilding industry.

In 1909 R. B. (later Lord) Haldane [q.v.], then secretary of state for war, asked the laboratory to undertake research in aeronautics, and the prime minister appointed an advisory committee on that subject. Thus was initiated the work to which Glazebrook devoted so much time and energy during his directorship and after his retirement. At the laboratory wind-tunnels were erected in which experiments on models of aeroplanes could be made in currents of air. Mathematical and experimental studies of the conditions of stability were carried out, to enable designers to plan aeroplanes that would fly steadily. This work was largely responsible for the superiority of British aircraft in the early days of the war of 1914–1918.

Another generous gift, this time from Sir J. C. Wernher [q.v.] in 1910, made possible a building for metallurgy. Delay was caused to this and other developments by a serious attack of typhoid fever which kept Glazebrook away from the laboratory for several months.

The outbreak of war in 1914 at first dislocated the work of the laboratory, which was deprived of a quarter of its staff. But new demands for research soon arose; the stability results had to be adapted to fresh types of aeroplane as they came forward, and gauges for the manufacture of munitions had to be tested for accuracy. Apparatus, formerly obtained from Germany, had to be examined, tested, and put into manufacture, and countless other applications of science had to be fitted into the war effort. As director, Glazebrook was responsible for the general supervision of all this work, and it is generally agreed that he did it supremely well.

Glazebrook reached the age limit in 1919 and retired. He had then done a full life's work; other men would have been content to rest, but Glazebrook filled his remaining years with endless activities. From 1920 to 1923 he was Zaharoff professor of aviation at the Imperial College of Science and Technology and director of the aeronautics department, and thereafter remained chairman of the aeronautical research committee, which in particular investigated aeroplane engines, greatly improving their reliability. He became a member of the statutory commission for the university of Cambridge in 1924, and was for a time chairman of a Home Office committee on the lighting of factories and workshops. He was also chairman of the executive committee of the National Physical Laboratory from 1925 to 1932, and did much good work for the Royal Society, of which he was elected a fellow in 1882 and was foreign secretary from 1926 to 1929; the society awarded him the Hughes medal in 1909 and a Royal medal in 1931. He received the gold medal of the Royal Aeronautical Society in 1933. He was appointed C.B. in 1910, and after being knighted in 1917, K.C.B. in 1920 and K.C.V.O. in 1934. Honorary degrees were conferred upon him by the universities of Manchester, Oxford, Edinburgh, and Heidelberg. His chief recreations were climbing in the Alps during his annual holiday, and golf at other times.

On his retirement from the National Physical Laboratory Glazebrook returned to live for a time at Cambridge, but most of his work was then in London and he found he must follow it. First he moved to Notting Hill Gate, but in 1924 he built himself a house at Limpsfield Common, Surrey.

Glazebrook combined scientific knowledge and ability with business sagacity, sound judgement of men, and general mental vigour. He was one of the foremost figures in the world of science in his time. Withal he had a kindly, lovable nature, and was held in affectionate regard by his many friends. He married in 1883 Frances Gertrude, daughter of John William Atkinson, of Leeds. They had one son and three daughters. He died at Limpsfield Common 15 December 1935.

A bas-relief of Glazebrook by John E. Cluysenaar is at the National Physical Laboratory. His portrait in oils (1919) by his cousin Hugh de T. Glazebrook was presented to him by the staff when he retired. He left it to Lady Glazebrook for life, with reversion to the laboratory.

[*The Times*, 17 December 1935; *Obituary Notices of Fellows of the Royal Society*, No. 5, December 1936 (portrait); *Proceedings* of the Physical Society, vol. xlviii, 1936; personal knowledge.]   W. C. D. DAMPIER.

GLENAVY, first BARON (1851–1931), Irish lawyer and politician. [See CAMPBELL, JAMES HENRY MUSSEN.]

GODLEY, (JOHN) ARTHUR, first BARON KILBRACKEN (1847–1932), civil servant, was born in London 17 June 1847, the eldest child and only son of the politician John Robert Godley [q.v.], of Killegar, co. Leitrim, by his wife, Charlotte, second daughter of Charles Wynne Griffith-Wynne, of Voelas, Denbighshire, and Cefnamlwch, Carnarvonshire. He was a first cousin of A. D. Godley [q.v.]. He was educated at Radley (1857–1861) and afterwards at Rugby, under Frederick Temple [q.v.]. In 1866 he went, as an exhibitioner, to Balliol College, Oxford, where he gained a reputation as a brilliant classical scholar. He was awarded a first class in classical moderations (1868) but was prevented by illness from entering for *literae humaniores*. He won the Hertford (1868) and the Ireland (1870) scholarships, and the chancellor's Latin verse (1867), the Gaisford Greek verse (1869), and the Gaisford Greek prose (1870) prizes. On leaving Oxford he studied law for a short time, but in 1872 he was appointed assistant private secretary to Gladstone, who was then prime minister, and held this post until the fall of the liberal government in 1874. Gladstone was struck with his abilities, and notwithstanding the difference in age and, later, on certain political questions, a warm and lasting friendship was established between the two men. On Gladstone's retirement from the leadership of the liberal party, Godley acted as private secretary to Lord Granville [q.v.]; he had already resumed his legal studies, and he won the Eldon law scholarship in 1874 and was called to the bar by Lincoln's Inn in 1876, but never practised. From 1874 to 1881 he was a fellow of Hertford College. On Gladstone's return to power in 1880, Godley was recalled, this time as his principal private secretary. In 1882 he was made a commissioner of inland revenue, and in 1883 succeeded Sir Louis Mallet [q.v.] as permanent under-secretary of state for India. In the words of a colleague, 'he set himself to mould the comparatively juvenile Office, to reform and simplify its procedure, and to establish its efficiency on a firm basis. It is not too much to say that the India Office, as it was known in later years, was largely his creation.' In the course of the twenty-six years during which he held office, Godley's recognized experience and judgement gave him a position of unusual influence; this was increased by great charm of manner, wit, and powers of expression, both in speech and in writing. He was appointed C.B. in 1882, K.C.B. in 1893, and G.C.B. in 1908. On his retirement in 1909 he was raised to the peerage as Baron Kilbracken, of Killegar.

Godley was a devoted Rugbeian, and served for thirty years (1902–1932) as chairman of the governing body. He was also a trustee of the British Museum and a director of the P. and O. and other companies. He was elected to an honorary fellowship at Hertford College in 1910 and at Balliol in 1912. In 1931 he published his *Reminiscences*. After his retirement he joined the conservative party, but took little part in public affairs, save for his membership in 1913 of the royal commission on Indian finance and currency. He died at Summerfield House, near Malvern, 27 June 1932.

Godley married in 1871 Sarah (died 1921), only daughter of Sir Walter Charles James, second baronet, afterwards first Lord Northbourne, and had two sons, the younger of whom died in childhood, and three daughters, the eldest of whom predeceased her father. He was succeeded as second baron by his elder son, Hugh John (born 1877).

There is a portrait of Kilbracken by R. E. Morrison at Rugby.

[*Reminiscences of Lord Kilbracken*, 1931; private information; personal knowledge.]

EVELINE C. GODLEY.

GOLDSMID-MONTEFIORE, CLAUDE JOSEPH (1858–1938), Jewish biblical scholar and philanthropist. [See MONTEFIORE.]

GOODENOUGH, FREDERICK CRAUFURD (1866–1934), banker, was born in Calcutta 28 July 1866, the third son of Frederick Addington Goodenough, of Calcutta, by his wife, Mary Lambert. He was grandson of Edmund Goodenough, headmaster of Westminster School and later dean of Wells, and great-grandson of Samuel Goodenough, bishop of Carlisle [qq.v.]. Frederick Goodenough was educated at Charterhouse and Zürich University. He studied law, served his articles, and was admitted a solicitor. He entered the Hudson's Bay Company as assistant secretary and subsequently joined the Union Bank of London in the same capacity. He was appointed secretary of Barclay & company, Ltd., on its incorporation as a joint stock company in 1896, and in 1903 became general manager. In 1913 he was elected to a seat on the board and was appointed chairman in 1917.

Goodenough, judged by any standard, adorned a generation rich in men of distinction in banking and finance. Possessed of great determination, with a clear grasp of affairs and administrative ability of a high order, he was admirably equipped to mould and shape the bank of which he was the chief architect and which, indeed, was the ruling passion of his working life. He saw it as a great national institution far transcending the stereotyped conception of a business enterprise, and so he made it. A convinced imperialist, he grasped the need for an Empire bank and, in spite of a good deal of head-shaking—not always kindly—amongst his contemporaries in the City, pressed forward with his project for the formation of Barclays Bank (Dominion, Colonial, and Overseas) which was to confound all the gloomy prognostications of its detractors and to vindicate in the most brilliant way the vision and faith of its author.

The heavy and insistent calls of a life devoted to business, and the handicap of poor eyesight, did not prevent Goodenough from rendering his full measure of service in public and charitable work. He was a member of the Council of India from 1918 to 1930; he was joint treasurer of Westminster Hospital; and for his services to Oxford University, notably in connexion with the Bodleian Library appeal, he received the honorary degree of D.C.L. in 1933. The deep sincerity of his belief in the Empire and his admiration for Oxford led him to the task of founding in 1930 London House, a hall of residence in London chiefly for Dominion students in the metropolis. His object was to create bonds of friendship between this country and the British Commonwealth and Empire and to bring to London something of the aroma of the older university. In this characteristically bold and imaginative project his concern for the cause of education achieved its highest expression, but he also gave it practical effect in other spheres: he was a governor of the Charterhouse foundation and a member of the governing body of the school, and he was a vice-president of the Institute of Bankers in the activities of which he took a lively interest.

Apart from all the preoccupations of business and public life, Goodenough's heart lay in the peace of the English country-side. His was no formal attachment, but a familiar love of the rural setting, its work, its interests, and its ways. But even the quietude of country life with its measured tread did not deflect him from exercising to the full the driving force at his command. Many years before his time, the vicissitudes of fortune had led to the loss of landed estate at Filkins in Oxfordshire held by earlier generations of the family, and for the restoration of these properties Goodenough devoted patient endeavour during a large part of his lifetime. He accomplished his purpose and had the well-merited satisfaction of enjoying possession for the last seventeen years of his life.

Goodenough's keen interest in agriculture made him a worthy champion in its cause at a time when the public consciousness of the significance of this, the greatest of all British industries, had not been awakened.

A commanding figure, Goodenough was a formidable man to meet, but behind the stern exterior there lay a charm of manner, and the young bank clerk who approached him with trepidation found his fears allayed by a disarming smile, which was all the more prized because it was rare and fleeting. But throughout his life, strict disciplinarian though he was, he was animated by a desire to help others; and many of the younger generation of his time have cause to be grateful to him for his helping hand and his sound advice.

Goodenough married in 1898 Maive, fifth daughter of Nottidge Charles Macnamara, F.R.C.S., of Calcutta and London, and had three sons and two daughters, the younger of whom predeceased her father. He died in London after a brief illness 1 September 1934.

[Personal knowledge.]   E. Fisher.

GORDON, CHARLES WILLIAM (1860–1937), divine, and author under the pseudonym of Ralph Connor, was born at Indian Lands, Glengarry county, Ontario, 13 September 1860, the fourth of the six sons of Daniel Gordon, a Free Church minister who had emigrated to Canada from Blair Atholl, by his wife, Mary Robertson. He was educated at public schools, the high school at St. Mary's, Ontario, and at the university of Toronto, where he graduated in 1883. He then taught for a year and a half at the high school at Chatham, Western Ontario, before entering Knox College, Toronto. After graduating there in 1887 he spent a further year studying theology at Edinburgh University; he was ordained in 1890 to the ministry of the Presbyterian Church and carried on missionary work among miners and lumbermen in the Rocky Mountains. After raising money in Great Britain for western missions (1893–1894), he settled down in 1894 as minister of St. Stephen's church, Winnipeg, where he remained until 1936. During part of the war of 1914–1918 he acted first as chaplain to the 43rd Cameron Highlanders and later as a senior chaplain in Flanders. In 1917 he served on a special commission sent by the British and Canadian governments to the United States of America to present the Allied view of the war, and in 1918 on a special commission from the Canadian government to Great Britain. He returned to Canada in 1919. In 1921 he was elected moderator of the general assembly of the Presbyterian Church of Canada and helped to form in 1925 the United Church of Canada. He was appointed C.M.G. in 1935 and he received honorary degrees from Glasgow University and from Queen's University, Kingston, Ontario. He married in 1899 Helen, daughter of the Rev. John King, of Manitoba College, Winnipeg, and had one son and six daughters. He died at Winnipeg 31 October 1937.

Gordon published his first book, *Black Rock*, in 1898, and as 'Ralph Connor' became the 'best-seller' among Canadian authors. He records in his autobiography, *Postscript to Adventure* (1938), that two of his early books, *The Sky Pilot* (1899) and *The Man from Glengarry* (1901), reached a sale of over five million copies. He adds modestly (in a book which is perhaps not excessively modest): 'I have often tried to analyse the reaction upon my mind of this unique experience. . . . I have attempted to explain this reception by a variety of reasons: *Black Rock* and *Sky Pilot* gave an authentic picture of life in the great and wonderful new country in Western Canada, rich in colour . . . the buffalo and his hunters . . . the land of the trapper . . . the Mounted Police, and that virile [*sic*] race of men and women. . . . The pictures were from personal experience. Another cause . . . and a very influential one . . . was the fact that though in fiction form they possess a definitely religious motif. . . . And it was this religious motif that started that vast host of religious folk who up to this time had regarded novel-reading as a doubtful indulgence for Christian people.'

Besides the four books mentioned Gordon wrote twenty-nine others, chiefly novels and devotional works, but he never again reached the level of his early years. He himself admits that he hardly attempted literary style or form. His recurring theme is that every human being has some good characteristics; his heroes are shown working miraculous 'conversions' through understanding this simple fact. His own popularity as young preacher, army chaplain, and conciliator in labour disputes probably sprang from a like simplicity. He is sensational, superficial, romantic. In his earlier books, recalling what he had seen and heard in youth, he can vividly describe fights in lumber camps, horse-racing, college football games, and log-driving. These are still popular children's books.

[C. W. Gordon, *Postscripts to Adventure: the Autobiography of Ralph Connor* (with a preface by his son, J. K. Gordon), 1938; V. B. Rhodenizer, *A Handbook of Canadian Literature*, Ottawa, 1930.]   CARLTON STANLEY.

GORDON, JOHN CAMPBELL, seventh EARL OF ABERDEEN and first MARQUESS OF ABERDEEN AND TEMAIR (1847–1934), statesman, was born in Edinburgh 3 August 1847, the third and youngest son of George John James Hamilton-Gordon, fifth Earl of Aberdeen, by his wife, Mary, second daughter of George Baillie, of Jerviswoode, of a family well known in Covenanting annals. His childhood was spent largely in the Ranger's House, Blackheath, and after studying at St. Andrews University he finished his education at University College, Oxford.

Four successive deaths between 1860 and 1870 brought Gordon unexpectedly to the peerage. (He changed his name back from Hamilton-Gordon in 1900.) His grandfather, the prime minister, George

Hamilton-Gordon [q.v.], the fourth earl, died in 1860, his father in 1864; in 1868 he lost his second brother by a rifle accident, while in 1870 his eldest brother, an adventurous young man with a passion for the sea, was swept overboard while working in the American mercantile marine under an assumed name. It was not until 1872 that the youngest brother's succession to the title was confirmed. A regular attendant thenceforth at the House of Lords, in 1878, after his marriage, he voted against Beaconsfield's government over the Afghan war. He became a constant liberal and in 1879 was one of the party at Lord Rosebery's house at Dalmeny for Gladstone's first Midlothian campaign. Appointment as lord-lieutenant of Aberdeenshire in 1880 was followed in 1886 by an offer, which was accepted, to go to Dublin as lord-lieutenant, a task requiring courage as the memory of the Phœnix Park murders was still fresh. One of his first acts was to renew relations with the lord mayor and corporation of Dublin, and shortly afterwards he and Lady Aberdeen travelled through the disturbed southern counties. On the defeat of the government in 1886, a great demonstration of affection and regret at their departure revealed the impression which they had made during their six months' stay at Dublin Castle.

In 1893, after the return of the liberals to office, Aberdeen went to Canada as governor-general. The five years' term was at first not easy, being marked by three changes in the premiership in two years, but with the victory of (Sir) Wilfred Laurier [q.v.] in 1895 tension was relaxed. Aberdeen returned home in 1898, and in 1906 he was appointed once more to the lord-lieutenancy at Dublin, this time for the longest term in its history. For nine years he laboured for a better understanding between the two countries, and his efforts seemed to be bearing fruit. Royal visits in 1907 and 1911 were of good omen, and when the home rule bill became law in 1914 and Aberdeen's impending retirement was announced, very numerous requests for an extension of his term were received from towns and other influential quarters, and a leading Irish member of parliament wrote that he had converted the lord-lieutenancy from a hateful into a popular institution and had thereby strengthened loyalty to the throne. On his retirement in 1915 he was advanced a step in the peerage as Marquess of Aberdeen and Temair (gazetted in 1916).

From early days Aberdeen had been interested in social welfare, and in 1874 he had served on a royal commission on railway accidents (he had a lifelong interest in railway matters) and had helped to bring to light the excessive hours worked by railwaymen; later he took part in a similar inquiry into loss of life at sea. Ably seconded in this side of his work by Lady Aberdeen, he put into effect several new ideas for the welfare of the farmers and labourers at Haddo House and the House of Cromar, which he built at Tarland, near Aboyne. The general tendency of the time was to combine small holdings into larger farms; but in 1920 he was able to say that during his fifty years as laird the holdings on his estates had increased from 935 to 958 and that 588 houses had been built. Another successful venture was evening classes for farm servants. This work in Aberdeenshire alternated with such efforts as the founding of the London Playing Fields Society and unceasing political and religious work. He was in constant association with the seventh Lord Shaftesbury [q.v.] and later with Henry Drummond [q.v.].

Aberdeen had three sons and two daughters; the younger daughter died in infancy and the youngest son was killed in a motor-car accident in 1909. The elder daughter married John Sinclair, afterwards first Lord Pentland [q.v.]. In 1920 he handed over the management of his Haddo estates to his heir, Lord Haddo, and spent the remainder of his life at the House of Cromar, where he died 7 March 1934. He was succeeded as eighth earl and second marquess by his eldest son, George (born 1879).

Aberdeen was sworn of the Privy Council in 1886, was appointed G.C.M.G. in 1886, K.T. in 1906, and G.C.V.O. in 1911. Honorary degrees were conferred upon him by the universities of Aberdeen and Oxford and by numerous universities in Canada and the United States of America. He served as lord high commissioner of the General Assembly of the Church of Scotland from 1881 to 1885 and again in 1915. He was elected an honorary fellow of University College, Oxford, in 1932 and was lord rector of St. Andrews University from 1913 to 1916.

In 1877 Lord Aberdeen married ISHBEL MARIA MARJORIBANKS (1857–1939), born in London 14 March 1857, the youngest daughter of Sir Dudley Coutts Marjoribanks, afterwards first Lord Tweedmouth, by his wife, Isabella, eldest daughter of Sir James Weir Hogg [q.v.] and sister of Quintin Hogg [q.v.]. Her character and ideals were moulded by her mother, whose influence was the strongest in her life. Educated privately, she entered upon her adult life with the endowment of a liberal education and a sense of social responsibility. In her home she came into contact with many great political and religious leaders, of whom Gladstone impressed himself most strongly on her mind, and she was early inspired to devote herself to religious and humanitarian pursuits. She became a devoted and ardent liberal and, in later years, president of the Women's Liberal Federations both in England and in Scotland. After her extremely happy marriage, 'We Twa' became the affectionate synonym for married felicity and abounding social service. The home of Lord and Lady Aberdeen became, wherever it was, the centre of generous hospitality and the birthplace of fruitful enterprises. One of the earliest of these was the Haddo House Association, developing later into the Onward and Upward Association. Beginning as an educational and recreational project for the tenants of the Aberdeenshire estates, it soon extended its membership throughout Great Britain and the Dominions. During her husband's first lord-lieutenancy, the setting up of cottage and village industry under the Irish Industries Association, the Women's National Health Association, founded in 1907, with its pioneer work for mother and child welfare, a remarkably successful crusade against tuberculosis, and the exhibitions of town and country planning, all owed much to her energy and guidance, and she contributed in a marked degree to the growth of confidence among the Irish people in the intentions of the British government. In Canada the same vigour was evident. Not only did she institute a Dominion-wide health service by the foundation in 1898 of the Victorian Order of Nurses, but she came into close contact with two movements which were thereafter to hold her affection: the Red Cross Society and the National Council of Women. In 1893 she was elected president of the International Council of Women (formed at Washington in 1888), and almost immediately she became its acknowledged leader. Under her guidance its efforts were directed to the improvement of the social and economic position of women and the promotion of peace. She was the leader and spokesman of a deputation of the council to a meeting of the League of Nations commission at the Peace Conference of Versailles in 1919 and she successfully advocated the opening of all posts on the secretariat of the League of Nations to women on equal terms with men. At the jubilee celebrations of the movement, held in Edinburgh in 1938, tribute was paid by representative men and women of many lands to the inspiration of her leadership which had brought the International Council to a place of power and influence.

Many honours, British and foreign, were bestowed on Lady Aberdeen. She was one of the first women to be nominated a justice of the peace. In 1931 she was appointed G.B.E., and she received the honorary degree of LL.D. from Aberdeen University and the Queen's University, Kingston, Ontario. In 1928 she received an honour which she perhaps esteemed as highly as any, the freedom of the city of Edinburgh.

Lady Aberdeen's activities were never allowed to interfere with her domestic duties. She entered fully and intimately into the upbringing of her children. A woman of deep religious conviction, she felt herself under divine guidance in all her undertakings. To the end of her life she maintained vigour of mind and body; she died at Aberdeen 18 April 1939, and was buried in the cemetery at Haddo House.

There is a portrait of Lord Aberdeen by Charles Furse at Dublin Castle, another, by James Sant, at Haddo House, and a third, by Baron Barnekow, in the Town and County Hall, Aberdeen. A cartoon by 'Spy' appeared in *Vanity Fair* 6 February 1902.

[*The Times*, 8 March 1934 and 19 April 1939; Lord and Lady Aberdeen, *We Twa*, 1925, and *More Cracks with We Twa*, 1929; Lady Aberdeen, *Musings of a Scottish Granny*, 1936, and *Through Canada with a Kodak*, 1892; private information; personal knowledge.]   G. F. Barbour.
        Matthew Urie Baird.

GORE, CHARLES (1853–1932), bishop successively of Worcester, Birmingham, and Oxford, the youngest son of Charles Alexander Gore (son of the second Earl of Arran), commissioner of woods and forests, by his wife, Lady Augusta Lavinia Priscilla, second daughter of John William Ponsonby, fourth Earl of Bessborough [q.v.], and widow of William Thomas Petty-Fitzmaurice, Earl of Kerry, was born at Wimbledon 22 January 1853. He was educated at Harrow and at Balliol College, Oxford (scholar, 1870): he ob-

tained a first class in classical moderations (1872) and in *literae humaniores* (1875), and a fellowship at Trinity College (1875). Both at Harrow, where he was deeply influenced by H. M. Butler [q.v.] and still more by B. F. Westcott [q.v.], and at Oxford he showed qualities and interests which marked his whole life—devotion to the Christian faith in its Anglo-Catholic expression, a radical temper, power of vigorous speech and argument, hatred of social injustice. No man was ever more clearly called to the ministry of the Church. After his ordination as deacon (1876) and priest (1878) he divided his time for two or three years between teaching, lecturing (notably on Plato), and other college duties at Trinity; curacies in vacation, and at week-ends at Christ Church, Bootle, and St. Margaret's, Princes' Road, Liverpool; and meetings of a group nicknamed the 'Holy Party' which included his old friend H. S. Holland, F. Paget [qq.v.], John Richardson Illingworth, and others and which was already ripening the seed of *Lux Mundi*.

A purely academic life never attracted him and in 1880, at the invitation of J. F. Mackarness [q.v.], bishop of Oxford, Gore began, as vice-principal of Cuddesdon College, 'to form the characters of young clergymen', a task for which he was admirably fitted. The distinction of his personality and the range of his influence were already well known, and when the Pusey Memorial Library (generally known as the Pusey House) was established, the committee, with H. P. Liddon [q.v.] as its leading figure, wisely invited him to become the first 'principal librarian' with the duty of studying and teaching theology and of acting as friend and adviser of Anglican undergraduates. Although Gore was not altogether willing to return to Oxford he was fortunately persuaded, largely through Holland's urgency, to accept the invitation (1883). His work was to begin in October 1884. In the interval he paid his first visit to India, where he was concerned in the work of the Oxford Mission to Calcutta to which he rendered great service then and later.

The years at the Pusey House (1884–1893) were perhaps the most important of Gore's life. It may be doubted whether any man save J. H. Newman has exercised so strong an influence on the religious life of the university. It was brought to bear not only or even mainly through sermons, lectures, and books but through personal relations with men of all kinds and ages. During these years too his main contributions to the making of modern Anglicanism took definite shape. He was active on behalf of the Christian Social Union (founded in 1889); although never a socialist in any strict sense of that term, he was profoundly convinced that socialist ideals could find countenance in the Gospel and he hoped to win the Church and the labour movement to share his conviction. Again, it was natural that to a man so determined to live and to draw others to live according to the spirit and precepts of that Gospel the revival of community life in the Church of England should make strong appeal. In 1892 the community of the Resurrection (established at Mirfield in 1898), an outgrowth of the society bearing that same name, and also the work of Gore, came into definite being as a brotherhood of celibate priests living under a simple rule and 'having all things in common': of this community he was superior until 1901. Meanwhile throughout these busy years he was deep in study and controversy, fighting on more than one front. A small book on *Roman Catholic Claims* (1888) was widely read: a much larger work, *The Ministry of the Christian Church* (1888, entitled *The Church and the Ministry* in the fourth and new editions, 1900 and 1919), is still a standard 'apology for the principle of the apostolic succession'. Interpretations of the creeds or of Christian history which he judged alike unorthodox and unfounded were opposed with an energy which to some degree explains the sorrowful amazement felt by Liddon and other friends of Gore on the appearance in 1889 of his famous essay in *Lux Mundi* on 'The Holy Spirit and Inspiration'.

Then and always Gore was an Anglo-Catholic. But then and always he was 'certain that (he) must be in the true sense a free thinker'. He might and did draw the line between orthodoxy and unorthodoxy sharply, even arbitrarily. But he held that he drew it at the dictation not of tradition but 'of the best judgment of (his) own reason'. He had become convinced when he wrote his essay that many of the critical conclusions about the Old Testament must be accepted and could not be dismissed by quoting against them the apparent authority in a few instances of Christ's words in the Gospels. No one, however, was more certain than he of the credibility of the Evangelists. Therefore he was driven to conclude that the true humanity of Christ entailed certain limita-

tions of consciousness. He maintained this conclusion not only in later editions of *Lux Mundi* and in his Bampton lectures on *The Incarnation of the Son of God* (delivered and published in 1891), but in the elaborate *Dissertations on Subjects connected with the Incarnation* (1895), appealing especially to St. Paul (Philippians ii. 7) as evidence for a certain *Kenôsis* or self-emptying by Christ at His Incarnation.

The distress of Liddon and his friends was unmeasured, and not less was Gore's own unhappiness when he became fully aware of their feelings. He was ready to explain but not to retract. During a second visit to India (1890) he offered to resign his position at the Pusey House, but this suggestion was for several reasons unacceptable. He was, however, becoming restless and anxious to give more time to reading and to the affairs of the community. In 1893 he moved to the small benefice of Radley, where for a year he was a devoted but often disappointed country parson. In 1894, after refusing the deanery of Winchester, he was wisely offered by Lord Rosebery and wisely accepted a Westminster canonry. His preaching and lecturing drew crowds to the Abbey: in London and in Oxford he became a great personal force. Some of his best work in biblical and doctrinal exposition was done at this time: *The Body of Christ: an Enquiry into the Institution and Doctrine of Holy Communion* (1901: fourth ed. 1907 with several subsequent reprints) is a good example of his vigorous, lucid theological teaching. Membership of the Synthetic Society, which he helped to found in 1895, brought him into close touch with minds of many casts, and in his house he was hospitable to all kinds of people. Schemes for church reform and vigorous pressing of his strict opinion on the 'ethics of subscription' engaged him in much public discussion. A visit to America with (Dr.) C. A. Alington in 1897 was a welcome change. On all hands he was now recognized as a power in the Church, and when he accepted Lord Salisbury's offer of the see of Worcester there was general expectation that the new bishop would show the qualities of 'fearless honesty, apostolic zeal, and personal sanctity' ascribed to him by his Westminster colleague Herbert Hensley Henson. His courage had indeed just been shown by his denunciation of the management of concentration camps in South Africa.

The nomination became public on 8

November 1901. The consecration arranged for 25 January 1902 had to be postponed until 23 February owing to objections on doctrinal grounds raised by the Church Association at the confirmation. The vicar-general rejected these, but appeal was made to the King's Bench and Gore refused to bend to Archbishop Temple's desire to anticipate the court's decision: it was given in his favour on 10 February.

Gore's Worcester episcopate was brief. The diocese was unwieldy: a generous gift of £10,000 by Canon T. H. Freer encouraged the revival of a project of division, creating Birmingham a separate see. Gore added £10,000 (almost his whole private fortune) and promised £800 per annum of the Worcester stipend: the bill went through parliament rapidly with Joseph Chamberlain's warm support, and Gore was enthroned bishop of Birmingham with general acclaim (March 1905). It was a happy translation. Birmingham promised a task more practicable and more congenial than Worcester. The promise was fulfilled. He established excellent relations with civic authorities, with Free churchmen, and with evangelicals as well as with men of his own churchmanship. His eloquence, wide interests, and care for the true progress of a great city won him a remarkable position in its public life. As a disciplinarian he was strong and generally successful in his diocese, although his characteristic attempt to prevent his friend Henson from preaching for Dr. John Henry Jowett in Carr's Lane chapel was a failure, and probably ill judged: fortunately a lawsuit was avoided. In politics he was sternly opposed to the education bill of 1906, but a strong supporter of the trade boards bill (1909) and of the famous budget of that year. His advocacy of the appointment of a royal commission to inquire into the affairs of the two ancient universities caused some resentment among their members. At this period and indeed ever after its foundation (1903) which he had inspired, his interest in the Workers' Educational Association was unfailing.

In 1908 Gore had hinted that he might be ready to go to India as bishop of Bombay. The offer was made but he finally refused it largely because he was then engaged in a stiff struggle with the opponents of the liberal government's licensing bill. But, perhaps unfortunately, he did not resist the pressure put upon him, chiefly by Randall Davidson, the arch-bishop of Canterbury, and H. S. Holland, to succeed Francis Paget in the see of Oxford. He left Birmingham in 1911 amid wide regret, for a rural diocese far larger in area and in the number of its parishes, far more conservative, and less readily responsive to a masterful personal influence. An effort to divide it failed. He had to deal with many questions of discipline and of criticism where his decisive temper often clashed with the suspended judgements characteristic of academic minds: thus his relations with the university were not easy. Active as he was, he was inevitably more remote at Cuddesdon than at Worcester (for he had refused to occupy Hartlebury Castle) or at Birmingham. And controversy was incessant. His inquiry (1913) into the affairs of the Benedictine community at Caldey led to most of its members joining the Church of Rome: it was 'his way even when ... most friendly to go straight to the point', and he cannot be fairly blamed. The indecision and sometimes the inactivity of other bishops in dealing with ritual irregularities or credal vagaries angered him: great as was his admiration for Randall Davidson as a man, and over-persuaded as he often was by him, he was impatient of his balancing diplomacy. When William Sanday [q.v.] threw his weight as a biblical scholar on to the liberal side of the controversy about miracles (1913) and when Gore's support of Welsh disestablishment alienated much diocesan opinion he seriously contemplated resignation. The Kikuyu strife (1913 onwards) involving the relations of the Church of England with Free churchmen was indeed partly quenched by the outbreak of war in 1914 and by the archbishop's 'opinion' (1915); but the latter was unsatisfactory to Gore, while the war brought new burdens.

Yet Gore's Oxford episcopate was no failure. His influence both as a spiritual force and as an organizer was great and lasting. His sermons, his confirmations, and his personal counsels were deeply valued. A mission to the university conducted by him early in 1914 made a profound impression; the National Mission of 1916 and the Life and Liberty movement (1917) owed much to his support. He paid two visits to the troops in France (1914, 1915) and another to America to speak about war aims (1918). The change of scene was a refreshment after diocesan labours and the 'crisis' of the Hereford bishopric. Gore had taken the lead in protesting that Henson fell 'outside the limits of tolerable conformity' recently recognized by Convocation, but withdrew his protest when, after Henson's letter to the archbishop (published 18 January 1918), he felt that the line drawn by Convocation had not been broken.

The actual occasion of Gore's resignation of his see (1 July 1919) was the decision of the Representative Church Council to make baptism (without confirmation) the qualification for a vote in elections to the Church Assembly. But the reasons for his decision were many. He was now sixty-six and tired: he had long been carrying on a triple struggle to check what he regarded as disloyalty to the creeds on the part of liberal churchmen, to prevent the disruption of the Church which would, he feared, result from compromise with the Free Churches upon the rule of episcopal ordination, and to restrain the 'Romanizing' tendencies of the extremer Anglo-Catholics (see *The Basis of Anglican Fellowship*, 1914). He had not found among the bishops or elsewhere that vigorous effort of corporate thinking and action along these lines which he had consistently urged. Above all he wanted time for thought and writing. He took a small house in London and entered upon thirteen more years of various activity. He lectured in theology at King's College, London, and was dean of the theological faculty there (1924-1928), preached regularly at Grosvenor Chapel, and travelled widely both for holidays and as a representative of the Church. In 1923 and 1925 he was in the Near East for the archbishops' Eastern Churches committee and in the same years at the Malines 'conversations' under Cardinal Mercier's chairmanship he showed that he was still a critic of Roman Catholic claims. The attempted revision of the Prayer Book (1927-1928) had his support, but some of his last battles were fought against suggestions of the Lambeth Conference of 1930 on South Indian Church reunion schemes and on the use of contraceptives.

Gore's writings in these years summed up the main interests and influences of his life. Chief among them is his trilogy *Belief in God* (1921), *Belief in Christ* (1922), *The Holy Spirit and the Church* (1924): a single volume *The Reconstruction of Belief* (1926) includes the whole. The book is a witness to the liberal orthodoxy of its author and his many followers. In 1929-1930 his Gifford lectures at St. Andrews University gave a broad and attractive survey of *The Philosophy of the Good Life*

(published in 1930). The *New Commentary on Holy Scripture* (1928), produced under his editorship, provided a widely used compendium of knowledge and generally moderate criticism. In *Christ and Society* he again enforced the social implications of Christianity, and his little volume on *Jesus of Nazareth* (1929), exhibits to the full his power of simple and persuasive exposition. This incomplete list is a remarkable record of literary vigour in the crowded life of an old man.

After a last visit to India in 1930-1931 Gore's health failed. He died in London 17 January 1932. His ashes rest in the church of his community at Mirfield.

Gore's influence on the Church of England was unequalled in his generation. He exercised it through a mind and character of singular force and through a complete and evident single-mindedness. Men knew where he stood. There were limits to his sympathies, but none to the devotion with which he served the truth as he saw it. His opinions on theology, criticism, and 'applied Christianity' were formed early and changed little. He led a great body of Anglicans to accept some fundamental results of biblical inquiry, and no one did more to convince Christians that their faith should direct and interpret the life of society. In his later years he repudiated the charge that he had followed the familiar course from liberalism to conservatism in thought; yet he hardly measured the degree in which New Testament criticism may fairly influence the interpretation of the creeds, and he was inclined to overstrain some favourite arguments. This tendency can be seen in the immense weight which he rested upon Old Testament prophecy and upon certain texts which seemed to him to justify his view of the early Christian ministry. His insistence on the duty of mental decision and of facing the consequences of it was salutary, but those who disagreed with his conclusions often thought that he treated the arguments leading to their own with some lack of sympathy and that he was too ready to prescribe the limits of legitimate diversity both in belief and in ecclesiastical order.

In person, Gore was of middle stature, gaunt and wiry: in manner, sometimes reserved and austere, often warmly affectionate and delightfully humorous. For comfort he cared little, but he enjoyed all good things, not least music, pictures, and architecture: he was always an admirable traveller, enthusiastic in sightseeing and interested in his fellows. All his life he was a great teacher of all sorts and conditions of men. His friends and hearers found unfailing pleasure in his many familiar turns of speech, in a voice peculiarly expressive of a natural and absolute sincerity, and in some engagingly characteristic attitudes of mind and body. All recognized in him a great Christian man.

Gore was elected an honorary fellow of his two Oxford colleges (Balliol and Trinity) in 1922 and 1903 respectively and of King's College, London, in 1922. He received honorary degrees from the universities of Edinburgh (1896), Oxford (1904), Cambridge (1909), Birmingham (1909), Durham (1919), and Athens (1924). There are portraits of him by Sir John Lavery at Hartlebury Castle; by Bernard Munns at Bishop's Croft, Birmingham; by Glyn Philpot at Cuddesdon College; and by A. U. Soord at Mirfield. Drawings of his head by John Mansbridge can be seen at the National Portrait Gallery, Mirfield, Balliol College, and Birmingham. There is a statue by T. Stirling Lee near the west door of Birmingham Cathedral.

[*The Times*, 18 January 1932; G. L. Prestige, *Life of Charles Gore*, 1935; A. Mansbridge, *Edward Stuart Talbot and Charles Gore*, 1935; G. Crosse, *Charles Gore*, 1932; W. R. Inge, *Bishop Gore and the Church of England*, 1908 (reprinted in *Outspoken Essays*, vol. i, 1919); G. K. A. Bell, *Randall Davidson, Archbishop of Canterbury*, 2 vols., 1935; H. H. Henson, *Retrospect of an Unimportant Life*, 2 vols., 1942–1943; personal knowledge.]

ALWYN DUNELM. (A. T. P. WILLIAMS.)

GOSSET, WILLIAM SEALY (known as 'STUDENT') (1876–1937), statistician and industrial research scientist, was born at Canterbury 13 June 1876, the eldest son of Colonel Frederic Gosset, R.E., of Watlington, Oxfordshire, by his wife, Agnes Sealy, daughter of Edward Urch Vidal. He was in turn a scholar of Winchester College and of New College, Oxford, where he obtained a first class in mathematical moderations in 1897 and in natural science (chemistry) in 1899. In the latter year he joined the scientific staff of Arthur Guinness, Son & company in Dublin and a few months before his death was appointed head brewer.

The original appointment followed a policy just initiated by Messrs. Guinness of attaching to their staff several university scientists. A mass of statistical data was available bearing on the relations between brewing methods, the characteristics of raw materials (barley and hops),

and the quality of the finished product. Gosset was the first to realize the value of this unused material to his firm and in attempting its analysis was soon drawn into the study of the theory of probability and error. His 1904 report to the brewery showed him already grappling with some of the problems needing solution in applying statistical methods to experimental and routine work of large-scale industry.

In 1905 Gosset made contact with Karl Pearson [q.v.] and studied during the session of 1906–1907 in his laboratory at University College, London. This period saw Gosset working on his first three papers, later published in *Biometrika*, on the Poisson limit to the binomial theorem and the sampling distributions of the mean, standard deviation, and correlation coefficient.

Gosset found in the Biometric School of Sir Francis Galton, W. F. R. Weldon, and Karl Pearson [qq.v.] a statistical technique developed for handling comparatively large samples. Forced in his brewery work to draw conclusions leading to executive action from the analysis of relatively small numbers, he introduced a new mathematical approach to the subject which opened the way to much of the rapid advance in statistical technique which soon followed.

Besides dealing with problems of the chemist and biologist Gosset was concerned, as a user of barley, with agricultural experimentation in which he carried out pioneer work in collaboration with Edwin Sloper Beaven. He also played a prominent part in the joint effort of Messrs. Guinness and the Irish Department of Agriculture to improve the Irish barley crop. Later he came into close contact with Professor Ronald Aylmer Fisher, then at Rothamsted. In 1935 he left Dublin in order to take charge of a new Guinness brewery in London.

Between 1907 and 1937 Gosset published twenty-two statistical papers which were re-issued by *Biometrika* in 1942 under the title of '*Student's' Collected Papers* (edited by E. S. Pearson and J. Wishart). His writings are characterized by a sound common sense based on practical experience; in his theoretical work he showed a power of brilliant guessing where his mathematics just failed to reach a solution. His influence spread widely in later years, not only through his written papers, but by a correspondence that linked him to experimenters all the world over.

In 1906 Gosset married Marjory Surtees, youngest daughter of James Surtees Phillpotts, sometime headmaster of Bedford Grammar School; she was a sister of Dame Bertha Newall [q.v.]. They had one son and two daughters. He died at Beaconsfield 16 October 1937.

[*The Times*, 19 October 1937; *Biometrika*, January 1939 (bibliography and portrait); *Annals of Eugenics*, January 1939 (portrait); *Nature*, 13 November 1937; personal knowledge.]   E. S. PEARSON.

GOUGH-CALTHORPE, SIR SOMERSET ARTHUR (1864–1937), admiral of the fleet. [See CALTHORPE.]

GRAHAM, HUGH, BARON ATHOLSTAN (1848–1938), newspaper proprietor, was born of Scottish parents at Athelstan in eastern Quebec 18 July 1848, the eldest son of Robert Walker Graham, by his wife, Marion, daughter of Colonel Thomas McLeay Gardner. At the age of fifteen his scanty education at Huntingdon Academy terminated when an uncle, E. H. Parsons, the editor of the *Evening Telegraph* of Montreal, gave him employment, first as office boy, later as business manager. After gaining a varied experience in journalism, he took the daring step of founding, in January 1869, with meagre resources, an evening paper, the *Montreal Star*. In its initial stages it specialized too much in sensational news and scandals to win favour with the educated public of Montreal but, after it had acquired a good circulation among the workers, Graham, who had great business ability, gradually transformed it into a reputable, influential, and prosperous paper. Later he established two weeklies, the *Family Herald* and *Weekly Star*, which had a nation-wide circulation in the rural areas, and the *Montreal Standard*, which catered for the urban population of Montreal; he also acquired control of the *Montreal Herald*, a liberal daily, and became president of the Montreal Star Publishing Company. A man of great vitality and immense energy, he retained active direction of his newspapers until he was well beyond his eightieth year, when he disposed of them. His education being deficient, he made no pretence of being a writer or editor, and the outstanding factors in his remarkable success as a newspaper publisher were his almost uncanny ability to appreciate and even foresee what the public would regard as important news and his energetic skill,

which he reinforced by a willingness to spend money freely for his purposes, in catering for its appetite as he gauged it from time to time.

Since Graham was a strong protectionist and keen imperialist, the political influence of his papers was usually, but not always, exercised on behalf of the Canadian conservative party. Indeed in political circles he was regarded as erratic and undependable and his habit of sending communications to political leaders in a curious cipher of his own invention exposed him to the charge of being an intriguer. But he never wavered in his ardour for the closer consolidation of the British Commonwealth, and it led him to take a leading part in the organization of the Empire Press Union, of the Canadian section of which he was president for many years.

In his later life Graham used his great wealth generously for philanthropic purposes. Among these, he was best known for the maintenance of a free soup-kitchen every winter for the poor of Montreal and the support of hospitals and medical research. He was knighted in 1908 and was raised to the peerage as Baron Atholstan, of Huntingdon, Quebec, and Edinburgh, in 1917; he was the first Canadian journalist to receive this latter honour. He received the honorary degree of LL.D. from Glasgow University in 1909. He married in 1892 Annie Beekman, second daughter of Edward Hamilton, of Montreal, and had one daughter. He died at Montreal 28 January 1938.

A portrait of Atholstan by Alphonse Jongers is in the possession of his daughter, the Hon. Mrs. B. M. Hallward, of Montreal.

[*The Times*, 29 January 1938; *Canadian Men and Women of the Time*, edited by Henry James Morgan, 2nd ed. 1912; *Who's Who in Canada*, 1937–1938; private information.]
                    JOHN A. STEVENSON.

GRAHAM, ROBERT BONTINE CUNNINGHAME (1852–1936), traveller, poet, horseman, scholar, Scottish nationalist, laird, and socialist, was born in London 24 May 1852, the eldest of the three sons of William Cunninghame Bontine, of Gartmore, Perthshire, and Ardoch, Dumbartonshire, a major in the Scots Greys, and a great-grandson of Robert Cunninghame Graham, the song writer [q.v.], by his wife, Anne Elizabeth, youngest daughter of Admiral Charles Elphinstone Fleeming, of Cumbernauld and Biggar,

Dumbartonshire. By an entail dating from 1770 the eldest son had to bear the surname and arms of Bontine during the lifetime of his father. Robert's real name reflects his descent from two ancient families, the Cunninghams, earls of Glencairn, and the Grahams, earls of Menteith, through whom he could claim descent from Robert II and his second consort, and, in view of the illegitimacy of the Stewart line, to antiquaries such as Andrew Lang he was the 'uncrowned king of Scots'. To his neighbours he was 'Gartmore', to South Americans he was 'Don Roberto', but revolutionary circles in London in the 'eighties knew him as 'Comrade'.

Cunninghame Graham spent two years at Harrow and a year at a private school in Brussels, but his real time and place were with Tudor courtly adventurers. At the age of seventeen he paid the first of several visits to Spanish America and rode with *gauchos* over the South American plains (where in 1873 he visited the relics of the social experiment of the Jesuits in Paraguay) and, later, with Indians in Mexico, where he formed a close friendship with 'Buffalo Bill'. So W. H. Hudson [q.v.], dedicating *El Ombú* to him in 1902, called him 'Singularísimo escritor inglés' because he 'alone of European writers has rendered something of the vanishing colour of that remote life'. He was in fact in Paraguay when that land had lost most of its male population in the four years' war waged by Francisco Solano Lopez upon Brazil, Argentine, and Uruguay, and he gave an account of the man in his *Portrait of a Dictator* (1933). In the war of 1914–1918 he was there again, buying remounts for the British government; in 1935 he went there once more, at the age of eighty-three, and at Buenos Aires, greatly respected by the people, he died 20 March 1936. In honour of him, a new city in the Argentine was named Don Roberto.

As befitted 'the most picturesque Scot' of his time, Cunninghame Graham's career at home was even more romantic. At the general election of 1886 he was elected as a liberal for North-West Lanarkshire (which had rejected him in the previous year), and he is said to have been the first member of the House of Commons to be suspended for using the word 'damn' in the House. His sense of fellowship and compassion, which included the lower animals, easily moved him to indignation at cruelty and injustice. His political sense was both erratic and acute. It went to the underdog wherever he found him. A single visit to Ireland converted him to devotion to Parnell, whose funeral he was the only non-Irish member to attend. He quickly developed into an ardent socialist devoted to William Morris [q.v.], and a friend of John Burns, although he was estranged from Burns when the latter avowed himself a pacificist in 1914. He contested unsuccessfully the Camlachie division of Glasgow in 1892, and in 1918, again unsuccessfully, Western Stirling and Clackmannan. When the national party of Scotland was founded in 1928 he was elected its first president. In the same year at the election for the lord rectorship of Glasgow University he polled only 66 votes fewer than Stanley Baldwin.

In height, appearance, and bearing, Cunninghame Graham looked a Spanish Don. When at the Old Bailey in 1887 he was sent to prison after the riot in Trafalgar Square in which he had been severely wounded by a policeman's baton and Burns had saved his life, a reporter who saw him in the dock thus described him: 'a striking figure, with a breezy head of hair and moustachios to match, and a sharply pointed beard, lighter than his hair. He took off his hat, laid down his stick, pulled off his coat and settled down.' The reporter, unaware of the truth, described him as having the appearance of a Spanish noble, and this was native to him, for his maternal grandmother (Catalina Paulina Alessandro) was a Spanish lady who gave birth to his mother in the admiral's cabin in a ship on the West Indies station. He himself, as a boy, lived much at Ryde with his grandmother who could remember Goya, and who taught him Spanish and brought him up in the Spanish way. He used a Mexican saddle when riding in Rotten Row, and he was as much at home in Spain and Morocco as in Scotland. His understanding of old Spanish life and of the Conquistadores is shown in nine volumes of historical and biographical studies. He wrote a little-known classic of travel, *Mogreb-el-Acksa* (1898), an account of a dangerous journey, when he travelled through southern Morocco; a local *cadi* imprisoned him, and he was released only after a painful experience. But perhaps his best work is to be found in his many volumes of stories, essays, and sketches. His style is in the tradition of the prose of King James's Bible, candid, direct, and vivid; his images are homely and apt. Nobody who has read such moving character studies as 'In a German Tramp' and 'A Hegira' from *Thirteen Stories* (1900), and 'Beattock for Moffat' from *Success* (1902), his noble tribute to William Morris on the occasion of the poet's funeral at Lechlade, 'With the North-West Wind' from *The Ipané* (1899), his sombre narrative of the passing of James Keir Hardie [q.v.] in *Brought Forward* (1916), or the picture of a Spanish dancer, Aurora La Cujiñi, in *Charity* (1912) but must respect and admire him for his contribution to English letters.

In 1879 Cunninghame Graham married Gabriela, daughter of Don Francisco José de la Balmondière. Born in Chile, of a French father and a Spanish mother, she was poet, water-colourist, botanist, and mystic. She died, childless, in 1906, and he himself dug her grave in the grounds of the ruined Augustinian priory on the isle of Inchmahome in the Lake of Menteith. He was buried beside her, and there is a memorial to him on a mound, reputed to be the spot where King Robert the Bruce died, adjoining the main road at Castlehill, Dumbartonshire, a site which he himself had presented to the National Trust of Scotland.

Cunninghame Graham used to say that he had been the 'victim' of at least a hundred artists. The best portrait is said to be the full length by (Sir) John Lavery (1906) in the Corporation Art Gallery, Glasgow. An earlier portrait by Lavery, also a fine picture, which shows him on his horse Pampa, is in the Museo de Bellas Artes, Buenos Aires. A painting by G. P. Jacomb-Hood (1887), two small portraits by Lavery, and a bust and a small equestrian statuette by Felix Weiss are in the possession of Vice-Admiral A. B. Cunninghame Graham of Ardoch, and a drawing by (Sir) William Rothenstein is published in *English Portraits* (1898). There are two copies of a bronze head and shoulders by Albert Toft (1891) in Edinburgh and Glasgow, and there are three copies of a head by Jacob Epstein (1923) in Aberdeen, Jerusalem, and in the artist's private possession.

[*The Times*, 23 March 1936; H. F. West, *Robert Bontine Cunninghame Graham*, 1932; A. F. Tschiffely, *Don Roberto*, 1937; personal knowledge.]   H. M. TOMLINSON.

GRAHAM, WILLIAM (1887–1932), labour leader, was born at Peebles 29 July 1887, the eldest son and child in the family of seven children of George Graham, master-builder, of Peebles and afterwards of Edinburgh, by his wife, Jessie Newton.

A scholarship from the Peebles public school took him to George Heriot's Hospital School in Edinburgh. Leaving at the age of sixteen, he spent two years (1903–1905) as a junior clerk in the War Office, but relinquished the civil service for a post on a Selkirk newspaper at £1 a week. Moving to Edinburgh, he earned sufficient by free-lance journalism to enter the university in 1911; here he graduated M.A. (1915), with honours in economic science, and LL.B. (1917), with honours in economic history, statistics and mathematical economics, forensic medicine, and administrative law.

Joining the independent labour party in 1906, and later the University Fabian Society, Graham combined his work and studies with socialist propaganda and was elected to the Edinburgh town council in 1913 while still a student. From 1915 to 1918 he was a lecturer in economics for the Workers' Educational Association.

At the general election of 1918 Graham won Central Edinburgh for the labour party and represented this constituency continuously until 1931. He was quickly marked out as a coming man. A master of figures, with a logical and well-trained mind, and an exceptional memory, his speeches were models of clarity and reasoning, devoid of any oratorical flourish. His gifts found full scope on the royal commissions on income tax (1919) and on the universities of Oxford and Cambridge (1920–1921); on the Speaker's conference on devolution (1919–1920); on Lord Colwyn's committee on railway agreements (1920); on the departmental committee on grants to local authorities (1922); on the joint committee on the British Broadcasting Corporation's charter (1925–1926); and on the departmental committee on native welfare in Kenya (1926). He also served on the Medical Research Council (1920–1928) and was chairman of the Industrial Fatigue Research Board (1921).

Outstanding among labour party experts on finance, Graham was appointed in 1924 financial secretary to the Treasury in the first labour government and was notable as chief assistant to Philip Snowden [q.v.], being responsible for piloting two intricate pensions bills through the House of Commons. Upon the fall of the government he was sworn of the Privy Council. While in opposition from 1924 to 1929 he was an assiduous member of the public accounts committee.

In the second labour government (1929–1931) Graham reached Cabinet rank as president of the Board of Trade and was responsible for the negotiations between the mine-owners and the miners which preceded the introduction of the coalmines bill and afterwards for its conduct through the House of Commons. The appointment of the overseas trade development committee, the missions of Lord Kirkley to South Africa and Rhodesia, Sir Ernest Thompson's mission to Japan and China, and Sir Arthur Balfour's mission to Egypt, as well as inquiries into the cotton, iron and steel, and fisheries industries, were all carried out on Graham's initiative. At the League of Nations Assembly in 1929 he sought to secure a 'tariff truce', as a preliminary to an agreement for freer trade, but the financial crisis frustrated his efforts. He took a considerable part in the discussions at The Hague and at Geneva over the revision of German reparation payments in kind and in endeavouring to establish greater international co-operation.

Occasionally, during Snowden's indisposition, Graham rendered valuable aid at the Treasury and served on various important Cabinet committees, including that set up to consider the recommendations on government economy made by the committee under the chairmanship of Sir George (afterwards Lord) May in 1931. Unconvinced of the necessity for the cuts in services and salaries that were demanded by the committee's report, Graham stood with those of his colleagues who opposed the 10 per cent. reduction in unemployment benefit which caused the resignation of the government. He declined office in Ramsay MacDonald's all-party administration (1931) and lost his seat at the general election of that year.

The break with his colleagues affected Graham greatly and very shortly after accepting a post as economic adviser to the firm of Messrs. Schwab & Snelling, he suddenly fell ill and died at his home at Hendon 8 January 1932 at the age of forty-four. He married in 1919 Ethel Margaret, only daughter of Henry Beardmore Dobson, cashier, of Harrogate; there were no children of the marriage.

Graham was an unusual type of labour member, belonging to the fourth generation of a family with traditions of public service. His sound Edinburgh training prepared him for hard study, wide economic reading, and the power of easy factual exposition. His writings were mainly in reviews and the general press, but in 1921 he published *The Wages of Labour*, and on various occasions indicated his adhesion to the guild system as a challenge to capitalist industrialism. In 1927 he received from Edinburgh University the honorary degree of LL.D.

[*The Times*, 9 January 1932; private information; T. N. Graham, *Willie Graham*, 1948; personal knowledge.]   J. S. MIDDLETON.

GRAHAME, KENNETH (1859–1932), author and secretary of the Bank of England, was born in Edinburgh 8 March 1859, the second son of an advocate, James Cunningham Grahame, by his wife, Bessie, daughter of John Ingles, of Hilton, Lasswade. He was doubly descended from Robert the Bruce. 'Anthony Hope', the novelist [Sir A. H. Hawkins, q.v.], was his first cousin. After education at St. Edward's School, Oxford, he spent two years in the Westminster offices of his uncle, John Grahame, a parliamentary agent.

In 1879 Grahame began work as a clerk in the Bank of England. He was competent and conscientious, but his literary bent found some outlet in the writing of poems and reflections in a small ledger. Much of his spare time was filled up by training in the London Scottish, with which he served for seven years. Sundry visits to the ship of his uncle, Commander Ingles, at Portsmouth, fostered his perennial interest in things nautical.

In 1886 Grahame met F. J. Furnivall [q.v.], who discouraged his poetic aspirations but urged him to write prose for the reviews. This he did, and gained an interview with W. E. Henley [q.v.], who printed a number of essays and sketches and tried to induce Grahame to leave the Bank for literature.

Too level-headed to do this, Grahame nevertheless continued writing, and in 1893 published his first book, *Pagan Papers*, essays reprinted from Henley's *National Observer*, which was well reviewed. Grahame wrote for *The Yellow Book* between 1894 and 1897, and in 1895 published *The Golden Age*, essays from this magazine and the earlier *Pagan Papers*, which revealed in this thirty-six-year-old bachelor a remarkably delicate appreciation of the child mind. It won from A. C. Swinburne the description of 'one of the few books which are well-nigh too praiseworthy for praise', and was a favourite with Theodore Roosevelt and the Emperor William II.

Grahame's business career had a success

parallel to that of his writings. He became secretary of the Bank in 1898, and filled that office with credit until his retirement for reasons of health in 1908. He was twice near death—from pneumonia in 1899 and from a lunatic's revolver-shot at the Bank in 1903. In 1899 he married Elspeth (died 1946), elder daughter of Robert William Thomson, of Edinburgh and Stonehaven, and step-daughter of J. F. Moulton, Lord Moulton [q.v.]. Their only child, Alastair, born in 1900, was killed by a train near Oxford in 1920, while an undergraduate at Christ Church.

Dream Days (1898) dealt with the same characters as *The Golden Age*. Then, in 1908, Grahame produced *The Wind in the Willows*, much of it written to the boy Alastair at Littlehampton in letter form. This book made a fortune for its author, and raised him to a status of mastery as a writer of children's books comparable with that of Lewis Carroll, Edward Lear, and J. M. Barrie. The famous animal characters, Mole, Badger, Rat, Toad, and the rest, remain equally popular with child and adult readers. The book was dramatized by Mr. A. A. Milne in 1929 as *Toad of Toad Hall*.

Grahame died suddenly at his home at Pangbourne 6 July 1932. He was a large, fair, genial, and dignified man, kindly, shy, and generous, who loved wit and good company and was beloved by many. His insight into child mentality has probably never been surpassed, and his subtle and evocative prose was an admirable vehicle for the poetry and pathos of his thought. A drawing of Grahame by J. S. Sargent (1912) is in the Bodleian Library.

[*The Times*, 7 July 1932; C. L. Hind, *Authors and I*, 1921; P. R. Chalmers, *Kenneth Grahame: Life, Letters and Unpublished Work*, 1933; D. M. Fyrth, *Étude littéraire Kenneth Grahame*, 1937.]

HERBERT B. GRIMSDITCH.

GRANT, SIR (ALFRED) HAMILTON, twelfth baronet, of Dalvey (1872-1937), Indian civil servant, was born in Edinburgh 12 June 1872, the fifth and youngest son of Sir Alexander Grant, tenth (sometimes reckoned eighth) baronet, principal of Edinburgh University [q.v.], by his wife, Susan, second daughter of the metaphysician James Frederick Ferrier [q.v.]. He was educated at Fettes and Balliol College, Oxford, and entered the Indian civil service in 1895. He was posted originally to the Punjab commission, but, when the North-West Frontier Province

was established by Lord Curzon as a separate unit, Grant was transferred there as a member of the foreign and political department (later the Indian political service) and held among other posts that of secretary to Sir Harold Arthur Deane, the first chief commissioner, and to Sir George Roos-Keppel [q.v.], who succeeded Deane on the latter's death. He also accompanied the mission of Sir Louis Dane to Kabul in 1904-1905 and was appointed C.I.E. in 1908. In 1912 he went to the foreign department of the government of India as deputy-secretary and in 1914 was appointed foreign secretary, which post he held with distinction throughout the years of the war of 1914-1918. In 1915 he was appointed C.S.I.

During the war years many difficult problems of policy connected with India's foreign relations fell to be decided, largely upon the advice which Grant gave to the viceroy and the government of India, and perhaps the most critical situation was that which arose in 1919, when Amir Amanullah made an unprovoked attack upon India and precipitated the third Afghan war. Although the initial attack was easily defeated and the strategic threat to India was never dangerous, the government of India was for political and internal reasons anxious to end the fighting as soon as possible and to procure a resumption of friendly relations with Afghanistan. The Amir was equally desirous of a solution and the difficulty lay in finding some device to save Amanullah's face with his own people. It was largely due to Grant's imagination and to his intimate knowledge of and sympathy with the Afghan point of view that a solution was found. He realized that the control of Afghan external relations exercised by His Majesty's government in virtue of a treaty concluded after the second Afghan war was a continual source of irritation to the Afghans, since it compromised their international independent status, and was at the same time of little practical benefit to His Majesty's government. He was appointed chief British representative of the delegation which met Afghan representatives at Rawalpindi in the summer of 1919 in order to enter upon preliminary negotiations for a treaty of friendship. In the course of these negotiations Grant, largely on his personal initiative and in anticipation of the full concurrence of His Majesty's government, undertook that Afghan external relations should in future be entirely free from any foreign control.

It was on this basis that a treaty was finally concluded in November 1921, and all subsequent relations between His Majesty's government and the Afghan government have been conducted with remarkable good will on both sides. This concession was hailed in Afghanistan as an Afghan victory over the British and was bitterly criticized both in the British press and by many British officers of experience on the North-West Frontier of India as an undignified surrender of principle and prestige. Time has, however, shown that Grant's intuition was not at fault and results have fully justified the advice that he gave.

Grant was appointed K.C.I.E. in 1918 and in 1919 succeeded Roos-Keppel as chief commissioner of the North-West Frontier Province, holding this post until his retirement from the service in 1922 after being appointed K.C.S.I. After retirement he became interested in commercial finance and served as director of a number of companies in London, which dealt with the development of Canadian silver mines and also with oil production. He was well known and popular as a member of White's Club, where his skill as a bridge player and unfailing resource and humour as a raconteur earned him a notable reputation. As a young man he represented Oxford at Rugby football and in later life maintained a robust interest in sport of all kinds, including golf. He succeeded his brother as twelfth baronet in 1936 and died in London 23 January 1937.

Grant was twice married: first, in 1896 to Mabel Bessie (died 1910), fifth daughter of Colonel Thomas Heaton Lovett, of Belmont (now Henlle Hall), Shropshire, and had a son and a daughter; secondly, in 1914 to Margaret Lucia, youngest daughter of Lieutenant Alexander Cochran, R.N., of Ashkirk, Selkirkshire, and had a son and two daughters. His elder son predeceased him and he was succeeded as thirteenth baronet by his grandson, Duncan Alexander (born 1928).

A portrait of Grant by Graham Glen belongs to Lady Grant; a better one is at Government House, Peshawar.

[*The Times*, 25 January 1937; Official records; personal knowledge.]

AUBREY METCALFE.

GRAVES, ALFRED PERCEVAL (1846–1931), author and educationist, was born in Dublin 22 July 1846, the second son of Charles Graves [q.v.], afterwards bishop of Limerick, by his wife, Selina, eldest daughter of John Cheyne [q.v.], physician-general to the forces in Ireland. The Graves family had for several generations contributed with distinction to scholarship and to the learned professions in Ireland, notably in the persons of Richard Graves (1763–1829), Richard Hastings Graves, Robert James Graves [qq.v.], and Graves's father, a fellow of the Royal Society and at the time of Alfred's birth fellow of Trinity College, Dublin, and professor of mathematics there. Between the ages of ten and fourteen Graves was educated at Windermere College, and was then prepared at home by private tutors for Trinity College, Dublin, where, after winning a classical scholarship, he obtained the equivalent of honours in classics and in English literature, history, and language. His first book, *Songs of Killarney*, appeared in 1873 when he was employed as a Home Office clerk and private secretary at £300 a year. In 1874 he married Jane (died 1886), eldest daughter of James Cooper Cooper, of Cooper Hill, co. Limerick, a member of a family renowned for its beauty. In 1875, after six years in the Home Office, he began his long and useful career as an inspector of schools. After serving successively in Manchester and Huddersfield, he was for many years stationed at Taunton, and while there published his *Songs of Old Ireland* (1882) and *Songs of Erin* (1892), both in collaboration with his friend (Sir) C. V. Stanford [q.v.]. Graves, who wrote and adapted the words to old Irish folk tunes chiefly derived from the collection of George Petrie [q.v.], parted with his musical rights to the publisher for £80, and he used to say that for his song 'Father O'Flynn' (which, written in 1875, and included in *Songs of Old Ireland*, attained world-wide fame after it was sung by (Sir) C. Santley [q.v.] at a concert in the early 'eighties) he had had but £1. 12s., his original fee when it was published in the *Spectator*. In 1891 he married as his second wife Amalie, eldest daughter of Heinrich Ritter von Ranke, professor of medicine at Munich University, and greatniece of the historian Leopold von Ranke, who had married Graves's aunt many years previously.

In 1895 Graves was appointed to the metropolitan district of Southwark and removed to London, where he founded the educational councils in several boroughs both within and without his own district. He now made some mark as a humorist by his contributions to *Punch*, a journal with which his younger brother Charles was closely associated; but he gained the greater part of his position in the world of letters as a poet of Irish nature and country life, and an essayist on Irish musical and literary subjects. He was a leading figure in the recently founded London Irish Literary Society, of which he was twice president, and as an editor and anthologist performed service in the cause of the understanding and appreciation of Ireland—her poets, her folk-lore, and her music. His 'translations', however, both from the Irish and the Welsh were based on other people's translations, for he had but a smattering of Gaelic and no Welsh; but in his *Celtic Psaltery* (1917) he rendered with success the spirit of the early Irish Christian poetry.

In 1910 Graves retired from the civil service, but remained active in the educational world as chairman of the representative managers of the London County Council schools (1911–1919). He promoted the supply of playing fields for children in urban schools and the educational use of the cinema. He had made his home at Wimbledon, but his last years were largely passed at Harlech in North Wales, where he organized and wrote the greater part of the books of the historical pageants of 1920, 1922, and 1927. Here he also wrote his autobiography, *To Return To All That* (1930), which was in the nature of a reply to an autobiography by his fourth son Robert, entitled *Good-bye To All That* (1929).

Graves died at Harlech 27 December 1931 and is buried there. He was survived by his second wife and by his ten children, three sons and two daughters of each marriage.

[*The Times*, 28 December 1931; A. P. Graves, *To Return To All That* (portrait and bibliography), 1930; private information; personal knowledge.]   JOSEPH HONE.

GREENE, HARRY PLUNKET (1865–1936), singer, was born at Old Connaught House, co. Wicklow, 24 June 1865, the son of Richard Jonas Greene, barrister, of Dublin, by his wife, Louisa Lilias, fourth daughter of John Plunket, third Lord Plunket, and granddaughter of William Conyngham Plunket, first Lord Plunket, lord chancellor of Ireland [q.v.]. He was educated at Clifton College, and afterwards studied singing at Stuttgart and Florence and in London. He was professor of singing at the Royal Academy of

Music (1911–1919) and at the Royal College of Music (1912–1919). He married in 1899 Gwendolen Maud, younger daughter of Sir C. H. H. Parry [q.v.], and had two sons and a daughter. He died in London 19 August 1936.

Greene's contribution to music in this country was due in equal proportions to his timely arrival as an adept interpreter for Sir C. V. Stanford [q.v.], Parry, Sir Arthur Somervell, and that generation of English composers, and to his native charm of character and vivid poetic imagination. He made his first appearance in England as a bass-baritone in 1888, and soon established his reputation as a singer, first by his 'joint partnership', from 1893 onwards, in recitals with the pianist Leonard Borwick in the classical repertory of German *Lieder* and Brahms songs, and secondly as a specialized interpreter of the regular series of cantatas and oratorios which Parry wrote for the Three Choirs festivals, especially 'Job' at Gloucester in 1892.

Music in that generation was only just becoming a profession for men of education and social position. Sir F. A. G. Ouseley [q.v.] had set a precedent despite discouragement from the dean of Christ Church, Oxford, who would not permit a baronet and a gentleman commoner to read for a degree in music. Parry further enlarged the bounds, but in the executive ranks of the profession, particularly among singers, Greene was an arrival from a new and welcome sphere, to be joined later by such men as Gervase Elwes [q.v.] and James Campbell McInnes. Each of these brought special gifts into the common purpose of establishing the rising generation of British musicians. Greene was the first in the field, and was in particular the 'creator' of the Stanford Irish song-cycles in which his native charm of manner was irresistible (before political differences had clouded the outlook) and he was a partner on equal terms in the Charles Stanford–Henry Newbolt combination of patriotic and sea songs which were of a far higher degree of merit than anything that had previously been set down.

The effect of Greene on his generation was remarkable: it was due to his charm and humour combined with his magnificent presence, his perfect diction in speech and song, now beguiling and now commanding, and, above all, to his fresh-air outlook which banished the hackneyed insincerities of the shop-ballad and raised the standard of public taste. In this campaign he was particularly influential as an adjudicator in the competition festival movement, both in this country and in Canada.

Greene was a writer of considerable distinction not only on music (*Interpretation in Song*, 1912) but on his favourite recreation of fishing (*Where the Bright Waters Meet*, 1924). He also wrote *Charles Villiers Stanford* (1935).

A portrait of Greene by James Gunn was commissioned by many of his friends on his seventieth birthday and is at present in the keeping of his family.

[*The Times*, 20 August 1936; *Grove's Dictionary of Music and Musicians*, 4th ed., vol. ii, edited by H. C. Colles; H. P. Greene, *From Blue Danube to Shannon*, 1934; personal knowledge.]   STEUART WILSON.

GREET, SIR PHILLIP BARLING BEN (1857–1936), actor-manager, was the younger son of Captain William Greet, R.N., by his wife, Sarah Barling. He was born 24 September 1857 on board the *Crocodile*, recruiting ship, which his father commanded, then lying off the Tower. Intended for the navy himself and educated at the Royal Naval School, New Cross, he became a master at a private school at Worthing, but was attracted to the stage. On this he made his first appearance in November 1879 with J. W. Gordon's stock-company at Southampton, afterwards joining Sarah Thorne at the Theatre Royal, Margate. There he remained for three years, making his London début at the Gaiety Theatre in March 1883 as Caius Lucius in *Cymbeline* with Miss Wallis. In the same year he joined Minnie Palmer in *My Sweetheart*, playing the comic 'dude'-character of Dudley Harcourt, with the catch phrase, 'Dash it all!' In the following year he made his first appearance at the Lyceum Theatre with Lawrence Barrett, and was the Apothecary in Mary Anderson's production there of *Romeo and Juliet*, thus beginning a lifelong friendship with Mary Anderson herself.

In 1886 Greet went into management and entered upon his principal lifework with a series of open-air—or, as he called them, 'pastoral'—performances of Shakespeare's plays. Apart from this, he toured the United Kingdom and the United States of America with a repertory company in which a large number of players who were afterwards well known made their first important appearances. In 1902, in association with William Poel

[q.v.], Greet revived the morality *Everyman* at the Imperial Theatre. It had been originally presented in 1901 by the Elizabethan Stage Society at an open grave in the Charterhouse. Greet played it afterwards in countless theatres, churches, halls, and open spaces on both sides of the Atlantic. Thereby he did much for the creating of a new interest in the study and presentation of pre-Shakespearian drama. From this time until 1914 he was a constant visitor to the United States, which he toured from coast to coast and which he revisited in the years 1929 to 1932.

In 1914 Greet returned to England and joined Lilian Baylis [q.v.] at the Old Vic. There his company became the nucleus of the Old Vic and Sadler's Wells organization, destined to win larger success than even he had anticipated. In 1918, at the desire of the committee of the Board of Education on Shakespeare for schools, he formed a company which gave performances in London County Council schools and other educational centres, thus initiating a movement which during four years was the means of presenting Shakespeare's plays before over a million children. From 1924 to 1926 he was associated with Mr. W. E. Stirling in the presentation of English plays in Paris and was awarded the diploma and gold medal for English productions at the Exhibition of 1926. From 1933 to 1935 he acted as master of the greensward at Mr. Sydney Carroll's open-air theatre in Regent's Park, the promotion of which was very largely inspired by his example. In February 1929 his fiftieth year on the stage was celebrated at a complimentary dinner given to him by actors and actresses who had appeared in his companies, and in June he was knighted for his services 'to drama and to education'.

Although he made no claims to great eminence as an actor, Greet appeared in character-parts with no little success. As a producer he was patient and painstaking, combining practicality with good taste. Although he owed much to the ideas of others—particularly to Poel in such productions as *Everyman*—his experience of the popular stage kept his own adventures within feasible limits. He was a sympathetic interpreter more than a profound scholar; but his love of the stage was a genuine enthusiasm. He was an assiduous playgoer, always preferring to pay for his seat in the pit or some other unreserved part of the house, than accept a complimentary stall. He died, unmarried, in London 17 May 1936.

[*The Times*, 18 May 1936; Cicely Hamilton and Lilian Baylis, *The Old Vic*, 1926; Sybil and Russell Thorndike, *Lilian Baylis*, 1938; E. J. Dent, *A Theatre for Everybody*, 1945; Russell Thorndike, *Sybil Thorndike*, 1929; personal knowledge.]   S. R. LITTLEWOOD.

GREGORY, ISABELLA AUGUSTA, LADY GREGORY (1852–1932), playwright and poet, the youngest daughter of Dudley Persse, of Roxborough, co. Galway, by his second wife, Frances, daughter of Colonel Richard Barry, was born at Roxborough 15 March 1852. Her father at one time owned an estate of more than 4,000 acres. Sir H. P. Lane [q.v.], the art collector and critic, was her nephew. She was educated privately. In 1880 she married, as his second wife, Sir W. H. Gregory [q.v.] whose house and property, Coole Park, Gort, were situated a few miles from her father's estate. Her husband died in 1892 leaving her with one son, who became a distinguished painter and was killed in action as an airman in Italy in January 1918.

In 1898 Lady Gregory became acquainted in London with W. B. Yeats [q.v.] who was beginning to write plays and had conceived the idea of opening a little theatre in London for the production of his own and his friends' plays, plays of a romantic kind in contrast to the realistic drama of Ibsen. Lady Gregory up to this time had taken little interest in the theatre, but she had always been deeply interested in her country, not in the usual patronizing manner of a big landowner's daughter; indeed, unlike most of her class, she was drawn to the humbler of her neighbours, to the dwellers in cottages, the inmates of workhouses. Yeats set her gathering folklore, and later in the year of their meeting he visited her at Coole, together with her neighbour Edward Martyn, who, like Yeats, had a play which he wanted to have produced. In an afternoon's talk it was decided, by Lady Gregory's influence, to have the plays performed in Dublin. A little later G. A. Moore [q.v.] joined the group, money was guaranteed for the first performance, and on 8 May 1899 with the production of Yeats's *The Countess Cathleen* the Irish Literary Theatre came into being.

If Lady Gregory began by having little interest in drama, save that she was a great admirer of Yeats's work, she quickly became, not the most dominant member of this group, for Yeats was bound to be that, but the element which, more or less, kept it together. The first three years' performances in Dublin were given by companies of players imported from England: later a purely Irish amateur company was formed and the nature of the plays changed. The Irish peasant as serious dramatic material was discovered by J. M. Synge [q.v.] and by Padraic Colum and others; he was no longer merely a creature of comic fiction or heroic political drama, and here Lady Gregory suddenly disclosed her talent as a dramatist. Hitherto her only literary work had been editing her husband's *Autobiography* (1894) and in *Mr. Gregory's Letter-Box* (1898) the letters of his grandfather, W. Gregory (1766–1840, q.v.). On 27 December 1904 the Abbey Theatre, Dublin, was opened. Lady Gregory was a co-director with Yeats and Synge, and she continued to be a director until the day of her death. She showed very marked administrative ability in all branches of the theatre's work, and it is not too much to say that, without her enthusiasm and determination, the theatre would not have survived its early years of struggle.

Lady Gregory wrote twenty-seven original plays, adapted four of Molière's, translating them into Irish country speech, translated a play by Goldoni as *Mirandolina*, and collaborated with Douglas Hyde and with Yeats. About the beginning of the century she became interested in Gaelic, learned the language, and put together old sagas which she published in English under the titles *Cuchulain of Muirthemne* (1902) and *Gods and Fighting Men* (1904). Other noteworthy non-dramatic works are *Poets and Dreamers* (1903) and *A Book of Saints and Wonders* (1907). But her chief claim to literary eminence lies in her dramatic work. She had a rich sense of humour and her early one-act plays, *Seven Short Plays* (1909), are masterpieces in dialogue and construction. Perhaps in her later, longer comedies, *The Image* (1910) and *Damer's Gold* (1913) for instance, she was apt to over-elaborate her dialogue. She wrote two series of what she styled 'folk-history plays' (1912 and 1923), that is to say, plays of Irish history seen through the eyes of Irish countrypeople and told in country speech, in the dialect which she called 'Kiltartan' after a village near her own home. The adjective has passed into Irish speech. These plays did not have the popularity which they deserved. More popular were her delightful fantastic plays, half realistic, half of fairyland: *The Golden Apple* (1916), *The Dragon* (1920), *Aristotle's Bellows* (1923). Nobility, tragic nobility, attracted her, and so she wrote a play about Don Quixote, *Sancho's Master* (1928), and a Passion play, *The Story Brought by Brigit* (1924).

Lady Gregory died at Coole Park 22 May 1932. A portrait by A. Mancini is in the Dublin Municipal Gallery of Modern Art, and there is a portrait of her by (Sir) Gerald Festus Kelly in a private collection. A bust by Jacob Epstein is in the Dublin Municipal Gallery, and the Abbey Theatre has an early portrait by 'A E' and a drawing by J. B. Yeats.

[*The Times*, 24 May 1932; Lady Gregory, *Our Irish Theatre*, 1914; *Lady Gregory's Journals, 1916–1930*, edited by Lennox Robinson, 1946; A. E. Malone, *The Irish Drama* (containing a list of Lady Gregory's plays to that date), 1929; George Moore, *Hail and Farewell. Ave*, 1911; private information; personal knowledge.]   LENNOX ROBINSON.

GREGORY, JOHN WALTER (1864–1932), geologist and explorer, was born in London 27 January 1864, the only son of John James Gregory, a wool merchant, of Bow, London, by his wife, Jane Lewis. He was educated at Stepney Grammar School, which he left at the age of fifteen. After eight years in the wool business, during which he graduated at the university of London, he joined (1887) the staff of the British Museum (Natural History) as an assistant in the geological department and so he remained until 1900. He was professor of geology and mineralogy at Melbourne University from 1900 to 1904 and of geology at Glasgow University from 1904 until 1929 when he retired to Essex. Throughout his active life he found time and opportunity to travel in all the continents, thus to supplement his great book-learning on the geology, geography, and peoples of the world with first-hand observation. In addition to the important expedition of Sir M. W. Conway [q.v.] to Spitsbergen (1896) others took him to Western Canada (1891), Austria, Cyrenaica (1908), Chinese Tibet (1922), and Peru (1932) to examine mountains, to East (1892–1893, 1919), West (1912), and South Africa, Australia, China, and Russia to study plains and plateaux, to New Zealand, Norway, and Dalmatia to see fjords, and to the West Indies for acquaintance with the smaller isles. He was eventually drowned in the rapids of the Uru-

bamba River called the Pongo de Mainique (lat. 11° 48′ S.; long. 72° 51′ W.) in Peru 2 June 1932.

Gregory's published work (consisting of over twenty books and more than 300 papers) covers fields of research involving museum, laboratory, and the countryside. At first he wrote mainly on palaeontology, and became the authority on bryozoa, corals, and echinoids, but soon his pen was busy with many other aspects of geology and geography. In particular, he sought the origin of things and brought his erudition, experience, and courage to bear when he presented some explanation of phenomena or championed a theory on rift valleys in East Africa, mountain chains in the Old or New World, deserts of Australia, fjords, ocean basins, land bridges, and submarine canyons. He discussed economic questions like water-supply and ore and coal deposits and the more dangerous questions of mankind, their races, population, distribution, migration, and immigration. Besides a great output of specialist works he wrote a few popular books on geology and geography which were widely read. Mankind's partial knowledge of the earth's surface and its crust has resulted in many controversies, few of which he did not investigate and embellish with thoughtful arguments. His *Geography, Structural, Physical, and Comparative* (1909) marks a new departure in such text-books, and his works on bryozoa are standard works of reference. Two other important books also deserve mention: *The Great Rift Valley* (1896) and *The Rift Valleys and Geography of East Africa* (1921).

Although slight in build and apparently diffident in manner, Gregory was wiry and tireless in body, tenacious and indomitable in purpose, and an indefatigable worker with a rare memory. As a teacher he was supreme and students thronged to hear him, whilst his stoutness of heart, enthusiasm, and geniality made him almost fanatically beloved by some who knew him best. No one came to him in vain for stimulus or inspiration.

Gregory received many academic and scientific honours. These included honorary degrees from the universities of London, Melbourne, and Lima, the fellowship of the Royal Society (1901), and the medals of various societies. He was president of the Geological Society from 1928 to 1930 and of Section C of the British Association in 1907 and 1931 and of Section E in 1924. He married in 1895

Audrey, daughter of the Rev. Ayrton Chaplin, of Woodham Walter, Essex, and had a son (who accompanied him to Chinese Tibet) and a daughter.

[*The Times*, 14 June 1932 and 2 May 1933; *Obituary Notices of Fellows of the Royal Society*, No. 1, December 1932 (portrait); private information; personal knowledge.]

J. V. HARRISON.

GREIFFENHAGEN, MAURICE WILLIAM (1862–1931), painter, was born in London 15 December 1862, the third and youngest son of August Greiffenhagen, by his wife, Helen Cundell. The family was of Danish origin, though the artist's grandparents had left Denmark and settled in Archangel before his father was born. Greiffenhagen received his early education at University College School: in 1878 he passed into the Royal Academy Schools, where he won the Armitage prize, the cartoon medal, and several other awards. He exhibited first at the Royal Academy in 1884, and continued to be an exhibitor until his death: his early exhibited paintings include some subject-pictures as well as portraits in oils, but it was not long before he came to concentrate on the latter. During the first part of his career he did a considerable amount of illustration work, for books and periodicals; his best-known examples in this sphere are his illustrations to the novels of Rider Haggard, which began to appear in 1887. He also contributed to the *Daily Chronicle*, the *Lady's Pictorial*, and occasionally to *Punch*.

In 1906 Greiffenhagen became headmaster of the life department of the Glasgow School of Art, a position which he held until 1929. Throughout this period his permanent home was in London, and his work in Glasgow was carried out on regular visits to that city. Apart from his teaching, Greiffenhagen's work thereafter fell into two main categories, of which the first was the more important; these were portrait-painting and large-scale decorative work. As a portrait-painter he made a considerable reputation; his robust sense of design and firm technique produced particularly striking results in his portraits of men. His talent for decorative work found its fullest expression in the historical panels which he designed for exhibition pavilions at Paris and Dunedin (1925) and Antwerp (1930). He also designed a travel-poster, 'The Gateway of the North', for the London, Midland, and Scottish Railway, in which his strong sense of colour

was seen to great advantage. He was elected A.R.A. in 1916 and R.A. in 1922, and received the honorary degree of LL.D. from Glasgow University in 1926. Paintings by him were acquired by the Tate Gallery, the Walker Art Gallery, Pittsburg, and other museums and art galleries.

Greiffenhagen married in 1889 Beatrice (died 1949), daughter of John Latham, of London, and had two sons, the elder of whom was killed in the war of 1914–1918. He died in London 26 December 1931.

A self-portrait of Greiffenhagen was in the possession of his widow.

[*The Times*, 28 December 1931; Ulrich Thieme and Felix Becker, *Allgemeines Lexicon der Bildenden Künstler*, vol. xiv, 1921; private information.]

JAMES LAVER.

GRENFELL, SIR WILFRED THOMASON (1865–1940), medical missionary and author, was born at Parkgate, Cheshire, 28 February 1865, the second of the four sons of the Rev. Algernon Sidney Grenfell, headmaster and proprietor of Mostyn House School, Parkgate, by his wife, Jane Georgina Hutchinson, daughter of a colonel in the Indian army. He was educated at Marlborough, and resided at Queen's College, Oxford, for the Michaelmas term of 1888, during which he played Rugby football for the university. He studied medicine at the London Hospital medical school and London University, under Sir Frederick Treves [q.v.], and qualified M.R.C.P. and M.R.C.S. in 1886. While studying medicine he came under the influence of Dwight Lynam Moody, the American revivalist, and of the brothers J. E. and C. T. Studd, and for a time conducted a Sunday school class, to which he gave instruction in the art of boxing. He was at the same time secretary in succession of the cricket, football, and rowing clubs in London University; and he thus became at an early age an exponent of that 'muscular Christianity' which Charles Kingsley had made popular.

In 1887, the year after qualification, Grenfell joined the Royal National Mission to Deep-Sea Fishermen as a medical missionary; and after serving for five years in this capacity from Iceland to the Bay of Biscay, he became a master mariner, and fitted out the mission's first hospital ship. In 1892 he visited Labrador, and he was so greatly shocked by what he later described as 'the poverty and ignorance and semi-starvation among English-speaking people of our own race' that he decided to devote the rest of his life to the betterment of the lot of the people of Labrador. In 1893 he established at Battle Harbour the first hospital of what came to be known as the Labrador Medical Mission; and as time went on he not only built other hospitals, but he also opened nursing stations, schools, orphanages, and social welfare centres. When, over forty years later, he retired, he had built up an organization that included six hospitals, seven nursing stations, four hospital ships, four boarding schools, fourteen industrial centres, twelve clothing distribution centres, a co-operative lumber mill, and a seaman's institute at St. John's, Newfoundland. What his lifework, as an example of practical Christianity, meant to the people of Labrador, whether whites, or Indians, or Eskimos, it would be difficult to exaggerate.

At first the Labrador Medical Mission was financed by the Royal National Mission to Deep-Sea Fishermen; but from an early date most of the necessary funds were raised by Grenfell himself. He made speaking tours through both Canada and the United States of America; and he roused such interest and support on these trips that the Labrador Medical Mission came to be almost better known in America than it was in England. In 1912 the Mission to Deep-Sea Fishermen withdrew its support; and Grenfell then organized the International Grenfell Association, with branches in England, the United States, Canada, and Newfoundland; and it was this association that stood behind Grenfell's work during the latter part of his life.

Not only by his lecture tours, but also by his books, Grenfell aroused interest in his work, and gained support for it. Beginning with *Vikings of To-day* (1895), he published between 1905 and 1938 a succession of books about Labrador and a number of religious books, which, although not outstanding for their literary qualities, have an engaging simplicity and modesty that endeared them to many people.

Recognition of Grenfell's work came to him in the form of numerous honours. The university of Oxford elected him her first honorary M.D. (1907), and he received honorary degrees from St. Andrews University and many universities and colleges both in the United States and in Canada; in 1915 he was elected an honorary fellow of the College of Surgeons of America, and in 1920 a fellow of the Royal College of Surgeons of England; he was appointed C.M.G. in 1906 and K.C.M.G. in 1927;

in 1928 he was elected lord rector of St. Andrews University; in 1935 he was awarded the gold medal of the Royal Empire Society; and in 1936 he was elected an honorary fellow of Queen's College, Oxford.

In 1935 ill health compelled Grenfell's retirement from active work; and he died at Charlotte, Vermont, 9 October 1940. In 1909 he married Anne Elizabeth Caldwell (died 1938), daughter of Colonel Edmund Burke MacClanahan, of Lake Forest, Illinois, and had two sons and a daughter.

[The chief source of information is Grenfell's autobiography first published in 1919 under the title *A Labrador Doctor*, and republished in 1932, in a revised and expanded form, under the title *Forty Years for Labrador*. See also: James Johnston, *Grenfell of Labrador*, 1908; A. G. Hall, *Doctor Wilfred Grenfell*, 1919; F. L. Waldo, *With Grenfell on the Labrador*, 1920, and *Grenfell*, 1924; D. Wallace, *The Story of Grenfell of the Labrador*, 1922; B. J. Mathews, *Wilfred Grenfell*, 1924; E. H. Hayes, *Forty Years on the Labrador*, 1930; Joyce Reason, *Deep-sea Doctor*, 1942; Genevieve May Fox, *Sir Wilfred Grenfell* (New York), 1947.]   W. S. WALLACE.

GREVILLE, FRANCES EVELYN, COUNTESS OF WARWICK (1861–1938), was born in London 10 December 1861, the elder daughter and co-heiress of Colonel Charles Henry Maynard (only son of the last Viscount Maynard), by his second wife, Blanche Adeliza, second daughter of Henry FitzRoy, of Salcey Lawn, Northamptonshire. She was educated at home. In 1881 she married Francis Richard Charles Guy Greville, Lord Brooke, who succeeded his father as fifth Earl of Warwick in 1893 and died in 1924. They had three sons, of whom the eldest became sixth Earl of Warwick and died in 1928, and the second died in infancy, and two daughters.

Lady Warwick was a celebrated late Victorian and Edwardian beauty and a member of the 'Marlborough House set' which grew up about the Prince of Wales (afterwards King Edward VII) as a reaction from the inflexible and limited social life of Queen Victoria's court. She inherited Easton Lodge, Dunmow, Essex, from her grandfather and at first made it a country retreat for fashionable Edwardians. After her husband had inherited Warwick Castle, Lady Warwick gave a ball there in 1895, the extravagance of which was criticized in *The Clarion*. As a result of this she met the editor, Robert

Blatchford, and under his influence she was converted to socialism. She recalled at the time that the motto of her husband's family was *Vix ea nostra voco*. Her devotion to the cause of labour and its champions was as complete as her early conquests in society. She established a school at Dunmow to encourage rural occupations, and the first college for training women in horticulture and agriculture at Studley Castle, Warwickshire. At the general election of 1923 she stood as labour candidate for Warwick and Leamington, but was defeated by the conservative, Mr. Anthony Eden, brother-in-law of her eldest son. In 1925 Lady Warwick wished the labour party to accept Easton Lodge as an international labour university, but the plan was considered impracticable and her offer was refused. Easton, however, became an unofficial meeting-place for labour reformers, and Lady Warwick's interest in the improvement of conditions among the working class continued to the end of her life. She was also solicitous for the preservation of birds and animals, and she formed a sanctuary at Easton where she collected a multitude of birds, domestic animals, and horses about her. She used her social position, her fortune, and her continuous vitality for all her charitable and social interests and achieved results equal to those of any woman of her class in her time.

Lady Warwick wrote with ease and an amiable interest in both the past and the present. Of her numerous books *Warwick Castle and its Earls* (1903) records the historical background of her married life: *A Woman and the War* (1916), *Life's Ebb and Flow* (1929), and *Afterthoughts* (1931) revealed her conversion from the luxurious standards of Edwardian society to care for the working classes. Her intelligent comprehension of problems made her a valuable advocate of the labour cause, and her kindness of heart no less than her opinions won for her regard from those ranks of society which she sought to help.

Lady Warwick died at Easton Lodge 26 July 1938. A portrait by Carolus-Duran is at Warwick Castle; another, by J. S. Sargent, is in America.

[*The Times*, 27 July 1938; private information; personal knowledge.]

HECTOR BOLITHO.

GREY, SIR EDWARD, third baronet, and VISCOUNT GREY OF FALLODON (1862-1933), statesman and bird-lover, was born in London 25 April 1862, the eldest of the seven children, four sons and three daughters, of Colonel George Henry Grey, by his wife, Harriet Jane, youngest daughter of Lieutenant-Colonel Charles Pearson. He was grandson of Sir George Grey, second baronet (1799-1882, q.v.), and succeeded him in the baronetcy and the ownership of Fallodon, Northumberland. His great-grandfather was Captain Sir George Grey, R.N., a younger son of General Sir Charles Grey, of Fallodon and Howick, afterwards first Earl Grey [q.v.], who was also father of Charles, second Earl Grey [q.v.], the prime minister of the Reform Bill.

Grey's father had served with the Rifle Brigade in the Crimea and the Indian Mutiny, and was chosen as one of the first equerries of the Prince of Wales. Having sold out of the army, Colonel Grey adopted a country life, he and his wife living in a very happy joint household with the older generation, Sir George and Lady Grey, at Fallodon. The colonel managed the home farm. Grey, therefore, was brought up from infancy at Fallodon.

Fallodon has no rare and peculiar beauty. It was a dignified and comfortable country house of moderate dimensions, standing among woods in the centre of a small estate, in a piece of unspoilt English countryside. The sea is visible two miles away to the east through a much-loved gap in the Fallodon trees: on that lonely shore of tufted dunes, reefs of tide-washed rocks, and bays of hard sand, between Dunstanborough and Bamborough castles, Grey would lie by the hour, both as boy and man, watching the various tribes of sea birds, or the woodcock immigrants landing tired from their voyage across the North Sea. On the other side of Fallodon, to the west, rise the heather-moors, crowned by Ros Castle Camp, Grey's favourite point of view, whence the Great Cheviot hill and most of north Northumberland are clearly visible. In the burns coming down out of these moors to the sea, Grey taught himself as a boy the rudiments of the art of fishing, on which he became so famous an authority.

At nine years old Grey was sent to a small preparatory school of thirty boys near Northallerton. Two years later (1873) he was sent to a larger and better school, Temple Grove, East Sheen, where he stayed until 1876: it was kept by a remarkable man, Ottiwell Charles Waterfield, for whom Grey had a great admiration. He rushed up the school and after one year found himself in the first class.

In December 1874 his father died suddenly at Sandringham, where he was in attendance on the Prince of Wales. Thus at twelve years old Grey passed out of his father's care, and came more than ever under the strong and gentle influence of his grandfather. Sir George Grey had just retired from parliament and he devoted much of the last eight years of his life to his grandchildren at Fallodon. 'He took my father's place with us', wrote Grey.

In September 1876 Grey went to Winchester. He got up the school rapidly at first, but being kept back from promotion into 'Sixth Book' after he had clearly deserved it, he lost interest in the regular work of the school. But he read poetry and pursued an intellectual life of his own, 'seemed rather solitary', and was regarded as the ablest boy in the school if he had chosen to exert himself, according to the testimony of his junior in Du Boulay's house, H. A. L. Fisher [q.v.]. While at Winchester he became very skilled in fishing the clear waters of the Itchen, where he learnt the art of the dry fly which he afterwards did much to introduce into northern streams. He became devoted to Winchester and its customs and in the last four years of his life one of his greatest pleasures was to revisit it as a fellow, even when he was too blind to see it.

Grey went up to Balliol College, Oxford, in 1880. His relations with Oxford are, perhaps, unique. After having been sent down for incorrigible idleness in 1884, he was in 1928 elected chancellor of the university. 'The life I led', he wrote of his time at Oxford, 'was one of pure pleasure and one of a kind that I could not have enjoyed at any other time of life. It led to nothing, but it left no scars, nothing to be regretted or effaced. It cleared the way for serious things.' He spent his time on expeditions into the country on foot and in dog-cart, on games of 'real' tennis at which he afterwards twice (1896 and 1898) became amateur champion, a little mild ragging, and very limited gambling. He admired Jowett, who appreciated his latent abilities but was unable to induce him to exert them.

The death of Sir George Grey in 1882 brought the formative influence of his grandfather over Grey's thought and character to an end, but the place was taken at the most critical juncture of his life, the time of his departure from Oxford, by an equally remarkable man, Mandell Creighton [q.v.], then engaged on writing his *History of the Papacy* in the rectory of Embledon, the parish in which Fallodon stood. The rector instilled into the young squire the same kind of moderate democratic liberalism and sense of public duty which he had first learnt from his grandfather, and which Creighton now purveyed through a more modern and a more intellectual medium.

Grey had been idle at Oxford. He was never idle again. He was sent down from Balliol in January 1884. Yet that year and the next may be called the formative years of his life, both in intellectual development and in power of action. The moment he left the university he proceeded to discover, by characteristically amateurish and unpretentious experiment, his genius for bird-observation in general and for wild-duck culture in particular. He put himself, as his note-books show, through a systematic course of reading in history, thought, and poetry by the best English authors. He entered official life in London and political life in Northumberland, winning at the age of twenty-three a resounding electoral triumph. And towards the end of 1885 he married.

In July 1884 Grey was initiated into public service as private secretary to Sir Evelyn Baring, afterwards first Earl of Cromer [q.v.], and in October he became private secretary to H. C. E. Childers [q.v.], then chancellor of the Exchequer. In the summer of 1884 he had made his first public speech as chairman at a liberal demonstration in Alnwick held to protest against the action of the House of Lords in delaying the passage of the county franchise bill. The impression which he made was so favourable that next year he was chosen to contest the Berwick-on-Tweed division in the liberal interest. Since his grandfather's defeat in 1852 it had been a conservative stronghold, but the extension of the franchise under the new Act enabled him to carry the seat, and he never lost it, even during the long period of liberal depression resulting from the home rule controversy. The mutual affection that grew up between the young member and the fishermen, shepherds, and others of his neighbours who supported him, was one of the chief things that kept him in political life, in many respects contrary to his inclinations. In the local language they 'thought that tarrable of Sir Edward', and he felt that he could not desert them. He had determined, if ever he lost the seat, not to re-enter parliament for any other constituency.

In October 1885 Grey married (Frances) Dorothy, eldest daughter of Shalcross FitzHerbert Widdrington, a squire of Newton-on-the-Moor, sixteen miles south of Fallodon. Her father was a moderate conservative, but the chief influence on her mind had been that of Creighton. The political opinions of husband and wife therefore coincided sufficiently, but she cared little for politics and, directly or indirectly, always tended to draw him back out of public life, into the occupations of country-lover, bird-watcher, and amateur naturalist—the life which they both at heart passionately preferred. The influence of his political friends H. H. Asquith and R. B. (afterwards Viscount) Haldane [qq.v.] had to be exerted to the utmost to keep him in politics, by appealing to his strong sense of public duty. Political ambition he had none.

The fact that the liberals were out of office from 1886 to 1906 for all except three years, enabled Edward and Dorothy Grey to realize their ideal of life while he remained an opposition member. They enlarged the famous Fallodon ponds and the variety of kinds of duck inhabiting them which Grey had begun to introduce in 1884. The birds were not pinioned but were wooed into an extraordinary tameness. The 'fox-proof fence' protected the ponds. The other place where the Greys found their happiness, as much as at Fallodon, was the tiny cottage in a meadow by the banks of the Itchen in Hampshire, where trout fishing and, still more, bird-observation could be carried on in solitude. No road led up to it: as Grey said, anyone who wanted to come there in a wheeled vehicle must come in a wheelbarrow. Even when Grey was in office, week-ends could be snatched here.

Grey, like his friends Asquith and Haldane, supported home rule for Ireland, but thought that Gladstone neglected English questions overmuch. They were also more interested in the British Empire than most liberals. From 1892 to 1895 the liberals were in office, and in August of the former year Grey was sent to the Foreign Office as parliamentary under-secretary, first under Lord Rosebery, and then under Lord Kimberley, when Rosebery became prime minister on Gladstone's retirement in 1894. The fact that his successive chiefs were both in the House of Lords threw on Grey the task of answering for foreign affairs in the House of Commons. It was this apprenticeship that first drew his mind away from domestic to foreign affairs, while his manner of speaking in the Commons won him a national reputation that rendered his return to private life more difficult. On 28 March 1895 Grey made in parliament a pronouncement, known as 'the Grey declaration', to the effect that French encroachment on the upper waters of the Nile would be viewed by England as an 'unfriendly act'. The declaration, to which some of the liberal ministers demurred, proved very serviceable at the time of the subsequent Fashoda incident.

In 1895 the liberal party lost power and remained in opposition for another decade. In 1897 Grey visited the British West Indian Islands as a member of a royal commission appointed to inquire into their economic circumstances. The commission in its report pointed out the danger which threatened those British Colonies where sugar was almost the only interest, and suggested various remedies, some of which were adopted.

The South African war divided the liberal opposition into supporters and opponents of the war policy of Alfred Milner and Joseph Chamberlain [qq.v.]. Rosebery, Asquith, Haldane, and Grey were the leading imperialist liberals, and Grey went even further than his friends in support of the war, thereby sowing the seeds of that distrust felt for him as foreign minister in later years by the more radical sections of the party.

The leadership of the divided liberal party at this time lay with Sir Henry Campbell-Bannerman [q.v.], who was a critic of the war. Rosebery had already retired from the leadership, but some thought that he might return to it. In December 1901 Rosebery made his famous speech at Chesterfield urging the government to negotiate with the Boers. By hastening peace, which followed next year, the speech helped to solve the difficulties of the liberal party, but for the moment it seemed to aggravate them, because the reappearance of Rosebery as a rival leader incensed the followers of Campbell-Bannerman. The year 1902 was a year of rival leagues and dinners, 'war to the knife and fork', within the liberal ranks. Already, before Chesterfield, a Liberal Imperial Council had been formed with Grey as president; after Chesterfield the Liberal League took its place with Rosebery as president, and Asquith, Grey, and Sir Henry Fowler as vice-presidents. If Rosebery had gone on with frequent speeches and active leadership, the split in the party might have become complete and permanent. But he sank back after the Chesterfield effort, as Grey had foretold.

With the return of peace the chief cause of liberal dissensions was removed; then A. J. Balfour's education bill of 1902 and Chamberlain's protectionist campaign united imperialists and 'pro-Boers' in hearty opposition. Grey was active and enthusiastic both as a free trader and a defender of the rights of nonconformists in education. So was every liberal of every hue, while the unionist party was split from top to bottom. In this new and joyous excitement the very existence of the Liberal League was forgotten by its vice-presidents, and by all men except its lordly president who thought it a force in politics long after it had ceased to be so.

In June 1904 Grey spoke in the House welcoming the agreement that Lord Lansdowne [q.v.] had made with France about Morocco and Egypt. Grey's experience in the Foreign Office from 1892 to 1895 had made him aware of dark and dangerous currents in German policy. He therefore now welcomed friendship with France as necessary for the security of Great Britain and as affording the best hope of European peace. On this subject, that soon proved to be of grave import, he differed from Rosebery who dissented from Lansdowne's policy.

The question whether Grey would take office on the return of the liberals to power was becoming urgent as the Balfour government tottered to its fall. Grey would have much preferred private life devoted to the study of birds in the society of his wife who cared little for politics. As a director since 1898, and as chairman since 1904, of the North-Eastern Railway he had just the kind and amount of public work that he liked. He had broken with Rosebery not only on foreign policy but on home rule, a cause which Rosebery now abandoned. But he still had little confidence in Campbell-Bannerman. An agreement had been made by Asquith, Haldane, and Grey in September 1905, before the formation of the liberal government, to take office only on condition that Campbell-Bannerman, when he became prime minister, should go to the House of Lords, leaving Asquith to lead the Commons. When the time came, Campbell-Bannerman refused to go to the Lords, and in consequence Grey declined to take the Foreign Office which Campbell-Bannerman offered him. His obstinacy lasted for three days (4–7 December 1905),

holding up the formation of the government and threatening the unity of the party on the eve of the general election. Asquith and Haldane had been more quick to see their error, and at the last moment Grey yielded to their solicitations, and accepted his destiny at the Foreign Office, at the head of which he remained until December 1916. He thus held the seals of office continuously for a longer period than even Grenville or Castlereagh.

From the moment of taking office Grey's relations with Campbell-Bannerman became most cordial. Contrary to his expectations, he found the prime minister a very able leader of the House of Commons and a strong supporter of his own policy of friendship with France. He also admired and warmly supported Campbell-Bannerman's boldly liberal policy in granting immediate self-government to South Africa, and resented Milner's opposition.

In the first days of February 1906, just two months after his becoming foreign secretary, occurred the tragedy of his private life, the death of Lady Grey, as the result of a carriage accident in Northumberland. It is quite possible that if this had not happened he would not have remained for eleven years in office. Work there was now an anodyne.

In January 1906, before his wife's death and while the general election was occupying the attention of other Englishmen, Grey had to meet alone the first great crisis of his policy, laying down the lines to which he adhered until the outbreak of war in 1914. Germany hoped and France feared that the change of government in England would reduce Lansdowne's agreement with France to a nullity. By that agreement Great Britain had undertaken to support France 'diplomatically' as to Morocco. How much that 'diplomatic' support would be worth was now the question. Germany, taking Morocco as a test, was trying by threats to break the newly formed Anglo-French *Entente*. The situation was highly critical, for Russia, weakened by her defeat in the Japanese war, was inclining to desert France and enter into the German orbit. If France were now to find British support purely academic, she would be compelled to follow Russia into the German orbit, and England would be friendless in face of a hostile Europe. In the winter of 1905–1906 the French ambassador in London, Paul Cambon, asked Grey whether in the case of

German aggression England would defend France in arms. Grey, with the full concurrence of Campbell-Bannerman, let both France and Germany know that in his opinion England would fight in such circumstances, although he could not pledge his country until the circumstances arose on which the country would judge. France had no positive pledge, but Germany had full warning.

Grey at the same time permitted the continuance in more official form of 'military conversations', initiated by Lansdowne, between French and British military chiefs as to the steps to be taken by Great Britain to aid France in the hypothetical case of this country being ready to aid France to repel a German attack. Campbell-Bannerman sanctioned these 'conversations', but failed to report them to the Cabinet, as he and Grey should no doubt have done. Neither prime minister nor foreign secretary saw the full political significance of these technical talks, which was better appreciated in Paris and, fortunately, also in Berlin. It was due to the further continuance of these 'military conversations' in later years, followed by Haldane's army reforms, that the British Expeditionary Force arrived in France in 1914 just in time to save Paris.

In March 1906 the conference of powers at Algeciras dealt with the Morocco question and reached a compromise that saved peace but did not grant the full German demands. Germany did not push the matter to war because England had rallied to France, because Russia had for that reason also rallied to her ally, and because President Theodore Roosevelt threw the diplomatic weight of the United States of America against the extravagant demands of Germany. A personal friendship and an intimate correspondence now grew up between Grey and Roosevelt, cemented by their common interest in bird-life. Grey's determination to secure the friendship of the United States as the first of British interests was an essential part of his policy both in peace and in war.

Grey was the principal author of the Anglo-Russian agreement of August 1907. Before he took office he had hinted at the desirability of such an agreement in a speech in the City on 21 October 1905. The agreement, although always unpopular with the advanced elements in the rank and file of the liberal party, had the warm approval of Campbell-Bannerman as prime minister and of John (afterwards Viscount) Morley [q.v.] as secretary of state for India. Morley gave Grey valuable assistance in overcoming the objections to any understanding with Russia traditional among the older school of British authorities in India.

There were two motives in Grey's mind for this logical extension of Lansdowne's policy into a new sphere. First, that Anglo-Russian understanding would be a work of liberalism and peace. The interests of the two Empires touched at so many sore points, Tibet, Afghanistan, and Persia, that Grey believed that only a friendly agreement, directly negotiated by the two governments, could avoid a clash. The second reason for such an agreement was brought strongly home to him during his first months in office by the Moroccan crisis between Germany and France. He had to consider what would be the consequence to this country and to Europe of war between Great Britain and Russia with such a power as Germany on the flank, and how it would be possible to remain friends with France while remaining at enmity with her ally. Friction with Great Britain in Asia might at any moment push the Tsar Nicholas II back into the policy of Björkö, where only a year before he had come to terms with the German Emperor in a pact that was intended to operate to the disadvantage of Great Britain.

It was relatively easy to agree that both Russia and England should abstain from interference in Tibet and that Russia should not interfere in Afghanistan. The real difficulty was Persia, where Russia had already violated Persian independence in the northern spheres where lay Teheran, the capital. This area was recognized by the agreement as being the sphere of Russian influence. The British sphere of influence was delimited to the south-east of Persia around Seistan and the approaches to British India. A neutral zone was left between the two, extending down to the Persian Gulf. Both countries recognized the independence of Persia, but put very different interpretations on the phrase. Whereas the British sent no troops into their sphere of influence, the Russians continued to impinge on Persian independence in the north. Until 1914 Grey was continually protesting to the Russian government, but in vain. Unless Great Britain was prepared to go to war, she could not eject the Russians from the position which they had occupied in north Persia before the agreement. The conduct of Russian officers in north Persia, and also the civil war of rival terrorisms raging in Russia itself between the tsardom and the revolutionaries, made the agreement increasingly unpopular in England, particularly with the radicals of Grey's own party.

If the Balkan question had not existed to divide Russia and Germany, the Anglo-Russian agreement might soon have broken down. But although its geographical scope was Asiatic only, it paved the way for Anglo-Russian friendship in Europe. As an integral part of the Triple *Entente* the agreement was successful, owing to the popular passion in Russia on behalf of the Slav races in the Balkans. On that question English policy in Grey's hands was merely that of a neutral peacemaker. But it was none the less the Balkan and Austro-Hungarian question, in which Grey took neither side, that attached Russia to the *Entente* and induced her government only partially to violate the Asiatic agreement with Great Britain.

While many liberals and labour men disliked the policy of the *Ententes* with France and Russia, later criticism has taken the opposite line, and Grey has often been blamed for not turning these understandings into alliances, in which case, it is argued, Germany would never have dared to go to war. Grey's answer to this was twofold. In the first place, he had not the power to make formal alliances either with France or Russia. He could not pledge Britain to fight before the actual occasion arose because the Cabinet, and the House of Commons, and the country were opposed to any such commitment. In the second place, he would not have made these alliances even if he could because he feared that if France and Russia were sure of British support under whatever conditions war arose, their policy towards Germany might become provocative and involve this country in a war which British and American opinion would regard as unjustified.

On the one hand Grey was ensuring that in case of war Great Britain would not be without friends, and on the other hand he was earnestly working and hoping to preserve peace. He therefore made large concessions to Germany in order to remove all grounds for her constant complaint of 'encirclement'. The Bagdad railway agreement of 1913 acknowledged Germany's right to extend her influence in Asiatic Turkey, delimiting it only at the

approaches to the head of the Persian Gulf, where British interests had been established long ago. Grey was also prepared to make an agreement allowing Germany a large share of the Portuguese Colonies in Africa, particularly Angola, in case they were put up for sale by Portugal, as at that time seemed not improbable. But Grey refused to make a secret treaty to this effect. When war broke out in August 1914, the contingent agreement about the Portuguese Colonies had been initialed by Grey, but he refused to sign it until Germany agreed that it should be published. Until war broke out, Grey, unlike his predecessors, refused to make secret treaties or secret clauses for treaties. His subsequent secret treaties were war-time measures.

In 1911 Grey renewed the alliance with Japan which Lansdowne had made in 1902 and renewed and extended in 1905. The question of the Congo atrocities had been raised under Lansdowne, but only came to a head in Grey's period of office. The Congo had long been, under an old international agreement, almost the private estate of Leopold II, King of the Belgians. Through the agency of various companies, he had turned it into a vast slave-farm, contrary to the treaties under which he held his powers. This state of things was exposed by the gallant and disinterested efforts of a private individual, Edmund Dene Morel. The British public had taken fire, and the foreign secretary too. But the foreign secretary knew that fire was not enough. His plan was to encourage the Belgian state to take over the Congo from King Leopold; but he would only recognize the transfer on condition of wholesale reform, and in particular the abolition of forced labour. British treaty rights in the Congo were in his hands the lever to secure humanitarian demands. Neither Germany nor France nor any great power save the distant United States cared about the matter. But thanks to Grey's firmness and tact, thanks also to the better elements in the Belgian people and parliament, and to the high character of King Albert, Leopold's successor on the throne, Congo reform was an accomplished fact before the war of 1914–1918, and Belgium and England had not fallen out.

In the rather similar affair of the Putumayo atrocities in South America, Grey's publication of the Putumayo Blue Book in July 1912, based on the reports of Roger Casement [q.v.], was a personal act of the foreign secretary, not suggested by the custom of his office but by his own indignation.

The severity and deadly importance of Grey's daily work at the Foreign Office prevented him from taking a very active part in domestic politics. He was fully in accord with the policy of Asquith's government over the budget of 1909 and the subsequent struggle with the Lords. Indeed he was more democratic than his colleagues in that he wished to abolish the hereditary element in the upper chamber: he had, however, on that point to be content with the preamble of the Parliament Act of 1911 which has never been implemented; it was inserted partly to appease him. He did not like the style of Lloyd George's oratorical appeals, the very opposite of his own restrained and almost conversational method of public speech. But the personal relations of the two men were friendly enough at this period. He opposed Lloyd George in the Cabinet on the question of the naval estimates, successfully supporting Reginald McKenna's demand for more ships in the Cabinet crisis of 1909.

Meanwhile crisis followed crisis in Europe. In 1908 Austria-Hungary annexed Bosnia-Herzegovina with its million Serb inhabitants. Grey in the name of international law and right demanded that the matter should be brought before a conference of the powers. He received no support and the idea of the Concert of Europe received another set-back.

In 1911 came the Agadir crisis. The Algeciras agreement of 1906 had proved only a temporary settlement; it had now been violated by France, or so Germany claimed. French influence and arms had penetrated into Morocco, to restore order in an oriental state falling into chaos. French action was not unreasonable, but neither was Germany's demand that she must receive compensation elsewhere in Africa. Her demand for practically all the French Congo, however, was excessive, and Germany had begun the negotiations with the warlike gesture of sending the warship *Panther* to Agadir. War seemed highly probable. But Lloyd George's unexpected speech in strong support of Grey's stand, although it caused wild indignation in Germany, in fact smoothed the road to peace. The Germans saw that a united Britain would fight if France were attacked. An agreement was reached by which France, in return for a free hand in Morocco, ceded two large strips of Congolese territory to the Germans. In fact Germany had received good terms, but her original demands had been so high and she had sought to impose them by such violent methods on France and Britain, that a fair agreement at the end seemed like a German defeat.

The situation remained most alarming. The great powers of Europe were ranged in two armed camps with Italy balancing between. British-German antagonism, owing to the building of the German fleet in rivalry to the British, came to the forefront of the picture. In 1912 Grey consented that his friend Haldane should go to Germany to try to arrange with the Emperor and his advisers for a limitation in the growth of the German fleet, as the only possible road to better relations with Britain. Haldane's mission was a complete failure.

Grey had constantly pressed the great powers to compel the Turks to make real reforms in Macedonia, but without success. The result was the war of 1912, when an alliance of the Balkan national states liberated Macedonia and Thrace by force of arms. The immediate consequence of the defeat of Turkey was a grave danger of a general European war in 1913. Austria-Hungary, furious at the growth of Serbia's power, meditated an attack upon her, while the Russian government and people were determined not to let her be crushed. Grey strove for peace in a spirit of real neutrality, and France and Germany both backed him up on this occasion. Consequently a general European war was just averted. But the price was the exclusion of Serbia from the outlet on the Adriatic which her arms had won from the Turks. Grey had actively supported this 'inferior settlement', as he himself called it, because the alternative was a general European war. How little then was there on his part a policy of 'encirclement', or rooted hostility to the claims of the central powers.

The next time that trouble arose between Austria and Serbia, over the murder of the Archduke Francis Ferdinand at Serajevo on 28 June 1914 and the Austrian ultimatum of 23 July, Grey's efforts to have the matter again referred to European arbitrament were unavailing, because on this occasion Germany refused a conference and backed Austria through thick and thin. The story of the outbreak of war in August is too well known and has been too often discussed to require repetition here.

Up to the last moment the Cabinet was divided on the issue of going to war to protect France, and the country at first was no more united. Grey, who was clear on the subject, advanced with very careful steps in the Cabinet, which came round to his side very gradually, but almost unanimously when Germany made it clear that she would attack Belgium. A similar change of opinion took place in the public mind. Grey's speech in the House of Commons on 3 August was therefore entirely successful; it was purposely restrained in tone, with no emotional appeal, which might have provoked more opposition than was aroused by his careful statement of the issue. It was the greatest and most tragic moment of his life. He felt the tragedy to the full. 'I hate war, I hate war', he said passionately to a friend. It was due to the way in which Grey had handled the crisis that Great Britain entered the war as a united people and that American opinion was largely on her side.

Perhaps Grey 'hated war' too much, and had too little interest in military affairs, to be as good a foreign minister in war-time as in peace. Yet even that is by no means certain. On the most important issue of all, the relations of Great Britain with the United States, he took the right line and adhered to it in spite of much outcry and opposition, and achieved complete ultimate success. The question was how far to press the blockade in disregard of American interests and demands. It was a narrow and winding path that he had to tread to avoid catastrophe. His personal friendships with Walter Page, the American ambassador in London, and with President Wilson's adviser, Colonel House, and with the British ambassador at Washington, Sir Cecil Spring-Rice [q.v.], kept him well informed as to American opinion. He was deliberately prepared to make some sacrifice of this country's direct military interest, as in the case of cotton export to Germany early in the war, in order to prevent a quarrel with America. If he had not considered American opinion as it then was, the United States would never have come into the war on the side of the Allies, and might have put an embargo on the export of munitions on which Great Britain's own war effort depended. The Contraband Department set up by the Foreign Office under Mr. Alwyn Parker functioned excellently. In February 1916 it became a department of state under Lord Robert Cecil who was of one mind with Grey.

Grey's war-time policy in the Balkans was less well informed and less definite. But it may be doubted whether anything except the military success denied to Great Britain at the Dardanelles in 1915 could have brought Bulgaria in on the right side. Grey's refusal of Greek military aid in September 1914 and March 1915, subsequently condemned by Lloyd George, was rendered absolutely necessary by Russia's veto.

The most severely criticized part of Grey's policy is the secret Treaty of London (26 April 1915) which he made with Italy, as the price of her entering the war on the side of the Allies. The promise to Italy of large portions of the Dalmatian coast inhabited by Yugo-Slavs caused trouble after the war. Grey regarded the Italian terms as extortionate, but he defended his acceptance of them because on no other terms would the Italian foreign minister, Baron Sonnino, agree to his country's joining the Allied side, and if Italy had adopted the alternative of entering the sphere of influence of the central powers the Allies would probably have lost the closely balanced war. Serbia in any case had been promised enormous expansion of territory if the Allies should win.

Meanwhile Grey's health and particularly his eyesight were rapidly deteriorating. He deliberately sacrificed the chance of preserving his eyesight to continuance of his duty as foreign secretary in war-time, although he would have been only too glad to lay down the burden. In July 1916 he was raised to the peerage as Viscount Grey of Fallodon, in order to reduce his work by retirement from the House of Commons. At length in December 1916 final release came by the break-up of Asquith's government and reconstruction under Lloyd George. In that complicated and embittered affair Grey took very little part. His attitude towards Lloyd George's aspirations was not the same as that of the closer bodyguard of Asquith. As between the two men, he greatly preferred his old friend the outgoing prime minister, but he had the suspicion that the country desired a change and that the fulfilment of its desire might perhaps help on the war. The way for the change of ministry had indeed been prepared by a campaign of abuse of which he had his share, but which fell off him like water from the back of one of his Fallodon ducks; he did not waste his small ration of eyesight in studying the productions of the gutter press.

One reason why Grey had no regrets was that he left foreign affairs in the hands of Balfour and Robert Cecil. He had been alarmed at Lloyd George's bellicose method of brushing aside President Wilson's feelers for peace, but he knew that Balfour and Cecil would never quarrel with America.

During the seventeen years that passed between Grey's resignation and his death, he was never again in the forefront of affairs. In September 1919 he consented at the request of the British government to go as ambassador on a special mission to the United States, in order to persuade President Wilson to compromise with the Senate so as to bring America into the League of Nations. But Wilson was ill and had quarrelled with House and would not even see Grey. The part played by Grey in his later years as president of the League of Nations Union from November 1918 onwards, his activities on the Liberal Council formed in 1926 in opposition to Lloyd George's later proceedings, and some of his speeches in the House of Lords were not unimportant, but he was too blind and often too ill to lead a party or to aspire to office.

Grey's blindness steadily increased as the years went on. To put it in terms of his favourite sport, first he had to give up the dry fly, then ordinary trout fishing, then salmon, until finally in 1932 he wrote from Fallodon to a friend: 'I cannot see whether I put my worm into the water or on to the bank. With my ducks I can at any rate feel when they take it out of my hand, and distinguish some of them when they are very close.' He was equally cut off from books, of which as life advanced he had grown very fond. Fortunately he knew much of the best poetry by heart, particularly his favourite Wordsworth. He could read to himself continuously only in braille.

Other disasters fell thick upon Grey. Fallodon was burnt down in May 1917. Only the furniture, pictures, and books on the ground floor were saved. After living in the kitchen wing until the war was over, he rebuilt the house, with the old bricks and in the same general style as before but with two stories instead of three and with some change in the ground plan of the rooms. In February 1923 the cottage on the Itchen was burnt, and was not rebuilt. These two breaches with the past grieved him sorely. In 1922 his second marriage gave him a brief period of real happiness. His second wife was Pamela Adelaide Genevieve, youngest daughter of Percy Scawen Wyndham, of Clouds, near Salisbury, sister of George Wyndham [q.v.], and widow of Edward Priaulx Tennant, first Lord Glenconner. But in 1928 Lady Grey died; in the same year his youngest brother Charles, of whom he had become almost as fond as formerly of his next brother George, was killed by a buffalo in Africa, as George in 1911 had been killed by a lion. And besides these private strokes, Grey lived to see his hopes for the pacification of the world shattered, America withdrawn into herself, Europe armed to the teeth, and Germany under the Nazi régime. He foresaw a grim future for mankind, the more so as he had less than no sympathy with the increasing mechanization of life.

But Grey's private afflictions and public disappointments never broke his courage or soured his serene and constant spirit. Neither in his letters nor in his talk was there any cry of personal pain or even of impatience. He was unfailing in his quiet, humorous observation of life, and his determination to make the daily best of what was left. All who saw him went away cheered and elevated by the strong, even current of his talk, delightful, easy, humorous, sustained without effort high above the level of his griefs. Visitors to Fallodon were always made happy. The spring in him was never dry.

Grey's principal achievement in these later years was the production of his books, a task which owed much to the encouragement of his wife. In *Twenty-five Years, 1892–1916* (2 vols., 1925) he told the story of his public career; blind as he was, he could not have searched the necessary documents without the devoted scholarly assistance of his friend John Alfred Spender. The publication of *Fallodon Papers* (1926) and *The Charm of Birds* (1927) put him in touch with a wide public on that side of thought and feeling for which he cared the most. His book on *Fly Fishing*, the art in which he was so great a master and which gave him so many hours of happiness, had first appeared in 1899. Taken together, these books place him in the category with Izaak Walton, White of Selborne, Richard Jefferies, and his own friend W. H. Hudson [q.v.].

In the summer of 1933 Grey's health gave way altogether and those who saw him at Fallodon that August felt him to be a dying man, although he could still stroll on the lawn and sit among the ducks.

He had no long period of confinement indoors. On 7 September he died. His ashes were placed beside those of his first wife under Fallodon trees which they had planted together in their youth. Grey was childless, and his peerage became extinct. His three younger brothers having predeceased him without issue, he was succeeded as fourth baronet by his second cousin, Charles George (born 1880). He left Fallodon to Captain Cecil Graves, son of his eldest sister.

Grey was sworn of the Privy Council in 1902 and elected F.R.S. in 1914. In 1912 he was appointed K.G., being the first commoner to receive that honour since it was bestowed upon Castlereagh in 1814.

The best portrait of Grey is that representing him in his robes as chancellor of Oxford University, by Harold Speed, in the Oxford and Cambridge Club. Another portrait by Speed is in the National Portrait Gallery, as is also a sketch in oils by Sir James Guthrie, a study for his group of 'Some statesmen of the Great War'. A cartoon by 'Spy' appeared in *Vanity Fair* 5 February 1903.

[The unrivalled source for the study of Grey's foreign policy is *British Documents on the Origin of the War, 1898–1914* edited by G. P. Gooch and H. W. V. Temperley, 13 vols., 1926–1938. His *Twenty-five Years* gives his own account of his public work. G. M. Trevelyan, *Grey of Fallodon*, 1937, gives many references to authorities both for his public and private life, as well as quotations from unpublished letters and documents. An autobiography covering his early years, quoted in *Grey of Fallodon*, has never been published.]

G. M. TREVELYAN.

GRIFFITH, FRANCIS LLEWELLYN (1862–1934), Egyptologist, was born at Brighton 27 May 1862, the youngest of the six sons of John Griffith, headmaster of Brighton College and later vicar of Sandridge, Hertfordshire, by his wife, Sarah Eliza, daughter of Richard Foster, banker, of Cambridge. Frank Griffith was mainly taught by his father until in 1875 he went to Sedbergh School, whence after two and a half years he was transferred to Highgate School, and there, apparently under the influence of a master, he acquired that interest in ancient Egypt which became his ruling passion. At Queen's College, Oxford, where he had gained an open scholarship in 1879, he divided much of his time between Egyptology, in which he was self-taught, and natural history. There, too, he came into contact with A. H. Sayce [q.v.], who gave him much encouragement. He refused to read for final honours but became nevertheless a sound classical scholar.

In 1882 Griffith was articled to a brother, a solicitor in Brighton, but on graduating in 1884 he was appointed official student of the Egypt Exploration Fund, thanks to financial help from an aunt and an old family friend, and in 1884–1885 he gave valuable assistance to (Sir) Flinders Petrie at the site of Naucratis. During the next three years, often working single-handed and making exploratory journeys, he gained a special knowledge of Lower Egypt, and in 1886 a journey through Upper Egypt with Petrie brought a rich harvest of copies of rock *graffiti* and tomb inscriptions.

In 1888 Griffith was appointed an assistant in the department of British and medieval antiquities and ethnography at the British Museum, where he remained for eight years, being allowed to devote to Egyptology every moment which he could spare from routine duties. His publications of inscriptions and his pleas for the better recording of monuments led to the creation in 1890 of a branch of the fund called the Archaeological Survey. Griffith was appointed its superintendent (from 1926 to his death director) and supervised, with the closest attention to detail, the publication of twenty-five volumes of records. From 1892 to 1901 he was assistant professor of Egyptology at University College, London; from 1896 to 1908 he was honorary lecturer in Egyptology at Manchester University; in 1901 he was made reader in Egyptology at Oxford; in 1924 he was appointed honorary professor there; and after his retirement in 1932 he continued for a year as deputy professor and in 1933 was given the rank of professor emeritus. In 1916 he was elected an honorary fellow of his own college, and in 1924 a fellow of the British Academy. Learned bodies in France, Germany, Denmark, Austria, Egypt, and the United States of America also recognized his achievements by electing him to membership, and he received honorary degrees from the universities of Leipzig (1909) and Aberdeen (1925). On his seventieth birthday in 1932 a stout volume of *Studies* by over seventy colleagues was presented to him; it contains a bibliography. He died at Boars Hill, near Oxford, 14 March 1934.

During nearly half a century Griffith showed himself a prolific and accurate scholar. His admirable edition of a unique sign-list in *Two Hieroglyphic Papyri from Tanis*, and the publication of some of the harvest from Upper Egypt in 1886 as *The Inscriptions of Siût and Dêr Rîfeh* (both in 1889) gave him an assured position in the field of international Egyptology. In 1892 he began to edit a series of annual *Archaeological Reports* containing surveys of the progress of Egyptology in all countries. These continued until shortly before the foundation in 1914 of the *Journal of Egyptian Archaeology*, to which he contributed exhaustive bibliographies. In *A Collection of Hieroglyphs* (1898) his interest in natural history, first acquired at Sedbergh, led him to identify accurately many animals and plants depicted by the signs.

Perhaps Griffith's most remarkable characteristic was a genius for decipherment, which led him to study with much success a number of scripts and languages only imperfectly understood. The first-fruits of this gift appeared in *Hieratic Papyri from Kahun and Gurob* (2 vols., 1897–1898), in which a mass of early papyri found by Petrie, many of them extremely cursive, were interpreted with a skill and accuracy which even to-day leave very little to add. His *Stories of the High Priests of Memphis* (1900) first established demotic on a firm scientific basis, and placed him at the head of living students of that script. This was followed by *The Demotic Magical Papyrus of London and Leiden* (with Sir Herbert Thompson, 3 vols., 1904–1909) and the *Catalogue of the Demotic Papyri in the John Rylands Library, Manchester* (3 vols., 1909), by far the most important work in the whole subject. He threw much light on the scanty and obscure remains of Old Coptic, and later devoted himself with valuable results to the interpretation of Meroitic, a language of pagan Nubia; and in *The Nubian Texts of the Christian Period* (Berlin Academy, 1913) he made a great advance on his predecessors' work in another Nubian tongue. His interest in Nubian matters led him in 1910 and after to undertake, with his second wife, expeditions known as the Oxford University Excavations in Nubia. The results from Faras and Sanam were published in the University of Liverpool *Annals of Archaeology and Anthropology* (viii–xv, 1921–1928); after digging at El-Amarna in 1923–1924 he laid bare three temples and many inscriptions at Kawa in ;Dongola province in 1930–1931.

Griffith was twice married: first, in 1896 to Kate (died 1902), daughter of Charles Timothy Bradbury, cotton-spinner, of Ashton-under-Lyne. She collaborated with him in translating Egyptian texts for *A Library of the World's Best Literature* (1897). On her father's death in 1907 Griffith inherited a considerable fortune which enabled him to create the Griffith Egyptological Fund by a gift of £8,000 to the university of Oxford. He married secondly in 1909 Nora Christina Cobban, daughter of Surgeon-Major James Macdonald, of Aberdeen, and sister of Sir J. R. L. Macdonald [q.v.]. Born 7 December 1870, she had been her future husband's pupil at Oxford, and a student of antiquities and texts in Aberdeen museums and in Egypt itself. For a time she was conservator of the Archaeological Museum, King's College, Aberdeen. Gifted with a strong intellect, a remarkable memory, and much skill with the pencil, she became her husband's devoted helper in all his activities. After his death she spared neither labour nor expense in completing two of his unfinished projects: a large corpus of over 500 *graffiti* from temples from Philae southwards to Maharraka, entitled *Catalogue of the Demotic Graffiti of the Dodecaschoenus* (1935, 1937) ('Les Temples Immergés de la Nubie'), all the folio plates of which she herself had drawn; and Griffith's part (the demotic) of *The Adler Papyri* (1939). She organized and largely financed further work of excavation in Nubia in 1934–1935 and 1935–1936. She died at Boars Hill 21 October 1937.

Griffith bequeathed the finest private Egyptological library in existence, all his papers, and his own considerable fortune, subject to his wife's life interest (there were no children by either marriage), to the university of Oxford, for the creation and endowment of an institute for Egyptological study and other departments of Near Eastern research. To this was added the bequest of his widow's own very considerable estate. The Griffith Institute, built as an annexe to the Ashmolean Museum, contains besides a large number of books on other oriental languages a mass of unpublished archaeological records, and is the chief centre in Great Britain for research and instruction in the languages and literatures of the ancient Near East.

Griffith was an ideal scholar, benevolent, full of praise for good work and of encouragement for beginners, with a passion for his subject, an astonishing gift of intuition leading to correct conclusions, and an unlimited capacity for patient drudgery.

Humility was an outstanding trait: in the war of 1914–1918 no task was too menial for him in the Oxford hospitals. He was tall and spare, of great energy, a tireless walker, and in later life a lover of outdoor games.

There is a portrait of Griffith by Kenneth Green (1932) in the Griffith Institute.

[A. H. Gardiner, *Journal of Egyptian Archaeology*, vol. xx, 1934; W. E. Crum, *Francis Llewellyn Griffith, 1862–1934* in *Proceedings* of the British Academy, vol. xx, 1934; private information; personal knowledge.]   BATTISCOMBE GUNN.

GRIFFITHS, ERNEST HOWARD (1851–1932), physicist, was born at Brecon 15 June 1851, the son of the Rev. Henry Griffiths, principal of the Memorial College, Brecon, by his wife, Mary Blake, a descendant of Admiral Blake. He was educated at the Owens College, Manchester, where he held a Whitworth scholarship, and at Sidney Sussex College, Cambridge. Having obtained a pass degree in 1873, he engaged in work as a private tutor and became a very successful university coach. The social side of the university greatly appealed to him; he was fond of music and rowing; he drove tandem, and later took to yachting. In 1897 he was elected a fellow, and in 1904 an honorary fellow of his college.

Griffiths's scientific work belongs to the period when the usual objective of the physicist was to carry the accuracy of physical measurements to another place of decimals. Although he had been occupied with the determination of the mechanical equivalent of heat by the electrical method since 1887, it was not until 1891 that he published his first work, 'On the Determination of some Boiling and Freezing Points by means of the Platinum Thermometer' (*Philosophical Transactions* of the Royal Society, vol. clxxxii). His interest in this subject arose out of an inquiry from C. T. Heycock and F. H. Neville who were searching for an instrument for the measurement of the freezing-points of alloys better than the so-called 'fixed zero' mercury thermometers then available. He constructed a number of platinum resistance thermometers and proceeded to calibrate them by reference to fixed points. He was unable to reconcile his results with those of H. L. Callendar, who had given an empirical formula for temperatures measured by a platinum resistance thermometer calibrated directly in terms of a gas thermometer. To clear

up the discrepancy, Callendar and Griffiths joined forces to redetermine the boiling-point of sulphur, and they showed that the value given by H. V. Regnault, which had been accepted by Griffiths, was about 4° too high (*Philosophical Transactions*, *ibid.*). In the course of this investigation they improved the technique for determining the boiling-point of sulphur, and also converted the resistance boxes of their day from crude appliances suitable for technical electrical measurements into instruments of precision.

Henry Augustus Rowland's classical paper on the determination of the mechanical equivalent of heat had been published in 1880, and Griffiths published in 1893 a paper on 'The Value of the Mechanical Equivalent of Heat, deduced from some Experiments performed with the view of establishing the Relation between the Electric and Mechanical Units; together with an Investigation into the Capacity for Heat of Water at Different Temperatures' (*Philosophical Transactions*, vol. clxxxiv). In this work Griffiths, who had built a small laboratory in his own grounds, was assisted by G. M. Clark. His final contribution to this subject will be found in Sir R. T. Glazebrook's *Dictionary of Applied Physics* (s.v. 'Mechanical Equivalent of Heat', 1922).

Other investigations carried out at Cambridge were 'The Latent Heat of Evaporation of Benzene' (with Miss Dorothy Marshall in *Philosophical Magazine*, vol. xli, 1896); 'The Influence of Temperature on the Specific Heat of Aniline' (*Philosophical Magazine*, vol. xxxix, 1895); and 'The Latent Heat of Evaporation of Water' (*Philosophical Transactions*, vol. clxxxvi, 1895). He regarded the last as one of his best pieces of work and in later years he submitted it as a thesis for the degree of D.Sc. at the university of Wales.

In 1901 Griffiths was appointed principal of the University College of South Wales and Monmouthshire, at Cardiff, with a chair of experimental philosophy. In this capacity he was elected to a fellowship at Jesus College, Oxford, for one year, in rotation with the other principals in Wales, in 1905, 1909, 1913, and 1917. Departure from Cambridge involved leaving incomplete an investigation into the accurate measurement of the freezing-points of dilute aqueous solutions, constants then of great importance in the thermodynamic and electrolytic theory of solutions. In his early years at Cardiff he was greatly hampered by the absence of laboratory facilities. He had to devote much time to the planning of the new college buildings in Cathays Park, and it was not until 1909 that the Viriamu Jones memorial research laboratory was completed. In this building Griffiths was deeply interested, and he insisted that it should be built of non-magnetic materials. Although he was three times vice-chancellor of the university of Wales, his life at Cardiff was marked by many disappointments, and problems of administration to one of his temperament proved irksome. But amid official work he was able, in conjunction with Dr. Ezer Griffiths, to carry out an investigation of the thermal capacities of metals from liquid air temperatures up to 100° C. and compare the results with the modern quantum theories (*Philosophical Transactions*, vols. ccxiii and ccxiv, 1913 and 1914).

In 1918 Griffiths retired, and the death in the same year of his wife, Elizabeth Martha, daughter of George Dall Clark, of Bowdon, Cheshire, whom he had married in 1877 and by whom he had no issue, meant for him a somewhat lonely life. But he retained his spirit of optimism, and during the last years of his life at Cambridge his main interests were his old college and the British Association, of which, when it met at York in 1906, he was president of the mathematical and physical sciences section, and in 1913, at Birmingham, of the educational science section. In 1920 he became general treasurer of the association, but resigned in 1928. He served on the executive committee of the National Physical Laboratory and took a keen interest in its work on electrical standards.

Griffiths was elected F.R.S. in 1895 and received the Hughes gold medal in 1907. He received honorary degrees from the universities of Aberdeen, Manchester, and Liverpool. He died at Cambridge 3 March 1932.

A portrait of Griffiths by Gabriel Thompson hangs in University College, Cardiff.

[*Obituary Notices of Fellows of the Royal Society*, No. 1, December 1932 (portrait); *Nature*, 26 March 1932; *Proceedings* of the Physical Society, vol. xliv, 1932; *The Times*, 4 March 1932; private information; personal knowledge.]   Ezer Griffiths.

GROSSMITH, GEORGE, the younger (1874–1935), actor-manager and playwright, was born in London 11 May 1874, the elder son of the entertainer and singer in light opera George Grossmith [q.v.], by his wife, Emmeline Rosa, only daughter of Edward Noyce, M.D. He was nephew of the comedian W. W. Grossmith [q.v.]. He was educated at University College School and in Paris, and it was originally intended that he should enter the army, but he failed in his examination at Woolwich. He first appeared on the stage at the Criterion Theatre, in July 1892, in *Haste to the Wedding*, a musical play adapted by (Sir) W. S. Gilbert [q.v.], with music composed by Grossmith's father. Engagements followed at several London theatres until November 1894, when for the first time he was seen at the Gaiety Theatre in *The Shop Girl*. In the autumn of 1895 he made his first appearance in New York in this play. He appeared at the Comedy Theatre in 1899 in one of his own plays, *Great Caesar*, and at the Globe Theatre in 1900 in another, *The Gay Pretenders*. After acting for a short period at other theatres and in the United States of America, he returned to the Gaiety in 1901, under the management of George Edwardes, with whom he remained in association until 1913, appearing in a succession of popular musical plays, notably in *The Toreador* (1901), *The Orchid* (1903), *The Spring Chicken* (1905), *The Girls of Gottenburg* (1907), and *Our Miss Gibbs* (1909). During this period he also appeared at the Hicks (later Globe) Theatre in 1908 in *A Waltz Dream*, at the Alhambra Theatre in 1914, and in the United States. In 1914 he entered into management with Edward Laurillard, his productions with whom included *Potash and Perlmutter* (Queen's Theatre, 1914), *To-night's the Night* (Gaiety, 1915), and *Theodore and Co.* (Gaiety, 1916).

During the war of 1914–1918 Grossmith was commissioned in the Royal Naval Volunteer Reserve (1916) and later served with the Royal Naval armoured cars. After the end of the war he became manager, with Laurillard, of the Winter Garden Theatre, which they opened in May 1919 with *Kissing Time*; this was followed by a number of other successful musical plays there and at the Adelphi Theatre, which, with other theatres, they also controlled. This partnership ended in 1921, when Grossmith entered into partnership with J. A. E. Malone. Grossmith appeared at His Majesty's Theatre in April 1923, under his own management, as Lord Quex in a revival of *The Gay Lord Quex* by Sir Arthur Pinero [q.v.], his first venture into serious comedy. At the Palace Theatre in March 1925 he scored one of the greatest successes of his career in *No, No, Nanette*, and he also appeared there in *Princess Charming* in 1926. In 1929 he again visited America and appeared in several plays. He made his last appearance on the stage at His Majesty's Theatre, during October 1934, as Talma in *Josephine*.

In 1931 Grossmith became managing-director of Drury Lane Theatre, but resigned the position after twelve months, and in 1932 he became chairman of London Film Productions, Ltd.; he had himself appeared on the screen in several pictures from 1929 to 1931.

Grossmith wrote (both alone and in collaboration) or adapted more than thirty plays, many of which were eminent successes, including *The Spring Chicken, Rogues and Vagabonds, The Girls of Gottenburg, Havana, The Dollar Princess, Everybody's Doing It, The Bing Boys are Here, Theodore and Co., A Night Out, The Cabaret Girl,* and *Primrose*.

Grossmith originated the 'dude' or 'dandy' in musical comedy when he appeared as Lord Percy Pimpleton in *Morocco Bound* at the Shaftesbury Theatre in 1893, and he continued to play that type of character for nearly thirty years with almost unvarying success. To Grossmith must also be accorded the credit of introducing the modern type of revue to London with *Rogues and Vagabonds* at the Empire Theatre in 1905; and he was also the first to introduce 'cabaret' entertainment to this country, at the Whitehall Rooms, Hotel Metropole, in 1922.

Always a fluent French speaker, Grossmith appeared in Paris, in revue at the Folies Bergère in 1910, and also acted with Réjane, the famous French actress, at her theatre in 1911. He was created a chevalier of the Legion of Honour and an officer of Public Instruction by the French government, and also received decorations from the Greek government and from the pope.

In appearance Grossmith was lanky and of angular physique. He made capital out of his physical peculiarities, which, combined with the curious carriage of his arms and hands, and the fixed smile of his large mouth, helped to create a stage personality which few could forget. Although he had no voice for singing, he had the faculty of putting his songs across the footlights in an inimitable manner, and he was a very nimble dancer.

Grossmith married in 1895 Gertrude, youngest daughter of Henry Rudge, actor, of Edgbaston; she was known on the stage as Adelaide Astor. They had a son and two daughters, the elder of whom, Ena, adopted her father's profession with some success. He died in London 6 June 1935.

A portrait of Grossmith in uniform by Weedon Grossmith was exhibited at the Royal Academy in 1917.

[George Grossmith, 'G. G.', 1933; *Morning Post* and *News Chronicle*, 7 June 1935; *Who's Who in the Theatre*, 1933; personal knowledge.]   JOHN PARKER.

GUEST, FREDERICK EDWARD (1875–1937), politician and promoter of aviation, was born in London 14 June 1875, the third of the five sons of Ivor Bertie Guest, first Baron Wimborne, by his wife, Lady Cornelia Henrietta Maria, eldest daughter of John Winston Spencer-Churchill, seventh Duke of Marlborough [q.v.], and sister of Lord Randolph Churchill [q.v.]. He was brother of Sir Ivor Churchill Guest, first Viscount Wimborne [q.v.].

Guest was educated at Winchester. In 1894 he obtained a commission in the East Surrey Regiment, and in 1897 he joined the first Life Guards. In the South African war he received the Queen's medal with five clasps. On the outbreak of war in 1914 he at once offered himself for service, and was appointed an extra aide-de-camp to Lord French. He was awarded the D.S.O. in 1917 and was appointed C.B.E. in 1919. He was a chevalier of the Legion of Honour.

A few years before the war Guest had turned to politics which had long attracted him. His first speech was made in 1905 in support of his cousin Mr. Winston Churchill, whom he had followed over to the liberal party, and whose private secretary he became. Guest, after four unsuccessful attempts to enter parliament, was returned for East Dorset at the general election of December 1910, and held the seat until 1922, when he was defeated. In 1917 he became chief whip to the liberal members of the coalition government, and in 1921 was appointed secretary of state for air. He was sworn of the Privy Council in 1920. In 1923 Guest was returned for the Stroud division of Gloucestershire, but his want of sympathy with the liberal party increased. He often abstained from voting, or voted with the conservatives. At the general election of 1924 he was returned for North Bristol largely through the support of conservative voters. So markedly independent was his attitude that, at the general election of 1929, he found another liberal, with the sanction of Lloyd George, standing against him at Bristol. The result was the return of the labour candidate. A year later he joined the conservative party, announcing his decision in a letter to Baldwin. He was returned at the general election of 1931 for the Drake division of Plymouth, and was re-elected in 1935.

In addition to his political work Guest carried on other activities as secretary of state for air in 1922, when he took a close interest in flying. He made the important appointment of Sir W. S. Brancker [q.v.] to the position of director of civil aviation, and it was with Guest's approval that the director organized the air pilots of the Empire into a body which should establish their professional status and protect it. When in 1930 Brancker lost his life in the accident to the airship R. 101, Guest succeeded him as deputy master of the newly established Guild of Air Pilots and Air Navigators, a position which the possession of a pilot's licence entitled him to assume. He became master in 1932.

However often he was at variance with the party organizers, 'Freddie', as his many friends called him, remained about the most popular man in the House of Commons. A good sportsman, he was a polo enthusiast in his younger days, fond of travel and big-game shooting, and, throughout his life a man of many interests, he was the most charming and attractive of companions.

Guest married in 1905 Amy, daughter of Henry Phipps, an ironmaster in the United States of America, and had two sons and one daughter. He died at Sunbury-on-Thames, after an illness of some months, 28 April 1937.

[*The Times*, 29 April 1937.]

ALFRED COCHRANE.

GUEST, SIR IVOR CHURCHILL, third baronet, and first VISCOUNT WIMBORNE (1873–1939), politician, was born in London 16 January 1873, the eldest of the five sons of Ivor Bertie Guest, first Baron Wimborne. He was brother of F. E. Guest [q.v.].

From Eton Guest went to Trinity College, Cambridge. His interest early centred in politics, and after contesting Plymouth unsuccessfully as a conservative in 1898, he was returned unopposed for that constituency at a by-election in February 1900, and held the seat at the general election later in that year. Before this he had served in South Africa as a captain in the Dorset Imperial Yeomanry. The tariff reform proposals of Joseph Chamberlain [q.v.] caused Guest to cross the floor of the House with his cousin Mr. Winston Churchill and others who adhered to free trade. As a result of this at the general election of 1906 Guest was returned as a liberal for Cardiff Boroughs by a majority then unprecedented. From 1906 to 1909 he was chairman of the royal commission on coast erosion and afforestation. In 1910 he was sworn of the Privy Council and accepted a peerage to strengthen the government representation in the House of Lords, and sat until his father's death in 1914 as Baron Ashby St. Ledgers. He was paymaster-general from 1910 to 1912.

Soon after the outbreak of war in 1914 Wimborne was appointed to the staff of Lieutenant-General Sir Bryan Mahon [q.v.], then commanding a division at the Curragh. Shortly afterwards he was offered by Asquith the post of lord-lieutenant of Ireland. His interest in Irish affairs led him to accept the viceroyalty and he held it during practically the whole war (1915–1918). His love of sport and generous hospitality made him popular, but events were too strong for him, and the rebellion of Easter 1916 followed. It was Wimborne's idea that the leaders, who were known to the police, should be arrested before trouble broke out, but unfortunately the approval of this sensible precaution by the absent chief secretary, Augustine Birrell [q.v.], could not be obtained in time, and nothing was done. After the event there was a public inquiry, at which the viceroy's evidence created a favourable impression, and he consented to withdraw the resignation which he had sent in. However, in 1918 he was asked by the government to report on the subject of conscription for Ireland, and on his refusal to support this measure his place was taken in May by Lord French. Wimborne was advanced to a viscountcy in the following June.

On his return to England Wimborne ceased to take any share in politics, and turned his attention to business activities. His sympathy with the labour party enabled him at the time of the General Strike in 1926 to accelerate a settlement by helping to get the leaders into touch with the government. In the crisis of 1931 he supported the all-party government, and he was elected the first president of the national liberal party.

Wimborne was a discriminating connoisseur of the arts. He was always fond of sports and games. He had a tennis court of his own at Canford Manor, and could play a good game; he hunted, and raced for a short time. But he was best known as a polo player, and as a patron of polo. He was captain of a team known as the 'Quidnuncs', which could hold its own with any of the best clubs, and in 1914 he financed a team which went out to the United States of America. It must have been a satisfaction to him that it secured one of the rare British victories in the depressing series of British matches with America.

In 1902 Wimborne married Alice Katherine Sibell, younger daughter of Robert Wellesley Grosvenor, second Lord Ebury: a son and two daughters were born of the marriage. Wimborne died in London 14 June 1939, and was succeeded as second viscount by his son, Ivor Grosvenor (born 1903), who was elected member of parliament for Brecon and Radnor in 1935.

A portrait of Wimborne by Sir William Orpen is in the possession of his widow.

[*The Times*, 15 June 1939.]

ALFRED COCHRANE.

GUNTHER, ROBERT WILLIAM THEODORE (1869–1940), zoologist and antiquary, was born at Surbiton, Surrey, 23 August 1869, the only son of the zoologist Albert Charles Lewis Gotthilf Günther [q.v.], by his first wife, Roberta, sixth and youngest daughter of Baillie John McIntosh, of St. Andrews, and sister of William Carmichael M'Intosh, also a well-known zoologist [q.v.]. His mother died ten days after his birth, and his father married again in 1879. He was educated at University College School, London, and at Magdalen College, Oxford, where he continued the biological tradition of his family by obtaining in 1892 a first class in animal morphology, as the school of zoology was then called. In 1893 he went to the Stazione Zoologica at Naples, where he made a useful study of the relative movements of land and sea. He then became lecturer (1894) and tutor (1896) in natural science at Magdalen College, and in 1897 he was elected to a fellowship which he held until 1928. He was elected a fellow of the Linnean Society in 1900 and was vice-president in 1927–1928. The university of St. Andrews conferred upon him the honorary degree of LL.D. in 1925.

Gunther's guiding motive was his veneration for the science of the past, and it is as an antiquary that he will be remembered. After the war of 1914–1918 he devoted himself to the collection and preservation of instruments and writings relative to the history of science, and it was largely through his agency that the Lewis Evans collection of scientific instruments was presented to the university of Oxford in 1924. For the welfare of this collection, of which he became the first curator, he used all his considerable powers of persuasion and polemic. He induced the university to house it in a part of the Old Ashmolean Building and he was most successful in extracting from rather apathetic university institutions their scientific treasures which might otherwise have been lost or dispersed, or at least would not have been available for study. The creation in 1935 of the Museum of the History of Science, in which various collections are now incorporated, and the obtaining for it of the whole of the Old Ashmolean Building—Oxford's principal monument of seventeenth-century science —was Gunther's worthiest work.

From 1934 to 1939 Gunther was university reader in the history of science. He published many works on this subject, amongst which may be mentioned his *Early British Botanists and their Gardens* (1922), the fourteen books, some original and some reprints, which constitute the series *Early Science in Oxford* (1920–1945), and his massive and beautifully produced *The Astrolabes of the World* (2 vols., 1932). Some of these are marred by inaccuracies, due to the author's haste to cover the vast field which he saw open before him and to his individualism that disinclined him to consult those with specialized knowledge, but none the less they supply information that can nowhere else be obtained.

Gunther died suddenly at South Stoke, Oxfordshire, 9 March 1940. He married in 1900 Amy, daughter of Eustace Neville-Rolfe, of Heacham, Norfolk, consul-general for southern Italy (1895–1908), and had two sons. The elder, Eustace Rolfe Gunther, a most promising oceanographer, died as the result of an accident in May 1940.

[*Nature*, 6 April 1940; *Proceedings* of the Linnean Society of London, 152nd session, 1939–1940, part iv; private information.]

F. SHERWOOD TAYLOR.

GUTHRIE, THOMAS ANSTEY (1856–1934), humorous writer under the pseudonym of F. ANSTEY, was born in London 8 August 1856, the eldest of the three sons of Thomas Anstey Guthrie, military tailor, of Cork Street, Burlington Gardens, by his wife, Augusta Amherst Austen. The Guthries came from Forfarshire two or three generations back. He was educated at a private school at Surbiton (the original of Crichton House in *Vice Versa*), at King's College School, and at Trinity Hall, Cambridge, where he read law. He was called to the bar by the Middle Temple in 1880, but never practised, and eagerly took the chance of becoming a writer given him by the great success of *Vice Versa* in 1882. In 1886 he began a connexion with *Punch* and in 1887 was 'called to the Table' at the *Punch* office. He there began sketches and stories and the series of 'Voces Populi', 'Mr. Punch's Young Reciter', 'Mr. Punch's Model Music-hall Songs and Dramas', 'Mr. Punch's Pocket Ibsen' (all of which were published in book form), developing an exquisite talent for burlesque and parody, for recording and subtly transmitting the quality of current entertainment and of the day-to-day talk of Londoners. From *Vice Versa* onwards he continued to write imaginative fiction in which no flights of fancy were barred. He plainly enjoyed the hurdles at which he set himself in having to make plausible the most astonishing transformations. But in his humorous reporting he stuck faithfully to reality and his parodies contain description and criticism which no social historian of the 'eighties and 'nineties should neglect.

In the twenty-five years following *Vice Versa* Anstey Guthrie produced a succession of fantastic novels, notably *The Brass Bottle* (1900) and *Only Toys!* (1903), and made one or two excursions into more serious writing with *The Giant's Robe* (1884) and *The Pariah* (1889). But his public knew very well the kind of books which it wanted from him. Two or three of his works were successfully produced on the stage, *The Man from Blankley's* (1893), *The Brass Bottle*, and *Vice Versa* as a Christmas play.

Anstey Guthrie wrote no novel after *In Brief Authority* (1915), but in 1925 he issued the last of his volumes of collected *Punch* sketches, *The Last Load*. It did not sell a thousand copies. By that time a new public had grown up which found his reliance on magic demoded; and when in 1931 the Book Society was encouraged by the enthusiasm of George Gordon,

president of Magdalen College, Oxford, to issue an omnibus volume of Anstey's work entitled *Humour and Fantasy*, although Anstey was gratified he was not in the least surprised to learn that the volume had not met the taste of 1931. His later literary work was largely devoted to translating and adapting the plays of Molière for the English stage. He died in Kensington 10 March 1934.

Anstey Guthrie's autobiography, prepared for the press by his sister and his sister's son, Dr. Eric Millar, of the British Museum, was published posthumously in 1936 under the title of *A Long Retrospect*; a bibliography of his writings is printed at the end of that volume.

Anstey Guthrie was a man of most equable disposition, of a sociable nature and with many friends, who was all his life grateful for having been endowed with a literary talent which had enabled him to live a much more agreeable and free life than he had ever expected when he had set out to qualify for the law. Being singularly free from the weaknesses and temptations that beset literary men, he was unruffled by his gradual eclipse, and surmounted the formidable test of character of achieving in his twenties an immense literary success and of never repeating it. He never appealed to the American public and his English public was never big; it was discriminating and faithful and sufficient, and he was grateful for it. He was a man of few wants, a dog-lover and a lifelong bachelor, whose pleasures were foreign travel with old friends, and in his later years he made exquisite miniature reproductions of great paintings. He lived all his life in London. In appearance he was slightly built with a prominent moustache; although he became bald, he never looked old, even when advanced in his seventies.

A painting of Anstey Guthrie at work in his home in Kensington by L. Campbell Taylor (1928–1929) is in the possession of Dr. Eric Millar, who also owns a crayon drawing by Laura Anning Bell.

[F. Anstey, *A Long Retrospect*, 1936; private information; personal knowledge.]

DOUGLAS WOODRUFF.

HADDON, ALFRED CORT (1855–1940), anthropologist, was born in London 24 May 1855, the second child and elder son of John Haddon, head of a firm of type-founders and printers, sprung from farmer stock near Naseby and with a strong Baptist tradition. From his mother,

Caroline Waterman, who published books for children under the name of 'Caroline Hadley', Alfred Haddon imbibed a great insight into natural history and skill in drawing patterns. His education was broken, as his father's means diminished, and he attended various schools in London, but, struggle as he might to follow his father's business and to take part in the religious activities of his family, his bent was always natural history. He eked out the family fortunes, after attending evening classes at King's College, London, by teaching; but all the time he was collecting specimens and teaching himself zoology. At length, his father having decided that his son would never be a business man, he was allowed to prepare for the university and in 1875 he entered Christ's College, Cambridge. His chosen masters were F. M. Balfour [q.v.], to whom he dedicated his first book, *An Introduction to the Study of Embryology* (1887), and (Sir) Michael Foster [q.v.]. In 1878 he obtained a first class in the natural sciences tripos (comparative anatomy), and in 1879 he was given a grant by the university to work for six months at the Stazione Zoologica at Naples, after which he was appointed curator of the Zoological Museum at Cambridge and a university demonstrator in zoology.

Haddon did not, however, at this time stay long in Cambridge, for in 1880 he was appointed professor of zoology at the Royal College of Science and assistant naturalist to the Science and Art Museum in Dublin. While doing pioneer work there in the scientific classification of sea-anemones, he developed an ethnographical interest in western Irish life. In 1888–1889, having given up his post at the museum owing to pressure of teaching, by the aid of a grant of £500 he went to the Torres Strait to study marine biology, and returned with many specimens, but determined to record as much as possible of the life of the people before contact with Europeans had extinguished native custom. The saving of vanishing data became his watchword, and important papers read before the British Association (1889) and at the Royal Institution (1890, published in *Nature*, 30 October) brought him into touch with (Sir) J. G. Frazer and (Sir) W. H. Flower [q.v.] and added to his links with T. H. Huxley [q.v.]. Since his work in Dublin occupied only a part of the year, Haddon accepted a part-time lecturership in physical anthropology at Cambridge (1894–1898) and planned the famous Cambridge anthropological expedition of 1898–1899 to the Torres Strait, New Guinea, and Sarawak. On his way back he stayed with Charles Hose [q.v.] in Borneo and made many observations for comparative purposes. In 1900 he was appointed university lecturer in ethnology at Cambridge, and in 1901 election into a fellowship at Christ's College permitted him to resign his Dublin chair: although he had to lecture in London (1904–1909) in order to add to his income, it enabled him to exercise a valuable influence at the Horniman Museum, while his friendships with (Sir) G. Laurence Gomme, Henry Woodd Nevinson, Edward Clodd [q.v.], and George Amos Dorsey widened his sphere of influence in this country and opened the way to a series of visits to the United States of America. In 1909 he was able to reduce his outside work on appointment to a readership in ethnology at Cambridge.

The meeting of the British Association in Australia in 1914 and a grant from the Percy Sladen Trust enabled Haddon to visit the Torres Strait and Papua once more, in the company and with the help of his younger daughter Kathleen (later Mrs. Rishbeth), who published several books on string figures: Haddon himself had given his data to Mrs. C. Furness Jayne, who published them as *String Figures* (1906). A piece of string was Haddon's scheme for making friends with Papuan and other children who eventually drew their mothers and even their fathers into his circle. Returning to Europe, Haddon worked at his Torres Strait Reports and in 1917 took up educational and welfare work with the British army in France until he was compelled to withdraw by temporary ill health. After the war, he acted as temporary curator of the Cambridge University Museum of Archaeology and Ethnology and organized his own South Sea collections. With his help the museum, where he continued to work until his death, became a primary centre for anthropological study and research.

The financial strain which had been faced by his wife with unwavering courage and by Haddon himself with boundless effort was now eased by the settlement in life of his children, and in 1925 he retired on completing his seventieth year. That same year Christ's College celebrated his birthday by a dinner in hall, the first occasion on which women dined in a men's college hall in Cambridge, an appropriate event for a champion of women's education, although he disliked the movement called feminism. For his eightieth birthday (1935), Mr. Louis Clarke, the curator of the museum, presented on behalf of many friends a case containing 10,000 anthropological photographs, most of them from Haddon's own negatives, which he placed in the Haddon library at the museum. The *Reports of the Cambridge Anthropological Expedition to Torres Straits*, of which volumes ii to vi had appeared between 1901 and 1912, were completed, after much consideration, in 1935 by the publication of volume i. But characteristically there was no cessation in planning new work. In the next five years Haddon published (with Miss L. E. Start) *Iban or Sea Dayak Fabrics and their Patterns* (1936), the result of years of study of textile designs, and *Canoes of Oceania* (with Mr. James Hornell, 3 vols., 1936–1938), and he completed *Smoking and Tobacco Pipes in New Guinea*, an important study of cultural diffusion which was published posthumously in 1946. His death took place at Cambridge a few weeks later 20 April 1940.

As a humanist, a great teacher, a scientific pioneer, and a keen champion of the underprivileged, Haddon left a gracious memory, salted with wit and illuminated by many friendships. The Torres Strait expedition of 1898–1899 marked an epoch in anthropological research, and it is characteristic of Haddon that it brought together a group of distinguished students who all kept their affectionate respect for their leader during their lifetime.

Haddon married in 1881 Fanny Elizabeth (died 1937), daughter of Thomas Rose, draper, of Bedford, and sister of his Cambridge friend John Holland Rose, the historian. They had a son and two daughters. He was elected F.R.S. in 1899 and received the honorary doctorate of science from the universities of Manchester and Perth (Western Australia). He was president of Section H (anthropology) of the British Association in 1902 and 1905, and in 1902–1904 of the Royal Anthropological Institute of Great Britain which appointed him Huxley memorial lecturer in 1920 and awarded him the first Rivers memorial medal in 1924.

Haddon's portrait was painted by P. A. de László in 1924 and hangs in the hall of Christ's College; the artist painted a copy for the Haddon library, and presented a third to the family.

[*The Times*, 22 April 1940; *Obituary Notices of Fellows of the Royal Society*, No. 9, January 1941 (portrait); List of over 600 books and articles by A. C. Haddon compiled by Miss E. S. Fegan and deposited in the Haddon library at the Museum of Archaeology and Ethnology, Cambridge; A. H. Quiggin, *Haddon the Head Hunter* (select bibliography), 1942; private information; personal knowledge.]   H. J. FLEURE.

HADFIELD, SIR ROBERT ABBOTT, baronet (1858–1940), metallurgist and industrialist, was born at Attercliffe, then a village adjoining Sheffield, 28 November 1858, the only son of Robert Hadfield, of Sheffield, by his wife, Marianne Abott, the daughter of a breeder of shire horses in Oxfordshire. He came of a family long associated with Edale in Derbyshire, which had given to Sheffield a member of parliament (George Hadfield, q.v.) and a master cutler. The elder Robert Hadfield entered the steel trade, and in 1872 set up a works for the production of steel castings, then a novelty in England. Large hydraulic cylinders and steel projectiles, until then only made in France, were among the products, and the foundations of a great armament industry were thus laid.

Hadfield was educated at the Collegiate School in Sheffield, where he became interested in chemistry and made experiments at home on the melting of steel, so that when, after a few months in the steel firm of Messrs. Jonas and Colver, he entered his father's works, his first act was to establish a laboratory. A problem arising in the works led him to make a systematic study of the alloys of iron with manganese and with silicon. In 1882 he discovered that whilst increasing the proportion of manganese beyond the usual limit made steel brittle and useless, a further increase reversed the effect, and a steel with 12–14 per cent. of manganese had remarkable properties. Although apparently soft, a file would slip over its surface without abrading it. Quenching in water from a white heat made the new alloy softer, whilst all previously known steels were hardened by such treatment. An indentation could be made with a chisel, but the steel could not be cut except by an emery disk. This steel has found wide application in crushing and grinding machinery, in tramway and railway crossings, and wherever resistance to abrasion is required. Its lack of brittleness also led to its adoption for helmets in the war of 1914–1918.

The silicon steels which were next examined proved to have interesting electrical properties, including a high resistance. (Sir) William Barrett found that with 3–4 per cent. of silicon and as little as possible of other elements the magnetic hysteresis was exceptionally low, and in 1899 these properties were described in a joint paper communicated to the Royal Society of Dublin. The new steel was difficult to roll, and it was some years before it was produced commercially. Its effect has been to reduce greatly the weight and bulk of electrical transformers.

From this time onwards Hadfield continued his researches on the alloys of iron, but no other novel steel resulted, although important additions were made to the knowledge of alloy steels. His work was always patient and systematic, a wide range of alloys being prepared and their physical and mechanical properties studied in detail. He often collaborated with physicists interested in the properties of metals, supplying them with series of alloys of graduated composition and having tests conducted in his own laboratories. In this way, in collaboration first with Sir James Dewar [q.v.] and then with the staff of the Cryogenic Laboratory at Leyden, he studied the properties of metals at low temperatures down to that of liquid hydrogen, the behaviour of manganese steel again proving to be anomalous. He was led by these researches to enter into the controversies as to the nature of the process of hardening of steel, maintaining the 'carbonist' view of his friend John Oliver Arnold against the insistance of most metallurgists on the importance of allotropy. The modern theory incorporates both views.

In 1888, on the death of his father, Hadfield became chairman and managing director of the company at the early age of thirty. He was brought into contact with manufacturing problems, and made important experiments on the production of sound steel ingots. The great development of the armament side of the business led him to give special attention to the deformation of steel at high velocities, and he made many experiments on armour-piercing shells. Much work on corrosion was carried out in his laboratories, and he was active in calling attention to the economic effects of wastage by corrosion. Interest in the subject was stimulated, but no novel results were obtained.

Hadfield was keenly interested in the history of metallurgy. In the course of a visit to Ceylon he studied a collection of Sinhalese objects of the fifth century A.D.

and demonstrated the method by which they had been hardened. He made a fuller study of the Delhi iron pillar, dated about A.D. 300. His most extensive work in this field was his examination of the alloys of iron prepared by Michael Faraday and James Stodart between 1818 and 1822, preserved at the Royal Institution. Of these he published a detailed series of analyses and micrographic studies, ultimately collected into a book, *Faraday and his Metallurgical Researches* . . . (1931). In 1925 he had published *Metallurgy and its Influence on Modern Progress*, containing a review of the past and present condition of the science and an account of his own researches, with reflections on the needs of education and research.

Hadfield was throughout his life one of the hardest of workers, and his capacity for sustained work was equalled by his ability to save labour by systematic organization. He was an enlightened employer, and in 1891 he was one of the first to introduce an eight-hour day into his works. He was proud of the reputation of his firm, and built up within it a strong organization for experimental work. New scientific devices, such as the thermo-electric pyrometer, were quickly introduced. After an extremely serious illness and an operation which would have incapacitated most men he resumed work, and until the last years of his life showed little sign of age. He died at his house on Kingston Hill, Surrey, 30 September 1940.

Hadfield had an exceptionally wide circle of scientific friends and correspondents and maintained particularly close connexions with his French colleagues. His hospitality contributed much to the success of international scientific meetings held in Great Britain, especially during his presidency of the Faraday Society from 1914 to 1920. For many years he rarely missed a council meeting of the Iron and Steel Institute, of which he was president from 1905 to 1907. His reputation as a scientific investigator rests mainly on his discovery of manganese steel, but his influence on the development of alloy steels, both through the activities of his own company and its research staff and also through his enthusiasm for the encouragement of metallurgical studies, was very considerable. He was knighted in 1908 and created a baronet in 1917. He was elected F.R.S. in 1909 and received several academic and numerous other honours, including the freedom of the City of London in 1917 and of Sheffield in 1939.

Hadfield married in 1894 Frances Belt, daughter of Colonel Samuel Morris Wickersham, of Philadelphia, but had no issue. Soon after the outbreak of war in 1914 the Hadfields founded a hospital at Wimereux, and Lady Hadfield's devoted services during the whole war were recognized by her appointment as C.B.E. in 1918. The Hadfield-Spears ambulance was again active in France in 1939.

[*The Times*, 2 October 1940; *Obituary Notices of Fellows of the Royal Society*, No. 10, December 1940 (portrait); private information.]   C. H. DESCH.

HADOW, GRACE ELEANOR (1875–1940), principal of the Society of Oxford Home-Students (afterwards St. Anne's Society) and pioneer in social work, was born at South Cerney vicarage, near Cirencester, 9 December 1875. She was the youngest child and fourth daughter of William Elliot Hadow, vicar of South Cerney, a noted preacher in his own district, by his wife, Mary Lang, second daughter of Henry Cornish, of Tavistock. Sir William Henry Hadow [q.v.] was the eldest child and was godfather to Grace.

Miss Hadow had no systematic early education, but her swift questing mind led her to read widely, and to take full advantage of every opportunity for learning and, largely through her close association with her eldest brother, she quickly developed a keen and scholarly interest in literature, music, and drama. In her twenty-fifth year she won her way to Somerville College, Oxford, and in 1903 was placed in the first class in the final honour school of English language and literature. After holding temporary academic posts at Bryn Mawr, Pennsylvania, and at Somerville College, she was appointed tutor in English at Lady Margaret Hall, Oxford, in 1906, and lecturer in 1909. In 1917 she became head of a subsection of the welfare department of the Ministry of Munitions and in 1920 secretary of Barnett House, Oxford, where she had further scope for her creative powers in social work, especially in rural districts. From its inception in 1915 the Women's Institute movement owed much to her, and from Barnett House she launched the movement for rural community councils by starting one in Oxfordshire. In 1929 she became principal of the Society of Oxford Home-Students. She combined with remarkable success the work of the head of an academic body with that of a pioneer in social work. The academic status of the society rose, a fine library was built, and a site for future central buildings secured. She established happy relations with her 220 scattered students and their many hostesses, and she was known by her colleagues not only as a great principal but as a great friend.

Meanwhile Miss Hadow's social and educational work continued. Her witty and brilliant speech, her ability as a chairman, her constructive ideas and zeal in carrying them out were valued not only by such bodies as the National Federation of Women's Institutes, of which she was vice-chairman from 1916 to 1940, or by the Conference on Commonwealth Relations held in Sydney in 1938 of which she was a conspicuous member, but by the innumerable little village communities to which she selflessly devoted her shining gifts, and which so largely owed their existence to her. She died in London 19 January 1940.

Miss Hadow's chief publications are *The Oxford Treasury of English Literature* (edited with W. H. Hadow, 3 vols., 1906–1908); *Ideals of Living* (an anthology, 1911); and *Chaucer and his Times* (1914).

[*The Times*, 22 January 1940; H. C. Deneke, *Grace Hadow*, 1946; *The Ship* (Year Book of the Society of Oxford Home-Students, Old Students' Association), No. 29, 1939 (Supplement); personal knowledge.]   L. GRIER.

HADOW, SIR (WILLIAM) HENRY (1859–1937), scholar, educationist, and critic and historian of music, was born at Ebrington, Gloucestershire, 27 December 1859, the eldest son of William Elliot Hadow, curate, afterwards vicar, of Ebrington, by his wife, Mary Lang, second daughter of Henry Cornish, of Tavistock. After more than seven years at Malvern College he went up in 1878 to Worcester College, Oxford, of which he was successively scholar, lecturer (1884), fellow, tutor, and dean (1889), and finally honorary fellow (1909). He obtained a first class in classical moderations (1880) and in *literae humaniores* (1882), and after taking his B.A. degree studied music in both Germany and England and took the B.Mus. degree in 1890. He lectured in both classics and music, and examined in the final schools of *literae humaniores*, modern languages, and English. He was a brilliant lecturer, speaking always without notes (in his lectures on Aristotle even without a text), and possessing a remarkable fund of apt and often witty illustration. He composed chamber music and songs (some of high merit), and stimulated the performance of music in Oxford at a time when the art was still of little account in the eyes of authority. But his practical knowledge of music was most important as the foundation of his critical and historical writings. The two small volumes of *Studies in Modern Music* (1892 and 1895) opened a new era in musical criticism. By setting music against a background of general culture Hadow broke down the barrier between the professional critic and the layman, and made clear the position, which he maintained throughout his life, that music has a rightful place in a liberal education. *Sonata Form* (1896) was ostensibly a text-book; but its luminous exposition in simple terms is adorned with the grace of style which marked all Hadow's writing. In 1897 came *A Croatian Composer*, in which the Slavonic origin of Josef Haydn is asserted. Later research disputes Hadow's conclusions, but the value of his work on Haydn's melodic style remains. His masterpiece, *The Viennese Period* (vol. v of the *Oxford History of Music*, of which he was general editor), was published in 1904. Between 1906 and 1908 he joined with his sister Grace Hadow [q.v.] in producing the three volumes of the *Oxford Treasury of English Literature*.

In later years Hadow wrote short books on *Music* (1924), *Church Music* (1926), *English Music* (1931), and *Richard Wagner* (1934); in 1928 he published a volume of *Collected Essays*. He was an enthusiastic admirer of the Tudor music brought to light by Dr. Edmund Horace Fellowes and others. 'They call William Byrd the English Palestrina', he once remarked; 'I shall not rest until Palestrina is called the Italian Byrd!'

In 1909 the current of Hadow's life was turned into a very different channel. He became principal of Armstrong College, Newcastle, a post which he held until 1919. Here he proved himself as able in administration as he had been in scholarship, and from 1916 to 1918 was vice-chancellor of the university of Durham. In 1918, the year in which he was knighted, he was made director of education for the Young Men's Christian Association on lines of communication in France, and shortly afterwards was appointed assistant director of staff duties (education) at the War Office. For his war-time services he was appointed C.B.E. in 1920.

From 1919 to 1930 Hadow was vice-chancellor of the university of Sheffield.

The times were difficult, and external duties entailed frequent absences; but Hadow's masterly powers of chairmanship expedited the dispatch of business, and he found time to serve many and varied causes in his new environment. As a public speaker he was unrivalled, whatever the audience or topic. During his tenure of office at Sheffield the chair of music was established (1927) and steps were taken towards the institution of degrees in music.

The fourteen years from 1920 to 1934 saw Hadow as a leading influence in national education. During this period he was chairman of the consultative committee of the Board of Education; and under his chairmanship no less than six valuable reports were issued. One of these, *The Education of the Adolescent* (1927), became known as the 'Hadow Report', and was for many years the indispensable handbook of teachers and administrators. In neither the theory nor the practice of education was Hadow a specialist; but his work on this committee and on others was far-reaching in its effects. Music, a subject especially dear to his heart, he was enabled to raise from the humblest place in the syllabus to one of full equality with the rest. His breadth of outlook and the range of his knowledge persuaded many who would have turned a deaf ear to professional appeals; the continuous and growing attention now paid to the training of the amateur in intelligent listening is due first and foremost to Hadow's efforts.

When about to retire from Sheffield in 1930, Hadow married a lifelong friend, Edith, second daughter of John Troutbeck, precentor of Westminster Abbey; she predeceased him by less than a month. He died in London 8 April 1937.

Hadow's honorary degrees were numerous: he was D.Mus. of Oxford (1909), Durham (1910), and Wales (1921); LL.D. of St. Andrews (1923), Liverpool (1925), and Birmingham (1930); D.Litt. of Bristol (1925), Leeds (1930), and Sheffield (1930).

In Hadow a brilliant and rapid mind and an exceptional memory were accompanied by great charm of manner and a ready wit. His academic range was remarkable enough; even more striking was the adaptability with which he turned from scholarship to administration. He had the wisdom to set others on the road rather than attempt everything himself; and the number of those inspired by his initiative, counsel, and encouragement must indeed be large.

There is a pencil drawing of Hadow by

Sir William Rothenstein (1920) in the university of Sheffield.

[*The Times*, 10 April 1937; *Grove's Dictionary of Music and Musicians*, 4th ed., vol. ii and supplementary volume, edited by H. C. Colles; *Musical Times*, May 1937; *Music and Letters*, July 1937; *Sheffield University Magazine*, June 1938; private information; personal knowledge.]   F. H. SHERA.

HALDANE, ELIZABETH SANDERSON (1862-1937), born in Edinburgh 27 May 1862, was the only daughter of Robert Haldane, of Cloan, Auchterarder, Perthshire, by his second wife, Mary Elizabeth, second daughter of Richard Burdon-Sanderson, of West Jesmond and Otterburn Dene, Northumberland, whose second son was Richard Burdon Haldane, Viscount Haldane, and the fourth, John Scott Haldane [qq.v.].

Elizabeth Haldane was educated in a highly cultivated atmosphere at home, where she shared her brothers' tutors and entered into their discussions on philosophy, science, and politics, which doubtless helped to develop her unusual mental attainments. About the age of fifteen she attended a private school in Edinburgh where her pre-eminence in literature, mathematics, and languages became rapidly apparent.

After the death of her father in 1877, Miss Haldane, with her mother, spent a winter in Paris, where she formed congenial friendships and gained a wider outlook on life, which ultimately led to her writing the life of Descartes. Her home life was afterwards spent partly in London and partly at Cloan, where her devotion to her mother somewhat curtailed her early activities, but in these comparatively quiet years she gained that experience and knowledge which were to fit her so admirably for dealing later with wider spheres of interest, and stimulated her efforts for the welfare of humanity, a trait inherited from both her parents.

During this early period Miss Haldane organized reading circles, and founded the Auchterarder institute and library of which she remained the honorary secretary for fifty-three years. This brought her into contact with Andrew Carnegie [q.v.], who personally appointed her a trustee of the United Kingdom Trust, the first woman to be so distinguished. Her unbroken attendance at meetings of the trust from 1914 to 1937 constitutes a fine record, and it is an illustration of her indefatigable interest in all that she undertook.

She was prominently associated with the formation (1890) of the Scottish Women's Benefit Society, the members of which were later admitted to the Ancient Order of Foresters, the pioneers of old age pensions for women in Scotland. She worked for some time in London under Octavia Hill [q.v.] in her well-known efforts to improve the housing conditions of the poor, and in 1884 she helped to establish a similar organization in Edinburgh. In the pioneer days of the Westminster Health Society (founded in 1903) she proved a tower of strength on the National Council for Maternity and Child Welfare, and Carnegie House owes its existence largely to her influence.

The Institute of Industrial Psychology, Aldwych House, where vocational guidance tests were carried out, interested Miss Haldane profoundly, while on the artistic side she was equally enthusiastic. The salvation by the Carnegie Trust of the Sadler's Wells Theatre and Ballet was inspired by her, and she maintained her interest in its activities. In the years before the war of 1914-1918, when her brother Richard was secretary of state for war, she played a large part in encouraging the extension of the nursing services, especially in connexion with the Territorial Associations. During the war she was mentioned in dispatches and received the Reine Elisabeth medal for work on behalf of Belgian soldiers and the housing of Belgian refugees.

Miss Haldane was the first woman to be made a J.P. in Scotland (1920), the first to receive the honorary degree of LL.D. from St. Andrews University (1911), and the first to become a member of the Scottish Savings Committee (1916). She was appointed C.H. in 1918. She was vice-chairman of the Territorial Forces Nursing Service and, among a host of other appointments, she was a member of Queen Alexandra's Imperial Military Nursing Service Board, the General Nursing Council (1928), the board of management of the Edinburgh Royal Infirmary, the Scottish Universities' Committee (1909), the royal commission on the civil service (1912), and the advisory committee under the Insurance Act of 1912. She was deputy-president of the Red Cross Society for Perthshire, and one of the governors of Birkbeck College.

When the women's suffrage movement was at its height, Miss Haldane was opposed to militant methods, but she worked steadily for enlightened freedom for women in education and the professions. Her political views—she remained a staunch liberal all her life—might be summed up in the words of her great-uncle Robert Haldane, of Airthrey, in a speech which he delivered at Stirling in 1794: 'The true character of a democrat was that of a friend of his country, a lover of peace, and one who cherished the sentiment of universal benevolence.'

In addition to her public work Miss Haldane was an author of distinction. Besides contributing articles to various periodicals and works of reference (including the notice of her brother Richard in this DICTIONARY) she published the following works: *Hegel's Lectures on the History of Philosophy* (translated with F. Simpson, 3 vols., 1892); *The Wisdom and Religion of a German Philosopher* (Hegel, 1897); *James Frederick Ferrier* (1899); *Descartes, his Life and Times* (1905); *The Philosophical Works of Descartes* (translated in collaboration with G. T. T. Ross, 2 vols., 1911–1912); *The British Nurse in Peace and War* (1923); *Mary Elizabeth Haldane* (edited 1925); *George Eliot and her Times* (1927); *Mrs. Gaskell and her Friends* (1930); *The Scotland of Our Fathers* (1933); *Scots Gardens in Old Times* (1934); and *From One Century to Another* (1937).

The outstanding features of Miss Haldane's character were love of humanity, courage, and ability, coupled with a clarity of vision, and force which enabled her to overcome any obstacles which she encountered in her way. Her life throughout was marked by an absence of self-consideration, and an abundant flow of little kindnesses which did much to lighten for many the daily path of life. There is no painted portrait of her; the best photograph is that in the Carnegie Trust memorial number. She was of medium height, rather thick set, not exactly good looking, but with a high forehead and an expression of extreme intelligence and benevolence. Her practical-shaped hands betokened capability in what they undertook. She died at St. Margaret's Hospital, Auchterarder, 24 December 1937.

[*The Times*, 28 December 1937; E. S. Haldane, *From One Century to Another*, 1937; private information; personal knowledge.]

ELLA R. CHRISTIE.

HALDANE, JOHN SCOTT (1860–1936), physiologist and philosopher, was born in Edinburgh 3 May 1860, the fourth, but third surviving, son of Robert Haldane, writer to the signet, of Cloanden (later called Cloan), Auchterarder, Perthshire, by his second wife, Mary Elizabeth, second daughter of Richard Burdon-Sanderson, of West Jesmond and Otterburn Dene, Northumberland. He was a younger brother of Richard Burdon Haldane (afterwards Viscount Haldane), and an elder brother of Elizabeth Sanderson Haldane [qq.v.].

Educated at Edinburgh Academy and University, and at the university of Jena, Haldane graduated in medicine at Edinburgh in 1884, and was appointed demonstrator in physiology at University College, Dundee. A few years later (1887) he joined his uncle, (Sir) John Burdon-Sanderson, Waynflete professor of physiology at Oxford [q.v.], as a demonstrator, and thenceforward Oxford was his home. He was elected a fellow of New College in 1901, and reader in physiology at Oxford in 1907, resigning the latter post in 1913.

At Dundee Haldane had investigated the composition of the air in dwellings and schools, and soon after reaching Oxford he began an investigation of the suffocative gases encountered in coal mines and wells, showing their dependence on spontaneous oxidation processes occurring in the coal and soil. Turning his attention to carbon monoxide, the deadly constituent of 'after-damp' resulting from a colliery explosion, he elucidated by experiments on animals and on himself the physiological action of this gas, and in 1896 submitted to the home secretary an important report on the causes of death in colliery explosions and underground fires, which clarified much that had previously been uncertain and gave a basis on which to develop means for overcoming the danger. He thus became associated with the mining profession, an association which he maintained throughout his life.

Between 1892 and 1900 Haldane introduced a number of new methods for investigating the physiology of the respiration and blood and for gas analysis; of these the most widely used were his haemoglobinometer, his apparatus for blood-gas analysis based on the reaction between oxyhaemoglobin and ferricyanide, and his apparatus for the accurate and rapid analysis of air or mixtures of gases.

Of Haldane's researches in pure physiology the most fundamental was published in the *Journal of Physiology* (vol. xxxii, 1905) in his classical paper on the regulation of the lung ventilation, in collaboration with John Gillies Priestley. In this he showed by experiments on man that the regulation of the breathing is in the main determined by the exquisite sensitiveness of the respiratory centre in the brain to variations in the tension of carbon dioxide in the arterial blood which reaches it, and thus gave a clue to the explanation of the automatic changes of the breathing which occur with changes in bodily activity. The further development of this subject was to occupy him for a number of years during which he investigated the influence on the breathing of deficiency of oxygen and of muscular exercise, and the part played by the vagus nerves in co-ordinating the respiratory rhythm, his work having an important bearing on the regulation of the reaction of the blood. During the course of this work he led, in 1911, a scientific expedition to Pike's Peak, Colorado, to study the effects of low barometric pressure and the process of acclimatization to high altitudes. His discoveries revolutionized current ideas about respiration, and the precise correlation of function which he had so clearly demonstrated had wide implications respecting the co-ordination of other bodily functions. This led him later to investigate the cardiac output and the function of the kidney in relation to the body's physiological requirements.

Haldane was an invaluable member from 1896 onwards of many advisory committees to government departments and was responsible for much of the experimental work on which the reports of these committees were based. At the request of the Admiralty he investigated the problem of deep diving with a view to reducing the risk of 'caisson disease' due to the liberation of bubbles of nitrogen in the blood during the ascent to the surface. Proving by experiments on animals and on man that it was safe to start decompression by halving the absolute air-pressure to which the diver had been exposed, he developed in 1907 a detailed method of 'stage decompression' by which the diver may be brought safely to the surface, and later extended these instructions to include other circumstances when the industrial worker is obliged to work in compressed air. The risks of 'caisson disease' were thereby practically abolished, and the method of stage decompression was universally adopted.

During the South African war Haldane's influence was largely responsible for the improvement of the inadequate diet at first provided in the concentration camps and thus abolished a serious menace to health. During the war of 1914-1918 he identified for the War Office the type of poison gas introduced by the Germans and the nature of the effects produced, and subsequently did further work on the pathology and treatment of cases of war-gas poisoning both in the acute and in the chronic stages, designing a portable oxygen administration apparatus for use in the field.

Throughout his life Haldane's researches continued on problems connected with mining. His demonstration in 1905 of the importance of the wet-bulb temperature in limiting man's power to withstand a high environmental temperature threw much light on the genesis of heat-stroke in the tropics and on the significance of the high temperatures encountered in the deep workings of mines. As director (1912) of a mining research laboratory founded at Bentley colliery, near Doncaster, by the Doncaster colliery owners and transferred in 1921 to Birmingham where it had the support of the British Colliery Owners' Research Association, and as a member of the Safety in Mines Research Board since its inception in 1921, he was engaged with questions concerned with hot and deep mines, mine ventilation, mine-rescue apparatus, underground fires due to spontaneous oxidation of coal, illumination at the coal face, and pulmonary disease caused by the inhalation of dust—all problems directly bearing on the safety and health of the miner. In 1921 he was made an honorary professor of mining in Birmingham University, and his great services to the mining profession were recognized when he was elected president of the Institution of Mining Engineers in 1924, a position which he held until 1928.

In his book *Respiration* (1922, new ed. 1935), founded on the Silliman memorial lectures delivered in Yale University in 1916, Haldane left a record of his achievements in pure and applied science from which an estimate can be formed of the profound influence which he had on physiology. He invariably made his experimental investigations both on himself and on those of his colleagues who were ready to act as his subjects, and the study of human physiology, and no less of medicine and hygiene, owes a lasting debt to him.

Destined for a life of active research in natural science, Haldane was greatly attracted by philosophy, which indeed may be said to have guided and, in its turn, to have been inspired by his scientific work in a search for a consistent theory which should offer an intelligible explanation of the phenomena of life. Biology he regarded as an independent science with axioms and modes of interpretation different from those appropriate to the physical sciences, since it includes an aspect of man's experience which cannot be interpreted in terms of the physical sciences alone. He himself showed in his own work how immensely valuable chemical and physical methods of research could prove in physiological investigations. Physiology implied to him the study of the living organism as a whole, and as his own researches threw into clear relief the astonishing delicacy with which the different functions of the body are correlated during normal life he was led to the conclusion that from the physiological standpoint the phenomena of life 'express the maintenance of a co-ordinated whole which includes within itself relations to environment as well as the mutual relationships of details of internal structure and activity'. These philosophical views were developed mainly in the last two decades of his life in a series of books which includes *The Sciences and Philosophy* (1929, the Gifford lectures delivered at Glasgow in 1927–1928), *The Philosophical Basis of Biology* (1931, the Donnellan lectures delivered at Dublin University in 1930), and *The Philosophy of a Biologist* (1935).

In his scientific investigations Haldane drew no sharp distinction between pure and applied science. Far reaching as were his contributions to academic science it was his practice to devote himself concurrently with his laboratory researches in this field to problems in applied science, either in connexion with mining or with questions on which his advice had been sought by government departments. A review of his work as a whole shows how closely interwoven were these two aspects. A study of the effects on man caused by breathing foul air foreshadowed his great work on the physiology of respiration; the investigation of the regulation of body temperature in a hot environment was the outcome of the working conditions which he encountered in the depths of a Cornish tin mine, and the use that he made of carbon monoxide for physiological research was initiated by his inquiry into the causes of death in colliery explosions.

Haldane's capacity for work was astonishing and he rarely took a holiday.

His outstanding personality, the simplicity and directness of his experimental methods, the clear reasoning which made the solution of the complex problems that he handled appear easy, his kindness and regard for others made an ineffaceable impression on those who worked with him. He continued working until the end, and it was but shortly after returning from a visit to Persia to investigate cases of heat-stroke in the oil refineries that his death occurred at Oxford from pneumonia at midnight 14–15 March 1936.

Haldane received honorary degrees from many universities. Elected F.R.S. in 1897, a Royal medallist of the society in 1916 and Copley medallist in 1934 in recognition of his discoveries in human physiology and their practical application, he was in 1928 appointed C.H. for his scientific work in connexion with industrial disease.

Haldane married in 1891 Louisa Kathleen, only child of Coutts Trotter, of Dreghorn, and he had a son, John Burdon Sanderson Haldane, F.R.S., Weldon professor of biometry at University College, London, and a daughter, the novelist Mrs. Naomi Mary Margaret Mitchison.

[*The Times*, 16 March 1936; *Nature*, 4 April 1936; *Transactions* of the Institution of Mining Engineers, vol. xci, 1936; *Obituary Notices of Fellows of the Royal Society*, No. 5, December 1936 (portrait); Sir J. A. L. Haldane, *The Haldanes of Gleneagles*, 1929; personal knowledge.]   C. G. Douglas.

HALIFAX, second Viscount (1839–1934). [See Wood, Sir Charles Lindley.]

HALLIBURTON, WILLIAM DOBINSON (1860–1931), physiologist and biochemist, was born in London 21 June 1860, the only son of Thomas Halliburton, a Yorkshireman, of Upper Norwood, by his wife, Mary Homan. He was educated privately and at University College School, London, and subsequently at University College where he graduated B.Sc. (Lond.) in 1879 and M.D. with gold medal in 1884.

In 1883 Halliburton became Sharpey scholar and later assistant to (Sir) E. A. Sharpey-Schafer [q.v.] at University College. He received the science research medal in 1885 and subsequently went to Vienna for a short period. In 1890 he succeeded Gerald Yeo [q.v.] as professor of physiology at King's College, London, where he remained until his resignation owing to ill health in 1923. He rapidly attracted to himself a large number of brilliant investigators, notably (Sir) F. W. Mott, W. E. Dixon [qq.v.], Dr. F. S. Locke, Thomas Gregor Brodie, (Sir) Charles James Martin, Dr. Otto Rosenheim, and Corrado Donato Da Fano, and almost every young biochemist of note of that time studied under him, including his great friends, (Sir) Frederick Hopkins and (Sir) Jack Drummond. He also became associated with (Sir) David Ferrier [q.v.], a physician at the then nearby King's College Hospital. At King's College he played a very important part, not only in the development of his department, which was rebuilt under his direction, but also in the college as a whole. He acted for many years as dean of the medical faculty and on his death endowed a chair, details of which are to be decided after the death of Mrs. Halliburton. A tablet to his memory has been placed in the laboratory which bears his name.

Halliburton was one of the first to appreciate the importance of chemical assay of biological materials. His textbook, *Chemical Physiology and Pathology* (1891), was the greatest work of the time, and contains information regarding the chemical constitution of every part of the body known at that date; it was translated into Spanish in 1917 and Portuguese in 1934. His own contributions were for the most part limited to the differentiation of the proteins of blood and muscle and the constitution of nerve tissue, and in his papers are to be found many facts which have been the basis of much later work. He also wrote *Essentials of Chemical Physiology* (1893), which reached its eleventh edition in 1922. His best-known book is 'Halliburton's' *Physiology*, which for the last thirty years has been the vademecum of the medical student. It was originally 'Kirke's' *Physiology*, but he made it more popular than it ever was before. During his authorship, which began in 1896, there were nineteen editions, and no fewer than 125,000 copies were published. It has twice been translated into Chinese. Under Professor Robert John Stewart McDowall, who succeeded him at King's College, it has now (1946) reached its thirty-ninth edition and has become 'McDowall's' *Handbook of Physiology*. In addition he published a vast number of scientific papers. In 1916 he was asked by the Physiological Society to edit *Physiological Abstracts*, which the society had decided to inaugurate; during his editorship of the first seven volumes

the journal became firmly established and a periodical of international importance. Halliburton had already shown his great facility at this kind of work in writing the physiological section of the annual report of the Chemical Society.

Halliburton was elected F.R.S. in 1891, and that society records his great value as a member of the physiological committee in virtue of the soundness of his judgement and equability of his disposition. He received the honorary degree of LL.D. from the universities of Aberdeen and Toronto. He was elected F.R.C.P. in 1892 and was awarded the Baly medal in 1911; to the college he gave the Goulstonian lecture (1893), the Croonian lecture (1901), and the Oliver-Sharpey lecture (1907).

As a man, Halliburton was ever lovable and approachable, and had a great sense of humour, although to the outside world he appeared a little serious. As a speaker, he had few equals, and when it was necessary to find a physiologist who could give a popular lecture, he was often selected for the task. He will be remembered as one of the pioneers in the establishment of biochemistry as a distinct branch of biology, a position which was recognized by his election as one of the first honorary members of the Biochemical Society. All his life his physical activities were very severely limited by an attack of infantile paralysis which in his first year lost him the use of his right arm, but with his left he accomplished much.

Halliburton married in 1886 Annie, daughter of James Dawes; there were no children of the marriage. He died at Exeter 21 May 1931.

[*The Times*, 23 May 1931; *Proceedings* of the Royal Society, series B, vol. cix, 1931-1932 (portrait); *British Medical Journal*, 1931, vol. i, pp. 957 and 1006 (portrait); *Lancet*, 1931, vol. i, p. 1263 (portrait); *Biochemical Journal*, 1932, vol. xxvi (i); *King's College Calendar*; private information; personal knowledge.]   R. J. S. McDOWALL.

HAMILTON, JOHN ANDREW, VISCOUNT SUMNER (1859-1934), judge, was born at Manchester 3 February 1859, the younger son of Andrew Hamilton, an iron merchant there, by his wife, Frances, daughter of Joseph Sumner, of Sharston, Cheshire. He was educated at Manchester Grammar School under F. W. Walker [q.v.]. In 1878 he won a scholarship at Balliol College, Oxford, was awarded a first class in classical moderations (1879) and in *literae humaniores* (1881), was president of the Union in 1882, and in the same year was elected to a prize fellowship at Magdalen. This made his subsequent career possible, for his only other endowment was his brain.

Hamilton was called to the bar by the Inner Temple in 1883, became a bencher there in 1909, and was treasurer in 1930. He was made K.C. in 1901, and was counsel to the university of Oxford from 1906 to 1909.

On being called to the bar Hamilton joined the Northern circuit, but work there for juniors mostly went to 'locals' and after a few years he gave up any attendance. He read as a pupil with J. C. Bigham (afterwards Viscount Mersey, q.v.) in Goldsmith Building, stayed on as his helper when Bigham took silk in 1883, and took over the chambers when Bigham was made a judge in 1897. Despite the consequent contact with Bigham's many clients Hamilton had to wait a long time before he made any way at the bar. In 1889 a brilliant young Balliol man, and fellow of All Souls, was advised by Jowett to go to Hamilton as a pupil. But Hamilton, on being asked, said that his practice was too small to justify his taking a pupil, and Cosmo Gordon Lang went instead to W. S. (afterwards Lord) Robson [q.v.]. Hamilton was perhaps consoled later on when another Scot from Oxford did become his pupil: John Buchan also deserted the law for better things.

It was only in his sixth year that Hamilton earned more than £100 in fees. Happily the Magdalen fellowship, which he held until 1889, gave him something to live upon, and he supplemented this by doing work as a university extension lecturer, by some journalism, and by contributions to this DICTIONARY. This last was due to his having been a contemporary at Balliol of (Sir) Sidney Lee; in fact there are only five out of the sixty-three volumes of the main work in which his initials do not appear. To the Supplement of 1912–1921 he contributed masterly lives of Lord Macnaghten and Lord Parker of Waddington. First and last he was one of the most voluminous contributors to this work.

The university extension lecturing had one undesigned result. It caused Hamilton's introduction to Maude Margaret Todd, second daughter of the Rev. John Wood Todd, D.D., of Forest Hill, near Sydenham, where she was the headmistress of a flourishing girls' school. In 1892 he married this lady, and went to live at the school. One of his younger friends at the bar cherishes the recollection of being present at a prize-giving party at the school, and of seeing the future lord of appeal in ordinary, in a frock coat, making himself agreeable to the parents. When her husband became a flourishing 'silk', and their united income must have been large, Mrs. Hamilton gave up the school: they moved to Streatham, and later to Gloucester Square, north of Hyde Park. They had no children.

By the time of his marriage the tide had turned, and Hamilton was rapidly developing a large practice, chiefly in the Commercial Court, and in competition with (Sir) T. E. Scrutton [q.v.]. They took silk on the same day in 1901, and continued their contests in the front row. Hamilton had the finer brain, was a better scholar, and much more gifted as a speaker; Scrutton perhaps outdid him in industry and pertinacity. The first fifteen volumes of *Commercial Cases* record their many forensic encounters.

Hamilton was the first of the two to be raised to the bench when, in February 1909, he was, by the selection of Lord Loreburn, made a judge of the King's Bench division. The vacancy was created by the promotion of his old master, Bigham, to be president of the Probate, Divorce, and Admiralty division.

So began Hamilton's career as one of the greatest judges of his time. He remained in the King's Bench division for three and a half years. While there he never once reserved judgement: but what he said at the close of every case, however complicated or difficult, when taken down in shorthand, was better than the laboured writing of other judges, while it scintillated with phrases that none of them could rival by the consumption of midnight oil.

In October 1912 Hamilton was promoted to the Court of Appeal, and sworn of the Privy Council. He only sat in that court for a year, and in October 1913 was made a lord of appeal in ordinary. The existence of other ennobled Hamiltons constrained him to resort to his mother's maiden name for his title, and he became Lord Sumner, of Ibstone, a village in the Chiltern Hills where he had, some years before, acquired a pleasant country house. In 1927, having no son to embarrass by the step, he exchanged his life peerage for an ordinary one and became Viscount Sumner.

The war of 1914–1918 provided far more legal problems than did that of 1939–1945.

The Prize Court was constantly at work under Sir Samuel Evans [q.v.], and appeals from it to the Privy Council were frequent and important. The other courts had also to solve many difficult questions, and there were many that were carried to the House of Lords. By contrast, from 1939 to 1945 the work of the Prize Court (chiefly from the absence of neutrals) was insignificant, and there was only one important appeal; and the business of the other courts was far less than in the earlier war. In all the appeals from 1914 onwards Sumner took a leading part. After the death of Lord Parker of Waddington in 1918 he usually presided at the appeals from the Prize Court before the Judicial Committee.

Apart from their legal merits the most striking thing about Sumner's judgements is their style. He was as great a master of language as any judge who has ever lived, both in speech and in writing. His power of delivering judgements extempore has already been noted. In the Court of Appeal, the Privy Council, and the House of Lords, some of his written judgements attain the highest level of English prose. Of the wit that adorned them perhaps these sentences may serve as samples: 'It is hard to see how infantile temptations can give rights, however much they excuse peccadilloes' (*Latham* v. *Johnson* (1913), 1 K.B. 409) and 'In *Ayre* v. *Craven* the plaintiff was an ordinary doctor at Hull, so did not belong to that class of medical practitioners which the appellant's counsel postulated, but never defined, for whose professional well-being a reputation at least for continence was said not to be a general requisite' (*Jones* v. *Jones* (1916), 2 App. Cas. 493). In the *Oxford Book of English Prose* (compiled by Sir A. T. Quiller-Couch, 1925) there is a part of his judgement in *Bowman and others* v. *The Secular Society* (1917, App. Cas. 466). The only other judicial utterances thought worthy of inclusion in that book are passages from Lord Bowen and Lord Macnaghten.

Sumner carried out several pieces of public work outside the law. He was chairman of the working classes cost of living committee in 1918, of the British and foreign legal procedure committee in the same year, of the royal commission on compensation for suffering and damage by enemy action in 1921, and of the House of Lords committee on abeyances in 1926. A more important service was rendered by him as a member of the British delega-tion to the reparations commission of the Paris Peace Conference in 1919, his colleagues being Lord Cunliffe and Mr. W. M. Hughes. For this he was appointed G.C.B. in 1920.

As an undergraduate, and at the Union, Sumner had been regarded as a formidable and aggressive radical. In the *Masque of B-ll-l* (1881, said to be by J. W. Mackail) are the lines

> I am Hamilton; my mission
> Is to be a politician.

But from leaving Oxford until he had been for some time in the House of Lords he was totally inactive in politics. From 1920 onwards he displayed most of the attributes of the 'die-hard' conservative. In July of that year he delivered a bitter speech, attacking the government, in the debate upon the action of General R. E. H. Dyer [q.v.] at Amritsar in April 1919, and in 1922 he fiercely opposed the 'treaty' which settled the fate of Ireland. When Bonar Law formed his ministry in October 1922 it was thought by many that Sumner might become lord chancellor. Lord Cave was perhaps a safer choice, but the best friends of that most amiable man could hardly think that he would make as great a lord chancellor as Sumner might have been.

Sumner received many academic honours. He was elected an honorary fellow of Magdalen in 1909, was an honorary D.C.L. of Oxford, and LL.D. of Cambridge, Edinburgh, and Manchester universities. He was a member of the Athenaeum and of the Carlton, but did not make much use of either club. Lady Sumner had not much liking for society. Her husband satisfied his more gregarious instinct, elsewhere than at home, by frequent attendance at dinners of The Club (to which he was elected in 1914), and at the benchers' table and in the smoking-room (although he never smoked) of the Inner Temple. It was a pleasure to discerning colleagues at either to get a seat by him, and be entertained by his brilliant talk. The epigrams and sallies had much of a cynical acidity. But the most discerning realized that there was a kind heart beneath the iron breast-plate. Once, when at the Temple, after his death, this was questioned, Sir Lancelot Sanderson said: 'When Sumner and I were briefless barristers on the Northern circuit we sat through the trial of Mrs. Maybrick at Liverpool. At the end of that tragedy we walked out in silence to the robing-room. Hamilton stood gazing out of the window

—and suddenly burst into an uncontrollable fit of weeping.'

In 1930, being warned of a weakness of his heart, Sumner resigned from his judicial duties. His wife and he had always been fond of European travel, and his leisure gave them an opportunity for longer visits to Italy. He died suddenly, from a heart attack, in London 24 May 1934, and was buried in the churchyard at Ibstone.

Sumner's portrait, painted in 1919 by Sir William Orpen, is in the National Portrait Gallery. The benchers of the Inner Temple are the happy possessors of a portrait of him by Oswald Birley. Those who rate portraits by the mysterious canons of art criticism may decry this picture, and possibly apply the epithet 'photographic' to it. But to those who knew Sumner well it is the very man himself. They might say before it, 'Hush! he will speak', and await the clearing of the throat that was commonly the prelude to some devastating fulmination.

[*The Times*, 26 May 1934; *Law Quarterly Review*, January 1945; personal knowledge.]

F. D. MacKinnon.

HANNAY, ROBERT KERR (1867–1940), Scottish historian, was born at Glasgow 31 December 1867, the eldest son of Thomas Hannay, iron master, of that city, by his wife, Elizabeth McDowall. He was educated at Albany Academy, Glasgow, the university of Glasgow (M.A., 1895), and University College, Oxford, where he obtained a second class in classical moderations (1891) and in *literae humaniores* (1893). In 1894 he was appointed lecturer in classics and ancient history at University College, Dundee, and in 1901 lecturer in ancient history at St. Andrews University. There he began those studies in Scottish history which were to constitute his life's work. *The College of St. Leonard* (1905) was followed by *The Archbishops of St. Andrews* (5 vols., 1907–1915), both written in collaboration with Professor (Sir) John Herkless; for these Hannay furnished the fresh material from manuscript sources. The reputation thereby gained led to his appointment in 1911 as curator of the historical department of the Register House, Edinburgh, where his scholarship maintained the high traditions of such predecessors as Joseph Robertson (1810–1866, q.v.). In 1919 he became Sir William Fraser professor of ancient (Scottish) history and palaeography in Edinburgh University, and in 1930 historiographer-royal for Scotland. His other distinctions included the fellowship of the Royal Society of Edinburgh (1922), the honorary degree of LL.D. of St. Andrews University (1923), and honorary membership of the Royal Scottish Academy (1933). In 1899 he married Jane Ewing (died 1938), second daughter of James Stewart Wilson, D.D., minister of New Abbey, Kirkcudbrightshire, and had one son. Mrs. Hannay was appointed O.B.E. (1918) and C.B.E. (1933) for her social services. He died in Edinburgh 19 March 1940.

Hannay was an unconventional and stimulating teacher of senior students, encouraging them, as fellow workers, to use original sources. No general history of Scotland came from his pen. In his view more research was necessary, especially in his own field of the later middle ages, before the rewriting of the existing narratives could be justified. But by his numerous contributions to the *Scottish Historical Review*, the *Juridical Review*, the publications of the Scottish History Society, the Stair Society, and the Old Edinburgh Club, and in his introductions to volumes ix to xiv (1684–1689) of the third series of *The Register of the Privy Council of Scotland* (1924–1933) and *The Acts of the Lords of Council in Public Affairs, 1501–1554* (1932), as well as in such typical works as the *Rentale Dunkeldense* (1915) and *The College of Justice* (1933), he successfully challenged many accepted views on the educational, ecclesiastical, and institutional history of his country. His complicated style was partly due to a supersensitive dread of inaccuracy in general statements. The style, however, was not the man. Tall and handsome, he was generous in communicating knowledge, genial and sociable, a born raconteur, an excellent golfer, and a musician of considerable gifts.

[*Scotsman*, 20 March 1940; *Proceedings* of the Royal Society of Edinburgh, vol. lx, 1941; *University of Edinburgh Journal*, vol. x, 1940; personal knowledge. A memorial volume, with bibliography, for the Scottish History Society is in preparation.]

Henry W. Meikle.

HANWORTH, first Viscount (1861–1936), judge. [See Pollock, Ernest Murray.]

HARDEN, Sir ARTHUR (1865–1940), chemist, was born at Manchester 12 October 1865, the second son and third of the

nine children of Albert Tyas Harden, a
Manchester manufacturer, by his wife,
Eliza, daughter of John MacAlister, of
Paisley. He was educated at Victoria Park
School, Manchester, and later at Tettenhall College, Staffordshire, until he was
sixteen years old, when he entered the
Owens College, Manchester, and studied
chemistry under Sir H. E. Roscoe [q.v.].
He graduated with first class honours in
chemistry in 1885 and forthwith embarked
upon an investigation of the action of
silicon tetrachloride on aromatic amide-
compounds under the guidance of Julius
Berend Cohen. The results of his first
research were published by the Chemical
Society and on its merits he was awarded
the Dalton scholarship by the university
in 1886. The next two years were spent
at the university of Erlangen where, under
Otto Fischer, he prepared a nitrosonaph-
thylamine and investigated its properties.
For his thesis on this subject he was
awarded a Ph.D. there.

In 1888 Harden was appointed a lecturer in chemistry at the university of
Manchester. He took his responsibilities
very seriously and for the next few years
was preoccupied with teaching. He published a few papers on chemical topics and,
with Roscoe, an interesting historical research on the genesis of the atomic theory
of John Dalton [q.v.]. From the study of
Dalton's note-books they concluded that
it was his observations on the diffusion of
gases which led him to formulate his
atomic theory.

In 1897 Harden became chemist to the
Lister Institute (known previously as the
British Institute of Preventive Medicine
until 1898, when it became the Jenner
Institute of Preventive Medicine until
1903) in London. He became head of the
new department of biochemistry in 1907
and held this position until his retirement
in 1930. There he made contact with
biology. His first venture in biochemistry
was to investigate the fermentation of
sugar by various bacteria. The observations were necessarily limited to a quantitative study of the products, and what
happened in the intermediate stages could
only be imperfectly deduced from their
nature and amounts. Notwithstanding,
his researches laid some of the foundations
of bacterial chemistry.

Shortly after Harden began work upon
bacterial metabolism, Eduard Büchner
published experiments from which he concluded that living yeast was not, as maintained by Pasteur, essential for alcoholic

fermentation but could be induced by an
expressed juice free from cells. Appreciating that if Büchner's contention were
true, his yeast juice would provide material
for the study of the conversion of sugar
to alcohol step by step, Harden repeated
his experiments and confirmed his results.
Büchner opined that yeast juice contained
an enzyme 'zymase' which broke up the
sugar, but the chemical transactions involved in the conversion of one molecule
of glucose into precisely two each of alcohol
and carbonic acid were mysterious.

For the next thirty years, Harden's
principal researches were directed to the
solution of the mystery. In this he was
powerfully supported by able pupils and
collaborators and notably by William
John Young and Robert Robison. He
discovered many new facts indicating that
in the transformation of sugars to alcohol
and carbonic acid a complex series of
reactions was involved and he made two
fundamental discoveries. The first was
that before any breakdown of the sugar
molecules occurred, combination with
phosphoric acid was necessary and that
it was only after this preliminary phosphorylation had been achieved that they
became susceptible to disruption by the
zymase in yeast. The second was that
yeast juice contained not one but several
enzymes which catalysed different reactions during the progress of conversion of
sugar into alcohol and carbonic acid. One
of these he supposed to activate the preliminary phosphorylation of the sugar
molecules; another, a phosphatase, effected
the separation of the phosphoric acid from
the first products of cleavage of the sugar
molecule after it had served its purpose.
Thus it became available for combination
with further sugar molecules. The essential part played by phosphorylation and
dephosphorylation in the breakdown of
sugars by yeast was soon found to apply
to fermentation by other micro-organisms
and provided a clue for the understanding
of the conversion of glycogen into lactic
acid in muscle during activity. Indeed,
recognition of the significance of Harden's
discovery constituted a turning-point in
the history of muscle chemistry.

During the war of 1914-1918 Harden
suspended his work on alcoholic fermentation in order to study the chemistry of the
two then known water-soluble vitamins.
Although he, like many others, did not
succeed in isolating these active principles,
some of his observations on their properties found immediate useful application

in the solution of nutritional problems confronting the far-flung armies, and they were a valuable contribution to the early knowledge of these accessory food factors.

Literary work occupied much of Harden's time. While a lecturer at Manchester, he wrote, in collaboration with Roscoe, an elementary text-book of chemistry and with F. C. Garrett one on practical organic chemistry for the use of students. He also revised and edited the *Treatise on Chemistry* (1894) by Roscoe and Carl Schorlemmer [q.v.]. The first edition of his monograph on *Alcoholic Fermentation* was published in 1911. He contributed the article on this subject to *Thorpe's Dictionary of Applied Chemistry*, and one on 'Bacterial Metabolism in the System of Bacteriology' published by the Medical Research Council in 1930. For twenty-five years he was joint editor of the *Biochemical Journal*.

The importance of Harden's contributions to biochemistry was recognized in 1909 by his election as a fellow of the Royal Society and as Nobel prizeman in chemistry with Hans von Euler, of Stockholm, for 1929. Honorary degrees were conferred upon him by the universities of Manchester (1931), Liverpool (1935), and Athens (1937), and the title of professor of biochemistry by the university of London (1912). In 1935 he was awarded the Davy medal of the Royal Society and he was knighted in 1936.

Harden married in 1900 Georgina Sydney (died 1928), elder daughter of Cyprian Wynard Bridge, of Christchurch, New Zealand; they had no children. He died at Bourne End, Buckinghamshire, 17 June 1940.

[*The Times*, 18 June 1940; *Biochemical Journal*, November 1941 (portrait); *Obituary Notices of Fellows of the Royal Society*, No. 11, November 1942; *Journal* of the Institute of Brewing, September 1940; private information; personal knowledge.]

CHARLES J. MARTIN.

HARDY, SIR WILLIAM BATE (1864–1934), biologist, was born at Erdington, Warwickshire, 6 April 1864, the only child of William Hardy, of Llangollen, North Wales, by his wife, Sarah, eldest daughter of William Bate. He was educated at Framlingham College and entered Gonville and Caius College, Cambridge, in 1884. He was elected scholar in 1885 and was awarded a first class in the natural sciences tripos (zoology) in 1888. He was elected a fellow of the college in 1892, and was a tutor from 1900 to 1918. He became university lecturer in physiology in 1913, specializing earlier in histology, later in colloid chemistry and biophysics.

In 1915 Hardy organized the 'Food (War) Committee' of the Royal Society which did very important work in advising the government. After the formation of the Department of Scientific and Industrial Research he became the first chairman of the Food Investigation Board (1917–1928), director of Food Investigation (1917–1934), and superintendent of the Low Temperature Research Station at Cambridge (1922–1934): he was responsible for creating the Torry research station and the Ditton laboratory. From 1919 to 1931 he was chairman of the advisory committee on fisheries of the Development Commission which issued a very valuable series of confidential reports on fisheries (including freshwater fisheries) whereby the fishery departments were strengthened and great progress was made. He was elected F.R.S. in 1902, and was biological secretary from 1915 to 1925; he gave the Croonian lecture in 1905 'On Globulins', and the Bakerian lecture in 1925 on 'Boundary Lubrication'. In 1931 he was Abraham Flexner lecturer at Vanderbilt University, U.S.A. At the time of his death he was president of the British Association, and had been a trustee of the National Portrait Gallery since 1922. He was knighted in 1925. He received honorary degrees from the universities of Oxford, Aberdeen, Birmingham, and Edinburgh.

Hardy's scientific life began with histology. Sceptical of the significance of much that was seen, after fixing and staining, under the microscope, he began to study for himself the effect of such treatment on colloidal systems. This led to his pioneer work in colloid chemistry and later in the molecular physics of films, surfaces, and boundary conditions. Thence he passed on to static friction and so to the action of lubricants. In presenting him with a Royal medal in 1926, the president of the Royal Society, Sir Ernest (afterwards Lord) Rutherford [q.v.] said: 'In colloid chemistry, his name is known . . . for the fundamental and pioneer work which he has accomplished in that field. The stability of colloid sols in relation to the electric charge, the theory of flocculation, the nature and importance of the iso-electric point, the theory of protein ampholytes, and the electric charges of the positive and negative colloid ions represent some of his important discoveries. . . . The modern theory of protein solutions . . . is very largely due to his pioneer work in that field.

'Hardy has also been a pioneer in the elucidation of the nature of surface forces and surface films and the orientation of molecules at surfaces. . . . As a natural outcome of this work, Hardy has turned his attention in recent years to the friction between surfaces and the nature of lubrication, and in a series of important investigations has thrown a flood of light on a subject which had long been neglected by both physicists and chemists. For the first time . . . the dependence of friction and lubrication on the structure and molecular orientation of surface films and the force-fields of molecules in relation to their structure and polarity have been elucidated.'

In spite, however, of the successful physical outcome of his work, the biological instinct can be seen throughout Hardy's activities and published papers. The organizations which he founded for research on food bear the stamp of his conviction that the science of food is not simply physics, chemistry, and engineering, but that of living material. Hardy 'never wavered in his conviction that no solution of a practical problem was worth while unless it was based on an adequate knowledge of the fundamental science that lay behind it': to him biology and molecular physics were equally fundamental. His *Collected Scientific Papers* covering the years 1891 to 1934, edited by Eric Keightley Rideal, were published in 1936.

All his life Hardy was an adventurer in new fields, finding joy in fresh discovery, content not to interfere with others if they wished to exploit and profit by what he had found. This adventurous spirit found an outlet in sailing and no estimate of Hardy would be adequate without a reference to his love of the sea. One of the finest yachtsmen of his time, he combined with perfect seamanship a capacity for instant decision in emergency. His first yacht, *Cockatoo*, was equipped as a floating laboratory for marine biology: his last, *Estrella*, served as a houseboat on the Helford river in his later years. To him, the world was a wonderful place. His own nature seemed to those who knew him well to have much of the strength, beauty, and consistency which he found in the natural world.

Hardy married in 1898 Alice Mary, eldest daughter of Gerard Brown Finch,

barrister, and had a son and two daughters. He died at Cambridge 23 January 1934.

A crayon portrait of Hardy by Francis Dodd, drawn (1941) from a photograph, hangs in the senior combination room of Gonville and Caius College, Cambridge.

[*The Times*, 24 and 25 January 1934; *Obituary Notices of Fellows of the Royal Society*, No. 3, December 1934 (portrait); private information; personal knowledge.]

A. V. HILL.

HARINGTON, SIR CHARLES (1872–1940), general, known to all as Tim, was born at Chichester 31 May 1872, the youngest son of Emanuel Thomas Voe, of London, an indigo planter of Behar, India, by his wife, Isabella Jane Crowdy. When Charles was four years old his father adopted his own mother's maiden name and thereafter the son became known as Charles Harington. He was educated at Cheltenham College, where he began to build for himself a not inconsiderable reputation as a cricketer. In 1890 he passed into the Royal Military College, Sandhurst, and two years later was posted to the 2nd battalion of the Liverpool (later the King's) Regiment, then stationed at Aden. He returned with his regiment to England in 1893 and was at Manchester and Colchester, where he himself admitted there was more sport than soldiering. Thence the regiment moved to Aldershot and subsequently to Holywood, near Belfast, where in 1897 he was appointed adjutant, and in the following year saw a fortnight of 'active service' in the streets during the Belfast riots. On the outbreak of the South African war he received orders for embarkation. He came home shortly after the relief of Ladysmith and for his services in the campaign he was appointed to the D.S.O. (1900).

Harington then went to Fermoy, Ireland, as adjutant to the newly raised 4th battalion of the King's Regiment. In 1903 he became an instructor to the Royal Military College and while there qualified (1906) for the Staff College, where he spent two years working hard and playing hard and making some lasting friendships. At the end of 1907 he left the college and, after a short time in Ireland, went, early in 1908, to the War Office, becoming G.S.O. 3, Staff Duties Branch, in 1909, dealing with promotion examinations. He moved to Aldershot two years later as brigade major to the 6th (later 2nd) brigade under Sir Horace Smith-Dorrien [q.v.] as commander-in-chief, and later, Sir Douglas Haig. In 1914, now a major, he again joined the staff at the War Office, this time to work on the revision of Field Service Regulations and in July was transferred to the Mobilization Branch.

Shortly after the outbreak of war in 1914 Harington was appointed G.S.O. 2 to the III Corps in France which was formed at the time of the retreat from Mons. Early the next year he was sent as G.S.O. 1 to the famous 49th (West Riding) division, newly arrived from England, and went with the division into the front line near Fleurbaix, and thence to the Ypres salient. Towards the end of 1915 he was appointed brigadier-general, General Staff, to the Canadian Corps then being formed and in the line near Messines, where it was engaged at Hill 60 and St. Eloi. In June 1916 he was selected as major-general, General Staff, Second Army under General (afterwards Viscount) Plumer [q.v.]. Together they made a splendid team, and their brilliant staff work was responsible for the surprise attack and capture of the Messines ridge in June 1917 with comparatively small losses, and in November for the action at Passchendaele, but this time with heavy losses due to the severe winter conditions. Shortly after Passchendaele Plumer and he were ordered to Italy, but returned to the Second Army at Cassel in March 1918, where the situation had deteriorated. Three months later during the great German spring offensive Harington was appointed deputy-chief, Imperial General Staff, but was allowed to remain in Flanders until the situation became stabilized. He came home in May 1918 and took up his new duties at the War Office, continuing there until, in October 1920, he was promoted lieutenant-general and left for Constantinople as general officer commanding-in-chief the Army of the Black Sea.

In Constantinople began the most arduous period of Harington's career, for he was called upon to prove himself a diplomat as well as a soldier. Insufficient credit has been given to his courage, tact, administrative skill, and almost superhuman efforts to avoid war in his handling of the Chanak crisis in 1922, when, as general officer commanding-in-chief the Allied forces of occupation in Turkey, he virtually won the key to victory and the friendship of Turkey. His handling of the situation was not altogether pleasing to Lloyd George, but was highly commended by Curzon and many others. In December 1923 he

returned home to become general officer commanding-in-chief, Northern Command, at York, where he spent the next three and a half years, receiving promotion to general in March 1927. He was sent to India the following October as general officer commanding-in-chief, Western Command, where he spent an uneventful but happy few years at Quetta. He came home early in 1931 to take up the post of general officer commanding-in-chief, Aldershot, and was made aide-de-camp general to the king (1930–1934). He was disappointed not to achieve his ambition, chief of the Imperial General Staff, but on being offered the governorship of Gibraltar in 1933 he gladly accepted. Here he found life very pleasant until the outbreak of the Spanish civil war in 1936 when he had to cope with problems of refugees and neutrality.

In 1937 ill health necessitated Harington's retirement and in October he came home and settled in Sussex, where he occupied himself with many interests including Toc H, boys' clubs, the Old Comrades' Association, and the committee of the Marylebone Cricket Club. He was appointed C.B. in 1917, K.C.B. in 1919, G.B.E. in 1922, and G.C.B. in 1933. He was given the freedom of the city of York (1927), and the honorary degree of D.C.L. was conferred upon him by Oxford University (1924), both of them honours which do not commonly fall to the lot of a soldier. While deputy chief of the Imperial General Staff he founded and became first president of the Army Sports Control Board. He wrote *Plumer of Messines* (1935) in memory of his former chief.

Harington was a spare, highly strung man, with a charming manner and remarkable clarity of vision. His organization for a battle was superb. He had a great sense of humour and was well known and liked in the services. In common with many great leaders he was a deeply religious man. In 1904 he married Gladys Norah, eldest daughter of Brigadier General O'Donnel Colley Grattan, of the King's Regiment; there were no children of the marriage. He died at Cheltenham 22 October 1940.

[*The Times*, 24 October 1940; Sir Charles Harington, *Tim Harington Looks Back*, 1940; Sir J. F. Maurice and M. H. Grant (Official) *History of the War in South Africa, 1899–1902*, 1906–1910; Sir J. E. Edmonds, (Official) *History of the Great War. Military Operations. France and Belgium, 1914–1918*, 1947; Philip Gibbs, *Realities of War*, 1920.]

C. V. OWEN.

HARKER, ALFRED (1859–1939), petrologist, was born at Kingston-upon-Hull 19 February 1859, the eldest son of Portas Hewart Harker, corn merchant, by his wife, Ellen Mary Tarbotton. He was educated at the Hull and East Riding College and at Clewer House School, Windsor. Admitted a sizar at St. John's College, Cambridge, in 1878, he graduated as eighth wrangler in the mathematical tripos of 1882 and was placed in the first class of both parts of the natural sciences tripos (1882 and 1883), with physics as his principal subject. The geological interests which he had acquired as a boy in his native Yorkshire were strengthened at St. John's, where he was elected a fellow in 1885, and led him eventually to a life study of petrology at Cambridge. He became demonstrator in geology in 1884 and university lecturer in 1904. In 1888 he was awarded the Sedgwick prize. In 1918 a readership in petrology was created for him, a post which he held until his retirement in 1931. His early researches dealt with slaty cleavage in rocks, on which he contributed an authoritative report to the British Association (1886), and later (with J. E. Marr, q.v.) he made a pioneer contribution on the thermal metamorphism of rocks in his studies of the mineral assemblages surrounding the Shap granite of Westmorland (1891 and 1893).

Seconded in 1895 to the Geological Survey of Scotland, for summer field-work in the Western Isles, Harker mapped in great detail the igneous mountain group of the Cuillins and the Red Hills of Skye and later surveyed Rum and Eigg. The outcome of his researches in Skye and Rum appeared in the Geological Survey memoirs *The Tertiary Igneous Rocks of Skye* (1904) and *The Geology of the Small Isles of Inverness-shire* (1908). These studies inaugurated a new era in the investigation of igneous rock complexes and rank among the great achievements in igneous geology. With the completion in 1905 of his official studies on the staff of the Geological Survey, he now found time to elaborate some of his early essays on theoretical petrology, and these were presented in his *Natural History of Igneous Rocks* (1909). Written in an extremely lucid style, this classic study, through its philosophical contributions to the major problems of igneous action, has come to exert a profound influence on petrological thought. In his later years he returned once more to the subject of the metamorphism of rock masses, in studies which

were eventually expanded in his treatise *Metamorphism* (1932, 2nd ed. 1939 and Russian translation 1937), enriched by illustration from the metamorphic fields of Great Britain which he knew so well, and now occupying a high place in the literature of petrology.

Harker's character was marked by great modesty and he valued research above any position. He was elected F.R.S. in 1902 and was awarded a Royal medal in 1935; he also received the Murchison medal (1907) and the Wollaston medal (1922) from the Geological Society of London, of which he was president from 1916 to 1918. He received honorary degrees from the universities of McGill (1913) and Edinburgh (1919). He died, unmarried, at Cambridge 28 July 1939.

[*Obituary Notices of Fellows of the Royal Society*, No. 8, January 1940 (selected bibliography and portrait); *The Eagle* (magazine of St. John's College, Cambridge), vol. li, 1939 (portrait); *The Times*, 31 July 1939; *Nature*, 19 August 1939; *Quarterly Journal* of the Geological Society, vol. xcvi, 1940–1941; personal knowledge.]   C. E. TILLEY.

HARMSWORTH, HAROLD SIDNEY, first VISCOUNT ROTHERMERE (1868–1940), newspaper proprietor, was born at Hampstead 26 April 1868, the second son of Alfred Harmsworth, barrister, of the Middle Temple, by his wife, Geraldine Mary, daughter of William Maffett, a land agent in county Down. He was a younger brother of Alfred Harmsworth, Viscount Northcliffe [q.v.]. Harold Harmsworth left St. Marylebone Grammar School at an early age and became a clerk in the Inland Revenue Office. Here he stayed for some years, apparently unambitious and contented. When his brother Alfred asked him to join the firm which he had founded to produce a number of periodicals such as *Answers, Comic Cuts*, and the *Sunday Companion* (1888). But as soon as he took in hand the business side of the organization which developed into the Amalgamated Press, he showed rare ability for financial management. He was inclined at first to advise caution when new ventures were mooted, but as all these prospered his attitude grew bolder, and when in 1894 a London daily newspaper was offered to the brothers they bought it for £25,000 and embarked on a career that was to make them millionaires many times over. The *Evening News* soon became a valuable property and they decided to launch a morning journal. In 1896 appeared the *Daily Mail*. Working on a small capital (£40,000) it won immediate popularity and, although sneers and abuse were lavished on the 'new journalism', as it was called, the revolution which the Harmsworths inaugurated in both the methods and material of newspapers was soon to set the standard for most of the organs of the daily press. So far as its editorial side was concerned, the elder brother received and merited most of the credit, but in the background there was always the younger's solid judgement and masterly handling of finance. From the one serious set-back which Northcliffe suffered Harold Harmsworth stood aloof. Later on, however, in 1914 when the *Daily Mirror* had been turned from a disaster into a success he took it over and made it an immensely profitable undertaking along with its satellite, the *Sunday Pictorial* (the first Sunday picture newspaper to appear in London), which he produced in 1915.

Being a shy man, Harmsworth had no wish to share in the public attention paid to Northcliffe, but he was known to a small circle as the financial brain of the business, an extremely astute investor, and a generous giver. In 1910, when he was created a baronet, he had already begun his series of munificent donations to universities, which included a professorship at Oxford and two at Cambridge, and to municipal art galleries, for which he bought pictures, not following so much his own taste as the advice of prominent critics. Four years later he was raised to the peerage as Baron Rothermere and with the war of 1914–1918 entered upon a new phase of his career. Emerging from the privacy in which he had lived so far, he accepted in 1916 the director-generalship of the Royal Army Clothing Department and in the following year was appointed air minister with the special task of amalgamating what were then the Royal Naval Air Service and the Royal Flying Corps. He met with a good deal of opposition; he disliked having to 'argue and wrangle in public as to the reasons for his business decisions'; and unhappily soon after his appointment his eldest son died of wounds received in battle (his second son had been killed in 1916), and the father's grief almost overwhelmed him. He resigned his office (1918) and for a time remained invisible even to his intimates. Lloyd George as prime minister paid a warm tribute to his 'inestimable service' and said that 'time will bring with it a full

recognition of your achievement'. Slowly the wound healed and Lord Rothermere, promoted a viscount in 1919, resumed his newspaper and financial activities. He had sold his *Daily Mail* interest in 1910, but had started a Glasgow paper, the *Record*, and bought the *Leeds Mercury*; these with the *Mirror* and *Pictorial* were at this time his principal press properties. He spent an increasingly large amount of time on financial operations and at one time estimated his wealth at twenty millions sterling; but it decreased heavily in value. His will was proved for not more than a few hundred thousand pounds.

Northcliffe's death in 1922 threw on Rothermere fresh responsibilities. He took over control of Associated Newspapers, owning the *Daily Mail*, *Evening News*, and the *Sunday Dispatch*; this he kept until 1932, when he passed it on to his son. He sold his brother's share of *The Times* to Major Astor, and the Amalgamated Press to the Berry brothers. To the latter he transferred also two Manchester papers bought by him after the death of Sir Edward Hulton [q.v.] in 1925. An attempt which he made to establish a chain of Northcliffe newspapers did not succeed.

Although still shy and shunning public appearances, Rothermere now signed frequent articles in the *Daily Mail* on the need for a strong Air Force and in praise of Mussolini and Hitler; with the latter he once stayed at Berchtesgaden. He favoured better understanding with the Nazi régime and seemed inclined to back Sir Oswald Mosley in Great Britain, but never came out as his supporter. He had taken a close interest in Magyar grievances at an earlier date and was believed to have been approached with an offer of the Hungarian crown. His activities at home were more fruitful than his excursions into foreign affairs. In conjunction with his mother (who died in 1925) he gave £40,000 to the Middle Temple, which elected him an honorary bencher; and in her memory he bought the site of Bethlehem Hospital for a playground; he was chief donor, too, to the fund for saving the Foundling Hospital. A man of few friends (his abrupt manner of speech seemed disconcerting), he was in the family circle affectionate and very generous. In May 1940 he was asked by Lord Beaverbrook, then minister of aircraft production, to undertake a mission to the United States. There his health suddenly failed, and he died in Bermuda, where he had gone to recuperate, 26 November 1940.

Lord Rothermere married in 1893 Mary Lilian (died 1937), daughter of George Wade Share. He was succeeded as second viscount by his youngest and only surviving son, Esmond Cecil (born 1898).

A bust of Lord Rothermere by Jacob Epstein and an oil-painting by John Cope (c. 1908) are in the possession of the second Lord Rothermere. Another portrait, by P. A. de László (c. 1936), was hung in the Parliament House at Budapest.

[*The Times*, 27 November 1940; personal knowledge.] HAMILTON FYFE.

HARRADEN, BEATRICE (1864–1936), novelist, born at Hampstead 24 January 1864, was the younger daughter of Samuel Harraden, musical instrument importer, by his wife, Rosalie Lindstedt. She was educated in Dresden; at Cheltenham, Queen's, and Bedford colleges; and graduated B.A. of London University. Her life—spent in study, in travel, and in devoted service to the cause of female suffrage and emancipation—was unobtrusive and outwardly uneventful.

Beatrice Harraden made her appearance in London literary circles in the 'nineties under the auspices of Eliza Lynn Linton [q.v.]. This formidable but warm-hearted lady introduced the girl at her Sunday afternoon gatherings as 'my little B.A.' and delighted to show her off as the learned young person which she undeniably was. Short and slight, with an olive complexion, a clever rather serious face, and beautiful dark eyes, Miss Harraden dressed in the fashion of five years earlier, that is to say, after the style of a Liberty aesthete of the 'eighties, in a gown (usually of sage-green velvet) which hung straight from the shoulders, topped by a mushroom-hat. She wore her hair short, with a fringe, and in outward appearance carefully eschewed the fashions of the moment. As a being she was natural, affectionate, and modest, had a considerable sense of humour, and was well loved throughout her life.

Miss Harraden, the novelist, had lofty principles, a deep feeling for beauty, and an uncritical sympathy with the rebel and the outcast. But she knew too little of ordinary human nature to be able to create real men and women. Now and again she depicted a conflict or a companionship with shrewdness or sympathy; but the relationship rather than the persons related was her interest. Similarly she was a passionate advocate of woman's rights; but the cause, not the individual woman, was what stirred her enthusiasm. A fatal strain of whimsy helped her to evade the actualities for which she had no taste. Continually she slipped into fantasy, into allegory, into fable. With her first story, *Ships That Pass in the Night* (1893), she had what to posterity must remain an inexplicable success. The book has delicacy and integrity; but it is rhapsodical, elusive, and deliberately parabolic.

None of her later novels achieved anything like its success. Through them there runs an almost mystical insistence on the significance of a fleeting contact between two strangers, one of whom, Excelsior-fashion, 'passes on'. This obsession probably arose from the one tragic experience of her life, for she fell deeply in love with a man who falsified his clients' accounts and whose body was found not long after in a crevasse on a Swiss glacier.

In 1930 Miss Harraden received a civil list pension in recognition of her literary work. She died at Barton-on-Sea, Hampshire, 5 May 1936.

[*The Times*, 6 May 1936; private information.] MICHAEL SADLEIR.

HARREL, SIR DAVID (1841–1939), Irish administrator and public servant, was born at Downpatrick, co. Down, 25 March 1841, the youngest son of David Harrel, of Mount Pleasant, co. Down, who was agent for the Ker estate in that county, by his wife, Jane, daughter of James Wharton, of Belfast. He was educated at the Royal Naval School, Gosport, intending to enter the Royal Navy, but was over age at the examination date and became a midshipman in the Dunbar Shipping Company. He left the sea in order to enter the Royal Irish Constabulary in 1859 but retained a lifelong affection for his first profession. He became interested in the Irish land question early, when, as a young police officer, he witnessed unfair treatment of tenants and evictions, and wrote a letter to Gladstone, stating what he had seen. In later years Harrel followed with constant interest the successive remedial measures which led to the settlement of the land question. He was appointed resident magistrate in 1879, serving during the Land League days in county Mayo, where his just and generous character established mutual trust and affection between him and the people. He was chief commissioner of the Dublin Metropolitan Police from 1883 to 1893. Harrel was an active member of the

Congested Districts Board, which brought much improvement to the poor western districts of Ireland. An Ulster Protestant, he worked for the Irish peasantry, in co-operation with Roman Catholic bishops and priests, with whom his relations were always those of mutual respect and friendship.

Although the two administrations represented differing political outlooks, Harrel, serving as under-secretary for Ireland (1893–1902) while John (Viscount) Morley and George Wyndham [qq.v.] were chief secretaries, maintained a lasting friendship with each statesman. After Harrel's retirement from Irish office, owing to ill health, Morley's opinion and influence were instrumental in the recognition by the government of his gifts as arbitrator, and he acted as chairman and member of various arbitration and conciliation boards dealing with trade disputes in England, as befitted one of his strength, sense of justice, and deep humanity, and his service in this respect was of special importance during the war of 1914–1918.

Harrel was sworn of the Irish Privy Council in 1900, was appointed C.B. in 1887, and, after being knighted in 1893, K.C.B. (1895), K.C.V.O. (1900), G.B.E. (1918), and G.C.B. (1920).

In 1863 Harrel married Juliana (died 1931), daughter of Richard Nugent Horner, rector of Killeeshill, co. Tyrone. It was a perfect marriage of two rarely matched characters, and Harrel's deep respect for his wife's judgement influenced and supported him throughout his career. They had three sons and two daughters. He died at Bath 12 May 1939.

[*The Times*, 13 May 1939; Katharine Tynan, *The Years of the Shadow*, 1919; private information; personal knowledge.]

PAMELA HINKSON.

HARRIS, GEORGE ROBERT CANNING, fourth BARON HARRIS, of Seringapatam and Mysore, and of Belmont (1851–1932), cricketer and administrator, was born at St. Ann's, Trinidad, 3 February 1851, the only son of George Francis Robert Harris, third Lord Harris [q.v.], governor of Trinidad, who was appointed governor of Madras in 1854. His mother, who died when he was two years old, was Sarah, younger daughter of George Cummins, archdeacon of Trinidad. He was grandson of George William Harris, second Lord Harris [q.v.], and great-grandson of George Harris, first Lord Harris [q.v.]. The Harris family had a remarkable record of service in the Indian army and in Indian administration, which was maintained by the fourth Lord Harris.

Harris entered Eton in 1864. He was in the eleven for his last three years, and was captain in 1870, when there was a very close struggle with Harrow which Eton won by only 21 runs. An incident occurred when as bowler he ran out the batsman at his end who was backing up too eagerly. He checked his delivery on the crease, and instead of bowling put the wicket down, an unusual mode of dismissal which evoked a noisy expression of disapproval from the Harrow partisans. In an atmosphere of tense excitement this action, while perfectly legitimate, required some courage, but courage was a quality in which Harris was never found wanting. His development as a batsman came later than his school and university days. He went up to Christ Church, Oxford, and was three years (1871, 1872, and 1874) in the university eleven, but except on one or two occasions his scores were modest. His best innings was, perhaps, his last, against Cambridge in 1874, when he made 43, described as an admirable display.

Harris's main interest was in his own county, Kent, where a county cricket club was formed early in 1870, and shortly after leaving Oxford, he became its moving spirit. His energy in collecting capable players, as well as in encouraging the interest of supporters, was invaluable. He accepted the captaincy in 1875, and held it until 1889, playing in most of the matches. The improvement in his own form was rapid, for before long he came to be regarded as one of the best amateur batsmen in England.

In early matches with Australia Harris played a prominent part. In the winter of 1878–1879 he took out to Australia an amateur team with two professional bowlers. The side played no test matches, and its programme contained only five eleven-a-side games, the remainder being against odds. The team won and lost against Victoria, and also against New South Wales. The fifth match, against a strong mixed eleven, also went against it. There was an unfortunate disturbance at Sydney, owing to an umpire's decision. The crowd rushed the ground, and for a time all was confusion. This affair, and some controversial correspondence which followed, may almost be said to have had a share in bringing about in 1880 the first test match ever played in this country between England and Australia.

When the Australians next visited England, in that year, it was found that, owing to some faulty arrangement, their programme was of the dullest and most unworthy kind. Although they brought quite a good side, they had only a few eleven-a-side matches, most of their engagements being with local twenty-twos and eighteens. Towards the end of the season some extra matches were played, and among these was one against the full strength of England. It was felt that in view of what had happened, the right man to collect and captain the English side was Harris. The match was an immense success. It took place at the Oval in the first week of September and, according to contemporary accounts, was attended by more people than had ever watched a game of cricket in England. England put almost, if not quite, its full strength into the field, and won by five wickets after a much closer struggle than at one time had looked probable. In 1884 Harris again captained England in two test matches, one at Lord's which England won, and the other, a huge run-getting affair at the Oval, which was drawn.

After his retirement from active play in first-class cricket, Harris continued his services to the game, and proved as valuable in the committee room as he had done in the field. A member of the Marylebone Cricket Club for over sixty years, he filled many important offices, as trustee (1888), treasurer (1896-1932), and president (1895). Everywhere respected and popular, at the end of his life he held a position of authority and influence in the cricket world to which cricket history can furnish no parallel.

It is no reflection upon Harris's record as a statesman to say that his name is remembered chiefly in connexion with cricket. He was under-secretary for India from June 1885 to February 1886, and under-secretary for war from 1886 to 1889. From 1890 to 1895 he was governor of Bombay, an office in which he showed robust common sense. He handled the troubles in some of the Kathiawar states with tact and vigour and he did valuable work by the keen interest which he showed in agriculture. But his chief service while governor was the popularization of cricket among Indians, and it was he who secured the first visit to India of a representative team from England under the captaincy of Martin Bladen Hawke, seventh Lord Hawke [q.v.]. On his return from Bombay Harris began a long connexion with

the City of London as chairman and director of various South African undertakings. He served in the South African war as assistant-adjutant-general with the Imperial Yeomanry.

Harris, who possessed handsome features and a fine physique, succeeded his father as fourth baron in 1872. He was appointed G.C.I.E. in 1890, G.C.S.I. in 1895, and C.B. in 1918. He married in 1874 Lucy Ada (died 1930), second daughter of Carnegie Robert John Jervis, third Lord St. Vincent. He died at his home, Belmont, near Faversham, 24 March 1932, and was succeeded as fifth baron by his only child, George St. Vincent (born 1889).

A portrait of Harris by Arthur Hacker is in the pavilion at Lord's Cricket Ground.

[*The Times*, 26 March 1932; Lord Harris, *A Few Short Runs* (portrait), 1921; Wisden's *Cricketers' Almanack*, passim.]

ALFRED COCHRANE.

HARRIS, JAMES THOMAS ('FRANK') (1856-1931), author, editor, and adventurer, the fourth child and third son of Thomas Vernon Harris, a seaman, by his wife, the daughter of a Baptist minister, was probably born 14 February 1856. The place of his birth was at various times stated by himself to have been Galway, Tenby, and Brighton. His father and mother were Welsh, and the boy's early years were spent in Ireland. At the age of fourteen he ran away to the United States of America, where, having worked as bootblack, labourer, hotel clerk, and cowboy, he joined an elder brother in Kansas in 1872, and attended the state university. Here he acquired the language, at least, of idealistic philosophy, and became, as he remained throughout life, a systematic amorist. By a subsequent return to Europe, brief experience as correspondent in the Russo-Turkish war of 1877-1878, and attendance at two German universities, he prepared himself for a grand assault upon London at the age of twenty-seven. The assault began with work on the *Evening News*, which he edited and sensationalized; but at the end of four years the position was lost or resigned, and in 1886, almost by force, he obtained the editorship of the *Fortnightly Review*. Harris used control of this periodical, which he filled with striking contributions from leading or rising men, for his own social advancement; and in 1887 he married a wealthy widow, Mrs. Edith Mary Clayton, whose house in Park Lane made ideal headquarters for a political campaign which was to end, he hoped, in the premiership. He was a socialist. The campaign failed, in spite of Harris's ferocious brilliance as talker and orator, and the marriage likewise failed. In 1894 he eloped with Miss Helen O'Hara, later Mrs. Harris, published a first book, *Elder Conklin and Other Stories*, and bought the *Saturday Review*, which he made for four years the most brilliant literary and political weekly of the time. This period (1886–1898) was without question the finest in his life, for he associated as an equal with the most distinguished contemporary writers and had tyrannic power over their minds; but it ended in the latter year, when he sold the *Saturday Review*, wasted his own and other people's money in an incompetent attempt to run luxury hotels on the French Riviera, and thenceforth became not so much a buccaneer as a petty opportunist of whose needs other men took advantage.

Harris continued to write. His play, *Mr. and Mrs. Daventry*, the idea for which he said that he bought from Oscar Wilde [q.v.], was produced in 1900. A second volume of short stories, *Montes the Matador*, containing his best work in fiction, was published the same year. He now began the most elaborate of all his writings, *The Man Shakespeare*, a book which anticipated the later vogue for psychoanalytical literary criticism and sought by ingenious quotation and conjecture to present Shakespeare as self-confessed not only in the Sonnets but in the characters of Romeo, Hamlet, Orsino, Jaques, etc. The book, published in 1909, has not influenced Shakespearian scholars; but some of its analyses, especially that of the character of Macbeth, are suggestive. It was followed in 1910 by a play, *Shakespeare and his Love*, and in 1911 by a study, *The Women of Shakespeare*. A short novel about anarchists in Chicago, *The Bomb* (1908), an historical tale, *Great Days* (1913), and further volumes of short stories practically concluded his work in fiction. Meanwhile one disastrous journalistic venture followed another, from a new weekly, the *Candid Friend*, in 1901, and the attempted revival of *Vanity Fair* in 1907, to a brief, ignominious flutter with a woman's journal, *Hearth and Home*, in 1911, and a shady exploit with *Modern Society* which led to imprisonment for contempt of court and the final eclipse of Harris as a reputable English journalist. He returned in 1914 to the United States, where he acquired and ran *Pearson's*

Magazine, using it during the war of 1914–1918 as a medium for vehement and scurrilous anti-British political writing.

In 1915 there began the last long phase of Harris's literary career, which was devoted to books and short pieces about men whom he had known, or pretended that he had known, in palmier days. The first of five series of *Contemporary Portraits* (1915–1930) was then published, and for the rest of his life these portraits, with biographies of Wilde (2 vols., New York, 1916) and Mr. Bernard Shaw (1931), and an immense serial autobiography, *My Life* (published in Germany, America, and France, 1925–1930; abridged version, under the title of *Frank Harris, His Life and Adventures*, published by Grant Richards in 1947), occupied his time. Such personal books all suffer from Harris's fantastic delusion of greatness, complete lack of humour, reckless unreliability of statement, and poor sense of character. But, while glib and untruthful, they contain valuable sidelights upon the men whom he knew or had read about; and they have more life than his fiction, which, extravagantly praised by early critics, is mechanical and without feeling. It was as a personality that Harris impressed; and every surviving testimony emphasizes his physical vigour, vehement (even outrageous) speech, rich bass voice, and piercing eyes. Mr. Shaw is quoted by Mr. Hugh Kingsmill as saying: 'He is neither first-rate, nor second-rate, nor tenth-rate. He is just his horrible unique self.' That uniqueness did not embrace literary genius. He lived, often in great straits for money, until 26 August 1931, and died at Nice.

[A. I. Tobin and Elmer Gertz, *Frank Harris: a Study in Black and White* (Chicago), 1931; Hugh Kingsmill, *Frank Harris*, 1932; Frederic Carrel, *The Adventures of John Johns* (for pre-*Fortnightly* career in London), 1897; Frank Harris, *My Life* (New York), 1925–1930.]   FRANK SWINNERTON.

HARRISON, MARY ST. LEGER (1852–1931), novelist under the pseudonym of LUCAS MALET, was born at Eversley, Hampshire, 4 June 1852, the younger daughter of the novelist Charles Kingsley [q.v.], by his wife, Frances, daughter of Pascoe Grenfell, of Taplow, Buckinghamshire. Henry Kingsley [q.v.] was her uncle. As a girl she studied at the Slade School of Fine Art under (Sir) Edward Poynter [q.v.] but abandoned any idea of an artistic career on her marriage to the

Rev. William Harrison, which took place in 1876. After a short period spent at Wormleighton, Worcestershire, her husband was appointed to the living of Clovelly in North Devon, a place which for many years remained the Harrisons' home.

Mrs. Harrison's first literary success came with the appearance of her second novel, *Colonel Enderby's Wife* (1885), written, like all her books, under the pseudonym of 'Lucas Malet', a name formed from the surnames of two families related to the Kingsleys and chosen because she did not want to profit by the literary fame of her own family. In 1891 she published *The Wages of Sin*, a novel dealing partly with artistic circles in London, partly with the fishing people of her own home at Clovelly. The book was stigmatized by many critics as being both daring and unpleasant, although, judging by later standards, it is difficult to make out the grounds for such objections. *The History of Sir Richard Calmady* (1901) provoked an even louder storm of criticism, partly owing to the fact that the book deals with the subject of deformity, but in spite of its realistic theme the novel is written throughout in the high romantic manner.

In 1897 William Harrison died, without issue, and in 1902 his widow was received into the Roman Catholic Church. In 1906 she bought a house in her father's old parish of Eversley, but she spent much of her time travelling abroad with her cousin and adopted daughter, Miss Gabrielle Vallings. She was especially at home in France, where she had many friends among the artists of the day. Her knowledge of French literature was extensive and she had a particular admiration for Flaubert. She lived in London throughout the war of 1914–1918, but in 1924 she moved to Montreux, where she made one of a literary circle which included such various writers as Romain Rolland, Mr. Robert Hichens, 'Sapper' (Cyril McNeile, q.v.), and Louis N. Parker. Part of each year she spent in England, and it was during one of these visits that she was taken ill, dying some eighteen months later at Tenby 27 October 1931. The previous year she had been awarded a civil list pension in recognition of her literary work.

A handsome woman and an excellent conversationalist, 'Lucas Malet' was a well-known figure in contemporary literary society, her friends including Henry James [q.v.] and the critic W. L. Courtney [q.v.].

She was among the most successful novelists of her day and was considered by her contemporaries to be extremely outspoken, but, writing always in an elaborate Meredithian style and in the romantic convention, she can hardly be considered a forerunner of the realistic school of twentieth-century novelists.

Two miniatures of 'Lucas Malet' by S. A. Lindsey are in the possession of Miss Vallings.

[*The Times*, 29 October 1931; private information.]   GEORGINA BATTISCOMBE.

HARTSHORN, VERNON (1872–1931), miners' leader and politician, was born at Pontywaun, Monmouthshire, 16 March 1872, the elder son of Theophilus Hartshorn, coalminer, by his wife, Helen Gregory, daughter of a farm labourer. He began to work in a pit as a boy, and later he was for a time employed as a clerk in a colliery company's office at Cardiff docks. Returning to work at Risca, he was elected by the miners as their checkweighman.

Hartshorn, who from an early age had taken a deep interest in industrial and political movements, was one of the pioneers of the independent labour party in Wales. In 1905 he was elected miners' agent of the Maesteg district of the South Wales Miners' Federation and in 1911 to its executive council and to the National Executive Council of the Miners' Federation of Great Britain. He took a leading part in the minimum wage strike of 1912 and was prominent in local government business. At the general election of 1918 Hartshorn, who had in 1910 twice unsuccessfully contested the Mid-Glamorgan division as a labour candidate, was returned unopposed as the first member for the newly formed Ogmore division of Glamorganshire, and he held the seat until his death. Notwithstanding parliamentary duties, he aided the miners in their strike in 1920, but he found himself so much at variance with his extremist colleagues that he resigned from both the miners' executive councils to which he belonged. He was soon afterwards re-elected and from 1922 to 1924 he was president of the South Wales Miners' Federation.

During the war of 1914–1918, Hartshorn served on the Coal Trade Organization Committee, the Coal Controllers' Advisory Committee, and the Industrial Unrest Committee in South Wales, and his services were recognized by appointment as O.B.E. in 1918.

In parliament Hartshorn was elected chairman of the Welsh labour group in 1923, and in the first labour administration in 1924 he was postmaster-general and sworn of the Privy Council. In 1927 he was appointed to the Indian Statutory Commission, which he regarded as one of the greatest works ever undertaken by any seven men. The chairman, Sir John (later Viscount) Simon stated that those portions of the commission's report which dealt with the franchise and the method of election were especially due to Hartshorn.

On the formation of the second labour administration in 1929, the prime minister announced that a place for Hartshorn would be found as soon as the commission had completed its work. Accordingly, in 1930 he was appointed lord privy seal with special responsibility for the government's policy on employment, but although a report handed to the prime minister by Hartshorn after two months of office earned Ramsay MacDonald's high praise, Hartshorn's death did not allow this promise to come to fulfilment.

Hartshorn owed his rise to his special knowledge of the mining industry, his outstanding ability as a negotiator, and his great power of leadership. He himself attributed his moral and mental development to Primitive Methodism, to Robert Blatchford, and to his own wife, Mary Matilda, daughter of Edward Winsor, coalminer, of Nailsea, Somerset, whom he married in 1899 and by whom he had two sons and a daughter. He died at Maesteg, South Wales, 13 March 1931.

[*The Times*, 14 March 1931.]

W. L. Cook.

HAWKE, MARTIN BLADEN, seventh BARON HAWKE OF TOWTON (1860–1938), cricketer, was born at Willingham, Lincolnshire, 16 August 1860, the second but eldest surviving son of Edward Henry Julius Hawke, sixth Lord Hawke, vicar of Coates and rector of Willingham from 1854 to 1875, by his wife, Jane, third daughter of Henry Dowker, of Laysthorpe, Yorkshire. He was great-great-grandson of Edward Hawke, first Lord Hawke [q.v.], the celebrated admiral. He was educated at Eton, where he gained his cricket colours in 1878, playing against Harrow that season, and again in 1879. On leaving he went for a time to a private tutor, and did not go up to Magdalene College, Cambridge, until the autumn of 1881. He was in the university eleven for

three years (1882–1883 and 1885). He did not play against Oxford in 1884, but he captained the Cambridge side in 1885.

In the late summer of 1881, before he went to Cambridge, Hawke was invited to play for Yorkshire, the county with which his name will always be associated. He appeared in two matches at the Scarborough festival, and in the second of these, against I Zingari, batted with some success. In 1882 as a Cambridge blue his assistance was welcomed by the Yorkshire executive, and as soon as the university season was over, he became a regular member of the county eleven, playing in thirteen matches. His batting had made a distinct advance, and with a number of useful double-figure scores, the highest of which was 60 against Gloucestershire, he fully justified his selection. His services to Yorkshire cricket in after years were so varied and important that his value as a playing member of the side is apt to be overlooked. But in point of fact, if never a very sound batsman, he became a very dangerous one, a powerful hitter, and at his best in an emergency. Apart from his captaincy he was well worth his place.

Yorkshire in those early days was regarded as one of the strongest opponents in the county competition, for the team contained some of the best professional cricketers to be found in the country. The need of the moment was a competent captain, able to control and direct the talent available. In 1883 Hawke was offered the captaincy, which he accepted, and he held it until 1910.

Hawke entered upon his duties with energy, and improved the organization in many ways, handling with tact and wisdom problems and difficulties as they arose. His relations with the professionals under his leadership were admirable. He could be firm in cases where discipline called for drastic action, but his kindly interest in those who served the side well was unfailing. It was at his suggestion that the system of winter pay was introduced, and that the large sums received for benefit matches were suitably and wisely invested. At the end of each season there was a friendly gathering of Yorkshire players at the captain's country house, Wighill Park, near Tadcaster. After his marriage he settled at Huttons Ambo Hall, near Malton.

With the continued supply of high-class professionals, and the aid of some amateurs, one of whom, (Sir) F. S. Jackson, was among the greatest of his generation, it is no wonder that Yorkshire soon reached the top of the tree. The team won the championship for the first time in 1893, and in the twenty-seven years of Hawke's captaincy it held the premier place eight times. Considering how often it had to let its best men off for test matches this is a good record.

Another notable service, even more valuable to the progress of the game, was rendered by Hawke. This was the arrangement and management of cricket tours from England to various parts of the world. He went to Australia in 1887, but owing to his father's death in December he was obliged to return home. Later he took teams to India (twice), the United States of America and Canada (twice), South Africa (twice), the West Indies, and South America. It is interesting to notice that he lived to see South Africa, India, and the West Indies admitted to full test-match status.

For many years Hawke served the Marylebone Cricket Club as a member of various committees. He was elected president of the club in 1914. Owing to the outbreak of war, no change was made, and he held office until 1918. On the death of George Harris, fourth Lord Harris [q.v.], in 1932 he became treasurer. He remained president of the Yorkshire county club until his death.

Lord Hawke died in Edinburgh after a few days' illness 10 October 1938. He married in 1916 Marjory Nelson Ritchie (died 1936), third daughter of William Peacock Edwards, J.P., of Edinburgh, and widow of Arthur J. Graham Cross. There was no issue of the marriage, and he was succeeded as eighth baron by his brother, Edward Julian (1873-1939).

[*The Times*, 11 October 1938; Lord Hawke, *Recollections and Reminiscences* (portraits), 1924; Wisden's *Cricketers' Almanack*, passim.]
ALFRED COCHRANE.

HAWKINS, SIR ANTHONY HOPE (1863-1933), novelist under the pseudonym of ANTHONY HOPE, was the younger son of the Rev. Edwards Comerford Hawkins, by his wife, Jane Isabella, daughter of Archibald Grahame, of Brighton. Kenneth Grahame [q.v.], the author, was his first cousin. He was born 9 February 1863 at Clapton where his father was headmaster of St. John's Foundation School for the Sons of Poor Clergy. There, at Leatherhead whither the school was moved, and at Marlborough, where he won the 100 yards and quarter-mile races,

Hawkins began his education, proceeding to Balliol College, Oxford, with an exhibition (which in his first term was raised to a scholarship) in 1881. He played in the college fifteen, obtained a first class in classical moderations (1882) and in *literae humaniores* (1885), and became president of the Union (1886). He was called to the bar by the Middle Temple in 1887. His father, now a widower, had been presented to St. Bride's church, Fleet Street; and with him Hawkins made his home for the next seventeen years. There were three careers for which he was equally equipped, politics, the law, authorship. A staunch liberal, he stood (1892) without success but without disgrace, for a conservative constituency, South Buckinghamshire. After six years at the bar he was holding briefs from such important bodies as the Great Western Railway. By June 1893 he had published five novels, of which *Mr. Witt's Widow* (1892) achieved as well as promised. To authorship he leaned most, and on 28 November 1893 his choice was made for him rather than by him. On that afternoon as he walked back to the Temple from the Westminster county court, where he had won a case, the story of *The Prisoner of Zenda* unrolled itself before him. He began it the next morning, and writing two chapters a day, finished it on 29 December. It was published in April 1894, a modern romance of adventure. The debonair chivalry of its hero, the fresh, vivid narration, and the tenderness of the love-story took more than the town by storm. Andrew Lang acclaimed it at the Academy banquet. R. L. Stevenson sent congratulations from far Samoa. The same summer saw *The Dolly Dialogues* published. Written with the most delicate wit and now and then touched with a shade of sadness, suggested as much as stated so that the reader to his pleasure must do a share of the work himself; these conversations between Dolly, Lady Mickleham, and Mr. Samuel Carter are so truthfully set in the London season of their day that the social historian would be unwise to neglect them. They enhanced the fame and profits gained by *The Prisoner of Zenda*; and on 4 July Hawkins, aware of the danger of a divided mind, wrote letters of farewell to his legal clients and gave twenty years to imaginative work.

The Chronicles of Count Antonio (1895) and *Simon Dale* (1898) are historical romances. *Rupert of Hentzau* (1898), a sequel to *The Prisoner of Zenda, The Heart*

of *Princess Osra* (1896), *Phroso* (1897), *Sophy of Kravonia* (1906) were of the Ruritania type, more fanciful but less compelling. Hawkins and others thought *The King's Mirror* (1899), a diary of disillusionment, and *Double Harness* (1904) his best work. But he had many interests and ways of expressing them. He would take some outstanding figure, an empire builder (*The God in the Car*, 1894), a politician (*Quisanté*, 1900), an actress (*A Servant of the Public*, 1905), build up the character carefully against its natural background, set it in contact with a woman or a man of high individuality, and work out the relationship, sometimes to failure, sometimes to contentment, never but once (*Tristram of Blent*, 1901) to the triumphal march. *The Great Miss Driver* (1908), a Queen Elizabeth in a modern county, is set to choose between independence and surrender, grasps and loses the advantages of both, and climbs courageously back to her independence. All these are thoughtful analytical novels of character rather than incident and graced with the felicitous dialogue of which he especially was master. But although they were well received, Anthony Hope remained the author of *The Prisoner of Zenda*.

The Prisoner of Zenda, dramatized by Edward Rose, was produced with great success by Sir George Alexander [q.v.] at the St. James's Theatre in January 1896. Hawkins, whose early ambition had been to act, turned playwright. *The Adventure of Lady Ursula* was produced in October 1898, with Evelyn Millard and Herbert Waring, and was followed in 1900 by *English Nell*, a version of *Simon Dale*, with Marie Tempest as Nell Gwyn. Both were profitable, but *Pilkerton's Peerage* (1903), a satire on the distribution of honours, also added to his reputation.

Hawkins married in 1903 Elizabeth Somerville (died 1946), daughter of Charles Henry Sheldon, of New York, and had two sons and a daughter. He lived thereafter at 41 Russell Square but, warned by ill health, he rented and subsequently bought Heath Farm, Walton-on-the-Hill, Surrey, exchanging the big London house for a smaller one in Gower Street. On the outbreak of war in 1914 he joined the Editorial and Public Branch Department (the original Ministry of Information), which was under the direction of Charles Frederick Gurney Masterman [q.v.] at Wellington House, and was knighted for his services in 1918. He was for twelve years on the committee of the Authors' Society, for four years its chairman, and a founder of its pension scheme. He published a modest volume of reminiscences (*Memories and Notes*) in 1927. He died at Heath Farm 8 July 1933.

[*The Times*, 10 July 1933; Anthony Hope, *Memories and Notes*, 1927; Sir Charles Mallet, *Anthony Hope and his Books*, 1935; private information; personal knowledge.]

A. E. W. MASON.

HAY, SIR HARLEY HUGH DALRYMPLE- (1861–1940), civil engineer, was born probably at Rawalpindi, India, 7 October 1861, the third son of Colonel George James Dalrymple-Hay, Bengal Staff Corps, by his wife, Amelia Emily, daughter of Colonel Henry Daniel Maitland, and grandson of Sir James Dalrymple-Hay, second baronet, of Park Place, Glenluce. Educated at a private school in Edinburgh and by army tutors, he began his engineering career as a pupil on the South Wales line of the Midland Railway, and later joined the engineering staff of the London and South Western Railway for which he was engaged for several years on various engineering works.

In 1894 Dalrymple-Hay became resident engineer for the Waterloo and City Railway for the construction of which he employed his own method of a hooded shield and clay pockets for driving tunnels under compressed air without requiring a heading or timbers outside the shield. This system and other improvements in the methods of constructing tube railways, originated by Dalrymple-Hay, have been used since both in this country and in the United States of America and have in fact become standard practice. In 1902 he took up the appointment of consulting civil engineer to the Underground Electric Railways Company of London, a position which he held for thirty-eight years and until his death; in 1907 he began his own private practice as a consulting civil engineer in Westminster.

It is impracticable to enumerate all Dalrymple-Hay's tube-railway works, consisting as they do of over sixty miles of tunnels in London alone, but they include the Bakerloo, Hampstead, and Piccadilly lines; the extensions from Golders Green to Edgware, from Finsbury Park to Cockfosters, and from Highgate to East Finchley; the stations at Piccadilly Circus, Leicester Square, Waterloo (Bakerloo line), King's Cross, Hyde Park Corner, Knightsbridge, the Elephant and Castle, and many others; also numerous escalator schemes, amongst which was the first escalator on the underground system, that at Earls Court, which was completed in 1911.

Dalrymple-Hay was asked in 1921 to report on a system of tube railways for Calcutta, and later designed a tunnel under the river Hugli. This tunnel, completed in 1931, was the first shield-driven iron-lined tunnel under a great tidal river in the East, and its construction was carried out under high air pressures, in difficult climatic conditions, and with the use of unskilled labour. Amongst other works outside London for which he was responsible were a system of culverts for the Bristol corporation's generating station at Portishead, and tunnels for the Edinburgh corporation under the Firth of Forth at Portobello.

Although Dalrymple-Hay's work was mostly concerned with the construction of tunnels and tube railways, a branch of civil engineering in which he was probably the greatest expert of his day, he also was concerned in other engineering projects of varying natures. Possibly the most interesting of these was the widening of Richmond bridge. The 150-year-old bridge was strengthened and widened by some 11 feet, without either the traffic over it or the water traffic under it being stopped for a single day, and without any alteration to the architectural design, the existing façade stonework and parapet being dismantled, numbered, and later replaced on the widened bridge.

Dalrymple-Hay was consulting engineer for the construction of the Post Office (London) Railway, a system of great interest and ingenuity, which was opened in 1928, and it was for the Post Office that he undertook his last major work. This was a secret system of deep-level tunnels beneath Whitehall to preserve from aerial bombardment intercommunication between government offices.

Dalrymple-Hay was knighted in 1933, and served on the council of the Institution of Civil Engineers from then until his death. As a student of the institution he was awarded a Miller prize in 1885 for a paper on 'Trigonometrical Surveying' and in 1900 he won a Telford gold medal and Telford premium for his paper on 'The Waterloo and City Railway'. A characteristic of Dalrymple-Hay was his strong belief in practice being preferable to theory and experience being more valuable than scholarship. He was intensely human, a quality which endeared him to men of all walks of life who worked under him. He married in 1891 Agnes Yelland, daughter of Frederick Waters, and had a daughter. He died at Chorley Wood, Hertfordshire, 17 December 1940.

[*Engineer* and *Engineering*, 27 December 1940 (portraits); *Journal* of the Institution of Civil Engineers, vol. xv, 1940–1941; *The Times*, 20 December 1940 and 3 January 1941; private information; personal knowledge.]   AGNES Y. DALRYMPLE-HAY.

HEAD, SIR HENRY (1861–1940), neurologist, was born at Stamford Hill, Stoke Newington, 4 August 1861, the eldest son of Henry Head, an insurance broker at Lloyds, by his wife, Hester, daughter of Richard Beck. He was educated for two years at Grove House School, Tottenham, and afterwards at Charterhouse. He then spent some time at the university of Halle before going to Trinity College, Cambridge, in 1880. From 1884 to 1886 he studied under Ewald Hering at the German university of Prague. On his return to Cambridge he studied physiology and anatomy and went to University College Hospital, London, for clinical work, before qualifying M.B. (Camb.) in 1890, later taking his M.D. (Camb.) in 1892. His principal teachers at Cambridge were (Sir) Michael Foster, W. H. Gaskell, and J. N. Langley [qq.v.].

After qualification Head became successively house-physician at University College Hospital, and Victoria Park Hospital for Diseases of the Chest, and clinical assistant (1894) at the County Mental Hospital, Rainhill, Liverpool. He then became registrar at the London Hospital and in 1896 assistant physician, becoming in due course physician and consulting physician. His M.D. thesis 'On Disturbances of Sensation, with special reference to the Pain of Visceral Disease', was extended and published in *Brain* (1893, 1894, and 1896). This piece of work established 'Head's Areas', the regions of increased cutaneous sensitiveness associated with diseases of the viscera. In 1894 he became M.R.C.P. and six years later F.R.C.P., and in 1897 he received the Moxon medal which is awarded every third year by the Royal College of Physicians to the person who is deemed to have distinguished himself by observation and research in clinical medicine. He gave the college's Goulstonian lecture in 1901 on 'Some Mental States associated with Visceral Disease in the Sane' and in 1911 the Croonian lecture to the college on

'Sensory Changes from Cerebral Lesions'. In 1899 he was elected F.R.S., and later served on the council (1915–1917) and as vice-president (1916–1917). In 1908 he was awarded a Royal medal for his work on neurology and in 1921 delivered the Croonian lecture to the society on the 'Release of Function in the Nervous System'. From 1905 to 1921 he was editor of the neurological journal *Brain* which had been founded in 1878. In 1920 he was president of the section of neurology at the annual meeting of the British Medical Association held at Cambridge.

The most interesting event in Head's life was the operation performed on him by James Sherren, an eminent surgeon attached to the London Hospital. At the time of the operation the circumstances were ideal. Head was then forty-two years old, in perfect health, he had not smoked for two years and no alcohol was taken during the time of observation. The operation, the details of which are described by William Halse Rivers Rivers under the title of 'A Human Experiment in Nerve Division' (*Brain*, vol. xxxi, 1908), consisted in exposure and excision of small portions of Head's left radial and external cutaneous nerves. To facilitate regeneration of the sensory fibres the ends of the excised nerves were united with silk sutures. The following results were observed: 'All forms of superficial sensibility were lost over the radial half of the forearm and the back of the hand. There was no interference with deep sensibility, as this is subserved by afferent fibres in the motor nerves. Head recognized two forms of superficial or cutaneous sensibility and called these "protopathic" and "epicritic". Protopathic sensibility, which returned about seven weeks after the nerve had been cut, included sensory response to pain, heat, and cold of a crude nature. Epicritic sensibility, which returned later, was finer and more discriminating; degrees of temperature could be distinguished, light touch was appreciated, and the subject was able to locate accurately the point touched.' Throughout the investigation the tests were applied by Rivers, while Head, whose eyes were closed, was unaware of the nature of the stimuli and of the correctness or error of his replies.

The work entitled *Studies in Neurology*, which appeared in two volumes in 1920, was written by Head in collaboration with Dr. Gordon Holmes, Dr. George Riddoch, J. Sherren, W. H. R. Rivers, and Theo-

dore Thompson. It consists mainly of seven articles which had appeared in *Brain* between 1905 and 1918. The work also contains an account of the methods employed in testing sensation, an introduction and an epilogue dealing with the common aims of the writers, and finally a consideration of the most serious criticisms.

Head's last important work, entitled *Aphasia and Kindred Disorders of Speech*, appeared in two volumes in 1926; this was based on the examination of a large number of men suffering from gunshot wounds of the brain. According to Dr. Holmes these volumes were 'devoted not merely to the clinical and symptomatic aspects of disturbances of speech, but were also an attempt to investigate the psychical processes concerned therein, and the physiological integrations necessary for the comprehension and expression of ideas in language'. It was characteristic of Head's loyalty to his former teachers that he dedicated his work on aphasia to Gaskell of Cambridge, Hering of the German university of Prague, and John Hughlings Jackson [q.v.], of the London Hospital.

Beyond delivering numerous lectures before medical or scientific societies already mentioned, Head did not receive many distinctions; he was knighted in 1927, elected an honorary fellow of Trinity College, Cambridge, in 1920, and received the honorary degree of LL.D. from Edinburgh University, and that of M.D. from Strasburg University.

Head's chief relaxations were music and literature, particularly poetry and prose of the eighteenth century, and later psychological novels such as those of Meredith, Hardy, and Henry James. He had two volumes printed for private circulation containing some of his own verse and a translation of some of Heine's poems; these were published in 1919 under the title *Destroyers and Other Verses*.

After a long illness Head died of pneumonia at Reading 8 October 1940. In 1904 he married Ruth (died 1939), the highly gifted eldest daughter of Anthony Lawson Mayhew, fellow of Wadham College, Oxford; they had no children. He left the greater part of his fortune to the Royal Society 'for the purpose of the advancement in England of the science of medicine in the widest sense' with the Royal Society as residual legatee.

In conclusion there may be quoted the following estimation by Dr. Holmes of

Head's character: 'Head was an outstanding personality, but in certain respects a complex one. Though he gave the impression of being a severe materialist, he was interested in certain forms of mysticism, probably due to the influence of the Quaker atmosphere in which he was brought up. A rigidly scientific and objective outlook on all matters which he studied was in him combined with a vivid imagination which at times seemed to carry his ideas beyond the bounds of probability. To casual acquaintances his talents in conversation and discussion often appeared extravagant, but they invariably contained a germ of truth. His published writings, on the other hand, were always subjected to a rigid criticism which assured an accurate and reasoned presentation of the conclusions to which he had come.'

[*The Times*, 10 October 1940; *Obituary Notices of Fellows of the Royal Society*, No. 10, December 1941 (portrait); *British Medical Journal*, 1940, vol. ii, pp. 539 and 577 (portrait); *Lancet*, 1940, vol. ii, p. 534 (portrait); *Brain*, vol. lxiii, 1940 (bibliography).]

J. D. ROLLESTON.

HEALY, JOHN EDWARD (1872–1934), journalist, was born at Drogheda 17 March 1872, the eldest child and only son of James Stanislaus Healy, solicitor, of that town, by his wife, Kate Mary, daughter of John Edward Appleyard, of Drogheda. He was educated at the local grammar school and in 1892 entered Trinity College, Dublin, as a sizar. There he developed remarkable gifts and found an enduring spiritual home.

Healy was not only a classical scholar in 1895 and in 1896 first senior moderator in modern literature, but also junior moderator in classics and was awarded the Brooke prize. He was in three successive years vice-chancellor's prizeman—twice for English verse and once for English prose. When, therefore, two years after graduation he was invited to join the staff of the Dublin *Daily Express* he was richly equipped and after a few years became its editor.

In 1906 Healy was called to the Irish bar, although he remained Dublin correspondent of *The Times* to which he had been appointed in 1899. In 1907, however, he returned to full-time newspaper work as editor of the *Irish Times*, and through the twenty-seven difficult and arduous years in this office proved himself a supreme journalist and leader-writer.

To Healy, at home among the main currents of European culture, Irish nationalism appeared a reedy backwater. He therefore threw himself whole-heartedly into the defence of the union and, when his cause was overwhelmed, fought on to keep the new Ireland as close as might be to the Empire. Although just and chivalrous in controversy he could strike shrewdly. The majority in his beloved country was against him and in the early nineteen-twenties his life—he refused protection of any kind—was in constant peril. Courage went, however, with the equanimity which was his outstanding characteristic.

Healy took an active part in Irish politics during some of the most critical years of the home rule controversy. He was associated closely with Sir Horace Plunkett [q.v.] in his economic campaign, and when the home rule bill reached the statute book, being convinced that without a united Ireland no form of self-government would be of any avail, he gave staunch support to the anti-partition movement, and he fought vigorously against any attempt to broaden the gap between Dublin and London. His real interests, however, were always scholarly rather than political. Sir J. P. Mahaffy [q.v.] had been his tutor at Trinity College, and it was to him that Healy looked for guidance and advice throughout his newspaper career. In 1923 his university conferred upon him the honorary degree of M.A.

In 1899 Healy married Adeline, daughter of James Poë Alton, of Limerick and later of Dublin, and sister of Dr. E. H. Alton, provost of Trinity College, Dublin. By her he had two sons. He died in Dublin 30 May 1934, respected even by his strongest opponents and regarded far beyond her shores as the most lucid of all interpreters of Ireland. A portrait, by Briana Alton, is in Mrs. Healy's possession.

[*The Times* and *Irish Times*, 31 May 1934; private information; personal knowledge.]

R. J. HERBERT SHAW.

HEALY, TIMOTHY MICHAEL (1855–1931), Irish political leader and first governor-general of the Irish Free State, the elder son of Maurice Healy, by his wife, Elizabeth, daughter of Daniel O'Sullivan, of Bantry, co. Cork, was born at Bantry 17 May 1855. His father, a scholarly man who could recite Homer, was successively clerk of the poor-law union at Bantry and after 1862 at Lismore. Bantry had been one of the most stricken districts in Ireland during the famine years, and Healy had therefore early occasion to be affected by a sense of the misgovernment of his country, and its misfortunes. He was educated at the Christian Brothers' School at Fermoy; but was largely self-taught, for he had to set out for Dublin to pick up a living at the age of thirteen. In 1871 he left Ireland to find employment in Newcastle-upon-Tyne as a shorthand clerk in the office of the North Eastern Railway Company. His spare hours at Newcastle were given to political work among the Irish population —he became secretary of the Home Rule Association after a visit of Isaac Butt [q.v.]—and to literary studies, these last assisted by his prodigious memory. He could repeat Shakespeare almost by heart, and knew enough French and German to be able to enjoy these literatures. Years later, during a spell in prison, he memorized the Bible. In 1878, after removing to London and becoming confidential clerk in a large floor-cloth factory, he began to frequent the lobby of the House of Commons, as the contributor at a guinea a week of a weekly parliamentary letter to the *Nation*, owned and edited by another Bantry man, Timothy Daniel Sullivan, who had married his aunt, his father's sister. He thus came into contact with the young members of the Parnellite party whom he astonished by his cleverness and accomplishments. In the *Nation* he 'wrote up Parnell and obstruction week after week with that bright, fiery, corrosive wit which we now all know; and the *Nation* newspaper was Parnell's first organ, and Tim Healy his first spokesman in the press' [T. P. O'Connor (q.v.), *Charles Stewart Parnell*]. Early in 1880 Parnell, when in America on an Irish mission, remembering what he had heard of Healy's secretarial abilities, cabled for the latter to come out and organize the Canadian end of the tour. In reference to this collaboration T. P. O'Connor [*ibid.*] says, 'If ever a man served another faithfully, Tim Healy was the faithful servant of Parnell.' That Parnell recognized Healy's ability there is no doubt; later he said that Healy had the only political head among his followers. As to Healy's early attitude towards the inscrutable leader against whom he afterwards turned so fiercely, it was one of mingled reverence, doubt, and affection. While in Canada he described Parnell as O'Connell's successor, 'the uncrowned King of Ireland'; yet in a letter of 1879 to his brother Maurice he had written of

the insecurity which he felt as regards Parnell's qualities of head and heart. Parnell, it has been generally considered by those who had the opportunity of observation, rather markedly failed to respond to the affectionate side of Healy's disposition. He never admitted him even to the limited intimacy which he extended to William O'Brien [q.v.] and a few of his colleagues.

After the general election of 1880 Gladstone, the new premier, found himself faced with the agrarian agitation which the Parnellites had sponsored. Healy threw himself heartily into this movement in the course of which he was arrested on a charge of intimidation. His arrest was immediately followed by his nomination for the borough of Wexford, where a vacancy had occurred, and he was returned without opposition. He was then tried by jury in Dublin under one of the acts in the ferocious Whiteboy code, but acquitted. On taking his seat in parliament he was at first ill at ease. The press reporters mocked at his brogue and even at the cut of his clothes. He responded to mockery by an almost superhuman diligence in acquainting himself with the weaknesses of parliamentary procedure and exploiting these to the profit of the policy of obstruction. Ministers had no more embarrassing questioner, for Healy was at pains to acquaint himself with details of every obscure scandal of public administration in the United Kingdom. His constructive ability first showed itself during the debates on the highly complicated Land Act of 1881. He was one of a half a dozen members, Irish or English, who could grasp the measure in its intricacies, and, indeed, the discussion of the measure was mainly carried on by him and two of Gladstone's law officers. His greatest triumph was the adoption of the 'Healy clause' which provided that no rent should in future be chargeable on tenants' improvements, and it is said to have been accepted by Hugh Law [q.v.], the Irish attorney-general, in a moment of absence of mind. 'I have added millions to the pockets of the tenants', Healy whispered to the nationalist member by his side.

Although the Land Act of 1881 represented a substantial victory for the tenants, agrarian agitation continued and was met by stringent measures of coercion and by the imprisonment without trial of hundreds of Land Leaguers. Healy himself was imprisoned in 1883 for six months.

When matters between the government and the Parnellites were about at their worst, a vacancy occurred in county Monaghan, and the author of the 'Healy clause' was put up as Parnellite candidate in order to attract the support of the Protestant farmers who had hitherto voted for the liberals. After an exciting struggle in which he had Parnell's personal support, he was returned at the head of the poll against a liberal and an Orangeman. At the general election of 1885 he made an even deeper incursion into Ulster, and succeeded in winning the seat in South Londonderry, which he held until the next year. He had been called to the Irish bar (King's Inns, Dublin) in 1884 (eventually taking silk in 1899) and was doing a fair business in the new land courts. His gain in self-assurance was accompanied by a growing distrust of Parnell, of whose entanglement with Mrs. O'Shea he was undoubtedly aware. Parnell, Healy felt, had as a consequence lost his fighting zest and grasp on strategy. It was never suggested by Healy's worst enemies that he himself intrigued for the leadership; and in his attitude towards Parnell's private fault he had more human understanding, and was more of a man of the world than has been supposed by some of his critics. The colleague in the party whom Healy most trusted and admired was the hunchback J. G. Biggar [q.v.], whose philanderings were indiscriminate and notorious. It was with Biggar that he travelled to Galway in February 1886 when he had his first open difference with Parnell. Parnell had proposed Captain O'Shea, not even a nominal home ruler, as member for Galway, and Biggar and Healy determined to oppose this irresponsible exercise of power. Both made speeches in favour of the popular candidate, Michael Lynch; but after Parnell's unexpected arrival in the town Healy succumbed to the old fascination, on Parnell's agreeing to find another seat for Lynch.

Healy stood in awe of but two men: Gladstone and Parnell—and of the two Gladstone after 1886 was in his political judgement the more important asset to the Irish cause. This helps to explain his volte-face in the crisis of Irish leadership which followed the divorce case of 1890. Healy at first supported Parnell's re-election to the chairmanship of the Irish party, saying 'we will teach these damned nonconformists to mind their own business'; but on the publication of Gladstone's refusal to co-operate further with the Irish leader he strongly, although with tears in his eyes, recommended Parnell's temporary retirement if satisfactory assurances regarding the coming home rule bill could be obtained from the British premier. 'My voice', he added, 'will be the first to call you back.' Parnell responded coldly by naming Gladstone the 'unrivalled sophist', and it was then that Healy flew at his throat. Healy asked if the Gladstone alliance was to perish 'in the stench of the Divorce Court', and in subsequent electoral struggles in Ireland he made frequent and very regrettable references to Mrs. O'Shea. It is to be remembered, as some excuse, that he regarded Mrs. O'Shea not merely as the 'woman in the case' but as a politician with an anti-Irish bias who had had a disastrous influence upon Parnell's public as well as private conduct. He was convinced (as appears in his autobiography, *Letters and Leaders of My Day*) that it was at Mrs. O'Shea's insistence that the retirement, suggested under stress of a sincere emotional regard for Parnell, was refused.

In 1892, when Parnell was dead, Healy, who had represented North Longford since 1887, captured North Louth for the anti-Parnellites. But he was a constant thorn in the flesh to the other anti-Parnellite leaders, John Dillon [q.v.] and T. P. O'Connor, whom he accused of subservience to English liberalism after the defeat of home rule and Gladstone's retirement. Eventually he was expelled from the National League in 1895; but it was found impossible to dislodge him from North Louth, where he was under the special protection of Cardinal Logue [q.v.] and the clericals, who rightly regarded him as the most able and resolute advocate at Westminster of Roman Catholic interests, educational and otherwise. He led a small political party of his own which had the financial support of William Martin Murphy, another self-made Bantry man and a captain of Irish industry. On the reunion of the nationalists in 1900 Healy supported the choice of John Redmond [q.v.] as chairman, but was a few months later shown the door of the league by William O'Brien and in 1902 was expelled from the party itself. During the chief secretaryship of George Wyndham [q.v.] he was on friendly personal relations with that minister, who was prepared, short of home rule, to come to terms with nationalist and Catholic sentiment. It was Healy's opinion that no British statesman would follow Gladstone in taking a serious risk for home rule, and the captious attitude of the Irish party, dominated by John Dillon's anti-tory prejudice, towards Wyndham's friendly gestures, appeared to him therefore to be a rejection of the substance for the shadow. Healy was now at the height of his powers, and his speeches, often as rich in pathos as in dexterity and wit, seldom failed to captivate the House. In 1910 he joined William O'Brien, his former foe, in the foundation of the 'All For Ireland' League, which had for its object the defence of Wyndham's Land Purchase Act and the promotion of the cause of Irish self-government by conciliation and consent among Irishmen rather than by parliamentary tactics. In the same year, after being defeated in North Louth, he found a seat in North-East Cork, an O'Brienite stronghold, and became a K.C. and was made a bencher of Gray's Inn. He appeared frequently in the English courts during the suffragette agitation as an advocate of the women prisoners, and in Ireland gave much of his time to working up the case of the Lough Neagh fishermen (see his *Stolen Waters, A Page in the Conquest of Ulster*, 1913, and *The Great Fraud of Ulster*, 1917). On the other hand, his conservatism showed forth when he acted for William Martin Murphy and the employers in the arbitration proceedings which followed the great Dublin strike of 1913.

During the situation created first by the Ulster revolt against H. H. Asquith's home rule bill of 1912, then by the war, and finally by the insurrection in 1916, Healy was unsparing in criticism of Redmond's management of national interests. After 1916 the Sinn Feiners were the rising power in Ireland, and although Healy differed from them in his view of the war, he fully shared their opinion of the inadequacy of the promises and performances of both the Asquith and coalition governments. His views were reflected in W. M. Murphy's *Irish Independent*, the most widely read newspaper in Ireland. In 1917 he made a speech in which he declared a general sympathy with Sinn Fein, not indeed in its aspect of a revival of the physical-force tradition, but as originally formulated by Arthur Griffith [q.v.], who had for twenty years advocated the abstention of Irish members from Westminster. At the general election of 1918 he took no part in what proved to be the death-struggle of the nationalist parliamentary movement, and resigned his seat

in Cork in favour of a Sinn Fein prisoner. In 1922 he was recommended, on the British side, by F. E. Smith, first Earl of Birkenhead [q.v.], a personal friend, and, on the Irish, by his wife's nephew and his own cousin, Kevin O'Higgins [q.v.], for the post of governor-general of the newly established Irish Free State. The appointment was resented by old Parnellites and brought some grist to the mill of the republican opponents of the settlement. Healy, no republican, accepted it with a good conscience and played the part of an Irish Talleyrand *au rebours* with good will if not with enthusiasm for the years (1922–1928) that he occupied the residence of former viceroys in Phoenix Park. He fulfilled his duties with a social tact which won respect especially from former Irish unionists. One characteristic utterance, showing the mood into which he had passed, may be recorded. At a public dinner in 1924 the poet W. B. Yeats [q.v.] had spoken with solemn eloquence about the condition of the world, and Healy, who followed, said, 'I think we should remind the bard of his own lovely lyric, "Down by the sally gardens my love and I did meet . . . She bid me take life easy".'

Three years after his retirement from the governor-generalship Healy died 26 March 1931 in the always brilliantly lighted villa which he had built for himself at Chapelizod, near Dublin. His wife, Erina, daughter of T. D. Sullivan and niece of A. M. Sullivan [q.v.], a first cousin, whom he had married in 1882, predeceased him in 1927; they had three sons and three daughters. His gifted younger brother Maurice, to whom he had been ever bound by the closest ties of political agreement as well as of fraternal affection, died in 1923. A portrait of Healy by Sir John Lavery is in the Dublin Municipal Gallery of Modern Art; another, by P. A. de László, belongs to Lord Devonport and a third, by Sir William Orpen, to Healy's daughter, Mrs. O'Sullivan.

[*The Times*, 27 March 1931; T. M. Healy, *Letters and Leaders of My Day*, 2 vols., 1928; D. P. Barton, *Timothy Healy: Memories and Anecdotes*, 1933; Joan Haslip, *Parnell*, 1936; St. John Ervine, *Parnell*, 1925; Barry O'Brien, *Life of Charles Stewart Parnell*, 1899; F. H. O'Donnell, *A History of the Irish Parliamentary Party*, 2 vols., 1910; William O'Brien, *An Olive Branch in Ireland*, 1910, and *Evening Memories*, 1920; T. P. O'Connor, *The Parnell Movement*, 1886, and *Charles Stewart Parnell*, 1892; private information; personal knowledge.]   JOSEPH HONE.

HEATH, SIR THOMAS LITTLE (1861–1940), civil servant and authority on ancient mathematics, was born 5 October 1861 at Barnetby-le-Wold, Lincolnshire, the third and youngest son of Samuel Heath, of Thornton Curtis, Ulceby, Lincolnshire, a farmer whose hobby was the classics, by his wife, Mary, daughter of Thomas Little, of Hibaldstowe in the same county. He was one of six children, all musically as well as intellectually gifted. After a period at Caistor Grammar School he went to Clifton, and thence, with a foundation scholarship, to Trinity College, Cambridge. He obtained a first class in both parts of the classical tripos (1881 and 1883); he was bracketed twelfth wrangler in 1882; and he was elected a fellow of Trinity in 1885 and an honorary fellow in 1920.

Heath passed first into the civil service in 1884, and entered the Treasury, where, after only three years' service, he became private secretary to Sir Reginald Earle (afterwards Lord) Welby [q.v.], then permanent secretary. From 1891 to 1894 he was private secretary to successive financial secretaries, and he became assistant secretary to the Treasury in 1907. In 1913 he was appointed permanent secretary, jointly with Sir John (afterwards Lord) Bradbury, and auditor of the civil list; Heath taking control of the administrative side of the Treasury, while the finance work fell to Bradbury. In 1919, however, when Bradbury retired from the civil service and the government decided to reorganize the Treasury on a much larger scale than before the war, Heath became comptroller-general and secretary to the commissioners for the reduction of the National Debt. His great knowledge of Irish land finance was valuable to the National Debt Office which dealt *inter alia* with this matter, for he had been intimately concerned with the financial details of the various Irish land bills which guaranteed loans to Irish farmers in order to enable them to purchase their holdings. He retired from the civil service in 1926. He was appointed C.B. in 1903, K.C.B. in 1909, and K.C.V.O. in 1916.

Heath was an excellent civil servant of the old type. He was quick, accurate, neat, painstaking, and thorough in all his written work, in which these qualities, together with his technical knowledge and his power of marshalling facts clearly and accurately for the decision of ministers, were of the greatest value. He was less at home in oral work and with the conference habit which grew to be an important method of transacting public business during and after the war.

After his retirement Heath, who had served as one of the Cambridge commissioners under the Universities of Oxford and Cambridge Act (1923), served from 1927 to 1929 on the royal commission on national museums and galleries. In 1927 he published an interesting and lucid monograph on *The Treasury*, in the 'Whitehall series', which contains a clear and accurate account of the British financial system.

It was, however, to his unofficial work on Greek mathematics that Heath owed his fellowship of the Royal Society (1912), on the council of which he served two terms; his presidency of the Mathematical Association (1922–1923); and his fellowship of the British Academy (1932). He was one of the select band of British public servants who have enriched scholarship by the judicious use of their scanty leisure. His training at Cambridge in classics and mathematics led him to take an interest in Greek mathematics, a subject explored by few at that time despite the unique place occupied by Euclid for generations in the education of English youth; and even Euclid was known only through imperfect versions of the simpler books of the *Elements*. Heath's labours in this field won for him the reputation of being one of the world's leading authorities on Greek mathematics; and he made accessible in a notation readily understood by all competent mathematicians the works of their leading Greek precursors.

Heath first gave his attention to Diophantus, whose *Arithmetica* had not previously been edited in England. His essay *Diophantus of Alexandria: a Study in the History of Greek Algebra*, published in 1885, was revised in 1910 so as to give not only a faithful rendering of the difficult Greek but a thorough history of Greek algebra; and he vindicated the high esteem in which the Alexandrian 'father of algebra' was held by Fermat and Euler. In 1896 he did a similar service for Apollonius of Perga, whose masterly treatise on the conic sections was a book sealed even for good Greek scholars by the prolixity of its rigid geometrical proofs. Heath successfully produced a work which was 'Apollonius and nothing but Apollonius', but which, thanks to skilful compression and the substitution of modern notation for literary proofs, occupied less than half the space of the original; it was prefaced by valuable essays on the previous history of conic sections among the Greeks. In 1897 Heath applied the same methods to an edition of the works of Archimedes; and a savant chiefly known through the picturesque stories of his leap from the bath and his death at the hands of a Roman soldier was recognized as one of the supreme mathematical geniuses of all time. The work was supplemented in 1912 by a translation of the *Method* of Archimedes, discovered a few years earlier by J. L. Heiberg. In the meantime Heath had turned his attention to Euclid, publishing in 1908 a monumental three-volume edition of the *Elements* in which he followed the same principles. In this edition the notable tenth book on irrational magnitudes was for the first time rendered into English in an intelligible form; and Heath justified against modern 'improvements' Euclid's rigidly logical choice of axioms and postulates and his order of proof. A second edition appeared in 1926. He hoped to be able to re-establish the teaching of Euclid in the schools, and to this end he produced in 1920 an edition of Book I of the *Elements* in Greek.

In 1913 Heath published with a translation and commentary the Greek text of the tract of Aristarchus of Samos *On the Sizes and Distances of the Sun and Moon*; he prefaced it with a thorough study of the history of Greek astronomy before Aristarchus, justifying the title of this author as the 'Copernicus of antiquity'. He wrote short popular works on Aristarchus and Archimedes in 1920.

In 1921 Heath crowned his separate studies with *A History of Greek Mathematics* in two volumes. Arranged partly according to chronology and partly according to subject-matter, it immediately became the standard work on the subject. Ten years later he condensed it into *A Manual of Greek Mathematics*, and in 1932 he published under the title *Greek Astronomy* a collection of translations covering the same ground as the prefatory matter of his Aristarchus. He also gave much help to the ninth edition of Liddell and Scott's *Greek Lexicon*, which had in earlier editions taken little notice of Greek mathematical terminology. At his death he was engaged on an edition (published in 1948) of the mathematical content of Aristotle's works.

Heath was a keen mountaineer and had made ascents of most of the Dolomites; he was also an enthusiastic musician. He married in 1914 Ada Mary, daughter of

Major Edward Charles Thomas, of Wandsworth Common, and had a son and a daughter. Lady Heath, who survived him, was herself a musician of professional standing. He died at Merry Hall, Ashtead, Surrey, 16 March 1940.

[*The Times*, 18 March 1940; M. F. Headlam, *Sir Thomas Little Heath, 1861–1940* in *Proceedings* of the British Academy, vol. xxvi, 1940 (portrait); *Obituary Notices of Fellows of the Royal Society*, No. 9, January 1941; private information; personal knowledge.]

MAURICE HEADLAM.
IVOR THOMAS.

HENDERSON, ARTHUR (1863–1935), labour leader and statesman, was born in Glasgow 13 September 1863, the younger son of David Henderson, a Scottish cottonspinner, who died when Henderson was nine years old; his mother, a Scotswoman, moved, on re-marriage, to Newcastle-upon-Tyne. He left school at the age of twelve and was apprenticed at the Robert Stephenson locomotive and foundry works, where he learned to be 'a good, clean moulder'. There, too, interest in politics awoke; during the dinner-hour he read the daily newspaper aloud to his fellow workers. At the age of eighteen, as a fully trained journeyman, he joined the Ironfounders Union and, before long, was unpaid secretary of the Newcastle lodge. This, even in the north-east, made him a marked man, as he realized during several spells of unemployment at Stephensons'. From the first, Henderson won and held the confidence of those with whom he worked; in 1892 he was elected district delegate for the area covering Northumberland, Durham, and Lancashire. In this capacity he succeeded in 1894 in getting effective conciliation machinery set up; he acted as secretary of the north-east coast conciliation board and later (1908) was chairman. As a member of the Newcastle city council, to which he was elected in 1892, he acquired a mastery of local government and the committee method. A fervent admirer of Gladstone, his first notable speech was in support of John Morley, and from 1895 to 1903, he acted as agent to Sir J. W. Pease [q.v.], radical member for the Barnard Castle division of Durham. As an active trade unionist, however, Henderson shared the new currents of opinion drawing many intelligent workmen away from liberalism towards a party of their own; he attended as a visitor in 1899 the historic London conference of socialists and trade unionists which set up the labour representation committee (1900). In 1903 he became its treasurer and was nominated by his union as independent labour candidate for Barnard Castle, and at a by-election in the same year he won the seat. Re-elected in 1906 he moved to Clapham, which was thenceforward his home.

On the labour representation committee Henderson worked in close association with James Keir Hardie [q.v.] and with James Ramsay MacDonald [q.v.], seeing in the latter the predestined leader of the new labour party. He presided over the 1906 conference which finally established the party, and in 1911 succeeded MacDonald as secretary, holding this arduous post until 1934. It was due to Henderson that the party held together, despite deep division, when war broke out in 1914. Like the majority of labour members, he threw himself whole heartedly into the war effort; when MacDonald on 4 August resigned his leadership in the House, Henderson replaced him. He was sworn of the Privy Council in January 1915 in recognition of his services to man-power, and he entered H. H. Asquith's Cabinet in May nominally as president of the Board of Education and later (1916) as paymaster-general, but his main work was as adviser on matters of labour, and this induced Lloyd George to include him in his original War Cabinet of five, without portfolio (December 1916). Resentment against the working of the Munitions Acts vented itself in vigorous criticism of Henderson at party conferences, but he held his own and told his opponents with typical directness: 'I am not here either to please myself or you; I am here to see the war through.' In 1917, after the first Russian revolution, he went on an official mission to Russia. Convinced that, if Russia was to be kept in the war, the British government should send delegates to the conference of international socialists proposed to be held at Stockholm, he commended this course not only to the Cabinet but to a special labour conference, an action which led to a breach with Lloyd George and resignation from the Cabinet in August. He subsequently refused to accept the C.H. at the hands of the premier, but his sense of public duty caused him in 1919 to act as chairman of the workers' side of the National Industrial Conference; its unanimous report in favour of a legal maximum working week of forty-eight hours, with minimum-time rates of wages, was largely due to his patient skill.

The Stockholm Conference marks a turning-point in Henderson's career. From this time onwards his outlook was to be predominantly internationalist. In close association with MacDonald and Sidney Webb, a democratic peace policy was worked out for labour. Whereas continental parties, split on the war, were further divided by the appeal of communism, as represented by Moscow, the British labour party remained united, and Henderson steadily converted it to the League of Nations. At the same time he set himself the task of strengthening the organization of the party and broadening its basis. A new constitution in 1918 specifically opened the party's ranks to 'workers by hand and by brain'. The structure remained federal, as an association of trade unions and socialist societies; but through the establishment of local labour parties which individuals could join from conviction, the purpose was accomplished which he had foreshadowed in 1904 in the words: 'What we want is to get away as far as possible from mere trade representation. We want labour representation in the proper sense of the term.' At the same time, Henderson strengthened the central machine, and brought in a wide range of experts to serve on advisory committees. It was largely owing to his thorough and sustained work that the vote cast for labour in the election of 1923 gave MacDonald the opportunity of forming a minority government.

Meanwhile Henderson's electoral career had been curiously chequered. In December 1918 he was defeated at East Ham (S.). In August 1919 he had been elected for Widnes, which rejected him in the general election of November 1922. In January 1923 at a by-election at East Newcastle he gained the seat, only to lose it at the general election at the end of that year, and it was not until February 1924 that a by-election at Burnley enabled him to take his seat in MacDonald's administration. Although home secretary, Henderson was mainly occupied in the international field; he played a large part in the London conference called to implement the Dawes plan in 1924, and at Geneva contributed notably to the working out of the protocol for the arbitral settlement of international disputes, acquiring thereby a thorough knowledge of the Covenant and of the League in all its aspects. The election of December 1924 severely reduced the number of labour members in the House of Commons; with great self-sacrifice, Henderson took on again (1925-

1927) the thankless task of chief whip, which he had held in 1914 and from 1921 to 1923, as well as that of re-constituting both the machinery and the confidence of the party. The statement of aims known as *Labour and the Nation* (1928), for the preparation of which he was responsible, helped in no small measure to make possible the second labour government of 1929.

By now Henderson was well prepared for the office of secretary of state for foreign affairs by his chairmanship of the Labour and Socialist International at Hamburg in 1923, and by constant other visits to the continent and to the various parts of the British Commonwealth. Although his tenure of the office of foreign secretary was brief, he succeeded, in the judgement of very many, in restoring the moral prestige of Great Britain and establishing her leadership in the effort to lay secure foundations for international peace. He chose his subordinates with skill and pursued a line of action as firm as it was clear. The House of Commons and the country recognized a strong hand at the helm, directed by experience and purpose. Courage marked his first public act when he forced the resignation in July of Lord Lloyd, high commissioner in Egypt, as part of a determined effort to reach an agreement which should lead on to the independence actually achieved in 1936. Further, for the first time since 1917, a British ambassador was sent to Russia (November). The major problem was, however, Franco-German relationships; Henderson saved The Hague conference of August 1929 from disaster and at Geneva, a month later, took an important step in the struggle for security by affixing a British signature to the Optional clause, an action supported later by the Dominions, with the representatives of which he established warm concord. On terms of personal friendship with both Briand and Stresemann, his impartiality was conspicuous in his handling of the Austrian issue in 1929, and the Silesian plebiscite in 1931. By 1930 he could state that Great Britain was ready to sign the General Act of Arbitration, and move on to the disarmament on which his heart was set. He believed in the League; he made it work. Sympathizing with the anxieties of France, he yet saw small hope of peace unless the pledge of article viii of the Covenant was honoured by all. To this end he strove with his whole energy; when, at last, 2 February 1932 was set as the date for the meeting of a world con-

ference on disarmament, he was, on the motion of Briand, unanimously nominated (May 1931) to preside over it.

The hopes thus raised were shattered by the financial crisis of the late summer of 1931. Henderson had, at no time, let his Foreign Office work absorb him; the House of Commons was never neglected; he was the most accessible of ministers, in constant friendly touch with the rank and file of members, whose concern with mounting unemployment at home and abroad he fully shared. He was one of the Cabinet sub-committee of five set up to examine the alarming financial diagnosis of the Economy Committee set up under the chairmanship of Sir George (later Lord) May. When the situation developed to the point at which drastic cuts in unemployment benefit were demanded in order to meet an anticipated budget deficit and safeguard the gold standard, Henderson was faced with a grim choice between long-standing loyalty to MacDonald and the principles of a lifetime. With a majority of his colleagues he held that the crisis was not being met in the right way; and when MacDonald, after tendering the resignation of the Cabinet as a whole, formed next day (24 August) a 'national government', the shock, as a colleague put it at the time, made Henderson suddenly an old man. Chosen by the labour party to lead it in opposition, he faced with fortitude a personal situation of acute pain in the harsh severance of long association. In the subsequent general election he was defeated, but in September 1933 he returned to parliament at a by-election as member for the Clay Cross division of Derbyshire. Although the crisis had caused him both distress and illness, he did not flinch from the superhuman task of presiding over the world disarmament conference. The greater the danger to world peace (and he saw it already as very great) the clearer the obligation to proceed with the work. From 1932 therefore until the summer of 1935 he remained at his post at Geneva. By the end of that summer an operation, long delayed, was performed and on 20 October 1935 he died in London.

So there closed a career which brought Henderson from the humblest beginnings to a commanding position in national and European affairs. Tall, massively built, fair skinned and fair haired, with keen-sighted three-cornered blue eyes, Henderson, in spite of his Scottish parentage, struck men of other lands as a typical Englishman. Those who did not penetrate below the surface thought him stolid; not so those who came to know the slow strength of his mind, the firm courage of his will, and the warm kindness of his nature, which won him the universal nickname of 'Uncle Arthur'. Wholly disinterested, he devoted his life to the ideas in which he believed. Indeed his character, which was as strong as a rock, owed much to his religion. His elder brother once said: 'for Arthur, life began with his conversion': in these words lies the key to an influence which puzzled the superficial. At sixteen he accepted fully the Wesleyan creed; its discipline of faithful co-operation and service coloured his whole life. As a Wesleyan lay preacher he learned to speak: from religious conviction came the anchored certainty which carried him through every disappointment and sustained both his trade union work, his patient building of a party, and his mastery of the complex problems which faced him as foreign secretary.

Henderson married in 1888 Eleanor, daughter of William Watson, of Newcastle and afterwards of Rotherfield, Sussex, a fellow member of his chapel. His home life was happy and the family—three sons and one daughter—singularly united. His eldest son was killed in action in 1916; the other children survived him, and it was a deep satisfaction to him that his two younger sons chose to follow in his political footsteps. Of the many distinctions showered upon him by public bodies at home and abroad, the most precious was the Nobel Peace prize, awarded in 1934.

[*The Times*, 21 October 1935; M. A. Hamilton, *Arthur Henderson*, 1938; personal knowledge.]   MARY AGNES HAMILTON.

HENDERSON, SIR REGINALD GUY HANNAM (1881–1939), admiral, was born at Mylor, near Falmouth, 1 September 1881, the second son of Commander John Hannam Henderson, R.N., of the Red House, Tenby, by his wife, Elizabeth, adopted daughter and niece of Henry May, of Honolulu. Of Scottish ancestry, he was a descendant of Andrew Henderson (*fl.* 1734–1775, q.v.) whose son John was secretary to Alexander Hood, Viscount Bridport [q.v.]. The family had settled in east Kent. Its strong naval ties are typified by Henderson's three admiral uncles of whom Sir William Hannam Henderson was founder and editor of the *Naval Review* (1913–1931), and Sir Reginald Friend Hannam Henderson devised the detailed scheme for the Royal Australian Navy.

Henderson entered the navy through the *Britannia* and in 1897 joined the *Mars* in the Channel Squadron under his uncle Reginald. In March following he was transferred to the *Hermione*, under Captain (Sir) G. A. Callaghan [q.v.], until promoted sub-lieutenant in November 1900. Having obtained first class certificates in all courses he was promoted lieutenant in May 1902 and served in the *Venerable*, flagship, in the Mediterranean until his appointment in 1903 to the gunnery school. He qualified as a gunnery expert in April 1905, and remained on the school staff until January 1906. He then served as gunnery officer in the *Euryalus*, flagship, on the North America and West Indies station and in the battleship *Britannia*, in the Channel Fleet, in 1910, rejoining as senior staff officer the gunnery school where he remained until his promotion as commander in June 1913; he was then specially selected to accompany Admiral Mark Kerr's naval mission to Greece where he was employed in instructing the Greek navy in modern gunnery.

On the outbreak of war in 1914 Henderson was sent to the *Erin* and served in her at Jutland. As one of the most brilliant of the younger officers, he was brought by Jellicoe to the Admiralty in 1916 and placed in the anti-submarine division, where he worked out a trial convoy plan for the protection of colliers sailing to France. Its success led to the general adoption of the convoy system, when the entry of the United States of America into the war provided the necessary destroyers. His imagination and enterprise at this time earned him special promotion to captain in October 1917, and he remained on the war staff as naval assistant to the assistant chief, Admiral Sir A. L. Duff [q.v.], until 1919. On appointment to the China command, Duff took Henderson as flag captain in the *Hawkins* for two years, and then, after a period (1923–1925) at the Royal Naval College, Henderson commanded the aircraft carrier *Furious* (1926–1928) and was promoted to flag rank in March 1929. His only flag command was as rear-admiral, aircraft carriers (1931–1933), flag in the *Courageous*, and there he did much to advance the development of the Fleet Air Arm, especially in the tactical use of carriers acting together.

In April 1934 Henderson (a vice-admiral since September 1933) was selected to join the Admiralty as third sea lord and controller. The Cabinet having at last awakened to the growing defencelessness of the country, agreed in 1935 to an increase in armaments, and this moment was an excellent opportunity to a man of Henderson's great administrative ability, infectious energy, and openness of mind. He took up his new post with buoyant enthusiasm, and during the two years before construction of battleships became possible in 1937 (under the Washington and London treaties), he was preparing, as controller, new designs for all classes of ships and providing for facilities for their construction and equipment. The great expansion projected after 1935 proved to be beyond the resources of the armament firms in Great Britain. Personal visits secured substantial supplies from Vitkovice in Czechoslovakia and also from other sources for armour-plates. In construction he showed the same advance, and under him were designed the *Illustrious* class of aircraft carrier with an armoured flight-deck, the J-class destroyers with only two boilers, and the all-welded minesweeper. His monument is the memory of a fleet ready for action when war broke out, but he did not live to see the result of his labours. He was promoted admiral in January 1939 and in March his strong physique broke down under the strain and he was forced to resign. He died in Haslar Hospital, Portsmouth, 2 May 1939.

Henderson was appointed C.B. in 1919 and K.C.B. in 1936, and specially promoted to G.C.B. by the King in 1939. He married in 1911 Islay, daughter of Rhoderick McNeil Campbell, of the Campbells of Dunstaffnage, and had two sons.

[Admiralty records; private information.]
VINCENT W. BADDELEY.

HENRY, SIR EDWARD RICHARD baronet of Campden House Court (1850–1931), commissioner of metropolitan police, was born at Shadwell, Middlesex, 26 July 1850, the only surviving son of Alexander Henry, M.D., of Lagaturn, co. Mayo, by his wife, Maria McDonnell. He was educated at St. Edmund's College, Ware, and at University College, London, whence he passed by examination into the Indian civil service, being posted as assistant magistrate-collector in Bengal, and rising through successive stages to be in 1890 secretary to the Board of Revenue.

It was Henry's appointment in 1891 as inspector-general of police in Bengal that proved to be the turning-point of his career, for it enabled him to begin that study of the use of finger-prints in the detection of crime which made his tenure of the commissionership of metropolitan police epoch-making. In the East, finger-prints had long been regarded as incontrovertible signatures to documents, and the publication by (Sir) Francis Galton [q.v.] of his work on *Finger Prints* (1892) had attracted much attention to this study, so that Henry, even before he had been seconded in 1900 from India for organizing the civil police of Pretoria and Johannesburg, had made an extremely valuable contribution to the solution of the most intractable problem of this study, namely, the method of classification of finger-prints, by evolving a system of his own. This had been adopted by the government of India in 1897 and he gave it to the world in *Classification and Uses of Finger Prints* (1900, printed by order of the government of India). In 1899 Henry gave evidence before a committee on the identification of criminals which decided on the adoption of his system in Great Britain, and the results proved extremely satisfactory, both in the reduction of the already small margin of error, and, much more so, in the astonishing rapidity with which the finger-prints could be classified. In the first year of the establishment of the Central Fingerprint Bureau, four times as many old criminals were identified as in previous years, and Henry's system has, with modifications, been adopted in most countries. Two outstanding cases, the Deptford (or 'Masked') murder in 1905 and a burglary in 1909, revealed the new system to the public which gave it its confidence, and finger-prints became an indispensable feature of modern detective stories.

In 1901 Henry resigned from the Indian civil service and was appointed assistant commissioner of the metropolitan police in charge of the Criminal Investigation Department. Two years later he succeeded Sir E. R. C. Bradford [q.v.] as commissioner. It was a period of no small anxiety. Trade depression encouraged processions of the unemployed; allegations of misconduct against the police were so rife that in 1906 a royal commission of inquiry into the police force was appointed. When it reported in 1908, Henry was proud to be able to say that practically every specific case of misconduct alleged was proved to be unfounded.

Henry had to deal with a situation marked by growing disorder in the public. In 1908 there was grave threat of a religious riot over the proposal that the Host should be carried round Ashley Gardens at the Eucharistic Congress of that year. This made Henry's personal position as a Roman Catholic difficult; but a far more lasting anxiety was caused by the agitation of the suffragists and the destructive violence of the suffragettes. However, neither movement was responsible for the bullet wound inflicted on Henry in 1912 by a crack-brained man whose application for a cab-driver's licence had been refused at Scotland Yard owing to inability to pass the tests. Henry's generous plea for mercy secured that a sentence of fifteen years' penal servitude was passed instead of one for life. Although he apparently recovered from the wound, it took its toll, and even before the outbreak of war in 1914 he had asked to be relieved of his post. But he was too valuable a servant to lose at such a moment, for his influence in the force was very great, as the men realized that he was making determined efforts to bring about better conditions, especially in respect of housing and single men's quarters; yet even he could not prevent the growth of discontent over the rate of pay, or ease the burden carried by the force with its numbers depleted by recruitment into the fighting services. At length, in August 1918, a strike broke out; Lloyd George intervened in favour of the men; the home secretary, Sir George (later Viscount) Cave [q.v.] and Henry both offered to resign; Henry's offer was accepted, and he was created a baronet.

This incident, in which Henry had no opportunity of making an open defence, brought his public career to an end. He spent his remaining years in active interest in local affairs as a Justice of the Peace of Berkshire, and he was a director of several companies. In 1890 he married Louisa Langrishe, daughter of the Rev. John Lewis Moore, vice-provost of Trinity College, Dublin, and besides two daughters, had a son, who died nearly a year before his father, so that on Henry's death at Ascot 19 February 1931, the baronetcy became extinct. His honours included appointment as C.S.I. in 1898, C.V.O. in 1905, K.C.V.O. in 1906, K.C.B. in 1910, and in 1911, after attending the King and Queen to the Imperial Durbar at Delhi, G.C.V.O.

A cartoon of Henry by 'Spy' appeared in *Vanity Fair* 5 October 1905.

[*The Times*, 21 February 1931; E. R. Henry, *Classification and Uses of Finger Prints*, 4th ed. 1913; Sir Charles Mallet, *Lord Cave, a Memoir*, 1931; private information.]

HENSCHEL, SIR GEORGE (1850–1934), musician, was born at Breslau 18 February 1850, the only son of Moritz Jacob Henschel, of Breslau, by his second wife, Henriette, daughter of Joseph Frankenstein, of Landshut, Silesia. His parents were Jewish and of Polish descent. He was converted to Christianity when young, and he never used the first of his two original names Isidor Georg. He was educated at St. Magdalen College, Breslau, and at the Wandelt Institute there. At the age of twelve (1862) he appeared as a pianist in Berlin: he entered the Leipzig Conservatorium in 1867 and the royal conservatorium at Berlin in 1870, developing a fine baritone voice which led in 1874 to his first important engagement, in Cologne, and to his first appearance in England in 1877. He had already made a mark as a singer and composer sufficient to attract the attention of Brahms as a personal friend, and to earn an entry in the first edition of *Grove's Dictionary of Music and Musicians*. It is safe to say that no other musician appears as a 'live entry' in the first three editions (1879, 1913, and 1927).

From 1881 until 1884 Henschel was the first conductor of the Boston Symphony Orchestra; he was the founder, organizer, and first conductor of the London symphony concerts (1886–1897), and was the first conductor of the Scottish Orchestra, Glasgow (1893–1895). His marriage in 1881 to the talented American singer Lillian June, only daughter of Lucien Champlin Bailey, of Columbus, Ohio, opened up the long and successful series of duet recitals, in which Henschel was invariably accompanist as well as singer. This remarkable artistic partnership, which was highly valued all over Europe and the United States of America, was terminated in 1901 by the death of Lillian Henschel. From then until 1907 he lived in retirement in Scotland, but in 1909, two years after his second marriage, he entered upon a second career as a conductor and as a concert singer accompanying himself, which continued until his farewell concert in 1914. He returned to broadcast during the Schubert centenary celebrations of 1928, and inquiries were received from Cologne for 'the young artist' whose singing had been so acceptable. This was the man of seventy-eight who had first sung in Cologne fifty-four years previously. His last broadcast was given in 1934 in his eighty-fourth year.

In his span of fifty years of professional

life Henschel established himself in Europe and the United States as composer, conductor, singer, as well as accompanist, showing a natural gift for music in every variety of form which was unusual then, but which would be unparalleled in these days of specialization. That a singer should in the late 'eighties form an orchestra in London, train and conduct it, organize its concerts, and carry them on for eleven years was a most noteworthy feat of pioneering which created the praiseworthy tradition of good orchestral playing continued in London under Sir Henry Wood. But it was above all as a singer that Henschel's genius impressed itself on the public for nearly sixty years, and his earlier contemporaries valued him more as the unique singer that he was; while those who knew him only in the last twenty-five years of his life remember the inextinguishable vitality and excitement of his singing, the inevitable sweep of his rhythm, and the singular authority of his style in the classical *Lieder*.

Of Henschel's numerous compositions of all kinds two songs, 'Morning Hymn' and 'Young Dietrich', are still favourites, while the Requiem Mass written in memory of his first wife, and two Masses written for All Saints' church, Margaret Street, London, show him to be more than the mere fluent writer.

Henschel married secondly, in 1907, Amy, eldest daughter of Alexander Louis, of New York, and had one daughter. He was naturalized as a British subject in 1890, and died at Aviemore, Inverness-shire, 10 September 1934. He was knighted in 1914, and received the honorary degree of Mus. Doc. from the university of Edinburgh in 1910. His only child by his first marriage, Helen Henschel (Mrs. Harold Claughton), carried on her father's musical tradition as a singer playing her own accompaniments.

Three portraits of Henschel by Sir Lawrence Alma-Tadema, J. S. Sargent (1889), and P. A. de László are in the possession of Lady Henschel.

[Sir G. Henschel, *Musings and Memories of a Musician*, 1918; Helen Henschel, *When Soft Voices Die*, 1944; *Grove's Dictionary of Music and Musicians*, 4th ed., vol. ii, edited by H. C. Colles; private information; personal knowledge.]   Steuart Wilson.

HERFORD, CHARLES HAROLD (1853–1931), scholar and critic, was born at Manchester 18 February 1853, the eldest son of Charles James Herford, wine-merchant, of that city, by his wife, Mary Jane, daughter of J. G. Robberds [q.v.]. He was nephew of Brooke Herford and of William Henry Herford [qq.v.], and was educated at Castle Howell School, Lancaster, founded by the latter. From 1867 to 1869 he was a regular student at the Owens College, Manchester. After working six years at architecture, he went up to Trinity College, Cambridge, in 1875. He was bracketed eighth classic in 1879, in which year he also obtained a second class in the moral sciences tripos: he won the Members' (1879), the Harness, and the Le Bas (1880), and the Hare (1881) essay prizes. He was professor of English language and literature at University College, Aberystwyth, from 1887 to 1901, and was first holder of the independent chair of English literature at Manchester University from 1901 until his retirement in 1921. In 1900 he was Percy Turnbull lecturer at Johns Hopkins University, Baltimore. He acted as literary critic of the *Manchester Guardian* until his death.

Herford's most notable works are a model edition of Spenser's *The Shepheards Calender* (1895); *The Age of Wordsworth* (1897); the 'Eversley' edition of Shakespeare (10 vols., 1899); and the life and critical studies which he contributed to the Oxford edition of Ben Jonson (vols. i and ii, 1925). He edited the 'Warwick' Shakespeare, contributing to it *Richard II* (1893), *Othello* (1920), and *The Winter's Tale* (1926). *Shakespeare's Treatment of Love and Marriage* (1921), *A Sketch of Recent Shakespearean Investigation, 1893–1923* (1923), and *A Sketch of the History of Shakespeare's Influence on the Continent* (1925) rounded off these larger studies. He wrote handbooks on *Browning* (1905), *Wordsworth* (1930), and the chapters on Keats and Shelley in the *Cambridge History of English Literature*, vol. xii. He edited *The Two Noble Kinsmen* (1897), *English Tales in Verse* (1902), Sir Thomas Browne's *Religio Medici, and other Writings* (1906), Lord Herbert of Cherbury's *Autobiography* (1928), and Southey's *Journal of a Tour in Scotland in 1819* (1929), and he revised and edited with a prefatory memoir Julia Wedgwood's *Life of Josiah Wedgwood* (1915).

Herford widened his range to embrace the literature of Germany, Italy, Norway, and Russia. His first book, *Studies in the Literary Relations of England and Germany in the Sixteenth Century* (1886), broke new ground. *The Influence of Goethe's Italian Journey on his Style* (1900) was the

Taylorian lecture delivered at Oxford in 1897. He helped to found the English Goethe Society (1885–1886) and gave a presidential address on *Goethe and Wordsworth* (1926). He championed the Ibsen movement with verse translations of *Brand* (1894) and *Love's Comedy* (1900). He wrote essays on Pushkin, *A Russian Shakespearean* (1925), and 'The Culture of Bolshevist Russia' (*The Post-War Mind of Germany and other European Studies*, 1927), and on *Gabriele d'Annunzio* (1920) and *Dante and Milton* (1924).

Herford was the most accomplished English scholar of his age. A humanist of the older type, he concentrated on the ideas and the characters of the men behind the books. His attitude is seen in such essays as *The Permanent Power of English Poetry* (1902), *Is there a Poetic View of the World?* (1916), 'National and International Ideals in the English Poets' (*Bulletin* of the John Rylands Library, 1916), *The Poetry of Lucretius* (1918), *William Blake* (1928). He contributed to this DICTIONARY lives of Ben Jonson, Thomas Middleton, Laurence Minot, and Hensleigh Wedgwood. He wrote memoirs of his uncle William Herford (1911), J. Estlin Carpenter (1929), and a full life of P. H. Wicksteed (1931).

Herford died 25 April 1931 at Oxford, where he had lived since 1927. He married in 1888 Marie (died 1930), daughter of Hermann Betge, chief postmaster of Bremen, and had one son, who was killed in the war of 1914–1918, and one daughter. He was elected a fellow of the British Academy in 1926, and received honorary degrees from the universities of Manchester (1899), Wales (1921), and Innsbrück, this last conferred in absence to recognize *The Case of German South Tyrol against Italy* (1927). A portrait by T. C. Dugdale belongs to Manchester University.

[*The Times*, 27 April 1931; *Manchester Guardian*, 29 October 1927 and 27 April 1931; J. G. Robertson, *Charles Harold Herford, 1853–1931* in *Proceedings* of the British Academy, vol. xvii, 1931; P. Simpson in the Oxford *Ben Jonson*, vol. iv, 1932; private information; personal knowledge.]

PERCY SIMPSON.

HERRINGHAM, SIR WILMOT PARKER (1855–1936), physician, was born at Guildford 17 April 1855, the elder son of William Walton Herringham, of Old Cleve, Somerset, then curate of St. Nicholas's church, Guildford, and later prebendary of Wells Cathedral, by his wife, Matilda Anne, youngest daughter of

Colonel John Boteler Parker, commandant, Woolwich. He was educated at Winchester and at Keble College, Oxford, where he was an exhibitioner and obtained a second class in classical moderations (1875) and in *literae humaniores* (1877). In 1931 he was elected an honorary fellow of his college.

After leaving Oxford, Herringham was for a few months a student of Lincoln's Inn, but gave up law for medicine when he entered St. Bartholomew's Hospital medical school in October 1877. He qualified M.R.C.S. in 1881, B.M. (Oxon.), and M.R.C.P. in 1882, and graduated D.M. (Oxon.) in 1888. He was elected F.R.C.P. in 1889. At St. Bartholomew's he was Kirkes gold medallist and house-surgeon to (Sir) Thomas Smith [q.v.], and medical registrar and demonstrator of anatomy in 1883. Herringham was not appointed to the staff as assistant physician until 1895. He was physician from 1904 to 1919. He was also physician to the West London Hospital (1883–1893) and to the Paddington Green Children's Hospital (1888–1900), and then consulting physician. After qualification he was in private practice until the war of 1914–1918.

In 1886 Herringham contributed to the *Proceedings* of the Royal Society (vol. xli) a paper entitled 'The Minute Anatomy of the Brachial Plexus' which was referred to with appreciation when in 1930 he received the second quinquennial award of the Osler bronze medal. In 1883 he succeeded F. H. H. A. Mahomed [q.v.] of Guy's Hospital as honorary secretary of the British Medical Association's organization for the collective investigation of disease, and in 1884 brought out the second volume of the reports containing the analysis of the collected cases of acute pneumonia. In 1894 he published with (Sir) Archibald Garrod [q.v.] and W. J. Gow *A Handbook of Medical Pathology, for the Use of Students in the Museum of St. Bartholomew's Hospital.*

Herringham's special interest was in diseases of the kidney, and he published many papers on this subject in the *Saint Bartholomew's Hospital Reports* and medical journals. In 1912 he wrote a monograph on diseases of the kidney which included chapters on renal disease in pregnancy by his colleague Herbert Williamson. At an informal meeting in May 1906, at Herringham's house, (Sir) William Osler [q.v.] suggested the formation of an Association of Physicians of Great Britain and Ireland. This association was formed a year later and Herringham agreed to act as its honorary general secretary. The other and related project which was discussed at this meeting, attended by Garrod and (Sir) J. Rose Bradford [q.v.] as well as by Osler, was the founding of the *Quarterly Journal of Medicine*, which is still the official journal of the Association of Physicians. Herringham was also active in the chief medical societies in London which became amalgamated into the Royal Society of Medicine in 1907. In 1929 he delivered the Harveian oration before the Royal College of Physicians without notes, a *tour de force*. This was published in the *Lancet* (1929, vol. ii), under the title of 'Circumstances in the Life and Times of William Harvey'; an extended version of this was printed in the *Annals of Medical History* (vol. iv, 1932), in which Herringham described his discovery of a hitherto unknown portrait of Harvey. He was vice-chancellor of the university of London from 1912 to 1915, and was knighted in 1914 for his services as honorary general secretary to the International Medical Congress held in 1913.

At the outbreak of the war of 1914–1918 Herringham was lieutenant-colonel in command of the medical unit of the London University Officers Training Corps. As temporary colonel, Army Medical Service, he went to France as consulting physician to the forces overseas and attended Lord Roberts in his last illness. He became attached to general headquarters, was made surgeon-general in 1917, and promoted major-general in 1918. He was appointed C.B. (mil.) in 1915, and K.C.M.G. in 1919. His book *A Physician in France* (1919) made a wide public aware of the part played by the medical services in an army at war. He was one of the four sectional editors of the *History of the Great War based on Official Documents. Medical Services* (1922–1924).

In 1918 Herringham unsuccessfully contested the London University seat as an independent. When he resigned his post as physician to St. Bartholomew's Hospital in 1919 he became chairman of the reconstruction committee of the hospital, which was responsible for the creation of the posts of directors (subsequently professors) of medicine and surgery in the hospital. After Osler's death in the same year Herringham was offered in the following year (1920) the regius chair of medicine at Oxford in succession to Osler, but he declined as he felt that he was unsuited for the position. He was chairman of the General Nursing Council for England and Wales (1922–1926) and of the governors of the Old Vic (1921–1929). He was also chairman of the council of Bedford College for Women. In 1909 he was made an honorary M.D. of Trinity College, Dublin.

Herringham married in 1880 Christiana Jane (died 1929), eldest daughter of Thomas Wilde Powell, stockbroker, of Piccard's Rough, Guildford; she was an accomplished artist in tempera and water-colour, who translated the *Book of the Art of Cennino Cennini* (1899). They had two sons, the elder of whom died in childhood, and the younger was killed at Messines in 1914. He died at Lymington, Hampshire, 23 April 1936.

Herringham was a classical scholar and spoke French and Italian well. With his pointed beard and deep voice he was a formidable personality who made his mark on medicine principally as an organizer, administrator, and teacher.

A portrait of Herringham by Sir William Rothenstein (1935) hangs in Keble College, Oxford.

[*British Medical Journal*, 1936, vol. i, p. 915 (portrait) and p. 965; *Lancet*, 1936, vol. i, p. 1030 (portrait); *Saint Bartholomew's Hospital Reports*, vol. lxix, 1936 (bibliography and portrait).]   HUGH CLEGG.

HEWINS, WILLIAM ALBERT SAMUEL (1865–1931), political economist, historian, and politician, was born near Wolverhampton 11 May 1865, the second son of Samuel Hewins, a merchant in the iron trade, by his wife, Caroline Green, of Wednesfield. He was educated at Wolverhampton Grammar School, and obtained the Hatherton scholarship which enabled him to go to Pembroke College, Oxford, where he came under the influence of (Sir) C. H. Firth [q.v.]. Firth testified that the pupil soon outran the master in an understanding of the economic and social facts of the seventeenth century. He graduated with a first class in mathematical moderations (1885) and a second class in the final mathematical school (1887). On leaving Oxford he took a large part in university extension work. He lectured to working class audiences, mainly in the north of England, on trade unionism, factory legislation, and other economic and social questions. In 1895, at the invitation of Sidney Webb amongst others, he organized the London School of Economics, of which he was director until

1903, and saw it achieve much success. He was Tooke professor of economic science and statistics at King's College, London (1897–1903), a member of the senate of London University (1900–1903), and he held the chair of modern economic history at that university (1902–1903).

Unmoved by the knowledge that other leading political economists of the day regarded his views as reactionary, Hewins welcomed in 1903 the invitation of Joseph Chamberlain [q.v.] to become secretary of the Tariff Commission, a body of representative industrialists who set themselves to work out Chamberlain's policy of safeguarding British industry and encouraging imperial economic unity. He held this post until 1917 and was chairman from 1920 to 1922.

Noteworthy as were his qualities as an historian and a lecturer, Hewins found only a limited scope for them in political and parliamentary life. He fought three unsuccessful elections, at Shipley (1910) and twice at Middleton (1910 and 1911), before being returned at a by-election in March 1912 as conservative member for Hereford City which he represented until 1918. In parliament he became especially attached to Walter Long [q.v.] who was colonial secretary from 1916 to 1918, and from 1917 to 1919 Hewins took part in realizing a policy which had much in common with Chamberlain's ideas. In 1918 the Hereford City constituency was merged in the South Herefordshire division. Hewins was not invited to stand for the new division, and, despite three attempts (1922, 1923, and 1924) in the Swansea West constituency, he failed to be returned again to Westminster.

In 1914 Hewins was received into the Roman Catholic Church and became one of the principal advisers of Cardinal Bourne [q.v.] in anything political concerning Roman Catholicism. He contributed copiously to current periodicals on economic and Empire matters, and wrote many books, notable among them being *Imperialism and its Probable Effects on the Commercial Policy of the United Kingdom* (1901) and *The Apologia of an Imperialist* (1929).

Hewins married in 1892 Margaret, eldest daughter of James Slater, of Bescot Hall, Staffordshire, and had a son and two daughters. He died suddenly at his home in Chelsea 17 November 1931.

[*The Times*, 18 November 1931; W. A. S. Hewins, *The Apologia of an Imperialist*, 2 vols., 1929.]   PERCY HURD.

HICHENS, (WILLIAM) LIONEL (1874–1940), man of business, was born at St. Leonard's 1 May 1874, the younger and posthumous son of John Ley Hichens, of St. Ives, Cornwall, by his wife, Catherine Bacchus, of St. Leonard's. He was educated at Winchester and at New College, Oxford, where he graduated in *literae humaniores*. After some further study of languages in France and Germany, he became a master at Sherborne School, but abandoned that post in the 'black week' in December 1899 in order to volunteer for a cyclist section organized by the Inns of Court and attached to the City Imperial Volunteers. With that force he went out to South Africa, serving mainly as a dispatch-rider on missions of risk and trust, until the entry of Lord Roberts into Pretoria in June 1900, when he returned to England. A chance visit to Egypt in the same year brought him into contact with Lord Cromer [q.v.], who appointed him to a post in the Egyptian Ministry of Finance. In the following year he was invited to South Africa by Lord Milner [q.v.] who was forming his 'kindergarten' for reconstruction work in the conquered colonies. Hichens was appointed town treasurer of Johannesburg and a year later colonial treasurer of the Transvaal. He earned much credit in both posts, to which was subsequently added that of treasurer of the inter-colonial council of the Transvaal and Orange River Colony. He retired from South Africa in 1907 when responsible government was substituted for crown colony rule.

After a short period of unemployment broken by service as a member of the royal commission on decentralization in India in 1907 and then in 1909 as chairman of a board of inquiry into the public service of Southern Rhodesia, Hichens became in 1910 chairman of the great shipbuilding firm of Cammell Laird & company which was on the point of closing. To this and other cognate business activities he gave the rest of his life, rebuilding and completely rehabilitating the firm, of which he was still chairman at the time of his death thirty years later. As a captain of industry he made his mark very rapidly, serving as chairman of the Central Council of the Association of Controlled Firms which co-ordinated the production of munitions in the war of 1914–1918 and also on a government mission to Canada where he assisted in the formation of the Imperial Munitions Board. The regard which he won thus early for breadth of judgement, clear grasp of essentials, and capacity for handling men increased steadily throughout his career; and he was always particularly distinguished for his understanding of labour.

The rare combination of vision, sympathy, and practical capacity which Hichens possessed was signally displayed in the many contributions which he made to public discussion of industrial problems in the period of reconstruction after the war of 1914–1918. He was a good speaker with a simple but incisive style, and was as much at home with working-class audiences as with those drawn from his own side of industry. His Watt anniversary lecture on *Some Problems of Modern Industry* (1918) created a wide stir at the time of its delivery earlier in that year; and that was but the first of many illuminating discourses on the relations between the state and industry, operatives and managers, capital and labour. He is indeed to be remembered as one of the pioneers who gave national thought a new direction at that critical time, insisting, in opposition to the growing materialism of the age, that 'the industrial problem is primarily a moral one' and setting in the conduct of his own life and business a shining example of the Christian principles in which he believed.

Hichens married in 1919 Mary Hermione, youngest daughter of General Sir Neville Gerald Lyttelton [q.v.]. He had three sons, the eldest of whom was killed in action during the first days of the landing in Normandy in 1944, and three daughters. Hichens was himself killed by a bomb which fell on Church House, Westminster, 14 October 1940.

[*The Times*, 17 October 1940; *Round Table*, December 1940; personal knowledge.]

ALTRINCHAM.

HICKS, WILLIAM JOYNSON-, first VISCOUNT BRENTFORD (1865–1932), statesman, born in Canonbury 23 June 1865, was the eldest son of Henry Hicks, merchant, later of Plaistow Hall, Kent, by his wife, Harriett, daughter of William Watts, of Oadby, Leicestershire. He was educated at Merchant Taylors School from 1875 to 1881. In 1882 he was articled to a firm of London solicitors, and was admitted as a solicitor in 1887. Partly through the influence of his father, who for twenty-one years was a prominent member of the City common council, but mainly by his own industry and insistence on looking into things for himself, he

acquired a considerable practice. He foresaw the revolution which road motor traction, then becoming a commercial possibility, would bring about, and he collaborated with (Sir) Montague Barlow in publishing in 1906 *The Law of Heavy and Light Mechanical Traction on Highways in the United Kingdom*.

In 1894 Hicks made the acquaintance of Richard Hampson Joynson, of Bowdon, Cheshire, a Manchester silk-manufacturer, whose only child, Grace Lynn, he married in 1895. Next year Hicks added the surname of Joynson to his own. He and his father-in-law had strong interests in common, both being conservative in politics and evangelical in religion. Hicks assisted Joynson in philanthropic work in Manchester, where he became well known. In 1906, after unsuccessfully contesting North Manchester in 1900, he stood for the North-West division, but was heavily defeated by Mr. Winston Churchill. Two years later, however, at a by-election necessitated by Mr. Churchill's appointment as president of the Board of Trade, the result was reversed. It was during this contest that the nickname of 'Jix' was applied to him by one of his supporters, (Sir) Ian Malcolm.

Joynson-Hicks lost his seat in the general election of January 1910 and in December was defeated at Sunderland but was returned unopposed for Brentford at a by-election in March 1911. In 1918 he was returned for Twickenham, and held the seat until his elevation to the peerage in 1929.

When Joynson-Hicks re-entered parliament in 1911 he showed improvement as a legislator and debater. He made use of his legal and technical knowledge of motor road traffic, of aviation in its infancy, of the telephone, and kindred subjects. In October 1912 he called attention to the inadequacy of the military air service, and Colonel J. E. B. Seely (later Lord Mottistone), then secretary of state for war, subsequently admitted that his criticism had made a considerable contribution to the efficiency displayed by the Royal Flying Corps in the early days of the war of 1914–1918. During the war he became a prominent member of a group in parliament which was interested in aviation, and in 1916 he published *The Command of the Air*. In 1919 he was created a baronet. At this time it seemed possible that his career was ended. He had a good position in the House and a secure seat, but he had never held office and the power of an old antagonist, Lloyd George, seemed firmly established. In 1920 he visited India and the Sudan. While in India he went to Amritsar in order to make investigations into the shooting, and subsequently in the House defended the action of Brigadier R. E. H. Dyer [q.v.]. He also made a formidable attack upon the administration of the secretary of state, E. S. Montagu [q.v.], in February 1922.

Although not a member of the government, Joynson-Hicks had a considerable following of private members in the conservative party, and he certainly contributed to the overthrow of Lloyd George's administration in October 1922 by his exposure of its increasing disregard of principle. He was now in rapid succession to fill important posts in the government, each of which enhanced his reputation. Bonar Law at once offered him the post of parliamentary secretary to the Department of Overseas Trade. In March 1923 he was transferred to the office of postmaster and paymaster-general, and after Bonar Law's resignation in May, his successor, Baldwin, made Joynson-Hicks financial secretary to the Treasury with the unusual addition of a seat in the Cabinet, being then sworn of the Privy Council. Three months later he went to the Ministry of Health.

At the close of 1923 the conservative party went out of office, and on its return in 1924 Joynson-Hicks became home secretary. His five years' tenure was eventful. In May 1926 he had to deal with the General Strike: his success in doing so was largely achieved by intelligent anticipatory organization. For the police force he displayed singular devotion, and won its confidence in a remarkable degree. A year later he was responsible for the raid on Arcos Limited which resulted in the severance of diplomatic relations with Great Britain by the Soviet government, represented by that firm.

Throughout his life Joynson-Hicks took a great interest in religious matters. He was a member of the Church Assembly and in 1921 became president of the National Church League. He took a prominent part in parliament in defeating the Prayer Book measure of 1927, and when the amended Deposited Book came before the House of Commons in June 1928, Joynson-Hicks again opposed it in an impressive speech, and the bill was rejected by a larger majority. In May he had published *The Prayer-Book Crisis.*

During the last year of his term of office as home secretary Joynson-Hicks was largely concerned in passing the Shops Act of 1928 and the Summer Time Act of 1928. The former has been described as the shop-assistant's charter. He was also preparing a factories bill for the amelioration of the conditions of the workers. But the general election of 1929 placed the labour party in office, and Joynson-Hicks, who did not stand for parliament, was created Viscount Brentford, of Newick in Sussex. Five years at the Home Office with a working day of twelve or fifteen hours had seriously impaired his health. He died in London 8 June 1932. He had two sons and a daughter, and he was succeeded as second viscount by his elder son, Richard Cecil (born 1896).

A portrait of Joynson-Hicks by Sir Arthur Cope, which was presented to him by the constabulary of the whole country on his retirement from the Home Office, hangs in Scotland Yard.

[*The Times*, 9 June 1932; H. A. Taylor, *Jix Viscount Brentford*, 1933.]

E. I. CARLYLE.

HILL, SIR (EDWARD) MAURICE (1862–1934), judge, was born at Tottenham 8 January 1862, the eldest of the five sons of the Johnsonian scholar G. Birkbeck N. Hill [q.v.], by his wife, Annie, daughter of Edward Scott, of Beech Hill, Wigan. Maurice Hill's sisters married Sir William Ashley and Charles George Crump [qq.v.]. He spent much of his childhood at Bruce Castle, Tottenham, where his father was headmaster of a school in which modern theories of education had been developed by his family. From Haileybury he went as an exhibitioner to Balliol College, Oxford, and graduated with a first class in classical moderations (1881) and in *literae humaniores* (1884). In 1888 he was called to the bar by the Inner Temple, took silk in 1910, and was elected a bencher of his Inn in 1917.

At the bar Hill built up a solid practice in commercial law, and became a prominent expert in all legal problems concerned with maritime matters. Apart from his work at the bar, he was keenly interested in politics and social reform. He was devoted to the liberal cause and often spoke at political meetings, but he never stood for parliament.

In January 1917 Hill was appointed a judge of the Probate, Divorce, and Admiralty division of the High Court. Until May 1925 the division was manned by a president and one puisne judge. In

September 1918 the president, Sir Samuel Evans [q.v.], died. His successor, William Pickford, Lord Sterndale, was president for only one year and was then succeeded by H. E. Duke, Lord Merrivale [qq.v.]. The result of these changes, coupled with the fact that the president's time was much occupied with prize cases (which he alone heard) was that Hill spent nearly the whole of the first eight years of his judicial life trying Admiralty cases. This work increased enormously in consequence of the war. The novel conditions of navigation in convoy, zigzagging without lights at full speed, and often in fog, combined to bring a constant stream of cases before the court. The right man is apt to appear when needed, and Hill certainly met, with complete satisfaction to all concerned, the need for a good Admiralty judge. The records in the Admiralty Registry indicate the amount of work done by him, often sitting on Saturdays. From 1917 to 1924, inclusive, he tried 1,313 Admiralty causes, the peak year being 1920 when he disposed of 308. Hill only succeeded in keeping abreast of the list and in getting the ships' witnesses away to sea as soon as possible by long hours of work after court. In 1925 an additional judge was appointed to the division to help Hill, whose health was breaking down under the continuous strain, but by that time the tide of Admiralty causes had begun to ebb.

Perhaps the most important of Hill's Admiralty judgements were those in which he dealt with claims to immunity from legal process by state-owned ships. The anomalies of this kind of claim were frequently pointed out by Hill. They have since been dealt with by an international convention, prepared in 1924 and re-examined in 1947. A significant stage in this department of maritime law was reached in England by the passage of the Crown Proceedings Act of 1947.

Hill, before the outbreak of war in 1914, with the help of his brother, (Sir Arthur) Norman Hill, first baronet, an eminent legal adviser to the shipping community, drafted the legal forms necessary to put into effect a scheme of national insurance in time of war. This scheme did much to enable the mercantile marine to carry on its essential work after the outbreak of war.

In his last years on the bench Hill had to try from time to time divorce and probate cases. Although he brought to these cases the same high standard of care and impartiality, the divorce work was always distasteful to him. His sympathetic mind hated the cruelty, and his deep sense of decency revolted from the repulsive evidence in some of these cases.

Before his appointment as a judge Hill did important work during the war as chairman of the Ship Licensing Committee which led to the formation of the Ministry of Shipping. At the request of the government he wrote a memorandum on the subject of freedom of the seas. This memorandum formed the basis of article 297 of the Treaty of Versailles, and the principle of equality of treatment of vessels of all flags as outlined in the memorandum was afterwards embodied in the Maritime Ports Convention of 1923.

Hill married in 1891 Susan Ellen Berta, fourth daughter of George Burgess Hadwen, silk-mill owner, of Kebroyd, Halifax, and had two sons. The elder son, Mr. Philip Maurice Hill, is general manager of the Chamber of Shipping of the United Kingdom. In 1924 the death of Hill's wife, and the prolonged strain of his judicial work, caused for a time a serious breakdown in his health. In October 1930 he resigned from the bench, and he died at Wimbledon 6 June 1934.

As a judge, Hill inspired confidence in all who appeared before him. He brought to each case obvious ability, utter impartiality, and a strenuous desire to be just. Although this desire may have seemed at the time to prolong the hearing when other cases were pressing, he never failed to be courteous and helpful to counsel or witness. In the result, Hill's power of discernment of what was true and just nearly always enabled him to decide the case aright.

In character Hill was modest and peculiarly free from any kind of vanity or self-seeking. He paid little attention to his personal appearance, and in court, as an aid to thought, usually discarded his wig when the argument became interesting. He seemed to care for simple beauty almost as much as he cared for truth. It is not surprising that he won the respect and affection of all who knew him.

A portrait of Hill, by (Sir) Walter Russell (1918), presented to him by the London and Liverpool War Risk Association, is in the possession of his elder son.

[*The Times*, 7, 16, 19, 28 June 1934; Admiralty Registry records; private information; personal knowledge.]

A. T. BUCKNILL.

HINKSON, KATHARINE (1861–1931), better known as KATHARINE

TYNAN, poet and novelist, was born in Dublin 23 January 1861, the fourth daughter of Andrew Cullen Tynan, by his wife, Elizabeth O'Reilly. Her father was a farmer who had purchased Whitehall, Clondalkin, co. Dublin, formerly the property of J. P. Curran [q.v.] whose daughter Sarah had been betrothed to Robert Emmet [q.v.]. Amid such associations and in this beautiful scenery Katharine Tynan spent her early years, and with her dog, her sugar stick, and her book under her arm, she 'learned all the mysteries of the fields'. She was a clever child, but her eyesight having been imperilled by an attack of measles, her school-days at the Sienna Convent, Drogheda, were curtailed. She grew up to be a woman full of gentle fun and sympathy, with the graciousness that she would herself have attributed to her convent schooling, and with an enchanting brogue. In her childhood she had heard talk about the Fenians: in her 'teens her father, a well-known nationalist, encouraged her to listen to the conversation of his political friends; in her girlhood she joined the Ladies' Land League, but according to her own statement that branch of the Irish movement did not greatly appeal to her, and, like her father, she supported Parnell both before and after the 'split'. But her future lay in letters rather than in politics. In her 'teens she was reading 'everything' from Rossetti and William Morris to Miss Braddon and Eugène Sue, and it was to her father that she showed her poems, and, when he had paid for the publication of her first book, Louise de la Vallière (1885), to him she brought the news of their success. This earned her the acquaintance of Wilfred and Alice Meynell [q.v.], of William and Christina Rossetti, of W. B. Yeats [qq.v.] and his family, of George Russell (AE) [q.v.], and of all the leaders of the Irish literary movement. From that time too, there began to flow a stream of more than a hundred novels by which she made a pleasant living, and at intervals she published collections of poems. During her married life and widowhood she wrote her autobiography in five volumes, Twenty-five Years: Reminiscences (1913), The Middle Years (1916), The Years of the Shadow (1919), The Wandering Years (1922), and Memories (1924), which, with the personal accounts of such figures as Parnell and Alice Meynell, gave her a claim to be considered a contemporary historian.

In 1883 Katharine Tynan married Henry Albert Hinkson, an open scholar of Trinity College, Dublin, a barrister, and a writer of novels. By him she had two sons, who both held commissions in the British Army during the war of 1914–1918, and a daughter, the novelist Miss Pamela Hinkson. After her marriage her home was in England until her return to Ireland in 1916. Her husband was appointed a resident magistrate in county Mayo in 1914, and when he died in 1919 she moved from place to place, living for a time on the continent and later partly in Ireland and partly in England. Of her work W. B. Yeats wrote: 'Mrs. Hinkson is happiest when she puts emotions that have the innocence of childhood into symbols and metaphors from the green world about her. She has . . . a devout tenderness like that of St. Francis for weak instinctive things', and in the preface to her Collected Poems (1930) George Russell (AE) described her as 'happy in religion, friendship, children', and 'instantly kindling to beauty'. She died at Wimbledon 2 April 1931.

A portrait of Katharine Tynan by John Butler Yeats (1896) is in the Municipal Art Gallery, Dublin.

[Katharine Tynan, Twenty-five Years, 1913, The Middle Years, 1916, The Years of the Shadow, 1919, The Wandering Years, 1922, and Memories, 1924; Collected Poems, 1930; private information.]   SYLVIA LYND.

HOBDAY, SIR FREDERICK THOMAS GEORGE (1869–1939), veterinary surgeon, was born at Burton-on-Trent 4 November 1869, the eldest son of Thomas Hobday, a brewer's manager for Messrs. Bass, by his wife; Mary Newbold. From Burton Grammar School he entered his uncle's coal business. Disliking office work he moved to Hanley for two years as an articled apprentice to Alfred Hodgkins, M.R.C.V.S. After three years (1888–1891) at the Royal Veterinary College and a further year with Hodgkins he graduated M.R.C.V.S. in 1892. He served six months as resident hospital surgeon before entering private practice with Arthur Blake, M.R.C.V.S., of Redhill. In October 1893 he returned to the Royal Veterinary College on appointment to a junior professorship with charge of the out-patients' department and the teaching of materia medica and hygiene. He took his F.R.C.V.S. in 1897 and was awarded the John Henry Steel medal in 1899. In the same year he resigned his professorship and joined Frank Ridler, M.R.C.V.S., in 1900 in practice in Kensington.

Hobday became a skilful surgeon, the craftsman rather than the reasoning diagnostician; the busy clinic and operating theatre rather than the library and classroom moulded him. Ambitious, energetic, restless, he spared neither himself nor his assistants. He was urbane with clients and invariably courteous to students. He entered fully and generously into projects for the advancement of his profession. Among the more durable products of his earlier work were the development and refinement of animal anaesthesia, the surgery of the reproductive system, and the surgical technique for small animals. His operating theatre attracted fellow practitioners and visitors from abroad. He invited Professor Walter Long Williams, of Cornell University, U.S.A., to demonstrate modifications of Professor Karl Adolf Kurt Günther's plastic operation for the relief of 'roaring' in horses. In Hobday's hands the operation became so successful that the hunting world eventually applied the term 'hobdayed' to horses which had been relieved of the impediment to their breathing. His second conspicuous aptitude was his journalism, on which his restless energy was imprinted. He compiled or edited four useful text-books and wrote numerous articles for the professional press, particularly for the *Veterinary Journal*, of which he was editor from 1906 to 1939. Lacking the disposition for reflection and critical study, he acquired the habit of seeking ideas of more informed minds, especially of Henry Gray, M.R.C.V.S., his neighbour and friend of over forty years.

In 1912 Hobday was gazetted honorary veterinary surgeon to Queen Alexandra; throughout his life he was retained in the royal appointment. On the outbreak of war in 1914 he joined the Army Veterinary Corps, and from 1915 to 1916 was in command of No. 22 Veterinary Hospital in France with the rank of major. At the end of 1916 he took his hospital to Italy. For his services he was twice mentioned in dispatches and appointed C.M.G. (1918); he also received French and Italian decorations. He retired from the army with the esteem of many influential veterinary surgeons of Allied countries; he was an honorary member of the veterinary associations of Paris, Belgium, Norway, Sweden, and the United States of America. By maintaining his friendships abroad he was the most widely known and travelled British veterinary surgeon. Later he received the honorary doctorate of veterinary medicine from Zürich University (1933), the foreign associateship of the Veterinary Academy of France, and corresponding membership of the Academy of Medicine of Rumania (1936).

In 1919 Hobday returned to his Kensington practice and numerous public activities. In appreciation of his work for the profession the Central Veterinary Society presented him with the Victory medal (1921). The idea of the unity of medicine as a biological study embracing men, animals, and plants had been fostered by several generations of discerning physicians and veterinary surgeons; a further step was taken by the Royal Society of Medicine in establishing a section of comparative medicine (1922). For his vigorous support of the new foundation Hobday was elected president of the section (1924–1926) in succession to Sir T. Clifford Allbutt [q.v.]; later for his work on behalf of medical and veterinary collaboration he was elected an honorary fellow of the Royal Society of Medicine (1937). He was prominent in the work of several animal welfare organizations, including the Universities Federation for Animal Welfare, of which he was president (1927–1939). As an examiner for the Royal College of Veterinary Surgeons for many years he was more effective than as a member of its council. In council he was amiable and avoided controversy; he took a minor part in the affairs of education and professional ethics. He had a *penchant* for social gatherings; he enjoyed seeing and being seen by everyone.

In 1927 the governors issued an appeal for £35,000 for the reconstruction of the Royal Veterinary College. Hobday, as chairman of the *ad hoc* committee, visited the continental centres of veterinary education and made up his mind that the college should be entirely rebuilt in a style worthy of the Empire. Within a few months his propaganda had attracted attention; he dominated the appeal fund organization. At the height of his influence the governors appointed him in 1927 principal of the college in succession to Sir John McFadyean, being thereby made responsible for the administration of the college, the professorship of surgery, and the appeal and planning for reconstruction; a burden too great for any one man. Hobday began his great task with enthusiasm and remarkable energy; in his inaugural address he declared the governors' scheme inadequate and called for £250,000. By 1936 he had won; the appeal fund totalled £285,000, the income and student entry had been more than doubled, the college staff had been enlarged, and the debt of 1927 had been cleared. In 1933 he was knighted, but his path to victory was marred with inevitable omissions and he was overwhelmed by misfortune.

In 1936 defects in the college administration were alleged; the governors appointed a committee of inquiry and, with unfeeling prudence, called upon Hobday to resign. Denied an opportunity of defending himself he refused to resign, whereupon the governors announced his resignation on the grounds of his having passed the age limit. When reminded at a subsequent meeting that no age limit had been specified in the appointment of the principal, the governors ruled that Hobday's salary would cease at the opening of the new buildings, until which date he would remain absent on leave. He was invited to the opening of the new buildings by the King and Queen in November 1937, and received their congratulations; but he was a broken man. Disillusionment embittered his forced retirement; resentment sapped his strength. He wrote his autobiography (1938) but his joyousness had gone. He aged very rapidly and died at Droitwich 24 June 1939.

Hobday married in 1895 Elizabeth, daughter of Thomas Evans, a farmer, and widow of William Chambers, of Bromyard, Herefordshire, who practised veterinary surgery. They had a son and a daughter.

A portrait of Hobday by John Hassall hangs in the library of the Royal Veterinary College.

[*The Times*, 26 June 1939; Sir Frederick Hobday, *Fifty Years a Veterinary Surgeon*, 1938; *Veterinary Journal*, July 1939 (portrait); *Nature*, 29 July 1939; private information; personal knowledge.]   T. Hare.

HOBHOUSE, HENRY (1854–1937), pioneer in local government, was born at Hadspen House, near Castle Cary, Somerset, 1 March 1854, the only son of Henry Hobhouse, by his first wife, Charlotte Etruria, youngest daughter of James Talbot, third Lord Talbot de Malahide. On his father's death in 1862 he became head of the younger branch of the Hobhouse family, which had been located at Hadspen House since 1785. He was a country squire with an inherited estate of about 2,500 acres. His father and grand-

father before him had set conspicuous examples of duty and public spirit in the unpaid work of petty and quarter sessions; and although he was not quite eight years old when his father died, the tradition was handed on to him by his uncle and guardian, Arthur (afterwards Lord Hobhouse, q.v.), the well-known judge. He was also first cousin to L. T. Hobhouse [q.v.]. Educated at Eton and at Balliol College, Oxford, of which he was a scholar, he was awarded a second class in classical moderations (1873) and a first class in *literae humaniores* (1875). In 1880 he was called to the bar by Lincoln's Inn, and in the same year was appointed a county magistrate: he practised as a parliamentary draftsman and counsel until 1885. In 1884 he collaborated with Sir Robert Wright [q.v.] in *An Outline of Local Government and Local Taxation in England and Wales*, which remained a standard legal text-book for over half a century, its eighth main edition appearing in the year of his death.

In 1885 Hobhouse entered parliament for East Somerset as a liberal, and in 1886 retained the seat as a liberal unionist. In the debates in 1888 on the county councils bill he was very influential. No member excelled him in direct knowledge of county administration, and the bill's policy—to transfer it from quarter sessions to elected county councils—was the one which he, unlike some rival specialists, entirely approved. When Lord Salisbury formed a coalition ministry with the liberal unionists in 1895, Hobhouse's standing was high enough to warrant his inclusion; but his party's eminent front-benchers were so disproportionate to its total membership, that no newer comer stood a chance. Repeatedly passed over in favour of conservatives, he evinced no sourness, but concentrated increasingly on county questions. In 1902 he gave weighty support to the Balfour education bill, which he helped to shape. Its passage perhaps partly determined his acceptance in 1904 of the chairmanship of the Somerset county council, a post which he filled with great distinction for twenty years. He took a leading part in forming in 1889 the County Councils' Association, of which he was an original member and from 1914 to 1920 chairman. He retired from parliament in 1906, having been sworn of the Privy Council in 1902.

Hobhouse was, in his day, the pattern of the public-spirited country gentleman. No aspect of local welfare escaped him, but his favourite subjects were education and agriculture. He started three secondary schools on private account, and after 1902 was keenly interested in the foundation of others by his county council. He was a member of the royal commission on secondary education (1894–1895), a notable governor and benefactor of the King's School, Bruton, and very influential in the conversion of University College, Bristol, into Bristol University of which (1909–1937) he was pro-chancellor and which conferred upon him the honorary degree of LL.D. His interest in farming had many sides. He was chairman of the Cider Institute at Long Ashton, and raised a fund for it. At one time he was much concerned to combat the urban bias in rural education; but had only moderate success. He cared much for painting, architecture, scenery, and literature, and took to learning foreign languages in order to study their masterpieces in the original. He was a devoted churchman; an ecclesiastical commissioner from 1890 and a member of the Church Assembly from 1920. He shot regularly, but not very well; he rode a good deal about his estate, but never hunted.

Hobhouse was twice married: first, in 1880 to Margaret Heyworth (died 1921), seventh daughter of Richard Potter, of Standish House, Gloucestershire; she was one of the well-known sisters who included Mrs. Sidney Webb and Lady Courtney of Penwith; secondly, in 1923 to Anne Mackessack, elder daughter of William Grant, of Forres, Morayshire. By his first marriage he had four sons and three daughters; the youngest son was killed in the war of 1914–1918 and the youngest daughter died in infancy. He died at Hadspen House 25 June 1937.

There is a portrait of Hobhouse by Hall Neile (c. 1924) at Hadspen House.

[*The Times*, 28 June 1937; private information; personal knowledge.]

R. C. K. ENSOR.

HOBSON, ERNEST WILLIAM (1856–1933), mathematician, was born at Derby 27 October 1856, the eldest son of William Hobson, founder, editor and part proprietor of the *Derbyshire Advertiser* and a prominent figure in municipal affairs, by his wife, Josephine Atkinson. J. A. Hobson [q.v.], the economist and publicist, was one of his brothers. His early education was obtained at Derby School. In 1871 he was elected to a scholarship at what is now the Imperial College of Science,

South Kensington, and studied physics for a time in London under Frederick Guthrie [q.v.]; but, although a versatile student with many interests, he was always primarily a mathematician whose ambition directed him naturally towards Cambridge. In 1874 he obtained a scholarship at Christ's College, and he remained a member of that foundation for the rest of his life.

Hobson was senior wrangler in January 1878, and was elected a fellow of his college in the autumn of the same year. In 1883 he was chosen as one of the first university lecturers in mathematics, and in 1903 as Stokes lecturer, a position of particular distinction. In 1910 he succeeded Andrew Russell Forsyth as Sadleirian professor of pure mathematics, and he held this position until 1931, dying at Cambridge soon after his retirement, 18 April 1933. He had long been a conspicuous figure in the international world of science, and had received many honours, a Royal medal (1907) of the Royal Society, of which he had been elected a fellow in 1893, and the De Morgan medal (1920) of the London Mathematical Society, honorary degrees, and memberships of foreign academies.

Hobson was for many years one of the first of English mathematicians, but his career in the years following graduation was not particularly distinguished. He was a singular exception to the rule that mathematicians do their best work when they are young, and it was not until he was nearly forty that he published the first of the works upon which his reputation rests. This, an elaborate memoir on 'spherical harmonics' in the *Philosophical Transactions* of the Royal Society for 1896, is a classic in its field, and its preparation may well have occupied him for several years; but, whatever allowances are made, his development as an original mathematician seems now to have been strangely slow.

The slow pace of Hobson's progress is no doubt largely explained by the Cambridge traditions of the time, the extravagant importance attached to position in the tripos, and the general indifference to research: it was one of Hobson's greatest services to Cambridge later to help to break down these traditions. It was then quite usual even for the best of Cambridge mathematicians to act as private coaches for the tripos, and Hobson for many years expended much of his energy in this way. He was a good and successful coach, although less notorious than E. J. Routh [q.v.] or Robert Rumsey Webb, and had one theatrical triumph, Miss Philippa Fawcett, who was placed 'above the senior wrangler' in 1890, being one of his pupils. John Maynard (afterwards Lord) Keynes, was another. It was not until 1903 that Hobson abandoned coaching in order to win more leisure for research, and not until he was fifty that he developed fully what were to prove the dominant interests of his life.

The modern theory of functions, as understood in Europe since the days of Riemann and Weierstrass, was hardly known in England before 1890. In particular it was unknown to Cambridge mathematicians, dominated as they were by the algebraical traditions of Cayley and Sylvester and by the depressing shadow of the tripos. The first steps towards enlightenment were taken by A. R. Forsyth, whose *Theory of Functions of a Complex Variable*, published in 1893, raised the first wave of interest in the subject. Forsyth, however, cared only for the 'complex' theory, and was in any case deficient in critical power; and the still more fundamental 'real' theory remained neglected. It was here that Hobson found the great opportunity of his life.

Hobson's *Theory of Functions of a Real Variable* was published in 1907, at first as a single volume. The modern theories of measure and integration, initiated in France by Bord and Lebesgue, were then still unfamiliar; and Hobson and William Henry Young (who never held a regular position in the university) were the first Cambridge mathematicians to grasp the significance of the new ideas. The subject expanded rapidly, and Hobson's book, in its various editions, occupied him for twenty years. In its final form of 1926–1927 it fills two volumes and over 1,500 pages, and the best tribute to the vitality of the subject and the author is that it is still possible to feel that many sections are too short. It is a fine book, written with full mastery of a vast subject and with many important contributions of Hobson's own; it probably ranks first among systematic treatises written by modern English mathematicians; and if English mathematics has now lost all its insularity, if these subjects, once neglected, are now widely understood and admirably taught, it is to Hobson and Young that the credit is primarily due.

Hobson wrote four other books. The most important is *Spherical and Ellipsoidal Harmonics*, published in 1931: this,

although it appeared so late, contains the substance of much of his early work, and in particular of his memoir of 1896. His first book, *A Treatise on Plane Trigonometry* (1891), is a 'text-book' of a much more elementary kind, although an important one which has run through many editions. This was the first English book, apart from the *Algebra* of George Chrystal [q.v.], to give any serious account of the elements of 'algebraical analysis'. *Squaring the Circle* (1913), a reprint of six lectures given in that year, is a 'popular' book, agreeably written and full of entertaining information, which inspires regret that Hobson did so little of this kind of exposition. Finally, in *The Domain of Natural Science* (1923), the Gifford lectures delivered at Aberdeen in 1921–1922, Hobson appears as a philosopher. He was an intimate friend of James Ward [q.v.] and philosophy had always been his strongest interest outside mathematics, so that his selection as lecturer was quite appropriate. The book itself, however, although competent and scholarly, is slightly disappointing, the position which he defends, a rather extreme and abstract form of the 'descriptive' view of natural science, being much more reasonable than exciting.

Apart from his position as a leading British mathematician, Hobson was a conspicuous and influential figure in Cambridge. He was proctor twice, served on the council of the senate and on important syndicates, and was a frequent speaker in senate-house discussions. He was, as was to be expected of a man of his temperament and upbringing a 'radical', as radicalism was understood in university circles thirty years ago, who was usually to be found on the *placet* side —the controversy over women's degrees was an exception; and he was one of the leaders in the movement for the reform of the mathematical tripos which resulted in 1910 in the abolition of the order of merit.

Hobson married in 1882 Selina Rosa, daughter of Rudolf Knüsli, a merchant, of Glarus, Switzerland, and had four sons, of whom one predeceased him. A portrait of him by Kenneth Green (1925) hangs in the combination room of Christ's College.

[*The Times*, 19 April 1933; *Obituary Notices of Fellows of the Royal Society*, No. 3, December 1934 (portrait); *Journal* of the London Mathematical Society, vol. ix, 1934; private information; personal knowledge.] G. H. HARDY.

HOBSON, JOHN ATKINSON (1858–1940), economist and publicist, was born at Derby 6 July 1858, the second son of William Hobson, founder, editor, and part-proprietor of the *Derbyshire Advertiser*, by his wife, Josephine Atkinson. The mathematician E. W. Hobson [q.v.] was his elder brother. He was educated at Derby School and at Lincoln College, Oxford, of which latter he was a scholar. From 1880 to 1887 he held posts as classical master in schools at Faversham and Exeter, and from 1887 to 1897 was a university extension lecturer for Oxford and London. He paid a series of long visits to the United States of America and Canada, and spent, at the request of the *Manchester Guardian*, some months in South Africa on the eve of the war of 1899–1902. His main energies were devoted, however, to economic and social studies, on which he published some thirty-five works, as well as numerous pamphlets and articles. He married in 1885 Florence, daughter of Jonathan Edgar, attorney, of New Jersey, and had a son and a daughter. He died at his home at Hampstead 1 April 1940.

Hobson's work as an economist was done at a time when the scope of the science was in process of enlargement, while its methods were being modified by the progress of realistic investigations into economic and social life. It is as an acute and original thinker, who made important contributions to both changes, that he will principally be remembered. He had been influenced by Ruskin, on whose social teaching he published a study (*John Ruskin, Social Reformer*, 1898). As explained in two of his later books, *Work and Wealth: a Human Valuation* (1914) and *Wealth and Life; A Study in Values* (1929), he approached economics as a humanist, but a humanist with an unusual power of logical analysis, and also with a firm grasp of a wide range of economic facts. From the beginning, he struck out on lines of his own. The theory of underconsumption formulated in *The Physiology of Industry* (1889), in which he collaborated with A. F. Mummery [q.v.], and developed in his subsequent works, asserted that economic health requires the maintenance of a correct balance between expenditure on consumption and on capital goods, and saw the principal cause of unemployment in a tendency to oversaving on the part of a wealthy minority, which was the inevitable consequence of extreme inequality in the distribution of income. When first advanced, the doctrine did not find favour with his fellow economists. The London University Extension Board, with surprising fatuity, refused to allow Hobson to lecture for it on political economy, and, to the discredit of English universities, he was never offered an academic post. Later work on trade depressions, however, reached conclusions which had an affinity with those suggested by him, and he lived to read the handsome tribute to his work as an intellectual pioneer paid by John Maynard (afterwards Lord) Keynes in *The General Theory of Employment, Interest and Money* (1936). Hobson's next important book, *The Evolution of Modern Capitalism: a Study of Machine Production* (1894), attacked the subject of industrial organization from a different angle. Offering an analytical account of the creation by modern machine industry of a proletariat divorced from control of the conditions on which its livelihood and welfare depend, and of the concentration of power in the hands of an oligarchy of capitalist entrepreneurs, it remains an indispensable introduction to nineteenth-century economic history. It was followed, after the appearance of *The Economics of Distribution* (1900) and several smaller works, by two books which reveal Hobson's originality and synthetic power at their best. *Imperialism: a Study* (1902, 3rd, revised ed. 1938) traces the drive for imperial expansion to the search for new markets and opportunities for investment on the part of wealth which, owing to the poverty of large sections of the population in capitalist countries, could not find profitable openings at home. *The Industrial System: an Inquiry into Earned and Unearned Income* (1909) found the principal source of inequality in surpluses accruing, after the necessary costs of production had been met, to the classes owning capital and land, or enjoying special educational and other advantages. The remedies prescribed in that book and in some of the author's later writings, such as *Democracy after the War* (1917), *Taxation in the New State* (1919), and *The Economics of Unemployment* (1922), include steeply graduated taxation, the extension of the social services, and the nationalization of monopolies.

Although, as an economist, Hobson for long travelled almost alone, he was far from being a recluse. He was keenly interested in public affairs; and his migration to London was a turning-point in his career. It introduced him to a group of thinkers and reformers who were preaching a modernized liberalism, and gave him an opportunity, which he was quick to seize, of promoting the causes which commanded his allegiance. The *Progressive Review*, in which he was associated with Ramsay MacDonald [q.v.] from 1896 to 1898, had a brief and troubled life; but the *Nation* supplied him with the platform which he required. The circle which its editor H. W. Massingham [q.v.] gathered about him included L. T. Hobhouse [q.v.], Henry Woodd Nevinson, Mr. John Lawrence Le Breton Hammond, C. F. G. Masterman [q.v.], and other well-known names. Some of them were Hobson's intimate friends; and from 1906 to 1920 much of his writing, not only on current politics, but on sociological subjects, was first published in the *Nation*. He was a vigorous opponent of the South African war; served on the Bryce committee which prepared a scheme for a League of Nations; helped to found the Union of Democratic Control; and published, in addition to his earlier study of imperialism, *The War in South Africa: its Causes and Effects* (1900); *The Psychology of Jingoism* (1901); *Towards International Government* (1915); and *Richard Cobden, The International Man* (1919). In addition to his books and articles, he found time for lecturing. Himself a convinced, though tolerant and undogmatic, rationalist, he was strongly attracted by the Ethical Movement. The addresses which for many years he delivered to South Place Ethical Society made a deep impression upon all who heard them.

Setting a high value on 'free and fragmentary intercourse . . . as a mode for the discovery and communication of truth', Hobson did not regard such activities as an impediment to his austerer studies, but as an assistance to them. It is, however, through his books that his widest and most enduring influence has been exercised. The best introduction to his work as a whole is to be found in two of his later volumes, *Free-Thought in the Social Sciences* (1926) and the autobiographical *Confessions of an Economic Heretic* (1938). While he made original and fruitful contributions to economic thought, his approach to the problems of society was that of a sociologist rather than an economic theorist. He refused to treat ethics, politics, and economics in isolation from each other, and his best work was done in the border region where studies, convention-

ally separated, intersect. Acutely conscious as he was of the tricks played by interest on reason, he rejected, as warped by an unconscious class-bias, both the individualist economics of his youth and the proletarian economics which attacked them. His own version of socialism drew a distinction between standardized industries, which could appropriately be nationalized, and those in which personal taste and skill play an important part. It proposed to secure the advantages of collective ownership where, as in the case of monopolies, that policy would best serve the public interest, while preserving a large field for individual initiative and ingenuity in meeting the demand for qualitative production.

[*Manchester Guardian* and *The Times*, 2 April 1940; *Derbyshire Advertiser*, 5 April 1940; J. A. Hobson, *Confessions of an Economic Heretic*, 1938; personal knowledge.]

R. H. TAWNEY.

HOCKING, SILAS KITTO (1850-1935), novelist and preacher, was born at St. Stephen in Brannel, Cornwall, 24 March 1850, the third son of James Hocking, part owner of a tin-mine, by his wife, Elizabeth Kitto, who was related to John Kitto, author of *The Pictorial Bible* [q.v.]. Through his mother he came of one of the oldest Cornish families. Educated privately and perhaps elsewhere, he intended to be a mine surveyor, but in 1869 was accepted as a candidate for the ministry of the United Methodist Free Church, and was ordained in 1870. He held pastorates at Pontypool, Spalding, Liverpool, and Manchester before going, in 1883, to Duke Street, Southport, where, during the next thirteen years, he preached to crowded congregations.

Hocking resigned from the ministry in 1896 in order to devote himself to writing, liberal politics (he unsuccessfully contested the Aylesbury division of Buckinghamshire in 1906 and Coventry in January 1910), lecturing, and journalism. He wrote his first book, *Alec Green*, at Liverpool in 1878, and a year later *Her Benny*, a tale of the Liverpool streets, for children, the copyright of which he sold for £20. It was translated into many languages and over a million copies were sold. In all, he wrote fifty books, including his reminiscences, *My Book of Memory* (1923), and at one time was said to be the best-selling English novelist. In 1894 he became editor of the *Family Circle*, and two years later established, with Frederick Anthony Atkins, the *Temple Magazine*, a sixpenny illustrated monthly journal for Sunday reading.

Hocking married in 1876 Esther May (died 1940), youngest daughter of Richard Lloyd, of Liverpool, and had a son and two daughters. He died at Highgate 15 September 1935. The secret of his success was that 'he wrote of what he knew for people he understood'. Sir Henry Campbell-Bannerman said that he had 'done more in providing healthy fiction for the young people of this country than any other man'. A cartoon of him by 'Spy' appeared in *Vanity Fair* 14 November 1906.

His brother JOSEPH HOCKING (1860–1937), novelist and preacher, the youngest son of James Hocking, was born at St. Stephen in Brannel 7 November 1860. 'My earliest recollections', he wrote, 'are of sitting in the old chimney corner, with a log on the fire, and my mother telling me ancient Cornish stories of wizards, wreckers, ghosts, and haunted houses.' He was educated privately and perhaps elsewhere, also at Crescent Range Theological College, Manchester, where he was first in his year, winning the Cuthbertson prize, and the Owens College, Manchester. He had read almost all Scott's works before he was twelve, and would walk twelve miles through the Cornish lanes to buy a cheap reprint of the classics. At the age of thirteen he wrote his first novel, which, he said, 'was not a success'. At sixteen he began to study land surveying, but after four years felt a call to the ministry of the United Methodist Free Church, and was ordained in 1884. In 1887 he travelled extensively in the Middle East, and on his return became minister of Woodford Green Union church in Essex. He resigned in 1910.

Jabez Easterbrook, the first of Hocking's fifty-three published books, appeared in 1891. Several came out serially in the *British Weekly* and other journals. He regarded fiction as an effective medium for conveying religious ideas to a popular public. His tales, sometimes set in the Cornwall of his childhood, were competently written, didactic, and make a good use of suspense. Perhaps the most successful were *The Woman of Babylon* (1906), *The Trampled Cross* (1907), and *The God That Answers by Fire* (1930). In 1887 he married Annie, eldest daughter of Joseph Brown, J.P., F.C.S., and had a son, who was killed on active service in 1918, and four daughters. He died at Perranporth, Cornwall, 4 March 1937.

[*The Times*, 16 September 1935 and 5 March 1937; S. K. Hocking, *My Book of Memory*, 1923; *Methodist Recorder*, 19 September 1935; *Tit-Bits*, 5 January 1909; *Men and Women of the Time*, 1899; private information.]

R. G. BURNETT.

HODGE, JOHN (1855–1937), labour leader, was born at Muirkirk, Ayrshire, 29 October 1855, the eldest son of William Hodge, a puddler, by his wife, Marian Henderson, who came from Dumfriesshire. In his fifth year he attended the school attached to the ironworks at Motherwell, where his father then laboured. After a strike in 1865 the father was victimized, and the family moving to Glasgow for a year, John was transferred for a short time to Hutcheson's Boys' Grammar School. Later, after returning to Motherwell, he passed an examination for a position as pupil teacher, but was disqualified as he was under thirteen. In 1868 he entered a solicitor's office at Hamilton where he earned £10 a year and gathered some smattering of Scottish law. After a turn at puddling at Parkhead ironworks, Glasgow, in addition to ventures in the grocery and provision trades, he was engaged as a stocktaker by the firm of David Colville & Sons, iron and steel makers, of Motherwell. But he quarrelled with one of the partners, and attracted by the high wages reputed to be earned by steel melters, he then got work as third hand at Blochairn steelworks, Glasgow, and while there, on account of his knowledge and skill, was invited to return to Colville's.

A demand by Colville's for a 20 per cent. reduction in wages and the dismissal of one in three men in the works led in November 1885 to a strike, which collapsed in a week, but gave rise to the formation in the following year of the British Steel Smelters' Association with Hodge as unpaid secretary and his wife as unpaid assistant. Within six months practically every steel smelter in Scotland had been enrolled. Smelters worked up to seventy hours a week under a system by which contractors received from £40 to £50 a week and the men 8s. 6½d. down to 5s. 9d. a shift of twelve hours. Sound organization and patient argument led to the substitution of 'payment by results', with the selling price of metal as a basis; and the conversion of twelve hours to three shifts of eight hours. Success in Scotland was followed by similar achievement south of the Border and particularly among the tinplate workers in South Wales.

Hodge held firmly to the principles of conciliation and arbitration. As the association grew in strength, and, absorbing other organizations, moved from Glasgow to Manchester and then to London, Hodge left his mark on those cities. In Glasgow he engaged in a successful campaign for bringing the city tramways under municipal control, and as president of the Glasgow trades council he presided over the Trades Union Congress in 1892; in Manchester he served on the city council, and in London he was appointed president of the British Iron, Steel, and Kindred Trades Federation, for the administration of friendly benefits, and of the Iron and Steel Trades Confederation which dealt with trade negotiations and legal questions; and he was president of both until he retired from them in 1931.

Greatly influenced by Henry George's *Progress and Poverty*, Hodge became imbued with the socialist ideas which J. Keir Hardie [q.v.] was promulgating, and he led his association in the formation of the labour party, serving on its national committee from 1900 to 1915. He stood unsuccessfully for Gower (1900) and Preston (a by-election, 1903), but, winning Gorton in 1906, he was an original member of the parliamentary labour party, and held this seat continuously until 1923. During the war of 1914–1918 he was the first minister of labour (1916–1917) and subsequently (1917–1919) minister of pensions in Lloyd George's coalition government. The present status of the Ministry of Labour owes much to his determination, and his sympathetic administration of the Ministry of Pensions marked a great advance in the treatment of service men and their dependants. He was sworn of the Privy Council in 1917.

When the General Strike in support of the miners took place in May 1926 Hodge was strongly opposed to the association taking part. The association suffered in finance and membership, and when meeting the iron and steel trades employers afterwards it required all Hodge's tact to secure reconciliation and the resumption of the broken agreements; but he went so far as to diagnose the strike as 'a great moral gesture, a great moral uplift for the purpose of helping the miners whom they believed were being ground down to conditions little better than slavery'.

Hodge's gifts were a native canniness, a wide knowledge of the trade, an acquaintance with men and affairs gained by visits to the United States of America, Canada, Australia, New Zealand, and the continent, as well as at home; together with a forthrightness mingled with good-natured humour. He was a constitutionalist, looking for his socialist ideals to be achieved by education and legislation, and anxious always that the agreements to which he put his hand should be honoured by all concerned.

Hodge married in 1885 Mary Lambie (died 1931), daughter of James Forsyth, of Lanark: he had first met her in 1877, and by her he had four daughters. He died at his home at Bexhill-on-Sea 10 August 1937.

[*The Times*, 11 August 1937; John Hodge, *Workman's Cottage to Windsor Castle*, 1931; private information; personal knowledge.]

J. S. MIDDLETON.

HOLLAND, SIR SYDNEY GEORGE, third baronet, and second VISCOUNT KNUTSFORD (1855–1931), hospital administrator and reformer, was born in London 19 March 1855, the elder of the twin sons of H. T. Holland (afterwards second baronet and first Viscount Knutsford, q.v.), and grandson of Sir Henry Holland, the physician [q.v.]. His mother, who died shortly after giving birth to the twins, was Elizabeth Margaret, elder daughter of Nathaniel Hibbert, of Munden, Hertfordshire, and a granddaughter of Sydney Smith. All through life the twins, Sydney and Arthur, were devoted and for long hard to tell apart. In 1858 their father remarried with Margaret Jean, elder daughter of Sir C. E. Trevelyan, sister of Sir G. O. Trevelyan [qq.v.], and niece of Lord Macaulay. She was a good mother to the twins, but their unconventional and even prodigal outlook was not learned at her knee. Their father, who was a busy lawyer and later statesman, was not able to see much of them, and they passed their summer holidays with their grandmother Mrs. Hibbert or at Knutsford with their great-aunts Mary and Lucy Holland, the prototypes of the ladies in *Cranford*. Sydney was sent to Wellington, where he came under the influence of the future historian Osmund Airy, who opened the boy's mind and humanized his outlook, turning his thoughts to social service. His father designed him for the army, but his educational standard proved too low for Woolwich. He fell back on the bar, to please his father, and in 1873 went up to Trinity Hall, Cambridge, where he made scores of friends, and spent his days in debates and rowing and swimming, in which last he became an expert. After leaving Cambridge in 1876 he read for the bar and was called by the Inner Temple in 1879. He then entered the chambers of George Baugh Allen, a well-known special pleader of the day. He began now to interest himself in boys' clubs, did some competitive swimming, and learned conjuring from professionals. He achieved moderate success in the criminal courts and later at the parliamentary bar, but a flair for business and a call to social service decided, and divided, his life's activities. In the cause of temperance, he helped to launch a scheme of coffee taverns. In 1882 he inherited a house and competence, and in 1883 married Lady Mary (died 1947), fourth and youngest daughter and tenth child of Bertram Ashburnham, fourth Earl of Ashburnham (born 1797).

Holland's name now began to be known through letters to the press and pamphlets on many social questions. In 1888 he was elected a director of the East and West India Dock Company, and in the dockers' strike of 1889 he took a leading part in voicing the employers' case, in which *The Times* and even John Burns acknowledged his fairmindedness. His interest in the dock labourers led him to visit them at the Poplar Hospital and thus launched him without previous experience into hospital management, but he never feared responsibility and was always at war with apathy and incompetence. As a dock company director and chairman of Poplar Hospital (1891) at critical junctures he quickly put both concerns on their feet again. In four and a half years he raised enough money to make the Poplar Hospital one of the best of the smaller London hospitals.

In 1896, at the suggestion of Miss Eva Luckes, matron of the London Hospital, Holland applied to be put on the committee and in the same year he was elected chairman and so continued until his death which took place in the hospital 27 July 1931. His fame rests on those thirty-five years. An obituary notice in *The Times* asserted 'He was much more than "the Prince of Beggars" who raised £5,000,000 for the "London". He was practically the founder of modern hospital efficiency. He raised the whole standard of nursing and hospital work from a very low to a very high level'; while a leading article said 'He gave his whole life to that work, and not his life only; his enthusiasm also, that rare and splendid gift of friendship which was as spontaneous and as simple as it was irresistible. ... He gave much more than he took from others. ... He spent the money so that every penny bought the

utmost possible benefit for his beloved patients. ... The London Hospital ... is the everlasting memorial to a great organizer and a great man.' Holland was no sentimentalist although he knew how to play on the emotions. Publicity was his first weapon. He did not despise 'stunts'. His resource was remarkable. He was a great showman, a telling and touching speaker, and, with the actor's arts, a notable broadcaster.

Lord Knutsford, as he became on succeeding his father in 1914, loved the good things of life, spent royally his City income on grouse-moors and forests, and made a pleasant home for his family at Kneesworth Hall, near Royston. His family life and friendships alike were ideally happy. He was survived by his wife and their two daughters. He wrote innumerable articles and letters to the press and was himself a constant subject for press 'stories'. In 1926 he published an autobiography, *In Black and White*, which had a popular success.

Lord Knutsford was succeeded as fourth baronet and third Viscount Knutsford by his twin-brother, Arthur Henry Holland-Hibbert (1855-1935).

A portrait of Lord Knutsford by Oswald Birley hangs in the London Hospital. A cartoon of him by 'Spy' appeared in *Vanity Fair* 25 August 1904.

[*The Times*, 28 July 1931; J. Gore, *Sydney Holland, Lord Knutsford*, 1936; N. Langton, *The Prince of Beggars*, 1921; Lord Knutsford, *In Black and White*, 1926; private information; personal knowledge.]   JOHN GORE.

HOLMES, SIR CHARLES JOHN (1868-1936), landscape painter and art critic, was born at Preston 11 November 1868, the elder son of Charles Rivington Holmes, vicar of St. Michael's church, Bromley-by-Bow, later vicar of Stratton, Cornwall, by his wife, Mary Susan, eldest daughter of Joseph Briggs Dickson, solicitor, of Preston. He was grandson of the antiquary John Holmes [q.v.] and nephew of Sir Richard Holmes [q.v.], librarian at Windsor Castle. After early schooling at St. Edmund's, Canterbury, Holmes went as a scholar to Eton in 1883, and as an exhibitioner to Brasenose College, Oxford, in 1887. From 1889 to 1903 he worked in London as publisher's and printer's assistant: with his cousin, Francis Rivington; at the Ballantyne Press; with John Cumming Nimmo; and Charles Ricketts and Charles Shannon [qq.v.] at the Vale Press. For some years he had been teaching himself to draw; now direction was given to his efforts by Ricketts, and he was made to etch by William Strang [q.v.]. Laurence Binyon prompted his first essay in art criticism—'Hiroshige' published in the *Dome* for September 1897. Other early publications, *Hokusai* (1899), *Constable* (1901), and art journalism in the *Realm* and *Athenaeum*, culminated in the major book, *Constable and his Influence on Landscape Painting* (1902), which is still the most authoritative work on that artist. In 1900, as landscape painter himself, Holmes began exhibiting with the New English Art Club.

In 1903 Holmes became co-editor, with Robert Dell, of the newly established *Burlington Magazine*; he resigned in 1909. In 1904 he was elected Slade professor of fine art at Oxford and he so continued until 1910. Some of his Slade lectures are the basis of *Notes on the Science of Picture-Making* (1909) and *Notes on the Art of Rembrandt* (1911). His standing as a painter was recognized in 1905, when, together with J. S. Sargent [q.v.], he was elected a member of the New English Art Club. The only other London art society which he joined was the Royal Society of Painters in Water-Colours, of which he was elected an associate in 1924 and a member in 1929. His paintings of mountain scenes and industrial subjects belong to no school or movement but his own. They were inspired by strong personal emotion, but in execution disciplined by constant analysis of the methods of his predecessors, European and oriental.

On the retirement of (Sir) Lionel Cust [q.v.] in 1909 Holmes became director of the National Portrait Gallery. His prime concerns were remodelling and rearranging the exhibition rooms, and starting a national photographic record. In 1916 he was appointed director of the National Gallery, 'in succession to Sir Charles Holroyd [q.v.]. The constitution of the gallery was still a vexed question. Alternative solutions were to give the director unfettered responsibility for the purchase of pictures, subject to Treasury control; or but one vote on a board of many amateurs. The second policy was in favour. The new director was hardly supple enough gladly to subordinate what he regarded as a trust of scholarship to the prejudice or taste of less exacting standards. Meanwhile his experience as critic, administrator, and publisher was focused on familiarizing the public with the contents and significance of the National Gallery.

Photograph and publications departments were organized, Holmes personally contributing the admirable *Illustrated Guide to the National Gallery* (1921) and *Old Masters and Modern Art in the National Gallery* (3 vols., 1923–1927). He was knighted in 1921 and appointed K.C.V.O. in 1928, the year in which he retired from the directorship of the National Gallery, continuing to write and paint. His last book was his autobiography, *Self and Partners* (1936). He received honorary degrees from the universities of Cambridge and Leeds, and was elected an honorary fellow of Brasenose College in 1931. He died in London 7 December 1936. In 1903 he married his cousin Florence Mary Hill, a violinist and composer, only daughter of Charles Robert Rivington, solicitor, of London; there were two sons of the marriage.

Holmes's achievement as a writer, and the distinction of his art, are due to unusual integration of theory and practice. He learnt to draw and paint through unremitting experiment and analysis of the old masters. His painter's insight gave him special grasp of those masters' problems and their ways of solving them. Other writings of his, *Leonardo da Vinci* (*Proceedings* of the British Academy, vol. ix, 1919); *An Introduction to Italian Painting* (1929); and *A Grammar of the Arts* (1931) are vital because of their lucid, concrete explanation of the great artists' thought and practice. Works by Holmes are in many public collections, including the Tate Gallery, British Museum, Victoria and Albert Museum, Fitzwilliam Museum, Ashmolean Museum, and the galleries of Manchester, Adelaide, Johannesburg, Melbourne, and Sydney.

[Sir C. J. Holmes, *Self and Partners*, 1936; *The Water-Colours of C. J. Holmes* (with foreword by Michael Sadleir), 1920; X. B. [C. H. Collins Baker], *Sir Charles Holmes* (*Contemporary British Artists*), 1924; *Sir Charles Holmes, K.C.V.O.*, Memorial Exhibition Catalogue (with foreword by A. M. Hind), Fine Art Society, February 1937; A. M. Hind, 'The Sketch-Books of Sir Charles Holmes', in *Burlington Magazine*, August 1940; A. M. Hind, 'The Water-Colours of Sir Charles Holmes', in the Old Water-Colour Society's Club, Twenty-first Annual Volume, 1943.]

C. H. COLLINS BAKER.

HOLMES, THOMAS RICE EDWARD (1855–1933), historian and classical scholar, was born at Waterstown House, near Athlone, co. Westmeath, 24 May 1855, the fifth son and seventh child of

Robert Holmes, owner of the property of Moycashel, in the parish of Kilbeggan, co. Westmeath, and tenant of Waterstown House, by his wife, Jane, daughter of William Henn, a master in Chancery, of Dublin. From Merchant Taylors School in London he passed in 1873 to Christ Church, Oxford, as a junior student. At Oxford, where he obtained a second class in classical moderations (1875) and a first class in modern history (1877), he fell under the influence of Sidney James Owen, then university teacher of Indian law and history.

In 1878 Holmes became a master at Lincoln Grammar School, whence in 1880 he moved to Blackheath Proprietary School. Six years later he went to St. Paul's School where he remained until in 1909, with the help of a civil list pension, he was able to retire. He received honorary degrees from the universities of Dublin (1904) and Oxford (1922), and was elected a fellow of the British Academy in 1925. In 1888 he married Isabel, daughter of Lionel Isaacs, of The Grove, Mandeville, Jamaica: they had no children. He died at Roehampton 4 August 1933, and was survived by his wife.

Throughout his career Holmes devoted his leisure, and during the twenty-four years of his retirement his whole working time, to learned research. First, he developed an interest acquired at Oxford by writing what until then did not exist—a comprehensive and critical account of the events in India during the years 1857 and 1858. His *History of the Indian Mutiny* appeared in 1883. Secondly, having published various subsidiary studies on the history of British India, he was led by the needs of his pupils at St. Paul's to turn his attention to the works of Julius Caesar. It was as a Caesarian scholar, one of whose greatest services was to challenge the more speculative doctrines of Napoleon III, and as an historian of Rome in the times of Caesar and Augustus, that he became most widely known. In these fields his main publications were *Caesar's Conquest of Gaul* (1899, 2nd ed. 1911), *Ancient Britain and the Invasions of Julius Caesar* (1907), *The Roman Republic and the Founder of the Empire* (3 vols., 1923), and *The Architect of the Roman Empire* (vol. i, 1928; vol. ii, 1931). The outstanding characteristics of Holmes's work are his extreme accuracy, the independence of his judgement, and his mastery of the literature of his subjects.

[*Thomas Rice Edward Holmes, 1855–1933* in *Proceedings* of the British Academy (bibliography), vol. xxii, 1936.]

HOLST, GUSTAV THEODORE (1874–1934), composer, whose original name was GUSTAVUS THEODORE VON HOLST, was born at Cheltenham 21 September 1874, the elder son of Adolph von Holst, a music teacher in Cheltenham, by his first wife, Clara, daughter of Samuel Lediard, solicitor, of Cirencester. The von Holsts were of Swedish origin though long settled in England. The painter Theodor von Holst [q.v.] was Gustav's great-uncle.

At an early age Holst began to learn the violin and the pianoforte. His favourite composer in these days was Grieg. Soon after entering Cheltenham Grammar School he read Berlioz's *Orchestration* and with no further instruction started to set Macaulay's 'Horatius' to music for chorus and orchestra. However, his father discouraged composition and wished him to be a virtuoso pianist, but neuritis prevented this and at the age of seventeen he was allowed to study counterpoint with G. F. Sims of Oxford.

In 1892 Holst obtained his first professional engagement as organist of Wyck Rissington, Gloucestershire. At the same time he conducted a choral society at the neighbouring Bourton-on-the-Water. Next year saw the first public performance of his work in Cheltenham, the music for an operetta, *Lansdowne Castle*. As a result of this success his father sent him to the Royal College of Music where he studied composition with (Sir) C. V. Stanford [q.v.]. At this time he got to know the later works of Wagner and heard Bach's B minor Mass; thenceforth Bach and Wagner became his passion until in later years the influence of English folk-song and of the Tudor composers tended to weaken the Wagnerian supremacy although Bach was never dethroned.

Meanwhile Holst had made himself proficient on the trombone and was able to eke out his modest allowance by playing on seaside piers and in a 'Viennese' dance band. The trombone took him right into the heart of the orchestra, an experience which was the foundation of his great command of instrumentation.

In 1895 the Royal College awarded Holst a scholarship. This meant free tuition but only £30 a year for 'maintenance' and his life at this time, partly on principle, but chiefly from necessity, was almost unbelievably frugal. Owing to this his neuritis became so bad that he could not hold an ordinary pen and his eyesight suffered severely. These two weaknesses persisted throughout his life. Out of his poverty, however, there grew indirectly his love of the English country. He could not afford train journeys and used to walk to his various destinations. His habit of long walks never left him. They were his relaxation after a spell of hard work and a prelude to new periods of inspiration.

In 1898 Holst became first trombone and *répétiteur* to the Carl Rosa Opera Company and shortly after joined the Scottish Orchestra as second trombone. Thus ended his *status pupillaris*. His student compositions had grown in competence but, although his intimate friends saw something beneath the surface, his work did not, in itself, show great originality or force. Strangely enough the germ of the future Holst seems to be found in his early children's operettas; otherwise he was content, unconsciously perhaps, to lay the foundations of that incomparable sureness of touch and clarity of texture which mark his mature writing.

It was now that Holst discovered the feeling of unity with his fellow men which made him afterwards a great teacher. A sense of comradeship rather than political conviction led him, while still a student, to join the Kelmscott House Socialist Club in Hammersmith. Here he met Isobel, daughter of an artist, Augustus Ralph Harrison, and he married her in 1901. They had one daughter, Imogen, who followed her father's footsteps as composer and teacher.

Mysticism had always attracted Holst, and he had read Walt Whitman and Ibsen. In 1899 with no other training than a little 'grammar school' Latin he learnt enough Sanskrit to make translations of the Vedic hymns for musical setting. On these followed the *opera di camera*, 'Savitri' (1908), also on a Sanskrit subject: this was first performed at the London School of Opera under Mr. Hermann Grunebaum in 1916. These works, although mature, were but a foreshadowing of something greater— 'The Hymn of Jesus'—written in 1917 and first performed at the Queen's Hall in 1920.

In 1903, although still comparatively unknown, Holst decided to give up the trombone and devote himself to writing music. He soon found that man cannot live by composition alone and he became music teacher at the James Allen Girls' School, Dulwich, and at the Passmore Edwards (later the Mary Ward) Settle-

ment, where he gave the first English performances of several Bach cantatas. In 1905 he was appointed director of music at St. Paul's Girls' School, Hammersmith. Here he did away with the childish sentimentality which schoolgirls were supposed to appreciate and substituted Bach and Vittoria; a splendid background for immature minds. In 1913 a sound-proof music room was built at the school where he could work undisturbed. The first work written in these rooms was the 'St. Paul's' suite for strings (1913) dedicated to the school orchestra.

St. Paul's was a clean slate, but at Morley College for Working Men and Women in South London, where Holst became musical director in 1907, a bad tradition had to be broken down. The results were at first discouraging, but soon a new spirit appeared and the music of Morley College, together with its off-shoot the 'Whitsuntide festival' held at Thaxted, Essex, and elsewhere, became a force to be reckoned with. The 'Holst' room stands as a memorial to his work there which was carried on in the same spirit by his successors.

The year 1914 marked the inception of Holst's most famous work, 'The Planets', a suite for orchestra, each movement being suggested by the astrological attribute of a planet. This was completed in 1917. A private performance was given in 1918 under (Sir) Adrian Boult as a parting present to the composer on his departure to the Near East. The war had brought Holst great misery; he tried in vain to enlist and he began to think that he was useless; then the Young Men's Christian Association invited him to organize music for the troops in Salonika. In view of this official appointment he decided to discard the prefix 'von' from his name. He returned after a successful year abroad to find, rather to his dismay, that he was becoming a popular composer. The American orchestras were fighting for the first public performance of 'The Planets' which was produced at the Queen's Hall in 1919 and followed there by 'The Hymn of Jesus' in 1920.

Holst went back to his sound-proof room and in 1919 composed the 'Ode to Death' (a setting of a poem by Whitman), considered by many to be his most beautiful choral work. He also finished in 1922 his opera *The Perfect Fool*. This was played to a crowded house at Covent Garden in 1923. The audience was puzzled and did not understand his peculiar sense of humour, so well appreciated by his friends. However, the splendid ballet music has remained in the repertoire.

From 1919 to 1924 Holst was professor of composition at the Royal College of Music and he held a similar post at University College, Reading, from 1919 to 1923. An accident while conducting at Reading caused concussion. Disregarding this he went to America in 1923 in order to conduct at the musical festival at the university of Michigan at Ann Arbor, but on his return his old enemy, insomnia, became alarming and he was ordered complete rest. This enabled him soon to re-start composing, first an opera, *At the Boar's Head*, founded on the Falstaff scenes of *Henry the Fourth*, and set almost entirely to English dance tunes (produced by the British National Opera Company at Manchester in 1925), and second and more important, the 'Keats' choral symphony, written for the Leeds festival of 1925. Its strength and power were obvious but it had no popular success and an entirely inadequate performance in London did not help it. Holst's dread of popularity seemed to drive him back upon himself. A certain aloofness appeared in his music; for instance, in 'Egdon Heath' (1927, first performed in 1928), written as a homage to Thomas Hardy. Even those who understood him best found it difficult to assimilate at first, although they are gradually coming round to the composer's own opinion, that this was his best work. However, some gracious smaller compositions belong to this period, notably the seven part-songs for women's voices (1925–1926), settings of poems by his friend Robert Bridges.

Holst's position as a composer is testified to by the Holst festival held in his native town of Cheltenham in 1927 and by the award of the gold medal of the Royal Philharmonic Society in 1930. He was also invited to lecture at Harvard University and to conduct his own compositions in Boston. This (his third) visit to the United States of America (1932) was interrupted by illness, but he recovered quickly and he returned to England apparently well though without some of his old energy. At this time he wrote the six choral canons which are a puzzle to many although some have succeeded in plucking out the heart of their mystery.

In these later years Holst's constant companion was his daughter, and whenever they could meet, he and his lifelong friend, Dr. Ralph Vaughan Williams, would spend whole days discussing their compositions. Holst declared that his music was influenced by that of his friend: the converse is certainly true.

Holst again fell ill in 1932, although he was able in 1933 to write the 'Lyric Movement' for Mr. Lionel Tertis, the violist. He died in London of heart failure following an operation 25 May 1934. His ashes were buried in Chichester Cathedral, close to the memorial to Thomas Weelkes [q.v.] whose music he greatly loved.

Holst's music has been called cold and inhuman: it is only cold from its burning intensity. It is true that he sometimes seemed to be living in a world removed from human beings, but he never lost touch with his fellow men.

A portrait of Holst, by Bernard Munns, is in Cheltenham Public Library, and a drawing, by Sir William Rothenstein (1920), is at Morley College.

[Imogen Holst, *Gustav Holst*, 1938 (chronological lists of compositions, and portraits); *Grove's Dictionary of Music and Musicians*, 4th ed., vol. ii, edited by H. C. Colles; *Music and Letters*, July and October 1920; *Musical Times*, July 1934; personal knowledge.]

R. Vaughan Williams.

HOPE, ANTHONY (pseudonym), novelist. [See Hawkins, Sir Anthony Hope.]

HOPKINSON, Sir ALFRED (1851–1939), lawyer, educationist, and politician, was born at Manchester 28 June 1851, the second son of John Hopkinson, mechanical engineer and sometime mayor of Manchester, by his wife, Alice, daughter of John Dewhurst, of Skipton, Yorkshire. His elder brother was John Hopkinson [q.v.].

Hopkinson was educated at a private school in Manchester and in 1866 went to the Owens College, thence in 1869, as a scholar, to Lincoln College, Oxford, where he was placed in the second class in *literae humaniores* in 1872 and in the first class in the B.C.L. examination in 1874. He was elected to the Stowell fellowship in civil law at University College in 1873, and to the Vinerian scholarship in 1875.

Hopkinson was called to the bar by Lincoln's Inn in 1873 and settling in Manchester as a barrister speedily acquired a considerable local practice on the Northern circuit, mainly in the Palatine Chancery Court. This he conducted in conjunction with the tenure of a lecturership and (later at the age of twenty-four) of the professorship of law at the Owens College. He resigned this chair in 1889.

In 1885 Hopkinson unsuccessfully contested the East division of Manchester as a liberal, and in 1892 the South-Western division as a liberal unionist; but, having moved to London in 1889 and having taken silk in 1892, he was elected member for the Cricklade division of Wiltshire in 1895, only to resign the seat in 1898 on his appointment as principal of the Owens College, the first constituent college of the newly formed Victoria University of which he became first vice-chancellor in 1900. In these offices he did his finest work.

Retiring from the vice-chancellorship in 1913, Hopkinson devoted himself unstintingly to public service, including a visit to India to report on the university of Bombay, and at a by-election in 1926 he was once more returned to parliament as unionist member for the Combined English Universities, finally retiring in 1929.

A man of striking physical appearance and great personal charm, Hopkinson was never known to act otherwise than in accord with the dictates of his own conscience, which in turn were based on a deep-rooted belief that 'the hope of mankind is in the Christian religion'. On his death he was described as 'above all else a Christian gentleman to whom religion was a thing which he recorded as vital not only in his own life but also in that of the nation'. In *Rebuilding Britain, a Survey of Problems of Reconstruction* (1918) he expounded his political ideas and views of English affairs, whilst in *Penultima* (1930) he gave frank and refreshing expression to the views which had guided him throughout his long and unselfish life.

Hopkinson was knighted in 1910 and elected an honorary fellow of Lincoln College, Oxford, in 1903. He received honorary degrees from the universities of Manchester, Glasgow, Aberdeen, Leeds, and Bristol, and was elected bencher of Lincoln's Inn in 1896; he was treasurer in 1921. In 1873 he married Esther (died 1931), youngest daughter of Henry Wells, of Nottingham, and had four sons and three daughters. Of his sons, the second became archdeacon of Westmorland and the third was member of parliament for the Mossley division of Lancashire. He died at Bovington, Hertfordshire, 11 November 1939.

[*The Times*, 13 November 1939; Sir Alfred Hopkinson, *Penultima*, 1930; *Alpine Journal*, May 1940; private information; personal knowledge.]   ALFRED T. DAVIES.

HORNE, ROBERT STEVENSON, VISCOUNT HORNE OF SLAMANNAN (1871–1940), lawyer, politician, and man of business, was born 28 February 1871 at the mining village of Slamannan, Stirlingshire, the youngest son of Robert Stevenson Horne, minister of the parish of Slamannan, by his wife, Mary, daughter of Thomas Lochhead, of Toward, Argyll. Throughout his varied and successful career he exhibited the characteristics which are commonly recognized as the birthright of the sons of the Scottish manse, a resolute ambition to get on in the world, the gift of forgathering easily and congenially with all sorts and conditions of men, and a well educated mind alive to the practical realities of life yet not devoid of imagination. Horne was educated at George Watson's College, Edinburgh, and at the university of Glasgow, where he combined the pursuit of academic studies in arts and law with strenuous undergraduate politics. In both he distinguished himself, for he graduated with first class honours in mental philosophy (1893) and became president of the university conservative club and of the students' representative council. For a man of his gifts the bar was an obvious choice, and, after lecturing for a year on philosophy in the University College of North Wales at Bangor, he was admitted a member of the Faculty of Advocates in 1896. His connexion with Glasgow, from which so much of the work of the Court of Session comes, assisted his early success, and his practice throve, especially in commercial and shipping cases. In 1910 he took silk.

Horne was not a dedicated lawyer, although he was proficient in knowledge of the law and efficient in its practice. The law was rather his means of livelihood and advancement than his delight, and he continued to cultivate his political interests and contacts, as if prescient that his real vocation lay in that sphere. The war of 1914–1918 gave him the opportunity of entering a wider field and he was quick to seize it. A minor appointment as secretary to the agricultural section of the National Service Department was followed by his association with Sir Eric Campbell Geddes [q.v.], in railway organization at the front with the rank of lieutenant-colonel. From transport Horne turned to the direction first (1917) of the department of materials and priority and then (1918) of the department of labour at the Admiralty, where he held the office of third civil lord from

1918 to 1919. In December 1918, on the conclusion of the war, he was returned to parliament as unionist member for the Hillhead division of Glasgow, and had the unusual honour of at once taking his seat on the front bench of the House of Commons as minister of labour, an appointment which he owed to the high opinion of his ability which the prime minister, Lloyd George, had formed and throughout retained. Here Horne found a sphere peculiarly suited to his gifts of good temper and persuasion and to his origin and upbringing. He handled with conspicuous success the labour disputes which were then rife in the mining and railway worlds. In 1920 he became president of the Board of Trade, and in the following year he attained the second position in the Cabinet as chancellor of the Exchequer. On the dissolution of the coalition government in 1922 his loyalty to Lloyd George deterred him from accepting office in the new administration formed by Bonar Law, and his political life may then be said to have ended, although he retained his seat in the House of Commons until he was raised to the peerage in 1937 as Viscount Horne of Slamannan.

An ex-Cabinet minister is often at a loss for employment compatible with his position, but Horne's versatility was equal to the situation. He is said to have thought of the possibility of a judgeship in the Court of Session, but for the successful Scotsman in London there are *vestigia nulla retrorsum*, and he turned to the City. Once more success attended him, and before long he found himself among the financial and commercial élite as a director of the Suez Canal Company, the Peninsular and Oriental Steam Navigation Company, Lloyds Bank, the Commercial Union Assurance Company, and other concerns. He was chairman of the Burmah Corporation and of other important undertakings. In 1934 he became chairman of the Great Western Railway Company.

Among the honours which Horne received were the freedom of the City of Edinburgh and the lord rectorship of Aberdeen University (1921–1924). He was appointed K.B.E. in 1918 and G.B.E. in 1920, and was sworn of the Privy Council in 1919. The universities of Glasgow, Edinburgh, Aberdeen, and Birmingham conferred honorary degrees upon him and he was a grand officer of the Order of the Crown of Italy.

Lord Horne died at Farnham, Surrey, 3 September 1940. As he was unmarried, the peerage became extinct. His career has been described as meteoric, but it had none of the eccentricities of a celestial vagrant. On the contrary, in each of its successive phases it attracted the rewards of a supreme conventional competence rather than of wayward genius. He could do well and sometimes brilliantly whatever task he tackled, but the mark which he left was not permanently distinctive. Debonair, alert, and sprightly, he was in much request socially, for he had the zest for good fellowship which accompanies the ability to shine in it, and his equipment included an inexhaustible stock of really amusing stories. The first Earl of Birkenhead wrote of him: 'Sir Robert Horne contributed much to the liveliness, to the charm, and to the good humour of English political life in those dark and lowering days when those who could offer these gifts were rare and shining figures.'

[*The Times*, 4 September 1940; personal knowledge.]   MACMILLAN.

HORNIMAN, ANNIE ELIZABETH FREDERICKA (1860–1937), pioneer of the modern theatre repertory movement, was born at Forest Hill, London, 3 October 1860, the only daughter of Frederick John Horniman [q.v.], founder of the Horniman Museum and liberal member of parliament for Falmouth and Penryn from 1895 to 1904, by his first wife, Rebekah, daughter of John Emslie, of Dalton. She was educated privately, and studied for five years at the Slade School of Fine Art under Alphonse Legros [q.v.], and for five years acted as secretary to W. B. Yeats [q.v.]. A woman of considerable wealth, with very determined views, she interested herself originally in the theatre merely because her relatives strongly disapproved of it. Doubtless, however, she was to some extent influenced by her association with Yeats.

Miss Horniman's first connexion with theatrical affairs was in March 1894 when, at the Avenue Theatre (on the site of the Playhouse), London, she produced John Todhunter's play *The Comedy of Sighs* and Yeats's *The Land of Heart's Desire*; these were followed in April by Mr. Bernard Shaw's comedy *Arms and the Man*. She incurred heavy financial loss in this initial venture, which she described as a 'fruitful failure'. She was not deterred by this early setback, and it in no way damped her enthusiasm, but it was ten years before she made her next move. It was an important decision. She determined to subsidize the Irish national theatre movement. In 1904 she took over the old theatre of the Mechanics' Institute in Abbey Street, Dublin, and lent it rent free for six years to the Irish National Theatre Society. The gift amounted to £12,000 and the Abbey Theatre, Dublin, presented many fine plays and produced several brilliant players.

Miss Horniman transferred her activities to Manchester in 1907, when she acquired the Midland Theatre, which she opened in September of that year with *David Ballard* and *His Helpmate* both written by Charles M'Evoy. She produced several modern plays here. Her policy was thoroughly catholic, her object being to produce plays by authors of all ages, with especial emphasis on new writers; they were to be performed by a permanent company of picked, front-rank artists, and at prices within the reach of all.

The immediate appreciation of Miss Horniman's efforts was such that in 1908 she purchased the old Gaiety Theatre, Manchester, and practically rebuilt the house. She opened the new Gaiety (the first modern repertory theatre in this country) in September with *When the Devil was Ill*, by M'Evoy, and *Marriages are made in Heaven*, by Mr. Basil Dean. From that date until 1921 she presented over 200 plays, more than a hundred of which were original. The early promise of catholicity in the selection of authors was amply fulfilled. Euripides, Shakespeare, Beaumont and Fletcher, Ben Jonson, Goldsmith, Sheridan, Ibsen, Sudermann, Maeterlinck, Galsworthy, St. John Hankin, Rostand, Arnold Bennett, Mr. Bernard Shaw, Harley Granville-Barker, Barrie, and Mr. St. John Ervine were all represented. Among the new writers of the 'Manchester school' whose works she presented were M'Evoy, W. S. Houghton [q.v.], Allan Monkhouse, Mr. Harold Brighouse, Mr. Basil Dean, Harold Chapin, and Miss Elizabeth Baker. Among the successful modern plays presented were *Hindle Wakes*, *The Mob*, *The Younger Generation, Jane Clegg, Chains*, and *Mary Broome*. She made one solitary appearance on the stage, when she 'walked on' in *Nothing Like Leather* at the Gaiety in September 1913.

To the great regret of lovers of the repertory movement all over the country the enterprise collapsed after fourteen years, and in 1921 Miss Horniman was forced to sell out. She received the sum of £52,000 for her interest, but out of this amount a large overdraft at the bank had to be met. When she relinquished her management, she presented her entire library of plays to the Drama League.

Manchester University recognized the value of Miss Horniman's work by conferring upon her the honorary degree of M.A. in 1910, and she was appointed C.H. 'for services to the drama' in 1933. She was deeply interested in astrology, had a great knowledge of Wagnerian opera, and a wide understanding of art and architecture. She was an interesting lecturer, and was widely esteemed as a generous personality. At one time she was an ardent supporter of the suffragette movement, but the stage was her ruling passion. She died at Shere, Surrey, 6 August 1937.

A portrait of Miss Horniman by Emma Magnus hangs in the Chorlton Repertory Club.

[*The Times*, 9 August 1937; *Who's Who in the Theatre*, 1936; personal knowledge.]

JOHN PARKER.

HORRIDGE, Sir THOMAS GARDNER (1857–1938), judge, was born at Haulgh Tonge with Haulgh, Bolton, Lancashire, 12 October 1857, the only son of John Horridge, manufacturing chemist of that town, by his wife, Margaret, youngest daughter of Robert Sharpe Barlow, of Bolton. He was educated at Nassau School, Barnes. He was admitted a solicitor in 1879 and practised at Southport. In 1884 he was called to the bar by the Middle Temple and joined the Northern circuit, practising as a member of the local bar at Liverpool, where his Lancashire associations secured him a start. He was endowed with a good presence and self-confidence as well as ability, and he soon acquired a substantial practice. In 1901 he took silk and was successful, especially in commercial cases, but his practice continued to be mainly on circuit. In 1907 he appeared for W. H. Lever (later Viscount Leverhulme, q.v.) in his successful action for libel against the Northcliffe newspapers, one of his juniors being F. E. Smith (later Earl of Birkenhead, q.v.). At the general election of 1906 Horridge had entered parliament as liberal member for East Manchester, defeating A. J. Balfour (later first Earl of Balfour, q.v.) by a substantial majority. F. E. Smith entered parliament at the same time and Horridge's election oratory became one of the targets for Smith's invective in his famous maiden speech. The two men crossed swords on the government's trades disputes bill (1906) which Horridge supported, as he did the old age pensions scheme.

Horridge did not stand at the general election of January 1910, and in October of that year was appointed a judge of the King's Bench division. He proved an excellent judge in both jury and non-jury cases, sound, competent, dignified, and expeditious. His only fault was an occasional brusqueness to counsel and witnesses. He frequently dealt with bankruptcy and divorce as well as the ordinary King's Bench cases. In 1916 he took part with Sir Rufus Isaacs (later Marquess of Reading, q.v.) and Sir Horace Avory [q.v.] in the trial at bar of Roger Casement [q.v.]. The court's construction of the Treason Act of 1351 was upheld in the Court of Criminal Appeal. From the legal point of view his most interesting decision was in the case of *Philips* v. *Brooks* (1919). In this case a man had induced a jeweller to sell him jewellery and to allow him to take it away, by passing himself off as a man of good financial position whom he named. Horridge held that pawnbrokers who had advanced money to the fraudulent customer in good faith, on the security of the jewellery, obtained a good title to it, since the jeweller had intended to sell the goods to the fraudulent customer and there was thus no error as to the identity of the contracting party. The sale was therefore voidable, but not void. Horridge, who had told a royal commission in 1935 that he was opposed to the introduction of a retiring age for judges, retained his position until his eightieth year, resigning in May 1937. He was sworn of the Privy Council on his retirement. In 1929 he had filled the office of treasurer of the Middle Temple. He died at Hove 25 July 1938.

Horridge was twice married: first, in 1901 to Evelyne (died 1920), youngest daughter of Melvill Sandys, of the Bengal civil service, of Lanarth, Cornwall; secondly, in 1921 to May Ethel Markham (by deed poll), daughter of Captain Francis Pavy, of London, and Wroughton, Wiltshire, and widow of Alfred Isenberg. There were no children by either marriage.

[*The Times*, 26 July 1938; *Law Journal*, 30 July 1938 (portrait); *Law Reports*.]

DAVID DAVIES.

HORTON, ROBERT FORMAN (1855–1934), Congregational divine and theological writer, was born in London 18 September 1855, the only son of Thomas Galland Horton, Congregational minister, by his wife, Sarah Ellen, second daughter of Robert Forman, hop merchant and maltster, of Derby. To Horton, as the son of a nonconformist minister, brought up in a nonconformist milieu, nonconformity of a definite but liberal type was bone of his bone and flesh of his flesh, and it was as a nonconformist minister that his own life-work was done.

Horton was educated at Tettenhall Proprietary School, Wolverhampton, at Shrewsbury, and at New College, Oxford, of which he was an open scholar. He obtained a first class in classical moderations (1875) and in *literae humaniores* (1878), was president of the Union (1877), and was elected a fellow of his college in 1879. He retained his fellowship until 1886, and until 1883 was lecturer in ancient and modern history. He was Lyman Beecher lecturer at Yale University in 1893, being invited, to his own great embarrassment, to lecture on preaching. For great preacher as Horton undeniably was, preaching was never to him, as he once declared, the 'delight that it was to most preachers'. Speaking in debate or on the platform was a pleasure to him; but in the pulpit he was overwhelmed by the sense of responsibility in being permitted to convey to men the message of God. That was characteristic of Horton's deep humility. Yet the Yale lectures, published in 1893 as *Verbum Dei* and later (1898) as *The Word of God*, must have been immensely helpful to several generations of ministers. Of all his books this is the likeliest to survive.

The main work of Horton's life was not, however, literary but pastoral, as pastor of the Lyndhurst Road Congregational church in Hampstead from 1884 to 1930. To this church, built for him, he attracted a very large and distinguished congregation, which included at times great statesmen and brilliant journalists. Yet it was not without a struggle that he decided in 1883 to leave Oxford for Hampstead and to be ordained (January 1884). At Oxford his official work in college was congenial and Oxford itself had laid on him her spell. More than that, this nonconformist of nonconformists knew that there was a special place for him in Oxford which only he could fill. There were some 200 nonconformists already in residence, and after the final removal of disabilities they were coming up in increasing numbers. But they still felt rather isolated and apart. Mansfield College had not yet come to

Oxford to provide them with a training college and a social centre. The latter Horton provided in his rooms in New College, where were held the meetings of a nonconformist union which he founded with James (afterwards Viscount) Bryce [q.v.] as president.

From Oxford Horton went frequently to preach as a lay pastor in a temporary church at Hampstead, and in 1883 he had to make a final choice between his two spheres of activity. He never regretted his decision, the less, perhaps, as his departure from Oxford coincided with his rejection as examiner in 'the Rudiments of Faith and Religion', an examination then a necessary preliminary to a degree. Unwisely nominated to the office, Horton refused to withdraw, but an angry mob of country clergymen vetoed the nomination in Convocation and Horton left Oxford, deeply resenting an act of 'bigotry and intolerance'.

Horton became a far more distinguished man in London than ever he could have been in Oxford. But ambition was the least of his temptations. All the great offices in his own denomination fell to him in due course: he was chairman of the London Congregational Union (1898) and of the Congregational Union of England and Wales (1903), and president of the National Free Church Council (1905). He declined more than once to leave Hampstead for a pulpit of even greater publicity. Fame came to him indeed but he never sought, and even shunned it. Casual auditors found his wit mordant, and his speech sarcastic; but these attributes, if obtrusive, were quite superficial; in his heart there was nothing but love and tenderness, coupled with deep humility.

Horton had a ready pen: the British Museum catalogue contains fifty items from it: many devotional and some controversial pamphlets; a few exercises in critical theology; some biographies (e.g. *Oliver Cromwell*, 1897). But Horton was too much of a preacher to be a completely successful teacher; he had too little detachment; the moral purpose is too obtrusive. It is, then, as the unconscious revelation of a saintly personality that his writings can to advantage be read.

Horton died at Hampstead 30 March 1934. He married in 1918 Isabel Violet, younger daughter of Duncan Frederick Basden, of Hampstead, and had one daughter.

[*The Times*, 2 April 1934; R. F. Horton, *An Autobiography*, 1917; Albert Peel and Sir J. A. R. Marriott, *Robert Forman Horton* (portraits and bibliography), 1937; private information; personal knowledge.]

J. A. R. MARRIOTT.

HOSKYNS, SIR EDWYN CLEMENT, thirteenth baronet (1884-1937), divine, the eldest child and only son of (Sir) Edwyn Hoskyns, afterwards twelfth baronet and second bishop of Southwell (whom he succeeded in 1925), by his wife, Mary Constance Maude, only daughter of Robert Benson, of London, was born at St. Clement's vicarage, Notting Hill, London, 9 August 1884. He was descended from John Hoskins [q.v.], lawyer and wit, and from Sir John Hoskyns [q.v.], second baronet and second president of the Royal Society.

Hoskyns was educated at Haileybury, Jesus College, Cambridge, the university of Berlin, and Wells Theological College. Ordained in 1908 to the title of St. Ignatius, Sunderland, he was appointed in 1912 warden of Stephenson Hall in the university of Sheffield. In 1915 he became a chaplain to the forces, and was awarded the M.C. and mentioned in dispatches.

While still serving overseas Hoskyns was elected into a fellowship at Corpus Christi College, Cambridge, and began his work early in 1919. Theological liberalism was then dominant in Cambridge. Hoskyns became a pioneer of a critical, evangelical Catholicism, intensely devoted to the Church of England and her formularies. He had studied under Harnack in Berlin, knew and had been influenced by Schweitzer, and found through Loisy an approach to the New Testament. His lectures on the theology and ethics of the New Testament began as an exposition of the religious experience of the primitive Church. It was that experience which lay behind and was reflected in the documents of the New Testament. To the authority of that experience he appealed, and only through the study of that experience would he approach the problem of Christian origins. Slowly his lectures changed. The *Römerbrief* of Karl Barth gave him a language. His friendship with Gerhard Kittel led to the adoption of the lexicographical method of the *Theologisches Wörterbuch*. In his most important book, *The Riddle of the New Testament* (1931), written in collaboration with his pupil the Rev. Francis Noel Davey, he reached his final position. No interpretation of the person and teaching of Jesus which failed to explain the faith of the primitive Church could be true to history.

This development of Hoskyns's thought can be traced in his *Cambridge Sermons* (1938), edited after his death with a biographical account by Canon Charles Hugh Egerton Smyth. It comes out in his occasional papers, *Christ and Catholicism* (1923), 'The Christ of the Synoptic Gospels' in *Essays Catholic and Critical* (1926) which marked a turning-point in English theology, and in 'Jesus the Messiah' in *Mysterium Christi* (1930). His largest books are his brilliant translation of Barth's commentary on *The Epistle to the Romans* (1933) and his unfinished commentary on *The Fourth Gospel* (1940), edited by the Rev. F. N. Davey.

Hoskyns was a teacher who inspired his pupils through his enthusiasm. In his college he exercised a profound influence as dean of chapel from 1919 and as librarian and president from 1929. His interests were wide and human—rowing, music, farming. His piety was natural and direct. In 1921–1922 he served the university as senior proctor. He was canon theologian of Liverpool Cathedral from 1932 to 1935.

In 1922 Hoskyns married Mary Trym, younger daughter of Edwin Budden, schoolmaster, of Macclesfield: she was a research fellow of Newnham College, Cambridge, from 1921 to 1924. By her he had four sons and a daughter. He died suddenly in London 28 June 1937, and was succeeded as fourteenth baronet by his eldest son, Chandos Wren Hoskyns (born 1923), who was killed in flying operations over Norway in 1945.

[*The Times*, 30 June 1937; E. C. Hoskyns, *Cambridge Sermons*, 1938; personal knowledge.]   J. O. Cobham.

HOUSMAN, ALFRED EDWARD (1859–1936), poet and classical scholar, was born at the Valley House, Fockbury, in the parish of Catshill, Worcestershire, 26 March 1859, the eldest child in the family of five sons and two daughters of Edward Housman, a solicitor practising in the neighbouring town of Bromsgrove, by his first wife, Sarah Jane Williams, who died in 1871. In the previous year Housman had been sent to Bromsgrove School, whence in 1877 he passed as a scholar to St. John's College, Oxford.

At Oxford Housman gained first class honours in classical moderations in 1879, but in 1881 he failed to obtain honours in *literae humaniores*. This failure, due to his neglect of philosophy and history, seriously affected his spirits. He worked at home for the civil service examination, at the same time helping his old headmaster in sixth form teaching. In 1882 he became a higher division clerk in the Patent Office, and took lodgings in Bayswater with his greatest friend, Moses John Jackson, to whom he later dedicated the first volume of his Manilius. Jackson went to India in 1887, and about the same time Housman settled in Highgate, whence in 1905 he moved to Pinner, which he did not leave until he went to Cambridge in 1911.

In the Patent Office Housman found time for classical study. At Oxford he had already worked on the text of Propertius, and had corresponded with the great Cambridge Latinist H. A. J. Munro [q.v.], but his first publication was in the year of his entry into the civil service. This was a powerful paper on Horace in the *Journal of Philology*, followed next year by a note on Ovid's *Ibis*, but he printed no more until 1887, when he contributed to the first volume of the *Classical Review* an article on passages of Sophocles and Euripides. In every later year, including that of his death, he published at least one classical article or review, and the output of the years following 1887 was especially striking. It dealt with textual problems in all three Greek tragedians and in half a dozen Latin poets.

In 1889 Housman became a member of the Cambridge Philological Society, and he contributed several papers to its *Proceedings* and *Transactions*, as well as to the *American Journal of Philology*. The high quality of his work attracted such wide attention that when in 1892 the death of Alfred Goodwin, professor of Greek and Latin at University College, London, gave him the chance of entering academic life, he obtained testimonials from fifteen British scholars, and also from Basil Lanneau Gildersleeve of Baltimore and Nikolaus Wecklein of Munich. In place of Goodwin's combined chair two professorships were now established. Housman stood in the first instance for the Latin chair, but desired to be considered, if the Latin went to another candidate, for the Greek chair. He obtained his first preference, and remained until his death a professor of Latin: thenceforward his published work was almost confined to that language. It is true that between 1897 and 1910 he made several brilliant contributions to the restoration of lost works of Greek poetry then coming to light in Egyptian papyri, and that in later years he was often consulted by the editors of the *Oxyrhynchus Papyri*, and of Liddell and Scott's *Lexicon*, but almost all his other classical work was concerned after 1892 with Latin. He remained, nevertheless, as his review (published in the *Classical Review*, vol. xxxix, 1925) of the text of Sophocles of A. C. Pearson [q.v.] suffices to prove, one of the best Grecians in Europe.

Housman's tenure of his London chair lasted until 1911. For most of that time University College was served by a professorial staff of great distinction in many departments, but in the words which Housman used of his colleague John Arthur Platt, 'much of the teaching which he was required to give was elementary, and he seldom had pupils who possessed a native aptitude for classical studies or intended to pursue them far'.

The work which Housman published while he was in London dealt with most of the chief Latin poets from Lucilius to Juvenal. Of these Propertius and Ovid had been among his earliest interests. He now published four masterly papers on the manuscripts of Propertius, a step towards an edition which he had contemplated at least as early as 1882, but which he never produced. Of Ovid he edited the *Ibis* for vol. i of the *Corpus Poetarum Latinorum* edited by J. P. Postgate [q.v.], published in 1894, and in 1897 he wrote a series of important papers on the text of the *Heroides*. His next publications concerned Manilius and Juvenal. In 1898 he printed a short paper emending without discussion some fifty passages in Book I of Manilius and three years later a similar paper on Book V. In 1903 he published an edition of Book I which showed every sign of long preparation. It became the first story of that 'monument', to borrow his own phrase, which he resolved to build himself, and which he completed twenty-seven years later with the publication of Book V in 1930.

The preface to Book I was a challenging assertion of Housman's views on scholarship. Its ruthless wit and unanswerable severities enchanted his juniors, although they were less pleasant reading to some of his seniors and contemporaries. The Latin commentary was designed 'to treat of two matters only: what Manilius wrote, and what he meant', without including 'the illustration of his phraseology and vocabulary'; but this restriction did not exclude single notes running to over a thousand words, or pages where a line or two of text stands above fifty of small-print commentary.

The text of Manilius in Postgate's *Corpus* had already been assigned to another, but in 1903 Housman was asked to edit Juvenal for a later fascicule. He had hitherto dealt in print with little except the new lines found in 1899 in a Bodleian manuscript, and he had 'no design of publishing or composing any such work', but he accepted the offer and produced in 1905 both this *Corpus* text, with a short Latin preface, and an independent edition, provocatively aimed *editorum in usum*. This was not on the scale of his Manilius, and the notes were much briefer, but it gave fresh proof of his learning and acuteness and has remained the standard text. The English preface, about half as long as that to Manilius I, was no less brilliant in expression and even broader in range, and Juvenal's greater popularity put the book into the hands of a larger public.

Housman's next classical work, the second volume of Manilius, appeared after his election to his Cambridge chair, but in 1896, four years after his London appointment, he startled his family and friends by the publication of *A Shropshire Lad*. He later revealed some facts about the dates of these sixty-three lyrics. In the foreword to *Last Poems* (1922) he spoke of 'the continuous excitement under which in the early months of 1895 I wrote the greater part of my other book', and he stated elsewhere that his most prolific period was the first five months of that year. The definite dates of twenty of the poems are known, and of these nine are assigned, at least in their inception, to the first six months of 1895, and three more to its second half. The other eleven are earlier, the earliest being of 1890, in which year he had contributed to Alfred William Pollard's *Odes from the Greek Dramatists* three lyric translations of Aeschylus, Sophocles, and Euripides. Housman also stated that he wrote verse at the age of eight or earlier, but very little until he was thirty-five. Some early verse survives showing little of his later power, but the characteristic piece which his brother Laurence printed as number xlviii of the posthumous *More Poems* (1936) had appeared in an Oxford periodical in 1881.

There has been speculation about the 'continuous excitement' of 1895, but it is likely that Housman referred simply to an unexplained outburst of creative activity: he said in 1933, in his Leslie Stephen lecture, that he had seldom written poetry unless he was rather out of health. His

English writing in his London period was not confined to verse, for he delivered in 1892, the year of his election, an admirable introductory lecture, defending classical studies, which happily survives, and at intervals he contributed papers on English and Scottish poets to the University College literary society, but he instructed his executors to destroy them.

Late in 1910 the death of J. E. B. Mayor [q.v.] threw open the Latin chair at Cambridge, and Housman was persuaded to stand. The election took place early in 1911: the field was strong, but Housman was successful, and Trinity College elected him into a fellowship. In May he delivered a striking inaugural lecture. His main theme was a sharp distinction between the functions of a classical scholar and those of a literary critic. He had no wish to suppress this lecture, and he often quoted from it, but unluckily he had stressed a textual point in Shelley's Lament' which he was unable to verify, and he never printed it.

The move to Cambridge was Housman's last, and, as he never married, he lived in Trinity until his death. He lectured regularly, almost always on some portion of a Latin poet, and he delivered between twenty and thirty distinct courses. Some dealt with books prescribed for textual study in part ii of the classical tripos: the poets whom he chose for himself were Lucretius, Catullus, Horace, Ovid, Lucan, and Persius.

Housman's most important classical publications after 1911 were the last four books of Manilius, which appeared in 1912, 1916, 1920, and 1930. The prefaces to the second, third, and fourth books, which lucidly explain the complex astronomical and astrological theories imperfectly expounded by the poet, contain flashes of brilliant wit, but little general criticism or discussion. In the fifth volume, however, he dealt trenchantly with the Manilian literature of the past three decades, winding up with a proud defence of his own methods and achievement.

Apart from an *editio minor* of Manilius, with short critical notes, which appeared in 1932, and a reprint of his Juvenal, with a second preface, in 1931, Housman published no more classical works, except an edition of Lucan in 1926, reprinted with corrections in the following year. This book, aimed, like the Juvenal, *editorum in usum*, is one of his best. The preface is brilliant, and the text and notes show an unerring grasp of Lucan's rhetorical modes of speech and thought. Here, as elsewhere, some of his most striking corrections are simple changes of punctuation.

In 1922 Housman published *Last Poems*, containing forty-one lyrics. He says in the foreword: 'About a quarter of this matter belongs to the April of the present year, but most of it dates between 1895 and 1910.' Some poems plainly refer to the death in action of his youngest brother Herbert in 1901. He contributed in 1927 a charming preface to J. A. Platt's posthumous *Nine Essays*. In 1932 he accepted the Leslie Stephen lecturership at Cambridge, and in 1933 delivered and printed a striking lecture, *The Name and Nature of Poetry*, which threw light on his tastes and on his own poetical creation.

At Cambridge Housman's regular habits included between luncheon and tea one or other of Cambridge's country walks, when he avoided company, but watched with a keen and subtle eye the progress of the seasons in tree and flower. He took many short holidays in England, and often went abroad. He always shunned Germany, but as a young man he went to Constantinople, and he paid a few visits to Italy, chiefly to Venice. He early formed the habit of spending three weeks or a month every summer in different parts of France.

Housman's health deteriorated in 1932, and three years later he was seriously ill. He was able, however, to visit France in the summer of 1935, and he lectured as usual in each term of that year and also in the Lent term of 1936, but in the Easter term he broke down after two lectures, and he died in a nursing home at Cambridge on 30 April.

Housman's will forbade any collection of his published classical papers, and any attempt to print what he had not published, and he extended the ban to all unprinted English prose but, happily, not to his unprinted poetry. Here, referring to his brother Laurence, he wrote: 'I permit him but do not enjoin him to select from my verse manuscript writing, and to publish, any poems which appear to him to be completed and to be not inferior to the average of my published poems; and I direct him to destroy all other poems and fragments of verse.' His brother found it possible to print forty-eight pieces, which appeared in 1936 under the title *More Poems*. A few of these scarcely deserved to be saved, but the average is high, and some may rank with his best. The same can hardly be said of the further eighteen serious poems which his brother appended to his memoir *A. E. H.* in 1937, but the light verse and parodies which accompanied them are delightful. The best text of the posthumous lyrics will be found in *The Collected Poems of A. E. Housman* (1939).

Housman was of slender build, with delicately sensitive features. His sensitiveness was indeed acute and it made him so reserved that most people found his company difficult; but he enjoyed social meetings, and his conversation, when he felt at ease, was full of wit and charm. He did not smoke, but was a connoisseur of food and wine. He had a powerful memory, which occasionally played him tricks, and decided views on most subjects. In classical scholarship his disciplined passion for truth made him ready to accept new evidence and to modify old conclusions, but in other matters he was not tolerant of opposition. In history and politics, especially, he was apt to pin his faith to a few not infallible authorities, and he often allowed his prejudices to warp his judgement. His antinomianism did not prevent him lending strong support to most established institutions, and he combined declared atheism with an hereditary attachment to the high church party. He admired Aristippus 'who was not afraid of words', and he sometimes professed a cult of ruthlessness, but his working philosophy was tinged with the Stoicism which he rejected, and he hated cruelty. He was deeply read in English literature and he had by heart an immense amount of poetry. His taste was catholic, but he had strong preferences, which are clearly shown in his Leslie Stephen lecture.

Housman was eminent in two fields, the distinctness of which he often emphasized, that of classical scholarship and that of original poetry. In the first his permanent rank was assured before his death, and it is among the highest. As he knew, he was not fully comparable to Bentley, whom he outshone in patience and intellectual honesty and closely approached in swiftness of insight and brilliant power, but whose scholarship had a sweep and range which he could not equal. To the rest of the giants we may extend what Housman said of himself matched with Porson: 'the comparison is not preposterous—he surpassed me in some qualities as I claim to surpass him in others'. Of contemporary scholars he most admired, and rated above himself, U. von Wilamowitz-Moellendorff,

a lesser man than Bentley, but cast in the same titanic mould. His admiration for Wilamowitz is one of many disproofs of the belief that he was unfair to German learning. He was pitiless to pretentious incompetence, of which he found too much in the contemporary scholarship of all countries, including England; and if Germany filled most space in his onslaughts this was because nine-tenths of the work in his special fields was done by Germans.

Housman's restriction to Latin after 1892 was a loss to Greek scholarship, but the choice is intelligible. His passion for perfection came nearer being satisfied in the narrower field, and as a textual critic he even preferred to concentrate his attention on writers not of the first rank, since their ideas and means of expression were in some degree predictable. His early notes on Aeschylus, always his favourite poet, are brilliant, but not equal to his best work in Latin, and, had he ever begun to edit him, he would probably have abandoned the task from the conviction that it was less difficult than impossible. Manilius, on whom he lavished his richest gifts, was, as he knew, a poor poet with a bad subject, but his edition throws invaluable light on Latin usage and on the facts of textual transmission, and the problems of this corrupt text exercised his highest faculties.

On Housman's rank as an English poet it would be rash to attempt a verdict. When *A Shropshire Lad* appeared it struck a new note in late nineteenth-century literature. The chief sources of which he declared himself conscious were Shakespeare's songs, the Scottish Border ballads, and Heine. Other influences have been noted, especially those of the English Bible and of Matthew Arnold, and there are many delicate reminiscences of Greek and Latin poetry, but his work remains unmistakably personal. He has been accused of monotony, and his favourite themes are not numerous, but he shows great variety in metre and a Horatian felicity of expression: every poem has phrases that no one else could have written. It is often said that *Last Poems* is inferior to *A Shropshire Lad*, but both are uneven, and some of his best work is in the later volume: one at least of the very finest ('Tell me not here') was composed in the year of its publication. Housman's low estimate of much of the verse of the seventeenth and eighteenth centuries angered some younger critics, and both the form and the content of his own poetry were out of fashion in the same circles before he died, but it can hardly be doubted that his best poems will always rank high, although perhaps, unlike his scholarship, not in the highest class of all. He refused almost all honours, including the Order of Merit, but accepted an honorary fellowship from his Oxford college in 1911.

There is no painted portrait of Housman, but there are several drawings: of these, two made by (Sir) William Rothenstein in 1906 are respectively in the National Portrait Gallery and at Trinity College, Cambridge. His appearance in later life is best shown in that made by Francis Dodd in 1926 for St. John's College, Oxford. Another drawing by Dodd (1936), and a plasticine medallion by Theodore Spicer-Simson (1924), are in the National Portrait Gallery.

[*The Times*, 2 May 1936; A. S. F. Gow, *A. E. Housman, A Sketch, together with a List of his Writings and Indexes to his Classical Papers*, 1936; Alfred Edward Housman Memorial Supplement to the *Bromsgrovian*, 1936; Laurence Housman, *A. E. H.*, 1937, and *The Unexpected Years*, 1937; Percy Withers, *A Buried Life*, 1940; F. T. Grant Richards, *Housman 1897–1936*, 1941; J. Carter and J. Sparrow, *A. E. Housman, An Annotated Check-List*, 1940; A. S. F. Gow, 'A. E. Housman at Oxford' in *Oxford Magazine*, 11 November 1937; R. W. Chambers, *Man's Unconquerable Mind*, 1939; private information; personal knowledge.]

D. S. ROBERTSON.

HOUSTON, DAME FANNY LUCY (1857–1936), philanthropist and eccentric, was born at Kennington, Lambeth, 8 April 1857, the fourth daughter of Thomas Radmall, warehouseman, by his wife, Maria Isabella Clarke. She grew up a beautiful woman who for a time earned her livelihood on the stage, and her portrait was painted by H. J. Thaddeus, an Irish artist. She married three times: first, in 1883 Theodore Francis Brinckman, later third baronet, whom she divorced in 1895; secondly, in 1901 George Frederick William Byron, ninth Lord Byron, who died in 1917; and thirdly, in 1924 Sir Robert Paterson Houston, baronet, member of parliament for the West Toxteth division of Liverpool from 1892 to 1924, of the Houston Shipping line, who in 1926 bequeathed to her four-fifths of a fortune of about £7,000,000. She had no children.

By the time of her second marriage, Lady Byron had become a strong advocate of women's rights and displayed a fervent interest in their welfare, founding, financing, and, during the war of 1914–1918, administering the first rest home for tired nurses, which earned her appointment as D.B.E. in 1917; but it was not until she became possessed of her third husband's bequest that her name became widely known.

Sir Robert Houston had been domiciled in Jersey, and a month after his death a Royal Court was convened there to determine 'the state of mind and body' of his widow, but by the time that the verdict was given in her favour, she had recovered something of her balance of mind. Her inheritance was indeed larger than might have been expected, for as the laws of Jersey provided for no statutory declaration of the value of an estate, no duties appeared to be payable on that of Sir Robert Houston. In 1927 Lady Houston, who refused to admit any liability, made an *ex gratia* payment of £1,500,000 to satisfy the demands of the Exchequer; and in 1933 she again made a voluntary payment of some £46,000 to cover, as she maintained, the amount of income tax which she would have had to pay in the previous five years, had she not been resident in Jersey.

Before this dispute had ended, Lady Houston had come to be regarded by her friends as 'a warm-hearted woman who would brook no contradiction, and demanded implicit obedience from those who served her'. She bestowed her largess on coal-miners, worshippers in Liverpool Anglican Cathedral, tramwaymen in Hull, persecuted Russian Christians; and her largest contribution to charity was £40,000 to King George's Jubilee Trust. But to the general public she was a strident, perhaps sincere, patriot, who painted her rooms in red, white, and blue, which she had adopted as her racing colours, kept a yacht, the *Liberty*, displaying the motto *Nemo me impune lacessit*, and aired her views with 'combative patriotism' in the *Saturday Review*, which she had purchased.

Lady Houston, however, deserves to be remembered for her gift of £100,000 to enable a British team to compete for the Schneider trophy in 1931, when the government had refused the funds. The trophy was won by Flight-Lieutenant George Hedley Stainforth, flying a supermarine Rolls-Royce S6, the direct predecessor of the Spitfires and Hurricanes of the battle of Britain. Two years later she financed the expedition which flew over Mount Everest. In 1932, being convinced that war was inevitable, she offered a contribution of £200,000 to the air defence of London, which was refused on the ground that parliament was sole judge of the sum to be spent in defence. She also offered to salvage the Finnish barque *Herzogin Cecilie*, to be used as a training ship in 'masts and sails'. This offer was also declined with thanks. By now she had become notorious rather than famous; nevertheless her intervention in the matter of the Schneider trophy remains, though indirectly, an act of the greatest service to the country.

Lady Houston died intestate at Hampstead 29 December 1936.

[*The Times* and *Daily Telegraph*, 31 December 1936; *Evening Standard*, 30 December 1936; Warner Allen, *Lucy Houston D.B.E.*].

H. A. ST. G. SAUNDERS.

HOWARD, ESME WILLIAM, first BARON HOWARD OF PENRITH (1863–1939), diplomatist, was born at Greystoke Castle, Cumberland, 15 September 1863, the youngest of the four sons of Henry Howard, of Greystoke, by his wife, Charlotte Caroline Georgiana, eldest daughter of Henry Lawes Long, of Hampton Lodge, Surrey. He was educated at Harrow, leaving in 1881 for further studies abroad. He joined the diplomatic service in April 1885, and in June of that year went on to the staff of his brother-in-law, H. E. M. Herbert, Lord Carnarvon [q.v.], who had just been made lord-lieutenant of Ireland. The country was in a state of great unrest, for the home rule agitation was at its height, and at the beginning of 1886, when Gladstone came into office, Carnarvon resigned. Howard was then sent to the embassy in Rome, where he remained until 1888 when he was transferred to Berlin under Sir Edward Malet [q.v.]. This year was one of great changes in Germany. The old Emperor, William I, died in March, and three months later his son and successor, Frederick III, also died and was succeeded by the Emperor William II. Howard watched the coronation of the new Emperor, and two years later his dismissal of the chancellor in 1890. He left the Berlin embassy at the end of 1890, and in 1892, while still under thirty, retired from the diplomatic service, unsuccessfully contesting Worcester as a liberal at the general election in the latter year.

For the next few years Howard led an adventurous life, travelling in various parts of the world. He then became assistant private secretary to John Wodehouse, Lord Kimberley [q.v.], secretary of state for foreign affairs in Lord Rosebery's government of 1894–1895. In 1900, during the South African war, he served with distinction as a trooper in the Imperial Yeomanry, joining a corps called the Duke of Cambridge's Own, the members of which waived their pay. He saw some fighting, was captured and escaped, and, after being eleven years absent from the diplomatic service, rejoined it in 1903.

Howard was now given his first independent post, being appointed consul-general for Crete, where he had a difficult task. In the island, nominally autonomous but actually controlled by the consuls-general of Great Britain, France, Russia, and Italy, trouble was caused by the Venizelist revolt in favour of union with Greece. Howard's firm and tactful handling of the situation gained him credit, and on his return to England in 1906 he was appointed C.V.O. and C.M.G.

After several short-term appointments Howard was promoted to be minister at Berne in 1911, and was transferred to Stockholm in 1913. He stayed there until after the armistice, and the history of his mission is that of the blockade. One of the chief difficulties in coming to an agreement with Sweden for an effective blockade of enemy countries was that the trade to Russia was through that country, and any attempt to put pressure on the Stockholm government was met by the threat of preventing supplies to Russia. Howard acted with great discretion, and the position was eased by the Russian revolution. Considering his difficulties, it is surprising to what an extent he had the foreign trade of Sweden under his control by 1918.

After the armistice Howard, who had been appointed K.C.M.G. in 1916 and K.C.B. in 1919, was attached to the British delegation of the Peace Conference in Paris. He was sworn of the Privy Council and became ambassador at Madrid in 1919. His career ended with the greatest of his many successes. In 1924, on the resignation of Sir Auckland (later Lord) Geddes, Howard was selected to be ambassador at Washington. He remained six years in office, his mission was a brilliant personal triumph, and he won the trust and regard of all shades of American opinion. The universities of Washington (1925) and Hartford (1929) conferred honorary degrees upon him.

In 1923 Howard was appointed G.C.M.G.

and in 1928 G.C.B. On his return home in 1930 he was raised to the peerage as Baron Howard of Penrith. In 1935–1936 he published his memoirs, *The Theatre of Life*, in two vivid and charming volumes. He married in 1898 Lady Maria Isabella Giovanna Teresa Gioachina, sixth daughter of Sigismondo Nicholas Venantius Gaetano Francis, Prince Giustiniani-Bandini and eighth Earl of Newburgh. Earlier in the same year he was received into the Roman Catholic Church. Five sons, the eldest of whom predeceased his father, were born of the marriage. Lord Howard died at his home at Hindhead 1 August 1939, and was succeeded as second baron by his second son, Francis Philip (born 1905).

A portrait of Howard, by H. Harris Brown, is in the possession of his widow.

[*The Times*, 2 August 1939; Lord Howard of Penrith, *The Theatre of Life*: vol. i, *Life seen from the Pit, 1863–1905*, 1935; vol. ii, *Life seen from the Stalls, 1905–1936*, 1936.]

ARTHUR COCHRANE.

HUNT, ARTHUR SURRIDGE (1871–1934), papyrologist, was born at Romford, Essex, 1 March 1871, the eldest son and third child of Alfred Henry Hunt, solicitor, later of Romford Hall, by his wife, Emily Pertwee, who was descended from a French Huguenot family originally named Pertuis. He was educated at Cranbrook School and Eastbourne College, whence in October 1889 he went as a classical scholar to Queen's College, Oxford. In 1891 he obtained a first class in classical moderations, but in 1893 only a second class in *literae humaniores*. In the first disappointment he abandoned his hope of a fellowship; but a project of being ordained and the winning of the Aubrey Moore studentship led, despite his father's death in 1893, to his remaining at Queen's, and in 1894 he was elected to the Craven fellowship. He chose as his field of study the palaeography of early Latin manuscripts in Spanish libraries, but after his return from Spain, on the invitation of his friend and older contemporary at Queen's, B. P. Grenfell [q.v.], he abandoned Latin palaeography for papyrology. In January 1896 he joined Grenfell and D. G. Hogarth [q.v.], who were excavating for papyri in the Fayum. Thus was formed a partnership memorable in the history of classical scholarship, which made the names of the 'Dioscuri of Oxford', as they were called, familiar throughout the learned world. Details of their joint work will be found in the notice of Grenfell.

From 1896 to 1900 Hunt was a senior demy of Magdalen College, Oxford, and from 1901 to 1906 a fellow of Lincoln, of which he was elected an honorary fellow in 1918; in 1906 he became research fellow of Queen's. In 1908, on Grenfell's election as professor of papyrology, Hunt was appointed lecturer in that subject. During Grenfell's absence from 1908 to 1913 he worked alone, and in the latter year, Grenfell's professorship having lapsed, Hunt was elected professor in his place. After his recovery, Grenfell was in 1919 appointed joint professor with Hunt, who, during the war of 1914–1918, served successively as an officer in the Oxfordshire and Buckinghamshire Light Infantry, in the War Trade Intelligence Department, in the War Office, and in the Intelligence Corps in France. From 1920, when Grenfell's health finally collapsed, Hunt was sole editor of the volumes of papyrus texts issued by the Egypt Exploration Society. He had previously edited alone volume i of the *Catalogue of the Greek Papyri in the John Rylands Library Manchester* (1911) and *Tragicorum Graecorum Fragmenta Papyracea* (1912).

Hunt married in 1918 Lucy Ellen, fourth daughter of Surgeon-Major-General Sir Alexander Frederick Bradshaw. His health had never been robust, and in 1932 the sudden death of his son, his only child, was a blow from which he never really recovered, although he made little show of grief. He died at Oxford 18 June 1934. He received honorary degrees from the universities of Glasgow, Dublin, Königsberg, Graz, and Athens, and was Drexel medallist of the university of Pennsylvania. He was elected a fellow of the British Academy in 1913, and was also a member of several foreign academies.

Hunt was a fine scholar, with a keenly critical intelligence, and unsparing in his devotion to accuracy. Beneath a reserved manner lay a fund of quiet humour, generous kindness, and deep religious feeling.

[H. I. Bell, *A. S. Hunt, 1871–1934* in *Proceedings* of the British Academy, vol. xx, 1934; F. de Zulueta, *Studia et Documenta Historiae et Iuris*, fasc. ii. 1935; private information; personal knowledge.] H. I. BELL.

HUNT, WILLIAM (1842–1931), historian, was born at Clifton, Bristol, 3 March 1842, the elder son of William Hunt, curate of Holy Trinity church, Hotwells, Clifton, later vicar of Holy Trinity church, Weston-super-Mare, and prebendary of Wells Cathedral, by his wife, Maria Simpson. Educated at Harrow and Trinity College, Oxford, he obtained a second class in classical moderations in 1862 and a first class in law and modern history in 1864. He was ordained in 1865 as curate to his father at Weston-super-Mare, and two years later was presented to the vicarage of Congresbury, Somerset. He held the living for fifteen years, in the course of which he restored the church, built a new day school, and occupied his leisure with historical work of which he had laid the foundations at Oxford. He was an examiner in the final school of modern history at Oxford from 1877 to 1879 and again in 1881 and 1882. In 1882 he resigned his living, came to London, and devoted the rest of his life to the writing of history and biography.

Hitherto, Hunt had concerned himself mainly with county and diocesan history, and with the activities of the Somersetshire Archaeological Society, of which he was a member from 1866 to the end of his life and an honorary general secretary from 1872 to 1879. Of these interests the fruits are his *Somerset Diocese, Bath and Wells* (1885), a history of *Bristol* (1887) in the 'Historic Towns' series, of which he was joint-editor with E. A. Freeman [q.v.], and an edition of *Two Chartularies of the Priory of St. Peter at Bath* (1893) for the Somerset Record Society.

In London Hunt was associated almost from its foundation with this DICTIONARY, for which he wrote nearly 600 articles, including the biographies of Edward I and Edward III and many medieval churchmen. In him (Sir) Leslie Stephen [q.v.] found an ideal contributor and sub-editor —learned, accurate, and impartial. It was, however, his share in two other historical enterprises which brought Hunt wider recognition. These were *A History of the English Church* in eight volumes (1899–1910) of which he was joint-editor with W. R. W. Stephens [q.v.], and to which he contributed the very successful first volume (1899), covering the period before the Norman Conquest; and *The Political History of England* in twelve volumes (1905–1910), written by leading historians, of which he and R. L. Poole [q.v.] were the general editors. Both series were fortunate in their editors, and both, especially the latter, have remained standard authorities up to the present time. The issue, within five years, of twelve volumes of the quality of the *Political History* was, indeed, a notable editorial achievement. Hunt him-

self wrote the tenth volume (1905), dealing with the reign of George III from his accession to the Act of Union. Lucid, careful, and dispassionate, Hunt was no merely 'safe' historian: he wrote with insight, decision, and a ripe knowledge of human affairs. He travelled widely, had a large acquaintance, and his figure, with flowing beard, was well known at the Savile Club. A staunch conservative, he contributed frequently to the *Saturday Review*, in which at one time he sought to acquire a joint controlling interest. He was president of the Royal Historical Society from 1905 to 1909, and in 1921 was elected an honorary fellow of Trinity College to which he was deeply attached and to which his library was presented by his widow. Although not in its front rank, Hunt holds an established position in the great school of English historians which dates from the time of Freeman and William Stubbs; its tradition he well understood and its standard of scholarship he worthily upheld.

Hunt was twice married: first, in 1865 to Emma (died 1893), daughter of the Rev. Arthur Ramsay; secondly, in 1895 to Katharine, daughter of Thomas Rae, merchant, of Melbourne, Victoria. He had no children. He died in London 14 June 1931.

[*The Times*, 16 June 1931; *Proceedings* of the Somersetshire Archaeological and Natural History Society for the year 1931, vol. lxxvii, 1932 (portrait); *History*, January 1932; private information.]   J. R. H. WEAVER.

HUNTER, SIR ARCHIBALD (1856–1936), general, was born in Kilburn, 6 September 1856, the son of Archibald Hunter, by his wife, Mary Jane Graham. Both his parents came of good Lowland families. He was educated at Glasgow Academy and Sandhurst and was gazetted to the 4th Foot (The King's Own) in June 1874, joining the 1st battalion at Gibraltar. He quickly made his mark as an efficient and zealous officer, serving as adjutant from April 1880 to November 1882; he had been promoted to captain in August 1882.

Hunter saw his first active service in 1884, being employed on the Nile expedition on intelligence duties and gaining a brevet as major (1885) besides being mentioned in dispatches. For fifteen years (1884–1899) he served with the Egyptian Army, gaining a great reputation for gallantry and efficiency and doing much to build up the army for the work before it. He was severely wounded at Giniss (December 1885), where the Dervish advance was effectively checked, and was awarded the D.S.O. At Toski in 1889 he did good service in command of a brigade, and was again wounded, gaining another brevet (lieutenant-colonel). From August 1892 to July 1894 he was governor of the Red Sea littoral and of Suakin, receiving command of the Sudan Frontier Field Force in the latter month and retaining it until November 1896. Promoted to substantive major in June 1892, he obtained a brevet as colonel in January 1894. In the operations of 1896 to 1898 which culminated in the recovery of Khartoum, Hunter was Kitchener's right-hand man. At Firket (7 June 1896) he commanded the infantry most successfully, and was specially promoted to major-general in November 1896, when aged only forty. In 1897 he led the flying column which defeated the Dervishes at Abu Hamed (7 August) and went on to occupy Berber (5 September). At the battles of the Atbara (8 April 1898) and of Omdurman (2 September) he was again in command of a division, which he handled with great ability, especially at Omdurman where his judicious dispositions and use of his reserves did much to ensure victory. His good services were repeatedly acknowledged in the Sudan dispatches and he received the thanks of both Houses of Parliament. After the fall of Khartoum he was appointed K.C.B. (1898).

May 1899 brought Hunter command of the Quetta division in India, but on the dispatch of troops from India to Natal he was appointed chief of staff to Sir George White [q.v.] and played a big part in the defence of Ladysmith, being more second in command than chief staff officer. He has been described as the life and soul of the defence and led and planned the successful sortie of 7 December in which two of the enemy's guns were disabled.

Shortly after the relief (1 March 1900), Hunter was promoted lieutenant-general and given command of the 10th division, composed of troops transferred from Natal to the western Transvaal. His column's advance over the Vaal at Windsorton and their defeat of the Boers at Rooidam (5 May 1900) contributed appreciably to the relief of Mafeking and to the diversion of the Boers from opposing Lord Roberts's advance on Pretoria. In June, owing to an accident to Major-General Sir Ian Hamilton, he was placed in command of the columns operating in the north-east of the Orange River Colony and was responsible for the manœuvres which culminated in the second great Boer surrender, that of General Marthinus Prinsloo and 4,000 men in Brandwater Basin (30 July), a success largely caused by his skilful combinations and inspiring leadership; he later commanded in the central Orange River Colony but was invalided home in January 1901.

From May 1901 to September 1903 Hunter was general officer commanding the Scottish District (later Command), after which he commanded first the Western and later the Southern Army in India until October 1908, assisting Lord Kitchener in the reorganization of the Indian Army. He was promoted general in December 1905. Appointed governor and commander-in-chief of Gibraltar in September 1910, his well-founded criticisms on the shortcomings of the civil administration, prompted by his zeal for the welfare and efficiency of the garrison, led to some friction with the civil authorities, and he relinquished the post in July 1913.

Shortly after the outbreak of war in 1914, Hunter was given command of the Aldershot Training Centre and later became general officer-commanding-in-chief, Aldershot Command. For the next three years (until September 1917) he laboured assiduously at the training of the New Armies, most of the divisions of which, as well as their drafts and reinforcements, did their final preparation under him. Always zealous for those under him, he was the right man for the place and the New Armies owed much to him. He retired from the army in October 1920.

Hunter was elected conservative member of parliament for Lancaster in 1918 but did not seek re-election in 1922. He was colonel of his old regiment, The King's Own, from 1913 until 1926. He was appointed G.C.B. in 1911 and was aide-de-camp general to the king from 1917 to 1919. He was also honorary colonel of the 5th (Territorial) battalion of the Highland Light Infantry and received the honorary degree of LL.D. from the universities of Glasgow and Cambridge. With Lord Kitchener as his best man, he married in 1910 Mary (died 1924), younger daughter of Hickson Fergusson, of The Knowe, Ayrshire, and widow of George Arbuthnot Burns, second Lord Inverclyde; there were no children of the marriage. He died in London 28 June 1936.

A vigorous, energetic, and capable soldier, Hunter was extremely popular with all ranks of the army, inspiring affection and respect. He played a notable part in the recovery of the Sudan for civilization and in South Africa he enhanced his reputation. It has been said of him that 'he never spoke ill of any man, was always seeking to do others kindnesses and never forgot a friend'.

A portrait of Hunter is included in the cartoon 'A General Group' by 'Spy' which appeared in *Vanity Fair* 29 November 1900.

[*The Times*, 29 June 1936; W. S. Churchill, *The River War*, 1899, new ed. 1902 (portrait); Sir J. F. Maurice and M. H. Grant, (Official) *History of the War in South Africa 1899-1902*, 1906-1910; *The King's Own, the history of a Royal Regiment*, edited by L. I. Cowper, 1939.]

C. T. ATKINSON.

HUNTER, SIR GEORGE BURTON (1845-1937), shipbuilder, was born at Sunderland 19 December 1845, the third son of Thomas Hunter, of Sunderland, by his wife, Elizabeth, eldest daughter of William Rowntree, also of Sunderland. After leaving school at the age of thirteen he was for two years a pupil of Thomas Meek, engineer to the River Wear commissioners. He was then apprenticed to the shipbuilding firm of W. Pile, Hay & company, of Sunderland, and was put in charge of the drawing office in 1865. Four years later (1869) he went to the Clyde as assistant to (Sir) William Pearce at the shipyard of Robert Napier [qq.v.] at Govan. In 1871 he returned to his old firm as manager, and on the closing of its yard in 1873 he joined S. P. Austin in establishing at Sunderland a yard for the construction of iron ships. That partnership was dissolved in 1880 and he went to Wallsend as principal partner of C. S. Swan. In 1895 the firm was formed into a limited company with Hunter as chairman, and by combining in 1903 with Wigham Richardson & company became under the style of Swan, Hunter, & Wigham Richardson one of the most important shipbuilding undertakings on the north-east coast, possessing also extensive interests in the Clyde area. Hunter remained chairman of the new company until 1928, and it was a tribute to the reputation which he had won for excellence of design and quality of workmanship that, in an area predominantly engaged in the construction of cargo tonnage, it was able to secure the order for a ship so elabo-

rately fitted as the famous Cunard liner *Mauretania*. He was a pioneer of the system, which was adopted for her, of building ships within large glazed sheds, which provided protection against the weather.

Habitually dressed in a blue reefer suit and often wearing a yachting cap, Hunter was a familiar figure on Tyneside. Regarded as a fair and just employer, he set an example of hard work, being in his office every day from 10 a.m. to 6 p.m. except on Saturdays, when his hour of departure was 4 p.m.; and besides taking a keen interest in industrial questions relating to the payment and training of workmen was president of the National Temperance Federation, treasurer of the United Kingdom Alliance, and chairman of the Simplified Spelling Society.

Hunter was appointed K.B.E. in 1918 in recognition of his services during the war of 1914-1918, and received the honorary degree of D.Sc. from Durham University in recognition of his work on the council of Armstrong College. In 1900 he unsuccessfully contested Sunderland as a liberal. He married in 1873 Ann (died 1927), daughter of Charles Hudson, of Whitby, and niece of George Hudson [q.v.], the 'railway king', and had two sons and three daughters. He died at Jesmond, Newcastle-upon-Tyne, 21 January 1937.

[*The Times*, 22 January 1937; *Engineer* and *Engineering*, 29 January 1937 (portrait).]

H. M. ROSS.

HUNTER-WESTON, SIR AYLMER GOULD (1864-1940), lieutenant-general. [See WESTON.]

HUTCHINSON, ARTHUR (1866-1937), mineralogist, was born in London 6 July 1866, the only child of George Hutchinson, of Woodside, Westmorland, silk merchant, of London, by his wife, Deborah Richardson, of Culgaith, Cumberland. He was educated at Clifton College and in 1884 went with a scholarship to Christ's College, Cambridge, where he was awarded first classes in both parts of the natural sciences tripos (1886 and 1888). After a year's research work in chemistry with Matthew Moncrieff Pattison Muir he went to Germany where he studied under Emil Fischer and W. K. Röntgen and obtained the degree of Ph.D. In 1891 he was appointed a demonstrator in the chemical laboratory at Gonville and Caius College, Cambridge, and in 1892 was elected into a fellowship at Pembroke College and appointed college lecturer in natural science.

Hutchinson's work as a mineralogist began in 1895 when he was appointed demonstrator in mineralogy in the university of Cambridge. In this capacity he conducted, almost unaided, for twenty-eight years the whole of the course in mineralogy for the first part of the natural sciences tripos. He was appointed university lecturer in crystallography in 1923 and finally in 1926 he succeeded William James Lewis as professor of mineralogy. He was then within five years of the age for retirement. During these years he devoted himself to the development of his department, encouraging research in X-ray crystallography and preparing for the organization of the two new departments of mineralogy and petrology and of crystallography which were established on his retirement from the professorship in 1931.

Hutchinson's first notable contribution to mineralogical research was the discovery of a new mineral, stokesite, in 1899. In the same year he began work on the diathermancy and optical characters of stibnite, showing that the mineral, ordinarily supposed to be opaque, transmitted light of long wave-length, and he successfully measured its refractive indices, and proved its orthorhombic symmetry. He devised an inverted form of goniometer for the determination of the crystallographic and optical characters of small crystals, and a protractor for the construction of stereographic and gnomonic projections, adapting this later (1925) to the interpretation of Laue X-ray photographs of crystals. Several charts for the graphical solution of crystallographic problems, for the correction of specific gravity determinations, and for the solution of some formulae in crystal optics were published between 1915 and 1925. For eight years (1904–1912) he wrote the section on mineralogical chemistry in the *Annual Reports* of the Chemical Society.

In addition to his mineralogical work Hutchinson took an active share in college and university life. He was assistant tutor of Pembroke College from 1901 to 1926, and was elected master of the college in 1928, a post from which he retired only five months before his death at Cambridge 12 December 1937. He was a governor of Gresham's School, Holt, for twenty-two years, and of St. Bees School, Cumberland, and he was an active member of the council of Clifton College.

Hutchinson was elected F.R.S. in 1922 and an honorary fellow of Christ's College in 1935; he was appointed O.B.E. for his research work on gas masks during the war of 1914–1918. In 1901 he married Evaline, second daughter of Alexander Shipley, of Datchet, Buckinghamshire, and sister of Sir Arthur Everett Shipley [q.v.]; they had two sons and a daughter. The elder son is professor of zoology in Yale University.

A portrait of Hutchinson by Sir William Rothenstein is in Mrs. Hutchinson's house at Culgaith.

[*The Times*, 13 December 1937; *Obituary Notices of Fellows of the Royal Society*, No. 7, January 1939 (bibliography and portrait); personal knowledge.]

W. CAMPBELL SMITH.

HUTCHINSON, HORATIO GORDON (HORACE) (1859–1932), golfer and author, was born in London 16 May 1859, the third son of General William Nelson Hutchinson, of the Grenadier Guards, by his wife, Mary, daughter of John Russell [q.v.], headmaster of Charterhouse and later rector of St. Botolph's church, Bishopsgate. In 1864 his father went to live near Northam in Devon. In that year the Royal North Devon Golf Club was founded and Hutchinson thus learnt golf as a boy. He went to school first at Charterhouse, which he left owing to ill health, and later at the United Services College, Westward Ho! In 1878 he went up to Corpus Christi College, Oxford. In that year the first university golf match was played and Hutchinson led the Oxford side, as he did in 1879, 1880, and 1882 (there was no match in 1881). In 1881 he won the university cue and played for Oxford in the doubles match at billiards. He was also a competent oarsman and cricketer. He intended to read for the bar and entered at the Inner Temple, but his health, always frail, temporarily broke down. Later, in 1890, he had thoughts of being a sculptor and worked for some time in G. F. Watts's studio, but this project was likewise abandoned; he embraced no regular profession but took gradually to authorship. In 1886 he wrote a small book *Hints on the Game of Golf*, which synchronized with the great increase in the popularity of the game in England, and had considerable success. In 1890 he edited and wrote a large part of the volume on golf in the Badminton Library, and from that time became a prolific writer on golf both in books and newspapers, as also on

Hutchinson, H. G.   D.N.B. 1931–1940

shooting, fishing, and natural history; he was himself a fine shot and fisherman. When *Country Life* was founded in 1897, he wrote regularly for it on all these subjects and edited several volumes in the *Country Life* Library. He wrote several not unsuccessful novels, among them *Peter Steele, the Cricketer* (1895), and *'Bert Edward, the Golf Caddie* (1903). He was essentially an essayist rather than a novelist, having a fluent, pleasant, and graceful style in which he could write rapidly and without effort on a variety of topics.

When in 1886 the amateur championship was formally instituted Hutchinson beat Henry Lamb in the final and in 1887 won against John Ball [q.v.] at Hoylake. In 1888 he played in an exhibition at the Meadowbrook Club near New York, one of the earliest occasions on which the game was seen in the United States of America. He played for England against Scotland in the first international match in 1902 and in each subsequent year until 1907, except 1905 when he was ill. In 1908 he was the first Englishman to be elected captain of the Royal and Ancient Golf Club of St. Andrews. As a golfer Hutchinson was for a long time one of the leading players in the country, with a dashing and characteristic style, and his career would have been even more successful than it was but for intermittent ill health. During the last eighteen years of his life he was incapacitated by grave illness: he then left his home at Forest Row in Sussex and moved to London where he died 27 July 1932.

Hutchinson married in 1893 Dorothy Margaret, younger daughter of Major Frederick Barclay Chapman, of the 14th Hussars; there were no children of the marriage.

A portrait of Hutchinson by Oswald Birley is in the possession of Mrs. Hutchinson.

[*The Times*, 29 July 1932; H. G. Hutchinson, *Fifty Years of Golf*, 1919; private information; personal knowledge.]

BERNARD DARWIN.

HUXLEY, LEONARD (1860–1933), biographer, poet, and editor of the *Cornhill Magazine*, was born in London 11 December 1860, the second, but elder surviving, son of the famous scientist Thomas Henry Huxley [q.v.], by his wife, Henrietta Ann, daughter of Henry Heathorn, of Bathurst, New South Wales. He was educated at University College School, at St. Andrews University, and at

Balliol College, Oxford, of which he was an exhibitioner and where he obtained a first class in classical moderations (1881) and in *literae humaniores* (1883). In 1884 he became an assistant master at Charterhouse and stayed there until in 1901 he joined the publishing firm of Smith, Elder, & company, becoming the close friend and literary adviser of Reginald John Smith [q.v.] and his assistant in the editorship of the *Cornhill Magazine*. After the death of Smith in 1916 and the amalgamation of his firm in the following year with John Murray's, Huxley willingly migrated to Albemarle Street and there continued his role of valued friend and adviser as well as becoming sole editor of the *Cornhill*, a position which gave him full scope for showing his kindness to, interest in, and almost paternal encouragement of honest literary effort.

In 1885 Huxley married Julia Frances (died 1908), daughter of Thomas Arnold and sister of Mrs. Humphry Ward [qq.v.]: she was the successful headmistress of Priorsfield School, near Godalming. By her he had a daughter and three sons, the second of whom died in 1914, while the other two, Dr. Julian and Mr. Aldous Huxley, are both well known for their scientific and literary works. In 1912 Huxley married as his second wife Rosalind, third daughter of William Wallace Bruce, and had two sons. He was brother-in-law of John Collier [q.v.], the well-known portrait-painter, with whom he was on terms of intimate friendship.

Huxley's generous nature, combined with his veneration for the memory of his father and his enjoyment of the successes of his sons, saved him from any sense of being overshadowed. Nevertheless, it was a great pleasure to him when in 1919 his old university of St. Andrews conferred upon him the honorary degree of LL.D. in recognition of his own literary achievements. He wrote an outstanding biography of his father, *The Life and Letters of Thomas Henry Huxley* (2 vols., 1900; 2nd ed. 3 vols., 1903), and also *The Life and Letters of Sir Joseph Dalton Hooker* (2 vols., 1918). His poetic talent, which he inherited from his mother, was proved by his volume *Anniversaries* (1920), and, among other works, he skilfully edited *Jane Welsh Carlyle: Letters to her Family, 1839–1863* (1924) and *Elizabeth Barrett Browning: Letters to her Sister, 1846–1859* (1929). He always maintained his inherited interest in biology, and was an enthusiast for music and the delights of open-air life. He died at Hampstead 3 May 1933.

Portraits of Huxley, by John Collier, one as a young, the other as an older, man, are in the possession of his widow. The head of the portrait as a young man was painted by Marian Collier and finished by her husband after her death.

[*The Times*, 4 May 1933; personal knowledge.]   JOHN MURRAY.

INCHCAPE, first EARL OF (1852–1932), shipowner. [See MACKAY, JAMES LYLE.]

INVERNAIRN, BARON (1856–1936), shipbuilder. [See BEARDMORE, WILLIAM.]

IQBAL, SIR MUHAMMAD (1876–1938), Indian thinker and poet, was born at Sialkot in the Punjab in February 1876. His forebears were Hindus, originally from Kashmir, who had been converted to Islam. He was educated at Murray (Scottish Presbyterian) College at Sialkot and Government College, Lahore (afterwards the university of Lahore), where his brilliance gained him a post as lecturer in philosophy, first in the Oriental College and later in Government College. During these years he came under the influence of (Sir) T. W. Arnold [q.v.], who introduced him to Western philosophy and the principles of critical scholarship. When Arnold left Lahore in 1904 Iqbal decided to continue his studies in England and in 1905 was admitted to Trinity College, Cambridge, where he read philosophy with J. M. E. M'Taggart [q.v.]. At the same time he attended law lectures at Lincoln's Inn and was called to the bar in 1908. From Cambridge he went to Germany and obtained the degree of D.Ph. from Munich University for a thesis published in 1908 under the title of *The Development of Metaphysics in Persia*. In 1908 Iqbal returned to India, and for the rest of his life practised as a barrister, a profession which he valued for its independence. In 1923 he was knighted, and from 1927 to 1929 was a member of the Punjab legislative council. Through his poems he had already won an outstanding position in the Indian Moslem community, and he served as president of the All-India Moslem League in 1930 (when the *Pakistan* project was definitely adopted as the political objective of the League) and as a delegate to the first Round Table Conference held in London in 1931 to frame a constitution for India. In his last years he took little part in politics. He died at Lahore 21 April 1938, and was buried there.

For the last twenty-five years of his life Iqbal stood in a class by himself as a Moslem thinker and poet. Impressed by the vigour and vitality of Europe and of Western thought, he saw in the social apathy of Moslem pantheism the cause of Moslem decadence, and in reaction against its negations he was drawn towards the evolutionary philosophy of Bergson and Nietzsche. It became his fixed purpose to infuse into Indian Islam the same spirit of activism. His first major work, a Persian *masnavi* sequence entitled *Asrār-i Khudī* (1915; translated into English, with an introduction, by Dr. Reynold Alleyne Nicholson as *The Secrets of the Self*, 1920), with its gospel of the creative ego striving to achieve freedom and the fuller development of personality, took the younger generation of Indian Moslems by storm. But together with this he insisted that the true development of personality could be achieved only by sinking the self in the service of a community inspired by common spiritual traditions and in the pursuit of its highest values. Such a society could not be found in the West because of the evils inherent in Western civilization and social order, in the materialism of Western thought, and the corrupting influences of nationalism and imperialism. In contrast to these he saw in Islam the pattern within which the social endeavour and spiritual life of the developing personality should be integrated. This was the theme of his second poetic work, *Rumūz-i Bēkhudī* ('The Symbols of the Non-Self'), issued in 1918.

These two doctrines, the sustained struggle of the awakened ego to raise humanity to a higher stage of evolution, and the moral, spiritual, and intellectual values of an idealized Islamic community, were developed and diversified in Iqbal's later poems. These were composed sometimes, like the first two, in Persian for the sake of a wider Moslem circle, although there is no indication that they were much read outside India: *Payām-i Mashriq* ('The Message of the East'), in reply to Goethe's *West-östlicher Divan* (1923); *Zabūr-i Ajam* ('Persian Psalms', 1927); *Jāvid-Nāmah* ('The Book of Eternity'), modelled after the *Divina Commedia* (1932). Sometimes they were composed in Urdu for his own Indian public: *Bāng-i Darā* (1924); *Bāl-i Jibrīl* (1935); and *Darb-i Kalīm* (1936).

A more systematic account of his thought was put together by Iqbal in a course of lectures delivered at Madras in 1928–1929 and published as *The Reconstruction of Religious Thought in Islam* (1930; second ed., with a supplementary chapter, 1934). Throwing aside the traditional transcendentalist dogmas of Islam, as the imposition of an alien Hellenistic philosophy, he set out to reinterpret the Koran in evolutionary and immanentist terms. As a thinker, his chief weakness was a failure to eliminate or reconcile the contradictions in his ethical teaching, where a dynamism of Western inspiration came into conflict with his insistence upon the cultural values of the Islamic tradition. Nevertheless, he had an immense influence upon the contemporary generation of Indian Moslem intellectuals, and after his death an 'Iqbal Academy' was founded at Lahore to expound and propagate his ideas.

[*The Times*, 22 April 1938; Sir M. Iqbal's works; S. Abdul Wahid, *Iqbal: his Art and Thought*, 1944; K. G. Saiyidain, *Iqbal's Educational Philosophy*, 1938; *Iqbal as a Thinker* by various writers, 1945; *Shād Iqbāl* (correspondence with Raja Sir Kishen Parshad), edited by S. M. Qadiri, 1942; private information.]

H. A. R. GIBB.

ISAACS, RUFUS DANIEL, first MARQUESS OF READING (1860–1935), lord chief justice of England, ambassador to the United States of America, and viceroy of India, was born in the parish of St. Mary Axe, London, 10 October 1860. He was the second son and the fourth of the nine children of Joseph Michael Isaacs, a Jewish fruit merchant, then carrying on business in Spitalfields, by his wife, Sarah, daughter of Daniel Davis, of London, a woman of strong character who wielded unchallenged sway over her growing household. Joseph Isaacs's daughter Esther Stella became the wife of Alfred Sutro [q.v.]; his brother Henry was lord mayor of London in 1889–1890. Rufus did not receive all the education which his father's income would have justified; after two years at a school in Brussels, which he left at the age of seven, he was for some years a boarder at an Anglo-Jewish academy in Regent's Park and then attended for some months at University College School in Gower Street. His schooldays were over before he was yet fourteen. It says much for the courageous determination and quick adaptability with which he faced some later stages of

his remarkable career that this initial handicap was so largely overcome.

At the age of fifteen Isaacs, after a period in Hanover spent in learning some German, entered the service of the family business, an occupation which he soon grew to dislike, while his spare time was given to many lively escapades. There is no truth in the story that he ran away to sea; his parents arranged for him to join the sailing-ship *Blair Athole* as an apprentice, but, scanning the apprenticeship deed, he refused to pledge himself to the stipulated two years of service and chose instead to sign articles for the round voyage as a ship's boy at the wage of ten shillings a month (October 1876). The experiment did not work out well; he tried to leave the ship at Rio de Janeiro, but was caught and in due course sailed in her up the Hooghly and, in April 1877, saw the country which he was next to revisit as viceroy forty-four years later. When the *Blair Athole* reached London Isaacs abandoned further employment at sea and for a time resumed the unattractive routine of work in the fruit trade. In 1880 he exchanged this drudgery for the Stock Exchange, where he carried on the business of a jobber in the foreign market, an enterprise which ended in the disaster of his being 'hammered' when overwhelmed by a sudden slump in August 1884. It was then proposed that he should endeavour to repair his finances and repay his creditors by going to seek his fortune in central America, but his mother intervened and insisted that, instead, he should read for the bar.

Isaacs studied law for six months in the office of Algernon Sydney, a solicitor who was a personal friend of his family. In January 1885 he was admitted as a student to the Middle Temple. He read for a year as a pupil in the chambers of (Sir) J. L. Walton [q.v.], then a rising Common Law junior, and was called to the bar in November 1887. Three weeks later he was married to Alice Edith, third daughter of Albert Cohen, a City merchant, at the West London synagogue.

Isaacs at once established himself in chambers of his own at 1 Garden Court, Temple. Work came quickly and his first year of practice produced £519. The establishment of the Commercial Court in 1895 provided him with a forum in which his inside knowledge of the Stock Exchange and his practical experience of commercial documents gave him unusual qualifications for successful argument, and another branch of the law in which he was specially occupied was that relating to trade unions. He became overwhelmingly busy, and after ten and a half years in a stuff gown, his application for silk was granted by Lord Chancellor Halsbury in April 1898.

Isaacs soon attained a position in the front row where he became the acknowledged equal of competitors as powerful and distinguished as Sir Edward Clarke and Sir Edward Carson [qq.v.]. His practice lay chiefly in heavy cases of a business kind or before special juries, with occasional excursions to the divorce court or the Old Bailey. It is impossible within reasonable limits of space to give a list of his chief forensic triumphs; amongst them were the Taff Vale litigation (1902), the prosecution of Whitaker Wright (q.v., 1904), the defence of Sir Edward Russell (1905), and the defence of Robert Sievier (1908). Such a burden could only have been discharged by a man of great physical and mental vigour. Isaacs's method was to start the preparation for the day's labours at a very early hour before breakfast; he made it his rule not to do legal work after dinner.

Isaacs's fine presence and handsome features, combined with a voice of rare quality, expressive hands, and an alert glance that compelled attention, made him an advocate of the first rank, while his complete mastery of the facts, his moderation in statement, and his firm but courteous attitude in argument, always secured him a friendly reception from the bench. Among his brethren at the bar he was a popular colleague, completely unspoiled by success. He was not a profound lawyer, but hard work and good sense made him the master of all the law that mattered for winning his case. His cross-examination was often very effective, although his questions had not the crispness of Carson's; and his speeches in court, expressed in commonplace language and directed strictly to the matter in hand, had a verdict-getting quality which showed how well he understood what the tribunal was thinking. Indeed, Isaacs's greatest asset at the bar was not eloquence (although he was popularly regarded as a fine orator) but a penetrating power of judgement, which enabled him to see the point on which the case would ultimately turn, the main difficulty of fact to be surmounted, and sometimes the moment when compromise could wisely be effected. Isaacs's political leanings had always

been to the liberal side. In the internal dissension which rent the liberal party during the South African war, his sympathies were with the liberal imperialists. After unsuccessfully contesting North Kensington at the general election of 1900, he was returned for Reading at a by-election in August 1904 and retained that seat, in spite of some close contests, until his appointment as lord chief justice in 1913. He became a bencher of his Inn in 1905 and served as treasurer in 1927.

In March 1910, when Sir Samuel Evans [q.v.] became president of the Probate, Divorce, and Admiralty division, Isaacs was appointed, amid universal approval, to succeed him as solicitor-general. In the following October, when Sir W. S. (later Lord) Robson [q.v.] left the House of Commons to become a lord of appeal, Isaacs succeeded to the attorney-generalship and thus, at the age of fifty, became the official head of the bar.

Isaacs was an excellent law officer and brought all his ability and industry to bear on the multifarious business of the Crown both in court and out of it. In 1911 he led for the prosecution in *Rex* v. *Mylius* when the defendant was convicted of criminal libel for circulating the utterly false story that King George V, whose coronation was approaching, was married before his marriage to Queen Mary. In 1912, in the only murder case in which he ever took part, he secured the conviction of the poisoner Frederick Henry Seddon at the Old Bailey, and later in the same year, at the height of the militant suffragette disturbances, he prosecuted (supporter though he was of votes for women as a constitutional reform) Mrs. Emmeline Pankhurst [q.v.] and others for conspiring to commit injury and damage.

Isaacs was also heavily occupied on the Treasury bench in aiding to pilot government bills through the House of Commons and in particular rendered strenuous help to the carrying of Lloyd George's Health Insurance Act (1911). His industry and geniality were everywhere appreciated, and he took great pains in the endeavour to make himself a successful parliamentarian. His speeches, however, did not catch the ear of the House as effectively as his innumerable friends hoped. He sometimes tended to continue at too great length and there was an absence of striking or memorable phrase. Isaacs's inclusion in the Privy Council was announced in the coronation honours of 1911. He was appointed K.C.V.O. in the same year.

In June 1912 Lord Loreburn resigned the office of lord chancellor and the attorney-general was deeply chagrined that, instead of himself, Lord Haldane was invited to occupy the woolsack. At first Isaacs was disposed to regard his being passed over as a reflection not only upon himself but upon his race. His ruffled feelings, however, were more than soothed by the prime minister's invitation that the attorney-general should become a member of the Cabinet—a new but questionable precedent, which has seldom been followed since. The result was that Isaacs had the great satisfaction of entering the inner circle of government without having to give up his membership of the House of Commons.

The even tenor of Isaacs's advancement was now grievously interrupted by the 'Marconi' controversy. When wireless communication, of which Guglielmo Marconi was one of the scientific pioneers, was in its first stage of commercial development, Isaacs's brother Godfrey became joint managing director of the Marconi Wireless Telegraph Company and, in March 1912, obtained for his company a contract with the Post Office for a long-distance service, subject to ratification by the House of Commons. In point of fact, neither of the law officers of the Crown was ever consulted about this contract, which was negotiated and settled departmentally. Rumours nevertheless began to arise in certain quarters that the monopoly obtained from the government by the Marconi Company was due to the influence exercised by the attorney-general in favour of his brother, and that he and certain other ministers who were his close friends—namely, Lloyd George and the liberal chief whip, the Master of Elibank— were seeking to make profits out of the shares of that company. There was no truth in this, but what was true was that when Godfrey Isaacs carried through negotiations with a different company, the American Marconi Company, and acquired as his personal holding a large block of shares in that company, he, on 9 April, offered to dispose of some of these shares to his brothers Rufus and Harry Isaacs. The American company had no interest in the profits of the English company, but Rufus refused, preferring to have no dealings with Godfrey in view of the English company's relations with the government, while Harry acquired a large shareholding. On 17 April—the *Titanic* disaster occurred in the interval and demonstrated the importance of wireless communication at sea—Harry independently offered to Rufus some of his American shares and the attorney-general bought 10,000 at the market price of £2, and later on the same day, transferred 1,000 of them to each of his two ministerial friends. There can be no question but that these transactions in the American shares, carried out as they were in the parties' own names, operated to confirm the unfounded rumour which began to be exploited in sections of the press, that ministers of a government which was making an agreement with the English Marconi company were improperly interesting themselves in the shares of that company.

It was not until 11 October that the postmaster-general, Mr. Herbert (later Lord) Samuel, could move for the appointment of a select committee to investigate and report upon the Marconi contract and the attorney-general intervened to deal with criticisms in the debate affecting himself. He repudiated completely the false insinuations made against him in regard to the English Marconi company, but did not think it necessary to refer to his holding in the American company, with which the British government had nothing to do. It was a lamentable error of judgement. The further information was made public in the course of an undefended action for libel against the Paris newspaper *Le Matin* in March 1913, and shortly afterwards (25 March) Isaacs at last got his opportunity of appearing before the select committee, which had already been sitting for six months. In the meantime he had had to endure fierce attacks from a portion of the press. His evidence extended over three days and completely disposed of any allegation of corruption. Whether his conduct involved impropriety was debated by the committee, but in the end the final Report, adopted by a majority, acquitted the ministers involved by declaring that they had acted throughout in the sincere belief that what they did was not in conflict with their public duty.

In the debate upon the Report on 18 June the attorney-general declared that, while at the time he considered that the purchase of these American shares was quite unobjectionable, he had come to realize that 'it was a mistake to purchase those shares'. The House adopted a motion accepting this expression of regret, reprobating any charge of corruption, and acquitting the ministers of acting otherwise than in good faith. Isaacs suffered acutely during this long and painful controversy, although none but the most credulous and most malignant could have supposed that he had acted from corrupt motives. He was sustained by the continued confidence reposed in him by his constituency and by the proofs that his friends of the bar knew him to be of unsullied character.

The dying embers of this unhappy dispute, which throughout had been inflamed by fierce party feeling, had hardly ceased to glow when the position of lord chief justice fell vacant through the retirement of Viscount Alverstone in October 1913. Asquith, the prime minister, had no hesitation in offering the post to Isaacs, who accepted it. At the swearing-in ceremony on 22 October, Lord Haldane spoke of him as 'a man of the highest honour' and the welcome which he received showed that the profession shared this opinion to the full. He was raised to the peerage as Baron Reading in the New Year's honours list of 1914.

Had it not been for the outbreak of war in August 1914, Lord Reading might have continued to discharge the functions of the head of the King's Bench division for a full span of judicial service, and have become an outstanding figure on the illustrious roll of chief justices. His wide experience and dignified bearing fitted him for such a part, and he gave general satisfaction while performing his duties in the lord chief justice's court. But at the outbreak of war his help was called for to assist the Treasury in framing financial and legislative plans for the domestic emergency, and although he retained the chief justiceship until 1921, and intermittently presided (for example, in settling the status of an enemy alien in *Porter* v. *Freudenburg*, 1915, and at the trial for treason of Roger Casement [q.v.], 1916) his statesmanlike qualities were throughout the war increasingly employed on special duties of the highest order imposed upon him by the successive governments of Great Britain.

In September 1915 Reading, who had been appointed G.C.B. at the New Year, led the Anglo-French mission to the United States to seek American credits for supplies urgently needed for carrying on the war. He achieved a brilliant success, and after immense efforts secured a loan, to be spent in the United States, of 500 million dollars. He returned in October and went back to the more limited scope of his judicial work, with an appetite whetted for wider responsibilities. The government continued to take constant advantage of his advice, and he was advanced to a viscountcy in the birthday honours of 1916.

The entry of the United States into the war in April 1917 made it more necessary than ever that the complicated strands of Anglo-American finance should be gathered together in the hands of the right man, and in September Reading again crossed the Atlantic with the special appointment of high commissioner, and a mandate which covered Canada also. He had expected that his absence would be brief, but the tasks which beset him were so intricate that he could not get back until November, and even then was kept engrossed in financial matters in London where the British War Cabinet required his assistance. An earldom was conferred upon him in that same month.

Reading's exceptional qualifications both as skilled negotiator and as promoter of good will between his own country and the United States were widely recognized on both sides of the Atlantic, and the successes that had attended his labours led to, and abundantly justified, his appointment in January 1918 as ambassador to Washington, in succession to Sir Cecil Spring-Rice [q.v.]. At the same time his authority to deal on Great Britain's behalf with every aspect of the war effort was emphasized by the additional title of high commissioner. He and Lady Reading, whose pluck in spite of ill health was unfailing, made an uncomfortable crossing in February. The new ambassador had to handle a host of delicate and urgent problems—amongst them the acceleration of food supplies to Great Britain, negotiations for the more rapid availability of American troops in the crisis of the war, the question of intervention in Russia and in the Far East, and complex financial arrangements of many kinds—and yet he found time for a series of public speeches well calculated to sustain Anglo-American co-operation. In June he received honorary degrees from the universities of Harvard, Yale, Princeton, and Columbia. He continued to work at intense pressure at Washington until July 1918, after which the ambassador's presence in England was required for the next six months. In the interval the armistice in Europe presaged the end of his war service and in May 1919 he was succeeded as ambassador by Viscount Grey of Fallodon.

The services which Reading rendered to his country and to the Allies as ambassador to the United States in the last year of the war were everywhere regarded as invaluable. Lloyd George addressed to him a letter (21 May) in which he declared: 'When the time comes...the leading part which you played in co-ordinating the war-effort of the United States and the other Allies, and, above all, in helping to bring about that dramatic movement of the American Army in Europe in the spring and summer of 1918, which contributed so strikingly to the Allied victory in the later autumn, will be understood in its true perspective.'

Reading's position while combining the positions of war-time ambassador and lord chief justice was exceedingly anomalous; the foreign secretary (A. J. Balfour), when urging him to continue at Washington longer than he had at first intended, recognized his difficulty. 'We cannot think', he had cabled in the summer of 1918, 'in the circumstances the judiciary would insist on your early return to your high office, as, however great their deprivation may be, it is after all domestic, while duties you are now executing are essential to effective prosecution of the War and cannot be performed by another.' Reading now returned to the lord chief justice's court. But at the end of 1920 his kaleidoscopic career included another call for wider service. In January 1921 it was announced that Reading had been chosen to succeed F. J. N. Thesiger, Lord Chelmsford [q.v.], as viceroy of India. He went to India at a critical time. The Montagu-Chelmsford reforms had been put into legislative shape by the Act of 1919 and it was a chief task of the new viceroy to watch over their early application. The frustration of the new plans was the object of Gandhi, who hoped by fomenting Mohammedan resentment at the terms of the Treaty of Sèvres to combine Hindu and Moslem on a common platform of non-co-operation. Agitation became rife and led to many violent demonstrations, but Reading showed much patience before resorting to extreme measures. In the summer of 1921 he was constrained to arrest the Ali brothers, and in March 1922 Gandhi was imprisoned. In August 1921 he had to deal with the ferocious rebellion of the Moplahs in the Madras Presidency. Notwithstanding the disturbed conditions, the visit of the Prince of Wales to India, planned to take place in November 1921, was carried through.

In the following year, Sikh agitation in the Punjab reached extreme heights, and the boycott by the Congress party of the reformed legislatures was accompanied by grave political tension. Not content with mere repression, Reading on 28 February 1922 sent to E. S. Montagu [q.v.], the secretary of state for India, a dispatch strongly representing the interest of Indian Moslems in the post-war treatment of Turkey and putting forward the government of India's request for a revision of the Treaty of Sèvres. Montagu agreed to make this dispatch public. He did so without obtaining the consent of the prime minister and foreign secretary, with the result that he had to resign his office. The viceroy was deeply stirred, although his own action had been unexceptionable, and for a time he hesitated whether he should not follow the minister into retirement. Second thoughts proved best; the value of his liberal outlook was preserved for India, and after Bonar Law's government had come into power, the negotiation of the Lausanne treaty went far to relieve Moslem anxieties.

The Indian elections of 1923 saw the abandonment by Congress of its previous boycott of the legislatures, although its policy of attacking the reforms from the inside brought consequences to meet which Reading felt compelled to authorize exceptional measures; but in February 1924 Gandhi was released. In May 1924 the committee on the working of the Government of India Act, presided over by Sir Alexander Muddiman [q.v.], was appointed and its Report, published in March 1925, led to much controversy. Reading hoped (although the hope was not realized until after his time) that one result might be to advance the setting up of the statutory commission which was due to be appointed not more than ten years from the passing of the Act of 1919. Reading left India in April 1926. He had discharged his viceregal duties with great distinction in most difficult years, avoiding all vague and high-sounding promises while applying his practical mind in a liberal spirit to every problem that came before him. In recognition of his services he was in April created a marquess, and in June he received the freedom of the City of London. He had been appointed G.C.S.I. and G.C.I.E. in 1921 and G.C.V.O. in 1922. The universities of Cambridge and Oxford (1926) conferred honorary degrees upon him.

After his return to England, Reading,

besides undertaking a number of business posts of which the most important was his association, first as director, and later as president, with Imperial Chemical Industries, played a dominating part in the Round Table Conference on the Indian constitution which was called by the labour government in 1930. In January of that year Lady Reading died. In August 1931 he married Stella, third daughter of Charles Charnaud; she had long acted as principal secretary in the Reading household. When, just afterwards, Ramsay MacDonald formed his all-party government, Reading, now aged nearly seventy-one, was appointed foreign secretary, but after the general election in October he resigned the post.

In 1934 Reading was appointed lord warden of the Cinque Ports, having held the captaincy of Deal Castle from 1926. He died in London 30 December 1935, and was succeeded as second marquess by his only child, Gerald Rufus (born 1889), who became a barrister of the Middle Temple (K.C., 1929) and had borne the courtesy title of Viscount Erleigh.

Reading was a man of impressive personality and winning charm. His courtesy and tact contributed powerfully to the success of everything which he undertook. While his manner was reserved and he detested undue effusiveness, the sweetness of his nature gave him a host of friends and admirers. He remained throughout a proud upholder of his race, without taking any part in Jewish observances. In his youth he was a fine boxer.

There is a striking portrait of Reading by P. A. de László in the viceroy's house at Delhi. Other portraits include a full-length in the robes of the Star of India, by Oswald Birley, which hangs in the Middle Temple, and an earlier one, by the same artist, in lord chief justice's robes in Reading Municipal Art Gallery. A chalk drawing by (Sir) William Rothenstein (1925) is in the National Portrait Gallery. C. S. Jagger [q.v.] executed a life-size statue of him which is at New Delhi; a bust by Lady Kennet (Kathleen Scott) is in the possession of the family. A cartoon of him by 'Spy' appeared in *Vanity Fair* 18 February 1904.

[*The Times*, 31 December 1935; Lord Reading (son), *Rufus Isaacs, first Marquess of Reading*, 2 vols., 1942–1945; personal knowledge.] SIMON.

ISHERWOOD, SIR JOSEPH WILLIAM, first baronet (1870–1937), ship de-signer, was born at Hartlepool 23 June 1870, the son of John Isherwood, by his wife, Mary Ellen Dobinson, of Stockton-on-Tees. He was educated at Luggs School, Hartlepool.

When about fifteen years of age Isherwood entered the drawing office of Edward Withy & company, shipbuilders, of Hartlepool, and, after serving in various other departments, left that firm to join the staff of the principal ship surveyor of Lloyd's Register of Shipping in 1896. It became his duty to examine day by day the plans of ships, and particularly cargo ships, for which that society's classification was desired. He soon came to the conclusion that ships for the carriage of dry cargo and oil could be designed which would be cheaper to build and would carry more cargo, and thus be more profitable in operation at sea. In 1907, when he resigned his position at Lloyd's Register, he published particulars of his new invention, which came to be known as the longitudinal system, in the *Shipping World*. It was at once recognized that Isherwood had made a notable contribution to the science of naval architecture. After a short association with the shipbuilding firm of Messrs. Craggs, at Middlesbrough, he began to practise as a naval architect in London. Later he developed an improved 'bracketless' system and later still introduced a new design of hull form, namely, the 'arcform'. Several ships of this type were immediately laid down and gave satisfactory results.

By 1937, 2,500 ships, cargo vessels, and oil tankers, the design of which incorporated one or more of Isherwood's special designs, had been built and upwards of fifty 'Isherwood' ships were under construction in the shipyards of this and other countries, representing the 'arcform' design and the 'combination' and 'bracketless' systems. He also introduced an ingenious type of steel hatch cover.

Isherwood, who was created a baronet in 1921 in recognition of his contributions to the progress of naval architecture and his work for the government during the war of 1914–1918, retained to the end of his life the enthusiasm of youth tempered by the experience of advancing years. He was always thinking out and testing new ideas and extending and improving the organization of his offices in London and New York, which dealt with orders from shipowners in all parts of the world. He was a member of the Worshipful Company of Shipwrights, of the Institution of Naval

Architects, of the North-East Coast Institution of Engineers and Shipbuilders, and of the Society of Naval Architects and Marine Engineers, New York. He was also a member for many years of the technical committee of Lloyd's Register of Shipping.

Isherwood married in 1892 Annie Mary, daughter of Matthew Robson Fleetham, and had a son and a daughter. He died in London 24 October 1937 and was succeeded as second baronet by his son, William (born 1898).

[*The Times*, 25 October 1937.]

ARCHIBALD HURD.

ISLINGTON, BARON (1866–1936). [See POYNDER, SIR JOHN POYNDER DICKSON-.]

ISMAY, JOSEPH BRUCE (1862–1937), shipowner, was born at Crosby, near Liverpool, 12 December 1862, the eldest son of Thomas Henry Ismay [q.v.], of Dawpool, Cheshire, senior partner in the firm of Messrs. Ismay, Imrie & company and founder of the White Star Line, by his wife, Margaret, daughter of Luke Bruce. He was educated at Elstree School and Harrow, and on leaving the latter went for a year to a tutor in France, after which he served an apprenticeship of four years in his father's office and then went on a year's tour round the world. He was then sent to New York where he worked in the White Star office for a year at the end of which time he was appointed agent for the White Star Line in New York. In 1891 he settled in England and the same year became a partner in the firm of Ismay, Imrie & company.

After his father's death in 1899, Ismay became head of the business and his management was most brilliant and successful. In 1901 he was approached by American interests towards forming an International Shipping Company, and after lengthy negotiations between him and J. P. Morgan (1837–1913), the International Mercantile Marine Company was formed. C. A. Griscom, president of the American Steamship Line, was then at the head, but was succeeded in 1904 by Ismay, who resigned this position in 1912 and was succeeded by H. A. Sanderson.

Ismay was also chairman of the Asiatic Steam Navigation Company, director of the Liverpool London and Globe Insurance Company, the Sea Insurance Company, the Birmingham Canal Navigation Company, and the London, Midland and Scottish Railway, of which he was offered the chairmanship but declined. He was chairman of the Liverpool Steamship Owners Protection Association, the Liverpool and London War Risks Association, and the Delta Insurance Company.

Ismay inaugurated the cadet ship *Mersey* for training officers for the merchant navy and he took the deepest interest in all ranks of the merchant service. He gave £11,000 to found a fund to benefit widows of seamen who lost their lives afloat and in 1919 presented £25,000 to establish a fund to 'mark his admiration of the splendid and gallant manner in which the officers and men of all ranks in the British Merchant Marine have carried on throughout the war'.

Ismay was a man of striking personality and in any company arrested attention and dominated the scene. Those who knew him slightly found his personality overpowering and in consequence imagined him to be hard, but his friends knew this was but the outward veneer of a shy and highly sensitive nature, beneath which was hidden a depth of affection and understanding which is given to but few. Perhaps his outstanding characteristic was his deep feeling and sympathy for the 'underdog' and he was always anxious to help anyone in trouble. Another notable trait was an intense dislike of publicity which he would go to great lengths to avoid. In his youth he won many prizes in lawn-tennis tournaments; he also played association football, having a natural aptitude for games. He enjoyed shooting and fishing and became a first class shot and an expert fisherman. Perhaps the latter was his favourite sport and he spent many happy holidays fishing in Connemara.

Ismay married in 1888 Julia Florence, eldest child of George R. Schieffelin, of New York, and had two sons and two daughters. He died in London 17 October 1937.

[*The Times*, 18 October 1937.]

ARCHIBALD HURD.

JACKSON, FREDERICK GEORGE (1860–1938), explorer, soldier, and big-game hunter, was born at Alcester, Warwickshire, 6 March 1860, the eldest son of George Frederick Jackson, landowner and agriculturist, by his wife, Mary Elizabeth, daughter of Frederick Alfred Crowe, rector of Alcester. After being at school at Denstone College, he spent three years on a Queensland cattle station, and then for a brief period attended classes at Edinburgh University.

In 1887 Jackson sailed for a summer voyage in the Greenland Sea in the sealer and whaler *Eric*. Inspired by Fridtjof Nansen's projected voyage in the *Fram*, Jackson published in 1892 his plans for an attempt on the Pole, using Franz Josef Land, then supposed to extend far north, as a base. In order to test equipment and gain experience he explored Vaigach Island, in Arctic Russia, and made a sledge journey from Khabarova to Kirkenes in 1893–1894. Finding a patron for his polar project in Alfred Harmsworth (afterwards Lord Northcliffe, q.v.) he organized the Jackson-Harmsworth polar expedition which sailed in the *Windward* in 1894. The expedition had its base at Cape Flora in Franz Josef Land for three years. Jackson and Albert Borlase Armitage explored British Channel and found to the north Queen Victoria Sea, which put an end to hopes of a poleward journey. Jackson's map revealed the main features of the western half of the group of islands. On 17 June 1896 he met Nansen and Fredrik Hjalmar Johansen returning from their northern record of latitude 86° 14′ N. They had wintered in the north of the group at Cape Norway, on an island subsequently named Jackson Island by Nansen, and were hoping to make their way to Spitsbergen. This chance encounter probably saved the lives of the two Norwegians. For his services Jackson was awarded in 1898 the Norwegian order of St. Olav.

Jackson, commissioned in the Manchester Regiment, served with distinction with the mounted infantry in the South African war from 1899 to 1902. In the war of 1914–1918 he transferred to the East Surrey Regiment and served on the western front. After the armistice he was in charge of Russian prisoners in Germany.

In 1925–1926 Jackson made a long journey in search of sport by rail and boat and on foot through tropical Africa from Beira to Matadi, via the Victoria Falls, Katanga district, the Lualaba river, Lakes Tanganyika and Kivu, and the Congo river. Soon after his return to England he was appointed a member of the international commission of inquiry into the existence of slavery and forced labour in the Republic of Liberia set up by the League of Nations. The report was published in 1930.

Jackson's travels were inspired chiefly by love of adventure and the opportunities of big-game hunting. His explorations were confined to his pioneer surveys in Franz Josef Land, where his scientific staff, including A. B. Armitage, Reginald Koettlitz, and W. S. Bruce [q.v.], were able to do much useful work.

Jackson was awarded a gold medal of the Société Géographique de Paris (1899) and the Royal Humane Society's medal (1885). He married, first, in 1898 Mabel (died 1918), youngest daughter of Colonel Dalrymple Bruce; secondly, in 1925 Marguerite Wigan, elder daughter of Albert Hernu, of Boulogne, and widow of Henry James Fisher. There were no children. He died in London 13 March 1938. A memorial tablet was unveiled in St. Paul's Cathedral in 1945.

There are two portraits of Jackson, painted in oils: one is in the possession of his widow; the other (with his bear dogs), by Frederick Stacpoole, hangs in the Scott Polar Research Institute, Cambridge.

[*The Times*, 14 March 1938; F. G. Jackson, *The Great Frozen Land*, 1895, *A Thousand Days in the Arctic*, 1899, and *The Lure of Unknown Lands*, 1935; private information.]

R. N. RUDMOSE BROWN.

JACKSON, SIR HERBERT (1863–1936), chemist, was born in Whitechapel, London, 17 March 1863, the only surviving son of Samuel Jackson, by his wife, Clementina Rebecca Grant. Educated at King's College School, in 1879 he entered King's College, London, where he worked for thirty-nine years, becoming successively demonstrator, lecturer, and professor of organic chemistry (1905), and Daniell professor of chemistry (1914). He was elected a fellow of the college in 1907.

Jackson covered an immense field in his investigations, but he committed very little to paper, and his publications give an entirely inadequate impression of the extent and importance of his work. About 1890, in the course of experiments on the excitation of phosphorescence by means of discharge tubes, he discovered that by using a concave cathode he could concentrate the phosphorescent response of material at the anti-cathode to a small area about the centre of curvature of the cathode. He also observed that phosphorescence was excited in screens held outside the tube. There is no doubt that, in this work, he came very near to anticipating W. K. Röntgen's discovery of X-rays in 1895. With a discharge tube having a concave cathode and inclined anti-cathode, Jackson found that he was able in 1896 to reproduce all Röntgen's effects; and this original Jackson 'focus-tube' became the prototype of later X-ray tubes.

Besides numerous investigations in pure chemistry, Jackson's inquiries extended to such subjects as the weathering of stone, and the action of soaps and solvents in laundry-work; his advice on chemical matters was freely sought by manufacturers. He was greatly interested in oriental ceramics, and his determinations of the colouring agents in glasses and glazes and reproduction of the effects gave much assistance to archaeologists and connoisseurs. In all his work he was a skilled user of optical instruments, and he was, particularly, a master of microscope technique; and his wide experience in the interpretation of microscopic observations was often the key to his success. He was also an expert photographer.

Early in the war of 1914-1918 this country was greatly handicapped by inability to produce glasses for special purposes. Jackson undertook an investigation, and working under great pressure, by 1915 had succeeded in determining the formulae for a number of different laboratory, heat-resisting, and other glasses, including a full range of optical glasses. In this work he put his knowledge at the disposal of the glass manufacturers and helped them in their production problems. For these and other invaluable war services he was appointed K.B.E. in 1917. In the same year he was elected F.R.S. In 1918 he resigned his professorship on being appointed the first director of research of the British Scientific Instrument Research Association, a post which he held, with conspicuous success, until his retirement in 1933, and in which he became the friend and scientific adviser of the optical industry. He was president of the Röntgen Society (1901-1903) and of the Institute of Chemistry (1918-1921); a member of the senate of the university of London and a governor of the Imperial College of Science; and he gave valuable service on many government and scientific committees. He died at Hampstead 10 December 1936. He married in 1900 Amy, elder daughter of James Collister, and had no children.

Jackson was a man of infinite resource, of very varied accomplishments, and great personal charm. As a young man he was a notable athlete. He was an entertaining talker, with a wealth of information on out of the way subjects. To those who worked with him, particularly the younger men, his help and encouragement were unfailing, and to all those who knew him there remains the memory of a generous and inspiring personality.

[*The Times*, 14 December 1936; *Obituary Notices of Fellows of the Royal Society*, No. 6, January 1938 (portrait); personal knowledge.]

THOMAS MARTIN.

JAGGER, CHARLES SARGEANT (1885-1934), sculptor, was born at Kilnhurst, Yorkshire, 17 December 1885, the elder son of Enoch Jagger, colliery manager, by his wife, Mary Elizabeth Sargeant. Educated at Kilnhurst national school and the Middle Class School, Sheffield, he left at the age of fourteen to learn the craft of engraving on silver with the Sheffield firm of Messrs. Mappin & Webb. He worked concurrently at the Sheffield School of Art, where he studied modelling and metal engraving and taught drawing in the evenings. In 1903 he won a scholarship to the Royal College of Art, South Kensington. After seven years there as student and assistant to Professor Edward Lanteri a travelling bursary enabled him to study for some months in Rome and Venice. In 1914 he won the Rome scholarship in sculpture, but was prevented from taking it up.

Jagger joined the Artists' Rifles, passing out early in 1915 with a commission in the 4th battalion of the Worcestershire Regiment with which he went to Gallipoli. He was later transferred to the 2nd battalion, serving in France and Belgium. He was three times wounded, and won the M.C. On demobilization he began work as a sculptor in London. He had been deeply impressed by the patience and solid valour of the average infantryman; and he translated this spirit so well into bronze that he was commissioned to execute many war memorials. He designed the British Memorial to Belgium, in Brussels, and his Artillery Memorial at Hyde Park Corner (with the architect, Mr. Lionel Pearson) won him the gold medal of the Royal Society of British Sculptors in 1926. He was elected A.R.A. in the same year and in 1921 a fellow of the Royal Society of British Sculptors, which in 1933 again awarded him its gold medal, for stone groups at Imperial Chemical House, Millbank. In 1932 he was appointed an additional member of the Royal Mint Advisory Committee on Coins, Medals, Seals, and Decorations.

Jagger executed (1922) a portrait statuette of the Prince of Wales (later Duke of Windsor) and statues of Lord Reading and Lord Hardinge of Penshurst. These last were for New Delhi, and Jagger was engaged on a figure of King George V for the same city when he died suddenly in London 16 November 1934.

Influenced in his early years by Sir Alfred Gilbert [q.v.] and Auguste Rodin, Jagger developed an individual style that was stronger than that of the former and far less romantic than that of the latter. He is seen best not in his Artillery Memorial, which was done in collaboration, but in the great, massive, monumental bronzes of soldiers, one of the most imposing of which is the Great Western Railway War Memorial at Paddington Station. Rigidly realistic, but obviously products of a master craftsman, these works epitomize the dour, stolid courage and endurance of the soldier of the war of 1914–1918 as perfectly as anything in graphic, plastic, or literary art which that war produced. Jagger also executed low reliefs, less realistic and more decorative, and was a stylish draughtsman in pencil and charcoal. For the 'How to do it' series published by *The Studio* he wrote a monograph on *Modelling and Sculpture in the Making* (1933).

Jagger was twice married: first, in 1916 to Violet Constance, daughter of Thomas Charles Smith, solicitor's manager; she divorced him in 1924; secondly, in 1925 to Evelyn Isabel Wade. By his first marriage he had a son, and by his second marriage two daughters.

Portraits of Jagger by his brother David are in the possession of the Graves Art Gallery, Sheffield, and of his second wife, who later married Mr. Quentin Clarke, of Buffalo, New York, U.S.A.

[*Burlington Magazine*, February 1922; *Studio*, November 1914; Ulrich Thieme and Felix Becker, *Allgemeines Lexikon der bildenden Künstler*, vol. xviii, 1925; *Catalogue of the Charles Sargeant Memorial Exhibition*, 1935; *The Times*, 17 and 20 November 1934; *Mexborough Times*, 23 November 1934; private information.]   HERBERT B. GRIMSDITCH.

JAMES, MONTAGUE RHODES (1862–1936), biblical scholar, antiquary, and palaeographer, was born 1 August 1862 at Goodnestone, Kent, the third son and the fourth and youngest child of Herbert James, perpetual curate of Goodnestone, formerly fellow of King's College, Cambridge, by his wife, Mary Emily, daughter of Admiral Joshua Sydney Horton. Three years later Herbert James was presented to the rectory of Livermere, near Bury St. Edmunds, where he died in 1909. His son started as a mere boy to make careful notes and plans of churches in the neighbourhood; he learned quickly and read much. In 1876 he gained a scholarship at Eton and there had for his 'tutor' Henry Elford Luxmoore. Prizes for classics, divinity, and French were not his only distinctions: he learned Italian in his spare time and even acquired enough Ethiopic to make an English version of the apocryphal *Rest of the Words of Baruch*; he explored unaided the early Western manuscripts in the college library, and devoured solid works on medieval art and architecture. Games (and mathematics) he viewed as a penance to be got through as quickly as possible. A visit to France in 1880 with Luxmoore disclosed to him the magnificence of French church architecture and painted glass, and forty years later he was able to claim that he had visited all but two of the 143 cathedrals in the land. In 1882 he crowned his Eton career by winning the Wilder divinity prize and the Newcastle scholarship. Later in the year he went up as an Eton scholar to King's College, Cambridge. There he presently used his influence in helping to break down the barriers of mistrust which at that time tended to separate Etonian and non-Etonian members of the college. He took part in three Greek plays and joined the Amateur Dramatic Club. These activities brought him into contact with J. W. Clark, the antiquary, and Charles Waldstein (afterwards Sir Charles Walston), the classical archaeologist [qq.v.], and of both he was the grateful and admiring disciple. Something too he owed to the profound and rigorous scholarship of Henry Bradshaw [q.v.]. Besides college prizes he won the Carus divinity prize in 1882, and a Bell scholarship in 1883; he was Craven scholar in 1884, and in the same year secured the first Jeremie Septuagint prize and a first class in part i of the classical tripos. Turning to classical archaeology he visited Greece and in 1885 obtained a first class in part ii of the tripos. In the following year he won the first chancellor's classical medal and was shortly after appointed assistant to Waldstein, director of the Fitzwilliam Museum, and afterwards to his successor, John Henry Middleton. In 1887 he was elected a fellow of King's for a dissertation on *The Apocalypse of St. Peter*. He was hesitating between classical and biblical studies when he visited Cyprus (1887–1888) and joined D. G. Hogarth and E. A. Gardner [qq.v.] in excavating the Temple of Aphrodite at Paphos. In three months he travelled over most of the island and learned modern Greek. His choice was determined by his appointment as lecturer in divinity at King's, but although he gave courses on the New Testament and Apocrypha he did so without feeling that he had any gift for instruction. His appointment as dean in 1889 made him in part responsible for the fabric of the chapel, and when the sixteenth-century painted windows were leaded afresh he was able with his exhaustive knowledge of Christian iconography to discover and to reconstruct pictures disordered by earlier 'restorers', a service which he was to repeat later for the Priory Church at Great Malvern. As director of the Fitzwilliam Museum (1893–1908) in succession to Middleton, he secured for the university some of its most splendid and precious manuscripts.

In 1895 James brought out the first of a long series of descriptive catalogues of the Western manuscripts at Cambridge and elsewhere which were soon to place him in the front rank of palaeographers. Between 1895 and 1932 he catalogued the manuscripts at Eton, Lambeth, Westminster Abbey, the John Rylands Library, Manchester, Aberdeen University Library, in every college in Cambridge, and those in the Fitzwilliam Museum and in the University Library (catalogue as yet unpublished), not to mention important collections in private hands. To these must be added nearly a score of volumes edited for the Roxburghe Club, the Walpole Society, and others, in which single manuscripts or families were described and their history and relations elucidated. 'My catalogues', he wrote, 'were on a scale that had not been tried before', adding with unaffected humility 'they may not unfairly be called superficial or at least preliminary.' He knew that there were omissions and slips (his writing was a sore puzzle and he was a negligent proofreader), that there was still much for others to glean after his reaping. Even so his achievement is prodigious: he was an explorer charting an unknown continent.

Hardly less remarkable is his work on Apocryphal literature, for which his name may fairly rank with that of Johann Albert Fabricius. He was the first scholar in England to cultivate this field, and he did for Apocrypha much what the Bollandists have done for hagiography: he brought it out of the category of literary lumber into being a comprehensible documentation of human thought and life for the modern educated reader.

Beside all this James wrote extensively on the arts and literature of the Middle Ages, editing and translating texts, and, in a lighter vein, composing ghost-stories and little plays for schoolboys. To his other languages he soon added Danish, Swedish, and Coptic, with a modicum of Hebrew and Syriac. His immense learning was the fruit of a memory exact and capacious as that of Porson or Macaulay, great powers of concentration, and a faculty for working continuously at high speed: his *Apocryphal New Testament* (1924) was composed in under three months. Yet there is no parade of learning; there is admirable coolness and sanity of judgement, whether of books or of persons; and the English is limpid and concise. Alike in all that he wrote or spoke or did there was a seemingly effortless grace, a telling simplicity which is 'the echo of a great mind'.

In 1900 James exchanged the office of dean for that of tutor, but after two years was glad to be free once more to devote his whole time to scholarship and the museum. In 1905 on the death of Augustus Austen Leigh he was elected provost of King's, and for all his dislike of administrative business proved that a scholar can also be a man of affairs. The office of vice-chancellor he filled with distinction in the difficult years 1913–1915.

In 1918 James was offered by the Crown the provostship of Eton, and was the first to preside in turn over both the foundations of King Henry VI. Both for the school and for James himself, steeped as he was in the sentiment and the history of the place, the appointment was a singularly happy one. He enjoyed the company of boys and entertained them frequently. His first concern was for the chapel: he had the modern stall-canopies removed so as to reveal the fifteenth-century wall-paintings, 'a treasure unrivalled in this country', and suggested designs in connexion with the war memorial, which, however, were not generally applauded. His real skill lay in inscriptions, and of the style known as 'lapidary' he was a master. He gave much thought to the ordering of the services in chapel and was himself an effective preacher. His gratitude to the founder amounted to an almost personal devotion, and in all that he did for Eton that thought was uppermost.

Until 1914 it was James's practice to spend a part of his holidays with friends bicycling in France, of which, excluding Paris and the Riviera, he knew every corner. Denmark and Sweden stood next in his affections; once he bicycled from Dieppe to Regensburg, but Germany, apart from her scholarship, had no great attraction for him. His tastes were simple: he 'collected' nothing, and gave little thought to his surroundings or personal comfort; he liked his food and loved his pipe. At King's he was always accessible and seemed never too busy to spend a social evening with younger friends, stimulating talk in others rather than himself talking, for although quite prepared to unlock his store of knowledge for any inquirer he was far too modest ever to 'hold forth'. If alone, he would devour the *State Trials*, the Victorian novelists, or modern detective fiction; poetry but seldom. Politics and the problems of philosophy did not interest him. Charitable in his judgements he disliked bitterness and fault-finding, preferring to dwell on whatever was good in men or things. He had a rich vein of humour and appreciated it in others. The spirit of youthfulness never left him; he desired to be and to see others happy; he 'kept his friendships in repair' and the circle of them was for ever widening.

James received honorary degrees from the universities of Dublin (1907), St. Andrews (1911), Oxford (1927), and Cambridge (1934), and the gold medal of the Bibliographical Society (1929). He was elected a fellow of the British Academy in 1903, and was an honorary member of the Royal Irish Academy, a commissioner for the Exhibition of 1851, and a trustee of the British Museum; he served on the royal commissions on public records, on historical monuments, and on the universities of Oxford and Cambridge; he was made officier de l'Instruction Publique (France), commander of the Belgian Order of Leopold, and in 1930 was appointed to the Order of Merit. He died, unmarried, at Eton 12 June 1936.

James was tall, with clear-cut features, and hands long and tapering. He had a natural dignity and his presence at any ceremony made it seem more august. There is a chalk drawing of him by William Strang (1909) in the Fitzwilliam Museum; an oil-painting by Glyn Philpot (1918) at King's College; and another oil-painting, by G. F. Kelly (1935), at Eton.

[*The Times*, 13 June 1936; M. R. James, *Eton and King's*, 1926; S. G. Lubbock, *A Memoir of Montague Rhodes James with a list*

of his writings by A. F. Scholfield, 1939; Stephen Gaselee, *Montague Rhodes James, 1862–1936* in *Proceedings* of the British Academy, vol. xxii, 1936; C. H. K. M[arten] and others in *Eton College Chronicle*, 18 June 1936; A. B. Ramsay, *ibid.*, 25 June 1936; J. H. C[lapham] in *Cambridge Review*, 9 October 1936; private information; personal knowledge.]   A. F. SCHOLFIELD.

JELLICOE, (JOHN) BASIL (LEE) (1899–1935), housing reformer, was born at Chailey, Sussex, 5 February 1899, the elder son of Thomas Harry Lee Jellicoe, rector of Chailey, by his wife, Bethia Theodora, youngest daughter of Sir John Boyd, of Maxpoffle, Roxburgh, lord provost of Edinburgh from 1888 to 1891. His father was a cousin of J. R. Jellicoe, first Earl Jellicoe [q.v.].

From an early age Jellicoe's heart was set upon the vocation of the priesthood. Through the generosity of his godmother, Mrs. Hepburn, he was educated at Haileybury and Magdalen College, Oxford. A few months before the end of the war of 1914–1918 he left Oxford to join the Royal Naval Volunteer Reserve and served for a short time in the Mediterranean. In 1920 he resumed his studies at Oxford and was ordained deacon in 1922 and priest in 1923.

Brought up in the Tractarian tradition, it was the social implications of sacramental Christianity which determined Jellicoe's outlook; as a schoolboy he had made a speech on Christian socialism to the Oddfellows at a village inn. For politics or social reform as such he had but little interest; it was the theological aspect of these matters in their direct relation to human beings which aroused in him an urgent desire to demonstrate the efficacy of the Christian gospel. This he achieved, not only by means of the great enterprises which he inspired, but also through the influence of his character and convictions on all types of people, especially the young. 'No man', wrote William Temple, 'ever so luminously exemplified the sacramental quality of the Christian religion as did Basil Jellicoe.' His opportunity came at an early age when in 1921, while still a layman, he was given charge of the Magdalen College mission in the Somers Town district of St. Pancras. In that overcrowded area, where more than 22,000 people were living at an average of two to three persons per room, Jellicoe realized that the value of clubs and camps was merely palliative; the fundamental need was better housing. The evils resulting

Jellicoe, J. B. L.

from slum conditions were to him 'the devil's work' and he described Somers Town as 'a gigantic theft'. So, towards the end of 1924, largely as a result of his initiative, the St. Pancras House Improvement Society was formed to re-house existing tenants. Beginning with a share capital of £250 it became the vanguard of a widespread campaign of voluntary housing. By 1930 the society's capital had reached £160,000, and some hundreds of the poorest families in London had been re-housed in blocks of flats at low but economic rents.

Jellicoe found the Magdalen College mission disorganized and heavily in debt. When in 1927 he resigned the headship owing to ill health he left it not only free of debt but in so flourishing a condition that, according to the *New Survey of London Life and Labour*, vol. ix (1935), 'nothing should be described in St. Pancras before the splendid work of the Magdalen College Mission . . . has been mentioned'. After his resignation he continued his work for housing in Somers Town and elsewhere, notably in the Isle of Dogs.

Jellicoe's ambition was not limited to the re-housing of the poor; it was to demonstrate the possibility of a Christian motive and environment for all human activities through the consecration of life to the service of God. A public house under Christian management was among the projects which he initiated.

In 1931 Jellicoe visited Canada, where his sermons and speeches made a profound impression. Illness frequently intervened during the last ten years of his short life, and he died, unmarried, in a nursing-home at Uxbridge 24 August 1935.

[*The Times*, 26 August 1935; Kenneth Ingram, *Basil Jellicoe*, 1936 (portraits); personal knowledge.]

PERCY MARYON-WILSON.

JELLICOE, JOHN RUSHWORTH, first EARL JELLICOE (1859–1935), admiral of the fleet, was born at Southampton 5 December 1859, the second of the four sons of John Henry Jellicoe, a captain in the Royal Mail Steam Packet Company and later its marine superintendent at Southampton, by his wife, Lucy Henrietta, daughter of John Rushworth Keele, of Southampton. It was natural that the future admiral should elect to follow a sea career; but there were other hereditary incentives; for his family had already contributed seven officers to the Royal Navy,

notably on his mother's side. One of her ancestors, Philip Patton, had fought at La Hogue, and her grandfather, Admiral Philip Patton [q.v.], had served as second-in-command to Lord Keith in the Downs when Napoleon had his camp at Boulogne, and he was second sea lord during the Trafalgar campaign.

Jellicoe spent much of his boyhood among the docks and on the waterfront; and at a very youthful age gained experience of small craft. From the age of six he attended a preparatory school at Southampton, passing at eleven (after a year at a larger school) to Field House, Rottingdean, where he was well grounded in mathematics. In 1872 he received a nomination for the Royal Navy, and in the summer of that year passed second into the *Britannia*, being twelve and a half years old, and four feet six inches high. In the summer of 1874 he passed out top of his term, gaining first class certificates in every subject, with consequent promotion to midshipman. In the autumn he joined the *Newcastle*, his first sea-going ship, an iron sailing frigate with auxiliary steam. As midshipman he had under him broad-shouldered, bearded men, whose agility in making and shortening sail required a combination of knowledge, muscle, and nerve which the youngster was expected to equal or excel. In October the *Newcastle* set sail from Sheerness, and dropped anchor at Plymouth two and a half years later after visiting Gibraltar, Rio de Janeiro, the Falkland Islands, the Cape of Good Hope, St. Helena, Ascension, Bombay, Singapore, Hong-Kong, Nagasaki, and Mauritius. During the long cruise Jellicoe added to his height five inches; and, to his experience of the unexpected always happening at sea, a range remarkable for his years.

In July 1877 Jellicoe joined the battleship *Agincourt* which shortly afterwards sailed to join Vice-Admiral (Sir) Geoffrey Phipps Hornby [q.v.], at the time under orders to prepare to force the Dardanelles during the Russo-Turkish war. Jellicoe had charge of two steamboats and four cutters; and on arrival at Gallipoli was employed ashore as a dispatch rider. A more daunting experience was the handling of the *Cruiser* (a sailing vessel attached to the fleet for instructional purposes) when the commander-in-chief came on board for inspection and ordered the sloop to take him back to his flagship. At the close of the trip Jellicoe was complimented on his performance, and on his

474

nineteenth birthday obtained a first class certificate in seamanship, and left the *Agincourt* for a period of study at the Royal Naval College, Greenwich.

Here and afterwards in the gunnery and torpedo courses at Portsmouth Jellicoe again obtained first classes, and, as a 'three one-er', was properly entitled to immediate promotion; but for technical reasons this encouragement was denied him, and for six months he served in the *Alexandra*, flagship of the Mediterranean Fleet, as signal sub-lieutenant. In September 1880 he was promoted lieutenant, and returned home through Italy, visiting Rome, and at Florence contracting dysentery. When he recovered he determined to qualify as a gunnery specialist; but before undertaking intensive study ashore for two years or longer it was necessary to complete at least one year's watch-keeping at sea; and in February 1881 Jellicoe returned to the *Agincourt*.

In May 1882, in consequence of the rebellion of Arabi Pasha, the *Agincourt* was ordered to Malta, where she embarked a battalion of infantry; and, despite her low speed and the overcrowding on board, reached Alexandria only thirty-six hours after the bombardment, bringing welcome reinforcements. Jellicoe was sent with a company of seamen to support the turning movement of Sir Garnet Wolseley [q.v.] from Ismailia; and from that base was entrusted with secret dispatches for the commander-in-chief, which, in the disguise of a refugee and amid a horde of verminous natives, he conveyed successfully to Port Said.

After a year of active service Jellicoe was released to qualify as a gunnery specialist. In the theoretical work at Greenwich he defeated all competitors and was awarded the £80 prize; and at Portsmouth he gained first class certificates in gunnery and torpedo. In May 1884, as a full-blown gunnery lieutenant, he was appointed to the staff of the *Excellent* gunnery school and participated in the far-reaching reforms instituted at that time by the dynamic commandant, Captain J. A. (later Lord) Fisher [q.v.].

In 1885 Admiral Sir Geoffrey Phipps Hornby hoisted his flag in the *Minotaur*. Fisher was appointed his chief of staff, and as his own staff-officer selected the most junior of those who had served under him in the *Excellent*, a very notable testimonial to Jellicoe's merits. The cruise was short, but enabled him to witness the first torpedo attack on a fleet, and the first modern attempt at a tactical fleet action. In September 1885 he was appointed gunnery lieutenant to the *Monarch*, an obsolescent turret ship; and in April 1886, in the same capacity, joined the *Colossus*, the most up-to-date battleship then afloat. At the end of the year he was back again in the *Excellent* as an experimental officer to superintend the gunnery tests of all ships commissioning. The monotony of the work was relieved by experiments which led to the adoption of the 4·7-in. (45-pounder) and 6-in. (90-pounder) guns.

In 1889 the passing of the Naval Defence Act allocated £21,000,000 to the long neglected task of increasing and modernizing the *matériel* of the fleet; and much of the unprecedented labour involved in the provision of ten battleships and forty-two cruisers fell upon Fisher, then director of naval ordnance. To assist him in his task he insisted that Jellicoe should be transferred from the *Excellent* to the Admiralty, although the step was contrary to precedent. Looking back on this period Jellicoe records that he was frequently at work until midnight in his efforts to keep pace with the daily influx of work. In June 1891 he was promoted commander; and in March 1892, in the *Sans Pareil*, commanded by Captain (Sir) A. K. Wilson [q.v.], joined the Mediterranean Fleet at Malta.

Early in 1893 Admiral Sir George Tryon [q.v.], then commander-in-chief, asked the captain of the *Sans Pareil* that Jellicoe might come as commander to his flagship, the *Victoria*, then recommissioning at Malta; and when preparations were complete, left for a cruise in the Levant. On 22 June, as he drew near to Tripoli, with his fleet in two lines ahead he prepared to anchor. Before doing so it was necessary to put about. But instead of the customary procedure, he signalled the leading ship of each column to turn inwards towards one another. For this manœuvre Tryon allowed insufficient sea-room; and the *Victoria*, rammed by the *Camperdown*, turned over and sank with the loss of her admiral and nearly 400 men. Jellicoe, who was suffering from a bout of Malta fever, hurried on deck, walked along the port side of the ship as it assumed a horizontal position; and, before the *Victoria* took the final plunge, committed himself to the water. Swimming as strongly as his condition allowed and receiving some assistance from a midshipman, he kept afloat until he was picked up. On his return to England the effects of his immersion declared themselves and he was for a time invalided.

In command of the Mediterranean Fleet Tryon was succeeded by Admiral Sir Michael Culme-Seymour, whose flag flew in the *Ramillies*, a new battleship successfully conforming to the requirements of the age of steel. The utmost care was exercised in the choice of her officers, and for commander the choice of the Admiralty fell upon Jellicoe who, later in life, looked back with pleasure to a commission which lasted three years (October 1893 to December 1896) and of which he retained delightful memories. The other ships of the fleet did their utmost to surpass the flagship in smartness and efficiency; but, thanks to her commander, the *Ramillies* excelled them all. At the close of the commission Jellicoe returned to England and in January 1897 was promoted captain.

After a year's work as a member of the Ordnance Committee Jellicoe set out for the Far East in company with Admiral Sir E. H. Seymour [q.v.] who, flying his flag in the *Centurion* on the China station, chose Jellicoe as his flag captain and chief of staff. The hour of their arrival coincided with a critical conjuncture in the Far East. The utter defeat of China by Japan two years earlier and the seizure by the victor of the key-points on the Gulf of Pe-chi-li led to the intervention of the great powers: the seizure of Port Arthur by Russia, of Kiaochow by Germany, and of Kwang-Chow-wan by France. It was impossible for Great Britain, with her vast interests in the Orient, to stand aside; and she secured from China a lease of Wei-hai-wei for a period co-extensive with the occupation of Port Arthur by Russia. In May 1898 Seymour occupied the place, and Jellicoe busied himself with the conversion of the harbour into a naval base. For the rest it was the duty of the British fleet to keep the peace. All the great powers had squadrons or ships to support their diplomacy in the event of further disputes; and further disputes seemed only too probable. The presence of a strong British fleet, it was hoped, would exercise a stabilizing effect upon the ocean-ways.

But it was not at sea that the storm was brewing. On 28 May 1900 a telegram from Peking, requesting a guard for the legations, communicated the first intelligence of the Boxer rising. Seymour, as commander-in-chief of a strictly naval force, was in no position to deal with a military crisis: but appeals for help left him no alternative; and he summoned a conference of international flag officers and invited them to send contingents ashore under his personal command. He selected Jellicoe as his chief of staff; and on 5 June sent him ahead to decide whether to advance by river, road, or railway. Jellicoe reported that the river was choked by sandbanks, the road a broken track, and the railway the only possibility. Assembling all the tugs and lighters in the neighbourhood he sent them to the ships, knowing that small craft only could bring the troops ashore. Signalling by searchlight, he apprised the admiral of the situation; and on 10 June an international naval brigade set out for Peking. The total, representing ten nations, numbered little more than 2,000 men, of whom 915 were British.

The difficulties that were soon to prove insuperable declared themselves at once. The day temperature of 95° sank at night to an icy chillness. The terrain was little better than desert; and the sand-laden wind parched the skin and irritated the throat. The railway was highly vulnerable; and although the imperial army permitted the force to pass the Taku forts and occupy Tientsin, in a few days it openly joined the rebels. Before long the railway was irreparably broken both ahead of the column and in its rear; and a council of war (19 June) decided to leave the railway and retreat by the river bank, towing the wounded in sampans. Serious opposition was encountered; and on 21 June, while leading an attack at Peitsang, Jellicoe received a bullet in the left lung, and fell dangerously wounded. After an injection of morphia he wrote his will on the battlefield and was placed in a sampan to die. But his strong constitution bore him up; moreover, as the last spark of strength flickered out of the expedition, reinforcements from the base had captured the Taku forts (17 June), and brought the exhausted crusaders to the comparative comforts of Tientsin (26 June). From here Jellicoe was removed to Wei-hai-wei to recover from his wound. Some fifteen months later, after a four years' commission, the *Centurion* was relieved by the *Glory* and Jellicoe returned home (September 1901), having accumulated most valuable Far Eastern experience and an insight into the capacities of various nations on active service.

In March 1902 Jellicoe was selected to fill a new post at the Admiralty, that of naval assistant to the controller. As such, his duty was to inspect all new ships under construction, and this took him to Clydeside. While in Scotland he renewed his acquaintance with Sir Charles William Cayzer (later first baronet, of Gartmore, Perthshire), from whom he had previously received hospitality. On this occasion Jellicoe's friendship with Cayzer's second daughter, Florence Gwendoline, ripened into an engagement; and in July 1902 they were married in London. Just over a year later Jellicoe was appointed to command the armoured cruiser *Drake*, and his happy home life was interrupted.

In November 1904 Fisher, who had become first sea lord in the previous October, recalled Jellicoe to the Admiralty, and in February 1905 he was appointed director of naval ordnance and to serve on the committee then assembling to determine the future design of battleships; the existing mixed armament of heavy and medium calibres was considered anachronistic; and the development of long-range firing certainly demanded a radical change. The outcome was the 'all big gun' battleship *Dreadnought*, which rendered all her predecessors obsolete. Jellicoe's duties were of paramount importance: in addition to stimulating the accuracy of long-range gunnery by battle-practice, he conducted a long-delayed reform of revolutionary significance—the transfer of responsibility for the output of naval ordnance from the War Office to the Admiralty. In February 1907 he was promoted rear-admiral; in August he hoisted his flag in the *Albemarle* as second-in-command of the Atlantic Fleet; and in October, on the occasion of the naval review at Spithead, was knighted and invested by King Edward VII with the insignia of the K.C.V.O. He had been appointed C.B. in 1900 and C.V.O. in 1906.

A commission which included a cruise off the coast of Portugal at the time of the assassination of King Carlos and his elder son, and participation in the tercentenary celebrations at Quebec can hardly be described as uneventful. But to a keen naval officer greater significance attached to battle-practice at a range of five miles in contrast with the one-mile maximum of some eleven years earlier when Jellicoe was commander of the *Ramillies*. Still more important for his future was the enforced absence of the commander-in-chief, which for a period put him in charge of the whole fleet. In August 1908, after just a year's sea-time, he returned to England, and in October rejoined the

Admiralty as controller and third sea lord.

Jellicoe became responsible for new naval construction at a moment of extreme difficulty. The *Dreadnought* admittedly surpassed all previous battleships; but in promoting a new type Great Britain of necessity had given other nations a better chance of drawing level than they had enjoyed for two and a half centuries. Not only were the Germans intent on seizing this opportunity; but the general election of 1906 brought in a government committed to the curtailment of armaments. When Jellicoe became controller there was a strong probability that by 1912 England would have eighteen dreadnoughts and Germany twenty-one. Jellicoe pointed out that if Britain's shipbuilding capacity might in an emergency enable her to overtake a German lead, the same argument did not apply to heavy ordnance, which could not be constructed against time. It was this hard fact that weighed down the balance and led to the inclusion in the 1909–1910 programme of the eight battleships which restored the lead to Britain. But the adoption of the *Dreadnought* brought another disadvantage. The ships were growing too large for existing docks; and the government was not prepared to face the excessive cost which new docks would entail. Its veto cramped the breadth of the new vessels, which in consequence were not sufficiently proof against underwater attack. The total displacement might compare favourably with that of German ships of the same class; but the German ships, mounting smaller guns and with greater beam, were heavily protected about their vitals; and the greater hitting power of the British ships would be seriously offset if one lucky shell from the enemy found their protection insufficient. The toughness of the German ships required an improvement in British armour-piercing shells; and for these the controller, after experimental firings at a ship, put forward insistent demands. The documented proofs of his foresight clear him of the blame for faulty Cabinet decisions, with which political apologists have tried to saddle him.

Concluding his term of office with the satisfaction of having seen ninety vessels, including twelve battleships, added to the fleet, Jellicoe, in December 1910, with the rank of vice-admiral, hoisted his flag in the *Prince of Wales* as vice-admiral commanding the Atlantic Fleet. The year that followed saw the coronation review of

King George V and the Agadir incident. During the latter Jellicoe took his fleet to a south Irish port to be ready for any eventuality. In December 1911 the steamship *Delhi*, with the Princess Royal and her family on board, suffered shipwreck off Cape Spartel, and Jellicoe earned the gratitude of the King for the effective steps taken to rescue them. The same month, to give him experience in handling a squadron of dreadnoughts, he was appointed to command the second division of the Home Fleet, and hoisted his flag in the *Hercules*. The two years of Jellicoe's command afloat passed uneventfully; and in December 1912 he was summoned again to the Admiralty. As second sea lord he became responsible for the discipline and manning of the fleet and all questions affecting officers and men.

Meanwhile the war cloud lowered over Europe; and in June 1914 the tragedy of Serajevo precipitated the crisis. The Admiralty had already ordered a naval mobilization; and at Spithead the King reviewed a fleet which included fifty-seven capital ships. At the close of the exercise the Admiralty cancelled the customary paying off and dispatched the fleet to Scapa Flow. Jellicoe followed overland, ostensibly as second-in-command; but on 4 August he received a telegram directing him to open a secret envelope which had been handed to him on leaving London. This proved to be his appointment as commander-in-chief, Grand Fleet, with the acting rank of admiral, flying his flag in the *Iron Duke*.

For the distant blockade of the German fleet Scapa Flow was not ill placed; but in August 1914 as a naval base it lacked every requisite. In its desire to avoid action calculated to increase the tension with Germany, the government had refrained from taking the measures necessary for the defence of the place or the maintenance of a fleet there. There were three entrances through which hostile torpedo-craft could gain ingress; and it was not until February 1915 that they were blocked. Jellicoe found it necessary to keep his fleet continually moving; and in August one day only was spent in harbour. When winter came the weather in those latitudes grew dark and tempestuous; and the swirl of waters through the Pentland Firth made return to harbour a hazardous proceeding. Although Jellicoe had a large floating dock towed up to the Cromarty Firth, and although Rosyth was put into full use, there were for some time

not sufficient facilities or docks and plant for minor repairs. The fleet was reduced by casualties and damage requiring repairs, for which ships had to be sent south to the Channel ports; and had the Germans been more venturesome they might in January 1915 have challenged Jellicoe's dreadnought strength on practically equal terms. But they preferred to stay snugly in harbour, while the Grand Fleet in the first four months of the war steamed 16,805 miles. The commander-in-chief balanced the rigours of his routine by a personal interest in the welfare of the 60,000 officers and men under his command. Admirals and captains were, in Nelson's phrase, a band of brothers; while the lower deck knew instinctively that Jellicoe thought more of their happiness than of his own.

During 1915 (the year in which he was promoted admiral) Jellicoe strengthened his grip on northern waters. By the middle of the year he had a preponderant margin of dreadnought strength; and, as a base, Scapa was in some degree equipped for repairs and put in a reasonable state of defence. No pains were spared to increase the Grand Fleet's fighting efficiency by evolutions and exercises. But it was no longer necessary to plough the seas as a precaution against torpedo attack; and time could be spent in harbour with comparative immunity. But, as in the days of Hawke, Jervis, Howe, and Nelson, the wearisome, monotonous blockade continued; and between the outbreak of war and the battle of Jutland the German admiral only five times emerged from harbour. After each modest sally of some hundred miles he hastened home with the mendacious assurance that he had vainly offered his opponent the chance of battle.

The King, at the outbreak of war, described the navy as the country's 'sure shield'; and this definition opportunely emphasized the necessarily defensive character of Jellicoe's blockade. So long as the Grand Fleet controlled all sea approaches to and from Germany, the enemy in a naval sense was immobilized. The raids of the German battle-cruisers on British fishing towns and seaside resorts, ethically indefensible and strategically ineffective, were intended to undermine the trust which this country reposed in its sea-governance. In this objective they failed signally, and unless the Germans were content with having built a dreadnought battle fleet to no purpose, it was for them to break Jellicoe's stranglehold;

it was for them to assume the offensive. The appointment early in 1916 of Admiral Scheer brought the chances of a collision perceptibly nearer. Not that his plans for reducing the British margin of dreadnought superiority came any nearer success than those of his predecessors, but they did involve him in the meshes of the net which Jellicoe set to catch him. On 31 May, the weather being thick for the time of year, he gave the word to attack a British detached force which Jellicoe had sent in the direction of the Skagerrak. The German battle-cruisers, under Admiral Hipper, were sent on ahead and were sighted at 2.20 p.m. by the British light cruiser *Galatea* wearing the broad pendant of Commodore E. Alexander Sinclair, and the first salvoes of the battle of Jutland were fired when the *Galatea*, in company with the *Phaeton*, opened fire on two enemy destroyers. At 2.35 Hipper's battle-cruisers were sighted, and at 3.48 the two squadrons opened fire on each other. [See also Beatty, David, Earl.]

Although the British battle-cruisers had with them four fast dreadnought battleships, their prime function was that of scouting; and when at 4.33 Scheer himself appeared in Hipper's wake, Beatty put about to join Jellicoe to the northward of the battlefield, drawing the enemy's forces after him. Jellicoe had intercepted the signals from the *Galatea* and other ships, and was making all speed to the south, sending ahead his own battle-cruisers to support those already engaged. But he was in no position to order a 'General Chase', the signal beloved by the navy in sailing days: for he was still some fifty miles away; and from those engaged had received no exact intelligence as to the enemy's position or formation. His own fleet, numbering twenty-four dreadnought battleships, was in sailing order, six lines-ahead disposed abeam. Before he accepted battle he had to deploy his six columns into single line ahead; and before deployment it was essential that he should know at what point on his front the enemy would appear.

At 6.14 the German battle-fleet was reported; not (as was expected) immediately ahead, but to the westward. Jellicoe, with no enemy yet in sight, instantly signalled deployment on his port (or easternmost) wing column. By doing so, he threw a mantle of invisibility over his own fleet, while the glare of the setting sun through the mist made silhouette targets of the enemy. As his six divisions drew into a perfect line ahead he crossed the enemy's T, compelling them to alter course and steer parallel to him. At 6.23 the leading British battleships opened fire, the salvoes of nine dreadnoughts converging on three of their opponents. Outmanœuvred, and outclassed except in *matériel*, Scheer turned and doubled on his tracks. By this time the murky evening was rendered more opaque by the pall of battle-smoke that hung above the combatants. It was thus impossible for Jellicoe to know whether Scheer had actually retreated, or fortuitously disappeared behind the curtain of mist. What he did know was that he had placed the British battle-fleet between the Germans and Germany; and that if they desired to see home again they must re-emerge.

For ten miles Scheer fell back to the inhospitable west. Then pulling his force together he came back in line ahead, hoping to work a passage past, or even through, his opponents, like a snake wriggling through a wire fence. At 7.10 he reappeared; and for the second time reeled backwards under the punishment of Jellicoe's devastating fire. Georg von Hase records that the *Derfflinger* was hit twenty-five times, often by 15-in. shells, and that the British battleships had the range to an inch. [*Kiel and Jutland*, translated by A. Chambers and F. A. Holt, 1921.]

For the second time accepting the necessity of retreat, Scheer ordered his destroyers to veil him with a smoke-screen, and to deliver a massed torpedo attack. In theory he could count on the discharge of 224 of those deadly projectiles; but as Jellicoe instantly launched an effective counter-attack on the enemy flotillas, only thirty-one torpedoes were actually fired, though these might have played havoc with a line of twenty-four ships broadside on. Jellicoe, however, turned his ships individually at an angle of 45° to the eastward of their advance; and the torpedoes thus ran harmlessly between the widened interstices in his line.

Night now sank upon the sea; and Jellicoe, who still stood between the Germans and Germany, took every step that ingenuity could suggest to block their natural avenues of escape. In a land campaign under similar circumstances the enemy would have been compelled to continue the action on the morrow; but in deep waters the entire surface of ocean is a path; and all that Scheer needed was the breadth of one ship where in Indian file the rest could follow. Darkness served him well in this his third and last attempt; and with heavy losses he brought his defeated ships back in dejection to their base. On 1 June Jellicoe found himself alone in German waters. If he had successfully sunk, burnt, or destroyed every vessel brought against him, he could not have been more completely master of the sea.

The immediate sequel to the action forms an interesting study in popular psychology. Jellicoe signed the Jutland dispatches on 18 June; and upon them any proper appraisal of the action hinged. Before he reached harbour, however, the Germans issued a *communiqué* representing Jutland as a glorious success for their arms; and this preposterous claim the Admiralty published on 2 June; supplementing it with a frank but inadequate statement which disclosed little beyond the serious British losses. The public, finding in the latter no hint of victory, at once conceived the idea that the engagement had been a disaster and were confirmed in their delusion when they discovered that the German losses, both in ships and men, were less heavy than the British. With good cause for annoyance with German publicity and Admiralty reticence, they visited their displeasure on Jellicoe and allowed their resentment to be fanned into flame by undiscerning critics who, not in club-land only, demonstrated what Nelson would have done. But there were two big differences. First, the close blockade, possible in Nelson's day but impossible in Jellicoe's, prevented any general action in home waters in 1805. Secondly, in 1805 Nelson was not even in command of the Grand Fleet. Had he been, he would probably not have taken the risks which he accepted at Trafalgar, where he was covered by the Grand Fleet under Cornwallis. Unhappily the critics of 1916 overlooked these important distinctions; and the mistaken tradition that, if not a defeat, Jutland was at best a drawn battle, for very many years lingered on.

Later events fully established the correctness of Jellicoe's judgement (formed on the battlefield of Jutland) that the Germans would not again risk such an encounter. More serious at the moment was the U-boat assault on British seaborne supplies; and Jellicoe modestly volunteered to serve on a committee to grapple with this baffling problem. It was not, however, until November 1916 that, on appointment as first sea lord, he left the perfect organization of the Grand Fleet for the mass of unsolved problems at headquarters. The merchantmen needing defence were privately owned and were run by private enterprise over which government had no control. The responsibility of the Board of Trade was unsuited to an hour when the vessels were no longer engaged in commerce, but in carrying the supplies on which the life of the nation depended. Some nationalization of the industry was inevitable; but that was for Cabinet action. Taking up his new duties on 4 December Jellicoe went straight to the heart of the problem and made it his first duty to see that the arming of the merchantmen was accelerated. By the end of February 1917 2,899 ships had guns to defend themselves; and depth-charges were daily accumulating. But these measures of protection, with others instituted before he accepted office, drove the Germans in February to unrestricted U-boat warfare; and shipping losses soared in April to the staggering total of 599,000 tons. Britain possessed 3,200 steamers. Of these 1,900 were engaged on war purposes only, leaving 1,300 to stock the country with food and raw material. How long could Britain hold out, if she continued (as in April) to lose ten merchantmen a day?

There is a widespread belief that salvation was found in the convoy system; and that this was evolved by amateurs and imposed from without upon a recalcitrant Admiralty. The first premiss is true; the second is unjust to Jellicoe: for he brought from the Grand Fleet the officers who, under his direction, organized the convoy system. 'The establishment and development of the convoy system', wrote Tirpitz, '(a tremendous achievement on the part of the English) involved years of work.' He was wrong in his time estimate; and yet nearer the truth than those who have claimed for this statesman or that the whole credit for an idea easy to suggest but which only the British Admiralty could implement. It is true that, in the hour of Jellicoe's arrival, the naval staff was opposed to the extension of the convoy system beyond the escort of troopships and other precious freights (which had been convoyed since the outbreak of hostilities): but such opposition (whatever the cause) serves only to emphasize the impossibility of expanding the system in December 1916. In the black days of April 1917 two compensatory factors adjusted the balance. The new Ministry of Shipping (inaugurated in December 1916) began to function, and brought unity of control and direction to the mercantile marine; unrestricted U-boat atrocities brought the United States of America into the war, and so permitted the release, for escort duties, of the tenth cruiser squadron (until then employed in preventing American goods from reaching Germany); the admission into American harbours of armed British merchantmen; and a substantial reinforcement of American escort vessels which were essential for the success of the convoy system. Within a matter of months (to quote Admiral Sims, U.S.N.) 'the whole gigantic enterprise flowed with a precision and regularity which it is hardly likely that any other transportation system has ever achieved'; and the credit, however able the contribution of colleagues and allies, belongs in chief to Jellicoe, whose lifelong sea-experience, administrative gifts, and grasp of technical minutiae were never employed to better advantage.

The tributes paid by the sailors Sims and Tirpitz may be contrasted with the views of the landsman who, in the month after Jellicoe's appointment as first sea lord, became prime minister, and whose impatient temper and utter ignorance of sea-conditions combined to make him chafe at any delay. The peril was indeed extreme; and Jellicoe was doing no more than his duty in demonstrating that there was no infallible panacea for U-boat troubles, and in recommending resort to rationing. But Lloyd George came to believe that the negligence of the Admiralty was proved and that Jellicoe was the embodiment of the maladministration which he denounced [*War Memoirs*, vol. iii, c. xl, 1934]. In July 1917 he translated to a higher political plane the then first lord of the Admiralty, Sir Edward Carson [q.v.], and put in his place Sir Eric Geddes [q.v.], the railway king, to teach the Admiralty their business. When, being totally ignorant of naval traditions, customs, and sentiments, Geddes trampled such trifles underfoot, it was Jellicoe's unpleasant task to remind him that the sea lords were his colleagues, not his subordinates; and on Christmas Eve 1917 he found in his office a curt note from Geddes dismissing him from government employ. He carried into the silence of exile the consoling thought that the submarine menace had been mastered and that he had provided the Grand Fleet with the armour-piercing shells which at Jutland would have made

the German losses five or six times as heavy. In January 1918 he was raised to the peerage as Viscount Jellicoe, of Scapa. In 1919 he received the thanks of both Houses of Parliament and a grant of £50,000, and was promoted admiral of the fleet.

At the Imperial Conference in March 1917 the Admiralty had been invited by the Dominions to consider the most effective manner in which they could share in the naval defence of the Empire; and when the war ended, this invitation was renewed with a clear hint to utilize Jellicoe's unquestioned status as one of the greatest living sailors. The Admiralty approved; and in February 1919 Jellicoe left Portsmouth for a cruise which included visits to India, Australia, New Zealand, and Canada. The tour lasted a year and involved an immense amount of work of an invaluable but unspectacular kind. The magnitude and secrecy of the recommendations preclude adequate appraisal; but among solid results must be counted the formation of the great naval base at Singapore, and the establishment of the royal Indian navy and of the New Zealand naval division. It was no fault of Jellicoe's if effect was not given to his earnest plea for a strong Pacific Fleet with accumulations of fuel to ensure its mobility. From the personal standpoint the most satisfying aspect of the cruise was the heart-stirring enthusiasm everywhere shown for Jellicoe himself. Such world-wide appreciation and spontaneous tributes of applause could hardly fail to make amends for the censure, contumely, and political persecution from which he had suffered at home.

After six months' leave, Jellicoe, with his household, sailed in August 1920 for New Zealand to take up his duties as governor-general. He held the appointment for four years; and during that time raised the office to a pinnacle of esteem previously unapproached. Unfailing ally of every charitable and philanthropic impulse, wise guide to the most sagacious of his own counsellors, idol of every child in the Dominion, he established between himself and those whom he governed strong ties of personal affection, and left behind him unfading memories of nation-wide gratitude. Importuned to stay and reluctant to leave, he re-embarked in November 1924, retiring from the service in December. In June 1925 he was advanced to the rank of Earl Jellicoe.

During the last eleven years of his life

Jellicoe patiently shouldered many voluntary tasks. Not only was he chairman of the National Rifle Association and grand president of the British Empire Service League; but he interested himself keenly in the Boy Scout movement and in 1925 became county commissioner for London. On the death of Lord Haig in 1928 the British Legion invited him to fill the vacant presidency. Thinking a soldier to be a more suitable choice, he asked permission to decline. The nomination was then referred to thirteen area conferences, all of which unanimously elected him, and he held office until 1932. In all these causes he laboured strenuously, never sparing himself or allowing himself the rest and recreation which his health demanded and his age condoned. On 9 November 1935 he caught a chill while planting poppies; and two days later attended the Armistice Day service at the Cenotaph. The infection spread to one lung; and on 20 November, fifteen days before his seventy-sixth birthday, he died at his home in Kensington. On 25 November the funeral procession passed through crowded streets to St. Paul's Cathedral, where his body was fittingly laid to rest beside those of Nelson and Collingwood.

Unaided by wealth or social prestige, Jellicoe rose to the head of his profession by sheer merit and force of character. He might have suffered from pride and over-confidence. But the key to his character was selflessness. A man of deep religious convictions, he never allowed personal considerations to affect his judgement; never spoke of himself; and instead of courting publicity, shunned it. When pilloried by the press and censured by politicians, he answered not a word and allowed no recriminations. In congenial company his shrewd, twinkling eyes radiated friendliness and sympathy; and his countless little acts of kindness to the needy, diffident, and distressed made all who served with him worship 'J. R. J.' with a touching doglike devotion, deepened by their unquestioning trust in his faultless leadership. Those who passed with him through the flame of battle testify to his imperturbable calm, and the lightning speed of his decisions. When, however, he found that ill-informed writers were unjustly attacking the reputations of officers who had served under his command, then and then only would he write to the proper authorities to call attention to the injustice.

In addition to the honours already mentioned, Jellicoe was appointed K.C.B. in 1911, G.C.B. in 1915, and G.C.V.O. in 1916: in the last-named year for his services at Jutland he was appointed to the Order of Merit. He also received the freedom of the City of London and honorary degrees from the universities of Oxford, Cambridge, St. Andrews, and Glasgow. His numerous foreign decorations included the grand cross of the Legion of Honour.

Jellicoe had one son and five daughters, the second of whom died in childhood. He was succeeded as second earl by his son, George Patrick John Rushworth (born 1918), who was awarded the D.S.O. and the M.C. in the war of 1939–1945.

A half-length portrait of Jellicoe, by R. G. Eves, is in the possession of H.M.S. *Excellent* and the United Services Club, and a quarter-length, by the same artist (1935), is in the National Portrait Gallery. A portrait of him is included in Sir A. S. Cope's picture 'Some Sea Officers of the Great War', painted in 1921, in the National Portrait Gallery. A cartoon of him by 'Spy' appeared in *Vanity Fair* 26 December 1906.

[Sir Reginald Bacon, *The Life of John Rushworth Earl Jellicoe*, 1936; Lord Jellicoe, *The Grand Fleet 1914–1916*, 1919, *The Crisis of the Naval War*, 1920, and *The Submarine Peril*, 1934; Sir Julian Corbett, (Official) *History of the Great War. Naval Operations*, vol. iii, 1923; C. E. Fayle, *Seaborne Trade*, vol. iii, 1924; Lord Chatfield, *The Navy and Defence*, 1942.]   GEOFFREY CALLENDER.

JENKIN, CHARLES FREWEN (1865–1940), first professor of engineering science in the university of Oxford, was born at Claygate, Surrey, 24 September 1865, the second son of Henry Charles Fleeming Jenkin [q.v.], by his wife, Anne, only child of Alfred Austin, permanent secretary to the Office of Works, and niece of John Austin the jurist [q.v.]. He was educated at Edinburgh Academy and at the university, where from 1868 his father was professor of engineering; he then went to Trinity College, Cambridge, where he was a senior optime in the mathematical tripos of 1886. On leaving Cambridge he entered the engineering workshops of Messrs. Mather & Platt at Manchester, whence he moved to the London and North Western Railway works at Crewe. In 1891 he became engineer to the Royal Gunpowder Factory at Waltham Abbey, where he designed machinery for a new factory of cordite. Later he pursued practical work in other fields: at Newport,

Monmouthshire (1893–1898), Blackheath (1898–1903), Stafford (1903–1905), and London (1905–1908). But enthusiasm for its technical side was blended with dislike of its more commercial aspects. His heart was always set upon research, and in London he found time for work—on calcareous sponges—which is recorded in two papers dated 1908. Although undertaken as a hobby, this work seems to have decided his election to the new chair at Oxford in that year, when he became a fellow of New College, migrating to Brasenose in 1912.

At Oxford for some years Jenkin had to strive against the handicaps of insufficient staff, space, and equipment: not until 1914 was his scattered department installed within one building, and by that time the war had brought him work of quite another kind. He had always had a passion for the sea, and it was natural that in 1914 he should join the navy as a lieutenant, Royal Naval Volunteer Reserve. More unexpectedly, on the amalgamation early in 1918 of the Royal Flying Corps and the Royal Naval Air Service, he became head of a group responsible for the preparation of specifications in regard to every kind of aircraft material, with the rank of lieutenant-colonel, Royal Air Force. That work, for which he was appointed C.B.E. in 1919, entailed much experimental study (never before had 'factors of safety' been cut so low) and brought him into association with the best-known British workers in this field. Its results are recorded in his *Report on Materials of Construction used in Aircraft and Aircraft Engines* published by the Stationery Office in 1920; its effect on his own outlook is shown by his presidential address to the British Association (Section G) in that year, and by his own research in post-war years. Jenkin's main concern was with the effects of cracks and notches on the strength of machine parts, and the influence of fatigue. With Mr. Alfred Maurice Binnie, G. D. Lehmann, and W. N. Thomas, he notably promoted understanding of 'corrosion fatigue', testing metals at rates of alternation far higher than had been usual (20,000 alternations per second in 1928, by a novel method in which the specimen itself was made the 'reed' of an acoustic resonator). Largely by reason of this work he was elected F.R.S. in 1931.

On retirement from his chair in 1929 Jenkin settled at St. Albans and joined the staff of the Building Research Station at Garston, near Watford, where he investigated the properties of granular materials and clay.

Jenkin married in 1889 Mary Oswald, youngest daughter of Donald Mackenzie (Hon. Lord Mackenzie), and had two sons and a daughter. Both sons predeceased him, the younger on active service in the navy in 1916. He died at St. Albans 23 August 1940.

[*The Times*, 26 August 1940; *Obituary Notices of Fellows of the Royal Society*, No. 10, December 1941 (portrait); R. L. Stevenson, Memoir of Fleeming Jenkin prefixed to his *Papers*, 1887; personal knowledge.]

R. V. SOUTHWELL.

JENKS, EDWARD (1861–1939), writer on law and history, was born at Stockwell in South London 20 February 1861, the eldest of the four sons of Robert Jenks, who traded in the City of London, by his second wife, Isobel Frances, daughter of Edward Jones, furniture manufacturer, of Nottingham. He was educated at Dulwich College (1874–1877), leaving in his seventeenth year in order to be articled to a solicitor. In 1883, the year after he had qualified, the death of his mother put money at his disposal, which made it possible for him to enter King's College, Cambridge, as a pensioner, in the Michaelmas Term. He read law, was awarded an exhibition in 1884, and was placed first in the first class in the tripos of 1886; in the same year he won the chancellor's medal for the encouragement of the study of English law. His college rewarded these successes with a scholarship. Next year (1887) he was bracketed second in the first class in the historical tripos. Concurrently, he was reading for the bar, to which he was called by the Middle Temple in 1887; he won a studentship in jurisprudence and Roman law (1886) and the Barstow scholarship of the four Inns of Court (1887). At Cambridge, he was awarded the Le Bas (1887) and the Thirlwall (1889) prizes for essays on *Thomas Carlyle and John Stuart Mill* and *The Constitutional Experiments of the Commonwealth. A Study of the Years 1649–1660*, published respectively in 1888 and 1890. He was director of studies in law and history at Jesus College and lecturer at Pembroke College in 1888–1889, and in the latter year was elected into a fellowship, which he held until 1895, at King's.

In 1889 Jenks left England on his appointment as professor and dean of the faculty of law in the university of Melbourne. In 1890, soon after his arrival, he married Annie Ingham, of Leeds, who had followed him from England. She died next year after having given birth to a son. Jenks, by nature combative, was soon engaged in public controversy with (Sir) John Madden, the vice-chancellor, over questions of university administration. [See Ernest Scott, *A History of the University of Melbourne*, 1936.] But this incident did not distract him from collecting material for *The Government of Victoria (Australia)*, published in 1891, a pioneer work of great merit, not yet superseded, nor from writing an essay, which won him the Yorke prize at Cambridge in 1891, on *The History of the Doctrine of Consideration in English Law*, published in 1892.

In November 1891 Jenks resigned his chair at Melbourne and, returning to England, was appointed next year to a professorship in the recently instituted faculty of law at University College, Liverpool, which three years later (1895) became the Queen Victoria chair of law in the Victoria University of Manchester, of which University College, Liverpool, was a constituent body. During his four years at Liverpool Jenks championed the cause of humanism in legal education in opposition to the view that a lawyer, in particular a solicitor, is perfectly equipped if he has learnt the technique of his trade. It often happens that the men who count for most in the profession belong to the latter school of thought. Jenks entered upon the fray with zest and considerable success. In his last report to the board of legal studies he wrote: 'To have taken even a modest part in founding an institution which has for its object, not merely the sharpening of technical faculties, but the production of wise and public-spirited men is, and must always be, a source of unmixed gratification.' This was written in 1895. Next year Jenks left Liverpool in order to take up the post of reader in English law in the university of Oxford with a tutorship and lecturership in law at Balliol College. In these capacities he made his mark as a competent and stimulating teacher. His *Law and Politics in the Middle Ages* was published in 1898 (2nd ed. 1913), his *Modern Land Law* in 1899, and in 1900 there appeared a small manual entitled *A History of Politics* which had a large sale and the distinction of translation into Japanese. Another work begun during this period was *A Digest of English Civil Law* arranged in the form of a code along the lines of the German civil code. It was the joint product of a team which included Jenks, as editor, and four other Oxford lawyers. It appeared in parts (1905–1917) and in a consolidated edition in 1921 (3rd ed. 1938).

In 1903 Jenks left Oxford for London on his appointment as principal and director of legal studies of the Law Society, a position which he held for twenty-one years. Here the problem was the same as at Liverpool, but on a nation-wide scale. Jenks fought the battle with indomitable courage and persistence. He gathered about him a staff of teachers of remarkable ability, many of whom were greatly distinguished in after life. He was an effective and sympathetic administrator. In 1924 he transferred his activities to the newly founded chair of English law in the university of London, attached to the London School of Economics and Political Science. In 1927 he became dean of the faculty of laws in the university. He had taken the degree of LL.B. in 1909 with a first class, no mean performance for a man in his forty-ninth year.

When his five-year tenure as professor expired in 1929 Jenks made his home at Bishop's Tawton, near Barnstaple, where he continued to take an undiminished interest in public affairs, and, in particular, in the Workers' Educational Association and the League of Nations Union. He was in the habit of visiting Geneva when the Assembly of the League was in session.

An activity in which Jenks took a prominent part was the foundation in 1909 of the Society of Public Teachers of Law, familiarly known at the time as 'Jenks's trade union'. He was for some years virtual, not titular, editor of the *Independent Review*, in which his own contribution 'The Myth of Magna Carta' (November 1904) made a considerable stir.

Jenks received honorary degrees from the universities of Wales (1928), Paris (1929), and Bristol (1933). He was elected a fellow of the British Academy in 1930.

In 1898 Jenks married as his second wife Dorothy Mary, fourth daughter of Sir William Bower Forwood, of Liverpool, who with their son and daughter survived him. The son of his first marriage won the M.C. and was killed in action in 1917. Jenks dedicated to his memory his book on *The Government of the British Empire* (1918). He himself died at Bishop's Tawton 10 November 1939.

Jenks was indefatigably active both in

mind and in body, a man of wide interests, obstinate to a fault in maintaining a view once formed, whether in the world of ideas or of practice. Above all he was a teacher. He might have won a higher position in literature if his work had been more concentrated, but he wanted the critical judgement to make a great historian.

There is a portrait of Jenks by Frank Bennett in the Law Society's School of Law, but a more satisfactory likeness will be found in the photograph prefixed to the memoir in volume xxvi of the *Proceedings* of the British Academy.

[R. W. Lee, *Edward Jenks, 1861–1939* in *Proceedings* of the British Academy, vol. xxvi, 1940 (bibliography and portrait); private information; personal knowledge.]

R. W. LEE.

JERRAM, SIR (THOMAS HENRY) MARTYN (1858–1933), admiral, was born at Chobham, Surrey, 6 September 1858, the second son of Samuel John Jerram, vicar of Chobham, by his wife, Grace, daughter of Thomas Hunt, of Hermitage, co. Waterford. He was a grandson of Charles Jerram [q.v.]. He entered the navigating branch of the Royal Navy through the *Britannia* in 1871. After service as navigating cadet and midshipman in the Channel Fleet he was promoted navigating sub-lieutenant in 1877; two years later he transferred to the executive branch and joined the sailing sloop *Seaflower*, employed in the training of boys. He was promoted lieutenant in 1881 and after a year in the *Iron Duke*, flagship on the China station, he returned to the *Seaflower* as first lieutenant for another year. In 1884 he was given command, for the passage to Australia, of the torpedo-boat *Childers* (65 tons), just completed by (Sir) J. I. Thornycroft [q.v.] for the government of Victoria. Although the *Childers*'s complement was only twelve all told, and her coal capacity but ten tons, she made the long voyage with complete success; Jerram received the appreciation of the Admiralty and a special letter of thanks from the Victorian minister of defence.

Jerram then became first lieutenant of the sloop *Reindeer* on the North America station for three and a half years and later, in 1889, of the cruiser *Conquest* on the China station. That ship was transferred the next year to the East Indies station, and was in the squadron commanded by Vice-Admiral Sir E. R. Fremantle [q.v.] from which a naval brigade, in which

Jerram commanded a battalion, was landed for the punitive expedition against the Sultan of Vitu, in East Africa. The next year (1891), while in command of the *Pigeon*, he was landed for a time at Beira to act as British vice-consul, afterwards receiving from the Foreign Office 'high appreciation and thanks for his services'. Returning home in 1892, he became first lieutenant of the *Ruby*, in the training squadron, thereby resuming the close association with the training service which was to last for many years more. He was promoted commander in 1894, and was for two years executive officer of the masted training ship *Northampton*, employed on the training of youths; he was then given command of the masted sloop *Curaçao*, tender to the *Northampton*, which he held until promoted captain in 1899. Command of the training ship *Boscawen* at Portland followed for the next three years, combined with his appointment as assistant to the inspecting captain of boys' training ships.

In 1902 Jerram returned to the China station for eighteen months in the battleship *Albion*, as flag captain to the second-in-command, Rear-Admiral Harry Tremenheere Grenfell, and to the Channel Fleet in May 1904 in command of the battleship *Russell*. In December 1905 he came ashore to command the Royal Naval Engineering College at Keyham until his promotion to flag rank in 1908. After a year as chief of staff to Sir George Neville in the reserve divisions of the Home Fleet, he was appointed in 1910 second-in-command in the Mediterranean, with his flag in the *Duncan*, until 1912, in which year he was appointed C.B. In 1913 he became commander-in-chief on the China station, as acting vice-admiral with his flag in the armoured cruiser *Minotaur*; he was promoted vice-admiral in June 1913 and appointed K.C.B. in 1914. His chief preoccupation on the outbreak of war in 1914 was the powerful German squadron under Admiral Graf Spee, which had been based on Tsing-Tao but of which the whereabouts was at first unknown. It soon became clear, however, that the German ships had left their peace-time station in the China Seas, and various other activities there developed for the Allied navies, of which by that time Jerram had under his command Russian, French, and Japanese ships as well as his own. German radio stations in the Caroline Islands and elsewhere were destroyed by bombardment, measures were taken to cope with commerce raiding by the German cruiser *Emden*, and to protect troop convoys from Australia. The flagship *Minotaur* being needed for these duties, Jerram first shifted his flag to the armed merchant cruiser *Empress of Japan*, but later found it necessary to remain ashore at Singapore in order adequately to control his composite and scattered forces.

In 1915 Jerram returned home to command the second battle squadron of the Grand Fleet. Since his squadron formed the starboard wing of the fleet, it fell to him, in the *King George V*, to lead the battle line in the battle of Jutland; and although in his official dispatch Admiral Sir John (afterwards Earl) Jellicoe [q.v.] paid a tribute to Jerram's qualities as a squadron commander, he became the target for a certain amount of criticism, much of it ill informed, on the score of lack of initiative in that position. For his services in the battle he was appointed K.C.M.G. (1916); but when Vice-Admiral Sir David (afterwards Earl) Beatty [q.v.] who was his junior succeeded to the command of the Grand Fleet at the end of 1916, he left the fleet and was appointed to the Admiralty for special service. He was promoted admiral in April 1917 and retired at his own request a few months later. He was appointed G.C.M.G. in 1919.

In September 1918, when the inadequacy of the current pay scales for officers and men became an urgent matter, Jerram was appointed president of a committee thereon; the rates recommended by his committee, somewhat whittled away by official parsimony, became the basis of the new scales then introduced. A permanent Welfare Committee was set up in 1919 and Jerram was appointed president of it. He became president of the Naval Prize Tribunal in 1925. After his retirement he lived at Alverstoke, Hampshire, where he died 19 March 1933.

Jerram was twice commended for jumping overboard and saving life at sea, in 1881, when lieutenant of the *Seaflower*, for which he received the bronze medal of the Royal Humane Society, and in 1902, when captain of the *Albion*. For his war services he received Japanese, French, Russian, Italian, and Chinese decorations. While not, perhaps, an outstanding leader of men, he was one in whose sympathy, fairness, and understanding of their needs in the difficult matters of their pay and conditions of service the men of the navy

had full confidence. He married in 1892 Clara Isabel (died 1926), second daughter of Joseph Parsons, of Ennox, Somerset, and had two sons.

A portrait of Jerram, by Neville Lytton, is in the Imperial War Museum.

[*The Times*, 21 March 1933; private information; personal knowledge.]

H. G. THURSFIELD.

JOACHIM, HAROLD HENRY (1868–1938), philosopher, was born in London 28 May 1868, the second child and only son of Henry Joachim, a London wool-merchant, who as a boy had come to England from Kitsee in Hungary, by his wife, Ellen Margaret, daughter of the organist and composer Henry Thomas Smart [q.v.]. He was educated at Harrow and at Balliol College, Oxford, where he won the senior classical scholarship in 1886. He was awarded a first class in classical moderations (1888) and in *literae humaniores* (1890), and in the latter year was elected to a prize fellowship at Merton College. He lectured on moral philosophy at St. Andrews University from 1892 to 1894, when he returned to Balliol as lecturer in philosophy under J. A. Smith [q.v.]. In 1897 he succeeded William Wallace as fellow and tutor in philosophy at Merton. In 1919 he was appointed to the Wykeham professorship of logic in succession to J. Cook Wilson [q.v.], and held the chair until his retirement in 1935.

Joachim's main publications are *A Study of the Ethics of Spinoza* (1901); *The Nature of Truth* (1906); and translations of Aristotle's *De lineis insecabilibus* and *De generatione et corruptione* (published respectively in vol. vi, 1908, and vol. ii, 1922, of the Oxford translation of the *Works of Aristotle*); the translation of the *De generatione* was followed in the same year by a revised text with introduction and commentary. His almost completed commentary on Spinoza's *Tractatus de Intellectus Emendatione* was published posthumously in 1940, and it is hoped that the very detailed manuscript of his lectures on logic may also appear in print.

These works, none of them lengthy and all of them written in a close but luminous style, to which his undergraduate pupil Mr. T. S. Eliot has acknowledged a great debt, were the fruit of a deep and finely discriminating scholarship. Joachim once dismissed as 'heavy and perishable' the writings of a certain German professor, and few men had a better right to criticize with such a phrase. None of Joachim's contemporaries ranked higher than he either as a Spinozist or as a textual critic and interpreter of Aristotle.

But to study minutely and scrupulously the meaning of the great thinkers was always for Joachim a means to the solving of his own problems. A pupil of R. L. Nettleship [q.v.] and, at Merton, a colleague of F. H. Bradley [q.v.], he shared in general the idealist views which then dominated Oxford philosophy. *The Nature of Truth* presents the most compact single statement of the coherence theory of truth. Joachim there proceeds by examining doctrines of Aristotle, Descartes, Spinoza, and Bradley, but he confesses himself in the main inspired by Hegel. Bradley he regarded as still tinged with the empiricism of his opponents and too much affected by Lotze's reaction from Hegel. But although he conceived himself as working in Hegel's shadow, he was always loth to attempt exposition of Hegel's system, and he offers his conclusions with none of Hegel's untroubled confidence. Very certain of his own way of thinking, he pursued it without compromise; but he was most cautious in estimating the distance which he had travelled. Despite his lifelong deference to the views of J. A. Smith, who in his later years acknowledged Benedetto Croce as his master, Joachim did not fully share Smith's enthusiasm for the Italian idealists. He would praise them for going straight to the point, but he did not regard their contribution to philosophy as fundamental.

The part which Joachim played in the life and affairs of the university was restricted by his intense devotion to philosophy. His pupils at Merton found him an exacting but infinitely patient teacher. His acquaintance with undergraduates studying other subjects was small, but at Merton and subsequently as Wykeham professor at New College his acumen both as advocate and as critic made him a most influential member of the governing body.

In 1907 Joachim married his first cousin Elisabeth, daughter of Joseph Joachim, the violinist. A son and two daughters were born of this extremely happy marriage. His admiration for his uncle was a deep influence on his life. He was himself a considerable musician and a violinist of great talent (though, characteristically, he for long gave up playing because he could not find time to practise sufficiently), and he did much to help Oxford music. It came naturally to him to illustrate the notion of a coherent whole in terms of a musical composition, and all his philosophic activity, his writings, his phrasing and diction when he lectured or discussed, showed something akin to the exact and delicate technique of the classical violinist.

The keenness of Joachim's mind, the quiet candour of his conversation, and that sense of the greatness of his subject which he always succeeded in conveying, gained him the devotion and high respect of all his friends, but of none more than of those who asked, and always obtained, his help. The generosity with which he would read and criticize, unsparingly but constructively, work presented for his advice was never stinted even in the last years of his life, when he had become almost blind from cataract.

Joachim was elected a fellow of the British Academy in 1922 and an honorary fellow of Merton in 1919 and of New College in 1936; he received the honorary degree of LL.D. from St. Andrews University in 1923. He died at Croyde, Devon, 30 July 1938.

[*The Times*, 2 August 1938; H. W. B. Joseph, *Harold Henry Joachim, 1868–1938* in *Proceedings* of the British Academy, vol. xxiv, 1938 (bibliography); personal knowledge.]

G. R. G. MURE.

JOEL, SOLOMON BARNATO (1865–1931), financier and sportsman, was born in London 21 December 1865, the youngest of the three sons of Joel Joel, of London, by his wife, Kate, daughter of Isaac Isaacs, and sister of Barnett Isaacs, known as Barney Barnato [q.v.]. His brothers were Woolf and Jack Barnato Joel [q.v.].

The relationship which was destined most materially to affect the course of Joel's life was that of being nephew to Barney Barnato, the young Jew who, sprung from very humble origins in Whitechapel, made his way out to Kimberley in South Africa soon after the first discoveries of diamonds there in the early eighteen-seventies, amassed a great fortune, and, at one time the rival, afterwards the colleague, of Cecil Rhodes [q.v.] in the diamond-mining industry, joined with him in the formation of De Beers Consolidated Mines in 1888.

'Solly' Joel, as he was generally nicknamed, went out to South Africa in the early 'eighties to join his uncle and his brother Woolf Joel in business at Kimberley. Later on he became a partner in the firm of Barnato Brothers, first established in London in 1880 by Barney and his brother Harry Barnato. In 1896, the interests of his firm having spread from the diamond mines of Kimberley to the gold mines of the Witwatersrand, Joel was a member of the 'reform committee' in Johannesburg, and along with other members of that committee was arrested in 1896, after the Jameson raid, by President Kruger's government, and released on payment of a heavy fine. In the following year (1897) he accompanied Barney Barnato on his last voyage to South Africa in the *Scot*, in the course of which Barnato fell overboard and was drowned.

Another tragedy, in 1898, the shooting of Woolf Joel at Johannesburg by one von Veltheim, left only Solly, his surviving uncle Harry Barnato, who died in 1909, and his brother Jack Joel in the business of Barnato Brothers.

At this date (1898) Joel, now aged thirty-three, had given proof of possessing much of his uncle's business acuteness and enterprise. As early as 1890 he had become a director of the Johannesburg Consolidated Investment Company, in which the gold-mining interests of Barnato Brothers were centred. He now became chairman of that company in succession to his brother Woolf and of many successful gold-mining companies on the Witwatersrand under its general control. In 1900 he was elected to the board of De Beers Consolidated Mines.

Joel's business activities were multifarious and incessant. They extended to coal and copper mining, and to banking, in which he engaged as director of the Standard Bank of South Africa. But his chief interests were always in gold and diamond mining: in regard to the latter, he followed through the Diamond Syndicate the policy of Rhodes and Barnato of monopolizing the production and controlling the sale of what was almost purely a luxury commodity, paradoxically sought after for its costliness hardly less than for its intrinsic beauty. The industrial use of diamonds had not, in Joel's day, reached the commercial importance which it has since attained. But Joel, business man and millionaire as he was, loved diamonds not only for the wealth which they brought him, but as an amateur with a genuine admiration for fine stones; a taste which sometimes led him to a display of them which, while it might provoke smiles, proceeded from a real artistic instinct.

After the South African war of 1899–1902 Joel, although he continued to visit South Africa from time to time, lived mainly in England, at his London house in Great Stanhope Street and at his country seats, Maiden Erlegh, near Reading, and Moulton Paddocks, near Newmarket. Although the head office of De Beers was moved to Kimberley from London he could look after his business interests very well from the latter: and in England he found full scope for his restless activity and for his tastes for lavish hospitality, for the theatre, and for sport.

Of these the first was proverbial: he was a most generous host. The second, combined with his business instinct, led him to take an interest in the management of several theatres, in particular of Drury Lane. The third covered the fields of yachting, cricket, and racing. He was fond of visiting the Riviera in his yacht *Eileen*. Of cricket he was not a player but a patron; and the visit in 1924 to South Africa of an English team under the captaincy of the Hon. Lionel (afterwards third Lord) Tennyson was due to his liberality. But his ruling passion in sport was for horse-racing.

Joel's first big success on the turf was in the Ascot Gold Cup of 1906, when his horse Bachelor's Button beat the celebrated Pretty Polly. He also bought Polymelus, which won him many races and was a conspicuous success at the stud. After that he achieved many other successes: Pommern, a son of Polymelus, in 1915 won him the Two Thousand Guineas, the New Derby stakes (the first war Derby ever held), and the St. Leger. He won many important handicaps, the Royal Hunt Cup at Ascot, the Cambridgeshire twice, and the Doncaster Cup amongst others. In 1921 he headed the list of winning owners.

Joel was twice married: first, to Ellen Ridley (died August 1919) by whom he had three sons and two daughters; secondly, in November 1919 to Mrs. Phoebe Benjuta, *née* Carlo, by whom he had one daughter. He died at Moulton Paddocks 22 May 1931. He was a man of kindly disposition and a devout Jew, in whose appearance and manner there was something that might give colour to the mainly mythical conception, popular in his day, of the South African millionaire raised by his own untiring efforts from lowly beginnings to a lofty pinnacle of success and wealth.

Alike in business and on the turf the career of JACK BARNATO JOEL (1862–1940), was in many respects similar to that of his more conspicuous and widely known younger brother Solly. Born 29 September 1862, the second son of Joel Joel, he too went out to South Africa at a tender age, in 1874, and later became a partner in Barnato Brothers. He too became a director of the Johannesburg Consolidated Investment Company in 1898. In 1931, after Solly's death, he was elected to the chair of that company, which he retained until his own death. He also was a director of several of the gold-mining companies of the Witwatersrand, and was largely interested in diamonds and in the copper mines of Northern Rhodesia.

Like Solly, Jack Joel lived the latter part of his life in England. His house was on the Childwick Bury estate, St. Albans, which he bought in 1907: it had previously belonged to Sir J. B. Maple [q.v.]. Again, like Solly, he was a prominent figure on the turf and was an authority on British bloodstock. He won in all eleven classic races, including the Derby twice (1911 and 1921), with horses of his own breeding, among them the well-known Dean Swift. In 1908, 1913, and 1914 he headed the list of winning owners.

Joel married Olive Coulson (died 1937), daughter of Thomas Sopwith, and had one son. He died at Childwick Bury 13 November 1940.

A cartoon of Joel appeared in *Vanity Fair* 20 January 1910.

[*The Times*, 23 May 1931 and 14 November 1940.] Dougal O. Malcolm.

JOHNSON, WILLIAM ERNEST (1858–1931), logician, was born at Cambridge 23 June 1858, the fifth child and second son of William Henry Farthing Johnson, proprietor and headmaster of Llandaff House School, Cambridge, by his wife, Harriet, daughter of Augustine Gutteridge Brimley, of Cambridge, and half-sister of the essayist George Brimley [q.v.]. He was the brother of the writers George William Johnson and Reginald Brimley Johnson. Educated at his father's school, at the Perse School, Cambridge, and at the Liverpool Royal Institution School, he entered King's College, Cambridge, as a mathematical scholar in 1879, and was eleventh wrangler in the mathematical tripos of 1882. His interests had now settled on philosophical subjects, and he was placed in the first class in the moral sciences tripos of 1883. For some years he gained his living as a mathematical coach in Cambridge, until openings were found for him in the teaching for the moral sciences tripos and as a lecturer in psycho-

logy and in the theory of education to the Cambridge Women's Training College and for the University Teachers' Training Syndicate. He had no permanent position, however, until 1902, when he was appointed to the newly created Sidgwick lecturership in moral science in the university and was elected into a fellowship at King's College. He held these positions for the rest of his life, continuing to lecture until a few months before his death which took place at Northampton 14 January 1931. He had married in 1895 Barbara Keymer, daughter of Charles William Heaton, lecturer in chemistry at Charing Cross Hospital, London. After his wife's death in 1904 his sister Fanny made a home for him and his two sons.

Johnson suffered all his life from ill health: bronchial troubles, together with a natural shyness, kept him to his house or college rooms. But he was always accessible and sociable: his pupils, who numbered a large proportion of those reading moral science in the university, and those who attended his lectures, which were delivered conversationally and with frequent digressions, were aware of a lovable personality and were infected with his exacting subordination of originality to clarity and truth.

As well as lecturing on logic Johnson lectured on philosophical psychology and on mathematical economics (he published a substantial article on 'The Pure Theory of Utility Curves' in the *Economic Journal* for December 1913); but it was as a logician that he became known to the learned world when the insistence and assistance of his pupils induced him to develop his ideas in three volumes of a treatise on *Logic* (part i, 1921; part ii, 1922; part iii, 1924). A fourth volume, to treat of probability, was projected; but this was never completed, its first three chapters being published posthumously in *Mind* (January, July, and October 1932). The *Logic* brought him fame outside Cambridge: the universities of Manchester (1922) and Aberdeen (1926) conferred honorary degrees upon him, and in 1923 he was elected a fellow of the British Academy.

Johnson wrote his *Logic* at a time when the subject was developing out of the traditional formal logic, with John Stuart Mill's empirical treatment superimposed, into the wider study made possible by the work of the symbolic logicians from George Boole to Mr. Bertrand (afterwards Earl) Russell. Johnson was not in full sympathy with these developments, and devoted time and energy to criticism of Russell; but his definition and exposition of the subject-matter of logic as 'the analysis and criticism of thought' did much to break down previous restrictions upon its scope. Johnson began with the proposition as the unit of thought, and introduced the logic of terms as subsidiary to the logic of propositions, a significant reversal of the customary order. He attached great importance to the relation of the thinker to the proposition which is the object of thought, and showed that this 'epistemic' aspect could not be ignored in logic. He introduced an illuminating distinction between properties of different degrees of generality; and in his discussion of deduction he emphasized, at a time when the symbolic logicians had not realized its importance, the difference between the premisses of a deduction and the logical principles in accordance with which the conclusion is drawn. His treatment of probability, as the field of rational but not certain belief, was similar to that of John Maynard (afterwards Lord) Keynes, who in his *Treatise on Probability* (1921) acknowledged his debt to Johnson. Johnson's mathematicological ingenuity was shown in his attempts to improve on the rule of succession in the theory of probability, as well as in a paper 'Sur la théorie des équations logiques' published in the *Bibliothèque du Congrès International de Philosophie*, vol. iii (1901).

A portrait of Johnson by Delmar Harmood Banner is in the possession of his elder son, Mr. Charles Johnson.

[C. D. Broad, *William Ernest Johnson, 1858–1931* in *Proceedings of the British Academy*, vol. xvii, 1931; *Cambridge Review*, 30 January 1931; private information; personal knowledge.]   R. B. BRAITHWAITE.

JOHNSTON, SIR CHRISTOPHER NICHOLSON, LORD SANDS (1857–1934), Scottish judge, was the second son of James Johnston, of Sands, in the parish of Tulliallan, formerly in the county of Perth, now in the county of Fife, by his wife, Margaret, youngest daughter of Christopher Nicholson, minister of the parish of Whithorn, in the county of Wigtown. He was born in the mansion-house of Sands 18 October 1857.

After being educated at Madras College, St. Andrews, and the universities of St. Andrews, Edinburgh, and Heidelberg, Johnston was admitted in 1880 to the Faculty of Advocates. His progress at the Scottish bar was steady, and, after holding appointments as junior counsel to various government departments, he entered the Crown Office in 1892 as an advocate-depute, a post which he was obliged to vacate on the change of government which followed the general election of that year. He returned, however, in 1895 when the conservatives regained power, and remained there until 1899 when he was appointed sheriff of Caithness, Orkney, and Zetland. In 1900 he was transferred to the sheriffdom of Inverness, Elgin, and Nairn; and in 1905 to that of Perth. In 1902 he took silk.

Johnston was always a keen politician. In 1892 he unsuccessfully contested Paisley as a conservative, but at a by-election held in December 1916, having resigned his sheriffdom, he was returned to parliament as member for the universities of Edinburgh and St. Andrews. In 1917 he was knighted and succeeded Lord Dewar as a senator of the College of Justice in Scotland, taking the judicial title of Lord Sands.

As a silk, Sands had never been in large practice, and he came to the bench unwearied by over-work, but with a wealth of experience. Interested always in what went on about him, he had been brought into contact with the ordinary people of Scotland in his work as a sheriff and as a churchman in a way which was not possible for a busy counsel. The value of this training was seen in his work as a judge. He had a wide knowledge of law and much common sense. He grasped quickly the essential points in a case and had a mastery over facts. To appear before him was stimulating, for he had a fondness for testing discussion by hypothetical cases, often fantastic, but always helpful. His written judgements are admirable in form and sound in substance, full of quaint illustrations and touches of humour which light up the argument and remain in the memory. Underlying them all is an understanding of the Scot and a human sympathy which were characteristic.

Outside the courts Sands found his chief interest in the work of the Church of Scotland. In 1907 he was elected procurator of the Church, and remained its official legal adviser until 1918. He served on its principal committees, and he was a licensed lay-preacher for many years. But his reputation as a churchman rests chiefly on his part in the long negotiations which in 1929 brought about the union of the Church of Scotland and the United Free Church of Scotland. In 1903 he had edited, and largely rewritten, John Morison Duncan's *Parochial Ecclesiastical Law of Scotland*, and was a recognized authority on that subject. He was also a theologian of considerable attainments. His views were listened to with respect, and a memorandum which he drew up became the basis on which union was effected. For his services the university of Edinburgh conferred upon him in 1928 the honorary degree of D.D., an unusual distinction for a layman. He received the honorary degree of LL.D. from the universities of St. Andrews in 1909 and Glasgow in 1930.

Sands was also interested in social and educational work, especially in that which concerned youth. Amongst other activities he was from 1921 chairman of the Carnegie Trust for the Universities of Scotland and from 1919 president of the Edinburgh battalion of the Boys' Brigade.

Sands wrote much on all kinds of topics, legal, theological, biographical, and general. His style was easy and pleasant; and, apart from contributions to periodical literature and manuals on the various Acts dealing with small-holdings, he was the author of a considerable number of books, such as *Major Owen and other Tales* and *St. Paul and his Mission to the Roman Empire* (1909), and *Off the Chain* (1924).

Sands married in 1898 Agnes Warren, second daughter of James Ebenezer Dunn, of Dunmullin, Strathblane, in the county of Stirling, and had two sons and two daughters. He died in Edinburgh 26 February 1934. His portrait, by Henry Lintott (1930), is in the vestibule of the Church of Scotland Assembly Hall, Edinburgh.

[*Scotsman* and *The Times*, 27 February 1934; personal knowledge.]

M. G. FISHER.

JOHNSTON, SIR REGINALD FLEMING (1874–1938), scholar, traveller, and administrator, was born in Edinburgh 31 October 1874, the son of Robert Fleming Johnston, W.S., by his wife, Isabella Anna Catherine Irving. Reginald Johnston was educated privately, at Edinburgh University, where he won the Gray prize, and at Magdalen College, Oxford, where he obtained a second class in modern history in 1898.

Johnston began his lifelong connexion with China when, having entered the Hong-Kong civil service, he arrived in the colony at the end of 1898. From 1899 to 1904 he was acting clerk of the councils and assistant colonial secretary in the colony, and from 1900 to 1902 he was also private secretary to the governor. Towards the end of 1902 he began, during one of his periods of leave, the series of journeys into the interior of China which were to make him such a fascinating authority on the country and its people. He travelled on this occasion through Tongking, ascending the Red River to the high plateau of Yunnan, traversing this province from east to west, and descending by way of the Chinese Shan states into the French-protected states of Upper Laos, from which he reached Bangkok. In 1904, on a second trip, he started from Kiaochou, then in German hands, travelling to Tsinanfu in Shantung, where he visited the tomb of Confucius and was entertained by the descendant in the seventy-sixth generation of the sage, and then proceeded to Korea. In 1906, on a third journey, he travelled alone with his bull terrier from Peking to Ichang, through the famous Yangtze gorges to the sacred Buddhist mountain of Omeishan in Szechuan. From here, via Tachienlu, he travelled through the borders of eastern Tibet, descending through southern Yunnan to cross the Mekong valley into Burma. From this journey emerged his delightful book *From Peking to Mandalay* (1908) which contains some valuable ethnological comments on these border regions.

In 1904 Johnston was seconded to Wei-hai-wei as assistant to the commissioner, (Sir) James Haldane Stewart Lockhart, to whom he dedicated his second book on China, *Lion and Dragon in Northern China* (1910). In this work, which is packed with information presented in a scholarly and readable form, he deals with the history and legends of Wei-hai-wei, its native chronicles, its village life and folklore. In Shantung, in which the province of Wei-hai-wei lies, he was near to the heart of ancient China, and in particular to the birthplace of Confucius, for whom he conceived an especial veneration. This is the secret to an understanding of Johnston's character, for, as time went on, he became to all intents and purposes a Confucianist. He could write sympathetically of Buddhism and Taoism, although he felt that either of these could be extinguished without loss, but Confucianism or rather the principles and doctrines which Confucius connotes, he felt could not be annihilated without irreparable harm to the soul and body politic of China. To this theme Johnston returns in book after book, and because of this and his subsequent relations with the last occupant of the Dragon throne he became *persona non grata* to the new China of the Kuomintang, which regarded him as an imperialist reactionary and as a *laudator temporis acti*. He was in fact something very much greater than either of these.

Throughout his life Johnston was highly critical of Christian missionary activities in China, and in two books, *A Chinese Appeal to Christendom concerning Christian Missions* (published in 1911 under his Chinese name Lin Shao Yang) and *Letters to a Missionary* (1918), he showed how painstaking and wide was his theological reading and how trenchant a critic he could be. Not unnaturally these volumes aroused considerable antagonism, and it was his belief that they cost him, at a later stage in his career, the governorship of Hong-Kong, and, what was much nearer to his heart, the vice-chancellorship of Hong-Kong University.

In 1913 Johnston, who from 1906 to 1917 was district officer and magistrate at Wei-hai-wei, published his *Buddhist China*. In this deep and sympathetic study he traces the early history of Buddhism in China, describes Buddhist pilgrimages to the sacred hills of Buddhism, and ends with some delightful chapters on the monks and monasteries of Chiu Hua Shan and Puto Shan, which he had visited in person.

In November 1918 Johnston, after administering for a year the territory of Wei-hai-wei in the absence of the commissioner, was offered and was permitted to accept the post of European tutor to the last of the Ch'ing Emperors, Hsüan T'ung, whose personal name was P'ui Yi, then still a boy in his 'teens. For the greater part of the next six years he actually lived within the walls of the Forbidden City, and for the rest of his life served with unswerving loyalty the interests of his imperial pupil. In the most absorbing of all his works, *Twilight in the Forbidden City* (1934), dedicated to the Emperor, he describes these years. His position as a member of the imperial household soon brought him into conflict with the Nei Wu Fu (the imperial household department), which he realized exploited its privileges at the expense of its imperial master, and vain intrigues were made to bring about his resignation.

Throughout this period he had the complete confidence of the Emperor who, in 1924, made him comptroller of the imperial household and head of the Nei Wu Fu itself. His book gives a most interesting description of the arrangement and life of the Forbidden City in its decline; of the imperial tutors and the Manchu aristocracy; and of the hopes and dreams of the monarchists after the Emperor's abdication and the establishment of the republic in February 1912.

Johnston was still at his post when, on 5 November 1924, the so-called Christian general Fêng Yü-hsiang seized the Forbidden City by a *coup d'état* and expelled the Emperor, who took refuge in the house of his father Prince Ch'un in the northern section of Peking, where he remained under close military surveillance, and in considerable personal danger. From this house on 29 November Johnston was able to contrive his flight to the legation quarter, where he took refuge in the Japanese Embassy. For this deed Johnston had to suffer a campaign of slander and abuse at the hands of the Chinese nationalist press.

In 1925 Johnston left the service of the Emperor to become (1926) secretary to the British China indemnity delegation, and in 1927 he returned to Wei-hai-wei as commissioner, remaining there until October 1930, when he returned to England after he had arranged the restoration of that territory to China. For this work he received the thanks of the secretaries of state for the Colonies and for foreign affairs, and, from the citizens of Wei-hai-wei itself, as a parting present, a white porcelain bowl, full of spring water, the highest compliment which could be paid by the Chinese to the integrity of an administrator. From the Emperor he had already received the button of the highest of the nine official grades and the Sable Court Robe. In 1931 he revisited China as chairman of the delegation of the Universities' China Committee.

The last phase of Johnston's career was his professorship of Chinese in the university of London, when he was head of the department of languages and cultures of the Far East at the School of Oriental Studies from 1931 to 1937. This work was not particularly congenial to him, but he did it faithfully, with flashes of enthusiasm, and his classes on T'ang poetry were attended by a small but devoted band of students.

In 1935 Johnston paid a visit to his old

pupil, then in Manchuria, and went on to study the Manchu archives at Mukden; unfortunately the results of his researches were never published, as by his wish all his unpublished papers were destroyed at his death. In the previous year (1934) he had published his *Confucianism and Modern China* (the Lewis Fry memorial lectures delivered at Bristol University in 1933–1934) in which he restated his early belief in the wisdom of the doctrine of Confucius.

Johnston, although a competent administrator, was by nature rather a scholar, theologian, and poet. In addition to the works already mentioned he published anonymously a volume of poems, *The Last Days of Theodoric the Ostrogoth and other Verses* (1904), and a slight but attractive book *The Chinese Drama* (Kelly and Walsh, 1921). He was by preference a recluse, and on every available occasion he used to retire to a small property, which he called the 'Cherry Glen', deep in the country to the north of Peking, where he built a shrine to the poet Shelley, to whom, as he was delighted to tell, the local country women came to pray for children. Here he could enjoy the scenery and introduce a few favoured friends to his wonderful collection of mountain chronicles. On his retirement he replaced this retreat by the purchase of a small island, Eilean Righ, in Loch Craignish, Argyll, where he built a house for his considerable oriental library, now at the School of Oriental Studies in London.

Despite his reserve, Johnston could be a gay, stimulating companion, and was most hospitable. Even those Chinese who did not agree with him politically could not but respect and admire his simplicity, his integrity, his wide sympathies, and his abiding loyalty to a lost cause. He died, unmarried, in Edinburgh 6 March 1938.

Johnston was appointed C.B.E. in 1918, C.M.G. in 1928, and K.C.M.G. in 1930. The university of Hong Kong conferred upon him the honorary degree of LL.D. in 1929. He was a member of numerous learned societies both British and foreign.

[*The Times*, 8 March 1938; Sir R. F. Johnston's writings; personal knowledge.]

R. SOAME JENYNS.

JOICEY, JAMES, first BARON JOICEY, of Chester-le-Street (1846–1936), colliery proprietor, was born in the hamlet of Kip Hill, near Tanfield Lea, co. Durham, 4 April 1846, the younger son of George Joicey, a mechanical engineer, a partner in the engineering firm of Joicey & company, Forth Banks engine works, Newcastle-upon-Tyne. George Joicey was one of four brothers who, in the year 1828, had embarked upon the adventure in coal-mining at Tanfield Moor which became the well-known coking coal firm of James Joicey & company. He had married Dorothy, daughter of Jacob Gowland, of Wrekenton, near Gateshead. George Joicey died when his son was nine years old, but his widow lived to a ripe old age. James Joicey, who was educated at Gainford School, West Darlington, entered the family business in 1863 at the age of seventeen and became a partner four years later, eventually rising to the position of chairman and managing director.

In 1885 Joicey was elected liberal member of parliament for the Chester-le-Street division of the county of Durham, and held the seat until he was raised to the peerage in 1906 as Baron Joicey, of Chester-le-Street. He had been created a baronet in 1893. In 1931 he joined the conservative party.

In 1896 Joicey purchased, from the Earl of Durham, the Lambton collieries, at a time when the coal industry was suffering from a deep depression, and made a remarkable success of the venture. In 1911 he added to the magnitude of his commercial interests by the acquisition, from the company of that name, of the Hetton collieries, also situated in the county of Durham; and in 1920 he purchased, from the Marquess of Londonderry, the Silksworth colliery in the same county. In 1924 the Lambton company purchased the shares of the Joicey company, and thereafter the firm became known as the Lambton, Hetton and Joicey Collieries Ltd., the largest coal mining concern in the great northern coalfield, with an output of upwards of six million tons of coal per annum.

Joicey did not confine his interests to the coal trade; he was for many years a director of the London and North-Eastern Railway Company and, until a few years before his death, was president of the Newcastle-upon-Tyne chamber of commerce. In business he was shrewd, sagacious, and far-sighted. He was of a handsome presence, an engaging personality, and had an optimistic outlook on life.

Lord Joicey acquired first the Longhirst estates near Morpeth, Northumberland, and later on, early in the century, purchased the Ford Castle estates in Northumberland, near the Border. He died at Ford Castle at the age of ninety 21 November 1936.

Lord Joicey was twice married: first, in 1879 to Elizabeth Amy (died 1881), only daughter of Joseph Robinson, J.P., of North Shields; secondly, in 1884 to Marguerite Smyles (died 1911), daughter of Colonel Thomas Drever, of the East India Company's service. By his first wife he had two sons, and by his second, two sons and a daughter, all three of whom predeceased their father, the elder son being killed in action in 1916. He was succeeded as second baron by his elder son by his first wife, James Arthur (1880–1940).

A portrait of Lord Joicey by Sir John Lavery, which was presented to him by the Newcastle-upon-Tyne and Gateshead chamber of commerce in recognition of his services as president, hangs in the Commercial Exchange, Quayside, Newcastle: another portrait, by Trevor Haddon, is in the possession of the family at Etal Manor, Berwick-on-Tweed. A cartoon of him by 'Spy' appeared in *Vanity Fair* 19 December 1906.

[*The Times*, 23 November 1936; private information; personal knowledge.]

R. A. S. REDMAYNE.

JOLY, JOHN (1857–1933), engineer, geologist, and physicist, was born at Holywood, King's County, 1 November 1857, the third and youngest son of John Plunket Joly, rector of Clonbulloge, co. Kildare, by his wife, Gräfin Julia Anna Maria Georgina, daughter of Graf Friedrich Wilhelm Ludwig August von Lusi. His father's family, of which Charles Jasper Joly [q.v.] was a member, was of French origin; through his mother he was a kinsman of Richard Lovell Edgeworth, the Abbé Edgeworth de Firmont, and Maria Edgeworth [qq.v.]. Except for a year spent in France, he was educated at Rathmines School, Dublin. In 1876 he entered Trinity College, Dublin, where he studied modern literature and engineering, and in 1883, on graduating with first class honours, he was appointed to a teaching post in the engineering school. In 1887 he was appointed to the chair of geology in the university of Dublin which he held until he died, unmarried, in Dublin 8 December 1933.

Joly had early shown his originality and inventive powers and had published papers on reading meteorological instruments at a distance, on the volcanic ash from Krakatoa, and on photometry, and from 1884 he maintained a constant flow of inventions and researches among which may be recorded a meldometer which determined the melting-points of minerals and other substances, a hydrostatic balance to determine the specific gravity of small quantities of dense or porous bodies, and a condensation method of calorimetry, by which he succeeded in determining by direct measurement the specific heats of gases at constant volume, a problem of great theoretical importance in the study of the gaseous state and hitherto insoluble; his simple electric furnace which reduced aluminium from topaz anticipated Henri Moisson's method of producing that metal. He made some of the earliest determinations of the volume-change of rocks upon fusion, ingeniously replacing the containing vessels by the surface-tension of the molten substances.

In 1893 Joly joined with (Professor) Henry Horatio Dixon in investigating the ascent of sap in trees, and their cohesion theory, after much criticism and discussion, remains the only generally accepted explanation of the rise of water to the tops of high trees. On natural-colour photography Joly's work was of great interest. He originated in 1894 the idea of making the positive image select from a particoloured transparent screen the correct amounts of three primary colours and by this invention produced transparent pictures of great beauty and true representation, which were exhibited at the Royal Society in 1895. They were the earliest pictures of the kind ever exhibited and are the starting-point of all that has since been accomplished. In a sense they are superior to anything done later, for Joly's method can allow for the actual sensibility of the eye for the three primary colours. In 1897 he showed that the 'canals' of Mars may be rationally attributed to the gravitational effects of satellites moving near the planet's surface.

During his tenure of the chair of geology Joly published some 150 papers. Being a keen yachtsman he was led to write on such subjects as synchronous signalling, a method for observing the altitude of a star when the horizon is obscure, a collision predictor, a method of measuring distances at sea in thick weather, an explosive seasounder, floating breakwaters, the age of the earth estimated by the accumulation of sodium in the ocean, and the radioactivity of sea-water. During the war of

1914–1918 he submitted sixteen inventions to the Admiralty. Other subjects were: the apophorometer for studying the sublimation products of minerals, pleochroic haloes, their radio-active origin and what they tell of the age of rocks, and a quantum theory of vision. To radio-activity in geology he paid much attention, pointing out how the distribution of radio-active substances in the earth must modify our views on its age, and by devising a new and accurate method of estimating the quantity of thorium in rocks, he showed that that element plays a part in earth-history almost as important as that of radium.

The radio-active explanation of the occurrence and the action of thermal cycles in earth-history was the outcome of Joly's prolonged researches on the radio-activity of the constituents of the outer crust. In *The Surface History of the Earth* (1925, 2nd ed. 1930) he shows that the slow accumulation of radio-active heat in the deeper layers of the earth's crust must in time lead to their melting and thus by establishing new isostatic conditions allow the subsidence of the continental masses and the consequent transgression of the oceans, which now deposit their sediments on the submerged tracts. Meanwhile the molten layers, losing their accumulated heat by convection, actuated by lunar tides, slowly return to their solid state. Heat accumulation recommences, expansion follows, raising the continents and buckling the sedimentary deposits on their lower levels. The continued accumulation of heat in the radio-active layers leads inevitably to the repetition of the same events, and one millennial beat of the radio-thermal timekeeper will follow another through the lapsing aeons, until the radio-activity of the deeper layers of the crust ultimately expires. Thus the grand geological problems of sedimentary succession interrupted by revolutions and unconformities, together with many lesser puzzles, find their solution and unification in Joly's theory of thermal cycles.

Scientific work by no means occupied all Joly's energy. In college life he was chiefly responsible for the appointment of the Trinity College Science Schools Committee which, under his inspiration during thirteen years of arduous work, and with benefactions from E. C. Guinness, Earl of Iveagh [q.v.], and others, built and equipped the schools of physics and botany and endowed the Iveagh geological laboratory. In 1907 he was one of the foremost champions in defence of Trinity College against the Bryce scheme, and undoubtedly the ablest defence of Trinity College came from Joly's pen. He gave impressive evidence before the Fry commission in 1905–1906 and in 1920 he was a member of the Geikie commission, the report of which, recommending a subsidy to Trinity College, had been adopted by the imperial parliament when the establishment of the Irish Free State put an end to the project. In university life his sympathy both with colleagues and students gave him great influence, and in teaching he inspired enthusiasm and affection by his originality of treatment and picturesque diction. During the Irish rebellion of Easter 1916 he took an active part in the defence of Trinity College. An account of his experiences then was published in *Blackwood's Magazine* (July 1916).

In conjunction with D. J. Cunningham [q.v.] and William Spotswood Green, Joly developed a scheme of marine research in order to improve the Irish fisheries, and became a commissioner of Irish Lights in 1901. Working with Walter Clegg Stevenson he devised the deep-seated application of radio-active preparations in hollow needles, and discussed the use of other radio-active methods in therapeutics. He was the originator of the formation in 1914 of the Royal Dublin Society's Radium Institute. He was president of this society from 1929 to 1932, having been its honorary secretary from 1897 to 1909, receiving its Boyle medal in 1911. He was elected F.R.S. in 1892 and was awarded a Royal medal in 1910. In 1905 he was president of the Photographic Convention of the United Kingdom. From the London Geological Society he received the Murchison medal in 1918, and in 1908 he was president of Section C (geology) of the British Association. He was elected a fellow of Trinity College, Dublin, in 1918, and in the same year he was selected by the Foreign Office to represent Irish universities on the Balfour mission to the United States of America. In 1924 he delivered both the Hugo Müller lecture at the London Chemical Society and the Halley lecture at Oxford. The universities of Cambridge and Michigan and the National University of Ireland conferred upon him the honorary degree of Sc.D.

Joly was a man of intensely vivid and varied personality. His poetic nature expressed itself in his diction and in some sonnets, his interest in art in a beautiful collection of modern pictures; and his unselfish consideration and sympathy for others more than matched these qualities and his inventive genius.

A portrait of Joly by Leo Whelan is in the possession of Professor Henry Dixon and a copy of it hangs in the council Room of the Royal Dublin Society. Professor Dixon also possesses a small drawing in water-colours by Sir Richard Paget and another by Mrs. Dixon.

[*Obituary Notices of Fellows of the Royal Society*, No. 3, December 1934 (bibliography and portrait); Henry H. Dixon, *John Joly, Presidential Address to the Dublin University Experimental Science Association, 1940*, 1941 (portrait); *Nature*, 20 January 1934; *Quarterly Journal of the Geological Society*, vol. xc, 1934; J. Joly, *Reminiscences and Anticipations*, 1920; *British Medical Journal*, 1933, vol. ii, p. 1132; *Philosophical Magazine*, 7th series, vol. xvii, 1934; personal knowledge.]

HENRY H. DIXON.

JONES, ADRIAN (1845–1938), sculptor, was born at Ludlow, Shropshire, 9 February 1845, the fourth son of James Brookholding Jones, of that town, by his wife, Jane Marshall. After leaving Ludlow Grammar School his early love of horses led him to study at the Veterinary College, Camden Town, and at the age of twenty-one he passed the examinations of the Royal College of Veterinary Surgeons. During his schooldays his other chief interest had been in water-colour painting, in which art he received some instruction. However, at this stage he had no intention of making art his career. In 1867 he was gazetted to the Royal Horse Artillery and served subsequently in the 3rd Hussars, the Queen's Bays, and the 2nd Life Guards. He served in several campaigns, including the Abyssinian war (1868), the first Boer war (1881), and the Nile expedition (1884), retiring as captain in 1890. During this period he was first active as a painter, chiefly of horses, and latterly received instruction in sculpture from C. B. Birch [q.v.]. He first exhibited a work of sculpture at the Royal Academy in 1884, and continued to be an exhibitor until 1935: he also exhibited at the Grosvenor Gallery, the Royal Institute, and the Paris Salon. In 1891 he exhibited at the Academy a small group representing a quadriga. This was admired by the Prince of Wales who proposed that a large group, based upon this model, should be placed on the top of Decimus Burton's arch on Constitution Hill. The full-size group, known as the Peace Quadriga, which was not completed and in position

until 1912, may be said to have set the seal upon Jones's reputation as a monumental sculptor. Among other large-scale works of his in public places are the Royal Marines Monument, St. James's Park (1903), the Soldiers' National War Memorial, Adelaide (1904), the Carabineers' War Memorial, Chelsea Embankment (1905), and the Cavalry War Memorial, Stanhope Gate (1924).

Jones's career as a whole was successful if unspectacular. His lengthy experience of the veterinary service had equipped him with a perfect understanding of horses, which were always his chief models. Although an excessive realism tends to mar some of his work, he undoubtedly excelled in this sphere and enjoyed a considerable reputation.

Jones was appointed M.V.O. in 1907 and was awarded in 1935 the gold medal of the Royal Society of British Sculptors. In 1933 he published his reminiscences, *Memoirs of a Soldier Artist*. He was twice married: first, in 1870 to Emma (died 1884), daughter of Thomas Beckingham, attorney, of Ross-on-Wye; secondly, in 1891 to Emma, daughter of Robert Wedlake, master mariner, of Watchet. There was one son of the first marriage. Jones died in London at the age of ninety-two, 24 January 1938.

A bust of Jones, by Roland Bevan, is in the possession of the family.

[*The Times*, 25 January 1938; Adrian Jones, *Memoirs of a Soldier Artist*, 1933.]

JAMES LAVER.

JONES, Sir HENRY STUART- (1867–1939), classical scholar, Roman historian, and lexicographer, the only child of Henry William Jones, vicar of St. Andrew's church, Ramsbottom, Lancashire, by his wife, Margaret Lawrance Baker, was born 15 May 1867 at Hunslet, Leeds, where his father was then curate. Stuart was his second Christian name, but after his marriage, he and his wife generally prefixed it to their surname: when he was knighted in 1933 he legally assumed the name of Stuart-Jones. He was educated at Rossall School, under Dr. Herbert Armitage James, and won a scholarship to Balliol College, Oxford, in 1886. His career at the university was distinguished. Besides obtaining first classes in classical moderations (1888) and *literae humaniores* (1890), he won the Hertford scholarship (1886), the Ireland and Craven scholarships (1888), and the Gaisford prize for Greek prose with a Platonic dialogue

'Δάμων ἢ περὶ μουσικῆς' (1890). In the last-mentioned year, Stuart-Jones was elected by competitive examination to a non-official fellowship at Trinity College, Oxford, and, as Craven fellow and Derby scholar, spent three years (1890–1893) on classical studies in Italy and Greece. He then returned to Oxford and began tutorial work by taking pupils in classics at Trinity, and in ancient history, in succession to Henry Francis Pelham [q.v.], at Exeter College. In 1894, after his marriage in that year to Ileen, only child of the Rev. Edwyn Henry Vaughan, a well-known Harrow house-master and a brother of Charles John Vaughan [q.v.], he was transferred to an official fellowship at Trinity, and became one of the three tutors in 1896.

Stuart-Jones's reputation as a scholar grew rapidly, and he was known to be the author of many brilliant reviews, such as those of Robinson Ellis's *Noctes Manilianae* and (Sir) R. C. Jebb's *Ajax* of Sophocles, in the *Oxford Magazine*, of which he was for a time review-editor under Charles Cannan [q.v.]. His earliest publications were an elaborate reconstruction of the chest of Kypselos (*Journal of Hellenic Studies*, vol. xiv, 1894) and a text-book of *Select Passages from Ancient Writers illustrative of the History of Greek Sculpture* (1895). He also revised (1898–1900) the text of Thucydides for the *Scriptorum Classicorum Bibliotheca Oxoniensis*, projected by the Clarendon Press, which he thus inaugurated. The value of such work and of his teaching was widely recognized; and it was felt that, if a vacancy occurred in any of the chairs of Greek, Latin, or ancient history at Oxford, he would be a very strong candidate, and, for the Lincoln and Merton professorship of classical archaeology, a certain choice. But after a serious breakdown in health from overwork, Stuart-Jones accepted in 1903 the directorship of the recently founded British School at Rome, with the financial assistance of a research fellowship from Trinity College. There he consolidated his profound knowledge of Roman history and antiquities, subsequently displayed in his principal books and articles for the next twenty years. In May 1905 he resumed his tutorship at Trinity; but he left Oxford in December for a country home at Saundersfoot, near Tenby, revisiting Oxford to examine in *literae humaniores* in 1909, 1910, and 1911, and during the war in 1916 and 1917, and again in 1919. He was probably the last

man to examine in this school as well as in classical honour moderations (1900 and 1901).

Between 1906 and 1912 Stuart-Jones published his principal books on Roman history and dealt with allied subjects in the *Quarterly Review, The Times Literary Supplement*, and many learned periodicals. But he was not forgotten at Oxford, and in 1911 the Clarendon Press invited him, and Trinity College by electing him to a fellowship enabled him, to undertake the long-wanted revision of Liddell and Scott's *Greek–English Lexicon*, then in its eighth edition. In this great task, not only his wide knowledge of Greek, but his practical ability and tact, were conspicuous. Putting aside the earlier suggestions for a *Thesaurus Linguae Graecae*, which would have extended over several lifetimes, Stuart-Jones at once organized a remarkable body of specialists as voluntary collaborators. Although incorporating in it a great amount of new material, from inscriptions, papyri, and comparatively unexplored writers, he kept the new edition within reasonable bounds as to size, print, and dates of issue in parts, by an ingenious scheme for abbreviation of references, and by drastic omission of ecclesiastical and Byzantine words. In 1920 he was supplied with an extremely efficient assistant in the person of an ex-scholar of Trinity College, Roderick McKenzie, afterwards Fereday fellow of St. John's College, whose death in June 1937 was a very serious blow. By 1939 Stuart-Jones had seen the last part (X) of the *Lexicon* through the press, and had the necessary *Supplement of Addenda* well in hand, in spite of his failing health.

During the war of 1914–1918 both Stuart-Jones and McKenzie had offered their services to the Foreign Office and had undertaken confidential work in London and Geneva, in which their acquaintance with Eastern European languages was of great value. But with this exception, Stuart-Jones made steady progress with the *Lexicon*, in spite of the fact that from 1919 to 1934 he also occupied important academic posts. In 1919 he was elected unanimously to the Camden professorship of ancient history in succession to F. J. Haverfield [q.v.]. This chair, to which is annexed a fellowship at Brasenose College, is now by custom appropriated to Roman history. After this date, apart from his inaugural lecture on *Fresh Light on Roman Bureaucracy* (1920), Stuart-Jones published important articles but no complete book except the *Catalogue of the Sculptures in the Palazzo dei Conservatori at Rome* (which he edited in 1926). His professorial lectures were mainly on Roman provincial bureaucracy, on which fresh light was being thrown by Egyptian papyri. He found much to interest him during term time in the life of his new college; and for some years he served usefully on the Hebdomadal Council, gaining administrative experience, but at the cost of overwork, and, as he was constitutionally unable to take anything quietly, some over-excitement.

This, together with the fact that his home was still at Saundersfoot, probably induced Stuart-Jones in 1927 to become a candidate for the principalship of the University College of Wales at Aberystwyth, although he was a strong churchman, only half Welsh by birth, and in no way Welsh by education. His election was due as much to his impressive personality as to his eminence as a scholar. His seven years of administration were sound although not sensational. He dealt with the status and salaries of the non-professorial staff, with the extension of the library and other new college buildings, and with the establishment of courses on arts and crafts at the intermediate and subsidiary stages for the B.A. degree. An able letter from him in *The Times* may be said to have produced the benefaction from Sir Julian Cahn for the development of the agricultural and plant-breeding station on 300 acres of hill land. Stuart-Jones acted as vice-chancellor of the university of Wales for the two years 1929 and 1930; and he was knighted in 1933. In spite of illness in 1933, he had consented to retain office for another year, but he was obliged, by medical advice, to resign at very short notice in March 1934.

As a devoted supporter of the Church in the diocese of St. David's, Stuart-Jones continued to serve assiduously on the Representative Council of the Welsh Church; he also attended the meetings of learned societies and committees. On his seventieth birthday the Society for the Promotion of Roman Studies, of which he had been president from 1926 to 1929, presented him with a special volume (xxvii, 1937) containing a photographic portrait, a full bibliography of his publications, and appropriate papers contributed by English and foreign scholars. He was elected to honorary fellowships at Brasenose (1928), Trinity (1935), and Balliol (1936) colleges, and received honorary degrees from the universities of Oxford, Wales, Leeds, and Liverpool. He was elected a fellow of the British Academy in 1915 and a member of the German Imperial Archaeological Institute in 1904. After a long, but not incapacitating, illness, he died at Tenby 29 June 1939, and was buried with his wife, who had died in 1931, at Saundersfoot. They had one son.

As a classical scholar Stuart-Jones was polymathic, with a ready and retentive memory, and a special flair for ascertaining and estimating in a very short time all the important points in any new publication on his subjects. He was a competent linguist and a lucid expositor, and among general interests he was fond of music. The bibliography of his books, articles, and signed reviews occupies nearly eight pages of the *Festschrift* mentioned above, but, as the prefatory note states, 'no single volume of any periodical could adequately represent all his activities and interests', and it is difficult to say to which branch of classical study his contributions, other than the *Greek Lexicon*, have been most important and illuminating. His best-known works, besides those already mentioned, are: *The Roman Empire, B.C. 29 to A.D. 476* ('Story of the Nations' series, 1908); *Companion to Roman History* (1912), an elaborate compendium published by the Clarendon Press; and *The Sculptures of the Museo Capitolino* (which he edited in 1912). But special articles such as those on 'Art under the Roman Empire' (*Quarterly Review*, vol. cciv, 1906) and on 'Mithraism' (Hastings's *Encyclopaedia of Religion and Ethics*, vol. viii, 1915), together with his chapters in vol. vii of the *Cambridge Ancient History* (x, xiv, and xvi, the last two in collaboration with Professor Hugh Last, and v, vi of vol. x) and revisions in the *Encyclopædia Britannica* (eleventh edition) are of conspicuous merit; and his reviews seldom fail to contain original suggestions.

[*The Times*, 30 June 1939; J. L. M[yres], *Sir Henry Stuart Jones, 1867–1939* in *Proceedings* of the British Academy, vol. xxvi, 1940 (portraits); personal knowledge.]

H. E. D. BLAKISTON.

JONES, SIR ROBERT, first baronet (1857–1933), orthopaedic surgeon, was born at Rhyl 28 June 1857, the eldest child and elder son of Robert Jones, a London free-lance journalist, by his wife, Mary, daughter of Edward Hughes, of Rhuddlan, Flintshire. He was educated at Sydenham College, and in 1870, five years before the death of his father, to whom he was deeply attached, an uncle by marriage, Hugh Owen Thomas, an orthopaedic surgeon, offered Jones residence in his home if he should decide to read medicine. The invitation was accepted and in 1873 he left London to study at the Liverpool School of Medicine, from which he graduated in 1878. The new life was strange and exacting, for his uncle was a man of genius and great powers of endurance, and had it not been for his vigorous constitution, Jones might not have been able to combine the arduous work of a medical student with eager participation in his uncle's life and work, a 'part-time' apprenticeship which was of great value to him, for it instilled into him his uncle's passion for effective service with complete disregard of self. To the serenity, affection, and religion of his aunt, Mrs. Thomas, he probably owed more than he knew, for without her cultured and kindly presence his uncle's home might well have proved unbearably restless.

Jones was appointed honorary assistant surgeon to the Stanley Hospital, Liverpool, in 1881, becoming surgeon in 1886 and in 1888 consulting surgeon to the Manchester Ship Canal Company. He collected and taught his surgical teams, and this experience among injured seamen and dockers was a valuable preparation for his work during the war of 1914–1918. In 1889 he was elected honorary surgeon and dean of the clinical school at the Royal Southern Hospital, Liverpool.

In 1891 his uncle died, and Jones had to decide whether he should continue with orthopaedic work or take the easier path of general surgery. Loyalty to Thomas and all that he stood for, with a determination to vindicate his teaching and bring honour to his name, dispersed any doubts which Jones may have entertained.

At some time in 1900 Jones met (Dame) Agnes Gwendoline Hunt, a nurse, and almost at once they were working together with perfect understanding in a system of orthopaedic surgery, nursing, and after-care, novel in character and superb in quality. Thus came into being the first country orthopaedic hospital (at Baschurch, Shropshire) for crippled children of every kind, with wards where fresh air, courage, and happiness combined to cure body and mind as one unit. But before this could come to full flower the war of 1914–1918 broke out. Jones was appointed inspector of military orthopaedics in 1916, and his teaching and influence spread not only in the army, but in the hospitals of Great Britain. The Thomas splint, invented by Jones's uncle, reduced the mortality of gun-shot wounds in the femur from 80 per cent. to 20 per cent., and a great orthopaedic organization had been set up. It was one of his chief sorrows that soon after the war most of the units of the organization were dispersed, and that his efforts to save the Shepherd's Bush unit as a centre for teaching and research were unavailing.

It remained to build up a new orthopaedic scheme. The Baschurch germ was working, and in 1919 the Central Council for the Care of Cripples was set up, from which has grown a system of regional orthopaedic hospitals throughout England and Wales, each linked with general and cottage hospitals and serving closely every village in its region, the first of the regional specialist services.

Honours came to Jones from many quarters. He was knighted and appointed C.B. in 1917, and K.B.E. in 1919 for his services in the war, and created a baronet in 1926. Among other distinctions he received honorary degrees from the universities of Liverpool, Wales, Aberdeen, McGill, Harvard, Smith's College, and Yale, together with that rare honour, the D.S.M. of the United States of America. He was president of the British Orthopaedic Association (1920–1925); he was the first president of the International Society of Orthopaedic Surgery, and he was elected an honorary fellow of the Royal College of Surgeons in 1918.

Jones's great qualities grew freely and were used without reserve. He remained pleasantly immune to worldly wisdom and made friends equally with duke or docker. He understood and enjoyed almost every form of sport; he was a formidable boxer in early manhood and always delighted in a game of cricket. Yet it was only necessary to be with him in hospital to know that his heart was in his work above all else. He was a surgeon of superb skill, a clinician of wide experience and resource, and an admirable teacher. He founded a school of orthopaedics, and, what is more, by his gift of friendship he brought together orthopaedic surgeons with a strong sense of fellowship so that they became eager to learn and as ready to discuss their failures as their successes, for he gave them his sense of values.

Jones married in 1887 Susannah, daughter of William Evans, merchant, of Liverpool, and had a son and a daughter.

The death in 1918 of Lady Jones, who had been deeply anxious about her son who was serving in the trenches, was a heavy blow, and towards the end of his life he spent much time with his daughter at Bodynfoel Hall, Llanfechain, Montgomeryshire, where he died 14 January 1933. He was succeeded as second baronet by his son, Arthur Probyn (born 1892), who changed his name by deed-poll to Probyn-Jones in 1933.

[*The Times*, 16 January 1933; Frederick Watson, *The Life of Sir Robert Jones*, 1934 (portrait); *British Journal of Surgery*, April 1933; personal knowledge.]

GATHORNE R. GIRDLESTONE.

JOURDAIN, FRANCIS CHARLES ROBERT (1865–1940), ornithologist, was born at Adenshaw Lodge, near Manchester, 4 March 1865, the eldest of the five sons of Francis Jourdain, later vicar of Ashbourne, Derbyshire, by his wife, Emily Clay. He was educated at Ashbourne Grammar School and at Magdalen College, Oxford, graduated in 1887, and was ordained in 1890. He was vicar of Clifton-by-Ashbourne, Derbyshire, from 1894 to 1914, and rector of Appleton, Berkshire, from 1914 until his retirement in 1925, after which he devoted most of his time to ornithology.

Jourdain's primary preoccupation in ornithology was the collecting and study of eggs, but he was interested in almost every aspect of the breeding habits of birds and was an excellent general field ornithologist. He travelled widely in Europe and North Africa collecting eggs and studying breeding habits and distribution. The very extensive first-hand experience which he thus acquired was combined with an encyclopaedic knowledge of the literature of his subject, and he became generally recognized both at home and abroad as the leading authority on the breeding biology of the birds of the palaearctic region, especially its western portion. He was one of the first fully to recognize the importance to scientific ornithology of accumulating accurate factual data on all phases of the breeding of birds, for example on incubation and fledgling periods, the share of the sexes in parental duties and so on, and he devoted much of his time for many years to this task. As a result when *A Practical Handbook of British Birds* appeared (2 vols., 1919–1924), in the authorship of which he collaborated with Harry Forbes Witherby, Ernst Johann O. Hartert, and others, his concise and systematic treatment of these matters set up a new standard in the literature. It also provided an effective stimulus to further investigation and was largely responsible for the remarkable increase in precise information on breeding biology recorded in *The Handbook of British Birds* (5 vols., 1938–1941), the enlarged successor of the work just mentioned.

His work in *The Handbook*, the product of a lifetime of study, was Jourdain's greatest contribution to ornithology, but he was also the author of important faunistic papers on Corsica, Spitsbergen (he was leader of the Oxford University expedition to Spitsbergen in 1921), Cyprus, Spain, and North Africa, and many other ornithological publications. The list of those under his own name, although extensive, perhaps hardly brings out to the full the importance of his contribution to British ornithology or the extent of his influence upon it. Apart from *The Handbook*, he supplied material to or actually collaborated in some of the principal standard works on British ornithology of the present century and was constantly assisting other ornithologists from his unique fund of knowledge. His 'Study of Parasitism in the Cuckoos' (*Proceedings of the Zoological Society*, 1925) deserves notice as a valuable contribution to general evolutionary biology, and his active interest in and encouragement of local faunistic work on birds in the British Isles should also be mentioned. He was also for many years assistant editor to his friend Witherby of the journal *British Birds*.

Jourdain's caustic style in controversy was famous in ornithological circles, but, characteristic though it was, it tended to give a misleading impression of him. His ready sympathy and helpfulness towards the younger generation of ornithologists in particular reflected his real character much more accurately. This attractive trait found full play through his close association with Oxford during the period when he was rector of Appleton and afterwards, and contributed greatly to the development of ornithological studies there.

Jourdain married in 1896 Frances Emmeline (died 1933), daughter of William Richard Smith, of Clifton, Derbyshire, and had two sons, the younger of whom predeceased his father, and a daughter. He died at Bournemouth 27 February 1940.

[*Ibis*, fourteenth series, vol. iv, 1940 (bibliography and portrait); *Nature*, 8 June 1940; *British Birds*, April 1940; personal knowledge.]

B. W. TUCKER.

JOYNSON-HICKS, WILLIAM, first
Viscount Brentford (1865–1932),
statesman. [See Hicks.]

KEARLEY, HUDSON EWBANKE,
first Viscount Devonport (1856–1934),
man of business, was born at Uxbridge,
Middlesex, 1 September 1856, the youngest
son of George Ewbanke Kearley, of Uxbridge, by his wife, Mary Ann, only
daughter of Charles Hudson, of Old Ford,
Essex, and widow of Josiah John Barrow.
He left Surrey County School, Cranleigh,
at the age of fifteen, and after serving,
without salary, for eight months in a City
coffee sale-room, he joined the firm of
Messrs. Tetley & Sons Ltd., tea merchants,
of Mincing Lane. In 1876 he successfully
founded the firm of Heseltine and Kearley
and opened his first shop at Brentford in
1878. From 1880 onwards many branches
were opened in town and country under
the name of International Stores. G. A.
Tonge joined the firm soon afterwards and
on Heseltine's retirement it changed its
name in 1887 to Kearley and Tonge.

Kearley then turned to politics, and at
the general election of 1892 was returned
to parliament as liberal member for
Devonport, which he represented until
January 1910. He was appointed in 1905
parliamentary secretary to the president
of the Board of Trade, and his services
were recognized by the conferment of a
baronetcy in 1908. In the same year he
conducted through the House of Commons
the Port of London bill, and in 1909 gave
up his political career in order to become
the first chairman of the newly constituted
Port of London Authority, a position
which he held until his retirement in 1925.
Sworn of the Privy Council in 1909, he
was raised to the peerage as Baron Devonport, of Wittington, Buckinghamshire, in
1910. In November 1916 he was appointed
first food controller by Lloyd George, with
the object of fixing maximum prices for
the principal foods and of securing the
economic use of food. During his tenure
of office a voluntary scheme of rationing
was developed. His proposals for setting
up the machinery for compulsory rationing had been accepted by the War Cabinet,
subject to approval by his successor, when
he resigned from office on grounds of ill
health in May 1917 and was advanced to a
viscountcy. During this time he was also
chairman of the royal commission on sugar
supplies.

Ambitious, courageous, and enterprising, Devonport possessed a forceful personality, which inevitably involved him in
acrimonious controversy, particularly with
the representatives of dock labour. He
was a successful pioneer of the modern
chain-store system, the shares of Kearley
and Tonge and the International Stores
being disposed of in 1927 for £4,000,000.
The modern Port of London, embracing
the far-sighted development programmes
which he inaugurated, represents the most
notable public service rendered by him.
He was a keen sportsman and an ardent
gardener.

Devonport married in 1888 Selina,
youngest daughter of Edward Chester, of
Blisworth, Northamptonshire; they had
two sons and one daughter. He died at
his Scottish estate of Kinloch, Perthshire,
5 September 1934, and was buried at
Hambleden cemetery, near Marlow. He
was succeeded as second viscount by his
elder son, Gerald Chester (born 1890).

There is a portrait of Devonport by
P. A. de László in the possession of the
Port of London Authority.

[*The Times*, 6 September 1934; Lord
Devonport, *The Travelled Road—Some
Memories of a Busy Life* (privately printed),
1934; official documents of the Port of
London Authority; personal knowledge.]

J. D. Ritchie.

KEITH, Sir WILLIAM JOHN (1873–
1937), administrator in Burma, was born
at Portobello, Edinburgh, 13 April 1873,
the eldest of the four gifted sons in the
family of six children of Davidson Keith,
an advertising agent in Edinburgh, by his
wife, Margaret Stobie Drysdale. Educated
at Edinburgh Royal High School, Edinburgh University, and Christ Church,
Oxford, he entered the Indian civil service
in 1896, heading the list in the final
examination. Of his brothers, Arthur
Berriedale Keith headed the combined
home and Indian civil services list in 1901
but remained in England; the other two
both served in Burma, Steuart being a
sessions judge in the Indian civil service
and Alan a barrister; they successively
died when nearing promotion to the bench
of the Rangoon High Court.

William Keith spent his entire service
in Burma, and save for a few years in the
districts, mainly as settlement officer, he
was always at headquarters. But he was
much more than a secretariat officer: he
never forgot a face or ceased to visit the
villages. All the posts which he held were
in revenue or finance; he wielded the
power of the purse and, combining an

unrivalled capacity for work with a remarkable knowledge of the country, he began to dominate the other departments in 1912, while still junior to their chiefs. For two decades there was hardly a project upon which he did not leave his creative mark, or a state paper of which he was not largely the author. He might have had a more spectacular career had he been less indifferent to his own claims. He was loyalty itself to men placed in invidious positions. When the Montagu–Chelmsford reforms were applied to Burma in 1923, and the first native ministers were appointed, he was one of the few Europeans to give them his real intimacy.

From 1923 to 1928 Keith was leader of the House in the legislative council (the Burmese parliament), as well as finance member and vice-president of the executive council, acting as governor in 1925. Appointed C.I.E. in 1917, knight bachelor in 1925, and K.C.S.I. in 1928, he was the only man ever to receive the K.C.S.I. solely for service in Burma.

Keith retired in 1928 to St. Margaret's, Dunbar, the home of his youth, where he died 22 January 1937, having served as a member of the burgh council (1929–1932) and as bailie and magistrate (1931). He married in 1915 Isabel, only daughter of Sir Harvey Adamson, lieutenant-governor of Burma, and had one son and two daughters.

[*The Times*, 25 January 1937; private information.]   G. E. HARVEY.

KELLY, SIR JOHN DONALD (1871–1936), admiral of the fleet, was born at Southsea 13 July 1871, the second son of Lieutenant-Colonel Henry Holdsworth Kelly, Royal Marine Artillery, by his wife, Elizabeth, daughter of John Collum, of Bellevue, co. Fermanagh. Entering the Royal Navy in 1884, he became a midshipman in 1886 and sub-lieutenant in 1891. Promoted lieutenant in 1893, he served for six years continuously on the Australia station, for the last three years in the flagship *Royal Arthur*; after qualifying as a gunnery officer he served in the cruiser *Forte*, on the Cape station, whence he was promoted commander in 1904. He served in that rank on the China station and at home; he was promoted captain in 1911 and was for eighteen months (1913–1914) superintendent of physical training before returning to sea service in command of the light cruiser *Dublin* in the Mediterranean, a month before the outbreak of war in 1914. There he greatly distinguished himself when the *Dublin*, together with her sister ship, the *Gloucester*, commanded by his younger brother, Captain (Sir) William Archibald Howard Kelly, were the only ships to keep touch with the German battle-cruiser *Goeben* when she eluded the British battle-cruiser squadron. He subsequently commanded the cruisers *Devonshire* and *Weymouth* in home waters and, from 1917 until the end of the war, the battle-cruiser *Princess Royal*.

In 1919 Kelly was appointed director of the Operations Division of the Naval Staff at the Admiralty, being promoted rear-admiral in 1921; from 1922 to 1923 he was rear-admiral in the Home Fleet, a detachment of which under his command spent many months in the Dardanelles and Bosphorus during the disturbances in Turkey. In 1924 he joined the Board of Admiralty as fourth sea lord; he was promoted vice-admiral in 1926, returning to sea service in 1927 in command of the first battle squadron and as second-in-command of the Mediterranean Fleet for two years, after which he had two years' further employment on shore as admiral commanding reserves; he was promoted admiral in 1930. On relinquishing that command, seeing no further prospect of employment, he sent the Admiralty a request to retire forthwith in order to facilitate the promotion of younger officers; but before this took effect, the political crisis of 1931 occurred, of which the repercussion in the navy was the mutiny in the Home Fleet at Invergordon in September, and Kelly was chosen as the man to take over the command-in-chief with the task of restoring discipline in the fleet. That task he performed with conspicuous understanding, firmness, and success, in recognition of which he was appointed G.C.V.O. in 1932.

After two years in the Home Fleet command Kelly was appointed first and principal naval aide-de-camp to the king (1934–1936), and commander-in-chief at Portsmouth. That command he held for two and a half years until July 1936, when, having reached the age of sixty-five, he was due for compulsory retirement; but the day before he was relieved, he was specially promoted to admiral of the fleet, and he flew his union flag in that rank for one day before hauling it down and retiring to his home at Greenham Hall, Taunton. Four months later he died in London 4 November 1936, and was buried at sea with full naval honours.

Kelly married in 1915 Mary (died 1937),

daughter of Thomas Hussey Kelly, of Glenyarrah, Sydney, New South Wales; they had one daughter. He was appointed C.B. in 1919, K.C.B. in 1929, and G.C.B. in 1935. He was a man of fine physique, a prime seaman, a man of strong common sense and sympathy, of great courage, determination, and strength of character. He earned, and was accorded, the respect and gratitude of all ranks in the navy, officers and men alike, for his rapid restoration of the discipline and morale of the Home Fleet in 1931.

[*The Times*, 5 November 1936; Admiralty records; private information; personal knowledge.]   H. G. THURSFIELD.

KENDAL, DAME MARGARET SHAFTO (1848–1935), better known as MADGE KENDAL, actress, was born at Grimsby, Lincolnshire, 15 March 1848. She belonged to a family, originally domiciled in Scotland, which had been connected with the stage for two hundred years. Her great-great-grandfather, James Shafto Robertson, was a theatre-manager at Peterborough, his company touring a circuit of towns in the vicinity of that city; her father, William Robertson, although he had been intended for a solicitor, managed this theatre after his father's death and, in addition, acted in a great many parts; her eldest brother, Thomas William Robertson [q.v.], originally an actor, became a celebrated dramatist, the founder of a new, naturalistic style of play, sometimes, derisively, described as 'the teacup and saucer drama', or 'bread and butter school', which included *Caste* (1867); and she herself, in addition to two of her brothers and four of her sisters, went on the stage. Her husband was an actor, and two of her daughters became actresses. Her father married a young actress, Margharetta Elisabetta Marinus, the daughter of a Dutchman who taught languages in London. It was while she was with her husband's company on the Lincoln circuit that Madge, her twenty-second and last child, was born.

The failure of the Lincoln circuit sent the Robertsons to London, where William Robertson became the partner of J. W. Wallack [q.v.] in leasing the Marylebone Theatre, and it was in this theatre, on 20 February 1854, that Madge, then not quite six years of age, made her first appearance as an actress. Her part was Marie in *The Struggle for Gold*. By the time she was fifteen she was a seasoned actress, and had performed in London,

Bristol, and Bath. It was while she was appearing at the reopening of the Theatre Royal, Bath, in March 1863 that Ellen Terry [q.v.], then aged sixteen, and she appeared together for the first time. The play was *A Midsummer Night's Dream*. Ellen Terry was Titania, Madge Robertson the second singing fairy. Her songs were 'Over hill, over dale' and 'I know a bank'. The Oberon of this production was Ellen's sister, Kate Terry. After another engagement at Bristol had ended, Madge, now turned seventeen, returned to London where, on 29 July 1865, she made her real London début, playing Ophelia to the Hamlet of Walter Montgomery [q.v.] at the Haymarket Theatre. This production was a failure, and was soon succeeded by *King John*, with Madge Robertson as Blanche of Spain. It, too, was a failure, and it was followed by *Othello*, with Madge as Desdemona, Montgomery as Iago, and a negro, named Ira D. Aldridge, as the Moor. This was strenuous training for a girl of seventeen, but it is not the entire tally of her training, for in the same year, or early in 1866, she played Lady Macbeth to the Macbeth of Samuel Phelps [q.v.] at Hull and later, in London, Lady Teazle to his Sir Peter at the Haymarket. By the time she was married, when she was twenty-one, she had acted over fifty parts in productions as various as Shakespeare and pantomime.

In 1869 Madge Robertson married the actor-manager William Hunter Kendal [q.v.], with whom thenceforth her whole life was identified. As an actor, he was in no wise comparable to his wife, as an actress: he was dull and pompous, both as a player and a private person, a solemn, sententious man whose heavy utterances were received by his wife as the most delicious sallies of wit; and he made a cult of respectability which, although it earned appreciation for him and his far abler wife, made them both disliked in many quarters because of the ostentation with which the respectability was displayed. Mrs. Kendal was called the 'matron of the English theatre', and the title sat very heavily upon her. Her marriage, so far as it related to Kendal and herself, was happy, but it was far from happy in respect of their five children, two sons and three daughters, the divorce of one being a heavy grief to Kendal. After Kendal's death the influence which he had exercised over his wife's opinions seemed to become more severe. She grew publicly censorious, and all her utterances, often witty, whether they referred to the times in general or to the theatre in particular, were acid and denunciatory. Acting had declined, the drama was degenerate, the young had neither morals nor manners. Her reproaches were rendered more grim by the style of dressing which she now affected; a style which was ostentatiously old-fashioned, but, nevertheless, suited her appearance and was attractive.

Madge Kendal was an accomplished, but not a great, actress. Her verve was immense, as a result, in part, of extraordinary vitality, and her gaiety, on occasions, was charming and infectious. It is arguable that she might have been a greater *comédienne* than she was, had she forgotten her husband's passion for respectability. But even under his oppressive influence she was delightful to watch, on the stage or off it. Her stature was tall, and she had a serene look that fitted her especially for elderly parts. Her character was firm and robust, too firm, perhaps, for family affection to survive, too robust to make her easy to work with. But the long line of actors and actresses who went to the making of her were able, at times, to resist and even to overthrow her husband's influence; and it was when they were in the ascendant that she was at her best. She was familiar to playgoers in her last years on the stage mainly in amiable, unexacting, sentimental pieces, such as *A Scrap of Paper*, *Still Waters Run Deep*, and *The Elder Miss Blossom*, but in June 1902, at His Majesty's Theatre, when she and Ellen Terry played respectively Mrs. Ford and Mrs. Page in *The Merry Wives of Windsor* to Beerbohm Tree's Falstaff, she showed her happiest spirit. Those who had the good fortune to see her and Ellen Terry in this production, realized what great *comédiennes* they were. As they had begun together, almost forty years earlier, so they ended together, in Shakespeare.

In 1908 Mrs. Kendal retired from public work. In 1926 she was appointed D.B.E. and in 1927 G.B.E. Her birthplace did not forget her: in 1932 she was made an honorary freewoman of Grimsby. Her autobiography, *Dame Madge Kendal*, in writing which she was assisted by Rudolph de Cordova, was published in 1933, but it is an untidy, inaccurate work, as was, perhaps, inevitable, for she was eighty-five when it appeared. She died at her home at Chorley Wood, Hertfordshire, 14 September 1935.

A portrait of Madge Kendal, painted in her eightieth year by Sir William Orpen, was presented to her on behalf of a number of old friends by Sir Johnston Forbes-Robertson, and is now in the Tate Gallery.

[*The Times*, 16 September 1935; *Dame Madge Kendal*, by herself, 1933; *Who's Who in the Theatre*, 1933; personal knowledge.]

St. John Ervine.

KENNEDY, HARRY ANGUS ALEXANDER (1866–1934), Scottish New Testament scholar, was born at Dornoch, Sutherland, 4 July 1866, the elder son of George Rainy Kennedy, Free Church minister in that town, by his wife, Mary Margaret McIntyre. Having won distinction as a classical scholar at the Edinburgh Academy and the university of Edinburgh, he proceeded to the study of theology at the New College in that city and at the German universities of Halle and Berlin. In 1893, the year in which he married Elisabeth (died 1928), daughter of George Gordon, flax-importer, of Donavourd, Perthshire, he was ordained as minister of the Free church at Callander, and remained in that charge until he was elected in 1905 to the chair of New Testament language and literature in Knox College, Toronto. Four years later he returned to Edinburgh, having been called to succeed the well-known biblical scholar Marcus Dods [q.v.] in the chair of New Testament language and literature in the New College. In this post he remained until premature ill health compelled him to retire in 1925. After a period of such growing weakness as rendered impossible the continuance of his scholarly pursuits, Kennedy died in Edinburgh 23 March 1934, survived by his three daughters.

It was during his twelve years of happy and fruitful ministry in Callander that Kennedy first made a name for himself among biblical scholars. His small volume on *The Sources of New Testament Greek*, published in 1895, was a pioneer in its kind. Its thesis was that the language of the Septuagint and of the New Testament was not, as had always been assumed, a Hebraic dialect of the Greek tongue, but the common speech of the contemporary Hellenistic world, a conclusion which was soon to be confirmed by the study of the Greek papyri found in Egypt, and by the further researches of scholars like Adolf Deissmann, George Milligan [q.v.], and J. H. Moulton [q.v.]. Having first followed up this notable achievement by the contribution of a learned article on the 'Old Latin Biblical Versions' to the third volume of Hastings's *Dictionary of the Bible*, Kennedy turned from the purely linguistic field to that of biblical ideas. In 1904 he published his Cunningham lectures (delivered in Edinburgh in 1902–1904) on *St. Paul's Conceptions of the Last Things*. Just at this time the eschatological problem was beginning to occupy the central place in biblical controversy, and Kennedy's wide acquaintance with Jewish apocalyptic literature combined with the conscientious exactitude of his New Testament scholarship to enable him to make a notable contribution to the discussion. This was followed nine years later by *St. Paul and the Mystery Religions* (1913), a volume no less timely in that it was devoted to the assessment of a further tendency then beginning to exercise a wide influence on biblical interpretation, namely, the tendency represented by Richard Reitzenstein and other scholars, mainly continental, to derive the most characteristic features of Paulinism from certain ideas widely current in the contemporary Hellenistic world. In 1919 there appeared *Philo's Contribution to Religion*, a first-hand investigation which, besides being of the greatest interest to students of Philo himself, is hardly less valuable for the understanding of the background of New Testament thought. In the same year Kennedy had published *The Theology of the Epistles*, a small book hardly surpassed in its field. A still smaller volume, more popular in style, on *The Vital Forces of the Early Church*, brought Kennedy's literary career to a virtual close in 1920; and this, together with his commentary on *The Epistle to the Philippians* in the 'Expositor's Greek Testament', which had appeared as early as 1903, completes the tale of the works published by him in volume form.

Although Kennedy's own theological position might be described broadly as that of the liberal evangelicalism which surrounded him in his mature years, the great merit of his work, as well as the source of its lasting usefulness, lies in its large measure of freedom from tendency. He was above all an exact and conscientious scholar, grounding his conclusions upon an impartial survey of his evidence, and following whithersoever the argument led him. In this, and in the guileless charm of his warm and genial personality, he set a noble example to the generation of Scottish ministers which it was his business to train.

[*The Times*, 29 March 1934; personal knowledge.]
JOHN BAILLIE.

KENNETT, ROBERT HATCH (1864–1932), biblical and Semitic scholar, was born at St. Laurence, Thanet, 9 September 1864, the only son of John Kennett, J.P. for the Cinque Ports and first mayor of Ramsgate, by his second wife, Jane Hatch, of Ulcombe, Kent. He was educated at Merchant Taylors School, where he learnt Hebrew under Charles James Ball. In 1882 he gained a scholarship at Queens' College, Cambridge, the president of which was the Syriac scholar George Phillips [q.v.], and where the distinguished orientalist William Wright [q.v.] was a fellow. He obtained a first class in the Semitic languages tripos of 1886, and in 1887, the year in which he was ordained, was awarded the first Tyrwhitt Hebrew scholarship and the Mason prize for biblical Hebrew. Elected a fellow of his college in 1888, Kennett was lecturer in Hebrew and Syriac there from 1887 to 1903, and chaplain from 1887 to 1893 and again from 1902 to 1908. He was also lecturer in Hebrew and Syriac at Gonville and Caius College from 1891 to 1893. He was appointed university lecturer in Aramaic in 1893, and ten years later was elected to the regius professorship of Hebrew and to the canonry of Ely Cathedral, then, for the last time, attached to the chair. In 1889 he married Emily Augusta, second daughter of Major-General Edward William Smythe Scott, Bengal Artillery, and granddaughter of Lieutenant-General Sir W. S. Whish [q.v.], and had two sons and a daughter. The younger son, Austin, an official in the government of Nigeria, and author of an important book on *Bedouin Justice* (1925), survived his father by only a few months. Kennett died rather suddenly at Ely 15 February 1932.

Among Kennett's contemporaries at school were G. A. Cooke [q.v.] and Charles Fox Burney, later respectively regius professor of Hebrew and Oriel professor of interpretation of holy scripture at Oxford; and at Cambridge, along with W. E. Barnes, A. A. Bevan, F. C. Burkitt [qq.v.], and Norman M'Lean, he was among the pupils of William Robertson Smith [q.v.]. It was a notable period in Cambridge biblical studies, and Kennett took a prominent part in interpreting the Graf-Wellhausen position in Old Testament criticism which was then winning its way. For forty years he was an earnest evangelical teacher and 'higher critic', and his most immediately effective work lay in bridging the gulf between biblical and modern modes of thought. As a critic he was independent and original, if not daring; and he attracted attention by his studies on the date of Deuteronomy (the first of which was published in the *Journal of Theological Studies* for January 1905), part of a brilliant treatment of Israelite history during the seventh to the fifth centuries B.C., and also by his defence of a Maccabean date for the Psalms and other portions of the Old Testament. He was twice (1909 and 1931) Schweich lecturer of the British Academy, his lectures being published respectively as *The Composition of the Book of Isaiah in the Light of History and Archaeology* (1910) and *Ancient Hebrew Social Life and Custom as indicated in Law, Narrative and Metaphor* (1933). His critical work, with the reconstruction of biblical history which it involved, was the subject of much discussion, although in many important respects his views were in harmony with certain trends of Old Testament research.

Of medium height, dark, with blue eyes, and of indifferent health, Kennett was a warm-hearted man with great personal charm, wide in his interests, and utterly unselfish in his efforts to help pupils and colleagues.

[Introduction by S. A. Cook to R. H. Kennett, *The Church of Israel*, 1933 (select list of writings and portrait); *Cambridge Review*, 26 February 1932; private information; personal knowledge.]   S. A. COOK.

KEOGH, SIR ALFRED (1857–1936), lieutenant-general, was born probably in Dublin 3 July 1857, the younger son of Henry Keogh, barrister-at-law. Educated at Queen's College, Galway, he qualified in medicine at the age of twenty-one, and entered the army in 1880, after serving as house physician at Brompton Hospital for Diseases of the Chest and as assistant at the Westminster Ophthalmic Hospital. He gained the Herbert prize and the Martin gold medal at Netley and was promoted surgeon-major in 1892. During the South African war he was in charge of a general hospital and was specially promoted lieutenant-colonel in 1900. From 1902 to 1905 he was deputy director-general, Army Medical Services, being promoted colonel in 1904 and surgeon-general the following day; and from 1905 until 1910 he was director-general. He was that year appointed rector of the Imperial College of Science and Technology. Shortly after the outbreak of war in 1914 Keogh acceded to Kitchener's request to return to the War Office, but only on con-

dition that he was granted exceptional powers. He retired finally in 1918 and resumed his rectorship, holding this appointment until 1922.

Keogh's reforms were far-reaching in extent and effect. During his first tenure of office he set himself to bridge the gulf between the military and civil branches of his profession, and to raise the standard of practice in the army. In 1907 the Royal Army Medical College was established at Millbank, London, for post-graduate teaching, including training in specialist subjects. He founded an army school of hygiene. The many station hospitals distributed over the country were replaced by central hospitals, equipped and staffed on a scale impossible in small establishments. When R. B. (later Lord) Haldane [q.v.] organized the Territorial army, it fell to Keogh to create a medical service for the New Armies. With the co-operation of the civil profession, the teaching hospitals were brought into the scheme, and the staffs trained in military duties. Thus when war came, the great machine that he had built up worked smoothly, and grew and developed under his guiding hand as the fighting fronts expanded.

Keogh was an organizer and administrator of the first rank. He had the gift of quick decision, and a firm grip of essentials. For all his resolute enthusiasm, he was unfailingly courteous and considerate, and never forgot the good work of others. His conspicuous services won him many distinctions: he was appointed C.B. in 1900, K.C.B. in 1906, G.C.B. in 1917, G.C.V.O. and C.H. in 1918. He received honorary degrees from the universities of Dublin, Aberdeen, Edinburgh, Leeds, and Oxford. He was elected F.R.C.P. in 1914 and honorary F.R.C.S. (England, Edinburgh, and Ireland). He was honorary physician to the king from 1907 to 1910. In 1922 he was awarded the gold medal of the Institute of Mining and Metallurgy.

Keogh was twice married: first, in 1880 to Elizabeth (died 1887), daughter of George Williams, M.D., of the Indian Medical Service, and had one son; secondly, in 1888 to Camilla Porterfield (died 1948), daughter of Captain William Hamilton Sheriff Hart, of the 105th Regiment, and had two daughters. He died in London 30 July 1936.

A portrait of Keogh by Arthur Hacker hangs in the Royal Army Medical College, London.

[*The Times*, 31 July 1936; *British Medical Journal*, 1936, vol. ii, p. 317 (portrait); *Lancet*,

1936, vol. ii, pp. 349 and 464; *Journal* of the Royal Army Medical Corps, vol. lxvii, 1936; private information.] W. P. MacArthur.

KERR, PHILIP HENRY, eleventh Marquess of Lothian (1882–1940), journalist and statesman, was born in London 18 April 1882, the elder son of Major-General Lord Ralph Drury Kerr, by his wife, Lady Anne, sixth daughter of Henry Granville Fitzalan-Howard, fourteenth Duke of Norfolk [q.v.]. He was nephew of Schomberg Henry Kerr, ninth Marquess of Lothian, and of Lord Walter Talbot Kerr [qq.v.]. He was educated at the Oratory School (then at Edgbaston), and New College, Oxford. After having been awarded a first class in modern history in 1904, he went to South Africa as private secretary to Sir Arthur Lawley (later sixth Lord Wenlock), then lieutenant-governor of the Transvaal, and soon afterwards became the youngest of that band of promising young men whom Alfred, Lord Milner [q.v.] gathered about him after the South African war.

As assistant secretary of the Inter-Colonial Council of the Transvaal and Orange River Colony and of the Railway Committee of the Central South African Railways (1905–1908), Kerr, working under Mr. R. H. (later Lord) Brand, drew up a report on railway rates which showed clearly that unless the South African colonies united, they must drift back into internecine quarrels, and this earned him his appointment in 1907 as secretary of the Transvaal Indigency Commission. Its Report, 'a milestone in the study of the colour question', found that the 'colour bar' created in South Africa, as in the United States of America, a class of poor whites, which represented a most serious problem, and brought into prominence the fundamental problems of the relations between the white and black races. A year later, one of his main bents appeared after his appointment as editor of *The State*, a monthly review founded by his colleagues and friends for the purpose of promoting union between the South African colonies. In this capacity he played an effective part in the campaign for federation. After he and others of his friends had returned to England on the coming into force of the Union constitution in 1909, they founded together in 1910 the *Round Table*, a quarterly magazine which had as its aim the organic union of the British Commonwealth, and Kerr was appointed its first editor. In that periodical, while purveying

sane information to its readers about imperial and American affairs, he did not fail to give serious warnings of the German danger which was impressed upon him by the writings of German professors no less than by the utterances of the military caste.

This work was interrupted in December 1916 by the call to Kerr from Lloyd George to become his private secretary, and the next five were the most controversial years of his life. He was more responsible than any one else for the document with regard to the German nation which forms a preface to the Treaty of Versailles. In *The Truth about the Peace Treaties* (1938) Lloyd George acknowledges the 'priceless help' given by Kerr to the prime minister, and emphasizes the importance of the part played by Kerr in dealing with the Dominions, India, and the United States. As an illustration of Kerr's literary gifts he singles out the reply sent by the Allies to Brockdorff-Rantzau's challenge of Germany's responsibility for the war, which was drafted by Kerr and won the admiration of both President Wilson and Clemenceau. He acknowledges also the help which Kerr gave in the matter of the Russian civil war which led the critics of the prime minister to use strong language about Kerr's influence; but he denies that Kerr was pro-Bolshevist. 'It was Kerr's activities, acting on my instructions, that gave rise to the legend that the Foreign Office had been transferred to "the garden suburb at 10 Downing Street"' (a temporary structure in the garden), but Lloyd George adds, 'I could not have kept fully in touch with events abroad without Mr. Kerr's intelligent and informed vigilance.'

In 1921 Kerr resigned his secretaryship and in 1922 gave up his directorship of United Newspapers (1918) which he had held for a year. He devoted his leisure to writing on imperial politics, and one fruit of it was his publication in conjunction with Mr. Lionel Curtis of *The Prevention of War* (1923), based on the lessons of American history from the covenant of Massachusetts Bay made by the Pilgrim Fathers on landing in New England to the achievement of federation. On this theme he was to speak frequently when ambassador to the United States of America.

In 1925 Kerr accepted the post of secretary to the Rhodes trustees. The work was entirely congenial to him. By giving him opportunity for travel all over the world, it deepened his acquaintance with the Dominions and the United States, and prepared him even further for the final climax of his career. To his imagination was due the short-lived experiment of the Rhodes travelling fellowships which, while they lasted, were of immense value to the fellows and tutors of Oxford colleges, by giving them personal acquaintance with overseas territories and problems which they could not otherwise have gained. How high a value Kerr attached to this position is shown by his retention of the post in spite of the ministerial duties which fell upon him in the financial crisis of 1931.

In August of that year Lord Lothian (as Kerr had become on the death of his cousin in 1930) joined the all-party Cabinet of Ramsay MacDonald [q.v.] as a representative of the liberal party, and received the chancellorship of the duchy of Lancaster. In November he became under-secretary of state for India and, as chairman of the Indian Franchise Committee (1932), he went to India to report on the question of electoral franchise. He prepared a very valuable Report and, characteristically, created friendly associations between the India Office and Indians in India. However, with the re-emergence after the Ottawa Conference of the issue of free trade, he, as a convinced free trader, reluctantly left the administration at the end of September 1932.

It was not, however, until his appointment as ambassador to the United States in 1939 that Lothian revealed to the public of both countries his persuasive powers, his statesmanlike qualities, and his breadth of vision. A series of speeches delivered by him to American audiences after July 1939 placed him in general esteem in the very forefront of public men. At a farewell dinner given to him in London by the Pilgrims of Great Britain, he emphasized the difficulties and complexities of Anglo-American relations in spite of the underlying unity, and avowed it to be his task to increase mutual confidence by making the British outlook better known to Americans. Arriving at his post on the eve of the outbreak of war, he gave in New York to the Pilgrims of the United States on 25 October an address which attracted universal attention. After pointing out the difference between totalitarian propaganda and British statements, he entered on an exposition of the origins of the war, the principles of British policy, and the reasons for the absence of universal war which had prevailed from 1815

to 1914. He claimed that the British had the right to tell their story, but that they felt that having done that it was for the Americans and the Americans alone to form their own judgement about the British and the war. The war was the outcome of the mistakes of the past, but the victorious democracies of 1919 could at any rate claim that they did apply their own principles, whereas Hitler was challenging the whole democratic conception of international life. If political errors had been committed at Versailles, they were small in comparison with the freeing of nations which that treaty had effected and, as a matter of fact, the greatest mistakes at Versailles were not political but economic. The principles of British policy he declared to be the right of all nations to autonomous freedom and the clearing out of the Gestapo from among them, without which there could be no lasting peace, and the establishment of some security against constantly renewed wars of aggression. At the same time he asked what were American aims, adding that Americans must think out the question for themselves and that it was inconceivable to him that the United States had no contribution of its own to make to the solution of the greatest problem ever presented to the genius of mankind. Then he turned to the century of peace in the nineteenth century, and attributed it to four factors: first, to the combination of the Monroe doctrine (suggested by Canning), with the power of the British navy which had prevented any attack from any European or Asiatic power; secondly, to a stable international currency based on gold; thirdly, to free trade and at worst low tariffs; fourthly, to free immigration into the New World. From these factors had sprung an unexampled expansion of human freedom and prosperity. He ended by agreeing that disarmament on a large scale was essential, but he added that 'peace comes from there being overwhelming power behind law'. The next day he added, at the *Herald Tribune* forum, his belief that progress to peace had come by stages in human history; from the Greek city state, from the Roman conception of a single law throughout the Empire, from the English representative system, and from the federation of the United States, all of which would lead eventually to a universal federation of mankind, a theme which he had already propounded in his Burge memorial lecture of 1935.

These beliefs Lothian put before the

American public in sixteen speeches and a broadcast during the remainder of his life. Only once again were they all combined in a single speech, an address to the Chicago Council of Foreign Relations (4 January 1940), but one or other recurs again and again, whether he is warning the students at Swarthmore that however attractive communism and fascism may appear to the young, totalitarianism is not the right remedy, or addressing the St. Louis Chamber of Commerce, or the *alumni* of Columbia University on the occasion of his receiving the honorary degree of LL.D. in June 1940. He continued to press his beliefs upon the American public even when the successive blows of the German invasions of Denmark and Norway, Holland and Belgium, the fall of France, and the evacuation at Dunkirk compelled him to turn to the immediate prospect and warn his hearers of the strategic consequences to themselves if the ports and factories of Great Britain and France should all pass into German hands and the guardianship of the waterways leading from Germany to the Atlantic and the Mediterranean be weakened by the transference of the British fleet to the western shores of the Atlantic, thus compelling the United States to guard both the Atlantic and the Pacific with a fleet designed for the control of only one ocean. Yet, while he made no secret of the fact that Great Britain desperately needed American munitions and destroyers, he was ever careful to say that the decision what their policy was to be was a matter for the Americans themselves and their responsibility.

In the last address, read for him on the day before his death, he came nearer to advising them what to do than ever before. 'If you back us you won't be backing a quitter. The issue now depends largely on what you decide to do. Nobody can share that responsibility with you.' He died at Washington, unmarried, 12 December 1940.

The death of Lothian was felt as a calamity of the first order, not only in Great Britain, where warm tributes were paid to him in both Houses of Parliament, but also in the United States, where he was awarded a state funeral, and his ashes were laid in the National Cemetery at Arlington, to be removed later to Jedburgh. No British ambassador had ever done so much to dissipate the traditional suspicion that clouded the relations between Great Britain and the United States,

and it is no disparagement to his successor to say that at the moment it was felt that no one could take Lothian's place.

In person, Lothian was well above medium height, and in youth was exceedingly handsome. No one, however, was less attentive to appearances: his clothes were untidy, his habit of running his fingers through his hair left it generally in an admired disorder, nor did he think it incongruous for a marquess to attend the coronation of his sovereign in an Austin Seven. All through his life, while he inspired the greatest affection and admiration in his friends, and while he both preached and practised the true Christian virtues, he always maintained a certain detachment himself. While profoundly interested in public affairs, he never showed any liking for party politics. His mind was both analytical and constructive. He had an exceptional measure of sympathy with new ideas, which was both a strength and sometimes a weakness. He would absorb and accept a new point of view, but then come back gradually to a sort of dead centre of sanity and common sense. When at Oxford, new vistas of thought were suddenly opened to him, and particularly he used to say, when he first read the works of Mr. Bernard Shaw, he lost and never regained his early Roman Catholic faith. But the need, so early implanted in him, for some definite faith remained compelling upon him, and after some years of indecision and indeed ill health, he became a sincere and convinced believer in Christian Science. There were not wanting those who said that a more orthodox treatment of the ailment from which he died would have saved his life. He retained a deep knowledge and love of the Bible, traces of which are clearly apparent in the speeches which he delivered in America. His character was therefore complex, a mixture of critical faculty and realism on the one side and, so to speak, in another compartment a deep and strong faith. He gave himself generously to all good causes. In his will he left Newbattle Abbey to Edinburgh for educational purposes and his magnificent Elizabethan house in Norfolk, Blickling Hall, to the National Trust.

Lothian, who was appointed C.H. in 1920 and was sworn of the Privy Council in 1939, was designated K.T. in 1940 in recognition of his services, but owing to his absence from the country he never was knighted and invested with the insignia. In addition to his honorary degree at

Columbia University, he had already received the honorary degree of LL.D. from Edinburgh University in 1936 and that of D.C.L. from Oxford University in 1939. In 1936 he was elected an honorary fellow of his college. He was succeeded as twelfth marquess by his cousin, Peter Francis Walter Kerr (born 1922), his younger brother, David Anselm Kerr, having been killed in action in 1914.

There is a posthumous portrait of Lothian by James Gunn at Rhodes House, Oxford, and a plaster death-mask is in the National Portrait Gallery.

[The American Speeches of Lord Lothian, edited by Lionel Curtis, with a preface by Lord Halifax and a memoir by Sir Edward Grigg (later Lord Altrincham), 1941; Lord Templewood, Ambassador on Special Mission, 1946; The Times, 13 and 17 December 1940; David Lloyd George, The Truth about the Peace Treaties, vol. i, pp. 263–265, 1938; private information; personal knowledge.]
BRAND.

KETTLE, EDGAR HARTLEY (1882–1936), pathologist, was born in London 20 April 1882, the son of Edgar Kettle, by his wife, Mary Austin, daughter of Edward Hartley, of Chipping Norton, Oxfordshire. He was educated at Skipton Grammar School, of which his uncle, Edward Tomson Hartley, was headmaster. At the age of sixteen he underwent an operation on the knee, and it was during his stay in St. Mary's Hospital as a patient that he decided to take up a medical career. Returning to St. Mary's in 1902, with an entrance scholarship, he became attracted to the study of pathology and before graduating M.B., B.S. (London) in 1907, was given the post of demonstrator in that subject. As a senior student he acted as temporary house-surgeon at the French Hospital. Here he formed a close friendship with Dr. James Alexander Murray, of the Imperial Cancer Research Fund, and acquired an enduring interest in cancer research. In 1908 he was invited to work in the new laboratories of the Cancer Hospital, Fulham, and there he remained until 1912, when he returned to St. Mary's as first assistant pathologist. In 1910 he obtained the M.D. degree and during part of 1911 he worked under Ludwig Aschoff at Freiburg.

At St. Mary's Hospital Kettle became successively assistant lecturer, joint pathologist with (Sir) Bernard Spilsbury, pathologist and lecturer in pathology (1918), and ultimately director of the Institute of Pathology and Medical Research. On the

outbreak of war in 1914 he was unable to join the Royal Army Medical Corps because of his stiff knee. In addition to his pathological work he taught students, shared the work of his clinical colleagues, and even acted for a time as resident obstetric officer. In 1916 he also became director of pathology to the Third London General Hospital at Wandsworth. In 1924 he left London for Cardiff to become the first whole-time professor of pathology and bacteriology in the Welsh National School of Medicine, and in 1927, on the retirement of Sir F. W. Andrewes [q.v.], he was chosen to succeed him in the chair of pathology at St. Bartholomew's Hospital. At this turning-point in his career the sudden perforation of a gastric ulcer placed his life in peril, but he fought his way back to health and was able to take up his new duties in the early summer of 1928. His years at St. Bartholomew's were the happiest of his life, but in 1934 he felt bound to accept a call to the newly instituted chair of pathology at the British Postgraduate Medical School at Hammersmith, a post for which he was particularly qualified by experience, standing, and personality. In 1935, when in the midst of enthusiastic planning of the new department, a serious recurrence of his old gastric trouble necessitated a radical operation. After a long and anxious convalescence, during which he showed indomitable courage, he was able to return to work for a short time, but he died at his home in London 1 December 1936.

Kettle's early publications were concerned with experimental rheumatism, cancer, splenomegaly, infection, and immunity. Histopathology was his special province and he devoted much attention to malignant disease. His classical monograph on The Pathology of Tumours (1916), illustrated by his own drawings, reached a second edition in 1925, and a third edition, edited by Professor W. G. Barnard and Dr. A. H. T. Robb-Smith, was published in 1945. In 1919 he was the first to describe in detail the actual lesions of gas gangrene. His outstanding contribution to medicine was the series of papers on silicosis and its association with pulmonary tuberculosis, published between 1922 and 1934. Kettle and his collaborator, Professor W. E. Gye, showed that the injurious qualities of silica depended on its solubility in the tissues and not, as had been generally assumed, on its great hardness and insolubility. Kettle's later investigations covered the whole problem of the relation of dust to infection. In collaboration with Dr. Reginald Hilton he devised a method of rapidly determining whether or not any given dust was capable of producing serious lung disease.

Kettle was a member of the Medical Research Council's committees on industrial solvents, industrial pulmonary disease, and radiology, and represented the council at the international conference on silicosis held at Johannesburg in 1930. At the invitation of the International Labour Office he attended the meetings of the international committee on pneumoconiosis at Geneva two months before his death. He was consulting pathologist to St. Bartholomew's Hospital and to Queen Alexandra's Military Hospital, Millbank, a member of the executive committee of the Imperial Cancer Research Fund, and treasurer (1928) of the Pathological Society of Great Britain and Ireland. He was president of the pathological sections of the British Medical Association (1928) and of the Royal Society of Medicine (1930–1932). As one of four representatives nominated by the British universities he gave evidence before a committee of the House of Lords on the 'Osteopaths bill'. He was elected F.R.C.P. (1931) and F.R.S. (1936).

Kettle's mastery of and enthusiasm for his subject and his gift of friendship won and retained the confidence and affection of all who worked with or under him. A Kettle memorial lecturership, to be held in rotation at the four medical schools with which he was associated, was founded by colleagues and pupils in 1938.

Kettle married in 1918 Marguerite Henrietta Pam, M.D. (died 1939), daughter of Leopold Pam, who was for many years a member of the editorial staff of the *Lancet*. They had no children.

[*The Times*, 2 and 4 December 1936; *Obituary Notices of Fellows of the Royal Society*, No. 6, January 1938 (portrait); *Journal of Pathology and Bacteriology*, March 1937 (bibliography and portrait); *British Medical Journal*, 1936, vol. ii, p. 1236 (portrait); *Lancet*, 1936, vol. ii, p. 1427 (portrait); *St. Bartholomew's Hospital Reports*, 1937 (bibliography and portrait); *St. Bartholomew's Hospital Journal*, January 1937; *St. Mary's Hospital Gazette*, vol. xliv, 1936–1937.]

W. J. BISHOP.

KILBRACKEN, first BARON (1847–1932), civil servant. [See GODLEY, (JOHN) ARTHUR.]

KING, SIR (FREDERIC) TRUBY (1858–1938), pioneer of the science known

as mothercraft, was born at New Plymouth, New Zealand, 1 April 1858, the third son of Thomas King, of New Plymouth, a manager of the Bank of New Zealand, by his wife, Mary Chilman. He was educated at New Plymouth, and went to Edinburgh University, where he was awarded the Ettles scholarship and graduated M.B., C.M. in 1886. After practising for a number of years in New Zealand, he founded in 1907 the Royal New Zealand Society for the Health of Women and Children, known as the Plunket Society. From 1921 to 1927 he was the director of child welfare in the Dominion.

In 1918, immediately after the end of the war, King established in London the Plunket Society Training Centre, having been sent over to England by the New Zealand government for that purpose. His mothercraft centres have since been imitated in every English-speaking country, as well as in various foreign countries, such as Russia, Poland, Palestine, and China, where his writings are read and their teaching is followed. His books, *Feeding and Care of Baby* (1913) and *The Expectant Mother and Baby's First Month* (1924), were for a long time the only authentic works on the subject, but some years before his death his daughter, Miss Mary Truby King, brought out a revised edition of his teachings with additional matter under the title of *Mothercraft* (1934). There are thousands of men and women in various countries who owe their healthy bodies, or even their lives, to the principles laid down by King.

The following impressive figures have been given of the results of King's philanthropic labours. In New Zealand in 1905 the annual mortality of infants under twelve months old was 8 per cent. By 1912 it had fallen to 5·1 per cent., and in 1934 to 3·16 per cent. In Dunedin, where the work originated, it was as low as 2·1 per cent. Thanks mainly to King and the adoption of his methods during the same period of about thirty years, the rate of infant mortality has fallen in a marked manner. At the time of his death, the New Zealand rate was still very much lower than it was in Great Britain and the United States of America.

It was said of King after his death that he combined infinite patience and accurate observation with flashes of imagination, but that the essence of his teaching was based upon respect for the laws of nature, and the rules of common sense. No compliment could have pleased him better than this. As a pioneer worker in welfare, he always declared that he regarded it as his greatest reward that so much of what he advocated so vigorously was accepted so generally as to become a commonplace. His admirers may well go farther and say that, however ordinary his work may appear, his infectious enthusiasm overcame many seemingly insuperable obstacles and produced benefits to humanity as valuable as those which flowed from the labours of Lister or Pasteur.

King was appointed C.M.G. in 1917, and knighted in 1925. In 1887 he married Isabella Cockburn (died 1927), daughter of Adam Millar, of Edinburgh, and had one daughter. He spent his last years in a small bungalow in the grounds of one of his mothercraft homes. His favourite recreation was gardening, and his love of flowers intense. He had much skill in growing them, especially rhododendrons. He died at Wellington, New Zealand, 9 February 1938.

[*The Times*, 10, 12, 14, and 17 February 1938; information from the Office of the High Commissioner of New Zealand.]

ARTHUR COCHRANE.

KIPLING, (JOSEPH) RUDYARD (1865–1936), author, came of farming stock in Yorkshire. His father, John Lockwood Kipling (1837–1911), the eldest son of Joseph Kipling, a methodist minister, worked as a potter in Staffordshire, studied at South Kensington, and was for some time employed as a designer at Burslem. He married Alice (1837–1910), daughter of George Browne Macdonald, a Wesleyan minister, of Wolverhampton. The Macdonalds were Highlanders who had migrated to Fermanagh after the 'Forty-Five'. Alice's grandfather, James Macdonald, who had become a preacher on the invitation of John Wesley himself, came to England in 1795. There his son was born. George Browne Macdonald had a large family, including four daughters who married and had children: Alice Kipling, Georgiana, wife of Sir Edward Burne-Jones [q.v.], Agnes, wife of Sir Edward Poynter [q.v.], and Louisa, wife of Alfred Baldwin and mother of Earl Baldwin of Bewdley.

John Kipling married (March 1865) on the strength of his appointment as architectural sculptor in the Bombay School of Art. The elder of their two children (a daughter followed three years later) was born in Bombay 30 December 1865, and named Joseph after his grandfather: his second name was chosen by his godmother Louisa Macdonald, to commemorate the place where his parents had first met, Rudyard Lake in Staffordshire. In 1871 his doctors advised that the boy should be sent home. He passed some years with a disagreeable and pious family at Southsea: but Christmas holidays were happily spent with the Burne-Jones family at The Grange, Fulham, and they knew nothing of the beatings and humiliations recorded in 'Baa, Baa, Black Sheep'. He remembered William Morris seated on a rocking-horse telling the children the story of Burnt Njal. In 1877 Mrs. Kipling came home, carried the boy away from Southsea, and in 1878 entered him at the United Services College, Westward Ho! In the latter year his father, now principal of the Mayo School of Art and curator of the museum at Lahore, spent some months on furlough in England, and took Rudyard to the Paris Exhibition. This visit was the beginning of a devotion to France which grew stronger to the end.

Kipling as a schoolboy showed no outstanding qualities except a passion for reading, to which Cormell Price, the headmaster, ministered wisely and generously. At Westward Ho! and in his holidays he began to build that knowledge of English literature which reveals itself so abundantly, by reference or allusion, throughout his work. The Bible, the Elizabethan translators, the poets indiscriminately, Defoe and the story-tellers, small and great: he drew his vocabulary from them all. He had, too, for a schoolboy, an unusually wide knowledge of French literature, and he made some slight progress in Russian, with a view, it may be suspected, to service some day on the Afghan frontier: it is not to be forgotten that these susceptible years were also the years of the Russo-Turkish war, of Indian troops at Malta, and the great Jingo song. Out of his friendships and the incidents of school life he was afterwards to weave the adventures of *Stalky and Co.* (1899). There has been much idle disputation over the verisimilitude of Kipling's school stories. The truth seems to be that, like Scott and Dickens, he at all ages possessed, and heartily enjoyed, the gift of transmuting the commonplace into drama or fairy tale. Add the exuberant sense of fun, which appears in 'Brugglesmith' (1891) and 'My Sunday at Home' (1895), and no further analysis or explanation seems necessary.

Kipling's extraordinary powers of reception and recollection made him in fact a reporter of genius: and it was as a reporter that he became known when he returned to India in 1882 and joined the staff of the Lahore *Civil and Military Gazette*: he was also associated with the Allahabad *Pioneer*. Here he was once more under the eye of his father, to whose standards of fine craftsmanship Rudyard loyally and enthusiastically adhered: to see everything with his own eyes; to experiment endlessly with 'the weight, colour, perfume, and attributes of words in relation to other words'; and to set down the results with the utmost precision of epithet and phrase. The vast and many-coloured pageant of India was his field, and, dominant over all, was the imperial race, 'picked men at their definite work' of doing justice and upholding the law, and, in the doing, misunderstood and sometimes reviled by the great, ignorant, liberal public in England. From his father he had the gift of mixing with all sorts and conditions: from his mother a vitality and imagination which led a viceroy to say 'Dullness and Mrs. Kipling cannot exist in the same room.' And these two were, and remained, his public.

Very soon, verses, mostly satiric with a secret meaning for the initiated, sketches, and stories began to be quoted and talked about, not always with approval, wherever English officials and their families met in India. There had been such things before but never of this vivid quality and wide range. They reached England: Sir William Hunter [q.v.], who knew both books and India, wrote in the *Academy* of a new star rising in the East; and by 1888, when the writer was only twenty-two, the literary world was asking 'Who is Rudyard Kipling?' The books which created this early fame were *Departmental Ditties* (1886), *Plain Tales from the Hills*, *Soldiers Three*, *The Story of the Gadsbys*, *In Black and White*, *Under the Deodars*, *The Phantom Rickshaw*, *Wee Willie Winkie* (all 1888), containing altogether over seventy stories. The next volume, *The Courting of Dinah Shadd* (1890), had for introduction a biographical sketch by Andrew Lang [q.v.], then at the height of his authority as a critic. No writer since Dickens had been exposed to so sudden a blaze of celebrity. But Kipling was unspoiled by praise, undisturbed by criticism. He was now and always his own taskmaster. He would declaim a paragraph or chant a poem (he had no ear and an unmusical voice) until he was satisfied that every phrase and cadence was doing its duty. 'A word', he said, 'should fall in its place like a bell in a full chime.' In the rising art of the short story England had found a master to rival Guy de Maupassant, and few things gave him more pleasure than to learn that a French critic had detected the phrase 'burdensome geniality' round which a whole story ('A Wayside Comedy', 1888) had been written. Some day his translators, headed by André Chevrillon, were to make him almost as popular in France as in England.

Late in 1889 Kipling left India for a long journey in Japan and the United States of America, and, with £300 to his credit, settled in London, in rooms in Villiers Street by Charing Cross. The critical journals, especially the *National Observer*, made much of him and he was soon taken into the circle of W. E. Henley, Thomas Hardy, (Sir) Edmund Gosse, (Sir) Waltes Besant, to whose novel, *All in a Garden Fair*, he owned a debt in craftsmanship, George Saintsbury [qq.v.], and Andrew Lang. R. L. Stevenson, whom he greatly admired, was at Vailima, and although they corresponded, they never met. But Kipling made it a matter of principle to join no literary coterie, and never, directly or by implication, to criticize another craftsman's work. In London also, Kipling made the acquaintance of Wolcott Balestier (son of Henry Wolcott Balestier, of Rochester, New York), an American journalist of French origin, with whom he wrote *The Naulahka* (1892), and his sister Caroline Starr, whom he married. Meanwhile he had published his one novel *The Light that Failed* (1891), visited America again, and made his first journey to the Cape: thence on to Australia and New Zealand; back, with 'General' William Booth [q.v.], to Colombo, visiting Lahore for the last time. Indefatigable traveller and observer as he was, he never saw the world again as he had seen India, with the eyes first of childhood and then of early manhood.

Immediately after their marriage in January 1892 the Kiplings started for America, on a journey round the world: a project brought to an uncomfortable stop by the failure of a bank in Yokohama. Returning eastward by Canada, they settled on the Balestier property at Brattleboro, Vermont. Here they lived for four years. Kipling did not like his neighbours, nor did they like him: his impressions of American society gave edge to the *Jungle Book* story of the *Bandarlog*. In the end a mischievous feud, provoked by a trifle and culminating in a lawsuit, so worked on his horror of publicity, and his dislike of interference, as to send him, sooner than he had intended, back to England. He had finished his best volume of stories, *Many Inventions* (1893), written the two *Jungle Books* (1894 and 1895), and drafted *Captains Courageous* (published 1897).

Kipling's fame was reaching its highest point—the fame, first, of a great story-teller and ballad-singer: then of a master of comedy and sentiment. True pathos came later with the death of his eldest child, Josephine, for whom the *Just So Stories for Little Children* (1902) were to have been written: he himself ranked them highest among his stories, the 'Recessional' (1897) among his poems. The choice is significant: the family and the Empire were the poles about which his genius turned: and between *Barrack-Room Ballads* (1892) and *The Seven Seas* (1896) Kipling had become the exponent of a political creed, a national philosophy, an imperial ethic. The note had been loudly struck in 'The English Flag' (1891) which the aged Tennyson approved, and *The Seven Seas* might be read as an overture to the celebrations of the year of jubilee. And although well sustained by *A Fleet in Being* (1898), the masterpiece of his craft as journalist and special correspondent, *Kim* (1901), *Puck of Pook's Hill* (1906), and *Rewards and Fairies* (1910), his popularity was never again so universal as it had been before the South African war.

In 1898–1899 the family—Josephine, Elsie, and John—were in New York visiting Mrs. Balestier. There Kipling fell dangerously ill of pneumonia: Josephine died, and alarm and sympathy were felt throughout the English-speaking world. He was a national figure, and his death would have been felt as a national calamity. But those who had stood aloof from the somewhat feverish exaltation of those years were not slow to remark a vein of brutality, of something at once noisy and showy, in his art; a love of violence and domination, an 'effete Philistinism' not in keeping with the new age of pacific democracy and government directed not by inherited experience but by liberal principles. The anti-imperial reaction, stimulated by the mismanagement of the South African war, was gathering strength, and the young intellectuals on that side were waiting, with parody, caricature, or sober protest, to put the great imperialist down. Never much affected by criticism of his

work, Kipling went on writing and travelling. He made his second journey to the Cape in 1898 and from 1900 to 1908 the family went there every year, leaving England in December and returning in April or May. Then the venue was changed to Switzerland: winter sports at Engelberg, followed by a trip to France or Italy, and a return to England for John Kipling's Easter holidays. In 1902 the Kiplings had bought Bateman's, at Burwash, in Sussex: and here for the first time he struck roots in the English soil which he worshipped. Here *Puck* was begun in the autumn of 1904, and, with *Rewards and Fairies* and *A School History of England* (1911), may be taken as 'a sort of balance to, as well as a seal upon, some aspects of my "Imperialistic" output in the past'. These volumes contain some of his most durable poetry, besides the much quoted 'The Glory of the Garden', and the last of his famous ballads, the verses called 'If', written with Dr. Jameson in mind, which 'snowballed themselves', as he ruefully acknowledged, and were translated into twenty-seven languages.

In 1907 Kipling was awarded the Nobel prize for literature. He had refused the laureateship when in 1895, after long delay, Lord Salisbury decided to fill the post vacant since the death of Tennyson and, on Balfour's urgent recommendation, offered it to Kipling. He felt, then and always, that he could do better work and be of more use to the country if he were free to write as he chose. Anticipating this reply, Asquith did not invite him to accept the office when next it fell vacant in 1913. In 1916 Robert Bridges suggested that the Order of Merit could not be more suitably bestowed: 'Kipling is the greatest living literary genius that we have: and it is generally thought that he has been passed over on account of his politics.' Five years later the proposal was renewed and the names of Kipling and Sir J. M. Barrie [q.v.] were discussed between the King and Lloyd George. The offer was made but Kipling prayed that he might be excused. To his great distress, the story became public. Finally, in 1924 the offer was made for the third time, and declined on the same grounds, that whatever he did or might do for the King or Empire in the troublesome times ahead would be most serviceably done without acknowledgement in the public eye.

From about his fortieth year onward more and more of Kipling's energy was given to imperial concerns. The menace of Germany grew ever nearer and more formidable: and he was equally ready to take arms for conscription or against women's suffrage, against democracy, or for the rights of Ulster. These vehement preoccupations, grounded upon an intense faith in discipline, and self-discipline, and recalling, in substance and expression, the vaticinations of Carlyle and of Tennyson in his later years, coincided with a new and, to the general public, a by no means attractive development of his literary manner. Of *Rewards and Fairies* he said that he 'loaded the book up with allegories and allusions'. This tendency to a cryptic, over-mannerized style of writing grew on him with the years and produced 'the Kipling whom nobody reads', the Kipling of *A Diversity of Creatures* (1917), *Debits and Credits* (1926), and *Limits and Renewals* (1932). He had made a rule for himself: 'Never follow up a success: when you have found what you can do, do something you can't.' But after forty-five, he was no longer in the full enjoyment of health, or of his old creative power, and the genius which might have told, what he once aspired to tell, 'the saga of the Anglo-Saxons', was deflected to a range of business which to his eye was of vastly greater importance: to warn, to exhort, to preach; some said to scold his countrymen. His style, drawing less and less on observation, and more and more on the notebook, had lost its magnetism for a generation which knew the formula: his political faith, authoritarian, hierarchic, feudal, embarrassed some as much as it exasperated others. Certain Irish members demanded his prosecution: one liberal organ described him as a 'vindictive maniac'.

From his fiftieth year until his death, moreover, Kipling suffered constant and often acute pain, accompanied by haemorrhage and sickness, from a duodenal ulcer, only diagnosed by a French surgeon in 1933. No treatment (and a score of doctors were consulted) gave him more than passing relief. It is against this background of wretchedness and bodily distress that the work of his last twenty years must be viewed. In order to keep the pain at bay, he drove his mind harder and harder: going always deeper, his handling always more tense, his style more abrupt. From allusive he became obscure, from obscure at times unintelligible.

The long-foreseen war of 1914–1918 gave Kipling a field of action not unwelcome. He poured out letters, verses, and speeches. He wrote of minesweepers and submarines:

of the training of the New Armies: he busied himself with the history of his son's regiment, the Irish Guards (published as *The Irish Guards in the Great War*, 2 vols., 1923). Above all he wrote of France, of France at war, when all were on his side: of France after the war, when England was not so whole-hearted; and his passionate antagonism to Germany, at a time when French policy was to most Englishmen a mystifying exasperation, and Germany a harmless and beaten enemy, involved him once more in a cloud of angry detraction.

Compensating honours came to Kipling from many quarters: most valued of all were the doctorates conferred upon him by the universities of Paris and Strasburg in 1921. In November 1922 he was elected lord rector of St. Andrews University, among the honorary graduates at his installation in the following October being his cousin Stanley (later Earl) Baldwin, then prime minister. In 1926 he was awarded the gold medal of the Royal Society of Literature, which only Scott, Meredith, and Hardy had received before him. He was elected an honorary fellow of Magdalene College, Cambridge, in 1932, received honorary degrees from the universities of McGill (1899), Durham and Oxford (1907), Cambridge (1908), Edinburgh (1920), and Athens (1924). In 1918, at the invitation of M. D. Caclamanos, he translated the Greek national anthem into English, and the version appeared in the *Daily Telegraph* on 17 October 1918. In return the Greek government presented him with an original gold *stater* of Alexander the Great in mint condition. In 1933 he was made a foreign associate of the Académie des Sciences Morales et Politiques. Twice only did he consent to broadcast—a short speech delivered at a luncheon given by the Royal Society of Literature to the Canadian Authors Association on 12 July 1933 (recorded) and his last speech to the Royal Society of St. George on 6 May 1935. His last completed book was *Souvenirs of France* (1933). An unfinished autobiography, *Something of Myself*, was published posthumously in 1937. He died after an operation in London 18 January 1936, and was buried in Westminster Abbey. His widow survived until 1939. She bequeathed Bateman's to the National Trust.

Kipling's only son was killed in action on the western front in 1915. Much of the father's energy was given in the years after the war to the War Graves Commission:

until 1939 the Last Post was sounded at the Loos Memorial by Kipling's endowment. His one surviving child, Elsie, married Captain George Bambridge, of Wimpole, Cambridgeshire.

Kipling, though short, was lithe and slim, with beautifully balanced movements. His most arresting feature was his heavy eyebrows, which shot up and down with his talk: under them twinkled bright blue eyes. Among the numerous portraits are: a pencil drawing by Lady Granby (Violet, Duchess of Rutland) (1891) at Bateman's; paintings by John Collier (1891) in the possession of Mrs. Bambridge and (1900) at Bateman's; a painting by Sir Philip Burne-Jones (1899) in the National Portrait Gallery, a replica of which is in the Victoria Memorial Hall, Calcutta; a painting by William Strang (1913) at Magdalene College, Cambridge, and a pencil drawing by the last-named artist (1937) in the National Portrait Gallery. A bronze bust by Henry Pegram (1909) is at Bateman's, and another, by Ginette Bingguely-Lejeune (1936–1937), is in the National Portrait Gallery. A plaque by Patrick Synge-Hutchinson is in the possession of Mrs. Bambridge. There are cartoons by 'Spy' (*Vanity Fair*, 7 June 1894), (Sir) Max Beerbohm (*The Poet's Corner*, 1904), and many others.

[Rudyard Kipling, *Something of Myself*, 1937; André Chevrillon, *Three Studies in English Literature: Kipling, Galsworthy, and Shakespeare* (translated from the French by F. Simmonds), 1923; Sir George MacMunn, *Rudyard Kipling: Craftsman*, 1937; Edward Shanks, *Rudyard Kipling*, 1940; L. R. Carpenter, *Rudyard Kipling. A Friendly Profile*, 1942; E. W. Martindell, *A Bibliography of the Works of Rudyard Kipling, 1881–1923*, 1923; F. V. Livingston, *A Bibliography of the Works of Rudyard Kipling*, 1927, and *Supplement* (containing lists of portraits, &c.), (Harvard), 1938; private information; personal knowledge.]   G. M. YOUNG.

KNOX, EDMUND ARBUTHNOTT (1847–1937), bishop of Manchester, was born at Bangalore, India, 6 December 1847, the second son of George Knox, by his wife, Frances Mary Anne, elder daughter of Thomas Forbes Reynolds, M.D., of Wallington, Surrey. The eldest son was Sir George Edward Knox [q.v.]. The father was one of the last chaplains in the East India Company's service; he retired in 1855 and became a secretary of the Church Missionary Society in 1857; but the connexion with India remained a close one throughout Edmund Knox's

earlier days. His own work, however, lay entirely in England. He was educated at St. Paul's School, and had a distinguished career at Oxford, as a scholar of Corpus Christi College and later as fellow (1868), dean (1872), and tutor (1875) of Merton College, posts which he held until 1884. His great ability was shown by his first classes in classical moderations (1867), *literae humaniores* (1868), and law and modern history (1869), and his versatility as a scholar by his election to the Boden Sanskrit scholarship (1867). But with his intellectual powers went great practical ability and a strong call to evangelism and pastoral work. He was accounted one of the most effective disciplinarians of his day as dean of Merton and in his year of office as proctor, but his strong sense of law and order, both then and later, when he had become a diocesan bishop, did not in any way conflict with his sense of spiritual responsibility for those with whom he had to deal. He was ordained deacon in 1870 and priest in 1872. In his old age he recalled the days when the fellows of Merton used to ride out on horseback to take the services at Wolvercote.

In 1884 Knox's real lifework began when he became rector of Kibworth Beauchamp, near Leicester, but his powers as an administrator first showed themselves fully when he became vicar of Aston, Birmingham, seven years later (1891). Shortly afterwards, in 1892, occurred the death of his wife, Ellen Penelope, eldest daughter of Thomas Valpy French, bishop of Lahore [q.v.], whom he had married in 1878. She left him with a family of four sons and two daughters, and in 1895 he married Ethel Mary, daughter of Canon Horace Newton, vicar of Redditch, to whose quiet support he owed much both in Birmingham and in Manchester. For twelve years he exercised a wide influence in Birmingham, becoming in 1894 suffragan bishop of Coventry and archdeacon of Birmingham and in 1895 rector of St. Philip's church, Birmingham, afterwards the cathedral. There he laid effective foundations for the new diocesan see of Birmingham before he himself became bishop of Manchester in 1903.

At Manchester Knox became, with whole-hearted Lancastrian backing, the acknowledged leader of the evangelical party. He took a prominent part especially in the controversies over the Church schools (1906) and the Church of England

Assembly (Powers) Act, commonly called the Enabling Act (1919), of which he was a vigorous critic. But as a diocesan bishop his great concern was to foster direct pastoral and evangelistic work by his clergy, and he was never more effective than in the efforts which he made with this end in view. Probably his own deepest joy was in the founding of the great annual mission to the holiday-makers upon the sands at Blackpool. His charges, later published as books such as *Sacrifice or Sacrament* (1914) and *On What Authority?* (1922), dealt mainly with the doctrinal statement of the evangelical case. But his ability was shown most of all in organization. It was said of him by a Manchester layman that he was worth any six business men on a committee. Yet throughout his career he was always a pastor and always found time for personal and individual work.

Knox retired in 1921 and spent a long old age at the house at Shortlands, Kent, bought for him by the diocese of Manchester. He was in his ninetieth year when he died there 16 January 1937. During his retirement his powers as a scholar reasserted themselves. Both his *Robert Leighton, Archbishop of Glasgow* (1930) and *The Tractarian Movement, 1833–1845* (1933) were considerable pieces of historical research. In 1935, only two years before his death, he published his *Reminiscences of an Octogenarian, 1847–1934*, a work which in its vigour and liveliness casts many illuminating sidelights upon nearly a century of the history of the Church of England.

A portrait of Knox, painted by A. T. Nowell in 1911, was presented by Mrs. Knox to the Old Rectory Club, 90 Deansgate, Manchester, where it now hangs.

[*The Times* and *Manchester Guardian*, 18 January 1937; E. A. Knox, *Reminiscences of an Octogenarian*, 1935; private information; personal knowledge.]   L. W. GRENSTED.

KNUTSFORD, second VISCOUNT (1855–1931), hospital administrator and reformer. [See HOLLAND, Sir SYDNEY GEORGE.]

KOTZÉ, SIR JOHN GILBERT (1849–1940), South African judge, born at Leeuwenhof, Cape Town, 5 November 1849, was a member of a well-known family which has lived in South Africa since 1691 when Jan Kotzé from Amsterdam settled there. He was the youngest son of Petrus Johannes Kotzé, who was twice mayor of Cape Town and who lived at Leeuwenhof on the slopes of Table Mountain, later the official residence of the administrator of the Cape Province. His mother was Susanna Maria, eldest daughter of Johannes Gysbert Blanckenberg. He was educated at the South African College (afterwards the university of Cape Town) from 1864 to 1868, and in 1869 he became a student at London University and the Inner Temple. He qualified for the LL.B. degree in 1872, and in 1874 he was called to the bar and returned to South Africa where he began to practise as a barrister, first in Cape Town and then in Grahamstown. In March 1877, when he was only twenty-seven, the office of chief justice of the South African Republic (Transvaal) was offered to him by President Burgers. He accepted it, but before he assumed duty the Transvaal was annexed by Great Britain and on Kotzé's arrival at Pretoria the administrator suggested that Kotzé should take his seat as sole judge of the High Court about to be constituted. He agreed but reserved his right to claim the position of chief justice.

In 1879 the high commissioner for South Africa, Sir Bartle Frere [q.v.], drew up a constitution for the Transvaal, based upon the principles of crown colony government. He submitted it to Kotzé, who told him that it was in conflict with the annexation proclamation and would not be accepted by the Boers. The constitution was nevertheless introduced and aroused widespread dissatisfaction. In the same year Kotzé drew up a minute in which he set out certain objections to the appointment of an attorney-general who had not been admitted as a barrister and signed it in his capacity as chief justice; he sent it to the governor, Sir Garnet Wolseley [q.v.], to be forwarded to the secretary of state. The governor declined to do so on the ground that Kotzé was not chief justice and had no right to sign in that capacity. This led to a controversy which the governor settled, temporarily at any rate, by appointing Jacobus Petrus de Wet as chief justice and Kotzé as puisne judge. Kotzé protested and petitioned the Privy Council but nothing further was heard of the matter because the Boers' dissatisfaction with the new constitution led to the establishment by them of their own government on 16 December 1880 and to the first Anglo-Boer war. After the war Kotzé was appointed (1881) chief justice of the Transvaal, but he found his position difficult. In 1882 he was offered a seat on the bench of the High Court of Griqualand West; he accepted the offer but did not take up the appointment because he was persuaded to continue as chief justice, and thereafter from 1882 to 1898 he presided over the Supreme Court of the South African Republic, the name which the country resumed in 1884.

In spite of the fact that he was on the bench, Kotzé took a surprisingly active interest in political questions and in 1893, without resigning from the bench, he became a candidate for the Presidency. But the secluded life which is necessarily led by a judge does not make him a popular figure on the hustings and Kotzé received only 81 votes, against 7,854 cast for Kruger.

In 1897 a constitutional crisis of the first magnitude arose out of certain judgements given by Kotzé. In 1884 he had, in a considered judgement, examined the constitutional powers of the Volksraad in relation to the *grondwet* (constitution) of 1858 and had decided that supreme power in the Republic was vested in the Volksraad, that it had power to make laws which were in conflict with the *grondwet*, that it could legislate by mere resolution (*besluit*) and that the Supreme Court had no jurisdiction to pronounce on the validity of its enactments. Subsequently he began to have doubts about the matter, and in 1895 he announced, by way of *obiter dictum*, that his views had changed and that he now regarded the *grondwet* as a rigid constitution on the lines of the American constitution and that the Supreme Court had jurisdiction to inquire into the validity of Acts of the Volksraad. On 22 January 1897 he carried these new views into effect in a judgement (*Brown v. Leyds*) which caused considerable embarrassment to the government. The Volksraad immediately passed a law authorizing the president to ask the judges whether they claimed the right to inquire into the validity of the Volksraad's legislative acts and, if they did not repudiate such a right, to dismiss them. The judges protested but the president put the fateful question. The chief justice of the Cape Colony, Sir John Henry (later Lord) de Villiers [q.v.], although his views on the constitutional issue differed from those of Kotzé, hastened to Pretoria to mediate in the dispute. A temporary compromise was effected, but after a while Kotzé considered that the president was not carrying out his side of it and communicated his views to him very pointedly. Kruger promptly acted under the provisions of the obnoxious law and dismissed Kotzé on 16 February 1898. An appeal to the people by Kotzé proved fruitless and the sensation caused by his dismissal was soon overshadowed by the outbreak of the second Anglo-Boer war in 1899.

In 1900 Kotzé was appointed attorney-general of Southern Rhodesia. In 1902 he took silk; in 1904 he was appointed to the bench of the Cape Eastern Districts Court at Grahamstown and on 8 July of that year he became its judge president. In 1913 he accepted a puisne judgeship in the Cape Provincial division of the Supreme Court of South Africa at Cape Town and in 1920 he became judge president of that court. In July 1922 he was appointed a judge of appeal and held that post until his retirement in 1927.

Kotzé was knighted in 1917, having in 1896 been appointed a Knight Grand Cross of the Order of the Conception by the King of Portugal. He received the honorary degree of LL.D. from the universities of the Cape of Good Hope (1912), Cape Town (1927), and Witwatersrand (1939). He was twice married: first, in 1872 to Mary Aurelia (died 1931), fourth daughter of Daniel Bell, of Milton House, Clapham; secondly, in 1933, to Margaretha Jeldina, daughter of Hendrik Doornbos of Groningen. One son and six daughters were born of his first marriage. He died at Cape Town at the age of ninety 1 April 1940.

Kotzé's best-known legal work is a translation, with valuable notes, of Simon van Leeuwen's *Commentaries on Roman-Dutch Law* (2 vols., 1881–1886; 2nd ed. 1921). He also published a monograph on *Causa in the Roman and Roman-Dutch Law of Contract* (1922) and contributed several learned articles to the *South African Law Journal*.

Kotzé had many endearing qualities. On the bench he was always patient and courteous and ready to listen with an open mind to the dullest of arguments, and his old-world courtesy was perfect in its simplicity and ease. He was proud of having been appointed to the bench at the early age of twenty-seven and of having been on it, with a short interval, for fifty years. He was ever a stout upholder of the principles of judicial independence. He was deeply imbued with the principles of Roman-Dutch law, and was an earnest student of the medieval authorities. He was undoubtedly one of the most distinguished judges and jurists that South Africa has produced, and his learned and lucid judgements will continue to be cited with the respect that they so fully merit. His valuable collection of legal works, some of great rarity, now forms part of the library of the Appeal Court of South Africa, which also contains his bust by Grace Wheatley.

[J. G. Kotzé, *Biographical Memoirs and Reminiscences* (incomplete), vol. i, 1934, *An Appeal to the Inhabitants of the South African Republic*, 1898, and *Documents and Correspondence relating to the Judicial Crisis in the South African Republic*, 1898; *The Memoirs of Paul Kruger told by himself*, 2 vols., 1902; E. A. Walker, *Lord de Villiers and His Times: South Africa, 1842–1914*, 1925, and *A History of South Africa*, 1928; M. Nathan, *Paul Kruger, his Life and Times*, 1941; personal knowledge.]   E. F. WATERMEYER.

KYLSANT, BARON (1863–1937), shipowner and financier. [See PHILIPPS, OWEN COSBY.]

LACEY, THOMAS ALEXANDER (1853–1931), ecclesiologist and controversialist, was born at Nottingham 20 December 1853, the younger child and only son of George Frederick Lacey, by his wife, Susan Woodward, a native of Stamford, Lincolnshire, who was ill treated and deserted by her husband, being left to bring up two infants. Lacey was nominated to a free place in the grammar school at Nottingham, founded in 1513, which in 1868 was re-established as the high school, and the excellence of his Latin paper in the Oxford senior local examination resulted in his being offered in 1871 an exhibition at Balliol College, Oxford, where he was awarded a second class in *literae humaniores* in 1875. He became one of the most accomplished Latinists of his time, and it is related that when he was in Rome in connexion with the inquiry into Anglican ordinations Pope Leo XIII said that he wished that he had a cardinal who could write such Latin as Mr. Lacey. In 1876 he was ordained while a master at Queen Elizabeth Grammar School, Wakefield. He married in 1888, while a master at Denstone College, Dorothy, only daughter of William Stott Banks, solicitor, of Wakefield. There were three sons and three daughters of the marriage. He was vicar of St. Edmund's church, Northampton, from 1892 to 1894, and of Madingley, near Cambridge, from 1894 to 1903.

In 1894 Lacey embarked upon the most important task of his life. It was notorious that misconceptions about Anglican ordinations existed in Rome. Discussion of the subject had begun in the previous year by the publication of the Abbé Portal's treatise upholding the validity of Anglican ordinations. Portal had also had important conversations with Charles Wood, Viscount Halifax [q.v.]. The Pope himself was bent on furthering reconciliation and took the initiative in appointing a commission on Anglican orders. In collaboration with Edward Denny, Lacey composed a *Dissertatio Apologetica de Hierarchia Anglicana* (1895). In March 1896 the commission appointed by Leo XIII to investigate the question assembled in Rome. In April, at the desire of the Abbé Duchesne and of Cardinal Gasparri, Lacey, accompanied by Frederick William Puller, of the Society of St. John the Evangelist, Cowley, went to Rome to give further help. He remained in Rome until June, and in *A Roman Diary* (1910) gave a graphic account of the comings and goings in the antechambers of the cardinals, the differences among the Roman theologians, the enthusiasm of Leo XIII, the high expectations, and finally the successful neutralizing efforts of the English Roman Catholics led by Cardinal Vaughan [q.v.] with inflexible determination to get Anglican ordinations condemned.

During the middle years of his life Lacey was a member of the editorial staff of the *Church Times*, the organ of the high church party. He contributed a weekly essay over the pseudonym 'Viator' and anonymously was the author of brilliant leading articles ranging over an immense variety of topics. As a proctor in convocation (1922–1929) his speeches were provocative, paradoxical, and disconcerting. He wrote learnedly on liturgical and historical subjects and in 1917 delivered the Bishop Paddock lectures at the General Theological Seminary, New York, published the same year as *Unity and Schism*. He was one of the editors of the *English Hymnal* (1906) to which he contributed many translations of ancient Latin hymns. His original hymn 'O Faith of England, taught of old' is widely used. In 1903 he became chaplain, and from 1910 to 1919 was warden, of the London Diocesan Penitentiary, Highgate. In 1918 he was appointed canon-residentiary of Worcester Cathedral and was treasurer from 1922 until his death at Worcester 6 December 1931. He received the honorary degree of

D.D. from St. Andrews University in 1926.

[*Church Times*, 11 December 1931; T. A. Lacey, *A Roman Diary*, 1910; Lord Halifax, *Leo XIII and Anglican Orders*, 1912; private letters; personal knowledge.]

C. B. MORTLOCK.

LAIDLAW, SIR PATRICK PLAY-FAIR (1881–1940), physician, was born at Glasgow 26 September 1881, the third of the six sons of Robert Laidlaw, M.D., at that time superintendent of the Glasgow Medical Mission and later a magistrate and medical officer in the Seychelles Islands, by his wife, Elizabeth, daughter of Patrick Playfair, a member of a family which has produced several men of eminence in science and medicine; among these were Sir Lyon Playfair, first Baron Playfair, and his brother W. S. Playfair [qq.v.], well known as a specialist in obstetrics and gynaecology.

Laidlaw first attended a private Quaker school in North London; from there he went to the Leys School, Cambridge, and in 1900 he began his medical studies as a scholar at St. John's College, Cambridge. In October 1904 he won a scholarship to Guy's Hospital, London, where he completed his medical course and then became a demonstrator in physiology in the medical school. From 1909 to 1913 he was engaged in research on problems of pharmacology and physiology in the Wellcome Physiological Research Laboratories at Herne Hill, together with (Sir) Henry Dale, with whom he investigated important pharmacological actions of histamine, the presence of which in ergot had recently been shown. Here he was also associated with George Barger [q.v.] and Arthur James Ewins. With the latter he investigated the fate of tyramine in the body and showed that it is both deaminized and oxidized to phenol acetic acid in the liver. In association with Ewins he later found a method of producing indol-ethylamine by synthesis and studied its metabolic breakdown.

In 1913 Laidlaw was appointed to the Sir William Dunn lecturership in pathology at Guy's Hospital. Since most of his interest up to this point had lain in pharmacology and physiology, he felt unprepared to tackle the new work without making a further study of the subject. Before taking up this appointment, therefore, he spent some months in Vienna and Freiburg studying pathology. The outbreak of war in 1914 found Laidlaw with a large hospital department to run and but little opportunity for research. He was very fully occupied in teaching and organizing the examination of post-mortem mater al at Guy's Hospital. Even these arduous duties could not suppress completely Laidlaw's ingenuity, and in 1915 he first described the use of hydrogen in spongy platinum to remove the last traces of oxygen from a culture tube and so greatly improve conditions for growing anaerobic bacteria, a method later developed by Dr. Paul Fildes and James McIntosh. In this war period also he collaborated again with Sir Henry Dale and with A. N. Richards, of Philadelphia, on the subject of histamine shock and its physiological relations. This work was widely acclaimed at the time, not only because of its intrinsic merit but also because it was thought to explain traumatic shock, a condition of the utmost importance in the war. While the investigation undoubtedly led to a great improvement in the treatment of wounded persons by transfusion of blood and other fluids, it has since become clear that the release of histamine from the injured tissue is not the cause of wound shock.

Laidlaw's work at Guy's Hospital ceased in 1922 when he joined the staff of the Medical Research Council at the National Institute for Medical Research. From then onwards he concentrated almost entirely on bacteriological and virus research. The virus disease first selected for investigation was dog distemper, because of the opportunity which it offered for experiment. With the assistance of George William Dunkin, M.R.C.V.S., he first found a means of transmitting the disease to ferrets, thus greatly widening the scope of the study, and before long conclusive evidence was obtained in support of Henri Carré's claim that the primary infective agent responsible for true dog distemper is a filterable virus. Two methods of inducing immunity to this disease in dogs were then developed. By the first method partial immunity was obtained by injection of the virus inactivated by treatment with formaldehyde, followed by a small injection of the active virus, which caused an abortive attack and left the animal with a strong and lasting immunity. By the second method the animal received simultaneous injections of the active virus and a serum rich in the protective antibodies. Again, permanent immunity was established.

Experience gained in this work laid the

foundation for Laidlaw's research on epidemic influenza. In collaboration with Dr. Christopher Howard Andrewes and Dr. Wilson Smith, he showed that the ferret was susceptible to the influenza virus as directly obtained from the human patient. By an accident one of the team became infected with influenza from one of the ferrets, thus completing the evidence that the infecting agent was transmissible in both directions. At a later stage the technique was modified and extended to mice. On the basis of this work Laidlaw and his colleagues proved that the infective agent of human epidemic influenza is a virus, a discovery which has been confirmed all over the world. The influenza work was not brought to the same satisfactory conclusion as the distemper research, partly because it was found that epidemics in different parts of the world are due to different viruses and partly because such epidemics are so unpredictable that large numbers of people have to be inoculated in order to be prepared for an outbreak which may or may not occur. American experience indicates, however, that some immunity can be built up by influenza virus vaccine.

Laidlaw was keenly interested in many other branches of medical science and he collaborated with Dr. Clifford Dobell in an investigation on parasitic amoebae. The first part of this investigation consisted in obtaining a new method for growing these amoebae profusely. The particular trick adopted was to use grains of rice starch in the medium as the supply of carbohydrate for the growing organisms. Having obtained rapidly growing cultures by this method, Dr. Dobell and Laidlaw then studied the action on such cultures of the alkaloids of ipecacuanha and thereby made an important contribution to knowledge of the treatment of amoebic dysentery by this drug. One of his chief characteristics was his ability and willingness out of his vast experience to advise and assist in research work those who consulted him on almost any problem. In 1936 he succeeded Stewart Ranken Douglas as deputy director of the National Institute for Medical Research and head of the department of pathology and bacteriology. Shortly after this time his health, never robust, began to fail, and he died suddenly in London of heart failure in the night of 19–20 March 1940, a day or two after his election into an honorary fellowship at St. John's College, Cambridge.

Laidlaw was elected F.R.S. in 1927, and received a Royal medal from the society in 1933 for his work on distemper in dogs; he was knighted in 1935 for his great contributions to medicine. He was unmarried. He had a modest and retiring nature and disliked publicity. Little of his work is published; he gave the Linacre lecture on 'Epidemic Influenza: a Virus Disease' in 1935, and the Rede lecture on 'Virus Disease and Viruses' at Cambridge in 1938.

[*The Times*, 23 March 1940; *Obituary Notices of Fellows of the Royal Society*, No. 9, January 1941 (bibliography and portrait); *British Medical Journal*, 1940, vol. i, p. 551 (portrait); *Lancet*, 1940, vol. i, p. 623 (portrait); personal knowledge.]

E. MELLANBY.

LAKE, SIR PERCY HENRY NOEL (1855–1940), lieutenant-general, was born at Tenby, Wales, 29 June 1855, the eldest son of Lieutenant-Colonel Percy Godfrey Botfield Lake, of Grenfell, Canada, 54th and 100th Regiments, by his wife, Margaret, second daughter of William Phillips, of Quebec. He was educated at Uppingham and gazetted to the 59th Foot (later the 2nd battalion, East Lancashire Regiment) in August 1873. His first experience of active service came in the first stage of the second Afghan war (1878–1879) where he became assistant field engineer, Southern Field Force, and gained a medal for the campaign. He passed into the Staff College as a captain and graduated with honours in 1884.

In the following year Lake accompanied the Sudan expedition as deputy-assistant-adjutant and later quartermaster-general with the forces of Sir Gerald Graham [q.v.], which were operating from Suakin against the dervishes, and he took part in the actions of Hasheen and Tofrek and in the advance on Tamai. For the campaign he was awarded the medal and clasp and the bronze star. Two years later (1887) he was appointed staff captain and deputy-assistant-adjutant-general for Intelligence at the War Office. After his three-year tenure of this office he acted as secretary to R. J. Lindsay, Lord Wantage [q.v.], chairman of the committee on terms of service in the army (1891); and he was promoted major in that year. In 1892 he was made deputy-assistant-adjutant-general at the headquarters of the Irish Command, Dublin district, but in 1893 he sailed for Canada to become quartermaster-general, Canadian Militia, and during the next five years did excellent work, receiving the brevet of colonel in 1899. The same year he went to India as assistant-quarter-master-general for intelligence duties at the headquarters of the army in India, but at the outbreak of the South African war in 1899 he was brought back to the War Office to become assistant-adjutant-general (afterwards assistant-quarter-master-general) for mobilization, and as chief staff officer II Army Corps. He was promoted colonel and appointed C.B. in 1902. He remained at the War Office until 1904, when he once more left for Canada to become chief of the General Staff, Canadian Militia. He was promoted major-general and appointed C.M.G. in 1905.

During the next three years Lake did much to increase the efficiency of the Militia and urged the formation of a general staff on the British army model. In 1908 he was appointed K.C.M.G. and nominated inspector-general, Canadian Militia, and chief military adviser to the Canadian government, appointments which he held until the end of 1910 when he returned to England. Early in 1911, with promotion to lieutenant-general, he was again sent to India as division commander (7th Meerut division), and in 1912 became chief of general staff, at Simla, India. During the next few years as a member of the 'army in India committee' he did much to build up that army and as a result a force was sent from India in 1915 to Mesopotamia to ensure the safety of the oilfields. After the first failure to relieve (Sir) Charles Townshend [q.v.], besieged in Kut el Amara, Lake became commander-in-chief in Mesopotamia and with the Tigris Force made a second attempt, which again failed. However, with large reinforcements he prepared for a fresh campaign, but in August 1916 (Sir) F. S. Maude [q.v.] took over and Lake came home to give evidence before the Mesopotamia commission. Maude testified to his excellent foundation work and he was appointed K.C.B. (1916) and given a post in the Ministry of Munitions in May 1917.

Two and a half years later, in November 1919, Lake retired from the army and returned to Canada to make his home in Victoria, British Columbia. From 1913 to 1920 he was honorary colonel of the East Lancashire Regiment. In 1891 he married Hester Fanny, only daughter of Henry Woodyer, architect, of Grafham, Surrey; there were no children of the marriage.

He died at his Canadian home 17 November 1940.

[*The Times*, 20 November 1940; F. J. Moberly, (Official) *History of the Great War. The Campaign in Mesopotamia 1914–1918*, 4 vols., 1923–1927; *Who's Who in Canada*, 1927.]

C. V. OWEN.

LAMB, SIR HORACE (1849–1934), mathematician, was born at Stockport, near Manchester, 27 November 1849, the second son of John Lamb (a cotton-mill foreman, of Stockport, and an inventor of an improvement of the spinning machine), who died while Horace was a child. His mother, whose maiden name was Elizabeth Rangeley, married again, and Horace was brought up by her sister Mrs. Holland, kind but severely puritan; she sent him to Stockport Grammar School, where he gained a lasting love for the Greek and Latin poets from his excellent headmaster, the Rev. Charles Hamilton, whose sister-in-law, Elizabeth, daughter of Simon Foot, merchant, of Blackrock, co. Dublin, he married in 1875.

After leaving school Lamb's main studies were in mathematics, first, for a year, under Thomas Barker [q.v.] at the Owens College, Manchester, and then at Cambridge, where he attended the lectures of J. Clerk Maxwell [q.v.] and (Sir) G. G. Stokes [q.v.], and in 1872 was second wrangler and second Smith's prizeman. His college was Trinity, of which he was successively scholar (1869–1872), fellow and lecturer (1872–1875), and honorary fellow (1920–1934). For recreation he took long country walks; later he travelled widely, especially in Italy and Switzerland, where he was an early climber of the Matterhorn. He read much in French, German, and Italian, and had many artistic interests.

After three years' teaching at Cambridge, where the rule of celibacy for college fellows was still in force, Lamb went out with his wife to Adelaide, Australia, as professor of mathematics at the newly founded university there. In 1885 he returned to the Owens College (which had become a constituent member of the Victoria University of Manchester) to succeed his old teacher Barker. There and at the university he served as professor of pure, and later also of applied, mathematics until 1920, remaining five years beyond the normal retiring age, because of the war of 1914–1918.

Lamb was a born teacher, and the excellence and inspiration of his lectures to successive generations of Manchester students of mathematics, engineering, and physics were an important factor in the career of many of his able pupils, of whom the most distinguished was Sir Arthur Eddington. When on his eightieth birthday his former students paid him a tribute, his reply included the words: 'I did try "to make things clear", first to myself (an important point) and then to my students, and somehow to make these dry bones live.' He was very lucid both in his lectures and in his many books, of which the most notable was his treatise *Hydrodynamics* (1895), first published in 1879 as *A Treatise on the . . . Motion of Fluids* and successively enlarged in several editions and translations. In lecturing and writing his choice of topics and mode of treatment were very judicious, equally in pure and in applied mathematics.

Lamb's special subjects were hydrodynamics, sound, elasticity, and mechanics, on all of which he wrote books, as well as many original memoirs. He wrote also an excellent elementary textbook *Infinitesimal Calculus* (1897), which combines great clarity with mathematical rigour. In his *Hydrodynamics* he selected the main researches and results from a great mass of publications, and brilliantly presented them in a unified elegant treatment, himself filling in many gaps and making many valuable improvements and extensions by his own researches, as, for example, in the theory of tides and waves.

Among the special problems to the solution of which Lamb made important contributions the following may be mentioned: the motion of perforated solids in a perfect liquid; the fortnightly tide; waves on deep water due to a local disturbance of its surface; tidal phase differences; the motion of a sphere or cylinder in a viscous liquid; the oscillations of a viscous spheroid; vibrations of elastic spheres and spherical shells; electromagnetic induction in spheres and spherical shells; the vibration of thin curved plates and shells; the deflection of gravity by tidal loading of the earth's surface; waves in air, allowing for the upward decrease of density; the propagation of earthquake tremors along the surface of an elastic solid; and the diffraction of light at the straight edge of a semi-infinite plane.

In the words of his contemporary A. E. H. Love [q.v.]: 'His writings call up before one the picture of an extremely acute and wonderfully alert mind, endowed with a profound knowledge of the facts of physics, especially on its dynamical side, keenly interested in the work of others, particularly when it had a bearing on any matter of mechanics or wave-transmission, equipped with an exceptionally varied and powerful mathematical technique, and ever on the look-out for topics on which his analysis could be employed for the promotion of natural knowledge.'

In 1884 Lamb was elected a fellow of the Royal Society, which later awarded him a Royal medal (1902) and its highest honour, the Copley medal (1923). Among his many other honours were a knighthood (1931) and the presidency of the British Association (1925) and of the London Mathematical Society (1902–1904), which latter awarded him its De Morgan medal in 1911, and of the Manchester Literary and Philosophical Society. He received honorary doctorates from the universities of Glasgow, Oxford, Cambridge, Dublin, St. Andrews, Manchester, and Sheffield.

On his retirement from Manchester Lamb returned to Cambridge, where the university made him an honorary (Rayleigh) lecturer; he lectured there for fourteen years. He retained his high mathematical powers, which in most mathematicians wane with age, and continued to produce elegant and important memoirs. During the war of 1914–1918 he had given valuable help to the Admiralty and to aeronautical research, and he continued to serve the latter for a time (1921–1927) as a member of the Aeronautical Research Committee. On many other councils and committees also, as previously at Manchester during his long membership of the university senate, his wide knowledge and the wisdom of his outlook were highly esteemed. He died at Cambridge 4 December 1934.

Lamb was a man of great personal dignity, somewhat awe-inspiring to youth, but on closer acquaintance kindly, humane, humorous, highly cultured, conservative in temper, with wide interests and many contacts. His wife, who had borne him three sons and four daughters, died in 1930. One of his sons, Henry, a distinguished artist, painted a notable portrait of him, which was presented in 1913 to the university of Manchester.

[*The Times*, 5 December 1934; *Obituary Notices of Fellows of the Royal Society*, No. 4, December 1935 (portrait); personal knowledge.]   S. CHAPMAN.

LAMINGTON, second BARON (1860–1940). [See BAILLIE, CHARLES WALLACE ALEXANDER NAPIER ROSS COCHRANE-.]

LANE POOLE, REGINALD (1857–1939), historian. [See POOLE.]

LANE-POOLE, STANLEY EDWARD (1854–1931), orientalist and historian. [See POOLE.]

LANGDON, STEPHEN HERBERT (1876–1937), Assyriologist, was born at Ida, near Monroe, Michigan, in the United States, 8 May 1876, the elder son of George Knowles Langdon, farmer, by his wife, Abigail Elizabeth Hassinger. He was educated at the high school at Monroe and the university of Michigan at Ann Arbor and also took degrees at the Union Theological Seminary and Columbia University in New York; he then (1904–1906) studied in Paris, where he was ordained deacon (1905) in the American Episcopal Church (never proceeding beyond that order), and (1906–1907) at Leipzig.

In 1908 Miss Mary Wallace Shillito offered £10,000 to the university of Oxford to found a readership in Assyriology on condition that Langdon was elected; appointed on these terms, he remained in Oxford for the rest of his life. In 1913 he became a naturalized British subject, and in 1919 was given the title of professor on the retirement of A. H. Sayce [q.v.]. He was a voluminous editor and interpreter of Sumerian and Assyrio-Babylonian texts, but his work was marred by inaccuracy caused by undue haste and a defective sense of language; he wrote fluently in French and German as well as English, but all his writing betrayed his mixed education. At the same time scholarship owes him a great debt for much pioneer work, especially in making an immense number of cuneiform tablets accessible for the first time; and many flashes of brilliance lit up if they did not always solve the numerous problems offered by these often exceedingly obscure texts. He also found time to raise funds for the excavation of Kish and spent two seasons (1923, 1925) personally directing the work at some risk to his health: these excavations not only made considerable additions to early Mesopotamian history but also greatly enriched the collections of the Ashmolean Museum at Oxford and the Field Museum at Chicago, which provided part of the funds. Further, before Langdon's time, all English Assyriologists were either self-taught or educated on the continent, and his chief merit was perhaps to have built up an English school of Assyriologists.

Langdon married in 1925 May Adelaide, younger daughter of Thomas Gregory, J.P., of Cardiff, owner of the Garth engineering works, but had no issue. He was elected a fellow of the British Academy in 1931 and a corresponding member of the Académie des Inscriptions et Belles-Lettres in 1933; he was also Schweich lecturer of the British Academy in 1933 and Singer-Polignac lecturer at the Collège de France in 1934. He died suddenly at Oxford 19 May 1937.

[*The Times*, 21 May 1937; *Oxford Magazine*, 27 May 1937; C. J. Gadd, *Stephen Herbert Langdon, 1876–1937* in *Proceedings* of the British Academy, vol. xxiii, 1937; personal knowledge.]   G. R. DRIVER.

LANSBURY, GEORGE (1859–1940), labour leader and politician, was born in a toll-house on the turnpike road between Halesworth and Lowestoft 21 February 1859. He was the second son of George Lansbury, a railway sub-contractor in the employment of Thomas Brassey [q.v.], by his wife, Mary Ann Ferriss, of Clyro, Radnorshire. His connexion with East London began in 1868 when his parents moved, after successive periods at Sydenham and Greenwich, to Bethnal Green. Later they settled in Whitechapel. His education, received at elementary schools in these four places, ended at the age of fourteen. For several years he was employed in unloading coal trucks for the Great Eastern Railway under a contract originally held by his father.

In 1880, when he was twenty-one, Lansbury married Elizabeth Jane (died 1933), elder daughter of Isaac Brine, owner of a sawmill and veneer works in Whitechapel, by whom he had four sons and eight daughters: two sons and two daughters predeceased him. With his wife and their three children he sailed in 1884 for Australia to seek his fortune. Next year, however, the young couple were back in London, where he accepted a partnership in his father-in-law's business, and made his home in Bow, where he lived for the rest of his life. Lansbury now came under the influence of the Christian socialists. This was to determine the whole course of his career, and he threw himself energetically into local politics, at first as a radical. In 1890, however, he was converted to socialism, and William Morris and H. M. Hyndman [qq.v.] soon took him into the earliest British group of socialists, which had been known since 1884 as the Social Democratic Federation. In 1892 he was elected to the local Board of Guardians; and three years later he made (at Walworth) the first of five unsuccessful attempts to enter parliament. He was, as a Poplar guardian, a moving spirit in the setting up of the Hollesley Bay (Suffolk) colony for unemployed men; as a member of the Central (Unemployed) Body for London he completed his remarkable knowledge of the conditions of life and labour in the metropolis, and from 1905 to 1909 was a member of the royal commission on the Poor Laws and was one of the four signatories of the famous minority Report. Returned to parliament as a labour member for the Bow and Bromley division of Poplar in December 1910, he resigned in 1912, in order to fight the seat as an independent on the straight issue of votes for women, a cause in which he was an ardent believer. This gallant effort failed and he was not back at Westminster until 1922, when he was again returned for Bow and Bromley and held the seat until his death. During the war, he was closely associated with the pacificist section of the labour party and a powerful defender of the conscientious objector. He had been one of those responsible for the creation of labour's first daily paper, the *Daily Herald* (1912); during the war, he edited a lively *Weekly Herald*, and in 1919 played a vigorous part in making it again a daily paper, which he edited during a series of difficult years.

For all his idealism Lansbury had a measure of practical sagacity and shrewdness; when the second labour government was formed in 1929, he was made first commissioner of Works, and the Lido in Hyde Park, among many other instances, will be a memorial of the work which he did for Londoners. As to the line he would take in the financial crisis of 1931, there could never be any doubt; on an issue which could be formulated as that of reducing or not reducing the allowances to the unemployed, he was for the unemployed. As the solitary survivor of Cabinet rank in the labour party after the election of 1931, he was chosen by the party to be leader of the opposition in the House of Commons; in that arduous post his warmth of heart and his unfaltering courage excited respect even from his opponents. In 1935, however, an issue arose which presented his pacificism with a formidable dilemma—that of the en-

forcement of sanctions against Italy in its attack on Abyssinia, a fellow member of the League of Nations. Although Lansbury had accepted the League as fundamental to the party's foreign policy, he now found it impossible to subscribe to the view that loyalty to the League might imply the use of force against an aggressor. At the conference held on the eve of the general election in 1935, finding himself in a small minority on this issue, he resigned the leadership. Opinions differed, and will continue to differ, about the wisdom of the policy of unilateral disarmament which he advocated on the ground that if Great Britain only would give a lead, other countries would be sure to follow. In 1935 in a volume of reminiscences entitled *Looking Backwards and Forwards*, his pacificist position is uncompromisingly set out; in another book, *My Quest for Peace* (1938), he describes a series of journeys to the capitals of Europe, in which, hoping against hope, he talked to the heads of states. As the shadow of war grew deeper, he retired more and more from active politics, and died in London 7 May 1940. He had been sworn of the Privy Council in 1929.

In his person, Lansbury was identified throughout his very active life with the East End of London, and was widely known as the John Bull of Poplar, a designation suggested in part by his appearance, the ruddy-complexioned face with its side-whiskers surmounting a tall, erect figure invariably clothed in a double-breasted blue serge suit, in part by the long battles associated with his public life in Poplar, when he and his colleagues on the council cheerfully went to prison rather than submit to the action of the Ministry of Health in surcharging the municipality for the high rates imposed during a period of severe unemployment. In his own person, and in the wide devotion which he inspired within the labour movement and beyond it, he represented the truth that the inspiration of British socialism is derived rather from the Bible than from Karl Marx. Whereas the lay-preachers in the movement are normally found among the nonconformists, Lansbury was throughout his life an Anglican whose links with theosophy and Indian religious movements made him sympathetic and tolerant to the most various creeds and faiths. Both his socialism and his pacificism sprang from strong spiritual conviction; both were potent rather than precise. His career can hardly be appreciated without some sense of his personality: this non-smoker and teetotaller was a man of powerful physique, genial, vigorous, companionable, hearty; the father of a large family, who attracted children and was attracted by them everywhere; a man who could arouse great popular audiences to enthusiasm as, without a trace of embarrassment, he talked, in a great booming voice, of love as the sole basis for national and international action.

[*The Times*, 8 May 1940; George Lansbury, *My Life*, 1928; personal knowledge.]

MARY AGNES HAMILTON.

LÁSZLÓ DE LOMBOS, PHILIP ALEXIUS (1869–1937), painter, whose original name was FÜLÖP ELEK VON LÁSZLÓ, was born in or near Budapest 28 April 1869, the eldest son of Adolphus László, tailor, and was brought up in poor circumstances, having very little formal education. While still a mere child, under thirteen years old, he worked for a scene-painter and learned photographic retouching. In his adolescence he studied at the Industrial Art School and the National Drawing School, Budapest.

At the age of nineteen László won a state scholarship which took him to Venice. After a brief stay he returned to Budapest, whence he went on to Munich Academy, studying there under Alexander von Liezen-Mayer: he subsequently won the Bavarian silver medal in 1892. There followed a spell at the Académie Julian, in Paris, under Jules Lefebvre and Benjamin Constant. Back in Hungary in 1891, he won the grand prize of the Hungarian Art Society. He specialized in portraiture, attracted attention in 1894 by his portrait of Prince Ferdinand of Bulgaria, and in 1899 painted the Emperor Francis Joseph and Prince Chlodwig Hohenlohe-Schillingsfürst, and in 1900 Pope Leo XIII. For the last two pictures he was awarded gold medals at the Paris Salon and the earlier one placed him *hors concours* there.

László now pushed rapidly forward into the position of a sought-after portrait-painter. He moved to London in 1907, and his services were soon in great demand among the famous. He painted King Edward VII in that year, and built up an enormous practice which in due course included such sitters as Theodore Roosevelt, Lord Roberts, and Lord Haldane. He was appointed M.V.O. in 1910, and an hereditary nobleman of Hungary in 1912; he was officially honoured by many other countries; and on his deathbed he was awarded the order of Matthias Corvinus, Hungary's highest honour for art.

László was not naturalized as a British subject until 29 August 1914. During the war of 1914–1918 he committed sundry indiscretions, such as sending money to his relatives in Hungary and using the Dutch diplomatic bag for correspondence. He was interned in September 1917, and in June 1919 a naturalization (revocation) committee sat to determine whether his certificate should be revoked. It found, however, no evidence of disaffection or disloyalty, and so the naturalization was upheld.

Once the passions of war had subsided, László quickly got into his stride again. Many of his friends felt that the accusations of disloyalty had been provoked by the spite of jealous rivals; in any event his life had for long been moulded in the British pattern. He had married in 1900 Lucy Madeleine, sixth daughter of Henry Guinness, of Burton Hall, Stillorgan, co. Dublin, and had five sons, who were all brought up to speak English only; his daughter died in infancy. He worked busily on at his Hampstead home until his death there 22 November 1937.

László had a pleasing, courteous, and exuberant manner, and was very popular in society. His status as a portrait-painter is not with the more eminent masters, for he had neither deep psychological penetration nor a highly nervous and individual line. But he was very far from being a mere journeyman. A rapid worker, who could throw off a stylish portrait in an hour or two, he used his rectangle of canvas to the best advantage, produced an impeccable likeness, and imparted an air of distinction to his sitters even though not all of them possessed it.

László held various one-man shows, at the French Gallery, Messrs. Agnew's, Messrs. Knoedler's, and elsewhere, and a posthumous exhibition was held at Messrs. Wildenstein's. He joined the Royal Society of British Artists in 1907 as an honorary member and for a time acted as president. He also belonged to the Royal Society of Portrait Painters, was a fellow of the Royal Society of Arts, and was elected a vice-president just before his death. To the 'How to Do It' series of *The Studio* he contributed (in collaboration with Mr. Alfred Lys Baldry) a monograph on *Painting a Portrait* (1934); and a paper on 'The Art of our Day' (read before the Royal Society of Arts in 1936) expressed outspoken views on the more eccentric schools.

László is represented at the Tate Gallery, the Luxembourg, and the Galleria d'Arte Moderna in Rome. In 1911 he painted a self-portrait, by the request of the Italian government, for the Uffizi Gallery, Florence.

[*The Times*, 24, 25, 26, 27, 28 June 1919, 23, 24, 25 November 1937; *Daily Telegraph*, 23 November 1937; Owen Rutter, *Portrait of a Painter. The Authorized Life of Philip de László*, 1939; *The Work of P. A. de László*, with a foreword by A. L. Baldry, 1921; *The Studio*, September 1923; Ulrich Thieme and Felix Becker, *Allgemeines Lexikon der Bildenden Künstler*, vol. xxii, 1928.]

HERBERT B. GRIMSDITCH.

LAWRENCE, ALFRED TRISTRAM, first BARON TREVETHIN (1843–1936), lord chief justice of England, was born at Pontypool 24 November 1843, the eldest son of David Lawrence, surgeon, of Pontypool, by his wife, Elizabeth, daughter of Charles Morgan Williams. Intending to study medicine, he left Mill Hill School early, but at nineteen, having watched Hardinge Giffard (later Lord Halsbury) and Henry Matthews (later Lord Llandaff, qq.v.) in a case in which some property of his father was concerned, he asked leave to go to the bar. He entered Trinity Hall, Cambridge (of which he was elected an honorary fellow in 1908), and was placed second in the first class in the law tripos of 1866. In 1869 he was called to the bar by the Middle Temple (of which he became a bencher in 1904 and treasurer in 1914) and in due course joined the Oxford circuit. He soon acquired a busy and varied practice on circuit and in London, and was accepted as a sound lawyer and a reasonable and adroit advocate, not only by his clients but by the judges before whom he appeared. From first to last he had a ready eye for the essential principles of his case, and a gift of clear and persistent exposition. In 1882 he was made junior counsel to the Admiralty and in 1885 recorder of the royal borough of Windsor. In this office, which he held until his elevation to the bench, he became the friend and unofficial adviser of the dean, Randall Davidson [q.v.]; and the future archbishop consulted him on many of the problems arising in the court of Queen Victoria. Indeed, throughout his life, a host of friends, young and old, sought and received Lawrence's wise and sympathetic counsel.

Family responsibilities were probably the reason why Lawrence delayed to take silk until 1897, and he was already in the sixties when in 1904 he was raised to the bench. The appointment received the cordial and unanimous approval of the profession and was amply justified in the result. His grasp of essentials both in fact and law was such that scarcely any of his decisions came up for criticism or revision to the House of Lords. His mind was clear and vigorous, and free from any trace of prejudice or eccentricity. His appreciation of principle was intuitive, and he had a thorough knowledge of human nature. His patience and deliberation ensured not only that every case was fully and thoroughly heard but that every litigant should feel that it was so. It was in April 1921, at the age of seventy-seven, that he was appointed to the office of lord chief justice of England, vacant owing to acceptance by R. D. Isaacs, Lord Reading [q.v.], of the viceroyalty of India. He was immediately sworn of the Privy Council and created Baron Trevethin, of Blaengawney, Monmouthshire, in August of the same year.

In March 1922, in his seventy-ninth year, Trevethin resigned his great office. His tenure of it had been too brief to leave any great mark on the history of the English justiciary, but it was long enough to enhance his reputation as a judge of sound wisdom and wide experience. He also rendered important public service as president of the Railway and Canal Commission, of the War Compensation Court from 1920 to 1922, and of the Admiralty Transport Arbitration Board from 1922. There can be no doubt that his gifts would have been of high value in the judicial functions of the House of Lords had not sensitiveness of his incipient deafness made him shrink from inflicting inconvenience on others. Accordingly, he retired to his beautiful home in Breconshire and lived a country life for fourteen more years. On 3 August 1936 he was fishing in the Wye above Builth Wells when he died at the great age of ninety-two.

In 1875 Trevethin married his cousin, Jessie Elizabeth (died 1931), daughter of George Lawrence, of Moreton Court, near Hereford, and sister of Sir Walter Lawrence [q.v.], and had four sons, the youngest of whom predeceased him. The eldest son, Alfred Clive, became Treasury solicitor and king's proctor, and died in 1926, leaving a daughter. The second son, Charles Trevor (born 1879), succeeded his father as second baron; and the third son, Geoffrey, made a judge of the King's Bench division in 1932, became a lord justice of appeal in 1945, and after presiding over the trial of the war criminals at Nuremberg was raised to the peerage as Baron Oaksey, and appointed a lord of appeal in ordinary in 1947. Lord Trevethin also had one daughter.

In his young days Trevethin won distinction as a horseman, not only in the hunting field but as a successful rider in point-to-point races and steeplechasing; in his middle years he was a well-known and popular figure on the golf links, particularly at Nairn and Woking; and in his retirement he was a devoted angler. It is sufficiently remarkable to record that, at the age of ninety-two, he was still capable of killing heavy salmon in the Wye.

A portrait of Lord Trevethin by R. G. Eves hangs in the Middle Temple; there are also portraits by Sir William Orpen and J. Hanson Walker at Abernant, Builth Wells, his home (now the residence of his son), and another, by A. Cluysenaar, at Middleton House, near Banbury. A cartoon of him by Spy' appeared in *Vanity Fair* 26 October 1907.

[*The Times*, 4 August 1936; private information; personal knowledge.]

NIGEL G. DAVIDSON.

LAWRENCE, THOMAS EDWARD (1888–1935), known as 'Lawrence of Arabia', was born at Tremadoc, North Wales, 15 August 1888, the second in a family of five sons. His father, Thomas Robert Chapman (who had assumed the name of Lawrence), the younger son of an Anglo-Irish landowning family, had followed up a sound classical schooling with an agricultural course and some years of continental travel and mountaineering; he lived on private means permitting of comfort though not luxury; became keenly interested in church architecture and in photography; and was an enthusiastic yachtsman, shot, and (from the early days of the safety bicycle) cyclist. His mother, Sarah Maden, the daughter of a Sunderland engineer, was brought up in the Highlands and afterwards in Skye. Both parents were devout, evangelical members of the Church of England.

Having learnt his letters from hearing his elder brother taught them, Lawrence read newspapers and books at the age of four, began Latin at six, and entered the Oxford High School at eight. From the age of twelve he covered his tuition expenses by scholarships at school and a Welsh exhibition at Jesus College, Oxford. Deep love of literature, archaeology, and architecture, particularly of the Middle Ages, led him to choose as a thesis for the modern history school 'The Influence of the Crusades on European Military Architecture—to the End of the XIIth Century' (published in 1936 as *Crusader Castles*). After bicycle tours throughout England and France he journeyed alone, on foot and without baggage, through Syria, Palestine, and the southern fringe of Turkey. In 1910 he obtained a first class in history, partly on his thesis, and was awarded a four years' senior demyship for travel by Magdalen College at the instance of D. G. Hogarth [q.v.], Lawrence's lifelong friend, who in 1911 sent him on the British Museum expedition that was excavating the Hittite city of Carchemish. There, after an interval in Egypt, he returned next year, assisting (Sir) C. Leonard Woolley until the outbreak of war in 1914; of this he wrote, 'it was the best life I ever lived'. He acquired some Arabic, together with the habit of eating Arab food and wearing Arab clothes. From January to March 1914 he and Woolley carried out an archaeological survey of the Negeb and country south of Beersheba for the Palestine Exploration Fund (which in 1915 published their report under the title of *Wilderness of Zin*), joining Captain Stewart Newcombe, who was already surveying that area for the War Office.

On the outbreak of war in 1914 Lawrence, being below standard height (then raised to 5 feet 5 inches) obtained but a sedentary commission in the Geographical Section, General Staff of the War Office. Dispatched to Military Intelligence in Egypt when Turkey joined the central powers, he spent two years in what was later called the Arab Bureau, which became by 1916 the Intelligence Service for the Arab campaign. In the October of that year he accompanied to Jidda (Sir) Ronald Storrs, who had initiated the negotiations which culminated in the Arab Revolt, and presented Lawrence to the Sharif Abdullah, second son of Husain, Grand Sharif of Mecca, and obtained from Husain an introduction to his third son, Faisal, who at that moment was retreating discomfited before a Turkish advance from Medina. Turkish strength in the Hejaz still amounted to nearly 15,000 rifles, 10,000 of which held

Medina, 2,500 the railway between Medina and Amman, including the strongly garrisoned port of Aqaba, and 1,200 the port of Wajh. The Arabs in their anxiety pressed for the dispatch to the Hejaz of a British brigade, which Lawrence, on his return to Egypt, opposed as too cumbersome, and was himself dispatched as liaison officer and adviser to Faisal, whose confidence he soon won and whose tribal levies he helped to organize.

The secret of Lawrence's ascendancy, physical, intellectual, and moral, is best explained in his own words: 'Among the Arabs there were no distinctions, traditional or natural, except the unconscious power given a famous shaikh by virtue of his accomplishment: and they taught me that no man could be their leader except he ate the ranks' food, wore their clothes, lived level with them, and yet appeared better in himself.' Preferring to contain rather than to assault or starve the 10,000 Turks in Medina and thus compel the enemy to tie down additional troops to maintain them, Lawrence induced Faisal to threaten their communications by moving north and attacking the Hejaz railway, which thenceforth passed progressively out of effective Turkish control. It was his theory and practice that the Arabs should become 'an influence (as we might be), an idea, a thing invulnerable, intangible, without front or back, drifting about like gas, a vapour, blowing where we listed' . . . 'tip and run: not pushes, but strokes . . . the smallest force in the quickest time at the farthest place'. After the storming of Wajh Lawrence left Faisal there to establish his headquarters, and rode on into the interior, rousing the northern tribes and passing behind the enemy lines in Syria. Returning, he fell in with a force of the Howaitat tribe, under the celebrated Auda Abu Tayi, with it routed a Turkish battalion near Ma'an, and in August 1917 took and occupied Aqaba for Faisal. Having thus brought the whole Hejaz south of Aqaba, excepting Medina, under Arab-British control, Lawrence was promoted major and was awarded British and French decorations which he subsequently refused.

The climax of Lawrence's campaign began when, hurrying to Egypt to obtain supplies for starving Aqaba, he offered Sir Edmund (later Viscount) Allenby [q.v.], the newly arrived commander-in-chief, 'to hobble the enemy by his preaching if given stores and arms and a fund of two hundred thousand sovereigns to con-vince and control his converts', and Allenby briefly replied: 'Well, I will do for you what I can.' Lawrence was given all he asked, and the fund was later increased to half a million pounds; thenceforward he directed Arab levies, now brigaded with the British Expeditionary Force and operating as a mobile right wing. Having defeated the Turks heavily in the model engagement of Tafila, he concentrated upon scientific train-wrecking with such success that Medina became virtually isolated, and the Turks, their rail-guards extended to Aleppo, offered a reward of £20,000 for the capture of 'al Urans, destroyer of engines', in whose protection sixty out of his bodyguard of ninety Arabs lost their lives. Towards the end of 1917, while reconnoitring alone the railway junction of Deraa, Lawrence was seized (but not recognized), forcibly enlisted in the Turkish army, and beaten senseless, but by dawn he had escaped. Next summer he persuaded Faisal to leave Aqaba in favour of Qasr Azrak for the advance upon Damascus. Finally, having broken up the Turkish Fourth Army east of the Jordan, Lawrence led the Arab troops up to Damascus on 1 October 1918, some hours ahead of the British, chivalrously allowing Sharif Nasir to precede his entry; and preserved it against serious threats of reverting to the Turks, until Allenby arrived three days later. 'In the crucial weeks while Allenby's stroke was being prepared . . . nearly half of the Turkish forces [some 2,000 sabres and 12,000 rifles] south of Damascus . . . were distracted by the Arab forces. With some relatively light assistance from Chaytor's Force these Turkish masses were paralysed by an Arab contingent that counted less than 3,000 men, and of which the actual expeditionary core was barely 600 strong. It would be difficult to find in the whole history of war as extraordinary a case of economy of force in distraction.' The whole payments for the Arab revolt amounted to four millions in gold, of which about half came back in purchases of food and clothing.

His task done, Lawrence retired. 'The East was sucked dry. Never outstay a climax' was his light self-dismissal, behind which, however, pressed heavily the physical toll of the sun, the snow, and the sand, battle, murder, and, never to be redeemed or forgotten, the climax of outrage in Deraa. He reached England on Armistice Day after four years' absence, and having done his utmost (though not to his own satisfaction) for Faisal and the Arab cause at the Peace Conference, settled down to the writing of his adventures. In November 1919 he was elected a research fellow of All Souls College, Oxford, and in 1921 was called by Mr. Churchill as political adviser to the newly formed Middle Eastern Department in the Colonial Office. The partnership was entirely successful. Faisal (whose ejection by the French from Damascus had been the culmination of Lawrence's disillusionment) was made king of Iraq, which was soon to become an independent state: and shortly afterwards the threat to Palestine of an unsettled Arab Transjordan was removed by the appointment of Faisal's elder brother, Abdullah, as its ruling prince on the condition that he, and his future subjects, did not interfere with French-mandated Syria. Feeling that (apart from Syria and Palestine, both already committed to the League of Nations) his 'Arab honour' was satisfied, and that he had gained his 'outlet' from public affairs, Lawrence insisted on his release from the Colonial Office in June 1922, and in August enlisted in the ranks of the Royal Air Force, changing his name to J. H. Ross to escape publicity, and again in 1923 to T. E. Shaw. This latter change was legalized by deed poll in 1927. Discharged from the Royal Air Force because his identity became disclosed, he sought refuge in the Tank Corps, but in August 1925 returned to the Royal Air Force. This took him in 1926 to the North-Western Frontier of India whence, in deference to Russian suspicions, he was recalled in 1928. As an aircraftman, neither attaining nor desiring officer's rank, he spent happily the last six years of his service, latterly testing, supervising, and even designing high-speed and power motor-craft at Plymouth, and later on the Solent. His service expired at Bridlington in February 1935, and he was retired at the age of forty-six, sad at leaving his work and comrades in the Royal Air Force. He bicycled to Clouds Hill, his three-roomed cottage at Bovington, Dorset, and remained there, unsettled, and evading the appointments thrust upon him in connexion with the expansion of the Royal Air Force, yet unable to enjoy his unaccustomed leisure which he planned to spend in exploring, by bicycle, the scenery and monuments of England. On 13 May, swerving on his powerful motor-cycle to avoid two boys bicycling abreast, he was violently thrown, and after lingering unconscious for five days, died in Bovington Camp Hospital 19 May 1935. He never married.

Lawrence was slightly but strongly built. His growth had been checked by breaking a leg in his 'teens. His forehead was high; the line of his face vertical and, in proportion to the depth of his head, long. His hair was long and fair and unruly, parted and brushed sideways. He had a straight nose, piercing blue eyes, a firm full mouth, strong square chin, and fine, careful, accomplished hands. He could be the best company in the world, holding his own with Mr. Churchill or Mr. Bernard Shaw: he could also retire within himself in any company. He preferred the society of men to that of women, with very few exceptions, and had friends in all classes. Books gave him almost as much companionship, and he was widely read in French, Latin, and Greek, as well as in English. He was a judge of painting, sculpture, architecture, and craftsmanship of every kind; and had a true appreciation of music, which he trained and gratified on a large collection of carefully tended gramophone records. He preferred neither to smoke nor to drink alcohol, and ate sparingly; but he yielded himself almost voluptuously to the 'dope' of high speed, on the swiftest motor-cycles. At eighty or ninety miles per hour he achieved 'a sense of moulding the hills and dales'.

Unique in kind as were Lawrence's exploits, their chance of historic survival would have been uncertain had he not himself recorded them in his brilliant and arresting *Seven Pillars of Wisdom* (1935) which was twice re-written during the years 1919 and 1920, after the original manuscript had been lost. Into his style, based originally upon *Travels in Arabia Deserta* (1888) by the venerated C. M. Doughty [q.v.], Lawrence poured the conscious, conscientious devotion of the artist-craftsman which he had lavished upon his maps, his machinery, and his plans for battle. 'Words', he wrote, 'get richer every time they are deliberately used … but only when deliberately used', and again, more significantly, 'Writing has been my inmost self all my life, and I can never put my full strength into anything else.' Lawrence would not have the book published in his lifetime, but issued in 1926 for subscription about a hundred copies superbly printed and illustrated by the best artists of the day. The loss of

£11,000 over this thirty guineas issue was more than covered by his abridged version, *The Revolt in the Desert*, published next year (1927) at thirty shillings: but the surplus was given to charity. Lawrence also organized the re-publication in 1921 (with an admirable introduction) of Doughty's *Arabia Deserta* (the only fruit of his residence at All Souls) and made in 1924 a pseudonymous version, *The Forest Giant*, of *Le Gigantesque* by A. le Corbeaux, and under his own name a prose translation of the Odyssey, commissioned from the United States of America and published in 1932. He wrote a remarkable, if sometimes brutal, picture of his early days in the Royal Air Force, entitled *The Mint*, of which, however, he forbade publication until 1950, although a copyright edition of fifty copies (ten of which were for sale, prohibitively priced) was arranged in America in 1926.

None can begin to realize the unsuspected, the bewildering variety and versatility of Lawrence, before as well as after his Arabian exploits, until he has read *The Letters of T. E. Lawrence*, selected and edited by Mr. David Garnett in 1938. It has indeed been said that he would have survived (as would Edward Fitzgerald without *Omar Khayyam*) if only as a letter-writer. The letters emphasize the strange blend of contrasts and oppositions that made up his elusive, enigmatic, and paradoxical personality. Imperious but retiring, logical yet intuitive, profoundly impressive and provokingly puckish, on equal terms with field-marshals and Cabinet ministers, great writers, mechanics, scholars, and slaves, he bequeathed the example of one who combined physical prowess and courage under the open sky with passionate self-dedication to the testament of the great humanities, which he chose to enjoy in poverty rather than hazard the artificiality and time-wasting servitude of high position; even without his work, without his book, he was a standard and a touchstone of reality in life.

Among the portraits of Lawrence are several by Augustus John, including a painting in the National Portrait Gallery, and a pastel by Eric Kennington at All Souls College, Oxford, made for *Seven Pillars of Wisdom*. The portrait painted by James McBey soon after Lawrence's entry into Damascus hangs in the Imperial War Museum. There is a bronze bust by Eric Kennington in the crypt of St. Paul's Cathedral, and a posthumous effigy, also by Eric Kennington, in St. Martin's church, Wareham.

[*The Times*, 20 May 1935; T. E. Lawrence, *Seven Pillars of Wisdom*, 1935, *Secret Despatches from Arabia*, 1939, *Oriental Assembly*, 1939, and *Men in Print*, 1940; B. H. Liddell Hart, *T. E. Lawrence*, 1934; *The Letters of T. E. Lawrence*, edited by David Garnett, 1938; Charles Edmunds, *T. E. Lawrence*, 1935; R. H. Kiernan, *Lawrence of Arabia*, 1936; Vyvyan Richards, *T. E. Lawrence*, 1939; Clare Sydney Smith, *The Golden Reign*, 1940; Elizabeth W. Duval, *T. E. Lawrence, A Bibliography*, 1938; B. H. Liddell Hart and R. Graves, *T. E. Lawrence to his Biographers*, 1938; Sir Ronald Storrs, *Orientations*, 1937; *T. E. Lawrence, by his Friends*, edited by A. W. Lawrence, 1937; personal knowledge.]

RONALD STORRS.

LAWRENCE, SIR WALTER ROPER, first baronet (1857–1940), Indian civil servant, was born at Moreton Court, near Hereford, 9 February 1857, the fifth son of George Lawrence, J.P., of Moreton, by his second wife, Catharine, daughter of Edward Lewis, of Wenvoe, Glamorganshire. He was educated at Cheltenham College and passed first into the Indian civil service in 1877. After two years' probation at Balliol College, Oxford, he went to India and began his official experience as assistant commissioner in the Kurram, where he saw the closing stages of the second Afghan war. With his brilliant record he escaped any long period of district work, which was apt to narrow the outlook of the Indian civil servant, and his opportunity came in 1889 when he was appointed settlement commissioner in Kashmir. A settlement—the adjustment of the revenue dues between the cultivator and the state—may well make or mar the career of any civilian, especially when carried out in an Indian state where the susceptibilities of the ruling house have to be weighed. Lawrence emerged triumphantly; his work was good and stood the test of time; the volume in which he recorded his experiences, *The Valley of Kashmir* (1895), remains a standard work.

When the highest offices in the service were opened to him, Lawrence abandoned his Indian career and returned to England in 1896 to be chief agent to H. A. B. Russell, Duke of Bedford [q.v.], until Lord Curzon recalled him to India at the end of 1898 to be his private secretary. Although less in the public eye, Lawrence's services in this post were of the highest order. He was the emollient between a great viceroy, impatient to carry through his first twelve reforms, and an administration which resented being hustled; yet his methods were unobtrusive; he never posed as the secretary who was 'running' the viceroy,

Five years later Lawrence again left India and embarked on active business and public work in England. India reclaimed him in 1905-1906, for in the previous year he had been appointed chief of the staff to the Prince and Princess of Wales on their visit, and his tact and accessibility, his wide knowledge of India and the ruling princes, contributed materially to the success of that long and exacting tour. There followed years of continuous activity in England, including a short period (1907-1909) as member of the Council of India; he resigned because it interfered on a narrow ruling with his business interests. He was one of the elder statesmen, always called in or consulted when Indian affairs were under consideration, the trusted counsellor of ministers and of all who sought guidance on India. He gathered up his experiences in a last book, *The India we Served* (1928), which is stamped with the mellow wisdom and generous appreciation of India and its peoples so characteristic of all his service.

Lawrence was appointed K.C.I.E. in 1903 and G.C.I.E. in 1906, in which year he was created a baronet in recognition of his work during the royal tour. In 1917 he was appointed C.B. and G.C.V.O. in 1918. He married in 1885 Lilian Gertrude (died 1929), daughter of John Gwynne James, of Ayleston Hill, Hereford, and had two sons. He died at Wokingham 25 May 1940, and was succeeded as second baronet by his elder son, Roland (born 1886).

A cartoon of Lawrence by 'Spy' appeared in *Vanity Fair* 15 June 1905.

[*The Times*, 27 May 1940; W. R. Lawrence, *The India we Served*, 1928; personal knowledge.]   STANLEY REED.

LAWS, ROBERT (1851-1934), pioneer missionary, the only son of Robert Laws, cabinet-maker of Aberdeen, by his first wife, Christian, daughter of Alexander Cruickshank, an Aberdeenshire crofter, was born at Aberdeen 28 May 1851. Apprenticed to his father's trade, he attended evening school. Later, combining half-day manual work with university classes, he studied arts at Aberdeen, followed by theology at Edinburgh, and medicine at Aberdeen and Glasgow, his steadfast purpose being to follow in the footsteps of David Livingstone.

Laws was ordained on 26 April 1875 to the ministry of the United Presbyterian Church of Scotland by the presbytery of Aberdeen and he was sent as medical officer, second in command, with a Scottish Free Church expedition on 21 May 1875, to found a mission in Central Africa to be named 'Livingstonia'. Under his supervision, a 48-foot sectional steamship was assembled at the mouth of the Zambezi River, dismantled at the Murchison Cataracts, and, after a seventy-mile portage, reconstructed on the Upper Shiré. It reached Lake Nyasa on 12 October, sixty-three days' voyage from the coast, the first steamship to float on any African lake. Contacts were made with tribes representing fifteen different languages, and for sixteen years missionary work was pursued beyond the jurisdiction of any European nation.

From 1877 Laws, now in full control, planned a series of mission stations along the western shore of Lake Nyasa and at strategic inland sites. He opened his first school in 1876; when he left Africa in 1927, there were over 700 primary schools, several secondary schools and teacher-training centres, and a central institution, the Overtoun Institution (of which he was principal), providing educational, theological, medical, technical, and agricultural instruction, which he visualized as the nucleus of a university. His goal was a Bible-reading, self-governing, self-supporting, self-extending Church, with schools, staffed by African Christian teachers, as the basic evangelizing agency. He baptized his first convert in 1881, the earnest of a Christian community which, by 1927, numbered 60,000 with thirteen ordained African pastors.

In the interests of missionary work Laws visited Canada, the United States of America, Germany, and Nigeria as well as carrying out extensive exploration of central African areas devastated by tribal warfare, slavery, superstition, and primitive savagery. He was moderator of the General Assembly of the United Free Church for 1908, and from 1912 to 1916 he served, at the governor's request, as senior unofficial member of the legislative council of Nyasaland. His achievements earned his appointment as C.M.G. in 1923 and he was elected F.R.G.S. in 1884, and F.R.S.G.S. in 1900. The university of Aberdeen conferred upon him the honorary degrees of D.D. in 1891 and of LL.D. in 1925, and the city of Aberdeen bestowed its freedom upon him in 1928. In 1929 Mount

Nyamkowa was officially re-named Mount Laws.

Laws married in 1879 Margaret Troup, daughter of Charles Gray, and had one daughter. He died in a London nursing home 6 August 1934.

A bronze plaque of Laws, produced under the direction of W. B. Fagan, was erected in 1936 at the Livingstonia Mission Station. A plaster cast of this is in Christ's College, Aberdeen.

[Laws's letters and diary, and *Reminiscenses of Livingstonia*, 1934; W. P. Livingstone, *Laws of Livingstonia*, 1921.]

LESLIE DUNCAN.

LAWSON, SIR HARRY LAWSON WEBSTER LEVY-, second baronet, second BARON and VISCOUNT BURNHAM (1862–1933), newspaper proprietor, was born in London 18 December 1862, the elder son of Edward Levy-Lawson, first Baron Burnham [q.v.], by his wife, Harriette Georgiana, only daughter of the actor-manager Benjamin Nottingham Webster [q.v.]. He was educated at Eton and Balliol College, Oxford, where he was awarded a first class in modern history in 1884. A successful speaker, he was elected secretary of the Union. Five months before his final examination he married Olive, eldest daughter of General Sir Henry Percival de Bathe, fourth baronet.

Politics rather than journalism attracted Lawson at first, and at the general election of 1885 he was returned as liberal member for West St. Pancras, being, at twenty-two, 'baby' of the new House of Commons. Losing that seat in 1892, he became member for the Cirencester division at a by-election in 1893 and was again defeated in the liberal débâcle of 1895. Not until ten years later, after he had left the liberal party on the home rule issue, did he re-enter parliament, at another by-election, as unionist member for the Mile End division of the Tower Hamlets, which seat, after losing it in 1906 and regaining it in January 1910, he held until he succeeded to the barony in 1916. He was called to the bar by the Inner Temple in 1891.

Lawson did not limit the sphere of his public work to parliament, for he never neglected an opportunity of usefulness. In 1889 he was elected to the first London County Council as representative of West St. Pancras, and served until 1892. He served again, as representative of Whitechapel, from 1897 to 1904, and was mayor of Stepney from 1907 to 1909.

In 1903, when his father was raised to the peerage, the managing-proprietorship of the *Daily Telegraph* was handed over to Lawson, and it became the principal interest and the pride of his exceptionally busy life. He retained it until 1928, when, after his appointment to the Indian Statutory Commission, he took with deep regret the step of making over the property to other owners. While he held it he had always declined to accept ministerial office on the ground that the independence of his newspaper might be compromised; for he took consistently the highest view of the functions and obligations of journalism. During the twenty-four years of his control he became, as his father had been, a leading figure in the London newspaper world and its chief spokesman throughout the Empire, holding for long periods the presidency of the Newspaper Press Fund, the chairmanship of the Newspaper Proprietors' Association, and the presidency of the Institute of Journalists and the Empire Press Union. He was president of the Imperial Press Conferences held in Ottawa and Melbourne in 1920 and 1925.

Lawson rejoiced in lending the energetic support of his newspaper to great purposes independent of politics. The firm foundation of Anglo-Belgian friendship, for example, owed much to the advocacy of the *Daily Telegraph*. Another cause which he did all that he could to forward was that of the Territorial army. For many years he had held a commission in the Royal Bucks. Hussars, and commanded the regiment from 1902 to 1913. On the outbreak of war in 1914 he rejoined, and took a leading part in training the second reserve regiment. In recognition of these services he was advanced to a viscountcy in 1919, having been a member of the Companionship of Honour since its foundation in 1917. He was appointed G.C.M.G. in 1927. He was also the recipient of numerous foreign decorations, and several universities, both at home and abroad, conferred honorary degrees upon him.

Both before and after his succession to the title Burnham enjoyed a notable reputation as the ideal chairman for public assemblies of every kind. He had served his apprenticeship as a member of such bodies as the royal commission on civil establishments (1889–1894), the Speaker's conference on electoral reform (1916), wherein he moved the resolution which led to the enfranchisement of women in the Reform Act of 1918, and the joint conference on the reform of the House of Lords under the chairmanship of Lord

Bryce (q.v., 1918). He had served, too, on various bodies dealing with imperial questions, which were among his special interests. Apart from his wide experience of public affairs he was fitted for the duties of chairmanship by his fair-mindedness, moderation, and genial temper. Governments in need of a workable report on a matter of difficulty turned naturally to Burnham.

Burnham's most signal work in this respect was done as chairman of the Standing Joint Committee representing teachers and local education authorities which in 1920 formulated new scales of pay for teachers in all state schools. In subsequent disputes he acted as arbitrator, and the result of his long and laborious work was the establishment of the 'Burnham scales', which still form the basis of the teachers' charter of remuneration.

Another notable success was Burnham's chairmanship of the third, fourth, and ninth International Labour Conferences held at Geneva in 1921, 1922, and 1926. His securing respect for the rules of order in this assembly was recognized as a triumph of personality. He was also president of the Public Health Congresses held at Bordeaux in 1924 and Ghent in 1927, and chairman of the first World Press Conference, held at Geneva in 1927.

Burnham's membership (1927–1930) of the Indian Statutory Commission under the chairmanship of Sir John (later Viscount) Simon was the last public service of his career. The incessant hard work entailed by two long visits to every part of India left their mark on his health. In 1933 he was one of eight peers who sat on the Joint Select Committee appointed to consider the government's proposals for Indian reform, and he had attended one of its meetings just before his death. He died in his sleep at his London house 20 July of that year.

For most of his life Burnham was active in the management and finance of hospitals and other works of charity; for many years he served on the council of King Edward's Hospital Fund for London. In 1921 he gave to the City of London, in memory of his father, the estate adjoining Burnham Beeches which he named Fleet Wood.

Burnham's only child was a daughter and the viscountcy became extinct on his death. He was succeeded as third baronet and third baron by his brother, William Arnold Webster (born 1864).

[*The Times* and *Daily Telegraph*, 21 July 1933; personal knowledge.]

E. C. BENTLEY.

LEATHES, SIR STANLEY MORDAUNT (1861–1938), historian and administrator, was born in London 7 May 1861, the elder son of Stanley Leathes [q.v.], prebendary of St. Paul's Cathedral, professor of Hebrew in King's College, London, and rector of Much Hadham, Hertfordshire, by his wife, Matilda, daughter of Martin Butt, rector of East Garston, Berkshire. He was educated at Eton, where he was a king's scholar from 1873 to 1880, and at Trinity College, Cambridge, of which he was also a scholar, and where he was awarded a first class in part i of the classical tripos of 1882 and was second chancellor's medallist in 1884. He was elected a fellow of Trinity in 1886, and served the college as lecturer in history from 1892 to 1903. As a teacher he is described by his pupils as accurate and lucid, and the same qualities appear in his writings.

With Lord Acton, Leathes helped to plan, and with (Sir) A. W. Ward and (Sir) G. W. Prothero [qq.v.] he edited (1901–1912), the *Cambridge Modern History*, and himself wrote the chapters on 'Italy and Her Invaders', 'France', 'Habsburg and Valois', 'Henry IV of France', 'Richelieu', 'Mazarin', 'Modern Europe', and 'Great Britain', a list which shows his own chief interests. During these years Leathes lived in college rooms (13 Nevile's Court). He took a full share in the business and social life of the college, being somewhat of a *bon vivant*. His chief recreation was riding and hunting; he was often out with the Cambridgeshire hounds on a Friday, their near day, and occasionally went by train to Huntingdon for a Cambridgeshire Tuesday or a Fitzwilliam Saturday.

In 1903 Leathes was offered and accepted the post of secretary to the civil service commission and left Cambridge. In 1907 he became a commissioner, and from 1910 to 1927 he was first commissioner. He also served as chairman of several government committees on special questions, and from January to November 1918 he was in charge of the staff and accommodation in the Ministry of Food. In 1911 he was appointed C.B. and K.C.B. in 1919.

Leathes also continued to write. In 1911 he published (under a pseudonym) *Vox Clamantis*, and later (under his own name) *The People of England* (3 vols., 1915–1923) and *Rhythm in English Poetry* (1935). He never married. For some time after leaving Cambridge he lived in the Temple, and afterwards shared with the

Rev. J. A. Nairn a house near Maidenhead. He died at Gloucester 25 July 1938.

[*The Times*, 27 July 1938; Trinity College, Cambridge, records; private information; personal knowledge.]   W. C. D. DAMPIER.

LEE, VERNON (pseudonym), author. [See PAGET, VIOLET.]

LE STRANGE, GUY (1854–1933), orientalist, was born at Hunstanton, Norfolk, 24 July 1854, the youngest of the three sons of Henry L'Estrange Styleman le Strange [q.v.], of Hunstanton Hall, an amateur decorative painter, by his wife, Jamesina Joyce Ellen, youngest daughter of John Stewart, M.P., of Belladrum, Inverness-shire. He was educated at Clifton and the Royal Agricultural College, Cirencester, and later spent long periods abroad, first with his mother in Paris and after his marriage in 1887 to Wanda Irene, eldest daughter of William Cornwallis Cartwright, M.P., of Aynho Park, Northamptonshire, he lived in Florence. Of this marriage there were no children.

It was while he was in Paris that le Strange's interest in oriental studies was awakened by his contact with Julius Mohl, professor of Persian at the Collège de France, the husband of Mary Mohl [q.v.], who persuaded him in spite of extremely bad sight to learn Persian. At the same time he also studied Arabic. In 1877 he travelled to Persia, where he remained until 1880, the first-fruits of the visit being an edition (with W. H. D. Haggard, 1882) of the *Vazir of Lankuran*, a Persian comedy, enlivened by some witty and racy notes. The title-page, which calls the work 'a text-book of colloquial Persian for the use of travellers', shows le Strange's preoccupation with the practical side of oriental scholarship; and it was always characteristic of him to be concerned more with subject-matter than with philology. It was not until many years later, in 1915, that he again published a Persian text, the *Nuzhat al-Qulub*. In the meantime he worked at the historical geography of the Middle Eastern Moslem lands, and it is in this field that he made his chief contribution to oriental scholarship. He began in 1884, while staying at Haifa with his brother-in-law Laurence Oliphant [q.v.], with a translation of Muqaddasi's *Description of Syria, including Palestine* (published in 1886), which was followed by *Palestine under the Moslems* (1890), *Baghdad under the Abbasid Caliphate* (1900), and *The Lands of the Eastern Caliphate* (1905).

After his wife's death in 1907 le Strange settled in Cambridge, becoming a member of Pembroke College, of which his friend E. G. Browne [q.v.] was a fellow. With Browne and others he became active in the affairs of the memorial fund to E. J. W. Gibb [q.v.], the publications of which include several works edited or translated by him—a remarkable achievement for a man with his degree of defective sight. In 1912 he became almost totally blind, yet refused to be overcome by his difficulties. Not only did he continue his oriental work but he took up the study of Spanish, publishing a selection of *Spanish Ballads* (1920) and translations of the *Relaciones* of Don Juan of Persia (1926) and of *Clavijo, Embassy to Tamerlane, 1403–1406* (1928). In 1890 he had published a three-volume edition and translation of *The Correspondence of Princess Lieven and Earl Grey*. He died at Cambridge 24 December 1933.

[*The Times*, 27 December 1933; *Journal* of the Royal Asiatic Society, April 1934; personal knowledge.]   R. LEVY.

LETHABY, WILLIAM RICHARD (1857–1931), author and architect, was born at Barnstaple 18 January 1857, the only son of Richard Pyle Lethaby, of Barnstaple, by his wife, Mary Rowe Crago. He gave early indication of artistic leanings. He passed from the local school of art into the office of Alexander Lauder, an architect in the town, and later into that of Richard Waite of Derby.

In 1879 Lethaby won the Soane medallion, for architectural study abroad, of the Royal Institute of British Architects, and in 1881 the Pugin studentship; an appointment in the office of R. N. Shaw [q.v.] followed. He thus had a share in the design of New Scotland Yard (1891). In this year he began independent practice, and his chief works were big country houses, including High Coxlease, Hampshire; Avon Tyrell on the borders of the New Forest; Melsetter, in the Orkneys; and a church at Brockhampton in Herefordshire.

Soon after joining Shaw, Lethaby became a member of the Society for the Protection of Ancient Buildings, coming into contact with William Morris and the architect Philip Webb [qq.v.], an association which was probably the strongest influence in his life. He and Webb were neighbours in Gray's Inn until 1900, and intimate friends until Webb's death in 1915. In 1922 Lethaby said: 'The happy chance of close intimacy with Philip Webb the architect, at last satisfied my mind about that mysterious thing we call "architecture". From him I learnt that what I was going to mean by architecture was not mere designs, forms, and grandeurs, but *buildings*, honest and human, with hearts in them.'

It is, however, as a teacher, author, and critic rather than as a practising architect that Lethaby is remembered. He was one of the organizers and a principal of the London County Council Central School of Arts and Crafts in 1894 and in 1900 became the first professor of design at the Royal College of Art, South Kensington. He was master of the Art Workers Guild in 1911.

In 1906 Lethaby was invited to become surveyor to the dean and chapter of Westminster Abbey, and in this year his book *Westminster Abbey and the King's Craftsmen* was published, a work that has ever since been recognized as the best foundation for the architectural and artistic study of the Abbey buildings. His single aim throughout his term of office (which closed in 1928) was to preserve the buildings by constant daily care, and to avoid the addition of new work. He was responsible for the skilful cleaning which revealed so much of the long-hidden colour of monuments and fabric. His influence in this sphere spread far beyond Westminster. He was the recognized supreme authority on the care of old buildings.

Lethaby's published works illustrate the width of his architectural and artistic interests. *Mediaeval Art . . . 312-1350* (1904, revised ed. 1912) covers art and architecture in north-west Europe, and the Mediterranean as far east as Palmyra and Baalbec. *Londinium, Architecture and the Crafts* appeared in 1923. A small volume entitled *Home and Country Arts* (also 1923) marks his keen interest and appreciation of the work of ordinary people. 'Art is best thought of as fine and sound ordinary work', he said at a gathering in his honour, and 'Life is best thought of as service'. His other works include *Architecture, Mysticism and Myth* (1892), *Leadwork* (1893), *The Church of Sancta Sophia* (with Harold Swainson, 1894), *Architecture* (1912), *Form in Civilization* (1922), *Westminster Abbey Re-examined* (1925), and *Philip Webb and his Work* (*Builder*, 1925; posthumously published in book form 1935). Numerous articles appeared in various journals, notably *Archaeologia*, and the *Journal* of the Royal Institute of British Architects.

A small man, slender, and delicate, Lethaby was a strong personality. He possessed high gifts as a lecturer, and the power of communicating his own enthusiasm to his audience. He disliked pretence and sham; but he was ever sympathetic towards all honest effort. The character of his literary work often suggests a mind so clear that it must have had the power to reject ideas which had no reasonable basis, and, as is the fact with so many ideas about architecture, are useless because they cannot be defined. Lethaby's strong grasp of his subject is a marked feature of his writings.

Lethaby married in 1901 Edith (died 1927), daughter of Howard Crosby, of New York, and had no issue. He died in London 17 July 1931 and was buried in the churchyard at Hartley Wintney in Hampshire: a stone in the pavement of the west walk of the Great Cloister at Westminster Abbey commemorates him there.

[*Journal* of the Royal Institute of British Architects, 20 February 1932; Lethaby's works; private information; personal knowledge.]   JOHN G. NOPPEN.

LEVY-LAWSON, SIR HARRY LAWSON WEBSTER, VISCOUNT BURNHAM (1862-1933), newspaper proprietor. [See LAWSON.]

LINDSAY, DAVID ALEXANDER EDWARD, twenty-seventh EARL OF CRAWFORD and tenth EARL OF BALCARRES (1871-1940), politician and art connoisseur, was born at Dunecht House, Aberdeen, 10 October 1871, the eldest of the six sons of James Ludovic, twenty-sixth Earl of Crawford and ninth Earl of Balcarres, astronomer, collector, and bibliophile [q.v.], by his wife, Emily Florence, second daughter of Colonel Edward Bootle Wilbraham. He was educated at Eton and Magdalen College, Oxford, where he was president of the Union in 1894. At the general election of 1895 he entered parliament as conservative member for the Chorley division of Lancashire (in which Haigh Hall, then the family seat, is situated), and he continued to represent it until his succession to the peerage in 1913, being known as Lord Balcarres before that date. He was an active politician, and served as a party whip from 1903 to 1913. On the outbreak of war in

1914 he enlisted, without disclosing his identity, as a private in the Royal Army Medical Corps, and served for several months before being identified and commissioned as second lieutenant. In July 1916 he was extracted from the army, much against his will, in order to enter the Cabinet as president of the Board of Agriculture and Fisheries, and was sworn of the Privy Council. Subsequently he became in succession lord privy seal (1916–1919), chancellor of the Duchy of Lancaster (1919–1921), first commissioner of Works (1921–1922), and unpaid minister of transport (1922). As party whip he was actively concerned in the negotiations with regard to the conservative party leadership in the House of Commons in 1911, and as first commissioner of Works he had the congenial task of administering the Ancient Monuments Act of 1913.

On the break-up of Lloyd George's government in 1922 Crawford resigned, and his active political life came to an end. But his more characteristic work as a representative of artistic interests then began. Art had always been one of his prime concerns. He had a fine collection of pictures in his house at 7 Audley Square, partly inherited, partly acquired by himself. In 1903 he had published a study of Donatello, and in 1909 a volume on *The Evolution of Italian Sculpture*. He became an elected trustee of the British Museum in 1923, and was an active member of the standing committee. He was chairman of the Royal Fine Art Commission, founded in 1924. He was also a trustee of the National Gallery and the National Portrait Gallery, a member of the royal commissions on historical manuscripts and historical monuments (of which latter he became chairman), chairman of the Council for the Preservation of Rural England, a member of the council of the British School at Rome, a member and eventually president (1936) of the Roxburghe Club, and a fellow (1900) and eventually president (1924–1929) of the Society of Antiquaries. To the Roxburghe Club he presented in 1926 an edition of the sixteenth-century school-book, the *Vulgaria Puerorum* of William Horman [q.v.], with an introduction by M. R. James [q.v.].

Crawford's position as the acknowledged representative of cultural interests in general was recognized by many distinctions. He was appointed K.T. in 1921, was chancellor of Manchester University from 1923, and received honorary doctor-

ates from the universities of St. Andrews, Manchester, Cambridge, Edinburgh, and Liverpool. He was elected a fellow of the Royal Society (1924), an honorary fellow of Magdalen College, Oxford (1923), and of the Royal Institute of British Architects, and was secretary for foreign correspondence of the Royal Academy.

Besides his early works on artistic subjects, Crawford contributed a very full article on 'Museums of Art' to the eleventh edition of the *Encyclopaedia Britannica* (1911), and presidential addresses to the Society of Antiquaries (*Antiquaries Journal*, vols. v–ix).

Although he occasionally appeared somewhat brusque and dictatorial in the expression of his opinions, Crawford was in fact open-minded and ready to accept the views of others. He was pleasant in social intercourse and quite devoid of self-assertion. He married in 1900 Constance Lilian (died 1947), youngest daughter of Sir Henry Carstairs Pelly, third baronet, member of parliament for Huntingdon, and had two sons and six daughters, the third of whom predeceased her father. He died at Haigh Hall, near Wigan, 8 March 1940, and was succeeded as twenty-eighth earl by his elder son, David Alexander Robert (born 1900).

The best portraits of Lord Crawford are a half-length by Glyn Philpot (1913), in the possession of his heir, and a more informal portrait, seated, by James Gunn (1939) in the National Portrait Gallery. Another portrait by Gunn is at Manchester University, and the family owns a head in charcoal by G. F. Watts, an etching by G. L. Brockhurst, and a three-quarter-length by G. Fiddes Watt.

[*Antiquaries Journal*, vol. xx, 1940; *Obituary Notices of Fellows of the Royal Society*, No. 9, January 1941 (portrait); Sir (Joseph) Austen Chamberlain, *Politics from Inside*, 1936; private information; personal knowledge.]   F. G. KENYON.

LINDSAY, WALLACE MARTIN (1858–1937), classical scholar, was born at Pittenweem, Fife, 12 February 1858, the fourth and youngest son of Alexander Lindsay, Free Church minister there, by his wife, Susan Irvine Martin, and brother of Thomas Martin Lindsay [q.v.]. From Edinburgh Academy he entered Glasgow University as first bursar at the age of sixteen. In 1877 he graduated with first class honours in classics and second class honours in philosophy and proceeded, as Snell exhibitioner, to Balliol College.

Oxford. There he obtained a first class in classical moderations (1878) and in *literae humaniores* (1881). He studied for a year at Leipzig University; on his return he was elected to a fellowship at Jesus College, Oxford, and, after spending two years as assistant in humanity at Edinburgh University, took up tutorial duty at Jesus in 1884. There he remained for fifteen years: in 1899 he was appointed professor of humanity in the university of St. Andrews, and he was holding that office at the time of his death at St. Andrews, as the result of a road accident, 21 February 1937. He was unmarried.

A rare combination of critical acumen and untiring industry made Lindsay one of the greatest of British Latinists; both in philology and in palaeography he was the outstanding figure of his time and his position was recognized by election to membership of many of the learned societies of Europe and America. The most striking characteristic of his work was method. He was an accomplished literary scholar of elegance and taste, but, although he valued these things, he devoted his life to the austere work of scientific scholarship. With intense concentration he confined himself to the course which was marked out for him as one inquiry led to another as its preliminary or its complement, shirking no labour, however tedious, in the determination to make each step of his advance secure.

Lindsay's philological studies in Germany had brought him into contact with the new comparative methods, and the first task which he set himself was a scientific treatment of Latin philology. *The Latin Language* (1894) was immediately accepted as a standard work and established his reputation both in Great Britain and on the continent. He had broken new ground in using Celtic to illustrate Latin, and in order to find new early Irish material he made a search for glosses in the Latin manuscripts in Italian libraries. These researches led to two large undertakings, critical editions of Martial (1903) and Plautus (1904–1905), and to several ancillary studies. Plautus involved the preparation of editions of the lexicographers, Nonius (1902) and Festus (1912), and of Isidore's *Etymologiae* (1911). Study of manuscripts had shown him that much detailed work in palaeography remained to be done, and in a series of monographs, culminating in *Notae Latinae* (1915), which collected the abbreviation-symbols of early Latin manuscripts, he continued the work of Traube and recorded the fruits of investigations in most of the continental libraries. Festus had suggested a new study, that of the medieval glossaries as a source for supplementing the text; pursuing this with characteristic thoroughness, he exposed the origin and nature of the glossaries and, with collaborators, produced the five volumes of *Glossaria Latina* (1926–1932). In the midst of this vast labour he found time to return not only to the dramatists, producing *Early Latin Verse* (1922) and an edition of Terence (1926), but also to palaeography, conducting from 1922 to 1929 a new journal, *Palaeographia Latina* (6 vols.), mostly written by himself, and in 1928 becoming co-editor of the Italian *Monumenti Palaeografici Veronesi*, of which Part II (1934) was almost wholly his work. To British and foreign journals he contributed a steady stream of articles and notes distinguished by alertness of observation and by verve of style.

Lindsay was always ready to help an interested student, but, although he sometimes knew more about his pupils than they imagined, he had little patience with routine teaching, and university business did not appeal to him. He loved the country and the open air, and in vacation, when he was not abroad, was always in the Highlands, taking long walks on the hills. He knew his own abilities, but never paraded them; he made no pretence to omniscience and was generous in appreciation of other men's work. He was no dry-as-dust pedant, but full of wit and in his young days a lively companion; after he left Oxford, deafness cut him off more and more from society and from the pleasures of golf and music, but he never lost his gaiety and zest. In his eightieth year he was as debonair as ever and had the vigour, in mind and body, of a young man.

Lindsay was elected an honorary fellow of Jesus College, Oxford, in 1928, and a fellow of the British Academy in 1905. He received honorary degrees from the universities of Glasgow, Heidelberg, Dublin, and Groningen.

[*The Times*, 22 February 1937; H. J. Rose, *Wallace Martin Lindsay, 1858–1937* in *Proceedings* of the British Academy (embodying a memorandum and a bibliography by Lindsay himself), vol. xxiii, 1937; personal knowledge.]   C. J. FORDYCE.

LIPTON, SIR THOMAS JOHNSTONE, baronet (1850–1931), grocer and yachtsman, was born in a tenement house in Glasgow 10 May 1850, the only surviving son of Thomas Lipton. The father, a poor labourer from Shannock Green Mills, near Clones, co. Monaghan, had left Ireland with his wife, Frances, daughter of Frank Johnstone, of Kilrid, Clones, because of the potato famine, and in Glasgow worked successively in a warehouse and as time-keeper in a cotton-mill, before opening a small grocer's shop. In this enterprise he was aided by his wife, a shrewd and kindly woman, whose salutary example was frequently praised by her son in the days of his prosperity.

Lipton was already at work in his father's shop at the age of nine. A year or two later he was employed at half a crown a week by a stationer. He quickly moved on to a shirt shop, where he earned four shillings, and at the age of fifteen sailed in a Burns liner for the United States of America, landing there with no more than thirty shillings in his pocket. He secured employment first on a Virginia tobacco plantation and later in the rice-fields of South Carolina. Tiring of this heavy drudgery, he eventually stowed away in a ship bound from Charleston to New York, revealing his presence en route with an offer to work. In New York he worked in a big grocer's shop; but at the age of twenty he became homesick, saved up his passage money, and returned to Glasgow. In keeping with that penchant for publicity which was later to contribute so much towards the foundation of his fortunes, he timed his return for a Saturday afternoon, when the neighbours, free from work, were able to see him drive up to his parents' door in a cab, with a rocking-chair and a barrel of flour ostentatiously displayed on the roof.

Lipton at once began work in his father's grocery store. Within the year he had raised £100, and on his twenty-first birthday (1871) he opened his own shop in Stobcross Street, Glasgow. By obtaining supplies of butter, bacon, and eggs from Ireland he was able to eliminate middlemen's profits and so to undersell his rivals. His premises were kept scrupulously clean and he worked long hours. He operated on a cash basis, made many journeys to Ireland for stock, and earned a reputation as an enterprising tradesman, supplying good food at a low price.

At the age of twenty-four Lipton opened his second shop, and others followed in rapid succession. He was a pioneer in the art of publicity, devising one advertising scheme after another, amusing the public and spreading his name abroad. He would stage an elaborate procession for the opening of a new shop, publicly parade through the streets of Glasgow a monster cheese, which, when cut by students, was found to contain gold coins, or hire a balloonist to drop leaflets entitling the holders to substantial prizes.

This publicity was backed up by sound stock and fair prices. Lipton opened up trade in London (to which he transferred his firm's headquarters in 1889), and so greatly expanded his business that at the age of thirty he was a millionaire. He ran his own printing and paper-bag works, and in Chicago set up a factory capable of killing and dressing 300 to 400 pigs a day. This was followed by another plant in the same city which had a daily output of 4,000 hogs. In 1889 Lipton acquired his own tea plantations in Ceylon.

Up to 1897 Lipton had given the whole of his energies to business and had had virtually no outside interests. He now began to dispense some of his great wealth in munificent charity, and to show that keenness for yacht-racing which was to win him an international reputation in sporting circles.

In this year (1897) the Princess of Wales had a scheme for the provision of meals for poor people, but was £25,000 short of the £30,000 which she needed. Lipton provided it, and a few years later when she sponsored a poor people's restaurant, he provided the whole cost of £100,000.

The year 1898 brought Lipton a knighthood and saw the formation of the limited liability company, Lipton, Ltd., and the purchase of the steam yacht *Erin*, on board which he was to entertain many distinguished people, including King Edward VII.

In 1899 Lipton issued his first challenge for the America's cup with the yacht *Shamrock I*. He was defeated then, and again year after year, but yacht-racing became an all-absorbing interest on which he lavished a fortune. His numerous attempts on the cup over a period of thirty years cost him something like £1,000,000. He did not take the helm himself, but employed professional skippers (notably Sycamore and Heard) and was represented on board by his friend Colonel Duncan Neill. Although Lipton never won the cup he earned from the Americans the reputation of being 'the world's best loser'; and in 1930, after his fifth challenge, with *Shamrock V*, they presented him with a gold cup and an album of signatures in appreciation of his sportsmanship.

Lipton was appointed K.C.V.O. in 1901 and created a baronet in the following year. During the war of 1914–1918 he plied the *Erin* between Marseilles and Salonica with medical supplies until she was sunk by a submarine. He kept up his connexion with Lipton, Ltd. until 1927, when he retired, retaining the title of life president. He died at his home in London 2 October 1931. He was unmarried, and bequeathed most of his fortune to charitable institutions in Glasgow.

Lipton will be remembered as one of the most successful business men of his time, and a devotee of the great sport of yachting, whose splendid hospitality, good humour, and inability to accept defeat made him virtually an ambassador of goodwill from Great Britain to America. In business he was shrewd, hard-working, and honest, but he owed his success to an association of those qualities with a perception of the power of advertising which far outstripped that of most of his contemporaries. During his yacht-racing period, which embraced the last thirty-three years of his life, he became known as a lavish and genial host, whose lifelong abstention from alcohol and tobacco in no way impaired his hospitality. His unusual insight into other men's mental processes was of the highest use in the business and social worlds alike. He was a member of the City lieutenancy, and was at one time honorary colonel of the 6th volunteer battalion, Highland Light Infantry.

Of a portrait of Lipton by (Sir) Hubert von Herkomer 1897 the present whereabouts are unknown; a drawing by Edouard Pizzella, of New York, hangs in the head offices of Lipton, Ltd., in London. A cartoon of him by 'Spy' appeared in *Vanity Fair* 19 September 1901.

[*The Times*, 3 October 1931; T. C. Bridges and H. H. Tiltman, *Kings of Commerce*, 1928; Sir T. J. Lipton, *Leaves from the Lipton Logs*, 1931; *Literary Digest*, 17 October 1931; *Allied Staff Magazine*, December 1931; private information.]   HERBERT B. GRIMSDITCH.

LOCK, WALTER (1846–1933), warden of Keble College, Oxford, and professor of divinity, was born at Dorchester, Dorset, 14 July 1846, the second son of Henry Lock, solicitor, of Dorchester, and a member of a well-known family there, by his wife, Susannah Ware, daughter of William May, of Bridgwater. He was educated at Marlborough, whence he gained a scholar-

ship at Corpus Christi College, Oxford. He was awarded a first class in classical moderations (1867) and in *literae humaniores* (1869), and won the Hertford (1867) and Craven (1870) scholarships. In 1871 he was president of the Union. In 1869 he had been elected to a fellowship at Magdalen College, which he held until 1892, and in 1870 to one of the first 'tutorships' of Keble College, of which he became sub-warden in 1881. The religious and theological standpoint of this very liberally minded follower of the original Tractarians is revealed in his essay on 'The Church' in *Lux Mundi* (1889), *John Keble, a Biography* (1893), and *The Bible and Christian Life* (1905). At the end of the century he was appointed the first general editor of the *Westminster Commentaries* on the Revised Version, but he best showed his own matured cautious (sometimes over-cautious) scholarship in his *Critical and Exegetical Commentary on the Pastoral Epistles* (1924). He was ordained deacon in 1872 and priest in 1873, and in 1895 was appointed Dean Ireland's professor of exegesis of Holy Scripture. He held the chair until 1919 when his election to the Lady Margaret professorship of divinity (with a canonry at Christ Church) heralded his resignation in 1920 of the wardenship of Keble College which he had held since 1897. From the Lady Margaret chair he retired in 1927, having been elected to an honorary fellowship at Magdalen in 1897 and at Corpus Christi in 1920, and to honorary membership of the council of Keble College in the last named year.

In 1892 Lock married Jane Cecil, eldest daughter of Charles Heathcote Campion, rector of Westmeston, Sussex, and had one son and four daughters. He died at Oxford 12 August 1933.

Whether as a member of the Hebdomadal Council, on which he served from 1896 to 1919, or as chairman of the board of faculty of theology, or as a member of the council of St. Hugh's Hall (later College), Oxford, Lock showed himself not unsympathetic to new ideas and new causes. He supported the higher education of women and strove successfully for the abolition of the denominational restrictions on admittance to the degrees of B.D. and D.D. He was to the end a lucid lecturer and a compelling preacher: his seminars were attended by most post-graduate theological students. At Keble College, throughout his fifty years of service, his lovable personality, determined tactfulness, and directive energy shaped its destiny and profoundly influenced its members.

A portrait of Lock by C. W. Furse (1895) hangs in the hall of Keble College.

[*The Times*, 14 August 1933; *The Clock Tower* (magazine of the Keble Association), November 1933; *Oxford Magazine*, 12 October 1933; personal knowledge.]

D. C. SIMPSON.

LODGE, ELEANOR CONSTANCE (1869–1936), historian and principal of Westfield College, London, was born at Hanley, Staffordshire, 18 September 1869, the youngest child and only daughter of Oliver Lodge, merchant, afterwards of Wolstanton, Staffordshire, by his wife, Grace, youngest daughter of the Rev. Joseph Heath. Of the eight brothers who preceded her the eldest was Sir Oliver Lodge [q.v.] and the fourth Sir Richard Lodge [q.v.]. Educated at private schools, the turning-point in her life came in 1890 when she went up to Lady Margaret Hall, Oxford, taking the final honour school of modern history in 1894. She found lasting happiness in her chosen subject, in out-door sports, and in congenial friendships. At the École des Chartes and the École des Hautes Études in Paris (1898–1899) she began researches into the English rule in Gascony, which resulted in several im-portant studies, especially 'The Estates of the Archbishop and Chapter of Saint-André of Bordeaux under English Rule', published in *Oxford Studies in Social and Legal History*, vol. iii (1912), and *The English Rule in Gascony* (1926). She also published other notable books as well as articles in *British Academy Social and Economic Records* (1927) and the *Cambridge Medieval History*, vol. v (1926). Many vacations were spent working in French archives and exploring the remote countryside on foot or bicycle. In the spring of 1918 she took charge of the Oxford Women's Canteens for French Soldiers in Champagne, shared in the re-treat before the Germans, and then nursed in Paris.

Appointed librarian of Lady Margaret Hall in 1895, Miss Lodge was history tutor from 1899 to 1921, becoming vice-principal also in 1906. She played an important part in the second stage of the develop-ment of university and college life for women in Oxford. She gave to her pupils her own ardent desire for knowledge and regard for thoroughness and truth; she worked wholeheartedly for the welfare of Lady Margaret Hall and furthered by her statesmanship the admission in 1920 of women as full members of the university.

From 1921 to 1931 Miss Lodge was principal of Westfield College, Hampstead, and here too she strengthened her college internally, furthering in particular the building of the chapel and the develop-ment of the library, and she helped to secure its recognition as one of eight col-leges forming the central part of the uni-versity of London. She gave public service on the Hampstead borough council and served also on the councils of educational and learned bodies, often as president. In 1928 she was the first woman to obtain the degree of D.Litt. of Oxford University and in 1932 she was appointed C.B.E. The university of Liverpool conferred upon her the honorary degree of Litt.D., and she was elected an honorary fellow of Lady Margaret Hall and of Westfield College. She died at Windsor after a long illness 19 March 1936. Her vivid and spontaneous book of memories, *Terms and Vacations* (published posthumously in 1938), was the expression of her gratitude for all that a university education had meant to her, and revealed the simplicity of her charac-ter, the quality of her unselfishness, her tireless energy, and her keen sense of humour. A portrait-head in chalk by L. Leslie Brooke (1916) and an oil-painting by J. B. Souter (1931) are at Lady Mar-garet Hall, and an oil-painting by (Sir) G. F. Kelly hangs at Westfield College.

[E. C. Lodge, *Terms and Vacations*, edited by Janet Spens, 1938; Sir Oliver Lodge, *Past Years*, 1931; *Lady Margaret Hall: A Short History*, 1923; University and college reports, calendars, registers, and journals; personal knowledge.]   EVELYN JAMISON.

LODGE, SIR OLIVER JOSEPH (1851–1940), scientist and first principal of Birmingham University, was born at Penkhull, Staffordshire, 12 June 1851, the eldest of the eight sons of Oliver Lodge, afterwards of Wolstanton, Staffordshire, who had built up a prosperous agency for the supply of materials used in the pottery industry. He was brother of Sir Richard Lodge and of Eleanor Constance Lodge [qq.v.]. On both the paternal and maternal sides, Lodge came of a family of school-masters and clergymen. His maternal grandfather, Joseph Heath, was head-master of a school at Lucton in Hereford-shire, and his paternal grandfather, Oliver Lodge (who was the father of a family of twenty-five children, Lodge's father being the twenty-third), was a native of Ireland

and became incumbent of Barking in Essex and headmaster of Barking School. Unremitting industry was the note of the Penkhull household: Lodge's mother, Grace, youngest daughter of Joseph Heath, was a remarkable woman who could find time to rear a large family, to manage a country house and farm, to keep the books of her husband's business, and to take up, as a hobby, photography by the wet process.

At eight years of age Lodge entered Newport Grammar School in Shropshire where he spent four unhappy years and was then transferred as a private pupil to the charge of the rector of Combs in Suffolk. At fourteen his schooldays ended; his father wished him to inherit the agency which he had established and, until his twenty-second year, Lodge was deeply immersed in the routine of business, but not wholly, for a maternal aunt, who had already introduced him to some knowledge of astronomy, invited him periodically to stay in London, where he attended classes in chemistry and geology and, above all, a course of lectures on heat given by John Tyndall [q.v.]. He used to call this course an eye-opener and it probably determined his future. He won an exhibition under the Science and Art Department and, his father unwillingly consenting, there followed a period of study at the Royal College of Science under T. H. Huxley, (Sir) Edward Frankland, and Frederick Guthrie [qq.v.], and at University College under W. K. Clifford [q.v.], Olaus Henrici, and George Carey Foster. For some years Lodge filled a post as demonstrator in physics in Carey Foster's laboratory. During this period he graduated D.Sc. (1877) and published papers on the flow of electricity in plane sheets, on models illustrating the flow of electricity through various media, on thermo-electricity, on the induction balance of D. E. Hughes [q.v.], on thermal conductivity, and on the foundations of mechanics. In 1881 Lodge was appointed to the chair of physics at the newly founded University College in Liverpool. During his tenure of this chair he carried out those researches which established his reputation as a physicist and for which the Royal Society (of which he had been elected a fellow in 1887) in 1898 awarded him its Rumford medal.

Forward-looking as was Lodge's mind, he was essentially a child of the nineteenth century, and in nothing is this more apparent than in his devotion to the concept of an ether. His great experiments are intimately related to this concept and fall into two categories, wireless and the relative motion of matter and ether.

Lodge's contributions to wireless were many and some of them were fundamental. There is little doubt that his early experiments would have led him to the discovery of electro-magnetic radiation had he not been anticipated by Heinrich Hertz; in his discourse to the Royal Institution in 1891 he showed experiments which foreshadowed the ultra short-wave advances of a later generation; his discovery that metals in loose contact tend to stick together when electro-magnetic radiation falls upon them formed the basis for the construction of a primitive receiver; and his famous patent of 1897 diagnosed the disease which afflicted early transmitters and prescribed the remedy therefor; it is not too much to say that his experiments and investigations were the major influence in making spark telegraphy possible.

So with Lodge's heroic experiments on the relative motion of matter and ether. Interest in the ether was reawakened by the announcement of the principle of interference by Thomas Young [q.v.] in 1801 and, until the closing years of the nineteenth century, it was considered a doubtful question whether the ether in the neighbourhood of moving matter was or was not carried along by the moving matter; an historic experiment by Albert Abraham Michelson and Edward William Morley in 1887 was considered to be decisive in favour of a convected ether. Lodge, however, in 1893 mounted two parallel steel disks, three feet in diameter and one inch apart, on a common vertical axis, and spun them round at a very high speed, sending two rays of light in opposite directions round the space between the disks and observing their interference. The experiment was sensitive and the answer was clear; the ether was *not* carried along in the space between the disks. This fundamental contradiction served to usher in a new era of theory, which culminated in the reign of relativity.

In 1900 Lodge was appointed principal of the new university of Birmingham— the first of the modern English civic universities to receive a charter—and his active career as an experimental physicist ended. His influence in shaping the development of the young university was profound and characteristic. He had neither taste nor capacity for the day-to-day details of routine administration, and, indeed, he made it a condition of his appointment that such matters should be left in the hands of the vice-principal. But Lodge had strong views on the framing of the general policy of a modern university, and it is in the main due to his wise and skilful guidance that the university of Birmingham has become the university of the Midlands and that its ideals have not been narrowed by over-devotion to specialization, whether in the sciences or in humanist studies.

The British Association played a considerable part in Lodge's scientific and social life, and between his first meeting, the Bradford meeting of 1873, and his last, the Blackpool meeting of 1936, there were very few meetings which he missed. In 1891 he was president of Section A (mathematics and physics), and at the Birmingham meeting of 1913 he was president of the association.

Two major interests dominated Lodge's intellectual life, physical and psychical research. His active interest in psychic phenomena dates from the Liverpool period where, about 1883, he carried out some pioneer experiments in thought-transference, and his investigations of the famous mediums, Mrs. Piper and Eusapia Palladino, are of great importance. Lodge paid close attention to the mental and physical sides of psychical research; in order to explain Mrs. Piper's results an appeal to telepathy at least was necessary, whereas in the investigation of Eusapia Palladino, Lodge and Charles Richet, with whom he worked, were convinced that they had witnessed instances of telekinesis. In the opinion of a competent judge Lodge's influence has been greater as a philosopher of psychical research than as a practical investigator. He concluded, on the evidence observed by him, that the mind survives the dissolution of the body, and he consistently expounded the instrument theory of the relation between body and mind.

Lodge wrote many books on many subjects. Of his scientific works mention may be made of *Signalling across Space without Wires* (1897), *The Ether of Space* (1909), *Talks about Wireless* (1925), and *Advancing Science* (1931): of his works on psychical research *Raymond* (1916) caught the public ear, but *My Philosophy* (1933) contains the latest expression of his considered views on life generally. He received honorary degrees from thirteen universities; was president of the Physical Society (1899–1900) and of the Society for

Psychical Research (1901–1904 and 1932); and was knighted in 1902. He resigned his post of principal of the university of Birmingham in 1919 when, proposing to devote the rest of his life to the study of the ether of space, he retired to Lake, near Salisbury. There he died 22 August 1940.

In 1877 Lodge married Mary Fanny Alexander (died 1929), daughter of a sea-captain, Alexander Marshall; they had six sons and six daughters. The youngest son, Raymond, was killed in the war of 1914–1918.

There are two portraits of Lodge painted by Sir George Reid; one is in the possession of the university of Birmingham, the other is at Flore House, Northampton. A third portrait, painted by Bernard Munns, is in the Birmingham City Art Gallery. A marble bust by C. J. Allen is in the University Library, Liverpool. A cartoon by 'Spy' appeared in *Vanity Fair* 4 February 1904.

[Sir Oliver Lodge, *Past Years. An Autobiography*, 1931; *Letters from Sir Oliver Lodge*, compiled and annotated by J. A. Hill, 1932; Theodore Besterman, *A Bibliography of Sir Oliver Lodge*, 1935; *Obituary Notices of Fellows of the Royal Society*, No. 10, December 1941 (portrait); *Proceedings* of the Physical Society, vol. liii, 1941 (portrait); private information; personal knowledge.] **ALLAN FERGUSON.**

LODGE, SIR RICHARD (1855–1936), historian and teacher, was born at Penkhull, Staffordshire, 20 June 1855, the fourth son of Oliver Lodge, merchant, afterwards of Wolstanton, Staffordshire, by his wife, Grace Heath. He was brother of Sir Oliver Lodge and Eleanor Constance Lodge [qq.v.]. Educated at Christ's Hospital, he came up in 1874 to Balliol College, Oxford, as an exhibitioner, being awarded a Brackenbury scholarship the following year. After winning the Stanhope (1875) and the Lothian (1876) essay prizes, he was awarded a first class in modern history in 1877 and elected a fellow of Brasenose College in 1878. He acted first as lecturer and then as tutor in modern history and became vice-principal in 1891. In 1894 he was appointed first professor of modern history at the university of Glasgow, remaining there until 1899, when he succeeded (Sir) G. W. Prothero [q.v.] in the chair of modern history at Edinburgh and retained the professorship until his retirement in 1925. From 1911 to 1925 he was dean of the faculty of arts.

Between 1878 and 1894 Lodge was one of a small group of college history tutors, which included Edward Armstrong [q.v.], A. L. Smith [q.v.], A. H. Johnson, and C. R. L. Fletcher [q.v.], who, by their lectures, teaching, organizing ability, and disciplined enthusiasm, made the honour school of modern history at Oxford. Lodge shared with his brother Oliver a superb gift of lucid exposition, which he took with him in the maturity of his powers both to Glasgow and to Edinburgh. His influence on, and his interest in, his students of every type and of both sexes were deep and sincere, notably in imparting a high standard of critical tests in the handling of historical material and a realization of the importance of truth in history as the basis of any sound citizenship. His tall, lean figure with its fine blue eyes and irresistible smile enhanced the spoken word whether in lecturing or in personal intercourse. Lodge had, also, a marked capacity for administration which he proved both in his college at Oxford and particularly at Edinburgh, where his impressive personality and capacity for work made him a notable influence both in the university and in many spheres of civic life. A convinced liberal all his life, he had become one of the leading public figures in Scotland by the time of his retirement.

Lodge left Edinburgh to reside at Harpenden, Hertfordshire. He employed his retirement up to his last illness in original and industrious research on the manuscript sources of British foreign policy from 1688 to 1760. His chief printed works are *A History of Modern Europe* (from 1453 to 1878), which went through many editions after its appearance in 1885; *Richelieu* (1896); *The Close of the Middle Ages, 1273-1494* (1901); vol. viii (1660-1702) of Longman's *Political History of England* (1910); *Great Britain and Prussia in the Eighteenth Century* (1923, the Ford lectures for 1921-1922); *Studies in Eighteenth-Century Diplomacy, 1740-1748* (1930); *The Private Correspondence of Sir Benjamin Keene* (1933); and 'The College under the Later Stuarts' (*Brasenose College Quatercentenary Monographs*, vol. ii, part i, 1909).

Lodge was knighted in 1917 for his academic and public services. He received honorary degrees from the universities of Glasgow (1905), Manchester (1912), and Edinburgh (1926), and was elected an honorary fellow of Brasenose College (1911), a distinction which gave him unqualified satisfaction, but he was certainly disappointed in 1916 at not being ap-

pointed principal of Edinburgh University as successor to Sir William Turner. The vacancy in the headship of Brasenose when Charles Henry Sampson succeeded Charles Buller Heberden as principal in 1920 came too late to cause Lodge disappointment. He was president of the Royal Historical Society from 1929 to 1933. He married in 1882 Annie Gwendoline, daughter of Henry Morgan, of Norwich, who survived him. They had three sons, of whom the eldest and youngest predeceased their father, the youngest having been killed in the war of 1914-1918, and four daughters, of whom the eldest predeceased her father. He died in London after an operation 2 August 1936.

On his retirement from Edinburgh Lodge was presented with his portrait (by William Nicholson), a replica of which now hangs in the university; it was subscribed for by several hundred contributors from both inside and outside the university, and a deserved tribute was paid on the occasion to his services to the university and city.

[*The Times*, 4 and 6 August 1936; *Scotsman*, 4 August 1936; *Oxford Magazine*, 29 October 1936; Margaret Lodge, *Sir Richard Lodge*, 1946; personal knowledge.]

CHARLES GRANT ROBERTSON.

LOTHIAN, eleventh MARQUESS OF (1882-1940), journalist and statesman. [See KERR, PHILIP HENRY.]

LOUISE CAROLINE ALBERTA (1848-1939), princess of Great Britain and Ireland, Duchess of Argyll, was born at Buckingham Palace 18 March 1848, the sixth child and fourth daughter of Queen Victoria. She was the most beautiful and not the least gifted of the Queen's daughters, and her intelligence and wit made her a favourite with her father and attracted the notice of Carlyle. In 1871 the Princess married John Douglas Sutherland Campbell, Marquess of Lorne, who in 1900 succeeded his father as ninth Duke of Argyll [q.v.]. She was the first member of the royal family for more than fifty years to contract matrimony with a subject of the sovereign, and the innovation (especially as the bridegroom was a Scotsman) had the strong approval of the Queen. There were no children of the marriage.

Princess Louise spent five years (1878-1883) in Canada as the consort of the governor-general, and a memorial of her stay is the name given to Lake Louise near

Laffan in the Rocky Mountains. After their return to this country, the princess and Lord Lorne were able to promote the causes which they had at heart with singular unanimity, as both were endowed with the same literary and artistic tastes. Leading an extremely quiet and retired life, giving only small parties, eschewing royal functions as far as possible, and not showing over-much attention to the conventions of her station, the princess wrote articles for magazines under the nom de plume of 'Myra Fontenoy', and made her home at Kensington Palace a rendezvous for artists and sculptors, of whom the chief was Sir J. E. Boehm [q.v.], and who also numbered among them (Sir) Alfred Gilbert [q.v.], J. Seymour Lucas, and Sir Lawrence Alma-Tadema [q.v.]. Of the causes to which the princess gave her support the Ladies' Work Society, which enabled poor ladies to gain a living from needlework, was perhaps nearest to her heart, but far more important was the impetus which she gave to the education of women, for under her strong encouragement the National Union for the Higher Education of Women was founded in 1872. She was its first president, and the growth and spread of high schools for girls all over the country will probably be her most lasting and influential work. She was not content to be a mere figurehead, but followed the work closely, and took an active share in it by means of speeches, letters to the press, and an especial interest in the teaching of art.

As a working artist, the princess early exhibited gifts as a sculptress, and she was instructed by Mary Thornycroft [q.v.]. Of the princess's works the best known is the marble statue of Queen Victoria at Kensington Palace overlooking the Round Pond. The monument to Prince Henry of Battenberg in Whippingham church, near Cowes, is also highly esteemed, and she designed the memorial in St. Paul's Cathedral to the Canadian soldiers who fell in the South African war.

After the Duke of Argyll's death in 1914, the princess lived a life yet more retired, and divided her time between London and Roseneath House in Dumbartonshire. In 1919 she was given the colonelcy-in-chief of the Argyll and Sutherland Highlanders. After long enjoyment of good health she died at Kensington Palace in her ninety-second year 3 December 1939.

[*The Times*, 4 and 8 December 1939; personal knowledge.]   DOROTHY CANTELUPE.

LOUISE VICTORIA ALEXANDRA DAGMAR (1867–1931), princess royal of Great Britain and Ireland, Duchess of Fife, was born at Marlborough House 20 February 1867, the third child and eldest daughter of the Prince and Princess of Wales. She was educated at home and developed a strong taste for outdoor life. In 1889 the princess married Alexander William George Duff, sixth Earl of Fife, who was eighteen years her senior and was created a duke on his marriage: by a special remainder of 1900, the dukedom of Fife passed to the princess's daughters and their male issue. This union enabled the princess to live in entire privacy, and, in the stretches of the Dee at Mar Lodge, near Braemar, and in the Deveron at Duff House, near Banff, to indulge freely in her favourite sport of salmon-fishing, in which she developed exceptional skill. In 1905 the princess was declared princess royal and her two daughters, Lady Alexandra Duff (later Princess Arthur of Connaught) and Lady Maud Duff (later Countess of Southesk), were created princesses with the title of 'highness'. On 13 December 1911, as the princess and her family were travelling to Egypt for the sake of her health, which was never robust, their ship was wrecked in a gale near Cape Spartel. The princess refused to leave until all the women and children on board had been taken off, and the hardships endured by the party were severe as the boat which was taking them to land was swamped. The death of the duke at Assuan 29 January 1912 was hastened by this misadventure. After continuing to live in retirement, the princess died at her house in Portman Square 4 January 1931.

[*The Times*, 5 January 1931; private information.]

LOVAT, fourteenth (sometimes reckoned sixteenth) BARON (1871–1933). [See FRASER, SIMON JOSEPH.]

LOVE, AUGUSTUS EDWARD HOUGH (1863–1940), mathematician and geo-physicist, was born 17 April 1863 at Weston-super-Mare, the second son of John Henry Love, surgeon, later police-surgeon to the borough of Wolverhampton, where the family lived until the death of the father in Love's later Cambridge days. His mother was Emily Serle. He had two sisters, with the younger of whom he was on terms of especial affection; after their father's death she kept house for him for the rest of his life. He was unmarried.

Love entered Wolverhampton Grammar School in 1874. He gave little indication whilst at school of the career which was to follow. In 1881 he was awarded a sizar-ship at St. John's College, Cambridge, to which he went up in 1882. He was at first doubtful whether to read classics or mathematics, but chose the latter and gradually came to the top of his year. He was elected scholar of the college in 1884, was second wrangler in the mathematical tripos of 1885, and was awarded the first Smith's prize in 1887, after being elected in 1886 into a fellowship at St. John's which he retained until 1899, occupying the post of college lecturer in mathematics most of that time. He was elected F.R.S. in 1894. In those Cambridge days began his long association with the London Mathematical Society, which he served as secretary (1895–1910) and as president (1912–1919). In 1926 he was awarded the society's De Morgan medal.

In 1898 Love was elected to the Sedleian chair of natural philosophy at Oxford, a position which he held until his death. He was elected a fellow of Queen's College, Oxford, in 1927, when he was also elected an honorary fellow of St. John's College, Cambridge. He was awarded a Royal medal of the Royal Society in 1909, and its Sylvester medal in 1937. He became an associate of the Italian Accademia dei Lincei, and a corresponding member of the Institut de France.

Love's chosen field of research was the theory of elasticity of solids in its mathe-matical setting, and its application to problems of the earth's crust. On this subject, and on problems of hydro-dynamics and electromagnetism involving kindred differential equations, he contri-buted to various journals some fifty odd memoirs. His main technical contribu-tions to mathematical theory are perhaps his discovery of what are known as 'Love waves' (1911) and his theory of bi-harmonic analysis (1929). The latter is unsuitable for description here, but 'Love waves' can briefly be sketched. His account of them was published in *Some Problems of Geodynamics* (1911), the essay for which he had been awarded the Adams prize of the university of Cambridge. J. W. Strutt, third Baron Rayleigh [q.v.], had discovered the possibility in a solid of a type of surface wave consisting of vertical and horizontal components which decayed exponentially with depth. These

seemed to be of importance for seismology, but difficulties arose in identifying them with the observed 'long waves' which occur late in a seismic disturbance. Love investigated the possibility of the propa-gation of a purely distortional surface wave, and found that such could exist in a heterogeneous medium. In these waves the disturbance is purely horizontal (transverse to the direction of propaga-tion), and the wave-velocity, unlike that of 'Rayleigh waves', depends upon wave-length. 'Love waves' have proved of con-siderable importance in the hands of later investigators, who have been able to infer, from their application to seismograms, indications of the thickness of the upper layer of the earth's crust.

Love, however, will be remembered chiefly as the author of what throughout his life was a standard work, *A Treatise on the Mathematical Theory of Elasticity* (1892–1893; later editions 1906, 1920, 1927). This is a fine, scholarly work, written with an historical sense; unhurried in style, massive in lecture, satisfying in its fullness. It gives the general theory of stress and strain; of the conditions of equilibrium and stability of elastic plates, shells, and solids; of torsion of rods and the bending and vibrations of beams; and of the transmission of force. It remains a permanent monument to the academic aspect of elasticity. The treatment is throughout severely analytical, but it took form too early to incorporate the tensor calculus.

Love had a certain whimsicality of manner and appearance which endeared him to his many friends. Although no experimenter, he was a typical repre-sentative of the characteristic English school of applied mathematics, and notably continued the mathematical tradi-tion of Sir G. G. Stokes, J. Clerk Maxwell, [qq.v.] and Lord Rayleigh. He died at Oxford 5 June 1940.

[*The Times*, 6 June 1940; *Obituary Notices of Fellows of the Royal Society*, No. 9, January 1940 (portrait and bibliography); *Nature*, 21 September 1940; *Journal* of the London Mathematical Society, vol. xvi, 1941 (biblio-graphy); personal knowledge.]

E. A. MILNE.

LOW, SIR SIDNEY JAMES MARK (1857–1932), author and journalist, was born at Blackheath 22 January 1857. His father, Maximilian Loewe, a Hungarian Jew, fled to England in 1848, established himself successfully in business in the City of London, and married Therese Schacherl, daughter of a Viennese rabbi. Sidney was the eldest child in their family of six sons and five daughters. He was educated at King's College School, Strand, and in 1876 went with a scholarship to Pembroke College, Oxford. But in 1877 he migrated to Balliol as an exhibitioner (he was later a Brackenbury scholar) and was awarded a first class in modern history in 1879. From boyhood he was attracted to literature and history. Between 1883 and 1885 he was lecturer on constitutional history at King's College, London; in 1884, with Frederic Sanders Pulling, he published his first book, *The Dictionary of English History*. About 1883 Low began contributing to the *St. James's Gazette*, and soon became its sub-editor under Frederick Greenwood [q.v.], whom he succeeded as editor in 1888. His editorship was brilliant; the circulation of the *St. James's* meagre; its influence immense. Low gathered round him such men as Andrew Lang, George Saintsbury, Gilbert Parker, H. D. Traill, Herbert and J. K. Stephen; and gave their earliest opportunities to Rudyard Kipling, J. M. Barrie, Anthony Hope, and many others. Resigning the editorship in 1897, Low was next year appointed by William Heseltine Mudford leader-writer on the *Standard*, of which Low was literary editor in 1904–1905. From 1898 his career was that of a hard-working, brilliant, and trustworthy journalist. He declined the editorship of the *Johannesburg Star*, was passed over for that of the *Morning Post*, and, because of age, missed the editorship of *The Times*.

Low's masterpiece, *The Governance of England* (1904), and *A Vision of India* (1906, the fruit of his visit as special correspondent on the royal tour of 1905) merited, and won, wide attention and proclaimed him an ardent imperialist. They were followed by volume xii (1837–1901) in Longman's *Political History of England* (with L. C. Sanders, 1907), *Egypt in Transition* (1914), *Samuel Henry Jeyes* (1915), and many important pamphlets. After the *Governance*, Low's most notable contribution to literature is his study of *De Quincey* (1911). He contributed regularly to all the leading monthly journals, specializing in biographical subjects such as Cecil Rhodes, on whom he published a miniature masterpiece in the *Nineteenth Century* for May 1902.

Low was called to the bar by the Inner Temple in 1892, and was knighted in 1918. He was twice married: first, in 1887 to Elsie (died 1921), daughter of John Davison; secondly, in 1924 to Ebba Cecilia, daughter of Captain Gustaf Hermann Emile Byström, of Stockholm. He had no children. He died at his home in Kensington 13 January 1932.

Low's friendships were wide and eclectic. He loved the theatre, society, and life. His admiration for the Empire, and understanding of it, were profound; he knew well and admired Rhodes, Cromer, H. M. Stanley, Curzon, Sir Reginald Wingate, and, above all, Milner, and won their intimate confidences. As a writer and journalist Low's place is very high; as an historian his place, if modest, is assured.

[Desmond Chapman-Huston, *The Lost Historian: A Memoir of Sir Sidney Low*, 1936; Low's diaries; unpublished letters addressed to Low; private information.]

DESMOND CHAPMAN-HUSTON.

LOWRY, THOMAS MARTIN (1874–1936), chemist, was born at Low Moor, Bradford, Yorkshire, 26 October 1874, the second son of Edward Pearce Lowry, afterwards senior Wesleyan chaplain at Aldershot, by his wife, Jemima Hofland. From Kingswood School, Bath, Lowry proceeded in 1893 with a Clothworkers scholarship to the Central Technical College, South Kensington, where he came under the influence of H. E. Armstrong [q.v.]. His chemical ability soon showed itself and in 1896 Armstrong appointed him his assistant. He held this office until 1913, combining it from 1904 to 1913 with that of lecturer in chemistry at the Westminster Training College.

In 1913 Lowry was appointed head of the chemical department of Guy's Hospital medical school with the title of professor of chemistry in the university of London. After occupying this position for seven years he was elected in 1920 to the newly established chair of physical chemistry at Cambridge, where W. J. Pope [q.v.], also a former pupil of Armstrong, was head of the department of chemistry, and during his sixteen years' tenure of this professorship he developed an active school of research, directed mainly to the investigation of optical rotatory power. He became a member of Trinity Hall.

In 1898 in Armstrong's laboratory Lowry discovered that freshly prepared solutions of nitro-d-camphor showed a change of rotatory power with time. He termed the phenomenon 'mutarotation' and referred it to the establishment of an equilibrium between nitro-d-camphor and an unknown isomeride. From this observation he was led on the one hand to the study of polarimetry and on the other to the investigation of reversible isomeric change (which he termed 'dynamic isomerism') and the greater part of his subsequent work lay in these two fields.

Lowry became particularly interested in the variation of rotatory power with wavelength and gave the Bakerian lecture to the Royal Society in 1921 on this subject, in collaboration with Dr. Percy Corlett Austin. His most noteworthy achievements in this connexion were his measurements of the rotatory dispersion of quartz from the infra-red to the far ultra-violet and his discovery that one of the characteristic frequencies in the Drude equation for the rotatory dispersion of camphor coincides with the characteristic frequency of the carbonyl group. To account for the latter observation he advanced his hypothesis of induced dissymmetry (1924). His studies on isomeric changes of the kind which he termed 'prototropic' yielded much information on the action of catalysts on these processes and led him to an extended definition of acids and bases, advanced simultaneously by J. N. Brønsted (1923).

During the war of 1914–1918 Lowry did valuable service in overcoming the difficulties in shell-filling caused by the polymorphism of ammonium nitrate and was director of shell-filling (1917–1919). He wrote several books, the most important of which was his treatise on *Optical Rotatory Power* (1935). He was elected F.R.S. in 1914, and appointed O.B.E. in 1918, and C.B.E. in 1920. He received honorary degrees from the universities of Dublin and Brussels. He married in 1904 Eliza, eldest daughter of Cornelius Wood, Methodist minister, and had two sons and a daughter. He died at Cambridge 2 November 1936.

[*The Times*, 4 November 1936; *Obituary Notices of Fellows of the Royal Society*, No. 6, January 1938 (portrait); private information; personal knowledge.] W. H. MILLS.

LUCAS, SIR CHARLES PRESTWOOD (1853–1931), civil servant and historian, was born at Glan-yr-Afon, Crickhowel, Brecknockshire, 7 August 1853, the fourth and youngest son of Henry John Lucas, M.D., of Glan-yr-Afon, by his wife, Elisabeth, daughter of George Bevan, vicar of Crickhowel. He was educated at Winchester where he was head of the roll in 1865 and became one of a contemporary trio of distinguished scholars and friendly rivals, the other two being (Sir) R. L. Antrobus and G. E. Buckle [q.v.]. Lucas himself won an open exhibition at Balliol College, Oxford, and, with a first class in classical moderations (1873) and in *literae humaniores* (1876), was awarded the chancellor's medal for a Latin essay (1877).

Having been placed first on the civil service examination list of 1877, Lucas was appointed to the Colonial Office and eventually became an assistant undersecretary of state in 1897. When the department dealing with the 'self-governing Colonies' was reorganized with increased dignity and importance as the Dominions Department in 1907 Lucas was appointed the first head of that department, which was the forerunner of the Dominions Office established in 1925. He retired in 1911. He was appointed C.B. in 1901, K.C.M.G. in 1907, and K.C.B. in 1912. He was called to the bar by Lincoln's Inn in 1885.

In addition to being a civil servant of very great distinction Lucas was the author of numerous valuable books about the British Empire. He projected *A Historical Geography of the British Colonies*, to which he contributed an *Introduction* (1887); he was also responsible for vols. i–v, part 1 (1888–1901). His other works include *The Canadian War of 1812* (1906), *A History of Canada, 1763–1812* (1909), *Greater Rome and Greater Britain* (1912), *The British Empire* (1915), *The Beginnings of English Overseas Enterprise* (1917), *The Partition and the Colonization of Africa* (1922), *The Story of the Empire* ('British Empire' series, vol. ii, 1924), and *Religion, Colonising and Trade* (1930). He edited and himself wrote much of the work entitled *The Empire at War* (5 vols., 1921–1926), a record of the part played by the Dominions and Colonies in war, particularly in the war of 1914–1918.

If 'proper words in proper places' is the true definition of style, as laid down by Swift, everything that Lucas wrote bore that hall-mark, and he was in fact a master of English prose. Election to a fellowship at All Souls College, Oxford (1920–1927), came as a fitting crown to his career as a scholar and a man of letters.

His simple and kindly nature, his sterling character and ability, and his unequalled knowledge of colonial affairs made Lucas liked and respected by all ranks in the Colonial Office and by officials and others from the Colonies who came to see him in London, and he was regarded with something more than liking by those of his colleagues whose work brought them into closest contact with him. For nearly fifty years from 1881 he gave much of his spare time to devoted and inspiring work at the Working Men's College in Great Ormond Street, founded by F. D. Maurice [q.v.] and Thomas Hughes [q.v.], of which he became principal in 1912. He died, unmarried, in London 7 May 1931.

[*The Times*, 8 May 1931; personal knowledge.]   JOHN RISLEY.

LUCAS, EDWARD VERRALL (1868–1938), journalist, essayist, and critic, was born at Eltham, Kent, 11 June 1868, the second of the four sons of Alfred Lucas, agent for insurance companies and building societies, by his wife, Jane Drewitt. Both his parents were Quakers, and members of families where interests had mainly been in farming, banking, and brewing, but on his mother's side he was related to Lord Lister and A. W. Verrall [qq.v.]. His parents moved to Brighton not long after he was born, so that he was able to call himself a Sussex man, and to give to that county not the least of his loyalties. Always devoted to his mother, he had less affection for the paternal regimen. 'I got from my father', he wrote, 'very little but knowledge of what to avoid . . . and learned . . . from his piety without works to be too much the unbeliever.' It is possible, however, that he derived from both parents his inclination to avoid, as a writer, the unpleasant realities of life, and to believe, even in war-time, that war was the worst of evils.

After having been sent to no less than eleven schools, Lucas was apprenticed at the age of sixteen to a Brighton bookseller, and after two years joined the staff of the *Sussex Daily News*. In 1892 he was enabled, through the gift of £200 from an uncle, to go to London and attend the lectures of W. P. Ker [q.v.] at University College. He read assiduously and in 1893 began his journalistic career on the *Globe*, a leading evening paper.

Lucas's early struggles left him something of a cynic, and he could be a bitter satirist, when he chose, of political and topical affairs. But he chose seldom, and emerged more and more as an apostle of the humanities, and if no optimist himself, a cause of optimism in others. He made it more and more his aim to communicate the delight which he found in art, travel, and letters to a rapidly growing circle of readers, and the manner that he cultivated for this purpose was, in appearance, so effortless, that only by its readableness could its craft be ascertained. As a young journalist, he spent many of his evenings translating Maupassant, not for publication, but as practice in style.

Lucas's publications include many anthologies and about thirty collections of light essays, on almost any subject that took his fancy, and some of the titles which he gave to them, *Listener's Lure* (1905), *One Day and Another* (1909), *Old Lamps for New* (1911), *Loiterer's Harvest* (1913), *Cloud and Silver* (1916), *A Rover I would be* (1928), indicate sufficiently the lightness, gaiety, and variety of their contents. Besides these, he wrote essays of travel in many places, *Highways and Byways in Sussex* (1904), *A Wanderer in Holland* (1905), *A Wanderer in Paris* (1909), *A Wanderer in Florence* (1912), *Zigzags in France* (1925), and short books on painters, notably *Vermeer of Delft* (1922), *John Constable the Painter* (1924), and *Vermeer the Magical* (1929). He produced an edition of *The Works of Charles and Mary Lamb* (7 vols., 1903–1905) and a *Life of Charles Lamb* (2 vols., 1905). 'Elia' indeed was his idol, but his devotion was rather to the urbane companion than to the learned and rather wistful recluse. He used occasionally the form of romance (*Over Bemerton's*, 1908, perhaps the best, *Rose and Rose*, 1921, and *Genevra's Money*, 1922, are examples in this kind, slight, sentimental, and charming), but he was accustomed to say that he could not write a novel, because no novel made out human beings as bad as they really were. Of the painters he praised, he remarked: 'I know very little about pictures, but I like to write about them for the benefit of those who know less.' To estimate the permanent value of his work is difficult, but he undoubtedly broadened the horizon of culture for a great number of readers by the easy introduction which he gave them to books that they would not otherwise have read, and pictures that they would not have seen; at the same time, he helped to liberate the language of the critic and the essayist from undue pedantry and affectation. Many writers in this field who followed him owe more than they realize to his clarity; many readers have a like debt to the liveliness of his sympathies. Often preferring the quaint to the profound, and claiming neither deep study nor creative imagination, he established himself by dint of good taste, observation, and wit as a man of letters, gaining friendship and admiration alike from the learned and the less critical. In his later years, a member of many social clubs, he added to the reputation of a writer that of a connoisseur who was also a *bon vivant* and a lavish host. He was, for a long time, a prolific contributor to *Punch* and a member of its staff, and in 1924 he became chairman of Methuen's Publishing Company, with which he had been long connected.

Lucas received honorary degrees from the universities of St. Andrews and Oxford. He was appointed C.H. in 1932. He married in 1897 Florence Elizabeth Gertrude, daughter of James Theodore Griffin, colonel in the United States army, and had a daughter. He died in London 26 June 1938.

There is a portrait of Lucas by Ralph Peacock in the offices of *Punch*. The plaster cast of a bust by John Tweed is in the possession of the sculptor's family.

[*The Times*, 27 June 1938; E. V. Lucas, *Reading, Writing and Remembering*, 1932; Audrey Lucas, *E. V. Lucas: A Portrait*, 1939; personal knowledge.]　　　E. V. KNOX.

LUNN, SIR HENRY SIMPSON (1859–1939), founder of the travel agency which bears his name, was born at Horncastle, Lincolnshire, 30 July 1859, the eldest son of Henry Lunn, afterwards of West Ashby House, Lincolnshire, by his wife, Susanna, daughter of Simpson Green, of Horncastle. He was educated at Horncastle Grammar School, and in 1881 entered Headingley College, Leeds, to prepare for the Methodist ministry; he left two years later to complete his course at Trinity College, Dublin, and was ordained in 1886. He hoped to be a medical missionary in India, and graduated in medicine and surgery in 1887. After his marriage in the last-named year he went to India, but ill health cut short his missionary career, and he returned to England in 1888. Some remarks on the standard of living of Methodist missionaries in India gave great offence to his brother ministers. As a consequence he contemplated taking orders in the Church of England, but no denomination was broad enough for him. In 1891 he founded a paper entitled *The Review of the Churches* devoted to the cause of reunion, and from this arose in 1892 the Grindelwald Conference of religious leaders, which became an annual event until 1896. The organization of these meetings interested Lunn

in travel and hotel work in Europe, and in 1892 he began to arrange tours: in 1909 there was founded the limited company which bears his name, with the associated organizations of the Hellenic Travellers' Club (1906) and Alpine Sports, Limited (1908).

During the South African war Lunn was an ardent pro-Boer, and his desire to be on good terms with all nations and peoples led to his being accused of having German sympathies, and brought him much unpopularity. He was constantly dispatching 'goodwill tours' about the globe, being misled by his humanitarian instincts into the belief, common among some earnest liberals until 1914, that friendly personal relations between the intelligentsia of various countries could avail against the forces of military and economic ambition. Lunn was a follower of Asquith, and twice stood unsuccessfully for parliament (January 1910 and in 1923).

After the war of 1914–1918 Lunn turned more to his religious activities, and sat upon many committees, and convened many conferences. In 1924 he travelled round the world with his wife in an ambitious effort to promote the union of the Churches, and to harness them to the League of Nations. Although he enjoyed unlimited hospitality, and delivered many speeches and sermons, he had to admit that he found no particular grounds for encouragement as regards the objects which he had at heart. He paid two subsequent visits to the United States of America, where his energy and powers of preaching were much appreciated.

Lunn maintained to the end of his life an infectious optimism on the subject of reunion, and a simple and sincere trust in Providence. If his opinions invited argument, at least he had the courage of them, and as a man his character never lost its charm. His own religious position was that of Wesley, a Methodist member of the Anglican Church.

Lunn, who was knighted in 1910, married in 1887 Ethel, daughter of Canon Thomas Moore, rector of Midleton, co. Cork, and had three sons, Arnold, Hugh, later known as Hugh Kingsmill, and Brian, and one daughter, who predeceased her father. He died in London 18 March 1939.

A portrait of Lunn by John Collier (1910) is in the possession of the family.

[*The Times*, 20 March 1939; Sir Henry Lunn, *Chapters from My Life*, 1918, and *Nearing Harbour*, 1934.]
　　　ALFRED COCHRANE.

LYGON, WILLIAM, seventh EARL BEAUCHAMP (1872–1938), politician, was born in London 20 February 1872, the elder son of Frederick Lygon, sixth Earl Beauchamp [q.v.], by his first wife, Lady Mary Catherine, only daughter of the historian Philip Henry Stanhope, fifth Earl Stanhope [q.v.]. He was educated at Eton and Christ Church, Oxford, and succeeded his father in 1891, the day before his nineteenth birthday.

From the first Beauchamp was precociously interested in public affairs. When he was twenty-three he was elected mayor of Worcester; at twenty-five he was a member of the London School Board. At twenty-seven (1899) he was appointed by Lord Salisbury governor of New South Wales. It was not a very successful experiment: for so responsible a post he was still rather too young.

Beauchamp returned to England in 1902 to find the Balfour government in the throes of a conversion to protection. Although brought up in the conservative, high church tradition of his family, he was personally an uncompromising free trader, and was soon so much alienated from the government's economic policy that he joined the liberals. Naturally they received him with open arms. He was wealthy and influential, a model landlord, a clear and competent speaker, an ideal chairman, and a popular and generous host.

Beauchamp's marriage in 1902 to the Duke of Westminster's beautiful sister, Lady Lettice Mary Elizabeth, younger daughter of Victor Alexander Grosvenor, Earl Grosvenor, and granddaughter of Hugh, first Duke of Westminster [q.v.], certainly added to his influence. Their magnificent receptions at Halkyn House, their big town mansion in Belgrave Square, were events of high importance in the London season, and a rallying point for liberals all over the country. After the liberal triumph of 1906, Beauchamp was sworn of the Privy Council, and he entered the Cabinet in 1910 as lord president of the Council. A few months later he was appointed first commissioner of Works. In August 1914, when Lord Morley [q.v.] and John Burns resigned on account of their opposition to the government's war policy, Beauchamp accepted the office of lord president of the Council held by the former, and retained the post until 1915. In 1916 he became president of the Free Trade Union. During the years after the war he played a considerable part in the efforts made to revive the fortunes of the liberal party, and from 1924 to 1931 he was leader of the party in the House of Lords. In 1931 he suddenly resigned all his offices but one and went to live abroad.

Lord Beauchamp was appointed K.C.M.G. in 1899 and K.G. in 1914. From 1913 to 1933 he was lord warden of the Cinque Ports, and from 1929 to 1931 chancellor of London University. He died in New York 15 November 1938, and was succeeded as eighth earl by his eldest son, William (born 1903). He was also survived by his youngest son and his four daughters. His wife and his second son both predeceased him in 1936.

[Private information; personal knowledge.]
STUART HODGSON.

LYNCH, ARTHUR ALFRED (1861–1934), author, soldier, and politician, was born at Smythesdale, Victoria, Australia, 16 October 1861, the fourth son of John Lynch, civil engineer and mining surveyor, a native of Tiermaclane, co. Clare, by his wife, Isabella, daughter of Peter McGregor: she was born at Perth in Scotland. He went to school at Ballarat, and at Melbourne University he graduated as M.A. and as a civil engineer. Coming to Europe, he first studied physics and psychology at the university of Berlin (1888–1889). He then took up medicine and studied at the Hôpital Beaujon in Paris. Later in life, during a parliamentary recess, he obtained the diploma of the École supérieure d'électricité in Paris.

In 1889 Lynch turned to journalism, and was thus engaged in London for six years, in the course of which he stood unsuccessfully for Galway city in 1892. In 1896 he was a war correspondent for the *Evening News* in the Ashanti campaign, and from that year until 1899 he was the Paris correspondent of the *Daily Mail*.

On the outbreak of the South African war Lynch went to Pretoria as the correspondent of the Paris *Le Journal*, and immediately on arrival in January 1900 joined the Boer side and was appointed colonel of 'No. II Irish Brigade', a group of seventy men drawn from every country in Europe except Turkey. When, however, he had done six months' active campaigning, he returned to Paris by way of New York after the republics had been over-run. These exploits gained him election to parliament as member for Galway city at a by-election in November 1901, but when he came to England in

June 1902 to take his seat, he was arrested, tried for high treason, and in January 1903 sentenced to death. This sentence was immediately commuted to penal servitude for life. Within twelve months he was released on ticket-of-leave and went to live in Paris. In July 1907 he was granted a free pardon. Having qualified from St. Mary's Hospital, Paddington, he began in 1908 to practise medicine in North London, and continued to do so until his death. At a by-election in September 1909 he was elected nationalist member for West Clare, for which he sat until 1918, his parliamentary activities during the war being chiefly directed towards a more vigorous prosecution of the hostilities against Germany, so that in 1918 this former rebel received the King's commission as a colonel for the purpose of conducting a recruiting campaign in Ireland.

Lynch's writings include literary and scientific criticism, philosophy, biographical studies, fiction, and verse, his output being in general characterized by disparagement of established contemporary figures. Intellectually an ambitious man, he believed himself to be one of the outstanding minds of the age, a fact which affords a clue to much of his career. Thus his 'deepest motive' in joining the Boers was, according to himself, to show that he, a thinker, was the equal or superior of men of action. His most considerable work is his *Principles of Psychology* (1923), which, in his opinion, 'is destined to be a lamp to the feet of men when the British Empire itself is forgotten'. This judgement has not received general endorsement.

Lynch married in 1895 Annie, daughter of the Rev. John Donor Powell. He died, without issue, in London 25 March 1934.

[A. A. Lynch, *My Life Story*, 1924; *The Times Law Reports* of treason trials; private information.]   DONAL O'SULLIVAN.

LYONS, JOSEPH ALOYSIUS (1879–1939), prime minister of Australia, was born at Stanley, Tasmania, 15 September 1879, the fourth son of the eight children of Michael Lyons, an estate-manager for the Van Diemen's Land Company in north-western Tasmania; later his father bought a butchery and a bakery at Ulverstone. His mother was Ellen, daughter of John Carroll. His parents had emigrated from Ireland.

When Lyons was nine years old his father failed in business and broke down in health. Young Lyons took a post to supplement the family income, but later his aunts, the Misses Carroll, enabled him to continue his schooling. At sixteen he became a student-teacher, and at twenty he was in charge of a small rural school. In 1907 Lyons underwent a year's training course at the new Teachers' College in Hobart, and qualified to enter the university. Soon afterwards his political activities became the subject of a debate in parliament, and a motion to 'discipline' him failed by one vote. He was then invited to stand as a labour candidate in the Tasmanian parliament, and in 1909 was returned for Wilmot, which he represented until 1929.

In 1914 the labour party took office in Tasmania and Lyons was appointed treasurer, and also minister for education and for railways; in this period he did much to extend the system of state high schools. When the government was defeated in 1916 he became leader of the opposition. Labour remained in opposition until 1923, when Lyons became premier and treasurer though without a majority in the House. By 1925 the budget showed the first surplus since 1918, and labour gained an absolute majority in the assembly for the first time. Besides being premier and treasurer, Lyons was also minister for railways from 1923 to 1924 and for mines from 1925 until 1928, when the labour government was defeated. In October 1929 he contested the Commonwealth elections, and was returned for Wilmot with a sound majority. He promptly became postmaster-general and minister for public works in Mr. Scullin's (labour) government.

In July 1930 the Commonwealth treasurer, Mr. Edward Granville Theodore, was forced to resign and Lyons became acting-treasurer. In November, while Mr. James Henry Scullin was in London, the labour caucus voted for the compulsory conversion of an internal loan of £28,000,000. Lyons defeated this move, and mainly by his own efforts carried out a successful voluntary conversion in December. In January 1931 Mr. Theodore was re-appointed treasurer, and Lyons at once resigned from the Cabinet. He was totally opposed to the treasurer's financial plans to bring the Commonwealth Bank under Treasury control. In March 1931 he opposed these plans in the House and was expelled from the party together with five supporters,

These members joined with the nationalist party in May to form the United Australia party under the leadership of Lyons. The rejection of its banking legislation by the Senate finally forced Mr. Scullin's government to reduce expenditure. In June 1931 the Commonwealth and all the states accepted the Premier's Plan, which combined deflationary measures to balance budgets with some expansionist measures to promote recovery. The plan had the support of both the government and opposition leaders, but a section of the labour party remained hostile to it and brought down Mr. Scullin's government in November 1931. In December the United Australia party won a sweeping victory, and Lyons became prime minister in the following January, pledged to carry out the Premier's Plan.

From 1932 to 1935 Lyons as prime minister and treasurer had the main responsibility for financial policy. Early in 1932 the New South Wales government of Mr. John Thomas Lang defaulted again on overseas interest payments; the Commonwealth assumed responsibility and took steps to recover the money. From 1933 economic conditions improved, and Australian recovery policy proved one of the most successful. Lyons's government was returned in September 1934, and, for the third time in succession, in October 1937 with reduced majorities. Besides the office of prime minister, Lyons was also minister for health (November 1935–February 1936) and vice-president of the Executive Council (November 1935–November 1937). He led the Australian delegation to the Imperial Conference in 1935, and with his wife attended the silver jubilee of King George V. In 1937 they again represented Australia at the coronation of King George VI, and the prime minister attended the Imperial Conference. For his services Lyons was sworn of the Privy Council (1932), and appointed C.H. (1936). He received the honorary degree of LL.D. from the universities of Cambridge and Melbourne and the freedom of the cities of Edinburgh, London, and Aberdeen. He died at Sydney 7 April 1939.

Lyons's break with the labour party was one of the most spectacular events in recent Australian history. It was the outcome of a disquiet that had been growing for a long time. As a Roman Catholic he had been perturbed in 1921 by the party's adoption of socialism as its aim. In Commonwealth politics he disliked the 'advanced' views of some of his colleagues, including Mr. Theodore's views on finance. To this was added a personal distrust, for Mr. Theodore had become wealthy; Lyons himself died poor. His break with his party was due to honest differences; most of the party agreed with Lyons in rejecting Mr. Lang's policy of repudiation, but accepted Mr. Theodore's plans. The Australian electorate supported Lyons, although Mr. Theodore's plans have later been realized. Economists have since doubted whether the deflationary measures of the Premier's Plan were altogether desirable, but they agreed then that it was the only practicable policy. The latter years of Lyons's government are more open to criticism. After 1933 a much bigger public works programme was desirable. While the international situation rapidly grew worse, defence expenditure increased very slowly. On the other hand, Lyons established the Department of External Affairs as an independent department in 1935 and began the system of Australian diplomatic representation abroad. Nothing was done to carry out the recommendations of the royal commission on the Australian monetary and banking systems (1937), although they were generally approved by economists. A National Insurance Act was passed (1938), but was shelved mainly because of opposition from the government's own supporters. Thus Lyons's later years were not marked by any great positive achievements. He was, however, very generally liked, for he was kindly and unostentatious. His personal relations with many former labour colleagues remained friendly, even after he had broken with them politically. He had the patience, tact, and tolerance necessary for the successful working of parliamentary democracy. But he is remembered chiefly for his leadership in the crisis of 1931. Ordinary men, confused by the differences within the labour party, and knowing little of economics, turned readily to Joseph Lyons, whose honesty and belief in economy they could easily understand.

Lyons married in 1915 Enid Muriel, daughter of William Charles Burnell, sawmiller, of Burnie, Tasmania. They had six sons, one of whom predeceased his father, and six daughters. His wife gave him valuable help in his work. She was elected to the Commonwealth parliament for Darwin (Tasmania) in 1943 and was appointed G.B.E. in 1937.

There is a portrait of Lyons by

W. B. McInnes in Parliament House, Canberra.

[*Argus* (Melbourne) and *Herald* (Melbourne), *passim*; *The Times*, 8 April 1939; E. O. G. Shann and D. B. Copland, *The Crisis in Australian Finance 1929 to 1931*, 1931, and *The Battle of the Plans*, 1931; D. B. Copland, *Australia in the World Crisis, 1929–1933*, 1934; R. I. Downing, 'The Planning of Public Investment in Australia', *International Labour Review*, October 1945; *Commonwealth Parliamentary Handbook, 1901–1930*, 1930; private information.] HERBERT BURTON.

LYTE, SIR HENRY CHURCHILL MAXWELL (1848–1940), deputy keeper of the public records and historian, was born in London 29 May 1848, the only son of John Walker Maxwell Lyte, of Berry Head, near Brixham, by his wife, Emily Jeannette, daughter of Colonel John Craigie, of the East India Company's service. He was grandson of the hymn-writer Henry Francis Lyte [q.v.], and through his mother was descended from the elder brother of the great Duke of Marlborough. Educated at Eton and Christ Church, Oxford, he graduated in the school of law and modern history in 1870.

In 1875 Lyte published his first book, *A History of Eton College, 1440–1875*, and in 1886 *A History of the University of Oxford from the Earliest Times to the Year 1530*, standard works which still retain their value. During the same period he wrote a number of reports for the Historical Manuscripts Commission, including notable accounts of the muniments belonging to the dean and chapter of St. Paul's Cathedral, and the Duke of Rutland's manuscripts at Belvoir Castle. In 1886, when he was still only thirty-seven, he was appointed, at a critical moment, to the deputy keepership of the public records, a post which he held with great distinction for forty years.

By this time the impulse given by the foundation in 1838 of the Public Record Office had died away. The schemes of Sir Francis Palgrave and Sir T. Duffus Hardy [qq.v.] to publish the records *in extenso* had broken down: the department was slack and riven by personal jealousies. With cautious persistence Lyte altered all this, and infused fresh energy into the office. The premises were rebuilt: the vast accumulation of documents was sorted: and the chief classes made available for reference in a new series of *Lists and Indexes*. Above all, he instituted and carried far towards completion the in-

valuable series of *Calendars of the Chancery Rolls*. Among his own publications, the great edition of the *Book of Fees* (part i, 1920, part ii, 1923) and *Historical Notes on the use of the Great Seal of England* (1926) are noteworthy.

In 1926, being then seventy-eight years of age, Lyte resigned to make way for a younger man. A shrewd administrator and an understanding chief (if somewhat aloof), he had long ere this turned the office into a vigorous and efficient department. A loyal staff of able men co-operated in a long series of publications which have at once assisted and profoundly influenced the development of modern historical research. Official recognition of his services came early, for he was appointed C.B. in 1889 and K.C.B. in 1897; he was an original fellow of the British Academy, and in 1929 his old university conferred upon him the honorary degree of D.Litt. A kindly man, keenly interested in genealogy, with artistic leanings and a taste for photography, he retained his good health and zeal for study to the last, dying after a short illness at Wells, Somerset, 28 October 1940, at the age of ninety-two. His lifework was the creation of a new and better tradition in the conduct of the Public Record Office and it remains as his monument.

Lyte married in 1871 Frances Fownes (died 1925), elder daughter of James Curtis Somerville, J.P., of Dinder House, Wells, and had three sons and three daughters.

[Charles Johnson, *Sir Henry Churchill Maxwell-Lyte, 1848–1940* in *Proceedings* of the British Academy, vol. xxvi, 1940 (portrait); personal knowledge.]

V. H. GALBRAITH.

LYTTELTON, SIR NEVILLE GERALD (1845–1931), general, was born at Hagley, Worcestershire, 28 October 1845, the third of the eight sons of George William Lyttelton, fourth Lord Lyttelton [q.v.], by his first wife, Mary, second daughter of Sir Stephen Richard Glynne, eighth baronet, and sister of Mrs. William Ewart Gladstone. He was brother of Arthur Temple Lyttelton [q.v.] and Alfred Lyttelton [q.v.]. He came from a home devoutly Anglican and was educated at Eton, whence in 1865 he joined the Rifle Brigade and went to Canada where he helped to suppress the Fenian rising of 1866. In 1867 he acted as secretary to the commission dealing with the Oregon boundary dispute,

After having been posted to various places in England, Ireland, and India (where he served in the expedition of 1877–1878 against the Jowaki Afridis), Lyttelton became private secretary to H. C. E. Childers [q.v.] who had been appointed secretary of state for war in the liberal government of 1880, but in 1882 he took part in the Egyptian campaign as aide-de-camp to Sir J. M. Adye [q.v.] to whom, as governor of Gibraltar, he became military secretary from 1883 to 1885. From the latter year until 1890 he was military secretary to Lord Reay [q.v.], governor of Bombay, and after joining the 3rd battalion of his regiment at Jullunder as second in command he returned to England in 1893, having shortly before been promoted to command the first battalion. He then commanded the second battalion in Ireland. In 1894 he was appointed assistant adjutant-general at the War Office and assistant military secretary in 1897. But the next year he went to the Sudan in command of a brigade, and was present at the battle of Omdurman. In 1899 he commanded the 2nd Infantry brigade at Aldershot.

At the outbreak of war in South Africa, Lyttelton, who was sent to Natal in command of the 4th brigade and successively thereafter commanded the 2nd and 4th divisions, was held to be one of the few senior officers who emerged with enhanced reputation from that unsatisfactory episode, credit accruing to him from his handling of his troops at Spion Kop, Vaal Krantz, and the relief of Ladysmith. He used to contrast the battle of Omdurman where '50,000 fanatics streamed across the open regardless of cover to certain death' with Colenso, 'where I never saw a Boer all day ... and it was our men who were the victims'. After having commanded in the eastern Transvaal, in the operations against General C. R. De Wet [q.v.], and in Natal once more, he became commander-in-chief in South Africa in succession to Kitchener from June 1902 until January 1904. These years saw little of military importance, but he and Lady Lyttelton exerted themselves to bring Briton and Boer together as much as possible, and he and General Louis Botha [q.v.] discussed the conduct of the war with great interest.

The most important phase of Lyttelton's military career opened on his appointment as chief of the General Staff and first military member of the Army Council in 1904. It was during his four years of office that the Expeditionary Force was built up. Lyttelton's preponderating interest was in the training of the staff and the formation of the Officers' Training Corps. In this and in two other matters, events were to justify him: in a dispute with H. O. Arnold-Forster [q.v.] over the introduction of a heavier type of artillery, wherein he won his point, and in his criticism of the changes in staff organization inaugurated by Kitchener in India, of which he strongly disapproved and to which he attributed the misfortunes of the Mesopotamian campaign.

In 1908 Lyttelton, who had been promoted full general in 1906, went to Ireland as commander-in-chief, and in 1912 he was appointed governor of the Royal Hospital, Chelsea, a post which he held until his death which took place there 6 July 1931.

Lyttelton was mentioned in dispatches and received a brevet of lieutenant-colonel after the battle of Tel-el-Kebir (1882), and he was again mentioned after Omdurman (when he was promoted major-general) and in the South African war (when he was promoted lieutenant-general). He was appointed C.B. in 1897, K.C.B. in 1902, G.C.B. in 1907, and G.C.V.O. in 1911, and he was sworn of the Irish Privy Council in 1908. He married in 1883 Katharine Sarah, youngest daughter of James Archibald Stuart-Wortley [q.v.], and was survived by her and by their three daughters, the eldest of whom married C. F. G. Masterman [q.v.], and the youngest, W. L. Hichens [q.v.].

There is a portrait of Lyttelton by Archibald Stuart-Wortley at Hagley Hall, and there are two by Harris Brown, the one at the Royal Hospital, Chelsea, and the other in the possession of his second daughter, Mrs. Arthur Grenfell. A cartoon of him by 'Spy' appeared in *Vanity Fair* 5 September 1901.

[*The Times*, 7 July 1931; Sir Neville Lyttelton, *Eighty Years*, 1927; personal knowledge.]

LUCY MASTERMAN.

LYTTON, SIR HENRY ALFRED (1865–1936), actor, whose original name was HENRY ALFRED JONES, was born in Kensington 3 January 1865 (he always gave the date erroneously as 3 January 1867), the only son of Henry Jones, jeweller, by his second wife, Martha Lavinia Harris. He was educated at St. Mark's School, Chelsea, where he took part in amateur theatrical performances and whence he ran away in an unsuccessful endeavour to become a professional actor.

A few years later, in 1882, Lytton made his first appearance on the professional stage at the Philharmonic Theatre, Islington, in *The Obstinate Bretons*, in the caste of which was his future wife, Louie, daughter of William Webber, of London, whom he married in 1884. Through her influence he secured an engagement with the D'Oyly Carte Opera Company, and made his first appearance at the Royalty Theatre, Glasgow, in February 1884 in the chorus of *Princess Ida*. He appeared under the name of H. A. Henri, his wife's stage name being Louie Henri. He remained with the D'Oyly Carte Company only a short time before joining another touring company, the London Comedy and Operetta Company.

Early in 1887 Lytton was engaged by Richard D'Oyly Carte [q.v.] at the Savoy Theatre, London, as understudy to George Grossmith, the elder [q.v.]. Fortune smiled on him almost immediately, for in January 1887, a week after the production of *Ruddigore*, by (Sir) W. S. Gilbert and Sir Arthur Sullivan [qq.v.], his principal fell ill, and Lytton made a great success in Grossmith's part of Robin Oakapple. It was after this success that, at the suggestion of Gilbert, he adopted the name of Lytton. He then toured with the D'Oyly Carte Company for several years, and it was not until April 1897 that he again appeared in London when, at the Savoy Theatre, he succeeded George Grossmith as Ferdinand the Fifth in *His Majesty*. From 1897 to 1899 he appeared at the Savoy in revivals of *The Yeomen of the Guard*, *The Grand Duchess*, *The Gondoliers*, *Trial by Jury*, and *H.M.S. Pinafore*, increasing his reputation very considerably.

In July 1899 Lytton undertook the management of the Criterion Theatre, London, producing a farcical comedy, *The Wild Rabbit*, by George Arliss which, however, was unsuccessful. He returned to the Savoy in the same year, and remained there until 1903, playing leading parts in *The Rose of Persia* (1899), *The Pirates of Penzance* (1900), *Patience* (1900), *The Emerald Isle* (1901), *Iolanthe* (1901), *Merrie England* (1902), and *A Princess of Kensington* (1903).

During the next six years Lytton was seen at various London theatres, in *The Earl and the Girl* (Adelphi, 1903), *The Talk of the Town* (Adelphi, 1905), *The White Chrysanthemum* (Criterion, 1905), *The Spring Chicken* (Gaiety, 1906), *The Little Michus* (Daly's, 1906), and *My Darling* (Hicks, 1907).

Lytton returned to the Savoy in April 1908 to appear for the first time at that theatre in *The Mikado*. From that date until his retirement in 1934 he played exclusively in the repertory, in London and the provinces. He played no fewer than thirty characters in these operas during his career, and appeared in all his famous parts during the seasons at the Prince's Theatre in 1919, 1921, 1924, and 1926, and again at the Savoy in 1929–1930 and 1932–1933. His performances as John Wellington Wells in *The Sorcerer*, Sir Joseph Porter in *H.M.S. Pinafore*, Major-General Stanley in *The Pirates of Penzance*, Reginald Bunthorne in *Patience*, the Lord Chancellor in *Iolanthe*, Ko-Ko in *The Mikado*, Robin Oakapple in *Ruddigore*, Jack Point in *The Yeomen of the Guard*, and the Duke of Plaza-Toro in *The Gondoliers* were unexcelled, either by his predecessors or his successors. It is remarkable that he was not the original exponent of any of these parts, but his popularity in them was extraordinary. Undoubtedly his best impersonation and his own favourite part was his Jack Point, which was full of intensely human appeal, romance, and pathos. He made his last appearance with the D'Oyly Carte Company at the Gaiety Theatre, Dublin, in June 1934.

For twenty-six years Lytton was the mainstay of the company, and in 1930, when he was knighted, he was entertained at luncheon by 500 men and women representative of the stage, literature, art, politics, the law, and commerce. After the celebration of his stage jubilee, he received a national testimonial, and among the signatories of the album which accompanied the gift were the prime minister, Ramsay MacDonald, Stanley Baldwin, and Lloyd George, the presentation being made by the last-named. At Christmas 1934 he entered on his last engagement when, at the Prince of Wales's Theatre, Birmingham, he acted as the Emperor in the pantomime *Aladdin*, his first and only part in pantomime.

According to his own confession Lytton could not read a line of music, and all his songs were taught him by his wife, who played them over and over again until he had mastered them. He possessed a light, pleasant voice with crystal-clear diction, a high sense of comedy, a remarkably keen sense of 'timing' which gave poise and distinction to every part which he undertook, and his acting always appeared to be perfectly spontaneous.

Lytton died in London 15 August 1936, and was survived by his wife (died 1947) and two sons and two daughters. A son was killed in 1917 while serving in the Royal Flying Corps; two others died in infancy. He was the author of two books, *The Secrets of a Savoyard* (1922) and *A Wandering Minstrel* (1933).

[*The Times* and *Daily Telegraph*, 17 August 1936; *Who's Who in the Theatre*, 1936; Sir H. A. Lytton, *The Secrets of a Savoyard*, 1922, and *A Wandering Minstrel*, 1933; private information; personal knowledge.]

JOHN PARKER.

MACALISTER, SIR DONALD, first baronet (1854–1934), physician, principal and vice-chancellor and, later, chancellor of the university of Glasgow, was born at Perth 17 May 1854, the second son of Donald MacAlister, by his wife, Euphemia, second daughter of Angus Kennedy, of Bowmore, Islay. The MacAlisters had long been settled on Lochfyneside as land-holders and later as crofters and fisher-men, but the elder Donald MacAlister had become a publishers' agent, living succes-sively in Glasgow, Perth, Aberdeen, and, from 1864 until his death in 1881, in Liverpool where he was with the firm of Blackie & Son. He had a large family and narrow means, so that his son had not only to provide for his own education but, in his early manhood, to bear the greater part of the maintenance and education of his younger brothers and sisters. After attending various schools, MacAlister went in 1866 to Liverpool Institute, then under the direction of the Rev. John Sephton, to whose teaching and guidance MacAlister owed much. In 1873 he entered St. John's College, Cambridge, as a scholar, though also elected elsewhere. He read mathematics and finished his course in January 1877 as senior wrangler and first Smith's prizeman. In November 1877 he was elected into a fellowship at St. John's. He remained a fellow of the college until the end of his life, and was senior tutor from 1900 to 1904.

After a brief and happy interlude as a mathematical master at Harrow, Mac-Alister turned to his original intention of studying medicine, first at Cambridge, later in 1879 at St. Bartholomew's Hospital, and for a short time at Leipzig. In 1881 he settled in Cambridge, and took up medical teaching, investigation, and practice: he held the positions of Linacre lecturer, of deputy to the regius professor of physic (Sir George Paget, q.v.), and in 1884, when he graduated M.D., of physician to Addenbrooke's Hospital. In this work he had great success, and won wide recognition in the Royal College of Physicians and in other schools. He was elected F.R.C.P. in 1886 and gave the Goulstonian lecture on 'The Nature of Fever' in 1887; a year later he delivered the Croonian lecture. He had been editor of the *Practitioner* since 1882, and held this post for thirteen years. His main energies were already drawn to organiza-tion and administration; he took an active part in college and university affairs. A decisive event was his election in 1889 as the representative of Cambridge on the General Medical Council. This became one of his chief fields of activity; he was a member for forty-four years, and for twenty-seven years (1904–1931) he was president.

In 1907 MacAlister was nominated for appointment by the Crown as principal of the university of Glasgow. In his twenty-two years of office, broken as they were by the war of 1914–1918, he pre-sided over a great expansion of the univer-sity. To a remarkable degree he gained the confidence of city and university alike, and gathered support both for his building programme and for the endowment of teaching posts. His health was never completely reliable; but he had immense resolution, industry, and staying power, and accomplished at Glasgow, in London, and farther afield a great volume of work. Apart from the affairs of the General Medical Council, he took a leading part in the general university business of the country. He was one of the founders of the Universities' Bureau of the British Empire, and was for many years chairman of the standing committee of vice-chancellors and principals of the British universities. He served on many govern-ment commissions, including the Treasury Committee of 1908 on the university of Wales, the commission on the Queen's University, Belfast, and the royal com-mission on the civil service (1912–1915). On medical matters, he was chairman of the British Pharmacopœia committee, and had a large share in the preparation of the *British Pharmacopœia* in 1898 and its revision in 1914. He was chairman of the medical consultative committee of the Scottish Board of Health and had a long and active association with the de-velopment of the Highlands and Islands medical service board. He was also vice-chairman of the Carnegie United Kingdom Trust.

MacAlister was fond of travel, and acquired languages with astonishing ease. His most widely known publication is *Echoes* (1907), a volume of translations in verse from and into most modern European languages. He had a special interest in Russian and Romani, and was president of the Gypsy Lore Society in 1915. In religion he was a staunch Presbyterian.

MacAlister held honorary doctorates from thirteen universities at home and abroad. He was appointed K.C.B. in 1908 and created a baronet in 1924. He received the freedom of the city of Glasgow in 1924, and after his resignation of the principalship in 1929 he was elected chancellor of the university.

MacAlister married in 1895 Edith Florence Boyle, eldest daughter of his distant kinsman Alexander Macalister, professor of anatomy at Cambridge; there were no children of the marriage. He died at Cambridge 15 January 1934.

A portrait of MacAlister was painted in 1924 by Maurice Greiffenhagen for the General Medical Council. Glasgow University commissioned one to be painted by George Henry, which is now in the senate room. A replica of the portrait by Greiffenhagen was presented to his wife, together with a bust by George Paulin.

[*The Times*, 16 January 1934; E. F. B. MacAlister, *Sir Donald MacAlister of Tarbet*, 1935; personal knowledge.]

H. J. W. HETHERINGTON.

McCARDIE, SIR HENRY ALFRED (1869–1933), judge, was born at Edgbaston 19 July 1869, the son of an Irishman, Joseph William McCardie, merchant, of Edgbaston. His mother, Jane Elizabeth Hunt, was English. He was called to the bar by the Middle Temple in 1894, and read in the chambers of (Judge) James John Parfitt, at Birmingham. He joined the Midland circuit and became a bencher of his Inn in 1916. In the same year he was appointed a judge of the King's Bench division.

McCardie had two characteristics which tended to place him in a category of his own among judges. Most judges keep in the forefront of their minds the reflection that their duty is to decide the case before them and not to deliver a dissertation on the whole of the law involved. This is the explanation of the loose phraseology sometimes employed by judges in their judicial pronouncements, which misleads students and necessarily drives them to supplement their study of original authorities by much resort to text-books. But McCardie's judgements read as though he had consciously prepared them for the host of law students, contemporary and future. Their prolixity was inspired, not by any vain wish to make a parade of his immense learning, but by a single-hearted desire to fulfil what he conceived to be the true judicial function. A certain lord chancellor aptly described him as 'the greatest master of case-law of our time'. His learning extended, too, outside the limits of English case-law. In *Cohen* v. *Sellar* (1926) he was faced with the curious question whether a man who has promised to marry a woman, and fails, without legal justification, to carry out his promise, can demand the return of the engagement ring. McCardie reached the negative conclusion through a long chain of intricate reasoning, based not only upon an exhaustive study of the English authorities, but also upon the most profound research into Roman and continental law. His second peculiarity, which he shared with the famous Louis Dembitz Brandeis, one of the ablest judges who ever graced the Supreme Court of the United States of America, was his conviction that the consideration of social problems, as well as that of judicial precedents, should form part of the tools of a judge's trade. In pursuance of this view, he delivered himself freely of all sorts of aphorisms on many burning topics of the day. This habit was by no means always popular either with his judicial brethren or with some outside the legal profession. Thus he held a firm opinion that it might sometimes be a moral duty to carry out an operation for abortion. His expression of this opinion from the bench in 1931 was much criticized, but it is worthy of note that it was, in effect, vindicated in the famous case of *R.* v. *Bourne* (1939), where it was held that in all abortion trials the onus is on the Crown to prove that the operation was not performed with the object of preserving the life of the mother. In *Place* v. *Searle* (1932), an action by a husband against the enticer of his wife, he gave vent to a long disquisition on the status of married women from the sociological point of view, for which he incurred the rebuke of Lord Justice Scrutton [q.v.] in the Court of Appeal. But the case which rendered him the target for much political rancour was *O'Dwyer* v. *Nair* in

1924. This was a libel action, arising out of the Amritsar disturbances in 1919, and especially the drastic action of Brigadier-General R. E. H. Dyer [q.v.], which was a cardinal point in the case. McCardie, who never lacked the courage of his convictions, took occasion to record deliberately his considered opinion that the action of Dyer was right, and that the secretary of state for India had acted wrongly in removing him from the army. He spoke with full knowledge that his remarks would cause great dissatisfaction in certain quarters. Nor was he disappointed, for George Lansbury [q.v.] put down a motion in the House of Commons for an address to the King praying for McCardie's removal from the bench. Although he was supported by the assurance that in calling the attention of the jury to the evidence on that particular point, he had done nothing but his plain duty, an assurance rendered doubly sure by the approval of many of his judicial brethren, nevertheless his heart was greatly wounded by the vindictiveness of the attacks upon him, which made him intensely unhappy. The whole episode must have inspired his written words, which might serve as a model for any aspirant to the bench, 'Judges seek no popularity. They will not yield to the passing winds of popular excitement.'

Among McCardie's most famous criminal cases should be mentioned the trials in 1922 of Henry Jacoby for the murder of Lady White, and of Ronald True for the murder of Olive Young. Among his many civil decisions it is difficult to make the proper selections. *Maclenan* v. *Segar* (1917) is a classic authority on the extent of an innkeeper's liability to his guest for the safety of his premises. In 1918, in *Naylor, Benzon and Co.* v. *Krainische Industrie Gesellschaft*, in which McCardie held a contract, entered into between a British and an Austrian company before the war, to have been dissolved, notwithstanding a suspension clause, by the outbreak of war, he expressed doubt of Lord Halsbury's view that no court can invent a new head of public policy, and said: 'Public policy is a variable thing. It must fluctuate with the circumstances of the time.' In *Jeffrey* v. *Bamford* (1921) he laid down that a partnership for the purpose of carrying on a bookmaker's business is not *per se* illegal. In *Phillips* v. *Britannia Hygienic Laundry Co.* (1923) he held that one who had broken a statutory order by bringing on a road a motor-car with a defective axle did not, by that mere breach, render himself liable to a civil action at the suit of a person injured thereby. In *Gayler and Pope* v. *Davies* (1924) he enunciated the principle that if a horse is left unattended in a public street and bolts, this is prima facie evidence of negligence against its owner. All these, and many others, represent vital contributions by a great and learned judge to the vast fabric of the Common Law, which he faithfully served with all his might.

The political attacks made upon him may have led to the deep fits of depression from which McCardie suffered, and in one of which he died by his own hand in London 26 April 1933. He never married.

[*The Times*, 27 and 29 April 1933; George Pollock, *Mr. Justice McCardie*, 1934.]

H. G. HANBURY.

McCORMICK, WILLIAM PATRICK GLYN (1877–1940), vicar of St. Martin-in-the-Fields, London, was born at Hull 14 June 1877, the fourth child and third son of Joseph McCormick, vicar of Holy Trinity church, Hull, afterwards canon of York Minster, rector of St. James's church, Piccadilly, and an honorary chaplain to the king, by his wife, Frances, daughter of Lieutenant-Colonel Gregory Haines, of the East India Company's service, and granddaughter of Hugh, first Viscount Gough [q.v.]. McCormick was educated at Llandaff Cathedral School, Exeter School, and St. John's College, Cambridge. He was ordained deacon in 1900 and priest in 1901, and in 1902 went to South Africa as an army chaplain, intending to make this his career. He soon realized the urgent need of a Christian ministry on the Rand, so in 1903 he went to Jumpers Deep Mine, Cleveland, and lived with the men in their quarters. It was very uphill work, but his warm friendliness, coupled with his prowess at Rugby football and at cricket soon made him very popular. He started the parish of St. Patrick's, Cleveland, raising the money for building the church and vicarage. In 1910 he was appointed rector of St. John's church, Belgravia, Johannesburg, and in the same year married Ada Miriam, daughter of George Herbert Shelton, of the Stock Exchange, a kinsman of William Morris. By her he had a son and three daughters.

McCormick was on leave in England at the outbreak of war in 1914, and joined the army as a chaplain one month later, seeing active service in France. From 1915 to 1917 he was senior chaplain to the

Guards division; from 1917 to 1918 deputy-assistant-chaplain-general to the XIV Corps; and from 1918 to 1919 assistant-chaplain-general at Boulogne. In 1917 he was awarded the D.S.O., and he was four times mentioned in dispatches. On his return to England in 1919 he was appointed vicar of Croydon; from 1923 to 1927 he was an honorary canon of Canterbury Cathedral; and from 1928 until his death he was an honorary chaplain to the king. When H. R. L. Sheppard [q.v.] resigned the living of St. Martin-in-the-Fields in 1927, McCormick was appointed vicar, and so remained until his death. It was no easy task to follow a man like Sheppard, but no one could have done it so successfully as McCormick. He carried on the work of his predecessor and extended it in many ways. At the end of his life he suffered from heart trouble, and the strain of the war, which involved turning the crypt into a shelter for use in air-raids, probably hastened his death in London 16 October 1940.

McCormick was an outstanding personality with a shrewd brain and the gift of bringing out the best in people. Although not a great orator, he could hold his congregations, whether in church or on the air, by his simplicity and utter sincerity. Apart from the warm friendliness of his manner, his most distinctive characteristics were his shining faith, his serenity, and his selfless humility.

A memorial plaque to McCormick is in the crypt of St. Martin-in-the-Fields.

[R. J. Northcott, *Pat McCormick*, 1941; private information; personal knowledge.]

C. JOYCE E. HOLLINS.

MACDONALD, SIR GEORGE (1862–1940), numismatist, classical scholar and archaeologist, and civil servant, was born at Elgin 30 January 1862, the third son of James Macdonald, a master at Elgin Academy and an antiquary, by his wife, Margaret Raff. He was educated at the Ayr Academy, of which his father was then rector, and at Edinburgh University, where he had a distinguished career. Thence he proceeded in 1884 to Balliol College, Oxford, obtaining a first class in classical moderations (1885) and in *literae humaniores* (1887). From 1887 to 1892 he was a member of the staff of the Kelvinside Academy, Glasgow, and was subsequently (1892–1904) a lecturer in Greek at the university. In 1904 he was appointed assistant secretary of the Scottish Education Department, ultimately becoming

secretary (1922–1928). A departmental connexion with the Royal Scottish Museum caused him to be nominated to the royal commission on museums and galleries (1927–1930) and following thereon to the standing commission (1931): he was re-appointed for a further period of seven years in 1938. He also became a member of the fine arts commission for Scotland on its institution in 1927. From 1918 onwards he was one of the two reporters for the Carnegie Trust for the universities of Scotland under the research scheme. He was also a member of the university grants committee from 1933 onwards.

Besides being a distinguished administrator, Macdonald was also a skilled numismatist and archaeologist and an eminent authority on Romano-British history and antiquities. The Hunterian collection of coins in Glasgow University had long claimed his attention, and between 1899 and 1905 he produced his catalogue of Greek and Roman coins in that collection, a work which placed him in the front rank of numismatists and which was 'crowned' by the Académie des Inscriptions et Belles-Lettres and which brought him the award of the Prix Allier de Hauteroche (1907). He was a frequent contributor to the *Numismatic Chronicle* and in 1905 he delivered in Edinburgh the Rhind lectures in archaeology which were published in the same year as *Coin Types, their Origin and Development*. Many numismatic societies, both British and foreign, claimed him as a member, and in 1935 he was president of the Royal Numismatic Society, which had awarded him its medal in 1913.

With an interest inherited from his father in the Antonine Wall between the Forth and the Clyde, Macdonald devoted much of his leisure to establishing its line and in excavating its forts. A course of Dalrymple lectures delivered in Glasgow in 1910 on this subject subsequently formed the main strand of his *Roman Wall in Scotland* (1911). A close friendship with F. J. Haverfield [q.v.] led to the publication in 1924, after Haverfield's death, of his Ford lectures in their joint names under the title of *The Roman Occupation of Britain*. His authoritative work on Romano-British history was fully recognized abroad and his reputation as a scholar was enhanced by his regular contributions to Pauly–Wissowa's *Real-Encyclopädie* from 1923 to the close of his life.

Many honours were conferred upon

Macdonald. He was appointed C.B. in 1916 and K.C.B. in 1927. He received honorary degrees from the universities of Edinburgh, Glasgow, Oxford, and Cambridge. He was elected a fellow of the British Academy in 1913, and an honorary fellow of the Royal Society of Edinburgh in 1933 and of Balliol College, Oxford, in 1936; he was also an honorary member of the Royal Scottish Academy and a trustee of the National Library of Scotland. He was president of the Society for the Promotion of Roman Studies from 1921 to 1926 and of the Classical Associations of England and Wales (1931) and of Scotland (1936). At the time of his death he was president of the Society of Antiquaries of Scotland, chairman of the royal commission on the ancient and historical monuments of Scotland, and a member of the advisory board for Scotland to the ancient monuments department of the Office of Works.

Macdonald married in 1897 Margaret Tannahill, daughter of George Younger, a Glasgow merchant, and had a son and a daughter who predeceased her father. He died in Edinburgh 9 August 1940.

Macdonald's portrait by Maurice Greiffenhagen, at present with the Scottish Education Department, will eventually be placed in the Scottish National Portrait Gallery.

[The Times, 12 August 1940; A. O. Curle, Sir George Macdonald, 1862–1940 in Proceedings of the British Academy, vol. xxvii, 1941 (portrait); personal knowledge.]

A. O. CURLE.

MACDONALD, HECTOR MUNRO (1865–1935), mathematical physicist, was born in Edinburgh 19 January 1865, the elder son of Donald Macdonald, originally of Kiltearn, Ross, by his wife, Annie, daughter of Hector Munro, of Kiltearn. His earliest education was in Edinburgh, but after the removal of his parents to Fearn in Easter Ross, he went to school there, and later to the Royal Academy, Tain, and Old Aberdeen Grammar School. He graduated at the university of Aberdeen in 1886 with first class honours in mathematics and was awarded a Fullerton scholarship. Proceeding to Clare College, Cambridge, as a foundation scholar, he graduated as fourth wrangler in 1889, was elected in 1890 into a fellowship at Clare, which he held until 1908, and in 1891 was awarded the second Smith's prize.

In the last years of the nineteenth century Macdonald published many papers of a pure-mathematical character, on the relations between convergent series and asymptotic expansions, the zeros and the addition theorem of Bessel functions, various Bessel integrals, spherical harmonics, and Fourier series. But his permanent reputation as a discoverer will probably rest chiefly on a group of researches in mathematical physics, the origin of which may be traced to the announcement by Cambridge University in 1899 of the Adams prize subject for 1901, 'The improvement of existing knowledge in respect of . . . the modes and periods of free electric vibrations in systems of charged bodies, and the radiation from them . . . the theory of wireless telegraphy'. Macdonald submitted an essay which won the prize. The great advance made in it was the solution of the problem of diffraction at the edge of a perfectly conducting (i.e. totally reflecting) prism, which was solved by a method admitting of extension to any transparent or metallic prism of which the optical constants are known.

Macdonald's essay was published under the title Electric Waves in 1902. About this time, Guglielmo (afterwards Marchese) Marconi succeeded in sending wireless signals across the Atlantic: and the problem of explaining the mechanism of such transmission attracted the attention of mathematicians. The question may be put thus: the electric waves generated by the sending apparatus differ from waves of light only by having a longer wave-length, which is, nevertheless, small compared with the radius of the earth; the curved surface of the earth may, therefore, be expected to form a sort of shadow, effectively screening the receiving apparatus at a distance; how, then, does it happen that in practice the waves penetrate into the region of the shadow?

To Macdonald belongs the credit of having been the first to formulate the problem as one of diffraction, and of having, in a series of papers published between 1903 and 1914, solved it. The fact that wireless signals are much stronger than his final theory would lead the student to expect, and that consequently the diffraction explanation cannot account for the facts, does not diminish the importance of his achievement: for it was necessary to find the answer to the diffraction problem before accepting the (physically) more complicated theory that a layer exists in the upper rarefied region of the atmosphere, which acts as a reflector for electro-magnetic waves of great wave-length, so that between this layer and the earth's surface the waves spread with only two-dimensional divergence.

Macdonald's later papers (eight were produced in his seventh decade) and his book *Electro-magnetism* (1934) continued the main study of his life, the radiation, transmission, and reflection of electric waves. He never seemed to be affected by the tremendous upheaval caused by the discoveries of the twentieth century—relativity and quantum-mechanics.

In 1904 Macdonald left Cambridge on being appointed to the chair of mathematics in his old university of Aberdeen, where his ability as an administrator soon made him the most influential member of the senatus. In 1907 he was elected as one of the representatives of the senatus on the university court, of which he remained a member (except when absent on government service during the war) for the rest of his life, attending his last meeting only a week before his death. Brought up on a farm, and with the further experience of estate management gained as acting senior bursar of Clare, he naturally took up specially the oversight of the university lands and buildings; his conception of a *cité universitaire* for the neighbourhood of King's College has left a permanent impress on that region.

The value of Macdonald's scientific work was recognized by his election in 1901 to the fellowship of the Royal Society, of which he was awarded a Royal medal in 1916. He was president of the London Mathematical Society in 1916–1918, was elected into an honorary fellowship at Clare in 1914, and received the honorary degree of LL.D. from Glasgow University in 1934. A portrait painted by R. G. Eves was presented by his friends to the university of Aberdeen in 1933.

Macdonald never married. He died at Aberdeen after a short illness 16 May 1935.

[*The Times*, 17 May 1935; *Obituary Notices of Fellows of the Royal Society*, No. 4, December 1935 (portrait); personal knowledge.]

EDMUND T. WHITTAKER.

MacDONALD, JAMES RAMSAY (1866–1937), labour leader and statesman, was born in a two-roomed 'but and ben' at Lossiemouth, Morayshire, a grey, lowland village of fishermen and farmworkers in the parish of Drainie, within a few hours' walk of the Highlands, 12 October 1866. Isabella Ramsay, his grandmother, a woman of exceptional courage and character, had successfully reared her four young children after being left penniless by an absconding husband. Of these, the youngest, Anne, said to have been the most intelligent of the family, when working at a farm in the parish of Alves, near Elgin, became with child by the head ploughman, John MacDonald, a Highlander from the Black Isle of Ross. She did not marry, and her son was born in her mother's cottage. The peculiar circumstances of MacDonald's childhood may well have accounted for the unusual later combination of mental toughness, physical courage, and extreme sensitiveness in his character.

At Drainie school, where the fees were eightpence a month, the boy studied Euclid and the ancient tongues, and devoured such books as were available in his grandmother's cottage or were lent him by a consumptive watchmaker, who introduced him to the works of Dickens. Before he was fifteen he was head of the school. For a short while, after leaving, he worked on a farm, but when he was about sixteen the 'dominie' of Drainie invited him to become a pupil teacher, at seven pounds ten shillings a year. With the free run of the 'dominie's' shelves he made the acquaintance of Shakespeare, of Carlyle's tory socialism, Ruskin's socialist aesthetics, and Henry George's then extremely influential *Progress and Poverty*. Although he was fundamentally of a religious turn of mind, with an unfailing reverence for what he called 'the grand, crowned authority of life', an obstinate streak of rationalism combined with that instinct of the insurgent, which sprang perhaps from his fatherless childhood, to prevent any of the rival Scottish orthodoxies from gaining his allegiance.

In 1885, at the age of eighteen, MacDonald obtained employment in Bristol from a clergyman who was inaugurating a boys' and young men's guild there. Chance thus brought him to what was at that time almost the only English city in which there was some nucleus of socialist activity. This was a branch of the Social Democratic Federation, founded in 1881 as the Democratic Federation by H. M. Hyndman [q.v.], which professed those Marxian doctrines which MacDonald was to spend so much of his later life in combating. He joined the branch, and took his share in its members' persistent but unsuccessful efforts at outdoor evangelism. Meanwhile he became an enthusiastic geologist, and spent on books money which should have gone on food and clothes. Before the end of the year, however, he had returned to Lossiemouth with the few pounds which he had contrived to save, and the resolve that, when he next left home, he would return successful, or not return at all.

A few months later MacDonald went south again, this time to London. The post which he had hoped to obtain was filled a day before his arrival, and for a while he nearly starved, tramping the city in search of work and living mainly on oatmeal sent from home—for which he scrupulously paid—and hot water. He is said to have found employment on the very day on which his last shilling was spent—the addressing of envelopes, at ten shillings a week, for the newly formed Cyclists' Touring Club. A little later, as an invoice clerk in a warehouse at fifteen shillings, he 'lived like a fighting-cock', helped his mother, paid fees at the Birkbeck Institute and other places of education, and saved money into the bargain. In later life he seldom spoke of these early struggles, but they certainly coloured his political creed and reinforced the belief, which he sometimes afterwards expressed, in the power of extreme poverty to breed 'the aristocratic virtues'. Before long, however, thanks to underfeeding and overwork—he was spending every spare moment on reading science—his health broke down completely and he was compelled to return home.

By 1888 MacDonald was back in London, and, after another period of unemployment, was fortunate enough to be chosen as private secretary to Thomas Lough, Gladstonian parliamentary candidate for West Islington, with whom he remained until 1891. Thus for the first time he came into contact with the politically minded middle class. He was still speaking at open-air meetings for the Social Democratic Federation, and in 1887 he was present in Trafalgar Square on the celebrated 'Bloody Sunday' (13 November). But, what was far more significant, in 1886 he joined the Fabian Society. Conscious that by now 'almost all organisations contain elements making for Socialism' this body had set its face, almost from the first, against 'revolutionary heroics', and concentrated upon conciliating and harnessing, instead of antagonizing, the latent forces of the age as did the social democrats, MacDonald found its middle class and eminently practical environment a novel and congenial atmosphere. In particular the Fabians had wisely resolved to eschew all the distracting shibboleths of those 'vague idealists, so prominent in the 'eighties and 'nineties, who were ready to embrace any cult, from vegetarianism to bimetallism, provided that it was labelled 'progressive'. MacDonald was never a crank.

Nevertheless, the Fabians were scarcely more qualified than the Social Democratic Federation to convert the man in the street, and it was not until 1893, with the foundation of the independent labour party, that there appeared a body capable both of fusing the working class, skilled and unskilled, into political unity, and of popularizing socialist doctrines. It stood both for independent labour representation as against alliance with one or other of the traditional parties, and for socialism. Of both aims MacDonald wholly approved and in 1894 he applied for membership in a personal letter to Keir Hardie. At the general election of 1895 he stood as independent labour party candidate for Southampton, polling only 886 votes. At this time he was earning a slender income by journalism, and it is remarkable evidence of the resolute process of self-education upon which he had embarked that he should have been invited to contribute a considerable number of articles to this DICTIONARY.

In the following year MacDonald married Margaret Ethel, daughter of John Hall Gladstone, F.R.S., of Pembridge Square, London, and a great-niece of Lord Kelvin [q.v.]. Her father was both a distinguished scientist and an active social and religious worker—he was one of the founders of the Young Men's Christian Association—and Margaret Gladstone had been attracted to socialism through her own social work in Hoxton and elsewhere. The marriage opened a new life for MacDonald. Not only did it mean financial independence, but the influence of his wife began insensibly to colour his own views. 'She saw spirit in everything', he wrote of her after her death; and thenceforth the faint streak of rationalism seems to fade out of him, and he was carried yet farther from the bleak materialism of Marx. Margaret MacDonald also possessed a genius for friendship which MacDonald himself had always lacked, and she made their new home at 3 Lincoln's Inn Fields the centre of a wide circle of friends. Here their six children were born, and despite the unceasing public activities of both parents their family life was exceptionally happy and united. The next few years were filled with expanding activities. There was foreign travel, which marriage had made possible, and for which Mac-Donald retained a passion to the end of his life. There were the regular gatherings in his home of labour and socialist prota-gonists, and friends and well-wishers from overseas. Moreover, in 1900 MacDonald had become secretary of the labour representation committee, the germ of the labour party: he held the post until 1912, and was treasurer from 1912 to 1924. Since 1896 he had been a member of the national administrative council of the independent labour party (where he was regarded as markedly cautious), and from 1894 to 1900 he served on the executive committee of the Fabian Society (which considered him a dangerous intransigent). From 1901 to 1904 he represented Central Finsbury on the London County Council. The acquisition through his marriage of an upper-middle-class social background un-doubtedly accelerated MacDonald's rise to prominence in the labour movement. It was, for example, a strong recommendation for his secretaryship of the labour repre-sentation committee that he was not depen-dent upon the trade unions for an income.

With Hardie, MacDonald drafted the resolution by which in 1899 the Trades Union Congress convened a special con-gress to devise plans for returning more labour members to the next parliament. He was largely responsible for next year's decision representing a compromise be-tween the traditional liberal-labourism of the Trades Union Congress and the class-war socialism of the Social Democratic Federation—to set up the labour repre-sentation committee, which in 1906 be-came the labour party. He had taken an active part in the resistance to the South African war, and his *What I Saw in South Africa* (1903) was based upon a journey undertaken with his wife on the morrow of the peace. More significant was *Social-ism and Society* (1905). the whole argument of which is characteristically based upon the analogy between politics and biology. Not unnaturally this book rejects, as anti-quated, Marxism and the doctrine of the class war, 'on the threshold of scientific sociology, but hardly across it'. At the general election of 1906 he was returned for Leicester, which he had unsuccessfully contested in 1900. All but five of the twenty-nine successful labour repre-sentation committee candidates, and Mac-Donald among them, owed their success to an electoral arrangement made with the liberals, a fact which goes far to explain labour political strategy during the next few years. The new party was bound to support the liberals because the liberals were now about to establish the new sys-tem of social insurance, which was sound collectivist doctrine, but it was also bound to support them because it owed most of its own seats to liberal complaisance.

From the first MacDonald attended regularly, and spoke frequently, in the House of Commons, and at once estab-lished his reputation; 'a born parlia-mentarian' was Lord Balfour's subsequent verdict. In public as in private life there was an impenetrable hinterland in Mac-Donald; it would often be his strength, and sometimes his weakness, that in a sense he was always a man of mystery. His writings—*Socialism* appeared in 1907 and *The Awakening of India*, which has been described as the best short book on India ever written by a tourist, in 1910—helped to mark him out as not only the most distinguished spokesman but the most distinguished thinker of the labour group in parliament. But perhaps it was his dominating influence in the indepen-dent labour party, at this time the 'prae-torian guard' of the labour movement, which was most significant for the fortunes of the country, and which eventually most affected his own career. As chairman from 1906 to 1909, and as a leading figure for many years, he did more than anyone else to implant in a society abounding with visionaries and extremists his own practical instinct for moderation. The triumph of moderation is never inevitable, unless moderates of sufficient stature are forthcoming, and but for the influence of MacDonald during this seminal phase the labour party between the two wars might have preferred revolution to evolution. Meanwhile the world-wide journeyings, which did much to give him his grasp of foreign affairs, were continuing. Each summer from 1907 to 1916 he was on the continent on a political mission; in 1906, with his wife, he embarked upon a world tour, and in 1909 they visited India.

MacDonald retained his seat at the two general elections of 1910, and in 1911 he became chairman of the parliamentary labour group. It was in this year that he suffered a crushing blow in the loss of his wife, which followed that of his youngest son eighteen months previously. With his wife's death MacDonald's social circle contracted; his natural sensitiveness and aloofness revived; thenceforth he was always in a sense a lonely man. The short memoir of his wife which he wrote for private circulation that year was expanded and published in 1912 as *Margaret Ethel MacDonald*. It is a most moving tribute and an unconscious portrait of the author as well as of his wife.

1911–1914 were years of international tension, and industrial strife. MacDonald was closely involved in negotiation over the great railway strike of August 1911, which was the climax of a series of savage industrial disputes. In parliament on 16 August he deplored the strikes but argued that the business of the House was not merely to talk law and order but to listen to the men's case, and to realize that behind it there was a long history of social injustice. Industrial unrest persisted into 1912 and MacDonald continued to put the case of the strikers to parliament, to exhort them to patience and discipline, and to advise on parliamentary tactics. Throughout these years, in which support in parliament for the liberal government had to be combined with socialist propaganda in the country, there were recurrent complaints of the moderation and 'subservience' of the parliamentary labour group, and in particular of MacDonald, its leader; but in spite of all he contrived to retain the confidence of the party, and even of the independent labour party. The successful struggle for moderation within his own party lent all the more force to his denunciation in 1914 of Sir Edward Carson and those conservatives who planned violent resistance in Ulster to the government's policy of home rule: 'let them start that sort of appeal to lawlessness and anarchy . . . and he would not like to prophesy as to who was going to write the last sentence'. In December 1912 he paid a second visit to India, as a member of the royal commission on the public services in India. He signed the subsequent Report with some reservations, but embodied what he had learnt at greater length in his *The Government of India* (1919).

On 5 August 1914, the day after the declaration of war on Germany, MacDonald resigned his chairmanship of the party, which declined to support his proposal that labour members should oppose the government's demand for a war credit of £100 millions. On the same day the executive and the parliamentary group had resolved '. . . that it has opposed the policy which has produced the war, and

that its duty now is to secure peace at the earliest possible moment on such conditions as will provide the best opportunities for the re-establishment of amicable feelings between the workers of Europe'. Both MacDonald and the majority of his colleagues could claim that throughout the years of war which followed he and they alike were faithfully discharging the duty thus defined; yet while they were to become loyal supporters of the war-time coalition, recruiting orators, and Cabinet ministers, he was soon to be the best-hated man in Great Britain, widely, although quite erroneously, regarded as a pro-German and a pacificist. Yet the views which, despite violence and misrepresentation, MacDonald continued to expound throughout the war accurately, if not always altogether lucidly, embodied the substance of the original resolution. Great Britain was wrong to enter the war; having entered it she must win it; yet even in war-time the rational temper of the moderate must somehow be preserved, lest the eventual peace be of that vindictive kind which must ensure further wars. That the war must be won he had no doubt; and although he would not join in the highly coloured oratory of the recruiting platform, he told his audiences that 'those who can enlist, ought to enlist, those who are working in munition factories should do so whole-heartedly'. Early in December 1914 he went to Belgium as a volunteer member of a British ambulance attached to the Belgian army —only to be promptly sent back to England on instructions from home. A fortnight later he returned, with a pass from Lord Kitchener, as an official visitor and showed much coolness under fire during an adventurous journey with Colonel John Edward Bernard Seely (later Lord Mottistone). But although he was always for winning the war, he did not cease to believe, and to say, that Great Britain had been wrong to embark upon it. Indeed the use to which German propagandists were able to put some of his strictures on British foreign policy did much to make him appear as an enemy of his country. But his main theme was the necessity for keeping alive, even in war-time, the generous and unimpassioned temper of peace. He was never a pacificist, yet, excluded from the platform of the official labour party, he necessarily worked closely with the independent labour party, the membership of which was overwhelmingly pacificist. Temperamentally a moderate, and now more than ever standing for a middle course, he was never wholly at ease with the violence and illogicality of much of the independent labour party propaganda. Partly no doubt for this reason he had been largely instrumental in founding, in September 1914, an *ad hoc* organization, the Union of Democratic Control, which included many liberals as well as socialists, and the object of which was to secure a democratic foreign policy. Another wartime organization on the platforms of which he was able to speak, the National Council for Civil Liberties, also included liberals as well as socialists in its membership. Whatever his platform, however, every meeting at which MacDonald spoke was a potential riot, and the popular press did much to provoke violence, by attributing to him provocative sayings invented by itself, and encouraging the public to break up his meetings. In comparison with MacDonald the other spokesmen of the opposition, including the pacificists, were ignored, and he became the personification of all that the average patriotic citizen disliked and mistrusted. The courage with which MacDonald sustained this concentration of venom did much to deepen the devotion of his followers, and earned him a new affection even among the orthodox labour majority. Indeed it was to his new hold over both wings of the party, and particularly over the independent labour party, that he was to owe his return to the leadership in 1922, and therefore the premiership in 1924.

The welcome extended by MacDonald and his friends to the first Russian revolution, that of Kerensky and the moderates, of March 1917 was long quoted against him as if it had been accorded to the later revolution of Lenin and the Bolsheviks. But the first revolution had appeared to herald the establishment of democracy, the disavowal of imperialism, and an early negotiated peace. When, however, a delegation from the labour party and the independent labour party, which included MacDonald, was about to sail from Aberdeen to visit the provisional government at Petrograd, with the permission of the British Cabinet, the crew of its ship refused to sail if MacDonald and two other members were to be allowed to travel. This incident, which was widely reported, served to discredit MacDonald yet further. It is just possible that if the delegation had been permitted to sail its visit might have assisted the Kerensky government

to resist the subsequent onslaught of the Bolsheviks. The two wings of the labour party, however, in which there had been no formal split, were brought closer together by the resignation that August of Arthur Henderson [q.v.] from the coalition War Cabinet, over the question of the socialist conference to be held in Stockholm. Thenceforth, until the end of the war, MacDonald and Henderson spoke very much the same language, and each helped the other to gain the ear of that wing of the party to which he had hitherto been suspect. MacDonald warmly welcomed President Wilson's Fourteen Points but was doubtful whether at this late hour the declaration would avail to stave off a 'military' peace. As the war ended he was respected by the bulk of his party, and was the object of the passionate devotion of an influential minority in it, but for the general public he was still the most unpopular and mistrusted man in Britain, and at the general election in December 1918 he was defeated at West Leicester by just over 14,000 votes.

In February of the following year MacDonald was active as a delegate to the International Socialist Conference at Berne, which he hoped to see paving the way to a conciliatory peace, but which was soon rent by that conflict between revolutionary communism and parliamentary socialism with which MacDonald was chiefly occupied during the next few years. In 1920 he succeeded in persuading the annual conferences of both the independent labour party and the labour party to reject communism. Thereafter the extremists seceded, and the subsequent concentration of their hostility upon MacDonald did much to restore his reputation with the general public. In March 1921 he was defeated by a narrow majority at a by-election at East Woolwich, in which his opponents made much play with his war record, but at the general election of 1922, with the rising tide of reaction against Lloyd George's coalition, he was returned with a comfortable majority for the Aberavon division of Glamorganshire. He was at once elected chairman of the parliamentary labour party, after a close contest with Mr. John Robert Clynes, thanks primarily to the enthusiastic support of the so-called Clydeside group of left-wing socialists, with whose extreme views MacDonald was to be constantly in conflict throughout the rest of his career. Since the labour members now outnumbered the liberals he at once became official leader of the opposition, and it was probably now that his gifts as a House of Commons man were most conspicuous.

At the general election of 1923 the labour party, with 191 seats, was again more powerful than the liberals, and the two together were strong enough to defeat the conservative government. A vote of no confidence having been carried on 17 January 1924, MacDonald did not hesitate to form the first labour government, although it could only exist upon sufferance. He was then sworn of the Privy Council. He made what was thought by many to be the mistake of himself filling the office not only of prime minister but of foreign secretary. Inevitably his preoccupation with foreign affairs made it difficult for him to do himself full justice as leader of the House, and it probably diminished his interest in the domestic programme of his government. Moreover, the twofold responsibility involved a severe physical strain: for MacDonald was conscientious almost to a fault, and he never acquired the art of delegating responsibility; it was said of him that he had been known, when prime minister, to look up trains for one of his secretaries. His diplomacy was on the whole successful. He found France and Germany disposed for conciliation, came to an understanding with the French prime minister, M. Herriot, whose outlook was much the same as his own, and accepted, on behalf of this country, the Experts' Report on German Reparations. The Allied Conference of July in London was summoned to translate this Report into action, and led to the settlement of the following month. In September, at Geneva, MacDonald and Herriot together proposed a protocol for security, arbitration, and disarmament, which was subsequently drafted, though never ratified.

In domestic affairs, however, MacDonald's touch appeared to be less certain. He made little attempt to conciliate the liberals, on whose support his government depended, and although he was in fact by no means comfortable with his Clydeside supporters, the impression got abroad that he was unduly subservient to them. The abrupt reversal in August of the government's previous intention not to guarantee a loan to the Russian government was ascribed to the intervention of backbench Russophils, and about the same time the abandonment of the prosecution of a journalist charged with inciting the armed forces to mutiny was also denounced by the opposition as a concession to forces outside the Cabinet, and brought about the defeat and resignation of the government. MacDonald's premiership had substantially increased his own reputation; and it was gratefully recognized, even by opponents, that in parliamentary tradition, in public ceremonial, and in the relations of Cabinet and Crown there had been no breach with tradition; but in the election which followed in October 1924 the public was prevented from pronouncing a clear-cut verdict on the record of his government by the publication a few days before polling-day of the so-called Zinoviev letter. The precise significance of this document was not understood by the public, even after MacDonald's explanation, delayed by the exigencies of a strenuous election tour, had reached it; but the letter, as presented by his opponents, served to strengthen the vague general impression that the labour government had been discreditably subservient to extremist influences. This was the charge of which MacDonald's whole career had been an emphatic repudiation, and after the election, in which his party lost forty-one seats, it was again his influence which secured the emphatic repudiation of communism by the labour party conference of 1925.

Extremist influences, however, were in the ascendant in the industrial wing of the movement, and the following year saw the abortive General Strike. MacDonald had always disapproved of 'direct action', and behind the scenes, although the extremists had not sought his advice, he did his best to avert the explosion. Having failed he felt bound, as leader of a party so closely allied to the Trades Union Congress, to acquiesce in what followed. In 1927 he just survived a severe illness contracted during a visit to the United States of America, but recovered rapidly enough to play a principal part in drafting the party manifesto *Labour and the Nation* (1928), a lengthy document which characteristically combined a comprehensive programme of reform with a restatement of theory and a renewed repudiation of communism. Before the general election in May 1929 he undertook an exacting nation-wide speaking campaign which contributed markedly to the victory of his party: he himself was returned for the Seaham division of county Durham. With 287 seats labour was for the first time the strongest party.

For the administration which he now formed MacDonald was mainly concerned to select colleagues whose outlook was akin to his own; trade unionism was not so strongly represented as in 1924, and the extremists were almost wholly excluded. This time he did not attempt to combine the office of foreign secretary with the premiership, but he continued to devote his attention chiefly to foreign affairs, on which, he believed, all else depended. After conversations with General Dawes, the American ambassador, and a visit to President Hoover in the United States— the first to be made by a prime minister of Great Britain—he succeeded in bringing about a revival of the Naval Conference, which was held in London in January 1930. Agreement was reached between Great Britain, the United States, and Japan and it seemed that a genuine advance towards naval disarmament had been made. Meanwhile the Hague Conference, at which Philip Snowden [q.v.] effectively represented Great Britain, had removed the obstacles to the application of the Young Plan for the payment of reparations. Once again, however, the government's domestic record was less satisfactory, at any rate to socialists. Its difficulties were due partly to the breach between MacDonald and the independent labour party, partly to the steady darkening of the general economic horizon. An informal understanding with the liberals meant that for the first time labour was not merely in office but in power. It was all the easier, therefore, for the government to disregard its left-wing critics, and, except that they persuaded it to relax the regulations governing unemployment insurance, they exercised scarcely any influence on domestic policy. At the annual conference of the party a vote of censure by the rebels was early defeated, thanks to a fighting speech by MacDonald. At the first Indian Round Table Conference, held towards the end of 1930, his skilful chairmanship was generally admired, although the gulf between Hindus and Moslems was not bridged. But throughout the year, with the deepening of the universal economic depression, unemployment rose, and its cost had been greatly increased by the more generous conditions of benefit. The Report of the economy committee set up under the chairmanship of Sir George (later Lord) May, published on 31 July 1931, estimated a deficit of £120,000,000 by April 1932. The Report, which made the financial position of the country appear even more precarious than it actually was, was followed by a flight of

foreign investors from the pound, and a serious drain on British gold reserves. Throughout the subsequent meetings of the special economy committee of the Cabinet, and of the Cabinet itself, MacDonald pressed for economies sufficient to balance the budget. Some of his colleagues, however, although ready to accept reductions of expenditure totalling more than £56,000,000 were not prepared to face a further saving of £22,000,000 on unemployment insurance, to which the general council of the Trades Union Congress, which was consulted on 20 August, had shown itself resolutely opposed. After prolonged discussions within the Cabinet, and negotiations which it had sanctioned with the leaders of the other parties, MacDonald had to report to the King on the morning of 23 August that his colleagues could not agree. Later that Sunday the King saw Sir Herbert Samuel and Baldwin separately, and at night again received MacDonald, who tendered the resignation of the labour government. The King urged MacDonald to reconsider his own position, and next morning, at MacDonald's request, the King held a conference of the three party leaders at Buckingham Palace, and within a few hours MacDonald had formed an all-party government in conjunction with the leaders of the conservative and liberal parties. Although Snowden, J. H. Thomas, and Lord Sankey followed him into the 'national' government, MacDonald had made no attempt to carry the bulk of his party with him, and he was at once succeeded in its leadership by Henderson. Yet at first he regarded the coalition as no more than a temporary expedient for overcoming the financial crisis, after which parties were to revert to their normal alinement. Inevitably, however, subsequent controversy, let alone the bitterness with which many of his former colleagues and followers now assailed him, made the breach permanent. Some of his critics, indeed, maintained that in forming the new government he had yielded to the temptations of what Lord Passfield called 'the aristocratic embrace', and even that he had himself long plotted to bring about the fall of his own government. There can be no doubt, however, that at the outset of the crisis he had expected to fall permanently from power, or that he did not at first desire the coalition to outlast the immediate crisis.

The exodus of short-term capital compelled the new government to abandon the gold standard which it had been formed to defend, but it was not long before confidence was restored and foreign capital was pouring in again. In the election which followed in October the government, appealing for a virtually free hand or 'doctor's mandate', secured all but fifty-nine seats. MacDonald himself won a remarkable personal triumph at Seaham, which had been hitherto as impregnable a labour stronghold as any in the country.

MacDonald now formed his fourth administration, with an unchallengeable majority composed of the conservative and liberal parties and a small 'national' labour group, which at first exercised an influence disproportionate to its size. MacDonald found himself at ease with his new colleagues, and is said to have done much to preserve harmony between them. Snowden and the free-trade liberals, although retained for a while by the 'agreement to differ' on tariffs announced on 22 January 1932, left the coalition after the preferential tariff agreements reached at Ottawa that summer. The government, however, pressed on with a programme of domestic retrenchment and reform, which included a number of socialist measures, notably in agriculture. MacDonald continued to regard the European situation as the key to domestic recovery, and despite operations for glaucoma in each eye in February and May of 1932 he presided at a Four Power Conference in London in April and was present at the Disarmament Conference in Geneva in the same month. He was mainly responsible for the summoning of the abortive World Economic Conference of 1933 in London, which was doomed by the refusal of President Roosevelt's government to agree to the stabilization of currency. MacDonald was also the author of the draft convention which saved the Disarmament Conference from collapse. He was always a believer in personal diplomacy, and his visits to Paris and Rome did much to bring about a consultative pact between Great Britain, France, Italy, and Germany. By now, however, the shadow of Hitler was beginning to fall across the European scene, and MacDonald, with his colleagues, was convinced that appeasement must thenceforth be pursued simultaneously with a restoration of Great Britain's dangerously impaired defences. The White Paper on National Defence of March 1935, which heralded a programme of rearmament,

bore not only his initials but clear evidence of his drafting. Three months later (7 June) he resigned the premiership, and assumed the sinecure office of lord president of the Council.

MacDonald's powers were clearly impaired by prolonged overstrain: he had probably worked longer hours than any previous prime minister. The remorseless vendetta waged against him by a few of his former associates had also had its effect. He had not played a prominent part in the House of Commons of late, partly because the government's huge majority rendered personal intervention seldom necessary and partly owing to his preoccupation with foreign affairs, but partly also because he was conscious that failing health had begun to make his speaking involved and obscure. At the general election in November 1935 his courageous decision to contest Seaham undoubtedly contributed to the victory of the 'national' coalition, and to the survival of the small 'national' labour group, but his own defeat was inevitable. He was returned, however, at a by-election in January 1936 for the Scottish Universities. He died suddenly 9 November 1937, on a holiday voyage to South America, and after his body had lain in state in the cathedral of Bermuda and after a funeral service in Westminster Abbey, he was buried beside his wife in Spynie churchyard, near Lossiemouth. He left two sons, of whom the younger, Malcolm, was at the time secretary of state for Dominion affairs, and three daughters.

MacDonald was somewhat above middle height. His face, with its sensitively chiselled features and large and luminous eyes, was that of an artist rather than a statesman. He had always been a handsome man, but in later life, when his dark waving hair had turned white, and there was a marked suggestion of strain and self-restraint about eyes and mouth, his appearance was particularly striking. He had a taste for physical hardship and danger and was a great walker. His two collections, *Wanderings and Excursions* (1925) and *At Home and Abroad* (1936), contain many of his travel experiences. He received honorary degrees from the universities of Glasgow (1924), Edinburgh (1925), Wales (1926), Oxford (1931), and McGill (1929). In the year of the General Strike it was proposed at Cambridge that an honorary degree should be conferred upon him, but he refused to accept one which at that time would certainly have been passed only by a majority.

Portraits of MacDonald by Solomon J. Solomon (presented to him in 1912 by the labour party) and by Ambrose McEvoy are in the possession of his family, who also own portraits by Augustus John and Sir John Lavery (unfinished), as well as two bronze busts by Jacob Epstein (1926 and 1931) and one by Felix Joubert (c. 1936). Another portrait by Lavery (1931), and a bronze bust by Epstein (1934), a copy of one of those mentioned above, are in the National Portrait Gallery.

[The Times and Manchester Guardian, 10 November 1937; Lord Elton, Life of James Ramsay MacDonald (1866–1919), 1939; Lord Snowden, An Autobiography, 2 vols., 1934; Reports of the annual conference of the labour party and independent labour party; private information; personal knowledge.]

ELTON.

MACDONELL, SIR PHILIP JAMES (1873–1940), colonial judge, was born in London 10 January 1873, the eldest son of the journalist James Macdonell [q.v.], by his wife, Annie, daughter of Daniel Harrison, of Beckenham, Kent, and niece of Mary Howitt [q.v.]. He was nephew of the jurist Sir John Macdonell [q.v.]. After being educated at Clifton under J. M. Wilson [q.v.], he went up to Brasenose College, Oxford, as a Hulme exhibitioner at the age of seventeen. He was president of the Union in 1895, after obtaining a first class in modern history in 1894. He took his B.A. degree in 1897, in which year he represented Oxford against Cambridge as a fencer.

In 1900 Macdonell was called to the bar by Gray's Inn (of which he was Bacon scholar), but the same year he went out to South Africa and was war correspondent of The Times until 1902. This proved to be a turning-point in his life and thenceforth he served the British Empire in three continents. Beginning his legal career in the Transvaal and continuing it in Northern Rhodesia, he was secretary to the Transvaal Native Commission in 1903 and assistant crown prosecutor (Witwatersrand Court) from 1907 to 1908. In the last-named year he was appointed public prosecutor and legal adviser to the Chartered Company in north-west Rhodesia, and from 1911 to 1918 filled the same posts in Northern Rhodesia. In 1911, during a visit to England, he took his B.C.L. degree. From 1918 to 1927 he was a judge of the Northern Rhodesia High

Court. Even after he had left Africa Macdonell retained to the end of his life a love of that country and an intense interest in its peoples and problems. He became chief justice of Trinidad and Tobago and president of the West Indian Court of Appeal in 1927, and from 1930 to 1936, when he retired, he was chief justice of Ceylon.

Macdonell was knighted in 1925, and in 1939 was sworn of the Privy Council and became a member of the Judicial Committee. In 1938, two years after his retirement, he was sent on a commission to report and advise (to the Colonial Office) on a complicated problem of inter-tribal jurisdiction in the Balovale District, Northern Rhodesia. He wrote characteristically of this work: 'I cannot tell you what a pleasure the work is—to get back into the old atmosphere; to be received on an equality by men who are absolutely au fait with native matters; the constant dialogues of experts day after day; and the having to try and master a most delicate and intricate problem—truly I am a lucky man to have been given this duty.'

Macdonell always keenly enjoyed his work; his memory was remarkable and his mind moved with extraordinary rapidity. 'I never knew a man who got through work faster', said a fellow judge. A natural impatience and vehemence—perhaps a Celtic inheritance from highland ancestors—were tempered by quick kindness and generosity. He had many and lasting friendships. He was a good classical scholar and was wont to take the Odyssey with him on his constant voyages. In 1940 he was elected an honorary fellow of Brasenose College. The later years of his life were spent in Scotland—for which he had a romantic attachment—at Gatehouse-of-Fleet, Galloway. Early in the war of 1939–1945 he undertook to preside over the tribunal dealing with military exemptions sitting in Manchester. Here, worn out by overwork, he fell ill and died at a nursing home in Southport 15 December 1940.

Macdonell married in 1910 Aline, youngest daughter of William Drew, chartered accountant, of Glasgow; they had no children.

[The Brazen Nose (magazine of Brasenose College, Oxford), November 1939 and June 1941; personal knowledge.]   AMICE LEE.

McDOUGALL, WILLIAM (1871–1938), psychologist, was born at Chadderton, Lancashire, 22 June 1871, the second son of Isaac Shimwell McDougall, manufacturing chemist, of Higher Broughton, Lancashire, by his wife, Rebekah Smalley. After attending a private school in Lancashire, he went at the age of fourteen to the Real-Gymnasium at Weimar for part of a year. He then proceeded to the Owens College, Manchester, where he first studied languages, history, and mathematics, but, influenced by the works of Herbert Spencer, Charles Darwin, and Thomas Huxley, soon turned to biology. In 1890, after graduating with first class honours (specializing in geology in his last year), he proceeded with a scholarship to St. John's College, Cambridge, and obtained first classes in both parts of the natural sciences tripos (1892, 1894). Having decided upon a medical career, McDougall entered St. Thomas's Hospital in 1894. Here he carried out experiments in the laboratory of (Sir) Charles Scott Sherrington, but after reading William James's *Principles of Psychology* he began to doubt whether medical practice would satisfy him. In 1898 he agreed to join the Cambridge anthropological expedition to the Torres Straits, and with William Halse Rivers Rivers he carried out a survey of the sensory endowment of the natives of that region. He also developed wide and lasting anthropological interests.

In November 1897 McDougall was elected into a fellowship at St. John's College, Cambridge, and began to make a systematic study of contemporary psychology. On the advice of James Ward [q.v.], professor of mental philosophy and logic at Cambridge, he joined G. E. Müller at Göttingen, and continued laboratory work on colour vision and on attention. On his return to England he lectured and demonstrated on psychology under James Sully at University College, London, from 1902 to 1904. During this period McDougall published papers on various problems of physiological psychology, especially on vision. He had helped to found the British Psychological Society in 1901. He also began to prepare for work on social psychology.

In 1903 McDougall was elected Wilde reader in mental philosophy at Oxford and soon opened an experimental research laboratory. Five years later (1908) he published his *Introduction to Social Psychology*. This book gained a great reputation throughout the whole civilized world, and probably did more than any other single publication to stimulate study of the foundations of social behaviour. His

views, strongly opposed to any mechanistic interpretation of human conduct, were further expressed in *Body and Mind* (1911) and *Psychology: the Study of Behaviour* (1912). During the war of 1914–1918 McDougall served as a major with the Royal Army Medical Corps and was fully occupied with the study and treatment of nerve cases among fighting men until the middle of 1919.

In 1920 McDougall became professor of psychology at Harvard University, and entered upon an extremely controversial period of his career. In books, articles, and lectures he advocated what he called 'hormic' psychology. He thought that the most fundamental feature of all human activity is 'goal searching', the simplest form of which he found in instincts. He opposed behaviourism, which was then flourishing, particularly in America. His second most influential work, *An Outline of Psychology*, was published in 1923, and was followed in 1926 by *An Outline of Abnormal Psychology*. Both were systematic treatises. Then, too, McDougall began his Lamarckian experiment, which was planned to demonstrate the inheritance of acquired characteristics through many generations of rats. This he regarded as his 'most important contribution to science'.

McDougall left Harvard in 1927 in order to become professor of psychology at Duke University, North Carolina. Here he continued his experiments on inheritance, and wrote many books of a more or less popular nature, some systematic, some dealing with current affairs, some on general problems of eugenics. He also more fully developed his long-standing interests in psychical research.

In 1912 McDougall was elected F.R.S. and a fellow of Corpus Christi College, Oxford. He received the honorary degree of D.Sc. from Manchester University in 1919 and was elected an honorary fellow of St. John's College, Cambridge, in 1938. He married in 1900 Annie Aurelia, daughter of Henry Hickmore, government contractor, of Brighton, and had three sons and two daughters: the eldest son, who was killed flying, and the younger daughter predeceased him. He died at Durham, North Carolina, 28 November 1938.

McDougall was tall and handsome, with an impressive voice and manner. In his early days he was no mean athlete. His influence upon contemporary psychology was very great. He can fairly be regarded as the real inspiration of a wide and intensive study of social psychology in the

English-speaking world. Among contemporary psychologists he was the most powerful advocate of an idealistic outlook upon human life and activity. Many excellent judges consider that his early work on physiological psychology was his best.

[*The Times*, 29 November 1938; *Obituary Notices of Fellows of the Royal Society*, No. 8, January 1940 (portrait and bibliography); *British Journal of Psychology*, vol. xxix, 1938–1939; a brief autobiography in *A History of Psychology in Autobiography*, edited by Carl Murchison, vol. i, 1930; personal knowledge.]

F. C. BARTLETT.

M'FADYEN, JOHN EDGAR (1870–1933), Scottish biblical scholar, was born in Glasgow 17 July 1870, the eldest child in the family of three sons and four daughters of James Hemphill M'Fadyen, of Glasgow, manager of the publishing department of the *Evening Citizen* and the *Weekly Citizen* newspapers, by his wife, Jane McKee. He received his early education at Hutcheson's Boys' Grammar School, Glasgow, and at Glasgow University, at which, after a distinguished career, he graduated M.A. with a first class in classics, being the most conspicuous graduate of his year (1890). He proceeded to Balliol College, Oxford, as Snell exhibitioner, and was awarded a first class in classical moderations (1892) and a second class in *literae humaniores* (1894). He won the junior (1893) and the senior (1896) Hall-Houghton Septuagint prizes and the Denyer and Johnson scholarship (1897). In 1894 he returned to Glasgow as a George A. Clark classical scholar, in order to take the theological course at the Free Church College (later Trinity College), where he came under the inspiring influence of A. B. Bruce [q.v.], (Sir) George Adam Smith, T. M. Lindsay [q.v.], James Stuart Candlish, and Henry Drummond [q.v.]. A semester spent during this period at Marburg increased his scholarly equipment, and when in 1898 he finished his theological course, he was appointed to the chair of Old Testament literature and exegesis in Knox College, Toronto, and took with him to Canada his newly married wife, Marie, daughter of Amtsgerichtsrat Wilhelm Scheffer, of Eschwege, Hesse. He remained in Toronto until 1910, when he was recalled to Glasgow, to occupy the chair of Old Testament language, literature, and theology in Trinity College where he remained until his death in Glasgow 24 December 1933. He had

two sons and a daughter, who predeceased her father. He received honorary degrees from Pine Hill Divinity Hall, Halifax (1910) and the university of Glasgow (1911).

In the second half of the nineteenth century, the scientific theory of evolution influenced deeply men's thoughts concerning the world and human life and destiny, and the prevalent belief in the steady progress of human thought and achievement made a vogue of philosophical materialism. It was inevitable that, at such a time, the books of the Bible should be examined in accordance with the canons of literary and historical criticism, with the result that many generally accepted ideas were severely disturbed and the doctrine of the verbal inspiration of Holy Scriptures was directly challenged. It was M'Fadyen's main work to be a mediator of the new learning, both to those who had been disturbed by it and to those who desired to profit by it.

It is intelligible, therefore, that one of M'Fadyen's early publications was a volume of apologetic with the title *Old Testament Criticism and the Christian Church* (1903). Apart from his repeated revisions (1914–1930) of the *Introductory Hebrew Grammar* of A. B. Davidson [q.v.], M'Fadyen did not devote himself to linguistic or philological studies; his work was predominantly exegetical, homiletical, and devotional. His translations of various books of the Old Testament into modern speech satisfied an urgent need; exegetical studies such as *A Cry for Justice* (1912) and *The Problem of Pain* (1917) were evidence of genuine scholarship and of living faith; whilst in volumes such as *The Use of the Old Testament in the Light of Modern Knowledge* (1922), *The Approach to the Old Testament* (1926), and *A Guide to the Understanding of the Old Testament* (1927), he showed the essential unity and the spiritual content of that collection of books.

Upon his own students M'Fadyen exercised a profound influence. His rich scholarship yoked to the grace and humility of his character made him a teacher beloved. But his influence extended far beyond the classroom. By the written and the spoken word he made many people his debtors, both in this country and on the other side of the Atlantic.

[*Glasgow Herald*, 26 December 1933; *Expository Times*, March 1934; W. I. Addison, *The Snell Exhibitions*, 1901.]

JOHN MAUCHLINE.

M'INTOSH, WILLIAM CAR-MICHAEL (1838–1931), zoologist, was born at St. Andrews 10 October 1838, the only son of John M'Intosh, builder and town councillor, of St. Andrews, by his wife, Eliza, third daughter of Robert Mitchell, linen manufacturer. His youngest sister, Roberta, married A. C. L. G. Günther [q.v.]; she was a gifted artist and executed many of the illustrations for her brother's works. After schooldays at Madras College, St. Andrews, he entered the university, but soon transferred to Edinburgh in order to study medicine. He graduated M.D. with distinction and gold medal in 1860 and specialized in the study of mental disease. In 1863 he became medical superintendent of Perth District Asylum at Murthly, a post which he held for the next twenty years. From his boyhood he had been interested in natural history, and at Edinburgh he was especially influenced by John Goodsir [q.v.], the anatomist, and G. J. Allman [q.v.], the zoologist, the latter of whom he accompanied on dredging excursions in the Firth of Forth. He began early the long series of faunistic papers which were continued until the last years of his life. A number of these papers were reprinted in *The Marine Invertebrates and Fishes of St. Andrews* (1875) with a supplement, *Additions to the Marine Fauna of St. Andrews* (1927). His most important work in pure zoology was his great *Monograph of the British Marine Annelids*, published in four folio volumes by the Ray Society; the first two parts of this work, published in 1873 and 1874, dealt with the nemertine worms, a group not now included in the annelida. Thereafter the work was laid aside, to be resumed in 1900 and completed in 1923. Hardly less important was his report on the polychaete worms obtained by the *Challenger* expedition, which appeared in two volumes in 1885, and a shorter report (1887) describing the greatest zoological novelty obtained by the expedition, the animal to which he gave the name *Cephalodiscus*.

In 1882 the chair of natural history in the university of St. Andrews became vacant and M'Intosh, abandoning his medical career, returned to his native city as professor of zoology, a position which he occupied until his retirement in 1917. In 1883 he was appointed to conduct investigations on behalf of a royal commission on Scottish sea fisheries, and for this purpose the first marine laboratory in this country was established at St.

Andrews. The results of this period of his work are summed up in *Life Histories of British Marine Food-Fishes* (with Arthur Thomas Masterman, 1897) and *The Resources of the Sea* (1898).

M'Intosh was elected F.R.S. in 1877 and was awarded a Royal medal in 1899. He was also elected F.R.S. (Edinburgh) in 1869, having been awarded the Neill medal in 1868; he was vice-president from 1927 to 1930. In 1924 he received the Linnean medal of the Linnean Society. He was president of the Ray Society from 1913 until his death. He received honorary degrees from the universities of St. Andrews, Edinburgh, Oxford, and Durham. He was primarily a descriptive zoologist, and, as such, his writings on the polychaete and especially the nemertine worms will long remain indispensable to the student of these groups. In fishery research he was one of the pioneers, and although many of his conclusions have been invalidated by later work, he had a clearer conception of the broad outlines of marine ecology than many of his contemporaries.

M'Intosh died, unmarried, at St. Andrews 1 April 1931. A portrait of him by James Caw, undated but probably painted soon after 1880, hangs in the rooms of the Linnean Society, Burlington House.

[*The Times*, 2 April 1931; *Proceedings* of the Royal Society, vol. cx, B, 1932 (portrait); *Nature*, 2 May 1931; personal knowledge.]

W. T. CALMAN.

MACKAY, JAMES LYLE, first EARL OF INCHCAPE (1852–1932), shipowner, was born at Arbroath 11 September 1852, the younger son of James Mackay, shipmaster and shipowner, of Arbroath, by his wife, Deborah, daughter of Alexander Lyle, of Canada. From his earliest years he lived in the world of shipping; at the age of eight he accompanied his father on a voyage to Archangel, narrowly escaping death by drowning. In 1862 his father was drowned crossing the Atlantic and his mother died two years later. Young Mackay was then at Elgin Academy and of his education he said, 'I was fonder of boats than of books, I was a froward sort of a boy ... extremely naughty ... who would never come to any good. . . . Eventually I was brought to heel by four years of the strict discipline of an office.' Leaving school at the age of fourteen he was employed for a few months as scrivener in a lawyer's office, then he was apprenticed to a rope-maker in Arbroath; at nineteen he went to London as an employee at £50 a year of Messrs. Gellatly, Hankey, Sewell & company, and it was his work there and at Gravesend which brought him into daily contact with ships, men of the sea, and the seaborne commerce of London. These interests were to dominate his life, and the first opportunity of satisfying them came when in 1874 he was appointed to the staff of Messrs. Mackinnon Mackenzie & company, of Calcutta.

Although the Suez Canal had been opened in 1869, the British mails in 1874 were still being sent by the 'overland' route, and Mackay, who was eventually to become vice-president of the Suez Canal Company, made his first voyage to India, not through the available canal, but by Alexandria, Cairo, and Suez. In 1878 he was appointed to Bombay, where once more a great opportunity awaited him. The failure in that year of the City of Glasgow Bank ruined the Bombay agents of the British India Steam Navigation Company, and Mackay was chosen by Mackinnon, Mackenzie & company to act in their place. Within two years he was given a partnership with an interest in the Bombay firm. Bombay was not only the port of entry to India but was the centre of a vast entrepôt trade extending from Durban to Basra and from Suez to Colombo; and it was characteristic of Mackay that he had already set himself by personal visits to the trading agents to build up a local and intimate knowledge of the conditions in the Persian Gulf. His knowledge thus acquired, cemented by his unusually tenacious memory, was of immense value in his task, varied as it was with demands for the carriage of troops and stores in connexion with the Russo-Turkish war of 1877–1878 and the Zulu war of 1879. This connexion with East Africa was perhaps more romantic than that with the Persian Gulf and the Red Sea, for a service from Aden to Zanzibar established in 1873 led to the foundation in 1888 by Sir William Mackinnon [q.v.] of the British East Africa Company, and the foundation of the British East African possessions, which, with promptitude on the part of the government, might have included the territory which came to be German East Africa and is now Tanganyika.

Returning to Calcutta in 1883, Mackay became president of the Bengal chamber of commerce, holding the post from 1890 to 1893, and was confronted with the burning question of the Indian currency.

From 1891 to 1893 he served on the legislative council, and in 1892, soon after having been elected president of the Indian Currency Association, the viceroy H. C. K. Petty-Fitzmaurice, Lord Lansdowne [q.v.], who had picked him out in British commercial circles, selected him to put their views before the Indian currency committee sitting in London under Farrer Lord Herschell [q.v.]. There is little doubt that his evidence was of great weight in framing the policy which led to the establishment of Indian currency on the gold standard. By the time he left India, he was senior partner in the firms of Mackinnon, Mackenzie, & company and of Macneill & company, and through his reorganization of Binny & company, of Madras, his field of enterprise embraced the jute, tea, and coal industries of Bengal, the cotton and wool industries of Madras, the seaborne trade between India and Burma, the Persian Gulf and East Africa and many ancillary companies in the hinterland of these areas. He also founded the Australian house of Macdonald Hamilton & company.

In 1893 Mackay came home for good to take charge of the London office of the British India Company, and his influence in the City rapidly grew as director and chairman of a host of companies, some connected with shipping, such as the Suez Canal Company of which he became vice-president and chairman of the London committee. Others were banking corporations such as the P. & O. and the National Provincial Banks. He was thrice president of the chamber of shipping of the United Kingdom (1903, 1918, 1919) and in 1926 president of the International Shipping Federation. Nevertheless, the government called on him for his services. From 1897 to 1911 he was a member of the council of the secretary of state for India as official member to represent the non-official point of view. In 1901 he was appointed by the British government special commissioner and plenipotentiary in the negotiations with China to secure uniform currency in that country, and to abolish *likin* and other duties which clogged the flow of goods between the interior of China and the treaty ports. Although the treaty of Shanghai was signed in 1902, it failed of its object, not from any fault of Mackay, who treated the Chinese negotiators with a patience and perseverance that were in startling contrast to the directness which marked his approach to all matters. On retiring from the India Council in 1911 Mackay was raised to the peerage as Baron Inchcape, of Strathnaver, in the county of Sutherland.

During and after the war of 1914–1918 Inchcape continued his services on a multitude of government committees: in 1917 he was made a member of the committee of imperial defence, from 1921 to 1922 he served on the national economy (Geddes) committee, and from 1922 to 1923 he was chairman of the committee on Indian retrenchment. His work for the government did not interfere with his business life which was chiefly centred on the London office of the British India Company, and in 1914 Inchcape, on becoming chairman, revived proposals for the fusion of the company with the P. & O. Company, with which the British India had always been on amicable terms, and carried them through. Under this agreement, the P. & O. Company purchased the whole ordinary stock of the British India Company and part of the preference stock, so that £12,600,000 sterling and 1,250,000 tons of shipping were now brought under one direct authority. In 1916 this was followed by the fusion of the New Zealand Shipping Company and its subsidiary the Federal Line; next year by that of the Union Steamship Company of New Zealand, the Hain and Nourse lines, and in 1920 by that of the General Steam Navigation Company, while in 1919 an interest had been obtained in the Orient Line. In its final form, the group unified a capital of twenty-three millions with a tonnage not far short of two millions.

In this remarkable fusion of different interests, each serving a particular trade and having its own special problems, Inchcape's claim, which he always pressed, to allow the individual full play to originate, develop, and achieve, was most amply and vividly illustrated. It was not amalgamation so much as unification, for to each of the constituent parts there was allowed full and untrammelled liberty to develop its own individuality. Each was left to seek and find its own objective, to secure it perhaps even in competition with another member of the group. The dead hand of uniform formalism, of seeking and sheltering behind a superior authority, was abhorrent to Inchcape, and wholly absent from his conception of the unification which he had thus established.

Inchcape was never a politician, although he was once nominated as a candidate for Plymouth and made one or two election speeches when, on his return home from India, he was induced for a very brief period to consider entering politics. He was a declared liberal, but in 1926 he crossed the floor of the House of Lords to the conservative benches. He was an ardent and convinced free trader, and he bitterly resented the encroachment of the activities of the state into the life of the individual, believing that its function should be limited to defence, the maintenance of law and order, and the strictest economy in finance, leaving to the citizen the opportunity of self-help and self-development, particularly in matters of trade, commerce, and industry. The curtailment of the liberties of the subject which was imposed during and after the war of 1914–1918 was particularly repugnant to him, and he found especial pleasure in his discharge, almost single-handed, of the stupendous task of selling for the Exchequer the fleet of ships built here or acquired from the enemy during the war, for £35,000,000, as against the expense of £850. He will go down to future generations as the most prominent figure of his time in British shipping.

Inchcape was appointed K.C.I.E. in 1894, G.C.M.G. in 1902, K.C.S.I. in 1910, and G.C.S.I. in 1924; he was advanced to the degree of a viscount in 1924 and to that of Earl of Inchcape and Viscount Glenapp in 1929. He married in 1883 Jane Paterson, daughter of James Shanks, of Rosely, Arbroath, a leading Scottish engineer. She survived him until 1937 with one son and three of their four daughters; the third daughter was lost at sea in 1928 in an attempt to fly the Atlantic. He died at Monaco, on board his yacht *Rover*, 23 May 1932, and was succeeded as second earl by his son, Kenneth (1887–1939).

Portraits of Inchcape by de László are at the P. & O. and the Chamber of Shipping.

[*The Times*, 24 May 1932; Hector Bolitho, *James Lyle Mackay, first Earl of Inchcape*, 1936; private information; personal knowledge.]   M. M. S. GUBBAY.

MACKENNAL, SIR (EDGAR) BERTRAM (1863–1931), Australian sculptor, was born in Melbourne 12 June 1863, the second son of John Simpson Mackennal, by his wife, Sarah Hyde. His father was an architectural sculptor, who was born in Ayrshire and, after being articled to a Liverpool sculptor, emigrated in 1852 to Melbourne, where he carried out work of an architectural character on several of its principal buildings. Bertram Mackennal studied first under his father and at the National Gallery School in Melbourne. At the age of eighteen he came to London, chiefly to study the Elgin marbles, and entered the Royal Academy Schools. Dissatisfied with the routine there, he left after a very short time and went to Paris, where he worked in several studios, acquiring variety and freedom of style. Returning to England, he secured a position as head of the art department in a pottery at Coalport, Shropshire. He first exhibited about 1886, and three years later he won the competition for the decoration of Government House, Melbourne. This took him back to Australia, but in two years he was again in Paris, where he gained his first great success with the figure of 'Circe', which received an honourable mention in the Salon of 1893, and attracted a good deal of attention at the Academy the following year. It is now in the National Gallery of Victoria, Melbourne.

The marble figure of 'Oceanus', commissioned by the Union Club of Sydney; the South African War Memorial for Islington; the memorials to Queen Victoria for Lahore, Blackburn, and Australia; and the pediment of the Local Government Board office, Westminster, followed at intervals, and in 1910 Mackennal was called upon to design the coronation medal of King George V, and also the obverse of the new coinage, to supersede the Edwardian design of G. W. De Saulles [q.v.]; in recognition of this he was in 1912 appointed M.V.O. He was then commissioned, with (Sir) Edwin Lutyens as architect, to execute the national memorial to King Edward VII in St. George's Chapel, Windsor. This was unveiled in 1921, when King George advanced him as K.C.V.O. Among other important works by Mackennal are the national memorial to Gainsborough at Sudbury, Suffolk; the tomb of Sir Redvers Buller in Winchester Cathedral; the equestrian statue of King Edward VII in Waterloo Place; the nude male figure, 'Here Am I', for Eton playing fields; and the war memorial to members of both Houses of Parliament in the porch of St. Stephen's Hall. In the last year of his life Mackennal was commissioned by King George to execute a portrait in marble of Queen Alexandra to be placed on the wall of Sandringham church. He was elected A.R.A. in 1909 and R.A. in 1922, but he did not exhibit at the Aca-

demy after 1929, when he was represented by the figures of a soldier and a sailor for the Anzac memorial at Sydney. He is represented at the Tate Gallery by 'The Earth and the Elements', a small group of four figures in marble, a Chantrey purchase of 1907, and 'Diana Wounded', a life-size marble figure, a Chantrey purchase of 1908. Mackennal revisited Australia in 1901 and again in 1926, when the sales at an exhibition of his work established a record for sculpture in the Dominion.

In forming an estimate of Mackennal's ability as a sculptor it is necessary to discount the artistically irrelevant circumstances that he was the first Australian artist—the first overseas artist, indeed—to be elected to the Royal Academy, the first to have a work purchased for the Tate Gallery, and the first to be knighted. But making full allowance for any discrepancy between his reputation and his powers, he must be pronounced to have been a brilliant 'all round' sculptor and a master of his craft, particularly in the treatment of marble, with poetical imagination and a peculiar elegance of style.

Mackennal married in 1884 Agnes (died 1947), daughter of Henry Spooner, of London, and had a daughter. He died suddenly at his home, Watcombe Hall, Watcombe, Torquay, 10 October 1931.

[*The Times*, 12 October 1931; William Moore, *The Story of Australian Art*, 1934; Kineton Parkes, *Sculpture of To-day*, vol. i, 1921; private information.]

CHARLES MARRIOTT.

MACKENZIE, Sir ALEXANDER CAMPBELL (1847–1935), composer and principal of the Royal Academy of Music, was born in Edinburgh 22 August 1847, the eldest son of Alexander Mackenzie, by his wife, Janet Campbell. He inherited musical talent, his great-grandfather having been a member of the Forfarshire militia band, his grandfather a professional violinist, and his father leader of the orchestra at the Theatre Royal, Edinburgh, and editor of the *National Dance Music of Scotland* (1859).

At the age of ten, after leaving Hunter's School, Edinburgh, Mackenzie was sent to study music at Sondershausen in Thuringia. He lived with the family of a member of the ducal orchestra, attended the Realschule, and entered the conservatorium where he studied under K. W. Ulrich and Eduard Stein; in 1861 he joined the ducal orchestra as second violinist. On coming to London in 1862 he won the king's scholarship at the Royal Academy of Music, and with P. P. C. Sainton [q.v.] as his master for the violin, Charles Lucas [q.v.] for composition, and Frederick Bowen Jewson for the piano, completed his training there in 1865.

Thus equipped Mackenzie settled (1866–1881) in Edinburgh, where he became known as a violinist, gave chamber concerts at which Schumann's pianoforte quartet and quintet were for the first time played in Scotland (1870), was organist of St. George's church, Charlotte Square, and was appointed in 1873 conductor of the Scottish Vocal Music Association. Meanwhile, he found time to compose a pianoforte trio and a string quartet, besides a pianoforte quartet in E flat published at Leipzig. Hans von Bülow, who had seen the proof-sheets of this work, later made the composer's acquaintance. It was through this meeting that Mackenzie's overture 'Cervantes', performed at Sondershausen in 1877, was produced at Glasgow two years later under von Bülow's direction. Soon after, two other orchestral works appeared, 'Rhapsodie Ecossaise' and 'Burns' (his second Scottish rhapsody), played at Glasgow in 1880 and 1881 respectively, (Sir) August Manns [q.v.] conducting. About this time choral works were also occupying his attention. One of these, a cantata entitled 'The Bride', received a hearing at the Worcester festival of 1881.

But overwork began to undermine Mackenzie's health. After a period of rest abroad he soon recovered and decided to remain in the warmer climate of Italy. Save for just over a year in England (1885) he made Florence his headquarters for seven years (1881–1888). There he settled down to compositions of larger scale. Besides purely instrumental works he wrote operas and oratorios, including the opera *Colomba* produced at Drury Lane, London, by the Carl Rosa Company in 1883, and the oratorio 'The Rose of Sharon', one of the successes of the Norwich festival of 1884. A violin concerto written for Sarasate was played at the Birmingham festival of 1885 and six pieces for the violin (including 'Benedictus') were a feature of Monday Popular Concerts at the St. James's Hall (1888) with Lady Hallé [q.v.] as soloist. During the season of 1885–1886 Mackenzie, as conductor of the Novello oratorio choir in London, met Gounod and Dvořák. He had already established a firm friendship with Liszt who paid his final visit to England primarily in order to hear

his 'Saint Elizabeth' performed under Mackenzie's direction at the Royal Academy of Music in 1886.

On the death of Sir George Macfarren [q.v.] in October 1887 Mackenzie was appointed to succeed him as principal of the Academy. From 1888 until his retirement in 1924 he was responsible for its administration. His first task was to set his house in order. Supported by royal patronage and by a sympathetic board of directors and committee of management, reforms were initiated. The professorial staff became a more cohesive body. Generous donors gave sums of money to found scholarships. The scope and influence of his own experience broadened the musical education which the Academy was meant to provide. He established links with the then recently founded Royal College of Music, which, with the friendly co-operation of (Sir) C. H. H. Parry [q.v.], culminated in the formation (1889) of the Associated Board of the Royal Academy of Music and the Royal College of Music—an examining body, later known as the Associated Board of the Royal Schools of Music the work of which in stimulating musical effort among boys and girls of school age has had far-reaching effects throughout Great Britain and the Dominions.

From 1892 to 1899 Mackenzie was conductor of the Philharmonic Society's concerts which brought him into close personal touch with composers, conductors, and executant *artistes* of international repute—Tschaikowsky (whose 'Pathetic' symphony Mackenzie introduced to London), Saint-Saëns, Grieg, Strauss, Busoni, and Joachim. His intimate knowledge of German and Italian made him quite at home with them. Such knowledge, coupled with his cosmopolitan musicianship, eminently fitted him to be president (1908–1912) of the International Musical Society: he presided over congresses at Vienna (1909) and London (1911), at the latter of which British music in its manifold aspects was performed.

The new national trend based on folk-song 'begun by Parry the Englishman, Mackenzie the Scot, and Stanford the Irishman' was manifest by the end of the century, and in 1903 Mackenzie himself undertook a six-weeks' tour of Canada at the invitation of Dr. Charles Harriss in order to study the possibilities of Canadian folk-song. Many contemporary British works then introduced by Mackenzie gave impetus to choral festival competitions throughout the Dominion. At the Academy he taught composition, conducted the students' orchestra, and lectured, besides attending to his administrative work. The move in 1911 from Tenterden Street to the new building at York Gate, Marylebone Road, and the centenary celebrations (1922), with a performance of his opera *The Cricket on the Hearth*, provide ample testimony to his gifts of organization. Many students, now distinguished members of their profession, remember his genial friendship and wise leadership with gratitude.

Of his works with *opus* numbers (they total 90) it is significant that nearly half were written before Mackenzie became principal of the Royal Academy of Music. It is probable that by these his merits as a composer will be assessed. 'The Cotter's Saturday Night', one of his most effective works for chorus and orchestra, was produced during the year of his appointment and finds him true to national folk-song tradition, as does also the music of the *Little Minister* (1897). His operas and oratorios might have achieved greater success had he been blessed with better librettists. Although among his instrumental works neither symphony nor sonata is to be found, what he did produce gives him an honoured place among the composers of his time.

Mackenzie was knighted in 1895 and appointed K.C.V.O. in 1922. His many academic distinctions included the honorary degree of doctor of music of the universities of St. Andrews, Cambridge, Edinburgh, and Oxford, the honorary LL.D. of Glasgow and Leeds, and the honorary D.C.L. of McGill. He was also a member of the Royal Swedish Academy and received the gold medals for arts and sciences of Hesse-Darmstadt and Saxe-Coburg. He married in 1874 Mary Melina (died 1925), daughter of John Burnside, of Edinburgh, and had a daughter. He died in London 28 April 1935.

A portrait of Mackenzie painted by René de l'Hôpital in 1923 is in the possession of the Royal Academy of Music. A cartoon of him by 'Spy' appeared in *Vanity Fair* 14 January 1901.

[*The Times*, 29 April 1935; Sir A. C. Mackenzie, *A Musician's Narrative*, 1927; *Grove's Dictionary of Music and Musicians*, 4th ed., vol. iii, edited by H. C. Colles; *Oxford Companion to Music*, edited by Percy Scholes, 6th ed., 1945.]   MOIR CARNEGIE.

MACKENZIE, JOHN STUART (1860-1935), philosopher, was born at Spring-burn, Glasgow, 29 February 1860, the younger son of Thomas McKenzie, by his wife, Janet Brown. He and a brother three years his senior comprised the whole family of Thomas McKenzie, an intrepid but not, in the worldly sense, specially successful Scotsman who, after having been in business in some branch of the clothing trade in Glasgow, emigrated in 1868 with his family to South America where he was overtaken by disaster. Within a short time of their arrival his wife, and, some months afterwards, he himself, died; and the children had to be brought back to Scotland to the care of relatives. The elder boy went into engineering in which he did well, while John, who was sent to the Glasgow High School, after a brilliant career at Glasgow University, and after having been awarded the Shaw fellowship at the university of Edinburgh, found himself urged by his chief philosophical teacher, Edward Caird [q.v.], to take up the subject of social philosophy, in preference to the study of Hegel, which, for him, had lain 'nearer to the heart's desire'. Thus it happened that his Shaw lectures, delivered during his tenure (1884-1889) of the fellowship, constituted an 'Introduction to Social Philosophy', and were published under that title in 1890.

Meantime, in 1886, Mackenzie had entered Trinity College, Cambridge, as a scholar. He obtained a first class in the moral sciences tripos of 1889. But much more important than any gaining of distinctions at Cambridge were the friendships which he contracted there; in particular that of a youth of kindred tastes, six years junior to him, whom he found much absorbed, as he himself had once been, in Herbert Spencer, and whom, not uncharacteristically, he would appear to have urged towards the Hegelian researches from which he himself had been led to abstain. This was J. M. E. M'Taggart [q.v.] whose later influence on his own pupils gave the impetus to much in the early development of those tendencies in philosophy which have since (during the first half of the twentieth century) been especially associated with Cambridge. In 1890 Mackenzie was elected into a fellowship at Trinity which he held until 1896. In 1895 he was appointed professor of logic and philosophy at University College, Cardiff, a post from which he retired in 1915 at the early age of fifty-five, in order, chiefly, 'to have time to write'.

It is not implied, of course, that Mackenzie had not already written. Besides his Shaw lectures, his *Outlines of Metaphysics* (1902), and his *Lectures on Humanism* (1907) he had produced, as far back as 1893, that notable *Manual of Ethics* which seemed, somewhat to his astonishment, to have made his name familiar almost wherever ethics were taught and English was spoken. But what he would probably have regarded as his chief works were published during and after the war of 1914–1918. They are *Elements of Constructive Philosophy* (1917), *Outlines of Social Philosophy* (1918), *Fundamental Problems of Life* (1928), and, finally, a small but comprehensive volume which should be included here, entitled *Cosmic Problems* (1931). His *Arrows of Desire* (1920) is in the nature of a collection of occasional essays on popular subjects, although it is perhaps his most readable book. The university of Glasgow conferred upon him the honorary degree of LL.D. in 1911 and he was elected a fellow of the British Academy in 1934.

Mackenzie married in 1898 Hettie Millicent, daughter of Walter William Hughes, of Bristol, herself an educationist and writer, who was head of the Department for the Training of Teachers at Cardiff both before her marriage and after. There were no children of the union. He died at Brockweir, near Chepstow, 6 December 1935.

As a representative of the later phase of the neo-Hegelian school of British idealistic philosophy, Mackenzie invites comparison, as a teacher and writer, with his early friend M'Taggart. Their ultimate metaphysical faith was the same; but Mackenzie had nothing of that intense need for precise statement and rigidly concatenated argument which characterized M'Taggart. He was not a 'dry light', as Caird had once remarked to him. He held the universe to be, indeed, an order; but creative imagination must be the key to it rather than logic. And this seems in later years, although the personal link was never broken, to have drawn him rather away from M'Taggart's thought, and to have led him to see the chief promise for the future of philosophy in such thinkers as, for example, Mr. Edward Douglas Fawcett who, although groping rather more in the dark, appealed to him as perhaps pointing nearer to the dawn.

[*John Stuart Mackenzie*, edited by his wife (portrait), 1936; J. H. Muirhead, *John Stuart Mackenzie, 1860–1935* in *Proceedings* of the British Academy, vol. xxi, 1935; personal knowledge.]   J. W. SCOTT.

McKENZIE, (ROBERT) TAIT (1867–1938), Canadian sculptor and expert in physical culture, was born at Ramsay, Ontario, 26 May 1867, the second of the three sons of William McKenzie, a minister of the Free Church of Scotland, by his wife, Catherine Shiells. His father soon moved to the neighbouring village of Almonte, where Tait McKenzie's youth was spent. He was educated at Ottawa Collegiate Institute and McGill University, where he graduated B.A. in 1889 and M.D. in 1892. After appointments as house surgeon at Montreal General Hospital (1893), and as a ship's surgeon (1894), he settled in practice at Montreal and was for a year house physician to the governor-general of Canada. While practising as an orthopaedic surgeon, McKenzie held many university appointments, all connected with his profession and some of them reflecting his interest in art and sport. He was in succession medical director of physical training, demonstrator, and later lecturer, in anatomy at McGill University; and he also acted as lecturer on artistic anatomy to the Montreal Art Association and at the Harvard University summer school and the Olympic lecture course at St. Louis (1904). From 1904 to 1931 he was professor of physical education in the university of Pennsylvania. During the war of 1914–1918 he served in the Royal Army Medical Corps with the temporary rank of major. He was president of the Society of Directors of Physical Education in Colleges (1912), and of the American Physical Education Association (1913–1915), and was a fellow of the Philadelphia College of Physicians and the American Medical Association. He published two books, *Exercise in Education and Medicine* (1910), a text-book, and *Reclaiming the Maimed*, a handbook on physiotherapy.

About 1902 McKenzie began to exhibit sculpture, chiefly athletic in character, at the Salon, the Royal Academy, and other art institutions in England and the United States of America. His earlier works might all be described as celebrations of youth in active exercise, but later he executed several memorials. The most important of these in Great Britain are the statue of General Wolfe in Greenwich Park, the gift of Canada to England, the model for which was exhibited at the Academy in 1929; the Scottish-American War Memorial in Princes Street Gardens, Edinburgh; and the Cambridge War Memorial. There are statuettes by him in the Fitzwilliam Museum, the Ashmolean

Museum, and the royal collection at Balmoral. His memorial statue of Lieutenant-Colonel G. H. Baker is in the House of Commons, Ottawa; there are heroic statues by him of 'The Youthful Franklin' and George Whitefield at the university of Pennsylvania, Philadelphia; and monumental portraits by him, chiefly plaques in relief, decorate the campus of more than one other American university. He is represented by smaller works at the Metropolitan Museum of Art, New York, and in the art galleries of Ottawa, Montreal, and St. Louis. For the stadium in Stockholm he designed a medallion, 'Joy of Effort', and for his distinguished services in sculpture at the Olympic games of 1912 King Gustavus V of Sweden awarded him the King's medal.

McKenzie's artistic, anatomical, and athletic interests were so closely connected that it is exceedingly difficult to form a just estimate of his rank as a sculptor. The combination of medicine or surgery with painting or sculpture is not uncommon in the history of art, but McKenzie differed fundamentally from all the instances that can be recalled in that in his case the connexion was direct. Sir Francis Seymour Haden [q.v.] was a landscape etcher, and Henry Tonks [q.v.] excelled in domestic genre, and their aims in representation were exclusively artistic. Even when the work of McKenzie is compared with antique sculpture concerned with muscular movement, such as the Discobolus and the Laocoön, a difference in approach is apparent, because in them the aim was formal, the difference being sharpened by the circumstance that McKenzie also executed a 'Discus Thrower'. He gave direct plastic expression to his ruling passion for bodily fitness, and in that respect he may be called unique.

McKenzie married in 1907 Ethel, eldest daughter of John O'Neil, of Hamilton, Ontario; there were no children of the marriage. He died at Philadelphia 29 April 1938.

A drawing was made of McKenzie at work on 'The Discus Thrower' by Violet Oakley, and a head was carved in mahogany by Boris Blai.

[C. E. C. Hussey, *Tait McKenzie, A Sculptor of Youth* (containing a chronological list of his works to 1929), 1929; William Colgate, *Canadian Art, 1920–1940,* 1943; Kineton Parkes, *The Art of Carved Sculpture,* vol. i, 1931; private information.]

CHARLES MARRIOTT.

McKERROW, RONALD BRUNLEES (1872–1940), scholar and bibliographer, was born at Putney 12 December 1872, the only son of Alexander McKerrow, civil engineer, and grandson of William McKerrow [q.v.]. His mother was Mary Jane, elder daughter of Sir James Brunlees [q.v.]. From Harrow he proceeded to King's College, London, and thence to Trinity College, Cambridge, where he won the chancellor's English medal in 1895 and graduated in medieval and modern languages in 1897. After three years (1897–1900) as professor of English in the Government School of Foreign Languages at Tokyo, he settled in London and engaged in literary and critical work, becoming in 1908 a director of the publishing firm of Sidgwick & Jackson, and in 1912 honorary secretary (jointly with Alfred William Pollard) of the Bibliographical Society. The society remained throughout one of his chief concerns, and for it he produced two exhaustive monographs on *Printers' and Publishers' Devices in England and Scotland 1485–1640* (1913) and *Title-page Borders used in England and Scotland, 1485 to 1640* (with Frederic Sutherland Ferguson, 1932). His edition of the works of the Elizabethan writer Thomas Nashe, undertaken at the suggestion of A. H. Bullen [q.v.], appeared in five volumes between 1904 and 1910, and was at once recognized as setting a standard in English editing. In 1925 McKerrow founded the *Review of English Studies,* which he continued to edit until his death, combining the task from 1934 to 1937 with the editorship of *The Library,* the organ of the Bibliographical Society. His *Introduction to Bibliography for Literary Students* (1927) is an authoritative guide to everything in the material production of printed books that can bear on the study and editing of English literature. The last ten years of his life were devoted to the great critical edition of Shakespeare that he undertook for the Clarendon Press. A substantial portion, comprising most of the early plays, was in fact prepared, but the only part published before his death was the slender but important volume of *Prolegomena for the Oxford Shakespeare* (1939), in which he laid down what he considered to be the principles of text-construction and explained his methods of applying them. In this and other works he probably did more than any man to place the editing of English literature upon a scientific basis. Such was in fact his ultimate aim throughout. In bibliography his powers of observation, memory, and inference combined to give him a sure insight into mechanical processes. But this and much else was for him ancillary to the critical study of literature, and his wide knowledge and experience were placed ungrudgingly at the service of others. If, as some thought, a certain intolerance of speculation where certainty was admittedly unattainable led him to impose too severe a curb on the liberty of an editor, he rendered invaluable service in keeping criticism sane and informed, and in basing it firmly on recognized and clearly defined principles.

McKerrow was Sandars reader in bibliography at Cambridge University in 1928–1929, was awarded the gold medal of the Bibliographical Society in 1929, was elected a fellow of the British Academy in 1932, and received the honorary degree of Ph.D. from Louvain University in 1927. He married in 1915 Amy, daughter of William Bonnet, of Conway, and had twin sons. He died at Picket Piece, Wendover, 20 January 1940.

[*The Times*, 22 January 1940; W. W. Greg, *Ronald Brunlees McKerrow, 1872–1940* in *Proceedings* of the British Academy, vol. xxvi, 1940 (portrait); *The Library*, 4th series, vol. xxi, 1941 (containing a list of his writings); private information; personal knowledge.]

W. W. GREG.

MACKINTOSH, HUGH ROSS (1870–1936), Scottish theologian, was born at Paisley 31 October 1870, the fourth child and younger son of Alexander Mackintosh, minister of the Gaelic Free church at Paisley, by his wife, Jannet Ross. Partly because of early delicate health, and partly because both his parents died before he was ten years old, a large part of his childhood and boyhood was spent in the Highlands, his second home being a country manse, at Edderton in Ross-shire, where he was brought up by an aunt. He was educated at the Neilson Institution, Paisley, the Royal Academy, Tain, and George Watson's College, Edinburgh. In 1888 he entered Edinburgh University, where he specialized in classics and philosophy, in the latter of which he graduated with first class honours, being awarded the Ferguson scholarship in 1893. There he was deeply influenced by Andrew Seth, afterwards A. S. Pringle-Pattison [q.v.]. Subsequently he studied theology at the New College, Edinburgh, where he was influenced by A. B. Davidson [q.v.] and Marcus Dods [q.v.], and at the universities of Freiburg,

Halle, and Marburg, at a time when Ritschlianism was in the ascendant in German theology. He was ordained to the ministry of the Free Church in 1897 and until 1901 was minister of Queen Street church, Tayport, and then for three years (1901–1904) first minister of Beechgrove church, Aberdeen. In the last-named year he was appointed professor of systematic theology at the New College, Edinburgh, and he held this chair, which after the union (1929) of the United Free Church with the Church of Scotland became in 1935 the chair of Christian dogmatics in the university of Edinburgh, until his death. He received honorary degrees from the universities of Edinburgh, Oxford, and Marburg. In 1899 he married Jessie, third daughter of David Air, of Dunmore, Dundee, and had one son and three daughters. He died after a very short illness at Stornoway, in the course of a conference of highland lay-missionaries, 8 June 1936.

While Mackintosh was a keen churchman, and preached very frequently, his main activity was theological teaching and writing. Beginning with a somewhat Calvinistic heritage, he was strongly affected by the new developments of biblical criticism that were causing such a stir in the Scotland of his youth, and also by the Ritschlianism which he had begun to imbibe at Marburg from the teaching of Wilhelm Herrmann, with whom he maintained a lasting friendship. He helped to introduce Ritschlianism to the English-speaking world by translating (in collaboration with Dr. A. B. Macaulay, 1900) the most important of the three volumes of Albrecht Ritschl's great work, *The Christian Doctrine of Justification and Reconciliation*. Mackintosh's own work plainly shows the influence of Ritschl. Yet he was critical of the Ritschlian theology at many points, and he cannot fairly be called a Ritschlian. In the matter of Christology, which is the subject of his *magnum opus*, *The Doctrine of the Person of Jesus Christ* (1912), his position is along the lines of the kenotic theories, with strong emphasis both on the actual personality of the human and historical Jesus and on the Incarnation of the Son of God. When the 'dialectical' theology of Karl Barth took the world by storm, Mackintosh was both appreciative and critical, as can be learnt from chapter viii of his *Types of Modern Theology, Schleiermacher to Barth* (published posthumously in 1937), a book in which his own position in theology may well be studied indirectly.

Mackintosh was never involved in hot theological controversy, nor did he found a school of thought. Yet it is not difficult to indicate his peculiar contribution and his distinctive influence. He heralded somewhat prophetically the return to dogma, the return to eschatology, and the return to church-consciousness which are now so unmistakable. From the start there ran through his thinking a strong sense of 'the divine initiative', and its priority over human effort, which the 'dialectical' theology has more recently been emphasizing. Most characteristic of all, perhaps, is Mackintosh's emphasis on the forgiveness of sins as the central boon offered in the Gospel. To him the divine forgiveness was the supreme miracle which ought to be the starting-point and norm of all man's thinking as to what miracle means; and indeed his whole interest in theology was conditioned by the constant reflection that Christian truth is a thing that has to be preached to sinful men in need of pardon; so that it is not surprising to find him devoting one whole book to this great subject, *The Christian Experience of Forgiveness* (1927).

Although keeping aloof from church politics Mackintosh took his share of ecclesiastical responsibility, and on two occasions when the General Assembly set up committees on the re-statement of the Faith, he was made convener and bore a large share of the burden. In 1932 he was elected moderator of the General Assembly of the Church of Scotland.

Mackintosh's portrait was never painted, but an enlarged photograph which hangs in the senate room of the New College, Edinburgh, gives an excellent likeness.

[*The Times*, 10 June 1936; H. R. Mackintosh, *Sermons, with Memoir by A. B. Macaulay*, 1938; personal knowledge.]

D. M. BAILLIE.

McLAREN, CHARLES BENJAMIN BRIGHT, first BARON ABERCONWAY, (1850–1934), barrister and man of business, was born at Edinburgh 12 May 1850, the eldest son of Duncan McLaren [q.v.], member of parliament for Edinburgh, by his third wife, Priscilla, daughter of Jacob Bright, of Green Bank, Rochdale, and sister of John Bright [q.v.], the radical statesman, after whom he was named. His elder half-brother John, Lord McLaren [q.v.], became a Scottish judge.

McLaren was educated at Edinburgh University, where he graduated in 1870 with first class honours in philosophy and won the Ferguson and Hamilton scholarships. After completing his education at the universities of Bonn and Heidelberg he took to journalism in Edinburgh and contributed numerous leading articles to the *Scotsman*. Soon, however, he turned to the English law and was called to the bar by Lincoln's Inn in 1874, developing in due course a solid Chancery practice.

In view of his family associations it was natural that McLaren should be attracted to the liberal cause in politics, and he entered the House of Commons at the general election in 1880 as member for Stafford. In 1886 he voted for Gladstone's home rule bill in the famous division on the second reading, but was defeated at the ensuing general election. In 1892 he was returned for the Bosworth division of Leicestershire, a constituency for which he sat continuously until 1910, when he was succeeded there by his elder son. He was created a baronet in 1902, was sworn of the Privy Council in 1908, and in 1911, on Asquith's recommendation, was raised to the peerage as Baron Aberconway, of Bodnant in the county of Denbigh.

In 1877 McLaren had married Laura Elizabeth, only daughter of Henry Davis Pochin, of Bodnant, Denbighshire, another radical member of parliament, and an associate of his father and his uncle John Bright. They had two sons, the younger of whom was killed in action in 1917, and two daughters. On her father's death she inherited his property in North Wales and the considerable fortune which he had acquired as a manufacturing chemist and industrialist. This circumstance had some effect in determining the later course of McLaren's career, for in 1897, the year in which he took silk, he gave up his practice at the bar and turned to the direction of various industrial companies in which his wife held an extensive interest; and as his legal experience had been largely in the field of company and mercantile law this transition came easily to him. He became chairman of John Brown & company, the Clydeside shipbuilders, who during his term of office launched many great warships and liners; chairman of the Metropolitan Railway Company; of the Tredegar Iron and Coal Company; of the Sheepbridge Iron and Coal Company; and of various other concerns. He was much interested in the historical side of the development of British heavy industries and wrote a book on the subject, *The Basic Industries of Great Britain* (1927).

582

Aberconway and his wife spent much time at their home at Bodnant, which commands a fine view over the mountains of North Wales. Lady Aberconway became an expert in gardening, and in collaboration with her elder son, Henry, developed the grounds both at Bodnant and at her other home at Antibes in the south of France into gardens of beauty and wide botanical fame. She also had talent as an artist in pastels. She was a shrewd woman of business and for long a keen supporter of the cause of women's rights and suffrage. During the war of 1914–1918 she turned her London house into a hospital for servicemen and directed it herself, for which services she was appointed C.B.E. She died at the Château de la Garoupe, Antibes, 4 January 1933.

Aberconway was a man of genial temperament whose abilities led him to a uniformly successful career. His associations being as they were, he may be called fortunate in having lived through the full tide of liberal political supremacy and freedom of industrial enterprise. He died in London 23 January 1934, and was succeeded as second baron by his elder son, Henry Duncan (born 1879).

There is a portrait of Aberconway by G. Fiddes Watt at Bodnant, where there are also portraits of himself and Lady Aberconway by P. A. de László.

[*The Times*, 24 January 1934; personal knowledge.]   MARTIN McLAREN.

MACLEAN, SIR DONALD (1864–1932), politician, was born at Farnworth, Lancashire, 9 January 1864, the elder son of John Maclean, a master cordwainer, of Farnworth, later of Kilmoluag on the island of Tiree, and Mounthill, Carmarthen. His mother, Agnes Macmellin, was a highland lady of good birth who habitually talked Gaelic in her family circle. She died in 1924 at the age of ninety-one.

Maclean, who was educated at Haverfordwest and Carmarthen grammar schools, was early devoted to a legal career. He was admitted as solicitor in 1887, and practised in Cardiff and London. His political career began in 1906, when, after three unsuccessful contests, he won a sensational victory for the liberals at Bath where he had been defeated six years before. He lost the seat in January 1910: from December 1910 to 1922 he was member for Peebles. He was a popular and respected but not particularly distinguished member until 1911, when he was appointed chairman of ways and means

and deputy Speaker, a position which he held until 1918, being the first solicitor to hold this office, for which his handsome presence, his cool judgement, and his imperturbable good humour and patience admirably qualified him. But he laid the real foundation of his reputation by the indefatigable diligence with which he handled during the earlier war years the rather dreary and technical odds and ends of war-time administration. In 1916 (when he was sworn of the Privy Council) he was made chairman of the Treasury committee on enemy debts, and of the London military appeals tribunal. The next year, in which he was appointed K.B.E., he was also chairman of the reconstruction committee of the Poor Law. In 1924 he was chairman of the committee on the registration of dock labour, and in 1926 of the inter-departmental committee on the effect of social insurance on migration. The Ministry of Health, established in 1919, owed its shape and form largely to a Maclean committee's report.

The dramatic climax of Maclean's career occurred in 1918, for he was one of the little band of twenty-nine independent liberals returned in the general election of that year. They met in such extreme dejection that it was seriously proposed to disband the party altogether. 'If we go out of that door without forming a party,' Maclean is reported to have said, 'Liberalism will go under for a generation.' Largely by his influence, the liberal parliamentary party was formed, with Maclean himself as chairman (1919–1922); and largely by his cool and able leadership it grew steadily in influence and numbers. In the general election of 1922 he himself was defeated, but his party carried fifty-nine seats. Like most liberals at that time, his electoral career was stormy. He was defeated at Kilmarnock in 1923, and at East Cardiff in 1924. But in 1929 he was elected for North Cornwall and retained the seat until his death. He was a member of the liberal 'shadow Cabinet' which helped to form the all-party government on 24 August 1931, and he was later one of the four ministers who threatened to resign when that government decided to adopt a tariff policy and were only with difficulty persuaded by the prime minister, Ramsay MacDonald, to 'agree to differ'.

Maclean had accepted the post of president of the Board of Education in the government. After the general election in October 1931 the appointment was confirmed with a seat in the Cabinet. He was not long enough at the Education Office to initiate any policy, or do more than help to soothe the teachers, at that time furious at the cuts in their salaries. Persistent overwork had undermined his strength, and he died suddenly in London 15 June 1932 as the result of a heart attack.

Maclean married in 1907 Gwendolen Margaret, eldest daughter of Andrew Devitt, of Oxted, Surrey. His wife and his four sons and one daughter survived him: the eldest son was killed on active service in 1943.

[*The Times*, 16 June 1932; personal knowledge.]   STUART HODGSON.

McLENNAN, SIR JOHN CUNNINGHAM (1867–1935), Canadian physicist, was born at Ingersoll, Ontario, 14 April 1867, the son of David McLennan, from Aberdeenshire, miller and later graindealer, by his wife, Barbara, daughter of John Cunningham, of Stewarton, Ayrshire. After receiving a sound primary education at the collegiate institutes in the towns of Clinton and Stratford, he taught in country schools for some years in order to obtain funds for entering the university of Toronto in 1888. After graduating as head of his class with first class honours in physics in 1892, he served for six years as assistant demonstrator in that subject and then spent a year (1898–1899) at Cambridge studying under (Sir) J. J. Thomson [q.v.] at the Cavendish laboratory, to which he returned in later years for intellectual refreshment. Thereafter eight more years of excellent work at Toronto, as demonstrator (1899), associate-professor (1902), and director of the physics laboratory (1904), gave him an unchallengeable claim to the chair of physics when it fell vacant in 1907. With characteristic energy he set himself to enlarge and invigorate his department; the McLennan laboratory in the fine modern physics building at Toronto, which has an equipment unexcelled anywhere, is his lasting monument. He was elected F.R.S. (Canada) in 1903.

A first-rate lecturer and tutor for his students, McLennan's influence was exerted continuously for the improvement of teaching standards and the encouragement of research in his university, of which he was throughout his life a very devoted son. He was the leading spirit in organizing an Alumni Association, which raised the $50,000 required to match the contribution of the government of Ontario for building a convocation hall, and he later (1913–1916) served as president of the association.

Even before the war of 1914–1918 McLennan's industrious energy in research had won for him recognition as an authority upon radio-activity and cosmic rays and, after the outbreak of war, a report which he made upon the helium resources of the British Empire, particularly of Canada, led to the construction from his designs of a plant at Calgary, Alberta, which successfully extracted helium from natural gases. But before it was running, he had been summoned to London in 1917 by the British Admiralty, and there, in collaboration with Ernest (later Lord) Rutherford [q.v.] and other scientists, he accomplished what the former described as 'work of outstanding importance . . . in combating the submarine menace' and in the same year was appointed O.B.E. for his services. In 1919 he acted as scientific adviser to the Admiralty.

After the war McLennan returned to his teaching work and having acquired a good supply of helium, set himself to develop low temperature research, to equip his laboratory for spectroscopic investigations, and create in it a cryogenic branch. In his post-war career he succeeded in 1923 in liquefying helium, but one of his most important achievements was when, in association with Professor G. M. Shrum, he reproduced in 1925 the well-known 'auroral green line', which had baffled earlier investigators. The high reputation of McLennan and the school of physics which he had built up attracted graduate students from all over the world, and it was a fitting reward for his work that in 1930 he was appointed dean of graduate studies two years before his retirement in 1932.

Idleness, however, was foreign to McLennan's nature, and his work on a royal commission in Ontario on the treatment of cancer had so greatly impressed him with the urgent need for remedies for this dread disease that he decided to migrate to Great Britain and embrace an opportunity offered there for studying the radium treatment of cancer by physical tests. A special laboratory and clinic were established for him and four grammes of radium were lent by the Radium Belge Corporation, and he was immersed in this work with his habitual ardour when he died suddenly near Abbeville, while travelling in a train from Paris to London, 9 October 1935.

In 1935 McLennan was appointed K.B.E. for his services to science; and honorary degrees were conferred upon him by the universities of Toronto, Manchester, Liverpool, and McGill. Elected F.R.S. in 1915, he was a Royal medallist in 1927 and Bakerian lecturer of the society in 1928 and its vice-president in 1933–1934; he was president of the Royal Canadian Institute (1915–1916) and of the Royal Society of Canada (1924–1925). He wrote no important book but was the author of numerous papers on such subjects as radio-activity, electrical conduction in gases, spectroscopy, and the liquefaction of helium and other gases.

McLennan was an eminent physicist; 'clear-sighted, swift in decision and energetic in action, his qualities stood him in good service, and many stories are current in illustration of his driving power and almost ruthless disregard of persons and difficulties that stood in his way'. He supplemented his marked abilities as a teacher and his unflagging zeal for research with a notable gift for the popular exposition of his scientific lore, which over the years made a great contribution to the education of the Canadian public about the value of scientific research. As president of the Royal Canadian Institute, which had this work as its objective, he was one of the prime movers in the successful campaign for the establishment at Ottawa of the magnificent national laboratories of the National Research Council, of which he was one of the most influential members. McLennan had his detractors, who accused him of a weakness for the well-to-do and of a fondness for self-advertisement, but he had also a wide circle of admirers and friends. He liked club life and social functions, being himself generous in his hospitality; in politics he was a strong conservative and imperialist. He married in 1910 Elsie Monro (died 1933), daughter and heiress of William Ramsay, whisky merchant, of Bowland, Midlothian; there were no children of the marriage.

A portrait of McLennan by Augustus John hangs in the physics building at the university of Toronto.

[*The Times*, 10 and 14 October 1935; H. H. Langton, *Sir John Cunningham McLennan. A Memoir* (bibliography and portrait), 1939; *Obituary Notices of Fellows of the Royal Society*, No. 4, December 1935 (portrait); *Transactions and Proceedings* of the Royal Society of Canada, third series, vol. xxx, 1936 (portrait); *Nature*, 23 January 1932 and 19 October 1935; *Proceedings* of the Physical Society, vol. xlviii, 1936; private information.]
J. A. STEVENSON.

MACLEOD, JOHN JAMES RICKARD (1876–1935), physiologist and biochemist, was born at New Clunie, near Dunkeld, Perthshire, 6 September 1876, the son of Robert Macleod, Free Church minister of New Clunie, by his wife, Jane Guthrie McWalter. He was educated at Aberdeen Grammar School and at Marischal College, whence he graduated M.B., Ch.B. with honours in 1898 and was awarded the Anderson travelling fellowship. He worked for a year at Leipzig and Berlin, and on his return was appointed demonstrator of physiology at the London Hospital Medical College under Sir Leonard Hill. In 1901 he was appointed to a Mackinnon research studentship of the Royal Society, and the following year he became a lecturer in biochemistry at the London Hospital. In 1903, at the early age of twenty-seven, he was appointed professor of physiology at the Western Reserve University, Cleveland, Ohio, where he remained until 1918 when he became professor of physiology at Toronto. During his last two years at Cleveland he had been engaged in various war duties and had acted for part of the winter session of 1916 as professor of physiology at McGill University, Montreal. In 1928 he was appointed regius professor of physiology at Aberdeen, a post which he held in spite of steadily increasing disability until his death there 16 March 1935. He married in 1903 Mary Watson, daughter of Robert McWalter, of Paisley; they had no children.

Macleod's name will always be associated with the discovery of insulin. His interest in diabetes began in 1905, and before the discovery of insulin in 1921 he had published some thirty-seven papers on problems connected with the metabolism of carbohydrates. Like many other workers in the field Macleod believed that there was probably an internal secretion of the pancreas which prevented the accumulation of sugar in the blood. When in October 1920 (Sir) Frederick Grant Banting came to him with a request for assistance in an attempt at the extraction of the hypothetical pancreatic secretion Macleod recognized the feasibility of the proposed experiments, but he had no reason to think that Banting would succeed when so many well-trained physiologists had failed. However, in May 1921

Macleod gave Banting the use of a laboratory, with experimental animals and the services of an assistant. Banting, in co-operation with Professor Charles Herbert Best, obtained in a few months a promising extract which did exert a beneficial effect on experimental diabetes. The original idea which started this particular fundamental research was certainly Banting's, but without the facilities, advice, and co-operation provided by Macleod and others it is doubtful if the investigation would have reached such early success. With a group of workers attacking various problems under Macleod's direction, clear-cut and speedy results were obtained, and the value of insulin in the control of diabetes was fully established. Macleod was responsible for the adoption of the name 'insulin', a name that had been suggested by Sir E. A. Sharpey-Schafer [q.v.] about 1916 for what at that time was the hypothetical secretion of the pancreas.

In an attempt to throw some light on the mode of action of insulin Macleod reverted to a line of research which had attracted him almost at the outset of his career. In 1908, stimulated by Claude Bernard's theories, he had studied the possible role of the nervous system in the causation of hyperglycaemia. His last serious research, published in the *Proceedings* of the Royal Society in 1932, was concerned with the possible existence of a diabetogenic centre in the brain. Problems of carbohydrate metabolism did not exhaust the range of his interests and he carried out much research in other fields. His earliest paper, in 1899, was on the phosphorus content of muscle, and was followed by papers on such diverse subjects as compressed-air sickness, the biochemistry of carbamates, lactic acid metabolism, chemistry of the tubercle bacillus, electric shock, purine bases, and the physiology of respiration. Between 1899 and 1933 he published, sometimes alone, but more often in collaboration, nearly 200 papers, and those of his pupils, working under his direction, amounted to another hundred. He was the author of books entitled *Practical Physiology* (1903), *Diabetes, its Pathological Physiology* (1913), *Fundamentals of Human Physiology* (with R. G. Pearce, 1916, 4th ed. 1936), *Physiology and Biochemistry in Modern Medicine* (1918, 7th ed. 1935), *Laboratory Manual in Physiology* (1919), *Insulin and its Use in the Treatment of Diabetes* (with W. R. Campbell, 1925), *Carbohydrate Metabolism and Insulin* (1926), and *The Fuel of Life* (1928).

Macleod was deeply interested in medical education and acted as associate dean of the medical faculty at Toronto and as dean at Aberdeen. His greatest achievement was as a teacher and director of research. His engaging personality and cheery optimism in the face of many trials inspired the affection and devotion of all who worked with him. He had many interests outside the laboratory, being well read and devoted to the arts, particularly painting; he was also a keen gardener and golfer.

Macleod's share in the discovery of insulin was recognized by the award of many honours. In 1923 he shared the Nobel prize for medicine jointly with Banting. Macleod divided his share of the prize with Professor James Bertram Collip, and Banting divided his with Best. He was Cameron prizeman at Edinburgh (1923), Beaumont lecturer at Detroit (with Banting, 1923), Vanuxen lecturer at Princeton (1928), and Herter lecturer at Johns Hopkins University (1933). He was president of the American Physiological Society (1922-1923) and of the Royal Canadian Institute (1925-1926); he was elected F.R.S. of Canada (1919), of London (1923), and of Edinburgh (1932), and F.R.C.P. (London) under the special by-law, in 1930. He was an honorary member of many learned societies and institutions at home and abroad. He received honorary degrees from the universities of Aberdeen, Pennsylvania, Toronto, and Western Reserve and the Jefferson Medical College.

There is a portrait medallion of Macleod in bronze by Emanuel Hahn (1928) in the medical building at Toronto University.

[*The Times*, 18 March 1935; *Lancet*, 1935, vol. i, p. 716 (portrait), *British Medical Journal*, 1935, vol. i, p. 624 (portrait); *Obituary Notices of Fellows of the Royal Society*, No. 4, December 1935 (portrait); *Biochemical Journal*, vol. xxix, 1935; *Quarterly Journal of Experimental Physiology*, vol. xxv, 1935. Both Macleod and Banting gave accounts of the researches leading to the discovery of insulin in their joint Beaumont foundation lectures (1923); Banting's Cameron prize lecture on 'The History of Insulin', *Edinburgh Medical Journal*, January 1929, should also be consulted.]   W. J. BISHOP.

MACMILLAN, SIR FREDERICK ORRIDGE (1851-1936), publisher, was born at Cambridge 5 October 1851, the elder son of Daniel Macmillan [q.v.], joint founder in 1843 with his younger brother, Alexander Macmillan, of the bookselling and publishing firm of Macmillan & company, by his wife, Frances, only daughter of Charles Orridge, a Cambridge chemist. He was educated at Uppingham under Edward Thring [q.v.], was trained in the family firm, then at Cambridge, and subsequently spent five years at its branch in New York where in 1874 he married Georgiana Elizabeth, daughter of Thomas Warrin, of Newtown, Long Island. In 1876 he returned to England as a partner to begin his long career in the London house then situated in Bedford Street. He had personal experience of printing and bookselling, as well as every side of publishing, including 'town travelling'; and was one of the few publishers with first-hand knowledge of all the technicalities of his exacting profession. He took a keen personal interest in the New York branch of the business which in 1890 became an independent firm under the name of the Macmillan Company, with the London partners as directors. Following his uncle's lead Macmillan built up a world-wide organization with branches in Canada, Australia, India, and elsewhere, and established for it an international reputation second to none. He was a man with genuine taste and sound judgement, seldom misled by the prejudices of his 'readers', but in selecting manuscripts for publication was inclined to shy at extremes whether of emotion or of manner. He had a natural courtesy; enjoyed the personal friendship of many of his distinguished authors; and maintained the generous and hospitable tradition set by his father and uncle.

Macmillan was president of the Publishers Association in 1900–1902 and 1911–1913, and played the leading part in establishing the 'net book agreement' (1890) now regarded as the Magna Carta of the trade. He took a share in framing the Copyright Act of 1911 and served on the royal commission on paper in 1916. He was a trustee of the Booksellers' Provident Institution, and was knighted in 1909 for his work as chairman (from 1903) of the board of management of the National Hospital for the Paralysed and Epileptic, Queen Square. He was appointed C.V.O. in 1928.

Macmillan exercised a dominating influence in the councils of the book trade, but at the end of his career he found himself, as a sturdy individualist, opposed to the new spirit of co-operation which followed the reports of the joint committee of publishers and booksellers in 1928–1929. Nevertheless at the age of eighty he was young enough to write to the leader of the new movement: 'I am sure you will believe me when I say that if I do not always agree with my juniors I do not take it for granted that they are wrong.'

Macmillan died in London 1 June 1936; he had no children and was succeeded in his business by his nephews, the sons of his brother, Maurice Macmillan.

[*The Times*, 2 June 1936; Charles Morgan, *The House of Macmillan, 1843–1943*, 1943; *The Net Book Agreement* (privately printed), 1924; F. A. Mumby, *Publishing and Bookselling*, 1930; F. D. Sanders, *British Book Trade Organization*, 1939; private information.] STANLEY UNWIN.

McMILLAN, MARGARET (1860–1931), educationist, was born at Westchester, New York State, 20 July 1860, the second of the three daughters of James McMillan, who had emigrated as a youth to the United States from Glen Urquhart, Inverness-shire. On one of his visits home he married (1858) Jean Cameron, from Dochfour, near Inverness, and settled with her at Westchester. The father, who came of crofter stock, interested himself in fibre manufacture, but died in 1865, and the mother, impoverished, returned with her two surviving daughters to Inverness.

Miss McMillan was educated at Inverness High School, and studied music at Frankfort-on-Main in order to fit herself for the career of a finishing governess: later she studied languages at Geneva and Lausanne. Subsequently she was trained for the stage, but her desire, inspired by the clan motto, *Miseris succurrere disco*, led her in 1892 to devote her activities to social reform, and in 1893 she was 'called' to the labour 'church' at Bradford in Yorkshire, where she became a member of the independent labour party (founded there in January of that year) and was widely known as the 'labour prophetess of the north'. However, she was diverted to interest in schoolchildren by her election to the local school board in November 1894, and about 1899 she compelled the first recorded medical inspection of schoolchildren, at the Usher Street schools, which was carried out in her presence by Dr. James Kerr, afterwards medical officer to the London County Council. This success, and her subsequent influence with the officials of the Board of Education, made her the undoubted founder of medical inspection in English elementary schools.

In 1902 Miss McMillan left Bradford for London, where she joined her elder sister, Rachel McMillan (1859–1917). After establishing at Bow in 1908 a children's clinic which had to be partially closed two years later, the sisters began work in 1910 at Deptford, where their new clinic met with immediate success: it received a grant from the London County Council in 1911 for dental treatment and in 1912 for eye and ear treatment. The McMillans also created camp schools for boys and girls and a nursery school for infants. During the war of 1914–1918 they completed the establishment of the pioneer open-air nursery school for children under five years of age, which attracted world-wide interest: the new building was opened by H. A. L. Fisher [q.v.] in 1917. In 1930 the new building of the Rachel McMillan College at Deptford (previously known as the Rachel McMillan Training Centre), for training students in nursery school work, was opened by Queen Mary. It was Margaret McMillan's last achievement.

In creative power and her influence in promoting legislation, Miss McMillan undoubtedly affected the education of elementary schoolchildren more than any other person. As a writer, she obtained renown at home and abroad; her speeches were compelling and eloquent; her organizing powers were used with efficiency and adventurous skill, and all her work for the welfare of the children was inspired by strong spiritual and religious motives.

Miss McMillan was appointed C.B.E. in 1917 and C.H. in 1930. She died at Harrow 29 March 1931. A portrait of her, painted by John Mansbridge, hangs in the Rachel McMillan College.

[*The Times*, 30 March 1931; A. Mansbridge, *Margaret McMillan, Prophet and Pioneer*, 1932; Margaret McMillan, *Life of Rachel McMillan*, 1927; D'Arcy Cresswell, *Margaret McMillan*, 1948; personal knowledge.]

ALBERT MANSBRIDGE.

McMURRICH, JAMES PLAYFAIR (1859–1939), Canadian anatomist, was born at Toronto, Canada, 16 October 1859, the son of John McMurrich, by his wife, Janet Dickson. He was educated at Upper Canada College and at the university of Toronto, whence he graduated B.A. (1879) and M.A. (1881). At the age of twenty-

three he became professor of biology at the Ontario Agricultural College (1882–1884), and then went to Johns Hopkins University as instructor in osteology and mammalian anatomy (1884–1886); at the same time he studied for his Ph.D., which he took in 1885. His early academic career was noted for numerous changes and a rapid rise. He held in succession the professorships of biology at Haverford College, Pennsylvania (1886–1889), of animal morphology at Clark University, Worcester, Massachusetts (1889–1892), of biology at the university of Cincinnati (1892–1894), and of anatomy at the university of Michigan (1894–1907). Having refused the chair of anatomy at Yale University, he was appointed to Toronto as professor of anatomy in 1907 and held this chair until his retirement in 1930, when he was made professor emeritus. He acted as dean of the school of graduate studies from 1922 until 1930. He died at his home at Toronto 9 February 1939. In 1882 he married Katie Moodie (died 1932), daughter of J. J. Vickers, of Toronto, and had a son and a daughter.

McMurrich was the author of *A Text-Book of Invertebrate Morphology* (1894, 2nd ed. 1896), *The Development of the Human Body* (1902, 7th ed. 1923), and of more than a hundred papers on morphology and embryology. He was a leading authority on the actiniaria or sea-anemones. He was keenly interested in the history of science and his *Leonardo da Vinci, the Anatomist (1452–1519)* (1930), is an authoritative estimate of da Vinci's position as an anatomist and physiologist, based on a thorough study of the facsimile reproductions of the manuscripts. He translated Johannes Sobotta's *Atlas and Text Book of Human Anatomy* (1906–1907), edited Henry Morris's *Human Anatomy* (4th ed. 1907), and wrote the sections on the muscular and vascular systems in George Arthur Piersol's *Human Anatomy* (1907).

McMurrich was elected F.R.S. (Canada) in 1909 and was posthumously awarded the Flavelle medal in 1939. He was president of the Society of Naturalists (1907), the American Association of Anatomists (1908), the Royal Society of Canada (1922), and the American Association for the Advancement of Science (1922), and was chairman of the Biological Board of Canada (1926–1934). He was also a member of the North American commission on fisheries investigations

(1921–1939). He received the honorary degree of LL.D. from the universities of Michigan (1912), Cincinnati (1923), and Toronto (1931).

A portrait of McMurrich by Kenneth Forbes is in the anatomy building at the university of Toronto.

[*Minutes of Proceedings* of the Royal Society of Canada, 1939 (portrait); *The Times*, 18 February 1939; *Canadian Medical Association Journal*, vol. xl, p. 409, 1939; *Lancet*, 1939, vol. i, p. 481; *Anatomical Record*, vol. lxxiv, supplement, 1939 (portrait).]

W. J. BISHOP.

MACNAMARA, THOMAS JAMES (1861–1931), politician, was born in the barracks at Montreal 23 August 1861, the only son of Thomas Macnamara, a Crimean veteran, a sergeant in the 47th Foot (later the Loyal North Lancashire Regiment). He came to England at an early age and was educated at St. Thomas's school, Exeter, and the Borough Road Training College for Teachers. He became a school-teacher, his last post being that of head of a board school in Bristol for eight years. In 1892 he came to London as editor of the *Schoolmaster*, the organ of the National Union of Teachers, of which he was elected president in 1896. In the general election of 1895 he unsuccessfully contested the borough of Deptford as a liberal, but he was returned in 1900 for North Camberwell, and represented that constituency (which in 1918 became North-West Camberwell) continuously for twenty-four years. In 1907 he was appointed parliamentary secretary to the Local Government Board and in the next year, parliamentary and financial secretary to the Admiralty. In 1911 he was sworn of the Privy Council.

During his parliamentary life Macnamara became associated more and more closely with Lloyd George who in 1920 made him a member of the Cabinet as minister of labour, a post which he held for two years during a period of severe industrial depression. He retained his seat in 1922 and 1923, but he was defeated in 1924. In 1929 he failed at Walsall and did not again enter parliament, but continued to be of service to Lloyd George as an organizer and a speaker on liberal platforms. As a speaker on platforms he earned a well known reputation and by his energy he deserved the nickname of 'Fighting Mac'. In some of the books which he wrote on his experiences as a schoolmaster,

he displayed a pleasant sense of humour, and he was a prolific writer on social questions.

Macnamara married in 1886 Rachel, eldest daughter of Angus Cameron, of Rannoch, Perthshire, and of Bristol, and had three sons and a daughter. In 1898 he received the honorary degree of LL.D. from the university of St. Andrews and in 1907 that of M.A. from the university of Oxford. He died in London 4 December 1931.

A cartoon of Macnamara by 'Spy' appeared in *Vanity Fair* 9 October 1907.

[*The Times*, 5 December 1931.]

E. I. CARLYLE.

McNEILE, (HERMAN) CYRIL (1888–1937), soldier, and novelist under the pseudonym of SAPPER, was born at Bodmin 28 September 1888, the son of (Captain) Malcolm McNeile, R.N., later governor of the Royal Naval Prison, Lewes, by his wife, Christiana Mary Sloggett. He was educated at Cheltenham College and at the Royal Military Academy, Woolwich. Joining the Royal Engineers in 1907, he was gazetted captain in 1914, and served throughout the war of 1914–1918, winning the M.C.

McNeile retired from the army in 1919 with the rank of lieutenant-colonel and his best known story, *Bull-dog Drummond*, published a year after his retirement, was sub-titled 'the adventures of a demobilised officer who found peace dull'. Writing under the pseudonym of 'Sapper', he had already published several books, most of them dealing with war-time experiences, but it was *Bull-dog Drummond* that made him famous as a writer of 'thrillers'. A dramatized version ran successfully at Wyndham's Theatre, London, in 1921–1922 with (Sir) Gerald du Maurier [q.v.] playing the title part, and was later given in New York with equal success, whilst in 1929 the production of a film version marked the beginning of a series of films of varying merit based on the *Bull-dog Drummond* stories which McNeile published almost every year until his death. None of these sequels has the merit of the original book, which, lacking any literary pretensions, is excellent as a straightforward story of exciting if improbable adventure.

McNeile married in 1914 Violet Baird, daughter of Lieutenant-Colonel Arthur Sholto Douglas, of the Cameron Highlanders, and had two sons. He died at West Chiltington, near Pulborough,

Sussex, 14 August 1937, of illness traceable to his war service.

[*The Times*, 16 August 1937; S. J. Kunitz and H. Haycraft, *Twentieth Century Authors: a Biographical Dictionary* (New York), 1942.]

GEORGINA BATTISCOMBE.

McNEILL, JAMES (1869–1938), Indian and Irish civil servant, was born at Glenarm, co. Antrim, 27 or 29 March 1869, the youngest son of Archibald McNeill, of Carnegies in the Glens, who had been trained as a shipbuilder, owned a bakery which served the coastal area between Cushendun and Cushendall, and also farmed in a small way. His mother was Rosetta Macauley, who on her mother's side traced an ancestry back to the O'Neills, Earls of Tyrone, chieftains of Catholic Ulster before the Plantations. In the once remote Glens of Antrim, justly celebrated for their wild beauty, the Roman Catholics have survived as a majority and constitute a little nationalist enclave in the unionist dominion of north-east Ulster. Like the Catholic populations in other parts of the north the people of the Glens possess a strong sentiment of local patriotism, and James McNeill always sustained strong nationalist and United Ireland opinions alongside of a pride in his Ulster descent and an appreciation of the Ulster character, without distinction of creed.

McNeill passed his early childhood in the Glens, and there acquired that love of nature and of out-door life which he ever combined with the tastes of a student. After attending the local national school for a year or two he was sent south to his uncle, the Rev. Charles Macauley, a professor at Maynooth, under whose care he remained while he was being educated at Belvedere, the large Jesuit day school in Dublin, where he met with so many successes, particularly in classics and history, that he was advised to direct his course towards the Indian civil service. He prepared for the examination at Blackrock College, near Dublin, and afterwards at Emmanuel College, Cambridge. In 1890 he went out to the Bombay Presidency. His first important work was the preparation of the general administration report for 1895–1896, the year of the beginning of the bubonic plague epidemic, and at the time of his retirement, during the winter of 1914–1915, he was commissioner of the central division of the presidency and an additional member of the imperial legislative council of India. In every respect,

including that of amusement—he became during these years a fine shot and horseman and an expert at pig-sticking—the life of India suited him; and if he left the service at forty-five, the earliest retiring age, it was not to seek leisure but to place his abilities at the disposal of his native country, then at a crisis of her history. His lively sense of Indian grandeur and destinies had won him the trust of the Indian leaders with whom his work brought him in contact. Yet he had not disguised his view that the evolution of India towards political freedom would be a long process owing to the racial and religious complications involved.

On his return to Ireland, McNeill made his home near Dublin with his brothers Charles and John, the latter a prominent figure in the Irish National Volunteers, in politics a leader of Sinn Fein, and, as a scholar, closely associated with the Gaelic revival. After the Easter rebellion of 1916, John McNeill, although not a participant, was compromised in its antecedents and was arrested, narrowly escaping execution. James McNeill, who had hitherto been chiefly interested in the political and economic aspects of the Gaelic revival, now threw in his lot with the political movement led by Mr. de Valera which triumphed throughout nationalist Ireland at the elections of December 1918, and in 1922, after the British government had come to terms in the previous December with the representatives of Dail Eireann (of which John McNeill was Speaker), James McNeill helped to draft the constitution of the new state. In the same year he was appointed chairman of the Dublin county council, and acted on several occasions as arbiter between employers and workmen. In 1923 he was sent to London as high commissioner of the Irish Free State, a position for which his long official experience in high administrative posts made him peculiarly fitted. The negative results of the Ulster Boundary Commission (1924–1925), upon which his brother presented the case for Irish unity, were a great disappointment to him, but he remained faithful to the 'Dominion' settlement of 1921, and in 1928 he accepted the governor-generalship of the Irish Free State.

It was explained at the time by one of the Irish ministers that, as a result of the Imperial Conference of 1926, the governor-general was no longer a representative or agent of the British government, but had been appointed by the King on the advice of the Irish government and held 'in all respects the same position in relation to the administration of public affairs in a Dominion as is held by His Majesty the King in Great Britain'. Unlike T. M. Healy [q.v.], his predecessor in the office, McNeill was a man of gentle speech who had made no personal enemies, and the appointment met with general approval, especially in literary and artistic circles, where Mrs. McNeill had been well known, both in Dublin and in London. But in 1931 the accession of Mr. de Valera's Fianna Fail, or republican party, to power made the position of a governor-general, however tactful and unassuming he might be, extremely uneasy. As an earnest of its ultimate intention to abolish the office altogether, the new government set about reducing it to obscurity, and at the Eucharistic Congress of 1932 McNeill was excluded from welcoming the visitors in his official capacity. For all the gentleness of his manner there was Ulster iron in McNeill's character and he challenged the conduct of the executive council towards his office in a correspondence which he printed in the *Irish Times* on 12 July 1932. Personally he would have been glad to resign but, as a matter of principle, he wished to force the executive council to get rid of him by means of the constitutional machinery at its disposal, and finally it was in accordance with advice tendered by Mr. de Valera to King George V that McNeill relinquished the office of governor-general in October 1932. He lived long enough to see the establishment of a new constitution in which the governor-general was replaced by a president and Eire (in English 'Ireland') defined as a republic in 'external association' with the British Commonwealth; but he would have preferred to such changes an approach to unity with Ulster. He enjoyed six years of retirement on a small estate near Dublin, and died in London 12 December 1938.

McNeill married in 1923 Josephine, daughter of James Aherne, of Fermoy, co. Cork; there was no issue of the marriage.

A crayon drawing of McNeill by Louis Raemakers is in the possession of Mrs. Josephine McNeill, and a portrait in oils by Sarah Purser is in the possession of Mr. J. J. Auchmuty.

[*The Times* and *Irish Times*, 13 December 1938; *Studies* (a biographical notice of John McNeill by Fr. John Ryan, S.J.), December 1945; Denis Gwynn, *The Irish Free State, 1922–1927*, 1928.]   JOSEPH HONE.

McNEILL, RONALD JOHN, BARON CUSHENDUN (1861–1934), Irish politician, was born at Torquay 30 April 1861, the only surviving son of Edmund McNeill, a landowner, of Craigdunn, Craigs, near Cushendun, co. Antrim, who held land agencies, by his wife, Mary, eldest daughter of Alexander Miller, of Ballycastle, co. Antrim. The McNeills, who had settled in Antrim in 1676, were of Scottish origin; they could trace their descent from Torquil MacNeill, chief of the Clan Neill (born c. 1380). Ronald McNeill was educated at Harrow and at Christ Church, Oxford, where he was awarded a second class in modern history in 1884. In 1888 he was called to the bar by Lincoln's Inn, but he abandoned the law for journalism and politics.

In 1899 McNeill was appointed assistant editor, and in 1900 editor, of the *St. James's Gazette*, a post which he held until 1904. He unsuccessfully fought four elections, in West Aberdeenshire (1906), South Aberdeen City (February 1907 and January 1910), and Kirkcudbrightshire (December 1910), before he was elected, unopposed, at a by-election in July 1911, conservative member for the East or St. Augustine's division of Kent, known since 1918 as the Canterbury division, a seat which he held for sixteen years. From 1906 to 1911 he was assistant editor of the eleventh edition of the *Encyclopaedia Britannica*, to which he contributed some remarkably diverse articles, on subjects ranging from recent legislation in Australia and the history of the Fenians to lawn tennis and rackets. In 1907 he published his first book, *Home Rule: its History and Danger*, which was followed in 1908 by two contributions to composite works, 'Socialism' in *The New Order*, edited by Lord Malmesbury, and 'The History of Australia and New Zealand' in *The Historian's History of the World*, edited by Henry Smith Williams. His last and most important work, published in 1922, was *Ulster's Stand for Union*, in which he stated the Ulster unionists' case with clarity, force, and precision.

McNeill belonged to the group of conservatives who were called 'die-hards', and was, as a result of his imperial studies, a 'whole-hogger' in the matter of tariff reform. His impulsive temper, which caused him, during the debates on home rule in November 1912, to hurl a Blue Book at the head of Mr. Winston Churchill, then first lord of the Admiralty, joined to his extreme opinions on controversial matters, made many persons under-estimate his ability; and surprise was expressed even by members of his own party when in 1922 after the downfall of Lloyd George's second coalition government, Bonar Law appointed him parliamentary under-secretary for foreign affairs. But his skill and patience in debate, and his general industry, soon won him regard from those most surprised; and no one murmured when Baldwin, in forming his first and second ministries (1923 and 1924), retained McNeill in that office. He was sworn of the Privy Council in 1924. In November 1925 he became financial secretary to the Treasury, his chief being no other than Mr. Winston Churchill. In October 1927 he succeeded Lord Cecil of Chelwood as chancellor of the duchy of Lancaster, which office, together with a seat in the Cabinet, he held until 1929. In November 1927 he was raised to the peerage as Baron Cushendun, taking his title from the village in Antrim where he held his property.

For a short time Cushendun held Lord Cecil's office as chief British representative to the League of Nations, and, during a sitting of the preparatory disarmament commission on 19 March 1928, he delivered a denunciation of the Russian scheme for the immediate abolition of all armed forces, which caused the conference, according to the *New York Times*, to break 'into scarcely precedented cheering. In the international arena, a new personage had arrived.' The London *Times*, describing the speech, said that 'every old Leaguer present declared it to be the greatest speech ever delivered at a League meeting. Lord Cushendun attacked the Russian scheme until the Soviet delegates seemed at one moment ready to rush from the room.' From August to December 1928, when Sir Austen Chamberlain, the foreign secretary [q.v.], was ill, McNeill was acting secretary of state for foreign affairs and chief British representative at the meetings of the Council and Assembly of the League of Nations. One of his functions during this time was to sign in Paris on 27 August the Kellogg pact under which war was outlawed.

McNeill, who, perhaps because of his impulsive, but generous, temper, was admired by his opponents little less than by his friends, was a tall man, but, since he was remarkably well-built, looked less tall than he actually was. He claimed, nor was his claim disputed, to be the tallest barrister of his time: he was just over 6 feet 6 inches. He was twice married: first, in 1884 to Elizabeth Maud (died 1925), fifth daughter of William Bolitho, of Polwithen, Penzance, and had three daughters, the second of whom predeceased her father; secondly, in 1930 to Catherine Sydney Louisa (died 1939), daughter of Sir Mortimer Reginald Margesson, and had no children. He died at Cushendun 12 October 1934.

[*Belfast Telegraph*, 12 October 1934; *Belfast News-Letter*, 13 October 1934; *The Times*, 13 October 1934; private information.]

ST. JOHN ERVINE.

MACPHAIL, SIR (JOHN) ANDREW (1864–1938), pathologist and author, was born at Orwell, Prince Edward Island, 24 November 1864, the third son of William Macphail, of Orwell, by his wife, Catherine Moore, daughter of Finlay Smith. Both came of highland Scottish stock. He was educated locally, at Prince of Wales College, Charlottetown, and at the age of seventeen was acting as headmaster of Fanning School, Prince Edward Island. At McGill University he graduated in medicine in 1891, afterwards studying for a time at the London Hospital. His success as a practising specialist and lecturer in pathology at Montreal at the Western Hospital and at the Protestant Hospital for the Insane (1895–1906) led to his appointment in 1907 to the chair of medical history in McGill University, which he held for thirty years. His academic duties left him time to undertake the editorship of both the *Canadian Medical Journal* and the *University Magazine* and in the latter, which he made the leading intellectual review of Canada, he found scope to express his own views fearlessly and to encourage promising young Canadian writers.

Macphail had published three volumes of essays and a novel, *The Vine of Sibmah* (1906), before the war of 1914–1918 called him to medical service in France with the sixth Canadian Field Ambulance and later at the Canadian Overseas Army's headquarters. During the war he published an anthology of tragic verse, *The Book of Sorrow* (1916), and a life of John McCrae, the Canadian soldier-poet, under the title *In a Flanders Field* (1918). In 1917 he delivered the Cavendish lecture at Cambridge. For his war services he was knighted in 1918 and appointed O.B.E. in 1919. He received the honorary degree of LL.D. from McGill in 1921. After the war he gave up editorial work but continued to write freely for Canadian and British reviews and to produce books. An English translation (1921) of Louis Hemon's well-known novel *Marie Chapdelaine* was followed by a volume on the medical services for the Canadian official history of the war (1925), *Three Persons* (1929), and *The Bible in Scotland* (1931). He also left for posthumous publication a semi-autobiographical volume, *The Master's Wife* (1939), which tells the story of the Macphail family in Canada and has been considered the best story ever written of pioneer life in Canada.

A man of marked individuality and great mental versatility, Macphail was a prominent figure in the literary world of Canada and in his later years a famous character in Montreal. He wrote with equal skill upon medicine, politics, economics, military affairs, and religion in a vivid, pungent style, spiced with an original vein of ironic wit. His views were also original, for, while he was a firm conservative and staunch imperialist, he was a keen free-trader and his rigid presbyterianism did not prevent him from being a steady champion of the Roman Catholic French-Canadians.

Macphail married in 1893 Georgina (died 1902), youngest daughter of George Bull Burland, of Montreal, and had a son and a daughter. He died at Montreal 23 September 1938.

A portrait of Macphail by Alphonse Jongers (1924) is in the possession of the family.

[*The Times*, 24 September 1938; *British Medical Journal*, 1938, vol. ii, p. 723 (portrait); *Lancet*, 1938, vol. ii, p. 807; *Canadian Men and Women of the Time*, 2nd ed. 1912; *Who's Who in Canada* (portrait); personal knowledge.] J. A. STEVENSON.

MACPHERSON, (JAMES) IAN, first BARON STRATHCARRON (1880–1937), was born near Newtonmore, Inverness-shire, 14 May 1880, the second son of James Macpherson, J.P., of Newtonmore, by his wife, Anne, daughter of James Stewart. Educated locally and at George Watson's College, Edinburgh, he graduated M.A. and LL.B. at Edinburgh University, where he was senior president of the Students' Representative Council and president of the Liberal Association. Called to the bar by the Middle Temple in 1906, he combined legal practice with journalism and politics, and after having unsuccessfully contested Wigtownshire and East Renfrewshire at the two general elections of

1910, he was returned at a by-election in 1911 as liberal member for Ross and Cromarty. He held the seat until his retirement at the end of 1935, for the last four years as a liberal national. A parliamentarian almost by instinct, he was soon prominent in the liberal land campaign and presided over the Scottish branch of the inquiry. From 1914 to 1916 he was parliamentary secretary to the under-secretary of state for war, from 1916 to 1918 under-secretary of state for war, and from 1918 to 1919 vice-president of the Army Council (deputy secretary of state for war). He was sworn of the Privy Council in 1918. When the government was reconstituted in January 1919, Macpherson, the youngest minister in the Cabinet, was chosen for the thankless and perilous post of chief secretary for Ireland. An ardent home ruler, although as a Presbyterian not forgetful of the North, he was convinced that repressive measures were not enough and he strove for a constructive policy. In daily danger, he carried on undaunted, but the situation grew steadily worse. After a year of increasing tension in Ireland, with doubts and vacillation at Westminster, Macpherson brought forward the Cabinet's legislative proposals. The bill passed its second reading on 31 March 1920 and reached the Statute Book in December, but Macpherson, frustrated in his hopes of a more liberal approach, had resigned on 3 April. His health had suffered under the strain, but with characteristic courage he went straight to the Ministry of Pensions where, with a task that appealed to his human sympathies, he accomplished his best administrative work, culminating in the Pensions Act of 1922, the keystone of pensions policy until the outbreak of the war of 1939–1945.

With the fall of the coalition government in 1922 Macpherson at the age of forty-two passed out of office. Service for Scotland had been the ruling passion of this warm-hearted Gael—regarded by many as the representative Highlander of his time—and although the Scottish Office eluded him, he made his mark in many other ways upon contemporary Scottish and especially highland life. His interest in Gaelic studies was both academic and practical, and Lord Alness has testified that it was Macpherson who induced him to insert the Gaelic clause in the Education Act of 1918. He became a K.C. in 1919, a bencher of his Inn in 1930, and recorder of Southend in 1931. Apart from his legal work he was interested in later years in imperial trade, abating the rigour of his free-trade principles to advocate the claims of primary producers.

Combining highland courtesy with the urbanity of a man of the world, Macpherson was popular alike with political friends and with opponents. He was an impressive speaker, and with his command of picturesque imagery and poetic phrase was especially welcome on highland platforms. He received the honorary degree of LL.D. from Edinburgh University and was a freeman of the royal burgh of Dingwall. Created a baronet in 1933, Macpherson was raised to the peerage as Baron Strathcarron, of Banchor, Inverness-shire, in 1936. In 1915 he married Jill, only daughter of (Sir) George Wood Rhodes, first baronet, and had a son and two daughters. He died suddenly in London 14 August 1937 and was succeeded as second baron by his son, David William Anthony Blyth (born 1924).

[*The Scotsman* and *The Times*, 16 August 1937.]   GEORGE A. WATERS.

MADDEN, SIR CHARLES EDWARD, first baronet (1862–1935), admiral of the fleet, was born at Brompton, Gillingham, Kent, 5 September 1862, the second son of Captain John William Madden, of the Fourth (King's Own) Regiment, by his wife, Emily, second daughter of John Busby, of Kingstown; he was descended from a long line of Anglo-Irish families. He entered the *Britannia* as a naval cadet in 1875 and on promotion to midshipman in 1877 was sent to the *Alexandra*, the flagship of (Sir) Geoffrey Hornby [q.v.], in the Mediterranean, and served in her throughout that famous command. In 1880 he went to the *Ruby*, a corvette in the East Indies squadron, for two and a half years, being promoted sub-lieutenant in her in 1881. Soon after promotion to lieutenant in 1884 he decided to specialize in torpedo and spent two years in the *Vernon* torpedo school with an additional six months as staff officer of that establishment. In 1892 he was appointed torpedo lieutenant of the *Royal Sovereign*, flagship of the Channel squadron, and in 1893 resumed his post as staff officer of the *Vernon* until promoted commander in 1896. After three years at sea as commander of the cruiser *Terrible* and the battleship *Caesar* he returned to the *Vernon* in 1899 for a further two years, being promoted captain in June 1901. A year later he became, for two years, flag

captain in the *Good Hope* (cruiser squadron) to Admiral (Sir) Wilmot Hawksworth Fawkes, who had been his captain in the *Terrible* and since been naval private secretary to the first lord. During this service he took Joseph Chamberlain [q.v.] on his memorable visit to South Africa at the end of 1902.

In February 1905 Captain (Admiral of the Fleet Sir) H. B. Jackson [q.v.] was brought by Lord Selborne from the command of the *Vernon* to the Admiralty as third sea lord and controller. Jackson was the greatest scientific naval officer of his generation, and asked for Madden, now a leading torpedo specialist, to be his naval assistant. It was the time of the great reforms of Sir John (afterwards Lord) Fisher [q.v.] in fleet redistribution, dockyard administration, and shipbuilding policy, and Madden soon became one of his most trusted instruments in carrying them out. Fisher had already, in the previous October, named Madden to Lord Selborne as one of the 'five best brains in the navy below the rank of admiral' and in December (1904) secured his appointment as a member of the epochmaking 'ships designs committee' which produced the *Dreadnought* and *Invincible* designs for battleships and armoured cruisers (later styled battle-cruisers). A year later he made Madden his own naval assistant, a post which he held until August 1907. During those stormy years Madden's sound judgement and cool common sense were of the utmost value to his great chief. He was then glad to get to sea again, this time as captain of the *Dreadnought* herself, and as chief of staff to Sir Francis Bridgeman [q.v.], commander-in-chief of the Home Fleet. In December 1908 he was brought back to Whitehall, first as naval private secretary to Reginald McKenna until January 1910 and then as fourth sea lord until December 1911.

Madden had reached flag rank in April 1911 with unusually short sea service as a post-captain, and only fourteen months' fleet experience, but he was now to be at sea continuously for over eleven years as a flag officer in the main British Fleet, including the whole period of the war of 1914–1918. He commanded the first division, Home Fleet (flag in the *St. Vincent*) during 1912, the third cruiser squadron (flag in the *Antrim*) during 1913, and then the second cruiser squadron (flag in the *Shannon*) until the eve of the outbreak of war. When Admiral Sir J. R.

(afterwards Earl) Jellicoe [q.v.] was appointed to take over the command of the Grand Fleet he asked for his wife's brother-in-law, Madden, who had been designated to rejoin the Board of Admiralty as third sea lord and controller, to accompany him as chief of staff. Madden was accordingly sent to the *Iron Duke* (Jellicoe's flagship) on 4 August 1914 and remained in her until Jellicoe became first sea lord in November 1916, having been promoted acting vice-admiral in June 1915 and confirmed in that rank immediately after the battle of Jutland. In Jellicoe's Jutland dispatch of 18 June 1916 Madden's brilliant work as his chief of staff was recorded thus: 'Throughout a period of twenty-one months of war his services have been of inestimable value. His good judgment, his long experience in fleets, special gift for organization, and his capacity for unlimited work, have all been of the greatest assistance to me, and have relieved me of much of the anxiety inseparable from the conduct of the fleet during the war. In the stages leading up to the fleet action and during and after the action he was always at hand to assist, and his judgment never at fault. I owe him more than I can say.'

On the change of chief command in 1916 Madden was appointed to the command of the first battle squadron, as second in command of the Fleet, with the acting rank of admiral (flag in the *Marlborough* and later in the *Revenge*), and retained it until April 1919, having been confirmed as admiral in February of that year. When Sir David (afterwards Earl) Beatty [q.v.] hauled down his flag as commander-in-chief of the Grand Fleet and the war organization of the navy was broken up, Madden was appointed to the command of the newly constituted Atlantic Fleet (flag in the *Queen Elizabeth*) which he held from 1919 to 1922.

In the autumn of 1919 Madden was created a baronet and granted £10,000 by a vote of parliament, and on finally coming ashore in August 1922 he received a letter of appreciation from the Board of Admiralty for 'the manner in which he exercised command of the Atlantic Fleet and for his services to the Royal Navy and to the Empire'. He was at once appointed first and principal naval aide-de-camp to the king and was promoted admiral of the fleet in July 1924. He served in 1923–1924 as chairman of the committee on the functions and training of royal marines, and in 1925, under the chairmanship of

Lord Chelmsford [q.v.], on that for the list of executive officers of the navy. He then retired to Broadstone, Forest Row, Sussex, until July 1927, when, on the recommendation of W. C. (afterwards Viscount) Bridgeman he was selected to succeed Lord Beatty as first sea lord. Two years later he would have been placed on the retired list, but, in order to retain him in office, Bridgeman procured a special order in council to secure his remaining admiral of the fleet on the active list supernumerary to establishment, so long as he held appointment as first sea lord.

Madden thus returned to the Board after over fifteen years to find very different responsibilities and problems awaiting him. Disarmament was in the air and very strong and persistent pressure was brought to bear on the Admiralty to restrict the shipbuilding programme, which was the principal cause of dispute with the United States of America at the abortive Geneva naval conference at the moment when he assumed office. The Admiralty contention had been and remained that seventy cruisers were required. But Madden had reluctantly to accept Cabinet decisions reducing the previously agreed programme of construction and by the time Ramsay MacDonald's labour government came into power in 1929 it had consequently become impracticable to reach the standard total. With much misgiving therefore Madden felt obliged under protest to assent to a lower standard of fifty which was confirmed in the London naval treaty of 1930. He finally retired from the Board and the active list in July 1930.

Madden was awarded numerous honours and decorations. He was mentioned in dispatches for service at Suez in 1883, and was appointed C.V.O. in 1907, K.C.B. in January 1916, and K.C.M.G. for his services at Jutland. He received the rank of commander of the Legion of Honour. The Russian Order of St. Anne, the military Order of Savoy, and the Japanese grand cordon of the Rising Sun were conferred upon him in 1917. He was admitted to the rank of grand officer of the Legion of Honour in 1918, and at the end of the war he was appointed G.C.B. and given the Belgian Order of Leopold, the French croix de guerre (bronze palms), and the Chinese Order of the Striped Tiger. He was appointed G.C.V.O. in 1920 and a member of the Order of Merit in 1931. The honorary degree of LL.D. was conferred upon him by Cambridge University in 1919, and that of D.C.L. by Oxford University in 1928.

Madden acquired during his long career an intimate knowledge of every detail of his profession and was universally esteemed as a man upon whom complete reliance could be placed in any task which he was set. His manner was modest and unassuming; he was popular and an excellent host: he had no enemies, but did not easily make friends. The parts which fell to him to play during the war of 1914-1918 he played to perfection. As chief of staff to Jellicoe he was responsible for much of the organization of the fleet, and by the care and tact with which he carried out his chief's instructions he contributed largely to its efficiency. While in the closest confidential intimacy with Jellicoe, he was more an interpreter of his views than a contributor to their formation. As second-in-command to Beatty, while kept fully informed of all developments and consulted on major problems, he was not a man to put forward or insist on strong views of his own, and difficulties which might have arisen had he been of less loyal personality or more ambitious character were non-existent, although he was over eight years older than Beatty.

As first sea lord Madden was ill at ease in dealing with politicians who, without directly challenging the validity of the Admiralty's assessment of the proper standards of naval defence, urged the undesirability of proceeding with ship construction in face of the opposition of the United States of America, and, when MacDonald began his proposals for the conference which produced the London naval treaty by accepting the reduction to a total of fifty cruisers, Madden did not feel justified on constitutional grounds in going to the length of resignation as a protest. In private life he was a devout churchman, a thorough sportsman, and was devoted to his family. During his retirement he was greatly interested in local affairs and gave much time to support of the British Legion.

Madden married in 1905 Constance Winifred, third and youngest daughter of Sir Charles Cayzer, first baronet, and sister of Countess Jellicoe, and had two sons and four daughters. He died in London 5 June 1935, and was succeeded as second baronet by his elder son, Charles Edward (born 1906).

Madden's portrait is included in Sir Arthur Cope's picture 'Some Sea Officers of the Great War', painted in 1921, in the National Portrait Gallery, and there is a charcoal and watercolour drawing of him by Francis Dodd in the Imperial War Museum.

[Admiralty records; private information.]
VINCENT W. BADDELEY.

MAITLAND, SIR ARTHUR HERBERT DRUMMOND RAMSAY-STEEL-, first baronet (1876-1935), politician and economist. [See STEEL-MAITLAND.]

MAITLAND, JOHN ALEXANDER FULLER- (1856-1936), musical critic and connoisseur, was born in London 7 April 1856, the only child of John Fuller-Maitland, by his wife, Marianne, only child of George Noble, of Duffryn, Glamorganshire. He was grandson of Ebenezer Fuller-Maitland, a prominent member of the Clapham Sect. In 1862 his father built the house in Phillimore Gardens, Kensington, which Fuller-Maitland inherited, and which was for fifty years his home and a very famous centre for musical gatherings.

Owing to delicate health, Fuller-Maitland was educated privately, except for three terms at Westminster, but in 1875 he entered Trinity College, Cambridge: this proved to be the turning-point in his career, for he then came under the influence of (Sir) C. V. Stanford and W. Barclay Squire [qq.v.] and entered upon what he called five or six years of 'musical amateurity'. He was invited about 1881 by (Sir) George Grove [q.v.] to contribute to his Dictionary of Music and Musicians, and in 1882 Grove introduced him to John (later Viscount) Morley [q.v.], editor of the Pall Mall Gazette, of which Fuller-Maitland then became the musical critic; but W. T. Stead [q.v.] succeeded Morley as editor in 1883, and in 1884 Fuller-Maitland was dismissed. The same year, however, he became the musical critic of the Guardian and in 1889 he succeeded Francis Hueffer [q.v.] as musical critic of The Times. This post he held until 1911 when he retired to Borwick Hall, near Carnforth. He married in 1885 Charlotte Elizabeth (died 1931), eldest daughter of William Squire, of Feltham Hill, Middlesex, and sister of Barclay Squire; there were no children of the marriage. He died at Borwick Hall 30 March 1936.

For many years Fuller-Maitland was a prominent figure in English musical life. Criticism was his chief activity; and the influence which he wielded was wide and wholesome. He was not endowed with originality of insight, nor with special gifts of style; but he had high ideals, extensive knowledge, and untiring enthusiasm. His tastes were in the main conservative; but he took a keen interest in many different kinds of music. He was an early researcher into folksong and medieval choralism, and (in collaboration with Squire) produced the authoritative edition of the *Fitzwilliam Virginal Book* (1894–1899); he was a Purcell scholar, and contributed vol. iv (*The Age of Bach and Handel*, 1902) to the *Oxford History of Music*. Among those who were, roughly speaking, his contemporaries, Brahms, Joachim, Parry, and Stanford were nearest to his heart; and he wrote books on all four. He also edited, with many personal contributions, the second edition of *Grove's Dictionary* (1904–1910). Perhaps the most significant book of his large output is *A Door-keeper of Music* (1929), an autobiography from childhood to retirement: attractively full of good sense and pleasant humour, it portrays in vivid fashion many varied scenes of the social and artistic life of Victorian and Edwardian England.

Fuller-Maitland received the honorary degree of D.Litt. from Durham University and was an associate of the Royal Academy of Fine Arts, Brussels.

[*The Times*, 31 March 1936; *Cambridge Review*, 30 October 1936; J. A. Fuller-Maitland, *A Door-keeper of Music*, 1929 (portrait); *Grove's Dictionary of Music and Musicians*, 4th ed., vol. ii, edited by H. C. Colles; personal knowledge.]

BRUCE L. RICHMOND.
ERNEST WALKER.

MALET, LUCAS (pseudonym), novelist. [See HARRISON, MARY ST. LEGER.]

MARGOLIOUTH, DAVID SAMUEL (1858–1940), classical scholar and orientalist, was born in London 17 October 1858, the only son of Ezekiel Margoliouth, of Bethnal Green, an Anglican missionary to the Jews, who, it is said, had been a rabbi. His mother was Sarah Iglitzki. After attending Hackney Collegiate School as a dayboy, he was elected to a scholarship at Winchester College in 1872, and was probably the most erudite boy who had ever passed through College. In 1877 he proceeded to New College, Oxford, of which as scholar, fellow (1881), and honorary fellow (1937), he remained an ornament until his death. He obtained a first class in classical moderations (1878) and

in *literae humaniores* (1880). In 1889 Margoliouth was elected Laudian professor of Arabic in the university of Oxford, a position which he held until his retirement in 1937. In 1899 he was ordained, and proved to be a preacher of curious dignity and eloquence. He travelled extensively abroad, especially in the Middle East, and in 1914, after escaping with difficulty from Switzerland, he immediately offered his services to the War Office, which sent him with his wife to India, to lecture, as it proved, with marked success. After 1918 he spent much time in Bagdad and the regions near, where he built up a reputation for knowing Islamic things better than most learned Moslems themselves, and also for great personal kindness towards Eastern scholars. In 1931, as his active teaching diminished, he gave up his house in Oxford and went to live on Boars Hill. Two years later (1933) by the death of his wife, Jessie Payne, daughter of Robert Payne Smith [q.v.], dean of Canterbury, whom he had married in 1896, he lost the close companion and fellow student of thirty-seven years, but continued his work undaunted. They had no children. He died in London 22 March 1940.

At the time of his death Margoliouth had among the Islamic peoples of the East, and indeed among oriental scholars in Europe, 'an almost legendary reputation'. Even as an undergraduate his contemporaries regarded him with a sort of stupefaction. It was intelligible that a Winchester scholar should win the Hertford and Ireland scholarships (1878) in his first year and proceed to sweep up the Craven (1881) and Derby (1882) scholarships; but when he went on to take the Pusey and Ellerton Hebrew scholarship (1879), the Houghton Syriac prize (1880), the Boden Sanskrit scholarship (1881), and the Kennicott Hebrew scholarship (1882), he ceased to be quite human. The impression was deepened by his exotic and vivid appearance—*Questo bel animal feroce*, as an Italian lady described him— and his deep, bell-like voice. Indeed, although not strikingly Jewish in appearance, he bore about him some marks of Eastern origin. His ancestors at one time lived in Poland, but had arrived there from the farther East.

As a classical tutor Margoliouth was too far removed from his pupils' standard. He might be inspiring, but he was not encouraging. His lectures were apt to set the few undergraduates who followed them off in pursuit of abstruse problems, reading scholia and 'poaching in Suidas for unlicensed Greek'. By 1884 he had published two little books on Greek tragedy, *Studia Scenica* (1883) and an edition of the *Agamemnon* (1884). It may have been disappointment at the reception of these books which led him to forsake Greek, at least temporarily, and since the chair of Arabic happened to fall vacant, to become a candidate for that. It was not that he specially admired Arabic literature: he was attracted by the survival of Arabic as a spoken language and the vast range of problems which it opened up. Unlike most scholars, he was a brilliant linguist, and although somewhat silent in English, he became full of conversation when addressed in Arabic or Turkish.

After his appointment as Laudian professor Margoliouth's main work was, of course, Arabic, although he wrote prefaces in vigorous Latin and published two or three parerga in Greek. He had already in 1887 published *Analecta Orientalia ad Poeticam Aristoteleam*, in which the Arabic and Syriac translations are edited and used for the textual criticism of the Greek text. This valuable little book was followed up twenty-four years later (1911) by an edition of *The Poetics of Aristotle*, translated from Greek into English and from Arabic into Latin, with a revised text, commentary, glossary, and *onomasticon*. This is a strange work. It seems as if Margoliouth, irritated at the mass of conventional criticism which has been showered upon the *Poetics*, was determined at every point to dig deeper, and even to exaggerate his corrections. His later venture in Greek scholarship was less fortunate. Always fond of puzzles and anagrams, he found in the first seven lines of the *Iliad* and the first ten of the *Odyssey* anagrams containing the name of Homer with details of his birth, life, and method. When a critic showed that by the same method of anagram the *Medea* and some other plays could be made to state that they also were written by Homer, he retorted by producing not merely 'signatures' by anagram but also dates, in the first three couplets of various tragedies. It is difficult to know how far he was serious in these exercises of ingenuity.

But, of course, his reputation rests not on these parerga but on his oriental studies. In the years following his appointment to the Laudian chair a series of erudite publications—*Arabic Papyri of the*

Bodleian Library (1893), a translation of part of Baidāwi's Koran-Commentary (*Chrestomathia Baidawiana*, 1894), and *The Letters of Abu'l-'Alā* (1898)—testified to his mastery of some of the most difficult and intricate branches of Arabic literature. After his marriage he was largely occupied in collaboration with his wife on *A Compendious Syriac Dictionary* founded on her father's *Thesaurus Syriacus* (1896–1903, supplement to *Thesaurus*, 1927) but found time to issue a series of biblical studies, mostly of a controversial kind. One controversy was concerned with the Hebrew fragment of Ecclesiasticus which was brought back from the East in 1896 by Agnes [Smith] Lewis [q.v.] and led to the discovery of further fragments among the Bodleian and British Museum papyri. Margoliouth insisted that the newly discovered text was not original but merely a translation from the Persian, which in turn had been translated from a corrupt text of the Greek. He also maintained that the original text of Ecclesiasticus was written in rabbinical Hebrew, a theory which involved the conclusion that other biblical books, written in classical Hebrew, must be far earlier than scholars have placed them. He published at this time *Lines of Defence of the Biblical Revelation* (1900), an edition of Proverbs, Ecclesiastes, and the Song of Solomon in the 'Temple' Bible (1902), and *The Synoptic Gospels as Independent Witnesses* (1903). Another controversy ranged round the famous Hebrew papyri discovered at Elephantine, which apparently prove the existence of a Jewish community in Upper Egypt as early as the fifth or even sixth century B.C. Margoliouth suspected that the papyri were modern forgeries, and although he made few converts to this view he produced some points difficult to answer.

With the appearance of *Mohammed and the Rise of Islam* in the 'Heroes of the Nations' series (1905) Margoliouth for the first time came before the wider public as an interpreter of Islam. This study was followed by *Mohammedanism* in the 'Home University Library' (1911) and by his Hibbert lectures on the *Early Development of Mohammedanism* (delivered in 1913, published in 1914), as well as a number of articles contributed to various encyclopaedias. All three books had a substantial success, and have stood for a generation as the standard English works on their subjects. Amongst orientalists, however, they had a somewhat mixed reception, and their ironical tone sometimes in-furiated his Moslem readers. A similar reception met the publication of his Schweich lectures on *The Relations between Arabs and Israelites prior to the Rise of Islam* (delivered in 1921, published in 1924). Even more startling was an article published in the *Journal* of the Royal Asiatic Society in 1925 denying the authenticity of all that pre-Islamic Arabian poetry which is regarded with such especial admiration by many experts in Arabic literature. In his last book, the volume on Mohammed in Blackie's 'What did they Teach?' series (1939), the views expressed in his earlier books are sturdily reasserted, but the careful reader may perhaps detect, in spite of the familiar irony and astringence of style, some slight softening of their harder edges.

It was in editing and translating Arabic texts that Margoliouth's scholarship found its most congenial field. His prodigious memory, which carried without effort the fruits of a vast range of reading in many languages, was an unequalled instrument for this task. The series of six volumes of Yāqūt's *Dictionary of Learned Men* (edited in Arabic 1907–1927), comprising volumes i and iii and an abstract of volume iv of the original (volume i and the full text of volume iv are apparently lost), was his most celebrated editorial achievement. But to some Arabists his less famous texts—the turgid and allusive *Letters of Abu'l-'Alā* and the discursive *Table-Talk* of at-Tanūkhi (*Table-Talk of a Mesopotamian Judge*, 1921)—gave a more brilliant exhibition of his powers. As a translator his scrupulous accuracy and ease of diction are seen in his versions of the Chronicle of Miskawaih (text by H. F. Amedroz) published under the title of *The Eclipse of the Abbasid Caliphate* (7 vols., 1920–1921), of the *Table-Talk* (1922), and the *Devil's Delusion* of Ibn al-Jauzī which appeared serially in *Islamic Culture* (vols. ix–xii, 1935–1938).

Margoliouth took an especial delight in subjects which called as much for ingenuity as for profound knowledge. Hence the particular appeal which Arabic papyrology had for him. He spent years in classifying and interpreting the mass of often fragmentary papyri in the Crawford collection belonging to the John Rylands Library at Manchester (preliminary edition, *Select Arabic Papyri of the Rylands Collection*, 1909; complete catalogue, 1933).

In England Margoliouth had many public interests and was by no means deficient in practical energy and ability. He worked zealously on the council of the Royal Asiatic Society, of which he was director in 1927 and president from 1934 to 1937, and which awarded him its gold medal in 1928. He was elected a fellow of the British Academy in 1915 and received the honorary degree of D.Litt. from Durham University in 1922. He was president of the Eastern Question Association in 1910; for many years he was chairman of the governing body of the Warneford Hospital for mental diseases, Headington, Oxford.

Margoliouth's irony, so alarming to strangers, came, it would seem, from the depths of his nature. It was part of a profound scepticism, against which in religious matters he defended himself by the assumption of an extreme and almost paradoxical orthodoxy, but which otherwise pervaded his general outlook. Never was a learned man less apt to wax enthusiastic over the value of learning. He liked solving abstruse problems. What really stirred him was pity for human suffering. When it came to that, all irony and scepticism fell away; he was ready to give most generously both of time and money. In his last years the persecution of the Jewish people, it may almost be said, 'haunted him like a passion'; he worked for them as he had worked before for the Assyrians and Armenians.

He was certainly a man of most massive learning and great ingenuity. In problems of literature his judgement seems often to have been unbalanced, a fault which was the more conspicuous because he never 'played for safety' or took refuge in vagueness. He had an immense memory. He was never slipshod, never unprepared. No scholar of his generation left so deep and permanent a mark on oriental studies.

The best portrait of Margoliouth is the drawing, made when he was a young man, by William Rothenstein in *Oxford Characters* (1896). There is a portrait of him by Harriet Halhed in the Griffith Institute, Oxford, painted about the time of his marriage.

[*The Times*, 23 March 1940; Gilbert Murray, *David Samuel Margoliouth, 1858–1940* in *Proceedings* of the British Academy, vol. xxvi, 1940; personal knowledge.] GILBERT MURRAY.

MARLOWE, THOMAS (1868–1935), journalist, born at Portsmouth 18 March 1868, was the eldest son of Thomas Henry

Marlowe, of Auchnacloy, co. Tyrone, by his wife, Kate, daughter of John Conway. He was educated at Queen's College, Galway, with a view to becoming a doctor, and at the London Hospital, but he changed his mind and entered journalism in Dublin. From there he went to Manchester as a reporter and in that capacity joined the staff of the *Star* when it was founded by T. P. O'Connor [q.v.] in 1888. Six years later he was engaged by Alfred and Harold Harmsworth [qq.v.] for service, still as a reporter, with the *Evening News*. Promoted to be news editor, he gave such solid proof of ability that in 1899 he was at the age of thirty-one made managing editor of the three-year-old *Daily Mail*.

Although little known to the public, Marlowe was soon a prominent figure in the newspaper world. The rapid increase in the circulation of the *Daily Mail* during the early part of the twentieth century was attributed largely to his sound judgement combined with a readiness to adopt new methods and a quick eye for fresh talent. With so active and all-pervading a chief proprietor as Alfred Harmsworth (Lord Northcliffe), the editor had of necessity to take second place, but his shrewd caution, tempering the bold enterprise of the other, was of great value, as Northcliffe testified, writing generously of Marlowe's grasp of world affairs, happy knack of avoiding monotony, and 'the mixture of English and Irish in him that gives both force and variety'.

With Harold Harmsworth (Lord Rothermere), who succeeded his brother as controller of the *Daily Mail* in 1922, Marlowe's relations were not at all times so smooth. In Northcliffe he recognized a newspaper genius and was willing to defer to the intuitions, even to fall in with the freaks, of so adventurous a spirit. Rothermere did not call himself a journalist and many of his vagaries in the field of foreign politics seemed to Marlowe so ill advised as to be damaging to the paper. In 1926, therefore, he decided to retire and went to live in the Isle of Wight. His health had suffered from the difficult periods through which he had gone. He had for some time been very deaf and his friends saw with regret that he had grown old beyond his years. He died at sea, returning from a visit to South Africa, 3 December 1935. He married in 1889 Alice Warrender, second daughter of John Morrison Davidson, barrister and journalist, and had four sons, of whom the two elder predeceased their father, and

four daughters, of whom two survived him.

[*The Times*, 6 December 1935; private information; personal knowledge.]

H. HAMILTON FYFE.

MARR, JOHN EDWARD (1857–1933), geologist, was born at Poulton le Sands, Morecambe, Lancashire, 14 June 1857, the third son and youngest of the nine children of John Marr, a partner in a silk mill and small trader, by his wife, Mary Simpson. His father was of Scottish descent, his ancestors belonging to the clan Macdonald. He was educated at Lancaster Grammar School, and in 1875 went to St. John's College, Cambridge, with an exhibition, which was later turned into a foundation scholarship. In 1878 he was placed in the first class of the natural sciences tripos, with geology as his main subject.

Marr then spent four years at Cambridge as a university extension lecturer. His lectures were on geology with particular attention to the relationship between geology and scenery, a subject which he developed later in his book *The Scientific Study of Scenery* (1900, 9th ed. 1943), in many ways a pioneer work in this branch.

For a short time Marr acted as deputy to A. H. Green [q.v.] at Leeds University before returning to Cambridge, and in 1881 he was elected into a fellowship at St. John's College, which he held until the end of his life. In 1886 he was appointed university lecturer in geology under Thomas McKenny Hughes, and was the leader of the team which raised the school of geology at Cambridge to pre-eminence amongst the universities of Great Britain. In 1917, on the death of Hughes, he was appointed to the Woodwardian chair of geology, from which he resigned in 1930 for reasons of ill health.

It was natural that Marr, who had spent his early life in the Lake District and North Wales, should be attracted to the study of the palaeozoic strata, particularly when working in Cambridge with the tradition of Adam Sedgwick [q.v.] still kept strongly to the fore by Hughes. One of his earliest pieces of work was to visit the lower palaeozoic rocks of Bohemia, then being worked upon by Joachim Barrande. It was here that Marr, as a young student, showed that Barrande's theory of 'colonies' was untenable, and that the explanation of the phenomena was to be found in the complex earth movements of the district.

Many other papers on the palaeozoic

rocks and their fauna appeared, and Marr acquired a worldwide reputation as the authority on the rocks of this age. Later he devoted much time to the elucidation of the glacial and postglacial deposits of the Cambridge area, again advancing a new interpretation, which in its major points has been upheld by later workers.

It was not, however, as a writer of scientific papers and books that Marr exerted most effect upon geology and geologists. As a teacher his influence was marked on a long series of pupils from Cambridge. In the lecture-room, but more particularly in his home and in the field, his teaching was of the highest quality; here his pupils soon became more his friends than mere pupils, and his humorous stories made them unconscious of receiving instruction. In the field Marr had a natural flair for picking out the most important features in a geological succession, and although in early life he lost one eye and his sight was poor, this facility stayed with him to the end. He was insistent upon accurate detail of observation, and demanded it from his pupils.

Besides his work at Cambridge, Marr spent much energy upon the work of the Geological Society of London, acting as a member of the council for thirty-four years in aggregate, and as president from 1904 to 1906. His advice and common-sense counsel smoothed over numerous awkward controversies. He received the Woolaston medal in 1914, the highest award of the society.

In 1891 Marr was elected F.R.S., and in 1930 received a Royal medal of the society. He received the honorary degree of Ph.D. from the university of Prague in 1908. In 1896 he was president of the geological section of the British Association meeting at Liverpool and he delivered the Tyndall lecture at the Royal Institution in 1906.

In 1893 Marr married Amy Birkett (died June 1933), daughter of John Stubbs, of Shap Wells, Westmorland, and had a son, who lost his life by enemy action in 1942. He died at Cambridge 1 October 1933.

A portrait of Marr by Kenneth Green (1925) hangs in the Sedgwick Museum, Cambridge.

[The Times, 2 October 1933; Obituary Notices of Fellows of the Royal Society, No. 3, December 1934 (portrait); Quarterly Journal of the Geological Society of London, vol. xc, 1934; Nature, 18 November 1933; Proceedings of the Geological Association, vol. xlv, 1934; Geological Magazine, July 1916; private information; personal knowledge.]
                                    W. B. R. KING.

MARSHALL, SIR WILLIAM RAINE (1865–1939), lieutenant-general, was born at Stranton, near Hartlepool, 29 October 1865, the younger son of William Marshall, of Foggy Furs, Stranton, solicitor, by his wife, Elizabeth Raine. Educated at Repton and at the Royal Military College, Sandhurst, he was commissioned to the Sherwood Foresters in January 1885. The first eight years of his service were spent with the 1st battalion of the regiment, mainly in Ireland, where he made a reputation as a horseman, which he had increased on the polo-ground and the race-course when in 1893 he was, on promotion to captain, transferred to the 2nd battalion in India. In 1897 he was chosen to fill a vacancy in the 1st battalion of The Queen's Own Royal West Kent Regiment in the Malakand campaign and was present at the action of Landakai (16 August). In October of that year he returned to the 2nd Sherwood Foresters for the Tirah expedition, in which he led his company with the Gordon Highlanders in the storming of Dargai and was at the capture of the Arhanga and Sampagha passes.

Marshall was with his battalion in Malta in 1899, when the Malta command was ordered to raise mounted infantry companies in the South African war, and his fame as a horseman marked him out for service with one of these. His company formed part of the 7th Mounted Infantry battalion, and he led it in the fighting round Bethlehem and the Witte Bergen, where he was slightly wounded, in the summer of 1900. In the following November he took a leading part in the actions round Bothaville, in which his commander, Lieutenant-Colonel P. W. J. Le Gallais, was killed. General Sir Ian Hamilton, who commanded the Mounted Infantry division in South Africa, wrote of this action in the introduction to Marshall's Memories of Four Fronts (1929): 'Marshall was awarded the rare distinction of a double Brevet. A fine reward, but could they have given him less when, by his cool yet desperate valour, he, and he alone, had saved the whole column from destruction? He would no doubt have got the Victoria Cross as well: also, afterwards, another Victoria Cross at the Dardanelles; only, being each time the senior on the spot, there never was anyone to recommend him.' The South African war brought Marshall the brevets of major and of lieutenant-colonel, and when in 1908 he became a substantive major, promotion to brevet-colonel followed automatically. In 1911 he was appointed assistant commandant of the Mounted Infantry School at Longmoor and in the February of the next year was given command of the 1st battalion of the Sherwood Foresters in India.

In October 1914 Marshall's battalion was ordered home to form part of the 8th division, with which he served in the winter of 1914–1915 in the water-logged trenches in front of Neuve-Chapelle, where he was slightly wounded. In January 1915 he was chosen to command the 87th brigade of the famous 29th division, then forming for the Gallipoli campaign. He was in command at the landing at 'X' beach on 25 April and, as at Bothaville, his coolness and quick decisions saved the situation when the Turks counter-attacked. He was again slightly wounded. Twice in the early operations on the peninsula he was in temporary command of the 29th division and, his reputation as a leader established, he was promoted major-general in June 1915, commanding successively the 42nd, 29th, and 53rd divisions. The 53rd, reduced to a skeleton by casualties, was sent in the late autumn to Egypt to refit, Marshall remaining to help in the evacuation.

From Gallipoli Marshall went to Salonika to command the 27th division, with which he served from January to September 1916, a period of stagnation on the Macedonian front. He was then given command of the III (Indian) Corps in Mesopotamia, where in August Sir F. S. Maude [q.v.] had been appointed commander-in-chief of a reorganized army. Marshall led this corps in the operations which culminated in the defeat of the Turks at Kut el Amara (24 February 1917) and the capture of Bagdad (11 March). When Maude died of cholera in November, Marshall was, to his surprise, appointed commander-in-chief of the Mesopotamia Expeditionary Force. His methods were different from those of his predecessor. He wrote in *Memories of Four Fronts*: 'No one knew what policy had been dictated to Maude nor what his plans were, but one could not well sit with folded hands so long as there were Turkish forces within possible striking distance. . . . When I first took over command I had felt it my duty to try to live up to the example of

my distinguished predecessor in the matter of work in the office, but, with my very able Staff to cope with the details of the various problems which presented themselves, and confining myself to major points on which a decision was required, I very soon began to curtail my office hours.' The time saved was spent mainly with his troops. Marshall's immediate task was to make Bagdad secure against a Turco-German counter-attack, and in this he succeeded. He realized that Palestine had become strategically the more important theatre and readily released a division to reinforce Sir Edmund (later Viscount) Allenby [q.v.]. Despite this he finished the war in Mesopotamia triumphantly by enforcing the surrender of the Turkish army on the upper Tigris (October 1918).

After being promoted lieutenant-general in January 1919, Marshall was appointed commander-in-chief, Southern Command, India, in the following August. He arrived in November. Peace-time administration made no appeal to him, and in 1924, the year after his term of command expired, he retired from the army and gave himself up to a life of country pursuits. He was colonel of the Sherwood Foresters from 1930 to 1935.

Marshall made no pretence of being a student of war. He was a natural leader of men, of imperturbable courage, with a quick eye for the essential in a critical situation, and the gift of coming to the right decision quickly.

Marshall was appointed C.B. in 1916, K.C.B. in 1917, K.C.S.I. in 1918, and G.C.M.G. in 1919, and was awarded many foreign orders. He married in 1902 Emmie, daughter of John Hett, of Headlam Hall, co. Durham, and widow of John Stephen-Stephen, of Edinburgh and Elgin. He had no children. He died of heart failure at Bagnoles de l'Orne, France, 29 May 1939.

There is a portrait of Marshall in the Officers' Mess, Sherwood Foresters, Derby, and another is included in J. S. Sargent's picture 'Some General Officers of the Great War', painted in 1922, in the National Portrait Gallery.

[*The Times*, 1 June 1939; Sir W. R. Marshall, *Memories of Four Fronts*, 1929; personal knowledge.]   F. MAURICE.

MASSON, SIR DAVID ORME (1858–1937), chemist, was born in London 13 January 1858, the only son of David

Masson [q.v.], the historiographer royal for Scotland, who was then professor of English literature at University College, London, by his wife, Emily Rosaline, eldest daughter of Charles Orme, of Hampstead. In London and then in Edinburgh Masson's childhood and youth were strongly coloured by the literary influences of his father's and mother's circles which included the Tennyson brothers, the pre-Raphaelite brotherhood, Coventry Patmore, Mazzini, Carlyle, Browning, and Huxley.

In Edinburgh Masson attended the Academy and then the University, graduating in both arts and science. After a period at Göttingen, he joined the staff of University College, Bristol, in 1880, engaging in work with (Sir) William Ramsay [q.v.] on atomic volumes. Returning in 1882 to Edinburgh to a research fellowship in chemistry, he published several papers on glyceryl trinitrite and trinitrate, and on salts of organic bases such as sulphines. In 1886 he married Mary, second daughter of (Sir) John Struthers (1823–1899, q.v.), professor of anatomy in Aberdeen University, and migrated to Australia, having accepted an invitation to the chair of chemistry in the university of Melbourne. For thirty-seven years he was a prominent figure in the academic life of a rapidly growing city.

Despite the handicaps of isolation and heavy teaching responsibilities, Masson's original scientific work was extensive and of a high order. Apart from studies associated with the periodic classification of the elements, his chief interests lay in the development of the theory of solution as originally put forward by Svante A. Arrhenius, Jacobus Hendricus van 't Hoff, Wilhelm Ostwald, and their school, and in interpreting the chemical dynamics of such reactions as that of hydrogen peroxide on potassium cyanide, the decomposition of cyanates, and the decomposition of persulphuric acid and its salts in aqueous solution. His paper on the velocity of the migration of ions was a particularly valuable contribution in its time (*Philosophical Transactions* of the Royal Society, vol. cxcii, 1899). A problem in theoretical interpretation always attracted him rather than one in design or manipulation of apparatus; and in his later years he contributed much to the development of ideas on the constitution of atoms, and again to the theory of dissociation of electrolytes in water.

From 1910 Masson became absorbed more and more in university administration and in outside public work. In 1911–1913, as president of the Australasian Association for the Advancement of Science, he took the leading part in organizing the visit of the British Association to Australia in 1914. He actively assisted the first expedition under (Sir) Douglas Mawson to the Antarctic in 1911–1914; and again in 1929–1931 he was chairman of the committee responsible for the British, Australian, and New Zealand Antarctic research expedition. During the war of 1914–1918 he served on many special committees dealing with munitions and naval matters and did notable work from 1915 onwards in drafting the scheme leading to the establishment of a Commonwealth Institute of Science and Industry, which in 1926 was reorganized as the Council for Scientific and Industrial Research, on which he served until his death. Retirement from active teaching in 1923 gave him increased opportunity for outside interests which included service on several business directorates.

The Melbourne University Chemical Society, the Society of Chemical Industry of Victoria, and the Australian Chemical Institute were all initiated by Masson and so (with Sir T. W. Edgeworth David, q.v.) was the Australian National Research Council. He presided over the second Pan-Pacific Scientific Congress held in Melbourne and Sydney in 1923.

Masson was elected F.R.S. in 1903, and appointed C.B.E. in 1918, and K.B.E. in 1923: he received the honorary degree of LL.D. from Edinburgh University in 1924. A Masson lecturership was established in his honour by the National Research Council, and a Masson memorial scholarship by the Australian Chemical Institute.

Personal charm, broad vision, originality and independence of mind, clarity of exposition, and perfect integrity made Masson a powerful influence in his adopted university and Dominion. To him and to his two colleagues Sir Walter Baldwin Spencer [q.v.], biologist, and Sir Thomas Lyle, physicist, the science schools of Melbourne University will be for ever deeply indebted. Masson died in Melbourne 10 August 1937. He had one son, who became vice-chancellor of the university of Sheffield, and two daughters, the younger of whom predeceased her father.

A portrait of Masson by W. B. McInnes

hangs in the Wilson hall of the university of Melbourne.

[*Obituary Notices of Fellows of the Royal Society*, No. 7, January 1939 (portrait); private information; personal knowledge.]

                                    DAVID RIVETT.

MATHEW, THEOBALD (1866–1939), lawyer and wit, was born in London 5 December 1866, the elder son of the judge Sir James Charles Mathew [q.v.], by his wife, Elizabeth, daughter of Edwin Biron, vicar of Lympne, Kent. He was a great-nephew of his namesake, Father Theobald Mathew [q.v.], the temperance advocate, and a brother-in-law of John Dillon [q.v.]. His parents, devout Roman Catholics and admirers of Cardinal Newman, sent him to the Oratory School, Edgbaston, and to the cardinal's old college, Trinity College, Oxford, where he matriculated in 1885 and graduated with a second class in modern history in 1888: throughout his life he remained greatly attached to his college and cherished the friendships which he formed there.

Mathew was called to the bar by Lincoln's Inn (his father's Inn) in 1890: he became a bencher of the Inn in 1916, and would have been treasurer, had he lived, in 1940. He was in chambers with (Sir) Joseph Walton [q.v.], afterwards judge of the High Court, and he there acquired a profound knowledge of English law and an unswerving respect for its traditions. He practised as a junior on the common law side until he was over seventy years of age, for, like his father, he never took silk; and he deliberately preferred to keep his forensic work within reasonable dimensions.

Mathew first came into public notice in 1896 as the editor, with (Sir) Malcolm Macnaghten, of the *Commercial Cases*, being the reports of proceedings before the Commercial Court, which began its existence, under the inspiration of Mathew's father, in 1895; the introduction to the first volume of this series has always been regarded as the most authoritative statement of the reasons that led to the formation of the Commercial Court. In 1902 he published a small volume entitled *Practice of the Commercial Court*. He was recorder of Margate from 1913 to 1927 and of Maidstone from 1927 to 1936.

But Mathew's fame amongst his contemporaries was not based upon his professional career. Far beyond legal circles he was well known as one of the great wits of his generation. He saw, with Irish intuition, the funny side of everything, and he had the rare gift of expressing himself, at the luncheon table, in chambers, at the Garrick Club, and elsewhere, in swift and in impromptu sayings which were treasured and repeated by his innumerable friends, and came, in course of time, to be an unwritten saga of *plaisanteries*. This rich endowment of humour was aided by his personal appearance: he was small and insignificant in stature, and wore pince-nez behind which his smile was concealed, and, with this background, he had a deep and resonant voice in which his witticisms were enounced. They always seemed to be spontaneous. One such remark may here be recalled, as typical of the rest. Visiting the library of another Inn, at that time notorious for its recruitment of students from equatorial Africa, Mathew had to make his way through ranks of these dusky lawyers. At length he saw the white face of a friend, held out his hand in greeting, and said: 'Dr. Livingstone, I presume.' That tale has become legendary, but it shows admirably how happily and quickly his mind reacted to the situation in which he found himself. And his jokes were never tainted by any kind of malice. That, no doubt, is one reason why, as was said in an obituary notice, 'no-one in the Temple was so widely known or so well-beloved'. For fifty years 'Theo', as he was universally called, could have laid claim to this unique position amongst his contemporaries. He was also a superb after-dinner speaker.

Happily Mathew's reputation as a wit is not solely dependent upon verbal tradition, for in 1925 he began to contribute to the *Law Journal* a weekly series of 'Forensic Fables', illustrated by his own skilful pen-and-ink sketches of the characters. These were subsequently published as a separate volume in 1926, and were followed by *Further Forensic Fables* (1928) and by two series of *Final Forensic Fables* (1929 and 1932). Never before, in the history of English law, has such brilliant and penetrating light been thrown upon the *cursus curiae* as it presents itself to the practising lawyer of the day. And Mathew did not hesitate to portray in his gallery, in the thinnest disguise, some famous personalities of the time: easily identifiable are the 'old hand' with his somewhat unprofessional methods; the fashionable leaders who settled the case when neither of them could understand the question addressed to them by the erudite judge; the 'tearful performer'; the sagacious solicitor who had 'Law for the Million' bound in a cover lettered with the name of an old law report. It is believed that Mathew's reputation for many years to come will be sustained by these four slender volumes.

Mathew also collected in a volume entitled *For Lawyers and Others* (1937) some learned articles which he contributed from time to time to periodicals, and he was a contributor to this DICTIONARY.

Mathew married in 1898 Ruth, daughter of the Rev. George Henry Rigby and niece of Sir John Rigby [q.v.]; he had five sons and two daughters. He died in London 20 June 1939.

Sir William Orpen [q.v.] made, on the back of a dinner menu, a sketch of Mathew which is in the possession of the family; it is a good example of Orpen's skill in portraiture.

[Private information; personal knowledge.]
P. A. LANDON.

MATHIESON, WILLIAM LAW (1868–1938), historian, was born at Wardie, Leith, 25 February 1868, the third surviving son of George Mathieson, shipowner, by his wife, Isabella Melrose. He was educated at Edinburgh Academy and University; at the latter he distinguished himself in the history classes and won the lord rector's prize in 1893. Possessed of modest means which he supplemented by tutoring, he settled down to a scholar's uneventful life in Edinburgh. In his early years he contributed to W. E. Henley's *National Observer* and reviewed for the *Athenaeum*. By his first historical work, *Politics and Religion, A Study in Scottish History from the Reformation to the Revolution* (2 vols., 1902), he stepped into the front rank of contemporary historians. *Scotland and the Union . . . 1695–1747* (1905), *The Awakening of Scotland . . . 1747–1797* (1910), and *Church and Reform in Scotland . . . 1797–1843* (1916) completed his interpretation of Scottish history. Primarily interested in movements, especially in the connexion between Church and State, Mathieson is the historian of the growth of the moderate tradition in Scotland. Based on a thorough study of the printed sources, his interpretation is distinguished by 'a philosophic charm and impartiality which humanized controversies and periods which are still too often the prey of partisan bitterness'. His generalities are vivified by apt illustration, brilliant historical portraiture,

and a certain 'demurely trenchant wit'. The same qualities characterize all his work, although his later style tended to be too concentrated. He next turned to cognate aspects of English history in *England in Transition, 1789–1832* (1920) and the more original *English Church Reform, 1815–1840* (1923), a sketch of a hitherto neglected subject. Finally, his studies of the slave trade, a virtually unworked field, won him a place among the historians of the British Empire. He published four volumes between 1926 and 1936, the first being *British Slavery and its Abolition, 1823–1838*, and the last *The Sugar Colonies and Governor Eyre, 1849–1866*. He also wrote the chapter on 'The Emancipation of the Slaves, 1807–1838' for the *Cambridge History of the British Empire*, vol. ii (1940).

A scholar of genial personality, Mathieson died at Wardie 26 January 1938. In 1910 he married Christian Mary (died 1941), third daughter of James Shaw, J.P., sheriff of London and Middlesex in 1874–1875; there was no issue of the marriage. He received the honorary degree of LL.D. from Aberdeen University in 1912. His portrait by D. Gordon Shiels is in the Scottish National Portrait Gallery, Edinburgh.

[*The Scotsman*, 27 January 1938; *The Times*, 3 February 1938; *Edinburgh Academy Register*, 1914; Bruce Dickins, 'Thumbnail Sketch of an Edinburgh Scholar', Edinburgh Bibliographical Society's *Transactions*, vol. ii (1938–1945), 1946; personal knowledge.]
HENRY W. MEIKLE.

MAUD CHARLOTTE MARY VICTORIA (1869–1938), princess of Great Britain and Ireland, Queen of Norway, was born at Marlborough House 26 November 1869, the fifth child and third and youngest daughter of the Prince and Princess of Wales. Her versatile and vivacious character took full advantage of the education of the time and the many distinguished visitors to Marlborough House and Sandringham gave her numerous friends and a very wide knowledge of world affairs, while she fully appreciated her mother's love of music and art.

Princess Maud's love of country life, her horses, and her dogs was fully gratified when in 1896 she married Prince Christian Frederick Charles George Valdemar Axel, second son of the Crown Prince (afterwards King Frederick VIII) of Denmark, and made her home at Appleton House, Sandringham, where her only child Alexander Edward Christian Frederick

(Crown Prince Olav) was born in 1903. When Prince Charles (as he was known) was elected to the throne of Norway in 1905, taking the name of King Haakon VII, Queen Maud entered into her duties and learnt the ways of her new country, which could not be better exemplified than in her upbringing of her son in the sports of the country, yachting and ski-ing, at which he excelled at a very early age. Very soon the Queen had laid out an English garden at Bygdo Kongsgaard, which she loved to show to all her friends, and whenever it was possible for her, she was to be seen riding and, when the snow came, running on skis.

Queen Maud's great love of children and animals led her to support any good cause, but quietly and almost shyly, according to her nature; many a musician and artist will remember her personal encouragement. Except during the war of 1914–1918 the Queen was able to visit Appleton every year: her last public appearance in this country was at the coronation of her nephew King George VI in 1937. She died in London 20 November 1938, and was buried in Oslo.

[*The Times*, 21 November 1938; personal knowledge.]

MAUDE, AYLMER (1858–1938), translator and expounder of the works of Count Leo Tolstoy, was born at Ipswich 28 March 1858, the younger son of Francis Henry Maude, perpetual curate of Holy Trinity church, Ipswich, by his wife, Lucy Thorp, who came of Quaker stock. Maude was educated at Christ's Hospital, but in 1874 he was sent to the Lyceum at Moscow for two years. After earning his living as a tutor in English from 1877 to 1880, he married in 1884 Louisa, daughter of James Stewart Shanks, a British business man in Moscow, and was employed in a large carpet factory there as business manager and later as director until 1897, when he and his wife returned to England and settled first at Purleigh in Essex, where there was a Tolstoyan colony, and, on the dispersal of the colony in 1901, at Great Baddow.

Before leaving Russia, however, Maude had made the acquaintance and close friendship of Tolstoy. He did not wholly accept Tolstoy's views, and he frankly disapproved of Tolstoy's suspicions of the motives of persons who differed from him. Nevertheless this friendship was the foundation of Maude's claim to be remembered, for he devoted the rest of his life almost entirely to the translation of all the works of Tolstoy and to expounding his ideas in Britain. In all this work he was substantially assisted by his wife, who in 1900 translated Tolstoy's *Resurrection*. Maude was manager of the migration of the persecuted Doukhobors from the Caucasus to Canada, to which Tolstoy had devoted the proceeds of that novel.

Of the works of Tolstoy, *Anna Karenina*, *War and Peace*, and *My Confession* were among those jointly translated by Maude and his wife. So too were in general the plays and the shorter stories. Maude himself translated the works on religion, art, and sociology, and after re-visiting Tolstoy at Yasnaya Polyana in 1902 he was authorized to write the *Life of Tolstoy* which appeared in two volumes (*The First Fifty Years*, 1908; *The Later Years*, 1910) and was completed shortly before Tolstoy's death. All these works, with Maude's notes and introductions, were included in the monumental edition of the works of Tolstoy published in twenty-one volumes from 1928 to 1937. For his work as an interpreter and translator of Tolstoy, he was awarded a civil list pension of £100 in 1932.

Besides the translations, Maude also wrote some independent treatises which include *Tolstoy and his Problems* (1901) and *A Peculiar People, the Doukhobors* (1905); and he appeared as a vigorous defender of Dr. Marie Stopes (*The Authorized Life of Marie C. Stopes*, 1924, and *Marie Stopes: her Work and Play*, 1933).

In the war of 1914–1918 Maude went with the expedition of the North Russian Relief Forces as a lecturer for the Young Men's Christian Association. His lectures, particularly on Tolstoy, were of the greatest value, not only to British but also to Allied troops in Russia, while his knowledge of Russian literature made him a most valuable liaison officer with the leading Russians, both military and civil.

Maude died at Great Baddow 25 August 1938, and was survived by his wife, who died in 1939. There were four sons of the marriage.

A portrait of Maude by Emily Shanks is in the possession of his son Mr. Arnold Maude.

[*The Times*, 26 August 1938; private information.]   JANKO LAVRIN.

MAXSE, LEOPOLD JAMES (1864–1932), journalist and political writer, was born in London 11 November 1864, the second child and younger son of Admiral Frederick Augustus Maxse [q.v.], by his wife, Cecilia, daughter of Colonel James Steel, who came of a family of Cumberland squires. He was a nephew of Sir H. B. F. Maxse [q.v.]. His father, who had had little education owing to service at sea, was determined that his children should have what he had missed. In his home every subject was questioned and discussed; there was no church-going, but great account was taken of character, and much attention paid to sport and exercise. The Maxses often went to France and were intimate with French people, but one friendship was noteworthy, for the admiral's eye for real value in human beings drew him to Clemenceau, friendship with whom, begun in 1872, developed into a family intimacy and affected Leo Maxse all his life, while it is known that Clemenceau in later years relied upon his judgement.

Maxse was educated at Harrow and at King's College, Cambridge, where he made a reputation for wit and independence of all, even undergraduates', conventions, but nevertheless became president of the Union. Although he was awarded a second class in the historical tripos of 1886, he never troubled to take his degree, and it was one of his sayings that he could never understand why people liked letters after their names or titles before them. After Cambridge, Maxse went on a grand tour for a year to India, Australia, New Zealand, Canada, and the United States of America, from which he returned a confirmed imperialist. His plans for being called to the bar and standing for parliament were ended by a serious illness, but after three years of frustration, Admiral Maxse in 1893 bought the *National Review* and gave it to his son, who, it was thought, could do as much or as little work on the review as his health allowed. Through interest in the work he recovered to better though never perfect health. Outwardly indeed his life was uneventful, but under him the *National Review* became an outstanding periodical, for not only had he a sure knowledge of human nature, but his wit, the pungency of his style, and his lack of vanity attracted journalists, politicians, and statesmen alike. In London, where he settled soon afterwards, he discovered a prodigious power of serious work; he began to influence public affairs, and his judgement was not often at fault. As early as 1899 he showed his prescience when, on being offered the editorship of a

great colonial newspaper, he refused, saying: 'I must stay in England to warn people of the German danger.' He attacked alike the scandals of the Dreyfus and the Marconi affairs, and in 1925 he was almost alone in deploring the return to the gold standard. His deep understanding and admiration for France led him to transports of indignation when he contemplated the efforts of this country towards a *rapprochement* with the Germans. He foresaw war after 1919 as he had foreseen it before 1914, and he believed that if the Germans were plainly told that this country would fight for what it cared for and maintain its armaments, war could be prevented. He deplored the waste of time and energy represented by the League of Nations, and his imperialism led him to denounce as treachery the proposed abdication of British imperial responsibilities in favour of Geneva. He was a confirmed democrat, believing in the excellence of ordinary men's judgement, and holding that if the public had been told the truth it would have rejected all this unsound doctrine.

Maxse married in 1890 Katharine, the gifted eldest daughter of Vernon Lushington, K.C., of Cobham. She died in 1922 without issue. Maxse himself died in London 22 January 1932.

[*The Times*, 23 January 1932; personal knowledge.]　　　　　　　V. MILNER.

MAXWELL, SIR HERBERT EUSTACE, seventh baronet, of Monreith (1845–1937), country gentleman, politician, and miscellaneous writer, was born in Edinburgh 8 January 1845, the fourth (but only survivor) of the five sons of Sir William Maxwell, sixth baronet, by his wife, Helenora, third and youngest daughter of Sir Michael Shaw-Stewart, fifth baronet, of Greenock and Blackhall. His early education at home and at private schools aroused his interest in natural history and allied subjects, and it was developed and extended by the tutor who prepared him for Oxford, after what he himself described as three years of 'insensate indolence' at Eton. During his year at Christ Church (1864–1865) he failed to pass responsions, the first step towards a commission in the Scots Fusilier Guards. Nevertheless, he had acquired much miscellaneous information outside the normal subjects of school and university, on which he was to base the self-education of later years. The lack of purpose in his early life was mainly due to the religious tenets of his parents. Belonging as they did to the Catholic Apostolic Church, and believing that the Second Advent was imminent, neither they nor their children felt the necessity for planning for the future. He settled at Monreith, helping his father to manage the estate, acquiring a unique knowledge of the people and countryside of Wigtownshire, of which he was lord-lieutenant from 1903 to 1935, and establishing his reputation as a sportsman in angling, shooting, and horsemanship.

After his father's death in 1877 Maxwell entered parliament as conservative member for Wigtownshire. He was an assiduous lord of the Treasury from 1886 to 1892, besides serving on various commissions. As chairman of the tariff reform party in the House of Commons in 1903, he was closely associated with the policy of Joseph Chamberlain [q.v.]. In 1906 he did not seek re-election owing to financial circumstances, which were also the stimulus of his literary work. Between 1887 and 1932, beginning with novels, he wrote, in addition to several biographies, books on topography, natural, local, and national history, archaeology, horticulture, and sport, as well as making numerous contributions to scientific and other periodicals. He had a charming, if too facile, pen, but such remarkable versatility precluded deep research. His *Memories of the Months* ran to seven series (1897–1922), of which the first three reached revised editions (1931–1932). *Robert the Bruce and the Struggle for Scottish Independence* (1897) and a *Life of Wellington* (1899) are typical of his historical work. His editing of the *Creevey Papers* (2 vols., 1903) provided a valuable supplement to the *Greville Memoirs*. His Rhind lecturerships in archaeology at Edinburgh (1893 and 1911), presidency of the Society of Antiquaries of Scotland (1900–1913), and chairmanship of the National Library of Scotland (1925–1932), testified to his services to learning. Other distinctions included that of privy councillor (1897), F.R.S. (1898), and K.T. (1933). He also received honorary degrees from the universities of Glasgow and Durham.

A personality of much charm, and the most prominent of scholarly country gentlemen in Scotland, Maxwell died at Monreith 30 October 1937 at the age of ninety-two. He married in 1869 Mary (died 1910), eldest daughter of Henry Fletcher-Campbell, of Boquhan, Stirlingshire, and had two sons and three daughters. Both his sons predeceased him

(the younger died of wounds received at Antwerp in 1914) and he was succeeded as eighth baronet by his grandson, Aymer (born 1911). A portrait by Oswald Birley is at Monreith.

[Sir H. Maxwell, *Evening Memories*, 1932; *Obituary Notices of Fellows of the Royal Society*, No. 6, January 1938 (portrait).]
HENRY W. MEIKLE.

MAXWELL LYTE, SIR HENRY CHURCHILL (1848–1940), deputy keeper of the public records and historian. [See LYTE.]

MELBA, DAME NELLIE (1861–1931), prima donna, whose married name was HELEN PORTER ARMSTRONG, was born 19 May 1861 at Doonside, Richmond, a suburb of Melbourne, Australia, the elder daughter and third child of David Mitchell, by his wife, Isabella Ann Dorn. Both parents were natives of Forfarshire; the mother was of Spanish descent. David Mitchell, a man of strong character, had arrived in Australia with one sovereign in his pocket and became a pioneer in a number of enterprises, in all of which he succeeded, and his children therefore grew up in good circumstances. Music was one of the interests and accomplishments of the household. Nellie Mitchell, encouraged to sing from her earliest childhood, sang at six years of age at a school concert organized by her aunts in the Richmond town hall, gaining an enthusiastic encore. Later she was sent to the Presbyterian Ladies' College in East Melbourne, where the professor of singing was Madame Christian, who, a former colleague of Sir Charles Santley [q.v.], had settled in Australia and later became a nun. Madame Christian was a pupil of the famous singing teacher Manual Garcia [q.v.], and from her Nellie Mitchell first learnt the principles of vocalism of the great school which Madame Mathilde Marchesi, also the pupil of Garcia, and at one time deputy for him, later unfolded fully to her, and to which, as she always insisted, she owed the development and preservation of her voice. Before leaving Australia she had some lessons from an old Italian opera singer, Signor Cecchi, but in her autobiography, *Melodies and Memories* (1925), she does not refer to them with satisfaction.

David Mitchell was averse to his daughter embarking on the career of a professional singer, but after her marriage in December 1882 (dissolved in 1900) to a young Irishman, Charles Nesbitt Frederick Armstrong, youngest son of Sir Andrew Armstrong, first baronet, of Gallen Priory, King's County, manager of a sugar plantation in Port Mackay, she lived a desolate and lonely life in the heart of the bush in a small house with a galvanized iron roof. At length her father paid her passage to England, and after giving a farewell concert Nellie Armstrong in the spring of 1886 sailed for England with her only child, a son. Her reception in London was by no means encouraging. She sang to Sir Arthur Sullivan [q.v.], who said that after a year's further study he might be able to offer her a small part in *The Mikado*. Wilhelm Ganz, however, accompanist and friend of Patti, arranged opportunities for her to sing at Prince's Hall, Piccadilly, and at the Freemasons' Hall in the City, but the audiences were small, and the experience, in spite of some congratulations, Mrs. Armstrong found disheartening. She therefore, having been given in Australia a letter of introduction to Madame Mathilde Marchesi, decided to go to Paris and present it. The famous teacher, testing her voice thoroughly, recognized its possibilities, and also found a character full of determination to pursue the hard path of a serious student of singing. So sure was Marchesi of the success in store for Nellie Armstrong that in the middle of the first interview she went out of the room to inform her husband that she had 'found a star'.

After a year's lessons, the famous *entrepreneur* Maurice Strakosch, hearing her in Madame Marchesi's studio, offered 'Melba'—as she called herself at her first appearance in Paris—a ten years' contract, which was duly signed. Immediately afterwards came a better offer from the management of the Théâtre de la Monnaie in Brussels. This Marchesi advised Melba to accept, assuring her that Strakosch, an old friend, would not make any difficulty. He did, however; but an *impasse* was dramatically solved by his sudden death, and Melba's appearance on 13 October 1887 as Gilda in Verdi's *Rigoletto* was an extraordinary triumph, the entire Brussels press proclaiming the advent of an artiste of the first rank.

Soon after this, (Sir) Augustus Harris [q.v.] engaged the successful débutante for his first season of Italian opera at Covent Garden, and Melba made her début there as Lucia in Donizetti's *Lucia di Lammermoor* on 24 May 1888. At the conclusion of the opera it was clear that she

had captured the public, and she had instantly won the suffrages of society, making more friends among the wealthy patrons of the Royal Italian Opera than any prima donna of the period. There was some reserve, however, on the part of the press from the point of view of complete operatic artistry, but the extraordinary beauty of the strikingly fresh voice, perfectly even through its compass of two and a half octaves (B flat to F^{III}), used with an art that seemed nature in perfection, was freely recognized.

On 8 May 1889 Melba made her first appearance at the Paris Opéra as Ophélie in Ambroise Thomas's *Hamlet* and studied the parts of Marguerite in *Faust* and Juliette with Gounod himself. Sarah Bernhardt also went to infinite pains in assisting Melba to realize, in a way suited to her individuality, the dramatic possibilities of the characters which she had to assume on the operatic stage, but she never became a really good actress. Yet the critics, on her first appearance, hailed her as such and did not appreciate her voice.

Less than a month later Melba returned to Covent Garden, largely through the influence of Lady de Grey (later Marchioness of Ripon), who overcame some hesitation on the prima donna's part, and she appeared (15 June) in the first performance ever given in England of Gounod's *Roméo et Juliette* in French, with Jean de Reszke as Romeo and Edouard de Reszke as the Friar. A marked advance in Melba's acting and singing had taken place: the association of Melba with the brothers De Reszke was an operatic landmark, and thenceforth she took part regularly in every Covent Garden season.

Melba's position was now assured, and her public life was passed in singing at various capitals of the world, although it was not until 1893 that she first visited the United States, where she sang at the World's Fair in Chicago. Her visit to St. Petersburg in 1891 was noted for two things; the Tsar's command to lay aside the tradition that only Russian should be sung at the Imperial Opera House, so that Melba and her colleagues could sing *Roméo et Juliette* in French, and the invitation given to her to sing in private to Anton Rubinstein, who was already in failing health. Again when in the following year she sang at the Scala at Milan at the beginning of a brilliant tour in Italy, Verdi went to hear her, and, inviting her to his house, went with her through the

Desdemona music in *Otello* and praised her rendering. In 1893, in fulfilment of a promise made to the composer, she introduced the part of Nedda in *Pagliacci* to the British public at Covent Garden. For her, Saint-Saëns composed the title-role of *Hélène* which she studied while travelling in the train during a tour of Canada and the United States in 1903, and in which she sang at Monte Carlo in 1904. The last opera which she added to her list of twenty-five was *La Bohème*, and she sang in it first at Philadelphia in 1898, having studied it with the composer in Italy earlier in the year. So much did the part appeal to her, that she exerted her personal influence and got *La Bohème* accepted at Covent Garden, and 'Melba nights' there became for a generation of opera lovers her appearance in that role.

It is not surprising that when she revisited her native land in 1902, after an absence of sixteen years, 'Australia's queen of song' was greeted with a rare enthusiasm. She never forgot Australia, visiting it not infrequently, and after her retirement in 1926 she settled there finally at Coombe Cottage near Coldstream in Victoria. In 1918 she was appointed D.B.E. and was thenceforth known as Dame Nellie Melba: in 1927 she received the G.B.E. Another order which she received was that of Science, Art, and Music, which was pinned on her breast in 1904 by Queen Alexandra after a state concert at Buckingham Palace in honour of the Archduke Francis Ferdinand.

Melba's kindness of heart was wide and her charitable acts many. When in 1906 Oscar Hammerstein's enterprise in grand opera at the Manhattan Opera House seemed doomed to disaster, and she was advised by friends in New York not to fulfil her engagement, she came to the rescue, although the circumstances called for considerable courage; but her success was greater than ever before, and the audiences were extraordinary. She raised over £100,000 for the Red Cross during the war of 1914–1918. Towards young singers she constantly showed interest, inculcating the method she used, which she held could alone bring out the full beauty of the human voice, and preserve it. She showed her *camaraderie* by appearing in 1922–1923 in London with the British National Opera Company, an organization which was making a praiseworthy effort to further the cause of opera in English.

Melba's voice was not of an instantly arresting strength, but it had that power of expansion in a large building which is a characteristic of beautiful singing. It was this 'Stradivari' quality which won the admiration of the violinists Joachim and Sarasate. The technique was invariably impeccable: scale passages were like strings of pearls, and Melba's shake was perfect in its distinctness, evenness, and limpidity. Melba was favoured in appearance by nature and she preserved her physical advantages by careful living. When she retired, her intonation was still perfect, her technique unimpaired, and her voice still wonderfully fresh and 'girl-like'. She died at Sydney 23 February 1931.

A bust of Melba was made by (Sir) Bertram Mackennal [q.v.] in September 1899. Melba presented it to the National Gallery, Melbourne, and it was unveiled by Lord Brassey, then governor of Victoria.

[Nellie Melba, *Melodies and Memories*, 1925; Agnes G. Murphy, *Melba. A Biography*, 1909; Herman Klein, *Great Women Singers of My Time*, 1931; *Grove's Dictionary of Music and Musicians*, 4th ed., vol. iii, edited by H. C. Colles; Arthur Mason in *Musical Opinion*, 1 April 1931; personal knowledge.]

J. MEWBURN LEVIEN.

MELLANBY, JOHN (1878–1939), physiologist, was born at West Hartlepool 12 June 1878, the second of the three sons of John Mellanby, manager of a shipbuilding yard at West Hartlepool, by his wife, Mary Isabella Lawson, of Edinburgh. From Barnard Castle School he won a scholarship at Emmanuel College, Cambridge, in 1896; he was placed in the first class in both parts of the natural sciences tripos (1899 and 1900, physiology). In 1902, after a year's post-graduate work, he was put in charge of the new research laboratories of Messrs. Burroughs, Wellcome & company, manufacturing chemists, at Brockwell Park, Herne Hill. After three years he went to Manchester in order to do the clinical work for the medical degree; he took his M.D. (Cantab.) in 1907.

Mellanby then worked as a G. H. Lewes research student at Cambridge until in 1909 he was appointed lecturer in charge of the physiological department at St. Thomas's Hospital medical school, a post which became a professorship in the university of London in 1920; there he stayed until he was appointed Waynflete professor of physiology in the university of Oxford in 1936, thereby becoming a fellow of Magdalen College.

Mellanby's work is contained in some sixty papers, mostly in the *Journal of Physiology* and the *Proceedings* of the Royal Society. The most important deal with three main subjects, the proteins of the blood, coagulation, and the secretion of the pancreas. His duties at Brockwell Park, connected with the preparation of diphtheria antitoxin, provided him with ample supplies of horses' blood and while there he laid the foundation of work to which he returned again and again throughout his life.

Mellanby's first paper, on 'Globulin' (1905), was important in showing, first, that in the solution of globulin by electrolytes bivalent ions are four times as efficient as univalent: secondly, that the conductivity due to the ions is not diminished by the presence of the globulin; thirdly, that the long current belief that globulin could be separated from albumin by fractional precipitation with neutral sulphates was mistaken; much more albumin than globulin is thrown down in serum by half saturation, for instance, with ammonium sulphate and also at lower concentrations: fourthly, that some eighty per cent. of the protein in serum is compounded with un-ionized salts; for if serum was frozen in a long vertical tube, then thawed and removed in a number of layers, each layer contained more solids than the layer next above it, protein and salts in the same proportion, the lowest maybe ten times as much as the uppermost. If the protein was coagulated and removed the conductivity at the original temperature increased in proportion to the amount of protein removed.

In work on coagulation Mellanby devised a method for isolating prothrombase, finally (1930) as a dry white powder that could be kept and retain its properties for months; and by a related method obtained refined preparations of thrombase (1933). With these purified products the study of coagulation was put on a surer basis, as his own work showed.

In work on the pancreas Mellanby showed that the curdling of milk in the stomach is due to pepsin, thus explaining the secretion of 'rennet' by fish, and that the curdling by pancreatic juice is due to trypsin. As this action on milk can be demonstrated with far smaller amounts of trypsin than any other action on proteins, he used it for a delicate method of estimating the amount of trypsin, which has proved valuable. He also added to exact knowledge of the other enzymes secreted by the pancreas. And in the matter of secretin he corrected many errors in the original description of its properties, formation, and mode of action, and especially showed that the secretion which it induced consisted of little more than an alkaline fluid, the appropriate medium for the action of the pancreatic enzymes, and contained none of those enzymes themselves. Finally in 1932 he succeeded in obtaining preparations of secretin as a fine white powder of which 1/40 of a milligram injected into the bloodstream of a cat gives unmistakable evidence of activity. One of his latest publications (1938) dealt with the action of secretin on the liver, which resembles that which it has on the pancreas. In this work he describes interesting observations on the formation and circulation of bile salts.

Mellanby was elected F.R.S. in 1929. He was editor of *Physiological Abstracts* for many years and had been a member of the Medical Research Council since 1936. He had a happy disposition, but he shrank from accepting any responsibility outside his own department. He married in 1911 Alice Mary, daughter of Joseph Watson, solicitor, of Barrhead, and had a daughter. He died at Oxford 15 July 1939.

[*The Times*, 17 July 1939; *Obituary Notices of Fellows of the Royal Society*, No. 8, January 1940 (portrait); *British Medical Journal*, 1939, vol. ii, p. 256; *Lancet*, 1939, vol. ii, p. 226.]   J. B. LEATHES.

MERCER, JAMES (1883–1932), mathematician, was born at Bootle, Liverpool, 15 January 1883, the son of Thomas Mercer, an accountant, by his wife, Sarah Alice Mercer. He was educated at University College, Liverpool, and at Trinity College, Cambridge, where he obtained a scholarship in 1902. He was bracketed senior wrangler with John Edensor Littlewood in 1905, was a Smith's prizeman in 1908, and was elected a fellow of Trinity in 1909. After a short period of service as an assistant lecturer in Liverpool University, he was recalled to Cambridge as a fellow and mathematical lecturer of Christ's College in 1912, and, up to the outbreak of war in 1914, was active in both teaching and research. He served as a naval instructor during the years 1914 to 1918, and was present in that capacity at the battle of Jutland.

The high hopes raised by Mercer's early mathematical work were never fully realized. He resumed his activity on his return to Cambridge, and was elected F.R.S. in 1922; but his health, which had always been uncertain, began to fail, and led to his resignation of his lecturership in 1926. He never recovered his powers, and died suddenly in London 21 February 1932. He married in 1911 Annie, fourth daughter of William Barnes, of Walton, near Liverpool, and left a son.

Mercer, although he wrote comparatively little, and almost all of it before he was thirty, was a mathematician of high originality and great skill, who made important advances in more than one branch of analysis. He was one of the first English mathematicians to occupy himself with the then novel theory of integral equations, to which, and to the closely related theory of orthogonal series, he contributed a number of striking theorems. One theorem in particular, concerning 'kernels' with positive 'eigenvalues', has become famous, and appears under his name in every treatise on the subject. A second 'Mercer's theorem', of an entirely different kind, plays an important part in the modern theory of divergent series; and these two theorems alone are enough to secure for him a permanent place in the history of mathematics.

[Obituary Notices of Fellows of the Royal Society, No. 2, December 1933 (portrait); Journal of the London Mathematical Society, vol. viii, 1933; private information; personal knowledge.]   G. H. HARDY.

MERRIVALE, first BARON (1855–1939), judge and politician. [See DUKE, HENRY EDWARD.]

MERZ, CHARLES HESTERMAN (1874–1940), electrical engineer, was born at Gateshead-upon-Tyne 5 October 1874, the eldest child of John Theodore Merz, a naturalized British subject of German descent, who was an industrial chemist and author of A History of European Thought in the Nineteenth Century (1896–1914). His mother was Alice Mary, daughter of Edward Richardson, a well-known Quaker of Newcastle-upon-Tyne. Charles Merz, his two brothers, and his sister, were brought up in a highly intellectual atmosphere at The Quarries, Benwell, Newcastle-upon-Tyne, which became the home of the Merz family. Here were to be met persons who took an active part in the affairs of the day, political, economic, religious, literary, and scientific, and this environment doubtless had an important bearing on the develop-

ment of the character and mental outlook of Charles Merz.

Owing to his mother's Quaker connexion, Merz was educated at Bootham School, York, after which he studied at the Armstrong College (later King's College), Newcastle-upon-Tyne. In 1893 he went as a pupil to the Pandon Dene generating station of the Newcastle-upon-Tyne Electric Supply Company which had been founded in 1889 by his father and Robert Spence Watson [q.v.], who had married his mother's sister. In 1894 he became a pupil at the Robey engineering works in Lincoln. Sometime later he was engaged at the Bankside station of the City of London Electric Lighting Company, superintending contracts for the British Thomson-Houston Company, manufacturers of electrical plant, of which company his father was at that time a director. At the age of twenty-three he was appointed manager and engineer to operate the plant which the British Thomson-Houston Company had provided for electricity supply in Croydon. So successful was he in this that he was given charge of a similar and larger contract at Cork which also included tramways. Here it was that he came into contact with William McLellan, who in 1902 became his partner in the well-known firm of Merz and McLellan, consultative electrical engineers (established first at Newcastle-upon-Tyne and later in London also), until the latter's death in 1934.

When the Walker and Wallsend Gas Company was seeking legal sanction for the establishment of an electricity supply for shipyards and other industrial works on Tyneside, young Merz was asked to assist the company in its parliamentary bill. On the successful conclusion of this application he and McLellan were appointed consulting engineers for the scheme and took up residence at Newcastle-upon-Tyne. Merz was only twenty-five years old when in 1899 this work was completed.

Merz and McLellan designed the Neptune Bank power station at Wallsend which was inaugurated by Lord Kelvin in 1902, this being the first station in Great Britain to generate 3-phase current at what was then the high voltage of 5,500. This pioneer electric power supply undertaking was shortly afterwards transferred to the Newcastle-upon-Tyne Electric Supply Company, and under Merz's guidance it and its sister companies were combined to constitute the North

Eastern Electric Supply Company which used to cover the whole of the north-east coast. Upon the obvious success of this undertaking were based the important Electricity Company Acts of 1902. The same year Merz was responsible for a second pioneer undertaking in the electrification of the North-Eastern Railway between Newcastle and Tynemouth.

Before a parliamentary committee Merz was a superb expert witness, calm, collected, lucid, accurate, and penetrating. These characteristics were conspicuously in evidence during the protracted proceedings of the Administrative County of London electric power bill in 1904–1905 when he was only thirty years of age. After passing all committee stages the bill failed through lack of parliamentary time, and a great opportunity for consolidating the chaotic London position was lost.

In 1907 Merz visited Australia in order to report on the electrification of the Melbourne suburban railway system which he supervised in 1912. This was the beginning of a widespread association with power supply and railway electrification abroad, and he made frequent visits in relation thereto to Australia, the Argentine, South Africa, India, and the United States of America.

In addition to carrying on his varied and extensive practice as a consultative electrical engineer, Merz served his country in several other respects. He was chairman of the electric power supply subcommittee of the coal conservation committee (1916), of the report of which a far-reaching outcome is the electric 'grid' system of Great Britain. Towards the end of the war of 1914–1918 he organized for the first lord, Sir Eric Geddes [q.v.], the new Department of Experiment and Research at the Admiralty, of which he became the first director.

Although Merz was a vice-president of the Institution of Electrical Engineers (1912–1915), his dislike of public speaking restrained him from accepting nomination for the presidency, but he greatly valued the bestowal (1931) of the Faraday medal by the institution, as well as the honorary degree of D.Sc. (1932) conferred upon him as 'a pioneer in the new era of three-phase electrical transmission in this country' by the university of Durham, and the vice-presidency of the Royal Institution, in which he took a deep interest. He characteristically declined all pecuniary recompense or titular honours in respect of his work for the government.

Merz married in 1913 Stella Alice Pauline, daughter of Edmund de Satur, of Dublin, and had a son and a daughter. He, his two children, and two servants were killed by an enemy bomb at his home in Kensington 15 October 1940. The house was completely demolished, only Mrs. Merz escaping, although injured.

Merz possessed a mind orderly to an extraordinary degree, as well as the faculty of dealing with both the broad essentials of a problem and the details of its execution, and his equable temperament was invaluable in matters of controversy. Taken all in all he has some claim to be regarded as in his own sphere as the principal electrical engineer of his time. He was an appreciative employer and a warm friend. He combined deep religious feeling with a strong love of nature, in particular of the Lake District, where he spent many happy holidays.

There is a portrait of Merz by Arnold Mason at the Institution of Electrical Engineers.

[Personal knowledge.]

R. A. S. REDMAYNE.

METHUEN, PAUL SANFORD, third BARON METHUEN, of Corsham (1845–1932), field-marshal, was born at Corsham Court, Wiltshire, 1 September 1845, the eldest of the three sons of Frederick Henry Paul Methuen, second Baron Methuen, by his wife, Anna Horatia Caroline, only child of John Sanford, vicar of Nynehead, Somerset. He was descended from a brother of John Methuen [q.v.], the negotiator of the 'Methuen treaty' with Portugal. His grandfather Paul Methuen, first Baron Methuen (1779–1849), represented Wiltshire in several parliaments.

Methuen was educated at Eton and, after two years' service in the Royal Wiltshire Yeomanry, joined the Scots Fusilier Guards as ensign and lieutenant in November 1864, being promoted lieutenant and captain in December 1867; captain and lieutenant-colonel in July 1876; and regimental major in October 1882, after serving as adjutant of the 1st battalion from August 1868 to November 1871. He held several staff appointments, as brigade major, Home District (1871–1876), as military attaché in Berlin (1878–1881), as assistant adjutant and quartermaster-general, Home District (1881–1884), and as deputy adjutant-general in South Africa (1888–1890). He saw active service at Amoaful in the Ashanti campaign of 1873–1874 on the staff of Sir Garnet (later Viscount) Wolseley [q.v.], and was commandant at headquarters in Egypt for three months in 1882, being present at the battle of Tel-el-Kebir. He had received his brevet-colonelcy in 1881. He served in the expedition of Sir Charles Warren [q.v.] to Bechuanaland in 1884–1885, where he commanded Methuen's Horse, a corps of mounted rifles raised for the expedition, and obtained his first experience of South Africa and of the Boers. He became a substantive colonel in November 1888, being promoted major-general in May of that year; he commanded the Home District from 1892 to 1897, having succeeded his father in the title in 1891. In 1897 he served as press censor at headquarters with the Tirah expedition and was promoted lieutenant-general in April 1898, and on the outbreak of the South African war he was given command of the 1st division.

By the time Methuen reached South Africa, early in November 1899, the original plans had had to be abandoned, and he found himself committed to relieving Kimberley with fewer than 10,000 men, including a mere handful of mounted troops. For lack of them, although he successfully dislodged the Boers from strong positions at Belmont (23 November) and Graspan (25 November) these successes could not be exploited by an effective pursuit. Attacking again on 28 November he found their skilfully chosen position at the Modder river difficult to capture, but his left eventually secured a passage over the river and in the night the Boers acknowledged defeat by retiring. He was slightly wounded in the engagement. It has been suggested (*German Official History*, vol. v, p. 851) that by pressing on at once before the 'much shaken' Boers could recover from three successive reverses much might have been gained. However, the troops needed rest, remounts, and reinforcements; difficulties over communications and supplies were serious and Kimberley was in no urgent need of immediate relief. But the suspension of the advance allowed the Boers to draw reinforcements from Kimberley and Natal and to make their next position, at Magersfontein, really formidable. Methuen's attack (11 December) miscarried, although for a time the issue hung in the balance; indeed, the German critic suggests that success might have been achieved by greater vigour in pressing the attack, especially on the part of the subordinate commanders. This repulse, together with the defeats of Lieutenant-General Sir William Gatacre at Stormberg (10 December) and of General Sir Redvers Buller [qq.v.] at Colenso (15 December), was a terrible shock to British complacency, and brought home to everyone the seriousness of the problem to be faced and the need for more substantial efforts. Methuen became the target for much foolish, ill-informed, and unjust criticism, mainly from civilians with little qualification for forming an opinion of any value; but Buller manfully resisted the proposal to make Methuen a scapegoat by superseding him and Lord Roberts not only retained him in his command but emphatically declared that the task set Methuen had been impossible with that force. Moreover, no army had as yet faced magazine rifles and smokeless powder and the training of the first troops to endure that ordeal was likely to leave room for improvement.

During the operations which ended in initial failure at Paardeberg (18 February 1900), Methuen at the Modder river helped to detain General Piet Cronje in his position. Subsequently he conducted operations in the Kimberley–Boshof area during the advance on Pretoria with considerable success and continued actively engaged, mainly in the Western Transvaal, until the end of the war. Most officers of his seniority had gone home, but he remained, chasing the elusive C. R. de Wet [q.v.] with untiring energy and persistence. He never spared himself; if he was assiduous for his troops, his unremitting efforts made no small contribution to the ultimate success. If he achieved no spectacular victory, he had many minor successes, notably against General Jacobus Hendrik de la Rey near Klerksdorp on 19 February 1901; he gave his opponents no rest, made many captures, thwarted them again and again, and gained their respect as well as the trust and affection of his own men. It was a cruel fate which led to his being beaten, badly wounded, and captured towards the end of the war, at Tweebosch (7 March 1902), through the misconduct of the undisciplined and half-trained irregulars who constituted the majority of his column.

Appointed colonel of the Scots Guards in May 1904, an appointment which gave both him and the regiment great pleasure, Methuen was promoted general the same month and in June received command of the IV Army Corps. This was transformed into the Eastern Command in 1905 and gave him the opportunity of putting into practice the lessons which he had learned in South Africa, particularly with regard to accurate rifle-fire. As a trainer and administrator he made a substantial contribution to the high standard of training attained by the British Expeditionary Force in 1914.

In April 1908 Methuen was appointed general officer commanding-in-chief in South Africa, a post which he held until 1912. He was most popular, particularly with his former opponents, and did much by improving relations between Boers and British to give the Union of South Africa a good start. He was governor and commander-in-chief of Natal in 1910. He was promoted field-marshal in June 1911.

Methuen's service did not end here: although in his seventieth year he was appointed governor and commander-in-chief of Malta in February 1915 and retained the post until May 1919. Here, as always, he was indefatigable and never spared himself, and it was thanks largely to his foresight that Malta found itself well equipped with hospitals and staff for the Dardanelles expedition. He received the honorary degree of LL.D. from the university of Malta, and after returning home he was appointed constable of the Tower at the end of 1919. But he lived chiefly at Corsham Court, doing much to help the British Legion, the Church Lads' Brigade, the Boy Scouts, the V.A.D. organization, and many local movements and causes, here, as in the army, winning the affection and respect of all whom he met. He was appointed C.B. in 1882, C.M.G. in 1886, K.C.V.O. in 1897, K.C.B. in 1900, G.C.B. in 1902, G.C.V.O. in 1910, and G.C.M.G. in 1919.

Methuen was twice married: first, in 1878 to Evelyn (died 1879), eldest daughter (by his second marriage) of Sir Frederick Hutchinson Hervey-Bathurst, third baronet, of Clarendon Park, Wiltshire, and had no children; secondly, in 1884 to his cousin Mary Ethel (died 1941), second daughter of William Ayshford Sanford of Nynehead Court, formerly in the Colonial Service, and had three sons and two daughters, the elder of whom predeceased her father. He died at Corsham Court 30 October 1932, and was succeeded as fourth baron by his eldest son, Paul Ayshford (born 1886).

Methuen's influence over the army was widespread, extending even beyond the Brigade of Guards, for whom he worked in every way, much as did Sir John Moore

for the Light Brigade. Chivalrous, kindly, generous, with the highest standards of duty and expecting others to be imbued with the same ideals, he got the best out of those with whom he dealt and who could not fail to profit by so fine an example. His great personal courage, which led him into the fighting line even when in high command, was never more conspicuous than at Tweebosch, and his unselfishness and his devotion to his calling were equally conspicuous along with dignified endurance of unreasonable criticism and an assiduous discharge of a great variety of public services.

A portrait of Methuen by John Shirley Shirley-Fox (1905) hangs in Corsham Court.

[*The Times*, 31 October 1932; Sir J. F. Maurice and M. H. Grant, (Official) *History of the War in South Africa 1899–1902*, 1906–1910; *German Official History of the War in South Africa*, 1904 (translated); private information.]   C. T. ATKINSON.

MEYRICK, EDWARD (1854–1938), entomologist, was born at Ramsbury, Wiltshire, 24 November 1854, the eldest son of the Rev. Edward Meyrick, formerly fellow of Magdalen College, Oxford, by his wife, Mary, youngest daughter of Alfred Batson. His ancestors came from Wales and he was collaterally related to Rowland, Sir Gelly, Sir John (died 1659), and Sir Samuel Rush Meyrick [qq.v.]. He was educated at Marlborough and at Trinity College, Cambridge, where he obtained a first class in the classical tripos of 1877. For ten years he taught in schools in Australia and New Zealand and from 1887 to 1914 was a classical master at his old school. From 1889 to 1914 he was president of the Marlborough College Natural History Society, and many of those whom he infected with his enthusiasm and love of accuracy remained keen naturalists while some achieved great distinction.

In the lepidoptera and particularly in the microlepidoptera of distant countries Meyrick found an almost unworked field. In hundreds of articles in many scientific periodicals, particularly in those of New Zealand, Australia, India, and South Africa, and also in a privately published periodical, *Exotic Lepidoptera*, begun in 1912, he described probably some twenty thousand species new to science. But he did not confine himself to description. He brought his exceptional knowledge of distribution to bear on problems of geological history and he undertook a comprehensive reclassification of the whole order lepidoptera on the basis of characters which he considered showed more adequately the natural relationships. These ideas he used in *A Handbook of British Lepidoptera* (1895) of which a revised edition appeared in 1928.

Pioneer work on so large a scale was naturally not immediately accepted in its entirety and not all has stood the test of later work, but Meyrick was the first to place the classification of insects on a scientific basis: he was one of the greatest lepidopterists there has ever been, and beyond doubt the foremost microlepidopterist of his time. He was a rapid worker and to the end he kept his astonishing activity, his eyesight, and his dexterity of hand. A fine scholar, he never allowed his knowledge and love of the classics to fade and the results may be seen in the clarity of his descriptions and the accuracy of his scientific nomenclature. To his many correspondents he was prompt, courteous, and generous, and he bequeathed to the British Museum (Natural History) his remarkable collection of some hundred thousand specimens, with his own watercolour illustrations.

Meyrick was elected F.R.S. in 1904. In 1927 he was awarded the Captain Scott memorial medal of the South African Biological Society for his contributions to South African entomology. In 1892 he married Antonia, daughter of Heinrich Eckhard, a lawyer in the Rhenish Palatinate, and had three sons, the eldest of whom was killed in the war of 1914–1918, and two daughters. He died at Marlborough 31 March 1938.

[*Obituary Notices of Fellows of the Royal Society*, No. 7, January 1939 (bibliography and portrait); *The Entomologist's Monthly Magazine*, vol. xxiv (3rd series), 1938; *The Entomologist*, vol. lxxi, 1938 (portrait); *Annual Reports* of the Marlborough College Natural History Society, No. 87, 1939; private information; personal knowledge.]

GUY PEIRSON.

MILLIGAN, GEORGE (1860–1934), Scottish divine and biblical scholar, was born at Kilconquhar, Fife, 2 April 1860, the eldest son of the parish minister, William Milligan [q.v.], who later in the same year became professor of biblical criticism in the university of Aberdeen. His mother was Anne Mary, daughter of the physician and essayist David Macbeth Moir [q.v.], known as 'Delta'. He was elder brother of Sir William Milligan [q.v.].

After attending the Gymnasium at Aberdeen he graduated at Aberdeen University in arts (1879) and divinity (1883), studying also at the universities of Edinburgh, Göttingen, and Bonn. He superintended the early development of St. Matthew's church, Edinburgh (1883–1894), becoming in 1887 its first ordained minister. In the country charge of Caputh, Perthshire (1894–1910), he added to the faithful performance of his parochial duties an assiduous devotion to biblical scholarship; and stirred by a lecture of Marcus Dods [q.v.] he took up zealously the study of the accumulating stores of non-literary Greek papyri, lecturing on the subject at Oxford (1899), Cambridge (1904), and in the United States of America (1909). As regius professor of biblical criticism in Glasgow University (1910–1932) and clerk to the senate (1911–1930), he won the confidence, honour, and affection of all with whom he had to do. He received honorary degrees from the universities of Aberdeen (1904), Durham (1919), Glasgow (1932), and Edinburgh (1933). He died in Glasgow 25 November 1934.

It was a notable pioneering achievement for Milligan to issue, while still at Caputh, a standard commentary on St. Paul's Epistles to the Thessalonians (1908), in which *inter alia* he applied the new papyrological evidence to a re-examination of the Pauline grammar and vocabulary. He began his *magnum opus*, *The Vocabulary of the Greek Testament* (1914–1929), in collaboration with J. H. Moulton [q.v.], and after the issue of part ii in 1915 completed it single-handed; its comprehensiveness and accuracy provided a foundation for successors to build upon, while in readableness and human interest it remains unsurpassed.

Milligan served the Church of Scotland with spontaneous and conscientious loyalty, more particularly in the field of religious education; and, like his father and his father-in-law, Dr. John Rankine, he became moderator of the General Assembly (1923). His simplicity and sympathy, which made him in private life so courteous and approachable, found early expression in his pastoral ministry and in collections of children's addresses, and later led him to make the results of scholarship more generally available in many courses of lectures and published volumes. By nature placid, receptive, fair-minded, he wrote and taught with admirable balance and lucidity.

Milligan was twice married: first, in 1891

to Janet Simpson (died 1898), daughter of John Rankine, D.D., minister of Sorn, Ayrshire; secondly, in 1902 to Margaret Catherine, daughter of William Ellis Gloag, Lord Kincairney [q.v.], senator of the College of Justice. One son was born of each marriage.

[*Glasgow Herald*, 26 November 1934; personal knowledge.]   G. S. DUNCAN.

MILLS, BERTRAM WAGSTAFF (1873–1938), circus proprietor, was born in London 11 August 1873, the son of Halford Lewis Mills, by his wife, Mary Fenn Wagstaff. His father, who was the proprietor of a coach-building works in Paddington, owned two small farms in the country, one at Harefield, near Rickmansworth, and the other at Chalfont St. Giles, where he sent his horses to rest. It was at one or other of these farms that Bertram spent much of his childhood, and it was on these horses that he was taught to ride. He left school before he was fifteen, and began work in his father's business, travelling from show to show, and exhibiting carriages all over Europe. During the war of 1914–1918 he served in the Royal Army Medical Corps.

It was after the war, when there was little coach-building work to be done, that Mills entered the circus business. A careless remark after seeing a circus at Olympia, that he was sure he could put on a better show, was taken up by a friend who was a director of Olympia, and who challenged him to make his words good. The result was that for eighteen years (1920–1937) at Christmas he put on a circus at Olympia which came to be recognized as a popular entertainment. It was built up on a large scale, and in 1929 he extended his activities by starting the Bertram Mills tenting circus, with which he toured the provinces from April to October.

Statistics of the organization are interesting. The tour required four special trains and about 75 lorries and tractors to transport the animals and circus equipment. To show the work necessary to secure first-class performers, it may be mentioned that in 1937 Mills and his son travelled something like 50,000 miles to collect new turns from all parts of the world. At Olympia alone the weekly expenses ranged between £15,000 and £20,000 for the five weeks' season, the attendance at which averaged 70,000 a week. Some 4,000 people in all were employed, and there was a permanent salary list of about 1,800 men and women in all

sorts of callings. The road show cost £40,000 to launch and the running expenses came to £2,500 a week. Among the friends of Mills who took a great interest in the concern was the fifth Earl of Lonsdale, who accepted the presidency of the circus company in 1921.

At the Richmond horse show, where for many years he was a successful exhibitor, Mills was a familiar figure. He always entered for the coaching Marathon from Hyde Park to the show ground with his 'Old Times' London to Brighton stage coach. He was the president of the Showmen's Guild from 1934 until his death. In addition to his labours as a showman and entertainer, he had considerable experience of local government work, for he was a member of the London County Council for ten years (1928–1938). A few months before he died he had been adopted as unionist candidate for the Isle of Ely.

In 1901 Mills married Ethel, daughter of William Notley, of Thorndon, Suffolk. He had two sons, Cyril Bertram and Bernard Notley. His last wish was that the circus should be carried on by his sons, and this wish they faithfully carried out. He died at Chalfont St. Giles 16 April 1938. A man of much ability and force of character, his popularity and powers of organization were remarkable. It can have been the lot of few to give so much pleasure to young and old alike.

[*The Times*, 18 April 1938.]
    ALFRED COCHRANE.

MILLS, SIR WILLIAM (1856–1932), engineer, was born at Sunderland 24 April 1856, the son of David Mills, shipbuilder, of Sunderland, by his wife, Sarah Ann Kirkaldy. The earlier part of his working life was occupied with marine engineering. On leaving school at the age of fourteen he began a seven years' apprenticeship with Messrs. George Clark, marine engineers, of Sunderland, and then spent a number of years at sea, obtaining a first class certificate as a marine engineer (1884) and gaining experience in the repair of submarine telegraph cables. For a short time he was a draughtsman with the Central Marine Engine Works at West Hartlepool and assistant outdoor manager with Messrs. J. Dickinson, of Sunderland. He was the inventor of a boat-disengaging gear which came into use in both naval and merchant ships.

Turning from marine engineering to metal-manufacturing Mills began business on his own account as a general engineer in Sunderland in 1885 and established the first aluminium foundry in the United Kingdom. There, and also at works which he set up in Birmingham soon afterwards (both later became limited companies under the style of William Mills Limited), he turned out castings for the motor-car and aircraft industries, taking out several patents for improvements in foundry technique. Early in 1915 he introduced and opened works in Birmingham (Mills Munitions Limited) for making the hand grenade for which his name is chiefly known and which was used in enormous quantities by the British and their allies during the war of 1914–1918. Its principle was derived from the Roland bomb, a Belgian invention, but by working out methods of preventing both premature explosion and failure to explode he contributed greatly to the practical efficiency of the weapon. He also prepared an instructional film demonstrating its use and delivered lectures on the subject. His services were rewarded by a knighthood in 1922 and he received £27,750 from the government, but he failed in his contention that he was not liable to pay income-tax on that sum and was wont to declare that he had lost money by the grenade. He was chairman of the James Watt Memorial Trust. He was a collector of pictures, china, and antiques. In 1891 he married Eliza (died 1930), daughter of William Vincent Hodgson, cotton spinner, of Manchester, and widow of John R. Gandy, of Warrington; there were no children of the marriage. He died at Weston-super-Mare 7 January 1932.

[*The Times*, 8 January 1932; *Engineer* and *Engineering*, 15 January 1932.]

H. M. Ross.

MILNE, Sir (ARCHIBALD) BERKELEY, second baronet (1855–1938), admiral, the younger but only surviving son of Admiral of the Fleet Sir Alexander Milne, first baronet [q.v.], by his wife, Euphemia, youngest daughter of Archibald Cochran, of Ashkirk, Roxburgh, was born at his father's official residence at the Admiralty 2 June 1855. He was grandson of Admiral Sir David Milne [q.v.]. At the time of his birth his father was junior naval lord and his godfather (Admiral Sir) M. F. F. Berkeley (afterwards Lord Fitzhardinge, q.v.) was senior naval lord. After a short period at Wellington College he entered the training ship *Britannia* as a naval cadet in 1869, passing out as midshipman in 1870. In that rank he served under Sir

E. G. Fanshawe [q.v.] in the flagship *Royal Alfred*, North America and West Indies station, and under Captain (afterwards Sir) George Tryon [q.v.] in the *Raleigh*. Promoted sub-lieutenant in 1875, he was advanced to lieutenant in 1876, with three first-class certificates. He then joined Commodore Sullivan, South Africa station, in the corvettes first *Tourmaline* and then *Active*. He remained on that station for three years, being transferred to the *Boadicea* when Captain (afterwards Sir) F. W. Richards [q.v.] succeeded Sullivan as commodore, but for most of the time he was lent for service on shore during the Transkei Kaffir rebellion of 1877–1878 and later throughout the Zulu war of 1879. He was appointed naval aide-de-camp to Lord Chelmsford, was wounded at the battle of Ulundi (3 July), and was several times mentioned in dispatches. After returning to England later in the year he joined the *Minotaur*, flagship of Vice-Admiral A. W. C. Hood (afterwards Lord Hood of Avalon, q.v.) in the Channel squadron. In June 1882 he was appointed to the *Orion* in the Mediterranean and a month later, on Admiral (Sir) Anthony Hoskins [q.v.] leaving the Board of Admiralty in order to bring reinforcements during the Egyptian war, he became his flag-lieutenant in the *Penelope* and was present at the battle of Tel-el-Kebir (13 September). Thus, since first going to sea he had had unusual opportunities of service under the most distinguished officers of the day, of whom three later filled his father's place as senior naval lord.

On his appointment to the royal yacht *Victoria and Albert* in October 1882, Milne now began a different career as a sea courtier. He rapidly won the affection and regard of the Prince and Princess of Wales, and spent eight of the next eighteen years in royal yachts, finishing as commodore and later (1903–1905) rear-admiral in charge of H.M. yachts.

Milne was promoted commander in 1884, and captain in 1891, and in the intervals between turns of yacht duty he was commander in the Channel squadron flagships *Minotaur* and *Northumberland* (1887–1889) and captain of the *Trafalgar* (flagship, 1894–1896), *Venus* (1897–1900) in the Mediterranean, and *Jupiter* (1900–1904) in the Channel squadron.

In his sea-going commands Milne had shown himself to be a competent and popular officer, so that after reaching flag-rank in April 1904, and leaving the command of H.M. yachts sixteen months later, he was selected to be second-in-command of the Atlantic Fleet (flag in the *Victorious*) under Admiral Sir William May [q.v.] (1905–1906) and of the Channel Fleet (flag in the *Hibernia*) under Lord Charles Beresford [q.v.] (1908–1909). He was then (having been promoted vice-admiral in May 1908) transferred to the command of the second division of the Home Fleet (flag in the *King Edward VII*) under May for another year.

Promoted admiral in September 1911, in November 1912 Milne hoisted his flag in the *Good Hope*, soon to be replaced by the great battle-cruiser *Inflexible*, as commander-in-chief in the Mediterranean. By July 1914, when war seemed imminent, his force had been much strengthened and included three battle-cruisers, four armoured cruisers, four light cruisers, and fourteen destroyers.

The naval situation in the Mediterranean was very obscure in those critical days. It was unknown whether Italy would join her allies of the Triple Alliance, or even whether Austria would come in at once. The fast new German battle-cruiser *Goeben* was at large, and it was presumed would try to get out into the Atlantic. Milne had been informed that his first task should be to assist the French in transporting their African army and to try to bring to action any fast German ship, particularly the *Goeben*, which might attempt to interfere. At the same time he had to keep a watch on the Adriatic until the decision of Italy and Austria was known. But he knew nothing of the actual intentions of the French authorities and all his attempts to communicate with them failed. In this dilemma he obtained Admiralty authority to concentrate his force at Malta. In the end the French African army was transported without incident under escort of the whole French Mediterranean fleet, but the *Goeben* and her escort, the cruiser *Breslau*, after coaling at Messina (a neutral port) turned east instead of west and slipped through to the Dardanelles and Constantinople, evading by her superior speed the cruiser squadron under Admiral (Sir) Ernest Troubridge [q.v.], but closely pursued as long as possible by the light cruiser *Gloucester*.

There was a tendency in the press and elsewhere to criticize Milne for his action or inaction in this confused and difficult situation. But he had faithfully carried out his instructions; he had no reason then to anticipate any understanding between Germany and Turkey, he had no communication from the French naval authorities about the transport of the African army; he knew that the *Goeben* was faster than any of his ships and much more powerful than all but his battle-cruisers, two of which had been ordered by the Admiralty to Gibraltar to prevent the *Goeben* escaping westwards, and he was uncertain until too late whether Italy would be neutral and Austria an enemy. On 30 August 1914 the Admiralty issued a statement that 'his conduct and dispositions in regard to the German vessels *Goeben* and *Breslau* had been the subject of the careful examination of the Board with the result that Their Lordships have approved the measures taken by him in all respects'.

As by diplomatic agreement the supreme command in the Mediterranean was to be assumed by the French, and Milne was senior to the French admiral, he returned home in his flagship on 18 August. He had been offered and had accepted the command of the Nore, but this post was subsequently filled by Sir George Callaghan [q.v.] who had been relieved in command of the Grand Fleet by Sir John (afterwards Earl) Jellicoe [q.v.]; and, no further opportunity of employment occurring, Milne was placed on the retired list at the end of the war.

In 1921 Milne published a small book *The Flight of the Goeben and the Breslau* in which he challenged the accuracy of Sir Julian Corbett's account of the affair in the (official) *History of the Great War. Naval Operations* and the implied censure of his conduct. Milne's book sets forth clearly and convincingly his own account of his proceedings and justifies the official approbation which had been repeated in the Admiralty's announcement of his retirement in 1919.

Milne was an able officer, well liked in the service and popular in London society where his long association with King Edward VII and Queen Alexandra made him a well-known figure. He was a keen fisherman and deer-stalker and a good shot, and devoted much of his half-pay time to horticulture at his ancestral residence of Inveresk Gate, Musselburgh. He bequeathed a collection of rare shrubs and orchids to the Edinburgh Botanical Gardens.

Milne's association with the court brought him a number of foreign distinctions, French, German, Greek, Spanish, and Norwegian, as well as the C.V.O. (1903), K.C.V.O. (1904), K.C.B. (1909), and G.C.V.O. (1912), and he held appointments as groom-in-waiting to King Edward VII and extra equerry to his three successors. He died, unmarried, in London 5 July 1938 leaving no heir to the baronetcy.

[Admiralty records; Sir Julian S. Corbett, (Official) *History of the Great War. Naval Operations*, vol. i, 1920; personal knowledge.]

VINCENT W. BADDELEY.

MITCHELL, REGINALD JOSEPH (1895–1937), aircraft designer, was born in the village of Talke, near Stoke-upon-Trent, 20 May 1895, the eldest of the three sons of Herbert Mitchell, a Yorkshireman who served as headmaster successively in three Staffordshire villages and later established a printing business in Hanley. His mother was Eliza Jane Brain, whose family lived at Longton, near Stoke-upon-Trent, where his childhood was spent. He was educated at an elementary school in Longton, and at Hanley High School. At the age of sixteen he became an apprentice in the shops of Messrs. Kerr, Stuart & company, makers of locomotives at Stoke; and during his apprenticeship went to night school at local technical colleges. His subjects there were engineering, mechanics, mathematics, and drawing. After a thorough training at the bench he passed on to the drawing office, and while he was becoming skilled as an engineer, he was already indulging his personal interest in aeroplanes by designing, making, and flying model gliders. That interest persisted, and in 1916, before he was twenty-two, he obtained employment at the Supermarine Aviation Works at Southampton, directed at that time by Hubert Scott-Paine, who was devoted to the cause of flying-boats. Within three years, Mitchell had been appointed chief engineer and designer. He remained with the firm, through a change in ownership in 1923, until his death at Southampton 11 June 1937, and for the last ten years was also a director. He was awarded the silver medal of the Royal Aeronautical Society in 1927 and was appointed C.B.E. in 1931. In 1918 he married a school-teacher, Florence, daughter of Henry James Dayson, farmer, and had a son.

Mitchell had a succession of military flying-boats to his credit, but his chief fame rests upon the design and development of high-speed float-seaplanes for Schneider trophy races between 1922 and 1931 and upon the ultimate emergence of the Spitfire fighter—the most renowned of all fighter aeroplanes in the war of 1939–1945. The Spitfire exemplified Mitchell's special quality of combining fine lines with great structural strength. In that sense it marked the union of practical engineering and aerodynamic knowledge in Mitchell. It also represented that orderly if brilliant progression in Mitchell's work which justified the kindly criticism since made that his 'second thoughts were best'. Before he built the Spitfire he had built another fighter to specifications laid down by the Air Ministry. Having finished that and satisfied himself as well as everybody else that it was mediocre, he went ahead with his own ideas and in 1936 made the beautiful aeroplane which was used to such deadly purpose from the beginning of the war to the end. Nearly 19,000 Spitfires were built. The Spitfire began its career with a top speed of 346 m.p.h. and, with more power and slight modifications, it went on to a top speed of 460 m.p.h. It remained delightful to fly right to the end as was always the way with Mitchell's high-speed aeroplanes. His first Schneider trophy winner covered the course at Venice in 1927 at 281 m.p.h.; his third flew the course at Calshot in 1931 at 340 m.p.h. During that period, the power at his disposal rose from 900 h.p. to 2,600 h.p. and with it came more weight to carry and more heat to be dissipated. His ingenuity surmounted these difficulties at little sacrifice in size. In the S.6 and the S.6 B. seaplanes of 1929 and 1931 respectively, fuel was carried in the floats, oil was cooled in channels under the skin of the fuselage, and there was no radiator. The liquid for the cylinder jackets was cooled in the false skin of the wings. In the same way there were no excrescences on the Spitfire when it appeared. The engine was completely cowled and the radiator was little more than a slot under the starboard wing. The wing was an almost perfect ellipse, gently tapered and diminishing in thickness towards the tips. The Spitfire looked a thoroughbred and, in a way, it had the limitations of a thoroughbred, for its duration was only 1¼ hours; but it carried eight guns in the wing and a reasonable amount of ammunition. It did what Mitchell expected of it and it delighted a hard-tried generation. Mitchell's merit was that he first produced a real racing aeroplane and then applied the same formula to the design of a fighter. He wedded good engineering to aerodynamic grace and made science his guide. In consequence he always knew what he was doing. His forecast of top speed was never wrong by more than 4 m.p.h.

[*The Times*, 12 June 1937; private information.]   E. COLSTON SHEPHERD.

MONASH, SIR JOHN (1865–1931), Australian general, was born of Jewish parentage in Melbourne 27 June 1865, the only son of Louis Monash, of St. James's Park, Hawthorn, Melbourne, by his wife, Bertha Manasse; his parents were born and married in Germany. He was educated at Scotch College and at the university, Melbourne, where he graduated in arts, engineering, and laws. He was Argus scholar with honours in engineering.

Monash began practice as a civil engineer in 1884, specializing in rail, road, bridge, and water-supply design and construction. From his earliest student days he had been a keen and enthusiastic member of the Australian Citizen Forces and in 1887 secured his first commission as a lieutenant with promotion to captain in 1895 and major in 1897. In this connexion his power of lucid exposition was noticed by (Sir) Ian Hamilton and other officers visiting Australia. From 1900 he concentrated on reinforced concrete construction and introduced his methods into Victoria, Tasmania, and South Australia. In 1901 he was given command of the North Melbourne Artillery. In 1905 he had been promoted lieutenant-colonel in the Citizen Forces and by 1913 had achieved his full colonelcy. He also served as an officer of the Intelligence Corps from 1907 to 1914. His progress in the engineering world had by then brought him to the presidency of the Victorian Institute of Engineers, which he held for two years.

On the outbreak of war in 1914 Monash was appointed chief censor for Australia but only held the post for a month as his services were required in a more active field of operations. He was put in command of the 4th Infantry brigade and accompanied it to Gallipoli in April 1915, and was promoted brigadier-general in July. During this campaign his brigade was engaged in defence of a sector which came to be named after him, Monash Valley, and later it was employed in the fighting at Suvla Bay. Towards the end of the year Gallipoli was evacuated and Monash was mentioned in dispatches three times for his services in the campaign.

Monash was then given command of the 3rd Australian division in July 1916 with the rank of major-general, and after training the division in England he proceeded with it to France (November 1916) where it took part in the battles of Messines (June 1917) and Passchendaele (October 1917), the third battle of Ypres (1917), and the defence of Amiens (1918). His great and obvious capacity, especially in the higher commands, was soon recognized and he succeeded General William (later Lord) Birdwood in command of the Australian Army Corps in France, assuming the command in May 1918 with the rank of lieutenant-general.

Monash's great *forte* was planning, and to this objective he brought to bear all his training and experience as a brilliant engineer. His plans for battle were blueprints of the most detailed construction complete to the last detail, and so well were his great qualities recognized and appreciated that it fell to him with the Australian Army Corps successfully to withstand the last offensive of the enemy in the late spring of 1918 and to launch the great Allied offensive of August 1918. To his masterly organization and his brilliance as a corps commander the Allies owed much for the success of the offensive and his great achievements with the corps during the ensuing battles earned for him recognition as one of the ablest corps commanders in the British army. After the armistice was signed he was appointed director-general of the Department of Repatriation and Demobilization of the Australian Imperial Forces in Europe, Africa, and Asia, and for his untiring devotion to this new field of service was mentioned in dispatches eight times. On his return to Australia he became a member of the Council of Defence. He was promoted full general in 1930 and retired from the army in the same year.

Monash's great organizing ability was still further recognized in a new field, when in 1920 he was appointed chairman of the Victorian Government State Electricity Commission set up by act of parliament. He accepted the invitation in 1923 to become vice-chancellor of Melbourne University and in the following year became president of the Australasian Association for the Advancement of Science, a post which he occupied for two years. In 1931 he acted as official representative of the Commonwealth of Australia at the inauguration of New Delhi, India; and at this time was director and chairman of several Indian and Commonwealth companies.

Monash was appointed C.B. in 1915, K.C.B. in 1918, and G.C.M.G. in 1919. In

1920 he published his book entitled *The Australian Victories in France in 1918* which was a tribute to the great merits of the Australian soldier in the field. In addition he published numerous scientific papers on engineering subjects which had been presented to Australian scientific societies, and also his presidential addresses. In 1920 Melbourne University conferred upon him the honorary degree of doctor of engineering, the first time such a degree was granted by an Australian university. He also received honorary degrees from the universities of Oxford (D.C.L.), Cambridge (LL.D.), and Melbourne (LL.D.).

Monash was without doubt the most prominent Australian soldier of the war of 1914-1918 and when he died at his home, Toorak, Melbourne, 8 October 1931 he was given a state funeral by the city, and many fine eulogies were paid to him. He married in 1891 Victoria (died 1920), youngest daughter of Moton Moss, of Melbourne, and had a daughter.

Portraits of Monash by Sir John Longstaff (1918) and by James Quinn are at the Australian War Memorial at Canberra where there is also a bust by Paul Montford. At the National Gallery, Melbourne, there is a portrait by I. M. Cohen.

[*The Times*, 9 October 1931; *Argus* (Melbourne), 9 October 1931; Fred Johns, *An Australian Biographical Dictionary*, 1934; *Australian Encyclopædia*, 1926; *War Letters of General Monash*, edited by F. M. Cutlack, 1934; Sir J. E. Edmonds, (Official) *History of the Great War. Military Operations. France and Belgium, 1918*, vols. ii–v, 1937–1947; C. F. Aspinall-Oglander, (Official) *History of the Great War. Military Operations. Gallipoli*, vols. i and ii, 1929–1932; C. E. W. Bean, *Official History of Australia in the war of 1914-1918*, 12 vols., 1922–1942.]

C. V. OWEN.

MOND, SIR ROBERT LUDWIG (1867–1938), chemist, industrialist, and archaeologist, was born at Farnworth, near Widnes, Lancashire, 9 September 1867, the elder son of Ludwig Mond [q.v.], by his wife, Frida, only child of Adolf Meyer Loewenthal, of Cologne. His younger brother was Alfred Moritz Mond, first Lord Melchett [q.v.]. He was educated at Cheltenham College, Peterhouse, Cambridge, Zürich Polytechnicum, Edinburgh University, and at Glasgow University under Lord Kelvin.

In his early days Mond worked in his father's factory at Winnington, Cheshire,

and published papers (1922) describing his researches on metallic carbonyls, one of which, that of nickel, was used for the commercial separation of that metal by the Mond Nickel Company, of which he became chairman in 1919. He also took part in the investigations which led to improvements in the production of zinc by the electrolysis of zinc chloride. Although a patient and resourceful experimenter, his special contribution was not so much in discovery, as in making possible the work of those whom he selected to assist him. For a time, after his father's death in 1910, he applied scientific method to farming at Combe Bank, Sevenoaks, where he was a pioneer in the production of pure milk from a selected herd of dairy cows. To the equipment of his father's benefaction, the Davy-Faraday research laboratory of the Royal Institution, he gave much thought and was its honorary secretary for life, while to that institution he contributed large sums for its reconstruction in 1931.

As much at home in France as in Great Britain, Mond contributed largely towards the acquisition of the Maison de la Chimie in Paris for meetings of French chemical societies and for documentation of chemical literature. He regarded it as a focus for chemistry generally, and he gave a large sum to the funds of the National Council for Chemistry. He also supported the cause of a 'Chemistry House' in this country. The Norman Lockyer Observatory at Sidmouth also had his support by the gift of buildings and a photographic equatorial telescope. He also made large benefactions to the universities of Liverpool and Toronto.

For forty years Mond had an abiding interest in archaeology. As a worker in the field and as a generous supporter and organizer of expeditions and of the preservation of antiquities, he was responsible in many cases for the publication of results. Early in the century he explored the mortuary chapels of the nobles at Thebes, working personally at the digging for three winters with Professor Percy Edward Newberry, Howard Carter [q.v.], Arthur E. P. B. Weigall, (Sir) Alan Gardiner, and Ernest J. Mackay as colleagues. The Theban Necropolis was restored and protected at his expense and a catalogue published by him; the famous tomb of the vizier Ramose was cleared and described: while later, in 1926, Armant, the site of Harmonthis, was attacked. For the excavation of the burial-place of the sacred

Buchis Bulls on this site Mond supported a large staff, including Dr. H. Frankfort, Frederick William Green, and Oliver Myers. Detailed descriptions were published by Mond and Myers in *The Bucheum* (3 vols., 1934) and *The Cemeteries of Armant* (2 vols., 1937); sixty-nine scholars contributed to these works. In the Eastern and Libyan deserts Mond financed the work of exploration of which accounts were published (1937, 1938). He was also the chief financial supporter of the British School of Archaeology in Palestine, under Professor John Garstang, and he aided the work of (Professor) Dorothy Garrod in her exploration of the cave deposits of Mount Carmel, where valuable evidence of the antiquity of man in the Near East has been obtained. In all these enterprises to which he gave generous financial support Mond's chief interest was the academic and instructional aspect, leading to the advancement of learning. In his London house he fitted up a 'Pharaoh Room' to display treasures which he had acquired, but for the most part he gave these to museums and universities.

Mond received the honorary degree of LL.D. from the universities of Liverpool and Toronto; he was president of the Faraday Society and of the Société de Chimie Industrielle; he was knighted in 1932 and elected F.R.S. in 1938. He received the Messel medal in 1936. He was twice married: first, in 1898 to Helen Edith (died 1905), third daughter of Julius Levis, in whose memory he founded the Infants' Hospital, Vincent Square, and had two daughters; secondly, in 1922 to Marie Louise, daughter of Guillaume Jean Le Manach, of Belle-Isle-en-Terre, Brittany, and widow of Simon Guggenheim. He died in Paris 22 October 1938.

There is a full-length portrait of Mond by Sir F. O. Salisbury in the possession of Lady Mond at Belle-Isle-en-Terre; copies belong to his daughters. A marble bust by W. C. A. King also belongs to Lady Mond, and a full-length marble recumbent statue by A. Circuscu is at Belle-Isle-en-Terre.

[*The Times*, 24 October 1938; *Obituary Notices of Fellows of the Royal Society*, No. 7, January 1939 (portrait); *Nature*, 12 November 1938; *Journal* of the Society of Chemical Industry, vol. lvii, 1938.]

R. ROBERTSON.

MONRO, HAROLD EDWARD (1879–1932), poet, editor, and bookseller, was born at St. Gilles near Brussels 14 March 1879, of Scottish ancestry, the son of Edward William Monro, civil engineer, by his wife, Arabella Sophia Margary. His childhood was spent in Brussels and for some years he was bilingual. At the age of seven he was living at Wells, Somerset. He was educated at Radley (1892–1896), and spent a year in France between leaving school and going up to Gonville and Caius College, Cambridge, in 1898. In 1901 he was awarded a third class in the medieval and modern languages tripos, and in the summer of 1902, during a walking tour in the Harz Mountains, he met his first wife, Dorothy Elizabeth, daughter of Frederick Herbert Browne, schoolmaster, whom he married in 1903. He had intended to read for the bar, and passed the first part of the examination, but the prospect of marriage upset these plans, and he became a land agent and poultry farmer in Ireland, where he stayed for two or three years.

Returning to England Monro took a house near Haslemere, and founded the Samurai Press (Cranleigh, Surrey), from which were published volumes of poems by Mr. Wilfrid Wilson Gibson and John Drinkwater [q.v.], and a little book by Monro himself, *Proposals for a Voluntary Nobility* (1907). This publishing business was not a success, and about 1907 Monro went abroad to Florence and Switzerland (where he bought a mill but was driven out in a few weeks by floods). Between 1906 and 1911 he published three volumes of verse and two of prose, *The Evolution of the Soul* (1907) and *The Chronicle of a Pilgrimage* (a walk from Paris to Milan, 1910). In the autumn of 1911 he came to London, founding first the *Poetry Review*, which he edited during 1912, and next (in January 1913) the Poetry Bookshop in Devonshire Street, Holborn, which he later moved to Great Russell Street. This was not a commercial success, but enjoyed a great reputation, and Monro maintained it until his death. Here he started a series of readings by poets of their own works or of their favourite poets, and these continued up to the time of Monro's death, and a large number of the poets famous during those years took part in the readings. He also founded a quarterly journal called *Poetry and Drama* of which eight numbers appeared during 1913 and 1914. On the outbreak of war in August 1914 Monro became an officer in an anti-aircraft battery, but was later drafted for duty in the War Office.

In July 1919 Monro founded the

(*Monthly*) *Chapbook* and edited it until it came to an end in 1925. After 1911 he published four further volumes of poetry, a book on *Some Contemporary Poets* (1920), *One Day Awake* (a morality, 1922), and an anthology of twentieth-century poetry (1929). The first two of these books, his two magazines, and the Poetry Bookshop expressed his unselfish enthusiasm for poetry quite unlike his own, which Mr. T. S. Eliot has said 'will remain as one variety of the infinite number of possible expressions of tortured human consciousness . . . remain because . . . he has not simply done something better than anyone else, but done something that no one else has done at all'.

Monro met Alida Klementaski in March 1913. She worked with him in the Poetry Bookshop and in 1920 became his second wife, his first marriage, by which he had a son, having been dissolved in 1916. He was crippled by increasing ill health and pain in his last two years, and died at Broadstairs 16 March 1932.

A portrait of Monro by Jacob Kramer is reproduced as the frontispiece to his *Collected Poems* (1933).

[*The Collected Poems of Harold Monro*, edited by Alida Monro (with a biographical sketch by F. S. Flint, a critical note by T. S. Eliot, and a bibliography), 1933.]

FREDERICK PAGE.

MONTAGUE, FRANCIS CHARLES (1858–1935), historian, was born in London 31 August 1858, the eldest son of Francis Montague, of St. Margaret's, Twickenham, by his wife, Rosa McCabe, daughter of a Drogheda merchant; he was brother of C. E. Montague [q.v.]. He was a precocious child, being able, it was said, to read Greek at the age of eight. From University College School and University College, London, he went to Balliol College, Oxford, as an exhibitioner in 1875. After gaining a first class in classical moderations (1877) and in *literae humaniores* (1879) he became a prize-fellow of Oriel College in 1881. On the advice of Benjamin Jowett he declined an offer of a position as leader-writer on *The Times* and tried his fortune at the bar, to which he was called in 1883 by Lincoln's Inn. In 1891 he returned to Oxford and, although he never married, he was not again elected to a fellowship, but lived in a house of his own and did a considerable amount of teaching. He lectured on law and was later (1893–1927) lecturer in modern history at Oriel having charge for many

years of historical tuition there, and also taking part in the training of candidates for the Indian civil service (1892–1920). From 1893 to 1927 he was professor of history in University College, London, of which he had become a fellow in 1880: he travelled between Oxford and London by train to give his lectures.

For about twenty years Montague maintained a steady output of historical books, all of them judicious, accurate, and written in excellent English; but he was unfortunate in never having the literary success that he deserved. Besides reviews, an elementary text-book on English constitutional history, contributions to the *Cambridge Modern History*, and editions of Bentham's *Fragment on Government* (1891) and Macaulay's *Essays* (1903), he published an essay on *The Limits of Individual Liberty* (1885), a *Life of Sir Robert Peel* (1888), and volume vii (1603–1660) in Longman's *Political History of England* (1907). In 1930 he was elected an honorary fellow of Oriel. He died at Oxford 8 April 1935.

Montague was a man of wide reading and of distinguished taste in literature and the arts. There was much of the eighteenth century in his mind and outlook; he was a tolerant rationalist and a blameless epicurean. Short in stature and naturally shy with strangers, he seemed ill-fitted for his first profession, nor did he enjoy lecturing or, except with his best pupils, teaching. In conversation he had few equals. He spoke in well-formed sentences, often with an elegant levity, each point sharpened by his appropriate but sometimes unexpected choice of words. 'There are two things', he said, 'of which my knowledge is derived entirely from books: they are love and war.'

[*The Times*, 9 April 1935; personal knowledge.]   G. N. CLARK.

MONTEFIORE, CLAUDE JOSEPH GOLDSMID- (1858–1938), Jewish biblical scholar and philanthropist, was born in London 6 June 1858. He was the younger son of Nathaniel Mayer Montefiore, of London, by his wife, Emma, daughter of Sir Isaac Lyon Goldsmid, first baronet [q.v.]. He was great-nephew of Sir Moses Haim Montefiore, first baronet [q.v.], nephew of Anna Maria Goldsmid and of Sir Francis Henry Goldsmid [qq.v.], and great-grandson of Mayer Amschel de Rothschild. He assumed the additional surname of Goldsmid by letters patent in 1883.

Claude Montefiore was educated privately and at Balliol College, Oxford, where he came under the influence of the religious liberalism of Benjamin Jowett [q.v.] and obtained a first class in *literae humaniores* in 1881. In 1881–1882 he studied in Berlin at the Anstalt für Wissenschaft des Judentums. Here he met a learned Rumanian Jew, Solomon Schechter, whom he brought back to England as his tutor in rabbinic literature. Jowett and Schechter were largely responsible in determining Montefiore's mental outlook and scholarly pursuits.

Amply endowed with wealth, learning, and leisure, Montefiore used these freely in the service of the Anglo-Jewish community, in furthering both Jewish and non-Jewish educational ventures, and in promoting the cause of liberal reform within English Jewry. He helped to maintain the Cambridge lecturership in rabbinic studies, thus fostering the fruitful work of Solomon Schechter, Israel Abrahams, and H. M. J. Loewe. He was joint editor from 1888 to 1908 of the *Jewish Quarterly Review*, and during a long working life he produced a steady stream of books and articles inculcating his own liberal conceptions of Judaism and spreading among Christian readers a knowledge of the rabbinic writings and their bearing on the teachings of the Gospels and St. Paul: *Liberal Judaism* (1903), *The Synoptic Gospels* (2 vols., 1909, 2nd ed. 1927), *Some Elements of the Religious Teaching of Jesus* (Jowett lectures, 1910), *Outlines of Liberal Judaism* (1912, 2nd ed. 1923), *Judaism and St. Paul* (1914), *Rabbinic Literature and Gospel Teachings* (1930), and *A Rabbinic Anthology* (with H. M. J. Loewe, published posthumously 1938).

From 1888 onwards Montefiore was active as the joint-founder, inspiration, and mainstay of the Jewish Religious Union for the Advancement of Liberal Judaism and of the Liberal Jewish synagogue in London, of which he was president from 1910 until his death and where he frequently preached. His educational work included a conspicuous share in the affairs of the Froebel Society and Institute, the Anglo-Jewish Association, of which he was president from 1896 to 1921, and the University College of Southampton, of which he was president from 1915 to 1934.

Montefiore delivered the Hibbert lectures in 1892, published in the same year as *The Origin and Growth of Religion as illustrated by the Religion of the Ancient Hebrews*; he received the honorary degree of D.D. from the university of Manchester (1921) and that of D.Litt. from the university of Oxford (1927); and in 1930 he was awarded the British Academy medal for biblical studies.

Claude Montefiore's most distinctive contribution was in the field of New Testament scholarship. To him was due in great measure that sympathetic and constructive use of rabbinic material which characterized British and American students during the first half of the twentieth century.

Montefiore was twice married: first, in 1886 to Thérèse (died 1889), daughter of Lazar Schorstein, of Reuter's Agency, London, and had a son; secondly, in 1902 to Florence Fyfe Brereton (died December 1938), youngest daughter of Richard James Ward; she had been vice-principal of Girton College, Cambridge. He died in London 9 July 1938.

There is a portrait of Montefiore, painted by Oswald Birley in 1925, in the New Liberal Jewish synagogue, St. John's Wood Road; and, in the library of University College, Southampton, a portrait by (Sir) William Rothenstein (1928) and a bust by Benno Elkan (1934).

[*The Times*, 11 July 1938; *Liberal Jewish Monthly*, September 1938; Lucy Cohen, *Some Recollections of Claude Goldsmid Montefiore 1858–1938* (with a foreword by H. A. L. Fisher and a bibliography), 1940; F. C. Burkitt in *Speculum Religionis* (a volume of essays presented to Montefiore on the occasion of his seventieth birthday), 1929; private information.]   H. Danby.

MONTMORENCY, JAMES EDWARD GEOFFREY DE (1866–1934), legal scholar. [See De Montmorency.]

MOORE, GEORGE AUGUSTUS (1852–1933), novelist, was born at Moore Hall, Ballyglass, on the shores of Lough Carra, co. Mayo, 24 February 1852. His family, which had good but not indisputable assurance of descent from the author of *Utopia*, was certainly old and distinguished, a Captain George Moore, of Ballina, having been 'vice-admiral of Connaught' under William III. The novelist's great-grandfather made a fortune at the end of the eighteenth century and built Moore Hall, which was burned by republicans in 1923. His son George, who had a tendency towards literature, married Louisa Browne, granddaughter of John Browne, first Earl of Altamont, thus linking the Moores with the marquessate of Sligo. Louisa having been brought up by nuns, her eldest son, George Henry Moore [q.v.], was educated at Oscott College, Birmingham, and in 1851 added to the family's Roman Catholic connexions by marrying Mary, eldest daughter of Maurice Blake, of Ballinafad, co. Mayo. Their eldest son, the novelist, although sent to Oscott in his turn, never took kindly to the Roman Church and, in later life, emphatically repudiated it.

Moore's childhood and early youth, spent chiefly in Ireland, provided him with little education of the kind which he could assimilate, but the countryside, the tenants, the servants, and the racing stables yielded to his curious and observant mind a rich store of memories. His father died in 1870, and in 1873, as soon as Moore was of age, he set out for Paris, determined to paint. Finding that he had not talent enough, and having the courage to admit defeat, he put away his brush for ever and began to write. The growing embarrassment of his estate recalled him from France, and by early 1880 he was struggling in London to earn a living by his pen. Little had been visibly accomplished during his years in Paris, but he had been admitted to the society of great artists, had absorbed the influences of impressionism in painting and of naturalism in literature, and was bursting with what were then, in England, aesthetically revolutionary ideas. What he lacked was discipline, which he was temperamentally incapable of accepting from others, and this, with an industry that never failed him, he now began to apply to himself.

Moore's first novel, *A Modern Lover*, appeared in 1883. It had, as a story, originality and boldness, but the treatment was crude, the writing incorrect. It succeeded in drawing attention to itself, but scarcely prepared Moore's acquaintance, who appear still to have regarded him as slightly ridiculous, for the firmness and intelligence of *A Mummer's Wife* (1885), which, owing something to Zola and in its principal female character even more to Emma Bovary, has good claim to be considered the first realistic novel in English since Defoe. But it was not a masterpiece; the writing was still flawed; Moore was still serving his long apprenticeship. Although *A Drama in Muslin* (1886) and *Confessions of a Young Man* (1888) added to his reputation, and two volumes of essays established him as a challenging critic, the nine years following

A Mummer's Wife were marked by the failure of four novels excluded by him from his collected works, and *Esther Waters*, his earliest book unquestionably of the first rank, did not appear until 1894.

There followed another doubtful period of nine years. In *Evelyn Innes* (1898) and *Sister Teresa* (1901) there was a garishness, produced by a social phase in the artist's life, which caused him afterwards to reject them from the canon. At the turn of the century Moore appears to have been conscious of his art having run into a barren patch and of a need to seek new pastures. This and the influence of an old friend, Edward Martyn, and of W. B. Yeats [q.v.] led to his leaving England in 1901 and settling in Dublin, hot with the notion of becoming a leader of an Irish renaissance. Politics, clericalism, and Yeats cooled his enthusiasm for this idealistic project and he returned to London after ten years; but his Dublin period served his purpose. It released him, at any rate for a time, from the rich and fashionable, and took him back to his native country and the deep perceptions of childhood. A volume of Irish stories, *The Untilled Field* (1903), and a short novel, *The Lake* (1905), were the foundation of his later style, and the three great volumes of autobiography, *Hail and Farewell: Ave, Salve,* and *Vale*, published in 1911, 1912, and 1914, had their root in Ireland.

From 1911 until the end of his life Moore lived at 121 Ebury Street. He seldom read for the pleasure of reading or lived for the pleasure of living; for him literature and life existed chiefly for what he could wring from them for his own books. Although impressionable for a time by any person or any aspect of art that seemed likely to serve as steel to his flint, he was of an almost ferocious independence. As a man he was unique. He could be on occasions tempestuously intolerant, and yet he commanded an elaborate and charming courtesy. No one to him was anonymous. He would learn about football from footmen, and, with an easy familiarity that belonged to the eighteenth century, was interested in his servants' personal lives; and yet, if a housemaid was clumsy, he could, with eighteenth-century directness, throw his boots at her. A corresponding candour and intimacy mark his autobiographical writing. It is unlike any other because what he chiefly cared for in it was to tell a story that should conform to his aesthetic principles of story-telling, and because, having this single purpose, he treated himself and his friends with a ruthless impartiality of grace, ridicule, insight, and indiscretion. The same approach to criticism gave to his writing in this kind—even to the mature *Avowals* (1919) and *Conversations in Ebury Street* (1924)—a mingled freshness and rashness, an air of proceeding newly minted from a wilful but fearless mind. Moore was never 'safe', seldom sure of himself for long even when writing, and, after his work was published, always eager to improve it. Certain ideas came up for treatment again and again. One, the idea of celibacy, may be watched in the volumes of short stories, *Celibates* (1895), *In Single Strictness* (1922), and *Celibate Lives* (1927). Another, the life of St. Paul and the death of Jesus, may be traced from 1911 onward through several versions of his play *The Apostle* to its culmination in *The Brook Kerith* (1916). This novel stands, together with *Héloïse and Abelard* (1921), at the peak of Moore's achievement in fiction, although good critics have given almost as high a place to *A Story-Teller's Holiday* (1918). But this brilliant treatment of old Celtic legends has neither the depth nor the lovely elegance of the two epics; nor has *Aphrodite in Aulis* (1930) their strength.

It is likely that Moore will be remembered best for three achievements: for *Esther Waters*, which has more warmth and compassion than any other work of his; for *Hail and Farewell* because no other book resembles it; and for the structural firmness and supple narrative of *The Brook Kerith* and *Héloïse and Abelard*. In these two books he accomplished the purpose of his later life—to escape from the rubbed jargon and journalistic subjects of ordinary novels, to treat in prose an epic theme, and to discover a language and a rhythm, beautiful and dignified, which should yet preserve the illusion of a story melodiously spoken. Landor, Pater, and Balzac were his masters, and, when he wrote *The Lake* and *The Untilled Field*, Turgenev. Such masters and such single-mindedness were unlikely to make him popular in England between the wars of 1914 and 1939. He sought lucidity and 'the melodic line' at a time when that quest was little valued, and fashionable criticism was therefore inclined to over-stress his limitations. Of these, the chief were a lack of mystical intuition and an impatience of metaphysics. By gigantic labour he did much to overcome them, and of this *The Brook Kerith* is honourable proof. When he had a subject that avoided, or enabled him to overcome, these faults, he was unrivalled, and his translation of *The Pastoral Loves of Daphnis and Chloë* (1924) which could not tempt him to them, is, as prose, of rare beauty. In *Esther Waters*, the first realistic masterpiece in the language, and in *Héloïse and Abelard*, he twice did what none other had done in the English romantic medium, and it is improbable that these services will be forgotten.

In his middle life Moore was regarded by many as a shocking or scandalous writer, for he made no concessions to Victorian prejudice. In his later years controversy died down; the school of sociological criticism then fashionable passed him by in silence. To a great mass of novel readers he was unknown even by name, and he received no honour from the universities or from the state. Nevertheless, on his eightieth birthday (1932), a memorial was addressed to him in which a group of distinguished men hailed him as 'a master of English literature', and, so long as he lived, he had, after Hardy's death, a strong claim to be considered the chief novelist of his day, Kipling's greatness being different in kind. He died, unmarried, in London 21 January 1933.

There is a drawing of Moore as a young man by Edouard Manet; an oil-painting by Richard Sickert is in the Tate Gallery; and a pastel ('The Red Dressing-Gown') by Henry Tonks is in the National Portrait Gallery. He also figures in the groups 'Hommage à Manet' (1909) by Sir William Orpen in the Manchester Corporation Art Gallery and 'Saturday Evening at the Vale' by Tonks in the Tate Gallery.

[*The Times*, 23 January 1936; G. A. Moore, *Hail and Farewell*, 1911–1914; Joseph Hone, *The Life of George Moore* (with bibliography), 1936; Charles Morgan, *Epitaph on George Moore*, 1935; personal knowledge.]

CHARLES MORGAN.

MOORE, MARY (1861–1931), actress and theatre manager. [See WYNDHAM, MARY, LADY.]

MORGAN, CONWY LLOYD (1852–1936), comparative psychologist and philosopher, was born in London 6 February 1852, the second son of James Arthur Morgan, solicitor, by his wife, Mary Anderson. He received his early education at the Royal Grammar School, Guildford, his parents having moved to Weybridge a few years after his birth. Here the discipline was mainly classical, with some mathematics but no science. He was, however, early attracted to scientific studies and at the age of seventeen he entered the School of Mines in London with the intention of becoming a mining engineer, and became increasingly interested in the pursuit of pure science. On finishing his course, in order to postpone the final decision about a career, he accepted a post as private tutor which gave him the opportunity of extensive travel in North and South America. On his return he resumed his scientific studies. at the Royal College of Science, where he worked, among other teachers, under T. H. Huxley [q.v.], whose influence upon him was profound.

During this later period as a student Lloyd Morgan undertook a certain amount of lecturing and teaching in schools, but his first regular professional post was in South Africa at the Diocesan College at Rondebosch, where he was appointed in 1878 to teach not only the physical sciences in general, but also English literature and, for a time, constitutional history. In 1884 he returned to England to succeed W. J. Sollas [q.v.] in the chair of geology and zoology at University College, Bristol, where he was destined to pass the rest of his professional career. Three years later he was elected principal of the college, a post which in the early days of the university colleges was regarded as compatible with the continued tenure of a chair. But as the college developed the administrative work grew with it, and when in 1909 the university charter was granted, Lloyd Morgan only accepted the vice-chancellorship of the new university in order to give it a start. In the following year, by his own wish, he resigned and resumed the work of his chair, now renamed the chair of psychology and ethics, from which he retired in 1919. He lived on in Clifton for some years and even on one or two occasions returned to the university to give temporary assistance in the department of philosophy, as it had now become. He finally retired to Hastings, where he died 6 March 1936.

As principal, Lloyd Morgan's impressive appearance, his upright and kindly personality, and his intellectual eminence commanded universal respect and liking, particularly among those most closely associated with him, but he had little taste for administration and was not parti-cularly well equipped to handle some of the more assertive academic politicians of the time. On the other hand there can be no reservations about the value of his services to learning. His main interest in the early days of his tenure of the chair at Bristol was on the side of geology, but that soon gave place to what for many years occupied the centre of his attention, the study of animal and comparative psychology. His contributions in this field were pre-eminent. Indeed, it would not be too much to say that, in the English-speaking world at any rate, he was one of the chief founders of the scientific study of animal psychology. He was among the first to apply systematically the methods of scientific experiment to the subject. But, besides that, his work was noteworthy for its philosophical analysis and clarification of the concepts used and its establishment of sound general principles of explanation and interpretation. The results of his investigations appeared in a long series of publications of which the most important are *Animal Life and Intelligence* (1890–1891), *Habit and Instinct* (1896), *Animal Behaviour* (1900), and *Instinct and Experience* (1912). He was elected F.R.S. in 1899, being the first fellow to be elected for psychological work, and he received the honorary degree of D.Sc. from Bristol University in 1910.

In his later years Lloyd Morgan's interest turned more to general philosophical and metaphysical speculation. In this field he developed and gave his own interpretation to the idea of the emergence of novelty which was being discussed by Samuel Alexander [q.v.] and others at that period. His most important works in this field of investigation are his two courses of Gifford lectures delivered at St. Andrews University in 1922 and 1923 and published as *Emergent Evolution* (1923) and *Life, Mind and Spirit* (1926).

Lloyd Morgan married in 1878 Emily Charlotte, daughter of Henry William Maddock, vicar of All Saints' church, St. John's Wood, and had two sons, the elder of whom predeceased him.

A portrait of Lloyd Morgan, painted by Anning Bell in 1921, hangs in the university of Bristol.

[*Bristol Times and Mirror*, 5 December 1904; *British Journal of Psychology*, July 1936; *Obituary Notices of Fellows of the Royal Society*, No. 5, December 1936 (portrait); private information.]　　　G. C. FIELD.

MORGAN, Sir GILBERT THOMAS (1872–1940), chemist, was born at Essendon, Hertfordshire, 22 September 1872, the son of Thomas Morgan, butler, of Essendon, by his wife, Marie Louise Corday, of French-Swiss nationality. He was educated at the Central Foundation School, Cowper Street, London, whence he passed in 1886 to the Technical College, Finsbury, as a certified student, and under the stimulus of Silvanus Phillips Thompson [q.v.], John Perry, and Raphael Meldola he had by the time he left the college in 1889 prepared a series of new derivatives of benzeneazo-β-naphthol and assisted in the extraction of ceria from cerite. That his early ventures in research were on various small problems of an entirely different nature was afterwards to have a far-reaching effect, since he never specialized in any one branch of chemistry, but was at home in the organic, inorganic, and physical branches of that science.

Morgan left Finsbury in 1889 and was employed as assistant chemist for five years in the firm of Read Holliday & company, dye manufacturers, at Huddersfield (later British Dyes, Ltd.), whence, for the sake of the acquisition of knowledge, he gave up a post of great promise in order to perfect himself in the new ideas of Jacobus Hendricus van't Hoff, Svante A. Arrhenius, and Wilhelm Ostwald, and became at a mature age a student at the Royal College of Science. Nomination to the staff was the prelude to appointment in 1912 as professor of chemistry at the Royal College of Science in Dublin; in 1916 he returned to Finsbury as professor in succession to Meldola, and in 1919 he was elected Mason professor of chemistry at Birmingham University. Six years later he crowned his career as the first director of the Chemical Research Laboratory which at the instance of Sir Richard Threlfall [q.v.] had been set up at Teddington. In 1937 he retired, but not into inactivity, for he had become chairman of the research fund committee of the Institute of Brewing, and had entered actively on a new and large field of research when he died at Richmond, Surrey, 1 February 1940.

Throughout his life Morgan had two main interests in his work: chemical reactions under high pressures and synthetic resins. The first of these arose from his use of the autoclave at Huddersfield, where he produced the dyestuff Titan Como Blue which enjoyed a brief period of high popularity. The second also made its appearance towards the end of his period as a commercial chemist, for he made an observation which in other hands assumed unusual importance. By the condensation of phenol with formaldehyde he obtained a clear amber resin, possessing unexpected physical properties but useless as a source of dyes; the experiment was therefore laid aside and forgotten, until in 1906 the first of the Baekeland patents for the manufacture of synthetic plastics showed how narrowly Morgan had missed a fortune. Research into colours and the improvement of autoclaves together with co-ordinated compounds were still his chief studies at Dublin and Birmingham, and when he was appointed director of the laboratory at Teddington, it was these two subjects, together with the examination of low-temperature tars, that he made its basic studies. But no man was less of a specialist than Morgan, and when in 1916 he went back to Finsbury he was in a position to place a wide knowledge of organo-metallic compounds at the disposal of the Chemical Warfare Committee. It was the same at Teddington, where the value of the laboratory was soon recognized and additional long-range investigations were undertaken in all manner of micro-biological problems, including those of water pollution and the chemical constituents of wood smoke.

Morgan's publications are still regarded as authoritative; they include *Achievements of the British Chemical Industry in the last Twenty-five Years* (Cantor lectures, Royal Society of Arts, 1939), *British Chemical Industry. Its Rise and Development* (1938), *Inorganic Chemistry, a Survey of Modern Development* (1936), and *Organic Compounds of Arsenic and Antimony* (1918). He also contributed alone or in collaboration over 350 original scientific papers, always being careful to acknowledge the work of others; and from 1903 to 1906 he was editor of the *Journal* of the Chemical Society.

Many honours were bestowed upon Morgan: he was appointed O.B.E. in 1920 and knighted in 1936; he was elected F.R.S. in 1915, and he received honorary degrees from the universities of Dublin, St. Andrews, and Birmingham. In 1921 he was awarded the gold medal of the Worshipful Company of Dyers; in 1931 he was president of the Society of Chemical Industry, which in 1939 awarded him its medal; and of the Chemical Society in 1933. He married in 1912 Kathleen Nembhard (died 1944), daughter of George Desborough. He had no issue.

Morgan possessed an extraordinarily retentive memory and his love of work was matched by his tireless energy and his devotion to thoroughness and efficiency. He was one of the very few men who are at once a brilliant research chemist, an inspiring teacher, and a good organizer.

[*Obituary Notices of Fellows of the Royal Society*, No. 9, January 1941 (portrait); *Journal* of the Chemical Society, July 1941; *Nature*, 17 February 1940; *The Times*, 2 February 1940; Sir G. T. Morgan, 'Personal Reminiscences of Chemical Research', *Journal* of the Society of Chemical Industry, vol. lviii, 1939, and (obituary notice) vol. lix, 1940; *Journal* of the Institute of Brewing, April 1940 (portrait); personal knowledge.]

J. C. IRVINE.

MORISON, SIR THEODORE (1863–1936), educationist and writer, was born in Malta 9 May 1863, the only son of the author James Augustus Cotter Morison, and grandson of James Morison (1770–1840) [qq.v.]. His mother was Frances Adelaide, daughter of the London publisher George Virtue and sister of James Sprent Virtue [qq.v.]. He was educated at Westminster and at Trinity College, Cambridge, where he obtained a second class in the classical tripos of 1885. The following year he went to India as tutor to the young Maharajas of Chhaturpur and Charkhari, and in 1889 was appointed a professor at the Mohammedan Anglo-Oriental College at Aligarh. The aim of Sir Sayyid Ahmed Khan, founder of the college, was to reconcile orthodox Mohammedan opinion to western methods of education based upon Islamic culture and religion. The college, later the Moslem University of Aligarh, played a great part in the Moslem renaissance in India, and Morison had much to do with its development during his sixteen years at Aligarh, the last six of which were spent as principal. Lord Curzon recognized his influence by nominating him as an additional member of his legislative council for 1903–1904, and in 1904 Morison was chosen to preside over the All India Mohammedan Educational Conference.

In 1905 Morison returned to England, and at the end of the following year John (later Viscount) Morley, the secretary of state for India, appointed him one of his advisers on the Council of India, a position which Morison filled until 1916. In 1913 Lord Crewe chose him to be a member of the royal commission on the public services in India under the chairmanship of Sir John Poynder Dickson-Poynder, Lord

Islington [q.v.]. The commission completed its work in 1915, and Morison, although over fifty, took a commission in the Cambridgeshire Regiment (Territorial Force) and saw service as a political officer in East Africa from 1916 to 1918.

In 1919, after demobilization, Morison became principal of Armstrong College (later King's College), Newcastle-upon-Tyne, where he remained until 1929, serving as vice-chancellor of Durham University from 1924 to 1926. Under his control the college made marked progress, and he devoted his attention especially to the improvement of student amenities. In 1933, although nearly seventy, he became director of the British Institute in Paris. There he established personal relations with the university and in other ways improved the academic standing of the institute. He died in Paris 14 February 1936.

Morison married in 1895 Margaret (died 1931), daughter of Arthur Cohen [q.v.], barrister, and had a son and a daughter, who predeceased her father. He was appointed K.C.I.E. in 1910, K.C.S.I. in 1917 in recognition of his services on the Islington commission, and C.B.E. in 1918. He was an officer of the Legion of Honour and of the Belgian Order of Leopold, and in 1920 the university of Durham conferred upon him the honorary degree of D.C.L.

A portrait of Morison by T. B. Garvie (1930) hangs in the library of King's College, Newcastle-upon-Tyne.

[*The Times*, 15 February 1936; *The Northerner* (magazine of Armstrong College, Newcastle-upon-Tyne), November 1929; private information.] J. C. POWELL-PRICE.

MORRELL, LADY OTTOLINE VIOLET ANNE (1873–1938), was born in London 16 June 1873, the only daughter and youngest child of Lieutenant-General Arthur Cavendish-Bentinck, by his second wife, the youngest daughter of Henry Montague Browne, dean of Lismore, Augusta Mary Elizabeth, who was created Baroness Bolsover. On Ottoline's half-brother succeeding in 1879 to the dukedom of Portland, the other children of Arthur Cavendish-Bentinck were granted in 1880 the precedence of the children of a duke. She never went to school but was educated by her mother at Welbeck. Brilliant, idealistic, and eccentric, she early found herself in rebellion against the orthodox traditionalism of her home: and in 1902 she married Philip Edward Morrell (died 1943), liberal member of parliament for South Oxfordshire (1906–1910) and

Burnley (1910–1918), who shared her aesthetic tastes and 'advanced' views. They had a son, who died in infancy, and a daughter. The Morrells settled in London where Lady Ottoline soon found her true *métier* as the centre and patroness of a bohemian and intellectual circle which was to include some of the most distinguished artists and writers of the age, notably Mr. Bertrand (afterwards third Earl) Russell, D. H. Lawrence [q.v.], W. B. Yeats [q.v.], Mr. Walter de la Mare, Mr. T. S. Eliot, Mr. Augustus John, Mr. Henry Lamb, (Giles) Lytton Strachey [q.v.], Virginia Woolf, Mr. Aldous Huxley, and Mr. Siegfried Sassoon. In 1913 the Morrells left London for Garsington Manor, Oxfordshire, where Lady Ottoline's social activities continued until they were abruptly broken into by the war of 1914–1918. Both she and Morrell were strong pacificists, and made their house a refuge for conscientious objectors, whom they generously befriended. After the war the circle revived to include new generations of genius, first at Garsington and after 1924 at 10 Gower Street, London, where Lady Ottoline lived until her death at Tunbridge Wells 21 April 1938. She was a character of Elizabethan extravagance and force, at once mystical and possessive, quixotic and tempestuous; with the result that those friendships in which her nature found fulfilment ended sometimes in violent quarrels. But she was a figure of the first importance in the literary and artistic history of her time. She did much to help her protégés, whose gifts she was often the first person to recognize: in the lives of several she played a crucial and dramatic role: and, indeed, her own personality was, in its way, a considerable work of art, expressing alike in her conversation, her dress, and the decoration of her houses, a fantastic, individual, and creative imagination.

There are portraits of Lady Ottoline (as a child, with her mother) by Alessandro Ossani (1875), by Violet, Duchess of Rutland (1883), and by James Sant (1883) in the possession of her daughter, Mrs. Vinogradoff; and another, by Jean Edouard Lacretelle (1879), is at Welbeck. A portrait and a drawing of her as a woman, by Augustus John, also belong to her daughter; and another, by Henry Lamb, is in the possession of Viscount Hambleden.

[Personal knowledge.]   DAVID CECIL.

MORRIS, EDWARD PATRICK, first BARON MORRIS, of St. John's and of the City of Waterford (1859–1935), premier of Newfoundland, was born at St. John's, Newfoundland, 8 May 1859, the third son of Edward Morris, of Waterford, Ireland, and later keeper of the poorhouse at St. John's, by his wife, Catherine, daughter of the Rev. John Fitzgerald, of Tipperary. Morris was a Roman Catholic and was educated first at St. Bonaventure's College in St. John's, and thereafter at the university of Ottawa. He entered upon the profession of the law, being admitted to the Newfoundland bar in 1885, taking silk there in 1896. But his life's work lay in politics. In the same year that he was called to the bar, he was elected at the age of twenty-six to the House of Assembly as liberal member for St. John's West, and he held the seat until 1919, that is, throughout his career. He first obtained office in 1889, at the age of thirty, when he entered the Cabinet of Sir William Whiteway [q.v.] as minister without portfolio, and was acting attorney-general from 1890 to 1892 and again in 1895.

In the years of Morris's political career Newfoundland had a stormy and troublesome history, and he was associated prominently with most of her critical experiences. In 1895, as a result of the disastrous fire in St. John's of 1892, the bad fishery season of 1893, and the banking collapse of 1894, negotiations were opened with Canada to discuss the terms upon which Newfoundland might enter the Dominion. Morris was appointed one of the delegates, being associated on this occasion, as upon others, with (Sir) Robert Bond [q.v.]. Morris was ready to be convinced that Newfoundland should join the federation, but the Canadian terms were not generous and there was strong opposition in Newfoundland, and especially in his own constituency, against union. In the result the negotiations were abandoned. In 1898 Morris, then in opposition, played a decisive part in the acceptance of the 'Reid contract'. The government of Sir James Winter [q.v.], which had assumed office on the defeat of Whiteway in 1897, signed a contract with (Sir) Robert Reid [q.v.], which virtually sold all the colony's means of communication to Reid. Bond strenuously opposed the contract, but Morris broke with his party and, taking seven others with him, assisted the passage of the measure.

From 1898 to 1900 Morris led a group called the independent liberal party. In 1900 internal dissensions led to the defeat of Winter's government. Bond took office and formed a coalition with Morris, who now supported a revision of the Reid contract. Bond remained premier until 1909 and Morris held office in his Cabinet until 1907, being attorney-general and minister of justice from 1902. He was associated with Bond as a delegate to the Colonial Office in 1901 (as he had been in 1897) to represent Newfoundland's interests in the negotiations with France on the difficult question of French fishing-rights on certain specified coasts of the colony. The negotiations broke down and a settlement had to await the conclusion of the *entente cordiale* in 1904. He was counsel for the British government in the North Atlantic fisheries dispute conducted at The Hague in 1910.

In 1907 Morris, who had been knighted in 1904, resigned from the Bond Cabinet owing to a disagreement with the premier on a trifling point, and in 1908 became leader of a group known as the people's party. But in March 1909 he became premier, leading a coalition of the liberals who had seceded with him and the conservative party, which he had opposed so long, under the name of the 'people's' party, and at a general election in May, following upon a period of extraordinary confusion and deadlock in the House of Assembly, he was well established in office. He remained premier continuously for nearly nine years. Old-age pensions were introduced by his government, the expansion of education and of agriculture was stimulated, and considerable railway development—later to prove a financial burden—was undertaken. He represented Newfoundland at the Imperial Defence Conference of 1909 and at the Imperial Conference and the coronation in 1911. But it was in the war of 1914–1918 that he made his greatest contribution. He was a leading figure in the movement which led to the organization of the Royal Newfoundland Regiment and the enlistment of Newfoundlanders in the Royal Navy. He brought Newfoundland prominently into the councils of the Empire, representing her at the Imperial War Conference of 1917 and acting as a member of the Imperial War Cabinet from 1916 to 1917. He was thus instrumental in leading Newfoundland forward to Dominion status, in association with the other nations of the British Commonwealth. In 1917 Morris reconstructed his government and formed a coalition to include representatives of the liberal opposition. Then

at the end of the year he decided to resign, and in January 1918 he was succeeded as premier by (Sir) William Lloyd, the liberal leader. In the same month he was raised to the peerage—a rare distinction for a Dominion statesman—as Baron Morris, of St. John's and of the City of Waterford, 'for his long and distinguished services to the Empire'.

On his retirement Lord Morris lived in England and took an active interest in imperial affairs and philanthropic institutions. He had found time while in office to edit (1897–1905) the *Newfoundland Law Reports* for the periods 1817–1828 and 1864–1903. He was sworn of the Privy Council and received honorary degrees from the universities of Oxford, Cambridge, Glasgow, and Edinburgh in 1911, and was appointed K.C.M.G. in 1913; he was an honorary freeman of London, Edinburgh, Glasgow, Manchester, and Bristol. He was a man of great vigour, a forceful and convincing speaker, of powerful physique, and of considerable personal charm. He was a staunch advocate of the rights of Newfoundland and at the same time an ardent supporter of the British Empire. He would be regarded by many as the greatest in the line of Newfoundland premiers; he is rivalled only by Bond.

Morris married in 1901 Isobel Langrishe (died 1934), daughter of the Rev. William Wellman Le Gallais, of Jersey and Newfoundland, and widow of James P. Fox. He died in London 24 October 1935, and was succeeded as second baron by his only child, Michael William (born 1903).

A portrait of Morris is included in Sir James Guthrie's picture, 'Some Statesmen of the Great War', painted in 1921–1930, in the National Portrait Gallery.

[*The Times*, 25 October 1935; *Newfoundland Royal Commission Report, 1933,* 1933; *Cambridge History of the British Empire,* vol. vi, 1930; private information.]

K. C. WHEARE.

MOTT, SIR BASIL, first baronet (1859–1938), civil engineer, was born at Leicester 16 September 1859, the youngest son of Frederick Thompson Mott, of Birstall Hill, near Leicester, by his first wife, Elizabeth Ann, daughter of Isaac Dobell. He was educated at Leicester Grammar School, the International College at Isleworth, at Solothurn in Switzerland, and the Royal School of Mines, South Kensington, where he won the Murchison medal in 1879. After some years as a mining engineer he became assistant and then partner to James Henry Greathead and at the age of twenty-five was appointed resident engineer for the construction of the City and South London Railway. The work was of a revolutionary nature, this being the first deep-level tube to be constructed and the first occasion on which the Greathead shield was used on a large scale. The line, from the Monument to Stockwell, was opened by the Prince of Wales in 1890. Electric traction was then in its infancy and Mott assumed responsibility for the running of the line until the many unforeseen difficulties of operation had been overcome. Some years later (in 1896) he entered into partnership with Sir Benjamin Baker [q.v.] and with him was responsible for the construction of the second deep-level tube, the Central London Railway, from the Bank to Shepherd's Bush, which was opened in 1900.

After Baker's death in 1907, Mott carried on his own practice as consulting engineer with his partners David Hay, Mr. David Anderson, and later Mr. G. L. Groves. He visited the United States of America and was responsible for the introduction of escalators into Great Britain and, as consulting engineer to the London Passenger Transport Board, for many large constructional works and extensions to the London tube railways.

Mott was associated also with many important bridge schemes; among others the widening of Blackfriars bridge, undertaken with Baker and carried out after the latter's death, the widening of Kingston and the reconstruction of Southwark bridges, the construction of Queensferry bridge at Chester, and the single-span high-level road bridge at Newcastle-upon-Tyne. During the war of 1914–1918 Mott served on several government committees, visiting France and India and advising on various defence schemes.

After the war Mott was consulted by the Ministry of Transport and made reports on the proposed Charing Cross bridge, road bridges over the Forth and the Tay, the Channel tunnel, and other important schemes. He was a member of the Severn Barrage Committee and of the government Economic Advisory Committee. In 1925 there was considerable anxiety as to the safety of St. Paul's Cathedral and Mott was appointed chairman of the works committee of engineers and architects entrusted with the preservation of the fabric; the method which

was adopted, that of grouting the piers, aroused some controversy at the time but proved entirely successful.

One of the most important projects for which Mott was primarily responsible was the Mersey road tunnel connecting Liverpool and Birkenhead; ventilated for petrol-driven traffic, it is in length and diameter the largest sub-aqueous tunnel in the world. It was opened by King George V in 1934.

Mott became a member of the Institution of Civil Engineers in 1895, and was elected vice-president in 1920 and president in 1924. He was appointed C.B. in 1918, created a baronet in 1930, and elected F.R.S. in 1932. He was an associate of the Royal School of Mines, a fellow of the Imperial College of Science and Technology, and a member of the Société des Ingénieurs Civils de France.

Mott married in 1887 Florence Harmar (died 1923), daughter of William Parker, and had two sons. He died in London 7 September 1938, and was succeeded as second baronet by his elder son, Adrian Spear (born 1889).

A portrait of Mott by Stanhope Forbes is in the possession of the Institution of Civil Engineers.

[*The Times*, 8 September 1938; *Obituary Notices of Fellows of the Royal Society*, No. 8, January 1940 (portrait); *Journal* of the Institution of Civil Engineers, vol. x, 1938; office records; personal knowledge.]

DAVID ANDERSON.

MOUNT TEMPLE, BARON (1867–1938), politician. [See ASHLEY, WILFRED WILLIAM.]

MOYNIHAN, BERKELEY GEORGE ANDREW, first BARON MOYNIHAN, of Leeds (1865–1936), surgeon, was born in Malta 2 October 1865, the only son, with two elder sisters, of Captain Andrew Moynihan, V.C., of the 90th Regiment, afterwards of the 8th Foot (the King's Regiment), by his wife, Ellen Anne, younger daughter of Thomas Parkin, cabinet-maker, of Hurst, near Ashton-under-Lyne. His father, who was Irish by descent, died of Malta fever, and his mother settled at Leeds with her sister, the wife of Police-Sergeant Alfred Ball.

Moynihan was educated at Christ's Hospital (1875–1881) and at the Royal Naval School, New Cross (1881–1883), where his chief success was at swimming, which remained his favourite recreation. He was a boy of spirit and ability, but made no mark at school. On his eighteenth birthday he entered the Leeds Medical School, then at the Yorkshire College, intending to become an army doctor. He soon discovered an aptitude for medicine and worked unremittingly with brilliant success. He was dresser to Arthur Fergusson McGill, who awakened his interest in surgery, and he qualified M.B. (London) in 1887. He was then appointed house-surgeon (1887–1889) to (Sir) William Mayo Robson at the Leeds General Infirmary. During the winter of 1889 he worked in Berlin and in April 1890 became resident surgical officer at the Leeds General Infirmary. There he attracted the attention of Thomas Richard Jessop, the leading practitioner and surgeon in the district. He was admitted F.R.C.S. (England) in 1890 by examination and in 1893 he graduated M.S. (London) with a gold medal. He set up as a consultant in Leeds in 1893, acting also as private assistant to Jessop. A vacancy occurred on the infirmary staff in 1894, but Moynihan was not elected. He was, however, appointed demonstrator in anatomy at the Yorkshire College and in 1909 became professor of clinical surgery in the university of Leeds. In 1896 he was elected assistant surgeon to the infirmary, becoming surgeon in 1906 and consulting surgeon on retirement in 1926.

Between 1896 and 1914 Moynihan gained a reputation as the most accomplished surgeon in England, and among the greatest of all surgeons. He aimed at perfection of technique, developing his unrivalled dexterity to assure the soundest, rather than the most brilliant work, although brilliance was his native gift. He also gave much thought to medical care before and after operation, 'making the patient safe for surgery'. In particular he practised and preached gentleness in manipulation. His work became widely known through the consummate showmanship with which he expounded it to visitors, until his clinic became an essential place of pilgrimage for British and American surgeons. His practice grew wide but he made time, by early rising, to write several important books, as well as numerous articles. He collaborated with Mayo Robson in *Diseases of the Stomach and their Surgical Treatment* (1901), and *Diseases of the Pancreas and their Surgical Treatment* (1902). He had lectured at the Royal College of Surgeons in 1899, but his pre-eminence was hardly recognized in England when in May 1903 he was invited by the American Surgical Association to read a paper at its meeting at Philadelphia. Here he formed lasting friendships with leading surgeons, especially William J. and Charles H. Mayo and George W. Crile. He had already made innovations towards absolute asepsis in the 'ritual' of his operating theatre and introduced from America the use of rubber gloves, which after some ridicule became universally worn by surgeons. In 1903 appeared *Surgical Treatment of Gastric and Duodenal Ulcers* and in 1904 *Gallstones and their Surgical Treatment*, which became a classic. His surgical doctrine was admirably set out in *Abdominal Operations*, published in America in 1905; he revised its fourth edition in 1926. Throughout this period Moynihan was studying the differential diagnosis of peptic ulcers. He gradually satisfied himself, by correlation of symptoms with pathologic changes found at operation, of the precise syndrome of the duodenal ulcer. His book *Duodenal Ulcer* (1910) established his reputation as a clinical scientist. His chain of reasoned observation and its conclusion have been compared to the discovery of a new star.

Moynihan was a dominant individualist with an eager determination to achieve his projects for his profession. In 1909 he formed a club for visiting surgical clinics; it proved successful and assumed the name 'Chirurgical Club', which in 1929 was altered to 'Moynihan Chirurgical Club'. He instigated the publication of the *British Journal of Surgery* in 1913; and he promoted the Association of Surgeons of Great Britain and Ireland, formed in 1920, with equal success.

Moynihan served in France from 1914 to 1915 as a consulting surgeon, rising to the rank of major-general in the Army Medical Service. Later he was chairman of the Council of Consultants (1916–1919) and a member of the Army Medical Advisory Board (1917–1936). In October 1917 he spent three weeks in America; he was admitted an honorary fellow of the American College of Surgeons and achieved a remarkable success as an orator at a series of patriotic meetings. He had a beautiful voice and was a master of clear, rhetorical English. He was again in America in 1920 to give the first J. B. Murphy lecture to the American College of Surgeons, at Montreal, in honour of the man whom he called the greatest surgeon of all time, and with whom he shared many characteristics.

Moynihan was elected to the council of the Royal College of Surgeons in 1912 and was president in 1926; his six years' rule gave the college new life and prestige. There in 1920 he gave the Bradshaw lecture on 'The Spleen and some of its Diseases' and in 1927 the Hunterian oration, speaking of the achievements of Hunter and Lister, who had based their surgery on physiological principles, an ideal which Moynihan had made familiar as 'the pathology of the living'. He insisted that medical science could be advanced by observation of disease in the operating theatre better than by post-mortem dissection. He gave the Romanes lecture at Oxford on 'The Advance of Medicine' in 1932.

He was made an honorary LL.D. of Leeds University in 1924 and was given the freedom of the city in 1926. He received honorary degrees from fourteen universities in many parts of the world.

Moynihan was knighted in 1912; appointed C.B. in 1917 and K.C.M.G. in 1918 and created a baronet in 1922, he was raised to the peerage as Baron Moynihan, of Leeds, in 1929. His oratory was less successful in the House of Lords than outside, but his influence secured the defeat of the registration of osteopaths bill in 1935. He was less welcome when he advocated the legalization of euthanasia.

Moynihan married in 1895 Isabella Wellesley, second daughter of Thomas Richard Jessop, F.R.C.S., of Leeds. Of this singularly happy marriage there were born a son and two daughters. He died of shock at Carr Manor, Meanwood, Leeds, his home since 1914, 7 September 1936, seven days after the death of Lady Moynihan. A burial in Westminster Abbey was offered, but since he had identified his career with Leeds he was buried there at Lawnswood cemetery. He was succeeded as second baron by his son, Patrick Berkeley (born 1906).

Moynihan was at all times self-aware and even histrionic; he was not impervious to flattery and latterly showed faults of judgement, probably incipient symptoms of the cerebral failure which caused his sudden death. He fulfilled his own description of the ideal surgeon: 'a handsome man of distinguished presence, a man of wide knowledge and general culture, a man of great technical skill and sound judgement, and a man of compassionate heart'. He stood six feet high and was broad in proportion; until middle life his hair was fiery red; his hands were blunt and muscular.

A portrait of Moynihan by Sir Hubert von Herkomer (1912) is in the possession of his family; one by Richard Jack (1927) is at the General Infirmary, Leeds, with a copy by the artist at the Royal College of Surgeons (reproduced in colour in the *British Journal of Surgery*, July 1936). A marble bust by Sir W. Reid Dick is at the infirmary (reproduced in the *British Medical Journal*, 1940, vol. i, p. 185), and another, by F. J. Wilcoxson, is at the Royal College of Surgeons; the Leeds Medical School has a bronze bust by the latter and a bronze cast of his hands.

[*The Times*, 8 September 1936; Donald Bateman, *Berkeley Moynihan, Surgeon*, 1940; *British Medical Journal*, 1940, vol. i, pp. 601 and 649; *University of Leeds Medical Society Magazine*, vol. vii, 1937 (bibliography); personal knowledge.]

W. R. LE FANU.

MUIRHEAD, JOHN HENRY (1855–1940), philosopher, the third son of John William Muirhead, writer to the signet, of Glasgow, by his wife, Mary Burns (who claimed a connexion with Susan Ferrier, the novelist, q.v.), was born at Glasgow 28 April 1855. Educated at the Glasgow Academy, he proceeded to the University where he graduated M.A. in 1875. The year previously he had won a Snell exhibition at Balliol College, Oxford, to which he went up in Trinity Term 1875. Amongst his intimate friends and contemporaries were (Sir) Henry Jones, J. S. Mackenzie [qq.v.], John MacCunn, and W. P. Ker [q.v.]. After obtaining a first class in classical moderations (1877) he was, to the surprise of the college, placed in the second class in *literae humaniores* in 1879. He was *proxime accessit* for the Gaisford prize for Greek prose and obtained the Chancellor's Latin essay prize in 1881. Failing to obtain a fellowship, he became assistant in Latin to Professor George Gilbert Ramsay at Glasgow University from 1879 to 1885, when he left to study philosophy and theology at Manchester New College in London, and thenceforward philosophy was the subject to which he devoted himself until his death.

In 1888 Muirhead was appointed lecturer in mental and moral science at the Royal Holloway College; he also lectured for Bedford College and the London Society for the Extension of University Teaching. In the same year he became editor of the 'Library of Philosophy', a position which he held until his death. In 1891 he helped James Bonar and others to found the Ethical Society, and in 1892 published his best known text-book, *The Elements of Ethics*, which found a wide public. He also edited the 'Ethical Library'. In 1896 he was appointed professor of philosophy and political economy in the Mason College at Birmingham. After the conversion of the college into the university of Birmingham (1900), political economy was, to Muirhead's relief, constituted as a separate chair, and he retained the chair of philosophy until his retirement in 1922.

Muirhead's mental and physical vigour continued unimpaired, and in two visits to the United States of America (1923 and 1925–1928) he held special positions as a lecturer and visiting professor in the universities of California (Berkeley and Los Angeles). Returning to Great Britain in 1929, he devoted himself to editing the 'Library of Philosophy', acting as chairman of the council of the newly founded British Institute of Philosophy, and maintaining an active interest in the modern developments of philosophy at home, on the continent, and in the United States. He was elected a fellow of the British Academy in 1931.

Muirhead was far from being simply a stimulating teacher of philosophy. Always a 'social reformer' in many spheres of civic endeavour, at Birmingham he played an important part in converting the Mason College into the first unitary civic university, and for twenty-six years was even more influential in the life of the city than in that of the classroom and senate. Here, as elsewhere, his simplicity of character, his devotion to realizing in action high ethical principles, his sympathy with thinkers and systems opposed to his own views, and his determination to find a common denominator underlying apparent antagonisms, earned for him in all quarters a deep respect and warm affection, increased by his work as editor of the 'Library of Philosophy' in which he introduced to English readers many notable works by the prominent leaders of every school of thought, British, continental, and American.

Philosophically, as a young man he had been deeply influenced by T. H. Green and R. L. Nettleship [qq.v.], as also by Edward Caird (q.v., whose life he wrote in 1921 in collaboration with his friend Sir Henry Jones), and later by F. H. Bradley and Bernard Bosanquet [qq.v.], so that, although his chief interest was ethics, in which his main problem was to state the

relations between the end or good and the rule or obligation for achieving it (in 1932 he published *Rule and End in Morals*), he continued to be throughout his career a prominent representative of the British school of idealists. This general attitude is maintained particularly in *Coleridge as Philosopher* (1930) which is the best account of Coleridge's philosophy with emphasis on the Platonic elements in it, linking up the exposition with *The Platonic Tradition in Anglo-Saxon Philosophy* (1931) which leads from the Platonists of the seventeenth century to Muirhead's own philosophical position and contains a study of Bradley's metaphysics.

Muirhead was twice married: first, in 1892 to Mary Talbot (died 1922), daughter of the Rev. Gilbert Innes Wallas, and sister of Graham Wallas [q.v.]; secondly, in 1927 to Pauline, daughter of George Bailey, who survived him. There was no issue from either marriage. He died at Rotherfield, Sussex, 24 May 1940, with mental powers unabated.

[*The Times*, 27 May 1940; Sir C. G. Robertson and Sir W. D. Ross, *John Henry Muirhead, 1855–1940* in *Proceedings* of the British Academy, vol. xxvi, 1940 (with bibliography and a portrait); private information; personal knowledge.]

CHARLES GRANT ROBERTSON.

MUNRO-FERGUSON, RONALD CRAUFORD, VISCOUNT NOVAR (1860–1934), politician. [See FERGUSON.]

MURISON, ALEXANDER FALCONER (1847–1934), jurist and author, was born at Walhowe, in the parish of Deer, Aberdeenshire, 3 March 1847, the eldest of the four sons of Alexander Murison, a crofter of Walhowe, by his wife, Elspeth, daughter of William Murison, a crofter of Bridge-foot, near Fraserburgh, Aberdeenshire. He was proud to recall that he had once acted as a herd-boy on his native hills. In his autobiography, written at the age of eighty-six, he has vividly described the struggles to obtain for him a better education than that afforded by village schools. Having won a bursary at Aberdeen Grammar School, he showed his gift for languages by winning school prizes for Latin and Greek, gaining the first bursary at Aberdeen University, and graduating with first class honours in classics. He then returned to his old school as head English master (1869–1877), and, as at London and Oxford, his passion for education and scholarship soon proved him to be an inspiring teacher. He then decided on the venture of going to London, where he was called to the bar by the Middle Temple in 1881 and supported himself by teaching and by journalism, practising before the Privy Council and the Chancery division. In 1883 he succeeded W. A. Hunter [q.v.], to whom he owed much, as professor of Roman law; in 1901 he was appointed professor of jurisprudence; and in 1913 deputy professor of Roman-Dutch law. These 'part-time' posts at University College, London, he held concurrently until he retired in 1925, having been in the service of the college as professor for forty-two years, during which he had also been dean of the faculty of laws (1912–1924), and a member of the senate of the university of London (1921–1924). In 1915 he was appointed deputy reader in Roman law at Oxford, and in 1916 deputy professor to Henry Goudy, on whose retirement from the regius chair of civil law in 1919 he was probably precluded by his advanced age from the succession, to which his friends, knowing his learning and admiring the moral greatness of his character, considered him fully entitled. In 1924 he was appointed K.C. by Lord Chancellor Haldane.

During the forty-two years in which he held office in London, Murison set himself the stupendous task of collating the codices of the text of Justinian's *Institutes*, and pursuit of this aim led him to all the great law libraries of Europe, always travelling third class (and on one occasion in a cattle-truck) because of the meagreness of his stipendiary pittance and the paucity of his private means. But his immense erudition, his mastery of practically every European language except Turkish, his accomplishment as a Latin, Greek, and Hebrew scholar, combined with his engaging modesty and charm, made him friends everywhere among foreign jurists, and acquired for him an international reputation for scholarship. Unfortunately the colossal undertaking was never completed, and the results remain in manuscript in voluminous notebooks in the library of University College, London. Almost the only published contribution in English made by Murison on the civil law is an historical introduction on 'The External History of Roman Law' prefixed to the second edition (1885) of Hunter's *Roman Law*. As his poverty diverted him from pursuing the success that might have been his at the bar, by enticing him into the production of educational text-books

and journalism (he joined the staff of the *Daily Chronicle* in early days and from 1902 to 1912 was editor of the *Educational Times*), so also the versatility of his mind led him to play truant to the cause of jurisprudence, for he translated the whole of Horace (1931) and of Pindar (1933) into verse, Virgil's *Bucolics and Georgics* (1932), and the first twelve books of the *Iliad* (1933) into English hexameters, and Schiller's *Wallenstein* (1931) into English verse with the original metres. A translation of Books xiii to xix of the *Iliad* remains in manuscript. In Italy, where his scholarship was highly esteemed, he published a characteristic treatise, *Il diritto nei poeti Latini* (1935) which was read at the International Congress of Roman Law held in Rome in 1933. His intellectual vigour remained unimpaired to the last.

The honorary degree of LL.D. was conferred upon Murison in 1893 by the university of Aberdeen, for the lord rectorship of which he stood against Lord Huntly in 1896 and was but narrowly beaten. In politics an ardent liberal, he unsuccessfully contested, at four general elections, in 1900, 1906, and 1910, three conservative strongholds, the Bridgeton division of Glasgow, the universities of Glasgow and Aberdeen, and, twice, the Central division of Glasgow. He married in 1870 Elizabeth (died 1924), elder daughter of William Logan, shopkeeper, of Fetterangus, Aberdeenshire, and had two sons; the younger, Sir (James) William Murison (died 1945), was sometime chief justice of Zanzibar and of the Straits Settlements. He himself died at Clapham Common 8 June 1934.

[A. F. Murison, *Memoirs of 88 Years* (1847–1934), edited by A. L. Murison and Sir J. W. Murison, privately printed 1935 (bibliography and portraits); personal knowledge.]

J. H. MORGAN.

MURRAY, SIR GEORGE HERBERT (1849–1936), civil servant, born at Southfleet, Kent, 27 September 1849, was the eldest son of George Edward Murray, fellow of All Souls College, Oxford, and rector of Southfleet, by his wife, Penelope Frances Elizabeth Pemberton, youngest daughter of Brigadier-General John Austin. He was great-grandson of Lord George Murray, bishop of St. David's [q.v.], second son of John, third Duke of Atholl [q.v.]. He was heir-presumptive to the dukedom from 1865 to 1871 and second heir-presumptive at the time of his death. Educated at Harrow and Christ

Church, Oxford, he obtained his degree in the school of *literae humaniores* in 1872, and entered the Foreign Office the next year under the old system of limited competition after nomination by the secretary of state, but he was transferred to the Treasury in 1880, and appointed a second class clerk in the department of the auditor of the civil list. Murray's services were utilized for several royal commissions: in 1886 he was secretary to the royal commission on the depression of trade, in 1887 to the royal commission on gold and silver; and in 1889 to the Western Highlands and Islands of Scotland commission, receiving high praise for his work. He was private secretary to the first lord of the Treasury (Mr. Gladstone) from August 1892 to March 1894, when the new first lord (Lord Rosebery) gave him the same appointment. In 1897 he was appointed chairman of the Board of Inland Revenue; in 1899 he was transferred to the Post Office as secretary; and in 1903, on the retirement of Sir Francis Mowatt, he was appointed permanent administrative secretary in conjunction with Sir Edward Walter Hamilton [q.v.], permanent financial secretary. On Hamilton's retirement in 1907 Murray became sole permanent secretary, and in 1909 auditor of the civil list. He retired from the civil service in 1911. He was appointed K.C.B. in 1899, G.C.B. in 1908, and G.C.V.O. in 1920, having been sworn of the Privy Council in 1910.

Murray was an excellent civil servant of the old type. The Treasury minute on his retirement recorded 'My Lords' expression of their gratitude' for 'his indefatigable industry, his quick and acute perception, his complete mastery of the most complex administrative problems, and his exceptional powers of lucid and pointed expression' which 'presented a combination of qualities rarely found in union, and, in his case, employed with single-minded devotion in the service of the State'. He was a man of great physical and constitutional strength which he was able to maintain in spite of his neglect of the usual methods of exercise. Although he was among the last of the generation which lunched not at all or on 'a biscuit and a glass of sherry', he enjoyed the good things of life and was a connoisseur of food, wine, and cigars. For many years he was a member of Grillions, The Club, and the Society of Dilettanti, and was a regular attendant at their dinners. He was a familiar figure at Brooks's, where he was for long chairman of the library committee. After his retirement the government made use of his services on several committees; and on the outbreak of war in 1914 he took a leading part in the management of the Prince of Wales's Fund. In 1915 he was chairman of the committee on the employment of soldiers and sailors disabled in the war. He also held directorships in several important companies, notably the Westminster Bank and the Southern Railway. He was elected an honorary student of Christ Church in 1913.

Murray died in London 4 April 1936. He married in 1879 Helen Mary (died 1932), eldest daughter of John Mulholland, afterwards first Lord Dunleath, and had a son, Sir Evelyn Murray, K.C.B., who was successively secretary to the Post Office and chairman of the Board of Customs and Excise, and a daughter.

[*The Times*, 6 April 1936; Treasury records; private information; personal knowledge.]

MAURICE HEADLAM.

MURRAY, GEORGE REDMAYNE (1865–1939), physician, was born at Newcastle-upon-Tyne 20 June 1865, the eldest son of William Murray, M.D., a physician with a reputation for shrewd common sense and forthrightness, and with a deeper wisdom which reflected itself in the guidance of his son to those men and those places by which he might best be trained for his chosen profession; his mother was Frances Mary, daughter of Giles Redmayne. He was educated at Eton and at Trinity College, Cambridge, where he graduated with first class honours in part i of the natural sciences tripos in 1886. He then joined a group of Cambridge medical students who had been attracted to University College Hospital, London, by the teaching of Sydney Ringer and (Sir) Victor Horsley [qq.v.]. He distinguished himself at his teaching hospital, and with the Fellowes and Senior gold medals passed his final examinations in 1888. He graduated M.B. (Camb.) in 1889 and proceeded M.D. (Camb.) in 1896. A man of his qualities was quickly affected by the research enthusiasm of his teachers, and this set his mind upon a career in experimental medicine. For this purpose he visited the most famous of the medical clinics in Berlin and Paris and then returned to his native city in 1891 to begin his work as pathologist to the Hospital for Sick Children and lecturer in bacteriology in the Durham University College of Medicine.

Within a few months of his return to Newcastle, and at the early age of twenty-six, Murray made the discovery which brought him fame. His friend Horsley, who himself was working on the physiology of the thyroid gland, suggested that myxoedema might be cured by grafts of animal thyroid. Murray preferred to use an extract of thyroid gland by hypodermic injection. This cured a myxoedematous woman, and he published his results in the *British Medical Journal* of 10 October 1891, under the heading 'Note on the Treatment of Myxoedema by Hypodermic Injections of an Extract of the Thyroid Gland of a Sheep'. With characteristic care he followed the fate of this woman and reported her progress in the *British Medical Journal* of 27 August 1892 and 13 March 1920.

This discovery opened up a field of interest and research in the medical sciences which led to a new knowledge of the endocrine glands and their influence on health and personality. With his reputation established Murray entered into the responsible posts of Heath professor of comparative pathology at Durham in 1893, and of physician to the Royal Victoria Infirmary at Newcastle-upon-Tyne in 1898. He held these posts until 1908. He moved to Manchester in circumstances which proved his charm and honesty of purpose. He was appointed by Manchester University to its chair of medicine which carried with it the privilege of being a physician to Manchester Royal Infirmary. The choice of Murray for the vacant post raised a storm of local opposition, but he entered on his duties with so quiet an unconcern, and so friendly an attitude, that his worth was immediately apparent and he lived out his professional life in Manchester until 1925, beloved by his colleagues and admired by his friends. The responsibilities of university and professional life deflected him from experimental medicine to teaching, medical practice, and university administration. His later writings were mainly on clinical subjects.

Murray received many honours: he was president of the Association of Physicians (1936), member of the Medical Research Committee (later Medical Research Council), Goulstonian (1899) and Bradshaw (1905) lecturer to the Royal College of Physicians, of which he had been a fellow since 1898. Honorary degrees were conferred upon him by Durham and Dublin Universities. In later years two of his most practical achievements were the work which he did as a member of the

departmental committee of the Home Office on dust diseases in card-room workers, and the service which he rendered in the war of 1914–1918 as a consulting physician to the British forces in Italy. He retired from active work a few years before his death, which took place at his home at Mobberley, Cheshire, 21 September 1939. He married in 1892 Annie, daughter of Edward Robert Bickersteth, a well-known Liverpool surgeon, a cousin of Edward Bickersteth, dean of Lichfield, and of Robert Bickersteth, bishop of Ripon [qq.v.]. They had three sons, two of whom were killed in the war of 1914–1918, and a daughter.

[*The Times*, 23 September 1939; *British Medical Journal*, 1939, vol. ii, p. 707; *Lancet*, 1939, vol. ii, p. 767 (portrait); personal knowledge.]   J. C. SPENCE.

MURRAY, SIR (JOHN) HUBERT (PLUNKETT) (1861–1940), Australian administrator of Papua, was born in Sydney, New South Wales, 29 December 1861, the eldest son of Sir Terence Aubrey Murray [q.v.], by his second wife, Agnes Anne, third daughter of John Edwards, of London. He was elder brother of Dr. Gilbert Murray.

Murray was educated at Sydney Grammar School, and in England at Brighton College and, after a year in Germany, at Magdalen College, Oxford, where he was a classical demy and graduated with a first class in classical moderations (1882) and in *literae humaniores* (1885). He was also a fine scholar in French and German. He was a tall man of fine physique, a good boxer (he held the Queensberry rules heavyweight championship), oarsman, and swordsman. After being called to the bar by the Inner Temple in 1886, he practised as a barrister in Australia. He was a crown prosecutor in New South Wales, and in 1901 and 1902 was an acting district court judge. A romantic feeling for Ireland influenced him in his reversion to the Church of Rome and led him to join the New South Wales Irish Rifles, of which he became the commander during the South African war. Because its bulk was small and the matter difficult, he carried a Pindar in his pocket throughout the campaign and read it five times through. On his return to Sydney in January 1901 he held the rank of major, retiring as lieutenant-colonel.

After his return to Australia Murray entered the service of British New Guinea as chief judicial officer, taking office in

September 1904. In April 1907 he was appointed acting administrator, and in November 1908 became lieutenant-governor. He held this position, together with that of chief judicial officer, until his death at Samarai, Papua, 27 February 1940. He was appointed C.M.G. in 1914, and K.C.M.G. in 1925. He was twice married: first, in 1889 to Sybil Maud (died 1929), fifth daughter of Richard Lewis Jenkins, M.D., of Nepean Towers, N.S.W., and had two sons and a daughter; secondly, in 1930 to Mildred Blanche Bloomfield, daughter of Henry Bloomfield Trench and widow of George Arthur Pomeroy Vernon.

On 1 September 1906 the administration of the colony was taken over by the Commonwealth of Australia under the Papua Act of 1905. Papua then had an area of about 93,000 square miles, with a European population in 1940 of less than 2,000 and about 300,000 natives, broken up into innumerable small tribes with different languages. There was little fertile ground, much was precipitous mountain, and in the west were extensive dismal swamps. The natives were savages of stone-age culture, many of them headhunters and cannibals chiefly for ritual purposes, with a strong tradition of warfare between the many small tribes or villages, but with great power of affection and fidelity. Murders of white men were formerly frequent when the island used to be visited by 'black-birders' who seized natives to be sold as labourers on other islands or in Queensland, but in the latter part of Murray's administration their activities had practically ceased.

It was during the first decade of Murray's administration that real development of European copra plantations took place. For many years, however, he incurred the hostile criticism of the traders, of the planters, and of the miners. He was charged with being the enemy of the white man and with being a foolish friend of the natives, but it was not long before he secured the confidence of the Protestant missions. Nevertheless as late as 1920 a public meeting in Port Moresby demanded his recall. Ultimately he lived down all opposition. He prescribed areas for each of the competing missions. He secured the exclusion of the Territory from the application of the Australian Navigation Act, which was threatening to strangle development. He introduced land and native labour ordinances which, after incurring much opposition, have been gener-

ally approved, and his government became a model administration of what is called a native community.

Murray built a strong and enduring administration upon foundations worthily laid by Sir William Macgregor [q.v.]. The basis of his administration rested upon an understanding of the mentality of the natives. He contended that the natives could be civilized without being spoilt, and that they must move towards civilization or disappear, but that civilization should not mean their assimilation to the white men or their subjugation. His annual reports are equally a store-house of humour and of information for the anthropologist and others. In these reports he described murder as the 'favourite crime' of the Papuan, but explained that what to a European was murder might to a Papuan be merely a high-spirited adventure or even a social duty. Murray had no prison for a long time; instead he made the murderers walk with him when he went on circuit, in order to educate them. He illustrated the point of view of the native by telling how a native, on realizing that he might be punished for the murder of a girl, exclaimed in astonishment, 'But there are plenty of girls left.'

Murray devoted himself in the first place to the establishment of the authority of the government and the administration of law upon a basis which would appeal to the native mind. He undertook and organized extensive patrols throughout the country, sometimes going to territory where no white man had been seen. He insisted on justice and mutual understanding. On some occasions he even responded to a shower of arrows by sitting down and smoking, and when the arrows stopped, putting out gifts for the attackers to come and take, thereby gaining a reputation for invulnerability. He absolutely prohibited punitive expeditions against communities. He always used the minimum of force, and ultimately the natives realized the benefits of law and order under an administration which was benevolent but not weak.

One of the difficulties which confronted the administration was the universal belief in sorcery. The influence of the sorcerers was so great that when a native believed that he was the object of a sorcerer's attentions he would pine away and die. Murray sometimes used these beliefs in the interests of the natives. When, for example, an epidemic of small-pox was threatened he had to consider how he could induce the natives, who are very much afraid of the knife, to submit to vaccination. He explained that there was a powerful sorcerer in the west who was proposing to attack the people, but that, if the people had a government mark on their arms, the sorcerer would retire discomfited and would not harm them. The result was that the people willingly and eagerly submitted to vaccination.

From the beginning of his administration, Murray not only declared that the object of Australian administration should be the welfare of the native, but he put this principle into practice. He strongly contended that this policy was the only policy that could wisely be adopted from an Australian point of view. The country is not suitable for any extensive European occupation, and if the natives disappeared it would be occupied by Asiatic, and probably hostile, races. He therefore insisted upon the exclusion of Asiatic immigrants and aimed always at the preservation of the native race.

When Commodore James Elphinstone Erskine annexed New Guinea in the name of the Queen in 1884 he declared, 'Your lands shall be secured to you. Your wives and children will be protected.' This declaration was taken as a fundamental principle in Murray's policy. He considered that the welfare of the natives demanded that they should retain the closest connexion with the land, so that they would not become a body of employees earning wages during their working lives and then falling into dull and helpless destitution. He was determined to prevent the creation of a landless proletariat. The Land Ordinance provides that no land can be purchased from a native except by the government, and not even by the government unless it is clear that the natives understand the transaction, and that the land is not used by the natives or required for them. The result is that, out of an area of about 57 million acres, 1,800,000 acres have been acquired by the government from the natives. Only about 24,000 acres have been alienated by the government in freehold, mainly to missions, and about 200,000 acres in leasehold.

The Native Labour Ordinance, in force from time to time, permitted indentured labour, which Murray regarded as a necessity for the time being in the ultimate interests of the natives. There is no compulsory recruiting of labour and the indenture of women is forbidden, as destructive of village life. No native could be indentured for a period longer than three years, and the system was very carefully policed.

In 1915–1916 Murray introduced a native tax, based on the village as the unit, with a maximum of £1 per head. The proceeds of this tax are used for the development of native plantations, and for health, educational, and recreational services for the natives. The imposition of the tax was received with enthusiasm by the natives, and villages which had been excluded because it was considered that they were too poor to pay any tax strongly resented their exclusion and insisted upon having the honour of paying the tax.

Murray introduced a system whereby education is in the hands of the missions, a subsidy being paid by the government. The English language is taught in the native schools. Instruction is carefully devised to meet the needs of the natives. No attempt has been made to introduce higher education. He declared that some higher developments must be regarded as non-essential while Papuan British subjects were still being roasted and eaten within twenty-four hours of Port Moresby.

At the end of his career, Murray's achievements met with wide recognition. In 1923 the following tribute was paid by the League of Nations: 'Papua leads the world in justice, wisdom, mercy, and the efficacy of her rule.' He had faced a problem of intense difficulty with high ideals which were derided by practical men. His active interest in the well-being of the natives was accompanied by patient sympathy and understanding. He was a reserved and modest man who abhorred the spectacular, but pursued a chosen course with determination and courage. Among his chief characteristics were self-discipline, mental and physical, humour, and a dislike of pretence. He was assiduous in training his staff and the men whom he trained were devoted to him. As a soldier he recognized the necessity for force behind the law in order to secure respect and obedience. As a lawyer he appreciated the basic importance of justice in dealing with primitive races. As a scholar and a humanist he had an insight into the native mind which has seldom been equalled. In his last annual report (1938–1939) he wrote of a dancing-ground in a native village far away in the mountains, where the open space was surrounded by casuarina trees 'planted apparently because the natives like "the whistling wind blowing through them"; and perhaps an old man, nurtured in the outworn scholarship of Greek literature, may be allowed to remember the pine tree that whispered to Thyrsis in the first Idyll of Theocritus'. In 1937 the natives presented an address to him in which they said: 'We people of Papua all know that in July, 1937, you completed thirty years as Governor of Papua. During all those years we have seen your good works, and all the helpful things you have done. When we have come to speak to you, you have not closed your ears, nor have you frowned on us, but have received us, and listened to us, and taken action for us. We have seen all the good things you have done and our happiness is great because of you.

'Therefore we all beg of you not to leave us, but stay here as our Governor for years to come. For we know you and how you have led us into the ways of your laws, treating white people and ourselves just the same. We know that you love us well, and we are full of love for you our Governor.'

[*The Times*, 29 February 1940; J. H. P. Murray, *Papua or British New Guinea*, 1912, *Papua of To-day*, 1925, Annual Reports to the Commonwealth Government, and 'The Scientific Aspect of the Pacification of Papua', presidential address (Sydney) 1932, Australasian Association for the Advancement of Science; *Australian Quarterly*, September 1940; *Proceedings* of the Royal Australian Historical Society, vol. xxxi, part 3, 1945 (portrait); Lewis Lett, *The Papuan Achievement*, 1942 (portrait), *Papua, its People and Promise*, 1943, and *Papuan Gold*, 1943; W. N. Beaver, *Unexplored New Guinea*, 1920; C. A. W. Monckton, *Some Experiences of a New Guinea Magistrate*, 3rd ed. 1921, and *Last Days in New Guinea*, 2nd ed. 1922; private information; personal knowledge.]

J. G. LATHAM.

MURRAY, SIR OSWYN ALEXANDER RUTHVEN (1873–1936), civil servant, was born at Mill Hill 17 August 1873, the fourth son of the lexicographer (Sir) James Augustus Henry Murray [q.v.], then a schoolmaster, by his second wife, Ada Agnes, daughter of George Ruthven, of Kendal. He was educated at the Oxford High School as a day boy and at Exeter College, Oxford, where he held a classical scholarship and was placed in the first class in classical moderations (1893), *literae humaniores* (1895), and jurisprudence (1896). In 1897 after the higher civil service competitive examination he was appointed to the Admiralty secretariat. Later in the year he won the Vinerian

(law) scholarship but declined the offer of a resident fellowship in law at St. John's College. As resident clerk at the Admiralty from 1898 until 1901 he came into close personal relation with G. J. Goschen [q.v.], then first lord, who made him his assistant private secretary; from 1901 to 1904 he served as private secretary to H. O. Arnold-Forster [q.v.] and E. G. Pretyman, when they were parliamentary and financial secretaries. He had been promoted to be assistant principal clerk in 1903, but he did not take up this post until 1904.

By that time Murray's exceptional ability was generally marked and in October 1904 he was selected for the post of assistant director of victualling and clothing with a view to his succeeding Sir Henry Yorke as director. This offer of novel and important work, with opportunities for effecting reforms long overdue, in a most important department, appealed to Murray, and in 1905 he succeeded to the directorship. During his six years in charge he brought about a veritable revolution in a department where urgent and drastic reforms were needed to bring conditions afloat into reasonable accord with modern standards prevailing ashore. The standard ration was thoroughly overhauled, the savings system (of money taken in lieu of portions of the ration) abolished, a messing allowance introduced, the contract canteen arrangement placed on a sound footing, a school of cookery established in the home ports, and the present general messing system, whereby complete daily meals are provided by the paymaster from general stores, experimentally inaugurated.

Murray was brought back to the secretariat in 1911 as the assistant (or deputy) secretary of the Admiralty, and was actively concerned with the preparations for war as the danger became more imminent and with the novel problems of administration that arose on its outbreak. In 1917 Sir Eric Geddes [q.v.] was made first lord with instructions to effect drastic changes in the government of the office. After a short hesitation he appointed Murray as permanent secretary in place of Sir Graham Greene who was transferred to the Ministry of Munitions. In the result Murray's patience and tactful advice, with his knowledge of the traditions of the service, were of great value in securing the smooth working of the reforms that were carried out. After the war he served as permanent secretary under eight ministers who relied increasingly on his ripe experience. It was then that Murray's most important, though unspectacular, work was accomplished. As accounting officer for naval expenditure from 1921, as well as permanent secretary, he was responsible for the supervision and criticism of all proposals involving cost, at a period when the impulse to cut down all military expenditure was strong. By his clear grasp of essentials he succeeded in so steering the course of navy estimates through successive administrations that a strong navy was existing and ready in 1939 when war again broke out.

After a serious illness in 1933, from which he never fully recovered, Murray died at Roehampton 10 July 1936, within a few months of his intended retirement.

Naturally reserved in manner, and not readily making friends, Murray was nevertheless universally respected not only for his remarkably fine intellect, but for his high character and devotion to duty. His share in preserving the navy on an adequate basis during the years that followed the war was very great, and he notably increased the prestige of his historic office at a time when a lesser man might easily have let it sink. His main outside interest was research in Devon family history, in which he became a recognized authority.

Murray was appointed C.B. in 1910, K.C.B. in 1917, and G.C.B. in 1931, and was elected an honorary fellow of Exeter College in 1919. He married in 1900 Mildred Octavia, fourth daughter of the Rev. Septimus March, and had a son and a daughter.

[Lady Murray, *The Making of a Civil Servant*, 1940; Admiralty records; personal knowledge.]   VINCENT W. BADDELEY.

MYSORE, SIR SHRI KRISHNARAJA WADIYAR BAHADUR, MAHARAJA OF (1884–1940), was born 4 June 1884, the elder son of Maharaja Sir Shri Chamarajendra Wadiyar. Ten and a half years later (February 1895) he succeeded his father as head of the state. During his minority, his mother, a woman of remarkable character, ruled the country as regent from behind the purdah. The young Maharaja was carefully educated; he owed much to the influence in his formative years of a distinguished member of the Indian civil service, (Sir) Stuart Fraser, who was appointed his tutor and guardian. The Maharaja was invested with full administrative powers by the viceroy in August 1902, and there opened a striking chapter in the history of India.

The young ruler found to his hand an administration well organized on modern lines, with an efficient civil service. The main element of Mysore, then as now, is a hardworking Hindu peasantry, loyal to the ruling house. On the great river Cauvery, a hydro-electric installation has been set up, the first of its kind in India, and the use of electricity, a state concern, has made deep mining possible in Kolar; its use in towns and villages has benefited industry, particularly the silk and textile industries, and agriculture.

Throughout the Maharaja's rule the people, especially the peasantry, were brought into close touch with the administration through the representative assembly, set up in 1882, a body of 250 members elected on a broad franchise, reflecting the opinion of the countryside, to which the government almost invariably gave full consideration. A growing political consciousness inspired by political movements in adjacent British provinces led to a demand for further reforms. The Maharaja did not hesitate to show his confidence in the loyalty of his people, and in 1922 he introduced a system of popular government approaching that which had been established in British India in 1920. Later on, popular control was further extended; a minister responsible to the elected majority in the legislative council, set up in 1907, was appointed to the executive; wide control over finance and administration was conceded to the people's representatives; in fact the system comes very near to constitutional monarchy.

The Maharaja's political sympathies extended beyond the frontiers of the state and he welcomed the prospect of a federal India in which the states would participate. Had a federation come into being, there is little doubt that he would have ensured that the authentic voice of Mysore would be heard in the federal assembly.

Loyalty to old friends was a pleasing characteristic of the Maharaja. This quality was shown in a marked degree in his life-long friendship with Mr. Mirza Ismail, a Moslem of Persian extraction (since 1930 Sir Mirza Ismail), who had been a companion of his boyhood, had shared his studies, and in 1925 became chief minister. The Maharaja gave a free hand and full support to Sir Mirza, to whose statesmanship and imagination the progress of the country, both in the political and in the economic field, is largely due.

With a finely developed character the Maharaja combined culture with perfect breeding. In his youth he played polo well; in his later years he excelled at rackets, squash rackets, and lawn tennis. A strictly orthodox Hindu, he did not share his table with Europeans; nevertheless his hospitality, especially on the occasions of the Birthday and Dussarah weeks, was widely appreciated. Only towards the end of his life, in 1936, did he visit Europe. Although a great patron of the Brahmins, he would not admit their claim to a monopoly of Sanskrit learning, and he encouraged its study among non-Brahmins. He did much to encourage Indian music, while, a violinist himself, he greatly appreciated the classical music of the West. His death, which took place at Mysore 3 August 1940, was a great loss to India and the British Commonwealth.

The Maharaja was appointed G.C.S.I. in 1907 and G.B.E. in 1917. In his youth he married a Kathiawar princess but had no children, and he was succeeded by his nephew, the son of his younger brother.

[Personal knowledge.]   W. P. BARTON.

NAIR, SIR CHETTUR SANKARAN (1857–1934), Indian jurist, etc. [See SANKARAN NAIR.]

NAIRNE, ALEXANDER (1863–1936), scholar, theologian, and mystic, was born at Hunsdon, Hertfordshire, 17 January 1863, the eldest child and elder son of Spencer Nairne, rector of Hunsdon, by his wife, Marion Walker, daughter of John Marshall, first Lord Curriehill [q.v.], and sister of John Marshall, second Lord Curriehill, both Scottish judges. He belonged to the Sandford branch of the Nairne family who had suffered for their Jacobite sympathies. His ancestors for several generations were Scottish ministers. His grandfather fought as a midshipman at the battle of Copenhagen.

Nairne was educated at Haileybury and Jesus College, Cambridge, of which latter he was a scholar. He obtained first classes in the classical (1884) and theological (1886) triposes, two university prizes, and a university scholarship. He was a fellow of Jesus from 1887 to 1893 and again from 1917 to 1932 and was elected an honorary fellow in the last-named year. He was ordained deacon in 1887 and priest in 1888, and was curate of Great St. Mary's and vice-principal of the Clergy Training School at Cambridge from 1887 to 1889. He was then successively an assistant master at Harrow (1890–1892), curate of Hadleigh, Suffolk (1892–1894), and rector of Tewin, Hertfordshire (1894–1912).

From 1900 to 1917 Nairne was professor of Hebrew and Old Testament exegesis in King's College, London. Here he had for the first time the opportunity of showing his special ability. His lectures were very popular, 'a curious and effective combination of detailed information and poetry, touched with mysticism'. It was the time when the religious world of England was learning about the 'higher' criticism of the Old Testament, and Nairne was one of the most successful of those who introduced this new aspect of the Bible. 'Nairne', writes one of his students, 'strengthened my faith because he made it clear that behind all the difficulties there was something very real which he himself believed.' 'I think', writes another, 'he succeeded in conveying the modern view of the Old Testament, without unduly disturbing the minds of men who had been brought up in the old fashioned belief about it and he did this partly by his power of making us feel the magnificence of the poetry, and partly by his own evident spiritual life. . . . I was always filled with wonder at the extent of his learning; no great literature seemed unknown to him.'

From 1914 to 1922 Nairne was a canon of Chester Cathedral, where the stimulating effect of his scholarship and his personality was warmly welcomed. In 1917 he returned to Cambridge as fellow and dean of his old college; he was vicar of All Saints' church until 1919, Hulsean lecturer in 1919–1920, and regius professor of divinity from 1922 to 1932.

Nairne's position at Cambridge was a remarkable one. He took no interest in the business of the university or of the theological faculty, but he had a wide personal influence upon undergraduates and dons alike. His lectures were found stimulating and inspiring by all except those who sought easy answers to examination questions. Men felt that they had seen a great light, which they could neither describe nor reflect, but which they were glad to have seen for a moment. His scholarship, his love of great literature, his wide range of knowledge, his sympathy with artists, poets, and men of science, made his influence wide. He treated all undergraduates as his intellectual equals, and spoke of Shelley, or Sir James Frazer, author of the *Golden Bough*, or J. M. E.

M'Taggart the philosopher, almost as good Christians, for they seemed to him to be in touch with spiritual realities. 'Because they had known Nairne not a few were led for the first time to believe that theology was a respectable study.' He formed a society for undergraduates called the 'Clouds', which met once a week to read Plato, and to find out what Plato really meant. His rooms were crowded. After some years the members of the 'Clouds' gave him a book written by all of them and inscribed to νεφελη-γερέτα.

Nairne's books are without the parapher-nalia of scholarship or criticism but they contain much fine scholarship and much insight. The pedants were a little scorn-ful. The Hebraists said that he did not know his grammar, but some felt that he understood the genius of the language better than the grammarians. The 'higher' critics said that he made no contribution to their studies. That was no doubt true. He was suspicious of their work, but to many his judgement often appeared better than theirs. His scholarly instincts, his poetic sense, his religious piety, taught him to avoid their blunders, but he was never afraid to trust his reason. He wanted to know what a book really meant, and he saw more deeply than most. His book on the Epistle to the Hebrews, *The Epistle of Priesthood* (1913), his Hulsean lectures, *The Faith of the New Testament* (1914), and *The Life Eternal: here and now* in parti-cular are books which take the reader deeper into truth than most theological literature.

Nairne was a canon of St. George's Chapel, Windsor, from 1921 until his death, which took place at Windsor 15 March 1936. In 1931 the university of St. Andrews conferred upon him the honorary degree of D.D. He married in 1889 Ethel (died 1921), daughter of Lambart Campbell Edwards, vicar of Kingsbury, Middlesex. He had no children.

Unworldly and not interested in worldly affairs, Nairne was a man of radiant charm and kindness, of alertness of sympathy, of a goodness which compelled almost all who met him not only to like him but to love him.

There is an etching of Nairne's head by Francis Dodd in the old library at Jesus College, Cambridge.

[*The Times*, 16 March 1936; *Cambridge Review*, 1 May 1936; private information; personal knowledge.]   A. C. HEADLAM.

NATHAN, SIR MATTHEW (1862–1939), soldier and civil servant, was born in Paddington 3 January 1862, the second son of Jonah Nathan, manufacturer, by his second wife, Miriam, daughter of Lewis Jacobs, of London, both of Jewish origin. He entered the Royal Engineers from the Royal Military Academy in 1880, and saw active service with the Sudan expedition of 1884–1885, and with the Lushai expedition in 1889, being pro-moted captain in the last-named year. In 1895 he was appointed secretary to the Colonial Defence Committee under Joseph Chamberlain, who was much struck by his ability. In 1898 he was promoted major, and in 1899 was sent to Sierra Leone to administer the government of that colony, and a year later was made governor of the Gold Coast, which at that time was un-settled. After three years of energetic reform, which was both prudent and popular, he was transferred to Hong-Kong, where the reputation which he had already made was confirmed. In 1907 he was promoted brevet lieutenant-colonel and made governor of Natal, a position which he held until 1909 when the four South African colonies were conjoined in the Union of South Africa. In that year he returned to England, and was appointed secretary to the General Post Office. His success led to his promotion in 1911 to the chairmanship of the Board of Inland Revenue.

Shortly before the outbreak of war in 1914 Nathan was selected by the govern-ment for the office of under-secretary for Ireland, and was sworn a member of the Irish Privy Council. His new duties proved more difficult than any that he had as yet undertaken. When the Easter rebellion broke out in 1916, the chief secretary, Augustine Birrell [q.v.], was in England and Nathan was in charge at Dublin Castle, under the lord-lieutenant, Lord Wimborne [q.v.]. Severe criticism was made on the Irish executive for its failure to warn the government of the danger. The lord-lieutenant and the chief secretary both resigned, but the former, who resented the charge of neglect, was persuaded with some difficulty to resume office. Nathan, however, was not re-instated, and he returned to England, where he was secretary to the Ministry of Pensions until 1919.

In 1920 Nathan was appointed governor of Queensland, a post which he held for five years. He had to deal with a restless labour government under Mr. Edward

Granville Theodore, which abolished the legislative council, extended the state railway system, and acquired the Brisbane tramways. Nathan found scope for his own tastes in promoting the cause of learning by setting up a sub-committee of the Civil Research Committee, the recommendations of which led to the Great Barrier Reef expedition of 1928–1929. He was chancellor of Queensland University from 1922 to 1926, and received the honorary degree of LL.D. in 1925. He also served on the special commission on the constitution of Ceylon (1927–1928) and as chairman of the colonial secretary's advisory committee on rubber (1926–1928). He was appointed C.M.G. in 1899, K.C.M.G. in 1902, and G.C.M.G. in 1908.

After retirement from public life, Nathan found zest in the study of local history and the administration of the county of Somerset where he made his home at West Coker. He died there, unmarried, 18 April 1939.

[*The Times*, 19 April 1939.]

ARTHUR COCHRANE.

NAWANAGAR, MAHARAJA SHRI RANJITSINHJI VIBHAJI, MAHA-RAJA JAM SAHEB OF (1872–1933), Indian ruler and cricketer, was born at the family village of Sarodar 10 September 1872, the son of Jadeja Jiwansinhji, a cadet of the ruling family. The ruling chief, Jam Vibhaji, was childless and an adopted son was sought in the Sarodar family. A youthful uncle having been adopted and shortly afterwards poisoned, the choice fell upon Ranjitsinhji, who was regularly adopted in 1879 but in secret, owing to the fate of his predecessor. His adoption was valid by law and custom, unless a son were later born to the adoptive father by an acknowledged wife. When in 1882 Jam Vibhaji asked that his son by a Moslem woman should be recognized as his heir, although she was not, nor could legally be, married to the ruler, the Bombay government refused the request. This decision was overruled by the governor-general, Lord Ripon, and the boy was recognized as heir. In spite of the change in his status, Ranjitsinhji continued his education at Rajkumar College at Rajkot, and showed promise of great proficiency at games, as well as qualities which led the principal to report that a better or manlier boy had never resided there; and in 1888 the principal took Ranjitsinhji to England, with a considerable allowance from the Nawanagar State.

Ranjitsinhji went to Trinity College, Cambridge, in 1890 and took up cricket with zeal, being coached by professionals and getting every game that he could, mainly from Cambridge clubs. His scores in Cambridge town cricket attracted some attention, and after playing in the seniors' match in 1892, he became a regular member of his college eleven. For the next few years his batting developed season by season; in 1893 he received an early trial for the university and made 40 in the next match, after which he was never dropped again, but continued to make useful scores, showing himself an admirable fieldsman in the slips and becoming an object of much popularity and interest.

On leaving Cambridge in 1893, Ranjitsinhji decided to remain in England and to qualify by residence for Sussex. In 1895 there began an association with that county which lasted until 1904, and he was captain of the team from 1899 to 1903. His first appearance for Sussex was at Lord's on 9 May against the Marylebone Cricket Club, and is noticeable because it was the first occasion when he gave an exhibition of the long innings afterwards characteristic of his batting. He scored 77 not out and 150 in a style which an observer described as that of a wizard. In 1896 a strong Australian team came to England for a rubber of three games (the number not being increased to five until the next Australian visit in 1899). After some discussion as to his qualification, Ranjitsinhji was chosen to play in the second test match, which was held at Manchester on 18 July. Australia won the toss and scored 412 to which England replied with 231 and had to follow on. England's second innings was the triumph of one man, Ranjitsinhji, who gave a superb display, making 154 not out, the next highest score being 41 from A. E. Stoddart [q.v.] and the total for the innings was 305. Thanks to some fine bowling by Tom Richardson, Australia lost seven wickets in getting the necessary 125, and the match, which looked at one time like a walk-over, ended in a most severe and exciting struggle.

In the winter of 1897–1898 Ranjitsinhji went to Australia with the second of the two teams taken out by Stoddart. The tour was a disappointment owing to illness and other causes, and of the five test matches England lost four. In the single match won by England, Ranjitsinhji scored 175 on a hard wicket at

Sydney. Many observers of his style and methods were impressed by the quickness of his eye and of his movements, and it is interesting to know that he said that the first few overs which the Australian fast bowler, E. Jones, sent down to him, were the fastest he ever tried to play. On being asked whether he could see them, he replied that he could see them well enough, but could not get his bat there in time to make connexion. On the whole, considering what a wonderful batsman he was, he was never as great a success in test matches as might have been expected, and a singular spell of misfortune befell him in 1902 when he made only 15 runs in four test match innings.

In run-getting, Ranjitsinhji set new standards, which remained until the era of (Sir) Donald Bradman and Walter Hammond thirty years later. He was the first batsman to score over 3,000 runs in a season, an aggregate which he reached in 1899 and again in 1900. He was absent in India in 1898, but in the nine seasons between 1895 and 1904 he was never lower than fifth in the averages and he headed them three times (1896, 1900, and 1904). He played seventy-two three-figure innings in which fourteen reached 200: with him in the Sussex team was Commander C. B. Fry, and the pair were a formidable obstacle to the attack.

Quite as impressive as the quantity of runs made by Ranjitsinhji was the style in which they were made. At the outset he relied chiefly upon back-play, watching the ball closely and being marvellously quick in dealing with the fastest deliveries. His cutting and gliding on the leg side were superb in their certainty. Later he became more orthodox in his methods and scored with plenty of power in front of the wicket. From first to last he remained known to the British public as one of the greatest, perhaps the greatest, cricketer of his generation.

After the season of 1904 reasons of state obliged Ranjitsinhji to return to India, but he came back to English cricket again in 1908 and 1912, playing for Sussex. In 1915 he had the misfortune to lose an eye in a shooting accident, and his last appearance in the cricket field was in 1920, when he wanted to show that it was possible to bat with only one eye.

Jam Jasvatsinhji, whose recognition disinherited Ranjitsinhji, died childless in August 1906. Ranjitsinhji's claim to succeed, never abandoned by him, and

warmly supported by other chiefs, was admitted by the government of India and he was installed in March 1907. His state, although moderately prosperous in years of good rainfall, was liable to scarcity, and generally backward. Although the new ruler's personal requirements were of the simplest, his private generosity and his view as to the need of maintaining the reputation of the state, especially on ceremonial occasions, added to the burden of the expenditure which he incurred for the improvement of the state. He did much to provide against seasonal scarcity by the construction of irrigation works, he re-built his capital town, Jamnagar, and he extended road and rail communications. For the bulk of the revenue thus required the Jam Saheb relied on the development of his ports, of which, like the other Kathiawar states, Nawanagar had retained control. This privilege had no great value so long as the facilities of the ports for ocean-going vessels were few and there were no communications by rail into the interior. The Jam Saheb, however, set himself to improve the ports and to take advantage of the great market afforded by British India. The land customs line which had, with the increase of import duties, been imposed in 1905 in order to separate the Kathiawar states from British India, was found to be so inconvenient in practice that in 1917 the government of India agreed to its abolition, on condition that the full rates of duty were levied at the state ports. The states were allowed to retain the sums collected by them, but the Indian government reserved the right to reconsider the arrangement if its fiscal interests were seriously affected. The imports at the Kathiawar ports, especially Nawanagar, increased so rapidly, assisted as they were by concessions of charges which could not be foregone at the British Indian ports, and also, it was believed, by a refund of some portion of the duty levied, that the loss to the British Indian revenue was considerable, and many complaints were received from Bombay and Karachi. These causes led to the re-imposition of the land customs line in 1927 and formed a subject of controversy for several years. The revenue thus received, however, enabled the Jam Saheb to maintain a high rate of expenditure, and to improve the resources of his state and the condition of his people.

The war of 1914–1918 gave the Jam Saheb the opportunity of showing his intense loyalty to the Empire and his affection for the British people. He threw the resources of the state into the struggle and himself served on the staff in France. The shooting accident which deprived him of an eye, although it terminated his active service and impaired his health, did not check his development as an Indian statesman. At Geneva he facilitated the recognition of India in the comity of nations by his personal qualities and his talents as a host.

In Indian affairs, the Jam Saheb's own tendency had always been liberal and he sympathized with the aspirations of British Indians for self-government, but he was convinced that the system of the Indian states was that most in accord with the real Indian tradition, and with the welfare of the state subjects. While, therefore, he agreed with the acceptance by the states' representatives at the Round Table Conference (1930) of the principle of an All-India federation, he realized the danger to the states, as well as to the continuance of India within the British Commonwealth which was involved in federation without due safeguards. His doubts as to the safety of the states in a federation increased as he realized the lack of unity among the princes themselves. He had taken an active part in the formation of the Chamber of Princes in 1921 and became its chancellor in 1932, a position involving, in his weakened health, much sacrifice. Although, in his own belief, a dying man, he attended the meeting of the chamber at Delhi in March 1933, and emphasized the danger to the princes unless they could establish unity in their ranks. The effort was too great, and on his return he died at Jamnagar 2 April 1933.

It was said of Ranjitsinhji that he first put India on the map for the ordinary Englishman. The position originally obtained by his prowess at cricket could not have been maintained without his qualities of patience, foresight, and understanding of men of all races and classes. Nor should his great personal charm be left unrecorded. He was not only the perfect host, but the perfect guest.

The Jam Saheb was appointed K.C.S.I. in 1917, G.B.E. in 1919, and G.C.S.I. in 1923.

There is a portrait of the Jam Saheb, painted by H. S. Tuke and exhibited at the Royal Academy of 1909, at Jamnagar, and a statue by Herbert Haseldine (1931) stands there also.

[Wisden's *Cricketers' Almanack, passim*; Official records; Roland Wild, *The Biography of Colonel His Highness Shri Sir Ranjitsinhji*, 1934; private information; personal knowledge.]
P. R. CADELL.
ALFRED COCHRANE.

NEHRU, PANDIT MOTILAL (1861–1931), Indian lawyer and Congress leader, was the posthumous son of a wealthy Kashmiri Brahmin, Pandit Gangadhar Nehru, who had been the *kotwal* (head of police) in Delhi city under the last of the Mogul emperors up to the Indian mutiny. Born at Agra 6 May 1861, Motilal was brought up there by an uncle, Nand Lal Nehru, and was educated at Muir College, Allahabad. He practised as a *vakil* from 1883, and in 1895 was enrolled as an advocate of the High Court, Allahabad. The very lucrative practice which he obtained enabled him to live luxuriously. The palatial house which he built, *Ananda Bhavan* (Joy's Abode), was the scene of lavish hospitality to British and Indian friends. He was president of the United Provinces provincial conference of the National Congress in 1907, and soon afterwards became a member of the local legislature.

Nehru presided at the session of the National Congress held at Amritsar at the end of 1919. Under Gandhi's influence he threw himself into the first non-co-operation movement, took to the wearing of *khaddar* (homespun cotton cloth), moved with his family into an outbuilding, and turned his fine residence first into a free public school, and then into the permanent headquarters of the All-India Congress organization. Suspending his practice at the bar, he travelled about the country in support of civil disobedience and boycott of the elections for the legislatures under the Montagu–Chelmsford reforms. In 1921 he underwent six months' imprisonment for taking part in an unlawful (Congress) assembly.

In the following year Nehru modified his attitude to the extent of forming with C. R. Das, the Bengali leader, the Swaraj party on a programme of fighting the general election at the end of 1923 in order to wreck the central legislative assembly from within. On the death of Das in 1925 (the year in which Nehru resumed his practice at the bar) he became president of the party, and under his leadership in the House it merged in 1926 with the Congress party. An astute tactician, an eloquent debater and orator, and a stern disciplinarian, with a dignified presence in his white homespun, he was a formidable opposition leader. Government measures were resisted and much delayed, but mere wrecking tactics were abandoned, and the party took its full share in the work of select committees.

The pandit actively promoted the boycott of the statutory (Simon) commission appointed at the end of 1927. In the following spring he became chairman of an 'All Parties Conference' and of the committee which it appointed to 'determine the principles of the constitution of India'. The resulting Nehru Report, published a few months later, outlined a plan of Dominion status, but aroused strong opposition from Moslem and other minority interests. The annual Congress session held at Calcutta under his chairmanship decided on intensified non-co-operation if the plan were not accepted by the British government within twelve months. Meeting at Lahore at the end of 1929, a year later, under the chairmanship of the pandit's extremist son, Jawaharlal, the Congress declared that the proposals of the report had lapsed and demanded complete independence.

The ageing leader, influenced by deep affection for his son, but with much misgiving, threw the weight of his support into the intensified civil disobedience campaign. On the proscription in 1930 of the Congress working committee, of which he was chairman, he was sentenced to six months' imprisonment, but after a few weeks' detention was released on grounds of ill health. He died at Lucknow 6 February 1931, and his ashes were consigned to the sacred Ganges at Allahabad. His wife, whom he had married in 1882 and who had given him the fullest political support, died in 1938. They had a son and two daughters.

[*The Times*, 7 February 1931; *All Parties Conference 1928* [*Nehru*] *Report*; Jawaharlal Nehru, *Jawaharlal Nehru, an Autobiography*, 1936 (portrait); *Annual Register*, 1927 to 1931.]   F. H. BROWN.

NEWALL, DAME BERTHA SURTEES (1877–1932), better known as DAME BERTHA PHILLPOTTS, educationist and Scandinavian scholar, was born at Bedford 25 October 1877, the second of the three daughters of James Surtees Phillpotts, headmaster of Bedford Grammar School, by his wife, Marian Hadfield, daughter of John Cordery, of Hampstead. She was a great-granddaughter of Henry Phillpotts, bishop of Exeter [q.v.]. Miss Phillpotts's early education was received from masters of the grammar school. She entered Girton College, Cambridge, as a scholar in 1898 and was awarded a first class (French and German) in the medieval and modern languages tripos of 1901. Between 1901 and 1913 she was acquiring, extending, and deepening her knowledge of Scandinavian languages, history, archaeology, and literature. She was Pfeiffer student of the college (1903–1904, 1905–1906), and in 1913 was elected first Lady Carlisle fellow of Somerville College, Oxford. When in Stockholm during the war of 1914–1918 she was appointed clerical assistant at H.M. Legation and also acted as private secretary to the British minister, Sir Esme Howard [q.v.], and was appointed O.B.E. in 1918.

Miss Phillpotts became principal of Westfield College, Hampstead, in 1919, but resigned in 1921 on being invited to return to her own college, which she served as mistress from 1922 to 1925, in succession to her first cousin Miss Katharine Jex-Blake. She retired on the grounds that her father had need of her, and she was thereupon elected a research fellow. In a year's time she found herself able to accept appointment as a university lecturer and became director of Scandinavian studies and head of the department of other languages in the university of Cambridge. In 1929 she was appointed D.B.E. She married in 1931, as his second wife, Hugh Frank Newall (died 1944), F.R.S., emeritus professor of astrophysics in the university of Cambridge, and youngest son of the engineer and astronomer Robert Stirling Newall [q.v.]. She died at Cambridge 20 January 1932, and was buried beside her parents in Tunbridge Wells cemetery. She was elected a fellow of the Royal Society of Northern Antiquaries, Copenhagen, in 1911.

At the head of two colleges in a time of change, Miss Phillpotts, during short terms of office, accomplished much: she improved their status in the outside world and stimulated their intellectual life within. During her mistress-ship Girton received its charter (1924). She was the only woman member of the statutory commission for the university of Cambridge (1923–1927), and was a member of the statutory commission for the university of London (1926–1928).

Dame Bertha Phillpotts was a scholar as well as an administrator. She was recognized as an authority on Scandinavian subjects. She journeyed to Iceland six times between 1903 and 1914, and worked in libraries and visited archives in Stockholm, Copenhagen, and a number of German cities. The range of her published works suggests but does not fully represent what she might have produced: she had planned, especially, a history of Iceland for which notes are extant. Her last book, *Edda and Saga*, which appeared in 1931 a few months before her death, perhaps shows most completely the nature of her mind and interest. Her first book, *Kindred and Clan in the Middle Ages and After* (1913), was her own answer to her own questions. *The Elder Edda and Ancient Scandinavian Drama* (1920) connects epic in poetry and early drama and touches on what appeared to be parallel problems in the origins of Greek tragedy, a theme to which the writer did not return, and which later research has considerably modified.

Dame Bertha Phillpotts possessed great vitality and a distinction of personality and appearance. A portrait of her by P. A. de László (1921) is at Westfield College, and another, by Howard Somerville (1927), is at Girton College.

[*The Times*, 21, 25, 29 January, 12 February 1932; *Manchester Guardian*, 21 January, 5 February, 7 May, 13 June 1932; *Cambridge Review*, 29 January 1932; private information; personal knowledge.]

M. G. LLOYD THOMAS.

NEWBOLT, SIR HENRY JOHN (1862–1938), poet and man of letters, was born at Bilston, Staffordshire, 6 June 1862, the elder son and eldest of the three children of Henry Francis Newbolt, vicar of St. Mary's church, Bilston, by his second wife, Emily, second daughter of George Bradnock Stubbs, of Walsall and Blymhill. He was educated at Clifton and in 1881 was awarded a scholarship at Corpus Christi College, Oxford, where he graduated with a first class in classical moderations (1882) and a second class in *literae humaniores* (1885). In 1887 he was called to the bar by Lincoln's Inn; he practised law for twelve years, and—'a real claim to immortality'—contributed largely to the *Law Digest*; but he was steadily tending the while towards literature. His first book, *Taken from the Enemy*, a tale of the Napoleonic wars, appeared in 1892 and was followed by *Mordred*, a tragedy in blank verse, published in 1895; in the following year Andrew Lang spontaneously printed six poems in *Longman's Magazine*, and 'Drake's Drum', immediately famous,

appeared in the *St. James's Gazette*. Newbolt himself relates how after reading this poem with silent absorption, his friend Robert Bridges [q.v.] declared, 'It isn't given to a man to write anything better than that. I wish I had ever written anything half so good.' It was included in a collection of twelve poems entitled *Admirals All* (1897) four editions of which raced into circulation within a fortnight. Many books followed from 1898 to 1932, various in theme and kind, but consistent in the diligent and fastidious care and thought expended upon their making; indeed, owing in part perhaps to his training in the law, but much more to native impulse, inclination, and character, he can seldom, if ever, have failed to master anything on which he set his mind and heart. During its brief lifetime (1900–1904) he edited the *Monthly Review*. He served at the Admiralty and the Foreign Office in the years of war, and was finally controller of wireless and cables. In 1923, at the request of the Committee of Imperial Defence, he undertook the completion in two volumes (iv and v) of the official *History of the Great War: Naval Operations*, of which the first three had been written by Sir J. S. Corbett [q.v.]. He was devoted in honorary service. In 1919 he was appointed chairman of the departmental committee on English in national education and wrote the introduction to the Report (1921). He served on many commissions, councils, and committees such as the Royal Literary Fund, the Central Council for the Care of Churches, the Royal Society of Literature, and he was a trustee of the National Portrait Gallery (1928–1937). He was knighted in 1915 and appointed C.H. in 1922. He received honorary degrees from the universities of Bristol, Glasgow, St. Andrews, Sheffield, Toronto, Oxford, and Cambridge, and in 1920 he was elected an honorary fellow of his college.

Newbolt's paternal grandfather was a naval officer, and his early ballads were naturally and at once labelled patriotic, and he himself a nautical Kipling. These spirited poems of the sea, however, were only a phase, and among the rest, which are both classical and romantic in form, such poems as 'The Non-Combatant', 'Moonset', 'Master and Man', and especially the lovely 'Nightjar', reveal gifts rich in promise, although only partially explored. His faith in Christianity and the influence of tradition, social, historical, and literary, was paramount in his mind and work. He was haunted too by the seductive problem of Time, not that of the clock but of the self within, and by a 'sense of the past' allied to the idea of the Supreme Consciousness, contained in a poem included in *A Perpetual Memory* (a collection of his later poems published posthumously in 1939). 'Pre-incarnation', so to speak, is indeed the theme of his *Aladore* (1914)—love-allegory, fantasy, reverie, fairy-tale; so simple and limpid in its imposed archaic style that it may conceal its depth and its full meaning. In part for this reason it was his Benjamin among his own books.

Newbolt was a full, ready, and lucid speaker, a vivifying conversationalist, a pregnant and delightful letter-writer. He was not a born story-teller; but his romances have a serene and imaginative grace now rare in English fiction. In his criticism, well equipped and both subtle and vigorous, he held true to tradition; but his mind never crystallized. Gifted with an imaginative and catholic taste, he welcomed and studied innovation in poetic form and content, was a zealous admirer of Thomas Hardy [q.v.], and to any promising novice he proved himself a friend in need, in word and deed. An enthusiast by nature, he could hardly avoid a tendency to optimism. Spare in figure, aquiline in face, with a finely moulded head, a small mouth, and a dominant nose, alert and ready in speech and laughter, he surveyed the world, friend, foe, or stranger, from grey-blue eyes at once intent, penetrating, and contemplative. Throughout his life he was faithful to his idea and ideal of England and Englishness. In spite of so many literary pursuits that called him away from it, poetry was his inmost and lifelong devotion.

Newbolt married in 1889 Margaret Edina, fourth daughter of the Rev. William Arthur Duckworth, of Orchardleigh, Frome, an estate which, old in lineage, appealed vividly to his imagination and gave him the legend enshrined in 'Fidele's Grassy Tomb' and, with its 'island church', the scene of his romance *The Old Country* (1906). At this time also two valuable friends and influences came into his life, Mary Coleridge [q.v.] and his wife's cousin Ella Coltman. There were a son and a daughter of the marriage. He died in London 19 April 1938.

There is an etching of Newbolt by William Strang (1898) in the Tate Gallery; a silverpoint by the same artist (1898), chalk drawings by E. H. Kennington (1920) and (Sir) William Rothenstein (1920), and an oil painting by Meredith Frampton (1930) are in Lady Newbolt's possession.

[Sir Henry Newbolt, *My World as in my Time*, 1932; *The Later Life and Letters of Sir Henry Newbolt*, edited by his wife Margaret Newbolt, 1942; personal knowledge.]

WALTER DE LA MARE.

NICKALLS, GUY (1866–1935), oarsman, was the third son of Tom Nickalls, of Horton Kirby, Kent, afterwards of Patteson Court, Nutfield, Surrey, an original member of the London Rowing Club, by his wife, Emily Quihampton. He was born at Horton Kirby 12 November 1866, and like his brother Vivian, also a prominent oarsman, was educated at Eton and Magdalen College, Oxford. In early youth he was considered to be of delicate constitution, but after he had been at Eton a short time he began to develop the physique and stamina which made him the outstanding oarsman that he eventually became. He had many other interests in life, especially in connexion with sport, although it is on account of his remarkable successes in boat-racing that his name will always remain a household word. He rowed for Eton two years, winning the Ladies' plate in 1885, and five years for Oxford (1887–1891), being a member of the winning crew the last two years. His Henley successes are likely to remain a record for all time. Over this course he rowed in all 81 races, of which he won 67 and lost 13, one being a dead heat. This extraordinary achievement includes the following victories: 5 Diamond sculls, 6 Goblets or pair-oared races, 7 Stewards' or four-oared races, 4 Grand Challenge cups, one Olympic eights, and one Ladies' plate. Probably the most notable of all these achievements was his rowing at No. 4 in the Leander Olympic eight at the age of forty-one years and eight months. In writing of them in his autobiography he comments: 'I do not wish for a moment to take any credit to myself. . . . Nature has endowed me with a fairly strong body, a constitution of iron, and a will power or stubbornness above the average. These I have tried my best not to abuse, and any man so built and constituted, given my opportunities, could no doubt have done the same.'

From 1891 to 1922 Nickalls was a member of the Stock Exchange. An enthusiast in all things, he forced his way into the army at the age of forty-seven without previous military experience. He went to France in 1917 as superintendent of the physical and bayonet training of a division (afterwards increased to three divisions), and remained abroad until the end of hostilities. Later in life he devoted a considerable amount of his time to work on behalf of the Worcester College for the Blind, and was successful in collecting a considerable sum as the foundation of a permanent endowment fund.

On 7 July 1935, while motoring north for his annual fishing holiday in Scotland, Nickalls met with a motoring accident, from the results of which he died at Leeds next day. It is unlikely that there will be seen again his equal as an oarsman in power and endurance.

Nickalls married in 1898 Ellen Gilbey (died August 1935), daughter of Henry Gold, J.P., of Hedsor, Buckinghamshire. There were two sons of the marriage, Guy and Rodney. The former was a member of the winning crew in the boat-race of 1923, when president of the Oxford University Boat Club, and created a record for the Grand Challenge Cup with seven wins, while the younger son was captain of the boats at Eton.

[*The Times*, 9 July 1935; Guy Nickalls, *Life's a Pudding* (published posthumously), 1939; personal knowledge.]

HARCOURT GOLD.

NOBLE, MONTAGU ALFRED (1873–1940), Australian cricketer, was born at Sydney 28 January 1873, the son of Joseph Noble, by his wife, Maria Collins. He came into notice in December 1894, when playing for eighteen Sydney Juniors against the first of the two English teams taken out to Australia by A. E. Stoddart [q.v.]. The visitors were without their best bowlers, but the batting of the Juniors was remarkable, Noble scoring 152 not out, and Victor Trumper, another great batsman of the future, 67. Noble then received a trial in the New South Wales team, and gradually established himself as a cricketer of extraordinary merit.

When, after an interval of three years, Stoddart's second team visited Australia in 1897–1898, Noble, after being left out of the first test match, was chosen for the remaining four. All the four matches in which he played were won by Australia, and although he did not make runs, his bowling accounted for 19 wickets at an average cost of 20 runs each.

Noble was an obvious choice for the next Australian tour in England, and in the season of 1899 he paid the first of his four visits to this country. It was a summer of fine weather with hard wickets, and only one of the tests was finished, the Lord's match, which England lost by ten wickets. In the fourth game the Australians owed their rescue from a precarious position to the stubborn defence of Noble. To the English total of 372 they replied with 196, and had to follow on nearly 200 runs behind. Noble, who had made 60 not out in the first innings, followed this up with 89 in the second. He was batting altogether for eight and a half hours, and at one time did not score a run for three-quarters of an hour. This performance, although tedious to watch, was remarkable as an example of endurance, and was effective in saving the game.

As a captain Noble's reputation stands high. Although he did not captain an Australian eleven in this country until he visited it for the fourth time in 1909, in Australia as far back as 1903 he had been appointed to lead the home eleven against both (Sir) Pelham Warner's team, and the team taken out by A. O. Jones in 1907–1908. After losing the first of these campaigns, he won the second, and in March 1908 a testimonial match was arranged at Sydney in his honour. The testimonial fund exceeded £2,000. In England in 1909 he is described as having shown himself a courageous and enterprising commander. He won the toss five times, and two out of the three test matches that were finished. English accounts of these matches that summer consist chiefly of violent denunciations of the English selection committee which, by putting in the wrong men and leaving out the right ones, ruined any chance that England might have had of winning.

As an all-round test-match player Noble is shown by his figures to have had no equal. Only one other Australian cricketer, George Giffen, can challenge comparison with him as a batsman and bowler combined. Noble played in 39 matches against England, scoring 1,905 runs and taking 115 wickets. Giffen in 31 matches scored 1,238 runs and took 103 wickets. Hitherto only one other cricketer, Wilfred Rhodes, has made over 1,000 runs and taken over 100 wickets in test matches between England and Australia.

On his return home after the tour of 1909 in England, Noble announced his intention of retiring from first-class cricket. It was shortly after this that differences arose between the Australian board of control and certain of its principal players, the consequence being that the triangular tournament held in England in 1912 lost much of its interest owing to the weak representation of Australia.

In his later years Noble was a well-known writer and lecturer on cricket. He married Elizabeth Ellen Ferguson and had three sons and a daughter. He died at Sydney 22 June 1940.

[*The Times*, 24 June 1940; Wisden's *Cricketers' Almanack, passim*; private information.]   ALFRED COCHRANE.

NORGATE, KATE (1853–1935), historian, was born in St. Pancras, London, 8 December 1853, the only child of Frederick Norgate, bookseller, later a partner in the firm of Messrs. Williams & Norgate, by his wife, Fanny, daughter of John Athow, statuary, stonemason, and surveyor of the Norwich city pavements. Her grandfather, Thomas Starling Norgate [q.v.], a friend of William Taylor (1765–1836, q.v.), gave her a link with the active literary group which throve in Norwich in the first half of the nineteenth century. When she fell under the spell of John Richard Green [q.v.], she was ready to use to the full the opportunities which he gave her. By 1877 she had already made some progress with her first book. Her mother is said to have accompanied her to the British Museum and to have sat by her in the reading-room. Green gave her every encouragement. *England under the Angevin Kings*, in two volumes, was published in 1887, four years after his death. Its merits were recognized at once, notably by E. A. Freeman [q.v.], who wrote a long appreciation of it in the *English Historical Review* (vol. ii, 1887). The book revealed a new historian. Miss Norgate's mastery of the original sources showed critical power and found expression in good, clear narrative. If she was affected by Green's strong preference for the chronicles and avoided unpublished material, she did not share his deliberate indifference to 'records' and used them assiduously in her later studies. In every way, except its neglect of manuscript evidence, her work marked a great advance upon that of Agnes Strickland [q.v.]. The appearance of this young woman who had trained herself made the distinction between men and women historians an anachronism.

England under the Angevin Kings carried the story down to 1206. It was continued in *John Lackland* (1902) and *The Minority of Henry the Third* (1912). In *Richard the Lion Heart* (1924) Miss Norgate retraced her steps to follow the life of Richard I, as a hero of the Christian West. All three books are careful, well arranged, clear, and spirited narratives. They give the best available history of great movements and great events, interesting to the general reader and useful to the scholar. In her younger days Miss Norgate was full of generous enthusiasm. She joined with her friend Thomas Andrew Archer in a passionate defence of Freeman against the attacks of J. H. Round [q.v.] (*English Historical Review*, vol. ix, 1894). Of her critical studies, the most important is her defence of the authenticity of Adrian IV's bull *Laudabiliter* (*English Historical Review*, vol. viii, 1893); here, although she exposed herself to some thrusts by Round, she was undoubtedly right.

In these early years Miss Norgate was happy, contributing to this DICTIONARY, working with Alice [Stopford] Green [q.v.] in the preparation of the illustrated edition of Green's *Short History of the English People* (1892–1894), and working on her next book in the society of learned friends like William Hunt [q.v.]; but she outlived them all, and was hardly known to the next generation. The only recognition which came to her was given by Somerville College, Oxford, which in 1929 elected her an honorary fellow. She died at Gorleston-on-Sea 17 April 1935.

[*The Times*, 6 May 1935; Walter Rye, *Norfolk Families*, vol. ii, 1913; *Letters of John Richard Green*, edited by Leslie Stephen, 1901; private information.]   F. M. POWICKE.
                                                P. MILLICAN.

NOVAR, VISCOUNT (1860–1934), politician. [See FERGUSON, RONALD CRAUFORD MUNRO-.]

NUTTALL, GEORGE HENRY FALKINER (1862–1937), bacteriologist, was born at San Francisco, California, 5 July 1862, the second son of Robert Kennedy Nuttall, M.D., formerly of Tittour, co. Wicklow, by his wife, Magdalena, daughter of John Parrott, of San Francisco. In 1865 the family returned to Europe, the children being educated in England, France, Germany, and Switzerland. It was to his cosmopolitan upbringing that Nuttall owed his ability to speak several languages, an accomplishment which was to help him greatly in his work and travels. He returned to America in 1878 and entered the university of California, obtaining the M.D. degree in 1884. In 1886 he went to Germany where he remained for four years studying mainly botany and zoology, subjects that led on to an interest in parasitology, which became the main scientific interest of his life. In 1891 he returned to America as assistant to W. H. Welch, professor of pathology at Johns Hopkins University, Baltimore. From 1892 to 1899 he worked on hygiene at Göttingen and Berlin, and in 1899 he gave a course of lectures on bacteriology at Cambridge, being appointed a year later university lecturer in bacteriology and preventive medicine.

In 1901 Nuttall founded the *Journal of Hygiene* and in 1908 *Parasitology*, the former of which he edited up to the time of his death, the latter until 1933. In his editorial work he displayed the same thoroughness as in his research. He considered that part of the duty of an editor is educational and spent much time in correcting and improving papers and in advising young and inexperienced workers. As editor he exerted great influence on workers scattered all over the world, and his journals became models upon which the publications of several scientific societies were based.

In 1906 Nuttall was elected the first Quick professor of biology at Cambridge and a fellow of Magdalene College, with the duty of devoting himself to the 'study of Protozoa, especially such as cause disease'. In 1919 he issued an appeal for funds with which to build an institute for parasitological research. As the result of this appeal, a generous gift, made by Mr. and Mrs. P. A. Molteno, provided funds for the erection of the Molteno Institute for Research in Parasitology (later known as the Molteno Institute of Biology and Parasitology), which was formally opened in 1921. In 1920 the 'study of Parasitology' was substituted for the 'Study of Protozoa' in the regulations concerning the duties of the Quick professor.

Nuttall's scientific work covered a very wide field; in addition to several books, he published papers on bacteriology, serology, hygiene, tropical medicine, and parasitology. Among his most valuable contributions to science was his discovery in 1888 that defibrinated blood possesses a strong bactericidal property against anthrax bacilli, and that this property disappears on heating the blood to 55° C.

This work founded the study of humoral immunity and was the forerunner of great discoveries such as that of anti-toxic immunity. In 1892 he studied in great detail in collaboration with Welch the anaerobic gas-forming micro-organism, now known as *Clostridium Welchii*, the great importance of which as a pathogenic agent was not fully appreciated until the war of 1914–1918. In collaboration with H. Thierfelder (1895–1897) he carried out the first successful experiments on life under aseptic conditions, experiments which solved one of the outstanding problems which preoccupied Pasteur.

In 1897 Nuttall turned his attention to the part played by arthropods in the spread of disease, a subject to which he devoted the later period of his life. In 1899 he published his well-known paper *On the role of Insects, Arachnids and Myriapods as carriers in the spread of Bacterial and Parasitic Disease of Man and Animals*, which contained an exhaustive critical and historical review of the whole subject. In 1901 he showed that the disappearance of malaria from England was not due to the extinction of *Anopheles* which in that year were still numerous in all formerly malarious districts.

In 1901 Nuttall became interested in the precipitin reaction, and in 1904 published his classical monograph, *Blood Immunity and Blood Relationship*, which demonstrated the existence of a distinct similarity in chemical structure of the blood in animals which are related phylogenetically. He then began his investigations on diseases transmitted to animals by ticks. By means of infected ticks (*Haemophysalis leachi*), sent to him from South Africa, he succeeded in infecting dogs with piroplasmosis, a disease unknown in England. This was the first case of investigation of a disease imported by means of an infected vector. An important result of this investigation, which had great economic importance, was the discovery of the curative property of trypan blue for piroplasmosis in dogs, cattle, and sheep. This study was followed by an extensive investigation of the anatomy, biology, life-history, and systematics of ticks, carried out in collaboration with Cecil Warburton and Louis Edward Robinson, which occupied him during the remaining years of his life.

Nuttall resigned the Quick professorship in 1931 and became emeritus professor of biology. He died suddenly in London 16 December 1937 on the eve of a dinner to be given by sixty colleagues in his honour on his retirement from his long and successful editorship of the *Journal of Hygiene*. He married in 1895 Paula (died 1922), daughter of Kammerherr Hans von Oertzen-Kittendorf, of Mecklenburg, and had two sons and a daughter.

Nuttall was of distinguished appearance, had great charm of manner, was an excellent raconteur, and was invariably at ease in whatever company he found himself. He was elected F.R.S. in 1904, received honorary degrees from several universities, and was elected corresponding member of many scientific societies. In 1932 he was presented by his colleagues and pupils with his portrait in oils by P. A. de László; this is in the possession of the family. A pencil portrait by the same artist is at Magdalene College, Cambridge.

[*The Times*, 18 December 1937; *Obituary Notices of Fellows of the Royal Society*, No. 7, January 1939 (portrait); *Parasitology*, vol. xxx, 1938; *Journal of Hygiene*, vol. xxxviii, 1938.]   G. S. GRAHAM-SMITH.

O'DWYER, SIR MICHAEL FRANCIS (1864–1940), Indian administrator, was the sixth son in a family of fourteen children of John O'Dwyer, of Barronstown, co. Tipperary, where the family sept had been settled for centuries and he himself was born 28 April 1864. His mother was Margaret, daughter of Patrick Quirk, of Toom, Tipperary. He was educated at St. Stanislaus College, Tullamore, and passed the open competition for the Indian civil service in 1882 and the final examination in 1884. The intervening two years of probation he spent at Balliol College, Oxford, where in a third year he obtained a first class in jurisprudence. Joining the service in India in 1885 he was first posted to Shahpur in the Punjab. His rise was rapid and was achieved by sheer character and ability. He greatly distinguished himself in land revenue settlement work, and was made director of land records and agriculture in the Punjab (1896); next year he was placed in charge of the settlements of the Alwar and Bharatpur States. He was a fine rider and sportsman, a warm sympathizer with the rural classes, and a master of the vernacular. After a long furlough which he spent largely on examination leave in Russia, passing for an interpretership, O'Dwyer was selected by Lord Curzon [q.v.] for a prominent part in the organization of the new North-West Frontier Province and its separation from the Punjab: he was revenue commissioner from 1901 to 1908. From 1908 to 1909 he was acting resident in Hyderabad, and agent to the governor-general in Central India from 1910 to 1912. In December 1912, while Lord Hardinge of Penshurst was viceroy, he was appointed to be lieutenant-governor of the Punjab, a post which he held until 1919. When he assumed charge in May 1913 he was cautioned by the viceroy 'that the Punjab was the Province about which the Government were then most concerned; that there was much inflammable material lying about, which required very careful handling if an explosion were to be avoided'. In his vivid book *India as I Knew It, 1885–1925* (1925), O'Dwyer explains this warning and shows how after the return of Sikh emigrants from America, Canada, and the Far East in the first few months of the war of 1914–1918 the Punjab narrowly escaped becoming a theatre of widespread disturbances. (Sir) Austen Chamberlain [q.v.], shortly after quitting the India Office, testified to the 'great skill, firmness and moderation' with which O'Dwyer had piloted the Punjab in the first two years of the war. It was generally acknowledged that his firm, fearless, but at the same time sympathetic administration had been the directing factor which turned the Punjab in very critical months from a theatre of danger into a great example of loyal recruiting for the cause of the British *raj*. At the same time, the very success that had attended his effort led to accusations of undue pressure on the part of subordinate officers, and was a cause, although possibly a minor one, of the unrest in the province in 1919. O'Dwyer's services were recognized by his appointment as G.C.I.E. in 1917 after he had been created K.C.S.I. in 1913.

Soon after the departure of Lord Hardinge, however, in the spring of 1916 and the arrival of Lord Chelmsford [q.v.] the 'home rule' agitation, under the leadership of B. G. Tilak and Mrs. Annie Besant [q.v.], gradually became more intense. Revolutionary crime having begun in Bengal, a special Defence of India Act had already been promulgated (1915). But that Act would come to an end with the war, and after more experience the government of India decided that more legislation would probably be needed to supply its place. The matter was inquired into by a special committee of five, presided over by Mr. Justice

Rowlatt, which began work in Calcutta in January 1917, and their report was embodied in an emergency bill, which passed into law as the Anarchical and Revolutionary Crimes Act in March 1919, and led to Gandhi's 'civil disobedience' and 'passive resistance' movement. This culminated in the Punjab and Guzerat riots and the tragedy of the Jalianwala Bagh at Amritsar in April. There is no doubt that the shooting there was ordered by the military officer in command, Brigadier-General Reginald E. H. Dyer [q.v.], because he thought it necessary to avert a highly dangerous impression that the government's arm was paralysed. Dyer reported his action to Lieutenant-General Sir William Beynon, his superior officer, and the latter asked the lieutenant-governor by telephone whether he approved. O'Dwyer, under the impression that what had been done was irrevocable, replied at once in the affirmative. Dyer had acted to the best of his judgement when in fact he was faced with a great and imminent danger. Strong measures had been required and had been taken; and the plague was stayed, but at a heavy cost, for many apparently innocent spectators had mingled with the crowd. In October the government of India appointed a committee of inquiry, of which Lord Hunter was chairman, and its report led to Dyer being ordered by the commander-in-chief in India, Sir C. C. Munro [q.v.], to resign his appointment as brigade-commander. O'Dwyer explains in his book all that he did to avert this conclusion. Attempts were made to involve him in Dyer's downfall, but without success. In 1922 Sir Sankaran Nair [q.v.], formerly a judge of the Madras High Court and member for education of the viceroy's executive council, published a book entitled *Gandhi and Anarchy* in which certain passages directed against O'Dwyer were challenged by him in London as libels. In 1924, after a trial before Mr. Justice McCardie [q.v.], who in summing up expressed his opinion that Dyer had acted rightly and had been wrongly punished, the jury, by a majority verdict of eleven to one, agreed to by the parties, found for the plaintiff and judgement was given for the agreed damages of five hundred pounds.

O'Dwyer served as a useful member of Lord Esher's committee on the administration and organization of the army in India (1919–1920) and often wrote letters to *The Times* on Indian affairs. After his retirement he welcomed to his house in London Indian visitors and his many friends. He believed, as he had always believed, in the necessity of British control in India for that country's welfare. His aim was always to benefit India. But he did not think that either of the constitutions promulgated in 1919 and 1935 would benefit India, and he opposed them both on important points with infinite pains and labour. His convictions were strong and he upheld them with all the energy and tenacity of his character. But with all his vigour and eloquence he was full of kindly humour and ready to see an antagonist's point of view. After his death it was truly said by the *Observer*: 'No servant of India formed his judgements more conscientiously nor expressed them with more frankness and courage, nor had it a more profound well-wisher than the man whose long life of devotion has been foully ended.'

O'Dwyer was shot from behind by an Indian assassin named Udhan Singh at the close of a crowded meeting of the Royal Central Asian Society in London on 13 March 1940. The murderer was tried and convicted. The tragedy was deeply mourned by his many friends and admirers. A memorial fund committee was formed and a brass was placed in the Church of Our Lady of the Annunciation, Warwick Street, in which, in 1896, he had married Una, daughter of Antoine Bord, of Castres, France, who survived him with their son and daughter.

[*The Times*, 14 and 15 March 1940; Sir M. F. O'Dwyer, *India as I Knew It, 1885–1925*, 1925; personal knowledge.] H. V. LOVETT.

OLIVER, FREDERICK SCOTT (1864–1934), man of business and publicist, was born in Edinburgh 20 February 1864, the elder son of John Scott Oliver, a merchant in Madeira, and later in Edinburgh, by his wife, Catherine, daughter of Duncan McLaren [q.v.], politician, and half-sister of John McLaren, Lord McLaren [q.v.], Scottish judge. The mother died in 1869, and Frederick and his brother were brought up by their father and their father's sister Beatrix Oliver.

Oliver was educated at George Watson's College, Edinburgh, Edinburgh University, and Trinity College, Cambridge, where from 1883 to 1886 he read for the moral sciences tripos. After taking his degree he studied law and was called to the bar by the Inner Temple in 1889, but three years later, on the invitation of his Cambridge friend

Ernest Debenham, he entered the firm of Messrs. Debenham & Freebody. In this career he was brilliantly successful. He played a leading part in developing what when he joined it was a comparatively small wholesale concern into one of the leading retail and wholesale businesses in London; and when he retired from the active conduct of its affairs to the estate which he had bought at Edgerston at the head of the Jed valley in the Cheviot Hills, whence his paternal forebears came, he had acquired a large fortune.

Above all, however, Oliver was a man of letters. He was a close student of history, particularly of the eighteenth century. He wrote English prose with the clear precision of Swift; and being at the same time keenly interested in the politics of his country and of his time, and the confidant of many men of high position in public affairs, he employed his learning and his talents for the practical furtherance of the causes which he had at heart. Foremost among these was that of Joseph Chamberlain [q.v.] and tariff reform, and Oliver's first published work, *The Statesman and the Bishop* (1904), which appeared under the pseudonym of 'John Draper', consisting of a letter indirectly addressed to John Percival, bishop of Hereford [q.v.], is a fine piece of controversial writing. Next came a brilliant biography of *Alexander Hamilton* (1906). This was written with the same cause in mind; but the life-story of the author of *The Federalist* had the effect, probably unforeseen by Oliver himself, of serving as a source of inspiration to the men who were then working for the Union of South Africa and who were afterwards to be numbered among his intimate friends.

Another cause which Oliver espoused was that of seeking a solution of the Irish question in the federalization of the institutions of the United Kingdom; and three books, *Federalism and Home Rule* (1910), consisting of letters written to *The Times* earlier in that year under the pseudonym of 'Pacificus', *The Alternatives to Civil War* (1913), and *What Federalism is Not* (1914), were devoted to this object. But the best known and most popular of Oliver's works was undoubtedly *Ordeal by Battle* (1915), a critical examination of the conduct of the first year of the war of 1914–1918. This was followed by *Ireland and the Imperial Conference* (1917). Then came *The Endless Adventure*, designed as a thesis on the art of politics, but narrowed down to a study of the career of Sir Robert Walpole as a great exponent of that art. Of this work the first two volumes were published in 1930 and 1931, and the third, which was left unfinished but contains Oliver's 'Political Testament', in 1935 after the author's death. Lastly *The Anvil of War*, consisting of letters exchanged between him and his brother W. E. Oliver (who was in Canada) from 1914 to 1918, was posthumously published in 1936, with an introductory memoir by Mr. Stephen Gwynn.

Oliver was a master of the art of living. The last years of his life were clouded by ill health, but no illness could blunt his pen, or dim the brilliance of his letters or of his talk, unfailing sources of joy to his host of friends.

Oliver married in 1893 Katharine Augusta, eldest daughter of his uncle, Lord McLaren, and had two sons and a daughter. He died at Edgerston 3 June 1934. A portrait of him with his wife (1903) by Charles Furse is at Edgerston, together with a bust by his sister-in-law, Mrs. Ottilie Wallace.

[*The Times*, 5 and 6 June 1934; *The Anvil of War*, edited by S. Gwynn, 1936; personal knowledge.]   Dougal O. Malcolm.

OMAN, JOHN WOOD (1860–1939), divine, was born on the farm of Biggins in the parish of Stenness, Orkney, 23 July 1860, the second son of Simon Rust Oman, a farmer who in earlier years had been master of a sailing vessel, by his wife, Isabella Irvine Rendall. He owed his early education mainly to a tutor engaged for a neighbouring family and shared by a few other boys. Many references in Oman's works reveal how deeply his mind was shaped by the freedom and simplicity of his boyhood—its close contacts with the soil and the sea and with the hardy and vigorous folk who gained their living from them. He himself described his father, in the dedication of his Kerr lectures, as 'a scholar only of life and action, but my best teacher'. He entered Edinburgh University in 1877, graduating in 1882 with first class honours in philosophy and winning the Gray and Rhind scholarships. Thence he proceeded to the theological college of the United Presbyterian Church in Edinburgh, and at the conclusion of the course there he studied at the universities of Erlangen, Heidelberg, and Neuchâtel. Returning to Scotland he served for a brief period as assistant minister at St. James's church, Paisley. In 1889 he accepted a call to be minister of Clayport Street church, Alnwick, thus passing into the Presbyterian Church of England, in the service of which he remained to the end of his life. Whilst at Alnwick he married in 1897 Mary Hannah, daughter of Henry Hunter Blair, J.P., of Gosforth, a very happy union broken only by her death in 1936. They had four daughters.

It was during his ministry at Alnwick that Oman's quality as an unusually learned, powerful, and original thinker in the field of theology—already known to his intimates—began to be more widely known, mainly through the publication in 1902 of *Vision and Authority; or, the Throne of St. Peter* (new and revised ed. 1928), and in 1906 of his Kerr lectures, *The Problem of Faith and Freedom in the last two Centuries*. The former revealed a mind singularly able to keep profound and informed theological reflection in close relation with the religious life and its problems; the latter showed an easy, first-hand mastery, issuing in penetrating and original judgements, of the works of every relevant writer of importance from Pascal to Ritschl. Before the publication of these two works he had issued in 1893 what is still the only translation into English (though out of print) of F. E. D. Schleiermacher's epoch-making *Reden über die Religion*.

In 1907 Oman was appointed professor of systematic theology and apologetics in Westminster College, Cambridge, the theological college of the Presbyterian Church of England, where he remained until his retirement in 1935, having become principal in 1922. At Westminster College he was one of a remarkably distinguished teaching staff, his colleagues being John Skinner, Charles Anderson Scott, and Dr. Patrick Carnegie Simpson. During this time Oman came to be recognized, first in Cambridge, and later more widely, as one of the most learned and original minds at work in theology. He was thrice (1913–1916, 1919–1922, 1929–1931) appointed Stanton lecturer in the philosophy of religion in the university of Cambridge, and served for many years on the board of the faculty of divinity and on its degree committee. In 1909 he became a member of Queens' College and in 1935 an honorary fellow of Jesus College; the honorary degree of D.D. was conferred upon him by the universities of Edinburgh and Oxford. In 1938 he was elected a fellow of the British Academy. His own Church honoured him by electing him

moderator of the General Assembly in 1931. He died at Cambridge 7 May 1939.

Oman's eminent position as a thinker was achieved partly through his work as a teacher, which greatly influenced all his students, but more through his published writings, among which, besides those already named, should be mentioned *The Church and the Divine Order* (1911), *Grace and Personality* (1917), *The Paradox of the World* (1921), *The Natural and the Supernatural* (1931), *Concerning the Ministry* (1936), and *Honest Religion* (published posthumously in 1941 with a memoir of the author by George Alexander and Herbert Henry Farmer). Of these *Grace and Personality* and *The Natural and the Supernatural* are the most important both as affording insight into Oman's characteristic teaching and as permanent enrichments of theological literature. Oman's theology was built round a strongly personalistic doctrine of man and of God's dealings with man. Man's true end can only be achieved through a reverence which never subordinates sacred values to expediency or profit, a freedom which accepts all the risks of freedom, a sincerity which walks steadfastly by its own insight. All these needs and prerogatives of personality God Himself unwaveringly respects, having Himself created and bestowed them. In *Grace and Personality* this theme is worked out in relation to the central Christian doctrines of grace and forgiveness with a thoroughness, consistency, and power which make it, in the words of a critic, 'one of the major treasures of theological literature'. In *The Natural and the Supernatural* the same basic thoughts are made the clue to the understanding of the nature and history of religion, of the processes of knowledge, of evolution, of the natural order, the whole constituting a sustained argument to justify the contention that there is direct awareness of the supernatural which leads on to fuller knowledge of God only as men live in loyalty to those sacred values through which He discloses Himself to their souls.

Oman's writing is not always easy to follow, demanding close attention and a willingness to weigh every sentence with care; but it rises at times to real, if restrained, eloquence, is interspersed with apt illustration, and always rests on a vast knowledge which is masked from the uninformed by a refusal to adorn his pages with references to other authors. His character, in its massive and at times almost formidable integrity, was an impressive embodiment of his own teaching. Physically also he was impressive, being tall and with a noble head. A fine portrait of him by H. G. Riviere is in the hall of Westminster College, Cambridge.

[F. R. Tennant, *John Wood Oman, 1860–1939* in *Proceedings* of the British Academy, vol. xxv, 1939 (portrait); Memoir by George Alexander and H. H. Farmer prefixed to J. W. Oman, *Honest Religion*, 1941; private information; personal knowledge.]

H. H. Farmer.

ORAGE, ALFRED RICHARD (1873–1934), editor, and exponent of social credit, whose original name was Alfred James Orage, was born at Dacre, near Bradford, Yorkshire, 22 January 1873, the younger son of William Steverson Orage, farmer, and later a teacher in his own school at Dacre, by his wife, Sarah Anne McQuire. William Orage died during the infancy of Alfred, who was brought up by his mother in poor circumstances at his father's native village, Fenstanton in Huntingdonshire. The benevolence of Howard Coote, the son of a local squire, enabled him to continue his education at the village school as a pupil teacher and to proceed to a teachers' training college at Culham, Oxfordshire. In 1893 he became a teacher in an elementary school at Leeds; but, although he was very able and enthusiastic in class, he soon developed wider outside interests which embraced literature and guild socialism. With Mr. Holbrook Jackson, whom he met in 1900, Orage founded the Leeds Arts Club, with the main object of fostering new standards in the arts.

In 1906 Orage came to London as a free-lance journalist. In 1907, with the financial backing of Mr. Bernard Shaw, Orage and Mr. Jackson bought a dying weekly review called the *New Age*. Although both were keen Fabians, they by no means limited the paper to socialist views. Among early contributors who later became famous were G. K. Chesterton [q.v.], H. G. Wells, and Arnold Bennett [q.v.]. Jackson relinquished his joint editorship in 1909, and the *New Age* was essentially an expression of Orage's personality. His incisive and illuminating political notes helped to give the journal high prestige, although it never attained a large circulation.

In 1918 Orage met Major Clifford Hugh Douglas, and soon became convinced that social credit was a sound economic scheme. He was to become a strong advocate of the theory, but meanwhile, just after the war of 1914–1918, he fell under the influence of the occultist P. D. Ouspensky, and, through him, became a disciple of the Russian mystic George Gurdjieff. In October 1922 Orage gave up the editorship of the *New Age* and spent rather more than a year at Gurdjieff's institute, Le Prieuré, at Fontainebleau, dividing his time between manual labour and the study of Gurdjieff's philosophy. From the end of 1923 until 1930 he was in the United States of America, holding meetings and giving lectures to raise funds for Le Prieuré, but occasionally visiting London or Fontainebleau.

Returning finally to England in 1930, Orage in 1932 founded the *New English Weekly*, which became the organ of social credit and also a forum for many good writers, established or newly discovered. He died suddenly at Hampstead early in the morning of 6 November 1934 after having given a broadcast address on the Douglas theory the previous evening.

Himself a forcible and persuasive writer, with a nice sense of word values, Orage was quick to detect and encourage talent in others, and was rightly proud of the great reputations later won by many contributors to the *New Age*. Optimistic, energetic, and intellectually fearless, he constantly pursued an ideal, the lineaments of which he saw, at different times, in guild socialism, the philosophy of Nietzsche on whom he did pioneer work, publishing two valuable monographs, the mysticism of Gurdjieff, and the economic doctrine of social credit. An unconventional thinker, a gifted lecturer, and an amusing and racy talker, he exercised a considerable literary influence and displayed high editorial virtues in the selection, presentation, and integration of literary teams.

Orage was twice married: first, in 1896 to Jean Walker (who divorced him in 1927); secondly, in 1927 to Jessie Richards, daughter of Harvey Lyman Dwight, dealer in building supplies, of Albany, U.S.A. There were a son and a daughter by the second marriage.

A drawing of Orage by F. Ernest Jackson (1909), and an oil-painting by T. C. Dugdale (1932), are in the possession of Orage's widow.

[*The Times*, 7 and 11 November 1934; *Manchester Guardian*, 7, 12, and 13 November 1934; Philip Mairet, *A. R. Orage: A Memoir*, 1936; S. G. Hobson, *Pilgrim to the Left*, 1938; private information.]

Herbert B. Grimsditch.

ORAM, Sir HENRY JOHN (1858–1939), engineer vice-admiral, was born at Plymouth 19 June 1858, the eldest son of John Joseph Oram, of Plymouth, by his wife, Jane Hall. He was educated at private schools and went in 1873 to the Royal Naval Engineering College at Keyham, Devonport, whence he entered the Royal Navy in 1879 as assistant-engineer. Subsequently during the three years higher engineering course at the Royal Naval College, Greenwich, he proved himself to be a brilliant student. Leaving Greenwich in 1882 he served as junior engineer in the troopships *Crocodile* and *Malabar* and, becoming engineer in 1884, he returned to London on appointment as assistant-engineer in the department of the engineer-in-chief at the Admiralty. In that department Oram was destined to spend a period of more than thirty-three years. Promotion came very rapidly; in 1889 he became chief-engineer, in 1893 staff-engineer, and in 1897 fleet-engineer. In that year he was specially promoted to the rank of inspector of machinery; he became chief inspector in 1901 (the title being changed to engineer rear-admiral in 1903); in 1902 he was made deputy engineer-in-chief; and in 1907 he succeeded Engineer Vice-Admiral Sir Albert John Durston as engineer-in-chief of the fleet, with the rank of engineer vice-admiral; he held this last post until he retired in June 1917.

Oram's period of office as engineer-in-chief was one of unusual activity in naval engineering as it saw the introduction of the water-tube boiler, oil fuel, and the turbine. These important innovations gave Oram a task exceeding that of his predecessors both in range and in engineering interest, and it was in no small measure due to his tenacity and skill that by 1902 the fleet was able to report that the vessels fitted with water-tube boilers had reached a satisfactory standard of performance. He was a member of the technical committee formed in 1903 to report on the designs for the machinery of the subsidized liners *Mauretania* and *Lusitania*, and he was responsible for the detailed investigations which enabled Durston confidently to recommend the use of steam turbines in 1905 for the *Dreadnought*. He also served on the royal commission on oil fuel and engines under the chairmanship of Lord Fisher [q.v.]. With Richard Sennett he was author of *The Marine Steam Engine* (1898) which has been the authorized text-book for naval engineers for many years.

Oram was elected F.R.S. in 1912, and was president of the Institute of Metals (1914), of which he was a founder-member, and of the Junior Institution of Engineers (1908–1909). He was appointed C.B. in 1906 and K.C.B. in 1910. For his collaboration with the United States navy during the war of 1914–1918 he received the American D.S.M.

Oram married in 1881 Emily Kate (died 1928), only daughter of John Bardens, of Plymouth, and had two sons and two daughters. He died at Cranleigh, Surrey, 5 May 1939.

[*The Times*, 6 May 1939; *Obituary Notices of Fellows of the Royal Society*, No. 8, January 1940 (portrait); *Nature*, 3 June 1939; personal knowledge.] W. M. Whayman.

        H. A. Brown.

ORPEN, Sir WILLIAM NEWENHAM MONTAGUE (1878–1931), painter, was born at Stillorgan, co. Dublin, 27 November 1878, the fourth and youngest son of Arthur Herbert Orpen, a Dublin solicitor, by his wife, Anne, eldest daughter of Charles Caulfeild, bishop of Nassau. The Orpens were a well-known Protestant family, claiming descent from the French; William's grandfather, Sir Richard Orpen, was president of the Incorporated Law Society of Ireland. His father and his eldest brother, the architect Richard Francis Caulfeild Orpen, were both skilful painters in water-colour.

William Orpen's own gift for drawing was evident at an early age and he was sent to the Metropolitan School of Art, Dublin, when only eleven. He became the prodigy of the school and at seventeen went on to study at the Slade School of Fine Art, London. Here the critical encouragement of Henry Tonks [q.v.] was a potent influence in revealing qualities of style and design in the work of the old masters. With such fellow students as Mr. Augustus John and Arthur Ambrose McEvoy [q.v.] Orpen expanded at once and was one of the chief of that brilliant band of young draughtsmen who made the high reputation of the Slade School. His large composition 'Hamlet', which won the Slade summer prize in 1899, was no mere student's exercise but a remarkably mature piece of picture-making: in its eclecticism—influences of Rembrandt, Watteau, Goya, and Hogarth may be traced—and in its passages of *bravura* execution it already displayed two of Orpen's essential qualities.

Orpen began to exhibit with immediate success at the New English Art Club, of which he was elected a member in 1900. 'The Mirror', shown that year and now in the Tate Gallery, was the first of a remarkable series of interiors with small figures, precisely drawn and painted with great justice of tone and lighting, often with a beautiful use of pigment. The detailed realism of these pictures was in no wise akin to that of the pre-Raphaelites but in atmospheric envelopment was related to the Dutch masters of the seventeenth century, while a flavour of anecdote linked them with the English tradition of Wilkie. Backed by the recommendation of J. S. Sargent [q.v.] commissions for portraits came quickly from Sir George Swinton, Percy Wyndham, George Moore [q.v.], and many others.

In 1901 Orpen married Grace, youngest daughter of Walter John Knewstub, of Highgate, the friend and assistant of Dante Gabriel Rossetti: they had three daughters. Her elder sister, Alice, was already married to (Sir) William Rothenstein, whose intimate pictures of interiors with figures may have given a lead to Orpen. He joined forces with Mr. John in a teaching studio in Chelsea, but the success of this became embarrassing and a menace to work. His style gained freedom in a number of nudes and in half-length figures in the open air, seen against a background of sky, finely spaced and broadly painted. For painter-like vision he did nothing better than these and some fanciful self-portraits such as 'The Dead Ptarmigan' (1909) and 'Myself and Venus' (1910). In its balance of portraiture and design, and by reason of its sitters— George Moore, Wilson Steer, Walter Sickert, Henry Tonks, Dr. D. S. MacColl, and Sir Hugh Lane—'Hommage à Manet' (1909, now in the Manchester Corporation Art Gallery) will probably prove to be the most satisfying and lasting in interest of his groups.

Orpen's affection for his native country was profound and leapt out spontaneously. Such pictures as 'Sowing the Seed for the Board of Agriculture and Technical Instruction in Ireland' (1913) and 'The Western Wedding' (1914) gave play to his gamin-like humour and satirical fantasy. For some years he visited Dublin to direct the life-classes at the Metropolitan School of Art, and his thoroughness and dislike of pose or humbug made him a most stimulating teacher. He was a member of the Royal Hibernian Academy, but resigned in 1915.

In 1908 Orpen sent a brilliant portrait of Mr. C. J. Wertheimer to the Royal Academy and two years later was elected an associate. After this his pictures were among the chief features of the exhibitions at Burlington House, but he abandoned private work for two years from April 1917 when he went to France as an official war artist, with the rank of major in the Royal Army Service Corps. He threw himself wholeheartedly into the recording of men, from commanders-in-chief to the humblest of privates, and of characteristic and fantastic incidents, and amassed an immense number of paintings and drawings most of which he presented to the nation, after an exhibition held at Messrs. Agnews in 1918. At the Imperial War Museum they form a remarkable record, detailed, accurate, and occasionally, as in 'Changing Billets, Picardy' and 'Bombing; Night', of grim intensity.

There followed nine months of intense activity at the Peace Conferences in Paris and at Versailles. Two pictures of the Quai d'Orsay and the Hall of Mirrors, Versailles, with small figures of the great leaders treated crisply, wittily, without deference, against brilliantly painted backgrounds, remain as evidence of the signing of peace. But Orpen's own feelings were expressed in 'To the Unknown British Soldier in France', a draped coffin placed in the empty Hall of Mirrors and guarded by two gaunt wraiths from the trenches. Orpen had a profound admiration for the British fighting man, for the half-bitter, half-humorous fortitude of the troops: he was not so much impressed with the behaviour of national politicians, nor by state occasions.

Orpen was appointed K.B.E. in 1918 and elected a Royal Academician in 1919. Thenceforward he was more than ever in demand as a fashionable portrait painter. He was fond of painting women sitters against a black background, lighting the figure from two sides, an arrangement which gave luminosity and a certain ethereal appearance to his unfaltering but matter of fact statement: portraits of Miss Lily Carstairs (1914) and Mrs. Melvill (1921) are examples of this treatment. It would be difficult to surpass such portraits of men as those of James Law of the *Scotsman* (1915) and Sir William McCormick (q.v., 1920) for characteristic likeness and descriptive rendering of detail. At this they stop, offering little to stir the spectator's sensibility or imagination.

A serious illness at Amiens in 1918 undermined Orpen's health. He drove himself hard at work and at play and in 1931 his robust constitution began to fail. Three slight and enigmatic canvases at the Academy in that year disquieted his friends; the end came quickly and he died in London 29 September 1931.

Orpen was probably the most successful British artist of his time. With nearly 600 portraits he assumed the position in the public eye which Sargent, and before him Millais, had occupied. From the outset he was the industrious apprentice and learned everything that study from the living model and the drawings and paintings of the masters could teach him. He was equipped to deal with any subject which demanded power in rendering the appearances of textures, colour, lighting, and the appurtenances of a scene, although his ordering of them in design remained conventional rather than creative or significant. For one so keenly alive to the present moment Orpen was curiously irresponsive to the art movements of his day, but his sanity and robustness were refreshing, and his complete certainty of hand and eye represented professional skill at a very high level. His two books, *An Onlooker in France, 1917-1919* (1921) and *Stories of old Ireland and Myself* (1924), show shrewd observation and an uncommonly graphic use of words. He was president of the International Society of Sculptors, Painters, and Gravers (from 1921) and of the Royal and National Societies of Portrait Painters; a member of many clubs, he was an extremely entertaining companion, high spirited, droll, and brimful of songs and stories.

There is a pencil and wash self-portrait of Orpen in the National Portrait Gallery. Another self-portrait is included in 'The Selecting Jury, New English Art Club' (1909) in the same collection.

[*The Times*, 1 October 1931; P. G. Konody and Sidney Dark, *Sir William Orpen* (containing a chronological list of his works and lists of his self-portraits and of his pictures in public galleries), 1932.]

H. L. WELLINGTON.

ORR, WILLIAM McFADDEN (1866-1934), mathematician, was born at Ballystockart, Comber, co. Down, 2 May 1866, the eldest son of Fletcher Blakeley Orr, farmer and corn and flax mill-owner, of Ballystockart, by his wife,

Elizabeth, daughter of David Lowry, farmer, of Ballymachashan, Killinchy, co. Down. He received his early training in mathematics at the local national school. After spending two years at an intermediate school in Newtownards, he entered the Methodist College, Belfast, where he came under the mathematical direction of James Adams McNeill, afterwards headmaster of Campbell College, Belfast. He obtained a scholarship in mathematics at the Royal University of Ireland in 1883, and graduated at that university in 1885, from Queen's College, Belfast, a constituent college of the Royal University. He proceeded to St. John's College, Cambridge, being senior wrangler in 1888 and obtaining the first place in part ii of the mathematical tripos of 1889. In 1891 he was both elected into a fellowship at St. John's and appointed professor of applied mathematics at the Royal College of Science for Ireland, Dublin, and when in 1926 this institution was absorbed by University College, Dublin, he was offered and accepted an equivalent position in that college as professor of pure and applied mathematics, from which he retired in 1933. In 1909 he was elected F.R.S., and he received the honorary degree of D.Sc. from Queen's University, Belfast, in 1919.

As professor of applied mathematics in the Royal College of Science Orr's teaching was characterized by accurate definition, logical rigour, and clear statements of underlying assumptions. The scrupulous style of his exposition is shown in his *Notes on Thermodynamics for Students* (1909), a model in its precision in the formulation of principles. He ever sought to furnish his students with the mathematical tools for dealing with the physical, chemical, and engineering problems which they met in the laboratories, where he was frequently to be seen modestly deploring his lack of experimental knowledge. Mathematics under his inspiring influence became, for staff and students alike, an integrating subject in the small college.

Orr's exemplar was McNeill, of whom he wrote an appreciation containing an unconscious self-portrait. 'Though McNeill was a thorough teacher of mathematics, still more thoroughly did he, like other great teachers I have known, teach—and rather to the man than to the boy—the more valuable lessons that our life's work, whatever it may be, should be done as well as we can do it and that difficulties are not to be evaded, but to be attacked and overcome. As may be imagined he was a strict disciplinarian; living the strenuous life himself, he had little sympathy with the idle or the purposeless.' Combined with this stoical austerity, Orr had a considerate generosity, exercised quietly and effectively, for students and teachers in difficulties of health or fortune.

Orr's mathematical outlook was fashioned in the Cambridge tradition of Lord Rayleigh, A. E. H. Love [qq.v.], and Sir Joseph Larmor, with whom he carried on an active correspondence. He will be best known for his work on the stability of the steady motions of a liquid. His statement of this difficult problem was accepted by Rayleigh and (Sir) Horace Lamb. His critical value for the Reynolds number, 177, was verified by Dr. Richard Vynne Southwell using an elastic analogue. He clarified the problems arising from the whirling of shafts in his 'Note on Mr. Lees' Paper on the Whirling of an Overhung Shaft' (*Philosophical Magazine*, vol. xlv, 1923), which was supplemented by correspondence and discussion with his colleagues. His highly developed critical faculty, directed with the fiercest intensity against his own work, was never at rest. It was especially active in dealing with text-books, as he rightly felt that clear thinking in applied science rests upon a sound grasp of fundamental principles. The climate of the quantum and relativity physics of the twentieth century was not congenial to him, but he never ceased to take an interest in these developments and to look forward to a reconciling synthesis with the classical dynamics.

Orr married in 1892 Elizabeth (died 1926), daughter of Samuel Watson Campbell, of Melbourne, who originally came from county Down, and had three daughters, the eldest of whom predeceased her father. He died at Douglas, Isle of Man, 14 August 1934.

[*Obituary Notices of Fellows of the Royal Society*, No. 4, December 1935 (portrait); *The Campbellian* (journal of Campbell College, Belfast), November 1907; private information; personal knowledge.]

FELIX E. HACKETT.

OTTLEY, SIR CHARLES LANGDALE (1858–1932), rear-admiral, was born at Richmond, Yorkshire, 8 February 1858, the seventh son of Lawrence Ottley, rector of Richmond and canon of Ripon, by his wife, Elizabeth, daughter of John Bickersteth, rector of Sapcote, Leicestershire, and sister of Robert Bickersteth,

bishop of Ripon [q.v.]. Robert Lawrence Ottley, canon of Christ Church, Oxford, was an elder brother. He entered the Royal Navy in 1871, and in 1877 was serving as a midshipman in the screw corvette *Amethyst*, when in company with the *Shah* she engaged the rebel Peruvian warship *Huascar* off the coast of Peru. He gained accelerated promotion to lieutenant by obtaining first class certificates in all his examinations, and in 1882, as lieutenant of the *Monarch* (Captain (Sir) George Tryon, q.v.), was present at the bombardment of Alexandria, receiving the Egyptian medal with clasp and the khedive's bronze star. Later in that year he returned home in order to qualify as a torpedo officer, and while serving in the *Vernon* he displayed marked technical ability and inventive capacity by devising a very successful automatic mooring gear for submarine mines which bears his name. In 1884 he became torpedo lieutenant of Rear-Admiral Tryon's flagship, the *Nelson*, on the Australia station for two years; he was later appointed torpedo lieutenant of the *Camperdown* and afterwards of the *Victoria*, flagships of the commander-in-chief Mediterranean, Admiral Sir Anthony Hoskins [q.v.], who was later relieved by Vice-Admiral Tryon. Ottley was promoted commander in 1892, but remained in the ship in that rank as executive officer until early in 1893, when he returned home in order to become commander of the *Vernon* for two and a half years. He resumed sea service in 1897, in command of the sloop *Nymphe* in the Mediterranean, employed chiefly as senior naval officer at Port Said in 1897 and at Constantinople in 1898.

Ottley relinquished command of the *Nymphe* on his promotion to captain in January 1899, and was then appointed naval attaché to various British embassies; he acted in that capacity during the next five years in Washington, Rome, Tokyo, St. Petersburg, and Paris, thereby gaining unique knowledge and experience of foreign navies and foreign policy. Towards the end of his service as naval attaché he contemplated adopting a political career, and he was chosen in 1903 as prospective conservative candidate for Pembroke Boroughs. But his special qualifications led to his appointment in 1904 to the staff of the recently established Committee of Imperial Defence, and in 1905 to his selection, although a comparatively junior captain, to succeed Rear-Admiral Prince Louis of Battenberg (afterwards Louis Mountbatten, first Marquess of Milford Haven, q.v.) as director of Naval Intelligence, then the most important post, other than membership of the Board, in the Admiralty; and he abandoned his parliamentary ambitions. As director of Naval Intelligence, he sat on a number of important commissions, notably that of 1906 on war risks to shipping. In 1907 he was the principal naval delegate to the second Peace Conference at The Hague, where he took a leading part in drawing up the convention limiting the use of submarine mines, to the development of which he had devoted so much ingenuity many years earlier. In that same year, when the original secretary of the Committee of Imperial Defence, Sir George Clarke (afterwards Lord Sydenham, q.v.), relinquished that office, largely owing to differences of view which had arisen between him and the first sea lord, Sir John (afterwards Lord) Fisher [q.v.], Ottley was selected to relieve him. In 1908 he was a delegate to the International Maritime Conference of London. He reached the top of the captains' list in that year, but not having served at sea in that rank, he was automatically placed on the retired list on promotion to rear-admiral (1908); but he remained secretary to the Committee of Imperial Defence until 1912, when he had completed five years in office. Those five years, largely as a result of Ottley's unostentatious but skilful organization and guidance, were the most important period in the development of the committee into a highly efficient instrument for the co-ordination of the nation's forces in the preparation for, and conduct of war.

On retirement from office, Ottley made his home at Coruanan, Fort William, Inverness-shire, and joined the board of Messrs. Armstrong, Whitworth & company, of Newcastle-upon-Tyne; he took an active part in the superintendence of that company's output of war material, particularly after the outbreak of war in 1914. He was appointed M.V.O. in 1903, C.B. in 1911, and K.C.M.G. in 1907 for his services at The Hague Peace Conference. He retired from the board of Armstrongs on the post-war reconstruction of the company. In 1892 he married Kathleen Margaret, daughter of Colonel Alexander Stewart, of the Royal Artillery, and had a son, who died of wounds in 1914. A few days before his death he moved from Coruanan to Creag, Tarbet, Argyll, where

he died 24 September 1932. He was a man of much charm and no little literary ability, a good linguist, and a fluent, convincing, and persuasive speaker.

[*The Times*, 26 September 1932; Admiralty records; private information.]

H. G. THURSFIELD.

OULESS, WALTER WILLIAM (1848–1933), painter, was born at St. Helier, Jersey, 21 September 1848, the third son of Philip John Ouless, marine-painter, of Jersey, by his wife, Caroline Marguette Savage. He was educated at Victoria College, Jersey. Coming to London in 1864, he entered the Royal Academy Schools the following year, at the early age of sixteen, and in 1869, when he was not yet twenty-one, he made his first appearance at a Royal Academy exhibition with two subject pictures, 'Home Again' and 'A Tender Passage'. He continued to exhibit regularly until 1928, when he was represented by a portrait of Sir Arthur Keith, which is now in the Royal College of Surgeons together with Ouless's portrait of Lord Lister, painted in 1897. He was elected A.R.A. in 1877 and R.A. in 1881, and in 1924 he became a Senior Academician.

At the beginning of his career Ouless painted subject pictures, and it was on the advice of Sir J. E. Millais [q.v.] that he concentrated on portraiture. This advice was justified by events, and Ouless was quickly recognized as one of the most trustworthy portrait-painters of the day, sure of getting a good and sympathetic likeness with a high degree of technical skill. At the same time his earlier practice in figure composition enabled him to give to his portraits a broadly pictorial effect that is not very commonly combined with veracity in detail, and his appreciation of character gained by sobriety of statement.

Ouless is represented in the National Portrait Gallery by portraits of John Bright (1879), (Sir) George Scharf (1885), Lord John Manners (later seventh Duke of Rutland, 1886), (Viscount) Morley (1891), and Thomas Hardy (1922). His portrait of Thomas Sidney Cooper [q.v.] is in the art gallery attached to the Royal Museum and Public Library at Canterbury. Ouless painted both King Edward VII (1900) and King George V (1905) as Prince of Wales, the latter for Lincoln's Inn, and among the other distinguished people who sat to him were Charles Darwin (painted for the family in 1875); Russell Gurney (1875, Fishmongers' Company); Cardinal Newman (1880–1881, Oriel College, Oxford); (Earl) Roberts (1882, for the Mess, Woolwich); Cardinal Manning (1888: the painting was destroyed by enemy action in 1940 but is represented by a replica at the Oratory, Birmingham); Bishop Edward King (1899, Bishop's House, Lincoln); and Sir (Henry) Evelyn Wood (1906, Fishmongers' Company). His portrait of Philip Westlake was presented by his daughters to the Tate Gallery in 1934. Towards the end of his life he painted a few landscapes, mostly in the county of Dorset.

Ouless was for a long time an active member of the council of the Royal Academy. He was a governor of Dulwich College, and he occupied himself a good deal with the affairs of the Dulwich Picture Gallery, which he helped to re-hang. For many years he devoted much time to the Artists' General Benevolent Institution, both as honorary secretary and vice-president. Personally he was much liked, although during his later years partial deafness kept him from mixing much in general society. 'No man could have had a more loyal and steadfast friend, nor wiser counsellor, while he also possessed the charming courtesy of a great gentleman' (*The Times*, 1 January 1934).

Ouless was a chevalier of the Legion of Honour and a member of the Order of Leopold, and during his long life he received gold and silver medals for his work at Berlin, Paris, Munich, and Vienna. In 1878 he married Lucy Maitland (died 1931), daughter of Thomas King Chambers, M.D., honorary physician to the Prince of Wales, of Shrubs Hill House, Sunningdale. The eldest of his three daughters is Miss Catherine Ouless, the landscape and portrait painter. He died after a short illness at his home in London 25 December 1933.

Ouless's self-portrait, exhibited at the Academy in 1918, is in the Uffizi Gallery, Florence; there is a replica in the Barreau Gallery, St. Helier. There was also a portrait of Ouless by his eldest daughter, but this was destroyed by enemy action in 1940. A portrait of him is included in Grenville Manton's 'Conversazione at the Royal Academy' (1891), in the National Portrait Gallery.

[*The Times*, 27 December 1933 and 1 January 1934; private information.]
CHARLES MARRIOTT.

PAGE, THOMAS ETHELBERT (1850–1936), classical scholar, teacher, editor, and political critic, was born at Lincoln 27 March 1850, the second son of William Tomlinson Page, of Stonebow, Lincoln, general manager of the Lincoln and Lindsey Banking Company, by his wife, Ann Watson. Both his father and his elder brother were prominent citizens of Lincoln. He was educated at Lincoln Grammar School, Shrewsbury, and St. John's College, Cambridge, of which last he was a scholar. He was second in the classical tripos of 1873, S. H. Butcher [q.v.] being first and A. W. Verrall [q.v.] third—a trio of famous scholars who were declared equal for the chancellor's medals that year. He was also Porson prizeman (1870), Porson scholar (1871), Browne medallist for a Latin ode (1870, 1871, 1872), Davies scholar (1872), and chancellor's medallist for an English poem (1872). Having been at once elected a fellow of his college, he turned immediately to school work, and for thirty-seven years (1873–1910) was sixth-form master at Charterhouse, where his brilliant scholarship and fine critical judgement, combined with exceptional gifts of voice and personality, made a vital and lasting impression upon his pupils. He was pre-eminent among the assistant masters of his day.

While still a schoolmaster Page produced what soon became the standard school editions of the *Odes* of Horace and the *Aeneid*, which made his name familiar to classical students everywhere, and in 1912, after he had retired from teaching, he was invited by James Loeb to be editor-in-chief of the 'Loeb Classical Library'. He held this position for the last twenty-five years of his life, editing the various translations with laborious care and fine critical judgement, and handling the translators, both English and American, with tact and considerateness.

Page's academic distinction was recognized when his college elected him an honorary fellow in 1931 and Manchester University conferred upon him the honorary degree of Litt.D. in 1913. But he was much more than a scholar. He served for thirty years on the town council of Godalming, generously applying his great intellectual powers to the problems of local administration, and was made an honorary freeman of that ancient borough. For many years he was a member of the Surrey county council and education committee, where his utterances were remembered for the shrewdness of his judgement and the incisive wit that drove his point home. He was a governor of Charterhouse and a member of the governing body of that school, as well as of Shrewsbury and Cranleigh. In 1934 the King appointed him C.H., and his selection for this distinction was warmly welcomed.

There are portraits of Page in the two places most closely associated with his life, one, by John Collier (1911), in the school at Charterhouse, the other, a better representation, by Clive Gardner (1927), in the Reform Club. But no portrait or short biographical record can make real to those who did not know him the distinction of his personality, which made him in any company, however eminent, the most striking figure. His magnificent presence, tall stature, and noble head, with the fine eyes and close-cropped beard, attracted the notice of strangers. Those who conversed with him found a courteous listener and a weighty and witty talker, who touched no subject that he did not illuminate. His friends knew him for a man of high principle, loyal, generous, sensitive, and fundamentally kind-hearted. At the Reform Club his commanding personality, arresting conversation, and on special occasions his oratory, made him throughout his later years a leading figure. To the general public he was best known by his letters to The Times, which compelled attention by their forceful criticism and political insight.

Page stood unsuccessfully for parliament as an independent at a by-election for Cambridge University in February 1911: in his later years he was a recognized exponent of liberalism, but rather as a political philosophy than a party label. For him it was 'an animating and informing spirit which seeks to mould and shape all political measures in accordance with a great ideal'; and that ideal was, so far as laws can avail, 'to establish and confirm two great principles, individual freedom and individual responsibility'. His letters to The Times show the discriminating judgement with which he interpreted this creed and the keen interest with which he followed public affairs up to the last days of his long life.

Page died at Godalming 1 April 1936. He married in 1875 Delamotte Caroline Eugenie, only daughter of Edward Toynbee, of Lincoln, a half-brother of Joseph Toynbee [q.v.]. There were two daughters of the marriage.

[The Times, 2 April 1936; private information; personal knowledge.]

FRANK FLETCHER.

PAGE, WILLIAM (1861–1934), historian and antiquary, was born in London 4 September 1861, the third and youngest son of Henry Page, of Norfolk Square, London, by his wife, Georgina Forrester. After a short time at a private school he went to Westminster from January to May 1875, but on his father's death that year he entered the office of a civil engineer, and was appointed to a post under the Queensland government in 1881. In 1885 he returned to England and joined his brother-in-law, William John Hardy, son of Sir William Hardy [q.v.], as partner in the firm of Hardy & Page, record agents and legal antiquaries. From 1896 to 1902 he made his home at St. Albans where his brother-in-law lived: he then removed to Battersea and in 1906 to Hampstead, where he remained until 1922, finally settling at Middleton, near Bognor, where he died 3 February 1934. He married in 1886 Kate Marion, youngest daughter of Charles William Roe, of Chiswick, and had a son and a daughter.

Page's first archaeological paper, 'Some Remarks on the Northumbrian Palatinates and Regalities', was printed in Archaeologia in 1888. His reputation as a learned and accurate scholar grew apace, and while he was still a young man a turn of events, for which he was in no way responsible, provided him with a unique opportunity. The Victoria History of the Counties of England, initiated at the end of Queen Victoria's reign, and intended to surpass all previous histories in thoroughness and accuracy, began its ambitious career under the best auspices and with ample funds. But not until it had been under way for some time did it become clear to its promoters that much of the material which they counted on their contributors to produce, such as topographical details and manorial descents, existed only in the national archives and needed much time and expert training to reduce to printable form. Fortunately, they turned to Page, who in 1902 became joint editor, with Herbert Arthur Doubleday, of the History and in 1904 sole editor, a position which he held until his death. By 1902 only one volume had appeared: by the end of 1910 there were forty-six volumes. Failure of funds and the war of 1914–1918 stopped the progress of the work and disorganized it almost entirely, so that in 1922 Page took the whole of the materials to his home at Middleton, and in 1928 became sole proprietor of the History. In order to ensure its continuance he made over all the materials in 1931 to the university of London, which set up a management committee of which he was chairman until his death.

In 1932 Oxford University conferred upon Page the honorary degree of D.Litt., the sole recognition that his great services to history received. He served on the royal commission on historical monuments for England from 1909 to 1934, as an inspector under the historical manuscripts commission, and on a number of special committees, while his output of archaeological and historical work, much of it devoted to St. Albans and Hertfordshire, is a clear index of the extent of his knowledge.

[*The Times*, 5 February 1934; *Victoria History of the Counties of England. Rutland*, vol. ii, pp. ix–xi, 1935 (portrait); personal knowledge.]   CHARLES PEERS.

PAGET, LADY MURIEL EVELYN VERNON (1876–1938), philanthropist, was born in London 19 August 1876, the only daughter and elder child of Murray Edward Gordon Finch-Hatton, twelfth Earl of Winchelsea and Nottingham, by his wife, Edith, only daughter of Edward William Harcourt, of Stanton Harcourt and Nuneham Park, Oxfordshire. In 1897 she married (Sir) Richard Arthur Surtees Paget, second baronet, of Cranmore Hall, Shepton Mallet, who succeeded his father in 1908.

Lady Muriel's first philanthropic achievement was the establishment in 1905 of the Invalid Kitchens of London, to which she remained honorary secretary until her death, and this led to her giving help to the Belgian Refugees Committee in London when the German armies overran Belgium in 1914. In the following year she organized and administered the Anglo-Russian Hospital with a base hospital in the Dmitri Palace at Petrograd and field hospitals at the front. In 1917 she went with the Russian army to Rumania, and set up a hospital at Durohoy during a grave epidemic of typhus. Returning to Russia she continued to work there until after the revolution she and her staff were withdrawn under Red Army escort by way of Siberia and Japan; but her return to Europe only brought fresh work, and in 1919 at the head of the mission that bore her name, Lady Muriel went to Czechoslovakia at the personal request of President Masaryk, and in that country, Latvia, Estonia, and Lithuania, she inaugurated and administered hospital and child welfare work. In 1919 also, as chair-

man of the Rumanian Red Cross in England, she went to Rumania, where she organized a child-welfare centre. In every case the authorities of these countries took over the work in 1922. In these countries her name came to be held in great honour and the news of her death was received with general emotion. The connexion with Russia was resumed in 1924, when she organized and maintained relief for the numerous distressed British subjects in Moscow and the provinces who had been ruined by the revolution, and in 1930 the work being extended to Leningrad, the organization became known as the British Subjects in Russia Relief Association. Her visits to her headquarters were frequent between 1924 and 1937, and when in March 1938 the British consul was withdrawn, her organization was the only official link between British subjects in Leningrad and their government until three months later they were expelled. An improbable charge of espionage made against her and her organization at the trial of Rakovsky was emphatically repudiated by Neville Chamberlain in March 1938.

If Russia was the most important scene of Lady Muriel's activities it was by no means her sole preoccupation. From 1926 to 1938 she was a governor of the People's Palace in Mile End Road. She travelled often to Geneva for Red Cross conferences, and in 1934 she went as British delegate to the fifteenth International Red Cross conference in Japan, but although during the last twelve years of her life she suffered from the illness from which she eventually died, she maintained her enthusiasm for the causes which she had at heart. It was characteristic of her that in the final phase she refused any opiate which might interfere with her powers of organizing her Russian relief work.

Lady Muriel died in London 16 June 1938. She was survived by her husband, her younger son, the elder having died in infancy, and three daughters. For her philanthropic work Lady Muriel was appointed O.B.E. in 1918 and C.B.E. in 1938. She also received decorations and medals from Belgium, Japan, Imperial Russia, Rumania, Czechoslovakia, Lithuania, and Latvia.

A pencil sketch of Lady Muriel by Brian Hatton (1912) is in the possession of Sir Richard Paget.

[*The Times*, 17, 18, 21, 22, 23 June 1938; private information; personal knowledge.]   GRACE H. PAGET

PAGET, VIOLET (1856–1935), author under the pseudonym of VERNON LEE, was born at Château St. Léonard, near Boulogne, 14 October 1856. Her father, Henry Ferguson Paget, having been educated in Warsaw, was involved in the Polish insurrection in 1848. Forced to fly the country, he became tutor to Eugene Lee-Hamilton [q.v.], whose widowed mother he married in 1855. Matilda Lee-Hamilton was the daughter of Edward Hamlin Adams, of Carmarthenshire, whose sons took the name of Abadam. Violet was the only child of her mother's second marriage, the companion of her youth and her earliest intellectual influence being her poet half-brother Eugene. Before she was fifteen she discovered the deserted meeting-place of the Arcadian Academy in Rome and began to collect materials for its history. These contributed to her first book, *Studies of the Eighteenth Century in Italy* (1880), a pioneer work which brought to light the significance of the contemporary efflorescence in music and drama, and made the fantastic world of eighteenth-century Italy live again. Her pseudonym of 'Vernon Lee' was chosen, with reference to her brother, in 1875. During the ensuing fifty years she published some thirty volumes. *Euphorion: being Studies of the Antique and the Mediaeval in the Renaissance* (1884) and its sequel, *Renaissance Fancies and Studies* (1895), won her a high place among the interpreters of the Italian Renaissance. Travel sketches such as *Genius Loci* (1899) and *The Spirit of Rome* (1906) reveal a unique power of conveying the essence of the places which she describes. Her sensitive delight in every detail of the Italian landscape prompted Browning's lines in *Asolando*:

'"No, the book
Which noticed how the wall-growths wave"
said she
"Was not by Ruskin."
I said "Vernon Lee?"'

Her works of fiction are eminently readable but her later excursions into philosophy are over-elaborate and obscure. *Satan the Waster* (1920) expressed her hatred of war, which, together with her cosmopolitan outlook, led her to write and speak in a way that incurred censure during the war of 1914–1918.

In 1881 Vernon Lee paid the first of many visits to England. Her tailor-made clothes, short hair, gleaming eyes, and brilliant talk made her a conspicuous figure in artistic circles. She received the honorary degree of D.Litt. from Durham University in 1924, and in 1934 saw the Italian version of her play *Ariadne in Mantua* (1903) performed in Florence before an enthusiastic audience. She died at Il Palmerino, San Gervasio, the Florentine villa which had long been her home, 13 February 1935. If her early promise was not wholly fulfilled, she stood to her many friends for the quintessence of European culture, conversing with equal ease and distinction in Italian, French, and English. 'Vernon Lee was by far the cleverest person I ever met'; wrote Maurice Baring; her culture was 'shot with imagination.'

Of the two portraits of Vernon Lee by J. S. Sargent, the sketch in oils done in 1881 was bequeathed to the Tate Gallery, the drawing made in 1889 is in the possession of the Ashmolean Museum.

[*The Times*, 14 February 1935; *Vernon Lee's Letters* (privately printed), 1937; Maurice Baring, *Lost Lectures*, 1932; private information.]   CECILIA M. ADY.

PAKENHAM, SIR WILLIAM CHRISTOPHER (1861–1933), admiral, was born in London 10 July 1861, the second son of Rear-Admiral Thomas Alexander Pakenham, third son of the second Earl of Longford, by his wife, Sophia Frances, third daughter of Sir Tatton Sykes, fourth baronet, of Sledmere [q.v.]. He entered the *Britannia* training ship as a naval cadet in 1874, and, having passed out two years later, he went to sea in the *Monarch* in the Mediterranean, being promoted midshipman in 1876. He was transferred to the frigate *Raleigh* next year. Together with an able seaman he was highly commended for gallantry in plunging into the sea and rescuing a coxswain who had fallen overboard as the ship was leaving Larnaka, Cyprus, in August 1878. In September 1879 he joined the *Alexandra*, flagship of Sir Geoffrey Hornby [q.v.], and remained in her when Sir F. B. P. Seymour (afterwards Lord Alcester, q.v.) succeeded to the command until promoted to sub-lieutenant in October 1880. Having undergone the usual gunnery course in the *Excellent* at Portsmouth he was in December 1882 again appointed to the *Alexandra* (still flagship of Lord Alcester); but soon after Lord John Hay had assumed the command he was transferred in April 1883 to the corvette *Canada*, destined to join the North America squadron. In this ship he was a strict though benevolent autocrat of the gun-room mess in which Prince George (afterwards King George V) was serving as midshipman. He was promoted lieutenant in October 1883, and was soon brought home again, having been chosen as flag-lieutenant by Rear-Admiral (Sir) George Tryon [q.v.] (flag in the *Nelson*) during the three years (1884–1887) of his command of the new Australia station.

Pakenham's remaining nine years as lieutenant were spent mainly as gunnery officer of the small cruisers *Calypso*, *Garnet*, and *Sybille* in the Training squadron, and on the Pacific and Mediterranean stations. While in the *Calypso* he again distinguished himself by a brave attempt to save the life of a petty officer who had fallen into the sea from the foreyard during drill in Kiel Harbour.

Promoted commander in June 1896, Pakenham served for nine months in the old *Galatea* (coastguard ship at Hull) and for eighteen months in the *Venus* under Sir (Archibald) Berkeley Milne [q.v.] in the Mediterranean. He had qualified as an interpreter in French while on half-pay in 1884, and was selected for duty in the Naval Intelligence Department from August 1899 until March 1901. Then he commanded the sloop *Daphne* on the China station, and, after being lent to Rear-Admiral Harry Tremenheere Grenfell's flagship *Albion* as acting captain early in 1902, returned home in June of that year. He was promoted captain in June 1903.

The outbreak of war between Russia and Japan was imminent and Pakenham's experience in intelligence work and his linguistic abilities (although he never learnt the difficult Japanese language) marked him out as the officer to succeed Captain (afterwards Admiral Sir Ernest) Troubridge [q.v.], who was due for relief in 1904 as naval attaché in Japan. War broke out on 6 February 1904 and Pakenham relieved Troubridge in March, taking his place on board the battleship *Asahi* in which he remained continuously until after the final Japanese victory at Tsushima on 27 May 1905. His reports to the Admiralty throughout the war were brilliantly written and revealed a thorough appreciation of the strategic, tactical, and technical implications of the events and situations which he described. His cool daring in exposing himself to danger in order more completely to observe the proceedings of the great battle much impressed the Japanese, and led the Emperor of Japan, on Admiral Togo's

recommendation, to confer on him the second class of the Order of the Rising Sun. He was specially appointed C.B. (military division) soon after the battle.

After returning to England in 1906 Pakenham commanded the cruiser *Antrim* for two years in the Atlantic Fleet, and then the *Glory* and *Triumph* (battleship bought from Chile in 1904) in the Mediterranean until January 1910, when he came home to take command of the new battleship *Collingwood* in the Home Fleet, until December 1911. Mr. Winston Churchill, in reconstituting his Board soon after taking office, selected Pakenham to be fourth sea lord, being impressed by his reputation as an officer of strong character and his unique experience of modern naval warfare. Before Pakenham left the Board two years later he had in June 1913 reached flag-rank, and in December he took command of the third cruiser squadron, Home Fleet, with his flag in his old ship *Antrim*. In March 1915, with his flag in the *Australia*, he took charge of one of the two battle-cruiser squadrons which belonged to the Australian Commonwealth and had been willingly lent for service in the Grand Fleet after the victory of the Falkland Islands (8 December 1914) had disposed of German danger in the Pacific. He thus had the titular appointment of rear-admiral commanding the Australian Fleet. In the battle of Jutland (31 May 1916) Pakenham's flag was flown in the *New Zealand*, the *Australia* being under repair at Devonport after a collision with the *New Zealand* in a fog on 22 April. His remaining ship the *Indefatigable* was blown up and lost early in the battle. Pakenham distinguished himself by able support of Vice-Admiral Sir David (later Earl) Beatty [q.v.] and was rewarded by appointment as K.C.B. (1916), being personally decorated with that order and also as K.C.V.O. by the King on the occasion of his visit to the fleet at Rosyth in 1917. In November 1916 Beatty became commander-in-chief in succession to Sir John (later Earl) Jellicoe [q.v.], and on his insistent recommendation Pakenham was appointed to succeed him in the command of the battle-cruiser force although there were many officers with strong claims senior to him but who had seen less service with battle-cruisers. He transferred his flag from the *Australia* to the *Lion* in January 1917 and retained the command until April 1919, having been promoted acting vice-admiral in June 1917 and confirmed in that rank in

September 1918, and having been present at the surrender of the German Fleet in the Forth at the end of the war.

After a well-deserved rest on half-pay Pakenham was appointed president of the Royal Naval College, Greenwich, in August 1919, but at his own request was given another command afloat as commander-in-chief, North America and West Indies station in October 1920. After two and a half years he returned home. He had been promoted admiral in April 1922 and retired at his own request in March 1926. He long maintained correspondence with his Japanese friends and made a great impression at Geneva in 1927 by travelling from England for the sole purpose of calling upon Admiral Viscount Saito who had been minister of marine in 1905. He was appointed G.C.B. in 1925 and succeeded Sir C. C. Monro [q.v.] as Bath King of Arms in 1930. He resigned from this post only a few days before his death, which took place at San Sebastian 28 July 1933. He was unmarried.

Pakenham was appointed K.C.M.G (1919), made commander of the Legion of Honour, and given the croix de guerre (bronze palms), the first class of the Japanese Order of the Rising Sun, the grand cordon of the Chinese Order of the Excellent Crop, and the D.S.M. of the United States of America in the post-war award of honours.

Pakenham was a strong-minded, somewhat austere, able, and well-read officer, wholeheartedly devoted to the service and something of a 'character' with his faultless care of his personal appearance and dress, his quiet sense of caustic humour, and his studiously polite, if somewhat elaborate, manners. Mr. Churchill paid him a notable tribute in *The World Crisis* (1923).

Numerous stories are told of Pakenham, as that during the battle of Tsushima the casemate on which he was stationed was struck by a shell with resulting casualties, and his white uniform was splashed with blood. He quietly left the deck and returned in a few minutes with spotless attire and resumed his notes of the battle. It is also related that while in the Grand Fleet he always slept fully dressed as in day-time and that he had all the furniture of the admiral's quarters burnt, together with all inflammable articles in the ship including the deck corticine and the companion-ladder, in order to prevent the danger of fire during an action; and he kept only a chair in his bridge cabin.

A portrait of Pakenham in oils by (Sir) William Nicholson and a charcoal and water-colour drawing by Francis Dodd are in the Imperial War Museum, and he is represented in Sir A. S. Cope's picture 'Some Sea Officers of the Great War', painted in 1921, in the National Portrait Gallery.

[Admiralty records; private information.]
VINCENT W. BADDELEY.

PARIS, SIR ARCHIBALD (1861–1937), major-general, was born at Lansdown, Bath, 9 November 1861, the youngest son of the Rev. Archibald Paris, of Ludgeon, Cornwall, by his wife, Caroline, second daughter of the Rev. Sir Henry Delves Broughton, eighth baronet. Educated at Eton and the Royal Naval College, Greenwich, he joined the Royal Marine Artillery in 1879.

Paris passed out of the Staff College, Camberley, in 1888, and, after a period afloat and five years as adjutant of the 1st Antrim Artillery Militia (1894–1899), was selected for service in South Africa in 1900. Initially employed in training field batteries in Rhodesia, he finally commanded, under Lord Methuen [q.v.], the 'Kimberley column', a mixed force, mostly mounted irregulars, which was attacked and forced to surrender near Tweebosch in March 1902 owing to the flight of most of the mounted troops. Paris was exonerated from blame and later commended for the gallant resistance organized by him. Thrice mentioned in dispatches, he was promoted brevet lieutenant-colonel in June 1902 for distinguished service in the field. From 1903 to 1906 he was instructor at the Royal Military Academy.

In September 1914 Paris relieved Sir G. G. Aston [q.v.] in command of the Royal Marine brigade, and in October was promoted temporary major-general and appointed to command the Royal Naval division which he led with distinction at Antwerp, throughout the Gallipoli campaign, and in France until severely wounded in October 1916, with the eventual loss of a leg. In June 1917 he was placed on the retired list as 'unfit for further service owing to wounds'.

Paris was five times mentioned in dispatches, and promoted major-general for services in the field in 1915. He was appointed C.B. in 1907 and K.C.B. in 1916. He also received many foreign decorations. He was honorary colonel commandant of the Portsmouth division,

Royal Marines (1923–1933), and was awarded a good-service pension in 1925.

Tall and spare, with a cast in one eye caused by an accident, Paris had a thorough grasp of his profession and proved himself a cool and trusted commander. In 1885 he married Lilian Jean, youngest daughter of General Henry Melvill, Bengal Cavalry, and had a son, Brigadier Archibald Charles Melvill, who was killed on active service in Malaya in 1942. He died at Montreux 30 October 1937.

A portrait of Paris by Miss Donald Smith hangs in the Officers' Mess, Royal Marine Artillery, at Eastney Barracks, Portsmouth.

[M. H. Grant, (Official) *History of the War in South Africa 1899–1902*, vol. iv, 1910; Official records at the Royal Marine Office, Admiralty; Cyril Field, *Britain's Sea Soldiers*, vols. i and ii (up to 1914, privately printed), 1924; Sir H. E. Blumberg, *Britain's Sea Soldiers 1914–1919*, 1927; E. Fraser and L. G. Carr-Laughton, *The Royal Marine Artillery, 1804–1923*, 2 vols., 1930; *The Times*, 5 November 1937; personal knowledge.]

R. C. TEMPLE.

PARKER, SIR (HORATIO) GILBERT (GEORGE), baronet (1862–1932), author and politician, was born at Camden East, Addington, Ontario, 23 November 1862, the eldest son of Joseph Frederick Parker, of Belleville, Canada, born in Ireland of English descent, by his wife, Samantha Jane, daughter of George Simmons, of United Empire Loyalist extraction. Proud of his ancestry and alluding frequently to its influence on his writings, Parker recorded little about his parents except that his father had emigrated to Quebec about 1834 and had become a captain in the Canadian militia. He was educated at the village school at Camden and the Normal School at Ottawa and became a school-teacher at the age of seventeen. He attended Trinity College, Toronto, in preparation for holy orders for two years, but he did not proceed beyond the diaconate, and after being a curate for a short time he returned to teaching. Owing to weakness of health he visited Australia in 1885 and became associate-editor of the Sydney *Herald*, and the income derived therefrom enabled him to travel and to indulge his interests in oratory and drama and to write verse. When in London in 1889, on the advice of a friend, he burnt all his manuscripts and made a fresh start with the Canadian 'North-West'. *Pierre and his People* (1892) was his first book of

tales. It is doubtful whether he had had more than a glimpse of the prairies, let alone of the remote north: certainly the geography, the flora, and the fauna, are exceedingly hazy, the characters unconvincing, and the plots and incidents sensational. But New York and London seemed to be hungry for this sort of writing. A vast, uncritical reading public could be played upon by phrases about the 'wide spaces', the 'frozen north', and 'tall yarns' about blue-blooded 'remittance-men'. It has been hinted that his marriage (1895) aided him to literary and social success, but Parker was now no novice; besides stories in periodicals, he had already published half a dozen books. He continued to write and publish until late in life. His industry enabled him to master a subject, such as French-Canadian history, and then, with no great attention to verisimilitude or style, he would write voluminous melodrama. *The Trail of the Sword* (1894) on French Canada and the American Colonies promised better things; in his later preface (imperial edition 1912–1923) he recorded W. E. Henley's comment: 'It is not just big, but the next one will get home.' Unfortunately next year he published *When Valmond came to Pontiac*. This silliest of all tales about Quebec, although it enhanced his reputation at the time, was unworthy of him. *The Seats of the Mighty* (1896), on the Colonies and the capture of Quebec, often called Parker's best novel about Canada, sometimes his best novel, is marred by the same faults, yet it displays, like *The Trail of the Sword*, one of his best features, a covert admiration for French Canadians. He now very deliberately turned to a new field, Jersey during the French Revolution, in *The Battle of the Strong* (1898); the subject was industriously studied and his description of the Channel tides seems truer to nature than his Canadian scenes. But here, as in *The Weavers* (1907), the long novel about England and Egypt, an immature reader might suspect that the villains are too villainous to be possible, and the heroines too good to be true. In all he wrote thirty-six books, of which several were dramatized and in that form enjoyed popular success; but he never cured himself of turgidity in his style nor of morbid interest in torture, mental and physical.

Parker entered the political arena in Great Britain when he was elected conservative and imperialist member for Gravesend in 1900, and he continued to represent the constituency until 1918. He took politics seriously, and was an active promoter of imperial unity, especially in South African and Egyptian affairs. He was chairman of the Imperial South African Association from 1903 to 1911, and was active in the cause of promoting small ownerships, being the founder of the Small Ownership Committee and chairman of the special committee on small ownership. For two and a half years during the war of 1914–1918 he was in charge of publicity for America.

Parker married Amy Eliza (died 1925), daughter of Ashley Van Tine, of New York; there were no children of the marriage. Many honours came to him; he was knighted in 1902, created a baronet in 1915, and sworn of the Privy Council in 1916. He received honorary degrees from the universities of Toronto, McGill, and Laval. He died in London 6 September 1932.

A cartoon of Parker by 'Spy' appeared in *Vanity Fair* 23 June 1909.

[*The Times*, 7 September 1932; Harold Williams, *Modern English Writers 1890–1914*, 3rd ed., 1925. The best clue to Parker and his work is to be found in the prefaces to his books, imperial edition, 23 vols. (New York), 1912–1923.]   CARLETON STANLEY.

PARSONS, SIR CHARLES ALGERNON (1854–1931), engineer and scientist, was born in London 13 June 1854, the youngest of the six sons of William Parsons, third Earl of Rosse [q.v.], by his wife, Mary, elder daughter of John Wilmer Field, of Heaton Hall, Yorkshire. His eldest brother was Laurence Parsons, fourth Earl of Rosse [q.v.]. He was brought up at the family seat, Birr Castle, Parsonstown, Ireland; he was never sent to school but had, along with his brothers, the benefit of private tuition by men of such scientific calibre as (Sir) R. S. Ball and G. Johnstone Stoney [qq.v.]. At the age of seventeen he entered Trinity College, Dublin, where he spent two years before proceeding to St. John's College, Cambridge, in 1873. There was at that time no engineering school at Cambridge, but Parsons attended lectures on mechanism and applied mechanics, and he studied mathematics with such effect that in 1877 he graduated as eleventh wrangler.

Parsons at once began his engineering training by a four years' apprenticeship at the Elswick works of Sir William Armstrong & company. This was followed by

two years (1881–1883) with Messrs. Kitson & company, of Leeds, where he developed a four-cylinder high-speed epicycloidal steam-engine that he had patented, and he also occupied himself with experiments on the propulsion of torpedoes by means of rockets.

In 1884 Parsons acquired a junior partnership in the firm of Clarke, Chapman & company, of Gateshead, and assumed charge of their newly organized electrical department. In those days electric dynamos were small machines driven usually at 1,000 to 1,500 revolutions per minute by a belt from the fly-wheel of a reciprocating engine. Parsons set himself the task of producing a machine which would drive the dynamos direct and concentrated on the development of a steam turbine. It occurred to him that by dividing the expansion of steam into a number of pressure drops it should be possible to run a turbine at a moderate speed and at the same time secure a proper relationship between the steam speed and blade speed. His first patents, taken out in 1884, show how thoroughly he considered all the difficulties in the path for the construction of such a high-speed turbine and the steps which he proposed to take to overcome them. The principle of subdividing the whole expansion of the steam into a number of stages, so that only comparatively moderate velocities have to be dealt with, still forms the basis of all efficient turbine design. The first Parsons turbo-dynamo constructed in 1884 developed an output of $7\frac{1}{2}$ kw. when running at a speed of 18,000 revolutions per minute, and was an immediate success. Many such machines were constructed almost exclusively for ship-lighting and by 1888 about 200 were in service.

Realizing the possibilities of the new type of prime mover, and in order to develop it to its fullest extent, Parsons in 1889 founded the firm of C. A. Parsons & company and established a small works at Heaton on a site about two miles from the centre of Newcastle-upon-Tyne. The first power-station in the world to employ turbo-generating plant was the Forth Banks power-station at Newcastle. This station went into commission in January 1890 with an initial equipment of two 75 kw. Parsons turbo-alternators. Other public lighting companies quickly followed this lead, and turbo-alternators were installed at Cambridge and Scarborough. The Cambridge station went into commission in 1892 with three 100 kw. turbo-alternators. These machines were the first turbine units to be operated with condensers, and tests showed their efficiency to be comparable with that of the best reciprocating engines of equal power.

As the size of turbo-alternators for power-station work gradually increased, so the efficiency of the sets was improved. By 1900, 1,000 kw. turbo-alternators with a steam consumption of 18·22 lbs./kw. hour were under construction; by 1912, 25,000 kw. sets taking 10·42 lbs./kw. hour; and by 1923, 50,000 kw. sets taking 8·19 lbs./kw. hour. Parsons lived to see an output of more than 200,000 kw. delivered by a single turbo-generator, and the reciprocating steam engine completely superseded by the turbine for central station work.

The growth of electricity supply consequent upon the invention of the turbine created a demand, not only for larger generating units but also for higher transmission voltages in order that more extensive areas might be economically served. In the early days the practice had been to generate at about 2,000 volts, and to increase the pressure when required by transformers. By 1905 Parsons had constructed turbo-alternators generating at 11,000 volts, and this voltage became the usual generating pressure for many years. In 1928 he again attacked the problem of generating at higher voltages and produced a 25,000 kw. turbo-alternator generating directly at 36,000 volts. The machine was entirely successful and Parsons had set a new standard in power-station practice. Many of the most important power stations, both in Great Britain and abroad, have adopted the practice of generating directly at 36,000 volts, thereby eliminating the large and costly step-up transformers necessary with the previous method.

The use of the steam turbine for the propulsion of ships was amongst the claims made by Parsons in his original patent of 1884, but he confined his energies at first to the task of establishing the position of the turbine on land, and it was not until 1894 that he decided to attack the problem of marine propulsion. He established a separate organization with works at Wallsend and formed a separate company which was later known as the Parsons Marine Steam Turbine Company. A small vessel, with a length of 100 feet and a displacement of 44 tons, was constructed and fitted with turbine machinery. This vessel, the *Turbinia*, after much experimental work, attained a speed of thirty-four knots. At the naval review held in 1897 to celebrate the diamond jubilee of Queen Victoria, the *Turbinia* created a sensation by racing down the lines of warships at a speed greater than that of any other vessel afloat, as at that time the fastest destroyers could hardly exceed twenty-seven knots. In 1899 the Admiralty entrusted Parsons with the construction of a thirty-knot turbine-driven destroyer, the *Viper*, which attained a speed of over thirty-seven knots when officially tested. A second destroyer, the *Cobra*, was also fitted with turbine machinery, but shortly afterwards both these ships were lost at sea by accidents.

In 1901 the first turbine-driven passenger vessel, the *King Edward*, was built for service on the river Clyde. This was followed by the *Queen Alexandra* for the same duties, and within the next year or two turbine propulsion had also been adopted for the cross-channel boats *Queen* and *Brighton*. The Parsons Marine Steam Turbine Company, in order to demonstrate to the Admiralty once more the advantages of turbines for warships, laid down in 1901 another turbine-driven destroyer, which was acquired in 1903 by the fleet under the name of *Velox*. This was followed in 1902 by the first turbine-driven cruiser, the *Amethyst*, which was one of four cruisers then under construction. The performance of the *Amethyst* was so remarkable that the last prejudices against turbine machinery in the Royal Navy were overcome and the way was open for its general adoption. In 1905 a committee on naval design appointed by the Admiralty advised that in future turbine machinery should be used exclusively in all classes of warships; the dreadnoughts were the first class of battleship to be affected by this decision [see FISHER, JOHN ARBUTHNOT].

Similar striking progress was made in the Mercantile Marine, the Cunard Company first adopting turbines in 1905 in the 30,000-ton liner *Carmania*. The *Lusitania* and *Mauretania* followed in 1906, the latter vessel holding the 'Blue Riband of the Atlantic' for nearly a quarter of a century. The success of the turbine at sea having been established, it was recognized as the prime mover for the navies of the world as well as for all the fastest ocean liners.

There remained yet to be met the demand of the immense fleets of low-speed tramp steamers and cargo vessels. Parsons realized that the only satisfactory solution was the introduction of mechanical reduction gearing between the turbine and the propeller shaft, thus enabling each vessel to run at its most efficient speed. In order to test this he bought in 1909 an old cargo vessel, the *Vespasian*, in which he replaced the 750 h.p. triple expansion engines by geared turbines, and after exhaustive tests the new machinery was proved to be entirely successful. This was another great advance, for not only did it diminish the size of the machinery and increase its efficiency, but it enabled the ordinary cargo vessel to profit equally by the employment of turbines.

Lastly, after the war of 1914–1918, the competition of the marine oil engine had to be met. Parsons felt very strongly that marine engineers ought to take advantage of the economies in fuel resulting from the use of higher pressures and temperatures as obtained in installations on land. Knowing that a practical demonstration was the surest and quickest way to convince the sceptics, he accordingly equipped a small passenger vessel, the *King George V*, with high-pressure geared turbines. This vessel was the pioneer of high-pressure steam at sea, and thereby opened up a new field for marine engineers, which, in both naval and mercantile practice, has led to great advance.

The activities of Parsons were not confined to the branch of engineering by which he earned his greatest fame. He took a keen interest in all matters connected with optics, and when he established the Heaton works in 1889 he organized a special department for the production of searchlight reflectors. He built up what was probably the most important business devoted to the manufacture of such reflectors. In January 1921 he acquired a controlling interest in the firm of Ross Ltd., of Clapham, well known as makers of binoculars and other small optical apparatus. Here he introduced various improvements in the methods of glass-grinding but soon turned his attention to the much larger question of the manufacture of optical glass itself. The following July he purchased the Derby Crown Glass Company and under the name of the Parsons Optical Glass Company produced about a hundred different kinds of glass for optical purposes. Parsons made many scientific and mechanical improvements in the processes employed in the manufacture of the glass. In 1925 he purchased the firm of Sir Howard Grubb &

Sons, makers of large astronomical telescopes, and under the name of Sir Howard Grubb, Parsons, & company built new works for it at Walkergate, adjacent to his turbine works at Heaton. Many notable instruments have been constructed at Walkergate, including 36-inch reflecting telescopes for Greenwich Observatory and for the Royal Observatory, Edinburgh, and two 74-inch reflectors, one for Toronto and the other for Pretoria.

Parsons also invented an 'auxetophone', a device for increasing the sound of stringed instruments, particularly of the double-bass. This was used at the Queen's Hall in 1906, and was generously supported by (Sir) Henry Wood, but otherwise not accepted by the musical profession.

Of Parsons's many inventions and experiments, an attempt to make diamonds was the only one in which he failed to achieve his aim.

Parsons was appointed C.B. in 1904 and K.C.B. in 1911, and was admitted to the Order of Merit in 1927. He was elected F.R.S. in 1898 and was vice-president in 1908, and Bakerian lecturer in 1918. He received the Rumford medal in 1902, and the Copley medal in 1928. From the Royal Society of Arts he received the Albert medal in 1911, and from the Institution of Electrical Engineers, the Faraday medal (1923) and the Kelvin medal (1926). He was elected an honorary fellow of his college in 1904, and received honorary degrees from the universities of Oxford, Cambridge, Edinburgh, Glasgow, Dublin, Durham, Liverpool, and Sheffield. In 1911 he delivered the Rede lecture at Cambridge and he was president of the British Association in 1919. The city of Newcastle-upon-Tyne made him a freeman in 1914.

In 1883 Parsons married Katherine (died 1933), daughter of William Frogatt Bethell, of Rise Park, East Yorkshire, and had a son, who was killed in action in 1918, and a daughter, who is one of the three women members of the Institution of Naval Architects. He died 11 February 1931 on board the *Duchess of Richmond* at Kingston, Jamaica.

Parsons is considered to be the most original engineer whom this country has produced since the days of James Watt. He lived to see the fruit of his labours in the complete transformation of the method of producing power from steam, on both land and sea. He took out over 300 patents. Outside his work, he was an enthusiastic fisherman; in society, he was shy and retiring.

A portrait of Parsons by Sir William Orpen (1921) hangs in the Laing Art Gallery, Newcastle-upon-Tyne, and a medallion by Sir William Reid Dick is at the Heaton works.

[*The Times*, 13 February 1931; Rollo Appleyard, *Charles Parsons, His Life and Work* (bibliography), 1933; *Proceedings* of the Royal Society, vol. cxxxi, A, 1931; Sir Charles A. Parsons, *Scientific Papers and Addresses*, 1934; R. H. Parsons, *The Steam Turbine and Other Inventions of Sir Charles Parsons* (British Council 'Science in Britain' series), 1942; Alexander Richardson, *The Evolution of the Parsons Steam Turbine*, 1911; *Reminiscences and Letters of Sir Robert Ball*, edited by W. V. Ball, 1915; private information.]

C. D. GIBB.

PATEL, VITHALBAI JHAVABHAI (1870–1933), first Indian president of the Indian legislative assembly, was born in 1870 in a yeoman family claiming descent from the founders of the Kunbi Patidar village of Karamsad in the Kaira district of the Bombay Presidency, which was famous for scientific farming. A rebel all his life, Patel began by breaking away from the family tradition, studied English, and became a lawyer. After a few years he went to England and was called to the bar by Lincoln's Inn in 1908. On his return to India he practised in Bombay and watched the growing political agitation under Tilak the extremist for independence, under Gokhale the moderate for dominion status. When Gokhale died in 1914, 'V. J.' entered politics as a member of the Bombay legislative council, and rose rapidly to prominence, for his vehement oratory appealed to the more violent. He made vigorous attempts to secure for Indians a wider scope in public life, and refused to confine himself to mere obstruction and criticism of government measures. He was undeterred by any obstacles or conventions, and during the war he went so far as to visit a member of government at midnight and ask to be prosecuted and imprisoned on the ground that rest was necessary for his health and a 'crown of martyrdom' would advance his political career.

Nominally a follower of Gandhi, Patel had a hearty contempt for the doctrines of *ahimsa* (non-violence) and *satyagraha* (the pursuit of truth), and when in 1917 E. S. Montagu [q.v.] came to India as secretary of state to prepare reforms which to the official mind were revolutionary,

Patel astonished him by his scorn for so petty a programme. Yet he had more sense how to surmount practical difficulties than most of his compatriots. When challenged on India's inability to defend herself he would reply acidly: 'In the eighteenth century we hired plenty of European adventurers to train our troops. Even now we would be able to hire some Germans or some Irish.'

In 1923 Patel joined the Indian legislative assembly as member for Bombay city. In defiance of the policy of the national congress to abstain from taking office, he stood and was elected president by a narrow majority in August 1925. Two years later he was re-elected unanimously. Of this phase of his activities it has been said that his venerable appearance concealed a considerable fund of sheer *gaminerie*. His position and his comparative leisure enabled him to devise innumerable tricks for harassing the leading officials in the assembly and making the government of India ridiculous. But his health gave way and he resigned in 1930, and in the year after resigning he was imprisoned but released on grounds of ill health. In search of medical aid he went first to London, where he enjoyed the company of men with similar unorthodox opinions, and in 1932 to Vienna, and later to Geneva where he died 22 October 1933.

Thus closed a stormy career of agitation for the independence of India. Despite their mutual antipathies, Patel, with Gandhi, to whom alone he was second in influence, awakened from slumber one-fifth of the people of the world, and, for good or for ill, inspired them with the spirit of national self-consciousness.

[*The Times*, 23 October 1933; E. J. Thompson and G. T. Garratt, *The Rise and Fulfilment of British Rule in India*, 1934; personal knowledge.]

H. S. LAWRENCE.

PATERSON, WILLIAM PATERSON (1860–1939), Scottish divine, was born at Skirling Mains, Peeblesshire, 25 October 1860, the eldest son of John Paterson, farmer, of Skirling Mains, by his wife, Mary, daughter of John Waugh, of St. John's Kirk. On his father's side he was descended from a line of Lanarkshire farmers, and through his mother was related to a family distinguished for its scholarship and literary talent.

From Skirling school and the Royal High School, Edinburgh, Paterson entered Edinburgh University, where he graduated

M.A. (with honours in classics) and B.D., and as Pitt scholar studied in Leipzig, Erlangen, and Berlin for two years (1883–1885), forming a lifelong interest in German theology, philosophy, and literature. After serving as assistant successively in Galashiels and at St. Columba's church, London, he was ordained to the ministry of the Church of Scotland in 1887, with the charge of St. Michael's church, Crieff, until 1894. In that year he was elected to the chair of systematic theology in Aberdeen University, and speedily became known as a thinker, speaker, and personality of exceptional gifts. In 1903 he succeeded his master, Robert Flint [q.v.], as professor of divinity in the university of Edinburgh; he resigned the chair in 1934. He was dean of the faculty of divinity from 1912 to 1928.

To theological learning Paterson contributed in 1903 *The Apostles' Teaching*, a compact and skilful exposition of the message of St. Paul and of the Epistle to the Hebrews. The Baird lecture for 1905 grew into the *Rule of Faith* (1912), an expository and critical survey of Christian conceptions of the seat and of the substance of doctrine. From the Gifford lectures given at Glasgow University in 1924 emerged in 1925 *The Nature of Religion*, an impressive review of the place and significance of religion in the history and experience of mankind, its immense diversity and apparent incoherence, its complex response to the natural varieties of human temperament and of individual and social motives. Marked by patient insight and scholarly equipment, it explores with judgement and perspective the historical background and the continuing environment against which the Christian system stands out in commingled affinity and contrast. 'The nature of religion, when it is understood, is its best apology. One of the weightiest of the arguments in support of the truth of religion is that which is founded on the consideration of its aims and provisions, and especially of the nature of the doctrine which has been transmitted to the later generations as the harvest from the spiritual history of mankind.'

Two volumes of sermons for the times, *In the Day of the Muster* (1914) and *In the Day of the Ordeal* (1917), express the vision of religious patriotism which animated Paterson in a world at war. A massive article on 'War' in Hastings's *Encyclopaedia of Religion and Ethics*

treats with learning and penetration of an evil so long established as to have become an institution. Three composite volumes, *German Culture* (1915), *Social Evils and Problems* (1918), and *The Power of Prayer* (1920), attest his initiative as editor and his skill as a contributor. His last work, a lucid and judicious study of *Conversion* (1939), is marked by the same powers of intellectual retrospect and critical analysis. Profoundly interested in the development of doctrine, he viewed it as a clear-eyed apologist with psychological insight as well as historical perspective, sympathetically weighing in the balance of a catholic judgement the gains and losses to spiritual truth in the successive phases of Christian thought. His writings constitute less a system than a harmonious illustration of scholarly method and standpoint. Fundamentally loyal to the substance of authoritative dogma, Catholic and Reformed, he exercised a teacher's liberty to re-interpret in modern terms without any desire to deviate from the central well-trodden way or break the sacred continuity of tradition. If no innovation in opinion or theory and no distinctive school of doctrine can call him father, his acute perception of the significant, his sanity and comprehensive tolerance of spirit, his sense of the pageant of human history and the continuity of Divine Providence, his ear for the rhythm of vigorous prose, and his unfailing devotion to the good, the beautiful, and the true, however manifested, pervade with a fine consistency the whole of his written work.

Paterson was appointed a chaplain-in-ordinary to the king in Scotland in 1916, and received honorary doctorates from the universities of Edinburgh (D.D. 1897, LL.D., 1937), Pennsylvania (1905), Trinity College, Dublin (1920), Glasgow (1926), and St. Andrews (1937).

In the chair of Robert Leighton, Thomas Chalmers [qq.v.], and Flint, Paterson exerted a far-reaching influence alike in theological education and in Church leadership, attracting and attaching pupils, British and foreign, promoting with his colleagues in the faculty a series of important academic reforms and the institution of a post-graduate school in theology, and playing a notable part in the negotiations which led in 1929 to the reunion of the Scottish Church. Deeply interested in social and moral welfare, he was catholic and irenic in his churchmanship, and quick to appreciate the varied attainments and capacities of other men.

No public figure in Scotland in his generation inspired more general admiration, pride, trust, and affection. Conscious of his own powers, he was touchingly alive to their limitations, upon occasion amusingly envious of the particular gifts of lesser men. With a tinge of endearing absent-mindedness he could be intensely practical in the management of affairs. Simple, direct, and unaffected in all relations, he ruled his life with Spartan austerity. Courteous, indeed courtly, in bearing, he was unobtrusive in personal religon. In nothing was he more distinguished than in his conversation, the eloquent overflow of a full mind and a patient observation of men and things. He was never so happy as when sharing talk on equal terms, although, as if the saturation-point had been reached, he would break off with whimsical abruptness, no matter in what company. But no one could withstand the appeal of the dark eyes which flashed or reflected the gleam of warm human interest and sympathy. In any gathering, domestic or public, his spare ascetic figure, of middle height, and his slightly stooping head with clear-cut, rugged features and unruly silvered hair, were carried with an individual poise, and commanded attention and expectancy. As moderator in 1919 of the first General Assembly of the Church of Scotland held after the war of 1914–1918 he acquitted himself with a dignity and mastery equal to the occasion, and he is commemorated in the picture of the scene painted by Robert Hope and preserved in the Offices of the Church in Edinburgh.

Paterson married in 1888 Jane (died 1928), daughter of Robert Sanderson, tweed manufacturer, of Galashiels, and had four sons, the second and third of whom were killed in the war of 1914–1918, and three daughters. He died in Edinburgh 10 January 1939 and was buried in Skirling churchyard.

A portrait in oils of Paterson by G. Fiddes Watt is in the New College, Edinburgh, and water-colour portraits by Henry Kerr are in the possession of his family.

[Hew Scott, *Fasti Ecclesiae Scoticanae*, new ed., vol. vii; personal knowledge.]

W. A. CURTIS.

PATIALA, SIR BHUPINDRA SINGH, MAHARAJA OF (1891–1938), born at Patiala 12 October 1891, was the eldest son of Maharaja Sir Rajindra Singh, and succeeded his father as ruler of Patiala State on the latter's death in November 1900. He was educated at the Aitchison Chiefs' College at Lahore and was invested with full powers over the state administration in 1910. He was appointed G.C.I.E. in 1911. On the outbreak of war in 1914 he offered all his military forces to His Majesty's government and one of his cavalry regiments was dispatched overseas on active service. The Maharaja was given the honorary rank of lieutenant-colonel and himself visited several areas of active operations. It is estimated that about 28,000 men from Patiala State enlisted in the Indian army during the war. The Maharaja also used to the full his great influence to help the government in dealing with revolutionary tendencies among the Sikhs. In 1918 he went to England as a representative of the Indian states at the Imperial War Conference. In the same year he was appointed G.B.E. and promoted to the rank of major-general. During the Afghan war of 1919 his desire to be of active assistance to the government was recognized by his being placed on the staff of the general officer commanding at Peshawar. In 1921 he was appointed G.C.S.I. and in 1922, on the occasion of the visit of the Prince of Wales to India, G.C.V.O. He attended the League of Nations Assembly as the representative of India in 1925, and in 1926 was elected chancellor of the Chamber of Princes, an office which he held continuously until 1930 and again from 1933 to 1935 and in 1937. It was as chancellor of Chamber that he led the delegation of the princes of India at the Round Table Conference held in London in 1930. The Maharaja died at Patiala 23 March 1938, and was succeeded by his eldest son, Yadavindra Singh.

As the foregoing record shows, the Maharaja played a distinguished part in public life and was always ready to give loyal service to the Empire and to India. Unfortunately his later years were clouded by scurrilous attacks upon both his private life and his conduct as ruler of his state. These attacks culminated in the publication in 1930 of a pamphlet, *The Indictment of Patiala*, which purported to be the report of a committee of investigation into Patiala affairs appointed by the Indian States People's Conference. This attracted so much public attention both in England and India that the Maharaja asked for an official inquiry into the allegations made in the pamphlet. An inquiry was held, which completely exonerated him and found that the publication was the outcome of a deliberate conspiracy between certain individuals and political organizations. All who knew the Maharaja were satisfied that this finding was correct, since they had personal knowledge of his simple and generous nature and were convinced that he was incapable of the vicious and cruel conduct attributed to him by his enemies. He was a notable cricketer and captained the Indian cricket team which visited England in 1911; he also played polo with considerable skill in his youth and did much to support and encourage both these games in India. The breeding and training of sporting dogs became one of his chief hobbies in later years. As a young man he was strikingly handsome, both in face and figure, and as he grew older his distinguished presence made him remarkable in all company.

A cartoon of the Maharaja by 'M. R.' appeared in *Vanity Fair* 4 January 1900.

[Official records; personal knowledge.]
AUBREY METCALFE.

PATTISON, ANDREW SETH PRINGLE- (1856–1931), philosopher, whose original name was ANDREW SETH, was born at Edinburgh 20 December 1856, the second, but eldest surviving, son of Smith Kinmont Seth, a clerk in the head office of the Commercial Bank of Scotland, by his wife, Margaret, daughter of Andrew Little, farmer, of Middle Blainslie, Berwickshire. He came of country stock on both sides of his family, for his paternal grandfather was a farmer in Fife. One of his brothers, James, was his colleague in the university of Edinburgh for twenty-one years (1898–1919), each brother occupying one of the two chairs of philosophy. Their mother encouraged her sons in their intellectual aspirations. She kept house for James for most of the twenty years of her widowhood, and was long remembered by many Edinburgh students for her exceptional charm and her lively understanding of her sons and of their pupils.

Seth showed high promise in classics at the Royal High School, Edinburgh, and in classics and philosophy at Edinburgh University. In 1878, after graduation with first class honours in both these subjects, he went to Germany with a travelling scholarship awarded by the Hibbert trustees. There he spent two years, first in Berlin (where he met Eva, daughter of Albrecht Stropp, of Bogi-

slavitz, Silesia, whom he married in 1884), and afterwards in Jena and Göttingen, studying under R. H. Lotze. His first book, *The Development from Kant to Hegel* (1882), was his scholarship dissertation. It was also the source from which his subsequent philosophy proceeded. To the end he was a liberal traditionalist in the Kant–Hegel tradition, but inclining away from Hegel by reason of his own moralistic individualism.

In 1880 Seth won the coveted but not very lucrative Ferguson scholarship and became assistant at Edinburgh University to Alexander Campbell Fraser [q.v.] at £40 a year. He was also a leader-writer for the *Scotsman*. After holding the chair of logic and philosophy at University College, Cardiff (1883–1887) and that of logic, rhetoric, and metaphysics at St. Andrews University (1887–1891), he achieved his ambition of succeeding Campbell Fraser as professor of logic and metaphysics. He held the chair for twenty-eight years (1891–1919).

Seth's appointment was due, in large measure, to the success of his books *Scottish Philosophy* (1885) and *Hegelianism and Personality* (1887). These were two sets of Balfour lectures, A. J. (afterwards first Earl of) Balfour having in 1883 established an *ad hoc* lecturership expressly for Seth at Edinburgh. For this, publication was a condition. A third set of these lectures, on 'Realism', appeared in four numbers of the American *Philosophical Review* (1892–1893). Forty years later (1933), in belated piety, after the author's death, they were published in book form with a memoir, by George Freeland Barbour. The success of the first two Balfour books was thoroughly deserved. Their style, helped, perhaps, but never cheapened, by the author's experience of journalism, was lively, lucid, and distinguished, their scholarship discriminating, their substance an attempt to show that idealists with the freshest German outlook might discover in Reid's answer to Hume something which even Kant had missed and might reasonably challenge Hegelian efforts to predigest man and the world in the insatiable maw of an impersonal logic.

Seth, who in 1898 added to his own name that of Pringle-Pattison as a condition of accepting the bequest of the estate of The Haining, near Selkirk, was a successful although scarcely a great teacher. A shy man, unready of speech, he hugged the shelter of his manuscript, reading it beautifully to large classes which sometimes were almost openly restive. No debater, he read still more polished lectures, almost entirely historical, to his smaller senior classes. In delicacy, persistence, and practical wisdom, his kindness to his students was very notable.

Except for some volumes of admirable essays, Pringle-Pattison published nothing round the turn of the century. In 1917 appeared *The Idea of God in the Light of Recent Philosophy*, his most important work. The book was an elaboration of his Gifford lectures delivered at Aberdeen in 1912–1913. It ripened the philosophy of the Balfour books, pursuing, as ever, the method of 'construction through criticism' and insisting that the construction dominated the criticism. He held that 'God, or the Absolute' was the source of individuation although not Himself an individual among others; and human selves were 'the apex of the principle of individuation by which the world exists'. A relative pluralism was secure; pantheism could and should be denied. Even if certain extreme ideas were placated rather than controlled, the book was a fine achievement. Pringle-Pattison supplemented it in 1922 with *The Idea of Immortality*, the first of the two series of his Edinburgh Gifford lectures, given after his retirement from his chair (1921–1923). In the second series, remarking privately that immortality was 'an unpleasant subject', he turned to more general topics, eventually publishing his *Studies in the Philosophy of Religion* in 1930.

Pringle-Pattison received honorary degrees from the universities of St. Andrews (1892), Princeton (1896), Durham (1902), and Edinburgh (1919). He was elected a fellow of the British Academy in 1904 and was Hibbert lecturer at Manchester College, Oxford, in 1921. He was a tall man, not very lithe, with a slight stoop, a majestic beard, and eyes which constantly troubled him. His ivory complexion harmonized with hair, abundant and very silky, which greyed early and silvered equally before middle life. In 1925 he was presented by friends and old pupils with his portrait by A. E. Borthwick which is now in the possession of his son.

Pringle-Pattison's wife died in 1928. They had four sons, of whom the youngest was killed in action in 1916, and three daughters, the eldest of whom died as an infant. He died at The Haining 1 September 1931.

[*The Times*, 2 September 1931; J. B. Capper and J. B. Baillie, *Andrew Seth Pringle-Pattison, 1856–1931* in *Proceedings of the British Academy*, vol. xvii, 1931; G. F. Barbour, Memoir prefixed to *The Balfour Lectures on Realism*, 1933; A. S. Pringle-Pattison, Memoir prefixed to James Seth's *Essays in Ethics and Religion*, 1926; personal knowledge.]
JOHN LAIRD.

PAUL, HERBERT WOODFIELD (1853–1935), author and politician, was born at Finedon, Northamptonshire, 16 January 1853, the eldest son of George Woodfield Paul, vicar of Finedon and honorary canon of Peterborough Cathedral, by his wife, Jessie Philippa, daughter of Lieutenant Herbert Mackworth, R.N. From Eton he won a scholarship at Corpus Christi College, Oxford, where he was president of the Union (1875), and obtained a first class in *literae humaniores* (1875). Called to the bar by Lincoln's Inn in 1878, he never practised, though he could be imagined as a formidable cross-examiner; but he devoted himself to literary work, largely in the political field, soon becoming a skilled leader-writer for the *Daily News*.

From 1892 until 1895 Paul sat as member for South Edinburgh. A devoted follower of Gladstone, he was a strong party man and in particular a convinced free-trader, but although a capable debater, did not win in parliament the reputation merited by his exceptional talents.

Besides *Men and Letters* (1901) and a valuable appreciation of Gladstone's career (*Life of William Ewart Gladstone*, 1901) Paul published in 1902 *Matthew Arnold*, with whom he had many literary sympathies, as he had with a very different figure, Lord Acton, whose letters to Mary Gladstone he edited in 1904, and in 1905 a defence of Froude as an historian (*Life of Froude*). His most solid and important work was the *History of Modern England* (1904–1906) which has been described as the *Annual Register* tempered by epigrams. Its five volumes should be on the shelves of every historical library. *Stray Leaves*, a collection of essays published in 1906, offers conclusive evidence of the breadth and variety of his knowledge. It includes two papers on Greek literature and religion, marked by fine scholarship and literary acumen; an affectionate appreciation of Charles Lamb, in the form of a review of the biography by E. V. Lucas [q.v.], of which he admired the thoroughness but deprecated the bulk as being unsuited to the subject; an obituary notice of Bishop Mandell Creighton, for whom both as an historian and as a man his admiration was unbounded; a sarcastic picture of Arthur James Balfour's attitude in the dilemma created by Joseph Chamberlain's outburst in favour of protection; and a review of Mr. Winston Churchill's life of his father, showing the fascination exercised by some of Lord Randolph's qualities, and boldly forecasting in a sentence or two the promise of the author's future. This book was followed by a study of the age of *Queen Anne*, for Goupil's illustrated monographs (1906, revised without illustrations, 1912), an epoch in which he felt completely at home, and *Famous Speeches* (1910).

Meanwhile the liberal triumph of 1906 had returned Paul for Northampton; but in 1907 a nervous collapse foreshadowed his retirement in 1909. By 1910 he had sufficiently recovered to undertake the office of second civil service commissioner (to which he had been appointed the previous year), and for which he was perfectly suited by his gifts and attainments, and which he held until 1918. The rest of his life was spent in retirement at Forest Row where he died 4 August 1935.

In 1883 Paul married Elinor, daughter of William Ritchie, legal member of the viceroy's council in India, and sister of Sir Richmond T. W. Ritchie [q.v.]. She was a lady of great charm. They had a son and a daughter.

Paul never sought or obtained popularity in the conventional sense; his comments, often sub-acid, but never captious or unfair, aroused the animosity of one or two fellow writers; but he was less contemptuous than he appeared to be, and recognized all work which was not slipshod or marred by prejudice. He ignored gossip and scandal, and despised those who found pleasure in discussing the weaknesses of men whom he deemed to be essentially great. He was no lettered recluse, but a delightful companion in leisure hours. Nurtured in a county for which fox-hunting was a religious exercise, he could appreciate the points of a well-bred horse; and he thoroughly enjoyed good cheer and a glass of choice wine. He had some enemies, but was the most loyal of friends, and it is sad that he left a slighter mark on his age than some who could not claim a tithe of his ability or his acquirements.

[*The Times*, 7 August 1935; personal knowledge.] CREWE.

PAYNE, HUMFRY GILBERT GARTH (1902–1936), archaeologist, was born at Wendover 19 February 1902, the only son of the historian Edward John Payne [q.v.], by his wife, Emma Leonora Helena Pertz, granddaughter of Georg Heinrich Pertz (editor of the *Monumenta Germaniae Historica*) and of James John Garth Wilkinson the Swedenborgian [q.v.]. He was educated at Westminster and at Christ Church, Oxford, of which he was an open classical scholar. At Oxford he obtained a first class in classical moderations (1922) and in *literae humaniores* (1924), and showed himself to be one of the ablest all-round classical men of his time. It was in his last year at Oxford that he became seriously interested in Greek art, partly under the influence of (Sir) J. D. Beazley and Alan Blakeway, and resolved to make himself an archaeologist. After taking his degree he continued his studies as university research scholar in Mediterranean archaeology (1924–1926), as assistant at the Ashmolean Museum (1926–1928), and as a senior scholar of Christ Church (1926–1931). He was awarded the Conington prize for classical learning in 1927.

In 1929 Payne was appointed director of the British School of Archaeology at Athens. In 1931 the publication of *Necrocorinthia*, a study of vase-painting and the other arts at Corinth, placed him at once, as all admitted, in the front rank of classical archaeologists. Two of his chief pieces of work as director were the publication of *Archaic Marble Sculpture from the Acropolis* (1936: a volume of photographs by Mr. Gerard Mackworth Young with text by Payne), and the excavation of Perachora, a small but rich archaic site opposite Corinth. The first volume of *Perachora*, edited by Mr. Thomas James Dunbabin, was published in 1940; most of it is by Payne. The second volume is to come. In 1936 a staphylococcic infection, which had been present in a minor form for some years, suddenly became acute; when he was removed to hospital it was too late, and he died in Athens 9 May. He was buried at Mycenae.

Most of Payne's work was done in the field of archaic art, which he loved and understood. *Necrocorinthia* collected and arranged a vast body of important material, and may be said to have furnished the study of archaic art with a new basis. It was supplemented in 1933 by *Protokorinthische Vasenmalerei*. *Archaic Marble Sculpture* not only sets many statues and fragments in a fresh light, but gives a truer account of the essential qualities of archaic Greek sculpture than can be found elsewhere. A fine eye, deep respect for the individual object, great structural power, wealth of detail combined with breadth of vision, perfect clearness of thought and expression, these qualities appear in all Payne's work.

Payne was six feet five inches in height, straight, slender, square-shouldered, with a small head, and small features (except the mouth), fair hair, a fresh complexion, eyes of a strong blue, and something boyish, yet resolute, in the face. He was a fine draughtsman, and took more and more pleasure, as time went on, in drawing and painting landscapes. He married in 1926 Elizabeth Dilys, daughter of Thomas Powell, bank manager, of Bridgnorth and Bournemouth; she wrote a good account of him, especially of his life in Greece. There were no children.

[*The Times*, 11 May 1936; Dilys Powell, *The Traveller's Journey is Done*, 1943 (portraits); personal knowledge.]

J. D. Beazley.

PEARSON, ALFRED CHILTON (1861–1935), classical scholar, was born in London 8 October 1861, the only child of Robert Henry Pearson, merchant, of London, by his wife, Georgina Boswood. He was educated at Highgate and King's College schools, and at Christ's College, Cambridge, which he entered as a scholar in 1879. After obtaining a first class in both parts of the classical tripos (1881 and 1883) he read for the bar and was called by Lincoln's Inn in 1885, in which year he married Edith Maud, fourth daughter of Reuben Green, solicitor and town clerk of Kensington, and settled in London. In 1890 he became a schoolmaster. After two years at Bury St. Edmunds and one at Ipswich he passed in 1893 to Dulwich College, which he left in 1900, in order to enter his late father's London business, moving at the same time to Warlingham in Surrey.

Pearson's publications began in 1887 with a note in the *Classical Review*, to which he continued to contribute articles and reviews on many Greek subjects: his first book was *The Fragments of Zeno and Cleanthes* (1891), an admirable work which had won him the Hare prize at Cambridge two years before. All his later books were editions of works of the Greek tragedians, although between 1908 and 1921 he contributed more than twenty articles to

Hastings's *Encyclopaedia of Religion and Ethics*. He began with a series of school editions of Euripides (*Helena*, 1903; *Heraclidae*, 1907; *Phoenissae*, 1909) and with an abridgement (1907) of the *Ajax* of Sophocles edited by Sir R. C. Jebb [q.v.]. Next, at the invitation of the syndics of the Cambridge University Press, he prepared for posthumous publication (1910) the verse translation and incomplete commentary on Aeschylus's *Agamemnon* left by W. G. Headlam [q.v.], and also undertook the completion of Jebb's Sophocles by editing the Fragments. Pearson spent several years on this difficult task, and in 1917 produced a masterly edition in three volumes. In 1919 he was elected Gladstone professor of Greek at Liverpool University, and in 1921 succeeded Henry Jackson as regius professor of Greek at Cambridge, becoming thereupon a fellow of Trinity College. His chief remaining work was the Sophocles which he added to the 'Oxford Classical Texts' series in 1924. Soon after this his health failed. He resigned his chair in 1928, and lived from 1932 to 1934 at Hunstanton before removing to London, where he died 2 January 1935 after five years of total incapacity. His wife had died in 1930. They had a son and two daughters, the elder of whom predeceased her father.

Pearson was a man of active habits, an oar and a cricketer in youth, and a keen golfer and walker in later life. Intensely loyal and generous, he combined deep modesty with strong opinions, carefully formed and not easily shaken. His scholarship was of a very high order, especially on the linguistic and grammatical side. All his books are models in their kind, and his masterpiece, *The Fragments of Sophocles*, shows a vast range of knowledge at the service of an acute and sober judgement. He was elected an honorary fellow of Christ's College in 1922 and a fellow of the British Academy in 1924.

Pearson was never painted, but there is a drawing by A. K. Laurence, made in 1927, at Trinity College, Cambridge.

[*The Times*, 3 January 1935; D. S. Robertson in *Cambridge Review*, 18 January 1935; G. C. Richards, *Alfred Chilton Pearson, 1861–1935* in *Proceedings* of the British Academy, vol. xxi, 1935 (bibliography); private information; personal knowledge.]

D. S. Robertson.

PEARSON, KARL (1857–1936), mathematician and biologist, was born in

London 27 March 1857, the younger son and second of the three children of William Pearson, Q.C., of the Inner Temple, and his wife, Fanny Smith, both of Yorkshire descent. He was educated at University College School, King's College, Cambridge, of which latter he was a scholar and where he was third wrangler in the mathematical tripos of 1879, and at the universities of Heidelberg and Berlin. Pearson's studies included mathematics, metaphysics, engineering, law, medieval languages, political science, and history; his first two publications (both anonymous), *The New Werther* (1880) and *The Trinity: a Nineteenth Century Passion Play* (1882), were literary and his original intention was to practise at the bar to which he was called by the Inner Temple in 1882. Like many other Templars, Pearson combined reading in chambers with lecturing and writing, on social, ethical, and historical subjects. A selection of lectures and essays was published in 1888 under the title *The Ethic of Free Thought*. These papers, together with another selection published in 1897 under the title *The Chances of Death and other Studies in Evolution*, and some papers largely historical which appeared in *Biometrika* much later, particularly his study of 'The Skull and Portraits of Henry Stewart, Lord Darnley' (vol. xx B, 1928), give a reader to whom mathematical or arithmetical subjects are repellent, an opportunity of understanding why, in his principal field of work, Pearson inspired both enthusiasm and opposition. There is more than a superficial likeness between his writings and those of Macaulay. He had a vivid literary style and wide knowledge, but also some failure to be just to men and ideas of which he disapproved.

(Sir) Alexander Kennedy [q.v.] persuaded Pearson, who regarded him as one of the greatest science professors of his day, to abandon law for mathematics, and in 1884 Pearson succeeded Olaus Henrici as Goldsmid professor of applied mathematics and mechanics in University College, London. The remainder of his working life was spent in University College. More than fifteen years before he was elected first Galton professor of eugenics (1911), statistics and eugenics had become Pearson's main intellectual interest, but he continued to be a highly efficient teacher and investigator of the subjects within the purview of the Goldsmid chair. Not content with this, he applied for and was appointed to the

Gresham professorship of geometry in 1891. His predecessors at Gresham College had either been sinecurists (like Sir William Petty, q.v.) or had used the endowment as an opportunity of giving popular instruction. Naturally Pearson chose the second alternative and out of two of his courses there grew the most widely read of his books, *The Grammar of Science* (1892), which was reprinted in 'Everyman's Library' in 1937. The influence of this book on the generation which was young at the end of the nineteenth century was great. Pearson's mockery of the current text-book definition of mass as 'quantity of matter', his insistence on the relativity of motion, on the nature of scientific 'laws' as primarily descriptive of the routine of perception and conceptually extended, his reiteration of the view that the man of science tries to answer the question 'How?' not the question 'Why?' were stimulating. To young readers now, much which was startling fifty years ago is commonplace and it is easy to criticize Pearson's rather light-hearted acceptance of the rule of succession based by Laplace on Bayes's postulate (actually Pearson never lost interest in attempts to make the logical basis of what is called inverse probability more secure); but even now a youth whose education has been primarily literary could learn a good deal about the aim of scientific method from the first edition of *The Grammar*.

In his courses at Gresham College Pearson taught the elements of the mathematical theory of probability with that wealth of illustration, diagrammatic and arithmetical, which characterized all his popular lectures, and within a few years he was to be absorbed in the application to biological data of the calculus of probabilities. The stimulus came from reading *Natural Inheritance* by (Sir) Francis Galton [q.v.] and from personal friendship with W. F. R. Weldon [q.v.] and, later, with Galton himself. 'It was Galton', he said, 'who first freed me from the prejudice that sound mathematics could only be applied to natural phenomena under the category of causation. Here for the first time was a possibility—I will not say a certainty—of reaching knowledge as valid as physical knowledge was then thought to be, in the field of living forms and above all in the field of human conduct.' Between Pearson and Weldon there grew up a partnership to test the Darwinian theory by measurement and Pearson's first mathematical contribution to the theory of evolution was published in 1894. Pearson's enthusiasm for the Darwinian theory of evolution by natural selection never flagged and his veneration for Darwin and Galton increased, if possible, as he grew older; statistical verifications of the Darwinian hypothesis remained throughout his later life a principal interest. But the statistical methods which he invented or improved were applicable in so many fields of scientific research that he attracted students of widely different tastes from all parts of the world, and his laboratory was for many years almost the Mecca of biostatisticians or biometricians. In 1901 he founded the journal *Biometrika*, which became a vehicle of publication of his own and his pupils' researches. In addition, series of separate memoirs, mathematical tables for the use of biometricians and other computers, and brochures on controversial topics came from his laboratory, largely the work of himself and his pupils, but including much contributed by other workers.

Pearson continued to control this immense output down to 1933, and after resigning his chair remained an indefatigable investigator and writer until his death, which took place at Coldharbour 27 April 1936. In 1890 he married Maria, daughter of William Sharpe, solicitor, brother of Samuel and Daniel Sharpe [qq.v.] and nephew of Samuel Rogers [q.v.]. By her he had a son, Egon, now professor of statistics at London University, and two daughters. She died in 1928, and in 1929 he married a fellow worker in his laboratory, Margaret Victoria, daughter of John Child.

Pearson was among the most influential university teachers of his time; he took great pains to be intelligible and could hold a large audience either of students or of merely casual hearers who were without special interest in his topics. In the smaller circle of his research pupils he inspired enthusiastic personal affection; no head of a department repaid loyal service more generously. It is, of course, impossible to give those who never came under the wand of the magician at an impressionable age an idea of his personal influence. He had some of the defects of his qualities; he was dominating. Like the great headmaster John Percival [q.v.], he had an intense and genuine belief in freedom of thought but was apt to attribute intellectual differences of opinion to stupidity or even moral obliquity. Personal relations between him and his pupils were sometimes painfully interrupted for years; but it is pleasant to record that eventually most of these broken friendships were happily resumed. Only intellectual differences disturbed harmony; in the ordinary social relations of life he was a charming host, guest, or travelling companion. Pearson's influence upon those who only knew him through his writings was also great. He was admired and feared, rather than loved, by many; in some he aroused bitter hostility. The Macaulay-like qualities of his mind explain this; his triumphantly clear exposition and his bitter or contemptuous controversial style. He treated many opponents as Macaulay treated Croker, James Mill, and Sadler.

Whatever may be the final estimate of his personal contributions to the science and art of statistics, there can be no doubt that in Great Britain, in the United States of America, and, to a less extent, in Europe, Pearson's demonic energy was a prime factor in the revolution which has led to the setting up of statistical laboratories not only in universities and government departments but in industrial concerns. A number of the leading statisticians of England and America were his pupils or pupils of his pupils; others may have been inspired by the very intensity of their opposition to Pearson's methods and conclusions. At least he convinced them that statistics were important.

What may be regarded as weaknesses were not caused by but correlated with the qualities which made Pearson an inspiring leader. He was impatient to reach conclusions, to measure the manifestations of life, to correlate one manifestation with another. He sought an organon which would work and tended to be a little more hasty in building the logical foundation of a process and more lax in marking its limitations than was to be expected in a mathematician of his school. He had also one of the defects that, perhaps inevitably, tend to be associated with a man who has developed a consistent series of methods entirely of his own devising. Any statistician or mathematician who followed the same lines as his, or lines similar to those which he followed, was sure to arouse his interest, but he was uninterested in or even hostile to those who had followed other paths. It was difficult to interest him in the work of continental mathematical statisticians;

he was contemptuously hostile to Ladislaus von Bortkiewicz and although he published a portrait of A. A. Tschuprow in *Biometrika* the inscription suggests that Tschuprow's chief title to fame was a small treatise on correlation.

It is, however, possible that had Pearson's statistical outlook been wider, his effective influence would have been less. If his drive for results sometimes led to waste of energy, it more often led to valuable discoveries. If he insisted overmuch on arithmetical exactitude to the nth place of decimals, at least his rule that, in a practical subject, algebra should never be divorced from arithmetic, has had a very good effect upon his pupils, even upon his critics.

Pearson was elected F.R.S. in 1896 and was awarded the society's Darwin medal in 1898. He received the honorary degree of LL.D. from the university of St. Andrews, and of D.Sc. from the university of London. He was elected an honorary fellow of King's College, Cambridge (1903), of the Royal Society of Edinburgh, and of University College, London.

There is a drawing of Pearson by F. A. de Biden Footner (1924) in the possession of University College, London.

[*Speeches . . . in honour of Professor Karl Pearson* (containing valuable autobiographical data, privately printed), 1934; *Obituary Notices of Fellows of the Royal Society*, No. 5, December 1936 (portrait); E. S. Pearson, *Karl Pearson*, 1938; personal knowledge.]

M. GREENWOOD.

PEEL, WILLIAM ROBERT WELLESLEY, first EARL and second VISCOUNT PEEL (1867-1937), statesman, was born in London 7 January 1867, the eldest of the four sons of Arthur Wellesley Peel, first Viscount Peel [q.v.], by his wife, Adelaide, second daughter of William Stratford Dugdale, of Merevale Hall, Warwickshire, and grandson of the statesman Sir Robert Peel [q.v.]. His early years were spent in London and at Sandy, Bedfordshire; he was educated at Harrow and at Balliol College, Oxford. He played a full part in the undergraduate life of the university, and his active mind, which made him delight in the company of gay and interesting people, was further nourished by the circle which he met under his father's roof at Speaker's House.

In 1893 Peel was called to the bar by the Inner Temple and for the next few years went on circuit, sometimes acting as marshal to (Sir) Roland Vaughan Williams

[q.v.]. In 1897 he served as special correspondent of the *Daily Telegraph* in the Greco-Turkish war; this gave him his first experience of foreign affairs, which remained a lifelong interest. These activities were cut short by an attack of typhoid. He gained his first experience of public affairs at home as a member of the royal commission on the Port of London. In 1900 he began his long connexion with the London County Council; he was a member successively for Woolwich, Westminster, and Kennington, becoming leader of the municipal reform party from 1908 to 1910, and chairman from 1914 to 1916. There he showed his qualities as a debater, and his zest for a tough fight. In 1900 he entered parliament as unionist member for the Southern division of Manchester but lost his seat at the great liberal victory of 1906. He was member for Taunton from 1909 until he succeeded his father in 1912. From 1906 onwards his party was in opposition and he did not therefore have the opportunity of winning his spurs in office until 1917, when he became joint parliamentary secretary to the National Service Department in the coalition government.

At the beginning of the war of 1914-1918 Peel was in command of the Bedfordshire Yeomanry, but was obliged to relinquish this post in 1915 owing to ill health. In 1919 he became undersecretary of state for war under Mr. Churchill, being sworn of the Privy Council. The relationship of chief and under-secretary might have been a difficult one when these posts were held by two men of such strong personality, the secretaryship actually being held by the younger man who happened to have had far more experience of office. But they solved the problem by dividing their spheres of influence.

In 1921 Peel became chancellor of the Duchy of Lancaster, an office usually looked upon as a mere rung in the ladder, but Peel, with his interest in the countryside, was energetic in the performance of his duties there, which were little more than those of the king's land agent. With this post was combined that of minister of transport. From 1922 to 1924 he was secretary of state for India; with his second term of office from 1928 to 1929, his membership of the India Round Table Conference of 1930-1931, his chairmanship of the Burma Round Table Conference from 1931 to 1932, and his membership of the joint select comnittee on Indian constitutional reforms n 1933, his career demonstrates his con- tinuous preoccupation with the problems of the Indian Empire. In his handling of these problems he showed his realistic grasp of things as they were and a commonsense point of view, which would not allow his judgement to be deflected by wishful thinking or too optimistic idealism. Between his two periods at the India Office he was first commissioner of Works (1924–1928), lord privy seal (1931), and chairman of the Wheat Com- mission (1932).

Although politics and the affairs of the nation were Peel's real interest, he played some part in the world of business and finance as chairman of James Williamson & company, to which he succeeded on the death of his father-in-law in 1929; he was also a director of Barclays Bank and of the Great Northern Railway. His record and qualifications would have justified other advancement, but the fact that he held no further major office after his second tenure of the India Office was, perhaps, due to his increasing want of sympathy with those in power. But in other directions he carried on his active career until his death. In 1934 he was chairman of the royal com- mission on the dispatch of business at common law, and in 1936 he went to Palestine to accomplish the last work of his life as chairman of the royal com- mission of 1936–1937. The report of this commission was widely commended. Always an excellent speaker, full of humour and lucid in explanation, he re- tained this power to the end, and only two months before he died he spoke in the House of Lords on the findings of the commission to the admiration of all who heard him. Possibly it was in the conduct of these commissions and round the con- ference table that Peel was at his best. He had a mind which delighted in getting to the heart of any new problem, in balancing conflicting ideas, and in hand- ling the men who held them. He had a quick grasp of essentials, the courage of his convictions, and, above all, humour.

Peel was created Earl Peel in 1929. For his services in the war of 1914–1918 he was awarded the American D.S.M. He was appointed G.B.E. in 1919 and G.C.S.I. in 1932. In 1899 he married Eleanor (Ella), elder daughter of James Williamson, first Lord Ashton, and had a son and a daughter. He died at Peters- field 28 September 1937, and was suc-

ceeded as second earl by his son, Arthur William Ashton (born 1901).

Peel was a big man, his most conspi- cuous features being his very bright blue eyes and his thick moustache, which became the joy of the caricaturist. There is a portrait of him by William Nicholson at County Hall, London.

[*Daily Telegraph*, 30 September 1937; per- sonal knowledge.]   DORIS BLACKER.

PEET, THOMAS ERIC (1882–1934), Egyptologist, was born at Liverpool 12 August 1882, the eldest son of Thomas Peet, corn-merchant, of that city, by his wife, Salome Fowler. He was educated at Merchant Taylors School, Crosby, and obtained a Jodrell scholarship at Queen's College, Oxford, where he was awarded a second class in classical and mathematical moderations (1903) and in *literae humaniores* (1905). During his last year there David Randall-MacIver interested him in the then unexploited Italian prehistoric period; on a small grant from the Craven fund he made a brief reconnaissance in Italy, and in 1906 easily gained a Craven fellowship. During the next three years he explored early Italian sites and wrote *The Stone and Bronze Ages in Italy and Sicily* (1909), still the best work of general reference on the subject. But Italian archaeology offering no permanent livelihood, Peet turned to Egypt. In 1909 he excavated at Abydos, first for the Liverpool Insti- tute of Archaeology, and afterwards for the Egypt Exploration Fund (later Society) from 1909 to 1913; the results of his work for the fund are contained in *The Cemeteries of Abydos*, parts i–iii (1913–1914). From 1913 to 1928 he was lecturer in Egyptology at Manchester University. His next literary task in book form was *The Inscriptions of Sinai*, part i (edited in collaboration with (Sir) Alan Henderson Gardiner, 1917). In 1915 he obtained a commission in the Royal Army Service Corps, and showed great ability at Salonika, where he and one other man supervised the whole of the landing of supplies in 1916–1917. By the summer of 1918 he was serving in France as a lieu- tenant in the 14th battalion of the King's Liverpool Regiment.

Demobilized early in 1919, Peet was elected in the following year to the Brunner chair of Egyptology at Liverpool Univer- sity. Early in 1921 he directed a season's excavations at El-Amarna for the Egypt Exploration Society. In 1923 he became Laycock student in Egyptology at

Worcester College, Oxford. After 1921 his life was outwardly uneventful (except for a visit as lecturer to Cairo University in 1929) until 1933, when he was elected reader in Egyptology at Oxford and a fellow of Queen's. His tenure of these positions was short-lived, for he died at Oxford 22 February 1934, shortly before the readership had been definitely converted into a chair. He married in 1910 Mary Florence, daughter of Richard Johnson Lawton, civil engineer, of Chiswick, and had a daughter.

At the outset of his Egyptological career Peet realized the importance of a good knowledge of the Egyptian language and writing; several of his works (e.g. *The Mayer Papyri*, 1920; *The Rhind Mathematical Papyrus*, 1923; *The Great Tomb-Robberies of the Twentieth Egyptian Dynasty*, 1930) deal with important texts in the often very difficult 'hieratic' script, of which he had exceptional mastery. His *Egypt and the Old Testament* (1922) discusses with rare critical skill the biblical records of Egyptian contacts. In 1929 the delivery of his Schweich lectures (published in 1931) on *A Comparative Study of the Literature of Egypt, Palestine and Mesopotamia* broke fresh ground. Among his many activities he found time to edit the university of Liverpool *Annals of Archaeology and Anthropology* from 1921 (from 1925 jointly), and the *Journal of Egyptian Archaeology* from 1923 until his death.

Peet's services to his science were many, and indeed he was the best example that England has produced of an all-round Egyptologist, equally able in the field, the study, and the lecture theatre, in archaeology and philology, in the historic and prehistoric periods. Two aspects of his subject in the interpretation of which he excelled were Egyptian history (he contributed largely to the *Cambridge Ancient History*) and mathematics.

As to Peet's character, the description given by a colleague who stood close to him may be quoted from: 'Intensely alive and vital.... His versatility was extraordinary. ... His scientific work was fundamentally solid, the expression of his conclusions crystal-clear. Perhaps he was slightly lacking in imagination, but he saw reality through and through. . . . No one ever found him shirking a responsibility, and his unobtrusive kindnesses were innumerable.'

[*Journal of Egyptian Archaeology*, vol. xx, 1934 (portrait); *Oxford Magazine*, 1 March 1934; personal knowledge.]

BATTISCOMBE GUNN.

PEMBREY, MARCUS SEYMOUR (1868–1934), physiologist, was born at Oxford 28 May 1868, the second son of John Cripps Pembrey, a learned proofreader in oriental languages at the Oxford University Press, by his wife, Annie Coster Tanner. He was educated at Oxford High School and at Christ Church, Oxford, which he entered in 1885, becoming a Fell exhibitioner in 1888 and obtaining a first class in natural science (physiology) in 1889. The award of the Radcliffe travelling fellowship in 1890 enabled him to visit the physiological laboratories at Kiel and Würzburg. After qualifying in medicine in 1892 from University College Hospital, he became a demonstrator in physiology at Oxford under (Sir) J. S. Burdon-Sanderson [q.v.]. In 1895 he was appointed lecturer in physiology at Charing Cross Hospital medical school, and vacated this post in 1900 for a similar position, which in 1920 became a professorship, at Guy's Hospital medical school.

Pembrey's first research on the respiratory exchange of mammals was soon coupled with an investigation of the regulation of body temperature, and experiments on the developing chick and newly born mammals did much to explain the characteristic difference between warm- and cold-blooded animals. This led him to an investigation of the respiratory process in hibernating mammals, which resemble cold-blooded animals during their winter sleep. After serving from 1906 to 1909 on a War Office committee which inquired into the physiological effects of food, training, and clothing on the soldier, he devoted much attention to the problem of general physical fitness and to the effects of muscular exercise on the respiration, circulation, body temperature, and kidneys.

Working in co-operation with the physicians at Guy's Hospital Pembrey showed how the physiologist can help the clinician and, with a quick appreciation of the significance of the discoveries of J. S. Haldane [q.v.], he made important observations on clinical cases of periodic or Cheyne-Stokes breathing, on the respiratory phenomena associated with diabetes and cardiac disability, on changes of temperature resulting from lesions of the spinal cord, and on the elimination of water by the kidneys and skin.

Pembrey was elected F.R.S. in 1922. He was a stimulating and original teacher, always ready to debate scientific problems, forthright in argument but never bitter.

Country life appealed to him—he farmed on a small scale at his home in Sussex whilst working at Guy's—and on relinquishing his chair he retired to a farm at Ramsden in Oxfordshire, but within a year he died unexpectedly at Oxford 23 July 1934.

Pembrey married in 1895 Bessie Cecily, daughter of Edward Ebenezer Crake, rector of Jevington, Sussex, and had five sons and five daughters.

[*Obituary Notices of Fellows of the Royal Society*, No. 4, December 1935 (portrait); *Lancet*, 1934, vol. ii, pp. 279–280; Guy's Hospital *Reports*, vol. lxxxv, 1935; personal knowledge.] C. G. DOUGLAS.

PERKIN, ARTHUR GEORGE (1861–1937), organic chemist, was born at Sudbury, Middlesex, 13 December 1861, the younger son of the chemist (Sir) William Henry Perkin [q.v.], by his first wife, Jemima Harriet, youngest daughter of John Lissett, who was of Huguenot descent. His elder brother, William Henry Perkin [q.v.], became Waynflete professor of chemistry in the university of Oxford. His mother died of consumption before he was a year old and he was very delicate. After his father's second marriage in 1866 he was sent to a boarding-school at Margate, and at the age of ten joined his brother at the City of London School, chosen as being the only school available where science was then taught. During their holidays, the boys carried out experiments in a hut fitted as a laboratory in the garden at Sudbury. Chemical research became the prime object of the working lives of both brothers and music was their principal recreation. Nine members of the family constituted an orchestra in which Arthur played the flute.

In 1878 Perkin entered the Royal College of Chemistry at South Kensington, where he studied under (Sir) Edward Frankland and Frederick Guthrie [qq.v.] and carried out the investigation leading to the publication of his first paper, which appeared in the *Journal* of the Chemical Society in 1880. After one year (1880–1881) at Anderson's College, Glasgow, he was awarded a clothworkers' scholarship tenable in the dyeing department of Yorkshire College, Leeds (afterwards Leeds University), and worked with J. J. Hummel on derivatives of brazilwood and logwood. In 1882 he became chemist, and in 1888 manager, at the alizarin factory of Messrs. Hardman & Holden of Manchester. In 1892 he joined the staff of the dyeing department, Yorkshire College, as lecturer and research chemist. This position was an ideal one for him because, apart from delivering one course of lectures and supervising the laboratory work of senior students, he could devote all his time to his own investigations. He was primarily interested in isolating numerous natural colouring matters and in investigating their constitutions, largely by degradative methods and by studying their dyeing properties. He left to others the confirmation of his deductions by synthesis. His profound knowledge of natural colouring matters established his international reputation in this field and brought many chemists from abroad to work with him. In 1918 he published, in collaboration with Dr. Arthur Ernest Everest, *The Natural Organic Colouring Matters*.

In 1916 Perkin was appointed professor of colour chemistry and dyeing in Leeds University, subsequently turning his attention again to the chemistry of anthraquinone derivatives. He retired in 1926. He was elected a fellow of the Royal Society in 1903, and was awarded its Davy medal in 1924. He received the honorary degree of D.Sc. from Leeds University in 1927. A great chemist in his generation, his attitude to his students was so fatherly that he was always referred to by them as 'Pa Perkin', a title independently conferred upon his brother in Manchester.

Perkin married in 1887 Annie Florence, daughter of James Bedford, of Leeds; there were no children of the marriage. He died at his home at Headingley, Leeds, 30 May 1937. An excellent portrait of him by Richard Jack was presented to the university of Leeds on his retirement and hangs in the great hall.

[*Journal* of the Chemical Society, October 1938; *Obituary Notices of Fellows of the Royal Society*, No. 7, January 1939 (portrait); personal knowledge.] F. M. ROWE.

PERKS, SIR ROBERT WILLIAM, first baronet (1849–1934), Methodist, industrialist, and politician, was born at Brentford 24 April 1849, the elder son of the Rev. George Thomas Perks, who was president of the Wesleyan Conference in 1873, by his wife, Mary, daughter of James Alexander Dodds, an Edinburgh architect of promise who died young.

Perks was educated at Kingswood School, Bath, which was then exclusively for Wesleyan ministers' sons, and at

King's College, London, where he won many open prizes mainly for English essays. He competed for four years in succession for the Indian civil service, missing entrance each year by one or two places. This was a great disappointment at the time, but he lived to regard it as the most fortunate escape of his life. Turning to law he qualified as a solicitor and in 1876 became the partner in London of (Sir) Henry Fowler (afterwards Viscount Wolverhampton, q.v.), with whom he remained for twenty-five years. The firm specialized in railway and parliamentary practice, and by sheer business acumen Perks made a reputation as a lawyer who could pilot company bills through parliament. He studied intensively all railway law, and had little difficulty in being appointed solicitor to the London Metropolitan District Railway Company, at the time of its expansion in the late 'seventies, and he was associated with Messrs. Walker of Westminster in building Barry docks and railway, the great harbour works that created the Buenos Ayres port, the Rio de Janeiro harbour works, and the tunnel through the Andes. With the same firm, with which he worked until 1912, he helped to build the Severn tunnel and he was one of the chief advocates of the English Channel tunnel scheme. After leaving Messrs. Walker he joined a firm of dock and railway contractors in Ottawa and New York.

As liberal member of parliament for the Louth division from 1892 to 1910 Perks was originator and chairman (1906–1908) of the parliamentary committee of 200 nonconformist members of the House of Commons, to whom may be attributed the recovery of nonconformist influence in politics at the end of the century. When in February 1902 the Liberal League was formed under Rosebery, Asquith, Grey, Fowler, and Haldane, Perks was the treasurer, and owing to his skill, they were never in financial difficulties.

But Perks's interest was Methodism, and his endeavours very largely contributed to the success of his Church during his lifetime. In 1878 he was one of the first batch of laymen to be admitted to the Wesleyan Conference, which had until then been confined to ministers. He agitated for years for the organic union of the three larger Methodist Churches and worked skilfully for its consummation. When it was accomplished in 1932 he was elected unanimously as the first vice-president of the united body.

The imaginative mind of Perks devised and carried to its successful conclusion the scheme of raising the sum of one million guineas to celebrate the opening of the twentieth century, with the cry of 'One million guineas from one million Methodists'. Nobody was to contribute more than one guinea in his own name, and when Lord Rosebery offered one hundred guineas, the offer was rejected until he had searched out ninety-nine village people and children connected with Methodism to whose names his money was attached. Part of the money thus raised was devoted to the founding of the Westminster Central Hall, on the site of the Aquarium.

Perks was a good Methodist, charitable in the extreme, doing humble as well as prominent work for his Church. He was a skilful debater both politically and religiously. He was contemptuous of ecclesiastical display or ornaments and a characteristic attitude was summed up in his remark that 'a Geneva gown is a poor equivalent for a feeble sermon'.

Perks was created a baronet in 1908. He married in 1878 Edith, daughter of William Mewburn, of Wykham Park, Banbury, and had one son and four daughters, of whom the eldest predeceased her father. He died in London 30 November 1934, and was succeeded as second baronet by his son, Robert Malcolm Mewburn (born 1892).

A portrait of Perks by A. T. Nowell is in the possession of Sir Malcolm Perks: a copy hangs in Westminster Central Hall.

[Denis Crane, *The Life Story of Sir Robert W. Perks*, 1909; *Sir Robert Perks, Baronet* (autobiographical notes printed for private circulation), 1936; *The Times*, 1 December 1934.]   O. A. RATTENBURY.

PERRY, Sir **(EDWIN) COOPER** (1856–1938), physician and administrator, was born at Castle Bromwich, Warwickshire, 10 September 1856, the only son of Edwin Cresswell Perry, who became vicar of Seighford, Staffordshire, in 1861, by his wife, Esther Cooper, daughter of Joseph Cockram, of Darlaston, Staffordshire. Perry's father, an all-round scholar and mathematician, was responsible for his entire education until he was thirteen. In 1870 he won a scholarship at Eton, where he was awarded the Newcastle scholarship in 1876 and whence he became a scholar of King's College, Cambridge, gaining the Bell university scholarship (1876), the Browne scholarship and medal (1878), and the Pitt scholarship (1879), and was senior classic in the tripos of 1880. While at Cambridge he was associated with A. H. Mann [q.v.], the organist of King's, in the revision (1879–1882) of the King's College anthem book.

In 1880, having been elected into a fellow-ship at his college, Perry set aside classics, became a medical student, and in 1883 was appointed assistant lecturer in medical subjects at King's and assistant demonstrator of anatomy in the Cambridge medical school. In 1885 he entered the London Hospital and qualified M.R.C.S. in October, and subsequently (1886–1887) held the posts of house surgeon to (Sir) Frederick Treves [q.v.] and house physician to (Sir) Stephen Mackenzie [q.v.] at the London Hospital.

In 1887 his fellowship ran out and Perry was appointed an assistant physician to Guy's Hospital and, in the following year, dean of the medical school. In conjunction with Mr. Frederick Newland-Pedley he was responsible for the establishment of a dental school at Guy's. In 1892, on the death of John Charles Steele, Perry was appointed superintendent of Guy's Hospital, an office which he held until 1920. He was a governor of Guy's Hospital from 1920 to 1937. He went twice to Egypt (1897 and 1926) in order to assist in the organization of the teaching of medicine in Cairo.

Perry, who in 1897 was appointed one of the first visitors for the Prince of Wales's Hospital Fund (later King Edward's Hospital Fund), served for many years as a member of its distribution committee of which from 1921 until his death he was chairman. He was appointed G.C.V.O. in 1935 in recognition of his services to the fund.

Perry was elected in 1900 to the senate of the university of London as a representative of the faculty of medicine. He resigned in 1905 but was re-elected in 1915. From 1917 to 1919 he was vice-chancellor, and in 1920 was appointed principal of the university and held this post until 1926. In 1929 he became a member of the committee which redrafted the statutes of the university and he was a Crown member of the court from 1930 until his death. In accordance with the recommendations of the Athlone Committee on Postgraduate Medical Education in London (1921) he took a leading part in the foundation of the London School of Hygiene and Tropical Medicine, instituted by royal charter in 1924, and

for many years was the chairman of the council.

After the South African war, Perry served on a commission appointed to reorganize the Army Medical Service. For his services in founding the Royal Army Medical College at Millbank he was knighted in 1903 ; he received the honorary degree of LL.D. from the university of London and that of M.D. from the university of Egypt.

At the end of 1938 Perry had a complete right-sided paralysis and he died at his home at Worthing twelve days later, 17 December. His body was cremated and his ashes were interred in the church of his old home at Seighford. He married in 1890 Caroline Maud (died 1935), second daughter of James MacManus, of Killeaden House, Kiltimagh, co. Mayo, and had one daughter.

Perry's life was full and many sided. A classical scholar, a musician, a sound physician and morbid anatomist, and an administrator of unusual quality, he would have made an ideal civil servant. Weighty, wise, deliberate in judgement, knowing just when to wait and watch and when to take decisive action, he could draft a document that could be subtle without deceit, and uncompromising yet courteous. He was a master of concise and lucid English prose. When in doubt as to the clarity of a sentence he had a habit of translating it into the more compact confines of Latin and then retranslating it.

Perry was little known to the public, for he was shy and had few social gifts, and did not care who got the credit for anything as long as it was done, usually by himself. He published practically nothing ; his life's work is embodied in minutes, memoranda, and charters. Those who worked behind the scenes knew his value, his massive intellect and constructive capacity. He lived his life as he wished it. Regardless of money, public applause, or preferment, he chose the reality of power and influence rather than the trappings of publicity, and he used his intellectual gifts entirely for the public good.

[*British Medical Journal*, 1938, vol. ii, p. 1339 (portrait) ; *Lancet*, 1938, vol. ii, p. 1493 (portrait) ; Guy's Hospital *Reports*, vol. lxxxix, 1939 (portrait) ; *The Times*, 19 December 1938 ; private information ; personal knowledge.] HERBERT L. EASON.

PETAVEL, SIR JOSEPH ERNEST (1873–1936), engineer and physicist, was born in London 14 August 1873, the younger son of Emmanuel Petavel, D.D., an eminent Hebrew scholar, who was minister of the Swiss church in London from 1864 to 1867, by his wife, Susanna, only daughter of William Olliff, of Great Missenden, Buckinghamshire. The father, who had come to England in 1863, sprang from a Protestant family (originally the name was Tavel) belonging to the district of Bôle in the canton of Neuchâtel, where it is known to have been settled in the middle of the sixteenth century and where its members became eminent as landowners, administrators, and scholars. In 1876 Emmanuel Petavel left England with his family for Geneva and later went to Lausanne. Joseph was educated and followed a course in engineering at the university; but in 1893 he returned to England, and studied science, including engineering, at University College, London.

In 1896 Petavel published his first paper, written in collaboration with (Sir) John Ambrose Fleming, of University College, on the alternating current arc, and he was able by means of an 1851 Exhibition grant to pass the next three years at the Royal Institution, where he made, for Fleming and (Sir) James Dewar [q.v.], accurate measurements of the physical properties of materials at low temperatures. He also worked in the Davy-Faraday laboratory of the Institution towards obtaining a primary standard of light, and designed an indicator for measuring pressures set up in exploding gaseous mixtures known as the 'Petavel gauge'. As John Harling research fellow at Manchester University (1901–1903), working in the newly erected physics laboratory of (Sir) Arthur Schuster [q.v.], he used this gauge for determining the pressures set up by the propellant cordite and in erecting electrical furnaces and apparatus for studying chemical action and high pressures and temperatures. In this work his capacity for design was illustrated, for many of its features have since been incorporated by other workers using high pressure apparatus.

After an interlude, during which he erected and demonstrated at the St. Louis International Exhibition (1904) a reproduction of Dewar's plant at the Royal Institution for the liquefaction of gases, Petavel returned in 1905 to Manchester, where three years later he was appointed to the chair of engineering, held from 1868 to 1905 by Osborne Reynolds [q.v.] whose ideals in regard to the importance of fundamental work Petavel respected and followed. In this chair, which he combined with the post of director of the Whitworth laboratories, he pursued such topics as standards of light, ventilation, structural stresses, the theory of gas engines and aeronautics, while proving himself an efficient administrator. During the war of 1914–1918 not only was his laboratory working at high pressure on the design of instruments and on testing of materials, but he also spent much of his time in London serving on committees for aeronautics, on which he became a recognized authority, and in 1919 was appointed director of the National Physical Laboratory. To this work he gave all his energies until his death, planning buildings for the study of physics, high-tension electricity, acoustics, a compressed-air tunnel, and many other new developments. By the various advances in knowledge made under his directorship he greatly extended the national and international authority and influence of his institution; but he will also be remembered for the beautifying of Bushy House and grounds, for which he left the Royal Society a large sum, and for his hospitality to the staff and to his friends.

Petavel, who had been elected F.R.S. in 1907, was appointed K.B.E. in 1920. He died, unmarried, at Bushy House 31 March 1936.

[*Obituary Notices of Fellows of the Royal Society*, No. 5, December 1936 (portrait); *The Times*, 1 April 1936; personal knowledge.]

R. ROBERTSON.

PETTY-FITZMAURICE, EDMOND GEORGE, BARON FITZMAURICE, of Leigh (1846–1935), better known as LORD EDMOND FITZMAURICE, statesman and historian, was born at Lansdowne House, London, 19 June 1846, the younger son and second child of Henry Thomas Petty-Fitzmaurice, Earl of Shelburne, afterwards fourth Marquess of Lansdowne [q.v.], by his second wife, Emily Jane Elphinstone de Flahault, Baroness Nairne, eldest daughter of the Comte de Flahault. His elder brother was Henry C. K. Petty-Fitzmaurice, fifth Marquess of Lansdowne [q.v.]. At Eton he won a Prince Consort's prize for French, which he knew perfectly, and at Trinity College, Cambridge, where he was a scholar, he was awarded the English essay prize and graduated with a first class in the classical tripos of 1868. He took pride in later life in having helped to revive football at the university. He was president of the Union in 1866. He was called to the bar by Lincoln's Inn in 1871, but never practised.

At the general election of 1868 Fitzmaurice was returned unopposed as liberal member for the family seat of Calne in Wiltshire, and in 1872 was appointed private secretary to Robert Lowe (later Viscount Sherbrooke, q.v.) his predecessor in the seat. In this parliament he betrayed those vigorous radical sentiments which distinguished him throughout his career, and he was the author of the amendment to the bill for the abolition of university tests, which extended its operation to heads of houses, thereby displeasing Gladstone, with whom, however, a common interest in theology was a link of continued friendship. But for the fall of the government in 1874 he would have been parliamentary undersecretary to the Home Office.

Fitzmaurice's parentage opened many doors to him on the continent, and during the years of Beaconsfield's administration he obtained a clear insight into French politics, and he formed a close connexion with the circle of the elder and younger Andrassy and of Apponyi, whom he warned against the danger of an intolerant policy towards the non-Magyar races of Hungary; in 1880 he was appointed commissioner at Constantinople for the reorganization of the European provinces of Turkey and Crete under the Treaty of Berlin. In this position, which he held until 1881, he greatly distinguished himself by drafting a scheme for organic reform of administration, which was frustrated by the play of Abdul Hamid II on the mutual jealousies of Austria and Russia. A similar fate befell his proposal for a greater Albania, but this was revived in 1913 by Berchtold when it was too late. It is by no means improbable that had these schemes been adopted in 1880, the whole subsequent history of the Balkans and of the world might have been changed.

Fitzmaurice, while serving as second plenipotentiary at the Danube Navigation Conference of 1882–1883 in London, was appointed, at the new year of 1883, undersecretary of state for foreign affairs in succession to Sir Charles Dilke [q.v.], and although suggestions were thrown out that he should go to higher posts, he remained at the Foreign Office under Lord Granville until the resignation of the liberal ministry in 1885. His tenure of office had proved his ability, and in July 1885 he delivered a speech in Glasgow advocating reform in local government, Commons procedure, land law, licensing law, and the House of Lords, which attracted considerable attention and resulted in his being adopted as liberal candidate for the Blackfriars division of Glasgow, his seat at Calne having been extinguished by the Redistribution Act. But a breakdown in health, the sequel to an accident in 1875, compelled his retirement, and it was not until November 1887 that he emerged, proclaiming at a liberal meeting at Old Cumnock in Scotland his faith in home rule. Neither when he stood for Deptford at the general election of 1892, nor for the Cricklade division of Wiltshire at that of 1895, was he successful, but at a by-election in February 1898 he recovered for the liberals the Cricklade division and held it again at the general election of 1900.

During these years of opposition, Fitzmaurice had taken the side of Sir Henry Campbell-Bannerman against the liberal imperialists, but to general surprise and no small indignation he was passed over for Cabinet rank when the new liberal administration was formed at the end of 1905. He was offered the secretaryship of state for foreign affairs should Grey refuse it, and on the latter accepting the post, Fitzmaurice was appointed to his old place as under-secretary of state and was raised to the peerage as Baron Fitzmaurice, of Leigh, in Wiltshire.

The situation thereby resulting at the Foreign Office might have been one of great difficulty. Compared with Grey, Fitzmaurice had far longer experience of politics and office, a greater command of European languages, and a wider acquaintance with foreign statesmen and countries, but it says much for the character of the two men that their association was one of perfect harmony, even though Fitzmaurice did not share Grey's enthusiasm for the Anglo-Russian *entente*, and warned Grey against Russian untrustworthiness, as can especially be seen in a remarkable memorandum of April 1907 (see *British Documents on the Origins of the War*, vol. v, no. 400, pp. 461–462) on the subject of Isvolsky's attempts to manœuvre the Foreign Office into most dangerous commitments to a revision of treaty stipulations concerning the Straits. Although his work was unknown to the public, he obtained the complete confidence of the House of Lords and he acquired a high reputation. In 1908, on becoming prime minister, Asquith offered him the chancellorship of the duchy of Lancaster, an office which he accepted, taking his place in the Cabinet, and being sworn of the Privy Council, but a recurrence of his malady compelled his resignation a few months later, and so in 1909 his public life came to an end.

During the years of opposition and exclusion from the House of Commons, Fitzmaurice had been building up the reputation as an historian which earned him election as a fellow of the British Academy in 1914. He had published in 1875–1876 a three-volume life of *William, Earl of Shelburne*, thereby securing the friendship of Disraeli who in *Sybil* had sought to vindicate the reputation of 'one of the suppressed characters of English history', and in 1905 he brought out another authoritative biography, in two volumes, that of his old chief, Lord Granville, which, like the life of Shelburne, ran through more than one edition. The earlier work successfully vindicated the character of his enigmatic but far-seeing ancestor; the later may be considered as the authoritative exposition of liberal foreign policy during the Victorian era, and is distinguished by a remarkable knowledge and a penetrating judgement in foreign affairs, while the Queen's correspondence with Granville at the time of the Schleswig-Holstein controversy throws much light on her policy, tactics, and influence with her ministers. Lesser works were a life of another of his ancestors, Sir William Petty (1895), and a monograph (1901) on Charles William Ferdinand, Duke of Brunswick, who led the Prussians at Valmy and was killed at Auerstädt, a brilliant piece of writing, strong in characterization and showing an uncommon insight into military problems.

As befitted the scion of a noble county family, Fitzmaurice took an active part in local affairs, being chairman of the Wiltshire county council (1896–1906) and of the Court of Quarter Sessions (1899–1905), never slackening in his zeal for the promotion of education, and a most devoted champion of public rights of way. In 1887 he was appointed one of the five boundary commissioners under the Local Government Act. He was a trustee of the National Portrait Gallery from 1881 to 1915, and received the honorary degree of D.Litt. from Bristol University in 1912. At Leigh, until crippled with arthritis, he

showed himself to American and English scholars as a brilliant conversationalist, inheriting the Scottish humour and French wit of his maternal ancestors. When at his best, he was a graceful and accomplished orator, and he was a master of the art of letter-writing. He had also the rare gift of being as much interested in the younger generation as in his own, and many a youth in Wiltshire schools owed his university career to Fitzmaurice's unobtrusive munificence.

Lord Fitzmaurice married in 1889 Caroline (died 1911), daughter of William John FitzGerald, of Litchfield, Connecticut, U.S.A.: there were no children of the marriage. Fitzmaurice died at his residence, Leigh House, Bradford-on-Avon, 21 June 1935. A cartoon of Fitzmaurice by 'Spy' appeared in *Vanity Fair* 14 June 1906.

[*British Documents on the Origins of the War*, edited by G. P. Gooch and H. W. V. Temperley, vol. v (1928); private information; personal knowledge.]   J. H. MORGAN.

PHELPS, LANCELOT RIDLEY (1853–1936), provost of Oriel College, Oxford, and authority on poor law administration, the third son of Thomas Prankerd Phelps, rector of Ridley, Kent, and honorary canon of Rochester Cathedral, by his wife, Laura, fourth daughter of Sir Percival Hart Dyke, fifth baronet, was born at Ridley 3 November 1853. He was educated at Charterhouse (of the governing body of which he was for many years a valuable member) and at Oriel College, Oxford. Admitted a scholar in 1872, he was elected a fellow (just before the new statutes came into force) in 1877, and ordained deacon in 1879 and priest in 1896. He was a lecturer (1880–1885) and vice-principal (1885–1893) of St. Mary Hall; and was tutor (1893–1914), provost (1914–1929), and honorary fellow (1929–1936) of Oriel. As successively scholar, fellow, provost, and honorary fellow, he was a member of Oriel for sixty-four years. On the occasion of the college sexcentenary in 1926 the university conferred upon him the honorary degree of D.C.L. He died, unmarried, at Oxford 16 December 1936.

As a tutor of the college, Phelps was responsible for the general supervision of one third of its undergraduates, and the friend of many more. He talked with them late into the night; he took them on reading parties to High Force, on the Tees, where he was the life and soul of long expeditions from which he alone returned untired; he kept up a lifelong correspondence with many of them. In all these ways he probably had as wide and deep an influence as any Oxford tutor of his time. He never became a specialist in any academic subject, but he had a very active and lively mind, and was an excellent and popular lecturer on classics and on political economy. In particular, his lectures on economics to Indian civil service probationers influenced many who became distinguished civil servants; and in later years he had an equally great influence on the members of the Sudan civil service.

Two matters in which Phelps was deeply interested were the fabric of the college and the college estates. It is mainly to his efforts that the college owes the adornment of the hall by panelling and stained glass windows executed by his friend John Ninian Comper; he was a frequent visitor to the estates, where he rode and shot with the farmers and could talk to them in their own language about crops and stock. To his colleagues he was perhaps most completely himself as steward of common room. An admirable talker and raconteur himself, he never monopolized the conversation; he insisted that this must be general, and his art in its management resembled nothing so much as that of a conductor who draws its best out of every instrument. Another side of Phelps's interests is illustrated by the notable collection of paintings by William Turner of Oxford which he formed and which he sold in 1929 after his resignation from the provostship.

While he was for many years a councillor and afterwards an alderman, Phelps's main activity outside the college was his work as chairman of the Oxford board of guardians of the poor, and later of the public assistance committee. He combined a great interest in the welfare of the poor with a truly Gladstonian economy and individualism. He was a member of the royal commission on the Poor Laws (1905–1909), and his views are writ large in the majority Report. In 1929–1930 he served as chairman of a departmental committee on the relief of the casual poor. The principles set forth at length in the Reports of these two bodies had been briefly and lucidly stated in a pamphlet, *Poor Law and Charity*, published by Phelps as early as 1887.

Phelps's vivid personality, his handsome, bearded face, his flow of animal spirits, his wit and love of paradox, will be long remembered in the college, the university, and the city which he served so well over a great span of years.

There is a portrait of Phelps by Briton Riviere, painted in 1916, at Oriel College.

[F. R. B[arry] in *Oriel Record*, January 1937 (portrait); *The Times*, 17 December 1936; *Oxford Magazine*, 21 January 1937; personal knowledge.]   W. D. Ross.

PHILIP, Sir ROBERT WILLIAM (1857–1939), physician and founder of tuberculosis dispensaries, was born at Glasgow 29 December 1857, the youngest son of George Philip, a minister of the Free Church of Scotland, whose charge was the Union church at Govan, by his wife, Margaret Josephine, daughter of Joseph Robertson. Educated at the Royal High School, Edinburgh, and at Edinburgh University, he graduated M.B., C.M. in 1882 and M.D. (gold medal) in 1887.

The life of Philip covers the first fifty-seven years of an era in the history of tuberculosis that began with Robert Koch's discovery of the tubercle bacillus in 1882. In that year, Koch communicated his discovery to the Berlin Physiological Society. At this time Philip was engaged in post-graduate study in Vienna, where he saw the tubercle bacillus for the first time. He was so much impressed by the potentialities of this discovery that 'Embryology, gynaecology, and all the other specialities that had drawn me to Vienna got the go-by', and, having decided to devote special attention to tuberculosis, he returned to Edinburgh in 1883. On confiding his intention to the professor of medicine, he was told: 'Don't think of such a thing. Phthisis is worn to a thin thread. The subject is exhausted.'

Undaunted, Philip established, with the assistance of his *fiancée* and of a few friends, what became in 1894 the Royal Victoria Hospital for Consumption, at Craigleith, near Edinburgh. Its out-patients' department in Bank Street, in the heart of the city, opened in 1887, was the first tuberculosis dispensary in the world. It was a centre for the treatment of ambulant cases, for the examination of contacts, and later a clearing house for the open-air school, the sanatorium, the tuberculosis colony, and the hospital for advanced cases, these being the essential components of what became known throughout the world as the co-ordinated Edinburgh system. In 1909 the first tuberculosis dispensary in England was established at Paddington through the work of Edith McGaw (later Lady Philip), who devoted herself for over thirty years to the prevention of tuberculosis.

In 1890 Philip joined the staff of the Edinburgh Royal Infirmary, becoming lecturer on chest diseases. When the new chair of tuberculosis was founded in Edinburgh in 1917, Philip was elected to fill the post, which he held until his death. He was an inspiring teacher although not a great clinician. Seldom are these gifts combined. His conception of pulmonary tuberculosis as a visceral lesion in a systemic disease was a conspicuous contribution to medicine. He was author of *Pulmonary Tuberculosis, Etiological and Therapeutic; based on an Experimental Investigation* (1891), and in 1911 *A Selection of Writings* appeared; he wrote *The Actual Position of Tuberculosis To-day* (1923) and *Collected Papers on Tuberculosis* (1937). Twelve of his former pupils, and many specialists in other lands, prepared a *festschrift*, *The Control and Eradication of Tuberculosis; a series of International Studies* (1911).

In 1912 Philip's conception of a uniform tuberculosis service was adopted by the British government, and in 1913 he was knighted. He was elected F.R.C.P. Edinburgh in 1887, was president from 1918 to 1923, and for fourteen years (1923–1937) he was curator of the research laboratory of the college; he was elected F.R.C.P. London in 1933. He was president of the British Medical Association in 1927. He received the honorary degree of LL.D. from the universities of Glasgow and Wales and that of M.D. from the university of Egypt. He was elected F.R.S. Edinburgh in 1889 and received several foreign medals and prizes.

Philip had a clear business head and was unrivalled as an organizer and administrator; as a chairman he was unsurpassed. He had leisure to cultivate culture; and was an excellent companion and an admirable host, not above the art of flattery; a diplomat in English, French, and German. His formal manner, often mistaken for vanity, was really the expression of a profound sense of occasion. He was an egoist, but having an ego that others could admire; an epicurean of the original school and one to whom millions will be indebted who will never hear his name.

Philip was twice married: first, in 1888 to Elizabeth (died 1937), youngest daughter of John Fenton Motherwell, of co. Sligo; secondly, in 1938 to Edith Josephine (died February 1939), eldest daughter of Joseph McGaw, of Kooba, New South Wales. Both marriages were without issue. He died in Edinburgh 25 January 1939.

A portrait of Philip by Sir James Guthrie is in the Royal College of Physicians, Edinburgh. A portrait of Edith McGaw by Hugh de T. Glazebrook (1900) is in the Paddington Tuberculosis Dispensary.

[*The Times*, 27 January and 24 February (Lady Philip) 1939; *British Medical Journal*, 1939, vol. i, p. 251 (portrait); *Lancet*, 1939, vol. i, p. 299 (portrait); *La Revue de la tuberculose*, April 1939; personal knowledge.]

HALLIDAY SUTHERLAND.

PHILIPPS, SIR IVOR (1861–1940), major-general and man of business, was born at Warminster 9 September 1861, the second of the six sons of (Sir) James Erasmus Philipps, twelfth baronet, vicar of Warminster and later prebendary of Salisbury Cathedral, by his wife, Mary Margaret, eldest daughter of Samuel Best, rector of Abbots Ann, Hampshire, and sister of the fifth Baron Wynford. At one time the family owned property at Picton in Pembrokeshire, but these lands had passed out of the possession of the male line early in the nineteenth century. He was a brother of John Philipps, Viscount St. Davids, and of Owen Philipps, Lord Kylsant [qq.v.]: these three eldest brothers and the youngest brother, Sir Laurence Philipps, all became prominent in the City. Ivor Philipps was educated at Felsted School. He served in the militia from 1881 until 1883, when he received his commission in the Indian army; four years later he first saw active service in the Burma campaign (1887–1889), for which he received the medal and two clasps. He later took part in the Chin Lushai (1889) the Miranzai (1891), and the Isazai (1892) expeditions. His promotion to captain followed in 1894, and two years later he served on the North West Frontier of India (receiving the medal and two clasps); from 1896 to 1897 in the Tirah campaign (being twice mentioned in dispatches); and in 1900–1901 with the China expedition (being mentioned in dispatches and receiving the medal and clasp). In 1900 he was awarded the D.S.O. and promoted major in the following year. He retired from the Indian army in 1903. Three years later he became liberal member of parliament for Southampton, retaining the seat until 1922. From 1908 to 1912 he was governor of Pembroke Castle and commanded the Pembroke Yeomanry, with the rank of lieutenant-colonel (1908) and honorary colonel (1909).

On the outbreak of war in 1914 Philipps was called to the War Office as G.S.O. 2, and in November 1914 was promoted brigadier-general and given command of the 115th brigade. He was promoted temporary major-general in January 1915 and for a short while in that year he was parliamentary secretary (military) to the minister of munitions. Later in the same year he raised the 38th Welsh division, went with it to France in December, and saw active service in the battle of the Somme in July 1916, in which month he was made honorary major-general. After the war he gave his attention to work in the City, where he was director of about twenty companies, his varied interests including chemicals, rubber, hotels, and insurance. He also spent much time and thought on the restoration of Pembroke Castle, for which the freedom of the city of Pembroke was conferred upon him in 1936. In 1900 he published *The Issue of Orders in the Field*.

Philipps was a tall, striking-looking man, of transparent sincerity and charm. He was appointed K.C.B. in 1917. He married in 1891 Marian Isobel, youngest daughter of James Buchanan Mirrlees, of Redlands, Glasgow, and had one daughter. He died in London 15 August 1940.

[*The Times*, 16 August 1940; Wilfred Mills, (Official) *History of the Great War: Military Operations, France and Belgium, 1916*, vol. ii.]
C. V. OWEN.

PHILIPPS, SIR JOHN WYNFORD, thirteenth baronet, and first VISCOUNT ST. DAVIDS (1860–1938), financier, was the head of the family of great antiquity in South Wales. He was born at Warminster 30 May 1860, the eldest of the six sons of (Sir) James Erasmus Philipps, twelfth baronet, vicar of Warminster and later prebendary of Salisbury Cathedral. He was brother of Major-General Sir Ivor Philipps [q.v. for parentage] and of Owen Cosby Philipps, Lord Kylsant [q.v.]: John Philipps was educated at Felsted and at Keble College, Oxford, where he graduated with honours in modern history in 1882. He was called to the bar by the Middle Temple in 1886.

As a young man Philipps's tastes lay in the direction of politics, sport, and society.

He sat as liberal member for Mid-Lanarkshire from 1888 to 1894, and for Pembrokeshire from 1898 to 1908. His connexion with finance seems to have been almost accidental. He had become interested in two moderate-sized investment trust companies, which at the time of the crisis in the affairs of Baring Brothers (1890) fell into difficulties. Although he was only thirty years old, Philipps was chosen chairman, and undertook the laborious task of guiding them back to prosperity. In the process he learned much about City affairs, and gradually became a power among trust companies. At the end of his life he was chairman of no fewer than twelve of them.

Philipps then passed on to more ambitious flights, and turned his attention to South American railways. The first company that he joined was the Costa Rica Railway Company, of which he became chairman, and the finances of which he greatly improved under very difficult circumstances. More important than this was his development of the Buenos Ayres and Pacific Railway. When (about 1900) he became its chairman this was one of the least successful of the large Argentine lines. Its mileage was little more than 400, and its finances were in a deplorable state. By amalgamation and extension Philipps built it up into a network of over 2,500 miles, extending from Buenos Ayres to the Transandine line connecting with Chile. Owing to prevailing conditions the outlay required had to be raised chiefly by debenture issues, and for some years the ordinary stock was unable to pay a dividend. There was a later period during which ordinary dividends were regularly paid, but exchange losses and other financial difficulties affected the finances adversely.

In 1908 Philipps was raised to the peerage as Baron St. Davids, and in 1918 was promoted to a viscountcy. In 1912 he succeeded his father as thirteenth baronet. He was sworn of the Privy Council in 1914 and appointed G.B.E. in 1922. His wealth enabled him to buy back some of the Welsh estates which had once been the property of his ancestors.

St. Davids was twice married: first, in 1888 to Leonora (died 1915), younger daughter of Isidor Gerstenberg, of London, founder and chairman of the Council of Foreign Bondholders; their two sons were both killed in the war of 1914–1918; secondly, in 1916 to Elizabeth Frances, second daughter of Paulyn Francis

Cuthbert Rawdon-Hastings, in whose favour in 1921 three ancient English baronies were called out of abeyance. Of this marriage there were a son and a daughter. St. Davids died in London 28 March 1938, and was succeeded as second viscount by his youngest son, Jestyn Reginald Austen Plantagenet (born 1917).

A portrait and a bust of St. Davids are in the possession of his son at Roch Castle, Pembrokeshire. Another portrait used to hang in the Board Room of one of his offices at 117 Old Broad Street, London.

[*The Times*, 29 March 1938.]

ALFRED COCHRANE.

PHILIPPS, OWEN COSBY, BARON KYLSANT (1863–1937), shipowner and financier, was born at Warminster 25 March 1863, the third of the six sons of (Sir) James Erasmus Philipps, twelfth baronet, vicar of Warminster and later prebendary of Salisbury Cathedral. He was a younger brother of Sir John Wynford Philipps, first Viscount St. Davids, and of Major-General Sir Ivor Philipps [qq.v.]. After serving his apprenticeship with a firm of shipowners and brokers at Newcastle-upon-Tyne, he accepted a position in Glasgow in 1886, and in 1888 founded a shipping company of his own, the King Line, on the Clyde. His early activities marked him out as a man of energy and enterprise, and when, on his coming to London in 1902, the Royal Mail Steam Packet Company was being reorganized, he was appointed a director and later chairman.

Philipps had already begun the policy of securing a controlling interest in other important shipping lines. He acquired the Pacific Steam Navigation Company, a transaction involving an expenditure of one and a half million pounds, a sum which seemed large at the time, but was small in comparison with some of his later deals. This company then concluded an agreement with the Royal Mail Steam Packet Company, a step justified by the fact that both companies served the South American republics, one on the east, and the other on the west coast. Controlling interests, too, numerous to mention, for some of which there was not the same obvious explanation, were also obtained in other concerns; it was always a consideration with Philipps to better the representation of British shipping services in the world's trade. An important step was the acquisition in 1912 of the Union-Castle Mail Steamship Company, which had been developed by the genius of Sir Donald Currie [q.v.].

In 1927 a very large transaction was carried out. This was the purchase, at the price of seven million pounds, of the entire share capital of the Oceanic Steam Navigation Company, the fleet of which was known as the White Star Line. This was in American hands, and it was said that others who had contemplated the deal had, on examination, disapproved of it. But Lord Kylsant, as he had then become, thought in very large figures, and he was so much impressed with the idea of Great Britain controlling this line that he carried the deal through. He financed the purchase in rather a singular way by inviting the public to subscribe for the preference shares, and the members of the various shipping companies of which he was the head to take up the ordinary shares. It was at this time that, reviewing the enormous responsibilities shouldered by Kylsant, his friends began to fear that he was carrying a burden which no single individual was capable of bearing: in 1924, on the death of Lord Pirrie [q.v.], he had added greatly to his commitments by assuming control of the vast concern of Messrs. Harland & Wolff, of Belfast. The position, already difficult, was aggravated by a severe depression of trade instead of the revival upon which Kylsant, optimist as he was, relied. Rumours were so rife that it became impossible to conceal the true nature of the position. He was given leave of absence by the Royal Mail Steam Packet Company, and on his return was arrested. At his trial at the Central Criminal Court in July 1931 he was charged with publishing false accounts of the Royal Mail Steam Packet Company for 1926–1927, and found not guilty, but on the charge of publishing and circulating a false prospectus in 1928 he was convicted and sentenced to a year's imprisonment in the second division. By his attitude at the trial, when he accepted entire responsibility, and blamed none of those who had served on his various boards, he earned sympathy. On his return home to his house in Wales his car was drawn by forty men under a special arch of welcome. For a brief period in 1933 he returned to public life.

Philipps was raised to the peerage as Baron Kylsant, of Carmarthen, in 1923. He was appointed K.C.M.G. in 1909 and G.C.M.G. in 1918. Before his elevation to the peerage he was liberal member of parliament for the Pembroke and Haverfordwest district from 1906 to December 1910; he was returned unopposed as conservative member for Chester at a by-election in February 1916 and represented the city of Chester division as a conservative from 1918 to 1922. He served as president of the London Chamber of Commerce, the Chamber of Shipping of the United Kingdom, and the Federation of Chambers of Commerce of the British Empire.

In 1902 Kylsant married Mai Alice Magdalen, daughter and co-heiress of Thomas Morris, of Coomb, Llangain, Carmarthenshire, and had three daughters. He died at Coomb 5 June 1937.

[*The Times*, 7 June 1937; *The Royal Mail Case*, edited by Collin Brooks, 1937.]

ALFRED COCHRANE.

PHILLIMORE, SIR RICHARD FORTESCUE (1864–1940), admiral, was born at Boconnoc, Cornwall, 23 December 1864, the eldest of the six sons of Admiral Sir Augustus Phillimore, commander-in-chief at Plymouth from 1884 to 1887, by his wife, Harriet Eleanor, second daughter of George Matthew Fortescue, and cousin of Hugh, third Earl Fortescue [q.v.]. He was a first cousin of Sir Walter Phillimore, first Lord Phillimore [q.v.]. He entered the Royal Navy in 1878, became midshipman in 1880, sub-lieutenant in 1884, and was promoted lieutenant from the royal yacht in 1886. He became a gunnery officer and was gunnery lieutenant of the *Invincible* and successively of the cruisers *Phaeton* in the Mediterranean, *Aeolus* in China, and *Furious* in the Channel squadron, whence he was promoted commander in 1899. As executive officer of the battleship *Goliath*, he took part in the operations against the Boxer rebels in China in 1900, receiving the China medal. From January 1904 he commanded the cruiser *Mohawk* in the Indian Ocean, and during the operations in Somaliland of that year he landed in command of the machine guns of the naval brigade and took part in the capture of Illig. Promoted captain in June 1904, he later commanded the cruiser *Juno* in the Home Fleet, *Aboukir* in the Mediterranean, and the battle-cruiser *Inflexible* in the Home Fleet. In 1912 he became chief of staff to Admiral Sir A. Berkeley Milne [q.v.], commander-in-chief, Mediterranean, with the rank of commodore, 2nd class, from 1913, and he was holding that post at the outbreak of war in 1914.

After the escape of the German battle-cruiser *Goeben*, Milne was recalled from the Mediterranean, and Phillimore took over command of the *Inflexible* as a private ship. In November 1914, with her sister ship the *Invincible*, she was sent to the South Atlantic under Vice-Admiral Sir F. C. D. Sturdee [q.v.], arriving at the Falkland Islands in the nick of time to intercept and annihilate the German squadron under Admiral Graf von Spee. The *Inflexible* then returned to the Mediterranean and became the flagship of Vice-Admiral (Sir) S. H. Carden [q.v.] at the Dardanelles. In the attack on the Turkish forts in March 1915 she came under heavy fire which wrecked her bridge and foretop, and she also struck a mine, so that she was in danger of sinking; but Phillimore managed to get her to an anchorage off Tenedos and to patch her up sufficiently for her to return to Malta for repair, making the passage stern first. While she was out of action he became principal beach master at the Gallipoli landing, earning a mention in dispatches; later, he was principal naval transport officer at Mudros, the advanced base for the Gallipoli operations.

Promoted rear-admiral in August 1915, Phillimore was sent to Russia as head of a British naval mission; in that capacity he was in constant close contact with the Tsar, travelled to every part of the Russian front, and was on board the Russian flagship at the bombardment of Varna in October 1916. He remained in Russia until the following December, when he was given command of the first battle-cruiser squadron of the Grand Fleet, with his flag in the *Repulse*. While holding that command he took a leading part in developing the use of aircraft carried in ships of the fleet; and he was also again in action. In November 1917, when his flagship was going to the support of British light cruisers chasing German light cruisers into the Heligoland Bight, he did not allow himself to be deflected from that duty by a warning against risking damage from German minefields, and was thus able to afford the needed support at the critical moment. In 1918 he took over command of the aircraft carriers of the Grand Fleet, with the title of admiral commanding aircraft, flying his flag in the cruiser *Furious*, which had been partially converted by the addition of a flying-off deck in place of her fore turret; he held that command for the remainder of the war.

That was Phillimore's last service at

sea. He was promoted vice-admiral in 1920 and then commanded the Reserve Fleet until 1922. From 1923 to 1926 he was commander-in-chief at Plymouth, being promoted admiral in 1924. He was not employed again, but was first and principal naval aide-de-camp to the king from 1928 until compulsorily retired in 1929. He was appointed M.V.O. in 1905, C.B. in 1914, K.C.M.G. in 1918, K.C.B. in 1919, and G.C.B. in 1929; he also held both Russian and Japanese orders. In 1905 he married Violet Gore, youngest daughter of Henry Hobhouse Turton, banker, and had three sons and one daughter. After his retirement he lived at Shedfield House, near Botley, Hampshire, and devoted his undiminished energies to local government work and agricultural organization.

Phillimore was a man of great energy, initiative, and imagination, with a very strong sense of duty. In action he was quite without fear; Sir Roger (later Lord) Keyes, no bad judge of energy and daring, wrote of him at the Dardanelles as 'the indomitable Phillimore'; and this quality he also displayed to an advanced age in the hunting field. He died at Shedfield House 8 November 1940.

[*The Times*, 11 November 1940; Admiralty records; private information; personal knowledge.]　　　　H. G. THURSFIELD.

PHILLPOTTS, DAME BERTHA SURTEES (1877–1932), educationist and Scandinavian scholar. [See NEWALL.]

PHILPOT, GLYN WARREN (1884–1937), painter, was born in London 5 October 1884, the younger son in the family of five children of John Philpot, surveyor, who was of Kentish stock, by his wife, Jessie Carpenter. His parents were strict Lutherans. From the age of seven he showed an aptitude for drawing, and at thirteen, without being instructed, printed a little book, illustrated with woodcuts influenced by the pre-Raphaelites. He went to school at Streatham, which at fifteen and a half he left on account of ill health, and his father in consequence sent him to the Lambeth Art School, to study with Philip Connard, thinking that the lessons might interest without tiring him. Here his facility for drawing and composition obtained him a scholarship for two years; this meant free tuition and materials, an important consideration at that time. At eighteen he transported himself to Rouen, where he painted his first picture to be hung at the Royal Academy (a church interior), and at twenty to Paris in order to work under Jean Paul Laurens. He was singularly unaffected by the current trend of art as displayed by his fellow students, which is remarkable because towards the end of his life he responded to the contemporary and unacademic. As much in the Louvre as in the school, his taste was moulded by hours spent in meditation over the old masters, Goya and Titian in particular. He became a brilliant exponent of their method of building up a picture with under-painting, of working the colour with successive glazes, and of finally floating varnish mixed with ivory black or sienna over the whole surface. Yet dexterity was never his chief concern.

In 1906, the year in which he became a Roman Catholic, Philpot took a small studio in Chelsea, soon to move to a larger one, where he was convinced that he could do better work. Although sales were few and his father could no longer help him, he was determined to risk the expense, and much hard work ensued before he had earned enough to travel to Spain in 1909. On his return he painted 'Manuelito', a picture that brought him immediate recognition. From then on he could have devoted himself to a stream of portraits ('Lord Glamis' and 'The Japanese Ambassador' are of this period) had not his sense of integrity stopped him. He was aware that hackwork leads to sterility, and his own inclination was to produce decorations that are always imaginative and often fantastic. He constantly drew from male models, mostly negro—'to keep my eye and hand in'—although he preferred his memory when painting a picture. Having barely saved sufficient money to last for two months, Philpot acquired an even larger studio and again went to Spain. As a result he painted 'Zarzarrosa' (1910) which was hailed as a masterpiece in the press. A spate of work followed broken by visits to Italy and France. 'The Marble Worker' (1912) won him the first prize of a gold medal and £300 at the International Exhibition at Pittsburg, while the subsequent year saw him painting portraits in the United States of America. When war was declared in 1914 he was living in Venice. Rolling up his half finished 'Under the Sea' (completed in 1919) he packed it at the bottom of his luggage and sailed for England in a crowded refugee ship in order to offer himself at a recruiting centre, only to be rejected on medical grounds. Eventually he was accepted by the Public School Corps, but after his health had twice broken down he was freed from further military service. The war had not altered Philpot's style, and with peace commissions for portraits poured in upon him. He was elected R.A. in 1923 and soon afterwards was chosen to paint King Fouad in Cairo (for which he was paid £3,000 and his fare). He was enthralled by North Africa. By 1927 Philpot had become restive under mounting obligations. In an attempt to escape he rented a house at Baynards, Surrey, and threw himself into making a large bronze 'Oedipus replying to the Sphinx'. Three years later he was back in America and a collection of his pictures was on view at the International Exhibition in Venice.

A long-standing dissatisfaction with his own work, a belief that it must develop into something spiritually more significant, and a desire to be rid of his few possessions culminated in 1931 in Philpot hiring a studio in Paris, where for a time he deserted painting altogether for sculpture. Upon resuming it he abandoned glazes, for he was now confident that richness of texture hindered rather than aided expression, and endeavoured by direct painting with brighter colours, by a simplification of form, and by a more sensitive line to reveal the essence of his vision. He warned a relative that this change might bring complete failure financially, but that he was prepared to starve rather than retract. The public was startled and inquiries for portraits almost ceased. He sent his new canvases to two 'one-man' exhibitions (1932 and 1934) at the Leicester Galleries, London. He had not relaxed in spite of his heart, which had begun to be troublesome. During 1935 he settled afresh in London, but from Christmas 1936 to the end of the succeeding summer, save for spells in England for portraits, he lived at Cannes, doing watercolours, shown in November 1937 at the Redfern Gallery. The greater number were sold on the opening day, which made him feel that success attended his venture. Just before the end of the exhibition he underwent a slight dental operation that necessitated an anaesthetic, after which he left for the country to stay the night with friends. Within an hour of his return to London the next day, 16 December 1937, he died suddenly of heart failure. Hardly had he been buried when his disciple, Vivian Forbes, prostrate with grief, committed suicide.

His career proved Philpot to be brave and unmercenary. He was also generous, gentle, shy, enthusiastic, and quick, with a great charm of manner, and a delicious sense of fun and of the ridiculous. He was unmarried and his life was governed by his art and by his deep affection for his sisters and close friends. Final recognition of his achievement was given in a memorial exhibition of his works held in 1938 at the Tate Gallery, of which he was a trustee for two periods beginning respectively in 1927 and 1935.

[Private information; personal knowledge.]
THOMAS LOWINSKY.

PINERO, SIR ARTHUR WING (1855–1934), playwright, was born in Islington 24 May 1855, the only son of John Daniel Pinero, a solicitor with a practice in London, who belonged to a family of Portuguese Jews—the name is said originally to have been Pin-heiro—which had, however, been settled in England for several generations. His mother was Lucy Daines. Of his early life little is known. He left no records and seems to have left no relations, other than a stepdaughter, who died before this account of him was written. His education appears to have been scanty and spasmodic. Part of it was received at private schools and in evening classes at the Birkbeck Institute, but the more important part was obtained from the age of ten in his father's office where, following the example of his paternal ancestors in England, he bound himself to the law. The law, however, attracted him little. His bent was towards the stage, but as an actor, not as a playwright; and the fact that he studied elocution at the institute more assiduously than he studied any other subject indicates what his intentions were about his career.

When he was nineteen Pinero was engaged as 'a general utility man' by Mr. and Mrs. R. H. Wyndham, of the Edinburgh Stock Company, and made his first appearance at the Theatre Royal, Edinburgh, on 22 June 1874. His salary was a guinea a week. His next employment, in 1875, was at the Alexandra Theatre, Liverpool, under the management of Edward Saker [q.v.], and here, while acting in *Miss Gwilt* by Wilkie Collins, he was confused by that author with another actor in the cast whom Collins admired. This mistake caused Pinero to be engaged for the London production of *Miss Gwilt* in 1876, and immediately afterwards he joined the Lyceum company on tour, playing Claudius to Henry Irving's Hamlet. He remained in this company, first under Mrs. S. F. Bateman [q.v.] and then under Irving, for more than five years. In 1881 he went to the Haymarket Theatre to join (Sir) Squire Bancroft and his wife [qq.v.]. In 1884 he ceased to act. Acting, in spite of his love of it, was not his work. He was competent in small parts, exact and industrious, but devoid of the spirit and vivacity of mood which actors require. A dramatic critic in Birmingham said of his King in *Hamlet* that it 'was the worst Claudius the city has ever seen'. His failure did not depress him. He knew that he was the thwarted actor who becomes a playwright, and could console himself with the heartening thought that if he was a poor Claudius, the creator of Claudius had been a poor Ghost in the same play.

It was not until 1877, when he was twenty-two, that Pinero began to write plays. A one-act play, entitled *£200 a Year*, was produced as a 'benefit' performance in aid of Francis Henry Macklin at the Globe Theatre on 6 October 1877. This small and forgotten piece, which brought him a set of shirt-studs from Macklin, was the first of a remarkably long and diversified series of works which established their author as one of the most distinguished playwrights of his era. In fifty-five years he wrote fifty-four plays of every sort, beginning with 'one-acters' and including a few adaptations from the French, a comic opera, *The Beauty Stone* (written in collaboration with Arthur Strettell Comyns Carr and with music by Sir Arthur Sullivan, 1898), and a mime, *Monica's Blue Boy* (with music by Sir F. H. Cowen, q.v., 1918). His productivity was not more remarkable than the variety and quality of the work thus rapidly composed. All his plays were written with superb technical skill. Some critics acclaimed him as the most accomplished craftsman of the English theatre since the time of Shakespeare, and held that that master alone could match and surpass him in construction, although Sheridan and Barrie were not far behind them. In sheer suspense, the bedroom scene in *The Gay Lord Quex* may be placed alongside of the trial scene in *The Merchant of Venice*, and the screen scene in *The School for Scandal*.

It was with farces that Pinero first attracted attention; and these farces were of a far finer and more intelligent type than was commonly found in farce at that time. The English theatre, after a great period in the eighteenth century, had fallen to a state so low that in the time of Macaulay a dramatist was regarded with contempt as a poor hack hired to throw mindless words together for undemanding audiences; and it was not until T. W. Robertson [q.v.] began to write his domestic comedies, of which *Caste* (1867) is the best known, that it raised its head again. Pinero's sense of Robertson's services to the English theatre is shown in his charming comedy, *Trelawny of the 'Wells'* (1898), in which Robertson figures as Tom Wrench. The farces had immense vitality, a fact amply demonstrated in 1943, when *The Magistrate*, which was performed for the first time in 1885, was revived.

Pinero's mind, however, now under the influence of Ibsen, was not likely to be limited to skilfully contrived farces; and a play called *The Profligate*, with (Sir) Johnston Forbes-Robertson [q.v.] in the principal part, which was produced by (Sir) John Hare [q.v.] at the Garrick Theatre on 24 April 1889, revealed a dramatist more gravely concerned than was the author of *The Magistrate*. Its end was sorrowful: the repentant profligate committed suicide; and this was an end which the public would not tolerate. Pinero, much against his will, made the ending happy. The public was not sentimentally foolish in demanding that Renshaw should dash the cup of poison from his lips: it showed a true instinct in its estimate of Renshaw's character. But, right or wrong, the fact that a different Pinero had arrived in the theatre was now plain; and this Pinero steadily rose in stature and esteem. The first performance of *The Second Mrs. Tanqueray* at the St. James's Theatre on 27 May 1893, when Pinero was thirty-eight, established his renown beyond a shadow of doubt; and it also established the renown of an actress, Mrs. Patrick Campbell [q.v.], until that night unknown. Pinero, whose eye for a player was uncommonly shrewd, found her. This play, which started the vogue of 'problem plays', extended Pinero's reputation far beyond his own country. It had faults which were acidly noted down, but it was serious and adult, and it was written with high skill and sincerity. The plays which followed it, notably *The Notorious Mrs. Ebbsmith* (1895), *The Gay Lord Quex* (1899), *Iris* (1901), *Letty* (1903), *His House in Order*

(1906), and *Mid-Channel* (1909), were nearly all works of gravity; and one of them, *His House in Order*, showed his craftsmanship at its highest. Among his last plays, *The Enchanted Cottage*, produced at the Duke of York's Theatre on 1 March 1922, was a charming and most tender comedy, in which his kindliness and humanity were abundantly revealed. Thirty of the plays (from 1891 to 1930) were published in twenty-nine volumes, of which the first eleven contain introductions by Malcolm Charles Salaman.

Pinero's dialogue was sometimes stilted, and his mind did not move easily among ideas. He had none of the grace of Barrie, nor any of the wit and audacity of Mr. Bernard Shaw. But within the convention which he followed his dialogue was serviceable, and his sense of situation and his skill in contrivance enabled him to use it very effectively. He was the first English dramatist to cast plays to type: that is to say, to employ actors and actresses because they were physically and intellectually suitable to the parts which they performed. He was opposed to the fashion of his time of expecting a player to be capable of performing almost any part. His experience as 'a general utility man' had cured him of that illusion. His star set as that of Mr. Shaw rose, but it will rise again, although not, perhaps, as high as once it did.

A portrait of Pinero by Joseph Mordecai (1891) is in the National Portrait Gallery. A sketch by Phil May is reproduced in Mr. Hamilton Fyfe's book, and there is a bust in the Garrick Club. A cartoon by 'Bulbo' appeared in *Vanity Fair* 1 February 1906. His appearance was extraordinary. Except for very heavy, black eyebrows, he was almost hairless; his features were sharp, but not in the least Hebraic. All his movements were slow and deliberate, not as of a man naturally lethargic, but as of one whose mind has been well made up in advance of action. He was courteous and kind and without long resentment or any rancour, but he was ruthless in casting a play and would discard actors or actresses without the slightest compunction if he thought them unsuitable to their parts. He was not content to take the second best or to manage with what was at once available, preferring to wait until he could obtain the best. Stoical virtues seemed to be highly developed in him, for he bore his prosperity with as much fortitude as his adversity. If he felt his decline from

popularity, he did not show his feeling, nor did he permit himself to become envious of those who displaced him. Shaw dislodged him from his pinnacle, but in spite of some wounding things Shaw had said, Pinero's friendship for Shaw deepened as the two men grew older.

Pinero was knighted in 1909. He died in London 23 November 1934. He married in 1883 Myra Emily Wood (an actress under the name of Myra Holme), daughter of Beaufoy A. Moore and widow of Captain John Angus Lushington Hamilton. She died in 1919, leaving, by her first husband, a daughter to whom Pinero was deeply attached.

[*The Times*, 24 November 1934; *Who's Who in the Theatre*; Clayton Hamilton, *The Social Plays of Sir Arthur Pinero*, 4 vols., 1917; Wilbur Dwight Dunkel, *Sir Arthur Pinero* (Chicago), 1941; H. Hamilton Fyfe, *Sir Arthur Pinero's Plays and Players* (written without Pinero's knowledge and inaccurate as to certain facts), 1930; personal knowledge.]

St. John Ervine.

PLAYFAIR, Sir NIGEL ROSS (1874–1934), actor-manager, was born in London 1 July 1874, the younger son of the obstetric physician William Smoult Playfair [q.v.], and nephew of Lyon Playfair, first Baron Playfair of St. Andrews, and Sir Robert Lambert Playfair [qq.v.]. He was a second cousin of the actor Arthur Wyndham Playfair (1869–1918). His mother was Emily, daughter of James Kitson, of Elmete Hall, Yorkshire, and sister of James Kitson, first Baron Airedale [q.v.]. He was educated at Harrow and at University College, Oxford, where he at once found his feet in the Oxford University Dramatic Society. He was called to the bar by the Inner Temple in 1900, but soon began to take part in the amateur productions of the 'Old Stagers' and the 'Windsor Strollers'. His first appearance on the professional stage was in 1902 at the Garrick Theatre in *A Pair of Knickerbockers*. For a short time he was a member of the Benson Repertory Company with which he toured in the West Indies and where he specialized in farcical Shakespearian parts. In 1904 at the Royalty Theatre he acted Ralph in *The Knight of the Burning Pestle*, his favourite part. He produced the play at the Kingsway Theatre in 1920. In 1907 he was at His Majesty's Theatre, and four years later was given a leading part in H. G. Granville-Barker's production of Arthur Schnitzler's *Anatol*. Thereafter he was continuously engaged, notably as Sir Benjamin Backbite in *The School for Scandal* and as Cutler Walpole in *The Doctor's Dilemma* (1913). Although by this time he had achieved a sure position by reason of his very individual gift for dry but good-humoured comedy, dry as the driest sherry and as pungent in private life as on the stage; it was not until after the war of 1914–1918 that his real lifework may be said to have begun.

In 1918, together with Arnold Bennett [q.v.] and Alistair Tayler, Playfair formed a syndicate of three which purchased a long lease of the Lyric Theatre, Hammersmith, a derelict playhouse in what was then little more than a slum. Although situated within a stone's throw of an important traffic centre, this theatre seemed the last place in the world where high-class entertainment could possibly succeed. But in his choice Playfair proved well justified.

For its opening performance, in February 1919, the theatre was cleverly let to (Sir) Barry Jackson, who brought from the Birmingham Repertory Theatre *Abraham Lincoln* by John Drinkwater [q.v.]. Contrary to expectation this play ran for over a year, thus laying the trail for that long series of Playfair's own productions which were to make the Lyric Theatre, Hammersmith, a household word. The first of these productions was the famous revival in 1920 of *The Beggar's Opera*, decorated by Claud Lovat Fraser [q.v.], which ran without a break for 1,463 performances. There followed *The Way of the World* and *The Duenna* (1924), *The Rivals* (1925), *Riverside Nights* (1926), *When Crummles Played* (1927), *She Stoops to Conquer* and *The Critic* (1928), and other plays of a similar type, a blend of eighteenth-century comedy and twentieth-century satire which was perfectly adapted to the taste of the time. Besides taking parts in many of these productions, Playfair gathered round him a company of young players, musicians, and stage designers who, under the inspiration of his genial leadership, made their own reputations as well as helping to make his. It was indeed a family party, the work of which had much of the impromptu charm of a family charade— but a charade with a difference, for nothing could exceed the neat finesse which characterized all Playfair's work as a producer. He combined scholarship with a native sense of 'style' which was something new in the theatre of those days,

and his essentially personal contribution was fitly recognized by the knighthood which was conferred upon him in 1928. Still at the height of his powers, he died in London after a short illness 19 August 1934, and there closed a unique if brief episode in the history of the English stage.

In 1905 Playfair married Annie Mabel, daughter of Francis Thomas Platts, district superintendent of police, Dacca: she was an actress under the name of May Martyn. She made his home a centre of welcome to artistic people, young and old. They had three sons.

There is a portrait of Playfair in the part of Tony Lumpkin by Walter Sickert in the Tate Gallery, and a drawing by George Belcher was at Singapore when Mr. Giles Playfair left his belongings there during the war of 1939–1945.

[Sir Nigel Playfair, *The Story of the Lyric Theatre Hammersmith*, 1925, and *Hammersmith Hoy*, 1930; Giles Playfair, *My Father's Son*, 1937; *The Times*, 20 August 1934; *Who's Who in the Theatre*, 1933; personal knowledge.]　　　GEOFFREY A. WHITWORTH.

PLUMER, HERBERT CHARLES ONSLOW, FIRST VISCOUNT PLUMER, of Messines (1857–1932), field-marshal, was born at Torquay 13 March 1857, the elder son of Hall Plumer, of Malpas Lodge, Torquay, by his wife, Louisa Alice Hudson, daughter of Henry Turnley, of Kensington. He came from an old Yorkshire family and was a great-grandson of Sir Thomas Plumer [q.v.], master of the Rolls. He was educated at Eton, and in the autumn of 1876 he passed direct into the 65th Foot (1st York and Lancaster Regiment) at Lucknow. At the unusually early age of twenty-two Plumer found himself adjutant: he was promoted captain in 1882. The Afghan war passed the 65th by, and after proceeding to Aden the battalion embarked for home in February 1884. Nevertheless, Plumer was to undergo a sharp baptism of fire in the Sudan campaign, for *en route* the 65th were summoned to Trinkitat near Suakin, where a force under Sir Gerald Graham [q.v.] had assembled to retrieve Osman Digna's massacre of the *gendarmerie* commanded by General Valentine Baker [q.v.] at El Teb on 5 February, and to rescue the Egyptian garrison of Tokar. Although too late to do this, the battalion won the fierce fight with hosts of Arabs at El Teb on 29 February, and a fortnight later (13 March) the still fiercer struggle at Tamai, where the 2nd brigade square was penetrated by the Arabs. In both battles the 65th were hotly engaged and suffered considerably. Plumer was mentioned in dispatches and received the third class Medjidie. Shortly afterwards the battalion resumed its voyage and went to Dover. Next year Plumer passed into the Staff College and in 1890 was appointed deputy-assistant-adjutant-general at Jersey in the days when that appointment covered war-training as well as administration. On its termination in 1893 he joined the 84th Foot in Natal, having been promoted major in January of that year.

Plumer now entered upon a period in which he was to found his reputation. After the defeat of the Jameson Raid (2 January 1896), he was one of the imperial officers sent to disarm the troops of the British South Africa Company and secure their ammunition before they could attempt a rescue of the imprisoned raiders. The mission was successful, and the best of the company's troops were withdrawn. But the severe outbreak of rinderpest, and the company's preventive measures, unsettled the Matabele, who broke out into rebellion under Lobengula and within a few days murdered over 200 settlers and their families. An irregular relief force consisting eventually of 750 men and 1,100 horses was hastily got together at Kimberley and Mafeking under the command of Plumer with the local rank of lieutenant-colonel, until Sir Robert Martin should arrive to take command in the area. Prompt action by Plumer, who had to train his irregulars and equip them while marching up to the front in Rhodesia, saved the settlers, and after seven months of continual marching and fighting, the Matabele were cowed and surrendered to Cecil Rhodes [q.v.] as a result of the famous meeting where he met them almost single-handed.

The Matabele relief force was now broken up, and Plumer, receiving many encomiums and a brevet lieutenant-colonelcy, returned home at the end of 1896. In a staff appointment at Aldershot he worked from 1897 until the summer of 1899 when, on the approach of war in South Africa, he was hastily dispatched with a number of officers to raise an irregular mounted infantry corps, the Rhodesian Horse, at Bulawayo, while other officers raised a similar force in Bechuanaland, both under Colonel (afterwards Lord) Baden-Powell. These two forces were to protect British territory until imperial troops could arrive. But

the Boers, waiting for the grass to grow on the veld for their horses, gave a breathing space to Plumer, who had received an enthusiastic welcome from his veterans. On 3 October the corps was sufficiently trained to go to its war stations; on the 11th war was declared, and the Boer armies invaded British territory, but their western strategy was disarranged by the magnets of Rhodes at Kimberley and the little force under Baden-Powell at Mafeking. Plumer was now in command of all the local forces in the west, north of Kimberley, and many guerrilla engagements followed until in May 1900 he was able to join hands with the southern Mafeking relief force under (Sir) Bryan Mahon [q.v.], and, Mafeking having been relieved, Plumer commanded the northernmost of the three columns that advanced on Pretoria from the west under General Sir Archibald Hunter [q.v.]. In the great 'De Wet hunt' which followed it was Plumer's column which hung on his heels day and night for 800 miles until, after a six weeks' ride, the guerrilla chief was compelled to bring his remnant back to the starting point. Plumer was appointed C.B., and in March 1902, now a brevet-colonel and brigadier-general, he came home on leave and was posted to a brigade at Aldershot; but being promoted major-general at the early age of forty-five, was transferred to the Colchester district, and then after a few months he was appointed in 1903, on Lord Roberts's recommendation, to be quartermaster-general in the newly formed Army Council. The new secretary of state for war, H. O. Arnold-Forster [q.v.], an enthusiastic if theoretical army reformer, wanted to provide a very short service army and to weld this country's too numerous uncorrelated military forces into a military organization that would earn her a place in the military opinion of the continent. Although his scheme was not generally acceptable to military thought, Plumer believed that it could be made to work, but when R. B. (afterwards Viscount) Haldane [q.v.] superseded Arnold-Forster, a new, and, as is now known, a better scheme, was carried into effect. But it was a severe and undeserved blow when Haldane, conceiving by some odd misunderstanding that Plumer would not support his plans, reconstituted the Army Council without him in December 1905. Nevertheless, he found fortune return to him when in 1906 he was appointed K.C.B. and placed in command of a fighting division (the 5th) in Ireland, where he remained until 1909. In 1908 he was promoted lieutenant-general and two and a half years later was appointed commander-in-chief at York.

At the Christmas following the outbreak of war in 1914, Plumer was appointed to the command of the II Corps in France, and in May 1915 to that of the Second Army. For two not very exciting years he held the fateful Ypres salient, training young troops and drafts and perfecting communications in complete harmony with Sir Douglas Haig. For long the British had sat in the low land with the enemy on the high land, and Haig had wished to seize the higher ground as far as the Dutch coast. The move had begun in 1916 with the protracted, costly, but not unsuccessful battle of the Somme, followed early in 1917 by the battle of Arras and Lens. To the north lay the Second Army under Plumer, who, knowing what was to come, was making far-sighted preparations against the Messines and Wytschaete Plateau. After the collapse in April 1917 of General Nivelle's offensive, an Allied conference held in Paris in May decided that the offensive must continue. On asking Plumer when he could attack, Haig promptly received the reply 'the 7th of June', and in effect at 3.10 a.m. on that day Plumer's offensive began with immense cannonades. By evening Messines and Wytschaete were carried and by next morning the Oostaverne line as well. All night the troops worked at consolidation in readiness for the counter-attack of three German divisions; but the plateau was carried and the battle was over, with a considerable number of prisoners and many guns captured, at a cost of one-fifth of the expected casualties. It was a triumph of wise preparation, and from all sides congratulations poured in upon the 'little man' whose hair had gone snow-white during the two anxious years just past.

Plumer had now shown that he and his staff could arrange and his troops carry out; and he and Sir Hubert Gough were told to continue as soon as possible the attack on the high ground running from near Messines to the far side of Passchendaele, beyond which the Fourth Army under Sir Henry Rawlinson [q.v.] had been collected. The great series of operations which began on 21 July cannot be described here, but the two commanders, acting in perfect unison, fought eight great battles with immense results despite the foulest weather. On 13 November the Passchendaele high ground was at last secured; but in the meantime the prospects of the Allies had suffered a grievous change. With the disappearance of Russia, the eastern German army was coming west, and in the late autumn Italian defeat at Caporetto (24 October) had to be retrieved at all costs.

On 7 November Plumer and his chief of the general staff, General (Sir) C. H. Harington [q.v.], were ordered to Italy to take over an Allied force of six French and five British divisions, behind which the Italian army was to re-form. On 3 December they had taken over the line which it was essential to make good, and were holding the Montello section which ran from Lake Garda to the Piave. As Allied divisions struggled into position, the situation was saved, and by Plumer's regrouping (with the cordial acquiescence of the Italians), by his robust common sense, and by the sturdy lesser fighting of the Allies, it was possible to bring back the Second Army to France after four months' absence.

Plumer and his staff reached Cassel on 13 March. On the 21st Gough's attenuated line was attacked and broken through. That very afternoon Haig sent for Plumer, showed him all the facts, and asked what he could do to help. The Second Army had fourteen fairly good divisions and at once Plumer said, placing his hand on his younger chief's shoulder, without even consulting Harington (who was present): 'I will give you twelve divisions in return for tired ones'. Haig said: 'That means giving up Passchendaele'. 'Not a bit of it', replied Plumer.

Haig's gratitude was great. But after the British had weathered the first storm, a second fell on Plumer himself. With the twelve good divisions gone south and their places taken by the tired ones, filled up with new officers and men, Messines and Wytschaete went, and finally Passchendaele itself. Yet in spite of almost desperate crises, Plumer calmly held the Ypres salient until, with the enemy exhausted and starving, the assault died down. It was the last German effort in the north, and it only remained for the Allies to make their victorious effort, when the British were restored and the Americans ready.

In the pursuit of the German army the Second Army took its full share in supporting the Fourth Army and the group under the command of the King of the Belgians.

Almost every day before the armistice Plumer's troops secured considerable captures of the enemy, and a month later his corps had crossed the Rhine, making a triumphant march through Cologne. Plumer was appointed to command the occupied territory and, although Germany was in great economic distress, Plumer was not the man to allow nonsense. As the industrial trouble spread, he put down internal riot and German strikes ruthlessly. At the same time by a telegram to the prime minister (8 March) he secured the immediate dispatch of food to the starving Germans. In 1919 he was raised to the peerage as Baron Plumer, of Messines and of Bilton, Yorkshire. He also received the thanks of parliament, a grant of £30,000, and was promoted field-marshal.

Even before peace had been signed, Plumer entered upon the third period of his life, the nine years as proconsul. It opened with his appointment as governor of a disturbed and, for a while, unhappy Malta, where famine and the fourteen points were breeding trouble, the former among the people, the latter among politicians. There had been severe riots and some rioters had been killed. When Plumer landed in June 1919 he found a large crowd awaiting him and a guard of 300 men from the navy. He at once ordered it to be reduced to twenty men. Seeing laurel wreaths on the ground, he asked the reason, and hearing that two rioters had been killed at that spot, he ordered their immediate removal, and proceeded with the formalities. The people were impressed, for it was clear that Plumer was a man who knew his own mind; and it was not long before they were to have ample evidence that their well-being and the removal of just grievances was the governor's first care. Plumer made great efforts to understand the people racially and historically, and he saw how little ground there was for Italian claims. The favourable impression which he had thus made was confirmed by the address delivered by this Anglican general to the clergy of the island (1924) when, in accordance with custom, they waited on him with candles at the palace on Candlemas Day. He showed sympathy, emphasizing how religion must be part of the people's lives and how the clergy were essential to their well-being, but there was also some scolding for indifference and neglect.

It was during Plumer's governorship that in 1921 the first representative government of Malta was introduced, and the legislative assembly [was inaugurated by the Prince of Wales. When Plumer left in 1924, the manifestations of esteem and affection were very great.

But civil affairs were not the only questions to which Plumer had to attend. Harington was commanding the Allied garrison in the Dardanelles and Constantinople with a small British contingent when in 1922 the Turks under Mustapha Kemal fell upon the Greeks in Asia Minor and seriously threatened the British garrison at Chanak. Plumer was by chance on his way to Constantinople in the admiral's yacht to meet his old chief of the general staff. Just as in 1918 he offered all his men to Haig, so did he come to the help of Harington, sending from Malta every man on whom he could lay hands.

In August 1925 Plumer accepted the office of high commissioner in Palestine, to which Transjordan was added in 1928, and again his personality helped considerably in making Jewish settlers and Arabs realize that, while sympathetically hearing their troubles, he would allow no disorder. The work was strenuous, especially when carried on with his thoroughness, and the years of war having taken their toll, in July 1928 he resigned, and was raised to the degree of a viscount in 1929.

Plumer died in London 16 July 1932, and was buried in Westminster Abbey. He married in 1884 his second cousin, Annie Constance (died 1941), younger daughter of George Goss, of Park Crescent, London, and was succeeded as second viscount by his only son, Thomas Hall Rokeby Plumer (1890–1944). Of his three daughters, who all survived him, the eldest became principal of St. Anne's Society, Oxford. His many honours included the G.C.M.G. (1916), G.C.V.O. (1917), G.C.B. (1918), and G.B.E. (1924). Cricket ever commanded his great enthusiasm and he was elected president of the Marylebone Cricket Club in 1929.

To ambition of service Plumer added energy and enterprise in military matters, and there were inherent in him those characteristics of good faith and robust common sense for which he was noted and which were responsible for his marked gift of endearing himself to all who came into contact with him, from general to private soldier.

A portrait of Plumer by René de

l'Hôpital is in the possession of the family. He figures in J. S. Sargent's picture, 'Some General Officers of the Great War', painted in 1922, which hangs in the National Portrait Gallery. A cartoon of him by 'Spy' appeared in *Vanity Fair* 13 November 1902. He is also included in the cartoon 'A General Group' by 'Spy' which appeared in *Vanity Fair* 29 November 1900.

[Sir Charles Harington, *Plumer of Messines*, 1935; Sir J. E. Edmonds, (Official) *History of the Great War. Military Operations. France and Belgium, 1914–1916*, 1922–1931, and Cyril Falls, *1917*, 1940; private information; personal knowledge.]   GEORGE MACMUNN.

PLUNKETT, SIR HORACE CURZON (1854–1932), Irish statesman, was born at Sherborne House, Gloucestershire, 24 October 1854, the third son in the family of four sons and three daughters of Edward Plunkett, sixteenth Lord Dunsany, admiral, by his wife, Anne Constance, younger daughter of John Dutton, second Lord Sherborne. She was a lady of great gentleness and courage who died of consumption in 1858 at the age of forty. Their home was at Dunsany, co. Meath, and family ties and the Irish home meant much to Plunkett. He was educated at Eton and at University College, Oxford, where he obtained a second class in modern history in 1877. Never robust and now threatened by lung trouble, in 1879 he sought health and fortune by sharing a ranch in Wyoming, on the foothills of the Rocky Mountains. His diary reveals the hardships and humours of those pioneering days. For ten years he followed ranching, coming back to Ireland each year for a short period. In September 1888 he published in the *Nineteenth Century* an article on 'Co-operative Stores for Ireland'. In 1889, partly for family reasons, he returned and made his home in Ireland, but continued every year to visit the United States of America where he still had property and where he kept in touch with public men and affairs.

In 1889 the campaign for agricultural co-operation opened. With strategic sense Plunkett saw that the best demonstration of the value of co-operation would be to organize co-operative creameries in the dairy districts of Southern Ireland. Despite great difficulties, by June 1891, at the second annual conference of dairy co-operative societies, held at Limerick, he reported that a thousand Irish farmers had between them subscribed £10,000 and formed eighteen co-operative societies. In 1891 the Congested Districts Board for Ireland was constituted, and Plunkett was appointed a member, a position which he held until 1918. In 1892 he entered parliament as unionist member for South County Dublin. In 1894 there was founded the Irish Agricultural Organization Society, the forerunner of similar organizations in England, Scotland, and Wales—a great landmark in Plunkett's life. He remained president until 1899. In 1895 on his initiation, the Recess Committee was convened, and Irishmen of differing political and religious views met to consider the agricultural and industrial welfare of Ireland. Within a year they issued a report which led in 1899 to the establishment by act of parliament of the Department of Agriculture and Technical Instruction for Ireland. In all this creative work Plunkett was a leader who knew how to choose and win men. Just as in the field of voluntary agricultural co-operation the Irish Agricultural Organization Society was the model, so in the sphere of statutory machinery of government the new department in Dublin deeply influenced subsequent developments in England, Scotland, and Wales.

Plunkett was appointed vice-president of the department and for seven years guided its policy and administration in this very critical period. The office was political, but when in 1900, shortly after the establishment of the department, he lost his seat in South County Dublin, he was retained as vice-president and, despite party political agitation, continued to hold this position until the spring of 1907.

Important as were these achievements alike in voluntary and in statutory organization, still more far-reaching was the philosophy of rural life which Plunkett's vision and experience were bringing into clearer expression. From early days in the movement Plunkett had emphasized, first that farmers must rely upon themselves, secondly that they must co-operate in the face of modern competition. Self-help justified state aid, but state aid must always be directed to calling out self-help. Gradually the wider significance of the movement revealed itself. Ireland was a demonstration centre, but the problem was world-wide. The industrial revolution needed to be redressed by an agricultural revolution through co-operation. It was more than a matter of technical business organization. Agriculture was a life, and from Plunkett's visionary, practical mind the new creed emerged, 'Better farming, better business, better living'. Theodore Roosevelt, president of the United States, in his conservation and country life policy, took over Plunkett's slogan and, as he said, 'megaphoned' it over his country. It was but one example of the wide influence which Plunkett had, in peace and in war, in building up Anglo-American understanding and co-operation. Here also he was a pioneer.

By 1907, when he resigned from the Irish Department of Agriculture, Plunkett's main constructive work was accomplished. The next twenty-five years were devoted to spreading the gospel. In December he was re-elected president of the Irish Agricultural Organization Society, and in 1908 public appreciation of his services was marked by the purchase and gift to him of 84 Merrion Square, Dublin, to be called 'The Plunkett House' and to become the headquarters of the agricultural co-operative movement. His main interest continued to centre in his work for co-operation, and he fought strenuously to maintain the independence of the movement. But he was deeply concerned at the growing acuteness of the Irish political situation and by the proposals to seek a solution by partition. The progress of land purchase and the experience of administering the Irish Department of Agriculture helped his conversion to home rule. But partition he hated, and he never ceased in his efforts to avert it. In 1914, at the height of the crisis, he made 'an appeal to Ulster not to desert Ireland'. In the Irish Convention of 1917–1918, of which he was chairman, his efforts were untiring to try to find a solution which would keep Ireland united. In 1919, when he founded the Irish Dominion League, his aim again was to keep Ireland united and to keep her within the British Commonwealth. His public-spirited efforts seemed to fail, but, as in the field of co-operation, they show a consistency of conviction and a tenacity of purpose which never yielded in the face of difficulties. In 1922 he accepted membership of the Senate of the Irish Free State, but he was seldom able to attend, and when he was in the United States in 1923 his house, Kilteragh, Foxrock, co. Dublin, was burned down by political extremists. He resigned after a year, and with failing health, and the growing influence overseas of his work, he decided to make his home in England at Weybridge. As early as 1919 he had established in London a foundation to advance study and research in agricultural co-operation. His work now reached far beyond Ireland and Great Britain. In 1924 a notable conference on agricultural co-operation in the British Empire was held at Wembley under Plunkett's presidency. In 1925 he visited South Africa, partly for his health but also in order to help the agricultural co-operation movement in that country. In 1927, unable to accept membership of the royal commission on agriculture in India, he submitted, at the special request of the chairman, an extensive memorandum on 'co-operation as a factor in the economic, social and political development of rural India'.

In the early years Plunkett had had to face first apathy, then opposition, and in his last years he had to combat what to him was a perversion of the pure gospel— 'compulsory co-operation'. Men could not be made true co-operators by act of parliament. Co-operation recognized the intelligent conviction and free loyalty of the individual. With that idea and with the mission of it he was possessed. It was so to the end, when, despite great physical suffering and weakness, the flame of his faith burned bright and clear. He died, unmarried, at Weybridge 26 March 1932.

Plunkett was sworn of the Irish Privy Council in 1897 and appointed K.C.V.O. in 1903. He was elected F.R.S. in 1902; received honorary degrees from the universities of Oxford (1906) and Dublin (1908); and was elected an honorary fellow of University College, Oxford, in 1909.

Plunkett published two books, *Ireland in the New Century* (1904) and *The Rural Life Problem of the United States* (1910), as well as a very considerable number of pamphlets. A collection of these and of memoranda, speeches, letters to the press, and private correspondence has been made in the Co-operative Reference Library, housed in the Horace Plunkett Foundation in Bloomsbury. Plunkett's diary (52 volumes, 1879–1932) has been preserved and is under the control of his literary executor.

A portrait of Plunkett by Dermod O'Brien and a bronze bust by Francis Derwent Wood are in the Plunkett House, Dublin; there are also two portraits in the Municipal Art Gallery, Dublin, the one by J. B. Yeats and the other by Sir John Lavery. Two crayon drawings by Yeats were at Kilteragh, but it is not known whether they have survived.

[*The Times*, 28 March 1932; Papers at the Plunkett House; R. A. Anderson, *With Horace*

Plunkett in Ireland, 1935; private information; personal knowledge.]

W. G. S. ADAMS.

POEL, WILLIAM (1852–1934), actor, stage-director, and author, was born in London 22 July 1852, the third son of William Pole [q.v.], engineer and musician, a friend and supporter of the pre-Raphaelites, by his wife, Matilda, daughter of Henry Gauntlett [q.v.], vicar of Olney, and sister of the organist and composer H. J. Gauntlett [q.v.]. His father's interest in the pre-Raphaelites strongly influenced the boy, who was to bring kindred ideals to bear upon the stage. He was chosen by William Holman Hunt [q.v.] to pose for the well-known picture in the Birmingham Art Gallery of 'The Finding of the Saviour in the Temple'. At an early age young Pole decided to become an actor, changing his name to Poel for stage purposes on the suggestion of a misprint in an early programme. He joined the company of C. J. Mathews [q.v.] in 1876, went to Italy with Tomaso Salvini, and in 1881 began a lifework which was to revolutionize stage-production by presenting the first quarto *Hamlet* without scenery at the St. George's Hall, himself playing Hamlet to the Ophelia of Helen Maude, afterwards Lady Tree. In the same year he became manager of the Royal Victoria Hall, Waterloo Road, afterwards known as the Old Vic, and two years later joined (Sir) F. R. Benson [q.v.] as his first stage-manager. In 1895 Poel founded the Elizabethan Stage Society, an outgrowth of the Shakespeare Reading Society to which he had been instructor for eight years. He presented Elizabethan and other classics in the halls of City companies, the Inns of Court, and elsewhere, in conditions approximating to those of their original performance, without scenery. The plays could thus be acted in accordance with the text, instead of being transposed and cut for scenic purposes, as had become the habit in spectacular revivals. Poel also insisted upon rapid and clear speaking of blank verse, with varied emphasis.

Altogether Poel produced seventeen of Shakespeare's plays under these conditions, notably *Romeo and Juliet*, with a Romeo (Esmé Percy) of sixteen and a Juliet (Dorothy Minto) of fourteen, the right ages according to the text; *Troilus and Cressida*, with (Dame) Edith Evans as Cressida; *Twelfth Night*, presented, as in Shakespeare's day, at the Middle Temple hall; and *The Comedy of Errors* at Gray's Inn. Among other memorable revivals of his were Marlowe's *Dr. Faustus*, the anonymous *Arden of Feversham*, Ford's *The Broken Heart*, Milton's *Samson Agonistes*, the Book of Job in dramatic form, and Jonson's *Sejanus; His Fall*. At the Playhouse, Oxford, in 1924, he gave the first performance in England of *Fratricide Punished*, a translation of what is probably an early German version of *Hamlet*. In 1901, in association with (Sir) P. Ben Greet [q.v.], he arranged the first modern production of the morality-play, *Everyman*, in the Charterhouse. He himself gave a remarkable grotesque study of the character of Death. This production brought new life to the old morality, which has been constantly presented ever since in all sorts of forms the world over. In 1909 Poel took over the part of Father Keegan in Mr. Bernard Shaw's *John Bull's Other Island*, lending to it a personal inspiration and dignity.

Apart from his work as actor and producer, Poel was the author of several plays, including *Priest or Painter*, adapted from William Dean Howell's novel, *A Foregone Conclusion*, and produced at the Olympic Theatre in 1884, and *Mehalah, or The Power of Will*, adapted from the novel by Sabine Baring-Gould [q.v.] and produced at the Gaiety Theatre two years afterwards (1886). In 1913 was published his *Shakespeare in the Theatre*, an invaluable exposition of his views both on the plays themselves and on their production. He published from time to time many pamphlets, notably *Prominent Points in the Life and Writings of Shakespeare* (1919), arranged in four tables, which originally appeared in the *Bulletin of the John Rylands Library, Manchester*.

Towards the close of his life Poel prepared a privately printed record of his productions, with inserted photographs and notes by himself, and presented it to twenty-five of his friends. Shortly before his death at Putney 13 December 1934 he was twice offered a knighthood, but declined it. His love for the theatre was entirely selfless. His initiative, imagination, learning, and kindly but strong personality never won in his lifetime the recognition which they deserved. He married in 1894 Ella Constance, eldest daughter of the Rev. Alfred Locock, and a devoted and understanding helpmeet. Their only child died some years before her father.

A portrait of Poel in the character of

Father Keegan, by Henry Tonks, was presented to him by his friends on his eightieth birthday and is now in the National Portrait Gallery.

[W. Poel, *Notes on Some of William Poel's Stage Productions* (privately printed), 1933, and *Shakespeare in the Theatre*, 1913; *The Times*, 14 December 1934; personal knowledge.]   S. R. LITTLEWOOD.

POLLOCK, ERNEST MURRAY, first VISCOUNT HANWORTH (1861–1936), judge, was born at Wimbledon 25 November 1861, the fifth, but fourth surviving, son of George Frederick Pollock, queen's remembrancer, by his wife, Frances Diana, daughter of Henry Herbert, rector of Rathdowney, Queen's county. He was grandson of Sir Jonathan Frederick Pollock, lord chief baron of the Exchequer, great-nephew of Sir David Pollock and Sir George Pollock, nephew of Sir William Frederick Pollock and Sir Charles Edward Pollock, and first cousin of Sir Frederick Pollock [qq.v.]. He was a scholar of Charterhouse, and passed from there to Trinity College, Cambridge, being called to the bar by the Inner Temple in 1885. He became a bencher in 1914 and treasurer in 1936. He had a fairly good practice as a junior, and took silk in 1905. At the general election of January 1910, after two unsuccessful efforts (1900 and 1906) at Spalding, he was elected conservative member of parliament for Warwick and Leamington and held the seat until 1923. He was appointed K.B.E. in 1917. In 1919 he was appointed solicitor-general, and in March 1922 attorney-general, resigning that office when the coalition government broke up in October. He had been sworn of the Privy Council in February.

As an advocate Pollock never attained the front rank. Indeed, he was deemed fortunate in being nominated law officer, there being a dearth of eminent advocates among politicians of the conservative party when he was appointed. Nor can it be said that as law officer he rose to the occasion so far as practice in the courts was concerned. Yet both his circumstances and his qualities were calculated to produce an advocate of the first class. He was born to one of the best-known legal names of the period, and inherited the Pollock face, which his great-grandmother Sarah Homeria Parsons, the wife of the saddler from Berwick, transmitted to so many of her descendants. Moreover, he had a fine presence, infinite zest, an excellent memory, and a quick, although not a deep, intelligence. He was never at a loss for a word, had plenty of confidence, and a resounding if somewhat strident voice. Finally, he was scrupulously honest, a quality which is more valuable to the advocate of to-day than is generally understood, at any rate outside the profession. Yet in the conduct of difficult and complicated cases such as fall to the lot of law officers, he was often obviously outclassed by the counsel who opposed him. Particularly in the Armstrong case (1922), an action in which the accused was charged with poisoning his wife, his handling of the prosecution was much criticized. He appeared to prefer intuition to close reasoning in his arguments, a course which did not assist the court.

When the revolt of the conservative party occurred in 1922, and the coalition was wrecked at the famous meeting of that party at the Carlton Club (19 October), Pollock stood by the coalition and went into exile. The new conservative prime minister, Bonar Law, when he formed his government, offered through Lord Cave to Pollock and Sir Leslie Scott, respectively attorney-general and solicitor-general in the coalition government, the posts of home secretary and attorney-general, leaving it to their choice which post each of them should occupy. Having formed and expressed a definite opinion against the break-up of the coalition, both preferred to stand aside on the ground that it was contrary to the public interest, and that it was inconsistent with constitutional propriety for them to accept office in the new government. Accordingly, Pollock returned to the bar, and to many it seemed that his career was at an end. He was neither essential to the government, nor a danger to it if left out. For he was too serious and loyal a conservative to be a nuisance to his party. He was consoled with a baronetcy in November.

A year later (1923) Pollock was offered by Baldwin the post of master of the Rolls, the third highest post in the legal hierarchy. The appointment was unexpected and the subject of considerable criticism both in the press and at the bar. Indeed, he was not legally or intellectually of the same calibre as the eminent holders of that office during the previous twenty years. Nevertheless, in the ordinary run of appellate work in the Court of Appeal over which he presided, he may be said to have disappointed his critics. He was a good president and courteous to the bar.

His wide knowledge of the world enabled him to pick up the facts of a case quickly. And if his judgements were sometimes rather long, they were decided and clear.

But Pollock's greatest service to his generation and to posterity lay in the industry and enthusiasm which he brought to the execution of his duty as custodian of records. The Law of Property Amendment Act (1924) by its second schedule added to section 144 of the Law of Property Act (1922) a new section (144 A) conferring on him powers which in other hands might have lain fallow. Here was a field in which Pollock's conservative outlook and veneration for the past found a welcome and useful outlet. He used these powers to the full, and inspired others to join in a movement to save, before it was too late, the contemporary records of manors which lay rotting in the offices of country solicitors, in manor houses, or on the rubbish heap. He was always willing to spend his leisure in addressing meetings far and wide as to the mine of contemporary medieval documents which this country was so fortunate as to possess. Scholars and historians owe much to his unflagging efforts in this direction. The awakening of interest and pride which resulted has not been confined to purely manorial records: and this country is no longer to be reproached for being the repository of medieval documentary evidence unique in quality and quantity, but cared for by none and explored mainly by the scholars of foreign countries.

In 1926 Pollock was raised to the peerage as Baron Hanworth, taking his title from the village in Middlesex where his grandfather, the lord chief baron, had bought an estate in 1834. In 1935 he resigned the mastership of the Rolls owing to increasing ill health, and was advanced to a viscountcy in January 1936. He died at Hythe, Kent, 22 October of that same year.

In 1929 Hanworth published a life of his grandfather, *Lord Chief Baron Pollock*, which supplies a key to his character. A tenacious memory, coupled with an exceptional gift of mimicry, made him an ideal raconteur and endeared him to his fellow benchers of the Inner Temple. He was a keen sportsman, fond of shooting and fishing, and of the country generally. He was a good and religious man, whose simple piety was not obscured by a slight tendency to pomposity. Indeed, Lord Hewart, an acute critic of his fellow men, described him as the model of a Christian gentleman. He married in 1887 Laura Helen, eldest daughter of Sir Thomas Salt, first baronet, a Staffordshire banker, and had a son and a daughter. He met his future wife at Stafford in 1884, when he was marshal to Mr. Justice Manisty. The other judge, Baron Huddlestone, insisted upon the lodgings being kept at a very high temperature, and the result was a fire. Salt entertained both judges and marshals at Weeping Cross, his home nearby. Hanworth's son was killed in action in France in March 1918, and he was succeeded as second viscount by his grandson, David Bertram Pollock (born 1916). His younger brother Bertram was bishop of Norwich from 1910 to 1942.

A portrait of Hanworth by J. M. Crealock hangs in the Inner Temple.

[*The Times*, 23 and 27 October 1936; private information; personal knowledge.]

FREDERIC WROTTESLEY.

POLLOCK, SIR FREDERICK, third baronet (1845–1937), jurist, was born in London 10 December 1845, the eldest of the three sons of Sir William Frederick Pollock, second baronet, queen's remembrancer [q.v.], by his wife, Juliet, daughter of Henry Creed, vicar of Corse, Gloucestershire. He was grandson of Sir Jonathan Frederick Pollock, first baronet, lord chief baron of the Exchequer [q.v.], and first cousin of Ernest Murray Pollock, first viscount Hanworth [q.v.]. He was educated at Eton, where he was a king's scholar, and at Trinity College, Cambridge, of which he was elected a scholar in 1865, and where he distinguished himself as Pitt scholar (1865) and as second in the classical tripos of 1867 and sixth among the senior optimes of the mathematical tripos of that same year. He was awarded the first chancellor's medal in 1867 and in 1868 he was elected a fellow of Trinity. In 1871 he was called to the bar by Lincoln's Inn, of which he was elected a bencher in 1906.

From this time onward, Pollock's main preoccupation was his activity as a legal writer, professor, and editor. His appearances in court were infrequent and soon ceased for professional purposes. His enthusiasm for the study of the principles of law had been kindled by the teaching of two great lawyers, Nathaniel Lindley, Lord Lindley [q.v.] and Sir James Shaw Willes [q.v.]. To Lindley he wrote: 'In your chambers and by your example I learnt the root of the matter which too many things in common practice conspired to obscure, that the law is neither a trade nor a solemn jugglery but a science.' He soon set to work to produce a series of books which marked a new era of thought in English law. In 1876 he published his *Principles of Contract at Law and in Equity*. It was not a mere text-book for practitioners, but a work for students of principles and legal thinkers. In 1887 appeared a companion work on *The Law of Torts*, marked by the same wealth of legal learning and thought, combining the philosophy of law with its practical aspects. Both these works have exercised a great influence on the theory and practice of law and have become classics and ought so to continue for long. They originated a new era in that they were literature, models of classical style of large planning, and accurate thought. They have been read both in England and in the United States of America and wherever the common law is studied and practised. In 1883 he published a small classic on *The Land Laws*.

In that same year Pollock became Corpus professor of jurisprudence at Oxford (with a fellowship at Corpus Christi College) and he held the chair until 1903. During these years he made important contributions to the subject of his chair. In 1890 he published his *Introduction to the History of the Science of Politics*. His *First Book of Jurisprudence for Students of the Common Law* (1896) has been described by a successor in the chair as probably the most original book on the subject published in England. In his volume on *Possession in the Common Law* (1888, to which (Sir) R. S. Wright, q.v., contributed part iii) he sought to show that English law had developed, in the cases, a theory of possession as logical as anything that Roman or civil law could produce. And he did not confine his lecturing to Oxford. He was professor of common law in the Inns of Court from 1884 to 1890; he lectured at the Royal Institution in 1884; and in 1894 he visited India where he delivered the Tagore law lectures, published in the same year as *The Law of Fraud, Misrepresentation and Mistake in British India*.

After he had resigned the chair at Oxford, Pollock lectured at Harvard in 1903 and at Columbia University in 1912. To these lectures we owe some of his most illuminating work such as *The Genius of the Common Law* (1912). A valuable collection of essays was published under the title *Essays in Jurisprudence and Ethics* (1882). Another collection, entitled *Essays in the Law*, of which that on the history of the law of nature is famous, was published in 1922. To *Select Essays in Anglo-American Legal History* (1907–1909) he contributed a valuable chapter. He also contributed to *Essays in Legal History* published in 1913 under the editorship of (Sir) Paul Vinogradoff [q.v.]. Pollock, however, did not fail to remark that the common law had its shortcomings, in that it has not fully satisfied the demands of a modern social conscience which has been compelled to call in the act of parliament to supplement or override the individualism of the common law: but he more often addressed his criticism to particular decisions than to the wider issues of policy.

Outside the limits of the common law, Pollock's activities were just as great. He added an introduction and notes to Maine's *Ancient Law* (1906), and in collaboration with Sir Dinshah Mulla he issued a very fully annotated edition of the *Indian Contract Act and Specific Relief Act* (1905), of which a sixth edition was brought out in 1931. But as an editor, his principal service was his editorship from 1885 to 1919 of the *Law Quarterly Review*. He was chiefly responsible for its foundation, and he was a constant contributor, several of his most important articles being first published in its pages, which also contained brief notes by him referring to current decisions of the courts. His essays were not ephemeral but were weighty additions to legal learning and thought and to comparative law and legal history. But a chief service of the *Review* was to set an example to all the law journals and reviews which have promoted the discussion and criticism of legal problems. And at the same time (from 1895 to 1935) he was also editor-in-chief of the *Law Reports*, that most essential part of the English legal machinery. In 1936 he was co-editor with Mr. Alfred Frank Topham, who became sole editor in 1937.

In the early years after F. W. Maitland [q.v.] had been called to the bar, Pollock met him, and between them a very fruitful friendship was to arise. They were both members of the Sunday Tramps Club which had been founded by (Sir) Leslie Stephen [q.v.] and Pollock, and Pollock took up Maitland's idea of the *History of English Law before the Time of Edward I* (2 vols., 1895, second ed. 1898), a work which, although it bears Pollock's name on the title-pages, Pollock himself fairly stated was almost entirely Maitland's (as the style shows). But the chapter on

Anglo-Saxon law is Pollock's, and to him must go the credit of having encouraged Maitland and taken his full share in the planning and revision of the book. Another fruitful friendship was that with Oliver Wendell Holmes, afterwards an associate justice of the Supreme Court of the United States, whom he first met in London in 1874, and with whom he corresponded closely until Holmes's death in 1935. In 1941 appeared a memorial of this friendship, entitled *The Holmes-Pollock Letters . . . 1874–1932*. The English edition, with an introduction by his son Sir John Pollock, appeared in 1942. This unique correspondence throws great light on the lives and ideas of these two men, so akin in their sympathies, tastes, and devotion to the common law, and embodies an intimate exchange of armchair confidences about their reading, their opinions on legal matters, and their general interests, which will prove for future historians an illuminating record how two cultivated men, each in his hemisphere, thought and lived in the decades covered by the correspondence.

Besides these specifically legal interests, Pollock's help was called upon by the government on various occasions. He prepared the draft of the Partnership Act of 1890 (in 1877 he had published a *Digest of the Law of Partnership*), and he drafted several Indian bills. He advised the government on the Venezuelan complication of 1895, and served on several royal commissions, such as that on labour from 1891 to 1894, and he was chairman of the royal commission on the public records in 1910.

It was natural that Pollock should receive many honours. Honorary degrees were conferred upon him by the universities of Edinburgh, Dublin, Harvard, Oslo, Columbia, Paris, and Cambridge: he became a corresponding member of the Institut de France and an associate member of the Royal Academy of Belgium. He was elected a fellow of the British Academy in 1902; and an honorary fellow of Corpus Christi College, Oxford, in 1906, and of Trinity College, Cambridge, in 1920. In 1911 he was sworn of the Privy Council. In 1914 he was appointed the Admiralty judge of the Cinque Ports, a post which, as he used to lament, however ancient and honourable, did not give him a single opportunity of showing his judicial talents. It is a curious fact that not until 1920, and then, it is said, only at the instance of Lord Birkenhead, did he take silk. He succeeded to his father's baronetcy in 1888.

This long catalogue gives no idea of Pollock's vivid, many-sided, and delightful life, full of diversified interests and accomplishments. He was deeply interested in philosophy which inspired his ambition to define the nature of legal concepts, and he was doubtless helped in this by his study of Savigny and Ihering. In 1880 he published a life of Spinoza with a full statement of his philosophy which Lord Samuel described as the best book written on the subject in English, and in 1935 Pollock published a brief brochure on Spinoza. Moreover, he was a keen, skilled, and expert fencer; in his younger days an enthusiastic mountaineer along with Holmes, Stephen, and many others. He contributed to the Badminton Library volume on *Mountaineering* (1892) and was honorary librarian of the Alpine Club. He travelled frequently on the continent of Europe and knew all the famous picture galleries, and was an ardent connoisseur in music. He was an accomplished linguist and wrote verses in Latin, Greek, French, German, and Italian. He had a keen sense of humour which used to escape in his serious legal writings. His *Leading Cases done into English* (1876) is a brilliant and by no means uninstructive series of parodies of the decisions. Of his lighter and non-legal publications there may be mentioned *The Etchingham Letters* (with E. Fuller Maitland, 1899), *Outside the Law* (1927), and, towards the end of his life, *For my Grandson. Remembrances of an Ancient Victorian* (1933), a little book containing much worldly wisdom and autobiographical material.

Pollock was most blessed in his marriage, which took place in 1873, to Georgina Harriet (died 1935), younger daughter of John Deffell, of Calcutta, an East India merchant. She was a very gracious hostess and a woman of wide intellectual interests. They had a son and a daughter. The son, (Frederick) John Pollock (born 1878), the historian and author, succeeded as fourth baronet on his father's death, which occurred in London in his ninety-second year 18 January 1937.

It is not easy to exaggerate the importance to historical and philosophical study of English law of Pollock's decision, made after some hesitation, not to return to Cambridge but to follow a vocation in a scholar's life and in the study of law in particular. In that vocation he performed a more lasting service to his country and to the world than would have been his lot in classical scholarship. He developed his ideal of a broad culture while pioneering, at least in England, new ideals of legal thought and theoretical progress in the region of Anglo-American law and of jurisprudence. Thus he not only found his *métier* but realized a happy, useful, and distinguished life, even more than if he had obtained the highest positions in the law, for he was granted good health and domestic felicity, and he lived surrounded by congenial friends, constantly engrossed in the interests and activities which he loved, moving about in the institutions dear to his heart like Cambridge, Oxford, and Lincoln's Inn, and drawing satisfaction from his diversified travels. He was cosmopolitan in sympathy and experience. It has indeed been said that his reputation was greater abroad than at home. In one sense that is true, because of the admiration felt in other countries for English law and for the ideal of the English gentleman and scholar. It may also be that in England, law appeals less to the ordinary man whether of higher or lower station. Pollock was certainly not 'popular' in his activities or way of life, which were choice and cloistered. It was enough for him to be given a figure in the selected circles of his choosing; but he was not a selfish dilettante. He worked hard and incessantly at his proper work, as a teacher of law. His legal writings advanced the study of English law and its prestige in the world, and helped to make it more fit for its high destiny. Our English law, which looks so crude in the Year Books, so pedantic in Coke, and so uninspired in the eighteenth and early nineteenth centuries, has nevertheless established itself as one of the two great legal systems of mankind and has become the law of the greater part of the world, more humane, sensible, and freedom-loving than any other system. This was Pollock's great inspiration, which he has expressed in several glowing and eloquent passages. He looked beyond the ordinary lawyer's insularity to the whole sweep in time and place of the common law, and he traced it from its earliest beginnings to its modern range and complexity.

This was a great ideal and allied to it was Pollock's ideal of the worth of the academic lawyer, the legal scholar and thinker, whose work was, as he thought, too much disparaged and discredited by the legal practitioner. He was proud to write and to lecture, and to stimulate others to do so. He described the poor state of legal research and teaching in England in his inaugural lecture as Corpus professor. He achieved much towards remedying those defects, and in that way, and by his writings, Pollock has earned a most conspicuous place in the history of English law.

[*The Times*, 19 January 1937; *Law Quarterly Review*, April 1937; Sir Frederick Pollock, *For My Grandson*, 1933; *The Holmes-Pollock Letters*, 1942; private information; personal knowledge.]   WRIGHT.

POLLOCK, HUGH McDOWELL (1852–1937), Irish politician, was born at Bangor, co. Down, 16 November 1852, the third and youngest son of James Pollock, master mariner, by his wife, Eliza McDowell. He was educated at Bangor Endowed School. Until the year 1917 his activities were wholly commercial, but this developed his vigorous mental gifts and fitted him for his belated public career. Long service as member and chairman (1918–1921) of the Belfast Harbour Board and the Belfast Ropeworks and as member and president of the council of the Belfast Chamber of Commerce enabled him to assimilate swiftly government administration and parliamentary procedure. Municipal administration did not attract him; this fact and his abstention from politics explain his late arrival on the public stage. The business of Shaw, Pollock, & company, flour importers, and the Lord shipping line involved journeys to North America, which, with travel in Europe, strengthened his natural bent for learning about the political, social, and business outlook of other countries. There were few subjects of discussion which he could not illuminate from a well-stored memory. A deep interest in education, wide reading, golf, and shooting also played their part in moulding an ideal minister of the Crown.

The turning-point of Pollock's career came in 1917 when he was nominated to represent the Belfast Chamber of Commerce, as a member of the abortive Irish Convention which met in Dublin in a desperate attempt to reconcile the divergent views of North and South. He was one of the few members of the convention who approached the home rule question dispassionately. Swayed by no political prejudices, he saw it as an economic problem and, having examined the data of Anglo-Irish finance, he concluded that the preservation of fiscal unity with Great Britain was essential.

On the formation of the Northern Ireland parliament in 1921, Pollock was elected a member for South Belfast, which he held until 1929 when he became member for Windsor, a new seat comprising part of his former constituency; he was appointed finance minister and deputy prime minister in June 1921, holding both these offices until his death. The crown of his career as minister was his success in securing the acceptance by the imperial government of the principle that equal taxation entitled the people of Northern Ireland to the same social benefits as those of Great Britain, and that only after these were provided should the statutory contribution towards imperial expenditure be assessed. His foresight is also recorded in the Loans Guarantee legislation which enabled ship-building yards in Belfast to secure orders over a period when British ship owners were unable to finance new construction from their unaided resources. He thus retained in being a nucleus of skilled craftsmen and at the same time provided the British merchant navy with many modern fast vessels of high strategical value in the war of 1939–1945.

Although Pollock had a ready and trenchant style in debate, he was no party man. His interests were of an imperial cast, those of a statesman rather than a politician. He was appointed C.H. in 1936.

In 1885 Pollock married Mrs. Annie Robinson, daughter of Andrew Marshall, of Brooklyn, U.S.A., and had four sons and a daughter. He died in Belfast 15 April 1937.

A portrait of Pollock by Frank McKelvey, in the possession of his daughter, Mrs. Cleaver, was destroyed by enemy action.

[*The Times*, 16 April 1937; Hansard, *Parliamentary Debates* (Northern Ireland); *Belfast Newsletter*, 16 April 1937; private information; personal knowledge.]

G. C. Duggan.

POOLE, REGINALD LANE (1857–1939), historian, was born in London 29 March 1857, the younger son of the Arabic scholar Edward Stanley Poole, whose mother was Sophia Poole and whose younger brother was Reginald Stuart Poole [qq.v.]. Reginald's mother, Roberta Elizabeth Louisa, daughter of Charles Reddelien, a naturalized German, died in 1866 and his father in 1867, so that he and his brother, Stanley Edward Lane-Poole [q.v.], were brought up by their grandmother and her brother, Edward William Lane, the orientalist [q.v.]. They

never went to school, but had efficient classical tutors. The atmosphere in their home at Worthing was one of evangelical religion and oriental learning. In 1874 Reginald went up to Balliol College, Oxford, as a commoner. At this time his main interest was in Hebrew, which in those days was studied in the honour school of theology. During his first term he won a theological prize at Balliol, and shortly afterwards he was elected to a Hebrew exhibition at Wadham College, whither he migrated. His Hebrew brought him into contact with the aged Dr. Pusey, for whom he felt 'the affection of a pupil' and whose 'spiritual force' he acknowledged. He spent the long vacation of 1876 at Leyden over a translation from the Dutch of Jan Pieter Nicolaas Land's *Principles of Hebrew Grammar* which was published the same year. In 1877 he returned to Balliol for the purpose of reading modern history, fortunately with William Stubbs as his tutor. His classes in the schools, a third in classical moderations and seconds in theology and modern history, by no means represented his intellectual quality, and in 1879 he won the Lothian essay prize which was published as *The History of the Huguenots of the Dispersion* (1880). Perhaps his examination record partly explains his not being elected to a college fellowship until long afterwards, but the chief reason for this was that he married as early as 1881 and so could not undertake to live in college.

After a year as an assistant in the department of manuscripts at the British Museum, Poole was appointed in 1881 to a Hibbert travelling scholarship: he was then passing through a phase of the 'liberal Christianity' which the Hibbert Trust represents. In 1882 he took the degree of Ph.D. at Leipzig and published the first of his numerous contributions to the history of music, Sebastian Bach. After a year in Zürich, he published some of the results of his studies in his *Illustrations of the History of Medieval Thought* (1884, 2nd ed. 1920). This excellent book had a marked influence in opening up in England the study of medieval learning and political thought.

By this time Poole had settled in Oxford, where he remained for the rest of his life. He took a full share in historical teaching and examining. From 1886 to 1910 he was a lecturer at Jesus College; from 1898 to 1933 a research fellow, and from 1933 an honorary fellow, of Magdalen College; from 1896 to 1927 university lecturer in diplomatic; and from 1909 to 1927 keeper of the university archives. The heavy routine work of the *English Histori-cal Review*, of which he carried the main burden from its foundation in 1886, when he was assistant editor, to his resignation of the editorship in 1920, although it enabled him to render signal services to historical scholarship, necessarily prevented him from writing long books. Nevertheless, although mainly consisting of articles, editions and calendars of manuscripts, his literary output was very large. In 1911–1912 he delivered the Ford lectures, published in 1912 as *The Exchequer in the Twelfth Century*. The *Lectures on the History of the Papal Chancery*, which he delivered as Birkbeck lecturer in Trinity College, Cambridge, in 1912–1913 and published in 1915, form his largest single contribution to diplomatic. A full bibliography of his works down to that date (compiled by his younger son, Mr. Austin Lane Poole, later president of St. John's College, Oxford) is printed in the volume *Essays in History* presented to him to celebrate his seventieth birthday in 1927. In the same year he published his admirable edition of John of Salisbury's *Historia Pontificalis*. At the age of seventy his health was already failing, and for several years at the end of his life he was unable to leave his house. He continued, however, to contribute to historical periodicals, and an important collection of his *Studies in Chronology and History* was edited by his son in 1934. In his later years he received the many academic honours which were his due, including honorary doctorates from Oxford, Cambridge, Louvain, and Leipzig, and the honorary membership of various learned societies, British and foreign. He was elected a fellow of the British Academy in 1904. He died at Oxford 28 October 1939.

Poole married Rachael Emily (died 1937), second daughter of Frank Rodbard Malleson, a pioneer in the cause of working-class education, and son of J. P. Malleson [q.v.]. She was a woman of many accomplishments and an authority on the history of art: her *Catalogue of Oxford Portraits* (3 vols., 1912–1925) is a work of permanent value. They were survived by their two sons and two daughters.

Poole's great learning would have been impossible but for exceptional industry and an exceptional memory: he knew the names and dates not only of all the popes but also of many other celebrities including all the Derby winners. He had a special power of tracing the connexions of related facts in widely distant fields. His mental processes were precise, and his knowledge, in spite of its wide range, was an organized whole, with nothing vague or loosely attached. Easily reading Latin, Greek, Hebrew, Arabic, and at least five modern European languages, he knew not only medieval Europe, but also the older literatures in which medieval Europeans read. His earlier studies illuminated the history of ideas. As he grew older his exact knowledge of chronology and the forms of documents became more and more the framework of his investigations. With no strong interest in philosophy or imaginative literature, he was musical, not only versed in the history and theory of music, but also playing the piano and 'cello.

An excellent portrait-drawing by William Strang, made in 1905, is reproduced in the volume of *Essays in History*. Poole was slightly built, of middle height and upright carriage. His finely-cut features were clean-shaven until his last invalid years, when he grew a full white beard. A most entertaining, and at times pungent, talker, he delighted in the amenities of civilized academic life, and especially in the historic traditions of Magdalen and of his university offices. From his middle age he was strongly conservative in all his views and he had 'settled down into a steady churchmanship of the old-fashioned Anglican type'. He never spared himself in helping other scholars, from his friend Lord Acton, planning the *Cambridge Modern History*, down to the clumsiest beginner in his class on diplomatic.

[*The Times*, 30 October and 3 November 1939; G. N. Clark in *English Historical Review*, January 1940; C. C. J. Webb, *Reginald Lane Poole, 1857–1939* in *Proceedings* of the British Academy, vol. xxv, 1939 (portrait); personal knowledge.]   G. N. CLARK.

POOLE, STANLEY EDWARD LANE- (1854–1931), orientalist and historian, was born in London 18 December 1854, the elder son of the Arabic scholar Edward Stanley Poole [q.v.] and brother of Reginald Lane Poole [q.v.]. Losing both parents at an early age, he and his brother were privately educated. Stanley entered Corpus Christi College, Oxford, as an exhibitioner in 1874. He was already proficient in oriental studies and working under his uncle, R. S. Poole [q.v.], in the coin department of the British Museum; indeed, the first of the fourteen volumes of his *Catalogue of Oriental and Indian Coins in the British Museum* appeared under his uncle's editorship in 1875. On the death of his great-uncle E. W. Lane [q.v.] in 1876 Lane-Poole (unlike his brother, he preferred to use the hyphen) undertook to complete his great Arabic lexicon, and issued the sixth part, with a memoir, in 1877; this was followed by the fragmentary seventh and eighth parts in 1885 and 1893. In 1877 he was awarded (not surprisingly) a third class in modern history and was appointed to the coin department, where he remained until 1892. During this period he displayed a phenomenal literary industry. In addition to the *Catalogue* (completed in 1892) and other numismatic works, he published several books on social life and art in Egypt (which he visited in 1883 on an archaeological mission), *The Moors in Spain* (1887), *Turkey* (1888), *The Barbary Corsairs* (1890), *The History of the Moghul Emperors of Hindustan* (1892), a handbook on *The Mohammedan Dynasties* (1894), editions of Swift's works (including his letters and journals, 1884, 1885), and biographies of Stratford Canning, Lord Stratford de Redcliffe (2 vols., 1888), and others. With his gift for condensing his sources in a simple and attractive style, several of these became standard works and were frequently reprinted. But Lane's lexicon remained unfinished, although it is only fair to say that the task required a scholar of Lane's long experience and concentration.

Between 1895 and 1897 Lane-Poole was engaged in archaeological research for the Egyptian government, and from 1898 until his retirement in 1904 he was professor of Arabic at Trinity College, Dublin, from which he received the degree of D.Litt. in 1900. Some of his best works were written at this time, notably his *Saladin and the Fall of the Kingdom of Jerusalem* (1898), *A History of Egypt in the Middle Ages* (1901), and *The Story of Cairo* in the 'Mediaeval Towns' series (1902). In 1879 he married Charlotte Bell, second daughter of David Wilson, of Ballymoney, co. Antrim, and great-niece of General Francis Rawdon Chesney [q.v.], whose biography he edited in 1885. There were three sons, the eldest of whom predeceased his father, and a daughter of the marriage. His wife died in 1905, and Lane-Poole lived in retirement in London until his death there 29 December 1931.

[*The Times*, 31 December 1931; private information.]   H. A. R. GIBB.

POPE, SIR WILLIAM JACKSON (1870-1939), chemist, was born in London 31 March 1870, the eldest son of William Pope, a City merchant, who came from Biggleswade, Bedfordshire, by his wife, Alice, daughter of William Hall, of Prudhoe, Northumberland. He was educated at the Cowper Street endowed schools in Finsbury, the Finsbury Technical College, and the Central Institution (afterwards the City and Guilds' College of the Imperial College of Science and Technology), where he was a pupil of H. E. Armstrong [q.v.]. After having been successively assistant to Armstrong, working with Professor Frederick Stanley Kipping, head of the chemistry department of the Goldsmiths' Institute at New Cross (1897-1901), and professor of chemistry in the municipal school and faculty of technology of the university of Manchester (1901-1908), he obtained the chair of chemistry in the university of Cambridge and was a professorial fellow of Sidney Sussex College until his death (1908-1939).

Although Pope's crystallographic studies leading to the announcement of the valency-volume theory (with William Barlow, 1906) and his investigations in general organic chemistry deserve attention, it is chiefly the advances which he made in stereochemistry, depending on the application of the principles of symmetry to molecular structure, which will remain associated with his name.

When Pope began his stereochemical investigations the phenomenon of optical activity among naturally occurring organic compounds had been correlated with the asymmetry of their molecular structure, whereby enantiomorphism or mirror-image isomerism of the molecule results. This had come to be interpreted narrowly in terms of the presence in the molecule of at least one 'asymmetric' carbon atom, i.e. a carbon atom around which four different univalent atoms or groups of atoms (radicals) are spatially arranged. It had also come to be assumed that at least one carbon atom, in addition to the 'asymmetric' one, must be present in the molecule of the compound exhibiting optical activity.

In 1897 Pope began his stereochemical investigations by introducing improvements in the methods and new strong acids (derived from camphor) for the resolution of externally compensated compounds, chiefly organic bases, into their optically active isomerides. By his resolution (1899-1902) of synthetic benzylphenylallylmethylammonium iodide, methylethyl-thetine bromide, and methylphenylselene-tine bromide, Pope demonstrated that a compound can exhibit optical activity which contains not an 'asymmetric' carbon atom but another atom, nitrogen, sulphur, or selenium, which has an asymmetric environment. During the same period he also showed that the atom of tin may be an asymmetric centre by obtaining methylethylpropylstannic iodide in an optically active form. The experimental proofs that nitrogen, sulphur, selenium, and tin could, like carbon, be centres of asymmetry and give rise to optically active compounds constituted the greatest advance in stereochemistry since the work of Pasteur and the later work of Jacobus Hendricus van't Hoff and Joseph Achille Le Bel.

Much later (1914), by his synthesis and resolution into its optically active forms of a compound containing one 'asymmetric' carbon atom and no other carbon atom in the molecule, namely, chloroiodomethanesulphonic acid, Pope established that a carbon atom attached to four different univalent atoms or radicals, none of which need contain a carbon atom, was sufficient to determine the possibility of a compound exhibiting optical isomerism.

Pope was the first to demonstrate and illustrate (1908–1935) the basic principles on which depend the enantiomorphism and hence the optical activity of chemical compounds. By his resolution into its optically active isomerides of 1-methyl-*cyclo*hexylidene-4-acetic acid, Pope proved that a compound, the molecule of which does not contain an asymmetric atom but the molecular structure of which, as a whole, exhibits no element of symmetry, has a non-superposable mirror image and therefore can give rise to optical activity. No less remarkable was Pope's demonstration of the persistence of optical activity through a series of derivatives of the optically active parent compounds. Some of these optically active derivatives also had asymmetric molecular structures. Extending this work, Pope successfully investigated the synthesis and optical resolution of the compound, 1 : 1'-diamino-*cyclo*butane*spirocyclo*butane, possessing an axis of twofold symmetry, and thereby established the mirror-image isomerism of molecules possessing certain elements of symmetry. This conclusion was emphasized by the results of the investigation of *spiro*-5 : 5-dihydantoin, *cis*-2 : 5-dialkyl-piperazines, and related substances. By

these investigations Pope established the broad principle concerning mirror-image isomerism, namely, that the molecular configuration may be 'dissymmetric' and may possess any elements of geometrical symmetry excepting a centre of symmetry and a plane of direct symmetry and that the molecular configuration of an optically active, or potentially optically active, compound need not be asymmetric or devoid of geometrical symmetry.

During the war of 1914–1918, Pope devoted himself entirely to the solution of problems of national importance. He studied the first organic compounds of gold and platinum and also co-ordination compounds of the metals of groups I and VIII of the periodic classification. He also made substantial contributions to knowledge of the photographic process and to colour photography.

Among Pope's collaborators were Professor Kipping, W. H. Perkin [q.v.], Stanley J. Peachey, Professor A. H. D. Neville, Professor Charles Stanley Gibson, Professor John Read, and Dr. Frederick George Mann. The results of Pope's investigations were published chiefly in the *Journal* of the Chemical Society, the *Proceedings* (A) of the Royal Society, and in various French and German chemistry journals.

Pope occupied a leading position in chemistry and he received numerous honours, including several medals. He was president of the Chemical Society (1917–1919), of the Society of Chemical Industry (1920–1921), of the Union internationale de Chimie (1922–1925), and of the Solvay chemical conferences in Brussels (1922–1936). In 1902 he was elected F.R.S., and was awarded the Davy medal in 1914. For his war services he was appointed K.B.E. in 1919 and grand officer of the Belgian Order of Leopold in 1937.

Pope died, unmarried, at Cambridge 17 October 1939. With his death the professorship of chemistry in the university of Cambridge came to an end. In its place the chair of organic chemistry was established. During Pope's tenure of his chair and through his influence the chairs of physical chemistry, theoretical chemistry, colloid science, and metallurgy within the department of chemistry in the university of Cambridge were established.

[*Obituary Notices of Fellows of the Royal Society*, No. 9, January 1941 (portrait); *Journal* of the Chemical Society, 1941, part ii (portrait); *The Times*, 18 October 1939; personal knowledge.]   C. S. GIBSON.

POSTAN, EILEEN EDNA LE POER (1889-1940), better known as EILEEN POWER, historian and teacher, was born at Altrincham, Cheshire, 9 January 1889, the eldest of the three daughters of Philip Ernest le Poer Power, a London stockbroker, by his wife, Mabel Grindley Clegg. She was educated at the Bournemouth and Oxford High Schools, and at Girton College, Cambridge. After obtaining a first class in both parts of the historical tripos (1909, 1910), she was awarded the Gilchrist research fellowship at Girton, and studied at the university of Paris and the École des Chartes from 1910 to 1911, afterwards working at the London School of Economics and Political Science as Shaw research student from 1911 to 1913. She was director of studies in history at Girton from 1913 to 1921. During her tenure of the last-named post she was Pfeiffer fellow of the college (1915-1918) and visited the Far East as Albert Kahn travelling fellow (1920-1921), producing on her return an account of her travels (*Report to the Trustees of the Albert Kahn Travelling Fellowship, September 1920-September 1921*, University of London Press). On resigning her position at Girton, of which she was elected an honorary fellow in 1938, she was appointed successively lecturer (1921), reader (1924), and professor of economic history (1931) at the London School of Economics in the university of London. She became in 1931 a corresponding member of the Mediaeval Academy of America, and was Ford's lecturer in English history at Oxford in 1938-1939, being the only woman so far to hold that position. She married in 1937 Michael Moissey Postan, son of Efim Postan, of Tighina, Bessarabia, and later professor of economic history at Cambridge, with whom she had long worked at the London School of Economics. She died very suddenly in London 8 August 1940.

At the time when Miss Power began her career, the department of history which she was to make her own still remained in England something of a parvenu. She had given her heart to the Middle Ages, not, as she later wrote, to 'those dear Middle Ages which the noodles praise', but to the everyday life of village and borough, market, counting-house, and farm. Much groping was needed, however, before she found her road. Her years as a student at the London School of Economics did something to help her to discover her true bent. The subject of her choice— the economic position of women in the

thirteenth and fourteenth centuries—bore fruit in a chapter on 'The Position of Women' later contributed by her to *The Legacy of the Middle Ages* (edited by C. G. Crump, q.v., and Dr. Ernest Fraser Jacob, 1926); but that topic, although a magnet to research, was too vast and heterogeneous to be compressed into a book. The result, therefore, as her thought matured, was not a single volume, but work on several fronts at once. It was a combination of books, articles, and editorial activities devoted to economic and social history, but striking into that field by a variety of converging paths.

The first of Miss Power's larger publications aroused some controversy. It is not, perhaps, surprising that *Medieval English Nunneries, c. 1275-1535* (1922) should have disappointed those readers who expected a discourse on the religious life, but complaints of lack of sympathy missed the mark. The object of the authoress, as she explained in her preface, was not to add another to the excellent books on the monastic ideal already in existence, 'but to give a general picture of English nunnery life during . . . the three centuries before the Dissolution'. That task, an important one, she performed to admiration. 'Incomparably better than anything of the kind that has been done before or since in any European language' was the verdict of a leading medievalist; nor, perhaps, would the ladies whose portraits she painted have been as shocked as their champions by the flashes of wit which enlivened her learning. Neither her lecture on Pierre du Bois (Fossey John Cobb Hearnshaw, *The Social and Political Ideas of Some Great Mediaeval Thinkers*, 1923), nor the three volumes of *Tudor Economic Documents* (edited with Professor Richard Henry Tawney, 1924) which include some discoveries of her own, err by excess of levity; but the union in her work of scholarship and high spirits is part of its charm, and *Some Medieval People* (1924), as later her translation, with an introduction, of *Le Ménagier de Paris* (1928), is conspicuous for both. Her interest during these years was increasingly focused on two central topics. A miniature of a family of Essex clothiers (*The Paycockes of Coggeshall*, 1920) had been the earliest of her works. In 'The English Wool Trade in the Reign of Edward IV' (*Cambridge Historical Journal*, vol. ii, no. i, 1926) and later in a more elaborate essay on 'The Wool Trade in the Fifteenth Century' (*Studies in English Trade in the Fifteenth Century,* edited with her future husband, 1933), she returned to her first love. She did not live to complete her history of the medieval wool trade; but her posthumously published Ford lectures, *The Wool Trade in English Medieval History* (1941), are an original and important contribution to the subject.

The second group of problems which especially appealed to Miss Power were those of medieval peasant life. She had long been in revolt against the static uniformities of the conventional legend. An invitation to contribute to the *Cambridge Medieval History* gave her the opportunity to demolish them. Her chapter on 'Peasant Life and Rural Conditions (*c.* 1100 to *c.* 1500)' (vol. vii, 1932) has as its note a realism which takes full account of natural diversities of climate and soil, heavily stresses varieties of economic type, and differs from most previous English writing in doing as ample justice to the relatively free pastoralists of the hill regions, from the Pennines to the Pyrenees, as to the manorialized cultivators of the cereal-growing lowlands. As a contribution to economic history, the part played by her in planning the great enterprise of the *Cambridge Economic History of Europe* was not less important. The design of the first volume, *The Agrarian Life of the Middle Ages* (1941), and the selection of contributors to it, were predominantly hers. Her death removed, in the words of her colleague, (Sir) John Clapham, 'the editor upon whom, as a medievalist, the main responsibility for the first three volumes rested'.

Miss Power's interests were not confined to her own special field. She had been captured, when Kahn fellow, by the charm of China, and a love for it, which was returned, remained with her throughout life. She lectured on the modern history of the Far East, which she revisited in 1929, as well as of Europe, was co-editor with the eminent orientalist Sir (Edward) Denison Ross [q.v.], of the 'Broadway Travellers' series, and produced an illuminating essay on 'The Opening of the Land Routes to Cathay' (Arthur Percival Newton, *Travel and Travellers of the Middle Ages*, 1926). She bore her fair share of the burdens which fall to a woman with a head for business, helping, in addition to the routine duties of academic life, to found the *Economic History Review* (the first volume of which appeared in 1927), and acting as secretary of the Economic History Society from its foundation in 1926

to her death. Her personal influence both on her colleagues and on a large circle of acquaintances was profound and lasting; but her students and their needs held the first place in her thoughts. In the art of exposition, from academic lectures to broadcasting for schools, she was generally recognized, not only in England but in the United States of America, where she taught in 1930 at Barnard College, as well as in China, to have few rivals; but, for all her brilliance as a lecturer, it was personal contacts which best revealed her magic. She possessed to an extraordinary degree the gift of not merely drawing out different personalities, but of fusing them into an organic group. 'Whenever she came in', remarked one of her pupils, 'the thing became a party', and to talk in later years to her former students was to realize that to not a few of those who looked back with happiness on their university days, the university meant above all Eileen Power. The honorary degree of D.Litt. conferred upon her in 1933 by the university of Manchester was a tribute to the teacher not less than to the scholar.

[*The Times*, 9, 13, and 19 August 1940; *Economic Journal*, December 1940; *Girton Review*, Michaelmas Term 1940; private information; personal knowledge.]

R. H. TAWNEY.

POWER, EILEEN EDNA LE POER (1889–1940), historian and teacher. [See POSTAN.]

POYNDER, SIR JOHN POYNDER DICKSON-, sixth baronet, and BARON ISLINGTON (1866–1936), politician and administrator, was born at Ryde, Isle of Wight, 31 October 1866, the only son of Rear-Admiral John Bourmaster Dickson, by his first wife, Sarah Matilda, third daughter of Thomas Poynder, of Hilmarton Manor, Calne, Wiltshire. On his father's side John Dickson came of a family which had distinguished itself in the two fighting services, the most notable member being his great-uncle Major-General Sir Alexander Dickson [q.v.]. He succeeded to his uncle's baronetcy in 1884. His mother's family had made its mark in commerce and had attained considerable wealth in the East India trade. From his uncle, Thomas Poynder, of Hilmarton, whom he succeeded in 1887, he inherited a large fortune, and in 1888 he assumed by royal licence the additional surname of Poynder. He was educated at Harrow and Christ Church, Oxford, settling down thereafter at Hartham Park, near

Chippenham, Wiltshire, where the Poynder lands were extensive. It was characteristic of him that, when he came of age, he remitted a year's rent to all his tenant-farmers.

After leaving Oxford Dickson-Poynder was commissioned in the 3rd Royal Scots Regiment and afterwards joined the Wiltshire Yeomanry, serving from 1900 to 1901 as aide-de-camp to P. S. Methuen, third Lord Methuen [q.v.], in the South African war. His services during the campaign, which involved a good deal of dispatch-riding in enemy country, won him the D.S.O. But he had not inherited from his Dickson ancestors their over-riding military proclivities, nor was he devoted to business like the Poynders. Apart from country life, in which he played the part of an active sportsman and a very conscientious landowner, his instincts drew him towards public service in parliament and in administration. He entered parliament very young, being elected conservative member for the Chippenham division of Wiltshire in 1892, and retaining the seat until his resignation in 1910, although he had in 1905 crossed the floor of the House on the tariff reform issue and joined the liberal party. Not content, moreover, with parliamentary work, and wishing to familiarize himself with the conditions of the working population in an urban area, he also served on the London County Council from 1898 to 1904 as member for St. George's, Hanover Square.

Dickson-Poynder had proved himself an effective public speaker with a natural appeal to many types of elector in his first parliamentary contest when, all untried, he had defeated a local opponent of experience and influence; and he won himself a position of considerable weight as a private member of the House of Commons in the early years of the century. But he never obtained office as a member of that House and in 1910 he left it for other fields, when he accepted the appointment of governor of New Zealand and was raised to the peerage as Baron Islington, of Islington.

From this point onwards Islington held successively a number of important posts and distinguished himself in all of them. In 1911 he was sworn of the Privy Council and appointed K.C.M.G. In 1912 he resigned his governorship in order to become chairman of the royal commission on the public services in India. These duties occupied him for two years, in the course of which he was appointed G.C.M.G.

(1913), and were followed by four years' office, from 1914 to 1915 as under-secretary of state for the Colonies and from 1915 to 1918 as under-secretary of state for India. From November 1917 to May 1918 the secretary of state, E. S. Montagu [q.v.], was absent in India, during which time Islington had sole charge of the office. Finally, in 1920 he undertook the chairmanship of the National Savings Committee, speaking on its behalf with marked success in all parts of the country until his resignation in 1926, when he was appointed G.B.E.

Islington had by then acquired a position of considerable authority in the House of Lords. The most signal example of the House's respect for his knowledge and judgement was perhaps the majority which he obtained on 21 June 1922 for a motion against acceptance of the mandate for Palestine 'until such modifications had been effected as would comply with British pledges to the Arabs'. This achievement was the more remarkable in that it was opposed by Lord Balfour, speaking for the first time in the House of Lords, with the high authority of an ex-prime minister and a famous House of Commons debater, and with all the eloquence of a convinced and devoted Zionist, who had given his name to the so-called Balfour Declaration of November 1917. Islington also made many speeches on India distinguished by great breadth of view and knowledge of the subject.

It was, however, earlier in his career, as a member of the London County Council, that Islington did his most effective work for liberal causes. Like Lord Rosebery, he was much in advance of his time in his advocacy of better housing and improved facilities for education, reforms more popular to-day than they were when he espoused them. Another example of his public spirit was his service for twenty-one years (1891–1912) as chairman of the board of management of the Royal Northern Hospital at Islington.

Islington married in 1896 Ann Beauclerk, third daughter of Henry Robert Duncan Dundas, of Glenesk, Midlothian, and granddaughter of Robert Cornelis Napier, first Baron Napier of Magdala [q.v.]. The issue of the marriage was an only daughter, so that on his death in London 6 December 1936 his honours became extinct. 'Unassuming without shyness, and able without a touch of intellectual aloofness' (*The Times*, 8 December 1936), he was in every way a noteworthy example of the public spirit and capacity brought by many members of the old landowning class to the service of the nation and the Empire.

[*The Times*, 8, 11, 12 December 1936; personal knowledge.]   ALTRINCHAM.

PRINGLE-PATTISON, ANDREW SETH (1856–1931), philosopher. [See PATTISON.]

PROTHERO, ROWLAND EDMUND, BARON ERNLE (1851–1937), administrator, author, and minister of agriculture, was born at Clifton-upon-Teme, Worcestershire, 6 September 1851, the third of the four sons of George Prothero, vicar of Clifton-upon-Teme, afterwards rector of Whippingham, Isle of Wight, by his wife, Emma, only daughter of the Rev. William Money Kyrle, of Homme House, Herefordshire, and Whetham House, Wiltshire. He was a younger brother of Sir George Prothero [q.v.]. He was educated at Marlborough, where he distinguished himself as a cricketer rather than as a scholar, and at Balliol College, Oxford. After being awarded a second class in classical moderations in 1873, and a first class in modern history in 1875, he was elected in the latter year to a fellowship at All Souls, which he held until 1891. Called to the bar by the Middle Temple in 1878, he joined the Oxford circuit. In 1880 serious eye trouble brought his legal career to an end, and, advised to give up reading, he spent three years 'in the wilderness', in France, acquiring an intimate knowledge of the French peasant and a love of that country which never left him. His sight recovered, and he turned to literature as a career, contributing anonymously to the *Quarterly* and *Edinburgh Reviews*. His first book, *The Pioneers and Progress of English Farming*, appeared in 1888. It showed an intimate knowledge of economic history and of rural life, and having been largely rewritten, it was republished in 1912 under the title *English Farming, Past and Present*, the classic work on agricultural history, which has gone through many editions. In 1893 he established his literary reputation as the author of *The Life and Correspondence of Arthur Penrhyn Stanley*. He had known Dean Stanley personally and the book, which was a great success, was supplemented two years later by *Letters and Verses of Arthur Penrhyn Stanley*. In 1889 he became associated with (Sir) James Knowles [q.v.] in editing the *Nineteenth Century*, and from 1893 to 1899

he was editor of the *Quarterly*. Continuing his own work at the same time, he edited *The Private Letters of Edward Gibbon* (2 vols., 1896) and *The Letters and Journals of Lord Byron* (6 vols., 1898–1901).

The circumstances of Prothero's life underwent a complete change when, late in 1898, he accepted an offer from the eleventh Duke of Bedford to become agent-in-chief of his great estates in town and country, a post which he held until 1918. His literary work continued, however, as a recreation for his spare time, and in due course he produced *The Psalms in Human Life* (1903), edited *The Letters of Richard Ford* (1905), and wrote *The Pleasant Land of France* (1908), the outcome of his early rambles in that country. The care of a great estate in its widest implications appealed to him as the opportunity for constructive work in administrative and social fields, and he played an active part in local government in the county of Bedford, and particularly in secondary education, being the first chairman of the higher education committee of the county council. As time went by he found himself more and more involved in public affairs. In January 1910 he unsuccessfully contested the Biggleswade division of Bedfordshire in the conservative interest. In June 1914, however, a few weeks before the outbreak of war, he was returned unopposed as a burgess of Oxford University at a by-election consequent on the death of Sir William Anson. He was again returned at the general election of 1918. No one, probably, was ever better fitted than Prothero, intellectually or socially, to represent his university, but he had entered parliament too late in life to make much mark in the House of Commons. Soon, however, the food situation of the nation became a major problem. He served on a committee set up in 1915 under the chairmanship of Lord Milner [q.v.] to advise upon measures for the increase of production, which recommended the guarantee to farmers of profitable prices for wheat. Asquith's coalition government was reluctant to go so far, but a year later, when Lloyd George's coalition ministry was formed, the principle was accepted. Prothero was appointed president of the Board of Agriculture and Fisheries in December 1916, and in 1917 he introduced and carried a corn production bill, the purpose of which was to make wheat-growing profitable and to improve the economic status of the farm worker by setting up an Agricultural Wages Board to regulate wages and conditions of employment. Powers to enforce proper cultivation of the land were also included. Prothero's sound knowledge of agriculture and rural life, and the advisers whose help he sought, particularly (Sir) Daniel Hall, then secretary of the Board of Agriculture, and E. G. Strutt [q.v.], a well-known land agent and farmer, ensured the success of his war-time food production campaign, but he aimed at more than this. He saw in the submarine menace and the fear of short commons an opportunity to re-establish agriculture under a system of state aid combined with safeguards which would secure good farming by the farmer and good estate management by the land-lord. At Lloyd George's request he continued in office for a short time after the end of the war, relinquishing his place in September 1919. The government, however, had accepted the war-time payment of subsidies for wheat and oats as the peace-time policy of the nation, and it was embodied in the Agriculture Act of 1920. The heavy fall in cereal prices which followed within the next few months led to its repeal, and Prothero's constructive work for farming passed into history merely as a war-time expedient.

Prothero's later years were affected by increasing blindness. In two charming homes, the one in Chelsea and the other at Ginge Manor, near Wantage, he continued his literary work, with the help of a reader, and saw his friends. These included men and women distinguished in the highest social and literary circles. The circumstances of his early days in the rectory at Whippingham had brought him into close contact with the Royal Family, and this had enabled him to render many services to the Princess Royal when, as Crown Princess and for a few brief weeks as German Empress, she was suffering greatly from public misunderstanding during her husband's last illness. Prothero's last days were occupied in the preparation of his autobiography, which was published posthumously (1938) under the title of *Whippingham to Westminster*. He died at Ginge Manor 1 July 1937.

In 1919 Prothero was raised to the peerage as Baron Ernle, of Chelsea; he took his title from the name of a Wiltshire family from which he was descended on his mother's side. He was appointed M.V.O. in 1901 and was sworn of the Privy Council on entering the Cabinet in 1916. He was a member of the royal commission on the universities of Oxford and

Cambridge from 1919 to 1922. Honorary degrees were conferred upon him by the universities of Athens (1924), Oxford (1926), and Wales (1929), and he was elected an honorary fellow of Balliol College in 1922. In 1935 the Royal Agricultural Society of England awarded him its gold medal 'for distinguished service to the farming industry'. He was president of the English Association in 1921–1922 and of the Marylebone Cricket Club in 1924–1925. He was twice married: first, in 1891 to Mary Beatrice (died 1899), daughter of John Bailward, of Horsington Manor, Somerset; secondly, in 1902 to Barbara Jane (died 1930), only daughter of Lieutenant-Colonel Charles Ogilvy Hamley, of the Royal Marine Light Infantry, and niece of General Sir E. B. Hamley [q.v.]. By his first marriage he had a son, who died of wounds received in action in Mesopotamia in 1918, and a daughter.

[Lord Ernle, *Whippingham to Westminster*, 1938; *The Times*, 3 July 1937; personal knowledge.] C. S. ORWIN.

PURCELL, ALBERT ARTHUR WILLIAM (1872–1935), agitator, whose name was registered at birth as Albert, was born at 29 Britannia Street, Hoxton New Town, 3 November 1872, the son of Albert Duncan Purcell, french-polisher, by his wife, Charlotte Alleway, and throughout his life carried the hard, rough characteristics of his early struggles. With little elementary education, he was put to french-polishing (a trade in which he remained a worker all his life), became active in trade union work, and was secretary of the Amalgamated Society of French Polishers in 1898. When that body merged in the National Amalgamated Furnishing Trades Association he found wider experience as an organizer in Lancashire. From 1907 to 1922 he was a delegate to the Salford trades council and in 1910–1911 and 1917–1919 president of the Manchester and Salford trades and labour council, of which he was for some-time secretary. He was elected to the general council of the Trades Union Congress in 1919 and served until 1928, presiding at the Hull congress in 1924, and was fraternal delegate to the American Federation of Labour at Atlantic City in 1925. As president of the International Federation of Trade Unions from 1924 to 1927 he had many contacts with the leaders of industrial movements in other countries and learned much of the conditions of foreign workers. Elected to parliament as labour member for Coventry in 1923, he was greatly concerned with the promotion of better relations with the Soviet Union, which he had visited as a member of a British labour delegation in 1919, and which he toured as chairman of a Trade Union Congress delegation in 1924. He was active in forwarding the negotiations upon the Anglo-Russian treaty which was the subject of much contention before the defeat of the labour government at the 'Red letter' election in that year. Industrial and social conditions of Indian workers were also subjects of his keen interest and study as the result of a visit to India on behalf of the Trades Union Congress in 1927. He stood unsuccessfully for Coventry at the general election of 1924, but was returned for the Forest of Dean division at a by-election in July 1925. He retired from parliament in 1929.

In 1926, as a member of the general council of the Trades Union Congress, Purcell was one of the chief advocates of the miners' demands and vigorously supported the General Strike proclaimed by other trade unions on May Day of that year. He was a member of the main strike committee and had much to do with its direction and strategy. Whilst never associating with the communist party in Great Britain, he possessed the revolutionary temperament and was one of the more prominent labour leaders of his time who had confidence in well-organized industrial action outside parliament being utilized in combination with political pressure to achieve drastic changes in the structure and purposes of industry. Forceful in speech and will, Purcell was an agitator in the accepted sense. He had come up from the proletarian depths and declared the class war as the most effective means of abolishing the poverty and hard conditions which he himself had suffered and which had shaped the destinies of so many of his fellows. He was fired by the achievements of the Russian revolution in the elimination of the capitalist and profit motive from industry and, while recognizing the different circumstances prevailing in Great Britain, he never slackened in pronouncing upon the solidarity of the workers of the two nations.

Purcell married in 1895 Sarah Elizabeth, daughter of George Thomas Fidler, engine-driver, of Edmonton, and had a son, who died in infancy, and three daughters. He died suddenly at his home in Manchester 24 December 1935.

[*The Times*, 27 December 1935; *Trade Union Congress Annual Report*, 1924.]

J. S. MIDDLETON.

PURSER, LOUIS CLAUDE (1854–1932), classical scholar, was born at Dungarvan, co. Waterford, 28 September 1854, the youngest son of Benjamin Purser, grain merchant, of Dungarvan, by his wife, Anne, daughter of John Mallet, iron, brass, and copper founder, of Dublin, who came from Devonshire, and sister of Robert Mallet [q.v.]. Louis Purser's grandfather was a partner in A. Guinness, Sons, & company, and he himself showed something of the scrupulousness of his uncle, John Purser, who, as a protest against 'gambling on the stock exchange', resigned when the firm was made into a joint-stock company. He was educated at Midleton College, co. Cork, at Portora Royal School, Enniskillen, and in 1871 he entered Trinity College, Dublin, where he was influenced by that brilliant group of fellows, (Sir) J. P. Mahaffy, Arthur Palmer, and R. Y. Tyrrell [qq.v.], then winning high repute for Dublin scholarship. A reverse in the family fortunes drove him into teaching before he graduated as senior moderator in classics in 1875, and between then and his election as a fellow in 1881 habits of industry and self-denial became a second nature to him. By this time he had been attracted to the main interest of his life. In 1882 he was collaborating with Tyrrell in the second volume of *The Correspondence of Cicero* (1886) and during the preparation of the subsequent volumes (1890, 1894, 1897, 1899) his contribution became predominant. In 1898 he was appointed professor of Latin at Trinity College but, amid protests from his colleagues, his modesty led him to resign in 1904, and he thenceforth confined himself to administrative duties in the college, where his influence, based on his executive ability, shrewd judgement, and inexhaustible kindness, made him valued by highest and lowest as a counsellor and friend, and not least as a constant helper and encourager of young scholars. When, after being appointed vice-provost in 1924, the ill health of the provost, J. H. Bernard [q.v.], put upon Purser at the age of seventy quasi-public duties, his anxious temper drove him, in three years, to resign once more a post the burdens of which he perhaps unduly felt. In 1927 he also resigned his fellowship, but he lived long enough to complete the revision of *The Correspondence of Cicero* for its second edition, and he left his house for the last time when he took to the University Press the corrected proofs of the sixth volume, which appeared in 1933. Five days later he died, unmarried, in Dublin 20 March 1932.

Purser was a man much beloved and trusted, genial, full of good stories, excellent company, liking feminine society, and popular with both women and children. On the other hand, he needed some sort of central privacy and this induced him to cling to his rather cheerless rooms in the college and make his study his hearthstone.

Purser's scholarship was marked by literary gift and historical grasp as well as by minute and exhaustive criticism of text and language, and he will be remembered by The Correspondence ('the very marrow of Roman cultural history'). The precise total of his labours cannot be established, for besides a critical text of Cicero's Letters in the 'Oxford Classical Texts' series (Ad familiares, 1901, and Ad Atticum, 1903), an edition of Apuleius' Story of Cupid and Psyche (1910), work on Sidonius Apollinaris and Prudentius in later years, and contributions to Hermathena and the Proceedings of the Royal Irish Academy, much of his work is inextricably involved with that of other scholars, whose books, when they were stricken by illness, he completed and revised. He often spent himself without thought of self on persons who had no claim upon him, and his purse was notoriously open to calls of friendship and distress.

Purser was elected a fellow of the British Academy in 1923, and received honorary degrees from the universities of Glasgow (1914), Oxford (1923), and Durham (1931). He refused the presidency of the Royal Irish Academy, of which he was secretary from 1902 to 1914 and vice-president in 1916, 1922, and 1927–1928.

A fine portrait of Purser by Leo Whelan (1926) hangs in the common room of Trinity College, Dublin, where his name is perpetuated in two entrance prizes and a lecturership in classical archaeology.

[A. C. Clark, Louis Claude Purser, 1854–1932 in Proceedings of the British Academy, vol. xviii, 1932; Tenney Frank, Cicero, ibid., p. 115; personal knowledge.]

OLIVE PURSER.

QUICK, SIR JOHN (1852–1932), lawyer, politician, and judge of the Commonwealth Arbitration Court, was born at Trevega, Towednack, near St. Ives, Cornwall, 22 April 1852, the only child of John Quick, who went to Victoria in October 1854 in order to seek for gold, by his wife, Mary, daughter of James Quick, of Trevega. The father died at Bendigo, however, a few months after his arrival, leaving his wife and child in poor circumstances. Quick attended private schools until the age of ten, and then helped to support his mother. He worked in a foundry, then with various gold-mining companies, and in a printing press; eventually, about the age of seventeen, he became a reporter on the Bendigo Independent and, later, on the Bendigo Advertiser. He decided to study law, and in 1873 matriculated and entered the university of Melbourne. He graduated LL.B. in April 1877, and was admitted to the Victorian bar in June 1878. While studying law he had worked as a reporter with The Age; he now became leader of the parliamentary staff of the paper, and so entered political circles. He became a strong supporter of the 'liberal' party of (Sir) Graham Berry [q.v.], advocating protection and land reform. Encouraged by Berry, he stood for the Victorian parliament in July 1880, and was returned as one of the three members for Sandhurst (Bendigo). He then began practice as a barrister at Bendigo, and in April 1882 was admitted to the degree of LL.D. by the university of Melbourne. As an independent member he played an active part in Victorian politics until he lost his seat in 1889, when Bendigo's representation was reduced to two members. He had, however, established his reputation, and became senior partner in the firm of Quick, Hyett, & Rymer in Bendigo.

After 1889 Quick became keenly interested in Australian federation. Sir Henry Parkes [q.v.], the premier of New South Wales, called a federal convention in Sydney in 1891, which drew up a draft constitution. But nothing was done to get this constitution adopted and the federal movement languished until, in July 1893, a conference was held at Corowa of delegates from many voluntary organizations. Of these none was more active for federation than the Australian Natives' Association, which Quick represented. At Corowa Quick was chiefly responsible for the adoption of the idea that each colony should pass an act for the election of representatives to a federal convention; the draft constitution was then to be submitted to a referendum of the people.

Quick drafted a model bill for submission to the six colonial parliaments, and for the next few years was tireless in getting these ideas adopted. He also proposed at a convention held at Bathurst in 1896 that the senate in the proposed federal constitution should be elected by the people, instead of by state legislatures. In 1897 he was one of the ten Victorian delegates elected to the Federal Convention which drafted the Commonwealth constitution, and his work for federation was recognized by his being knighted in January 1901.

In 1901 Quick was returned unopposed to the Commonwealth parliament for Bendigo, and held the seat until he was defeated in 1913. From December 1904 to July 1907 he was chairman of a royal commission which made a thorough investigation of Commonwealth tariffs; its Reports were followed by higher duties, with preferential rates to Great Britain, in 1908. Quick was largely instrumental in bringing about the Deakin-Cook 'fusion' government of 1909, in which he held the position of postmaster-general from June 1909 to April 1910. In 1911 he was one of eighteen representatives elected by the Commonwealth parliament to attend the coronation of King George V. Upon his defeat in 1913 he retired from politics, and devoted himself to his practice and business interests until June 1922, when he became deputy president of the Commonwealth Arbitration Court. He retired from this position in 1930, and died in Melbourne 17 June 1932. Quick married in 1883 Catherine, daughter of Joseph Harris, mine-manager, of Eaglehawk, Victoria, formerly of Liskeard, Cornwall; they had no children.

Quick's chief publications are: *The History of Land Tenure in the Colony of Victoria* (1883), *The Annotated Constitution of the Australian Commonwealth* (with Sir Robert Randolph Garran, 1901), *The Judicial Power of the Commonwealth* (with Sir Littleton Ernest Groom, 1904), and *Legislative Powers of the Commonwealth and the States of Australia* (1919).

The prominent characteristics of Quick's work were his capacity for taking pains, his mastery of detail, and his tenacity of purpose. These qualities probably enabled the federal movement to achieve success earlier than it would have done without his leadership. They were demonstrated also by his work on the royal commission on tariffs, and in the Commonwealth Arbitration Court. His work in the latter sphere won him respect and recogni-

tion from all parties for his judicial fair-mindedness.

There is a portrait of Quick by W. B. McInnes in the Bendigo Art Gallery.

[*Bendigo Advertiser, Argus* (Melbourne), *Age,* 18 June 1932, and *Herald* (Melbourne), January 1926; *The Times,* 18 June 1932; J. Quick and R. R. Garran, *The Annotated Constitution of the Australian Commonwealth* (especially pp. 153–163), 1901; *Commonwealth Parliamentary Handbook, 1901–1930,* 1930; Charles Daley, 'Sir John Quick' in the *Victorian Historical Magazine,* December 1934 (portrait); private information.]

HERBERT BURTON.

RACKHAM, ARTHUR (1867–1939), illustrator, was born in London 19 September 1867, the eldest of the five surviving sons of Alfred Thomas Rackham, admiralty marshal, of South Lambeth, by his wife, Anne, daughter of William Stevenson, draper, of Leicester and Nottingham. Leaving the City of London School at the age of sixteen owing to delicate health, he took a voyage to Sydney, Australia. Finding both physical and imaginative stimulus in this journey, he returned to London and embarked upon an evening art course at the Lambeth School of Art. His days were occupied in business, but he gradually sold work to periodicals, first appearing in *Scraps* (1884) and later contributing to the *Pall Mall Budget,* the *Westminster Budget,* and *Cassell's Magazine.* His first work in book form consisted of drawings from photographs for a travel brochure called *To the Other Side* (1893). These were conventional and gave no hint of the highly individual style which he was later to develop.

Rackham's powers expanded and flowered during the 'nineties, when photo-process engraving was revolutionizing the art of book-illustration. He adapted himself well to the half-tone technique, but over and above this technical dexterity he soon displayed an imaginative resource that was in tune with the adventurous strivings of the age and before long placed him ahead of such established favourites as Randolph Caldecott, Kate Greenaway, and Walter Crane [qq.v.]. His edition of the Grimm brothers' *Fairy Tales,* published in 1900, was the beginning of his real renown. He was elected an associate of the Royal Society of Painters in Water-Colours in 1902 (reaching full membership in 1908) and in 1905 issued a limited signed edition of Washington Irving's *Rip van Winkle* which carried his name across the Atlantic. Later in the same year he sold all the drawings for this book when they were shown at an exhibition held at the Leicester Galleries, London.

The Christmas gift-book proved an excellent market for Rackham. His sensitive and agile line earned him the appreciation of the connoisseurs, while his care for the spirit of each text commended him alike to children and adults. He received gold medals at Milan (1906), Barcelona (1911), and from the Société Nationale des Beaux Arts (1912), which made him an associate. He was master of the Art Workers' Guild in 1919, and was honoured by purchases of his drawings for the Tate Gallery, the Musée du Luxembourg, Paris, and the galleries of Vienna, Barcelona, Melbourne, Preston, and Bradford.

Rackham's style had, in its angularity, high imagination, and plethoric detail, a certain Gothic flavour; and indeed it was to old German artists like Albrecht Dürer and Albrecht Altdorfer that he turned, rather than to the more fashionable Frenchmen. He habitually took his holidays in South Germany and the Alps; he was interested in opera and attended the Wagner festivals at Bayreuth. Although not unappreciative of his material success he was modest, cheerful, and generous, and was a methodical and businesslike man.

Rackham married in 1903 Edyth, youngest daughter of William Robert Starkie, J.P., R.M., of Cregane Manor, Rosscarbery, co. Cork, and had a daughter. Mrs. Rackham was herself an artist. He died at Limpsfield, Surrey, 6 September 1939.

A self-portrait of Rackham (1892) is in the possession of his sister-in-law, Mrs. Harris Rackham, at Cambridge. Another (1919) hangs in the hall of the Art Workers' Guild, Queen Square, London.

[S. B. Latimore and G. C. Haskell, *Arthur Rackham: a Bibliography*, 1936; A. S. Hartrick, 'Arthur Rackham', in the Old Water-Colour Society's Club, Eighteenth Annual Volume, 1940; private information.]

HERBERT B. GRIMSDITCH.

RAIT, SIR ROBERT SANGSTER (1874–1936), historian and principal of Glasgow University, was born at Narborough, Leicestershire, 10 February 1874, the fourth child and elder son of David Rait, of the Inland Revenue Department, by his wife, Elizabeth Sangster. Soon afterwards departmental duties took his father back to Scotland and ultimately to Aberdeen, to which city both parents had originally belonged. Rait was educated at Oldmeldrum village school, at the grammar school (familiarly known as 'The Barn'), and at King's College, Old Aberdeen, where he matriculated in 1890 and graduated M.A. in 1894. For two sessions thereafter he acted as assistant to the professor of logic, whilst attending classes in the Free Church Divinity Hall. There was then no provision at Aberdeen for the teaching of history, a subject for which Rait showed unusual aptitude, but strenuous private preparation enabled him, being then too old to compete for a scholarship, to win an exhibition in history at New College, Oxford, in December 1896. There, in 1899, he won the Stanhope essay prize for an essay on 'The Scottish Parliament' which was published in 1901 as *The Scottish Parliament before the Union of the Crowns* and gained praise from F. W. Maitland [q.v.]. He was awarded a first class in modern history in 1899, and in the following October was elected to a fellowship at his college by examination. He threw himself with great vigour into the social and academic life of a young tutor, and his gifts of friendship and ready repartee found full scope during the years in which he was dean. He was also very popular among the senior members of the university.

The success of the Scottish Exhibition of National History, Art, and Industry, held at Glasgow in 1911, having provided funds for the establishment of a chair of Scottish history and literature in the university, Rait was appointed the first holder in 1913; his work was interrupted from 1915 to 1918 by his membership of the War Trade Intelligence Department in London, but from 1918 until 1929 he developed the work of his chair. He wrote accounts of Scotland for various series; and although his interests lay mainly in political history and biography, his chief contribution to historical learning was his constitutional work *The Parliaments of Scotland* (1924) in which he dealt clearly with the perplexing subject of Scottish parliamentary origins. His *Life and Campaigns of Hugh, first Viscount Gough, Field-Marshal* (2 vols., 1903) should not, however, be overlooked, for the book was a long-delayed and effective answer to the criticisms levelled at Gough as a general. Writing easily and forcefully, he contributed many reviews and leaders anonymously to the *Glasgow Herald*; and by these and by public addresses and broadcast talks on literary and historical subjects, he exercised a profound influence upon the intellectual life of Scotland. In 1929 he was appointed principal and vice-chancellor of the university of Glasgow in succession to Sir Donald MacAlister [q.v.] and resigned the post of historiographer-royal for Scotland which he had held since 1919. The great period of university expansion, which had set in after 1918, had ended, and Rait's task was to conserve and consolidate. He made a dignified and popular head of the university. Always courteous and approachable, he introduced a new warmth and friendliness into university life in Glasgow. This was the great contribution of his brief tenure of office.

Appointed C.B.E. for his war services in 1918, Rait was knighted in 1933. He received honorary doctorates from the universities of Aberdeen (1921), Glasgow (1930), Edinburgh (1933), and Lyons (1933), and was elected an honorary fellow of New College in 1933. Having been a member of the Board of Trustees of the National Library of Scotland since its foundation in 1925, he became the second chairman of the Board in 1932.

Rait was struck down by serious illness in September 1935, and died at the Principal's Lodging, Glasgow, 25 May 1936. In 1908 he married Ruth Edith Mary, elder daughter of John Charles Edward Bridge, of Peverel Court, Aylesbury, and had two daughters. The university of Glasgow possesses a posthumous portrait, painted by James Gunn.

[Private information; personal knowledge.]
W. R. Cunningham.

RAMSAY, Sir WILLIAM MITCHELL (1851–1939), classical scholar and archaeologist and the foremost authority of his day on the topography, antiquities, and history of Asia Minor in ancient times, was born in Glasgow 15 March 1851, the youngest son of Thomas Ramsay, by his wife, Jane, daughter of William Mitchell, both of Alloa. Ramsay's family had been bred to the law for three generations, his father, grandfather, and great-grandfather having all been advocates, his grandfather also procurator-fiscal of Clackmannanshire. His father died in 1857, and the family returned to its native shire to settle in a rural home near Alloa. In his education his eldest brother and his maternal uncle, Andrew Mitchell, of Alloa, took an active interest. From the Gymnasium, Old Aberdeen, he went on to the university of Aberdeen and then won a scholarship at St. John's College, Oxford: there he obtained a first class in classical moderations (1874) and in literae humaniores (1876). In his second year at Oxford (1874), he was enabled by the generosity of his maternal uncle to spend the long vacation at Göttingen, studying Sanskrit under a great scholar, Theodor Benfey. This was a critical period of his life: then for the first time, in his own words, he 'gained some insight into modern methods of literary investigation', and his 'thoughts ever since turned towards the border lands between European and Asiatic civilization'. A further stimulus was received from Henry Jardine Bidder, of St. John's, a man of incisive mind and speech, who first opened his eyes to the true spirit of Hellenism and so helped to fit him for the work which he had in view.

The opportunity of embarking on what Ramsay desired to make his lifework—exploration in Asia Minor for the study of its antiquities and history, with special reference to the influence of Asia on Greek civilization and the Greco-Roman administration—was afforded by his election in 1880 to an Oxford studentship for travel and research in Greek lands. At Smyrna he had the good fortune to meet (Sir) C. W. Wilson [q.v.], then British consul-general in Anatolia, who advised him to explore the unknown inland regions of the country and in whose company he made two long journeys in 1881–1882. So started an exploration that was to be continued, save for one break (1891–1899), until 1914. Further funds were provided by his election to a research fellowship at Exeter College, Oxford, in 1882, and by the establishment of an Asia Minor Exploration Fund supported by individuals and societies. From 1885 to 1886 he held the newly created Lincoln and Merton professorship of classical archaeology and art at Oxford and became a fellow of Lincoln College; he was then appointed regius professor of humanity at Aberdeen, where he remained until 1911. After his retirement he continued to devote himself to Anatolian studies up to the very end of his long life.

Ramsay was knighted in 1906 and received many academic distinctions: three honorary fellowships of Oxford colleges (Exeter, 1898, Lincoln, 1899, and St. John's, 1912) and honorary degrees from six British universities and from New York, Bordeaux, and Marburg. He was an original fellow of the British Academy but resigned in 1924. In 1893 he was awarded the gold medal of Pope Leo XIII, and in 1906 the Victoria medal of the Royal Geographical Society. He paid several visits to the United States of America to deliver courses of lectures, most of which were afterwards published.

Ramsay married first, in 1878, Agnes Dick (died 1927), second daughter of the Rev. William Marshall, of Leith, and granddaughter of the Rev. Dr. Andrew Marshall, of Kirkintilloch, Dumbartonshire, one of the Original Seceders from the Church of Scotland. She shared with her husband the discomforts of travel in Turkey and aided him in his work. By her he had two sons, the younger of whom was killed in action in 1915, and four daughters. He married secondly, in 1928, Phyllis Eileen, daughter of Alfred Ernest Thorowgood, of Old Bosham, Sussex, who survived him. He died at Bournemouth 20 April 1939.

Ramsay's title to distinction is the immense advance, based upon a rich harvest of new evidence, which he achieved in the knowledge of the geography and topography of Asia Minor and of its political, social, and cultural (including religious) history. In his *Historical Geography of Asia Minor* (1890) and in subsequent articles he worked out a topographical scheme which, while leaving much to be settled by discovery, laid a sure foundation for historical study. Topography and history are combined in his local history of Phrygia (*The Cities and Bishoprics of Phrygia*, 1895, 1897), uncompleted for lack of adequate evidence. The value of his historical work as a whole, largely scattered in journals and elsewhere (listed down to 1923 in *Anatolian Studies* presented to him), cannot be set forth here. Most widely known are his contributions to early Christian history, beginning with *The Church in the Roman Empire before A.D. 170* (1893) and continuing in a series of books devoted mainly to St. Paul and St. Luke. His basic contention, supported by a wealth of argument, that St. Luke is a first-class historian of the first century A.D., has won wide acceptance, although the statements in the passage dating the birth of Christ (ii. 1–2) present problems which still elude a favourable solution. Another thesis which Ramsay firmly established is that the Galatians to whom St. Paul addressed his Epistle were those, not of Galatia proper, but of the southern part of the Roman province. The value of his New Testament studies is enhanced by the

fact that he approached the subject, not as a theologian, but as a Roman historian versed in the working of Roman institutions in the provinces and possessing an intimate knowledge of the country which figured so prominently in the early history of the Church.

[Autobiographical data contained in Sir W. M. Ramsay's own publications; *The Times*, 22 April 1939; private information; personal knowledge.]   J. G. C. ANDERSON.

RAMSAY-STEEL-MAITLAND, SIR ARTHUR HERBERT DRUMMOND, first baronet (1876–1935), politician and economist. [See STEEL-MAITLAND.]

RAMSDEN, OMAR (1873–1939), goldsmith, was born at Nether Hallam, near Sheffield, 21 August 1873, the eldest son of Benjamin Woolhouse Ramsden, artist-craftsman, by his wife, Nora, daughter of John Driver Ibbotson, a member of the firm of S. D. & R. Ibbotson, ivory-cutters and dealers, of Sheffield. Omar Ramsden was educated in Illinois and at Sheffield and completed his training at the Royal College of Art, South Kensington, where he won several distinctions. He then travelled for more than a year on the continent, his itinerary including France, Spain, Italy, and Germany, and he made good use of the opportunity of studying fine examples of applied art work in the churches and public buildings of those countries. For he had decided to follow his father's calling, and his next step was a period of apprenticeship in the elder Ramsden's studio.

About 1904 Omar Ramsden set up an independent practice in London. He had come to the conclusion that craftsmanship in the precious metals had sunk to a mediocre level, and he determined to do what he could towards raising its standards. As time went on the admirable quality of his work brought him many commissions, and by the 'twenties of this century he was esteemed one of the very best goldsmiths in England.

Ramsden worked on modest tasks as well as on ceremonial plate for churches and public bodies, and to every project, great and small, he brought the same feeling for material, the same finish in detail and opulence in design. Ecclesiastical crafts naturally figured largely in his output. He was working on silverware for three cathedrals—those of Coventry, Bermuda, and Colombo—at the same period; and he carried out the reconstruction of one entire end of Whitstable parish church. Among his chief works are the great mace presented to the city of Sheffield by the fifteenth Duke of Norfolk, the monstrance of Westminster Cathedral, the entire plate and ornaments for the sanctuary of St. Bartholomew the Great, London, and the badge and chain of office of the master of the Honourable Company of Master Mariners.

Ramsden's life was dominated by the desire to show that even in a utilitarian and mechanical age there was still a place for craftsmanship in the precious metals. His joy in his material was evident, as was the humility of his approach; and some of his works, like the mazer bowl made in 1937 to mark the fact that Great Britain had had three kings in one year, earned international appreciation. In 1937 also he printed privately a brochure on *Mazers*, in which several examples of his work are reproduced. He was a member of the Royal Society of Miniature Painters, on the council of which he served, as well as of the Art Workers' Guild, a liveryman of the Worshipful Company of Goldsmiths, and chairman of the Church Crafts League, and his work is represented in the Victoria and Albert Museum and various other museums in England and abroad. A number of objects, ecclesiastical and secular, designed by him were shown at the Exhibition of Modern Silverwork held at Goldsmiths' Hall in July 1938 and will be found listed in the catalogue. He married in 1927 Annie Emily, daughter of Charles James Berriffe, coach-builder, of Brightlingsea, Essex, and widow of Charles Downs-Butcher, of London and Whitstable. They had no children. He died in London 9 August 1939.

A drawing of Ramsden by van Duindsson is in the possession of his widow.

[*The Times*, 15 and 17 August 1939; private information.]   HERBERT B. GRIMSDITCH.

RANJITSINHJI, MAHARAJA JAM SAHEB OF NAWANAGAR (1872–1933), Indian ruler and cricketer. [See NAWANAGAR.]

RAPSON, EDWARD JAMES (1861–1937), Sanskrit scholar, was born at Leicester 12 May 1861, the son of Edward Rapson, who later opened a school at Ledbury and afterwards became vicar of West Bradley, Somerset. His mother was Eleanor McArdle from county Dublin. He was educated at Hereford Cathedral School, where he formed a lifelong interest in music, and from there went up to St. John's College, Cambridge, in 1879, being elected to a foundation scholarship in 1883. He was awarded a first class in the classical tripos of 1883 and in the Indian languages tripos (Sanskrit and comparative philology) of 1885. He studied Sanskrit under E. B. Cowell [q.v.]. His first published work, *The Struggle between England and France for Supremacy in India* (1887), had gained for him the Le Bas prize in 1886, and in 1887 he was elected into a fellowship at his college, which he held until 1893. In 1887 also, after a short period as assistant to Sir Monier Monier-Williams [q.v.] at the newly founded Indian Institute at Oxford, he was appointed assistant keeper in the department of coins and medals at the British Museum. The rich collections of the museum provided ample scope for Rapson's talents and industry, and he soon established himself as a leading authority on Indian numismatics. His two major publications in this field are *Indian Coins* (1898), which appeared as one of the volumes of J. G. Bühler's 'Grundriss der Indo-arischen Philologie und Altertumskunde', and the *Catalogue of the Coins of the Andhra Dynasty, the Western Kṣatrapas, the Traikūṭaka Dynasty and the 'Bodhi' Dynasty* (1908). The latter work is a masterpiece of reconstruction, and established for the first time some degree of clarity in a very obscure period of Indian history.

From 1903 to 1906 Rapson occupied, concurrently with his post in the British Museum, the chair of Sanskrit in University College, London. He left the museum in 1906 on his election to the professorship of Sanskrit at Cambridge in succession to Cecil Bendall. A born teacher and never sparing of his own time and efforts, Rapson applied himself to his new duties with conspicuous energy and success. His duties as a teacher were by no means light, but they did not prevent him from continuing his literary and scholarly work. In 1914 appeared his *Ancient India from the Earliest Times to the First Century A.D.* which provided for the general reader an excellent summary of all that was then known about the early history and culture of India. Two major works occupied his attention during his tenure of the professorship at Cambridge. In 1901 (Sir) Aurel Stein had discovered in Chinese Turkestan a collection of ancient documents written in a variety of the Indian Kharoṣṭhi script. Rapson's preliminary decipherment appeared in 1905, and for many years, in conjunction with two French scholars, Auguste M. Boyer and Émile Senart, he worked on the task of editing the texts. The publication appeared in three parts between 1920 and 1929. His second important undertaking was editing the first two volumes of the *Cambridge History of India*. The first volume was published in 1922. Preparation of the second volume occupied him for the rest of his life, but the difficulties inherent in a subject where so few collaborators can be found prevented him from realizing the project.

As a scholar Rapson was distinguished by great thoroughness and strict adherence to scientific method. The same virtues characterized his teaching. He was elected a fellow of the British Academy in 1931. After holding his chair for thirty years he resigned it in 1936. A little over a year later he died suddenly at Cambridge 3 October 1937. He married in 1902 Ellen Daisy (died 1921), daughter of William B. Allen, of West Bradley; there were no children of the marriage.

[L. D. Barnett, *Edward James Rapson, 1861–1937* in *Proceedings* of the British Academy, vol. xxiii, 1937; *Journal* of the Royal Asiatic Society, October 1938; personal knowledge.]   T. BURROW.

READING, first MARQUESS OF (1860–1935), lord chief justice of England, etc. [See ISAACS, RUFUS DANIEL.]

REED, EDWARD TENNYSON (1860–1933), caricaturist, was born at Greenwich 27 March 1860, the only son of the naval architect (Sir) Edward James Reed [q.v.], by his wife, Rosetta, eldest daughter of Nathaniel Barnaby, of Sheerness, and sister of (Sir) Nathaniel Barnaby [q.v.]. He was educated at Harrow, and at the age of twenty had visited Egypt, China, and Japan. He had very little early training as a draughtsman, but conceived the idea of applying a burlesque of prehistoric life to contemporary events and persons. Thus 'A Quiet Game of Whist in Early Times' demonstrates the inconvenience caused to card-playing cave-dwellers by the presence of the *stegosaurus ungulatus*, the *triceratops*, and the *pterodactyl*, and 'Prehistoric Coaching for the Boat Race' shows the same kind of intrusion on woad-stained raft-paddlers of the Thames. The drawings, which were executed in a spirit of broad and riotous comedy, had a considerable vogue, and no doubt the fact that the Natural History Museum at South Kensington had not been open long enough for the skeletons of ancient monsters to lose the charm of novelty, greatly added to their appeal. It is certain that scientific lecturers bore witness at the time to their probable verisimilitude, and that schools applied for the use of the pictures as instructional magic lantern slides.

Nearly all Reed's work was done for *Punch*. He joined the staff in 1890, under the editorship of (Sir) Francis Burnand [q.v.], and for many years used palaeontology, archaeology, and heraldry as the basis of his humour. He combined the ability to seize the likeness of living persons with that of reanimating the bones of extinct beasts, and for this reason was asked in 1894 to succeed Harry Furniss [q.v.] as the illustrator of *Punch*'s parliamentary pages, a post which he held for eighteen years.

Many of Reed's drawings were published in collections, notably *Mr. Punch's Prehistoric Peeps* (1896), *Mr. Punch's Animal Land* (1898), *Mr. Punch's Book of Arms* (1899), and *The Tablets of Azit-Tigleth-Miphansi the Scribe* (1900), the last-named (as the portentous paronomasia implies) being a mock historical record of current politics illustrated in the Assyrian monumental manner.

Reed left the staff of *Punch* in 1912, and subsequently drew for the *Bystander*. His style of caricature was far too insistently facetious for the taste of a later period, but he was probably the originator of antediluvian pictorial fun. He married in 1891 Beatrice, daughter of William Bullen, of Earlsfield, and had a son and a daughter. He died in London 12 July 1933.

[*Punch*, 19 July 1933; personal knowledge.]
E. V. KNOX.

RENDLE, ALFRED BARTON (1865–1938), botanist, was born at Lewisham 19 January 1865, the only son of John Samuel Rendle, secretary to a London building society, by his wife, Jane Wilson, daughter of John Barton, of Rotherfield, Sussex; both were of Cornish stock. From his local school he gained a scholarship to St. Olave's Grammar School, Southwark, and from thence in 1884 a sizarship at St. John's College, Cambridge. At that time the direction of botanical teaching was practically in the hands of S. H. Vines [q.v.] who had recently been appointed reader.

Rendle, inspired by Vines's teaching,

after obtaining a first class in botany in the natural sciences tripos of 1887, wished to continue as a research worker, but the removal of Vines to Oxford in 1888 upset Rendle's plans, and he successfully applied for an assistantship in the department of botany, British Museum (Natural History). Although he had entered fully into the spirit of the new academic botany, he had been attracted by taxonomy from his schooldays, and had continued this study in the Botanic Garden at Cambridge.

At the Museum Rendle was given charge of gymnosperms, monocotyledons, and apetalae. Ever careful and conscientious, he did not hurry into print, and his first important work was the section on monocotyledons and gymnosperms in the *Catalogue of the African Plants collected by Dr. Friedrich Welwitsch in 1853–61* (1899). That same year his monograph on *Naias* gained him his D.Sc. (London), and led to his being invited to write the account of the Naiadaceae for the *Pflanzenreich* (1901) edited by Adolf Engler. Throughout his career he was engaged on the description of plants from collections received at the Museum.

Rendle was always interested in botanical education, and in 1894 was appointed head of the botany department at the Birkbeck Institute, where he lectured two or three evenings a week until his appointment as keeper of botany at the British Museum in 1906. He had a style of lecturing which was both attractive and successful with beginners, but somewhat uninspiring both in manner and method for more advanced audiences. His work at Birkbeck led to his writing his best-known work, *Classification of Flowering Plants*, the first volume of which, dealing with gymnosperms and monocotyledons, was published in 1904 (2nd ed. 1930); the second volume did not appear until 1925.

Rendle gave great service to systematic botany by his interest in the thorny topic of nomenclature. At the international botanical congress held at Vienna in 1905 he was appointed one of the four editors of the rules agreed on to unravel the tangle created by O. Kunze on this subject, and he continued to act until 1935. In 1931 he published a revised edition of James Britten and George Simonds Boulger's *Bibliographical Index of Deceased British and Irish Botanists*; he was the botanical editor of the eleventh edition of the *Encyclopaedia Britannica* (1911), and from 1924 to 1937 he was editor of the *Journal of Botany*. But, because of its accuracy

and scholarship, his most lasting memorial is the *Flora of Jamaica* (with William Fawcett), planned in seven volumes, of which five have appeared.

Rendle, who was elected F.R.S. in 1909, was a regular attendant at meetings of the British Association, visiting Australia (1914), Canada (1925), and South Africa (1929). In 1916 he was president of the botanical section, and in 1936 president of the conferences of the delegates of corresponding societies. He was botanical secretary of the Linnean Society from 1916 to 1923, and president from 1923 to 1927. Moreover, he was ever ready to help amateur botanists and natural history societies, and was president of the Quekett Microscopical Society (1919–1921), of the South Eastern Union of Scientific Societies (1927), and of the South Western Union of Naturalists (1931–1932). He also helped A. O. Hume [q.v.] with his scheme for the endowment of the South London Botanical Institute; he was its first president in 1911 and continued in office until his death. Much of his systematic work touched on horticulture and arboriculture and in 1919 he became honorary professor of botany of the Royal Horticultural Society, which awarded him the Victoria medal of honour in 1917 and the Veitch memorial medal in 1929.

After his retirement from the keepership in 1930, Rendle continued to work regularly in the department, and now that he was relieved of official duties, he could apply himself more assiduously to his own special interests. Although his health had given rise to anxiety, he accompanied a delegation from the British Association to the silver jubilee of the Indian Science Association. But a chill which he contracted on the voyage compelled his return from Bombay; three days after his return he died at Leatherhead 11 January 1938.

Rendle was twice married: first, in 1892 to Alice Maud (died 1896), daughter of James Armstrong, and had two sons and one daughter; secondly, in 1898 to Florence (died 1929), daughter of George Brown, and had five sons and one daughter. One son of each marriage died in infancy.

[*Obituary Notices of Fellows of the Royal Society*, No. 7, January 1939 (portrait); *Proceedings* of the Linnean Society, 150th session 1937–1938 (portrait); *Journal of Botany*, vol. lxxvi, 1938 (portrait); *Gardeners' Chronicle*, 19 November 1921; *The Times*, 13 January 1938; *Nature*, 5 March 1938; private information; personal knowledge.]   J. RAMSBOTTOM.

RICKETTS, CHARLES DE SOUSY (1866–1931), painter, printer, stage-designer, writer, and collector, was born at Geneva 2 October 1866, the son of Charles Robert Ricketts, a naval officer, by his wife, Hélène de Sousy, a French-woman. His mother and her father were amateur musicians of distinction. Having spent his infancy in London he left England at an early age to wander through France and Italy with his mother, who was in search of health. Upon her death at Genoa in 1879 he returned to London hardly knowing English. Being himself too delicate for school he spent the next three years eagerly reading any chance book, and 'basking' in the museums. At sixteen he was apprenticed to Roberts, the wood-engraver at the City and Guilds Technical Art School. There he met C. H. Shannon [q.v.] with whom, for the remainder of his life, he was to share everything. Inheriting £500 from his grandfather, Ricketts embarked upon the eighty-three volumes of the Vale Press (1896–1904) for which he designed founts (three in all), paper, and bindings, besides initials, borders, and illustrations, cut by himself. Of these *De Cupidinis et Psyches amoribus* and *The Parables from the Gospels* were masterpieces of their decade. In his approach Ricketts owed much to his older contemporary, William Morris [q.v.]. His work was less robust, less archaic, yet in beauty more calculated, more delicate. Besides the Vale books, of which he printed a *Bibliography* in 1904, he issued with Shannon *Daphnis and Chloe* (1893), a fine enterprise influenced by the *Hypnerotomachia*, and *Hero and Leander* (1894). For this each artist designed illustrations, which, for unity, were redrawn by Ricketts upon the blocks, and then cut by both. In 1894 Ricketts made exquisite pen-drawings, this time reproduced by a mechanical process, for *The Sphinx* by Oscar Wilde. In addition to his finely printed books Ricketts owned and edited with Shannon a periodical devoted to painting and literature, *The Dial* (1889–1897), which at the time was considered revolutionary. After 1904 he abandoned printing and gave himself up to painting and occasional modelling. It would seem that his books expressed in their pre-Raphaelitism the English side of his character, whilst his pictures, with their debt to Delacroix and Gustave Moreau, the French. In general his mood was tragic, melancholy, and romantic. On canvases such as 'The Betrayal', when he displayed poetic emotion, he was deeply moving. But on others, despite his remarkable knowledge of the medium of oil paint, his respect for it, and his command of composition, he fell short of his high intention because he leaned too heavily upon the artists of the past for inspiration. He was elected R.A. in 1928.

It was as a designer for the stage (from 1906) that Ricketts was pre-eminent. He anticipated by some years the work of Leon Bakst whose first undertaking was a collaboration for *Judith* in 1909. Both men revolutionized décor in the theatre, and made possible much that was later taken for granted. They realized that it was essential that one colour should prevail in each 'set' and that large pattern, when rightly placed on scenery and dresses, was effective upon the stage. Bakst obtained an international reputation, largely owing to Russian enthusiasm, whilst Ricketts suffered from British indifference. But W. B. Yeats [q.v.] called him 'the magician' and Mr. Bernard Shaw employed him for the first presentation of *The Dark Lady of the Sonnets* (1910) and for *Saint Joan* (1924) which, with his sumptuous, scholarly, and imaginative *Henry VIII* (1925), was Ricketts's most powerful achievement. Amongst many other productions were Wilde's *Salome* (boycotted by the press, 1906), Laurence Binyon's *Attila* (1907), *King Lear* (1909), Yeats's *The King's Threshold* and John Masefield's *Philip the King* (1914). Ricketts always felt happy when working for the theatre. He invented with speed, often finishing whole 'sets' with their accompanying dresses in a few hours. He did not enjoy this freedom when painting. Indeed, notwithstanding his skill, he often sat in front of a picture for two or three days before daring to add another touch.

It can be said of Ricketts that he always aimed at the highest and that both he and Shannon lived for art. When students they were poor, Ricketts receiving £25 quarterly and Shannon having no private means. Ignoring this they laid the foundation of their collection, then mostly photographs. During 1898 they began in earnest with the acquisition of Hokusai drawings for £60. Although even when most prosperous they together never had more than £1,000 a year, upon Ricketts's death they possessed a collection of old-master drawings, pictures, Egyptian and Greek objects, gems, Japanese drawings and prints, etc., that was valued for probate at £36,203. This includes neither the medallion by Masaccio, bought by Ricketts in the

Queen's Road, Bayswater, for 35s. in 1908, and presented by him to the National Gallery, nor the Persian miniatures which he was forced to sell for £4,000 when in 1929 Shannon met with an accident. They bequeathed all their treasures to museums and galleries.

Ricketts wrote three profound books, *The Prado and its Masterpieces* (1903), *Titian* (1910), and *Pages on Art* (1913). Other publications were *Beyond the Threshold* (1929), for which he invented an author, *Recollections of Oscar Wilde* (1932), *Unrecorded Histories* (1933), and *Self-Portrait* (1939), a selection from his letters and journals. The last three appeared posthumously. He was art expert and adviser to the National Gallery of Canada from 1924 until his death. Ricketts, himself a generous and faithful friend, was a man of masterful personality, dominating a circle of fervent admirers. A brilliant conversationalist, he was witty and ready to laugh at other people's jokes; he was courageous and intolerant of injustice, often championing liberty in the press. Undoubtedly out of sympathy with the painters of his time (this was largely due to his abhorrence of opaque paint) he was excited by the work of the poets, playwrights, and musicians, many of whom he claimed as his closest friends. Mr. Bernard Shaw described him as 'the noble and generous Ricketts, who always dealt *en grand seigneur*, a natural aristocrat as well as a loyal and devoted artist'. Throughout his life music was his solace, and flowers his only extravagance. He was found dead in his bed, from *angina pectoris*, at his home in London on 7 October 1931. He was unmarried.

There are portraits of Ricketts by Shannon (1898 and 1899) in the National Portrait Gallery, which also has, on loan from the National Gallery, a pencil drawing by Laura Anning Bell.

[*Self-Portrait, Letters and Journals of Charles Ricketts*, collected and compiled by T. Sturge Moore, edited by Cecil Lewis, 1939; personal knowledge.] THOMAS LOWINSKY.

RIDDELL, GEORGE ALLARDICE, BARON RIDDELL, of Walton Heath (1865–1934), newspaper proprietor, was born at Brixton, London, 25 May 1865, the only son of James Riddell, photographer, of Brixton, by his wife, Isabel Young. He was educated privately in London, and began work as a boy clerk in the office of a Bloomsbury solicitor, who, impressed by his ability and promise, gave him his articles. He passed his final examination first in all England, and was admitted a solicitor in 1888. He then joined the firm which was later known as Riddell, Vairey, & Smith, the clients of which included the corporations of Cardiff and Huddersfield and the *Western Mail*, Cardiff. When Lascelles Carr, proprietor of that newspaper, purchased the *News of the World*, a London Sunday journal, Riddell, already attracted to Fleet Street, became its legal adviser and later (1903), relinquishing law for journalism, was elected its chairman. It had not at one time a very savoury reputation; he was sensitive about this and improved it in many directions, and by skilful management put it in a position to reach some years after his death a circulation of seven millions, the highest of any newspaper in the world. He was also virtual head of the firm founded by Sir George Newnes [q.v.] and added to its publications *Country Life* and *John O' London's Weekly*.

Knighted in 1909, Riddell, who had played a large part in the settlement of the coal strike of 1912, became a prominent figure during the war of 1914–1918. Being very friendly with Lloyd George and useful to him, especially in connexion with the press, he was in 1919 appointed liaison officer between the British delegation and the press at the Paris Peace Conference: his success in carrying out his task was acknowledged by the press at a dinner of thanks and congratulation held in London in the autumn of that year. He performed the same duties at the later peace conferences, at the Naval Conference held at Washington in 1921, and at the International Press Conference held in Geneva in 1927. He was created a baronet in 1918, and in 1920 was raised to the peerage as Baron Riddell, of Walton Heath, in Surrey.

For a number of years Riddell was occupied chiefly with his business concerns, which included shrewd deals in real estate, although he made occasional appearances as a speaker, often on medical jurisprudence, which he had studied deeply; and he wrote articles of a reflective or reminiscent character. In 1933 he came prominently into view with *Lord Riddell's War Diary 1914–1918*. This was instantly welcomed as a useful contribution to history, throwing light on many events not before fully elucidated, as well as being an entertaining collection of portraits drawn from first-hand knowledge. It was followed, in the same year, by *Lord Riddell's Intimate Diary of the Peace Conference and After 1918–1923,* which has the same merits; and just before he died at Tadworth, Surrey, 5 December 1934, there appeared *More Pages from My Diary 1908–1914.* All these volumes reveal in their author insight, sound judgement, and humour. He was also very generous. He gave £100,000 and much of his time to the Royal Free Hospital, of which he was elected president in 1925, and a like sum to the Eastman Dental Clinic. He helped, too, to bring golf, which he played a great deal himself, within the reach of artisans. He was twice married: first, in 1888 to Grace Edith, daughter of Thomas Williams; secondly, in 1900 to a cousin, Annie Molison (died 1946), daughter of David William Allardice, of Valparaiso, Chile, and Rockferry, Cheshire. There were no children of either marriage. By his will, apart from making ample provision for his widow and bequests to friends and employees, he left the entirety of his very large estate to newspaper and other charities.

A portrait of Riddell by Sir William Orpen is in the National Galleries of Scotland: a bust by Sir W. Reid Dick is at the Royal Free Hospital, London.

[*The Times,* 6 December 1934; *Lord Riddell's War Diary 1914–1918* and *Lord Riddell's Intimate Diary of the Peace Conference and After 1918–1923,* 1933; Lord Riddell, *More Pages from My Diary 1908–1914,* 1934; private information.]   HAMILTON FYFE.

ROBERTSON, ARCHIBALD (1853–1931), bishop of Exeter, was the eldest son of George Samuel Robertson, by his wife, Helen, daughter of William Charles Kerr junior, physician, of Northampton, and grandson of Archibald Robertson [q.v.], physician, of Northampton. He was born 29 June 1853 at Sywell, Northamptonshire, where his father served the curacy. He was educated at Bradfield and at Trinity College, Oxford, of which he was in turn scholar (first class, *literae humaniores,* 1876), fellow (1876–1886), and after ordination (1878, 1882) dean (1879–1883), until his appointment as principal of Bishop Hatfield's Hall, Durham (1883–1897). In 1897 he became principal of King's College, London, and filled the office of vice-chancellor of London University in 1902–1903. From 1900 to 1902 he was Boyle lecturer. In 1903 he became bishop of Exeter, but was compelled to resign owing to ill health in 1916 when he retired to Oxford where he died 29 January 1931.

In academic life Robertson had gained some reputation as a careful, fair-minded, and patient teacher and administrator whose austerity of manner was underlaid by real kindliness, and if rather a hard taskmaster of others one who was not less unsparing of himself. Nor was it otherwise in a difficult diocese where he followed another head of a college (H. E. Ryle, q.v.), also without parochial experience, but where he had the aid of a much beloved suffragan, Robert Edward Trefusis, bishop of Crediton (1897–1930). His own attitude in ecclesiastical matters appears in his charges *English Churchmanship, an Invitation to Brotherly Union on the Basis of the Book of Common Prayer* (1905), and *The Church of England* (1910) no less than in his handling of difficulties at Plymouth, and he exerted himself without stint in the effort to raise funds for church-extension in the Three Towns. At the Lambeth Conference of 1908 he served on the committees on Christian faith and modern thought, on marriage problems, and on reunion, and was chairman of the committee on reorganization within the Anglican communion which recommended reforms in the consultative committee on representative lines and affirmed that 'the authority of the Diocesan Bishop as the Minister of the Church is not absolute but constitutional, being limited on the one hand by the canons applicable to Province and Diocese, and on the other by the analogy of the ancient principle that he should act after taking counsel with his clergy and people', a highly characteristic utterance.

It is, however, as a contributor to patristic and historical studies that Robertson is most frequently remembered. The needs of Oxford teaching prompted the issue of a Greek text of *St. Athanasius on the Incarnation* (1882, 2nd ed. based on Codex Seguerianus 1893, 4th ed. 1910) and a translation (1885 [1884], 2nd ed. revised and enlarged 1891). The fascination of Athanasian studies led to the production while he was at Durham of the large book entitled *Select Writings and Letters of Athanasius,* with prolegomena in Henry Wace and Philip Schaff's 'Library of Nicene and Post-Nicene Fathers' (1892). If the modest preface suggests great indebtedness to the work of J. H. Newman, W. Bright, and H. M. Gwatkin [qq.v.] it does not conceal marked independence of judgement, and the prolegomena together with the introductions to the several books are masterly summaries of permanent value. The same features of conciseness combined with clarity of exposition are seen in his articles on New Testament subjects in Smith's and Hastings's Dictionaries of the Bible and in a notable study of St. Augustine of Hippo written in 1901 and published in Henry Wace and William Coleman Piercy's *Dictionary of Christian Biography* (1911). To the Durham period belongs also his *Roman Claims to Supremacy* (1896). His appointment as Bampton lecturer (1901) afforded him an opportunity of subtle interweaving of history, political theory, and theology in a volume entitled *Regnum Dei* (published in the same year). In 1911 he published in conjunction with Alfred Plummer a commentary on the First Epistle to the Corinthians in the 'International Critical Commentary' series.

Robinson received the honorary degree of D.D. from Durham University (1893) and of LL.D. from Glasgow University (1901). He was elected a fellow of King's College, London, in 1899 and an honorary fellow of Trinity College, Oxford, in 1903. In 1885 he married Julia Eleanor Louisa (died 1925), daughter of Charles Noel Mann, rector of St. Mawgan in Meneage and vicar of St. Issey, Cornwall, by whom he had three sons.

[*The Times*, 31 January 1931; personal knowledge.]   CLAUD JENKINS.

ROBERTSON, GEORGE MATTHEW (1864–1932), alienist, was born at Simla 15 May 1864, the son of Colonel John Robertson, C.I.E., Indian Army, of Liddington Hall, Guildford, by his wife, Marie Frédérique Gumbert, of Colmar, Alsace, a descendant of General Jean Rapp, one of Napoleon's generals and a prominent figure during the closing years of the First Empire. His school days were spent at Madras College and at St. Andrews, and he entered Edinburgh University, graduating M.B., Ch.B. in 1885. Towards the end of his clinical studies he came under the influence of (Sir) Thomas Smith Clouston, physician-superintendent of the Royal Edinburgh Asylum for the Insane, at Morningside, who offered him a place on his staff on condition that he prepared himself by post-graduate study and research. After a short period spent as resident physician at the Edinburgh Royal Infirmary and in the pathological laboratories of the university, he went to London, where he studied at Bethlem Royal Hospital and at the National Hospital, Queen Square. The teaching of J. Hughlings Jackson [q.v.] left a lasting impression upon him.

After acting for a few years as assistant physician at Morningside, Robertson held in succession the posts of physician-superintendent of Perth District Asylum at Murthly (1892–1899), and of the Stirling District Asylum at Larbert (1899–1910). He became M.R.C.P. Edinburgh in 1891 and was elected a fellow in 1893. He did not take the M.D. degree until 1913, when, however, he received a gold medal for his thesis, which dealt with general paralysis of the insane. In 1908 he succeeded Clouston as physician-superintendent of the Morningside asylum, or, as it came to be called later, the Royal Edinburgh Hospital for Mental and Nervous Disorders. At the same time he became lecturer on mental diseases in the university of Edinburgh. In 1919 the lecturership was raised to the status of a chair, and Robertson became the first professor of psychiatry in 1920. He died in Edinburgh 28 March 1932, after a somewhat prolonged illness. He married in 1898 Lilias Catherine (died 1914), daughter of Daniel Ritchie, of Blackwood, Victoria, and widow of George Buchanan of Arden, and had a son.

Robertson continued the work of Clouston in transforming asylums, which were largely places of detention, into hospitals where mental disease was to be treated on much the same lines as in hospitals for physical disease. He was responsible for the adoption at Murthly of the separate or 'villa' system of housing patients; the introduction of hospital-trained nurses into asylum service; the care of certain classes of male patients by female nurses; and the reorganization of the night supervision of patients. A further reform which he originated, and which was carried through in the face of considerable criticism, was the institution in Edinburgh of nursing homes for the treatment of doubtful or early mental cases which could not be treated satisfactorily at home, but which hardly required actual certification. The Jordanburn Nerve Hospital was opened in 1929 at his instigation in order to provide similar facilities for the poorer class of patients. Robertson was deeply interested in the psychology of childhood and opened a special residential clinic for the investigation and treatment of 'problem' children.

He gave evidence before the royal commission on lunacy (1924), and took a prominent part in the discussions which preceded the passing of the Mental Treatment Act for England in 1930.

In addition to his annual reports, Robertson wrote numerous articles in the *Journal of Mental Science* and the *Edinburgh Medical Journal*. He was president of the Royal College of Physicians of Edinburgh (1925–1927), Morison lecturer (1911, 1913, 1927), and Cullen prizeman (1930). He was president of the Royal Medico-Psychological Association in 1922, Maudsley lecturer in 1926, and in 1927 was elected as honorary member of the association. An active member of the British Medical Association, he was president of the Edinburgh branch in 1926 and of the section for mental diseases at the annual meetings in 1922 and 1927. He was a corresponding member of the Société Médico-Psychologique and vice-president of the Centenaire de Bayle at Paris in 1922. In 1931 the university of St. Andrews conferred upon him the honorary degree of LL.D., and the Royal College of Surgeons of Edinburgh elected him an honorary fellow in 1927.

[*Journal of Mental Science*, vol. lxxviii, 1932 (portrait); *Edinburgh Medical Journal*, vol. xxxix, 1932 (portrait); *Annales Médico-Psychologiques*, vol. xc, 1932; *British Medical Journal*, 1932, vol. i, p. 688 (portrait); *Lancet*, 1932, vol. i, p. 805 (portrait); *The Times*, 30 March 1932.]　　W. J. Bishop.

ROBERTSON, JOHN MACKINNON (1856–1933), writer and politician, was born at Brodick in the Isle of Arran 14 November 1856, the second son of John Robertson, by his wife, Susan, daughter of John Mackinnon, of Brodick. He went to school at Stirling and left at the age of thirteen, and may therefore be said to have been almost entirely self-educated. His first important work was on the staff of the *Edinburgh Evening News*, which he joined as a leader writer in 1878, having the critic William Archer [q.v.] as a colleague. His articles created enough interest for him to be invited to London by Charles Bradlaugh [q.v.] with whom, from 1884, he worked on the *National Reformer*, the leading organ of the radical free thinkers. On Bradlaugh's death in 1891 he became sole editor until the demise of the journal in 1893, when he started the *Free Review* which he edited until 1895. After 1895 he earned his living by writing and lecturing, making a notably successful

tour over most of the United States of America in 1897–1898. In 1900 he was sent by the *Morning Leader* to South Africa to report upon the operation there of martial law. In 1906 (having stood unsuccessfully for Northampton as an independent in 1895) he was returned to parliament as a liberal for the Tyneside division, retaining his seat without difficulty until the 'coupon' election of 1918, when he was defeated. Robertson was a success in the House of Commons, and was made parliamentary secretary to the Board of Trade by Asquith in 1911, holding that office until 1915, when he retired and was sworn of the Privy Council. After his defeat in 1918, he devoted himself to writing until his death, which occurred in London 5 January 1933. He married in 1893 Maude, daughter of Charles Mosher, of Des Moines, Iowa, U.S.A., and had a son and a daughter.

Few people since the great French Encyclopaedist Bayle can have had so wide a range of significant knowledge as Robertson. He wrote the two classic histories of free thought (1899 and 1929). He was recognized as one of the leading Shakespearian scholars of his time. He was a literary critic of distinction, and his *Modern Humanists* (1891) contains some of the best work done in Great Britain since Matthew Arnold. His contributions to the history of Christianity, although they aroused great antagonism among orthodox scholars, were admitted everywhere to be based upon profound knowledge. He did work of great importance in social science; his studies of H. T. Buckle [q.v.], of the evolution of states, of German racial theories, of free trade, and thrift, are all remarkable alike for their insight and learning. It is, indeed, difficult to know what field of humanistic studies was outside his competence.

As a man, Robertson made some enemies both by his militant unorthodoxy in religious views, and by a certain irritated bluntness of manner. But he was the centre of a devoted circle of friends mostly, like himself, militant free thinkers, but also including John (Viscount) Morley, Augustine Birrell, and the historian J. B. Bury [qq.v.]. He was a man conspicuous for intellectual courage, direct, candid, and of complete integrity. He spoke admirably, and was a conversationalist of charm and power. Being both by training and by outlook aloof from the academic circles which he would have adorned, he received less recognition in his lifetime than was his due. But almost all who knew him had an affectionate reverence alike for his character and for his scholarship. It is not improbable that his intellectual position will be much higher in the next generation than it was during his lifetime.

[*The Times*, 7 January 1933; *Manchester Guardian*, 6 January 1933; *Literary Guide*, February 1935; personal knowledge.]

HAROLD J. LASKI.

ROBERTSON, SIR JOHNSTON FORBES- (1853–1937), actor, was born in Crutched Friars, London, 16 January 1853, the eldest child and eldest of the six sons of John Forbes-Robertson, by his wife, Frances, daughter of John Cott, of London. The father was a Scot who came from Aberdeen and won some success in London as an art critic and journalist: environment gave the son a single-minded ambition to become a famous painter. He was educated at Charterhouse, then still a London school, and was sent for a great part of his holidays for over six years to Rouen. On leaving school he qualified in 1870, at the age of seventeen, for a student-ship at the Royal Academy Schools, and at the end of three years' hard work had shown so much promise that his future as a painter seemed assured. Instead, he turned for his profession to the stage, where he was later joined by two of his brothers and one of his sisters.

By his own account Forbes-Robertson never liked acting, and considered himself temperamentally unfitted for it; but a desire to relieve his not very prosperous family of the expense of his upkeep made him take an unexpected opportunity. He had appeared in an amateur production, and the ascetic beauty of his face—he had sat to D. G. Rossetti, Ford Madox Brown, and other artists—and the resonance of his deep voice led to an offer from W. G. Wills [q.v.] in March 1874 of a part in his play *Mary Stuart*, then running at the Princess's Theatre, at a salary of £4 a week. The characteristic quality of Forbes-Robertson's playing was always to be beauty rather than intellectual or emotional strength, and this may fairly be ascribed to his idea of himself as essentially a painter.

In April 1874 Forbes-Robertson appeared with Ellen Terry [q.v.] in Charles Reade's *The Wandering Heir*, and after a tour with her he played a round of parts in Manchester under C. A. Calvert [q.v.]. By the end of the year, no longer quite a novice, he was back in London, playing

with Samuel Phelps [q.v.] at the Gaiety Theatre. Forbes-Robertson afterwards paid affectionate tribute to Phelps as his master, and painted the portrait of Phelps as Wolsey in the Garrick Club collection. Perhaps he owed it as much to Phelps's teaching as to his own natural graces that he surely and speedily made a name. Engagement followed engagement until in September 1876 he made his first notable personal success as Geoffrey Wynyard in (Sir) W. S. Gilbert's *Dan'l Druce, Blacksmith*. From that time onwards his name appears constantly in stage records, now with the Bancrofts, now with Wilson Barrett and Madame Modjeska, now with (Sir) Henry Irving, and now with (Sir) John Hare; and the list of his parts is as remarkable for its variety as for its growing importance.

Forbes-Robertson made the first of many appearances in the United States of America in October 1885 as Orlando with Mary Anderson in New York; and after a long tour there he appeared with her in London at the Lyceum Theatre in September 1887 as Leontes in a famous production of *The Winter's Tale*, for which he designed the dresses. He was by now recognized as one of the leading London actors, and for eight more years he continued in constant demand until in 1895 he decided to go into management for himself. Here again, as at the beginning of his stage career, he was taking an opportunity rather than realizing an ambition.

Forbes-Robertson's first season, at the Lyceum with Mrs. Patrick Campbell [q.v.] as his leading lady, was only a moderate success; it reflected a high-minded devotion to the cause of art rather than an ability to gauge the taste of playgoers. Indeed, his venture did not begin to ride on an even keel until, at the same theatre and with much misgiving, he presented himself as Hamlet in September 1897. This was not only the greatest artistic success of his career; it also established his fortunes. His Hamlet was acclaimed as the greatest of his time—some boldly said of any time. Thenceforward playgoers would always be eager to see him in the part, and even in his farewell season, when he was sixty years of age and the fire of youth had burnt itself out, the dignity and the poetic beauty of his interpretation were not to be forgotten.

During the next decade Forbes-Robertson continued to enjoy high artistic prestige and a modest prosperity. His choice of plays reflected his own taste, which sometimes ran far ahead of that of the public. For instance, he gave an early hearing, in days when the name of Mr. Bernard Shaw was still unpopular, to *The Devil's Disciple* (1900) and *Caesar and Cleopatra* (U.S.A., 1906). Success, when it came his way, was won with productions of the calibre of *The Light That Failed* (1903), a dramatization of Rudyard Kipling's sombre novel. He seemed not to be in search of easy success in less distinguished plays, although once, in *Mice and Men* (1902), which ran for nearly a year, he achieved it. The most important event in his life during this time was the engagement for a tour in the autumn of 1900 of a young American actress, May Gertrude, daughter of Thomas Dermot, of Rockland, Maine; her stage name was Gertrude Elliot, and she was sister of a more famous actress, Maxine Elliott. In December of the same year he married her, and she remained his leading lady until his retirement, and his devoted companion until his death. They had four daughters, the second of whom, Jean, followed her parents on to the stage and achieved distinction.

Then in 1908 there came to Forbes-Robertson that stroke of material good fortune for which every great actor must hope but which might easily have been denied to one of his fastidious spirit; he found a play which combined strong popular appeal with a chief part exactly suited to his personality. Jerome K. Jerome's *The Passing of the Third Floor Back* has little artistic merit, but the part of the Christ-like 'Stranger' who puts to shame the petty human failings of his fellow guests in a boarding-house brought out the sweetness and goodness that formed the basis of Forbes-Robertson's character. The appeal of play and actor to religious sentiment was irresistible. People for whom the theatre had normally no message flocked to see the piece in both England and America.

When at last this tide of fortune had spent itself, Forbes-Robertson found himself able and ready to retire from the stage. During his farewell London season, in June 1913, he was knighted by King George V. His last professional appearance was given at Harvard University in April 1916 as Hamlet. After more than twenty years of contented retirement he died at his home at St. Margaret's Bay, near Dover, 6 November 1937. In 1925 he published his autobiography *A Player Under Three Reigns*. He received honorary

degrees from the universities of Columbia (1915) and Aberdeen (1931), being the first actor of any nationality upon whom an American degree was conferred.

A portrait of Forbes-Robertson by Alfred Collins (1885) is in the possession of Lady Forbes-Robertson; another portrait by Meredith Frampton is at the Shakespeare Memorial Theatre, Stratford-on-Avon; and a drawing of him as Hamlet was made by J. P. Gülich (1897). A cartoon by 'Spy' appeared in *Vanity Fair* 2 May 1895.

[*The Times*, 8 November 1937; Sir J. Forbes-Robertson, *A Player under Three Reigns*, 1925; *Who's Who in the Theatre*, 1936; personal knowledge.]   W. A. DARLINGTON.

ROBERTSON, SIR WILLIAM ROBERT, first baronet (1860–1933), field-marshal, the eldest son of Thomas Charles Robertson, a villager of Welbourn, Lincolnshire, by his wife, Ann Rosamund Johnson, was born at Welbourn 29 January 1860. He was educated at a private school. In November 1877, giving his birthday as 16 January, he enlisted in the 16th Lancers, and being a strong, well-grown lad he quickly became adept in the many exercises then required of a lancer. He set earnestly to work to educate himself, paying a comrade a few pence an hour to read to him while he was cleaning his kit, and so he gained promotion quickly. He says in his autobiography that, while in the ranks, he was 'crimed' three times, once because a deserter whom he was escorting escaped, once because a horse which he was leading broke loose, and the third time because one of a party in his charge got drunk and was unhorsed. Despite these setbacks he was promoted troop-sergeant-major in 1885, when he had over seven years' service. Then, encouraged by his officers and by the rector of Welbourn, he set to work on the examination for a commission, which he passed in 1887, and in 1888 he was gazetted second-lieutenant in the 3rd Dragoon Guards, then serving in India.

Despite every economy a subaltern's pay in those days could not be made to cover the expenses of an officer in a cavalry regiment, and in order to eke it out Robertson took up the study of native languages, awards being offered to those who passed the examinations. He discovered that he had a gift for languages and in a few years he qualified in Urdu, Hindi, Persian, Pushtu, Punjabi, and Gurkhali. He did most of his work in the hot weather, when there were few military duties and most people slept in the middle of the day. His achievements as a linguist brought him to the notice of army headquarters and in 1892 he was appointed a junior officer of the Intelligence department at Simla. There he was chiefly concerned with the problems of the North-West Frontier. The advance of Russia towards India was a dominating factor in the military situation and Robertson was sent to explore the routes leading into India from the Pamirs. His reports were of such value that when in 1894 Umra Khan raised the tribes of Chitral and besieged the British garrison in the capital of that state, forcing us to send a relief expedition, he was appointed to the Intelligence staff of the force.

In this little campaign Robertson was severely wounded, was mentioned in dispatches, and awarded the D.S.O. While in hospital he was promoted captain and when he recovered from his wound he began to work for the Staff College. He qualified for admission—being the first ranker to do so—in 1896 and was nominated by the commander-in-chief in India for one of the vacancies at his disposal. At the Staff College he was much influenced by Lieutenant-Colonel G. F. R. Henderson [q.v.], the professor of strategy and tactics. When he passed out of the college there was need in the Intelligence department of the War Office for an officer who knew the North-West Frontier of India and Robertson, after a short period of probation, was appointed staff captain in the colonial section of that department. He was serving in it when President Kruger precipitated war in South Africa by invading the Cape Colony and Natal. On his appointment as commander-in-chief in South Africa, after the 'black week' of December 1899, Lord Roberts chose Henderson to be director of his Intelligence department and Henderson chose Robertson to serve under him. There was under the staff system which then prevailed, and of which Robertson was critical, little scope for an Intelligence department at headquarters, and in October 1900, after the occupation of Pretoria, he was sent back to the War Office, having in the meantime been promoted major. In the *Gazette* of November 1901 he was mentioned in dispatches and awarded the brevet of lieutenant-colonel.

Back in the Intelligence department, Robertson was appointed head of the foreign section, which he found to be ill equipped and badly organized, and with the full support of his chief, Sir William Nicholson [q.v.], he set about remedying these defects. As part of this process he spent some months in each year in visiting the principal foreign countries which were the charge of his section. He was promoted colonel in 1903 and thus caught up with and even passed most of his contemporaries, who had entered the army in the normal way, through the military colleges. He was appointed C.B. in 1905 and, in order that he might complete the re-organization of the foreign section, his appointment was extended for two years, to January 1907, when he was placed for a short time on half pay, using his leisure to translate German and Austrian military hand-books for his old section.

In May 1907 Robertson was appointed assistant quartermaster-general of the Aldershot Command and at the end of the year he became brigadier-general, general staff of the same command, under General Sir Horace Smith-Dorrien [q.v.]. R. B. Haldane's reform of the army was then in full development, the general staff was in being, an expeditionary force had been formed, and the creation of the Territorial army was in progress. This clearly indicated that the main task of the army was to prepare for the possibility of war on the continent of Europe. Robertson and his chief devoted themselves to making the training at Aldershot as realistic as possible, and in this Robertson's practical mind and his prolonged study of the army of Great Britain's most probable enemy proved to be of real value. His reputation in the army grew rapidly. None the less it came as a surprise to him and to the army in general when in June 1910 Nicholson, then chief of the imperial general staff, selected him for promotion to major-general and appointed him commandant of the Staff College; a ranker officer in that position was indeed a novelty. Shortly before this the King, on the occasion of a visit to the Aldershot Command, appointed Robertson a C.V.O.

At the Staff College Robertson applied to his students the same methods which he had used at Aldershot and set himself to make the study of war there less theoretical and more practical. He endeavoured to reproduce in his exercises the strain which falls upon a staff in times of crisis in war, then an entirely new development in training. He told the students 'direct your studies to a special and definite end—that of fighting the most probable and most formidable adversary for the time being'. His sound judgement and critical mind—he had an uncanny knack of spotting at once the weak points in a plan—deeply impressed his students and when he left the Staff College in October 1913 in order to become director of military training at the War Office, he was given a great ovation. Twice during his time as commandant he was in attendance on the King at army manœuvres and on the second occasion, in June 1913, he was appointed K.C.V.O. His long study of the problems which war with Germany would involve had led him to the conclusion that the enemy would invade Belgium in force with the object of turning the left of the Allied line and that the natural place of the British would be where this blow would fall. 'Hope for the best, prepare for the worst' was one of his favourite maxims, and while at the Staff College he made his students study how to conduct a retreat from an enemy in superior force. The last army manœuvres which as director of military training he planned in 1914, were arranged to deal with the same problem, and this study bore fruit when in August 1914 British troops were retreating from Mons. On mobilization he was appointed quartermaster-general at general headquarters in France. He did not share the optimism of the general staffs at French and British headquarters and agreed with Kitchener that the British area of concentration in France was dangerously advanced. When the German invasion of Belgium developed he had plans ready for the transfer of British bases from the Channel to the Atlantic coast, before the troops had fired a shot, and it was thanks to this foresight that he succeeded in keeping the army supplied during the long retreat. His handling of this difficult task inspired confidence in his ability and energy and when in January 1915 the health of Sir Archibald Murray, chief of the general staff at general headquarters, broke down, he was welcomed as his successor. He was appointed K.C.B. later that year.

The Allies in the West, having defeated the German attempts to reach Paris and the Channel ports, had to determine their strategy for 1915. French military and public opinion was eager to drive the enemy out of France and was convinced that this was possible. No French commander-in-chief who proposed a defensive strategy could have held his position. The Germans had transferred large forces from the northern to the eastern front and were driving back the Russians, who had come gallantly to the aid of France and Britain in the crisis of 1914. Robertson held that the first essential was to make the co-operation of the Allied forces effective and that therefore the British had no alternative but to aid the offensive campaign of the French to the utmost of their power, in accordance with the instructions of the British government to the commander-in-chief in France. Further he regarded it as very important that the British should drive the Germans farther away from the Channel ports and from Paris, before they brought back troops from the East. Realizing that Britain had not the power to conduct more than one offensive campaign at a time, he was opposed to the plans for attacking the Gallipoli peninsula. He had studied this operation when in charge of the foreign section, and had come to the conclusion that success was doubtful because it was not easy to provide artillery support for landings and he was sceptical of the opinion of the Admiralty that improvements in naval ordnance had overcome this difficulty. So began the prolonged controversy between 'Westerners' and 'Easterners', in which Robertson was a convinced 'Westerner'.

As the summer of 1915 wore on and British commitments grew, Robertson became anxious about the conduct of the war and sent to the War Office a memorandum in which he urged the setting up of an organization for the control and direction of Allied strategy. As a result of this General Joffre called in November 1915 the first conference of Allied commanders and chiefs of staff to consider the Allied campaign for 1916. This Robertson welcomed as a useful beginning. He was no less anxious to improve British arrangements for the control of military operations, and when in the autumn Kitchener told him that he wanted him to come to the War Office as chief of the imperial general staff he prepared for him a memorandum setting out the conditions upon which he was prepared to accept this appointment.

Robertson pointed out that the War Office was responsible for campaigns in France and the Dardanelles, India conducted the campaign in Mesopotamia without the resources to do this effectively, the Foreign Office was responsible for operations against the Senussi in Western Egypt, and the Colonial Office for the campaign in West Africa, a division of responsibility fatal to efficiency. He urged the setting up of a small war council charged with the co-ordination of policy and strategy in every theatre of war in which Great Britain was concerned; that the chief of the imperial general staff should be the responsible military adviser of this council and should issue its instructions to commanders-in-chief, and be in direct touch with these commanders without the intervention of the army council. He also asked for a reorganization of the general staff at the War Office in order to enable it to operate as the general headquarters of the Empire. Kitchener was at first disposed to consider these proposals to be an undue curtailment of the authority of the secretary of state for war, but after a personal interview he accepted them and Robertson became chief of the imperial general staff in succession to Murray in December 1915.

Before he re-entered the War Office Robertson had been asked by the government for his views on the situation in the Gallipoli peninsula and had strongly supported the proposal to evacuate Suvla Bay. This operation was completed before he assumed office and his first act as chief of the imperial general staff was to urge that Helles should also be evacuated. When this was done he created in Egypt a general reserve composed of the troops released from the Dardanelles. This he used to provide reinforcements for the campaign of 1916 in France, a very necessary step in view of the German attack on Verdun. Murray, who had become commander-in-chief in Egypt, materially increased the available reserve by occupying the wells in the Sinai peninsula, a more economical defence against attack from the East than was provided by lining the Suez Canal. This released further reinforcements for Mesopotamia, where Robertson selected General Sir F. S. Maude [q.v.] for the chief command.

The new arrangement began smoothly. Kitchener and Robertson, who was promoted general in June 1916, worked well together and when, on Kitchener's death that same month, Lloyd George became secretary of state for war, he expressed his agreement with the reorganization of the higher command. The successful evacuation of the Gallipoli peninsula, the ending of the campaigns in West Africa and Western Egypt, the occupation of the Sinai peninsula and, early in 1917, when Robertson was appointed G.C.B., the

defeat of the Turks at Kut-el-Amara, followed by the occupation of Bagdad, materially improved the British military situation. But against this had to be set the disastrous defeats of the Russians, the heavy cost of the battles of the Somme, the exhaustion of the French army, the over-running of Serbia and Rumania, and growing doubts as to the possibility of breaking through the German lines in the West. These led in December 1916 to the fall of Asquith and the accession of Lloyd George as prime minister.

Lloyd George, horrified by the long casualty lists of the Somme battles, was determined to secure greater political control of Allied strategy and to find an easier road to victory than was provided by assaults on German trenches. He was essentially an opportunist, and Robertson a firm believer in principles; the prime minister liked to form his conclusions after personal discussions; Robertson distrusted his powers of argument with statesmen and preferred to present his views in reasoned memoranda, so that from the first there were incompatabilities of temperament between the two. Friction increased when, at a conference of the Allies held in Rome in January 1917, Lloyd George, without consulting Robertson, put forward a plan for an Allied attack on Austria. This plan overlooked the limitations of communication between France and Italy and the superiority in this respect of the centrally placed enemy. The Allied ministers naturally referred it to the chiefs of staff for examination and report.

The French government, like Lloyd George, was alarmed by the losses of the campaigns of 1916 and it too sought greater political control. Joffre was removed and Nivelle took his place. Lloyd George met Nivelle on his return from Italy and, before the report on the Austrian plan was received, approved Nivelle's proposal for a quick break through the German lines in the West, on the understanding that, if this failed, operations would be broken off. To further this plan, the prime minister, again without consulting the chief of the imperial general staff, encouraged the French government to propose that Nivelle should have operational and administrative control of the British army in France. When, to the surprise of Robertson and Haig, this proposal was produced at an Allied conference held at Calais in February 1917, they held it to be dangerous in view of the many British commitments, and a compromise was reached by which Nivelle was given operational control in France for the campaign of 1917.

The failure of Nivelle's campaign, followed by serious mutinies in parts of the French army, produced a crisis which, it was agreed, could only be met by British attacks on a scale sufficient to keep the Germans occupied. The situation was further complicated by the probability of the collapse of Russian resistance, against which could be set the entry into the war of the United States of America. A conference of Allied commanders-in-chief and chiefs of staff held in June computed the rate at which German troops could be transferred from the eastern to the western front and came to the conclusion that between February and July 1918 the enemy might be in a dangerous superiority on the western front. In order to meet this it was agreed that a defensive attitude should be adopted in all secondary theatres of war and that as many men as possible should be transferred to the western front.

Robertson agreed with this recommendation and in order to implement it he prepared plans for the transfer of troops from Egypt and Salonika to the western front and urged the army council to press for a greater allocation of manpower to the army. This brought him again into conflict with the prime minister, who feared that these reinforcements would be used for another costly attack in France. Delay occurred in meeting the army council's request for more men, and Lloyd George returned to his advocacy of an attack on Austria as preferable to Haig's proposal for an offensive campaign on the Ypres front. When the Austrian plan proved to be impracticable the prime minister urged an invasion of Palestine as likely to provide a stimulus to public morale during the difficult period which was foreseen for the spring of 1918.

The heavy defeat of the Italian army at Caporetto in October 1917 and the disappointing results of the Passchendaele campaign brought about a fresh crisis. Lloyd George, who had been for some time in touch with the French prime minister, M. Painlevé, and had secured his agreement, proposed at a conference held at Rapallo the creation of a supreme war council composed of the prime ministers and one other minister from each Ally, provided with a permanent staff and with military representatives to furnish tech-

nical advice. Robertson cordially approved of the supreme council as a means of receiving better co-ordination of Allied policy, but he strongly disapproved of the military representatives having power to give technical advice independently of their chiefs of staff, who, he held, having behind them their general staffs organization, and particularly their intelligence services, were alone competent to give their governments responsible advice. Nivelle's failure had shaken confidence in an Allied supreme command and Lloyd George had expressly stated that this was, at the time, impracticable, but Robertson regarded the multiplication of military advice as a sorry alternative.

The differences between the two men came to a head at a meeting of the Supreme War Council held at Versailles from 30 January to 2 February 1918. There Lloyd George obtained approval, despite Robertson's objections, for an offensive campaign in Palestine in the spring. In the event this had to be postponed when the Germans attacked the western front in March. It was also decided to create an Allied general reserve on the western front controlled by the military representatives with Foch as chairman. Robertson had no faith in command by committee and said so, and in fact this committee was never able to get to work. It had become clear that he and the prime minister could not work together and Lloyd George proposed to bring in Sir Henry Wilson [q.v.] as chief of the imperial general staff, offering Robertson the post of military representative at Versailles. This Robertson refused on the ground that the appointment was wrong in principle. In February he left the War Office for the Eastern Command at home.

In the Eastern Command Robertson undertook a reorganization designed to release men for the fighting fronts and after the armistice he was concerned with the disturbances which arose from the dissatisfaction of the troops with the arrangements for demobilization. In this his firmness and tact avoided serious trouble. In June 1918 he became commander-in-chief, Home Forces, and in April 1919 of the British army of occupation on the Rhine. In this year he was appointed G.C.M.G., and for his eminent services during the war received the thanks of parliament and a grant of £10,000 and was created a baronet. In March 1920 he was promoted field-marshal and retired from active employment in the following year. He was appointed G.C.V.O. in 1931 and died in London 12 February 1933.

Robertson wrote two books; the first, an autobiography *From Private to Field-Marshal*, was published in 1921; the second, *Soldiers and Statesmen 1914–1918*, published in two volumes in 1926, was a reasoned account of the advice which he gave to the government. He was appointed in 1916 colonel of the Scots Greys, in 1925 of the 3rd Dragoon Guards, and in 1928 of the Royal Horse Guards. He received many foreign decorations, including that of grand officer of the Legion of Honour.

Robertson married in 1894 Mildred Adelaide, second daughter of Lieutenant-General Charles Thomas Palin, of the Indian Army, and had two sons, the younger of whom died at the age of eighteen, and two daughters. He was succeeded as second baronet by his elder son, Lieutenant-General Sir Brian Hubert Robertson (born 1896).

There is a portrait of Robertson in the Cavalry Club by R. C. Petre, and in the Imperial War Museum by Sir William Orpen; a portrait of him as colonel of the Royal Horse Guards by Mediria is in the possession of his daughter, Mrs. Locket-Agnew; a portrait of him is also included in J. S. Sargent's picture, 'Some General Officers of the Great War', painted in 1922, in the National Portrait Gallery.

[Sir William Robertson, *From Private to Field-Marshal*, 1921, and *Soldiers and Statesmen 1914–1918*, 2 vols., 1926; personal knowledge.]   F. MAURICE.

ROBINSON, JOSEPH ARMITAGE (1858–1933), dean of Westminster Abbey and of Wells Cathedral, was the third son among thirteen children of George Robinson, of Monaghan, Ireland, vicar in turn of the poor parishes of Keynsham, near Bath, and St. Augustine's, Everton, near Liverpool, by his wife, Henrietta Cecilia, daughter of Arthur Forbes, of Craig-a-vad, co. Down. He was born at Keynsham co. 9 January 1858 and educated under George Butler [q.v.] at Liverpool College and, like three of his brothers, at Christ's College, Cambridge, of which he was scholar (1877, fourth classic and second chancellor's medallist, 1881), fellow (1881–1899), and honorary fellow (1905). After ordination (1881, 1882) he became for a time (1883–1884) domestic chaplain to J. B. Lightfoot [q.v.], whose custom of

gathering young men to live under his roof at Auckland Castle Robinson adopted later at Westminster. On returning to Cambridge he engaged in teaching and research varied by a curacy at St. Mary the Great (1885–1888) and the vicarage of All Saints (1888–1892). On the way to Patmos in 1887 he met at Athens Dr. S. P. Lambros, who, in discussing the problem of a famous forgery by Constantine Simonides, showed him an essay that he had written and a new collation which he had had made of the Athos manuscript of the *Shepherd of Hermas*. For these Robinson secured publication by the Cambridge University Press (1888) with an English translation and valuable preface and appendices of his own. In 1890 he discovered in MS. Brit. Mus. 11884 the original Latin of the Acts of the Scillitan martyrs and shortly after, while in Vienna in search of a lost manuscript of the Passion of St. Perpetua, he detected in the Buddhistic romance of Barlaam and Joasaph (or Josaphat) the original Greek of the *Apology* of Aristides, of which a text and translation from a Syriac version found by James Rendel Harris at Mount Sinai were passing through the press. The result appeared in 1891 as the first of a new series of Cambridge 'Texts and Studies' under Robinson's editorship with an elaborate appendix by himself, which helped 'to open a new field before the student of Christian Apologetics'. In 1891 as vol. i, no. 2 in the series were issued the new texts of St. Perpetua, 'the most beautiful of all the records of Christian martyrdom' and of the Scillitan martyrs, and in 1893, separately, the revised text of Origen's *Philocalia*. The interest aroused by such work was marked abroad by the bestowal of the honorary degree of Ph.D. by Göttingen University (1893) and of the honorary degree of D. Theol. by Halle University (1894) and at home by his election to the Norrisian professorship of divinity at Cambridge (1893), which he held until 1899. From 1894 to 1899 he held the prebend of Compton Bishop in Wells Cathedral. In 1895 he published *Euthaliana* (Cambridge 'Texts and Studies', vol. iii, no. 3), a work of some importance for New Testament criticism, which shows that he had already begun those Armenian studies which led to his translation of St. Irenaeus: *The Demonstration of the Apostolic Preaching* (1920), 'a handbook of Christian evidence . . . as it presented itself to a master-mind at the end of the second century'.

Meantime Robinson's reputation had been growing as a scholar who was also a preacher, and his appointment to the rectory of St. Margaret's with the annexed canonry of Westminster Abbey was welcomed in 1899, the stall being exchanged for another in 1900. The approach of the coronation of Edward VII gave the new canon, with the approval of Archbishop Temple, on whom the responsibility for the service lay, an opportunity of suggesting modifications of the disastrous changes in the coronation rite introduced by William Sancroft with his ill advised alterations for James II, followed by those of Henry Compton for William and Mary, until the ceremony reached its lowest liturgical level in the form adopted for William IV. This process of restoration and repair was carried still further in the service for George V prepared by the Lambeth librarian under Robinson's supervision in 1911. After King Edward's coronation (9 August 1902), the octogenarian Dean Bradley resigned and Robinson was appointed to succeed him at the age of forty-four. He came to office at a difficult time when energetic action and even drastic decisions might seem to be called for. If allowed for the most part to go his own way he was by no means a difficult man to work with, even if he appeared at times freakish and provoking. The powers of a dean of Westminster are very extensive and in the hands of a masterful man the exercise of them might only too easily wear the appearance of despotism. Examples were seen in his treatment of the Athanasian Creed and his rejection of a strongly urged proposal that George Meredith should be buried in the Abbey in 1909, as to which he always contended that later ages would approve his literary estimate. He was an unflinching upholder of the rights of the Abbey which he loved, and of which, although he has been described as 'tall, gaunt, long-haired and prematurely bent', he was the most stately and, as the years passed, probably the most picturesque, as he was certainly the most learned, head that it had known for centuries. But undeniably his tenure (1902–1911) was marked at times by serious tension with a chapter not less desirous of handing on unimpaired to their successors their right to an adequate share in government. How much was gained by appeal to the visitor has not been disclosed, but some of the most important decanal prerogatives seem to have been affirmed. The dean,

however, partly on the ground of eye-trouble, decided not to undergo the strain of the approaching coronation, and accepted nomination to the deanery of Wells, retaining the office of lord high almoner to which he had been appointed in 1906.

Robinson's writings while at Westminster followed two distinct lines, theological and historical. In the one class were vivid and stimulating essays and addresses such as *Unity in Christ* (1901) and *The Vision of Unity* (published in 1908, the year of the Lambeth Conference), *The Study of the Gospels* (1902), *Some Thoughts on the Incarnation* (1903), *On Inspiration* (1905), *On the Athanasian Creed* (1905), and *The Advent Hope in St. Paul's Epistles* (1911), together with an elaborate commentary on the Epistle to the Ephesians (1903) in the Cambridge tradition and a conservative study of *The Historical Character of St. John's Gospel* (1908, enlarged ed. 1929). To the other category belong four works, which lay students of Abbey history under lasting obligation to him: *An Unrecognized Westminster Chronicler, 1381–1394* (1907), *The History of Westminster Abbey by John Flete* (1909), *Gilbert Crispin, Abbot of Westminster*, and *The Abbot's House at Westminster*, both published in 1911. To these should be added his share in *The Manuscripts of Westminster Abbey* by Montague Rhodes James [q.v.] (1909).

At Wells the new dean was in familiar surroundings and able to renew contact with friends, especially at Downside. The medieval deanery pleased him after the removal of evidence of modern 'taste', and he found additional happiness in his marriage (1914) to an old friend at Lambeth, Amy Edith, daughter of Francis Grantham Faithfull, of Broxbourne, Hertfordshire, clerk to the Merchant Taylors Company. The care of another great church of peculiar architectural features, to which he added a rood in the nave, stimulated and re-invigorated his antiquarian interests to the great advantage of his native county. His work on *The Saxon Bishops of Wells* (1918), his *Somerset Historical Essays* (1922) and contributions to the Somerset Record Society's *collectanea*, his Ford lectures delivered at Oxford in 1922 on *The Times of St. Dunstan* (published in 1923), the studies of *Two Glastonbury Legends* (1926), and *St. Oswald and the Church of Worcester* (1919) are not always easy to read since he disclaimed the intention of writing history, being content with the modest aim of 'collecting materials out of which others more competent will some day write it', but they are invaluable for their purpose. In other fields he published the work on Irenaeus already mentioned, a very long and notable article on the early history of Canterbury convocation (*Church Quarterly Review*, October 1915), an essay equally suggestive and deliberately provoking on *Barnabas, Hermas and the Didache* (1920), and sermons entitled *Giving and Receiving* (1928). His deep interest in liturgical questions, strongly influenced by long friendship with Edmund Bishop [q.v.], lent urgency to his views on Prayer Book revision which failed to secure favour in convocation, and his last days were clouded by recurrent ill health. Resigning in March 1933 he died, childless, at the Manor House, Upton Noble, Somerset, 7 May, and was buried at Wells.

Robinson was one of the early elected fellows of the British Academy (1903) and was appointed K.C.V.O. in 1932. He received the honorary degree of D.D. from the universities of Dublin (1908) and Glasgow (1910).

[*The Times*, 9 May 1933; J. M. Creed, *Joseph Armitage Robinson, 1858–1933* in *Proceedings* of the British Academy, vol. xx, 1934; John Peile, *Biographical Register of Christ's College*, vol. ii, 1913; private information; personal knowledge.]

CLAUD JENKINS.

ROGERS, ANNIE MARY ANNE HENLEY (1856–1937), educationist, was the eldest child and only daughter of the political economist James Edwin Thorold Rogers [q.v.], of Oxford, by his second wife, Anne Susanna Charlotte, second daughter of Henry Revell Reynolds, solicitor to the Treasury, and great-granddaughter of the physician Henry Revell Reynolds [q.v.]. Joseph Rogers [q.v.] was her father's brother. She was born 15 February 1856 at Oxford, where she died at the age of eighty-one, as the result of having been struck by a lorry, 28 October 1937. Her life, which was spent in Oxford, coincided with important developments in the position of women, in which she herself played a leading part. She was first brought into prominence by heading the list of successful candidates in the Oxford senior local examinations of 1873, thus becoming eligible, but for her sex, for exhibitions at Balliol and Worcester Colleges. In 1879 she joined the

Committee of the Association for the Higher Education of Women in Oxford (familiarly known for many years as the A.E.W.), organized privately in the previous year to promote facilities for teaching and examination by university standards, and was honorary secretary from 1894 until its dissolution in 1920. The success of this unofficial body led, through partial recognition by the university, to the institution in 1910 of the Delegacy for Women Students, and in 1920 women were admitted to all the privileges and obligations of actual membership of the university. Miss Rogers had been throughout the moving spirit; and although she never hesitated to attribute a due share of the result to the general advance in the position of women during the war of 1914–1918 and to the liberal attitude of the then chancellor, Lord Curzon, it is certain that the conservatism of the university would not have been overcome so steadily and so smoothly without the attention to detail, sound judgement, and intellectual grasp which characterized her own leadership.

Miss Rogers's energies were not exhausted by this absorbing lifework but found congenial scope from 1893 to 1930 in the administration, as honorary secretary to its successive governing bodies, of the Society of Oxford Home-Students (afterwards St. Anne's Society), as tutor in classics in the early days to all the women students, and as a member for forty-two years after 1894 of the council of St. Hugh's College, Oxford, which was granted its charter in 1927 and owes much to her talent for constitution-making. Her latter years, after she had retired from her last tutorial position—at St. Hugh's—in 1921, were devoted to the care of the college garden, and revealed a genius for horticulture not inferior to her skill in draftsmanship. She was elected an honorary fellow on the occasion of the college jubilee in 1936. In 1938, after her death, a memorial garden was laid out and endowed in her memory in the churchyard of the university church of St. Mary, where a Latin inscription on a garden seat recalls her services to education, administration, and horticulture.

Degrees by Degrees (published posthumously in 1938), her own narrative of forty-two years' labour (in forty-one of which she herself had participated) in a society which, perhaps above all others, displays England in her favourite illogicalities, shows Miss Rogers's strong intelligence, lively humour, and firm grasp of a most intricate subject.

A portrait drawing of Miss Rogers by Leslie Brooke is in the possession of St. Hugh's College.

[*The Times*, 29 October 1937; Introductory Memoir by B. E. Gwyer prefixed to A. M. A. H. Rogers, *Degrees by Degrees*, 1938; *Oxford Magazine*, 18 November 1937; personal knowledge.]   B. E. Gwyer.

ROGERS, LEONARD JAMES (1862–1933), mathematician, was born at Oxford 30 March 1862, the second of the five sons of James Edwin Thorold Rogers [q.v.], by his second wife. He was brother of Annie Rogers [q.v.]. Because of illness he was educated privately, but in 1880 he went up as a mathematical scholar to Balliol College, Oxford. Besides gaining a first class in mathematical moderations (1881) and in the final school of mathematics (1884) together with both the junior and senior university mathematical scholarships (1881, 1885), he also obtained a second class in classical moderations in 1882 and two years later graduated B.Mus. In 1888 he became professor of mathematics at the Yorkshire College, afterwards the university of Leeds, retiring, because of severe illness, in 1919. He returned to Oxford, where he remained free of official appointments, and died 12 September 1933. He served on the council of the London Mathematical Society in 1901 and was elected F.R.S. in 1924. He was unmarried. His abilities were many and his interests diverse. He was a musician of uncommon skill with a faultless ear and a tenacious memory. These gifts made him also a ready linguist and an engaging mimic, especially of broad Yorkshire. He was a first-class skater, an excellent knitter, and an amateur of rock-gardens.

Among these competing aptitudes music easily held first place, perhaps even as against mathematics. Rogers was a very good pianist and he sang well, taking an active part in choral music at both Leeds and Oxford. He combined a scholar's knowledge and a performer's love of the works of J. S. Bach and he carried in his memory a wide repertory of Chopin's pianoforte music. For composers of a more recent tradition he had no appreciation and little patience. So necessary was music to him that in 1917, bed-ridden and paralysed, he taught himself to play the concertina, the only instrument then possible to him. His mathematical

writings appeared mostly in the *Proceedings* of the London Mathematical Society (some twenty-two papers), but he also contributed to the *Messenger of Mathematics* and the *Proceedings* of the Cambridge Philosophical Society. He did not write a book. His first work was in the theory of reciprocants, that is of differential expressions unaltered by specified transformations of the variables, a subject that J. J. Sylvester [q.v.] had made popular at Oxford. But subsequently Rogers's chief work and interest lay in the associated fields of elliptic functions, theta functions, and basic hypergeometric series, called shortly q-series. Here his work crossed that of the remarkable Indian mathematician Srinivasa Ramanujan, and it was to the circumstances of this interconnexion that Rogers owed a good deal of his fame and recognition as a mathematician. Ramanujan in 1913 had conjectured a pair of identities important in partition-theory:

$$1+q/(1-q)+q^4/(1-q)(1-q^2)+q^9/(1-q)(1-q^2)(1-q^3)+\ldots$$
$$= 1/(1-q)(1-q^4)(1-q^6)(1-q^9)(1-q^{11})(1-q^{14})\ldots$$

and

$$1+q^2/(1-q)+q^6/(1-q)(1-q^2)+q^{12}/(1-q)(1-q^2)(1-q^3)+\ldots$$
$$= 1/(1-q^2)(1-q^3)(1-q^7)(1-q^8)(1-q^{12})(1-q^{13})\ldots$$

and they had been published without proof. It was only later and by accident that Ramanujan himself discovered that Rogers had already proved and published these identities nineteen years before, as particular cases of more general theorems.

It was typical of Rogers that his work should go unrecognized: a contemporary wrote of him 'no one paid much attention to anything he did'. He seemed strikingly unprofessional even among English mathematicians, whom their continental colleagues often find stubbornly amateur. He cared much for particular problems in mathematics and their solution, just as he cared for individual species in his rock-garden: that is, if they were sufficiently beautiful. But a full *corpus* of mathematical theory interested him as little as botany after Linnaeus. He was probably better read as a musician than as a mathematician. The president of the Royal Society described him after his death as 'remarkable among our Fellows, in that, according to a well-informed biographer, science was to him almost distasteful'. This is doubtful, but it is certain that he would have reckoned mathematics among the fine arts rather than with the sciences. It was the compulsion of beauty that informed his work here as in his other devotions and formed the common link between them. Of his personal charm, his grace of manner, the wit and sparkle of his conversation his friends were gratefully aware, and it is perhaps his greatest distinction to have spent freely on them what a harsher economy would have wished to conserve for posterity.

[*The Times*, 14, 16, and 26 September 1933; *Obituary Notices of Fellows of the Royal Society*, No. 3, December 1934 (portrait); *Nature*, 4 November 1933; private information; personal knowledge.]   T. CHAUNDY.

RONALD, SIR LANDON (1873–1938), musician, was born in London 7 June 1873, the younger son of Henry Russell [q.v.], well known in contemporary circles as a writer of ballads. From early boyhood Ronald, who was educated at St. Marylebone Grammar School and Margate High School (afterwards Margate College), was clearly marked out for a musical career; his mother directed his first lessons, which were followed by private instruction from Franklin Taylor (piano) and Henry Holmes (violin). At the age of fourteen he entered the Royal College of Music, and studied composition with (Sir) Charles Hubert Parry [q.v.], for whom he retained the utmost veneration.

At the age of seventeen Ronald was chosen to play piano solo in André Alphonse Toussaint Wormser's wordless play *L'Enfant Prodigue* at the Prince of Wales's Theatre (31 March 1891) and on tour. Appointed subsequently as coach and *répétiteur* at Covent Garden Theatre, he met Madame Melba [q.v.], and became her accompanist for a number of years, besides conducting the orchestra for her American tour in 1895. There followed a spell of some discouragement, during which Ronald conducted a succession of theatre bands and many of the smaller orchestras in the provinces. An engagement to direct a series of concerts in Birmingham led to his meeting Max Mossel, an association that proved to be of immense mutual value. Mossel persuaded him to conduct abroad, and this venture became the turning-point in his career. He toured the capitals of Europe in 1908–1909, meeting with success wherever he went, the critics comparing his work favourably with that of the great German conductors. Ronald has been acclaimed a fine exponent of the music of Sir Edward Elgar [q.v.], and it was on this tour that he introduced the A flat symphony to Rome (1909). News of these concerts having reached London, he was invited to conduct the Royal Philharmonic Orchestra in place of Hans Richter who was ill. From that time his reputation was established. In 1909 he was appointed permanent conductor of the Royal Albert Hall Orchestra (founded in 1905 as the New Symphony Orchestra), and there followed 'Harrison' concerts in the North, symphony concerts at the Queen's Hall (March 1909 until 1914), and Sunday afternoon concerts at the Royal Albert Hall (begun in October 1909).

In 1910 Ronald was appointed principal of the Guildhall School of Music, a post which he retained almost up to the time of his death. There he established the curriculum system, and brought the standard of teaching into line with that of the leading schools. He also formed a professors' club in order to bring a more corporate spirit into the building. The combination of this work with such musical commitments as conducting, journalism, and gramophone recording told on his health, and the Albert Hall concerts came to an end after the season of 1918–1919. The conductorship of the Scottish Orchestra was offered to him, and the committee of the Guildhall School of Music granted him leave of absence to undertake it. Ill health constantly handicapped his career, however, and although he conducted at the Albert Hall and the Palladium down to 1927, he had to give up much of his orchestral work from that time onwards.

Ronald's compositions, generally, were of the ballad type, and many of his songs achieved much popularity; but it was by conducting and as principal of the Guildhall School that he made his greatest contribution to music.

Ronald took no academic degrees, but the diplomas of F.R.A.M. (1921), F.G.S.M. (1922), and F.R.C.M. (1924) were conferred upon him, and in 1922 he was knighted in recognition of his services to music. He died in London after a long illness 14 August 1938. He was twice married: first, in 1897 to Mimi (died 1932), daughter of Josef Ettlinger, wholesale cloth merchant, and had a son; secondly, in 1932 to Mary (Mollie), daughter of Richard Dobson Callison.

A portrait of Ronald by John Collier

was presented to the Guildhall School of Music by members of the Corporation of the City of London.

[*Musical Times*, September 1938; Sir L. Ronald, *Variations on the Personal Theme*, 1922, and *Myself and Others*, 1931; *Grove's Dictionary of Music and Musicians*, 4th ed., vol. iv, edited by H. C. Colles.]

EDRIC CUNDELL.

ROPES, ARTHUR REED (1859–1933), lyric writer and librettist under the pseudonym of ADRIAN ROSS, was born at Lewisham 23 December 1859. He was the youngest son of William Hooper Ropes, a Russia merchant, by his wife, Ellen Harriet, daughter of J. Drinkrow Hall, of Scarborough, and was a nephew of John Codman Ropes, the well-known military historian. He was educated at Priory House School, Clapton, Mill Hill School, and the City of London School, and won an exhibition at King's College, Cambridge, where in 1881 he was awarded the chancellor's medal for English verse (for a poem on 'Temple Bar') and the members' prize for English essay. In 1882 he was bracketed eleventh wrangler, and he obtained a first class in the historical tripos and was awarded the Lightfoot scholarship for history and a Whewell scholarship for international law, all in the year 1883. In 1884, as the natural result of this distinguished academic career, he was elected into a fellowship at King's, which he held until 1890, teaching history and applying himself to the affairs of his college.

Ropes began writing verse, serious and comic, while still at school. The first of his works for the stage was the libretto of a vaudeville entertainment, *A Double Event*, written under the name of 'Arthur Reed' in collaboration with Arthur Law, and produced at the St. George's Hall in February 1884. This was followed by a comic opera, with music by F. O. Carr, which, under the title of *Faddimir*, was produced at the Opéra Comique Theatre in April 1889. It was announced as 'by Arthur Reed, music composed by Oscar Neville'. This effort led to a commission to Ropes and Carr from George Edwardes, then manager of the Gaiety Theatre, to write a burlesque on the subject of Joan of Arc, which they did, in collaboration with John Lloyd Shine, the actor. Produced at the Opéra Comique in January 1891, with the author using for the first time his pseudonym of 'Adrian Ross', *Joan of Arc* proved an immediate success

and ran for nearly a year. In 1892 Ropes collaborated with James T. Tanner in the authorship of *In Town*, which was, in many respects, the first of the modern musical comedies. In 1893 he wrote the lyrics for *Morocco Bound*, and it is estimated that from that date he wrote over 2,000 lyrics and had a hand in the production of sixty-odd musical plays. Graceful lyrics and humorous ditties flowed from his facile pen in a continuous stream, and his work contributed, in a great measure, to the success of most of the famous musical comedies of more than three decades, notably *The Circus Girl* (1896); *A Greek Slave* (1898); *San Toy* (1899); *Kitty Grey* (1900); *The Toreador* (1901); *A Country Girl* and *The Girl from Kay's* (1902); *The Orchid* (1903); *The Cingalee* (1904); *The Merveilleuses* (1906); *The Merry Widow* (1907); *The Dollar Princess* and *Our Miss Gibbs* (1909); *The Quaker Girl* (1910); *The Count of Luxembourg* (1911); *Gipsy Love* and *The Dancing Mistress* (1912); *The Marriage Market* (1913); *Betty* (1915); *The Happy Day* (1916); *Airs and Graces*, *Arlette*, and *The Boy* (1917); *Monsieur Beaucaire* (1919); *A Southern Maid* (1920); *Lilac Time* (1922); *The Beloved Vagabond* (1927); and *The Toymaker of Nuremberg* (1930).

Ropes had studied German specially in order to lecture on the life of Frederick the Great, and his knowledge of the language was of immense help to him in adapting the lyrics of *The Merry Widow*, *The Dollar Princess*, *The Count of Luxembourg*, *Lilac Time*, and other German and Viennese operettas. His association with the numerous musical productions of George Edwardes extended over twenty years, until the death of the latter in 1915.

In addition Ropes engaged in journalism, was on the staff of *Ariel* (1891–1892) and contributed to *Punch*, the *Sketch*, the *Sphere*, and the *World*. For some time he contributed 'Bran Pie' to the *Tatler*. He was also an author of repute under his real name. His *Short History of Europe* was published in 1889; he edited a selection of *Lady Mary Wortley Montagu's Letters* (1893); collaborated with Mary Emily Ropes in *On Peter's Island* (1901); wrote *The Hole of the Pit* (1914); compiled an historical manual on Napoleon I; and edited many French texts for the Pitt Press series. In 1914 he was one of the founders of the Performing Right Society and was a vice-president from 1924.

Ropes married in 1901 an actress, Ethel,

youngest daughter of Charles John Wood, a civil engineer, and had a son and two daughters. He died from heart failure, after a somewhat lengthy illness, at his home in Kensington 10 September 1933. In appearance he was a burly, good-tempered-looking man, bearded and bespectacled. He was a brilliant conversationalist with a fund of good stories, and an excellent companion.

[*The Times*, 12 September 1933; *Who's Who in the Theatre*, 1933; personal knowledge.]   JOHN PARKER.

ROSENHAIN, WALTER (1875–1934), metallurgist, was born in Berlin 24 August 1875, the only son of Moritz Rosenhain, business man, of Rosenberg, West Prussia, by his wife, Friederike, daughter of Rabbi Benjamin Yosman Fink, of Posen, whose Hebrew library was made over to the Staatsbibliothek in Berlin. Ernst Lissauer, poet and author of the 'Hymn of Hate', was a second cousin. In order that the boy should not be liable for military service, the family emigrated to Australia when he was five years old. He was educated at Wesley College, Melbourne, and passed into Queen's College in the university of Melbourne, where he graduated with first class honours in physics and engineering in 1897. He had been naturalized in Australia at the age of eighteen.

Rosenhain came to England in 1897 as the holder of an 1851 Exhibition scholarship and entered St. John's College, Cambridge, working with (Sir) Alfred Ewing [q.v.]. In order to study the deformation of metals he learned the technique of preparing metallic specimens for the microscope under Sir William Roberts-Austen [q.v.] at the Royal Mint. Observing that a strip of metal being strained while under the microscope showed dark lines changing in direction from one crystal grain to another, Ewing and Rosenhain correctly interpreted these as due to successive slips, as of cards in a pack, each line representing a step on the surface. By simple and ingenious experiments Rosenhain showed that the slip was a simple motion of translation. The term 'slip bands' has been generally adopted.

On leaving Cambridge in 1900 Rosenhain was appointed a scientific adviser to the glass-works of Messrs. Chance Brothers at Smethwick, near Birmingham, where he produced several papers on optical glass, and in 1908 a text-book on *Glass Manufacture*, which was revised in 1920. He also continued to work on the deformation of metals, making use of the conception of the hardening of deformed metals as due to the formation of a vitreous phase, put forward by Sir G. T. Beilby [q.v.].

In 1906 Rosenhain was invited to succeed (Sir) Harold Carpenter [q.v.] as superintendent of the Metallurgy and Metallurgical Chemistry Department (later the Metallurgical Division) of the National Physical Laboratory. In the twenty-five years during which he held this post he greatly enhanced the reputation of the department as a centre of metallurgical research. A new building was provided, and the staff and equipment were considerably increased.

The systematic investigation of the constitution of metallic alloys, begun under Carpenter, was continued by Rosenhain, special attention being given to the alloys of iron, which, on account of their high melting-point and great reactivity, present special difficulties. This also involved the preparation of several alloying metals in a state of purity not before attained. He showed much ingenuity in devising new instruments of research, including a plotting chronograph for registering thermal changes, and laboratory furnaces for very high temperatures. In studies of dental amalgams he devised methods of polishing, etching, and photographing specimens at very low temperatures. In his theoretical work he adopted an earlier suggestion that at the boundaries between adjacent crystal grains there was a disordered region, usually called the 'amorphous phase', and this hypothesis was ingeniously developed to explain many features of metallic behaviour. After having rendered useful service in furnishing provisional explanations and in suggesting new lines of research the hypothesis has been abandoned in the light of the new information derived from the use of X-rays.

Rosenhain was an inspiring leader of a team of investigators. He had a great gift of clear exposition and showed remarkable skill in controversy. His many papers, and his *Introduction to the Study of Physical Metallurgy*, published in 1914 (3rd ed. 1935), influenced metallurgical research in all countries. He retired in 1931 and went into private practice. A good linguist, he was well known on the continent and in the United States of America. He was elected F.R.S. in 1913, and was awarded the Carnegie silver medal in 1906 and the Bessemer medal of the Iron and Steel Institute in 1930. He was president

of the Institute of Metals (1928–1930) and
delivered the May lecture in 1923.

Rosenhain was naturalized in England
at the beginning of the war in 1914, and
although not a professing Jew he resigned
his honorary membership of several German scientific societies as a protest against
the treatment of Jews in the early years of
Hitler's régime.

Rosenhain married in 1901 Louisa,
daughter of Louis Monash and sister of
Sir John Monash [q.v.]. They had three
daughters, the eldest of whom predeceased
her father. He died at Kingston Hill,
Surrey, after a long illness 17 March 1934.

[*Obituary Notices of Fellows of the Royal
Society*, No. 3, December 1934 (portrait);
Journal of the Institute of Metals, vol. liv,
1939 (portrait); *Journal* of the Iron and Steel
Institutes, vol. cxxx, 1934; *The Times*, 22
March 1934; *Nature*, 5 May 1934; private
information; personal knowledge.]

C. H. DESCH.

ROSS, ADRIAN (pseudonym), lyric
writer and librettist. [See ROPES, ARTHUR
REED.]

ROSS, SIR (EDWARD) DENISON
(1871–1940), orientalist, was born in
Stepney 6 June 1871, the younger son of
Alexander Johnstone Ross, formerly a
minister of the Church of Scotland, who
in 1869 succeeded J. R. Green, the historian, as vicar of St. Philip's church,
Stepney, by his second wife, Adelaide,
daughter of William Collett Sandars, of
Hemel Hempsted, and sister of T. C.
Sandars [q.v.], editor of Justinian.

In 1887 the father, who was then vicar
of Snelston, Derbyshire, died from the
effects of a fall while Ross was still at
Marlborough. Ross was so backward as
to owe his promotion from the bottom
class to its abolition, but he sang in the
choir and picked up some skill in playing
both the flute and the organ. A crammer
pronounced him incapable of passing the
previous examination at Cambridge, so he
attended lectures at University College,
London, on French and English literature
and studied under Arturo Farinelli, soon
to find his Italian more fluent than his
preceptor's English. While studying
oriental languages under Ernest Renan,
Charles Henri Auguste Schefer, Theodor
Nöldeke, and Victor Rosen he quickly
learnt French, German, and Russian, and
at Strasburg he graduated Ph.D., his
thesis being an account of the early years
of Shah Isma'il.

Ross travelled extensively even before
he went to India, but the visit of which he
has left the fullest record is that in 1897
to Bokhara and Samarkand, which had
seldom been entered by an Englishman.

In 1896 Ross was appointed professor
of Persian at University College, London,
the receipts from which, like his father
before him, he supplemented by reviewing. In 1901 Lord Curzon secured his
appointment as principal of the Calcutta
Madrasah, a post which he held until 1911;
in 1906 he became officer in charge of the
records of the government of India and
assistant secretary in the department of
education; but on a visit to Berlin in 1907
he became deeply interested in the work
being done there on the old Turkish manuscripts that Alexander von Le Coq had
excavated in Turfan, and, when there
were added the texts found by (Sir)
Aurel Stein in Tun-huang and elsewhere,
Ross decided to devote himself to Chinese
and Uighur. This brought him to the
British Museum in 1914 as a first assistant
with special charge of the Stein collections,
but the outbreak of war put an end to his
Central Asian studies, for he was called
into the postal censorship where he worked
until in 1916 he was appointed director
of the School of Oriental Studies and professor of Persian in the university of
London; he resigned both posts in 1937.
His influence was shown in the number of
distinguished scholars whom he encouraged and started on their studies.

Save for one visit to Peking in a furlough year (he would gladly have exchanged his years in India for as many in
China) the travels of Ross between the
wars were undertaken as an orientalist
giving lectures in the United States of
America, Persia, Egypt, and Scandinavia.
But he also visited Persia in 1934 for the
millenary of the birth of Firdawsi, and he
was on another occasion the guest of the
Turkish government which desired to
purge Turkish of its accretion of Arabic
and Persian words, a notion which Ross
regarded as somewhat childish. In 1938
he delivered the Lowell lectures at Boston,
Massachusetts, with Mahmud, Tamerlane,
Bayazid, and Babur as some of the subjects. He took a leading part in the organization of the International Exhibition of
Persian Art held at Burlington House in
1931. In 1939 he was sent to Istanbul as
counsellor to the British Embassy to assist
in the development of Anglo-Turkish
commercial relations, and there, after a
short illness, he died 20 September 1940.

When principal of the Madrasah, Ross found in the library an Arabic manuscript which had escaped the notice of all his predecessors during the sixty years or so during which it had lain there. It proved to be 'Zafar ul Wálih bi Muzaffar wa Álih' by 'Abdallah Mohammed bin 'Omar al-Makkí al-Ásafí, known as Al-Makki, the scribe. The work is a draft of an unfinished history of Gujarat, recording also contemporary events elsewhere in India, written in honour of Zafar Khan, appointed to be nawab of Gujarat in A.H. 793, and founder of the Muzaffari dynasty there. On this text Ross laboured for twenty-five years and afterwards compiled an extensive analytical index (the whole being published in three volumes, 1910–1928, in the Indian Text series). In comparison with this labour Ross's other publications are slight, even occasional, but they cover a very wide field. He himself spoke of the Bankipur catalogue of Arabic and Persian manuscripts as his monument in India, but, except for his part in training the cataloguers, his share in the work was comparatively slight. His works include a translation of the *Tarikh-i-Rashidi: A History of the Moghuls of Central Asia* (1895), *The Heart of Asia* (with Francis Henry Bennet Skrine, 1899), a *Polyglot List of Birds in Turki, Manchu and Chinese* (1909), editions of the *diwans* of Babur and Baram Khan (*Journal* of the Royal Asiatic Society of Bengal, 1910), *Sir Anthony Sherley and his Persian Adventure* (1933), and *This English Language* (1939), a study-book for teachers of the language abroad. His autobiography *Both Ends of the Candle* was posthumously published in 1943, after he had worked at it reluctantly and fitfully since 1930 at the instigation of E. V. Lucas [q.v.].

In 1904 Ross married, at Venice, Dora, daughter of William Thomas Robinson, of Hull. She was a brilliant pianist, and, according to a leading London critic, knew more about music than anyone whom he had ever known. The marriage was a very happy one, as she continually added to the number of her own and her husband's friendships while preserving not a few that he might have lost had he been left to himself. She died, childless, in Istanbul, five months before Ross.

Many honours came to Ross: he was appointed C.I.E. in 1912, and was knighted in 1918; he was honorary lecturer in the department of Portuguese studies at King's College, London, a fellow of Cal-

cutta University and of London University, foreign corresponding member of the Hungarian and Portuguese Academies and of the Royal Batavia Society of Arts and Letters; and he received the gold medal of the Royal Asiatic Society in 1935.

There is a portrait of Ross by Frank Beresford, presented in 1937, at the School of Oriental and African Studies. A cartoon by 'Spy' belongs to Mr. A. Denison Ross.

[Sir Denison Ross, *Both Ends of the Candle*, 1943; private information; personal knowledge.]   J. A. CHAPMAN.

ROSS, SIR JOHN, first baronet, of Dunmoyle (1853–1935), last lord chancellor of Ireland, was born at Londonderry 11 December 1853, the eldest son of Robert Ross, minister of the Fourth Presbyterian church, Londonderry, by his wife, Margaret, daughter of Stuart Christie, of Londonderry. Early in the 'sixties he was sent to Foyle College, Londonderry. In 1873 he entered Trinity College, Dublin, where in 1874 he gained a sizarship and in 1876 won the first classical scholarship. He graduated B.A. in 1877 and LL.B. in 1879 when he was called to the Irish bar (King's Inns, Dublin). He took silk in 1891 and became a bencher of the King's Inns in 1893. He was conservative member of parliament for Londonderry City from 1892 until his defeat in 1895, and was appointed land judge in the Chancery division of the High Court of Justice in Ireland in 1896, and in 1921 lord chancellor of Ireland for life. But the office of lord chancellor of Ireland was abolished by statute in December 1922. He was sworn of the Irish Privy Council in 1902 and created a baronet in 1919. In 1882 he married Katherine Mary Jeffcock (died 1932), only daughter of Lieutenant-Colonel Deane Mann, of Dunmoyle and Corvey Lodge, co. Tyrone, and had one son and two daughters, the younger of whom predeceased her father. He died at Dunmoyle 17 August 1935, and was succeeded as second baronet by his son, Ronald Deane (born 1888).

Ross has been fitly described as a lawyer of great ability and learning, whose judgements were marked by much independence of thought. In his time Irish students were obliged to join an English Inn. So it was that, as a member of Gray's Inn, Ross became acquainted with the methods of the great English judges whose decisions it might become his duty to cite. Furthermore, in the course of his immense practice he acquired a great knowledge of the series of complex statutes passed to redress the agrarian grievances of Ireland; and thus it came about that when he was promoted to the bench as land judge he soon attained the eminence attested by the fact that during the twenty-six years of his judicial career the House of Lords never differed from his views, although after he ceased to be lord chancellor it did twice reverse his decisions.

Ross's versatility was astonishing. When an undergraduate he was no mean athlete; always a witty and forceful speaker, in 1877 he was elected president of the university philosophical society and in 1878 auditor of the college historical society, of which latter he was elected president in 1913; in 1914 his many services to his country and to his alma mater brought him the honorary degree of LL.D. of Dublin University, while his interest in the classics received recognition by his election to the presidency of the Classical Society of Ireland in the same year.

Ross was the embodiment of courage, fairness, and good sense; his affectionate loyalty to his friends earned him their sincere devotion, and even his political opponents readily admitted that in temperament he was never other than Irish in the best acceptation of the term.

[*The Times* and *Irish Times*, 19 August 1935; Sir John Ross, *The Years of my Pilgrimage: Random Reminiscences*, 1924, and *Pilgrim Scrip: More Random Reminiscences*, 1927; personal knowledge.]   R. W. Tate.

ROSS, Sir RONALD (1857–1932), discoverer of the mosquito cycle in malaria, was born at Almora, a hill station in the North-Western provinces, 13 May 1857, the eldest child in the family of ten of (General Sir) Campbell Claye Grant Ross, of the Indian Army, by his wife, Matilda Charlotte, eldest daughter of Edward Merrick Elderton, a London lawyer. On both sides his family seems to have been well to do, gifted, and successful, with more than usual intellectual endowments. His father's family, which had had a long connexion with India, was according to his *Memoirs* descended by junior branches from the Rosses of Balnagowan and Shandwick, Ross-shire.

At the age of eight (1865) Ross was sent to England for his education. His first four years in this country were spent at two small schools at Ryde, but on the return of his mother to India after a two years' visit home, he was sent in 1869 to

a boarding-school at Springhill, near Southampton, where he remained until the age of sixteen. His schooldays seem to have been very happy and it is characteristic of Ross's keen intellectual interests throughout life, as he records, that at this time he was deeply interested in zoology and in working out the elementary laws of harmony and experimenting in metre, lyrics, and epics. On leaving school he desired to be an artist, but deferred to his father's wishes and in 1874 became a medical student at St. Bartholomew's Hospital. He obtained the M.R.C.S. in 1879 but failed to pass the L.S.A. and so was unable to practise. As a single qualification sufficed for surgeoncies on board ship, he went for four or five voyages as a ship's surgeon (during which he wrote a Spanish drama 'Isabella' in blank verse and a novel 'The Major'). In 1881 he passed the L.S.A. and entered the Indian Medical Service. He arrived at Bombay in October of that year, and for several years held temporary appointments either attached to various Madras regiments or doing duty at station hospitals. Some six months were spent at Vizianagram, a short time at Pallaveram, both in the Madras Presidency. From September 1882 to August 1884 he was at Madras itself. In September 1884 he brought a detachment of Madras Pioneers from Quetta to Madras, and in January 1885 spent a week in Burma taking a regiment to Thyetmyoo. On two occasions he was with detachments of Indian troops at Port Blair in the Andamans. From May 1885 to May 1886 he was at Moulmein in Burma. Mainly, however, he speaks of Madras during this time and records that the sunlight and the air of India filled him with an extraordinary vigour. Having for the most part plenty of leisure to follow his own pursuits, he studied with characteristic intensity the world's poets and the classics, took up Italian, French, and German, wrote poems, dramas, and novels, and became deeply interested in mathematics, a subject which in later life entered into many of his writings on malaria. In 1888 he left Madras for his first leave in England, and in 1889 he married Rosa Bessie, daughter of Alfred Bradley Bloxam. So far Ross appears as a young officer leading an intensely intellectual, and it might almost be said emotional, life, adopting pursuits as the fancy took him with violent enthusiasm, studying, and writing—above all writing—filled with imagination and imagery and the dramatic sense. Beyond his taking the diploma in public health and studying bacteriology under Edward Emanuel Klein, there is no indication that he had at this time any special feeling for medicine and it was not until five years later that his name figured for the first time in the literature on malaria.

In 1894 Ross again came to England on leave. It was on this second leave to England that he was introduced to (Sir) Patrick Manson [q.v.]. Thenceforth the association of these two famous men was to be one of the great romances of tropical medicine. Ross next year returned to India fired with the ambition to solve the problem of the aetiology of malaria. Two years and four months later, on 20 August 1897, he saw the first significant sign of success that he had so far obtained, namely, the now familiar characteristic pigmented oocysts of the malaria parasite in an unusual kind of mosquito, Ross's 'dapple-winged mosquito', now well known as the anopheles mosquito. It was, however, not until the following year (1898), after he had taken up the study of *Proteosoma*, a parasite in the blood of birds closely resembling the parasite of human malaria, and had found these same pigmented cysts and, later, further stages in the development, that the discovery that malaria is an infectious disease transmitted from man to man by the mosquito was fully and for all time established. On 28 July 1898, when Manson announced Ross's results at the Edinburgh meeting of the British Medical Association, the whole astounding cycle of development had been demonstrated for bird malaria and hence by very obvious probability for malaria of man.

In February 1899 Ross left India on being invited by the Liverpool School of Tropical Medicine to take up the position of lecturer (later, 1902–1912, professor) in tropical medicine at that school: in July he retired from the Indian Medical Service. His mind was now turned almost wholly to the application of his discovery to the eradication of malaria by destruction of the anopheles mosquito. Success was not at first so great as had been anticipated, for although the method was clearly logical enough, difficulties in carrying it out were at first underestimated. Ross, nevertheless, lived to see his methods applied with increasing success all over the world and, as organization and experience increased, universally recognized as the way in which man might eventually rid

himself of this most deadly of all diseases of the tropics.

Ross died at the Ross Institute, Putney, after a long illness 16 September 1932. He was buried beside his wife (died 1931) at Putney Vale cemetery. He had two sons and two daughters. The elder son was reported missing in 1914 and the younger daughter also predeceased her father.

It has always been difficult to assess the relative part in Ross's great discovery that should be ascribed to Manson, upon whose original ideas regarding the transmission of malaria by the mosquito the work of Ross was founded and whose constant stimulus and help Ross always fully acknowledged. Undoubtedly, however, it was Ross who, unaided by any previous researches in this untrodden field, was the actual discoverer of the quite unsuspected mechanism of transmission which once and for all exploded the view, so far universally held, that malaria was contracted from air or water. The cycle in human malaria was not worked out by Ross but by Battista Grassi and his Italian colleagues, a fact that led to a very bitter controversy between Ross and Grassi on the question of priority.

Although in relation to his earlier work in India Ross's later contributions to medical science were less spectacular, further evidence of his originality and genius abound in his later work. He was the first to employ the counting of parasites in the assessment of the intensity of malarial infections, the first to lay the foundations of the study of malarial communities, the first to draw attention to the importance of the 'average enlarged spleen' in malaria studies, the first to employ the 'thick film' technique now universally adopted. Moreover, in the time between his retirement from India and his death he not only carried out many investigations in expeditions (most of which he organized and led) to various malarious countries but added materially to what was known of malarial epidemiology. It was during this latter period of his life that Ross wrote many of his more mature works. These include not only his *Prevention of Malaria* (1910), now a classic, and many other contributions dealing with malaria, but also his *Memoirs* (1923), various mathematical studies (1901–1931), papers on pathometry (1911–1929), plays, dramas, novels, and poems. The *Memoirs* give a very complete and fascinating account of his life, thoughts, and feelings, and the facts relating to his great discovery. That Ross was not a trained observer, indeed very far from this, makes it all the more remarkable that he should, in a subject for which he was seemingly so little equipped, have made one of the greatest discoveries in medicine. Ross's poems (published in a collected edition in 1928) have been highly spoken of, as also his novel *The Child of Ocean* (1889), and, although to some readers it seems rather confused, the sense of stress and storm and the imagery and descriptions of scenery remain even after many years. There can be no doubt that Ross had all the qualities of genius and some of its faults, for in many of his writings he shows a degree of self-centredness in complaints of obstruction in his work, which cannot be taken altogether at their face value by those who know the circumstances.

Within a few years of his discovery honours of every kind were conferred upon Ross by scientific institutions of many countries. In 1901 he was elected a fellow of the Royal Society, which awarded him a Royal medal in 1909: in 1902 he was awarded the Nobel prize for medicine: he was appointed C.B. in 1902 and K.C.M.G. in 1911. He also received honorary degrees from several universities. During 1912 he moved to London and became physician for tropical diseases at King's College Hospital, an appointment which he combined (1912–1917) with the chair of tropical sanitation at Liverpool. From 1913 until his death he was editor of *Science Progress*. During the war of 1914–1918 he was appointed (1917) consultant in malaria to the War Office and later (1925) to the Ministry of Pensions. When in 1926 the Ross Institute and Hospital for Tropical Diseases at Putney Heath was founded in his honour he became its first director-in-chief. In December 1933 the institute was united with the London School of Hygiene and Tropical Medicine.

There is a bronze bust of Ross by Lady Welby at the London School of Hygiene.

[*The Times*, 17 September 1932; *Transactions* of the Royal Society of Tropical Medicine and Hygiene, vol. xxvi, 1932–1933 (portraits); *Obituary Notices of Fellows of the Royal Society*, No. 2, December 1933 (portrait); *Science Progress*, vol. xxvii, 1932–1933 (portraits); Sir Ronald Ross, *Memoirs*, 1923; R. L. Megroz, *Sir Ronald Ross: Discoverer and Creator* (with bibliography), 1931; J. O. Dobson, *Ronald Ross, Dragon Slayer*, 1934.]

S. R. CHRISTOPHERS.

ROTHERMERE, first VISCOUNT (1868–1940), newspaper proprietor. [See HARMSWORTH, HAROLD SIDNEY.]

ROTHSCHILD, SIR LIONEL WALTER, third baronet, and second BARON ROTHSCHILD, of Tring (1868–1937), was born in London 8 February 1868, the elder son of Nathan Meyer Rothschild, first Baron Rothschild [q.v.], by his wife, Emma Louisa, daughter of Baron Karl von Rothschild, of Frankfort-on-Main. Educated at home, owing to delicate health, he studied for a year at Bonn University and then entered Magdalene College, Cambridge, until June 1889.

Following family precedent Rothschild joined the bank of N. M. Rothschild & Sons in order to study finance, under the tutelage of his father. His interests, however, were elsewhere. In early boyhood he had begun to collect and purchase insects, which fascinated him, and unlike most boys had persevered in his hobby. At Cambridge he came under the influence of the renowned ornithologist Alfred Newton [q.v.]; his zoological horizon became much widened and his ambition stimulated, the amateur collector developing into a naturalist who aimed at achieving something noteworthy in zoology. Collections of birds and mammals were acquired, on a corner of his father's estate at Tring a small house was built (1889) for the insects and books, and sheds were requisitioned on the estate for the provisional storage of the other zoological material. A larger building was added, with a display of specimens of all orders of the animal kingdom, and opened as a public museum in 1892. Gradually the museum grew to a considerable size, the aggregate floor-space, inclusive of the basements for storage, covering in 1913 nearly an acre and a half. As his duties in the City left him with too little time for his museum, Ernst Johann O. Hartert, an ornithologist, was put in charge of it in 1892 and in the spring of 1893 Dr. Karl Jordan was engaged as curator of the insect collections. In 1908 Rothschild gave up his work in the City. From 1894 the museum has issued its own periodical, *Novitates Zoologicae*, of which forty-one volumes have appeared, which are largely based on zoological collections received from explorers who had gone out for Rothschild to regions of which the fauna was not, or but little, known; he himself travelled in Europe and North Africa.

In 1898 the university of Giessen conferred upon Rothschild the honorary degree of D.Phil. In 1899 he became a trustee of the British Museum and in 1911 he was elected F.R.S. He was president of Section D (zoology) at the York meeting (1932) of the British Association; and was elected an honorary member by most of the more important societies of entomology and ornithology. His interest in natural history embraced botany as well; he was awarded the Victoria medal of honour in horticulture and was an honorary member of the American Orchid Society. Outside his scientific activities his services and obligations were numerous. From 1899 to 1910 he represented the Aylesbury division of Buckinghamshire in parliament as a conservative; he succeeded to the titles on the death of his father in 1915. He was chairman of the Tring urban district council for many years and president of various societies and institutes. In a codicil to his will he left the museum and all its contents to the British Museum, the greatest accession which that institution has ever received. He died, unmarried, at Tring 27 August 1937, internationally famous for his numerous contributions to our knowledge of mammals, birds, and insects and as the founder and owner of a large zoological museum. He was succeeded as fourth baronet and third baron by his nephew, Nathaniel Mayer Victor Rothschild (born 1910).

A portrait of Rothschild by René de l'Hôpital hangs in the board room of the Manchester Great Synagogue.

[*Obituary Notices of Fellows of the Royal Society*, No. 6, January 1938 (portrait); *Novitates Zoologicae*, vol. xli, 1938 (bibliography and portrait); *Nature*, 2 October 1937; *The Times*, 28 August 1937; personal knowledge.]
KARL JORDAN.

ROYCE, SIR (FREDERICK) HENRY, baronet (1863–1933), engineer, was born at Alwalton, near Peterborough, 27 March 1863, the younger son of James Royce, flour miller, by his wife, Mary, third daughter of Benjamin King, farmer, of Edwin's Hall, Essex. His father's death compelled him to earn his own living at the age of ten, and he was in turn selling newspapers, a post office messenger boy, and at the age of fourteen an apprentice in the Great Northern Railway Company's locomotive works at Peterborough. Being unable to complete his apprenticeship for lack of funds, he found employment in 1881 at Leeds in a tool factory, often working for sixteen hours a day. In 1882

he became a tester with the London Electric Light and Power Company, and advanced his wider education by going to the night classes of the City and Guilds Technical College and at the Polytechnic. So full of promise did he show himself that in the same year the London company appointed him chief electrical engineer for its pioneer scheme for the electric lighting of the streets of Liverpool.

In 1884, at the age of twenty-one, Royce, together with E. A. Claremont, founded the firm of F. H. Royce & company (entitled Royce Limited from 1894 until 1933), manufacturers of arc lamps, dynamos, and electric cranes at Cooke Street, Manchester, and later at Trafford Park; their original capital was only £70. In 1903 he bought his first motor-car, a 10 h.p. Decauville, the noise and untrustworthiness of which (as with other cars of the period) determined him to design and make motor-vehicles himself, and at the end of the year he had his first two-cylinder engines running for many hundreds of hours, coupled to dynamos. Every detail of the car, no matter how small, was designed with the same minute care, with ruthless testing, and even in those early days the slender resources of the company were spent on multifarious experiments, metallurgical research, and heat treatment. So when, on 31 March 1904, the first 10 h.p. two-cylinder Royce car was driven out of the factory at Cooke Street, it at once gave an impression of silence, smoothness, and flexibility and so fired the enthusiasm of C. S. Rolls [q.v.] who had a selling agency (C. S. Rolls & company) in London for continental cars of high repute, that late in 1904 he, with his able partner Claude Johnson, contracted to buy the entire output of cars produced by Royce Limited and to sell them under the name of Rolls-Royce. These two firms were combined in 1906.

Royce had soon perceived that it was a mistake to manufacture a wide range of models. He took as his motto 'Organise and specialise' and concentrated entirely on one car, the 40–50 h.p. 'Silver Ghost', the first of which was completed by the end of 1906. This type remained in production, with numerous improvements of detail, until 1925, when it gave place to 'Phantoms' and 'Wraiths'. The qualities of the 'Silver Ghost' so much increased the demand for it that in 1908 the motor section of the firm was separated from Cooke Street and transferred to Derby.

Royce was now at the height of his powers, but habitual overwork and lack of interest in his meals led to a breakdown in 1911 from which he was not expected to recover. Recovery was indeed only partial, but although he was never able to return to the factory, he continued to control the main designs, keeping in close contact with experiments and other activities for another twenty years. In motor-car design the original features of his work are the silent cam form of the valve-gear, the friction-damped slipper flywheel and spring drive for the timing gears, his battery ignition, the Royce expanding carburettor, and the wear-proof steering.

Royce, however, did not confine himself to designing motor-cars. Although Rolls had often pressed him to design an aero engine, he took no practical interest in the matter until the outbreak of war in 1914, when, after investigating various types of air-cooled engines at the request of the government, he at length characteristically made up his mind not to deviate from liquid cooling; so, starting from a 12-cylinder V, he produced the 'Eagle' early in 1915, which played an important part in the war, and was followed by the 'Falcon', the 'Hawk', and the 'Condor'. It was mainly his determination that led the Rolls-Royce Company to enter for the Schneider cup competitions, in which they won the trophy in 1929 and in 1931, setting up the world speed record at 408 m.p.h. Shortly before his death, Royce laid down the prototype designs of the 'Merlin' engine, making use of the experience gained in the Atlantic flight of 1919 and the Schneider cup competitions. True to his principles he here again stood firm in his decision to adhere to a 12-cylinder V engine, and that this type of engine persisted all through the war of 1939–1945 with extensive use on all types of aircraft is a standing witness to the correctness of Royce's policy.

For his services to engineering and the country, Royce was appointed O.B.E. in 1918 and created a baronet in 1930. There was no issue of his marriage, which took place in 1893, with Minnie Grace (died 1936), third daughter of Alfred Punt, of London. He died at West Wittering, near Chichester, 22 April 1933.

At the time of the Schneider cup competition it was said of him that 'Mr. Royce is not a man who prides himself upon inventing things. He likes to perfect things already in existence.' Apart from his genius as an engineer, Royce's most marked characteristic was an extraordinary modesty. In appearance he resembled a farmer, and his chief recreation was the cultivation of roses and fruit-trees. His remarkable memory he attributed to his night-school education, which 'made it imperative that I should never forget anything worth remembering, and I have never outgrown that habit'.

A life-size bronze statue of Royce by F. Derwent Wood was erected in the Arboretum at Derby in 1923. A bust by William McMillan is in the main offices of Rolls-Royce Limited at Derby. A cartoon by 'Spy' appeared in Mayfair, January 1919.

[The Times, 24 April 1933; Sir Max Pemberton, The Life of Sir Henry Royce, 1935; G. Geoffrey Smith, Frederick Henry Royce (British Council 'Science in Britain' series), 1945; Harold Nockolds, The Magic of a Name, 1938; H. Massac Buist, Rolls-Royce Memories (privately printed), 1926; Engineering and Engineer, 28 April 1933 (portraits); private information; personal knowledge.]

N. R. CHANDLER.

RUDOLF, EDWARD DE MONTJOIE (1852–1933), philanthropist, was born in Lambeth 11 April 1852, the second son of Major William Edward Rudolf, by his second wife, Susan Amy Goodin. He was educated mainly at home, as the failing sight of his father obliged him from a very early age to act as his amanuensis in translation work. Owing to the straitened circumstances of the family Rudolf began work as an office-boy in his thirteenth year. He managed to continue his education, denying himself even meals to buy books, and in 1871 gained entrance to the Office of Works at the first open examination. He became official private secretary to the first commissioner, G. J. Shaw-Lefevre (afterwards Lord Eversley, q.v.) and to his successor, Lord Rosebery.

Rudolf devoted all his spare time to work among young people in South London, and in 1872 became superintendent of the Sunday school at St. Anne's church, South Lambeth. Here his experience convinced him of the pressing need within the organization of the Church of England for a central home to which homeless children could be sent with no conditions save that of destitution, and then to be boarded out with families and thus kept from institutionalism. Rudolf's enthusiasm was infectious, and in March 1881 a meeting was held in the library of

Mark Hanbury Beaufoy, afterwards member of parliament for Kennington. Rudolf was resolute that the society should be regarded as an integral part of the Church's organization, and accordingly a deputation waited upon the archbishop of Canterbury (A. C. Tait, q.v.), who, after inquiry, showed his approval by becoming president in August. His chaplain, Randall Davidson [q.v.], remembered Tait saying, 'If the thing is to be done this man Rudolf is the man to do it. I have never heard a plan more admirably urged.' So came into being the Church of England Waifs and Strays Society (now the Church of England Children's Society), which by the time of the founder's death had provided homes for 37,000 children.

By the end of the first year there were two homes, containing thirty-four children. From the first Rudolf insisted on the children having as normal a life as possible. When they were not boarded out they were to be housed in small homes, not segregated or distinguished by any uniform. He was heartily in favour of emigration under proper supervision, and the first little party left for Canada in 1883. Later on the society opened two homes in Canada, and Rudolf made a number of visits, and spoke of himself as 'an Englishman who loves Canada'.

Rudolf acted as honorary secretary, but the work grew so rapidly that in 1890 the executive committee asked him to give his full time to it. He showed himself a remarkably able administrator, but, busy as he was, Rudolf never allowed organization to obscure his personal contact with the children. Whenever he visited a home, he always tried to get an hour with the children, and entered naturally into their games. Moreover, he did his best to keep in touch with the old boys and girls, and to make them feel that in him they still had a friend long after they had left the homes. He was strongly in favour of registration and inspection of all voluntary institutions for children. At the International Conference for the Welfare and Protection of Children held in London in 1902 he spoke in favour of this, adding that 'it might become a stepping-stone to the greatest advantage of all—the establishment of a State Children's Department'. Considerations of health led to his resignation of the secretaryship in 1919, but as founder he remained a keen member of all committees.

Rudolf's activities were not confined to the Waifs and Strays Society. He took part with Benjamin Waugh [q.v.] in the founding in 1884 of the National Society for the Prevention of Cruelty to Children, and gave evidence in support of the daylight saving bill. But his main interest, apart from children, was the League of Nations Union, and he was a member of both the executive and finance committees. He had himself in 1915 started a movement in favour of the establishment after the war of an international tribunal with power to enforce its decisions.

Since his early youth Rudolf had hoped to be ordained, and he was ordained deacon in 1898, but it was not until 1907 that he was ordained priest; in 1911 he became a prebendary of St. Paul's Cathedral. He was appointed C.B.E. in 1931 and in the same year the honorary degree of M.A. was conferred upon him by Oxford University.

Rudolf married in 1881 Emma Bulmer (died 1929), and had four sons, two of whom predeceased their father, and three daughters. He died at Eastbourne 29 May 1933, and by his own wish his body was cremated and the ashes buried in his wife's grave in Ocklynge cemetery.

Of his work, Archbishop Lord Lang of Lambeth wrote that it 'was the more remarkable because he had no conspicuous gifts of intellect and speech and not much of that strange magnetic quality that sometimes draws people into allegiance to some particular individuality. He had great and remarkable organizing ability, but his work was done mainly through the great qualities of a single-hearted and disinterested devotion to the children and to the Church of which he was a devoted son. . . .'

[*The Times*, 30 May 1933; [E. de M. Rudolf], *The First Forty Years, A Chronicle of the Church of England Waifs and Strays Society 1881–1920*, 1922 (portraits); C. H. Dant, *Distinguished Churchmen*, 1902; *Our Waifs and Strays*, June 1936; private information; personal knowledge.]

C. DE M. RUDOLF.

RUGGLES-BRISE, SIR EVELYN JOHN (1857–1935), prison reformer, was born at Spains Hall, Finchingfield, Essex, 6 December 1857, the second son in a family of five sons and seven daughters of Sir Samuel Brise Ruggles-Brise, of Spains Hall, who was member of parliament for East Essex from 1868 to 1884, by his wife, Marianne Weyland, fourth daughter of Sir Edward Bowyer-Smijth, tenth baronet, of Hill Hall, Essex. After being educated at Eton and at Balliol College, Oxford, where he was awarded a first class in *literae humaniores* in 1880, he gained the sixth place in the competitive examination for entrance to the administrative grade of the home civil service, and was appointed to the Home Office in 1881. From 1884 to 1892 he served as private secretary to four successive home secretaries, and was then appointed a prison commissioner. In 1895 he was promoted to be chairman of the Prison Commission, the administrative body which assists the home secretary to manage the prisons of England and Wales, and he held this position until he retired in 1921.

Just before Ruggles-Brise's appointment in 1895 a committee, of which Herbert (later Viscount) Gladstone [q.v.] was chairman, had issued a report recommending a number of changes in the prison system. To the task of bringing these changes into operation Ruggles-Brise devoted himself with the enthusiasm of a reformer and the wisdom of a practical administrator.

Power to make changes in the prison system was obtained by a provision in the Prison Act of 1898 that the mode in which sentences of penal servitude or imprisonment are to be carried out may be regulated by rules which are made by the secretary of state and become statutory unless they are disapproved by parliament. Use was made of this new power to abolish the old forms of 'hard labour' prescribed by the Prison Act of 1865, such as the tread-wheel and crank, and to modify the requirement in that Act that every criminal prisoner should either be kept in a separate cell by day as well as by night or 'subjected to such superintendence during the day as will . . . prevent his communicating with any other prisoner'. The rules of 1899 provided that 'the labour of all prisoners shall, if possible, be productive, and the trades and industries taught and carried on shall, if practicable, be such as will fit the prisoner to earn his livelihood on release'. Workshops were constructed and prisoners were not employed singly except during the early weeks of a hard-labour sentence. Thus the rigours of separate confinement were mitigated, and labour was treated not as an instrument of punishment but as a stimulus to effort, interest, and application. Reforms were also made in the classification of prisoners, in the treatment of the mentally defective and unstable, in the medical care of prisoners, in the de-velopment of prisoners' aid societies, and in the training of the prison staffs. One of the rules of 1899 laid down: 'It is the duty of all officers to treat prisoners with kindness and humanity. . . . The great object of reclaiming the criminal should always be kept in view by all officers, and they should strive to acquire a moral influence over the prisoners by performing their duties conscientiously, but without harshness.'

A recommendation of the Gladstone committee that 'a new form of sentence should be placed at the disposal of the judges, by which habitual criminals might be segregated for long periods of detention during which they would not be treated with the severity of first-class hard labour or penal servitude, but would be forced to work under less onerous conditions' was implemented by a provision in the Prevention of Crime Act (1908), authorizing sentences of 'preventive detention'. Comparatively little use has been made by the courts of this type of sentence, but the arrangements made by Ruggles-Brise for the treatment of prisoners so sentenced had beneficial effects on the prison system. The construction at Camp Hill in the Isle of Wight of an establishment intended for this class of prisoner set a new standard of prison accommodation, and experience of the rules framed for the purpose of subjecting these prisoners to 'less onerous conditions' showed that to confer privileges which are liable to be lost by misconduct is a more effective method of maintaining discipline than a harshly punitive régime.

Ruggles-Brise felt strongly that the prison system ought not to be applied to young offenders between the ages of sixteen and twenty-one. In 1897 he went to the United States of America in order to study the working of the state reformatories, and on his return began to devise special treatment for the young prisoners in the London prisons. A small society of voluntary workers (which later developed into the Borstal Association) was formed to visit these lads, to make arrangements for their employment on discharge, and to help and befriend them. In 1901 these young prisoners were collected together in the old convict prison at Borstal, near Rochester, and their treatment was regulated by new rules designed to effect rehabilitation by good disciplinary methods, hard work, and inducements to good conduct by a system of grades and rewards. Experience, however, showed that the sentences passed on these young offenders were generally too short to give sufficient time for their training, and in 1906 Ruggles-Brise made a strong representation to the secretary of state about the need for an alteration of the law. In 1908 the Prevention of Crime Act, which authorized sentences of Borstal detention for not more than three years, gave statutory effect to the principles that the object should be to subject the young offender to 'such instruction and discipline as appears most conducive to his reformation', that the length of his sentence should be related not merely to the facts of the particular crime of which he happened to be convicted but to his need of training, that the actual period of detention should, subject to the limits of the Borstal sentence, depend on his response to the training and instruction given to him, and that on his release on licence he should be subject to supervision and liable to recall should he misbehave. On the gateway of Borstal is an inscription in honour of Ruggles-Brise which says: 'He determined to save the young and careless from a wasted life of crime. Through his vision and persistence a system of repression has been gradually replaced by one of leading and training. We shall remember him as one who believed in his fellow men.'

Ruggles-Brise's influence extended to other countries. He was an active member of the International Prison Commission, of which he became chairman in 1910. In 1924 he published *Prison Reform at Home and Abroad*.

Ruggles-Brise was appointed C.B. in 1899 and K.C.B. in 1902. He was twice married: first, in 1914 to Jessie Philippa (died 1928), daughter of Robert Russell Carew, of Carpenders Park, Watford, and widow of Francis Robert Stonor, fourth Lord Camoys; secondly, in 1933 to Sheelah Maud Emily, daughter of Captain Francis Algernon James Chichester, and widow of Essex Edgeworth Reade. He died at Peaslake, Surrey, 18 August 1935.

A portrait of Ruggles-Brise by John Collier, which was presented to him in 1921, is in the possession of his widow at Ramsbury, Wiltshire. A cartoon of him by 'Spy' appeared in *Vanity Fair* 10 February 1910.

[Shane Leslie, *Sir Evelyn Ruggles-Brise. A Memoir of the Founder of Borstal*, 1938; Sir E. Ruggles-Brise, *The English Prison System*, 1921; *Annual Reports* of the prison commissioners; *Annual Volumes of Statutory Rules and Orders*, 1899.]   A. MAXWELL.

RUNCIMAN, WALTER, first BARON RUNCIMAN, of Shoreston (1847–1937), shipowner, was born at Dunbar 6 July 1847, the fourth son of Walter Runciman, master of a schooner, and later of the coastguard service, by his wife, Jean, eldest daughter of John Finlay, shipowner, of Dunbar. He was elder brother of James Runciman [q.v.]. In 1853 the family moved to the coastguard station at Cresswell, Northumberland, to which the father had been appointed. In 1859 young Walter ran away from home to seek a career at sea.

Runciman was bound apprentice for six years in the brig *Harperley*, 450 tons, which sailed with coal from the Tyne to Mozambique. After a few voyages he broke his indentures and tramped from Troon to the Tyne and there joined the brig *Maid of Athens*. He later served in four sailing ships, attended a nautical school in 1867, and obtained a mate's certificate. After further sea service he gained a master mariner's certificate in 1871. In 1873 he was appointed master of the barque *F. E. Althausse*, a command which he held for four years. In 1877 he transferred from sail to steam in order to become master of the steamer *Coanwood*, 1,650 tons, which he commanded for eight and a half years.

In 1884, having then sailed the seas for twenty-five years, Runciman was urged by his medical adviser to live ashore, and he began business as a shipowner at South Shields in 1885, when shipping was in a very depressed state. His first purchase was the steamer *Dudley*, 1,200 tons, which had been laid up in the Tyne for three and a half years. His training in both sail and steam proved of great value to him when he entered the shipowning business. The *Dudley* did well for him and with the flowing tide of better trade he bought at various times eleven other second-hand steamers. In 1889 he had built at South Shields his first new steamer, the *Blakemoor*, which was the foundation of the Moor Line, Ltd., the head office of which was in due course removed from South Shields to Newcastle. By 1895 the Moor Line owned twenty-five steamers and by 1914 the number had risen to about forty. After the war of 1914–1918 the Moor Line was wound up, and reserves and invested assets were distributed among the shareholders. From 1919 to 1921 the Runciman Company had no vessels, but a new Moor Line was started and by 1924 a fleet of twenty-three steamers was in service.

Runciman was senior partner in the firm of Walter Runciman & company; chairman and managing director of the Moor Line, and chairman of the Anchor Line, in which he acquired a controlling interest in 1935. He was president of the Chamber of Shipping of the United Kingdom in 1910–1911, and in 1932, on the death of James Lyle Mackay, Earl of Inchcape [q.v.], he succeeded to the presidency of the Shipping Federation until his death. This body had been formed in 1890 to combat the activities of the Seamen's and Firemen's Union under their secretary Joseph Havelock Wilson [q.v.], whose courage Runciman admired and towards whom he was sympathetically disposed.

In middle life Runciman was a strong liberal of independent attitude. For twenty-two years he was chairman of the Northern Liberal Federation Executive, and was sometime president of the Northern Liberal Federation. He represented the Hartlepools division in parliament from 1914 to 1918; but in 1931 he declared that 'free trade had outlived its usefulness' and favoured tariff reform.

Runciman was a keen yachtsman. His first yacht of note was the *Sunbeam*, bought in 1922, famous throughout the world for the voyages of her former owner, Thomas, Lord Brassey [q.v.]. She was succeeded by *Sunbeam II*, an auxiliary three-masted schooner built for Runciman and launched in 1929. He was a member of several yacht clubs and commodore of the Royal Northumbrian Yacht Club. When in his ninetieth year he intimated to the Admiralty that he would like to join the Royal Naval Volunteer Supplementary Reserve, and was appointed honorary commodore to date from 1 February 1937.

Early in the twentieth century Runciman bought Doxford, a beautiful estate in Northumberland. A subsequent purchase was Shoreston, also in Northumberland. He married in 1869 Ann Margaret (died 1933), daughter of John Lawson, of Cresswell, Northumberland. He was created a baronet in 1906 and was raised in 1933 to the peerage as Baron Runciman, of Shoreston. He died at Newcastle-upon-Tyne 13 August 1937. His only child, Walter, having been raised to the peerage as Viscount Runciman, of Doxford, in the previous June, the barony of Shoreston became merged in the viscountcy.

Runciman was respected throughout the shipping industry for his independence of thought, his geniality, and his kindliness. In addition to his autobiography *Before the Mast and After* (1924), he wrote several books on the sea. An ardent Methodist, of old Methodist stock, he spoke in many Methodist pulpits in Northumberland.

[*The Times*, 14 August 1937; Sir Walter Runciman, *Before the Mast and After*, 1924; personal knowledge.]   A. E. JOHNSTONE.

RUNDLE, SIR (HENRY MACLEOD) LESLIE (1856–1934), general, was born at Newton Abbot, Devon, 6 January 1856, the second son of Captain Joseph Sparkehall Rundle, R.N., by his wife, Renira Catherine, daughter of Commander Walter Wemyss Leslie, R.N. On leaving the Royal Military Academy, Woolwich, he was gazetted to the Royal Artillery in 1876. He first saw active service in 1879, taking part in the Zulu war at the battle of Ulundi (4 July), and being mentioned in dispatches. Two years later (1881), he took part in the Boer war and was wounded at Potchesfstroom.

Rundle's high military reputation rests mainly upon his services in Egypt and the Sudan. In 1882 he was present at the battle of Tel-el-Kebir, and received the medal with clasp and the bronze star. In 1883 he joined the Egyptian army, serving in it for fifteen years. He then served under (Lord) Kitchener with the Nile expedition (1884–1885), where he was engaged in guarding the Nubian Desert with a force of Ababdeh Arabs. For his services he was mentioned in dispatches and received promotion to captain and brevet-major in 1885. It was during this time that he formed a lasting friendship with Kitchener. In the same year he was posted to the Sudan Frontier Field Force (1885–1887), and while with that formation he was awarded the D.S.O. (1887) and the Osmanieh medal (3rd class). In 1889, on the Sudan frontier, he commanded the artillery at the decisive engagement at Toski, was mentioned in dispatches, promoted to brevet-lieutenant-colonel, and awarded the Medjidie medal (2nd class). In 1891, as assistant adjutant-general, he was engaged in the operations which resulted in the re-capture of Tokar, and the next year became adjutant-general in the Egyptian army, and spent nearly five years at Cairo, receiving his brevet-colonelcy in 1894. With the Dongola Expeditionary Force, as Kitchener's chief of staff, in 1896 he was present at the engagements of Firket and Hafir and was promoted major-general (supernumerary) in November 1896 and the same year was appointed C.M.G. After the battle of Omdurman (2 September 1898) he took Kitchener's place during his absence at Fashoda and led a column up the Blue Nile to relieve Gedaref, and for these services was appointed K.C.B. and received two medals and the special thanks of parliament in 1898. In this year he returned home to command the South-Eastern District (1898–1899) and the following year (1899–1900) became deputy adjutant-general to the forces, at the War Office. In 1900 he was given command of a division at Aldershot, but in March of that year was ordered to South Africa, where he served under Lord Roberts, in command of the 8th division of the South African Field Force (1900–1902). During this campaign he conducted the Dewetsdorp operations and commanded at the battles of Biddulphsberg and Wittebergen, and later fought with Lieutenant-General Sir Archibald Hunter [q.v.] in the Brandwater Basin, where he was slightly wounded. In 1900 he was appointed K.C.M.G. and for his services in the campaign gained the Queen's medal with three clasps and the King's medal with two clasps.

In 1902 Rundle returned again to England and assumed command of the 5th division, II Army Corps. In November 1903 he was appointed major-general in command of the North-Eastern District and acting general officer commanding-in-chief Northern Command until April 1905, when he was promoted lieutenant-general and general officer commanding-in-chief (2nd class). On relinquishing the Northern Command in November 1907, he remained unemployed until in July 1909 he was made governor and commander-in-chief of Malta, being promoted general in September of the same year. In 1911 he was appointed G.C.B., in 1912 G.C.V.O., and in 1914 G.C.M.G. He remained at Malta until February 1915, when he returned to England and succeeded Sir Ian Hamilton as commander-in-chief, Central Force, which comprised ten divisions and mounted territorials organized for home defence. He relinquished this post in May 1916 and became once more unemployed until his retirement from the army in May 1919. He was honorary colonel, 3rd battalion, the Buffs, from 1899 to 1907, and colonel commandant, Royal Artillery, in 1907.

Rundle married in 1887 Eleanor Georgina, eldest daughter of Captain Henry Jermyn Montgomery Campbell,

R.A., of Thurmaston Hall, Leicestershire. There was no issue of the marriage.

Rundle was an active man of smart appearance, possessed of remarkable keenness and efficiency, and during his long military career earned a reputation for thoroughness and caution. He never took a risk, and was rewarded by never meeting with a reverse. He was outwardly somewhat frigid and unapproachable, except to children, but known for his scrupulous fairness and justice, qualities essential in a good soldier. He died in London 19 November 1934.

[*The Times*, 20 November 1934; Sir J. F. Maurice and M. H. Grant, (Official) *History of the War in South Africa 1899–1902*, 1906–1910; private information.]   C. V. Owen.

RUSSELL, ARTHUR OLIVER VILLIERS, second Baron Ampthill (1869–1935), was born at the Palazzo Chigi in Rome 19 February 1869, the second son of Lord Odo William Leopold Russell, afterwards first Baron Ampthill [q.v.], by his wife, Lady Emily Theresa, third daughter of George William Frederick Villiers, fourth Earl of Clarendon [q.v.]. He succeeded his father in 1884. He was educated at Eton and New College, Oxford, where he continued the distinguished rowing career which he had had at Eton by rowing in the winning university eights of 1890 and 1891, in the winning Leander eight for the Grand Challenge Cup at Henley in 1891, and, with Guy Nickalls [q.v.], winning the Silver Goblets at Henley in 1890 and 1891. In 1891, the year in which he was awarded honours in modern history, he was president both of the Oxford University Boat Club and of the Oxford Union Society.

In 1895 Joseph Chamberlain [q.v.] selected Ampthill as his assistant-secretary at the Colonial Office, and in 1897 as his private secretary. In 1900 Ampthill succeeded Sir A. E. Havelock [q.v.] as governor of Madras, being appointed G.C.I.E. Lord Curzon, then viceroy, said that in matters of administration Ampthill had an old head on young shoulders, and when Curzon was absent in England in 1904 Ampthill was appointed acting viceroy and G.C.S.I. After returning to Madras for a few weeks in 1906 he came to England to represent the interests of the Indian settlers in East and South Africa, and afterwards did good service for Indian students in Great Britain as chairman of the advisory committee set up by (Lord) Morley on their behalf. Lack of sympathy with the reform proposals put forward by the liberal government prevented his return to India as viceroy, but he did valuable service at home in the organization of the Territorial army. During the war of 1914–1918 he went on active service in France, commanding a battalion of the Leicestershire Regiment and later two battalions of the Bedfordshire Regiment. For a year (1917–1918) he was Indian labour corps adviser at general headquarters on the western front. For these services he was thrice mentioned in dispatches, and was promoted brevet-colonel in 1919.

When in 1919 the government introduced the India bill giving authority to the Montagu–Chelmsford reforms, Ampthill was one of the few members of either House of Parliament who spoke and voted against the bill. On the second reading he reproached the Lords for the scant support which he had received in pressing the claims of Indians to be treated as British subjects throughout the Empire, and claimed that in India his views on reform were much in advance of those underlying the Morley–Minto proposals. He also strenuously opposed the government of India bill of 1935.

Ampthill was a prominent freemason from his undergraduate days, and in 1908 he was appointed by the Duke of Connaught to be pro-grand master of English freemasonry. This office he held until his death, which took place in London from pneumonia 7 July 1935. He married in 1894 Lady Margaret, third daughter of Frederick Lygon, sixth Earl Beauchamp [q.v.]. He had four sons and a daughter, and he was succeeded as third baron by his eldest son, John Hugo (born 1896).

A portrait of Ampthill by Sir A. S. Cope was presented to him by the Grand Lodge in 1933, and hangs in Freemasons' Hall. There is a copy by Dorofield Hardy in private possession.

[The Times, 8 July 1935.]

E. I. Carlyle.

RUSSELL, GEORGE WILLIAM (1867–1935), better known by his pseudonym 'AE' (AEon), Irish poet, painter, economist, and journalist, was born at Lurgan, co. Armagh, 10 April 1867, the youngest of the three children, two sons and a daughter, of Thomas Elias Russell, by his wife, Mary Anne Armstrong. The father was book-keeper in a firm of cambric manufacturers at Lurgan, and attended both the parish church and the Primitive Methodist chapel. When George was about ten years old the family moved to Dublin, where, at the age of fifteen, he became a pupil at Rathmines School, of which he used to say that it had 'at least produced two heretics', George Tyrrell [q.v.], an earlier pupil, and himself. A rather incongruous episode in his early life some time after he left school in 1884 was his employment in the Phoenix brewery in Dublin. He had begun attendance as a student at the Metropolitan School of Art before he was turned thirteen, and there, about 1886, began his memorable friendship with W. B. Yeats [q.v.], through whom he became acquainted with theosophy. Theosophy supplied him, a natural mystic, with a framework for his instinctive beliefs, and joining its inner circle, he renounced his ambition to become a painter: a very important event in his life, for his distinctive gift was painting. A good judge has asserted that 'had he painted day in and day out there can be no doubt that he would have taken rank as one of the most noteworthy painters of his age'. His natural vocation was thenceforth his main relaxation.

Having given up the brewery, 'as my ethical sense was outraged', Russell gained his living for some six years from 1890 as a clerk in Pim's drapery business in Dublin. His verses had interested Yeats and others, and in 1894 his friend Charles Weekes persuaded him to allow the publication (under the pseudonym of 'AE') of a little volume, Homeward: Songs by the Way. It attracted wide attention, and AE was thenceforth a leading figure in the new Irish literary movement. In 1897 came a great change in his life, when, with Yeats as intermediary, he joined the Irish Agricultural Organization Society, which had been founded some three years earlier. Normal life now claimed him more and more, and in 1898 he married a fellow theosophist of English parentage, Violet, daughter of Archibald North, and had two sons. His powers as a writer soon became invaluable to the Irish Agricultural Organization Society, and he made of its organ, the Irish Homestead—of which he remained editor from 1906 until its amalgamation with the Irish Statesman in 1923—a unique journal, read at least as much by British and American intellectuals as by Irish farmers. His interest in economics overflowed in various writings, of which the most notable are Co-operation and Nationality (1912) and The National Being (1916). His great conversational gifts and radiant presence attracted many visitors, and few of the distinguished people who came to study Ireland's problems thought their errand accomplished until they had had a talk with AE.

He came into much prominence during the labour disputes in Dublin in 1913, and, 'doing violence unto himself', was one of the principal speakers at a great meeting held in London at the Albert Hall on 1 November to protest against the obstinacy of the employers and the arrest of James Larkin for sedition. His belief in the economic interdependence of England and Ireland kept him aloof from the Sinn Fein rising of Easter 1916, but of those who served in the convention which was set up in 1917 he was by all accounts one of the most practical in his recommendations, although he greatly disappointed Plunkett, who was chairman, by his sudden withdrawal. He claimed in later life to have had some share in expediting the settlement of December 1921 by suggesting, in an interview with Lord Northcliffe, that the latter should give 'dominion home rule' the support of his newspapers. From 1923 to 1930 he edited the *Irish Statesman* which he strove to make the organ of reasonable opinion in the Irish Free State. In order to raise funds for its continuance he paid in 1928 the first of several visits to the United States, where he responded buoyantly to American hospitality, talked with the President and most of those prominent in politics, literature, and science, and discovered a faculty for addressing large audiences which pleased and surprised himself. In that year Yale conferred upon him the honorary degree of Litt.D., an example followed by Dublin University in 1929. Life in a self-governing and of course mainly Catholic Ireland brought some disillusionment; the censorship in particular drew his vigorous protests; and after his wife's death in 1932 he lived mostly in London. During a last lecturing tour in the United States his health broke down, and he died at Bournemouth 17 July 1935.

AE looked consistently to the antiquity of all races for the oracles of a universal wisdom-religion, and in Irish mythology he sought for hints of an ancestral lore identical with that of the sages of the East. These beliefs were called in Ireland, somewhat irreverently, 'AEtheism', but were not without influence on the idealism of Sinn Fein. His religious philosophy is expounded most fully in *The Candle of Vision* (1918), and his political idealism in two fictional fantasies, *The Interpreters* (1922) and *The Avatars* (1933). *Song and its Fountains* (1932), a prose commentary on his poems, is written in a tone of wondering confidence in his gift; for it was as a poet that AE wished to be remembered. His poems are not for everyone, and it has been truly said that there is nothing quite like them in English poetry; in them the reader listens to one who remembers past lives, exults rather eerily in cosmic happenings, and, more consolingly, in the divinity of man. To many they have brought comfort and encouragement. Perhaps his best-known poem, 'On behalf of some Irishmen not followers of tradition', is also, objectively, his best. *The House of the Titans and other poems* (1934) includes a curious poem, 'The Dark Lady'. His *Collected Poems* were published in 1913 (2nd ed. 1926).

In person Russell was a large, bearded man, and was the subject of many portraits. These include paintings in oils by Sarah Purser (c. 1902) formerly in the artist's possession; John Butler Yeats (1903) formerly in the John Quinn collection, New York; and Dermod O'Brien (c. 1914) at the Abbey Theatre, Dublin. There are two drawings by Sir William Rothenstein, of which the first (1914) is published in *Twenty-four Portraits*, first series (1920), and the second (1921) was formerly in the artist's possession; also busts, by John Hughes (1885–1886) in the Municipal Gallery of Modern Art, Dublin; Oliver Sheppard (1916) in the National Gallery of Ireland; Jerome Connor (c. 1930), and others.

[John Eglinton (W. K. Magee), *A Memoir of AE George William Russell* (containing lists of his writings and of his portraits), 1937; Monk Gibbon, *The Living Torch* (containing selections from AE's journalistic work), 1937; George Moore, *Hail and Farewell*, 1911–1914; E. A. Boyd, *Ireland's Literary Renaissance*, 1916; personal knowledge.]

W. K. MAGEE.

RUSSELL, HERBRAND ARTHUR, eleventh DUKE OF BEDFORD (1858–1940), was born in London 19 February 1858, the younger son of Francis Charles Hastings Russell, ninth Duke of Bedford [q.v.], by his wife, Lady Elizabeth, eldest daughter of George John Sackville-West, fifth Earl De La Warr. He was educated at home and at Balliol College, Oxford. In 1879 he joined the Grenadier Guards and served in the Egyptian campaign of 1882. He was, at Tel-el-Kebir, the last officer to carry the colours of his regiment into battle. From 1884 to 1888 he was aide-de-camp to the viceroy of India, Frederick Temple Hamilton-Temple Blackwood, first Marquess of Dufferin and Ava [q.v.]. In 1893 he succeeded his elder brother as Duke of Bedford. Seven years later he was called upon to make a decision which set the key-note for his subsequent career. In October 1900 Lord Salisbury, reconstructing his Cabinet after the general election, submitted to the Queen the name of the duke for the office of under-secretary of state for war. In his memorandum Lord Salisbury spoke highly of the duke's practical and military abilities, but in refusing this, and at least one subsequent offer of office (a colonial appointment) the duke was acting upon a conviction already reached, and one which grew stronger with years, that personal management of his estates and a political career could not be combined.

The Duke of Bedford was undoubtedly influenced by his almost passionate feeling for the lands which he held, and for the countryside in general. He was, as he himself recognized, no townsman, despite his important London properties; and although he was proud of his office of lord lieutenant of Middlesex (1898–1926), and of being chosen in 1900 as first mayor of Holborn, neither appointment gave him the same degree of pleasure and the same opportunities as did his chairmanship (1895–1928) of the Bedfordshire county council. All this was typical enough of a well-known English type, but the duke was a countryman who was also profoundly interested in science. This early interest had been much stimulated by the kindness shown him as a boy by F. T. Buckland [q.v.] and even more by his visits to T. H. Huxley [q.v.], with whom he studied physiology. After his succession to the dukedom the vast inheritance afforded opportunity for the practical application of science to the estates, particularly to the principal property of Woburn Abbey in Bedfordshire. There, in addition to the care given to the estate itself with utilization of every modern method, research stations were established in forestry and arboriculture. But expert as the duke proved himself in these, his chief scientific interest had been from the earliest days and remained in zoology. Here all that was done at Woburn was closely associated with work for the Zoological Society of which, after having been elected a fellow in 1872, he became president in 1899, holding that office for a period of thirty-seven years. During that time the development and care of the private collection of living creatures in the park at Woburn went along with the development and care of the collection in Regent's Park, where by his share in a guarantee of a sinking fund the construction of the aquarium in the gardens of the society was made possible. To the duke was due the introduction into the gardens of Prjevalsky's horse, the only genuine wild horse in existence. He also secured for Woburn park, in the years following the Boxer riots, the only surviving specimens of Père David's deer, a species of unknown origin, which had formerly been the property of the Emperors of China. In 1908 his work was recognized by election as F.R.S., for his patronage of research and his contribution to the increase of zoological knowledge.

The outbreak of war in 1914 caused an inevitable interruption to the work nearest the duke's heart; and he returned, as a matter of duty, to his earlier military interests. For many years he had commanded the 3rd (militia) battalion of the Bedfordshire Regiment. On war being declared, he established a Bedfordshire training depot in Ampthill park, which became, after the Military Service Act of 1916, a command depot with the duke as colonel-commandant. At the same time part of the Abbey and adjacent buildings were turned into a base hospital for wounded men direct from the firing-line. Provision made, at the sole expense of the duke, in both camp and hospital, for special and new methods of treatment testified to the importance which he, and no less the Duchess of Bedford, attached to medical and surgical, as to other research. In this connexion it may be added that the duke held for twenty-six years (1910–1936) the presidency of the Imperial Cancer Research Fund. For his war services the duke, who had received the Garter in 1902, was in 1919 appointed K.B.E.

The period after 1918 saw the duke more than ever quietly absorbed by his country interests. The pre-eminent achievement of the latter years of his presidency of the Zoological Society was the creation, conceived in 1926, of a zoological park at Whipsnade in Bedfordshire. To this work, in conjunction with the council and with the secretary, Sir Peter Chalmers Mitchell, the duke brought his whole heart; and his personal delight in the new project, as he watched it come to completion, was, as those around him noted, something akin to love. A lesser but still notable work during these years was his share in saving from extinction the survivors of the European bison herds which the war had nearly exterminated in their native haunts in Lithuania and the Caucasus.

As Lord Herbrand Russell the duke married in 1888 at Barrackpore Mary du Caurroy, younger daughter of Walter Harry Tribe, archdeacon of Lahore, by his wife, Sophie, daughter of Admiral Sir Henry Ducie Chads [q.v.], and sister of Sir Henry Chads [q.v.]. The marriage gave the duke a companion whose interest in science equalled his own.

MARY DU CAURROY RUSSELL, Duchess of Bedford (1865–1937), was born at Stockbridge, Hampshire, of which her father was then rector, 26 September 1865, and educated at Cheltenham Ladies' College and in Zürich. The duchess had as a young girl greatly desired to take up the profession of nursing. From the possibility of that career she was deflected by her marriage. But that marriage and the sympathies of the duke enabled her to accomplish work which might otherwise have been impossible for her; more particularly since in the early years of her married life she became the victim of a severe and distressing form of deafness. This affliction, however, strengthened her will to turn her interest in hospital work to account. In 1898 a small cottage-hospital was opened in Woburn; and in 1903 this was replaced by a model hospital, medical and surgical. The latter, like the former, was under the personal direction of the duchess, to fit her for which she had taken a course at the London Hospital. Gradually, however, both she and the professional men with whom she came into contact saw that her true bent was surgical rather than medical. The war of 1914–1918 offered her, in middle age, the opportunity for which she herself said that she had long waited. Her model hospital became the military hospital working in conjunction with the base hospital at the Abbey. The duchess supervised both and at the same time trained in theatre work, so that in 1917 she was able to undertake the post of surgeon's assistant. From this she proceeded to train in radiography and radiology, in both of which, already a photographer, she attained a remarkable degree of pro-

ficiency. After the closing of the Abbey hospital in 1920, the duchess devoted all her attention to her own model hospital, determined that it should profit by all that she had learned in her war service. It was accordingly reorganized as a civilian hospital for surgical cases; the duchess, whose attendance has been described as like clockwork, acting as chief theatre sister and as radiologist. Throughout in this work the duchess had the encouragement and support of the duke, as she had in her particular hobby of bird-watching, which she followed with zeal and great competence. In the latest of her achievements, the art of flying, she had indeed the support of the duke, but hardly, however, his sympathy, for he definitely disliked aeroplanes. The duchess, on the contrary, had long cherished a secret desire to fly when, at the age of sixty, in June 1926 she took her first flight and began to receive instruction as a pilot. Flights with a co-pilot to India in 1928 and 1929 and to South Africa in 1930, the last two being record flights, were rightly regarded as pioneer ventures in travel by air. But the principal service of the duchess was undoubtedly her hospital work, particularly on the surgical side, to which, labouring under a severe physical disability, she brought alike skill and devotion.

The duchess was lost at sea, in her aeroplane, off the East coast, 22 March 1937. The duke died at Woburn Abbey 27 August 1940. He was succeeded as twelfth duke by his only child, Hastings William Sackville (born 1888).

There is a portrait of the duke, in parliament robes, by John Collier (1913) in the Middlesex Guildhall; another portrait by the same artist is in the Shire Hall, Bedford; and portraits of the duke and of the duchess, and a bust of the duke, are at Woburn Abbey.

[Sir P. C. Mitchell, *Centenary History of the Zoological Society of London*, 1929; *Obituary Notices of Fellows of the Royal Society*, No. 9, January 1941 (portrait); John Gore, *Mary, Duchess of Bedford* (printed for private circulation), 1941; private information; personal knowledge.] Gladys Scott Thomson.

RUTHERFORD, ERNEST, Baron Rutherford of Nelson, of Cambridge (1871–1937), physicist, was born at Spring Grove (later called Brightwater), near Nelson, New Zealand, 30 August 1871. His father, James Rutherford, was a son of George Rutherford, a wheelwright of

Perth, Scotland, who emigrated to New Zealand in 1842, when James was three years old. New Zealand then had only about 2,000 white settlers. James married Martha, daughter of Charles Edwin Thompson, who died at Hornchurch, Essex, in 1853. His widow decided to settle in New Zealand with her young daughter, then ten years old. James and Martha Rutherford had twelve children, of whom Ernest was the fourth child and second son. The family moved to Foxhill in 1875, to Havelock in 1882, and finally to Pungarehu in the North Island in 1886. There James, who had previously worked as a wheelwright, farmer, timber contractor, and engineer, concentrated on the large-scale production of flax. He developed his own flax-milling operations, and planted specially selected native varieties. He died in 1928, in his ninetieth year, and his widow in 1935, at the age of ninety-two. Ernest Rutherford owed his strong constitution not only to the good stock of which he came, but also to the vigorous life on the farms where he spent his boyhood. He was a normal, healthy boy, clever but not precocious, a voracious reader, physically active and vivacious, skilled in many kinds of handiwork, and noted, even in early days, for the loud laugh which was one of his chief characteristics through life.

Rutherford attended the primary state schools at Foxhill and Havelock until he was fifteen years old, when he won a Board of Education scholarship and went to Nelson College in January 1887. There he soon displayed his all-round ability, carrying off in succession the chief prizes in all the main subjects of classics, history, English literature, French, and mathematics. Physics and chemistry were also taught, but not to any great extent. Much of the science that Rutherford learned at Nelson College came through informal instruction by one of the masters, W. S. Littlejohn, later principal of the Scotch College at Melbourne. In 1889, when he was head of the school, Rutherford gained a junior university entrance scholarship, which took him to Canterbury College, Christchurch, early in 1890.

There were only about 150 students at Canterbury College then, but Rutherford was fortunate in having several very able contemporaries. The university regulations compelled every student to take a pass degree before reading for honours in a special subject. Latin and pure mathematics were compulsory, and four other subjects had to be offered, only two of which might be scientific. As a result, Rutherford did not begin to study advanced physics seriously until 1892, when he was over twenty years of age. In the autumn of that year he took the B.A. pass degree, and won the university senior scholarship in mathematics. At the end of 1893 he graduated M.A. with first class honours in mathematics and in physics. Within a month he had begun his first serious investigation, in a cold, draughty cellar which was used as a cloakroom by the students. The results of this research were published in the *Transactions* of the New Zealand Institute (now the Royal Society of New Zealand) for 1894, under the title 'Magnetization of Iron by High-frequency Discharges'. A second paper, on 'Magnetic Viscosity', followed in the same journal in 1896. The intrinsic scientific interest of these papers was considerable at the time; but what is more important to record is that they revealed unmistakably Rutherford's remarkable ability to make accurate observations and measurements with primitive equipment.

In 1894, the year in which he graduated B.Sc., Rutherford had been a candidate for an 1851 Exhibition scholarship. The examiners placed him second on the list, but the first choice decided not to take up his scholarship, which was then awarded to Rutherford. He arrived in Cambridge in October 1895 to work under (Sir) J. J. Thomson [q.v.], and was admitted a member of Trinity College. He was the first post-graduate student to be accepted under a new statute which provided that graduates of other universities could qualify for a M.A. degree of Cambridge after two years' residence on the submission of a record of original work of sufficient merit. One month after his arrival W. K. Röntgen announced his discovery of X-rays, the first strong breeze of discovery which blew the science of physics out of the doldrums in which it had lingered for many years. Other exciting events quickly followed; in 1896 Antoine Henri Becquerel showed that uranium compounds emit radiations similar in some respects to X-rays, and in 1897 Thomson provided experimental proof of the existence of the electron, and thus the first definite indication that all the different kinds of matter might have a common origin.

In the exhilarating atmosphere of the Cavendish laboratory at this time Rutherford's genius blossomed. He began by continuing some of his own experiments on the detection of 'wireless' waves. When he was investigating the magnetic properties of iron in New Zealand, he had studied the original work of Heinrich Hertz on the transmission and detection of electromagnetic waves. Using a magnetized steel needle as a detector of oscillatory discharges, he had succeeded, before he left New Zealand, in sending and receiving signals through obstacles over the length of the physics laboratory. In Cambridge he developed this method, and was soon able to detect in his lodgings signals transmitted from the laboratory over half a mile away. This was the record at the time. He did even better later on, and demonstrated his methods at the meeting of the British Association held at Liverpool in September 1896. An account of the work was published in the *Philosophical Transactions* of the Royal Society (vol. clxxxix, 1897); this, his first communication to the society, was made in June 1896. But then he deserted the subject, although he never lost interest in it; there were more fundamental things to do, and at the suggestion and with the warm encouragement of his professor, who was the first fully to recognize his genius, he turned his whole attention to the conduction of electricity through gases. He began by using X-rays as the ionizing agent, and devised methods of great ingenuity and simplicity for determining the velocity and rate of recombination of gaseous ions. He then examined by similar methods the nature of the ionization caused by exposure of gases to the radiation from uranium, and quickly proved that uranium radiation is different in nature from X-rays, and consists of at least two distinct types of radiation, one which he called the α radiation, which is highly effective in causing ionization but easily absorbed; and the other, the β radiation, which is less effective but far more penetrating. Before he left Cambridge in 1898 he had published four papers, and sent a fifth to the press, all of which contained results of the highest scientific importance.

At the end of 1897 Rutherford was elected to the Coutts Trotter studentship at Trinity College, his 1851 Exhibition scholarship having been exceptionally renewed for a third year. But in the early summer of 1898 the Macdonald research professorship of physics at McGill University, Montreal, fell vacant, and Rutherford was advised to apply for it. He was

elected, although not yet turned twenty-seven, and sailed from England in September. By the end of the month he was already busy in his new laboratory, and the firstfruits of his famous work in Montreal appeared in May 1899 in a paper entitled 'Thorium and Uranium Radiation', communicated to the Royal Society of Canada.

Rutherford first lived in rooms in a boarding-house close to the university, and then moved to Union Avenue where he lived with his friends E. W. MacBride [q.v.], professor of zoology, and J. W. Walker, professor of chemistry. In the early summer of 1900 he paid a visit to New Zealand to be married. He had long been engaged to Mary Georgina, only daughter of Arthur Charles Newton, of Christchurch, New Zealand, and a friend of his undergraduate days. They were married in September, returned to Montreal by way of Honolulu and Vancouver, and settled in a house in Ste. Famille Street. There was a daughter of the marriage, who became the wife of (Sir) R. H. Fowler, and predeceased her father.

The laboratory at Montreal was new and good; 'the best of its kind in the world', wrote Rutherford to his mother. Its cost had been largely defrayed by Sir William Macdonald, who had also endowed the professorship. Rutherford was not overburdened with teaching, or other routine duties, and was able to spend most of his time in the laboratory. Nevertheless, he soon began to feel isolated and out of touch with scientific colleagues. He found it difficult to get suitable material for his work, and impossible to get enough, soon enough, to satisfy him. He felt that he might stagnate if he did not get away, and in 1901 seriously considered applying for the vacant chair of natural philosophy at Edinburgh University. Fortunately for McGill University, and perhaps fortunately for himself, no application was made. Later in the same year he rejected a suggestion that he should become a candidate for the chair of physics at University College, London, and during the next six years he refused many tempting offers from the United States of America. His temporary feeling of isolation and frustration had gone; younger men journeyed to Montreal to work under him; and he found himself the leader of a team, gaining as well as giving intellectual stimulus from the companionship and enthusiasm of its members. Rutherford differed from his great predecessors Newton and Faraday in that respect. He was not by nature a lone worker; he needed companionship, and enjoyed the responsibilities and triumphs of leadership.

One of the first of Rutherford's younger colleagues was Mr. (later Professor) Frederick Soddy, who was appointed to a junior post in the chemistry department in 1900. Early in 1901 Mr. Soddy joined Rutherford to help in the chemical investigation of radioactive material. By then Rutherford had proved that thorium compounds continually emit minute amounts of a gas or emanation which itself remains radioactive for some minutes after separation from the parent compound. He showed too that all solid substances in the neighbourhood of a thorium compound become themselves temporarily radioactive under certain conditions, and thought this to be due in some way to the action of the emanation, although he provided no proof at that time. He made a fine platinum wire strongly active by leaving it, when negatively charged, near a thorium compound. Heating the wire to a red heat, or dipping it in water or a solution of caustic soda, had no appreciable effect on its temporary radioactivity, which was, however, largely destroyed if the wire was dipped into a dilute solution of hydrochloric acid. Rutherford then evaporated the solution to dryness, and showed that the invisible residue on the glass surface was strongly radioactive. It was this brilliant investigation, typical of Rutherford's genius, that was the clue which led, with Mr. Soddy's invaluable help, to the final explanation of the cause of radioactivity after three more years of arduous experiment.

The revolutionary theory that radioactivity is a phenomenon accompanying the spontaneous transformation of the atoms of radioactive elements into different kinds of matter was first put forward by Rutherford and Mr. Soddy in a paper published by the London Chemical Society (*Transactions*, vol. lxxxi, 1902), and was supported by further evidence published in the *Philosophical Magazine* for September and November 1902. In his first book (*Radio-activity*, 1904) Rutherford gave a brilliant exposition of the methods and results of investigation on radioactivity up to that date. He based the disintegration theory mainly on the following experimental evidence. (1) Radioactivity is unaffected by any change in external conditions, whether by extreme heat or cold, or by the action of any chemical reagent. In these respects it differs from any known chemical reaction. It must be an atomic phenomenon. (2) The radioactivity of uranium, thorium, and radium is maintained by the production at a constant rate of new kinds of matter which themselves possess temporary radioactivity. The constant activity of the radio elements is due to a state of equilibrium where the rate of production of new matter is equal to the rate of decay of that already produced. (3) In many cases the active products possess well defined chemical properties different from those of the parent elements. (4) In some cases the new products, e.g. of thorium and radium, have the properties of inert gases of high molecular weight. (5) Radioactive change is accompanied by an emission of heat of quite a different order of magnitude from that observed in ordinary chemical reactions.

Rutherford was confident of the essential truth of the new theory, but cautious in his advocacy. In *Radio-activity* he wrote: 'In this book the experimental facts of radio-activity and the connection between them are interpreted on the disintegration theory . . . the agreement of any theory with the facts, which it attempts to explain, must ultimately depend upon the results of accurate measurement. The value of any working theory depends upon the number of experimental facts it seems to correlate, and upon its power of suggesting new lines of work. In these respects the disintegration theory, whether or not it may ultimately be proved to be correct, has already been justified by its results.'

The new theory was so completely at variance with the long accepted views of the indestructibility of matter that it was received with extreme scepticism, and even with contempt, by many prominent scientific men. Nevertheless, the distinction of Rutherford's work was recognized by his election as a fellow of the Royal Society in 1903, and by the award of the Rumford medal of the society in 1904; and opposition to his theories soon gave way under the mass of accurate evidence which accumulated in his laboratory. Before he left Montreal in 1907 the disintegration theory was generally accepted, and only a few of the older sceptics remained unconvinced. Popular interest in the work was of a nature and extent rarely excited by any scientific discovery. The most fantastic stories appeared in the newspapers, and journalists besieged the physics laboratory until their presence became so embarrassing that, to discourage them, authoritative statements had to be issued to the press.

A second edition of Rutherford's *Radioactivity* appeared in 1905, half as large again as the original edition, and in the same year he gave the Silliman lectures at Yale University, which were published in 1906 under the title *Radioactive Transformations*. He was strongly pressed to accept a professorship at Yale, but decided to remain at Montreal, where he felt so settled and happy that he bought some land on the north-west heights of the West Mountain, intending to build a house. Before the house was begun his future plans were changed. (Sir) Arthur Schuster [q.v.], Langworthy professor of physics at Manchester University, resigned his professorship, and Rutherford was invited to succeed him. He accepted and sailed for England in May 1907. At McGill University there is preserved with pride much of the simple, primitive apparatus and equipment which Rutherford used in effecting the greatest revolution in scientific thought since the days of Darwin and Faraday.

After a short summer holiday Rutherford settled in Withington, nearly two miles from the laboratory, where he embarked in October on the final stages of his researches on the nature of the 'alpha particle'. There is nothing more illustrative of his genius, experimental skill, and extreme caution in arriving at conclusions than the story of these researches. It was the so-called α-rays, discovered by him in 1899, which notably distinguished uranium radiation from other forms of ionizing radiation, such as X-rays. He soon formed the opinion that these rays consisted of minute particles of matter projected with great velocity. He suspected that the particles were positively charged, but it was not until 1903 that he obtained impure samples of radium active enough to demonstrate the deviation of the rays in a strong magnetic field. From his observations he deduced that if the α-particle consisted of any known kind of matter it must be either helium or hydrogen. The proof by Sir William Ramsay [q.v.] and Mr. Soddy, in the same year, that helium is a product of the decay of radium emanation, and the invariable presence of helium in all radioactive minerals, led him to express the view that the α-particle is in fact a positively charged atom of helium. But the evidence at that time did not satisfy him, and even in 1907, after much further work, he wrote 'it may still turn out that the alpha particle is hydrogen. . . . The whole question is still sub judice.' Within a year of his arrival at Manchester he had succeeded, by the use of a device invented by (Professor) Hans Geiger, in counting the number of α-particles produced in the disintegration of radium, and thus, by comparison with the measured total charge, deducing the electric charge on each particle. This masterly investigation provided at the same time an accurate determination of the number of molecules in a unit volume of gas (Avogadro's number) and of the elementary charge of the electron. This turned out to be much higher than the accepted figure, based on previous experiments by Thomson and others, but agreed closely with the figure deduced by Max Planck in the development of his quantum theory eight years before. Finally, Rutherford provided a convincing direct proof by showing, with the help of Mr. Thomas Royds, that, if radium emanation is contained in a tube with glass walls thin enough to permit the passage of α-particles, but strong enough to be gas tight, helium gradually appears in an evacuated space round the tube. He gave a full description of this work in a lecture delivered at Stockholm in December 1908, when he received the Nobel prize for chemistry.

The happiest time of Rutherford's happy life was spent at Manchester. Still young—he was only thirty-six when he went there—with position secure and reputation unassailable, he showed not the slightest sign of relaxation; on the contrary, he doubled his efforts. His energy was prodigious. He gathered round him a band of able young workers, many of whom distinguished themselves in after life and gratefully acknowledged how much they owed to Rutherford's inspiring force. He dominated his laboratory like a benevolent despot, and drove, or rather led, his team to the point of exhaustion, so much so that its members were glad to sit back a little when he was absent for a day. And yet, in the surge of new discovery, he found time to do many other things. A third, greatly enlarged and modified, edition of *Radioactivity* appeared in 1913, under the title *Radioactive Substances and their Radiations*. He went to Winnipeg in 1909 as president of Section A of the British Association, and after the meeting lectured in the United States. He spent nearly a fortnight in

Munich in 1910, seeing many of his old students, and then went to Brussels for the Radiology Congress, where he was the centre of attraction and took the most active part in the discussions. He went again to Brussels for the Solvay Conferences in the autumns of 1911 and 1913. He frequently attended the meetings of the Royal Society in London, and was elected a member of the council in 1910. His public lectures and addresses during the Manchester period, as well as during the later part of his life, are too numerous to mention. His fame spread far and wide; everyone wanted to see and hear him, and he did his best to comply with the demand by keeping in a state of readiness diagrams, lantern slides, and experimental equipment to illustrate his latest discoveries. The many public recognitions of his work during this period included a knighthood bestowed in 1914.

The great scientific event of the Manchester period was the development of the nuclear theory of the atom. In 1906, when Rutherford was investigating the deflection of α-rays in a strong magnetic field, he noticed that whereas the photographic records had sharply defined edges when the containing vessel was highly evacuated, they became broader, and the edges more diffuse, in the presence of air, or when a thin sheet of matter was interposed between the radioactive material and the photographic plate. A sheet of mica three-thousandths of a centimetre in thickness caused a 'scattering' of two degrees or more. Rutherford seized upon the great importance of this small effect, writing in 1906 that 'such a result brings out clearly the fact that the atoms of matter must be the seat of very intense electrical forces'. In his early days at Manchester, when, through the generosity of the Vienna Academy, he at last had sufficient radium for his work, (Professor) Geiger, under his direction, made a more careful examination of the scattering effect through small angles. Rutherford then asked (Professor) Geiger and (Dr.) Ernest Marsden in 1909 to see if any α-particles were scattered through very large angles. He said afterwards that he never expected that they would be; if so, this is the most remarkable example of Rutherford's instinct in choosing the right experiment to do. The unexpected happened, and within a few months it had been proved that about one particle in ten thousand had its path deflected through more than a right angle in passing through a thin sheet of matter.

For a full year Rutherford pondered, testing and rejecting various hypotheses. Then, just before Christmas 1910, he came into his laboratory in high spirits, saying that he knew exactly what the atom looked like. The only hypothesis that would satisfactorily account for all the facts was that nearly all the mass of an atom was concentrated on a positively charged central nucleus, the diameter of which was very small compared with the apparent radius of the atom, and that the positive charge must be balanced by outer electrons, a relatively long distance away. On this hypothesis he calculated the general laws of scattering, which were confirmed in detail by further observations within a few months. The theory was published in a classic paper in the *Philosophical Magazine* for May 1911.

The nuclear theory, rapidly developed during the next few years, was quickly accepted, and long before Rutherford's death had influenced the progress of nearly every branch of science. It was true that it did not fit in with the current electromagnetic theories, but that showed, said Rutherford confidently, 'that there must be something wrong with the theory of electromagnetic radiation, not of the atom'. The famous Danish physicist Niels Bohr, who visited Rutherford first in 1912, and became reader in mathematical physics at Manchester in 1914, devoted himself, soon after his first visit, to the application of Planck's quantum theory to Rutherford's atom, and showed how, with certain bold assumptions, the spectrum of hydrogen could be calculated. Bohr's theories, and the investigations of the X-ray spectra of the elements carried out by H. G. J. Moseley [q.v.], added strength to Rutherford's views, and by 1914 it was established that the chemical properties of the elements are determined not by their atomic weight, but by the charge on the central nucleus, and hence by the number and arrangement of the surrounding electrons. The total number of possible elements, distinct in their chemical properties, up to the heaviest, uranium, was known; and the idea was gaining ground that the different elements might exist in stable forms, differing in atomic mass, but with the same chemical properties and nuclear charge. The constitution of the nucleus itself remained the great fundamental problem of physics, a problem which Rutherford thought at the time must be left to the next generation to solve.

In April 1914 Rutherford went to America to deliver the first course of William Ellery Hale lectures at Washington on 'The Constitution of Matter and the Evolution of the Elements'. In July he travelled to Australia, with his wife and daughter, for the meeting of the British Association. War with Germany was declared before they arrived, but he decided to go through with his programme and, after leading a discussion at Melbourne on 'The Constitution of the Atom', and giving a public lecture at Sydney on 'Atoms and Electrons', he went on to New Zealand, visited his parents and friends in the North Island, and lectured at Canterbury College on the 'Evolution of the Elements', which was the title of his first address to an unofficial scientific society of the college when he was an undergraduate in 1891. He returned to England in January 1915 to find a laboratory rapidly emptying of his research staff and students. In the following July he became a member of a committee of the Admiralty Board of Invention and Research which had been appointed to develop new methods of dealing with the menace of submarine warfare. Within a short time his laboratory at Manchester was devoted to a study of under-water acoustics, and a large tank was installed on the ground floor. The Admiralty established a full-scale research station at Aberdour, near Rosyth, and Rutherford spent much of his time travelling to Aberdour to take part in trials, and to London for meetings of the committee. When (Sir) William Henry Bragg was put in charge of the work at Aberdour, Rutherford concentrated his attention more on the small-scale work. In the early summer of 1917 he went to America as one of the two British representatives on a Franco-British scientific commission, in order to give the United States scientists full information on the detection and location of submarines, and to discuss joint plans for improvement of methods. He took the opportunity to visit Yale University again, where he received an honorary degree, and to go to Montreal to renew friendships. When he returned to Manchester in July he felt that his main contributions to the war effort were coming to an end, and that he was justified in turning his attention again to fundamental problems of physics. With no one now to help him but his laboratory steward he started in September to investigate more closely than before what happens when α-particles collide with atoms of the lighter gases. He found some unexpected effects with air, which were soon shown to be caused by collisions of α-particles with nitrogen atoms. A long series of carefully controlled experiments, which involved the laborious and tiring counting of scintillations on a fluorescent screen, convinced him that the nucleus of the nitrogen atom is disintegrated under the intense forces developed in a close collision with an α-particle, and that the nucleus of a hydrogen atom is liberated, which must therefore be a constituent part of the nitrogen nucleus. In June 1919 his evidence for the first artificial transmutation of matter was published in the *Philosophical Magazine*. This was the culminating triumph of the Manchester period.

In April 1919 Rutherford was elected to the Cavendish professorship of experimental physics in the university of Cambridge in succession to Thomson, and into a fellowship at Trinity College, and the last great period of his life and work began. He settled in the autumn at Newnham Cottage, Queen's Road, where he lived until his death. He found a department crowded with graduate and undergraduate students, but deficient, in his view, in staff, space, and equipment. He spent some time in developing a plan for re-organization and extension, for which, unfortunately, money was not available until 1936. But he soon began to follow up vigorously his experiments on the disintegration of the light elements, and by the time that he gave his second Bakerian lecture to the Royal Society in June 1920 (he had given his first in May 1904) had provided conclusive proof, by measuring their deflection in a magnetic field, that the long range particles from nitrogen are indeed hydrogen nuclei. This was the lecture that contained his famous speculation on the existence of the neutron, and of an isotope of hydrogen of mass 2.

The next few years were years of consolidation and general progress, rather than of any major discoveries. Rutherford spent some time vainly searching for evidence of the existence of the neutron, and, with the help of (Sir) James Chadwick, then one of his research students, continued to explore, by the laborious scintillation method, the transmutation of atoms of the lighter elements by collision with α-particles. The Wilson Cloud chamber, that 'most original and wonderful' instrument, as Rutherford called it, was extensively used in the Cavendish laboratory to study the tracks of single α-particles, protons, and electrons. But it became clear to Rutherford that the days when so much could be discovered by the simplest means were passing, and that rapid progress in knowledge of the constitution of the nucleus could only be expected if he had more powerful means of experiment at his command. The years 1925 to 1930 were largely spent in encouraging the study of methods of producing fast charged particles by the application of high voltages to vacuum tubes, and the Cavendish laboratory gradually became equipped with elaborate electrical machinery. This period of preparation for the next major advance coincided with Rutherford's presidency of the Royal Society, to which he was elected in 1925. Earlier in the same year he had been appointed to the Order of Merit; and soon after his term of office was over he was in 1931 raised to the peerage as Baron Rutherford of Nelson, of Cambridge, the title being taken from the town near to which he was born, and at which he went to school.

In 1930 there appeared, under the title *Radiations from Radioactive Substances*, and with the collaboration of (Sir) James Chadwick and of (Dr.) Charles Drummond Ellis, another of his research students, a book in which the authors, after summarizing early work on radioactivity, dealt exhaustively and critically with the investigations of the last twelve years. It marked the end of an epoch; two years later, in 1932, Rutherford's forward policy was amply justified, and his predictions triumphantly fulfilled. In that year (Dr.) John Douglas Cockcroft and (Dr.) Ernest Thomas Sinton Walton succeeded in transforming lithium atoms into helium by bombarding them with protons accelerated through 600,000 volts; (Professor) Carl David Anderson in America discovered the positive electron, or positron; and (Sir) James Chadwick proved that the penetrating radiation which had been observed by Professor Walther Bothe to result from the bombardment of beryllium by α-particles consists of a stream of the long-expected and sought-for neutrons. In the next year Professor Harold Clayton Urey, of Columbia University, discovered heavy hydrogen, later named deuterium, and the Curie-Joliots in France produced the first artificially radioactive element. The way was set for another great advance, on a broad front.

Rutherford, then over sixty years of age, seemed to recover all the fire and enthusiasm of his youth. Many of the spectacular discoveries of the next few years were due to his direct inspiration; many others were made by workers in other countries. In 1936 he gave an account of all the recent work on the transmutation of elements in his Henry Sidgwick memorial lecture at Newnham College, Cambridge, which was published in expanded form in 1937 under the title *The Newer Alchemy*. In this little book he referred to the most recent discovery that even the heaviest elements, uranium and thorium, are transformed by slow neutrons; but, he added, 'the exact interpretation of these transformations is still sub judice'. The true interpretation was found only after his death. He did not live to see the failure of his hope, expressed in 1916, that man would not learn how to use atomic energy for practical purposes until the world was at peace. He died at Cambridge 19 October 1937, after a few days' illness, and was buried in Westminster Abbey on 25 October. With his death his peerage became extinct.

Rutherford received innumerable honours in addition to those already mentioned. In all, he was awarded honorary degrees from thirteen British, four Dominion, and eight foreign universities. His other distinctions included the Copley medal of the Royal Society (1922), and the honorary fellowship of the Royal College of Physicians. He was also honorary or foreign associate of most of the well-known foreign scientific societies and academies.

In the whole course of the history of science no one has surpassed Rutherford in his influence on his contemporaries; few have equalled the volume and accuracy of his experimental work. In upwards of 150 original papers and addresses published by him in scientific journals, alone or with collaborators, the careful reader can detect some mistakes in facts as well as in judgement; but they are so few as to be negligible. Nor do the papers published under his name represent the sum of his contributions to science; many others, in which his name does not appear in the title, owe their existence to his fertile mind, and much of their value to his skill in experiment. He himself attributed much of his success to his continuous efforts to improve accuracy of observation in every possible direction. There is much truth in this, but it is not the whole truth.

It was not only experience, based on hard, honest work, that taught him to concentrate on things that really mattered, and to avoid irrelevant side issues; this was a quality that he had from the very beginning. He was highly imaginative, rather than speculative. He was apt to underrate the more metaphysical inquiries of mathematical physicists; 'they play games with their symbols,' he said, 'but we in the Cavendish turn out the real solid facts of Nature'. But when abstruse theory led to conclusions which could be tested and confirmed in the laboratory, his scepticism turned quickly into enthusiasm. He was the severest critic of his own work, testing and re-testing his theories, and exhaustively examining alternatives, until he was satisfied that what he said or wrote could not easily be shaken. Neither in youth, nor as he grew old, did he ever try to save his face by complicated hypotheses: indeed he had no need to try. With all his abundant vitality, he knew how to curb his imagination, and how also to restrain his natural impatience with those whose work fell short of his own high standard. In the early days of radioactivity there were men, of more established reputations than his, who were inclined to be rash in speculation, and careless in experiment. Whatever Rutherford might say in private—and he was outspoken with his friends—he combined politeness with firmness in public discussion, though sometimes with a sly sarcasm that delighted his younger supporters.

Rutherford took great pains over his writings, holding that no scientific discovery is complete until it has been expressed in clear and concise language. As a speaker he was unpolished and hesitant. Words did not come easily to him before an audience. Long practice never made him perfect; but the power of his personality, his wide knowledge, and his robust common sense always made a great impression on those who heard his public utterances in the House of Lords, or in his capacity as chairman of the Advisory Council of the Department of Scientific and Industrial Research, an office which he held from 1930 until his death. When he lectured to scientific audiences on his own work he was unique and irresistible. The minor faults of diction were completely swamped by interest in what he had to say and by the infection of his enthusiasm and joy in his subject. A sound record exists of a lecture that he gave at Göttingen in December 1931, when he received an honorary degree from the university. It reveals him in a most characteristic and happy mood.

Rutherford's influence on his students was well described after his death by his son-in-law, (Sir) R. H. Fowler. 'Ideally equipped for directing a physical laboratory, he was capable at once of intense sustained individual research, of suggesting and inspiring with his own fire cognate researches of others over a very wide field, and, particularly in later years, of organising the team work for elaborate attack on many modern problems. His genial but dominant personality, his exacting demands for the best, the inspiration of his personal research, and the generosity with which he suggested and directed the work of his staff and students, created an atmosphere in any laboratory he directed which no one who experienced it will forget, or, alas, ever hope to meet again.' But it was not only his students whom Rutherford influenced. No man, old or young, great or small, who was striving in whatever way to enlarge the boundaries of science, ever came away from a talk with Rutherford without an added zest in his own work, and a feeling that he was a partner in a great adventure.

In person Rutherford was a big, heavily built, but loosely limbed man. His light blue eyes were shrewd and penetrating, his voice loud and resonant, his conversation animated and vivid. Supremely confident in his own powers, there was yet no trace of vanity in him: he was simple in all his ways, and unassuming and even boyish in behaviour. Athletic in his youth, a rheumatic condition of one knee caused him to be physically rather lethargic in middle age, when, in his own words, he 'took no more exercise than was consistent with self respect'. He enjoyed games of all kinds, so long as they were not taken too seriously and did not interfere with conversation. He had the characteristic of going to sleep for short periods during the daytime, waking up suddenly, and going on with a conversation where he had left off. He was seldom ill, although chronic, but not serious, throat trouble persisted through life. He was nearly always in high spirits, but he had occasional fits of anger when it was 'as if the sky was darkened by a thunder cloud. . . . In such moments everyone is of course afraid of him, but not more so than we dare to confess' (Niels Bohr).

An excellent portrait in oils of Rutherford by Oswald Birley (1932) hangs in the rooms of the Royal Society: there are copies in the Cavendish laboratory, Cambridge, and at Canterbury College, Christchurch, New Zealand. Another oil portrait, by P. A. de László, is at Trinity College, Cambridge; a third, by F. L. Emanuel (1936), belongs to Nelson College, New Zealand; and a fourth, by Jozef Jannsens (1917), is in the possession of Lady Rutherford. Other portraits include an oil sketch by James Gunn (1932) in the National Portrait Gallery, and pencil sketches by Francis Dodd in the Fitzwilliam Museum, and by Randolph Schwabe (1928) at Trinity College.

[*The Times*, 20, 22, and 25 October 1937; *Obituary Notices of Fellows of the Royal Society*, No. 6, January 1938 (portrait); A. S. Eve, *Rutherford*, 1939; Norman Feather, *Lord Rutherford*, 1940; private information; personal knowledge.]   H. T. TIZARD.

RYRIE, SIR GRANVILLE DE LAUNE (1865–1937), major-general and high commissioner for Australia, was born on the sheep-station of Micalago, Michelago, New South Wales, 1 July 1865, the second of the six sons of Alexander Ryrie, a well-known grazier and member of the legislative Council, by his wife, Charlotte, elder daughter of Captain Alured Tasker Faunce, of the 4th King's Own Regiment.

Educated at a preparatory school at Mittagong and at King's School, Parramatta, Ryrie, at the age of sixteen, went as jackeroo to Goonal station in north-west New South Wales. He became an excellent bushman and judge of horses, and gained considerable skill at carving and throwing a boomerang. Returning to Micalago as manager, Ryrie entered fully into the local life. His interests were sporting and social rather than intellectual and bookish, for his formal education had been meagre. He bred good horses and raced them, played football, and contested the finals of the New South Wales amateur heavyweight boxing championship, being narrowly defeated. His excellent physique, his fine tenor voice, and his clever mimicry of the lyre-bird were gifts that won him wide popularity.

Ryrie also worked hard, and was a member of the local Light Horse. In 1900 he embarked for South Africa as a captain in the 6th (N.S.W.) Imperial Bushmen, and was wounded at Wonderfontein (September), promoted major (November), and awarded the Queen's medal with four clasps. In June 1901 he returned home with his regiment.

From 1906 to 1910 Ryrie held the Queanbeyan seat in the New South Wales legislative assembly, but failed to gain the Cootamundra seat in 1910. In 1911 he was elected to the Commonwealth parliament for North Sydney, holding the seat until 1922. He remained, however, a citizen soldier, commanding the 3rd Light Horse regiment from 1907 to 1914 as lieutenant-colonel. He embarked for Egypt in December 1914 as brigadier-general commanding the 2nd Light Horse brigade. Serving through the Gallipoli campaign from May until the evacuation in December 1915, he was severely wounded on 29 September. With little love for military forms or text-books he nevertheless gained a reputation as a skilful soldier, with a sure sense of the possibilities of a situation and a marked unwillingness to waste the lives of his troops. These same qualities marked Ryrie's leadership of his brigade in Sinai and Palestine from 1916 to 1918, and in the latter year he took command of the Australian division of the Light Horse in Syria. Throughout he achieved steady consistent success for which he was five times mentioned in dispatches, and appointed C.M.G. in 1916, C.B. in 1918, and K.C.M.G. in 1919. He was again wounded, and in 1919 promoted major-general commanding the Australian troops in Egypt. His success rested not only on his military gifts, but perhaps equally on the devotion which this brusque, humorous, sixteen-stone giant inspired in his men, for he shared their rough life, their rations, and their dangers.

Back in Australia, Ryrie held the position of assistant minister for defence from 1920 to 1923. In 1922 he was returned unopposed to the Commonwealth parliament for Warringah, a seat which he held until he became high commissioner in London. He occupied this latter position from July 1927 until July 1932. In these years his health was not good, and on his return to Australia he retired from public life.

Ryrie married in 1896 Mary Frances Gwendolyn, second daughter of Alfred McFarland, judge of the District Court of New South Wales; they had a son and twin daughters. He died in Sydney 2 October 1937.

Ryrie's greatest contribution to Australian public life was probably as a military leader. Honest and fearless in politics, his outspokenness did not help his advancement. As high commissioner he worked hard; he was bent on making a success of the great scheme of British migration which came to nothing in the depression of 1929. His belief in 1927 that Australia could take 100,000 British immigrants a year proved unfounded. But Ryrie is remembered as a fine type of Australian countryman and as a military leader of the kind most fitted to get the best out of the Commonwealth's citizen forces. The value of his work in this field has been fully recognized in the official records of Australia's part in the war of 1914 to 1918.

There is a portrait of Ryrie by Charles Wheeler in the Australian War Memorial, Canberra, as well as one in a group of 'Sir Harry Chauvel and his Brigade Commanders in Palestine in 1918' by H. Septimus Power; the best portrait is probably a pencil drawing by George Lambert in possession of the family.

[*Sydney Morning Herald*, 4 October 1937; *Argus* (Melbourne), 4 October 1937; *The Times*, 4 October 1937; *Official Records of the Australian Military Contingents to the War in South Africa*, compiled by P. L. Murray, 1911; *Official History of Australia in the War of 1914–1918*, C. E. W. Bean, vol. i, 1933, vol. ii, 1924, and H. S. Gullett, vol. vii, 1923 (portrait); *Commonwealth Parliamentary Handbook, 1901–1930*, 1930; private information.]
HERBERT BURTON.

ST. DAVIDS, first VISCOUNT (1860–1938), financier. [See PHILIPPS, Sir JOHN WYNFORD.]

SAINTSBURY, GEORGE EDWARD BATEMAN (1845–1933), literary critic and historian, was born at Southampton 23 October 1845, the second son of George Saintsbury, secretary and superintendent of the docks, by his wife, Elizabeth Wright. Educated at King's College School, London, he entered Merton College, Oxford, as a classical postmaster in 1863, was awarded a first class in classical moderations (1865) and a second class in *literae humaniores* (1866), and, having failed to obtain a fellowship, left Oxford in 1868, and became a schoolmaster. His chief college friend was Mandell Creighton [q.v.]. After a few months at Manchester Grammar School he was for six years senior classical master at Elizabeth College, Guernsey, where he read widely in French literature, and sent his first reviews to the *Academy*. In 1874 he moved to Elgin as headmaster of the newly founded Elgin Educational Institute. It

did not prosper, and he returned to London in 1876 to live by his pen.

Saintsbury's first essay of note, on Baudelaire, was printed by John (afterwards Viscount) Morley [q.v.] in the *Fortnightly Review* for October 1875, and on Morley's invitation was followed in 1878 by eight essays on contemporary French novelists. It was as a critic of French literature that he began to make his name. He contributed over thirty articles on it to the *Encyclopaedia Britannica* (9th ed. 1875–1889), and wrote both a *Primer of French Literature* (1880) and a *Short History of French Literature* (1882), besides editing selected *French Lyrics* (1882) and *Specimens of French Literature from Villon to Hugo* (1883). His views, always his own, often ran counter to the accepted verdicts of the French critics. But he was also at work on English literature. His *Dryden* ('English Men of Letters' series, 1881) was a much needed study of a favourite of whom he always wrote, and spoke, with fervour. It brought the invitation to re-edit Scott's *Dryden*, but the edition suffered by delays in publication (18 vols., 1882–1893). He was more fortunate in his *Specimens of English Prose Style from Malory to Macaulay* (1885), and when he wrote his *History of Elizabethan Literature* (1887) his main interests had turned from French to English, although he was still to collect his *Essays on French Novelists* (1891), and to superintend, with his own critical matter superadded, the translation of Balzac (40 vols., 1895–1898). From 1886 onwards he contributed a series of articles on English authors to *Macmillan's Magazine*, and these, and some others, he collected in *Essays in English Literature, 1780–1860* (1890) and *Miscellaneous Essays* (1892), two of his best books. Then for a few years his criticism mostly took the form of introductions to editions—Swift's *Polite Conversation* and Florio's Montaigne (1892), Fielding and Herrick (1893), *The Heptameron* and Sterne (1894), Smollett (1895)—and to the selections from over thirty authors in Craik's *English Prose* (1893–1896). His *History of Nineteenth-Century Literature, 1780–1895* (1896) was published a few months after his appointment to the English chair at Edinburgh. About the same time he brought out his *Corrected Impressions: Essays on Victorian Writers* (1895) and a second series of *Essays in English Literature* (1895), and two other editions remained to be completed with his introductions, Peacock (1896–1897) and Donne (1896). During this period he had also written *Marlborough* ('English Worthies' series, 1885), *Manchester* (1887), and *The Earl of Derby* (1892).

This great body of critical work had been exceeded in sheer bulk by his work as a journalist. For some months in 1877 Saintsbury was on the staff of the *Manchester Guardian*, for which, as for the *Daily News*, his work was non-political. With Andrew Lang and Robert Louis Stevenson [qq.v.] he was a main contributor to *London* (1877–1879, edited by W. E. Henley, q.v.). He wrote for the *Pall Mall Gazette* while Morley remained its editor, and for the *St. James's Gazette*. But his main work as a journalist was on the *Saturday Review*, of which he was assistant editor from 1883 to 1894, when he left on a change of its ownership. The independent toryism of the *Saturday* was never more vigorous than in those years. He entered with zest into the fight against Gladstone's Irish policy, and saved the paper from the 'Parnell Letters' before they duped *The Times* (*Scrap Book*, iii, p. 274). 'In my twenty years of journalism', he says, 'I must have written the equivalent of at least a hundred volumes of the "Every Gentleman's Library" type —and probably more' (*Scrap Book*, i, p. x).

In September 1895 Saintsbury was appointed to the regius chair of rhetoric and English literature in the university of Edinburgh in succession to David Masson [q.v.]. This was a turning-point in his career, as he had to exchange the excitement and uncertainty which he had found in 'the charm of journalism' for the more staid duties of a Scottish professor. He may not at first have been well adapted to the ways of the Scottish student, but his influence grew steadily until he became a power in the university, and the twenty years of his professorship form one of the most notable periods in the history of a famous chair. The big books which he had long wanted to write now followed one another with surprising rapidity. His *Short History of English Literature* (1898), a wholly new book alike in design and substance, was written in less than a year. With its completion he was free to begin what he had long hoped would be his chief work, his *History of Criticism and Literary Taste in Europe from the Earliest Texts to the Present Day* (3 vols., 1900–1904), the first and still the only survey of critical theory and practice from ancient Greek to modern times. He supplemented it with *Loci Critici* (1903), a collection of

illustrative passages. Then came his *History of English Prosody from the Twelfth Century to the Present Day* (3 vols., 1906–1910), supplemented by his *Historical Manual of English Prosody* (1910); and then its natural but novel sequel *A History of English Prose Rhythm* (1912), a treatise on the structure and modulation of our best prose. These four big books, or their volumes, had appeared regularly at intervals of two years, and he had made time for much else even while a busy professor. Before he was appointed he had planned the 'Periods of European Literature' in twelve volumes, and of these he wrote three, *The Flourishing of Romance and the Rise of Allegory* (1897), *The Earlier Renaissance* (1901), and *The Later Nineteenth Century* (1907). He wrote a book on *Sir Walter Scott* (1897), and another on *Matthew Arnold* (1899). He edited selected plays of Dryden (2 vols., 1904) and Shadwell (1912), both in the 'Mermaid' series; a collection of *Minor Poets of the Caroline Period* (3 vols., 1905–1921); and the *Oxford Thackeray* (17 vols., 1908). He took a main part in the discussion on 'the grand style' in his address to the Dante Society on Dante (1905, published in *Essays and Studies of the English Association*, 1912), in his lecture (delivered in 1908) to the Royal Society of Literature on Milton (1909), and in his presidential address to the English Association on Shakespeare (1910). He delivered before the British Academy the Warton lecture on *The Historical Character of English Lyric* (1912). He wrote a book on *The English Novel* (1913). He was the chief contributor to the *Cambridge History of English Literature* (21 chapters, 1907–1916). When he retired from his chair in 1915, at the age of seventy, his unremitting energy had enabled him to accomplish much more than the tasks which he had foreseen on his appointment. He signalized his retirement by writing *The Peace of the Augustans; a Survey of Eighteenth-Century Literature as a Place of Rest and Refreshment* (1916).

On leaving Edinburgh, where he had resided at Murrayfield House (1896–1900) and 2 Eton Terrace (1900–1915), Saintsbury lived for some months at Southampton, and then settled in rooms at 1 Royal Crescent, Bath. Once he had completed his last big book, *A History of the French Novel* (2 vols., 1917–1919), he was free to relax, and to write his *Notes on a Cellar-Book* (1920). It gave him many new readers and led to the foundation of the

Saintsbury Club. In 1922, on his seventy-seventh birthday, he was presented with an address by over 300 friends and admirers, among them Frederic Harrison and Robert Bridges [qq.v.]. In acknowledging it he said that he had learned early that he was not destined to create great literature but that he had perhaps some faculty of appreciating it, and as he took the address to tell him that he had not merely flattered himself, he declared that he desired no higher praise. He forbade a biography, but supplied what he thought worth recording in his three *Scrap Books* (1922–1924), collections of reminiscences and observations. A high churchman, he never spoke or wrote about his religion; but a tory who gloried in the name and admitted that he would have opposed every great reform since the Reform bill, he did not conceal his distrust of what is called progress. To the end he remained a voracious reader, and writing he could not abandon. 'The professor ceasing, the reviewer revives', he said in print in 1923. Apart from his *Scrap Books* the main publications of his later years were *A Letter Book* (1922), with an introduction on the history and art of letter-writing, and *A Consideration of Thackeray* (1931), a collection of earlier writings on the novelist for whom his admiration was constant. In 1923–1924 he brought out, in four volumes, his *Collected Essays and Papers*, which was only a selection. Other *Prefaces and Essays* were collected by Oliver Elton in 1933; still more are collected in *George Saintsbury*. The *Memorial Volume* which appeared in 1945, and in *French Literature and its Masters*, edited by Huntington Cairns (New York, 1946).

As a critic Saintsbury was pre-eminently a 'taster' who said what it was he liked, and why he liked it. He looked for the characteristic quality and found it in style rather than in form or substance. The true and only test of literary greatness, he said, was the *transport*, the absorption of the reader. He never ceased, in his own words, 'to accentuate the importance of treatment over that of mere subject'. Interested as he was in the lives of authors, as his many introductory memoirs show, his attention never strays from the works by which they deserve to be remembered. His historical backgrounds are kept in their place as backgrounds; and we do not go to him for a philosophy of literature. As an historian of literature he had to deal with movements and tendencies, and here his remarkable knowledge made the task

easy for him, and congenial. While never subordinating style to substance, he enjoyed tracing the fortunes of a literary form and showing the changes in its appeal to the reader. Yet there are many who hold that even in his histories he is never better than when dealing with individual works or authors. He has a wider range than any other English critic, and when he is at his best no critic since Hazlitt has written with greater gusto.

In 1868 Saintsbury married Emily Fenn (died 1924), daughter of Henry William King, surgeon. They had two sons, the elder of whom predeceased his father. He died at Bath 28 January 1933 and was buried at the Old Cemetery of his native Southampton.

Saintsbury received honorary degrees from the universities of Aberdeen (1898), Durham (1906), Oxford (1912), and Edinburgh (1919), and was elected a fellow of the British Academy in 1911. In 1909 he was elected an honorary fellow of Merton College, where his portrait by William Nicholson (1925) hangs in the common room. The college has a collection of his letters.

[George Saintsbury, *A Scrap Book*, 1922, *A Second Scrap Book*, 1923, and *A Last Scrap Book*, 1924; *The Times*, *Scotsman*, and *Morning Post*, 30 January 1933; *London Mercury*, March 1933; Oliver Elton, *George Edward Bateman Saintsbury, 1845–1933* in *Proceedings of the British Academy*, vol. xix, 1933; *Life and Letters*, June 1933; Adam Blyth Webster, *George Saintsbury*, 1933; Helen Waddell, Preface to reprint of the chapters on Shakespeare in the *Cambridge History of English Literature*, 1934; *George Saintsbury. The Memorial Volume*, 1945 (a second volume, *A Saintsbury Miscellany*, with a full bibliography, is in preparation); Louise Creighton, *Life of Mandell Creighton*, 1904; personal knowledge.]   D. NICHOL SMITH.

SAKLATVALA, SHAPHURJI (1874–1936), politician, was born in Bombay 28 March 1874, the son of Dorabji Shapurji Saklatvala, a Parsee merchant, of Bombay and later of Manchester, and Jerbai Tata, a sister of J. N. Tata [q.v.], who, with his brother, founded the Tata Iron and Steel Works in India. Receiving his early education at St. Xavier's School and College in Bombay, Saklatvala studied law and was a member of Lincoln's Inn. For three years he prospected for coal, iron, and limestone in the Indian jungle, and considerably aided the production of the Tata firm. Welfare work in the plague hospitals and the slums of Bombay led to interest in Indian labour problems and association with the Indian Trade Union Congress. On accepting a position on behalf of the firm in London in 1905 (he did not resign his position of departmental manager until 1925), Saklatvala joined the National Liberal Club, but subsequently turned socialist, and in 1910 became active in the independent labour party, then affiliated to the labour party. He also joined the British socialist party and, for trade union association, the General Workers' Union and the National Union of Clerks. After the Russian revolution he assisted in the formation of a People's Russian Information Bureau and the communist party of Great Britain. In 1922 he first entered parliament as labour member for North Battersea, being the third member from India to be elected to the House of Commons, after Dabadhai Naoroji, a liberal, in 1892, and Sir M. M. Bhownagree [q.v.], a conservative, in 1895. After the formation of the Third (Communist) International in 1919, Saklatvala sought to secure the adhesion of the independent labour party, and upon his failure concentrated upon communist activity. He was a founder member of the Workers' Welfare League of India, which aimed at the equalization of European and Asiatic labour standards. In 1923 he lost his seat, but regained it as a communist in 1924. Appointed in 1925 a member of an inter-parliamentary delegation to the United States of America, his visa was revoked by the United States secretary of state, Kellogg, on the ground that the United States did not admit revolutionaries.

Active in agitation during the General Strike in 1926, Saklatvala was imprisoned for two months on a charge arising out of a May Day speech in Hyde Park. In 1927 he visited India, but was refused permission to stay in Egypt en route. He was a strong critic of the Indian National Congress and of Gandhi's methods, in particular of the re-introduction of the spinning-wheel and the weaving of khaddar cloth. Upon his return to England his permit to re-enter India was cancelled at the request of the Indian government. At the general election of 1929 he again contested North Battersea, but was defeated. In 1934 he visited Russia, travelling widely through the territory bordering on India, and was greatly impressed by the developments in industry, agriculture, education, and general culture among its backward peoples.

Saklatvala married in 1907 Sehri, daughter of Henry Marsh, of Tansley, Derbyshire; their three sons and two daughters were initiated into the Parsee religion in 1927, a ceremony for which the father was censured by the communist party. He died in London 16 January 1936.

Although a cultivated man and personally popular among a wide circle of friends, Saklatvala figured as 'a stormy petrel' throughout the later years of his life in London. He viewed social conditions in Great Britain with abhorrence and was extreme in his utterances about the continuance of British rule in India.

[The Times, 17 January 1936; Review of Reviews, December 1922.]

         J. S. MIDDLETON.

SALMOND, SIR (WILLIAM) GEOFFREY (HANSON) (1878–1933), air chief marshal, was born at Hougham, Dover, 19 August 1878, the elder son of Major-General Sir William Salmond, R.E., of Whaddon House, Bruton, Somerset, by his wife, Emma Mary, youngest daughter of William Fretwell Hoyle, of Hooton Levet Hall, Yorkshire. He was educated at Wellington College and the Royal Military Academy. He received his first commission in the Royal Artillery in 1898, and served in the Royal Regiment until 1913, seeing during these years active service in South Africa and in China (1900); he graduated at the Staff College in 1914.

Salmond was among the first of the army officers to give his attention to flying, and while a captain received his Royal Aero Club certificate in 1912. In 1913 he was appointed G.S.O. 3 at the Directorate of Military Aeronautics in the War Office; in August 1914 he was promoted major and went to France a few days after the outbreak of war, on the staff of Major-General (Sir) David Henderson [q.v.], later commanding the Royal Flying Corps. During the early months of the war he devised the method of 'pin-pointing' the enemy's guns. In January 1915 he returned to England to raise a new No. 1 Squadron and was back in time to take part with it in the battle of Neuve Chapelle. He commanded it at the capture of Hill 60 and in the battle of Aubers Ridge. In August 1915 he was promoted lieutenant-colonel and recalled to England.

The following November Salmond was given command of the 5th Wing, Royal Flying Corps, in Egypt. In July 1916 he was promoted temporary brigadier-general with command of the Middle East Brigade,

Royal Flying Corps, which had developed out of his original force of one wing, an extra squadron, and an aircraft park. He was rapidly gaining a reputation for accomplishing difficult tasks and for inspiring the most unlikely material to do first-class work. The conditions in which the brigade worked were arduous and unpleasant. Operations had to be organized over the deserts of Mesopotamia and among the mountains of Greece. Salmond set himself to deal with every variety of obstacle and made sure, by means of personal visits, that he understood the peculiar troubles of every unit in his brigade. These visits invariably contributed something to efficiency, partly because they led to useful improvements in equipment or methods, and not least because they were essentially friendly and stimulating in character. His knack of maintaining good human relationships, added to the zest and devotion with which he sought practical solutions for the many problems, created in the Middle East Brigade an intense *esprit de corps*. The help given by the Royal Flying Corps in the campaigns was warmly acknowledged by the army commanders in Salonika, East Africa, Egypt, and Palestine. It had consisted of all kinds of tactical support from artillery spotting and reconnaissance to the pursuit of retreating columns and the heavy bombing of Turkish transport behind the front. Salmond applied the principles afterwards developed in the tactical air forces of the war of 1939–1945, in circumstances and with air equipment which demanded the highest spirit and a genius for improvisation and adaptation. He recognized clearly the strategical implications and arranged his principal air bases with so sure an eye that many of them remained in use right up to the rearrangement of 1946 when British forces were removed from Egypt. By the middle of 1917 his brigade was fully organized, well sited, and well served. In August of that year he returned to England in order to take command of a training brigade, but this respite lasted only until the following January. Then he went back to the Middle East, as major-general, to take over the Middle East Command, Royal Flying Corps, a post which he held until 1921. This command was preserved during the interval between the wars; it served the Allied cause well in the war of 1939–1945; and it was the creation of Salmond who, with a prescience and breadth of outlook uncommon among air officers of his day, understood

its full significance and possibilities. As a command, it embraced all the territory covered by the earlier brigade, but it also spread itself beyond to the Persian Gulf and India.

While the war was still in progress Salmond laid out a line of air communications between Cairo and South Africa, making a chain of aerodromes which were used later by the flying pioneers and finally adopted by Imperial Airways. After the armistice he remained for three years in the Middle East consolidating the plan of which he was the author and chief engineer.

Salmond returned to England in 1922 as air member for supply and research, Air Council. He was given a permanent commission in the Royal Air Force as air vice-marshal in 1919. In 1927 he took over the command in India; at the end of 1928, when there was a revolution in Afghanistan, he arranged for the evacuation of Europeans from Kabul by air. He was promoted air marshal in 1929. In September 1931 he returned to England in order to become air officer commanding-in-chief Air Defence of Great Britain. He was promoted air chief marshal in January 1933, and became chief of Air Staff on 1 April of the same year.

Salmond was appointed C.B. in 1918, C.M.G. and K.C.M.G. in 1919, and K.C.B. in 1926; he was awarded the D.S.O. in 1917. The honorary degree of LL.D. was conferred upon him by Cambridge University in 1919. He married in 1910 Margaret Mary, eldest daughter of William Carr, of Ditchingham Hall, Norfolk, and had a son and three daughters. He died in London 27 April 1933.

[*The Times*, 28 April 1933; private information.]   E. COLSTON SHEPHERD.

SAMPSON, JOHN (1862–1931), Romani scholar, was born at Skull, co. Cork, 25 February 1862, the eldest son and third child of James Sampson, a chemist and mining engineer, who came of old Cornish stock, by his wife, Sarah Anne Macdermott, an Irishwoman, who was of Huguenot descent. His father died in 1871, leaving the family in straitened circumstances, and Sampson was apprenticed at the age of fourteen to Alexander Macgregor, a lithographer and engraver in Liverpool. His schooling had been brief, but he was all the more on his mettle to acquire scholarly accuracy, and resolutely taught himself, reading widely. In 1888 he tried, without financial success, to start a printing business. Four years later, in 1892, he was appointed the first librarian of University College, Liverpool, which afterwards became Liverpool University. For thirty-six years Sampson developed and enriched the library; and, while firm in maintaining discipline, spared no pains for, or encouragement to, genuine students, even the youngest. On his arrival he found gifted and inspiring friends, among them (Sir) Walter Alexander Raleigh [q.v.] and Kuno Meyer. As librarian, he sat *ex officio* on the senate, and in academic affairs always sided with the progressive party.

'Influenced', he says, 'by Borrow's inspiring romances', Sampson had long forgathered with gipsies and had begun to collect 'their language, folk-lore, and superstitions' (*The Welsh Gypsies*, a lecture delivered to the Liverpool Welsh National Society in 1901). In 1894 he encountered Edward Wood, a Welsh gipsy harpist and fiddler, from whom he heard the pure Welsh Romani dialect, 'an Indian language spoken in the heart of Wales'; 'a veritable mother-tongue miraculously preserved from corruption', and rapidly dying out. Sampson devoted the better part of his life to the study and interpretation of this language and of its speakers. He roamed amongst them, noting their sayings, tales, and customs, drew them out with instinctive sympathy, and became *par excellence* 'the Romano Rai' (gentleman-scholar, scholar-gipsy). Slowly, he amassed material; trained himself in phonetics, Sanskrit, and comparative philology; and poured out articles, chiefly in the *Journal* of the Gypsy Lore Society, of which he was long a pillar (see, for example, 'On the Origin and Early Migrations of the Gypsies', 3rd series, vol. ii, pp. 156–169, 1923). A notable series is that on 'Forty-Two Welsh Gypsy Folk-Tales' (Romani texts and translations; new series, vols. i–xii, 1907–1932). The final fruit of these labours was *The Dialect of the Gypsies of Wales* (1926), which was hailed by the experts as a masterpiece. 'He has already given to posterity what has aptly been described as the "canon" of their [the Welsh gipsies'] literature in the long series of his *Welsh Gypsy Tales*; and in his massive and scholarly *Dialect of the Gypsies of Wales* furnished us with a sure philological foundation for the intensive study of their idiom and its wide historical and ethnical relations' (Sir Donald MacAlister in *Journal* of the Gypsy Lore Society, 3rd

series, vol. xi, p. 38, 1932). 'A splendid volume, epoch-making in Gypsy and in Indo-Aryan studies', according to Jules Bloch in the *Bulletin de la Société de Linguistiques* (1926). In the lexicon itself the examples, taken straight from the unlettered speakers and accompanied by translations, are rich in entertainment even for the layman and reveal the gipsy temper and way of life. Sampson's *Romane Gilia* ('Romani Poems', 1931) are charged with his intense temperament and with the wild humour and fancy which are also rampant in the posthumous volume *In Lighter Moments* (1934). *The Wind on the Heath* (1930) is an attractive 'Gypsy anthology' in prose and verse from authors in many tongues. *Omar Khayyam* (1902) is a Romani version of twenty-two of Fitzgerald's quatrains, in the well-known metre. For Shelta, the hybrid tinkers' jargon, Sampson collected texts and a vocabulary (printed in Robert Alexander Stewart Macalister, *The Secret Languages of Ireland*, 1937, pp. 134 ff.).

Sampson's other great service to letters was the restoration of the text, long overlaid and 'improved' by editors, of William Blake's lyrics. In the *Poetical Works* (1905) he provided this definitive text with much critical and bibliographical apparatus. The edition of 1913 included 'The French Revolution', never before published, and long selections from the 'prophetic books'.

Sampson retired from office in 1928. He received many honours, which included honorary degrees from the universities of Oxford and Liverpool. He died 9 November 1931 at West Kirby, Cheshire, and by his own wish his ashes were scattered on Foel Goch, a height above the village of Llangwm, Denbighshire, to the sound of gipsy music. A Romani elegy, which Sampson had long before written on another 'Romano Rai', Francis Hindes Groome [q.v.], was recited.

Sampson was strongly built; his speech and tread were slow and deliberate. Very shy, he seemed at first, and despite his courtesy, somewhat formidable; but among his friends, to whom he showed a rare devotion, he was a great companion and free-minded humorist. Equally at home in a college and in the nomad camp, he brought a waft of the 'wind on the heath' into every atmosphere.

Sampson married in 1894 Jessie Margaret, daughter of David Sprunt, who lived successively near Runcorn and at Port Sunlight, Cheshire. He had two sons and a daughter; his younger son was killed in the war of 1914–1918.

[*The Times*, 10 and 14 November 1931; *Manchester Guardian*, 23 November 1931; R. A. Scott Macfie ('Andreas') in *Journal of the Gypsy Lore Society*, 3rd series, vol. xi, 1932; private information from Miss D. E. Yates, especially for Romani matter; personal knowledge.]   OLIVER ELTON.

SAMPSON, RALPH ALLEN (1866–1939), astronomer, was born 25 June 1866 at Skull, co. Cork, the third son in the family of five children of James Sampson, metallurgical chemist, by his wife Sarah Anne Macdermott. He was the younger brother of John Sampson [q.v.] When Ralph was five years old the family removed to Liverpool, where James Sampson, who was a Cornishman, lay ill for two years. At his death the income had fallen to £50 a year. Sampson had but little education until he was fourteen, when it became possible to send him to the Liverpool Institute: there he soon came to the front, and in June 1884 he was admitted as a sizar of St. John's College, Cambridge, going into residence at the following Easter, and being elected scholar of the college at the end of his first term. In 1888 he graduated as third wrangler. In the spring of 1890 he was awarded the first Smith's prize, and in November was elected into a fellowship at St. John's.

From 1889 to 1891 Sampson held a lecturership in mathematics at King's College, London, and during this period he published a hydrodynamical investigation 'On Stokes' Current-Function' in the *Philosophical Transactions* of the Royal Society (vol. clxxxii, 1891). In 1891 he returned to Cambridge as the first holder of the newly founded Isaac Newton studentship in astronomy and physical optics: here for two years he worked on astronomical spectroscopy with H. F. Newall, and in 1893 he published a memoir 'On the Rotation and Mechanical State of the Sun' (*Memoirs* of the Royal Astronomical Society, vol. li), which is notable as being the first treatment of the subject in which prominence was given to the effects of radiation and absorption (as compared with convection) on the sun's internal temperature.

In the autumn of 1893 Sampson left Cambridge on his election to the chair of mathematics in the Durham College of Science at Newcastle-upon-Tyne. In 1896 he removed to Durham itself, as professor of mathematics in the university, where he concurrently held the revived chair of astronomy from 1908 to 1910. In the latter year he was appointed professor of astronomy in Edinburgh University and astronomer royal for Scotland. Failing health led to his resignation from these posts in 1937. He died suddenly at Bath 7 November 1939.

Sampson's most important contributions to science, which occupied most of his time and energy from 1900 to 1920, are his *Tables of the Four Great Satellites of Jupiter* (1910) and his 'Theory' of these satellites (*Memoirs* of the Royal Astronomical Society, vol. lxiii, 1920). He was elected F.R.S. in 1903, was awarded the gold medal of the Royal Astronomical Society for his work on the satellites of Jupiter in 1928, and received honorary degrees from the universities of Durham and Glasgow.

Sampson married in 1893 Ida, daughter of Hudson Atkinson Binney, of St. Helens, Lancashire, and had a son and four daughters.

[*The Times*, 11 November 1939; *Obituary Notices of Fellows of the Royal Society*, No. 8, January 1940 (portrait); personal knowledge.]   E. T. WHITTAKER.

SAMSON, CHARLES RUMNEY (1883–1931), air commodore, was born at Manchester 8 July 1883, the second son of Charles Leopold Samson, solicitor, by his wife, Margaret Alice Rumney. He passed into the *Britannia*, joined his first ship as a midshipman in 1898, and served in the *Pomone* during the Somaliland operations of 1903–1904. As first lieutenant in the cruiser *Philomel* he took part in the suppression of gun-running in the Persian Gulf in 1909–1910.

In 1911 Samson was selected by the Admiralty as one of the first four naval officers to be trained to fly; he qualified for his pilot's certificate in six weeks of bad weather. From then onwards his life was devoted to flying. By December 1911 he had persuaded the Admiralty to equip the *Africa* with a launching platform which projected over the bows, and in the following year with similar apparatus he took off in a Short biplane from the *Hibernia* while the ship steamed at full speed. This was the first flight from a ship's deck to be made in Europe and marked the beginning of the idea of the aircraft-carrier: Samson contributed largely by experiment and demonstration to the growth of this project. He collaborated with Horace Short in designing a seaplane, and was a pioneer in aerial wireless communication and in bomb-dropping. On the formation of the Royal Flying Corps he was given command of the naval wing, and as commandant of the new naval air station at Eastchurch from 1912 to 1914 he practised cross-country flying and night-flying as exercises in air navigation, and had so much advanced naval flying during the early months of 1912 that he and four of his officers were allowed to fly over the naval review at Portland in May.

On the outbreak of war in 1914 Samson and his squadron were sent to Dunkirk with a brigade of marines. When the brigade was withdrawn to England a week later, he contrived to remain behind, linked up with the French forces in northern France, fitted out some of the squadron's motor-cars and lorries with machine-guns, and subsequently with a 3-pounder gun, and proceeded to help the French with a mixture of cavalry operations, infantry attack, and air reconnaissance. Self-reliance, dash, and ingenuity gave an air of buccaneering to these operations which delighted the French and produced results which, although on a small scale, could not be ignored by the British authorities. His mixed collection of aircraft also engaged in bombing the Zeppelin sheds at Düsseldorf and Cologne; and by the end of the year, when mobile warfare took its place, and trench warfare took its place, his squadron had won four D.S.O.'s, among them his own, and he was given special promotion and the rank of commander. He spent the next few months bombing gun positions, submarine depots, and seaplane sheds on the Belgian coast.

In March 1915 Samson's unit was moved to the Dardanelles. He was allotted a base made out of vineyards on the island of Tenedos. He was later moved to Imbros where he rejected the existing aerodrome and made a new one, using seventy Turkish prisoners as labourers. His squadron patrolled the Straits, spotted for the battleships, attacked the Turkish communications, including railway bridges, and ultimately covered the Allied evacuation. He even made his own brand of large bomb out of a twenty-six-gallon petrol tank, when he considered the regulation 20-lb. bombs inadequate.

At the end of this campaign Samson's unit was disbanded and he was given command of the Ben My Chree, a former Isle of Man passenger steamer fitted out as a seaplane carrier, and attended by two slower ships as escorts. Based on Port Said, he ranged the coasts of Palestine, Syria, and Arabia, sometimes bombarding Turkish positions, sometimes sending his seaplanes on reconnaissance and offensive tasks, and always demanding more work from the naval and military commanders. In January 1917 he sailed to Kastelorizo to carry out some operations with the French, and in the harbour there the Ben My Chree was sunk by Turkish gunfire. His two escort ships, already equipped to carry a few seaplanes, were now fitted out for independent air operations, and from Aden and later Colombo he searched among the islands and over the expanses of the Indian Ocean for enemy raiders.

Early in 1917 Samson was given command of the aircraft group at Great Yarmouth which was responsible for anti-submarine and anti-Zeppelin operations over the North Sea. He remained in this position until the end of the war and during that time his group shot down five Zeppelins. In order to bring fighter aircraft into action near the enemy coasts, he devised lighters to be towed behind naval ships and used as take-off platforms by fighter aircraft. He made the first trial take-off himself, but his Camel tumbled over the bows and the lighter passed over both aeroplane and pilot; he saved his life with some difficulty, and afterwards modified the design of the platform so that it served satisfactorily. In October 1918 the group at Great Yarmouth became a wing and was made part of a new group at Felixstowe under the control of the Royal Air Force; Samson became commanding officer of this group, and in August 1919 he gave up his naval commission and received a permanent commission in the Royal Air Force with the rank of group captain.

During 1920 Samson served in the Coastal Area as chief staff officer, and in the following year he became air officer commanding Royal Air Force units in the Mediterranean, with headquarters at Malta. In 1922 he was promoted air commodore and given command of a fighter group at Kenley. At this period his domestic affairs caused him much grief and anxiety and seemed to shake the buoyant self-assurance which was part of the secret of his success. He had married in 1917 Honor Oakden Patrickson, daughter of Herbert Storey, of Lancaster; he divorced her in 1923. He did excellent work a few years later, but the incident left its mark and probably had some influence on his early retirement from the service. In June 1926 he became chief staff officer, Middle East Command, and in that position he did the last of his pioneering work. He organized and led the first flight of a Royal Air Force bomber formation over Africa from Cairo to the Cape. This involved making and supplying the necessary bases and surveying an undeveloped route. The flight succeeded. Where Samson had led, other formations followed in succeeding years, and, later, commercial air transport for the most part used the trail which Samson had blazed in 1926. He remained with the Middle East Command until August 1927, but the great flight through Africa was his last big task.

Samson's chief qualities were his energy, his skill in improvisation, his personal courage, and his ability to pick the right men and to inspire them to intense and efficient effort. He was short, thick-set, and continued to wear a pointed beard after his transfer to the otherwise beardless Royal Air Force. His 'Captain Kettle' temperament accorded with his appearance, and his superiors, continually bombarded with well thought out if advanced proposals, were never allowed to forget his existence for long. He married secondly in 1924 Winifred, daughter of Herbert Kempson Reeves, solicitor, of Leatherhead. By his first marriage he had a daughter, and by his second marriage a son and a daughter (who was born posthumously). He resigned his commission in 1929 and died at Cholderton, Wiltshire, 5 February 1931. He was awarded the D.S.O. (1914) and bar (1917), the A.F.C. (1919), and the French Croix de Guerre with palm (1914); he was appointed C.M.G. (1919) and chevalier of the Legion of Honour (1915).

Portraits of Samson are included in two paintings, one by Fleming Williams, the other by Donald Maxwell, at the Imperial War Museum.

[*The Times*, 6 February 1931; C. R. Samson, *Fights and Flights*, 1930, and *A Flight from Cairo to Cape Town and Back*, 1931; *The Aeroplane*, 11 February 1931; C. F. S. Gamble, *The Story of a North Sea Air Station*, 1928.]
E. COLSTON SHEPHERD.

SANDERSON, BARON (1868–1939), educationist. [See FURNISS, HENRY SANDERSON.]

SANDS, LORD (1857–1934), Scottish judge. [See JOHNSTON, Sir CHRISTOPHER NICHOLSON.]

SANKARAN NAIR, SIR CHETTUR (1857–1934), Indian jurist, administrator, and politician, was born 11 July 1857 into the matriarchal Nair community of the west coast of India, and was educated at the Madras Presidency College.

After a successful career at the Madras High Court bar, which he finally led as advocate-general, Nair was promoted to the High Court bench in 1907, a post which he relinquished in 1915 in order to serve as member for education on the viceroy's executive council. Four years' rather uneasy tenure of this appointment ended in his resignation in 1919, and later in the same year he accepted the invitation of E. S. Montagu [q.v.] to serve upon the secretary of state's council. He remained in Whitehall until 1921, when he left the service of the government and returned to India as adviser to the Indore State.

While at the bar, Nair founded and edited the *Madras Review* and helped to conduct the *Madras Law Journal*, perhaps the best of the unofficial reports. His interest in social and political reform in those days culminated in his presidency of the Congress held at Amraoti in 1897. Years later, after severing his connexion with the British government, he issued a manifesto denouncing Gandhi's first non-co-operation movement, and published a book entitled *Gandhi and Anarchy* (1922). Dealing in this with the Punjab 'atrocities' of 1919 he bitterly attacked the then lieutenant-governor, Sir Michael O'Dwyer [q.v.]. The libel action which ensued was tried in 1924 by Mr. Justice McCardie [q.v.] and resulted in a verdict for O'Dwyer, with agreed damages.

In 1928 Nair accepted the chairmanship of the Indian central committee appointed to co-operate with the Simon statutory commission. The committee, however, failed to reach even a moderate degree of agreement, so that its work was largely unfruitful.

Nair was an Indian patriot of an unusual type. Strong and fearless in character and always ready to face unpleasant facts, he cared little whether his rugged bluntness of speech caused offence; and the defects of his qualities were apt to offend his official colleagues, who found him combative and lacking in reticence. Montagu, who toured India in 1917–1918 as a step in the preparation of his reforms, has left a very unflattering portrait, difficult to reconcile with his subsequent selection of Nair for a seat on his council.

As a High Court judge, Nair's exceptional independence of outlook and intimate knowledge of the systems of law prevailing on the west coast enabled him to contribute some valuable judgements. His chairmanship of the Indian central committee has been severely criticized, but the task of reconciling its discordant elements was indeed no easy one.

Nair was appointed C.I.E. in 1904 and knighted in 1912. He died at Madras 24 April 1934.

[*The Times*, 25 April 1934; E. S. Montagu, *An Indian Diary*, edited by Venetia Montagu, 1930; private information.]

A. J. CURGENVEN.

SASSOON, SIR PHILIP ALBERT GUSTAVE DAVID, third baronet, of Kensington Gore (1888–1939), politician and connoisseur, was born in Paris 4 December 1888, the only son of (Sir) Edward Albert Sassoon, second baronet, by his wife, Aline Caroline, daughter of Baron Gustave de Rothschild, of the French branch. He was grandson of Sir Albert Abdullah David Sassoon, first baronet [q.v.], who had been born at Bagdad in 1818 and had accompanied his father, David Sassoon, when he moved to Bombay and there founded the great merchant house of David Sassoon & company. The Sassoons had been settled in Mesopotamia for many centuries, and local tradition claimed that they had been driven out of Spain in the fifteenth century.

Philip Sassoon was educated at Eton and Christ Church, Oxford. At nineteen years of age he chose British nationality, having, on account of his birth in France, the right to elect for one country or the other. In 1912 his father, who had been unionist member for Hythe since 1899, died, and he was returned to parliament in the same interest for the same constituency. He represented it without a break for twenty-seven years, until his death. In 1933 he received the freedom of the borough. When war broke out in 1914 he held a commission in the Royal East Kent Yeomanry, and in December 1915 he was appointed private secretary to (Field Marshal) Sir Douglas (later Earl) Haig [q.v.], commander-in-chief of the British armies. In this important position, which he held until after the armistice, his cosmopolitan social gifts were fully called into play, and he obtained a unique view of the war, and of the statesmen and generals who were conducting it. It was to Sassoon that Haig handed the piece of paper on which he had written the famous 'Backs to the Wall' order of the day, and the field-marshal subsequently gave it to him. He retained it until his death, when he bequeathed it to the British Museum.

In the years immediately following 1918 Sassoon busied himself with politics, with travelling, and with entertaining. He completed Port Lympne, near Hythe, the country residence which he had begun before the war, and on which he spent freely his great fortune. This house soon became famous for its meetings between the various statesmen and soldiers who were conducting the lengthy Peace Conference in Paris, and their host showed his own particular qualities of tact and considerateness. In 1924 Sassoon was appointed under-secretary of state for air, a post which he held until 1929, and again from 1931 until 1937. During the second period the secretary of state for air sat in the House of Lords, and in consequence Sassoon represented his ministry in the House of Commons. His annual speech on the introduction of the air estimates, invariably delivered without a single written note, was followed with attention by members of all parties, because of its careful reasoning and mass of skilfully presented detail. Sassoon's quick comprehension of the meaning of air power did much to rouse the public: while the personal interest which he took in the Royal Air Force and the enthusiasm with which he always sought to promote its welfare were of great service to the country. In 1929 appeared his only book, *The Third Route*, notable for its descriptive skill and for its power of humorous exaggeration, both of which distinguished equally his conversation. In 1937 he was appointed first commissioner of Works, a post which synthetized many of his energies, and wherein he was most happy. Although death cut short his tenure of this office, several memorials remain to his taste: notably his restoration of Sir James Thornhill's Painted Hall at Greenwich Hospital.

Honours, like great wealth, came to Sassoon early. He was sworn of the Privy Council in 1929, held numerous orders and decorations, British and foreign (including the G.B.E., 1922), and was for many years a trustee of the National Gallery (chairman of the board from December 1932 to 1936), the Tate Gallery, the Wallace Collection, and the British School at Rome. But, despite his successful career, his gifts were perhaps more those of an artist than of a politician. His kindnesses were, like his wit, creative, and in Port Lympne and Trent Park, New Barnet, he made works of art. The first preserved the qualities of his fire and brilliance as a young man, while the second reflected his more mature judgement. Besides being a judge of pictures, he was a connoisseur of furniture, china, and old silver—in fact of all beautiful or decorative objects. The exhibitions, such as 'Conversation Pieces' and 'The Age of Walnut', which were held, in aid of charity, each spring for many years in his London house were famous among art-lovers. These exhibitions were organized by Sassoon and by his cousin Mrs. David Gubbay, who acted as hostess for him at Trent and Port Lympne. No picture of life between the wars is complete without some account of one of these houses, filled always with politicians, painters, writers, professional golfers, and airmen. His great entertainments were imbued with his personality and with imagination, as if with a kind of magic, and he seemed to be surrounded by a constant activity in house and garden.

Sassoon died, after a month's illness, at his London house, 45 Park Lane, 3 June 1939. He was unmarried, and the baronetcy became extinct. His only sister married the fifth Marquess of Cholmondeley.

There are several portraits of Sassoon, notably a painting and a charcoal-drawing by J. S. Sargent, and a painting by Glyn Philpot, all three of which are in Lady Cholmondeley's possession.

[Sir P. Sassoon, *The Third Route*, 1929; private information; personal knowledge.]
OSBERT SITWELL.

SAVAGE, ETHEL MARY (1881–1939), better known as MISS ETHEL M. DELL, novelist, was born at Streatham 2 August 1881, the younger daughter of John Vincent Dell, who was on the staff of the Equitable Life Assurance Company, by his wife, Irene Parrott. She was educated at a private school in Streatham and spent most of her early life at Knockholt, near Sevenoaks. The family moved to Ashford, Middlesex, where the father and mother died, and subsequently the two Misses Dell settled in Guildford. In 1922 the younger married Lieutenant-Colonel Gerald Tahourdin Savage, Royal Army Service Corps, who survived her. She died in a nursing home at Hereford 17 September 1939.

Ethel Dell showed a facility for writing as a child, and throughout her youth she contributed to various fiction magazines of the more elementary sort. She had a huge success with her first novel, *The Way of an Eagle* (1912), and there was hardly one of her subsequent thirty-four works of fiction (of which the last is dated 1939) which was not enormously popular. Her naturally retiring disposition was rendered doubly so by her nation-wide reputation; and she insisted on living a withdrawn, unpublicized life, motoring in the country and enjoying her garden and her dogs. Physically she was a handsome woman, rather above the average in height. Casual acquaintances have spoken of her unusual charm and simplicity of manner. She was generous to a fault with the large income brought in by her books.

As a popular novelist, Ethel Dell belongs to the class of Charles Garvice, Mrs. Florence Barclay, and Miss Edith Maude Hull: that is to say, her public was an ingenuous and uncritical one, which asked only for a well-sustained, romantic narrative, with dangers averted, innocence unsmirched, and characters recognizable from the first for what they proved to be. All of these she provided. She could tell with speed and deftness a story which was always wholesome, frequently dramatic, and certain of a happy ending. Her heroes (often short of stature and rather plain) are whipcord or tempered steel. Her heroines are proud, unhappy, and inclined to be fierce before marriage, although when at last they yield to their faithful lovers' pleas they become utterly submissive. Her villains are unmistakable 'Sir Jaspers', in whatsoever guise they appear. There is a curious strain of almost sadism in a number of the books: possibly her writing-self sought to redress the balance of her other self's timidity and gentleness. The children are rough and ill mannered; young women are subjected to tyrannies and insolence; male characters, otherwise commendable, take pleasure in being rude to ladies.

Miss Dell's work is free from the mawkishness of Garvice and Mrs. Barclay. Also it is noticeable that her characters are all more or less of the same social class. She rises above the *Peg's Paper* formula of duke and dairymaid, and also above the pure and lovely woman whose radiant influence transforms an unconvincing sinner into an intolerable saint. Indeed her plots have the liveliness, and promise something of the fevered tension, of a Cynthia Stockley novel. But the promise is unfulfilled. Passion is under ultimate control, and, however black things may look, deviation from the path of propriety is checked in time. This insistence on virtue in circumstances only explicable in terms of frailty makes her stories unreal. *The Hundredth Chance* (1917) is a good specimen of her qualities and her defects.

[*The Times*, 19 September 1939; private information.]   MICHAEL SADLEIR.

SAYCE, ARCHIBALD HENRY (1845–1933), orientalist and comparative philologist, was born at Shirehampton, near Bristol, 25 September 1845, the eldest son of Henry Samuel Sayce, perpetual curate of Shirehampton, by his wife, Mary Anne Cartwright. The father came of a Glamorganshire family. From birth Archibald Sayce was very delicate, and until over the age of seven suffered from pulmonary tuberculosis; during this time he did not even learn the alphabet. But at ten he was reading Virgil and Xenophon and attacking Homeric Greek and English literature with a tutor. In 1858, when his father migrated to Batheaston, Archibald became a day boy at Grosvenor College, Bath. There oriental studies (especially Hebrew) and comparative philology awakened his keen interest; when he was fourteen he learned the hieroglyphic alphabet and the names of the Pharaohs, and drew oriental inscriptions and works of art. During an attack of typhoid fever he studied cuneiform, laying the foundations of his career as an Assyriologist. At sixteen he developed an interest in theology; and while still at school he worked enthusiastically at Assyrian, as well as at Persian, Arabic, and Sanskrit, hoping for an Indian civil service appointment.

In 1865 Sayce went to Oxford; although entered for Brasenose he won a scholarship at Queen's College at the time of his matriculation. His first year saw the beginning of lifelong friendships with Friedrich Max Müller (with whom he read the Vedic hymns) and (Sir) John Rhŷs [qq.v.]. Just after he had gained a first class in classical moderations (1866) his eyesight broke down (not to be really cured until 1874) and his old lung trouble returned; for this he was sent to Pau and Biarritz, where he learned Basque. In 1868, while suffering from pneumonia, he obtained a first class in *literae humaniores*; but a second attack prevented his sitting for the honour school of law and modern history the following year. In 1869, shortly after taking his degree, he was elected a fellow and classical lecturer of Queen's; in 1870 he became a college tutor, and was also

ordained. In the early 'seventies he was a regular weekly contributor to *The Times* and the New York *Independent*. In 1874 he gave the first translations of the very difficult astronomical and astrological tablets from Nineveh, in a lecture to the Society of Biblical Archaeology, of which he was president from 1898 until it ceased to be an independent body in 1919. He was one of the Oxford representatives in the Old Testament revision company from 1874 to 1884; in 1876, after taking up Indo-Germanic philology, he became deputy professor of comparative philology.

From 1872 onwards Sayce spent most of his vacations travelling in Europe. In 1877–1878 he was in Greece as special correspondent of *The Times*, and in 1878 was nominated by the Italian government as delegate from Oxford to the Fourth Oriental Congress at Florence. He resigned his tutorship in the following year, and was then free to devote all his time to his special interests, including exploration of the East. Thereafter, almost until his death, he spent much of each year in travel, partly for his health's sake; he visited most of the countries of Europe and Asia (Major and Minor) including the Far East, also North Africa and the United States of America. In 1879 he helped to found the Society for the Promotion of Hellenic Studies. Two years later he copied and published as *The Ancient Hebrew Inscription Discovered at the Pool of Siloam in Jerusalem* the important inscription cut perhaps during the reign of Hezekiah in a tunnel which brought water into Jerusalem. One of his greatest triumphs was the decipherment (without any bilingual text) of the ancient Armenian ('Vannic') inscriptions, which he published in two articles in the *Journal* of the Royal Asiatic Society (vol. xiv, 1882) under the title of 'The Cuneiform Inscriptions of Van, deciphered and translated'.

In 1890, after his father's death, Sayce resigned his professorship and other university offices, retaining only his college fellowship, and planned to spend the rest of his days in Egypt. On arriving there he helped to found the Alexandria Museum, and was also instrumental in securing for the British Museum two important Greek works previously believed to be lost: Aristotle's *Constitution of Athens* and the *Mimes* of Herondas. In 1891, however, Oxford offered Sayce an extraordinary professorship of Assyriology; he accepted it gladly, and this led to his still living part of each year in Oxford. But from then on he spent much of his time in a large Nile-boat which he fitted up with his considerable library. In the following year he gave up his London flat and took a house in Edinburgh, which he occupied at intervals until his death. The years 1908–1910 were devoted to the exploration of the Sudan; during this period be brought about the excavation of Meroë, the ancient capital of Ethiopia, by Professor John Garstang for Liverpool University. The winter of 1911–1912 saw him in the Far East. In 1915 he resigned his professorship. Thereafter he lived quietly, dividing his time among Edinburgh, Oxford, and Egypt, and writing many articles and reviews. He died, unmarried, at Bath 4 February 1933, having bequeathed his oriental books to his college, his notes and copies to the Bodleian Library, and his collections, Near and Far Eastern, of antiquities, ceramics, etc., to the Ashmolean Museum.

Sayce's many publications showed forth an original mind, and a very active imagination. As early as 1870 a paper on 'An Accadian Seal', published in the *Journal of Philology*, laid the foundations of Sumerian grammar. With his *Assyrian Grammar* (1872), *Elementary Grammar with Reading-Book of the Assyrian Language* (1875), and *Lectures upon the Assyrian Language and Syllabary* (1877) he was the first to give in English the means of mastering the Assyrian language and writing, and he directed the serious attention of many Semitic scholars to the 'new' language. From 1874 onwards he contributed a number of Assyrian translations to *Records of the Past*, the second series of which (1888–1893) was also edited by him. General linguistics were represented by his *Principles of Comparative Philology* (1874–1875) and *Introduction to the Science of Language* (2 vols., 1880; 2nd ed. 1883; 3rd ed. 1890); in the former he insisted on the principle of analogy, which was to become a corner-stone of linguistic science. Several books were devoted to the Hebrew race and literature; such were *The Early History of the Hebrews* (1897), *Early Israel and the Surrounding Nations* (1898), and introductions to, and commentaries on, certain books of the Old Testament. In *The 'Higher Criticism' and the Verdict of the Monuments* (1894) he appealed from current theories, especially German ones, concerning the Old Testament to the evidence of archaeological remains and discoveries. Here may be mentioned his edition, with (Sir) A. E. Cowley [q.v.], of the *Aramaic Papyri Discovered at Assuan* (1906).

In 1882 Sayce devoted a long article to 'The Bilingual Hittite and Cuneiform Inscriptions of Tarkondêmos' (*Transactions of the Society of Biblical Archaeology*, vol. vii), and from then to the end of his life published many studies of the Hittites and their language, and was the first to introduce the forgotten empire of that people to the modern world in the face of almost universal ridicule; his repeated attempts at decipherment of the Hittite hieroglyphs, however, were not fruitful. In 1885 he published a decipherment, which has stood the test of time, of the texts of Mal-Amir, and so helped to place Elamite studies on a sound basis. Over a period of many years he published books and articles on the countries, peoples, history, religion, and literature of the Babylonians and Assyrians, and it was as an Assyriologist that he was chiefly known. In the ninth edition (1896) of Murray's *Handbook for Travellers in Egypt* his detailed knowledge of that country was utilized to good purpose; and he published many useful copies of Egyptian inscriptions. He wrote several books on the general archaeology of the Near East. A translation of Herodotus, Books I–III (1883) contained a number of philological errors, and was severely criticized. His last book was a stout volume of *Reminiscences* (1923), in which the doings of seventy-eight years are chronicled.

Sayce was an excellent and active lecturer, and gave addresses in many parts of the world. He often chose this form for the communication of important discoveries made by him. He published in 1887 his Hibbert lectures on Babylonian religion; in 1902 his Gifford lectures on Egyptian and Babylonian religion; and in 1907 his Rhind lectures on *The Archaeology of the Cuneiform Inscriptions*. He received honorary degrees from the universities of Oxford, Edinburgh, Aberdeen, Dublin, and Oslo, and the triennial gold medal of the Royal Asiatic Society (1925). In 1919 he was elected a corresponding member of the Institut de France; with this, he tells us, the chief ambition of his life was realized.

Sayce was a great *vulgarisateur*, especially in opening people's eyes to the importance of oriental archaeology for the understanding of the Bible. He both read and wrote enormously, and his great activity (including a number of excavations) was one of his most striking features. It was said that no man of his time (Jules Oppert perhaps excepted) had such a linguistic equipment, and that he could write good prose in at least twenty ancient and modern languages. His memory was extraordinary. He was a veritable clearing-house of archaeological learning and news, conversing and corresponding freely with the orientalists of three generations. In Assyriology he was one of the most remarkable figures of what has been called the heroic age of that subject. He was a great decipherer, and on his attainments in that direction his reputation will no doubt chiefly rest. He was a pioneer in other ways: he was among the first to appreciate the significance of Heinrich Schliemann's discoveries, and he demonstrated the existence of pre-Hellenic civilization in Greek lands long before the Mycenean age was accepted by scholars. But his widespread interests (embracing many Pacific cultures and cults) and vivid imagination made it impossible for him to specialize, and his conclusions were often vitiated by hasty judgements; indeed his critical faculty was inferior to his others. His repeated attacks on the 'higher criticism' were deprecated by many of his well informed colleagues. Nevertheless, he made important and lasting contributions to oriental philology and archaeology.

Few men so active and long-lived can have been so continually dogged by ill health as was Sayce. Weak lungs (his first utterance was a cough) and weak eyes were lifelong banes; the first, with their tuberculous tendency, forced him to live out of England most of his time, and gave him four attacks of pneumonia; the second hampered his work by making the reading of cuneiform tablets difficult. Typhoid, blood-poisoning, a fractured knee-cap, haemorrhage, sciatica, a snake-bite which he cauterized himself with his cook's red-hot tongs, thus saving his life, and a collision with a motor-car were among his set-backs, to which he opposed a wiry physique and great powers of recuperation.

Sayce had a very lovable character, and never spoke harshly of those who denounced his work. His charm was deeply felt by his colleagues and a large circle of other friends and acquaintances, by his pupils, to whom he devoted much time and attention, and by the natives of Egypt and Mesopotamia.

A portrait of Sayce by G. Fiddes Watt (1919) hangs in Queen's College, Oxford.

[A. H. Sayce, *Reminiscences*, 1923; Sir E. A. W. Budge, *The Rise and Progress of Assyriology*, 1925; *The Times*, 6 February 1933; *Journal* of the Royal Asiatic Society, April 1933; *Oxford Magazine*, 16 February 1933.]   BATTISCOMBE GUNN.

SCHAFER, SIR EDWARD ALBERT SHARPEY- (1850–1935), physiologist, was born at Hornsey 2 June 1850. He was the third son and fifth child of James William Henry Schäfer whose father was a noted musician at Hamburg, and who came to England as a young man and was shortly afterwards naturalized, settling in Highgate as a City merchant: he married Jessie, daughter of W. H. Brown, of London.

Schafer, after attending small schools in early childhood, was educated at Clewer House School, Windsor, and later at University College School, Gower Street, and University College. His elder brothers, like the other members of his family, had gone into business, but Schafer astonished his parents by saying that he wished to continue his education and study medicine. This was a break with the family tradition, but his parents agreed, and when he showed his capacity and won prizes and medals they were proud of him. In due time he became qualified as a medical practitioner. He was elected the first Sharpey scholar at University College in 1871. This award carried with it teaching duties, William Sharpey [q.v.], who was professor of general anatomy and physiology, being the first to institute classes in the practical side of these subjects. Schafer owed much to Sharpey, who has been described as the founder of English physiology, and when in 1918 he prefixed Sharpey's surname to his own he did so in order to emphasize this indebtedness. He became assistant professor of physiology in 1874 on (Sir) J. S. Burdon-Sanderson [q.v.] succeeding Sharpey, and was appointed Jodrell professor in 1883 when Burdon-Sanderson went to Oxford. Schafer was also Fullerian professor at the Royal Institution from 1878 to 1881. He resigned his professorship at University College in 1899 on being elected to the chair of physiology in the university of Edinburgh. He held this post until 1933 when he became emeritus professor, having completed more than sixty years as a teacher.

Schafer's early research work was in histology, and he maintained his interest in this subject throughout his life, holding that it is essentially a part of physiology, being necessary for a proper understanding of functional activity. His investigations on the wing structure of insects and on the absorption of fat by the villi of the small intestine of mammals attracted considerable notice. He was fond of recalling the fact that his first paper, which was on the nerves of the jellyfish and their mode of working, was rejected by the Royal Society (Ray Lankester said that it was nonsense), but when Oscar and Richard Hertwig made identical discoveries which were printed in a foreign journal, Schafer's paper was hurriedly published, and (as if to make amends) he was elected F.R.S. in 1878 a few days after his twenty-eighth birthday.

In 1883 Schafer published the results of his first researches on cerebral localization and in the following year he showed how photography could be successfully applied to record the beat of the frog's heart, and he also made use of a piston recorder. In 1886 in conjunction with (Sir) Victor Horsley [q.v.] he studied muscular contraction produced by stimulation of different parts of the motor tract, and he recorded the muscular rhythm that resulted from volitional impulses in man. Furthermore, with Sanger Brown, he investigated the effect of ablation of portions of the cortex of the brain and the effect of stimulating the visual area in monkeys and the working of the ciliary muscle. These investigations occupied him until about 1893.

The remarkable effect of an extract of the suprarenal gland when injected into the circulation in causing a constriction of the arterioles and a marked rise of the blood-pressure was discovered by George Oliver and Schafer in 1894. It led to the opening up of a field of research which has proved of the greatest importance to practical medicine. Schafer subsequently published further papers on the internal secretions (with Oliver, Benjamin Moore, Swale Vincent, and P. T. Herring). The study of these secretions, by E. H. Starling [q.v.], subsequently called 'hormones', is now known as endocrinology and Schafer did much to develop it. Before leaving University College he also did work (with Moore) on the innervation and contraction of the spleen and on the alleged sensory function of the motor cortex.

After going to Edinburgh Schafer continued his researches and published papers on the effects of partial transection of the spinal cord and circumsection of the motor cortex. In 1902 he demonstrated a direct communication of canaliculi with blood capillaries in the liver. Later he did work (with H. J. Scharlieb) on the action of

chloroform on the heart and vessels, (with A. N. Bruce) on the cerebellar tracts of the spinal cord, and (with Walker May) on the effects of section of the vagus and cervical sympathetic nerves. He also investigated the pulmonary circulation, and the influence of the vagus nerve on respiration and the action of the intercostal muscles. Among his latest researches on nerve function was one which involved the cutting of a nerve in his own arm.

Mention must also be made of Schafer's prone-pressure method of employing artificial respiration on persons apparently drowned. In a paper communicated to the Royal Society of Edinburgh in 1903, he showed that by this method the respiratory exchange was much greater than that occurring under the Marshall Hall, Howard, and Sylvester methods; it was subsequently adopted by the Royal Life Saving Society, which awarded him its Distinguished Service medal in 1909.

Schafer was the author of the following books, some of which have been widely used by students: *A Course of Practical Histology* (1877), *The Essentials of Histology* (1885), vol. ii, part i of the eleventh edition of *Quain's Elements of Anatomy* (1912), *Experimental Physiology* (1912), an *Advanced Text-book of Physiology* (of which he was editor and part-author, 2 vols., 1898–1900), *The Endocrine Organs* (1916), and a *History of the Physiological Society* (1927). Of this society Schafer was one of the founders in 1876, and at its jubilee the sole survivor of its original members. He also founded in 1908 the *Quarterly Journal of Experimental Physiology*. He was editor until his retirement in 1933, when a bound volume was presented to him, containing a vellum interleaf on which twenty-nine of his past and present assistants who contributed articles to it signed their names. It constitutes vol. xxiii of the *Journal*.

Schafer received many distinctions and held many posts. He was general secretary to the British Association from 1895 to 1900 and was president in 1912. He was president of the International Congress of Physiologists in 1923, and of the Royal Society of Edinburgh in 1933. He received honorary degrees from several British and various other universities, including Berne, Groningen, and Louvain. He obtained the highest award of the Royal Society of London, the Copley medal, in 1924, and numerous other medals. In 1913 he was knighted.

Schafer had a strictly evangelical upbringing and although he relinquished his religion he maintained throughout his life the high ethical standards of conduct and outlook which his parents had taught him, and he never forgot his Bible, which he could quote in such a way as to astonish even students of religion. He had a sincere regard for the truth and a hatred of intellectual dishonesty. At the same time he was liberal and tolerant as is shown, for example, by his championship of the rights of women, especially in the matter of their admission to the medical profession. He earned the appreciation of all members of his staff, many of whom themselves became distinguished workers. Moreover, he was a fine lecturer and won the admiration of his students. With a somewhat stern exterior he was one of the kindliest of men, and with those who came to know him well initial respect grew to permanent affection. He took a delight in hospitality and he invited every member of his class to large student parties which gave him unfeigned pleasure. At North Berwick, where he lived during his Edinburgh days, he was a regular player on the golf links. He married twice: first, in 1878 Maud (died 1896), daughter of Adolphus William Dixey, head of the firm of opticians of that name in Bond Street, and sister of Frederick Augustus Dixey, F.R.S., the entomologist; secondly, in 1900 Ethel Maude, youngest daughter of John Henry Roberts, F.R.C.S. By his first wife he had two sons, both of whom were killed in the war of 1914–1918, and two daughters, the elder of whom died young. He died at North Berwick 29 March 1935.

[*Obituary Notices of Fellows of the Royal Society*, No. 4, December 1935 (portrait); *The Times*, 30 March 1935; private information; personal knowledge.]   F. H. A. MARSHALL.

SCHILLER, FERDINAND CANNING SCOTT (1864–1937), philosopher, was born at Ottensen, near Altona, 16 August 1864, the second son of Ferdinand Schiller, a German merchant, of London and Calcutta, by his wife, Rosa De Castro. He was educated at Rugby (scholar) and at Balliol College, Oxford (exhibitioner), where he obtained a first class in classical moderations (1883) and in *literae humaniores* (1886) and was Taylorian scholar in German (1887). He became instructor in philosophy at Cornell University in 1893, and formed a friendship with William James which had a great influence upon his intellectual development. In 1897 he was appointed to a tutorial fellowship at

Corpus Christi College, Oxford, a post which he held until 1926 when he resigned after a severe illness, remaining a fellow until his death. He became professor of philosophy in the university of Southern California in 1929, and emeritus professor in 1936. He was elected a fellow of the British Academy in 1926. In 1935 he married Mrs. Louise Luqueer Griswold, eldest daughter of S. Bartow Strang, of Denver, U.S.A., and settled in California. There were no children of the marriage. He died at Los Angeles 6 August 1937.

Schiller's chief publications are *Riddles of the Sphinx* (1891, revised edition 1910), *Studies in Humanism* (1907, 2nd ed. 1912), *Formal Logic* (1912, 2nd ed. 1931), and *Logic for Use* (1929). His first book, *Riddles of the Sphinx*, was a brilliant effort to combine the ideas of Darwinian evolution with those of philosophic idealism. Herbert Spencer had already treated philosophic problems from an evolutionary standpoint, but he was far from being an idealist.

Soon after Schiller settled at Oxford in 1897 he became conspicuous as the advocate of what was called by himself and William James 'pragmatism'; this meant an insistence upon the importance of action in human affairs and upon the formation of human opinions. The main feature in Schiller's 'pragmatism' was the doctrine that truth was a kind of valuation which meant that truth can be equated with usefulness and that an opinion can be regarded as true so far as it is practically useful. The majority of Schiller's contemporaries refused to accept this definition of truth; it seemed to neglect the fact that real things have a nature and qualities of their own. If an opinion is to be regarded as true, it must correspond to objective reality, whether it is useful or not. Whatever may be thought of Schiller's definition of truth his general position that action is one of the main features of human experience cannot reasonably be disputed. No one can refute his arguments that men are creatures of action; that they take an interest in things and learn about things mainly for the sake of action; and that action is the supreme test of truth, because if a man fails in action, he can feel assured that the scheme of thought which guided him was false.

If Schiller's work is looked at broadly it can be said that his main service was to promote the humanization of philosophy. He saw clearly that the business of philosophy is to explain human experience as it is exemplified in ordinary persons, and that no important element of human experience should be omitted in the philosopher's survey. In defending this standpoint he attacked vigorously thinkers who, like Plato and Hegel, regarded imaginary beings, such as Ideas or the Absolute, as more real and more important than ordinary human experience and therefore produced systems which are useless and inhuman. Another object of Schiller's attack was formal logic, which he regarded as useless and false, and as having no value as a guide to action or as an explanation of human thinking.

Schiller had many of the gifts of a first-rate thinker: intellectual enthusiasm, vivid imagination, keen critical acumen, great originality and fertility of ideas; but his powers of analysis and synthesis were less remarkable. Although he did not produce a satisfactory comprehensive synthesis in any department of philosophy, he did good service in impelling British thought powerfully in the direction of a revival of the empiricist tradition.

Schiller had many interests outside philosophy. He was an ardent mountaineer, a persevering though unskilful golfer, and an inveterate punster. He was an excellent linguist, knew a great deal about physical science, wrote on eugenics, and took a deep and lifelong interest in that region of the supernormal and supernatural which is investigated by the Society for Psychical Research, of which he was president in 1914. He was for thirty-five years the able treasurer of the Mind Association.

[*The Times*, 9 August 1937; R. R. Marett, *Ferdinand Canning Schiller, 1864–1937* in *Proceedings* of the British Academy, vol. xxiii, 1937; personal knowledge.]   H. STURT.

SCHUSTER, SIR ARTHUR (1851–1934), mathematical physicist, was born at Frankfort-on-Main 12 September 1851, the second son of Francis Joseph Schuster, merchant and banker, of Frankfort, by his wife, Marie, daughter of Hofrath Max Pfeiffer, of Stuttgart. He was an elder brother of Sir Felix Otto Schuster [q.v.]. Both parents were of pure Jewish race and were converted to Christianity when their children were quite young. Arthur received his early education at the Gymnasium at Frankfort and in 1868 was sent to Geneva, where he studied at the academy and obtained a thorough mastery of French.

The annexation of Frankfort by Prussia in 1866 made life there so uncomfortable that in 1869 Arthur's father decided to transfer his family to Manchester, where he had a partnership in the family firm of Schuster Brothers, merchants. Thus, on leaving Geneva in 1870 Arthur returned to a home in England instead of Germany, and in 1875 he became a naturalized British subject.

For some months in 1870 and 1871 Schuster served in his father's firm; but the work was entirely uncongenial to one whose interests were scientific. His parents consulted (Sir) H. E. Roscoe [q.v.], and on his advice Schuster entered the Owens College, Manchester, where he studied physics under Balfour Stewart [q.v.] and mathematics under Thomas Barker [q.v.]. After spending a year at the Owens College he went, again on the advice of Roscoe, to Heidelberg to study under Gustav Robert Kirchoff, and took his Ph.D. degree there in 1873 at the end of a year's work. He spent the summer and autumn of 1874 working under Wilhelm Weber and Eduard Riecke at Göttingen and under Hermann von Helmholtz at Berlin, and in 1875 he led an expedition sent by the Royal Society to Siam to observe the total solar eclipse. This was the first of four eclipse expeditions in which he took part, the others being to Colorado in 1878, to Egypt in 1882, and to the West Indies in 1886.

Schuster spent the greater part of the years 1876 to 1881 at the newly established Cavendish laboratory, Cambridge, working first with James Clerk Maxwell [q.v.] and later collaborating with J. W. Strutt, third Lord Rayleigh [q.v.], in a determination of the ohm in absolute measure, an investigation on the results of which the Board of Trade fixed the value of the legal ohm.

From 1881 to 1907 Schuster was on the staff of the Owens College: first as professor of applied mathematics; then, from 1888, in succession to Balfour Stewart, as Langworthy professor of physics. Scientifically, this was Schuster's most productive period, and it will be convenient to summarize here the whole of his scientific work.

This work lay mainly in the field of spectroscopy, electricity in gases, terrestrial magnetism, optics, and the mathematical theory of periodicity. In spectroscopy he was very successful on eclipse expeditions and in 1882 he obtained the first photograph of the spectrum of the solar corona. While investigating the passage of electricity through gases he was the first to show that an electric current passes through a gas by means of gaseous ions and concluded that cathode rays are gaseous ions accelerated in the strong field near the cathode. He was also the first to show that the ratio e/m can be obtained by deflecting cathode rays in a magnetic field. Schuster became interested in terrestrial magnetism through his association with Balfour Stewart, who had suggested that the periodic variations of terrestrial magnetism were due to electric currents in a conducting layer of the upper atmosphere, the first suggestion of what is now known as the 'Heaviside layer' [see HEAVISIDE, OLIVER]. Schuster developed this idea mathematically and showed that the currents of air in the upper atmosphere caused by tidal motion are such as would produce the suggested effect. He wrote *An Introduction to the Theory of Optics* (1904) in which he introduced the idea that a beam of white light does not consist of a bundle of monochromatic rays which are spread out by a prism; but that white light consists of an irregular disturbance which is 'analysed' by the prism in a way analogous to that by which a mathematician uses Fourier's analysis to split up an irregular function into harmonic series. This led on to his work on the 'periodogram' which is a mathematical device for determining whether a series of data (for example, the annual sunspot numbers) contains any periodical recurrences of real significance. Although Schuster made no contributions to meteorology he was extremely interested in that science and for thirty-two years represented the Royal Society on the Meteorological Council which is the advisory body of the London Meteorological Office.

While professor at Manchester Schuster took an active part in the administration of the college and university and served on the committee of the Municipal School of Technology. He was a leader in the movement to replace the old Victoria University by three separate universities in Manchester, Liverpool, and Leeds, a movement which achieved success in 1903. In 1897 it was decided that the accommodation for physics in the Owens College was too small and that a new physical laboratory should be built. After visiting most of the physical laboratories on the continent he designed, in co-operation with Mr. Beaumont the architect, the new physical laboratories in Coupland Street which were opened by Lord Rayleigh in 1900.

Schuster was elected F.R.S. in 1879;

he served three periods on the council (1885–1887, 1898–1899, and 1912–1924); during the last period he was secretary (1912–1919), foreign secretary (1920–1924), and vice-president (1919–1924). He was awarded by the society a Royal medal in 1893, the Rumford medal in 1926, and the Copley medal (its highest award) in 1931. As secretary he not only proved an exceptionally able administrator, especially during the difficult war years, but he made possible several desirable projects by personally providing large sums of money, amongst which were £1,000 to the fee reduction fund, £3,000 to form the nucleus of a fund to provide pensions for the staff, and £3,500 as a fund to facilitate the international work of the society. As he found difficulty in carrying on the duties of secretary whilst living in Manchester he purchased in 1913 an estate at Twyford, near Wargrave-on-Thames, which became his home for the rest of his life. He was knighted in 1920, mainly for his work as secretary of the Royal Society.

By birth, training, and inclination Schuster was well qualified to take a leading part in the organization of international science. He represented the Royal Society in the preliminary negotiations leading to the formation in 1900 of the International Association of Academies, of which in 1905 he became a member of council. The association was disrupted on the outbreak of war in 1914; but before the end of the war he had taken steps to re-create international co-operation in science; and mainly as the result of his energy and influence the International Research Council was formed in 1919, with Schuster as secretary, a position which he held until 1928. During these years of strained international relations Schuster's organizing ability, his command of European languages, and his personal acceptability to men of science of both the Allied and central powers were important factors in ensuring the success of the new international organization.

Schuster took an active part in the work of the British Association: he was president of Section A in 1892, presided over the subsection of astronomy and cosmical physics in 1902, and was president of the whole association at its meeting at Manchester in 1915. He received honorary degrees from several universities and was a corresponding and honorary member of various British and foreign learned societies and academies.

Schuster was of a reserved nature and

it was not easy to know him intimately; but he took a personal interest in his students and went to much trouble to find suitable posts for those in whom he had confidence. His mind was very open to new ideas and he was amongst the first to make use of the 'safety bicycle' and to take up motoring. Although he was never a robust man and had bad health for the last part of his life, he enjoyed walking and cycling and was a keen mountaineer in his youth. He was fond of travel and made several journeys off the beaten track. He was a generous man and gave large sums, in addition to those mentioned above, to further scientific work. His principal recreation throughout life was sketching and painting. In 1887 he married Caroline, eldest daughter of George Loveday, of Wardington, Oxfordshire, and niece of (Sir) A. W. Ward [q.v.]. They had a son and four daughters. He died at Twyford, Berkshire, 14 October 1934.

[Sir A. Schuster, *Biographical Fragments* (portraits), 1932; *Obituary Notices of Fellows of the Royal Society*, No. 4, December 1935 (portrait); *Monthly Notices* of the Royal Astronomical Society, vol. xcv, 1935; *The Times*, 15 and 17 October 1934; private information; personal knowledge.]

GEORGE C. SIMPSON.

SCHUSTER, SIR FELIX OTTO, first baronet (1854–1936), banker, was born at Frankfort-on-Main 21 April 1854, the third son of Francis Joseph Schuster, merchant and banker, of Frankfort, by his wife, Marie, daughter of Hofrath Max Pfeiffer, of Stuttgart. He was a younger brother of Sir Arthur Schuster [q.v.]. The connexion of the family business with English commerce had begun in the eighteenth century, and a branch of it had been established in England since 1811. Accordingly, after the annexation in 1866 of Frankfort to Prussia, Francis Joseph Schuster migrated in 1869 with his family to Manchester, where he had a partnership in the firm of Schuster Brothers, and became naturalized. Felix received his early education at the Gymnasium of his native town and at the university of Geneva, and pursued it at the Owens College, Manchester. He was naturalized in 1875. Entering the family business he became a partner in 1879, and soon afterwards a director of the Imperial Bank. When in 1887 the connexions of Schuster, Son & company were taken over by the Union Bank of London, he became a director, in 1894 deputy governor, and in the follow-ing year governor in succession to C. T. Ritchie [q.v.], a position which he held until 1918.

As governor of the Union Bank, Schuster considered it to be his duty, in addition to the general supervision of policy, to keep himself informed about every detail in the daily administration of the bank. He had an intimate knowledge of every account of any size, and kept a close watch week by week on every branch. This, coupled with his most scrupulous care for the interests of the bank's shareholders and depositors, involved him in exceptionally heavy work, to which he brought a rare knowledge of the technical side of banking and bill-broking, both English and foreign. But he cherished certain worthy ambitions: to achieve distinction in his own field, and to help in the direction of the country's financial policy. By nature and training a Victorian liberal, he was by theory and experience a free trader. In the tariff reform controversy he stood for parliament at the general election of 1906 as free trade candidate for the City of London, but was unsuccessful. In recognition of his efforts he received in July 1906 a baronetcy from the liberal government.

Schuster was prominent among those bankers at the end of the nineteenth century who believed that concentration of the resources of banking concerns was necessary in the national interest, and with this aim he carried through in 1902 the amalgamation of the bank of Smith, Payne, and Smiths with the Union Bank. The measure was a great success and greatly increased Schuster's reputation. Similar operations with the London and Yorkshire Bank, Prescott's, and some smaller private banks followed, until in 1919 Schuster and Lord Inchcape [q.v.] united the National Provincial Bank of England and the Union of London and Smith's Bank in one institution. But thenceforth, although he continued his daily attendance in Princes Street, he ceased to be the all-dominating figure. Not only had ideas on sound banking policy greatly changed, but the war years had left their mark upon him. He was a devoted citizen of this country, but the break with friends and associates in Germany was naturally a grief to him. Yet he had no doubt where the right lay, and he did not hesitate to say that 'the present war was brought about by the deliberate action of the German government'. Also, during these years he lost not only his two younger daughters and two sons-in-law, but also, in 1918, his wife, Meta, daughter of (Sir) Hermann Weber, F.R.C.P., whom he had married in 1879.

Schuster served as finance member of the Council of India from 1906 to 1916: he was chairman of numerous banking associations and committees, and during the war of 1914–1918 he worked with Lord Cunliffe on the Foreign Exchange Committee. Although the association of two such strong personalities was at first difficult, their relationship soon became and remained harmonious.

Towards the end of his life Schuster's views on fiscal policy were modified. In a speech at Lincoln in October 1930 he said: 'I am still of the opinion that free trade would be best for us—best for the world', but, if foreign nations obstinately maintained their tariff walls, 'we, their best customers, may be compelled to use defensive measures. . . . Our present system is not free trade as Cobden conceived it.' He hoped, however, that the problem of British trade policy would be solved on non-party lines by a 'truly national government consisting of the leading men of all parties'.

Schuster's true bent in life was towards music as a main interest and to mountaineering as a relaxation. He might have attained great proficiency as a pianist, his taste being cultivated and severe and his technical skill great. His mountaineering began when he was a student at Geneva, and he became successively honorary secretary and vice-president of the Alpine Club, and, if he had not thought it his duty to avoid controversy, he might well have been its president. In person he was sturdily built and until late in life he enjoyed an excellent constitution. His appearance was striking. His face, which was most unusually pale, was framed by a square, black beard, grizzled as age advanced, and from it there looked out very deep brown eyes. He held strong views on right and wrong both in business and the affairs of ordinary life; and this, coupled with an extreme shyness of disposition, made him formidable in intercourse and conversation. He habitually overworked himself and he had very little tolerance of slackness, either in his colleagues or his subordinates, but inwardly his spirit was gentle and his mind tolerant, and he was a good and kindly friend.

Schuster died at Ruthin Castle, Denbighshire, after a long and painful illness, 13 May 1936. He was succeeded as second baronet by his son, Felix Victor (born 1885): his two elder daughters also survived him.

A portrait of Schuster by (Sir) Hubert von Herkomer, presented to him by the shareholders of the Union of London and Smith's Bank in 1903, is in the possession of his son. Another portrait, by an unknown artist, presented to him by the directors of the bank in 1915, belongs to his daughter Miss Evelyn Schuster. A cartoon by 'Spy' appeared in *Vanity Fair* 28 June 1906.

[*The Times*, 15 May 1936; *Alpine Journal*, November 1936; personal knowledge.]

SCHUSTER.

SCOTT, CHARLES PRESTWICH (1846–1932), journalist, was born at Bath 26 October 1846, the eighth child and fourth son of Russell Scott, a partner in Cory's coal company, by his wife, Isabella Civil, daughter of Joseph Prestwich, wine merchant, of Lambeth, and sister of the geologist Sir Joseph Prestwich [q.v.]. His paternal grandmother was a daughter of William Hawes [q.v.], the founder of the Royal Humane Society. He was educated successively at Hove House, Sussex, a school kept by a Unitarian minister, and at Clapham Grammar School, then in the hands of Charles Pritchard [q.v.], whence he was removed for reasons of health to a private tutor in the Isle of Wight. When he was of university age, Christ Church and Queen's College, Oxford, refused to admit him, requiring certificates of baptism, but he was accepted at Corpus Christi College, where he lived a full life, rowing, debating, and being awarded a second class in classical moderations (1867) and a first class in *literae humaniores* (1869). Among the friends whom he made at Corpus were two with whom he kept in touch in later life, Robert Bridges and (Sir) Samuel Dill [qq.v.]. He tried unsuccessfully for a fellowship at Merton College.

Scott left Oxford not only with his intellectual and moral outlook determined by influences exerted upon him as an undergraduate (the chief was J. R. Seeley's *Ecce Homo*), but with his career determined as well. His cousin John Edward Taylor [q.v.], the proprietor of the *Manchester Guardian* and the son of its founder John Edward Taylor [q.v.], after seeing some of Scott's essays, offered him a post which he accepted.

Scott arrived in Manchester in February 1871 and eleven months later Taylor made him editor. He was then twenty-five. Under him were men who were serving on the paper before he was born. He grew a beard to disguise his youth and showed himself a strict disciplinarian, gaining a reputation for severity which those who only knew him outside the office found it hard to understand. He soon made his mark by giving the paper for the first time a serious standing as a critic of arts and letters, but he did not change its whig tone in politics until the liberal crisis of 1886. Scott was converted to Gladstone's home rule policy by a series of articles that E. A. Freeman [q.v.] contributed to the paper. Scott's chief leader writer, W. T. Arnold [q.v.], was a convinced home ruler from the first and the power and quality of his articles created a great impression. Engaged now in a struggle that excited the deepest emotions on both sides, Scott was shaken out of his constitutional conservatism and for the rest of his life he was ready to consider new ideas without the inhibitions that had cramped his earlier liberalism. Like Gladstone he moved steadily to the left in his middle years. By its bold handling of the questions raised in the struggles of the dockers in 1889, the miners in 1893, and the engineers in 1897, the *Manchester Guardian* prepared opinion for the great constructive reforms of the two liberal administrations of the twentieth century. When the South African war broke out Scott found himself for the second time engaged in a struggle that excited the deeper passions of politics. At great cost to its material fortunes the paper defended an unpopular cause with the courage and dignity that marked its treatment of bitterly controversial issues.

Scott was at this time a great deal in London. After unsuccessful contests in North-East Manchester in 1886, 1891, and 1892, he had been elected for the Leigh division of Lancashire in 1895. He kept his seat in the 'khaki' election of 1900. Taylor had encouraged him to enter the House of Commons, but at this time he became very anxious about the fortunes of the paper and began to think that the editor was not giving it enough attention. Relations between the two men lost their former cordiality. Taylor died in October 1905 and it was found that he had made a will in uncertain terms. Scott, who had always understood that the paper would be left to him, had to purchase it, with the help of relatives and friends, for £242,000, after long and anxious negotiations. Hard upon this blow came a calamity in the death of his wife (November 1905). She had given him not only the happiness of a perfect marriage but also valuable help in the expansion of the paper's interests.

Scott left parliament in 1905, but he was in close touch with several of the new ministers, notably Loreburn and Lloyd George. His intimacy with Loreburn was especially important because Loreburn was the strongest critic in the government of Grey's foreign policy. Loreburn, like Scott, had differed sharply from Grey over the South African war. Scott, who had the traditional British mistrust of foreign commitments, paid great respect to the opinions and suspicions of his friend. He was thus confirmed in his view that it was his duty to present in the paper a reasoned criticism of a foreign policy that seemed to him provocative and adventurous. On women's suffrage, on the other hand, he found a warm ally in Grey, with whom he discussed plans for overcoming obstacles that proved insuperable until they were removed by war.

In 1914 Scott was, to the very last, against British participation in the war, but when war came he held that all criticism of pre-war diplomacy should be suspended and the whole energy of the nation thrown into the struggle. Early in the war he decided that the two most effective men of action in the government were Mr. Churchill and Lloyd George, and he used all his influence to strengthen their hands. He helped Lloyd George publicly and privately to bring about the change of government in December 1916. But he was never an uncritical supporter of Lloyd George. He attacked him for extending conscription to Ireland and for holding the election in December 1918, and during the campaign of the 'Black and Tans' in Ireland he broke off all personal relations. They were reconciled when negotiations for an Irish peace began and Scott was able to use his influence in the discussions that produced the Irish 'treaty' of December 1921.

During the last ten years of his life Scott watched with sorrow the declining fortunes of his party, but his natural optimism never broke down and he was hopeful about the labour movement. In 1923 and 1929 he urged the liberal leaders to support the labour government, while doing what he could to promote liberal reunion. By this time his position was that of an elder statesman, discussing politics with the leaders of all parties and enjoying the respect of men who disagreed with his politics.

Scott's conduct of the *Manchester*

Guardian was governed by his view that a newspaper should be a public organ serving the community as consciously and directly as a department of the civil service. He allowed himself a modest fixed salary and used the profits of its prosperous days to develop the paper and to build up a reserve fund in order to maintain its independence. During and after the war he himself wrote a great many leading articles. As an editor he could use and guide the force and fire of others, but as a writer he excelled in dispassionate and considered argument. He never lost his power of analysing and mastering the most complicated documents. His personal tastes were simple and almost austere; he bicycled to and from the office nearly to the end of his life. His later years brought him honours that he valued: Manchester University bestowed upon him the honorary degree of LL.D. in 1921; his college elected him an honorary fellow in 1923, and the city of Manchester admitted him a freeman in 1930. He declined more than once the offer of a knighthood. On his eightieth birthday his bust by Jacob Epstein was presented to the city of Manchester by a large body of subscribers which included three ex-premiers and notable names from foreign countries. He had raised a respectable but undistinguished Manchester paper to a leading place as a moral force in world politics.

Scott married in 1874 Rachel, youngest daughter of John Cook [q.v.], professor of ecclesiastical history in St. Andrews University. She was one of the original students of Girton College, Cambridge. They had three sons and a daughter. The eldest son died as a young man in 1908; the second (d. 1949) became manager of the *Manchester Guardian* after Taylor's death; the youngest succeeded his father as editor in July 1929, but was drowned accidentally less than four months after his father's death, which took place at Manchester 1 January 1932. The daughter became the wife of C. E. Montague [q.v.].

A portrait of Scott by T. C. Dugdale was presented to the Manchester Press Club.

[*Manchester Guardian*, 2 January 1932; W. Haslam Mills, *The Manchester Guardian: A Century of History*, 1921; J. L. Hammond, *C. P. Scott*, 1934; Sir William Haley (ed.), *C. P. Scott, 1846–1932. The Making of the 'Manchester Guardian'*, 1946; private information; personal knowledge.]   J. L. HAMMOND.

SCOTT, DUKINFIELD HENRY (1854–1934), parlaeobotanist, was born in London

28 November 1854, the youngest of the five sons of (Sir) George Gilbert Scott [q.v.], by his wife, Caroline Oldrid. Scott was educated by tutors at home, and under the influence of his mother took to field botany before he was fourteen years old. He soon passed to the more scientific aspect of the subject through the *Micrographic Dictionary* (1854) of John William Griffith and Arthur Henfrey [q.v.], whereby his attention was directed to plant structure, the study of which eventually became his main occupation. Thence he proceeded to a number of technical German works, which at that period were becoming available in translation, such as that of Wilhelm Friedrich Benedict Hofmeister on the higher cryptogamia. All this study, and certain efforts at microscopy, took place before Scott was sixteen, but there was then a period of some nine years during which his interest in botany remained dormant. At Christ Church, Oxford, he read classics (1872–1876); after this he spent three years training as an engineer.

In the autumn of 1879 botanical fervour stirred again, and, at the suggestion of (Sir) W. T. Thiselton-Dyer [q.v.], Scott decided to study the subject in Germany, then the centre of the botanical world. He worked, intermittently, over a period of two and a half years (1880–1882) in the university of Würzburg under Julius von Sachs, to whom Karl Goebel was then assistant. Scott, on his return to England, was instrumental in creating in this country an atmosphere of research, such as he had enjoyed in Sachs's laboratory. In 1882 Scott succeeded Frederick Orpen Bower as assistant to Daniel Oliver at University College, London, but in 1885 he was transferred to the Normal School (later Imperial College) of Science, taking charge, under T. H. Huxley [q.v.], of all the botanical work. Scott was not compelled to work for his living and his career of regular teaching lasted for a decade only, being given up in favour of unimpeded research when in 1892 he became honorary director of the Jodrell laboratory at Kew. When he left this post, fourteen years later, he retired to East Oakley House, near Basingstoke.

The moment of Scott's scientific life which determined its main course came in 1889, when he first met W. C. Williamson [q.v.], who, as professor of natural history at Manchester, had interested himself for forty years in the fossil plants of the carboniferous rocks. A visit with Bower to Manchester, where they spent many hours in the room known as Williamson's 'coal-hole', examining his slides of fossil plant structure, opened Scott's eyes to the field that he was to make his own. In his words: 'my work, since I knew Williamson, owes its inspiration to him.' At about the time that Scott was appointed to the Jodrell laboratory, Williamson removed to London; thenceforth the two men worked in concert. Williamson had come to recognize that he needed the help of a colleague with a more modern outlook, and in Scott he found the ideal collaborator. After Williamson's death in 1895 Scott continued these investigations alone, recording the results in a succession of memoirs dealing with the structure and affinities of the fossil plants of the palaeozoic rocks. The sections used by Williamson and Scott are in the British Museum (Natural History); the Scott collection includes more than 3,000 slides of carboniferous plants.

In addition to research papers, Scott published books on broader lines, such as *Studies in Fossil Botany* (1900, 3rd ed. vol. i, 1920, vol. ii, 1923) and *Extinct Plants and Problems of Evolution* (1924). He also wrote an elementary text-book, *An Introduction to Structural Botany* (1894), of which from the eleventh edition (1927) onwards, Professor Frederick Tom Brooks became joint editor. All Scott's books are of a type wholly distinct from that of the average work intended for students; there is a complete avoidance of dogmatic statement, and as much stress is laid upon what we do not know, as upon what we know. In everything which he wrote, Scott's attitude towards his problems was orientated to the Darwinian and phylogenetic outlook of his period; he stated explicitly in 1900 that 'the ultimate object of morphological inquiry is to build up the genealogical tree of the organic world'. Nevertheless, after a quarter of a century's further work, his modest conclusion in his latest book was that 'we know a good deal about extinct plants, but not enough, as yet, to throw much light on the problems of their evolution'. Modern research has underlined this deduction. The genealogical tree, which Scott hoped might be revealed, veils itself ever more and more inscrutably; but the partial disappointment of early expectations in no way impairs his standing as a structural palaeobotanist. His flair for divining the 'build' of a plant, a variant of the architectural trend in the Scott family, fostered by his engineering training; his just and simple

mode of presentation, disciplined by the Latin and Greek of his Oxford days; his balanced judgement, and his readiness to sacrifice cherished ideas, as soon as the evidence was shown to weigh against them: these factors combine to endow his work with lasting life.

Scott was elected F.R.S. in 1894 and received a Royal medal in 1906 and the Darwin medal in 1926. He was president of the Linnean Society (1908–1912) and received the society's gold medal in 1921. He was president of the Royal Microscopical Society (1904–1906), of the South-Eastern Union of Scientific Societies (1909), of Section K (botany) of the British Association (1896 and 1921), and of the palaeobotanical section of the International Botanical Congress (1930). He received the Wollaston medal of the Geological Society in 1928. Honorary degrees were conferred upon him by the universities of Manchester and Aberdeen. He married in 1887 one of his earliest students, Henderina Victoria (died 1929), daughter of Hendericus Martinus Klaassen, F.G.S., whose family was of Dutch extraction. There were three sons, the eldest of whom was killed in the war of 1914–1918, the second died at school, and the third died in infancy; there were also four daughters. He died at East Oakley House 29 January 1934.

A portrait of Scott by J. Kerr-Lawson hangs in the Jodrell laboratory, Kew Gardens.

[*Obituary Notices of Fellows of the Royal Society*, No. 3, December 1934 (portrait); *Annals of Botany*, vol. xlix, 1935 (bibliography and portrait); *Journal of Botany*, vol. lxxii, 1934; *Nature*, 3 March 1934; *Proceedings* of the Linnean Society, session cxlvi, 1933–1934; *New Phytologist*, vol. xxiv, 1925, and vol. xxxiii, 1934; *Current Science*, vol. ii, 1934 (portrait); private information; personal knowledge.]   AGNES ARBER.

SCOTT, SIR (JAMES) GEORGE (1851–1935), administrator in Burma and author, was born at Dairsie, Fife, 25 December 1851, the younger son of George Scott, minister of Dairsie from 1850 until his death in 1861, by his wife, Mary, daughter of Robert Forsyth, miscellaneous writer and advocate [q.v.]. In 1864 George and his elder brother (Sir) Robert Forsyth Scott, later master of St. John's College, Cambridge, were taken by their widowed mother to school at Stuttgart for three years, returning only when they were bilingual. George showed promise at King's College School, London, and at Edinburgh University, but, missing a scholarship by one place, left Lincoln College, Oxford, without taking a degree, owing to lack of means.

In 1875–1876 Scott accompanied a punitive expedition to Perak, Malaya, as special correspondent of the *Standard*. Thence he went in 1879 to Burma as headmaster of St. John's College, Rangoon, an Anglican mission school, and in a tropical climate succeeded in introducing association football, hitherto regarded as impossible among so hot-tempered a people: it is now an established game. In 1881 he returned home and read for the bar, but missed, again by one place, the law scholarship at the Inner Temple which might have enabled him to practise. The publication (under the name of Shway Yoe) of his first book, *The Burman: His Life and Notions* (2 vols., 1882), revealed a closer knowledge of the people than was usual at the time, and gave him an immediate reputation, not only among those concerned with Burma, but among employers in England. Hence, in 1884, he went out again as a war correspondent of the *Standard*, this time with the French armies engaged in the conquest of Tongking, and he wrote his second book, *France and Tongking: a Narrative of the Campaign of 1884, and the Occupation of Further India* (1885).

Invalided home, Scott was at the Inner Temple (by which he was eventually called to the bar in 1896) when the annexation of Upper Burma towards the end of 1885 gave him his supreme chance. The senior cadre in Burma, hitherto drawn from the Indian civil service, had to be expanded at short notice, and he was appointed to it, spending his time not in the sweltering plains but in the cool hills, the lovely Shan States plateau. These three dozen states had only a million people, but they covered an area larger than that of England and Wales; they were subdivided into even more numerous tribes, each speaking its own language; and they were unexplored. Some of the chiefs were engaged in civil war, others resented the overthrow by the British of their suzerain, the King of Burma. Half a dozen civil officers, escorted by small parties of British or Indian troops, had to spend the years 1886–1890 marching hard in all weathers to establish British rule. If there was little bloodshed it was largely due to Scott: he had an iron physique and a quick, masterful temper, but he also had a warm heart and he seldom failed to win men over. Thus, on one occasion, he and his troops,

emerging suddenly from the jungle, found their way barred: they had emerged under the walls of a fortified village in the country of the head-hunting Wa tribes, and the walls were already manned. Other officers would have either retreated, abandoning the expedition, or fought their way through, leaving a legacy of hatred. Scott made his men halt while he went forward, unarmed, almost within bowshot, and although he could only speak through four successive interpreters, as the language was at five removes, in a few minutes he had those angry savages on the wall laughing at his jokes.

Scott was appointed resident for the Northern Shan States at Lashio in 1891 and for the Southern at Taunggyi in 1902. He was chargé d'affaires at Bangkok in 1893 and 1894, and a member of the three boundary commissions which, between 1889 and 1900, delimited the Burma frontier along Siamese, French, and Chinese territory. He was appointed C.I.E. in 1892 and K.C.I.E. in 1901. He retired in 1910.

Throughout his life Scott wrote incessantly, newspaper columns, articles, stories, a score of books. His *Gazetteer of Upper Burma and the Shan States* (5 vols., 1900–1901) is still of value. His oriental manuscripts were given to Cambridge University.

An all-round athlete, Scott was proudest of having kicked 300 goals in first class football, mostly for the Harlequins and the London Scottish. He was a disobedient subordinate and an ideal chief, a living disproof of the dictum that before a man can command, he must learn to obey. He settled in London and haunted the Savage Club, but did not relish his retirement until in 1920 his marriage to the authoress G. E. Mitton gave him a collaborator and brought him much happiness. He then moved to Graffham, near Petworth, Sussex, where he died 4 April 1935.

Scott was married three times: first, in 1890 to Elizabeth Dora (died 1896), daughter of James Campbell Connolly, chaplain of Woolwich Dockyard; secondly, in 1905 to Eleanor Sarah, only child of John William M'Carthy, county court judge, by whom he had a daughter (the marriage was dissolved in 1918); thirdly, in 1920 to Geraldine Edith, third daughter of the Rev. Henry Arthur Mitton, master of Sherburn House, Durham.

A portrait of Scott by a German artist, Lomer, is in the possession of his widow.

[*The Times Literary Supplement*, 14 November 1936; G. E. Mitton (Lady Scott), *Scott of he Shan Hills. Orders and Impressions* (bibliography and portraits), 1936; private information.]   G. E. HARVEY.

SCRUTTON, SIR THOMAS EDWARD 1856–1934), judge, was born 28 August .856 in the East India Dock Road, Poplar, he elder son of Thomas Urquhart Scrutton, a prosperous shipowner, later of Buckhurst Hill, Essex, by his wife, Mary, daughter of the Rev. Edward Hickman. His father's family had for several generations run a line of vessels, originally under sail, between the United Kingdom and the West Indies. The father was a stalwart adherent of Congregationalism, in the days when that persuasion and the Liberation Society were a political force. Scrutton was accordingly educated at Mill Hill School.

On leaving school the relentless industry that he displayed throughout life spurred Scrutton to a pursuit of academic honours that can rarely have been equalled. At London University he took the degrees of B.A., M.A., and LL.B. (1882), with honours. He also won a scholarship at Trinity College, Cambridge, obtained a first class in the moral sciences tripos and was awarded the senior Whewell scholarship for international law in 1879, and was placed first in the first class of the law tripos of 1880. He won the Barstow scholarship of the Inns of Court in 1882. Finally, he won at Cambridge the Yorke prize for a legal essay in 1882, 1884, 1885, and 1886: to win it four times is a feat which no one else has hitherto achieved. With such a record he may have hoped for a fellowship at Trinity. A remark made by Sir J. J. Thomson [q.v.] shortly after Scrutton's death may explain why he did not get one. 'I remember Scrutton. A very clever man, and of immense industry, *but*—no originality.'

As an undergraduate Scrutton was lanky and rather uncouth. He was possibly the only Englishman of his time who never shaved in his life. Somewhere in the Cambridge Union, of which he was president in 1880, there is, or was, a photograph of him with a downy beard. One of the few diversions from his books that he allowed himself was riding the old high bicycle, and he represented Cambridge in a contest with Oxford men of a like reckless courage.

Scrutton was called to the bar by the Middle Temple in 1882, and formally joined the South-Eastern circuit: but he never went on it again. He became a K.C. in 1901, and a bencher of his Inn in 1908.

He never took much part in the social life, or in the business, of the Inn, and did not hold office.

Scrutton read in chambers with Sir A. L. Smith [q.v.] and was at the same time discharging the duties of professor of constitutional law and legal history at University College, London. After leaving Smith he had chambers for a time in Essex Court, and when his practice began to grow, as it soon did, moved to a large set of chambers at 3 Temple Gardens. The growth of his practice in commercial matters was hastened by the publication in 1886 of his book *The Contract of Affreightment as expressed in Charterparties and Bills of Lading*. This having been repeatedly, and carefully, revised by him and by others has remained the leading text-book on the subject: the fourteenth edition appeared in 1939. The subject for the Yorke prize which he won in 1882 was the laws of copyright. He turned his prize essay into a text-book, *The Laws of Copyright* (1883), and this was the source of another side of his practice. That was always mainly in commercial law, but his copyright business was considerable and lucrative.

In 1892 a case of extreme technicality about general average came before Mr. Justice J. C. Lawrence in the non-jury list. That unlearned judge (one of the political promotions of Lord Halsbury) was so palpably unfitted for such a task that it led to a movement for the establishment of a Commercial Court. This was achieved in 1895, and under Sir J. C. Mathew [q.v.] and his successors, who had a like qualification, the court for many years enjoyed its greatest prosperity. For some fifteen years Scrutton and his great rival, J. A. Hamilton (afterwards Viscount Sumner, q.v.), were the busiest practitioners in it.

In those years Scrutton got through an immense amount of work in the courts, or in the hideous room which he occupied in the hideous block called Temple Gardens, and in which it was characteristic of the man that a Spartan rigour reigned. He used to sit on a windsor chair, without a cushion, at a battered writing-table, to the side of which was a table, loaded with papers, that had come out of one of his father's ships, with a rough piece of wood filling the hole that had enclosed the mast. When darkness set in the only source of light was a Victorian chandelier with fishtail gas-burners. The other two rooms were filled with 'devils' and pupils: among them from time to time were the future

Lord Atkin, Lord Wright, Lord Justice MacKinnon, Mr. Justice Fraser, and Mr. Justice Henn Collins. At 4.15 all the party met in one of the rooms for tea. The liquid was repulsive: and the only form of food was Bath Oliver biscuits. Scrutton, silently absorbed in thinking about his work, would stride about the room until, almost daily, the top of his head crashed into the knob of the chandelier that hung from the ceiling.

In February 1909 Scrutton's rival, Hamilton, was promoted to the bench. Soon afterwards Scrutton was sent as special commissioner on the North-Eastern circuit, and discharged the duty to the general approval. In April 1910, on the recommendation of Lord Loreburn, he was appointed a judge of the King's Bench division, upon the resignation of Mr. Justice Sutton.

Scrutton soon proved himself a very efficient judge, but not a popular one. He never had good manners (partly because he was really a very shy man), and he indulged in petulant rudeness to counsel, and to solicitors' clerks on summonses. Eventually all the chief City solicitors, his former clients, gave a joint retainer to Alfred Chaytor, then a leading junior who took silk in 1914, to make a protest to the judge in court. Chaytor discharged this novel task with much tact, but with equal firmness. Scrutton listened without comment, but showed proof of his penitence in his subsequent conduct.

For six years Scrutton discharged with success the work of a judge of first instance in London (often in the Commercial Court), and upon circuit. He was very efficient in trying prisoners, although he had had no experience of such work at the bar. In 1915, at the Old Bailey, he had to try a notorious murderer, George Joseph Smith, in the sensational 'Brides in the Bath' case, and the man in the street came to agree with professional opinion that he was a great judge.

In October 1916, on the resignation of Lord Justice Phillimore, Scrutton was promoted to the Court of Appeal, and sworn of the Privy Council. During eighteen years in that court he displayed ever increasing judicial powers, and when for the last seven years he presided over one of its divisions, he had had few, if any, superiors in that position. When at the bar he was, if anything, hampered by an immense knowledge of case law. Towards the end of his career he came to see the wood rather than the trees, and developed a mastery of legal principles. Indeed he achieved no little of that originality which Thomson failed to discover in his younger days. In 1936 an American professor published an article about him, in which he uses the phrases 'a matchless commercial lawyer', 'among the noblest of the judicial bench', 'a greater commercial judge than Mansfield', 'the greatest English-speaking judge of a century'.

With age Scrutton became much more mellow. There was in 1932 an unhappy incident when he was very rude to H. A. McCardie [q.v.] (whom he probably despised intellectually) upon an appeal from him. McCardie was even more injudicious, and unjudicial, in his protest in court by way of rejoinder. But the younger barristers, who only knew Scrutton as presiding in the Court of Appeal, would regard him as a dignified, imposing, and kindly person.

Scrutton's intellectual interests besides the law were chiefly poetry, travel (before he was forty he had visited Palestine, Greece, Spain, and Italy), music, and church architecture. His only incursion into politics was in 1886, when, following the family tradition, he stood (but without success) as liberal candidate for the Limehouse division. When an undergraduate he became engaged to Mary, daughter of Samuel Crickmer Burton, solicitor, of Great Yarmouth, and they were married in 1884. They lived, a very devoted couple, at Westcombe Park, a suburb near Blackheath, and only moved to a flat in Piccadilly when Scrutton was on the bench. They had four sons, of whom the youngest was killed in the war of 1914–1918, and a daughter. He and his wife were devoted to music and the opera. Keen attendants at orchestral concerts in London, they were never prevented by claims of work from attending throughout the season at Covent Garden, and in his travels in Germany his lodestar was the music at Bayreuth and Munich. He was a member of the Reform Club and, when a judge, of the Athenaeum: but he was rarely seen in either club; if he had any spare time he spent it at home.

Early in life Scrutton took to bicycling and was a keen watcher of Rugby football, cricket, and athletic sports, and an enthusiastic, if not very skilful, golfer. He presented the Scrutton cup for an annual competition between the Inns of Court. It was in the course of a golfing holiday at Sheringham in the long vacation of 1930 that he was found to be suffering from a strangulated hernia. He was taken to hospital at Norwich and died there 18 August. He was buried in the Rosary cemetery at Norwich.

In addition to his books already mentioned Scrutton produced in 1891 *The Elements of Mercantile Law* and in 1895 an annotated version of *The Merchant Shipping Act, 1894*. The other three Yorke prize essays, all of which were printed, are *The Influence of the Roman Law on the Law of England* (1885), *Land in Fetters* (1886), and *Commons and Common Fields* (1887). He also wrote a valuable article on 'The Work of the Commercial Courts' (*Cambridge Law Journal*, vol. i, no. 1, 1921).

Scrutton was a fine figure of a man. There can never have been a court of so many united inches as when he sat with Lord Sterndale and Lord Justice Bankes. As it had never been shaved, his beard became a feature rather than an appendage, and was so clipped as to give him the look of an Elizabethan. His portrait was never painted, but an excellent photograph is reproduced as the frontispiece to the fourteenth edition of his *Charterparties and Bills of Lading*. A cartoon of him by 'Ape Junior' appeared in *Vanity Fair* 28 June 1911 : this depicts him in a characteristic pose.

[*The Times*, 21 August, 1 September, and 3 October 1934; *Manchester Guardian*, 21 August 1934; K. N. Llewellyn in *Columbia Law Review*, May 1936; private information; personal knowledge.]　　F. D. MacKinnon.

SEAMAN, Sir OWEN, baronet (1861–1936), poet, satirist, and parodist, was born in London 18 September 1861, the only son of William Mantle Seaman, a dressmaker of Suffolk yeoman stock, by his wife, Sarah Ann Balls. He had a distinguished academic career both at Shrewsbury, where he was captain of the school, and as a scholar of Clare College, Cambridge, where he was university Porson prizeman in 1882 and was awarded a first class in part i of the classical tripos of 1883. As a schoolmaster at Rossall (1884), professor of literature at Durham College of Science, Newcastle-upon-Tyne (1890–1903), and a barrister of the Inner Temple (1897), he had shown so remarkable a gift for the composition of light verse that he was asked to join the staff of *Punch* in the last-named year. He became assistant editor in 1902 and was editor from 1906 to 1932. *Horace at Cambridge* (1895) was a brilliant undergraduate exercise in parody, and during the interregnum in the poet laureateship which followed the

death of Lord Tennyson in 1892, Seaman enlivened the period of suspense with a number of brilliant parodies of elder and contemporary poets, following an almost established tradition in English letters. *The Battle of the Bays* (1896) preserves some of the best of these imitations.

Seaman continued to write parodies and was as successful with the blank verse of Tennyson as in the more difficult mode of George Meredith; but a great deal of his verse, in whatever form, was set to a political tune, as he followed the South African war, the embarrassments of the liberal party with regard to home rule and free trade, and the pretensions of Imperial Germany. His aptitude for ridicule within the severest forms of rhymed parody was unfailing; and in this respect he was a worthy successor of J. K. Stephen and C. S. Calverley [qq.v.], although his vein was too robust to be so tenderly mocking to his models as the latter, and he did not attempt to follow or assail the poets of a less adaptable idiom who deserted the Victorian and Edwardian styles. In a number of memorial pieces and during the war of 1914–1918 he composed verses of so great a dignity and earnestness that he often seemed a true poetic spokesman of the patriotic mood.

As an editor, Seaman was assiduous in the encouragement of talent, sparing no pains in the task of amendment and criticism, and was accustomed to write long manuscript letters on the use of a word or the turning of a phrase. A wit and a raconteur, he was a social success and in 1914 he was knighted, a testimony rather to the genuine merit of his satire than to the gratitude of a government which he had certainly not followed with his pen. In *In Cap and Bells* (1899), *Borrowed Plumes* (1902), and *A Harvest of Chaff* (1904) he followed his earlier parodies; more serious verses were evoked by more serious events and collected in *War-Time* (1915), *Made in England* (1916), and *From the Home Front* (1918). In 1929 he published *Interludes of an Editor*, in which his technique remained as skilful as ever, although the occasions which prompted his muse were less memorable. In 1934 he wrote a prologue for the performance of Milton's *Comus* at Ludlow Castle, where the masque had been first produced 300 years before. He did not allow the levity of this occupation to interfere with his sense of public duty, or with his graver preoccupations. He frequently lectured on Browning, of whom he was an enthusiastic admirer, gave much time to the training ship *Implacable*, and to the board of Putney Hospital for Incurables, and was an enthusiastic Volunteer. No satirist can have been less Bohemian in his habits; he set great store by social activities, shot and swam well, and had been captain of the Clare boats. He was elected an honorary fellow of his college in 1909, received honorary degrees from the universities of Durham (1906), Edinburgh (1924), and Oxford (1933), and was created a baronet (also in 1933) He died, unmarried, in London 2 February 1936.

A portrait of Seaman by H. A. Olivier hangs in the offices of *Punch*.

[*The Times*, 3 February 1936; *Punch*, 12 February 1936; private information; personal knowledge.]   E. V. KNOX.

SELIGMAN, CHARLES GABRIEL (1873–1940), ethnologist, was born in London 24 December 1873, the only child of Hermann Seligmann, by his wife, Olivia Mendez da Costa. From St. Paul's School he gained an entrance scholarship to St. Thomas's Hospital, where in 1896 he obtained his first medical qualification and was awarded the Bristowe medal in pathology. In 1897 he served as house-physician there. His earliest research, published while at hospital in 1896 and 1898, was concerned with tropical diseases and with abnormalities of bodily form. These two interests long continued with him, but they were soon dominated by anthropology. In 1898 he joined the Cambridge anthropological expedition to the Torres Strait and Borneo under the leadership of A. C. Haddon [q.v.]. The *Reports* of this expedition contain his important contributions to its work. On his return to England in 1899 he resumed his pathological research, often in collaboration with S. G. Shattock [q.v.], at St. Thomas's Hospital, where in 1901 he was appointed superintendent of the clinical laboratory.

In 1904, however, Seligman returned to ethnology. In that year he persuaded a wealthy American man of business, Major Cook-Daniels, to entrust him with the scientific leadership of an anthropological expedition to New Guinea, the results of which he published six years later in a monumental volume entitled *The Melanesians of British New Guinea* (1910). In 1906 he and his wife received an invitation from the government of Ceylon to make an ethnographic study of the Veddas, and in 1911 they published *The Veddas*, which is still the standard work on this primitive, aboriginal people. Seligman's elaborate

third volume on ethnological field-work, *The Pagan Tribes of the Nilotic Sudan*, appeared in 1932, the result of a survey undertaken by him and his wife during several visits (beginning in 1909–1910) to that country, thus laying, as they justly claimed, 'the foundations of a scientific study of the peoples of the Sudan '.

In 1913 Seligman was appointed to the chair of ethnology in the university of London. This he held until 1934 when he was compelled by ill health to resign. From 1923 to 1925 he served as president of the Royal Anthropological Institute, of which he was Rivers medallist (1925), Huxley memorial lecturer and medallist (1932), and Frazer lecturer (1933). In 1919 he was elected F.R.S. He died at Oxford from infective endocarditis 19 September 1940. In the abundance, breadth, and systematic thoroughness of his ethnological field-work he was unsurpassed.

Seligman married in 1905 Brenda Zara, youngest daughter of Myer Salaman. She survived him with their son.

A chalk drawing of Seligman by (Sir) William Rothenstein is in the possession of Mrs. Seligman.

[*Obituary Notices of Fellows of the Royal Society*, No. 10, December 1941 (bibliography and portrait); *Essays presented to C. G. Seligman*, edited by E. E. Evans-Pritchard and others (appreciation by A. C. Haddon and bibliography), 1934; personal knowledge.]
                CHARLES S. MYERS.

SETH, ANDREW (1856-1931), philosopher. [See PATTISON. ANDREW SETH PRINGLE-.]

SEXTON, SIR JAMES (1856–1938), politician and labour leader, is said to have been born at Newcastle 13 April 1856. His father, James Sexton, was Irish and his mother, who was born at Warrington, was of Irish extraction. They were hawkers, and after tramping to Birkenhead, set up as umbrella-menders in St. Helens when Sexton was six months old. The eldest of a family of six children, he was educated at Low House school (the fees were threepence a week, with sixpence monthly for coke for heating), and on Saturdays helped at his parents' stall in the market-place next to the original pitch where Thomas Beecham [q.v.] first sold his pills. At eight years of age, just before leaving school, Sexton was punching holes in clog-irons, and at nine was earning half a crown a week at the local glassworks, working on twelve-hour shifts. His father's association with the Irish Republican Brotherood and the Fenian movement coloured he boy's outlook.

In 1868 Sexton drifted to Liverpool nd stowed away in a sailing-ship bound or San Francisco, a four months' voyage. After some experience of gold-digging and ervice in a lumber ship, he and others vere drugged and kidnapped, to awake in , vessel bound for London via Cape Horn. On reaching Lancashire again, he laboured t a chemical works for fifteen shillings a week for three years before returning o sea, this time on the Atlantic passage. One adventure was the salving of Cleopatra's Needle, which had been cast adrift n the Bay of Biscay in a steel case.

Dockside work at Liverpool followed, nd in 1881 defective tackle flung Sexton nto a ship's hold, smashing his right cheek-one, displacing his right eye, and slightly racturing his skull. He spent nearly two months in hospital and on recovery his mployers disclaimed liability for injury as his application should have been made within six weeks. However, they found aim work as a winch-driver at a lower wage and deducted half a crown from his first week's money for the cab-fare to the hospital when he was injured. Not long afterwards he was dismissed and became a asual dock labourer before being able to et up a small business of his own.

Sexton early began agitating among the dockers to secure better conditions, and, joining the National Union of Dock Labourers in 1889, he became its secretary in 1893, and so continued until the union, with twenty-three others, was absorbed in the Transport and General Workers' Union in 1922. In 1892 Sexton, with Ben Tillett, gave evidence before the government commission on accidents at docks, which led to their inclusion in the Factory Acts, and influenced the introduction of the Workmen's Compensation Act of 1897.

Sexton was a founder-member of the independent labour party in 1893, and at the Trades Union Congress held at Plymouth in 1899 he seconded the resolution that inaugurated the labour party. He served on the parliamentary committee (1900–1905, 1907, 1909–1921) and on the general council of the Trades Union Congress (from 1923), and presided over the congress held at Hanley in 1905.

While seeking to organize continental dockers in 1896, Sexton was expelled from Antwerp and Ghent, but afterwards associated with the International Transport Workers' Federation, and in 1919 attended the first conference of the International Labour Organization at Washington. In 1914 he organized Liverpool dockers' battalions under the command of the Earl of Derby, and was a member of the government's transit committee.

Sexton fought unsuccessful parliamentary contests at Ashton-under-Lyne (1895) and West Toxteth (1906 and January 1910), but he was returned for St. Helens in 1918 and retained the seat until 1931, when he was defeated. He was appointed C.B.E. in 1917, was knighted in 1931, and received the freedom of the city of Liverpool in 1934, after serving as a councillor from 1905 and as an alderman from 1930.

Sexton was the first labour correspondent of the Board of Trade's *Labour Gazette,* and was a contributor to the *Seaman's Gazette,* the *Clarion,* and the *Liverpool Weekly Post,* and under the pseudonym of 'Tatters, M.P.' was the author of several parliamentary and other rhymes. An amateur actor in his youth, he wrote, besides several serial stories, a play entitled *The Riot Act* (1914); this last, based on the Liverpool transport strikes of 1911, was produced at the Liverpool Repertory and the Manchester Gaiety theatres.

Sexton married in 1881 Christina, daughter of William Boyle, painter, of Everton; she predeceased him, and there were no children of the marriage. He died at Wavertree, Liverpool, 27 December 1938.

[*Sir James Sexton, Agitator, The Life of the Dockers' M.P. An Autobiography,* 1936.]

J. S. MIDDLETON.

SEXTON, THOMAS (1848–1932), Irish politician, the son of J. Sexton, a constable in the Royal Irish Constabulary, was born at Ballygannon, co. Waterford, in 1848. The Christian Brothers undertook his education and found in him a clever pupil, quick at figures and a ready writer. His first employment, at the age of twelve, was a railway clerkship on the Waterford and Limerick Railway; in this he remained until, at the age of nineteen, he found a position in Dublin as a leader-writer on the *Nation,* then the chief organ of left-wing nationalism. A little later he entered political life as a member of the Home Rule League, where his abilities attracted the attention of T. M. Healy [q.v.], who recommended him to C. S. Parnell [q.v.] after the latter had displaced Isaac Butt [q.v.] in the leadership.

At the general election of 1880, as representative of Parnellism and the Land League, Sexton ousted Captain E. R. King Harman, one of the great Irish landlords, and a home ruler of the conservative school, from his seat in county Sligo. Sexton, who held this seat until 1885, and was member for South Sligo from 1885 to 1886, was quickly recognized as one of the half-dozen or so notable men of the untried party that Parnell had gathered about him. His parliamentary manner was suaver than that of most of his colleagues, and he could deliver in a musical voice an endless stream of well-balanced if not always expressive sentences—a power which was useful for the party's policy of obstruction. On Wednesday 2 February 1881 he spoke for three hours and a half towards the close of the record forty-one and a half hours' continuous sitting of the House of Commons which had begun on Monday 31 January, thus provoking Parnell to remark, 'Get Sexton wound up and he will go on for ever.' At the same time, his ardour for the movement, especially on its agrarian side, was not in doubt: he signed the 'No Rent' manifesto of 1881 and was for a while with Parnell in Kilmainham jail. His great triumphs were the winning of the new constituency of West Belfast for the nationalists in 1886, when he was also returned unopposed for South Sligo, and his interventions in the same year in the home rule debates. Gladstone described his speech at the second reading of the home rule bill as the most eloquent that he had heard in a generation of great orators. He was high sheriff of Dublin in 1887 and lord mayor in 1888–1889. After the Parnellite split Sexton represented the anti-Parnellites in North Kerry for over three years (1892–1896), having lost his seat at West Belfast in 1892; but he had little heart for internecine controversy, and in the last year he retired from parliament after having had an opportunity to display his remarkable talent for financial detail on the royal commission on financial relations between Great Britain and Ireland (1894–1896).

Sexton conducted the affairs of the *Freeman's Journal* from 1892 to 1912; but this was his only connexion with politics after he left parliament, and of the events which changed the face of his country after 1916 he seemed to be a detached spectator. He was chairman of a successful bakery and of a successful Roman Catholic insurance society, but apart from these business interests and his service on the viceregal

commission on Irish railways (1906–1910) he cherished up to the time of his death at the age of eighty-three a singular solitude, eschewing social as well as political contacts. He died, unmarried, at his home in Dublin 1 November 1932.

[*The Times* and *The Irish Independent*, 2 November 1932; F. H. O'Donnell, *A History of the Irish Parliamentary Party*, 2 vols. 1910.]   Joseph Hone.

SHACKLETON, Sir DAVID JAMES (1863–1938), labour leader, politician, and civil servant, was born at Accrington 21 November 1863, the only son of William Shackleton, a Nelson watchmaker, by his wife, Margaret Gregory. He attended the Haslingden elementary school. At the age of nine he began work as a 'half-timer' in a weaving-shed and continued to work as a cotton operative up to the age of twenty-nine. He was secretary of the Ramsbottom Weavers' Association (1893–1894) and of the Darwen Weavers' Association (1894–1907); and was president of the Weavers' Amalgamation and a member of the legislative council of the Textile Workers' Association. In these offices he displayed qualities of leadership, governed by wisdom and sound judgement, recognition of which established his reputation in Lancashire and led to his unopposed return as labour member of parliament for the Clitheroe division at a by-election in 1902.

In parliament, as on the trade union platform, Shackleton made no pretence at oratory; but he was an able and forceful speaker, simple and direct, and his fair and reasonable attitude in debate (for example, on the much-discussed trade disputes bill, 1906) and his knowledgeable contributions on workmen's compensation and on factory legislation gained for him the respect of all sections of opinion in the House of Commons. By assisting the passage of the Trade Disputes Act (1906) Shackleton, with other members of the then small labour group (James Keir Hardie [q.v.], Richard Bell, and Arthur Henderson [q.v.]), helped to secure the reversal of the Taff Vale judgement, which had gravely disturbed the trade union movement. He also took part in the early stages of the women's suffrage movement, introducing in 1910 the conciliation bill, which, after a free debate in which government and opposition benches were equally sharply divided, secured a second reading. Meanwhile, Shackleton remained a prominent and well-respected figure in the trade union movement. He was a member of he parliamentary committee of the Trades Union Congress from 1904 to 1910, and president of the congress in 1908 and 1909. He became chairman of the national labour party in 1905 and did much to mould the policy of what, after the general election of 1906, was an important group in the House of Commons.

In 1910 Shackleton resigned his seat in parliament and gave up his trade union activities in order to join the civil service: he became senior labour adviser to the Home Office, an appointment designed to assist that department with advice upon industrial problems. He vacated this post in 1911 on being appointed a national health insurance commissioner, an office which he held until 1916. He served as member of two royal commissions, on the Land Transfer Acts (1908–1910) and on railways (1913–1914). In 1916, when the Ministry of Labour was established, Shackleton was appointed its first permanent secretary. It was an unorthodox appointment, for he had had no administrative experience and no experience of the management of a large organization: the difficulties of the labour situation during the war period and in the early post-war years were, however, such as to need in the permanent secretary of the Ministry of Labour not so much a knowledge of administration as wisdom and familiarity with the traditions and habits of mind of the leaders of the trade union movement. In these respects, as in ability to gain the loyal and warm-hearted support of his civil service colleagues, Shackleton was well qualified, and in the result the appointment proved to be a good one. Ministers of labour so diverse as John Hodge and G. H. Roberts (both former trade union officials), Sir Robert (afterwards Viscount) Horne (conservative), and T. J. Macnamara (liberal) [qq.v.] relied on his advice with well-merited confidence. The control of the Ministry of Labour was rearranged in 1921, Shackleton becoming chief labour adviser, an office which he held until his retirement from the public service in 1925. After retirement he served as a member of the Industrial Transference Board (1928) and of the South Wales Coal Mines Arbitration Board (1934).

Shackleton died at St. Anne's, Lancashire, 1 August 1938. He was appointed C.B. in 1916 and K.C.B. in 1917. He married in 1883 Sarah, daughter of John Broadbent, of Accrington, and had a son and a daughter. He was a hard worker, a teetotaller and non-smoker, and a pleasant,

imperturbable colleague, replete with profound knowledge of the ordinary man.

[*The Times*, 2 August 1938 ; personal knowledge.]   HORACE WILSON.

SHANNON, CHARLES HASLEWOOD (1863–1937), lithographer and painter, was born at Quarrington, Lincolnshire, 26 April 1863, the second son of Frederick William Shannon, rector of Quarrington with Old Sleaford, by his first wife, Catherine Emma, daughter of Dr. Daniel Manthorp, of Thorpe Abbey, Thorpe-le-Soken, Essex. On leaving St. John's School, Leatherhead, he was apprenticed to one of the last of those wood-engravers upon whom then depended the existence of illustrated books and periodicals. In his employer's workshop he was joined by Charles Ricketts [q.v.] with whom he entered and attended the Lambeth School of Art; and eventually they shared lodgings.

This early companionship decided the future circumstances of the lives of Shannon and Ricketts ; for they kept house together until the death of the latter in 1931, pursuing the plastic arts in almost every form with single-minded, ardent intensity. By the time that they had qualified in their specific art it was dead, killed by photo-engraving. Turning wholly to creative art, they worked at first at illustration, Shannon's principal drawings being done for Quilter's *Universal Review*, but culminating in four plates for Oscar Wilde's *A House of Pomegranates* (1891), a book mainly illustrated by Ricketts. But being consummate wood-engravers, they were not content to work thus for publishers ; their aim was to engrave their own design, controlling all the circumstances of book-production ; and so to create a complete harmony with their blocks. The first book thus essayed was George Thornley's translation of *Daphnis and Chloë* (1893), in which Shannon's share was to produce a series of idylls in line which affected his pictorial invention throughout his first period. In the second, *Hero and Leander* by Marlowe and Chapman (1894), Shannon's share, if smaller, was of a maturing delicacy. Their last joint enterprise was *The Dial*, of which five numbers were issued between 1889 and 1897 with the help of the poets John Gray and Thomas Sturge Moore, and to which Shannon contributed a number of lithographs, examples of an art then in danger of falling to trade-printers ; and the great series of Shannon's prints in this medium later came to be recognized as one of the major British manifestations of that art. His early prints were almost wholly begun on the stone; later he would often work with a transfer throughout; the most desirable proofs are those which came from his own hand. Of this period Ricketts listed fifty-four prints; they are idyllic in theme, like his wood engravings. Some may be echoes of his boyhood, most are studies from the nude; but there are also a few portraits. Throughout there is a pervasive silvery quality, an illumination and beauty that was his secret.

When this work had apparently come to an end, Shannon was in full career as a painter of large canvases in oils, that brought him European consideration. Many of these were worked out from his lithograph designs: the spare, austere figures and cool silvery light gained in the richer medium. At the same time the subtle qualities of contour and texture found equal felicity of expression in a number of portraits and self-portraits, especially in Hon. Mrs. Chaloner Dowdall ('The Lady with the Cyclamen', 1899); while some of his most successful other works of this time, such as 'Tibullus in the House of Delia' (1898) (in which there are portraits of himself and his friends Ricketts, Lucien Pissarro, and Sturge Moore), were developed from his first period of lithography.

From 1904 to 1919 Shannon returned to lithography, producing forty-six catalogued prints. These, with their opulent contours and rich darks, showed a change of purpose and conception; and this was further manifested in his painting, which was then stabilized.

Throughout his full working life Shannon had followed his friend's interest in connoisseurship in the arts: like the brothers Goncourt, by their flair and deeply founded taste they had formed outstanding collections. This brought its own kind of fine reputation, but it may be that it distracted them in their creative art. At any rate, Shannon spent his later years realizing projects that had their origin in the imaginative excitement of youth, and did not proceed to further achievement.

In 1928 Shannon's native county tardily paid him the tribute of a one-man exhibition at Lincoln. On certain of the works shown there being returned to his studio in January 1929, he was re-hanging them on the principal staircase when he fell from the ladder, striking his head on the marble

pavement of the entrance hall. No fracture could be found, and after hovering for several weeks between life and death he made an apparent physical recovery but he was never again conscious of his environment, nor even recognized the friends who ministered to him until his death which took place at Kew 18 March 1937.

Shannon was elected A.R.A. in 1911 and R.A. in 1921. There are important works of his in the Tate Gallery, the Musée du Luxembourg, Paris, the Metropolitan Museum, New York, and in public galleries at Bremen, Munich, Venice, Liverpool, and Manchester. Of the early lithographs the following may also be mentioned: 'Shepherd in a Mist' (1892) 'Apple-Gatherers' (1895), 'The Bathers (1904); of his portraits 'Mrs. Dowdall (1899), 'Mrs. Patrick Campbell' (1908) 'Princess Patricia of Connaught' (1918-1919); among the self-portraits 'The Man in a Black Shirt' (1897) and 'The Man in a Striped Shirt' (1901); and of the other paintings 'A Wounded Amazon' (1896) 'The Bath of Venus' (1898-1904), 'The Romantic Landscape' (1904), 'Summer (1905).

There are self-portraits of Shannon (1897 and 1918) in the National Portrait Gallery.

[C. Ricketts, *A Catalogue of Mr. Shannon's Lithographs*: this contains an engraving by the author of an admirable medallion of Shannon's head modelled by Alphonse Legros (Vale Press), 1902; Georges Derry (Rainforth Armitage Walker), *The Lithographs of Charles Shannon*, 1920; *Masters of Modern Art, Charles Shannon* (containing a list of his works up to 1919), 1920; E. B. George, *Charles Shannon* (*Contemporary British Artists*), 1924; C Ricketts in *L'Art et les artistes*, vol. x, 1910 *The Times*, 19 March 1937; personal knowledge. See also, for much illuminating detail about the early working life of the two friends Sir Charles Holmes, *Self and Partners*, 1936 and Sir William Rothenstein, *Men and Memories*, 3 vols., 1931-1939.]

GORDON BOTTOMLEY.

SHARPEY-SCHAFER, SIR EDWARD ALBERT (1850-1935), physiologist [See SCHAFER.]

SHAW, THOMAS, BARON SHAW, later first BARON CRAIGMYLE (1850-1937) lawyer and politician, the only son of Alexander Shaw, of Dunfermline, by his wife, Isabella Wishart, was born there 23 May 1850. His father, who was of highland origin, and carried on business as a baker, died when Thomas was in his sixth year, and thereafter his upbringing was in the hands of one of those inestimable and self-sacrificing Scottish mothers who know so well how to combine for their sons affection with ambition. He attended the High School of Dunfermline of which he became dux and on leaving it was apprenticed to a local solicitor. He decided on adventuring to the Scottish bar and proceeded to the university of Edinburgh where he pursued his studies in the faculties of arts and law with ardour and distinction. He was awarded the Hamilton fellowship in mental philosophy and the lord rector's historical prize, and for a time acted as assistant to Professor Henry Calderwood [q.v.] in the class of moral philosophy. In 1875 he was admitted a member of the Faculty of Advocates.

The generous and democratic fraternity of the Parliament House is always ready to extend a welcome to ability, however humble in origin, but at the price of conformity with its high professional standards. This price Shaw was not invariably disposed to pay. He early recognized that for him the path of advancement lay in politics. He did not, however, neglect the law and soon acquired a considerable practice, especially in jury trials, civil and criminal, which provided a more congenial sphere for the exercise of his gifts of advocacy than the more exacting tasks of legal argument. He first entered parliament in 1892 as liberal member for the Hawick District of Burghs, a seat which he continued to hold until 1909, that is, throughout the whole of his political life. He was a home ruler, an opponent of the South African war, an ardent land law reformer, and in Church connexion an irreconcilable dissenter. His highly effective gifts as a political orator rendered him a valuable asset to the advanced wing of the liberal party in Scotland. In 1886 he set foot on the first rung of the ladder of official preferment by being appointed an advocate-depute in the Crown Office, and from 1894 to 1895 he was solicitor-general in succession to Alexander Asher and became a Q.C. in the former year. In December 1905 his political services were rewarded by his appointment as lord advocate in the government of Sir Henry Campbell-Bannerman, and in January 1906 he was, as is customary, sworn of the Privy Council.

In 1909 Shaw was appointed on the nomination of Asquith a lord of appeal in ordinary in circumstances which the contemporary press described as 'not par-

ticularly auspicious'. On 2 February 1909 Lord Robertson died suddenly in the South of France, thus causing a vacancy in the appellate tribunal. Shaw, who was at the time engaged as leading counsel for one of the parties in a divorce case which had attracted much public notice and was then being heard in the Court of Session, abandoned his client at a critical stage of the proceedings and departed to London in order to urge personally upon the prime minister his claims to the vacant office. He was successful and received the appointment and a life peerage with the title of Lord Shaw, of Dunfermline. Among other distinctions he was an honorary bencher of the Middle Temple (1910) and he received the honorary degree of LL.D. from the universities of St. Andrews (1902), Aberdeen (1906), Edinburgh (1908), and Pennsylvania.

From 1909 to 1929, when he resigned, Shaw discharged his judicial duties in the House of Lords and the Privy Council with competent assiduity. The judgements which he delivered have literary style and lucidity, but it cannot be said that he made any distinctive contribution to the law. His best-known effort was his dissent from all his colleagues and all the judges below in *Rex* v. *Halliday* (1917), in which with much vigour he condemned as illegal a defence of the realm regulation authorizing internment made during the war of 1914–1918. So far as the treatment of Scottish appeals is concerned he was from 1913 onwards overshadowed by the presence and authority of Lord Dunedin.

On several occasions Shaw rendered useful service by presiding over public inquiries, notably the royal commission on the importation of arms into the Dublin district (1914), the Scottish committee on the state purchase of the liquor trade (1917), and a court of inquiry concerning the wages and conditions of employment of dock labour in the United Kingdom (1920). In an article which he contributed to the *Fortnightly Review* in 1900 on 'The Scottish University Crisis' he made a strong plea for extending free education in Scotland to the universities by the abolition of class fees. This article attracted the attention of Andrew Carnegie [q.v.], a fellow native of Dunfermline, and undoubtedly greatly influenced him in founding (1901) the Carnegie Trust for the Universities of Scotland, with its twofold object of assisting students by the payment of their fees and of improving the equipment of the universities.

Shaw always retained his early interest in literature and was himself the author of a number of books. The best known is his *Letters to Isabel* (1921), an unconventional autobiography in the guise of a series of letters written to one of his daughters, in which he describes the leading features of his career as he wished it to be appreciated by posterity. So far as it purports to narrate facts and to convey impressions it must be read with considerable reservations. A sequel in similar vein, entitled *The Other Bundle*, appeared in 1927. In 1911 he published a lecture on *Legislature and Judiciary* which he had given at University College, London; an account of his visits to the annual meetings of the American and Canadian Bar Associations in 1922 and the addresses which he there delivered are to be found in a volume entitled *The Law of the Kinsmen* (1923); in 1928 he published a short study of *The Trial of Jesus Christ* and in 1933 *John Marshall in Diplomacy and in Law*, a sketch of the life of Chief Justice Marshall of the United States Supreme Court. Plays in verse on *Darnley* (1925) and *Leicester* (1931) further testify to his versatility.

On his resignation in 1929 Lord Shaw's life peerage was converted into an ordinary barony and, taking his new title from the estate which he had bought in Aberdeenshire, he was thenceforth known as Lord Craigmyle.

However much controversy attended his public career Craigmyle was singularly happy in his domestic life where he was assured of admiration and affection. He married in 1879 Elsie Stephen (died 1939), daughter of George Forrest, of Ludquharn, Aberdeenshire, and had a son and three daughters. He died at Glasgow 28 June 1937, and was succeeded as second baron by his son, Alexander (1883–1944), who married the eldest daughter of James Lyle Mackay, first Earl of Inchcape [q.v.].

[*The Times*, 30 June 1937; *Scotsman*, 15 February 1909; Lord Shaw, *Letters to Isabel*, 1921, and *The Other Bundle*, 1927; *Journal of Comparative Legislation*, July 1921; *Thomas Shaw (First Lord Craigmyle). A monograph by his son*, 1937; personal knowledge.]

MACMILLAN.

SHAW, THOMAS (1872–1938), labour leader and politician, commonly known as Tom Shaw, was born at Waterside, Colne, Lancashire, 9 April 1872, the eldest son of Ellis Shaw, miner, of Colne, by his wife, Sarah Ann Wilkinson. Tom Shaw was educated at St. James's elementary school at Waterside, and when ten years old entered a textile factory as a half-time worker: he left school finally at the age of twelve. Night schools and technical classes made up to some extent for his lack of early education and developed in particular a linguistic ability unusual in such circumstances: his aptitude for French and German served him greatly in later life. Before he was twenty-one he was a member of the Colne Weavers' Association, subsequently becoming its secretary: he also promoted the formation of the Northern Counties' Textile Federation, which embraced all the main sections of the cotton trade unions, and he was its first secretary. From 1911 to 1929, and again from 1931 until his death, he was secretary of the International Federation of Textile Workers and in the course of his duties visited every country in Europe except Spain and Portugal, combining an intimate knowledge of the technicalities of the developing industry with a grasp of industrial politics both at home and abroad. During the war of 1914–1918 he was director of national service for the West Midland region, and afterwards urged the claims of the King's Roll for the employment of ex-servicemen. He was appointed C.B.E. in 1919.

An enthusiastic supporter of the labour party from its inception (as the labour representation committee) in 1900, Shaw was returned to parliament for Preston in 1918 and held the seat continuously until his defeat in 1931. He was junior labour whip in 1919; minister of labour in the first labour government (January–October 1924); and secretary of state for war in the second labour administration (1929–1931). In the former period he introduced measures which enhanced the benefits of the Unemployment Insurance Acts. He was sworn of the Privy Council in 1924.

Upon the reconstruction of the Labour and Socialist International at Hamburg in 1923, when Arthur Henderson [q.v.] was appointed chairman, Shaw was elected joint secretary with Friedrich Adler, the Austrian socialist, its former secretary, with whom he served until 1925. In that capacity he visited the Ruhr and reported against its continued occupation by French troops. He stressed the impossibility of enforcing the German reparations laid down in the Treaty of Versailles, and forecast the probability of another war in twenty years' time.

In 1926 Shaw headed a delegation to investigate conditions in the Indian textile industry; and he was also an informed member of the Holman Gregory commission on workmen's compensation (1917–1920). A convinced champion of the League of Nations and the International Labour Organization, he was diligent in promoting the Washington convention for a forty-eight hours working week (1919) and was highly critical when in 1923 the British government declined to follow the lead of France, Belgium, and Holland in ratifying the proposal. A bill in Shaw's name for implementing the convention was before parliament in 1924, when the labour government fell.

While disagreeing fundamentally with communist principles and the Russian Soviet system, Shaw favoured friendly political and trade relations with Russia and supported the council of action representing the British trade union movement in its efforts to prevent British intervention in the Russo-Polish conflict in 1921.

From 1931 Shaw devoted his energies to the International Federation of Textile Workers, and it was in his capacity as secretary of that body that he attended as fraternal delegate the anniversary congress held in Brussels in 1938. There he was taken suddenly ill, and, returning to London, died there 26 September. He married in 1893 Susannah Whitaker Sterne Ryan, daughter of Charles Woodhead, tackler, and had four daughters, two of whom predeceased their father.

Possessed of a gift of plain, blunt speech, and a clear and logical mind, Shaw was a popular figure in his native county as well as in the wider world. He had no particular hobby beyond the collection of 'tacklers' tales'—unique examples of Lancashire factory humour—which he told and retold with unfailing and infectious enjoyment.

[*The Times*, 27 September 1938; *Colne Times*, 30 September 1938; private information; personal knowledge.]

J. S. MIDDLETON.

SHEPPARD, HUGH RICHARD LAWRIE (1880–1937), dean of Canterbury, was born at Windsor 2 September 1880, the younger son of Edgar Sheppard, later sub-dean of the Chapels Royal and canon of St. George's Chapel, Windsor, by his wife, Mary, daughter of Richard White, of Instow, Devonshire. He was educated at Marlborough and Trinity Hall, Cambridge (1901–1904), and after periods at Oxford House, Bethnal Green, as lay-

secretary to Cosmo Gordon Lang, then bishop of Stepney, and at Cuddesdon College, was ordained (1907, 1908) as chaplain of Oxford House of which he became head (1909). Resigning through over-strain, he again became secretary to Lang, then archbishop of York, until he was given charge of St. Mary's, Bourdon Street, London, and the chaplaincy of the newly founded Cavendish Club (1911), and then of Grosvenor Chapel, South Audley Street (1913).

In July 1914 Sheppard accepted the vicarage of St. Martin-in-the-Fields, Trafalgar Square, and on the outbreak of war the chaplaincy (for three months) of Lady Dudley's Australian hospital in France. Despite recurrent attacks of illness, his work at St. Martin's brought it world-wide fame through the development of religious broadcasting and the use of its position as a church open day and night. To great organizing ability, intuitive sympathy, and simple, kindly, often humorous directness of speech, Sheppard united an irresistible desire to make others happier and to enlist them in a fellowship of service. In 1917 with William Temple (afterwards successively archbishop of York and Canterbury) he inaugurated the Life and Liberty Movement which led in 1919 to the establishment of the National Assembly of the Church of England. In 1924 he published, as *The Human Parson*, the pastoral theology lectures which he had delivered at Cambridge in 1921, and in 1927 *The Impatience of a Parson*, after his resignation of St. Martin's through ill health. He was then appointed C.H., having already been a chaplain of the Order of St. John of Jerusalem since 1910. In 1929 he became dean of Canterbury, and exercised remarkable influence but was compelled by asthma to resign in February 1931. From 1934 until his death he was a canon and precentor of St. Paul's Cathedral, and in 1936 one of the founders of the Peace Pledge Union to which he devoted much energy. In 1927 the university of Glasgow conferred upon him the honorary degree of D.D., and in 1937 the students there elected him lord rector in preference to Mr. J. B. S. Haldane and Mr. Winston Churchill. He died suddenly in London 31 October 1937 and was buried at Canterbury.

Sheppard married in 1915 Alison Lennox, only daughter of William Oswald Carver, J.P., of Cranage Hall, Holmes Chapel, Cheshire, and had two daughters. A portrait by (Sir) G. F. Kelly is in the vestry-hall of St. Martin's, and there is another in the deanery at Canterbury.

[*The Times*, 1 November 1937; *Dick Sheppard by his Friends*, 1938; R. Ellis Roberts, *H. R. L. Sheppard. Life and Letters*, 1942; personal knowledge.]   CLAUD JENKINS.

SHORTT, EDWARD (1862–1935), politician, was born at Byker, Newcastle-upon-Tyne, 10 March 1862, the second son of Edward Shortt, vicar of St. Anthony's church, Byker, who was descended from an Irish family in county Tyrone, by his wife, Josepha, daughter of Joseph Rushton, of Alderley Edge. Shortt was educated at Durham School and at Durham University, where he was Lindsay scholar and graduated in classics in 1884. In 1890 he was called to the bar by the Middle Temple, of which he was elected a bencher in 1919, and joined the North-Eastern circuit. He was recorder of Sunderland from 1907 to 1918 and took silk in 1910. Elected as a liberal for Newcastle-upon-Tyne in January 1910, he retained the seat (Western division, 1918–1922) throughout his parliamentary career.

Shortt made no great success at the bar, but in parliament he was more successful. He was a clear and lucid debater, and as a private member he was as popular in the House as he had been on circuit. On the home rule bill of 1912 he spoke frequently, and his mastery of the details of the measure served him well. In June 1917 he was appointed chairman of a select committee set up to review the general administration of the Military Service Acts, which reported in August, recommending that medical examinations should be transferred from the War Office to a civilian authority. By his firm and tactful handling of a subject bristling with difficulties, he recommended himself to Lloyd George, who in April 1918 appointed Shortt to succeed Henry Edward Duke (afterwards Lord Merrivale, q.v.) as chief secretary for Ireland. In that post Shortt was confronted by serious trouble, but after acting promptly and arresting 150 Sinn Feiners he was able to report in July that the situation was much improved. In January 1919 he was transferred to the Home Office in order to deal with the threatened police strike. In that year there were two strikes, in March and in August, of which the second was the more serious in the provinces. Shortt showed skill and courage as well as sympathy in remedying genuine grievances, and a satisfactory settlement was reached.

His personal popularity with the force was shown on his resignation by a remarkable tribute from the constabulary in which full recognition was made of the work which he had done for them during his term of office.

With the fall of the coalition government in October 1922, Shortt's political career came to an end. Not so his activity. He was chairman of the committees on the rating of machinery, on trusts, and on heavy motor traffic, as well as others. In November 1929 he succeeded T. P. O'Connor [q.v.] as second president of the British Board of Film Censors, a salaried appointment but independent of trade control. In November 1933 he was appointed chairman of the committee of investigation into the Agricultural Marketing Act.

Shortt married in 1890 Isabella Stewart, daughter of A. G. Scott, of Valparaiso, and had a son, who was killed in action in 1917, and three daughters. He died in London of septicaemia following influenza 10 November 1935.

Shortt was sworn of the Privy Council and of the Irish Privy Council in 1918. The honorary degree of D.C.L. was conferred upon him by Durham University in 1920.

[*The Times*, 11, 12, 15 November 1935.]   E. I. CARLYLE.

SIDEBOTHAM, HERBERT (1872–1940), journalist, was born at Manchester 21 December 1872, the only son of Edmund Sidebotham, of Hyde and Manchester, by his wife, Agnes Greaves Dixon. Educated at Manchester Grammar School, he went in 1891 as a scholar to Balliol College, Oxford, where he was awarded a first class in classical moderations (1893) and in *literae humaniores* (1895), won a Craven scholarship (1892) and the Gaisford prizes for Greek verse (1893) and prose (1894), and was *proxime accessit* for the Ireland scholarship (1894). Thence he passed (1895) into the office of the *Manchester Guardian* as a leader-writer under its famous editor, C. P. Scott [q.v.], and so remained for over twenty-two years. Having made a hobby of military history, he became during the South African war the paper's military critic under the pen-name 'Student of War'; and the great credit with which he filled that role became even greater when he filled it again during the war of 1914–1918. In 1918 he transferred to London to be the military critic of *The Times*; but before he got into his stride, the war ended.

He remained with *The Times* until July 1921 as 'Student of Politics', writing a series of brilliant political character-sketches, reprinted in 1921 as *Pillars of the State*. For a short time (1922–1923) he became (at Lloyd George's suggestion) political adviser to the *Daily Chronicle*; but the paper could not offer sufficient scope for his pen, and he transferred to the service of the brothers Berry, who owned conjointly the *Sunday Times*, the *Daily Sketch*, and (later) the *Daily Telegraph*. On the first he wrote as 'Scrutator', on the second as 'Candidus', and on the third as 'Student of Politics'. In the 'Scrutator' articles he reached his highest level; they combine a style of brilliant maturity with a wealth of knowledge and often an almost uncanny insight; no others then written were more widely and attentively read by influential people. His 'Candidus' articles, in a lighter vein, were also original; in 1938 he made a book of them, *The Sense of Things*. A personal outside interest was Zionism; for over twenty years he wrote articles in its British organs, and he also published two books on the subject, *England and Palestine; Essays towards the Restoration of the Jewish State* (1918) and *Great Britain and Palestine* (1937).

Sidebotham's conversation mirrored a broad, deep culture; he never forgot his classics (as late as 1937 he printed privately twenty difficult Shakespearian sonnets done into Latin elegiacs); he also read foreign books voraciously. He was a good amateur pianist, early addicted to Liszt, but later to Mozart, and always to Beethoven. He was called to the bar by the Inner Temple in 1912, but did not practise. He married in 1899 Florence, daughter of Thomas Stephens, a Salford alderman, and had three daughters. He died at Roehampton 19 March 1940.

[Private information; personal knowledge.]
R. C. K. Ensor.

SIDGWICK, ELEANOR MILDRED (1845–1936), principal of Newnham College, Cambridge, was born at Whittinge-hame, East Lothian, 11 March 1845, the eldest daughter and eldest of the eight surviving children of James Maitland Balfour, of Whittingehame, by his wife, Lady Blanche Harriet, second daughter of James Brownlow William Gascoyne-Cecil, second Marquess of Salisbury. Among her five brothers were Arthur James, first Earl of Balfour, Francis Maitland Balfour [qq.v.], and Gerald William, second Earl of Bal-

four. Lady Frances Balfour [q.v.] was the wife of her youngest brother, Eustace James Anthony Balfour.

Eleanor Balfour's own intellectual gifts fitted her for this brilliant family circle. The closest bonds united her with her eldest brother, and each had great influence upon the other's thoughts and interests. In early years her bent was towards mathematics and scientific research, stimulated by her brother-in-law J. W. Strutt, third Lord Rayleigh, the joint discoverer of argon [q.v.], in some of whose work she collaborated.

In 1876 Miss Balfour married Henry Sidgwick, then praelector on moral and political philosophy at Trinity College, Cambridge [q.v.]. Their marriage was one of great happiness and shared work, broken only by his death in 1900. They had no children. Even before her marriage Mrs. Sidgwick was practically interested in the two main activities with which her name is associated, the higher education of women, and the Society for Psychical Research. Sidgwick was one of the pioneers through whose exertions Newnham College was founded at Cambridge, and in 1880 Mrs. Sidgwick became its sole treasurer, a post which she held until 1919. From 1880 to 1882 she was vice-principal, and in 1892 she succeeded Anne Jemima Clough [q.v.] as principal, and so remained until her resignation in 1910. The growth and success of the college were largely due to the wisdom and generosity of Henry and Eleanor Sidgwick: it is calculated that the latter's own gifts to it amounted to over £30,000. In 1894 Mrs. Sidgwick was one of the first three women to serve on a royal commission, being appointed to that on secondary education under the chairmanship of James (afterwards Viscount) Bryce [q.v.].

In 1916 Mrs. Sidgwick left Cambridge, and went to live with her brother Gerald and his wife at Fisher's Hill, near Woking, until her death there in her ninety-first year 10 February 1936. During these years, in collaboration with Gerald Balfour, she concentrated chiefly upon her study of psychical phenomena, and evidences of continuing personality after death, conducting her investigations with the rare degree of objectivity characteristic of her approach to all life's problems. She was elected president of the Society for Psychical Research in 1908, and named 'president of honour' in 1932, when she relinquished the honorary secretaryship which she had held for twenty-five years.

Her last address to the society was read in her absence by Lord Balfour, whom she authorized to state that she had reached personal conviction of the fact of survival.

Mrs. Sidgwick's writings are chiefly contained in the *Proceedings* of the Society for Psychical Research. In 1906 she published, in collaboration with her brother-in-law Arthur Sidgwick, *Henry Sidgwick, a Memoir*, and she contributed a lecture on 'War in its Ethical and Psychological Aspects' to *The International Crisis* (1915). She received honorary degrees from the universities of Manchester, Birmingham, St. Andrews, and Edinburgh.

A portrait of Mrs. Sidgwick as a young woman by J. J. Shannon hangs in the dining hall of Clough Hall, Newnham College.

[Ethel Sidgwick, *Mrs. Henry Sidgwick*, 1938; Blanche E. C. Dugdale, *Arthur James Balfour, First Earl of Balfour*, 2 vols., 1936; *Newnham College Letter*, January 1937; *Proceedings* of the Society for Psychical Research, June 1936; personal knowledge.]

BLANCHE E. C. DUGDALE.

SIMPSON, SIR JOHN WILLIAM (1858–1933), architect, was born at Brighton 9 August 1858, the eldest son of Thomas Simpson, architect, of Brighton, by his wife, Clara Hart. He was great-grandson of Robert Simpson [q.v.]. He was educated at private schools and subsequently attended the Royal Academy Schools, qualifying A.R.I.B.A. in 1882. After his election as a fellow in 1900 he became closely associated with the Royal Institute of British Architects: he was twice elected vice-president and was president from 1919 to 1921; and he was nominated to represent the institute on the council of the British School at Rome. He held this appointment for sixteen years, being one of the original members under the royal charter.

This association with a school of architecture abroad was but one of several enjoyed by Simpson, who was president of the Union Franco-Britannique des Architectes (1922–1923), and a corresponding member of the Institut de France, the Sociedad Central de Arquitectos, Buenos Ayres, and the Centralvereinigung der Architekten, Vienna.

At home Simpson held many public appointments, including that of secretary-general of the Town Planning Conference held in London in 1910. He specialized in the design of public buildings, planning (in collaboration) the Grafton Street Hospital, Liverpool, the National Hospital for the Paralysed and Epileptic, Queen Square, London, the Art Galleries for the Corporation of Glasgow, and the Victoria Institute, Worcester. He was solely responsible for the Offices of the Crown Agents for the Colonies at Millbank and for schools as diverse in character as Roedean, Gresham's School, Holt, and West Downs School, Winchester, and for new buildings at Lancing College and Haileybury College. He also undertook the design of several memorials, including the Queen Victoria memorial at Bradford; the Royal Sussex Regiment memorial at Brighton; the Onslow Ford memorial in St. John's Wood; and the Cartwright Memorial Hall at Bradford. In domestic architecture his skill in the solution of difficult technical and engineering problems found less scope. He was best known to the public for his work at the British Empire Exhibition held in 1924 at Wembley, where, in collaboration with his partner, Mr. Maxwell Ayrton, he was responsible for the general layout, the stadium, and the palaces of industry and engineering.

As architect to the Honourable Society of Lincoln's Inn, Simpson restored the Old Hall of the Inn and in 1928 published *Some Account of the Old Hall of Lincoln's Inn*. He wrote only two other books, *Essays and Memorials* (1923) and *Paris Rosemary* (1927), but published many professional papers devoted to such subjects as 'The Planning of Cities' and 'Open Spaces'.

Simpson died, unmarried, at his home at Highgate 30 March 1933. He was appointed K.B.E. in 1924, was a chevalier of the Legion of Honour, and was awarded the gold medal of the Société des Artistes Français in 1922.

A portrait of Simpson by Sir A. S. Cope (1922) is at the Royal Institute of British Architects.

[*Journal* of the Royal Institute of British Architects, 29 April and 13 May 1933; *The Times*, 1 April 1933; Sir J. Simpson's own writings.]   W. GODFREY ALLEN.

SIMPSON, SIR WILLIAM JOHN RITCHIE (1855–1931), physician and pioneer in tropical medicine, was probably born 27 April 1855, the only child of John Simpson, by his wife, whose maiden name was Arthur. Both were of Scottish descent, and died when he was young. The place of his birth is unknown: family tradition says that it was Edinburgh:

he himself at matriculation entered his birthplace as Glasgow, but neither statement is confirmed by official records. He was sent to school in Jersey; graduated M.B., C.M. at Aberdeen University in 1876; and in 1880 proceeded M.D. (Aberdeen) and took the diploma of public health at Cambridge. The same year he became medical officer of health at Aberdeen and lecturer on hygiene at the university.

After studying at King's College, London, Simpson became in 1886 the first medical officer of health for Calcutta, where, during his twelve years there, he found almost the whole range of problems in public health. With this wide experience gained, he was well qualified for the chair of hygiene at King's College, London, to which he was appointed in 1898 and which he occupied until his retirement in 1923. It was natural that he should co-operate with (Sir) Patrick Manson [q.v.] and (Sir) James Cantlie in founding the London School of Tropical Medicine, which was opened in October 1899; there he lectured on tropical hygiene from 1898 until 1923. In 1926 he was one of the founders of the Ross Institute and Hospital for Tropical Diseases at Putney, where he became the first director of tropical hygiene, and physician to the attached hospital.

Besides his regular work at London University, Simpson undertook many other important tasks. In 1900 he was a member of a commission to inquire into the dysentery and enteric fever among the troops in South Africa. He had hardly completed this task when, in the following year, plague broke out among the dense mass of refugees from the war area living in overcrowded and insanitary huts in the suburbs of Cape Town. Simpson had such success with his control of the disease that it was found unnecessary to cancel the visit of the Duke and Duchess of Cornwall and York. The disease was soon stamped out.

His wide experience of hygiene and his success at Cape Town placed Simpson in the front rank of sanitarians, and the government was not slow to recognize his value. He was appointed commissioner to investigate plague in Hong-Kong in 1902; sanitation in Singapore in 1906; plague on the Gold Coast, and public health in Sierra Leone, the Gold Coast, and Southern Nigeria in 1908; to report on plague and public health in East Africa, Uganda, and Zanzibar in 1913; and on sanitation and plague in the mines and mining villages

in the Gold Coast and Ashanti in 1924. His last visit to the tropics was in 1929 to the Chester-Beatty group of copper mines in Northern Rhodesia. From 1903 onwards he advocated the policy of (Sir) Ronald Ross [q.v.] for the control of malaria by reducing the mosquito. In 1913 he was a member of the commission on yellow fever in West Africa.

Simpson was a prolific writer, not only of official reports. He was editor of the *Indian Medical Gazette* (1889-1896), and joint editor of the *Journal of Tropical Medicine* (London) from its inception. He was author of *A Treatise on Plague* (1905), *The Principles of Hygiene in relation to Tropical and Sub-Tropical Climates* (1908), and *Maintenance of Health in the Tropics* (1916). He also wrote several papers on vaccination.

For his public services Simpson was appointed C.M.G. in 1909, and knighted in 1923. He received the Order of St. Sava in 1918 for work in Serbia during the war of 1914–1918. He gave the Croonian lectures in 1907 at the College of Physicians of which he was elected a fellow in 1899, and he was president of the Royal Society of Tropical Medicine and Hygiene in London from 1919 to 1921.

In 1888 Simpson married Isabella Mary Jane, fourth daughter of George Jamieson, D.D., minister of St. Machar's Cathedral, Old Aberdeen, and had a son, who was killed in the war of 1914–1918, and a daughter. He died at the Ross Institute, Putney, 20 September 1931.

Light in build, with delicately chiselled features, quiet, courteous, and charming in manner, Simpson displayed his core of native granite when he was working for some public good. It was characteristic of him that his last efforts were directed towards retaining open spaces in London for recreation, particularly the site of the Foundling Hospital.

There is a bust of Simpson by Frank Boucher in the School of Hygiene and Tropical Medicine in London.

[*British Medical Journal*, 1931, vol. ii, pp. 633 and 682 (portrait); *Journal of Tropical Medicine*, vol. xxxiv, 1931; *Lancet*, 1931, vol. ii, p. 712 (portrait); *The Times*, 22 September 1931; personal knowledge.]

MALCOLM WATSON.

SMILLIE, ROBERT (1857–1940), labour leader and politician, was born of working-class Scottish parents 17 March 1857 in Belfast. He and his elder brother were left orphans at an early age and were brought up by their grandmother. He left school for labour at the age of nine, but continued part-time schooling for three years more. Subsequently he joined his brother in southern Scotland as a lad of fifteen already broken in to hard manual work, and he retained, to the end of his life, the North Irish accent of his boyhood. He spent the whole of his adult life in Lanarkshire, and was by most regarded as a typical Scot. From 1878, when he married Anne Hamilton, he lived at Larkhall, in the same house.

Smillie's first post in the mines was that of pumpman, thanks to unusual physical strength; within four years he was a checkweighman and rising to recognized leadership among his fellows. Having consolidated the local union, he worked, first, to bring it into association with other unions in the area to form a single body for Lanarkshire; next, to get the Lanarkshire miners federated with other mining unions in Scotland; finally, to bring all mining unions in Great Britain into a single all-embracing federation, with close international affiliations. By 1888 these aims were accomplished; as representative of the Lanarkshire miners, he went to an all-British conference called to discuss the demand for an eight hours' legal working day. From 1894 to 1918 he was president of the Scottish Miners' Federation (founded 1886–1887). He played a leading part in bringing into being the Miners' Federation of Great Britain (1888); as its vice-president, he bore a large responsibility for the national coal strike of 1912, which established the principle of a national minimum wage, although the Coal Mines (Minimum Wage) Act of that year left the figures to be determined locally.

For Smillie, trade unionism was, in the last resort, an instrument for raising the status of the miner; he was always clear that if their ideas of social justice were to be realized the working classes had to organize politically as well as industrially. For twelve years he was an active member of the Larkhall school board; owing to his efforts, this was one of the first places in Scotland to supply its school children with free books; he campaigned for James Keir Hardie [q.v.] in many an election, and himself stood no less than six times as a candidate before he succeeded at Morpeth in 1923, a seat which he held until 1929. He was a foundation member of the Scottish parliamentary labour party (1888) and of the independent labour party (1893). The independent labour party was

indeed spiritually his political home; in 1914 he was a pacificist of that brand, and so remained. Two of his sons served in the army; another was a conscientious objector; but there was no breach in the Smillie home. Moreover, even those who disagreed most sharply with him respected his transparent sincerity; his power among the working classes was such that in 1917 Lloyd George invited him to be food controller, but he refused.

Smillie's great opportunity came in 1919, when his evidence before the royal commission on the coal industry under the chairmanship of Mr. Justice (afterwards Lord) Sankey, the force with which he stated the miners' case, and the skill and profound knowledge displayed in his penetrating cross-examination, conducted, without apparent passion, in a low and gentle voice, made plain the calibre of the man. The strain of his labours with the commission, and the disappointment caused by the failure of the government to implement the Report, seriously affected his health; in 1921 he resigned his post as president of the Miners' Federation of Great Britain, which he had held since 1912, although in the same year he again became president of the Scottish Miners' Federation (a post which he retained until his death) and continued active work in the general counsels of the labour party. He refused office in the first labour government (1924), and after its fall in the same year retired from active life, although, to the last, the simple house at Larkhall was the bourne of all sorts and conditions of men in search of guidance. He died at Dumfries 16 February 1940. His family life—he had six sons and two daughters —was singularly happy.

Smillie published in 1924 *My Life For Labour*; it is rather a picture of mining conditions and the miners' struggle than of himself; but when he says 'I was hot-blooded and warm hearted—not always the same thing', he gives a hint of the secret of his immense influence. He was a man of transparent integrity, in whom pity and indignation were passions wholly selfless: and he inspired entire confidence and respect in those who disagreed with him. Bound in close friendship to Keir Hardie, he resembled him in vision and force of character. Indifferent to worldly success and contemptuous of its outward signs, he used his power over his fellows in the furtherance of the ideas in which he believed, the welfare of the mining community in the first instance, and thence, in extension, the promotion of his general conception of social justice.

[*The Times*, 17 February 1940; R. Smillie, *My Life for Labour*, 1924; personal knowledge.]   MARY AGNES HAMILTON.

SMITH, SIR CHARLES EDWARD KINGSFORD (1897–1935), air-pilot, was born at Hamilton, Brisbane, 9 February 1897, the youngest of the four sons of William Charles Smith, bank manager, of Brisbane, by his wife, Catherine Mary Kingsford. After attending an elementary school in Vancouver, British Columbia, where his parents lived from 1903 to 1907, he was educated at Sydney Cathedral School and Sydney Technical College. In 1913 he became an engineering apprentice at the Colonial Sugar Refining Company, Sydney, and he enlisted in 1915 for the duration of the war, serving as a dispatch-rider in Egypt and Gallipoli in 1915 and in France in 1916. Within two months he was recommended for a commission and went to England for training, but before the end of his course he was transferred to the Royal Flying Corps, and was commissioned early in 1917, joining No. 23 squadron in France. After three months' service he was wounded in the foot; a long convalescence followed and he became an instructor in the Royal Air Force with the rank of captain.

On leaving the Royal Air Force in 1919 Kingsford Smith remained in England with the intention of winning the prize of £10,000 offered by the Australian government for the first flight from England to Australia. But the Australian government insisted on his abandoning his plans and he returned by way of the United States of America, spending more than a year in California, flying for the films and in flying circuses. He reached Sydney in 1921, and after giving exhibitions at fairs and country shows for Diggers Aviation Limited, he eventually joined West Australian Airways. He now had two main purposes before him: to develop inter-state communication by air in Australia and New Zealand by means of private companies, and to fly across the Pacific. In order to make money to realize the latter he joined another pilot, Keith Anderson, in the Gascoyne Transport Company at Carnarvon, and when in 1926 he had acquired sufficient means to buy two small aeroplanes, he founded the Interstate Services as a 'taxi' firm with Charles T. P. Ulm as manager, and next year flew with him round Australia in less than eleven days.

This feat, in half the previous record time, induced the New South Wales government to grant £3,500 towards the cost of the flight across the Pacific. With Ulm, he at once went to California in search of an aeroplane that was within the compass of their meagre resources.

In the event, by loans and financial help from Mr. Sidney Myer, of Melbourne, and finally from Captain G. Allan Hancock, the airframe of the Fokker used by Sir Hubert Wilkins in the Arctic was bought, then re-equipped, re-engined, and renamed the *Southern Cross*. With Ulm as second pilot and two Americans as navigator and radio-operator, Kingsford Smith set out on 31 May 1928 from Oakland, San Francisco, for Honolulu, about 2,000 miles away. The next stage to Fiji was a distance of 3,150 miles, and the *Southern Cross* was so heavily loaded with fuel that it had to take off from a beach on a flight that lasted nearly thirty-three hours. After some delay at Fiji, he set out on 7 June for the last 1,780 miles to Brisbane, and after passing through violent storms, he made his landfall 110 miles south of Brisbane, and so won £20,000 for the first trans-Pacific flight.

This was only the first stage in the enterprise of flying round the world which was Kingsford Smith's aim, and on 31 March 1929 a false start nearly cost him and his companions their lives, for they got off course and were forced to land in the Northern Territory, where food had to be dropped to them by aeroplane. Only two months later, on 25 June, he reached London in less than thirteen days, and next year he took the *Southern Cross* from Ireland to Newfoundland, and thence to San Francisco, thus completing his flight round the world on 1 July 1930, a little more than two years after he had begun it. These ocean flights, circling the earth at its greatest circumference, together with a flight from Melbourne to Perth and the first crossing of the Tasman Sea in 27 hours 52 minutes in 1928, were the most notable achievements of Kingsford Smith's flying career; but they were not his last. In October 1933 he made a solo flight from England to Australia in a Percival Gull, in seven days five hours. The following year he bought the single-engined Lockheed Altair in which he was to lose his life, and flew with Captain P. G. Taylor from Brisbane to San Francisco, with halts at Fiji and Honolulu; in August 1935 attempted his seventh crossing of the Tasman Sea in the *Southern Cross*, but had to turn back; on 6 November 1935 he set out in the Altair from England, accompanied by J. Thomas Pethybridge, a former mechanic, and then flying instructor at Sydney. They passed over Calcutta about midnight on 7 November and were never seen again. One of the wheels of the Altair was washed up on the coast of Burma in 1937.

It may well be that the great flight in which Kingsford Smith was lost would have been his last in any event, for he was anxious to settle down and devote himself to operating air-lines. The flight round Australia in 1927 was designed to promote a scheme for inter-state travel, and he founded in 1929 Australian National Airways, but the undertaking lived for only a year. The abortive flights of 1935 were intended to improve the prospects of the Trans-Tasman Air Service Development Company of which Kingsford Smith was a director.

Kingsford Smith's temperament was a disadvantage in business. He inspired confidence and loyalty in those who were associated with him personally and was always willing to take his share of the drudgery, but he had neither the inclination for nor the skill in the dull and routine processes of business organization. At the end, he believed he could obtain air-line contracts by undertaking spectacular flights and suspected intrigue when he failed to get them.

Kingsford Smith was twice married: first, in 1921 to Thelma McKenna, only daughter of a pastoralist, of Meentheena Station, Western Australia; this marriage was dissolved in 1930; secondly, in 1930 to Mary, only daughter of Arthur Powell, merchant and manufacturer, of Melbourne, and had a son. He was decorated with the M.C. in 1917, and was appointed honorary air-commodore in the Royal Australian Air Force in 1930 and K.B.E. in 1932. He was the author of *The Old Bus* (1932), the story of the *Southern Cross*, which was bought by the Australian government in October 1933 for £3,000, the sum which Kingsford Smith had paid for the airframe in 1927.

[*The Times*, 7 December 1935; Sir C. E. Kingsford Smith, *My Flying Life*, 1937; Beau Shiel (with Colin Simpson), *Caesar of the Skies*, 1937; Sir C. E. Kingsford Smith and C. T. P. Ulm, *The Great Trans-Pacific Flight*, 1928.]
E. COLSTON SHEPHERD.

SMITH, SIR GRAFTON ELLIOT (1871-1937), anatomist and anthropolo-gist, was born at Grafton, New South Wales, 15 August 1871, the second son of Stephen Sheldrick Smith, an English schoolmaster at Grafton and later at Sydney, by his wife, Mary Jane Evans, of Carmarthen. He was educated at his father's school at Sydney, and in 1888 entered the medical school in the university of Sydney, where he attracted the attention of Anderson Stuart and John Thomson Wilson, two enthusiasts of the Edinburgh school. After graduating M.B., Ch.M., in 1892, Elliot Smith held various clinical posts and in 1894 began his career as an anatomist and investigator. His intuition may be seen in the four papers published in 1894, dealing with a hydatid cyst in a congenital hernia, the significance of rare anomalies of nerves, muscles, and blood-vessels, and the cerebral commissures of the mammalia, with special reference to the monotremes and marsupials. In 1895 he gained a European reputation and gold medal by his M.D. thesis on the brain of non-placental mammals, and eleven papers dealing with the evolution of the cerebrum, cerebellum, and olfaction in primitive mammals.

In 1896 Elliot Smith came to England and continued his research-work in Cambridge under Alexander Macalister. In 1896 and 1897 he published eight papers on cerebral morphology, and began the descriptive catalogue of the brain collection in the museum of the Royal College of Surgeons, which became the source book for a generation of neurologists. In 1900 Elliot Smith became the first professor of anatomy in the new Government Medical School at Cairo. In the next nine years he published about fifty anatomical papers on the brains of living and extinct forms; but his mighty intellect, to quote Montaigne, was 'a tool adapted to all subjects and meddles with everything'. He became a critic of the methods of anthropologists, classical scholars, and Egyptologists. With Sir Gaston Maspero, George Andrew Reisner, Dr. (Frederic) Wood Jones, and others he began the Archaeological Survey of Nubia involving the examination of 20,000 burials, and he was able to throw light on ancient customs, religion, mummification, palaeopathology, and comparative anatomy.

In 1907 Elliot Smith was elected F.R.S. and in 1909 he was appointed to the chair of anatomy in Manchester University. He became involved with William Halse R. Rivers and Dr. William James Perry in the investigation of the early origins of magic and religion, the early migration of man, and the diffusion of culture. His belief in the newer inductive methods of human biology brought him into conflict with the older anthropologists and historians trained in the classical tradition.

The discovery of the Piltdown skull in 1912 brought Elliot Smith into close contact and occasional differences with (Sir) Arthur Smith Woodward and (Sir) Arthur Keith. In 1909, 1911, and 1920 he delivered the Arris and Gale lectures before the Royal College of Surgeons on the evolution of the brain; he served on the General Medical Council as representative of Manchester University from 1913 to 1919, he collaborated with Rivers and Professor Tom Hatherley Pear in the treatment of shell-shock during the war of 1914–1918; he inspired the Manchester Literary and Philosophical Society with his radical outlook. He received a Royal medal of the Royal Society in 1912, and delivered the Croonian lectures at the Royal College of Physicians in 1919 on 'The Significance of the Cerebral Cortex'. With Pear and G. G. Campion he divorced psychology from sexology.

In 1919, persuaded by E. H. Starling [q.v.], Elliot Smith accepted the chair of anatomy at University College, London. From 1919 to December 1932 he devoted himself to the new Institute of Anatomy made possible by the benefaction of the Rockefeller Foundation and put into practice his views on the significance of anatomy. Practical courses in histology, embryology, neurology, and radiological anatomy were instituted. Physical anthropology and, to a certain extent, cultural anthropology were taught and fostered. Liaisons were formed with University College Hospital and with the prosectorium of the Zoological Society. He scattered his demonstrators to chairs in the English-speaking world; he attracted post-graduate research workers; he welcomed overseas resident magistrates, medical officers, and men of varied interests. He championed John Irvine Hunter and Norman Dawson Royle, of Sydney, when they revived surgical interest in the sympathetic system. He interpreted discoveries in relation to the early history of man. He stimulated research in many fields and prepared his assistants to profit by the unexpected: Professor Raymond Arthur Dart in South Africa discovered the Taungs ape, Davidson Black in Peking the Peking skull. He visited the United States of America, Indonesia, Java, and China. He was largely responsible for winning the interest of the Rockefeller Foundation in anthropological and anatomical research in China, India, and Australia. He was Fullerian professor of physiology at the Royal Institute in 1933.

Of his numerous publications *The Ancient Egyptians* (1911), *The Migrations of Early Culture* (1915), *Evolution of the Dragon* (1919), *Elephants and Ethnologists* (1924), *The Evolution of Man: Essays* (1924), *Human History* (1930), and *Diffusion of Culture* (1933) prove Elliot Smith's intellectual stature and childlike simplicity of approach to scientific truth. His work was done in spasms, periods of idleness alternating with bursts of intense activity. From 1932, when he was partially incapacitated by a stroke, until his retirement from the chair of anatomy in September 1936, he contended cheerfully with much disability. He was knighted in 1934 for services to the Empire and to science. In 1911 he received the Prix Fauvelle of the Anthropological Society of Paris and in 1935 the Huxley medal of the London institute. He was elected a fellow of St. John's College, Cambridge, in 1899 and an honorary fellow in 1931. He married in 1900 Kathleen, daughter of William Latimer Macredie, of Sydney, and had three sons, the youngest of whom predeceased his father. He died at Broadstairs 1 January 1937.

[*The Times*, 2 January 1937; *Sir Grafton Elliot Smith. A Biographical Record by his Colleagues*, edited by W. R. Dawson, 1938 (bibliography); *Obituary Notices of Fellows of the Royal Society*, No. 6, January 1938 (portrait); personal knowledge.] H. A. HARRIS.

SMITH, HERBERT (1862–1938), Yorkshire miners' leader, was born in the workhouse at Great Preston, Kippax, in the West Riding of Yorkshire, 17 July 1862. His father had been killed in a mining accident a few days earlier and his mother died shortly afterwards. He remained at the workhouse until he was adopted by a childless miner and his wife, Samuel and Charlotte Smith, whose surname was his own. After education at a dame's school at Glass Houghton, near Castleford, and at a British school at Pontefract, when he was ten years old the boy went into the pit, at once joining the Yorkshire miners' movement, then known as the West Yorkshire Association. It was said of him as a youth: 'He was frightened of nowt!' and that remained the key-note of his character throughout his life. He served for thirty years (1891–1921) on the Glass Houghton school board; in 1894 he was elected to the local parish council, and in 1895 to the Pontefract rural district council and Board of Guardians, learning from the last the problems of local workhouse administration. From 1896 to 1904 he was president of the Castleford trades council. During his twenty-two years' residence in the Barnsley district he was a councillor and in 1932 was mayor of Barnsley; in 1903 he won a seat on the West Riding county council, where he specialized in public health and education. He also served as a magistrate.

In 1894 Smith was chosen a checkweighman, and as a delegate to the Yorkshire Miners' Association he became active in trade union affairs. Attracted by the independent political policy of James Keir Hardie [q.v.], he agitated for the miners' eight hours' day, for socialism, and for the labour party. In 1902 he was appointed to the Joint Board of the South and West Yorkshire Coalowners and Workmen. For forty-six years he was an official of the Yorkshire Miners' Association and was president from 1906. From that year he represented the association on the Miners' Federation of Great Britain, and was president from 1922 to 1929. The federation unified the district associations behind a demand for a minimum wage, an eight hours' day, the nationalization of the mines, and the abolition of mining royalties. He was involved in the formation of the triple alliance of railwaymen, transport workers, and miners, which proved completely ineffective when tested in 1914. He stood unsuccessfully for Morley as a labour candidate at the general election of January 1910.

Six great colliery explosions in six successive years (1908–1913) brought mining conditions vividly before public attention, and Smith achieved considerable fame in connexion with rescue work at the Whitehaven disaster (1910) and his cross-examination at the government inquiry which followed. Throughout his life he was foremost in rescue work in French and Belgian, as well as British mines.

Government war-time control of the mining industry ceased in 1921. Chaotic conditions ensued, and within a few years government subsidies totalled £30,000,000. The cessation of this assistance led to the lock-out and the subsequent sympathetic General Strike called by the Trades Union Congress in May 1926. In the national strike of miners, with A. J. Cook [q.v.],

secretary of the federation, Smith was prominent up to the conclusion of the dispute on 20 November, when the owners insisted upon all negotiations for settlement, including an extension of hours, being conducted in the separate districts. Local agreements were made, but the federation was kept in being. Smith resigned the presidency in 1929 in protest against any lengthening of the mining hours. He served for various broken periods between 1913 and 1931 on the general council of the Trades Union Congress, and on its behalf visited Russia in 1924, giving special attention to mining developments in the Soviet Union. He was president of the International Miners' Federation from 1921 to 1929.

In 1931 Smith was again prominent in rescue work after the Bentley explosion, when forty-five men were killed, and, although in his seventieth year, he was as daring as ever he had been. Four years later he was insistent on searching the workings after an explosion at Hemsworth and found a missing man. When attending an International Miners' Conference at Prague in 1936 he received a telegram stating that a disaster had overtaken fifty-six men at Wharncliffe Woodmoor; by 6 a.m. next day he had landed by air in Yorkshire, and by 9 a.m. was down the pit.

At a by-election held at Barnsley on 16 June 1938 Smith was the first to vote for the labour candidate, Mr. Frank Collindridge, and, returning to his office, sat down to his desk and died. His funeral took place on the day of the Yorkshire miners' demonstration and the twenty miles' route from Barnsley to Castleford was lined by miners and their families and the people to whose service he had devoted his life.

In 1885 Smith married Sarah Ann Ripley, of Castleford, by whom he had four sons and five daughters.

A bust of Smith by Jacobi, unveiled in 1931, is in the Miners' Hall at Barnsley.

[J. J. Lawson, *The Man in the Cap. The Life of Herbert Smith*, 1941.]

J. S. MIDDLETON.

SMITH, JOHN ALEXANDER (1863–1939), philosopher and classical scholar, the second son of Andrew Smith, of Dingwall, solicitor and county clerk of Ross, by his wife, Jane Eliza Fraser, was born at Dingwall 21 April 1863. He was educated at Inverness Academy, at the Collegiate School, Edinburgh, at Edinburgh University (where he was Ferguson classical scholar in 1884), and at Balliol College, Oxford, to which he was admitted as Warner exhibitioner and honorary scholar in Hilary term 1884. He obtained a first class in classical moderations (1885) and in *literae humaniores* (1887). After acting for some years as assistant to S. H. Butcher [q.v.], professor of Greek in Edinburgh University, he was elected a fellow of Balliol in 1891, and appointed Jowett lecturer in philosophy in 1896. In 1910 he was elected Waynflete professor of moral and metaphysical philosophy at Oxford, and became thereby a fellow of Magdalen College. He was elected to an honorary fellowship at Balliol in 1924. He retired in 1936, and died, unmarried, at Oxford 19 December 1939.

At Balliol Smith served under three distinguished masters—Benjamin Jowett, Edward Caird, and J. L. Strachan-Davidson [qq.v.]—and was one of a very able company of fellows, which included R. L. Nettleship, Evelyn Abbott, W. R. Hardie, A. A. Macdonell, H. W. C. Davis, and A. L. Smith [qq.v.]. Of all that band he was perhaps the most variously accomplished. The subject which he taught was philosophy, and many Balliol men could bear witness to the width and exactness of his knowledge of the subject and the stimulating quality of his teaching. He was a very fine Aristotelian scholar, and in 1908 succeeded Ingram Bywater [q.v.] as president of the Oxford Aristotelian Society. He worked for many years at an edition of the *De Anima*, and translated this work for the Oxford translation of *The Works of Aristotle* (vol. iii, 1931); he was joint-editor of the volumes published between 1908 and 1912. He lectured regularly on the *Ethics*, and in order to get to the bottom of Aristotle's theory of justice studied deeply in Greek law: the first volume (1920) of the *Historical Jurisprudence* of Sir Paul Vinogradoff [q.v.] owes much to Smith's learning and ingenuity. He made extensive preparations for an edition of the *Poetics*, which appealed to his literary as well as to his philosophical interest. In his general philosophical views he maintained on the whole the idealist tradition established by T. H. Green [q.v.] and Caird, but while much influenced by Hegel he was always a critical disciple.

As a professor Smith had a wider but probably not so deep an influence, since he was in less close contact with his hearers than he had been with his pupils. He came very much under the influence of Benedetto Croce, and in the opinion of some of

his friends adopted Croce's views too implicitly. The diversity of interests which made him a fascinating companion militated against the continuous effort needed for the working out of a consistent system of thought, and his self-critical temper prevented him from writing much for publication. There are, however, articles by him in the *Proceedings* of the Aristotelian Society (new series, vols. xiv, xvii, xviii, xx, xxv, xxvi, suppl. vols. v, vii, vii), in the *Journal of Theological Studies* (vol. xxxi) in *Papers read before the Synthetic Society, 1896–1908* (1909), in the *Classical Quarterly* (vols. xiv, xviii), in *Progress and History* (ed. F. S. Marvin, 1916), in the *Proceedings* of the Sixth International Congress of Philosophy (1926), and in S.P.E. Tract No. xxxiv (1930). He published separately in 1910 his inaugural lecture on *Knowing and Acting*, and in 1924 a paper on *The Nature of Art*. In 1916 he delivered the Hibbert lectures, on 'The Nature of Spirit and its Life', and in 1929–1931 gave the Gifford lectures at Glasgow on 'The Heritage of Idealism'. In 1930 he presided over the seventh International Congress of Philosophy, held at Oxford. He left behind him a very large number of valuable unpublished papers; a selection of those on Greek philosophy is deposited in Balliol library, and a selection of those on other subjects in Magdalen library.

The best account of Smith's later position in philosophy is to be found in his contribution to *Contemporary British Philosophy* edited by J. H. Muirhead [q.v.] (second series, 1925). After giving an account of his earlier views and interests he describes himself as having received his greatest illumination from Croce and Giovanni Gentile, and states a creed, or rather a set of 'suppositions', of which the chief are that the real is essentially in change, and is an event which occupies the whole of time; that history is throughout spiritual, and yet contains a distinction (of degree rather than of kind) between the mental and the non-mental; that reality manifests itself most fully in self-consciousness; that self-consciousness is not a fact but a process, a process of self-making; and that in making itself it reveals its own meaning.

Smith was not only a philosopher; he was an admirable classical scholar. A conspicuous instance of this is supplied by the testimony of an eminent scholar to the effect that he had often 'discovered unerringly what Pindar meant, where every one else was unconvincing'. He was deeply versed in philology (and, as became a

Highlander, not least in Celtic philology), and acquired with extraordinary facility at least a reading knowledge of many languages. He had a very acute feeling for the precise meaning, and the development of the meaning, of words. His ingenuity in conjecture was very great, but a growing love of paradox sometimes led him to views which a calmer judgement would have rejected. It should be added to the tale of his accomplishments that he was an admirable talker and raconteur, and skilful at card tricks and other forms of legerdemain; he was never happier than when he was entertaining children.

A pencil-sketch of Smith, drawn by Gilbert Spencer in 1936, is at Balliol College.

[*The Times*, 20 December 1939; *Oxford Magazine*, 18 January 1940; personal knowledge.]　　　　　　　W. D. Ross.

SMITHELLS, ARTHUR (1860–1939), chemist, was born at Bury, Lancashire, 24 May 1860, the third son of James Smithells, railway manager, by his wife, Martha, daughter of James Livesey. After two years at Glasgow University, he went to the Owens College, Manchester, in 1878, and, under the influence of (Sir) Henry Roscoe [q.v.], became a chemist. This training was extended by a short period abroad with J. F. von Baeyer at Munich and R. B. von Bunsen at Heidelberg, after which he returned to the Owens College as assistant lecturer in 1883, but, at the early age of twenty-five, he was appointed to the chair of chemistry at the Yorkshire College in Leeds. There he was well to the fore in the effort which resulted in the establishment of the university of Leeds (1904). The object of broadening the cultural basis of the Yorkshire College was attained while developing its special character as a school of applied science with university standards. As a trusted member of senate and council, Smithells placed himself unsparingly at the service of the university in this pioneering work, which is now receiving wide recognition by imitation.

Meanwhile Smithells was also engaged on that series of researches on flame structure which was his most eminent contribution to pure science. His instinct for the practical application of science led him in notable lectures and by productive conversations to make contacts with the gas industry. Of this activity one outcome was the endowment of the Livesey professorship at Leeds in 1910 and another,

the formation of a joint research committee of the gas industry and the university, with Smithells as chairman, securing thus a fruitful co-operation of unique character. In 1911 he was elected president of the Society of British Gas Industries. Other activities were marked by his presidencies of the Society of Chemists and Colourists and of the Science Masters' Association (1923), and not less distinctively by his appointment in 1907 as education adviser on home science and household economics at King's College for Women, London, where the subject later acquired degree status. In 1910 he was appointed president of the Indian Guild of Science and Technology and in 1913 was invited as special lecturer to the Punjab University; he accepted willingly, since it provided an opportunity to demonstrate how chemistry might be made to appeal to the Indian student and carry him from theory to practice.

Smithells was greatly shocked by the outbreak of war in 1914, but he felt impelled to help and, as visiting lecturer to the Northern Command in 1915 and later (1916–1919) as chief chemical adviser on anti-gas training of the Home Forces, he rendered services which were recognized by the honorary rank of lieutenant-colonel and appointment as C.M.G. (1918).

In 1923 Smithells resigned his professorship to take up the congenial duties of the director of the Salters' Institute of Industrial Chemistry in London, including the selection and supervision of promising graduates in chemistry who might receive a further training carefully planned to fit them for responsible work in industry. In this period he interested himself especially in the Institute of Chemistry, being president from 1927 to 1930; he received the honorary degree of D.Sc. from the universities of Manchester and Leeds in 1923. He was elected F.R.S. in 1901 and vice-president of the society in 1916. Failing health dictated his retirement in 1937 and his death at Highgate 8 February 1939 ended a career largely spent in continuous and successful effort to break down the barrier between an academic science too isolated and self-satisfied and a community not yet conscious of its own needs. A life so full of other activities left little time for writing, but a selection of his addresses with the title *From a Modern University* was published in 1921. These show the same gifts of lucidity and cogency as his speech, but cannot reproduce the effect of their spoken delivery and the impact of his distinguished personality. His letters too were valued by their recipients for the same qualities and intimate human touches.

Smithells was twice married: first, in 1886 to Constance Marie (died 1907), daughter of Frederic Mawe, and had two sons and one daughter; secondly, in 1908 to Katharine, daughter of Arthur Booth, and had one son. A portrait in oils by G. Fiddes Watt hangs in the great hall of the university of Leeds.

[*The Times*, 9 February 1939; *Obituary Notices of Fellows of the Royal Society*, No. 8, January 1940 (portrait); *Journal* of the Chemical Society, July 1939; *Nature*, 25 February 1939; personal knowledge.]

JOHN W. COBB.

SNELL, SIR **JOHN FRANCIS CLEVERTON** (1869–1938), electrical engineer, was born at Saltash, Cornwall, 15 December 1869, the son of Commander John Snell, R.N., by his wife, Mary Henrietta, only daughter of Frederick William Pouget Cleverton, of Saltash. He was educated at Plymouth Grammar School and at King's College, London, of which he was a fellow from 1929. After a four years' pupilage with the electrical firm of Messrs. Woodhouse & Rawson he became associated first, in 1889, with Colonel R. E. B. Crompton [q.v.], who employed him on electricity supply work at Kensington and Notting Hill and also at Stockholm; and then, three years later, with Major-General C. E. Webber [q.v.], for whom he carried out many country-house and other installations.

In 1893 Snell entered municipal service as an assistant electrical engineer to the (then) St. Pancras Vestry, and three years later went to Sunderland as borough electrical engineer, becoming also borough tramways engineer in 1899. In 1906 he began to practise in Westminster as a consulting engineer, and in 1910 he joined the firm of Messrs. Preece & Cardew. During this partnership, which lasted until 1918, he was in request as an expert witness, the most notable case in which he was engaged being the arbitration in 1912 concerning the terms on which the state should take over the National Telephone Company. In that arbitration he was chief technical witness for the Post Office and was under examination for thirteen days.

During the war of 1914–1918 Snell was a member of a number of government committees, including the water-power re-

sources committee of the Board of Trade and the Ministry of Agriculture's committee on electroculture, of both of which he was chairman. In 1919 he became electrical adviser to the Board of Trade and was appointed chairman of the electricity commission established by the Electricity (Supply) Act passed at the end of that year. In that position, which he held until the beginning of 1938, he took a leading part in shaping the electrical policy of the country and in bringing about the co-ordinated system of generating electricity and transmitting it by the 'grid' which was provided for by the Electricity (Supply) Act, 1926.

Snell was knighted in 1914 and appointed G.B.E. in 1925. He was president in 1902–1903 of the (Incorporated) Municipal Electrical Association; in 1914 of the Institution of Electrical Engineers, which awarded him its Faraday medal in 1938; and in 1926 of the engineering section of the British Association at its Oxford meeting. From 1926 to 1931 he was a vice-president of the Institution of Civil Engineers, but for reasons of health was obliged to decline nomination as president in 1930 and again in 1931. Besides many technical papers he was the author of *The Distribution of Electrical Energy* (1906) and *Power House Design* (1911 and 1921). He was fond of music, particularly the organ, took a keen interest in geology (he was a fellow of the Geological Society), and was a great lover of birds and animals. He married in 1892 Anne Glendenning, second daughter of Henry Bayly Quick, of Biscovey, Cornwall, and had a son. He died in London, after an operation, 6 July 1938.

[*The Times*, 7 July 1938; *Engineer* and *Engineering*, 15 July 1938 (portrait); *Nature*, 27 August 1938; *Journal* of the Institution of Electrical Engineers, vol. lxxxiii, 1938; *Journal* of the Institution of Civil Engineers, vol. x, 1938–1939.]

H. M. ROSS.

SNOW, SIR **THOMAS D'OYLY** (1858–1940), lieutenant-general, was born at Blandford, Dorset, 5 May 1858, the eldest son of the Rev. George D'Oyly Snow, of Langton Lodge, Blandford, by his wife, Maria Jane, daughter of Robert Barlow. He was sent to Eton, and passed thence to St. John's College, Cambridge. A year later, in 1879, he obtained a direct commission in the 13th Foot (Somerset Light Infantry) then in South Africa, and thus at once saw active service in the Zulu war.

Snow served with the Mounted Infantry in the Nile campaign of 1884-1885, and was severely wounded at Gubat. He was promoted captain in 1887. Having received a nomination, he spent the years 1892-1893 at the Staff College. In 1895 he was appointed a brigade-major at Aldershot, and, after promotion in 1897 to a majority in the Royal Inniskilling Fusiliers, accompanied Major-General (Sir) W. F. Gatacre [q.v.] as his brigade-major in the Nile campaign of 1898 (Atbara). He received a brevet lieutenant-colonelcy, and in April 1899 was transferred to the 2nd battalion Northamptonshire Regiment as second-in-command, and thus spent in India the whole period of the South African war. He returned home on promotion to substantive lieutenant-colonel in March 1903, but never commanded his battalion; for in June he was promoted colonel and appointed assistant quartermaster-general of the IV Corps (subsequently renamed the Eastern Command). There he remained until 1914, as assistant adjutant-general (1905) and later brigadier-general, General Staff (1906), until October 1909, when he was given command of the 11th infantry brigade. He held it for only a few months, being promoted major-general in March 1910.

Early in the following year Snow became general officer commanding, 4th division. In this appointment his gifts for training and command of troops were clearly manifested. He concentrated particular attention upon making junior officers criticize each other's work, on movement by night, on march discipline, then in its infancy, and on concealment from the air, an even younger matter, and produced a set of standing orders for war which were made use of by other divisions in the war of 1914-1918. The 4th division, detained in England for a few days in order to guard the east coast, had its first battle at Le Cateau, where Snow, agreeing with General Sir H. L. Smith-Dorrien [q.v.] that they must fight, covered the left flank of the II Corps, and then successfully brought away his division.

During the battle of the Marne Snow's tired horse (he was a big man of six feet four inches) fell and rolled on him, and cracked his pelvis; before he had completely recovered, at Lord Kitchener's request he took command in November 1914 of the newly formed 27th division, made up of regular troops from overseas garrisons. When the Germans launched the first gas attack in April 1915 Snow was the only divisional general with headquarters east of Ypres, and to him fell in a great measure the conduct of the defence. The same year he was promoted to the command of the VII Corps. In the battles of the Somme in 1916 it was his task to divert the Germans' attention to the Gommecourt salient, a task which he performed with thoroughness. In the battles of Arras in 1917 his corps was engaged as right wing of the Third Army. At the battle of Cambrai (1917) it was the right pivot of the operations, and unfortunately Snow's warnings of the German counter-attack were either overlooked or disregarded. The effects of his fall at the Marne were lasting, his lameness had increased, and as the winter of 1917-1918 approached he requested to be relieved, and was appointed general officer commanding-in-chief, Western Command at home, and promoted lieutenant-general. He resigned in September 1919. Forced to use a bath-chair, he left Blandford and settled down in Kensington, where he devoted much time to charitable work and became chairman of the Crippled Boys' Home for Training.

Snow was appointed C.B. in 1907, K.C.B. in 1915, and K.C.M.G. in 1917. From 1919 to 1929 he was colonel of the Somerset Light Infantry. He married in 1897 Charlotte Geraldine, second daughter of Major-General John Talbot Coke, of Trusley, Derbyshire, and had two sons and two daughters. He died in London 30 August 1940.

[Sir J. E. Edmonds, (Official) *History of the Great War. Military Operations. France and Belgium, 1917*, vol. iii, 1949; *The Times*, 31 August 1940; personal knowledge.]

J. E. EDMONDS.

SNOWDEN, PHILIP, VISCOUNT SNOWDEN (1864-1937), statesman, was born in a two-roomed cottage in the hamlet of Ickornshaw, Cowling, near Keighley, in the West Riding of Yorkshire, 18 July 1864, the only son and the youngest of the three children of John Snowden, of Cowling, by his wife, Martha, daughter of Peter Nelson, also of Cowling. His father was a weaver in a mill, who had begun his working life on a handloom at home and still used it to make pieces for his family. Both parents had abilities above their station in life; and as showing the quality of the local Yorkshire stock it may be noted that the row of thirty to forty moorland cottages known as Middleton, which included Snowden's birthplace, included also those of two other labour members who sat with him at different times in parliament. The atmosphere was strongly radical and Wesleyan Methodist; and the boy imbibed early a familiarity with the Bible and an admiration for Gladstone, neither of which ever left him. Educated at a very elementary local school which the Act of 1870 turned into a board school, he escaped the weaving-mill by becoming a pupil-teacher; but, after three years this career was cut short by his parents' migration across the Lancashire border to Nelson, following the failure of the firm which employed them. The boy, then fifteen, became a clerk in an insurance office, where he remained for seven years. At twenty-two he passed a civil service examination, and was appointed a junior exciseman, serving subsequently at Liverpool, in the Orkneys, at Aberdeen, and at Plymouth.

It was not until 1891, when he was twenty-seven, that the event occurred which changed Snowden's life. Until then he had been physically active and powerful above the average; but a small cycling accident led to acute inflammation of the spinal cord and rendered him a chronic cripple. After two years he was invalided out of the civil service. During convalescence he studied socialism with a view to reading a paper on it at the local liberal club, and in the process he became a socialist. This was not very long after the birth of the independent labour party (at Bradford in January 1893); and in 1894 Snowden addressed a meeting for the party's Keighley branch. He scored a great hit, and for the following ten years (1895–1905) settled down to the career of an independent labour party propagandist. Before long his reputation became national, and in a particular kind of idealistic, semi-religious eloquence he had no superior. As a 'draw' at meetings where admission was charged for, he was second to Keir Hardie alone. About 1899 he settled at Keighley in order to serve on the town council and the school board, and to act as editor (for 8s. a week) of a local socialist paper. For the years 1903–1906 he was national chairman of the independent labour party. But it was a grinding struggle. His impaired physique had come near breaking-point, when in 1905 he married Ethel, daughter of Richard Annakin, of Harrogate, a lady who not only cared for him devotedly, but had sufficient means to enable him to work at less strain.

Meantime, in the 'khaki' general election of 1900, Snowden had made at Blackburn his first bid for parliament. With the tide running strongly for the conservatives he was defeated, but achieved great personal popularity and polled over 7,000 votes. He stood as an independent labour party candidate under the auspices of the labour representation committee, a body which he had helped to found at the famous Memorial Hall conference in London earlier in the year, and which in 1906 changed its name to the labour party. In 1902 he unsuccessfully fought a by-election at Wakefield; but in 1906, with the tide in his favour, he was elected for Blackburn and remained of its two members until 1918. No less than fifty-two other labour members were elected with him, of whom twenty-eight were, like him, returned under the labour representation committee to sit as an independent party.

Snowden in the House of Commons was at first handicapped by his physical infirmity, which precluded his jumping up to catch the Speaker's eye. But when once arrangements had been made to get round this, he proved himself a debater of the first rank. His style in the House differed from his platform style, in that the latter had been warming and idealistic and had helped materially to make British socialism a gospel of love, not hate; whereas in parliament he became much harder and terser, and developed along with remorseless logic a very formidable gift of sarcasm. Two subjects he especially made his own—the drink question and national finance. His authority on the latter became much enhanced in 1909, when Lloyd George in framing his famous budget appeared to have gone to Snowden for some of its ideas. When war came in 1914 Snowden happened to be out of the country; but on his return he worked hard to rally that minority in the labour movement which opposed the war. He succeeded in especially identifying with it the independent labour party, of which he once more became chairman for three years (1917–1920); and he was a constant champion of conscientious objectors. He paid for these unpopular courses by losing his seat at Blackburn in 1918.

For four years Snowden was out of parliament, but at the general election of 1922 he was returned for the Colne Valley division of his native county. When in January 1924 Ramsay MacDonald [q.v.] formed the first labour government,

Snowden inevitably became chancellor of the Exchequer in it, and was sworn of the Privy Council. His budget was free trade and Gladstonian rather than specifically socialist. He abolished the protective 'McKenna duties', the corporation profits tax, and the inhabited house duty, besides lowering various taxes on commodities. He also lowered the taxes on popular entertainments, which he regarded as valuable rivals to the public-house. From November 1924 to June 1929 he and his party were out of office, although Snowden retained the Colne Valley seat. During this period occurred the General Strike of 1926. Snowden had no sympathy with it whatever, but in 1927 he made one of his most effective speeches against the government's trade union bill arising out of it. In the same year he quitted the independent labour party, which he regarded as having changed over from evolutionary to revolutionary socialism. When MacDonald formed his second Cabinet in 1929, Snowden almost automatically resumed his place at the Exchequer, such was his prestige in that field. His first task was to attend at The Hague an international conference upon the Young Plan. Taking the view that it fleeced Great Britain for the benefit of her continental allies, he demanded and eventually obtained large changes in it. The preponderance of expert opinion has since been that his view was wrong and the changes unfortunate; but the John Bullish vigour with which he urged and carried them won the acclaim of his fellow countrymen, even in quarters hitherto hostile. His return was that of a conquering hero, and in due course he received the freedom of the City of London.

But the rest of Snowden's period as chancellor was darkened by the great depression, which began to reach Europe from the United States of America towards the end of 1929. In his 1930 budget he confronted an estimated deficit of £42,264,000. He met it chiefly by raising the income-tax from 4s. to 4s. 6d. in the £ and increasing the surtax to yield £12½ millions extra; while at the same time he spent £5 millions on regraduating the income-tax, so that about three-quarters of those paying it paid no more than before. Thus almost the whole of the new burdens were borne by incomes of over £1,000 a year. But the fall in trade and unemployment continued to grow; and in a debate on 11 February 1931 Snowden took parliament into his confidence, disclosing the extreme gravity of the country's situation and appealing to the parties for a common effort to overcome its difficulties. His appeal caused a great sensation, and was well received all over the House, except by the left wing of his own party. A three-party committee of seven was set up, with Sir George (later Lord) May as chairman, to review expenditure and explore possible economies. Three weeks later Snowden had to undergo a serious internal operation, which kept him away from the House for seven weeks. But it was completely successful, and he presented his budget on 27 April.

This time Snowden estimated a deficit of £37,366,000. But as the numbers of the unemployed had now grown to 2,600,000, he did not wish to impose new taxes, nor could he well propose economies pending the Report of the May Committee. He therefore raised the money by stopgap devices—mainly by taking £20 millions from the Exchange Account. The controversial side of the budget lay elsewhere. Snowden included in it certain land tax clauses, providing for a valuation with a view to an eventual tax on land values. Here he had trouble with the liberals, who if they voted with the conservatives could oust the government; but at last he got his clauses through. Meanwhile the economic crisis grew rapidly worse; foreigners with sterling balances tended to withdraw them, and the country's stock of gold fell. The run was stimulated by the publication on 1 August of the May Committee's Report, which estimated the probable deficit by the following April at £120 millions, and advised an immediate saving of £96 millions—over £80 millions out of social services. On 12 August the Economy Committee of the Cabinet met and the opposition leaders were summoned to London; and for the ensuing twelve days a many-sided negotiation went on, Snowden's version of which is given at length in his *Autobiography*. The upshot was the resignation of the labour ministry and the formation by MacDonald on 24 August of a new three-party 'national' ministry, in which three other members of the old Cabinet—Snowden, J. H. Thomas, and Lord Sankey retained their places. Snowden took part without enthusiasm, but from a strong sense of duty. He was assured that the ministry was not to be a coalition, but would deal with the immediate crisis only.

Snowden's own main contribution was a new budget, introduced by him on

10 September 1931. He estimated that the deficit on the current financial year would be £74,679,000, and the deficit on the following one would (on the same basis) reach £170 millions. A drastic scheme balanced both the figures—about half by cuts and half by new taxation. The speech in which he asked for and obtained these sacrifices was worthy of the occasion, and in it he perhaps touched his highest level. Incidentally the finance bill included clauses to facilitate the conversion of the £2,000 millions of 5 per cent. war loan; and it was by using these that in 1932 Neville Chamberlain [q.v.] was able to convert the loan. But Snowden's troubles were not over, and on 21 September he had to suspend the gold standard, the speech in which he did so being again one of his best. There followed in October the general election. Snowden did not stand in it; after his severe illness in the spring he had decided not to; instead, he went to the House of Lords, being in November created Viscount Snowden, of Ickornshaw. But by two election letters and a broadcast address he made perhaps a larger contribution than anyone else to the government's victory at the polls.

In the reconstituted ministry Snowden became lord privy seal, and held that position until 28 September 1932. But a division soon developed in the Cabinet between protectionists and free traders, Snowden being particularly strong for free trade. An attempt was made to preserve unity by the famous 'agreement to differ', announced on 22 January 1932; but when in August the Ottawa Economic Conference was held and resulted in a scheme of preferential tariffs, the free traders felt their position to be impossible. The liberal party was split between Simonites and Samuelites, and the latter resigned with Snowden. It was the virtual end of his career in politics. He completed a valuable two-volume autobiography, which appeared in 1934, when he was seventy; and three years later he died at Tilford, Surrey, 15 May 1937. He had no children. He received the honorary degree of LL.D from the universities of Leeds (1927), Bristol (1929), and Manchester (1930).

Snowden's stature was curtailed by his infirmity, but he was very broad-shouldered, and gave an impression of his former strength. He was noticeably blond, with pale hair, a pale skin, and light-blue 'steely' eyes. Perhaps his most marked feature was his thin-lipped mouth, tightly pursed to utter his terse, hard phrases.

Although a man of fundamental generosity and capable of great charm, he was not always over-easy to get on with; in the party it used to be said that he was not a good committee-man. In other respects he was very 'Yorkshire', with the uprightness, downrightness, and impatience of sloth or crookedness which that conveys. He was a clear rather than a profound thinker, but his party owed much to him for the sure instinct with which he presented socialism in an English dress, rejecting the unassimilable elements of continental doctrine. No one in the movement could have been more completely working-class in origin; but he differed from most of his colleagues in not having graduated in the trade-union machine, and was never inclined, as some of them were, to put its claims above those of the democratic parliamentary state.

A bust of Snowden was made by the Hungarian sculptor Aloyse Ströbl, of which two castings exist: one is at the Treasury, the other at Leeds University library. A massive cairn of rough granite marks the spot on the wild moorland above Ickornshaw where in 1937 Snowden's ashes were scattered to the wind.

[Lord Snowden, *An Autobiography*, 2 vols., 1934; *The Times*, 17 May 1937; private information; personal knowledge.]

R. C. K. Ensor.

SOLLAS, WILLIAM JOHNSON (1849–1936), geologist, was born at Birmingham 30 May 1849, the eldest son of William Henry Sollas, shipowner, by his wife, Emma Wheatley. He was educated at the City of London School, the Royal College of Chemistry, and the Royal School of Mines, where he was taught by John Tyndall, (Sir) A. C. Ramsay, and T. H. Huxley [qq.v.], and in 1870 went to St. John's College, Cambridge, receiving an open scholarship there in 1872. On the advice of T. G. Bonney [q.v.] he took up geology and obtained a first class in that subject in the natural sciences tripos of 1873, and in 1882 was elected a fellow of his college. After six years as a university extension lecturer, he was appointed curator of the Bristol Museum, and lecturer in geology at the University College, becoming in 1880 professor of zoology and geology. In 1883 he went to Trinity College, Dublin, as professor of geology and mineralogy, and from 1893 to 1897 he was petrologist to the Geological Survey of Ireland. In 1897 he was appointed professor of geology and palaeontology at Oxford, and he held the chair until his death at Oxford 20 October 1936. He was elected a fellow of University College in 1901.

The research work which Sollas began as an undergraduate led him to the subject of sponges in general, including living forms, culminating in a monograph on the *Tetractinellidae* collected during the voyage of the *Challenger*, and in papers on the origin of flints and of freshwater fauna. While holding the chair at Dublin he became interested in the glacial features of Ireland, and in pleochroic haloes in the biotite of the Leinster granites and the igneous rocks of Carlingford. In view of later discoveries these researches showed a remarkable foresight.

In 1896 Sollas was sent by the Royal Society in charge of an expedition to Funafuti in the South Pacific to test the rival theories of the origin of the coral reefs by boring, and his work there prepared the way for (Sir) T. W. Edgeworth David [q.v.]. He applied with success the zoological method of serial sections to fossil reptiles and other organisms and devised his ingenious 'diffusion column' of heavy liquid for the determination of the specific gravity of mineral fragments. In later life he devoted most of his time to the study of palaeolithic man, on which he became recognized as a leading authority, making first-hand explorations of the Paviland cave and other caves and river terrace sites in western Europe. In 1911 he published what will perhaps remain the best known of his works, *Ancient Hunters and their Modern Representatives*. He also wrote an essay on geological time which was published with others in *The Age of the Earth* (1905) and he supervised the translation by his daughter, Hertha, of Eduard Suess's *Das Antlitz der Erde* (*The Face of the Earth*, 1904).

Sollas was elected F.R.S. in 1889 and was awarded a Royal medal in 1914. He was president of the Geological Society from 1908 to 1910, and he received the Bigsby medal in 1893 and the Wollaston medal in 1907. He was elected an honorary fellow of the Imperial College of Science and Technology in 1934, and he received honorary degrees from the universities of Dublin, Bristol, Oslo, and Adelaide.

Sollas was twice married: first, in 1874 to Helen (died 1911), daughter of William John Corin, of Redruth, Cornwall, and had two daughters; secondly, in 1914 to Amabel Nevill (died 1928), youngest daughter of John Gwyn Jeffreys [q.v.] and widow of H. N. Moseley [q.v.].

In his prime, Sollas was a man of great erudition, who wrote on almost every branch of geology from the intimate structure of crystals to the form and figure of the earth itself, with clarity, vigour, and humour. He was a gallant and doughty foe, a formidable controversialist, an investigator of untiring energy and unimpeachable accuracy, and a constant friend. At Oxford he was discouraged by the severe inadequacy of the equipment in his department, and in later years he suffered from extreme deafness.

[*Obituary Notices of Fellows of the Royal Society*, No. 6, January 1938 (bibliography and portrait); *Quarterly Journal* of the Geological Society, vol. xciii, 1937–1938; *The Times*, 24 October 1936; *Nature*, 5 December 1936; personal knowledge.]

W. W. WATTS.
J. A. DOUGLAS.

SOMERVILLE, SIR WILLIAM (1860–1932), agriculturist, was born at Cormiston, Lanarkshire, 30 May 1860, the only child to survive infancy of Robert Somerville, of Cormiston, by his wife, Margaret Alexander. The Somerville family seems to have settled in Lanarkshire in the twelfth century, and at one time held very extensive landed estates; but the 400 acre farm of Cormiston, bought in 1820, was Robert Somerville's only land. He farmed it until his death in 1879.

William Somerville was educated at the Royal High School, Edinburgh, and soon after leaving attended a short course of lectures in agriculture at Edinburgh University. Succeeding to Cormiston at the age of nineteen, he spent the following six years as a farmer. The experience of running a poor farm in a period of acute agricultural depression was an important part of his education, serving to develop the cautious business outlook on farming matters that was later to win for him the complete confidence of practical men.

In 1885, when Robert Wallace succeeded John Wilson [q.v.] in the chair of agriculture at Edinburgh, and when the university instituted a degree in the subject, Somerville returned to college and graduated in 1887 as one of the first small group of agricultural students. He then went to Munich in order to study forestry under Heinrich Mayr and Robert Hartig, and graduated D.Œc. in 1889. In the same year he returned to Edinburgh as the first lecturer in forestry. During his brief stay in that post he did much to awaken interest in the new German scientific approach to forest problems both by his contacts with foresters and by his translation of Hartig's book on *Timbers, and How to Know Them* (1890) and afterwards of his *Text-Book of the Diseases of Trees* (1894).

In 1891 Somerville passed on to the Durham College of Science (later King's College, Newcastle-upon-Tyne) as professor of agriculture and forestry, and at once began the big programme of field experimental work that was to prove so fruitful a means towards better farming. In 1899 he moved to Cambridge as the first Drapers' professor of agriculture, and was elected a fellow of King's College. Next, in 1902 he joined the Board of Agriculture and Fisheries as assistant secretary, but found the work of a government department far less satisfying than that of the lecture room and the experimental plot. In 1906 he accepted the Sibthorpian chair of rural economy at Oxford, and thereby became a fellow of St. John's College. At Oxford he spent the rest of his working life, retiring in 1925.

As a teacher of agriculture Somerville made a strong and lasting impression on his pupils, many of whom continued to look to him for inspiration long after they had left his lecture room. In middle life he was probably the most effective, among all academic agriculturists, as a speaker at farmers' gatherings. Indeed, no one contributed more than Somerville to removing the suspicion of research in agriculture which was entertained by farmers at the outset of his career. Moreover, he was a notable 'improver', for he bought two derelict farms ('Poverty Bottom', near Hastings, and Compton Cassey, near Northleach, in Gloucestershire) and brought both back into full and profitable production.

Among Somerville's many contributions to agricultural progress three deserve special mention. The first is the evidence which he produced that phosphate deficiency was the commonest cause of low productivity in pasture land, and that in basic slag (until then regarded as a worthless by-product) lay the means of improvement. As was said at the time, he made two blades of grass grow where one grew before, and also made them better. The second is the development of the simple field experiment as a means of discovering the responses to fertilizers of crops and grass, of testing the adaptability, in particular environments, of different species and varieties, and of compar-

ing the long-term results from various systems of cropping. The third is the use of the animal as a direct measure of the feeding value of pasturage. In all his experiments Somerville so contrived the layout that the plots provided striking visual demonstrations, and he invariably stated his results in terms of profit and loss. His method is illustrated by the now classical plots in Tree Field, Cockle Park, Northumberland.

Although agriculture became Somerville's main concern, his interest in trees was maintained to the end. He was twice (1900–1901 and 1922–1924) president of the Arboricultural Society, and was editor of its *Journal* for thirteen years (1910–1923). His last book, published in 1927, bears the title *How a Tree Grows*.

Somerville was a very complete countryman: among other things a competent field botanist, a student and a lover of birds, and a notable fisherman. Even after his health gave way, he maintained his lifelong interest in Alpine gardening.

Somerville was appointed K.B.E. and elected an honorary fellow of St. John's College, Oxford, in 1926. He received the honorary degree of LL.D. from Edinburgh University in 1922. In 1888 he married Margaret Elizabeth, fourth daughter of George Gaukroger, of Southfield, East Lothian, and had two daughters, the younger of whom predeceased her father. He died at Boars Hill, near Oxford, 17 February 1932.

A fine portrait of Somerville by G. Hall-Neale, presented to him by his pupils, hangs in the School of Rural Economy, Oxford. A replica is in the hall of St. John's College.

[*The Times*, 18 February 1932; *Nature*, 12 March 1932; *Agricultural Progress*, vol. x, 1933; private information; personal knowledge.]   J. A. S. WATSON.

SORLEY, WILLIAM RITCHIE (1855–1935), philosopher, was born at Selkirk 4 November 1855, the younger son of William Sorley, a minister of the Free Church of Scotland, by his wife, Anna Ritchie. He was educated at a school kept by an uncle at Birkenhead, and entered Edinburgh University when about fifteen years old. After taking his degree, he studied theology for several years at Edinburgh, Tübingen, and Berlin, with a view to entering the ministry, but was not ordained. At the age of twenty-four he began a further course of study, in moral science, at Trinity College, Cambridge, obtaining a first class in the moral sciences tripos of 1882.

Sorley was elected into a fellowship at Trinity in 1883, and from 1882 until 1887 he lectured in the university and elsewhere on ethics. In 1888 he became professor of logic and philosophy at University College, Cardiff, where he remained until 1894, in which year he was appointed regius professor of moral philosophy at Aberdeen University. In 1900 he succeeded Henry Sidgwick in the Knightbridge chair of moral philosophy at Cambridge: this post he held until his resignation in 1933. He was elected a fellow of King's College, Cambridge, in 1901.

Sorley inherited from his father both administrative and literary ability. At Cardiff he took an active part in the formation of the university of Wales, and at Cambridge he served on the council of the borough as well as on that of the senate of the university: he welcomed the experience which various kinds of business brought him, despite the distraction from literary pursuits. Besides editing works by Robert Adamson and James Ward, and being the author of several books, he wrote more than fifty articles, in which is to be found some of his most original thought. His chief work, containing the Gifford lectures delivered at Aberdeen in 1914-1915 and published in 1918 as *Moral Values and the Idea of God*, has played an important part in the education of students of philosophical theology. Among his other works mention may be made of *The Ethics of Naturalism* (1885) and *A History of English Philosophy* (1920). Sorley's philosophical and theological position was that of theism. His main theistic argument was based on considerations concerning moral values. These, he maintained, are objective in that they are not constituted by feeling or desire and in that they form one of the factors which a comprehensive philosophy should co-ordinate: the relations between moral values and reality he believed to be inexplicable by any non-theistic theory. A measure of the value of his writings as a contribution to knowledge and thought in the estimation of Sorley's contemporaries is to be found in the fact that they procured for him the degree of Litt.D. of Cambridge University (1905), the honorary LL.D. degree of Edinburgh University (1900), and the fellowship of the British Academy (1905).

Sorley married in 1889 Janetta Colquhoun, daughter of George Smith, journalist and author, of Edinburgh, and sister of

(Sir) George Adam Smith, the Old Testament scholar. They had twin sons, or whom the elder, Charles Hamilton, a young poet of genius, was killed in action in 1915, and a daughter. He died at Cambridge 28 July 1935.

[F. R. Tennant, *William Ritchie Sorley, 1855-1935* in *Proceedings* of the British Academy, vol. xxi, 1935; *The Times*, 30 July 1935; private information; personal knowledge.]   F. R. TENNANT.

SPEYER, SIR EDGAR, baronet (1862-1932), financier, philanthropist, and patron of music, was born in New York 7 September 1862, the second son of Gustavus Speyer, a Jewish banker, of Frankfort-on-Main, by his wife, Sophia, daughter of Rudolph Rubino, of Fritzlar, Prussia, and Frankfort.

Educated at the Realgymnasium, Frankfort, at the age of twenty-two Speyer became a partner in his father's three associated companies in Frankfort, London, and New York. In 1887 he came to London as director of Speyer Brothers, who were interested in exchange arbitrage with the continent and the United States of America and in railway finance.

This connexion with railways brought Speyer into prominence in the business life of London and contributed towards his great fortune. Electric traction had obvious possibilities of application to London transport; and under Speyer, who was naturalized in 1892, the firm was mainly instrumental in financing the Metropolitan District Railway Company. He became chairman of that company in 1906, and in July of that year was created a baronet. In 1903 he had joined the board of the Underground Electric Railways Company of London, becoming chairman in 1906, a post which he held until 1915. Speyer was active in liberal politics, and a friend of Asquith. He was sworn of the Privy Council in 1909.

In 1902 Speyer married a widow, Leonora, daughter of Ferdinand, Count von Stosch, of Mantze, Silesia. She had been a professional violinist, and he shared her musical interests, becoming chairman of the Queen's Hall Concert Board, and paying out some £2,000 a year for many years to make up the deficit on the promenade concerts. At his home in Grosvenor Street there were many concerts, at several of which Strauss and Debussy conducted their own works. Speyer also took a lively interest in philanthropic and cultural causes. He was on the board of King

Edward's Hospital Fund, president of Poplar Hospital, and a trustee of the Whitechapel Art Gallery. In the years before the war of 1914–1918 he led the life of a wealthy banker, socially well considered and lavish in entertainment, whether at Grosvenor Street or at Overstrand, near Cromer.

But in 1914 Speyer's origins were remembered, his patriotism was called into question, and he was even accused of signalling to German submarines from his Norfolk home. His brother James in New York was known to be pro-German, and Lady Speyer, incensed by the ostracism of those who had claimed to be her friends, spoke scathingly of their ingratitude. On 17 May 1915 Speyer wrote to Asquith, offering to resign his baronetcy and membership of the Privy Council, but Asquith replied that the King was unwilling to accept the offer, and added: 'I have known you long and well enough to estimate at their true value these baseless and malignant imputations upon your loyalty to the British Crown.' In November 1915 Sir George Makgill obtained a rule *nisi* calling upon Speyer and Sir Ernest Cassel [q.v.] to justify their membership of the Privy Council. In December a divisional court discharged the rule, and the decision was reaffirmed on appeal. Nevertheless, Speyer resigned all his offices and joined his brother in New York. In December 1921, as a result of proceedings of the Nationalization (Revocation) Committee, his name was struck off the list of Privy Councillors, and his naturalization, and those of his wife and three daughters, were revoked. A White Paper, published in January 1922, accused Speyer Brothers of engaging in 1915 in exchange arbitrage with the firm of Teixeira, of Amsterdam, knowing that this would involve traffic with Germany. There were other charges, but in a long statement to Reuter's agency Speyer characterized them as 'trivial beyond words'.

Speyer lived on in New York, and at the time of his death in Berlin 16 February 1932, was a director of the banking house of Speyer-Ellissen there. His services to London's transport, music, and hospitals need not be obscured by the events of 1915, and it may well be that he was guilty of no more than minor technical offences against the laws of his adopted country.

A portrait of Speyer by (Sir) William Orpen (1914) is in private possession. A caricature of him by (Sir) Max Beerbohm is reproduced in that artist's *Fifty Caricatures* (1913).

[*The Times*, 18 February 1932; *Daily Telegraph*, 17 October 1921, 9 January 1922; *Daily Herald*, 14 December 1921, 7 January 1922; *Morning Post*, 18 February 1932; E. F. Benson, *As We Are*, 1932; private information.]　　　HERBERT B. GRIMSDITCH.

SPRIGGE, SIR (SAMUEL) SQUIRE (1860–1937), medical editor and author, was born at Watton, Norfolk, 22 June 1860, the eldest son of Squire Sprigge, a doctor and small landowner, by his wife, Elizabeth, daughter of John Jackson, solicitor, also of long-established East Anglian stock. He was educated at Uppingham, at Gonville and Caius College, Cambridge, and at St. George's Hospital. After graduating in medicine in 1887 he cultivated his natural taste for letters and for the company of writers and artists, by becoming secretary to (Sir) J. Russell Reynolds [q.v.], and at the same time was persuaded by (Sir) Walter Besant [q.v.] to become secretary of the newly formed Society of Authors, of which he was later chairman (1910–1913). In those years he made many valuable friendships at the United University and Savile clubs. He proceeded M.D. in 1904.

The turning-point in his career came in 1893, when Sprigge accepted an invitation to join the *Lancet* as assistant editor. He had not been with them long when the editors, T. H. Wakley and Thomas Wakley [qq.v.], son and grandson of the founder, Thomas Wakley [q.v.], gave him the congenial task of tracing the origin and early fortunes of the paper; the result was a book *The Life and Times of Thomas Wakley* (1897). He published in 1905 his Cambridge M.D. thesis in book form under the title *Medicine and the Public*. The senior editor of the *Lancet* died in 1907, the junior survived him by only two years, and in 1909 Sprigge took over the editorship in name as well as in fact. His tenure of it during the next twenty-eight years proved him a diplomat and man of the world, upholding the traditions of medicine and keeping on close terms with its leading figures. Unlike the founder of the paper he preferred urbanity to combativeness, and his advice on public medical affairs was increasingly sought.

Sprigge wrote an enormous number of unsigned articles on medical politics and kindred subjects, which came out week by week in the *Lancet*. His wit and pungency of phrase, so well known in private life, were firmly checked in these careful and balanced writings and in public speech; but flashes of them shone through his early books *Odd Issues* (1899) and *An Industrious Chevalier* (1902), and in *Physic and Fiction* (1921). Quick judgement of men and an all-round view of situations were notable in his work as an editor, reinforced by many social and intellectual contacts beyond the world of medicine. Under his guidance the paper outlived the echoes of its violent adolescence and harsh middle age and moved into a period of renewed but sober youth.

The position which Sprigge came to hold in professional life was recognized by a knighthood in 1921, by election as F.R.C.S. in the same year, and as F.R.C.P. in 1927. In 1928 he delivered the Hunterian lecture to the American College of Surgeons. He also showed considerable talent as a water-colour artist and was an excellent judge of this branch of art. His kindness and readiness to help, financially and by his advice, his friends and those who worked with him, endeared him to all.

Sprigge was twice married: first, in 1895 to Mary Ada Beatrice (died 1903), daughter of Sir Charles Moss, chief justice of Ontario, and had a son and a daughter; secondly, in 1905 to Ethel Coursolles, daughter of Major Charles Jones, R.A., and had a daughter. He died in London 17 June 1937, still nominally in harness and still able to employ his alert and penetrating mind and keep up his friendships.

[*The Times* and *Manchester Guardian*, 18 June 1937; *Lancet*, 1937, vol. i, p. 1550 (portrait); *British Medical Journal*, 1937, vol. i, p. 1346 (portrait); personal knowledge.]

N. GERALD HORNER.

STAMFORDHAM, BARON (1849–1931), private secretary to King George V. [See BIGGE, ARTHUR JOHN.]

STEEL-MAITLAND, SIR ARTHUR HERBERT DRUMMOND RAMSAY-, first baronet (1876–1935), politician and economist, whose original name was ARTHUR HERBERT DRUMMOND STEEL, was born in India 5 July 1876, the second son of Colonel Edward Harris Steel, Bengal Staff Corps, by his wife, Emmeline, daughter of General Henry Drummond. He was nephew by marriage of Flora Annie Steel, the novelist [q.v.]. From Rugby School, where he gained many distinctions as a classical scholar, he passed with a classical scholarship to Balliol College, Oxford. His career there was unusually brilliant,

his versatility being as unbounded as his energy and industry. Concurrently with obtaining a first class in classical moderations (1897), in *literae humaniores* (1899), and in jurisprudence (1900), he became successively secretary, junior treasurer, and president of the Union (1899), and in the athletic field he obtained a place in the Oxford boat in 1899.

Leaving Oxford in 1900, with an Eldon scholarship and a fellowship at All Souls, Steel's intention was to be called to the bar and later to enter politics. His marriage in 1901 to Mary, only surviving daughter and heiress of Sir James Ramsay-Gibson-Maitland, fourth baronet, of Barnton and Sauchie, wrought a change in his plans, and at once opened the way to a political career. Upon his marriage he changed his surname to Ramsay-Steel-Maitland by royal licence. From 1902 to 1905 he was private secretary to two chancellors of the Exchequer, C. T. (afterwards Lord) Ritchie and (Sir) Austen Chamberlain. His first important piece of public work was the investigation which he carried out as special commissioner (1906–1907) to the royal commission on the Poor Laws, concerning casual employment, seasonal trades, dangerous occupations, and bad housing. This investigation, which he made jointly with Miss Rose Elizabeth Squire, is embodied in an appendix (published 1907) to the Report of the royal commission. In 1906 he unsuccessfully contested the Rugby division, but succeeded in January 1910 in obtaining a seat as conservative member for East Birmingham. In 1911 he became chairman of the unionist party, a post for which his marked ability in organization and administration admirably fitted him. He continued to represent East Birmingham (which on redistribution of seats in 1918 became the Erdington division) until 1929, when he lost his seat by a narrow margin to the labour candidate. He was returned for Tamworth at a by-election in December of the same year, and continued to represent it until his death.

Steel-Maitland's first official appointment was as parliamentary under-secretary for the Colonies from 1915 to 1917. During the next two years he held office as joint parliamentary under-secretary of state for the Foreign Office and, in his capacity as head of the Department of Overseas Trade, as parliamentary secretary to the Board of Trade. Whilst in control of this department he did much to improve the status and usefulness of the consular service. In 1919, with a view to acquiring a first-hand knowledge of business and finance, he accepted an invitation to join the board of the Rio Tinto Company, of which he subsequently became managing director, a position which he relinquished in November 1924 when Baldwin asked him to take charge of the Ministry of Labour. This office he held until June 1929. He was sworn of the Privy Council on joining the Cabinet. To his task as minister of labour he brought a combination of qualities which obviously equipped him for the post; an exceptionally wide and intimate knowledge and experience of the conditions of labour, a tireless energy and inexhaustible appetite for work, and, what is perhaps most essential of all, an ability to see both sides of a question and, in negotiation, to handle opposition or objection with good temper and tact. It has been truly said of him that he regarded the great problem of unemployment as something with which it was peculiarly his own personal duty to deal successfully. He laboured incessantly to bring about a better understanding and closer co-operation between employers and the trade union organizations; and even where he failed, his obvious integrity and sincerity won him the respect of all with whom he came in contact. One of his heaviest preoccupations was the chronic trouble in the coalfields, which in May 1926 developed into the General Strike. His chief legislative measure as minister of labour was the Unemployment Insurance Act of 1927. He was also responsible for the proposal to set up an Industrial Transference Board for placing unemployed workers in distressed mining and other areas in employment elsewhere.

Although a fluent speaker and debater and always completely master of his subject, Steel-Maitland somehow missed being altogether a successful House of Commons man. There was perhaps something a little too didactic and academic in his manner to suit the taste of the House, and with his nicely balanced judgement he would often in the heat of party controversy fail to make debating points which would have been helpful to his political friends.

In 1933, at the invitation of the Rockefeller Foundation, Steel-Maitland went to the United States for four months to examine into the economic measures which were then being introduced to relieve and counteract the industrial depression. The conclusions resulting from this investiga-

tion are contained in his book entitled *The New America* published in 1934.

Steel-Maitland was created a baronet in 1917. He received the honorary degree of LL.D. from the universities of Edinburgh and St. Andrews. He was an elder of the Church of Scotland and a delegate to the General Assembly for many years. His chief recreations, after he gave up rowing, were lawn tennis and golf. In the latter game he acquired considerable proficiency. It was on the golf links at Rye on 30 March 1935 that, after making a good drive from the tee, he instantaneously collapsed and died.

Steel-Maitland's wife and two sons and two daughters survived him. He was succeeded as second baronet by his elder son, Arthur James Drummond (born 1902).

[*The Times*, 1 April 1935; private information.]　　　　KENNETH R. SWAN.

STEVENS, MARSHALL (1852–1936), one of the founders and first general manager of the Manchester Ship Canal Company, was born at Plymouth 18 April 1852, the eldest son of Sanders Stevens, a shipowner and coal-merchant there, by his wife, Emma Ruth, daughter of James Marshall, a builder in the same town. He was educated at the Mansion House School, Exeter, and in his early years he entered his father's business. His grandfather, Thomas Stevens, was the head of one of the oldest shipping families in the West of England, and his great-uncle, Robert White Stevens, was the author of a book *On the Stowage of Ships and their Cargoes* (1858, 7th ed. 1878). Another great-uncle, John Lee Stevens, was one of the original proprietors and for many years editor of the *Shipping Gazette*. Stevens's interest in the affairs of his native town was shown in his scheme for making the Cattewater into an open seaport where the largest liners could berth; his adventurous spirit appeared when at the end of the siege of Paris, in 1871, he made his way through the German lines in order to obtain a consignment of hides, only to find that they had been consumed by the hard-pressed population.

In the late 'seventies Stevens settled at Garston on the Mersey, trading with general cargo steamers to the continent and thereby beginning the diversion of trade with the continent from east coast to west coast ports. On 27 June 1882, however, his long connexion with the Manchester Ship Canal began when he attended the initial meeting of the undertaking. He played a leading part in the enterprise, and by his determination and his special knowledge of railway and shipping conditions he, more than any one else, persuaded parliament to grant the necessary powers, and the bill for the construction of the canal became an act in 1885.

In that year Stevens was appointed provisional manager of the undertaking and later became general manager, a post which he held until 1896. The company's difficulties were not over with the passing of the Act, for unforeseen engineering difficulties used up all the subscribed capital. It was this period of his life more perhaps than any other which called upon those qualities of great determination, perseverance, and persistent energy which Stevens possessed. It was he who persuaded the Manchester corporation to find the remaining capital, and the canal, constructed, as he proudly stated, without a penny of Treasury money, was opened by Queen Victoria in 1894.

This transformation of inland Manchester into one of the greatest ports in Great Britain was Stevens's most important achievement for the country as a whole. Manchester itself has to thank him for changing a scheme for developing Trafford Park as a residential and sporting area into that for its growth into the great industrial and commercial centre which it has now become. He was the first managing director of Trafford Park Estates, and was interested in the Port of Manchester Warehouses, the Trafford Park Cold Store, and other allied undertakings. On matters of transport of goods and storage, Stevens's great knowledge raised him to a position of international importance, and his evidence was influential before many parliamentary committees, notably those considering the establishment of the Port of London Authority (1909) and the amalgamation of the railways (1921). He was a supporter of free trade, but not blind to its difficulties, advocating national granaries and the imposition of customs duties to countervail the burden of rates and taxes on home manufactures. Another scheme was the formation of an international bank, the bonds of which should be guaranteed by all nations, and the interest on which should form a sinking fund to cover default by any country. He sat in parliament from 1918 to 1922 as coalition unionist member for Eccles.

In 1873 Stevens married Louisa Blamey (died 1932), daughter of Philip Blamey, of Cusgarne and St. Blazey, Cornwall, and lady of the manor of St. Blazey. He was survived by three of his six sons, one of whom, Colonel T. H. G. Stevens, succeeded him as managing director of Trafford Park Estates; his only daughter died in infancy. In his later years Stevens was an invalid, but he showed characteristic courage in his illness, and divided his time between his villa at Roquebrune and his home in Cheshire. Desiring to visit once more his native town, in July 1936 he journeyed thither and died there 12 August that year.

[Sir Bosdin Leech, *History of the Manchester Ship Canal*, 1907; *Plymouth Comet*, 3 March 1894; *Manchester Guardian, The Times*, and *The Western Morning News*, 13 August 1936; personal knowledge.]

G. K. S. HAMILTON-EDWARDS.

STEWART, SIR HALLEY (1838–1937), founder of the trust which bears his name, was born at Barnet 18 January 1838, the tenth child and fifth son of Alexander Stewart, Congregational minister, of Barnet, by his wife, Ann Kezia White. Like his brothers before him, he went to his father's school at Barnet, later at Holloway.

Stewart went to Hastings and began the long career in which the ministry and business, journalism and politics, were interwoven. From 1863 to 1874 he was pastor, although never ordained, of Croft Church, Hastings; from 1874 to 1877 of Caledonian Road Church, London; in 1877 he was founder and first editor of the *Hastings and St. Leonards Times*. On the sale in 1900 of Stewart Brothers & Spencer, the Rochester and London oil-seed crushers and refiners, a firm which he had founded in 1870, he turned his attention to bricks, ultimately becoming vice-chairman of the London Brick Company.

Meanwhile Stewart had been taking an active part in politics. An advanced liberal, he advocated adult suffrage for both sexes, the land for the people, religious equality, and the abolition of hereditary legislators. He was president of the Society for the Liberation of Religion from State Patronage and Control, and also of the Secular Education League, deeming it contrary to the principles of Christianity and democracy to tax all and sundry for the teaching of a particular religion. He contested the Spalding division of Lincolnshire unsuccessfully in 1885 and 1886, but his victory there at a by-election in 1887 heartened the divided liberal party. He lost his seat in 1895, contested Peterborough unsuccessfully in 1900, but was member for Greenock in 1906, until he retired in January 1910. An incisive speaker and a good debater, his independence was as manifest within the House of Commons as without: he was never afraid to take his own line: T. M. Healy [q.v.] said to Stewart's son, 'So you're a son of Halley Stewart. We respect him here—he never trims his sails, and we always know where he stands.'

A deeply religious man, Stewart called himself not a Congregationalist but 'an independent of Independents'. To his own denomination he was a generous benefactor, especially for Church extension in Hertfordshire and for the education of ministers' children, but the conventional ways of giving left him unsatisfied. With a keen sense of stewardship, he felt that his wealth, much of which he held had 'accrued' not through his own labours, should be used for the benefit of mankind. He had a strong aversion to endowing existing institutions, and to supporting organizations with a theological basis, and he gave much thought to the terms of his trust, established in 1924 for 'research towards the Christian ideal in all social life', with the special objects of advancing religion and education and relieving poverty. He invited his three sons and four others to join him as trustees, and guided the trust's administration until his death, invariably revealing the belief in independence, the passion for freedom, and the financial acumen which had marked his life. He made many large gifts to the trust, which was also the residuary legatee of his estate. In 1933 the Halley Stewart laboratory was opened at Hampstead, a benefaction to King's College, London.

Stewart declined many honours, but accepted a knighthood in 1932; he was elected a fellow of King's College, London, in 1936. In 1865 he married Jane Elizabeth (died 1924), daughter of Joseph Atkinson, of Upper Norwood, and had seven sons, five of whom predeceased their father, and a daughter. He died at Harpenden 26 January 1937.

[*The Times*, 28 January 1937; personal knowledge.]   ALBERT PEEL.

STEWART, JOHN ALEXANDER (1846–1933), philosopher, was born at Moffat 19 October 1846, the elder son of Archibald Stewart, later minister of Glasserton, Wigtownshire, by his wife, Magdalene, daughter of Henry Goodsir. After his schooldays, he was educated at Edinburgh University, whence he gained a scholarship at Lincoln College, Oxford. He obtained a first class in classical moderations (1868) and in *literae humaniores* (1870), and was awarded the Newdigate prize for a poem on the Catacombs in 1868. In 1870 he was elected a senior student of Christ Church, a position which he held, together with lecturerships in philosophy at Lincoln and Oriel colleges (1874–1875), until his marriage in 1875. He remained at Christ Church as classical lecturer until 1882, when new statutes enabled him to be re-elected a student and appointed a tutor. In 1897 Stewart was elected White's professor of moral philosophy, thereby becoming a fellow of Corpus Christi College, and he continued some of his tutorial work at Christ Church until 1907. He resigned his chair, which he had filled with marked success, in 1927. He was elected an honorary student of Christ Church (1907) and an honorary fellow of Lincoln (1920) and of Corpus (1929); he received the honorary degree of LL.D. from the universities of Edinburgh (1896) and Aberdeen (1934). He married Helen (died 1925), only daughter of John Macmillan, and had no children. He died at Oxford 27 December 1933.

Stewart published two noteworthy books. His *Notes on the Nicomachean Ethics of Aristotle* (2 vols., 1892) is a work of permanent value from the exact scholarship, the very wide reading, the scrupulous and objective judgement, and the temperamental sympathy brought to bear upon it, and for many years it held its place as a definitive edition. The other was *The Myths of Plato* (1905) in which the mystic and the poet in Stewart came vividly alive. The book revealed the range of his powers and showed at the core of his thought an illuminative appreciation of life at its highest and best. His *point de départ* in philosophy was neither mathematics nor natural science. He relished the quasi-biological presentation in Aristotle of individual and group life, and the sublimation of it in Platonic teaching. His absorbing topic was life throughout its phases and implications as he conceived them. In a very pertinent sense life for him was drama. *The Myths of Plato* opens with a statement of his views of what poetry and art in general and also imaginative contact with nature effect in the 'patient', namely, that they give rise to transcendental feeling, by which he means experience of a uniting and reconciliative and virtually apocalyptic sort that reaches deeper than conceptual thinking. In explaining his views Stewart avails himself of the Kantian distinction between categories of the understanding and ideas of the reason as illustrating what was implicit in Platonic doctrine. This novel approach, which may be said to outflank the absolutist trends of his time, is elaborated in a detailed discussion of the myths which reveals unusually wide sympathies.

Stewart, a Scotsman of imagination who found his truest home in Oxford, and a Victorian imbued with the urbane optimism of the time and strongly interested in the advances of modern science, had gifts of scholarship, a versatile and searching culture, and an unfailing memory. He travelled widely, and he thought prophetically of North America as the ultimate citadel of western civilization. Distrusting philosophic dogmatism and the technical and scholastic trends of the study, he pursued a personal path, the adherent of no school and the friendly judge of any that answered his sense of humanity. He had little confidence in discussion, believing that its votaries lack the directer power of vision to bring them into one. His lecturing method, while outwardly austere, proceeded in a gentle rapture of belief and persuasion. With a tragic sense of evil veiled by a serene and stately courtesy, he combined an old-world grace, flavoured with humour and a delicate irony. To his fineness age added something of greatness.

[*The Times*, 29 December 1933 and 1 and 3 January 1934; *Oxford Magazine*, 18 January 1934; personal knowledge.]

JOHN MURRAY.

STOCKS, JOHN LEOFRIC (1882–1937), philosopher, was born at Market Harborough 26 October 1882, the sixth son among twelve children of John Edward Stocks, vicar of Market Harborough and afterwards archdeacon of Leicester, by his wife, Emily Jane, third daughter of Thomas Mallam, solicitor, of Oxford. He was educated at Rugby and at Corpus Christi College, Oxford, where he won a scholarship and obtained a first class in classical moderations (1903) and in *literae humaniores* (1905), and was captain of university hockey (1904–1905). In 1906 he was elected fellow and tutor of St. John's College, Oxford, where he remained, except for war service, until 1924. In 1913 he married Mary Danvers, eldest daughter of Roland Danvers Brinton, M.D., of

London: she was great-grand-daughter of J. M. Rendel [q.v.] and great-niece of G. W. Rendel [q.v.]. There were a son and two daughters of the marriage. During the war of 1914–1918 Stocks served from July 1915 in the King's Royal Rifle Corps. He was awarded the D.S.O. for gallantry at Beaucourt during the battle of the Ancre in November 1916 when he was wounded and subsequently sent home to instructional service. In 1924 he was elected professor of philosophy in the university of Manchester in succession to Samuel Alexander [q.v.]. He delivered the Riddell memorial lectures in the university of Durham in 1933 (*On the Nature and Grounds of Religious Belief*, 1934) and the Forwood lectures in Liverpool in 1935 (*Time, Cause, and Eternity*, 1938). During all this period he was also actively interested in public work, and stood, unsuccessfully, as labour candidate for the university of Oxford at the general election of 1935. In 1936 he was appointed vice-chancellor of the university of Liverpool, but he died suddenly while on a visit to Swansea 13 June 1937. His wife and children survived him.

Stocks's main technical philosophical interests were in Aristotelian studies and in Epicureanism. He contributed *De Caelo* to volume ii (1922) of the Oxford translation of *The Works of Aristotle*, and certain studies of the later Epicureans to the first series of the *New Chapters in the History of Greek Literature* (1921) by John Undershell Powell and Dr. Eric Arthur Barber. In his wider philosophical work he was concerned to make explicit the principles at work in different kinds of moral and political activity. Here he brought a philosophical judgement to bear on his practical experience in university administration, in guiding the policy of the Manchester University Settlement, and in other work for political and social reform. Instances of such judgement are to be found throughout the two volumes of his occasional essays and addresses, *The Limits of Purpose* (1932) and *Reason and Intuition* (edited by D. M. Emmet, 1939). These also reveal something of the character of the man: a disciplined and analytic temper of mind combining with a deep underlying concern for justice and for the good of his fellow men. His strength of character may have owed much to the latter; the former gave him the disinterested detachment which made him a fighter for causes without a trace of personal bitterness.

[*The Times* and *Manchester Guardian*, 14

June 1937; Introduction by D. M. Emmet, and Note by Sir W. D. Ross on Stocks's contributions to studies in Greek philosophy prefixed to J. L. Stocks, *Reason and Intuition*, 1939; foreword by William Temple to J. L. Stocks, *Time, Cause, and Eternity*, 1938; private information; personal knowledge.]

DOROTHY M. EMMET.

STRACHEY, Sir EDWARD, fourth baronet, and first Baron Strachie, of Sutton Court (1858–1936), politician and landowner, was born at Clifton, Bristol, 30 October 1858, the eldest of the three sons of Sir Edward Strachey, third baronet [q.v.], whom he succeeded in 1901. The baronetcy had been created in 1801, in favour of Edward's great-grandfather, the politician Sir Henry Strachey [q.v.]. His mother, who was his father's second wife, was Mary Isabella, daughter of J. A. Symonds, M.D., and sister of the author J. A. Symonds [q.v.]. He was brother of the journalist John St. Loe Strachey and first cousin of the author (Giles) Lytton Strachey [qq.v.]. He was educated privately and at Christ Church, Oxford.

Strachey's family, like those of most West Country landowners in the nineteenth century, had been staunch supporters of the liberal tradition, and he himself, after unsuccessfully contesting North Somerset (1885) and Plymouth (1886), represented South Somerset as a liberal from 1892 until his elevation to the peerage as Baron Strachie, of Sutton Court, in Somerset, in 1911. The whole of his life was devoted to the public service, with particular attention to home affairs and to the landed interest. As a politician, he was responsible for carrying the Outdoor Relief Friendly Societies Act (1894), the Post Office Amendment Act (1895), and the Post Office Guarantee Amendment Act (1898). In 1905 Campbell-Bannerman appointed him the spokesman of the Board of Agriculture and Fisheries in the House of Commons, a position which he held during four of the five years in which he acted as junior government whip, and from 1909 to 1911 he was parliamentary secretary to the Board, when Lord Carrington (afterwards Marquess of Lincolnshire) was president. In the former capacity it devolved upon Strachey to pilot the agricultural holdings amendment bill of 1906 and the small holdings bill of the following year through the Commons, when he displayed so much tact and consideration that it was admitted by his political opponents in the House that two

good acts had (in 1908) been made out of two bad bills. In the House of Lords he served as paymaster-general for three years (1912–1915), and was spokesman for Asquith's government on various occasions. He was sworn of the Privy Council in 1912. In 1925 he was involved in a controversy with Lloyd George over the liberal land policy, which he thought did considerable injury to liberalism and did not reflect the desires of the rural community.

In local administration Lord Strachie was equally zealous. He was an original member of the Somerset county council, of which he became an alderman; and he was a vice-president of the County Councils Association and of the Rural District Councils Association. As a landowner, his work for agriculture in parliament was supplemented by service in many voluntary organizations. At various times he was chairman of the Central Chamber of Agriculture and president of the Central Landowners Association, besides being a member of the governing bodies of several more local organizations for the betterment of farming.

Strachie married in 1880 Constance (died 1936), only child of Charles Bampfylde Braham, musician, granddaughter of the singer, John Braham, and niece of Frances, Countess Waldegrave [qq.v.]. They had a son, and a daughter who predeceased her father. Strachie died at Sutton Court, Pensford, Somerset, 25 July 1936, and was succeeded as second baron by his son, Edward (born 1882).

[*The Times*, 27 July 1936; *West Somerset Free Press*, 1 August 1936; personal knowledge.]

C. S. ORWIN.

STRACHEY, (GILES) LYTTON (1880–1932), critic and biographer, was born in London 1 March 1880, the fourth of the five sons of Lieutenant-General (Sir) Richard Strachey [q.v.], by his second wife, Jane Maria, second daughter of Sir John Peter Grant (1807–1893, q.v.), of Rothiemurchus. He was first cousin of Sir Edward Strachey, fourth baronet, and first Baron Strachie, and of J. St. L. Strachey [qq.v.]. Lytton Strachey evinced a precocious taste and talent for literature, which were sedulously fostered by his mother. After a short period at Abbotsholme School, Derbyshire, and a longer at Leamington College, he was sent in 1897 to Liverpool University, where until 1899 he studied history. This was followed by four years at Trinity College, Cambridge.

Here, largely under the influence of Dr. George Edward Moore, he formed his ideas, and also made some distinguished lifelong friends, including John Maynard (later Lord) Keynes, Dr. Edward Morgan Forster, Mr. Desmond MacCarthy, Mr. Leonard Woolf, and Mr. Clive Bell. He won the chancellor's English medal in 1902, and obtained second classes in both parts of the historical tripos (1901, 1903). After failing to secure a fellowship, he took up residence in London, where he worked regularly on the *Spectator* under the editorship of J. St. L. Strachey and also contributed to the *Edinburgh* and the *New Quarterly Reviews*. This work, although he disliked it, trained him in his craft. Meanwhile he became a prominent member of the celebrated 'Bloomsbury' literary and artistic circle, composed mainly of his Cambridge friends with the addition of the daughters of Sir Leslie Stephen [q.v.], Vanessa Bell and Virginia Woolf, and in which a culture of extreme refinement was combined with open rebellion alike against the beliefs and the habits of orthodox middle-class Victorianism.

Strachey's first book, *Landmarks in French Literature*, commissioned by H. A. L. Fisher [q.v.] for the 'Home University Library' series, came out in 1912. After this, his friends and family subscribed to make him financially independent of journalism, so that he might retire to the country and write books. His activities were not interrupted by the war of 1914–1918, for he was a conscientious objector; and *Eminent Victorians* appeared in 1918. This, although fiercely attacked as irreverent to the illustrious dead, at once put him in the front rank of contemporary authors. It was followed by *Queen Victoria* (1921), *Books and Characters, French and English* (1922), *Elizabeth and Essex* (1928), and *Portraits in Miniature, and Other Essays* (1931). The university of Edinburgh conferred upon him the honorary degree of LL.D. in 1926. In 1924 he settled at Ham Spray House, near Hungerford, where he was looked after by his friends Mr. and Mrs. Ralph Partridge until his death there from cancer 21 January 1932. He never married. *Characters and Commentaries*, a posthumous volume of collected studies, published and unpublished, appeared in 1933.

Strachey was a conspicuous figure wherever he appeared, with his wit and his silence, his tall, emaciated figure, and his red beard. Fastidious and ill-adjusted to the commonplace, he was in youth often melancholy; but literary success and the friendships which he cultivated so intensely made his later years agreeable. He was a sensitive, sensible critic, particularly remarkable for the work which he did in awakening Englishmen to the appreciation of the classical French authors, notably Racine. But his most memorable achievement was in biography. Here he sometimes showed the limitations of his civilized Voltairean rationalism, which made him unable to enter into the wild or mystical aspects of human nature. Nor was he a profound psychologist: before complex characters he was apt gracefully to confess himself baffled. But his economical mastery of design, his faculty of vivid story-telling, and the mingled elegance and vitality of his style are alike eminent; and they are made exhilarating by the continuous sparkle of an impish and adroit irony. He is also important historically, first, as the leader of that reaction against the Victorians which followed the war of 1914–1918, and, secondly, as the inaugurator of a new type of biography, brief and brilliant, in which fact and reflection are fused together into a work of art, individual and creative as a novel.

A portrait of Strachey by Henry Lamb is in the Tate Gallery, and a chalk drawing by Nina Hamnett belongs to the National Portrait Gallery.

[Guy Boas, *Lytton Strachey* (English Association Pamphlet No. 93), November 1933; Sir (H.) Max(imilian) Beerbohm, *Lytton Strachey* (Rede lecture), 1943; private information; personal knowledge.] David Cecil.

STRACHIE, first Baron (1858–1936). [See Strachey, Sir Edward.]

STRATHCARRON, first Baron (1880–1937). [See Macpherson, (James) Ian.]

STREETER, BURNETT HILLMAN (1874–1937), divine, was born at Croydon 17 November 1874, the only son of John Soper Streeter, solicitor, by his wife, Marion Walker. He was educated at King's College School in London, and from the time when in 1893 he went up to Oxford with a classical scholarship at Queen's College, his life was that of a typical Oxford don, the one college, of which he became successively fellow, dean, and praelector (1905), chaplain (1928), and provost (1933), claiming practically the whole of his academic loyalty. The only break was from 1899 to 1905, when he was fellow and dean of Pembroke College. In 1910 he married Irene Louisa, daughter of Captain Edward Cuthbert Brookes Rawlinson, formerly of the Bengal Cavalry, and then living at Slough. The marriage was childless.

Streeter's academic career was brilliant, with a first class in classical moderations (1895), *literae humaniores* (1897) and theology (1898), and a series of theological prizes and scholarships. It was his work at this time which laid the foundation of his studies in the New Testament, but he himself would probably have regarded the philosophy of religion as his main interest, viewing the various fields into which his inquiring mind was led as all subsidiary to the one central theme of the interpretation and presentation of religion in the modern world. The background of this was his intense concern and care for people. Although never of strong physique he rowed for his college as an undergraduate, and throughout his life retained an interest both in rowing and in undergraduates which was very closely linked in his mind with his academic work. His numerous writings were in almost every case conceived and written with the student world in view.

It was this pastoral and human interest which led Streeter to be ordained in 1899, despite the fact that his faith had always something of the character of a quest. He was more than once attacked as a modernist, especially after his contribution to *Foundations* in 1912, but the obvious sincerity of his religion and its practical applicability to human problems were a sufficient answer, and the attacks were never pressed far. He was, indeed, a regular speaker and a most popular figure at Student Christian Movement conferences. This same interest in human movements of thought and the search for a vital answer to the problems of life led him to undertake lengthy visits abroad. He made two long tours in China and Japan, lecturing both there and in India, and he visited the United States of America several times. In his closing years, after he had become provost of Queen's and a scholar with a world-wide reputation, he joined, with Mrs. Streeter, in the work of the movement founded by Dr. Frank N. D. Buchman, widely known as the Oxford Group, and it was as he was returning by air from Switzerland, where he had spent a long convalescence with some of its members, that his aeroplane crashed into a mountain near Basle in a fog, and he and his wife were killed, on 10 September 1937.

Streeter was one of the most distinguished New Testament scholars of his day, and a man beloved and respected by many generations of Oxford undergraduates, but apart from his Oxford life few honours came his way, although he was a member for nearly fifteen years (1922–1937) of the Archbishop's Commission on Doctrine in the Church of England, and was also appointed to a canonry in Hereford Cathedral, which he held from 1915 to 1934. This latter office led to the writing of one of his most interesting and most learned books, *The Chained Library* (1931), a study which revealed his astonishing power of assimilating large masses of detail in a subject quite remote from those which had already made him famous. He was elected a fellow of the British Academy in 1925 and an honorary fellow of Pembroke College in 1933. He was Dean Ireland's professor of exegesis from 1932 to 1933, and received the honorary degree of D.D. from the universities of Edinburgh, Durham, and Manchester.

Probably Streeter's best work was that on the New Testament, which attracted world-wide attention. He came into the front rank of scholars with his essay in the Oxford *Studies in the Synoptic Problem* (1911), and this was followed in 1924 by *The Four Gospels: a Study of Origins* which has become a standard and authoritative treatment of the problems of New Testament criticism. In particular he developed two new hypotheses of great importance, arguing in favour of an early Caesarean text of the Gospels and of an original source lying behind St. Luke's Gospel in its present form. The great value of his work lies in its entirely first-hand character. Whether he was dealing with chained libraries or with the Gospels and the manuscripts he went direct to the sources and owed very little to the work of other scholars.

Streeter's other writings, some of which reached a very large circulation, were in part essays in apologetics and the philosophy of religion, such as *Reality: A New Correlation of Science and Religion* (1926) and his Bampton lectures, *The Buddha and the Christ* (1932), and in part contributions to composite volumes of essays, of which the earliest and that which caused most stir was *Foundations . . . by Seven Oxford Men,* a work which, when it was published, seemed to some critics alarmingly modernist, a judgement which time has reversed.

Streeter's total literary output was considerable and its influence was very great among theological students and in university circles generally. But apart from the solid scholarship of *The Four Gospels* the main secret of that influence lay in his own personality with its great sincerity and its attractiveness to students of every type.

A good portrait of Streeter by Delmar Harmood Banner hangs in the provost's lodging at Queen's College, Oxford.

[*The Times*, 13 September 1937; *The Queen's College Record*, November 1937; *Oxford*, Winter 1937; College records; private information; personal knowledge.]

L. W. GRENSTED.

STRICKLAND, GERALD, BARON STRICKLAND, of Sizergh Castle (1861–1940), colonial administrator and politician, was the eldest son of Commander Walter Strickland, Royal Navy, by his wife, Louisa, daughter of Cavaliere Peter Paul Bonici, of Malta, and niece and heiress of Sir Nicholas Sceberras Bologna, fifth Count della Catena in Malta, whom he succeeded as sixth count in 1875, validity of succession being confirmed by the Privy Council in 1882. He was born in Malta 24 May 1861, and educated at Oscott College, Birmingham, and at Trinity College, Cambridge (1884–1887), where he graduated in law and was president of the Union in 1887. In the latter year he was called to the bar by the Inner Temple. He was elected a member of the Maltese council of government in 1886, and in 1887 represented the island at the first colonial conference and played a part in framing the Maltese constitution (known as the Strickland-Mizzi constitution) of that year. He also organized the committee which succeeded in stamping out a serious epidemic of cholera in Malta, and for his services he was appointed C.M.G. in 1889.

As assistant secretary (1888) and chief secretary (1889–1902) in Malta, Strickland introduced many reforms, always working for equality of opportunity for Maltese within the British Empire. He initiated drainage and electricity works, the construction of the great breakwater across the Grand Harbour at Valetta, and secured to parents the right of choice of English as a second language in the schools, of which he built twenty-six.

Strickland was appointed K.C.M.G. in 1897, and in 1902 became governor of the Leeward Islands, where he successfully fostered cotton-growing and co-operative sugar refineries. In 1904 he was promoted to Tasmania, going to Western Australia in 1909 and to New South Wales in 1913, in which year he was appointed G.C.M.G. On retiring from the colonial service in 1917 he resumed his interest in Maltese politics, assisting to draft the Milner–Amery constitution of 1921.

Having in 1896 acquired Sizergh in Westmorland from his cousin under a family settlement, Strickland now divided his time between his English and Maltese estates. He was a member of the Maltese legislative assembly from 1921 to 1930, and formed the Anglo-Maltese (later styled the Constitutional) party. After two parliaments in which he had been leader of the opposition, in 1927 he became prime minister of a constitutional-labour coalition government and minister of justice. In the meanwhile, in England, at the general election of 1924 he was returned as conservative member of parliament for the Lancaster division. Difficulties might have arisen owing to this dual status, and in January 1928 he was raised to the peerage as Baron Strickland, of Sizergh Castle. His premiership, during which he narrowly escaped assassination, proved a stormy battle against the influence of fascism and Italian interference in the domestic affairs of Malta. Unfortunately, this was aggravated by trouble which arose when the ecclesiastical senators, who held the balance of power in the senate, refused to pass the first coalition budget. Words used by Strickland in the heat of debate, as well as obstruction to the Church authorities in certain measures of discipline which they claimed to exercise over members of their religious orders, but which Strickland argued infringed the civil right of the individual, brought down the censure of the Church upon him and his party. Later, on 1 May 1930, on the eve of a general election, although Strickland was himself a member of an ancient Roman Catholic family, he was confronted by a pastoral from the bishops of Malta and Gozo forbidding their flocks to vote for him or for his followers. The Colonial Office was obliged to suspend the constitution on 24 June. In 1932 Strickland made his peace with the Vatican with an apology for his offending words, but nevertheless, when an amended constitution was restored that year, he failed to retain the premiership, and returned, as a member of the senate, to leadership of the opposition against a pro-Italian government. In 1933 the Italian influence began to interfere so flagrantly that once more the constitution was withdrawn. Strickland still worked hard for a limited representation to maintain contact between the British government and the people in case of war, and in 1939, succeeded, becoming leader of the elected members of the new council of government, his supporters holding a two-thirds majority.

In order to assist his unceasing efforts to combat Italian influence Strickland founded the *Times of Malta* (daily), *Berka* (the first vernacular daily in Malta), and the *Times of Malta* (weekly) newspapers. His publications include the article on Malta contributed to the thirteenth edition of the *Encyclopædia Britannica* and a monograph entitled *Malta and the Phoenicians* (1925).

Lord Strickland was twice married: first, in 1890 to Lady Edeline (died 1918), eldest daughter of Reginald Windsor Sackville, seventh Earl De La Warr, and had two sons, both of whom died in infancy, and six daughters, of whom all except the fourth, who died as an infant, survived him; secondly, in 1926 to Margaret, fourth daughter of Edward Hulton, of Ashton-on-Mersey, Cheshire, and sister of Sir Edward Hulton, baronet [q.v.]. He died in Malta 22 August 1940, when the barony became extinct.

Strickland, perhaps from his early struggles to secure his Maltese inheritance, and partly no doubt from his Maltese blood—to which race legal polemics seem almost necessary to existence—developed a personality, at any rate in his political career, which merited the description given to it of dominating and aggressive. In private life he was a genial host and brilliant controversialist, but the very ardency of his patriotism, both as an Englishman and as a Maltese, brought out a pugnacity of manner which went far to antagonize his would-be sympathizers, and to obscure the merit of his argument.

There are portraits in oil of Lord Strickland by C. Thorp at Sizergh and by E. Caruana Dingli in Malta. A cartoon in racing colours by 'Hay' appeared in *Vanity Fair* 4 May 1893. A statue sculptured by Anton Sciortino and subscribed for by the Maltese people stands in the Upper Barracoa Gardens at Valetta.

[*The Times*, 23 August 1940; H. Hornyold, *Genealogical Memoirs of the Family of Strickland of Sizergh*, 1928; private information; personal knowledge.]

HENRY HORNYOLD-STRICKLAND.

STUART-JONES, SIR HENRY (1867–1939), classical scholar. [See JONES.]

SUMNER, VISCOUNT (1859–1934), judge. [See HAMILTON, JOHN ANDREW.]

SUTRO, ALFRED (1863–1933), playwright and translator of Maurice Maeterlinck, was born in London 7 August 1863, the third and youngest son of Sigismund Sutro, M.D., an authority on continental spas and their cures, who had come to England from Germany as a young man and become naturalized, and the grandson of a German rabbi of Sephardi (Spanish-Jewish) ancestry. Sutro was educated at the City of London School under E. A. Abbott [q.v.] and in Brussels. While still a boy he became a clerk in the City, and at the age of twenty joined his elder brother, Leopold, in partnership as wholesale merchants. It was while in this business that he made the acquaintance of Alexander Teixeira de Mattos, like Sutro of Sephardi Jewish origin, who later devoted himself to the translation of works of continental writers, but was at that time the representative in England of a Dutch firm. After fourteen years in the City, and soon after his marriage in 1894 to Esther Stella, daughter of Joseph Michael Isaacs, of Upper Norwood, a fruit broker and importer in Covent Garden, and sister of Rufus Daniel Isaacs, first Marquess of Reading [q.v.], Sutro gave up business and lived for a time in Paris with his wife, who was an artist and later became a writer on art.

Among the friends whom they made there was Maeterlinck, with whom Sutro's relations continued very close throughout their joint lives. While still in Paris, recognizing the value of Maeterlinck's work, Sutro constituted himself his translator into English. Almost all of Maeterlinck's works were introduced by him to English readers, the most noteworthy being *The Treasure of the Humble* (1897), *Wisdom and Destiny* (1898), and above all *The Life of a Bee* (1901). How thoroughly he worked on these is shown by the fact that the translation of the last-named occupied six months of six or seven hours a day. Seven times he re-wrote the translation. This masterpiece had in the first instance been dedicated to Sutro, to whose play *The Cave of Illusion* (1900) Maeterlinck also wrote an introductory essay.

Apart from his translations of Maeterlinck and desultory journalism, Sutro turned to the writing of plays. In this he had many disappointments and about ten years passed before he achieved a real success. He even collaborated with George Meredith in the dramatization of *The Egoist*, but this also was never produced. Almost despairing of success as a dramatist Sutro took to writing duologues, a volume of which appeared in 1902 under the title of *Women in Love*. His first play to be produced, in 1895, was a joint adaptation with Arthur Bourchier [q.v.] of *Monsieur le Directeur* by Alexandre Bisson, entitled *The Chili Widow*, in which Bourchier, who produced it, appeared with Violet Vanbrugh. This proved a moderate success. His great success came nine years later with *The Walls of Jericho* (1904). Thenceforth Sutro was accounted one of the leading English dramatists, no year being complete for theatre-goers without a new play from his pen, sometimes more than one. The best-known of these are *Mollentrave on Women* and *The Perfect Lover* (1905), *The Fascinating Mr. Vanderveldt* (1906), *John Glayde's Honour* (1907), *The Builder of Bridges* (1908), *The Perplexed Husband* (1911), *The Two Virtues* and *The Clever Ones* (1914), *Uncle Anyhow* (1918), *The Choice* (1919), *The Laughing Lady* (1922), *A Man with a Heart* (1925), *The Desperate Lovers* (1927), and his last to be acted *Living Together* (1929). Most of these plays, as well as a few others, were published in book form. In addition there were *The Foolish Virgins* (a volume of stories, 1904), *About Women* (a series of sketches, 1931), and *Celebrities and Simple Souls* (a volume of reminiscences, 1933), in which he wrote with a kindly pen more of others than himself. This book was published a few days after his death. Some of his plays were serious, others light comedies, all were equally attractive to the theatregoing public. He looked on the drama as a popular art and strove to keep it so.

Before his marriage Sutro had been active and successful in the direction of working-men's clubs. During the war of 1914–1918, although over fifty years of age, he enlisted in the Artists Rifles. Later, he was on the staff of the 'War Trade Intelligence Department', for his services in which he was appointed O.B.E. (1918). Sutro died after a few days' illness at his home at Witley, Surrey, 11 September 1933. He was survived until 1934 by his widow. They had no children.

[*The Times*, 13 September 1933; *Jewish Chronicle*, 15 September 1933; A. Sutro, *Celebrities and Simple Souls*, 1933.]

ALBERT M. HYAMSON.

SUTTON, SIR JOHN BLAND-, baronet (1855–1936), surgeon, was born at Enfield Highway, Middlesex, 21 April 1855, the second child and eldest son of Charles William Sutton, of Enfield Highway, farmer, market-gardener, and amateur taxidermist, from whom he acquired that keen interest in natural history which is so apparent in his writings. His mother was Elizabeth, eldest daughter of Joseph Wadsworth, farmer, of Long Buckby, Northamptonshire. His second name was given him in memory of his maternal grandmother's family, and in 1899 he assumed by deed-poll the prefix surname of Bland.

Bland-Sutton's parents were poor, and being originally intended for the profession of schoolmaster he qualified as a pupil teacher during his last two years at an elementary school at Enfield Highway and afterwards in London. But he was determined to become a surgeon, and by thrift and hard work he managed after four years to save enough money, with help from his mother's family, to pay the fees of a medical school. In 1878 he began work at Thomas Cooke's school of anatomy in Brunswick Square, the last of the private anatomical schools, and a little later in the same year he joined the medical school of the Middlesex Hospital. His progress was rapid; he won prizes and scholarships, became a demonstrator of anatomy, and in 1881 was appointed prosector and pathologist to the Zoological Society.

Bland-Sutton was admitted a member of the Royal College of Surgeons of England in 1881 and rented a house in Gordon Street where he took resident pupils. He was admitted a fellow of the college in 1884 and in 1886 was appointed assistant surgeon to the Middlesex Hospital, becoming surgeon nineteen years later (1905). In 1892 he won the Jacksonian prize of the college, and in 1896 was appointed surgeon to the Chelsea Hospital for Women, a post which he held until 1911. This gave him the opportunity of developing his chief surgical interest, which had been aroused by the subject set for the Jacksonian prize, the surgery of the female generative organs, and he speedily became known as the leading exponent of gynaecological surgery of the day.

Bland-Sutton married in 1886 Agnes Hobbs (died 1898), of Didcot. In 1899 he married as his second wife Edith, youngest daughter of Henry Heather-Bigg, a lady of great social accomplishments. They lived from 1901 to 1929 at 47 Brook Street (now pulled down) and at the back of the house he built a remarkable hypostyle hall after the pattern of the Apadana (hall of honour) built by Darius at Susa, the roof of which was supported by thirty-two bull-columns of specially constructed enamelled bricks.

Bland-Sutton was knighted in 1912 and was created a baronet in 1925. He was president of the Royal College of Surgeons of England (1923–1926), and was Hunterian orator (1923). Many other honours, including numerous honorary degrees, were conferred upon him. He died in London 20 December 1936, having had no children by either marriage.

The amount of research work which Bland-Sutton accomplished in his younger days was very great. Between 1882 and 1895 he made 152 communications to various medical societies dealing with comparative anatomy, comparative embryology, and comparative pathology. Of these the most noteworthy are *Ligaments, their Nature and Morphology*, expanded into a small book in 1887, and 'On Odontomes' which has formed the basis of all subsequent work on the subject. He was an original and arresting writer, and his best known book, *Tumours Innocent and Malignant* (1893), has long since become a classic. Towards the close of his life he wrote a book about himself, *The Story of a Surgeon* (1930).

As an operator Bland-Sutton possessed brilliant dexterity of hand and the faculty of instant appreciation and decision, but most of all a splendid self-reliance which overrode all obstacles of place and circumstance. This is a quality less essential to-day when a surgeon enjoys so many aids, but it remains the first attribute of a really great surgeon.

His conviction that a wide knowledge of pathology is the hub of all medical teaching led Bland-Sutton in 1913 to present to the Middlesex Hospital the Institute of Pathology which bears his name, and his widow at her death in 1943 made bequests both to it and to the Royal College of Surgeons, the latter taking the form of a scholarship in memory of her husband.

Bland-Sutton was a small man with features strongly recalling Napoleon Bonaparte to whom his mental make-up also bore a decided resemblance. He was terse and decisive in speech; his humour was puckish in quality and quite peculiar to himself, and his mind betrayed a genius of a very uncommon type. In his later years he entertained lavishly, but there was a certain aloofness about him and he had very few intimate friends; amongst these was Rudyard Kipling, with whom he maintained affectionate relations for many years. He had the gift of bestowing inspiration on those who worked under him, for he invested all that he did with a halo of drama and romance, and many of his pupils have reason to be very grateful to him.

Bland-Sutton was the product of an age greatly influenced by Darwin, Huxley, and Tyndall and, possessing a mind avid for discovery, he himself made the means of prosecuting it. In his earlier days he walked more nearly in the footsteps of John Hunter than anyone else since Hunter's time.

An oil painting of Bland-Sutton by John Collier (1925) hangs in the hall of the Royal College of Surgeons. An earlier painting of him, also by Collier, belongs to the Royal Society of Medicine. There is a marble bust of him by Sir George Frampton in the Institute of Pathology, Middlesex Hospital, and a bronze replica of it is at Chelsea Hospital for Women. There is also a drawing by George Belcher (1925) which hangs in the common room of the Middlesex Hospital medical school. A cartoon of him by 'Elf' appeared in *Vanity Fair* 3 February 1910.

[Sir J. Bland-Sutton, *The Story of a Surgeon*, 1930; G. H. A. Comyns Berkeley, 'The Seven Stages of Sir John Bland-Sutton' (Supplement to *Journal of Obstetrics and Gynaecology of the British Empire*, April 1937; *The Times*, 21 December 1936; personal knowledge.]   VICTOR BONNEY.

SWIFT, SIR RIGBY PHILIP WATSON (1874–1937), judge, was born 7 June 1874 at St. Helens, Lancashire. He was the eighth child, and the eldest child by the second marriage, of Thomas Swift, solicitor, of St. Helens, who was called to the bar late in life and had a considerable practice on the Northern circuit chiefly in criminal and licensing work in and around Liverpool, where he lived during his later years. His mother was Emily, daughter of Philip Daft, of Nottingham.

Swift was educated at Parkfield School, Liverpool, and later obtained the LL.B. degree of London University. His training in the law was unusual: he left school at the age of seventeen and entered his father's chambers in Harrington Street, Liverpool, and father and son remained together until the death of the former in 1899. Swift was called to the bar by

Lincoln's Inn in 1895 within a month of reaching the age of twenty-one. His proposer was Sir John Rigby [q.v.], a cousin of his father. In due course he joined the Northern circuit. At that time, and for the next twenty or thirty years, the circuit was probably stronger than at any other period in its history. Swift soon got work: he was faithful in his attendance in the Crown Court at assize time and was always ready to undertake a dock defence or to look after the interests of an accused at the request of the judge, and from this he gained invaluable experience in advocacy. In the early years of the century he made rapid progress, and in 1910 he applied to the lord chancellor for silk and moved to London, taking chambers at 1 Garden Court. His claims to silk were great: he had made for himself a very substantial practice and had held it; his work was varied; on the *nisi prius* side it may well be said that he had attained a position seldom reached by any junior on the circuit; he was recognized as an eminent advocate. He was still young, however, and probably for that reason he had to wait two years for silk; it was not until 1912 that he was appointed in the same list as Gordon Hewart (afterwards lord chief justice) who had practised up to that time in Manchester. The appearance of these two new King's Counsel meant a great change on the Northern circuit. For a few years, until the claims of London called, they were opposed to each other in nearly all the work of importance. Swift's powers as an advocate grew and it would have been difficult to find a better jury advocate anywhere; and his practice was by no means confined to jury work.

Meanwhile Swift had been elected to parliament as conservative member for St. Helens in December 1910, after having been defeated in January of that year. He remained member until his defeat at the general election of 1918, but he did not take an active part in debate. He was recorder of Wigan from 1915 to 1920.

For some years Swift had an extensive practice in London and his services were in great demand. It was no surprise, therefore, when, on the recommendation of Lord Birkenhead, he was appointed a judge of the King's Bench division of the High Court in June 1920, and his appointment was welcomed. He was forty-six years old and for a time was the youngest judge on the bench. He certainly added strength to the judiciary: a sound knowledge of the law, wide experience of courts

and of procedure, a quick brain, a great knowledge of human nature, and a keen sense of humour enabled him to fill the position in a way that made everything appear easy.

During his seventeen years on the bench Swift was frequently in the public eye and presided over many trials of general interest. His power over juries was soon apparent; this was chiefly due to his ability to marshal the facts of any case, however complicated, and to put them before the jury in an attractive way. He had not long been appointed when in 1921 there came before him a case in which seventeen members of the Irish Republican Army were charged with treason-felony at Manchester. It was no easy task, but his handling of it showed him at his best. In *Nunan* v. *Southern Railway Company* (1923), the widow of a workman sued the company for damages under Lord Campbell's Act in respect of the death of her husband who had been killed in an accident on the railway. The husband was travelling on a workman's ticket upon which was printed a condition to the effect that 'the liability of the Company is limited to a sum not exceeding £100'. Swift decided that, although the condition would have prevailed in an action by the husband, it did not avail in an action by the widow, and his judgement was upheld in the Court of Appeal. In *R.* v. *Woolmington* (1935) a young husband was tried at Bristol for the murder of his wife by shooting. At an earlier trial at Taunton before Sir William (afterwards Viscount) Finlay the jury had failed to arrive at an agreement. Swift told the jury: 'All homicide is presumed to be malicious, and murder, unless the contrary appears from circumstances of alleviation, excuse or justification. In every charge of murder the fact of killing being first proved, all the circumstances of accident, necessity, or infirmity, are to be satisfactorily proved by the prisoner unless they arise out of the evidence produced against him, for the law presumeth the fact to have been founded in malice until the contrary appeareth' (a quotation from Archbold, citing Foster). Later he said: 'The Crown has to satisfy you that this woman died at the prisoner's hands. They must satisfy you beyond any reasonable doubt. If they satisfy you of that, then he has to show that there are circumstances to be found in the evidence which has been given from the witness box in this case, which alleviate his crime so that it is only manslaughter or which excuse the homicide altogether by showing that it was a pure accident.' The jury convicted the prisoner and he was sentenced to death. After an appeal to the Court of Criminal Appeal had failed, the House of Lords quashed the conviction, holding that the direction to the jury was wrong, and that the onus of proof always remained on the prosecution in such a case. Although Swift was held to be wrong there was considerable authority in support of his view, and he had followed a principle laid down 150 years before.

Swift was a man of great kindness of heart and he gave away much of the money which he earned: seldom did he turn down an appeal, and many a member of the bar who fell on hard times had cause to be grateful to him. He liked above all things to see a young man doing his work well, and he never forgot one who showed promise. No one did more to encourage the young advocate than he did: he often said that there ought to be something in the nature of a school of advocacy; it was just as necessary, he urged, to teach men how to speak and how to present a case as to teach them the law.

Swift always liked to go his old circuit and until the end of his career he went the far north at least every two years. From 1917 he lived at Crowborough, where he took a keen interest in the golf club and in his farm. He was fond of meeting old friends; he enjoyed entertaining, and he lived well. This no doubt affected his health, and during the last few years of his life he showed signs of failing and was apt to become somewhat testy. Yet he remained all the time a personality, strong and fearless.

Swift was made a bencher of Lincoln's Inn in 1916 and would have been treasurer had he lived a little longer. In 1935 he received the honorary degree of LL.D. from Liverpool University. He married in 1902 Beatrice, daughter of John Banks Walmsley, a Liverpool shipowner. They had no children. Her death in April 1937 was a blow from which he never really recovered, and he died at Crowborough on the following 19 October.

[E. S. Fay, *Life of Mr. Justice Swift*, 1939; *The Times*, 20 October 1937.]

JOHN E. SINGLETON.

SYDENHAM OF COMBE, BARON (1848–1933), administrator. [See CLARKE, GEORGE SYDENHAM.]

SYMONDS, SIR CHARTERS JAMES (1852–1932), surgeon, was born at Dal-housie, New Brunswick, 24 July 1852, the second son of Charles Symonds, barrister, by his wife, Margaret, eldest daughter of John Maltby, of New Brunswick. The family was of pioneer stock from Massachusetts (1635); Symonds's great-grandfather had settled in 1764 at St. John, New Brunswick, and established the school where Charters was educated; his grandfather had been Speaker of the house of assembly of the province in 1828. His father died in 1860; nine years later his mother brought Charters to London and struggled with poverty while he studied first at University College and then at Guy's Hospital, which he entered in 1870. After gaining the treasurer's gold medal (1875) and first class honours in medicine, he was from 1876 to 1879 demonstrator of anatomy at Guy's, and was elected F.R.C.S. in 1881. An early interest in higher medicine, shown by his taking the M.D. (Lond.) in 1878, was held by many to be a potent cause of his excellence as a surgeon, for, while he was a skilled and courageous operator in an era of expanding surgery, it was in the diagnosis and decision before an operation, and in care after it, that he excelled until the end.

Appointed assistant surgeon to Guy's in 1882, Symonds became one of the greatest bedside teachers that this hospital, and perhaps any, has ever known. From 1882 to 1888 he was surgeon to the Evelina Hospital for Sick Children, where he worked in close association with (Sir) Thomas Barlow; he was in charge of the new throat department at Guy's from 1886 until 1902, when he surrendered the post on becoming full surgeon. As with all great teachers there was a bit of the showman in him, though never of the mountebank. To a Monday 'round' of thirty students he could make a patient put out his tongue, swallow, and say 'ee-ee' in order that many students could arrive at the diagnosis more usefully than the teacher with a single pupil. After retiring from the active staff of Guy's in 1912, he taught fortnightly at Lambeth Hospital until a few months before his death.

Symonds will be remembered as the first surgeon to deal (1885) with the appendix vermiformis, between attacks of inflammation, by the removal of a concretion from within it, an operation that was superseded by taking out the whole structure. He laid down a classification of cancer of the gullet which still holds good and introduced his treatment for this disorder by intubation which is only now being superseded by more radical methods. In medical literature 110 contributions stand to his credit.

In 1915 Symonds was sent to Malta as consulting surgeon, with the rank of colonel, to the Mediterranean Expeditionary Force, and dealt with the cases from Suvla Bay; for the last two years of the war he was consulting surgeon at Netley and at Southern Command. He continued the great tradition of the Victorians in the width of his activities, being chairman of the executive committee of the Invalid Children's Aid Association, treasurer of the Royal Medical Benevolent Fund, and a member of the advisory committee to the home secretary on vivisection, as well as taking part in many affairs closely concerned with his profession.

Elected to the council of the Royal College of Surgeons in 1907, Symonds served a second period (1915–1923), becoming vice-president (1916–1918) and delivering the Bradshaw lecture (1916) and the Hunterian oration (1921), in which he broke new ground by speaking about Sir Astley Paston Cooper [q.v.] and his debt to Hunter rather than on Hunter himself. In 1929 the university of New Brunswick conferred upon him the honorary degree of LL.D. He was appointed C.B. in 1916 and K.B.E. in 1919.

In 1889 Symonds married Fanny Marie (died 1930), daughter of Lieutenant-General David Shaw, of the Madras Army, and had two sons, the elder of whom is Sir Charles Putnam Symonds, F.R.C.P., physician for nervous diseases at Guy's Hospital. He died at Harrow 14 September 1932.

[Guy's Hospital Reports, vol. lxxxiii, July 1933 (portrait); British Medical Journal, 1932, vol. ii, p. 611 (portrait); Lancet, 1932, vol. ii, p. 709 (portrait); The Times, 16 September 1932; personal knowledge.]

T. B. LAYTON.

TALBOT, EDWARD STUART (1844–1934), bishop successively of Rochester, Southwark, and Winchester, the younger son of John Chetwynd Talbot, Q.C., son of the second Earl Talbot and a leader of the parliamentary bar, by his wife, Caroline Jane, only daughter of James Archibald Stuart-Wortley-Mackenzie, first Lord Wharncliffe [q.v.], was born in London 19 February 1844. The Talbot family is an ancient one, many of whose members, including Edward Talbot's nephew Sir G. J. Talbot [q.v.], have reached legal and political eminence. His father, who was

a strong supporter of the Oxford movement, died in 1852, and his widowed mother formed a close friendship with the two sisters Lady Lyttelton and Mrs. Gladstone. Sent as a day boy to Charterhouse, he was compelled by illness to leave in 1858. He proceeded to Christ Church, Oxford in 1862, obtained a first class in literae humaniores (1865) and in law and modern history (1866), and was elected in the last-named year a senior student of Christ Church, where he remained for four years as modern history tutor. In 1869 he was appointed first warden of Keble College, Oxford, and was ordained deacon. In 1870 he was ordained priest and married Lavinia, third daughter of George William Lyttelton, fourth Lord Lyttelton [q.v.]: her eldest sister was the wife of his brother J. G. Talbot.

In the autumn of 1870 Talbot went into residence at Keble. The university as a whole regarded the new foundation with contempt. To meet the situation no better warden than Talbot could have been found, and for eighteen years he presided successfully over the college. He aimed at giving it a sure foundation as a college in the university where men of limited means might lead a full common life under the influence of the Church of England. A true son of the Oxford movement, Talbot acknowledged the Tractarians as his spiritual fathers. He contributed to Lux Mundi in 1889, but in contrast to that of Charles Gore [q.v.] his essay on 'The Preparation in History for Christ' did not provoke controversy. Like all the Lux Mundi school, Talbot was concerned to bring Tractarian principles into relation with the thought of the later nineteenth century. It was mainly due to his initiative that Lady Margaret Hall was founded at Oxford in 1878 as a definitely Church of England college for women.

In 1888 Talbot accepted the vicarage of Leeds, where he remained for six years (1889–1895). It was a profound change to a busy Yorkshire parish, where he found himself in contact with hard-headed business men, the crowds of the working classes, and many members of the Free Churches. Once when asked to which political party he belonged, he replied: 'Conservative with a bad conscience.'

Leeds was sorry to lose him when in 1895 Talbot became bishop of Rochester. To the episcopate he brought high academic distinction as well as educational and parochial experience. He continued the scheme inaugurated by his predecessors of dividing his unwieldy diocese, thus separating the agricultural area round Rochester from the populous area of south London, where he had always had his bishop's house. After protracted negotiations the work was accomplished, and Talbot was able to complete the other task which he had inherited, namely, that of making the old church of St. Saviour's, Southwark, the cathedral of the new diocese. He was enthroned there in 1905. His relationship with his clergy was friendly, although breaches of Prayer Book order by some of them placed him in a difficult position. The evangelical party suspected him as a Tractarian bishop, while high churchmen resented his efforts to restore order. As time passed he was understood, and won the respect and love of all his clergy. Not a ready speaker, at times he was hesitating, and in his anxiety to make his points clear addressed his audience at too great a length. He showed that a high churchman could work with evangelicals and liberals, and could understand Free churchmen also.

In 1911 Talbot was translated to the bishopric of Winchester, which he held for twelve years. It was the autumn of his life, but it was still a full and busy life. His prestige stood high and he spoke with great authority in the councils of the Church. One of Archbishop Davidson's staunchest supporters, he was noted for his width of view and his great gift of fairness. The last ten years of his life were spent in retirement in Kensington, where he died 30 January 1934. As *The Times* obituary notice rightly says, 'he helped to create, as well as to maintain, a tradition essential both to religious and to national life'.

Talbot celebrated his golden wedding while bishop of Winchester in 1920. Mrs. Talbot survived him until 1939. They had three sons and two daughters. Of the sons, Edward became superior of the community of the Resurrection; Neville (died 1943) became bishop of Pretoria and was afterwards vicar of St. Mary's church, Nottingham; and Gilbert, in whose memory the original Toc H was founded, was killed in action in 1915.

A portrait in oils of Talbot by George Richmond, painted in 1876, hangs in the hall of Keble College, of which he was elected the first honorary fellow in 1931. There is another portrait in Christ Church, painted by H. Harris-Brown. A cartoon of him as bishop of Rochester by 'Spy' appeared in *Vanity Fair* 21 April 1904.

[E. S. Talbot, *Memories of Early Life*, 1924; Gwendolen Stephenson, *Edward Stuart Talbot, 1844–1934*, 1936; A. Mansbridge, *Edward Stuart Talbot and Charles Gore*, 1935; The *Times*, 31 January 1934.]

SANKEY.

TALBOT, SIR GEORGE JOHN (1861–1938), judge, was born in London 19 June 1861, the eldest son of John Gilbert Talbot, conservative member of parliament for West Kent (1868–1878) and for Oxford University (1878–1910), by his wife, Meriel Sarah, eldest daughter of G. W. Lyttelton, fourth Lord Lyttelton [q.v.], and sister of A. T. Lyttelton [q.v.] and Alfred Lyttelton [q.v.]. He was a nephew of E. S. Talbot [q.v.], bishop of Winchester. Talbot's father was at Charterhouse, but his disapproval of the migration of that school to Godalming caused him in 1873 to send his son to Winchester, for which the son was ever grateful. In 1880 he gained a junior studentship at Christ Church, Oxford, obtained a first class in classical moderations (1882) and in *literae humaniores* (1884), and in 1886 was elected to a fellowship at All Souls.

A career in the Church or at the bar was obvious for Talbot. Perhaps the claims of heredity prevailed for the latter. On his father's side he was sixth in descent from Charles, Lord Talbot [q.v.], lord chancellor from 1733 to 1737: while on his mother's side he was thirteenth in descent from Sir Thomas Littleton [q.v.], judge of the Common Pleas (1466), and ninth in descent from Sir Thomas Bromley [q.v.], lord chancellor from 1579 to 1587. His grandfather, John Chetwynd Talbot (a son of the second Earl Talbot, whose ample law library he inherited), had a highly successful career at the parliamentary bar in its busiest days of railway promotions. As all these ancestors were members of the Inner Temple Talbot naturally followed them, and was there called to the bar in 1887. He took silk in 1906, became a bencher of his Inn in 1914, and was its treasurer in 1936. Until late in his career at the bar his busy practice was mainly before parliamentary committees, and in work of a like character, e.g. in the Railway and Canal Commission Court. He was also a learned ecclesiastical lawyer, and was eventually chancellor of six dioceses. He was counsel to the university of Oxford from 1915 to 1923.

In October 1916 Lord Buckmaster was minded to recommend Talbot for a vacant judgeship of the King's Bench division. Most unhappily the lord chancellor thought it right to consult the prime minister, Asquith, who dissuaded him on the ground that promotion from the parliamentary bar would not be popular with the profession, and H. A. McCardie [q.v.] was appointed instead. This was a misfortune. If Talbot had been appointed at the age of fifty-five, instead of having to wait as he did until he was sixty-two, there is little doubt that his judicial career would have ended in the House of Lords. At this time, and increasingly, Talbot's services were being sought in wider circles of the law, especially before the House of Lords, and the Judicial Committee of the Privy Council, e.g. in *Bowman* v. *The Secular Society* in 1917, and in Lady Rhondda's petition before the Committee of Privileges in 1922. In the latter, it is the opinion of Lord Greene, M.R., that Talbot's argument, before a troublesome and divided tribunal, was the finest effort of advocacy which he ever heard.

In November 1923, on the retirement of Mr. Justice Darling [q.v.], Lord Cave, as lord chancellor, redressed the mistake of 1916: Talbot became a judge of the King's Bench division. It would be hard to decide whether he was in every way more different from McCardie, who had supplanted him, or from Darling, whom he succeeded. On the bench he displayed every quality of the ideal judge. He had learning, dignity, industry, patience, and courtesy: his decisions were invariably right, and on most occasions were thought to be so by the Court of Appeal. And (although he tried at least one sensational murder case) his name was unknown to the readers of the cheap newspapers. The only occasion on which he made a mistake was when, being appointed to sit in the Commercial Court, he started there with a protest against one with so little experience of that class of work being selected. That, however, was the fault of a very needless modesty—he did the work as well as he did everything else. In the trial of criminals on circuit, of which he had had little experience at the bar, he had no contemporary superior.

Towards the end of 1936 Talbot's powers, both physical and mental, began to fail. In June 1937 he resigned, and thereupon was sworn of the Privy Council. His resignation would probably have taken place earlier if he had not waited in order to be present at Winchester, on 29 May, when seven Wykehamist judges were received *ad portas*. He died at Falconhurst, near Edenbridge, the pleasant estate created by his grandfather, 11 July 1938, and was buried at Markbeech near by.

Talbot was a tall, handsome man with a fresh complexion. He was ever a tireless walker in the country; and his pleasure in that was increased by his being an ardent and very learned botanist. He had a cold bath every morning, and was never known to wear an overcoat in town or country. His reading was widespread, and he remained a fine scholar all his days. When leaving Oxford he set himself a great programme of Greek and Latin literature, and by the strict devotion of a fixed daily time he completed the task in upwards of thirty years. He was a great lover of music, especially of the music of Handel, although he never played any instrument. Nature endowed him with a very hot temper, but such was the rigour of his self-discipline that those who knew him as a man did not readily detect that fact. He was a very devout churchman, who went to the early Communion on every Sunday and all major saints' days. There is a story that some foolish person once asked Charles Gore whether the law was a suitable career for a man of high ideals: the bishop answered: 'Do you know George Talbot?'

In 1897 Talbot married Gertrude Harriot, fourth daughter of Albemarle Cator, of Woodbastwick Hall, Norfolk. They were a happily devoted couple, who wrote to one another daily when parted. They had two sons and a daughter. Their only great sorrow was the death of the elder son in 1922. The younger son followed his father to the Inner Temple and the bar.

Next to his wife and family Talbot's greatest object of devotion was Winchester College. He was a fellow from 1930 until he resigned shortly before his death, and for a time was sub-warden. To be with him at Winchester was to see him at his happiest. In 1935 he was elected an honorary student of Christ Church, and he served for thirty-five years on the council of Keble College, Oxford.

There is a portrait of Talbot by W. G. de Glehn at Falconhurst.

[*The Times*, 14 October 1936 and 13 July 1938; *The Wykehamist*, 25 July 1938; *Law Quarterly Review*, July 1945; private information; personal knowledge.]

F. D. MACKINNON.

TANNER, JOSEPH ROBSON (1860–1931), historian, was born at Frome, Somerset, 28 July 1860, the eldest son of

Joseph Tanner, J.P., head of the firm of Butler and Tanner, printers, of Frome, by his wife, Fanny Robson. He was educated at Mill Hill School and entered St. John's College, Cambridge, in 1879. Thenceforth his life was associated with the college; he became successively scholar (1881), lecturer (1883–1921), fellow (1886–1931), tutor (1900–1912), and tutorial bursar (1900–1921). He obtained a first class in the historical tripos of 1882 and was president of the Union in 1883. Having a natural aptitude for business, he was drawn a good deal into university administration as a member of the council of the senate, chairman of the special board for history and archaeology, and a syndic of the University Press, for which he edited the *Historical Register of the University of Cambridge* (1917), and, for some years, the *University Calendar* and the *Student's Handbook of the University*; he was also treasurer of the Union (1902–1915). He retired from college work at the end of the war of 1914–1918, and shortly afterwards ceased to lecture, leaving Cambridge for Aldeburgh, Suffolk, in 1921, although he was pleased to be recalled to act as deputy for the regius professor of modern history, J. B. Bury, in 1926 and 1927: 'It is like being taken down off the shelf and dusted.'

As a historian Tanner's interests lay primarily in English naval history of the seventeenth century, in which he broke new ground, and the modern constitutional history of England. In 1896 he edited *Two Discourses of the Navy* by John Hollond [q.v.] for the Navy Records Society, and in 1903 he brought out the first volume of his *Descriptive Catalogue of the Naval Manuscripts in the Pepysian Library at Magdalene College, Cambridge,* a work which ran into four volumes and occupied him until 1923.

Tanner's retirement from teaching and administrative duties gave him leisure for the literary and historical activities that filled the last decade of his life. In 1918 he had become one of the editors of the *Cambridge Medieval History.* Although he was not a medievalist, his gifts as an editor and his organizing ability were invaluable to this great co-operative history; and the association in the editorial work with two other members of the college, former pupils of his, Charles William Previté Orton and Zachary Nugent Brooke, gave him much pleasure. He had lectured chiefly on English constitutional history, and three books represent the fruit of years of labour in this field: *Tudor Constitutional Documents* (1922), *English Constitutional Conflicts of the Seventeenth Century* (1928), and *Constitutional Documents of the Reign of James I* (1930).

At the same time Tanner continued his work in naval history, particularly on the life of Samuel Pepys. The Lees Knowles lectures, which he delivered at Trinity College in 1919, were published the following year as *Samuel Pepys and the Royal Navy.* These were followed by *Mr. Pepys. An Introduction to the Diary, together with a Sketch of his Later Life* (1925), *Samuel Pepys's Naval Minutes* (for the Navy Records Society, 1926), the *Private Correspondence of Samuel Pepys, 1679–1703* (2 vols., 1926) and *Further Correspondence of Samuel Pepys, 1662–1679* (1929).

Large as was the volume of his historical work, the best energy of Tanner's life was given to his college and his pupils. By them he will always be remembered for his sympathy, humour, and inspiration. His popularity as a tutor was due to a genuine interest in men and a wise and kindly understanding. In the teaching and administration of the history school he played a considerable part during the years in which it was rising to be one of the largest schools in Cambridge. He was an excellent chairman—effective, conciliatory, and constructive. His lectures, always read, and read admirably, were enlivened with happy quotations, and for generations attracted large classes. Distinguished alike as teacher, scholar, and administrator, 'his many gifts and activities', in the words of an old pupil, 'were bound together by an artistic faculty which he possessed without the burdensome artistic temperament'. For recreation he played a steady game of golf; he was a happy raconteur, and always good company in work or leisure.

Tanner married in 1888 Charlotte Maria, second daughter of George James Larkman, J.P., of Belton, Suffolk, and his hospitable home was a second centre of his genial influence. There were no children of the marriage. He died at Aldeburgh 16 January 1931, a generous benefactor of the college to which he was devoted. A portrait of Tanner by Mrs. Lewis Erle Shore is in the possession of his widow.

[*The Eagle* (magazine of St. John's College, Cambridge), vol. xlvi, pp. 184–187, 1931; *The Times,* 17 January 1931; *Cambridge Review,* 30 January 1931; personal knowledge.]

E. A. Benians.

TATA, Sir DORABJI JAMSETJI (1859–1932), Indian industrial magnate and philanthropist, was born in Bombay 27 August 1859, the elder son of Jamsetji Nasarwanji Tata [q.v.], pioneer of Indian industries, by his wife, Heerabai, daughter of Kharsetji Daboo. Shapurji Saklatvala [q.v.] was his first cousin. In 1875, after attending the Bombay Proprietary School, he was sent to England to a private tutor in Kent, and in 1877 he entered Gonville and Caius College, Cambridge, where he obtained his colours for cricket and football. He returned to Bombay in 1879, studied further at St. Xavier's College, and obtained the B.A. degree of Bombay University in 1882. His father then placed him as an apprentice in the office of the *Bombay Gazette* in order that he might gain experience of men and affairs. Two years later he was sent first to Pondicherry and then to the Empress cotton mills, Nagpur, for training, and in 1887, together with his cousin R. D. Tata, was taken into partnership in the newly formed company of Tata & Sons. Under his father's wise guidance he gained greatly in knowledge and understanding of Indian industry and finance, and on J. N. Tata's death in 1904 was well fitted to become the head of the firm. During the next twenty-five years the firm (reconstituted in 1907 as Tata Sons & company, and again in 1917 as Tata Sons Limited) expanded and became the largest industrial concern in India, with aggregate funds estimated in 1945 at £54,000,000 and giving employment to 120,000 men and women.

Tata's great contributions to Indian progress are, on the one hand, the successful completion with the able assistance of his cousin R. D. Tata, his brother (Sir) Ratan Tata (died 1918), and the chosen lieutenants of J. N. Tata, of the three bold and far-sighted projects planned and initiated by his father and, on the other, his munificent public benefactions. Through his keen personal interest in the early work and his energy and drive in finding the capital, the first project, the Tata iron and steel works, was established at Jamshedpur in 1911. To his father's bold plan for harnessing the heavy monsoon rainfall of the western *ghauts* he brought the same energy and resource and by 1919 three companies were in being. The endowment and establishment in 1911 of the Indian Institute of Science at Bangalore at an initial cost of £200,000 was a work of filial devotion for the two sons of J. N. Tata. Their father died before he could make

the bequest and his sons after protracted negotiations entered into a tripartite agreement with the government of India and the government of Mysore whereby, in accordance with the plan of J. N. Tata, young Indians could receive scientific training at a high level in India and by the practical applications of science advance the industrial development of their country.

In recognition of his services Tata was knighted in 1910. He was president of the Indian Industrial Conference in 1915 and a member of the Indian Industrial Commission from 1916 to 1918. From early manhood he took a keen interest in Indian cricket and athletics and did much to bring about India's participation in the Olympic Games. He was a patron of learning as well as of sport. He endowed a chair of Sanskrit at the Bhandarkar Institute, and helped many deserving scholars in their researches. About 1920 he gave £25,000 to the university of Cambridge for the equipment of the laboratories in the School of Engineering, and in 1922 he was elected an honorary fellow of his old college. His private charities are said to have totalled £150,000. After his wife's death in 1931 he set apart a sum of nearly £200,000 for the Lady Tata Memorial Trust, the object being to provide prizes and scholarships for research in any part of the world on diseases of the blood, and for work in India on subjects related to the alleviation of human suffering. In the last year of his life he created the trust which bears his name and endowed it with the whole of his private fortune. In accordance with his wishes it has rendered help without distinction of caste or creed. The endowment, estimated at £2,000,000 in 1945, had expended £800,000 in a wide range of charities including the endowment and maintenance of the Tata Memorial Hospital for Cancer, the Tata Institute of Social Sciences, and the Tata Institute of Fundamental Research (the last-named being jointly established by the government of Bombay and the trust).

After executing the trust deed Tata left India in April 1932. He was taken seriously ill in Europe and died at Kissingen, Bavaria, 3 June 1932. His remains were taken to England and laid beside his wife in the Parsi cemetery at Brookwood, Woking.

In 1898 Tata married Meherbai, daughter of a distinguished educationist, Hormasji Jehangir Bhabha, inspector-general of education in Mysore. There were no children of the marriage.

[*The Times* and *The Times of India*, 4 June 1932; F. R. Harris, *Jamsetji Nusserwanji Tata. A Chronicle of his Life*, 1925; records of the Sir Dorabji Tata Trust; private information.]

R. CHOKSI.

TAYLOR, WILLIAM (1865–1937), designer of scientific instruments, was born at Hackney 11 June 1865, the second son of Richard Taylor, hosier, by his wife, Marian Smithies, the daughter of a draper of York. He and his brother were mechanics from childhood, learning their crafts from a blacksmith and a wheelwright, and with a small lathe made by themselves the boys learnt the elements of turning. They gained their first knowledge of science from the *Edinburgh Encyclopædia*, but under Richard Wormald, a pioneer of the teaching of science in schools, their knowledge was widened at the Cowper Street School, Finsbury, where they even learnt turning, joinery, and cabinet-making under competent instructors. In these school workshops the brothers made a pair of the first telephones ever made in England and one of the first copies of Edison's tinfoil phonograph, and at home they built and fitted up a workshop.

Taylor spent his last term at school learning as much as he could about optics and in practising the use of logarithms in order to learn how to design lenses, in which he at this time became interested. He became one of the first students at the Finsbury Technical College under H. E. Armstrong, W. E. Ayrton [qq.v.], and John Perry. He was then apprenticed to Messrs. Paterson & Cooper, and while with them he made for Ayrton and Perry their famous ammeter, the actual instrument now in the Science Museum, South Kensington. In 1885 the family moved to Leicester, and within two years (1886) the brothers had founded the firm of T. S. & W. Taylor (afterwards Taylor, Taylor, & Hobson). From the outset William Taylor did most of the designing, and it was his remarkable talent as a designer which determined the character of the products of the firm and their mode of production. His inventiveness secured interchangeability in screws for the mountings of lenses, for Taylor had been much impressed by the degree to which it had been raised in America, but it was not until the ideas of the British lens-

makers had been proved, by experiment, to be wrong that the trade accepted the specification which, embodying Taylor's suggestions, was published by the Royal Photographic Society in 1901.

Although Taylor did much work for the government and for various committees, it was the example set by the firm under his direction which did most to raise the standard of mechanical and optical manufacture in Great Britain. It produced the epoch-making camera lens designed by Harold Dennis Taylor, and adopted methods of mass production which made possible the manufacture of very large numbers of camera lenses of such high quality that they acquired a commanding position all over the world. In this achievement Taylor's study of factory organization and skill in design, coupled with the novel range of machines for grinding and polishing lenses devised and patented by him, were all essential factors.

Besides this, Taylor's interest in the game of golf led him to study the form and flight of the golf ball, and he designed the 'Dimple' ball and a mechanical driving machine for testing the balls. He also produced an engraving machine which is in use all over the world.

The distinguishing features of Taylor's ability were a comprehensive knowledge of engineering practice, an authoritative grasp of the result desired, and, most marked of all, untiring patience and inexhaustible stamina in persevering to the end in view.

Taylor was appointed O.B.E. in 1918 and was elected F.R.S. in 1934. He married in 1892 Esther Margaret, daughter of John Coy, of Leicester, who survived him with their son and four daughters. He died in a snowdrift at Laughton Hills, Leicestershire, 28 February 1937.

[*Obituary Notices of Fellows of the Royal Society*, No. 6, January 1938 (portrait); *Nature*, 27 March 1937; *The Times*, 2 March 1937; personal knowledge.]　　　F. TWYMAN.

TEMPERLEY, HAROLD WILLIAM VAZEILLE (1879–1939), historian, was born at Cambridge 20 April 1879, the third son of Ernest Temperley, fellow, bursar, tutor, and mathematical lecturer of Queens' College, Cambridge, by his wife, Marion, daughter of Thomas Wildman, D.D., episcopalian chaplain at Callander. He was a younger brother of Major-General Arthur Cecil Temperley. After being educated at Sherborne, he entered King's College, Cambridge, in 1898 and obtained a first class in both parts of the historical tripos (1900, 1901). In 1905 he became a fellow of Peterhouse and published a *Life of Canning*. Between 1907 and 1909 he wrote five chapters in the *Cambridge Modern History* on Great Britain in the seventeenth, eighteenth, and nineteenth centuries. His interest in the Near East began with a journey to Serbia in 1905. A visit to Slovakia in 1907 introduced him to the racial problems of Hungary, and in 1910 he contributed a long introduction to a translation of Henry Marczali's *Hungary in the Eighteenth Century. Senates and Upper Chambers*, published in the same year, was suggested by the rejection of the budget of 1909 by the House of Lords. *Frederic the Great and Kaiser Joseph*, published in 1915, described the war of the Bavarian Succession in 1778. A *History of Serbia* was almost completed in 1914 although not published until 1917.

The general war of 1914–1918 revealed Temperley as a man of action. His knowledge of the Near East was utilized in various missions; he saw active service with the Serbian army at Salonica; and his services were recognized by appointment as O.B.E. in 1920 and by decorations from several countries. In 1919 he was a member of the British delegation to the Peace Conference, the record of which he was invited to prepare. The authoritative but unofficial *History of the Peace Conference of Paris*, to which he contributed nine chapters, appeared in six volumes (1920–1924) under the auspices of the newly founded Institute of International Affairs. *The Second Year of the League*, a study of the second Assembly of the League of Nations, published in 1922, may be regarded as a postscript.

After the war Temperley resumed his duties at Cambridge. He was appointed university reader in modern history in 1919 and was the first occupant of a chair of modern history created in 1931. He was founder and first editor (1923–1937) of the *Cambridge Historical Journal*, was joint editor of 'Helps to Students of History', and edited for the Historical Association its *Annual Bulletin of Historical Literature* (1922–1928). He collaborated with Arthur James Grant in *Europe in the Nineteenth (and Twentieth) Century, 1789–1914* (1927), which went through five editions, the last of which (1939) brought the story up to the Munich crisis of 1938. He wrote the chapter on Canning in the second volume

of the *Cambridge History of British Foreign Policy, 1783–1919*, published in 1923, and in 1925 he completed his masterpiece, *The Foreign Policy of Canning, 1822–1827*. His edition of the *Unpublished Diary of Princess Lieven*, illustrating the same period, also appeared in that year. He collaborated with George Peabody Gooch in selecting and editing *British Documents on the Origins of the War, 1898–1914* (published in thirteen volumes, 1926–1938). When the task was nearing completion Temperley embarked upon his largest enterprise, *England and the Near East*, designed to cover the years 1827 to 1878, of which the first and only volume, *The Crimea*, appeared in 1936. *Foundations of British Foreign Policy from Pitt, 1792, to Salisbury, 1902*, and *A Century of Diplomatic Blue Books, 1814–1914*, both published in 1938, compiled with the aid of Miss Lillian Penson, were intended to facilitate the study of diplomacy. Among his later interests were the International Historical Congress, of which he was the second president (1933–1938); the new Commonwealth Institute, of which he was the first president (1934); the Royal Commission on Historical Manuscripts; and the British Academy, of which he was elected a fellow in 1927. He initiated a *Cambridge History of Poland* and planned supplementary volumes to the *Cambridge Modern History*. He was elected master of Peterhouse in 1938, and died at Cambridge 11 July 1939.

Temperley married twice: first, in 1913 Gladys (died 1923), daughter of Job Bradford, barrister of Lincoln's Inn; secondly, in 1929, his cousin, Dorothy Vazeille, daughter of Arthur Temperley, prebendary of Lincoln Minster. He had a son by his first wife. The universities of Durham and St. Andrews conferred honorary degrees upon him and he was a corresponding member of many foreign academies. A man of boundless energy and wide sympathies, Temperley possessed friends in many countries. None of his contemporaries did more to secure international co-operation in historical research.

[*The Times*, 12 July 1939; G. P. Gooch, *Harold Temperley, 1879–1939* in *Proceedings* of the British Academy, vol. xxv, 1939 (portrait); *Some Historians of Modern Europe*, edited by Bernadotte E. Schmitt, 1942; L. M. Penson in *History*, September 1939; personal knowledge.]
             G. P. GOOCH.

TEMPLE, SIR RICHARD CARNAC, second baronet, of The Nash (1850–1931), soldier and oriental scholar, was born at

Allahabad, India, 15 October 1850, the elder son of the Anglo-Indian administrator (Sir) Richard Temple, first baronet [q.v.], of The Nash, Kempsey, Worcestershire, by his first wife, Charlotte Frances, daughter of Benjamin Martindale. He was educated at Harrow and at Trinity Hall, Cambridge, of which in 1908 he was elected an honorary fellow, and in 1871 he obtained a commission in the Royal Scots Fusiliers and embarked with them for India. Transferred to the Indian Army in 1877, he was first posted to the 38th Dogras, and with them took part in the second Afghan war (1878–1879). He next served in the 1st Gurkha Regiment. Having been mentioned in dispatches for his services in the Afghan campaign, he was selected in 1879 for the post of cantonment magistrate in the Punjab, where his lifelong study of Indian history, folk-lore, and ethnology was initiated, witness his *Legends of the Panjâb* (3 vols., 1883–1890) and contributions to *Panjab Notes and Queries*. In 1880, while stationed with a detachment of his regiment at the penal settlement of Port Blair in the Andaman Islands, he married Agnes Fanny, second daughter of Major-General George Archimedes Searle, Madras Staff Corps. The outbreak in 1885 of the third Burmese war brought him once more on active service, and led in 1887 to his being placed in charge of King Thibaw's capital on this monarch's deposition. From Mandalay he was promoted in 1891 to be president of the municipality and port-commissioner of Rangoon, and the last nine and a half years of his service were passed in the scene of his early romance, as chief commissioner of the Andaman and Nicobar Islands.

After succeeding to his father's baronetcy in 1902, Temple retired in 1904, having reached the rank of lieutenant-colonel in 1897, and entered upon the most fruitful period of his literary activities. His editorial labours produced *A Geographical Account of the Countries Round the Bay of Bengal, 1669–1679* by Thomas Bowrey (1905), *The Travels of Peter Mundy, in Europe and Asia, 1608–1667* (5 vols., 1907–1928), *The Diaries of Streynsham Master, 1675–1680* (1911), *The Papers of Thomas Bowrey, 1669–1713* (1927), and *New Light on the Mysterious Tragedy of the 'Worcester', 1704–1705* (1930), to mention only a few of his best known works. In 1913 he was president of the anthropological section of the British Association, and in 1925 he was elected a fellow of the British Aca-

demy. For his services in India he was appointed C.I.E. in 1894, and, for work connected with the joint committee of the St. John Ambulance Association and the British Red Cross Society during the war of 1914–1918, C.B. in 1916. He was also a Bailiff Grand Cross of the Order of St. John of Jerusalem (1927).

In his later years, from 1921 until his death at Territet, Switzerland, 3 March 1931, Temple was greatly inconvenienced by domestic troubles and ill health, which led him to an enforced exile, mostly spent at Territet. Here, undismayed by his numerous trials, and in touch with many devoted friends, he continued his literary activities, including the editorship of the *Indian Antiquary*, of which he had been sole editor since 1892. A literary colleague described as his principal characteristics 'his indefatigable industry, amounting to a joy of work, his exceptional range of knowledge and interests, covering almost all branches of Oriental research, his wide personal experience of almost all provinces of the Indian Empire, and his liberal and broad-minded outlook that enabled him better to understand and appreciate the cultures of the East as a whole'. He wielded sword and pen with equal skill and courage. He was survived by his wife, by his only son, Richard Durand Temple, D.S.O. (born 1880), who succeeded him as third baronet, and by his two daughters.

[R. E. E[nthoven], *Sir Richard Temple, Bt., 1850–1931* in *Proceedings* of the British Academy, vol. xvii, 1931; personal knowledge.]   R. E. ENTHOVEN.

TERRY, CHARLES SANFORD (1864–1936), historian and musician, was born at Newport Pagnell, Buckinghamshire, 24 October 1864, the elder son of Charles Terry, a physician there, by his wife, Ellen Octavia, daughter of Octavius Thomas Prichard, physician, of Abingdon Abbey, Northamptonshire. Both his grandfathers and two of his great-grandfathers were medical men. He was educated at St. Paul's Cathedral Choir School, King's College School, Strand, Lancing, and at Clare College, Cambridge, where he obtained a second class in the historical tripos of 1886. From 1890 to 1898 he was lecturer in history at Durham College of Science (later Armstrong College), Newcastle-upon-Tyne. Thereafter he became lecturer in history in Aberdeen University. In 1903 the lecturership was raised to a chair, which he held until his retirement in 1930. He died at his home, Westerton of Pitfodels, near Aberdeen, 5 November 1936. In 1901 he married Edith, eldest daughter of Francis Allfrey, brewer, of Newport Pagnell; there were no children of the marriage.

Among those Englishmen who have served Scotland, Terry takes a high place. He was not greatly concerned with the ideas which give rise to history, or with personalities: his interest lay in the pure course of events, which he set forth not only with sound scholarship, but with a remarkable clarity and conciseness and the power of marshalling intricate masses of detail into a lucid and balanced narrative. These gifts, with his warm and attractive personality, made him an excellent and beloved teacher. His considerable bulk of published work includes several useful collections of material concerning the various Jacobite movements and an important edition of the *Albemarle Papers, 1746-1748* (2 vols., 1902). His most valuable historical work, however, deals with the seventeenth century in Scotland. The chief of it is contained in his *Life and Campaigns of Alexander Leslie, first Earl of Leven* (1899) and *John Graham of Claverhouse, Viscount of Dundee* (1905), and in his editorial work on *The Cromwellian Union* (1902) and *Papers Relating to the Army of the Solemn League and Covenant* (2 vols., 1917). These books, exploring involved and neglected material, served to undermine a number of classic misstatements: and at a time when Scottish history was only too commonly seen with narrow scope, he dealt with Scotland always as part of Europe.

Terry was also a very fine musician, with a special interest in Johann Sebastian Bach. His *Bach: A Biography*, published in 1928 (revised ed. 1933), was received with enthusiasm in Germany. He also wrote on the Bach family, and his other editorial and critical work on J. S. Bach includes important editions of the *Chorals* (3 parts, 1915-1921), *Original Hymn-Tunes for Congregational Use* (1922), and *Cantata Texts, Sacred and Secular* (1926), and critical analyses for the 'Musical Pilgrim' series, founded in 1924. He also contributed to the third edition of *Grove's Dictionary of Music*. At Aberdeen he virtually created the University Choral and Orchestral Society, acting for many years as its conductor.

Terry received honorary doctorates of music from the universities of Oxford and Edinburgh, and other honorary degrees from Glasgow, Aberdeen, Durham, and

Leipzig. This German degree (Ph.D.) was conferred upon him in 1935 on the occasion of the two hundred and fiftieth anniversary of the birth of Bach. He was elected an honorary fellow of Clare College in 1929.

There is a portrait of Terry by Allan Sutherland at King's College, Aberdeen, but the likeness is not so good as in the pencil drawing by J. B. Souter, which hangs above the Bach Collection bequeathed by Terry to the library of the Royal College of Music, London. A photograph of him in old age, of admirable liveliness, is reproduced in vol. xxiv of the *Aberdeen University Review*.

[*Grove's Dictionary of Music and Musicians*, 4th ed., vol. v, edited by H. C. Colles; *The Times*, 6 November 1936; C. S. Terry's own writings; private information.]

AGNES MURE MACKENZIE.

TERRY, FRED (1863-1933), actor, was born in London 9 November 1863, the youngest son of Benjamin Terry, actor, by his wife, Sarah Ballard, actress, daughter of a Scottish minister at Portsmouth. Among his elder sisters were the actresses Kate, Ellen [q.v.], Marion, and Florence Terry; and Fred, after education in London, France, and Switzerland, sustained the family tradition by going on the stage at the age of sixteen. He 'walked on' in a celebrated revival of *Money*, with which the Bancrofts opened their management of the Haymarket Theatre on 31 January 1880. After experience on tour Terry appeared at the Lyceum Theatre in July 1884, in the revival by (Sir) Henry Irving [q.v.] of *Twelfth Night*, as Sebastian to the Viola of his sister Ellen whom he resembled remarkably. 'I don't think', Ellen Terry wrote in later years, 'that I have ever seen any success so unmistakable and instantaneous.' More touring followed, in this country and in the United States of America, but from the summer of 1887 the young actor, with his fine voice and presence, was found consistently in London. He was successful as Dr. William Brown in *Dr. Bill* at the Avenue Theatre (February 1890), and in a variety of parts for (Sir) H. Beerbohm Tree [q.v.] at the Haymarket Theatre between the years 1890 and 1894. These included D'Aulnay in *Comedy and Tragedy* (1890), John Christison in *The Dancing Girl* (1891)—Julia, daughter of Alexander Ritchie Neilson, of London, whom he married later in that year, was in the cast—and Laertes in *Hamlet*. Early in 1896 he was touring with (Sir) John

Hare [q.v.] in the United States; in June of the same year he was Charles Surface in the revival at the Lyceum by (Sir) Johnston Forbes-Robertson [q.v.] of *The School for Scandal*.

Don Pedro in *Much Ado About Nothing* (St. James's Theatre, 1898), and Squire Thornhill in *Olivia* (Lyceum, June 1900) were among the numerous performances which preceded Terry's own venture into management, with his wife. This took place at the Haymarket on 30 August 1900; Terry, superbly made up, appeared as Charles the Second in *Sweet Nell of Old Drury*, one of two parts with which his name became inseparably connected. During the next twenty-seven years Terry and Julia Neilson kept almost entirely to romantic-historical plays. Much of their time was spent in the provinces; but from 1905 to 1913 they had annual London seasons of six months at the New Theatre. During these they introduced to London such plays as *The Scarlet Pimpernel* (1905), with Terry in his other famous part of Sir Percy Blakeney; *Dorothy o' the Hall* (1906); and *Henry of Navarre* (1909). Terry retired from the stage in 1927.

Terry, who could be a character actor of high skill, is likely to be remembered best for his command of the romantic flourish and for his manliness, gaiety, and unfailing Terry charm, qualities evident in his various performances of Benedick (not seen in central London) and of Charles Surface. In 1918, when his portrait as Sir Percy Blakeney, painted by Frank Daniell (now in the possession of Julia Neilson), was presented to him by the managers of the United Kingdom (some sixty in number) whose theatres he visited, it was stated that he had never appeared in a variety theatre or acted for the cinema. He died in London 17 April 1933. He had a son, Dennis Neilson-Terry, whose early death in 1932 cut short a promising stage career, and a daughter, Phyllis Neilson-Terry, an actress of distinction.

It was unfortunate that Terry never used his powers to the full. He was equipped technically and physically for more testing work than the cape-and-sword parts in which he established his name; but once he was accepted as an actor of the romantic-historical school, he did not attempt to escape from the convention. All his productions were set in the same popular mould.

[*Ellen Terry's Memoirs*, with notes and additional chapters by E. Craig and C. St.

John, 1933; *The Times*, 18 April 1933; *Who's Who in the Theatre*, 1933.]

J. C. TREWIN.

TERRY, SIR RICHARD RUNCIMAN (1865–1938), musician and musical antiquary, was born at Ellington, Northumberland, 3 January 1865, the elder son of Thomas Terry, schoolmaster, of Newcastle-upon-Tyne, by his wife, Mary Ballard, daughter of Walter Runciman, of Dunbar, and sister of Walter, later first Lord Runciman, of Shoreston [q.v.]. His career as a professional musician opened in 1887 when he abandoned a choral scholarship at King's College, Cambridge, after two years only at that university, and one year previously at Oxford. Leaving Cambridge he went as music master to Elstow School, near Bedford, and three years later as organist to St. John's Cathedral, Antigua. He came home from the West Indies in 1893 at a time of spiritual crisis; his decision then to join the Roman Catholic Church reset the course of his life, and the career that gave him international fame had its inception in 1896 when he was appointed to direct the music at the Benedictine school of Downside. Here his supreme talent for choir training enabled him to present the liturgical music by sixteenth-century Catholic composers that he thenceforth made his lifelong study, bringing to light through unremitting researches the hitherto unknown masters of the Tudor polyphonic school which culminated in William Byrd [q.v.].

In 1901, at the instigation of Cardinal Vaughan, Terry came to London to direct the new choir of Westminster Cathedral, and during his twenty-three years there he initiated the Tudor music revival by presenting to the public through living performance almost the entire corpus, then only existent in obsolete manuscript notation, of early English works for the Roman rite. The perfection of his choir and the musical importance of his services at Westminster made the cathedral a focus of attention, and his work there in Tudor polyphony was a powerful motive force to the young composers of his day, a fact publicly recognized in the honorary degree of doctor of music conferred upon him by Durham University in 1911 and in the knighthood of 1922. Terry's research in early manuscripts left its mark primarily upon performance, and his vitality of mind and heart, allied to an unerring musical taste and scholarship, made him a potent

853

influence, although his legacy to the world in print is by comparison exiguous.

As a Roman Catholic Terry contributed materially to the improvement of church music by his published works on hymnology, carols, and plainsong, but it is as the father of the Tudor music revival that he has a permanent place in history. His public success in other musical spheres was considerable, as journalist, lecturer, examiner, and shanty-collector, which last owed much to his seafaring Runciman inheritance.

Terry married in 1909 Mary Lee (died 1932), daughter of Jasper Stephenson, of Aydon-Castle, Northumberland, and had a son and a daughter. He died in London 18 April 1938.

A portrait of Terry in doctor's robes, by Philip Hagreen, is in private hands.

[Hilda Andrews, *Westminster Retrospect. A Memoir of Sir Richard Terry*, 1947; *Grove's Dictionary of Music and Musicians*, 4th ed., vol. v, edited by H. C. Colles; personal knowledge.]   HILDA ANDREWS.

THESIGER, FREDERIC JOHN NAPIER, third BARON and first VISCOUNT CHELMSFORD (1868–1933), viceroy of India, was born in London 12 August 1868, the eldest of the five sons of Frederic Augustus Thesiger, second Lord Chelmsford [q.v.], by his wife, Adria Fanny, eldest daughter of Major-General John Heath, of the Bombay army. He was grandson of Frederic Thesiger, first Lord Chelmsford [q.v.]. He was educated at Winchester and Magdalen College, Oxford. He obtained a first class in jurisprudence and was elected to a fellowship at All Souls College in 1892, and for four years played cricket for the university, being captain of the eleven in 1892. He was called to the bar by the Inner Temple in 1893, but by tradition and temperament he was drawn to a public rather than to a professional career. Recognizing the importance of education in a modern democracy, he began to study the British educational system and from 1900 to 1904 he served as a member of the London school board. In 1904 he was elected to the London County Council, but next year, which was also the year of his succession to the title, he was given the opportunity of public service in a wider field than local government. He was offered and accepted the governorship of Queensland (1905–1909) and then the governorship of New South Wales (1909–1913). Tall, well built, good-looking, dignified, sociable and easy-mannered, he was admirably qualified for the personal and ceremonial duties of the King's representative in one of the overseas Dominions; and he soon proved himself more than a figurehead in the politics of Australia. He made friends with the party leaders, and their recognition of his honesty and disinterestedness enabled him to deal firmly and successfully with the crisis in Queensland in 1907 over the grant of a dissolution and to lighten the task of the first inexperienced labour government which took office in New South Wales in 1910.

Chelmsford was back in England when war broke out in 1914. A captain in the 4th Dorset Territorials, he at once joined his regiment and went with it to India. He had seen no fighting when, in the spring of 1916, he was appointed to succeed Lord Hardinge of Penshurst as viceroy of India. It was an unexpected choice, for he was only forty-seven, and the successful governor of two Australian States was not necessarily qualified for an office so much greater and more difficult. Nor were the difficulties eased by the war. The prestige of the government of India had been seriously damaged by the mismanagement of the Mesopotamian campaign, and, although the loyalty of India as a whole to the Allied cause was not in doubt, the new viceroy was confronted with a growing demand among the intelligentsia for constitutional advance, and in one or two areas, particularly in Bengal, with a terrorist conspiracy so dangerous that, in the first half of 1917, as the result of the report of a committee presided over by Mr. Justice Rowlatt, an Emergency Act was passed to equip the government with temporary powers of repression. Chelmsford quickly recognized that the claim for more self-government could not be left unanswered until the war was over, and he was corresponding on the subject with (Sir Joseph) Austen Chamberlain [q.v.] before the latter's resignation of the secretaryship of state for India in July 1917. Chamberlain's successor, E. S. Montagu [q.v.], was a more forcible character. Within a few months he obtained the agreement of the British and Indian governments to the historic announcement of 20 August 1917, which defined the goal of Indian policy as 'the progressive realization of responsible government'; and he spent the following winter in India discussing what the first step in the process was to be. Chelmsford was the antithesis of Curzon: he made no attempt to dominate his executive council; and since, with a few notable exceptions, most of his official advisers were opposed to the immediate concession of any radical measure of self-government, his response to Montagu's proposals was cautious and hesitating. Ultimately he signed the Montagu–Chelmsford *Report* (1918) which inspired the Government of India Act of 1919 and so set British India on the path towards full parliamentary 'home rule'.

Meantime a wave of unrest was passing over India, and the launching of Gandhi's first 'passive resistance' movement in protest against the Anarchical and Revolutionary Crimes Act of 1919 was followed by murderous disorder in the Punjab, the danger of which was enhanced by the simultaneous outbreak of the third Afghan war. The crisis was mastered, but it left behind it 'the shadow of Amritsar'. Brigadier-General R. E. H. Dyer [q.v.] was eventually censured by the government of India and other authorities, but for the long delay in conducting an inquiry into the tragedy Chelmsford and his colleagues must bear their share of blame.

Back in England in 1921 Chelmsford resumed his early interest in education. He was chairman of the University College (London) Committee from 1920 to 1932 and of the statutory commission appointed in 1923 to draft revised statutes for Oxford University which were promulgated in 1926. In 1924 he accepted Ramsay MacDonald's invitation to join the first labour government as first lord of the Admiralty. Thirteen years of political neutrality oversea had freed him from party ties; and he believed that as regards the navy directly and India indirectly his inclusion in the Cabinet would strengthen public confidence. The government fell before he had had time to prove his quality in administration or debate. He was again elected a fellow of All Souls College, Oxford, in 1929, and in 1932 he was elected warden. In his college and in the university he was as warmly liked and respected as he had been elsewhere, but the prospect of several years of useful and congenial work was cut short by a sudden and fatal heart-attack at Ardington House, near Wantage, 1 April 1933.

Chelmsford was created a viscount on his return from India in 1921; he was also appointed K.C.M.G. (1906), G.C.M.G. (1912), G.C.S.I. and G.C.I.E. (1916), and G.B.E. (1918), and was sworn of the Privy Council in 1916. He received honorary degrees from the universities of Birmingham (1927), Oxford (1929), Edinburgh

and Sheffield (1932), and was elected an honorary fellow of Magdalen College, Oxford, in 1917. He married in 1894 Frances Charlotte, eldest daughter of Ivor Bertie Guest, first Lord Wimborne [q.v.], and had two sons, the elder of whom died of wounds received in action in Mesopotamia in 1917, and four daughters. He was succeeded as second viscount and fourth baron by his younger son, Andrew Charles Gerald (born 1903).

There is a portrait of Lord Chelmsford by David Kelly at All Souls College, Oxford.

[*The Times*, 3 April 1933; *Oxford Magazine*, 27 April 1933; *Report on East India Constitutional Reforms* [Cmd. 9109 of 1918]; E. S. Montagu, *An Indian Diary*, edited by Venetia Montagu, 1930; personal knowledge.]

R. COUPLAND.

THOMAS, HERBERT HENRY (1876–1935), geologist, was born at Exeter 13 March 1876, the younger son of Frederick Thomas, of Exeter and later of Harrow, by his wife, Louisa Pickford. He was at school at Exeter and went to Cambridge in 1894 as an exhibitioner, becoming later a scholar, of Sidney Sussex College. He obtained a first class in both parts of the natural sciences tripos (1897, 1898) and won the Harkness scholarship for geology in the latter year.

From Cambridge Thomas went to Oxford in 1898 as assistant to W. J. Sollas [q.v.] and entered Balliol College. In 1900 he joined a party of scientists and geographers on a journey described in *Across Iceland* (1902) by William Bisiker. He was appointed geologist to the Geological Survey of Great Britain in 1901 and worked mainly in South Wales until his promotion as petrographer to the survey in 1911.

Much of Thomas's scientific work is incorporated in memoirs of the Geological Survey and in papers by other geologists. With Donald MacAlister he published in 1909 *The Geology of Ore Deposits*, and he contributed during the war of 1914–1918 to numerous reports on mineral resources, refractories, silica-bricks, and the material for their manufacture. Among his separately published papers several are of considerable importance. His earliest work dealt with the 'heavy' minerals of the Bunter Pebble-Bed (1902) and with the New Red Sandstone of the west of England (1909) and his essay on this subject won the Sedgwick prize of Cambridge University in 1903. This was pioneer work and established methods since widely used in sedimentary petrography.

A paper on 'The Skomer Volcanic Series' describing the igneous rocks of the islands off Wooltack Point and the adjacent Pembrokeshire coast (published in 1911) was Thomas's first important contribution to this branch of petrography. In 1922 he published an important paper on the sapphire-bearing xenoliths from minor intrusions in Mull, and in his address as president of the geological section of the British Association in 1927 he gave a *résumé* of the state of knowledge of tertiary igneous activity in Great Britain, embodying the results of the work done with Sir Edward Battersby Bailey and Dr. James Ernest Richey in Mull and Ardnamurchan. His last purely petrographic paper (with W. Campbell Smith) on 'Xenoliths . . . in the Trégastel-Ploumanac'h granite . . .' was published in 1932, the result of field work in Brittany.

Thomas was frequently called upon to identify materials for archaeologists, and when he was asked to investigate the stones of the inner circle of Stonehenge his knowledge of the rocks of South Wales enabled him to recognize the 'blue stones' as identical with the spotted dolerites of the Prescelly Mountains in Pembrokeshire. This identification, firmly established in his paper published in 1923, settled a problem that had baffled petrologists for fifty years.

Thomas was one of the secretaries of the Geological Society of London for ten years (1912–1922). He was awarded the Murchison medal of the Geological Society in 1925 and was elected F.R.S. in 1927. He was probably one of the best known and most able of the British geologists of his time. Gifted with a genial spirit and a warm heart he had a large circle of devoted friends. He was a keen fisherman and enjoyed sketching, and frequently illustrated his papers with his own drawings. He married in 1904 Anna Maria, eldest daughter of Oswald Henry Mosley, rector of Wentworth in the Isle of Ely, and had a son and a daughter. He died suddenly in London 12 May 1935.

[*Obituary Notices of Fellows of the Royal Society*, No. 4, December 1935 (portrait); *Quarterly Journal* of the Geological Society of London, vol. xcii, 1936; *Mineralogical Magazine*, vol. xxiv, 1937 (portrait); *Nature*, 20 July 1935; *The Times*, 13 May 1935; personal knowledge.]

W. CAMPBELL SMITH.

THOMSON, ARTHUR (1858–1935), anatomist, was born in Edinburgh 21 March 1858, the youngest son of John Thomson, fleet surgeon, R.N., by his wife, Mary Arthur. He was educated at Edinburgh Collegiate School and studied medicine at Edinburgh University, graduating M.B. in 1880, and subsequently serving as demonstrator of anatomy to (Sir) William Turner [q.v.].

In 1885 Thomson was appointed to the new post of university lecturer in human anatomy at Oxford, where hitherto anatomical teaching had been undertaken by the professor of comparative anatomy. The medical school at Oxford, the creation of Sir H. W. Acland [q.v.], was then in its infancy; Thomson's first class, consisting of seven students, worked in a tin shed. The new anatomical department, largely of his design, was opened eight years later. From 1893 he held the title of extraordinary professor of human anatomy, and in 1919 became the first Dr. Lee's professor, a post which carried with it a studentship at Christ Church. This process was part of the development of the whole medical school, in which Thomson came to take a leading share, in the face of considerable opposition. The work of organization was eminently congenial to him; and to it he devoted much of his energies for the greater part of his life. He brought to the task a slow and cautious mind, remarkable tenacity, and a fine sense of loyalty. He took keen personal interest in his pupils; and the advice and help which he was always ready to give were especially valuable in the early days of the school, when there was no dean and few of the colleges had medical tutors. He resigned his chair in 1933.

In pure research, mainly in the early development of the human embryo, Thomson was indefatigable, but he opened up no new field of inquiry, although he made several fresh observations; his work on 'squatting facets' on the knee and ankle bone is well known. Outside his own subject of anatomy he was greatly interested in ophthalmology, being the author of *Anatomy of the Human Eye* (1912), and anthropology, being co-author, with David Randall-MacIver, of *The Ancient Races of the Thebaid* (1905); and the establishment of a diploma in each of these subjects, at his instigation, gave him great satisfaction. As a lecturer he was conscientious and competent rather than brilliant, his lectures being principally memorable for their magnificent ambidextrous blackboard illustrations. For Thomson was a born artist and lover of painting; sketching in water-colour was his chief recreation. In 1900 he was appointed professor of anatomy at the Royal Academy, a position which he held for over thirty years, and delighted in the opportunities thus afforded for meeting other artists. In 1896 he published *A Handbook of Anatomy for Art Students*.

Thomson received honorary degrees from the universities of Edinburgh (1915), Durham (1919), and Oxford (1933). He was elected F.R.C.P. in 1907, and was a representative of Oxford University on the General Medical Council from 1904 to 1929. In 1888 he married Mary Walker, daughter of Norman Macbeth, R.S.A., and had two daughters. He died at Oxford 7 February 1935.

[*British Medical Journal*, 1935, vol. i, p. 334; *Lancet*, 1935, vol. i, p. 405 (portrait); *The Times*, 8 February 1935; *Nature*, 23 February 1935; private information; personal knowledge.]   T. B. Heaton.

THOMSON, Sir BASIL HOME (1861–1939), colonial governor and assistant commissioner of the metropolitan police, was born at Queen's College, Oxford, 21 April 1861, the third of the four sons of William Thomson [q.v.], provost of Queen's, afterwards archbishop of York, by his wife, Zoë, daughter of James Henry Skene, British consul at Aleppo, and granddaughter of James Skene [q.v.], of Rubislaw. He was educated at Eton and New College, Oxford, and served in the colonial service for ten years in Fiji, Tonga, of which he was prime minister, and British New Guinea. Having been called to the bar by the Inner Temple in 1896, he was that year appointed deputy governor of Liverpool prison and was successively governor of Northampton, Cardiff, Dartmoor, and Wormwood Scrubs prisons. In 1908 he was appointed secretary to the prison commission and in 1913 assistant commissioner of the metropolitan police. It therefore fell to his lot to combat suffragettes and, even before the outbreak of war in 1914, enemy espionage, and such was the completeness of the preparations made to meet that emergency that it was possible for the police to lay their hands on almost all enemy agents and thereby completely to baffle the German intelligence service in this country. He was appointed C.B. in 1916 and in 1919 director of intelligence at Scotland Yard and K.C.B. for his services, but in November 1921 he

resigned owing to his objection to a reorganization of the office which would have placed him under the immediate control of Brigadier-General Sir William Horwood, the commissioner of metropolitan police.

Thomson was a prolific writer whose works include books on the customs of the people of Oceania and historical subjects and fiction. Among these may be mentioned *The Diversions of a Prime Minister* and *South Sea Yarns* (1894); *A Court Intrigue* (1896); *The Indiscretions of Lady Asenath* (1898); *Savage Island* (1902); and *The Fijians* (1908): his numerous publications after his retirement include *Queer People* (1922) and *Mr. Pepper, Investigator* (1925).

Thomson married in 1889 Grace Indja, only daughter of Felix Stanley Webber, R.N., of Shroton House, Blandford, Dorset, and had two sons and a daughter. He was the recipient of several foreign orders. He died suddenly at Teddington 26 March 1939.

[*The Times*, 27 March 1939.]
                E. I. Carlyle.

THOMSON, Sir JOSEPH JOHN (1856–1940), physicist, was born at Cheetham Hill, near Manchester, 18 December 1856, the elder son of Joseph James Thomson, who carried on his father's business as publisher and bookseller, by his wife, Emma Swindells. So far as is known the ancestors of Joseph James Thomson were entirely lowland Scottish, and those of Emma Swindells came from the neighbourhood of Manchester. Thomson was educated at a private day school; when he was sixteen years old his father died and his mother moved to Fallowfield, nearer to the Owens College. She has been described by one who knew her as small, with bright dark eyes beaming with kindness, and dark hair hanging in clusters of ringlets over her ears. Her two sons were devoted to her and the three always spent their summer holidays together until her death in 1901.

It was intended that Thomson should be an engineer, and it was by a mere accident that he became a physicist. 'In those days', he wrote, 'the way of entering the [engineering] profession was to be apprenticed. . . . It was arranged that I should be apprenticed to Sharp-Stewart & Co., who had a great reputation as makers of locomotives, but they told my father they had a long waiting list. . . . My father happened to mention this to a friend, who said, "If

I were you, ... I should send him while he is waiting to the Owens College: it must be a pretty good kind of place, for young John Hopkinson who has just come out Senior Wrangler at Cambridge was educated there." My father took this advice, and I went to the College.' This, as Thomson points out, could only have happened in Manchester, because in no other English town was there anything similar to the Owens College. Thomson was then only fourteen, and on hearing that a student of this tender age had gained admission, the college authorities made a regulation raising the age limit for entrance.

When Thomson entered the Owens College in 1871, its professoriate could compare not unfavourably with that of any contemporary university. It included Thomas Barker, Balfour Stewart, (Sir) H. E. Roscoe, W. C. Williamson, Osborne Reynolds, W. S. Jevons, (Sir) Adolphus Ward, and James (later Viscount) Bryce [qq.v.]. At that period the college was in a struggling and formative stage. The natural development of the students was not restricted by manifold regulations and organization. The feast was, so to speak, spread on the table and they were invited to help themselves. These surroundings, with the background of Manchester itself in the middle of the nineteenth century, a centre of great scientific achievement with its Literary and Philosophical Society, suited Thomson, and he stayed there five years. He obtained a certificate and a prize in engineering, and some scholarships which helped to defray expenses; but he did not enter for any degree examination. During his last year he wrote an experimental paper 'On Contact Electricity between Non-Conductors', which was communicated to the Royal Society by Balfour Stewart and published in the *Proceedings* (vol. xxv, 1876). Towards the end of his time at Manchester he became acquainted with (Sir) Arthur Schuster [q.v.]. He also met J. H. Poynting [q.v.] and thus entered on a friendship which Thomson has described as one of the greatest joys of his life and which endured until Poynting's death in 1914.

On the advice of Thomas Barker, Thomson in 1875 entered for a scholarship at Trinity College, Cambridge, but was unsuccessful; in the following year, however, he obtained a minor entrance scholarship and came into residence immediately. As an undergraduate, he exhibited many of the characteristics which he had shown in childhood and youth, no great skill with his hands (he was reported to be of little use about the house) and no aptitude for open air sports, although to the end of his life he was very fond of watching good cricket and Rugby football. For exercise he relied on the usual afternoon walk or 'grind', and in this limited field he excelled both for speed and endurance. But in intellect and personality, according to A. R. Forsyth, his contemporaries at Cambridge, like those at Manchester, looked upon him as outstanding. In the mathematical tripos of 1880 (for which he coached with E. J. Routh, q.v.) he was second wrangler and was second Smith's prizeman with (Sir) Joseph Larmor at the head of the list.

That same year Thomson was elected a fellow of Trinity, the award being made for a thesis on the transformation of energy. In 1883 he was awarded the Adams prize for an essay on 'A general investigation of the action upon each other of two closed vortices in a perfect incompressible fluid': the subject for this prize is set by the examiners, not chosen by the candidate. This was published as *A Treatise on the Motion of Vortex Rings* (1883). The subject of his fellowship thesis seems to have developed as a kind of by-product of a train of thought arising from a course of lectures by Balfour Stewart on the principle of the conservation of energy, which he had attended at Manchester some years earlier. Thomson found very perplexing the idea of one kind of energy being transformed into something different —kinetic into potential energy, for example. It seemed to him simpler and otherwise equally satisfactory to suppose that all energy was of the same kind and that the transformation of energy could be more correctly described as the transference of kinetic energy from one 'home' to another, the effects which it produced depending on the nature of its home. This had been recognized in the case of the transformation of the kinetic energy of a moving body into heat on striking a target, the energy of the heated body being the kinetic energy of its molecules, and it seemed to him that the same thing might apply to other kinds of energy.

In a situation where there is a possibility of this kind it is very helpful if a method can be found of calculating the effects of such transformations independent of the nature of the mechanism involved. The thesis consisted of an account of the discovery of such a method based on the generalized mechanics of Sir W. R. Hamilton [q.v.] and of Joseph Louis Lagrange, and its various applications. It was never published in its original form but constituted the basis of two papers in the *Philosophical Transactions* of the Royal Society (vol. clxxvi, 1885 and vol. clxxviii, 1887) and of a book *Applications of Dynamics to Physics and Chemistry* (1888). The scope of the method is very wide.

In 1881 Thomson published a theoretical paper in the *Philosophical Magazine* (5th series, vol. xi) in which he proved that an electric charge must possess inertia and showed how to calculate its mass. Subsequent history shows that even had this achievement stood alone it would have established him as a scientist of the first rank. It also implied a deep insight into the problem of the measurement of the mass of a moving charged particle, a matter not then fully appreciated. This was of great importance for his subsequent experimental work. In 1882 he was appointed a lecturer in mathematics at Trinity and became a university lecturer in the following year, and in December 1894 he succeeded J. W. Strutt, third Lord Rayleigh [q.v.], as Cavendish professor of experimental physics in the university. The Cavendish professorship was not founded until 1871. Its first four holders were in turn James Clerk Maxwell [q.v.], Rayleigh, Thomson, and Ernest (later Lord) Rutherford [q.v.], a succession of great and varied talent probably unequalled among the occupants of any similar chair. It was no light task to follow two such predecessors, but it was made easier for Thomson by the fact that the foundations of the methods of teaching physics in the laboratory had been well laid in Rayleigh's time owing chiefly to the exertions of (Sir) R. T. Glazebrook [q.v.] and (Sir) William Napier Shaw.

Even before he had taken his chair, Thomson was occupied largely in consolidating the position in which electromagnetic theory had been left by Clerk Maxwell. One result of these labours was the appearance in 1893 of *Notes on Recent Researches in Electricity and Magnetism*, a volume intended as a sequel to Clerk Maxwell's treatise. This dealt in the main with the solution of various electrical problems presenting great mathematical difficulty, but it included also a comprehensive account, the first in the English language, of the discharge of electricity through gases. The compilation of this and the reflexions which it induced led Thomson to a suspicion or intuition that the next

great advance in our knowledge of the relationship between electricity and matter would be derived from a study of these phenomena, and he set to work vigorously attacking the problem by experiment. The results were rather disappointing. There was plenty to investigate and the phenomena were often very striking, but they were also very complex and, not infrequently, uncontrollable. There was nothing that one could pick out and say 'this is simple, we will begin by finding out what is causing it'. However, the results caused Thomson to take the view—it could not be put any higher—that the current in these discharges was carried by positively and negatively charged particles (ions) formed by the disruption of the chemical molecules of the gas.

This situation suddenly changed in 1895 when Wilhelm Konrad Röntgen discovered the X-rays and found that they caused the surrounding air, which is ordinarily an insulator of electricity, to become conducting. This method of producing a conducting gas was, from an experimental point of view, simpler and more metrical than anything hitherto available. Thomson immediately recognized this and seized the opportunity thereby presented to investigate the mechanism of the conduction. In this and subsequent work he had much help from the increased number of research students, many of them holders of the recently instituted 1851 Exhibition scholarships, who, under the new university regulations, were being, in effect, invited to come to the Cavendish laboratory. Several, coming from all parts of the world, were men of great ability who afterwards became eminent, such as Paul Langevin (from France) and Rutherford (from New Zealand).

The results of this work showed that, as Thomson expected, the electric currents were carried by positive and negative ions generated in the gas by the X-rays. Their physical properties were ascertained and measured and found to be such as would be expected if they were generated by the disruption of the molecules of the gas.

This achievement, important though it was, dealt only with the fringe of the matter. In contrast to the air rendered conducting by X-rays, the electric discharges in rarefied gases under high voltages were luminous, often strikingly so. From 1859 to 1862 Julius Plücker had shown that in these discharges radiation, called by Eugen Goldstein in 1876 cathode rays (*Kathodenstrahlen*), emanated from the negative pole and had various interesting properties. Among others it caused the walls of the glass bulbs, in which experiments of this kind are usually made, to glow with a greenish yellow light at the places where the radiation fell on them and these spots of light could be made to move about by changing the local magnetic field, for example, by shifting the position of a magnet outside the discharge bulb. For half a century a sharp controversy, which had a curious national demarcation, raged as to the nature of these cathode rays. The German physicists were unanimous in claiming that they were undulatory like light, while the English, led by C. F. Varley and (Sir) William Crookes [qq.v.], held that they were swiftly moving material projectiles. It is sufficient here to say that in this war, as in others, there was much to be said for both sides.

Thomson's experiments were largely instrumental in proving that the rays were rapidly moving material particles projected from the negative pole. But he was not content with this; he decided to settle once and for all the nature of these electrified particles by measuring their masses. He was not only able to measure the speeds of the particles but also the values of their specific charge (e/m), that is to say, the proportion which the electric charge of a particle bears to its mass. The mass of any one of these particles was proved to be a minute fraction, about one eighteen-hundredth part of that of the atom of hydrogen, the lightest chemical element. He also showed that similar particles originated in a number of different ways and that all had the same mass whatever the chemical nature of the matter from which they originated.

This was not merely a discovery, it was a revolution. The chemical atom had stood for nearly a century as an indivisible unit in the structure of matter. It now appeared that there was a more fundamental unit, an atom of pure electricity, a common constituent of all the chemical atoms. They were originally called corpuscles by Thomson, but later this was dropped in favour of electron, a word suggested many years earlier by G. Johnstone Stoney [q.v.], an Irishman with prophetic gifts. The first public announcement of their existence was made, by Thomson, in a Friday evening discourse delivered at the Royal Institution on 30 April 1897 and published in the *Philosophical Magazine* in the following October.

At this stage it was not proved with absolute certainty that the masses of the atoms and electrons were different, although it was highly probable. The masses themselves had not been measured and compared. The measurements gave the ratio of the mass of the particle concerned to the electric charge that it carried. It was still possible that the masses of the particles might be the same and the charges very different, although, had this been the case, it would have been difficult to understand the facts of electrochemistry. Still, this uncertainty existed, and it had to be dealt with. Thomson set about this problem with his characteristic energy and proceeded to measure directly the magnitudes of the charges on the particles. The method used was one the general development of which was due to Dr. Charles Thomson Rees Wilson, with important contributions by (Sir) John Sealy Edward Townsend towards this particular application. It consisted in inducing the charged particles to load themselves with a drop of water of known weight and then to observe the rate of fall of these drops in electric fields of various strengths. Thomson's experiments left no doubt that the charge of each of the particles was identical with that of a hydrogen ion in electrolysis within the (rather considerable) limits of experimental error. The conclusion as to the identity of the charges was confirmed about the same time by Townsend who used an entirely different method. After that there was no room for further doubt as to the truth of Thomson's revolutionary discovery.

The advent of the electron provided Thomson with more than ample material for the subsequent exercise of his great intellectual gifts. The problem of the structure of matter and of the chemical atoms in terms of electrons at once became pressing and towards the solution of this he contributed many original ideas. Older branches of physics such as optics, magnetism, and spectroscopy were found to be clothed with new life and interest, and new branches of knowledge like radioactivity, photo-electricity, and thermionics sprang up out of the fertile soil. In all these new developments Thomson played a great part.

Space does not permit a survey of all Thomson's contributions to this new knowledge, but two should here be mentioned. For the rest of his life most of his personal experimental work was directed towards improving the technique which had succeeded so well with the electron, and applying it to ascertain the masses, energies, and electric charges of the other particles occurring in electric currents through gases, and especially those which were positively charged and called by him positive rays. These were found to be atoms and molecules, singly or multiply charged (in terms of the electronic charge), but a large proportion of them were quite unknown to ordinary chemical science. They moved very fast and lasted just long enough to leave a track on a photographic plate. This method has hardly begun to be exploited yet, but when it has it seems bound to shed a vast illumination on the very intricate subject of the inner mechanism of chemical reactions. Not only the molecules but the atoms also were found to be peculiar or unexpected. Thus, with the inert elementary gas, neon, the most abundant track, as indicated by the photographic intensity, was that of a singly charged atom of mass 20, but this was always accompanied by a fainter one with an atomic mass 22. Thus was discovered the first pair of isotopes (elements with the same chemical properties but different atomic masses) except for those which had been known for some time to be present among the products of atomic decay (radio-activity).

Thomson's other outstanding achievement, this time theoretical, was the calculation of the amount of scattering of X-rays by the electrons in atoms. When combined with Charles Glover Barkla's experimental data, this showed that the number of electrons in an atom was close to one half the atomic weight for all the heavy elements. With the lighter elements the fraction increased gradually to unity for hydrogen, the lightest element. When reinterpreted later in terms of atomic numbers (the numbers attributed to the elements when they are arranged in order of increasing atomic weight, starting with hydrogen as number 1) this conclusion became simplified into saying that the number of electrons in an atom is equal to its atomic number. These discoveries and that of the neon isotope were important milestones near the beginning of the road that led to the theory of nuclear, as well as of atomic, structure.

As president of the Royal Society from 1915 to 1920, of which he had been elected a fellow in 1884, as well as in other capacities, for example, as a member of the Admiralty Board of Invention and Research, Thomson was deeply engaged throughout the war on government work. He was active in the formation of the Department of Scientific and Industrial Research, and was a member of the advisory council from its inception in 1919 until 1927. He presided over the royal commission set up in 1916 to inquire into the state of secondary education. In 1918 he was appointed by the Crown to succeed H. Montagu Butler [q.v.] as master of Trinity College. The appointment of the leading man of science to succeed a long list of distinguished men of letters was to some a startling departure from tradition, but Thomson, who throughout his life was generous and hospitable, proved well fitted for the post. Unlike some of his predecessors he was equally at home with the fellows, undergraduates, and servants of the college, and it prospered under his wise counsel. Although in infancy he had not been expected to live, he enjoyed uninterrupted good health, and he stated in his autobiography *Recollections and Reflections* (published in 1936) that he could not remember any day in the last sixty years when his work had been interrupted by bad health. It was not until the last four years of his life that a progressive decline in his memory heralded his death, which took place at the Master's Lodge 30 August 1940. His ashes were buried in the nave of Westminster Abbey hard by the graves of Newton, Darwin, Herschel, Kelvin, and Rutherford.

In the Cavendish laboratory Thomson built up the greatest research school in experimental physics yet seen. He was the man for the opportunity. The high level of his achievement is shown by the fact that to no less than seven men, who were trained and first made their mark under him there, the Nobel prize has been awarded, and this is an achievement which has never yet been equalled. What made him the inspiring leader that he was, came from his vital personality, his enormous mental energy, and his conviction that what he and his associates were doing was something very important. This was so patent that he communicated it to them without any apparent effort on his part. His great fertility in suggestion, if not always practical, and an uncanny insight into the parts of the literature likely to be useful were also valuable factors. Moreover others, seeing what important results he obtained with rather poor apparatus, were encouraged to persevere in their efforts. He had, in a degree seldom equalled, the gift of understanding the working of complicated apparatus, without using it himself. He was accessible to everyone and never out of temper.

The growth of Thomson's intellect seems to have been almost complete by the time he left Manchester. Associated though he was with physicists and mathematicians of great eminence at Cambridge there was no one there with whom he came into personal contact who had any influence upon him comparable with that of Clerk Maxwell (whom he never met). What Cambridge did for him was to supply the mathematical knowledge, skill, and discipline which enabled him to understand Maxwell's writings. These profoundly affected him and the resultant struggle to harmonize the view of the physical universe which he had formed at Manchester with those of Maxwell led him to the discovery of the electron. He was assisted in his labours by a very comprehensive memory embracing a great variety of subjects from science to athletic records. But it was liable at times to fail him and he was known to repeat the same story to the same people in a matter of minutes. But there were other instances, not uncommon in the laboratory, which were not capable of easy explanation. A researcher would explain to 'J. J.' (as he was universally and affectionately known) what he believed was the theory of the experimental results which he was getting. 'J. J.' would counter this by propounding quite a different view, and the argument would continue day after day and would finally cease, both sides being unconvinced. Then, perhaps a month later, 'J. J.' would tell the researcher that he had found the explanation of the results they had discussed, and would give a detailed account of the very theory the researcher had propounded. If generally this was dismissed as an instance of the vagaries of great minds, it did from time to time lead to difficulties and misunderstandings.

Being a man of very varied tastes and interests, often unexpectedly pronounced or unusual, Thomson would talk with anyone about almost anything, and seemed to be bored by no subject except philosophy, to which he was once heard to refer as a subject in which you spent your time trying to find a shadow in an absolutely dark room. Yet he was at times keenly interested in psychical research, telepathy, and water divining, particularly in cases where he thought that they could be investigated by physical methods.

In person, Thomson was of medium height, very slightly under the average, and well built. His head was large and squarish, the forehead wide and high, the face strong with well-marked features, including a broad nose and pronounced chin. One of his characteristic traits was a peculiar grin with which he concluded many of his utterances as though challenging dispute. He was most careless in his attire and appearance, and behaved as though it were a matter of no interest either to himself or others. Withal, he had a marked aptitude for finance and business. He was sincerely religious, a churchman with a dislike for Anglo-Catholicism, a regular communicant, who every day knelt in private prayer, a habit known only to Lady Thomson until near the end of his life. A ready speaker, with a remarkable command of English, he could, when occasion demanded, define a complex, difficult, or delicate situation with a precision and tact which few could equal. Travel as a recreation did not in itself appeal strongly to him, and before his old age he travelled little save for some honorific occasion such as to deliver a course of lectures, or receive an honorary degree, a medal, or a prize. Throughout his mature life it was to Cambridge that he ever wished to return, and from the day when he entered Cambridge as a scholar, he never missed a term. He married in 1890 Rose Elizabeth, second daughter of Sir George Edward Paget [q.v.], and had a son, Sir George Paget Thomson, also a physicist, and a daughter.

Practically all the honours which can fall to a man of science were bestowed upon Thomson. He was knighted in 1908, and admitted to the Order of Merit in 1912. He was appointed professor of natural philosophy at the Royal Institution in 1905, and a year later received the Nobel prize at Stockholm. He was awarded the Copley medal of the Royal Society in 1914, having previously received from it a Royal medal in 1894, and the Hughes medal in 1902; he was twice Bakerian lecturer (1887 and 1913), the first fellow to be so since 1879. He was an honorary member of all the leading foreign scientific academies, and he received honorary degrees from twenty-three universities. He was president of the British Association in 1909. After resigning his chairs at the Cavendish laboratory in 1919 and the Royal Institution in 1920, he was appointed honorary professor at each place in 1921, but he did not cease to come to the Cavendish laboratory.

Among Thomson's most important books these others may be mentioned: *Elements of the Mathematical Theory of Electricity and Magnetism* (1895, 5th ed. 1921), *Conduction of Electricity through Gases* (1903, 3rd ed., 2 vols., with G. P. Thomson, 1928 and 1933), *Electricity and Matter* (the first Silliman lecture, 1904), *The Corpuscular Theory of Matter* (1907), and *Rays of Positive Electricity and their Application to Chemical Analysis* (1913, 2nd ed. 1921).

There are portraits of Thomson by Arthur Hacker (1903) in the Cavendish laboratory, Cambridge; by G. Fiddes Watt (1922) in the Royal Society's apartments; by René de l'Hôpital (1923) at the Royal Institution; and by William Nicholson (1924) in the hall of Trinity College, Cambridge. There is a bust by F. Derwent Wood (1920) in the library of Trinity College, Cambridge; and there are drawings by William Strang (1909) in the Royal Library, Windsor Castle; by Francis Dodd (1920) in the Fitzwilliam Museum, Cambridge; by Walter Monnington (1932) at the National Portrait Gallery; and by Hendrik Lund (1932) in Oslo. There is also a talking 'film portrait' (1934) in the keeping of the Royal Institution of Electrical Engineers.

[Lord Rayleigh, *The Life of Sir J. J. Thomson*, 1942 (list of distinctions); Sir J. J. Thomson, *Recollections and Reflections*, 1936 and 'Survey of the Last Twenty-five Years', in *A History of the Cavendish Laboratory, 1871–1910*, 1910; *Obituary Notices of Fellows of the Royal Society*, No. 10, December 1941 (bibliography of his scientific papers and portrait); *Nature*, 14 September 1940; *The Times*, 31 August and 4 September 1940; personal knowledge.]

OWEN W. RICHARDSON.

THORNTON, ALFRED HENRY ROBINSON (1863–1939), painter, was born at Delhi 25 August 1863, the only child of Thomas Henry Thornton, chief secretary to the government of the Punjab from 1864 to 1876, by his wife, Alfreda, daughter of J. C. Spender, of Bath and Englishcombe. Sent home from India at the age of seven, he was educated at Harrow and at Trinity College, Cambridge, where he graduated in 1886.

Travel in Germany and France aroused in Thornton a lively interest in painting. Destined for a career in the Foreign Office, he worked there from 1888 to 1890, but at the same time he was studying at the Slade School of Art; and in 1890 he went to Le Pouldu, in Brittany, to paint. At this village (where Paul Gauguin was then at work) he spent three summers, studying each autumn and winter under Frederick Brown at the Westminster School of Art and at the Slade School.

The year 1893 saw Thornton launched as a practising artist in London and (for one session only) a teacher, in partnership with Walter Richard Sickert. Later he became a contributor to the *Yellow Book*, founded in 1894, and in 1895 a member of the New English Art Club. He made a wide acquaintance among prominent artists of the day, including J. M. Whistler and Charles Conder [qq.v.] and Wilson Steer. Roger Fry [q.v.] gave him a great deal of technical information about the methods of the old masters.

Thornton was primarily a landscape painter, in some degree influenced by the French Impressionists, but never dissolving form in light as did some members of that school, and remaining fundamentally English. He was a man of wide culture and alert intellect, who, as he worked, became more and more keenly interested in the philosophical implications of painting and in the underlying motives that produce art. In 1911 he first learned of the psychological theories of Sigmund Freud and proceeded to relate them to aesthetics. With the psychologist Dr. Ronald Gordon, of Bath, he collaborated in three articles on this subject published in the *Burlington Magazine*: 'The Influence of Certain Psychological Reactions in Painting' (May 1920) and 'Art in Relation to Life' (July and August 1921).

Always alive to innovation, although not himself an innovator, Thornton joined the London Group in 1914. His association with the New English Art Club continued throughout his working life, and he was honorary secretary of the club from 1928 until his death. In 1932 he acted as examiner and moderator in drawing to the Training Colleges' Delegacy of the University of London, continuing as moderator from 1933 to 1935.

Thornton married in 1900 Hilda, daughter of Thomas Walker, of Seaton Carew, co. Durham; there were no children of the marriage. He died at Painswick, Gloucestershire, where he had settled in 1920, 20 February 1939.

Thornton had a quiet, naturalistic style and believed in a high degree of simplification without approaching the extreme generalization of Cézanne and his school. He had a subtle appreciation of tone-values, which is especially apparent in those strong monochromes that are among his best works. He was adept in the difficult art of rendering the character of trees. His work is represented in the Tate Gallery, the British Museum, the Musée du Luxembourg, and the public collections of Bath, Bradford, Leeds, and Manchester.

A pen and ink drawing of Thornton by Cecily Hey is in the possession of Miss Laura Sapsford.

[*The Times*, 21 February 1939; *Artist*, May 1936; Alfred Thornton, *The Diary of an Art Student of the Nineties*, 1938; private information; personal knowledge.]

HERBERT B. GRIMSDITCH.

THRELFALL, SIR RICHARD (1861–1932), physicist and chemical engineer, was born at Hollowforth, Woodplumpton, near Preston, 14 August 1861, the eldest son of Richard Threlfall, of Hollowforth, wine merchant, who was mayor of Preston in 1885, by his second wife, Sarah Jane, daughter of Joseph Mason, of Stanmore, Middlesex. He was educated at Clifton College, and in 1880 won an entrance scholarship at Gonville and Caius College, Cambridge. After obtaining a first class in part i of the natural sciences tripos of 1882, he worked for nearly a year at Strasburg under August Adolph Eduard Ernest Kundt. He then returned to Cambridge, and was awarded a first class in part ii of the tripos of 1884.

In 1886, at the early age of twenty-five, Threlfall was elected professor of physics at Sydney University. He arrived to find no experimental laboratory; but through his pertinacity and persuasiveness funds were provided by the government, and a good laboratory was completed in June 1888. There Threlfall remained for thirteen years, busy with a variety of researches, among which may be specially mentioned the construction of an accurate portable instrument for comparative measurements of gravity. He travelled over 6,000 miles in Australia and Tasmania taking observations with this instrument. He was president of the Royal Society of New South Wales in 1895, and chairman of the royal commission on the spontaneous heating of coal cargoes in 1896. His energy and enthusiasm for scientific work, his wide range of knowledge and interests, and his powers of leadership, left a lasting impression in Australia. He may justly be called the father of physics in Sydney University. In 1899 Threlfall resigned his professor-

ship, and joined the firm of Messrs. Albright & Wilson, chemical manufacturers, of Oldbury, Birmingham, where he remained for the rest of his life. For the next fifteen years he devoted himself entirely to the affairs of the firm. He introduced many improvements in the production of phosphorus, worked out a method for the electrolytic manufacture of sodium chlorate, which was operated on a large scale at Niagara Falls, and designed and installed at Oldbury a gas engine plant for the production of electric power. In the course of this work he devised new and accurate methods for determining the efficiency of electric generators, and for the measurement of the rate of flow of gases in tubes and ducts.

Soon after the outbreak of war in 1914 Threlfall, on his own initiative, arranged for the exploration of sources of helium in gas wells in America, and worked out a scheme for the production of helium in quantity, and its use in balloons and airships. As a result he was invited by the Admiralty to serve on the Board of Invention and Research, which was formed in 1915. A little later (1916) he became one of the original members of the government Advisory Council on Scientific and Industrial Research; he served for ten years on the council, and remained closely associated with its work until his death. He was chairman of the Fuel Research Board and of the Chemical Research Board, and acted as the first (part-time) director of the Chemical Research Laboratory at Teddington, for the establishment of which he was largely responsible.

Threlfall was appointed K.B.E. in 1917 and G.B.E. in 1927. He was elected F.R.S. in 1899 and an honorary fellow of Gonville and Caius College in 1905; he received the honorary degree of D.Sc. from Manchester University in 1919 and the gold medal of the Society of Chemical Industry in 1929.

Threlfall married in 1890 Evelyn Agnes (died 1929), fourth daughter of John Forster Baird, of Bowmont Hill, Northumberland. His wife was an accomplished woman who published three books of poems. They had four sons and two daughters. He suffered from a stroke in 1929 and was in poor health until his death at Edgbaston 10 July 1932.

Threlfall was noted among his contemporaries for his ingenuity, accuracy, and persistency in experimental work, and for his manipulative skill; and this in spite of the loss of two fingers of his right hand, and of injury to others, in the course of experiments on explosives when he was a boy. While still an undergraduate he made a contribution of the first importance to biology by designing and constructing the first automatic microtome. In 1898 he published a book on *Laboratory Arts* which remained for many years a standard work on the subject.

In person Threlfall was short, sturdy, and muscular. In youth he was a famous athlete, and he retained throughout life his love of the countryside and his skill at country sports: he was a good shot and a keen fisherman. No portrait of him exists, but the photographs published in the *Journal* of the Chemical Society for January 1937 are excellent likenesses.

[*Obituary Notices of Fellows of the Royal Society*, No. 1, December 1932 (portrait); *Journal* of the Chemical Society, 1937, vol. i (portraits); *Nature*, 13 August 1932; *The Times*, 11 and 14 July 1932; private information; personal knowledge.]

H. T. TIZARD.

TOMLIN, THOMAS JAMES CHESSHYRE, BARON TOMLIN, of Ash (1867–1935), judge, was born at Canterbury 6 May 1867, the elder son of George Taddy Tomlin, of Combe House, Canterbury, by his wife, Alice, daughter of the Rev. William John Chesshyre, of Barton Court, Canterbury. He was educated at Harrow and at New College, Oxford, where he obtained a first class in jurisprudence (1889) and a second class in the B.C.L. examination (1891). He was called to the bar by the Middle Temple in 1891, being subsequently (1892) called *ad eundem* by Lincoln's Inn, becoming a bencher of the latter Inn in 1918.

Tomlin read as a pupil of R. J. Parker (later Lord Parker of Waddington, q.v.) and continued with Parker as his 'devil' until Parker (who became junior equity counsel to the Treasury in 1900 and never took silk) was appointed to the bench in 1906. While he was Parker's 'devil', Tomlin's practice was but moderate. On Parker's elevation to the bench Tomlin came into his own. His experience while Parker's 'devil' had equipped him to cope more than adequately with the large practice that immediately came his way. In drafting pleadings and in advising on evidence he had few equals. To that technical skill there was added a wide knowledge of law and a neat method of advocacy. His clearness of exposition on both fact and law was as convincing to the bench as it was appealing to his professional and lay clients. Tomlin was ap-

pointed junior equity counsel to the Board of Inland Revenue and certain other government departments but although more than one vacancy occurred while he was a junior, he was not, somewhat surprisingly, offered the post of junior equity counsel to the Treasury when (Sir) C. H. Sargant, then junior equity counsel, was elevated to the bench in 1913. In that year Tomlin took silk. He attached himself first to the court of Sir M. I. Joyce [q.v.] and on Joyce's resignation in 1915 he attached himself to the court of Sir Arthur Frederic Peterson. In 1919 he 'went special'. Tomlin's venture as a silk was successful from the beginning. His practice was by no means confined to the Chancery division. He was often engaged in the House of Lords and the Privy Council in a wide variety of cases.

In 1923, on Sargant's promotion to the Court of Appeal, Tomlin was appointed a judge of the High Court, Chancery division. In 1929 he was appointed a lord of appeal in ordinary without having served as a lord justice in the Court of Appeal—a course for which at that time precedents could be found only in the cases of Lord Blackburn and Lord Parker of Waddington. He was created a life peer and took the title of Baron Tomlin, of Ash, in Kent. A few days earlier he had been sworn of the Privy Council and became a member of the Judicial Committee. He died in harness at Canterbury 13 August 1935.

Tomlin proved himself a sound judge in the court of first instance. He was learned and, while quick and intolerant of irrelevance, remained courteous. He was indeed prone to interrupt an advocate, but his interruptions were those of a careful and knowledgeable judge and were directed either to getting clear in his own mind the point that the advocate was trying to make or making clear to the advocate the point that in Tomlin's view was involved. His interruptions did not give the impression that the case was not being heard with an open mind. The good reputation of the Chancery division was enhanced as well by his judgements as his methods. As a lord of appeal he was no less successful than as a judge of first instance. His personal charm secured the goodwill of his fellow law lords and he earned their respect as a lawyer and judge by his learning, industry, and skill of statement. When he differed from the majority he took his points firmly but always courteously.

Tomlin's judgements and opinions are marked by learning, clear thinking, and lucidity of statement. The point at issue is always made clear and the right solution is sometimes made to appear obvious. It is a curious fact—due perhaps to Tomlin's continuous care and wide knowledge—that few of his judgements stand out from the others. He was versatile. At the bar he had handled but few patent cases; as a judge he showed remarkable qualities in trying them. His success as a patent judge attested the correctness of his view that the best tribunal for such cases is the legal, not the scientific, mind. His decisions were admirable. A good judge contributes as well to the betterment of practice as to the elucidation of the law. Among Tomlin's lasting contributions to better practice are his directions on the role proper to be played in patent actions by expert witnesses (see *British Celanese* v. *Courtaulds*, 52 R.P.C. 171, 1935).

Tomlin's mind struck those who knew him best as being the incarnation of pure common sense, an uncommon quality. He never seemed to leave the firm ground of fact. He had but little of that speculative interest in the history and philosophy of the law which was so marked in the mind of his master Parker. The case to be dealt with was to Tomlin the matter of interest.

Tomlin undertook the chairmanship of various commissions. In 1923 he became chairman of the royal commission on awards to inventors and continued in that office until the commission's labours came to an end in 1933. In 1925 he became chairman of the Child Adoption Committee; in 1926 chairman of the University of London Commissioners; and in 1928 chairman of the Home Office Advisory Committee on the Cruelty to Animals Act. From 1929 to 1931 he was chairman of the royal commission on the civil service. This commission was an important one. The reference required the commission to report on the structure and organization of the civil service, the conditions of service, and retirement. The MacDowell commission (1912–1915) had dealt with much the same subject but the service had in the meantime undergone considerable change. Its functions had been extended; the position of women had been altered materially; new methods of wage negotiation had been introduced; and there had been dislocation of normal methods of recruitment. The Report was a valuable reasoned document. Much matter, some of which involved considerable detail, was adequately dealt with, but on some important matters, in particular the position of women and equal pay, the commission failed, to Tomlin's disappointment, to reach agreement.

Tomlin was elected an honorary fellow of New College in 1929 and he received the honorary degree of LL.D. from the universities of London, Toronto, and Columbia. He was president of the Harrow Association from 1933 until his death. He married in 1893 Marion Olivia, elder daughter of Colonel William Garrow Waterfield, C.S.I., and had two sons, the elder of whom predeceased his father, and two daughters.

[*The Times*, 14 August 1935; personal knowledge.]   UTHWATT.

TONKS, HENRY (1862–1937), painter and teacher of art, was born at Solihull, Warwickshire, 9 April 1862, the second son and the fifth of the eleven children of Edmund Tonks, brass-founder, of Birmingham, by his wife, Julia, youngest daughter of Henry Johnson, wine merchant, of London, who was of Northumbrian descent. He entered Clifton College in 1877, and later studied medicine, first at the Royal Sussex County Hospital, Brighton, in 1880, and then, in 1881, at the London Hospital. Here he was demonstrator of anatomy and enjoyed the close friendship of (Sir) Frederick Treves [q.v.], to whom he acted as house-surgeon in 1887; he was elected F.R.C.S. in 1888 and was later senior medical officer at the Royal Free Hospital.

Since youth Tonks had had a certain interest in art and towards 1890 this interest became very strong. About this time he had the good fortune to be introduced to Frederick Brown, who had for some while been a very successful art teacher, especially with regard to drawing; briefly, his idea was to return to a free and intelligent manner, as opposed to the sterile conventionality of the work being done in art schools of the period. Tonks studied under Brown as a part-time student at the Westminster School of Art, and when in 1893 Brown began to teach as Slade professor of fine art at University College, London, he invited Tonks in 1894 to be his assistant teacher there; so Tonks forsook surgery and began a famous teaching partnership. He and Brown were shortly joined by Wilson Steer as teacher of painting at the Slade School of Art; their students were imbued with a new sense of art, and especially draughtsmanship. In time a widespread change, largely due to this partnership, was effected in British art. Among their early pupils were Mr. Augustus John, (Sir) William Orpen [q.v.], and other distinguished students.

Tonks now had the opportunity to develop his painting, first working mainly in water-colour, then turning to oils. As an artist he was essentially English in outlook, loving a beautiful and elegant subject, tinctured with something of the spirit of the pre-Raphaelites, and the illustrators of the 'sixties. Besides his search for beauty of drawing, he gradually became intensely interested in the possibilities of the broken handling of oil-paint, being influenced to some extent by the French Impressionists, but mainly impelled by his fervent search for tone values. Among his chief works are 'Strolling Players' (Manchester Corporation Art Gallery), 'The Birdcage' (Ashmolean Museum), and a number of pictures in the Tate Gallery. In 1895 he was elected a member of the New English Art Club, and from 1891 was a constant contributor to its exhibitions. In 1936 a special exhibition of his works was held at the Tate Gallery.

In 1917 Brown retired, and Tonks, his obvious successor, became the Slade professor. He was the outstanding teacher of the age; in appearance tall, gaunt, and severe, his criticisms were sometimes the most scathing possible, yet his students loved him, and his ultimate love was for them. He never tired of striving to inculcate in them something of his own passion for drawing. Indeed, the particular historical significance of Tonks is that during the period from 1917 to 1930 he conducted a most vigorous defence of the traditional spirit in art in general, and in draughtsmanship in particular, at a time when futurism, abstraction, and so on, were assailing all that he held most dear. He retired from the Slade School in 1930, and the present (1945) energetic strength of the traditional movement is, in a considerable degree, due to his work.

Tonks had a host of friends, with an intimate circle including Steer, Dr. D. S. MacColl, J. S. Sargent [q.v.], George Moore [q.v.], and Sir Augustus Daniel. He engaged in fierce controversies, as was inevitable, and the fierceness was increased by the tenacity with which he held his views, and the vehemence with which he expressed them. He died,

unmarried, at his home in Chelsea 8 January 1937.

A self-portrait of Tonks, painted in 1909, is in the Tate Gallery, and a pencil drawing, with P. A. Grainger, by G. W. Lambert, is in the National Portrait Gallery. Portraits of Tonks are included in (Sir) William Orpen's picture 'The Selecting Jury of the New English Art Club' (1909), and D. G. Maclaren's 'Some Members of the New English Art Club', both in the National Portrait Gallery.

[Joseph Hone, *The Life of Henry Tonks*, 1939; Henry Tonks, 'Notes from "Wander-Years"', *Artwork*, Winter 1929; *The Times*, 9 January 1937; personal knowledge.]

GEORGE CHARLTON.

TOVEY, SIR DONALD FRANCIS (1875–1940), musician, was born at Eton 17 July 1875, the youngest son of Duncan Crookes Tovey, at that time an assistant master at Eton, later rector of Worplesdon, Surrey, by his wife, Mary Fison, who came from Norfolk. Both parents were unmusical, but had remarkable literary gifts. Donald's prodigious musical aptitude was apparent at a very early age; when eight years old he is said to have embarked on composition on an extended plan. It was the acuteness of his 'ear' in childhood, and the correlation of pitch heard and pitch sung, that attracted the notice of Miss Sophie Weisse, later headmistress of a girls' school at Englefield Green. To her Tovey owed his entire upbringing and education until he was nineteen, for he never went to an ordinary boys' school; moreover it was Miss Weisse who launched him on the open seas of public music-making. These early years were more than usually important in the making of the musician, for Tovey had shown, even in childhood, his remarkable power of absorbing music, both from score and from performance, with great rapidity and an almost mathematical accuracy. It was wise policy that sent the boy to (Sir) Walter Parratt [q.v.], then organist at St. George's Chapel, Windsor, for counterpoint lessons; later to James Higgs, for whom Tovey never lost his admiration; and later still at the age of thirteen to (Sir) Charles Hubert Parry [q.v.], to whom he always referred as 'my master'. A visit at the age of eight or nine to Berlin, where he heard the great violinist Joseph Joachim play the Beethoven violin concerto, and also spoke with him, was an important event. Another early influence dating from boyhood which Tovey publicly acknowledged was that of the great scholar of the keyboard A. J. Hipkins [q.v.]. In this formative period his mind was mainly occupied by music, without, however, neglect of other spheres of knowledge; for Tovey had a strong philosophical power of thought, and more than a leaning towards astronomy and the higher mathematics, retaining to his death a fine general learning which he was able to use as a background for even his most specialist writings. That he studied the piano with Ludwig Deppe appears to be untrue, but he was brought up on his methods and supported them.

In 1894 Tovey went to Balliol College, Oxford, as the first holder of the Lewis Nettleship memorial scholarship in music, and in that same year he appeared in public at Windsor as a pianist with Joachim. At Oxford Tovey entered what was for him a new, comparatively unsheltered world. Although by nature and training shy, his abounding natural humour and an ingrained kindliness found him a place even among the athletes. He read voluminously, scores especially, and never forgot what he read. At Balliol he came into close touch with Dr. Ernest Walker, who even at that time was astonished by the accuracy and readiness of his memory in the wide range of classical music. In 1898 he graduated B.A. with classical honours; in 1921 he was awarded a doctorate of music by decree of convocation and he was elected an honorary fellow of Balliol in 1934.

No familiar musical pattern in the England of his time seemed to fit this immensely learned, deeply thinking, energetic, if absent-minded young musician. The problem of opening Tovey's career was solved by Miss Weisse who arranged for him a series of classical chamber concerts in November 1900 at the St. James's Hall, London, at which he gave not only some quite unusual chamber works of the classical school, but also played a trio and quintet of his own, with many piano solos, and wrote a series of programme notes, many of which have been reprinted. This series and another in London in 1901 were followed by recitals in Berlin and Vienna, at which Tovey played with Joachim. The year 1903 witnessed an orchestral concert, under (Sir) Henry Wood, at which he played his pianoforte concerto; this work was repeated by Hans Richter in 1906 and Tovey also played it at Aachen in 1913. All through this second period

Tovey, the pianist, was playing classical chamber music with Lady Hallé [q.v.], Robert Hausmann, and others. The Chelsea Concerts Society was formed in 1906 and lasted until 1912, to be succeeded by the Classical Concert Society, which was revived after the war of 1914–1918. In the middle of all this concert work came a request from the *Encyclopædia Britannica* to write the articles on music for the eleventh edition, published by the Cambridge University Press. It was a turning-point in Tovey's life, and that was a seed time for his later activities. His friendship with Mr. R. C. Trevelyan from 1905 had also brought to the surface his lifelong interest in the problems of opera, and in correspondence with the poet he was discussing 'The Bride of Dionysus' from which emerged the opera produced in Edinburgh in 1929.

In 1914 Tovey successfully applied for the Reid professorship of music in the university of Edinburgh, in succession to Frederick Niecks. He was appalled by the conflict between Germany and England, bitterly regretting the break in the exchange of musical culture between the two countries. A new venture, started in 1917, had important effects—his founding of the Reid Orchestra in Edinburgh, with students and professionals playing the great masterpieces. Tovey conducted, played, and wrote numerous occasional commentaries for programmes—now famous in their reprinted form of *Essays in Musical Analysis* (6 vols., 1935–1939). The selection was widely representative of every phase of classical music, and also of the newer developments of Elgar, Dr. Ralph Vaughan Williams, Dr. W. T. Walton, and Mr. Paul Hindemith. He originated an entirely new system of university training in music, worked enthusiastically at his lectures and his orchestra, kept up his active pianoplaying, and in short blossomed out into one of the greatest personalities in the musical world of his day. He visited California in 1924-5-6, New York and Boston in 1926 and 1928, Barcelona in 1928 and 1934. He conducted a voluminous if sporadic correspondence. He lectured at Glasgow, Liverpool, Oxford, and elsewhere; broadcast several series of talks; edited (1931) Bach's 'Kunst der Fuge', finishing the last incomplete fugue and writing a rich commentary on the whole; continually absorbing music by some process of study unknown to ordinary musicians. He finished the opera, and he wrote in 1933 a 'cello concerto for Señor Paulo Casals (performed in 1934 and 1937). All this, added to his constant university work, brought on illnesses and an increasing rheumatic disability of the hands, which crippled him in his last years. He died in Edinburgh 10 July 1940. A previous union was declared null; he married in 1925 Clara Georgina, youngest daughter of Richard Wallace, merchant, of Edinburgh: there was no issue of the marriage. He was knighted in 1935.

As a pianist Tovey was without question in the first rank among players of his day, though he never embarked upon a virtuoso's career. He played chamber music with the most eminent artists only (Joachim and his quartet, Lady Hallé, Hausmann, Casals, Madame Suggia, the sisters d'Aranyi), and covered a wide area in his performances. Interested in the problems of piano-playing (one of the first indeed to play the double-keyboard-action piano of Emanuel Moor) he seemed to unfold and expound each work—its history, shape, and meaning—as he played. His philosophy of art held that each work can have perfection, and, if a great work, is perfect. As a composer he wrote, consciously, in the idiom of the German classics and has been, perhaps, unduly neglected. Yet good judges have accounted his opera to be a masterpiece of dramatic declamation and of instrumentation, and the 'cello concerto, long though it is, has magnificence.

Although five years after his death he is known chiefly as a musical historian and commentator, the writing of prose was always a secondary interest in Tovey's mind. He planned books, but never made a whole one himself. He had dreams of a complete treatise of musical instruction in four volumes, but wrote none of it. He wrote prose to assist the occasion of music, to expound music, or to clarify it, and he was surprised, and not entirely pleased, at his universal acceptance as a writer. Actually he wrote for the moment, and his writings should be classed as 'occasional', although, collected, they make a large corpus of musical learning. Apart from his profound knowledge, his sense of exploration, his deep beliefs, and examples, always apt, illustrating what he knew were more than theories, Tovey's writings are characterized, like his talk, by a brilliant and allusive humour, by reference to authors before unthought of as contributing to the practice of his art

(e.g. Lewis Carroll), by the creed already mentioned that a work can, and ought to be, perfect, and by that rare continuity of thought which comes from an ever-ready mind.

Those who were not able to be his pupils at Edinburgh University may get some sense of Tovey as a teacher by reading his books assiduously and with proper humour. His work at Edinburgh was conspicuous in the history of musical instruction in Great Britain, for it was alike theoretical (in the learned meaning) and practical (in the musical). His conducting of the Reid Orchestra, not always with very good forces to command, was vivid and intensely musical.

Joachim accounted Tovey the most learned man in music that had ever lived: on the ground that he knew it all, and that nowadays there is more to know. He was capable at any moment of playing any printed classical work on the piano, whether it were written for five or ten or a hundred instruments, and whether he could ever have heard it or not. But he was far removed from the antiquary, nor did he care greatly for musicians' lives.

Tovey was a tall, large man, in youth slender and ascetic-looking, but becoming in appearance more robust as he grew older. His eyes would wander at times, as if he were thinking of something else than the subject under discussion (for Tovey discussed interminably). Yet this was not inattention: he was seeking for the modern instance, in literature or elsewhere. When he digressed from his arguments (as he did at enormous length) it was found that the deviations were perfectly apposite and illuminating. His reading, outside music, consisted of detective stories, humorous works of all grades, especially verse (he set Lear and Hilaire Belloc brilliantly to music), the Encyclopædia Britannica, and any book containing information about the arts. His upbringing led him towards Beethoven as the principal star in his galaxy; but in the end he came to love Haydn most of all, and he was very sympathetic towards the less formally rhythmic music of Palestrina and of the English Tudor masters.

A portrait of Tovey by Otto Schlapp hangs in the music classroom of Edinburgh University. Two portraits by P. A. de László and other pictures hang in the Donald Tovey Memorial Rooms in Buccleuch Place, Edinburgh, dedicated by Dr. Sophie Weisse to his memory, with an endowment in the keeping of the university. His library is also there, in classrooms used by the faculty of music.

[Preface by E. Walker to Sir D. F. Tovey, *A Musician Talks* (edited by H. J. Foss), 2 vols., 1941; *Music Review*, February 1942; private information; personal knowledge.]

HUBERT J. FOSS.

TOYNBEE, PAGET JACKSON (1855–1932), Dante scholar, was born at Wimbledon 20 January 1855, the third of the four sons of the aural surgeon Joseph Toynbee [q.v.], by his wife, Harriet, daughter of Nathaniel Holmes and niece of the antiquary John Holmes [q.v.]. He was a younger brother of Arnold Toynbee and a second cousin of Sir C. J. Holmes [qq.v.]. Educated at Haileybury and Balliol College, Oxford, he worked for some years as a private tutor, but in 1892 he abandoned teaching and devoted himself entirely to research, more especially to the study of Dante. Noteworthy among his massive contributions to Dante scholarship are the *Dictionary of Proper Names and Notable Matters in the Works of Dante* (1898) which, with its revised and abbreviated edition, the *Concise Dante Dictionary* (1914), became the indispensable handbook of Dante students; *Dante in English Literature from Chaucer to Cary* (2 vols., 1909) which brought together practically all that was written in English about Dante; and his very valuable emended text of Dante's *Epistolae* (1920) with introduction and notes. Although he confined himself to the accumulation and elucidation of facts, making no attempt at literary appreciation, his exhaustive memory and tireless energy won for him a world-wide reputation as a Dantist. He was one of the very few Englishmen to be made a corresponding member of the Italian Reale Accademia della Crusca.

In 1894 Toynbee married Helen, second daughter of Edwin Grundy Wrigley, of Bury, Lancashire, who devoted herself to editing the letters of Horace Walpole. After her death in 1910, Toynbee took up the unfinished task and Horace Walpole, to whom Dante resembled 'a Methodist parson in Bedlam', thenceforth shared Dante's place in his activities. Three supplementary volumes of *Letters* (1918–1925) and the *Correspondence of Gray, Walpole, West and Ashton* (2 vols., 1915) are representative only of his achievements in this new sphere. Latterly Toynbee, who had no children, lived the life of a recluse at 'Fiveways', the house

which he built at Burnham, Buckinghamshire, his principal companion being a tame robin. He emerged occasionally to stay with his friend and fellow Dantist, William Walrond Jackson, for meetings of the Oxford Dante Society, of which he was for long the moving spirit. Among his last services to Dante scholarship were the revision of the *Oxford Dante* for its fourth edition (1924) and the bequest of a valuable collection of books to the Bodleian Library to which he had made notable benefactions in 1912–1917 and in 1923. He died at 'Fiveways' 13 May 1932. With him passed the last of the great English Dantists.

Toynbee was elected a fellow of the British Academy, of which he was Serena gold medallist, in 1919, and an honorary fellow of Balliol College in 1922. In 1923 the university of Edinburgh conferred upon him the honorary degree of LL.D.

[*The Times*, 16 May 1932; E. G. Gardner, *Paget Toynbee, 1855–1932* in *Proceedings* of the British Academy, vol. xviii, 1932; *Oxford Magazine*, 26 May 1932; personal knowledge.]

CECILIA M. ADY.

TRENT, first BARON (1850–1931), man of business and philanthropist. [See BOOT, JESSE.]

TREVETHIN, first BARON (1843–1936), lord chief justice of England. [See LAWRENCE, ALFRED TRISTRAM.]

TROTTER, WILFRED BATTEN LEWIS (1872–1939), surgeon, physiologist, and philosopher, the third son of Howard Birt Trotter, merchant, of Coleford, Gloucestershire, by his wife, Frances Lewis, was born at Coleford 3 November 1872. His childhood was one of ill health and invalidism until at the age of sixteen; his father having moved to London, he entered University College School. He passed thence in 1891 to University College and University College Hospital, and after a brilliant career as a medical undergraduate he qualified in 1896, thereafter rapidly taking the higher medical and surgical degrees and qualifications.

During his student years and in the ensuing period Trotter was fortunate in coming under the influence of some of the eminent men who at that time adorned the medical faculty at University College. His reflective mind responded to the stimulus of such teachers as (Sir) Victor Horsley and (Sir) J. R. Bradford [qq.v.], themselves distinguished scientists and clinicians of the first rank. On the technical side of his work as a surgeon he owed a great deal to his chief, Arthur Barker, who was a pioneer in the development of those refined methods that distinguish modern surgery.

In these congenial surroundings and in this inspiring atmosphere, Trotter developed those balanced and harmonious qualities of mind and heart which marked him out as at once the superbly skilled surgical craftsman, the clinician of fine judgement and deep human insight, the exact and imaginative experimentalist, the inspiring teacher and philosopher. Throughout his active life his range of interests did not diminish, and at his death he had achieved an influence amongst his professional brethren in this country that has scarcely been equalled by any man since the days of John Hunter.

In the opening years of the present century a delay in the occurrence of a vacancy on the surgical staff of University College Hospital gave Trotter, then a young man of just over thirty, the leisure to follow his scientific and philosophical bent, and in 1908 and 1909 there appeared two papers by him in the *Sociological Review* entitled 'The Instincts of the Herd', which were the first major exposition of herd psychology. These, together with additional essays in amplification of his original theme, were published in book form in 1916 under the title of *Instincts of the Herd in Peace and War*. In the two European wars of the present century, the remarkably penetrating analysis of German mass psychology revealed by these essays was widely recognized, and they have been amongst the formative influences in the growth of the study of social psychology.

During the same period, with a collaborator, Mr. Hugh Morriston Davies, Trotter was engaged upon an extensive and minute investigation of the physiology of cutaneous sensation in man. Considerably amplifying the earlier studies on this subject of (Sir) Henry Head [q.v.], the two workers divided no less than five cutaneous nerves in themselves, doing this in such a time-sequence that every stage of nerve regeneration and sensory restoration could be studied contemporaneously. This investigation added considerably to that of Head in the matter of the actual information obtained, and, in virtue of the inferences to be drawn from it, may be said to have replaced entirely the

hypothesis as to the constitution of the afferent nervous system postulated by Head. There is a brilliance and minute accuracy about this study, and a masterly breadth of interpretation of the facts of observation, that make of it one of the principal pieces of modern medical research. It bears the hall mark of scientific genius.

While engaged upon these diverse activities, Trotter, who was surgeon to University College Hospital from 1906 to 1939, was also building up a reputation as a leader amongst practising surgeons and teachers of surgery. His diagnostic acumen, his gift for handling the human material of his work, and his refined surgical technique marked him out amongst the surgeons of the opening years of the century, and by the time of his death had gained for him an almost legendary fame within the ranks of his profession and of those who were his patients. Much new work in surgery came from him; a technique for dealing with a particularly difficult form of malignant disease, advances in the surgery of the brain and spinal cord, together with original papers in which nosological entities were disentangled and clearly described. Trotter's teaching of surgery was one of his finest gifts. He maintained it on what Newman would have regarded as a true university level, and it was never mere technical instruction. It was characteristic of him that in 1935 he should have retired from his large private practice and devoted his remaining years entirely to his work at University College Hospital. He took over the professorship of surgery and the directorship of the surgical unit there, and for the three years of active professional life that were left to him set himself to the training of a few young surgeons.

During the last fifteen years of Trotter's life there came from his pen, usually to be delivered as addresses, a series of essays on the role of general principles and of abstract thought in the development of medicine, the relations of clinical and experimental study, the nature and limitations of the intellect, and upon divers aspects of nervous activity. Couched in a clear and lively English, informed by a humane and philosophical spirit, and not without a fine wit, these essays have come to exert a profound influence upon the thought of those young men who will be the leaders of medical science and art. Published under the title of *The Collected Papers of Wilfred Trotter* (1941), they promise to join the select list of classics which, like Osler's *Aequanimitas*, have come from the pens of medical men to whom they are particularly addressed.

Although attaining the highest place in the regard and respect of his colleagues and juniors, Trotter remained a naturally simple and modest man. He lived a life apart and few were admitted to his intimacy, yet in company his conversation was a delight, his wit of rapier quality, and his range of subjects inexhaustible. He was a lover of English prose, and possessed a wide familiarity with English literature. When he could be induced to discuss it, he displayed a keen interest in the modern schools of philosophy, and his critical mind moved easily and with delight in this difficult field of human thought.

Many academic honours, including honorary degrees from the universities of Liverpool and Edinburgh, were conferred upon Trotter. He was elected F.R.S. in 1931 (the only surgeon of his generation to be so distinguished), later becoming vice-president of the Royal Society and of the Royal College of Surgeons, of which latter he was Hunterian professor in 1913 and Hunterian orator in 1922. In 1928 he was appointed honorary surgeon to King George V, and in 1932 serjeant surgeon. From 1929 to 1933 he was a member of the Medical Research Council. All public honours he declined, out of a sense that a man should be content with the judgement of his professional and scientific peers and seek no other formal distinctions. In the councils of his profession he held a unique place, and he was one of those rare men around whose name and character legend begins early to gather. He may be judged the greatest surgeon of the present century in this country, and one sure of a permanent place in the record of British medicine.

Trotter married in 1910 Elizabeth May, daughter of Thomas Jones, colliery owner, and had a son. He died at Blackmoor, Hampshire, 25 November 1939. A portrait of him by M. Ayoub hangs in the medical school of University College Hospital.

[*Obituary Notices of Fellows of the Royal Society*, No. 9, January 1941 (bibliography and portrait); *British Medical Journal*, 1939, vol. ii, pp. 1117–1119; *Lancet*, 1939, vol. ii, pp. 1244–1246; *University College Hospital Magazine*, vol. xxv, 1940; personal knowledge.]   F. M. R. WALSHE.

TROUP, ROBERT SCOTT (1874–1939), forestry expert, was born at Neithrop, near Banbury, Oxfordshire, 13 December 1874, the second son of James Troup, consul-general at Yokohama, by his wife, Hannah Scott. Educated successively at the Gymnasium, grammar school, and university of Aberdeen, he went in 1894 to the Engineering College at Coopers Hill for training for the Indian forest service. He passed out at the head of his year and was posted to Burma in 1897. As a relatively junior officer he was put in charge of the important Tharrawaddy division, where he contributed much towards the technical advance in the raising and management of teak forests. When the Forest Research Institute was founded at Dehra Dun, India, in 1906, he filled at first the post of forest economist, and spent two fruitful years collecting and publishing information on the utilization of timbers and other forest products. He then changed to the study of Indian silviculture in which he was especially interested and in which he became the acknowledged leading authority. He travelled extensively in India and Burma recording detailed observations on the forests and trees, and initiating experiments on many forest problems, particularly on the growth and regeneration of the main tree species. This experimental work marked the introduction into India of systematic research in these subjects, whilst the collected information, supplemented by the results of his experiments in the provinces and in Dehra, ultimately appeared in 1921 as his most important publication, the three volumes on the *Silviculture of Indian Trees*. Troup did not publish much statistical work, as the measurement plots which he initiated could only yield the desired growth data after a considerable lapse of time, but most of the later studies have been in part based on his plots and methods and would have been considerably delayed without them.

In 1915 Troup left Dehra in order to become assistant inspector-general of forests, serving with (Sir) George Hart, and in 1917 he was appointed war controller of timber supplies to the Indian Munitions Board, a post which he held until February 1918. His services to India were recognized in 1920 by his appointment as C.I.E.

On the retirement of Sir William Schlich [q.v.] from the Oxford chair of forestry in 1920, Troup, one of Schlich's own pupils, was elected professor and held this post until his death at Oxford 1 October 1939. During this period he was a fellow of St. John's College. His interests were now widened to include the forests of the Colonies and the Empire, and he took a leading part in successive Empire Forest Conferences in London (1920), Canada (1923), Australia (1928), and South Africa (1935), as well as in the International Forest Congress at Rome (1926) and at Budapest (1936). It was largely on account of his representations that the Imperial Forestry Institute was founded at Oxford in 1924 for higher studies and research in forestry, he himself being its first director until the end of 1935. Subsequently, all members of the Colonial forest service have attended the institute for advanced study. Troup also gave courses on colonial forestry to probationers of the Colonial administrative service at both Oxford and Cambridge and his lectures were published post-humously in book form under the title *Colonial Forest Administration* (1940). He paid official visits to several Colonies in order to examine the forest position and problems and his reports on Kenya and Uganda (1922), Cyprus (1930), and Tanganyika (1935) are important historical documents. For this work for the Colonies he was appointed C.M.G. in 1934. He was elected F.R.S. in 1926.

Troup's specialized knowledge and experience of tropical forestry did not preclude a keen interest in British and temperate forestry. He made a useful contribution towards an understanding of a major problem through one of his last publications, on *Forestry and State Control* (1938), whilst his book on *Silvicultural Systems* (1928) is the standard work on the subject.

Troup married in 1901 Elizabeth Campbell, elder daughter of John Mortimer, an Aberdeen merchant, and had two sons and a daughter.

There is a portrait of Troup by P. A. Hay (1932) at the School of Forestry, Oxford.

[*The Times*, 3 October 1939; *Obituary Notices of Fellows of the Royal Society*, No. 8, January 1940 (portrait); *Empire Forestry Journal*, December 1939; private information; personal knowledge.] H. G. CHAMPION.

TUCKER, SIR CHARLES (1838–1935), general, was born at Ashburton, Devon, 6 December 1838, the younger son of Robert Tucker, of The Hall, Ashburton,

by his wife, Livinia, daughter of William Hancock, banker, of Wiveliscombe, Somerset. He was educated at Marl-borough, and, when barely seventeen, was commissioned in 1855 as an ensign in the 22nd (later the Cheshire) Regiment. Thus early began an army career which was to last almost continuously for eighty years. He always retained a regard for the rank of ensign and late in his life was urging its restoration in place of second lieutenant, to which he strongly objected. When over ninety he acknowledged a regimental telegram of birthday greetings with the reply: 'Aged ensign appreciates.' In May 1860 he was promoted captain and in November transferred to the 80th Staffordshire Volunteers (later the 2nd South Staffordshire Regiment). Thus began a connexion which ended more than seventy-five years later, when he died as colonel of the South Staffordshire Regiment.

In 1865 Tucker first saw active service, when his battalion was engaged in the Bhootan expedition which avenged the massacre of a British post at Diwangari. Ten years later the battalion was stationed in the Straits Settlements: during the minor operations at Perak in 1875 he held his first staff appointment on active service as brigade major. He was promoted brevet major in 1872 and to the substantive rank in 1877. In the following year he was second-in-command of his battalion in South Africa during the early operations against Sekukini, the Kaffir chieftain. Before the year was out he was officiating in command of the 80th Regiment in the valley of the Pongolo when the full-scale operations against the Zulus began. He was among the first on the spot after the disaster which befell one of his companies at the Intombi River Drift. He later saw that disaster avenged, for the 80th was on the front face of the square at Ulundi (4 July 1879) and bore the full impact of the charges of the Zulu impis in that action which, culminating in the destruction of the town and the chief's kraal, brought the operations to a close. He was promoted lieutenant-colonel and, with two mentions in dispatches to his credit, was appointed C.B. in 1879. After some seven months on half-pay as brevet colonel he was appointed commander, Middlesex regimental district, Hounslow, in February 1885, and in 1891 after another year on half-pay, he was first colonel on the staff and later brigadier-general with the troops in Natal. He was promoted major-general in 1893 and in 1895 left Natal for India where he commanded the Secunderabad district.

In December 1899 Tucker was sent to command the 7th division under Lord Roberts in South Africa. His division fought with distinction during the operations for the relief of Kimberley, the rounding up of General Piet Cronje, and particularly at Poplar Grove (7 March 1900) during the advance on Bloemfontein. After the fall of Pretoria he commanded a mixed force which, based on Bloemfontein, occupied a section of the lines of communication, and he was also in charge of a group of mobile columns. His services gained the high praise of Roberts and were recognized by his appointment as K.C.B. in 1901. In 1902 he was promoted lieutenant-general and in the following year was appointed commander-in-chief, Scottish district (later Command). He retired in 1905 and, being a close personal friend of King Edward VII, he was appointed G.C.V.O. in that year. He spent many years of his retirement at Biarritz: but soon military duties brought him home every year, for he was colonel of the Cheshire Regiment from 1909 to 1911 and thereafter colonel of the South Staffordshire Regiment, an honour of which he was extremely proud. He was appointed G.C.B. in 1912.

Tucker was twice married: first, in 1865 to Matilda Frederica (died 1897), daughter of John Hayter, younger brother of Sir George Hayter [q.v.], painter-in-ordinary to Queen Victoria, and had two sons and a daughter; secondly, in 1902 to Ellen Mary (died 1945), only daughter of Sir Maurice James O'Connell, second baronet. He died at Biarritz 22 December 1935, and was buried with full military honours at his Devon home, Ashburton.

Tucker is probably best known for his forcefulness of expression; tales about him are legion and his reputation on this score is legendary. But he was no less forceful in action. A firm disciplinarian, he hated red tape; he could stand up to higher authority if he thought that the services of his subordinates or the welfare of his men were receiving inadequate recognition or consideration. Hence, during his eighty years' service, he was both greatly loved and highly respected, combining, as he did in a most marked degree, the qualities of humour and humanity.

Two portraits of Tucker in the mantle of a Knight Grand Cross of the Bath, by H. A. Olivier, are in the possession of the South Staffordshire Regiment, and one of them is to be seen in the regimental museum at Davidson House, Lichfield.

[*The Times*, 24 December 1935; regimental papers; J. P. Jones, *History of the South Staffordshire Regiment*, 1923; personal knowledge.]   G. DAWES.

TURNOR, CHRISTOPHER HATTON (1873–1940), agricultural and social reformer, was born at Toronto, Canada, 23 November 1873, the only child of Christopher Hatton Turnor, whose family had been seated at Stoke Rochford, near Grantham, since the second half of the seventeenth century. He was great-grandson of the antiquary Edmund Turnor [q.v.]. His mother was Alice Margaret, eldest daughter of Hamilton H. Killally, of Toronto, whose family had Canadian blood on one side, a fact of which the subject of this notice was proud. His parents were ardent Plymouth Brethren, and he acquired an unconventional education with them as a boy, while they crusaded up and down North America, from Canada to Florida. There followed a period of residence at the Royal Agricultural College, Cirencester, after which he matriculated at Christ Church, Oxford, and graduated in 1896. On leaving the university, he studied architecture, and the Watts Picture Gallery at Compton, in Surrey, and a few private houses are evidence of the quality of his work.

In 1903, however, on the sudden death of his uncle, Turnor succeeded to Stoke Rochford Hall and the family estates in Lincolnshire of some 24,000 acres, and architecture had to be relegated to the background. It was a difficult time for the young heir, for agriculture had hardly then emerged from the great depression, and he had to take over some 4,000 acres of land in hand, which was being farmed at a loss. Turnor set himself to study the problems of administration. He was not prepared to acquiesce in the conventional attitude of many of his contemporaries towards their estates. He did not believe that there was no future in the land, nor could he rest content in the mere enjoyment of its amenities. The ownership of land was a trust, and he was convinced that there was a great work to be done by anyone prepared to devote himself to it in the spirit of adventure. Over most of England agricultural development had been at a standstill for five-and-twenty years, and he threw himself with zest into the inauguration of a new era of estate management on his property. One half of the land in hand was soon re-let, and highly qualified farm managers, one of them a Dane, were placed in charge of the rest. A tenant was found for the mansion at Stoke Rochford and for much of the shooting. Housing for the rural worker, the evolution of the stereotyped local agriculture, and the provision of small holdings as stepping stones for enterprising farm workers emerged as Turnor's particular interests. But he did not confine himself to agriculture, and in later years, when he had resumed occupation of his great mansion at Stoke Rochford, he devoted most of it to summer schools for teachers and for Workers' Educational Association students, and to conferences, both organized and informal, on social and religious questions. The development of education, indeed, might be regarded as his most enduring work. His agricultural activities made few converts, but he was a convincing speaker at any gathering at which educational reform was the subject for discussion, and he gave his time and services extensively to this cause. The fruits of his enthusiasm are to be seen in the teachers' training college which has been established in the mansion at Stoke Rochford. He was the author of the following books, which embody not only his theories but also his experience: *Land Problems and National Welfare* (1911); *Our Food Supply* (1916); *The Land and the Empire* (1917); *The Land and its Problems* (1921); *Yeoman Calling* (1939), and of some pamphlets and articles.

Turnor married in 1907 Sarah Marie Talbot, only child of Admiral Walter Cecil Carpenter, of Kiplin, Northallerton, Yorkshire; there was no issue of the marriage. He died at Torquay 19 August 1940, and was succeeded at Stoke Rochford by his first cousin, Major Herbert Broke Turnor.

[*The Times*, 22 August 1940; personal knowledge.]   C. S. ORWIN.

TUTTON, ALFRED EDWIN HOWARD (1864–1938), crystallographer and alpinist, was born at Stockport 22 August 1864, the only child of James Tutton, Venetian blind manufacturer, by his wife, Martha Howard. Leaving the national school, Edgeley, at the age of thirteen Tutton entered the office of the town clerk of Stockport, and in the evenings attended classes at the Mechanics Institute and chemistry lectures by (Sir)

Henry Roscoe [q.v.] at the Owens College, Manchester. In 1883 on the results of examinations of the Science and Art Department he gained a royal exhibition to the Normal School (later Royal College) of Science and Royal School of Mines at South Kensington, where he won the Murchison medal for geology and the prizes for physics and chemistry. After a fourth year, with a teaching scholarship, he became an assistant demonstrator in chemistry, being promoted full demonstrator and lecturer in 1889.

During the years 1886 to 1892 Tutton assisted (Sir) Edward Thorpe [q.v.] in research work on the oxides of phosphorus in relation to the 'phossy jaw' disease of match-makers. The beautiful crystals of the new tetroxide (P_2O_4) turned his attention to crystallography which then in private laboratories at his successive homes became his life's work. He specialized on the precise measurement of the morphological, optical, elasticity, and thermal expansion constants of artificially grown crystals of various isomorphous series. One large series of hydrated double sulphates and selenates of alkali and bivalent metals came to be known as 'Tutton salts'. He demonstrated that in each series these physical constants vary with the atomic weights of the replacing chemical elements. All his work was marked by the highest degree of accuracy down to the minutest detail. With a modified form of his interferometer the length of the imperial standard yard was determined in 1931 in terms of the wave-length of light, his result being 1,420,210 wave-lengths of the red cadmium line at 62 degrees Fahrenheit.

In 1895 Tutton was appointed inspector of technical schools under the Board of Education, being located successively in Oxford, London, and Plymouth. While in Oxford he took the degrees of D.Sc. (1903) and M.A. by decree of convocation (1905). On retiring from the Board of Education in 1924, Tutton lived in Cambridge, lecturing on chemical crystallography until 1931 when he settled at Dallington, Sussex, where he died 14 July 1938. He married in 1902 Margaret Ethel MacLannahan, youngest daughter of William Loat, of Cumnor Place, near Oxford, and had two sons and four daughters.

Tutton wrote five books on crystals and crystallography; his *Crystallography and Practical Crystal Measurement* (1911; 2nd ed., 2 vols., 1922) remains a standard treatise. His recreations were music and alpine photography. For thirty years holidays were spent in the Alps and from his numerous photographs lantern slides were made for his lectures. He wrote *The Natural History of Ice and Snow*, illustrated from the Alps (1927) and *The High Alps* (1931). He was a fellow of the Chemical Society for fifty years, was elected F.R.S. in 1899, and was president of the Mineralogical Society from 1912 to 1915. He received the honorary degree of D.Sc. from Manchester University in 1926.

[*Obituary Notices of Fellows of the Royal Society*, No. 7, January 1939 (portrait); *Mineralogical Magazine*, June 1939 (portrait); *Nature*, 20 August 1938; personal knowledge.]   L. J. SPENCER.

TWEED, JOHN (1869-1933), sculptor, was born in Glasgow 21 January 1869, the elder son of John Tweed, publisher, of Glasgow, by his second wife, Elizabeth Montgomery. He was educated at Hutcheson's Boys' Grammar School, Glasgow. In 1885 his father's death necessitated his leaving school in order to take his part in the family business. His natural talent for drawing and modelling occupied his leisure hours, and a little later a teaching scholarship at the Glasgow School of Art gave him the opportunity to develop this more seriously. During these years he worked with the sculptors G. A. Lawson [q.v.], J. A. Ewing, and J. Pittendrigh Macgillivray.

Setting his heart upon the career of a sculptor, Tweed was able to sell the publishing business, and in 1890 he left Glasgow for London, where he had been promised a teaching appointment. This appointment, however, came to nothing, and instead Tweed was taken into the studio of (Sir William) Hamo Thornycroft [q.v.]. During the next two years he received instruction first at the Lambeth School of Art and then at the Royal Academy Schools. Success in a competition for a group of figures on the façade of a public building in Edinburgh, and several private commissions for portrait busts enabled Tweed to visit Paris in 1893 and to make the acquaintance of the sculptor Auguste Rodin, whom he especially admired. This acquaintance quickly developed into a warm friendship, to be terminated only by Rodin's death in 1917. While in Paris Tweed worked for a few months at the École des Beaux Arts under Jean Alexandre Joseph Falguière. In

October 1893 he returned to London in order to execute his first important commission. This came from Cecil Rhodes and was for a relief representing 'The Landing of Van Riebeck', destined to decorate Rhodes's residence at Groote Schuur. The model for this work was exhibited at the Royal Academy in 1894. Although Tweed's dealings with Rhodes were marked by some differences of feeling on either side, this South African commission was followed by others, notably for full-length statues of Van Riebeck in Cape Town (1899) and of Rhodes himself at Bulawayo (1902).

During the next ten years Tweed made a considerable name as a portrait and memorial sculptor. In 1902 he was offered a commission which resulted in an acrimonious controversy; this was to carry to their conclusion the designs of Alfred Stevens [q.v.] for the memorial to the Duke of Wellington in St. Paul's Cathedral. The controversy was too involved and drawn out to be described here; but when the memorial—a bronze equestrian statue —was unveiled in 1912, it met with general approval. In the meantime Tweed had carried out several important memorial statues, including those to the third Lord Chesham at Aylesbury (1910), Captain James Cook at Whitby (1912), and Lord Clive in Charles II Street, St. James's Square (1912).

Tweed spent the greater part of the years of the war of 1914-1918 in London. During this period he executed a memorial bust of Joseph Chamberlain [q.v.] which was unveiled in Westminster Abbey in 1916, and the recumbent marble effigy of Sir William Anson [q.v.] for All Souls College Chapel, Oxford (1918). In the last named year he spent some months in France, commissioned by General Smuts to make sketches for a South African war memorial; this scheme, however, was not carried out. After the armistice he was more than ever occupied with memorial statuary: he executed in all twelve large-scale works between this date and 1930, notably war memorials for the King's Royal Rifle Corps at Winchester (1922) and for the Rifle Brigade in Grosvenor Place, London (1925); a memorial to Lord Kitchener on the Horse Guards Parade (1925); and two memorials to Cecil Rhodes, at Salisbury, Rhodesia (1928), and Mafeking (1932). He also executed a statue of Lord Ronaldshay for Calcutta (1923). During this period he found time to travel abroad, twice to Egypt, and, in

1928, to South Africa, where he was able to see for the first time many of his works in their final situations.

Tweed's last large-scale undertaking was the Peers' war memorial in the House of Lords, which was unveiled in 1932. In June 1933 a comprehensive exhibition of his work was held at Messrs. Knoedler's Galleries, London. His heart had been failing for some time and he died in London 12 November 1933. He married in 1895 Edith, second daughter of William Clinton, auctioneer, of Aldershot, and had a son and two daughters. A memorial exhibition of his work was held at the Imperial Institute, South Kensington, in June 1934.

Although Tweed's work is chiefly notable for its rugged power, some of his female portrait busts have considerable grace and charm. The influence of Rodin is sometimes apparent.

A portrait of Tweed by Theodore Roussel is in the possession of the family.

[*The Times*, 13 November 1933; Lendal Tweed and Francis Watson, *John Tweed, Sculptor. A Memoir*, 1936 (with list of works); Ulrich Thieme and Felix Becker, *Allgemeines Lexikon der Bildenden Künstler*, vol. xxxiii, 1939; *Art Journal*, February 1910; private information.]　　　　　　JAMES LAVER.

TWEEDSMUIR, first BARON (1875–1940), author and governor-general of Canada. [See BUCHAN, JOHN.]

TYNAN, KATHARINE (1861–1931), poet and novelist. [See HINKSON.]

UNWIN, SIR RAYMOND (1863–1940), architect, was born at Rotherham, Yorkshire, 2 November 1863, the younger son of William Unwin, an Oxford private coach, by his wife, Elizabeth, daughter of James Sully, of Bridgwater. He was educated at Magdalen School and was afterwards trained for the professions of engineering and architecture, in the latter of which he began to practice in 1896 in partnership with Richard Barry Parker. In this association he first came into prominence by their planning in 1904 the New Earswick model village, near York, for the Joseph Rowntree Village Trust [see ROWNTREE, JOSEPH, 1836–1925]; and afterwards, on a larger scale, the partners designed the first Garden City at Letchworth and the Hampstead Garden Suburb, which was opened in 1907. After 1910, when he organized the Town Planning Conference of the Royal Institute of British Architects, the architectural side of Unwin's life was almost wholly devoted to town planning. From 1911 he was lecturer in town planning at the university of Birmingham until in 1914 he became chief town planning inspector under the Local Government Board. The war of 1914–1918 gave him fresh opportunities, for under the Ministry of Munitions he designed the towns growing round such munition factories as Gretna Green, and thereafter he returned to the Ministry of Health as chief architect and later chief technical officer for building and town planning. His most widely influential contributions to planning may be considered to be in the report drawn up by the Committee on Housing of which Sir (John) Tudor Walters was chairman (1918) and in the Ministry of Health's *Housing Manual* (1918), and these led to his serving on a great number of planning committees such as the Building Research Board of the Department of Scientific and Industrial Research. He retired from the civil service in 1928, but his activities were not reduced. From 1929 to 1933 he served as technical adviser to the Greater London Regional Town Planning Committee, and from 1931 to 1933 as president of the Royal Institute of British Architects, the gold medal of which he was awarded in 1937. But in 1936 he was appointed visiting professor of town planning at Columbia University, and this to some extent severed his connexion with Great Britain, for he was still holding the post when he died at Lyme, Connecticut, 29 June 1940.

There was a political side to Unwin's life. In his young days he joined the Fabian Society and spoke frequently for the labour 'church' and the Ancoats 'brotherhood', and this led him during the war of 1914–1918 to become a member of a small group which aimed at promoting a league of nations. The fusion of this group with another, quite independent of it, under H. G. Wells, brought about the League of Nations Union, of the committee of which Unwin was an active and constructive member.

Unwin received many honours: he was knighted in 1932, and the universities of Prague, Toronto, Manchester, Trondhjem, and Harvard conferred honorary degrees upon him. He married in 1893 Ethel, elder daughter of Robert Parker, bank manager, of Chesterfield and Buxton, and sister of his partner. By her he had a son, who predeceased him, and a daughter. His work on *Town Planning in Practice* (1909) is a classic in its subject, and has been translated into French, German, and Russian. There is a portrait by Sir George Clausen in the rooms of the Royal Institute of British Architects.

[*The Times*, 1 July 1940; *Annual Register*, 1940; private information; personal knowledge.]   BARRY PARKER.

UNWIN, WILLIAM CAWTHORNE (1838–1933), engineer, was born at Coggeshall, Essex, 12 December 1838, the eldest son of William Jordan Unwin, pastor of the Congregational chapel at Woodbridge, Suffolk, and later principal of the Congregational theological college at Homerton, by his wife, Eliza Davey, daughter of J. Bailey Tailer, of Woodbridge. He attended the City of London School (1848–1854) and studied science for a year at New College, St. John's Wood, passing the London matriculation examination in 1855 with honours in chemistry, and by dint of study in the evenings he graduated B.Sc. (London) in 1861.

By personal introduction Unwin obtained in 1856 his first appointment as scientific assistant in Manchester to (Sir) William Fairbairn [q.v.], who was then devoting increasing attention to research. During the next six years he assisted Fairbairn in important researches, including those on the strength of boiler flues, on the laws governing the density and expansion of steam at higher temperatures, and on the properties of saturated steam. Unwin took a leading part in the trials of the Fay and Newall continuous mechanical railway brakes in 1859, which resulted in the general application of continuous brakes to all passenger rolling stock. He was also largely concerned with Fairbairn's famous early experiments on the fatigue of wrought iron girders (1860–1862), and the work of the Admiralty special committee on iron for shipbuilding. In 1862 Unwin became works manager to Messrs. Williamson & Brothers, of Kendal, but continued to correspond with Fairbairn on technical matters. At Kendal he was concerned with the construction of turbines and waterwheels and initiated his subsequent work on hydraulics. In the winter of 1864–1865 he gave to the Royal Engineers at Chatham, on Fairbairn's recommendation, his first engineering lecture. In 1866 he returned to Manchester as manager of the engine department of the Fairbairn Engineering Company.

Unwin's inclination was towards teaching, and in 1867 he returned to Homerton. Between 1868 and 1871 he prepared and delivered five different courses of lectures to the Royal Engineers on a wide range of civil and mechanical engineering subjects. In 1869 he was appointed an instructor in marine engineering at the Royal School of Naval Architecture and Marine Engineering at South Kensington, the forerunner of the present Royal Naval College, Greenwich.

The Royal Indian Engineering College was opened at Coopers Hill, Egham, in 1871, for the training of engineers for the public services in India. Unwin was appointed professor of hydraulics and mechanical engineering in 1872. Here, in addition to his teaching duties, he carried out much original work. The first edition of his famous text-book, *The Elements of Machine Design*, was published in 1877. He contributed the article on hydraulics to the *Encyclopædia Britannica* (1881), which was for many years a foremost English authority; it was reprinted separately as a *Treatise on Hydraulics* in 1907. Another work which became a leading text-book was his *Testing of Materials of Construction*, published in 1883, with further editions in 1899 and 1910.

In 1884 the Central Institution of the City and Guilds of London was being completed and Unwin was appointed professor of civil and mechanical engineering. He served as dean of the college from 1885 to 1896 and again from 1902 to 1904. When the Central Technical College was incorporated into London University in 1900 he became the first London University professor of engineering. The general organization which he then established was changed but little until the incorporation of the college into the larger Imperial College in 1910. In addition to administration and teaching he continued research on strength of materials, hydraulics, and steam power. In 1890 he was appointed, by the promoters of the Niagara Falls Power Company, secretary of the international commission established to assess the competitive designs for the first major hydro-electric power scheme. He took a prominent part in the development of the project and was appointed one of the three foreign consulting engineers to the company. In connexion with this work he visited the United States of America in 1892 and subsequent years, as well as Germany and France. He did much work on the Canadian Niagara Falls project, but refused an invitation to go to America permanently in charge of the work, preferring to retain his 'London work'. A development of his earlier work on pneumatic transmission in 1877, was his establishment of the principles of power transmission by compressed air.

At the same time Unwin took a prominent part from 1890 in the introduction and application of the internal combustion engine. He tested several, including the Priestman (1890), the Hornsby–Ackroyd (1894), and the Diesel (1897). His report on the last was a striking forecast of the development that has since taken place. He took up in 1893 the study of the stability of masonry dams for the water storage reservoirs then under construction, for hydro-electric power schemes for India, the Coolgardie water pipeline, and others. In his last paper before his retirement from his professorship in 1904 he developed the principles and formulae that have since been used generally for determining flow in gas mains. He undertook some of the earliest work for the Engineering Standards Committee and established dimensions for standard tensile test pieces.

After 1904, when he attended the International Engineering Congress at St. Louis, Unwin continued to be consulted on important projects and to give his services freely for the advancement of engineering practice. He took a principal part in the masonry dam controversy of 1905–1908, when his practical rational analyses were vindicated fully against the incorrect mathematical premises of his opponents. He was a British representative at the meeting in New York of the International Society for the Testing of Materials in 1912. He was a principal influence in fixing membership qualifications by examination for the leading technical institutions. For many years he gave much time to this work, in addition to serving on the governing bodies of London University, the Imperial College, and the City and Guilds College. During the war of 1914–1918 Unwin served on a number of technical committees of the Ministry of Munitions. After the war he curtailed his activities but continued to serve occasionally on government committees and to produce original contributions on engineering and educational problems. He was the first recipient, in 1921, of the Kelvin medal. His last important work was a report for the consulting engineers on the stresses in the Mersey Tunnel in 1922.

Unwin's technical interests were re-markably widespread and he attained eminence in all. His work on strength of materials, hydraulics, and water and steam power started at the beginning of his career; he continued to produce original work in them throughout his life. His work on masonry dams and on the establishment of the principles of design of reinforced concrete is balanced by his research work on steam and steam engines. He investigated the work of the pioneers of the internal combustion engine and was a leader in the advancement of engineering education and training.

Unwin was elected F.R.S. in 1886 and received the honorary degree of LL.D. from Edinburgh University in 1905. He was president of the Institution of Civil Engineers in 1911 and of the Institution of Mechanical Engineers in 1915; he was an honorary member of eight technical societies, and wrote numerous papers, lectures, and addresses. He died, unmarried, in Kensington 17 March 1933.

A portrait in oils of Unwin by Wilfred Waters is in the Institution of Civil Engineers; another, by Harold Speed, is in the Institution of Mechanical Engineers. A copy of the etching by Alphonse Legros is in the Imperial College of Science and Technology.

[E. G. Walker, *The Life and Work of William Cawthorne Unwin* (with bibliography), 1947 (privately 1938); *Obituary Notices of Fellows of the Royal Society*, No. 3, December 1934 (portrait); *Minutes of Proceedings* of the Institution of Civil Engineers, vol. ccxxxvi, 1934, p. 514; *Proceedings* of the Institution of Mechanical Engineers, vol. cxxiv, 1933, p. 789; *Transactions* of the American Society of Civil Engineers, vol. xcix, 1934, p. 361; *The Times*, 18 March 1933; personal knowledge.] E. G. WALKER.

VAUGHAN, WILLIAM WYAMAR (1865–1938), schoolmaster, was born at Hampstead 25 February 1865, the younger son of Henry Halford Vaughan [q.v.], regius professor of modern history at Oxford, by his wife, Adeline Maria, daughter of John Jackson, M.D., of the East India Company's service, the leading English physician in Calcutta. He was grandson of the judge Sir John Vaughan (1769–1839, q.v.), great-nephew of the physician Sir Henry Halford [q.v.], and first cousin through his mother of H. A. L. Fisher and Sir W. W. Fisher [qq.v.]. He was educated at Rugby, New College, Oxford, and the university of Paris. After fourteen years (1890–1904) spent as assistant master at Clifton College, where he was for long head of the modern side, he was appointed headmaster of Giggleswick School. Six years later (1910) he became master of Wellington College and in 1921 returned to his old school, Rugby, as the first lay headmaster since its very early days. He retired in 1931, and went to live at Princes Risborough.

Vaughan was president of the Modern Language Association in 1915, of the Incorporated Association of Headmasters in 1916, of the Science Masters Association in 1919, of the educational section of the British Association in 1925, and after his retirement his services were ever in great request on educational bodies. In 1932 he presided over the International Congress of Secondary Teachers and in 1935 he became chairman of the Central Council for School Broadcasting. He also served on the Consultative Committee of the Board of Education (1920–1926), on the government committee for considering the place of science in education, and on the Teachers' Registration Council (1928–1932), and he visited the Gold Coast as a member of the Advisory Committee on Education in the Colonies. It was as a delegate to the Indian Science Congress that he went to Agra in December 1937. While visiting the Taj Mahal he fell and broke his thigh. His leg was amputated, but he died of pneumonia at Agra 4 February 1938.

Broad-shouldered, broad-minded, large-hearted, Vaughan would have been a prominent figure in any walk of life: but that which he chose was particularly well suited to bring out his qualities. In him a rapid and sometimes explosive reaction to folly, neglect, or wrong-doing was tempered by a strong sense of justice, deep sympathies, and a keen sense of humour. He was fond of boys and understood them and he had a remarkable power of remembering their names and characteristics. In a time of much searching of heart in the educational world he showed that new ideas and methods can be assimilated without sacrificing what is valuable in the old, that freedom is not incompatible with discipline nor science with the humanities, and that school education is only the beginning of what should be a lifelong activity.

Vaughan was twice married: first, in 1898 to Margaret (died 1925), daughter of John Addington Symonds (1840–1893, q.v.), and had two sons, and a daughter who became principal of Somerville College, Oxford; secondly, in 1929 to Elizabeth, daughter of John Geldard, of Settle. He was appointed M.V.O. in 1920 and received the honorary degree of D.Litt. from Oxford University in 1931.

A portrait of Vaughan by Glyn Philpot is at Rugby.

[*The Times*, 5 February 1938; personal knowledge.]   H. C. BRADBY.

VESTEY, WILLIAM, first BARON VESTEY, of Kingswood (1859–1940), director of the Union Cold Storage Company, was born at Liverpool 21 January 1859, the eldest of the six sons of Samuel Vestey, provision broker, of Liverpool, by his wife, Hannah, daughter of William Uttley, of Westbar-in-Stansfield, Yorkshire. He was educated at the Liverpool Institute.

When he was seventeen years old Vestey was sent to the United States of America by his father to buy and ship home goods for him. Later he gave his attention to the canning business, and at thirty he had made so much money that he was able to retire and build himself a house at Freshfield near Southport. After a few years he grew tired of leisure, and went out to Argentina in order to study the preservation and storage of food by refrigeration. In conjunction with his brother, (Sir) Edmund Vestey, he started a cold store at Liverpool, and soon operations were extended to London. From this beginning the Union Cold Storage Company grew, with connexions in every part of the world. Having in 1906 begun to ship eggs, chickens, and other produce from China, the brothers acquired one or two boats, and converted them into refrigerated steamers. These were the beginnings of the Blue Star Line. One of the most difficult periods of Vestey's career was his attempt to start freezing works at Port Darwin in Australia. Large tracts of land and many cattle were bought, with the intention of developing the meat industry in Australia, but labour difficulties arose, and after a struggle which lasted over eight years, the works were closed and others built in Argentina. There the shipping companies found themselves unable to guarantee sailings to England with the output of the factory. It was therefore decided that the Cold Storage Company should be its own carriers by increasing the number of ships of the Blue Star Line, which eventually owned the largest number of refrigerated steamers in the world. The Vesteys also acquired many retail shops in England. In the war of

1914–1918 the vast resources controlled by the company in ships, stores of cattle, and cold storage accommodation were freely placed at the disposal of the government.

Vestey and his brother deserve to be remembered as having done valuable service by improving the carriage by sea of meats and other perishable goods, and thus increasing the food supply of this country. In 1934 they made a notable gift to Liverpool, by offering to defray the cost, estimated at £220,000, of the tower of the cathedral: this gift was made in memory of their parents.

In 1913 Vestey was created a baronet, and in 1922 was raised to the peerage as Baron Vestey, of Kingswood, Surrey. He was twice married: first, in 1882 to Sarah (died 1923), daughter of George Ellis, of Tranmere, Birkenhead, and had four sons; secondly, in 1924 to Evelyn, daughter of Hans Brodstone, of Superior, Nebraska, U.S.A. Vestey died at Gerrards Cross 11 December 1940, and was succeeded as second baron by his eldest son, Samuel (born 1882).

[*The Times*, 12 December 1940.]
ALFRED COCHRANE.

VICTORIA ALEXANDRA OLGA MARY (1868–1935), princess of Great Britain and Ireland, was born at Marlborough House 6 July 1868, the fourth child and second daughter of the Prince and Princess of Wales. Living constantly at home as the only unmarried daughter, the princess was never much in the public eye except as the companion of her father and mother, but both at Marlborough House and at Buckingham Palace she made herself their indispensable helpmeet. During Queen Alexandra's widowhood she was her mother's inseparable companion, and it was not until her death that at the age of fifty-seven the princess gained independence in a household of her own at Coppins, Iver, in Buckinghamshire. There during the last ten years of her life she found rest in her favourite recreations of music and gardening, and gave full rein to her kindly feelings towards animals. She inherited to the full her mother's endless generosity and sympathy for those in need. If this benevolence seemed to others misplaced, such a consideration was never allowed to stand in the way of a benefaction, once she had decided to make it. She was a true and lovable friend, and no common bond of affection united her to her brother King George V, with whom scarcely a day passed without communication, and whose precarious health was further impaired by the shock of her death at Coppins 3 December 1935.

[*The Times*, 4 December 1935; personal knowledge.]   EDWARD SEYMOUR.

VINES, SYDNEY HOWARD (1849–1934), botanist, was born at Ealing 31 December 1849, the only child of William Reynolds Vines, a schoolmaster, by his wife, Jessie Robertson. For part of his early life he lived in Paraguay where his father had a sheep ranch. His formal education began at a Moravian school in Germany, where he acquired a command of the language, and was concluded at Dr. Dawes's school at Surbiton. Under paternal persuasion Vines began in 1869 a medical course at Guy's Hospital, but he disliked certain aspects of the work and, influenced by (Sir) Michael Foster [q.v.], decided to specialize in physiology, reading for a London science degree. In 1872 he won an entrance scholarship at Christ's College, Cambridge; the following year he took his London B.Sc. with first class honours and in December 1875 was placed first in the natural sciences tripos at Cambridge. He was elected to a fellowship and lecturership at Christ's in 1876. It was during the tenure of this fellowship that he 'personally may be said to have founded the new School of Botany soon to expand under the hands of those who were, for the most part, his own pupils'.

In 1870 academic botany in Great Britain was moribund. There were no laboratories and the microscopical and experimental methods, which had already yielded brilliant results on the continent, were unknown. In that year T. H. Huxley [q.v.] began a short practical class in biology for intending school-teachers at the Royal School of Mines, South Kensington. As the course expanded the plant section of the work was handed over to (Sir) W. T. Thistleton-Dyer [q.v.], who invited Vines to assist him during the summer sessions of 1875 and 1876. When Vines began his college lectures at Christ's in the autumn of 1876 it was his practical acquaintance with his subject-matter that made his presentation a revelation to the small, but very able, group of men attending them. But there was no laboratory work and Vines, wishing to gain further experience before he organized such courses, spent the summer of 1877 working with Julius von Sachs at Würzburg. During the following Michaelmas term laboratory work was started at Cambridge in a room lent by Foster and equipped with microscopes and apparatus bought at the lecturer's own expense. It was a personal venture; the elderly professor, Charles Cardale Babington, did not approve and the university officially stood by and watched. The venture was a great success. In 1881 some room was allotted at the Botanic Gardens; two years later Vines was made a reader; and by 1887 a building large enough to take classes of up to a hundred had been provided. But Vines, full of enthusiasm, ready to repeat his practical classes two or three times because of limitation of space, and prepared to work the whole night through, if need be, lecturing, teaching, translating, and writing, may have overtaxed his strength and laid the foundations of ill health that influenced his subsequent long life.

Vines was elected to the Sherardian professorship at Oxford (including a fellowship at Magdalen College) in 1888, with the further responsibilities of a botanic garden and a herbarium, but without the stimulus of numbers of enthusiastic students; he had, moreover, to be careful of his health. During the short tenure of the chair by (Sir) Isaac Bayley Balfour [q.v.] a degree of reorganization of the small department had been made. It was thought to be sufficiently equipped for the needs of its small elementary classes, but facilities for research did not exist, and it was not until twenty-three years later that Vines was able to secure any considerable addition to the laboratory. The energy which he had displayed at Cambridge seemed to have exhausted itself, and except for his period of office as president of the Linnean Society (1900–1904), notable for the decision to admit women to fellowship in 1903, he was rarely seen by his contemporaries. He did not go to congresses; illness prevented him from attending the British Association meeting of 1900 when he was president of the botanical section; and he became almost a legendary figure to the younger men. He retired in 1919 and shortly afterwards went to live at Exmouth where he died 4 April 1934.

Vines had an acquisitive and critical rather than a constructive mind. He translated the second English edition of Sachs's *Textbook of Botany* (1882) and in 1886 published his own *Lectures on the Physiology of Plants*. He was not an experimenter, and although he contributed an important series of papers on proteolytic enzymes in plants, literary work appealed to him more strongly than laboratory experimentation. He found pleasure in the historical treasures of the Oxford department and collaborated with George Claridge Druce [q.v.] in books on the Dillenian (1907) and Morisonian (1914) herbaria. He was one of the group of botanists whose memorial to the Clarendon Press led to the foundation of the *Annals of Botany* in 1887, and he edited that journal for the first eleven years (1887–1899) of its existence.

Vines was elected F.R.S. in 1885 at the early age of thirty-five. In 1897 he was elected an honorary fellow of his Cambridge college. He had been an honorary fellow of the university of London since 1892.

Vines married in 1884 Agnes Bertha, eldest daughter of Walter Woodcock Perry, brewer, of Chelmsford. He had two sons, of whom the elder, Walter Sherard, became professor of English language and literature at University College, Hull, and a daughter. By his contemporaries and friends he was regarded as a man of exceptional ability with social charm, wide interests, and a delight in music. Although not a mountaineer, he regularly visited the Engadine and took a delight in alpine botany.

A portrait of Vines by John Collier (1905) is in the possession of the Linnean Society.

[*Obituary Notices of Fellows of the Royal Society*, No. 3, December 1934 (portrait); *Proceedings* of the Linnean Society, October 1933–May 1934 (portrait); *Journal of Botany*, vol. lxxii, 1934; J. Reynolds Green, *A History of Botany*, 1914; F. O. Bower, *Sixty Years of Botany in Britain*, 1938 (portrait); *Kew Bulletin*, 1934; *New Phytologist*, vol. xxiv, 1925; *The Times*, 6 April 1934; *Nature*, 5 May 1934; private information.]

T. G. B. OSBORN.

WADDELL, LAWRENCE AUGUSTINE (later AUSTINE) (1854–1938), medical officer in the Indian government service, traveller, and orientalist, was born at Cumbernauld, Dumbartonshire 29 May 1854, the son of Thomas Clement Waddell, D.D., schoolmaster and author, by his wife, Jean, youngest daughter of John Chapman, of Banton, Stirlingshire. From a private school he entered the university of Glasgow, where in 1878 he graduated (M.B., M.Ch.) with the highest honours. After being resident surgeon in the Western Infirmary, Glasgow, he entered the Indian medical service in

1880. For ten years from 1885 he was assistant sanitary commissioner and from 1888 to 1895 he was medical officer for the Darjeeling district. From 1896 for six years he was professor of chemistry and pathology in the Calcutta Medical College, and for four years editor of the *Indian Medical Gazette*. Accompanying military operations in Burma (1886–1887), Chitral (1895), Peking (1900), and the Mahsud blockade (1901–1902), he won military decorations on each occasion. In 1903 he served with the Malakand expeditionary force. His scientific publications include a memoir 'Are Venomous Snakes Autotoxic?' (*Scientific Memoirs by Medical Officers of the Army of India*, 1889), and an article on the 'Birds of Sikkim' (*Sikkim Gazette*, 1893).

Interest in Buddhism, first perhaps kindled by the time in Burma, led to Waddell's explorations of sites in the founder's country, in particular of the ancient capital, Pātaliputra, the Palibothra of the Greeks, and the identification of Buddha's birthplace, on the Nepal border: also in the course of his military services on the North-Western Frontier he acquired material for papers on the early 'Indo-Grecian' Buddhist art of Gandhāra.

Visits to Darjeeling from 1884 and Waddell's subsequent official connexion with the district, besides leading up to a charming descriptive work, *Among the Himalayas* (1899), drew him to the study of Tibet and Tibetan Buddhism, concerning which he contributed numerous papers to orientalist journals and published a highly substantial and valuable treatise, entitled *The Buddhism of Tibet or Lamaism* (1894, 2nd ed. 1934). As chief medical officer accompanying the Tibetan expedition of 1904, and with a special commission, he superintended the official collections of literature and art, which were later distributed, together with one private collection of his own, to libraries in Calcutta, London, Oxford, and Cambridge. He published in 1905 *Lhasa and its Mysteries*. On his return to England he was from 1906 to 1908 professor of Tibetan at University College, London. His retirement to Scotland was marked, until about 1915, by contributions to European journals and encyclopædias, continuing his studies of Buddhism and Tibet.

In 1917 Waddell began to display interest in a new field, that of ancient relations of India to the Mesopotamian world. This led to large volumes such as *Indo-Sumerian Seals Deciphered* (1925) and a theory of an 'Aryan' origin of the Sumerian and Egyptian civilizations, and, more generally, of the 'Aryans' as *The Makers of Civilization in Race and History* (1929) and the ultimate source of *The British Edda Reconstructed from Mediaeval MSS.* (1930). These works, containing much painstaking research and impressive to many, did not win the approval of experts.

Waddell received in 1895 the honorary degree of LL.D. from the university of Glasgow. He was appointed C.I.E. (1901) and C.B. (1904). He married in 1895 Amy Louise Reeves, and had a son, who was killed in the war of 1914–1918, and a daughter. He died at Craigmore, Rothesay, 19 September 1938.

[*Glasgow Herald*, 20 September 1938; *Journal* of the Royal Asiatic Society of Great Britain and Ireland, 1939; personal knowledge.]   F. W. Thomas.

WAGGETT, PHILIP NAPIER (1862–1939), divine and preacher, was born in London 27 February 1862, the second of the three sons of John Waggett, a distinguished London physician, by his wife, Florence Whitchurch, who was descended from non-juring ancestors. His younger brother, Ernest, followed his father's profession and became consulting surgeon to the Charing Cross Hospital. Waggett was educated at Charterhouse and at Christ Church, Oxford, where, as an exhibitioner, he was awarded a first class in natural science (1884) and, after a year's work, a second class in theology (1885). His interest in natural science never died away, and at the end of the century he impressed so exacting a critic as S. J. Gee [q.v.] with the width of his reading and the thoroughness of his knowledge of the latest medical theories. At Oxford he came under the influence of such leaders as Charles Gore, E. S. Talbot, Francis Paget, and H. S. Holland [qq.v.], whom he astonished by his intellectual quickness.

Waggett was ordained deacon in 1885 and priest in 1886. Drawn like very many of the young Anglo-Catholic clergy of the time to work in slums, he joined the staff of Henry Luke Paget, later bishop of Chester, at St. Frideswide's church, Poplar, accompanying him in 1887 to St. Pancras church. In 1889 Waggett accepted the headship of the Charterhouse mission in Southwark, where he proved a keen and tireless parish worker, although he found some of his duties uncongenial and confessed to a 'constitutional dislike of high spirits' which made the management of boys' clubs very difficult. The evangelical bishop of Rochester, A. W. Thorold [q.v.], heartily disliked the services, cassocks, and birettas of his Anglo-Catholic clergy, but he yielded to the brilliance of Waggett's conversation. In 1892 Waggett joined the Society of St. John the Evangelist, Cowley, and four years later went to South Africa as priest-in-charge of St. Philip's church, Cape Town; after three years he returned to England to gain fame as a preacher, missioner, and conductor of 'retreats'.

In 1911 Waggett was made head of St. Anselm's House, an unsuccessful attempt to establish a Pusey House at Cambridge; and on the outbreak of war in 1914 he immediately offered himself as a chaplain in the army. These years as an army chaplain were probably the happiest of his life: he was twice mentioned in dispatches and in 1918 he was sent to Palestine to fill a special position on Sir Edmund Allenby's staff. Among his duties was negotiation with the many, and always difficult, ecclesiastics in the Levant, and he used to relate with particular zest the story of his relations with the Catholicos of Kut. The war over, he delivered the Hulsean lectures at Cambridge in 1920 (he had been appointed lecturer for 1914-1915) and, after going to India with the Mission of Help in 1922-1923, he was lecturer to the General Theological Seminary in New York in 1924. At home, he had been elected a proctor in convocation for the diocese of Oxford in 1922, and he took part in the debates on the revision of the Prayer Book. In 1927 his community allowed him to accept the living of St. Mary's the Great, Cambridge, but by now he was physically a broken man, and he failed to exercise the influence in the university which had been expected. So, when he resigned in 1930, he retired to spend most of the nine remaining years of his life at Cowley, unable to take any part in the services and easily wearied by the visits of the friends whom he cherished. He died in a nursing home at Parkstone, Dorset, where he had been living with his sisters, 4 July 1939.

From his own university Waggett received the honorary degree of D.D. in 1921. During the years before the war he published two notable books; *The Heart of Jesus* (1902), a series of Holy Week sermons delivered at St. Paul's Cathedral, and *The Scientific Temper in Religion* (1905). He was one of the most gifted figures in what may be called the third period of the Catholic revival in the Church of England. He was a scientist, a theologian, a philosopher, a monk, and withal a brilliant and witty conversationalist with a love of paradox that startled and sometimes shocked. In common with many other of her outstanding sons, he was a priest whom his Church delighted not to honour.

[*The Times*, 6 July 1939; private information; personal knowledge.]

SIDNEY DARK.

WAIN, LOUIS WILLIAM (1860-1939), artist, notable for his drawings of cats, was born in London 5 August 1860, the eldest son of William Matthew Wain, embroiderer, of Leek, Staffordshire, by his wife, Felicia Marie Boiteux, who came from Paris. He was educated by the Christian Brothers at St. Joseph's Academy, Kennington, and by private tutors. At first he intended to make music his profession, but from 1877 to 1880 he also studied at the West London School of Art, where he was an assistant master from 1881 to 1882, and he came to devote his energies more and more to drawing. In 1882 he joined the staff of the *Illustrated Sporting and Dramatic News* and in 1886 that of the *Illustrated London News*; from 1907 to 1910 he visited New York, where he worked for the *New York American*.

Wain first drew cats, of which he was a devotee, in 1883, and these became a few years later the principal subject of his art. A rapid worker, he could produce as many as 600 drawings in a single year, and the list of his cat books occupies several columns of the British Museum Catalogue. His original treatment of cats, which he usually depicted as human beings in comical situations, quickly took the public fancy, and by the 'nineties his name had become a household word. In 1901 he started *Louis Wain's Annual*, which he ran for many years. But during the war of 1914-1918 he lost his popularity; there was hardly any demand for his drawings; and although he did some film cartoon work he sank into poverty. Lacking business acumen, when he sold his drawings he parted with his rights in them; moreover, he had squandered his savings in a rash commercial enterprise while he was living in New York.

In 1884 Wain had married Emily Marie, daughter of Thomas Richardson, fruiterer.

His wife died, childless, two years later after a long and painful illness. This bereavement cast a heavy shadow over his life and induced a melancholy which was in striking contrast to his mirthful drawings. After the war mental illness, largely the result of financial anxiety on account of his sisters with whom he had long made his home at Brondesbury, gradually declared itself, and in 1923 he was certified as insane. Two years later, he was rescued from the pauper ward of an asylum and, by the aid of a fund which was raised on his behalf, was transferred to the Bethlem Royal Hospital, where, among other amenities, he was supplied with the materials of his art. An exhibition of his work was held in London at the Twenty-One Gallery in October and November 1925. He died at Napsbury, near St. Albans, 4 July 1939.

[*The Times*, 7 July 1939; *Souvenir of Louis Wain's Work*, 1925 (portrait).]

M. R. TOYNBEE.

WALKER, SIR EMERY (1851–1933), process-engraver and typographical expert, was born in Paddington 2 April 1851, the eldest of the three sons of Emery Walker, a coachbuilder, originally from Norfolk, who was compelled owing to blindness to relinquish his business when they were still children. His mother was Mary Anne Barber. After receiving a little schooling at St. Mark's College, Chelsea, he began at the age of fourteen to earn his living. He was engaged in a succession of more or less laborious occupations until the trend of his life was fixed by a chance encounter with a man of remarkable inventive gifts named Alfred Dawson, who perfected a form of etching devised in the 'forties by a certain Palmer, who called the process glyptography. In 1872 Dawson founded at 23 Farringdon Street the Typographic Etching Company, which was by far the oldest firm of process-engravers in this country. In the following year Walker joined him and remained with him until 1883, when he went into business with his brother-in-law, Robert Dunthorne, as a printseller. But finding this change uncongenial he returned in 1886 to his old pursuit and, in partnership with Walter Boutall, founded the firm of 'process and general engravers, draughtsmen, map-constructors, and photographers of works of art' known under the successive names of Walker & Boutall, Walker & Cockerell, and finally Emery Walker, Limited. Its office was at 16 Clifford's Inn,

next door to the chambers of Samuel Butler [q.v.], which led to much friendly intercourse. The works were at a Georgian house at Hammersmith, not far from Walker's own home in Hammersmith Terrace.

By good fortune there was another riverside dweller at Hammersmith who shared Walker's tastes to the full. This was William Morris [q.v.]. Their acquaintance, begun in 1883, quickly ripened into an affectionate comradeship which grew only the stronger as long as Morris lived. Although Morris was the more forceful character, each could tell the other much that he did not know, and they saw eye to eye on all important topics. Among the subjects in which they were both deeply interested was the art of typography, then at a low ebb. Out of their eager talks and some preliminary experiments arose the Kelmscott Press, which was established early in 1891 in modest premises close to Morris's Kelmscott House. Its output during the seven years of its existence was astonishing. It comprised fifty-two works in sixty-six volumes, all printed by hand, with type and ornaments designed by Morris. Walker had to decline to be a partner in this costly enterprise, as he had no capital to risk. Nevertheless, he was all the while a virtual partner, and no important step was taken without his advice and approval. This was not the only field in which he co-operated with Morris. In 1888 they joined Walter Crane [q.v.] and others in founding the Arts and Crafts Exhibition Society, the parent stock from which many kindred societies sprang. To the catalogue of its first exhibition Walker contributed an article on typography in which important principles were laid down for the first time. At about the same period he was elected to the committee of the Society for the Protection of Ancient Buildings, founded in 1877 by Morris and the architect Philip Webb [q.v.]. These men were prominent in a group supporting the then young and unpopular socialist movement. As secretary to the Hammersmith branch it was Walker's duty to organize Sunday evening lectures, some of them by men afterwards famous, in the little hall adjoining Morris's house.

Morris's death in 1896 was a crushing blow, but Walker braced himself to continue his artistic labours more persistently than ever. In 1900, in conjunction with T. J. Cobden-Sanderson [q.v.], he founded the Doves Press in a house in Hammersmith Terrace, a few doors from where they both lived. For this renowned press a type of great beauty and legibility, based on the fifteenth-century Venetian type used by the Frenchman Nicolas Jenson, was cut from drawings made under Walker's eye. Unfortunately, after nearly twenty volumes had appeared, including the five volumes of an English Bible (1903–1905), a disagreement caused a severance of the partnership, and from 1909 to the close of the press in 1916 Cobden-Sanderson carried on the Doves Press alone.

The Kelmscott and Doves presses will go down to typographical history, together with the Ashendene Press, as the stately precursors of the numerous private presses that have since come into being, and Walker's name will be inseparably connected with them. But his great reputation among students of typography rests on a far wider basis, for he was keenly preoccupied with the appearance of the everyday book, and not only with its rich relations. It is scarcely too much to say that his influence, direct or indirect, can be discerned in nearly every well-designed page of type that now appears, and that to him more than to any other man this century's great improvement in book production has been due.

Walker was knighted in 1930, and in May 1933, shortly before his death, was elected an honorary fellow of Jesus College, Cambridge. He was Sandars reader in bibliography at Cambridge University for 1924–1925. Although his schooling ended at the age of thirteen, his erudition was extraordinary. It was combined with great modesty and a most lovable nature. He married in 1877 Mary Grace (died 1920), daughter of William Jones, supervisor of inland revenue, Hammersmith, and had one daughter. He died at his home in Hammersmith 22 July 1933.

A portrait of Walker by Sir George Clausen hangs in the hall of the Art Workers' Guild in Queen Square, London.

[Sir Emery Walker (privately printed, with portrait), 1933; London Mercury, September 1933; personal knowledge.]

SYDNEY COCKERELL.

WALKER, SIR JAMES (1863–1935), chemist, was born at Dundee 6 April 1863, the only son of James Walker, a flax merchant in Dundee, by his wife, Susan Hutchison, daughter of Arthur Cairns, also of Dundee. His early education at Dundee High School awakened in him an interest in science, largely owing to the enthusiasm of a young master.

Although Walker passed the entrance examination for St. Andrews University at the age of sixteen he did not proceed there, but became an apprentice to a flax and jute spinner for three years; yet his early interest in science remained and he finally entered Edinburgh University in 1882. Here he met a galaxy of talent in his teachers, George Chrystal [q.v.], P. G. Tait [q.v.], and Alexander Crum Brown. In those days specialization had hardly been dreamed of, but Crum Brown soon diverted Walker's enthusiasm towards chemistry. Graduating B.Sc. in 1885, he intended to proceed to a doctor's degree but was discouraged in view of his youth. He overcame the difficulty by performing the necessary experimental work in University College, Dundee, during his vacations and graduated D.Sc. (Edin.) in 1886. At that time German chemistry was in its ascendancy and a chemist's training was not complete without taking a Ph.D. at a German university. Walker therefore proceeded in 1887 to Johann von Baeyer's laboratory in Munich, a stronghold of organic chemistry. The 'eighties saw, however, the vigorous growth of the new science of physical chemistry, its leading exponent being Wilhelm Ostwald who went to Leipzig in 1887. Walker succumbed to the attraction and joined heartily in the rapid development of this new branch of chemistry. Having obtained his Ph.D. at Leipzig, in 1889 he carried his new-found enthusiasm back to Edinburgh where he had been appointed research assistant to Crum Brown: he held this post for three years, his chief work being on electrolytic synthesis. After a year Walker's interest wandered again, this time to the laboratory of (Sir) William Ramsay [q.v.] in University College, London, at that time the leading centre for physical chemistry in the United Kingdom. He entered the laboratory in 1892, and in 1893 became Ramsay's second assistant.

In 1894 Walker was elected professor of chemistry at University College, Dundee, and threw himself immediately into the task of conducting extensive researches in aqueous solutions and to furthering the cause of physical chemistry in this country. He succeeded Crum Brown as professor of chemistry in Edinburgh University in 1908. The war of 1914–1918 interfered with academic work, and Walker devoted himself wholly to the war by setting up in Edinburgh in 1915 the manufacture of trinitrotoluene (T.N.T.), then in great demand as a high explosive. In 1918 he returned to the manifold problems of the post-war period. He planned and saw built one of the finest university chemical laboratories in the country and established a research school in it in order to provide the higher training for chemistry now required for the greatly increased British chemical industry. He retired in 1928.

Walker received many honours, both for his academic and his industrial work. The honorary degree of LL.D. was conferred upon him by the universities of St. Andrews (1909) and Edinburgh (1929). In 1900 he was elected a fellow of the Royal Society by which he was awarded the Davy medal in 1926. He was knighted in 1921. From 1921 to 1923 he was president of the Chemical Society. His book, *Introduction to Physical Chemistry* (1899, 10th ed. 1927), did much to further the cause of physical chemistry in the English-speaking world. His advice was widely sought on a great variety of matters and given with equal readiness.

Walker married in 1897 Annie Purcell, elder daughter of Lieutenant-Colonel William Sedgwick, of Godalming, and had one son. He died in Edinburgh 6 May 1935.

[*Obituary Notices of Fellows of the Royal Society*, No. 4, December 1935 (portrait); *Nature*, 25 May 1935; personal knowledge.]
H. W. MELVILLE.

WALLACE, (RICHARD HORATIO) EDGAR (1875–1932), novelist, playwright, and journalist, was born in Greenwich 1 April 1875, the son of Richard Horatio Edgar, an actor, and Mary Jane (Polly) Richards (née Blair), an actress. He was brought up by George Freeman, a Billingsgate fishporter, and his wife, kindly and respectable people who cared for the boy within their limited means. At the age of eleven he played truant to sell newspapers in Ludgate Circus a few yards from the site of the bronze plaque which now commemorates him, and from the age of twelve, when he left an elementary school in Peckham, he was successively employed as a printer's boy, as a newsboy, in a shoe shop, in a mackintosh cloth factory, in a Grimsby trawler, as a milk roundsman, and as a road-maker and builder's labourer. At eighteen he enlisted in the Royal West Kent Regiment from which he transferred to the Medical Staff Corps and was drafted with it to South Africa in 1896. By this time he had produced his earliest work, a song for the comedian Arthur Roberts. In South Africa he wrote poems and articles for the *Cape Times* and other papers and later became successively a Reuter's correspondent and correspondent of the *Daily Mail*. In 1902 he became the first editor of the *Rand Daily Mail* in Johannesburg, and on his return to England again worked for the *Daily Mail*.

The first of the novels that were to make Wallace famous was *The Four Just Men* (1905), and this was followed by a series, most of which were sold outright for small sums, before he started on his West African stories, of which two were *Sanders of the River* (1911) and *Bones* (1915). Throughout his life he was interested principally in three activities; the stage, newspapers, and novel writing, and it would be true to say that he regarded them in that order of importance. His only relaxation was racing, and in the last few years of his life he owned and enjoyed a singularly unsuccessful string of race-horses. Graduating from music-hall songs and review sketches, he began to write plays, and his first dramatic success, *The Ringer* (Wyndham's Theatre, May 1926), marked the beginning of a phase in which his novels, such as *The Crimson Circle* (1922) and *The Green Archer* (1923), were being sold in their tens and hundreds of thousands, and he sometimes had two or three plays running in London at the same time. The novels for which he was most widely known were those detective stories in which, without the use of false clues or supernatural circumstances, a mysterious crime was solved and the criminals brought to justice: a simple formula on which the freshness and ingenuity of his invention worked a new pattern in every volume. His writing had simplicity, vigour, and pace, but it was the variety and originality of his plots that made his reputation: that, and his prolific output, since in twenty-eight years of authorship more than a hundred and seventy books of his were published. They were universally translated and his plays were produced in Europe, the British Empire, the United States of America, and the Scandinavian countries. His daily flow of magazine and newspaper articles was generally dictated to one of his secretaries, his novels were dictated to a dictaphone, and his plays were written by hand. He worked fast, and the best of his plays, *On the Spot* (1931), was written by him during a week-end.

Wallace married in South Africa in 1901 Ivy Maud (died 1926), daughter of William

Shaw Caldecott, a Wesleyan minister, of Simon's Town, and had two sons and a daughter. Their marriage was dissolved in 1918, and in 1921 he married Ethel Violet King (died 1933), by whom he had a daughter. At the general election of 1931 he stood unsuccessfully as liberal candidate for Blackpool. He died suddenly 10 February 1932 at Hollywood, California, where he had been writing motion picture stories. The first of these, *King Kong*, was produced shortly after his death. He was chairman of the Press Club from 1923 to 1925, inaugurated the Press Club Fund, and was one of the founder members of the Company of Newspaper Makers.

A portrait of Wallace by Tennyson Cole is at the Press Club. A bust was made by Jo Davidson.

[*The Times*, 11 February 1932; Edgar Wallace, *People. A Short Autobiography*, 1926; Margaret Lane, *Edgar Wallace*, 1938; E. V. Wallace, *Edgar Wallace*, 1932.]

FRANK DILNOT.

WALLAS, GRAHAM (1858–1932), political psychologist, was born at Monkwearmouth, Sunderland, 31 May 1858, the fifth child and elder son of Gilbert Innes Wallas, by his wife, Frances Talbot Peacock. His father, who in 1858 was curate at Bishopwearmouth, became in 1861 vicar of Barnstaple and later rector of Shobrooke, Devon.

Wallas was educated at Shrewsbury and went as a scholar to Corpus Christi College, Oxford, where he obtained a second class in classical moderations (1879) and in *literae humaniores* (1881). On leaving Oxford he became a classical schoolmaster, but resigned from the staff of Highgate School in 1885 'on a question of religious conformity', and in 1890 gave up school teaching for university extension lecturing. In 1886 he joined the Fabian Society, and in 1889 contributed to *Fabian Essays on Socialism*. He resigned from the society in 1904 in disapproval of its support of Joseph Chamberlain's tariff policy. In 1894 he was elected a member of the London school board, becoming chairman of its school management committee in 1897. In 1904, when the school board was merged in the London County Council, he was elected to that body, remaining a member for one three-year period. His experiences of London electioneering are reflected in his writings.

Already in 1895 Wallas had become a lecturer in the recently founded London School of Economics and Political Science, having previously been one of those who had planned the creation of that institution. In 1914 he was appointed to the newly created chair of political science, which he held until 1923. Between 1890 and 1928 he paid four visits to the United States of America, where he lectured. He received honorary degrees from the universities of Manchester (1922) and Oxford (1931).

Wallas published five books during his lifetime: *The Life of Francis Place* (1898), *Human Nature in Politics* (1908), *The Great Society* (1914), *Our Social Heritage* (1921), and *The Art of Thought* (1926): to these there must be added the half-finished *Social Judgment* (1934), a volume of collected essays entitled *Men and Ideas* (1940), and the essay on 'Property under Socialism' in *Fabian Essays*, already referred to. Of these, the *Life of Francis Place* is a work of historical research, based on Place's own records. The other four completed works are seminal in the true sense of that word. Wallas spent upon a single chapter the labour that most men spend on a book, and this has made his work a storehouse of suggestion for inquirers in many fields. In *Human Nature in Politics* he criticized the intellectualist assumptions current amongst political thinkers at that time, and pleaded for a closer association between psychological and political studies. He warned his readers that, until this had been brought about, the future of democracy would be in greater peril than was then realized. By 1914 the anti-intellectualist forces had shown themselves more clearly, and in the *The Great Society* Wallas urged the need for sustained thought in the task of humanizing modern large-scale life. In *Our Social Heritage*, a term of which he was the first to fix the meaning, he examined that part of human personality which is transmitted by the social process of teaching and learning. In *The Art of Thought* he examined the less conscious factors in thought in the light of his own experience as a teacher and administrator and of accounts given by poets and others who were not professed psychologists.

Wallas liked to describe himself as 'a working thinker', and much of his work was directed to the attempt to improve the mental processes of those who occupy their minds with public affairs. In this he marked a break with the prevailing radical and socialist tendency of his time which was more concerned with institutions and systems than with human beings. But he was also a lifelong promoter of the cause of social and political invention, deliberately using that term so as to mark the need for its extension from the purely mechanical field. As a teacher Wallas excelled equally with individual students or small groups, and as a platform lecturer. Through his books, his teaching, and his conversation he exerted a powerful influence over the thought of his time, and as the importance of the many issues to which he was the first to draw attention became more widely realized, his writings have gained increasing influence with the passing of the years.

Wallas married in 1897 Ada, daughter of George David Radford, draper, of Plymouth, a member of a family well known in the public life of that area. Herself an authoress, she shared in her husband's work and interests. They had one child, a daughter. He died at Portloe, Cornwall, 9 August 1932.

In the rooms at the London School of Economics dedicated to the memory of the 'founders' hang drawings of Wallas by Sir William Rothenstein and Robert Austin.

[Biographical note prefixed to *Men and Ideas*, edited by May Wallas, 1940; *Graham Wallas 1858–1932*: addresses given at the London School of Economics and Political Science, 19 October 1932; *The Times*, 11 August 1932; private information; personal knowledge.]   ALFRED ZIMMERN.

WARD, JOHN (1866–1934), politician and soldier, was born at Walton, Surrey, 21 November 1866, the son of Robert Ward, plasterer, by his wife, Caroline Edmonds. He was self-educated, and was considerably influenced by Kropotkin's *Appeal to the Young* and Henry George's *Progress and Poverty*. Beginning work at the age of twelve as a navvy on the Andover and Weyhill Railway, he was employed on many public works, including the Manchester Ship Canal. Volunteering for the Sudan campaign in 1885, he was engaged on the abortive military railway from Suakin to Berber, and received the Khedive's bronze star, with medal and clasp. In 1886 he joined the Social Democratic Federation and was selected to test the legality of the proclamation of the chief commissioner of the London metropolitan police, Sir Charles Warren [q.v.], prohibiting demonstrations of the unemployed in Trafalgar Square. The meeting was held on Lord Mayor's

Day (9 November) 1887, and Ward was arrested and sentenced. He founded the Navvies' Union in 1889, and exposed several serious sewer contract scandals. On the foundation of the General Federation of Trade Unions in 1901, Ward was elected to the management committee and served until 1929, for the last sixteen years as treasurer.

As a liberal-labour candidate Ward unsuccessfully contested Aston Manor in 1892. Although he attended the early conferences of the labour party in 1903, he declared his opposition to its independent political policy. Thereafter he associated with the liberal party and was returned to parliament for Stoke-upon-Trent from 1906 until he was defeated in 1929 by the labour candidate, Lady Cynthia Mosley (Lord Curzon's daughter and first wife of Sir Oswald Mosley).

When war broke out in 1914 Ward was gazetted lieutenant-colonel of the 21st Middlesex Regiment, for which he recruited five labour battalions, and served with them for a time in France. On 16 February 1917, on the way to the Far East, the troopship *Tyndareus* was mined off South Africa, but he and his men were rescued, and afterwards trekked over 6,000 miles of Russian territory from Vladivostock. During the campaign of intervention after the Russian revolution Allied armies sought contact with the Don Cossacks, who, under General Kaledin and General Krasnov, broke away from the Moscow government; and in May 1918 a force of Czecho-Slovakian prisoners of war and volunteers, under Kerensky, initiated the first revolt against the Bolsheviks and threatened the Siberian railway from the Volga to the Urals. Admiral Koltchak, with Allied assistance, with which Ward was associated, instigated a rising in Vladivostock and a new anti-Bolshevik government was established there and also at Omsk; both were later suppressed.

While in Hong-Kong in 1917, Ward had urged the home government to abolish the sale of Chinese women and children in the colony, but, although representations were continued for several years, no immediate success attended his efforts.

Ward was appointed C.M.G. in 1918 and C.B. in 1919; he received the French, Italian, and Czecho-Slovakian Croix de Guerre, and was created a Cossack Ataman.

Ward was exceptionally tall and retained his soldierly bearing throughout his life. An effective speaker, he engaged in most of the campaigns of the liberal party. The Navvies' Union passed out of existence, the newer generation of necessity employing mechanical appliances in place of the pick and shovel that distinguished the old-time navvy, and being catered for by the larger general labourers' unions.

Ward married in 1892 Lilian Elizabeth (died 1926), daughter of George Gibbs. She shared actively in his political work. Their son served in the navy during the war of 1914–1918. Ward died at his home at Andover 19 December 1934. A cartoon appeared in *Vanity Fair* (29 January 1908), which depicted the stalwart figure of Ward, with the wide awake hat which he affected, looking down at the diminutive Ben Tillett of the Dockers' Union.

[*The Times*, 20 December 1934; *Reports* of the General Federation of Trade Unions.]

J. S. MIDDLETON.

WARD, WILLIAM HUMBLE, second EARL OF DUDLEY (1867–1932), lord-lieutenant of Ireland and governor-general of Australia, was born at Dudley House, Park Lane, London, 25 May 1867, the eldest of the six sons of William Ward, first Earl of Dudley, by his second wife, Georgina Elizabeth, third daughter of Sir Thomas Moncreiffe, seventh baronet. He was educated at Eton, and succeeded his father in 1885. He made a three years' tour round the world from about 1884 to 1887.

In 1891 Lord Dudley married Rachel Anne, younger daughter of Charles Henry Gurney, a partner in Saunderson's Bank, London, and one of the Gurneys of North Runcton Hall, Norfolk. His wife, a lady of beauty and talent, had a great influence in turning his mind and energies to public service. He sold Dudley House and a part of the magnificent collection of pictures and china formed by his father. He began to take a part in local affairs and was elected mayor of Dudley in 1895 and 1896. He also began to speak in the House of Lords and in 1895 Lord Salisbury made him parliamentary secretary to the Board of Trade. He served in the South African war with the Worcestershire Yeomanry and was on Lord Roberts's staff as deputy-assistant-adjutant-general for the Imperial Yeomanry. In 1902 he was appointed lord-lieutenant of Ireland and sworn of the Privy Council. His tenure of the lord-lieutenancy was a great social success, but his belief in the 'devolution'

policy of his friend the chief secretary, George Wyndham [q.v.], aroused the hostility of Ulster towards him. But, although Wyndham was obliged to resign, Dudley continued to hold office until the fall of Balfour's administration in 1905. Thereafter, from 1906 to 1908, he served as chairman of the royal commission on congestion in Ireland.

In 1908 Dudley was appointed governor-general of the Commonwealth of Australia. He held office until 1911, and his years in Australia were most successful. He and his wife were popular, and he maintained the impartiality which the office demanded. In the war of 1914–1918 Dudley commanded the Worcestershire Yeomanry and saw service in Egypt and Gallipoli in 1915. Lady Dudley died in 1920, and in 1924 Lord Dudley married Gertrude, daughter of John Millar, and widow of Lionel Monckton (better known under her stage name of Gertie Millar). Dudley was appointed G.C.V.O. in 1903, G.C.M.G. in 1908, and G.C.B. in 1911. He died in London 29 June 1932, and was buried in the family burial ground at Himley Hall, Staffordshire. By his first wife he had four sons and three daughters, and was succeeded as third earl by his eldest son, William Humble Eric (born 1894), who, as Viscount Ednam, had been conservative member of parliament for Hornsey (1921–1924) and for Wednesbury (since 1931), and had served with distinction in the war of 1914–1918.

There was a portrait by Arthur Ellis, at Himley Hall, of Lord Dudley as a young man, just before he went to the South African war; a charcoal drawing of him by P. A. de László (1914) is in the possession of his widow. There is also a portrait by the Australian artist (Sir) John Longstaff in Parliament House, Canberra.

[*The Times*, 30 June 1932; private information.]

K. C. WHEARE.

WARNER, SIR GEORGE FREDERIC (1845–1936), palaeographer and scholar, was born at Winchester 7 April 1845, the fourth son of Isaac Warner, solicitor, of Winchester, by his wife, Susanna, daughter of John Witt, who held a high position in the shipping business at Southampton. He was educated at Christ's Hospital and at Pembroke College, Cambridge, of which he was a scholar: he obtained a second class in the classical tripos of 1868. In 1871 Warner entered the department of manuscripts in the British Museum, where he served for forty years, becoming assistant keeper in 1888 and keeper and Egerton librarian in 1904. He acquired an exceptionally thorough knowledge of all branches of the department, and from the time of his becoming assistant keeper he in effect directed most of the general administration of it.

Warner's special interests were in palaeography and illuminated manuscripts. He was associated with his senior colleague and friend Sir Edward Maunde Thompson [q.v.] in the publications of the Palaeographical Society (1873–1894) and in 1903 founded the New Palaeographical Society, of which he remained an editor until 1915. For many years he revised and edited the quinquennial volumes of the *Catalogue of Additions to the Department of Manuscripts* and himself superintended the volume for 1900–1905 (1907). In 1894 he initiated *A Catalogue of Western Manuscripts in the Old Royal and King's Collections*, which was published, in conjunction with his successor in the keepership, Julius Parnell Gilson [q.v.], in four volumes in 1921. In the sphere of illuminated manuscripts, Warner's principal official publications were the facsimile of the Sforza Book of Hours (1894), two sets of facsimiles of the best manuscripts in the Museum (the first comprising four series in colours, 1899–1903, and the second three series in black and white, 1907–1908), and *Queen Mary's Psalter* (1912). Unofficial publications included the *Miracles de Nostre Dame* (1885), the *Benedictional of St. Æthelwold* (1910), the *Gospels of Matilda, Countess of Salisbury* (1917), and the *Guthlac Roll* (1928), all for the Roxburghe Club, of which he became a member in 1911; also a French version of Valerius Maximus with miniatures of the school of Jean Fouquet (1907), and a catalogue of the illuminated manuscripts in the collection of C. W. Dyson Perrins (2 vols., 1920).

Warner's most important works of scholarship were his edition of the travels of Sir John Mandeville (*The buke of John Maundeuill*, Roxburghe Club, 1889), in which he identified the author and traced the sources from which he derived his romance, and the *Libelle of Englyshe Polycye* (1926), in which he elucidated the authorship of this plea for English sea-power. He was an exceedingly careful and accurate scholar, with a minimum of display. He was an admirable administrator of his department, thorough, courteous, and helpful; but an embarrassing stammer

precluded him from public appearances. He was elected a fellow of the British Academy in 1906, and an honorary fellow of Pembroke College in 1911, and received the honorary degree of D.Litt. from the university of Oxford on the occasion of the tercentenary of the Bodleian Library in 1902.

After retiring from the Museum in 1911, in which year he was knighted, Warner lived successively at Beaconsfield, Ealing, and Weybridge, and at Weybridge he died 17 January 1936. He married in 1884 Marian Amelia, daughter of Richard Budd Painter, M.D., of Brompton, and had a son, who died young, and a daughter. A good photograph is prefixed to a volume of *Miniatures and Borders from a Flemish Horae* presented to him on his retirement.

[*The Times*, 18 January 1936; Sir F. G. Kenyon, *Sir George Warner, 1865–1936* in *Proceedings* of the British Academy, vol. xxii, 1936; personal knowledge.]

F. G. KENYON.

WARRINGTON, THOMAS ROLLS, BARON WARRINGTON OF CLYFFE (1851–1937), judge, was born in London 29 May 1851, the only son of Thomas Warrington, a partner in the firm of Messrs. Garrard & company, silversmiths and jewellers, of London, by his wife, Mary Jane, daughter of Henry George Radclyffe. He was educated at Rugby and at Trinity College, Cambridge, where he was elected to a foundation scholarship and obtained a second class in the classical tripos of 1873. He was called to the bar by Lincoln's Inn in 1875, and became a pupil of F. C. J. Millar, Q.C. He soon acquired a reputation as a junior and, to quote from the letterpress of the cartoon of him in *Vanity Fair*, 'by dint of care, industry and ability acquired a large practice on the Chancery side'. He took silk in 1895, and, in accordance with the system then in force, attached himself to the court of Sir Arthur Kekewich [q.v.]. He soon established a considerable influence over that judge. The possibility of such influence was one of the main objections to the 'tied silk' system, but it can be said with certainty that Warrington never abused the influence which he obtained and thoroughly deserved the confidence of the judge. To other counsel he set a fine example. He knew his papers thoroughly; he treated his junior with a courtesy almost amounting to deference and his opponent, whether experienced leader or young junior, with exemplary politeness and respect. He was elected a bencher of his Inn in 1897.

In April 1904 Warrington was appointed a judge of the Chancery division of the High Court. His appointment was universally approved and he at once gained, and retained, the respect and affection of those who practised before him. In 1915 he was promoted to the Court of Appeal and sworn of the Privy Council. He retired in October 1926. On his retirement he was raised to the peerage as Baron Warrington of Clyffe, of Market Lavington, in Wiltshire, and continued for many years to render valuable service in a judicial capacity both in the House of Lords and in the Privy Council.

Warrington's contribution to legal literature was not comparable with that of Sir George Jessel, Lord Macnaghten, or Lord Parker of Waddington [qq.v.], but he was a sound equity judge and it was said of him with truth that 'the higher he went the better he got'. It did not often fall to his lot to adjudicate upon cases which attracted popular interest, but among important cases with which he was associated were *Hammerton* v. *Earl of Dysart* (1915), *de Keyser's Royal Hotel* (1919), and *Banco de Portugal* v. *Waterlow & Sons Ltd.* (1932). The first case related to an ancient ferry at Twickenham, and Warrington's judgement in the Chancery division, reversed by the Court of Appeal, was restored by the House of Lords. In the de Keyser case Warrington, in the Court of Appeal, helped to establish the important principle that the Crown is not entitled as of right, either under the prerogative or by statute, to take possession of the land or buildings of a subject for administrative purposes in connexion with the defence of the realm, without paying compensation. The Portuguese Bank case gave rise to much divergence of judicial opinion as to the measure of damages for breach of contract for which the printers of bank notes were liable by reason of their delivery of some of the notes to an unauthorized person who had placed them in circulation without authority. Warrington in the House of Lords was one of a dissentient minority who held that, on the facts of the case, the bank had proved no loss beyond the cost of printing notes to replace those which it had had to withdraw.

Warrington had interests outside the law. During his early years at the bar he was an enthusiastic member of the Inns of Court Rifles. His principal private interest was his house and garden at Clyffe Hall, to which he was devoted. In 1883 he married Emma Maud, eldest daughter of Decimus Sturges, barrister, of Lincoln's Inn. He had no children. He died at Clyffe Hall 26 October 1937. A cartoon by 'Spy' appeared in *Vanity Fair* 27 November 1907.

[*The Times*, 27 October 1937; *Law Reports*; private information.]   LIONEL L. COHEN.

WARWICK, COUNTESS OF (1861–1938). [See GREVILLE, FRANCES EVELYN.]

WATKINS, HENRY GEORGE, 'GINO' (1907–1932), Arctic explorer, was born in London 29 January 1907, the eldest child and elder son of Colonel Henry George Watkins, of the Coldstream Guards, by his wife, Jennie Helen, third daughter of Colonel Bolton Monsell, of the 73rd Highland Regiment. He was educated at Lancing and at Trinity College, Cambridge, where he came in contact with many young polar explorers at a period when Arctic travel had become a Cambridge enthusiasm. He had already become a skilled climber in the Alps and a flying enthusiast when in 1927 he organized and led a small but useful expedition to Edge Island, Spitsbergen (Svalbard). Next year, eager for more Arctic experience, he turned his attention to Labrador, which had become prominent owing to the boundary arbitration with Canada. He spent a year with Mr. J. M. Scott and various trappers exploring and surveying in the upper reaches of the Hamilton (Grand) River system. On his return, Watkins's interest in flying led him to organize and carry through a large expedition to eastern Greenland in the hope of investigating the possibilities of an air route between England and Canada across southern Greenland. The British Arctic Air Route expedition of 1930–1931 was marked by originality in conception and efficiency in execution. All the members were young, and few had previous polar experience. The expedition learnt from the Eskimo the technique of living off the land, including skill in hunting and dog-driving. Two parties crossed the ice-sheet of the interior and others did much survey work on a boat journey along the south-east coast. The boldest feat was the successful maintenance of an observatory on the ice-sheet at an altitude of 8,000 feet by Augustine Courtauld throughout the winter. On his return from

Greenland Watkins planned an Antarctic expedition but failed to find the money and so returned in 1932 to his work in Greenland. On or about 20 August 1932, although he had acquired the skill of an expert Eskimo in the handling of a kayak, he lost his life by drowning in Lakefjord when engaged alone on a seal hunt. The work of the expedition was continued under Mr. John Rymill.

A zest for living and a joy in overcoming difficulties, in which he showed a rare combination of daring and caution, made Watkins an ideal polar explorer. Although not a specialist himself, he had full appreciation of the scientific problems to be solved. The value of his work is shown by the many awards which he received, all of them in 1932 and most of them never previously given to so young a man. They included the Polar medal, the Hans Egede medal of Denmark, the Founder's medal of the Royal Geographical Society, and the Bruce medal of the Royal Society of Edinburgh. He was unmarried.

A portrait in oils of Watkins by his father is in the keeping of the family, and there is a bas-relief by Cecil Thomas at the Scott Polar Research Institute, Cambridge.

[J. M. Scott, *Gino Watkins*, 1935, and *The Land God Gave Cain*, 1933; F. S. Chapman, *Northern Lights*, 1932, and *Watkins's Last Expedition*, 1934; *Geographical Journal*, October 1932; *Polar Record*, Nos. 1–5, 1931–1933; *The Times*, 25 August 1932; private information.]   R. N. RUDMOSE BROWN.

WATSON, SIR (JOHN) WILLIAM (1858–1935), poet, was born at Burley-in-Wharfedale, Yorkshire, 2 August 1858, of Yorkshire ancestry on both sides. He was the son of John Watson, master grocer, afterwards a merchant in Liverpool, by his wife, Dorothy Robinson.

Educated at a school at Southport, he began to contribute verse to the newspapers at the age of fourteen. His first volume of verse, *The Prince's Quest*, published at his father's cost, appeared in 1880: this was followed by twenty-seven other works, mostly poetry. It was not, however, until 1890 that, with the appearance of *Wordsworth's Grave and Other Poems*, Watson began to attract public notice. *Lachrymae Musarum* (1892), a dirge for Tennyson, gave its name to another volume of poems in 1893. His work was greatly admired by Gladstone, and Watson was undoubtedly one of the few poets who were considered for the

laureateship when Robert Bridges [q.v.] was appointed in 1913. At the end of 1894 Watson commemorated his recovery from a serious illness in one of the most beautiful of his poems, 'Vita Nuova', published in the volume entitled *Odes and Other Poems*. This in turn was succeeded by *The Father of the Forest* (1895), by *The Purple East* (1896), and by the well-known *Ode on the Day of the Coronation of King Edward VII* (1902).

Watson complained in prose, and frequently in his verses, that modern life had moved away from poetry, but he himself was constantly inspired by current events, and was able to claim, without anyone being able to find fault with the claim, of a certain association that troubled the Near East:

'Who among singers sang for Man but me?'

It is perhaps for the reason that he fought so courageously with his pen among the dust of passing events that recognition of his work was fitful, for no man can take a vigorous part in political affairs without making enemies. Indeed the vigour with which he championed oppressed Armenians must have caused some anxiety to the British Foreign Office, when it led him to write in the *Westminster Gazette* of:

'Abdul the Damned on his infernal throne'.

There was, in fact, a *saeva indignatio* in Watson, which did not decrease with age. William Archer [q.v.] in his *Poets of the Younger Generation* (1902), in an ample estimate of Watson, complains that he might possibly have been a greater poet 'had the imaginative in his composition been less exactly balanced by the logical element'. This balance in the poet was accurately perceived, yet it seems hardly a thing to regret, but rather to resemble the ideal collaboration between a diamond-miner and a diamond-cutter, the one to find a fine stone and the other to cut it perfectly: so Watson would find a truth and, making it sparkle to its utmost by his art, would lay it before the public with all the radiance due to it.

By the year 1913 two troubles obviously oppressed Watson, the one that is shown in the very title of the book which he published in that year, *The Muse in Exile*, by which he deplored, in no mere personal sense, the neglect of poetry at that time in England; and the other, those influences that he feared were weakening the British Empire. But immediately the war of 1914–1918 broke out he wrote what was probably the finest sonnet produced by that war:

'At last we know you, war-lord. You that flung
The gauntlet down, fling down the mask you wore,'

wherein he showed his faith and trust in British strength.

Watson's own verses reveal an estimate of himself, as a singer pledged to the muses, which is a just one, and which is well borne out by his fine appreciations of other singers, not all of them human, as in his poems to Wordsworth, Shelley, Keats, Tennyson, Burns, and the skylark. One of his sonnets is a curious example of how a poet may gather his material from the future as well as from the present or the past, a poem to France, in which he says, amongst other things that are observed to-day:

'Nation whom storm on storm of ruining fate
Unruined leaves.'

It was written in 1894. He published *Selected Poems, with Notes by the Author* in 1928, and *The Poems of Sir William Watson* appeared posthumously in 1936.

Watson visited the United States more than once and lectured there with success; several of his poems show gratitude for recognition generously given to him there. In 1917 he was knighted. He married in 1909 Adeline Maureen, daughter of Harry Pring, of Dundalk, co. Louth, and many of his poems record that it was a very happy marriage. They made their home at Rottingdean. He died at Ditchling Common, Sussex, 11 August 1935, and was survived by his wife and their two daughters.

[*The Times*, 14 August 1935; W. Archer, *Poets of the Younger Generation*, 1902.]

DUNSANY.

WELLCOME, SIR HENRY SOLOMON (1853–1936), manufacturing chemist and patron of science, was born in a log cabin at Almond in the State of Wisconsin, United States of America, 21 August 1853, the younger son of the Rev. Solomon Cummings Wellcome, farmer and itinerant missionary to the Dakota Indian tribes, by his wife, Mary Curtis. His early education was received at frontier schools. Much of his boyhood was spent in Garden City, Minnesota, where, under the influence of William Worrell Mayo, he began to take a lively interest in pharmacy. He

qualified at the Philadelphia College of Pharmacy and served his apprenticeship with various reputable American firms, during which period he explored the cinchona forests of Peru and Ecuador, where he first became interested in the history of medicine. His progress was rapid and in 1880, at the age of twenty-seven, he came to England, where he entered into partnership with S. M. Burroughs, also an American by birth. The firm of Burroughs, Wellcome & company were manufacturers of fine chemicals, alkaloids, and pharmaceutical products including a special range of compressed drugs for which the trade-mark 'tabloid' was invented. The firm prospered and, on his partner's death in 1895, Wellcome acquired the whole business.

Wellcome was now a wealthy man and in a position to carry out his long cherished schemes for the advancement of medical research and education. He was essentially a patron of science; he provided the conditions necessary for successful medical research. In 1894 he founded the laboratories known as the Wellcome Physiological Research Laboratories, in 1896 the chemical research laboratories in London which bear his name; in 1901 he inspired the creation (1903) under the direction of (Sir) Andrew Balfour [q.v.] of the tropical research laboratories in connexion with the Gordon Memorial College at Khartoum, providing all the necessary equipment. In 1913 he founded in London the Wellcome Historical Medical Museum for which he had been collecting for many years. In 1913 also, the Wellcome Bureau of Scientific Research was established in London for the investigation in England of tropical diseases, and with this in 1914 was associated a museum which later became the Wellcome Museum of Medical Science (1923). All these were subsequently incorporated in the Wellcome Research Institution as a part of the Wellcome Foundation established in 1924 to unite the business of Burroughs, Wellcome & company with the various laboratories and museums. To crown his many benefactions Wellcome left practically the whole of his wealth to scientific research and education.

Wellcome's activities, however, were not confined to the establishment of medical research laboratories and museums: he encouraged and supported archaeological research in Africa and Palestine. At Gebel Moya, in the Sudan, he selected a late neolithic site where extensive excavations, which he himself directed for a number of years up to the outbreak of war in 1914, were carried out. It is probable that his interest in geographical exploration was stimulated by his friendship with Sir H. M. Stanley [q.v.], of whom he was an ardent supporter. He took an active interest in medical missionary work and was a devoted champion of General W. C. Gorgas in his pioneer sanitary efforts which made possible the construction of the Panama Canal. Wellcome's early contact with American Indians bred in him a lifelong sympathy for them, and for many years he was engaged in a thankless and costly legal struggle on behalf of a dispossessed tribe from Fort Simpson, British Columbia, whose history he published in *The Story of Metlakahtla* (1887).

When in 1928 the senate of Edinburgh University conferred upon Wellcome the honorary degree of LL.D., the dean of the faculty said: 'Mr. Wellcome has a threefold claim to academic distinction: he is a princely patron of medical research, a generous friend of missionary enterprise, and an enthusiastic promoter of geographical and archaeological exploration. . . .' This tribute covers to a large extent the range of Wellcome's activities.

Wellcome was a fellow or member of numerous learned societies, and in later life he was the recipient of many honours. In 1932 he was elected one of the few lay honorary fellows of the Royal College of Surgeons of England and was also elected F.R.S. The same year he was knighted in recognition of all that he had done for science and the British Empire, and he was made an officer of the Legion of Honour in 1936. He married in 1901 Gwendoline Maude Syrie, daughter of the philanthropist Thomas John Barnardo [q.v.], and had one son. The marriage was subsequently dissolved. He was naturalized in 1910. He died in London 25 July 1936.

[*Obituary Notices of Fellows of the Royal Society*, No. 6, January 1938 (portrait); *The Times*, 27 July 1936; original documents; personal knowledge.]   S. H. DAUKES.

WELLDON, JAMES EDWARD COWELL (1854–1937), successively headmaster of Dulwich and of Harrow, bishop of Calcutta, and dean of Manchester and of Durham, was born at Tonbridge 25 April 1854, the eldest son of the Rev. Edward Ind Welldon, second master of Tonbridge School, by his wife, Ellen Laura, second daughter of Samuel Byles Cowell, head of a printing firm in Ipswich. After being at school at Eton, of which he was a scholar and where he won the Newcastle scholarship in 1873, he went as a scholar to King's College, Cambridge. Here he won the Bell and Craven university scholarships (1874 and 1876) and was Browne's medallist (Greek ode, 1875 and 1876) and senior classic and senior chancellor's medallist (1877). In 1878 he was elected into a fellowship at his college, where he remained until he was appointed master of Dulwich College in 1883. In that year he was ordained deacon, and priest in 1885. He raised Dulwich from a low ebb to the position that it has since retained. The school song, 'Pueri Alleynienses', was his composition. But at Harrow he established his fame as a great schoolmaster. His lifelong love for Harrow and his undying interest in the careers of his pupils revealed the depth of his affection for the school, which he ruled with the masterly force of an infectious personality for thirteen years (1885–1898). The dinner which 200 old Harrovians gave to him on his eightieth birthday was a fitting response to his large-hearted interest in 'his old boys'. At Calcutta, as metropolitan of the Indian Church (1898–1902), he diligently tried to master Indian problems and travelled to every part of the country in order to get in touch with Indian Christians, but ill health and an unfortunate disagreement on missionary questions between him and the viceroy, Lord Curzon, led to his resignation. This setback, if it can be so called, probably prevented him from gaining that position in the Church to which his personality and abilities pointed, but his complete lack of resentment was nobly sealed by his magnificent bequest to the work of the Indian Church and he gave himself wholeheartedly to the considerable offices to which he was successively appointed. His health was re-established by an operation and by four and a half years of quiet work as canon of Westminster (1902–1906). The history of Westminster Abbey appealed to him strongly and he enjoyed showing parties of visitors from the Dominions and other parts of the Empire over the Abbey. The coronation of King Edward VII, in which he took an important part, was the leading event at the Abbey in his time.

As dean of Manchester (1906–1918) Welldon devoted himself zealously to the cathedral, which became a centre of spiritual and civic influence. His overflowing humanity compelled him to get into touch with all sorts and conditions of men. The story, which he told against himself, of an old Lancashire woman in a tram, who tapped him on the knee and said: 'Dean, I tell you what it is, you spout too much', is to his credit in more ways than one.

When Welldon went to the deanery of Durham in 1918 he was past the age for initiating new undertakings, but he administered the cathedral with due regard to its traditions and took a deep interest in the work of the university. His serene composure was manifested on one occasion when by some mistake he had been severely jostled by a party of miners and very nearly rolled into the river. After changing his clothes before preaching he delivered to the same men a sermon full of kindliness without an allusion to the subject. A serious fall, which crippled him for the rest of his life, led to his resignation in 1933 shortly after the death of a faithful servant who had been with him in close companionship for nearly fifty years. He retired to Sevenoaks, where he died 17 June 1937. He was unmarried.

Welldon's brilliant scholarship gave to the world translations of Aristotle's *Politics* (1883), *Rhetoric* (1886), and *Ethics* (1892). Aristotle coloured both his style and his manner of reasoning. He had a wide knowledge of English, French, German, and Italian literature. His historical sense was keen: his theological outlook both orthodox and human (*The Hope of Immortality*, incorporating his Hulsean lectures delivered at Cambridge in 1897 and 1898, 1898; *The Revelation of the Holy Spirit*, 1902; an edition of St. Augustine's *De Civitate Dei*, 2 vols., 1924). As an ecclesiastic it is impossible to give him a party label. Brought up in the strict evangelical tradition, he shook himself free of all narrow conceptions, retaining that sense of individual relationship to the Person of Jesus which was the keynote of his thinking. He was a frank but friendly critic of all parties and denominations, measuring them by a robust common sense and untarnished sincerity. He was a believer in the national character of the Church of England (*The Religious Aspects of Disestablishment and Disendowment*, 1911; *The English Church*, 1926) but nourished the hope of reunion, first with the British nonconformists and ultimately with all Christian Churches. He was an impressive preacher and several volumes of sermons mark the stages of his ministry. His autobiographical writings, *Recollections and Reflections* (1915) and *Forty Years On* (1935), are a storehouse of his views on various topics.

Welldon was a great personality. His stature and physical bulk, his mental strength, his emotional fervour all denoted power. There was no finesse about him. A professor once said of his examination work: 'I can't say much for his style, but it is like his fives-playing. The ball always nicks.' A great traveller, he was a real citizen of the world. He was a genial host, a good talker, a reservoir of choice stories, packed with humour. Of malice or resentment he was incapable.

A portrait of Welldon by John Collier (1898) hangs in the Vaughan library at Harrow.

[*The Times*, 19 June 1937; J. E. C. Welldon, *Recollections and Reflections*, 1915, and *Forty Years On*, 1935; private information; personal knowledge.]   J. W. S. TOMLIN.

WEMYSS, ROSSLYN ERSKINE, BARON WESTER WEMYSS (1864–1933), admiral of the fleet, was born in London 12 April 1864, the youngest and posthumous son of James Hay Erskine Wemyss, of Wemyss Castle, Fife, by his wife, Millicent Ann Mary, daughter of Lady Augusta Kennedy Erskine, the fourth daughter of the Duke of Clarence (later King William IV) by Mrs. Dorothy Jordan [q.v.]. His paternal grandfather, Rear-Admiral James Erskine Wemyss, was great-great-grandson of David, third Earl of Wemyss [q.v.], vice-admiral of Scotland, and his own maternal great-grandfather, King William, had been the last holder of the office of lord high admiral of the United Kingdom; thus the naval strain in his ancestry was strong.

Wemyss entered the training ship *Britannia* in 1877 with his third cousins, the Royal Princes Albert Victor (later Duke of Clarence) and George (later King George V). On passing out in 1879 with distinction he was appointed to the *Bacchante* under Captain Lord Charles Thomas Montagu-Douglas-Scott [q.v.], in which the princes were to spend three years on a memorable cruise round the world. On its termination he was sent to the *Northumberland* in the Channel squadron for eight months, and then was appointed senior midshipman of the *Canada* on the North America and West Indies station in which Prince George was his next junior. While in her he was promoted sub-lieutenant and in August 1884 came home for the normal twelve months' courses at Portsmouth and Greenwich. He then spent eighteen months in the *Hecla*, torpedo depot ship, in the Mediterranean, being promoted lieutenant in her in March 1887. In October of that year he was, naturally from his early associations, selected for service in the royal yacht *Osborne* for two years, after which he became flag-lieutenant in the *Anson* to Rear-Admiral (Sir) R. E. Tracey [q.v.], second-in-command of the Channel squadron, and left her in March 1890 to spend two years in the *Undaunted* (serving under Captain Lord Charles Beresford, q.v.) in the Mediterranean. He then returned to the Channel squadron for two years in the *Empress of India*, flagship of Rear-Admiral (Sir) Edward Seymour [q.v.] and after one year as first-lieutenant of the *Astraea*, 2nd class cruiser, in the Mediterranean, resumed royal yacht duty as first-lieutenant of the *Victoria and Albert* in 1896. On completion of this service he was promoted commander in August 1898 in accordance with established custom. He was commander of the cruiser *Niobe*, detached from the Channel squadron for special service at the Cape during the first year of the South African war. He was disappointed in having no opportunity for fighting service ashore, his ship being employed on ancillary duties, including that of transporting Boer prisoners to St. Helena and guarding them there. On return to England at the end of 1900 he was invited by the Duke of York (later King George V) to accompany him as second-in-command of the *Ophir* (a specially commissioned passenger ship) on his tour to the overseas Dominions, which was arranged mainly for the opening of the first parliament of the Commonwealth of Australia. Queen Victoria's death temporarily delayed the preparations for this cruise, but it took place from March to November 1901. Wemyss won golden opinions from all concerned and was specially promoted captain and appointed M.V.O. on its conclusion.

At Christmas 1902 the second Lord Selborne's memorandum launched the new scheme of naval education promoted by Sir John Fisher [q.v.]. Its first and most important part provided for the establishment of a new cadets' college on novel lines and Fisher had already marked down Wemyss as the ideal man to be its first captain. He was accordingly employed at the Admiralty in working out

the details of the new organization and of the building of the college in the grounds of Queen Victoria's house at Osborne until August 1903 when he was appointed to its command. The initial and continued success of this remarkable enterprise was largely due to his qualities of energy, resource, and tact, and his buoyant good temper and infectious enthusiasm. He won the respect and admiration of civilian masters, officers, and cadets alike, and the entire approval of the Board in Whitehall.

After two years at Osborne Wemyss was glad to return to the sea as captain of the *Suffolk* in the Mediterranean where Beresford was then commander-in-chief. He paid her off in April 1908 and, after a few months command of the *Albion*, flagship in the Atlantic Fleet, next year was appointed commodore, 2nd class, of the royal naval barracks at Devonport.

Wemyss's service there was interrupted for several months in 1910 while he commanded the *Balmoral Castle* which was commissioned to take the Duke and Duchess of Connaught to South Africa for the opening of the first Union parliament. He had accepted the offer of this command in April when the Prince of Wales had intended to undertake the ceremony, but the death of King Edward VII necessitated a change. King George made him extra naval equerry after his accession and he was appointed C.M.G. after the voyage. In April 1911 he reached flag rank, only twelve and a half years after promotion to commander, and in October 1912 he was appointed for a year rear-admiral in the second battle squadron of the Home Fleet (flag in the *Orion*).

On 1 August 1914, when war became imminent, Wemyss was appointed to the command of the twelfth cruiser squadron (flag in the *Charybdis*) with orders to act in concert with the French Admiral Rouyer in charge of the western patrol in the English Channel for the protection of the transports conveying the British Expeditionary Force to France. Constantly at sea in an old uncomfortable ship without any sign of the enemy, Wemyss found this a tiresome task, and was glad when in September his squadron was sent to Canada to escort the first contingent of 30,000 Canadians to England. This duty was successfully accomplished, although Wemyss himself considered that old slow cruisers were a risky protection to a convoy. He then resumed charge of the western patrol, transferring his flag to the

Euryalus until February 1915, when he hauled it down on the dispersal of his cruiser force.

Wemyss was at once selected for a new duty as governor of the island of Lemnos and to take charge of a naval base to be created at Mudros for the impending naval and military Dardanelles campaign, although occupying a most anomalous position in foreign territory without staff or detailed orders to guide him. He was required to organize and equip a base for a great army and fleet on an island which had no facilities for landing troops or discharging cargo, no water supply, and no native labour. He set to work at once with great energy and resourcefulness and in a few weeks troops were able to land and assemble for the attack on the Gallipoli peninsula. In March Vice-Admiral (Sir) S. H. Carden [q.v.], the commander-in-chief, had to give up the command through ill health. His second-in-command, Rear-Admiral (Sir) J. M. De Robeck [q.v.], was junior to Wemyss, although older, but Wemyss with great public spirit himself proposed that De Robeck should succeed Carden with the acting rank of vice-admiral, remaining himself in charge of Mudros.

In April Wemyss was able to take an active part in the landing operations in command of the first naval squadron, being in charge of the Helles section, with his flag in his former flagship *Euryalus*, and having Lieutenant-General Sir Aylmer Hunter-Weston [q.v.] and his staff on board. Throughout this critical and dangerous work he maintained close co-operation with the military authorities, readily accepted ideas from his own officers, such as the celebrated beaching of the cargo ship *River Clyde*, and helped to maintain the morale of the whole expedition by his indomitable cheerfulness and imperturbability. In August he was mentioned in dispatches for his invaluable services in the Gallipoli landing.

In November, during De Robeck's absence on leave, Wemyss was appointed acting vice-admiral, transferring his flag to the *Lord Nelson*. Commodore (afterwards Admiral Lord) Keyes, De Robeck's chief of staff, had obtained his admiral's leave to go to London to urge one more naval attempt to get through the Straits before the evacuation recommended by General Sir Charles Monro [q.v.] was effected. De Robeck himself did not advise this proposal, but Wemyss enthusiastically pressed it upon the generals

on the spot and by telegrams to A. J. Balfour [q.v.], the first lord. But military opinion was adverse and the Admiralty did not support him. In the actual evacuation of Suvla and Anzac Wemyss, although detesting the decision to effect it, threw himself into the naval direction of the operation with courage and optimistic determination, thereby sustaining the spirits of doubting generals, and deserved a full share of credit for its being carried out almost without loss.

In January 1916 Wemyss was appointed K.C.B. for his Dardanelles service and commander-in-chief of the East Indies and Egypt station. The *Euryalus* was again his flagship and he soon found opportunities of effective co-operation with the military commanders in the defence of Egypt against the Turks and the Senussi rising and in the support of General Sir Archibald Murray's advance to Sinai. He then took his squadron to the Persian Gulf and went himself up the Tigris in a river-gunboat to try to relieve the critical situation in Mesopotamia. In a forlorn hope of saving the garrison of Major-General Sir C. V. F. Townshend [q.v.] at Kut from surrender he attempted to get a food ship through to the town; it failed, but he could not rightly refuse the military appeal for help. He then completed his tour of his station, visiting both India, where he saw the viceroy, Lord Chelmsford, and Ceylon, and, after meeting Rear-Admiral (Sir) W. L. Grant, commander-in-chief, China station, at Penang, he returned to Egypt in August in time to support the advance by General Sir Edmund Allenby [q.v.] into Palestine, and foster the Arab revolt by his patrols in the Red Sea. He established cordial relations with the Emir Feisal and T. E. Lawrence [q.v.], as well as with the generals. He was promoted vice-admiral in 1916.

In June 1917 under an agreement between Great Britain, France, and Italy it was decided to appoint a vice-admiral as commander-in-chief of the British ships in the Mediterranean with headquarters at Malta. Wemyss was offered and accepted the appointment, but on returning to London for instructions he was invited by Sir Eric Geddes [q.v.], who had just succeeded Sir Edward Carson [q.v.] as first lord, to join his Board as second sea lord; that official had hitherto been expected to take the place of the first sea lord in his absence. But on further reflection Geddes decided to leave the second sea lord to carry on his personnel work and in September created a new office of deputy sea lord for Wemyss.

Geddes had been instructed by Lloyd George to proceed at once with the development of the war staff, already inaugurated by Mr. Churchill in 1912 on a much more extensive scale and on the lines of the General Staff of the army. Wemyss had no previous experience of Admiralty administration but entered with zest upon his new duties and arranged for Keyes to join him as director of the new Plans Division. Admiral Sir John Jellicoe [q.v.], the first sea lord, did not feel justified in handing over responsibilities to his new deputy and his differences with both Geddes and the prime minister led to his being replaced at the end of the year (1917) by Wemyss himself. Thus at the age of fifty-three Wemyss had reached the highest position in the naval service. Throughout 1918 he worked in complete unity with Geddes. He disliked office work but believed thoroughly in devolution of duties to trusted colleagues and subordinates and was able, by co-ordinating the several divisions of the war staff into a team, to inspire all with his own infectious enthusiasm. His success in dealing with the prolonged submarine menace was mainly due to this, and the dramatic exploit of Zeebrugge (April 1918) was an enterprise after his own heart. He was appointed G.C.B. in June 1918 and promoted admiral in 1919.

Wemyss's intimate knowledge of foreign affairs and friendships with the leading French admirals with whom he served in the Allied naval command were of great advantage as the armistice with its international problems drew near, and he represented the Allied navies with conspicuous distinction together with Marshal Foch at the final capitulation of the Germans at Compiègne. His success in securing what he considered to be the minimum of naval terms in the settlement was only obtained after vigorous resistance to the readiness of some members of the War Cabinet to weaken them, and to the blank ignorance of the French generals about the naval conduct of the war. With the new year preparations for the Peace Conference began in Paris and Wemyss was charged with the difficult task of maintaining the naval interests of this country: as at the armistice he succeeded in spite of many obstacles in getting his terms accepted by both the Allied statesmen and the Germans.

At home Wemyss took a leading part in securing substantial increases in the remuneration of the naval service. His new chief in Whitehall was Walter Long [q.v.], and, much hurt by an anonymous press agitation demanding his replacement by Sir David Beatty [q.v.] and by his exclusion in July from the list of peerages and money awards to the principal war leaders, in that month he asked his leave to resign. Long refused, but a few months later feeling himself out of sympathy with the government's attitude to the revolutionary Russian régime and to the maintenance of this country's naval supremacy, Wemyss decided definitely to resign and left office on 1 November 1919, being specially promoted admiral of the fleet and raised to the peerage as Baron Wester Wemyss, of Wemyss, co. Fife, the title of an ancient Scottish barony in his family. He remained on half pay until he reached the age limit and retired in 1929, having received no further government employment as a governor or ambassador which he felt he had a right to expect, and lived mainly at Wemyss and at Cannes. But he was actively engaged as director of the Cables and Wireless Company and the British Oil Development Company, conducting a successful mission on behalf of the latter to the Middle East in 1927 and to South America on behalf of the former in 1929. He maintained his intense interest in foreign affairs and occasionally expressed his views in the House of Lords and in the press, particularly his hostility to the Turkish treaty of 1920, and to the Washington naval treaty of 1922.

Wester Wemyss much enjoyed his duties as president of the Institution of Naval Architects, which he became in 1928. He received honorary degrees from the universities of Oxford, Cambridge, and St. Andrews, and the freedom of the last named city. His foreign decorations included the grand cordon of the Legion of Honour, the French médaille militaire (conferred by President Millerand at the unveiling of the Armistice monument in 1922), the United States D.S.M., and the highest distinctions of the other Allied countries.

Wester Wemyss possessed the great advantage of a most attractive courageous personality, although with no claim to deep technical knowledge in his profession. Nicknames are said to be some guide to a man's character, and the fact that he was universally known as 'Rosy' since childhood is a tribute to his bright and sunny disposition. He was a man of the world in the best sense of the phrase, with a simple faith in his own star and a cheerful optimism which carried him through many difficulties. A genial and generous host, he made friends readily and won the loyal devotion of his staff and subordinates. He had no opportunity of showing his qualities as a fleet leader, but as a naval statesman he deserved well of his country in maintaining to the full the great traditions of his post in Whitehall. His knowledge of French, much enhanced after his marriage by his wife's foreign connexions, contributed greatly to his intimate friendship with many of the great French officers of his time and made him a popular figure at many international meetings. He published in 1924 *The Navy in the Dardanelles Campaign*, a lively account of his own experiences and views.

Wester Wemyss married in 1903 Victoria, the only daughter of Sir Robert Burnett David Morier [q.v.], the eminent diplomat, and had one daughter. He died at Cannes 24 May 1933 and was buried in the chapel garden of Wemyss Castle after preliminary services at Cannes and Westminster Abbey, at which naval honours were officially accorded to him.

There is a drawing of Wester Wemyss by Francis Dodd in the Imperial War Museum, and his portrait is included in Sir A. S. Cope's picture 'Some Sea Officers of the Great War', painted in 1921, in the National Portrait Gallery.

[Admiralty records; Sir H. Newbolt, (Official) *History of the War. Naval Operations*, vol. iv, 1928; C. F. Aspinall-Oglander, (Official) *History of the Great War. Military Operations, Gallipoli*, vols. i and ii, 1929–1932; Lady Wester Wemyss, *The Life and Letters of Lord Wester Wemyss*, 1935; private information; personal knowledge.]

VINCENT W. BADDELEY.

WESTER WEMYSS, BARON (1864–1933), admiral of the fleet. [See WEMYSS, ROSSLYN ERSKINE.]

WESTON, SIR AYLMER GOULD HUNTER- (1864–1940), lieutenant-general, was born at Hunterston, West Kilbride, Ayrshire, 23 September 1864, the elder son of Lieutenant-Colonel Gould Read Hunter-Weston, twenty-sixth laird of Hunterston, by his second wife, Jane, elder daughter of Robert Hunter, twenty-fifth laird of Hunterston. After his maternal grandfather's death in 1880, his father assumed by royal licence the prefix surname of Hunter. He was

educated at Wellington College and the Royal Military Academy, and was commissioned in the Royal Engineers in 1884.

Hunter-Weston served in the Miranzai expedition (1891) and was promoted captain in 1892. He was wounded while in command of the Bengal Sappers with the Waziristan Field Force (1894–1895), receiving the medal and clasp, and was made brevet major. In 1896 he served in Egypt on the staff of Lord Kitchener [q.v.], in the battle of Firket (7 June), receiving the Queen's medal and the Khedive's medal with clasp. He entered the Staff College in 1898. The following year he commanded the first Mounted Engineers in South Africa, participating in many engagements, his most conspicuous exploit being the cutting of the railway near Bloemfontein, capturing valuable railway stock, and preventing General Piet Joubert from reinforcing the Boers in that town. His reckless courage combined with technical skill and great coolness in emergency carried him through this and other adventurous undertakings. In 1900 he received his brevet lieutenant-colonelcy and the D.S.O., and on his return home was appointed general staff officer, Eastern Command (1904–1908), gaining his brevet colonelcy in 1906. From this he was promoted colonel and chief general staff officer, Scottish Command, in 1908, and three years later became assistant director of Military Training at the War Office, where he remained until 1914.

In this year Hunter-Weston was given command, as brigadier-general, of the 11th Infantry brigade at Colchester. He took the brigade to France in 1914, and for his magnificent handling of his troops at Le Cateau and on the Aisne in the same year was promoted major-general. Early in 1915, in command of the 29th division, his successful landing at Cape Helles earned him promotion to temporary lieutenant-general and the command of the VIII Corps, but severe sunstroke necessitated his leaving this area and he returned to France still in command of the VIII Corps; for his distinguished service he was mentioned in dispatches ten times and confirmed as lieutenant-general in 1919. He retired from the army in 1920, and became colonel-commandant of the Royal Engineers in 1921.

At a by-election in October 1916 Hunter-Weston was elected unionist member of parliament for North Ayrshire and for the next nineteen years gave his attention to public affairs, representing Buteshire and North Ayrshire from 1918 to 1935. He was appointed C.B. in 1911 and K.C.B. in 1915. He married in 1905 Grace Strang, only daughter of William Strang Steel, of Philiphaugh, Selkirkshire, and founder of W. Strang Steel & company merchants in Burma. He died, childless, as the result of a fall from a turret at his home, Hunterston, 18 March 1940.

[*The Times*, 19 March 1940; C. F. Aspinall-Oglander, (Official) *History of the Great War. Military Operations, Gallipoli*, vols. i and ii; Sir J. E. Edmonds, (Official) *History of the Great War. Military Operations, France and Belgium, 1914–1918*, vols. i–v.]

C. V. OWEN.

WHITE, SIR (CYRIL) BRUDENELL (BINGHAM) (1876–1940), general, was born at St. Arnaud, Victoria, Australia, 23 September 1876, the third son of John Warren White, of Brisbane and co. Clare, Ireland, by his wife, Maria, second daughter of Robert Nassau Gibton, of Tallaght, co. Dublin. He was educated at Brisbane Normal School and at Eton School, Nundah, Queensland. From 1892 to 1899 he was in the service of the Australian Joint Stock Bank, Brisbane. In 1899 he joined the Queensland permanent artillery and saw service in the South African war in 1902, receiving the Queen's medal and three clasps. In 1906 he was the first Australian to be chosen for entry into the Staff College, Camberley. From 1908 to 1911 he was at the War Office (captain, 1908; major, 1911) whence he was appointed director of Military Operations, Australian Military Forces (1912–1914), being promoted lieutenant-colonel in 1914. He was responsible for the scheme which was successfully implemented when the Australian Imperial Forces were mobilized in August 1914. As chief of staff he landed the first division of the Australian Imperial Forces at Gallipoli (April 1915) and later he planned the historic evacuation of the Anzacs and the subsequent expansion of the Australian Imperial Forces in Egypt. He was promoted colonel in 1915, and received the D.S.O. He was promoted brigadier-general in 1915 and went to France as chief of staff to the I Anzac Corps under General William (later Lord) Birdwood. He was promoted major-general in 1917 and as temporary lieutenant-general accompanied General Birdwood as chief of the General Staff when the latter took over command of the British Fifth Army in 1918.

White returned to Australia in 1919 and was appointed chief of the General Staff, Australian Military Forces (major-general, 1920), retiring in 1923 to become chairman of the Public Service Board. In 1928 he retired from the army and entered business, becoming chairman, vice-chairman, and trustee of many Australian undertakings.

White was one of the ablest British staff officers produced by the war of 1914–1918, and soon after the outbreak of war in 1939 he was given the rank of lieutenant-general and recalled to resume his post as chief of the General Staff, Australia. His age and long retirement occasioned some criticism, but he soon proved that he was well equipped and able to resume high responsibilities and was promoted full general in March 1940. His services to his country were, however, to be of short duration, for he was killed in an air crash at Canberra 13 August 1940.

In 1916 White was appointed C.B., C.M.G. in 1918, K.C.M.G. in 1919 (and aide-de-camp to the king), K.C.V.O. in 1920, and K.C.B. in 1927. For his services in the war of 1914–1918 he also received many military decorations including those of France, Belgium, Portugal, Montenegro, and Japan. In 1905 he married Ethel, eldest daughter of Walter Davidson, of Coliban Park, Elphinstone, Victoria, and had two sons and two daughters.

[*The Times*, 14 August 1940; Fred Johns, *An Australian Biographical Dictionary*, 1934; *Australian Encyclopædia*, 1926; C. F. Aspinall-Oglander, (Official) *History of the Great War. Military Operations. Gallipoli*, vol. i, 1929.]

C. V. OWEN.

WHITE, HENRY JULIAN (1859–1934), Latin biblical scholar and dean of Christ Church, Oxford, was born at Islington 27 August 1859, the younger son of Henry John White, of the Mercantile Marine service, and afterwards on the staff of a local bank at Islington, by his wife, Susannah Wadeson. Educated at the Islington Proprietary School and privately, White went up to Christ Church, Oxford, in 1878, and after graduating in classics was awarded a first class in theology in 1883. He obtained the Denyer and Johnson theological scholarship in 1884 and the senior Greek Testament prize in 1885. In the latter year he was ordained deacon, and priest in 1886. One of his examiners in the theological school was John Wordsworth [q.v.], who as early as 1884 had appointed White as his assistant in the great critical edition of the Vulgate New Testament upon which he had embarked six years previously. Thus began the association which was to mean much.

In 1885 Wordsworth was consecrated to the see of Salisbury; and in 1886, after a year as curate at Oxted, Surrey, White followed him in order to become his domestic chaplain and (in 1887) vice-principal of the Theological College. At Salisbury White remained until he became theological lecturer and chaplain of Merton College, Oxford, in 1895; and it was these years which saw not only his main contributions to the series of *Old Latin Biblical Texts* but also the first-fruits of the partnership—the 'Wordsworth and White' Vulgate Gospels, published in separate parts from 1889 onwards. The Acts did not appear until 1905 when White was exchanging a fellowship at Merton, which he had held for eight years, for the professorship of New Testament exegesis at King's College, London, which he was to hold for fifteen. Throughout this period, although nearly all his spare time was devoted to the Vulgate, the rate of progress declined; for as the work proceeded a great deal more Old Latin and patristic evidence was included, and after Wordsworth's death in 1911 White was alone responsible. Small wonder that after his nomination to the deanery of Christ Church in 1920 progress became even slower. His spare time was now severely limited, and publication had advanced only as far as Ephesians when he died at Oxford 16 July 1934.

White was neither a great ecclesiastic nor an exceptional administrator: his colleagues at Christ Church were impressed mainly by his humility and his courage. But his scholarship was recognized by the bestowal of several distinctions. He received the honorary degree of D.D. from the universities of St. Andrews (1910) and Dublin (1927), and he was elected a fellow of the British Academy in 1932 and an honorary fellow of Merton College in 1921. In 1909 he married Clara Miller, daughter of George Berkeley White, and widow of Lieutenant-Colonel C. J. H. Warden, of the Indian Medical Service. There are two portraits at Christ Church, both painted by Ernest Moore in 1928, the one in the hall, and the other in the room in the library where his Vulgate books are preserved.

[S. C. E. Legg, *Henry Julian White, 1859–1934* in *Proceedings* of the British Academy,

vol. xxii, 1936; E. W. Watson, *Life of Bishop John Wordsworth*, 1915; *The Times*, 17 July 1934; *Oxford Magazine*, 25 October 1934; *Journal of Theological Studies*, January 1912 and January 1935.]　　H. F. D. SPARKS.

WHITLA, SIR WILLIAM (1851–1933), physician, was born at Monaghan 15 September 1851, the fourth son of Robert Whitla, woollen draper, of Monaghan, by his wife, Anne, daughter of Alexander Williams, of Dublin. He was educated at the Model School at Monaghan and also had a private tutor. Soon after leaving school he was apprenticed to Messrs. Wheeler & Whitaker, a leading firm of dispensing chemists in Belfast, an experience which was of considerable value to him in his subsequent career. In 1872 he began his medical training at Queen's College (afterwards University), Belfast, where he qualified the following year and graduated M.D. in 1877 with first class honours and a gold medal. He became physician at the Royal Victoria Hospital before he was thirty years old and physician to the Belfast Ophthalmic Hospital and also to the Belfast Hospital for Women and Children. He then set up in Belfast a private practice which soon became very successful.

In 1887 Whitla became president of the section of therapeutics and pharmacology at the annual meeting of the British Medical Association held in Dublin, and seven years later he was the British president of the therapeutic section of the International Congress of Medicine held in Rome. In 1890 he was elected professor of materia medica and therapeutics at Queen's College, Belfast. In 1909 he was president of the British Medical Association at the annual meeting held in Belfast, and was elected at different times president of the Irish Medical Schools and Graduates' Association and of the Ulster Medical Society. In 1910 he was elected representative of Queen's University on the General Medical Council and held that office for six years, during which time he gave valuable advice not only on therapeutics but also on matters of training and discipline. In 1908 he delivered the Cavendish lecture before the West London Medico-Chirurgical Society on the 'Etiology of Pulmonary Tuberculosis', in which he suggested that at no distant date Léon Calmette's contention would be accepted that in the immense majority of cases primary tuberculosis was not contracted by inhalation but entered through the intestinal tract. In 1913 he delivered the annual oration before the Medical Society of London in which he surveyed the whole field of therapeutics and indicated the lines along which progress would be made.

Whitla was the author of three principal works, namely *Elements of Pharmacy, Materia Medica and Therapeutics* (1882, 13th ed. 1939), *Dictionary of Treatment* (1891, 7th ed. 1923), and *Manual of the Practice and Theory of Medicine* (2 vols., 1908). It was characteristic of his generosity that he presented a copy of his *Dictionary of Treatment* to every member of the British Medical Association who attended the Belfast meeting in 1909.

In 1902 Whitla was knighted and appointed honorary physician to the king in Ireland. In 1918 he was elected first member of parliament for Queen's University, Belfast, and held the seat until 1923. He was a senator of Queen's University and in 1924 pro-chancellor. In 1902 the Medical Institute which he had built to house the Ulster Medical Society was opened. He received honorary degrees from the universities of Glasgow, Dublin, and Belfast and from the Accademia Fisico-Chimica Italiana, Palermo, in 1908.

Whitla married in 1876 Ada (died 1932), daughter of George Bourne, of Drakenage, Stafford. There were no children of the marriage. He died in Belfast 11 December 1933, after a prolonged illness.

[*The Times*, 12 December 1933; *British Medical Journal*, 1933, vol. ii, p. 1193 (portrait); *Lancet*, 1933, vol. ii, p. 1451 (portrait); *Ulster Medical Journal*, 1934, vol. iii.]

J. D. ROLLESTON.

WHITLEY, JOHN HENRY (1866–1935), Speaker of the House of Commons, was born at Halifax 8 February 1866, the eldest son of Nathan Whitley, of Halifax, by his wife, Sarah Rinder. He was educated at Clifton, to which he ever remained devoted, and London University. He joined his father in the family business of S. Whitley & company, cotton spinners, of Halifax. Practical interest in the working of the business was accompanied by close interest in social work in the town, especially on behalf of youth: this latter interest developed as he grew older and continued throughout his life and in 1921 he became president of the National Council of Social Service. He was a member of the Halifax town council from 1893 to 1900. In 1916 he gave money to be spent in premiums to architects for plans to guide public building and town planning.

Whitley was elected liberal member of parliament for Halifax in 1900 and represented that constituency until 1928. He was a liberal whip from 1907 to 1910, when he became deputy chairman of ways and means. A year later he became chairman of ways and means and deputy Speaker, an office which he held until 1921, when he was elected Speaker. As a private member, in opposition from 1900 to 1906, Whitley made many contributions to the Commons debates, particularly during the long and controversial discussions on the education bill of 1902, the details of which he had mastered with great thoroughness. His careful, closely reasoned speeches, based upon exact knowledge, compelled the attention of the House and influenced the final form of the bill. In this way and through his work as a whip, Whitley acquired a parliamentary reputation which was recognized by his selection as deputy chairman of ways and means.

When in 1921 Speaker Lowther retired, Whitley had been deputy Speaker for ten years and it was obvious that he had strong claims to succeed to the chair. His knowledge of the rules, usages, and traditions of the House of Commons was profound and he knew the tempers of members generally and their peculiarities. There was some questioning of his selection on the part of the conservatives, who contended that the chairmanship of committees should not be regarded as a stepping-stone to the speakership. The opposition went so far as to select Sir Frederick Banbury (afterwards Lord Banbury of Southam, q.v.) as its nominee, but before the day of election the opposition died down and Whitley was unanimously elected. His occupancy of the chair—there were five administrations in the seven years—was a disturbed and anxious one. Many of the subjects discussed excited the feelings of a number of members (wages, unemployment, miners' unrest, the General Strike of 1926) and the customary calm of the House of Commons was frequently disturbed: the Speaker was obliged to order the withdrawal or suspension of members and even on occasion to suspend the sitting. Throughout, Whitley maintained an unruffled demeanour, calling unruly members to order in quiet, measured tones. At the time of his retirement in 1928, the leader of the opposition (Ramsay MacDonald) said: 'We shall always remember your great kindness and the infinite pains you have taken to accommodate yourself to us and us to you. You have shown us in a most remarkable way how to be patient and courteous without being lax, how to be strict and severe without being mechanical and formal; and you have also demonstrated to us . . . how gentleness can rule and how persuasiveness can subdue.'

Despite the unprecedented scenes of disorder, Whitley fully maintained the traditions of the chair. If some members considered that he should have shown greater firmness, others—and they represented the more general view—thought that the Speaker had been wise in allowing very full play to the strong emotions of members, many of whom were new to the House of Commons, felt deeply about the matters in dispute, and were unaccustomed to the niceties and time-honoured traditions of parliamentary procedure. That he could be firm was shown during the General Strike: he arranged for parliamentary votes and proceedings to be produced by emergency means: and, in reply to a threat to withdraw workmen from the Houses of Parliament, he declared that he would not allow the work of the House of Commons to be interfered with and would, if necessary, conduct the business of the House without printing and by candlelight. Whitley was keenly interested in the Palace of Westminster, its fabric and its decoration, and he did much to promote knowledge and appreciation of it. He supported enthusiastically the Empire Parliamentary Association, and devoted much time to the entertainment of visiting members of Dominion legislatures.

In industry Whitley's name is associated with the joint consultative machinery (national joint councils, district councils, works committees) which was recommended by the committee on relations between employers and employed (one of the reconstruction committees) of which he was chairman from 1917 to 1918. Readjustment of labour conditions after the war was clearly likely to be a difficult process, and the recommendations in the Whitley reports were designed to secure regular consultation, co-operation, and conciliation between the two sides in industry. Joint machinery of varying types was recommended, adapted to suit the different degrees of organization in the various trades. The recommendations were strongly supported by the government of the day and were widely adopted by industry. After his retirement from

the speakership, Whitley served as chairman of the royal commission on labour in India (1929-1931). In the conduct of the commission's inquiry and in the framing of the Report, he showed characteristic thoroughness: he displayed, just as characteristically, sympathetic understanding of the viewpoints of Indian employers and employed. The publication of the Report was followed by the introduction of ameliorative legislation into the Indian Assembly. In 1930 Whitley was appointed by Ramsay MacDonald chairman of the board of governors of the British Broadcasting Corporation, a post which gave him much pleasurable interest and afforded scope for the exercise of those qualities of impartiality and imperturbability of outlook which long experience in the chair had developed in him to so marked a degree. He held this office until his death, which took place in London 3 February 1935.

Whitley was sworn of the Privy Council in 1911: he was allowed to decline the customary peerage on retiring from the speakership. In 1932 he was awarded the Kaisar-i-Hind medal (first class) for his services to India, having asked permission to decline the K.C.S.I. He married twice: first, in 1892 Marguerita Virginia (died 1925), daughter of Giulio Marchetti, one of Garibaldi's officers, who settled in Halifax and became manager of Crossley's carpet works; secondly, in 1928 Helen, daughter of John Albert Clarke, of Hunstanton and Fransham, Norfolk. By his first wife he had two sons and two daughters.

A portrait of Whitley by Glyn Philpot was presented to him by members of the House of Commons in 1929 and hangs in the dining-room of the Speaker's house.

[*The Times*, 4 February 1935; Hansard, *Parliamentary Debates*; personal knowledge.]

HORACE J. WILSON.

WHITNEY, JAMES POUNDER (1857-1939), ecclesiastical historian, was born at Marsden, near Huddersfield, 30 November 1857, the only son of Thomas Whitney, perpetual curate of Marsden, by his wife, Ann Jane, daughter of James Morice. Both parents were of South Welsh extraction. A precocious boy, he was reading history, not of the schoolboy sort, at eleven years old. He was educated at King James' Grammar School, Almondbury, and was a student (1874-1877) at the Owens College, Manchester, under Sir A. W. Ward [q.v.], who remained his mentor and friend. As a foundation scholar of King's College, Cambridge (1877), he was a wrangler in the mathematical tripos of 1881 and was also bracketed senior in the first class in the historical tripos of that year. Next year he won the Lightfoot scholarship for ecclesiastical history and the Whewell scholarship for international law. Ordained deacon in 1883 and priest in 1885, he became, after holding three curacies, rector of Hempstead-with-Lessingham, Norfolk (1890), and then rector of Milton, near Cambridge (1895). He was all the time amassing a singular knowledge of ecclesiastical history, and had been assistant lecturer in history at the Owens College from 1882 to 1887. In 1900 he was appointed principal of Bishop's College, Lennoxville, Canada, and held the office, along with a canonry of Quebec Cathedral, for five years. He came back to Cambridge as Hulsean lecturer (1906) and chaplain of St. Edward's church (1906–1909). From 1908 to 1918 he was professor of ecclesiastical history at King's College, London, and after a tenure of the rectory of Wicken Bonhunt, Essex (1918–1919), was elected in the latter year Dixie professor of ecclesiastical history and fellow of Emmanuel College at Cambridge. He held these two latter posts until his death, which took place at Cambridge 17 June 1939.

Whitney was an inspiring teacher more by personal and abiding influence on his pupils than by lectures. He always appreciated good work and generously recognized younger scholars. The attraction of his character and his wide sympathies, no less than the range and depth of his learning, made him invaluable both as joint-secretary of the Historical Congress held in London in 1913, and as joint-editor of the *Cambridge Medieval History* from 1907 to 1922. To him the resoldering of links broken by the war of 1914–1918, and the renewal in vol. iii of a severely lamed enterprise were in large measure due. His own writings reveal an historian of high distinction, judicious, comprehensive, fair-minded, sympathetic, to whom impartial learning gave originality. He possessed the power of seizing with a swift ease the gist of a question or of a book. But his works were scanty: the *coup d'œil*, exact, luminous, and instructive, was his forte. Combined with his lovable nature, the same gifts deepened the impression of his *obiter dicta* in conversation, which ranged over past and present with gay, humorous wit and wisdom. Sensitive as

he was to slights, on debated questions he thought of institutions rather than of men. Himself a devout Anglican, he had friends in all the Churches. He married in 1891 Roberta Frances Anne, daughter of Robert Champley, of Scarborough; she gave his valuable collection of books to the Seeley Historical Library at Cambridge. There were no children of the marriage.

Whitney's chief publications are: *The Reformation ... 1503–1648* (1907, revised as *The History of the Reformation*, 1940); *The Episcopate and the Reformation* (Hulsean lectures 1906–1907, published 1917); *The Second Century* (1919); *Hildebrandine Essays* (1932); *Reformation Essays* (1939); and contributions to the *Cambridge Medieval History*, vols. ii, iii, and v, to the *Cambridge Modern History*, vol. ii, and to the *Cambridge History of English Literature*, vols. ii and iii.

[*The Times*, 19 and 22 June 1939; Memoir by R. E. Balfour (with bibliography) prefixed to J. P. Whitney, *The History of the Reformation*, 1940; private information.]

C. W. PREVITÉ-ORTON.

WILD, (JOHN ROBERT) FRANCIS (1873–1939), antarctic explorer, was born at Skelton in Cleveland, Yorkshire, 18 April 1873, the son of Benjamin Wild, schoolmaster, of Newcastle-upon-Tyne, who later kept a school at Eversholt in Bedfordshire. His mother was Mary (Pollie), daughter of Robert Cook, of Sheriff Hutton, Yorkshire. Robert Cook may have been a grandson of Captain James Cook, the circumnavigator [q.v.], through the latter's son James who, according to the unconfirmed family tradition, was not drowned, as officially reported, but deserted from the Royal Navy and had therefore every inducement to conceal his identity. He abandoned his wife, and a man, representing himself to Robert Cook as his father, was in later years turned away from his putative son's door. At the age of sixteen Frank Wild went to sea in the merchant service, which he left as a second officer, transferring to the navy as a rating in 1900.

In 1901 Wild was accepted as ableseaman for the Antarctic Expedition of R. F. Scott [q.v.] in the *Discovery*. He was a member of A. B. Armitage's sledge party to the high plateau reaching an altitude of 8,900 feet, the first high level journey on the antarctic plateau, and when a member of the party was lost over an ice-cliff in a blizzard, Wild kept his head and led the party back to safety. In

1907 on (Sir) E. H. Shackleton [q.v.] returning to the Antarctic in the *Nimrod*, Wild was invited to join him and was one of the party of four that made the long southern sledge journey across the Ross Barrier, up the Beardmore Glacier, and over the high plateau to the record latitude of 88°23′ S., one of the greatest sledge journeys ever made. He showed himself to be an incomparable sledger, wiry, energetic, and buoyant, with great lasting powers and unusual muscular strength. In 1911 (Sir) Douglas Mawson chose Wild as a member of his Australian Antarctic Expedition in the *Aurora* and put him in charge of a party of eight which occupied the Western Base on the Shackleton Ice Shelf from which useful sledge journeys were made into Queen Mary Land and to Kaiser Wilhelm Land. This was one of the most daring winterings in antarctic history, since the base camp was seventeen miles from the land on floating ice. Wild's next antarctic expedition was in Shackleton's *Endurance* to the Weddell Sea in 1914, as second in command, a position in which he excelled. After the wreck of the ship by ice pressure, the explorers reached Elephant Island whence Shackleton and five others made a boat journey to South Georgia for help while Wild remained in charge of the rest of the party. To Wild's energy, initiative, and resource Shackleton attributed the survival of the party under most adverse conditions.

On his return to England Wild was commissioned as temporary lieutenant R.N.V.R. early in 1917, and served as a transport officer on the North Russian front. In 1918–1919 he wintered in Spitsbergen with a small party in charge of an English coal mining property. An attempt at tobacco planting in Nyasaland was cheerfully abandoned when in 1921 Shackleton prepared a new expedition to the Weddell Sea in the *Quest*. On the way south Shackleton died suddenly at South Georgia on 5 January 1922 and Wild took over command although by temperament he was unsuited as a leader. The ship was low-powered and far from satisfactory and ice conditions were bad, and Wild returned with nothing more than a few soundings, although without knowing it he was within sixty miles of the Antarctic continent. This was Wild's last expedition and reluctantly he settled in South Africa and resumed for a time his farming, eventually moving to Klerksdorp, where, after a period of ill health, he died 20 August 1939.

The Royal Geographical Society awarded Wild the Back grant in 1916 and the Patron's medal in 1924. He was appointed C.B.E. in 1920, and was awarded a civil list pension of £170 in May 1939.

Wild married in 1922 the widow of Granville Attman, a tea planter, of Borneo. He had rescued her from Russia while stationed there. There was no issue of the marriage.

[R. F. Scott, *The Voyage of the Discovery*, 1905; E. H. Shackleton, *The Heart of the Antarctic*, 1909, and *South*, 1919 (portrait); D. Mawson, *The Home of the Blizzard*, 1915; Frank Wild, *Shackleton's Last Voyage*, 1923; *Geographical Journal*, March 1940; *The Times*, 21 August 1939; private information.]

R. N. RUDMOSE BROWN.

WILKIE, SIR DAVID PERCIVAL DALBRECK (1882–1938), surgeon, was born at Kirriemuir, Angus, 5 November 1882, the younger son of David Wilkie, jute manufacturer, by his wife, Margaret Lawson Mill. He was educated at the Edinburgh Academy and the university of Edinburgh, whence he graduated M.B. in 1904 and M.D. in 1908. He was elected F.R.C.S. (Edinburgh) in 1907 and F.R.C.S. (England) in 1918. After graduation he held house appointments in the Royal Infirmary, the Royal Hospital for Sick Children, and the Chalmers Hospital, Edinburgh, and spent some time visiting surgical clinics at Bonn, Berne, and Vienna.

On his return to Edinburgh Wilkie became assistant to F. M. Caird, one of the pioneers of abdominal surgery in Scotland, and under his inspiring guidance Wilkie served an apprenticeship in the field of work of which he was to become an acknowledged master. At this time also he began to undertake research work into the causes and treatment of various abdominal disorders, including peritonitis, appendicular obstruction, peptic ulcer, and affections of the biliary passages. These researches were recognized by the award of the Liston Victoria Jubilee prize of the Royal College of Surgeons of Edinburgh in 1918. Hospital appointments came in due course. Wilkie joined the surgical staff of Leith Hospital in 1910 and in 1912 became assistant surgeon to the Royal Infirmary, Edinburgh. By 1914 he was well launched on his surgical career.

As a member of the Royal Naval Volunteer Reserve Wilkie was called up shortly after the outbreak of war in 1914. He was posted to the hospital ship *St. Margaret of Scotland* as acting staff surgeon and subsequently as surgeon commander and saw service in the Mediterranean. In 1918 he was for a time attached to the army in France. He was appointed O.B.E. in 1919.

On his return to civil life Wilkie resumed his hospital work and practice. His reputation as a surgeon and teacher now grew rapidly, so that in 1924, when the chair of systematic surgery at Edinburgh fell vacant through the death of H. Alexis Thomson, he was clearly marked for the succession. Hitherto the chair had been a part-time appointment but now its scope was widened to include the supervision of a department of experimental research and the conditions of tenure were modified to enable the professor to give the greater part of his time to university work. Wilkie threw himself into his new duties with characteristic zeal. His gift of lucid expression stood him in good stead as a lecturer, while his cheerful, dignified, yet modest presence won the hearts of his students. His particular interest was in the development of the research department and here he gathered around him a group of young surgeons, eager to learn from him and each proud to be known as one of 'Wilkie's young men'. Despite the preoccupations of his later years he always regarded this department as his main interest, and by his will he bequeathed funds towards its permanent endowment. After his death the university court, in recognition of his services, caused it to be known as the 'Wilkie Laboratory'.

In 1932 Wilkie accepted further responsibilities as director of the surgical unit of the municipal hospitals which were then being brought into association with the university as teaching hospitals. In addition, from 1934 until the time of his death he served as a senate's assessor on the university court.

Wilkie took a notable part in both the administrative affairs and social activities of the university. His equanimity and moderation, his charm of manner and, not least, the pleasing sonority of his voice, carried great weight in the council chamber, and he could smooth the rough places of controversy or press a point with a grace which was wellnigh irresistible. As chairman of the university settlement movement he came in contact, during the period of depression, with many workless men, which led him to found and endow a social establishment where they could spend their time in educational and recreational pursuits. From the historic association of its site he gave this establishment the name of Kirk o' Field College.

Wilkie's expert knowledge and sage counsel were in great demand. He served on many public committees, including the Army Medical Advisory Board, the scientific advisory committee of the British Empire Cancer Campaign, and the Medical Research Council (1933–1937). He was also chairman of the clinical advisory committee of the Scottish Board of Health and of the committee on burns set up by the Ministry of Mines. Among the professional honours conferred upon him were the honorary fellowship of the American College of Surgeons (1926), the Murphy lecturership, and the presidency of the Association of Surgeons of Great Britain and Ireland in 1936. In 1930 he had the distinction of being invited by the governors of St. Bartholomew's Hospital to assume for a time the duties of surgeon to the hospital and director of the surgical professorial unit. Later, in response to a similar invitation he took temporary charge of Harvey Cushing's Clinic at the Peter Bent Brigham Hospital in Boston, Massachusetts. In 1936 he was knighted.

Apart from his achievements as a surgeon and teacher, Wilkie's greatest contribution was in the influence of his personal qualities on all his associates. A man of liberal principles and religious in the broadest sense, he held the affectionate regard of his elders and coevals and inspired in younger men something akin to reverence. His modest bearing and frank open manner, and his warm sympathy for the troubles, anxieties, and ambitions of others endeared him alike to colleagues, students, and patients, while his simple almost boyish charm commanded a positive joy in sharing service with him. With such personal characteristics allied as they were to a progressive mind and scientific habit of thought he exercised an immense influence which extended far beyond the confines of his own school.

Wilkie married in 1911 Charlotte Ann Erskine, eldest daughter of James Middleton, M.D., of Stow, Midlothian; there were no children of the marriage. He died in London 28 August 1938.

[*University of Edinburgh Journal*, vol. ix, 1938; *British Journal of Surgery*, vol. xxvi,

1938 (portrait); *British Medical Journal*, vol. ii, 1938, p. 598 (portrait); *Lancet*, vol. ii, 1938, p. 645; *Edinburgh Medical Journal*, vol. xlv, 1938; *The Times*, 30 August 1938; personal knowledge.]

C. F. W. ILLINGWORTH.

WILKINSON, (HENRY) SPENSER (1853–1937), military historian and journalist, was born at Manchester 1 May 1853, the second son of Thomas Read Wilkinson, banker, of that city, by his first wife, Emma, youngest daughter of John Wolfenden. From the Owens College, Manchester, he won a classical postmastership at Merton College, Oxford, where he was awarded a second class in classical moderations (1875) and in *literae humaniores* (1877).

The chance perusal in 1874 of an Austrian pamphlet on the armies of Europe first awoke in Wilkinson that deep interest in military affairs which was to become the inspiration of his life. A keen volunteer at Oxford, where he initiated the University Kriegspiel Club, he devoted himself to the study of war and to convincing this country of the importance of the subject. It is principally for his prolonged and fruitful efforts in this direction that he will be remembered.

In 1880 Wilkinson was called to the bar by Lincoln's Inn, and practised in Manchester. Here he maintained his keen interest in the Volunteers and founded the Manchester Tactical Society, of which he remained the leader for some years. Turning to journalism in 1882, he wrote a series of articles on the Egyptian campaign for the *Manchester Guardian*, and served on the staff of that paper as leader writer and special correspondent until 1892. During this period he translated a number of German military works and wrote a succession of books on military subjects, the first of which was *Citizen Soldiers* (1884).

Wilkinson's most far-reaching contribution to British military thought was his book *The Brain of an Army* (1890), in which he described the German General Staff system. Both this and *The Brain of the Navy*, which followed in 1895, had an immense influence.

In 1894 Wilkinson was the moving spirit in the foundation of the Navy League. He brought out a series of works (the first in collaboration with Sir Charles Dilke, q.v.), directed to arousing a public sense of responsibility in regard to imperial defence. During the South African war his remarkable critical and constructive articles in the *Morning Post*, the staff of which he had joined as dramatic critic in 1895, attracted much attention. He became leader writer on military matters and international affairs to the *Morning Post*, and so continued until 1914. From 1909 to 1923 he was first Chichele professor of military history at Oxford, thereby becoming a fellow of All Souls College. In 1919 the university of Manchester conferred upon him the honorary degree of Litt. D.

Wilkinson's authority on the subject which he had made his own was now universally recognized, and his opinion was sought by many senior service men. In his later years he was the author of classical studies on *The French Army before Napoleon* (1915) and *The Rise of General Bonaparte* (1930). Shortly before his death he completed a translation in blank verse of the *Odyssey*.

Wilkinson married in 1888 Victoria (died 1929), daughter of the historian of painting (Sir) Joseph Arthur Crowe [q.v.], and sister of the diplomat (Sir) Eyre A. B. W. Crowe [q.v.]. They had two sons, the elder of whom was killed in war of 1914–1918, and four daughters. He died at Oxford 31 January 1937.

[*The Times*, 1 February 1937; H. S. Wilkinson, *Thirty-five Years, 1874–1909*, 1933; private information.]   E. D. SWINTON.

WILKINSON, SIR NEVILE RODWELL (1869–1940), soldier, herald, and artist, was born at Highgate 26 October 1869, the third son of Colonel Josiah Wilkinson, barrister, of Highgate, by his wife, Alice Emma, daughter of Thomas Smith, of Highgate. Educated at Harrow, he passed on to the Royal Military College, whence he was gazetted to the Coldstream Guards in 1890. His first service abroad was in India, but on the outbreak of war in 1899 he was sent to South Africa, serving with credit and winning a medal and four clasps. Illness caused him to be invalided home early in 1900, but he recovered sufficiently to be sent out again in 1902.

During the years of peace that preceded the war of 1914–1918 Wilkinson's interests turned more and more strongly to the decorative arts in general and to the art and lore of heraldry in particular. He entered the National Art Training School (later the Royal College of Art), South Kensington, and took his studies seriously. From his earliest days as a practising artist he conceived an extreme interest in working in miniature, and as early as 1907 he projected a model palace for the Queen of the Fairies on the scale of one inch to the foot.

So expert did Wilkinson become in heraldry that in 1907 he was able to resign his commission in the Guards (he had attained the rank of captain) and in 1908 to take up the post of Ulster King of Arms and registrar of the Order of St. Patrick. He shared with A. F. Winnington Ingram, bishop of London, the honour of officiating at two coronations, those of King George V and King George VI. Meanwhile he was proceeding slowly with Titania's palace and exhibiting regularly at the Royal Academy. On the outbreak of the war of 1914–1918 he rejoined the army and served on the staff first in France and later in Macedonia, earning a mention in dispatches and a brevet majority.

Returning to peaceful avocations, Wilkinson at length finished Titania's palace, a sixteen-roomed house which was opened by Queen Mary in 1923. For its decoration he had evolved a technique which he called 'mosaic painting'. By the use of an etcher's glass he laid on minute dabs of water-colour, irregular in shape like mosaic tesserae, and numbering 1,000 or more to the square inch. The palace was completely furnished with every conceivable detail, and was greatly admired by the public. It was exhibited all over the United Kingdom and in the United States of America, Canada, Newfoundland, Holland, Australia, New Zealand, and the Argentine.

Wilkinson continued his career as a decorative craftsman, and a collective exhibition of his works was held at the galleries of the Fine Art Society in 1937. He also wrote several books, including his reminiscences (1925), *Wilton House Pictures* (2 vols., 1907), *Wilton House Guide* (1908), and *The Guards Chapel, 1838–1938* (1938).

Wilkinson had his own niche in the art world, and his services to art and heraldry were recognized by his being appointed C.V.O. in 1911, knighted in 1920, and appointed K.C.V.O. in 1921. He married in 1903 Lady Beatrix Frances Gertrude, elder daughter of Sidney Herbert, fourteenth Earl of Pembroke. There were two daughters of the marriage. He died in Dublin 22 December 1940.

[*The Times*, 24 December 1940; Sir N. R. Wilkinson, *To All and Singular*, 1925.]

HERBERT B. GRIMSDITCH.

WILKINSON, NORMAN (1882–1934), stage designer, was born at Handsworth Wood, Birmingham, 8 August 1882, the second son of Howard Wilkinson, of Handsworth Wood, a partner in the firm of Messrs. Wilkinson & Riddell, textile wholesalers in Birmingham, by his wife, Jessie Caroline Bragg. Norman Wilkinson was educated at the New School, Abbotsholme, Derbyshire, which had Swedenborgian affiliations. Here he benefited from an enlightened policy which replaced the usual patriotic heroes by the great thinkers and artists. He thus early obtained an acquaintance with the works, among others, of Shakespeare, Blake, and Bach, and was familiar with the writings of Edward Maitland, Anna Kingsford [qq.v.], and other mystics.

On leaving school Wilkinson entered the Birmingham School of Art, which was then at its peak under the able administration of Edward R. Taylor. The brilliant staff included Arthur Gaskin and Henry Payne, who were both at that time working with William Morris, and Ernest Treglown, who was in touch with Edward Johnson.

Able to indulge unusual tastes, Wilkinson early acquired such things as a sixteenth-century harpsichord, a Kelmscott *Chaucer*, and old Welsh furniture with which he furnished in part a house designed for the family by W. R. Lethaby [q.v.]. Although he already had a small room fitted up as a model theatre, on the stage of which he produced scenery for Shakespearian dramas, his bent was really that of the collector and producer. He composed charming musical settings for the early lyrics of W. B. Yeats, and for old carols, and he played with taste. Naturally of a generous and affable disposition, he was shy and self-conscious, and, in common with other artists of this character, possessed of great and diverse talents, he lacked the intense application and ability necessary to correlate the detail required for technical mastery in any direction.

There followed periods spent in Paris and Italy with an especially intensive study of Gothic art and Tudor design. Wilkinson's enthusiasm for Elizabethan drama did not, however, rule out the work of Maeterlinck, Stephen Phillips, and Mr. Bernard Shaw, and he naturally turned to the less commercial stage. Beginning his designing of costumes in 1910 for Charles Frohman's repertory season at the Duke of York's Theatre, he followed this up with sets for *A Winter's Tale* and *Twelfth Night* (1912), and *A Midsummer Night's Dream* (1914) for Harley Granville-Barker at the Savoy Theatre. His settings for Granville-Barker's production of *The Dynasts* at the Kingsway Theatre in 1914 were among his major successes.

After the war of 1914–1918 Wilkinson for a time continued his work at the Lyric Theatre, Hammersmith, which was then under the management of (Sir) Nigel Playfair [q.v.], designing sets for *The Rivals*, *Lionel and Clarissa*, and *The Would-be Gentleman* in 1925–1926. To this period also belong his designs for plays produced by the Phoenix Society, the Stage Society, and the Stratford Festival (*A Midsummer Night's Dream*, 1932, and *Romeo and Juliet*, 1933.)

The war, however, really put an end to Wilkinson's work, for he never recovered from the effects of its brutalities upon his essentially pacificist nature. He died, unmarried, in London, 14 February 1934. He left the bulk of his drawings to the Courtauld Institute: there is no published record of them.

A water-colour portrait of Wilkinson by Maxwell Armfield (*c.* 1901) is in the possession of the artist.

[*The Times*, 16 February 1934; *Who's Who in the Theatre*, 1933; private information; personal knowledge.]

MAXWELL ARMFIELD.

WILSON, SIR ARNOLD TALBOT (1884–1940), soldier, explorer, civil administrator, author, and politician, was born at Clifton 18 July 1884, the eldest child and eldest son of the second marriage of James Maurice Wilson [q.v.]. He was educated at Clifton College and the Royal Military College, Sandhurst, from which he passed out first, being awarded the king's medal and the sword of honour. He was commissioned in 1903, posted to the 32nd Sikh Pioneers in 1904, and transferred to the Indian Political Department in 1909. He had already spent two years in south-west Persia, and he continued to serve there until 1913, holding the appointments of consul at Mohammerah (1909–1911), and second assistant at Bushire (1912–1913). During the period of his service in south-west Persia he explored and surveyed districts in Luristan and Fars, which were previously unknown. These districts were disturbed and the tribes turbulent. Travelling without regular escort, he wore Persian dress in order to make himself less conspicuous, but he was attacked on three occasions, being twice captured. It was owing to his tact and courage that he escaped alive and without being held for ransom. The value of his work was recognized by the grant in 1912 of the Macgregor memorial medal of the united services of India and also his appointment as C.M.G. Later (1937) he received the Richard Burton memorial medal.

In 1913, upon the formation of a commission representing Persia, Turkey, Russia, and Great Britain to settle the boundary between Persia and Turkish territory, Wilson was appointed deputy British commissioner, and in July 1914 he was promoted commissioner. The completion of the work near Mount Ararat coincided with the outbreak of the war of 1914–1918, and he made his way back to England via Archangel. Wilson's work and travels between 1907 and 1914 are described in his book *South-West Persia* (1941).

The Indian Expeditionary Force 'D' occupied Basra in November 1914, and early next year Wilson joined it as deputy chief political officer. He was employed temporarily in the dangerous work of reconnoitring the Turkish positions. At Nasiriya, where the enemy were entrenched behind a canal, Wilson was ordered to find out whether it was fordable. He carried out this duty successfully by swimming and crawling at night a great distance along the canal in the course of which he was exposed to enemy fire. For this exploit he was awarded the D.S.O. (1916).

Upon the formation in 1916 of a civil administration for the occupied country Sir Percy Cox [q.v.] and Wilson were appointed respectively civil commissioner and deputy civil commissioner. In March 1918 upon Cox's appointment as temporary British minister in Persia, Wilson succeeded him as acting civil commissioner and political resident in the Persian Gulf. In the short space of three years an efficient civil administration was established. The chief credit for this was due to Wilson. 'A.T.', as he was called by his colleagues, was an inspiring leader who won the confidence and affection of his subordinates. He kept in touch with them, however remote, by visiting them in an aeroplane, which at that time was a novel form of transport. He was appointed C.S.I. and a knight of the Order of St. John of Jerusalem in 1919 and K.C.I.E. in

1920. The peace of the country was widely disturbed by the insurrection which broke out in May 1920, and Wilson was subjected to severe criticism. In fact the main causes of the rising were complex and outside his control. He faced the crisis with characteristic courage and determination. The events are fully described in his book *Mesopotamia, 1917–1920, A Clash of Loyalties* (1931).

Upon Cox resuming the civil commissionership in October 1920, Wilson resigned from government service and in 1921 he accepted an appointment as resident director in Persia of the Anglo-Persian Oil Company. He returned to England in 1926, but continued in the service of that company until 1932. Soon after his return to England he took up his residence at Wynches in the village of Much Hadham, Hertfordshire, and he continued to live there for the remainder of his life. During the years 1930 and 1931 he held the position of chairman and took a principal part in the organization of the International Exhibition of Persian Art held at Burlington House.

Wilson was elected member of parliament for the Hitchin division of Hertfordshire as a national conservative at a by-election in June 1933, and was again returned at the general election of 1935. He soon gained a distinctive place in politics by his independent attitude and the extent of his interests and sympathies, and he served as chairman of a number of departmental committees. He was not a party man, and he did not hesitate to advocate policies which were unpopular and exposed him to unfriendly criticism. From 1933 onwards he pressed for rearmament and for compulsory military service. In 1935 he opposed the imposition of sanctions against Italy. Believing that neither the German nor the Italian peoples wanted war, he advocated, even after the occupation of Czechoslovakia, that further attempts should be made to bring about an agreed settlement: but he insisted that it must be made clear to the German and Italian authorities that the British nation would fight, if the negotiations failed. He inherited from his father a zeal for improving the conditions of the working classes, and this was strengthened by his having spent much of his boyhood in the industrial town of Rochdale, of which J. M. Wilson was vicar from 1890 to 1905. He made a close study of industrial assurance and workmen's compensation and was the joint author with Professor

Hermann Levy of two important works on those subjects, *Industrial Assurance* (1937) and *Workmen's Compensation* (2 vols., 1939–1941), which criticized the existing systems. These criticisms anticipated and were subsequently confirmed by Sir William (later Lord) Beveridge's Report on the social services. He also wrote a book in collaboration with Professor Levy on *Burial Reform and Funeral Costs* (1938).

In order to obtain information at first hand, Wilson tramped through his constituency and visited Germany, Italy, and Spain and questioned everyone he met ranging from Hertfordshire gamekeepers to Hitler and Mussolini. He recorded these conversations in a series of books entitled *Walks and Talks* (1934), *Walks and Talks Abroad* (1936), *Thoughts and Talks* (1938), and *More Thoughts and Talks* (1939). He was favourably impressed by some aspects of the Nazi and Fascist policies, but, as he stated, he was no believer in Nazism or Fascism as a policy for this country.

Wilson was a devout member of the Church of England and a confirmed believer in the British Empire as a power to preserve peace and civilize backward races. He studied languages and was proficient in Persian, Arabic, French, and Spanish and in three Indian languages. He read widely and revelled in quoting from sacred and profane literature, not only in his books, but also in his official reports and dispatches. In addition to those works to which reference has already been made, the following deserve mention: *The Persian Gulf* (1928), *Loyalties: Mesopotamia, 1914–1917* (1930), *Persia* (1932), and *The Suez Canal* (1933). He edited the *Nineteenth Century and After* from 1934 to 1938.

Wilson possessed qualities of body and mind which are rarely combined in one person. He was over six feet in height and correspondingly broad and he was strong and very hardy ; he took pride in performing feats of endurance. His character was forceful and his memory extraordinarily retentive. He possessed both physical and moral courage, fearlessly facing death on the battlefield and unhesitatingly expressing opinions which were unpopular if he believed them to be right. He was very industrious, but quick in decision. While his judgement was generally sound, he was sometimes led astray by an excess of self-confidence. His human sympathies were wide and generous. Above all he was guided throughout his life by a strong sense of duty and by a desire to help his fellow men.

It was characteristic of Wilson that upon the outbreak of war in September 1939, although fifty-five years of age, he should have volunteered for service in the Royal Air Force. He was appointed pilot officer in October and posted to a squadron of heavy bombers as air gunner. That same month he had announced to his constituents that he would not shelter himself behind the bodies of young men. He was killed 31 May 1940, when the aeroplane in which he was serving was shot down and crashed behind the German lines.

Wilson's last speech in the House of Commons on 7 May made a profound impression on the members who heard it. He urged the House to take as its motto the words carved on its cross benches *Numini et patriae adsto* (I stand by God and my Country).

Wilson married in 1922 Rose Caroline, daughter of Charles Henry Ashton, of Ellesmere, Shropshire, and widow of Lieutenant Robin Creswell Carver, Royal Air Force. His son and daughter survived him; his widow married Sir Humphrey Milford in 1947.

[*The Times*, 28 November 1940; *Daily Telegraph*, 5 June 1940; *Citizen of Letchworth*, 7 June 1940 and 12 February 1943; Hansard, *Parliamentary Debates*, 7 May 1940; *Journal of the Royal Central Asian Society*, April 1941; Wilson's own writings; personal knowledge.]   E. BONHAM-CARTER.

WILSON, HERBERT WRIGLEY (1866–1940), writer on naval matters and journalist, was born at Linthwaite, near Huddersfield, 25 October 1866, the eldest son of the eleven children of George Edwin Wilson, vicar of Linthwaite, by his wife, Cecilia Wrigley, a distant cousin of the first Lord Oxford and Asquith. He was a king's scholar of Durham School and a scholar of Trinity College, Oxford, where he was placed in the first class in classical moderations (1887) and in the second class in *literae humaniores* (1889).

Throughout his life Wilson struggled to bring home to his countrymen the essential importance of sea-power, and in 1896 he published his book *Ironclads in Action* which 'had an important influence on public opinion in favour of a stronger Navy', and to which Captain (later Admiral) A. T. Mahan contributed an introduction. Thirty years later the book, which had passed through many editions, was extended and republished in two volumes, under the title *Battleships in Action*, which included detailed analyses of the naval engagements during the war of 1914–1918. Of the agitation of 1908–1909 for the increasing of the battleship strength of the fleet, Wilson was one of the chief inspirers, and the justification for his action may be found in the overwhelming strength of the battle fleet at Jutland.

Wilson was a prodigious worker. Besides this very important book, he wrote in conjunction with his intimate friend Lord Charles Beresford [q.v.] a popular work *Nelson and His Times* (1897–1898); he was a contributor to the monumental work *The Royal Navy. A History from the Earliest Times to the Present* (1897–1903), by Sir William Laird Clowes [q.v.], and some chapters on naval history from his pen appear in the *Cambridge Modern History*. *With the Flag to Pretoria* (2 vols., 1900–1901) was an immensely popular history of the South African war. *The War Guilt* (1928), by a survey of international documents from 1871 to 1914, refuted the skilfully conducted propaganda by which the Germans strove to divest themselves of responsibility for the outbreak of war.

As a journalist, Wilson contributed leading articles to *The Times* and the *Standard* before accepting in 1898 the invitation of Alfred Harmsworth (later Lord Northcliffe) to join the staff of the *Daily Mail* as assistant editor and leader writer. He subsequently (1926) became a director of Associated Newspapers, Limited. After forty years' service he retired in 1938, but not before he had given repeated warnings to his countrymen of their danger through weakness in air power.

When Joseph Chamberlain [q.v.] opened his campaign for tariff reform in 1903, he enlisted the help of Wilson, who was able to overcome the initial opposition of the *Daily Mail*, and it was Wilson who was the means of persuading (Sir) Cyril Arthur Pearson [q.v.] to support Chamberlain in the *Daily Express*. He was one of the original members of the Navy League, and honorary editor of the *Navy League Journal* from 1895 to 1908. By the time of his death, unmarried, at Hitchin 12 July 1940, Wilson had raised himself into a position of international reputation on naval and foreign affairs.

[*The Times*, 13 July 1940; personal knowledge.]   J. B. WILSON.

WILSON, JAMES MAURICE (1836–1931), scholar, mathematician, astronomer, schoolmaster, divine, and antiquary, was born at King William's College, Isle of Man, 6 November 1836, the younger son (twin with his brother Edward Pears) of Edward Wilson, first principal (1833–1838) of King William's College, later (1846–1876) vicar of Nocton, Lincolnshire, by his first wife, Elizabeth (died 1842), eldest daughter of James Pears, rector of Charlcombe, near Bath, and headmaster of the grammar school. He was educated at King William's College and at Sedbergh. When in 1855 he went up to St. John's College, Cambridge, he had read a good deal of Latin and Greek, but little else, except that his early training in an evangelical household had given him a very thorough knowledge of the Bible.

In March 1856 Wilson was bracketed second with Henry Sidgwick [q.v.] for the Bell university scholarship: in the following term, in order to compete for a college scholarship in which advanced mathematics were required, he took a short but intensive course in that subject, and showed so much promise that he was pressed to read for the mathematical tripos, in which he came out senior wrangler (1859). A nervous breakdown followed, the result of overwork, which erased from his mind all the advanced mathematics so triumphantly acquired. This loss he afterwards repaired; but it meant, not revising, but learning again from the start. He stood for a fellowship at his college a year later and was elected on his classics.

Wilson had already in 1859 been appointed to a mathematical mastership at Rugby by Frederick Temple [q.v.], his chief duty being to organize the teaching of science there. The subject was new to him, and new to the school's curriculum, but he tackled the problem with enthusiasm, being especially attracted to astronomy. He was soon engaged in schemes for developing science teaching throughout the country, and served with T. H. Huxley and John Tyndall on a committee appointed to study the question. He was one of the original promoters of the Association for the Improvement of Geometrical Teaching which eventually (1897) became the Mathematical Association: he was president in 1921. In 1863 he succeeded to a boarding-house, and five years later (1868) he married Annie Elizabeth, daughter of Edward Moore, bank clerk, of Douglas, Isle of Man.

Wilson was devoted to Temple, but was not happy under his two successors, and on the sudden death of his wife in July 1878 he decided to give up schoolmastering and to take orders. Temple, now bishop of Exeter, was willing to ordain him and to find him work; but in October a letter from John Percival [q.v.], who was shortly leaving Clifton, opened a new prospect. Percival had been asked to recommend a successor and was anxious that Wilson, with whom he had worked at Rugby, should be the man. Wilson was reluctant, but pressure was brought from various quarters, and Temple, when consulted, urged him to accept. He finally agreed. He was ordained deacon and priest in 1879.

Twenty years at Rugby were followed by eleven years (1879–1890) as headmaster of Clifton. These were perhaps the happiest years of Wilson's life. He had been deeply influenced by one great headmaster, Temple, and was following another, Percival, the maker of Clifton, and found there an unusually able staff, including his old friend the poet T. E. Brown [q.v.]. He returned to his old love, the classics, and his lessons in Plato and Thucydides were an inspiration and revelation to his sixth form. He was a born teacher and preacher, and his influence on the school was probably exerted more through his sermons than by any other means. Simple, direct, and stimulating, they came home to boys of every age and temperament.

The busy life of a school did not monopolize Wilson's energies; biblical criticism became a main interest, and the neighbourhood of a great city introduced him to new and absorbing problems. Percival had started a school mission in the poorest part of Bristol, and this work was greatly extended by Wilson, who felt that education which ignored social duties and responsibilities was of little value. He was the first headmaster to introduce a summer camp for boys from the working class, run by members of the school, where the two classes might learn to know one another better.

In 1890 the bishop of Manchester, James Moorhouse [q.v.], offered Wilson the living of Rochdale with the archdeaconry of Manchester, and his growing interest in social work decided him to accept the invitation. Fifteen years of strenuous service followed. There was bitter rivalry between Church and Chapel, and his efforts to introduce more charity and to secure co-operation excited suspicion in both camps. But there was much to do in stimulating church life in a growing industrial district; large sums were raised for building or enlarging schools and churches, and a strong Lay Helpers Association was formed. In spite of exacting duties he found time for lectures on many subjects, and nearly fifty sermons, addresses, and other papers appeared in print during these years, including his Hulsean lectures delivered at Cambridge in 1898–1899 and published in the latter year as *The Gospel of the Atonement.*

In 1905, when he was in his sixty-ninth year, Wilson was offered and accepted a canonry at Worcester. At last the leisure which he had never known seemed to have come, with time to sift and arrange his ideas on the great problems of life in the mellow light of experience. But while there was work to be done, he could not rest. He became governor of the College for the Blind; as receiver-general he took over the accounts of the chapter; as librarian he discovered a new field of activity. There were scores of old manuscripts which had never been properly examined; he learnt how to decipher the abbreviations and medieval script; nearly 6,000 items were catalogued, and a series of publications followed, until failing eyesight put an end to his study of manuscripts. In 1908 a characteristic interlude occurred. The headmaster of the King's School was ordered a prolonged holiday; Wilson volunteered to fill the gap, moved with his wife (he had married again in 1883) into the headmaster's boarding-house, and resumed the strenuous life of teaching and organizing that he had known at Clifton. Civic work claimed his attention; the infantile death-rate was high; he became president of a committee formed to find a remedy, and in six years' time the rate was halved. Another cause which he championed was that of play-grounds and open spaces.

In 1926 growing deafness and blindness forced Wilson to resign his canonry. His much-loved second wife, Georgina Mary, eldest daughter of Admiral John Thomas Talbot, of Clifton, died later in the same year. But neither loneliness nor physical infirmities could quench his mental vigour or his interest in life; they survived unimpaired until his death, which took place at his home at Steep, near Petersfield, 15 April 1931 at the age of ninety-four. By his first wife he had two sons, of whom the elder was killed in action in 1915 and the younger was killed by an accident in youth, and two daughters; by his second wife he had three sons, of whom the eldest was Sir A. T. Wilson [q.v.] and the second was killed in action in 1916, and one daughter. A portrait by Sir William Richmond from which several mezzotints were made was accidentally destroyed in Clifton College chapel crypt during the war of 1939–1945.

'No scientific discovery can be contrary to religion. The mere apprehension that this could be so is itself a deep infidelity.' These words give the key to much of Wilson's theological writings, for to him one of the tasks of the age in which he lived was to present the underlying truth in terms not inconsistent with the new knowledge, and to separate the essential from the unessential in traditional theology. 'The essence of Christianity is the individual experience of Christ, but God reveals himself in the physical laws of the universe as well as in the voice of conscience, so that any contradiction between them is impossible.' On such problems Wilson tried to throw light, and many, even if they could not agree with his conclusions, would recognize in him not only a fearless, honest, and deeply earnest thinker, but a warm-hearted human being to whom religion was the great reality of life.

Wilson's intellectual gifts and inexhaustible energy, his intuition and imagination, his omnivorous curiosity and swift power of mastering the essentials of a problem, would have made him a prominent figure in any profession; and had he confined himself to any one field, he might have been remembered as one of the greatest thinkers or discoverers of his times.

[*The Times,* 16 April 1931; *James M. Wilson: an Autobiography 1836–1931,* edited by A. T. and J. S. Wilson, 1932; private information; personal knowledge.]

H. B. MAYOR.

WILSON, SAMUEL ALEXANDER KINNIER (1874–1937), neurologist, was born at Cedarville, New Jersey, United States of America, 6 December 1874, the only son of the Rev. James Kinnier Wilson, of county Monaghan, Ireland, by his first wife, Agnes Legerwood Hately. At an early age he was taken to live in Great Britain and was educated in Edinburgh at George Watson's College and the university. He graduated M.A. in 1897, M.B. in 1902, and B.Sc. (with first class honours in physiology) in 1903. After serving (1902–1903) as house physician to (Sir) Byrom Bramwell [q.v.] at the Edinburgh Royal Infirmary he studied in Paris for a year (1903–1904) as a Carnegie fellow. Among his teachers were Pierre Marie at the Bicêtre and J. F. F. Babinski at the Pitié. This period was important in laying the foundations of a French method of thought and approach to neurology. After a shorter interlude in Leipzig he became (1904) a resident medical officer at the National Hospital for the Paralysed and Epileptic, Queen Square, London. Thus began a thirty-three years' association which was ended only by death, for in turn he was house officer, registrar, pathologist, and honorary physician. At this period Wilson formed a friendship with the ageing J. Hughlings Jackson [q.v.], and he also came under the influence of Sir William Gowers [q.v.], C. E. Beevor [q.v.], Henry Charlton Bastian, and other great figures in neurology.

Wilson's monograph on progressive lenticular degeneration, contributed to *Brain* (1912), gained him not only the degree of M.D. with gold medal of Edinburgh University, but also international repute, for he was the first to detect the relationship between liver disease and putaminal destruction. His paper also afforded the first clue to the functions of the corpus striatum. The term 'Wilson's disease' became—and still often is—applied to what is to-day more often spoken of as 'hepato-lenticular degeneration'.

Elected in 1912 to the honorary staff of the Westminster Hospital, Wilson left in 1919 in order to join King's College Hospital as junior neurologist: he became senior neurologist in 1928. In 1920 he founded the *Journal of Neurology and Psychopathology* and became its first editor. He delivered the Croonian lectures of the Royal College of Physicians of London in 1925, on disorders of motility and muscle tone, and in 1930 the Morrison lecture of the sister college in Edinburgh. He was president of the neurological section of the Royal Society of Medicine for the two years 1933–1935, and was secretary-general of the second International Congress of Neurology (1935).

Wilson's neurological studies were diverse but particularly concerned with extra-pyramidal disorders; epilepsy, narcolepsy, affections of speech, and apraxia. He published a concise account of aphasia (1926) and a collection of papers in his *Modern Problems in Neurology* (1928). His *Neurology*, edited by Alexander Ninian Bruce, appeared posthumously in two volumes in 1940.

Wilson's strength as a neurologist lay in his philosophic clinical approach to a vexed problem; and in his brilliance as a teacher and writer. He had an unusual capacity of pointing out concepts and ideas which were always stimulating and arresting, and often provocative. In this way he appealed to the imagination of a great number of pupils, and fired in them the zeal for original investigation. His mind was of a highly speculative order and he was not interested in mere descriptive approaches to neurology, although himself an observer of the very keenest sort. Opportunity for experimental and laboratory research was not at his command, but his scientific training enabled him to assay and to criticize the work of others.

Unusually fluent in speech and with his pen, Wilson was in demand as a lecturer and speaker, and as a medical writer, critic, and contributor to periodicals. His clinics at Queen Square were always highly popular with students from all over the world, and abroad his name was probably the best known among British neurologists. World-wide academic honours were accorded him. He was made officier de l'Instruction Publique (France), an honorary fellow of the medical academies of Italy and Belgium, and an honorary member of the neurological societies of most European countries as well as of the United States of America and of Japan.

Wilson married in 1913 Annie Louisa, daughter of Alexander Bruce, M.D., of Edinburgh, and had two sons and a daughter. He died in London after a short illness 12 May 1937.

[*British Medical Journal*, 1937, vol. i, p. 1094; *Lancet*, 1937, vol. i, p. 1253 (portrait); private information; personal knowledge.] MACDONALD CRITCHLEY.

WIMBORNE, first VISCOUNT (1873–1939), politician. [See GUEST, Sir IVOR CHURCHILL.]

WISE, THOMAS JAMES (1859–1937), book-collector, bibliographer, editor, and forger, the eldest child and elder son of Thomas Wise, 'manufacturing traveller' and later tobacconist, by his wife, Julia Victoria Dauncey, was born at Gravesend 7 October 1859. Owing to early delicacy, which he outgrew, he was educated at home, and while still a youth joined the staff of Messrs. Rubeck & company, essential oil merchants, of London, of which firm he became before he was thirty chief clerk and cashier and eventually a partner, retiring in 1912.

Wise's first interest in the English poets he later attributed to having, while a boy, read poetry, and especially Shelley's, aloud to his invalid mother. He soon began to haunt the bookshops, and at eighteen bought a copy of *The Cenci*. Practising economy, and perhaps already a seller as well as a buyer, he was able by the age of twenty-five to pay £45, then the record price, for a fine copy of *Adonais* (Pisa, 1821). He also sought out the families of poets and bought manuscripts from them, so buying from Leigh Hunt's daughter the copy of *Epipsychidion* which Shelley had given him. In 1883 he had himself published *Verses*, but this, although in his list of 1895, was not included in the later Ashley Library catalogues.

Shelley led him naturally to Browning, and in 1886, when the Shelley and Browning societies were formed, Wise was active in both, taking charge of all the printing done by the former body. As time went on his interests and scope of collecting widened, and he came to take in the works of all the major, and many of the minor, English poets from the Elizabethan period, but omitting Shakespeare, whose folios and quartos were already beyond the purse of any but a really rich man, which Wise never was, nor one willing without rare necessity to pay high prices dictated by fashion. With the poets he included some primarily prose writers, and withal he paid particular attention (later, though not at first) to the pristine condition of the copies, as facilitating examination of such points as reissues or cancels, affecting the history of the text. He also hunted for small and privately issued pamphlets, and holograph manuscripts. In the sixteenth and early seventeenth century writers his library, as it finally stood, was of moderate, in the late seventeenth and the eighteenth of very great, and in the nineteenth century of unapproached completeness; he was in particular described as 'the literary heir of the pre-Raphaelite movement', and he might well have been called the same of the romantic movement. At the death in 1909 of Swinburne, the last survivor of both, he added greatly to his collection by buying from W. T. Watts-Dunton [q.v.]

whatever he needed from the poet's library and unregarded accumulations at Putney. He really set the fashion of collecting the works of contemporary authors. In forming the library Wise received much help from Richard Garnett [q.v.] and Alfred Pollard, of the British Museum, and from other collectors, such as George Atherton Aitken and Sir Edmund Gosse [q.v.]. In his turn he made his books freely available to students. In collecting books he probably took Frederick Locker's Rowfant Library as his model.

By his will (codicil dated 6 January 1933) Wise directed his trustees to offer the collection for sale to the British Museum at a price to be fixed by his wife; she accepted in 1937 a price (not yet made public) equivalent to certainly less than half its market value. But some 200 books entered in the catalogue were missing. He named the collection, from one of his homes (52 Ashley Road, Crouch End), the Ashley Library.

Wise paid great attention to the minute bibliographical examination of his copies, and in this lies much of the value of his catalogues, especially the latest. He issued short lists in 1893 and 1895; his full catalogues appeared in 1905–1908 and in 1922–1936 (11 vols.). He also between 1924 and 1931 produced 'Libraries', i.e. even fuller sectional catalogues of his collections of several great writers, including books about them: Shelley (1924), Swinburne (1925), Byron, Conrad, Landor (1928), the Brontës, the Brownings (1929), Dryden (1930), and Pope (1931): he had, between 1889 and 1908, produced small bibliographies of Ruskin (with J. P. Smart), Browning, Swinburne, and Tennyson. Larger bibliographies appeared of Coleridge (1913 and 1919), Borrow (1914), Wordsworth (1916), the Brontës (1917), Landor (with S. Wheeler, 1919), Swinburne (1919–1920), Conrad (1920, 2nd ed. 1921), and Byron (1932–1933). He also edited the catalogue (5 vols.) of the library (which he had largely formed) of J. H. Wrenn, of Chicago (1920). Independently of his library he edited (with Gosse) the works of Swinburne (1919) and (with Mr. J. A. Symington) the *Shakespeare Head Brontë* (4 vols., 1932). As early as 1895–1896 he had edited, with (Sir) William Robertson Nicoll [q.v.], *Literary Anecdotes of the Nineteenth Century*. Throughout his career, until about 1922, he produced some 250 'privately printed' reprints of small rare pieces.

Wise constantly and loudly denounced

piracies and forgeries, and also denied that he was a dealer. The shock was the greater when in 1934 there appeared *An Enquiry into the Nature of Certain Nineteenth Century Pamphlets*, by John Carter and Graham Pollard, proving that between forty and fifty pieces, commanding high prices, were forgeries, many bearing dates earlier than the known first editions, and all by type, paper, or imprint, or all three, not genuine; all were traced back to Wise, who had sold many copies of most through an ex-clerk in the business, whom he had helped to set up as a bookseller. These and others since exposed appear to have been produced roughly between 1886 and 1905. Wise claimed that some at least had been passed to him by Henry Buxton Forman [q.v.], with whom he had directed the printing for the Shelley Society, but he produced no evidence, and some explanations offered by him were demonstrably false. This book has been followed by a mass of evidence convicting Wise, not merely of printing forgeries, but of taking all occasions, some very subtle, of promoting their market values, of piracy, of inserting (in one important case at least) a forged cancel in a book, and, worse still, of habitually selling books which he knew to be forgeries and worthless at high prices to collectors whom he advised and who trusted him, notably to Wrenn, whose collection, now in the university of Texas, is the only one to contain all Wise's forged pamphlets (*Letters of Thomas J. Wise to John Henry Wrenn*, 1944, ed. Fannie E. Ratchford). A great deal of this evidence is to be found, marred by much unnecessary and unpleasant innuendo, couched in a style which the title would suggest, in *Forging Ahead, the True Story of the Upward Progress of Thomas James Wise, etc.*, by Wilfred Partington (1939), which is the authority for the details of Wise's birth (on which he himself was reticent) and early life.

In 1924 Wise was elected an honorary fellow of Worcester College, Oxford, and in 1926 received the honorary degree of M.A. of Oxford University. He was president of the Bibliographical Society in 1922–1924. He was twice married: first, in 1890 to Selina Fanny Smith, who deserted him in 1895 and whom he divorced in 1897; secondly, in 1900 to Frances Louise (died 1939), daughter of Francis Greenhalgh, of Bolton. The latter gave him devoted help with his catalogues, but there is no reason to suppose her guilty of complicity in his frauds; she was beloved by all who knew the pair. On leaving Crouch End he moved to Hampstead, where he was near his friends Gosse and Aitken, living successively at 23 Downside Crescent (1900–1910) and 25 Heath Drive (1910–1937). When he was exposed by Carter and Pollard he was a sick man. He died, childless, at Hampstead 13 May 1937.

Wise was very genial, if unrefined, in character as in aspect. His vanity in his library and its, and his own, repute was childlike and engaging. Indeed this, rather than desire of money (which anyhow was for the library), may well have been what first drove him to invent his ingenious and original type of forgery (if indeed he did invent it). He lived for his library, and his industry was colossal.

[The Ashley Library (catalogues, see above); Wilfred Partington, *Forging Ahead* (New York), 1939, and *T. J. Wise in the Original Cloth*, 1948; J. Carter and G. Pollard, *An Enquiry into the Nature of Certain Nineteenth Century Pamphlets*, 1934; and *The Firm of Charles Ottley, Lander & Co.*, 1948; *Letters of Thomas J. Wise to John Henry Wrenn*, edited by F. E. Ratchford, 1944; *The Times Literary Supplement*, various dates; *Between the Lines: Letters and Memoranda interchanged between H. Buxton Forman and Thomas J. Wise*, with a foreword by Carl H. Pforzheimer, edited by F. E. Ratchford, 1945; Correspondence with Sir Edmund Gosse (unpublished) in the Brotherton Collection, University of Leeds library; personal knowledge.]

ARUNDELL ESDAILE.

WOLFE, HUMBERT (1886–1940), poet and civil servant, whose name was changed from UMBERTO WOLFF in 1918, was born in Milan 5 January 1886, of Jewish parentage, the younger son and third child of Martin Wolff, of Mecklenburg-Schwerin, by his wife, Consola Terracini, of Genoa. The family settled in Bradford where his father pursued his wool business and the boy his education at Bradford Grammar School, whence he went as a scholar to Wadham College, Oxford, and was awarded a second class in classical moderations (1905) and a first class in *literae humaniores* (1907). In 1908 he passed by examination into the civil service, and in the Board of Trade his unusual personality, with his solidity and brilliance of mind, soon brought him to the fore, so that from 1912 to 1915 he was among the band of able civil servants who, with (Sir) William (later Lord) Beveridge, organized the labour exchanges and unemployment insurance schemes, a task which called out all Wolfe's powers. In

1915 he was transferred to the newly formed Ministry of Munitions as a controller of labour regulations, serving under Lloyd George and later Mr. Churchill, and Lord Beveridge reported that the contribution of Wolfe was 'of first class importance'. After the armistice Wolfe reverted to the employment exchanges (by then incorporated in the Ministry of Labour) and from 1919 to 1921, as director of services and establishments, he distinguished himself especially in international labour questions. He was regularly present at conferences at Geneva, where his command of languages, urbanity as chairman of a committee, sincerity, agreeable, sometimes impish, humour, eloquence, and constructive sense made him a most valuable delegate for Great Britain. In 1934 he became head of the whole of the department of employment and training, and when in 1937 the department was divided, he chose to go to the employment division, and in March 1938 became deputy secretary to the Ministry.

As war loomed nearer, the problem of manpower became increasingly more urgent, and in January 1939 the call was made for the recruitment of national services. As in 1915, Wolfe's sagacity and experience were of the utmost value, and six months after the opening of the campaign which aimed at raising a million men for civil defence, the Territorial Army, and the Auxiliary Fire Service, the King reviewed 2,000,000 recruits in Hyde Park. By the time war broke out in September, the home defences were manned and Wolfe saw his efforts rewarded. But it was at the cost of his life, for he worked suffering from high blood pressure and advanced arterio-sclerosis and with full knowledge of the consequences. The strain told and he died in London, on his birthday, 5 January 1940. He was appointed C.B.E. in 1918, and C.B. in 1925. In 1910 he married Jessie Chalmers, daughter of Joseph Graham, an Edinburgh schoolmaster, and had a daughter.

Wolfe will be longer remembered for his literary work. He devoted himself mainly to the study and practice of poetry. He had a visionary faith in its power to convey good, and, through satire, to rebuke evil. He took an artist's delight in form, arrangement, line, colour, and cadence, a craftsman's in the skilled employment of words, rhymes, and metres. His first poems, *London Sonnets* and *Shylock reasons with Mr. Chesterton* (1920) and *Kensington Gardens* (1924), sounded the

manner and matter of themes which he developed later, with characteristic grace and irony. In the course of the next twenty years, besides contributing noteworthy reviews to papers like the *Saturday Westminster Gazette* and the *Observer*, he wrote or edited over forty books, all of them reflecting the paradoxical qualities of his rich and complex nature. In prose he was always happy, even in an official report on *Labour Supply and Regulation* (1923). His critical essays, *Dialogues and Monologues* (1928), *Notes on English Verse Satire* (1929), *Signpost to Poetry* (1931), as well as his thoughtful and vivid studies of Herrick (prefixed to the *Poetical Works of R. Herrick*, 4 vols., 1928), Tennyson (1930), George Moore (1931), and Shelley (prefixed to *The Life of P. B. Shelley*, 1933), surprise yet satisfy by their independent and penetrating intelligence as well as by their lucidity of style. He deplored pomposity, and lit and pointed his own seriousness with peculiar turns of gay or sardonic humour. *Now a Stranger* (1933), *Portraits by Inference* (1934), *P.L.M.* (1936), and *The Upward Anguish* (1938) are excursions in reminiscence wayward and detached, but warmly alive. They show him a master in a sensitive art.

Wolfe's translations reveal his natural sympathy. He was very successful in using every device in an expert technique of verse to render the genius of the Greek Anthology in *Others Abide* (1929); or the knack and heart of simple-seeming German lyrics in *Portrait of Heine* (1930); or Ronsard's exquisite courtesy of form and phrase in *Sonnets pour Hélène* (1934). He also put into spirited English verse Rostand's *Cyrano de Bergerac* (1937), which was broadcast, and a beautiful Hungarian play, *The Silent Knight* (1937), which was produced at St. James's Theatre in the same year.

Wolfe's poetry has both lovers and haters. His crooked, philosophical smile would reconcile them, like the winners and losers in his *Requiem* (1927), indicating that it was all one—'no need for blame, no cause for praise'. He was a romantic in direct succession to Shelley and Byron, and even nearer to Hugo, de Musset, and Heine. He wrote defying contemporary trends, had an urgent belief in goodness and beauty, and, in a disillusioned age, was unashamed of idealism and pathos. Inevitably, then, he invited attack, which made him suffer. But wit and a sombre courage enabled him to face it, while, provided it were unbiased, he welcomed fair and honest criticism. His brains were apt sometimes to defeat his daemon, trammelling his meaning, marring his vision, and clouding communication, but at his best, when speaking straight out, he achieved inspired poetry in moods ranging from lyric and satiric to tragic. Passages and whole poems in *The Unknown Goddess* (1925), *Humoresque* and *News of the Devil* (1926), *Requiem* (1927), with which he reached the peak of his success, *This Blind Rose* (1928), *The Uncelestial City* (1930), *Snow* (1931), *Reverie of Policeman* (a poetic ballet, 1933, produced at the Mercury Theatre in 1936), *X at Oberammergau* (1935), *Out of Great Tribulation* (1939), and the wistful departing notes of *Kensington Gardens in Wartime* (1940) place him among the most genuine poets of his day.

A portrait of Wolfe by William Shackleton is in the Bradford City Art Gallery: a drawing of him was made by Sir William Rothenstein.

[*The Times*, 6 January 1940; *The Times Literary Supplement*, 13 January 1940; *Journal of the Ministry of Labour*, January 1940; Humbert Wolfe, *Now a Stranger*, 1933, and *The Upward Anguish*, 1938; private information; personal knowledge.]

VIOLA GARVIN.

WOOD, SIR CHARLES LINDLEY, fourth baronet, and second VISCOUNT HALIFAX (1839–1934), was born in London 7 June 1839, the eldest son of Sir Charles Wood, third baronet, and first Viscount Halifax [q.v.], by his wife, Lady Mary, fifth daughter of Charles Grey, second Earl Grey [q.v.], the prime minister of the Reform Bill. He was educated at Eton and at Christ Church, Oxford, where in 1861 he graduated with honours in law and modern history. After leaving Oxford in April 1862 he was, in September, appointed a groom of the bedchamber in the household of the Prince of Wales, whom five years earlier he had accompanied on a journey in the Lake District and subsequently on a tour through Germany.

At Oxford, Wood came into contact with some of the men and books of the Catholic revival in the English Church, which quickly captured his sympathies and thereafter commanded his loyalty throughout the whole of his long life. Interested as he became in the devotional and doctrinal side of the Oxford movement, he acquired some insight into the work of the Church among the poor and distressed, through the House of Charity in Soho, and in Whitechapel during the cholera epidemic of 1886. The same anxiety for service led to an adventure of a rather different kind in 1870, when he joined the International Red Cross and served for three weeks as storekeeper in a hospital at Sedan.

Rejecting the political career which was open to him through his family connexions, in 1868 Wood accepted the presidency of the English Church Union, a society founded in 1860 to defend the doctrine and discipline of the Church, to extend Tractarian teaching to the parishes, and to give advice and protection to prosecuted priests. Wood's acceptance at first dismayed his father, for the affairs of the Church appeared to be rapidly approaching a crisis and an appeal to the courts, in which, from the standpoint of an old-fashioned evangelical, the English Church Union would be on the wrong side. But Wood never regretted his decision, even when subsequently (1877) he felt that his presence in a storm centre of ecclesiastical politics made it desirable for him to resign his post as groom of the bedchamber—an event to which many years later his change in the family motto from *Perseverando* to 'I like my choice' is an allusion. He retained the presidency of the union until 1919, when he resigned. He was re-elected in 1927 and held the office until his death.

Wood's long tenure was notably associated with two enterprises. The first was his defence of the Anglo-Catholic position, both against the ritual prosecutions which accompanied the Act for the Regulation of Public Worship of 1874, and also against anything that from the Tractarian angle might be held to impair the doctrine or prejudice the Catholic heritage of the Church. The second was his work for the reunion of Western Christendom through a reopening of relations between the sees of Rome and Canterbury.

The battle of the Act lasted for twelve years, and ended in the complete defeat of those who hoped to kill the Oxford movement in the courts. It was of the greatest consequence that during these crucial years the Anglo-Catholics should have been led by a man with the courage, tenacity, and gifts of lucid exposition possessed by the president of the English Church Union. These same qualities were much in evidence during the ecclesiastical controversies of more than sixty years, through which Lord Halifax (as Wood became on the death of his father in 1885) led the Anglo-Catholic forces with varying success but unvarying vigour.

Halifax's work for reunion was a more personal enterprise. In 1894, with the help of his friend the Abbé Portal, he tried to initiate conversations between Rome and Canterbury. The attempt, which had a not unpromising start, developed into an inquiry at Rome into the validity of Anglican orders. Eventually the commission of cardinals appointed by Leo XIII submitted an adverse report, which was followed in 1896 by the Bull *Apostolicae Curae*, condemning the orders. There, for twenty-five years, the matter rested. But in 1920 the movement towards reunion received a new impetus from the 'Appeal to all Christian People' adopted by the sixth Lambeth Conference. Halifax, at Portal's suggestion, visited Cardinal Mercier, the venerated archbishop of Malines, and this meeting led to the initiation in 1921 of a series of 'conversations', conducted under the chairmanship of Mercier, between representatives of the Roman and Anglican communions. The conversations were interrupted by the death of Mercier in January 1926, and in June Portal, Halifax's most faithful ally, also died. With the passing of these two men, the fifth and last conversation, held in October, was little more than a liquidation. The whole story of this remarkable adventure in reunion has yet to be told. Its immediate consequences may have been slight, but it had the significance of a precedent. For the first time since the Reformation responsible Anglicans and Roman Catholics had met to discuss their differences, and in bringing about these meetings Halifax, despite his years, deafness, and partial blindness, played a great part, not so much perhaps in the debates as in the negotiations that preceded and followed them.

Malines was Halifax's last great work for the Church; although in 1933 his prompt and dramatic intervention brought about the amalgamation in the following year of the two Anglo-Catholic societies, the English Church Union and the Anglo-Catholic Congress. For more than fifty years he occupied a unique position in the Church of England. His authority among Anglo-Catholics, although not always unquestioned, was for a layman unrivalled. He had innumerable opponents, but no enemies. Those who were most affronted by his intractability on ecclesiastical matters usually succumbed to his friendliness, his charm, and his gaiety. Above all, whatever their religious allegiance might be, they could not fail to be attracted by the simplicity and strength of his devotional life.

Apart from his constant concern with the affairs of the Church, from the troubles of parish priests to the attempts to secularize education, from the revival of the religious orders, which he staunchly supported, to the defence of the Athanasian Creed, Halifax had a wide range of interests. He was a Yorkshire country gentleman, entertaining largely and variously in his Yorkshire home, Hickleton Hall, near Doncaster, and at Garrowby, near York, and delighting in country pursuits. He travelled a great deal, mostly in Europe. He made occasional incursions into politics. He accumulated an interesting collection of ghost stories, subsequently published by his son as *Lord Halifax's Ghost Book* (1936) and *Further Stories from Lord Halifax's Ghost Book* (1937). Although he survived many of the disputes in which he was involved and most of his earlier friends, such as Pusey, Liddon, Portal, Gore, W. J. Birkbeck, and Lord Stanmore, to the end of his life he continued to form new friendships and to follow with unabated zest the events of the day.

Halifax married in 1869 Lady Agnes Elizabeth (died 1919), only daughter of William Reginald Courtenay, eleventh Earl of Devon. They had four sons, of whom the three elder died when young, and two daughters. He died at Hickleton 19 January 1934, and was succeeded as fifth baronet and third viscount by his youngest son, Edward Frederick Lindley (born 1881), who was created Baron Irwin in 1925 and Earl of Halifax in 1944.

Halifax was the author of a considerable number of books and pamphlets on ecclesiastical questions of the day. Most of these are of ephemeral interest, but his well-written book, *Leo XIII and Anglican Orders* (1912), has a lasting value in the history of the divided Church.

A drawing of Lord Halifax by (Sir) W. B. Richmond (1880) and an oil-painting by McLure Hamilton (1929) are at Garrowby. Another oil-painting, by William Logsdail (1909), is at Hickleton. At Garrowby, in November 1932, at the age of ninety-three, Halifax appeared for the last time in the hunting field. He was accompanied by his son and eldest grandson, and the scene was painted by

Lionel Edwards. This picture hangs at Garrowby.

[*The Times*, 20 January 1934; J. G. Lockhart, *Charles Lindley, Viscount Halifax*, 2 vols., 1935–1936; personal knowledge.]

J. G. LOCKHART.

WOOLAVINGTON, BARON (1849–1935), philanthropist and race-horse owner. [See BUCHANAN, JAMES.]

WORDSWORTH, DAME ELIZABETH (1840–1932), principal of Lady Margaret Hall, Oxford, was born at Harrow-on-the-Hill 22 June 1840, the eldest of the seven children of Christopher Wordsworth, headmaster of Harrow, afterwards bishop of Lincoln [q.v.], by his wife, Susanna Hatley, daughter of George Frere, solicitor, of Twyford House, Hertfordshire, and first cousin of Sir Bartle Frere [q.v.]. She had two brothers, of whom the elder was John Wordsworth, bishop of Salisbury [q.v.]. Her childhood and girlhood were passed at her father's residence in Little Cloister as canon of Westminster and at his Berkshire vicarage of Stanford-in-the-Vale. Save for one year (1857) at a boarding-school at Brighton, she was educated by her father and able governesses in classics, history, English, modern languages, and music, and with her keen sense of colour and beauty she developed a vigorous style in painting. Knowledge of the Bible, strengthened by laboriously making fair copies of her father's vast *Commentary*, and daily training in the faith and worship of the Church bred a deep personal conviction and an unchanging devotion, which for her became second nature. She grew up under the stimulus of the free and equal discussion in which her father delighted; and her wit, quick mind, and original outlook gave her a place in a wide circle in London, Cambridge, and Oxford, devoted to scholarship, art, Church expansion, and social betterment. Travel abroad began early and continued through life. A long and close friendship with E. W. Benson, later archbishop of Canterbury [q.v.], and his wife was a broadening and liberating influence, and experience in statesmanship was gained as her father's secretary after his consecration in 1869 as bishop of Lincoln. There she made her home, even after his death and her appointment to Lady Margaret Hall, and it was not until 1899 that she went to live altogether at Oxford.

The turning-point in Miss Wordsworth's life came in 1878, when she was appointed the first principal of Lady Margaret Hall, Oxford, founded in that year by E. S. Talbot [q.v.], then warden of Keble College, and opened in 1879. Here Miss Wordsworth found her lifework and during the thirty years of her principalship she imprinted on the hall the indelible mark of her personality. Her character in its gaiety and serenity, its sanity and depth, was singularly unified, but because it was a bundle of opposite qualities a different aspect was revealed with every unexpected thing that she did or said. She was a true representative of her upbringing, but her fearless mind and spirit freed her from any bondage to it, and allowed play for her humour and critical intuition, as well as her power of warm affection and sympathy, which had no trace of sentimentality. She never suffered fools or bores gladly and the faculty of judging every person and thing on their merits tempered her firm adherence to principle, which was sometimes indeed prejudice. With a family tradition of dignified living she combined a genius for personal discomfort, and an instinctive austerity provided the means for endless generosity. Her Sunday Bible classes and her topical Christmas plays were equally expressive of her individual outlook: and she spoke at times with the compelling force of inspiration.

During Miss Wordsworth's long principalship the number of students increased from nine to fifty-nine; resident tutors were appointed; suitable buildings were added, and a hall and library had been begun. Her dearest hope of a permanent chapel was longer deferred, but she lived to see the foundation-stone laid in 1930. In the university at large her family connexions and her wide sympathies enabled her to reconcile the more conservative elements with those who supported the higher education of women, while her common sense did much to forward their admission to the university. She was convinced that if they did the work they must sooner or later get credit for it. But she was no feminist; that men and women should be side by side in the natural relationships of the family was her ideal, combined none the less with her father's profound belief in their equality as human beings, both alike with minds to be developed. To the last indeed she would have preferred for girls a home education such as hers had been, but since that was generally impossible a university training must take its place. In 1886, therefore, on her own initiative she opened St. Hugh's Hall, later St. Hugh's College, and so was unconsciously the formative influence in one college and the founder of another. With all her mental alertness and intellectual curiosity, Miss Wordsworth cared little for learning for its own sake; it must offer some beauty, entertainment, or usefulness. For this reason she did much to encourage the opening in 1897 of the Lady Margaret Hall Settlement for social service in Lambeth.

In 1909 Miss Wordsworth retired from office, and in full vigour of mind and spirit she passed the rest of her long life in Oxford, where she died 30 November 1932, in the length and width of her interest perhaps the greatest of the Oxford leaders of women's education. She received from Oxford University the honorary degree of M.A. in 1921, after degrees had been granted to women in the previous year, and the honorary degree of D.C.L. in 1928 on the occasion of the jubilee of Lady Margaret Hall, which was further marked by her appointment as D.B.E. She was elected an honorary fellow of Lady Margaret Hall and of St. Hugh's College in 1926.

Like her illustrious great-uncle, Miss Wordsworth would have had to admit having 'written verses', and some of her lighter pieces have become current coin. Under the pseudonym of Grant Lloyd two novels appeared in 1876 and 1883. In 1912 she published Glimpses of the Past, followed in 1919 by Essays Old and New and in 1931 by Poems and Plays, volumes in which her most characteristic writing was collected. But her chief publication was the biography of her father, written in collaboration with J. H. Overton [q.v.], which appeared in 1888.

A portrait in oils of Miss Wordsworth by (Sir) J. J. Shannon (1891) is at Lady Margaret Hall, which also possesses drawings by A. G. Walker (1909) and T. Binney Gibbs (1922).

[Elizabeth Wordsworth, Glimpses of the Past, 1912; J. H. Overton and Elizabeth Wordsworth, Christopher Wordsworth, Bishop of Lincoln, 1888; E. W. Watson, Life of Bishop John Wordsworth, 1915; A. C. Benson, Life of Edward White Benson, sometime Archbishop of Canterbury, 2 vols., 1899; The Brown Book, Lady Margaret Hall Chronicle, Wordsworth Memorial Number, June 1933; Lady Margaret Hall; a Short History, 1923; Annual Reports, minutes, and records of Lady Margaret Hall; Annual Reports of St. Hugh's College; St. Hugh's College Chronicle, 1932–1933; A. M. A. H. Rogers, Degrees by Degrees, 1938; private information; personal knowledge.]   EVELYN M. JAMISON.

WORTHINGTON, SIR PERCY SCOTT (1864–1939), architect, was born at Crumpsall, near Manchester, 31 January 1864, the elder son of Thomas Worthington, architect, of Alderley Edge, Cheshire, by his first wife, Elizabeth Anne Scott. He was educated at Clifton and Corpus Christi College, Oxford, and after a period spent in a London office and in studying at the Royal Academy Schools and University College, London, he travelled abroad and then joined his father in architectural practice in Manchester. From 1895, the year of his marriage, he gradually assumed sole charge of the practice: thenceforward, until he was joined twenty-four years later by his youngest half-brother (Sir John) Hubert, the work of Thomas Worthington & Son was done by the son—an anonymity somewhat characteristic.

Of Worthington's work, comprising a hundred or more building projects between the year 1895 and his death forty-four years later, the most notable examples are the London, Liverpool and Globe Insurance Office in Albert Square, Manchester (1918); Ashburne Hall of residence for women (1909–1931) and the Faculty of Arts building (1919), both for Manchester University; buildings for the Manchester Royal Infirmary (1912–1938); Manchester Masonic Temple (1929); Manchester Grammar School, in collaboration with Francis Jones (1931), and the Royal Eye Hospital out-patients' department and nurses' home, and the Dental Hospital and School (1939), both in Manchester. His work also included, besides school and college buildings, commercial premises and church details, thirty or more houses, and some forty hospitals and ancillary works.

On broad lines Worthington's work follows the general development of his time, progressing from an early emphasis on materials and craftsmanship to a confident employment of the column and entablature and the shapes associated with that tradition, and proceeding from that manner to a conspicuously massive form of expression, plain walls, great cornices, the interplay of solid and void, little ornamented. Trained by a classical education (wherein little relevant will have been learnt about architecture) he developed into a skilful and successful solver of competition problems and an expert on hospital building, in which he was a pioneer.

No work of architecture is purely personal. The initial inspiration needs patient labour and the help of others for its completion; and the co-operation of client, builder, craftsman, and specialist during many months. In such, the every-day activity of the architect, Worthington showed eminent qualities of leadership, a critical judgement sometimes perhaps over-acute, and at all times an obstinacy not to be satisfied by anything less than the best as he saw it.

Worthington was knighted in 1935 and received the honorary degree of Litt.D. from Manchester University in 1919. He was awarded the Royal gold medal of the Royal Institute of British Architects in 1930. From 1925 to 1927 he was a member of the Royal Fine Art Commission. He married Lucy Juliet, daughter of Charles Henry Wolff, of Hale, Cheshire, and had a son and a daughter. He died at Mobberley, Cheshire, 15 July 1939.

[*The Times*, 17 July 1939; *Journal* of the Royal Institute of British Architects (containing a list of his works), 14 August 1939; private information; personal knowledge.]

WILLIAM G. NEWTON.

WORTHINGTON - EVANS, SIR (WORTHINGTON) LAMING, first baronet (1868–1931), politician. [See EVANS.]

WRENBURY, first BARON (1845–1935), judge. [See BUCKLEY, HENRY BURTON.]

WRIGHT, SIR CHARLES THEODORE HAGBERG (1862–1940), librarian, was born at Middleton Tyas, near Richmond, Yorkshire, 17 November 1862, the third son of the Rev. Charles Henry Hamilton Wright, Hebraist and theologian [q.v.], by his wife, Ebba Johanna Dorothea, daughter of Nils Wilhelm Almroth, governor of the Royal Mint, Stockholm. After being educated privately in Russia, France, and Germany, and at the Royal Academical Institution, Belfast, he took the degrees of B.A. (1885), LL.B. (1888), and LL.D. (1899) at Trinity College, Dublin, and from 1890 to 1893 served as assistant librarian in the National Library of Ireland. In 1893 he was appointed secretary and librarian of the London Library, which thenceforward formed his life's work for forty-seven years. He was almost immediately called upon to plan and carry out the rebuilding

of the main building in St. James's Square; and acquisitions of adjoining land in 1913, 1923, and 1931 made possible extensions of the library in 1922 and 1934 under his guidance and close control. During his rule the number of books rose from 167,000 to 475,000. An author-catalogue was produced in 1903 and enlarged in 1913–1914, and supplements (*1913–1920* and *1920–1928*) were added in 1920 and 1929. A subject-index followed in three volumes published in 1909, 1923, and 1938. All these were planned by him and produced under his direction, and the whole classification of the library was devised by him.

Besides his administrative work as librarian, Wright was a scholar, particularly in Russian literature. He translated some of Tolstoy's posthumous works, and contributed articles on Russian subjects to periodicals. He was elected a member of the Roxburghe Club in 1916, and contributed to its publications a memoir of *Nicholas Fabri de Peiresc* (1926). In the same year he produced a brochure, *The London Library: a Sketch of its History and Administration*; and a second, *The London Library: a Survey, 1913–1940*, prepared with a view to the centenary of the library, was completed and published after his death, in 1941.

In person Wright was tall and handsome, with something of a Scandinavian appearance, which he may have derived from his mother. He was courteous in manner, but a firm administrator, who earned the confidence of his governing body and the affection of his staff. In 1919 he married Constance Metcalfe, daughter of Horace Lockwood, of Nunwood, Yorkshire, and widow of Tyrell Lewis. He died in London 7 March 1940, failing by one year to see the centenary of the library, but being spared the pain of witnessing the damage done to it by a German bomb in 1944. He was knighted in 1934.

A portrait of Wright by (Sir) William Orpen was sold at a British Red Cross sale in 1915, and was presented anonymously to the London Library, where it has since hung. A collection of his contributions to newspapers and periodicals, covering a wide range of subjects, was formed by an admirer and is preserved in the library.

[*The Times*, 8 March 1940; private information; personal knowledge.]

F. G. KENYON.

WYLLIE, WILLIAM LIONEL (1851–1931), painter, was born in London 5 July

1851, the eldest son of William Morison Wyllie, artist, of London and Wimereux, France, by his wife, Catherine, daughter of John Henry Benham. He was brought up in London and at Boulogne, and early showed artistic tastes, so that he was entered very young at Heatherley's art school in Newman Street. Leaving there at the age of fifteen he went on to the Royal Academy Schools, and won the Turner medal at the age of eighteen. He was first represented at the Royal Academy in 1868 with 'Dover Castle and Town'. Meanwhile he did a great deal of boating at Wimereux and soon manifested that love of the sea which was to be the main directive force in his life and art.

In the early 'seventies Wyllie obtained employment on the *Graphic*, his connexion with that journal continuing for some twenty years. A definite step was taken in 1883, when the Bond Street art dealer, Robert Dunthorne, showed an interest in his work. Wyllie's association with Dunthorne's firm was lifelong, and he also often held one-man exhibitions at the galleries of the Fine Art Society and elsewhere. He was elected an associate of the Royal Academy in 1889 and his exhibits there in 1901 did much to establish his reputation. He was elected a member of the Royal Society of Painter-Etchers and Engravers in 1904, and R.A. in 1907. In 1905 he published a book on *J. M. W. Turner* and produced what is perhaps his strongest picture, 'L'Entente Cordiale', showing the arrival of the French fleet in Cowes Roads. Wyllie spent much time at sea and did a good deal of work for the White Star shipping line, as well as for the navy, with which he sailed during most of the war of 1914–1918. His 'Blocking of Zeebrugge Waterway, St. George's Day, 1918' is full of drama and worthy of a great occasion.

Wyllie's favourite medium was water-colour (he was a member of the Royal Institute of Painters in Water Colours) and he could make stylish sketches even in a small boat on a choppy sea. Oils and etching were his other media. In his latter days his etchings of the busy life of the Port of London brought him widespread popularity. A rapid and prolific worker, he had salt water in his blood, and the golden-wedding greeting which he prized most was a telegram running: 'The navy loves you—Acland.' Active, vigorous, brisk, and kindly, he worked and sailed right up to the time of his sudden death at Hampstead 6 April 1931.

Wyllie married in 1879 Marian Amy, daughter of Captain William O'Brien Carew, of the Indian Marine, and had five sons, the second and fourth of whom were killed in the war of 1914–1918, and two daughters, the elder of whom predeceased her father. His wife, who shared the passion for boating and yachting which were always, apart from painting, Wyllie's main interests, survived him until 1937 and in 1935 published a biography of him entitled *We Were One*.

A portrait of Wyllie by Lionel Percy Smythe, called 'On the Way to Holland', showing him aboard a boat with his wife at the tiller, was destroyed by enemy action but is reproduced in *We Were One*.

[M. A. Wyllie, *We Were One—A Life of W. L. Wyllie, R.A., R.E., R.I.*, 1935; *Mariner's Mirror*, April 1931; *The Times*, 7 April 1931; *Art Annual*, 1907; private information.]

HERBERT B. GRIMSDITCH.

WYNDHAM, MARY, LADY (1861–1931), better known as MARY MOORE, actress and theatre-manager, was born in Islington 3 July 1861, the fifth child and third and youngest daughter of Charles Moore, of Dublin, by his wife, Haidée Sophie Acland. In 1861 Moore was a prosperous London parliamentary agent; but a financial disaster in 1873 brought him to ruin. The eldest daughter went on the stage, and Mary, who was educated at Warwick Hall, Maida Vale, followed her example as soon as she was sixteen. She had good looks, great charm, and a pretty singing voice, and made a start without difficulty at the Gaiety Theatre in light opera and pantomime; but in 1878, before her seventeenth birthday, she married James Albery [q.v.], a brilliant but erratic dramatist of forty, and left the stage.

Mary Moore returned to it in March 1885 as a sad young wife with an invalid husband and three little sons to support. (Sir) Charles Wyndham [q.v.], manager of the Criterion Theatre, gave her a touring engagement as understudy out of friendship for her husband and pity for her plight, but her worn looks gave him no hope that she would make an actress. Release from anxiety soon restored her youth and vivacity, and after astonishing Wyndham in two small parts she became his leading lady in a revival of John O'Keeffe's *Wild Oats*, in May 1886, which made her name overnight. A revival of T. W. Robertson's *David Garrick* in the following November sealed her success, and her acting partnership with Wyndham became one of the most famous partnerships of its time.

Mary Moore's particular talent for playing silly and helpless but attractive women was especially well served in parts written for her by H. A. Jones [q.v.] and Hubert Henry Davies. Jones's *The Case of Rebellious Susan* (1894), *The Liars* (1897), and *Mrs. Dane's Defence* (1900), and Davies's *Mrs. Gorringe's Necklace* (1903) and *The Mollusc* (1907) showed her at her best, and all were repeatedly revived. In herself, however, she was neither silly nor helpless. From the time of her husband's illness (he died in 1889) she managed her own affairs with wisdom. In 1896 Wyndham, recognizing that her head for business was better than his own, took her into partnership. The new management flourished exceedingly, and Wyndham's Theatre was opened in 1899 and the New Theatre in 1903.

The acting partnership continued until 1913, and was acclaimed in the United States of America, Germany, and Russia. Wyndham preserved a youthful spirit and figure until failing memory compelled his retirement at the age of seventy-six. Mary Moore acted little without him. In 1916, after the death of his wife, she married her partner in order to be able to take care of him. After his death in 1919 she made one successful appearance in a new play, and then devoted herself to managing her theatres (she founded Wyndham Theatres, Limited, in 1924) with the assistance of her stepson Mr. Howard Wyndham and her son Mr. Bronson Albery until her death in London 6 April 1931.

[*The Times* and *Daily Telegraph*, 7 April 1931; Mary Moore, *Charles Wyndham and Mary Moore* (privately printed), 1925; *Who's Who in the Theatre*, 1930.]

W. A. DARLINGTON.

YAPP, SIR ARTHUR KEYSALL (1869–1936), national secretary of the Young Men's Christian Association, was born at Orleton, near Leominster, 12 March 1869. For many generations his forebears had farmed in Herefordshire, and his father, Richard Keysall Yapp, lived there on his own land. All his life he retained the simplicity and instincts of a countryman. His mother, Jane, youngest child of Timothy Gammidge, a Congregational minister, exercised a great influence on the lives of her three children. The father died when his elder son, Arthur, was four years old, and the family moved to Leominster. Educated at home and at the Hereford County College, Yapp entered a local firm of agricultural engineers, devoting his spare time to temperance and mission work. It was not until he was twenty-one, however, that he was first attracted to the Young Men's Christian Association when the local branch invited him to become its honorary secretary. To this work he gave his leisure, and two years later (1892) came a call to service as a full-time general secretary of the Derby Y.M.C.A. In 1898 he left Derby in order to undertake the extension of the Y.M.C.A. work in Lancashire, where he became a pioneer in developing Y.M.C.A.s in Volunteer camps (1901), and, later, initiated a programme with the Territorial Force. Yapp's leadership extended throughout the north of England where in fields of widely different character he was gradually building up an experience that was to give him unique equipment for his later responsibilities. In 1907 he was invited by the Manchester Y.M.C.A. to superintend its new building enterprise and to become its first general secretary.

In 1912 Yapp went to London as secretary of the National Council of Y.M.C.A.s, Incorporated. The movement had already gone some way towards freeing itself from its rather narrow early traditions and at the outbreak of the war of 1914–1918 he inaugurated the war emergency service which was to spread throughout the world, bringing the association into a new phase of opportunity and responsibility. The red triangle sign, symbolizing spirit, mind, and body, was introduced in 1914 by Yapp. Through his inspiration, within ten days of the outbreak of war, 250 centres of rest and recreation were at the service of the forces, and before it had run its course there were more than 10,000 centres on the fighting fronts.

In 1917 Yapp was appointed K.B.E. and was invited by Lloyd George to take charge as honorary director of the food economy campaign, and for six months a heavy programme of travel and public speaking was added to his work. In 1918 he visited the United States of America, and in the post-war years went twice to India and once round the world. After the war there was a steady development of new branches at home, and in the days of industrial depression he threw the weight of the national movement behind the work in distressed areas.

For not less than fifteen years Yapp worked eighteen hours a day and seven days a week. In 1929 he retired owing to ill health from active leadership and became deputy president of the Y.M.C.A., which position he held until his death which took place suddenly at Woking 5 November 1936 after visiting the Y.M.C.A. there. He was buried at Orleton. In 1901 he married Alice Maude, second daughter of Thomas Hesketh Higson, of Southport, and had a son and a daughter.

An evangelical churchman from early youth, Yapp preached in churches and chapels of all denominations, and was the first layman to speak from the pulpits of Canterbury and other cathedrals. He had a fine presence with an attractive personality and a keen sense of humour, and was a lifelong teetotaller and non-smoker. An eloquent speaker and an admirable organizer with unbounded energy and initiative, he gave his life to Christian service, with a devotion to youth in which he firmly believed.

[Sir Arthur Yapp, *In the Service of Youth*, 1929, and *The Romance of the Red Triangle*, 1919; *British Y.M.C.A. Review*, December 1936; private information; personal knowledge.]   G. L. CLAPPERTON.

YARROW, SIR ALFRED FERNANDEZ, first baronet (1842–1932), marine engineer and shipbuilder, was born in London 13 January 1842, the elder son of Edgar William Yarrow, of Barnsbury, by his wife, Esther, daughter of Moses Lindo, the head of a firm of West India merchants in London. He was of Scottish descent on his father's side and Jewish on that of his mother, who was connected with Disraeli.

Yarrow, who was educated at University College School, London, early showed a talent for mechanics, and on leaving school at the age of fifteen he was apprenticed to the firm of Messrs. Ravenhill, Salkeld, & company, marine-engine builders, undergoing with them the usual thorough training of his time, whilst his leisure hours were spent in additional work and study in his own workshop. With a young friend, James Hilditch, who shared his interests, he attended lectures delivered by Michael Faraday [q.v.] at the Royal Institution and conducted varied experiments in engineering. As early as 1857 the two boys amused themselves by installing between their homes what was probably the first private telegraph line in England. Together they took out a number of patents, the most successful

being a new type of steam plough (1860–1862) made eventually at Chelmsford by Messrs. Coleman & Sons, who, after the termination of his five years' apprenticeship with Ravenhill, engaged Yarrow as their London representative. The friends had also explored the possibilities of the use of steam for road traction, and in 1861 their proposals were taken up by T. W. Cowan of Greenwich. In the same year, at the age of nineteen, Yarrow read a paper entitled 'Steam on Common Roads' before the Society of Engineers at Exeter Hall.

Hilditch left London to join his father in the north of England, and in 1866 Yarrow entered into partnership with a man named Hedley to establish a small works on the Isle of Dogs at Poplar. This was the modest enterprise which, after an inauspicious beginning, developed into one of the most famous engineering firms in the world, owing to the unremitting energy, confidence, and ability of Yarrow. The new firm's first activities were confined to the repair of river craft, until in 1868 his inventive and alert mind evolved the idea of improving the design and performance of steam launches. Steadily he overcame setbacks and losses, and in the following six years (1869–1875) the fast-expanding works turned out 350 small vessels of varying types. It is worthy of note that many of these were built by methods of prefabrication; they could be taken to pieces for transport overland, and reassembled without mechanical aid wherever they were required. Later Yarrow concentrated on the smaller types of war vessels, and in 1876 produced his first torpedo-boat, built for the Argentine fleet. This was quickly followed by another for the Netherlands fleet, and in 1877 the firm of Yarrow, with a growing international reputation, was constructing vessels for the British, French, Greek, and Russian navies.

During the next five years the design of torpedo-boats underwent considerable modification, increasing rapidly in power and speed, and by 1892 a speed of 27·3 knots, the highest then known, was attained by the *Hornet*, one of the new torpedo-boat destroyers, with the aid of water-tube boilers. Two years later Yarrow supplied to the Russian navy the *Sokol*, a torpedo-boat with a speed of 30 knots, and he next (1899) accepted an order from the Japanese government for boats 220 feet in length, of 6,000 horse power, and with a speed of over 31 knots. He was one of the first designers to carry out really systematic experiments and speed trials, and to see the advantages of the use of high tensile steel and aluminium, thus reducing considerably the thickness of plating and the weight of hull and fittings. At this time Yarrow collaborated with Dr. Schlick of Hamburg and Mr. Tweedy of Newcastle in the Yarrow-Schlick-Tweedy system which reduced vibration of machinery, and developed the Yarrow straight-tube boiler which was widely adopted for both small and larger vessels of the Royal Navy and is still installed in His Majesty's ships.

After forty years at Poplar, in view of prevailing industrial difficulties, high rates, and cost of labour, Yarrow transferred his works from the Thames to the Clyde in 1907, and in 1908 the first destroyer was launched from the new yard at Scotstoun. In 1913 he retired from business and made his home in Hampshire, but when war broke out next year, he immediately presented himself at the Admiralty to offer his services, and in Lord Fisher [q.v.], who returned there as first sea lord in October, he met a kindred spirit. Between them they shortly agreed upon and planned the rapid construction of additional destroyers for the navy, and an adequate supply of shallow-draught gunboats for use in Mesopotamia. For these latter vessels Yarrow accepted entire responsibility: although technically under Admiralty supervision, they were practically completed in every respect by the Yarrow firm and sent out to Mesopotamia, some as completed structures and some in parts for assembly at their destination. This great fleet of river gunboats assembled at Abadan to work in co-operation with General Maude's forces, whilst in other theatres of war the Yarrow destroyers were playing a prominent part. The *Landrail* was the first British ship to fire a shot at the enemy (5 August 1914). During the four years of war the Yarrow shipyards turned out 29 destroyers, all but two for the British navy, of speeds ranging from 35 to 40 knots. They were highly efficient and valuable ships, and gained the warm commendation and affection of their crews.

The character and personality of Yarrow were evident in all that he did and in every one of the craft constructed under his supervision. Designs showed originality and continuous improvement under his hand; details of hull, fittings, and machinery bore the marks of ingenuity and foresight; not the smallest detail escaped his notice. His particular interest in research led to his many munificent gifts to further this aspect of industrial development. In 1908 he presented £20,000 to the National Physical Laboratory for the construction of the Yarrow tank for testing ships' models: in 1923 he gave £100,000 to the Royal Society for the creation of a fund for the foundation of research professorships: and among countless other gifts were grants to the British Association and the Institution of Naval Architects. Another example of his generosity, in a different direction, is his endowment in 1895 of the Yarrow children's convalescent home at Broadstairs.

As an employer, whilst thoroughly versed in the technical and scientific side of his profession, Yarrow showed a keen and human interest also in all his staff, always advocating a closer intercourse between employer and employed in order to inspire mutual understanding and confidence. Frequently he invited one of his workmen to stay with him as his guest, and at the age of eighty he could walk through his workshops and speak to several hundred of his men, calling each by name. His great vitality never flagged. At the age of eighty-nine he made an air tour of Europe, and up to the very end of his life in his ninety-first year he was delighted to welcome and discuss any new invention or idea that might benefit the profession of which he was so great a master.

Yarrow was created a baronet for his war services in 1916, and was elected F.R.S. in 1922. He was elected a member of the council of the Institution of Naval Architects in 1887 and a vice-president in 1896; he was a corporate member of the Institution of Civil Engineers for sixty-two years and in 1929 was made an honorary life member. He was twice married: first, in 1875 to Minnie Florence (died 1922), daughter of Frank Franklin; secondly, in 1922 to Eleanor Cecilia, daughter of William Goodwin Barnes, of Foxley, Bishop's Stortford. By his first wife he had three sons, the youngest of whom was killed in action in 1915, and two daughters. He died in London 24 January 1932, and was succeeded as second baronet by his eldest son, Harold Edgar (born 1884).

A portrait of Yarrow by Hugh Riviere hangs in the Yarrow Home at Broadstairs.

[Eleanor C. Barnes, *Alfred Yarrow, His*

Life and Work, 1923; Obituary Notices of Fellows of the Royal Society, No. 1, December 1932 (portrait); The Times, 25 January 1932; personal knowledge.]

E. H. Tennyson-d'Eyncourt.

YATE, Sir CHARLES EDWARD, baronet (1849–1940), Indian administrator and British politician, was born at Holme-on-Spalding Moor, York, 28 August 1849, the eldest of the four sons of Charles Yate, fellow and dean of St. John's College, Cambridge, and vicar of Holme-on-Spalding Moor, by his wife, Jane Ann, daughter of Arthur Campbell, writer to the signet, of Catrine House, Ayrshire. He was educated at Shrewsbury under B. J. Kennedy [q.v.]. Yate was gazetted ensign and went out to India in 1867 to join the 49th Royal Berkshire Regiment. On admission to the Bombay Staff Corps in 1871 he was transferred to the Indian political service. In the second Afghan war, however, he commanded a detachment of the 29th Bombay Infantry. He was on the staff of Sir Frederick (afterwards Lord) Roberts [q.v.] in the celebrated march from Kabul to the relief of Kandahar in August 1880, and he was the political officer in charge of the city until its evacuation in May 1881. Attached to the Afghan boundary commission of 1884–1886, he was in charge at Pandjeh and showed intrepidity and resource when the Russian attack on the Afghan troops there (1885) brought this country to the verge of war. He was appointed C.S.I. in 1887 and C.M.G. in the following year after the completion of the demarcation of the frontier.

The varied appointments which followed suited a man of Yate's energetic temperament. He was consul at Muscat (1889); political agent in Baluchistan (1890–1892); commissioner for the settlement of the Kushk canals question on the Russo-Afghan frontier (1893); agent for the governor-general of India, and consul-general for Khorassan and Sistan at Meshed (1894–1898); and resident at Jodhpur (1898) and at Udaipur (1899), and acting agent to the governor-general for Rajputana (1898–1899). Finally Lord Curzon selected him to be agent to the governor-general and chief commissioner of Baluchistan, where he remained from 1900 to 1904, and he won the warm regard of the chiefs and peoples of the province. On his departure a clock tower and a fountain were erected in his honour at Quetta by public subscription. He pub-

lished Northern Afghanistan (1888), Khurasan and Sistan (1900), and gazetteers of parts of Rajputana. He was gazetted colonel in 1901 and retired from the army in 1906.

After two unsuccessful contests, at Pontefract (1906) and Melton Mowbray (January 1910), Yate was elected in December 1910 conservative member of parliament for the Melton division. His breezy speeches on varied topics at least had the merit of brevity. His robust conservatism was shown in his attachment to the old standards of administration in India and by his severe criticism of the methods and policy of E. S. Montagu [q.v.], then secretary of state for India. His blunt directness and honesty of purpose were in no way deflected by the baronetcy conferred upon him in 1921. With much reluctance he retired before the general election at the close of 1924. He moved from Asfordby House, Leicestershire, where he had made his home, to the Queen Anne mansion in Shropshire, Madeley Hall, which had belonged to the Yate family for three previous generations. He died there 29 February 1940 at the age of ninety.

Yate married in 1899 Charlotte Heath (died 1936), youngest daughter of Joseph Hume Burnley, chargé d'affaires at Dresden. He had an only son, who died in childhood, and two daughters. The portrait of Yate by John Collier which was presented to him when he left Baluchistan is in the possession of the family: a replica is in the Quetta museum.

[The Times, 2 March 1940; Sir Percy Sykes, Sir Mortimer Durand, 1926, and A History of Afghanistan, vol. ii, 1940; personal knowledge.]   F. H. Brown.

YEATS, WILLIAM BUTLER (1865–1939), Irish poet and playwright, the eldest son of John Butler Yeats, painter, by his wife, Susan, daughter of William Pollexfen, shipowner, was born in Dublin 13 June 1865. He was predominantly of Irish Protestant origin. His Yeats grandfather and great-grandfather had been Church of Ireland clergymen, and on his mother's side he sprang from a little community of shipowners and traders, long established in Sligo, with which county his father's family was also associated. Shortly after his birth his father, who possessed some small independent means, moved to London to study art. The children were frequently in Sligo with their Pollexfen grandparents, and the first verses which Yeats read with delight were from an Orange song-book found in his grandfather's stables. In 1877 he became a day boy at the Godolphin School, Hammersmith; but his holidays were spent in Sligo with his grandparents, and Sligo was the home to which his imagination constantly returned. In 1881 his father, now become a pre-Raphaelite portrait-painter, left London and took a house at Howth, near Dublin. Yeats's education was continued at the Dublin High School, where he was singled out as a clever and original lad, with a taste for natural history and English composition, but no scholar. He was about sixteen when he began to write verse under the eye of his father, who instructed him in Shakespeare and Balzac and directed his ambition towards dramatic poetry. The outlook of the elder Yeats, compounded of a humane aestheticism and the philosophy of J. S. Mill, did not wholly satisfy the spiritual needs of his son, who, while a student at the Metropolitan School of Art, fell readily into the company of a group of mystics. Of these the most remarkable was AE (George William Russell, q.v.)— afterwards a collaborator in the Irish literary movement—and with AE Yeats began to study the lore of the East at a theosophical society which Madame Blavatsky had established in Dublin. Even then in his wanderings about Sligo his imagination had been enticed by the common people's stories of magic, clairvoyance, and ghost-seeing. An introduction to Irish saga in the poetry of Sir Samuel Ferguson [q.v.] and his friendship with an astrological uncle in Sligo were other notable influences of this period.

Soon after the publication of his first book, *Mosada*, a dramatic poem reminiscent of Spenser and Shelley (Dublin, 1886), Yeats joined his parents in Bedford Park, London, where they had again settled in 1887. He continued to write lyrics and plays, and received encouragement from W. E. Henley and William Morris, at whose houses he met many men of note. He also moved in theosophical and spiritualistic circles and wrote with E. J. Ellis a far-ranging interpretative work on the esoteric William Blake (*The Works of William Blake, Poetic, Symbolic and Critical*, 1893). He had to live very frugally, even when with the charming folk-stories of *The Celtic Twilight* (1893) and with his *Poems* (1895), he had gained a distinguished position among the younger imaginative writers. When in 1895 he took up quarters of his own, they were in a very modest locality near Euston; and indeed he was fifty years of age before his income from his books exceeded £200 a year.

After the death of Parnell there was a movement in Ireland towards imaginative nationalism, Gaelic, and the ancient stories, and Yeats tells in his *Autobiographies* (1926) how he hoped to create some new *Prometheus Unbound*, with Patrick, Oisin, or Fionn, in Prometheus' stead, and how on visits to Ireland he went about organizing literary societies among the Fenians and supporters of the Parnellite tradition. His Irish activities were greatly stimulated by friendships with two remarkable persons; the Fenian John O'Leary [q.v.], 'one of Plutarch's people', and Maud Gonne (Madame Gonne MacBride), 'a woman Homer sung', and the subject of his own love poetry. He figured with them in the '98 commemoration movement and was thus brought into contact with Irish revolutionary politics. As Henry Woodd Nevinson noted, 'violent rebellion to the dominating power was contrary to his nature'; yet such politics were not so far removed as might at first appear from Yeats's main preoccupation, for he looked for some accepted authority which would convince the people that 'the more difficult pleasure is the nobler pleasure'. His first concern was with culture and civilization, for which he perceived that some high code of morality was the necessary support, and he hoped to find that support in the Fenian tradition. In London, by contrast, his chief companions were men who were remote from active life, such as Arthur Symons, Lionel Johnson, and the aesthetes of the Rhymers' Club, whose masters had been Pater and Mallarmé. The mark of this companionship was apparent in some of the verse in his *Wind Among the Reeds* (1899) and in the stories *The Secret Rose* (1897), where the fresh Celticism of such lyrics as the well-known 'Lake Isle of Innisfree' and the 'Man Who Dreamed of Faeryland' had given place to something more stylized and sophisticated. 'Yeats took his small colleen to London', someone is made to say in the Irish trilogy *Hail and Farewell* by George Augustus Moore [q.v.], 'and put paint upon her cheeks and dye upon her hair.' He was rescued from the fate of becoming a London-Irishman of letters by Isabella Augusta, Lady Gregory [q.v.], who made a theatre of poetry in Dublin seem possible to him. By the social influence which she could exert and the moral impetus with which she took up his ideas, Lady Gregory brought about, with Edward Martyn and George Moore, two Irish writers interested in the stage, the first performance in Dublin of the poet's beautiful verse-play *The Countess Cathleen*, which had been published in the *Poems* of 1895. This event of 1899 marked the occasion of the foundation of an Irish theatre. It was also the occasion for Yeats of his first notable conflict with the opinions of his fellow countrymen, for the theme of the play aroused Catholic suspicion by seeming to imply an heretical purpose. O'Leary had told Yeats that to succeed in Ireland he must have either the Fenians or the Church on his side; in his subsequent experience as director of the celebrated Abbey Theatre—established by the generosity of an Englishwoman, Annie Elizabeth Fredericka Horniman [q.v.]—he encountered the hostility of the Fenians, or, as it seemed to him, their degenerate successors, whose literal patriotism was offended by J. M. Synge's pictures of peasant life. In giving so much of his energy to the defence of Synge and other prose writers Yeats perhaps renounced an ambition to found a great imaginative tradition in an Irish theatre. Although he provided the gifted Irish players with a series of short blank-verse plays on heroic subjects, it was not these but the work of younger men, social and political satirists, that finally established the Abbey Theatre as a national institution. His most popular play was an early one, his patriotic *Cathleen ni Houlihan*, first performed in 1902 when Maud Gonne, in the part of the old woman who is Ireland, seemed, as he wrote at the time, 'a divine being fallen into our mortal infirmity'. His later work for the stage, or that part of it which he wrote under the influence of the Japan *Noh* plays 'performable in the drawing-room', seemed designed to conceal his real dramatic gift from the multitude.

Yeats's sensibility changed and expanded as a result of his experience of 'theatre business and management of men'. In *Responsibilities* (1914) and *The Wild Swans at Coole* (1917) he seemed to repudiate the wavering moods and rhythm of the 'Celtic Twilight' school, as leader of which he had made his reputation, both in England and in Ireland. It had come to be his conviction that what currently passed as the Celtic note in literature reflected the sentimentality of the cities and was remote from the folk spirit, which is at once concrete and romantic. In this new work he kept close to particulars. He was no longer afraid of eloquence, and wrote of

'Merchant and scholar who have left me blood
That has not passed through any huckster's loin;'

composed epigrams on Synge's enemies; and found themes in the Irish events in which he had figured. Donne (with his fury of self-control) and Landor had replaced Spenser and Shelley as his English masters. The Irish insurrection of Easter 1916, with its aftermath of executions, moved him and revived his tender feeling for his country:

'our part
To murmur name upon name,
As a mother names her child.'

For many years Yeats divided his time, when he was not occupied with the theatre in Dublin, between his London rooms (18 Woburn Buildings, later 5 Woburn Walk) and Coole Park, Lady Gregory's home in the county Galway plain. He spent many weeks each summer at Coole, praised for its hospitality to poets, scholars, and travellers in his two stately poems, 'Coole Park' and 'Coole and Ballylee',

'Where none has reigned that lacked a name and fame
Or out of folly into folly came.'

In 1917, when he was fifty-two, Yeats married a young English girl, Georgie, only daughter of William Gilbert Hyde Lees, of Pickhill Hall, Wrexham, and settled temporarily at Oxford (4 Broad Street, since demolished). He now plunged into the astrologico-historical speculations which were subsequently embodied in *A Vision* (1925, revised edition 1937). These speculations had a genesis in what Yeats called 'an incredible experience'; but Plato, Plotinus, and modern idealist philosophies, as well as Spengler, were ingeniously introduced to corroborate the argument of the book, which was based in part at least on what appeared to be preternatural communications. To the experience and beliefs set out in *A Vision* are traceable certain dominant preoccupations of Yeats's later poetry, which reveal the monstrous impact of eternity in time. Such poetry as 'I saw a staring virgin stand . . . And tear the heart out of his side', 'In Galilean turbulence', 'Those terrified vague fingers', and (his version of *The Magnificat*)

'The terror of all terrors that I bore
The Heavens in my womb',

was religious in its vivid apprehension of supernatural forces, but certainly not Christian in tone.

The young men, almost all orthodox Catholics, who were building up the Irish Free State during the closing stages of the civil war of 1922–1923, overlooked Yeats's antinomianism and offered him in 1922 a position as a senator. He had seen something of the fighting from Ballylee in county Galway, where he had made a house out of an old Norman tower; and although the Irish senators at this moment ran some physical risks, he readily accepted the invitation. At the end of 1923 he was awarded the Nobel prize for literature, which he received in person at Stockholm, where he greatly impressed the audience by his fine manners. On his return to Dublin he became a diligent member of the senate, which certainly possessed in him its most distinguished figure. He liked to entertain in his house at 82 Merrion Square and discuss with the new politicians Irish problems from an imaginative and philosophical point of view. He did some useful work in committees; but in his speeches often threw discretion to the winds, notably in 1925, in a passionate and sardonic attack on a change in the divorce law, which he considered unjust to the Protestant minority—'the people of Burke and of Grattan', now represented by him as the true founders of Irish nationalism. He had gone on several American lecture tours and was a practised speaker. His voice was musical, touched with melancholy. When emphasis was needed he would introduce a hard metallic note, and this at moments of passion was like the clash of swordblades. His myopic gaze as he spoke was turned within, looking into the darkness where, as he said, 'there is always something'. In appearance he was remarkable, having a pugnacious lower lip, olive complexion, and a magnificent head of hair which turned white in his sixties but never lost its vigour. He stood just over six foot, was careful if unconventional in his dress, and took regular exercise for his health, which had never been robust.

In 1928 Yeats's term of office as a senator came to an end, and he did not seek to renew it. In the same year he published *The Tower*; with this volume and *The Winding Stair* (New York, 1929) he was generally considered to have reached the peak of his poetic achievement. It was as if he had recovered his first vision, having become in the interval a great artist, master of many forms of expression, and possessed of many and varied themes. As compared with a Hardy, or a Housman, he had not a wide public, and did not command from his readers the same affection as these poets did from theirs. But the general consensus of critical opinion now assessed him not only as the greatest poet of English-speaking Ireland, but as one who would occupy a sure position among the greater poets of the English-speaking world. Most remarkable perhaps was the deference shown to him by members of the young modernist school. Writers who had grown up in a climate of opinion and feeling, the reverse of that which had prevailed in his youth, recognized in Yeats the most exciting and many-sided personality of the older generation of poets.

The honours which Yeats had won and his happy personal circumstances brought no complacency into his outlook, whether on himself or on society. The most rarefied and metaphysical lines of his poetry were interrupted by emphatic confessions that he found little consolation for the loss of the pride of youth in 'argument and abstract things', in the friendship of Plato and Plotinus ('I mock Plotinus' thought And cry in Plato's teeth'); and he sang of the eternal cross-purposes and the tragic ambivalence of all that touches man and of the impossibility of bringing life before the bar of reason. For an admirable prose play on Swift, *The Words upon the Window Pane* (1934), he wrote a preface in which he urged his countrymen, Catholic or communist, or both, to reject the belief in progress, 'the only myth of modern man', and admit the circular movement of history

'The Primum Mobile that fashioned us,
Has made the very owls in circles move.'

The only politics to the immediate issues of which he had ever been attentive were Irish; but in his last years, when catastrophe loomed over the world, he was ready to discuss international questions, not wholly *sub specie aeternitatis*. As early as 1923 he had declared on a public occasion that 'we do not believe that war is passing away, or that the world is getting better and better', and in a poem of 1919,

'The Second Coming', he had associated a brazen winged beast with approaching public disaster.

In 1932, although in failing health, Yeats made a last lecture tour in the United States in the course of which he collected funds for the Irish Academy of Letters, which he and Mr. Bernard Shaw and Russell had founded in that year. His *Collected Poems* and *Collected Plays* were published in 1933 and 1934 respectively. Installed at home in a little country house near Dublin he frequently visited London. A few of his early English friends survived, and he found himself in imaginative understanding with some of the younger English poets, in particular Walter James Redfern Turner, the Sitwells, Lady Gerald Wellesley (later Duchess of Wellington). A meeting with an Indian religious man, Shri Purohit Swami, revived his old interest in Eastern philosophies, and at the beginning of 1935 he went to Majorca with the Swami, who was engaged under his eye in an English translation of the *Upanishads*. Here a dropsical condition clearly revealed itself. But no flagging of his mental powers could be detected and he remained to the end the indefatigable artist. He had dreamed since his youth of bringing poetry to the people by its recital to music without any loss of its immediate intelligibility; and two years before his death he began to supervise radio broadcasts of modern verse, 'In the Poet's Parlour', 'In the Poet's Pub', with the help of musicians who had a sensitive ear for the sound of words (see V. Clinton Baddeley's *Words for Music*, 1941). The spirited ballads, patriotic and amatory, which filled his last book (*Last Poems and Plays*, a posthumous publication, 1940) were no doubt conceived as a contribution to an art in which music should be the handmaid of poetry. At the end of 1938 his wife brought him to Cap Martin, near Mentone, where he had friends near by. He was his gay social self at a Christmas party; but wrote on 14 January 1939 to a friend that he knew for certain that his time would not be long. 'I am happy', he added, 'and it seems to me I have found what I wanted.' He died of myocarditis on 28 January at the little rock-town of Roquebrune, overlooking Monaco, and was buried in the cemetery there until in 1948 his remains were brought to the churchyard of his great-grandfather's parish, Drumcliffe, near Sligo. He had a son and a daughter, who both survived him.

Yeats received honorary degrees from the universities of Dublin (1922), Oxford (1931), and Cambridge (1933). Among portraits in public galleries are a pencil drawing by John Butler Yeats, and a red chalk drawing by William Strang, in the National Gallery, Dublin, and paintings, by Augustus John in the Corporation Art Gallery, Glasgow, and in the Corporation Art Gallery, Manchester. A pastel by A. Mancini is in the possession of Mr. M. B. Yeats. Other portraits by John, Charles Shannon, and J. S. Sargent are reproduced in the *Autobiographies* and other of Yeats's books.

[*The Times*, 30 and 31 January 1939; John Eglinton (W. K. Magee), *Irish Literary Portraits*, 1935; Stephen Gwynn, *Irish Literature and Drama in the English Language*, 1936; Joseph Hone, *W. B. Yeats*, 1942; W. B. Yeats, *Autobiographies* (*Reveries over Childhood and Youth*, 1914, *The Trembling of the Veil*, 1922), 1926, and *Dramatis Personae*, 1935; F. L. Macneice, *The Poetry of W. B. Yeats*, 1941; *Letters on Poetry from W. B. Yeats to Dorothy Wellesley*, edited by D. Wellesley, 1940; *London Mercury*, March 1939; personal knowledge.]

JOSEPH HONE.

YOUNG, SYDNEY (1857–1937), chemist, was born at Farnworth, near Widnes, Lancashire, 29 December 1857, the third and youngest son of Edward Young, J.P., a Liverpool merchant, by his first wife, Anne Eliza Gunnery.

Young was educated privately at Southport and at the Royal Institution, Liverpool. At the Owens College, Manchester, he worked under Sir Henry Roscoe and Carl Schorlemmer, and then with his lifelong friends Arthur Smithells [qq.v.] and Julius Berend Cohen under Rudolf Fittig at Strasburg. He matriculated at London University in 1877 and obtained the degree of D.Sc. there in 1883. In those days he was a good swimmer and skater, did some climbing, and made some beautiful water-colour sketches.

In 1882 Young was appointed lecturer in chemistry under (Sir) William Ramsay [q.v.] at University College, Bristol. He had already published some work, but he now joined Ramsay in a most fruitful partnership which lasted until 1887, when Ramsay was appointed to the chair of chemistry at University College, London, and Young succeeded him at Bristol. Their researches on the vapour pressures of solids and liquids, and the thermodynamical relations which they proved to exist, have become chemical classics.

These and many of the authors' other papers are of as much importance now as when first published, for they deal with fundamental properties determined with the highest degree of accuracy.

The work with Ramsay on the critical constants had brought home to Young the necessity of dealing with pure substances; so attention was devoted to methods of purification and a systematic study was undertaken of the behaviour of mixed liquids when distilled. He collaborated with G. Thomas on further determinations of critical constants and on the study of hydrocarbons from American petroleum. For this they devised a most efficient 'bubbling still-head'. In Germany Young had become an expert glass-blower, and he made his beautiful still-heads himself. He continued this work with Thomas, F. R. Barrell, Hamilton Jackson, Francis Francis, John Rose-Innes, and Miss E. C. Fortey.

In 1893, while still in his thirty-sixth year, Young was elected F.R.S.: his youngest half-brother, the Rev. Alfred Young, was elected in 1934 as a mathematician. In 1904 Young succeeded J. E. Reynolds [q.v.] in the chair of chemistry at Dublin University. Teaching duties largely stifled his research work while at Trinity College, but he wrote books and articles. His *Fractional Distillation* had already appeared in 1903. *Stoichiometry* followed in 1908, and a second edition in 1918. In 1922 came *Distillation, Principles and Processes* with

chapters by Ernest Briggs, T. Howard Butler, Thomas Harold Durrans, F. R. Henley, James Kewley, and Joseph Reilly. Young also wrote for the revised edition (1921–1927) of *Thorpe's Dictionary of Applied Chemistry* the articles on 'Distillation', 'Sublimation', and 'Thermometers'. His publications extended from 1880 to 1928.

In 1904 Young was president of the chemical section of the British Association's meeting at Cambridge. He received the honorary degree of Sc.D. from Dublin University in 1905 and that of D.Sc. from Bristol University in 1921. Of the Institute of Physics he was a founder fellow, and became a fellow of the Institute of Chemistry in 1888. He was vice-president of the Chemical Society from 1917 to 1920, and a member of the 'Advisory Council of the Department of Scientific and Industrial Research' from 1920 to 1925. From 1921 to 1926 he was president of the Royal Irish Academy. In 1928 he resigned from his chair and retired to live outside Bristol. He died at Bristol 8 April 1937.

Young married in 1896 Grace Martha, daughter of James Kimmins, of Stonehouse, Gloucestershire, and had twin sons of whom Sydney Vernon was killed in action in 1915 and Charles Edgar became headmaster of Rossall.

[*Obituary Notices of Fellows of the Royal Society*, No. 6, January 1938 (bibliography and portrait); *The Times*, 9 April 1937.]

W. R. G. ATKINS.

CUMULATIVE INDEX

TO THE BIOGRAPHIES CONTAINED IN THE SUPPLEMENTS OF THE DICTIONARY OF NATIONAL BIOGRAPHY 1901–1940

Abbey, Edwin Austin . . 1852–1911
Abbott, Edwin Abbot . . 1838–1926
Abbott, Evelyn . . . 1843–1901
À'Beckett, Arthur William . 1844–1909
Abel, Sir Frederick Augustus . 1827–1902
Aberconway, Baron. See Mc-Laren, Charles Benjamin Bright.
Abercorn, Duke of. See Hamilton, James.
Abercrombie, Lascelles . . 1881–1938
Aberdeen and Temair, Marquess of. See Gordon, John Campbell.
Aberdeen and Temair, Marchioness of. See under Gordon, John Campbell.
Abney, Sir William de Wiveleslie 1843–1920
Abraham, Charles John . . 1814–1903
Abraham, William . . . 1842–1922
Acland, Sir Arthur Herbert Dyke 1847–1926
Acton, John Adams-. See Adams-Acton.
Acton, John Emerich Edward Dalberg, Baron . . . 1834–1902
Acworth, Sir William Mitchell . 1850–1925
Adam, James 1860–1907
Adami, John George . . . 1862–1926
Adams, James Williams . . 1839–1903
Adams, Sir John . . . 1857–1934
Adams, William Davenport . 1851–1904
Adams-Acton, John . . . 1830–1910
Adamson, Robert . . . 1852–1902
Adderley, Charles Bowyer, Baron Norton 1814–1905
Adler, Hermann . . . 1839–1911
A E, pseudonym. See Russell, George William.
Agnew, Sir James Willson . 1815–1901
Agnew, Sir William . . . 1825–1910
Aidé, Charles Hamilton . . 1826–1906
Aikman, George . . . 1830–1905
Ainger, Alfred 1837–1904
Aird, Sir John 1833–1911
Airedale, Baron. See Kitson, James.
Aitchison, George . . . 1825–1910
Akers-Douglas, Aretas, Viscount Chilston 1851–1926
Albani, Dame Marie Louise Cécilie Emma . . . 1852–1930
Alcock, Sir John William . . 1892–1919
Aldenham, Baron. See Gibbs, Henry Hucks.
Alderson, Sir Edwin Alfred Hervey 1859–1927

Alderson, Henry James . . 1834–1909
Aldrich-Blake, Dame Louisa Brandreth 1865–1925
Alexander, Boyd . . . 1873–1910
Alexander, Sir George . . 1858–1918
Alexander, Samuel . . . 1859–1938
Alexander, William . . . 1824–1911
Alexander, Mrs., pseudonym. See Hector, Annie French.
Alexandra, Queen . . . 1844–1925
Alger, John Goldworth . . 1836–1907
Alington, Baron. See Sturt, Henry Gerard.
Alison, Sir Archibald . . 1826–1907
Allan, Sir William . . . 1837–1903
Allbutt, Sir Thomas Clifford . 1836–1925
Allen, George 1832–1907
Allen, John Romilly . . . 1847–1907
Allen, Percy Stafford . . 1869–1933
Allen, Reginald Clifford, Baron Allen of Hurtwood . . 1889–1939
Allen, Robert Calder . . 1812–1903
Allenby, Edmund Henry Hynman, Viscount Allenby of Megiddo 1861–1936
Allerton, Baron. See Jackson, William Lawies.
Allies, Thomas William . . 1813–1903
Allman, George Johnston . . 1824–1904
Alma-Tadema, Sir Lawrence . 1836–1912
Almond, Hely Hutchinson . 1832–1903
Alverstone, Viscount. See Webster, Richard Everard.
Ameer Ali, Syed . . . 1849–1928
Amherst, William Amhurst Tyssen-, Baron Amherst of Hackney 1835–1909
Amos, Sir (Percy) Maurice (Maclardie) Sheldon . . . 1872–1940
Ampthill, Baron. See Russell, Arthur Oliver Villiers.
Anderson, Alexander . . 1845–1909
Anderson, Elizabeth Garrett . 1836–1917
Anderson, George . . . 1826–1902
Anderson, Sir Hugh Kerr . . 1865–1928
Anderson (formerly Macarthur), Mary Reid 1880–1921
Anderson (formerly Benson), Stella 1892–1933
Anderson, Sir Thomas McCall . 1836–1908
Anderson, Sir Warren Hastings . 1872–1930
Andrewes, Sir Frederick William 1859–1932
Andrews, Thomas . . . 1847–1907
Angus, Joseph 1816–1902
Annandale, Thomas . . . 1838–1907

Baring-Gould, Sabine	1834–1924
Barker, Thomas	1838–1907
Barling, Sir (Harry) Gilbert	1855–1940
Barlow, William Hagger	1833–1908
Barlow, William Henry	1812–1902
Barnaby, Sir Nathaniel	1829–1915
Barnardo, Thomas John	1845–1905
Barnes, George Nicoll	1859–1940
Barnes, John Gorell, Baron Gorell	1848–1913
Barnes, Robert	1817–1907
Barnes, William Emery	1859–1939
Barnett, Dame Henrietta Octavia Weston	1851–1936
Barnett, Samuel Augustus	1844–1913
Baroda, Sir Sayaji Rao, Maharaja Gaekwar of	1863–1939
Baron, Bernhard	1850–1929
Barr, Archibald	1855–1931
Barrett, Wilson	1846–1904
Barrie, Sir James Matthew	1860–1937
Barrington, Rutland	1853–1922
Barry, Alfred	1826–1910
Barry, Sir John Wolfe Wolfe-. See Wolfe-Barry.	
Bartholomew, John George	1860–1920
Bartlet, James Vernon	1863–1940
Bartlett, Sir Ellis Ashmead	1849–1902
Bartley, Sir George Christopher Trout	1842–1910
Barton, Sir Edmund	1849–1920
Barton, John	1836–1908
Bashforth, Francis	1819–1912
Bass, Michael Arthur, Baron Burton	1837–1909
Bates, Cadwallader John	1853–1902
Bateson, Sir Alexander Dingwall	1866–1935
Bateson, Mary	1865–1906
Bateson, William	1861–1926
Battenberg, Prince Louis Alexander of. See Mountbatten.	
Bauerman, Hilary	1835–1909
Baxter, Lucy, 'Leader Scott'	1837–1902
Bayley, Sir Steuart Colvin	1836–1925
Baylis, Lilian Mary	1874–1937
Baylis, Thomas Henry	1817–1908
Bayliss, Sir William Maddock	1860–1924
Bayliss, Sir Wyke	1835–1906
Bayly, Ada Ellen, 'Edna Lyall'	1857–1903
Bayly, Sir Lewis	1857–1938
Beach, Sir Michael Edward Hicks, Earl St. Aldwyn. See Hicks Beach.	
Beale, Dorothea	1831–1906
Beale, Lionel Smith	1828–1906
Beardmore, William, Baron Invernairn	1856–1936
Bearsted, Viscount. See Samuel, Marcus.	
Beattie-Brown, William	1831–1909
Beatty, David, Earl	1871–1936
Beauchamp, Earl. See Lygon, William.	
Beckett, Edmund, Baron Grimthorpe.	1816–1905
Beddoe, John	1826–1911
Bedford, Duke of. See Russell, Herbrand Arthur.	
Bedford, Duchess of. See under Russell, Herbrand Arthur.	
Bedford, William Kirkpatrick Riland	1826–1905
Beecham, Thomas	1820–1907
Beeching, Henry Charles	1859–1919
Beevor, Charles Edward	1854–1908
Bégin, Louis Nazaire	1840–1925
Beilby, Sir George Thomas	1850–1924
Beit, Alfred	1853–1906
Beit, Sir Otto	1865–1930
Belcher, John	1841–1913
Bell, Alexander Graham	1847–1922
Bell, Charles Frederic Moberly	1847–1911
Bell, Sir Francis Henry Dillon	1851–1936
Bell, Gertrude Margaret Lowthian	1868–1926
Bell, Horace	1839–1903
Bell, Sir Isaac Lowthian	1816–1904
Bell, James	1824–1908
Bell, Valentine Graeme	1839–1908
Bellamy, James	1819–1909
Bellew, Harold Kyrle	1855–1911
Bellows, John	1831–1902
Bemrose, William	1831–1908
Bendall, Cecil	1856–1906
Benham, William	1831–1910
Bennett, Alfred William	1833–1902
Bennett, Edward Hallaran	1837–1907
Bennett, (Enoch) Arnold	1867–1931
Benson, Arthur Christopher	1862–1925
Benson, Edward Frederic	1867–1940
Benson, Sir Francis Robert (Frank)	1858–1939
Benson, Richard Meux	1824–1915
Benson, Robert Hugh	1871–1914
Benson, Stella. See Anderson.	
Bent, Sir Thomas	1838–1909
Bentley, John Francis	1839–1902
Benton, Sir John	1850–1927
Beresford, Lord Charles William De La Poer, Baron	1846–1919
Bergne, Sir John Henry Gibbs	1842–1908
Berkeley, Sir George	1819–1905
Bernard, Sir Charles Edward	1837–1901
Bernard, John Henry	1860–1927
Bernard, Thomas Dehany	1815–1904
Berry, Sir Graham	1822–1904
Bertie, Francis Leveson, Viscount	1844–1919
Besant, Annie	1847–1933
Besant, Sir Walter	1836–1901
Betham-Edwards, Matilda Barbara. See Edwards.	
Bevan, Anthony Ashley	1859–1933
Bevan, William Latham	1821–1908
Bewley, Sir Edmund Thomas	1837–1908
Bhownaggree, Sir Mancherjee Merwanjee	1851–1933
Bickersteth, Edward Henry	1825–1906
Biddulph, Sir Michael Anthony Shrapnel	1823–1904
Biddulph, Sir Robert	1835–1918
Bidwell, Shelford	1848–1909
Bigg, Charles	1840–1908
Bigge, Arthur John, Baron Stamfordham	1849–1931
Bigham, John Charles, Viscount Mersey	1840–1929
Biles, Sir John Harvard	1854–1933

Brett, Reginald Baliol, Viscount Esher	1852–1930
Brewer, Sir Alfred Herbert .	1865–1928
Brewtnall, Edward Frederick .	1846–1902
Bridge, Sir Cyprian Arthur George	1839–1924
Bridge, Sir John Frederick .	1844–1924
Bridge, Thomas William . .	1848–1909
Bridgeman, Sir Francis Charles Bridgeman	1848–1929
Bridges, Sir (George) Tom Molesworth	1871–1939
Bridges, John Henry . .	1832–1906
Bridges, Robert Seymour .	1844–1930
Bridges, Sir William Throsby .	1861–1915
Briggs, John	1862–1902
Bright, James Franck . .	1832–1920
Bright, William . . .	1824–1901
Brightman, Frank Edward .	1856–1932
Brightwen, Eliza . . .	1830–1906
Brise, Sir Evelyn (John) Ruggles-. See Ruggles-Brise.	
Broadbent, Sir William Henry .	1835–1907
Broadhurst, Henry . . .	1840–1911
Brock, Sir Thomas . .	1847–1922
Brodribb, William Jackson .	1829–1905
Brodrick, George Charles .	1831–1903
Bromby, Charles Hamilton. See under Bromby, Charles Henry.	
Bromby, Charles Henry .	1814–1907
Brooke, Alan England .	1863–1939
Brooke, Sir Charles Anthony Johnson . . .	1829–1917
Brooke, Rupert . . .	1887–1915
Brooke, Stopford Augustus .	1832–1916
Brooking Rowe, Joshua. See Rowe.	
Brotherhood, Peter . .	1838–1902
Brough, Bennett Hooper .	1860–1908
Brough, Lionel . . .	1836–1909
Brought, Robert . .	1872–1905
Broughton, Rhoda . .	1840–1920
Brown, Ernest William .	1866–1938
Brown, George Douglas, 'George Douglas'	1869–1902
Brown, Sir George Thomas .	1827–1906
Brown, Gerard Baldwin .	1849–1932
Brown, Horatio Robert Forbes .	1854–1926
Brown, Joseph . . .	1809–1902
Brown, Peter Hume .	1849–1918
Brown, William Haig-. See Haig-Brown.	
Browne, Edward Granville .	1862–1926
Browne, George Forrest .	1833–1930
Browne, Sir James Crichton-	1840–1938
Browne, Sir James Frankfort Manners . . .	1823–1910
Browne, Sir Samuel James .	1824–1901
Browne, Thomas . .	1870–1910
Browning, Oscar . .	1837–1923
Bruce, Alexander Hugh, Baron Balfour of Burleigh . .	1849–1921
Bruce, Charles Granville .	1866–1939
Bruce, Sir David . .	1855–1931
Bruce, Sir George Barclay .	1821–1908
Bruce, Victor Alexander, Earl of Elgin	1849–1917
Bruce, William Speirs .	1867–1921
Brunton, Sir Thomas Lauder .	1844–1916

Brushfield, Thomas Nadauld .	1828–1910
Bryce, James, Viscount . .	1838–1922
Brydon, John McKean .	1840–1901
Buchan, Alexander . . .	1829–1907
Buchan, John, Baron Tweedsmuir	1875–1940
Buchanan, George . . .	1827–1905
Buchanan, Sir George Cunningham	1865–1940
Buchanan, Sir George Seaton .	1869–1936
Buchanan, Sir George William .	1854–1924
Buchanan, James, Baron Woolavington . . .	1849–1935
Buchanan, Robert Williams .	1841–1901
Buckle, George Earle .	1854–1935
Buckley, Henry Burton, Baron Wrenbury	1845–1935
Buckmaster, Stanley Owen, Viscount	1861–1934
Buckton, George Bowdler . .	1818–1905
Budge, Sir Ernest Alfred Thompson Wallis . . .	1857–1934
Bulfin, Sir Edward Stanislaus .	1862–1939
Bullen, Arthur Henry . .	1857–1920
Buller, Sir Redvers Henry .	1839–1908
Buller, Sir Walter Lawry .	1838–1906
Bulwer, Sir Edward Earle Gascoyne	1829–1910
Bunsen, Ernest de . . .	1819–1903
Bunsen, Sir Maurice William Ernest de. See De Bunsen.	
Bunting, Sir Percy William .	1836–1911
Burbidge, Edward . . .	1839–1903
Burbidge, Frederick William .	1847–1905
Burbury, Samuel Hawksley .	1831–1911
Burdett-Coutts, Angela Georgina, Baroness . . .	1814–1907
Burdon, John Shaw . . .	1826–1906
Burdon-Sanderson, Sir John Scott	1828–1905
Burge, Hubert Murray .	1862–1925
Burgh Canning, Hubert George De, Marquess of Clanricarde .	1832–1916
Burkitt, Francis Crawford .	1864–1935
Burn, Robert . . .	1829–1904
Burn-Murdoch, John .	1852–1909
Burnand, Sir Francis Cowley .	1836–1917
Burne, Sir Owen Tudor .	1837–1909
Burnet, John . . .	1863–1928
Burnet, Sir John James .	1857–1938
Burney, Sir Cecil .	1858–1929
Burnham, Baron. See Levy-Lawson, Edward.	
Burnham, Viscount. See Lawson, Harry Lawson Webster Levy-.	
Burns, Dawson . . .	1828–1909
Burnside, William . .	1852–1927
Burroughs (afterwards Traill-Burroughs), Sir Frederick William	1831–1905
Burrows, Montagu . .	1819–1905
Burt, Thomas . . .	1837–1922
Burton, Baron. See Bass, Michael Arthur.	
Bury, John Bagnell . .	1861–1927
Bushell, Stephen Wootton .	1844–1908
Busk, Rachel Harriette . .	1831–1907
Butcher, Samuel Henry .	1850–1910

Channell, Sir Arthur Moseley	.	1838–1928	Clery, Sir Cornelius Francis	.	1838–1926
Channer, George Nicholas.	.	1842–1905	Cleworth, Thomas Ebenezer	.	1854–1909
Chaplin, Henry, Viscount .	.	1840–1923	Clifford, Frederick	. .	.	1828–1904
Chapman, Edward John .	.	1821–1904	Clifford, John .	.	1836–1923
Charles, James	.	1851–1906	Clodd, Edward	. .	.	1840–1930
Charles, Robert Henry	.	1855–1931	Close, Maxwell Henry	.	1822–1903
Charley, Sir William Thomas	.	1833–1904	Clowes, Sir William Laird .	.	1856–1905
Charrington, Frederick Nicholas	1850–1936	Clunies-Ross, George	.	1842–1910
Charteris, Archibald Hamilton .	1835–1908	Clutton, Henry Hugh	. .	1850–1909
Chase, Drummond Percy .	.	1820–1902	Clutton-Brock, Arthur	.	1868–1924
Chase, Frederic Henry	.	1853–1925	Cobb, Gerard Francis	.	1838–1904
Chase, Marian Emma	.	1844–1905	Cobbe, Sir Alexander Stanhope .	1870–1931
Chase, William St. Lucian	.	1856–1908	Cobden-Sanderson, Thomas James	1840–1922
Chavasse, Francis James .	.	1846–1928	Cochrane, Douglas Mackinnon	
Cheadle, Walter Butler	.	1835–1910	Baillie Hamilton, Earl of	
Cheatle, Arthur Henry	.	1866–1929	Dundonald	1852–1935
Cheetham, Samuel .	.	1827–1908	Cochrane-Baillie, Charles Wallace	
Chelmsford, Baron. See Thesiger,		Alexander Napier Ross, Baron	
Frederic Augustus.		Lamington. See Baillie.	
Chelmsford, Viscount. See Thesi-		Coghlan, Sir Charles Patrick John	1863–1927
ger, Frederic John Napier.		Cohen, Arthur. . . .	1829–1914
Chermside, Sir Herbert Charles .	1850–1929	Coillard, François . .	1834–1904
Chesterton, Gilbert Keith .	.	1874–1936	Cokayne, George Edward .	.	1825–1911
Chevalier, Albert .	.	1861–1923	Coke, Thomas William, Earl of	
Cheylesmore, Baron. See Eaton,		Leicester . . .	1822–1909
Herbert Francis.		Coleman, William Stephen	.	1829–1904
Cheylesmore, Baron. See Eaton,		Coleridge, Bernard John Sey-	
William Meriton.		mour, Baron	1851–1927
Cheyne, Thomas Kelly	.	1841–1915	Coleridge, Mary Elizabeth	.	1861–1907
Cheyne, Sir (William) Watson	.	1852–1932	Coleridge, Stephen William	
Child, Thomas	.	1839–1906	Buchanan . .	1854–1936
Child-Villiers, Victor Albert		Coleridge-Taylor, Samuel .	.	1875–1912
George, Earl of Jersey. See		Coles, Charles Edward (Pasha) .	1853–1926
Villiers.		Coles, Vincent Stuckey Stratton	1845–1929
Childers, Robert Erskine .	.	1870–1922	Collen, Sir Edwin Henry Hayter	1843–1911
Childs, William Macbride .	.	1869–1939	Collett, Sir Henry	. .	1836–1901
Chilston, Viscount. See Akers-		Collier, John . .	1850–1934
Douglas, Aretas.		Collings, Jesse . . .	1831–1920
Chirol, Sir (Ignatius) Valentine .	1852–1929	Collingwood, Cuthbert	.	1826–1908
Chisholm, Hugh .	.	1866–1924	Collins, John Churton	.	1848–1908
Cholmondeley, Hugh, Baron		Collins, Michael .	.	1890–1922
Delamere . . .	1870–1931	Collins, Richard Henn, Lord	.	1842–1911
Christie, Sir William Henry Ma-		Collins, William Edward .	.	1867–1911
honey	1845–1922	Colnaghi, Martin Henry .	.	1821–1908
Chrystal, George .	.	1851–1911	Colomb, Sir John Charles Ready	1838–1909
Church, Sir William Selby	.	1837–1928	Colton, Sir John . .	1823–1902
Clanricarde, Marquess of. See		Colvile, Sir Henry Edward	.	1852–1907
Burgh Canning, Hubert George		Colville, Sir Stanley Cecil James	1861–1939
De.		Colvin, Sir Auckland	.	1838–1908
Clanwilliam, Earl of. See Meade,		Colvin, Ian Duncan .	.	1877–1938
Richard James.		Colvin, Sir Sidney .	.	1845–1927
Clark, Albert Curtis .	.	1859–1937	Colvin, Sir Walter Mytton. See	
Clark, John Willis .	.	1833–1910	under Colvin, Sir Auckland.	
Clarke, Sir Andrew .	.	1824–1902	Commerell, Sir John Edmund .	1829–1901
Clarke, Sir Caspar Purdon	.	1846–1911	Common, Andrew Ainslie .	.	1841–1903
Clarke, Charles Baron	.	1832–1906	Compton, Lord Alwyne Frederick	1825–1906
Clarke, Sir Edward George	.	1841–1931	Conder, Charles .	.	1868–1909
Clarke, George Sydenham, Baron		Conder, Claude Reignier .	.	1848–1910
Sydenham of Combe	.	1848–1933	Congreve, Sir Walter Norris	1862–1927
Clarke, Henry Butler	.	1863–1904	Connemara, Baron. See Bourke,	
Clarke, Sir Marshal James	.	1841–1909	Robert.	
Clarke, Maude Violet	.	1892–1935	Connor, Ralph, pseudonym. See	
Clasper, John Hawks	.	1836–1908	Gordon, Charles William.	
Clayden, Peter William .	.	1827–1902	Conquest, George Augustus	.	1837–1901
Clayton, Sir Gilbert Falkingham	1875–1929	Conrad, Joseph . .	.	1857–1924
Clerk, Sir Dugald .	.	1854–1932	Conway, Robert Seymour.	.	1864–1933
Clerke, Agnes Mary .	.	1842–1907	Conway, William Martin, Baron	
Clerke, Ellen Mary. See under		Conway of Allington	.	1856–1937
Clerke, Agnes Mary.		Conybeare, Frederick Cornwallis	1856–1924

Dale, Sir David	1829–1906	De László, Philip Alexius. See	
Dallinger, William Henry	1842–1909	László de Lombos.	
Dalrymple-Hay, Sir Harley		Delius, Frederick	1862–1934
Hugh. See Hay.		Dell, Ethel Mary. See Savage.	
Dalziel, Davison Alexander,		Deller, Sir Edwin	1883–1936
Baron	1854–1928	De Montmorency, James Edward	
Dalziel, Edward	1817–1905	Geoffrey	1866–1934
Dalziel, George	1815–1902	De Montmorency, Raymond	
Dalziel, James Henry, Baron		Harvey, Viscount Frankfort	
Dalziel of Kirkcaldy	1868–1935	de Montmorency	1835–1902
Dalziel, Thomas Bolton Gilchrist		De Morgan, William Frend	1839–1917
Septimus	1823–1906	Denney, James	1856–1917
Daniel, Charles Henry Olive	1836–1919	Denny, Sir Archibald	1860–1936
Daniel, Evan	1837–1904	Dent, Joseph Malaby	1849–1926
Danvers, Frederic Charles	1833–1906	Derby, Earl of. See Stanley,	
Darbyshire, Alfred	1839–1908	Frederick Arthur.	
D'Arcy, Charles Frederick	1859–1938	De Robeck, Sir John Michael	1862–1928
Darling, Charles John, Baron	1849–1936	De Saulles, George William	1862–1903
Darwin, Sir Francis	1848–1925	Des Vœux, Sir (George) William	1834–1909
Darwin, Sir George Howard	1845–1912	Detmold, Charles Maurice	1883–1908
Darwin, Sir Horace	1851–1928	De Vere, Aubrey Thomas	1814–1902
Daubeney, Sir Henry Charles		De Vere, Sir Stephen Edward	1812–1904
Barnston	1810–1903	De Villiers, John Henry, Baron	1842–1914
Davenport-Hill, Rosamond. See		Devlin, Joseph	1871–1934
Hill.		Devonport, Viscount. See Kear-	
Davey, Horace, Lord	1833–1907	ley, Hudson Ewbank.	
David, Sir (Tannatt William)		Devonshire, Duke of. See Caven-	
Edgeworth	1858–1934	dish, Spencer Compton.	
Davids, Thomas William Rhys	1843–1922	Devonshire, Duke of. See Caven-	
Davidson, Andrew Bruce	1831–1902	dish, Victor Christian William	
Davidson, Charles	1824–1902	Dewar, Sir James	1842–1923
Davidson, James Leigh Strachan-.		De Wet, Christiaan Rudolph	1854–1922
See Strachan-Davidson.		De Winton, Sir Francis Walter	1835–1901
Davidson, John	1857–1909	De Worms, Henry, Baron Pirbright	1840–1903
Davidson, John Thain	1833–1904	Dewrance, Sir John	1858–1937
Davidson, Randall Thomas,		Dibbs, Sir George Richard	1834–1904
Baron Davidson of Lambeth	1848–1930	Dibdin, Sir Lewis Tonna	1852–1938
Davies, Charles Maurice	1828–1910	Dicey, Albert Venn	1835–1922
Davies, John Llewelyn	1826–1916	Dicey, Edward James Stephen	1832–1911
Davies, Robert	1816–1905	Dickinson, Goldsworthy Lowes	1862–1932
Davies, (Sarah) Emily	1830–1921	Dickinson, Hercules Henry	1827–1905
Davies, William Henry	1871–1940	Dickinson, Lowes ('Cato')	1819–1908
Davis, Charles Edward	1827–1902	Dicksee, Sir Francis Bernard	
Davis, Henry William Carless	1874–1928	(Frank)	1853–1928
Davitt, Michael	1846–1906	Dickson, Sir Collingwood	1817–1904
Dawber, Sir (Edward) Guy	1861–1938	Dickson, William Purdie	1823–1901
Dawkins, Sir William Boyd	1837–1929	Dickson-Poynder, John Poynder,	
Dawson, George Mercer	1849–1901	Baron Islington. See Poynder.	
Dawson, John	1827–1903	Digby, William	1849–1904
Day, Sir John Charles Frederic		Dilke, Sir Charles Wentworth	1843–1911
Sigismund	1826–1908	Dilke, Emilia Francis Strong,	
Day, Lewis Foreman	1845–1910	Lady	1840–1904
Day, William Henry	1823–1908	Dill, Sir Samuel	1844–1924
Deacon, George Frederick	1843–1909	Dillon, Emile Joseph	1854–1933
Deakin, Alfred	1856–1919	Dillon, Frank	1823–1909
Deane, Sir James Parker	1812–1902	Dillon, Harold Arthur Lee-,	
Dearmer, Percy	1867–1936	Viscount	1844–1932
De Bunsen, Sir Maurice William		Dillon, John	1851–1927
Ernest	1852–1932	Dimock, Nathaniel	1825–1909
De Burgh Canning, Hubert		Dines, William Henry	1855–1927
George, Marquess of Clanri-		Dixie, Lady Florence Caroline	1857–1905
carde. See Burgh Canning.		Dixon, Sir Robert Bland	1867–1939
De Ferranti, Sebastian Ziani. See		Dixon, Walter Ernest	1871–1931
Ferranti.		Dobbs, Sir Henry Robert Con-	
Delamere, Baron. See Cholmon-		way	1871–1934
deley, Hugh.		Dobell, Bertram	1842–1914
De la Ramée, Marie Louise,		Dobson, (Henry) Austin	1840–1921
'Ouida'	1839–1908	Dods, Marcus	1834–1909
De la Rue, Sir Thomas Andros	1849–1911	Doherty, Hugh Lawrence	1875–1919

Elliot, Gilbert John Murray Kynynmond, Earl of Minto	1845–1914
Elliot, Sir Henry George	1817–1907
Elliott, Sir Charles Alfred	1835–1911
Elliott, Edwin Bailey	1851–1937
Ellis, Frederick Startridge	1830–1901
Ellis, Henry Havelock	1859–1939
Ellis, John Devonshire	1824–1906
Ellis, Robinson	1834–1913
Elsmie, George Robert	1838–1909
Elwes, Gervase Henry [Cary-]	1866–1921
Elwes, Henry John	1846–1922
Elworthy, Frederick Thomas	1830–1907
Emery, William	1825–1910
Emmott, Alfred, Baron	1858–1926
Ernle, Baron. See Prothero, Rowland Edmund.	
Esher, Viscount. See Brett, Reginald Baliol.	
Esmond, Henry Vernon	1869–1922
Etheridge, Robert	1819–1903
Euan-Smith, Sir Charles Bean	1842–1910
Eumorfopoulos, George	1863–1939
Eva, *pseudonym*. See O'Doherty, Mary Anne.	
Evan-Thomas, Sir Hugh	1862–1928
Evans, Daniel Silvan	1818–1903
Evans, Edmund	1826–1905
Evans, Sir (Evan) Vincent	1851–1934
Evans, George Essex	1863–1909
Evans, Sir John	1823–1908
Evans, John Gwenogvryn	1852–1930
Evans, Sir Samuel Thomas	1859–1918
Evans, Sebastian	1830–1909
Evans, Sir (Worthington) Laming Worthington-	1868–1931
Eve, Sir Harry Trelawney	1856–1940
Everard, Harry Stirling Crawfurd	1848–1909
Everett, Joseph David	1831–1904
Everett, Sir William	1844–1908
Eversley, Baron. See Shaw-Lefevre, George John.	
Ewart, Alfred James	1872–1937
Ewart, Charles Brisbane	1827–1903
Ewart, Sir John Alexander	1821–1904
Ewart, Sir John Spencer	1861–1930
Ewing, Sir (James) Alfred	1855–1935
Eyre, Edward John	1815–1901
Faed, John	1819–1902
Fagan, James Bernard	1873–1933
Fagan, Louis Alexander	1845–1903
Fairbairn, Andrew Martin	1838–1912
Fairbairn, Stephen	1862–1938
Fairbridge, Kingsley Ogilvie	1885–1924
Falcke, Isaac	1819–1909
Falconer, Lanoe, *pseudonym*. See Hawker, Mary Elizabeth.	
Falkiner, Cæsar Litton	1863–1908
Falkiner, Sir Frederick Richard	1831–1908
Falkner, John Meade	1858–1932
Fane, Violet, *pseudonym*. See Currie, Mary Montgomerie, Baroness.	
Fanshawe, Sir Edward Gennys	1814–1906
Farjeon, Benjamin Leopold	1838–1903
Farmer, Emily	1826–1905
Farmer, John	1835–1901
Farnell, Lewis Richard	1856–1934

Farningham, Marianne, *pseudonym*. See Hearn, Mary Anne.	
Farquhar, John Nicol	1861–1929
Farquharson, David	1840–1907
Farrar, Adam Storey	1826–1905
Farrar, Frederick William	1831–1903
Farren (afterwards Soutar), Ellen (Nellie)	1848–1904
Farren, William	1825–1908
Farrer, William	1861–1924
Farwell, Sir George	1845–1915
Fausset, Andrew Robert	1821–1910
Fawcett, Dame Millicent	1847–1929
Fayrer, Sir Joseph	1824–1907
Felkin, Ellen Thorneycroft	1860–1929
Fenn, George Manville	1831–1909
Ferguson, Mary Catherine, Lady	1823–1905
Ferguson, Ronald Crauford Munro-, Viscount Novar	1860–1934
Fergusson, Sir James	1832–1907
Ferranti, Sebastian Zianti de	1864–1930
Ferrers, Norman Macleod	1829–1903
Ferrier, Sir David	1843–1928
Festing, John Wogan	1837–1902
Field, Walter	1837–1901
Field, William Ventris, Baron	1813–1907
Fife, Duchess of. See Louise Victoria Alexandra Dagmar.	
Figgis, John Neville	1866–1919
Fildes, Sir (Samuel) Luke	1844–1927
Filon, Louis Napoleon George	1875–1937
Finberg, Alexander Joseph	1866–1939
Finch-Hatton, Harold Heneage	1856–1904
Finlay, Robert Bannatyne, Viscount	1842–1929
Finlayson, James	1840–1906
Finnie, John	1829–1907
Firth, Sir Charles Harding	1857–1936
Fisher, Andrew	1862–1928
Fisher, Herbert Albert Laurens	1865–1940
Fisher, John Arbuthnot, Baron	1841–1920
Fisher, Robert Howie	1861–1934
Fisher, Sir William Wordsworth	1875–1937
Fison, Lorimer	1832–1907
Fitch, Sir Joshua Girling	1824–1903
FitzAlan-Howard, Henry, Duke of Norfolk. See Howard.	
Fitzclarence, Charles	1865–1914
FitzGerald, George Francis	1851–1901
FitzGerald, Sir Thomas Naghten	1838–1908
FitzGibbon, Gerald	1837–1909
Fitzmaurice, Baron. See Petty-Fitzmaurice, Edmond George.	
Fitzmaurice, Sir Maurice	1861–1924
Fitzmaurice-Kelly, James	1857–1923
Fitzpatrick, Sir Dennis	1837–1920
FitzPatrick, Sir (James) Percy	1862–1931
Fleay, Frederick Gard	1831–1909
Flecker, Herman Elroy (James Elroy)	1884–1915
Fleming, David Hay	1849–1931
Fleming, George	1833–1901
Fleming, James	1830–1908
Fleming, Sir Sandford	1827–1915
Fletcher, Charles Robert Leslie	1857–1934
Fletcher, James	1852–1908
Fletcher, Sir Walter Morley	1873–1933
Flint, Robert	1838–1910
Floyer, Ernest Ayscoghe	1852–1903

George William Frederick Charles, Duke of Cambridge . 1819–1904
George, Sir Ernest . . . 1839–1922
George, Hereford Brooke . . 1838–1910
Gerard (afterwards de Laszowska), (Jane) Emily . . 1846–1905
Gerard, Sir Montagu Gilbert . 1842–1905
German, Sir Edward . . 1862–1936
Gertler, Mark 1891–1939
Gibb, Elias John Wilkinson . 1857–1901
Gibbins, Henry de Beltgens . 1865–1907
Gibbs, Henry Hucks, Baron Aldenham 1819–1907
Gibbs, Vicary 1853–1932
Gibson, Edward, Baron Ashbourne 1837–1913
Giffard, Hardinge Stanley, Earl of Halsbury. . . . 1823–1921
Giffen, Sir Robert . . . 1837–1910
Gifford, Edwin Hamilton . . 1820–1905
Gigliucci, Countess. See Novello, Clara Anastasia.
Gilbert, Sir Alfred . . . 1854–1934
Gilbert, Sir Joseph Henry. . 1817–1901
Gilbert, Sir William Schwenck . 1836–1911
Giles, Herbert Allen. . . 1845–1935
Giles, Peter 1860–1935
Gill, (Arthur) Eric Rowton . 1882–1940
Gill, Sir David 1843–1914
Gillies, Duncan . . . 1834–1903
Gilmour, Sir John . . . 1876–1940
Gilson, Julius Parnell . . 1868–1929
Ginsburg, Christian David . 1831–1914
Girouard, Désiré . . . 1836–1911
Girouard, Sir (Edouard) Percy Cranwill 1867–1932
Gissing, George Robert . . 1857–1903
Gladstone, Herbert John, Viscount 1854–1930
Gladstone, John Hall . . 1827–1902
Glaisher, James . . . 1809–1903
Glaisher, James Whitbread Lee 1848–1928
Glazebrook, Michael George . 1853–1926
Glazebrook, Sir Richard Tetley . 1854–1935
Gleichen, Lady Feodora Georgina Maud 1861–1922
Glenavy, Baron. See Campbell, James Henry Mussen.
Glenesk, Baron. See Borthwick, Algernon.
Gloag, Paton James. . . 1823–1906
Gloag, William Ellis, Lord Kincairney 1828–1909
Godfrey, Daniel . . . 1831–1903
Godkin, Edwin Lawrence. . 1831–1902
Godlee, Sir Rickman John . 1849–1925
Godley, Alfred Denis . . 1856–1925
Godley, (John) Arthur, Baron Kilbracken 1847–1932
Godwin, George Nelson . . 1846–1907
Godwin-Austen, Henry Haversham 1834–1923
Goldie, Sir George Dashwood Taubman 1846–1925
Goldschmidt, Otto . . . 1829–1907
Goldsmid, Sir Frederick John . 1818–1908
Goldsmid-Montefiore, Claude Joseph. See Montefiore.
Gollancz, Sir Hermann . . 1852–1930

Gollancz, Sir Israel . . . 1864–1930
Goodall, Frederick . . . 1822–1904
Goodenough, Frederick Craufurd 1866–1934
Goodman (formerly Salaman), Julia 1812–1906
Gordon, Arthur Charles Hamilton, Baron Stanmore . . 1829–1912
Gordon, Charles William, 'Ralph Connor' 1860–1937
Gordon (formerly Marjoribanks), Ishbel Maria, Marchioness of Aberdeen and Temair. See under Gordon, John Campbell.
Gordon, James Frederick Skinner 1821–1904
Gordon, John Campbell, Marquess of Aberdeen and Temair 1847–1934
Gordon, Sir John James Hood . 1832–1908
Gordon, Sir Thomas Edward . 1832–1914
Gordon-Lennox, Charles Henry, Duke of Richmond . . 1818–1903
Gore, Albert Augustus . . 1840–1901
Gore, Charles 1853–1932
Gore, George 1826–1908
Gore, John Ellard . . . 1845–1910
Gorell, Baron. See Barnes, John Gorell.
Gorst, Sir John Eldon . . 1835–1916
Gorst, Sir (John) Eldon . . 1861–1911
Goschen, George Joachim, Viscount 1831–1907
Gosling, Harry . . . 1861–1930
Gosse, Sir Edmund William . 1849–1928
Gosselin, Sir Martin le Marchant Hadsley 1847–1905
Gossett, William Sealy, 'Student' 1876–1937
Gott, John 1830–1906
Gough, Sir Charles John Stanley 1832–1912
Gough, Sir Hugh Henry . . 1833–1909
Gough, John Edmond . . 1871–1915
Gough-Calthorpe, Augustus Cholmondeley, Baron Calthorpe . 1829–1910
Gough-Calthorpe, Sir Somerset Arthur. See Calthorpe.
Gould, Sir Francis Carruthers . 1844–1925
Gould, Nathaniel . . . 1857–1919
Goulding, Frederick. . . 1842–1909
Gower, (Edward) Frederick Leveson-. See Leveson-Gower.
Gowers, Sir William Richard . 1845–1915
Grace, Edward Mills . . . 1841–1911
Grace, William Gilbert . . 1848–1915
Graham, Henry Grey . . 1842–1906
Graham, Hugh, Baron Atholstan 1848–1938
Graham, Robert Bontine Cunninghame 1852–1936
Graham, Thomas Alexander Ferguson 1840–1906
Graham, William . . . 1839–1911
Graham, William . . . 1887–1932
Grahame, Kenneth . . . 1859–1932
Grant, Sir (Alfred) Hamilton . 1872–1937
Grant, Sir Charles. See under Grant, Sir Robert.
Grant, George Monro . . 1835–1902
Grant, Sir Robert . . . 1837–1904
Grant Duff, Sir Mountstuart Elphinstone 1829–1906
Grantham, Sir William . . 1835–1911
Graves, Alfred Perceval . . 1846–1931

Harcourt, Augustus George Vernon	1834–1919
Harcourt, Leveson Francis Vernon-. See Vernon-Harcourt.	
Harcourt, Lewis, Viscount	1863–1922
Harcourt, Sir William George Granville Venables Vernon	1827–1904
Harden, Sir Arthur	1865–1940
Hardie, James Keir	1856–1915
Hardie, William Ross	1862–1916
Hardwicke, Earl of. See Yorke, Albert Edward Philip Henry.	
Hardy, Frederic Daniel	1827–1911
Hardy, Gathorne Gathorne-, Earl of Cranbrook. See Gathorne-Hardy.	
Hardy, Herbert Hardy Cozens-, Baron Cozens-Hardy. See Cozens-Hardy.	
Hardy, Thomas	1840–1928
Hardy, Sir William Bate	1864–1934
Hare, Augustus John Cuthbert	1834–1903
Hare, Sir John	1844–1921
Harington, Sir Charles ('Tim')	1872–1940
Harker, Alfred	1859–1939
Harland, Henry	1861–1905
Harley, Robert	1828–1910
Harmsworth, Alfred Charles William, Viscount Northcliffe	1865–1922
Harmsworth, Harold Sidney, Viscount Rothermere	1868–1940
Harper, Sir George Montague	1865–1922
Harraden, Beatrice	1864–1936
Harrel, Sir David	1841–1939
Harrington, Timothy Charles	1851–1910
Harris, Frederick Leverton	1864–1926
Harris, George Robert Canning, Baron	1851–1932
Harris, James Thomas ('Frank')	1856–1931
Harris, Thomas Lake	1823–1906
Harrison, Frederic	1831–1923
Harrison, Jane Ellen	1850–1928
Harrison, Mary St. Leger, 'Lucas Malet'.	1852–1931
Harrison, Reginald	1837–1908
Hart, Sir Robert	1835–1911
Hartington, Marquess of. See Cavendish, Spencer Compton.	
Hartley, Sir Charles Augustus	1825–1915
Hartshorn, Vernon	1872–1931
Hartshorne, Albert	1839–1910
Hastie, William	1842–1903
Hastings, James	1852–1922
Hatton, Harold Heneage Finch-. See Finch-Hatton.	
Hatton, Joseph	1841–1907
Havelock, Sir Arthur Elibank	1844–1908
Haverfield, Francis John	1860–1919
Haweis, Hugh Reginald	1838–1901
Haweis, Mary. See under Haweis, Hugh Reginald.	
Hawke, Martin Bladen, Baron Hawke of Towton.	1860–1938
Hawker, Mary Elizabeth, 'Lanoe Falconer'.	1848–1908
Hawkins, Sir Anthony Hope, 'Anthony Hope'.	1863–1933
Hawkins, Henry, Baron Brampton	1817–1907

Hawtrey, Sir Charles Henry	1858–1923
Hay, Sir Harley Hugh Dalrymple-	1861–1940
Hayes, Edwin	1819–1904
Hayman, Henry	1823–1904
Hayne, Charles Hayne Seale-. See Seale-Hayne.	
Hayward, Robert Baldwin	1829–1903
Hazlitt, William Carew	1834–1913
Head, Barclay Vincent	1844–1914
Head, Sir Henry	1861–1940
Headlam, Walter George	1866–1908
Headlam-Morley, Sir James Wycliffe	1863–1929
Healy, John Edward	1872–1934
Healy, Timothy Michael	1855–1931
Hearn, Mary Anne, 'Marianne Farningham'	1834–1909
Heath, Christopher	1835–1905
Heath, Sir Leopold George	1817–1907
Heath, Sir Thomas Little	1861–1940
Heathcote, John Moyer	1834–1912
Heaton, Sir John Henniker	1848–1914
Heaviside, Oliver	1850–1925
Hector, Annie French, 'Mrs. Alexander'.	1825–1902
Hector, Sir James	1834–1907
Heinemann, William	1863–1920
Hellmuth, Isaac	1817–1901
Hemming, George Wirgman	1821–1905
Hemphill, Charles Hare, Baron	1822–1908
Henderson, Arthur	1863–1935
Henderson, Sir David	1862–1921
Henderson, George Francis Robert	1854–1903
Henderson, Joseph	1832–1908
Henderson, Sir Reginald Guy Hannam	1881–1939
Henderson, William George	1819–1905
Henley, William Ernest	1849–1903
Hennell, Sara. See under Bray, Caroline.	
Hennessey, John Bobanau Nickerlieu.	1829–1910
Hennessy, Henry	1826–1901
Henry, Sir Edward Richard	1850–1931
Henry, Mitchell	1826–1910
Henschel, Sir George	1850–1934
Henty, George Alfred	1832–1902
Herbert, Auberon Edward William Molyneux	1838–1906
Herbert, Auberon Thomas, Baron Lucas.	1876–1916
Herbert, George Edward Stanhope Molyneux, Earl of Carnarvon	1866–1923
Herbert, Sir Robert George Wyndham	1831–1905
Herdman, Sir William Abbott	1858–1924
Herford, Brooke	1830–1903
Herford, Charles Harold	1853–1931
Herford, William Henry	1820–1908
Herkomer, Sir Hubert von	1849–1914
Herring, George	1832–1906
Herringham, Sir Wilmot Parker	1855–1936
Herschel, Alexander Stewart	1836–1907
Hertslet, Sir Edward	1824–1902
Heseltine, Philip Arnold, 'Peter Warlock'	1894–1930
Hewins, William Albert Samuel	1865–1931

Howland, Sir William Pearce	1811–1907	Irby, Leonard Howard Loyd	1836–1905
Hubbard, Louisa Maria	1836–1906	Ireland, William Wotherspoon	1832–1909
Huddart, James	1847–1901	Irvine, William	1840–1911
Hudleston (formerly Simpson),		Irving, Sir Henry	1838–1905
Wilfred Hudleston	1828–1909	Isaacs, Rufus Daniel, Marquess	
Hudson, Charles Thomas	1828–1903	of Reading	1860–1935
Hudson, Sir Robert Arundell	1864–1927	Isherwood, Sir Joseph William	1870–1937
Hudson, William Henry	1841–1922	Islington, Baron. See Poynder,	
Hueffer, Ford Hermann. See		John Poynder Dickson.	
Ford, Ford Madox.		Ismay, Joseph Bruce	1862–1937
Hügel, Friedrich von, Baron of		Iveagh, Earl of. See Guinness,	
the Holy Roman Empire. See		Edward Cecil.	
Von Hügel.		Iwan-Müller, Ernest Bruce	1853–1910
Huggins, Sir William	1824–1910		
Hughes, Arthur	1832–1915	Jacks, William	1841–1907
Hughes, Edward	1832–1908	Jackson, Sir Cyril	1863–1924
Hughes, Hugh Price	1847–1902	Jackson, Frederick George	1860–1938
Hughes, John	1842–1902	Jackson, Sir Frederick John	1860–1929
Hughes, Sir Sam	1853–1921	Jackson, Henry	1839–1921
Hulme, Frederick Edward	1841–1909	Jackson, Sir Henry Bradwardine	1855–1929
Hulton, Sir Edward	1869–1925	Jackson, Sir Herbert	1863–1936
Hume, Allan Octavian	1829–1912	Jackson, John	1833–1901
Hume, Martin Andrew Sharp	1843–1910	Jackson, John Hughlings	1835–1911
Hunt, Arthur Surridge	1871–1934	Jackson, Mason	1819–1903
Hunt, George William. See under		Jackson, Samuel Phillips	1830–1904
Macdermott, Gilbert Hastings.		Jackson, Sir Thomas Graham	1835–1924
Hunt, William	1842–1931	Jackson, William Lawies, Baron	1840–1917
Hunt, William Holman	1827–1910	Jacob, Edgar . [Allerton	1844–1920
Hunter, Sir Archibald	1856–1936	Jagger, Charles Sargeant	1885–1934
Hunter, Colin	1841–1904	James, Henry, Baron James of	
Hunter, Sir George Burton	1845–1937	Hereford	1828–1911
Hunter, Sir Robert	1844–1913	James, Henry	1843–1916
Hunter, Sir William Guyer	1827–1902	James, James	1832–1902
Hunter-Weston, Sir Aylmer		James, Montague Rhodes	1862–1936
Gould. See Weston.		Jameson, Andrew, Lord Ardwall	1845–1911
Huntington, George	1825–1905	Jameson, Sir Leander Starr	1853–1917
Hurlstone, William Yeates	1876–1906	Japp, Alexander Hay, 'H. A. Page'	1837–1905
Hutchinson, Arthur	1866–1937	Jardine, Sir Robert	1825–1905
Hutchinson, Horatio Gordon		Jayne, Francis John	1845–1921
(Horace)	1859–1932	Jeaffreson, John Cordy	1831–1901
Hutchinson, Sir Jonathan	1828–1913	Jebb, Eglantyne	1876–1928
Huth, Alfred Henry	1850–1910	Jebb, Sir Richard Claverhouse	1841–1905
Hutton, Alfred	1839–1910	Jelf, George Edward	1834–1908
Hutton, Frederick Wollaston	1836–1905	Jellicoe, (John) Basil Lee	1899–1935
Hutton, George Clark	1825–1908	Jellicoe, John Rushworth, Earl	1859–1935
Hutton, William Holden	1860–1930	Jenkin, Charles Frewen	1865–1940
Huxley, Leonard	1860–1933	Jenkins, Ebenezer Evans	1820–1905
Hwfa Môn. See Williams, Rowland.		Jenkins, John Edward	1838–1910
Hyndman, Henry Mayers	1842–1921	Jenkins, Sir Lawrence Hugh	1857–1928
		Jenkinson, Francis John Henry	1853–1923
Ibbetson, Sir Denzil Charles Jelf	1847–1908	Jenks, Edward	1861–1939
Ibbetson, Henry John Selwin-,		Jenner-Fust, Herbert	1806–1904
Baron Rookwood. See Selwin-		Jephson, Arthur Jermy Mounte-	
Ibbetson.		ney	1858–1908
Ignatius, Father. See Lyne,		Jerome, Jerome Klapka	1859–1927
Joseph Leycester.		Jerram, Sir (Thomas Henry)	
Ilbert, Sir Courtenay Peregrine	1841–1924	Martyn	1858–1933
Image, Selwyn	1849–1930	Jersey, Earl of. See Villiers,	
Ince, William	1825–1910	Victor Albert George Child-.	
Inchcape, Earl of. See Mackay,		Jessopp, Augustus	1823–1914
James Lyle.		Jeune, Francis Henry, Baron	
Inderwick, Frederick Andrew	1836–1904	St. Helier	1843–1905
Inglis, Elsie Maud	1864–1917	Jex-Blake, Sophia Louisa	1840–1912
Ingram, John Kells	1823–1907	Jex-Blake, Thomas William	1832–1915
Ingram, Thomas Dunbar	1826–1901	Joachim, Harold Henry	1868–1938
Innes, James John McLeod	1830–1907	Joel, Jack Barnato. See under	
Invernairn, Baron. See Beard-		Joel, Solomon Barnato.	
more, William.		Joel, Solomon Barnato	1865–1931
Iqbal, Sir Muhammad	1876–1938	Johns, Claude Hermann Walter	1857–1920

Lambourne, Baron. *See* Lockwood, Amelius Mark Richard.	
Lamington, Baron. *See* Baillie, Charles Wallace Alexander Napier Ross Cochrane-.	
Lane, Sir Hugh Percy	1875–1915
Lane, John	1854–1925
Lane Poole, Reginald. *See* Poole.	
Lane-Poole, Stanley Edward. *See* Poole.	
Lang, Andrew	1844–1912
Lang, John Marshall	1834–1909
Langdon, Stephen Herbert	1876–1937
Langevin, Sir Hector Louis	1826–1906
Langford, John Alfred	1823–1903
Langley, John Newport	1852–1925
Lankester, Sir Edwin Ray	1847–1929
Lansbury, George	1859–1940
Lansdowne, Marquess of. *See* Petty-Fitzmaurice, Henry Charles Keith.	
Lascelles, Sir Frank Cavendish	1841–1920
László de Lombos, Philip Alexius	1869–1937
Laszowska, (Jane) Emily de. *See* Gerard.	
Latey, John	1842–1902
Latham, Henry	1821–1902
Laughton, Sir John Knox	1830–1915
Laurie, James Stuart	1832–1904
Laurie, Simon Somerville	1829–1909
Laurier, Sir Wilfrid	1841–1919
Law, Andrew Bonar	1858–1923
Law, David	1831–1901
Law, Sir Edward FitzGerald	1846–1908
Law, Thomas Graves	1836–1904
Lawes (afterwards Lawes-Wittewronge), Sir Charles Bennet	1843–1911
Lawes, William George	1839–1907
Lawley, Francis Charles	1825–1901
Lawrence, Alfred Tristram, Baron Trevethin	1843–1936
Lawrence, David Herbert	1885–1930
Lawrence, Thomas Edward (Lawrence of Arabia)	1888–1935
Lawrence, Sir Walter Roper	1857–1940
Laws, Robert	1851–1934
Lawson, Edward Levy-, Baron Burnham. *See* Levy-Lawson.	
Lawson, George	1831–1903
Lawson, George Anderson	1832–1904
Lawson, Harry Lawson Webster Levy-, Viscount Burnham	1862–1933
Lawson, Sir Wilfrid	1829–1906
Leach, Arthur Francis	1851–1915
Leader, Benjamin Williams	1831–1923
Leader, John Temple	1810–1903
Leaf, Walter	1852–1927
Leake, George	1856–1902
Leathes, Sir Stanley Mordaunt	1861–1938
Lecky, Squire Thornton Stratford	1838–1902
Lecky, William Edward Hartpole	1838–1903
Ledwidge, Francis	1891–1917
Lee, Frederick George	1832–1902
Lee, Rawdon Briggs	1845–1908
Lee, Sir Sidney	1859–1926
Lee, Vernon, *pseudonym. See* Paget, Violet.	
Lee-Hamilton, Eugene Jacob	1845–1907
Lee-Warner, Sir William	1846–1914
Lefroy, William	1836–1909
Legg, John Wickham	1843–1921
Legros, Alphonse	1837–1911
Lehmann, Rudolf	1819–1905
Leicester, Earl of. *See* Coke, Thomas William.	
Leighton, Stanley	1837–1901
Leiningen, Prince Ernest Leopold Victor Charles Auguste Joseph Emich.	1830–1904
Leishman, Thomas	1825–1904
Leishman, Sir William Boog	1865–1926
Le Jeune, Henry	1819–1904
Lemmens-Sherrington, Helen	1834–1906
Lempriere, Charles	1818–1901
Leng, Sir John	1828–1906
Leng, Sir William Christopher	1825–1902
Lennox, Charles Henry Gordon-, Duke of Richmond. *See* Gordon-Lennox.	
Leno, Dan	1860–1904
Le Sage, Sir John Merry	1837–1926
Leslie, Sir Bradford	1831–1926
Le Strange, Guy	1854–1933
Lethaby, William Richard	1857–1931
Lever, William Hesketh, Viscount Leverhulme	1851–1925
Leverhulme, Viscount. *See* Lever, William Hesketh.	
Leveson-Gower, (Edward) Frederick	1819–1907
Levy-Lawson, Edward, Baron Burnham	1833–1916
Levy-Lawson, Harry Lawson Webster, Viscount Burnham. *See* Lawson.	
Lewis, Agnes	1843–1926
Lewis, Bunnell	1824–1908
Lewis, David. *See* under Lewis, Evan.	
Lewis, Evan	1818–1901
Lewis, Sir George Henry	1833–1911
Lewis, John Travers	1825–1901
Lewis, Richard	1821–1905
Lewis, William Thomas, Baron Merthyr	1837–1914
Liberty, Sir Arthur Lasenby	1843–1917
Lidderdale, William	1832–1902
Lincolnshire, Marquess of. *See* Wynn-Carrington, Charles Robert.	
Lindley, Nathaniel, Baron	1828–1921
Lindsay, David	1856–1922
Lindsay, David Alexander Edward, Earl of Crawford	1871–1940
Lindsay, James Gavin	1835–1903
Lindsay, James Ludovic, Earl of Crawford	1847–1913
Lindsay (afterwards Loyd-Lindsay), Robert James, Baron Wantage	1832–1901
Lindsay, Thomas Martin	1843–1914
Lindsay, Wallace Martin	1858–1937
Lingen, Ralph Robert Wheeler, Baron	1819–1905
Linlithgow, Marquess of. *See* Hope, John Adrian Louis.	
Lipton, Sir Thomas Johnstone	1850–1931
Lister, Arthur	1830–1908

MacDonald, James Ramsay	1866–1937
Macdonald, Sir James Ronald Leslie	1862–1927
McDonald, John Blake	1829–1901
Macdonald, Sir John Denis	1826–1908
Macdonald, Sir John Hay Athole, Lord Kingsburgh	1836–1919
Macdonell, Arthur Anthony	1854–1930
MacDonell, Sir Hugh Guion	1832–1904
Macdonell, Sir John	1845–1921
Macdonell, Sir Philip James	1873–1940
MacDonnell, Antony Patrick, Baron	1844–1925
McDonnell, Sir Schomberg Kerr	1861–1915
McDougall, William	1871–1938
Mace, James (Jem)	1831–1910
McEvoy, Arthur Ambrose	1878–1927
Macewen, Sir William	1848–1924
Macfadyen, Allan	1860–1907
M'Fadyen, John Edgar	1870–1933
Macfarren, Walter Cecil	1826–1905
McGrath, Sir Patrick Thomas	1868–1929
MacGregor, Sir Evan	1842–1926
MacGregor, James	1832–1910
Macgregor, Sir William	1846–1919
Machell, James Octavius	1837–1902
Machray, Robert	1831–1904
M'Intosh, William Carmichael	1838–1931
Macintyre, Donald	1831–1903
Mackay, Æneas James George	1839–1911
Mackay, Alexander	1833–1902
Mackay, Donald James, Baron Reay	1839–1921
Mackay, James Lyle, Earl of Inchcape	1852–1932
Mackay, Mary, 'Marie Corelli'	1855–1924
McKechnie, William Sharp	1863–1930
Mackennal, Alexander	1835–1904
Mackennal, Sir (Edgar) Bertram	1863–1931
Mackenzie, Sir Alexander	1842–1902
Mackenzie, Sir Alexander Campbell	1847–1935
Mackenzie, Sir George Sutherland	1844–1910
Mackenzie, Sir James	1853–1925
M'Kenzie, Sir John	1836–1901
McKenzie, John Stuart	1860–1935
McKenzie, (Robert) Tait	1867–1938
Mackenzie, Sir Stephen	1844–1909
Mackenzie, Sir William	1849–1923
McKerrow, Ronald Brunlees	1872–1940
MacKinlay, Antoinette. See Sterling.	
Mackinnon, Sir William Henry	1852–1929
Mackintosh, Charles Rennie	1868–1928
Mackintosh, Hugh Ross	1870–1936
Mackintosh, John	1833–1907
McLachlan, Robert	1837–1904
Maclagan, Christian	1811–1901
Maclagan, William Dalrymple	1826–1910
Maclaren, Alexander	1826–1910
M'Laren, Charles Benjamin Bright, Baron Aberconway	1850–1934
Maclaren, Ian, pseudonym. See Watson, John.	
McLaren, John, Lord	1831–1910
Maclean, Sir Donald	1864–1932
Maclean, Sir Harry Aubrey de Vere	1848–1920
Maclean, James Mackenzie	1835–1906
Maclear, George Frederick	1833–1902
Maclear, John Fiot Lee Pearse	1838–1907
McLennan, Sir John Cunningham	1867–1935
Macleod, Fiona, pseudonym. See Sharp, William.	
Macleod, Henry Dunning	1821–1902
Macleod, John James Rickard	1876–1935
Maclure, Edward Craig	1833–1906
Maclure, Sir John William. See under Maclure, Edward Craig.	
McMahon, Charles Alexander	1830–1904
MacMahon, Percy Alexander	1854–1929
Macmillan, Sir Frederick Orridge	1851–1936
Macmillan, Hugh	1833–1903
McMillan, Margaret	1860–1931
McMurrich, James Playfair	1859–1939
Macnaghten, Edward, Baron	1830–1913
McNair, John Frederick Adolphus	1828–1910
Macnamara, Thomas James	1861–1931
McNeile, (Herman) Cyril, 'Sapper'	1888–1937
McNeill, James	1869–1938
McNeill, Sir John Carstairs	1831–1904
MacNeill, John Gordon Swift	1849–1926
McNeill, Ronald John, Baron Cushendun	1861–1934
Macphail, Sir (John) Andrew	1864–1938
Macpherson, (James) Ian, Baron Strathcarron	1880–1937
Macpherson, Sir John Molesworth	1853–1914
McQueen, Sir John Withers	1836–1909
Macrorie, William Kenneth	1831–1905
M'Taggart, John M'Taggart Ellis	1866–1925
McTaggart, William	1835–1910
MacWhirter, John	1839–1911
Madden, Sir Charles Edward	1862–1935
Madden, Frederic William	1839–1904
Madden, Katherine Cecil. See Thurston.	
Madden, Thomas More	1844–1902
Magrath, John Richard	1839–1930
Maguire, James Rochfort	1855–1925
Mahaffy, Sir John Pentland	1839–1919
Mahon, Sir Bryan Thomas	1862–1930
Mair, William	1830–1920
Maitland, Agnes Catherine	1850–1906
Maitland, Sir Arthur Herbert Drummond Ramsay-Steel-. See Steel-Maitland.	
Maitland, Frederic William	1850–1906
Maitland, John Alexander Fuller-	1856–1936
Malet, Sir Edward Baldwin	1837–1908
Malet, Lucas, pseudonym. See Harrison, Mary St. Leger.	
Mallock, William Hurrell	1849–1923
Mallory, George Leigh	1886–1924
Malone, Sylvester	1822–1906
Manley, William George Nicholas	1831–1901
Mann, Arthur Henry	1850–1929
Manners, (Lord) John James Robert, Duke of Rutland	1818–1906
Manning, John Edmondson	1848–1910
Manns, Sir August	1825–1907
Mansel-Pleydell, John Clavell	1817–1902
Mansergh, James	1834–1905
Mansfield, Katherine, pseudonym. See Murry, Kathleen.	
Mansfield, Robert Blachford	1824–1908
Manson, Sir Patrick	1844–1922

Orr, Alexandra Sutherland	.	1828–1903
Orr, William McFadden	.	1866–1934
Osborne, Walter Frederick	.	1859–1903
O'Shea, John Augustus	.	1839–1905
O'Shea, William Henry	.	1840–1905
Osler, Abraham Follett	.	1808–1903
Osler, Sir William	.	1849–1919
O'Sullivan, Cornelius	.	1841–1907
Otté, Elise . . .	.	1818–1903
Ottley, Sir Charles Langdale	.	1858–1932
Ouida, *pseudonym*. See De la Ramée, Marie Louise.		
Ouless, Walter William	.	1848–1933
Overton, John Henry	.	1835–1903
Overtoun, Baron. See White, John Campbell.		
Owen, John . . .	.	1854–1926
Owen, Robert . . .	.	1820–1902
Oxford and Asquith, Earl of. See Asquith, Herbert Henry.		
Page, H. A., *pseudonym*. See Japp, Alexander Hay.		
Page, Thomas Ethelbert	.	1850–1936
Page, William . .	.	1861–1934
Paget, Francis . .	.	1851–1911
Paget, Lady Muriel Evelyn Vernon	.	1876–1938
Paget, Sidney Edward	.	1860–1908
Paget, Stephen . .	.	1855–1926
Paget, Violet, 'Vernon Lee'	.	1856–1935
Pain, Barry Eric Odell	.	1864–1928
Pakenham, Sir Francis John	.	1832–1905
Pakenham, Sir William Christopher	.	1861–1933
Palgrave, Sir Reginald Francis Douce	.	1829–1904
Palles, Christopher .	.	1831–1920
Palmer, Sir Arthur Power .	.	1840–1904
Palmer, Sir Charles Mark .	.	1822–1907
Palmer, Sir Elwin Mitford	.	1852–1906
Palmer, George Herbert	.	1846–1926
Palmer, George William	.	1851–1913
Pankhurst, Emmeline	.	1858–1928
Paris, Sir Archibald .	.	1861–1937
Parish, William Douglas	.	1833–1904
Parker, Albert Edmund, Earl of Morley . . .	.	1843–1905
Parker, Charles Stuart	.	1829–1910
Parker, Sir (Horatio) Gilbert George . . .	.	1862–1932
Parker, Joseph . .	.	1830–1902
Parker, Robert John, Baron	.	1857–1918
Parkin, Sir George Robert	.	1846–1922
Parr (formerly Taylor), Louisa .		d. 1903
Parratt, Sir Walter . .	.	1841–1924
Parry, Sir Charles Hubert Hastings . . .	.	1848–1918
Parry, Joseph . .	.	1841–1903
Parry, Joseph Haydn. See under Parry, Joseph.		
Parsons, Alfred William .	.	1847–1920
Parsons, Sir Charles Algernon	.	1854–1931
Parsons, Laurence, Earl of Rosse	.	1840–1908
Patel, Vithalbai Jhavabhai	.	1870–1933
Paterson, William Paterson	.	1860–1939
Patiala, Sir Bhupindra Singh, Maharaja of. . .	.	1891–1938
Paton, Diarmid Noël	.	1859–1928

Paton, John Brown . .	.	1830–1911
Paton, John Gibson . .	.	1824–1907
Paton, Sir Joseph Noël	.	1821–1901
Pattison, Andrew Seth Pringle (formerly Andrew Seth)	.	1856–1931
Paul, Charles Kegan	.	1828–1902
Paul, Herbert Woodfield .	.	1853–1938
Paul, William . . .	.	1822–1905
Pauncefote, Julian, Baron	.	1828–1902
Pavy, Frederick William .	.	1829–1911
Payne, Edward John	.	1844–1904
Payne, Humfry Gilbert Garth	.	1902–1936
Payne, Joseph Frank	.	1840–1910
Peacocke, Joseph Ferguson	.	1835–1916
Peake, Arthur Samuel	.	1865–1929
Pearce, Ernest Harold	.	1865–1930
Pearce, Stephen . .	.	1819–1904
Pearce, Sir William George	.	1861–1907
Pears, Sir Edwin .	.	1835–1919
Pearson, Alfred Chilton .	.	1861–1935
Pearson, Charles John, Lord	.	1843–1910
Pearson, Sir Cyril Arthur .	.	1866–1921
Pearson, Karl . . .	.	1857–1936
Pearson, Weetman Dickinson, Viscount Cowdray	.	1856–1927
Pease, Sir Arthur Francis .	.	1866–1927
Pease, Sir Joseph Whitwell	.	1828–1903
Peek, Sir Cuthbert Edgar .	.	1855–1901
Peel, Arthur Wellesley, Viscount		1829–1912
Peel, Sir Frederick . .	.	1823–1906
Peel, James . . .	.	1811–1906
Peel, William Robert Wellesley, Earl . . .	.	1867–1937
Peet, Thomas Eric . .	.	1882–1934
Peile, Sir James Braithwaite	.	1833–1906
Peile, John . . .	.	1837–1910
Pelham, Henry Francis	.	1846–1907
Pélissier, Harry Gabriel .	.	1874–1913
Pell, Albert . . .	.	1820–1907
Pember, Edward Henry .	.	1833–1911
Pemberton, Thomas Edgar	.	1849–1905
Pembrey, Marcus Seymour	.	1868–1934
Penley, William Sydney .	.	1852–1912
Pennant, George Sholto Gordon Douglas-, Baron Penrhyn. See Douglas-Pennant.		
Penrhyn, Baron. See Douglas-Pennant, George Sholto Gordon.		
Penrose, Francis Cranmer.	.	1817–1903
Pentland, Baron. See Sinclair, John.		
Percival, John. . .	.	1834–1918
Percy, Alan Ian, Duke of Northumberland . .	.	1880–1930
Percy, Henry Algernon George, Earl . . .	.	1871–1909
Pereira, George Edward .	.	1865–1923
Perkin, Arthur George	.	1861–1937
Perkin, Sir William Henry .	.	1838–1907
Perkin, William Henry	.	1860–1929
Perkins, Sir Æneas .	.	1834–1901
Perks, Sir Robert William	.	1849–1934
Perowne, Edward Henry .	.	1826–1906
Perowne, John James Stewart .	.	1823–1904
Perry, Sir (Edwin) Cooper	.	1856–1938
Perry, Walter Copland .	.	1814–1911
Petavel, Sir Joseph Ernest	.	1873–1936
Peterson, Sir William	.	1856–1921

Ramsay, Sir James Henry .	1832–1925
Ramsay, Sir William . .	1852–1916
Ramsay, Sir William Mitchell .	1851–1939
Ramsay-Steel-Maitland, Sir Arthur Herbert Drummond. See Steel-Maitland.	
Ramsden, Omar . . .	1873–1939
Randall, Richard William.	1824–1906
Randegger, Alberto . .	1832–1911
Randles, Marshall . .	1826–1904
Randolph, Francis Charles Hingeston-. See Hingeston-Randolph.	
Randolph, Sir George Granville .	1818–1907
Ranjitsinhji, Maharaja Jamsaheb of Nawanagar. See Nawanagar.	
Ransom, William Henry .	1824–1907
Raper, Robert William .	1842–1915
Rapson, Edward James .	1861–1937
Rashdall, Hastings . .	1858–1924
Rassam, Hormuzd . .	1826–1910
Rathbone, William . .	1819–1902
Rattigan, Sir William Henry .	1842–1904
Raven, John James . .	1833–1906
Raverty, Henry George .	1825–1906
Rawling, Cecil Godfrey .	1870–1917
Rawlinson, George . .	1812–1902
Rawlinson, Henry Seymour, Baron . . .	1864–1925
Rawlinson, William George .	1840–1928
Rawson, Sir Harry Holdsworth.	1843–1910
Rayleigh, Baron. See Strutt, John William.	
Read, Sir Charles Hercules .	1857–1929
Read, Clare Sewell . .	1826–1905
Read, Walter William .	1855–1907
Reade, Thomas Mellard .	1832–1909
Reading, Marquess of. See Isaacs, Rufus Daniel.	
Reay, Baron. See Mackay, Donald James.	
Redesdale, Baron. See Mitford, Algernon Bertram Freeman-.	
Redmond, John Edward .	1856–1918
Redmond, William Hoey Kearney	1861–1917
Redpath, Henry Adeney .	1848–1908
Reed, Sir Edward James .	1830–1906
Reed, Edward Tennyson .	1860–1933
Reeves, Sir William Conrad .	1821–1902
Reich, Emil . . .	1854–1910
Reid, Archibald David .	1844–1908
Reid, Sir George Houstoun .	1845–1918
Reid, James Smith . .	1846–1926
Reid, Sir John Watt . .	1823–1909
Reid, Sir Robert Gillespie .	1842–1908
Reid, Robert Threshie, Earl Loreburn . . .	1846–1923
Reid, Sir Thomas Wemyss .	1842–1905
Rendel, Sir Alexander Meadows	1829–1918
Rendel, George Wightwick .	1833–1902
Rendle, Alfred Barton .	1865–1938
Repington, Charles à Court .	1858–1925
Reynolds, James Emerson .	1844–1920
Reynolds, Osborne . .	1842–1912
Rhodes, Cecil John . .	1853–1902
Rhodes, Francis William .	1851–1905
Rhondda, Viscount. See Thomas, David Alfred.	

Rhys, Sir John . . .	1840–1915
Richards, Sir Frederick William	1833–1912
Richmond, Duke of. See Gordon-Lennox, Charles Henry.	
Richmond, Sir William Blake .	1842–1921
Ricketts, Charles de Sousy .	1866–1931
Riddell, Charles James Buchanan	1817–1903
Riddell, Charlotte Eliza Lawson (Mrs. J. H. Riddell), 'F. G. Trafford'	1832–1906
Riddell, George Allardyce, Baron	1865–1934
Ridding, George . .	1828–1904
Ridgeway, Sir Joseph West .	1844–1930
Ridgeway, Sir William .	1853–1926
Ridley, Matthew White, Viscount	1842–1904
Rieu, Charles Pierre Henri .	1820–1902
Rigby, Sir John . . .	1834–1903
Rigg, James Harrison .	1821–1909
Rigg, James McMullen .	1855–1926
Ringer, Sydney . .	1835–1910
Ripon, Marquess of. See Robinson, George Frederick Samuel.	
Risley, Sir Herbert Hope . .	1851–1911
Ritchie, Anne Isabella, Lady. See under Ritchie, Sir Richmond Thackeray Willoughby.	
Ritchie, Charles Thomson, Baron Ritchie of Dundee . .	1838–1906
Ritchie, David George .	1853–1903
Ritchie, Sir Richmond Thackeray Willoughby . . .	1854–1912
Rivaz, Sir Charles Montgomery	1845–1926
Riviere, Briton . .	1840–1920
Robeck, Sir John Michael De. See De Robeck.	
Roberts, Alexander . .	1826–1901
Roberts, Frederick Sleigh, Earl.	1832–1914
Roberts, George Henry .	1869–1928
Roberts, Isaac. .	1829–1904
Roberts, Robert Davies .	1851–1911
Roberts-Austen, Sir William Chandler . . .	1843–1902
Robertson, Archibald . .	1853–1931
Robertson, Douglas Moray Cooper Lamb Argyll .	1837–1909
Robertson, George Matthew .	1864–1932
Robertson, Sir George Scott .	1852–1916
Robertson, James Patrick Bannerman, Baron . .	1845–1909
Robertson, John Mackinnon .	1856–1933
Robertson, Sir Johnston Forbes-	1853–1937
Robertson, Sir William Robert .	1860–1933
Robinson, Frederick William .	1830–1901
Robinson, George Frederick Samuel, Marquess of Ripon .	1827–1909
Robinson, Sir John . .	1839–1903
Robinson, Sir John Charles .	1824–1913
Robinson, Sir John Richard .	1828–1903
Robinson, Joseph Armitage .	1858–1933
Robinson, Sir Joseph Benjamin.	1840–1929
Robinson, Philip Stewart (Phil)	1847–1902
Robinson, Vincent Joseph .	1829–1910
Robinson, William Leefe .	1895–1918
Robson, William Snowdon, Baron	1852–1918
Roby, Henry John . .	1830–1915
Rogers, Annie Mary Anne Henley	1856–1937
Rogers, Benjamin Bickley .	1828–1919
Rogers, Edmund Dawson .	1823–1910
Rogers, James Guinness .	1822–1911

Santley, Sir Charles . . .	1834–1922
Sargeaunt, John . . .	1857–1922
Sargent, John Singer . .	1856–1925
Sassoon, Sir Philip Albert Gustave David	1888–1939
Satow, Sir Ernest Mason . .	1843–1929
Saumarez, Thomas . .	1827–1903
Saunders, Edward . . .	1848–1910
Saunders, Sir Edwin . .	1814–1901
Saunders, Howard . . .	1835–1907
Saunderson, Edward James .	1837–1906
Savage (formerly Dell), Ethel Mary	1881–1939
Savage-Armstrong, George Francis	1845–1906
Savill, Thomas Dixon . .	1855–1910
Saxe-Weimar, Prince Edward of. See Edward of Saxe-Weimar.	
Sayce, Archibald Henry . .	1845–1933
Schafer, Sir Edward Albert Sharpey-	1850–1935
Scharlieb, Dame Mary Ann Dacomb	1845–1930
Schiller, Ferdinand Canning Scott	1864–1937
Schlich, Sir William . . .	1840–1925
Schreiner, Olive. See under Schreiner, William Philip.	
Schreiner, William Philip . .	1857–1919
Schunck, Henry Edward . .	1820–1903
Schuster, Sir Arthur . .	1851–1934
Schuster, Sir Felix Otto . .	1854–1936
Scott, Archibald . . .	1837–1909
Scott, Charles Prestwich . .	1846–1932
Scott, Lord Charles Thomas Montagu-Douglas- . .	1839–1911
Scott, Clement William . .	1841–1904
Scott, Dukinfield Henry . .	1854–1934
Scott, George Herbert . .	1888–1930
Scott, Hugh Stowell, 'Henry Seton Merriman' . . .	1862–1903
Scott, Sir (James) George . .	1851–1935
Scott, John	1830–1903
Scott, Sir John . . .	1841–1904
Scott, Leader, *pseudonym.* See Baxter, Lucy.	
Scott, Sir Percy Moreton . .	1853–1924
Scott, Robert Falcon . .	1868–1912
Scrutton, Sir Thomas Edward .	1856–1934
Seale-Hayne, Charles Hayne .	1833–1903
Seaman, Sir Owen . . .	1861–1936
Seccombe, Thomas . . .	1866–1923
Seddon, Richard John . .	1845–1906
Sedgwick, Adam . . .	1854–1913
See, Sir John . . .	1844–1907
Seebohm, Frederic . . .	1833–1912
Seeley, Harry Govier . .	1839–1909
Selby, Thomas Gunn . .	1846–1910
Selby, Viscount. See Gully, William Court.	
Seligman, Charles Gabriel . .	1873–1940
Selous, Frederick Courteney .	1851–1917
Selwin-Ibbetson, Henry John, Baron Rookwood . . .	1826–1902
Selwyn, Alfred Richard Cecil .	1824–1902
Semon, Sir Felix . . .	1849–1921
Sendall, Sir Walter Joseph .	1832–1904
Sergeant, (Emily Frances) Adeline	1851–1904
Sergeant, Lewis . . .	1841–1902

Seth, Andrew. See Pattison, Andrew Seth Pringle-.	
Seton, George	1822–1908
Severn, Walter . . .	1830–1904
Sewell, Elizabeth Missing . .	1815–1906
Sewell, James Edwards . .	1810–1903
Sexton, Sir James . . .	1856–1938
Sexton, Thomas . . .	1848–1932
Seymour, Sir Edward Hobart .	1840–1929
Shackleton, Sir David James .	1863–1938
Shackleton, Sir Ernest Henry .	1874–1922
Shadwell, Charles Lancelot .	1840–1919
Shand (afterwards Burns), Alexander, Baron . . .	1828–1904
Shand, Alexander Innes . .	1832–1907
Shandon, Baron. See O'Brien, Ignatius John.	
Shannon, Charles Haslewood .	1863–1937
Shannon, Sir James Jebusa .	1862–1923
Sharp, Cecil James . . .	1859–1924
Sharp, William, writing also under the pseudonym of Fiona Macleod	1855–1905
Sharpe, Richard Bowdler . .	1847–1909
Sharpey-Schafer, Sir Edward Albert. See Schafer.	
Shattock, Samuel George . .	1852–1924
Shaughnessy, Thomas George, Baron	1853–1923
Shaw, Alfred	1842–1907
Shaw, Sir Eyre Massey . .	1830–1908
Shaw, James Johnston . .	1845–1910
Shaw, John Byam Lister . .	1872–1919
Shaw, Richard Norman . .	1831–1912
Shaw, Thomas, Baron Craigmyle	1850–1937
Shaw, Thomas . . .	1872–1938
Shaw-Lefevre, George John, Baron Eversley . . .	1831–1928
Shearman, Sir Montague . .	1857–1930
Sheffield, Earl of. See Holroyd, Henry North.	
Sheffield, Baron. See Stanley, Edward Lyulph.	
Shelford, Sir William . .	1834–1905
Shenstone, William Ashwell .	1850–1908
Sheppard, Hugh Richard Lawrie	1880–1937
Sherborn, Charles William .	1831–1912
Sherrington, Helen Lemmens-. See Lemmens-Sherrington.	
Shields, Frederic James . .	1833–1911
Shipley, Sir Arthur Everett .	1861–1927
Shippard, Sir Sidney Godolphin Alexander . . .	1837–1902
Shirreff, Maria Georgina. See Grey.	
Shore, William Thomas . .	1840–1905
Shorter, Clement King . .	1857–1926
Shorthouse, Joseph Henry .	1834–1903
Shortt, Edward . . .	1862–1935
Shrewsbury, Arthur . . .	1856–1903
Shuckburgh, Evelyn Shirley .	1843–1906
Sidebotham, Herbert . .	1872–1940
Sidgwick, Eleanor Mildred .	1845–1936
Sieveking, Sir Edward Henry .	1816–1904
Sifton, Sir Clifford . .	1861–1929
Simmons, Sir John Lintorn Arabin	1821–1903
Simon, Sir John . . .	1816–1904
Simonds, James Beart . .	1810–1904
Simpson, Sir John William .	1858–1933

Stephen, George, Baron Mount Stephen	1829–1921
Stephen, Sir Leslie	1832–1904
Stephens, Frederic George	1828–1907
Stephens, James	1825–1901
Stephens, James Brunton	1835–1902
Stephens, William Richard Wood	1839–1902
Stephenson, Sir Frederick Charles Arthur	1821–1911
Stephenson, George Robert	1819–1905
Sterling (afterwards MacKinlay), Antoinette	1843–1904
Sterndale, Baron. See Pickford, William.	
Stevens, Marshall	1852–1936
Stevenson, David Watson	1842–1904
Stevenson, James, Baron Stevenson	1873–1926
Stevenson, John James	1831–1908
Stevenson, Sir Thomas	1838–1908
Stevenson, William Henry	1858–1924
Stewart, Charles	1840–1907
Stewart, Sir Halley	1838–1937
Stewart, Isla	1855–1910
Stewart, James	1831–1905
Stewart, John Alexander	1846–1933
Stewart, Sir William Houston	1822–1901
Stirling, Sir James	1836–1916
Stirling, James Hutchison	1820–1909
Stocks, John Leofric	1882–1937
Stoddart, Andrew Ernest	1863–1915
Stokes, Adrian	1887–1927
Stokes, Sir Frederick Wilfrid Scott	1860–1927
Stokes, Sir George Gabriel	1819–1903
Stokes, Sir John	1825–1902
Stokes, Whitley	1830–1909
Stoney, Bindon Blood	1828–1909
Stoney, George Johnstone	1826–1911
Stopford, Sir Frederick William	1854–1929
Story, Robert Herbert	1835–1907
Story-Maskelyne, Mervyn Herbert Nevil	1823–1911
Stout, Sir Robert	1844–1930
Strachan, John	1862–1907
Strachan-Davidson, James Leigh	1843–1916
Strachey, Sir Arthur. See under Strachey, Sir John.	
Strachey, Sir Edward	1812–1901
Strachey, Edward, Baron Strachie	1858–1936
Strachey, (Giles) Lytton	1880–1932
Strachey, Sir John	1823–1907
Strachey, John St. Loe	1860–1927
Strachey, Sir Richard	1817–1908
Strachie, Baron. See Strachey, Edward.	
Strang, William	1859–1921
Strathcarron, Baron. See Macpherson, (James) Ian.	
Strathclyde, Baron. See Ure, Alexander.	
Strathcona, Baron. See Smith, Donald Alexander.	
Streeter, Burnett Hillman	1874–1937
Stretton, Hesba, pseudonym. See Smith, Sarah.	
Strickland, Gerald, Baron	1861–1940
Strong, Sir Samuel Henry	1825–1909

Strong, Sandford Arthur	1863–1904
Struthers, Sir John	1857–1925
Strutt, Edward Gerald	1854–1930
Strutt, John William, Baron Rayleigh	1842–1919
Stuart-Jones, Sir Henry. See Jones.	
Stubbs, William	1825–1901
Sturdee, Sir Frederick Charles Doveton	1859–1925
Sturgis, Julian Russell	1848–1904
Sturt, George	1863–1927
Sturt, Henry Gerard, Baron Alington	1825–1904
Sumner, Viscount. See Hamilton, John Andrew.	
Sutherland, Alexander	1852–1902
Sutherland, Sir Thomas	1834–1922
Sutro, Alfred	1863–1933
Sutton, Henry Septimus	1825–1901
Sutton, Sir John Bland-	1855–1936
Sutton, Martin John	1850–1913
Swain, Joseph	1820–1909
Swan, John Macallan	1847–1910
Swan, Sir Joseph Wilson	1828–1914
Swayne, Joseph Griffiths	1819–1903
Swaythling, Baron. See Montagu, Samuel.	
Sweet, Henry	1845–1912
Swete, Henry Barclay	1835–1917
Swift, Sir Rigby Philip Watson	1874–1937
Swinburne, Algernon Charles	1837–1909
Swinfen, Baron. See Eady, Charles Swinfen.	
Swinton, Alan Archibald Campbell	1863–1930
Sydenham of Combe, Baron. See Clarke, George Sydenham.	
Sykes, Sir Mark	1879–1919
Syme, David	1827–1908
Symes-Thompson, Edmund	1837–1906
Symonds, Sir Charters James	1852–1932
Symons, William Christian	1845–1911
Synge, John Millington	1871–1909
Tadema, Sir Lawrence Alma-. See Alma-Tadema.	
Tait, Frederick Guthrie. See under Tait, Peter Guthrie.	
Tait, Peter Guthrie	1831–1901
Talbot, Edward Stuart	1844–1934
Talbot, Sir George John	1861–1938
Tallack, William	1831–1908
Tangye, Sir Richard	1833–1906
Tanner, Joseph Robson	1860–1931
Tarte, Joseph Israel	1848–1907
Taschereau, Sir Henri Elzéar	1836–1911
Taschereau, Sir Henri Thomas	1841–1909
Tata, Sir Dorabji Jamsetji	1859–1932
Tata, Jamsetji Nasarwanji	1839–1904
Taunton, Ethelred Luke	1857–1907
Taylor, Charles	1840–1908
Taylor, Charles Bell	1829–1909
Taylor, Helen	1831–1907
Taylor, Henry Martyn	1842–1927
Taylor, Isaac	1829–1901
Taylor, Sir John	1833–1912
Taylor, John Edward	1830–1905
Taylor, Louisa. See Parr.	

Vallance, William Fleming	1827–1904	Waller, Lewis	1860–1915
Vandam, Albert Dresden	1843–1903	Waller, Samuel Edmund	1850–1903
Vane-Tempest-Stewart, Charles Stewart, Marquess of Londonderry	1852–1915	Walpole, Sir Spencer	1839–1907
		Walsh, Stephen	1859–1929
		Walsh, William Pakenham	1820–1902
Van Horne, Sir William Cornelius	1843–1915	Walsham, Sir John	1830–1905
Vansittart, Edward Westby	1818–1904	Walsham, William Johnson	1847–1903
Vaughan, Bernard John	1847–1922	Walter, Sir Edward	1823–1904
Vaughan, David James	1825–1905	Walton, Sir John Lawson	1852–1908
Vaughan, Herbert Alfred	1832–1903	Walton, Sir Joseph	1845–1910
Vaughan, Kate	1852 ?–1903	Wanklyn, James Alfred	1834–1906
Vaughan, William Wyamar	1865–1938	Wantage, Baron. See Lindsay (afterwards Loyd-Lindsay), Robert James.	
Veitch, Sir Harry James	1840–1924		
Veitch, James Herbert	1868–1907		
Venn, John	1834–1923	Ward, Sir Adolphus William	1837–1924
Verney, Margaret Maria, Lady	1844–1930	Ward, Sir Edward Willis Duncan	1853–1928
Vernon-Harcourt, Leveson Francis	1839–1907	Ward, Harry Leigh Douglas	1825–1906
		Ward, Harry Marshall	1854–1906
Verrall, Arthur Woollgar	1851–1912	Ward, Henry Snowden	1865–1911
Vestey, William, Baron	1859–1940	Ward, James	1843–1925
Vezin, Hermann	1829–1910	Ward, John	1866–1934
Vezin (formerly Mrs. Charles Young), Jane Elizabeth	1827–1902	Ward, Sir Joseph George	1856–1930
		Ward, Sir Leslie, 'Spy'	1851–1922
Victoria Adelaide Mary Louise, Princess Royal of Great Britain and German Empress	1840–1901	Ward, Mary Augusta (Mrs. Humphry Ward)	1851–1920
		Ward, Wilfrid Philip	1856–1916
Victoria Alexandra Olga Mary, princess of Great Britain	1868–1935	Ward, William Humble, Earl of Dudley	1867–1936
Villiers, John Henry De, Baron. See De Villiers.		Wardle, Sir Thomas	1831–1909
		Waring, Anna Letitia	1823–1910
Villiers, Victor Albert George Child-, Earl of Jersey	1845–1915	Warington, Robert	1838–1907
		Warlock, Peter, pseudonym. See Heseltine, Philip Arnold.	
Vincent, Sir (Charles Edward) Howard	1849–1908		
Vincent, James Edmund	1857–1909	Warne, Frederick	1825–1901
Vines, Sydney Howard	1849–1934	Warneford, Reginald Alexander John	1891–1915
Vinogradoff, Sir Paul Gavrilovitch	1854–1925	Warner, Charles	1846–1909
		Warner, Sir George Frederic	1845–1936
Von Hügel, Friedrich, Baron of the Holy Roman Empire	1852–1925	Warre, Edmond	1837–1920
Voysey, Charles	1828–1912	Warre-Cornish, Francis Warre	1839–1916
		Warren, Sir Charles	1840–1927
		Warren, Sir Thomas Herbert	1853–1930
Wace, Henry	1836–1924	Warrender, Sir George John Scott	1860–1917
Waddell, Laurence Augustine (later Austine)	1854–1938	Warrington, Thomas Rolls, Baron Warrington of Clyffe	1851–1937
Wade, Sir Willoughby Francis	1827–1906	Warwick, Countess of. See Greville, Frances Evelyn.	
Waggett, Philip Napier	1862–1939		
Wain, Louis William	1860–1939		
Wakley, Thomas. See under Wakley, Thomas Henry.		Waterhouse, Alfred	1830–1905
		Waterhouse, Paul	1861–1924
Wakley, Thomas Henry	1821–1907	Waterlow, Sir Ernest Albert	1850–1919
Walker, Sir Byron Edmund	1848–1924	Waterlow, Sir Sydney Hedley	1822–1906
Walker, Sir Emery	1851–1933	Watkin, Sir Edward William	1819–1901
Walker, Frederick William	1830–1910	Watkins, Henry George ('Gino')	1907–1932
Walker, Sir Frederick William Edward Forestier-. See Forestier-Walker.		Watson, Albert	1828–1904
		Watson, Sir Charles Moore	1844–1916
		Watson, Foster	1860–1929
Walker, Sir James	1863–1935	Watson, George Lennox	1851–1904
Walker, Sir Mark	1827–1902	Watson, Henry William	1827–1903
Walker, Sir Samuel	1832–1911	Watson, John, 'Ian Maclaren'	1850–1907
Walker, Vyell Edward	1837–1906	Watson, Sir Patrick Heron	1832–1907
Walkley, Arthur Bingham	1855–1926	Watson, Robert Spence	1837–1911
Wallace, Alfred Russel	1823–1913	Watson, Sir William	1858–1935
Wallace, Sir Donald Mackenzie	1841–1919	Watts, George Frederic	1817–1904
Wallace, (Richard Horatio) Edgar	1875–1932	Watts, Henry Edward	1826–1904
		Watts, John	1861–1902
Wallace, William Arthur James	1842–1902	Watts, Sir Philip	1846–1926
Wallas, Graham	1858–1932	Watts-Dunton, Walter Theodore	1832–1914
Waller, Charles Henry	1840–1910	Waugh, Benjamin	1839–1908

Wilson, William Edward . .	1851–1908
Wimborne, Viscount. See Guest, Ivor Churchill.	
Wimshurst, James . . .	1832–1903
Windus, William Lindsay . .	1822–1907
Winter, Sir James Spearman .	1845–1911
Winter, John Strange, *pseudonym.* See Stannard, Henrietta Eliza Vaughan.	
Winterstoke, Baron. See Wills, William Henry.	
Winton, Sir Francis Walter De. See De Winton.	
Wise, Thomas James . .	1859–1937
Wittewronge, Sir Charles Bennet Lawes-. See Lawes-Wittewronge.	
Wodehouse, John, Earl of Kimberley	1826–1902
Wolfe, Humbert (formerly Umberto Wolff). . .	1886–1940
Wolfe-Barry, Sir John Wolfe .	1836–1918
Wolff, Sir Henry Drummond Charles . . .	1830–1908
Wollaston, Alexander Frederick Richmond . . .	1875–1930
Wolseley, Garnet Joseph, Viscount . . .	1833–1913
Wolverhampton, Viscount. See Fowler, Henry Hartley.	
Wood, Charles . .	1866–1926
Wood, Charles Lindley, Viscount Halifax . . .	1839–1934
Wood, Francis Derwent .	1871–1926
Wood, Sir (Henry) Evelyn .	1838–1919
Wood, Matilda Alice Victoria, 'Marie Lloyd' . .	1870–1922
Wood, Thomas McKinnon .	1855–1927
Woodall, William . .	1832–1901
Woodgate, Walter Bradford .	1840–1920
Woods, Sir Albert William .	1816–1904
Woods, Edward . .	1814–1903
Woodward, Herbert Hall .	1847–1909
Woolavington, Baron. See Buchanan, James.	
Wooldridge, Harry Ellis . .	1845–1917
Woolgar, Sarah Jane. See Mellon.	
Wordsworth, Dame Elizabeth .	1840–1932
Wordsworth, John . .	1843–1911
Worms, Henry De, Baron Pirbright. See De Worms.	
Worthington, Sir Percy Scott .	1864–1939
Worthington-Evans, Sir (Worthington) Laming. See Evans.	
Wrenbury, Baron. See Buckley, Henry Burton.	
Wright, Charles Henry Hamilton	1836–1909
Wright, Sir Charles Theodore Hagberg	1862–1940
Wright, Edward Perceval .	1834–1910
Wright, Joseph . .	1855–1930
Wright, Sir Robert Samuel .	1839–1904
Wright, Whitaker . .	1845–1904
Wright, William Aldis . .	1831–1914
Wroth, Warwick William .	1858–1911
Wrottesley, George . .	1827–1909
Wylie, Charles Hotham Montagu Doughty-. See Doughty-Wylie.	
Wyllie, Sir William Hutt Curzon	1848–1909
Wyllie, William Lionel . .	1851–1931
Wyndham, Sir Charles .	1837–1919
Wyndham, George . .	1863–1913
Wyndham (formerly Moore), Mary, Lady . . .	1861–1931
Wyndham-Quin, Thomas Windham, Earl of Dunraven and Mount-Earl. See Quin.	
Wynn-Carrington, Charles Robert, Baron Carrington and Marquess of Lincolnshire .	1843–1928
Wyon, Allan . . .	1843–1907
Yapp, Sir Arthur Keysall . .	1869–1936
Yarrow, Sir Alfred Fernandez .	1842–1932
Yate, Sir Charles Edward . .	1849–1940
Yeats, William Butler .	1865–1939
Yeo, Gerald Francis . .	1845–1909
Yonge, Charlotte Mary .	1823–1901
Yorke, Albert Edward Philip Henry, Earl of Hardwicke .	1867–1904
Youl, Sir James Arndell . .	1811–1904
Young, Sir Allen William .	1827–1915
Young, Mrs. Charles. See Vezin, Jane Elizabeth.	
Young, George, Lord . .	1819–1907
Young, Sir George . .	1837–1930
Young, Sydney . .	1857–1937
Young, Sir William Mackworth .	1840–1924
Younger, George, Viscount Younger of Leckie . .	1851–1929
Yoxall, Sir James Henry .	1857–1925
Ypres, Earl of. See French, John Denton Pinkstone.	
Zangwill, Israel . . .	1864–1926